PENGUIN HANDBOOKS

The Penguin Guide to Compact Discs, Cassettes and LPs

This book is primarily about **compact discs** and the reader will immediately discover the remarkable range of music available in this new medium by quickly scanning through its pages. The **C Ds** stand out clearly, as their catalogue numbers are printed in **bold** type, while *cassettes* are numbered in *italics* and LPs are given a roman typeface. But no survey of recordings available in a new medium, however revolutionary, can be made in a vacuum, for in the world of recorded music the legacy of the past is as fundamental as the promise for the future. So our survey first looks closely at the available compact discs and then considers whether a less expensive *cassette* alternative might be the 'best buy'. Finally, where appropriate we compare distinguished earlier recordings, which may be found only in the LP format.

EDWARD GREENFIELD has been Record Critic of the *Guardian* since 1954 and from 1964 Music Critic too. At the end of 1960 he joined the reviewing panel of *Gramophone*, specializing in operatic and orchestral issues. He is a regular broadcaster on music and records for the BBC and has a weekly record programme on the BBC World Service. In 1958 he published a monograph on the operas of Puccini. More recently he has written studies on the recorded work of Joan Sutherland and André Previn. He has been a regular juror on International Record awards and has appeared with such artists as Elisabeth Schwarzkopf and Joan Sutherland in public interviews.

ROBERT LAYTON studied at Oxford with Edmund Rubbra for composition and with the late Egon Wellesz for the history of music. He spent two years in Sweden at the universities of Uppsala and Stockholm. He joined the BBC Music Division in 1959 and has been responsible for such programmes as *Interpretations on Record*. He has contributed 'A Quarterly Retrospect' to *Gramophone* for a number of years and he has written books on Berwald and Sibelius and has specialized in Scandinavian music. His recent publications include a monograph on the Dvořák symphonies and concertos for the BBC Music Guides, of which he is General Editor, and the first two volumes of his translations of Erik Tawastsjerna's definitive study of Sibelius. In 1984 he was awarded the Finnish State Literary Prize.

IVAN MARCH is an ex-professional musician. He studied at Trinity College of Music, London, and later at the Royal Manchester College. After service in the RAF Central Band, he played the horn professionally for the BBC and has also travelled with the Carl Rosa and D'Oyly Carte opera companies. Now director of the Long Playing Record Library, the largest commercial lending library for classical music on compact discs in the British Isles, he is a well-known lecturer, journalist and personality in the world of recorded music. He is a regular contributor to *Gramophone*.

The Penguin Guide to Compact Discs, Cassettes and LPs

Edward Greenfield, Robert Layton and Ivan March

Penguin Books

Penguin Books Ltd, Harmondsworth, Middlesex, England
Viking Penguin Inc., 40 West 23rd Street, New York, New York 10010, U.S.A.
Penguin Books Australia Ltd, Ringwood, Victoria, Australia
Penguin Books Canada Limited, 2801 John Street, Markham, Ontario, Canada L3R 1B4
Penguin Books (N.Z.) Ltd, 182–190 Wairau Road, Auckland 10, New Zealand

First published 1986

Made and printed in Great Britain by
Richard Clay (The Chaucer Press) Ltd,
Bungay, Suffolk
Typeset in 9 on 10½ pt Times

Contents

Preface

The newcomer to CD is usually amazed by the magnetism and uncanny presence of a clear and realistically balanced digital recording the first time it is heard against a background of total silence. After this dramatic experience it is only a short step to discovering that a first-class analogue recording from the pre-digital era can be digitally remastered so that its (inevitable) background hiss is much subdued, often virtually silenced, while the quality of the sound is considerably enhanced.

However, the compact disc is not the only modern sound-carrier which gives excellent reproduction. The prerecorded chrome cassette offers an alternative technology that is in essence more casual, and is equally valid in a different way. It too provides music against a quiet background which, if not absolutely silent, is free from arbitrary intrusions and disturbances. The best 'bargain' cassettes can offer up to an hour and a half of listening while costing about a third as much as a compact disc.

It may be thought that the LP is now potentially obsolete, having served us faithfully for three and a half decades, yet at the present time many of the more esoteric issues at the edge of the repertoire are still offered to the musical public only in LP format. (It is salutary to remember that at the beginning of the 1950s Vivaldi's *Four Seasons* was considered esoteric repertoire. Now it is the most frequently recorded piece of classical music.) So the experienced collector should not contemplate ignoring this still important format, if he wants to continue to explore and expand his musical awareness. It will be some years yet before the CD catalogue can encompass the range of music currently available on black vinyl discs.

The Penguin Guide to Compact Discs, Cassettes and LPs has been compiled independently of our previous surveys. It includes *all* major CD issues and all the important bargain-priced chrome cassettes which seem competitive. In making assessments, considerable reference is made to older recordings on LP and tape. Moreover, the authors discuss key issues in all three media made since the *Complete Penguin Stereo Record and Cassette Guide* went to press during 1984. This earlier *Complete Guide* remains in print for those readers who wish to gain further background knowledge of earlier recordings.

About the Compact Disc

The compact disc (CD) has caught the public imagination in a way its creators could hardly have anticipated when the first CDs were made available to the general public in the early months of 1983, nor could it have been guessed how quickly the new medium would come to dominate the world of recording. Perhaps more surprisingly, the general awareness of something new and special was slower to make its initial impact in the United States than in Europe, but American collectors soon made up for lost time and quickly generated a degree of enthusiasm for the silver disc to match that of any other part of the western world.

The CD – developed jointly by Philips and Sony – is a quite different conception from previous recording systems, with its technology firmly planted in the second half of the twentieth century. The disc is truly compact in size, measuring 12 cm (4·75 inches) in diameter. While it does have potential for containing music on both sides, in the event only the underside is used for the recording, the upper face featuring label details. The earliest 78 r.p.m. discs were single-sided, so one can sense here an almost sentimental link with the gramophone's original development. However, while the first shellac discs contained only about four minutes of information, the CD offers up to about eighty minutes' playing time, long enough to contain Beethoven's *Choral symphony* – although only a small minority of those currently available approach this maximum time-space.

The CD's recorded information is cut on to a single spiral track in the form of pits instead of wave forms, and this information is read by a laser beam. The speed at which the disc rotates is very fast (300–500 r.p.m.) and the recorded information is read at a constant velocity. The laser beam starts at the inner radius where the disc is revolving at its highest r.p.m. As the beam moves outwards, the angular speed is reduced to maintain constant track speed. The disc itself is moulded in clear PVC, but has additional covering laminations of mirrorlike micro-thin aluminium, and a final protective coating of lacquer. There is no wear or deterioration in use and, given reasonable handling care, the lifetime of a compact disc has no foreseeable limit. It was originally thought that CDs were robust enough to withstand unfriendly treatment of any kind, but experience suggests that the playing surface should be treated with care and kept free of grease and dust. A diametrical scratch could well offer no problems, but grease-bonded foreign matter running parallel with the groove, or a deep indentation (or manufacturing flaw), can, in certain circumstances, interrupt the pulse code modulation in the groove which maintains the tracking laser beam on its course. Curiously, such a fault can bring problems on some CD players but not on others which are technologically better equipped to resist misinformation of this kind, nor is this resistant ability necessarily related to the cost of the CD player.

The main features of digital reproduction using the CD system give the following advantages:

a silent background for the music;
a breadth of dynamic range to equal that experienced at a live concert;
a frequency range covering the complete audio spectrum discernible by the human ear;
an absence of non-linear and other distortions;
absolute pitch security;
no loss of quality in the mastering or pressing process.

The very positive (though by no means uncritical) welcome given to the compact disc, spearheaded by the British magazine *Gramophone*, was balanced by a less enthusiastic response from some other sections of the hi-fi press, but much of this adverse reaction was misdirected. CDs brought an obvious new degree of fidelity and tangibility, emphasized by their background silence, so that any flaws and misjudgements deriving from the recording sessions became only too readily apparent. During the analogue era, recording engineers had evolved techniques to compensate for the loss of fidelity which appeared within the recording chain, from the moment the sound was picked up by the microphones until, after various mastering, pressing or copying processes, it appeared as an end-product in LP or cassette form. The object of such artificial enhancement was to sharpen the aural focus, refine detail and improve presence. However, with the arrival of digital recording, this 'touching up' of the sound image by special microphone placement and complicated remixing of an essentially multi-track recording often became counter-productive: its artifice became apparent to the ear, bringing an unrealistic sharpness of outline and a clinical quality to internal definition. Moreover, close microphones often brought an added edge in the upper range, particularly unattractive when applied to orchestral violins playing loudly.

It is a credit to the recording staff of the major production companies that they quickly adjusted to this new situation. Perhaps even more remarkably, in some instances the problems were anticipated. Among recordings dating from the earliest digital era, those initiated by the pioneering American Telarc Company and engineered by Jack Renner demonstrated an awareness that, with the digital process, natural concert-hall acoustics presented with simple microphone techniques would yield an excellent impression of realism.

The compact disc system has proved very sensitive to hall ambience. In the analogue era, the finest LPs were notable for a perceptive choice of recording venue in relation to the music. CD communicates the ambient coloration even more distinctively. A studio recording becomes readily distinguishable from one made in a concert hall; where the choice is flattering to the music making in the right way, the listener's pleasure is greatly enhanced. One thinks, for instance, of

St Eustache, Montreal, where many of Decca's famous Dutoit recordings have been made with such success. Alternatively, where the acoustic effect is dry and relatively unflattering, as with recordings made in the Mann Auditorium, Tel Aviv, the added definition of the CD gives the listener a concert-hall projection, and the truthfulness of the sound-image makes the relative lack of bloom acceptable. With Karajan's recent digital recordings made in the Berlin Philharmonie the ear is aware of a lack of sumptuousness in the sound-picture, compared with earlier analogue LPs made in a different venue; but the ears adjust when the overall definition is positive. Sometimes a specific concert hall can seem ideal for certain repertoire, as in the series of Tchaikovsky *Symphonies* recorded in Oslo – although perceptive microphone placing also plays an important part in the success of these recordings. In the world of Opera, problems often arise from the complicated multi-microphone techniques favoured by some producers. Here the truthfulness of CD can expose and even emphasize uncomfortable changes of perspective, which interfere with listening continuity.

With solo instrumental recordings or small groups, balance is of critical importance. A guitar can all too readily sound jumbo-sized, while both piano and harpsichord need to be placed within a room perspective, without the impression that the microphones are hanging over the keyboard. The presentation of a string quartet demands a sense of space round the players: there must be no feeling of constriction, nor of the dominance of any one instrument; and the ears will resist excessive resonance, in which textures are blurred or inflated.

One of the most pleasurable surprises of CD has been the degree of enhancement possible with the digital remastering of older analogue records. While comparatively recent recordings show a consistent improvement in definition, the benefit seems even greater with issues deriving from the vintage 1960s or even earlier. One thinks of the inspirational Jacqueline du Pré/Dame Janet Baker/Barbirolli coupling of the Elgar *Cello concerto* and *Sea pictures*, and of Elisabeth Schwarzkopf's operetta recital from EMI; or, even more remarkable, the superb 1959 Decca set of *Peter Grimes*, one of the great recordings of all time. Not only does the removal of nearly all the background noise contribute greatly to the sense of immediacy, but also we can now for the first time hear everything that the recording team was able to capture on the master tape. In the case of *Peter Grimes*, the feeling of tangibility and realism is little short of astonishing, while the ambience brings a bloom and evocation to the overall sound-picture beyond anything one would expect to experience in the opera house.

It has been fascinating, while compiling this book, to discover how much the mid-1980s have in common with the mid-1960s, the great expansion era of the stereo LP. The very beginning of that decade was distinguished by Bruno Walter's Indian summer in the CBS studios, recording Beethoven, Brahms, Dvořák and Mozart, and Klemperer's set of Beethoven *Symphonies* with the Philharmonia. Karajan's first Beethoven cycle was soon to follow from DG, together with the Kempff Beethoven *Concertos* and *Sonatas*. Meanwhile, Rubinstein was recording Chopin for RCA, and at Decca Solti had already begun his great *Ring* cycle. And there was much else besides. All these remarkable achievements remain with us, and now many are reappearing on CD to stimulate and satisfy a new generation who are rediscovering not only the unique qualities of these performances, but also the skill of an earlier generation of balance engineers. In certain cases it has also been found possible to improve on a sound-balance that was originally far less than ideal. Heifetz's RCA recording of the Brahms *Violin concerto* with Fritz Reiner dates from an experimental period at the very beginning of the stereo era. When first issued on LP, it suffered from harshness due to a combination of treble emphasis and a too-close microphone placing for the soloist. The digital remastering for CD has both softened the background noise and at the same time smoothed the upper range. The attractive Chicago ambience remains and the improvement in sound is striking.

When CD looks further back, to the mono era or, even before that, to the age of 78s, the results are inevitably more uneven. Recording equipment was comparatively primitive; and in recordings of any scale, allowances usually have to be made. This applies to many of the Furtwängler records made for DG and EMI and the Mengelberg Philips reissues, which also can offer problems of adjustment because of changes in styles of performance. Nevertheless, here as elsewhere the immense value of these reissues is to give the collector of the 1980s a glimpse into a past age of music making so that he or she may discover how well the legendary musicians of long ago can stand alongside the interpreters of our own time.

Introduction

The object of *The Penguin Guide to Compact Discs, Cassettes and LPs* is to give the serious collector a comprehensive survey of the finest recordings of permanent music, primarily on compact discs, but also on cassettes and LPs. As most CDs are issued almost simultaneously on both sides of the Atlantic and use identical international catalogue numbers, this *Guide* should be found to be equally useful in Great Britain and the USA. The internationalization of repertoire and numbers is increasingly applying to cassettes and LPs (though EMI/Angel remains an exception to this practice). The major European labels are imported in their original formats; thus we have BIS from Scandinavia, Erato from France, Harmonia Mundi from France and Germany, Hungaroton from Hungary, Supraphon from Czechoslovakia, Telefunken from Germany, all providing important recordings of international repertoire, often rare and uniquely valuable. The (relatively) smaller labels like ASV, Chandos, Hyperion, Meridian from Britain and Arabesque, Nonesuch and Pro Arte from the USA are marketed independently and, like the European issues, have international catalogue numbers. Though these small recording companies are obviously suffering at present from difficulties in obtaining CD pressings in large numbers (with demand far outstripping supply), they are able to compete with the majors on both artistic and technical terms and, by imaginative choice of repertoire, have established a firm and expanding presence in the market place. Special mention must be made of Pickwick International, the British firm which has provided the first 'bargain-priced' compact discs, retailing at about two-thirds of the premium price with no apparent loss of standards, either artistic or technical, even if the artists' roster contains some presently unfamiliar names.

DG's justly famous Walkman series continues to dominate the field of extended-length chrome cassettes by continuing to produce some astonishing bargains. The technology of cassette transfer has now become highly sophisticated and, where chrome stock is used, the difference in sound between tape and equivalent LP is minimal, any minor disadvantage in range being more than offset by the security from extraneous background noises offered by the former. With major issues and reissues the back-up documentation is now generally adequate, though sometimes suffering from miniaturization, with librettos often printed in a minuscule typeface. Yet CDs, too, are not always entirely free from this fault. Unfortunately many double-length bargain-priced cassettes incorporate only minimal documentation, offering merely a list of titles and performers. This represents a lamentable deterioration in standards, which is also reflected by the three-language presentation of musical notes with premium-priced issues, in all three media, thus limiting the space available.

EMI/Angel currently manufacture all their cassettes using iron-oxide tape stock – a doubly curious fact, when one remembers that the British company did much to pioneer and promote the use of chrome in the early 1980s. With this change of policy came the introduction of the XDR process which seeks to maximize the fidelity of the transfer. However, experience has shown that iron-oxide stock, however skilfully manipulated, has problems with the focus of a recording made within reverberant acoustics, and the ear readily notices a loss of definition in the upper range, especially when an A/B comparison is made with the equivalent LP.

The sheer number of records of artistic merit available causes considerable problems in any assessment of overall and individual excellence. While in the case of a single popular repertoire work it might be ideal for the discussion to be conducted by a single reviewer, it was not always possible for one person to have access to every version, and division of reviewing responsibility inevitably leads to some clashes of opinion. Also there are certain works and certain recorded performances for which one or another of our team has a special affinity. Such a personal identification can often carry with it a special perception too. We feel that it is a strength of our basic style to let such conveyed pleasure or admiration for the merits of an individual recording come over directly to the reader, even if this produces a certain ambivalence in the matter of choice between competing recordings. Where disagreement is profound (and this has rarely happened), then readers will find an indication of this difference of opinion in the text.

We have considered and rejected the use of initials against individual reviews, since this is essentially a team project. The occasions for disagreement generally concern matters of aesthetics, for instance in the manner of recording balance, where a contrived effect may trouble some ears more than others, or in the matter of style, where the difference between robustness and refinement of approach produces controversy, rather than any question of artistic integrity.

EVALUATION

Most recordings issued today by the major companies, whether on compact disc, LP or cassette, are of a high technical standard and offer performances of a quality at least as high as is heard in the average concert hall. In deciding to adopt a starring system for the evaluation of records, we have decided to make use of from one to three stars. Brackets round one or more of the stars indicate some reservations about its inclusion and readers are advised to refer to the text. Brackets round all the stars usually indicate a basic qualification: for instance, a mono recording of a performance of artistic interest, where considerable allowances have to be made for the sound quality, even though the recording may have been digitally remastered.

Our evaluation system may be summarized as follows:

*** An outstanding performance and recording in every way.
** A good performance and recording of today's normal high standard.
* A fair performance, reasonably well or well recorded.

Our evaluation is normally applied to the record as a whole, unless there are two main works, or groups of works, on each side of the disc, and by different composers. In this case each is dealt with separately in its appropriate place. In the case of a collection of shorter works, we feel there is little point in giving a different starring to each item, even if their merits are uneven, since the record can only be purchased as a complete programme.

ROSETTES

To a very few records and cassettes we have awarded a rosette: ❀.

Unlike our general evaluation, in which we have tried to be consistent, a rosette is a quite arbitrary compliment by a member of the reviewing team to a recorded performance which, he finds, shows special illumination, a magic, or spiritual quality that places it in a very special class. The choice is essentially a personal one (although often it represents a shared view), and in some cases it is applied to an issue where certain reservations must also be mentioned in the text of the review. The rosette symbol is placed immediately before the normal evaluation and record number. It is quite small – we do not mean to imply an 'Academy award' but a personal token of appreciation for something uniquely valuable. We hope that, once the reader has discovered and perhaps acquired a 'rosette' CD, tape or LP, its special qualities will soon become apparent.

COMPACT DISC ACCOLADE

To another group of recordings we have awarded a compact disc accolade: ©.

This suggests that the recording gives a sense of natural presence and realism beyond that which we have previously experienced, and that balance problems have been satisfactorily solved, liberating the musical image to give a convincing illusion of a real performance within a believable acoustic.

At the time of going to press, a small number of recordings which we have already sampled in their LP and tape formats are scheduled for release on CD. Where the catalogue numbers are known, we have listed them. Obviously some might deserve an accolade but this could not be given without an audition. However, if a recording is highly praised in its LP and cassette formats, the compact disc will almost certainly reflect a similar degree of excellence.

DIGITAL RECORDINGS

Many compact discs are actually recorded digitally, but an increasing number of digitally remastered analogue recordings are now appearing, and we thought it important to include a clear indication of the difference:

Dig. This indicates that the master recording was digitally encoded.

BARGAIN ISSUES

With the honourable exception of Pickwick's mid-priced series (issued on the aptly named 'Innovative Music Productions' label – IMP for short) all CDs are issued at premium price. During the period of the preparation of this book, as world demand has continued to outstrip supply we have seen that price rise rather than fall, so that a CD now costs nearly twice as much as an equivalent premium-priced LP, and approximately four times as much as a bargain-priced record or cassette. With a wide range of first-class recorded repertoire now also available on LPs and tapes in a medium-price range, the collector has plenty of scope to decide how much to pay for a recorded performance.

The symbols (M) or (B), placed first before the starring, indicate whether a record or tape is issued in the UK at medium or bargain price. Where no bracketed initial precedes the starring, it can be taken that the LP or tape is on a premium-priced label, usually ranging from about £5.50 to £7.00. CDs are currently offered at a list price of between £11.00 and £12.00.

The key to our indications is as follows:

(M) Medium-priced label: in the price-range between £3.50 and £4.50.
(B) Bargain-priced label: about £2.50.

In the case of double-length cassettes, which contain the equivalent of the contents of two normal LPs, we have taken this into account in choosing the appropriate symbol. For instance, DG Walkman tapes have a list price in the region of £3.50 but usually offer up to ninety minutes of music.

It is possible that, in current inflationary times, prices may rise during the life of this book, so that the above limitations become unrealistic, but the major manufacturers usually maintain the price ratios between labels when an overall increase is made.

LAYOUT OF TEXT

We have aimed to make our style as simple as possible, even though the catalogue numbers of recordings are no longer as straightforward as they once were, and we are now often dealing with a triple format of CD, LP and cassette, all relating to the same recording. So, immediately after the evaluation and before the catalogue numbers, the record make and label are given, usually in abbreviated form (a key to the abbreviations is provided on pages xxi–xxiii).

The compact disc catalogue number comes first in **bold type** (unless there is no CD available at the time of going to print); then comes the LP number in roman type, and finally the cassette is indicated in *italics*.

In certain cases, the digits are the same for both LP and cassette; in a more limited number of instances, the digits are the same for CD, LP and cassette, and the alphabetical prefixes indicate the format.

Here are some typical examples:

Decca Dig. **400 055-2**; SXDL/*KSXDC* 7562.

This indicates that the **CD** number is **400 055-2**; the LP is SXDL 7562 and the cassette is *KSXDC 7562*.

Sometimes the cassette uses the full record number with an added prefix, e.g.

HMV Dig. **CDC 747002-2**; ASD/*TCC-ASD* 4059; or CBS **CD 35826**; 35826/*40-*.

Here the **CDs** are: **CDC 747002-2** **CD 35826**
the LPs: ASD 4059 35826
and the cassettes: *TCC-ASD 4059* *40-35826*

Where the catalogue number is entirely in digits, often the first four change to indicate the cassette, e.g. DG Priv. 2535/*3335* 176. This means that the LP number is 2535 176 and the tape equivalent *3335 176*.

With the move towards international numbering of recordings, further complications have arisen. For instance the Polygram group (Decca, DG and Philips) now use the same basic catalogue number for the recording in all three media, indicating which by the final additional digit:

1 = LP; 2 = CD; 4 = cassette.

In this case our listing might be, for example: DG Dig. **410 507-2**; 410 507-1/*4*. To complicate matters even further, EMI use different final digits to indicate a set. Here is an example where two LPs have as equivalent a single double-length cassette: HMV Dig. SLS/*TC-SLS* 143484-3/*9*. This means that the LP number is SLS 143484-3 and the cassette number *TC-SLS 143484-9*.

The numbers which follow in square brackets are US catalogue numbers; here a similar differentiation is made between disc (in roman type) and cassette issue (in italics), while the abbreviation [id.] indicates that the American number is identical with the European.

ABBREVIATIONS

To save space we have adopted a number of standard abbreviations in listing orchestras and performing groups (a list is provided below), and the titles of works are often shortened, especially where they are listed several times. Artists' christian names are sometimes not included where they are not absolutely necessary for identification purposes. We have also usually omitted details of the contents of operatic highlights collections. These can be found in the *Gramophone Compact Disc* and *Classical Catalogues* published by *Gramophone* magazine.

We have followed common practice in the use of the original language for titles where it seems sensible. In most cases, English is used for orchestral and instrumental music and the original language for vocal music and opera. There are exceptions, however; for instance, the Johann Strauss discography uses the German language in the interests of consistency.

ORDER OF MUSIC

The order of music under each composer's name broadly follows that adopted by the *Gramophone Catalogues*: orchestral music, including concertos and symphonies; chamber music; solo instrumental music (in some cases with keyboard and organ music separated); vocal and choral music; opera; vocal collections; miscellaneous collections.

The *Gramophone Catalogues* now usually include stage works alongside opera; we have not generally followed this practice, preferring to list, for instance, ballet music and incidental music (where no vocal items are involved) in the general orchestral group. Within each group our listing follows an alphabetical sequence, and couplings within a single composer's output are *usually* discussed together instead of separately with cross-references. Occasionally and inevitably because of this alphabetical approach, different recordings of a given work can become separated when a record is listed and discussed under the first work of its alphabetical sequence. A cross-reference is then usually given (either within the listing or in the review) to any important alternative versions. The editor feels that alphabetical consistency is essential if the reader is to learn to find his way about.

CONCERTS AND RECITALS

Most collections of music intended to be regarded as concerts or recitals involve many composers, and it is quite impractical to deal with them within the alphabetical composer index. They are grouped separately, at the end of the book, in three sections. In each section, recordings are usually arranged in alphabetical order of the performers' names: concerts of orchestral and concertante music under the name of the orchestra, ensemble or, if more important, conductor or soloist; instrumental recitals under the name of the instrumentalist; operatic and vocal recitals under the principal singer or vocal group, as seems appropriate.

In certain cases where the compilation features many different performers it is listed alphabetically under its collective title, or the key word in that title (so *Favourite operatic duets* is listed under 'Operatic duets'). Sometimes for complicated collections only brief details of contents and performers are given; fuller information can usually be found in the *Gramophone Compact Disc* and *Classical Catalogues*.

RECORD NUMBERS

Enormous care has gone into the checking of record and cassette numbers and contents to ensure that all details are correct, but the editor and publishers cannot be held responsible for any mistakes that may have crept in despite all our zealous checking. When ordering records or cassettes, readers are urged to provide their record-dealer with full details of the music and performers as well as the catalogue number.

DELETIONS

Although, for the moment, CDs still seem relatively impervious to the deletions axe, it is likely that some records and cassettes will have been withdrawn in the period before we appear in print, and others are likely to disappear during the lifetime of the book. Sometimes copies may still be found in specialist shops, and there remains the compensation that most really important and desirable recordings are eventually reissued.

SUPPLY PROBLEMS

Because the limited manufacturing capacity for CDs is a worldwide problem, collectors often find it frustratingly difficult to obtain the recordings they want. Although a number of new factories are due to open in the next twelve months, demand is also increasing and it seems likely that the supply situation will get worse before it gets better. We can only counsel patience and perseverance. Usually it is possible to obtain a desired CD if one tries long and hard enough.

ACKNOWLEDGEMENTS

The editor and authors express herewith their gratitude to Roger Wells for his help in the preparation of this volume, and also to E. T. Bryant, M.A., F.L.A., for his assistance with the task of proof-correcting. The editor also wishes to thank his wife, Kathleen March, both for her zealous checking of the finished copy before it was delivered to Roger Wells and thence to the printers, and for her eagle eye in dealing with the proofs. Without her untiring efforts, this book would have been a good deal less accurate than it is. He would also like to acknowledge the expert assistance of Raymond Cooke, O.B.E., the Managing Director of KEF Electronics, in the preparation of the information about the compact digital disc. The authors would also like gratefully to acknowledge many letters from readers which have helped to make the present text freer from errata than its predecessor.

For American Readers

American catalogue numbers are included throughout this survey where they are known at the time of going to press. In each case the American domestic listing is given in square brackets immediately after the British catalogue number. The abbreviation [id.] indicates that the American and British numbers are identical, or nearly so. For instance, a CBS number could use the same digits on both sides of the Atlantic, but have different alphabetical prefixes, and EMI/Angel use extra digits for their British compact discs. Thus the US number **CDC 47001** becomes **CDC 747001-2** in Britain (the **-2** is the European indication that it is a compact disc). The addition of (d.) immediately before the American number indicates some difference in the contents of the American issue. We have taken care to check catalogue information as far as is possible, but as all the editorial work has been done in England there is always the possibility of error; American readers are therefore invited, when ordering records locally, to take the precaution of giving their dealer the fullest information about the music and recordings they want.

The indications (M) and (B) immediately before the starring of a disc refer only to the British record, as pricing systems are not always identical on both sides of the Atlantic.

Where no American catalogue number is given, this does not necessarily mean that a record is not available in the USA; the transatlantic issue may not have been made at the time of the publication of this *Guide*. Readers are advised to check the current *Schwann* catalogue and to consult their local record store.

One of the more significant roles played by the international recording industry is to provide recordings of contemporary scores, and in this way the gramophone record becomes fundamental in establishing the reputation of music written in our own time. However, for understandable commercial reasons, the greater part of this output is permanently accessible only in its country of origin. Those recordings that are exported seldom remain available abroad for long periods (although there are honourable exceptions). A great deal of important twentieth-century American music is not readily obtainable in recorded form in Great Britain, whilst modern British and European composers are much more generously favoured. The reflection of this imbalance within these pages is obviously not the choice of the authors.

An International Mail-order Source for Recordings

Readers are urged to support a local dealer if he is prepared and able to give a proper service, and to remember that many CDs, LPs and tapes involve a great deal of perseverance to obtain. If, however, difficulty is experienced locally, we suggest the following mail-order alternative, which operates world-wide:

Squires Gate Music Centre,
Squires Gate Station Approach,
Blackpool,
Lancashire FY8 2SP,
England.

Compact disc orders are patiently extended until they finally come to hand and scrupulous care is taken in the visual inspection of LPs exported by this organization (which is operated under the direction of the Editor of *The Penguin Guide to Compact Discs, Cassettes and LPs*). A full guarantee is made of safe delivery of any order undertaken. Please write for more details, enclosing a stamped, addressed envelope if within the UK.

American readers seeking a domestic mail-order source may write to the following address where a comparable supply service has been set up (to handle both American and imported European labels). Please write for more details (enclosing a stamped, addressed envelope) to:

Squires Gate (USA),
PO Box 406,
Fairfax,
Virginia 22030,
USA.

Abbreviations

Ac.	Academy
AAM	Academy of Ancient Music
Acc.	Accolade
Amb. S.	Ambrosian Singers
Ang.	Angel
Ara.	Arabesque
Arc.	Archiv
arr.	arranged
ASMF	Academy of St Martin-in-the-Fields
ASV	Academy Sound and Vision
Bar.	Baroque
Bav.	Bavarian
BPO	Berlin Philharmonic Orchestra
Cal.	Calliope
Cap.	Caprice
CBSO	City of Birmingham Symphony Orchestra
CfP	Classics for Pleasure
Ch.	Choir; Choral; Chorus
Chan.	Chandos
CO	Chamber Orchestra
COE	Chamber Orchestra of Europe
Col.	Cologne
Coll.	Collegium
Coll. Aur.	Collegium Aureum
Coll. Mus.	Collegium Musicum
Con.	Contour
Concg. O	Concertgebouw Orchestra of Amsterdam
cond.	conductor, conducted
Cons.	Consort
Dept	Department
DG	Deutsche Grammophon
Dig.	digital recording
E.	England, English
ECO	English Chamber Orchestra
Em.	Eminence
Ens.	Ensemble
Fest.	Festival

Fr.	French
Gal.	Galleria
GO	Gewandhaus Orchestra
Gold	Gold Label
Green.	Greensleeve
HM	Harmonia Mundi
HMV	His Master's Voice
Hung.	Hungaroton
Hyp.	Hyperion
Jub.	Jubilee
L.	London
Lon.	London (Record Company)
Lon. Ent.	London Enterprise
LACO	Los Angeles Chamber Orchestra
LAPO	Los Angeles Philharmonic Orchestra
Liszt CO	Liszt Chamber Orchestra
LOP	Lamoureux Orchestra of Paris
LPO	London Philharmonic Orchestra
LSO	London Symphony Orchestra
Lyr.	Lyrita
Mer.	Meridian
Met.	Metropolitan
Moz.	Mozart
movt	movement
Mun.	Munich
Mus. Ant.	Musica Antiqua
N.	North
nar.	narrated
Nat.	National
None.	Nonesuch
NY	New York
O	Orchestra, Orchestre
Odys.	Odyssey
O-L	Oiseau-Lyre
Op.	Opera
orch.	orchestrated
Ph.	Philips
Phd.	Philadelphia
Philh.	Philharmonia
PO	Philharmonic Orchestra
Pres.	Presence
Priv.	Privilege
PRT	Precision Records & Tapes
Qt	Quartet
R.	Radio
Ref.	Référence

ROHCG	Royal Opera House, Covent Garden
RPO	Royal Philharmonic Orchestra
RSO	Radio Symphony Orchestra
S.	South
Salz.	Salzburg
Sar.	Sarabande
SCO	Stuttgart Chamber Orchestra
Seq.	Sequenza
Ser.	Serenata
Sera.	Seraphim
Sig.	Signature
Sinf.	Sinfonietta
SNO	Scottish National Orchestra
SO	Symphony Orchestra
Soc.	Society
Sol. Ven.	I Solisti Veneti
SRO	Suisse Romande Orchestra
Sup.	Supraphon
Tel.	Telefunken
V.	Vienna
Van.	Vanguard
Var.	Varese
VCM	Vienna Concentus Musicus
VPO	Vienna Philharmonic Orchestra
VSO	Vienna Symphony Orchestra
W.	West

Adam, Adolph (1803–56)

Giselle (ballet): complete recording of original score.
(M) ** Decca Jub. 411 848-1/*4* (2). Monte Carlo Op. O, Bonynge.

We still await a compact disc of the first of the great Romantic ballets. Bonynge's analogue recording makes a serviceable stopgap. He directs with some flair, the Monte Carlo orchestra is competent, and the result is certainly dramatic. Unfortunately the wind playing is without the beauty of timbre that the music ideally needs. However, the Decca recording, from 1960, is certainly vivid and brilliantly lit, notably so on the chrome tapes; it is a pity that in the cassette format a better turnover point was not chosen between sides three and four. Martinon's famous 1959 recording is currently out of the catalogue; Fistoulari's complete Mercury set (SRI 77003), although much more beguilingly played by the LSO, suffers from over-resonant and bass-heavy recording. At the moment the best buy in this repertoire would seem to be Karajan's Decca Jubilee reissue (JB/*KJBC* 14) from 1962; he offers highlights from the older European score, with the Vienna Philharmonic responsive, but somewhat suave in their elegance. The Decca recording has a pleasingly warm ambience, but the atmosphere of the music making is not very French. However, as the legend of the Wilis (the ghosts of dead girls jilted by their lovers) on which *Giselle* is based is a German one, this is perhaps not wholly inappropriate.

Adams, John (born 1947)

Shaker loops.
*** Ph. **412 214-2;** 412 214-1/*4* [id.]. San Francisco SO, De Waart – REICH: *Variations for winds.****

Shaker loops is one of the more appealing of minimalist works. John Adams adapted the piece from an earlier string septet when he became composer-in-residence to the San Francisco orchestra. The inspiration was from the Shakers, the religious sect whose devotions regularly led to shaking and trembling. (The shaking was a substitute for sex, which they didn't believe in – so perhaps it is not surprising that the Shakers are no longer numerous. They are now best remembered for their hymnal – the source of inspiration for Copland's *Appalachian spring* – and also a much-admired cookery book.) In his four linked movements Adams reproduces the shaking in prolonged ostinatos and trills, making the result sound like Sibelius stuck in the groove. Whatever the limitations, there is a genuine poetic imagination here; both performance and recording are outstanding, with an excellent chrome tape – lively and full-bodied.

Grand pianola music.
*** HMV Dig. EL 270291-1/*4* [Ang. DS/*4XS* 37345]. Feinberg, Oppens, Wood,

Bryden, Wheeler, Solisti New York, Wilson – REICH: *8 Lines; Vermont counterpoint.****

Even more than Adams's *Shaker loops*, this ambitious work seems likely to achieve a crossover between the worlds of concert and 'pop' music. It is in three sections, the first possessing the most fascinating aural detail, dominated by the piano filigree, but with vocal, orchestral and percussive interjections making a kaleidoscopic texture which is hypnotically compulsive in its climactic progress. After a more serene central movement the finale builds to a huge climax, using a simple but indelible phrase as its basis. Indeed the emotional and structural scope of the work is belied by its title, and one could imagine this piece creating a sensation at a promenade concert. The performance here has the spontaneity of a live occasion and the recording is very impressive, although on tape the bass drum occasionally swamps the overall sound-picture. Tape collectors should not be put off by this, however; the work is extremely telling, makes an immediate impact, and does not pall with repetition.

Addinsell, Richard (1904–77)

Warsaw concerto.

/// Ph. Dig. **411 123-2**; 411 123-1/*4* [id.]. Dichter, Philh. O, Marriner (with *Concert of concertante music* ***).

*** Decca Dig. **414 348-2**; 414 348-1/*4* [id.]. Ortiz, RPO, Atzmon – LITOLFF: *Scherzo*; GOTTSCHALK: *Grande fantaisie*; RACHMANINOV: *Concerto No. 2.****

Richard Addinsell's pastiche miniature concerto, written for the film *Dangerous moonlight* in 1942 – after Rachmaninov had been approached first, to no avail, it is said – remains the most indelible of all genre pieces of its kind. It is perfectly crafted and its atmosphere combines all the elements of the Romantic concerto to great effect; moreover it has a truly memorable main theme. It is beautifully played here, with Marriner revealing the most engaging orchestral detail. His warmth and the stylish commitment of the soloist combine almost to convince one it is a masterpiece. It will certainly outlive a great many twentieth-century works whose aspirations are more pretentious. The sound is first rate, with a kindly acoustic, admirably suited to the music, superbly caught on the CD. But the LP too is excellent, and the chrome cassette is vivid and well balanced.

The alternative from Cristina Ortiz is a warmly romantic account, spacious in conception, with the resonant ambience of Walthamstow Assembly Hall providing beguilingly rish string timbres. Although the opening is leisurely, Cristina Ortiz plays the main theme very tenderly; her approach is given an added evocation by the slightly backward balance of the piano. If the couplings are suitable, this is a rewarding collection, more substantial than Dichter's.

Albéniz, Isaac (1860–1909)

Piano concerto No. 1 (*Concierto fantastico*), orch. Trayter.
** HMV Dig. ASD/*TC-ASD* 163588-1/4 [Ang. DS/*4XS* 38038]. Ciccolini, RPO, Bátiz – FALLA: *Nights.***

Albéniz's *Piano concerto* is an early work dating from 1887, neither very characteristic nor very Spanish in its harmonic and melodic idiom. It possesses a certain charm, although the finale is empty. It is given a persuasive performance here and is very well recorded, with a good XDR tape. However, the Falla coupling is not outstanding among the versions available.

Cantos de España: Córdoba, Op. 232/4; Mallorca (*Barcarola*), *Op. 202; Piezás caracteristicás: Zambra Granadina; Torre Bermaja, Op. 92/7, 12; Suite española: Granada; Sevilla; Cádiz; Asturias, Op. 47/1, 3–5.*
*** CBS Dig. **CD 36679** [id.]; 36679/*41*- [M/*HMT* 36679]. John Williams (guitar).

Some of Albéniz's more colourful miniatures are here, and John Williams plays them most evocatively. His mood is slightly introvert, and the underlying technical skill is hidden in his concern for atmosphere. A most engaging recital, recorded with great faithfulness and not over-projected. The CD has striking presence, although it is not as beguiling as Julian Bream's RCA recital – see below – in catching the surrounding ambient effect. There is a good cassette.

Cantos de España: Córdoba, Op. 232/4; Mallorca, Op. 202. Suite española, Op. 47: Cádiz; Granada; Sevilla.
❀ ☾ *** RCA Dig. **RCD 14378**; RS/*RSK* 9008 [ARL 14378]. Julian Bream (guitar) – GRANADOS: *Collection.**** ❀ ☾

Julian Bream is in superb form in this splendid recital, his own favourite record, vividly recorded in the pleasingly warm acoustic of Wardour Chapel, near his home in Wiltshire. The normal LP and cassette both convey the illusion of live music-making very convincingly, but the compact disc, with its background of complete silence, is electrifying, giving an uncanny impression of the great guitarist sitting and making music just beyond the loudspeakers. Perhaps the image is a fraction larger than life, but the effect is remarkable, and this issue is undoubtedly a landmark in recorded realism. The playing itself has wonderfully communicative rhythmic feeling, great subtlety of colour, and its spontaneity increases the impression that one is experiencing a 'live' recital. The performance of the haunting *Córdoba*, which ends the group, is unforgettable.

Suite española, Op. 47.
(*) ASV ALH/*ZCALH* 949 [id.]. Alma Petchersky (piano) – FALLA: *Fantasia baetica*; GRANADOS: *Allegro de concierto.*

Alma Petchersky is an Argentine pianist, a sensitive and musical player of excellent credentials. Hers is at present the only available version of these justly popular salon pieces, and she is obviously thoroughly at home with them. She plays engagingly and with a natural spontaneity that gives pleasure. The playing is distinctly feminine in its guile (much more so than that of Alicia de Larrocha), and one occasionally feels the need of more flamboyance and temperament, particularly in *Cádiz*. But the *Asturias* is particularly successful and the Albéniz *Suite* is undoubtedly the most successful of the three works included in this recital. The recording is generally faithful, without being in the top bracket; the cassette is well balanced, but the use of iron-oxide stock means that there is some loss in the upper range, even though the image is quite believable.

Albinoni, Tommaso (1671–1750)

Adagio in G min. for organ and strings (arr. Giazotto).

*** Ph. Dig. **410 606-2**; 6514/*7337* 370 [id.]. I Musici – (with *Concert of Baroque music* ***).

(M) *** Pickwick **PCD 802**; CC/*CCTC* 7597. Scottish CO, Laredo (with string masterpieces ***).

(*) Decca Dig. **411 973-2; 411 973-1/*4* [id.]. SCO, Münchinger (with *Concert of Baroque music* **(*)).

** DG **415 301-2** [id.]. BPO, Karajan – CORELLI: *Concerto grosso, Op. 6/8*; VIVALDI: *Four seasons.* **(*)

(M) ** DG Sig. 415 201-1/*4*. BPO, Karajan – PACHELBEL: *Canon and gigue* **; VIVALDI: *Four seasons.* **(*)

There are already a number of different versions on CD of Albinoni's *Adagio*, in the notoriously anachronistic Giazotto arrangement, which continues to attract the attention of the public, despite the groans of the scholars. They include a rather sombre new digital version, beautifully recorded, by Karajan and the Berlin Philharmonic (DG **413 309-2**) and a less opulent but strongly expressive account from Münchinger and his Stuttgart Chamber Orchestra, also technically first class. Both of these, which are from collections of Baroque music, will be found in the Concerts section. Karajan's earlier analogue version has been digitally remastered to make a generous bonus, alongside Corelli's *Christmas concerto grosso*, for his 1973 account of Vivaldi's *Four Seasons* (with Michel Schwalbé). The remastering has not been entirely advantageous, however, and the sound quality is now less smooth and less alluring. The Albinoni and Vivaldi performances are also available on a mid-priced Signature LP and cassette, and this seems a better investment at less than half the cost, offering Pachelbel instead of Corelli.

I Musici gave the famous *Adagio* its CD début; collectors who, understandably, have a soft spot for the piece will find this performance thoroughly recommendable, with nicely judged expressive feeling, giving the melodic line a restrained nobility. The sound is excellent too, and the rest of the programme is equally successful.

No less telling is the strongly contoured account, most responsively played by the Scottish Chamber Orchestra under Jaime Laredo. This is offered on a superbly recorded medium-priced Pickwick compact disc, or alternatively on a bargain-priced Contour LP or cassette, in a collection of baroque 'String masterpieces'.

Il nascimento dell'Aurora (complete).
**(*) Erato Dig. NUM/*MCE* 751522 (2). Anderson, Zimmermann, Klare, Browne, Yamaj, Sol. Ven., Scimone.

Albinoni's instrumental music has ridden into popularity on the Baroque wave – not least the inescapable *Adagio* – but this is the first major vocal piece to be recorded. Written as a court celebration, probably on the birth of Princess Maria-Theresa, daughter of Charles VI of Austria, its 26 movements, mostly brief and lively, make up a substantial and attractive two-hour stage entertainment or 'festa pastorale'. This well-balanced live recording, made at Vicenza in Italy in 1983, puts forward a persuasive case despite some roughness in the choral singing (which is particularly distracting in the first chorus) and some intrusive audience applause. Soloists are first rate, the orchestra generally stylish.

Alkan, Charles (1813–88)

30 Chants: Allegretto, Op. 38/2; 2 Barcarolles, Op. 65/6, Op. 70/6. Esquisses, Op. 63/4, 10, 11, 20, 21, 28, 29, 41. Gigue, Op. 24. Marche No. 1, Op. 37; Les mois: Gros temps; Carnaval; Promenade sur l'eau, Op. 74/1–3. Nocturne No. 1, Op. 22. Petit conte. Préludes, Op. 31/11, 12, 13, 15, 16. Le tambour, Op. 50/2. Toccatina, Op. 75.
(M) *** HMV EG 270187-1/*4* [Ara. (M) 6523]. Ronald Smith (piano).

This collection of Alkan miniatures is certainly varied, though no one would choose to listen to it all at one sitting. Alkan collectors should note that most of these pieces have appeared before, though not in quite such realistic sound. Ronald Smith gives a dazzling account of *Carnaval* from *Les mois* at the beginning of the record, and he is in good form throughout. A useful complement to the larger-scale works Mr Smith has given us. (A fuller collection is available on HMV SLS 5100 (3) [Ara. 8127-3/*9127-3*]; the *Grande sonate*, Op. 33, is separate: HMV HQS 1326 [Ara. 8140/*9140*].)

Allegri, Gregorio (1582–1652)

Gustate et videte; Miserere mei; Missa Vidi turbam magnam.
**(*) Mer. 45 r.p.m. E45 77058. St John's College, Cambridge, Ch., Guest.

The brilliant and popular setting of the *Miserere* is here attractively coupled with two other examples of Allegri's church music which give a much fuller idea of his work. They are both impressive, the setting of the Mass sounding grandly sonorous (rather like late Palestrina) and the motet, *Gustate et videte*, more elaborate in its detail, with organ accompaniment. Performances go for strength and vigour rather than purity and polish, with trebles convincingly adopting forthright 'continental' tone. Good, wide-ranging recording.

Miserere.
*** Gimell **CDGIM 339** [id.]; CfP CFP/*TC-CFP* 40339 [Ang. RL/*4RL* 32122]. Tallis Scholars, Phillips – MUNDY: *Vox Patris caelestis*; PALESTRINA: *Missa Papae Marcelli.****
(M) *** Argo 417 160-1/*4* [id.]. King's College Ch., Willcocks (with *Collection****).
(*) DG Arc. Dig. **415 517-2; 415 517-1/*4* [id.]. Westminster Abbey Ch., Preston – PALESTRINA: *Missa Papae Marcelli* etc.****
(M) ** Pickwick Dig. **PCD 806**; CC/*CCTC* 7602. Pro Cantione Antiqua, Mark Brown – TALLIS: *Lamentations* etc.**
** HMV Dig. **CDC 747065-2**; EL 270095-1/*4* [Ang. DS/*4DS* 38086]. King's College, Cambridge, Ch., Cleobury – (with *Concert* **(*)).

Allegri's Renaissance motet has now achieved a popular status to rank it alongside Albinoni's *Adagio* and Pachelbel's *Canon*. Its admirers are, however, in good company, for the fourteen-year-old Mozart was so impressed when he heard it in the Sistine Chapel that he wrote the music out from memory so that it could be performed elsewhere. Neither the Pickwick nor the HMV performance is ideal. Both have good strong treble soloists, and the medium-priced Pickwick CD, although rather forwardly balanced, is very well recorded. The King's recording is acoustically mistier, but still lacks the ethereal radiance of the earlier King's performance on Argo with its arresting account of the treble solo by Roy Goodman. This has now been reissued within a splendid collection of King's recordings, mostly dating from the mid-1960s, including Tallis's 40-part motet, *Spem in alium* – see Concerts (Vocal Collections), below.

Finest of all is the Gimell/CfP version in which the treble solo is taken by a girl, Alison Stamp, and her memorable contribution is enhanced by the recording itself. The Tallis Scholars are ideally balanced, in Merton College Chapel, Oxford, and their conductor, Peter Phillips, emphasizes his use of a double choir by placing the solo group in the echoing distance, and the main choir directly in front of the listener. The contrasts are dramatic and hugely effective, with the solo treble soaring up, as if into the heavens. This superbly atmospheric account is even more telling against the background quiet of CD, and the firmer focus adds to the tangibility of the clearly separated double chorus and the magic of Alison Stamp's solo. However, on LP and tape the price of this issue is quartered and the cassette transfer is first class.

Preston's account with the Westminster choristers is not recorded in the Abbey but in the more intimate acoustic of All Saint's, Tooting. The performance is a fine one and, like the Argo and Gimell/CfP versions, uses the device of a double perspective to add evocation to the second group. The treble solo, though sung confidently, is more positive, less easeful in style; and the result is not quite so memorable as with its two main competitors. However, the coupling includes an outstanding performance of Palestrina's *Missa Papae Marcelli*. While the CD adds an extra sense of tangibility, the chrome cassette too is of the very highest quality, every bit the equal of the LP.

Alwyn, William (1905–85)

(i) *Rhapsody for piano quartet; String quartet No. 3; String trio.*
*** Chan. Dig. ABRD/*ABTD* 1153 [id.]. (i) David Willison; Qt of London.

These three works encompass half a century: the thick-textured *Rhapsody* comes from 1938, when Alwyn was in his thirties, while the *Third Quartet* was composed in 1984, the year before his death. The *String trio* comes in between, at a time when serial techniques were in vogue – but Alwyn's serialism (like Frank Martin's or Benjamin Frankel's) is skin deep and never strays far from a fundamentally tonal language. As one would expect, it is more expertly written than the earlier work and has many moments of real eloquence. The *Third Quartet* is the most important work on this record; like its two predecessors, it is a concentrated and thoughtful piece of very considerable substance, elegiac in feeling. The playing of the Quartet of London throughout (and of David Willison in the *Rhapsody*) is both committed and persuasive. As a recording, this is in the very first flight, and brings the musicians vividly into one's living-room.

Fantasy-Waltzes; 12 Preludes.
(*) Chan. Dig. **CHAN 8399; ABRD/*ABTD* 1125 [id.]. John Ogdon (piano).

The *Fantasy-Waltzes* were written after a visit to Troldhaugen, Grieg's home near Bergen. They are highly attractive pieces, particularly the haunting *Third in E minor* and are excellently played by John Ogdon, who is also responsible for a perceptive sleeve-note. There is very occasionally a trace of roughness in his *forte* tone (in the Eighth piece, for example), but there is great delicacy elsewhere and a command of colour and atmosphere. The *12 Preludes* are fluent, inventive, beautifully wrought pieces that ought to be better known and well repay investigation. The recording, made at the Maltings, Snape, is first rate and carries the imprimatur of the composer in whose presence it was made. Recommended.

Reminder. Alwyn's symphonies are still available on Lyrita: the *First* on SRCS 86; the *Second* and the *Sinfonietta* on SRCS 85; the *Third* with *The Magic Island* on SRCS 63; the *Fourth* and *Fifth* on SRCS 76; and the two *String quartets* on Chandos (ABRD/*ABTD* 1063 [id.]).

(i) *Invocations;* (ii) *A Leave-taking* (song cycles).
*** Chan. Dig. ABRD/*ABTD* 1117 [id.]. (i) Jill Gomez, John Constable; (ii) Anthony Rolfe-Johnson, Graham Johnson.

Almost as an offshoot from his opera, *Miss Julie* (Lyrita SRCS 121/2), Alwyn wrote these two song-cycles for the two singers who sang the principal roles of Julie and the Gamekeeper. In each, with a distinctive and unexpected choice of poems, Alwyn shows a keen ear for matching word-movement in music with a free arioso style. Notable in the tenor cycle, *A Leave-taking* (to words by the Victorian, John Leicester Warren), is *The ocean wood*, subtly evocative in its sea inspirations. The soprano cycle (to words by Michael Armstrong) is almost equally distinguished, leading to a beautiful *Invocation to the Queen of Moonlight*, which suits Jill Gomez's sensuous high soprano perfectly. Excellent performances, not least from the accompanist, and first-rate recording.

Arensky, Anton (1861–1906)

Piano trio No. 1 in D min., Op. 32
*** CRD CRD 1109/*CRDC 4109* [id.]. Nash Ens. – RIMSKY-KORSAKOV: *Quintet for piano and wind.****

Apart from the *Tchaikovsky variations*, Arensky is probably best known for this D minor *Piano trio*, published in 1894. The shades of Mendelssohn, Borodin and Tchaikovsky can be clearly discerned; while the invention is fertile and has an endearing period charm, at the same time the ideas have undoubted freshness. This account by members of the Nash Ensemble is so far the best we have encountered on record – and it has the benefit of first-class engineering, with the chrome cassette in the demonstration class. These fine players capture the Slav melancholy of the *Elegia*, and in the delightful scherzo Ian Brown is more delicate than – and every bit as nimble-fingered as – either Eileen Joyce on the pre-war Parlophone set or Leonard Pennario in Heifetz's celebrated RCA recording.

Rimsky-Korsakov's *Quintet for piano and wind* makes a most winning coupling.

Arne, Thomas (1710–78)

Thomas and Sally (ballad opera), complete.
(B) ** PRT GSGC/*ZCGC* 7059. Hazel Holt, Temperley, Taylor, Langridge, Northern Sinf., Preston.

This is the most famous of ballad operas, and rightly so. Its fresh simplicity –

both musical and dramatic – is hard to resist (sailor lover returns just in time to save his beloved from a fate worse than death), and since the early mono version disappeared from the catalogue many years ago, a stereo version is welcome. This one, recorded with excessive reverberation in a church, is not as polished as it might be, and the singing cast is not strong, but Simon Preston's direction is understanding. It is a pity that the libretto issued with the original recording (in 1970) has been omitted, without even a synopsis provided in its place. The sound is fully acceptable.

Arnold, Malcolm (born 1921)

Clarinet concerto No. 1; Horn concerto No. 2; Oboe concerto; Trumpet concerto.
(M) *** HMV EL 270264-1/*4*. Hilton, Civil, Hunt, Wallace, Bournemouth Sinf., Del Mar.

Malcolm Arnold has more than eighteen concertos to his credit, the one for guitar having both depth and atmosphere. Having been a trumpeter, Arnold writes with uncommon skill for the instrument, and the same brilliance characterizes John Wallace's dazzling playing. The work is relatively recent, following the *Eighth Symphony* (1979); like so much of his music, it has broad appeal, but touches a richer vein of imagination in the slow movement. The *Oboe concerto* (1952), written for Leon Goossens, is played with quite superb panache and virtuosity by Gordon Hunt who is surely second to none among present-day players; Janet Hilton in the *First Clarinet concerto* (1948) and Alan Civil in the *Second Horn concerto* (1956) are hardly less brilliant. This music is well crafted, enormously facile and at times glib, but Arnold has many admirers and they will find much to delight them in these performances. The recordings on both LP and tape are in the best tradition of the house.

Reminder. Julian Bream's pioneering 1961 recording of the *Guitar concerto* is still available, coupled with Giuliani (RCA GL/*GK* 13883); while John Williams's more recent account paired with Brouwer makes a splendid alternative on CBS (76715/*40*- [M/*MT* 36680]).

(i) *Symphony No. 2, Op. 40;* (ii) *Symphony No. 5, Op. 74.*
(M) *** HMV ED 290461-1/*4*. (i) Bournemouth SO, Groves; (ii) CBSO, composer.

This imaginative recoupling of two of Arnold's most impressive symphonies can be warmly welcomed. Both recordings date from the 1970s. They are here refurbished on long sides and the sound is wide in range, with plenty of presence. The *Second Symphony* is one of Malcolm Arnold's best pieces, far more complex in structure than it may initially seem. Like Shostakovich, Arnold opts in the first movement for an easy-going *Allegretto*, but the undemanding open-air manner conceals genuine symphonic purpose. So with the rest of the symphony, including the beautiful slow movement – much the longest – where a haunting tune with a distant echo of the second subject of Tchaikovsky's *Pathétique* builds to a formidable climax. Arnold has developed the habit of hiding his deeper emotions behind a bright, extrovert manner, and his *Fifth Symphony* brings out this dichotomy very clearly. It is a consciously elegiac work, written in memory of friends who died young; it contains some of his most intense and emotional music but remains easily approachable. The *tempestuoso* first movement, starting with a solitary oboe, is punctuated with bursts of anger and with percussion adding brilliance; it is both tenderly valedictory and nostalgic. So too the gratefully lyrical slow movement before the dazzling scherzo and the drum-and-fife finale. The composer secures an excellent response from the Birmingham orchestra, as Groves, in Bournemouth, is equally dedicated. The first-rate sound-balance is also well captured on the cassette, which is of EMI's finest XDR quality.

Arriaga, Juan (1806–26)

String quartets: Nos 1 in D min.; 2 in A; 3 in E flat.
(M) *(*) Ph. 412 054-1/*4*. Rasumovsky Qt.

Previous issues of the quartets, including the pioneering account of Nos 1 and 2 by the Guilet Quartet on Nixa, have never accommodated them on less than a side each. (The Chilingirians take four sides.) But the Rasumovskys' brisk tempi inevitably affect character, and the wonderfully thoughtful slow movement of the *D minor* sounds almost casual at this pace. Similarly, the opening of the *A major* sounds breathless and wanting in grace. If it must be taken with such brio, the lightest articulation and keenest sensitivity are needed if the music is to sparkle: here, the first part of the *Andante* is completely thrown away. At mid-price this will have its attractions for many collectors, but there is much more to Arriaga's genius than we are offered here. Excellent engineering.

Still recommended: The performances by the Chilingirian Quartet are polished and stylish, full of character and very well recorded (CRD CRD 1012/3; *CRDC 4012/3* [id.]).

Auber, Daniel (1782–1871)

Fra Diavolo (complete).
**(*) HMV Dig. EX 270068-3/*5* (2). Gedda, Mesplé, Dran, Berbié, Corazza, Baston, Laforge Ch. Ens., Monte Carlo PO, Soustrot.

In 1933 *Fra Diavolo* was turned into a film, with Laurel and Hardy featured as the inept pair of bandits, Beppo and Giacomo – but even that failed to bring it back into the general repertory. This lively complete recording presents it as a jolly romp, depending largely on a pastime which is evidently older in France than is generally realized: baiting the English tourist, a Milord and his wife.

With Fra Diavolo himself as a kind of swaggering Don Giovanni figure (as the name itself implies, 'Brother Devil'), the twists and turns have a Rossini-like sparkle without quite the same individuality of invention. Ensembles and choruses – well sprung by Soustrot – are generally more important than arias, though Diavolo has his big heroic piece at the opening of Act III and the second tenor, Lorenzo, has a charming Romance, once a favourite of Richard Tauber, but here done rather clumsily by Thierry Dran. Gedda in the name part is also strained, but the voice still rings well, and Mady Mesplé is less shrill than usual as the bright, pert Zerline (more overtones of *Don Giovanni*). Other singing too is flawed, but it is the teamwork that brings the fun. Atmospheric recording is, however, a little distant for capturing the full humour. There are excellent matching XDR tapes.

Auric, Georges (1899–1983)

Overture.

(M) *** Ph. Seq. 412 028-1/*4*. LSO, Dorati – FRANÇAIX: *Concertino*; MILHAUD: *Le Boeuf sur le toit*; SATIE: *Parade*.***

Georges Auric's *Overture*, although it seems to use part of a theme from Debussy's *Petite suite*, has more of the Montmartre atmosphere of Gershwin's *American in Paris*. It is irrepressibly gay, and its melodic freshness and a vivacious performance help to dispel the suspicion that it is a shade too long for its content. Vivid recording, on disc and tape alike. With splendid couplings this collection is more than the sum of its parts.

L'Eventail de Jeanne: (complete ballet, including music by Delannoy, Ferroud, Ibert, Milhaud, Poulenc, Ravel, Roland-Manuel, Roussel, Florent Schmitt).
Les Mariés de la Tour Eiffel: (complete ballet, including music by Honegger, Milhaud, Poulenc, Tailleferre).
❀ ₠ *** Chan. Dig. **CHAN 8356**; ABRD/*ABTD* 1119 [id.]. Philh. O, Simon.

Composite works, such as *Les Vendredis*, or the *Sellinger's Round* of Britten, Lennox Berkeley, Tippett and others, rarely prove a satisfactory whole; such is undoubtedly the case in both of the ballets recorded here – but what a delightful and exhilarating assortment they make! Only two of the pieces in *Les Mariés de la Tour Eiffel*, the product of a collaboration between Cocteau and *Les Six*, are longer than three minutes and most are much shorter; similarly, the longest of the feathers in *L'Eventail* (*Jeanne's Fan*), the *Kermesse valse* of Florent Schmitt, runs to barely five minutes (and, incidentally, is the weakest). This ballet was the idea of a Parisian society hostess who presented ten composers with a feather from her fan and invited them to write a piece each for her ballet pupils to dance to. A carefree spirit and captivating wit run through both these inventive scores. The Ravel *Fanfare* is among the shortest and most original of the contributions to *L'Eventail de Jeanne*, and there are many other charming things apart from the best-known number, Poulenc's *Pastourelle*. Roland-Manuel's inventive

Canarie is a real discovery and so, too, is Roussel's *Sarabande* – a haunting and lovely piece. Honegger's contribution to *Les Mariés*, a highly effective *Funeral march*, will also be new to most collectors; it incorporates the theme from Milhaud's *Wedding march* as well as the Waltz from Gounod's *Faust*. In fact these pieces are full of imagination and fun – even the Ibert *Valse* quotes the Ravel *Valses nobles*. Geoffrey Simon and the Philharmonia Orchestra give a very good account of themselves and the Chandos recording is little short of spectacular. Its detail is quite marvellously sharp on CD, and the chrome cassette is remarkably good, too.

Bach, Carl Philipp Emanuel (1714–88)

Flute concertos: in A min.; in B flat; in A; in G, Wq. 166/9.
(M) ** Ph. 412 043-1/*4* (2). Aurèle Nicolet, Netherlands CO, Zinman.

Aurèle Nicolet's set has the advantage of being complete. All four concertos derive from the 1750s and, as a glance at the Wotquenne numbers will show, they exist in alternative versions for cello and keyboard. The present arrangement was probably made at the behest of Frederick the Great. Nicolet uses a modern instrument. Both soloist and orchestra play extremely well, but with rather lively tempi these performances are less than ideal; with fresh recording they still give a good deal of pleasure, however, for they are always alive. On tape the layout is over a single double-length cassette and the transfers are of first-class quality.

Harpsichord concertos, Wq. 43/1–6.
*** HMV Dig. SLS 143486-3/*9* (2) [Ang. S/*4X2X* 3929]. Asperen, Melante '81 O.

Interesting repertoire. These six concertos come from 1771 during Bach's Hamburg period, and they are disturbingly original and volatile in temperament. Period instruments are used to produce an excellently light and transparent texture. The playing of Bob van Asperen is a delight: bright, vital and intelligent; and the recording is very fine indeed. An indispensable issue for collectors interested in this intriguing composer. The XDR-tape transfer places three concertos on each side of a single extended-length cassette. The high level catches the harpsichord clearly, but the orchestral focus is less sharp. A pity that chrome stock was not used.

Harpsichord concerto in G, Wq. 43/5.
(*) CRD **CRD 3411 [id.]. Pinnock, E. Concert – VIVALDI: *Trial between harmony and invention* etc.**(*)

An excellent performance of an attractive work, using original instruments, nicely balancing the claims of modern ears and total authenticity. This is a bonus for a pair of CDs containing all the concertos of Vivaldi's Op. 8 except *The Four Seasons*. The CD transfer smooths the treble a little but maintains most of the original focus.

6 Hamburg sinfonias, Wq. 182/1–6 (complete).
*** DG Arc. **415 300-2**; 2533 449 [id.]. E. Concert, Pinnock.

The sharp originality of C.P.E. Bach was never more apparent than in these symphonies, written after he had left the employ of the King of Prussia and at a time when he could at last please himself in adventurous writing. They are particularly striking in their unexpected twists of imagination, with wild, head-reeling modulations and sudden pauses which suggest the twentieth century rather than the eighteenth. The performing style of the English Concert is less abrasive than that of its principal rival, the Academy of Ancient Music, under Christopher Hogwood (whose Oiseau-Lyre set – DSLO 557/8 – has yet to appear on CD); it has more concern for eighteenth-century poise and elegance, without losing any degree of authenticity. All six symphonies are fitted on to one CD and LP (65 minutes), and the excellent 1980 analogue recording sounds splendidly fresh and clear in its remastered format.

4 Hamburg sinfonias, Wq. 182: Nos 1 in G; 2 in B flat; 3 in C; 5 in B min.
*(*) Tel. Dig. **ZK8. 42843**; AZ6/*CX4*. 42843. Liszt CO, Rolla.

All six symphonies are accommodated on Pinnock's Archiv record, whereas the Telefunken CD offers only four. By far the most interesting and unpredictable is the *B minor*, which also receives the liveliest advocacy. The performances are very expert – as one would expect from this ensemble – but a little dry, as are the recordings, which are bright but clinical. An inauspicious CD début.

Trio sonatas: in A min., Wq. 148; in D, Wq. 151.
(*) Denon Dig. **C37 7093 [id.]. Nicolet, Holliger, Jaccottet – J. S. BACH: *Trio sonatas.* **(*)

Originally written for flute and violin (or two violins) and continuo, these *Trio sonatas* sound attractive enough in the combination of flute and oboe, although one would have welcomed a greater degree of dynamic variation in the playing. This effect, however, is partly caused by the resonance. In spite of the catalogue numbering, the *D major Sonata* was probably written about a decade before the *A minor* work, yet it is undoubtedly the finer piece, showing Carl Philipp Emanuel's originality and flair to good effect. Both playing and recording are admirably vivid.

Trio sonata in G, Wq. 157.
*** CBS Dig. **MK 37813**; 37813/*40*- [id.]. Rampal, Stern, Ritter, Parnas – J. C. F., J. S. and W. F. BACH: *Trio sonatas.* ***

A particularly attractive work, opening with a fine *Adagio* and with a memorably spirited central movement. The playing is distinguished and the balance excellent. The CD is very clear and believable, but could have been improved with a shade more ambience. A recommendable and rewarding collection, with a good matching chrome tape.

Bach, Johann Christian (1735–82)

Oboe concerto in F.
(M) *** Ph. 412 354-1/*4*. Heinz Holliger, ECO, Leppard – FIALA: *Cor anglais concerto*; HUMMEL: *Introduction, theme and variations.****

The manuscript for this work was rediscovered in the British Museum and its authenticity is not certain. It is an attractive, if not an especially individual work, but with an appealing *Larghetto* and a florid finale, which Holliger despatches effortlessly. Indeed the playing is of the highest quality and Holliger contributes his own cadenzas. The sound is fresh, full and well balanced, not quite as transparent on tape as on disc, but still good.

Six 'favourite' overtures: Nos 1–3 in D; 4 in C; 5–6 in G.
*** 0-L **417 148-2**; DSLO/*DSLC* 525 [id.]. AAM, Hogwood.

J. C. Bach's *Six 'favourite' overtures* were published as a set in London in 1763 for use in the concert hall, although their original derivation was theatrical. They are all short and succinct Italian-style pieces in three movements (fast–slow–fast), and they show great variety of invention and imaginative scoring (using double wind, horns and strings). The performances here are characteristically alert and vivid and there are many features to stay in the mind: the trio for wind instruments in the finale of No. 1; the attractively robust outer movements of No. 3; the Vivaldi-like figuration of the finale of No. 4; the tripping strings in the *Andante* of No. 5. This is not an issue to play all at once; when dipped into, however, it offers delightful music played in a refreshingly spirited (and stylish) way. The analogue recording dates from 1978. It sounds impressively fresh, and there is also an excellent cassette.

Sinfonias, Op. 18/1–6.
(M) *** Ph. 412 045-1/*4*. Netherlands CO, Zinman.

The six *Sinfonias*, Op. 18, date from 1781. Some of the music derives from stage works, but the writing shows Bach at his most consistently inventive. The vigour of the music is exhilaratingly conveyed here and the element of contrast with slow movements, which are played with attractive simplicity, is strong. The recording is bright, fresh and clear, on both disc and the excellent tape.

Oboe quartet in B flat, Op. 8/6.
*** Denon Dig. **C 37 7119** [id.]. Holliger, Salvatore Qt – Michael HAYDN: *Divertimenti*; MOZART: *Adagio.****

The unpretentious elegance of J. C. Bach's *Oboe quartet* is beautifully caught by the incomparable Holliger and his stylish partners. An excellent coupling for even more compelling works, all vividly recorded.

Bach, Johann Christoph Friedrich (1732–95)

Sonata for fortepiano, flute and violin in C, HWV II/7.
*** CBS Dig. **MK 37813**; 37813/*40*- [id.]. Rampal, Stern, Ritter, Parnas – C. P. E., J. S. and W. F. BACH: *Trio sonatas.****

An engagingly inventive piece throughout its three movements, with the role of the fortepiano important enough to imply a solo concertante chamber piece. The artists play expertly and readily convey their enjoyment, while the balance is very adroit. The clarity of the recording is emphasized on CD without artificiality, but a little more ambient glow would have been welcome. The cassette is slightly smoother on top.

Bach, Johann Sebastian (1685–1750)

The Art of fugue, BWV 1080.
(M) ** Decca 414 326-1 (2). Stuttgart CO, Münchinger.

The Art of fugue; Canons, BWV 1072/8 and 1086/7; Musical offering, BWV 1079.
** DG Arc. Dig. **413 642-2** (3). Col. Mus. Ant., Goebel.

The Art of fugue; Canons, BWV 1072/8; 1086; Goldberg canons, BWV 1087.
**(*) DG Arc. 413 728-1/*4* [id.]. Col. Mus. Ant., Goebel.

There is no doubt that these Cologne performances sound wonderfully clean and present in the CD medium, and that they are for the most part brilliantly executed; however, the digital recording for *The Art of fugue* and the *Canons* is marginally more vivid and immediate than the analogue recording for the *Musical offering*. The three-disc volume in DG Archiv's Bach Edition on CD aptly gathers his two most towering examples of contrapuntal mastery and adds some attractive chips from the master's workbench in a collection of tiny canons discovered only recently. The rhythmic vigour of the playing of Musica Antiqua confounds the scholarly idea that this is music not intended for performance, though the bite of the authentic string-tone in *The Art of fugue* makes it inadvisable to hear the whole piece at a single sitting. In slow movements the expressiveness of the playing is welcome, though the expressive bulges of tone are at times exaggerated. In both the big works the movements are played in an unusual order, but effectively so.

In *The Art of fugue* the movements are divided between strings and solo harpsichord, and the two harpsichord players are often imaginative and expressive. Generally, this is much to be preferred to the somewhat joyless *Musical offering* with which it comes in harness. Here Reinhard Goebel places the *Canons* together and follows them with the *Trio sonata*. The *Ricercars* are played on the harpsichord by Henk Boum, an impressive artist who is somewhat austere in making no registration changes, but who has a strong grasp of the architecture. The six-part *Ricercar* is particularly fine, and the *Canons* are also very successful. However, the centrepiece of the *Musical offering* is the *Trio sonata*, and this reading is mannered and self-conscious (particularly in the slow movement). Marriner is greatly preferable.

Those concerned with Goebel's *Art of fugue* in its LP or cassette format are offered the newly found *Canons* but are not hampered with the *Musical offering*. The recording on LP is first rate, not quite so clean as on CD. The cassettes are generally smoothly transferred, a fully acceptable alternative.

For those seeking a mid-priced set, Münchinger's version from the mid-1960s has been reissued on Decca, and the sound is a good deal mellower than the newer Archiv recording. Its very sobriety has a cumulative impact, and the instrumentation is not without colour, with the fugues generally given to the strings and the canons to solo woodwind, varied with solo strings. After the incomplete quadruple fugue, Münchinger rounds off the work with the chorale prelude, *Vor deinen Thron*, in principle quite wrong, but moving in practice. The recording, from a vintage Decca period, is excellent.

Still recommended: Marriner's style of performance of *The Art of fugue* with the ASMF is profoundly satisfying, with finely judged tempi, unmannered phrasing and resilient rhythms. The recording is beautifully refined on disc, rather less reliably so on cassette, although still impressive (Ph. 6747 172/*7699 007* (2) [id.]).

Brandenburg concertos Nos 1–6, BWV 1046/51; Orchestral suites Nos 1–4, BWV 1066/9; (i) *Triple concerto in A min., BWV 1044*.

(*) DG Arc. **413 629-2 (4) [id.]. E. Concert, Pinnock; (i) with Beznosiuk, Standage.

This package of four CDs continues the DG Archiv Bach Edition. The merits of Pinnock's *Brandenburg concertos* are enhanced on the present CD transfer which is made at a high level, giving the impression of vivid presence. As performances, the orchestral *Suites* are somewhat more controversial and, as so often in performances on period instruments, there is a distinct loss of breadth and grandeur. In the *Triple concerto*, for the same forces as the *Fifth Brandenburg* (flute, violin, harpsichord and strings), Lisa Beznosiuk and Simon Standage are both excellent and Pinnock himself is at his very best. There is no doubt that the CD has wonderful clarity here.

Brandenburg concertos Nos 1–6.

*** DG Arc. Dig. **410 500/1-2**; 410 500/1-1/*4* [id.]. E. Concert, Pinnock.

*** Ph. **400 076/7-2**; 6769/*7654* 058 (2) [id.]. ASMF, Marriner.

*** HMV Dig. **CDC 747045-2** (Nos 1, 2, 6); **747046-2** (Nos 3, 4, 5) [id.]; EX 290005-3/*5* (2) [Ang. DSB/*4X2S* 3930]. Linde Cons., Linde.

*** Erato Dig. **ECD 88054** (1–3); **88055** (4–6); NUM/*MCE* 751342 (2). Amsterdam Bar. O, Koopman.

(*) Ph. Dig. **412 790-2; 412 790-1/*4* (2) [id.]. I Musici.

(*) O-L Dig. **414 187-2; 414 187-1/*4* [id.]. AAM, Hogwood.
(M) **(*) HMV ED 290374/5-1/*4* [Ang. SB/*4X2S* 3787]. Bath Fest. O, Menuhin.
(M) *(*) DG 413 185-1/*4* (2) [2707 112/*3370 030*]. BPO, Karajan.
*(*) Tel. Dig. **ZK8[CDT]42823**; AZ6/*CX4* 42823 (Nos 1, 2, 4); **ZK8[CDT]42840**; AZ6/*CX4* 42840 (Nos 3, 5, 6) [2635 620 (2)]. VCM, Harnoncourt.
(B) *(*) CfP CFPD 41 4448-3/*5* (2). Virtuosi of England, Davison.

Pinnock's is the most exhilarating set of the *Brandenburgs*, whether on original or modern instruments. It represents the very peak of his achievement as an advocate of authentic performance, with sounds that are clear and refreshing but not too abrasive. Interpretatively he tends to opt for fast speeds in outer movements, relatively slow in *Andantes* with a warm but stylish degree of expressiveness – as in the lovely account of the slow movement of *No. 6* – but from first to last there is no routine. Soloists are outstanding, and so is the recording. The chrome cassettes too are vivid and clear, if marginally less cleanly focused than the LPs, especially in *Concerto No. 5*. The CDs are transferred at a very high level, giving the sound great immediacy.

For those who still cannot quite attune their ears to the style of string playing favoured by the authentic school, Marriner's ASMF set should prove a fine alternative. Above all, these performances communicate warmth and enjoyment. In three of the concertos Marriner introduces such distinguished soloists as Henryk Szeryng, Jean-Pierre Rampal and Michala Petri, adding individuality without breaking the consistency of beautifully sprung performances. George Malcolm is an ideal continuo player. With superb playing, well-chosen speeds and refined recording, this is an excellent choice for those not insisting on the use of period instruments. The sound is equally natural on both LP and cassette. The compact discs, available individually, appear to have been separately mastered. The first, containing *Concertos Nos 1–3*, has each concerto separately banded, whereas the second has additional bands for individual movements. The sound is first class, but very slightly more refined in the later concertos, with *No. 5* sounding exceptionally realistic and the strings in *No. 6* captured more successfully than ever before on disc. In the earlier concertos the ear more readily notices artificial balances, and the trumpet in *No. 2* is rather too bright and forward; the strings in *No. 3* sound very natural, however; taken as a whole, this analogue recording has responded well to its digital remastering.

The Linde Consort is one of the most stylish and responsive of authentic performing groups working in Europe and their set of *Brandenburgs* sounds very fresh and vivid on CD. It can be warmly recommended with its sprung rhythms and generally well-chosen tempi, and these compact discs deserve to rank alongside Pinnock's set. The recorded sound is also first rate on LP, with matching tapes.

Relaxed and intimate, Koopman's account is also among the most attractive using period instruments, another good alternative to Pinnock's outstanding version for those who prefer expressive contrasts to be less sharply marked.

Like Pinnock, Koopman is not afraid to read *Affettuoso* on the slow movement of *No. 5* as genuinely expressive and warm, though without sentimentality. As with Pinnock, players are one to a part, with excellent British soloists included in the band. In the *Third Concerto*, Koopman effectively interpolates the *Toccata in G*, BWV 916, as a harpsichord link between the two movements. The sound on CD is immediate, but not aggressively so. There are good chrome cassettes but the quality is marginally less clean on top than in the disc versions.

I Musici are joined by distinguished soloists. Heinz Holliger brings expressive finesse (and nicely judged embellishments) to the principal oboe role, while Hermann Baumann leads the superb horn playing in *No. 1*. Guy Touvron's trumpet bravura is as arresting in *No. 2* as it is stylish, and the recording balances him effectively with the oboe and recorder. The readings are strong and direct, with allegros powerfully energetic at generally fast speeds, the string playing heard at its finest in the extremely energetic finale of *No. 3*, which also reveals clear antiphonal detail. The sound is very vivid, close and immediate, without being aggressive, matching the performances. Where I Musici fall short is on rhythmic imagination in slow movements, with bass lines at times too evenly stressed, perhaps owing to the absence of a director, but the plainness and honesty of these invigorating accounts will appeal to many. The digital recording is strikingly 'present' on CD, but the slightly smoother chrome cassettes also make an excellent impression.

Though Hogwood's set of *Brandenburgs* is notably less persuasive than Pinnock's, also on period instruments, with often brisk speeds, more metrical and less well sprung, the distinctive point is that unlike most rivals he has chosen the original Cothen score rather than the usual text as sent to the Margrave of Brandenburg. Besides many detailed differences, this version has no *Polonaise* in the *First Concerto*, and the harpsichord cadenza in *No. 5* is much less elaborate, 'more convincingly proportioned' as Hogwood himself suggests. Some may prefer the extra directness of Hogwood's approach over Pinnock's, with charm never a part of the mixture, more abrasive string-tone and brisker, less expressive slow movements. Excellent recorded sound, with the expected added presence on CD. The chrome cassettes match the LPs fairly closely, although there is slight loss of refinement in the upper range.

Menuhin's 1969 set with the Bath Festival Orchestra was reissued for the Tercentenary on two separate discs and tapes. The remastered recording still sounds well and has not lost its bloom. The hint of overloading from the horns in *No. 1* is perhaps slightly more noticeable (especially on the cassettes, which have less upper range than the discs), but otherwise the sound is well balanced and clean. Rarely have the *Brandenburg* rhythms been sprung more joyfully, and tempi are uncontroversially apt. The soloists are outstanding, and there is a spontaneity here that is consistently satisfying.

Karajan's polished and lively performances are certainly not for authenticists. They are, of course, beautifully played and represent an orchestral tradition now likely to disappear. The recording is full and vivid, the sound smooth and sleek rather than sharply detailed.

It is a sign of the maturing art of authentic performance that Harnoncourt – once a pioneer in the field – in his newest digital recording for Telefunken now sounds so laboured. Speeds are slow, rhythms heavy. There is some expert playing, both solo and ensemble, but the artificially bright and clinically clear recording gives an aggressive projection to the music making.

Reissued in a double album, the bargain-priced CfP set by the Virtuosi of England (recorded in 1972) offers robust and lively playing. The brisk, unfussy approach of the conductor, Arthur Davison, is impressive, but these performances in the last analysis lack individuality.

(i) *Brandenburg concertos Nos 1, 4 and 6;* (ii) *Concerto for flute, violin and harpsichord, BWV 1044;* (iii) *Double violin concerto in D min., BWV 1043.*

(B) * DG Walkman *413 421-4* [id.]. (i) Mun. Bach O, Karl Richter; (ii) Nicolet, Baumgartner, Kirkpatrick, Lucerne Fest. Strings; (iii) Melkus, Rantos, Vienna Capella Academica.

Brandenburg concertos Nos 2, 3 and 5; Orchestral suites Nos 2–3.

(B) * DG Walkman *413 143-4* [id.]. Mun. Bach O, Karl Richter.

There are many splendid bargains in DG's much-lauded Walkman series of double-length chrome tapes, but these are not among them. Karl Richter here perpetuates the heavy German style. In the *Brandenburg concertos* he is rhythmically rigid and, though there is some fine solo playing – notably the horns in *No. 1* – these performances cannot be recommended in a crowded market. In the *Suites* (with Aurèle Nicolet making a distinguished contribution to *No. 2*) the metronomic approach is consistent and the lack of double-dotting in the overtures makes them sound heavier still. The performance of the *Double violin concerto* by Eduard Melkus and Spiros Rantos, with the Vienna Capella Academica, which is included on the first tape, is in a different class altogether, fresh and stylish; but the *Triple concerto*, BWV 1044, is acceptable rather than distinctive. The sound throughout is very good.

(i) *Brandenburg concerto No. 5;* (ii) *Concerto for oboe and violin, BWV 1060;* (iii) *Double violin concerto in D min., BWV 1043;* (i) *Suites Nos 2 in B min.; 3 in D, BWV 1067/8.*

(B) **(*) Ph. On Tour *412 895-4*. (i) ASMF, Marriner; (ii) Holliger, Grumiaux, New Philh. O, De Waart; (iii) Szeryng, Rybar, Winterthur Coll. Mus., Szeryng.

The Philips 'On Tour' double-length chrome tape series is the Philips equivalent to DG's Walkman series, offered at a comparable bargain price. This generous Bach collection is infinitely preferable to the Walkman/Richter offering (see above) and makes an attractive concert. With distinguished soloists – William Bennett in the *B minor Suite* and Holliger and Grumiaux in BWV 1060 – the performances are consistently stylish and spirited. The sound too is generally excellent, though the faithfulness of the tape transfers reveals the much earlier recording date of the *Double violin concerto*, where the quality is less ample in texture than the other recordings, which all come from the 1970s.

Flute concertos: in C (from *BWV 1055*)*; in E min.* (from movements of *Cantata No. 35*)*; in G min.* (from *BWV 1056*).
**(*) CBS Dig. IM/*IMT* 39022 [id.]. Rampal, Ars Rediviva, Munclinger.

If you enjoy transcriptions of Bach for the flute – and they are easy to enjoy here – it is difficult to imagine them being better played than by Jean-Pierre Rampal. The *C major* and *G minor Concertos* derive respectively from the *A major* and *F minor Harpsichord concertos*. Rampal is wonderfully nimble in the opening allegro of BWV 1055 and gives a radiantly beautiful account of the slow movement cantilena of BWV 1056. Munclinger, who made the arrangements, provides sympathetic accompaniments with the Ars Rediviva of Prague, although rhythmically he does not quite display Rampal's lightness of touch. The recording is very good indeed and beautifully balanced. It sounds especially well on the chrome tape.

Concerto for flute, violin and harpsichord in A min., BWV 1044; Concerto for oboe and violin in C min., BWV 1060; Concerto for oboe d'amore in A, BWV 1055.
*** DG Arc. Dig. **413 731-2**; 413 731-1/*4* [id.]. Beznosiuk, Standage, Reichenberg, Pinnock, E. Concert.

As in their other Bach concerto recordings for DG Archiv, Pinnock and the English Concert prove the most persuasive practitioners of authentic performance, both vigorous and warm with consistently resilient rhythms. This collection of works transcribed from better-known originals features two wind soloists with tone warmer and less abrasive than many using baroque instruments. The recorded sound is exceptionally vivid in its sense of presence, particularly on CD.

Guitar concerto in E (arr. from *Violin concerto, BWV 1042*). *Aria from BWV 1003.*
** CBS Dig. **MK 39560**; IM/*IMT 39560* [id.]. John Williams, ASMF, Sillito – HANDEL and MARCELLO: *Concertos.***

This is not an especially effective arrangement: the guitar has to be artificially balanced with the modern string texture. Williams makes the strongest impression in the *Adagio* and in the *Aria* from the *A minor Sonata for unaccompanied violin*, which is offered as an encore. The recording is good. The chrome tape is not as extended in the upper range as the LP.

Harpsichord concertos Nos 1 in D min., BWV 1052; 5 in F min., BWV 1056; Double harpsichord concertos Nos 1–2, BWV 1060/1; Triple harpsichord concertos Nos 1–2, BWV 1063/4; Quadruple harpsichord concerto, BWV 1065. Violin concertos Nos 1–2; Double violin concerto, BWV 1041/3.
(*) DG Arc. Dig. **413 634-2 (3). Pinnock, Gilbert, Mortensen, Kraemer, Standage, Willcock, E. Concert.

Pinnock's Bach has undoubted panache, offering scholarship tempered with excellent musicianship, even if there are times when his playing can be too fast and unrelenting. This compilation, which Archiv prepared for their tercentenary Bach Edition on CD, collects the major keyboard concertos plus the two violin concertos and the *Double concerto* in what are for the most part brilliant performances. In the violin concertos the tempi will be too extreme for some tastes, though these accounts are generally to be preferred to those of Jaap Schröder/Christopher Hogwood, in which slow movements are fast and shorn of romanticism, and the nasal and raw string-tone is unpleasing. Of the period-instrument performances, this still leads the field, and the CD has great lucidity and presence.

Harpsichord concertos Nos 1 in D min., BWV 1052; 2 in E, BWV 1053; 5 in F min., BWV 1056.

(M) *** HMV ED 290361–1/*4* [(d.) Ang. Sera. 4XG 60410]. George Malcolm, Menuhin Fest. O, Menuhin.

George Malcolm's set of the concertos was made in the early 1970s. The individuality of the solo playing is splendidly matched by Menuhin's imaginative accompaniments, warm and energetic, and the recording balance is first class, with the harpsichord image most believable in its relationship with the accompanying group. The serene performance of the famous *Largo* from the *F minor Concerto* is characteristic of the inspirational music-making, while Malcolm's dexterity in allegros is exhilarating. The cassette is especially successful, and this offers one of the most desirable collections of Bach's keyboard concertos currently available. Highly recommended, except to those who must have acerbic string timbre.

Clavier concertos Nos 1 in D min., BWV 1052; 4 in A, BWV 1055; 5 in F min., BWV 1056.

*** Denon Dig. **C37 7236**. András Schiff (piano), ECO, Malcolm.

If Bach's keyboard concertos are to be given on the piano rather than the harpsichord – and there are many listeners for whom the substitution is an agreeable one – they could hardly be more persuasively presented than here. The recording is beautifully balanced, the sound absolutely truthful, fresh, vivid and clean. András Schiff never tries to pretend that he is not using a modern piano, and the lightness of his touch and his control of colour are a constant delight to the ear. Malcolm's accompaniments are both alert and resilient, and the actual sound of the strings is perfectly in scale. Outer movements have splendid vigour and transparency; slow movements are expressive and evocative in their control of atmosphere. Schiff's decoration in the *Larghetto* of the *A major* is admirable, as is his simple eloquence in the famous cantilena of the *F minor Concerto*. This is highly recommended, and it is an example of digital recording at its most believable, although it is more noticeable on CD that the upper strings are soft-grained and not brightly lit.

Clavier concertos Nos 2 in E, BWV 1053; 4 in A, BWV 1055.
(M) ** CBS 60036/*40*- [MS 7294]. Glenn Gould (piano), Columbia SO, Golschmann.

Clavier concertos Nos 3 in D, BWV 1054; 5 in F min., BWV 1056; 7 in G min., BWV 1058.
(M) ** CBS 60028/*40*- [MS 7001]. Glenn Gould, Columbia SO, Golschmann.

Gould's recordings date from the end of the 1960s and the microphones were rather too close to put much air round the strings; the clear piano timbre is precisely caught. Allegros are forcefully energetic; slow movements have imaginative touches, and the famous cantilena of BWV 1056 is attractively cool. Gould's crisp articulation, effectively and cleanly decorated, is unique, and the spare piano timbre is obviously recorded as he intended. In their way these performances are refreshing, although the vocalise remains an irritant.

Double harpsichord concertos Nos 1–3, BWV 1060/2; Triple harpsichord concertos 1–2, BWV 1063/4; Quadruple harpsichord concerto in A min., BWV 1065.
*** Ph. 6769/*7654* 075 [id.]. Koopman, Mathot, Ernst, Collyer, Amsterdam Bar. Ens.

Koopman's collection of concertos for two, three and four harpsichords and strings was one of the first issues which established the vigour and stylishness of the talented Amsterdam Baroque Ensemble. For anyone wanting a complete set of authentic performances of these consistently refreshing works this is an excellent choice, with speeds well considered, refined playing – not least from the soloists – and first-rate recording, on both disc and tape.

Double harpsichord concertos: Nos 1 in C min.; 2 in C; 3 in C min., BWV 1060/2.
(*) DG Arc. Dig. **415 131-2; 2534/*3311* 002 [id.]. Pinnock, Gilbert, E. Concert.

The character of the Pinnock performances is robust, with the balance forward and the performances very strongly projected. The combination of period instruments and playing of determined vigour certainly makes a bold impression, but the relatively unrelaxed approach to the slow movements will not appeal to all ears. The third of the double concertos, BWV 1062, is an alternative version of the *Concerto for two violins*, BWV 1043; though the keyboard format has a certain fascination, it is no match for the original, especially in the beautiful slow movement, with – as here – squeezed accompanying chords. The lively recording has very striking presence on CD, but is also very effective on LP and cassette.

Double clavier concertos Nos 1 in C min., BWV 1060; 2 in C, BWV 1061; Triple clavier concerto in D min., BWV 1063; Quadruple clavier concerto in A min., BWV 1065.
*** DG Dig. **415 655-2**; 415 655-1/*4* [id.]. Eschenbach, Frantz, Oppitz, Schmidt (pianos), Hamburg PO, Eschenbach.

Helmut Schmidt, the famous German politician, has been in the recording studio before to record, very creditably, Mozart's *Triple piano concerto* for EMI. Here, as fourth soloist in the *Quadruple concerto*, he again joins his friends, Eschenbach and Frantz, alongside Gerhard Oppitz. This work opens the concert – and very enjoyable it is, with soloists and musical director Eschenbach showing they appreciate the colour of the Vivaldi work (Op. 3/10, originally for four violins) on which it is closely based. The other concertos are presented with comparable vigour (the finale of the *Triple concerto* is particularly exhilarating) with slow movements correspondingly thoughtful and responsive. The accompanying notes make the point that these artists came together to celebrate Bach's Tercentenary. Their appreciation and identification communicate vividly here, and all those who enjoy Bach played on the piano cannot fail to respond. The recording is rather resonant but it attractively bathes the music making in a genial glow, and the spirit of this record is the very opposite of that atmosphere of scholarly rectitude that too often pervades more authentic Bach playing. On CD the reverberation offers no problems and, although detail is not sharp, the overall sound-picture is very believable.

Triple harpsichord concertos Nos 1 in D min.; 2 in C, BWV 1063/4; Quadruple harpsichord concerto in A min., BWV 1065.

(*) DG Arc. Dig. **400 041-2; 2534/*3311* 001 [id.]. Pinnock, Gilbert, Mortensen, Kraemer, E. Concert.

Like the *Double concertos* above, this music was originally conceived for other instruments. The *C major Concerto*, BWV 1064, was based on a triple violin concerto, and in the *Quadruple concerto* Bach drew on Vivaldi's Op. 3/10, originally for four violins. The slightly aggressive style of the music making – everything alert, vigorously paced and forwardly projected – emphasizes the bravura of Bach's conceptions. The sound too has striking presence and clarity, yet is not without atmosphere. The cassette matches the disc very closely. The CD adds to the feeling of presence and the sound has added depth, but the aggressive feeling remains and the listener is the more conscious that the balance is artificial and microphone-aided.

Triple clavier concertos Nos 1 in D min., 2 in C, BWV 1063/4; Quadruple clavier concerto in A min., BWV 1065.

(*) EMI **CDC 747063-2 [id.]; 2C 069 73064 [Ang. DS/*4XS* 37897]. Béroff, Collard, Tacchino, Rigutto, Paris Ens., Wallez.

Another record for those who prefer their Bach on the piano, and very enjoyable it is too, given such spirited and refreshing playing from this distinguished French team. The balance is skilfully managed and enables the keyboard part-writing to be heard with the utmost clarity and to vivid effect. The orchestral playing is not particularly distinguished; however, but the excellence of the pianists who dominate the proceedings outweighs any reservations. The sound quality has additional clarity in CD, though in both formats this record gives pleasure.

Oboe concertos: in A (from BWV 1055); in D min. (from BWV 1059); in F (from BWV 1053).
*** Ph. Dig. **415 851-2**; 6514/*7337* 304 [id.]. Heinz Holliger, ASMF, Iona Brown.

Stylish, pointed performances – leaning at times towards Romantic expressiveness in slow movements – of two concertos better known in their harpsichord versions (BWV 1053 and 1055) and a third reconstructed from seemingly independent movements. The outer movements of the latter owe their origins to the *Cantata No. 35* – Bach was always transcribing cantata movements for his concertos – while the lovely slow movement is well known in two forms: as the central movement of the *F minor Harpsichord concerto* and as the *Sinfonia* from *Cantata No. 156*, where the oboe is soloist. Excellent recording, with the CD gaining from the silent background; but both the LP, with immaculate surfaces, and the chrome cassette are also first rate in all respects.

(i) *Violin concertos Nos 1–2, BWV 1041–2;* (ii) *Violin concerto in G min.* (from *BWV 1056*); (i; ii) *Double violin concerto, BWV 1053;* (i; iii) *Double concerto for violin and oboe in D min., BWV 1060.*
(M) *** HMV EG 290530-1/*4* [(d.) Ang. S/*4XS* 37076; S/*4XS* 36841]. (i) Perlman, (ii) Zukerman, (iii) Black; ECO, Barenboim.

This mid-priced reissue in the HMV Master series offers exceptional value in combining the Perlman/Zukerman recordings of BWV 1041–3, and also including Zukerman as soloist in the *G minor Concerto* (arranged from the *F minor Harpsichord concerto* with its sublime *Arioso* slow movement). The two famous soloists, with their friend and colleague Barenboim, are inspired to give a magic performance of the *Double violin concerto*, one in which their artistry is beautifully matched in all its intensity. The slow movement in particular has rarely sounded so ravishing on record. Perlman is also impressive in the slow movement of the *E major* solo *Violin concerto*, but in BWV 1056 neither he nor Zukerman is quite so impressive without the challenge of the other. The other double concerto, for violin and oboe, is a transcription of the *C minor Concerto for two harpsichords*, and here oboist Neil Black makes a distinguished contribution. The outer movements tend to be fastish and the slow movement is expressive and eloquent. Barenboim provides the most sympathetic support throughout, and this is a Bach record to cherish. The engineers provide a full and agreeable ambience that preserves an excellent balance between soloists and orchestra. This is in every way greatly to be preferred to Perlman's latest CD (see below). The remastered recording sounds somewhat dry but the balance remains good.

Violin concertos Nos 1 in A min.; 2 in E; Double violin concerto in D min., BWV 1041/3.
*** HMV Dig. **CDC 747011-2** [id.]; ASD/*TC-ASD* 143520-1/*4* [Ang. DS/*4XS* 37989]. Mutter, Accardo, ECO, Accardo.

*** DG Arc. Dig. **410 646-2**; 410 646-1/*4* [id.]. Standage, Wilcock, E. Concert, Pinnock.
(M) *** HMV ED 290146-1/*4* [Ang. Ser. S/*4XG* 60258]. Menuhin, Ferras, Fest. CO, or Robert Masters CO.
(M) **(*) Pickwick Dig. **PCD 808**; CC/*CCTC* 7607. Laredo, Scottish CO.
(B) **(*) CfP CFP 41 4465-1/*4*. Sillito, Bean, Virtuosi of England, Davison.
(M) ** Ph. 412 915-1/*4*. Szeryng, Hasson, ASMF, Marriner.
*(**) O-L Dig. **400 080-2**; DSDL/*KSDLC* 702 [id.]. Schröder, Hirons, AAM, Hogwood.
*(*) Denon Dig. **C 37 7096** [id.]. Kantorow, Cenariu, Mun. CO, Stadlmair.
*(*) Ph. Dig. **411 108-2**; 411 108-1/*4* [id.]. Kremer, ASMF.

It is not currently fashionable to play Bach with the degree of romantic warmth that Anne-Sophie Mutter adopts, but her range of tone as well as the imagination of her phrasing is extremely compelling. Her performance of the slow movement of the *E major Concerto* is finer than any other version, with marvellous shading within a range of hushed tones. Accardo's accompaniment here (as throughout this collection) is splendidly stylish and alert, as the opening of the first movement of BWV 1042 readily shows. In principle the slow movement of the *Double concerto* – where Accardo takes up his bow to become a solo partner, scaling down his timbre – is too slow, but the result could hardly be more beautiful, helped by full EMI recording which gives richness and body to the small ECO string band. The soloists are rather forwardly balanced, but in all other respects this issue is technically impressive. The CD is strikingly fresh and clear and gives the artists great presence. The equivalent cassette (though not chrome) is one of EMI's best. The level drops slightly on side two, but the sound remains full and vivid.

If you want the three favourite Bach *Violin concertos* on original instruments, then Pinnock's disc is the one to go for. Rhythms are crisp and lifted at nicely chosen speeds – not too fast for slow movements – but, as so often with authentic performances of violin concertos, the edge will not please everyone. Good clear recording.

Menuhin's (1960) record was made when he was in excellent technical form. He directs the orchestra as well as appearing as principal soloist, and it is in the accompaniments that these accounts fall slightly short, with outer movements not as rhythmically resilient as Accardo's. Nevertheless Menuhin's playing still gives great pleasure, with its balance of humanity and classical sympathy. Ferras matches his timbre to Menuhin's perfectly in the *Double concerto* and their playing cannot be faulted on minor points of style. HMV have freshened the recording, losing something in bass resonance, but providing a sound-picture that belies the record's age. The cassette too is admirably managed, the sound wide-ranging, yet full-bodied.

On the mid-priced Pickwick CD, Laredo directs sympathetic traditional performances of the three concertos, which are lively in outer movements, warmly expressive without being sentimental in slow movements. The excellent Scottish Chamber Orchestra is well recorded with a realistic, well-judged balance except for the rather too prominent harpsichord continuo which, at times, in its relentlessness detracts from the generally well-sprung rhythms. Laredo's tone is a little thin at times, but that is a fault on the right side of Bach.

Kenneth Sillito and Hugh Bean, both of them distinguished orchestral leaders as well as fine virtuosi, are outstandingly successful as soloists in the *Double concerto*. This is one of the most beautiful accounts of the lovely slow movement of that masterpiece on record, deeply felt but pure and restrained. Though the accompaniments are not always ideally resilient, the performances can all be warmly recommended for a well-recorded bargain issue. The solo concertos are shared, Kenneth Sillito playing the *A minor Concerts* and Hugh Bean the *E major*.

Szeryng's mid-1970s performances with Marriner – reissued at mid-price on Philips – have the advantage of full-bodied modern recording which produces an excellent balance between soloists and orchestra and a warm spread of sound. In spontaneity and depth of feeling, however, they do not displace Menuhin's HMV reissue, nor indeed the Classics for Pleasure set by Sillito and Bean. The Philips issue includes the *Air* from the *Orchestral suite No. 3* as a short encore. The sound is equally vivid on disc and cassette.

With authentic sound uncompromisingly abrasive and speeds generally brisk and inflexible, the Academy of Ancient Music's version of the *Violin concertos* is the opposite of Mutter's expressive approach. For some it apparently stands as a refreshing revelation, but sample the slow movement of the *Double concerto* – like a siciliana – before you buy. Bright and clear recording to match, with the edge of string sound unrelenting. There is little to choose between LP and cassette, while the compact disc with its silent background puts the music making into even sharper relief.

Kantorow is an excellent violinist with fine imagination and pure, sweet tone; however, when Stadlmair's accompaniments are rhythmically so stodgy and the speeds so leaden, particularly in the slow movements of the two solo concertos, it provides poor competition in a much-recorded coupling. Sigrid Cenariu, the second violinist in the *Double concerto*, has a tight but pronounced vibrato which brings a marked contrast with Kantorow.

Kremer adopts (by electronic means) both solo roles in the *Double concerto* and thus the interplay of human personality is lost in this most human of works. Kremer also directs the accompanying ensemble, so these interpretations cannot be accused of any kind of artistic inconsistency – indeed, they have the forward thrust of a determined advocate, in slow movements as well as allegros which are extremely vigorous. The end effect is relentless and, in spite of excellent recording – the CD is exceptionally vivid – this collection offers only limited musical rewards.

Violin concertos: in D min., BWV 1052; in G min., BWV 1056; (i) *Double concerto for violin and oboe in D min., BWV 1060.*

*(*) HMV Dig. **CDC 747073-2**; EL 270149-1/*4* [Ang. DS/*4XS* 37971]. Perlman; (i) Ray Still; Israel PO.

All three concertos are better known in harpsichord versions. These recordings, dry and close to the point of aggressiveness, are far less acceptable than Perlman's own earlier versions of the two D minor works with the ECO under Barenboim. Though he plays with imagination, he is heavier this time. The other concerto, the violin version of the *F minor Harpsichord concerto*, is even heavier in the first two movements, with the *Largo* almost coming to a halt. The recordings probably sound best in their XDR-cassette transfers, which smooth the treble somewhat.

Double violin concerto, BWV 1043; Double concerto for violin and oboe, BWV 1060.

** CBS Dig. **MK 37278**; 37278/*40*- [id.]. Zukerman, Stern, Killmer, St Paul CO, James – VIVALDI: *L'estro armonico: Double concerto.***

Zukerman – who is the music director of the St Paul Chamber Orchestra – has made this group a fair rival in its musical achievement to the Minneapolis Orchestra in the other city of the yoked pair of 'twins'. Unfortunately, the recording of his CBS digital collection underlines the weightiness of the bass which is uncomfortably heavy for Bach. Solo work is a delight, but there are better versions of all these concertos.

Double concerto for violin and oboe in D min., BWV 1060; Easter oratorio: Sinfonia.

*** Ph. Dig. **411 466-2**; 6514/*7337* 311 [id.]. Holliger, Kremer – VIVALDI: Oboe, Violin concertos.***

Double concerto for violin and oboe; Triple concerto for flute, violin and harpsichord in A min., BWV 1044.

(*) Denon Dig. **C37 7064 [id.] Kantorow, Bourgue, Adorján, Dreyfus, Netherlands CO, Bakels.

Holliger is at his distinguished best in the *Double concerto* and Kremer makes a good partner in a fresh performance with a serene central *Adagio*. But what makes this coupling memorable is the improvisatory quality which Holliger brings to his beautiful account of the solo in the *Sinfonia* from the *Easter oratorio* which sounds just like the slow movement of a concerto. The recording is first class, the ambience nicely judged, and the oboe is especially tangible in the CD format, though both LP and tape are also excellent.

Maurice Bourgue is also an outstanding artist and in the Denon version the *Double concerto* is dominated by him, with phrasing and tonal nuances that consistently ensnare the ear. Jean-Jacques Kantorow, winner of many international prizes, proves another outstanding artist, not quite so individual but producing immaculate playing. The *Triple concerto* is less compellingly done, and there one is more aware of the often inappropriately beefy style of the Netherlands Chamber Orchestra, as recorded here. The flautist, András Adorján, Hungarian-born but trained in Denmark, is the leader, with Kantorow matching his rhythmic freshness and evenness of tone. Huguette Dreyfus's harpsichord is rather aggressively recorded, but otherwise the sound is first rate.

The Musical Offering, BWV 1079.
*** Ph. **412 800-2**; 9500 585 [id.]. ASMF, Marriner.
*** HMV Dig. EL 290341-1/*4*. Linde Consort.
** Tel. AZ6.41124 [id.]. VCM, Harnoncourt.

Sir Neville Marriner uses his own edition and instrumentation: strings with three solo violins, solo viola and a solo cello; flute, organ and harpsichord. He places the three-part *Ricercar* (scored for organ) at the beginning and the six-part *Ricercar* at the very end, scored for strings. As the centrepiece comes the *Trio sonata* (flute, violin and continuo), and on either side the *Canons*. Thurston Dart advocated playing the three-part *Ricercar* on the fortepiano (as it was probably heard in Potsdam). The actual performance here is of high quality, though some of the playing is a trifle bland. It is, however, excellently recorded and overall must be numbered among the most successful accounts of the work. Although originally an analogue master (1980), in its CD format it is given additional presence and clarity.

Hans-Martin Linde draws on the thinking of the American scholar, Ursula Kirkendale, whose conclusion favours the same sequence of movements as that adopted by Spitta – not that this is necessarily a first consideration since, with a little effort, the listener can exercise his own preferences in playing the disc. Generally speaking, Linde is as stylish and accomplished as any of his rivals, and he and his six colleagues are to be preferred to the Musica Antiqua, Köln, and have a warmer sound, too. The cassette, transferred at a very high level indeed, is most vivid and clear.

On Telefunken a remastering of the 1970 recording by the Vienna Concentus Musicus. The textures emerge with marginally greater transparency and lucidity. This is an eminently acceptable version, and offers some excellent keyboard playing from Herbert Tachezi in the two *Ricercari*. That Harnoncourt is pragmatic and not ultimately purist emerges in his choice of a cello rather than viola da gamba, and a viola and tenor viola for some of the *Canons*. The general consensus of opinion seems to favour this version in preference to the Musica Antiqua, Köln, which DG chose for their Bach Edition – and rightly so.

Orchestral suites Nos 1–4, BWV 1066–9.
*** Erato Dig. **ECD 88048**/9; NUM/*MCE* 750762 (2) [id.]. E. Bar. Soloists, Gardiner.
*** HMV Dig. EX 270310-3/*5* (2). ASMF, Marriner.
(M) *** Decca Jub. 414 248-1/*4* (2) [id.]. ASMF, Marriner.
(B) *** CfP CFPD 41 4440-3/*5* [Ang. Sera. SIB/*4X2G* 6085 (2)]. Bath Fest. O, Menuhin.
(*) German HM **1C 567 199930-1; 1C 165 99930-1. Petite Bande, Kuijken.
(*) DG Arc. **410 708-2; 410 708-1/*4*. E. Concert, Pinnock.

(*) Capriccio **10 011/2 (available separately). Leipzig New Bach Coll., Pommer.
*(*) Decca Dig. **414 505-2**; 414 505-1/*4* (2) [id.]. SCO, Münchinger.
*(*) Tel. Dig. **Z K8 43051/2**; AZ6/*CX4* 43051/2. VCM, Harnoncourt.

Gardiner's is an outstanding set using period instruments. In his characteristic manner allegros tend to be fast and lightly sprung, with slower movements elegantly pointed. Though the edginess of baroque violins using a squeeze technique on sustained notes makes for some abrasiveness, Gardiner avoids the extremes which mark even Pinnock's English Concert version on CD. Thanks to full and immediate recording, textures are fresh and clear, with trumpet and timpani biting through but not excessively. If you want slightly mellower sound and manner along with period instruments, go to the Linde Consort on HMV Reflexe, not yet available on CD (SLS/*TC-SLS* 14384-3/*9* [Ang. SB/*LX2S* 3943]), but otherwise Gardiner is a first choice. There are good equivalent chrome cassettes, but the upper range, notably the violin timbre, is rather less refined on tape.

Marriner's third and most recent version of the Bach *Suites* uses an edition prepared by Clifford Bartlett and shows notable differences from both his earlier versions, the first one for Argo fresh, bright and brisk under the influence of Thurston Dart, the second for Philips far slacker and sometimes too smooth. The third one reveals some influence from the authentic movement; on one textual point, the double-dotting in the introduction to *Suite No. 3* in D, he takes a more extreme view than the authentic specialists, turning the three semiquavers at the end of each half-bar into precise demi-semiquavers. In the other introductions too, there is a return to the clipped, clear manner of his first version – but not to speeds quite so fast. At times the new version may not be quite so precise of ensemble as the very first; but, with a slightly more relaxed manner and more spacious recording, it is more genial, a good choice for anyone wanting modern instruments and outstanding digital recording. As in both previous versions, William Bennett is the brilliant flute soloist in *Suite No. 2*.

Marriner's Argo recording, dating from the beginning of the 1970s, dominated the catalogue for over a decade. It has now been reissued on Decca's mid-priced Jubilee label. The remastered sound is even more vivid than the original, especially on the cassettes which are brightly lit in the treble. Thurston Dart was very much involved in this performance; the exuberance of the music making makes a fitting memorial to his scholarship which always sought to enhance, never to deaden, the music's spirit. William Bennett is the agile and sensitive soloist in the *Second Suite*, even providing decoration in the famous *Badinerie*, with splendid bravura. For those not insisting on original instruments, this is still an excellent recommendation, very competitively priced.

Menuhin's set was recorded at the beginning of the 1960s. The sound was first class in its day, full, clear and well balanced, and it does not seem dated now, with excellent cassettes to match the LPs. Those who respond to Bach from the 'pre-authentic era' will find Menuhin's humanity shows an admirable balance between freshness and warmth, conveying the music's spirit and breadth without inflation. A first-rate bargain.

Kuijken with La Petite Bande shows that authentic performance need not be acidly over-abrasive. Set against a warm acoustic – more comfortable for the trumpet-sound if not always helpful to clarity – these are brightly attractive performances with their just speeds and resilient rhythms. Solo work is most stylish, though ensemble is not always immaculate and intonation is somewhat variable. Nevertheless a good alternative to Pinnock and the English Concert if you are looking for performances on original instruments. The CDs are certainly preferable to the Archiv set in their added spaciousness, and definition is better than on LP. The single extended-length cassette is generally satisfactory, but the trumpets offer problems in the *Third Suite*.

Trevor Pinnock boldly encourages a more abrasive style than most in the Bach *Suites*, with string tone which within its lights is beautifully controlled, but which to the unprepared listener could well sound disagreeable, with a bright edge to the squeezed, vibratoless timbre. Any feeling of Baroque grandeur is minimized here. Nevertheless, with a refreshingly alert approach to each movement in turn – not least to the slow introductions which, as one would expect, are anything but ponderous – these are invigorating performances, beautifully sprung and spendidly recorded on disc. In the *B minor Suite*, although there could be more contrast in feeling, there is no sense that reverence for supposed authenticity is stifling musical spontaneity. On CD, the sharpness of focus is even more striking than on LP or cassette.

Pommer's version, issued as part of the Leipzig Bach Edition to celebrate Bach's Tercentenary, brought the first complete set of the *Suites* on CD using modern pitch. Anyone not wanting authentic performance might consider these lively and fresh versions with generally brisk but not unfeeling speeds, rhythmically buoyant. Karl-Heinz Passin, the flute soloist in *Suite No. 2*, is not specially imaginative, but he gives a brilliant account of the dashing *Badinerie* at the end, in which Pommer encourages a hint of accelerando. Good atmospheric recording, but with a slightly boomy bass.

Münchinger and his Stuttgart players were among the pioneers in recording Bach on an apt scale, so it is sad that his latest version of the *Suites* – for all the fullness and brilliance of the digital recording – is unattractively heavy, with rhythms unlifted.

When one remembers that it was Harnoncourt more than anyone on record who broke new ground with his authentic performances from the late 1960s onwards, it is disappointing that this new digital version is so lacking in finesse. No match for the finest authentic versions, despite excellent recording.

CHAMBER MUSIC

(Unaccompanied) *Cello suites Nos 1–6, BWV 1007/12.*

*** HMV Dig. **CDS 747471-8** (2) [id.]; EX 270077-3/*5* (2), Heinrich Schiff.

*** DG Dig. **415 416-2** (3); 415 416-1/*4* [id.]. Mischa Maisky.

*** HMV Dig. **CDC 747090** (1–2). **747091** (3–4), **747092** (5–6) [id.]; SLS 107772-3/*5* (3). Paul Tortelier.

(*) Decca Dig. **414 163–2; 414 163-1/*4* (2) [id.]. Lynn Harrell.
(*) CBS Dig. **M2K 37867 (2); 3-37867/*40*- (3) [13M/*13T* 37867]. Yo-Yo Ma.
(M) **(*) Ph. 6725 030 (3). Maurice Gendron.

Schiff blows any cobwebs away from these dark and taxing works, not with consciously authentic performances that risk desiccation but with sharply direct ones, tough in manner and at speeds generally far faster than usual. For once one is constantly reminded that these are suites of dance movements, with Schiff's rhythmic pointing a delight. So even the *Sarabandes* emerge as stately dances, not unfeeling but freed of the heavy romanticism which is often plastered on them. Equally, the fast movements are given a lightness and resilience which make them sound fresh and new. Strong and positive, producing a consistent flow of beautiful tone at whatever dynamic level, Schiff here establishes his individual artistry very clearly. He is treated to an excellent recording, with the cello given fine bloom against a warm but intimate acoustic. The cassette transfer, made at the highest level, gives a very realistic impression, the cello image full and tangible. The compact discs are announced just as we go to press.

Mischa Maisky is undoubtedly a master cellist; he produces an altogether sumptuous tone which is beautifully captured by the DG engineers. His issue is handicapped by being spread over three records, which is no doubt tidy and logical, but is also uneconomical in view of the fact that Decca with Harrell, CBS on CD with Ma and HMV in their recording of Schiff manage to squeeze them on to two. (There are only two DG chrome tapes – of high quality – but without a corresponding reduction in cost.) Maisky's performances are beautifully cultured and at a high emotional temperature. He is rather less inclined to let the music speak for itself than some of his rivals and is at times even self-indulgent. The *Sarabande* of the *D minor Suite* is a little narcissistic and the impatient may find it interminable; nor is that of *No. 5 in C minor* free from affectation. There are times in the quicker dance movements when one longs for him to move on – the *Allemande* of *No. 6* is taken so slowly that on the LP the second repeat has to be omitted to accommodate it comfortably on one side. However, there is no doubt that he makes an absolutely glorious sound and commands an unusually wide range of colour and tone. In its LP format the movements are unbanded.

Recorded in the reverberant acoustic of the Temple Church in London, Tortelier's 1983 performances of the *Suites* present clear contrasts with his version of twenty years earlier. His approach remains broadly romantic by today's purist standards, but this time the rhythms are steadier, the command greater, with the preludes of each suite strongly characterized to capture the attention even in simple chattering passagework. Some will prefer a drier acoustic than this, but the digital sound is first rate, with striking presence on CD and little to choose in quality between the discs and the excellent XDR cassettes.

The spareness and restraint of Harrell's performances contrast strongly with the more extrovert manner of most virtuosi, but rarely if ever is he guilty of understatement. The simple dedication of the playing, combined with cleanness of attack and purity of tone, bring natural, unforced intensity. One might disagree with the occasional tempo, but the overall command is unassailable. Excellent, aptly intimate recorded quality. (Note that all six *Suites* are contained on two discs only, whether CD or LP, as against the usual three.) The realism of the sound is very striking in all three media, with the silent background giving a marginal advantage to the CD format.

Yo-Yo Ma gives deeply satisfying performances, not generally as weighty or improvisational as Tortelier's epic readings, less direct and positive than Schiff's, yet not as restrained as Lynn Harrell's. The effect is both strong and thoughtful. Ma commands the highest artistry, and his playing invariably offers both technical mastery and elevation of spirit. Moreover, the CBS engineers have given him truthful and well-balanced sound, effective on both disc and the lavishly packaged tape set. However, his intonation is not always absolutely impeccable. This is not serious but, all the same, in so lofty a movement as the *Sarabande* from *Suite No. 5 in C minor* one does not want to be aware of any blemishes. In years to come, one feels Ma may find even more to say on these intensely demanding works – just as Tortelier has developed over the years – but although there is much to admire, his present set cannot be counted a first recommendation, although it is successfully fitted on to a pair of CDs, against three LPs and cassettes.

Maurice Gendron has the advantage of excellent and truthful analogue recording, plus the economy of a successful mid-priced reissue, on LP only. He plays with consistent beauty of tone and his phrasing is unfailingly musical; although these readings have an element of sobriety (save, perhaps, for *No. 6* which is superbly done), their restraint and fine judgement command admiration. They can be recommended to those seeking a minimum financial outlay combined with high artistic merit. The surfaces remain impeccable.

(Unaccompanied) *Cello suites Nos 1 in G, BWV 1007; 4 in E flat, BWV 1010* (arr. for flute).
(*) Denon Dig. **C 37 7383 [id.]. Aurèle Nicolet (flute).

Understandably, exponents of instruments other than the violin and the cello cast envious eyes on the violin partitas and the cello suites; Aurèle Nicolet, an excellent artist, makes a good case for translating two of the suites to the needs of an instrument with a compass two octaves higher. The one real gain is the extra flexibility, with brisk dance movements the most effective – but even there the extra ease is hardly consistent with what Bach intended. Nicolet overcomes the problem of the double-stopped chords with deft arpeggios. Good, undistracting recording.

Flute sonatas (arr. from *Trio sonatas*): *in G, BWV 525; in D min., BWV 527; in G, BWV 1038; in C min., BWV 1079.*
(*) Denon Dig. **C37 7058 [id.]. Aurèle Nicolet (flute), Michio Kobayashi (harpsichord).

These are all arrangements (BWV 525 and 527 come from organ sonatas), but effective enough. The playing is flexible and lively, and this duo certainly work well together as a team. The balance of the flute is a shade close, so that Nicolet dominates the proceedings, but the keyboard detail is not masked and the instrument is realistically recorded. The acoustic is resonant, but agreeable. The performances are very positive; a little more light and shade from the flute would have made them even more attractive, but allegros are never aggressive, and Kobayashi nimbly matches Nicolet in dexterity.

Flute sonatas Nos 1–3 (for flute and harpsichord), *BWV 1030/2; 4-6* (for flute and continuo), *BWV 1033/5.*
*** DG Arc. Dig. 413 789-1/*4* (2) [id.]. Hazelzet, Jaap ter Linden, Boumann.

Flute sonatas Nos 1–6, BWV 1030/5; Partita in A min. for solo flute, BWV 1013; Sonata in G min., BWV 1020.
*** Ph. Dig. 410 404-1/*4* (2) [id.]. Hüntler, Jaap ter Linden, Koopman.
** CBS Dig. 12M/*12T* 39746 (2) [id.]. Rampal, Pinnock, Pidoux.

Readers who are allergic to period instruments should sample the slow movement of the *B minor Sonata*, which Wilbert Hazelzet plays with a gentle authority and sensitivity that are most persuasive. He and his accomplished partner also play the finale with unobtrusive virtuosity that is appealing. Hazelzet and Boumann are members of the Cologne Musica Antiqua, and these two LPs derive from their admired 7-record set of Bach's chamber music. The *E flat Sonata*, BWV 1031, at one time thought to be the work of Carl Philipp Emanuel, despite evidence to the contrary in the latter's handwriting, is also beautifully played. There is much felicitous music-making here – the finale of the *E major Sonata*, BWV 1035, is particularly delicate. The Archiv recording is very natural indeed and in every way well balanced, with the single double-length chrome cassette also in the demonstration class.

Konrad Hüntler has been a member of both the Collegium Aureum and the Capella Coloniensis and is obviously a marvellous player. Both he and Ton Koopman are vivid and outgoing artists and they project all this music very strongly. In addition to the usual six *Sonatas* they offer the solo *A minor Partita* and the *G minor Sonata*, BWV 1020. According to Alfred Dürr and other scholars, the latter is probably the work of Carl Philipp Emanuel. The opening *Andante* of the *C major Sonata*, BWV 1033, is given without continuo support, and it was at one time believed that this was a solo sonata, but whether this compromise is a satisfactory solution is another matter. The recording is as lively and bright as the performances, with disc and tape sounding virtually identical, and well balanced too. Honours are evenly divided between this and the Archiv group. Hüntler's tone is warmer and bigger, though Hazelzet shows the greater sensibility, particularly in the *B minor Sonata*, and the DG recording is slightly more recessed and more subtle. The Philips set, however, includes two extra works, and that may well be the deciding factor.

Rampal plays fluently and in good style. He is particularly impressive in his phrasing of slow movements, and his performance of the solo *Partita* is eloquent.

The snag is the recording balance, with the flute timbre rich and forward, while the harpsichord (an attractive American instrument, after Hemsch) is relegated to the background. When Roland Pidoux's cello is added to the continuo, the combined sound tends to congeal and detail is opaque.

Lute suites (arr. for guitar) *Nos 1–4, BWV 995/7 and 1006a; Prelude in C min. and fugue in G min., BWV 999/1000.*
(B) *** CBS *MGT 39487* [M2-33510]. John Williams (guitar).

Lute suites (arr. for guitar): *Nos 1–4, BWV 995/7 and 1006a; Prelude in C min. and fugue in G min., BWV 999/1000; Prelude, fugue and allegro in E flat, BWV 998.*
(M) *** DG Dig. 419 099-1/*4* (2) [id.]. Göran Söllscher (guitar).

John Williams shows a natural feeling for Bach; the flair of his playing with its rhythmic vitality and sense of colour is always telling. His is a first-class set in every way; the control of line and ornamentation are equally impressive. The transfer on to a single double-length iron-oxide tape offers good presence and, although the quality is not as refined as on Söllscher's chrome cassettes, many will count this excellent value.

Göran Söllscher is completely at home in this repertoire, and his performances are thoughtful, highly musical and have the semi-improvisatory quality of a live recital. The *Suite in G minor* derives from the *Fifth Suite for unaccompanied cello*, while the *Suite in E flat* is an arrangement of the *Partita in E for solo violin*. Söllscher uses an eleven-stringed guitar especially made for Renaissance and Baroque repertoire; it is beautifully recorded here, within an agreeably warm acoustic. This is most distinguished, the quality equally impressive on LP and the excellent chrome tapes. Söllscher is especially impressive in the *Prelude, fugue and allegro in E flat*, BWV 998, a marvellously controlled performance. As sound, the DG recording is far more noteworthy than the CBS for John Williams, but the layout is much more expensive.

Lute suites (arr. for guitar) *Nos 1 in E min., BWV 996; 2 in A min.* (originally *C min.*), *BWV 997*; (i) *Trio sonatas Nos 1 in E flat, BWV 525; 5 in C, BWV 529* (ed. Bream).
(*) RCA **RD 89654. Julian Bream (guitar/lute); (i) with George Malcolm.

Bream's compilation comes from records made in the 1960s: the *Lute suites* were recorded in Kenwood House in 1965 and the *Trio sonatas* at Bishopsgate Institute in 1969. The *Lute suites* are played with great subtlety and mastery on the guitar; the *Trio sonatas* are usually heard on the organ, but Bream's arrangement for lute and harpsichord is effective, even if one may prefer the originals. They are elegantly played and crisply recorded; the digital remastering provides a quiet background and adds to the sense of presence, though the harpsichord remains a shade less well defined in the bass register than is ideal.

Lute suites Nos 3 in G min., BWV 995; 4 in F (trans. of *Solo Violin partita in E*), *BWV 1006a; Prelude in C min., BWV 999, and Fugue in G min., BWV 1000.*
(*) Saydisc Amon Ra **CD-SAR 23 [id.]. Nigel North (baroque lute).

Nigel North plays this music on a baroque lute and he is convincingly recorded in a slightly dry acoustic which is yet not too enclosed. These works lie awkwardly for the lute, and his style is freer and less rhythmically precise than Göran Söllscher using the guitar; some may prefer the firmer outline of the latter's playing, especially in the *Prelude and fugue*, BWV 999/1000. Nigel North is at his finest in the transcription of the *E Major Violin partita*, which he plays in the key of F (even though the autograph is in the key of the original), as apparently E major offers problems for the lute. (Söllscher plays the work in E flat.) Certainly it is both enjoyable and very convincing in North's arrangement where there are a few minor changes in the chordal layout.

Trio sonatas: in G min., BWV 1029; in D min., BWV 1036; in F, BWV 1040 (for flute, oboe and continuo).
(*) Denon Dig. **C37 7093 [id.]. Nicolet, Holliger, Jaccottet – C. P. E. BACH: *Trio sonatas.***(*)

The *Sonata in D minor*, BWV 1036, although attractive, is almost certainly spurious; indeed, its content seems too mellifluously *galant* to come from the pen of Johann Sebastian. BWV 1029 certainly is Bach, as its opening movement makes obvious, deriving from a sonata for viola da gamba. All three are enjoyable when given performances so spirited and polished. One would have welcomed rather more light and shade, but the resonant ambience has contributed to this. In all other respects the recording is excellent.

Trio sonatas: in C, BWV 1037; in G, BWV 1038; in G, BWV 1039; Movement in F, BWV 1040.
*(*) HMV Dig. EX 27 0083-3/5. Linde Consort – HANDEL: *Trio sonatas.**(*)

The Linde Consort number some expert players among their ranks, but even so one is aware of the imperfections and vulnerability of period instruments, and intonation and ensemble are not always perfect here. Well recorded though they are, these performances do not give unqualified pleasure and cannot be given a strong recommendation.

Trio sonatas: in C min. (from *The Musical Offering, BWV 1079*)*; in G, BWV 1038.*
*** CBS Dig. **MK 37813**; 37813/*40*- [id.]. Rampal, Stern, Ritter, Parnas – C. P. E., J. C. F. and W. F. BACH: *Trio sonatas.****

In this splendidly played group of *Trio sonatas* the *G major*, BWV 1038, is especially welcome, the excerpt from *The Musical Offering* less so (as it will make a duplication for many collectors), even though the performance is full of vitality. The balance is good, but the CD suggests the microphones were just a shade too close to the violin. The chrome tape smooths this touch of edginess satisfactorily.

Viola da gamba sonatas Nos 1–3, BWV 1027/9.

*** CBS Dig. **MK 37794**; 37794/*40*- [id.]. Yo-Yo Ma (cello), Kenneth Cooper (harpsichord).

*** DG Dig. **415 471-2**; 415 471-1/*4* [id.]. Mischa Maisky, Martha Argerich (piano).

Yo-Yo Ma plays with great eloquence and natural feeling. His tone is warm and refined and his technical command remains as ever irreproachable. Kenneth Cooper is a splendid partner; and collectors who prefer the cello to a gamba need not hesitate. The colour of the harpsichord does not blend with the cello quite as naturally as with a gamba and there is still a case to be made for the modern piano as a more appropriate partner. The CD has wonderful clarity and presence, and admirers of this cellist will undoubtedly want to acquire this issue. On cassette the quality varies a little between sides, with side two rather sharper in focus than side one.

Mischa Maisky is also a highly expressive cellist and, unlike Yo-Yo Ma, he opts for the piano – successfully, for Martha Argerich is a Bach player of the first order. In fact the sonority of the cello and the modern piano seems a happier marriage than the compromise Ma and Kenneth Cooper adopt. The recording is extremely well balanced too, and although the acoustic has struck some commentators as a little too reverberant, others will find it pleasingly warm. A most enjoyable account for collectors who do not care for period instruments. The reverberation means that the chrome cassette loses a little of the definition of the versions on discs, but it still produces very good sound.

(Unaccompanied) *Violin sonatas Nos 1–3, BWV 1001, 1003 and 1005; Violin partitas Nos 1–3, BWV 1002, 1004 and 1006.*

*** Denon Dig. **C37 7405/7** [id.]. Jean-Jacques Kantorow.

(*) DG Dig. **413 810-2; 413 810-1/*4* (3/*2*) [id.]. Schlomo Mintz.

Jean-Jacques Kantorow won the Carl Flesch Prize in 1962 at the age of seventeen but has made relatively few records until quite recently. This playing is refreshingly clean, and his well-paced and fluent accounts have much to commend them. They are vital, satisfying performances; though the recording lacks warmth, it is clear and present, even if there is a trace of edge at the very top. This gifted French artist may lack the grace and smoothness of Grumiaux, but the playing is in eminently good style and he does justice to Bach's contrapuntal writing. A highly recommendable set.

Schlomo Mintz takes all the technical difficulties in his stride and his excellently recorded accounts give much musical satisfaction. His playing has youthful vitality and power, but the famous *Chaconne* from the *D minor Partita* finds him wanting. Intonation is generally secure but goes seriously awry in the middle of the *G minor Fugue*. The sound is bold and clear, with no loss of quality on the excellent chrome tapes, and admirers of this artist need not hesitate.

Still recommended: Shumsky on ASV (ALHB 306) has a wisdom that is rather special, and in its way his set (on LP only) remains unchallenged – big-scale playing, full of flair and imagination. However, the dry, close acoustic reduces the appeal of this version, which is not as aurally attractive as either the Kantorow or Mintz CDs.

Violin sonatas (for violin and harpsichord) *Nos 1–6, BWV 1014/9.*
*** Ph. Dig. **410 401-2**; 410 401-1/*4* (2) [id.]. Monica Huggett, Ton Koopman.
(M) *(*) DG 413 515-1/*4* [id.]. David Oistrakh, Hans Pischner.

Violin and harpsichord sonatas Nos 1–6; in G, BWV 1019a; Violin and continuo sonata in G, BWV 1021.
**(*) DG Arc. Dig. 413 326-1 (2). Reinhard Goebel, Robert Hill, Col. Mus. Ant.

Monica Huggett, one of the outstanding exponents of authentic performance and first violin of Koopman's Amsterdam Baroque Soloists, plays with refined expressiveness in a beautifully unified conception of these six endlessly inventive works. Other versions may be more vigorous but, with excellent recording, detailed and well balanced, period instruments are presented most persuasively. The sound is strikingly 'present' in its CD format. Two alternative versions are given of the slow movement of BWV 1019. The cassette transfer seems to emphasize the edge of the baroque violin: its upper range is not as clean as on the LP and CD.

Originally issued as part of an anthology of Bach chamber works, the Goebel/Hill version brings fresh vigorous performance also on period instruments, pleasantly abrasive in the violin tone, bringing dance-based movements, in particular, vividly to life. The *E minor Sonata* and the alternative version of BWV 1019 make important additions to the regular six sonatas. The sound is first rate.

Oistrakh plays with his incomparable mastery, but his style is at variance with the music. His approach is that of the nineteenth-century concert hall, and his accompanist, Hans Pischner, is relegated very much to the background.

KEYBOARD MUSIC

The Art of fugue, BWV 1080 (see also orchestral versions).
*** HM **HMC 901169/70**; HM/*40* 1169/70 [id.]. Davitt Moroney (harpsichord).
** Ph. **412 729-2**; 412 729-1/*4* [id.]. Zoltan Kocsis (piano) (with Ferenc Rados).

Kocsis plays *The Art of fugue* on a full-timbred piano, boldly and clearly, but often favouring considerable cadential ritenutos. This will not be to all tastes, although the part-writing is made admirably clear. It must be said that the purposeful approach, coupled with the forward projection of the sound, can become a little wearing, and there is little variety of dynamic. The fugues are followed by the four canons and then, by way of supplement, the augmentational canon and the transcription for two keyboards of the three-part mirror fugue. Kocsis is joined here by Ferenc Rados, but they do not make a convincing case for the use of piano textures, as detail is not well defined. The recording itself is natural, with good chrome tapes.

After Kocsis, it is a relief to turn to Davitt Moroney's account of *The Art of fugue* on the harpsichord. He commands not only the intellectual side of the work but also the aesthetic, and his musicianship is second to none. Moroney makes some alterations in the order of the various contrapuncti but he argues his case persuasively. If you want an account of this work on CD, played on a keyboard instrument, this is unlikely to disappoint – and he is eminently well served by the engineers. Davitt Moroney has imagination as well as scholarship.

Capriccio in B flat, BWV 992; Chromatic fantasia and fugue in D min., BWV 903; French suite No. 5 in G, BWV 816; Italian concerto in F, BWV 971. Toccata and fugue in D min., BWV 914.
(M) ** Pickwick Dig. **PCD 817** [id.]. Robert Aldwinkle (harpsichord).

Robert Aldwinkle is a brilliant player, as the *Chromatic fantasia* immediately demonstrates; he is also thoughtful, and his articulation is the model of clarity. But his style lacks idiosyncrasy; thus the famous *Gavotte* in the *French suite* is very positive, yet is rather too sober. The harpsichord is faithfully recorded, but the microphones capture a bright treble and a lighter response from the bass. This may be the character of the instrument, which is not named; however, unless the volume control is set at *mezzo forte* there is at times a touch of aggressiveness.

Capriccio in B flat, BWV 992; Fantasia and fugue in A min., BWV 904; Prelude, fugue and allegro in E flat, BWV 998; Suite in E min., BWV 996 (originally for lute); *Toccata in E min., BWV 914.*
*** Ph. Dig. **416 141-2**; 416 141-1/*4* [id.]. Gustav Leonhardt (harpsichord).

Gustav Leonhardt plays a William Dowd harpsichord, modelled on an instrument by Mietke of Berlin dating from 1715. The sonorities are rich and the great Dutch player exploits them with characteristic resourcefulness. His well-planned recital has vitality, freshness and imagination, and everything comes vividly to life, thanks perhaps to a splendidly articulate recording. Both LP and (more particularly) CD collectors are advised to play at a low level setting for the most natural effect. There is a very good cassette, but it lacks the ultimate presence of the disc versions.

Chromatic fantasia and fugue in D min., BWV 903; Chorale Preludes: Ich ruf zu dir, BWV 639; Nun komm' der Heiden Heiland, BWV 659 (both arr. Busoni); *Fantasia in A min., BWV 922; Fantasia and fugue in A min., BWV 904; Italian concerto in F, BWV 971.*
*** Ph. **412 252-2**; 9500 353 [id.]. Alfred Brendel (piano).

Brendel's fine Bach recital originally appeared in 1978 and has been digitally remastered for the CD format. The performances are of the old school with no attempt to strive after harpsichord effects, and with every piece creating a sound world of its own. The *Italian concerto* is particularly imposing with a finely sustained sense of line and beautifully articulated rhythms. The recording is in every way truthful and present, bringing the grand piano very much into the living-room before one's very eyes. Masterly.

Chromatic fantasia and fugue in D min., BWV 903; Fantasia in C min., BWV 906; Italian concerto in F, BWV 971; Prelude and fugue in A min., BWV 894.
(*) *Denon Dig.* **C37 7233 [id.]. Huguette Dreyfus (harpsichord).

Eminently straightforward accounts, perhaps a little unyielding at times but cleanly and truthfully recorded. Huguette Dreyfus plays with an admirable style and taste, without any ostentatious changes of registration. The recording is processed at a high level and for best results should be played at a low volume setting.

English suites Nos 1–6, BWV 806/11.
*** HMV Dig. EX 270243-3/*5* (2). Gustav Leonhardt (harpsichord).

Gustav Leonhardt uses a 1755 instrument by Nicholas Lefebvre of Rouen recently restored by Martin Skowronneck, and very beautiful it is, too. The *English suites* are thought to come from 1715, the year of Carl Philipp Emanuel's birth, or possibly a few years later, and to pre-date the *French suites*. Leonhardt's playing has a flair and vitality that one does not always associate with him, and there is no doubt that he makes the most of the introspective *Sarabande* of the *G minor Suite*. He is better served by the engineers than he was when he last recorded these for Philips, where he was too forward. His performances, too, are more flexible and relaxed. This makes an excellent (and equally acceptable) three-star alternative to that of Kenneth Gilbert on Harmonia Mundi (HM 1074-5/*40* [id.]).

French suites Nos 1–6, BWV 812/7.
**(*) HMV Dig. EX 270173-3/*5* (2) [Ang. DS/*4X2S* 3971]. Andrei Gavrilov (piano).

French suites Nos 1–6; Suites: in A min., BWV 818a; in E flat, BWV 819; Allemande, BWV 819a.
*** O-L Dig. **411 811-2**; 411 811-1/*4* (2) [id.]. Christopher Hogwood (harpsichord).

French suites Nos 1–6; Overture in the French style, BWV 831.
*(*) CBS M/*M2T* 39099 (2) [id.]. Glenn Gould (piano).

Christopher Hogwood uses two harpsichords now in the possession of the Paris Conservatoire collection, a Ruckers of 1646 enlarged and modified by Taskin in 1780, and a 1749 instrument, basically the work of Jean-Jacques Goujon and slightly modified by Jacques Joachim Swanen in 1784. They are magnificent creatures and sound splendid here, even if the recording is very slightly bottom-heavy and the level high. Hogwood coaxes superb sounds from them: his playing is expressive, and the relentless sense of onward momentum that disfigures so many harpsichordists is pleasingly absent. On CD, the added tangibility and presence bring also a more successful balance of sound. These performances have both style and character, and can be recommended with some enthusiasm. The genesis of the so-called *French suites* is a complicated matter which Hogwood discusses in his scholarly notes, included with this set. To the *French suites* themselves he adds the two others that Bach had obviously intended to include as Nos 5 and 6. The useful notes describe the tuning which was adopted for each suite.

Gavrilov's set is full of interesting things, and there is some sophisticated, not to say masterly, pianism. The part-writing is keenly alive and the playing full of subtle touches. He draws a wide range of tone colour from the keyboard and employs a wider dynamic range than might be expected. There is an element of the self-conscious here and a measure of exaggeration in some of the *Gigues*, but there is much that is felicitous, too. One thinks longingly of Adolf Busch's dictum that the artist should draw attention to the beauty of the music and not to his own artistry. The recording is excellent, though the XDR cassettes lack the ultimate degree of upper range.

Brilliant though Glenn Gould's playing is, it is far too idiosyncratic to justify an unqualified recommendation. Needless to say, there are revealing touches; marvellously clear part-writing and much impressive finger dexterity. There are some odd tempi and a lot of very detached playing that inspires more admiration than conviction. The recording is acceptable, rather dry and close. The chrome cassettes match the discs closely and are lavishly packaged.

Goldberg variations, BWV 988.

*** DG Arc. **415 130–2**; 2533 425 [id.]. Trevor Pinnock (harpsichord).

*(**) CBS **CD37779**; 37779/*40*- [id.]. Glenn Gould (piano).

Trevor Pinnock uses a Ruckers dating from 1646, modified over a century later by Taskin and restored most recently in 1968 by Hubert Bédard. He retains repeats in more than half the variations – which seems a good compromise, in that variety is maintained yet there is no necessity for a third side. The playing is eminently vital and intelligent, with alert, finely articulated rhythm. If tempi are generally brisk, there are few with which listeners are likely to quarrel; Pinnock shows himself flexible and imaginative in the inward-looking variations such as No. 25. The recording is very truthful and vivid, especially in its CD format, though it benefits from a slightly lower level of setting than usual. In any event this can be recommended alongside Leonhardt's Harmonia Mundi version (1C 065 99710) which is preferable to his earlier Telefunken recording (AQ6 41198).

Glenn Gould made his recording début with the *Goldberg variations* way back in the mid-1950s; this latest version was among the last records he made. As in his earlier account, there are astonishing feats of prestidigitation and the clarity he produced in the part-writing is often little short of extraordinary. In his earlier record he made no repeats; now he repeats a section of almost half of them and also joins some pairs together (6 with 7 and 9 with 10, for example). Yet, even apart from his vocalise, he does a number of weird things – fierce staccatos, brutal accents, and so on – that inhibit one from suggesting this as a first recommendation even among piano versions. The recording is, as usual with this artist, inclined to be dry and forward (he engineered his own records and admired this kind of sound) which aids clarity. A thought-provoking rather than a satisfying reading – an award-winning disc, too; however, for all that, many readers will find the groans and croons intolerable and will be bewildered by many things he does. The withdrawn, rapt opening *Aria* is rather beautiful – but why, one wonders, does he emphasize the third part in many of the canons? The chrome cassette matches the disc faithfully. The CD has admirable presence but emphasizes the vocalise.

Italian concerto in F, BWV 971; 4 Duets, BWV 802/5; Partita No. 7 in B min., BWV 831.
*** Ph. Dig. **416 410-2**; 416 410-1/*4* [id.]. Jean Louis Steuerman (piano).

Jean Louis Steuerman's recital stands out among recent issues offering Bach's keyboard music on the piano. His playing is free without seeming out of style, consistently imaginative and alive in every bar of the music. The outer movements of the *Italian concerto* have infectious buoyancy, the finale irresistible in its vigour; while the *Andante*, like the serene *Sarabande* in the *B minor Partita*, has a simple beauty which is most affecting. In both movements the sustaining powers of the piano are used to great effect, yet the music is not romanticized. The *Duets* (which derive from the so-called *Organ mass* in the third volume of the *Clavierübung*) are delightfully fresh, the rhythmic articulation consistently deft. The performance of the *B minor Partita* crowns the recital: this is Bach in terms of the modern instrument with no concessions to the harpsichord. With excellent, natural Philips recording, this is strongly recommended, though the chrome cassette brings a sound-balance that is fuller in the middle range and slightly less fresh on top.

15 2-part Inventions, BWV 772/786; 15 3-part Inventions, BWV 787/801.
*** Denon Dig. **C37 7566** [id.]. Huguette Dreyfus (harpsichord).
*** DG Arc. Dig. **415 112–2**; 415 112-1/*4* [id.]. Kenneth Gilbert (harpsichord).
(*) Decca Dig. **411 974-2; 411 974-1/*4* [id.]. András Schiff (piano).

The title Bach gave these pieces clearly denotes their pedagogic purpose: to impart an ability to play clearly in two and three parts and 'above all to attain a singing style of playing'. Begun in 1720 for his eldest son, ten-year-old Wilhelm Friedemann, they were originally placed in order of difficulty, but Bach subsequently arranged them in ascending key order. For those wanting a recording of these works played on the harpsichord, choice rests between Huguette Dreyfus and Kenneth Gilbert's Archiv set which is first class in every way. Dreyfus, however, is hardly less impressive; in some ways her playing is more relaxed, though no less rhythmically vital. Her instrument is a Hemsch and her recording was made at Notre Dame in 1978. To achieve a realistic result it is essential to reduce the dynamic level to the lowest point if the instrument is not to seem out of scale. Mme Dreyfus is a shade warmer and freer than Gilbert and some will prefer her record.

Kenneth Gilbert plays a magnificent 1671 harpsichord by the Antwerp maker, Jan Couchet, which was later enlarged, first by Blanchet and then by Taskin in 1778, and which was restored in 1980 by Bédard. It has a rich, almost pearl-like sound, which is enhanced by the acoustic of Chartres Museum where it was recorded. Once again the CD needs to be played at a much lower level of setting than usual if the dynamic capacity of the instrument is to register truthfully. Gilbert's playing has exemplary taste and sense of musical purpose. The cassette too is successfully transferred at a very high level. Strongly recommended, alongside the Denon version.

Readers who prefer their Bach on the piano – at least sometimes – will welcome András Schiff's excellent recording on Decca. His playing is very much of the old school, rather generous with rubato (some of it in questionable style) and other expressive touches, but elegant in the articulation of part-writing. This is at times a bit overdone; such is his musicianship and pianistic sensitivity, however, that the overall results are likely to persuade most listeners. There is a lot of life and colour in the playing and much to enjoy. The recording is excellent in all three formats, and the instrument sounds extraordinarily lifelike, as if in one's very room, on CD.

Partitas Nos 1–6, BWV 825/30.

*** DG Arc. Dig. **415 493-2**; 415 493-1/*4* (2) [id.]. Trevor Pinnock (harpsichord).
(*) HM Dig. **HMC 901144/6; HMC/*40* 1144/6 [id.]. Kenneth Gilbert (harpsichord.
*** Hyp. A 66041/3. Elizabeth de la Porte (harpsichord).
*** Decca Dig. **411 732–2**; 411 732-1/*4* [id.]. András Schiff (piano).
*(*) Denon Dig. **C37 7333/5.** Huguette Dreyfus (harpsichord).

Trevor Pinnock has the advantage of economy, as Archiv have astutely fitted all six *Partitas* on to two discs. In order to do so, Nos 1, 2 and 4 are on the first record, 5, 3 and 6 on the second, each CD taking about 65 minutes. He uses a copy of a Hemsch (*c.* 1760) by David Jacques Way, tuned to unequal temperament and sounding marvellously present in this recording. Tempi are generally well judged, rhythms vital yet free, and there is little to justify the criticism that he rushes some movements. He also conveys a certain sense of pleasure that is infectious. Elizabeth de la Porte, where we have sampled the two side by side, is at times more poetic, but Pinnock has great spirit and panache. There are excellent chrome cassettes, although the harpsichord image loses a little of its sharpness of focus.

There is no doubting the excellence of Kenneth Gilbert's set on Harmonia Mundi which, in terms of scholarship and artistry, has much to recommend it. All the same it is handicapped, like that of Elizabeth de la Porte, by being spread over three discs or cassettes. Professor Gilbert uses a Couchet-Taskin-Blanchet

(1671–1778) and is well enough recorded – but most readers will doubtless want to know whether the differences between the Gilbert and the Pinnock versions justify the additional outlay, and it is difficult to argue that they do.

Elizabeth de la Porte plays the six keyboard *Partitas* with such natural understanding and sensitivity that one hopes she will go on to record more. This is the opposite of an aggressive, clangorous harpsichord style, yet the range of expression in these virtuoso pieces is never underplayed, either in the power of display movements or in tender, melodic writing. The recording is faithful and easy on the ear, never overmodulated as many harpsichord recordings are.

Schiff is a most persuasive advocate of Bach on the piano, consistently exploiting the modern instrument's potential in range of colour and light and shade, not to mention its sustaining power. Though few will cavil at his treatment of fast movements, some may find him a degree wayward in slow movements, though the freshness of his rubato and the sparkle of his ornamentation are always winning. The sound is outstandingly fine, particularly on CD, but the chrome cassette is in the demonstration class too.

Huguette Dreyfus gives strong, purposeful performances which, with the harpsichord recorded close, quickly sound too heavyweight. Her rhythmic style is rather relentless, lacking the tonal variety, charm and point which make rivals such as Elizabeth de la Porte so persuasive. The six *Partitas* are extravagantly laid out, with only two on each disc, where on CD three are perfectly easily possible.

The Well Tempered Clavier (*48 Preludes and fugues*), *BWV 846/983* (complete).
*** DG Arc. Dig. 413 439-1 (5) [id.]. Kenneth Gilbert (harpsichord).
** Ph. **412 794-2** (4); 412 794-1 (5) [id.]. Friedrich Gulda (piano).

The Well Tempered Clavier, Book 1: Nos 1–24, BWV 846/69.
*(*) Erato STU 715212 (2) [id.]. Ton Koopman (harpsichord).
*(*) Ph. 6769/*7654* 106 (2) [id.]. Daniel Chorzempa (clavichord, harpsichord and organ).

Gilbert has made some superb harpsichord records, but his set of the '48' crowns them all. By a substantial margin it now supplants all existing versions, with readings that are resilient and individual, yet totally unmannered. Though Gilbert deliberately refuses to use the sort of wide changes of registration which are now thought unauthentic, the range of his expression and the beauty of his instrument, made originally in Antwerp in 1671 and later enlarged in France, give all the variety needed. There is a concentration and purposefulness about each performance over the widest range of moods and expression, and the quality of recording, immediate without being too aggressive, adds to that.

Gulda's recording of the 48 was originally made in 1973. The digital transfer on CD brings out all the more sharply not only the dryness of the acoustic but the pianist's commendable reluctance to use the sustaining pedal. His approach is generally severe, with articulation bright and clean and with ornamentation crisp and precise. From time to time his idiosyncratic musical personality emerges in eccentric speeds: so the organ-like fugue of the *C minor* of the second book is funereally slow and the *E major* of the same book unremittingly loud. In both he rightly sees grandeur, but his mode of achieving it is hardly apt or stylish. Using such a set on CD is particularly convenient, with separate bands for the *Fugues* as well as the *Preludes*.

Koopman's keenly responsive playing has been very successful on many Bach concerto recordings, but, with generally brisk speeds relentlessly pursued, this set of the first book of the '48' is disappointing, even though he uses a fine copy of a Ruckers instrument.

Daniel Chorzempa's recording seeks variety of texture by dividing up the music between clavichord, harpsichord and organ. This seems a good idea but, in the event, is not entirely successful, for the clavichord (which, if reproduced at a realistic level, has a very small voice) proves to lack tonal substance and produces a good deal of action noise. Moreover, Chorzempa's playing throughout, although very positive and clean, is very matter-of-fact, with less inherent vitality than Koopman, and with much less musical imagination than Kenneth Gilbert.

COLLECTION

(i) *Chromatic fantasia and fugue, BWV 903; French Suite in B min., BWV 831; Italian concerto, BWV 971; Toccata in D min., BWV 913.* (ii) *Allabreve in D, BWV 589; Canzona in D min., BWV 588; Passacaglia in C min., BWV 582; Pastorale in F, BWV 590; 6 Schübler chorales, BWV 645–50; Toccata, adagio and fugue in C, BWV 564; Toccatas and fugues: in D min., BWV 565; in D min. (Dorian), BWV 538; in F, BWV 540.*

(*) DG Arc. **413 638-2 (3). (i) Trevor Pinnock (harpsichord): (ii) Ton Koopman (organ).

Trevor Pinnock's performances come from the late 1970s and have been digitally remastered to excellent effect. He is impressive in the *Chromatic fantasia and fugue*, where his sense of style is matched by his technical expertise. A certain literalness of approach is less evident in the *Chromatic fantasy* than in the finale of the *Italian concerto*, which is relentless, and in the *Toccata*. Ton Koopman is allotted two of the three records here and his recordings are of more recent provenance. He uses two instruments, the Grote Kerk, Massluis, on which all but the *Schübler chorales* are recorded, and the Waalse Kerk, Amsterdam, whose reeds are a good deal more strident. There is no want of vitality, but he can be austere in matters of registration and, at times, a little unyielding rhythmically. However, admiration far exceeds reservations, and the clarity of sound on CD is really quite outstanding.

ORGAN MUSIC

Organ music (complete recording).

(B) *** Argo 414 206-1 (25) [id.]. Peter Hurford (various organs).

Also available separately as follows:
(M) *** Argo D120 D3/*K120 K32* (3/2) [id.]. Volume 1: *Chorale preludes, variations*, etc.
(M) *** Argo D138 D3/*K138 K32* (3/2) [id.]. Volume 2: *Clavierübung*, etc.
(M) *** Argo D150 D3/*K150 K32* (3/2) [id.]. Volume 3: *Canonic variations*; *Chorale partitas*, etc.
(M) *** Argo D177 D3/*K177 K32* (3/2) [id.]. Volume 4: *Chorale variations*; *Fugues*, etc.
(M) *** Argo D207 D3/*K207 K33* (3) [id.]. Volume 5: *Fantasias and fugues*, etc.
(M) *** Argo D226 D3/*K226 K33* (3) [id.]. Volume 6: *Chorale preludes*; *Preludes and fugues*, etc.
(M) *** Argo D227 D3/*K227 K33* (3) [id.]. Volume 7: *18 Leipzig chorales*; *Preludes*, etc.
(M) *** Argo D228 D4/*K228 K44* (4) [id.]. Volume 8: *Orgelbüchlein*, etc.

Peter Hurford's integral recording of Bach's organ music – made over a four-year period between 1978 and 1982 – is a major achievement of recording history. Using several organs in each programme, Hurford planned a series of linking recitals, usually spread over three discs, so that each musical grouping offered a diverse range of contrasting repertoire. Throwing off the cobwebs of the German tradition, he took an essentially orchestral approach, seeking to bring out the colouristic possibilities as well as the full emotional resource of the music. His choice of instruments was an important part of the overall scheme, and the support of the Argo engineers ensured consistently superb sound quality, as impressive on cassette as on disc. His complete set is now issued on twenty-five LPs at what amounts to bargain price (not much over £2 per disc), but the original groupings remain available in the mid-price range. They are a splendid investment, and no doubt a CD edition will follow.

33 Arnstadt chorale preludes (from Yale manuscript).
*** HM Dig. **HMC 905158**; HMC/*40* 5158 [id.]. Joseph Payne (organ of St Paul's, Brookline, Mass.).

38 Arnstadt chorale preludes (Yale); *8 Short preludes and fugues, BWV 553/60.*
*** HMV Dig. EX 270331-3/*5* [id.]. Werner Jacob (Silbermann organ, Arlesheim).

These pieces recently came to light in a volume of 82 chorale preludes in the Lowell Mason collection at Yale. Of the 38 Bach chorale preludes in the MS, 33 were previously unknown, and it is these that Joseph Payne gives us on his compact disc. As he points out, these were not intended to be heard consecutively; and he has arranged them in 'a sequence chosen for musical interest and contrast and not in the order of the manuscript'. The obvious advantage of CD, apart from clarity and presence, is of course the fact that one can isolate a short group to suit one's personal preference. Payne uses the 1983 Bozeman-Gibson organ at St Paul's Church, Brookline, near Boston, which makes very suitable noises.

The sound has a splendid definition, though the acoustic is not particularly warm.

In addition to the 33 newly discovered chorale preludes authenticated by Christoph Wolff, Werner Jacob gives us the other five present in the collection but known from other sources. This entails going on to a second LP, and offering a fill-up, the *Eight Short preludes and fugues*, BWV 553–60, attributed to Bach. Werner Jacob uses the Silbermann organ of Arlesheim Cathedral in Switzerland and has the advantage of an altogether more pleasing acoustic. It may not match the American recording in terms of clarity, but in every other respect it has much to recommend it, including a much warmer ambience and sense of atmosphere. It costs the same as Payne's compact disc, but it is, of course, less easy to isolate individual chorale preludes, particularly on cassette. The choice may be left to individual taste: both offer illumination and neither will disappoint. The acoustic of Arlesheim Cathedral will sway many collectors in favour of the EMI recording.

Allabreve in D, BWV 589; Canzona in D min., BWV 588; Fantasia in G, BWV 572; Passacaglia in C min., BWV 582; Pastorale in F, BWV 590; Prelude in A min., BWV 569.

**(*) DG Arc. Dig. 413 162-1/*4*. [id.]. Ton Koopman (organ of Grote Kerk, Massluis, Netherlands).

This recital opens with a massively conceived, well-structured account of the *C minor Passacaglia*; then comes a refreshing contrast as Ton Koopman registers the *Pastorale* with great charm, featuring the Massluis organ's flute stops to engaging effect. There is remarkable unforced bravura in the brilliant *G major Fantasia*, and again Koopman shows his appreciation of the diverse and, at times, piquant colouristic possibilities of his instrument. Although there is an element of sobriety in the playing here, it never suggests lack of imagination; with superb recording on both disc and chrome tape, this varied programme can be recommended.

Chorale partita on Sei Gegrüsset, Jesu gutig, BWV 768; Fantasia in G, BWV 572; 6 Schübler chorale preludes, BWV 645/50.

€ *** Ph. **412 117-2**; 412 117-1/*4* [id.]. Daniel Chorzempa (Silbermann organ, Arlesheim Cathedral).

Both the *Sei gegrüsset Partita* and the *Schübler chorales* are admirably designed to demonstrate the palette of a fine organ in the hands of an imaginative player; and here Daniel Chorzempa is on top form, in matters of both registration and musical judgement. His playing is always alive rhythmically (the famous opening *Schübler chorale* has a characteristically genial articulation). The *Fantasia* is comparatively sober but ends with impressive, almost orchestral flair. The Silbermann organ at Arlesheim is justly famous for its colours and bright focus; it sounds splendid on the superbly balanced CD, but also very impressive on the LP and especially on the chrome tape which, like the CD, is in the demonstration league.

Chorale partita on Sei gegrüsset, Jesu gutig, BWV 768; Prelude and fugue in D, BWV 532; Prelude in G, BWV 568; Sonata No. 4 in E min., BWV 528.

© *** Denon Dig. **C37 7376** [id.]. Jacques Van Oortmerssen (organ of Walloon Church, Amsterdam).

The organ of the Waalse Kerk is a magnificent instrument, dating originally from 1680 but extended in 1734 by Christian Müller. After various modifications through the years, in the mid-1960s the organ was restored as closely as possible to Müller's conception. The opening *Prelude in G* massively demonstrates the power and variety of timbre it commands and Jacques Van Oortmerssen, although not an international virtuoso, is fully its master in the buoyant performance of the *Prelude and fugue in D*. His registration in the *Andante* of the *E minor Sonata* is a delight; in the extended variations of the *Sei gegrüsset Partita* he is consistently imaginative in his choice of colouring. The playing, always alive, is traditional in the best sense, and the CD recording is superbly realistic. A most rewarding recital. The separate sections of the *Sei gegrüsset* variations are separately banded; in many ways, this is more effective than Chorzempa's performance (see above), partly because the various mixtures of Van Oortmerssen's registration are so naturally well defined.

Chorale preludes: Ach bleib' bei uns, BWV 649; Liebster Jesu, BWV 731; O Mensch, bewein, BWV 622; Wachet auf, BWV 645; Fantasia in G, BWV 572; Fugue in E flat (St Anne), BWV 552; Prelude and fugue in C, BWV 545; Toccata and fugue in D min., BWV 565.

(B) **(*) CfP CFP 41 4479-1/*4*. Noel Rawsthorne (organ of Liverpool Cathedral).

Those who like their Bach on a really big organ, with a distinctly non-baroque flavour, will find that Noel Rawsthorne's performances have plenty of vigour, and they are effectively registered too, especially the better-known chorale preludes. The two larger works have the right balance of momentum and controlled tension, and although the sound has a sense of spectacle, inner detail is only slightly blurred. As sheer sound this is undoubtedly exciting. The tape transfer is impressive too and uncongested.

Chorale preludes: Alle Menschen müssen sterben, BWV 643; Vater unser in Himmelreich, BWV 737; Fantasia and fugue in G min., BWV 542; Passacaglia and fugue in C min., BWV 582; Toccata in F, BWV 540.

(*) Telarc Dig. **CD 80049; DG 10049 [id.]. Michael Murray (organ at Methuen Memorial Hall, Mass.).

The sound here is first class, of course, especially on CD, though not more impressive and certainly not clearer than Peter Hurford's analogue Argo records. The acoustic is fairly reverberant, and this is an organ obviously intended by its builders to produce a wide panoply of sound rather than crystal-clear inner detail. It reproduces naturally; one feels the engineers have not sought spectacle for its own sake. The most impressive performance is of the *Passacaglia and fugue in C minor*, well placed and powerful with an effectively wide dynamic range. Michael Murray's approach to the *Fantasia and fugue* and *Toccata* is rather measured. However, clearly he understands the structure of all this music. The *Chorale preludes* are given serene and, it must be admitted, slightly static performances, but the sense of repose of *Alle Menschen müssen sterben*, which ends the recital, is enhanced by the clean focus of the CD, although the background is not quite silent, for the organ contributes its own characteristic sound as the air goes through the pipes.

Chorale preludes: Christ unser Herr, BWV 684; Nun freut euch, BWV 734; Nun komm' der Heiden Heiland, BWV 659; Wo soll ich fliehen hin, BWV 646; Preludes and fugues: in A, BWV 536; in C and C min., BWV 545/6; in D, BWV 532; in E min., BWV 548; in G, BWV 541; Toccata and fugue in D min. (Dorian), BWV 538; Trio sonata No. 6 in G, BWV 530.
(B) * HMV *TCC2-POR 290113-9*. Lionel Rogg (various organs).

This comes in HMV's 'Portrait of the Artist' series of bargain-priced double-length tapes, but the choice of iron-oxide rather than chrome tape has led to a loss of focus and minor transfer problems caused by the reverberation. Rogg uses an impressively wide range of Andersen and Metzler organs; and the readings are thoughtful, well structured and sometimes powerful in effect. The lack of inner clarity, however, is serious.

Chorale preludes: Kommst du nun, BWV 650; Schmucke dich, BWV 564; Wachet auf, BWV 654; Fantasia and fugue in G min., BWV 542; Prelude and fugue in A min., BWV 543; Toccata and fugue in D min., BWV 565; Trio sonatas Nos 1 in E flat; 2 in C min.; 5 in C, BWV 525–6 and 529.
(M) **(*) DG 413 514-1/4 (2). Karl Richter (organ of Jaegersborg Church, Copenhagen).

This pair of discs (or tapes), expertly engineered, summarizes Karl Richter's 1960s recordings in Copenhagen on a splendid Danish organ, superbly recorded. The performance of the *Toccata and fugue in D minor* shows Richter at his very best, matching weight with vigour, and excellently paced. The *Trio sonatas* are rather sober but attractively registered, and the *Chorale preludes* are presented with effective simplicity. Richter's approach is scholarly without being pedantic, relaxed enough to let the music breathe, yet perhaps lacking the final touch of imagination to be really memorable.

Concertos (after Vivaldi) *Nos 2 in A min.* (from *Op. 3/8*), *BWV 593; 3 in C* (from *Op. 7/11*), *BWV 594; 5 in D min.* (from *Op. 3/11*), *BWV 596; Fugue in B min.* (on a theme of Corelli, *Op. 3/4*), *BWV 579.*
*(*) Ph. Dig. **412 116-2**; 412 116-1/4 [id.]. Daniel Chorzempa (Silbermann organ of Domkirche, Arlesheim).

A disappointing collection. Chorzempa's approach to this music is too serious by far, containing little of the joy of Bach's revelling in the music of his Italian contemporary. The tread is heavy and the chosen registration unwieldy, with the pedals often adding to the weighty manner of presentation. The recording is excellent, with the CD projecting everything forcefully and the LP and cassette marginally less sharply defined.

Concerto in A min. (after Vivaldi), *BWV 593; Fantasia and fugue in G min., BWV 542; Fugue in G min., BWV 578; Passacaglia and fugue in C min., BWV 582; Toccata and fugue in D min., BWV 565.*
** Erato Dig. **ECD 88004**; NUM/*MCE* 75052. Marie-Claire Alain (organ of Collégiale of Saint-Donat).

After a lively account of the famous *D minor Toccata and fugue* Marie-Claire Alain is heard at her most individual in the *Fugue in G minor*, BWV 578, which she registers delicately, giving the impression of orchestral woodwind. At the other end of the scale, she is weightily imposing in the *Passacaglia in C minor*, but a similarly massive approach to the *G minor Fantasia* seems a little overdone. The *Concerto* is buoyant in the outer movements, but the *Adagio* (again nicely registered) rather hangs fire. Mme Alain is undoubtedly an individualist and a fine player, but she is not convincing in all she does, even if every performance is obviously carefully considered. The organ sounds attractive with its throaty reeds and sonorous pedals which support but never confuse the texture.

Concerto in A min. (after Vivaldi), *BWV 593; Preludes and fugues: in D, BWV 532; in B min., BWV 544; Toccata and fugue in D min., BWV 565.*
(*) Telarc **CD 80088; DG 10088 [id.]. Michael Murray (organs at Congregational Church, Los Angeles).

The paired Skinner-Schlicker organs at the First Congregational Church of Los Angeles are widely separated, situated at opposite ends of the nave. They are controlled by twin consoles of four manuals; the effect in this recording is to spread the point source of the sound (there are no exaggerated antiphonal effects) in the most attractive way. The acoustics of the church are such that detail in the *Toccata and fugue* and the *Concerto* is never blurred, though in the *B minor Prelude and fugue* Michael Murray's mellifluous presentation produces over-smooth articulation. He and the organ both sound splendid in BWV 565, where the fast pacing generates lively bravura. The arrangement of the Vivaldi *Concerto* is pleasingly registered, especially the central *Adagio*, and is played with an agreeably light touch. In both preludes and fugues, however, the approach is more conventional.

Fantasia in C, BWV 570; Fugue in G min., BWV 578; Preludes and fugues: in C, BWV 545; in G min., BWV 535; 6 Schübler chorales, BWV 645/50; Toccata and fugue in D min., BWV 565; Trios: in C min., BWV 585; in D min., BWV 583.
** Denon Dig. **C37 7004** [id.]. Hans Otto (Silbermann organ, Freiberg).

A generous recital (55′ 37″) very well recorded. The attractively bright, reedy characteristic of the Freiberg organ is well suited to Bach's music, and the balance ensures inner clarity as well as a convincing overall perspective. Hans Otto, however, is a rather didactic player. He does not make a distinctive impression with the opening *Toccata and fugue in D minor*, and is rhythmically over-assertive in the famous opening *Schübler chorale*, *Wachet auf*. He is at his best in the *Prelude and fugue in G minor* (BWV 535) and the closing *Fugue* of the recital (BWV 578) which are presented simply and straightforwardly.

Fantasia in G, BWV 572; Passacaglia in C min., BWV 582; Toccata, adagio and fugue in C, BWV 564; Trio sonata No. 1 in E flat, BWV 525.

(M) *** Decca Viva 414 075-1/*4*. Gillian Weir (organ of St Lawrence Church, Rotterdam).

By the side of Peter Hurford on Argo, Gillian Weir is less flamboyant, less ripe in her feeling for colour. Her registration in the slow movement of the *Trio sonata* is engagingly cool and in complete accord with the clear poised playing. The bravura in the *Fantasia in G* cannot escape the listener, yet there is no sense of the virtuosity being flaunted, and in consequence the closing pages are somewhat withdrawn in feeling. The remorseless tread of the *Passacaglia in C minor* is immensely compelling, and the companion *Toccata, adagio and fugue* is hardly less telling in its sense of controlled power. The recording of this characterful Dutch organ is marvellous, with a dry sparkle at the top, yet with a full, clean, bass that never clouds the texture. The cassette is similarly vivid and clear.

Fantasia and fugue in G min., BWV 542; Fugue in G min., BWV 578; Passacaglia and fugue in C min., BWV 582; Prelude and fugue in B min., BWV 544; Toccata and fugue in D min., BWV 565.

* Denon Dig. **C37 7039** [id.]. Helmuth Rilling (organ of Gedächtniskirche, Stuttgart).

Helmuth Rilling's account of the famous *Fugue* of BWV 565 lacks the necessary volatile quality; these deadly serious performances, although all well played technically, are very deliberate indeed. Rilling's approach best suits the *C minor Passacaglia*, but in his hands it seems interminable. Those who enjoy the traditional German style of Bach playing will find the recording of the Stuttgart organ very good, with the brightness of the reeds predominating.

Passacaglia and fugue in C min., BWV 582; Preludes and fugues: in A min., BWV 543; in D, BWV 532; Toccata and fugue in D min., BWV 565.

(M) *** Ph. 9502/*7313* 080 [id.]. Daniel Chorzempa (organ of Our Lady's Church, Breda, Holland).

A beautifully recorded analogue recital with notable depth, clarity and resonance. The tape is in the demonstration class. The *Passacaglia and fugue in C minor* is impressively sustained, while the *Prelude and fugue in D* is especially buoyant. A most desirable medium-priced recital.

Passacaglia and fugue in C min., BWV 582; Toccata and fugue in C, BWV 564; Toccata and fugue in D min. (Dorian), BWV 538; Toccata and fugue in D min., BWV 565.

*** Argo **411 824-2**; 411 824-1/*4* [id.]. Peter Hurford (organs of Ratzeburg Cathedral, West Germany, and Church of Our Lady of Sorrows, Toronto, Canada).

An excellent sampler of Hurford's Bach recordings, opening with his massively extrovert *Toccata and fugue in D minor*, BWV 565, but with a variety of mood in the other works, the *Dorian fugue* quite relaxed, the *C minor Passacaglia and fugue* unhurried but superbly controlled. The sound is first class in all three formats, with the CD having that extra degree of presence, but the cassette is also demonstration-worthy.

Prelude and fugue in E flat, BWV 552; Prelude, Largo (BWV 529/2) and fugue in C, BWV 545; Toccata and fugue in D min., BWV 565.

*(*) Ph. Dig. **410 038-2**; 6514/*7337* 274 [id.]. Daniel Chorzempa (organ).

Daniel Chorzempa is splendidly recorded on CD, LP and the excellent chrome tape; but the performances are very measured, as is obvious from the famous *D minor Fugue*. In the big E flat work, the effect is massive but static, and the performance is too deliberate by half. The CD with its silent background creates a most spectacular impression on the listener and it is a pity that this recital offers playing of relatively little flair.

6 Schübler chorale preludes, BWV 645/50; Chorales: Jesu, joy of man's desiring (from *Cantata 147*)*; Erbarm dich, BWV 721; Ich ruf' zu dir, Herr Jesu Christ, BWV 639; Nun freut euch, BWV 734a; Nun komm' der Heiden Heiland, BWV 659; O Mensch bewein, BWV 622; Wir glauben all an einen Gott, BWV 680.*

** Erato Dig. **ECD 88030**; NUM/*MCE* 75064 [id.]. Marie-Claire Alain (organ of Collégiale of Saint-Donat, Drôme).

Marie-Claire Alain's style here is often impulsive, and she registers exuberantly in the faster chorales. However, in the slower ones there are hints of romanticism. The rhythm of the first *Schübler chorale*, *Wachet auf*, could be smoother, but at least the playing here is never dull. The organ is given striking presence on CD.

Toccata, adagio and fugue in C, BWV 564; Toccatas and fugues: in D min. (Dorian), BWV 538; in D min., BWV 565; in F, BWV 540.

(*) DG Arc. Dig. **410 999-2; 410 999-1/*4* [id.]. Ton Koopman (organ of Massluis Grote Kerk).

Ears will prick up at the opening flourishes of the famous *D minor Toccata and fugue*, BWV 565, as Ton Koopman, who favours plenty of ornamentation, has added a brief trill. When this eccentricity is past, the performance is attractively buoyant and the *Toccata, adagio and fugue*, BWV 564, also goes well. However, a good deal of the fast passagework in the programme as a whole tends to get slightly blurred by the acoustic resonance, even on CD. On cassette, the opening pedal of BWV 540 causes momentary muddying of the texture. The performances throughout are very positive, even if the last degree of imagination is missing in both execution and registration. If one accepts the spacious presentation and accompanying lack of sharp inner definition, the tangibility of the organ image is impressive.

VOCAL MUSIC

Cantatas Nos 1: Wie schön leuchtet uns der Morgenstern; 2: Ach Gott, vom Himmel; 3: Ach Gott, wie manches Herzeleid; 4: Christ lag in Todesbanden.
*** Tel. **ZL8 35027**; DM6 48191 (2) [id.]. Treble soloists from V. Boys' Ch., Esswood, Equiluz, Van Egmond, V. Boys' Ch., Ch. Viennensis, VCM, Harnoncourt.

This remarkable project – to record all the church cantatas of Bach – got under way in the early 1970s during the life of the first *Penguin Stereo Record Guide*, and it is appropriate that during the tercentenary year the earlier volumes should reappear digitally remastered, but with simpler presentation in their CD formats. The LPs too are being reissued at a lower price, with the documentation modified. The CD packaging omits the musical scores, but includes English translations of the texts and the excellent notes by Alfred Dürr. The remastering is remarkably successful and there is no background noise worth speaking of, while the sound is clarified and refined, with an overall gain in presence for voices and accompaniment alike.

The authentic character of the performances means that boys replace women, not only in the choruses but also as soloists, and the size of the forces is confined to what we know Bach himself would have expected. The simplicity of the approach brings its own merits, for the imperfect yet otherworldly quality of some of the treble soloists refreshingly focuses the listener's attention on the music itself. Less appealing is the quality of the violins, which eschew vibrato – and, it would sometimes seem, any kind of timbre!

Generally speaking, there is a certain want of rhythmic freedom and some expressive caution. Rhythmic accents are underlined with some regularity, and the grandeur of Bach's inspiration is at times lost to view. Where there are no alternatives for outstanding cantatas, such as the marvellously rich and resourceful sonorities of the sinfonia to *Ach Gott, vom Himmel* (No. 2), with its heavenly aria, *Durchs Feuer wird das Silber rein*, choice is simple, and here the performance too is a fine one. There is slightly more grandeur to Richter's account of *Christ lag in Todesbanden* (No. 4), but there is so much fine music in Cantatas 2 and 3, not otherwise obtainable on record, that the first of these volumes is a must.

Cantatas Nos 4: Christ lag in Todesbanden; 26: Ach wie flüchtig, ach wie nichtig; 51: Jauchzet Gott in allen Landen; 56: Ich will den Kreuzstab gerne tragen;

61: Nun komm, der Heiden Heiland; 80: Ein feste Burg ist unser Gott; 106: Gottes Zeit ist die allerbeste Zeit (*Actus tragicus*)*; 147: Herz und Mund und Tat und Leben.*

** DG Arc. **413 646–2** (3) [id.]. Soloists, Mun. Bach Ch., Mun. Bach O, Karl Richter.

As part of their CD Bach Edition issued in the tercentenary year, Archiv have collected eight cantatas from the vast number recorded by Karl Richter over the years. Thanks to him, we had the most comprehensive survey of the Bach cantatas to be put on record before the ambitious Harnoncourt–Leonhardt venture got into its stride. The earliest recording here, *Herz und Mund und Tat und Leben*, comes from 1962 and is among the best, while the most recent, *Ach wie flüchtig, ach wie nichtig*, comes from 1979. The choice seems quite arbitrary, though it does garner a particularly rich variety of singers including Edith Mathis, Ernst Haefliger, Peter Schreier and Dietrich Fischer-Dieskau. The digitally remastered transfers sound very good indeed, and collectors need not worry on this score. Richter, of course, was rather heavy-handed at times – no one who puts his 1966 account of *Gottes Zeit* alongside the infinitely more imaginative and sensitive version made by Jürgen Jürgens with the Leonhardt Consort at about the same time would have any doubts on that score! Recommended, but with modified rapture.

(i) *Cantatas Nos 5: Wo soll ich fliehen; 6: Bleib bei uns;* (ii) *7: Christ unser Herr zum Jordan kam; 8: Liebster Gott.*

*** Tel. **ZL8 35028**; DM6 48192 (2) [id.]. Esswood, Equiluz, Van Egmond, (i) Treble soloists from V. Boys' Ch., Ch. Viennensis, V. Boys' Ch., VCM, Harnoncourt; (ii) Regensburg treble soloists, King's College Ch., Leonhardt Cons., Leonhardt.

This is generally up to the standard of the series, although Richter's old recording of No. 8, *Liebster Gott*, on Archiv (now deleted) had greater breadth and vision than the Leonhardt version. No. 6, *Bleib bei uns*, has a fine alto solo with oboe obbligato, which is very well done; the solo treble also distinguishes himself. The wind embroidery for the opening chorus of No. 8 again shows the character of the early instruments to good effect, and Kurt Equiluz's solo, *Was willst du dich, mein Geist, entsetzen*, eloquently sung, is given an effective oboe d'amore decoration. The presence of the remastered sound is striking in these excellent CDs.

(i) *Cantatas Nos 9: Es ist das Heil; 10: Meine Seele erhebt den Herrn;* (ii) *11: Lobet Gott in seinen Reichen.*

*** Tel. **ZL8 35029**; DM6 48203 (2) [id.]. Esswood, Equiluz, Van Egmond; (i) Regensburg treble soloists, King's College Ch., Leonhardt Cons., Leonhardt; (ii) Treble soloists from V. Boys' Ch., Ch. Viennensis, V. Boys' Ch., VCM, Harnoncourt.

Cantata No. 9 has a memorable opening chorus with a background embroidery by flute and oboe d'amore. Later there is a striking tenor aria, *Wir waren schon zu tief gesunken*, and a duet for soprano and alto, *Herr, du siebst statt, guter Werke*, again decorated by the flute and oboe d'amore. *Lobet Gott*, the Ascension cantata, is a large-scale work (extending to two sides) in which the joyful introductory chorus (with trumpets) sets the mood for a strong performance that brings out the best in all the soloists.

Cantata No. 10: Meine Seele erhebt den Herrn.
(M) *** Decca Ser. 414 322–1/*4*. Ameling, Watts, Krenn, Rintzler, V. Ac. Ch., SCO, Münchinger – *Magnificat.****

An excellent coupling for a first-rate account of the D major *Magnificat*. This fine cantata is very well sung and played, with all the performers at their best. The recording too is freshly vivid, notably so on the excellent chrome tape. A bargain.

Cantatas Nos 12: Weinen, klagen; 13: Meine Seufzer, meine Tränen; 14: Wär Gott nich; 16: Herr Gott, dich loben.
*** Tel. **ZL8 35030**; DM6 48204 (2) [id.]. Gampert, Hinterreiter, Esswood, Equiluz, Van Altena, Van Egmond, King's Coll. Ch., Leonhardt Cons., Leonhardt.

Cantata No. 12, *Weinen, klagen, sorgen, zagen* (Weeping, lamenting, worrying, fearing) written for the third Sunday after Easter, has an understandable melancholy. The alto aria is particularly fine (*Kreuz und Krone sind verbunden*) and the oboe obbligato is beautifully done. No. 14, *Wär Gott nich mit uns diese Zeit*, has a splendid extended opening chorus, of considerable complexity and striking power. There is much wonderful music in all three works here; performances and recordings are first class.

Cantatas Nos 17: Wer Dank opfert; 18: Gleich wie der Regen; 19: Es erhub sich ein Streit; 20: O Ewigkeit, du Donnerwort.
*** Tel. **ZL8 35031**; DM6 48205 (2) [id.]. Treble soloists from V. Boys' Ch., Esswood, Equiluz, Van Egmond, V. Boys' Ch., Ch. Viennensis, VCM, Harnoncourt.

Another fine set including superb music which is very little known. No. 17 has a long sinfonia and opening chorus combined; and in No. 19, the introductory fugal chorus is magnificent in its tumultuous polyphony. The closing chorus is simpler, but trumpets add a touch of ceremonial splendour. No. 20 also features trumpets not only in the choruses but no less effectively in the bass aria, *Wacht auf*. This work also includes a memorable alto/tenor duet, *O Menschenkind, hör auf geschwind*. The sound is first class, fresh, vivid and clear.

(i) *Cantatas Nos 21: Ich hatte viel Bekümmernis;* (ii) *22: Jesus nahm zu sich die Zwölfe; 23: Du wahrer Gott.*
(*) Tel. **ZL8 35032; DM6 48217 (2) [id.]. Esswood, Equiluz, (i) Walker,

Wyatt, V. Boys' Ch., Ch. Viennensis, VCM, Harnoncourt; (ii) Gampert, Van Altena, Van Egmond, King's College Ch., Leonhardt Cons., Leonhardt.

The magnificent *Ich hatte viel Bekümmernis* lacks something in flair and Leonhardt is a little rigid in No. 22, *Jesus nahm zu sich die Zwölfe*. Harnoncourt tends in general to be freer, but a constant source of irritation through the series is the tendency to accent all main beats. This was the final appearance of the King's College Choir which made a worthwhile contribution to many of the early performances in the series. The CD transfers are well up to the standard already set by this rewarding enterprise.

Cantatas Nos 24: Ein ungefärbt Gemüte; 25: Es ist nichts gesundes; 26: Ach wie flüchtig; 27: Wer weiss, wie nahe mir.
*** Tel. **ZL8 35033**; EX6.35033 (2) [2635033]. Esswood, Equiluz, Van Egmond, Siegmund, Nimsgern, V. Boys' Ch., Ch. Viennensis, VCM, Harnoncourt.

This volume is worth having in particular for the sake of the magnificent *Es ist nichts gesundes*, a cantata of exceptional richness of expression and resource. No. 27, *Wer weiss, wie nahe mir mein Ende*, is altogether magnificent too, and the performances are some of the finest to appear in this ambitious and often impressive survey. Certainly for those dipping into rather than collecting all this series, Volumes 1 and 7 would be good starting points, even though in the case of the latter all the cantatas are exceptionally short.

Cantatas Nos 28: Gottlob! nun geht das Jahr zu Ende; 29: Wir danken dir, Gott; 30: Freue dich, erlöste Schar!
(*) Tel. **ZL8 35034; EX 6.35034 (2) [2635034]. Esswood, Equiluz, Van Egmond, Nimsgern, V. Boys' Ch., Ch. Viennensis, VCM, Harnoncourt.

(i) *Cantatas Nos 31: Der Himmel lacht, die Erde jubilieret;* (ii) *32: Liebster Jesu, mein Verlangen; 33: Allein zu dir, Herr Jesu Christ;* (i) *34: O ewiges Feuer.*
*** Tel. EX 6.35035 (2) [2635035]. (i) Esswood, Equiluz, Nimsgern, V. Boys' Ch., Ch. Viennensis, VCM, Harnoncourt; (ii) Gampert, Jacobs, Van Altena, Van Egmond, Hanover Boys' Ch., Leonhardt Cons., Leonhardt.

Cantatas Nos 35: Geist und Seele wird verwirret; 36: Schwingt freudig euch empor; 37: Wer da glaubet und getauft wird; 38: Aus tiefer Not schrei ich zu dir.
*** Tel. EX 6.35036 (2) [2635036]. Esswood, Equiluz, Ruud Van der Meer, V. Boys' Ch., Ch. Viennensis, VCM, Harnoncourt.

These three albums continue the high standard that has distinguished this enterprise. Of the new names in the roster of soloists one must mention the stylish singing of René Jacobs, and Walter Gampert is the excellent treble soloist in *Liebster Jesu*. No. 34 is an especially attractive cantata and here, as throughout, one notes the liveliness as well as the authenticity of the performances. EX 6.35036 is another set where the listener is struck again and again by the fertility of Bach's imagination. No. 35 features an outstanding concertante organ solo;

No. 36 features a pair of oboi d'amore, and there are oboes in duet in No. 38. Most enjoyable, with excellent solo singing.

(i) *Cantatas Nos 39: Brich dem Hungrigen dein Brot;* (i; ii) *40: Dazu ist erschienen der Sohn Gottes;* (iii) *41: Jesu, nun sei gepreiset; 42: Am Abend aber desselbigen Sabbats.*

*(*) Tel. EX 6.35269 (2) [2635269]. (i) Jacobs, Van Egmond, Hanover Boys' Ch., Leonhardt Cons., Leonhardt; (ii) Van Altena; (iii) Esswood, Equiluz, Van der Meer, V. Boys' Ch., VCM, Harnoncourt.

This is one of the less distinguished sets in this long and successful project. No. 41, *Jesu, nun sei gepreiset*, probably fares best: one admires the light tone of the baroque brass instruments and the general sense of style that informs the proceedings, even if intonation, as inevitably seems to happen with authentic instruments, is not always true. The music is quite magnificent. So, too, is Cantata 42, *Am Abend aber desselbigen Sabbats*, but these artists do little to convey the feeling of the opening sinfonia, the oboe melody losing much of its expressive fervour. There is a loss of breadth too in No. 39, *Brich dem Hungrigen dein Brot*, which is not altogether offset by the authenticity to which these performers are dedicated. There is some very stylish and well-prepared singing but, taken by and large, the performances radiate greater concern with historical rectitude (as these artists conceive it) than with sheer musical pleasure. The recordings are exemplary.

(i) *Cantatas Nos 43: Gott fähret auf mit Jauchzen; 44: Sie werden euch in den Bann tun;* (ii) *45: Es ist dir gesagt; 46: Schauet doch und sehet, ob irgend.*

*** Tel. EX 6.35283 (2) [2635283]. (i) Jelosits, Esswood, Equiluz, Van der Meer, V. Boys' Ch., VCM, Harnoncourt; (ii) Jacobs, Equiluz, Kunz, Hanover Boys' Ch., Leonhardt Cons., Leonhardt.

Not all the volumes in this ambitious series have equal claims on the collector's pocket, but this is among the finest yet to appear. Cantata 43, *Gott fähret auf mit Jauchzen*, and its succcessor are for the Sunday of Ascension Day and the Sunday following, while No. 46 is the one that includes the original *Qui tollis peccata* of the *B minor Mass*. This and No. 43 are not otherwise available, and though the texture could be more revealingly laid out in 46, this is the only technical blemish in a very fine recording. The performances are of the highest standard and young Peter Jelosits, the boy treble, copes manfully with the very considerable demands of Bach's writing. He is really astonishingly fine, and his companions in these records are no less accomplished. Leonhardt takes the chorale in No. 46 a bit on the fast side; but enough of quibbles – this is really a first-class box.

Cantatas Nos 47: Wer sich selbst erhöhet; 48: Ich elender Mensch; 49: Ich geh' und suche mit Verlangen; 50: Nun ist das Heil.

*** Tel. EX 6.35284 (2) [2635284]. Jelosits, Esswood, Equiluz, Van der Meer, V. Boys' Ch., Ch. Viennensis, VCM, Harnoncourt.

This fine (if uneven) series continues its progress and reaches almost a quarter of the way through the complete cantatas. The same stylistic features of the set are to be found as in earlier boxes along with the same excellent presentation, though here the scores are printed in black and not brown. The treble soloist in No. 49, *Ich geh' und suche mit Verlangen*, Peter Jelosits, really is remarkable. Perhaps the chorus in No. 50, *Nun ist das Heil*, is a shade overdriven, but by and large this is one of the best of the series, and the riches the music unfolds do not fail to surprise and reward the listener.

Cantata No. 51: Jauchzet Gott in allen Landen.
*** Ph. Dig. **411 458-2**; 411 458-1/*4* [id.]. Emma Kirkby, E. Bar. Soloists, Gardiner – *Magnificat.****

Jauchzet Gott is one of Bach's most joyful cantatas; Emma Kirkby follows the example of the opening trumpeting (Crispian Steele-Perkins – in excellent form) when she begins. It is a brilliantly responsive performance, admirably accompanied and very well recorded in all three formats.

Cantatas Nos 51: Jauchzet Gott; 52: Falsche Welt; 54: Widerstehe doch der Sünde; 55: Ich armer Mensch; 56: Ich will den Kreuzstab gerne tragen.
*** Tel. EX 6.35304 (2) [2635304]. Kweksilber, Kronwitter, Esswood, Equiluz, Schopper, Hanover Boys' Ch., Leonhardt Cons., Leonhardt.

A stunning set, arguably the most remarkable in the series so far. *Jauchzet Gott*, the most familiar, has an altogether superb soprano soloist in Marianne Kweksilber as well as a no less impressive Don Smithers as trumpet obbligato. There have been some splendid records of No. 51 in the past, but this eclipses them all. There is no need for less enthusiasm in the case of the remaining cantatas in this box, all of which are done with great distinction. Readers should not miss this collection.

Cantatas Nos 52: Falsche Welt, die trau' ich nicht!; No. 84: Ich bin vergnügt mit meinem Glücke; No. 209: Non sa che sia dolore.
*** Ph. Dig. 6514/*7337* 142 [id.]. Elly Ameling, London Voices, ECO, Leppard.

A delightful record. The opening of *Falsche Welt, die trau' ich nicht!* is a transcription of the first movement of the *Brandenburg Concerto No. 1*, omitting the violino piccolo and modifying a few bars of the horns' part; and the aria, *Ich halt es mit dem lieben Gott*, bears some resemblance to *V'adore pupile* in Handel's *Giulio Cesare*. Elly Ameling is in wonderful voice and Neil Black's oboe playing both here and in the first Cantata on the disc, *Ich bin vergnügt mit meinem Glücke*, is eloquent. Indeed, the obbligato playing throughout gives much pleasure, including William Bennett's flute in the Italian cantata *Non sa che sia dolore*. Sensitive and alert contributions from the ECO and Raymond Leppard, as well as a first-class recording, make this a most desirable issue. There is a good, though not perhaps outstanding, cassette.

Cantatas Nos 56: Ich will den Kreuzstab gerne tragen; 82: Ich habe genug.
(M) *** Decca Ser. 414 055-1/*4*. Shirley-Quirk, St Anthony Singers, ASMF, Marriner.

An earlier edition of the *Stereo Record Guide* was somewhat (and perhaps unjustly) dismissive of this performance when it appeared in 1965. It wears its age lightly, and both the solo singing and the obbligato playing of Roger Lord are to be admired. The sound is remarkably fresh and, at its highly competitive price, this issue should enjoy a wide currency. However, it faces formidable competition at this price from Gérard Souzay and Winschermann, who are on good form and well recorded (Ph. 9502/*7313* 094) but where the alternation of organ and harpischord accompaniment is a minor irritant.

Cantatas Nos 57: Selig ist der Mann; 58: Ach Gott, wie manches; 59: Wer mich liebet; 60: O Ewigkeit, du Donnerwort.
**(*) Tel. EX 6.35305 (2) [2635305]. Jelosits, Kronwitter, Esswood, Equiluz, Van der Meer, Tölz Boys' Ch., VCM, Harnoncourt.

All these cantatas are short, and No. 59, *Wer mich liebet*, is particularly beautiful. *O Ewigkeit, du Donnerwort* is a fine cantata, too. The performances here are well up to the standard of the series.

Cantatas Nos 61: Nun komm, der Heiden Heiland; 62: Nun komm, der Heiden Heiland; 63: Christen, ötzet diesen Tag; 64: Sehet, welch' eine Liebe.
**(*) Tel. EX 6.35306 (2) [2535306]. Jelosits, Kronwitter, Esswood, Equiluz, Van der Meer, Tölz Boys' Ch., VCM, Harnoncourt.

These volumes maintain their high standard, even if they are unlikely to appeal to all tastes. The boy soloist in *Nun komm, der Heiden Heiland* (No. 61) is not the equal of Peter Jelosits, and sounds short-breathed, while the vibratoless strings at the opening invite unfavourable comparison with the Richter recording. Still, these slight inadequacies are a small price to pay for the general excellence and scholarship this set exhibits, and it will give undoubted pleasure.

Cantatas Nos (i) *65: Sie werden aus Saba alle kommen;* (ii) *66: Erfeut euch, ihr Herzen; 67: Halt' im Gedächtnis Jesum Christ;* (i) *68: Also hat Gott die Welt geliebt.*
**(*) Tel. EX 5.35335 (2) [2635335]. (i) Jelosits, Equiluz, Van der Meer, Tölz Ch., VCM, Harnoncourt; (ii) Esswood, Equiluz, Van Egmond, Hanover Boys' Ch., Ghent Coll. Vocale, Leonhardt Cons., Leonhardt.

The best thing in this volume is Leonhardt's broad and spacious account of No. 66, which also offers some stunning playing on the natural trumpet. Harnoncourt's versions of Nos 65 and 68 are a little wanting in charm and poetry (the dialogue between the voice of Christ and the chorus in No. 67 is also prosaic).

But there is fine solo singing, and that and the instrumental playing outweigh other considerations. The recording too is well focused and clean.

Cantatas Nos 69 and 69a: Lobe den Herrn, meine Seele; 70: Wachet, betet; 71: Gott ist mein König; 72: Alles nur nach Gottes Willen.
*** Tel. EX 6.35340 (2) [2635340]. Equiluz, Van der Meer, Visser, Tölz Ch., VCM, Harnoncourt.

Gott ist mein König, No. 71, is the earliest cantata of this set, dating from 1708 and written for the inauguration of the Mühlhausen town council. It is the only Bach cantata to have been printed during his lifetime and is an enchanting piece, full of invention and variety. This set also includes both versions of Cantata 69, *Lobe den Herrn, meine Seele*. Originally written for one of the town council election services in Bach's first year at Leipzig, it was adapted in 1730 and new material was added; only the numbers which differ or are new are re-recorded in this set. No. 72 employs more modest forces than the others and is an Epiphany cantata dating from 1726. Wilhelm Wiedl is the excellent treble throughout, and the other soloists and instrumentalists cannot be too highly praised. The choral singing is not above criticism but is still more than acceptable. Excellent recorded sound.

Cantatas Nos 73: Herr, wie du willst; 74: Wer mich liebet; 75: Die Elenden sollen essen.
** Tel. EX 6.35341 (2) [2635341]. Erler, Klein, Esswood, Equiluz, Kraus, Van Egmond, Hanover Boys' Ch., Ghent Coll. Vocale, Leonhardt Cons., Leonhardt.

All three of these cantatas come from the period 1723–5; *Die Elenden sollen essen*, No. 75, was the one Bach chose for his inaugural composition at St Nicholas's Church in Leipzig in 1723. No. 73 is an Epiphany piece written in the following year and has some strikingly original invention. No. 74 is a cantata for Whit Sunday, the second of two with this title. The merits of the Telefunken series are well enough established, but some of its weaknesses emerge here: some sedate and really rather weak choral work and a reluctance to permit 'expressive' singing deprive the music of some of its eloquence, and the boy trebles, though possessed of musical and pleasing voices, are not fully equal to Bach's taxing writing. However, none of these cantatas is otherwise available, and the music really is worth getting to know.

Cantatas Nos 74: Wer mich liebet, der wird mein Wort halten; 147: Herz und Mund und Tat und Leben.
*** Ph. 9502/*7313* 110. Cotrubas, Hamari, Equiluz, Reimer, Netherlands Vocal Ens., German Bach Soloists, Winschermann.

We thought these to be highly musical performances on their first appearance in the early 1970s, and liked No. 147, the cantata from which *Jesu, joy of man's desiring* comes, far better than Karl Richter's Archiv record. With the passage of time, this version seems even finer and a welcome and refreshing change from the Leonhardt–Harnoncourt approach. Of course, their Telefunken cycle conditions modern ears but it is not the only way, and it is a joy to hear firm, well-focused timbres from the wind and strings. There is warmth and vitality in the Philips coupling, and the singers are not frightened to colour the words. *Wer mich liebet, der wird mein Wort halten* is a most inventive and rewarding piece. The sound is excellent and the balance admirable on disc; the cassette is of acceptable quality, though the choral focus is less than ideally sharp, especially in No. 147.

Cantatas Nos (i) *76: Die Himmel erzählen die Ehre Gottes;* (ii) *77: Du sollst Gott, deinen Herrn, lieben;* (i) *78: Jesu, der du meine Seele;* (ii) *79: Gott, der Herr, ist Sonn' und Schild.*

**(*) Tel. EX 6.35362 (2) [2635362]. Esswood, (i) Wiedl, Equiluz, Van der Meer, Tölz Ch., VCM, Harnoncourt; (ii) Bratschke, Kraus, Van Egmond, Hanover Boys' Ch., Leonhardt Cons., Leonhardt.

Two of the cantatas in Volume 20 are not otherwise recorded at present, and all four are of outstanding interest. As always in authentic performances one is aware of constraints, and the ear longs for the bolder colours and greater power of modern instruments. However, there is too much good music here for such reservations to worry us for long.

Cantatas Nos 80: Ein' feste Burg; 81: Jesus schläft; 82: Ich habe genug; 83: Erfreute Zeit.

*(*) Tel. EX 6.35363 (2) [2635363]. V. Boys' Ch. treble soloists, Esswood, Equiluz, Van Egmond, Huttenlocher, Van der Meer, Ch. Viennensis, Tölz Ch., VCM, Harnoncourt.

This is one of the less successful issues in the Telefunken series. *Ich habe genug* has been performed more impressively on other recordings, and Philippe Huttenlocher, though intelligent and thoughtful, is not always secure. Some of the choral singing elsewhere in this volume could do with more polish and incisiveness too.

Cantatas Nos 80: Ein' feste Burg ist unser Gott; 140: Wachet auf, ruft uns die Stimme.

(M) **(*) HMV ED 290150-1/*4*. Ameling, Baker, Altmeyer, Sotin, S. German Madrigal Ch., Cons. Musicum, Gönnenwein.

€ **(*) Decca Dig. **414 045-2**; 414 045-1/*4* [id.]. Fontana, Hamari, Winbergh, Krause, Hymnus Boys' Ch., SCO, Münchinger.

The HMV performances are conducted by Wolfgang Gönnenwein and not Karl Forster as stated on the spine of the cassette. They are distinguished by some fine singing from Elly Ameling and Dame Janet Baker; the direction throughout is musical through and through and is also nicely recorded. We liked them on their first appearance in the late 1960s, and at mid-price they become even more competitive. There is plenty of space round the sound, and balance between the soloists and instrumentalist is well judged.

Münchinger, who uses the trumpets and timpani added by Bach's eldest son, Wilhelm Friedemann, has the advantage of excellently transparent and well-detailed Decca digital recording and a fine team of soloists: both Gösta Winbergh and Tom Krause make positive contributions. Karl Münchinger does not bring quite the warmth or musicality that distinguishes Gönnenwein, but there is little of the pedantry that has at times afflicted his performances. On CD, extra pleasure is afforded by the attractive ambience – the concert-hall balance is expertly managed – and by the tangibility of the chorus, whose vigorous contribution is given striking body and presence. All the movements are separately banded. There is an excellent chrome cassette.

Cantatas Nos 82: Ich habe genug; 169: Gott soll allein mein Herze haben.
(B) *** HMV *TCC2-POR 154592-9*. Baker, Amb. S., Bath Fest. O, Menuhin – *Arias.****

Ich habe genug is one of the best-known of Bach's cantatas, while No. 169 is a comparative rarity. The performances are expressive and intelligent, though Dame Janet Baker does not achieve quite the same heights of inspiration here as in her Decca record of No. 159. Recording is admirably lifelife and reproduces smoothly, with a natural bloom on the voice. The disc version is now withdrawn, but the coupling of this special double-length cassette issue is very attractive – see below.

Cantatas Nos (i) *84: Ich bin vergnügt; 85: Ich bin ein guter Hirt; 86: Wahrlich, wahrlich, ich sage euch; 87: Bisher habt ihr nichts gebeten in meinem Namen;* (ii) *88: Siehe, ich will viel Fischer aussenden; 89: Was soll ich aus dir machen; 90: Es reifet euch ein schrecklich Ende.*
** Tel. EX 6.35364 (2) [2635364]. Esswood, Equiluz, (i) Wiedl, Van der Meer, Tölz Ch., VCM, Harnoncourt; (ii) Klein, Van Egmond, Hanover Boys' Ch., Ghent Coll. Vocale, Leonhardt Cons., Leonhardt.

If the performances here are of variable quality, the musical inspiration is not, and the set is worth acquiring for the sake of this neglected music, much of which is otherwise unobtainable.

Cantatas Nos (i) *91: Gelobet seist du, Jesus Christ; 92: Ich hab' in Gottes Herz und Sinn;* (ii) *93: Wer nur den lieben Gott lässt walten; 94: Was frag' ich nach der Welt.*
*** Tel. EX 6.35441 (2) [2635441]. Esswood, Equiluz, (i) Bratschke, Van Egmond, Hanover Boys' Ch., Ghent Coll. Vocale, Leonhardt Cons., Leonhardt; (ii) Wiedl, Van der Meer, Huttenlocher, Tölz Boys' Ch., VCM, Harnoncourt.

One of the most desirable of these Bach sets, with assured and confident playing and singing from all concerned.

Cantatas Nos (i) *95: Christus, der ist mein Leben; 96; Herr Christ, der ein'ge Gottessohn; 97: In allen meinen Taten;* (ii) *98: Was Gott tut.*
*** Tel. EX 6.35442 (2) [2635442]. (i) Wiedl, Esswood, Equiluz, Huttenlocher, Van der Meer, Tölz Ch., VCM, Harnoncourt; (ii) Lengert, Equiluz, Esswood, Van Egmond, Hanover Boys' Ch., Ghent Coll. Vocale, Leonhardt Cons., Leonhardt.

These cantatas are not otherwise represented in the current catalogue. There are occasional weaknesses here (Philippe Huttenlocher is not altogether happy in No. 96), but the set is still well worth having.

Cantatas Nos (i) *99: Was Gott tut;* (ii) *100: Was Gott tut;* (i) *101: Nimm von uns, Herr; 102: Herr, deine Augen sehen nach dem Glauben.*
** Tel. EX 6.35443 (2) [2635443]. (i) Wiedl, Esswood, Equiluz, Huttenlocher, Tölz Ch., VCM, Harnoncourt; (ii) Bratschke, Esswood, Equiluz, Van Egmond, Hanover Boys' Ch., Ghent Coll. Vocale, Leonhardt Cons., Leonhardt.

With this album Telefunken come to the twenty-fifth volume of the cantatas and pass the century! This is no mean achievement, and though inevitably there is unevenness in the series, it is still one of the triumphs of the recording industry. In this volume, Cantata No. 99 fares less well than the others, but it would be curmudgeonly to dwell on the shortcomings of this box – or of the series as a whole, for it serves to introduce collectors to unfamiliar works.

Cantatas Nos (i; ii) *103: Ihr werdet weinen und heulen;* (iii; iv) *104: Du Hirte Israel, höre;* (v; vi) *105: Herr, gehe nicht ins Gericht;* (vi; ii) *106: Gottes Zeit* (*Actus tragicus*).
*** Tel. EX 6.35558 (2) [2635558]. (i) Esswood, Equiluz, Van Egmond; (ii) Hanover Boys' Ch., Ghent Coll. Vocale, Leonhardt Cons., Leonhardt; (iii) Esswood, Huttenlocher; (iv) Tölz Boys' Ch., VCM, Harnoncourt; (v) Wiedl, Equiluz, Van der Meer; (vi) Klein, Harten, Van Altena, Van Egmond.

The best-known and most deeply moving cantata here is the 'Actus tragicus' (*Gottes Zeit ist die allerbeste Zeit*). *Ihr werdet weinen und heulen* has rarely been put on disc and is a poignant and expressive piece that rewards attention. Both these performances are among the very finest to have reached us in this series. No. 105, *Herr, gehe nicht ins Gericht*, is arguably one of the very deepest of all Bach cantatas. Harnoncourt is perhaps wanting in expressive weight, but neither this fact nor the reservations one might feel about his account of No. 104, which is not otherwise available, diminishes the value of this excellent box, which comes with the usual notes and score.

Cantatas Nos (i) *107: Was willst du dich betrüben;* (ii) *108: Es ist euch gut; 109: Ich glaube, lieber Herr; 110: Unser Mund sei voll Lachens.*
*** Tel. EX 6.35559 (2) [2635559]. (i) Klein, Equiluz, Van Egmond, Hanover Boys' Ch., Ghent Coll. Vocale, Leonhardt Cons., Leonhardt; (ii) Wiedl,

Frangoulis, Stumpf, Lorenz, Esswood, Equiluz, Van der Meer, Tölz Ch., VCM, Harnoncourt.

The high standards of this series are maintained throughout this volume, and that applies to performance, recording, pressings and presentation.

(i) *Cantatas Nos 111: Was mein Gott will; 112: Der Herr ist mein getreuer Hirt;* (ii) *113: Herr Jesu Christ, du höchstes Gut; 114: Ach, lieben Christen, seid getrost.*
**(*) Tel. EX 6.35573 (2) [2635573]. Equiluz, (i) Huber, Esswood, Van der Meer, Tölz Boys' Ch., VCM, Harnoncourt; (ii) Hennig, Jacobs, Van Egmond, Hanover Boys' Ch., Ghent Coll. Vocale, Leonhardt Cons., Leonhardt.

None of the cantatas included in this volume is otherwise available, so the set is in one sense self-recommending. The performances are also good, with some fine singing. The opening chorus of *Der Herr ist mein getreuer Hirt* is among the most beautiful of Bach's choral fantasias and it must be said that Harnoncourt does it justice. Both *Herr Jesu Christ, du höchstes Gut* and *Ach, lieben Christen, seid getrost* are cantatas for Trinity, and Leonhardt's accounts of them are free from pedantry, well shaped and unaffected. This is one of the sets that lovers of the Bach cantatas should acquire even if they have ambivalent feelings about this series. The usual high standards of recording and presentation are maintained.

Cantatas Nos (i; iii; iv) *115: Mache dich, mein Geist, bereit; 116: Du Friedefürst, Herr Jesu Christ:* (ii; v; vi) *117: Sei Lob und Ehr dem höchsten Gut;* (i; iii; vii) *119: Preise, Jerusalem, den Herrn.*
*** Tel. EX 6.35577 (2) [2635577]. (i) Tölz Ch., VCM, Harnoncourt; (ii) Hanover Boys' Ch., Ghent Coll. Vocale, Leonhardt Cons.; (ii) directed Leonhardt, with Equiluz; (iii) Esswood; (iv) Huttenlocher; (v) Jacobs; (vi) Van Egmond; (vii) Holl.

Cantatas Nos 120: Gott, man lobet dich in der Stille; 121: Christum wir sollen loben; 122: Das neugebor'ne Kindelein; 123: Liebster Immanuel, Herzog der Frommen.
*** Tel. EX 6.35578 (2) [2635578]. Treble soloists from Tölz Ch., Esswood, Equiluz, Huttenlocher or Holl, Tölz Ch., VCM, Harnoncourt.

No serious grumbles about any of the performances here, even if one or two numbers fall short of perfection. The recordings are exemplary in every way and those who have followed the series – and at present there is no other way of acquiring these cantatas – need not hesitate.

Cantatas Nos (i) *124: Meinen Jesum lass ich nicht; 125: Mit Fried und Freud ich fahr dahin; 126: Erhalt uns, Herr, bei deinem Wort;* (ii) *127: Herr Jesu Christ wahr' Mensch.*
*** Tel. EX 6.35602 (2) [2635602]. (i) Bergius, Rampf, Esswood, Equiluz, Thomaschke, Tölz Ch., VCM, Harnoncourt; (ii) Hennig, Van Egmond, Hanover Boys' Ch., Ghent Coll. Vocale, Leonhardt Cons., Leonhardt.

These all come from the second cycle of cantatas that Bach wrote for Leipzig and which, until Easter 1725, consisted entirely of chorale cantatas, and they are very well performed. This is another set that collectors who are not automatically acquiring the complete series should not overlook.

Cantatas Nos (i) *128: Auf Christi Himmelfahrt allein; 129: Gelobet sei der Herr, mein Gott;* (ii) *130: Herr Gott, dich loben alle wir; 131: Aus der Tief rufe ich, Herz zu dir.*

**(*) Tel. Dig. EX 6.35606 [2635606]. Hennig, Bergius, Jacobs, Rampf, Equiluz, Van Egmond, Heldwein, Holl; (i) Hanover Boys' Ch., Ghent Coll. Vocale, Leonhardt Cons., Leonhardt; (ii) Tölz Boys' Ch., VCM, Harnoncourt.

Cantatas Nos (i) *128: Auf Christi Himmelfahrt allein; 129: Gelobet sei der Herr;* (ii) *130: Herr Gott.*

(*) Tel. Dig. **ZK8.42840 [id.]. Soloists, (i) Hanover Boys' Ch., Ghent Coll. Vocale, Leonhardt Cons., Leonhardt; (ii) Tölz Boys' Ch., VCM, Harnoncourt (from above).

Auf Christi Himmelfahrt allein is an Ascension cantata and is quite richly scored, with trumpet, two horns, oboe, oboe d'amore, oboe da caccia; while its companions, *Gelobet sei der Herr, mein Gott* and *Herr Gott, dich loben alle wir*, are even more elaborate, with three trumpets and timpani. The singers are excellent and the trumpeter admirable, but the strings have an edge that is more than razor-sharp and not pleasing. The brass playing in *Gelobet sei der Herr* is pretty rough but the treble, Sebastian Hennig, acquits himself excellently in the glorious aria that forms the centrepiece of the cantata. *Herr Gott, dich loben alle wir* was composed for Michaelmas Day (29 September) 1724; it has a powerful opening chorus whose trumpets proclaim the Kingdom of God. All three cantatas are short and are comfortably accommodated on the CD. *Aus der Tief rufe ich, Herz zu dir* (Out of the deep have I called unto Thee, O Lord) is the earliest of Bach's cantatas written at Mühlhausen in 1707, and is a more extended work than its companions in this box. It is a marvellous, inspired piece, whose grave beauty is eloquently conveyed by Harnoncourt, and it is almost worth the price of the volume alone. The recording and pressings are of the high standards set by this series; those collecting the series will need no further encouragement to invest in this.

Cantatas Nos 132: Bereitet die Wege; 133: Ich freue mich in dir; 134: Ein Herz, das seinem Jesum lebend weiss; 135: Ach Herr, mich armen Sünder.

** Tel. Dig. EX 6.35607 (2) [2635573]. Hennig, Jacobs, Van Altena, Van Egmond, Hanover Boys' Ch., Ghent Coll. Vocale, Leonhardt Cons., Leonhardt.

Of the four cantatas recorded here, *Bereitet die Wege, bereitet die Bahn!* is probably the best performance. The young treble, Sebastian Hennig, is both secure and in tune, and the cantata itself has grandeur. There is, incidentally, no final chorale, Leonhardt substituting a chorale setting from Cantata No. 164

which the score included with the set, naturally enough, does not reproduce. The balance of the recording is felicitous and collectors will find little to quarrel with here. *Ich freue mich in dir* comes off less well, thanks to an indifferent contribution from the Ghent Collegium Vocale, just as in its companion, *Ein Herz, das seinem Jesum lebend weiss*, the tenor's intonation is not always absolutely firm. But there is a lot to admire in his singing in the final cantata in this box, *Ach Herr, mich armen Sünder*, and much in Leonhardt's performance that gives pleasure and profit.

Cantatas Nos 136: Erforsche mich, Gott; 137: Lobe den Herren; 138: Warum betrübst du dich; 139: Wohl dem, der sich auf seinem Gott.
** Tel. EX 6.35608 (2) [2635608]. Bergius, Rampf, Esswood, Equiluz, Holl, Heldwein, Hartinger, Tölz Ch., VCM, Harnoncourt.

In playing time this collection represents poor value for money: No. 137 is only 14 minutes, 136 is a mere 16′ 43″ and the longest of the four cantatas is only 18′ 39″. There is some relatively routine playing in this set, which emerges straight away in *Erforsche mich, Gott, und erfare mein Herz*. The singing is another matter: Paul Esswood's contribution in the aria, *Es kömmt ein Tag*, is very distinguished indeed, as is Robert Holl. Its successor, *Lobe den Herren, den mächtigen König der Ehren*, is probably the best-known and it prompts some lovely singing from Alan Bergius of the Tölz choir. No. 138, *Warum betrübst du dich, mein Herz*, is a particularly beautiful cantata, arguably the finest of the four. Written for the Fifteenth Sunday after Trinity, it opens with a strikingly poignant chorus which makes less effect than it might, thanks to some undistinguished singing and direction. The treble, Stefan Rampf, sounds distinctly insecure in the third section, *Er kann und will lasse nicht*. Nor can one say that *Wohl dem, der sich auf seinem Gott*, another Trinity cantata, is given a performance really worthy of it. The two oboi d'amore sound a little fragile at one point in the opening chorus. Still, the music is worth having and is not otherwise available.

Cantatas Nos 140: Wachet auf; 147: Herz und Mund und Tat und Leben.
(*) Tel. **ZK 8 43203 [id.]. Bergius, Rampf, Esswood, Equiluz, Hampson, Tölz Boys' Ch., VCM, Harnoncourt.

A coupling of two familiar cantatas, both made famous by their chorales. In No. 147, some may be a little disconcerted by the minor swelling effect in the phrasing of *Jesu, joy of man's desiring*, but otherwise the authentic approach brings much to enjoy. In No. 140 there are two beautiful duets between treble and bass soloists, representing dialogues between Jesus and the human soul, which are memorably sung. The production and recording are well up to the usual Telefunken standard.

Cantatas (i) *Nos 147: Herz und Mund und Tat und Leben; 148: Bringet dem Herrn Ehre seines Namens;* (ii) *149: Man singet mit Freuden vom Sieg;*

150: Nach dir, Herr, verlanget mich: 151: Süsser Trost, mein Jesus kommt.
*** Tel. Dig. **ZL8 35654**; EX6 35654 (2). Bergius, Hennig, Esswood, Equiluz, Van Egmond; (i) Tölz Boys' Ch., VCM, Harnoncourt; (ii) Ghent Coll. Vocale, Leonhardt Cons., Leonhardt.

The compact discs sound absolutely first class, with splendid definition and clarity in their favour. However, on LP the surfaces are inaudible and in addition to the price advantage many collectors will be swayed by the fact that the LP set also offers the miniature scores. The best-known cantata here is the festive No. 147, *Herz und Mund und Tat und Leben*, part of which derives from Weimar; but 148, *Bringet dem Herrn Ehre seines Namens*, is relatively little heard and proves an inventive and rewarding score. Paul Esswood's aria, *Mund und Herz steht dir offen*, scored for two oboi d'amore and oboe di caccia, is a delight and is beautifully played (much better than in No. 154 in the next volume). No. 149, *Man singet mit Freuden vom Sieg*, is another festive cantata whose opening chorus draws on 208, *Was mir behagt*. Generally good playing here and some fine singing, particularly from the young treble, Sebastian Hennig. No. 150, *Nach dir, Herr, verlanget mich*, is not assigned to any specific Sunday or feast-day; if doubt has been cast on its authenticity, surely there can be none as to its merit. There is a marvellous bassoon obbligato in the bass aria, *Krafft und Starke sei gesungen Gott*, which is expertly played. (Not all the instrumental playing is flawless or tidy.) No. 151, *Süsser Trost, mein Jesus kommt*, is a Christmas cantata, and a delightful one, too.

Cantatas Nos 152: Tritt auf die Glaubensbahn; 153: Schau lieber Gott, wie meine Feind; 154: Mein liebster Jesus ist verloren; 155: Mein Gott, wie lang, ach lange; 156: Ich steh' mit einem Fuss im Grabe.
(*) Tel. Dig. **ZL8 35656; EX6 35656 (2). Wegmann, Bergius, Rampff, Esswood, Equiluz, Hampson, Tölz Boys' Ch., VCM, Harnoncourt.

The five cantatas in this box are designed for the two Sundays after Christmas and the first three of Epiphany. None are otherwise currently available in either LP or compact disc format. Unlike the majority of these boxes, all five cantatas are given to the Vienna Concentus Musicus under Nikolaus Harnoncourt. No. 152, *Tritt auf die Glaubensbahn*, is the earliest, dating from 1714, and has some particularly felicitous instrumental invention: the *Sinfonia* is a delight. The playing of the Concentus Musicus is eloquent and the performance as a whole very enjoyable. Unfortunately the young Christoph Wegmann is obviously beset by nerves, though the voice, if unsteady, is admirably pure. No. 153, *Schau lieber Gott, wie meine Feind*, is a rarity and is unusual in that it discards the usual opening chorus in favour of a simple chorale: indeed, the cantata has three chorales in all. No. 154, *Mein liebster Jesus ist verloren*, is a powerful and emotional piece. The oboi d'amore suffer from imperfect intonation in the fourth number, *Jesu, lass dich finden*. Generally speaking, however, this is an acceptable performance. No. 155, *Mein Gott, wie lang, ach lange*, is another early cantata (1716) and shares the fourth side of the LP with No. 156, *Ich steh' mit einem*

Fuss im Grabe. The recording is very clean indeed, but perhaps a trifle dry, with relatively little ambience. As with its predecessor, the surfaces are very quiet; in addition to the price advantage over the compact discs, the LP set also offers the miniature scores along with copious and scholarly notes.

Cantata No. 205: Der zufriedengestellte Äolus.
*** Tel. Dig. **ZK8. 42 915**; AZ6. 42 915 [id.]. Kenny, Lipovsek, Equiluz, Holl, Arnold-Schönberg Ch., VCM, Harnoncourt.

There is no alternative recording of *Der zufriedengestellte Äolus* (or *Aeolus propitiated*) which Bach composed in 1725 for the name-day of August Müller, a botanist at the University of Leipzig. Bach calls it 'Dramma per musica', and some of its invention comes as close to opera as anything he wrote. It is a long piece of fifteen numbers and is written for ambitious forces: three trumpets, two horns, drums, two flutes, two oboes, string continuo with obbligato parts for viola d'amore, viola da gamba and oboe d'amore, plus four solo voices and choir, all of whom serenaded the learned scholar. Picander's libretto is slight, as for that matter is the plot. Aeolus plans to release the autumn gales, and resists the pleas of Zephyrus and Pomona to desist; however, Pallas finally persuades him that to do so will spoil the festivities she plans for August Müller. The performance is very good indeed, though the heavy accents in the opening chorus of the winds and the wooden orchestral tutti in the second number must be noted. Alice Harnoncourt's obbligato in *Angenehmer Zephyrus* (Delightful Zephyr) is a model of good style and is beautifully articulated. The singers, particularly Yvonne Kenny's Pallas and Kurt Equiluz's Zephyrus, are good; the recording has a decently spacious acoustic and no lack of detail. Recommended.

Cantatas (i) *Nos 208: Was mir behagt, ist nur die muntre Jagd* (Hunt cantata); (ii) *211: Schweigt stille, plaudert nicht* (Coffee cantata).
(M) ** HMV ED 290370-1/4. (i) Kupper, Köth, Wunderlich, Fischer-Dieskau, Berlin SO; (ii) Otto, Traxel, BPO, Forster.

Both recordings date from the early 1960s and benefit from new cutting techniques: the *Hunt cantata*, which takes 35 minutes, is accommodated in this EMI transfer on one side. Fischer-Dieskau is the finest of the soloists here; Erika Köth suffers from a consistent vibrato and Karl Forster does not bring the lightest touch to the proceedings. The *Coffee cantata* is another matter and again finds Fischer-Dieskau at his most persuasive. So conditioned are we to period-instrument performances that these accounts now seem distinctly overweight and the style heavy-handed, but there is a good deal of musical life in them. The recording sounds fresh and full-blooded.

Cantatas Nos 211: Schweigt stille, plaudert nicht; 212: Mer hahn en neue Oberkeet (Peasant cantata).
** Hung. Dig. **HCD 12462** [id.]. Laki, Gati, Fülöp, Capella Savaria, Németh.

In the *Coffee cantata* the famous aria, *Hat man nicht mit seinen Kindern*, goes much faster than usual – so as to reinforce the grumbling, snappish character of

Schlendrian, no doubt, but oddly serving only to diminish it. (Fischer-Dieskau has infinitely more character here in Karl Forster's EMI reissue – see above). The Capella Savaria under Philip Németh use authentic instruments and, if the strings sound badly in need of a massive blood transfusion in the admired (but not by us) manner of 'authentic' groups, there is an accomplished flautist. These are decently recorded performances, not outstanding but eminently serviceable and, at times, quite spirited.

Christmas oratorio, BWV 248.

(*) Tel. **ZB8 35022; FK6 35022 (3) [id.]. Treble soloists from V. Boys' Ch., Esswood, Equiluz, Nimsgern, V. Boys' Ch., Ch. Viennensis, VCM, Harnoncourt.

** Erato Dig. **ECD 880593**; NUM/*MCE* 751373 (3) [id.]. Schlick, C. Watkinson, Equiluz, Brodard, Lausanne Ens. and Ch., Corboz.

** DG Arc. **413 625-2** (3) [id.]. Janowitz, Ludwig, Wunderlich, Crass, Mun. Bach Ch. and O, Karl Richter.

(M) ** Decca 414 445-1/*4* (3). Ameling, Watts, Pears, Krause, Lübeck Kantorei, SCO, Münchinger.

* Eurodisc Dig. 610134 (3) [id.]. Augér, Burmeister, Schreier, Adam, Dresden Kreuzchor and PO, Flamig.

(*) CBS Dig. 13M/*13T* 39229 (3). Augér, Schreier, Muckenheim, Hamari, Schöne, Gächinger Kantorei and Bach Coll., Stuttgart, Rilling.

Harnoncourt in his search for authenticity in Bach performance has rarely been more successful than here. It will not be to everyone's taste to have a boy treble and male counter-tenor instead of women soloists, but the purity of sound of these singers is most affecting. Above all Harnoncourt in this instance never allows his pursuit of authentic sound to weigh the performance down. It has a lightness of touch which should please everyone. The sound, as usual from this source, is excellent and has transferred to CD with conspicuous success.

Festive with trumpets, superbly played, Corboz's version begins exceptionally well with fresh and beautifully balanced sound from chorus and orchestra. All six cantatas are presented very attractively, with bright sound set within an intimate but helpful acoustic; however, Corboz falls too often into a rhythmic jogtrot to undermine the imaginative singing and solo playing. The four soloists all have clean, very attractive voices, marred only by Michel Brodard's heavily aspirated style. Carolyn Watkinson is outstanding, but the tenderness of her singing in the Cradle song in the second cantata is minimized when the accompaniment is pedestrian.

Richter's recording comes up impressively in the CD transfer prepared for DG Archiv's Bach Edition, but the performance as well as the recording have dated. Relatively stiff, Richter takes an unvarying view of the chorales; fine solo singing and good choral work are, however, some compensation, with Christa Ludwig especially beautiful in the Cradle song. The contribution of the late Fritz Wunderlich too is glowingly beautiful, but Franz Crass, the bass, is coarse and unyielding.

Münchinger directs an admirably fresh performance, sharper in tone, brighter in recording (which dates from 1967) than Richter's set on DG Archiv. With an excellent team of soloists and with Lübeck trebles adding to the freshness, this is a good middle-of-the-road version, representative of modern scholarship as determined in the immediate pre-authentic era.

Despite bright choral singing and first-rate solo contributions from Augér and Schreier, the Eurodisc version is ruined by the stodgy conducting of Flamig. The digital recording is more successful with voices than with instruments.

With excellent soloists – including Peter Schreier as an outstanding and keenly imaginative tenor – the Rilling performance yet fails to win any recommendation on account of its rhythmic heaviness at whatever speed and its rough, thin recording. Choral sound is particularly disagreeable.

Easter oratorio, BWV 249.

(M) **(*) Decca Ser. 414 054-1. Ameling, Watts, Krenn, Krause, V. Ac. Ch., SCO, Münchinger.

(M) ** HMV ED 100255-1/*4*. Zylis-Gara, Johnson, Altmeyer, Fischer-Dieskau, S. German Madrigal Ch., SW German CO, Gönnenwein.

With a thrift common among eighteenth-century composers, Bach reworked secular material for this attractive oratorio. The opening sinfonia is dramatic with its hints of 'thunders and lightnings' in the style of the *St Matthew Passion*; but in the main it is a genial work and a genial performance is what is called for. Münchinger gives a spacious and impressive reading, and is well served by his splendid team of soloists. Given such fine recording, too, this is a reliable recommendation for the work, if lacking the last degree of imagination.

Gönnenwein has good soloists and the sound has an authentic feel – the 1964 recording re-emerges freshly in the present remastering – although he does not entirely avoid an over-scholarly impression. But the music making is spirited, with a committed and lively contribution from the chorus. This makes a good alternative choice to Münchinger, with the bright clean cassette transfer every bit the equal of the LP.

Magnificat in D, BWV 243.

*** Ph. Dig. **411 458-2**; 411 458-1/*4* [id.]. Argenta, Kwella, Kirkby, Brett, Rolfe-Johnson, David Thomas, E. Bar. Soloists, Gardiner – *Cantata No. 10.****

(M) *** Decca Ser. 414 322-1/*4*. Ameling, Watts, Krenn, Bork, Krause, V. Ac. Ch., SCO, Münchinger – *Cantata No. 10.****

* Tel. Dig. **ZK8 42955**; AZ6/*CY4* 42955 [id.]. Heichele, Esswood, Equiluz, Holl, V. Boys' Ch., Schoenberg Ch., VCM, Harnoncourt – HANDEL: *Utrecht Te Deum.**(*)

The better-known D major version of the *Magnificat* receives an exhilarating performance from John Eliot Gardiner. Tempi are consistently brisk, but the vigour and precision of the chorus is such that one never has the feeling that the pacing is hurried, for the singing has fervour as well as energy and, when there is need to relax, Gardiner does so convincingly. A splendid team of soloists, and the accompaniment is no less impressive, with a memorable oboe d'amore obbligato to embroider the *Quia respexit*. This is first class in every way, and the recorded sound is well balanced, fresh and vivid. The CD has that extra degree of presence, but the chrome cassette is outstandingly well managed, too.

Münchinger's Stuttgart recording dates from 1969 and was one of his finest Bach performances. It is still as impressive as any in the catalogue after the Gardiner version, which has a more authentic overall feel. But in its day, Münchinger's version was highly regarded. The soloists are uniformly good and so are the contributions of the Vienna Academy Choir and the Stuttgart Chamber Orchestra. Münchinger tends to stress the breadth and spaciousness of the *Magnificat* – though his reading has plenty of spirit – and the Decca engineers have captured the detail with admirable clarity and naturalness. Even though this is in Decca's lowest price range (and thus costs about a third the price of Gardiner's CD), the cassette is transferred on chrome stock. It is admirably focused and extremely vivid, with the trumpets sounding resplendent. A fine bargain.

Harnoncourt's version is generously coupled with a major Handel piece, but the squareness of rhythm, with repeated quavers chugging instead of lifting, makes the result pedestrian, despite some excellent solo singing. The chorus is far less imaginative, pedestrian like the playing. The sound is clear but on the dry side, not at all atmospheric.

Magnificat in E flat (original version), *BWV 243a*.

*** O-L **414 678-2** [id.]. Nelson, Kirkby, C. Watkinson, Elliot, D. Watkinson, Christ Church Ch., AAM, Preston – VIVALDI: *Gloria*.***

The original version of the *Magnificat* is textually different in detail (quite apart from being a semitone higher) and has four interpolations for the celebration of Christmas. Preston and the Academy of Ancient Music present a characteristically alert and fresh performance, and the Christ Church Choir is in excellent form. One might quibble at the use of women soloists instead of boys, but these three specialist singers have just the right incisive timbre and provide the insight of experience. The compact disc is now paired with Vivaldi's *Gloria*, a much more generous coupling than the original LP.

Mass in B min., BWV 232.

© *** DG Arc. Dig. **415 514-2**; 415 514-1/*4* [id.]. Argenta, Dawson, Fairfield, Knibbs, Kwella, Hall, Nichols, Chance, Collin, Stafford, Evans, Milner, Murgatroyd, Lloyd-Morgan, Varcoe, Monteverdi Ch., E. Bar. Soloists, Gardiner.

*** HMV Dig. **CDS 747293-8** [id.]; EX 270239-3/*5* (2). Kirkby, Van Evera, Iconomou, Immler, Kilian, Covey-Crump, David Thomas, Taverner Cons. and Players, Parrott.

*** Ph. **416 415-2** (2); 6769 002/*7699 076* (3) [id.]. Marshall, Baker, Tear, Ramey, Ch. and ASMF, Marriner.

*** Eurodisc **610 089** (2). Popp, C. Watkinson, Bluchner, Lorenz, Adam, Leipzig R. Ch., New Bach Coll. Mus., Schreier.

*** None. Dig. **CD 79036-2**; D 79036/*D4* [id.]. Nelson, Baird, Dooley, Minter, Hoffmeister, Brownless, Opalach, Schultze, Bach Ens., Rifkin.

(*) Tel. **ZA8 35019; FK6 35019 (2) [id.]. Hansmann, Iiyama, Watts, Equiluz, Van Egmond, V. Boys' Ch., Ch. Viennensis, VCM, Harnoncourt.

(M) **(*) Decca Jub. 414 251-1/*4* (2). Ameling, Minton, Watts, Krenn, Krause, Stuttgart Chamber Ch. and O, Münchinger.

(M) ** DG 413 948-1 (3). Stader, Töpper, Haefliger, Fischer-Dieskau, Mun. Bach Ch. and O, Karl Richter.

(M) ** DG 415 622-1/*4* (2) [id.]. Janowitz, Ludwig, Schreier, V. Singverein, BPO, Karajan.

John Eliot Gardiner makes an impressive start to his projected series of Bach choral works for DG Archiv with this magnificent account of the *B minor Mass*, one which attempts to keep within an authentic scale but which also triumphantly encompasses the work's grandeur. Where latterly in 'authentic' performances we have come to expect the grand six-part setting of the *Sanctus* to trip along like a dance movement, Gardiner masterfully conveys the majesty (with bells and censer-swinging evoked) simultaneously with a crisply resilient rhythmic pulse. The choral tone is luminous and powerfully projected. In the earlier parts of the *Mass*, Gardiner generally has four voices per part, but key passages – such as the opening of the first *Kyrie* fugue – are treated as concertinos for soloists alone. The later, more elaborate sections, such as the *Sanctus*, have five voices per part, so that the final *Dona nobis pacem* is subtly grander than when it appears earlier as *Gratias agimus tibi*. The regular solo numbers are taken by choir members, all of them pure-toned and none of them hooters, making a cohesive whole. The alto, Michael Chance, deserves special mention for his distinctively warm and even singing in both *Qui sedes* and *Agnus Dei*. On CD, the recording is warmly atmospheric but not cloudy, very well designed to present both breadth and clarity. There are excellent chrome cassettes.

Prompted by Joshua Rifkin's argument for one voice per part even in this most monumental of Bach's choral works, Parrott very effectively modifies that absolute stance – hoping to re-create even more closely the conditions Bach would have expected in Leipzig – by adding to the soloists a ripieno group of five singers from the Taverner Consort for the choruses. The instrumental group is similarly augmented with the keenest discretion. Though there was no live performance of the *Mass* in Bach's lifetime – it was considered a work of theory like the *Art of fugue*, a summation of a lifetime of study – this aims 'to adopt the conventions of a hypothetical performance by Bach himself at Leipzig'. Parrott's success lies in retaining the freshness and bite of the Rifkin approach while creating a more vivid atmosphere. Speeds are generally fast, with rhythms sprung to reflect the inspiration of dance; however, the inner darkness of the *Crucifixus*, for example, is intensely conveyed in its hushed tones, while the *Et resurrexit* promptly erupts with a power to compensate for any lack of traditional weight. Soloists are excellent, within the new conventions of authentic performance, with reduction of vibrato still allowing sweetness as well as purity. The three boy altos from the Austrian Tölzerchor are very well matched, sharing the alto solo role between them. If you want a performance on a reduced scale, Parrott scores palpably over Rifkin in the keener, more dramatic sense of contrast, clearly distinguishing choruses and solos. The recording, made in St John's, Smith Square, is both realistic and atmospheric. The compact discs are impressively clear and generously cued. They emphasize the comparatively forward balance and intimacy of scale.

For Neville Marriner this was a larger recording project than he had undertaken before, and he rose superbly to the challenge. Predictably, many of the tempi are daringly fast; *Et resurrexit*, for example, has the Academy chorus on its toes, but the rhythms are so resiliently sprung that the result is exhilarating, never hectic. An even more remarkable achievement is that in the great moments of contemplation such as *Et incarnatus* and *Crucifixus* Marriner finds a degree of inner intensity to match the gravity of Bach's inspiration, with tempi often slower than usual. That dedication is matched by the soloists, the superb soprano Margaret Marshall as much as the longer-established singers. This is a performance which finds the balance between small-scale authenticity and recognition of massive inspiration, neither too small nor too large, and with good atmospheric recording, not quite as defined as it might be on inner detail; this is fully recommendable. The remastering for CD has been able to improve the definition only marginally: the choral textures are realistically full but not ideally transparent. The layout is on two CDs against three LPs, and good access is provided by the cueing.

The refreshing distinctiveness of Schreier's reading is typified by his account of the great *Sanctus*, dancing along lightly and briskly, not at all weighty in the usual manner. His speeds are consistently fast, but that does not prevent Schreier from capturing a devotional mood, as for example in the final *Dona nobis pacem* which, in powerful crescendo, begins in meditation and ends in joy. Though Schreier has opted for modern pitch and instruments, his performance gains from experience of the authentic movement; in the bass aria, *Quoniam*, for example, he has a corno di caccia playing the horn obbligato an octave higher than usual. With bright, keen choral singing and very good work from the soloists (Theo Adam occasionally excepted, with his sour tone), this is an excellent version for anyone wanting a resilient, lightweight view, using authentically small forces but without the problems of authentic performance. Good, spacious recording.

Whether or not you subscribe to the controversial theories behind the performance under Joshua Rifkin, the result is undeniably refreshing and often exhilarating. Rifkin – best known for playing Scott Joplin rags but a classical scholar too – here presents Bach's masterpiece in the improbable form of one voice to a part in the choruses. There are scholarly arguments in favour of suggesting that Bach, even for such grand choruses, employed that smallest possible ensemble. Certainly one gets a totally new perspective when, at generally brisk speeds, the complex counterpoint is so crisp and clean, with original (relatively gentle) instruments in the orchestra adding to the freshness and intimacy.

The soprano, Judith Nelson, is already well known in the world of authentic performance; the other soloists also sing with comparable brightness, freshness and precision, even if lack of choral weight means that dramatic contrasts are less sharp than usual. An exciting pioneering set, crisply and vividly recorded, which rightly won *Gramophone*'s choral award in 1983. However, the newer set from Parrott's Taverner Consort, which has followed on directly from Rifkin's pioneering approach, will probably be preferred by most readers for its greater sense of drama and atmosphere.

Harnoncourt's version marked a breakthrough in the development of the authentic movement. The compact disc version of his performance is not just clearer but carries more impact. It confirms that, in parallel with his account of the *Christmas oratorio*, this is one of his most effective Bach performances on a chamber scale, with the choir, including boys' voices, projecting keenly. Rhythmically he is not so imaginative as his finest authentic rivals, and the brisk *Sanctus* is disappointing, but he rises warmly to the final *Dona nobis pacem*, given a real sense of occasion. First-rate solo singing, notably from Helen Watts, not normally associated with authentic performances, but aptly firm and even. Nicely balanced recording, good for its late-1960s vintage.

Münchinger's is a strong, enjoyable performance with an exceptionally fine quintet of soloists and first-rate recording. That it comes on four sides instead of six adds to its attractiveness, and on balance it makes a fair recommendation; however, with fastish tempi and a generally extrovert manner it is efficient rather than inspiring. The chorus sings well but is placed rather backwardly. The recording dates from 1971 and has been successfully remastered, with the cassettes particularly successful in their vividness. The chorus sounds vibrant and clear and the trumpets offer no transfer problems.

Though Richter's performance dates from the early 1960s it is still worth considering, for the choral work is well focused, firm and distinct. Among the soloists, Hertha Töpper is disappointing, but the others, Fischer-Dieskau in particular, are most impressive. However, although now reissued at mid-price, it is on three discs against Münchinger's two.

Karajan's performance is marked by his characteristic smoothness of Bach style. He conveys intensity, even religious fervour, but the sharp contours of Bach's majestic writing are often missing. The very opening brings an impressive first entry of the choir on *Kyrie* but then, after the instrumental fugue, the contrapuntal entries are sung in a self-consciously softened tone. There is a strong sense of the work's architecture, however, and the highly polished surfaces do not obscure the depths of the music. The reissue – at mid-price – has successfully remastered the recording to fit on to two discs and matching chrome cassettes (in a DG flap-pack), the sound quality smooth to match the performance.

Masses: in F, BWV 233; in A, BWV 234; in G min., BWV 235; in G, BWV 236.

* HMV Dig. EX 270029-3/5 (2). Åkerlund, Weller, De Mey, Varcoe, Basle Madrigalists, Linde Cons., Linde.

(M) * Ph. 6725 038 (2). Giebel, Ameling, Litz, Finnila, Altmeyer, Prey, Reimer, Mun. Pro Arte Ch. and O, Redel; Westphalian Singers, German Bach Soloists, Winschermann.

All Bach's Lutheran masses have the same ground plan: the *Kyrie* is distinguished by contrapuntal writing of some ingenuity, while the *Gloria* falls into two larger-scale movements that provide a festive framework for three solo sections. All the material is borrowed or 'parodied' from the cantatas BWV 72, 102, 179 and 187, only the recitatives and choruses being newly composed. These Linde performances are dutiful, neither vital nor particularly imaginative – and at times less than distinguished. The *Qui tollis* of the *A major Mass*, for example, suffers from frail intonation from the flutes and some insecurity from Lina Åkerlund, who phrases sensitively. There is some good singing, particularly from Sharon Weller and Stephen Varcoe, but these *Masses* need more persuasive advocacy and commitment. The recordings are well balanced and lifelike; the cassettes too are of good quality, with a satisfactory choral focus.

On Philips, the *F major* and *A major Masses*, BWV 233–4, were recorded in 1965 under Kurt Redel, and the remaining two five years later with Helmut Winschermann. No nonsense about period instruments or contemporary performance practice here – but little joy for those who like old-fashioned Bach either! Redel is uninspired and the choral singing laborious. Winschermann has greater warmth and is less heavy-handed; moreover, he has a better choir and the advantage of Elly Ameling among his soloists. All the same, well recorded though these performances are, they are not really recommendable.

St John Passion, BWV 245.

(M) **(*) Decca 414 068-1/*4* (2) [id.]. Ellenbeck, Berry, Ahrans, Ameling, Hamari, Hollweg, Prey, Stuttgart Hymnus Boys' Ch., SCO, Münchinger.

(M) ** Ph. 412 415-1/*4* (3/*2*). Giebel, Hoffgen, Haefliger, Young, Berry, Crass, Netherlands R. Ch., Concg. O, Jochum.

** DG **413 622-2** (2); 413 944-1 (3) [id.]. Lear, Töpper, Haefliger, Prey, Engen, Mun. Bach Ch. and O, Karl Richter.

Münchinger's set dates from 1975, and the recording is excellent: no loss seems to have occurred in the remastering on to two instead of three discs. The dynamic range is strikingly wide and the sound itself fresh and full, with the tapes also bright and clear. Münchinger's reading matches his other recordings of Bach's choral works, with a superb line-up of soloists, all of them clear-toned and precise, and with a fresh and young-sounding tenor, Dieter Ellenbeck, as Evangelist. The musical balance of the score is pointed most satisfyingly without idiosyncrasy, using organ continuo with no harpsichord. This is preferable to Richter and is priced at not much more than a third of the cost of the DG CDs.

While Jochum and his Dutch group offer the relatively conventional interpretation that one would expect from him, there is a splendid warmth and musical spontaneity about the set which is recorded in a spacious acoustic. The performance has some outstanding contributions from the soloists, particularly from Giebel and Haefliger, and some eloquent instrumental playing. It is not, however, particularly concerned with authenticity; forces are not scaled down and the continuo role is divided between harpsichord and organ. The 1968 recording still sounds quite well, with the choral tone full-bodied; while the focus is less than sharp, the effect is reasonably convincing within the chosen acoustic. The tapes match the discs closely in this respect.

The CD version of Richter's 1964 recording (on two discs) freshens and clarifies the inevitably limited sound. Though choral passages remain less well focused, the recitatives and arias have fine immediacy. This is a typical example of Richter's Bach style, sober and weighty and obviously dedicated, but wearing badly as the trend towards lightening the performance of Bach gains ground. Haefliger is outstanding among the soloists. On LP, the set runs to three discs but is now offered at medium price.

St Matthew Passion, BWV 244.

(*) Ph. Dig. **412 527-2 (3); 412 527-1/*4* (4) [id.]. Schreier, Adam, Popp, Lipovsek, Holl, Dresden Children's Ch., Leipzig R. Ch., Dresden State O, Schreier.

(M) **(*) HM **HMC 901155-7**; HMC/*40* 1155-7. Crook, Cold, Schlick, Jacobs, Blochwitz, Kooy, Paris Chapelle Royale, Ghent Coll. Mus., Herreweghe.

(*) DG Arc. **413 613-2 (3); 413 939-1 (4) [id.]. Schreier, Fischer-Dieskau, Mathis, Baker, Salminen, Regensburger Domspatzen, Mun. Bach Ch. and O, Karl Richter.

(M) **(*) Decca 414 057-1/*4* (3). Pears, Prey, Ameling, Höffgen, Wunderlich, Krause, Stuttgart Hymnus Boys' Ch., SCO, Münchinger.

** Erato Dig. **ECD 880633**; NUM 750553 (3) [id.]. Equiluz, Faulstisch, Margaret Marshall, C. Watkinson, Rolfe-Johnson, Huttenlocher, Lausanne Vocal Ens. and CO, Corboz.

(*) Ph. mono **416 206-2** (3) [id.]. Erb, Ravelli, Vincent, Durigo, Van Tulder, Schey, Zanglust Boys' Ch., Amsterdam Toonkunst Ch., Concg. O, Mengelberg.

It is an astonishing achievement of Peter Schreier to conduct this most exacting of choral works as well as taking the leading vocal role of the Evangelist. As in his recording of the *B minor Mass* for Eurodisc using the same choir and some of the same soloists, his aim in Bach interpretation is to bring new lightness without following the full dictates of authentic performance and in this he succeeds superbly. Compared with the *B minor Mass*, where some of Schreier's speeds come near to being eccentrically fast, his fondness for brisk speeds is here kept in check. Such meditative arias as the contralto's *Erbarme dich* or the soprano's *Aus liebe* bring a natural gravity and depth of expression, though Marjana Lipovsek has a tendency to sit on the flat side of the note, and Lucia Popp's silvery soprano is not always caught at its sweetest. The end result is a refreshing and cohesive performance, ideal for records, when there is no tendency for the piece to drag. The recording is first rate, with the choral forces well separated. The CD version takes only three discs as against four LPs, and the extra convenience offered by copious banding adds to the enjoyment of using the set. The cassettes are also well managed with a good choral focus, though not as impressively vivid and clear as on Münchinger's Decca tapes.

With an outstanding team of solo singers, all clear-toned and mostly new to records, and with bright, immediate sound full of presence, Herreweghe's version presents a good choice for anyone wanting a performance on period instruments at lower pitch. Howard Crook is an excellent, fresh-toned Evangelist, and the other tenor, Hans-Peter Blochwitz, is first rate too. The alto part is taken by the celebrated counter-tenor, René Jacobs, rather hooty in *Erbarme dich*; but the soprano, Barbara Schluck, with her bright clear voice sings radiantly. The instrumental group plays in authentic style but not abrasively so; Herreweghe's control of rhythm, however, tends to be too heavy. Chorales are often slow and over-accented, and heavy stressing mars the big numbers too. In lightness and point the Schreier version on Philips, which is only just on the other side of the authenticity barrier, at modern pitch and with modern instruments but adopting many authentic performance practices, is consistently preferable.

Richter's version, replacing an earlier account, was the last of his major Bach recordings and arguably the finest, with an outstanding team of soloists and excellent choral singing (including splendid treble contributions from the 'Cathedral Sparrows' of Regensburg). Dame Janet Baker's singing of *Erbarme dich* crowns a totally dedicated performance, but the heaviness of Richter's approach to Bach is becoming more and more difficult to accept in an age when the extra illumination gained from treating Bach more lightly and resiliently is universally recognized. The CD transfer for the DG Archiv Bach Edition brings many benefits in convenience as well as in sound quality but, if anything, the extra immediacy adds to the heaviness.

Münchinger's direction does not attain the spiritual heights of an interpretation such as Klemperer's, but his version is consistently fresh and alert, and it has the degree of authenticity of its period (1965) – although much has happened to Bach performances since then. All the soloists are excellent, and Peter Pears shows that no tenor of his generation rivalled his insight as the Evangelist. Elly Ameling is sweet-toned and sensitive. The recording is first class, clear and brilliant and very well balanced. The cassettes are particularly successful, with the chorus sounding incisive and well defined, with just the right degree of weight. Some may object to the deliberate closeness with which the voice of Hermann Prey as Jesus has been recorded.

The scale and liveliness of the story-telling are very much in favour of the Corboz version. This is the *Matthew Passion* presented as a narrative rather than as a grand, spiritual event; it is enjoyable within limits but misses a sense of occasion and, with it, the spiritual depth of the work. Though the chorales are done lightly and expressively, it does not help that the choral sound is much cloudier than that of the solo voices, a first-rate team with Kurt Equiluz as ever an outstanding, lively and distinctive Evangelist. Chief blame for the limitations of the performance must rest with Corboz, who too often keeps rhythms too evenly stressed.

Mengelberg's performances of the *St Matthew Passion* were legendary in their day and this account, recorded in the Concertgebouw, Amsterdam, on Palm Sunday 1939, has great period interest as well as an obvious poignancy. However, the great German-born conductor indulges in ritardandos that are positively horrendous. The alto aria, *Buss und Reu*, is constantly pulled out of shape – indeed, it is altogether insupportable – and *Blute nur* which follows it is hardly less grotesque. Jo Vincent's glorious singing is also subject to totally ruinous ritardandi. It is good to have Karl Erb's Evangelist; but the passionate choral response is the best thing about this set – apart from Jo Vincent, of course – and is really gripping in its intensity. There are cuts; however, given what happens to much of what survives (including *Ich Will Dir mein Herze schenken*, where yet again Jo Vincent is not permitted to sing without the brakes grinding), this is of small account. With these singers participating there are obviously wonderful things, but for the non-specialist collector this is far too eccentric a performance to gain acceptance.

St Matthew Passion: excerpts.
** Erato Dig. **ECD 88017** [id.] from above recording, cond. Corboz.

Some collectors may like to have a CD sampler of Corboz's version of the *St Matthew Passion*, which tries to achieve a balance between tradition and the 'authentic' approach, using small forces but in a relatively relaxed way. The soloists are each given an opportunity to shine, and the highlight is Carolyn Watkinson's *Erbarme dich*. The snag is that the choral recording, although digital, is not as sharp in focus as one might have expected.

Vocal collections

Aria: *Bist du bei mir*. Cantata arias: *No. 6: Hochgelobter Gottessohn; No. 11: Ach bleibe doch; No. 34: Wohl euch ihr auserwählten Seelen; No. 129: Gelobet sei der Herr; No. 161: Komm, du süsse Todesstunde; No. 190: Lobe Zion, deinen Gott. Christmas oratorio: Bereite dich. Easter oratorio: Saget, saget mir geschwinde. Magnificat: Et exultavit. St John Passion: Es ist vollbracht.*
(M) *** HMV EG 290489-1/4. Dame Janet Baker, ASMF, Marriner.
(B) *** HMV *TCC 2-POR 154592-9*. (As above) – *Cantatas Nos 82 and 169.****

Predictably, Dame Janet Baker gives beautiful and deeply felt performances of a fine (mid-price) collection of Bach arias. Sweet contemplative arias predominate, and an excellent case is made for including the alternative cantata version, *Ach bleibe doch*, of what became the *Agnus Dei* in the *B minor Mass*. The accompaniments could hardly be more understanding (the gamba solo in *Es ist vollbracht* adding extra poignancy), and the recording is rich and warm. The alternative tape-only issue in HMV's 'Portrait of the Artist' series is even better value. Here the arias are coupled with two fine performances of Cantatas which are not otherwise available.

Arias: Mass in B min.: Agnus Dei; Qui sedes. St John Passion: All is fulfilled. St Matthew Passion: Grief for sin.

(***) Decca mono **414 623-2**; stereo 414 623-1/*4*. Kathleen Ferrier, LPO, Boult – HANDEL: *Arias*.(***) ❀

On 7th and 8th October 1952, Kathleen Ferrier made her last and perhaps greatest record in London's Kingsway Hall, coupling four arias each by Bach and Handel. The combined skill of John Culshaw and Kenneth Wilkinson ensured a recording of the utmost fidelity by the standards of that time; with the advent of stereo, Sir Adrian Boult and the LPO, who provided the original accompaniments, were persuaded by Culshaw to return and record a new orchestral backing, over the old, and the result was something of a musical and technological miracle. It might seem perverse, therefore, that for the CD issue Decca have returned to the original mono master tape, yet the results fully justify that decision. Close comparison between mono CD and stereo LP shows that in masking the earlier recording the voice became very slightly clouded, particularly in its upper range. Now it re-emerges with extraordinary naturalness and presence. The mono accompaniments were beautifully balanced and orchestral detail is clarified further, with the harpsichord continuo coming through the more transparent texture in *Grief for sin* and Ambrose Gauntlett's viola da gamba obbligato for *All is fulfilled* more tangible. Of course the upper strings sound thinner, but that adds an 'authentic' touch, and they are given a far more dramatic bite in the climax at the words: *The Lion of Judah fought the fight*. In stereo, on LP and tape, the overall effect is richer, but the digitally remastered mono original, apart from enhancing the vocal realism, undoubtedly emphasizes the freshness of Boult's contribution. The pre-Dolby background noise is still apparent but is in no way distracting. The compact disc documentation, however, is inferior to that provided with the medium-priced LP, offering only a chatty biographical note about Kathleen Ferrier and nothing about the circumstances surrounding the recording, or its subsequent history. The excellent cassette carries the stereo version, like the LP.

COLLECTION

'90-Minute anthology': (i) *Brandenburg concerto No. 2; Suite No. 3: Air;* (ii) *Italian concerto:* 1st movt; (iii) *Chorale prelude: Wachet auf;* (iv) *Toccata and fugue in D min., BWV 565;* excerpts from *Cantatas Nos 82; 147* (*Jesu, joy of man's desiring*)*;* (v) *208* (*Sheep may safely graze*)*;* (i) *Christmas oratorio; Magnificat in D; Mass in B min.; St Matthew Passion.*

(B) *** Decca *414 047-4*. Various artists including (i) SCO, Münchinger, with soloists and chorus; (ii) George Malcolm; (iii) Simon Preston; (iv) Karl Richter; Kirsten Flagstad.

Centred on Karl Münchinger's Bach recordings from his vintage Decca period, this is a most rewarding anthology, perhaps not quite as enticing as the comparable Handel compilation, but including the essence of Bach's greatness and many popular favourites. Münchinger is heard at his best in the *Second Brandenburg* and in the major choral works. Other attractive items include Kathleen

Ferrier's *Agnus Dei* from the *B minor Mass* (preceded by the *Sanctus*) and Kirsten Flagstad as soloist in *Schafe können sicher weiden*, better known as *Sheep may safely graze*. The concert opens and closes joyfully with choruses from the *Christmas oratorio* and side one ends with the glorious *Setzen uns mit Tränen nieder* from the *St Matthew Passion*. A happily conceived and well-executed 'popular' contribution to the Tercentenary. The sound – though only iron-oxide tape is used – is consistently good throughout.

Miscellaneous arrangements

'Switched-on Bach' (electronic realizations by Wendy Carlos and Benjamin Folkman): *Brandenburg concerto No. 3 in G. Cantatas Nos 29: Sinfonia; 147: Jesu, joy of man's desiring. Chorale prelude: Wachet auf. Suite No. 3 in D: Air. Two-part inventions in B flat; D min.; F. The Well-tempered Clavier: Preludes and fugues Nos 2 in C min.; 7 in E flat.*
(*) CBS **MK 63501; 63501 [**MK 7194**; MS 7194]. Wendy Carlos (Moog synthesizer).

The Moog synthesizer has now become quite an accepted item in the recording studio, but this highly individual record was the one which above all established Moog's claims as a popularizer in the classical field. The purist will certainly wince, but almost any of these arrangements for computer sound has a hypnotic quality, attested by the phenomenal success the disc had in America and by the way that non-Bachians tend to take to it. The interpretation of the *Third Brandenburg* is allegedly based – with all the subtleties of rubato and phrasing – on two classic recordings of the past, though Carlos rightly takes ultimate responsibility. The stereo effects are elaborate, many of them not just gimmicks but attempts to clarify what Bach wrote without altering his notes. In most ways this is a brilliantly successful record, the best of its kind. The CD transfer, although vivid, has moments when the focus slips, and the originally resonant sound has obviously resisted the clarifying process in places, bringing roughness to the sound-image. The LP is in the mid-price range and so costs about a third as much as the CD.

Bach, Wilhelm Friedemann (1710–84)

Trio sonata in A min. (incomplete).
*** CBS Dig. **MK 37813**; 37813/*40*- [id.]. Rampal, Stern, Ritter, Parnas – C. P. E., J. C. F. and J. S. BACH: *Trio sonatas.****

This comes at the end of an attractive and very well-played recital of music by Bach and his musical sons. We are offered a tempting opening movement and then, after a few bars, the *Larghetto* peters out in a mood of gentle melancholy. Whether the rest of the piece was lost or never actually written, we are not told. Admirably clear recording, and a good tape.

6 Duets for 2 flutes.
** Denon Dig. **C37 7287** [id.]. Aurèle and Christiane Nicolet.

Sixty minutes of flute duets is a daunting prospect but, taken individually and, it must be added, very occasionally, these pieces can give pleasure. Four of the six (F54, 55, 47 and 59) were composed while Wilhelm Friedemann was at Dresden (1733–46), and the remaining two after 1770 when he was unsettled. Aurèle Nicolet and his wife, Christiane, give highly accomplished and vividly recorded accounts of all six pieces, which are far from uninventive but hardly of great significance.

Baermann, Heinrich (1784–1847)

Adagio for clarinet and orchestra.
*** ASV Dig. **CDDCA 559**; DCA/*ZCDCA* 559 [id.]. Emma Johnson, ECO, Groves – CRUSELL: *Concerto No. 2**** ❀; ROSSINI: *Intro. theme and variations*; WEBER: *Concertino.****
*** HMV Dig. EL 270220-1/*4*. Meyer, Württemberg CO, Faerber – MENDELSSOHN: *Concert pieces*; WEBER: *Clarinet quintet.****

Heinrich Baermann was one of the greatest clarinettists of his day, admired both by Mendelssohn and by Weber, who must have had him in mind when composing the clarinet solo in the *Freischütz overture*. His rather beautiful *Adagio*, once attributed to Wagner, is offered here by two young clarinettists, both of whom have recently sprung to fame, Emma Johnson as the BBC's 'Young musician of the year' in 1984, and Sabine Meyer, who was involved in a tussle between Karajan and the Berlin Philharmonic when she was appointed principal in 1983. Both artists play the work warmly and sympathetically – Emma Johnson is particularly languorous – and both are well accompanied and recorded. Couplings should dictate choice here.

Balakirev, Mily (1837–1910)

Symphonies Nos 1 in C; 2 in D min.; Overture on three Russian folksongs; Russia; Tamara (symphonic poems).
** Eurodisc 300045 (3). USSR State Ac. O, Svetlanov.

Balakirev occupied a dominant position in Russian musical life for many years after the death of Glinka, yet his reputation rests on a distinctly meagre output. Indeed, there are two rather than three periods: the first from the 1850s to the 1860s embraces the *King Lear* music and various overtures, including the one recorded here; the second, the last dozen or so years of his life, begins with the appearance of the *First Symphony* in 1898. In between, Balakirev withdrew from active musical life into a world of intense religious preoccupations. In his music, then, we have what Gerald Abraham once called 'the dawn and sunset of genius with little of its full day'. Yet there is surely no questioning the appeal of his ideas or the skill and richness of their presentation. Balakirev's representation in the current catalogue is somewhat scanty and, apart from the *First Symphony*, none of his orchestral music, not even his masterpiece, *Tamara*, is currently available elsewhere. The *C major Symphony*, over which he laboured so long and painfully (a large part of it was already written in the 1860s), has been recorded by the City of Birmingham Symphony Orchestra under Neeme Järvi (see below), and the greater clarity and presence of the HMV recording makes it the stronger contender, even if the playing of the USSR Symphony Orchestra for Svetlanov has much to recommend it: their strings certainly have greater sonority and weight, though the brass and wind are not always to Western tastes. Nor is the quality of the recorded sound here outstanding, or anywhere near it. The much later *Second Symphony* is an attractive piece, here given a generally fine performance. The drawback is that the ample acoustic hampers definition. The idiom of this late work does not differ from the earlier one – indeed, some of the material of the scherzo was actually intended for the *First Symphony*. Yet the ideas (particularly the first movement and the final polonaise) are very engaging.

Svetlanov conveys the exotic hothouse atmosphere of *Tamara* excellently, if a little hampered by the reverberation. This performance is very persuasive until the *L'istesso tempo* passage 8 bars before fig. 18, where Svetlanov encourages the violas and then the violins to do some swooning portamenti that make one feel positively queasy. However, for those prepared to overlook this vulgarism, this is a very good *Tamara* and every bit as colourful and mysterious as the famous Beecham record. Climaxes in *Russia* suffer from some distortion, and the recorded sound here calls for some measure of tolerance. Nevertheless, this set fills an obvious gap.

Symphony No. 1 in C.
*** HMV Dig. EL 270050-1/*4* [Ang. DS/*4XS* 38090]. CBSO, Järvi – LIADOV: *Polonaise*.**(*)

Balakirev's *First Symphony* is rarely heard in the concert hall and is relatively neglected by the gramophone. This HMV version is only the fourth ever to appear. Järvi gives a very good performance of it, well prepared, with excellent ensemble and responsive woodwind phrasing. Perhaps the strings are just a little wanting in sonority and weight by comparison with the classic Karajan/Philharmonia recording (currently deleted), but this is a minor reservation. Järvi secures an excellent sense of momentum in the first two movements, and if the tension drops a little in the slow movement – by comparison with Karajan and Beecham – it is still convincingly shaped. The recording is extremely fine. The balance is a little close, but in truthfulness of timbre, richness of bass sonority and range the sound is altogether first class.

Bantock, Granville (1868–1946)

The Pierrot of the Minute: overture.
(*) Chan. **CHAN 8373; CBR/*CBT* 1018 [id.]. Bournemouth Sinf., Del Mar – BRIDGE: *Summer* etc.; BUTTERWORTH: *Banks of green willow.****

Bantock's overture comes from 1908 and was one of his most popular works. It is concerned with Pierrot's dream in which he falls in love with a Moon Maiden who tells him their love must die at dawn, but he will not listen. He wakes to realize that his dream of love lasted a mere minute. The writing is often delicate and at times Elgarian, and the piece is well worth investigating. The recording – originally issued on RCA – has now passed back to Chandos. It has been digitally remastered with great success and sounds remarkably fresh on CD. The cassette is excellent too and (like the LP) is offered at mid-price, so costs a great deal less than the CD.

Oedipus Colonnus: overture.
(*) Lyr. SRCS 123. Philh. O, Braithwaite – STANFORD: *Irish rhapsody No. 4.**

Bantock's very Straussian work, more a symphonic poem than an overture, is richly scored and well argued, starting with a fate theme in a slow 5/4, apt for a tragic Greek subject. Nicholas Braithwaite conducts a persuasive performance, outstandingly well recorded, but he cannot make the material sound really distinctive.

Barber, Samuel (1910–81)

Adagio for strings.
*** DG Dig. **413 324-2**; 2532/*3302* 083 [id.]. LAPO, Bernstein – BERNSTEIN: *Candide overture*; COPLAND: *Appalachian spring*; SCHUMAN: *American festival overture.****

An outstandingly eloquent account of Barber's famous *Adagio* from Bernstein. His reading has something of the expansiveness of his interpretation of another slow movement with valedictory associations forced on it, *Nimrod* from Elgar's *Enigma variations*. In Barber, Bernstein's expressiveness is more restrained and elegiac, but his control of the climax – in what is substantially a live recording – is unerring. The recording balance is somewhat close, but full and clear. The enormous advantage on CD of complete background silence is emphasized by the dynamic range of the climactic point, which is thrilling. There is also an extremely vivid chrome cassette. Bernstein's couplings are all highly desirable. Other versions – listed in the Concerts section – by the St Louis Symphony Orchestra under Slatkin, and the Milwaukee Orchestra conducted by Lucas Foss, are comparatively tensionless compared with Bernstein.

Adagio for strings; (i) *Piano concerto, Op. 38; Medea's meditation and Dance of vengeance, Op. 23a.*

*** ASV Dig. **CDDCA 534**; DCA/*ZCDCA* 534 [id.]. (i) Joselson; LSO, Schenck.

In this fine new recorded performance, Barber's *Concerto* emerges as a much stronger work than it previously seemed. Tedd Joselson is marvellously and dazzlingly brilliant, as well as being highly sensitive and poetic. What also shows this score to greater advantage than before is the greater richness and detail of the ASV recording and the unforced and poetic orchestral contribution from the LSO under Andrew Schenck. The *Concerto*'s ideas are exuberant, neo-romantic and, if not quite as fresh as the *Violin* or *Cello concertos*, they have an abundant warmth; needless to say, the piano writing is as expert as one would expect from the composer of the celebrated *Sonata*. The LSO also give a singularly fine account of the *Medea* excerpt (not to be confused with the Suite) and a restrained and noble one of the celebrated *Adagio*. On cassette the resonance has caused problems and led to a relatively low transfer level, which means that detail is clouded.

Cello concerto, Op. 22.

Ꞓ *** Chan. Dig. **CHAN 8322**; ABRD/*ABTD* 1085 [id.]. Wallfisch, ECO, Simon – SHOSTAKOVICH: *Cello concerto No. 1.****Ꞓ

It has taken three decades for the Barber *Cello concerto* to resurface on record: the pioneering record by Zara Nelsova and the composer (Decca mono LX3048) has long been a collectors' item. A new version by Raphael Wallfisch and the ECO under Geoffrey Simon comes in harness with the *Cello concerto No. 1* of Shostakovich and is all the more welcome for being so very much overdue. Of course the first movement is discursive and the invention throughout could be more strongly held together – but what invention! It has a vernal freshness and an affecting youthful innocence which never fails to exert its charm. It is an impressive and eloquent reading, and the elegiac slow movement is especially fine. Wallfisch is forwardly balanced, but otherwise the recording is truthful; the orchestra is vividly detailed on both LP and the excellent chrome tape. In its compact disc form, the sound is outstandingly realistic; given the excellence of the coupling, this must receive the strongest recommendation.

Bartók, Béla (1881–1945)

Concerto for orchestra.

(M) **(*) HMV ED 290134-1/*4* [id.]. Chicago SO, Ozawa – LUTOSLAWSKI: *Concerto.***(*)

(M) **(*) RCA Gold GL/*GK* 85220 [AGL1 2909]. Chicago SO, Reiner.

(M) ** DG 410 993-1/*4* [id.]. Boston SO, Kubelik – JANÁČEK: *Sinfonietta.***(*)

Concerto for orchestra; Dance suite.

*** Decca Dig. **400 052-2**; SXDL/*KSXDC* 7536 [Lon. LDR/5- 71036]. Chicago SO, Solti.

Concerto for orchestra; 2 Images, Op. 10.
(*) Ph. Dig. **411 132-2; 411 132-1/*4* [id.]. Concg. O, Dorati.

Concerto for orchestra; Music for strings, percussion and celesta.
(*) DG **415 322-2 [id.]. BPO, Karajan.

Solti gave Bartók's *Concerto for orchestra* its compact disc début, repeating the success of a similar coupling, made with the LSO in the mid-1960s. The brilliantly clear recording was an early demonstration of the advantages of CD, with the silent background increasing the projection of the music making and (with superb definition in the bass) helping to create the listener's feeling of anticipation in the atmospheric opening bars. The upper range of the sound, however, is very brightly lit indeed, which brings an aggressive feeling to the upper strings. This undoubtedly suits the reading, fierce and biting on the one hand, exuberant on the other. With superlative playing from Solti's own Chicago orchestra and such vivid sound – also impressive on LP and the strikingly brilliant chrome tape – this will be an obvious choice for most readers, particularly as Decca offer in addition a generous and apt coupling in the *Dance suite*, performed with a similar combination of sympathy and incisiveness. In the *Concerto* Solti has consulted original sources to suggest a faster speed than usual in the second movement, and this he makes entirely convincing. Otherwise, these are marginally straighter readings than those in his 1966 coupling of these same works, now reissued on Jubilee (JB/*KJBC* 144 [Lon. JL/*5*- 41037]).

Dorati's is a surprisingly lyrical account of Bartók's most popular work, consistently bringing out the folk-dance element along with the fun of the inspiration. The bite and excitement are less prominent than in more brilliant and extrovert readings, but there is a clear place for this, warmly rather than brilliantly recorded, and well coupled with the two atmospheric *Pictures: Blossoming* and *Village dance*. The CD version is a degree clearer and more faithful than the LP; the cassette – not transferred at the highest level – is of good quality: the resonance does not blur the focus.

Karajan's recording of the *Concerto for orchestra* comes from 1966 and of the *Music for strings, percussion and celesta* from 1973; they have been very successfully remastered digitally for compact disc which offers a more generous coupling than either of the original LPs. In the *Concerto*, the Berlin Philharmonic, in superb form, give a performance that is rich, romantic and smooth – for some ears perhaps excessively so. Karajan is right in treating Bartók emotionally, but comparison with Solti points the contrast between Berlin romanticism and earthy red-blooded Hungarian passion. With Solti, any rubato is linked with the Hungarian folksong idiom, where Karajan's moulding of phrases is essentially of the German tradition. The *Music for strings, percussion and celesta* also has well-upholstered timbre, and here Karajan's essentially romantic view combines with the recording to produce a certain urbanity. He avoids undue expressiveness in the opening slow fugue (except in a big rallentando at the end), but the third movement is given a performance in soft focus. Nevertheless, the playing of the Berlin strings is a pleasure in itself, and the sound is impressively rich and atmospheric.

Reiner's pioneering stereo recording was made in October 1955 and released the next year in its mono format. It has now been digitally remastered, with a gain in definition and a slight – only slight – loss of bloom: the quality is a little drier in texture, but the spaciousness of the Chicago acoustic produces an effect which is both vivid and yet with a good overall perspective. There is little to choose between the disc and the chrome tape. The performance is most satisfying, surprisingly straightforward from one brought up in central Europe, but with plenty of cutting edge. It is a pity that a coupling could not have been introduced for the reissue, which has now been raised from the bargain status of its last appearance to the mid-price range.

Ozawa's version of the Bartók on HMV makes a most competitive mid-priced LP coupling. Paired with Lutoslawski's virtuosic *Concerto* written in the following decade, it is given dazzling playing from the Chicago orchestra and bright but well-balanced recording. There are more searching and more atmospheric performances, but none more brilliant. With its generous coupling, this is undoubtedly a bargain, with an excellent matching tape, full and vivid, with the bright recording slightly tempered to advantage. The performance is full of life and energy.

Rafael Kubelik's account with the Boston Symphony, who premièred it under Koussevitzky – and that performance has never been surpassed! – comes from the mid-1970s. It is well recorded and has plenty of warmth without loss of detail. Kubelik's is, perhaps, a less exciting but more humane reading than Ozawa's, though it is less logically coupled. However, this is a reliable mid-price LP recommendation. On tape, the Boston acoustic is smoothly caught, with good detail.

Piano concertos Nos 1 in A; 3 in E.

(M) *** Ph. Seq. 411 001-1/*4*. Stephen Bishop-Kovacevich, LSO, Sir Colin Davis.

(i) *Piano concerto No. 1 in A;* (ii) *Sonata for 2 pianos and percussion.*

**(*) Decca Dig. 410 108-1/*4* [id.]. Vladimir Ashkenazy, (i) LPO, Solti; (ii) Vovka Ashkenazy, David Corkhill, Andrew Smith.

On Philips, Bishop-Kovacevich's readings of the *Concertos*, direct and incisive, are especially impressive for the pianist's handling of Bartók's often spare and always intense slow movements, here given concentrated power to compare with late Beethoven. The recording, of mid-1970s vintage, is firm and clean with a vivid matching cassette, the resonance well caught.

Both the *First Concerto* and the *Sonata* are given tough, even aggressive performances by Ashkenazy and Solti, urgent and biting, with the widest range of dynamics, never relaxing. Originally Solti planned to play the second piano part of the *Sonata*, but realized that this would mean he would have to practise a lot! In the end the choice of coupling was maintained, but instead Ashkenazy's son was invited to play the piano part with his father, a neat solution that worked out well.

Piano concerto No. 3 in E.
(*) Decca **411 969-2 [id.]. Vladimir Ashkenazy, LPO, Solti – PROKOFIEV: *Concerto No. 3.****

This Ashkenazy/Solti performance is a recoupling for CD (the original pairing was with the *Second Concerto*). The character of the performance follows very much the tone of voice of the tougher, earlier works, rarely relaxing. Tempi tend to be fast but, with the red-blooded Hungarian fire of the conductor matched by the Slavonic bite of the pianist, this performance sparks off the kind of energy and dash one would expect at a live performance, with the slow movement bringing hushed inner concentration. The transfer to CD is well managed, for the brilliance of the sound is the more striking, even if inner textures are not ideally detailed.

Violin concerto No. 1, Op. posth.
*** Decca Dig. **411 804-2**; 411 804-1/*4* [id.]. Kyung Wha Chung, Chicago SO, Solti – BERG: *Concerto.****

In Bartók's early *Concerto* – inspired, like Berg's late one, by a woman – the tender intensity of Chung's playing is established in the opening phrase, and the whole performance is comparably magnetic, brimming with poetry to make one forget the relative immaturity of the writing. Solti and the Chicago orchestra could not be more understanding, and the recording is brilliant and warm to match, whichever medium is chosen.

Violin concerto No. 2 in B min.
(M) *** HMV EG 290322-1/*4* [Ang. AM/*4AM* 37418]. Perlman, LSO, Previn.

Violin concerto No. 2; Rhapsody No. 1 (for violin and orchestra).
(M) *** Ph. Seq. 412 355-1/*4*. Szeryng, Concg. O, Haitink.
(M) *(**) CBS 60292/*40*- [MP/*MPT* 38886]. Stern, NYPO, Bernstein.

Perlman's is a superb performance, totally committed and full of youthful urgency, with the sense of spontaneity that comes more readily when performers have already worked together on the music in the concert hall. The contrasts are fearlessly achieved by both soloist and orchestra, with everyone relishing virtuosity in the outer movements. The slow movement is deliberately understated by the soloist, with the fragmentation of the theme lightly touched in, but even there the orchestra has its passionate comments. With no coupling, the disc is rather short measure, but no finer version of this masterly concerto has ever been available. The 1974 recording is full and lively, and there is a very good XDR cassette, closely matched to the disc.

Unlike Perlman, in the same price-range, Szeryng offers a worthwhile bonus. His too is a strong performance. Haitink keeps a firm grip on the proceedings, and there is a genuine excitement. The orchestra play with panache and brilliance, yet there is no lack of mystery in the more reflective passages of the first movement or in the marvellously poetic slow movement. The balance is not absolutely ideal, with Szeryng a bit forward in relation to the orchestra – but then, so is Perlman – and the sound is not quite as fine as the HMV disc; but the general astringency of this performance and its fire make it a viable alternative. The cassette too is extremely vivid.

Stern's classic version dates from 1958. It is grippingly intense and has a steely strength, emphasized by the balance which is extremely close. Indeed, the spikily brilliant sound-picture needs taming for complete comfort (though the tape is slightly smoother than the disc). The superbly assured playing of the soloist easily survives such aural scrutiny. Both *Rhapsodies* are offered, and here the underlying romanticism of the playing is more overt. Considerable reservations, then, about the sound quality, but not about the playing, which is magnificent, with passionate support from Bernstein's New York Philharmonic Orchestra in their halcyon period of excellence.

Dance suite.

*** ASV Dig. DCA/*ZCDCA* 536. LSO, Nowak – RAVEL: *Daphnis et Chloé: suites 1 and 2.****

Grzegorz Nowak in a finely pointed account with the LSO brings out a surprising range of mood, witty in the third movement, affectionate in the fourth. The recording, made at the EMI No. 1 Studio, is biting and brilliant without any harshness. The pity is that the Ravel coupling is far less imaginatively done.

Divertimento for strings; Music for strings, percussion and celesta.

*** Hung. Dig. **HCD 12531**; SLPD/*MK* 12531 [id.]. Liszt CO, Rolla.

Divertimento for strings; Rumanian folk dances.

(*) DG **415 668-2; 415 668-1/*4* [id.]. Orpheus CO – JANÁČEK: *Mládi.***(*)

The *Music for strings, percussion and celesta* (1936) and the *Divertimento for strings* (1939) were both written for Paul Sacher's Basle Chamber Orchestra. The Liszt Chamber Orchestra comprises seventeen players, including Janos Rolla who directs from the first desk. These are both expert performances, and distil a powerful atmosphere in the slow movements of both pieces. They command beautifully rapt pianissimo tone and keen intensity. The sound is less reverberant than some rivals, but there is no lack of ambience. Readers who want an account that would not have greatly differed from Sacher's at the first performance will not be disappointed: indeed, this is one of the best available.

The American Orpheus Chamber Orchestra also give an eminently well-prepared account of the *Divertimento*, but they are not as sensibly (or competitively) coupled as the Liszt Chamber Orchestra on Hungaroton. Good though their performance is, it is not quite as idiomatic in its sense of mystery or intensity of feeling as the Hungaroton, even if it possesses both in good measure. The recording, though very clean and well balanced, is not so atmospheric. The differences are minute and to emphasize them would be wrong.

The DG issue deserves a recommendation none the less, and readers attracted to the coupling can confidently invest in it. The popular *Rumanian folk dances* begin side two of the LP and cassette, which is completed by *Mládi*. The cassette transfer is of DG's finest quality, particularly vivid and clear.

(i) *The Miraculous Mandarin* (complete ballet), *Op. 19; Music for strings, percussion and celesta.*
(*) Decca Dig. **411 894-2; 411 894-1/*4* [id.]. (i) Kenneth Jewell Chorale; Detroit SO, Dorati.

The Miraculous Mandarin: concert suite; *Music for strings, percussion and celesta.*
(*) HMV **CDC 747117-2 [id.]; ED 290297-1/*4* [Ang. AM/*4AM* 34271]. Phd. O, Ormandy.

The range and brilliance of Decca's Detroit recording are spectacular, with the formidable bass response particularly impressive on CD. That makes up for any lessening of tension in the actual performance compared with Dorati's previous recordings of both works. Though the playing in the early ballet – the complete score, not the truncated text sanctioned in the so-called suite – is polished enough, it finally lacks the flamboyance needed, the bold display of controlled barbarism. The *Music for strings, percussion and celesta* lacks the final degree of intensity too. Nevertheless, such an apt, attractive and generous coupling presented in superb sound should not be dismissed. The chrome cassette is highly spectacular also, although the bass focus is less sharp than the CD.

Ormandy and the Philadelphia Orchestra have recorded *The Miraculous Mandarin* before, but this 1979 version of the suite does full justice to the opulence of the Philadelphia strings and the rich sonorities of their cellos and basses. *The Miraculous Mandarin* suite is dazzling; the only reservation to be made concerns the *Music for strings, percussion and celesta*, where greater mystery is needed (at least in the first and third movements). There is no want of eloquence and passion, but the dynamic range at the pianissimo end of the spectrum leaves something to be desired. That apart, there is so much to enjoy and admire here that this issue can be strongly recommended: the orchestral playing as such and the recording, too, are of the very first order. The LP has now been reissued in EMI's Master series at mid-price, so costs about a third as much as the CD and, truth to tell, the difference in definition (apart from the almost silent background) is only marginal; the cassette sounds well too, though the use of iron-oxide stock means that the upper range is not as far-reaching as in the other formats.

Music for strings, percussion and celesta; Rumanian folk dances (arr. Willner).
* Denon Dig. **C37 7122** [id.]. Tokyo Met. SO, Atzmon.

Atzmon's version not only offers exceptionally poor value but plain and uninvolved performances, redeemed only by some lively rhythms in the two fast movements of the *Music for strings, percussion and celesta*. Acceptable recording, not brilliant enough for this music.

CHAMBER MUSIC

(i) *Sonata for 2 pianos and percussion;* (ii) (Solo) *Violin sonata.*
ℭ *** Accord Dig. **149047**. (i) Janka and Jurg Wyttenbach, Schmid, Huber; (ii) Schneeberger.

(i) *Sonata for 2 pianos and percussion. Mikrokosmos, Vol. 6; Sonatina.*
❀ (M) *** Ph. Seq. 412 376-1/*4*. Bishop-Kovacevich; (i) with Argerich, De Goudswaard, De Roo.

The Accord recordings were made in Basle in the wake of the Bartók centenary celebrations. Hansheinz Schneeberger is little known outside Switzerland, though he has recorded Willy Burkhard's beautiful *Concerto*. He is obviously an accomplished artist and his account can withstand comparison with most if not all rivals. The *Sonata for 2 pianos and percussion* receives an exhilarating performance though Janka and Jurg Wyttenbach are neither as subtle nor as imaginative pianistically as Argerich and Bishop-Kovacevich on Philips. The CD recording is astonishingly good and is also very natural. There is impressive range and the percussion players sound as if they are there in one's living-room. Well worth paying money for!

Argerich and Bishop-Kovacevich still remain a strong first choice in the *Sonata*. Theirs is a subtle and atmospheric performance and receives a refined and truthful recording to match. On its first appearance it was coupled with an inspiring account of Debussy's *En blanc et noir* and some Mozart; but it is now more sensibly coupled with some of the solo Bartók record Bishop-Kovacevich made in 1969. The cassette does not quite match the LP in sharpness of detail but faithfully captures the recording's wide dynamic range. It is fully acceptable in the *Sonata* and even better in the solo piano music, which is transferred at a slightly higher level.

String quartets Nos 1–6.
** Hung. Dig. **HCD12502-4**; SLPD12502-4. Takács Qt.

The Takács Quartet is a Hungarian ensemble of high quality. They bring a youthful ardour and vitality to the Bartók quartets, and have excellent ensemble and attack to commend them. Theirs is the first complete cycle to appear on CD. No doubt in sheer beauty of sonority and tonal blend the Takács are outclassed by the Tokyo or the Lindsay on LP, and they do not distil the same sense of mystery and atmosphere. There is, however, much more to admire than to cavil at: they have ample fire and are certainly not short on virtuosity, as the coda of the *Third Quartet* shows – one can understand why they have collected plenty of prizes since they came together as students in the mid-1970s. All the same, there is more to the last movement of the *Sixth* than emerges in their hands – and those who recall the pioneering Hungarian (HMV) and Gertler (Decca) sets will find them wanting in that quality of repose and reflection those ensembles achieved. Nevertheless, there is some fine expressive playing here. The recording is a trifle forward and has plenty of presence, though it is not as refined as the DG. There is plenty of body in the CD format; collectors wanting a Bartók cycle will find a great deal here to reward them.

Still recommended: The recordings by the Tokyo Quartet with their balance of Bartókian sparkle and wit remain first choice in this repertoire (DG 2740 235 [id.]) while the alternative set by the Lindsay Quartet, searching and powerfully expressive, has the advantage of first-class digital sound and an extremely good cassette equivalent (ASV DCAB 301/*ZCDCA 504*, *509* and *510* [Van. 25011/3]).

String quartets: Nos 1 in A min; 5.
*** Tel. Dig. AZ6 42983. Eder Qt.

The Eder Quartet, a much-respected Hungarian ensemble, is a very formidable contender in what is a highly competitive field. Its account of No. 1 has real character and individuality and is full of insights. There is a marvellous intensity and sense of onward movement, without the slightest sense of the music being over-projected or held on the tight rein; on the contrary, one is barely aware of the bar line. And what wonderful quality of sound they produce in No. 1 at the Debussy-like episode (fig. 9), and such rapt tone and concentration of atmosphere at the *pianopianissimo possibile* passage into which it leads. A marvellous performance which makes one hear this music with fresh ears. The same must be said for No. 5, which is superbly played. The recording is in the demonstration class.

String quartet No. 3.
** Delos Dig. **D/CD 3004**. Sequoia Qt – RAVEL: *String quartet in F.***

The Sequoia Quartet comes from California, and this coupling shows it to better advantage than earlier recordings have done. However, it is an odd and not particularly generous coupling. The Bartók is played with great attack and splendid unanimity of ensemble, and they show a scrupulous attention to detail. It is well enough recorded, but does not displace either the Takács on compact disc, which comes as part of a complete cycle, or the Tokyo set on LP. It can only be a matter of time before the Eder Quartet records this for the new medium.

Dance suite; Hungarian peasant songs; 3 Rondos on folk tunes; Rumanian dances.
*** Denon Dig. **C37 7092** [id.]. András Schiff (piano).

András Schiff, whose reputation rests on his keenly imaginative readings in the classical repertory, here demonstrates his red-blooded Hungarian fervour. In the

Dance suite his range of mood, tone and expression makes up for the lack of varied orchestral colours, and the popular *Rumanian dances* have rarely been played with such infectious rhythms, often light and witty. The other collections are just as persuasively played, and the piano sound is first rate, with plenty of bite and only losing inner clarity with the heaviest textures of the *Dance suite*. Though the CD has only four bands, it is most generously indexed with even the 15 tiny *Peasant songs* all separated.

OPERA

Bluebeard's Castle (sung in Hungarian).
(M) *** Decca Lon. Ent. 414 167-1/*4* [id.]. Ludwig, Berry, LSO, Kertesz.
(*) Hung. Dig. **MCD 12254; SLPD/*MK* 12254 [id.]. Obraztsova, Nesterenko, Hungarian State Op. O, Ferencsik.

Bartók's idea of portraying marital conflict in an opera was as unpromising as could be, but in the event *Bluebeard's Castle* is an enthralling work with its concentration on mood, atmosphere and slow development as Bluebeard's wife finds the key to each new door. Its comparative absence of action makes it an ideal work for the gramophone, and there have been a surprising number of attempts to record it. Kertesz set new standards in his version with Christa Ludwig and Walter Berry, not only in the playing of the LSO at its peak, in the firm sensitivity of the soloists and the brilliance of recording, but in the natural Hungarian inflections inspired by the conductor. The reissue of this 1966 recording is one of the first on Decca's mid-price London Enterprise label, which now offers an equivalent cassette of high quality – indeed, it is in the demonstration class, refined as well as clear and vivid.

With two distinguished Soviet singers taking the roles of Bluebeard and Judith, Ferencsik's Hungaroton version (his fourth recording of the work) is vocally resonant and delicately atmospheric with the hushed pianissimo of the opening tellingly caught. Yet in musical weight and intensity, not to mention dramatic detail and technical virtuosity, this inevitably yields before the finest versions using Western orchestras. The digital recording is full and faithful.

Bax, Arnold (1883–1953)

The Garden of Fand; The Happy forest; November woods; Summer music.
ℭ *** Chan. Dig. **CHAN 8307**; ABRD/*ABTD* 1066 [id.]. Ulster O, Bryden Thomson.

November woods (symphonic poem).
(*) Lyr. SRCS 37. LPO, Boult – HOLST: *Fugal overture*; MOERAN: *Sinfonietta*.*

This excellent, highly enjoyable Chandos collection of Bax tone-poems is intended as the first of a series and represents the work of the Ulster Orchestra at its very finest. The Celtic twilight in Bax's music is ripely and sympathetically caught in the first three items, while *Summer music*, dedicated to Sir Thomas Beecham and here given its first ever recording, brings an intriguing kinship with the music of Delius. The Chandos recording is superb, full, vivid and natural with no unnatural close-ups. The chrome cassette has striking range and projection, but the massed upper strings lack body compared with the LP. The compact disc is outstanding, the bass firm and clean, while the sound has exceptional detail and range.

The reissue of the 1968 Lyrita recording of *November woods* (still at full price) restores Boult's admirably sympathetic performance to the catalogue. The LPO play the music with natural understanding, but this disc is now of greater interest for its Holst and Moeran couplings, which are otherwise not available.

In the faery hills; Into the twilight; Roscatha; The Tale the pine-trees knew.
Ͼ *** Chan. Dig. **CHAN 8367**; ABRD/*ABTD* 1133 [id.]. Ulster O, Bryden Thomson.

Outstanding as Bryden Thomson's records of Bax and others have been, this second collection of Bax tone-poems caps them all. With recording of demonstration quality, exceptionally vivid and well balanced on CD, Bryden Thomson draws from the Ulster Orchestra playing not just of keen commitment but of great refinement and finesse, too. *The Tale the pine-trees knew*, written in 1931, is one of the better known as well as one of the most evocative of Bax's tone-poems, here done with total sympathy. The other three tone-poems, written between 1908 and 1910, form an Irish trilogy which Bax – long before the Irish Republic ever used the name – collectively called *Eire*. The first two are filled with typically Baxian Celtic twilight, but the last (*Rosc-Catha* meaning 'battle hymn') presents the composer in vigorous, extrovert mood, making an excellent contrast.

Symphony No. 2 in E min. and C.
*** Lyr. SRCS 54. LPO, Fredman.

The *Second* is arguably the most richly imaginative of all Bax's symphonies. The ideas are copious and vividly conceived, and the music has a wild, imaginative intensity that is wholly compelling. Its richness of texture and powerful sense of atmosphere are obvious from the very outset. Many Bax scores have suffered the handicap of indifferent performance or recording. Myer Fredman has secured a first-class account: the LPO sound as if they have been playing it all their lives, and the recording, which dates from 1971, is a demonstration of analogue technique at its finest. This reissue, however, remains at full price.

Symphony No. 3.
(M) (***) HMV mono EX 290107-3/5 (2). Hallé O, Barbirolli – DELIUS: *Aquarelles*; IRELAND: *Mai-Dun; Forgotten rite; These things shall be;* QUILTER: *Children's overture*.(***)

This, the pioneering version of Bax's *Third Symphony*, is given with an intensity and feeling that completely eluded its only LP successor under Edward Downes, and admirers of this composer should not hesitate! The overall atmosphere is so enveloping and keenly felt that the odd imprecisions of ensemble are a small price to pay. The *Third Symphony* is a powerful work, arguably Bax's masterpiece, and well worth getting to know. Although some allowance has to be made for the sound, it is still remarkable for its period and an indispensable acquisition for those whose memories are excited by the record scene in the 1940s.

Symphony No. 4; Tintagel.
ℭ *** Chan. **CHAN 8312**; ABRD/*ABTD* 1091. Ulster O, Bryden Thomson.

The *Fourth Symphony* was written in 1930–31; part of the first movement was worked out at Bax's Irish refuge in Glencolumcille, but the seascapes that the score brings to mind are mainly those of the coast and islands of the Western Highlands where Bax spent each winter during the 1930s. The copious flow of ideas in the best of his symphonies (2, 3, 5 and 6) does not always go hand in hand with organic coherence, and the overall impression remains of a series of related episodes rather than a growing musical organism. This is not to belittle their power or originality but merely to underline what one critic has said, that a Bax symphony is 'like an instinctive drama of the emotions rather than a logically sustained argument'. The *Fourth* is the least concentrated and most hedonistic of the seven and flaunts the 'unashamed Romanticism' which Bax so often proclaimed. The ideas may not be quite as memorable as those of the *Third* and *Fifth* but the moods are still powerful and the colours vivid. The performance is altogether splendid; Bryden Thomson encourages his players to a scrupulous observance of dynamic nuance as well as a sensitive projection of atmosphere. The CD is one of the best now on the market: it has an altogether striking presence and a vivid detail that does full justice to Bax's sumptuous orchestral textures and opulent sonorities. Both the *Fourth Symphony* and *Tintagel* deserve an enthusiastic welcome to the CD catalogue; this is a demonstration disc even by the high standards Chandos have established in this field. The LP and the chrome tape are also first class.

Symphony No. 5 in C sharp min.
*** Lyr. SRCS 58. LPO, Leppard.

The *Fifth* is considered by some critics to be Bax's finest. Dedicated to Sibelius, it was first performed in January 1934 under the Finnish master's most eloquent champion, Sir Thomas Beecham. The symphony shows Bax holding in check the purely lyrical impulse to which he could give such generous vein, in favour of a greater degree of motivic integration. In some ways this is the most symphonic of the seven, though it has the same brooding intensity and powerful atmosphere that distinguish the first three symphonies. Raymond Leppard gives a dedicated and indeed inspired account which should go far to persuade anyone who doubts the power of Bax's imagination or the strength of his symphonic instinct. The LPO are at their very best, and so too are the Lyrita engineers. The recording dates from 1972 and this reissue, like that of the *Second Symphony*, is still in the premium price bracket.

Beethoven, Ludwig van (1770–1827)

Piano concertos Nos 1–5.
(*) Telarc Dig. **CD 80061 (3) [id.]. Rudolf Serkin, Boston SO, Ozawa.
*(*) Ph. Dig. **411 189–2** (3); 411 189-1/*4* (4/*3*) [id.]. Alfred Brendel, Chicago SO, Levine.

Piano concertos Nos 1–5; Andante favori in F, WoO 57; 6 Bagatelles, Op. 120; Für Elise, WoO 50.
**(*) Decca Dig. 411 899-1/*4* [id.]. Vladimir Ashkenazy, VPO, Mehta.

Piano concertos Nos 1–5; Andante favori; Polonaise in C, Op. 89.
(***) Arabesque mono **Z 6549** (*Nos 1–2*); **Z 6550** (*Nos 3–4*); **Z 6551** (*No. 5, Andante,* and *Polonaise*) [id.]. Artur Schnabel, LSO or LPO, Sargent.

Squeezed on to three CDs merely, Serkin's cycle for Telarc is not just a bargain, it presents a deeply satisfying series of performances. More clearly than his younger rivals, Serkin brings those moments of total magic which are the mark of live performance from a master, here caught in the studio. Technically the playing of the octogenarian is flawed – there is one amazing slip of finger in the second subject of the *First Concerto* – but where in his late Mozart recordings for DG the lack of polish is distracting, here one consistently registers certainty and power. The accompaniments have comparable spontaneity, and the sound is excellent, full, warm and natural.

On LP and cassette, Ashkenazy's cycle with Mehta and the Vienna Philharmonic has been issued in box format, a satisfying collection, easier and more spontaneous-sounding than his previous Chicago series for Decca with Solti. If Mehta's accompaniments are not always very positive, he is dealing with a pianist who in concert has directed all these concertos from the keyboard. The fill-ups, taken from varied earlier sources, are the same as on the individual LPs and CDs, but sound reasonably consistent. The LP sound is excellent in the concertos but cannot quite match the bright clarity of the CDs (available separately – see below).

Brendel's Chicago version was intended to prove how much more effective live recording is than studio performance, but the results – recorded at Orchestra Hall, Chicago – belie that. Anything Brendel does has mastery and distinction but, compared with his earlier studio recording of the concertos with Haitink and the Concertgebouw, this sounds self-conscious, less rather than more spontaneous-sounding. He did after all know that the tape was rolling, and that in itself must have affected the performances. The recorded sound gives a good sense of presence but is badly balanced, and loud applause at the end of each concerto is most intrusive. The tape layout with the *Emperor* first movement beginning on side two after the finale of the *First*, and the *Third Concerto* split between sides three and four is quite unsatisfactory. The sound is basically clear, but the string focus roughens in tuttis, especially in the *Emperor*.

Schnabel's performances fall into a special category. The concertos were recorded in 1932–3, save for the *B flat*, which dates from 1935; the solo pieces come from 1938 and some were unpublished. They are not to be confused with Schnabel's post-war cycle with Galliera and Dobrowen or his wartime accounts of Nos 4 and 5, made in Chicago. His playing has such enormous character that it transcends the limitations of sound that are inevitable at this period. The orchestral playing is occasionally lacking the finesse that we take for granted nowadays, but Schnabel's impulsive, searching and poetic playing offers special rewards. Not everything is equally successful: there is some roughness in the first movement of No. 3, but there are some marvellously spirited touches. Schnabel may not be so illuminating in the concertos as he was in, say, the late *Piano sonatas*, but that is comparing one peak with another higher one. The CD transfers are crystal clear and very little of the 78 r.p.m. hiss is apparent. However, for modern ears some adjustment is necessary to the dry orchestral texture, especially for the listener beginning with No. 1, where there is no bloom on the strings. The *Second* is rather fuller. In the *Fourth* there are some minor insecurities of texture; the *Emperor* sounds surprisingly well. Such is the electricity of the playing, however, that one soon forgets the primitive recording and succumbs to Schnabel's spell. The three CDs are available separately.

Piano concerto No. 1 in C, Op. 15.
(*) Nimbus Dig. **NIM 5003 [id.]. Mary Verney , Hanover Band – *Symphony No. 1.***
** DG Dig. **410 511-2**; 2532/*3302* 103 [id.]. Pollini, VPO, Jochum.

Piano concerto No. 1; 6 Bagatelles, Op. 26.
(*) Decca Dig. **411 900-2; 411 900-1/*4* [id.]. Ashkenazy, VPO, Mehta.

Ashkenazy gives a sparkling and relaxed reading of the *First Piano concerto*, with Mehta's tactful accompaniments adding to the open joyful manner of the first movement. Significantly, Ashkenazy opts not for Beethoven's biggest cadenza but for the much briefer first option of the three; though the slow movement is thoughtful in an unmannered way, this is a reading which stays within the brief of early Beethoven. Good, bright, finely detailed recording to match the performance. The six *Bagatelles* make an attractive fill-up, but not a generous one. The high-level cassette is brightly lit to the point of fierceness.

Mary Verney is a most persuasive advocate of playing Beethoven on a fortepiano. Though speeds are fast in all three movements of the *Concerto*, there is a gentleness and charm about the performance, intensified by the small scale of the solo instrument. Even with period instruments, the problems of balance are considerable, not just between soloist and orchestra but within the band. With CD clarifying the warmly reverberant sound – recorded in St Giles', Cripplegate – the unexpected perspectives are attractive, the extra clarity of the wind contrasting with the gentle, softly focused string sound.

Pollini is sometimes wilful but, with refreshing clarity of articulation, his is a performance, brisk rather than poetic, which vividly reflects the challenge of an unexpected partnership between pianist and conductor. The recording was taken from live performances but betrays little sign of that. The CD was an early issue and provides excellent presence, but this record does not really compete with Ashkenazy's disc, either musically or technically.

Still recommended: The combination of Bishop-Kovacevich and Sir Colin Davis produces an exceptionally satisfying (mid-priced) reading, among the finest versions ever recorded of this concerto (Ph. 6527/*7311* 174 [id.]) although we hope DG have plans to reissue the Kempff Beethoven cycle on CD.

Piano concertos Nos 1–2.
*(*) Ph. Dig. **412 787-2** [id.]. Brendel, Chicago SO, Levine.

It is a paradox that, so far from sounding more spontaneous in his live recording of the *First Piano concerto* with Levine, Brendel appears more self-conscious and mannered, and Levine also makes matters worse in the first movement with phrases over-lovingly held back. The slow movement is much slower than in Brendel's 1979 studio recording and the finale less crisp. In this and much else the penalties rather than the benefits of live recording are emphasized. The *Second* brings a similar reading with comparable flaws: a mannered first movement, a second movement (complete with groans from the soloist) less spacious than in Brendel's studio performance, and a finale sounding slightly rushed; imperfectly focused recording, not well balanced. The mastery of Brendel is never in doubt, but too much is stacked against it, not least the deafening applause at the opening and close. Despite the generous coupling, this is not recommended, with sound inevitably flawed and the piano slightly disembodied.

Still recommended: Radu Lupu's coupling of the two early concertos combines sparkle and sensitivity, and the digital recording is first rate (Decca SXDL 7502 [Lon. LDR 10006]).

Piano concerto No. 2 in B flat, Op. 19.
(*) Telarc Dig. **CD 80064 [id.]. Serkin, Boston SO, Ozawa – *Concerto No. 4.***(*)
(*) Decca Dig. **411 901-2; 411 901-1/*4* [id.]. Ashkenazy, VPO, Mehta – *Concerto No. 4.***(*)
** DG **413 445-2** [id.]. Pollini, VPO, Jochum – *Concerto No. 4.***

The natural gravitas of Serkin's view of Beethoven's earliest piano concerto – presaging last-period gravity at the end of the *Adagio* – is lightened by the humour of the playing, the inescapable sense of a great musician approaching the music afresh, spontaneously and without a hint of routine. Excellent support from Ozawa and full, vivid recording.

Ashkenazy's Vienna account of the *Second Piano concerto* is at once restrained and sparkling, thoughtful in the amazingly prophetic quasi-recitative which closes the slow movement, yet keeping the whole work well within an apt scale for early Beethoven. Excellent recording, bright and atmospheric, with a clean matching tape.

Pollini's version, taken from a live performance, is one of the more attractive of his Beethoven concertos series. But though it is well coupled on CD, it cannot match its finest rivals.

Piano concertos Nos 3–5 (*Emperor*).
(**) HMV mono RLS/*TC-RLS* 290001-3/*5* (2). Edwin Fischer, Philh. O; *No. 5* cond. Furtwängler.

The *Third* and *Fourth Concertos*, which Fischer conducted from the keyboard, do not find this great pianist at his most illuminating although, as always with this artist, there is still much to learn. His account of the *Fifth*, however, is one of the classics of its day. Recorded in 1951, this *Emperor* is grand in conception and majestic in execution. It has a warmth and vision that mark it off from many of its contemporaries, and the orchestral playing under Furtwängler is magnificent. Although it first appeared in the days of 78s, the quality of the sound is remarkably fresh and derives from the original mastertape. The cassettes match the LPs in clarity.

Piano concerto No. 3 in C min., Op. 37.
(*) Telarc Dig. **CD 80063 [id.]. Serkin, Boston SO, Ozawa – *Choral fantasia.***(*)
** DG **413 446-2** [id.]. Pollini, VPO, Boehm – *Piano sonata No. 31.***(*)

Piano concerto No. 3. Andante favori, WoO 57; Für Elise, WoO 50.
(*) Decca Dig. **411 902-2; 411 902-1/*4* [id.]. Ashkenazy, VPO, Mehta.

All the performances in Ashkenazy's Vienna series with Mehta are more relaxed than in his earlier Chicago set with Solti, but the first movement of the *Third Piano concerto* brings the most striking contrast of all, noticeably slower and less forceful. The result remains compelling, because it sounds so spontaneous and with fewer distracting agogic hesitations than before. Even Beethoven's big cadenza is presented relaxedly, not as a firework display. The slow movement is more easily lyrical than before, the finale lighter, more sparkling and with more charm than Ashkenazy usually allows himself. The two fill-ups come from much earlier sessions with less bright sound. The concerto, like the others in the series, has excellent sound, atmospheric as well as brilliant. The high-level cassette brings added brightness on top.

Serkin's Telarc version of the *Third Concerto* comes with the substantial bonus of the *Choral fantasia* as coupling. Though the octogenarian soloist's playing lacks some of its old fire, and the *Adagio* – taken relatively fast – is a little casual, the mastery of Serkin's conception is not in doubt, with his combination of ruggedness and flights of poetry, not least in the G minor and F minor passages at the beginning of the first-movement development. Though piano tone is a little twangy, the recording is outstandingly vivid and full.

The concentration of the playing and the single-minded clarity of Pollini's reading are matched by Boehm's strong, clear-minded accompaniment, but the performance is on the sober side for a youthful concerto that should sparkle more than it does here. On CD, the closeness of piano balance is more apparent than on LP, even though there are obvious gains in clarity. Unlike the original LP, the CD offers a sizeable bonus in the Op. 110 *Piano sonata*, an eloquent performance of considerable authority, which is (like the concerto) transferred impressively from an analogue original.

Still recommended: As in the *First Concerto*, Bishop-Kovacevich and Sir Colin Davis offer a highly satisfying account of the *Third* on Philips's mid-priced Sequenza label (6527/*7311* 176 [id.]).

Piano concertos Nos 3–4.

*** CBS Dig. **MK 39814**; IM/*IMT* 39814 [id.]. Murray Perahia, Concg. O, Haitink.

*(*) Ph. **412 788-2** [id.]. Brendel, Chicago SO, Levine.

Perahia, in a generous coupling which promises great things for his Beethoven series when it is completed, gives readings that are at once intensely poetic and individual, but also strong. In many ways he gives reminders of Wilhelm Kempff, a supreme Beethovenian of his time, with pointing and shading of passage-work that consistently convey the magic of the moment caught on the wing. As with Kempff, the diamond clarity and the touches of poetry may suggest for some an approach not rugged enough for Beethoven; but with Haitink and the Concertgebouw giving firmly sympathetic support, power is conveyed through sharpness of contrast, helped by fine, spacious and open recorded sound. Also as with Kempff, the magic never diminishes, with thoughtfully lyrical slow movements and delectably sparkling finales that are in no way mannered.

Brendel's CD coupling of Nos 3 and 4 provides generous measure, but is subject to all the reservations made concerning the complete cycle. Though Brendel's mastery and highly individual imagination are never in doubt, live performances are here, if anything, less spontaneous-sounding and more self-conscious than his earlier studio recordings. The audience noises, odd balances and intrusive applause are also obvious penalties.

(i) *Piano concertos Nos 3–4; Piano sonata No. 21 in C (Waldstein), Op. 53.*

(B) *** DG Walkman *419 086-4* [id.]. Wilhelm Kempff, (i) with BPO, Leitner.

Almost simultaneously with the appearance of Perahia's coupling, DG made available together Kempff's performances of the *Third* and *Fourth Concertos* on a bargain Walkman tape, offering the *Waldstein sonata* as a generous bonus. In the *C minor Concerto* Kempff's approach is relatively measured, somewhat serious in mood; but in its unforced way, happily lyrical, brightly sparkling in articulation, it is refreshingly spontaneous. Kempff may characteristically adopt a flowing speed for the slow movement, but this natural thoughtfulness gives it the necessary gravity and intensity. Again, in the *Fourth Concerto* Kempff's delicacy of fingerwork and his shading of tone colour are as effervescent as ever, and the fine control of the conductor ensures the unity of the reading. In both concertos the recording of the orchestra is full and resonant, the piano tone warm as well as clear. The change of timbre for the *Sonata* (which begins after the *Third Concerto*, the turnover coming after the first movement) is a little disconcerting, as here the recording quality is much drier. But the ear soon adjusts and the playing is what counts.

Piano concerto No. 4 in G, Op. 58.
(*) Telarc Dig. **CD 80064 [id.]. Serkin, Boston SO, Ozawa – *Concerto No. 2.***(*)
(*) Decca Dig. **411 902-2; 411 902-1/*4* [id.]. Ashkenazy, VPO, Mehta – *Concerto No. 2.***(*)
** DG **413 445-2** [id.]. Pollini, VPO, Boehm – *Concerto No. 2.***

Serkin in his eighties may lack some of the brio which made his earlier recordings of the *Fourth Piano concerto* so memorable, but his concentration and sense of spontaneity are as powerful as ever. Though strength is the keynote of his view in the outer movements, and the compression of the slow movement finds him at his most intense, the detailed poetry comes as the magic of the moment, a studio performance that captures the essence of what a live account should be. Excellent recording.

The relaxation and sense of spontaneity which mark Ashkenazy's Vienna cycle bring a performance of the *Fourth* which may lack something in heroic drive, but which in its relative lightness never loses concentration and brings a captivating sparkle to the finale. Though this may not be so powerful as Ashkenazy's earlier Chicago recording with Solti, it is fresher and more natural, with fewer expressive hesitations. Excellent recording to match the rest of the series, with a bright, clean cassette transfer.

There is an aristocratic feeling about Pollini's account, with classical poise and poetic sensitivity delicately balanced. Boehm is a faithful accompanist, but the end result is somewhat chilly; both Ashkenazy and Serkin are more spontaneously communicative. The CD has been successfully remastered from an analogue original.

Still recommended: Kempff's DG mid-priced coupling of the *Second* and *Fourth Concertos* with Leitner reigns supreme, the 1962 recording balance having stood the test of time, though the disc sounds fresher than the tape (DG Accolade 2542/*3342* 136 [id.]).

Piano concertos Nos 4 and 5 (Emperor), Op. 73; Piano sonatas Nos 14 (Moonlight), Op. 27/2; 19, Op. 49/1.
(B) *** HMV *TCC2-POR 154594-9*. Gieseking, Philh. O, Galliera.

These Gieseking stereo recordings from the late 1950s of the *G major* and *Emperor concertos* are here issued for the first time, in EMI's 'Portrait of the Artist' series on one double-length tape. The sound is astonishingly good, and Gieseking's incandescently bright timbre is captured truthfully, while the orchestra is full-bodied and well detailed. The performances are admirably fresh and imbued with classical feeling. Gieseking's playing is appealingly spontaneous and, with such impressive recording, admirers of this artist will not be disappointed, although the two *Sonatas* are rather cool. Each concerto is complete on one cassette side, with a sonata used as a balance.

Piano concerto No. 5 in E flat (Emperor), Op. 73.
*** Ph. Dig. **416 215-2**; 416 215-1/*4* [id.]. Arrau, Dresden State O, Sir Colin Davis.
*** Telarc Dig. **CD 80065**; DG 10065 [id.]. Serkin, Boston SO, Ozawa.
(*) Decca Dig. **400 050-2; SXDL/*KSXDC* 7503 [Lon. LDR/*5*- 10005]. Lupu, Israel PO, Mehta.
(*) RCA **RD 89389. Rubinstein, LPO, Barenboim.
(M) **(*) Ph. 412 917-1/*4* [id.]. Brendel, LPO, Haitink.
*(**) Decca Dig. **411 903-2** [id.]. Ashkenazy, VPO, Mehta.
** DG **413 447-2**; 2531/*3301* 194 [id.]. Pollini, VPO, Boehm.
*(*) Ph. Dig. **412 789-2**. Brendel, Chicago SO, Levine – *Piano sonata No. 31.***(*)

The wonder is that Arrau, for long an inhibited artist in the studio, should in his newest *Emperor* recording, made when he was over eighty, sound so carefree. The technical flaws are many, and the digital recording is rather resonant in bass, but with Sir Colin Davis and the Dresden State Orchestra as electrifying partners, the voltage is even higher than in his earlier versions of the mid-1960s. One would expect Arrau in his eighties to become more reflective, but the opposite is the case. The slow movement flows more freely, less hushed and poised than before, while the finale at a relaxed speed is joyful in its jaunty rhythms. Intensely individual, the very opposite of routine, this is from first to last a performance which reflects new searching by a deeply thinking musician. There is an excellent chrome cassette, full and wide-ranging.

With extraordinarily vivid recording, Serkin's Telarc *Emperor* is very satisfying. The great pianist is almost as commanding as ever, with fire and brilliance in plenty in the outer movements; yet there is also a degree of relaxation, of conscious enjoyment, that increases the degree of communication. The hushed expressive pianism that provides the lyrical contrast in the first movement is matched by the poised refinement of the *Adagio*; the finale is vigorously joyful. Ozawa's accompaniment is first class.

Lupu's version was the first to be issued on compact disc and the clarity of detail is impressive. The upper range is over-bright but the orchestral layout is convincing, and if the piano image seems a trifle near it gives a commanding presence to the solo playing. Lupu gives a performance which, without lacking strength, brings thoughtfulness and poetry even to the magnificence of the first movement, with classical proportions made clear. The slow movement has delicacy and fantasy, the finale easy exhilaration, though neither conductor nor orchestra quite matches the soloist's distinction. The cassette (unusually for Decca) is disappointing, with a lack of refinement in the orchestral tuttis of the first movement.

Rubinstein plays with spontaneous inspiration, compelling attention in every phrase, and the London Philharmonic under Daniel Barenboim accompany with keen understanding. The balance, however, is contrived, with the piano given an excessively forward balance. The timbre is truthful and fuller than Rubinstein often received, but the piano sounds larger than life. Orchestral wind solos emerge effectively and the strings are laid out fairly convincingly within a reverberant acoustic, but the bass response, though ample, is rather woolly.

As a recording, Brendel's 1977 *Emperor*, with the LPO under Haitink, was an outstanding example of analogue techniques. The sound is beautifully balanced with a wide range and warmth, although the strings are not quite so cleanly focused on tape as on disc. The piano timbre is outstandingly natural in both formats and is infinitely more successful than on the more recent CD (to say nothing of the merciful absence of audience participation). It goes without saying that there is much to admire from the artistic point of view, too. The reading is spaciously conceived, and the phrasing has no lack of eloquence. This version will undoubtedly give pleasure, but there is a studied quality about the music making that keeps this performance from being at the top of the list.

Though Ashkenazy's whole series with Mehta is easy and relaxed, only in the finale of the *Emperor* does that approach bring a slackening of tension to reduce the impact of the reading. The spaciousness of the first movement combined with clarity of texture is most persuasive, and so is the unusually gentle account of the slow movement. Excellent sound, warm and brilliant. On cassette the sound is very bright, especially the upper strings.

The clarity of Pollini's vision in his dedicated reading is never in doubt, and if at times his playing verges on the chilly, the strong and wise accompaniment of Boehm and the Vienna Philharmonic provides compensation. The slow movement is elegant, lacking the depth which the finest versions give it, and the finale is urgent and energetic rather than joyful. The analogue recording is acceptably transferred to CD but, by the standards of later issues, the quality is comparatively muzzy. The piano image is brilliant but close. The cassette is very successful.

In Brendel's 'live' Chicago recording, the CD emphasizes the snags, including the wild applause at the end. At the start there is a sudden switch-on of 'atmosphere', almost like tape-hiss starting; though in this more than in the earlier concertos Brendel's command and individuality come over powerfully, the relative constriction of the sound is distracting, with the piano aggressively clear. The *Sonata*, Op. 110, makes a generous fill-up; however, those wanting Brendel's performance of the *Emperor* would do better to stay with his earlier analogue version with Haitink.

Still recommended: Among outstanding vintage analogue *Emperors*, Kempff leads the field (DG Accolade 2542 190), although Bishop-Kovacevich, Gilels and Arrau can also be strongly recommended. All are at mid-price, and tape collectors will probably find the Arrau cassette the best buy, where the sound is splendidly bold and full (Ph. 6527/*7311* 055 [id.]). However, see also the On Tour and Walkman tapes discussed below.

(i; ii) *Piano concerto No. 5* (*Emperor*); (iii; iv) *Violin concerto in D;* (v) *Fidelio: overture, Op. 72b.*

(B) *** Ph. On Tour *412 897-4*. (i) Arrau; (ii) cond. Haitink; (iii) Grumiaux; (iv) cond. Sir Colin Davis; (v) Jochum; Concg. O.

(i) *Piano concerto No. 5* (*Emperor*); (ii) *Violin concerto, Op. 61;* (iii) *Fidelio: overture, Op. 72b.*

(B) *** DG Walkman *413 145-4*. (i) Eschenbach, Boston SO, Ozawa; (ii) Schneiderhan, BPO, Jochum; (iii) Dresden State O, Boehm.

It was DG who, with their Walkman series, pioneered the idea of bargain-priced double-length chrome tapes, specifically designed to capture the rapidly expanding market offered by the miniaturized cassette reproducer with headphones. Philips soon followed with a comparable label called On Tour, nattily illustrated with pictures of vintage cars, each placed longways on the front of the liner-leaflet, to make optimum use of the available space. Both the present issues were among the first releases in their respective series, and each offers outstanding versions of two of Beethoven's greatest concertos with the *Fidelio* overture used to fill out the space at the end of side two.

On Philips comes Arrau's authoritative 1964 recording of the *Emperor* with Haitink, notable for its splendidly realistic piano timbre. Arrau is at his most commanding; the slow movement in particular conveys the tension of a live performance – it sounds as though it might have been made in a single unedited take. Grumiaux's 1974 version of the *Violin concerto* with Sir Colin Davis admirably combines poetry with strength, and the solo playing itself has a characteristically restrained lyrical grace in the slow movement, to balance the sparkle of the finale. The Concertgebouw Orchestra is featured throughout (Jochum conducts the overture); though the reverberation brings at times a very slight loss of refinement in the orchestral focus, overall the quality is excellent.

On DG, Eschenbach too gives a deeply satisfying interpretation of the *Emperor*, helped by the equally youthful urgency of his accompanist, Ozawa. With thoughtfulness, power and bravura nicely balanced, this interpretation is also very acceptable – if not, perhaps, quite as strong as Arrau's account. The high-level transfer conquers the reverberant acoustic; although detail is not as sharp as in some versions, the sound has fine weight and richness, with the piano timbre appropriately firm and bold. The recording dates from 1974, whereas the coupling – sounding hardly less full-bodied – is from 1962. Schneiderhan's stereo version of the *Violin concerto* is among the greatest recordings of this work: the serene spiritual beauty of the slow movement, and the playing of the second subject in particular, have never been surpassed on record; the orchestra under Jochum provides a background tapestry of breadth and dignity. It is a noble reading with an innate sense of classicism, yet the first movement offers wonderful lyrical intensity. As an added point of interest, Schneiderhan uses cadenzas that were provided for the transcription of the work for piano and orchestra. The first-movement cadenza is impressive in scale and adds a solo part for the timpani. Both these tapes are genuine bargains. There are no disc equivalents.

Violin concerto in D, Op. 61.
*** HMV Dig. **CDC 747002-2**; ASD/*TCC-ASD* 4059 [Ang. DS/*4XS* 37471]. Perlman, Philh. O, Giulini.
*** Denon Dig. **C37 7508** [id.]. Kantorow, Netherlands CO, Ros-Marba.
*** DG **413 818-2**; 2531/*3301* 250 [id.]. Mutter, BPO, Karajan.
(*) RCA **RD 85402 [RCD1 4502]. Heifetz, Boston SO, Munch – BRAHMS: *Concerto.**** ❀
(***) HMV mono **CDC 747119-2** [id.]. Menuhin, Philh. O, Furtwängler – MENDELSSOHN: *Concerto.*(***)
(M) **(*) Chan. CBR/*CBT* 1024 [None. 71381]. Gruenberg, New Philh. O, Horenstein.
C ** Decca Dig. **400 048-2**; SXDL/*KSXDC* 7508 [Lon. LDR/*5*- 10010]. Kyung Wha Chung, VPO, Kondrashin.
** RCA Dig. **RD 70496**. Ughi, LSO, Sawallisch.
** CBS **MK 42018** [id.]. Francescatti, Columbia SO, Bruno Walter.
*(*) Ph. Dig. **410 549-2**; 6514/*7337* 075 [id.]. Kremer, ASMF, Marriner.

Violin concerto in D; Romances Nos 1–2, Opp. 40 and 50.
*** Ph. **416418-2**; 416237-1/*4* (without *Romances*) [id.]. Szeryng, Concg. O, Haitink.

Perlman's outstanding HMV digital recording of Beethoven's *Violin concerto* must be counted among the great recordings of this work. Perlman's is the most commanding of readings. The violin emerges in the first movement almost imperceptibly, rising gently from the orchestra, but there and throughout the performance the element of slight understatement, the refusal to adopt too romantically expressive a style, makes for a compelling strength, perfectly matched by Giulini's thoughtful, direct accompaniment. Steadiness of pulse is a hallmark of this version, but there is never a feeling of rigidity, and the lyrical power of the music making is a vital element. The beautiful slow movement has a quality of gentle rapture, almost matching Schneiderhan's sense of stillness and serenity in his recording of 1953; and the finale, joyfully and exuberantly fast, is charged with the fullest excitement. The digital recording is satisfyingly full and spacious, yet admirably clear, with an outstanding matching cassette. The CD disc is one of the finest so far to come from EMI, adding extra presence and refining detail, although emphasizing the forward balance of the soloist.

Kantorow, who has also recorded a very successful set of the Mozart concertos for Denon, follows a performing tradition in the Beethoven *Violin concerto* whose most distinguished recent advocate was Wolfgang Schneiderhan. Kantorow's playing has a comparable incandescent classical lyricism and unforced naturalness of line and phrasing, and his reading takes its place alongside the very finest recorded versions. There are many moments of great beauty, not least the hushed reprise of the main theme at the end of the first-movement cadenza. The slow movement too is very moving in its gentle sustained intensity, while the finale is nimble in articulation, yet with lyrical feeling still very much to the fore. The use of a chamber-sized accompanying group enhances the classical scale of the performance, with Ros-Marba providing an understanding if relaxed supporting role. The orchestral wind playing is particularly fine and the principal bassoon must receive special mention. The recording is first class, very well balanced in a spacious acoustic framework which never clouds detail, while the background silence of the CD gives the soloist a very tangible presence.

The slow basic tempi of Anne-Sophie Mutter's beautiful reading on DG were her own choice, she claims, and certainly not forced on her by her superstar conductor. The first two movements have rarely, if ever, been more expansively presented on record, but the purity of the solo playing and the concentration of the whole performance make the result intensely convincing. The finale is relaxed too, but is well pointed, at a fair tempo, and presents the necessary contrast. Good atmospheric recording against the warm acoustic of the Philharmonie Hall in Berlin. On CD, the closeness of balance is emphasized, but the digital transfer of an analogue original brings attractively warm sound, with more bloom on it than is usual in the Philharmonie. The cassette is somewhat variable in focus.

Szeryng's 1974 recording with Haitink brings a superb balance between lyricism and power. The orchestral introduction is immediately riveting in its breadth and sense of scale, and throughout the first movement Szeryng's playing has great beauty. His use of the Joachim cadenza is an added attraction. The slow movement blossoms with a richly drawn line, the glorious second subject phrased with great intensity; after this emotional climax, the link into the finale is managed with a fine sense of spontaneity. The dance-like mood which follows completes an interpretation that is as satisfying in its overall shape as in its control of mood and detail. The recording is full and resonant – inner orchestral definition is not always absolutely sharp – but the ambience is attractively warm, and the solo violin is beautifully caught. On CD, fine performances of the *Romances* (recorded two years earlier) are offered as a bonus, but the mid-priced cassette is extremely well managed and, costing very much less, seems an admirable way of acquiring this version of the *Concerto*.

RCA's digital transfer of a recording originally made in the very earliest days of stereo is astonishingly vivid on CD, with a fine sense of realism and presence, and the soloist only a little closer than is natural. The extra immediacy of CD reinforces the supreme mastery of a performance which may adopt fast speeds but never sounds rushed, finding time for individuality and imagination in every phrase. For some listeners, the comparative lack of serenity in the first movement (though not in the *Larghetto*) will be a drawback, but the drama of the reading is unforgettable. Heifetz's unique timbre is marvellously captured; the assured aristocracy of the playing confounds criticism.

Recorded only months before the conductor's death, Menuhin's version with Furtwängler is a classic which emerges with extraordinary freshness in its new CD format. The bond between the wrongly-reviled conductor and his Jewish champion brought an extra intensity to a natural musical alliance between two inspirational artists, here both at their peak. Rarely if ever has the Beethoven *Violin concerto* been recorded with such sweetness and tenderness, yet with firm underlying strength. With its generous coupling, it is a compact disc which defies the years. One hardly registers that this is mono recording.

Originally recorded for *Reader's Digest* around 1970, Gruenberg's refreshingly spontaneous-sounding version was finally issued on a regular label some fifteen years later. With Horenstein inspired and with Gruenberg on his mettle (having been brought in as a late replacement), the outer movements are clean, fresh and athletic, intensifying the inward meditation of the central *Larghetto*. It is not the most polished version, but it carries unusual conviction and is well recorded for its period, with a good matching cassette.

Miss Chung gives a measured and thoughtful reading which lacks the compulsion one would have predicted. That is largely due to the often prosaic conducting of Kondrashin. There is poetry in individual moments – the minor-key episode of the finale, for example, which alone justifies the unusually slow tempo – but with too little of the soloist's natural electricity conveyed and none of her volatile imagination, it must not be counted her final statement on a masterpiece. The digital recording is impressive on LP, but outstanding on the compact disc which is wonderfully transparent and real. The clarity and presence – and the silent background – are a joy and the balance is most natural. The cassette too is of demonstration quality and it is a pity that the performance is so relatively uninvolving.

Ughi's version, with excellent, beautifully balanced sound, most impressive in its CD format, is unexceptionable: a first-rate performance, fresh and unaffected, marked by consistent purity of tone in every register, which yet fails to grab the imagination, lacking magic.

Francescatti's recording dates from 1961; the digital remastering has smoothed the upper range of its original tendency to spikiness, yet has retained the vividness and clarity, with the brightness on top well supported with a firm, rich bass. Francescatti often produces a beautiful sound with a silvery upper register, although his intonation is just occasionally slightly suspect. There is much to admire, however, and there are many passages of lyrical beauty in the first movement. The emotional tension is well held. Walter's orchestral contribution is on the heavy side and sometimes misses a lightness of touch (as important in this work as a sense of grandeur). Perhaps it is that neither soloist nor conductor seems to relax and simply enjoy the music, which brings a slight sense of disappointment at the end, even though the slow movement is often most beautiful and the finale has an attractive feeling of the dance about it.

The point of controversy which for most will completely rule out the Kremer version is his use of the Schnittke cadenza with its facile avant-garde effects – including what one supposes are imitations of electronic music – which is totally out of style. Otherwise, the soloist's playing is sweet and generally sympathetic and the playing of the Academy under Sir Neville Marriner admirably transparent, not at all lacking in power. The sound on the CD is first rate, clear, refined and well balanced, but the cassette is bass-heavy.

Concerto movement in C, WoO 5; Romance No. 1, Op. 40.

(M) *** DG Sig. 410 985-1/*4* [id.]. Kremer, LSO, Tchakarov – SCHUBERT: *Konzertstück* etc.***

The early *Concerto movement in C* reveals Beethoven at twenty writing on an amibitious scale but rarely if ever achieving the touches of individuality which mark his mature concertos. This first movement is performed in a completion by Wilfried Fischer, effective enough; and the mixed bag of trivial coupling items is certainly apt, all of them beautifully played by Kremer and splendidly recorded, on disc and tape alike.

Triple concerto for violin, cello and piano in C, Op. 56.
(B) *** CfP Dig. CFP 41 4495-1/*4*. Zimmermann, Cohen, Manz, ECO, Saraste.
(B) ** DG Walkman *415 332-4* [id.]. Schneiderhan, Fournier, Starker, Berlin RSO, Fricsay – BRAHMS: *Double concerto*; MOZART: *Violin concerto No. 3.***

Triple concerto, Op. 56; Overtures: Coriolan; Egmont; Fidelio.
(*) DG **415 276; (d.) 2531/*3301* 262 [id.]. Mutter, Zeltser, Yo-Yo Ma, BPO, Karajan.

Triple concerto, Op. 56; Romances for violin and orchestra Nos 1 in G, Op. 40; 2 in F, Op. 50.
*** HMV Dig. EL 270079-1/*4*. Hoelscher, Schiff, Zacharias, Leipzig GO, Masur.

Triple concerto, Op. 56; Piano sonata No. 24 in F sharp, Op. 78; Fantasia in G min., Op. 77.
(M) ** CBS 60295/*40*- [MP/*MPT* 38895]. Rudolf Serkin, Laredo, Parnas, Marlboro Fest. O, Schneider.

Led by the cellist, Heinrich Schiff – a balance of responsibility suggested by Beethoven's own priorities in this work – the soloists in Masur's version make a characterful but finely integrated trio. Their rhythmic flair prompts Masur in turn to give one of his most sparkling Beethoven performances on record, and even the opening tutti is better sprung than those of their principal rivals. The long span of the first movement is firmly held together, the brief slow movement has inner intensity without being overweighted, while the finale is ideally clean and light. The sound is both full and detailed, far preferable to Karajan's DG. The two *Romances* are persuasively done and make a generous fill-up, with the most engaging orchestral detail in the accompaniment. There is a first-class cassette – one of EMI's best, firmly focused.

On Classics for Pleasure, with first-rate modern digital recording and with Robert Cohen leading an excellent team of prize-winning young soloists (his solo in the slow movement is superb), this makes an outstanding bargain version, keenly competitive with almost any full-priced issue, if not always so elegantly pointed as some. Jukka-Pekka Saraste and the ECO provide a lively, understanding accompaniment and the performance has splendid spontaneity throughout, with the finale sparkling in its sense of occasion. The recording is exceptionally well balanced, with most of the problems solved: the soloists forward, but not exaggeratedly so, and the orchestral backing given fine impact within the convincing acoustics of London's Henry Wood Hall. The high-level cassette, too, is very successful, matching the LP very closely.

For their CD issue, DG have added three overtures as a reasonably generous makeweight, while the detail of the analogue recording has been sharpened, but the point is emphasized that after Karajan's formidable crescendo, within his very positive opening tutti, the soloists seem rather small-scale. But there are benefits from the unity brought by the conductor when each of the young players has a positive contribution to make, no less effectively when the recording balance for once in this work does not unduly favour the solo instruments. Yo-Yo Ma's playing is not immaculate, and he does not dominate each thematic statement, but the urgency, spontaneity and – in the slow movement – the depth of expressiveness make for an enjoyable version, well recorded. On cassette the orchestral tuttis are rather opaque (this is most noticeable at the opening of the first movement) but the solo detail matches the LP closely.

The soloists in the 1962 Marlboro Festival version that CBS have happily restored to circulation in their mid-priced 'Portrait' series are more closely balanced than in the DG version, and the recording is obviously dated. Orchestral detail suffers a little and the solo timbres are not as natural as we would expect today, but the performance itself has considerable stature. It is dominated by Serkin (who also gives authoritative accounts of the two piano works) but the playing of Jaime Laredo and Leslie Parnas in the slow movement is memorable.

On the Walkman tape of Fricsay's 1961 recording, the balance is very similar, with the soloists again placed well forward. The performance has breadth and a genuine grasp of structure, with excellent solo playing. Only in the first movement does one sense a slight want of spontaneity, but in all other respects this is satisfactory and the sound is fuller than on CBS. The couplings are generous and of comparable quality.

12 Contredanses, WoO 14; 12 German dances, WoO 8; 12 Minuets, WoO 7.
(M) *** Ph. Seq. 412 356-1/*4* [id.]. ASMF, Marriner.

Even as a composer of light music Bethoven was a master, and this collection, beautifully played and superbly recorded, can be warmly recommended on disc. The cassette is disappointing, the sound thick and opaque at the bass end.

12 German Dances, WoO 8; 12 Minuets, WoO 7.
** HM **HMC 901017** [id.]. Bella Musica of Vienna Ens., Dittrich.

The CD by the Bella Musica of Vienna Ensemble offers all the advantages of the medium: truthful reproduction and excellent presence within a warm ambience. But the playing has the nonchalance of a background café group and, although it is in good style, it does not readily hold the attention.

The Creatures of Prometheus: Overture and ballet music: Nos 5, Adagio; 16, Finale, Op. 43. Overtures: King Stephen, Op. 117; Leonora No. 1, Op. 138; Leonora No. 2, Op. 72a; Leonora No. 3, Op. 72b.
(M) **(*) HMV ED 290401-1/*4* [Ang. AE/*4AE* 34441]. Philh. or New Philh. O, Klemperer.

This disc generously collects together some major performances of Beethoven's overtures, though curiously *Fidelio* is omitted. The approach to the three *Leonoras* – as one expects with Klemperer – uses measured tempi to bring out the architectural strength. Such is the conductor's control over tension, however, that no unbiased listener could find the results dull or heavy, even if one must turn elsewhere for the full drama of the opera house. Klemperer invests the extra items from the *Prometheus* ballet with an unexpected nobility of contour (if at the expense of their terpsichorean feeling), and the comparatively slight *King Stephen* is given strength. The remastered recording is clear, with textures less ample than the originals. The cassette, transferred at the highest level, is bright and clean but with the strings a little lacking in body.

Overtures: The Consecration of the house, Op. 124; Coriolan, Op. 62; The Creatures of Prometheus, Op. 43; Egmont, Op. 84; Fidelio, Op. 72c; King Stephen, Op. 117; Namensfeier, Op. 115; Leonora Nos 1–3, Opp. 138; 72a; 72b; The Ruins of Athens, Op. 113.
(M) *** DG 413 516-1/*4* (2) [id.]. BPO, Karajan.

Karajan's versions of the Beethoven overtures were recorded in the middle and at the end of the 1960s. There is a fastidiousness about some of the phrasing (for example in *Leonora No. 2*) and a smoothness that sometimes seem out of character, although this comment does not apply to *Egmont* and *Fidelio* and certainly not to *Leonara No. 3* with its electrifying coda. Throughout, one cannot but marvel at the superlative playing of the Berlin Philharmonic Orchestra, without a suggestion of routine in pieces that must be almost over-familiar. Taken as a whole, this is an impressive set and it has undoubted atmosphere. The recordings sound fresh and there is little to choose between the tapes (presented in one of DG's 'flap-packs') and the discs.

Overtures: Consecration of the house, Op. 124; Coriolan, Op. 62; Fidelio, Op. 72c; Leonora Nos 1–3, Opp. 138; 72a; 72b.
(*) HMV **CDC 747190-2 [id.]. Philh. O, Klemperer.

This seems a more satisfyingly arranged collection than Klemperer's LP (above) which also includes the three *Leonora overtures*. Here *Fidelio* is properly added, a performance more serious than usual, and *Consecration of the house*, a magnificent account, perhaps the finest ever recorded. The CD transfers are remarkably fresh. The three *Leonora overtures* (1964) are more forwardly balanced and the effect is vividly dramatic. The ear immediately notices the more recessed perspective at the opening of *Fidelio* (1962) and, because of this, the earlier recordings, *Consecration* (1960) and *Coriolan* (1959), do not sound more dated. Indeed, they are evidence of the excellence of Walter Legge's judgement in the early days of stereo.

Overtures: Coriolan, Op. 62; The Creatures of Prometheus, Op. 43; Egmont, Op. 84; Fidelio, Op. 72c; Leonora No. 3, Op. 72b.
** HMV Dig. **CDC 747086-2** [id.]; EL 270110-1/*4* [Ang. DS/*4XS* 38045]. LPO, Tennstedt.

Fidelio is the most successful performance here, with an exciting closing section, but *Egmont* has a lower voltage. Although the approach is crisply dramatic, the slightly distanced trumpet call in *Leonora No. 3* produces little frisson of anticipation; and generally, although the orchestral playing is alert and polished, there is nothing to resonate in the memory. The CD is well balanced, and clear and bright, but slightly lacking in ambient atmosphere.

Overtures: Coriolan, Op. 62; Creatures of Prometheus, Op. 43; Egmont, Op. 84; Leonora No. 1, Op. 138; Leonora No. 3, Op. 72a; The Ruins of Athens, Op. 113.
*** CBS Dig. **MK 42103**; IM/*IMT* 42103 [id.]. Bav. RSO, Sir Colin Davis.

This collection is superbly recorded – the sound is spacious and beautiful, full yet refined, and has a remarkably wide dynamic range. In *Leonora No. 3* the dynamic contrast is electrifying and adds to the drama of the performance. Both here and in *Leonora No. 1*, Sir Colin Davis secures playing of great distinction from the Bavarian orchestra; and the lighter pieces, *The Ruins of Athens* (which opens the concert engagingly) and *Creatures of Prometheus*, are played with obvious enjoyment and flair. *Egmont* is weighty, and in *Coriolan* Davis's broad tempo brings a hint of heaviness. It was a pity *Leonora No. 2* was omitted in favour of these two, but this remains a distinguished collection.

Romances for violin and orchestra Nos 1 in G, Op. 40; 2 in F, Op. 50.
(B) *** DG Walkman *413 844-4* [id.]. D. Oistrakh, RPO, Goossens – BRAHMS: *Violin concerto* **(*); BRUCH: *Concerto No. 1.***
* CBS Dig. **MK 37204**; 37204 [id.]. Stern, Boston SO, Ozawa – MENDELSSOHN: *Violin concerto.**

David Oistrakh's performances of the Beethoven *Romances* are of high quality and are well recorded. If the other works on this generous Walkman tape are attractive, this is excellent value. Readers might also like to consider an alternative Philips On Tour chrome tape, which includes first-class performances by Grumiaux of these Beethoven pieces within a very attractive anthology of short concertante works for violin and orchestra called '*Romance*' and including music by Chausson, Saint-Saëns, Svendsen, Tchaikovsky and Wieniawski (see under 'Romance' in the Concerts section, below).

Stern's performances cannot be recommended. They are anaemic in timbre, and the clarity of the CD only serves to emphasize the lack of warmth in the playing.

Symphonies Nos 1–9.
(M) * Denon Dig. **C 37 7251/6**. Berlin State O, Suitner (with soloists and chorus).

Symphonies Nos 1–9; Overtures: Consecration of the house; Coriolan; Egmont (with incidental music); *Fidelio. Grosse Fuge.*
**(*) HMV EX 290379-3/9 (6/5) [Ang. AEW 34469]. Soloists, Philh. Ch. and O, Klemperer.

Symphonies Nos 1–9; Overtures: Coriolan; Egmont; Fidelio; Leonora No. 3.
(*) DG Dig. **415 066-2 (6); 415 066-1/4 (7/6) [id.]. Soloists, V. Singverein, BPO, Karajan.
(M) **(*) Ph. **416 274-2**; 416 274-1/4 (6) [id.]. Leipzig GO, Masur (with soloists and chorus).

Symphonies Nos 1–9; Fidelio overture.
(**) Ph. mono **416 200-2** (*Nos 1–2*); **416 201-2** (*No. 3*); **416 202-2** (*Nos 4–5*); **416 203-2** (*No. 6* and *Fidelio overture*); **416 204-2** (*Nos 7–8*); **416 205-2** (*No. 9*) (available separately). Concg. O, Mengelberg (with soloists and Ch. in *No. 9*).

It should have been pure gain having Karajan recording a cycle of the Beethoven symphonies with new technical developments in mind, in the shape of digital recording, CD and video. Instead, the sound seems to have been affected by the need to have a video version recorded at the same sessions. The gain is that these performances have keener spontaneity, the loss that they often lack the brilliant, knife-edged precision of ensemble one has come to regard as normal with Karajan: the opening of No. 1 brings an obvious example. Similarly in sound, the recording engineers seem not to have been so careful in their balancing. Though there is relatively little homing-in of microphones to spotlight individual detail, the sound too often grows thick and congested in big fortissimo tuttis. Arguably it would have been preferable to have either the 1977 or, better still, the 1963 cycles transferred to CD with their cleaner, if less wide-ranging, sound. There is still a case for counting Karajan's cycle the finest on CD at the time of its issue. The easy power and massive command of his conducting in Beethoven make for magnetic readings, which will disappoint only those who make close comparisons with the past. Interpretatively, with speeds generally a little less extreme, there are a number of movements which sound more persuasive than before. Though the choral finale of the *Ninth* is let down by the soprano, Janet Perry, that culminating symphony sets the seal on a cycle that in interpretation is certainly satisfying in its consistency.

The separate discs in Klemperer's Philharmonia cycle, collected in a box, make up a set which, for all its flaws (see the separate reviews), has a weight and compulsion beyond all but the finest rivals. The overtures, like the symphonies, in their magisterial way have the Klemperer imprint firmly implanted. The six-disc layout is exceptionally generous, with direct metal mastering allowing sides of around forty minutes to bring out the original excellence of the engineering, helped by the new digital transfers.

Although it is probably not as satisfying all round as Klemperer's set, Kurt Masur's Beethoven cycle with the Leipzig Gewandhaus Orchestra has a very great deal to recommend it. In sheer naturalness of utterance, unforced expressiveness and the superlatively disciplined response of the orchestral playing, the Gewandhaus set is among the very finest on the market. The first two *Symphonies* are attractively fresh, with the slow movement of the *Second* memorable. The *Eroica* is uncommonly fine, particularly its nobly paced slow movement which is totally free from excessive emphasis in expression. The Philips recording has a natural perspective, a full acoustic ambience and great refinement. In the *Fourth Symphony* Masur is particularly successful, and the Gewandhaus Orchestra respond with marvellously alert playing. In the slow movement Masur brings great imagination and poetry to his reading; the homogeneous, cultured orchestral sound of the Gewandhaus Orchestra and its rhythmic resilience and vitality are in themselves a source of pleasure. The wind intonation is absolutely perfect and there is a natural exuberance that is very satisfying. The digital remastering now places the nine symphonies and four overtures on six compact discs, LPs and cassettes. The sound is considerably livelier than the originals, and on CD the violins above the stave are very brightly lit, though not edgy. On the splendid chrome tapes the treble, while still admirably fresh, is slightly smoother and more natural, and the bass is weightier and more expansive, yet inner detail remains very good. There will be many who prefer the sound balance on the tape to CD, for the high-level transfers bring very little background. Moreover, although the CDs are priced at six for the price of five, the tapes and LPs come in the lower medium-price range and cost a third as much overall. They are well packaged and the only minor drawback to the cassette layout is that on tape four the *Egmont overture* comes before the *Pastoral symphony* to even up the side-lengths. Not that these performances are all equally recommendable. Neither Masur's *Fifth* nor his *Pastoral* matches the finest in the catalogue: the former does not have the blazing intensity of Carlos Kleiber, and the latter does not eclipse Boehm. There are some details which will not have universal appeal (he tends to slow down for the trio sections of scherzos, and the horns are somewhat recessed at that point in the *Eroica*); nor can one say that the *Ninth Symphony* has the stature of, say, Karajan's reading. However, the Masur set wears well and is eminently sound and reliable; at times it is very much more than that.

Recorded in 1939 and 1940, before and after the invasion of Holland (when Mengelberg was a Nazi collaborator), these performances – with one serious exception – capture the live atmosphere of the Concertgebouw with astonishing freshness. They were taken from Hilversum radio recordings, and balances are often very odd, with woodwind tending to be distant but with the strings well enough recorded to reveal a polish rare, if not unique, at that time. Mengelberg's approach to Beethoven was romantic and wilful – unacceptably so for today – but, even more than Furtwängler, essentially a thinker among Beethoven interpreters, Mengelberg was urgently dramatic, often racing ahead at high speed. This is a set very much for specialists in interpretation; anyone wanting to sample it might try the *Ninth* with its electric sense of occasion and fine singing from the Toonkunst Choir. It is sad that the *Eroica* – the only one of the series which appeared on commercial disc – has dim, muffled sound, originally processed by Telefunken.

Suitner's is a workaday cycle of the Beethoven symphonies, only notable because it arrived so soon in the CD catalogue. The playing is competent, but the string section is less polished than one might expect of Berliners, even from the East. Scherzos tend to come off best, brisk and well sprung; but that only underlines the plodding qualities which afflict rhythms in both fast and slow movements. Nor is there much dramatic tension in these performances; the studio recording is variable, generally less cleanly defined in the symphonies recorded in 1980, rather fuller if never brilliant as the series progressed.

Symphony No. 1 in C, Op. 21.
(*) Ph. Dig. **416 329-2; 416 329-1/*4* [id.]. O of the 18th Century, Brüggen – MOZART: *Symphony No. 40.***(*)
** Nimbus Dig. **NIM 5003**. Hanover Band, Huggett – *Piano concerto No. 1.***(*)

Symphonies Nos 1 in C; 2 in D, Op. 36.
*** CBS Dig. IM/*IMT* 39707 [id.]. ECO, Tilson Thomas.
*** CBS **MK 42009** [id.]. Columbia SO, Bruno Walter.
(*) O-L Dig. **414 338-2; 414 338-1/*4* [id.]. AAM, Hogwood.
** DG Dig. **415 505-2**; 415 505-1/*4* [id.]. BPO, Karajan.
* Capriccio **10001**. Dresden PO, Kegel.

With his talented band of 45 players, Frans Brüggen directs an individual and compelling reading of Beethoven's *First*, which gains interpretatively from being recorded live. This will appeal to many who do not normally enjoy authentic performance, and has a degree of warmth and expressiveness not normally associated with recordings on period instruments. One snag is that recording balances are not ideal, and the timpani booms away very loudly. On the high-level tape, the focus is not absolutely sharp in fortissimos.

The coupling of the *First Symphony* with the *First Piano concerto* adds point to the Hanover Band's Nimbus issue of Beethoven on period instruments. With Monica Huggett directing from the leader's desk, the reading is less distinctive than that of the *Concerto* but, with rhythms fast, light and resilient, it has many of the same qualities, and the distinctive sound is comparably attractive, even if its relatively soft focus will not please everyone.

Michael Tilson Thomas's project of recording all the Beethoven symphonies with the English Chamber Orchestra brings excellent accounts of the first two symphonies, both apt in scale but with no sense of loss of weight because of the reduced number of players. Pacing is admirable, with vigour and urgency never leading to aggressiveness in outer movements. Slow movements are graciously phrased and fresh; and alert, clean articulation brings a buoyant scherzo in No. 2 and delicately traced string detail in the trio of the minuet of No. 1. The recording is well balanced internally, although the forward projection does mean that the difference between *piano* and *pianissimo* is reduced. Nevertheless, these are spirited and involving performances which give much pleasure. Both first-movement exposition repeats are made to seem an essential part of the structure.

Bruno Walter's set of Beethoven symphonies on CBS dates from the beginning of the 1960s, and the recordings have been remastered with striking success: the ambient warmth brings an attractive richness without blurring detail, and the upper string timbre remains fresh and lively. In the *First Symphony* Walter achieves a happy medium between the eighteenth-century quality of Karajan's analogue versions and the turgidity of Klemperer. Walter has his idiosyncrasies, notably in the speed changes within movements, the *Andante* being the most flagrant instance, yet he remains convincing. One odd textual point is the addition of trumpets to two of the groups of 'Halleluja' syncopations in the finale, where none are marked. The most controversial point about his interpretation of the *Second Symphony* is the slow movement which is taken very slowly indeed, with plenty of rubato. But the rich warmth of the recording makes the effect very involving. For the rest, the speeds are well chosen, with a fairly gentle allegro in the finale which allows the tick-tock accompaniment to the second subject to have a delightful lift to it. On technical grounds this reissue can stand alongside any of the more recent competition and the remaining hiss is not disturbing.

In his coupling of the first two Beethoven symphonies, Hogwood makes a promising start for his projected cycle of all nine using period instruments and authentic-sized forces. Though these performances do not have quite the exhilaration of his Haydn recordings, they avoid the over-abrasive manners of some of his Mozart symphony recordings. Some may want more positive, individual readings of this music; however, with sensible speeds, often fast but not gabbled, and with clean, finely balanced recording bringing out the freshness and transparency of authentic textures, the results are undistractingly attractive. The cassette is brightly lit and the upper range is more abrasive than on disc, especially in No. 2.

Karajan's new Beethoven series, digitally recorded with video included as part of the project, brings some surprisingly slack ensemble in this coupling of the first two symphonies. The performances are relaxed in good ways, too, with Karajan's flair and control of rhythm never leading to breathless speeds. Not unexpectedly, there are moments when detail is magically revealed, but the heavy reverberation of the recording makes the result arguably too weighty for these works, and pianissimos are rarely gentle enough. The sound balance of the CD is preferable to the LP which in some respects is less effective than the chrome tape – one of DG's best.

Kegel's heavy style is little suited to Beethoven's two earliest symphonies. Unlike Klemperer's comparably weighty readings, these lack rhythmic subtlety. Fair recording.

Symphonies Nos 1 in C, Op. 21; 4 in B flat, Op. 60.
(*) DG Walkman *419 085-4* [id.]. VPO, Boehm – MOZART: *Symphony No. 39.*(*)

Symphonies Nos 1 in C, Op. 21; 4 in B flat, Op. 60; Overture: Coriolan, Op. 62.
(M) **(*) HMV ED 290270-1/*4* [Ang. AE/*4AE* 34423]. Philh. O, Klemperer.

Symphonies Nos 1 in C, Op. 21; 4 in B flat, Op. 60; Egmont overture.
(M) *** DG Gal. 419 048-1/*4* [id.]. BPO, Karajan.

Symphonies Nos 1 in C, Op. 21; 8 in F, Op. 93.
* Denon Dig. **C37 7128** [id.]. Berlin State O, Suitner.

Karajan's 1977 series of Beethoven symphonies is being reissued in new couplings on Galleria, digitally remastered, clear, yet still weighty, ready for future appearance on CD. No. 1 is just as exciting, polished and elegant as in his first stereo version of 1962; in No. 4 the balance is close, exposing every flicker of tremolando. Yet the precision of the Berlin Philharmonic is a thing of wonder; if anything, Karajan conveys more weight and strength than before, with greater emphasis on the *Adagio*. Only the extremely fast tempo for the finale marks a questionable development, but even there the brilliance and excitement are never in doubt.

The LP coupling of Klemperer's digitally remastered versions matches one of the very finest of the set, the *Fourth*, with one of the less attractive, when the *First Symphony* is made to sound too heavy in the first and third movements. Even so, the concentration of the conductor and his characterful consistency are never in doubt. With an overture too, the coupling is as generous as the others in the series, with sound equally agreeable, remarkably fresh for its age. Tape and disc are closely matched, the tape, if anything, livelier on top in the *First*. Readers will note that with the LPs and tapes of this Klemperer series in the medium-price range, they cost about a third the price of the differently coupled CDs.

Boehm's recordings come from his Vienna cycle of the early 1970s, centrally satisfying readings, smoothly recorded, though with a good deal of resonance in the lower range. What these mature readings may lack is the sort of sharp idiosyncrasy which makes for dramatic memorability. So the first movement of the *C major Symphony* is spacious and mellow (the effect emphasized by the richly upholstered sound). The *Andante* is beautifully played, and the remaining movements have both character and vitality although there is comparatively little extrovert excitement. In the *Fourth*, Boehm's reading notes the kinship with the *Pastoral symphony*. The *Allegro vivace* is relatively easy-going, but with big, satisfying contrasts; the slow movement is warmly lyrical, and the last two movements bounce along joyfully. If Boehm misses some of the tensions, there is no lack of strength or weight.

The introduction sets the pattern of Suitner's performance of the *First* with tension low; though the allegro is much fresher, stodgy rhythms afflict all movements except the scherzo. The *Eighth* is better except in the plodding account of the third-movement Minuet but, even in the brisk and light account of the second-movement *Allegretto*, violins sound thin. Acceptable recording, none too cleanly defined.

Symphony No. 2 in D, Op. 36; Overtures: Coriolan, Op. 62; Egmont, Op. 84; Leonora No. 3, Op. 72a.
* Denon Dig. **C37 7367** [id.]. Berlin State O, Suitner.

Symphonies Nos 2 in D; 4 in B flat, Op. 60.
*** HMV **CDC 747185-2** [id.]. Philh. O, Klemperer.

Symphonies Nos 2 in D; 5 in C min., Op. 67.
(M) **(*) HMV ED 290252-1/*4* [Ang. AE 34425]. Philh. O, Klemperer.

Symphonies Nos 2 in D, Op. 36; 7 in A, Op. 92.
(M) *** DG Gal. 419 050-1/*4* [id.]. BPO, Karajan.

Symphonies Nos 2 in D, Op. 36; 7 in A, Op. 92; Creatures of Prometheus overture.
(B) ** DG Walkman *415 614-4* [id.]. VPO, Boehm.

The different couplings for CD emphasize the consistency of Klemperer's approach to Beethoven, with both the *Second* and *Fourth* symphonies sounding the more powerful through weighty treatment, and the former looking forward, even more clearly than usual, to the later symphonies, rather than back to the eighteenth century. Only in the finale is the result rather too gruff. The *Fourth* brings one of the most compelling performances of all, with Klemperer's measured but consistently sprung pulse allowing for persuasive lyricism alongside power. Exposition repeats are observed in the first movements of both symphonies. The sound on CD is fresh yet full.

The stereo version of the *Fifth* is plainly less electric than Klemperer's earlier mono version but, with exposition repeats again observed in both the outer movements, the epic magnificence of this most concentrated of Beethoven's symphonies is tellingly brought out, with resilient rhythms lightening speeds that are slower than usual. Welcoming freshening of well-balanced 1960 sound in the new digital remastering, with a very good matching tape.

A generous coupling for the reissue on Galleria, digitally remastered, of Karajan's 1977 performances. In No. 2 the manner is a degree weightier than in the earlier, 1962 version, but with firm lines giving the necessary strength. The tempo for the slow movement, as with No. 1, is less controversial than before; the recording, now clearer in its newest format, brings close-up effects which are less believable. The *Seventh* is tense and exciting, with the conductor emphasizing the work's dramatic rather than its dance-like qualities. The slow introduction, taken at a fastish tempo, is tough rather than monumental, and the main *Allegro* is fresh and bright, and not very lilting in its 6/8 rhythm, though it is more pointed here than in the earlier (1962) version. The *Allegretto* is this time a little weightier, but consistency with the earlier reading is the point to emphasize. The recording is clearer than the newer digital version, yet still full-bodied.

There was a time when a coupling like Boehm's in the bargain range, on chrome tape, would have seemed remarkable value for money, but EMI's comparably priced Klemperer series offers similar side-lengths with the option of LP or tape (as well as CD). Boehm's rather plain-spun view of Beethoven has undoubted character and the recordings (from 1972) are excellent, just as clear and with rather more body than the digitally remastered Klemperer versions. The *Second* was one of the finest performances in Boehm's Vienna set. After a brisk and dramatic view of the first movement, he gives genial readings of the remaining movements, affectionately expansive in the slow movement, joyful yet weighty in the scherzo and finale. Boehm's straight approach is less successful in the *Seventh*. The style is lighter, with well-articulated playing throughout, and the slow movement is undoubtedly eloquent in its slightly restrained way. But the outer movements lack the last degree of electricity, and many will find the slow basic tempo of the finale – a performance that keeps within itself – lacking in adrenalin, or indeed the spirit of the dance. The overture makes an agreeable fill-up.

The sound in Suitner's version of the *Second Symphony* is fuller and warmer than in most of his cycle, but then the overtures, recorded in a different year, bring thick sound, not well defined. The first-movement allegro, taken very fast, is fresh enough, but the violin passagework is often scrappy, and the slow movement brings a moulded style, unlike Suitner's usual manner.

Symphonies Nos 3 (Eroica); 5 and 7; Overtures: Consecration of the house; Fidelio; Leonora Nos 1 and 3.
❀ (M) (***) HMV mono EX 200457-3/*5* (2). Philh. O, Klemperer.

These mono recordings were the first of the Beethoven series which Klemperer recorded with the Philharmonia Orchestra from 1954 onwards, and in many ways they surpass the stereo versions made a few years later, when Klemperer was a degree more staid. When they were first reissued, they appeared in synthetic stereo, but the new digital transfers bring a striking improvement, with sharper focus in every register, notably in the firm, full bass. Violin tone is also markedly more realistic. There is no finer memorial for Klemperer on record than these incandescent performances of the three great odd-numbered symphonies, and the *Overtures* provide an attractive makeweight. It is remarkable that this mono recording of the *Consecration of the house* overture of 1956 has fuller (if less spacious) sound than the 1960 stereo version, reissued in coupling with the *Pastoral symphony*, and the performance is markedly more electrifying.

Symphony No. 3 in E flat (Eroica), Op. 55.
ℭ *** Ph. Dig. **410 044-2**; 6514/*7337* 314 [id.]. ASMF, Marriner.
(***) Decca mono **414 626-2**; 414 626-1/*4* [id.] VPO, Erich Kleiber.
** DG Dig. **410 028-2**; Sig. 413 979-1/*4* [id.]. LAPO, Giulini.
** Ph. 412 064-1/*4* [id.]. Concg. O, Kondrashin.
*(*) Telarc Dig. **CD 80090** [id.]. Cleveland O, Dohnányi.
(*) Denon Dig. **C37 7011** [id.]. Berlin State O, Suitner.
(*) Capriccio **10002** [id.]. Dresden PO, Kegel.

Symphony No. 3 (Eroica), Op. 55; Overture Coriolan, Op. 62.
(*) CBS **MK 42010 [id.]. Columbia SO, Bruno Walter.

Symphony No. 3 (Eroica), Op. 55; Egmont overture.
(*) DG Dig. **415 506-2; 415 506-1/*4* [id.]. BPO, Karajan.
** DG **413 778-2** [id.]. VPO, Bernstein.

Symphony No. 3 (Eroica); Grosse Fuge, Op. 133.
*** HMV **CDC 747186-2** [id.]; ED 290271-1/*4* [Ang. AE/*4AE* 34424]. Philh. O, Klemperer.

Symphony No. 3 in E flat (Eroica), Op. 55; Overture Leonora No. 3.
(M) **(*) DG Gal. 419 049-1/*4* [id.]. BPO, Karajan.

The digital remastering of Klemperer's spacious 1961 version reinforces its magnificence, keenly concentrated to sustain speeds slower than in his earlier mono account. The stoically intense account of the *Funeral march* is among the most impressive on record, and only in the coda to the finale does the slow tempo bring some slackening. Despite the extra length of sides – with the stereo version of the *Grosse Fuge*, dating from 1957, issued for the first time – the LP sound is first rate, vivid and well balanced, though the CD is even cleaner and more natural on top. The excellent high-level cassette matches the LP closely.

Sir Neville Marriner's version is in every way outstanding, for although the Academy may use fewer strings, the impression is of weight and strength, ample for Beethoven's mighty inspiration, coupled with a rare transparency of texture and extraordinary resilience of rhythm. The dance-rhythms of the fast movements are brought out captivatingly with sforzandos made clean and sharp to have one applying to the *Eroica* Wagner's famous remark about the *Seventh*, 'the apotheosis of the dance'. The *Funeral march* may emerge as less grave and dark than it can be, but Marriner's unforced directness is most compelling. The recorded sound is among the best ever in a Beethoven symphony, most impressive of all in the compact disc version, which in the slow movement gains greatly from the absence of background noise.

The gain in Karajan's latest digital version of the *Eroica* over his previous recordings lies most of all in the *Funeral march*, very spacious and intense, with dynamic contrasts intensified, even compared with his 1977 version. Here, and even more noticeably in the allegros, the playing is marginally less polished than before, lacking something of the knife-edged bite associated with Karajan. As with others in the series, the oddly balanced recording grows congested in big tuttis. Nevertheless, the power and concentration make it an epic reading, fully matching the scale of the argument, with tempi in the outer movements more relaxed and spacious than in the 1977 version. The sound in *Egmont*, given an urgently dramatic reading, is marginally more agreeable. LP and cassette are fairly closely matched.

It is a pleasure to turn from other accounts of this symphony and hear as beautiful and sympathetic a performance as Walter's. He is not monumental in the different ways of Klemperer and, before him, Toscanini. His handling was much gentler than Szell who followed the Toscanini pattern. (Szell's Cleveland version, coupled with No. 1, is available in the USA on a Japanese CD imported from CBS/Sony – **32DC 483**. It is a fine performance, exciting and dramatic, hard driven, but with the slow movement more searingly felt than in the Walter version.) With Walter one must not expect rip-roaring excitement at every possible moment; but on each page one detects the hand of a master who has thought and felt the symphony for a lifetime: this interpretation has all the ripeness of the best of Walter's work with the Vienna Philharmonic Orchestra between the wars. This sometimes leads to mannered touches, such as the slight pause to emphasize the chord at bar 75 in the first movement – but, even there, Walter makes it sound natural. The digitally remastered recording has all the amplitude one needs for such a reading: its expansive qualities bring rich horns as well as full-bodied strings. There is a slight excess of bass resonance at moments in the *Adagio*, but this can be adjusted with the controls and, although the upper range has a lower ceiling than a modern recording, the violins sound bright and fresh. The disc opens with a superb account of the *Coriolan overture*, spacious, warm and dramatic, and the sound-balance is especially telling, even if here (as throughout) there is a small residue of background noise. The pause between the end of the overture and the beginning of the symphony might have been longer.

Erich Kleiber's Vienna Philharmonic record of the *Eroica* was made in 1955 but not issued until 1959 because the woodwind balance was imperfect and the horns also rather backward. That said, few apologies need be made for this CD. Decca have rightly returned to the mono master and ignored the stereo transcription issued on their Eclipse label at the beginning of the 1970s. The quality is vivid and the spacious acoustics of the Musikvereinsaal spread the sound and help to cushion the violins above the stave. The performance is in every way outstanding – even more wonderfully intense and dramatic than his earlier, Concertgebouw version, and it includes the repeat of the exposition in the first movement to make the whole structure more powerfully monumental. The electricity of the performance is maintained throughout, with the *Funeral march* deeply felt, the mood lightened in the scherzo, the finale making an apotheosis. The musical notes appear to derive from the French LP issue and are not translated very felicitously.

Not everyone will identify readily with the fiery intensity of fast tempi in the outer movements of Karajan's 1977 performance, now reissued, digitally remastered, on Galleria. Contrasts are heightened with, if anything, a more intense account of the *Funeral march* than in earlier recordings. A point to consider is the absence of the exposition repeat in the first movement; but this is among the most polished as well as the most dramatic accounts available. An exciting performance of *Leonora No. 3* makes a very generous bonus. The sound, although not lacking fullness and weight, is better defined than the newer digital version.

Bernstein's 1980 Vienna Philharmonic recording of the *Eroica* brings a degree of disappointment compared with his earlier (1966) CBS record which was electrically intense. There is less incandescence in the first movement and a hard, clattering sound for the opening chords, which is emphasized in the digital remastering for CD. The first-movement exposition repeat is still observed and this is undoubtedly a strong and dramatic reading with a dedicated account of the *Funeral march*. This emerges as more clearly a march than before, yet very measured indeed, but its intensity is enhanced by the presence of an audience. The CD offers the *Egmont overture* as a bonus item, but the shallowness of the recording comes out more clearly than on the original LP (now deleted).

Giulini's refined and individual reading, with its almost eccentrically measured view of the first movement, was an early product of his love affair with the Los Angeles orchestra. It remains an extraordinary example of a conductor transforming an orchestra's usual character, and at mid-price can be valued for its new revelations, even if it is hardly a general recommendation. It is available on CD (remastered successfully from the analogue original) but the Signature reissue, costing a third as much and with an excellent equivalent cassette, would seem the most sensible way to approach this performance.

Kondrashin's version, recorded live at the Concertgebouw in 1979, is a fascinating memorial of a conductor whose recorded repertory was generally to be found in other areas, a surprisingly understated reading with many detailed points of illumination. Not a general recommendation but worth attention, with atmospheric sound, more acceptable than most live recordings.

Matched by clean, bright recording, Dohnányi's Telarc version brings a fresh and direct reading at consistently fast speeds. The playing of the Cleveland Orchestra is superb, reinforced by the wide-ranging sound, but the plainness of the interpretation diminishes the power of the argument; thus, even in the *Funeral march* the contrasting C major section with its triplets is made to sound trivial.

Suitner fails to measure up to the greatness of the *Eroica*. The first movement sounds cautious, and though the *Funeral march* is admirably hushed to the point of reticence the fast speed makes it lightweight. The 1980 recording is among the less well defined in Suitner's cycle.

Kegel's reading is, if anything, duller than the others in his complete cycle, recommendable only for the quality of sound.

Symphonies Nos 3 (Eroica); 8 in F, Op. 93.
(B) ** DG Walkman *415 331-4* [id.]. VPO, Boehm.

Symphonies Nos 3 (Eroica); (i) *9 in D min. (Choral), Op. 125.*
(M) ** DG 413 221-1/*4* (2) [id.]. VPO, Boehm, (i) with soloists and chorus.

Except in the *Funeral march*, Boehm is not quite at his finest in this Vienna performance of the *Eroica*, dating from the early 1970s; other symphonies in the cycle have more intense playing. But the *Funeral march*, without undue moulding of phrase, is still deeply devotional. On Walkman, with full, resonant sound it is paired with a straightforward, characterful account of the *Eighth*; alternatively there is mid-priced coupling with the excellent, if similarly straight view of the *Choral symphony*, notable for its dramatic yet controlled finale. This latter performance is also available on a Walkman tape, coupled with *Leonora No. 3* – see below.

Symphony No. 4 in B flat, Op. 60.
*(*) Orfeo Dig. **C 100841A**; S/*M* 100841B [id.]. Bav. State O, Carlos Kleiber.
* Denon Dig. **C37 7077** [id.]. Berlin State O, Suitner.

Symphonies Nos 4 in B flat, Op. 60; 5 in C min., Op. 67.
(*) CBS **MK 42011 [id.]. Columbia SO, Bruno Walter.

Symphonies Nos 4 in B flat; 7 in A, Op. 92.
** DG Dig. **415 121-2**; 415 121-1/*4* [id.]. BPO, Karajan.

Symphonies Nos 4 in B flat; 9 in D min. (*Choral*).
*(*) Capriccio **10006/7** [id.]. Hargan, Walther, Büchner, Kováts, Leipzig R. Ch., Dresden PO, Kegel.

Bruno Walter's reading of the *Fourth* is splendid, the finest achievement of his whole cycle. There is intensity and a feeling of natural vigour which makes itself felt in every bar. Sometimes in Walter's readings of the other symphonies, sensitive and humane though they are, one feels a lack of a sense of urgency. This performance is a triumphant refutation of any such criticism. The first movement may not have quite the monumental weight that Klemperer gives it, but it is livelier. The slow movement gives Walter the perfect opportunity to coax a genuinely singing tone from his violins as only he knows how; and the finale allows the wind department its measure of brilliance. All aspects of this symphony – so much more varied than we have realized – are welded together here and show what depths it really contains. The recording is full, yet clear, sweet-toned with a firm bass. Here as in the *Fifth* the sound-balance is richer and more satisfying than in many modern recordings. In Walter's reading of the *Fifth*, the first movement is taken very fast, yet it lacks the kind of nervous tension that distinguishes Carlos Kleiber's famous version. The middle two movements are contrastingly slow. In the *Andante* (more like *adagio*) there is a glowing, natural warmth, but the scherzo at this speed is too gentle. The finale, taken at a spacious, natural pace, is joyous and sympathetic, but again fails to convey the ultimate in tension. Perhaps coupled with a performance less outstanding than the *Fourth*, this would make a greater impact; and, providing one is not looking for something really electric, it is satisfying in its own way. The digital remastering for CD has left behind a residue of pre-Dolby background hiss, but it is not too distracting.

Karajan's generous coupling of the *Fourth* and *Seventh* symphonies comes from his most recent series of Beethoven symphony recordings, done with video cameras present. The impression is of more spontaneous, less meticulous performances than in his previous versions of these works, presumably recorded this time with longer takes. The bravura is most compelling, and there is no doubt about the command of Karajan's never-routine view of Beethoven – but too much is lost. The slow movement of the *Fourth* is fresh, sweet and beautifully moulded but is never hushed; and the *Allegretto* of No. 7, taken characteristically fast, is so smooth that the dactylic rhythm at the start is almost unidentifiable. Recording, not as detailed or analytical as usual, is undistracting.

Carlos Kleiber's version on Orfeo certainly captures the conductor's characteristic electricity, in a live performance in Munich, but, with rhythms jammed home hard, largely unsprung except in the slow movement, and speeds exaggeratedly fast, it cannot be recommended. The recording is full and immediate, but in playing-time few CDs offer poorer value for money. Even the first-movement exposition repeat is omitted, and there are no bands between movements.

Though the allegros in Suitner's performance bring brighter and cleaner playing than in most of his cycle, and the recording is fuller than usual, the disc could hardly provide worse value with only 35 minutes of music.

Over the years, Kegel has done some first-rate work with the Leipzig Radio Chorus, but his stodgy account of the *Ninth Symphony* cannot be recommended, with even the choral finale variably sung. The two-record format with No. 4 as coupling is extravagant, and the performance of the *Fourth* is in no way remarkable.

Symphony No. 5 in C min., Op. 67.
*** DG Dig. **410 028-2**; 2532/*3302* 049 [id.]. LAPO, Giulini.
*** DG **415 861-2**; 2530 516/*3300 472* [id.]. VPO, Carlos Kleiber.
(*) Denon Dig. **C37 7001** [id.]. Berlin State O, Suitner.
CBS **CD 36711** [id.]. VPO, Maazel – SCHUBERT: *Symphony No. 8.**

Symphony No. 5; Creatures of Prometheus: overture.
(*) Nimbus Dig. **NIM 5007. Hanover Band, Huggett.

Symphony No. 5; Overture: Leonora No. 3.
*** Decca Dig. **400 060-2**; SXDL/*KSXDC* 7540 [LDR/*5*- 71040]. Philh. O, Ashkenazy.

Symphonies Nos 5; 6 in F (Pastoral), Op. 68.
(*) DG Dig. **413 932-2 [id.]. BPO, Karajan.

Symphonies Nos 5–6 (Pastoral); Overture: Egmont.
(B) *** DG Walkman *413 144-4* [id.]. VPO, Boehm.

Symphonies Nos 5; 8 in F, Op. 93.
(*) HMV **CDC 747 187-2 [id.]. Philh. O, Klemperer.
** Capriccio **10003** [id.]. Dresden PO, Kegel.
** Erato Dig. **ECD 88043** [id.]. NHK O, Sawallisch.

Symphonies Nos 5 in C min., Op. 67; 8 in F, Op. 93; Fidelio overture.
(M) *** DG Gal. 419 051-1/*4* [id.]. BPO, Karajan.

Symphonies Nos 5; 9 in D min. (Choral).
**(*) DG 413 933-1/*4* (2) [id.]. BPO, Karajan (with soloists and chorus).

For those willing to accept the extravagance of a CD version of the *Fifth* with no coupling, choice rests between Giulini and Carlos Kleiber. Giulini has the advantage of an excellent modern digital recording and his performance is undoubtedly very satisfying. It possesses majesty in abundance and conveys the power and vision of this inexhaustible work. The sound is impressively full and brilliant on both LP and cassette; but the CD, with its combination of added clarity of detail and truthful textures, makes all the more impact, heard against a background of silence.

Carlos Kleiber's version dates from the mid-1970s and was originally highly praised as a recording, on both LP and tape. Textures are slightly dry and have been further clarified in the remastering for CD; here the upper range of the strings has less body than in the Giulini version. In Kleiber's hands the first movement is electrifying, but has a hushed intensity. The slow movement is tender and delicate, with dynamic contrasts underlined but not exaggerated. The horns, like the rest of the VPO, are in superb form, and the finale, even more than usual, releases the music into pure daylight. The gradation of dynamics from the hushed pianissimo at the close of the scherzo to the weight of the great opening statement of the finale has not been heard on disc with such overwhelming effect since Toscanini.

Karajan's 1977 recording of the *Fifth*, now issued digitally remastered on Galleria, is magnificent in every way, tough and urgently incisive, with fast tempi, bringing weight as well as excitement but no unwanted blatancy, even in the finale. The recording is satisfyingly wide-ranging in frequency and dynamic. The coupling of an electrically intense performance of the *Eighth* plus the *Fidelio overture* is certainly generous. Perhaps Karajan misses some of the joy of Beethoven's 'little one', but justifies his brisk tempi in the brilliant playing of the orchestra. No doubt this recording will appear on CD within the lifetime of this book.

Ashkenazy's is a vivid and urgent reading of the *Fifth*, with well-adjusted speeds for all four movements, as the *Andante con moto* is on the slow side and the finale is on the fast side, with joyful exuberance a fair substitute for grandeur. The overture, also fast, finds Ashkenazy at his freshest, too. The impact of these performances is enhanced by the richness and ample spread of the recording, set against a warm Kingsway Hall acoustic. The compact disc is a degree richer than the LP (there is an impressively full bass), but only marginally clearer. Here the symphony comes before the overture, whereas on the LP it is the other way about. The chrome cassette is lively and full-bodied and possesses excellent detail.

Karajan's CD coupling of the *Fifth* and *Sixth* presents characteristically strong and incisive readings, recorded – with video in mind – in longer takes than previously. The sound may not be so cleanly focused as in his earlier Berlin versions, but the feeling of spontaneous performance is most compelling, so that the typically fast speed for the first movement of the *Pastoral* no longer sounds too tense. However, with Karajan's approach the power of No. 5 is more effective than the atmospheric poetry of No. 6. On LP, with sound not quite so clean, the *Sixth* comes on a separate disc, and the *Fifth* is used as a fourth-side fill-up for the *Ninth*, discussed below.

On LP, Klemperer's *Fifth* is coupled with No. 2 (see above) and the *Eighth* with No. 7. For once the CD coupling is less generous than the LP although, as with the others in the series, CD brings a cleaner, more natural sound on top, notably in violin tone.

Boehm's Walkman coupling is exceptionally generous in offering the *Egmont* overture as well as the *Fifth* and *Sixth Symphonies*, on a single cassette. Boehm's account of the *Fifth* may not be the most powerful available, but the excellent playing and recording, rich and weighty in the bass as well as lively on top, makes it a good version to live with. It pairs naturally with Boehm's splendid account of the *Pastoral* (see below) in its display of positive feeling and absence of neurosis. The chrome-tape transfers of both works are very successful; in offering nearly ninety minutes of music, this tape is a bargain in every sense of the word.

The Hanover Band's recording on period instruments of the *Fifth Symphony* is its most successful yet. Balances at first seem strange with such gentle string tone, sharply focused (unlike some of the wind), but the extra clarity and pointedness of Beethoven on this scale is most refreshing. Speeds are all unexceptionable, not at all hurried as in many authentic performances of other music. Warm reverberation gives a pleasant bloom to the ensemble, but with brass made to sound washy.

Kegel's account of No. 5 is one of the best of his Beethoven cycle, well sprung rhythmically and tonally resonant, but even that lacks variety of expression, as does No. 8 with none of the lightening needed. Good faithful recording.

Sawallisch's coupling brings strong and undistracting readings of both symphonies, lacking something in individuality, but mainly falling short of the finest standards in the limitations of the Japanese string section. First-rate recording.

Suitner's is a small-scale reading, easy and ordinary, hardly individual at all. For once the scherzo is sluggish, and only the finale brings some liveliness. Thin, ill-defined sound and, at 36 minutes, poor value.

Recorded in Japan during a concert tour, Maazel's version of the *Fifth* is singularly unsuccessful. The performance is without any kind of distinction and only rises from the routine in the finale. The recording does not sound like a digital master: it is thick and opaque, and detail is sometimes inaudible. The VPO string timbre is virtually unrecognizable. Not recommended.

Symphony No. 6 in F (Pastoral), Op. 68.
*** Decca Dig. **410 003-2**; SXDL/*KSXDC* 7578 [Lon. LDR/*5*- 71078]. Philh. O, Ashkenazy.
(M) *** DG **413 721-2** (2) [id.]. VPO, Boehm – *Symphony No. 9.****
(***) Decca mono 592 105 [id.]. Concg. O, Erich Kleiber.
(*) Delos **D/CD 3017 [id.]. New York 'Y' CO, Schwarz.
** DG Dig. 413 936-1/*4* [id.]. BPO, Karajan.
(**) HMV mono **CDC 747121** [id.]. VPO, Furtwängler.
*(*) Denon Dig. **C37 7040** [id.]. Berlin State O, Suitner.
* Capriccio **10004** [id.]. Dresden PO, Kegel.

Symphony No. 6 (Pastoral); Overture: Coriolan.
(M) *** DG Sig. 413 977-1/*4* [id.]. VPO, Boehm.

Symphony No. 6 (Pastoral); Overtures: Coriolan; Creatures of Prometheus; Ruins of Athens.
(M) **(*) DG Gal. 415 833-1/*4* [id.]. BPO, Karajan.

Symphony No. 6 in F (Pastoral); Overture: The Consecration of the house; (i) *Egmont: Overture; Die Trommel geruhet; Freudvoll und leidvoll; Klarchens Tod, Op. 84.*
(M) *** HMV ED 290253-1/*4* [Ang. AE/*4AE* 34426]. Philh. O, Klemperer; (i) with Birgit Nilsson.

Symphony No. 6 (Pastoral); Overture: Creatures of Prometheus; (i) *Egmont: Overture and incidental music* (as above).
*** HMV **CDC 747188-2** [id.]. Philh. O, Klemperer; (i) with Birgit Nilsson.

Symphony No. 6 (Pastoral); Overture: Creatures of Prometheus.
** ASV ALH/*ZCALH* 961 [id.]. Northern Sinf. of E., Hickox.

Symphony No. 6 in F (Pastoral), Op. 68; Overture Leonora No. 2, Op. 72a.
*** CBS **MK 42012** [id.]. Columbia SO, Walter.

Symphony No. 6 (Pastoral); Overture: Leonora No. 3.
** DG **413 779-2** [id.]. VPO, Bernstein.

Beethoven's much-loved *Pastoral symphony* is very well served in all price ranges – on CD, LP and tape. Boehm's famous 1972 recording has been remastered, and on CD the fact that it was recorded a decade and a half ago is convincingly disguised. However, Klemperer's idyllic, deeply satisfying performance (to which we awarded a Rosette in our first *Penguin Stereo Record Guide*) is beginning to sound its age. It dates from 1958, and originally the string tone was not recorded as sweetly as Boehm's. Although refreshed by digital remastering, the upper range is noticeably a little thin; nevertheless, with its generous and worthwhile bonuses, it should be seriously considered by all collectors, especially as the LP and matching tape are most competitively priced. But the greater range and naturalness of Ashkenazy's Decca recording places it at the top of the list, even if the interpretation has less individuality than Klemperer's or Walter's and is somewhat more urbane than Boehm's conception.

Ashkenazy's is essentially a genial reading, almost totally unmannered. But the performance has a beguiling warmth and it communicates readily. With generally spacious tempi, the feeling of lyrical ease and repose is most captivating, thanks to the response of the Philharmonia players and the richness of the recording, made in the Kingsway Hall. After a *Storm* that is civilized rather than frightening, the performance is crowned by a radiant account of the *Shepherds' thanksgiving*. The sound, with its fairly reverberant acoustic, is particularly impressive on compact disc, but the chrome cassette too is of demonstration quality. On tape, there is slightly less edge on the strings, yet no loss of detail, and the balance suits the music making admirably.

Boehm's recording is available in a choice of formats. On CD, it is coupled with an outstanding version of Beethoven's *Choral symphony*; moreover, the pair of compact discs is offered at less than full price. The remastering has brought a softer focus to the upper strings, while the bass remains expansively resonant and full. There is glowing woodwind detail and the beauty of the sound overall is enhanced. Background noise has all but disappeared. On LP, still sounding fresh, it comes with an excellent performance of the *Coriolan overture* on DG's mid-priced Signature label. For tape collectors, however, there is an outstanding Walkman bargain – appreciably cheaper than the Signature tape – which includes Boehm's not earth-shaking but thoroughly respectable account of the *Fifth Symphony*. Both recordings sound excellent, and are not interrupted with side-breaks – see above. The reading of the *Pastoral* has a natural, unforced beauty, and is very well played (with strings, woodwind and horns beautifully integrated). In the first movement Boehm observes the exposition repeat (not many versions do); although the dynamic contrasts are never underplayed and the phrasing is affectionate, there is a feeling of inevitable rightness about Boehm's approach, no sense of an interpreter imposing his will. Only the slow movement with its even stressing raises any reservation, and that is very slight.

Bruno Walter was always famous for his interpretation of the *Pastoral symphony*. It was the only Beethoven symphony he recorded twice in the 78 r.p.m. era (although his second version with the Philadelphia Orchestra was disappointing). The present version dates from the beginning of the 1960s and, like his recording of the *Fourth Symphony*, it represents the peak of his Indian summer in the American recording studios. The whole performance glows, and the gentle warmth of phrasing is comparable with Klemperer's famous version. The slow movement is taken slightly fast, but there is no sense of hurry, and the tempo of the *Peasants' Merrymaking* is less controversial than Klemperer's. It is an affectionate and completely integrated performance from a master who thought and lived the work all his life. The sound is beautifully balanced, with sweet strings and clear, glowing woodwind, and the bass response is firm and full. The quality is very slightly shallower in the *Overture Leonora No.* 2 which opens the disc, but this splendid performance shows Walter at his most dramatically spontaneous, and it is superbly played. There is no better version in the catalogue. The digital remastering has left a small residue of background hiss, but it is never distracting. The sound is more transparent than Boehm's, with no less bloom, and Walter's CD has the advantage of being available separately.

Klemperer's account of the *Pastoral*, one of the very finest of all his records, prompted a legendary incident with the great recording producer, Walter Legge, when he queried the slow speed for the scherzo. 'You will get used to it,' the conductor drawled back; he even added insult to injury by picking up the phone to the control room five minutes later with the question: 'Have you got used to it yet, Walter?' That movement may in principle be eccentrically slow but, with superbly dancing rhythms, it could not be more bucolic and it falls naturally into place within the reading as a whole. The exquisitely phrased slow movement and the final *Shepherds' hymn* bring peaks of beauty, made the more intense by the fine new digital transfer, reinforcing the clarity and fine balance of the original sound, with violin tone amazingly fresh and clean for 1958. The ruggedness of Klemperer is well suited to the *Consecration of the house overture* which on LP precedes the symphony. The *Egmont* music follows it at the end of side two, an unusual but valuable coupling with Nilsson in her prime, unexpectedly but effectively cast in the two simple songs, the first made to sound almost Mahlerian. Cassette and LP are virtually identical in quality. The CD offers the *Creatures of Prometheus overture* instead of *Consecration of the house*, but retains the *Egmont* coupling. As usual, there is added refinement, and the *Symphony* gains much from the background quiet.

Kleiber's glorious account of the *Pastoral* comes from 1954 and is a performance of stature. The sound is less dated than one might expect, and the recording is so well balanced that sonic limitations are soon forgotten. The Concertgebouw wind excel themselves and are marvellously blended, while the quality of the string playing is hardly less eloquent. In all five movements one feels immediately that not only is this the 'tempo giusto' but that it is the only possible speed. The first movement is marvellously held together, with just the right balance between momentum and flexibility, and there is some wonderfully imaginative string phrasing in the slow movement. This is worlds removed from the brisk canter of the 1982 Karajan version. The *Peasants' merrymaking* seems to have just the right gait and character; all in all, this is inspiring for its architecture and command of musical detail: in short, a profoundly classical reading.

Although Schwarz uses a relatively small group of players, they are recorded in a warmly reverberant acoustic so that textures are glowingly full. His pacing of the first movement is very brisk (even with exposition repeat, it takes only 10′ 10″), but the lightness of the articulation prevents any sense of breathlessness. By contrast, the *Shepherds' hymn* is quite relaxed, with the feeling of serenity pleasingly maintained. After the climax, which is well prepared, there is an engaging simplicity in the coda itself. The central movements are more conventional: the brook flows easily and the robust vitality of the peasants gives way to an impressive but not cataclysmic thunderstorm. Although the tempo for the first movement takes a bit of getting used to, overall this performance has a great deal of character; the beauty of the string playing is enhanced by the richness of the recording, with the distanced balance providing a convincing overall picture, even if inner definition is never sharp.

Like Gerard Schwarz and the New York 'Y' Chamber Orchestra, Richard Hickox uses a smaller body of strings than usual, yet while the ASV recording is less resonant than that of the Delos CD and its detail is better defined, the ambience is still reverberant enough to inflate the chamber scale of the music making. Hickox's first movement is particularly attractive, fresh and lithe, the tempo brisk but never forced. The slow movement flows well enough, although there is an element of heaviness here which returns in the finale; the central movements are strongly contrasted. The overture is brilliantly done. The sound has an agreeably full bass response, while the upper range is attractively bright. There is a good cassette.

The issue of Karajan's newest (1982) recording on LP and cassette offers no coupling and, although the orchestral playing is first class, the performance, with its brisk tempi, suggests an invigorating walk, eyes firmly fixed on the horizon, rather than any loving dalliance to admire the surrounding natural beauty. The sound is good, with plenty of body; on cassette, however, the resonant lower range tends to out-balance the upper strings (though their timbre is not muffled).

Karajan's 1977 performance brought a more congenial reading than his earlier, excessively tense 1962 recording with the same orchestra. It is fresh, alert, consistent with the rest of the cycle, a good dramatic version, with polished playing, and recording which is wide-ranging but suffers from the odd balances which mark the 1977 cycle. The digitally remastered Galleria issue adds three overtures from 1970: *Coriolan* comes before the symphony and the others follow on after. The sound is fuller in these earlier recordings, but in the *Symphony* there is still plenty of bloom and weight, as well as more refined detail. Disc and chrome cassette are virtually identical.

Bernstein's reading has plenty of character and, with its combination of joy and serenity, is persuasive, even if the performance fails to bite in the *Storm* sequence. But the inevitable inconsistencies of live recording – even with discreet editing between performances – come out on CD in the discrepancy between the symphony and the overture, with *Leonora No. 3* – recorded earlier, in 1978 – treated to fuller, more agreeable sound than the *Pastoral*.

As digitally transferred to CD, the sound of the Vienna Philharmonic under Furtwängler is reasonably fresh and full, with plenty of detail but occasional oddities of balance. The reading is a very personal one, with eccentrically slow speeds in the first two movements which, unlike those of Klemperer, sound wayward, when the style is additionally so flexible. The quirks would no doubt have sounded more natural in a live Furtwängler performance.

Suitner's reading is plain and – except in the stodgy account of the *Peasants' merrymaking* – fresh. The recording is fuller than most in his series, but cannot compare with the finest rivals.

Kegel's dogged approach may be earthy in a generalized pastoral way, but more is needed if the full beauty of Beethoven's inspiration is to be appreciated. Fair recording.

Symphony No. 6 (Pastoral) (arr. Liszt).
** Tel. **ZK8.42781**; AZ 6/*CY4* 42781 [id.]. Cyprien Katsaris (piano).

Katsaris, using an instrument with the ideal combination of weight and clarity, makes an excellent exponent of Liszt's transcription of the *Pastoral symphony*, direct and fresh, if not specially illuminating interpretatively. The recording is rather resonant, which blurs the focus of the chrome tape just a little.

Symphony No. 7 in A, Op. 92.
(*) Lodia Dig. **LO-CD 786 [id.]. Philharmonic SO, Païta.
(*) DG **415 862-2; Sig. 410 932-1/*4* [id.]. VPO, Carlos Kleiber.
**(*) CBS Dig. M/*MT* 39052 [id.]. ECO, Michael Tilson Thomas.
(*) Denon **C37 7032** [id.]. Berlin State O, Suitner.

Symphony No. 7 in A; Overture: Coriolan.
** ASV ALH/*ZCALH* 952 [id.]. Northern Sinf., Hickox.
** Capriccio **10005** [id.]. Dresden PO, Kegel.

Symphony No. 7 in A, Op. 92; Overtures: Coriolan; Egmont.
Ͼ *** Decca Dig. **411 941-2**; 411 941-1/*4* [id.]. Philh. O, Ashkenazy.

Symphonies Nos 7 in A; 8 in F, Op. 93.
(M) **(*) HMV ED 290328-1/*4* [Ang. AE/*4AE* 34427]. Philh. O, Klemperer.
** CBS **MK 42013** [id.]. Columbia SO, Walter.
(*) DG **415 666-2** [id.]. BPO, Furtwängler.

Ashkenazy directs a warmly spontaneous, generally direct reading, taken steadily at unexaggerated speeds, and the result is glowingly convincing, thanks to fine playing and recording that sets new standards in this work, full and spacious yet warmly co-ordinated. The CD is marginally finer than the LP or the very lively, if slightly less refined, cassette, with the bass more crisply focused. After a grave, simple account of the slow introduction, the allegro at first sounds deceptively relaxed in pastoral mood, until the dramatic urgency of the movement takes over, its dance rhythms nicely lifted. The finale is a shade slower than usual, but effectively so. The two coupled overtures are contrasted: *Coriolan* is given a weighty reading at a measured speed, while *Egmont*, equally dramatic, is on the fast side.

The digital remastering of Klemperer's stereo versions of the *Seventh* and *Eighth* symphonies offers an outstandingly generous coupling with well-balanced sound (from 1961 and 1958 respectively), made remarkably fresh and with no penalty from the long sides. Although in No. 7 that incandescence which marked his superb earlier mono recording with the Philharmonia is missing, the power and concentration at broad speeds still make for a memorable performance. In No. 8 Klemperer's weighty approach is tempered by delightfully well-sprung rhythms. There is virtually nothing to choose between LP and cassette in sound quality.

Carlos Païta's CD was recorded in the Kingsway Hall, and the balance is excellent, the quality bright and vivid, with excellent detail and a convincing overall perspective. With apt tempi, his comparatively relaxed introduction leads naturally into a buoyant allegro, its rhythmic spring certainly catching the spirit of the dance. The *Allegretto* is eloquently shaped, with an impressive but not histrionic climax; the scherzo is taken fast and has an exhilarating lightness of touch, helped by neat articulation. The change of mood for the firmly contoured Trio is very smoothly handled; the finale is extremely volatile, producing an accelerando almost immediately after the opening statement, with the conductor again pressing on excitingly in the closing sections, to give the feel of a live performance. With excellent playing – the woodwind contribution to the first movement is strikingly fresh – this is very enjoyable, not a performance offering the deepest insights, perhaps, but one that is always satisfyingly alive.

Tilson Thomas's performance with chamber forces has extra crispness and toughness as a result of the compact scale, as well as extra clarity; so, in the first-movement allegro, the relaxed speed allows for delightful dotting of the compound time, with the woodwind unforcedly clear. The *Allegretto* flows briskly, though the thinness of violin tone does not always sound quite comfortable in CBS's rather dry recording. As a chamber account this certainly makes its distinctive mark, the more so when the conductor is both characterful and individual, and the unrushed finale makes a satisfying culmination. On the chrome cassette the sound remains vivid and well detailed, with the violins made to seem somewhat fuller in timbre than on LP. Fortissimos are slightly less refined, but generally the overall balance is both clear and weighty.

When it was first issued in 1976, Carlos Kleiber's record excited considerable controversy, and certainly this is a performance where symphonic argument never yields to the charms of the dance. Kleiber's incisively dramatic approach is marked instead with sharp dynamic contrasts and thrustful rhythms. Another controversial point is that Kleiber, like his father, maintains the pizzicato for the strings on the final brief phrase of the *Allegretto*, a curious effect. The digital remastering, however, has greatly improved the recorded sound, with the constriction noticed on the original LP now opened up so that the effect is much more spacious than before, with more resonance and weight in the middle and lower strings. This could not sensibly be suggested as a first recommendation for an only purchase, but it is not a record to ignore. The LP and cassette versions are on the mid-priced Signature label, which may seem a more sensible investment than the much more expensive CD, even though the latter offers superior sound.

Walter's *Seventh* has a comparatively slow first-movement allegro, but he had rehearsed his players well in the tricky dotted 6/8 rhythm and the result dances convincingly, even if the movement seems to lumber somewhat. The *Allegretto* also seems heavier than usual (partly because of the rich, weighty recording). It is rather mannered, with *marcato* emphases on most of the down beats, but the important point is that genuine tension is created with the illusion of an actual performance. The scherzo is also rather wayward: after a slow start, Walter suddenly livens up the middle with a faster pace, and this speed-change occurs in each repetition of the scherzo section. The trio also takes its time, but in contrast the finale goes with a splendid lift to the playing and very brilliant horns and trumpets in the exciting coda. With its full and spacious recording, this is clearly the version for those who enjoy a mellow and comparatively romantic view of the work. The coupled *Eighth* has similarly slow speeds, especially in the inner movements. The first goes well enough, but after that the pacing hampers the sustaining of any high degree of intensity. The reading is of course interesting and sympathetic, but there is a lack of grace, as though the players were not strongly involved; and the finale, though revealing many points with unusual clarity, has a tendency to dullness. Again the sound is full and well balanced, but – as in the rest of the series – the digital remastering has not been able to remove all the background noise.

With refined, slightly distanced recording of players set in a warm acoustic, you might not immediately realize that Hickox's is a version strictly on a chamber scale. The *Allegretto* is slow and at times over-expressive, but otherwise this is a sensible and invigorating account. *Coriolan* is on the sober side.

Kegel gives a firm, straightforward reading of No. 7, well recorded, but there are preferable alternatives with more generous couplings.

Any extension of the Furtwängler repertory is valuable, but these performances of Nos 7 and 8 in radio recordings of low fidelity find him at his most wilful, particularly in No. 8, where the first movement is pulled around with frequent and mannered tenutos, and the slow movement is leaden. The *Allegretto* of No. 7 is also funereal.

Suitner takes a characteristically plain view. The introduction has no grandeur, and the slow speed for the main allegro, though initially attractive in its lyrical spring, grows leaden. The scherzo is much the brightest movement, but the very fast speed for the finale finds the Berlin players sounding breathless. Unclear recording.

Symphony No. 7 in A (arr. *Liszt*).

(*) Tel. Dig. **ZK8.43113; AZ6/*CY4* 43113 [id.]. Cyprien Katsaris (with SCHUMANN: *Exercises on Beethoven's Seventh Symphony***).

(*) Nimbus **NIM 5013 [id.]. Ronald Smith (with BACH/BUSONI: *Chaconne****).

Cyprien Katsaris does wonders in translating Liszt's transcription into orchestral terms. His is very clean, precise playing, often powerful, with textures commendably clear and with generally steady, unexceptionable tempi. He observes the exposition repeat in the first movement. The *Schumann Exercises* make an apt if hardly inspiring fill-up, based on the main theme of the symphony's *Allegretto*. But the symphony is another matter, providing an unexpectedly illuminating listening experience. The sound is excellent, in all three media.

Ronald Smith, much more than Katsaris, turns the Liszt transcription into a pianistic essay, treating the music with more expressive freedom, often more seductively. He is daring in the Presto scherzo, then unexpectedly light and easy in the finale, with an attractive spring in the rhythm. The performance is not technically flawless but here, and even more in the superb Bach–Busoni transcription, he consistently plays with virtuosic flair. The reverberant recording is pleasantly atmospheric, but not every note is clear.

Symphony No. 8 in F, Op. 93.

(*) Telarc Dig. **CD 80090 [id.]. Cleveland O, Dohnányi – SCHUBERT: *Symphony No. 8*.**

Symphony No. 8 in F; Overtures: Coriolan; Fidelio; Leonora No. 3.

*** DG Dig. **415 507-2**; 415 507-1/*4* [id.]. BPO, Karajan.

Karajan's more relaxed view of the *Eighth* (compared with his 1977 Berlin version) is almost always pure gain. The second subject of the first movement, for example, is eased in more persuasively, while the second-movement *Allegretto* is made happily lyrical at a markedly slower speed than before. Nevertheless, Karajan's is a massive view of what has often been dubbed Beethoven's 'little symphony', taking it well into the powerful world of the nineteenth century, with fierceness part of the mixture in the outer movements. The three overtures are made massively Olympian too, with *Coriolan* especially impressive. The recording is marginally brighter and clearer than in most of the series, though there is still some congestion in fortissimos, and the cassette sounds rather opaque in tuttis.

Dohnányi, with the Cleveland Orchestra of which he is now principal conductor, is more successful in No. 8 than he is in the more challenging *Eroica*. This is a lively, resilient performance, exceptionally well played. The recording is not as bright as one expects from this source, but is acceptable. The coupling – once adopted in a classic Beecham record – could be, for some, an extra attraction.

Symphony No. 9 in D min. (*Choral*), *Op. 125.*

(M) *** DG Gal. 415 832-1/*4* [id.]. Tomowa-Sintow, Baltsa, Schreier, Van Dam, V. Singverein, BPO, Karajan.

(M) *** DG Dig. **413 721-2** (2) [id.]. Norman, Fassbaender, Domingo, Berry, Concert Singers of V. State Op., VPO, Boehm – *Symphony No. 6.****

(*) DG Dig. **410 987-2 [id.]. Perry, Baltsa, Cole, Van Dam, V. Singverein, BPO, Karajan.

** (*) Ph. Dig. **416 353-2**; 416 353-1/*4* [id.]. Donath, Schmidt, König, Estes, Bav. R. Ch. and SO, Sir Colin Davis.

(*) Telarc Dig. **CD 80120; DG 80120 [id.]. Vaness, Taylor, Jerusalem, Lloyd, Cleveland Ch. and O, Dohnányi.

(***) HMV mono **CDC 747081-2** [id.]. Schwarzkopf, Höngen, Hopf, Edelmann, Bayreuth Fest. Ch. and O, Furtwängler.

(***) RCA [mono **RCCD 1005**]. Farrell, Merriman, Peerce, Scott, Shaw Chorale, NBC SO, Toscanini.

(B) **(*) Pickwick Con. CC/*CCTC* 7592 [Lon. STS/*5*- 15089]. Sutherland, Procter, Dermota, Van Mill, Ch. de Brassus, Ch. des Jeunes de L'Eglise Nat. Vaudoise, SRO, Ansermet.

** Ph. Dig. **410 036-2** [id.]. Janet Price, Finnila, Laubenthal, Rintzler, Concg. Ch. and O, Haitink.

(M) ** Ph. 412 916-1/*4* [id.]. Tomowa-Sintow, Burmeister, Shreier, Adam, Leipzig R. Ch. and GO, Masur.

** HMV **CDC 747189-2** [id.]. Lövberg, Ludwig, Kmentt, Hotter, Philh. Ch. and O, Klemperer.

** CBS **MK 76999**; 76999 [id.]. Popp, Obraztsova, Vickers, Talvela, Cleveland Ch. and O, Maazel.

(M) (**) CBS 60003/*40*-. Arroyo, Safarty, Virgilio, Scott, Juilliard Ch., NYPO, Bernstein.

** CBS **MK 42014**; 60506/*40*- [MP/*MPT* 39029]. Cundari, Rankin, Da Costa, Wildermann, Westminster Ch., Columbia SO, Bruno Walter.

* RCA Dig. **RD 84734** [(d.) **RCD1 5020**]. Margaret Price, Horne, Vickers, Salminen, NY Ch. Artists, NYPO, Mehta – *Choral fantasia.**(*)

(*) Denon Dig. **C37 7021** [id.]. Hajossvova, Priew, Buchner, Schenk, Berlin R. Ch., Berlin State O, Suitner.

Denon Dig. **C37 7574** [id.]. Smičková, Soukupová, Přibyl, Novák, Czech Philharmonic Ch. and PO, Neumann.

Symphony No. 9 (Choral); Overtures: Coriolan; Egmont.
(B) *(*) Ph. On Tour *412 896-4* [id.]. Bode, Watts, Laubenthal, Luxon, LPO Ch., LPO, Haitink.

(i) *Symphony No. 9 (Choral);* (ii) *Overture: Leonora No. 3.*
(B) ** DG Walkman *413 843-4* [id.]. (i) Gwyneth Jones, Troyanos, Jess Thomas, Ridderbusch, V. State Op. Ch., VPO, Boehm; (ii) with Dresden State O.

Symphony No. 9 (Choral); Overture: Fidelio.
(M) ** HMV ED 290272-1/*4* [Ang. AE/*4AE* 34428]. Lövberg, Ludwig, Kmentt, Hotter, Philh. Ch. and O, Klemperer.

Fine as was Karajan's earlier recording of the *Ninth* with the Berlin Philharmonic, his 1977 performance reveals even greater insight, above all in the *Adagio*, where he conveys spiritual intensity at a slower tempo than before. In the finale the concluding eruption has an animal excitement rarely heard from this highly controlled conductor; the soloists make an excellent team, with contralto, tenor and bass all finer than their predecessors. The balance is not entirely satisfactory, with the solo voices in the finale unnaturally close; but, taken overall, this is the finest of Karajan's three DG versions, with no flaws in the solo singing as in the recent digital version. The digital remastering on to a single LP is extremely well managed, with no feeling of loss of depth and range, but it has necessitated a break in the slow movement. The chrome cassette, however, puts two movements uninterrupted on each side and matches the quality of the LP very closely to make a clear first choice, irrespective of price, except for those irrevocably committed to compact disc.

Boehm was one of the select handful of conductors who made records of the *Choral symphony* during the 78 r.p.m. era. Later he recorded it on mono LP for Philips and more recently as part of his 1972 complete set for DG. Just a few months before he died, he made his final statement on the work in his resplendent digital set. With generally slow tempi, his reading is spacious and powerful – the first movement even has a certain stoic quality – and in its broad concept it has much in common with Klemperer's version. Yet overall there is a transcending sense of a great occasion; the concentration is unfailing, reaching its peak in the glorious finale, where ruggedness and strength well over into inspiration, and that in spite of a pacing nearly as individual as that of Stokowski, notably in the drum and fife march, which is much more serious in feeling than usual. But with an outburst of joy in the closing pages, the listener is left in no doubt that this recording was the culmination of a long and distinguished career. With a fine, characterful team of soloists and a freshly incisive chorus formed from singers of the Vienna State Opera, this is strongly recommendable; its issue on CD, appropriately coupled to another outstanding Beethoven recording of the *Pastoral symphony*, is very welcome indeed, especially as the pair of CDs are offered at a reduced price, and the clarity of the sound is enhanced.

The high point of Karajan's most recent version of the *Ninth* is the sublime slow movement, here exceptionally sweet and true, with the lyricism all the more persuasive in a performance recorded – with video in mind – in a complete take.

The power and dynamism of the first two movements are striking too, but the choral finale is flawed above all by the singing of the soprano, Janet Perry, far too thin of tone and unreliable. The sound of the choir has plenty of body but is rather ill defined. As in the others in the series, CD helps to clarify recording which is less analytical than that usually given to Karajan.

Sir Colin Davis's easy manner makes for a relaxed view of the *Ninth*, one which underplays the apocalyptic power but which at a lower voltage presents a strong and enjoyable performance. The first movement – at a Furtwängler speed – is spacious but not overwhelming, lyrical with minor-key tensions underplayed, warm not tragic. The scherzo is light and lilting (with the long second repeat observed), and the slow movement has Elysian sweetness, though violin tone is not always ideally pure. In the choral finale, the drum-and-fife passage with tenor is easy and jaunty to contrast with the rough tones of the soloist, Klaus König. By contrast, the 6/4 *Allegro energico* is exceptionally fast and very exciting, helped by incandescent choral sound. Naturally balanced recording, with the soloists not sharply focused. There is an excellent cassette.

Starting on tremolos exceptionally precise in their definition of triplet rhythm, Dohnányi gives a crisp and direct reading which in its brisk, plain manners is consistently satisfying in the first two movements as well as the choral sections of the finale which are thrillingly done, with an excellent chorus and quartet of soloists. Jerusalem sings the big tenor solo superbly with 6/8 rhythms made to skip infectiously. Before that, in the finale speeds are hectic, with the quasi-recitatives rattled off mercilessly and the quotations from previous movements sounding perfunctory. The slow movement inspires refined playing from the Cleveland Orchestra, but there is no mystery. The manner is chilly if not the sound, which is warmly atmospheric with fair reverberation.

It is thrilling to have a CD transfer of the historic recording made at the re-opening of the Festspielhaus in Bayreuth in 1951. The chorus may sound washy in the distance, almost as though placed at the bottom of the Rhine, and the lack of perspective in the mono sound is brought out the more on CD (along with audience noises), but the extra clarity and freshness enhance impressively a reading without parallel. The spacious, lovingly moulded account of the slow movement is among Furtwängler's finest achievements on record and, with an excellent quartet of soloists, the finale crowns a great performance. EMI have also issued on a mono LP (ED 270123-1) Furtwängler's 1937 recording which may, in its dim imagery, give a very imperfect idea of the performance at Queen's Hall in London during the Coronation season of that year; with all the mistiness, curious balances, and even the occasional 'drop-out' of sound, the flavour of a live performance is still vividly caught, as though one is witnessing a great occasion from behind a curtain. Compared with the post-war Bayreuth performance of fourteen years later, this is more volatile in fast movements, but less flexible in the slow movement. The quartet of soloists is superb, while the British chorus is very variable, and the final coda brings a rush that can only be described as hysterical. Seriously flawed, but totally fascinating.

At a period when Toscanini was widely counted the top conductor of the world, his version of the *Ninth*, which appeared in the early 1950s, was awaited as no other. It proved just as apocalyptic in its vision as had been expected, but the sound was too dry to convey full grandeur. On CD, the digital transfer cannot correct faults in the original recording, but the immediacy and sense of presence are shattering, with the clarity and bite of the Shaw Chorale – a relatively compact band mainly of professional singers – adding to the impact. The clarity and precision of the soloists also put many later versions to shame; though the recording never allows a true pianissimo even in the slow movement, the style is more flexibly expressive than in most later Beethoven performances from this conductor, not hushed but warm and intense. This CD has only limited availability in the USA and is still awaiting issue in the UK.

Pickwick have recently reissued on their bargain-priced Contour label Ansermet's recording from the beginning of the 1960s which became famous later as the first technically successful one-disc stereo version of the *Choral symphony*. It is now also available on an exceptionally vivid chrome tape, transferred at the highest level, and giving the choral sound plenty of bite. The clarity of recording suits the interpretation, which lacks the weight of more traditional readings but has a freshness which makes it consistently enjoyable and interesting. The first two movements are clear-cut and dramatic, and the slow movement is restrained. The finale, if a little lightweight, gains from the clarity and from the quality of the soloists, with Joan Sutherland at her most beautiful. The choir is energetic but not always perfectly disciplined, yet this is still a performance of considerable character and is welcome back in the catalogue. The quality of Ansermet's Beethoven interpretations was often underestimated; this record shows his approach at its most effective.

Haitink's digital recording was made at a live concert in the Concertgebouw, but one would not know that; there are few if any signs of an audience, and – disappointingly – the performance rather fails to convey the feeling of an occasion, lacking a little in tension, even in comparison with Haitink's earlier studio version with the LPO. The reading, as before, is satisfyingly unidiosyncratic, direct and honest; but with this work one needs more. Happily, the clarity and precision of CD give a bite missing in the earlier LP and tape formats. But other CD versions convey more of the work's greatness.

Masur gives a spacious, well-proportioned and noble account that is certainly worth hearing. Soloists and chorus make a good team and the orchestral playing is first class. This might be considered as a single-disc medium-price version (and there is an excellent, vivid, high-level tape), but with Stokowski's inspired account (undoubtedly a great performance) available even more cheaply on Decca Viva (VIV/*KVIC 1* [Lon. JL/*5*- 41004]) Masur's Philips reissue seems relatively uncompetitive.

Klemperer's digitally remastered single disc goes one better by avoiding a turnover break in the slow movement and adding as a bonus his characteristically strong, serious version of the *Egmont overture*. The sound is amazingly good for its period (1958), with the finale fresher and better-balanced than many recent recordings. There is an excellent equivalent tape. However, Klemperer's weighty vision is marred by a disappointing quartet of soloists; and the slow speeds for the first two movements – the scherzo seems to go on for ever – come to sound ponderous. Yet the refined, flowing account of the slow movement is Klemperer at his finest. The CD omits the overture but offers compensating extra refinement, with the choral sound in the finale given astonishing presence and tangibility.

The monumental grandeur of the *Ninth* stands up well to Maazel's urgent and often aggressive Beethoven style. His is a strong performance, but one which misses warmer, deeper feelings. The solo quartet is a fine one – Vickers characterful, if miscast – and the choral singing is energetic. The recording matches the reading in its clarity and forwardness, but the extra clarity and brightness of the CD version underline the less attractive characteristics of the reading, making it uncompetitive with the finest rivals.

Bernstein's 1964 recording is let down by the shrill recording. It is a performance of some stature, combining eloquence with excitement (the scherzo must be the fastest on record), with a finale that is both intense and dramatic. However, the engineering is plainly inadequate, and the slow movement break is managed by a quick fade.

The remastering of Walter's 1959 recording brings striking improvement, especially in the choral finale, with a spacious orchestral balance and full, well-focused choral tone. The performance has fine moments but suffers from a rather low level of tension and slow tempi. The jog-trot speed for the scherzo sustains itself by the beauty and thoughtfulness of the general shaping, but the choral finale fails to rise to the sense of occasion. The soloists are not particularly impressive and the choir finds it hard to stay alert at Walter's relaxed pacing, all of which shows up most strikingly in the final pages.

'Live from Lincoln Center' is the ominous boast of Mehta's RCA version, designed in tribute to conductor and orchestra on their return to that company. The Avery Fisher Hall is no kinder here to the work of the engineers than it was before its acoustics were so expensively 'improved'. The sound is edgy and confused, with a boomy, ill-defined bass. As for Mehta's interpretation, it is generally plain and precise, but lacks mystery, with an over-sweet account of the slow movement. The excitement of the occasion comes over in the choral finale with its star quartet of soloists, but by far the most satisfying music-making comes in the *Choral fantasia*. In the USA, the recording is issued more economically on a single CD.

Boehm's earlier 1970 Vienna recording of the *Choral symphony* is available both on a bargain-priced Walkman tape and also at medium-price, coupled with the *Eroica symphony* – see above. The Walkman has the first three movements laid out on side one and the choral finale plus *Leonora No. 3* on side two. It costs about the same as Stokowski's inspirational version on Decca Viva (see above), only the latter is without the overture and has the disadvantage of a slow-movement turnover break. Boehm's reading has a natural, unforced quality. He chooses unusually slow tempi for both the *Adagio* and *Andante* themes of the slow movement, which are therefore given less contrast than usual. But the tone of voice is dedicated and the work ends with a dramatic, if controlled, account of the finale, with excellent singing from both chorus and soloists, who are forwardly balanced. The chrome-tape transfer might have been made at a higher level, but the focus is good. Undoubtedly the CDs of Boehm's later version offer a more compulsive experience, but this Walkman issue is certainly good value.

Haitink's 1976 LPO performance has much in common with his later digital CD version. It is a thoughtful and concentrated reading, warm and confident in the first movement, never cataclysmic, a shade lacking in weight. The slow movement, too, is easy and warm, and the finale not quite the culmination required, though very exciting at the close. The sound of this Philips bargain-priced chrome-tape equivalent to Boehm's Walkman issue is resonantly rich and full, though a little bass-heavy, with a rather woolly focus for the chorus. The Boehm cassette is clearly preferable.

Suitner's performance of the *Choral symphony* brought the first compact disc lasting over seventy minutes. Otherwise it is as undistinguished a version of this supreme masterpiece as could be imagined, plodding and unimaginative, indifferently played and poorly recorded. Indeed, the sound is among the least well defined in Suitner's cycle, particularly in the choral finale.

Neumann's Denon version is even poorer. Recorded live in Tokyo in 1976, it has very little sense of atmosphere or presence, set against a dry acoustic which exaggerates the flaws of a pedestrian performance, with the Czech violins – normally an excellent band – made to sound thin and harsh. Only the scherzo, light and crisp, rises above mediocrity; and the soloists are as poor a quartet as can be heard on disc, with even Vilem Přibyl, a good tenor, sounding over-strained.

Symphony No. 9 in D min. (*Choral*), *Op. 125* (arr. *Liszt*).
(*) Tel. Dig. **ZK8 42956; AZ6/*CY4* 42956 [id.]. Cyprien Katsaris (piano).

Liszt made no attempt to create pianistically 'effective' arrangements, yet in his transcription of the *Ninth Symphony* he conveys so much of the character of an orchestra storming the heavens. Initially, one's thoughts turn to the pianistic melodramas of the silent movies, but one is soon drawn into the symphonic argument. Cyprien Katsaris's performance is nothing short of a *tour de force*: his virtuosity is altogether remarkable and there is a demonic Beethovenian vehemence and drive. He must have as many hands as an octupus has tentacles, for his ability to convey the teeming activity of the finale, to bring various strands into the foreground and then disappear into the mêlée, is astonishing. In its CD form, the image is firm in focus, but there must be a minor reservation on account of the sound: the piano is closely observed in a reverberant acoustic ambience and listeners may at times be disturbed by its somewhat jangly quality. The chrome tape is excellently managed, with the resonance offering no problems.

Wellington's victory, Op. 91.
** Telarc Dig. **CD 80079**; DG 10079 [id.]. Cincinnati SO, Kunzel – LISZT: *Hunnenschlacht*.**
** CBS **CD 37252**; 37252 [id.]. VPO, Maazel – TCHAIKOVSKY: *1812*.*(*)

With a characteristically natural overall sound-balance, Kunzel's Telarc recording is the most sophisticated presentation of Beethoven's 'Battle' Symphony on record, though the real musketry and cannon featured in the recording sound curiously like a fireworks display. The performance is musically conceived and well played, but has no special individuality.

Maazel's version on CBS has more flair than Kunzel's and the CBS special effects are realistically interpolated. The opening sequence with the opposing forces lining up opposite each other is not as effectively conveyed here as on Morton Gould's old RCA recording (which, alas, was ruined by distortion), but the acoustic is well judged and this is certainly enjoyable. On compact disc, detail is clarified, but the drawback to this issue is the coupling, which is harshly recorded.

CHAMBER MUSIC

Cello sonatas Nos 1–5, Op. 5/1–2; Op. 69; Op. 102/1–2.
*** Ph. **412 256-2**; 412 256-1/*4* [id.]. Mstislav Rostropovich, Sviatoslav Richter.
(M) *** DG 413 520-1/*4* [id.]. Wilhelm Kempff, Pierre Fournier.

Cello sonatas Nos 1 in F; 2 in G min., Op. 5/1–2.
(*) CBS **CD 37251; 37251/*40*- [id.]. Yo-Yo Ma, Emanuel Ax.

Cello sonatas Nos 3 in A, Op. 69; 5 in D, Op. 102/2.
*** CBS **MK 39024**; IM/*IMT* 39024 [id.]. Yo-Yo Ma, Emanuel Ax.
(B) *** CfP CFP 41 4494-1/*4* [RL/*4RL* 32060]. Jacqueline Du Pré, Stephen Bishop-Kovacevich.

Made in the early 1960s, these classic Philips performances by two of the instrumental giants of the day have withstood the test of time astonishingly well and sound remarkably fresh in this compact disc transfer. Apart from the usual gains in continuity and freedom from surface clicks, there is so much greater presence and realism. The *Sonata*, Op. 5, No. 1, and the two *Sonatas*, Op. 102, are accommodated on the first disc and the remaining two on the second. There are good tapes, but the sound is less fresh and transparent and the analogue source more obvious. The tapes and LPs are offered at mid-price.

In the coupling of the two Op. 5 *Sonatas*, Yo-Yo Ma plays with extraordinary sensitivity and imagination – so, for that matter, does Emanuel Ax who has the more brilliant part. Unfortunately, the CBS engineers have not been wholly successful in balancing these artists. The piano often masks the refined lines that Yo-Yo Ma draws. Though the artists have the benefit of truthful digital recording in every other respect, the dominance of the piano is an irritant. However, having heard this partnership in the concert hall, we are unsure that the criticism attached to the CBS engineers is fully reasonable, for Emanuel Ax produces a big, wide-ranging tone which must have posed problems. A pity that his dynamic range was not scaled down for, in every other respect, he inspires the listener with his keenness of intelligence, clean articulation and powerful musicianship. In Opp. 69 and 102, No. 2, the internal balance is much better judged, and there is much to delight the listener. Yo-Yo Ma plays with all the beauty of tone and refinement of feeling we have come to expect from him, while Emanuel Ax's playing has vibrant personality and sure musical instincts. Both artists are heard at their most searching in the slow movement of the *D major*. There are still one or two things that prompt reservations: the pianist's sforzati in the main theme of the scherzo are aggressive to the point of being ugly – but there is so much that is felicitous that these moments of exuberance do not prove unduly worrying. The sound quality is well focused and truthful on LP, good on tape, and has the greatest presence in the CD format, where the silent background makes its own contribution.

The partnership of Fournier and Kempff was joined in the mid-1960s when their performances were recorded at live festival performances. The Paris audience is not seriously intrusive, and though the balances are not ideal the compulsion of the playing is such as to make the listener less critical than usual. The recording has been remastered and sounds remarkably fresh, notably so on the cassettes, which are offered in one of DG's cardboard 'flap-packs'. Kempff can always be relied on, in his inspirational way, to produce memorable results; here, the clarity of his style balances perfectly with the relatively delicate timbre of Fournier's cello. These are performances marked by light, clear textures and rippling scale work, even in the slow introductions, which are taken relatively fast. Some of the weight found by Rostropovich and Richter is missing, but there is a mercurial quality here which is attractive in a different way. Like the Philips set, this is available at mid-price on both LP and tape.

The Du Pré/Bishop-Kovacevich recordings come from 1966, the year after Jacqueline had made her definitive record of the Elgar *Concerto*. Comparing this Beethoven coupling with rival versions, one cannot help noting the extra expressive urgency which marks the interpretations and makes them intensely vivid. The very opening of the *D major Sonata* underlines an unbuttoned quality in Beethoven's writing and when, after the hushed intensity of the slow introduction of Op. 69, the music launches into the allegro, both artists soar away fearlessly. More remarkable still is the range of expressiveness in the slow movement of Op. 102/2. Du Pré's tone ranges from full-blooded fortissimo to the mere whisper of a half-tone, and with Beethoven providing the indication *Adagio con molto sentimento* it is completely fitting that these artists allow the freest range of expressive rubato. There may be one or two technical faults, but rarely have artists so young plumbed such depths of expression on record. With excellent recording, this is an obvious bargain. There is a good cassette, though the focus of sound is perceptibly sharper on side one (Op. 69).

Clarinet trio in B flat, Op. 11.

*** Decca **414 576-2** [id.]. Peter Schmidl, New V. Octet (members) – *Septet*.***

The New Vienna Octet make a better case for the Op. 11 *Trio* than most previous rivals. The playing is wonderfully alert and has both sparkle and warmth. Taken on artistic merit alone, this is second to none, but the coupling brings an added inducement. The 1981 analogue recording is admirably balanced and has transferred smoothly and realistically to CD.

Piano trios Nos 1 in E flat; 2 in G, Op. 1/1–2.
*** Sup. Dig. **C37 7490** [id.]. Suk Trio.

Piano trios: Nos 4 in B flat, Op. 11; 5 in D (Ghost), Op. 70/1; 10 Variations on 'Ich bin der Schneider Kakadu', Op. 121a.
(M) *** Ph. 412 395-1/*4* [id.]. Beaux Arts Trio.

Piano trio No. 5 in D (Ghost), Op. 70/1.
(B) ** DG Walkman *413 854-4* [id.]. Kempff, Szeryng, Fournier – SCHUBERT: *Trout quintet* **; MOZART: *Hunt quartet.****
(M) ** EMI Em. EMX 41 2078-1/*4*. Hephzibah and Yehudi Menuhin, Gendron – SCHUBERT: *Trout quintet.***

The fine Supraphon performances were recorded in the House of Artists in Prague in 1983, and the reverberant acoustic and forward balance lend liveliness to the sound without there being any loss of detail. The playing is lively and sparkling, that of the pianist, Josef Hala, being particularly felicitous. The Suk players also seem to have the knack of finding just the right tempi and do not rush either of the finales. The exposition repeats in the first movements are observed; and the CD is copiously indexed so that one can find the opening of the development in the first movements, should one wish to skip the repeat. A very good record.

The Beaux Arts reissue is an economical and attractive arrangement of performances that originally appeared in different couplings. The Op. 11 trio, which is split over two sides of the disc, is usually heard in its clarinet version. The Beaux Arts players are on excellent form here, and they project the drama and intensity of the *Ghost trio* to brilliant effect. The *Kakadu variations* are played with characteristic elegance too. The recordings date from the mid-1960s (when Daniel Guilet was the violinist) but they still sound fresh and lifelike. Good value, particularly at medium price. The cassette transfer is natural and well balanced.

The performance of the *Ghost trio* by Kempff, Szeryng and Fournier is comparatively restrained, sweet and lyrical rather than dramatic. The chrome-tape transfer is of high quality. The couplings are worthwhile and this makes quite a good Walkman bargain issue.

On the HMV mid-priced disc the *Ghost trio* makes a generous coupling for the *Trout quintet*. This performance dates from the mid-1960s, and on its first appearance we deplored the fact that the piano part was outweighed by the closer balance given to violin and cello; and we still feel that this diminishes the attractions of a good performance. The sound is also rather dry.

Piano trios Nos 5 in D (Ghost); 6 in E flat, Op. 70/1–2.
** Sup. Dig. **C37 7284** [id.]. Suk Trio.

(M) *(*) CBS 60296/*40*- [MP/*MPT* 38891]. Istomin, Stern, Rose Trio.

Piano trios Nos 5 (Ghost); 7 in B flat (Archduke), Op. 97.
(*) Ph. **412 891-2 [id.]. Beaux Arts Trio.

Piano trio No. 7 in B flat (Archduke), Op. 97.
(B) **(*) DG Walkman *415 333-4*. Kempff, Szeryng, Fournier – SCHUBERT: *Quartets Nos 12 and 14*.**(*)

Piano trio No. 7 (Archduke); 9 in B flat, WoO 39.
*** HMV Dig. **CDC 747010-2** [id.]. ASD/*TCC-ASD* 4315 [Ang. DS/*4DS* 37818]. Ashkenazy, Perlman, Harrell.

No need for hesitation in considering the Ashkenazy/Perlman/Harrell recording of the *Archduke*. This is in every respect a most musical and masterly performance and is excellently recorded. It is very much a front runner; there is spontaneity, warmth and a feeling for architecture. These artists also give us a small bonus in the form of a two-movement *Trio*, written in 1812 and also in the key of B flat. It is a gracious and unpretentious piece which, on the face of it, is backward-looking in style. Yet there are many subtle touches that leave no doubt of its later provenance. The recording is wide-ranging and vivid on both tape and LP, but the compact disc has a wonderful clarity and presence, and in sheer naturalness and definition makes a striking effect.

On Philips, the Beaux Arts Trio offer a popular coupling and they are realistically recorded. The *Archduke* was made in 1979 at La Chaux-de-Fonds in Switzerland and the *Ghost* two years later in London. The *Ghost trio* comes off marvellously and sounds very fresh, though the *Archduke* is not quite as spontaneous as their 1965 version, which is still available on LP and tape and does not sound its age (Ph. 6570/*7310* 917). All the same, this is an enjoyable coupling and more generous than the HMV alternative.

On Supraphon, the *Ghost trio* is given a closer balance and a slightly less open sound than that offered in the Opus 1 set (above). It certainly does not create as natural an effect as the Philips/Beaux Arts CD. Both works are very well played, though the Suk Trio are steadier and less crisp.

Kempff and his colleagues give a crystalline reading of the *Archduke*. It is the clarity and imagination of Kempff's playing which set the tone of the whole performance. He it is who grips the listener's attention with his individual touches of genius, so that by comparison Szeryng and Fournier sound less than inspired. However, the recording is expertly transferred to chrome tape and many will feel that this Walkman bargain coupling with the Amadeus performances of Schubert's *Quartettsatz* and *Death and the Maiden quartet* is excellent value.

The Istomin/Stern/Rose pairing of Op. 70, Nos 1 and 2, comes from a complete set of the trios recorded at the end of the 1960s. The balance is close but clear and realistically separated. The playing is of high calibre with strong personalities unsubmerged, yet working well together as a team. These are much bolder performances than those dominated by Kempff but they have less charm, partly because the piano timbre is shallower while there is a relative lack of ambient bloom, though the sound is not untruthful.

Piano trios Nos 8 in E flat, WoO 38; 9 in B flat, WoO 39; 14 Variations on an original theme in E flat, Op. 44; Variations on 'Ich bin der Schneider Kakadu'.
*** Sup. Dig. **C37 7562** [id.]. Suk Trio.

A delightful and well-filled compact disc: it lasts longer than an hour. These Beethoven works are given lively performances by the Suk Trio and, as in the Opus 1 *Trios*, the playing of the pianist, Josef Hala, is particularly fresh. Moreover, the recording is very good indeed, articulate and transparent. These are very enjoyable and inspiriting performances, as good as any on LP and thoroughly recommendable.

Piano and wind quintet in E flat, Op. 16.
*** CBS Dig. **MK 42099**; IM/*IMT* 42099 [id.]. Perahia, members of ECO – MOZART: *Quintet.****
** Telarc Dig. **CD 80114**; DG 10114 [id.]. Previn, V. Wind Soloists – MOZART: *Quintet.***
* Denon Dig. **C37 7090** [id.]. Kontarsky, BPO Wind Qt – MOZART: *Quintet.**

The view that Beethoven's *Piano and wind quintet* is less interesting than its Mozartian predecessor (which plainly inspired it) is almost confounded by Perahia's new CBS version, recorded at The Maltings with Neil Black (oboe), Thea King (clarinet), Tony Halstead (horn) and Graham Sheen (bassoon). The first movement is given more weight than usual, with a satisfying culmination. In the *Andante*, Perahia's playing is wonderfully poetic and serene and the wind soloists are admirably responsive. The pacing of the finale is ideally judged; and with the recording most realistically balanced, this issue can be recommended with all enthusiasm.

Previn is at his finest in the slow movement which he opens most persuasively; throughout, his wind colleagues emphasize the work's robust character, however, and the playing fails to sparkle as it might, although the finale goes well enough. Ensemble is good, if not immaculate; the recording, made in a rather resonant acoustic but naturally balanced, is faithful.

On Denon, clear, if rather dry, recording and playing to match – which is somewhat surprising, given the distinction of the wind players. Everything is very crisp and cleanly articulated, but the performance is at best business-like and straightforward and it cannot be given a positive recommendation.

Septet in E flat, Op. 20.
*** Decca **414 576-2** [id.]. New V. Octet (members) – *Clarinet trio.****
(M) ** Ph. 412 394-1/*4*. Berlin Philharmonic Octet (members).

The earlier recording of Beethoven's *Septet* by the older Vienna Octet held sway in the analogue stereo catalogue for more than two decades. In 1981 Decca replaced it with a more modern recording, also analogue, but of the highest quality. Like the earlier ensemble, the New Vienna Octet consists of the first desks of the VPO. This later version has all the elegance of the earlier one, but also conveys a sparkle and a sense of enjoyment that are thoroughly exhilarating. In terms of spirit and exuberance it is altogether special. The CD transfer is very successful.

A refined performance from this excellent Berlin Philharmonic group, with plenty of life in the outer movements, but with rather a solemn view taken of the slow movement. The recording quality is first class on both tape and disc, but there is greater character in the bargain-priced Contour version recorded at the beginning of the 1960s by the Melos Ensemble (CC/*CCTC* 7589).

Serenade in D for flute, violin and viola, Op. 25; Serenade in D for string trio, Op. 8.

(M) *** Ph. 6503/*7303* 108. Maxence Larrieu, Grumiaux Trio.

The light and charming combination of flute, violin and viola inspired the youthful Beethoven to write in an unexpectedly carefree and undemanding way. The sequence of tuneful, unpretentious moments reminds one of Mozart, and the playing here, polished and refined, brings out all the music's charm. With a sensible and almost equally enjoyable coupling, this is strongly recommended, especially in its cassette version, secure from background interference, for the transfer is of Philips's best quality.

(i) *String quartets Nos 1, Op. 18/1; 9 (Rasumovsky), Op. 59/3; 11, Op. 95; 12, Op. 127; 14–16, Opp. 131–2 and 135;* (ii) *Violin sonatas Nos 3 in E flat, Op. 12/3; 5 in F (Spring), Op. 24; 7 in C min., Op. 30/2.*

❀ (M) *** HMV mono EX 290306-3 (5). (i) Busch Quartet; (ii) Adolf Busch, Rudolf Serkin.

An indispensable set: the Busch are to the Beethoven *Quartets* what Schnabel is to the *Piano sonatas*. The musical insight of these players, their wisdom and humanity and total absorption in Beethoven's art, has never been surpassed and only sporadically matched. These performances are so superb that, despite their sonic limitations, it is possible to recommend them to younger non-specialist collectors even in these days of the compact disc. There are occasional portamenti that were in general currency in the 1930s but are unfashionable now, but few will find them irksome. The transfers made by Keith Hardwick are altogether magnificent. The three *Violin sonatas* from Busch and Serkin are hardly less illuminating. The violin is placed rather forward, though no more so than in the Kreisler set made a few years later. Serkin's piano sounds a little frail at times, but there is nothing frail about the playing! Kreisler has an incomparable tone but Busch the more classical spirit. Whichever set you may already have, you will not regret adding this one to your collection. It is very competitively priced, too – but is available only on LP, not in cassette form!

String quartets Nos 1–6, Op. 18/1–6.
*** HMV Dig. **CDS 747127-8** (3) [id.]; SLS/*TC-SLS* 5217 [Ang. SIC/*4X3G* 6121]. Alban Berg Qt.
** DG Dig. 410 971-1/*4* (3) [id.]. Melos Qt of Stuttgart.

String quartets Nos 1 in F; 2 in G, Op. 18/1–2.
(M) *** Ph. 6503/*7303* 059 [(d.) in 6703 081 (3)]. Italian Qt.

String quartets Nos 3 in D; 4 in C min., Op 18/3–4.
(M) *** Ph. 6503/*7303* 107 [(d.) in 6703 081 (3)]. Italian Qt.

String quartets Nos 5 in A; 6 in B flat, Op. 18/5–6.
(M) *** Ph. 412 056-1/*4* [(d.) in 6703 081 (3)]. Italian Qt.

While alternative versions of the *Quartets*, Op. 18, abound on LP, the Alban Berg Quartet still have the field to themselves on compact disc, though it can only be a matter of time before DG transfer the Melos set. The Alban Berg undoubtedly offer a polish and tonal finesse that put them in a class of their own. The affectation we noted in their set of the *Rasumovskys* (the tendency to exaggerate dynamic extremes) is less obtrusive here, and the overall sense of style is so sure that few will be disappointed. For the time being, CD collectors are unlikely to do better than this. The playing is immaculate and the sound has all the usual advantages of the new medium, excellent definition, presence and body. There are excellent cassette transfers, too.

The performances by the Melos Quartet offer a refined blend, impeccable intonation and superb ensemble. However, admiration rather than unalloyed pleasure is one's final reaction. Speeds are on the fast side, and too often this group does not convey a sufficient sense of pleasure in the courtly exchanges that take place among the four instruments, while at times their playing has an aggressive edge. There are of course some very good things in the set: the *Quartet* No. 6 in B flat is given with wit and grace; and the *Quartet* No. 5 is very fine, too: its minuet comes off excellently and there is elegance and charm in evidence. There is no question as to the finesse and mastery of the playing nor the vividness of the recording, but the Melos do not displace the Alban Berg on HMV or the Italian Quartet on Philips.

The Italian Quartet's performances have now been reissued on three separate LPs with excellent equivalent tapes. The sound is fresh and clean but a trifle more astringent than before, notably so in the *Quartets* Nos 5 and 6. Their performances are in superb style and continue to make an excellent choice at mid-price.

String quartets Nos 7–9 (Rasumovsky Nos 1–3), Op. 59/1–3; 10 in E flat (Harp), Op. 74; 11 in F min., Op. 95.
*** ASV ALHB/*ZCALHB* 307 (3) [id.]. Lindsay Qt.
(*) HMV Dig. **CDS 747131-8 (3) [id.]; SLS/*TC-SLS* 5171 [Ang. SIC/*4X3G* 6122]. Alban Berg Qt.

String quartets Nos 7–9 (*Rasumovsky Nos 1–3*)*; 10–11; Quartet in F* (after *Piano sonata No. 9 in E, Op. 14/1*).
** DG Dig. **415 342-2**; 415 342-1/*4* [id.]. Melos Qt of Stuttgart.

Whatever the respective merits of current rivals, the Lindsays on ASV will be hard to beat in this repertoire. Their set contains performances of real stature; and though they are not unrivalled in some of their insights, among modern performances, they are not often surpassed. The *F major*, Op. 59/3, is very impressive indeed, with tempi sounding completely right throughout and the slow movement more penetrating than with the Quartetto Italiano. Again, in each movement of the *E minor*, Op. 59/2, the Lindsays find the 'tempo giusto' and all that they do as a result has the ring of complete conviction. The development and reprise of the first movement are repeated as well as the exposition – and how imaginatively the development is played, too! The opening of the *C major*, Op. 59/3, has real mystery and awe. They move the second movement on quite smartly and are much faster here than the famous Busch account, though they do not match the intensity of the Busch *Allegro molto*. Yet how splendidly do they convey the pent-up torrent of energy released in this fugal onrush. The *Andante con moto quasi Allegretto* is too brisk, and as a result the movement is not quite as fresh or as strongly felt as the outer movements; nor does the minuet attain the distinction of its companions. All the same, this is a fine account. The two remaining quartets, Opp. 74 and 95, are not new: they were recorded in 1979 and are highly competitive. Certainly as a recording, this set is superior to most previous versions, and artistically it can hold its own with the best.

As with Opus 18, the Alban Berg gave Beethoven's 'middle-period' Quartets their compact disc début, although they were soon followed by the Melos set. The HMV recordings have great presence and immediacy in their CD format (some ears may feel too much so), and there is no doubt as to the realism of the recorded sound. The cassette transfers too are of admirable quality, rich and clear. But, unlike their Opus 18 set, these performances cannot be welcomed without certain reservations. Generally speaking, they favour rather brisk tempi in the first movements, which they dispatch with exemplary polish and accuracy of intonation. Indeed, an almost unsmiling momentum is maintained when they reach the quaver theme in thirds in the first movement of Op. 59/1, where almost every other quartet relaxes just a little. The slow movement of Op. 59/1 is free from excessive point-making, and throughout this quartet and its companions there is much perceptive music-making. Rhythms are marvellously sprung and every phrase is vividly characterized. One generalization can be made: there is a distinct tendency to exaggerate dynamic extremes. The introduction to Op. 59/3 suffers in this respect, and the results sound self-conscious. In the first movements of Op. 59/2 and Op. 95 the brilliance of the attack almost draws attention to itself, and perhaps the recording quality, which is a little closely balanced, gives it a slightly more aggressive quality than it really has. As quartet playing, however, this is superlative and in some respects (such as ensemble and intonation) it would be difficult to fault. But this is not the whole picture, and while this remains most accomplished and generally successful it does not displace the recordings by the Lindsay Quartet on ASV, which we hope will be made available on compact disc before too long.

The Melos set on DG differs from its rivals in offering Beethoven's own transcription of the *Sonata*, Op. 14, No. 1, which is not otherwise available. In the middle-period *Quartets* proper, the Melos adopt a generally sound approach and eschew unnecessary interpretative eccentricities. Dynamic nuances and other markings are scrupulously observed, though they do not attract attention to themselves as do the Alban Berg. But far too many of the finales are too fast, as they were in their Op. 18 set. Their sheer virtuosity is not in question and they are more than equal to any of the technical demands posed by this music. However, they are by no means as searching or humane as the Lindsays in Op. 59, No. 1 – the first movement is terribly rushed. Although they perhaps offer performances of the others that are as finely played as any, theirs is superb quartet playing rather than great Beethoven. The recording is strikingly real and the chrome cassettes are only marginally less impressive than the CDs.

String quartet No. 7 in F (Rasumovsky No. 1), Op. 59/1.
❀ *** ASV Dig. **CDDCA 553** [id.]. Lindsay Qt.

Now that this is available on compact disc, doubts concerning recommendations in the new format can be resolved. This is the most masterly account of the *F major Rasumovsky* for many decades, with exactly the right feeling and pace, inwardness and effortlessness. This version brings the listener closer to Beethoven than any of its rivals.

String quartet No. 8 in E min. (Rasumovsky No. 2), Op. 59/2.
*(*) Denon **C37 7033**. Smetana Qt.

The playing of the Smetana Quartet is good and the performance thoroughly musical. But the playing time here is little over 30 minutes, and frankly this is uncompetitive.

String quartets Nos 12 in E flat, Op. 127; 13 in B flat, Op. 130; 14 in C sharp min., Op. 131; 15 in A min., Op. 132; 16 in F, Op. 135; Grosse Fuge in B flat, Op. 133.
(*) HMV Dig. **CDS 747135 (4) [id.]; EX 270114-3/9 (4/3) [Ang. DDC/*4D3S* 3973]. Alban Berg Qt.

Some listeners may find the sheer polish of the Alban Berg Quartet gets in the way, for this can be an encumbrance: late Beethoven is beautified at its peril. Others dig deeper into the soul of this music – the Busch and the Lindsays do – and this tells in movements like the *Heiliger Dankegesang* of Op. 132 or the *Cavatina* of Op. 130. The CDs have greater clarity of focus, particularly at the bottom end of the spectrum, and a distinct gain in presence by comparison with the LPs. There are excellent cassettes. The new medium does full justice to the magnificently burnished tone that the Alban Berg command and the perfection of blend they so consistently achieve. No single version of the Late Quartets can give us the complete truth, and no set is more magnificently played and recorded. Indeed, in this respect, it is likely to remain unchallenged – yet, at the same time, it is difficult to suppress the feeling that others convey even more of the stature and depth of these great and profound works.

Still recommended: The Lindsays get far closer to the essence of this great music than many more illustrious rivals, and they have the benefit of excellent recording. They seem to find tempi that somehow strike the listener as completely right and which enable them to convey so much of both the letter and the spirit of the music (ASV ALHB 403 (4)).

String quartet No. 13 in B flat, Op. 130; Grosse Fuge, Op. 133.
*** Decca Dig. **411 943-2**; 411 943-1/4 [id.]. Fitzwilliam String Qt.
** Tel. Dig. **ZK8. 42982**; AZ6. 42982 [id.]. Vermeer Qt.

The Fitzwilliam version of Op. 130, characteristically wide in dynamic and tonal range, is remarkable above all for a sublime account of the fifth movement, *Cavatina*. Normally taken at a flowing pace, it emerges rather as a songful interlude than as the meditation which it is here, taken at a genuine *Adagio* with the marking *sotto voce* made breathtaking. At a steady pulse and with restrained phrasing, the result completely avoids heavy sentimentality; equally in the *Grosse Fuge*, given as the first option of the two finales Beethoven wrote, the unusually measured speeds in all sections bring a hushed contrast in the meno mosso sections that makes the bravura allegros the more dramatically intense and weighty. Good, warm recording, particularly on CD, full of presence. The chrome cassette, although extremely vivid, is, however, excessively bright on top.

In terms of refinement of tonal blend and unanimity of approach, the Vermeer performances are of a high order; moreover, they are artists of keen sensitivity and awareness. They are also the beneficiaries of excellent engineering and, in terms of sound quality, there is little to quarrel with. The image is clear and well focused, albeit forwardly balanced, even if the acoustic is on the dry side. They give a perceptive and technically impeccable account of the first movement, but some collectors might find them just a shade didactic here – and even more so in the finale, which is also a little too measured. The *Alle tedesca* movement and the *Cavatina*, on the other hand, will perhaps be a little fast for some tastes. An excellent performance all the same, even if not a first choice.

String quartet No. 14 in C sharp min., Op. 131.
*** ASV ACA/*ZCACA* 1014 [id.]. Lindsay Qt.
*** HMV Dig. ASD/*TC-ASD* 143664-1/*4*. Alban Berg Qt.

What strikes the listener most forcibly on this ASV record is the total conviction of the performance: the Lindsays always seem to find exactly the right tempo and to convey the illusion while one listens to them that this is the only way this music can be played. Their musical priorities always seem just right: while the Alban Berg set great store by beauty as well as truth, the Lindsays' sights are set on truth first and beauty second and, in so doing, they achieve both. A distinct first choice on disc and tape.

In terms of sound quality the Alban Berg version is the best recording as such of Op. 131, and probably the best-played version on the market. But there is, of course, more to late Beethoven than beautiful sound or superb playing; indeed, in this repertoire, surface beauty can be an encumbrance, drawing attention to the playing rather than to the music. Tempi here are invariably sensibly judged and, in the very opening, the *Adagio* is not too slow (it is qualified with a *ma non troppo*) and has a strong sense of forward movement, though there could perhaps have been more *piano*. There is a greater 'Innigkeit' in the Lindsay version and a greater spirituality, even if it is not quite as well played or recorded.

String quartet No. 15 in A min., Op. 132.
*** ASV ACA/*ZCACA* 1015 [id.]. Lindsay Qt.
*** Decca Dig. **411 643-2**; 411 643-1/*4*. Fitzwilliam Qt.
**(*) HMV Dig. EL 2700053-1/*4*. Alban Berg Qt.

The Lindsays penetrate to the heart of this score as few other ensembles do, and they have pretty unerring musical judgement. Although their rivals – the Fitzwilliams and the Alban Berg – offer many insights, the Lindsays' sights are set on truth first and beauty second, and in so doing they achieve both. They are very well recorded and there is a good tape.

Fearlessly adopting the widest expressive range, the Fitzwilliam Quartet build a formidable structure round the central *Heiliger Dankegesang*, a genuine *molto adagio* with an exceptionally slow speed superbly sustained and with the most hushed pianissimos. The extremes of the first movement equally are contrasted against the relaxation of the other movements, whether of ebullient joy or songfulness. With a pleasantly reverberant background (Kingsway Hall), the sound is warm and true; the balance is a little close, perhaps to counter the hall's resonance, but there is no doubting the realism and immediacy offered by the CD format. The cassette too reproduces smoothly.

Few accounts are more superbly played than the Alban Berg's peformance or, for that matter, more beautifully recorded; but others convey even more of the stature and depth of this great and profound work, and leave the listener more moved and enriched. The first movement is a shade fast, and in the mysterious opening bars many of their rivals are slower and more searching. However, the pianissimo right at the very end of the movement is a little affected, painted on rather than arising naturally. In the second movement the pace is fractionally brisker than is ideal and, indeed, that might be said of the whole work. Of course, the heart of the matter is the *Heiliger Dankegesang* and, as Schnabel said of the late sonatas, however good the performance is, it can never be good enough. This is marvellously played and there is genuine feeling but, superb though this is, it does not have the 'Innigkeit' of the rival Fitzwilliam version, nor indeed of the Lindsay performance, not yet available outside their boxed set of the Late Quartets.

String quartets: No. 16 in F, Op. 135; in F, Op. 14/1 (arr. of *Piano sonata*).
*(*) Sup. Dig. **C37 7694** [id.]. Smetana Qt.

On LP, Op. 135 is usually coupled with the *E flat*, Op. 127. As it is, at 37 minutes this CD is hardly well filled. Even were it to contain another substantial late quartet, it would still not compete seriously in terms of insight or musical polish with either the Lindsays or the Alban Berg. These are serviceable performances, but not as outstanding as one would expect from so illustrious an ensemble.

Violin sonatas Nos 1–10.
*** CRD Dig. CRDD 1115/9; *CRDCD 4115/7* [id.]. Erich Gruenberg, David Wilde.
(*) Ph. **412 570-2 (3); 6768 036 (4) [id.]. David Oistrakh, Lev Oborin.

On CRD, Erich Gruenberg and David Wilde can hold their own with distinguished rivals. Their performances have sparkle and freshness; they are very attentive to minutiae of nuance and dynamics without for one moment losing their grasp of the overall architecture. Gruenberg produces a good tone, too; both he and his intelligent partner have the benefit of excellent recording that conveys the sense of a real concert-hall experience. These readings have a spontaneity and vitality that will not disappoint collectors on LP, while on cassette they have the advantage of added economy, being issued complete on three separate double-length chrome tapes, each at normal premium price. The only snag is that this means the *Kreutzer* has to break between sides to accommodate the four works allotted to the final cassette. The quality of the transfers is outstandingly real and vivid.

The Philips set was made in the early 1960s and sounds a trifle plummier than is usual nowadays. There is not a great deal of air round each of the instruments, though the recording is not dry. There is a relaxed, almost effortless quality and lyricism about these performances that is winning. Oistrakh's tone is warm and lines are finely drawn; there is admirable rapport throughout between the two partners. Some critics found these accounts a little bland when they first appeared, but dipping into them again, while they would not necessarily be a first choice in every sonata, there is a selfless, musicianly quality that cannot fail to win over the listener. Other versions have more electricity or have gone deeper, but few are as natural. It is good to have them with the advantage of continuity and a silent background, and in such good transfers.

Still recommended: The Ashkenazy/Perlman set offers a blend of classical purity and spontaneous vitality that is irresistible. These performances sound equally well on LP or the splendid cassettes (Decca D92 D5/*K92 K53* [Lon. CSA/5- 2501]).

Violin sonatas Nos 1 in D; 2 in A; 3 in E flat, Op. 12/1–3.
*** DG Dig. **415 138-2**; 415 138-1/*4* [id.]. Gidon Kremer, Martha Argerich.

The partnership of Kremer and Argerich, two inspirational artists, works superbly in the first three sonatas. Each sparks the other into individual, but never wilful, expression, with the to-and-fro exchanges typical of early Beethoven consistently delightful. Argerich is marginally the more dominant, but from the challenging opening of No. 1 onwards the sense of two individual musicians enjoying a new experience is irresistible. Argerich feared that she might sound self-conscious in Beethoven when pinned down on record, but she need not have worried. The CD gives an even keener sense of presence than the LP. The chrome cassette too is extremely vivid and clearly focused.

Violin sonatas Nos 5 in F (Spring); 9 (Kreutzer).
*** Decca **410 554-2**; SXL/*KSXC* 6990. Itzhak Perlman, Vladimir Ashkenazy.
(B) *** DG Walkman *415 615-4* [id.]. Yehudi Menuhin, Wilhem Kempff – BRAHMS: *Violin sonata No. 2.****
** Ph. **412 255-2** [id.]. David Oistrakh, Lev Oborin.
** RCA Dig. **RD 70430**. Ughi, Sawallisch.

An obvious recoupling from the Perlman/Ashkenazy series. The manner has a youthful freshness, yet the style is classical. The dynamism is there but never becomes too extrovert, and the music unfolds naturally and spontaneously. The recording quality is outstanding, especially on the excellent compact disc; but the cassette is very successful too.

The Walkman tape also offers a recoupling, from the Menuhin/Kempff recordings of the early 1970s. Their reading of the *Spring sonata* has the magic which characterizes the whole cycle, and the performance of the *Kreutzer* is also unique. In many ways it is not as immaculate as earlier accounts, but the spontaneous imagination of the playing, the challenge between great artists on the same wavelength, is consistently present. The recording too is admirably 'live'. The bonus is a persuasively lyrical version of Brahms's *A major Violin sonata* by Christian Ferras and Pierre Barbizet. This is placed on side one, after the *Spring sonata*, and makes an admirable contrast to it. Undoubtedly this Walkman tape is a real bargain.

Philips have paired two of the most popular sonatas from the 1962 Oistrakh/Oborin recordings for those who do not want to invest in the complete set. The first movement of the *Spring sonata* could perhaps have had more sparkle, but there is musicianship here, and a selfless quality that is most appealing. Oistrakh's is playing of the old school, leisurely and civilized, and in sheer character and zest must yield to Perlman and Ashkenazy on Decca. The transfer of the Decca analogue recording is also more realistic.

Sawallisch and Ughi give satisfying if rather plain readings of Beethoven's two most popular violin sonatas. Though Sawallisch is an ever-sympathetic pianist, he rarely prods his immaculate soloist into flights of individuality. The one clear advantage over the Perlman/Ashkenazy version is the observance of the exposition repeat in the first movement of the *Kreutzer*. Well-balanced digital recording.

Violin sonatas Nos 7 in C min., Op. 30/1; 10 in G, Op. 96.
*** Decca **411 948-2** [id.]. Itzhak Perlman, Vladimir Ashkenazy.

Like the companion coupling of the *Spring* and the *Kreutzer*, these performances emanate from the 1977 set and have been digitally remastered and recoupled. The sound is improved, firmer and fresher than ever; no phrase is unimaginatively handled, and the playing of these artists is masterly.

7 Variations on Bei Männern; 12 Variations on Ein Mädchen (both from Mozart's *Die Zauberflöte*); *12 Variations on See the conquering hero comes* (from Handel's *Judas Maccabaeus*).
(M) ** Ph. 412 061-1/*4*. Maurice Gendron (cello), Jean Françaix (piano) – SCHUBERT: *Arpeggione Sonata*.**

Civilized performances of some elegance and finesse from Gendron, well supported by Jean Françaix. At mid-price these are well worth considering; the recordings, though not of recent provenance, are eminently serviceable on both disc and cassette. There is, however, a more illuminating account of the Schubert coupling from Maisky and Argerich on CD.

Wind octet in E flat, Op. 103; Rondino in E flat for wind octet, G.146; Wind sextet in E flat, Op. 71; March in B flat for two clarinets, two horns and two bassoons; Quintet for three horns, oboe and bassoon.
(B) *** Con. CC/*CCTC* 7604. London Wind Soloists, Brymer.

This collection originated in the Decca vaults but has now been reissued at bargain price on Pickwick's Contour label. Trivial and unexacting, it is a joy from beginning to end. The *Octet* was written before Beethoven left Bonn for Vienna, and the *Sextet* followed soon after he arrived there. The *Quintet* is the mystery work. Beethoven probably completed it, but the only known score has the beginning and end missing. But some astute analytical work by the nineteenth-century scholar Leopold Zellner brought a performable version of the movements as far as the minuet (trio missing). The work proves of far more than antiquarian interest, and the playing throughout the disc is masterly, with Alan Civil gloriously confident on the horn. The recording is of outstanding Decca quality, vintage 1965. The high-level chrome cassette is fresh and clean and gives the ensemble excellent presence.

Piano sonatas Nos 1–32.
(M) *(*) Ph. **412 193-2** (9) [id.]. Friedrich Gulda.

Piano sonatas Nos 1–32; Andante favori in F, G.170.
(*) Ph. **412 575-2 (11); 6768 004/*7699 080* (13) [id.]. Alfred Brendel.

Piano sonatas Nos 1–15.
(*) DG Dig. **413 759-2; 413 759-1 (6) [id.]. Daniel Barenboim.

Piano sonatas Nos 16–32.
(*) DG Dig. **413 766-2; 413 766-1 (6) [id.]. Daniel Barenboim.

With eleven hours of music on eleven CDs, the Brendel cycle makes full use of the extra convenience of the new medium, not just in playing-length, but in ease of use, when any movement can be selected more readily than was ever the case with LP. The new format actually encourages more listening, and though the CD transfers bring out the discrepancies between different recordings made between 1970 and 1977, tape-hiss is minimal and the sound good with plenty of percussive bite. As to the performances, though they lack some of the fighting spontaneity of the young Brendel many years ago on Turnabout, they have a dark, thoughtful, deeply satisfying quality that consistently gives pleasure.

Spontaneity and electricity, extremes of expression in dynamic, tempo and phrasing as well as mood, mark Barenboim's DG cycle, as they did his much earlier one for HMV. Some of his more extreme readings – such as the sleep-walking tempo for the finale of the *Waldstein* – have been modified to fall short of provocation or eccentricity. This time spontaneity is even more evident, though that means he has a tendency at times to rush his fences, particularly in the early sonatas, giving a hint of breathlessness to already fast speeds. That is exceptional, and so is the hint of technical stress. The first movement of the *Appassionata* is given with all his old flair, even more a vehicle for display thanks to dramatic extremes of light and dark. Conversely, the second and third movements are now plainer and simpler. The plainness in the first movement of the *Moonlight* is disappointing, however, less poetic, with little veiled tone; but the light, flowing finale of the *Tempest*, Op. 31 No. 2, is now more magically Mendelssohnian than ever. All three movements of the *Waldstein* this time are more lyrical, and that applies in the late sonatas too, not just in slow movements but equally strikingly in the great fugal movements, where inner parts are brought out more clearly and warmly. Only in the final Adagio variations of Op. 111 does a hint of self-consciousness develop, thanks to agogic hesitations at a tempo even slower than before. The lyrical opening movement of Op. 101 in A is delectably done, flowing and simple. The role of such a cycle as this is not to set Barenboim's readings as though in amber, fixed for ever, but to act more nearly as a living document of a performer at a particular point in his career. The sound is warm and spacious, much more consistent than before. The CD transfers – taking the sonatas in consecutive order but on one more CD than Brendel's rival set – come in two separate boxes.

Recorded in the mid-1960s, Gulda's CD set has the merit of being squeezed on to fewer discs than its direct rivals (at the expense of some repeats), but the readings are sadly erratic, a failing which grows ever more irritating as the sequence progresses. So in the early sonatas Gulda's energy and alertness are enough to carry conviction, even if deeper qualities are missing. The first movement of the *Moonlight* brings a measure of poetry, simple and intense; but otherwise that is a quality almost totally absent, when Gulda seems incapable of playing at anything less than mezzo forte. In the later and often greater sonatas, however, Gulda grows increasingly wilful, often adopting speeds which are nothing less than hectic and completely missing any inner intensity in the last-period masterpieces. The recording is dry but not aggressive, relatively undistracting. The nine CDs are offered for the price of six, but the apparent bargain must be weighed against the consideration that the alternative boxes from Barenboim and Brendel will give far greater musical satisfaction and offer much finer recordings, too.

Piano sonatas Nos 1–3, Op. 2/1–3; 5–7, Op. 10/1–3; 8 (Pathétique), Op. 13; 9–10, Op. 14/1 and 2.
** CBS M3P/*3PT* 39647 (3). Glenn Gould.

Fascinatingly individual piano playing, somewhat dominated by the artist's vocalise. The performances are full of eccentricities, yet they remain spontaneous (the listening experience is rather like eavesdropping on the artist playing for his own pleasure). Slow movements are often very slow, but marvellously sustained; the articulation of fast passages has superb clarity. Sometimes Gould is too fast, as in the breakneck account of the prestissimo finale of Op. 10/1 and in the *Pathétique* (a disappointing account). But the strong character of the playing always holds the attention, for Gould's thoughtfulness and dedication are everywhere obvious. The recording is truthful and close. The cassettes too have admirable presence, though the transfer level varies, and with it the actual quality of the timbre.

Piano sonatas Nos 1 in F min.; 2 in A, Op. 2/1–2; Bagatelles, Op. 33/4 and 7.
* Hyp. A/*KA* 66174 [id.]. Linda Nicolson (fortepiano).

Linda Nicolson uses a Schantz fortepiano from around 1797, restored by Adlam in 1982. She phrases sensitively and colours her tone imaginatively, although at times in the *F minor Sonata* one feels she is a shade too genteel, though she captures the spirit of the minuet well. She also has the measure of the *Bagatelles*, which she plays with character. Unfortunately the acoustic of the recording does not flatter the instrument: it is too resonant and not well focused.

Piano sonatas Nos 2 in A, Op. 2/2; 4 in E flat, Op. 7.
*** DG Dig. **415 481-2**; 415 481-1/*4* [id.]. Emil Gilels.

Gilels's magisterial Beethoven sonatas are one of the glories of the catalogue, and his leonine strength was tempered by a delicacy and poetry that few matched and none have surpassed. What marked Gilels off from other pianists was not just his aristocratic polish (Richter and Firkusny have that as well) or his commanding virtuosity, which in his case was a vehicle for deep musical insights, but his very special and totally individual tonal world. His accounts of the *A major Sonata* and the *E flat*, Op. 7, are as masterly as one expects and silence criticism. The recording is clear and well lit in the DG fashion, and does not perhaps do the fullest justice to the sound he produced in the concert hall; but, given such playing, there is no need to withhold the strongest recommendation. On CD, the piano image is very tangible; the chrome cassette too is one of DG's best.

Piano sonatas Nos 7 in D, Op. 10/3; 23 in F min. (Appassionata), Op. 57.
*** CBS Dig. **MK 39344**; IM/*IMT* 39344 [id.]. Murray Perahia.

Perahia is more than just a fine Mozart interpreter, as this remarkable record shows. Intense, vibrant playing in the *D major Sonata* with great range of colour and depth of thought. The slow movement is a model of sensitivity and keyboard colour, and Perahia's *Appassionata* is a performance of comparable stature. These are among the few interpretations to have appeared in recent years that can be recommended alongside Gilels. The recorded sound is truthful and present.

Piano sonatas Nos 8 (Pathétique); 13; 14 (Moonlight).
*** DG Dig. **400 036-2**; 2532/*3302* 008 [id.]. Emil Gilels.

Gilels is served by good sound and, as always, his performances leave the overriding impression of wisdom. Yet this compact disc, coupling the two Op. 27 sonatas and the *Pathétique*, does not quite rank among his very best (such as the *Waldstein* and Op. 101). The opening movement of the *Moonlight* is wonderfully serene, and there are many felicities. But the first movement of the *E flat Sonata* is strangely reserved (the wonderful change to C major so subtly illuminated by Schnabel goes relatively unremarked here), as if Gilels feared the charge of self-indulgence or out-of-period sentiment. However, such are the strengths of this playing that few will quarrel with the magnificence of his conceptions of all three pieces. The digital recording is very lifelike on the compact disc: the background silence benefits the opening of the *Moonlight* very strikingly. This would have earned a technical accolade, were not the balance so close (which brings a touch of hardness on fortissimos), but even so the presence of the piano is remarkable. The chrome tape is first class also.

Piano sonatas Nos 8 (Pathétique), Op. 13; 14 (Moonlight), Op. 27/2; 15 (Pastoral), Op. 28; 23 (Appassionata), Op. 57; 26 (Les Adieux), Op. 81a.
(B) *** DG Walkman *413 435-4* [id.]. Wilhelm Kempff.

Piano sonatas Nos 8 (Pathétique); 14 (Moonlight); 15 (Pastoral); 24 in F sharp, Op. 78.
(M) *** DG Gal. 415 834-1/*4* [id.]. Wilhelm Kempff.

Piano sonatas Nos 8 (Pathétique); 14 (Moonlight); 17 in D min. (Tempest), Op. 31/2; 21 in C (Waldstein), Op. 53; 23 in F min. (Appassionata), Op. 57; 26 in E flat (Les Adieux), Op. 81a.
(M) *** DG 414 519-1/*4* (2) [id.]. Wilhelm Kempff.

Piano sonatas Nos 8 (Pathétique); 14 (Moonlight); 21 (Waldstein); 23 (Appassionata).
(B) *** Ph. On Tour *412 217-4* [id.]. Claudio Arrau.

Piano sonatas Nos 8 (Pathétique); 14 (Moonlight); 21 (Waldstein); 26 (Les Adieux).
(B) **(*) HMV *TCC2-POR 54285*. Daniel Barenboim.

Piano sonatas Nos 8; 14; 23; 26; 5 Bagatelles, Op. 119/1–5.
(B) * CBS *MGT 39486*. Rudolf Serkin.

All these compilations rest under the shadow of Kempff's masterly recordings which show so well his ability to rethink Beethoven's music within the recording studio. Everything he does has his individual stamp, and above all he never fails to convey the deep intensity of a master in communion with Beethoven. The Walkman collection of five favourite named sonatas is an obvious bargain, yet the two-disc set (with excellent cassette equivalents) offers also the *Waldstein*, one of Kempff's most magical performances. However, the *Waldstein* is also available on Walkman, coupled with the *Third* and *Fourth Piano Concertos* (see above). The Galleria collection of four sonatas has been digitally remastered and the piano quality has undoubtedly gained in firmness. The chrome cassette gives excellent presence.

Arrau's collection is also very worth while (especially at bargain price). His performances are essentially more serious, less chimerical than Kempff's; they also have slightly less spontaneity. He is aided by characteristically full-timbred Philips piano sound, and as it happens the *Waldstein* is also memorable in his hands. Aristocratic poise and strength are balanced by a thoughtful understanding of Beethoven's overall scheme.

Barenboim's performances, taken from his earlier HMV cycle, combine impetuosity with a confident control of line. There is a rhapsodic feel to his approach which is often very convincing. In his hands *Les Adieux* is made to sound much stronger than usual, but the *Waldstein* is more controversial in its choice of excessively slow tempi in the outer movements. The sound is full and clear.

Rudolf Serkin is let down by the CBS engineers for, while these performances are undoubtedly authoritative, incisive and dramatic, the clattery piano tone precludes much enjoyment and robs the *Bagatelles* of the least suggestion of charm.

Piano sonatas Nos 8 (*Pathétique*)*; 14* (*Moonlight*)*; 23* (*Appassionata*).
*** Decca **410 260-2**; SXL/*KSXC* 7012 [Lon. CS/5- 7247]. Vladimir Ashkenazy.
*** Ph. **411 470-2**; 9500/*7300* 899 [id.]. Alfred Brendel.

For those wanting a compact disc of the three most popular named sonatas, Ashkenazy's readings will be found very satisfactory. The *Pathétique* is perhaps slightly understated for so ebulliently youthful a work, with the finale unusually gentle; nevertheless the performance conveys the underlying power. The *Moonlight* is generally successful, and the *Appassionata* is admirable. He is well served by the engineers and the analogue recordings are very well transferred to CD. There is also an excellent chrome tape.

Brendel's performances, too, are undoubtedly impressive, the *Moonlight* beautifully played, the others strong and thoughtful, yet not lacking power. The sound is full-bodied and clear, although plainly from an analogue source.

Piano sonatas Nos 15 in D (Pastoral), Op. 28; 17 in D min. (Tempest), Op. 31/2.
*(**) DG Dig. **419 161-2** [id.]. Emil Gilels.

This is a recoupling for CD, but in both recordings the DG engineers elect for a very close balance. It is as if one is observing the instrument from the vantage point of the keyboard itself, or at least very near it. There is clarity and impact, but the percussive qualities are emphasized. It is very different from the sound one remembers hearing at a Gilels recital in the concert hall, and there is a hardness in fortissimo passages that one is less aware of in a less forward balance. The *Pastoral* is a strange performance – a laboured, almost hectoring first movement, very deliberate in tempo and character, with little sense of flow and only occasional glimpses of the wisdom and humanity one associates with this great artist. The *Tempest sonata*, Opus 31, No. 2, is another matter; this performance has excited universal acclaim, and rightly so.

Piano sonatas Nos 21 in C (Waldstein); 23 in F min. (Appassionata), Op. 57; 26 in E flat (Les Adieux), Op. 81a.
❀ *** DG **419 162-2** [id.]. Emil Gilels.

This recoupling for CD offers three of Gilels's finest analogue recordings dating from 1972–5. The piano is believably present, but much less closely observed than in his later digital recordings, to great advantage. The *Waldstein* sounds particularly well and only a hint of hardness creeps into fortissimos in Opp. 57 and 81a. The account of the *Appassionata* has previously been hailed by us as among the finest ever made, and much the same must be said of the *Waldstein*. It has a technical perfection denied even to Schnabel, and though in the slow movement Schnabel found special depths, Gilels is hardly less searching and profound. Moreover, Gilels's fastidiously sensitive yet commanding *Les Adieux* is also one of the most impressive ever committed to disc. These are all performances to relish, to study and to keep for special occasions.

Piano sonatas Nos 21 in C (Waldstein), Op. 53; 26 in E flat (Les Adieux), Op. 81a; 27 in E min., Op. 90.
*** Decca **414 630–2** [id.]. Vladimir Ashkenazy.

Taking a broadly lyrical view, Ashkenazy gives a deeply satisfying reading of the *Waldstein sonata*. His degree of restraint and his occasional hesitations intensify his thoughtful approach, while never interrupting the broader span of argument. *Les Adieux* brings a vehement first movement and memorable concentration, while the account of the *E minor Sonata*, Op. 90, is masterly. The analogue recordings are first class and sound full, firm and clear in their CD transfer. There is slight variation in quality between the three works, with No. 27 in E minor (recorded in 1981, whereas the other two date from 1975) slightly fuller in timbre.

Piano sonatas Nos 23 in F min. (Appassionata), Op. 57; 32 in C min., Op. 111.
(*) Delos Dig. **D/CD 3009** [id.]. Carole Rosenberger.

Carole Rosenberger possesses both musical intelligence and technique, but already on compact disc the field is highly competitive, and these performances would have to be very special indeed to overcome the handicap of the inadequate recorded sound, which is very bottom-heavy and unpleasing.

Piano sonatas Nos 24 in F sharp, Op. 78; 29 in B flat (Hammerklavier), Op. 106.
(*) Ph. **412 723-2; 412 723-1/*4* [id.]. Alfred Brendel.

Piano sonatas Nos 26 (Les Adieux); 29 in B flat (Hammerklavier), Op. 106.
(M) **(*) Ph. 412 918-1/*4*. Alfred Brendel.

Piano sonata No. 29 (Hammerklavier).
*** DG Dig. **410 527-2**; 410 527-1/*4* [id.]. Emil Gilels.
(M) *** DG Sig. 413 989-1/*4* [id.]. Maurizio Pollini.

Gilels's *Hammerklavier* is a performance of supreme integrity, Olympian, titanic, subtle, imperious, one of the finest accounts ever recorded. Speeds for the outer movements are surprisingly spacious and relaxed, with clarity of texture and refinement of detail brought out. Yet the concentration brings the most powerful impact – not just in those movements but in all four. The recording is close and bright and harder than ideal: hearing Gilels play the work in London in 1984 left one in no doubt that there is more to the sound he produced in real life than the overlit quality the DG engineers have achieved. The recording is at its most effective on compact disc, but there is also an excellent chrome tape. Whichever format is chosen, this is still an indispensable issue and no collector need hesitate on artistic grounds.

Pollini's is also among the finest *Hammerklaviers* of recent years. Some details may be more tellingly illuminated by other masters such as Gilels or Brendel but, apart from Gilels, no one currently before the public has greater rhythmic grip, or such alert articulation and sensitivity to line, as well as a masterly control of the long paragraph. Moreover, the sound is most impressive, wide-ranging and realistic, and there is scarcely any difference between disc and cassette.

Brendel's 1972 LP recording of the *Hammerklavier* for Philips came early in his re-recording of the whole Beethoven sonata cycle, and there are still signs of a self-consciousness which make it less powerful than his earlier recording for Vox [Turnabout 34392]. Yet, thanks to fine recording, he conveys a deep, hushed concentration in the slow movement. Though this may not be quite worthy of a pianist who has become one of the great visionary Beethovenians of our time, it remains a fine version, more attractively coupled than on its first issue, with *Les Adieux*. There is an excellent, full-bodied cassette transfer.

The CD coupling of the *Hammerklavier* and Opus 78 comes not from Brendel's complete sonata cycle but from a live recording made at the Queen Elizabeth Hall in London a decade later. Though there is greater urgency and dramatic tension in the allegro movements, the great *Adagio* of the *Hammerklavier*, intense as it is, lacks the spacious sublimity of the earlier version, taken even more slowly. The audience make their presence felt only between movements and the recording, especially on CD, is very believable. The atmospheric ambience of the hall is well caught and the piano image is not too forward. There is an excellent chrome cassette.

Piano sonatas Nos 28 in A, Op. 101; 29 (Hammerklavier); 30 in E, Op. 109; 31 in A flat, Op. 110; 32 in C min., Op. 111.
(M) *** DG 419 102-1/*4* (2) [id.]. Wilhelm Kempff.

Kempff's *Hammerklavier* performance represents his interpretative approach to Beethoven at its most extreme and therefore controversial. Here his preference for measured allegros and fastish andantes gives a different weighting to movements from the usual, but in each the concentration of the playing is inescapable. If the slow movement flows more quickly than is common, there is a thoughtfulness of utterance which gives it profundity, while in the finale Kempff's clarity of fingerwork brings a new freshness that lacks nothing in excitement. The reading of Op. 109 sets the style for Kempff's other performances of the late sonatas, intense in its control of structure but with a feeling of rhapsodic freedom too, of new visions emerging. The second movement of Op. 110 is not as fast as it might be, but the result is cleaner for that, and in typical Kempff style the great *Arietta* of Op. 111 is taken at a flowing tempo, not nearly so slowly as with many a recorded rival. These are all great performances; and the remastered recording is clean and firm, on disc and tape alike.

Piano sonata No. 31 in A flat, Op. 110.
(*) DG **413 446-2 [id.]. Maurizio Pollini – *Piano concerto No. 3.***
(*) Ph. **412 789-2 [id.]. Alfred Brendel – *Piano concerto No. 5.**(*)

Both Pollini's and Brendel's performances are fill-ups for less successful concerto recordings. The Pollini account originates from his earlier set of the late sonatas in which his sober manners are more apt than in the concerto. Purity is the keynote here, rather than mystery or meditation. A good CD transfer from an analogue original.

Having the *Sonata*, Op. 110, as fill-up to the *Emperor concerto* is generous. Brendel's account comes from a 1975 analogue recording made in the studio, and is much preferable to the live recording for the concerto, with mellow but realistic piano sound and little perceptible tape-hiss. The thoughtfulness of the reading is most compelling.

Piano sonata No. 32, Op. 111.
(*) DG Dig. **410 520-2; 2532/*3302* 036 [id.]. Ivo Pogorelich – SCHUMANN: *Études symphoniques* etc.**(*)

Ivo Pogorelich produces consistent beauty of tone throughout the sonata, and his account of this masterpiece contains many felicities. It is imposing piano playing and impressive music-making. At times he seems to view Beethoven through Lisztian eyes, but there is much that is powerful here. Pogorelich has a strong personality and will provoke equally strong reactions. There are self-indulgent touches here and there, but also moments of illumination. The compact disc is admirably clear and realistically balanced, but the clarity of the recording and its background silence tend to emphasize the slightly dry bass quality.

Miscellaneous piano music

7 Bagatelles, Op. 33; 11 Bagatelles, Op. 119; 6 Bagatelles, Op. 126.
(M) *** Ph. Seq. 412 357-1/*4*. Stephen Bishop-Kovacevich.

Beethoven's *Bagatelles*, particularly those from Opp. 119 and 126, have often been described as chips from the master's workbench, but rarely if ever has that description seemed as apt as in these searchingly simple readings by Bishop-Kovacevich. The memorability and sparkle of each idea come over with astonishing freshness, and the recording is excellent, despite the length of sides. The cassette needs a bass cut but then sounds well, for the upper range is natural.

6 Bagatelles, Op. 126; 6 Ecossaises, WoO 83; Für Elise, WoO 59; 15 Variations and fugue on a theme from Prometheus (Eroica variations), Op. 35.
ℭ *** Ph. **412 227-2**; 412 227-1/*4* [id.]. Alfred Brendel.

Brendel may lack some of the sheer bravura of his own early playing in this collection of shorter pieces, but his consistent thoughtfulness and imagination bring out the truly Beethovenian qualities of even the most trivial pieces. The *Eroica variations*, not as flamboyant as with some, plainly point to the magnificence of their culminating development in the *Eroica* finale. Excellent recording, with the CD outstandingly realistic. The cassette is good too, but lacks the extra degree of presence of the compact disc.

VOCAL MUSIC

An die ferne Geliebte (song cycle), *Op. 98; Lieder for male voice* (complete recording).
*** HMV EX 270042-3 (3). Dietrich Fischer-Dieskau, Hartmut Holl.

Though Fischer-Dieskau's EMI collection of Beethoven's complete songs for male voice (other than folksong settings) may betray some of the harsher timbres that have come into his voice with age, their breadth of imagination, in detail as well as over the broadest span, is far keener than in an earlier set he recorded for DG (see below). This is in fair measure due to the consistently imaginative accompaniment of Hartmut Holl, far more sympathetic than Joerg Demus on DG. First-rate recording.

An die ferne Geliebte, Op. 98. Lieder: *Adelaide; L'amant impaziente; Es war einmal ein König; In questa tomba oscura; Maigesang; Zartliche Liebe.*
(*) DG **415 189-2 [id.]. Dietrich Fischer-Dieskau, Joerg Demus – BRAHMS: *Lieder*.**(*)

Recorded in 1966, Fischer-Dieskau's DG Beethoven selection finds him at his vocal peak, and though Demus's accompaniment is not as imaginative as the singer received in other versions of these songs, the singer's individuality is as positive as ever, with detail touched in as with no one else. The coupling with the Brahms is very generous, adding up to over seventy minutes of music, with transfers hardly betraying the age of the recording.

An die ferne Geliebte, Op. 98. Lieder: *Adelaide; Andenken; An die Hoffnung; Aus Goethes Faust* (*Song of the flea*)*; Busslied; Ich liebe dich; Der Kuss; Mailied; Neue Liebe; Resignation; Der Wachtelschlag; Der Zufriedene.*
(*) Amon Ra **CDSAR 15. Ian Partridge, Richard Burnett.

Partridge, accompanied on an 1800 fortepiano, gives delightful performances of a wide-ranging and generous collection of Beethoven songs, including the song-cycle *An die ferne Geliebte*. The honeyed tones of Partridge's tenor and his finely detailed feeling for words come over well – particularly suited to such soaring lyrical songs as *Adelaide* and *An die Hoffnung*. The twangy fortepiano is recorded much more dully.

Choral fantasia (for piano, chorus and orchestra), *Op. 80*.
(*) Telarc Dig. **CD 80063 [id.]. Serkin, Boston Ch. and SO, Ozawa – *Piano concerto No. 3.***(*)
*(*) RCA Dig. **RD 84734** (2). Ax, NY Choral Artists, NYPO, Mehta – *Symphony No. 9.**

As a generous fill-up for Serkin's version of the *Third Piano concerto*, the *Choral fantasia* is most welcome, even though the long opening solo lacks something in brio, the necessary evocation of Beethoven himself improvising. But Ozawa draws committed performances from chorus and orchestra, though vocal balances are odd, with the chorus close and the soloists rather distant in a believably reverberant acoustic.

Ax gives a beautifully concentrated and expressive account of the solo piano part, and Mehta's performance overall is a good one. But the 'live' recording in the Avery Fisher Hall is ill defined at both ends of the spectrum. Moreover, this is coupled with an unrecommendable two-CD set of the *Choral symphony*.

Folksong arrangements: Again my love; Bonnie laddie; The deserter; Helpless woman; Judy lovely; March Megan; Oh! who, my dear Dermot; The parting kiss; The sweetest lad was Jamie.
*** HMV Dig. EL 270323-1/*4* [Ang. DS/*4DS* 37352]. Robert White, Sanders, Peskanov, Rosen, Wilson – WEBER: *Folksong arrangements.****

Robert White follows up the success of his earlier RCA disc of Beethoven settings of folksongs with another delightful and often unusual collection. Beethoven may not even have seen the words – the publisher George Thomson often fitted new words to old tunes – but the charm and imagination of each one are delightful. In *Helpless woman* we even have a Beethoven setting of a Robert Burns poem. White's heady tenor and sharply expressive delivery are ideally suited to this music, and he is warmly accompanied by his instrumental ensemble. Warm recording.

Folksong arrangements: Bonnie laddie, highland laddie; Come fill, fill my good fellow; Could this ill world have been contriv'd; Faithfu' Johnie; La gondoletta; Good night, The morning air plays on my face; Oh had my fate been joined with thine; Oh, harp of Erin; Oh sweet were the hours; Once more I hail thee; The parting kiss; The pulse of an Irishman; The return to Ulster; The soldier's dream; Sunset.
*(*) HMV EL 270045-1/*4*. Fischer-Dieskau, Menuhin, Heinrich Schiff, Holl.

Fischer-Dieskau's latest HMV collection of folksong arrangements is one of his more disappointing records. The grit in his voice and the frequent expressive overemphasis remove all the charm without adding compensating qualities, not helped even by an exceptionally distinguished trio of accompanists. Good recording.

Missa solemnis in D, Op. 123.
*** DG **413 780-2**; 2707 110/*3370 029* (2) [id.]. Moser, Schwarz, Kollo, Moll, Netherlands Ch., Concg. O, Bernstein.

Bernstein's DG version with the Concertgebouw was edited together from tapes of two live performances, and the result has a spiritual intensity matched by very few rivals. Edda Moser is not an ideal soprano soloist, but the others are outstanding, and the *Benedictus* is made angelically beautiful by the radiant playing of the Concertgebouw concertmaster, Hermann Krebbers. The recording is a little light in bass, but outstandingly clear as well as atmospheric. The CD clarifies the sound still further, and there is also a good tape set. A firm primary recommendation for Beethoven's choral masterpiece in all formats.

OPERA

Fidelio (complete).
** Decca **410 227-2** (2) [id.]; D 178 D3/*K 178 K32* (3/*2*) [Lon. LDR/*5*- 10017]. Behrens, Hofmann, Sotin, Adam, Ghazarian, Kuebler, Howell, Chicago Ch. and SO, Solti.

Solti's set was the first-ever digital recording of an opera. The sound is full, clean and vividly atmospheric, matched by the conductor's urgent and intense direction. With fine choral singing the ensembles are excellent, but the solo singing is too flawed for comfort. Hildegard Behrens seems ungainly in the great *Abscheulicher*, the voice sounding less beautiful than usual; and both Peter Hofmann as Florestan and Theo Adam as Pizarro too often produce harsh unattractive tone. The compact discs can be recommended strongly for their sound quality, with balances fresher and cleaner; the pair of cassettes are very successful, too. But this version must be regarded as a stop-gap only, until Klemperer's famous set with Ludwig, Vickers, Frick and Berry appears on CD.

Bellini, Vincenzo (1801–35)

I Capuleti ed i Montecchi (complete).
(*) HMV **CDS 747388-8 [id.]; EX 270192-3/*9* (2) [Ang. DSB/*4D2S* 3969]. Baltsa, Gruberova, Howell, Raffanti, Tomlinson, ROHCG Ch. and O, Muti.

Muti's set was recorded live at a series of performances at Covent Garden when the production was new, in March 1984. With the Royal Opera House a difficult venue for recording, the sound is hard and close, far less agreeable and well balanced than in the previous EMI version of this opera, recorded in the studio with Beverley Sills and Dame Janet Baker, and now deleted. On the later version, Agnes Baltsa makes a passionately expressive Romeo and Edita Gruberova a Juliet who is not just brilliant in coloratura but sweet and tender, too. It is an unlikely but very successful matching of a Zerbinetta with a Carmen, but it is the masterful conducting of Muti that, more than anything, makes one tolerant of the indifferent sound. If (for good reasons) he has often been considered something of a sprinter in opera, here he is superb with the pacing, balancing fast and incisive choruses against passages of warmth, relaxation and repose. That mastery is especially striking at the end of Act I, when the five principals sing a hushed quintet in which Romeo and Juliet musically reveal their understanding, singing sweetly in thirds. With excellent contributions from the refined tenor, Dano Raffanti (Tebaldo), Gwynne Howell and John Tomlinson, it is a performance to blow the cobwebs off an opera that – even in the earlier recording – seemed one of Bellini's less compelling pieces.

Norma (complete).
(***) HMV mono **CDS 747304-8 [CDCB 47303]**; EX 290066-3/*5* (3). Callas, Filippeschi, Stignani, Rossi-Lemeni, La Scala, Milan, Ch. and O, Serafin.

Though the flatness of the 1954 mono recording is emphasized by the precision of CD, the sense of presence gives wonderful intensity to one of Callas's most powerful performances, recorded at the very peak of her powers, before the upper register acquired its distracting wobble. Balance of soloists is close, and the chorus could hardly be dimmer, but as a perfect re-creation of a classic, irreplaceable recording this is one of the jewels of the CD catalogue. This must not of course be confused with the later stereo recording which Callas made, also with Serafin; for not only is Callas in much fresher, firmer voice with electric intensity in every phrase, the casting of the veteran, Ebe Stignani, as Adalgisa gives Callas a worthily characterful partner in the sisters' duets. Filippeschi is disappointing by comparison, thin-toned and at times strained, and Rossi-Lemeni is not well treated by the microphone either.

La Sonnambula (complete).

(***) HMV mono **CDS 747378-8 [CDCB 47377]**; EX 290043-3/*5* (2). Callas, Monti, Cossotto, Zaccaria, Ratti, La Scala, Milan, Ch. and O, Votto.

Substantially cut, the Callas version was recorded in mono in 1957, yet it gives a vivid picture of the diva at the peak of her powers. By temperament she may not have related closely to Bellini's heroine, but the village girl's simple devotion through all trials is touchingly caught, most of all in the recitatives. The recording has transferred remarkably well to CD. There is a fair amount of atmosphere, and both orchestra and chorus are well caught. Nicola Monti makes a strong rather than a subtle contribution but blends well with Callas in the duets; and Fiorenza Cossotto is a good Teresa. Callas admirers will find this enjoyable as an overall performance.

Berg, Alban (1885–1935)

Violin concerto.

*** DG **413 725-2**; 2531/*3301* 110 [id.]. Itzhak Perlman, Boston SO, Ozawa – STRAVINSKY: *Concerto.****

*** Decca Dig. **411 804-2**; 411 804-1/*4* [id.]. Kyung Wha Chung, Chicago SO, Solti – BARTÓK: *Concerto.*

Violin concerto; 3 Orchestral pieces, Op. 6.

Ɛ **(*) Ph. **412 523-2**; 412 523-1/*4* [id.]. Gidon Kremer, Bav. RSO, Sir Colin Davis.

As far as the musical public is concerned, Berg has always been seen, rightly or wrongly, as the acceptable face of dodecaphony, the human side of the tone-row, though it is only the *Violin concerto* that has made real inroads into the concert repertory. Even so, it is remarkable that the CD catalogue already offers three different versions of this work.

Perlman's performance is totally commanding. The effortless precision of the playing goes with great warmth of expression, so that the usual impression of 'wrong-note Romanticism' gives way to total purposefulness. The Boston orchestra accompanies superbly and, though the balance favours the soloist, the recording is excellent. It has been convincingly remastered for CD, although the resonance of the Boston acoustic and the backward balance for the orchestra mean that detail is inevitably less sharp than in either the Decca or Philips alternative.

Perlman may be tougher, more purposeful in his performance of the Berg *Concerto*, but he does not excel Chung in tenderness and poetry. Played like this, it makes an excellent coupling for the Bartók on the reverse, another two-movement concerto. Despite the official two-movement layout, the Decca CD thoughtfully provides bands for the two sections in each. The violin is placed well in front of the orchestra, but not aggressively so. The recording is brilliant in the Chicago manner, but more spacious than some from this source.

Kremer's performance of the *Concerto* is more problematic, for it too is often intensely felt and enormously accomplished. However, there is an element of narcissism here, and Kremer often stresses the music's self-pity. The solo posturing at bars 43–57 of the second movement is unappealing and so is the withdrawn, nasal tone of the chorale. Besides providing an admirable accompaniment for the *Concerto*, the Bavarian Radio Orchestra give a fine account of themselves in the Op. 6 *Pieces*, and Sir Colin makes much of their refined textures and powerful atmosphere. This is a really compelling performance. The Philips recording is of altogether remarkable clarity and definition, completely truthful, while in the *Concerto* the balance between violin and orchestra is perfectly judged. In this respect it far surpasses Perlman's. In its combination of clarity, atmosphere and ambient warmth this CD is in the demonstration class, and the chrome cassette too is very successful.

Lieder: Abschied; Am Strande; Erster Verlust; Es klagt; Es wandelt; Ferne Lieder; Grabschritt; Geliebte Schöne; Grenzen der Menschheit; Ich liebe dich; Im Morgengrauen; Regen; Schattenleben; Schlummerlose Nächt; Sehnsucht II & III; Spaziergang; Traurigkeit; Uber den Bergen; Vielgeliebte schöne Frau; Winter; Wo der Goldregen steht.
*** HMV Dig. EL 270195-1. Dietrich Fischer-Dieskau, Aribert Reimann.

Fischer-Dieskau has here recorded for the first time a fascinating series of songs which Berg wrote in his teens and early twenties. Most of them give little indication of the mature style to come. Far from showing adventurous leanings towards atonality, the main influence is more Brahms and Schumann than Wolf; but then, as Berg's studies with Schoenberg progressed, so one begins, in a handful of later songs, to relate the writing to the Berg one knows. Fischer-Dieskau with highly sensitive accompaniment from Reimann makes no apology for even the simplest songs, and uses the sequence to develop a vivid character-study of the young composer. Excellent recording.

Berkeley, Michael (born 1948)

Oboe concerto.
*** Pearl SHE 583 [id.]. Nicholas Daniel, Southern Pro Arte, Marcus Dods – PALLIS: *Nocturne.***

Michael Berkeley's *Oboe concerto* is a work which is at once elegant and warmly expressive. Written in 1977, when the composer was still studying with Richard Rodney Bennett, it is uninhibitedly lyrical with predominantly slow outer movements framing a dashing central scherzo, which itself enfolds a charming waltz for trio. The final *Elegy* was written in memory of Benjamin Britten, Berkeley's godfather, and in its pure beauty conveys warmth as well as sadness. In his first major recording, Daniel gives a richly sympathetic performance full of individuality, and is admirably accompanied. Good, undistracting recording.

The Romance of the rose (Theme and variations); Uprising (Symphony in one movement).
*** Hyp. A 66097 [id.]. Southern Pro Arte, Charles Peebles – LEIGHTON: *Organ concerto.***(*)

Uprising, subtitled *Symphony in one movement*, may have found its inspiration like the oratorio, *Or shall we die?*, in the composer's response to current events, but it emerges in purely musical terms as a strong and dramatic piece largely in Berkeley's extrovert style. The *Theme and variations* show him at his most immediately engaging, writing fun music, warm, lyrical and catchy. Committed playing and fine recording.

(i) *3 Moods for unaccompanied oboe; String quartet; String trio.*
*** Hyp. A 66109 [id.]. (i) Keith Marshall; Amphion Quartet – FINZI: *Interlude* etc.***

Berkeley's *String quartet* in one movement, written in 1981 to commemorate the twenty-fifth anniversary of Gerald Finzi's death, is the most formidable example of his music yet put on record, a tough but immediately attractive piece that is the more sharply dramatic from having been intended not just as absolute music but to accompany a ballet. The *String trio*, written partly as an exercise in economy during a period of study with Richard Rodney Bennett, is tough and intense in a comparable way, the first of the two movements pure and restrained, the following allegro sharp and compact, with a lyrical central section and a slow meditative coda, leading to a brief pay-off. Economy even more obviously marks the oboe pieces, ingeniously varied in expression and mood and, like the string music, beautifully played and recorded here. The Berkeley works on the disc alone span 48 minutes, making the two Finzi items attractive bonuses.

Or shall we die? (oratorio).
*** HMV Dig. EL 270058-1/*4*. Harper, Wildon-Johnson, LSO Ch., LSO, Hickox.

Or shall we die?, Michael Berkeley's oratorio on the pain and problems of a nuclear world, is a flawed work; but few would deny its power or sincerity, splendidly caught in a recording by the original performers. Over his 50-minute span, using a text by the poet Ian McEwan, which relies heavily on resounding aphorisms (profound or sententious, depending on your viewpoint), Berkeley confidently uses an openly eclectic style that communicates immediately to any listener. The pity is that the biggest blemish comes at the very peak of the work, where the Woman's agony as the mother of a nuclear bomb victim is most tenderly brought home, only to be resolved in banality, when doggerel verses are set in pop parody, intended bathos which defeats its own object. Despite the flaws it is a strong, confident and colourful work which it is good to have on record, where the detailed message of the words can be more readily appreciated than in live performance. The recording is first rate, and there is an excellent cassette.

Berlioz, Hector (1803–69)

Harold in Italy, Op. 16.
** Sup. **C37 7244** [id.]. Lubomír Malý, Czech PO, Jílek.

(i) *Harold in Italy, Op. 16; Overture: Le Carnaval romain, Op. 9.*
*** DG Dig. **415 109-2**; 415 109-1/*4* [id.]. (i) Christ, BPO, Maazel.

Maazel's *Harold* was recorded at a public performance at the Philharmonie, Berlin, in April 1984 and is the first new recording of Berlioz's masterpiece to appear since the late 1970s. It is undoubtedly very fine; the structure is well held together, and there is a well-paced sense of forward movement in all four movements and no lack of poetic feeling. Maazel secures a nicely judged internal balance, there is some imaginative phrasing and he invariably finds the 'tempo giusto'. Wolfram Christ is an eloquent and dignified protagonist. There is no want of magic in the *March of the Pilgrims* where the delicacy of Berlioz's textures is fully realized. In the *Orgy of the brigands*, too, there is plenty of excitement. The recording is well balanced, with the wind laid well back and good perspective between the various orchestral sections. Maazel's fill-up deserves special mention: in his hands the overture, *Le Carnaval romain*, has exhilaration and momentum, as well as an infectious sparkle. The DG recording is marvellously clean and vivid. Incidentally, readers preferring the cassette format can be assured that the differences between it and the LP are minimal. But CD offers the usual advantages of the new medium over the old, and CD collectors have no occasion to hesitate, for Maazel does justice to this splendid work.

A warm enjoyable account on Supraphon, very much dominated by Lubomír Malý, a fine violist with a strong instrumental personality. He is balanced well forward, so we can enjoy his richly coloured timbre and supple phrasing. The performance is affectionate rather than electrifying, although it is convincingly paced, and the finale does not lack impetus. Orchestral detail comes through and the studio recording has a pleasing ambience, not overlit. However, the DG version has more character.

Overtures: *Béatrice et Bénédict; Le Carnaval romain, Op. 9; Le Corsaire, Op. 21; Rob Roy; Le Roi Lear, Op. 4.*
(*) Chan. Dig. **CHAN 8316; ABRD/*ABTD* 1067. SNO, Gibson.

Rob Roy is the rarity of Sir Alexander Gibson's Berlioz collection. It adds an aptly Scottish tinge to the record, even when traditional melodies – *Scots wha hae* at the opening – are given distinctly Berliozian twists. It is if anything even wilder than the other pieces, and with its anticipations of *Harold in Italy* finds Gibson and the SNO at their most dashingly committed. *King Lear*, another rarity, also comes out most dramatically, and though *Béatrice et Bénédict* is not quite so polished, the playing is generally excellent. With first-rate digital recording, outstanding on CD, this can be generally recommended. The chrome tape is strikingly vivid but lacks something in the middle range.

Romance, rêverie et caprice, Op. 8.
*** DG Dig. **400 032-2**; 2532/*3302* 011 [id.]. Perlman, O de Paris, Barenboim – LALO: *Symphonie espagnole.****

Berlioz's short concertante work for violin and orchestra uses material originally intended for *Benvenuto Cellini*. Perlman's ripely romantic approach to the *Rêverie* brings out the individuality of the melody, and with a sympathetic accompaniment from Barenboim the work as a whole is given considerable substance. First-rate digital recording, with disc and cassette closely matched. The sound on the compact disc is very similar to the standard LP, with the additional advantage of background silence.

Symphonie fantastique, Op. 14.
*** Ph. **411 425-2** [id.]. Concg. O, Sir Colin Davis.
(*) HMV Dig. **CDC 747278-2 [id.]; EL 270235-1/*4* [Ang. DS/*4DS* 38210]. Phd. O, Muti.
(*) DG **415 325-2; 2530 597/*3300 498* [id.]. BPO, Karajan.
(*) DG Dig. **410 895-2; 410 895-1/*4* [id.]. Chicago SO, Abbado.
(*) Decca Dig. **414 203-2; 414 203-1/*4* [id.]. Montreal SO, Dutoit.
(*) Erato Dig. **ECD 88028; NUM/*MCE* 75106 [id.]. O Nat. de France, Conlon.
** Telarc Dig. **CD 80076**; DG 10076 [id.]. Cleveland O, Maazel.
** Decca Dig. **400 046-2**; SXDL/*KSXDC* 7512 [Lon. LDR/*5*- 10013]. NYPO, Mehta.
*(*) Lodia **LO-CD 777** [id.]. LSO, Païta.
*(*) Sup. Dig. **C37 7722** [id.]. Czech PO, Košler.
* CBS Dig. **MK 39859**; IM/*IMT* 39859 [id.]. BPO, Barenboim.
* CBS **76652 [MK 35867**]. Cleveland O, Maazel.
* HMV **CDC 747372-2** [id.]. O de Paris, Munch.

Sir Colin Davis chose the *Symphonie fantastique* for his first recording with the Concertgebouw Orchestra, and the CD transfer of the 1974 analogue master is very impressive. There is a very striking improvement in the firmness of focus and detail is clearer – much more so than in the Abbado/Chicago digital version. If this does not quite match the finest rivals in brilliance and definition, the overall balance is very satisfying and believable, while the authority of the reading itself is paramount. The interpretation is very similar to Sir Colin's earlier account with the LSO, except that the Concertgebouw performance has more life and colour. The slow movement is more atmospheric than before and superbly played, and with CD the crude side-break of the original LP format is eliminated. The final two movements are very exciting, with a fine rhythmic spring given to the *March to the scaffold*, and the finale gripping to the last bar.

The balance of fierceness against romantic warmth in Muti's own personality works particularly well in this symphony, so that he holds the thread of argument together firmly without ever underplaying excitement. The sound is among the best which Muti has had in Philadelphia – full in range, if not always ideally clear in texture – but cannot equal Dutoit on Decca in realism or fidelity of balance. There is a good, though not outstandingly refined, XDR tape.

Karajan's reading is highly individual in its control of tempo in the first movement, but the Berlin Philharmonic are fully equal to his quixotic pacing, and the effect is certainly compelling. In the slow movement, the intensity of pianissimo playing is enhanced by the beautiful orchestral sound; this analogue recording from 1975 has a much more attractive ambience than many of Karajan's later digital records. The Waltz has characteristic panache and the spacious yet immensely dramatic finale sends the adrenalin racing. Here the recording is very vivid throughout and it brings out every nuance of the Berlin orchestra's subtle tone-colours. Unlike Sir Colin Davis, however, Karajan does not observe the first-movement repeat, and there is no doubt that Davis's structural control and overall pacing are more convincing.

Abbado brings the right dreamy atmosphere and feverish intensity to this score and the playing of the Chicago Symphony Orchestra has all the polish and finesse one could expect. There is much poetic feeling and the slow movement is outstandingly fine. There are two special points of interest: first, Abbado observes the exposition repeat in the first movement (also in the *March to the scaffold*); secondly, he, like Davis, incorporates the cornet part, which Klemperer was the first to include in his Philharmonia version. The DG recording is rich in texture but the balance is less than ideal (notably so in the oboe solo at fig. 16 in the first movement and at the opening of the *March*). The effect is recessed and while the background silence of the CD allows the magical pianissimo playing in the slow movement to register effectively, the resonance sometimes clouds finer points of detail.

The spectacular wide-ranging recorded sound is the first point to note with the Dutoit version, the fullest yet on CD, with excellent detail and a rich ambience, too. The performance is more controversial, if only because Dutoit tends to prefer speeds slower than usual, and in direct comparison that sometimes makes him seem less exciting than his finest rivals. Yet by keeping the pulse steady, he adds to structural strength while never limiting expressive warmth in lyrical passages or the crisp lifting of rhythm in allegros. Though the final *Dies irae* passage of the finale may seem rather stolid next to a faster, more frenetic reading, the power is most impressive. On the chrome cassette – a state-of-the-art Decca transfer – the recording quality is outstandingly fine, strikingly vivid, but with a glowing bloom on the overall sound-picture.

James Conlon is convincingly volatile in the first movement, and his reading has a fine sense of spontaneity. The Waltz is engagingly *galant*, yet the element of neurosis is present and rises to the surface in a dazzlingly effective accelerando at its close. The slow movement brings beautifully serene playing from the strings, with textures radiant. The *March to the scaffold* has a jaunty air, and the exuberant finale is less overtly satanic than in some hands. The fairly close balance gives more detail and projection than with Abbado, but the overall effect lacks the ambient beauty of the Decca recording. Even so, this is a very enjoyable account, impetuously sensitive to the work's charismatic mood changes.

The Telarc record is the second of two which Maazel recorded with the Cleveland Orchestra within two years – and much the better. The first, from CBS, has coarse, heavyweight sound, which goes with a performance that lacks finesse, the opposite of volatile. For Telarc, the sound is far more refined, and the performance is more naturally expressive in a spontaneous-sounding way, without losing anything in precision of ensemble. Even so, this rather plain account cannot quite compete with the finest rivals.

Mehta's reading is fresh and direct but not specially illuminating. The disc's chief claim to attention lies in the digital recording (Decca's first with this orchestra), which is wide-ranging and atmospheric. The compact disc was outstanding among early issues of the work. The clarity and transparency of detail are very striking indeed and the *March to the scaffold* has demonstration potential. However, the performance overall is stronger on extrovert brilliance than on poetic feeling and it has little sense of fantasy.

Païta draws some exciting playing from the LSO, but he whips up the frenzy of the work, its hysterical element, to undermine any sense of structure. The recording is bright and immediate but brings some odd balances, with the 'laughing' bassoon in the *March to the scaffold*, for example, presented almost as a concerto soloist.

On Supraphon, the Czech Philharmonic play beautifully – the cor anglais solo in the slow movement is particularly fine. The recording too is faithful and well balanced, if acoustically a little dry. Throughout, however, the voltage of the music making is too low for such a temperamental work, and in the *March to the scaffold* Košler is slow and deliberate to the point of being square.

Barenboim's Berlin version is disappointing, not helped by washy, ill-focused recording. In interpretation, his heavily expressive manner is little different from his earlier reading with the Paris Orchestra for DG. The Berlin solo playing is often very fine (the first oboe particularly so), but the result too often sounds self-conscious and mannered, lacking bite.

Charles Munch, France's top conductor at the time, made his first recording in 1967 with the then newly formed premier orchestra of Paris, and the result was a total disappointment, both as a performance and in sound. It did not deserve to be resurrected on CD.

Symphonie fantastique; Le Carnaval romain: overture; La Damnation de Faust: excerpts; *Romeo and Juliet*: Love scene.
(B) *(*) DG Walkman *413 847-4* [id.]. O de Paris, Barenboim.

(i) *Symphonie fantastique*; (ii) *Le Corsaire: overture; La Damnation de Faust: Danse de follets. Les Troyens: Trojan march*; (iii) *Royal hunt and storm*.
(B) *** EMI *TCC2-POR 290115-9*. (i) French Nat. RO; (ii) RPO; (iii) with Beecham Choral Society, Beecham.

Beecham's account still enjoys classic status, though it dates from 1961. The sound is amazingly fresh and vivid, while the performance has a demonic intensity that is immediately compelling. Gounod wrote that 'with Berlioz, all impressions, all sensations – whether joyful or sad – are expressed in extremes to the point of delirium', and Beecham brought to this score all the fire and temperament, all the magic and affection in his armoury. He drew from the French National Radio Orchestra playing of great rhythmic subtlety. The present reissue in EMI's 'Portrait of the Artist' series also includes other outstanding Beecham recordings, notably the *Royal hunt and storm*, which sound uniquely atmospheric in his hands. All the recordings come up well on this double-length tape which is an unquestionable bargain.

Barenboim's comparable Walkman cassette is much less attractive. Although it has the advantage of modern sound and excellent chrome transfers, his reading of the *Symphonie fantastique* is disappointing, with the first movement hectic and erratic. Only in the *March to the scaffold* and the finale does the performance suddenly acquire the necessary sharpness of focus. The other pieces included are much more successful, but the Beecham tape is overall a greatly superior investment.

La Damnation de Faust, Op. 24.
(M) *** DG 413 197-1/*4* [id.]. Mathis, Burrows, McIntyre, Paul, Tanglewood Fest. Ch., Boston Boys' Ch. and SO, Ozawa.

La Damnation de Faust: highlights.
(*) Decca Dig. **410 181-2 [id.]. Von Stade, Riegel, Van Dam, King, Chicago SO, Solti.

Ozawa's 1975 complete set is one of this conductor's most successful recordings, although the moulded style of his direction is very different from Solti's extrovert sense of drama. The relative softness of focus is underlined by the reverberant Boston acoustic which casts a glowing aura over superb orchestral playing and generally fine singing, the results seductively beautiful. Both on disc and on tape, this mid-priced reissue is highly successful.

Starting with the *Hungarian march* in spectacular wide-ranging sound, Solti's CD of highlights may give only a limited idea of the complete work, but the selection is intelligently made and there are warmly expressive moments, too. Certainly the recording on CD is immediate and vivid.

(i) *La Mort de Cléopâtre*; (ii) *Les Nuits d'été, Op. 7* (see also below).
*** DG Dig. **410 966-2**; 2532/*3302* 047 [id.]. (i) Jessye Norman, (ii) Kiri Te Kanawa, O de Paris, Barenboim.

The coupling of Jessye Norman in the scena and Dame Kiri Te Kanawa in the song-cycle makes for one of the most ravishing of Berlioz records with each singer at her very finest. Norman has natural nobility and command as the Egyptian queen in this dramatic scena while Te Kanawa compasses the challenge of different moods and register in *Les Nuits d'été* more completely and affectingly than any singer on record in recent years, more so than Norman in her beautiful but rather bland recording with Davis. Excellent DG recording for Barenboim and first-rate playing from the Paris Orchestra. The CD adds to the sense of presence and realism of both singers, intensifying the warmth and compulsion of the performances. There is also a good chrome tape, though the chosen transfer level brings a degree of background hiss.

Les Nuits d'été (song cycle), *Op. 7* (see also above).

(*) Ph. **412 493-2; 9500 783/*7300 857* [id.]. Jessye Norman, LSO, Sir Colin Davis – RAVEL: *Shéhérazade.***(*)

** Telarc Dig. **CD 80084** [id.]. Elly Ameling, Atlanta SO, Shaw – FAURÉ: *Pelléas et Mélisande.***

*(*) Decca Dig. **411 895-2**; 411 895-1/*4* [id.]. Hildegard Behrens, VSO, Travis – RAVEL: *Shéhérazade.***

*(*) CBS Dig. IM/*IMT* 39098 [id.]. Frederica von Stade, Boston SO, Ozawa – DEBUSSY: *La damoiselle élue.**(*)

Jessye Norman is in fine voice here but does not get fully inside this most magical of orchestral song-cycles. There is no lack of voluptuousness, but the word meanings are less subtly registered than in the finest rival versions. Davis's tempi too are sometimes over-deliberate. The CD transfer of a 1979 analogue recording has been well done, with extra presence of voice and orchestra, but cannot match the finest.

Very realistically recorded in a relatively intimate acoustic, Elly Ameling's version concentrates on pure beauty. Emotionally the performance is restrained, cautious even, with crisp, calculated, rather reticent playing from the orchestra.

Behrens has too uncomfortably cumbersome a voice for the opening *Villanelle*, and though the weight is apter for later songs this is a disappointing coupling for a warmly convincing account of the Ravel on the reverse. The Decca recording is outstandingly vivid, with lustrous orchestral detail, especially on the CD. The cassette too is in the demonstration class.

Frederica von Stade, always intelligent and naturally musical, yet sounds less spontaneous than usual in a disappointing version, not helped by Ozawa's cool and uninvolved accompaniment. Good recording.

Requiem mass (*Grande messe des morts*), *Op. 5.*

** Telarc Dig. **CD 80109**; DG 80109 (2) [id.]. Aler, Atlanta Symphony Ch. and SO, Robert Shaw – BOITO: *Mefistofele: Prologue*; VERDI: *Te Deum.***

(M) ** DG 413 523-1/*4* [id.]. Schreier, Bav. R. Ch. and SO, Munch.

(M) *(*) Decca Jub. 410 267-1/*4* [id.]. Riegel, Cleveland Ch. and O, Maazel.

(i) *Requiem mass*: (ii) *Symphonie funèbre et triomphale, Op. 15.*

(*) Ph. **416 283-2 (2) [id.]. (i) Dowd, Wandsworth School Boys' Ch., LSO Ch.; (ii) John Alldis Ch.; LSO, Sir Colin Davis.

Sir Colin Davis's recordings of the *Requiem* and the *Symphonie funèbre* both date back to 1970, so the CD coupling is logical and quite generous. For the recording of the *Requiem* Philips went to Westminster Cathedral, which should have been atmospheric enough, but then the engineers managed to produce a sound which minimizes the massiveness of forces in anything but the loudest fortissimos, thanks to the closeness of the microphones. In many passages one can hear individual voices in the choir. Once that is said, the performance is impressive, if not ideally expansive. In the *Rex tremendae* for example, Davis's clean taut account is less than tremendous, while the *Lacrymosa* is precise – even angular – in its precision. The large-scale brass sound is formidably caught and the choral fortissimos are glorious, helped by the fresh cutting edge of the Wandsworth School Boys' Choir. It was Davis's idea, not Berlioz's, to have boys included, but it is entirely in character. The LSO provides finely incisive accompaniment, and there is no doubt that the CD remastering has added to the overall impact and tangibility, in spite of the balance.

The *Symphonie funèbre et triomphale* is a fascinating product of Berlioz's eccentric genius, designed as it was to be performed not just in the open air but on the march. The *Funeral march* itself provides the most haunting music, but it needs more persuasive handling than Sir Colin's if it is not to outstay its welcome. The apotheosis too can be made to sound more effective than this.

Robert Shaw directs a fresh and straightforward reading of Berlioz's monumental score with attractively clean and well-disciplined choral singing. The Telarc recording, though not ideally clear in the massive fortissimos which bring some clouding, has a better sense of presence on instruments than on voices, with the massive forces contained in a pleasant but not at all ample acoustic. Male voices in the choir lack bite in exposed passages. More seriously, what the performance lacks is grandeur and a sense of occasion, such as is found on earlier recordings by Davis, Bernstein or Previn. So the *Tuba mirum* lacks weight and dramatic bite, for all the power of fortissimo; fresh and bright though the choral sound is in *Rex tremendae*, with strands well defined, the impression is not powerful enough. John Aler makes an excellent tenor soloist in the *Sanctus*, but the following *Hosanna* is pedestrian. The CD version was the first to arrive in the catalogue and brings exceptionally generous makeweights in the substantial Verdi and Boito items.

Munch recorded the *Requiem* twice in stereo, first for RCA (currently out of the catalogue) and then for DG. In many ways this second attempt is less successful than the first, for the playing of the Bavarian Radio Symphony Orchestra does not match that of the Boston orchestra on RCA; though the Bavarian Radio Chorus sing with professional precision, the result is not massive enough. The recording quality, although cleaner and more precise than the earlier American one, has less atmosphere. However, at medium price this is a fair recommendation. The chrome cassettes handle the *Tuba mirum* without problems but do not match the Decca tapes of the Maazel set.

Maazel's version has clean Decca recording, but the result is strangely unatmospheric, with the choir set at a distance. The performance too is uninvolving and, at times, prosaic. The cassette transfer shows Decca's engineering at its most impressive; the *Tuba mirum* with its spectacular brass is specially effective.

Still recommended: Previn's version of Berlioz's great choral work remains the finest so far put on disc and tape, and no doubt this will appear on CD in due course (HMV SLS/*TCC-SLS* 5209).

Te Deum, Op. 22.
*** DG Dig. **410 696-2**; 2532/*3302* 044 [id.]. Araiza, LSO Ch., LPO Ch., Woburn Singers, Boys' Ch., European Community Youth O, Abbado.

The newest DG recording from Abbado is very impressive. The sound is wide-ranging with striking dynamic contrasts and a much greater sense of presence than its predecessors. Artistically, too, it is of considerable merit: Abbado brings great tonal refinement and dignity to this performance, and the spacious sound helps. Francisco Araiza is altogether first class and has eloquence as well as tonal beauty to commend him. The choirs are responsive as are the young players Abbado has assembled, and there is no need for readers to hold back. Memories of Beecham in mono and Colin Davis on the Philips label are not banished, however; Sir Colin has a natural feeling for the pace of this work and his reading is perhaps the more moving. In some respects Abbado's version is superior (certainly as far as the soloist is concerned) and collectors acquiring it are unlikely to be disappointed. On compact disc the quality is very impressive, bringing extra gain in definition and spatial feeling. In its cassette format, the wide dynamic range poses some problems and the copies we sampled had varying quality between the two sides.

Les Troyens à Carthage: ballet music.
** Decca Dig. **411 898-2**; 411 898-1/*4* [id.]. Nat. PO, Bonynge – LECOCQ: *Mam'zelle Angot;* WEBER: *Invitation to the dance.****

Berlioz's ballet music sounds insubstantial heard away from its source. Although it has characteristic fingerprints it does not show its composer at his finest. It is very well played here and the brightly lit recording is vivid, marginally more so on CD than on LP. The cassette is first class, too.

Bernstein, Leonard (born 1918)

Candide: overture.
*** DG Dig. **413 324-2**; 2532/*3302* 083 [id.]. LAPO, Bernstein – BARBER: *Adagio;* COPLAND: *Appalachian spring;* SCHUMAN: *American festival overture.****

Candide: overture; Fancy free (ballet): excerpts; *West Side story: Symphonic dances.*
(M) *(*) Decca Viva 414 382-1/*4*. RPO, Eric Rogers – GROFÉ: *Grand Canyon suite.***

Bernstein's *Candide overture* is one of the most dazzlingly brilliant of the century, and the composer directs it in this live recording with tremendous flair, his speed a fraction slower than in his New York studio recording for CBS. One item in an outstanding collection of American music, brilliantly recorded in all formats.

On the generously full Decca Viva issue Eric Rogers directs his performances with gusto and obvious enjoyment. He understands the idiom, but he is never subtle, and the (ex-Phase 4) recording though extremely vivid is very close, which allows only a relatively restricted range of dynamic. The music is all spirited (especially the overture), but cannot compare with the composer's own performances. Tape and disc sound much the same.

Divertimento for orchestra; (i) *Halil* (*Nocturne*); (ii) *3 Meditations from Mass; On the Town* (*3 dance episodes*).
(*) DG **415 966-2 [id.]. (i) Rampal; (ii) Rostropovich; Israel PO, Bernstein.

This compact disc has been compiled from two separate LPs of shorter works. At just under an hour of music, the measure is generous enough, but the selection could easily have included one or more other pieces. Early Bernstein is well represented in the colourful and vigorous dances from *On the Town*, one of the most memorable of all musical films, while the other three works show the later Bernstein sharply sparked off by specific commissions. The *Divertimento* in its eight brief movements was intended as a tribute to the Boston Symphony Orchestra on its Centenary, easily and cheekily moving from one idiom to another. It is often jokey, but amiably so. The two concertante pieces, *Halil* for flute and strings and the *Meditations* for cello and orchestra, both beautifully reflect the individual poetry of the two artists for whom they were written and who perform masterfully here. The aggressive digital sound of the original recording bites even more on CD, with a brilliant top and spectacular bass leaving the middle light. With Bernstein, such sound does little harm.

Symphonies Nos 1 (*Jeremiah*); (ii) *2* (*The age of anxiety*) for piano and orchestra.
*** **DG 415 964-2** [id.]. Israel PO, Bernstein; (i) with Lukas Foss.

Bernstein's musical invention is always memorable, if at times a little too facile to match the ambitiousness of his symphonic aim; but the compelling confidence of his writing speaks of a genius stretching himself to the limit. The *Jeremiah symphony* dates from Bernstein's early twenties and ends with a moving passage from Lamentations for the mezzo soloist. As its title suggests, the *Second Symphony* was inspired by the poem of W. H. Auden, with the various movements directly reflecting dramatic passages from it, though no words are set in this work for orchestra alone. These performances with the Israel Philharmonic are not always quite as polished or forceful as those Bernstein recorded earlier in New York, but with excellent recording they never fail to reflect the warmth of Bernstein's writing. In No. 2 the concertante piano part is admirably played by Lukas Foss, and in both works the remastering for CD has brought vivid sound, clear and well balanced.

Piano music: *2 Anniversaries; 4 Anniversaries; 5 Anniversaries; 7 Anniversaries; Moby dyptich; Song without words; Touches;* Arr. of COPLAND: *El salón México*.
** Pro Arte **CCD 109**; PAD/*PCD* 140. James Tocco.

James Tocco won the 1973 Munich Piano Competition and has made a reputation for himself as an exponent of modern American music. This record collects Bernstein's complete output for piano, together with his transcription for one piano of Copland's *El salón México* on to one disc. Apart from the *Seven Anniversaries*, a beautiful set of pieces which Bernstein himself recorded for RCA, these are all new to the catalogue. Nearly all these miniatures are of high quality and are very sensitively played by James Tocco. Bernstein has used some of the material elsewhere in his output: the *Five Anniversaries*, for example, found their way into the *Serenade for violin, strings and percussion*. Unfortunately the recording does not do him justice: the instrument sounds imperfectly tuned and the acoustic in which it is recorded is too small. Nevertheless, in the absence of any rival, this must carry a cautious recommendation.

(i) *Songfest* (cycle of American poems); (ii) *Chichester Psalms*.
*** DG **415 965-2** [id.]. (i) Dale, Elias, Williams, Rosenshein, Reardon, Gramm, Nat. SO of Washington; (ii) Soloist from V. Boys' Ch., V. Jeunesse Ch., Israel PO; composer.

Songfest, one of Bernstein's most richly varied works, is a sequence of poems which ingeniously uses all six singers solo and in various combinations. Not only the plan but the writing too is ingenious, one song using strict serialism in the most approachable, idiomatically American way. Characteristically, Bernstein often chooses controversial words to set, and by his personal fervour welds a very disparate group of pieces together into a warmly satisfying whole, comparable with Britten's *Serenade*, *Nocturne* or *Spring symphony*. The coupling with the *Chichester Psalms* is new for CD. The latter was recorded live in 1977. One might have slight reservations over the treble soloist from the Vienna Boys' Choir, but otherwise the performance is first class, with the music's warmth and vigour compellingly projected. This makes a fine pairing with the near-definitive account of the *Songfest* which is superbly sung by all the participating artists. CD adds to the feeling of immediacy in both works.

Songs: La bonne cuisine (French and English versions); *I hate music* (cycle); *2 Love songs; Piccola serenata; Silhouette; So pretty; Mass: A simple song; I go on. Candide: It must be so; Candide's lament. 1600 Pennsylvania Ave: Take care of this house. Peter Pan: My house; Peter Pan; Who am I; Never-land.*
*** Etcetera Dig. ETC 1037 [id.]. Roberta Alexander, Tan Crone.

Trivial as most of these songs are – no fewer than 27 of them – they make a delightful collection, consistently bearing witness to Bernstein's flair for a snappy idea as well as his tunefulness. There is a charming artlessness about the four songs he wrote for a 1950 production of *Peter Pan* with Jean Arthur and Boris Karloff; even earlier is the cycle of five *Kid songs*, *I hate music*, first performed by Jennie Tourel in 1943. It is good to have the haunting number from the unsuccessful, bicentennial musical, *1600 Pennsylvania Avenue*, not to mention the two songs from the brilliant Voltaire-based *Candide*. Roberta Alexander's rich, warm voice and winning personality are well supported by Tan Crone at the piano.

West Side story: complete recording; *On the Waterfront* (symphonic suite).
❀ ℂ *** DG Dig. **415 253-2** (2). [id.]. Te Kanawa, Carreras, Troyanos, Horne, Ollman, Ch. and O, composer.

West Side story (only).
*** DG Dig. 415 253-1/*4* (2) [id.]. as above, cond. composer.

Bernstein's recording of the complete score of his most popular work – the first time he had ever conducted the complete musical himself – takes a frankly operatic approach in its casting, but the result is highly successful, for the great vocal melodies are worthy of voices of the highest calibre. Dame Kiri Te Kanawa may not be a soprano who would ever be cast as Maria on stage, but even in the kittenish number, *I feel pretty*, the magnificence of the voice adds a dimension, when the girlishly coy lines of each stanza, sparklingly done, explode with vitality for the pay-off phrase. José Carreras, the only Spanish-speaking member of the cast, but ironically the one in the story who has to be a real American guy, may be apparently miscast, but the beauty of such songs as *Maria* or *Tonight*, or even a sharp number like *Something's coming*, with floated pianissimos and subtly graded crescendos, has one admiring the score the more. Tatiana Troyanos, herself brought up on the West Side, spans the stylistic dichotomy to perfection in a superb portrayal of Anita, switching readily from full operatic beauty to a New York snarl and back, and Kurt Ollmann as Riff equally finds a nice balance between the styles of opera and the musical.

The clever production makes the best of both musical worlds, with Bernstein's son and daughter speaking the dialogue most affectingly. If patently more mature voices take over when the music begins, one readily adjusts when the singing itself so gloriously captures the spirit of the piece. The Balcony scene, which continually mixes dialogue and singing, is one of the highlights of the set, the touching first tryst of the lovers, set against the backcloth of the New York brownstones, where the fire-escape takes the place of the balcony.

Anyone who saw the extended television programme on the making of the recording will have realized that this was an extraordinary occasion, with all the participants deeply involved, and the composer electrifyingly re-creating his score from the rostrum. He conducts a superb instrumental group of musicians 'from on and off Broadway', and they are recorded with a bite and immediacy that is captivating, whether in the warm, sentimental songs or, above all, in the fizzing syncopated numbers, sounding even more original when precisely played and balanced as here.

The story is told of a principal viola player, a colleague from Bernstein's years as maestro of the New York Philharmonic, ringing up the composer to ask if he could be found a place for the sessions. 'Not possible,' was the reply, 'I had no room for violas in the theatre pit, so there are none in the score.' The musician chose to join the desks of second fiddles instead.

On CD, the power of the music is greatly enhanced by the spectacularly wide dynamic range of the recording (the chrome cassettes are more restricted and, though they sound well, there is much less bite). With a relatively dry acoustic keeping the sound-picture within an apt scale without losing bloom, the two humorous ensembles, *America* for girls, and *Gee Officer Krupke* for the boys, are given tremendous vitality and projection, with the chorus (and the exuberant orchestral percussion) adding colour most winningly. On CD only, the two-disc set includes, besides the musical, the vivid *Symphonic suite*, which was arranged from Bernstein's film music for the Marlo Brando film, *On the Waterfront*, written about the same period.

West Side story: highlights.
*** DG Dig. **415 963-2**; 415 963-1/*4* [id.] (from above recording cond. composer).

By cutting the dialogue, all the main numbers are included here, presented as vividly as on the complete set, and with just over 53′ of music included this is very good value. But the moving *Tonight* loses much without the spoken interchanges between the lovers, although the 'mock marriage' sequence is included in *One hand, one heart*, as is the introductory interchange which sets the scene for *Gee Officer Krupke*. As with the complete set, the cassette has less presence and bite than the LP and does not begin to match the CD.

West Side story: excerpts. *On the Town: Subway ride; Some other time. Mass: A simple song; Pax* (*Communion*).
*(*) CBS Dig. FM/*FMT* 39535 [id.]. Sasson, Hofmann, LAPO, Tilson Thomas.

Prompted by the success of the Bernstein complete set, this CBS anthology is distinctly less attractive. Deborah Sasson's voice has a soubrette quality, and *Tonight* is made to sound cosy in its intimacy, with the limited dialogue much less well handled than in the composer's own version. *One hand, one heart* with its quavery soprano line sounds sugary, and Peter Hofmann extends the sentimentality to his account of *A simple song* from the *Mass*. Michael Tilson Thomas's accompaniments are affectionate but the whole presentation lacks dramatic bite. The sound is good, more lively on disc than on tape.

West Side story: Symphonic dances.
*** DG Dig. **410 025-2**; 2532/*3302* 082 [id.]. LAPO, composer – GERSHWIN: *Rhapsody in blue* etc.**(*)
(B) *** DG Walkman *413 851-4* [id.]. San Francisco SO, Ozawa – GERSHWIN: *American in Paris* etc.***

Bernstein, recorded live, is at his most persuasive conducting a highly idiomatic account of the orchestral confection devised from his most successful musical. It may not be quite so crisp of ensemble as his earlier New York version, but it has more spirit with the players contributing the necessary shouts in the *Mambo* representing a street fight. Vivid if close-up sound, with the compact disc showing no marked difference from the standard LP and tape issues, although the resonance is controlled more cleanly.

Ozawa's performance is highly seductive, with an approach which is both vivid and warm, yet conceals any sentimentality. The sound is very good in this new chrome-tape transfer, and the Gershwin couplings are generous and attractive. A bargain.

Bertrand, Anthoine de (1540–81)

Amours de Ronsard, Book 1: *Amours de Cassandre:* excerpts.
** HM Dig. **HMC 901147** [id.]. Clément Janequin Ens.

Anthoine de Bertrand was born in the Auvergne and died in Toulouse in 1581. His settings of the First Book of Ronsard's *Amours* appeared in 1576, twenty-five years after they had first appeared in print and had come to occupy a dominant position in the history of the French chanson. The interest Bertrand took in chromaticism and enharmonic procedures is known to historians rather than to the non-specialist listener. However, the chansons recorded here by the Clément Janequin Ensemble show him to be, if not a great master, at least a composer of feeling and considerable resource. *Mon Dieu, mon Dieu que ma maistresse est belle* (No. 10 on the CD) is a touching and memorable piece. The fourteen chansons recorded here are interspersed with four short pieces by the French lutenist and composer, Guillaume de Morlaye, active in the 1550s. The performances are excellent throughout, as one would expect from this distinguished group; and Claude Debôves makes out a good case for the rather anonymous Morlaye pieces. Good performances and admirable recording make this a worthwhile (if not, perhaps, indispensable) addition to the catalogue.

Berwald, Franz (1797–1868)

Symphonies Nos 1 in G min. (*Sérieuse*)*; 2 in D* (*Capricieuse*)*; 3 in C* (*Singulière*)*; 4 in E flat.*
*** DG Dig. **415 502-2**; 415 502-1/*4* [id.]. Gothenburg SO, Järvi.

Franz Berwald has neither the range nor the stature of a Sibelius, but he is incontestably the leading Scandinavian symphonist of the first half of the nineteenth century. His first four symphonies receive a distinguished and auspicious CD début. The present set of recordings outclasses the previous Björlin versions on HMV and almost all previous rivals. First, the orchestral playing has abundant spirit and energy: this is music that is wholly in the life-stream of the Gothenburg orchestra; and secondly, the excellent acoustic of the Gothenburg Hall shows the scores to great advantage. Neeme Järvi sets generally brisk tempi, yet the pacing feels right; if the account of the *Capricieuse* seems mercurial, it is exhilarating and fresh. Although this is not the finest of Berwald's symphonies, Järvi almost convinces us that it is. Even if the slow movement is taken too fast its distinctive eloquence is not lost. The same could be said for the *Singulière* – and indeed the others in the set, which are given a similar bracing treatment. The sound, particularly on CD, is altogether superb, with every detail coming through with great clarity, and this can be strongly recommended. The chrome tapes are not quite as wide-ranging at the top as the LPs but are satisfyingly balanced.

Bizet, Georges (1838–75)

L'Arlésienne (incidental music): *suites Nos 1–2; Carmen: suites Nos 1–2.*
** Ph. **412 464-2**; 9500 566/*7300 715* [id.]. LSO, Marriner.

L'Arlésienne: suites Nos 1–2; Carmen: suite No 1; suite No 2: excerpts.
(B) *** DG Walkman *413 422-4* [id.]. LSO, Abbado (with CHABRIER: *España*; DUKAS: *L'apprenti sorcier*; RIMSKY-KORSAKOV: *Capriccio espagnol***(*)).

L'Arlésienne: suites Nos 1 and 2. Carmen: extended suite.
* HMV Dig. **CDC 747064-2** [id.]; EL 270024-1/*4* [Ang. DS/*4DS* 38096]. O Nat. de France, Ozawa.

L'Arlésienne: suites Nos 1 and 2: Carmen: suite No 1.
(*) DG Dig. **415 106-2; 415 106-1/*4* [id.]. BPO, Karajan.

Carmen: suites Nos 1–2.
(*) Telarc Dig. **CD 80048; DG 10048 [id.]. St Louis SO, Slatkin – GRIEG: *Peer Gynt.***(*).

Carmen: suite No 1.
(M) **(*) DG Sig. 413 983-1/*4*. BPO, Karajan – OFFENBACH: *Gaîté Parisienne***(*); RAVEL: *Boléro.****

Bizet's delightful incidental music for *L'Arlésienne* is not yet adequately served on CD. None of the available versions is in the class of the Beecham or Stokowski analogue sets, and readers would be well advised to wait and perhaps invest in the bargain-priced Walkman tape of the 1981 Abbado performances. His account of the *Carmen* suite is supplemented with two extra items, well played by the Hague Philharmonic Orchestra under Willem van Otterloo. The other highlight of this tape is Lorin Maazel's famous 1960 recording of Rimsky-Korsakov's *Capriccio espagnol*, lustrously played by the Berlin Philharmonic Orchestra in sparkling form, and there are also lively accounts of *L'apprenti sorcier* (Fiedler and the Boston Pops) and Chabrier's *España*, in a spirited performance by the Warsaw Philharmonic Orchestra under Jerzy Semkow. Among recent couplings of *L'Arlésienne* and *Carmen*, Abbado's recording undoubtedly stands out. The orchestral playing is characteristically refined, the wind solos cultured and eloquent, especially in *L'Arlésienne*, where the pacing of the music is nicely judged. A vibrant accelerando at the end of the *Farandole* only serves to emphasize the obvious spontaneity of the music making. There is warmth too, of course, and in the opening *Prélude* of the *Carmen suite* plenty of spirit. With vivid and truthful recording, this is very attractive if the couplings are suitable, for the tape transfers are well managed.

The Berlin Philharmonic Orchestra is superbly recorded on Karajan's CD (there is a demonstration-worthy chrome tape, too) and the orchestral playing combines polish with undoubted flair. The recording has the widest possible dynamic range, but the effect seems rather inflated in the tuttis. Tempi are not always ideally apt (notably the *Pastorale* and *Intermezzo* from the second suite) and Karajan sounds too languid at times. The *Carmen* suite, taken from his complete opera recording of 1983, is vividly played throughout. There is no doubt that this record makes a spectacular impact in its CD format, but one's reservations remain. Karajan's earlier recording of the *Carmen* suite is also available on a Signature reissue, interestingly recoupled, but which, like the later digital version, ends somewhat inconclusively with the Act IV Entr'acte. The sound is very good.

Marriner's collection is exceptionally generous, offering eleven items from *Carmen* and both *L'Arlésienne suites*, missing out only the *Intermezzo* from the second. The recording too is attractively rich and naturally balanced. But the musical characterization – in spite of fine LSO solo playing, notably from the flautist, Peter Lloyd – is sometimes lacking in flair and indeed brio. There are minor touches of eccentricity – Marriner's tempo suddenly quickens for the middle section of the *Minuet* from the *Second L'Arlésienne suite*, and although there is much to ravish the ear, the orchestration of the vocal numbers from *Carmen* is not always convincing. The digital remastering of the 1979 analogue recording is well done, but this cannot compare in vividness with Karajan's CD, nor in its sense of spectacle with Slatkin's Telarc disc.

Ozawa's collection does not compete. The performances sound too much like a rehearsal and refuse to spring to life. The direction is totally lacking in flair. The recording is good, but this cannot be recommended even with the extra vividness of CD.

The Telarc digital recordings of the *Carmen* orchestral suites made in St Louis have a self-conscious glittering brilliance. But there is a natural perspective, and the orchestral colour is very telling, helped by good playing, if with no special sophistication. Audiophiles will undoubtedly respond to the range and vividness of the sound: the only snag is that the bass drum is over-recorded and on LP muddies the texture at one or two climaxes. On CD this is less of a problem, although the drum-balance remains over-prominent.

PIANO MUSIC

2 Caprices; Les chants du Rhin; La chasse fantastique; 3 Esquisses musicales; Magasin des familles; Marine; Nocturnes Nos 1 in F; 2 in D; 4 Préludes; Romance

sans paroles; Thème; Variations chromatiques; Waltz in C; Grande valse de concert.
* Chant du Monde **LDC2 78776/7**; LDX 78776/7 [id.]. Par Setrak.

Bizet was a formidable pianist but his output for the instrument is not extensive. As Winton Dean puts it in his study of the composer, it suffers from a double disadvantage: 'it is too clumsy to reward the concert pianist and too difficult for the moderate amateur'. The early pieces (and this two-record set includes three recently discovered juvenilia) derive from the pyrotechnics of Thalberg and Liszt, while the *F major Nocturne* obviously uses Chopin as a model. By far the most interesting pieces are the *Variations chromatiques*, which Glenn Gould recorded, and the *Trois Esquisses musicales*, but neither begins to match the quality of *Jeux d'enfants*. Perhaps they would make a more positive impression, were they in the hands of a more subtle and sensitive player. Setrak is not persuasive nor does his recording enjoy the advantage of a sympathetic acoustic.

OPERA

Carmen (complete).
*** DG Dig. **410 088-2**; 2741/*3382* 025 (3) [id.]. Baltsa, Carreras, Van Dam, Ricciarelli, Barbaux, Paris Op. Ch., Schoneberg Boys' Ch., BPO, Karajan.
(*) Decca **414 489-2 [id.]; D 11 D 3/*K 11 K 33* (3) [Lon. OSA/*5*- 13115]. Troyanos, Domingo, Van Dam, Te Kanawa, Alldis Ch., LPO, Solti.
(M) *** DG 413 279-1/*4* (3/*2*) [id.]. Horne, McCracken, Krause, Maliponte, Manhattan Op. Ch., Metropolitan Op. O, Bernstein.
** Erato Dig. **ECD 880373**; NUM/*MCE* 751133 (3) [id.]. Film soundtrack recording with: Migenes Johnson, Domingo, Raimondi, Esham, Watson, Fr. R. Ch. and Children's Ch., Fr. Nat. O, Maazel.

On CD, Karajan's newest DG set of *Carmen* makes a clear first choice among currently available versions, with the performance combining affection with high tension and high polish. Where in his earlier RCA version he used the old text with added recitatives, here he uses the Oeser edition with its extra passages and spoken dialogue; this may account in part for the differences of approach, more intimate in the presentation of the drama, less extreme over certain controversial tempi. In Carreras he has a Don José, lyrical and generally sweet-toned, who is far from a conventional hero-figure, more the anti-hero, an ordinary man caught up in tragic love. The *Flower song* is exquisitely beautiful in its half-tones. The Micaela of Katia Ricciarelli is similarly scaled down, with the big dramatic voice kept in check. José van Dam – also the Escamillo for Solti – is incisive and virile, the public hero-figure, which leaves Agnes Baltsa as a vividly compelling Carmen, tough and vibrant yet musically precise and commanding. Where on stage (as at Covent Garden) Baltsa tends to exaggerate the characterization, here Karajan encourages her to be positively larger than life but still a believable figure, with tenderness under the surface. In her brief exchanges with Escamillo before the final scene, you are made to believe her love for the bullfighter. As for Karajan, he draws richly resonant playing from the Berlin Philharmonic, sparkling and swaggering in the bullfight music but delicate and poetic too. The digital recording is bright and atmospheric, if not always ideally balanced. The spoken dialogue distractingly sounds like the soundtrack of a French film. The compact discs bring benefit in extra clarity, but also bring out more noticeably the degree of close-up aggressiveness in the recording, with a tendency to bass-lightness. The cassette layout follows the discs. The transfer is refined and truthful, but the upper range is less telling than on LP and the focus is softer than the CD quality.

By the side of the digital Karajan recording, the Solti discs sound less strikingly brilliant than they seemed on first appearance. But this Decca performance, apart from making a satisfactory solution to the vexed question of text, is remarkable for its new illumination of characters whom everyone thinks to know inside out. Tatiana Troyanos is quite simply the subtlest Carmen on record. The blatant sexuality which is so often accepted as the essential ingredient in Carmen's character is here replaced by a far more insidious fascination, for there is a degree of vulnerability in this heroine. You can understand why she falls in love and then out again. Escamillo too is more readily sympathetic, not just the flashy matador who steals the hero's girl, in some ways the custodian of rationality, whereas Don José is revealed as weak rather than just a victim. Troyanos's singing is delicately seductive too, with no hint of vulgarity, while the others make up the most consistent singing cast on record to date. Solti, like Karajan, uses spoken dialogue and a modification of the Oeser edition, deciding in each individual instance whether to accept amendments to Bizet's first thoughts. Fine as other versions are of a much-recorded opera, this dramatic and sensitive account from Solti holds its place among recommended versions, but though the CD transfer brings out the generally excellent balances of the original analogue recording, it exaggerates the bass to make the sound boomy. The voices retain their fine realism and bloom, but orchestral textures are heavier and less clear than they should be, unless controls are adjusted. The cassettes are better balanced, with plenty of immediacy and excellent definition.

Bernstein's 1973 recording – now reissued at mid-price – was made at the New York Metropolitan Opera, the first major opera recording undertaken there for many years. It was based on the Met's spectacular production, with the same cast and conductor as on record, and the sessions plainly gained from being interleaved with live performances. Bizet scholars may argue about details of the text used in the performances: Bernstein adopted the original version of 1875, with spoken dialogue but with variations designed to suit a stage production. Some of his slow tempi will be questioned too, but what really matters is the authentic tingle of dramatic tension which impregnates the whole entertainment. Never before, not even in Beecham's classic set, had the full theatrical flavour of Bizet's score been conveyed, and Marilyn Horne – occasionally coarse in expression – gives a fully satisfying reading of the heroine's role, a great vivid characterization, warts and all. The rest of the cast similarly works to Bernstein's consistent overall plan. The singing is not all perfect, but it is always vigorous and colourful, and so (despite often poor French accents) is the spoken dialogue. The sound is good, but the chrome tapes are less brilliant in the treble than the LPs, though quite acceptable.

The glory of Maazel's Erato version is the Don José of Placido Domingo, freer and more spontaneously expressive than in his two previous recordings, not least in the lovely account of the *Flower song*. Julia Migenes Johnson is a fresh-toned Carmen, often exaggerating detail but presenting a vibrant, sexy character as she does in Francesco Rosi's brilliantly atmospheric film. Ruggero Raimondi sings cleanly and strongly as Escamillo, but Faith Esham is a shrill, thin-toned Micaela, vocally quite out of character. Maazel's conducting is bright and dramatic, if not always tender enough. The recording is clean, well balanced and natural, and very well reproduced on CD, less brilliant than Karajan's DG but arguably the best yet in the new medium. A recommendable set for those who have enjoyed the film.

Carmen: highlights.

*** DG Dig. **413 322-2**; 413 322-1/*4* [id.] (from above recording with Baltsa, Carreras, cond. Karajan).

(*) Erato Dig. **ECD 88041; NUM/*MCE* 75113 [id.]. (from above recording with Migenes Johnson, Domingo, cond. Maazel).

Good representative selections from both sets, with recording to match. The Erato CD will seem, for many, a better way of remembering the film than the complete set. It includes most of the key numbers and the sound is strikingly refined and clear.

La jolie fille de Perth (complete).

*** HMV Dig. EX 270285-3/*9* (3/*2*). Anderson, Kraus, Quilico, Van Dam, Zimmermann, Bacquier, Ch. and New PO of R. France, Prêtre.

Based on Scott's *Fair Maid of Perth*, the plot of Bizet's opera is as improbable as many others of the romantic period, yet it inspired Bizet to one delectable number after another, not just the famous *Serenade* for the tenor hero, Henry Smith. Even that *Serenade* has generally been done in a corrupt version with two parallel verses; in the original score, faithfully reproduced on this fine first recording, the restatement of the melody in the second verse is developed dramatically. Some of the other numbers – not just arias but choruses too, including some of the finest – were either modified or cut entirely. One of the many delights of the piece lies in relating it to Bizet's supreme masterpiece of eight years later. Here, as in *Carmen*, you have a principal gypsy role for mezzo soprano contrasted against a purer-toned soprano heroine; but this time it is the soprano who is the deliberately provocative one, leaving Henry Smith almost as wounded as Don José in *Carmen*. Unlike *Carmen*, however, this piece ends happily, with the crazed heroine delivering a Lucia-like mad song (coloratura delightfully done by June Anderson) before being shocked into sanity for the final curtain. As the hero, Alfredo Kraus sings stylishly – even if at times the voice shows its age. Gino Quilico is superb as the predatory Duke of Rithsay; José van Dam as the apprentice Ralph is aptly lugubrious in his drunken song, and the veteran Gabriel Bacquier makes a delightfully bluff figure of the heroine's father. Margarita Zimmermann (not always well treated by the microphone) as Mab, queen of the gypsies, makes an equivocal role convincing. Georges Prêtre's conducting is warm and understanding, even if ensemble is not always ideally crisp. Pleasingly warm recording to match which sounds most attractive in its tape, as well as its disc, format.

Bliss, Arthur (1891–1975)

Conversations; Madame Now; (i) *Oboe quintet; Rhapsody; Rout; The women of Yueh.*
*** Hyp. A 66137. Gale, Rolfe-Johnson, (i) Hulse, Nash Ens., Lionel Friend.

All the works on this record date from the same decade (1918–27), and all but two (*The Women of Yueh* and the *Oboe quintet*) pre-date the *Colour symphony*. With the exception of the *Quintet* and *Conversations*, part of which was recorded for the old *History of Music in Sound*, this is repertoire new to the catalogue. *Rout* and the *Rhapsody* are strongly Gallic in feeling, much influenced by Ravel, and attractively laid out for the instruments and the wordless voices. *Conversations* is inventive and often witty, and among the best pieces on the record. The *Oboe quintet* is a well-argued, finely sustained work that wears its years lightly. Throughout this interesting programme, the playing is as accomplished as one expects from this ensemble, and the recording quality is altogether excellent. Along with the *Clarinet quintet* and the *Music for strings*, the music recorded here represents Bliss at his best.

Meditations on a theme by John Blow; Music for strings.
**(*) Lyr. SRCS 33. CBSO, Hugo Rignold.

Music for strings, which was written at the same time as another particularly memorable piece by Bliss, the music to the H. G. Wells film *Things to Come*, represents one in the long series of successful works for strings by British composers. It was first heard in Salzburg in 1935. Boult conducted that first performance and though his HMV stereo version with the LPO is at present out of the catalogue, his earlier mono set is still available in a BBC Symphony Orchestra anniversary compilation (PRT BBC 4001 (4)). The performance by the City of Birmingham Symphony Orchestra does not quite match either of the Boult accounts, but Hugo Rignold's interpretation is an expressive one, with a tendency to slower tempi than usual. The result sounds convincing and committed. The *Meditations on a theme of John Blow* was written for the Birmingham orchestra in 1955. It is a series of variations designed to illustrate the different verses of the 23rd Psalm. The result is an amiable but rather rambling piece lasting about 35 minutes.

String quartets Nos 1 in B flat; 2 in F min.
*** Hyp. A 66178 [id.]. Delmé Qt.

Bliss's first essay in the quartet medium comes from 1914 but was suppressed, as indeed was a second, composed in California in 1923. The two quartets he acknowledged were both much later works, No. 1 dating from 1940 and its successor from 1950. They were recorded by the Griller Quartet on Decca not long after their completion, but both sets soon disappeared from circulation. These performances by the Delmé Quartet are not only thoroughly committed but enormously persuasive, and can be recommended even to readers not normally sympathetic to this composer. Both are fine pieces: the *First* is a work of strong character, well proportioned and not dissimilar in quality of inspiration to the *Music for strings*, written a few years earlier. Bliss regarded the *Second* as his finest chamber work, and the Delmé do it justice. The Hyperion recording is first rate.

(i; ii) *Hymn to Apollo*; (iii; iv) *A Prayer to the Infant Jesus*; (i; ii; v) *Rout*; (i; vi; vii) *Serenade*; (iii; iv) *The World is Charged with the Grandeur of God.*
*** Lyr. SRCS 55. (i) LSO; (ii) cond. composer; (iii) Amb. S.; (iv) cond. Ledger; (v) Woodland; (vi) Shirley-Quirk; (vii) cond. Priestman.

Although this is primarily a vocal collection – issued to celebrate the composer's eightieth birthday – it is in fact the orchestral writing that one remembers most vividly. Besides the short orchestral prelude *Hymn to Apollo* (written in 1926), the major work here, the *Serenade*, has two purely orchestral movements out of four. The second, *Idyll*, shows Bliss's lyrical impulse at its most eloquent. The orchestra is almost more important than the voice in *Rout*. One can see why Diaghilev admired this short cantata, for its music has a splendid vigour and spontaneity together with a certain *chic* quality, characteristic of the period during which the great ballet impresario made his reputation. The solo vocal performances throughout the disc are of high quality, and John Shirley-Quirk's swashbuckling account of the gay finale of the *Serenade* must have pleased the composer greatly. In *The World is Charged with the Grandeur of God*, the invention is less memorable, and it is again the orchestration that shows the composer's imagination at work, notably the atmospheric scoring for the flutes in the second section. The recording is first rate.

Bloch, Ernest (1880–1959)

Schelomo: Hebrew rhapsody (for cello and orchestra); *Voice in the wilderness.*
(M) *** Decca Lon. Ent. 414 166-1/*4* [id.]. Starker, Israel PO, Mehta.

This coupling – reissued in the new London Enterprise series – comes from 1970, a vintage period for Decca analogue recording, and the sound is first rate and very well balanced. Now there is a chrome tape, too; that also is extremely vivid, with transparent textures and a wide range. The *Voice in the wilderness*, a symphonic poem with cello obbligato, is diffuse in layout but has its imaginative moments. *Schelomo* is the more disciplined work, arguably Bloch's masterpiece. It is finely played by Starker, and Mehta proves sympathetic in both works, even if the last degree of passionate intensity is missing.

Blomdahl, Karl-Birger (1916–68)

Aniara (complete).
*** Cap. **CAP 22016:1/2**; CAP 2016:1/2 [id.]. Noel, Anderberg, Saeden, Arvidson, Haugan, Swedish R. Ch. and SO, Westerberg.

Karl-Birger Blomdahl was a dominating figure in Sweden during the 1950s and early 1960s; his opera, *Aniara*, was much acclaimed in his native country on its first appearance in 1959. *Aniara* was inspired by a long poem by Harry Martinson (1904–78), a figure of considerable substance in Swedish literary life who was awarded the Nobel Prize for Literature in 1974. The action of the opera takes place in the remote future when inteplanetary travel is almost commonplace. *Aniara* is a space-ship bound for Mars with some 8,000 people on board who are escaping from the poisoned, radio-active atmosphere of the Earth. Soon, the *Aniara* is thrown off course by a shower of meteorites, and her passengers are panic-stricken to learn that they are doomed to travel for ever into inter-galactic space. The years of travel and the immensities of space take their toll: various sects emerge; the ship's evil master, Chefone, establishes a tyranny over the passengers. Ultimately, one by one they perish, until the only survivor, the woman pilot, remains to dance her sad and lonely swan song.

There is no doubt that Blomdahl possessed a sophisticated aural imagination and a vital sensibility. What he does lack is real thematic vitality: it is not just a matter of good tunes – most contemporary operas suffer a similar handicap – but the fact that the lines lack both real direction and interest and the stamp of a commanding personal idiom. *Aniara* adds up to a good deal less than the sum of its parts: there is good craftsmanship rather than white-hot inspiration, and expertise rather than mastery. No masterpiece then, but not wholly negligible either. There are some highly effective and imaginative passages in its course. This persuasive and totally committed account by this wonderful cast certainly shows it to best advantage. The recording is in the demonstration class, with remarkable range and altogether superb definition.

Boccherini, Luigi (1743–1805)

Cello concerto in B flat (arr. Grützmacher).
** Denon Dig. **C37 7023** [id.]. Fujiwara, Netherlands CO, Inoue – HAYDN: *Cello concerto in D.***

Mari Fujiwara plays with eloquent phrasing, much musical intelligence and beauty of tone. Hers is the only account of the concerto currently in the CD catalogue; were the orchestral playing under Michi Inoue of equal quality, this would deserve a wholehearted recommendation. The recording is faithful and well balanced, and it is a pity that the orchestral contribution is not as distinguished.

Cello concerto No. 2 in D.
*** DG Walkman *415 330-4* [id.]. Rostropovich, Zurich Coll. Mus., Sacher – HAYDN**; DVOŘÁK: *Cello concertos.****

This is among the most worthwhile of DG's series of bargain-priced double-length Walkman tapes, for it includes a superb account of the Dvořák *Cello concerto* partnering Fournier and Szell. Fournier's account of the Haydn is less memorable, perhaps, but Rostropovich in Boccherini also offers a highly individual musical experience. Although essentially a performance in the grand manner (with Rostropovich providing his own cadenzas), the music making has tremendous vitality, with extremely lively outer movements to balance the eloquence of the *Adagio*. The forceful nature of the performance is short on charm and so perhaps a little out of character for an essentially elegant composer like Boccherini; but Rostropovich is so compelling that reservations are swept aside. He is given an alert accompaniment by Sacher, and the recording has fine body and presence. The chrome tape has excellent range and detail.

Boieldieu, François (1755-1834)

La Dame Blanche (opera): complete.
** Accord **149501** (2) [id.]. Sénéchal, Legros, Doniat, Héral, Louvay, Berbié, Baudoz, Ch. and O de Paris, Stoll.

With a hero named Georges Brown, Boieldieu's opéra-comique is set in eighteenth-century Scotland, a jolly romp of a piece with plenty of lively ensembles in a light-hearted style that anticipates Offenbach or Gilbert and Sullivan. The hero's big aria in Act I even anticipates the Gendarmes' duet by Offenbach; Michel Sénéchal as the hero sings superbly, with a light, clear, very French tenor. The male principals are better than the women, who tend to be shrill, but ensembles are well pointed and lively. Choruses are less polished. This CD transfer dampens down what was originally an unnaturally bright 1964 recording. It sounds rather boxy and limited, but is undistracting. The extensive

French dialogue on the original set has been omitted for CD, making the result more apt for repeated listening.

Boito, Arrigo (1842–1918)

Mefistofele (complete).
(*) Decca Dig. **410 175-2 [id.]; D270 D3/*K270 K32* (3/2) [Lon. LDR/*5*-73010]. Ghiaurov, Pavarotti, Freni, Caballé, L. Op. Ch., Trinity Boys' Ch., Nat. PO, Fabritiis.

Boito's *Mefistofele* is a strange episodic work to come from the hand of the master-librettist of Verdi's *Otello* and *Falstaff*, but it has many fine moments. The modern digital recording given to the Fabritiis set brings obvious benefits in the extra weight of brass and percussion – most importantly in the heavenly prologue. With the principal soloists all at their best – Pavarotti most seductive in *Dai campi, dai prati*, Freni finely imaginative on detail, Caballé consistently sweet and mellifluous as Elena, Ghiaurov strongly characterful if showing some signs of strain – this is a highly recommendable set, though Fabritiis in his last recording lacks a little in energy, and the chorus is placed rather distantly.

Mefistofele: Prologue.
** Telarc Dig. **CD 80109**; DG 80109 [id.]. John Cheek, Young Singers of Callanwolde, Atlanta Ch. and SO, Shaw – BERLIOZ: *Requiem*; VERDI: *Te Deum.***

Along with Verdi's *Te Deum*, the whole of the *Prologue* from *Mefistofele* makes a generous and attractive fill-up to the CD version of the Telarc Berlioz *Requiem*. Despite some excellent choral singing, finely disciplined, the performance remains obstinately earth-bound, though the heavenly choirs are more convincing than their infernal counterparts, which lack demonry. Fine, clear recording, with massed forces all precisely placed.

Nerone (complete).
ℭ **(*) Hung. Dig. **HCD 12487/9-2**; SLPD/*MCSLPD* 12487/9 [id.]. Nagy, Tokody, Dene, Miller, Takács, Gregor, Hungarian R. and TV Ch., Hungarian State Op. O, Queler.

Eve Queler conducts a powerful and atmospheric performance of Boito's massive, uncompleted opera. It occupied the composer for the last fifty years of his life, and though (not surprisingly) it hardly matches his earlier *Mefistofele* in freshness and variety and presents an unsatisfyingly episodic plot, there are dozens of marvellous ideas, starting with the strikingly original opening, sliding in like *Aïda* updated. Later too the piece is full of prayers and ceremonial music, all of it richly colourful and superbly performed by the company of the Hungarian State Opera whose soloists are far less afflicted with Slavonic wobbles than is common in Eastern Europe. Notable in the cast are Ilona Tokody as the heroine, Klara Takács, Lajos Miller as the Christian leader, and Janos Nagy as a disconcertingly engaging Nero, a tenor role. The recording is of outstanding quality, with the atmospheric perspectives demanded by the score most realistically conveyed.

Bolling, Claude (born 1930)

California suite: excerpts; Picnic suite; Suite for flute and jazz piano.
(B) **(*) CBS *MGT 39494*. Laws, Lagoya, Rampal, composer, with Ens. and rhythm.

Claude Bolling writes slight but engagingly inventive music which successfully makes the crossover from the idiom of rhythm and blues to that of the mainstream classical tradition. Three of the best numbers are included from the attractive incidental music for Neil Simon's film, *California Suite*, but the main substance is provided by the *Suite for flute and jazz piano*. Here the composer is joined by Jean-Pierre Rampal, whose phrasing of the lyrical movements is very persuasive. The rhythmic background has something in common with a baroque continuo and the writing looks back nostalgically and rather skilfully to that era. All the performances here are first rate and the sound vivid, though the double-length tape is transferred on iron-oxide stock and the results are slightly less refined than the original LP versions.

Suite for cello and jazz piano trio.
** CBS Dig. **MK 39059**; FM/*FMT* 39059 [id.]. Yo-Yo Ma, composer, Dayan.

This particular crossover music moves easily backwards and forwards. The opening *Baroque in rhythm* is lively and inventive but the *Concertante* which follows (11′ 50″) is too long; while in the fourth movement, *Ballade*, the composer produces a quite attractive lyrical idea, each of the score's six sections outstays its welcome. With Yo-Yo Ma participating and the composer at the piano, the performance could hardly be more persuasive, although the forwardly balanced recording does not help to make the music making seem evocative, for all its nostalgic melodic and rhythmic eclecticism.

Suite for violin and jazz piano.
(*) CBS **MK 73833; 73833/*40-* [M/*MT* 35128]. Zukerman, composer, Hédiguer, Sabiani.

Bolling's *Suite* displays characteristic facility and melodic fluency. Its style verges on pastiche, notably in the *Ragtime*, where the evocation of Scott Joplin is unmistakably accurate. There are eight movements altogether, the *Valse lente* (No. 7) is rather engaging in its evocatively old-fashioned way, like the opening

Romance and the *Caprice* which follows. The writing moves easily from the manner of the pre-jazz-era salon to Grappelli-like syncopations. The lively closing *Hora* is especially effective. It is superbly played by Zukerman, who is given expert support and good recording with a forward balance. On CD the relationship between violin and piano is much more tangible, with the violin to the front and left and the piano behind and on the right.

Bononcini, Giovanni (1670–1755)

Griselda (opera): abridged version.
(M) *** Decca Ser. 411 719-1. Elms, Sutherland, Elkins, Sinclair, Malas, Amb. S., LPO, Bonynge.

Bononcini is remembered well enough as Handel's rival as an opera-composer, but how rarely has one the chance to study his music. This one arrived originally in 1968, but had a short catalogue life, so those interested should snap up this budget-priced reissue on Decca's Serenata label before it disappears again; there is no tape. All credit to Richard Bonynge for resurrecting what by all accounts is the composer's most impressive work and providing here a generous sample in a score of numbers. By no stretch of the imagination does this music match Handel's in inspiration, but the numbers are nicely varied with several lovely arias for the patient Griselda (sung by Lauris Elms), several simpler pastoral airs, and a couple of jolly bass arias. Joan Sutherland's contribution in the castrato role of Ernesto is limited to four arias and a duet but, with bright and lively conducting from Bonynge and an agreeable orchestral sound which does not include 'authentic' astringencies, or bulges, this is most enjoyable. The recording is of vintage Decca quality.

Borodin, Alexander (1833–87)

Symphonies Nos 1 in E flat; 2 in B min.; 3 in A min.; In the Steppes of Central Asia.
** Chant du Monde LDX 78781/2; *K 331/2.* USSR Ac. SO, Svetlanov.

Symphonies Nos 1 and 3.
** Chant du Monde **LDC 278 781.** USSR Ac. SO, Svetlanov.

Symphony No. 2 in B min.
*(*) Ph. 412 070-1/*4* [id.]. Concg. O, Kondrashin – PROKOFIEV: *Symphony No. 3.**

Symphony No. 2 in B min.; In the Steppes of central Asia; (i) *Prince Igor: Polovtsian dances.*
(*) Chant du Monde **LDC 278 272 [id.]. USSR Ac. SO; (i) and Ch.; Svetlanov.

Symphony No. 2 in B min.; Prince Igor: Overture; Polovtsian dances.
(B) *** ASV Dig. ABM/*ZCABM* 761 [id.]. Mexico State SO, Bátiz.

Svetlanov gives vivid and well-characterized readings of the Borodin symphonies which may not be the most subtle performances but none the less have plenty of spirit as well as acceptable recording to commend them. His accounts are the first Borodin symphonies to reach CD. Glazunov completed the first two movements of the *Third* relying on his memory of Borodin's peformances on the piano, aided by sketches; whatever their authorship, the results are highly attractive. Svetlanov gives a convincing account of both it and the little-heard *First Symphony*, though there could perhaps be more subtlety at times, notably in the scherzo. The sound is very acceptable, without being in any way outstanding. On the second of the two CDs the *Polovtsian dances* make a vivid and exciting bonus. The recording dates from 1966.

Bátiz's bright, modern digital recording – clearly superior to the sound Chant du Monde provide for Svetlanov – certainly makes a vivid impression and the performances are extremely spirited. The first movement is taken very fast and reminds us of Martinon's famous version with the LSO (still available, on Decca SPA 281). The slow movement is undoubtedly eloquent, with a fine horn solo, but in the vivacious scherzo (and again later in the *Prince Igor overture*) one is made to realize that the Mexican State orchestra, though impressively rehearsed, cannot match the finest European orchestras in virtuosity and finesse. Even so, Bátiz has the gift of bringing music alive in the recording studio, and this applies to the *Overture* also (though at times he drives rather hard). The *Polovtsian dances* are without a chorus, and the effect is slightly shrill, but the energy of the performance is arresting. This is issued in the bargain range and is excellent value, with a good matching tape.

Kondrashin's rather brisk account of the *Symphony* has the advantage of fine orchestral playing, though it is let down by some intrusive audience noise and a lapse of intonation in the slow movement. In so competitive a field, this is not really a front-runner.

Prince Igor: Overture; Polovtsian dances.
(M) *** Decca Viv. 411 838-1/*4* [Mobile 517]. LSO Ch., LSO, Solti – GLINKA: *Russlan overture*: MUSSORGSKY: *Khovantschina: Prelude*, etc.***
*** Telarc Dig. **CD 80039**; DG 10039 [id.]. Atlanta Ch. and SO, Shaw – STRAVINSKY: *Firebird suite*.**(*)
** Decca **414 124-2** [id.]. Lausanne R. Ch. and Children's Ch., SRO, Ansermet – RIMSKY-KORSAKOV: *Scheherazade*.**

Originally issued in 1967 as a collection entitled 'Romantic Russia', this is one of Solti's very best records. The version of the *Polovtsian dances* is among the finest ever recorded. The chorus in the opening dances is lyrical and polished in a characteristically English way but, when the music warms up, the performance is exciting as anyone could wish. The *Overture*, too, has fine dash and spontaneity, and is less overtly Romantic than Solti's other account with the Berlin Philharmonic (also for Decca, but currently withdrawn). The sound, from a vintage

Decca period, still approaches the demonstration class, and the tape is first rate too.

It would be churlish not to give the remarkable Telarc digital recording of the *Polovtsian dances* a full recommendation. The choral singing is less clearly focused in the lyrical sections of the score than at climaxes, but the singers undoubtedly rise to the occasion. The entry of the bass drum is riveting and the closing section very exciting. The vivid sound-balance is equally impressive in the *Overture*, and if the Atlanta orchestra does not possess the body of string timbre to make the very most of the sweeping second subject, the playing has vitality and spontaneity in its favour. Robert Shaw's overall direction is thoroughly musical.

Ansermet's performance is a reliably good one, though the tension tends to sag in the passages where the choir – which is not outstanding – is expected to carry the music with only slight support from the orchestra. The end goes well. The recording is bright and clear.

Boulez, Pierre (born 1926)

(i) *Le Marteau sans maître;* (ii) *Livre pour cordes;* (iii) *Pli selon pli.*
(B) *** CBS Diamond DC 40173 (2). (i) Minton Ens. Musique Vivante; (ii) New Philh. O Strings; (iii) Lukomska, Bergmann, BBC SO, cond. composer.

Originally offered on two separate records this CBS reissue is effectively now at bargain price, with the two discs together in a double-sleeve, costing the same as a single premium-priced LP. Unfortunately, through bad planning, the use of a single double-length chrome cassette (instead of two separate cassettes to match the discs) means there was not enough space to include all the music. *Livre pour cordes* is omitted in the tape equivalent, which is not recommended. *Le Marteau sans maître* was the work with which Pierre Boulez as a composer first revealed a new world of sound. His method may have been rigorously serial, but the end result had an almost sensuous charm to it with its jingling, clinking percussion surrounding the stylized vocal line. It is still not an easy work but, with a fine performance under the composer's direction and with excellent immediate recording, it should be sampled both by Boulez's admirers and by all who want to venture into post-war serial development. *Livre pour cordes*, adapted from an early string quartet, is a far less demanding piece, but one equally worth studying. *Pli selon pli* is a grandly conceived work to refute the idea that serialists and their progeny are necessarily cramped in their inspiration. The title (literally 'fold upon fold') comes from the poet Mallarmé, and Boulez's layers of invention are used to illuminate as centrepieces three Mallarmé sonnets. Neither these craggy vocalizations nor the purely instrumental passages are at all easy to understand in a conventional sense, but the luminous texture of Boulez's writing is endlessly fascinating, and for the listener with an open mind there are few more rewarding records on which to widen experience of the avant-garde. Superb performance and recording under the composer's sharp-eared and electrifying direction.

Boyce, William (1710–79)

Symphonies Nos 1–8.
*** CRD **CRD 3413**; CRD 1056/*CRDC 4056* [id.]. Bournemouth Sinf., Ronald Thomas.

Even against such strong competition as the catalogue provides in these superb symphonies, Thomas and the Bournemouth Sinfonietta are outstanding, with buoyant playing set against a recording which captures the full bloom of the orchestra. The tempi are often rather brisker than those adopted by Marriner. This is an excellent set, highly recommendable. The CD is fully worthy of inclusion in CRD's first release in that format. With the orchestra placed at a believable distance – though the harpsichord fails to make a strong impression – the balance is truthful and detail is enhanced. The cassette too is first rate, the sound vivid and full, with only marginal loss of inner transparency.

Brahms, Johannes (1833–97)

Piano concertos Nos 1–2; Violin concerto; Double concerto for violin and cello; Academic festival overture.
*(*) DG Dig. 415 578-1 (4). Zimerman, Maisky, Kremer, VPO, Bernstein.

This box is offered at slightly less than full price (though at more than mid-price). It includes controversial but rewarding versions of the two *Piano concertos*, but neither Kremer's account of the *Violin concerto* nor the Maisky/Kremer recording of the *Double concerto* are among principal recommendations – see below. The digital recording is extremely vivid, but readers will find Gilels's medium-priced coupling of just the two *Piano concertos* an altogether more worthwhile investment.

Piano concertos Nos 1–2; Fantasias, Op. 116.
*** DG **419 158-2** (2); (without *Fantasias*) 413 229-1/*4* (2). Gilels, BPO, Jochum.

From Gilels comes a combination of magisterial strength and a warmth, humanity and depth that are altogether inspiring. Jochum is a superb accompanist; while the recording is very resonant and does not focus the piano in truthful proportion, it is full in an appropriately Brahmsian way. The excellent chrome cassettes and LPs are offered at mid-price; by way of compensation, the CDs offer the *Fantasias*, Op. 116, where Gilels displays artistry of an order that silences criticism.

Piano concerto No. 1 in D min, Op. 15.
*** Decca Dig. **410 009-2**; SXDL/*KSXDC* 7552 [Lon. DR/*5*- 71052]. Ashkenazy, Concg. O. Haitink.
(*) DG Dig. **413 472-2; (M) 413 472-1/*4* [id.]. Zimerman, VPO, Bernstein.

The new Ashkenazy digital recording of the Brahms *First Concerto* was obviously intended by Decca to provide a version for the 1980s to compare with Curzon's famous record made two decades earlier. However, for all its merits it fails to displace current recommendations, and the sound on the compact disc, although for the most part admirably faithful, only serves to emphasize the forward balance and the not quite convincing quality of the piano timbre as recorded. Ashkenazy gives a commanding and magisterial account of the solo part that is full of poetic imagination. All the different facets of the score – its combative energy, its strength and tenderness – are fully delineated. In the slow movement the atmosphere is not quite as rapt or hushed as in the Zimerman version; taken as a whole, however, the performance is very impressive indeed and there is superlative playing from the Concertgebouw Orchestra. The recording is enormously vivid, though the balance may worry some collectors. The forward placing of the soloist gives the lower and middle registers of the piano a disproportionate amount of aural space, and one or two octaves appear not to be absolutely true. The cassette is extremely lively, though the very forward balance brings a slightly aggressive quality to the strings and the piano timbre hardens on fortissimos.

Zimerman's remarkable partnership with Bernstein brings the most spacious reading, in which slow speeds are pursued steadily with rapt concentration. The atmosphere of a live recording is captured without intrusive noises and flawed detail, to make this a unique experience – not one to which every listener will respond in its departure from accepted convention, but powerful in its magnetism. There are signs that Bernstein wanted to indulge more overtly Romantic expressiveness than Zimerman's thoughtful style allows, although the pianist himself uses generous rubati in the second subject of the first movement, relaxing a good deal more than the composer's marking, *poco più moderato*, might be thought to imply. Undoubtedly Zimerman dominates the performance and the slow movement is lovingly played. His purity of timbre is remarkable, the effect hushed and intense. But there is a tendency to lay greater store by beauty of detail than coherence of structure, while the element of self-indulgence by both artists is inescapable. The generosity of spirit that informs many passages commands admiration, but comparison with Gilels, or with Curzon (Decca Jub. JB/*KJBC* 102 [Lon. 411 579-1/*4*]), is not to the advantage of the present performance. The CD, however, has impressive presence, while the recording is more natural than is often obtained in the Vienna Musikvereinsaal.

Piano concerto No. 2 in B flat, Op. 83.

(B) *** DG Walkman *419 087-4* [id.]. Gilels, BPO, Jochum – SCHUMANN: *Concerto.****

(*) DG Dig. **415 359-2; 415 359-1/*4* [id.]. Zimerman, VPO, Bernstein.

(*) Decca Dig. **410 199-2; 410 199-1/*4* [id.]. Ashkenazy, VPO, Haitink.

*(*) Decca **414 142-2** [id.]; Jub. JB/*KJBC* 94 [Lon. JL/*5*- 41032]. Backhaus, VPO, Boehm.

Piano concerto No. 2; Tragic overture.
(***) RCA **RD 85406 [RCD1 5406]**. Gilels, Chicago SO, Reiner.

On DG Walkman, Gilels's performance is coupled with Wilhem Kempff's 1974 recording of the Schumann *Concerto*, which is no less desirable. In the Brahms the partnership of Gilels and Jochum produces music making of rare distinction; if the resonant recording has some want of sharpness of focus, the spacious acoustic and rich piano timbre seem well suited to this massive concerto.

Bernstein and Zimerman open the first movement of Brahms's *B flat Concerto* at a measured *Andante*, and while there follows an impulsive burst from the soloist, the tempo only reaches *Allegro non troppo* at the orchestral tutti. Throughout the performance there is a constant ebb and flow in the music's momentum – even more striking than in these artists' approach to the *First Concerto* – and while the mastery of both soloist and conductor is never in doubt, the self-conscious nature of the reading is likely to prove more worrying with the repetition possible on the gramophone than it would at a live concert. Yet there is a sense of both power and grandeur here and moments of real magic – as at the gentle re-entry of the horns to introduce the recapitulation. The *Andante*, with its warmly expressive cello solo, has undoubted poetry, increasing in intensity at the closing pages when (with the *più*, of the composer's *più Adagio* marking, emphasized) the rapt hush of the pianissimo is very telling. The balance of brilliance and lyricism in the finale is effectively highlighted by the flux in the playing, and here the partnership is at its most convincing, although the grazioso character of the movement is not always apparent. The recording is spacious and wide-ranging, with the forwardly balanced piano very tangible in the CD format. The string timbre is brightly lit but there is a balancing weight. The LP and cassette are smoother in outline, but still vivid.

Gilels's RCA recording of the Brahms *B flat Piano concerto* dates from the early stereo era, first appearing in 1959 – although nowhere does the CD presentation make this clear, and the copyright date is given optimistically as 1985. That would not be so bad, had the recording sounded more modern, but in its present incarnation the orchestral sound is very shrill (even worse in the *Overture*) and the piano timbre shallow and clattery. However, with a large treble cut and matching bass boost, an acceptable sound can be obtained. The performance is another matter, and of its kind is unlikely to be surpassed. Though power and brilliance are the watchwords (no one has recorded the scherzo with more breathtaking command), the more relaxed side of the work is also managed well, with the slow movement suitably contrasted and the sparkling Hungarian ideas of the finale given an engaging lightness of touch. Above all, both Gilels and Reiner do not seek to interfere with the music's momentum; for all its excitement, the reading is firm and unmannered. If only the recording had more body, this would be unbeatable.

Ashkenazy's new performance with Haitink, spacious in conception and thoughtful in detail, is curiously lacking in impulse in the first movement, with cautious speeds, and overtly expressive in the lyrical episodes of the second movement. The slow movement is very beautiful and the finale offers the proper contrast; but in the last resort, in spite of excellent recording, this is slightly disappointing, even though the CD has striking presence.

Backhaus made his record of the *B flat Concerto* when he was in his eighties; whether or not one responds to his sober and unsmiling performance, there is no question of its magisterial grandeur or his massive technique. He has been surpassed in terms of poetic insight, inwardness of feeling and spirituality by such artists as Gilels, Arrau and Curzon in the slow movement, nor does he command their fire or sparkle in the scherzo. In the finale there is too little real warmth, poetic feeling or sense of joy. There is a certain marmoreal splendour about it all the same, and there is first-class orchestral playing under Boehm. Admirers of these artists can be assured of the excellence of the digital re-mastering that Decca have made. The CD is more than twice the price of the LP or the cassette, but the gain in presence is striking.

Violin concerto in D, Op. 77.
❀ *** RCA **RD 85402 [RCD1 5402]**; (d.) GL/*GK* 84909 [ARPI/*ARTI* 4445]. Heifetz, Chicago SO, Reiner – BEETHOVEN: *Concerto*.**(*)
*** DG Dig. **400 064-2**; 2532/*3302* 032 [id.]. Mutter, BPO, Karajan.
*** HMV **CDC 747166-2** [id.]; ASD/*TC-ASD* 3385 [Ang. S/*4XS* 37286]. Perlman, Chicago SO, Giulini.
(M) **(*) CBS 60043/*40*- [MY/*MYT* 37262]. Stern, Phd. O, Ormandy.
(*) Decca **411 677-2; Jub. 411 677-1/*4* [id.]. Belkin, LSO, Ivan Fischer.
(B) **(*) DG Walkman *413 844-4* [id.]. Ferras, BPO, Karajan – BRUCH: *Violin concerto No. 1* **; BEETHOVEN: *Romances*.***
(M) **(*) Ph. 412 919-1/*4* [id.]. Szeryng, Concg. O, Haitink.
** DG Dig. **410 029-2**; 2532/*3302* 088 [id.]. Kremer, VPO, Bernstein.

Heifetz's 78 r.p.m. gramophone performances were always something of an occasion, and his compact disc début in the Brahms *Concerto* is certainly cause for celebration. Like the Beethoven on the reverse, the CD transfer of this dazzling performance makes vivid and fresh what originally on LP was a rather harsh Chicago recording, more aggressive than the Boston sound in the Beethoven. With the CD, the excellent qualities of RCA's Chicago sound for Reiner come out to the full, giving a fine three-dimensional focus to display this high-powered partnership at its most formidable. The speeds for all three movements may be fast, but Heifetz's ease and detailed imagination make them more than just dazzling. Genuine allegros in the outer movements give a totally refreshing slant on a work often regarded as more lyrical than urgently dramatic, while the central *Andante*, at a flowing speed, is delectably songful. Anyone who wants to hear this great virtuoso, counted to be the master of masters, at his very peak cannot do better than obtain this superb CD. The two concertos together play for rather more than 72 minutes and therefore just fit within the possible time-span; it seems unlikely that any other contemporary artist will match this achievement and yet provide performances that remain entirely convincing. The Brahms *Concerto* is also available on mid-priced Gold Seal label on both disc and LP, but the sound does not compare with the compact disc.

It is an extraordinary achievement that the youthful Anne-Sophie Mutter should, so early in her career, provide a performance of the Brahms *Concerto* as commanding as any, matching fiery bravura with a glowing expressive quality, in a reading that is freshly spontaneous in every bar. In many ways her playing combines the unforced lyrical feeling of Krebbers (whose highly recommendable version is currently out of the catalogue) with the flair and individuality of Perlman. There is a lightness of touch, a gentleness in the slow movement that is highly appealing, while in the finale the incisiveness of the solo playing is well displayed by the clear (yet not clinical) digital recording. Needless to say, Karajan's accompaniment is strong in personality and the Berlin Philharmonic play beautifully, but he is by no means the dominant musical personality; the performance represents a genuine musical partnership between youthful inspiration and eager experience. The recording on disc is matched by the excellent chrome cassette, but the compact disc is finest of all, although its clarity emphasizes the close balance of the soloist, and there is a touch of fierceness in the orchestral upper range in tuttis. There is no increase in bass response, compared with the LP.

A distinguished account of the solo part from Perlman, finely supported by Giulini and the Chicago Symphony Orchestra, a reading of darker hue than is customary, with a thoughtful, searching slow movement rather than the autumnal rhapsody which it so often becomes. Giulini could be tauter, perhaps, in the first movement, but the songful playing of Perlman always holds the listener. The recording places the soloist rather too forward, and the orchestral detail could be more transparent. Admirers of Perlman, however, need not hesitate; granted a certain want of impetus in the first movement, this is an impressive and convincing performance. There is a good cassette.

Stern's 1960 recording, with Ormandy, made when he was at the peak of his career, is undoubtedly a great performance and deserves to be digitally remastered for CD to stand alongside the Heifetz version. On its newest LP and tape issue, the orchestral sound has been clarified but has lost some of its body. Yet the solo playing still emerges as ripely full-blooded, and Ormandy contributes a wonderfully positive Brahmsian warmth to a reading that carries the listener forward in its expressive spontaneity and fire. It is undoubtedly a performance which one can return to again and again with increasing satisfaction. The musical rewards of this account are slightly undermined by an artificially forward balance which highlights the soloist. Nevertheless, this must be numbered among the very finest of all available recorded performances, with the inspiration of the occasion caught on the wing.

Boris Belkin's performance with the LSO and Ivan Fischer was issued almost simultaneously on the mid-priced Jubilee label in its LP and tape format and then on CD, which costs nearly three times as much. The recording is excellent in all three media, but on CD it is especially impressive and a strong contender on technical grounds. The performance is direct and spontaneous. The tempo of the first movement is measured and spacious (especially alongside Heifetz), but the reading is deeply felt and makes a strong impression. This is far more than a routine performance without being of real stature but, fine though it is, it is outclassed by several other versions.

Much depends on one's attitude to Ferras's tone colour whether the Ferras/Karajan Walkman version is a good recommendation or not. DG have placed him close to the microphone so that the smallness of tone that in the concert hall is disappointing is certainly not evident here. Moreover, there is a jewelled accuracy about the playing that is most appealing, and Karajan conducts vividly. The recording is of good quality and the high-level transfer is of striking liveliness.

Although he chooses comparatively slow tempi for the outer movements, Szeryng has the advantage of a superb accompaniment from the Concertgebouw Orchestra under Haitink who holds the whole structure spaciously together. Szeryng's playing is lyrically passionate and assured, and communicates strongly. The reading has undoubted breadth – if few of the mercurial qualities for which his famous 1959 RCA account, partnered by Monteux (RCA VL/*VK* 89032 [AGL1/*AGK1* 5216]), was justly famous. However, this older version has very dated sound, whereas the Philips recording (from 1974) is first class, on both LP and cassette.

Gidon Kremer's version of the Brahms is powerful in attack and has remarkably clean articulation and fine rhythmic buoyancy. His view of the first movement is considerably tauter than in his earlier version, made in the mid-1970s with Karajan. He replaces the Joachim cadenza with a longer one by Reger (his *Prelude in D minor*, Op. 117, No. 6 for solo violin) – at least it isn't Schnittke – but this will undoubtedly diminish its appeal for many collectors. His second movement is hardly a true *Adagio*, and Bernstein is much broader than the soloist who tries to move things on. His finale is very fast indeed – the '*ma non troppo vivace*' marking being ignored. Bernstein generally produces sumptuous results from the Vienna Philharmonic and the recording has plenty of body, but ultimately Kremer is too narcissistic and idiosyncratic to carry a firm recommendation.

(i) *Violin concerto in D;* (ii) *Symphony No. 1 in C min., Op. 68; Hungarian dances Nos 1–2.*

(B) * Ph. On Tour *416 216-4* [id.]. (i) Grumiaux, New Philh. O, Sir Colin Davis; (ii) Leipzig GO, Masur.

Grumiaux's performance of the *Concerto*, it goes without saying, is full of insight and lyrical eloquence and Sir Colin Davis lends his soloist the most sympathetic support. It is well recorded too: the sound is firm and well detailed, with good presence. This On Tour chrome tape is the least expensive way of acquiring it, but alas it is encumbered with a lifeless version of the *First Symphony* (recorded in 1979). The playing of the Leipzig orchestra is of a high order, but the actual performance is inert and boring. The bass-heavy sound makes things worse.

Double concerto for violin and cello in A min., Op. 102.

(*) CBS **MK 42024 [id.]. Francescatti, Fournier, Columbia SO, Bruno Walter – SCHUMANN: *Piano concerto.* **(*)

(M) **(*) HMV EG 270268-1/*4*. Menuhin, Tortelier, LPO, Berglund.

(B) ** DG Walkman *415 332-4* [id.]. Schneiderhan, Starker, Berlin RSO, Fricsay – BEETHOVEN: *Triple concerto*; MOZART: *Violin concerto No. 3*.**

Double concerto in A min., Op. 102; Academic festival overture, Op. 80.
* DG Dig. **410 031-2**; 410 031-1/*4* [id.]. Kremer, Maisky, VPO, Bernstein.

Double concerto; Tragic overture.
*** DG Dig. **410 603-2**; 410 603-1/*4* [id.]. Mutter, Meneses, BPO, Karajan.

The Brahms *Double concerto* has been lucky in its recordings since the earliest days of stereo, as records conducted by Galliera, Fricsay and Bruno Walter readily demonstrate. Now the era of the digital compact disc produces a version which sets new standards. With two young soloists Karajan conducts an outstandingly spacious and strong performance. If from Antonio Meneses the opening cello cadenza seems to lack something in urgency and command, that is a deceptive start for, from then on, the concentration and power of the piece are built up superbly. As in her commanding performance of the Brahms *Violin concerto* – also with Karajan and the Berlin Philharmonic – Anne-Sophie Mutter conveys a natural authority comparable to Karajan's own, and the precision and clarity of Meneses' cello as recorded make an excellent match. (The chrome cassette is equally clear.) The central slow movement in its spacious way has a wonderful Brahmsian glow, and all these qualities come out the more vividly in the CD version, though the relatively close balance of the soloists – particularly the cellist – is more evident, too.

Bruno Walter's recording with Francescatti and Fournier dates from 1959 and the compact disc represents another astonishing example of digital remastering which enhances the original to extraordinary effect, with solo instruments most tangible and orchestral detail consistently vivid within an attractively warm ambience. The timbre of the violins is particularly agreeable. As the commanding opening shows, Fournier is magnificent and, if one can adjust to Francescatti's rather intense vibrato (caught more flatteringly here than in the Beethoven *Violin concerto*), this can stand among the most satisfying of available versions. Walter draws playing of great warmth from the Columbia orchestra and oversees the reading as a whiole with his customary humanity, yet tuttis are thrillingly expansive and vital. With an unexpected but rewarding coupling and 62 minutes of music, this is excellent value when the music making has such distinction.

The version by Menuhin and Tortelier, rather following the pattern set in EMI's outstanding earlier version with Perlman and Rostropovich, with Haitink conducting (ASD/*TC-ASD* 3905 [Ang. SZ/*4ZS* 37680], presents two outstandingly warm and individual soloists against the background of strong accompaniment, steadily paced. As in the earlier recording, the soloists are placed well forward, but this time the result is more genial as well as big and positive. The challenge between two volatile, inspirational artists brings the best out of both of them, with the slow movement sweet and relaxed and the finale slower than usual but nicely lilting and crisply pointed. Excellent, full recording, debatable only on the question of the forwardness of the soloists. There is a first-class cassette, strikingly well focused.

We have always enjoyed the Schneiderhan/Starker/Fricsay version of the *Double concerto* ever since it first came out on a ten-inch LP in the early 1960s. It still sounds fresh and warm, although again the two soloists are rather forwardly placed. Fricsay shapes the work splendidly; if the couplings are attractive, this well-engineered Walkman chrome tape is excellent value.

Recorded at concerts in the Vienna Musikvereinsaal in 1981–2, the Kremer/Maisky record originally formed part of the DG Brahms Edition. Mischa Maisky is a superb player with wonderful tonal finesse but some of the dynamic extremes are somewhat self-conscious, while Kremer's playing is often posturing and narcissistic. The playing of the Vienna Philharmonic for Bernstein is marvellous and the reading is expansive and warm. The excellence of the recording is not in question: there is plenty of concert-hall ambience and a wide dynamic range with real body and presence. There is an admirable breadth about much of it, but this is outweighed in the first two movements by a want of real momentum.

Hungarian dances Nos 1–21 (complete).
*** Ph. Dig. **411 426-2**; 6514/*7337* 305 [id.]. Leipzig GO, Masur.
*** DG Dig. **410 615-2**; 410 615-1/*4* [id.]. VPO, Abbado.
*** Decca Dig. SXDL/*KSXDC* 7585 [411 703-1]. RPO, Weller.

In Nos 5 and 6 Masur uses Parlow's scoring instead of Martin Schmelling (as preferred by Abbado) and in Nos 7 and 8 he opts for Schollum rather than Hans Gál. Masur is just a shade more relaxed and smiling and the timbre of the strings is generally richer and warmer than that achieved by the DG engineers in Vienna. Abbado has great sparkle and lightness, but the Leipzig orchestra is hardly less dazzling than the Viennese. The Philips issue has the finer sound (though the chrome tape has less sparkle than the disc and tends to be slightly middle-orientated) and sounds glowingly full on CD.

The RPO can hold its own with its illustrious rivals: the strings may not have the weight and depth of sonority that the Vienna orchestra command, nor are their clarinets so creamy and wind so finely tuned perhaps, but they still play with wonderful spirit, as if they enjoy every moment and indeed as if their lives depended on it. Walter Weller secures excellent playing from every department of the orchestra. The Decca recording is lively and bright, eminently truthful in timbre and with good, natural perspective. If pressed to a choice, the Masur which wears a natural charm and offers splendidly civilized recorded sound is the one to have, but Weller's is a thoroughly acceptable alternative.

Hungarian dances Nos 1–7; 19–21.
(B) ** Ph. On Tour *416 219-4* [id.]. LSO, Dorati – DVOŘÁK: *Slavonic dances.***

Dorati's selection, reissued in Philips's bargain-priced On Tour series, has a Mercury source. His conducting is fierce but captures a true Hungarian spirit. When his pacing is livelier than expected, one does not feel he is being wilful or intent on showing off, but simply that he and his players are enjoying it better that way. The recording has been remastered and the sound is both bright and full, if not especially transparent. However, the coupling is generous – the complete set of Dvořák's sixteen *Slavonic dances*, Opp. 46 and 72, which begin and end the tape, with the Brahms selection sandwiched between.

Serenade No. 2 in A, Op. 16; Academic festival overture.
(M) *(*) Ph. Seq. 412 002-1/*4*. Concg. O, Haitink.

This Philips record offers rather short measure: Decca accommodate the *A major Serenade* on one side (Jub. JB/*KJBC* 87) as did HMV in the now deleted version from Sir Adrian Boult. Accordingly, they are able to offer more substantial couplings than Philips do. Haitink's account of the *Academic festival overture* comes from 1972, though the *Serenade* is more recent. The performance is sound in conception and well shaped, but Kertesz offers a more strongly characterized performance. The Philips recording is excellent, however, and sounds especially well in its tape format.

Symphonies Nos 1–4.
*** CBS M3P/*3PT* 39631 [id.]. Columbia SO, Bruno Walter.

Walter's performances of the Brahms *Symphonies*, recorded at the beginning of the 1960s, represent the peak of his Indian summer in the CBS recording studios, not long before he died. The recording has been remastered for this reissue, but its spacious warmth of texture is not lost – and this is especially striking on the chrome cassettes which, with their ample bass response (almost over-resonant), produce glowing string textures without losing the brightness at the top. The performances are discussed under their separate CD issues.

Symphony No. 1 in C min., Op. 68.
*** CBS **MK 42020** [id.]. Columbia SO, Bruno Walter.
(*) German HM Dig. **1C 567 199974-2; 1C 067 99974 [Pro S SCS 626]. N. German RSO, Wand.
(*) Decca **414 458-2 [id.]; SXL/*KSXC* 6924 [Lon. CS/5- 7198]. Chicago SO, Solti.
(*) DG Dig. **410 023-2; 2532/*3302* 056 [id.]. LAPO, Giulini.
** DG Dig. **410 081-2**; 410 081-1/*4* [id.]. VPO, Bernstein.
** HMV Dig. **CDC 747029-2** [id.]; EL 270019-1/*4* [Ang. DS/*4DS* 38091]. LPO, Tennstedt.
(M) (**) HMV mono ED 270124-1. VPO, Furtwängler.
(**) Ph. mono **416 210-2** [id.]. Concg. O, Mengelberg – SCHUBERT: *Rosamunde* excerpts.(**)
** Ph. 412 064-1/*4* [id.]. Concg. O, Kondrashin.
*(*) ASV Dig. DCA/*ZCDA* 531 [id.]. Royal Liverpool PO, Janowski.

Symphony No. 1 in C min.; Variations on a theme of Haydn, Op. 56a.
(**) RCA [mono **RCCD 1007**]. NBC SO, Toscanini.

Walter's first two movements have a white-hot intensity that shows this conductor at his very finest. The first movement combines the best of all possible worlds. It is as magisterial and dramatic as Klemperer's famous record (no doubt to appear on CD in due course) – less forceful at the opening, perhaps, but with great underlying tension – and at the same time by adhering to a fairly consistent speed (barely any rallentando for the second part of the second subject) it conveys the architecture of the movement strongly. The second movement too is most impressive, warm with natural, unforced phrasing. But then comes a slight change. The third movement begins with a less than ravishing clarinet solo and, though the 6/8 section is lively enough, the playing is not as crisp as in the first two movements and there is not quite the same feeling of spontaneity. Things are back to normal in the last movement, however, though some might find the big string tune too slow. How beautiful the remastered recording makes the strings sound here, though; and later the brass is comparably sonorous. The coda is slower than in Walter's two earlier versions. The 1960 recording is full and well balanced; as sound, this is preferable to many more recent versions.

Wand's is an individual and refreshing reading, which explains his belated recognition as a thinker among conductors, the opposite of a showman. In the first movement, like Toscanini, Wand brings fierce intensity to the slow introduction by choosing an unusually fast speed, then leading naturally by modular pacing into the main allegro. The extra unity is clear. There is comparable dramatic intensity in the finale, though the choice of a tempo for the main marching melody, far slower than the rest, brings uncomfortable changes of gear. With a sense of spontaneity as in a live performance, the individuality of the reading is most convincing, helped by fresh recording which is made even clearer on CD.

With the Chicago orchestra's playing as refined as any on record, Solti here directs a performance both spacious and purposeful, with the first movement given modular consistency between sections by a single pulse preserved as far as possible. Some will want more relaxation, for the tension and electricity remain here even when tempi are expansive. The recording is both atmospheric and clear. However, on CD there is excessive bass resonance to cut back; otherwise, the original analogue sound is freshened. The bass emphasis is equally apparent on the otherwise excellent cassette.

Giulini takes a spacious view of the *First*, consistently choosing speeds slower than usual. Generally his keen control of rhythm means that slowness does not deteriorate into heaviness, but the speed for the big C major theme in the finale is so slow that it sounds self-conscious, not *Allegro ma non troppo* at all. As a result, that movement loses its concentration, even with Giulini's magnetic control. It remains a noble, serene view of a heroic symphony, beautifully played and well recorded. The compact disc is strikingly free and clear. The chrome cassette too is of excellent quality, although at the very opening the resonant bass brings a slight ripple in the texture from the drum beats.

The finale in Bernstein's version, even more than with Giulini, brings a highly idiosyncratic reading, with the great melody of the main theme first presented at a speed very much slower than the main part of the movement. On reprise it never comes back to the slow tempo until the coda brings the most extreme slowing for the chorale motif. These two points are exaggerations of accepted tradition, and though Bernstein's electricity makes the results compelling, this is hardly a version for constant repetition. Good recording, with the compact disc bringing the usual extra refinement.

As a recording, Tennstedt's EMI account is among the very finest; the CD version has well-defined detail and impressive body and presence. The LPO strings, however, are less sumptuous in tone or sophisticated in colour than some rival accounts and, if sheer beauty of orchestral sound is a first consideration, this will probably not be a good first choice. Tennstedt's reading is plain and unadorned and has something of Klemperer's integrity and directness. The first movement is broad and spacious in approach (and, at times, some listeners may find it a bit laboured and wanting in tension). Both Bernstein and Giulini invest detail with more loving care – perhaps too much so for all tastes – but there is nobility in both, and magnificent orchestral playing too! But Tennstedt's is an honest and sober account rather than an inspired one, and those who do not respond to either Bernstein or Giulini may well be tempted, particularly in view of the excellence of the recorded sound. The cassette is somewhat bass-heavy and there is some clouding at the very opening from the repeated drum strokes.

Furtwängler's recording dates from 27 January 1952 and presumably comes from the archives of the Austrian Radio. It is not ideally rich tonally, with hard-edged upper strings, and there is some distortion. Nevertheless, what a magnificent performance it is. Of course, Furtwängler pulls the the symphony out of shape; yet these disruptive changes of flow are no more disturbing than the illusion created when one gazes at a river some of whose waters appear to move more rapidly than others. At times, indeed, the flow seems to come to a complete standstill, as our perspective changes. It does this more than once in the symphony. But above all, it is the gloriously full and glowing textures as well as the sensitivity of the wind playing that disarm criticism. From the very outset the listener is left in no doubt that weighty issues are at stake, every note matters, yet the intensity is never unrelieved but carefully measured.

In Mengelberg's Concertgebouw recording from the 78 r.p.m. era, narrative power and dramatic eloquence are in strong evidence from first to last, and one is struck by the electricity and the sense of occasion that is communicated. Of course, there is the characteristic rhythmic flexibility – but this is not unduly disruptive, save in the famous main theme of the finale, which grinds to a virtual halt several times in its course. But what singing tone Mengelberg produces from the Concertgebouw strings, and what a shining quality the brass possess. The Philips engineers retain the natural concert pauses between movements, which is infinitely more civilized than the meagre few seconds we are allowed on some modern records; we can also hear the peremptory taps of the baton.

Kondrashin's is one of the series of live radio recordings which have appeared on Philips, a volatile reading with textures and rhythms surprisingly light. The atmosphere is well conveyed in a generally well-balanced recording, and the

Concertgebouw playing is good, spoilt only by a seriously flat-sounding horn in the finale.

Janowski's is a plain yet sympathetic reading, meticulous over dynamic levels; but neither the timbres produced by the Liverpool orchestra nor the unrounded digital recording matches up to the standards one requires on a full-price disc. The cassette sounds much the same. Janowski, unlike most, does observe the exposition repeat in the first movement.

Toscanini's CD is a disappointment when the transfer is even less clear in big tuttis than in most of his late NBC recordings, and even more harsh. The aggressiveness of the opening, taken very fast, is underlined by such edgy and confused sound, and though the electricity of the very dramatic readings comes over vividly, there is little relaxation. This American RCA issue is not currently available in the UK.

Still recommended: Karajan's latest version (DG 2531/*3301* 121 [id.]) or, at mid-price, his 1964 recording (DG Acc. 2542/*3342* 166) remain at the top of the list, although Klemperer's monumental Philharmonia record remains very competitive (HMV SXLP 30217).

(i) *Symphonies Nos 1;* (ii) *4 in E min., Op. 98.*
(B) *** DG Walkman *413 424-4* [id.]. (i) BPO; (ii) VPO, Boehm.

Boehm's set of Brahms symphonies, issued in excellent transfers on a pair of chrome tapes, at bargain price, make one of the outstanding bargains in the Walkman catalogue. Anyone learning their Brahms from these performances cannot go far wrong. Boehm's Berlin Philharmonic version of the *First* comes from the early 1960s (he recorded it again later, rather less successfully with the VPO). It is a centrally recommendable version, with tempi that are steady rather than volatile; but with polished playing from the Berliners, the performance is undoubtedly effective, and the well-balanced recording emerges here to excellent effect.

Older readers may remember that one of the glories of the Brahms discography in the wartime HMV 78 r.p.m. catalogue was a marvellous account of Brahms's *Fourth Symphony* by Boehm with the Saxon (Dresden) State Orchestra. As a performance, that has never been surpassed, but Boehm's 1976 account within his Vienna cycle very nearly matches it, with a spacious and noble reading of the first movement and a finely contrasted view of the final passacaglia, lyrical and dramatic elements sharply defined. There is heavy underlining in the great string melody of the slow movement, but this and other idiosyncrasies never interfere with the consistency of the reading. It may lack a little in weight and incisiveness, but overall it is very satisfying. Boehm's Vienna versions of the *Second* and *Third Symphonies* are considered below.

Symphony No. 2 in D, Op. 73.
(*) DG Dig. **400 066-2 [id.]. LAPO, Giulini.
**(*) Ph. 412 066-1/*4*. Concg. O, Kondrashin.
** German HM Dig. 1C 067 169519-1. N. German RSO, Wand.

Symphony No. 2; Academic festival overture, Op. 80.
*** CBS **MK 42021** [id.]. Columbia SO, Bruno Walter.
(*) DG Dig. **410 082-2; 410 082-1/*4* [id.]. VPO, Bernstein.

Symphony No. 2; Tragic overture, Op. 81.
(*) Decca **414 487-2 [id.]; SXL 6925 [Lon. CS/*5*- 7199]. Chicago SO, Solti.
* ASV Dig. DCA/*ZCDCA* 547 [id.]. Royal Liverpool PO, Janowski.

Walter's performance is wonderfully sympathetic, far more affectionate than his earlier mono version with the New York Philharmonic. The performance has an inevitability, a rightness which makes it hard to concentrate on the interpretation as such, so cogent is the musical argument. As though to balance the romanticism of his approach on detail, Walter – as in the *First Symphony* – keeps his basic speeds surprisingly constant: in the first movement he refuses to accelerate the strong soaring melody towards the end of the second subject, yet little of the passion is lost in consequence. In the finale, too, Walter refuses to be hurried (or, for that matter, to be slowed down by such markings as *tranquillo*) and the measured general tempo succeeds in creating a most satisfying whole. It is a masterly conception overall and one very easy to live with. The CD opens with a vigorous and yet expansive account of the *Academic festival overture*, sumptuously recorded; when the *Symphony* begins, the ear notices that in the remastering there is some loss in the lower middle and bass, which is less richly resonant than in the *First Symphony*. But the bloom remains and it is only when the strings soar loudly above the stave that one feels need of rather more support at the bottom end. This is a marginal point; on the plus side, detail is remarkably clear, and the middle string timbre is always fresh and warm, an important point in this symphony.

The restraint which made Giulini's recording of Beethoven's *Eroica symphony* with the same orchestra so individual yet so compelling is evident in Brahms, too. The result is less immediately magnetic, particularly in the first movement, and the recording is not one of DG's most vivid; but admirers of this conductor will find many points of fresh illumination. However, this is an example where the compact disc is markedly superior in sound to either LP or chrome cassette (which are both now deleted): the quality is much fresher and more transparent, and the effect is to give more projection and much better detail to the first movement and to give the whole performance something of a lift.

A powerful, weighty performance from Solti, its lyrical feeling passionately expressed in richly upholstered textures. The reading displays a broad nobility, but the charm and delicately gracious qualities of the music are much less a part of Solti's view. Yet the lyric power of the playing is hard to resist, especially when the recording is so full-blooded and brilliant. Solti includes the first-movement exposition repeat and offers a splendidly committed account of the *Tragic overture* as a bonus. On CD, the heavy bass has to be tamed if boominess is not to spoil the otherwise pleasing analogue sound, as digitally remastered.

In his live recording, Bernstein directs a warm and expansive account of the

Second, notably less free and idiosyncratic than the others in the series, yet comparably rhythmic and equally spontaneous-sounding. Good recording, considering the limitations at a live concert. The compact disc sounds well and there is a good chrome tape, though the transfer level is not especially high.

Kondrashin's account of the *Second Symphony* derives from a public concert recorded in 1975, and musically it is really rather special – a performance from another and better age. Its first movement unfolds with great naturalness and is wonderfully unforced and unhurried. In the slow movement the *Adagio* is distinctly *non troppo* and rightly so, but he moves things on very early in the movement, a little more than is consistent with his view of the work as a whole. However, in almost every respect, this is a lovely reading whose glowing textures linger in the mind and whose wisdom and humanity are enriching. The recording itself is eminently acceptable, but not outstanding; for all its insights, which are many, some collectors may think it uncompetitive – at least at full price. However, readers more concerned with musical rather than sonic values will find it well worth investigating. There is an excellent chrome cassette with a lively upper range that yet fully captures the rich Amsterdam acoustic.

Wand, belatedly appreciated outside Germany, directs a thoughtful reading with a broad and songful first movement at a slow basic tempo. In its plainness the third movement too is made to sound like a song of innocence, and the finale, starting gently, brings a fresh, well-articulated performance. The digital reading is not ideal, with strings lacking transparency and with occasional odd balances – as for example in the over-prominence of the horn solo at the end of the first movement.

A live concert performance in Liverpool at the time Janowski made this recording revealed that the harsh sounds – with string timbre tightened to super-brilliance – that emanate from the recording are not altogether to be blamed on the engineers. Janowski's plain style is least convincing in this most lyrical of the Brahms symphonies, with rhythms tending to sound too rigid, whether in his metrical view of the slow movement or the unsprung and charmless account of the third. The reverberant ambience brings congested textures in tuttis, with the edge on high violins unpleasantly emphasized. The overture, perhaps recorded at another time, is much more successful in both performance and recording.

Still recommended: As with the *First Symphony*, on LP and cassette Karajan remains a prime recommendation, alongside Boult who – at mid-price – offers Dame Janet Baker's memorable account of the *Alto rhapsody* as a fill-up (HMV SXLP/*TC-SXLP* 30529). In the case of Karajan, his earlier 1964 account (DG Acc. 2542/*3342* 167) – also offered at mid-price – competes well with the latest version (2531/*3301* 132 [id.]), although tape collectors not requiring the Boult will find Karajan's full-priced cassette – a first-class transfer – superior to the Accolade tape issue, which is bass-heavy.

(i) *Symphonies Nos 2–3;* (ii) *Academic festival overture.*
(B) **(*) DG Walkman *415 334-4*. (i) VPO, Boehm; (ii) BPO, Abbado.

Boehm's readings of the two middle symphonies will seem to most Brahmsians more idiosyncratic than those of Nos 1 and 4, though the conductor himself might have pointed out that he learnt his Brahms interpretations from the composer's friend, Eusebius Mandyczewski. His approach to the *Second Symphony* is certainly volatile in the first movement, with the *Adagio* very expansive indeed. But here the conductor's moulded style rivets the attention and one quickly accepts the extra spaciousness. After a gracefully phrased *Allegretto*, the finale is strong. The *Third Symphony* is very broadly conceived, the reins held comparatively slackly throughout until the finale, where the increased momentum creates a sense of apotheosis. The recordings date from 1976 and sound well, with the Vienna strings given more body than in the original LP issue of No. 2. The excellent account of the *Academic festival overture* by Abbado makes a generous bonus for a chrome cassette already offered at bargain price.

Symphony No. 3 in F, Op. 90.
*(*) DG Dig. **410 083-2**; 410 083-1/*4* [id.]. VPO, Bernstein.

Symphony No. 3; Academic festival overture.
(*) Decca **414 488-2 [id.]; SXL 6902 [Lon. CS/*5*- 7200]. Chicago SO, Solti.

Symphony No. 3; Tragic overture.
(M) *** Ph. Seq. 412 358-1/*4*. Concg. O, Haitink.

Symphony No. 3 in F; Variations on a theme of Haydn, Op. 56a.
*** CBS **MK 42022** [id.]. Columbia SO, Bruno Walter.

Bruno Walter's *Third* is highly recommendable both as a performance and as a recording. His pacing is admirable and the vigour and sense of joy which imbues the opening of the first movement (exposition repeat included) dominates throughout, with the second subject eased in with wonderful naturalness. The central movements provide contrast, though with an intense middle section in II. There is beautifully phrased string and horn playing in the *Poco Allegretto*. The finale goes splendidly, the secondary theme given characteristic breadth and dignity, and the softening of mood for the coda sounding structurally inevitable. The CD transfer brings soaring upper strings, excellent detail with glowing woodwind, and a supporting weight. The account of the *Variations* is relaxed and smiling, with deft and affectionate detail, moving forward to a majestic restatement of the chorale. The recording is clear and spacious.

Haitink's 1971 analogue recording shows how rich the LP and tape catalogue is in first-class accounts of this work. Haitink's is second to none: the orchestral playing of the Concertgebouw is distinguished by unanimity of attack and chording, wonderfully true intonation and homogeneity of tone; and Haitink's firmness of grip and lyrical eloquence make this a very satisfying mid-priced choice, either on LP or on the excellent cassette. Karajan's Berlin Philharmonic performance should not be forgotten, although characteristically he refuses to observe the first-movement repeat (DG 2531/*3301* 133 [id.]), but Haitink's Philips reissue is excellent value.

Solti takes a big-scale view of the *Third*, by far the shortest of the

Brahms symphonies. The epically grand opening, Solti seems to say, demands an equivalent status for the rest; and the result, lacking a little in Brahmsian idiosyncrasy, is most compelling. Solti's Brahms should not be underestimated and, with strikingly rich sound, this gives much satisfaction. However, as in the others of the cycle, there is too much bass emphasis on the CD transfer, although this can be tamed.

Bernstein's account of the *Third* was recorded live like the others in the series but, with speeds in the first three movements so slow as to sound sluggish, it lacks the very quality of flow one hopes to find in a concert performance. The result is disappointingly self-conscious, and only the finale at an aptly fast speed brings Bernstein's usual incisiveness. There is a satisfactory chrome tape, and the compact disc brings the usual advantages.

Symphony No. 3 in F (arr. for piano duet). *Variations on a theme of Schumann, Op. 23.*
** CRD CRD 1114/*CRDC 4114* [id.]. Bracha Eden and Alexander Tamir.

Even though it cannot compare with Liszt's piano transcriptions of the Beethoven symphonies, there is a certain interest in Brahms's own version of his *Third Symphony* for two pianos, four hands. There is evidence to suggest that the piano score preceded the orchestration; whether or not this is so, the piano arrangement is quite effective in its own right. It is given a sturdy, forthright performance by Eden and Tamir. Sometimes they allow the tension to flag a little in the lyrical writing, but they do their best to make up for the absence of sustained string tone. The *Variations on a theme of Schumann* (for one piano, four hands) are based on part of the Adagio of Schumann's *Violin concerto*, and the work (written five years after Schumann's death) has a valedictory quality, ending with the principal idea transformed into an elegiac funeral march. Eden and Tamir are eloquent at this point, but earlier in the work their directness of approach is sometimes a shade unyielding. This effect is accentuated by the bright, clear piano tone which has a touch of hardness on top. Disc and chrome tape are closely matched.

Symphony No. 4 in E min., Op. 98.
(*) DG Dig. **400 037-2; 2532/*3302* 003 [id.]. VPO, Carlos Kleiber.
(*) Decca **414 563-2 [id.]; SXL 6890 [Lon. CS 7201]. Chicago SO, Solti.

Symphony No. 4; Academic festival overture.
** ASV Dig. DCA/*ZCDCA* 533 [id.]. Royal Liverpool PO, Janowski.

Symphony No. 4; Tragic overture.
*** CBS **MK 42023** [id.]. Columbia SO, Bruno Walter.
*** DG Dig. **410 084-2**; 410 084-1/*4*. [id.]. VPO, Bernstein.

Walter's opening is simple, even gentle, and the pervading lyricism is immediately apparent; yet power and authority are underlying. The conductor's refusal to linger by a wayside always painted in gently glowing colours adds strength and impetus, building up to an exciting coda, the unanimity and cutting edge of the strings bringing a cumulative effect. A beautifully moulded slow movement, intense at its central climax, is balanced by a vivacious, exhilarating scherzo. The finale has an underlying impetus so that Walter is able to relax for the slow middle section. Walter's account of the *Tragic overture*, with its characteristic breadth, opens the record powerfully, so that the relaxed opening of the *Symphony* is the more striking. The CD brings full, well-balanced sound in an attractively spacious ambience, with glowing wind detail. The upper strings – as throughout this 1960 series – have not always quite the body of the finest modern recordings, but their freshness and the absence of edge, combined with the natural ambient warmth in the middle range, is appealing, and there is a full resonance in the bass. In the scherzo, the balance is superbly managed in its combination of sparkle and weight. The set is a remarkable achievement overall – one of the highlights of the CD catalogue.

Bernstein's Vienna version of Brahms's *Fourth*, recorded live, is exhilaratingly dramatic in fast music, while the slow movement brings richly resonant playing from the Vienna strings, not least in the great cello melody at bar 41, which with its moulded rubato comes to sound surprisingly like Elgar. This is the finest of Bernstein's Vienna cycle and, with good sound on both LP and cassette, is well worth considering. Like the others in the set, the compact disc gains in clarity, definition and range and gives the orchestra fine presence, although in the slow movement the LP offers slightly more warmth.

Any record from Carlos Kleiber is an event, and his is a performance of real stature. Everything is shaped with the attention to detail one would expect from this great conductor. Apart from one moment of expressive emphasis at bar 44 in the first movement, his reading is completely free from eccentricity. A gripping and compelling performance, though not more impressive than Karajan's last Berlin version (2531/*3301* 134 [id.]). With the more critical medium of CD, the limitations of the early digital recording, less clean and detailed than it might be, are more exposed. The strings above the stave sound a little shrill and glassy, while at the other end of the spectrum there is a want of opulence in the bass. The Bernstein CD, with the same orchestra on the same label, is both more refined and more atmospheric. Those wanting Kleiber's version might well consider the chrome tape, which is slightly kinder than the CD or LP to the upper string timbre, yet still retains the body and clarity of the recording.

The *Fourth* was the first of Solti's Brahms cycle to be recorded. The most distinctive point about the reading, after a very direct, fast and steady first movement, is that the *Andante moderato* of the second movement is very slow indeed, more an *Adagio*. It is not just that it starts slowly, as in some other versions; Solti characteristically maintains that speed with complete concentration. Not everyone will like the result, but it is unfailingly pure and strong, not only in the slow movement but throughout. The playing of the Chicago orchestra is magnificent – note the cellos in the second subject of the first movement, and the articulation of the anapaestic rhythms in the scherzo – and the recording is full and precise. However, on CD the very resonant bass needs cutting well back.

Janowski's is a refreshingly direct reading, treated to refined but rather recessed digital recording. Speeds are unexceptionable with the second-movement *Andante* slower than usual. The weight of the final passacaglia is undermined by the recording, and the distancing of strings in particular, though the final coda is exciting, as is the overture following. Ensemble is not so polished as in the finest versions. Disc and cassette sound very much the same.

Variations on a theme of Haydn (*St Anthony chorale*), *Op. 56a.*
(M) *** Ph. Seq. 412 005-1/*4*. Concg. O, Haitink – ELGAR: *Enigma variations.***
(M) *** CBS 60298/*40*- [MP/*MPT* 38889]. Columbia SO, Bruno Walter – DVOŘÁK: *Symphony No. 8.****

Haitink's account of the *Variations* is altogether satisfying, a beautiful and exciting reading, with the recording effectively remastered, to sound equally fresh on disc or tape. The coupling, however, is rather less memorable.

Walter's recording comes from the beginning of the 1960s and is coupled to an outstanding version of Dvořák's *G major Symphony*. It is beautifully played, the reading marked with Walter's own brand of affectionate lyricism, with orchestral playing that is both deft and gracious. The performance has a cumulative effect, moving the music onwards to a majestic re-statement of the chorale at the close. The recording is fresh and surprisingly full.

Variations on a theme of Haydn, Op. 56a (arr. for piano duet).
** CRD CRD 1113/*CRDC 4113* [id.]. Bracha Eden and Alexander Tamir (2 pianos) – *Waltzes.***

There is some evidence that, like the piano transcription of the *Third Symphony*, which these artists have also recorded, Brahms wrote out his *Variations* in piano score (for two pianos, four hands) before completing the orchestration. Both versions were written in the late summer of 1878. Much more than in the Symphony, the textural clarity of the piano arrangement is highly effective in bringing out the detail of the writing, and in this direct, robust performance, recorded with considerable presence, the music communicates strongly. As usual with CRD, there is little to choose in realism between the LPs and the excellent chrome tape.

CHAMBER MUSIC

Cello sonatas Nos 1 in E min., Op. 38; 2 in F, Op. 99.
*** DG Dig. **410 510-2**; 2532/*3302* 073 [id.]. Rostropovich, Rudolf Serkin.
*** Decca **414 558-2** [id.]; SXL/*KSXC* 6979 [Lon. CS/*5*- 7208]. Lynn Harrell, Vladimir Ashkenazy.
*** Hyp. Dig. **CDA 66159**; A/*KA* 66159 [id.]. Steven Isserlis, Peter Evans.

Cello sonatas Nos 1–2; Sonata in D (after *Violin sonata, Op. 78*).
*(*) Ph. **412 962-2** (2) [id.]. Pierre Fournier, Jean Fonda – GRIEG: *Sonata.***

The partnership of the wild, inspirational Russian cellist and the veteran Brahmsian pianist is a challenging one. It proves an outstanding success, with inspiration mutually enhanced, whether in the lyricism of Op. 38 or the heroic energy of Op. 99. Good if close recording. The balance is emphasized by the clarity of the compact disc, and the cello sounds almost as if coming from immediately inside the speakers. The various grunts and noises made by the participants also come over only too clearly. But the music making, with all its fervour, is tellingly projected, and listening becomes a very involving experience. There is an excellent chrome cassette.

Harrell and Ashkenazy give almost ideal performances of the two Brahms *Cello sonatas*, strong and passionate as well as poetic. However, although they are naturally recorded and well balanced, the acoustic is resonant and the imagery lacks the last degree of sharpness of focus. This is far less distracting with the clarification brought by CD, making the result attractively atmospheric. There is a very good tape, but the focus is most believable on compact disc.

Isserlis is one of a talented generation of young cellists, not just a fine technician but an able communicator. Using gut strings – which he always prefers – he produces an exceptionally warm tone, here nicely balanced in the recording against the strong and sensitive playing of his regular piano partner. In every way this perceptive and well-detailed reading stands in competition with the finest. The heroic power of the opening of the *F major* is presented with all the projection – if at less sheer volume – that Brahms himself would have expected. Warm, unaggressive Hyperion sound.

Fournier was seventy-eight when he made these recordings; although there are moments of distinction, they are relatively rare and the performances are dominated by his son, Jean Fonda, an effect emphasized by the balance: the piano is very tangible indeed, while Fournier's timbre is relatively meagre. At times Fournier's assurance seems to have deserted him – the opening of the transcription (by the composer) of the *Violin sonata*, Op. 78, doesn't sound very comfortable. Jean Fonda's pianism is forceful, angular in the first movement of Op. 38, almost hectoring in the opening movement of Op. 99. There are moments when the partnership finds special illumination, notably in the *Adagio* of the *F major*, but overall this is disappointing – and as two CDs are involved it is an expensive disappointment, although the Grieg coupling offers much more to give pleasure.

Clarinet quintet in B min., Op. 115.
(*) Orfeo **C 068831** [id.]. Leister, Vermeer Qt.

(i) *Clarinet quintet in B min., Op. 115;* (ii) *Clarinet trio in A min., Op. 114.*
*** Hyp. **CDA 66107**; A/*KA* 66107 [id.]. King, (i) Gabrieli Qt; (ii) Georgian, Benson (piano).

(i) *Clarinet trio in A min., Op. 114;* (ii) *Horn trio in E flat, Op. 40.*
**(*) Decca Dig. 410 114-1/*4* [id.]. (i) Schmidl, (ii) Hogner; András Schiff, members of New Vienna Octet.

Thea King and the Gabrieli Quartet give a radiantly beautiful performance of the *Clarinet quintet*, as fine as any put on record, and generously provide the ideal coupling in Brahms's other ensemble work for clarinet. Expressive and spontaneous-sounding, with natural ebb and flow of tension as in a live performance, this reading very surely resolves the perennial interpretative problem, when even the fast music is as much lyrical as dramatic. Not only does Thea King produce heavenly pianissimos, above all in the slow movement, she plays with exceptional bite and point in such a passage as the central Hungarian section in that movement. The *Trio*, a gentler work, brings a less positive performance – but still a most sensitive one. The recording of the strings is on the bright side, very vivid and real, particularly on cassette.

With members of the New Vienna Octet joining Schiff, the *Clarinet trio* is given a delightful performance, relaxed and warm, with a glowing account of the slow movement and Viennese lilt in the scherzo. The *Horn trio* has less urgency, though dramatic contrasts of dynamic are strongly brought out. Schiff's incisive playing is brightly caught on the full and realistic digital recording.

Karl Leister's Orfeo version of the *Quintet* is most disappointing, lacking lustre compared with the distinguished Berlin Philharmonic clarinettist's earlier DG recording. The Vermeer ensemble is well below form, and the recording surprisingly cloudy for CD.

Horn trio in E flat, Op. 40 (see also above).
*** Decca **414 128-2** [id.]; SXL/*KSXC* 6408 [Lon. CS 6628]. Tuckwell, Perlman, Ashkenazy – FRANCK: *Violin sonata.****

A superb performance of Brahms's marvellous *Horn trio* from Tuckwell, Perlman and Ashkenazy. They realize to the full the music's passionate impulse, and the performance moves forward from the gentle opening, through the sparkling scherzo (a typical Brahmsian inspiration, broad in manner as well as vivacious, with a heart-warming trio), the more introspective but still outgiving *Adagio* and the gay, spirited finale. The recording is worthy of the playing, although the engineers in their care not to out-balance the violin with the horn have placed the horn rather backwardly. They should have trusted Brahms: he knew what he was doing when he invented this unusual but highly effective combination. The relatively early recording date (1969) means that one must expect, even on CD, an essentially analogue sound-picture, atmospheric, rather than sharp in detail. But certainly the naturalness is enhanced when there is so little background noise. On cassette, the rather low transfer level has brought some loss of definition.

Piano quartets Nos 1 in G min., Op. 25; 2 in A, Op. 26; 3 in C min., Op. 60.
**(*) DG Dig. 413 194-1/*4* (2) [id.]. Vásáry, Brandis, Christ, Borwitzky.

The Brahms *Piano quartets* are not generously represented on disc at present, and these performances are commanding. Tamás Vásáry is particularly impressive throughout, and the string playing from the three principals of the Berlin Philharmonic is hardly less magnificent. These artists have a thorough grasp of these unfailingly rich and inventive scores and penetrate their character completely. The only reservation concerns recording quality: the players are forwardly balanced as if one were listening to them in the confines of an enclosed space, without there being sufficient room for the sound to expand. The bright, forward timbre of the strings is achieved at the expense of a natural tonal bloom. The tape layout splits all three works between sides, beginning with the *A major*, Op. 26. The first movements of both Opp. 25 and 60 are the last bands of the sides, which presents no problem on LP but is tiresome on cassette. The sound on tape is good but lacks the last degree of freshness in the upper range.

Piano quartet No. 1 in G min., Op. 25 (orch. Schoenberg).
*** HMV Dig. **CDS 747301-8** (2) [id.]. CBSO, Rattle – MAHLER: *Symphony No. 10.****
*** HMV Dig. EL 270169-1/*4*. as above, cond. Rattle.
** MMG **MCD 10018** [id.]. Baltimore SO, Comissiona.

Schoenberg's orchestral transcription of the Brahms *Piano quartet* was a labour of love and sprang from his dissatisfaction with the concert performances he heard in which the pianist was all too dominant. It has excited much – and distinguished – admiration, and it obviously enjoys Simon Rattle's devotion and commitment. Schoenberg went so far as to call it Brahms's fifth symphony and was at pains to redistribute the piano writing with all the skill at his command. The use of a xylophone in the finale strikes some listeners as bizarre, but it is the thickness of some passages that seems surprising, given Schoenberg's mastery of the orchestra. However, these are doubtless matters of opinion; the playing of the Birmingham orchestra for Rattle is so inspiriting that many doubts are silenced. Readers who want this transcription can rest assured that this performance is first class and the EMI recording natural and wide-ranging. There is an excellent XDR cassette. On CD, the transcription forms a generous bonus for Rattle's account of Mahler's *Tenth Symphony*.

A persuasive performance from the Baltimore orchestra under Comissiona, particularly by the strings, and a warm acoustic which produces an admirably Brahmsian sound. However, by present-day standards this is distinctly short measure (just over 40 minutes), particularly when one can get the Rattle version as a fill-up to Deryck Cooke's performing version of the sketch of Mahler's *Tenth Symphony*, which has the benefit of a more transparent and well-detailed recording.

Piano quintet in F min., Op. 34.
*** Ph. **412 608-2**; 412 608-1/*4* [id.]. André Previn, Musikverein Qt.

André Previn recorded this work before with the Yale quartet for HMV, but his new account with the much-admired Musikverein (the old Küchl) Quartet is far superior in every way. It is also much better recorded than its chief modern rival (Pollini and the Quartetto Italiano on DG) and the balance between pianist and quartet is very well judged. The work is beautifully shaped; the only reservation that might worry some collectors is the rather sweet vibrato of the leader, Rainer

Küchl. However, this is generally a safe recommendation and a first choice in this work in all three formats. The playing has fine vigour, warmth and spontaneity.

Piano trios Nos 1 in B, Op. 8; 2 in C, Op. 87; 3 in C min., Op. 101.
*** Chan. Dig. **CHAN 8334/5**; DBRD/*DBTD* 2005 (2) [id.]. Borodin Trio.

Piano trios Nos 1 in B, Op. 8; 3 in C min., Op. 101.
*** CRD **CRDC 3432**; CRD 1132/*CRDC 4132* [id.]. Israel Piano Trio.

Piano trio No. 2 in C, Op. 87.
*** CRD **CRDC 3433**; CRD 1133/*CRDC 4133* [id.]. Israel Piano Trio – SCHUMANN: *Piano trio No. 1.***(*)

The Borodin Trio give most musical and sensitive accounts of the three trios that convey the sense of music making in the home. Theirs are not high-powered performances in the manner of the Israel Piano Trio and they are accorded strikingly natural recording. There is strength when it is called for, lightness of touch and a sense of repose. They are not always perfectly in tune (the opening of the slow movement of Op. 8 is an example – and there are suspicions elsewhere) and this might well prove tiresome on repetition. However, the odd imperfections should not stand in the way of a recommendation in the new medium. The sound is extremely lifelike and present. The chrome cassettes have no lack of body and range and reproduce the piano tone most beautifully, but there is some fizziness at the very top.

The Israel Piano Trio give powerful accounts of all three *Trios*. They are recorded with great clarity and presence by the CRD team and play with sparkle and lightness of touch in the scherzo of Op. 8, and real sensitivity and inwardness of feeling in the slow movement. In the first movements they tend towards 'public' rather than chamber performances, the pianist at times sounding as if he is tackling a concerto, but they have no lack of eloquence or feeling. They give a fine muscular account of the opening of the *C major Trio*, though they tend to pull back somewhat self-indulgently for the second group. Throughout, however, the intensity is such that they always hold one's attention. They are very different in style from the Borodins, and their intonation is very accurate. As chamber-music making, the Chandos performances are less high-powered and in some ways more sympathetic, but the Israel group show a Brahmsian feel and their playing is commanding and spontaneous. The CDs offer fine presence and tangibility. The cassettes too are first class, and the firm focus and rich textures of the CRD tapes are preferable to the Chandos alternatives, though on CD the Chandos recording more than holds its own. However, Chandos only offer the three *Trios*, while CRD offer a substantial Schumann makeweight.

String quartets Nos 1 in C min.; 2 in A min., Op. 51/1 and 2.
*(*) Tel. **ZK8 43115** [id.]. Alban Berg Qt.

The Alban Berg Quartet play Brahms with their usual musical intelligence and offer a sophisticated blend of timbre, and immaculate ensemble. The playing has many subtleties, but the necessary Brahmsian warmth is missing. The 1978 analogue recording has good presence but is inclined to produce shrillness when the violin timbre reaches above the stave in fortissimo. There is much to admire here in the playing itself, but this is not really satisfying; the recordings by the Italian Quartet on LP and tape at medium price (Philips 6570/*7310* 919) are a safer recommendation.

Violin sonatas No. 1 in G, Op. 78; 2 in A, Op. 100; 3 in D min., Op. 108; F.A.E. Sonata: Scherzo.
(M) *** DG 415 003-1/*4* (2) [id.]. Pinchas Zukerman, Daniel Barenboim.

Violin sonatas Nos 1–3; F.A.E. Sonata: Scherzo; Hungarian dances Nos 1, 2, 7 and 9 (arr. Joachim).
*** HMV Dig. **CDC 747403-2** [id.]; EX 270010-3/*9* (2). Itzhak Perlman, Vladimir Ashkenazy.

Perlman and Ashkenazy bring out the trouble-free happiness of these lyrical inspirations, even in the *D minor Sonata* where the melody which opens the second-movement *Adagio* finds Perlman broad and warm, weighty yet avoiding underlying tensions. In their sureness and flawless confidence at generally spacious speeds, these are performances which carry you along cocooned in rich sound. One result is that, even more than with Zukerman and Barenboim, all three sonatas sound more alike than they usually do. Some may miss the bite of tension, even with Perlman's violin placed rather too close, in otherwise excellent recording, but the Hungarian or Slavonic tang of the first contrasting episode of the 'raindrop' finale of No. 1 or the contrasting vivace passages in the second movement of No. 2 are delectably pointed. The fill-up of four *Hungarian dances* is apt and delightful but not generous, with these Joachim arrangements bringing the most carefree playing. On a single extended-length tape (in a slimline box) *Sontas Nos 1* and *2* are complete on side one with *Sonata No. 3* plus the other pieces on side two. The high-level transfer has brought good presence but also a hint of edginess to the violin timbre at higher dynamic levels. The compact disc is announced as we go to press – we have not been able to sample it.

From Zukerman and Barenboim, warmly expressive performances, highly polished too, but with an easy spontaneity. Speeds are generally spacious, and Barenboim is particularly strong and thoughtful in this repertoire. Zukerman's approach tends to be much the same in all three works, and some listeners may find him a shade too elegant and sweet. Yet the *Third Sonata* has added tensions and proves particularly successful. At medium price, with faithful chrome-tape equivalents, these well-recorded performances are good value. One remembers, however, that the much-admired Suk/Katchen Decca set (currently out of the catalogue) managed to get all three *Sonatas* on a single disc.

Violin sonata No. 2 in A, Op. 100.
*** DG Walkman *415 615-4* [id.]. Christian Ferras, Pierre Barbizet – BEETHOVEN: *Violin sonatas 5 and 9.****

This intimately lyrical performance of the *A major Sonata* is most enjoyable. It is placed on side one of the Walkman cassette, immediately following the Menuhin/Kempff version of Beethoven's *Spring sonata*, and acts as an excellent foil to it. The recording is truthful and the transfers excellent.

PIANO MUSIC

4 Ballades, Op. 10.
*** DG Dig. **400 043-2**; 2532/*3302* 017 [id.]. Michelangeli – SCHUBERT: *Sonata No. 4.***

4 Ballades, Op. 10; 8 Pieces, Op. 76; Scherzo in E flat, Op. 4.
ℭ *** Ph. Dig. **411 103-2**; 411 103-1/*4* [id.]. Stephen Bishop-Kovacevich.

4 Ballades; 2 Rhapsodies, Op. 79; Waltzes, Op. 39.
*(*) CBS Dig. **CD 37800**; 37800/*40*- [id.]. Glenn Gould.

Michelangeli plays an instrument made in the 1910s that produces a wonderfully blended tone and a fine mellow sonority. The *Ballades* are given a performance of the greatest distinction and without the slightly aloof quality that at times disturbs his readings. Gilels had the greater insight and inwardness, perhaps, but there is no doubt that this is very fine playing, and it is superbly recorded. The compact disc is very impressive and approaches demonstration standard. The chrome cassette is also of high quality.

We know from his (now-deleted) accounts of the concertos that Bishop-Kovacevich is a distinguished Brahmsian. His fine performances of both the *Ballades* and the Op. 76 *Klavierstücke* have both fire and tenderness, and are most truthfully recorded. The Philips engineers seem to be particularly fortunate with the piano, and this record is no exception. The CD is wonderfully realistic and has the utmost presence. One hopes that Philips will encourage this artist to go on to record the complete piano music. The chrome cassette is naturally balanced and handles the wide dynamics of the recording without stress; the focus, however, is softer-grained and the CD image has greater tangibility.

Glenn Gould seems reluctant to let the *D minor Ballade* speak for itself and indulges in much exaggeration, lingering over cadences and losing any sense of natural movement. He has many insights of interest to offer but, overall, his view is too idiosyncratic to be widely recommended, and certainly not as an only version. The sound is dry and shallow, which is presumably what this artist liked, since his name is billed as co-producer. LP and chrome cassette sound very similar. The CD has added presence.

7 Fantasias, Op. 116; 3 Intermezzi, Op. 117; 4 Pieces, Op. 119.
*** Ph. **411 137-2**; 411 137-1/*4* [id.]. Stephen Bishop-Kovacevich.

This further issue in Stephen Bishop-Kovacevich's Brahms series for Philips can be strongly recommended. He finds the fullest range of emotional contrast in the Op. 116 *Fantasias*, but is at his finest in the Op. 117 *Intermezzi* and four

Klavierstücke, Op. 119, which contain some of Brahms's most beautiful lyrical inspirations for the keyboard. Some readers might feel that his slightly hesitant articulation of the first *E flat major Intermezzo* is a little self-conscious. (Brahms prefaced this marvellous piece with a quotation from a Scottish folk-poem: *Balou, my boy, lye still and sleep, it grieves me sore to hear thee weep*, and the opening phrase is like a vocal setting of these words.) But the poetic feeling of the playing is never in doubt and the serenity of the nostalgic second *Intermezzo in B flat minor* and the first *Piece*, (*Adagio*) of Op. 119 is very touching. The *Allegro risoluto* of the finale *Rhapsodie*, of Op. 119, which ends the recital, has splendid flair and passion. The recording is well up to Philips's usual high standard on CD, but the softer focus of the chrome tape brings occasional slight blurring of the image.

Hungarian dances for piano, 4 hands Nos 1–3; 5; 6; 11; 14; 16; 17; 19; 20.
(M) *** DG Sig. 413 984-1/*4* [id.]. Alfons and Aloys Kontarsky (piano duet) – DVOŘÁK: *Slavonic dances*.***

The Kontarsky Duo are given a crisp, modern DG recording and their performances are brilliant and full of character. For this mid-priced Signature reissue, some of the dances have been omitted from the complete set to make way for their no less attractive accounts of the Dvořák *Slavonic dances*, Op. 8. With an excellent chrome cassette, matching the LP in clarity and realism, this is a bargain.

Piano sonata No. 3 in F sharp min., Op. 5.
(*) Hung. Dig. **HCD 12601; SLPD/*MK* 12601 [id.]. Zoltán Kocsis.
(*) ASV ALH/*ZCALH* 948 [id.]. Shura Cherkassky – SCHUBERT: *Sonata No. 13*.(*)

Piano sonata No. 3; Theme and variations in D min. (from *String sextet, Op. 18*).
*** Decca Dig. **417 122-2**; SXDL 7561 [Lon. LDR 71061]. Radu Lupu.

Noble, dignified and spacious are the adjectives that spring to mind when listening to Lupu's Op. 5. He does not, perhaps, have the youthful ardour of Kocsis or the communicative qualities of Krystian Zimerman's account (which DG will surely make available on CD during the lifetime of this book). At times in the first movement one feels the need for a greater sense of forward movement: Lupu's view is inward, ruminative and always beautifully rounded. The *Variations* are at present only otherwise available in Zimerman's DG version. The recording is most realistic, the piano set slightly back, the timbre fully coloured, and the focus natural.

Kocsis gives an ardent account of the *F sharp minor Sonata*. Though this is not quite in the same flight either artistically or technically as his Debussy CD on Philips, it still has much to recommend it. His performance is spacious and expansive, and there is no lack of warmth. The slow tempo (an *adagio* rather than *andante*) he adopts in the second and fourth movements may worry some listeners – though this is not quite as disturbing as the small agogic exaggerations in which he indulges. The last few bars of the exposition of the first movement are pulled out of shape and the music comes to a virtual standstill at bar 24 of the second. Yet what wonderful points he makes elsewhere: never have those forward-looking harmonies in the *Intermezzo* (bars 19–23) sounded more Debussian, and he brings an almost nightmarish intensity to the gaunt, powerfully charged opening. For all one's reservations, this is playing of great imagination and artistry, and the recording is eminently truthful.

Cherkassky's recording was made in 1968 at a recital in London's Queen Elizabeth Hall with an unusually unobtrusive audience whose presence is only disclosed by the final applause. The performance is a magnificent one and shows a warmth and wisdom that resound in the memory. The *Andante* has wonderful inwardness and imagination, and only the fourth movement, *Rückblick*, lets it down with some agogic eccentricities and a terribly slow tempo. There is an insecure moment in the first movement but, all in all, this performance has such eloquence and humanity that criticism is disarmed. The sound is very truthful, like a well-balanced broadcast, but is not as full-bodied as the most recent Decca or Philips studio recordings, and the tape judders very slightly at bar 38 of the *Andante* of the *F minor Sonata*. Strongly recommended all the same, particularly in view of the bonus in the form of the Schubert *A major Sonata*. The cassette transfer has plenty of life, but the upper range of the piano timbre is somewhat shallow in fortissimos.

Waltzes Nos 1–16, Op. 39.
** CRD CRD 1113/*CRDC 4113* [id.]. Bracha Eden and Alexander Tamir – *Variations on a theme of Haydn.***

Spirited performance of these engaging miniatures from Eden and Tamir who play with flair, if not always a great deal of charm. Rhythms are strong rather than seductive. The recording is very realistic, on both LP and tape, but this issue is of primary interest for Brahms's own piano score of the *St Anthony Variations* (see below).

VOCAL MUSIC

Lieder: *Alte Liebe; Auf dem Kirchhofe; Feldeinsamkeit; Nachklang; O wusst' ich doch; Verzagen. Vier ernste Gesänge (4 Serious Songs), Op. 21.*
(*) DG **415 189-2 [id.]. Dietrich Fischer-Dieskau, Joerg Demus – BEETHOVEN: *Lieder.***(*)

Recorded in the late 1960s, Fischer-Dieskau's Brahms selection on CD brings consistently imaginative singing. His darkness and intensity in the *Four Serious Songs* are hardly matched in the relatively lightweight accompaniments from Demus – placed at a disadvantage by the recording balance; this is, however, an attractive choice of repertoire and, with excellent transfers presenting an ageing recording in the best possible light, the disc can be warmly recommended, particularly when the measure of music (over 70 minutes) is so generous.

(i) *Alto rhapsody, Op. 53; Funeral ode, Op. 13; Nänie, Op. 82; Song of the Fates, Op. 89.*
(*) HM Orfeo **C 025821A; S 025821A [id.]. (i) Alfreda Hodgson; Bav. R. Ch. and SO, Haitink.

Alfreda Hodgson and Bernard Haitink make a good partnership in the *Alto rhapsody*. Both respond to the work with an element of restraint, but there is also eloquence; though there is some lack of warmth, a natural response to the words brings dramatic articulation, too. The other works combine refinement with moments of fervour in much the same way, and there is some splendid singing from the Bavarian choir, especially in the *Funeral ode*. The 1981 analogue recording was made within a resonant acoustic, with the chorus and orchestra slightly backward in a concert-hall setting. Not everything is crystal clear, but the overall impression suits the music admirably and gives a convincing sense of realism.

Alto rhapsody, Op. 53; Song of destiny (Schicksalslied), Op. 54.
** CBS **MK 42025** [id.]. Mildred Miller, Occidental College Concert Ch., Columbia SO, Walter – MAHLER: *Lieder eines fahrenden Gesellen.***

Mildred Miller is a fresh rather than inspirational soloist in the *Alto rhapsody*, and in spite of coaching from Walter (who had decided views on the interpretation of this fine work) she gives a somewhat strait-laced account of the opening pages. The *Song of destiny* is very satisfactory, however, and displays the capabilities of the chorus to good effect. The CD transfers are well managed, with the orchestral detail in the *Rhapsody*, and the fine choral singing in both works, showing that Walter's directing hand has a special contribution to make.

Die Botschaft. (i) *2 Songs with viola, Op. 91 (Gestillte Sehnsucht; Geistliches Wiegenlied). Immer leiser; Die Mainacht; Meine Liebe ist grün; O komme, holde Sommernacht; Ständchen; Therese; Der Tod das ist die kühle Nachte; Von ewiger Liebe; Wie Melodien zieht es mir.*
(*) Ph. **416 439-2; 9500 785 [id.]. Norman, Parsons, with (i) von Wrochem.

The scale and tonal range of Jessye Norman's voice are ideal for many of these songs, but in some of them there is a studied quality which makes the result a little too static. That is particularly so in the most ambitious of the songs, *Von ewiger Liebe*, which mistakenly is put first. Nevertheless, there is much distinguished singing and playing here, and it is superbly recorded. The CD remastering adds presence and the effect is most realistic.

German Requiem, Op. 45.
(*) DG Dig. **410 521-2; 410 521-1/*4* [id.]. Hendricks, Van Dam, V. Singverein, VPO, Karajan – BRUCKNER: *Te Deum.***
(*) RCA Dig. **RD 85003 [RD-1 5003]. Battle, Hagegard, Chicago Ch. and SO, Levine.

(M) **(*) DG 415 000-1/*4* (2) [id.]. Mathis, Fischer-Dieskau, Edinburgh Fest. Ch., LPO, Barenboim – BRUCKNER: *Te Deum.****

** Telarc Dig. **CD 80092** [id.]. Augér, Stilwell, Atlanta Ch. and SO, Shaw.

German Requiem; Song of destiny, Op. 54.

(*) Ph. Dig. **411 436-2; 6769/*7654* 055 (2) [id.]. Janowitz, Krause, V. State Op. Ch., VPO, Haitink.

(i) *German Requiem; Variations on a theme of Haydn, Op. 56a.*

** Decca **414 627-2** [id.]; D 135 D 2/*K 135K 22* (2) [Lon. OSA/5 12114]. Te Kanawa, Weikl, Chicago Ch. and SO, Solti.

*(*) Orfeo SO 38924H (2) [id.]. (i) Margaret Price, Thomas Allen, Bav. R. Ch., Mun. Hochschule Chamber Ch., Bav. RSO, Sawallisch.

The chorus of the Vienna Singverein sounds disappointingly opaque in Karajan's latest version of a work which he has now recorded four times, but that is the only serious shortcoming of a reading which persuasively brings out the warmth of Brahms's writing, not merely its devotional or monumental qualities. The performance is not quite so polished as previous versions, but the sense of spontaneity is all the keener, and the soloists provide characterful contributions, even if the rapid vibrato of Barbara Hendricks detracts from a feeling of innocence in *Ihr habt nun Traurigkeit*. The relative closeness of the orchestra in the recording balance adds to the feeling of constriction in the sound. The cassettes match the discs closely, but the CDs have extra definition, although this serves to emphasize the faults of balance.

Haitink chooses very slow tempi in the *German Requiem*. There is a rapt quality in this glowing performance that creates an atmosphere of simple dedication; at slow speed *Denn alles Fleisch* (*All flesh is grass*) is made the more relentless when, with total concentration, textures are so sharply clarified. The digital recording offers beautiful sound and, with outstanding soloists – Gundula Janowitz notably pure and poised – this is very persuasive. The fill-up is the rarely recorded *Schicksalslied* (*Song of destiny*), which is most welcome and is admirably sung and played. On CD, with extra clarity and natural bass response, the warm and atmospheric qualities of the recording are all the more impressive, but the cassettes, transferred at a low level, are disappointingly amorphous and bass-heavy.

Levine's version starts with two big assets: it is contained complete on a single CD of over 70 minutes' length, and Margaret Hillis's celebrated Chicago Symphony Chorus is probably the finest in America. In addition, the two soloists both prove excellent, Kathleen Battle pure and sweetly vulnerable-sounding, Hagegard clear-cut and firm. Nor does Levine race the music to get it down to CD length. The outer movements of the seven may be faster than usual so that the first is hardly meditative, but there is no sense of haste. More serious is Levine's choice of an exceptionally slow speed for the second movement, *Denn alles Fleisch*, even slower than Haitink's and, unlike his, sounding rhythmically stodgy if undeniably powerful in impact. Levine may not be the most illuminating conductor in this work, and the recording is not ideal – with inner textures growing cloudy in tuttis – but for a 'bargain' CD version it will give much pleasure.

The reissue of Barenboim's 1973 recording offers a fine mid-price recommendation. The chorus is much clearer than in Karajan's digital set and, with the soloists forwardly balanced, the recording – on both disc and the excellent matching chrome tapes – captures the widest dynamic range. Barenboim's interpretation, individual to the point of being idiosyncratic, is very persuasive and often thrillingly dramatic (as in Parts Six and Seven which includes words familiar from Handel's *Messiah*: *Behold, I show you a mystery; we shall not all sleep, but we shall all be changed, in a moment, in the twinkling of an eye* – but sounding very different in Brahms's setting). Though the reading cannot be said to copy Furtwängler, there is something about Barenboim's approach to Brahms which here recalls the older master; while it is partly to the credit of the excellent engineering that the textures are clarified, the conductor's skill in balancing his forces and retaining choral incisiveness, while still achieving a warmly beautiful sound, is consistently impressive and makes this performance very enjoyable. Moreover, the coupled Bruckner *Te Deum* is much more successful than the new Karajan version, and adds to the attractions of this set. The tapes are offered in one of DG's flap-pack cardboard boxes.

Even more strikingly than in his set of the Brahms symphonies, Solti here favours very expansive tempi, smooth lines and refined textures. There is much that is beautiful, even if the result overall is not as involving as it might be. Kiri Te Kanawa sings radiantly, but Bernd Weikl with his rather gritty baritone is not ideal. Fine recording, glowing and clear, with an excellent tape equivalent.

Robert Shaw's experience as a leading choirmaster – working with his Chorale for Toscanini during the maestro's last years – makes for some exceptionally fresh and well-disciplined singing. The superb definition of the Telarc recording – more successful here than in the parallel recording of the Berlioz *Requiem* – brings even Brahms's murkiest passages into the light of day; and the firmness and clarity of the organ pedal at the very start demonstrates the quality of the engineers' work, though in places the very weight of the bass might be counted too heavy, even though it brings no boominess or distortion. This means that even in murmured choral pianissimos there is nothing hazy, but the very plainness underlines a limitation in the interpretation. For all its freshness and innocence, it does not convey the sense of occasion or detailed imagination of Karajan or – to take the other single-disc version – Levine on RCA, which is notably more individual. Good solo singing, with Arleen Augér superbly silvery and true in *Ihr habt nun Traurigkeit*.

The best point about Sawallisch's Orfeo version is the noble singing of Thomas Allen as baritone soloist. Margaret Price also sings powerfully in her one solo but misses the innocent purity of expression needed. The rest is disappointing, often too slow and heavy, and the recording brings thin violin tone and choral sound that tends to overload.

Still recommended: Klemperer's EMI version of the *German Requiem* with Schwarzkopf and Fischer-Dieskau is measured and characteristically monumental, but the solo singing is superb; although the chorus is backwardly balanced, the Phiharmonia Chorus were at the peak of their form. This is announced for CD issue as we go press (HMV **CDS 747238-3**).

5 Ophelia Lieder from 'Hamlet'; 2 Songs with viola, Op. 91. Lieder: *Dort in den Weiden; Gold überwiegt die Liebe; Der Jäger; Klage; Die Liebende schreibt; Liebesklage des Mädchens; Des Liebsten Schwur; 2 Mädchenlied; Mädchenfluch; Spanisches Lied; Todessehnen; Die Trauernde; Vorschneller Schwur.*
*** DG Dig. 413 787-1/*4* [id.]. Jessye Norman, Daniel Barenboim.

Like Jessye Norman's other selection of Brahms Lieder with Barenboim for DG (see below), this one was originally part of the Brahms Edition; it brings richly expressive performances of a wide-ranging group. Specially notable are the five *Ophelia Lieder* and the two *Songs with viola.* First-rate recording. There is an excellent cassette which gives the artists vivid presence, although some of the consonants are made to sound slightly edgier than on LP.

Romanzen und Lieder, Op. 84; Sapphische ode, Op. 94/4; Zigeunerlieder, Op. 103; Lieder: Dein blaues Auge; Klage I and II; Liebestreu; Das Mädchen; Das Mädchen spricht; Regenlied; Salome; Der Schmied; Therese; Vom Strande.
*** DG Dig. 413 311-1/*4* [id.]. Jessye Norman, Daniel Barenboim.

Jessye Norman is at her finest in this delightful and strongly contrasted selection from DG's Lieder box in the Brahms Edition. The task of recording a complete set of women's songs seems in this instance to have added to the warmth and sense of spontaneity of both singer and pianist in the studio. The heroic scale of *Der Schmied* is superb, as is the open simplicity of the *Zigeunerlieder*, while the gentler songs find the gloriously ample voice exquisitely scaled down. First-rate recording on both disc and cassette.

Bridge, Frank (1879–1941)

Lament for string orchestra; Two Old English songs (1, Sally in our alley; 2, Cherry ripe); Rosemary (Entracte No. 1); Sir Roger de Coverley (Christmas dance); Suite for string orchestra.
*** Lyr. SRCS 73. LPO, Boult.

All these pieces are expertly crafted and, though light in character, they are far from insignificant. They are nicely played by the LPO under Sir Adrian and recorded with great clarity and presence. A useful though not essential part of the Frank Bridge discography.

Suite for strings; Summer; There is a willow grows aslant a brook.
*** Chan. **CHAN 8373**; CBR/*CBT* 1018 [id.]. Bournemouth Sinf., Del Mar – BANTOCK: *Pierrot of the minute*; BUTTERWORTH: *Bank of green willow.****

The recording comes from 1979 and subsequently was digitally remastered.

Summer, written in 1914 just before the outbreak of the First World War, is one of Bridge's most evocative and imaginative scores, and it is beautifully played by the Bournemouth Sinfonietta under Norman Del Mar. The same images of nature permeate the miniature tone-poem, *There is a willow grows aslant a brook*, written in 1927. Both are inspired pieces and they are sensitively played. The *Suite for strings* is a somewhat earlier piece (1909–10) and is less impressive, though its third movement, a *Nocturne*, is lovely. The CD transfer is excellent and one can relish its finer definition and presence. There is also a very good (mid-price) cassette.

Britten, Benjamin (1913–76)

An American overture, Op. 27; Occasional overture, Op. 38; Sinfonia da Requiem, Op. 20; Suite on English folk tunes: A time there was, Op. 90.
*** HMV Dig. **CDC 747343-2** [id.]; EL 270263-1/*4* [Ang. DFO 38236]. CBSO, Rattle.

Although concentrating on early works, this collection spans Britten's composing career. Both the *Sinfonia da Requiem* (1940) and the *American overture* (1941), with its attractive whiff of Copland, belong to the composer's wartime residence in the USA. The *Occasional overture* (1946) with its brilliant orchestral command was commissioned by the BBC for the opening of the Third Programme. The *Suite on English folk tunes* was not completed until 1974, although one movement, the quirky *Hankin Booby* – for wind and drums – dates from 1966, another commission, this time for the opening of the Queen Elizabeth Hall. While the most ambitious piece is the *Sinfonia da Requiem*, written after the death of Britten's parents, the *Folk tunes suite* is a good deal more diverse in mood than one might expect, with the eloquent last movement, *Lord Melbourne*, with its beautiful cor anglais evocation, the longest and most memorable. The whole programme is splendidly played by the City of Birmingham orchestra under Rattle, whose passionate view of the *Sinfonia da Requiem* is unashamedly extrovert, yet finding subtle detail too. The recording is admirably vivid and clear, especially in its CD format; the cassette is one of EMI's best and is very well balanced, but the compact disc has an extra dimension of presence.

Violin concerto in D min., Op. 15.
(M) *** HMV ED 290353-1/*4*. Ida Haendel, Bournemouth SO, Berglund – WALTON: *Concerto.****
(B) *** CfP CFP 41 4489-1/*4*. Rodney Friend, LPO, Pritchard – TIPPETT: *Concerto for double string orchestra.****

Miss Haendel's ravishing playing places Britten's concerto firmly in the European tradition. She brings much panache and brilliance to the music, as well as great expressive warmth. This is a reading very much in the grand manner, and it finds Paavo Berglund in excellent form. His support is sensitive in matters of detail and full of atmosphere. The recording is most realistic, with a spacious perspective and warm string tone that is positively Mediterranean in feeling. The soloist is balanced a little close, but generally the security of her technique can stand up to such a revealing spotlight. The tape transfer must be accounted as successful as the disc, catching the full bloom of the violin timbre and managing the resonant orchestral acoustic without problems.

The rival version is also highly competitive. Originally coupled with the *Serenade*, it is now linked with Vernon Handley's outstanding performance of Tippett's string concerto. Rodney Friend, at the time leader of the LPO, later concert-master of the New York Philharmonic, proves a masterful soloist, less seductive than Ida Haendel, but magnificently incisive and expressive. With a first-class accompaniment from the LPO under Sir John Pritchard, this makes an excellent bargain issue, equally impressive on disc or tape.

Matinées musicales, Op. 25; Soirées musicales, Op. 9.
*** Decca Dig. **410 139-2**; SXDL/*KSXDC* 7539 [Lon. LDR/5- 71039]. Nat. PO, Bonynge – ROSSINI: *La Boutique fantasque*.*** ₵

Bonynge's versions of the two sets of *Musicales* are brightly played and extremely vividly recorded in the Decca manner, and on the compact disc the sparkle in the upper range and the vivid orchestral detail are very striking indeed. The balance is forward but there is no lack of ambience. The chrome tape, transferred at a modest level for Decca, is disappointing – there is much less glitter than on the LP, to say nothing of the compact disc.

Prelude and fugue for 18 solo strings, Op. 29; Simple symphony, Op. 4; Variations on a theme of Frank Bridge, Op. 10.
(*) Chan. **CHAN 8376; CRB/*CBT* 1018 [id.]. Bournemouth Sinf., Ronald Thomas.

Though inevitably comparisons with Britten's own recordings of these three string works reveal felicities that are missing here, the coupling is most attractive, the performances have a natural expressive warmth which is most engaging and, not least, the recording has a ripeness and resonance which are most satisfying, particularly in the bass registers, especially telling in the *Variations* in their CD format. The cassette too is extremely successful.

(i) *Symphony for cello and orchestra, Op. 68; Death in Venice: suite, Op. 88* (arr. Bedford).
₵ *** Chan. Dig. **CHAN 8363**; ABRD/*ABTD* 1126 [id.]. (i) Wallfisch; ECO, Bedford.

This is the first account of Britten's *Cello symphony* since Rostropovich's pioneering LP with Britten himself conducting, and the first version to reach CD. It is a marvellous piece, very much a new landscape in Britten's world. The example of the dedicatee, Rostropovich, in the concert hall as well as on record has been so commanding that any rival has to be very daring. Here it is astonishing how closely Wallfisch – in collaboration with the conductor who carried on the Aldeburgh tradition when Britten ceased to conduct – manages to match that unique artist. If Wallfisch's tone is not so resonant as Rostropovich's the slight help from the recording balance gives it all the power needed, and there is a case for preferring Wallfisch's rather more direct approach to the craggily fragmentary first movement. Sounding less improvisatory than Rostropovich, he and Bedford give a more consistent sense of purpose, and the weight and range of the brilliant and full Chandos recording quality add to the impact. If in the brief central scherzo Wallfisch does not achieve the lightness and fantasy of the dedicatee, the differences are minimal. Equally the power and purpose of the finale are formidable, with Bedford's direction even more spacious than the composer's, the effect emphasized by the Chandos ambience, spacious and warm.

Steuart Bedford's encapsulation of Britten's last opera into this rich and colourful suite makes a splendid coupling. It brings together most of the richest and atmospheric passages from an outstandingly intense and moving work which has never enjoyed the currency of his earlier stage masterpieces. The sequence of movements exactly follows the dramatic order in the opera, but by happy chance the result makes an exceptionally cogent and well-integrated musical structure in a continuous movement. Even so, it is a pity that the CD does not have bands between the separate sections. Otherwise performances and recording can hardly be faulted, and in its compact disc format the clarity and definition are outstanding.

The Young person's guide to the orchestra (*Variations and fugue on a theme of Purcell*), *Op. 34.*

** RCA **RD 82743 [RCD1 2743]**; RL/*RK* 12743 [ARL1/*ARK1* 2743]. Phd. O, Ormandy – PROKOFIEV: *Peter.***(*)

A 1978 analogue recording provides the CD début for the Britten *Young person's guide to the orchestra*. Ormandy's performance is straightforward and very well played. It has no special individuality except, perhaps, for the clarinets, whose contribution is attractively genial. The digital remastering tends to emphasize the brilliance of the sound. There is a hint of shrillness in the upper strings and no supporting weight in the bass. The brass and percussion, however, add a touch of spectacle. But there is nothing really distinctive here. There is a wide choice of recordings available on LP and cassette, including the composer's own on Decca, and excellent versions by Previn and Groves on HMV; the latter has the advantage of economy and very generous couplings (ESD/*TCESD* 7114).

VOCAL MUSIC

A boy was born, Op. 3; Festival Te Deum, Op. 32; Rejoice in the Lamb, Op. 30; A Wedding anthem, Op. 46.

*** Hyp. **CDA 66126**; A/*KA* 66126 [id.]. Corydon Singers, Westminster Cathedral Ch., Best; Trotter (organ).

Britten's brilliant set of choral variations, atmospheric and strikingly varied in character, was completed when he was only nineteen, a masterly work here beautifully performed and recorded, and generously coupled with a group of other small Britten choral works. All of them are sharply inspired, usually to match the requirements of particular occasions, as for example the *Wedding anthem* written for the wedding of Lord Harewood and Marion Stein, and never recorded before. *Rejoice in the Lamb* is the most masterly of the pieces, poignantly matching the pain as well as the innocence of the words of the mad poet, Christopher Smart. The refinement and tonal range of the choirs could hardly be more impressive, and the recording is refined and atmospheric to match.

Folksong arrangements: *The ash grove; Avenging and bright; La belle est au jardin d'amour; The bonny Earl o'Moray; The brisk young widow; Ca' the yowes; Come you not from Newcastle?; Early one morning; How sweet the answer; The last rose of summer; The minstrel boy; The miller of Dee; Oft in the stilly night; The plough boy; Le roi s'en va-t' en chasse; Sweet Polly Oliver; O waly, waly.*
(M) *** Decca 411 802-1/*4*. Peter Pears, Benjamin Britten.

Folksong arrangements: *The ash grove; La belle est au jardin d'amour; The bonny Earl o'Moray; The brisk young widow; Ca' the yowes; Come you not from Newcastle?; The foggy, foggy dew; The Lincolnshire poacher; Little Sir William; The minstrel boy; O can ye sew cushions; Oliver Cromwell; O waly, waly; The plough boy; Quand j'étais chez mon père; Le rois s'en va-t' en chasse; The Sally Gardens; Sweet Polly Oliver; The trees they grow so high.*
(M) *** HMV ED 290352-1/*4*. Robert Tear, Philip Ledger.

The reissue of the Pears/Britten collection reminds us of the *Punch* jingle:

> There's no need for Pears
> To give himself airs;
> He has them written
> By Benjamin Britten.

We must be grateful for such bounty. *Earl o'Moray* has almost too much Britten, and the accompaniment for *Early one morning* is unnecessarily clever and almost distracting. But others are delightful, especially *The ash grove* and the French song about the king going hunting. The recording is admirably faithful.

Close as Robert Tear's interpretations are to those of Peter Pears, he has a sparkle of his own, helped by resilient accompaniment from Philip Ledger. In any case, some of these songs are unavailable in Pears' versions, and the record is a delight on its own account. *Oliver Cromwell* is among the most delectable of pay-off songs ever written. Fine recording.

(i) *Les Illuminations* (song cycle), *Op. 18*; (ii) *Serenade for tenor, horn and strings, Op. 18*; (iii) *Nocturne*.
*** Decca **417 153-2** [id.]. Peter Pears, (i; ii) ECO; (ii) with Barry Tuckwell; (iii) wind soloists, LSO strings; composer.

Peter Pears's voice is so ideally suited to this music, his insight into word-meaning as well as phrase-shaping so masterly, that for once one can use the adjective 'definitive'. With dedicated accompaniments under the composer's direction, *Les Illuminations* and the *Serenade* (with its superbly played horn obbligato by Barry Tuckwell), which both come from the mid-1960s, make a perfect coupling. For the CD release, Decca have added the recording of the *Nocturne* from 1960. In this wide-ranging cycle on the subject of night and sleep, Britten chose from a diverse selection of poems – by Coleridge, Tennyson, Wordsworth, Wilfred Owen and Keats, finishing with a Shakespeare sonnet. It is a work full – as so much of Britten's output is – of memorable moments. One thinks of the 'breathing' motif on the strings which links the different songs, the brilliant dialogue for flute and clarinet in the Keats setting, and above all the towering climax of the Wordsworth excerpt. Each song has a different obbligato instrument (with the ensemble unified for the final Shakespeare song), and each instrument gives the song it is associated with its own individual character. Pears as always is the ideal interpreter, the composer a most efficient conductor, and the fiendishly difficult obbligato parts are played superbly. The recording is brilliant and clear, with just the right degree of atmosphere.

War requiem, Op. 66.

*** Decca **414 383-2** [id.]; SET 252-3/*K 27 K 22* [Lon. OSA/*5*- 1255]. Vishnevskaya, Pears, Fischer-Dieskau, Bach Ch., LSO Ch., Highgate School Ch., Melos Ens., LSO, composer.

*** HMV Dig. **CDS 747034-8** [id.]; SLS/*TC-SLS* 107757-3/*9* (2) [Ang. DSB/*4X2S* 3939]. Söderström, Tear, Allen, Trebles of Christ Church Cathedral Ch., Oxford, CBSO Ch., CBSO, Rattle.

The vivid realism of Britten's own 1963 recording of the *War Requiem*, one of the outstanding achievements of the whole analogue stereo era, comes over the more strikingly in the CD transfer, with uncannily precise placing and balancing of the many different voices and instruments. John Culshaw's contribution as producer is all the more apparent, but the penalty of CD precision is that the tape hiss is high, to the point of being at times distracting. Indeed it is more noticeable here than on the equivalent cassettes. Britten pointed the contrast between the full choir and orchestra in the settings of the *Requiem* and the tenor, baritone and chamber orchestra in the intervening settings of the Wilfred Owen poems. But what a recording can do that is impossible in a cathedral or concert hall is to modify the acoustic for each, and this has been done most sensitively and effectively by the Decca engineers. The Owen settings strike one more sharply than the Latin settings, but gradually as the work progresses the process of integration is accomplished, and the way the soloists' cries of *Let us sleep now* fade into the final chorus is almost unbearably moving on record as in performance. The recorded performance comes near to the ideal, but it is a pity that Britten insisted on Vishnevskaya for the soprano solos. Having a Russian singer was emotionally right, but musically Heather Harper would have been so much better still. The cassette issue, too, offers sound of remarkable depth and clarity. The work's closing pages are wonderfully effective heard against an almost silent background, with no possible danger of intrusive clicks and pops.

The HMV recording for Rattle, much closer in its perspectives and wider in frequency range but not more realistic than Britten's own set, is all the more immediate on CD, and with a fully digital recording there is no problem over background noise. The most striking difference between Rattle's interpretation and that of Britten himself lies in the relationship between the settings of Owen's poems and the setting of the liturgy in Latin. With Söderström a far more warmly expressive soloist than the oracular Vishnevskaya, the human emotions behind the Latin text come out strongly with less distancing than from the composer. One registers the more clearly the meaning of the Latin. Tear and Allen are fine soloists, though at times balanced too forwardly. If Tear does not always match the subtlety of Pears on the original recording, Allen sounds more idiomatic than Fischer-Dieskau. Rattle's approach is warm, dedicated and dramatic, with fine choral singing (not least from the Christ Church Cathedral trebles). The dramatic orchestral contrasts are superbly brought out as in the blaze of trumpets on *Hosanna*. The various layers of perspective are impressively managed by the superb digital recording with little to choose in definition between the LPs and the first-rate XDR tape, except that the layout on cassette has the advantage of added continuity with the music spaced over two sides (as against four on LP and CD). Yet in its combination of imaginative flair with technical expertise, the Culshaw recording of two decades earlier is by no means surpassed by this new HMV venture; indeed in sophistication of acoustic and detail it remains in a class of its own.

OPERA

Peter Grimes (complete).

❀ ℭ *** Decca **414 577-2** [id.]; SXL 2150-2/*K 71 K 33* (2) [Lon. OSA/5-1305]. Pears, Claire Watson, Pease, Jean Watson, Nilsson, Brannigan, Evans, Ch. and O of ROHCG, composer.

The Decca recording of *Peter Grimes* was one of the first great achievements of the stereo era. Few opera recordings can claim to be so definitive, with Peter Pears, for whom it was written, in the name part, Owen Brannigan (another member of the original team) and a first-rate cast. One was a little apprehensive about Claire Watson as Ellen Orford, a part which Joan Cross made her own, but in the event Miss Watson gives a most sympathetic performance, and her voice records beautifully. Another member of the cast from across the Atlantic, James Pease, as the understanding Captain Balstrode, is brilliantly incisive musically and dramatically; but beyond that it becomes increasingly unfair to single out individual performances. Britten conducts superbly and secures splendidly incisive playing, with the whole orchestra on its toes throughout. The recording, superbly atmospheric, has so many felicities that it would be hard to enumerate them, and the Decca engineers have done wonders in making up aurally for the lack of visual effects. Moreover, the digital remastering for CD miraculously has improved the sound still further. The striking overall bloom remains, yet solo voices and chorus are vividly clear and fully projected. Owen Brannigan sounds wonderfully ripe and present in the Prologue, while the orchestral sound is glorious. Some background noise remains, of course, but it is not really intrusive and, apart from that, one might think this a modern digital set. The 44 cues bring access to every item in the score. A marvellous sampler is provided by trying band 5 on the first disc; this brings the evocative *First Sea Interlude*, glowing with atmosphere, the very slight edge on the upper strings adding to the sense of bleakness.

Bruch, Max (1838–1920)

Violin concerto No. 1 in G min., Op. 26.
*** DG Dig. **400 031-2**; 2532/*3302* 016 [id.]. Mutter, BPO, Karajan – MENDELSSOHN: *Concerto.****
(*) Denon Dig. **C37 7123 [id.]. Kantorow, Netherlands CO, Ros-Marbà – MENDELSSOHN: *Violin concerto.***(*)
** RCA Dig. **RD 70111**. Ughi, LSO, Prêtre – MENDELSSOHN: *Concerto.***
(B) ** DG Walkman *413 844-4* [id.]. Yong Uck Kim, Bamberg SO, Kamu – BRAHMS: *Violin concerto***(*); BEETHOVEN: *Romances.****
* HMV Dig. **CDC 747074-2** [id.]; EL 270105-1/*4* [Ang. DS/*4DS* 38150]. Perlman, Concg. O, Haitink – MENDELSSOHN: *Concerto.**
(M) Ph. 412 929-1/*4* [id.]. Accardo, Leipzig, GO, Masur – MENDELSSOHN: *Violin concerto.***

Violin concerto No. 1 in G min.; Scottish fantasia, Op. 46.
(B) *(*) Ph. On Tour *416 227-4* [id.]. Accardo, Leipzig GO, Masur – TCHAIKOVSKY: *Violin concerto.*

In Anne-Sophie Mutter's hands the concerto has an air of chaste sweetness, shedding much of its ripe, sensuous quality but retaining its romantic feeling. There is a delicacy and tenderness here which is very appealing and, although the tuttis have plenty of fire, Karajan sensitively scales down his accompaniment in the lyrical passages to match his soloist. There is no doubting the dedication and conviction of the solo playing or its natural spontaneity. The digital recording provides a natural balance and a vivid orchestral texture. Though not as rich in timbre as Mintz's performance (available on LP only), this has a pervading freshness that gives much pleasure. While the compact disc does not bring the degree of improvement over the normal issue that the finest examples of this new medium readily provide, the opening of the concerto obviously gains from the background silence. There is a first-class tape.

Kantorow proves an outstanding soloist in one of his first major concerto recordings, fully living up to the reputation he has acquired after winning a unique collection of international prizes. The tone is pure and, even with the double-stopping in the finale, not only incisive but sweet and smooth with no scratch. Though his natural artistry makes for expressive phrasing, his is a plainer, less individual view than some. The accompaniment is reliable if not inspired. The sound is first rate: technically, this is the most impressive CD of this coupling.

Ughi gives a fresh and direct reading, very well recorded. It may not have the individuality of Mutter in the same coupling, but with well-chosen tempi and excellent accompaniment it makes a fair alternative.

Yong Uck Kim's performance impresses by its purity of style and understated feeling. But such an approach is not entirely successful in this ripely romantic work which does not always respond to such delicacy of feeling. Unfortunately, the orchestral accompaniment does not match the solo playing in finesse, but the recording is good and well balanced; the tape is well transferred. If the Brahms and Beethoven couplings are suitable, this Walkman reissue is certainly good value.

Perlman in his version with Haitink at once commands attention with his half-tone withdrawn manner, but then, as in the Mendelssohn on the reverse, the performance is heavily expressive, not nearly so spontaneous-sounding as his earlier version with Previn. The recording brings out a touch of acidity in the soloist's tone and, though the orchestra is backwardly balanced, the ensemble is harsh and relatively thin, a point underlined the more on CD. The XDR cassette tempers the upper range, but tuttis still remain somewhat fierce. Readers wanting Perlman in this coupling are urged to consider the earlier (analogue) LP which has opulent, full recording. The cassette sounds very similar but, because of the resonance, its internal focus is less sharp (HMV ASD/*TC-ASD* 2926 [Ang. S/*4XS* 36963]).

Accardo's 1978 recording (originally coupled with the *Second Concerto in D minor*, Op. 44) is now paired with a fine performance of the Mendelssohn. The playing in the Bruch is persuasive in its restrained eloquence, but the recording has been ruined in its remastering and the sound is unacceptably shrill, with the tape, if anything, worse than the disc. The element of shrillness exists also, though to a lesser extent, on the companion Philips 'On Tour' issue, which includes a most attractive performance of the engaging *Scottish fantasia*.

Kol Nidrei, Op. 47.

(*) Decca Dig. **410 144-2; SXDL/*KSXDC* 7608 [Lon. LDR/5- 71108]. Harrell, Philh. O, Ashkenazy – DVOŘÁK: *Cello concerto.***(*)

The withdrawn, prayerful Bruch piece finds a natural response in Lynn Harrell whose musical personality is often comparatively reticent, and his account with Ashkenazy is both eloquent and atmospheric and certainly very well recorded, especially in its compact disc format. There is a good cassette, too.

Scottish fantasia for violin and orchestra, Op. 46.

(*) RCA Gold GL/*GK* 89832. Heifetz, New SO, Sargent – SIBELIUS: *Violin concerto.**

Reissued in RCA's 'Legendary performers' series, Heifetz's recording shows its age far more than the Sibelius coupling. The balance favours the soloist to a distracting degree, and the digital remastering has left the violin's upper harmonics sounding a little edgy. The chrome tape is smoother than the LP, without loss of overall vividness. Heifetz plays with such supreme assurance that all lovers of great violin playing should seek out this coupling. After a little trimming at the top, the sound is far from unacceptable and the panache and subtlety of bowing and colour bring a wonderful freshness to Bruch's charming Scottish whimsy.

Symphony No. 2 in F min., Op. 36; Swedish dances, Op. 63.
**(*) Ph. Dig. 411 121-1/*4* [id.]. Leipzig GO, Masur.

For most music-lovers Max Bruch means the *G minor Violin concerto* and *Kol Nidrei*, but he was a many-sided and prolific composer with two mature symphonies to his credit, written in quick succession (1868; 1870). The *Second* is an ambitious three-movement work, very much in the Leipzig tradition, with strong overtones of Schumann. The ideas may not be as memorable, though none lack dignity, and the score is very well laid out for the orchestra. It has, like most Bruch, a certain nobility and seriousness of purpose, but does not really sustain its length. The performance by the Leipzig Gewandhaus Orchestra under Kurt Masur is persuasive, and readers wanting something off the beaten track might find it worth investigation. The recording has warmth and a natural perspective without being analytical. The high-level chrome cassette is of excellent quality and matches the disc closely.

Bruckner, Anton (1824–96)

Symphony No. 3 in D min.
*** DG Dig. **413 362-2**; 2532/*3302* 007 [id.]. BPO, Karajan.
** CBS Dig. **MK 39033**; IM/*IMT* 39033 [id.]. Bav. RSO, Kubelik.

Karajan's account of the *Third Symphony* is very impressive indeed. He opts for the Nowak edition of 1888–9, as opposed to the fuller 1878 version favoured by such Bruckner authorities as Robert Simpson and the late Deryck Cooke. One is awe-struck by the eloquence and beauty of the orchestral playing and the command of architecture that Karajan shows. His digital recording is spacious and refined. Karajan achieves a sense of majesty in the opening movement and an other-worldliness and spirituality in the slow movement that cannot fail to move the listener. We are not short of superb accounts of this score, yet the Karajan is second to none and will be a first choice for many. Haitink used the 1878 edition in his set but must yield to Karajan in terms of sheer atmosphere. In the CD format, the usual gains can be noted and few readers are likely to be disappointed. At the same time, fine though it is, this is not a state-of-the-art recording and it is not as transparent or detailed as, say, Chailly's Bruckner *Seventh* on Decca. The LP and cassette are closely matched.

Kubelik uses the 1978 edition (edited by Fritz Oeser) but compensates with brisk tempi in the outer movements, especially the finale. Although the performance has an attractive freshness, it is – like his Mahler – essentially lightweight, though with an eloquent slow movement. The bright, clear recording emphasizes that impression, although the resonance brings the odd moment when clarity of focus slips, even on CD. The cassette offers a fuller sound, but much less sharply defined.

Symphonies Nos 3 in D min. (*1873*)*; 4 in E flat* (*1874*)*; 8 in C min.* (*1887*).
**(*) Tel. Dig. GK6/*CX4*. 35642 (4) [id.]. Frankfurt RSO, Inbal.

This four-record set offers the 1873 text of the *Third*, the 1874 version of the *Fourth* and the 1887 edition of the *Eighth*. No one has recorded them commercially in these editions before. The keen student of Bruckner will already possess the thorough exegesis of their provenance by Deryck Cooke in the posthumously published essays, *Vindications*, or by Hans-Hubert Schönzeler and Dr Robert Simpson in their respective books. The differences are considerable: the scherzo of No. 4, for example, was completely rewritten for the definitive version, and No. 3 can at last be heard in the form in which it was presented to Wagner. The performances themselves are hardly of real stature, but they are perfectly acceptable and readers will find that they can spend many hours of fascination. Obviously this is a set for dedicated Brucknerians and will mean little to those who do not know the symphonies well, but it is of above-average interest and should not be overlooked. The *Fourth Symphony* from this set has been issued separately on an excellent CD (Tel. **ZK8 42921**).

Symphony No. 4 in E flat (*Romantic*).
*** DG **415 277-2**; 2530/*3300* 674 [id.]. BPO, Karajan.
*** Decca Dig. **410 550-2**; SXDL/*KSXDC* 7538 [Lon. LDR/*5*- 71038]. Chicago SO, Solti.
(M) *** HMV EG 290566-1/*4*. BPO, Karajan.
*** CBS **MK 42035** [id.]. Columbia SO, Bruno Walter.
(*) HMV Dig. **CDC 747352-2 [id.]; EL 270379-1/*4*. BPO, Muti.
(*) Denon Dig. **C37 7126. Dresden State O, Blomstedt.
(*) Decca **411 581-2 [id.]; Jub. JB/*KJBC* 120 [Lon. JL/*5* 41039]. VPO, Boehm.
(B) **(*) CfP Dig. CFP 41 4471-1/*4*. Hallé O, Macal.
(*) DG mono **415 664-2** [id.]. VPO, Furtwängler.

Karajan's opening has more beauty and a greater feeling of mystery than almost anyone else on CD. As in his earlier EMI record, Karajan brings a keen sense of forward movement to this music as well as showing a firm grip on its architecture. His slow movement is magnificent and is much brisker than either Boehm or Blomstedt. The DG analogue recording lacks the transparency and detail of the Decca or the bloom of the Dresden, but there is no doubt that this is a performance of considerable stature.

Karajan's 1972 EMI recording has now been reissued at mid-price in EMI's

Master series. This earlier reading has both simplicity and strength and the playing of the Berlin Philharmonic is very fine. Some might prefer the more atmospheric sound-balance, even if it is not so clearly detailed as the new DG version, recorded five years later. The DG performance is tauter and more crisply disciplined, while keeping all the qualities of strength and mystery. In the slow movement Karajan's lyricism is less consciously expressive than before. Even so, this reissue costs about a third as much as the later CD and remains a very satisfying experience.

As a Brucknerian, Solti can hardly be faulted, choosing admirable tempi, keeping concentration taut through the longest paragraphs, and presenting the architecture of the work in total clarity. Raptness is there too, and only the relative lack of Brucknerian idiosyncrasy will disappoint those who prefer a more loving, personal approach. Like Blomstedt and Boehm, Solti prefers the Nowak edition with the opening motif brought back on the horns at the end of the finale. The compact disc immediately establishes its advantage at the atmospheric opening horn call over shimmering strings, the more magnetizing when heard against silence. The slow movement gains similarly and the overall clarity and presence are the more striking in climaxes. Yet the slightly artificial brightness of the sound-picture is more apparent, too; this is not a mellow, cultured aural tapestry that one expects, for instance, from the Concertgebouw. Those who like plenty of brilliance from their Bruckner, however, will find Solti's version meets their needs admirably. There is an excellent cassette.

Although not quite as impressive as the Bruckner *Ninth*, Bruno Walter's 1960 recording is transformed by its CD remastering, with textures clearer, strings full and brass sonorous. It is not quite as rich as the Blomstedt Dresden recording on Denon, but is still pretty impressive, and the superbly played 'hunting horn' scherzo is wonderfully vivid. Walter makes his recording orchestra sound remarkably European in style and timbre. The reading is characteristically spacious. Walter's special feeling for Bruckner means that he can relax over long musical paragraphs and retain his control of the structure, while the playing has fine atmosphere and no want of mystery.

With warm, slightly distanced sound, the sensuous beauty of the Berlin Philharmonic string section has rarely been caught so beautifully in recent recordings. Muti as a Brucknerian has a fine feeling for climax, building over the longest span, and his flexible phrase-shaping of Brucknerian melody, very different from traditional rugged treatment, reflects a vocal style of expressiveness. With that extra warmth and high dramatic contrasts, Muti takes Bruckner further south than usual. For those fancying such treatment, this is an excellent version – but it will not suit everyone. The cassette copes remarkably well with the resonant acoustic and the wide dynamic range.

Blomstedt, like Boehm, opts for the Nowak edition, and the spacious and resonant acoustic in which his version is recorded lends it a pleasing sense of atmosphere. The dynamic range is wide and this performance has a certain ardour and conviction that impress. The slow movement has more feeling and poetry than one normally associates with this conductor, and the sumptuous tone produced by the Dresden orchestra is a joy in itself. This is less bright and analytical than either of the Decca rivals, but it is a beautiful sound none the less, and many will prefer it to the greater detail of the Decca. The performance, if not a great one, has much to recommend it and is both eloquent and dignified.

Boehm's record was made in 1974 and the sound in the CD format is very 'present' indeed – though whether this in itself is sufficient to encourage collectors to pay almost three times as much for the CD version as for the LP or cassette format is another matter. However, the gain is incontestable. The performance is based on the Nowak edition and is finely shaped with the benefit of beautiful orchestral playing. There was always a sobriety about Boehm and he was occasionally *kapellmeister*-ish. Good though this is, it would be idle to pretend that this reading is as fresh and inspired as Walter or Karajan.

A bargain version of this favourite Bruckner symphony is welcome, and in many ways Zdenek Macal's CfP disc fills the bill admirably. The opening may be slightly disappointing, with little feeling of power in reserve, but from there on the spacious, sympathetic dedication is compelling. The Hallé violins are not always sweet-toned, but the slow movement in particular is beautifully done. The scherzo bites hard at a fast speed, while the Laendler trio (taken slower than usual) has a delightful lilt. The well-balanced recording is first rate, both on disc and on the excellent XDR cassette which loses remarkably little in upper range and definition.

With a horn crack on the very first note, Furtwängler's 1951 Stuttgart radio performance can be recommended only with severe reservation except to committed devotees. They will relish the towering passion and unflagging intensity behind the rendering which, with extreme unmarked accelerandi, might be counted hysterical from any other conductor. The sound is thin, but in the digital transfer on CD the ear can readily adjust.

Symphony No. 4 (*Romantic*); (i) *Te Deum*.

(B) *(*) DG Walkman *415 616-4* [id.]. Chicago SO, Barenboim; (i) with Norman, Minton, Rendall, Ramey and Chicago SO Ch.

Although it is linked to a majestic account of the *Te Deum* with the Chicago soloists, chorus and orchestra singing and playing with heart-warming resonance, this Walkman coupling must be passed over. Barenboim's performance of the *Fourth Symphony* offers excellent sound and the Chicago orchestra play magnificently, but Barenboim's reading is very mannered and its insights confined to the surface. Barenboim's fine version of the *Te Deum* is also available linked to the Brahms *Requiem* on two medium-priced LPs and tapes – see below.

Symphony No. 7 in E.

€ *** Decca Dig. **414 290-2**; 414 290-1/*4*. Berlin RSO, Chailly.

*** Denon Dig. **C37 7286**. Dresden State O, Blomstedt.

(M) **(*) Ph. Seq. 412 359-1/*4* [id.]. Concg. O, Haitink.

(M) ** DG Sig. 413 978-1/*4* [id.]. VPO, Boehm.

** CBS **M2K 42036** (2) [id.]. Columbia SO, Walter – WAGNER: *Siegfried idyll.***(*)

(M) *(*) HMV ED 290004-1/*4* [Ang. AE/*4AE* 34420]. Philh. O, Klemperer.
* Sup. Dig. **C37 7419** [id.]. Czech PO, Matačič.

Riccardo Chailly's account of the *Seventh Symphony* ranks among the best now before the public. He obtains some excellent playing from the Berlin Radio Symphony Orchestra and, though he may not attain the warmth and, indeed, spirituality of Karajan and Jochum, his is a committed performance, and the apparent lack of weight soon proves deceptive. He has a considerable command of the work's architecture and controls its sonorities expertly. The recording, made in the Jesus-Christus Kirche, Berlin, is outstanding in every way. It is splendidly balanced, having realistic string tone with a nice bloom and a natural perspective. Warm, full tone throughout all the departments of the orchestra, yet a clean and refined sound which registers in both LP and CD formats, but is especially impressive on CD. On the chrome tape the sound is first class, but the slow-movement break of the LP remains.

A well-shaped account of the *Seventh* comes from Herbert Blomstedt and the Staatskapelle, Dresden. It is not quite as moving as his version of the *Fourth*, but it is still very fine, and the beautiful playing of the Dresden orchestra and the expansive acoustic of the Lukaskirche are strong points in its favour. The recording is finely balanced, the strings having a natural warmth and the orchestra being placed in well-judged perspective. The reading is totally dedicated and Blomstedt has both strength and imagination to commend him. It has rather more gravitas than the Chailly version, and many will prefer it on this account.

Haitink's one-disc version of the *Seventh* has the merits of directness and grasp of architecture. It is by no means as expansive, spacious – or, for that matter, expensive – as his two-record version made in 1979; though this is well recorded and finely conceived, the later version has more grip and greater sensitivity to atmosphere. However, this remains a very satisfying reading and is the least expensive way of acquiring the symphony. The cassette is every bit the equal of the disc but, unlike Klemperer's tape, it follows the disc layout with a turnover break in the *Adagio*.

Boehm's *Seventh* was originally issued in harness with the *Eighth*, but is now reissued on a single 'Signature' disc and tape. It goes without saying that the playing of the Vienna Philharmonic is of the highest order, but the performance taken as a whole is plain to the point of being dour. There is a fine sense of architecture and the music is firmly held together, but Boehm's phrasing is often prosaic and lacking in magic. The recording is admirably vivid and clear on both disc and cassette.

Though clearly preferable to Klemperer's version, Walter's reading shares the same basic fault of concentrating on detail at the expense of structure. The outer movements bring many illuminating touches and the final climax of the first is imposingly built, but overall the tension is loosely held. In the *Adagio*, which is kept moving by Walter far more convincingly than by Klemperer, the climax is disappointing, and made the more so by the absence of the famous cymbal clash as Walter uses the original text. The 1963 recording has been opened up in its remastering for CD and sounds fuller and more spacious than the original LPs;

indeed, on technical grounds there is little to complain of, although this cannot compare in richness of texture with Chailly's modern Decca version, which also has a far more economical format.

Klemperer's *Seventh* is beautifully played, and the remastered 1962 recording sounds well, with plenty of body and good detail. But with the first two movements very deliberately paced indeed, the performance is difficult to recommend. The tension is not especially high and it is stretched over structures that are made to seem almost interminable. At times the music making has an attractive lyrical feeling, and the scherzo is not ponderous; but overall this is not a success. The cassette matches the disc closely, losing only a little of the freedom of the upper range, and its one distinctive quality is that – unlike the LP – it offers the *Adagio* without a turnover break.

Fine playing from the Czech Philharmonic Orchestra, but Matačič, like Klemperer, is very spacious and the *Adagio* simply doesn't have enough grip. The scherzo too is very relaxed and fails to provide the needed contrast. Good, naturally balanced sound.

Symphony No. 8 in C min.

*** Ph. Dig. **412 465-2**; 6769/*7654* 080 (2) [id.]. Concg. O, Haitink – WAGNER: *Siegfried idyll.****

*** DG Dig. **415 124-2**; 415 124-1/*4*. VPO, Giulini.

(*) Lodia Dig. **LOCD 783/4 [id.]. Philharmonic SO, Païta – WAGNER: *Tristan: Prelude and Liebestod.***(*)

**(*) German HM 1C 153 99853/4 [id.]. Col. RSO, Wand.

Haitink's is a noble reading of this massive symphony, using the extended Haas edition. Never one to force the pace, Haitink's degree of restraint will please those who find Karajan too powerfully concentrated. The spaciousness of the slow movement brings a rare clarity and refinement; the tempo is relentlessly steady, even slower than Karajan's. On compact disc, the resonant Concertgebouw ambience has all the more atmospheric bloom, as well as fine detail, an aptly beautiful sound. Moreover, Haitink's fine performance of Wagner's *Siegfried idyll* is offered as a considerable bonus. Both the LPs and the cassettes are impressively clear and spacious, but the CDs are well worth their extra cost.

Giulini's account of Bruckner's *Eighth Symphony* has stature and will be eagerly sought out by his many admirers. He elects to use the Nowak edition, which may worry some collectors and incline them to opt for Haitink or Wand who both opt for the Haas. If these considerations do not worry you, the Giulini will be a strong contender, for he is a conductor of vision and the Vienna orchestra give him wonderful support. This reading has undoubted spirituality and power, and the DG recording is spacious and clean.

With speeds generally faster than usual, particularly in the first movement, the power and urgency of Païta's reading with a selected band of London sessions musicians is impressive. Nor is the meditative side of the reading lacking in intensity, making the whole sound unusually fresh. The brightness of top in the recording adds to that, though in some big tuttis there is a touch of aggressiveness.

Wand's version, using the Haas edition with its very full text, has a massive granite strength. His simple dedication comes over powerfully, building the structure involvingly. The playing is not always quite so refined as in some rivals, but with warm, spacious recording very apt for this music, this version can be recommended on LP, but note that there is no fill-up.

Symphony No. 9 in D min.
❀ *** CBS **MK 42037** [id.]. Columbia SO, Bruno Walter.
*** Ph. Dig. **410 039-2**; 6514/*7337* 191 [id.]. Concg. O, Haitink.
(M) *** HMV ED 290492-1/*4*. BPO, Jochum.
*(*) Sup. Dig. **C37 7420** [id.]. Czech PO, Matačič.

The remastering for CD of Bruno Walter's 1959 recording of Bruckner's *Ninth* is a superb achievement. This was one of the most beautiful results of Walter's Indian summer in the CBS studio, and now the results are immeasurably enhanced, with a blend of rich, clear strings and splendidly sonorous brass. Walter's mellow, persuasive reading leads one on through the leisurely paragraphs so that the logic and coherence seem obvious where other performances can sound aimless. Perhaps the scherzo is not vigorous enough to provide the fullest contrast – though the sound here has ample bite – yet it exactly fits the overall conception. The final slow movement has a nobility which makes one glad that Bruckner never completed the intended finale. After this, anything would have been an anticlimax.

The extremely measured speed of the first movement in Haitink's pure and dedicated reading may be taken as a deciding factor; he underlines the elegiac mood. Though the great dynamic contrasts are superbly and fearlessly caught – with compact disc even more immediate and involving than LP or cassette – this is not so thrustful an interpretation as Jochum's or Karajan's. The spaciousness of the sound against an ambient Concertgebouw acoustic gives a degree of distancing which matches the interpretation. It is the more effective on CD, adding to the feeling of tangible presence. On CD, the absence of background and the bite of fortissimos are specially impressive, as well as the clarity and refinement of light textures. The chrome cassette is fresh and refined too, spacious and full, but registers detail rather less sharply than the CD and LP versions.

The warmth as well as the power of Jochum in Bruckner set his readings apart, and this Dresden account of the last, uncompleted symphony is a splendid example of his art, with the Dresden strings made to sound weighty and sonorous in a fine digital recording. Jochum far more than is fashionable these days allows himself a wide degree of flexibility over tempi. Here he is at his most persuasive, giving an impression of spontaneity such as you would expect in the concert hall.

Recorded at a live concert (though the audience hardly makes its presence felt at all, and not very vociferously at the end) Matačič's account of the *Ninth*, although wayward, has rather more grip than his disappointing version of the *Seventh*. After an almost aggressive scherzo he conveys the splendour of the finale, with the strings of the Czech Philharmonic making an eloquent response. But this performance lacks the structural grasp of Karajan, and Matačič's expansive flexibility of tempo is much less convincing than Jochum's performance. Fair recording made in the House of Artists, Prague.

VOCAL MUSIC

Motets: *Afferentur regi; Ave Maria; Christus factus est; Ecce sacerdos magnus; Inveni David; Locus iste; Os justi medititur; Pange lingua; Tota pulchra es; Vexilla regis; Virga Jesse.*

(*) Hyp. **CDA 66062; A 66062. Salmon, Corydon Singers, Best; Trotter (organ).

A much more resonant acoustic setting than the one which DG provided for Jochum in the late 1960s: his erred on the side of dryness but, were it restored to circulation, it would take precedence over this record. The Corydon Singers under Matthew Best are not quite as well blended or as homogeneous in tone as were the Bavarian Radio Chorus, but Best's direction is often imaginative and he achieves a wide tonal range. The motets span the best part of Bruckner's creative life, though, given their devotional character, they are best heard two or three at a time rather than at one sitting.

Te Deum.

(M) **(*) DG Dig. 415 000-1/*4* (2) [id.]. Norman, Minton, Rendell, Ramey, Chicago Ch. and SO, Barenboim – BRAHMS: *German Requiem*.**(*)

** DG Dig. **410 521-2**; 410 521-1/*4* (2) [id.]. Perry, Müller-Molinari, Winbergh, Malta, V. Singverein, VPO, Karajan – BRAHMS: *German Requiem*.**(*)

Barenboim's *Te Deum* – here reissued at mid-price and coupled, like Karajan's set, with the Brahms *Requiem* – was recorded as recently as 1981, and is in every way preferable to the Karajan version. The digital recording is not wanting in atmosphere, but the choral timbre is fresh and clear and the overall balance is convincing. Among the soloists David Rendell is too tight in tone to be ideal, but they make a good team; Barenboim's direction, urgent and volatile, but expansive too, provides a reading which overall has convincing spontaneity and plenty of life. The excellent chrome tape matches the disc in body and clarity.

With Janet Perry a shrill soprano soloist, and with the big choral tuttis constricted in sound, the Bruckner *Te Deum* makes a disappointing fill-up for Karajan's latest version of the Brahms *Requiem*, though the majesty of the vision is never in doubt.

Burgon, Geoffrey (born 1941)

At the round earth's imagined corners; But have been found again; Laudate Dominum; Magnificat; Nunc dimittis; A prayer to the Trinity; Short mass; This world; Two hymns to Mary.
**(*) Hyp. A/*KA* 66123 [id.]. Chichester Cathedral Ch., Alan Thurlow.

Thanks to being used in a popular BBC television serial, John le Carré's *Tinker, tailor, soldier, spy*, Burgon's *Nunc dimittis* became temporarily a top hit with its haunting tune. Here it is well matched with the *Magnificat* that Burgon later wrote to complement it and a series of his shorter choral pieces, all of them revealing his flair for immediate, direct communication and well performed here. First-rate recording, with an equally impressive matching cassette.

Bush, Alan (born 1900)

(i) *Violin concerto, Op. 32*; (ii) *Dialectic, Op. 15*; (iii) *Six short pieces, Op. 99*.
**(*) Hyp. A 66138. (i) Parikian, BBC SO, Del Mar; (ii) Medici Qt; (iii) Alan Bush (piano).

Alan Bush, now in his mid-eighties, has suffered grievous neglect in his home country, though the *Dialectic* for string quartet was recorded by Decca on 78 r.p.m. records. The three works on the present disc come from different times in his life, the *Dialectic* from 1929, the *Violin concerto* from 1948 and the piano *Pieces*, which the 84-year-old composer plays himself, from 1983. The most substantial of these uncompromisingly tonal, but far from plain, works is the *Dialectic*, his second essay into the genre which is finely argued and well laid-out for the quartet medium. The sleeve note makes extravagant claims for the composer, and hails the *Violin concerto* as a 'major achievement', which is questionable, and 'quite devoid of padding or orchestral wizardry', which is undoubtedly the case. There is no question of this composer's integrity and skilled musicianship; if the whole work were as searching as much of its slow section, it would be an important addition to the repertory. But the ideas of the opening are really not strong enough and the orchestral writing lacks density of musical incident. Alan Bush's neglect has been attributed by his admirers to his political allegiance but, with the best will in the world, he does not match the lyrical sweep or orchestral expertise of, say, Benjamin Frankel, who also held strongly left-wing sympathies. The octogenarian composer has remarkably supple fingers and gives a very creditable account of his six *Pieces*, though he is recorded in an unsympathetic acoustic. The recording of the *Concerto*, made in the BBC Maida Vale studios, is a trifle dry but admirably clear, and the *Quartet*, if forwardly balanced, is given very acceptable sound. Even if one is not wholly convinced by the *Concerto*, this disc makes a welcome and long overdue visiting card for this widely respected figure.

Busoni, Ferruccio (1866–1924)

Divertimento for flute and orchestra, Op. 52.
*** Ph. Dig. **412 728-2**; 412 728-1/*4* [id.]. Nicolet, Leipzig GO, Masur – NIELSEN; REINECKE: *Concertos.****

Busoni's highly individual *Divertimento*, with its bitter-sweet mixture of wit and lyricism, is in three brief linked movements. The whole piece plays for only 9′ 19″, but the engaging quirkiness of the invention and diversity of mood are nicely controlled within an appealingly concise structure. The performance here is first rate, always responsive and freshly spontaneous, with the gentle but dark melancholy of the *Andante* acting as a foil to the spirited outer sections. There is an element of the unexpected in this score which is especially enticing. The recording is beautifully balanced on LP and CD, with a first-class matching tape.

Butterworth, George (1885–1916)

The Banks of green willow.
*** Chan. **CHAN 8373**; CBR/*CBT* 1018 [id.]. Bournemouth Sinf., Del Mar – BANTOCK: *Pierrot of the minute*; BRIDGE: *Suite for strings* etc.***

The Banks of green willow; 2 English idylls; A Shropshire lad.
*** Lyr. SRCS 69. New Philh. O, Boult – HOWELLS: *Elegy* etc.***

Boult's noble and radiant performances of these lovely pieces, which are fitted neatly on to a single LP side, come from 1976. His natural feeling for the pastoral inflections and the refinement of texture was unique, and with delicately atmospheric recording this Lyrita reissue is most welcome.

On Chandos, Del Mar too gives a glowingly persuasive performance of *The Banks of green willow*, which comes as part of a highly interesting programme of English music, devoted to Butterworth's somewhat older contemporaries, Bantock and Frank Bridge. The new digital transfer of a 1979 analogue recording has the benefit of even greater clarity without loss of atmosphere. There is a first-class cassette which, like the LP, has the advantage of being in the mid-price range.

Buxtehude, Diderik (*c.* 1637–1707)

Ciacona in E min, BuxWV 10; Durch Adams Fall ist ganz verderbt, BuxWV 183; Ein feste Burg, BuxWV 184; Gelobet seist du, BuxWV 189; Herr Christ, der einig Gottes Sohn, BuxWV 199; Komm Heiliger Geist, Herre Gott, BuxWV 199; Prelude and fugue in G min., BuxWV 149; Prelude, fugue and ciacona in C, BuxWV 137; Der Tag, der ist so freudenreich, BuxWV 182; Toccata and fugue in F, BuxWV 157; Wie schön leuchtet der Morgenstern, BuxWV 223.
*** Decca Dig. 410 106-1/*4* [id.]. Peter Hurford (organ).

Peter Hurford's recital is recorded in the Church of Our Lady of Sorrows, Toronto, and the Decca engineers succeed in conveying its grandeur to striking effect. This is a state-of-the-art recording which does full justice to the splendours of the instrument as, indeed, Peter Hurford does to the music. This does not duplicate Marie-Claire Alain's Erato recital more than minimally (they overlap on three chorale settings) and together they make a useful introduction to Buxtehude's organ music.

Chorales: *Ach Herr mich armen Sunder, BuxWV 178; Durch Adams Fall ist ganz verderbt, BuxWV 183; Gott der Vater wohn uns bei, BuxWV 190; In dulci jubilo, BuxWV 197; Komm, Heiliger Geist, Herre Gott, BuxWV 199; Wie schön leuchtet der Morgenstern, BuxWV 223; Passacaglia in D min., BuxWV 161; Preludes: in C, BuxWV 137; in G min., BuxWV 149; Toccata in D min., BuxWV 155.*
*** Erato Dig. NUM/*MCE* 75095. Marie-Claire Alain (organ).

The organ is that of the Sainte Chapelle of the château of the Dukes of Savoie, in Chambéry, which was rebuilt in 1975 by Haerpfer using as much of the 1675 original of Etienne Sénot as practicable. The sound has charm and Marie-Claire Alain shows characteristic ingenuity and taste in her presentation of this refreshing music. The extent of Buxtehude's originality is often underrated: he is far more than just a precursor of Bach, possessing a powerful and fertile musical imagination. Marie-Claire Alain is no less commanding an exponent of this repertoire than Hurford on Decca, and her excellently recorded LP can be recommended alongside his.

Byrd, William (1543–1623)

Ave verum corpus; Christe qui lux es et dies; Laetentur coeli (motets); *Lamentations; Masses for 3, 4 and 5 voices.*
** HMV Dig. EX 270096-3/*9* (2). Hilliard Ens., Paul Hillier.

Ave verum corpus; Defecit in dolore; Infelix ego; Masses for 3, 4 and 5 voices.
*** Gimell Dig. BYRD 345/*ZCBYRD 345* (2/*1*) [id.]. Tallis Scholars, Phillips.

Ave verum corpus; Masses for 3, 4 and 5 voices.
*** Gimell Dig. **CDGIM 345** [id.]. Tallis Scholars, Phillips.

Ave verum corpus; Great service: Magnificat and Nunc dimittis. Mass for five voices.
(M) *** Argo 414 366-1/*4*. King's College Ch., Cambridge, Willcocks.

Mass for three voices; Mass for four voices.
(M) *** Argo 411 723–1/*4*. King's College Ch., Cambridge, Willcocks.

Peter Phillips's performances are altogether more volatile than those recorded by Argo at King's, and some might prefer the greater serenity of the latter. But Phillips is a master of this repertoire; undoubtedly these performances have more variety and great eloquence so that, when the drama is varied with a gentler mood, the contrast is the more striking. This enormously rewarding music lends itself to an imaginatively varied treatment, and certainly the sound made by the Scholars in Merton College Chapel is beautiful, both warm and fresh. The CD omits two of the motets included on the pair of LPs (which cost about the same), and ends with a movingly simple account of the *Ave verum corpus*. The excellent cassette includes everything, so offers the best of all worlds.

In the Argo King's performances of the *Mass for five voices*, *Ave verum* and *Great service*, which were recorded in 1960, the style is more reticent, less forceful than in the famous coupling of the *Masses for three* and *four voices*, made three years later. These beautiful settings are sustained with an inevitability of phrasing and a control of sonority and dynamic that completely capture the music's spirit and emotional feeling. The recording of all this music is wonderfully clean and atmospheric, the acoustic perfectly judged so that the music seems to float in space yet retain its substance and clarity of focus. In the absence of compact disc this is better suited to cassette than to LP, with its freedom from extraneous noises. Unfortunately, the tape coupling the *Masses for three* and *four voices* is on iron-oxide stock, and the high-level transfer approaches saturation point and brings some loss of focus at peaks. The coupling of the *Mass for five voices* and music from the *Great service* uses chrome tape and the results are very impressive, with the resonant acoustic admirably caught.

The Hilliard Ensemble, using one voice per part, present pure and detached readings, recorded in an intimate rather than an ecclesiastical acoustic. Arguably, these were works which when they were written in Elizabethan times would be sung in private recusant chapels rather than openly, but that situation itself argues a more involved response. The motets on the fourth side, sung in a very similar style, make a suitable complement. The recording is full yet clear, and in this respect the XDR cassettes match the discs closely.

Cantiones sacrae: Aspice Domine; Domine secundum multitudinem; Domine tu iurasti; In resurrectione tua; Ne irascaris Domine; O quam gloriosum; Tristitia et anxiestas; Vide Domine afflictionem; Virgilate.

(*) CRD Dig. **CRD 3408; CRDD 1120/*CRDCD 4120* [id.]. New College, Oxford, Ch., Higginbottom.

Though the New College Choir under its choirmaster Edward Higginbottom does not sing with the variety of expression or dynamic which marks its finest Oxbridge rivals, it is impossible not to respond to the freshness of their music making. The robust, throaty style suggests a Latin feeling in its forthright vigour, and the directness of approach in these magnificent *cantiones sacrae* is most attractive, helped by recording which is vividly projected, yet at once richly atmospheric. While CD brings the usual obvious advantages, both LP and cassette are very impressive, the latter a demonstration of CRD's characteristically high standard of transfer.

Campion, Thomas (1567–1620)

Songs: *Come cheerful day; Come you pretty false-ey'd wanton; Fire, fire; Her rosie cheekes; I care not for these ladies; It fell on a sommers daie; Never weather-beaten sail; Shall I come sweet love to thee; The Cypres curtain; There is none, O none but you; Thinkest thou to seduce me.*
**(*) Hyp. A 66095 [id.]. Ian Partridge, Jakob Lindberg (lute).

The variety of expression in the songs of this inspired Elizabethan, a poet as well as a composer, comes over strongly in these fine performances, marred only by a degree of aggressiveness, not in the singer but in the closeness of the recording. Otherwise, full and vivid sound.

Canteloube, Marie-Joseph (1879–1957)

Chants d'Auvergne: Series 1–5.
*** HMV EL 290802-1/*4*. Victoria de los Angeles, LOP, Jacquillat.

It was Victoria de los Angeles who made the pioneering stereo recordings of the Auvergne arrangements (alongside Natania Davrath's justly admired two-disc Vanguard set). The warmth and sweetness of Los Angeles' tone when the recordings were made (1973 and 1975) exactly matches the allure of Canteloube's settings. Now the 24 songs have been reissued, squeezed on to one LP and a matching tape (playing for over seventy minutes), without any real loss of quality. Los Angeles' style is wonderfully fresh yet more robust in the famous *Baïlèro* than Kiri Te Kanawa's famous version; throughout, her experience in singing folksongs brings an extra degree of authenticity and an attractive rhythmic sparkle, which is matched by Jacquillat in the accompaniments. A bargain.

Chants d'Auvergne: L'Antouèno; Baïlèro; 3 Bourrées; 2 Bourrées; Brezairola; Lou coucut; Chut, chut; La Delaïssádo; Lo Fiolairé; Oï ayaï; Passo pel prat; Pour l'enfant; Tè, l'co, tè; Uno jionto postouro.
(*) CBS Dig. **CD 37299; 37299/*40*- [id.]. Frederica von Stade, RPO, Almeida.

Fine as Frederica von Stade's singing is, she is stylistically and temperamentally far less at home in Canteloube's lovely folksong settings than Kiri Te Kanawa, whose record of a slightly different selection appeared almost simultaneously with this (see below). Words are clearer here but, thanks in part to the more abrasive recording, the result is far less persuasively sensuous. The CD is clean and immediate but not as richly beautiful as the Decca, nor indeed as vividly atmospheric as Jill Gomez's Classics for Pleasure LP.

Chants d'Auvergne: L'Antouèno; Baïlèro; 3 Bourrées; 2 Bourrées; Brezairola; La Delaïssádo; Lo Fiolairé; Lou Boussu; Malurous qu'o uno fenno; La pastrouletta è lou Chibalie; Passo pel prat; La pastoura als camps; Pastourelle.

❀ ◖ *** Decca Dig. **410 004-2** [id.]; SXDL/*KSXDC* 7604 [Lon. LDR/5-71104]. Dame Kiri Te Kanawa, ECO, Tate.

Kiri Te Kanawa's is a ravishing recording of a selection from Canteloube's luscious settings. *Baïlèro*, the most famous of the songs, is taken extremely slowly, but one hardly registers that when, with sumptuous recording against a warm background, the result is hypnotically compelling. In such an atmosphere the quick songs lose a little in bite but, thanks in great measure to masterful and sympathetic accompaniment from the ECO under Jeffrey Tate, the compulsion of the whole sequence is irresistible. One wallows in Canteloube's uninhibited treatment, worrying little over matters of authenticity. The recording is of demonstration quality, most vivid and atmospheric. There is a splendid chrome cassette too.

Chants d'Auvergne: L'Antouèno; Baïlèro; 3 Bourées; Lou Boussu; Brezairola; Lou coucut; Chut, chut; La Delaïssádo; Lo Fïolairé; Jou l'pount d'o Mirabel; Malurous qu'o uno fenno; Passo pel prat; Pastourelle; Postouro, sé tu m'aymo; Tè, l'co tè.
(M) *** EMI EMX 41 2075-1/*4* [Ang. AE/*4AE* 34471]. Jill Gomez, Royal Liverpool PO, Handley.

Jill Gomez's selection of these increasingly popular songs, attractively presented on a mid-price label, makes for an intensely beautiful record, which as well as bringing out the sensuousness of Canteloube's arrangements keeps reminding us, in the echoes of rustic band music, of the genuine folk base. Jill Gomez's voice could not be more apt, for the natural radiance and the range of tone-colour go with a strong feeling for words and feeling, helped by her intensive study of Provençal pronunciation. Vernon Handley's accompaniments have a directness as well as a warmth which supports the voice admirably, and the recording is outstandingly full and vivid. For sample, try the tender and gentle *La Delaïssádo*, just as beautiful as the well-known *Baïlèro*. There is an excellent tape, though side two, with a higher level of transfer, is markedly more vivid than side one.

Chants d'Auvergne: Hé! beyla-z-y dau fé; Jou l'pount d'o Mirabel; Là-haut, sur le rocher; Lou boussu; Lou diziou bé; Malurous qu'o uno fenno; Obal din lo coumbèlo; La pastoura al camps; Pastorale; Pastourelle; La pastrouletta è lou chibalie; Postouro sé tu m'aymo; Quand z'eyro petitoune. Triptyque: Offrande à l'été; Lunaire; Hymne dans l'aurore.
*** *CBS Dig.* **MK 37837**; IM/*IMT* 37837 [id.]. Frederica von Stade, RPO, Almeida.

Frederica von Stade's second collection not only has more charm and personal identification than the first but also includes Canteloube's haunting *Triptyque*, written in 1914. It is very much in the tradition of twentieth-century French song-cycles in its colourful expressionism, but also anticipates the orchestral style to be made famous by his folk settings. The second of the three, *Lunaire*, is particularly evocative. This is its first recording in stereo. Von Stade's performance is eloquent and the recording suitably atmospheric, if not quite so sumptuous as the Decca sound for Kiri Te Kanawa.

Chants d'Auvergne, 4th and 5th series (complete).
*** Decca **411 730-2**; 411 730-1/*4* [id.]. Dame Kiri Te Kanwa, ECO, Tate – VILLA-LOBOS: *Bachianas Brasileiras No. 5.****

This second collection of Canteloube folksong arrangements from Kiri Te Kanawa, again with Jeffrey Tate providing richly beautiful accompaniments, fills in the gaps left in the first, and presents all remaining items in the five sets of the songs. They are not all as inspired as those in the earlier collection, and there is less variety, partly a question of Dame Kiri's preference for producing a continuous flow of sensuously beautiful sounds rather than giving a folk-like tang. The orchestral playing and the ripely atmospheric recording add to the richness of the mixture.

Caplet, André (1878–1915)

The Masque of the Red Death.
(*) HMV Dig. EL 270158-1/*4* [Ang. DS/*4DS* 38168]. Cambreling, Monte Carlo PO, Prêtre – DEBUSSY: *La chute de la Maison Usher*; SCHMIDT: *Haunted palace.**

André Caplet's association with Debussy was close: he helped prepare the scores of *La boîte à joujoux* and *Le martyre de Saint-Sébastien.* His *Conte fantastique* for harp and strings inspired by Poe's *The masque of the red death* makes an ideal companion for Debussy's *The fall of the house of Usher* fragment. Caplet's is a highly imaginative and evocative score, dating in its original form from 1908: he later transcribed it for chamber forces. It is eminently well played here by Frédérique Cambreling and the Monte Carlo orchestra under Georges Prêtre; the only reservation concerns the recorded balance which places the harp far too closely, thus diminishing the sense of mystery and atmosphere of this score.

Castelnuovo-Tedesco, Mario (1895–1968)

Guitar concerto in D, Op. 99.
(B) **(*) CBS *MGT 39017.* John Williams, ECO, Groves – RODRIGO: *Concierto; Fantasia*; VILLA-LOBOS: *Concerto.****

John Williams's more recent version of the *Concerto* with Groves is more vividly recorded than his earlier account with Ormandy and the Philadelphia Orchestra, but that was fresher and had more pace. He is placed far forward here, so that it is not always possible to locate him in relation to his colleagues. But if the sound is synthetic as far as perspective is concerned, it is by no means unpleasing. These artists make the most of the slow movement's poetry and the *Concerto* has no lack of charm. The generous couplings and distinguished performances (about which there are few reservations) make this extended-length tape issue a real bargain, for the transfers are well managed.

Cavalli, Francesco (1602–76)

Messa concertata (1656).
* Tel. AQ6 41931 [id.]. Mun. Vocal soloists, Bav. State O Chamber Ens., Hirsch.

Cavalli's *Messa concertata* from the *Musiche sacrae* is arguably his most important sacred work after the *Requiem*. The *Musiche sacrae* appeared in twelve separate part-books when he was at the height of his career as an opera composer. There are six canzone, five elaborate hymns, fifteen motets, a *Magnificat* for double choir, and this *Mass*. The work is more important historically than aesthetically and needs very persuasive advocacy if it is to make a strong impression. This performance, which dates from the mid-1970s but has only just reached the UK catalogues, is really rather lack-lustre, and the recording is not particularly distinguished either. This is little more than a stopgap until Raymond Leppard, whose performing edition appeared in the mid-1960s, commits it to disc.

OPERA

Xerse (complete).
*** HM **HMC 901175/8**; HMC/*40* 1175/8 [id.]. René Jacobs, Nelson, Gall, Poulenard, Mellon, Feldman, Elwes, De Mey, Visse, Instrumental Ens., Jacobs.

Ombra mai fù, sings King Xerxes in the opening scene, addressing a plane tree, and most listeners will have a double-take, remembering first Handel's *Largo*, and then that Cavalli set the same libretto 84 years earlier than Handel in 1654. Handel's *Serse* (note the difference of spelling) is a perky comedy, full of sparkling ideas, as the inspired English National Opera production made clear on stage, but Cavalli's opera, even longer but just as brisk in its action, can be presented just as winningly, as here in the first ever recording. Authentic performances of Cavalli have often sounded bald after Raymond Leppard's ripe renderings for Glyndebourne, but Jacobs's presentation is piquant to match the plot, often genuinely funny, sustaining the enormous length very well. As well as directing his talented team, Jacobs sings the title role, only one of the four counter-tenors, nicely contrasted, who take the castrato roles. The fruity alto of Dominique Visse in a comic servant role is particularly striking, and among the women – some of them shrill at times – the outstanding singer, Agnès Mellon, takes the other servant role, singing delightfully in a tiny laughing song. Most of the text is set to fast-moving recitative, but Cavalli flexibly introduces charming and concise songs and the occasional duet. The three Acts of the opera are preceded by an allegorical prologue taken from *Il Ciro*, an opera Cavalli wrote at about the same time. Excellent sound, which consistently allows the fresh, young voices of the principals to make every word plain. Notes and libretto are first rate.

Arias: *La Calisto: Ardo, sospiro è piango. La Didone: Cassandra's lament. L'Egisto: Clori's lament. L'Orimonte: Numi ciechi più di me. Scipione Africano: Non è, non è crudel. Xerse: La bellezza è un don fugace.*
(*) Erato Dig. **ECD 288100; NUM/*MCE* 75183 [id.]. Frederica von Stade, Scottish CO, Leppard – MONTEVERDI: *Arias.***(*)

Frederica von Stade, in excellent voice, sings *Cassandra's lament* (which opens the group) with a dignified simplicity, and she finds a similar direct eloquence for Clori's *Amor, che ti diè l'alti* from *L'Egisto*. The recital is well planned so that between them comes the delightful *La bellezza è un don fugace* (given attractively light articulation), and then follows Clori's lament, *Numi cieci più di me*, which – with a deliciously pointed accompaniment from Leppard and the Scottish Chamber strings – really sparkles. This is a most attractive programme, well balanced and recorded (there is an excellent chrome cassette alongside the CD and LP); the music itself is so appealing that one can forgive some lack of variety in timbre and dramatic presentation. Italian vocal texts are provided, without translations, and documentation is poor.

Chabrier, Emmanuel (1841–94)

Bourrée fantastique; España; Gwendoline overture; Marche joyeuse; Le Roi malgré lui: Danse slave. Suite pastorale.
*** Erato Dig. **ECD 88018**; NUM/*MCE* 75079 [id.]. Fr. Nat. PO, Jordan.

A sparkling collection to provide Chabrier's compact disc début. The playing is admirably spirited, even boisterous in the *Marche joyeuse*, and the melodramatic *Gwendoline overture* is relished with proper gusto. Perhaps Paray's account of the engaging *Suite pastorale* (on Mercury) was that bit more distinctive, but here the tempo of the third movement, *Sous bois*, is less controversial. *España* has infectious élan, yet rhythms are nicely relaxed so that the gaiety is never forced. The recording is generally first class, with the body and range of the CD especially telling. The balance of sound on tape is thinner, although there is no lack of liveliness.

OPERA

L'Étoile (complete).
❀*** HMV Dig. EX 270086-3/9 (2) [Pathé id.]. Alliot-Lugaz, Gautier, Bacquier, Raphanel, Damonte, Le Roux, David, Lyon Opéra Ch. and O, Gardiner.

This fizzing operetta is a winner. Musically a cross between *Carmen* and Gilbert and Sullivan, with plentiful Offenbach thrown in, the subtlety and refinement of Chabrier's score go well beyond the usual realm of operetta, and Gardiner directs a performance that from first to last makes the piece sparkle bewitchingly.

Improbably, it was the poet, Paul Verlaine, who suggested the original idea to his friend, Chabrier, when he wrote some naughtily sado-masochistic Impalement Verses. As they emerge in the finished operetta, they are no more improper than the Mikado's song in G. & S., and the exotic plot about King Ouf I who enjoys the spectacle of a little capital punishment has plenty of Gilbertian twists.

Central to the story, the star of *L'Étoile* is the pedlar, Lazuli, a breeches role, and Gardiner has been lucky to include in his company at the Lyon Opéra a soprano with just the personality, presence and voice to carry it off, Colette Alliot-Lugaz. Except for Gabriel Bacquier as the Astrologer, Sirocco, the others are not well known either, but all are first rate. The helpful French dialogue adds to the sparkle (just long enough to give the right flavour), and numbers such as the drunken duet between King and Astrologer are hilarious. Outstandingly good recording. On cassette, the opera is conveniently laid out on two sides of a single extended-length tape. The quality is first class in all respects, the sound fresh and clear, the voices caught with excellent presence and bloom.

Le roi malgré lui (complete).

**(*) Erato Dig. NUM/*MCE* 751623 (3) [id.]. Hendricks, Garcisanz, Jeffes, Quilico, Lafont, De Moor, R. France Ch., Nouvel PO, Dutoit.

This long-neglected opera is another Chabrier masterpiece, and Erato (in collaboration with French Radio) is to be congratulated on putting it on record, albeit in flawed form. Ravel said that he would rather have written this piece than Wagner's *Ring* cycle, and though the plot is an impossible muddle, the music makes one understand that extravagant remark. The reluctant king of the title is Henry of Valois, elected to the throne of Poland, who rather sympathizes with those who are plotting against him and adds to the muddle by changing places with his friend, Nangis. The result is a modified Cinderella story, ending happily, which prompts a series of superb numbers, some *Espãna*-like in brilliance (the well-known Waltz of Act II transformed in its choral form) and some hauntingly romantic, with even one sextet suggesting a translation of Wagner's Rhinemaiden music into waltz-time.

The pity is that the linking recitatives have been completely omitted from this recording, and in addition the score has been seriously cut. But Charles Dutoit is a most persuasive advocate. Star among the singers is Barbara Hendricks as the slave-girl Cinderella figure, Minka, who is finally united with Nangis (well sung by the light tenor, Peter Jeffes). Gino Quilico is the king, Isabel Garcisanz (rather shrill-toned) is Alexina, the ambitious wife of the buffo character, Fritelli, who is sung by Jean-Philippe Lafont. First-rate sound, but the chrome cassettes transferred at a high level, although vivid, are somewhat shrill in the treble. Interestingly, the recording is transferred on five sides only, with the last side left blank. The libretto is admirably clear. We look forward to the CD.

Chaminade, Cécile (1857–1944)

Concertino for flute and orchestra, Op. 107.
*** RCA Gold GL/*GK* 85448 [AGL1/*AGK1* 5448]. Galway, RPO, Dutoit – FAURÉ: *Fantaisie*; IBERT: *Concerto*; POULENC: *Sonata.****

A warm welcome back to the catalogue, at medium price, for the Chaminade *Concertino*, which undoubtedly has great charm. The principal theme of the first movement is of the kind that insinuates itself irresistibly into the subconscious, and the work has a delightful period atmosphere. It is splendidly played by James Galway, who is given excellent support by the RPO under Charles Dutoit. The recording, admirably spacious and finely detailed, has been digitally remastered since its last appearance. Definition on disc has been further improved without loss of bloom, but on the chrome tape the quality is slightly edgy at the top (though tameable).

Charpentier, Marc-Antoine (1634–1704)

Motets: *Alma Redemptoris; Amicus meus; Ave regina; Dialogus inter Magdalenam et Jesum; Egredimini filiae Sion; Elevations: O pretiosum; O vere, o bone. Magdalena lugens; Motet du saint sacrement; O vos omnes; Pour le passion de notre Seigneur* (2 settings); *Salve regina; Solva vivebat in antris Magdalena lugens.*
*** HM **HMC 901149**; HMC/*40* 1149 [id.]. Concerto Vocale.

Half of the motets on this record are for solo voice and the others are duets. All were intended for liturgical use. Among the best and most moving things here are the *O vos omnes* and *Amicus meus* which are beautifully done. Another motet to note is *Magdalena lugens* in which Mary Magdalene laments Christ's death at the foot of the Cross. This Harmonia Mundi series continues to go from strength to strength and serves to establish Charpentier as a really major figure in French music. Expressive singing from Judith Nelson and René Jacobs, and excellent continuo support. Well worth having in any format, but the image is naturally clearer and cleaner on CD. Worth a strong recommendation.

Caecilia, Virgo et Martyr; Filius prodigus (oratorios); *Magnificat.*
*** HM Dig. **HMC 90066**; (d.) HM 10066 [id.]. Grenat, Benet, Laplenie, Reinhard, Studer, Ars Florissants, Christie.

As the sleeve-note puts it, these Latin oratorios or dramatic motets of Charpentier occupy 'an isolated, if elevated position in French seventeenth-century music'. The two works recorded here come from different periods of his life: *Caecilia, Virgo et Martyr* was composed for the Duchesse de Guise in 1675, when he wrote a number of works on the subject of St Cecilia; the second, on the theme of the Prodigal Son, dates from the later period when Charpentier was *maître de chapelle* at St Louis-le-Grand (1684–98), and is richer in expressive harmonies and poignant dissonances. The music could scarcely find more eloquent advocates than these artists under William Christie; its stature and nobility is fully conveyed here. Included on the CD, though not on the LP, is another setting of the *Magnificat*, different from either of those recorded by Devos or Ledger – see below. It is a short piece for three voices and has an almost Purcellian flavour. One thing that will immediately strike the listener is the delicacy and finesse of the scoring. All this music is beautifully recorded; the present issues can be recommended with enthusiasm.

Laudate Dominum; 3rd Magnificat; Te Deum.
** Erato Dig. **ECD 88027**; NUM/*MCE* 75100 [id.]. Degelin, Jansen, Nirouet, Caals, Widmer, Ghent Cantabile, and Madrigal Ch., Musica Polyphonica, Devos.

Many readers will know the *Te Deum* from the Eurovision fanfare. It has been recorded a number of times, but this account from Louis Devos is as good as, if not better than, any of its predecessors. The two companion pieces, the setting of Psalm 116, *Laudate Dominum*, and the present setting of the *Magnificat* (one of many), are also from the mid-1690s and are comparative rarities. The performances are very good indeed and the standard of the singing more acceptable than the recording, which balances the team of soloists rather forwardly while the recording is not perhaps state-of-the-art. Nevertheless, a recommendation, even if collectors embarking on a Charpentier collection on CD might start elsewhere.

Leçons de ténèbres.
*** HM **CD 901005**; HM/*HM40* 1005/7. Jacobs, Nelson, Verkinderen, Kuijken, Christie, Junghänel.

Charpentier was an almost exact contemporary of Lully whom he outlived but whose shadow served to obscure him during his lifetime. These *Leçons de ténèbres* are eloquent and moving pieces, worthy of comparison with Purcell and more substantial musically than Couperin's later setting. Since the falsetto tradition was weak, it seems unlikely that any of the music was intended for male alto, a fact that the counter-tenor René Jacobs readily concedes in his notes. Yet his performance (like that of his colleagues) is so authentic in every respect that it is difficult to imagine it being surpassed. The pursuit of authenticity often produces inhibited phrasing and over-careful voice production, but here the results are a tribute to both musicianship and scholarship. This music has depth and these artists reveal its stature to fine effect. The recording is as distinguished as the performances; the cassette transfer too is admirable (although it needs a bass cut).

Magnificat; Te Deum.
(M) *** HMV EG 290301-1/*4* [Ang. AM/*4AM* 34719]. Lott, Harrhy, Brett, Partridge, Roberts, King's College Ch., ASMF, Ledger.

This is the best known of Charpentier's *Te Deum* settings written for the Sainte-Chapelle. It is also included on Devos's Erato CD (see above). There is a mixture of choruses, solo numbers and concertante movements, for which Charpentier provides invention of no mean distinction. The *Magnificat* is in D minor, for double choir, and has a good deal of antiphonal writing. Although none of this music has the depth of Purcell, it has a *douceur* and a freshness that makes it highly appealing. The performances have vitality and boldness, and the singing is stylish. The sound is excellent, well balanced and atmospheric; the cassette is much less clearly defined than the disc and is not recommended.

In navitatem Domini nostri Jésus Christi (*canticum*); *Pastorale sur la naissance de notre Seigneur Jésus Christ.*
*** HM **HMC 901082**. Les Arts Florissants Vocal and Instrumental Ens., Christie.

This CD appropriately re-couples two attractive works, both associated with Christmas and both composed for Marie de Lorraine, Duchesse de Guise, whose ensemble Charpentier directed until her death in 1688. This *Canticum* has much of the character of an oratorio (indeed, the word 'canticum' was loosely used to indicate both the motet and the oratorio) and affirms the composer's debt to his master, Carissimi. The invention has great appeal and variety and the artists who give so convincing an account of *Actéon* (see below) are no less persuasive here.

The *Pastorale* is not new to the gramophone, but this version supersedes its predecessor (in the edition of Guy Lambert) from which William Christie departs. The present issue contains music that was not included in the Guy Lambert edition which contained a different second part that had been intended for use at the Jesuit College in the Rue Saint-Antoine, Paris. It is a most rewarding piece and the grace and charm of the writing continue to win one over to this eminently resourceful composer. This series, undertaken by William Christie, seems almost self-recommending, so high are the standards of performance and recording, and so fertile is Charpentier's imagination. A momentary lapse of intonation fairly early on by the shepherdess should not put anyone off, for it is a minor blemish on an otherwise delightful achievement. The CD remastering is very successful; the only snag in the CD presentation is the minuscule print of the accompanying texts.

OPÉRA

Actéon (complete).
*** HM **HMC 901095**; HM 1095/*40* [id.]. Visse, Mellon, Laurens, Feldman, Paut, Les Arts Florissants Vocal and Instrumental Ens., Christie.

Actéon serves to confirm the growing impression that Charpentier was very much the greatest French composer of his day. It is a short work in six scenes, and the exact date of its composition remains unknown. As in so many other works which Harmonia Mundi and Erato are now investigating, the sheer fecundity and, above all, quality of invention take one by surprise though, by this time, one should take for granted Charpentier's extraordinarily rich imagination. Actéon is particularly well portrayed by Dominique Visse; his transformation in the fourth tableau and his feelings of horror are almost as effective as anything in nineteenth-century opera! William Christie has devoted such energy and scholarship to this composer that the authority of his direction ensures the success of this venture. Although scholarship is an important ingredient in this undertaking, musicianship and flair are even more important, and these are in welcome evidence. The other singers are first rate, in particular the Diane of Agnès Mellon. Alert playing and an altogether natural recording which is truthfully balanced and sounds splendidly fresh, as well as excellent presentation, make this a most desirable issue. The chrome cassette too is outstanding.

Medée (complete).
❀ *** HM **HMC 901139/41**; HM 1139/41 [id.]. Feldman, Ragon, Mellon, Boulin, Bona, Cantor, Les Arts Florissants Ch. and O, Christie.

Few records of early Baroque opera communicate as vividly as this, winner in 1985 of the International record critics' award and the Early Music prize in the *Gramophone* record awards. Despite the classical conventions of the libretto and a strictly authentic approach to the performance, Christie's account has a vitality and a sense of involvement which brings out the keen originality of Charpentier's writing, his implied emotional glosses on a formal subject. This was Charpentier's only tragédie-lyrique, and richly extends our knowledge of a long-neglected composer. Les Arts Florissants, in the stylishness of its playing on period instruments, matches any such group in the world, and the soloists are all first rate. Excellent recording, whether on LP or CD.

Chausson, Ernest (1855–99)

Concert for piano, violin and string quartet, Op. 21.
*** CBS Dig. **MK 37814**; 37814 [id.]. Perlman, Bolet, Juilliard Qt.

(i) *Concert for piano, violin and string quartet, Op. 21;* (ii) *Piece for cello and piano, Op. 39.*
** HM **HMC 901135**; HM/*40* 1135. (i) R. Pasquier, Daugareil, Simonot, B. Pasquier; (ii) Ridoux; (i; ii) Pennetier.

Since the pioneering records of Thibaud and Cortot, versions of the Chausson *Concert* for violin, piano and string quartet have hardly been thick on the ground. Ironically, things have improved to the extent that there have been three digital versions in recent years. The CBS version is not only artistically most satisfying but also gives the best-integrated aural picture. The sound is natural yet well observed, and the playing of Perlman and Bolet is quite exemplary. In short, this rather beautiful work has never been better served on record. It sounds even better on CD, although the violin timbre on compact disc suggests that Perlman was a little too close to the microphones.

On Harmonia Mundi there is an added inducement in the form of the Op. 39 *Piece* for cello and piano, which is not included on either the LP or the cassette. But good though Régis Pasquier and Jean-Claude Pennetier are, the distinction of the CBS team does tell. The French account is by no means wanting in imagination, but it is less poetic; the CBS recording is in every way superior.

Poème for violin and orchestra, Op. 25.
*** Decca **417 118-2**; SXL/*KSXC* 6851 [Lon. CS/5- 7073]. Kyung Wha Chung, RPO, Dutoit – RAVEL: *Tzigane*; SAINT-SAËNS: *Havanaise* etc.***
** Erato Dig. NUM 75052 [id.]. Mouillère, Monte Carlo PO, Jordan – LEKEU: *Adagio for strings* etc.; RABAUD: *La Procession nocturne*.***

Chung's performance of Chausson's beautiful *Poème* is deeply emotional; some may prefer a more restrained approach but, with committed accompaniment from the RPO and excellent recording in all three media, this makes an admirable foil for the virtuoso pieces with which it is coupled.

Mouillère's account is well played but there is nothing special about this performance; the interest of this disc lies in the couplings.

Symphony in B flat min., Op. 20.
** Sup. Dig. 1110 3404 [id.]. Czech PO, Kŏsler – ROUSSEL: *Le festin de l'araignée*, Op. 17.**

Symphony in B flat min., Op. 20; Soir de Fête, Op. 32; The Tempest, Op. 18: 2 Scenes.
(*) Chan. Dig. **CHAN 8369; ABRD/*ABTD* 1135 [id.]. RTB SO, Serebrier.

The Chandos recording is a co-production made in collaboration with RTB (Radio-Télévision Belge), and the sound is certainly natural. Serebrier succeeds in drawing playing of real conviction and some sensitivity from his players. He also offers the *Soir de Fête*, which Chausson wrote in the year before his death and had intended to revise, and which makes an excellent effect in this recording. In addition, the Chandos disc includes two dances from incidental music he composed for *The Tempest*, unlisted in most reference works on the composer. They are slight but attractive. The recording is very good indeed, without being in the demonstration class. The chrome cassette, too, is wide-ranging and brightly lit.

In terms of sheer orchestral playing the Kŏsler version can more than hold its own with its current rival. The Czech Philharmonic Orchestra are in excellent form: the woodwind and brass are beautifully blended and the balance throughout is finely judged. Kŏsler gives a thoroughly straightforward and well-characterized account of the *Symphony* with alert, well-articulated rhythms and a good feeling for proportion. His reading is free from mannerisms or point-making. The trumpet line in the final peroration can easily sound vulgar if there is excess vibrato, but here it is done with much greater restraint and dignity than is usual; and the accompanying wind chorus blends superbly. However, although the balance between the various sections of the orchestra is beautifully judged, and while the digital recording has clarity, it is top-heavy and suffers from glare.

Piano trio in G min., Op. 3.
*** Ph. Dig. **411 141-2**; 411 141-1/*4* [id.]. Beaux Arts Trio – RAVEL: *Trio in A min.****

The *G minor Trio* was written under the immediate influence of Franck, of whom Chausson had just become a pupil, and it will come as a pleasant surprise to most collectors, for its beauties far outweigh any weaknesses. There are many glimpses of the promise to come, and the invention is strong. The playing of the Beaux Arts Trio is superbly eloquent and the recording is very impressive on CD, even if the piano looms a little too large in the picture. A distinguished issue. There is an excellent chrome cassette.

Chávez, Carlos (1809–1978)

Symphonies Nos 1; 2 (Sinfonia India); 3.
*** MMG Dig. **MCD 10002.** LSO, Mata.

Though several generations younger than Chávez, Eduardo Mata was a personal friend of the composer and studied these symphonies with him, when Chávez himself was earlier recording them for CBS. This coupling of the first three, the most approachable, including the colourful *Sinfonia India* (more a symphonic poem than a symphony), provides an attractive sample from the complete cycle, very well played and recorded.

Cherubini, Luigi (1760–1842)

Symphony in D.
(M) *** Ph. Seq. 412 374-1/*4*. New Philh. O, Boettcher – WEBER: *Symphony No. 1.****

Since Toscanini's classic account, recordings of Cherubini's fine symphony have been few and far between. This is undoubtedly the best both in terms of performance, which is solid, lively and well thought-out, and recording, which is well balanced and truthful in timbre. Readers who do not know the symphony are strongly urged to investigate this admirable disc. Cherubini earned the admiration of no less a judge than Beethoven, and this work deserves more frequent hearings. The cassette is one of Philips's best, offering attractively lively and wide-ranging sound.

Coronation mass for King Charles X; Marche religieuse.
*** HMV Dig. EL 270283-1/*4*. Philh. Ch. and O, Muti.

Beethoven's warm admiration for Cherubini has not prevented his music from falling into neglect. Berlioz, too, spoke with enthusiasm of this *Mass* – as well he might, for one can almost sense his voice in the beautiful opening pages. Born ten years earlier than Beethoven, Cherubini survived him for fifteen years. This *Mass* dates from 1825 and there are signs in the *Gloria* that Cherubini was influenced by both *Fidelio* and the *Ninth Symphony*, and in the *Incarnatus* and *Crucifixus* by the *Missa solemnis*. But Cherubini's church music has a character of its own, beautifully crafted, with moments of real inspiration, such as the closing bars of the *Kyrie*. Muti presents the music with an intensity to hide any limitations, and both chorus and orchestra respond superbly. He secures the widest dynamic refinements (some may feel his dynamic range too extreme) and the digital sound is bold and full, with ceremonial trumpets braying magnificently, particularly in the *Et Resurrexit*. There is an instrumental appendix in the form of a *Marche religieuse*, written for Charles X at communion, which Berlioz described as 'mystic expression in all its purity', and it is indeed a very fine piece. The EMI recording is excellent in every respect; there is a first-class cassette, very well balanced with the chorus full and clear in focus. We look forward to its issue on compact disc.

Chopin, Frédéric (1810–49)

CONCERTANTE AND ORCHESTRAL MUSIC

Andante spianato and Grande polonaise brillante, Op. 22.
(B) ** Ph. On Tour *412 906-4* [id.]. Orozco, Rotterdam PO, De Waart – GRIEG; SCHUMANN: *Concertos**(*); WEBER: *Konzertstück.***

A generally well-played and recorded account of the concertante version of Op. 22 from Orozco, generously coupled on this extended-length 'On Tour' Philips chrome tape, although the other performances of music by Grieg, Schumann and Weber are of variable quality. Orozco has no lack of sparkle in the *Polonaise brillante*.

Piano concertos Nos 1 in E min., Op. 11; 2 in F min., Op. 21.
*** DG **415 970-2** [id.]. Zimerman, LAPO, Giulini.
** RCA **RD 85317 [RCD1 5317]**. Ax, Phd. O, Ormandy.

(i) *Piano concertos Nos 1 in E min.;* (ii) *2 in F min.; Piano sonatas Nos 2 in B flat min.* (*Funeral march*), *Op. 35; 3 in B min., Op. 56.*
(M) **(*) DG 413 235-1/*4* (2) [id.]. Argerich, (i) LSO, Abbado; (ii) Washington Nat. SO, Rostropovich.

Piano concertos Nos 1–2; Krakowiak (*Rondo*), *Op. 14.*
(B) ** Ph. On Tour *412 216-4* [id.]. Arrau, LPO, Inbal.

Piano concerto No. 1 in E min., Op. 11.
(*) DG **415 061-2 [id.]. Argerich, LSO, Abbado – LISZT: *Concerto No. 1.***(*)
(M) **(*) CBS 60033/*40*- [(d.) MY/*MYT* 37804]. Gilels, Phd. O, Ormandy.

(i) *Piano concerto No. 1; Andante spianato et Grande polonaise brillante, Op. 22; Piano sonata No. 3 in B min., Op. 58; Mazurka in F sharp min., Op. 59/3; Prelude in C sharp min., Op. 45.*
(B) **(*) DG Walkman *419 089-4* [id.]. Argerich; (i) LSO, Abbado.

Piano concerto No. 1; Ballade No. 1 in G min., Op. 23; Nocturnes Nos 4 in F; 5 in F sharp, Op. 15/1 and 2; 7 in C sharp min.; 8 in D flat, Op. 27/1 and 2; Polonaises Nos 5 in F sharp min., Op. 44; 6 in A flat, Op. 53.
(B) *** HMV *TCC2-POR 54275*. Pollini, Philh. O, Kletzki.

The CD coupling of Zimerman's performances of the two Chopin *Concertos* with Giulini will be hard to beat. This is arguably the finest version of the *First Concerto* to have appeared in the 1970s and is worthy to stand alongside Pollini's classic account. Zimerman is fresh, poetic and individual in his approach; this is a sparkling, beautifully characterized reading. His reading of the *F minor Concerto* has also won much acclaim, and rightly so. Elegant, aristocratic, sparkling – all these epithets spring to mind; this has youthful spontaneity and at the same time a magisterial authority, combining sensibility with effortless pianism. Both recordings are cleanly detailed. While the balance favours the soloist too much, in this respect the *F minor* is an improvement on the *E minor*, although the piano is still made to sound marginally too close. This leads the field, without question.

Emanuel Ax is the only other artist to offer both concertos on the same CD. His account of the *F minor* has admirable taste and finesse though not quite the sense of character of his finest rivals. The RCA recording, too, is not quite top-drawer though it is perfectly acceptable. In the *E minor Concerto* Ax and Ormandy are rather better served by the engineers and he is fresh and full of character. Not a first choice, perhaps, in either concerto, but there is still a lot to admire here.

Arrau's performances are available at bargain-price on the Philips extended-length 'On Tour' chrome tape. In his hands the concertos are immaculately aristocratic, though the expressive hesitations do not always grow naturally out of what has gone before, and Arrau's rubato will inevitably convince some listeners more than others. Moreover, the balance gives the distinguished soloist undue prominence, though the overall sound is pleasing and the piano timbre eminently realistic. The *Krakowiak* rondo makes an attractive bonus.

Pollini's classic recording, made shortly after he won the Warsaw Prize in 1959 as a youth of eighteen, still remains the best available of the *E minor Concerto*, particularly now that the sound has been improved. This is playing of such total spontaneity, poetic feeling and refined judgement that criticism is silenced. It is so marvellously sparkling and the rubato so superbly judged that one forgets about the performers and thinks only of Chopin. This performance is now issued on a double-length cassette which couples the *Concerto* with Pollini's first solo recital for HMV (also available separately – see below) which is as well planned as it is superbly played. One of EMI's 'Portrait of the Artist' series, this tape certainly encapsulates the distinctive quality of Pollini's playing. The transfer is well managed. The LP remains in the catalogue (without the solo items) and costing slightly less (SXLP 30160 [Ang. Sera. S/*4XG* 60066]). A CD is announced as we go to press, including most of the items on the tape (**CDC 747492-2**).

Martha Argerich's recording dates from 1969 and helped to establish her international reputation. The distinction of this partnership is immediately apparent in the opening orchestral ritornello with Abbado's flexible approach. Martha Argerich follows his lead and her affectionate phrasing provides some lovely playing, especially in the slow movement. Perhaps in the passage-work she is sometimes rather too intense, but this is far preferable to the rambling style we are sometimes offered. With excellent recording this is one of the most satisfactory versions available of this elusive concerto. The recording was originally of high quality, and it sounds remarkably fresh in its CD format. Definition is still good, and the ambient warmth of the analogue recording is preserved, although there is very slight recession of the image in pianissimo passages. There is very little background noise. However, there is an alternative Walkman tape, generously coupled with fine performances of the *B minor Sonata*, the *Andante spianato* plus two other pieces. This sounds extremely well and costs much less than the CD.

Argerich's performance is also available within a medium-priced set of two LPs and chrome tapes, coupled with her rather less successful version of the *F minor Concerto* in which she is partnered by Rostropovich. It is a strong but not always very romantic performance. Although the slow movement has an eloquent climax, its full poetry does not emerge until the closing pages; the finale, though vivacious, is not really memorable. Also included in the package are the *B flat minor Sonata* (from 1975) and the *B minor* (from 1968). Both are fiery, impetuous and brilliant performances, with no want of poetic vision to commend them. They hold their own with many in the catalogue, though both have a highly-strung quality that will not be to all tastes. The sound in the *Concertos* is excellent; the solo piano timbre in the *Sonatas* is somewhat drier. Discs and cassettes are closely matched.

It is good to see the Gilels recording returning to circulation, even if the sound does not flatter either him or the Philadelphia Orchestra. This is one of the most poetic and thoughtful accounts of the *Concerto* currently before the public. Gilels does not match the youthful fire of Argerich; but the lambent quality and sensitivity of his playing, with every phrase breathing naturally, make it one of the most desirable of records. Ormandy gives good support, but the engineers do not succeed in capturing the rich sonority of the Philadelphia strings. The cassette matches the disc closely. In the USA this performance is offered in a more generous format, coupled with the Liszt *E flat Concerto.*

Piano concerto No. 2 in F min., Op. 21.

(*) CBS Dig. **MK 39153; IM/*IMT* 39153 [id.]. Cécile Licad, LPO, Previn – SAINT-SAËNS: *Concerto No. 2* **(*).

** Decca Dig. **411 942-2**; 411 942-1/*4* [id.]. András Schiff, Concg. O, Dorati – SCHUMANN: *Concerto*.**(*)
** Ph. **416 443-2** [id.]. Clara Haskil, LOP, Markevitch – FALLA: *Nights*.**

Piano concerto No. 2; Krakowiak (rondo), Op. 14.
** Ph. Dig. **410 042-2**; 6514/*7337* 259 [id.]. Davidovich, LSO, Marriner.

Piano concerto No. 2; Polonaise No. 5 in F sharp min., Op. 44.
* DG **410 507-2**; 410 507-1/*4* [id.]. Pogorelich, Chicago SO, Abbado.

(i) *Piano concerto No. 2; Piano sonata No. 2 in B flat (Funeral march).*
(M) ** DG Sig. 413 976-1/*4* [id.]. Argerich, (i) Washington Nat. SO, Rostropovich.

Cécile Licad gives a very impressive account of the *F minor Concerto*: she has the appropriate combination of fire and delicacy. Comparisons with the most distinguished versions now before the public are not to her disadvantage; moreover, her sense of style earned her the imprimatur of the International Chopin competition in Warsaw, who chose this for their concerto record prize in 1985. She has excellent support from the LPO under Previn and the benefit of very natural recording, which sounds particularly refined on CD.

Intensely poetic and individual, Schiff's expressiveness has full room to breathe at generally spacious basic speeds. This is gentle Chopin, given an even softer focus by the recorded balance, with piano as well as orchestra placed at a distance against a warmly reverberant acoustic. However, the piano sound is rather boomy at the bottom and twangy at the top, while Concertgebouw ensemble is less crisp than usual. The chrome cassette is up to Decca's usual high technical standard.

Clara Haskil's recording dates from 1960 and last appeared, on a mid-priced LP, at the end of that decade. It is well recorded but overpriced on CD. The playing has undoubted freshness, but Clara Haskil gives the impression at times in the first movement that she is playing Mozart. While the *Larghetto* has genuine sensibility, this is not very competitive with Zimerman's CD offering outstanding performances of both concertos.

Bella Davidovich's is a very musical reading, and there is undoubted poetry in the slow movement. She is beautifully recorded, on both LP and cassette, and the compact disc offers a particularly natural sound-picture, warmly ambient, yet with excellent definition and detail. This is a pleasure to listen to, yet it must be admitted that the performance is somewhat undercharacterized. However, the attractions of this issue are increased by Davidovich's delightful account of the engaging *Krakowiak rondo*, sparkling and fresh, a very real bonus.

Argerich's performances, discussed above, are also available on this medium-priced Signature reissue, and certainly these performances have her musical personality strongly imprinted on them.

Listening to Pogorelich's account of the *Second concerto*, one can well understand what antagonized the jury at the Warsaw Chopin Competition in 1980, for they did not admit him to the finals (just as his Prokofiev *Sixth Sonata* makes one appreciate Argerich's championship of him on that occasion). This is pianism of no mean order – 'charismatic' is the word one is tempted to use – but at the service of a wholly narcissistic sensibility. It is Pogorelich's keyboard command and beauty of tone that his every gesture invites us to admire, while Chopin doesn't get too much of a look-in. It is all superbly played and recorded; however, the prospect of repeating the experience of hearing it is not to be contemplated without mixed feelings. True, one cannot but be bowled over by the sounds he produces, but it is difficult to be persuaded by their sense.

Still recommended: Zimerman's DG version combines qualities of freshness and poetic sensibility with effortless pianism (DG 2531/*3301* 126 [id.]). He offers the *Andante spianato and Grande polonaise brillante* as a bonus, whereas Ashkenazy's hardly less distinguished account includes a recital of favourite solo pieces (Decca SXL 6693 [Lon. CS/*5*- 6440]). Alicia de Larrocha too offers a fine performance in the lower-medium-price range, coupled with Backhaus's fascinating version of the Schumann *Concerto* (Decca Viva VIV/*KVIC* 43).

(i; ii) *Piano concerto No. 2 in E min.;* (iii) *3 Mazurkas, Op. 59;* (i) *Nocturnes Nos 1 in B flat min., Op. 9/1; 9 in B; 10 in A flat, Op. 32/1–2; in C sharp min., Op. posth.;* (iv) *Waltzes Nos 2, 4, 8–10, 11, 13–14.*
(B) *** DG Walkman *413 425-4* [id.]. (i) Vásáry; (ii) BPO, Kulka; (iii) Argerich; (iv) Zimerman.

This Walkman collection is excellent value. Tamás Vásáry's performance of the *Concerto* is one of his finest Chopin recordings and the 1964 sound remains first class. The balance is exceptionally convincing. The slow movement is played most beautifully, and in the other movements Kulka's direction of the orchestra has striking character and vigour. Side one is completed by four *Nocturnes* and side two includes a generous selection from Zimerman's distinguished set of the *Waltzes*, with performances as fine as any in the catalogue. It ends with Martha Argerich characteristically volatile in three *Mazurkas*. The transfers to chrome tape are first class throughout. A bargain.

Les Sylphides (ballet; orch. Douglas).
(M) *** DG Sig. 413 981-1/*4*. BPO, Karajan – DELIBES: *Coppélia.****

Karajan has the advantage of limpid and svelte playing from the Berlin Philharmonic Orchestra, and he evokes a delicacy of texture which consistently delights the ear. The woodwind solos are played gently and lovingly, and one can feel the conductor's touch on the phrasing. The upper register of the strings is bright, fresh and clearly focused, the recording is full and atmospheric, and this is one of Karajan's finest lighter discs. At medium price it is unbeatable. The chrome cassette is admirably managed, slightly more vivid than the disc in the upper range.

SOLO PIANO MUSIC

Ballades Nos 1–4; Impromptus Nos 1–3; Fantasie-impromptu, Op. 66.
(*) Ph. Dig. **411 427-2; (d.) 6514/*7337* 099 [id.]. Bella Davidovich.

Ballades Nos 1–4; Polonaise in A flat, Op. 53; Polonaise-fantaisie, Op. 61.
Erato Dig. **ECD 88023**; NUM/*MCE* 75088. François-René Duchable.

Ballades Nos 1–4; Scherzi Nos 1–4.
*** RCA **RD 89651**. Artur Rubinstein.
*(**) Tel. Dig. **ZK 43053**; AZ6/*ZK8* 43053 [id.]. Cyprien Katsaris.

Ballades Nos 1–4; Scherzi Nos 1–4; Sonatas Nos 2–3.
*** RCA RL/*RK* 85460 (3) [ARL3/*ARK3* 5460]. *Artur Rubinstein.*

Ballades Nos 1–4; Sonata No. 2 in B flat min. (Funeral march), Op. 35.
*(*) HMV **CDC 747344-2** [id.]; EL 270303-1/*4* [Ang. DS/*4DS* 37699]. Andrei Gavrilov.

Rubinstein's readings are unique and the digital remastering has been highly successful. The piano timbre now has more warmth and colour in the middle register, and the slight loss of brightness in the treble must be counted an improvement. The layout on CD is generous, but the discs and chrome tapes share the improvement in sound. The performances of the *Ballades* are a miracle of creative imagination. From the romantic splendour of the main theme of the *G minor* to the hushed half-tones of the tiny coda of the *F major*, Rubinstein is at his most inspired. The *Scherzi*, which gain most of all from the improved sound (they were originally very dry), are both powerful and charismatic. The readings of the *Sonatas* are unsurpassed, with a poetic impulse that springs directly from the music and a control of rubato to bring many moments of magic, not least in the second subject of the first movement of the *B flat minor Sonata*, and later in the central section of the *Funeral march*.

Bella Davidovich's CD differs from the LP in offering more music. We have three additional *Impromptus*, Opp. 29, 36 and 51, on the CD, enhancing the not inconsiderable attractions of this issue. First, there is the excellence of the piano sound, and secondly, the unaffected sensitivity of Bella Davidovich's interpretations. After Rubinstein, she leads the field on compact disc and is among the best in the inevitably much more competitive LP market.

Cyprien Katsaris is a player with an impressive technique and considerable power. He is a fiery interpreter of Chopin, but displays no lack of poetic feeling. The *B minor Scherzo* is very brilliant indeed, though the virtuosity never distracts attention away from composer to interpreter. Unlike Gilels or Perahia, one is quite aware that the piano has hammers! The LP of these performances was awarded a prize at the 1985 Warsaw Chopin Competition as 'the finest recital of the last five years' (though one does not know what other Western recordings were available to the jury). As piano playing it is certainly very good, at times even distinguished, but the recording as such leaves much to be desired. The acoustic is not really big enough and the climaxes are overwhelming. At times one has the feeling that the attention of a tuner might not have come amiss, and while this is a subjective comment, the sound certainly does not compare with the best recordings of, say, Philips or Decca of pianos. Moreover, on CD Katsaris's coupling comes into direct competition with Rubinstein.

Andrei Gavrilov has undoubted flair and his account of the *B flat minor Sonata* sets out in grand and mighty fashion. Moreover, on the face of it his record offers excellent value in that we are given the *Four Ballades* as well. There are some moments of tenderness (not too many, mind you), and his reading is at least free from the idiosyncratic posturing that mars Pogorelich's DG version. However, there is some ugly percussive tone in the devlopment section of the first movement and in the scherzo, and the climax of the slow movement is positively brutal. He gabbles the finale at the same speed as Rachmaninov (if not faster), but without the great pianist's elegance and finesse. Of course he is a strong personality, and there are some good things in some of the *Ballades*: there is plenty of fire in the *G minor*. In the *F major* he begins with appropriate poetry and tenderness, but the *A minor* outburst is horribly aggressive. This is undoubtedly an excellent recording, but the playing of Gavrilov will not suit all tastes.

Duchable's *G minor Ballade* is barn-storming and brilliant without being sensitive to the finer, aristocratic side of Chopin's sensibility. Admittedly, the recording is close and the instrument, a Bösendorfer, sounds thunderous. Even so, the beginning of the *A flat Ballade* leaves no doubt that tenderness is not this artist's strong suit. Indeed, it is a long time since those melting bars, marked *sotto voce* and at one point *pianissimo*, can have been so insensitively played.

Barcarolle, Op. 60; Berceuse, Op. 57; Fantaisie in F min., Op. 49; Impromptu No. 1 in A flat, Op. 29; Impromptu No. 2 in F sharp, Op. 36; Impromptu No. 3 in G flat, Op. 51.
*** CBS Dig. **MK 39708**; IM/*IMT* 39708 [id.]. Murray Perahia.

Perahia confirms the impression made in his *Sonata* record and his account of the *Préludes* that he is a Chopin interpreter of the highest order. There is an impressive range of colour and an imposing sense of order. This is highly poetic playing and an indispensable acquisition for any Chopin collection. The CBS recording does him justice. There is an excellent cassette, losing only a little of the upper range of the LP and CD.

Études, Op. 10, Nos 1–12; Op. 25, Nos 1–12.
*** Decca **414 127-2** [id.]; SXL/*KSXC* 6710 [Lon. CS/*5*- 6844]. Vladimir Ashkenazy.
*** DG **413 794-2**; 2530 291/*3300 287* [id.]. Maurizio Pollini.
** Erato Dig. **ECD 88001**; NUM/*MCE* 75001 [id.]. François-René Duchable.

Ashkenazy's 1975 version sounds wonderfully vivid in its CD form and, although there is little to choose between his performances and those of Pollini, the warmer sound that Decca provide for Ashkenazy might well make this a first choice for many collectors. However, honours are very evenly divided between them.

Pollini's record also comes from 1975 and sounds splendidly fresh in its digitally remastered form. This is playing of much stature. These are vividly characterized accounts, masterly and with the sound eminently present and seeming freer than in its original LP form.

François-René Duchable proves the equal of his rivals technically and brings considerable finesse and polish to the *Études*. He is not perhaps quite as imaginative in the more inward pieces as his distinguished colleagues, but he is obviously an artist to reckon with, and is generally well recorded. This is very much more successful than his *Ballades*.

Études, Op. 10/1–12; Op. 25/1–12; Piano sonatas Nos 2–3.
(B) ** CBS DC 40176 (2). Fou Ts'ong.

Fou Ts'ong is at his best in the *Études* and gives an impressive demonstration of his fine musicianship and expressive powers. Indeed, many individual studies compare well with the very finest available on record, though no easy equation emerges from comparisons. His insights are considerable, and his powerful technique is not in question either. He is also both perceptive and brilliant in both sonatas. His sensitivity is always in evidence, and there is poetry when required. The two discs are offered in a folding sleeve at the cost of a single premium-priced issue and, though the recorded sound is acceptable rather than distinguished, this is certainly good value. The 'equivalent' double-length chrome tape is not recommended as it omits the *Second Piano sonata*.

Mazurkas Nos 1–51.
*** RCA **RD 85171** (2); RL/*RK* 85171 (3). Artur Rubinstein.

The *Mazurkas* contain some of Chopin's most characteristic music. That they are often ignored by virtuoso pianists simply reflects the fact that as a rule they are less tricky technically, and concert pianists prefer to show off. Yet, as Rubinstein continually demonstrates, they contain some wonderfully pianistic ideas, none the worse for being simply expressed. At the one end you have certain *Mazurkas* which are first cousins to Chopin's *Polonaises*, and at the other end some that might almost be *Nocturnes*, while a lot in the middle could almost as readily have been included with the *Waltzes*. All are delightful, even if there is no need to linger very long over some of them. Rubinstein could never play in a dull way to save his life, and in his hands these fifty-one pieces are endlessly fascinating, though on occasion in such unpretentious music one would welcome a completely straight approach. As with the *Ballades* and *Scherzi*, the digital remastering has brought a piano timbre much more pleasing to European ears. The clarity of articulation is not dimmed, yet the quality is softer-grained than with the original LPs, slightly more so on the chrome cassettes (which are excellent) than on the pair of CDs.

Nocturnes Nos 1–19.
*** RCA **RD 89563** (2). Artur Rubinstein.
*** RCA RL/*RK*85018 (3) [ARL3/*ARK3* 5018]. Artur Rubinstein – *Waltzes.****

Nocturnes Nos 1–21.
*** Ph. **416 440-2** (2); 6747 485/*7699 088* [id.]. Claudio Arrau.

Rubinstein in Chopin is a magician in matters of colour; again and again throughout these two discs, there are moments of sheer perfection where the timing of a phrase exactly catches the mood and atmosphere of the composer's inspiration. His magical sense of nuance and the seeming inevitability of his rubato demonstrate a very special musical imagination in this repertoire. The recordings were the best he received in his Chopin series for RCA, and the quality is now finer still in these excellent CD transfers. The LPs and tapes – coupled with the *Waltzes* – are very impressive, too. There is no appreciable background noise on the CDs, and it is only very slight on the chrome cassettes, which are offered in a box. The only irritant is that the labels of the actual tapes offer no details of which *Nocturnes* each side contains. On LP and tape these recordings are available at mid-price on two separate discs or cassettes.

Arrau's approach clearly reflects his boyhood training in Germany, creating tonal warmth coupled with inner tensions of the kind one expects in Beethoven. In this he has something in common with Barenboim (see below). With the *Nocturnes* it can be apt to have an element of seriousness, and this is a very compelling cycle, full of poetry, the rubato showing an individual but very communicable sensibility. This is among Arrau's very finest Chopin recordings. It was made in the Amsterdam Concertgebouw in 1977/8; the analogue recording sounds wonderfully natural in its new CD format, though the rich refined sound-balance also projects well on the LPs and the excellent cassettes.

Nocturnes Nos 2 in E flat, Op. 9/2; 4 in F; 5 in F sharp; 6 in G min., Op. 15/1–3; 7 in C sharp min., Op. 27/1; 9 in B, Op. 32/1; 11 in G min.; 12 in G, Op. 37/1–2; 13 in C min.; 14 in F sharp min., Op. 48/1–2; 15 in F min., Op. 55/1; 18 in E, Op. 62/2; 19 in E min., Op. posth.
(*) DG Dig. **415 117-2 [id.]. Daniel Barenboim.

Barenboim's performances, taken from his complete set, are intense, thoughtful and poetic readings, the phrasing lovingly moulded, following rather in the mid-European tradition. Compared with Rubinstein, they lack a mercurial dimension, and the chosen selection tends to emphasize their repose. The sound is first class.

Polonaises Nos 1–6; 7, Polonaise-fantaisie, Op. 61.
*** DG **413 795-2**; 2530/*3300* 659 [id.]. Maurizio Pollini.

As with the *Préludes*, DG have been the first to enter the CD field. The engineers have made a decent job of the transfer, and in the absence of competition – and, it must be admitted, even in its presence in the future – this disc is likely to be well sought after. This is magisterial playing.

24 Preludes, Op. 28.
*** DG **413 796-2**; 2530/*3300* 550 [id.]. Maurizio Pollini.

24 Preludes, Op. 28; Preludes Nos 25 in C sharp min., Op. 45; 26 in A flat, Op. posth.; Barcarolle in F sharp min., Op. 60; Polonaise No. 6 in A flat, Op. 53; Scherzo No. 2 in B flat min., Op. 31.
(M) *** DG Gal. 415 836-1/*4* [id.]. Martha Argerich.

So far there is no alternative on CD, but the DG engineers have been very successful with the present transfer, and those investing in it can do so with confidence. In so far as one can speak of the best in artistic matters, this account and those by Ashkenazy and Perahia lead the field; until the latter's respective companies remaster theirs, this has the field to itself.

Martha Argerich's 1977 set of *Preludes* is generously supplemented on her Galleria reissue with other pieces recorded between 1961 and 1975. The *Preludes* show her at her finest, spontaneous and inspirational, though her moments of impetuosity may not appeal to all tastes. But her instinct is sure and the music making flows onwards compellingly with many poetic individual touches. The recording is resonant and full in colour. It has been digitally remastered, and disc and chrome tape sound very similar; if anything, the focus is fractionally firmer on cassette, without loss of warmth. The other pieces are splendidly played and the *Scherzo* impressively demonstrates her technical command, if that were not already apparent from the *Preludes*.

Scherzos Nos 1–4; Fantasie-impromptu, Op. 66. (See also above with *Ballades*.)
*** Ph. Dig. **412 610-2**; 412 610-1/*4* [id.]. Claudio Arrau.

Arrau's last recording of the four *Scherzi* was in the 1950s; this new one was made in Munich, just after the artist's eightieth birthday. There is little sign of age, even if he would have produced a greater weight of sonority at the height of his prowess. However, these accounts are full of wise and thoughtful perceptions and remarkable pianism, recorded with great presence and clarity. The middle section of the *First Scherzo* may strike some collectors as unusually slow and a trifle mannered, but there are magical things elsewhere, notably in the *Fourth*. Arrau's fire may have lost some of its youthful charisma, but the gains in wisdom and delicacy of feeling are adequate compensation. The Philips engineers seem to produce piano quality of exceptional realism. However, Ashkenazy's set should not be forgotten (Decca SXL 6334 [Lon. CS/*5*- 6562]). They offer dazzling playing of the highest order and first-rate Decca recording. Richter's electrifying versions are offered by HMV at mid-price and have the advantage of a tape alternative (SXLP/*TC-SXLP* 30510). The recorded timbre is, however, rather dry.

Piano sonatas Nos 1 in C min., Op. 4; 2 in B flat min. (Funeral march), Op. 35; 3 in B min., Op. 58.
(M) (*) Ph. Seq. 6527/*7311* 184 [id.]. Adam Harasiewicz.

Adam Harasiewicz was first prize-winner at the 1955 Warsaw International Competition. Subsequent prize-winners have included Pollini, Argerich and Zimerman; unlike them, Harasiewicz has not gone on to record repertoire other than Chopin. These recordings were made some years later, No. 2 appearing in the UK in 1960. To accommodate all three sonatas on one mid-price LP, exposition repeats are omitted – and (one is tempted to add) poetic feeling as well. These are surprisingly routine accounts and can be recommended only for those primarily concerned with economy. The cassette closely matches the LP.

Piano sonata No. 2 in B flat min. (Funeral march), Op. 35; Études Op. 10/8 and 10; Nocturne in E flat, Op. 55/2; Prelude, Op. 45; Scherzo No. 3 in C sharp min., Op. 39.
*(*) DG **415 123-2**; 2531/*3301* 346 [id.]. Ivo Pogorelich.

This record does not wear well, and though the sound is amazingly good in this CD transfer the interpretations seem more self-conscious than ever. There is no doubting the masterly pianism nor the extraordinary feeling for colour, but Pogorelich's self-aware reading of the *Sonata* does not grow more endearing.

Piano sonatas Nos 2 in B flat min. (Funeral march), Op. 35; 3 in B min., Op. 58.
*** DG Dig. **415 346-2**; 415 346-1/*4* [id.]. Maurizio Pollini.
(*) Erato **ECD 88083; NUM/*MCE* 75168 [id.]. François-René Duchable.

Pollini's performances are enormously commanding; his mastery of mood and structure gives these much-played *Sonatas* added stature. The slow movement of Opus 35 has tremendous drama and atmosphere, so that the contrast of the magical central section is all the more telling. Both works are played with great distinction, but while the CD gives plenty of presence, the balance is just a shade close, and the sound is good rather than special, as with many others of Pollini's DG records.

Duchable's readings are strongly impulsive and have strong character. His account of No. 3 is among the finest to have appeared in recent years, commandingly eloquent, with a memorable slow movement, rhapsodic in feeling, and a brilliantly articulated finale, exhilarating in its bravura. A similar sense of drama pervades the *B flat minor Sonata*, with its stormy first movement. The *Funeral march* is immediately commanding in its intensity, with the middle section elegiacally simple (much straighter than with Rubinstein). The return of the main theme is dramatic. The finale, by contrast, is under-articulated. Duchable is given a bold, full piano image. Some might find his reading of Op. 35 too intensely volatile – Rubinstein's performance has an aristocratic poise which is not part of Duchable's vocabulary – but his playing is commandingly spontaneous and has different insights to offer. There is an excellent cassette.

Waltzes Nos 1–19.
*** HMV Dig. EL 270289-1/*4*. Dimitri Alexeev.
** Ph. Dig. **412 890-2** [id.]. Zoltán Kocsis.
* Tel. Dig. **ZK8.43056**; AZ6.43056 [id.]. Cyprien Katsaris.

Waltzes Nos 1–14.
*** RCA **RD 89564**; GL/*GK* 89835. Artur Rubinstein.
*** RCA RL/*RK* 85018 (3) [ARL3/*ARK3* 5018]. Artur Rubinstein – *Nocturnes.****
*** Ph. **400 025-2**; 9500 739/*7300 824* [id.]. Claudio Arrau.
** Erato **ECD 88067**; NUM/*MCE* 75144 [id.]. Maria Joao Pires.

Dimitri Alexeev on an excellently engineered HMV recording brings us the best account of the *Waltzes* since Zimerman's DG set. He has personality, a genuinely aristocratic feeling, and a natural sense of style. This music making is unforced and the varied moods of these pieces are always successfully projected. It is a pity that this is not yet on CD, but it is scheduled to appear in the new format during the lifetime of this volume, as, one assumes, will the Zimerman (DG 2530/*3300* 965 [id.]). There is a good HMV cassette.

When we first discussed the original LP of Rubinstein's performances, we spoke of their chiselled perfection, suggesting the metaphor of finely cut and polished diamonds, emphasized by the crystal-clear, rather hard quality of the RCA recording. The digital remastering has softened the edges of the sound image, and there is an illusion of added warmth. Rubinstein's pacing is always perceptive, his rubato subtle and his phrasing elegant, and now the playing seems less aloof, more directly communicative. The CD is a separate issue with a companion mid-priced LP and cassette; the LPs and cassettes are also available coupled with the *Nocturnes* in a box. On tape, the quality is slightly softer-grained but still very pleasing.

Arrau produces his own specially rich, rounded tone-colours and is accorded beautiful sound by the Philips engineers. These are performances of elegance and finesse, though there are, as always, moments when the great pianist invests detail with a heavier significance than some listeners may feel is justified. But these are readings of real personality and, however the individual collector may respond, they are searching and considered. The compact disc is very fine indeed, and there is virtually no appreciable background noise stemming from the analogue master.

Unlike many of her rivals, Maria Joao Pires does not include the posthumously published pieces. She has a real sense of style, good musical judgement and taste, along with an impeccable technique. Moreover, she is well recorded, and it is only rarely (in the *A minor*, Op. 34, No. 2) that she falls short of real poetic distinction. The Erato recording has fine realism and presence, and there is an excellent chrome tape.

Zoltán Kocsis is full of fire and temperament but just a little too concerned to dazzle us with his superb technical prowess. Many of these are breathlessly fast and rushed, though there is no want of poetry in some of them. He includes five of the posthumous waltzes omitted by Arrau, Rubinstein and Zimerman. Kocsis is vividly – albeit too closely – recorded, but his playing is too eccentric and rushed to displace Zimerman.

Brilliant but unsympathetic playing from Cyprien Katsaris who allows his technical fluency to run away with him. There are moments of poetry, of course, but the aristocratic quality that a Zimerman, Ashkenazy or Lipatti bring to this repertoire is missing here. As with his account of the *Ballades and Scherzi*, the sound, despite the benefits of CD, does not compare with the best piano recording from Philips or Decca.

RECITAL COLLECTIONS

Albumblatt in E; Ballade No. 4 in F min., Op. 52; 2 Bourrées; Fugue in A min. Galop marquis, Impromptu No. 3 in G flat, Op. 51; Mazurkas, Op. 56/1–3; in F min., Op. 68/4 (revised version); *Polonaise No. 6 in A flat, Op. 53; Scherzo No. 4 in E, Op. 54; Waltzes: in F min., Op. 70, No. 2; in A min., Op. posth. Wiosna* (arr. from *Op. 74/2*).
*** Decca Dig. 414 465–1/*4* [id.]. Vladimir Ashkenazy.

This recital concerns itself with the works Chopin composed during the years 1841–3, when his relationship with George Sand was at its height. It shows to excellent advantage the strategy of Decca's planners in offering mixed recitals in this project, for the result is to contrast larger-scale pieces with miniatures, and to put the familiar alongside the rarities. On this LP we have such masterpieces as the *Fourth Ballade*, the *E minor Scherzo* and the Op. 56 *Mazurkas*, framed by some valuable rarities, the chromatic *Albumblatt* and the little *A minor Fugue*, and other posthumously published pieces. Among them, the unaffected simplicity of the *A minor Waltz*, published as late as 1955, and the piano transcription of his song, *Wiosna*, are particularly fetching. As usual, Ashkenazy's playing is authoritative and poetic, and the recordings excellent.

Andante spianato and Grande polonaise, Op. 22; Contredanse in G flat; Mazurkas, Op. 6/1–4; Polonaise in A flat, Op. 53; Tarantelle in A flat, Op. 43; Variations brillantes on a theme from Ludovic by Halévy.
* Telarc Dig. **CD 80040**. Malcolm Frager.

Although the programme is enterprising and Malcolm Frager's keyboard command is impressive, the performances here are not distinguished enough to reward continued re-listening. Frager plays the *Andante spianato* sensitively, but the *Polonaise brillante* is not convincing rhythmically, and the Op. 6 *Mazurkas* lack the instinctive feeling for rubato that Rubinstein, for one, can bring to them. The Bösendorfer is recorded in a resonant acoustic and the sound focus is cushioned – this was one of Telarc's early (1979) digital recordings and not one of their clearest.

Ballade No. 1 in G min., Op. 23; Nocturnes Nos 4 in F; 5 in F sharp, Op. 15/1–2; Nocturnes Nos 7 in C sharp min.; 8 in D flat, Op. 27/1–2; Polonaises Nos 5 in F sharp min., Op. 44; 6 in A flat, Op. 53.
(M) *** HMV EG 290263-1/*4* [Ang. AM/*4AM* 34703]. Maurizio Pollini.

A welcome separate reissue of Pollini's 1970 début recital. The playing is consistently distinguished, stirringly romantic in the *G minor Ballade* and the two *Polonaises*, while the *Nocturnes* show the finest sensibility and have the most delicate tonal shading. The recital is very well planned, and the recording is first class on disc and tape alike. (However, tape collectors will note that it is also available on a double-length issue, coupled with the *First Piano concerto* – see above.)

Ballade No. 1 in G min., Op. 23; Mazurkas Nos 19 in B min., 20 in D flat, Op. 30/2–3; 22 in G sharp min., 25 in B min., Op. 33/1 and 4; 34 in C, Op. 56/2; 43 in G min., 45 in A min., Op. 67/2 and 4; 46 in C; 47 in A min., 49 in F min., Op. 68/1–2 and 4; Prelude No. 25 in C sharp min., Op. 45; Scherzo No. 2 in B flat min., Op. 31.
(*) DG **413 449-2; 2530 236/*3300* 349 [id.]. Arturo Benedetti Michelangeli.

Although this recital somehow does not quite add up as a whole, the performances are highly distinguished. Michelangeli's individuality comes out especially in the *Ballade*, a very free rhapsodic performance which nevertheless holds together by the very compulsion of the playing. Michelangeli's special brand of poetry is again felt in the *Mazurkas*, which show a wide range of mood and dynamic; and the *Scherzo* is extremely brilliant, yet without any suggestion of superficiality. The piano tone is real and lifelike, and has been most realistically transferred to CD. There is also a good cassette.

'Favourite Chopin': Ballade No. 3 in A flat, Op. 47; Barcarolle in F sharp, Op. 60; Études, Op. 10, Nos 3 in E (Tristesse); 5 in G flat (Black keys); 12 in C min. (Revolutionary); Op. 25, No. 11 in A min. (Winter wind); Nocturne in F min., Op. 55/1; Polonaise in A, Op. 40/1; Preludes: in D flat (Raindrop), Op. 28/15; in C sharp min., Op. 45; Waltzes: in D flat; C sharp min., Op. 64/1 and 2.
*** Decca **410 180-2** [id.]. Vladimir Ashkenazy.

Digitally remastered from recordings made between 1975 and 1982, the sound here is slightly variable, but has striking vividness and presence. The upper range is less soft-grained than on the original LPs, with the treble brightly lit and often producing an edge on top in fortissimos, notably in the *Revolutionary study* and the *Polonaise*, while the *Black keys study* is somewhat clattery. The background silence serves to enhance this effect. Yet the middle range is warm and the bass firm and resonant. As can be seen, the selection is generous (nearly an hour of music) and popular. Ashkenazy is shown at his most commanding, though perhaps the inclusion of more *Nocturnes* would have given a better-balanced picture of his special sensibilities in this repertoire.

Barcarolle, Op. 60; Berceuse, Op. 57; Étude No. 3 in E, Op. 10/3; Fantaisie-impromptu, Op. 66; Mazurkas: Nos 5 in B flat, Op. 7/1; 37 in A flat, Op. 59/2; Nocturnes Nos 5 in F sharp, Op. 15/2; 13 in C min., Op. 48/1; Polonaises Nos 3 in A (Military), Op. 40/1; 6 in A flat, Op. 53; Scherzos Nos 2 in B flat min., Op. 31; 3 in C sharp min., Op. 39; Sonata No. 2 in B flat min. (Funeral march), Op. 35; Waltzes Nos 1 in E flat (Grande valse brillante), Op. 18; 6 in D flat (Minute), Op. 64/1.
(B) * Ph. On Tour *412 898-4* [id.]. Adam Harasiewicz.

This is a very generous selection, including many favourites, and the chrome tape offers excellent sound quality. But the performances, though unfailingly musical, are undercharacterized and lacking in projection and charisma.

Fantasia in F min., Op. 49; Nocturne in D flat, Op. 27/2; Polonaise No. 5 in F sharp min., Op. 44; Piano sonata No. 3 in B min., Op. 58.
(B) ** Con. CC/*CCTC* 7606. Peter Katin.

This collection combines all the virtues and vices of a 'live' recital. The audience is quiet during the playing (although there is one unfortunate cough in the *Sonata*) but provides applause at the end of each piece so sudden and vociferous as to make one jump, and certainly spoil any mood engendered by the playing. What a pity this was not edited out. The recording, made in The Maltings, Snape, is backwardly balanced but very believable: on grounds of timbre the piano image can hardly be faulted. The performances too have that special electricity of a public recital; indeed, with playing so wayward, especially in the *Sonata*, it is the atmospheric concentration that holds the performance together. Katin takes a little while to warm up in the opening *Polonaise*, then does the *Nocturne in D flat* very beautifully and is at his most convincing in the rhapsodic account of the *Fantasia in F minor*. There is genuine poetry here, and the articulation in the finale of the *Sonata* is most impressive. Disc and chrome tape sound virtually identical.

Fantaisie-impromptu in C sharp min., Op. 66; Mazurkas, Op. 24/1–4 and Op. 67/1–3; Mazurka in A flat; Nocturnes: in C sharp min. and D flat, Op. 27/1–2; Polonaises: in C sharp min. and E flat min., Op. 26/1–2; Prelude in A flat; Waltzes: in A flat, Op. 69/1; in G flat, Op. 70/1.
*** Decca Dig. 410 123-1/*4* [id.]. Vladimir Ashkenazy.

The tenth of Ashkenazy's historical recitals of Chopin's music is devoted to the years 1834–5 when the composer was in his mid-twenties, based in Paris and at the height of his success. Ashkenazy is wonderfully poetic in the two *Nocturnes*. There are two works without opus numbers: the *Prelude in A flat* and the *Mazurka* in the same key only came to light in the present century. Ashkenazy is often at his most affecting and revealing in the most familiar pieces: his account of the *A flat Waltz*, Op. 69, No. 1, is an instance in point, which finds him very imaginative in his command of nuance and colour. The recording, made at Kingsway Hall, London, is most truthful. Recommended in both LP and tape formats.

Fantaisie-impromptu in C sharp min., Op. 66; Polonaise No. 6 in A flat, Op. 53; Scherzo No. 2 in B flat min., Op. 31; Sonata No. 3 in B min., Op. 58.
*(*) HMV Dig. EL 270272-1/*4*. Andrea Lucchesini.

Andrea Lucchesini is a young Italian pianist who was not twenty when this record was made; his is a considerable talent and he possesses the requisite fluency and technical equipment to take all this repertoire in his stride. However, he has not fully surmounted the interpretative challenges these works pose – except, perhaps, in the case of the *B minor Sonata* which is rather impressive. The recording is very good indeed, but these readings do not displace those by the many great pianists on record. Let us hope that the next release from this gifted artist will encompass less familiar repertoire.

Impromptu in A flat, Op. 29; Largo in E flat, Op. posth.; Mazurkas: Op. 30/1–4; Op. 33/1–4; Nocturnes: Op. 32: Nos 1 in B; 2 in A flat; in C min., Op. posth.; Scherzo in B flat min., Op. 31; Variation No. 6 in E (from Hexameron); Waltz in F, Op. 34/3.
*** Decca Dig. **410 122-2**; 410 122-1/*4*. Vladimir Ashkenazy.

Volume Eight in Ashkenazy's continuing historical series is the first to be issued on compact disc (apart from the separate anthology of 'favourite' items – see above). It is well up to the high standard of the series, both in sensibility and in recording, with a splendid chrome tape, every bit the equal of the LP. The opening *Impromptu* is thrown off with a marvellous unaffected insouciance and the programme (which is concerned with music written in 1836–8) includes a memorably serene account of the *Sylphides Nocturne*, Op. 32/2. The playing is full of mercurial contrasts, the *B flat minor Scherzo* a fine example of Ashkenazy's current style combining bold drama with subtlety of inner feeling. The virtually unknown *Largo* is a rather solemn piece, but fits splendidly into a recital that is as well planned as it is expertly played. The variety of nuance within the eight *Mazurkas* included gives special pleasure. The CD itself is of the highest quality, and readers collecting this series need not hesitate.

Impromptu No. 3 in G flat, Op. 51; Nocturnes Nos 5 in F sharp min., Op. 15/2; 8 in D flat, Op. 27/2; 14 in F sharp min., Op. 48/2; Polonaise-fantaisie, Op. 61; Waltzes Nos 4 in F, Op. 3/3; 6 in D flat (Minute), Op. 64/1; 11 in G flat, Op. 70/1.
** RCA Dig. **RD 84437**. Peter Serkin.

Peter Serkin, unlike his famous father, Rudolf, has something of the reputation of a tearaway pianist; but here, in a well-chosen if hardly generous mixed bag of Chopin pieces, he gives sensitive and tasteful, almost classical readings, well recorded and believably transferred to CD.

Mazurkas, Op. 6/1–4, Op. 7/1–5; Nocturnes, Op. 15/1–3; in C sharp minor, Op. posth.; Scherzo No. 1 in B min., Op. 20; Waltzes: in E flat, Op. 18; A min., Op. 34/2.
*** Decca Dig. 411 896-1/*4* [id.]. Vladimir Ashkenazy.

The music on this disc comes from the period 1830–32, not long after the composer's first important public recital in Warsaw. It saw his journey to Vienna and then to Paris, where he met two musicians who were to be important for him, Liszt and Hiller. The *Four Mazurkas* of Op. 7 already show a great stride forward, compared to their predecessors; Ashkenazy plays No. 4 with particular sensitivity and strength. As usual, a skilfully planned and well-presented recital, and admirably recorded. The cassette quality is bold and clear, but at times there is a touch of hardness on the timbre, notably in the *Mazurkas*.

VOCAL MUSIC

Songs: *The bridegroom; The double end; Enchantment; Handsome lad; I want what I have not; Leaves are falling; Lithuanian song; Melody; Merrymaking; The messenger; My darling; Out of my sight; Reverie; The ring; The sad river; Spring; The warrior; What she likes; The wish.*

*** Decca Dig. **414 204-2**; 414 204-1/*4* [id.]. Elisabeth Söderström, Vladimir Ashkenazy.

The magic partnership of Elisabeth Söderström and Vladimir Ashkenazy, which has brought intense illumination to the songs of Rachmaninov, Tchaikovsky and Sibelius, is here just as revealing. Nothing establishes Chopin more clearly as a red-blooded Pole than these generally simple, unsophisticated songs with their plain folk melodies and sharp Slavonic rhythms. Söderström and Ashkenazy find an ideal balance, bringing out endless niceties of expression in pointing of word, phrase and rhythm, but keeping the essential freshness of inspiration. The excellent note of the late Martin Cooper points the listener to the special qualities of each of the 19 songs which are here strongly constrasted. They build up to three of the most individual, *The bridegroom* with its dramatic picture of a lover finding his bride dead, the *Lithuanian song* with its innocent folk-style exchanges, and *Leaves are falling*, more extended than the rest, a Pole's response to the Russians' callous treatment of his country in 1830. Well-balanced sound, full of presence.

Cimarosa, Domenico (1749–1801)

Il Maestro di Capella.

*** Hung. Dig. SLPD 12573 [id.]. József Gregor, Boys of Schola Hungarica, Corelli CO, Pál – TELEMANN: *Der Schulmeister*.***

Gregor's firm rich bass goes with a comparably strong personality and a striking ability to act the buffoon in this romp of an intermezzo with its comic conflict between the maestro di cappella and the orchestra. Plainly, Gregor's performance has benefited from stage experience. Though his comic style is on the broad side, his magnetism pulls the piece together very effectively, with Thomás Pál a responsive conductor. It is aptly if ungenerously coupled with the more heavily Germanic Telemann cantata. First-rate recording.

Coates, Eric (1886–1958)

By a sleepy lagoon; Cinderella (phantasy)*; Dambusters march; From meadow to Mayfair suite; London suite; London again suite; Saxo-rhapsody; The three bears* (phantasy)*; The three Elizabeths suite: Springtime in Angus.*
(B) ** EMI *TC2-MOM 154651-9*. Royal Liverpool PO, Groves.

On the whole, Groves proves a persuasive advocate, although occasionally his approach is slightly bland. Jack Brymer is the excellent soloist in the *Saxo-rhapsody*, and the other piece with a diluted jazz element, *Cinderella*, also goes with a swing. On tape the recording is smooth and pleasing, with the upper range a little restricted. In the car – at which the 'Miles of Music' series is directed – it makes an entertaining ninety minutes, though best heard in two separate parts; however, the performances lack the distinction of those of Sir Adrian Boult (see below), nor does the recorded sound match that provided by Lyrita – at full price.

Cinderella; London suite; London again suite; The three bears.
(*) Ara. **Z 8036** [id.]. Royal Liverpool PO, Groves.

Groves's Coates recordings were originally made in EMI's often unsuccessful hi-fi-conscious Studio Two sound-balance which provided an exaggerated brilliance at the expense of the bass response. On the Arabesque CD, the digital remastering has amplified this effect and though *Cinderella* triumphs over the sound by its sheer energy, elsewhere the orchestra seems emaciated, with its very bright, clear upper range unsupported by any weight from the lower strings.

From meadow to Mayfair suite: In the country; Evening in town; The Merrymakers overture; Summer days suite; The three bears (phantasy)*; The three Elizabeths suite: March.*
*** Lyr. SRCS 107. New Philh. O, Boult.

Dame Ethel Smyth once described Eric Coates (then at the end of his career as orchestral violist and in his early days as a composer) as 'the man who writes tunes'. And so he did, a profusion of memorable ones. But his music had great craftsmanship, too; lightweight though it is, it lies firmly within the English tradition. Here Boult finds its affinities with Elgar in delicacy of scoring and hints of nostalgia. *Summer days*, written during the summer of 1919, was the first work that Coates composed as an ex-orchestral player. It includes a justly famous waltz, *At the dance*, graciously elegant and with hardly any Viennese influence. It is a joy to hear this engaging music played with such finesse by a first-class orchestra obviously enjoying the experience; the only reservation about Boult's approach is his slowing down for the central section of the famous march from *The three Elizabeths*, which is out of character. The 1979 recording is splendid, matching Lyrita's predictable high standards. This reissue remains at full price.

Coleridge-Taylor, Samuel (1875–1912)

(i) *Hiawatha's wedding feast; The Bamboula* (rhapsodic dance).
*** HMV Dig. EL 270145-1/*4* [Ang. DS/*4DS* 38186]. (i) Rolfe-Johnson, Bournemouth Ch.; Bournemouth SO, Alwyn.

In its day *Hiawatha's wedding feast* blew a fresh breeze through a turgid British Victorian choral tradition; since then, the work has been kept alive in fairly frequent performances by amateur choral societies. The newest digital recording is first class in every way, and Kenneth Alwyn – who enters the recording studios too infrequently – secures a vigorous and committed contribution from his Bournemouth forces, with Anthony Rolfe-Johnson an excellent soloist in the famous *Onaway! Awake, beloved!* The music throughout is delightfully melodious and extremely well written for the voices, and this can be recommended strongly. There is an excellent equivalent cassette. Sir Malcolm Sargent's 1962 version remains in the catalogue at mid-price. It was a landmark of choral recording in its day and, with its spectacular choral ambience, is hardly inferior, in freshness or weight, to the new version. Moreover the coupling, an elegant account by George Weldon of the engagingly slight *Petite suite de concert*, with the Philharmonia Orchestra relishing the delicate *Demande et response* (a favourite of Palm Court era) is more desirable than *The Bamboula*, although that too is agreeable enough (HMV ESD/*TC-ESD* 7161 [Ara. 8005/*9005*]). However, the earlier cassette, transferred at a disappointingly low level, is no match for the tape of the newer issue.

Copland, Aaron (born 1900)

Appalachian spring: ballet suite.
€ *** Decca **414 457-2**; 414 457-1/*4* [id.]. Detroit SO, Dorati – STRAVINSKY: *Apollon musagète.****
*** DG Dig. **413 324-2**; 2532/*3302* 083 [id.]. LAPO, Bernstein – BARBER: *Adagio*; BERNSTEIN: *Candide overture*; SCHUMAN: *American festival overture.****

Appalachian spring: ballet suite; El salón México; Rodeo (ballet)*: 4 dance episodes.*
** HMV Dig. ASD/*TC-ASD* 143650-1/*4* [Ang. DS/*4DS* 38048]. Minnesota O, Marriner.

Appalachian spring: ballet suite; Fanfare for the common man; Rodeo: 4 Dance episodes.
€ **(*) Telarc **CD 80078**; DG 10078 [id.]. Atlanta SO, Lane.

Appalachian spring: ballet suite; Short symphony.
*** Pro Arte Dig. **CCD 140**; (d.) PAD 140 [id.]. St Paul CO, Russell Davies – IVES: *Symphony No. 3.****

Dorati has the full measure of Copland's masterly score, creating a marvellous evocation at the opening and a feeling of serene acceptance at the close, while the affectionately witty portrayal of *The Revivalist and his flock* is presented with sparklingly precise rhythms and splendid string and woodwind detail. The *Solo dance of the Bride* is equally characterful; throughout, Dorati finds a balance between the nicely observed interplay of the human characters and the spacious and lonely grandeur of the Appalachian backcloth. The Decca recording is superb in its range and vividness and again confirms the excellence of the acoustic of the Old Orchestral Hall, Detroit. The cassette is splendid too, amazingly close to the CD in its definition, although the latter has that extra touch of presence and tangibility that we have come to expect from the Decca engineers.

Bernstein's newest version was recorded at a live performance, and the conductor communicates his love of the score in a strong, yet richly lyrical reading. Some might feel that, carried away by the occasion, he pushes the climax of the variations on the haunting Shaker theme, *Simple gifts*, too hard, but the compulsion of the music making is obvious. The recording is close but not lacking atmosphere, and it sounds extremely vivid in all three formats.

The Telarc coupling is given recording of demonstration quality, naturally balanced and with glowing ambient warmth and vivid woodwind colouring. Lane's account of *Appalachian spring*, without missing the score's lyrical qualities, has an attractive feeling of the ballet theatre about it, with the strings lightly rhythmic. *Rodeo* too is not so bitingly dramatic and incisive as Bernstein's version (see below), but is more lyrical and atmospheric. The recording is even more vivid on the compact disc and the silent background is a great boon. The snag, however, is the extremely forward balance of the bass drum and tam tam at the opening of the *Fanfare for the common man*. The sheer force and amplitude of that simultaneous opening crash is unnerving. The level of transfer is extremely high; apart from making the listener jump (to say the least), if the volume control is set too high, one fears for the safety of the loudspeaker cones! This is more suitable for hi-fi demonstration than for the living-room.

Using a smaller ensemble than is usual, Russell Davies conducts fresh and immediate performances of both the *Short Symphony* of 1933, one of several early works, and the well-known suite from *Appalachian spring*, the latter included only on the CD version. The recording is bright and forward to match the performances.

Sir Neville Marriner's performances are amiable rather than rhythmically biting. He is at his most persuasive – helped by beautiful recorded sound – in atmospheric opening and closing sections of *Appalachian spring* and in the *Corral nocturne* of *Rodeo*. However, in movements like *Buckaroo holiday* and *Hoe down*, there is a folksy quality rather than the irrepressible zest that Bernstein generates in this music. The syncopated lilt in *El salón México* is engaging, and throughout there is fine orchestral playing (particularly from the strings in *Appalachian spring*). But these performances are not distinctive. The XDR cassette does not match the disc in sharpness of focus, though it is well balanced.

Appalachian spring: suite; Billy the Kid: suite; Danzón Cubano; Fanfare for the common man (from *Symphony No. 3*)*; Rodeo: 4 Dance episodes; El Salón México.*
(B) *** CBS *40-79020.* NYPO, Bernstein.

This excellent double-length tape gathers together Bernstein's vintage recordings of Copland's most popular works, and it was a good idea to feature the famous *Fanfare* by using an extract from the *Third Symphony.* The playing of the New York orchestra, on peak form, is superb and the music making is full of electricity. The sound is slightly less sharply defined at the top than the LP originals, but that is not an aural disadvantage, for there is no lack of atmosphere. The only drawback is the lack of documentation, consisting solely of a list of titles on the front of the box.

Billy the Kid (complete ballet); *Rodeo* (complete ballet).
*** HMV Dig. EL 270398-1/*4* [Ang. DS/*4DS* 37357]. St Louis SO, Slatkin.

Slatkin's coupling is particularly valuable for providing a first recording, very vivid and idiomatic, of Copland's complete ballet, *Billy the Kid.* The ballet suite usually recorded omits about ten minutes of music, including two delightful waltzes, the first a quick waltz based on the tune *Old Smokey*, used a moment earlier, and the second using the same idiom as the *Mexican dance*. That is a red-blooded pas de deux representing Billy's finding refuge with his Mexican sweetheart. The complete ballet *Rodeo* consists essentially of the usual four colourful movements but includes also a piano interlude (an old upright piano of 'doubtful' lineage was used for the recording, we are told). Both works are played and recorded with similar brilliance, with the St Louis orchestra responding to Slatkin's sympathetic and vigorous direction. The recording, made in the orchestra's own hall, is lively and well focused, with an attractive ambience.

Dance symphony; Danzón cubano; Fanfare for the common man; The Red Pony: suite.
(M) **(*) HMV Green. ED 270375-1/*4.* Mexico City PO, Bátiz.

Copland's *Red Pony* suite, written for Lewis Milestone's film, is among his most endearing lighter scores. The composer summed up the film and thus the music as 'a series of vignettes concerning a teenage boy called Jody and his life in a Californian ranch setting'. The music's nostalgia is well caught by this excellent performance by the Mexico orchestra under Bátiz, the best recording they have yet made together. The playing is notable both for its understanding and for its excellent ensemble. The *Dance symphony* is derived from an unperformed ballet composed with Diaghilev in mind. It was devised to fit a bizarre scenario involving dancing corpses, coffins and a vampire called Grohg, but was stillborn; the music turned up in its present format in 1929. If the orchestral ensemble is less impressive here, the playing is again alert and committed, as it is in the *Danzón cubano*, where the orchestra catches the element of colourful vulgarity with nice flair. Excellent sound and a mid-priced format make this issue worth getting for *The Red Pony* alone. A very good high-level cassette, though our copy brought a momentary discoloration in the brass in the spectacular opening *Fanfare*.

Dance symphony; El salón México; Fanfare for the common man; Rodeo (ballet): *4 dance episodes.*
(*) Decca Dig. **414 273-2 [id.]; SXDL/*KSXDC* 7547 [Lon. LDR/5-71047]. Detroit SO, Dorati.

There is a bright, extrovert brilliance about Dorati's attractive collection of Copland works, chosen for their immediate, cheerful, wide-open-spaces qualities. The playing demonstrates very clearly that orchestral virtuosity in the United States extends to orchestras other than the big five, and the digital recording has a clarity and impact that suit the music. The only reservation is that, rather surprisingly, Dorati's treatment of jazzy syncopations – an essential element in Copland of this vintage – is very literal, lacking the lift we think of as idiomatic. As usual, the transfer to CD brings added presence; as sound, this is very impressive.

El salón México; 3 Latin American sketches; Quiet city; Rodeo (ballet): *4 Dance episodes.*
(M) *(*) HMV ED 270254-1/*4*. Mexico City PO, Bátiz.

Bátiz is a lively interpreter of Copland in this attractively devised selection of his most colourful and atmospheric music, but the orchestra is not ideally polished, and the sound is harsh and aggressive, with lack of body. On the whole, the XDR tape sounds better than the LP, fuller yet not lacking brightness at the top.

Piano sonata; 4 Piano blues; Variations.
** Chan. ABR/*ABT* 1104 [id.]. Gillian Lin.

Gillian Lin is a Singapore-born pianist who recorded the Copland and Britten concertos successfully some time ago. Her performances here are eminently acceptable, particularly in the *Four piano blues*; she also gives a good account of the *Sonata*, which is not otherwise available at present since the deletion of Leo Smit's authoritative account. These recordings were made in association with the Australian Broadcasting Commission and are truthful and well balanced.

Corea, Chick (born 1941)

Fantasy for 2 pianos.
** Tel. Dig. **ZK8.42961**; AZ6/*CX4*.42961. Corea, Gulda – MOZART: *Double concerto*; GULDA: *Ping-Pong*.*(*)

This curious and inept coupling derives from the Munich Klaviersommer Festival of 1982. Chick Corea's jazz-inspired *Fantasy* is a rather agreeable piece, opening lyrically and unadventurously, but later becoming jazzier in feeling. The degree of aleatory content is not clear. The performance is certainly spontaneous and it is given a close, clear recording.

Corelli, Arcangelo (1653–1713)

Concerti grossi, Op. 6/1–12.
*(*) Chan. Dig. **CHAN 8336/6**; DBRD/*DBRT* 3002 (3) [id.]. Cantilena, Shepherd.

The first complete set of Corelli's Op. 6 to reach CD is the Chandos set from Cantilena directed by Adrian Shepherd. The performances are genial enough, but are at times a little rough-and-ready, and collectors are advised to stick to Marriner and his ASMF on Argo, or Kuijken's Petite Bande on Harmonia Mundi (if original instruments are required). The Chandos set is technically impressive, but it is expensive, on three CDs, while the alternatives cost far less.

Concerti grossi, Op. 6/5, 6, 7, 8 (Christmas concerto).
** Erato **ECD 88080** [id.]. Sol. Ven. Scimone.

I Solisti Veneti offer more polished accounts of the set than Cantilena on Chandos and are well enough recorded by the Erato engineers. They bring a robust vitality to some of the quicker movements – but are heavy-handed on occasion. On CD, the sound is fresh and full-bodied and the recorded image is very realistic; however, more transparency of texture and a lighter touch are needed in this repertoire, if modern stringed instruments are to be used.

Concerto grosso in G min. (Christmas), Op. 6/8.
** DG **415 301-2** [id.]. BPO, Karajan – ALBINONI: *Adagio***; VIVALDI: *Four seasons.***(*)

This is a bonus for Karajan's 1973 set of Vivaldi's *Four seasons*. It is beautifully played, although the style is hardly authentic. The sound is acceptable, but this is not one of DG's most impressive examples of digital remastering.

Violin sonatas, Op. 5/1, 3, 6, 11 and 12 (Follia).
*** Accent Dig. **ACC 48433D** [id.]. Sigiswald and Wieland Kuijken, Robert Kohnen.

When authenticity of spirit goes hand in hand with fine musical feeling and accomplishment, the results can be impressive, as they undoubtedly are here. In *Sonatas 1, 3* and *6* Sigiswald Kuijken bases his ornamentation on those of the Roger edition, adding his own for *No. 11*. Indeed, in terms of liveliness and imagination, this eclipses the earlier version on Archiv from Melkus. The results are not only convincing in terms of sonority but draw one into the sensibility of the period. This is a thoroughly recommendable issue which deserves to reach a wider audience than early music specialists; the recording is natural and the musicianship refined and totally at the service of Corelli.

Couperin, François (1668–1733)

Les Nations (ordres 1–4) complete.
* DG Arc. Dig. 410 901-1 (2) [id.]. Col. Mus. Ant.

This account by the Musica Antiqua, Cologne, has the benefit of recent scholarship which suggests that many of the dance movements were faster than had been previously thought. They certainly seem faster; yet, paradoxically, each of these suites feels longer. Perhaps this is due to the want of tonal variety and generosity. This group is greatly respected and revered in early music circles but, to be frank, their playing conveys little sense of the nobility and grandeur of this music, nor does it bring any sense of pleasure. The recording is satisfactory without being top-drawer. Recommended only to followers of this ensemble.

Pièces de clavecin (Harpsichord suites): Ordres 11 and 13.
*** Denon Dig. **C37 7070** [id.]. Huguette Dreyfus (harpsichord).

The representation of Couperin's keyboard music on compact disc is somewhat meagre at present, this Denon record being the first in the field. Huguette Dreyfus plays a Dowd and shows herself yet again to have great understanding of this style. Couperin has been called the 'Chopin of the harpsichord'; Mme Dreyfus certainly has the poetic sensibility and the grasp of rubato so necessary in the interpretation of his art. She is impeccably recorded – though to get a truthful aural picture of the instrument, readers would be well advised to play this at a very low-level setting.

Motets: *Domine salvum fac regem; Jacunda vox ecclesiae; Laetentur coeli; Lauda Sion salvatorem; Magnificat; O misterium ineffabile; Regina coeli; Tantum ergo sacramentum; Venite exultemus Domine; Victoria, Christo resurgenti.*
** HM **HMC 901150**; HMC/*40* 1150 [id.]. Feldman, Poulenard, Reinhart, Linden, Moroney.

This record explores unfamiliar ground: indeed, four of the items have only recently been discovered; the only exception is the Easter motet, *Victoria, Christo resurgenti*, which has been recorded before. The consensus of informed opinion is that the *Tenebrae* represent Couperin's sacred music at its best, but there is much here that is well worth investigating, and the motets on this record cover a wider spectrum of feeling and range of expressive devices than might at first be imagined. The performances are eminently acceptable, with some particularly good singing from Jill Feldman; the recording is made in a spacious and warm acoustic. The CD represents a distinct gain over its LP rival which sounds a shade congested towards the end of the sides; but there is no doubting that this is an issue of special interest to all lovers of French Baroque music.

Messe pour les couvents.
*** Argo Dig. 411 827-1/*4*. Peter Hurford, Ladies of Oxford Chamber Ch., Higginbottom.

Messe pour les paroisses.
*** Argo Dig. 411 826-1/*4*. Peter Hurford, New College, Oxford, Ch., Higginbottom.

The organ mass is a practice in which short organ pieces, called variously verses, versets or couplets, are played in alternation with verses sung by the choir and congregation. Couperin's two collections (*pour les paroisses* and *pour les couvents*) were published in the early 1690s when he was in his early twenties. In earlier issues (Gillian Weir and Lionel Rogg in recent years), Couperin's organ masses have been recorded without any liturgical reference point. Here the various pieces he composed for use during Mass at St Gervais are interspersed with appropriate plainsong. Peter Hurford, who plays with consummate sense of style, is recorded on the newly restored organ, designed by Robert Delaunay in 1683, of Saint-Pierre des Chartreux at Toulouse. The engineers have made an excellent job in marrying the acoustic with that of the Chapel of New College, Oxford, and capture the atmosphere of both to splendid effect. In the *Messe pour les couvents*, women's voices are an obvious choice to provide the appropriate plainchant, whereas the male voices of New College Choir are featured in the companion work. The same high standards of performance style and recording are common to both issues.

Couperin, Louis (1626–61)

Suites de pièces and complete keyboard music.
*** HM HM 1124/8 [id.]. Davitt Moroney (harpsichord).

Louis Couperin was a pupil of Chambonnières, and his keyboard output comprises enough individual dance pieces to make sixteen suites, as well as other pieces. Couperin did not organize his music into fixed suites and the main source, the Bauyn manuscript which contains almost all of his pieces, groups them in order of ascending tonality: fifteen pieces in C major, followed by five in C minor, twenty-three in D minor, and so on. Contemporary players would have put together their own suites from this, as did the compiler of the Parville manuscript which includes about half of them. The most famous of Louis Couperin's pieces are the unmeasured preludes, which Davitt Moroney plays with great idiomatic understanding, as he does the remaining works. Three instruments are used (an Albert Delin of 1768, a Couchet of 1671 and a Bellot of 1729), all restored in the workshop of Hubert Bédard and all tuned to the temperaments in use in France in the middle of the seventeenth century. This comprehensive survey by Davitt Moroney makes out a strong case for this repertoire; readers expecting it to be greatly inferior in quality to the clavecin music of François-le-Grand will be pleasantly surprised – though, of course, there is less of the poetic fantasy of his nephew at his best. The recording is eminently truthful, and the box is impressively presented; but there is no cassette or CD version.

Cowie, Edward (born 1943)

(i) *Clarinet concerto No. 2, Op. 5; Concerto for orchestra.*
*** Hyp. Dig. A 66120 [id.]. (i) Hacker; Royal Liverpool PO, Howard Williams.

Cowie richly deserves these first recordings of major works, two pieces which shower notes on the page with an exuberance that is daunting, reminding one somewhat of an amateur artist painting an abstract. Perhaps significantly, Cowie himself has been a painter, and some of his works have been directly inspired by paintings. The *Clarinet concerto No. 2* of 1975 is the more communicative of the two works here, with the broad image of sun eliminating fog well realized. Hacker makes a powerful, incisive soloist, as he needs to if he is to hold his own against Cowie's heavy orchestration. The *Concerto for orchestra* of 1979–80 is more problematic, depending on wild, thick textures that are hard to analyse. But the purposefulness of the writing is superbly brought out in this committed performance, very well recorded.

Crusell, Bernhard (1775–1838)

Clarinet concertos Nos 1 in E flat, Op. 1; 3 in E flat, Op. 11.
*** Hyp. **CDA 66055**; A/*KA* 66055 [id.]. King, LSO, Francis.

Crusell, born in Finland in 1775 but working in Stockholm most of his career, was himself a clarinettist. Most of the works, which on record and in the concert hall have latterly been infiltrating the repertory, include that instrument, and these two delightful concertos are among the most impressive. The echoes are of Mozart, Weber and Rossini with a hint of Beethoven, and though the writing is demanding for the soloist, Crusell generally avoided cadenzas. Thea King with her beautiful liquid tone makes an outstanding soloist, well accompanied by Francis and the LSO. The recording is first class, with an attractive ambient effect, well caught on CD. The cassette is vivid and wide-ranging, to match the LP.

Clarinet concerto No. 2 in F min., Op. 5.
❀ *** ASV Dig. **CDDCA 559**; DCA/*ZCDCA* 559 [id.]. Emma Johnson, ECO, Groves – BAERMANN: *Adagio*; ROSSINI: *Intro., theme and variations*; WEBER: *Concertino*.***
*** Hyp. **CDA 66088**; A/*KA* 66088 [id.]. Thea King, LSO, Francis – WEBER: *Concerto No. 2*.***

Emma Johnson chose Crusell's *Second Concerto* for the final of the BBC's 'Young Musician of the Year' contest in 1984. It made her a star, and in return she put Crusell's engagingly lightweight piece firmly on the map. Her delectably spontaneous performance is now caught on the wing, for she seems quite un-intimidated by the recording studio and this recording sounds very like a live occasion. There is an element of daring in the music making, the sparkling virtuosity of the outer movements bringing a lilting bravura that has one relishing the sense of risks being taken and brought off with ease. The songful *Andante* is no less appealing; throughout, it is the imaginative individuality of the phrasing and the natural feeling for dynamic light and shade that make this performance special. Groves is a lively and sympathetic accompanist, and the balance is a natural one. There is a good tape, but the CD and LP versions have slightly sharper detail.

Thea King's wide range of tone-colour and her unfailing artistry make this so-called *Grand concerto*, dedicated to Alexander I of Russia, seem even finer than it is with its Beethovenian first movement, its *Andante pastorale* slow movement in the warm key of D flat and its jaunty *Allegretto* finale. Not the obvious coupling for the better-known Weber concerto, but an attractive one. The digital recording is full and atmospheric with the soloist balanced forward. The CD, vividly clarifying a reverberant acoustic, is exceptionally realistic. There is also an outstandingly faithful cassette.

Divertimento in C, Op. 9.
*** Hyp. A 66143 [id.]. Francis, Allegri Qt – KREUTZER: *Grand quintet*; REICHA: *Quintet*.***

Crusell has become something of a light industry at Hyperion, who seem to be recording his complete works. (All three clarinet concertos and quartets enrich their enterprising list.) His music certainly has charm and grace, and the *Divertimento*, Op. 9, is no exception. It is available on the Finlandia label – hardly surprisingly since he was born in Finland – but no one wanting this slight but charming piece and its companions need look further than this nicely played and well-recorded account.

Debussy, Claude (1862–1918)

Berceuse héroïque; La Boîte à joujoux (ballet)*; Children's corner suite* (both orch. Caplet)*; Images pour orchestre; Marche écossaise.*
(B) *** EMI *TCC2-POR 290112-9*. O Nat. de l'ORTF, Martinon.

A generous and welcome double-length tape taken from Jean Martinon's complete set of the orchestral music. Martinon draws some extremely fine playing from the ORTF orchestra, and these performances can hold their own with any in the catalogue. *La Boîte à joujoux* is not so delicately articulated or quite so atmospheric as was Ansermet's, though there is no doubt that this is the better orchestral playing. The recordings have transferred well to tape, with only slight loss in the extreme upper range; the *Images* sound particularly vivid. A bargain.

Images; Prélude à l'après-midi d'un faune.
C *** HMV Dig. **CDC 747001-2**; ASD/*TCC-ASD* 3804 [Ang. DS/*4ZS* 37674]. LSO, Previn.

Previn's account of *Images* was the first EMI digital record to appear, and understandably it was also included in the first release of HMV compact discs. Detail emerges more clearly than in any of its LP rivals, yet there is no highlighting and no interference in the natural perspective one would expect to encounter in reality. Every colour and sonority, however subtle, registers; so vivid is the picture that there seems no intermediary between the musicians and the listener. Such is the clarity that this factor outweighs such reservations as one might have (it won both the *Gramophone* awards for the best sound and the best orchestral record of 1979). There is much to admire in Previn's performance, too. Dynamic nuances are carefully observed; there is much felicitous wind playing and no want of intelligent and musical phrasing. By the side of some of Previn's rivals there does seem to be a want of atmosphere in *Gigues*. Nor is that last ounce of concentration and electricity that is the hallmark of a great performance present in the other movements, particularly *Rondes de printemps*. Previn himself has given us more atmospheric accounts of the *Prélude à l'après-midi d'un faune* than this, though none is more vividly captured by the engineers. The chrome cassette is hardly less demonstration-worthy than the disc, with the widest range, a natural balance and vivid detail. The CD confirms the triumphant technical success, with the silent background enhancing the tangibility and refinement of the orchestral texture.

Jeux; (i) *Nocturnes.*
ℭ *** Ph. **400 023-2**; 9500 674/*7300 769* [id.]. Concg. O, Haitink, (i) with women's ch. of Coll. Mus.

However overstocked the catalogue may be, there must always be a place for performances and recording of the quality of this Philips issue. The playing of the Concertgebouw Orchestra is of the highest order, and Haitink's *Jeux* far surpasses any recent rivals. Indeed, it even matches such historic accounts as those of Cluytens and the Paris Conservatoire Orchestra and de Sabata's pioneering set of 78s. His reading is wonderfully expansive and sensitive to atmosphere, and *Jeux* undoubtedly scores over Boulez's much (and rightly) admired version from the more measured tempo and pensive approach that Haitink chooses. Competition is even stiffer in the *Nocturnes*, but this great orchestra and conductor hold their own. The cruel vocal line in *Sirènes* taxes the women of the Collegium Musicum Amstelodamense, but few versions, even those of Abbado and Giulini, are quite as beguiling and seductive as Haitink's. Add to this an equally admirable recorded quality, with transparent textures, splendidly defined detail and truthful perspective – in short, demonstration sound – and the result is very distinguished indeed. So is the handsome presentation, which reproduces Whistler's *Nocturne in Blue and Silver* to striking effect. In its ordinary LP format this received a twin *Gramophone* award, for the best orchestral and best engineered record of 1980. It is, of course, an analogue recording; but it has been digitally remastered for its compact disc issue, which brings just a little greater sense of concert-hall presence, with the bass also somewhat better defined.

The quality on cassette is richly atmospheric too, but there is a slight loss of range at the top compared with the LP.

La Mer; (i) *Danses sacrée et profane; Prélude à l'après-midi d'un faune.*
*(*) Telarc Dig. **CD 80071**; DG 10071 [id.]. St Louis SO, Slatkin; (i) with Tietov.

La Mer; Marche écossaise; Prélude à l'après-midi d'un faune; (i) *Rhapsody for clarinet and orchestra.*
(M) *** Ph. 412 920-1/*4* [id.]. Concg. O, Haitink; (i) with Pieterson.

La Mer; (i) *Nocturnes.*
*** HMV Dig. **CDC 747 028-2**; ASD/*TC-ASD* 143632-1/*4* [Ang. DS/*4DS* 37929]. LSO, Previn; (i) with Amb. S.
(*) Ph. Dig. **411 433-2; 6514/*7337* 260 [id.]. Boston SO, Sir Colin Davis; (i) with Tanglewood Fest. Ch.
** CBS Dig. 37832 [id.]. Philh. O, Tilson Thomas; (i) with Amb. S.
** Decca **414 040-2** [id.]. SRO, Ansermet; (i) with female ch.

Previn's *La Mer* is not quite as fine as Karajan's (DG 2542/*3342* 116), but it is a considerable achievement. His reading is more overtly passionate than Davis's; his ocean is clearly in the southern hemisphere, with Debussy's orchestral colours made to sound more vividly sunlit. The playing of the LSO is extremely impressive, particularly the ardour of the strings. There is less restraint and less subtlety than with Davis or Haitink, emphasized by the recording which has glittering detail and expands brilliantly at climaxes (though, even on CD, there is a slight loss of refinement at the very loudest peaks). The *Nocturnes* have even greater spontaneity. Some might feel that the *Sirènes* are too voluptuous (Davis's restraint is telling here), but this matches Previn's extrovert approach. The spectacular qualities of the EMI sound-picture certainly provide both works with a highly effective CD début, for, though definition is very clear, there is no lack of ambient atmosphere. The cassette is also very successful, full-bodied and well defined.

Sir Colin Davis's *La Mer* is a great success, too. The waters that this reading evokes are colder and greyer than Previn's, and there is always the sense of tremendous power used with restraint. One critic was reminded of Sibelius here – and Sir Colin does grasp the essentials of both. The set of *Nocturnes* is also very fine. Some will be surprised at Sir Colin's measured approach to *Sirènes*, but it is a convincing one, marvellously sustained in both feeling and atmosphere. *Nuages* is hardly less concentrated in poetic feeling, slow and ethereal. This is a very different view of *Nocturnes* from that of Haitink and the Concertgebouw Orchestra, but it is no less valid and is sumptuously played and recorded. The snag is that the acoustics of the Boston Hall tend to blur inner detail; although the definition of the CD is better than that of the LP, compared with Previn's HMV recording the effect is less than ideal, though the recording faithfully reflects the hall ambience (albeit without an audience).

Michael Tilson Thomas and the Philharmonia give highly sensitive and atmospheric performances of both scores, and it would be a pleasure to recommend them with enthusiasm. Unfortunately, the recording is not up to the much higher standards we have come to expect in the last few years from CBS, in that the engineers have elected for a clarity that negates all that impressionism stands for. Comparing this with Previn, Karajan or Haitink is rather like observing a landscape by Manet alongside a sharply focused photograph of the same scene. Artistically, however, there is a lot to admire.

Technically the transfers of the Ansermet recordings are remarkable: the *Nocturnes* and *Prélude à l'après-midi d'un faune* date from 1957 and *La Mer* from 1964; indeed, *Fêtes* sounds amazing. Whatever his failings, Ansermet secured a rather individual sound from his orchestra, and he is faithful to Debussy's scores, though the orchestral playing does not have the tonal bloom and finesse of the LSO under Previn. These readings have undoubted electricity, and the wind and brass playing radiates a vivid colouristic palette, partly the result of the unique partnership Ansermet established with the Decca recording engineers over his long recording career. This CD is clearly aimed at Ansermet aficionados, and it is a pity it could not have been put out at a reduced price. For all its undoubted merits, it cannot be recommended over and above its more recent rivals.

The restoration of Haitink's 1978 collection to the catalogue at medium price is most welcome, with the remastered sound more vivid than before, yet retaining its natural perspective and realistic colour, a marvellously refined sound. The cassette too has been re-transferred at the highest level and matches the disc closely in body and definition. Haitink's reading of *La Mer* is much closer to Karajan's tempo in his 1965 recording than in his more recent EMI version. Both conductors pay close attention to dynamic gradations and both secure playing of great sensitivity and virtuosity from their respective orchestras. *De l'aube à midi sur la mer* has real atmosphere in Haitink's hands. The *Jeux de vagues* is no less fresh; the *Dialogue du vent et de la mer* is both fast and exciting. An interesting point is that the brief fanfares that Debussy removed eight bars before fig. 60 are restored (as they were by Ansermet), but Haitink gives them to horns. (Karajan, who omitted them in the DG version, restored them in his HMV record, but on trumpets.) The *Prélude à l'après-midi d'un faune* and the undervalued *Clarinet rhapsody* are atmospherically languorous in Haitink's hands.

Although sumptuously, though not very clearly, recorded, Slatkin's Telarc CD must be counted an also-ran. There is too little electricity here, and the backward balance helps to make a minimal impression, although the orchestral playing is accomplished and the body of tone produced by the St Louis strings is impressive.

COLLECTION

(i) *Danses sacrée et profane; La Mer; Nocturnes; Prélude à l'après-midi d'un faune; Rêverie* (arr. Smith)*; Suite bergamasque: Clair de lune* (arr. Caillet).
(M) **(*) CBS *40-79023*. Phd. O, Ormandy; (i) with M. Costello.

A double-length cassette to show the Philadelphia Orchestra at the height of its powers during the Ormandy regime. The sound is remarkably good, with a slight smoothing at the top to mellow the excessively bright lighting from which CBS recordings of this orchestra have often suffered. Detail remains quite clear and the music making is vividly projected. The overall impression is one of languor, the *Nocturnes* especially atmospheric and *La Mer* evocative, though the last movement, the *Dialogue of the wind and the waves*, is as exciting as anyone could wish for, with superb unselfconscious bravura from all departments of the orchestra. With ninety minutes' music offered, this is excellent value and the arrangements at the end of the concert make attractive *bonnes-bouches*: they are beautifully played and warmly recorded. The documentation, however, is a disgrace, with just a list of titles at the front of the hinged plastic box.

CHAMBER MUSIC

Cello sonata; Petite pièce for clarinet and piano; Première Rapsodie for clarinet and piano; Sonata for flute, viola and harp; Violin sonata; Syrinx for solo flute.
*** Chan. **CHAN 8385**; ABR/*ABT* 1036 [id.]. Athena Ens.

This set scores over rival LPs in being more generously filled. In addition to the three late sonatas and *Syrinx*, we are given the two clarinet pieces (the *Rapsodie* is better known in its orchestral form). The most ethereal of these pieces is the *Sonata for flute, viola and harp*, whose other-worldly quality is beautifully conveyed here; indeed, this version can hold its own with the best in the catalogue. In the case of the other sonatas, there are strong LP competitors (Kyung Wha Chung and Lupu in the *Violin sonata*, Rostropovich with Britten in the *Cello sonata*). The works for wind are especially successful in the cassette version, which sounds admirably fresh; the string pieces are slightly less immediate.

Cello sonata in D min.
** Denon Dig. **C37 7563** [id.]. Fujiwara, Rouvier – STRAVINSKY: *Suite italienne*; SHOSTAKOVICH: *Cello sonata.***
** ASV Dig. DCA/*ZCDCA* 522 [id.]. Colin Carr, Francis Grier – FAURÉ: *Élégie* etc.; FRANCK: *Sonata.***

Mari Fujiwara and Jacques Rouvier give an elegant and idiomatic account of the Debussy *Sonata*, with plenty of fire in the finale. So far this is the only CD version. It is not superior to some of the rival LPs but is worth a recommendation in its own right. Well-balanced recording.

Colin Carr's account of this elusive work is one item on a disc of French cello music called 'The virtuoso cello', and he certainly lives up to the title in the sureness of his playing which allows the free fantasy of the central *Serenade*, with its strange pizzicatos, to come over with seeming spontaneity. Good recording, if rather dry in ambience, with a closely matching tape.

Still recommended: The classic version by Rostropovich and Britten has now been restored to the catalogue at mid-price and is self-recommending (Decca Jub. 410 168-1/*4* [Lon. JL/*5*- 41068]).

Sonata for flute, viola and harp.

(M) *** Decca 414 063-1/*4*. Ellis, Melos Ens. (members) – RAVEL: *Introduction and allegro*; ROPARTZ: *Prelude, marine and chansons*; ROUSSEL: *Serenade*.***

This Oiseau-Lyre 1960s anthology of French chamber music is more than welcome back to the catalogue. The age of the recording hardly shows, and now there is a vivid tape. Debussy's *Sonata*, one of a set of three written late in his career, needs just the kind of performance it receives here at the hands of three fine chamber music players, its ethereal atmosphere well caught. The couplings are hardly less desirable.

String quartet in G min.

(*) HMV **CDC 747347-2 [id.]; EL 270356-1/*4*. Alban Berg Qt – RAVEL: *Quartet*.**(*).

** Ph. Dig. **411 050-2**; 6514/*7337* 387 [id.]. Orlando Qt – RAVEL: *Quartet*.**

There have been abundant alternative LP versions of this coupling, though none is played more beautifully and superbly than by the Alban Berg on EMI. Technically they are in a class of their own, yet, strangely enough, one finishes listening to this with greater admiration than involvement. Not that they are in any way outside Debussy's world; rather, the performance beautifies the work and has little spontaneous feeling. It is superbly recorded but, for sheer musical pleasure, the Melos Quartet of Stuttgart on DG still remains a first choice. Despite these qualifications, it would be difficult not to give this a recommendation in preference to its current rival on CD. There is an excellent cassette, smooth and full, yet freshly detailed, though the upper range is not so wide as on LP and CD.

The Orlando Quartet is a superlative ensemble and they throw themselves into this work with complete dedication. They have a wide dynamic range, yet rarely does one feel that any detail is exaggerated and their tonal blend is magnificent. However, seven bars after fig. 1 comes a sudden drop in pitch and, later on (6 bars before 5), there is another discernible pitch change. The playing itself is so characterful elsewhere and so vividly recorded that one would want to report that these discrepancies are of no moment – but, alas, they are. The compact disc is extraordinarily realistic and, for those undisturbed by the momentary lurches in pitch, both here and another in the Ravel, it will be much admired. It is only fair to say that it collected much praise and a prize on the Continent, and the playing is otherwise of the highest order. There is a satisfactory cassette.

Still recommended: The DG recording by the Melos Quartet (to which we gave a Rosette in our last edition) offers playing that is distinguished by perfect intonation and ensemble and which has a natural sense of flow and great tonal beauty (2531/*3301* 203 [id.]).

PIANO DUET

Ballade; Cortège et air de dance (from *L'enfant prodigue*)*; En blanc et noir; Six épigraphes antiques; Lindaraja; Marche écossaise; Petite suite; Prélude à l'après-midi d'un faune; Symphony in B min.*
(M) *(*) DG 415 006-1/*4* (2). Alfons and Aloys Kontarsky – RAVEL: *Ma mère l'oye; Rapsodie espagnole* etc.*(*)

En blanc et noir; Six épigraphes antiques; Lindaraja; Marche écossaise; Petite suite.
❀ (M) *** Ph. Seq. 412 375-1/*4*. Werner Haas and Noël Lee.

En blanc et noir; Petite suite. Fêtes (from *Nocturnes*, arr. Ravel).
*(*) CRD CRD 1125/*CRDC 4125* [id.]. Bracha Eden and Alexander Tamir.

This Philips record collects all of Debussy's music for two pianos, played by Werner Haas and Noël Lee, and must be accounted one of the most treasurable Debussy records. The *Petite suite* and the *Six épigraphes antiques* are given with all the subtlety, expertise and atmosphere that one could wish; the performance of *En blanc et noir* is hardly less magical than the classic account by Martha Argerich and Stephen Bishop-Kovacevich on the same label. On its first appearance, at full price, this was worth every penny; now at mid-price, it should not be missed. The recording is atmospheric and refined. As this repertoire tends not to stay in circulation for very long, readers should not hesitate to snap this up. The cassette is in the demonstration class and every bit the equal of the disc.

The Kontarsky brothers offer an interesting and valuable anthology that supplements the Philips version by the late Werner Haas and Noël Lee by including a movement of a symphony that Debussy composed at the age of eighteen, when he stayed with Mme von Meck, and the two-piano version of the *Prélude à l'après-midi d'un faune*. They also offer the 1890 *Ballade*, better known in its solo piano form, though it is possible that Debussy intended to score it for piano and orchestra, like Fauré's. The interest and value of the set are diminished by the very dry and brittle sound and the somewhat unmagical performances, which do not begin to compare with those of Haas and Lee or Argerich and Bishop-Kovacevich.

The acoustic of the CRD recording is reverberant and tends to rob the music of subtlety. In any case, Eden and Tamir do not display the lightest touch, and even the *Petite suite* does not really sparkle as it might. There is no incandescence in the middle section of *Fêtes* (arranged for two pianos by Ravel) which is made to sound heavy by the resonance.

SOLO PIANO MUSIC

Arabesques Nos 1–2; Ballade; Images, Book 1: Reflets dans l'eau; Mouvement. Book 2: Poissons d'or. L'isle joyeuse; Préludes, Book 2: Feux d'artifice. Suite bergamasque.
(M) *** EMI EMX 41 2055-1/*4*. Daniel Adni.

This collection dates from 1972 and was a follow-up for a similarly successful Chopin recital which had served as Daniel Adni's gramophone début the previous year. It is outstanding in every way: this young Israeli pianist proves himself a Debussian of no mean order. His recital is well planned and offers playing that is as poetic in feeling as it is accomplished in technique. The HMV engineers have provided piano tone of satisfying realism, and readers seeking this particular compilation need not hesitate. There is an excellent cassette, too.

Berceuse héroïque; Children's corner suite; Danse; D'un cahier d'esquisses; Mazurka; Morceau de concours; Nocturne; Le petit nègre; La plus que lente; Rêverie.
*** Denon Dig. **C37 7372** [id.]. Jacques Rouvier.

An enjoyable and interesting Debussy recital from Jacques Rouvier which has the advantage of very truthful recording. There is no current alternative to the *Children's corner suite* – nor, for that matter, for most of the other pieces, though this state of affairs will doubtless soon be rectified. In the meantime this serves as a very useful addition to the catalogue and can be thoroughly recommended.

Children's corner; Estampes; La Fille aux cheveux de lin; L'Isle joyeuse; La plus que lente; Suite Bergamasque.
DG Dig. **415 510-2**; 415 510-1/*4* [id.]. Alexis Weissenberg.

One of the most insensitive – indeed, brutal – accounts of Debussy to have been committed to disc. Dynamic nuances are totally ignored and such subtleties as pianissimo unknown. Totally unacceptable artistically, though well enough recorded. Not recommended.

Children's corner; Images, Sets 1 and 2.
ℭ *** DG **415 372-2**; 2530 196/*3300 226* [id.]. Michelangeli.

Michelangeli's CD is outstanding in this repertoire. It is a magical and beautifully recorded disc. Michelangeli has made few records, but this is one of his best. It is also among the most distinguished Debussy playing in the catalogue. The remastering of the 1971 recording has been wonderfully successful. Although just a trace of background noise remains, it is not disturbing, and the tangibility of the piano image is remarkable.

Estampes; Images oubliées (1894); Pour le piano; Suite bergamasque.
❀ ℭ *** Ph. Dig. **412 118-2**; 412 118-1/*4* [id.]. Zoltán Kocsis.

An exceptionally well-played and intelligently planned recital from Zoltán Kocsis. He gives us *Pour le piano* together with its 1894 precursor, the *Images oubliées*, and adds the *Estampes*, whose last movement is also related to the third of the set, *'Quelques aspects de "Nous n'irons plus au bois" parcequ' il fait un temps insupportable'*. Beautifully alert playing in which every nuance is subtly graded. Although the recording in all three formats is excellent, this is repertoire that benefits enormously from the totally silent background that compact disc can offer, and the Philips engineers have captured the piano with exceptional realism and fidelity. As one expects from Kocsis, the playing is enormously refined and imaginative. The cassette is one of Philips's best: the transfer is strikingly successful and offers piano timbre of great naturalness.

Estampes; Préludes, Books 1 and 2; Images: Reflets dans l'eau.
**(*) HMV Dig. EX 270034-3/*5* (2) [Ang. DSB/*4D2S* 3954]. Youri Egorov.

This HMV set has the advantage of economy since it brings us the *Estampes* and the first of the *Images, Reflets dans l'eau*, as well as the two Books of *Préludes*. Egorov is a very fine player indeed; he gives performances of commanding keyboard technique, exquisite refinement and atmosphere. The recording is good, a shade too reverberant perhaps, and not quite as clear as Arrau (Philips) or Rogé (Decca). However, this must rank high in current LP sets of the *Préludes*.

Préludes, Book 1.
(*) DG **413 450-2; 2531/*3301* 200 [id.]. Arturo Benedetti Michelangeli.
(*) Denon Dig. **C37 7121 [id.]. Jacques Rouvier.

It goes without saying that Michelangeli's account reveals the highest pianistic distinction; it is in many ways a wholly compelling and masterful reading of these miniature tone-poems, with hardly a note or dynamic out of place, and it can be confidently recommended. However, in its CD format, this playing seems even cooler and more aloof and, while one remains lost in admiration for Michelangeli's actual playing, it must be conceded that not all collectors will find his readings sympathetic.

Jacques Rouvier comes from Marseilles and is an unostentatious and faithful interpreter of Debussy. In Book 1 he has to face formidable competition from Michelangeli – which he survives. His playing has atmosphere and elegance; though Michelangeli exhibits the greater keyboard control and (at times) evocation of character, Rouvier has greater warmth and a pleasing humanity. He is given an excellent recording, too.

Préludes, Book 2.
(*) Denon Dig. **C37 7043 [id.]. Jacques Rouvier.

There is some beautiful playing here, a rather steady but atmospheric and well-controlled *Brouillards* and a highly accomplished reading of *Les fées sont d'exquises danseuses*. The staccato and forte markings in *La puerto del vino* are a trifle exaggerated, but there are very few points with which one would quarrel. *La terrasse des audiences de clair de lune* is more measured than many interpreters on record, but it is marked *lent*, and Rouvier succeeds in shaping it with considerable mastery and makes the most of its different moods. At the time of writing, there is no alternative CD account, so this well-presented and -recorded version has the field to itself. The playing may not have the imagination and stature of Arrau or Gieseking, but it is still very fine indeed.

VOCAL MUSIC

Mélodies: *Beau soir; 3 Chansons de Bilitis; 3 Chansons de France; Les cloches; Fêtes galantes, Set 2; Mandoline.*
*** Unicorn **DKPCD 9035**; DKP/*DKPC* 9035 [id.]. Sarah Walker, Roger Vignoles – ENESCU: *Chansons****; ROUSSEL: *Mélodies*.**(*)

Sarah Walker's Debussy collection, three fine groups of songs plus three separate songs from much earlier (*Les cloches*, *Mandoline* and *Beau soir*), comes from an outstandingly fine disc of French songs. With deeply sympathetic accompaniment from Roger Vignoles, Sarah Walker's positive and characterful personality comes over vividly, well tuned to the often elusive idiom. Excellent recording, with CD adding realism in the warm acoustic.

La damoiselle élue.
⊂ *** Ph. Dig. **410 043-2**; 6514/*7337* 199 [id.]. Ameling, Taylor, women's voices of San Francisco Symphony Ch., San Francisco SO, De Waart – DUPARC: *Songs*; RAVEL: *Shéhérazade*.*** ⊂
*(*) CBS Dig. IM/*IMT* 39098 [id.]. Frederica von Stade, Boston Ch. and SO, Ozawa – BERLIOZ: *Nuits d'été*.*(*)

The purity of Elly Ameling's voice makes for a ravishingly beautiful account of Debussy's early cantata. Other versions have either been more sensuous or more brightly focused, but the gentleness of this is certainly apt for such a pre-Raphaelite vision. Radiant recording to match, which is enhanced by the compact disc. This has a remarkable translucent richness of texture, with the chorus slightly distanced yet naturally focused. The chrome cassette offers generally faithful sound, but does not begin to match the compact disc, which is an outstanding demonstration of the advantages of the new medium.

Coupled with a disappointing version of Berlioz's *Les nuits d'été*, von Stade's reading of *La damoiselle élue* is only marginally more recommendable, failing to create the necessary atmosphere. That is less due to von Stade's singing than to the unidiomatic narrator and the chorus. Good recording.

(i) *La damoiselle élue;* (ii) *L'enfant prodigue.*
*** Orfeo Dig. S/*M* 012821A [id.]. (i) Cotrubas, Maurice; (ii) Jessye Norman, Carreras, Fischer-Dieskau; Stuttgart R. Ch. and SO, Bertini.

Debussy's two early and evocative cantatas make an excellent and enjoyable coupling, particularly in performances as fine as these under Gary Bertini, recorded very beautifully. The earlier of the two, *L'enfant prodigue*, the work with which Debussy belatedly won the Prix de Rome at the third attempt, is here superbly characterized by the three soloists, Carreras as the prodigal son himself, rather too warmly Italianate for this music, but movingly expressive, Jessye Norman rich-toned yet graceful as the mother (the well-known *Air de Lia* superbly done), and Fischer-Dieskau as the forgiving father. *La damoiselle élue* is not nearly so rare on record, but Cotrubas gives a memorable reading, girlish and winning, pure and radiant. The chorus is rather too distant in the later cantata, but otherwise the sound is excellent.

OPERA

La chute de la Maison Usher (unfinished opera, arr. Blin).
*** HMV Dig. EL 270158-1/*4* [Ang. DS/*4DS* 38168]. Barbaux, Lafont, Le Roux, Le Maigat, Monte Carlo PO, Prêtre – CAPLET: *Masque***(*); SCHMIDT: *Haunted palace.****

In the last years of his life, Debussy was obsessed with the idea of writing two one-act operas on stories by Edgar Allan Poe, a more potent force in France than in the English-speaking world, thanks above all to the superb prose translations of Poe made by Baudelaire. When Debussy died, even the sketches for his Poe project had disappeared; but in the 1970s the Chilean scholar and composer, Juan Allende Blin, put together the rediscovered fragments of one of the two operas, *The Fall of the House of Usher*, and managed to reconstitute four hundred bars of music. Debussy left the scantiest indications concerning orchestration, and the scoring is the work of Allende-Blin himself. As Harry Halbreich points out in his notes, the music has extraordinary novelty, great harmonic freedom and a liberty of prosodic treatment far surpassing *Pelléas*. The music that Allende-Blin rescued amounts to a little under a half of the projected work, which would have taken just under an hour. The score has a great sense of mystery in the manner of *Jeux* and, perhaps, *Le martyre*, and is a real discovery. It makes, if not a full dramatic entertainment, at least a fascinating cantata, very original indeed, and very well performed here in this first commercial recording, in which Jean-Philippe Lafont is outstanding in the baritone role of Roderick, the doomed central character. The direction of Georges Prêtre is dedicated and the recording is suitably atmospheric, with a good matching tape. The documentation is excellent, including a libretto. Apt couplings have been chosen in two other works inspired by Poe. Lovers of Debussy should snap this up without delay.

Delibes, Léo (1836–91)

Coppélia (ballet): complete.
*** Decca Dig. **414 502-2**; 414 502-1/*4* (2) [id.]. Nat. PO, Bonynge.

Delibes wrote a marvellous score for *Coppélia*. There is never a dull bar, and the sparkling succession of tunes, orchestrated with consistent flair and imagination, provides a superb musical entertainment away from the theatre. Bonynge has recorded the ballet previously for Decca with the Suisse Romande Orchestra, but clearly the National Philharmonic with its personnel of expert British sessions musicians is able to provide more polished and no less spirited ensemble, and the wind solos are a constant delight. The only slight drawback is the relatively modest number of violins which the clarity of the digital recording makes apparent. In moments like the delicious *Scène et valse de la poupée*, which Bonynge points very stylishly, the effect is Mozartian in its grace. But the full body of strings above the stave lacks something in amplitude and the fortissimos bring a digital emphasis on brilliance that is not wholly natural. Having said that, the recording in all other respects is praiseworthy, not only for its vividness of colour, but for the balance within a concert-hall acoustic (Walthamstow Assembly Hall). In the many colourful and elegantly scored interchanges for woodwind and strings the tangibility of the players is very striking. Bonynge has the full measure of the music, and the orchestra obviously enjoy it, too. With 31 cues, the CDs provide admirable access for anyone wanting to make up a personally chosen suite.

Coppélia (ballet): suite.
(M) *** DG Sig. 413 981-1/*4* [id.]. BPO, Karajan – CHOPIN: *Les Sylphides*.***

Karajan secures some wonderfully elegant playing from the Berlin Philharmonic Orchestra, and his lightness of touch is delightful. The *Valse de la poupée* is beautifully pointed and the variations which follow have a suave panache which is captivating. The *Czárdás*, however, is played very slowly and heavily, and its curiously studied tempo may spoil the disc for some. The recording is even better than on the reverse and can be made to sound very impressive. The cassette also offers sparkling quality.

Sylvia (ballet): complete.
(M) *** Decca Jub. 414 275-1/*4* (2). New Philh. O, Bonynge.

The ballet *Sylvia* appeared five years after *Coppélia* and was first produced at the Paris Opéra in 1875. While confirming the success of the earlier work, *Sylvia* has never displaced it in the affections of the public, and understandably so. It is an attractive score with some memorable tunes but, to be honest, nearly all of these are contained in the suite, and in the full score we hear them more than once. If the work is not as consistently inspired as *Coppélia*, it does contain some delightful music and characteristically felicitous scoring. It is played here with wonderful polish and affection under Bonynge, and the recording is brilliant and sparkling in Decca's best manner. The chrome tapes are extremely vivid, but the violin timbre in the upper register lacks richness.

Delius, Frederick (1862–1934)

Air and dance for string orchestra; On hearing the first cuckoo in spring; Summer evening; Summer night on the river.
ℂ *** Chan. **CHAN 8330**; ABRD/*ABTD* 1106 [id.]. LPO, Handley – VAUGHAN WILLIAMS: *Serenade* etc.*** ℂ

Handley as an interpreter of Delius generally takes a more direct, less gently lingering view than is common, but here that refusal to sentimentalize – which can miss the more sweetly evocative qualities of the music – goes with the most subtle nuances in performance, fresh as well as beautiful and atmospheric. *Summer evening* is little more than a salon piece, but no less attractive for that. The tonal richness of the LPO's playing is superbly caught in the outstanding Chandos recording, which is all the more vividly real-sounding on CD. The chrome tape also reflects the highest state of the art, refined in every respect.

Two Aquarelles (arr. Fenby).
(M) (***) HMV mono EX 290107-3/5 (2). Hallé O, Barbirolli – BAX: *Symphony No. 3*; IRELAND: *Mai-Dun*; *Forgotten rite*; *These things shall be*; QUILTER: *Children's overture*.***

These exquisite performances were recorded by Sir John Barbirolli and the Hallé Orchestra in the 1940s, and their overall atmosphere is so enveloping and keenly felt that sonic limitations are soon forgotten.

2 Aquarelles (arr. Fenby); *Fennimore and Gerda: Intermezzo* (arr. Beecham); *Hassan: Intermezzo and Serenade* (arr. Beecham); *Irmelin: Prelude; Late swallows* (arr. Fenby); *On hearing the first cuckoo in spring; Song before sunrise; Summer night on the river.*
*** Chan. **CHAN 8372**; CBR/*CBT* 1017 [id.]. Bournemouth Sinf., Del Mar.

There are few finer interpreters of Delius today than Del Mar, once a protégé of Beecham, and this nicely balanced collection of miniatures is among the most broadly recommendable of Delius collections available. The performances are warmly atmospheric and have a strong sense of line. Full recording to match, and a highly successful digital transfer, the sound fresh yet with an excellent overall bloom. The analogue master dates from 1977, but this is not apparent in the sound quality. However, the reissue on LP and tape is at mid-price and costs considerably less than the CD. The cassette transfer, made at the highest level, is splendidly managed.

Brigg Fair; Dance rhapsody No. 2; Fennimore and Gerda: Intermezzo. Florida suite; Irmelin: Prelude; Marche-caprice; On hearing the first cuckoo in spring; Over the hills and far away; Sleigh ride; Song before sunrise; Summer evening; Summer night on the river; (i) *Songs of sunset.*
❀ (M) *** HMV EM 290323-3/5. RPO, Beecham; (i) with Forrester, Cameron, Beecham Choral Society.

Brigg Fair; Fennimore and Gerda: Intermezzo; Florida suite; Irmelin: Prelude; Marche-caprice; On hearing the first cuckoo in spring; Sleigh ride; Summer evening; Summer night on the river.
(B) *** HMV *TCC2-POR 154601-9.* RPO, Beecham.

All Beecham's stereo orchestral recordings plus the choral *Songs of sunset* are gathered together in this very reasonably priced two-disc (or tape) set. It is a unique and treasurable collection. His fine-spun magic with Delius's orchestral textures is apparent from the delicate opening bars of *Brigg Fair*; the string playing in *On hearing the first cuckoo in spring* and, more especially, in *Summer night on the river* is ravishing yet never too indulgent. The recording of these shorter pieces was the finest Beecham ever received; though the originals date back to 1960, the ear would hardly guess. The *Florida suite*, Delius's first orchestral work, is lightweight, but strong in melodic appeal and orchestral colour; the tune we know as *La Calinda* appears in the first movement. Elsewhere the negro influences absorbed by the composer even suggest a Dvořákian flavour. In the *Songs of sunset*, the choral recording is not very sharply focused and the soloists are backwardly balanced, but the performance itself remains indispensable. The notes provided with the set, drawn from the original issues, are less than ideal, but otherwise the presentation is good and the tape box is particularly attractive. One day this compilation will undoubtedly appear on compact disc, but until then the well-engineered tapes would seem to be an obvious best buy. The sound is beautiful, smooth yet well detailed, and there is freedom from intrusive background noise, so essential in this repertoire. For those not wanting the *Songs of sunset* the alternative double-length cassette in EMI's 'Portrait of the Artist' series can be recommended, although it lacks proper back-up documentation.

Cello concerto.
*** RCA RL/*RK* 70800. Lloyd Webber, Philh. O, Handley – HOLST: *Invocation*; VAUGHAN WILLIAMS: *Fantasia.****

Lloyd Webber is inside the idiom and plays the *Concerto* – not one of Delius's strongest works perhaps, though it was the composer's own favourite among his four concertos – with total conviction. Its lyricism is beguiling enough but the *Concerto* proceeds in wayward fashion, and the soloist must play every note as if he believes in it ardently – and this Lloyd Webber and his partners do. Though he does not produce a big sound in the concert hall, the RCA balance is ideal and conveys an almost chamber-like quality at times, with great warmth and clarity. One of the strengths of this version, apart from its technical excellence, is the interest of the coupling, which brings a first recording of Holst's *Invocation*. There is a recommendable chrome cassette, the sound fresh yet atmospheric, to match the disc closely.

Violin concerto; Légende for violin and orchestra; Suite for violin and orchestra.

Ⓒ *** Unicorn Dig. **DKPCD 9040**; DKP/*DKPC* 9040 [id.]. Ralph Holmes, RPO, Handley.

Shortly before his cruelly premature death, Ralph Holmes went to the studio and recorded this strong and beautiful performance of one of Delius's supreme masterpieces, the *Violin concerto*. Though the structure superficially may seem rhapsodic, it is in fact closely co-ordinated, as the late Deryck Cooke amply illustrated. Holmes and Handley, an ideal partnership, bring out the Delian warmth in their shaping of phrase and pointing of rhythm, while keeping firm control of the overall structure. The *Légende* – long forgotten in this orchestral form – and the early *Suite* make ideal couplings, played with equal understanding. Holmes's beautifully focused playing is nicely balanced against the wide span of the orchestra behind him in first-class digital recording, particularly impressive on CD. There is also an excellent tape.

Florida suite; North country sketches.
*** Chan. Dig. ABRD/*ABTD* 1150 [id.]. Ulster O, Handley.

Having taken over Sir Adrian Boult's mantle in recording the works of Elgar, Vernon Handley here turns back to Delius to evoke the spirit of Sir Thomas Beecham. In the delicacy of the orchestral playing (the muted Ulster strings create some exquisite textures) and the easy rhapsodic freedom of the melodic lines, this is music making in the Beecham mould, but of course the readings are Handley's own. His choice of tempi is always apt and it is fascinating that in the *North country sketches* which evoke the seasons in the Yorkshire moors Debussian influence is revealed. The delicious tune we know as *La Calinda* appears in the first movement of the *Florida suite*; elsewhere, the local influences absorbed by the young composer in America bring parallels with Dvořák. But Handley's refined approach clearly links the work with later masterpieces. The recording is superbly balanced within the very suitable acoustics of the Ulster Hall; one's only real criticism is the lack of sumptuous weight to the violins when they have an eloquent musical line in the *Florida suite*; but otherwise tuttis are superbly expansive. The chrome tape represents the highest state of the art and will serve until the CD appears.

Life's Dance; North Country sketches; Song of summer.
(M) **(*) HMV ED 290026-1/*4*. RPO, Groves.

This attractive Delius disc contains a virtually unknown piece, *Lebenstanz*, or *Life's dance*, which was written in the 1890s immediately before the tone-poem *Paris*. It presents a fascinating contrast, beginning with an urgency not always associated with this composer. *Song of summer*, a typically evocative piece, comes from the other end of Delius's career; it was conceived just before he lost his sight and was subsequently dictated to his amanuensis, Eric Fenby. The *North Country sketches*, depicting with Delian impressionism the seasons of the year, make an apt coupling. Groves is a sensitive interpreter, even if he rarely matches the irresistible persuasiveness of a Beecham. The balance is vivid and warm, almost too close in sound to do justice to such delicately atmospheric music. However, the recordings have transferred particularly successfully to cassette.

(i) *Dance rhapsody No. 1; Eventyr; Paris, the song of a great city;* (ii) *Song of summer;* (iii) *Cynara;* (iv) *Sea drift.*
(B) *** HMV *TCC2-POR 54295.* (i) Royal Liverpool PO, (ii) RPO; Groves with (iii) Shirley-Quirk; (iv) Noble, Royal Liverpool PO.

For any conductor attempting to interpret Delius today, the first thing is to try to forget the ghost of Sir Thomas Beecham and to produce spontaneous-sounding performances that may or may not correspond to his. Groves does just this in the magnificent picture in sound *Paris*, as well as in the shorter works. The tempi are less extreme than Beecham's, but refreshingly persuasive. *Cynara* (1907) is a setting of Dowson. John Shirley-Quirk does the solo part impressively and the performance of this work is very fine. *Sea drift* is by comparison disappointingly matter-of-fact, failing to convey the surge of inspiration that so exactly matches the evocative colours of Walt Whitman's poem about the seagull, a solitary guest from Alabama. However, taken as a whole this 'Portrait of the Artist' double-length cassette certainly shows Groves as a persuasive Delian, and none of the performances are otherwise available, except *A Song of summer* (see above). The recording is generally excellent.

String quartet.
*** ASV Dig. DCA/*ZCDCA* 526 [id.]. Brodsky Qt – ELGAR: *Quartet.****

The young members of the Brodsky Quartet in their first commercial recording give a richly expressive performance of Delius's *String quartet* of 1916 with its evocative slow movement, *Late swallows.* In this music the ebb and flow of tension and a natural feeling for persuasive but unexaggerated rubato is vital; with fine ensemble but seeming spontaneity, the Brodsky players consistently produce that. First-rate recording, and an excellent cassette.

VOCAL AND CHORAL MUSIC

(i) *Appalachia. Brigg Fair.*
(M) *** EMI EMX 41 2081-1/*4*. Hallé O, Barbirolli, (i) with Jenkins, Amb. S.

The reissue on EMI's Eminence label of Barbirolli's account of *Appalachia* is most welcome. Beecham's famous LP was marred by an unconvincing soloist but in every other respect was totally magical. Barbirolli dwells a little too lovingly on detail to suit all tastes, but for the most part he gives an admirably atmospheric reading that conveys, with the help of a richly detailed recording, the exotic and vivid colouring of Delius's score. The performance of *Brigg Fair* is no less evocative. The cassette is full and pleasing, but the upper range is strikingly more restricted than the LP, and the choral focus has little bite.

Idyll (*Once I passed through a populous city*); (i) *Requiem*.
(M) *** HMV ED 290027-1/*4*. Harper, Shirley-Quirk, RPO, Meredith Davies, (i) with Royal Choral Society.

The reissue of this 1968 record is particularly welcome since it couples two Delius rarities. The *Requiem* is not only new to the gramophone, but until recently had remained unperformed since the 1920s. It was written during the First World War, and Delius's well-known atheism as well as his disillusion with life did not find a responsive echo at the first performance; indeed, the work was written off. Though it is not an austere work, it is far sparer than most other Delius works of the period and much of it is rewarding, particularly in so fine a performance as this. The *Idyll* is much earlier, or at least its material is. The music, though uneven in inspiration, is often extremely impressive, and readers need have no reservations about either performance or recording. There is a good XDR cassette, with the upper range of the chorus not too seriously cushioned, although the disc is clearer.

English songs: *I-Brasil; So white, so soft; To daffodils;* French songs: *Avant que tu ne t'en ailles; Chanson d'automne; Le ciel est pardessus le toit; La lune blanche; Il pleure dans mon coeur.* Scandinavian songs: *Autumn; In the garden of the Seraglio; Irmelin rose; Let springtime come; Silken shoes; Twilight fancies; The violet; Young Venevil.*
*** Unicorn Dig. DKP/*UKC* 9022 [id.]. Lott, Sarah Walker, Rolfe-Johnson, Fenby.

This collection of English, French and Scandinavian songs – almost all of them slow and dreamy – provides a charming sidelight on Delius's art. Apart from the early *Twilight fancies*, they are little known, but all reflect the composer's sympathy for words. Except for three in German, the Scandinavian songs are sung in English. The three soloists all sing most understandingly, warmly supported by Eric Fenby's piano accompaniments. Excellent recording.

Song of the high hills; Songs: *The bird's story; Le ciel est pardessus le toit; I-Brasil; Il pleure dans mon coeur; Let springtime come; La lune blanche; To daffodils; Twilight fancies; Wine roses.*
❀ *** Unicorn Dig. **DKPCD 9029**; DKP/*DKPC* 9029 [id.]. Lott, Sarah Walker, Rolfe-Johnson, Amb. S., RPO, Fenby.

Even among Delius issues, this stands out as one of the most ravishingly beautiful of all. Eric Fenby, as a young man the composer's amanuensis and a lifelong advocate, draws a richly atmospheric performance from Beecham's old orchestra in one of the most ambitious and beautiful, yet neglected, of Delius's choral works. Inspired by the hills of Norway, Delius evocatively conveys the still, chill atmosphere above the snow-line by episodes for wordless chorus, here finely balanced. The coupling of Delius songs in beautiful, virtually unknown orchestral arrangements is ideally chosen, with all three soloists both characterful and understanding.

OPERA

Irmelin (complete).
**(*) BBC Dig. 3002 (3). Hannan, Rippon, Mitchinson, Rayner Cook, BBC Singers and Concert O, Del Mar.

'The best first opera by any composer,' said Sir Thomas Beecham of *Irmelin*, and this recording, conducted by one of Beecham's most individual and inspired pupils, goes a long way towards confirming that. The piece – a strange amalgam of *Parsifal*, *Turandot* and *Pelléas et Mélisande* (those last two operas postdating this) – is dramatically flawed, with Rolf the Robber hardly a convincing figure, but the love music here for Irmelin and Nils is among the most sensuously beautiful that Delius ever wrote. Though the plot disconcertingly prevents the two meeting until Act III, each continually dreams of an ideal of love, finally found. That draws from Delius his warmest writing, as is well known from the so-called *Prelude* which, with the help of Eric Fenby, the composer confected from salient motifs in the then unperformed opera. The soaring arc of the main love-motif hauntingly recurs in every conceivable transformation, finally returning as the lovers depart, unconcerned, into the sunset, fast and rhythmic with orchestral jingles adding a trimming of silver. Outstanding in the cast is Eilene Hannan in the name part, singing radiantly. Sally Bradshaw sings sweetly as the heavenly Voice in the Air, the messenger to Irmelin that her ideal of a prince is on his way. It is a pity that, for all the power of his singing, John Mitchinson does not sound younger as the hero, Nils, and a darker voice is needed for Rolf than Brian Rayner Cook's light baritone, but with Del Mar drawing warmly committed playing from the BBC Concert Orchestra (not quite sumptuous enough in the string section) this is a richly enjoyable set, beautifully balanced and recorded.

A Village Romeo and Juliet (complete).
(M) ** HMV EM 290404-3/*5* (2). Luxon, Mangin, Tear, Harwood, Shirley-Quirk, John Alldis Ch., RPO, Meredith Davies.

There are some wonderfully sensuous moments in this highly characteristic opera of Delius, written at the turn of the century. The famous *Walk to the Paradise Garden* with its passionate orchestral climax (superbly performed here) is the most memorable passage, but the music of the Dark Fiddler and much of the music for the two ill-starred lovers is intensely expressive. Unfortunately there is too little mystery in Meredith Davies's performance. He fails to persuade one to listen on when Delius's inspiration lets him run on dangerously long. Nevertheless there is some excellent singing and playing, and first-rate recording. The reissue comes on a pair of LPs against the original three, and is reasonably priced, so this is well worth exploring. The tapes are satisfactory but the sound is less transparent than on the discs and the upper range is more restricted, though the balance is good.

Donizetti, Gaetano (1797–1848)

Don Pasquale: highlights.
** Hung. Dig. **HCD 12610**. Gregor, Kalmar, Hungarian R. and TV Ch., Hungarian State O, Ivan Fischer.

As many Hungaroton releases have witnessed, opera is thriving in Budapest. Ivan Fischer conducts an energetic and well-drilled team in a generous collection of highlights, which brings particularly enjoyable singing from the bass, Jozsef Gregor, in the name part and from Istvan Gati as Malatesta, both clear and agile. The soprano, Magda Kalmar, and the tenor, Janos Bandi, are less stylish but are reliable enough. What is missing – largely thanks to the conductor – is lightness and the sparkle of comedy. The relative heaviness is underlined by the recording which brings out the voices well but makes the orchestra sound woolly.

L'Elisir d'amore (complete).
*** Decca **414 461-2** (2) [id.]; SET 503-5/*K 154 K32* [Lon. OSA 13101]. Sutherland, Pavarotti, Cossa, Malas, Amb. S., ECO, Bonynge.
(*) Eurodisc **601 097; 301 904 (3). Popp, Dvorsky, Weikl, Nesterenko, Mun. R. Ch. and O, Wallberg.
*(*) Ph. Dig. **412 714-2**; 412 714-1/*4* (2) [id.]. Ricciarelli, Carreras, Nucci, Trimarchi, Rigacci, Turin R. Ch. and O, Scimone.

Joan Sutherland's comic talents in a Donizetti role came out delectably in her performances on stage and on record of *La Fille du régiment*. Here she repeats that success, making Adina a more substantial figure than usual, full-throatedly serious at times, at others jolly like the rumbustious Marie. Malibran, the first interpreter of the role, was furious that the part was not bigger, and got her husband to write an extra aria. Richard Bonynge found a copy of the piano score, had it orchestrated, and included it here, a jolly and brilliant waltz song. Though that involves missing out the cabaletta *Il mio fugor dimentica*, the text of this frothy piece is otherwise unusually complete, and in the key role of Nemorino Luciano Pavarotti proves ideal, vividly portraying the wounded innocent. Spiro Malas is a superb Dulcamara, while Dominic Cossa is a younger-sounding Belcore, more of a genuine lover than usual. Bonynge points the skipping rhythms delectably, and the recording is sparkling to match. The CD transfer brings out the fullness, brilliance and clean focus of the 1971 sound, which has more presence than many modern digital recordings.

Wallberg conducts a lightly sprung performance of Donizetti's sparkling comic opera, well recorded and marked by a charming performance of the role of Adina from Lucia Popp, comparably bright-eyed, with delicious detail both verbal and musical. Nesterenko makes a splendidly resonant Dr Dulcamara with more comic sparkle than you would expect from a great Russian bass. Dvorsky and Weikl, both sensitive artists, sound much less idiomatic, with Dvorsky's tight tenor growing harsh under pressure, not at all Italianate, and

Weikl failing similarly to give necessary roundness to the role of Belcore. Like other sets recorded in association with Bavarian Radio, the sound is excellent, naturally balanced with voices never spotlit. Though this does not displace the Sutherland/Pavarotti/Bonynge set on Decca, it makes a viable alternative on LP, especially for admirers of Lucia Popp.

Scimone's set is disappointing. In a gentle way he is an understanding interpreter of Donizetti; but with recording that lacks presence, the chorus and orchestra's sound is slack next to rivals on record, and none of the soloists is on top form, with even Carreras in rougher voice than usual, trying to compensate by overpointing. Leo Nucci too as Belcore produces less smooth tone than normal, and Domenico Trimarchi as Dulcamara, fine buffo that he is, sounds too wobbly for comfort on record. Katia Ricciarelli gives a sensitive performance, but this is not a natural role for her and, unlike Sutherland, she does not translate it to her own needs. The chrome cassettes are very well transferred, matching the LPs closely.

Lucia di Lammermoor (complete).

*** Decca **410 193-2**; SET 528-30/*K2 L22* (3/*2*) [Lon. OSA/*5*-13103]. Sutherland, Pavarotti, Milnes, Ghiaurov, Ryland Davies, Tourangeau, ROHCG Ch. and O, Bonynge.

**(*) HMV EX 270064-3/*9* (3) [Ang. DXCS/*4D3X* 3951]. Gruberova, Kraus, Bruson, Lloyd, Amb. Opera Ch., RPO, Rescigno.

It was hardly surprising that Decca re-recorded Sutherland in the role with which she is inseparably associated. Though some of the girlish freshness of voice which marked the 1961 recording disappeared in the 1971 set, the detailed understanding was intensified, and the mooning manner, which in 1961 was just emerging, was counteracted. No one today outshines Sutherland in this opera; and rightly for this recording she insisted on doing the whole of the Mad scene in a single session, making sure it was consistent from beginning to end. Power is there as well as delicacy, and the rest of the cast is first rate. Pavarotti, through much of the opera not so sensitive as he can be, proves magnificent in his final scene. The sound quality is superb, though choral interjections are not always forward enough. In this set, unlike the earlier one, the text is absolutely complete. The analogue recording is greatly enhanced by the compact disc remastering, with balance and focus outstandingly firm and real. The silent background is particularly valuable in the pauses and silences of the Mad scene, the opera's powerful climax.

Edita Gruberova brings dramatic power as well as brilliance and flexibility to the role of Lucia, and rises well to the challenge of the Mad scene, where her rather overemphatic manner suits both the music and the drama best. Elsewhere, a degree of gustiness in the vocal delivery and the occasional squeezed note, together with noisy breathing, detract from the purity needed. Legato lines, too, tend to be overpointed. Kraus conceals his age astonishingly well, with finely controlled singing (no problems over legato), but with an occasional over-emphasis to match his heroine. Bruson and Lloyd are both first rate, but Rescigno's conducting lacks point, rather matching the plainness of the recorded production. Full, unremarkable sound.

Dowland, John (1563–1626)

Songs: *Awake sweet love, thou art returnd; Fine knacks for ladies; If my complaints, could passions move; I saw my lady weepe; Now, O now I needs must part; Say love if ever thou didst find; Shall I sue, shall I seeke for grace; Sweet stay awhile; What if I never speed.*
(*) Hyp. A 66095 [id.]. Ian Partridge, Jacob Lindberg (lute) – CAMPION: *Songs.*(*)

Partridge's admirable choice of Dowland songs makes an attractive coupling for the even rarer Campion songs on the reverse. As always, his pure, light tenor is most beautiful, but the close placing of the voice brings some unwanted forcing of sound, not the fault of the singer. The tasteful lute accompaniments from the talented Swedish lutenist are made to sound too reticent.

Dukas, Paul (1865–1935)

L'apprenti sorcier (*The sorcerer's apprentice*).
(*) RCA Dig. **RCD 14439 [id.]. Dallas SO, Mata (with Concert.***)
(*) Ph. Dig. **412 131-2; 412 131-1/*4* [id.]. ASMF, Marriner (with Concert of French music.**(*))
(B) ** CBS DC 40149 (2). O Nat. de France, Maazel – OFFENBACH: *Gaîté Parisienne*; RAVEL: *Alborada*; *Boléro* etc.; SAINT-SAËNS: *Danse macabre.***

Mata's performance comes from an outstanding early RCA CD which was one of the first demonstration records of the compact disc era. The orchestral balance, set back naturally within the attractive Dallas concert-hall ambience, remains very impressive, even if detail is less sharp than on some digital recordings. The performance of Dukas's justly famous orchestral scherzo is spirited and affectionately characterized, with a nicely paced forward momentum. There is little sense of calamity at the climax, but this fits in with Mata's genial conception.

Marriner's version has a lighter touch, with its scherzando springing of Dukas's jaunty principal melody and immaculate string ensemble. But there is a lack of consistency of tempo, which is not altogether convincing. The Philips recording is rich yet transparent, and the boom of the bass drum is impressive on CD.

Maazel's account is lively enough and characterful, but he loses something by broadening the climax. This is part of a two-disc set of popular French orchestral music, offered at the cost of a single premium-priced LP. The drawback is that the four Ravel items are overpowered and lacking in subtlety, although the rest of the performances are quite attractive. The recordings are modern. The equivalent tape version is not recommended as the Ravel *Alborada* and Saint-Saëns' *Danse macabre* are omitted, though the price is the same.

Symphony in C; La Péri (*poème dansée*).
(*) Erato Dig. **ECD 88089; NUM/*MCE* 75175 [id.]. SRO, Jordan.

This is the first account of either the Dukas *Symphony* or *La Péri* to reach CD. Neither is generously represented on LP at present, the only alternative to the symphony being the LPO account on Decca (SXL 6770). Armin Jordan offers good value and the Suisse Romande Orchestra play very well for him. Weller, on Decca, perhaps secures more cultured response from the LPO strings, but Jordan's reading has the greater musical conviction, and he is equally sensitive to atmosphere in *La Péri*. The Erato recording is eminently satisfactory and can hold its own alongside the Decca; and in any of the three formats this can be recommended to readers wanting this coupling. On the high-level tape, the sound is clear and vivid but rather dry and hard on top.

Dunstable, John (died 1453)

Motets: *Agnus Dei; Alma redemptoris Mater; Credo super; Da gaudiorum premia; Gaude virgo salutata; Preco preheminenciae; Quam pulcra es; Salve regina misericordiae; Salve scema sanctitatis; Veni creator; Veni sancte spiritus.*
**(*) HMV Dig. ASD/*TC-ASD* 146703 [Ang. S/*4XS* 38082]. Hilliard Ens., Hillier.

In the time of Henry V, Dunstable (or Dunstaple, which is historically more correct) was not only the leading English composer of his day but one of the most influential figures in Europe. His music has not been well served by the gramophone in recent years; this record by the Hilliard Ensemble of nine motets and mass movements is perhaps the most important contribution to his discography to have appeared for some time. These motets give a very good idea of his range, and they are sung with impeccable style. The Hilliard Ensemble has perfectly blended tone and impeccable intonation, and their musicianship is of the highest order. Some readers may find the unrelieved absence of vibrato a little tiring on the ear when taken in large doses, but most collectors will find this a small price to pay for music making of such excellence. There is a particularly informative note by Paul Hillier. The XDR cassette is of first-class quality and matches the disc in naturalness.

Duparc, Henri (1848–1933)

Chanson triste; L'Invitation au voyage.
€ *** Ph. Dig. **410 043-2**; 6514/*7337* 199 [id.]. Ameling, San Francisco SO, De Waart – DEBUSSY: *La damoiselle élue*; RAVEL: *Shéhérazade*.*** €

L'Invitation au voyage gains from being orchestrated, with Ameling's pure and lovely voice warmly supported. *Chanson triste* is beautifully sung too, but it sounds slightly overblown with orchestral rather than piano accompaniment. An apt, unusual coupling for the two bigger works, beautifully recorded. There is a good chrome cassette, but it is the splendid compact disc that shows these performances off to best advantage: it is wonderfully atmospheric, with a natural balance for the voice and a beguilingly rich orchestral texture.

Mélodies: *Au pays où se fait la guerre; Chanson triste; L'invitation au voyage; Le manoir de Rosamonde; Phidylé; Testament; La vie intérieure.*
** HMV Dig. **CDC 747111-2** [id.]; EL 270135-1/*4* [Ang. DS/*4DS* 38061]. Kiri Te Kanawa, Belgian Nat. Op. O, Pritchard – RAVEL: Shéhérazade.**

Dame Kiri often produces a most beautiful sound and is excellently supported by Sir John Pritchard and the Belgian Opera Orchestra; for all this, however, she is not wholly successful in terms of characterization. The EMI recording is very well balanced and her admirers may want to sample this, but she is not at her best here.

Still recommended: Dame Janet Baker's outstanding recital of the Duparc mélodies was given a Rosette in our last edition. As Baker and her accompanists (André Previn and the LSO) present them, each one of these songs is a jewelled miniature of breathtaking beauty (HMV ASD 3455 [Ang. S 37401]).

Duruflé, Maurice (born 1902)

Requiem; Danse lente, Op. 6/2.
*** CBS 76633/*40*- [M 34547]. Te Kanawa, Nimsgern, Amb. S., Desborough School Ch., New Philh. O, Andrew Davis.

(i) *Requiem, Op. 9;* (ii) *4 Motets, Op. 10.*
*** Erato Dig. **ECD 88132**; NUM/*MCE* 75200 [id.]. (i) Berganza, Van Dam, Colonne Ch. and O; (ii) Jean Sourisse, Philippe Corboz (organ); (i; ii) Audite Nova Vocal Ens., cond. Michel Corboz.

Those who have sometimes regretted that the lovely Fauré *Requiem* remains unique in the output of that master of delicate inspiration should investigate this comparably evocative *Requiem* of Duruflé. The composer wrote it in 1947, overtly basing its layout and even the cut of its themes on the Fauré masterpiece. The result is far more than just an imitation, for (as it seems in innocence) Duruflé's inspiration is passionately committed. Andrew Davis directs a warm and atmospheric reading, using the full orchestral version with its richer colourings. Kiri Te Kanawa sings radiantly in the *Pie Jésu*, and the darkness of Siegmund Nimsgern's voice is well caught. In such a performance Duruflé establishes his claims for individuality even in the face of Fauré's comparable setting. The fill-up is welcome too, and the recording is excellent, nicely atmospheric. Since our last edition, CBS have been encouraged by the success of this record to issue an excellent chrome tape equivalent.

Corboz conducts a warmly idiomatic reading of Duruflé's hauntingly evocative *Requiem* with its overtones of Fauré's masterpiece. He uses the full orchestral version; the slight haziness of the sound, merging textures richly, adds to the sense of mystery, where the very clarity of Andrew Davis on CBS might be counted a disadvantage. Excellent soloists.

Dvořák, Antonin (1841–1904)

American suite, Op. 98b.
*** Decca Dig. **411 735-2**; 411 735-1/*4* (2) (id.). RPO, Dorati – *Slavonic dances.***(*)

Dvořák's *American suite*, which has clear influences from the New World, was written first in a piano version (1894) but turned into an orchestral piece the following year. It is slight but charming music. Dorati has its measure and the RPO are very responsive. The Kingsway Hall recording balance seems to suit the scoring rather well, and all three formats are attractively vivid.

Overtures: Carnaval, Op. 92; In Nature's realm, Op. 91; Othello, Op. 93. Scherzo capriccioso, Op. 66.
*** Chan. Dig. **CHAN 8453**; ABRD/*ABTD* 1163 [id.]. Ulster O, Handley.

In what one hopes may be the first of a series of Dvořák symphonic poems, Vernon Handley – in his premier recording with the Ulster Orchestra, of which he is now Musical Director – couples a brilliant and beguiling account of the *Scherzo capriccioso* with the three linked *Overtures*, Opp. 91–3. Dvořák wrote this triptych immediately before his first visit to America in 1892. Until now, Opp. 91 and 93 have tended to be eclipsed by the just public acclaim for the *Carnaval overture*. Handley's superb performances put the three works in perspective. The opening of *Othello* is particularly beautiful, with the Ulster strings radiantly serene; later, Handley minimizes the melodrama, yet, with a fine overall grip, provides plenty of excitement. The idyllic *In Nature's realm* immediately introduces the linking motif which is most memorable when magically taken up by the cor anglais in the mysterious central episode of *Carnaval*. Handley does not seek breathless brilliance in this piece but brings breadth as well as excitement, ensuring that his excellent players can articulate cleanly without being rushed off their feet. In the *Scherzo capriccioso* his subtly lilting treatment of the lyrical secondary theme on the strings gives special pleasure. A splendid issue, superbly recorded in the attactive ambience of Ulster Hall, Belfast. The CD is announced as we go to press; the chrome cassette is richer in body than the brilliant LP (which is fresher on top).

Cello concerto in B min., Op. 104.
*** DG **413 819-2**; 139 044/*923 098* [id.]. Rostropovich, BPO, Karajan – TCHAIKOVSKY: *Rococo variations.****
(B) *** DG Walkman *415 330-4* [id.]. Fournier, BPO, Szell – BOCCHERINI***; HAYDN: *Cello concertos.***
(*) Decca Dig. **410 144-2; SXDL/*KSXDC* 7608 [Lon. LDR/*5*- 71108]. Harrell, Philh. O, Ashkenazy – BRUCH: *Kol Nidrei.***(*)
** Ph. **412 880-2** [id.]. Heinrich Schiff, Concg. O, Sir Colin Davis – ELGAR: *Concerto.***(*)

Cello concerto in B min., Op. 104; Silent woods (Waldesruhe), Op. 68.
(*) BIS **CD 245; LP 245 [id.]. Helmerson, Gothenburg SO, Järvi.

The collaboration of Rostropovich and Karajan in Dvořák's *Cello concerto* makes a superb version, warm as well as refined in reflection of the finest qualities in each of the two principals. If Rostropovich can sometimes sound self-indulgent in this most romantic of cello concertos, the degree of control provided by the conductor gives a firm yet supple base, and there have been few recorded accounts so deeply satisfying. The result is unashamedly romantic, with many moments of dalliance, but the concentration is never in doubt. Splendid playing by the Berliners, and a bonus in the shape of Tchaikovsky's glorious variations. The analogue recording dates from 1969 and its warm resonance does not lend itself to much clarifying in its new CD format. However, the original sound was both rich and refined, and that effect is certainly enhanced when the background is considerably reduced. There is also a good cassette.

Fournier's reading has a sweep of conception and richness of tone and phrasing which carry the melodic lines along with exactly the mixture of nobility and tension that the work demands. Fournier can relax and beguile the ear in the lyrical passages and yet catch the listener up in his exuberance in the exciting finale. The phrasing in the slow movement is ravishing, and the interpretation as a whole balances beautifully. DG's recording is forward and vivid, with a broad, warm tone for the soloist. It dates from 1962 and sounds newly minted on this Walkman chrome tape transfer. With couplings of Haydn (Fournier stylish but less impressively accompanied) and Rostropovich's larger-than-life version of Boccherini, this is another fine DG bargain.

Frans Helmerson is a young Swedish cellist who caused a stir in London some years ago when he replaced Rostropovich in this concerto. His version with Neeme Järvi and the Gothenburg orchestra faces – and survives – stiff competition in both the CD and LP catalogues from Rostropovich and others. Helmerson may not have the outsize personality of Rostropovich but he plays with eloquence and feeling, and the orchestra provide exemplary support. Although the Rostropovich–Karajan version remains a clear first choice, this makes a very fine CD alternative.

Lynn Harrell's newest recording of the Dvořák *Concerto* for Decca is a little disappointing and does not match his earlier RCA version, with the LSO under James Levine, at present out of the catalogue. The RCA collaboration proved powerful and sympathetic, with richly satisfying accounts of the first and second movements, culminating in a reading of the finale which proved the most distinctive of all. Here again the finale is the most successful, but the performance, though still impressive in its strength and detail, generally lacks the spontaneous power and incisiveness of the RCA account. The Decca digital sound is richly vivid (though forwardly balanced) and the compact disc, as usual, adds refinement of detail. The effect is more realistic than Rostropovich's much older recording, but Harrell's performance has less emotional weight.

Heinrich Schiff, who made such a promising start to his recording career in the Saint-Saëns concerto (now deleted), is disappointing in the bigger challenge of the Dvořák. The confidence of his concert appearances is here muted and the result is wayward, with Sir Colin Davis less at ease than usual in Dvořák. However, on CD the generous coupling with his more successful account of the Elgar *Cello concerto* may make this issue worth considering for some readers.

Czech suite, Op. 39; Nocturne for strings in B, Op. 40; Polka for Prague students in B flat, Op. 53a; Polonaise in E flat; Prague waltzes.
*** Decca Dig. **414 370-2** [id.]; SXDL/*KSXDC* 7522 [Lon. LDR/5- 71024]. Detroit SO, Dorati.

A collection of Dvořák rarities exhilaratingly performed and brilliantly recorded. The *Czech suite* can sometimes outstay its welcome, but certainly not here. The other items too have the brightness and freshness that mark out the Dvořák *Slavonic dances*, especially the *Polka* and *Polonaise*. The most charming piece of all is the set of *Waltzes* written for balls in Prague – Viennese music with a Czech accent – while the lovely *Nocturne* with its subtle drone bass makes an apt filler. The recording has an attractive warmth and bloom to balance its brightness, and this is the more striking on CD, which also emphasizes a momentary excess of resonance contributed by the bass drum to the *Polonaise*. The tape notices this too, but is impressively well transferred.

Czech suite, Op. 39; Serenade for strings in E, Op. 22.
*** Erato Dig. NUM/*MCE* 75124 [id.]. Lausanne CO, Armin Jordan.

Though the *Wind serenade* is the most obviously apt coupling for Dvořák's Op. 22, this Erato version can safely be recommended to anyone wanting another delightful, undemanding piece for coupling. The *Czech suite* may be less memorable than either *Serenade* but, in its undemanding, gently pastoral way, it is a charmer too. First-rate playing and recording, though the chrome cassette is not acceptable, being very shrill in the treble.

Serenade for strings in E, Op. 22.
*** DG Dig. **400 038-2**; 2532/*3302* 012 [id.]. BPO, Karajan – TCHAIKOVSKY: *String serenade.**** ⊂

Serenade for strings in E, Op. 22; Nocturne, Op. 40; (i) *Silent woods, Op. 68.*
** Delos Dig. **D/CD 3011** [id.]. (i) Douglas Davis; LACO, Schwarz.

Serenade for strings; Serenade for wind in D min., Op. 44.
⊂ *** Ph. **400 020-2**; 6514/*7337* 145 [id.]. ASMF, Sir Neville Marriner.
*(*) DG Dig. **415 364-2**; 415 364-1/*4* [id.]. Orpheus CO.

An obvious primary recommendation lies with Sir Neville Marriner's newest version of the Dvořák *String serenade* which is aptly joined with the lesser-known, but equally delightful, wind piece. This latest issue is also far preferable as a performance to his Argo account. Earlier mannerisms (as at the start) are eliminated, with speeds ideally chosen and wonderfully refined yet spontaneous-sounding and resilient playing. The *Wind serenade* on the reverse is just as stylish and beautifully sprung, and the recording is outstandingly vivid. With a gloriously rich and firm bass, the compact disc brings the best sound of all, for there the brightness of the treble is nicely balanced against the ample lower register. The *Wind serenade* has an uncanny sense of immediacy, set against a rather drier acoustic. The chrome tape is full but lacks range in the work for strings; Op. 44 is livelier.

Karajan's digital version is given a recording of striking finesse. The brilliance of the LP is tempered on the compact disc, which is transferred at a marginally lower level than the Tchaikovsky coupling. The recording has plenty of atmosphere and a very wide dynamic range, plus a slight tendency for the image to recede at pianissimo level. Karajan's approach is warmly affectionate in the opening movement and there is greater expressive weight than with Marriner, with the colouring darker. Yet the playing is both sympathetic and very polished and, though the focus is slightly more diffuse and less firm in the bass than the Tchaikovsky coupling (which earns a technical accolade), many will feel that the softer delineation suits the music. The chrome cassette too is of DG's best quality, matching the compact disc quite closely.

The Los Angeles Chamber Orchestra phrase very musically and play with elegant polish, while the resonant acoustic produces beautiful sound, the opening of the *Serenade* given an attractive serenity. But the performance, though quite well characterized, is emotionally cool and lacking in charm. The *Nocturne* makes an attractive if insubstantial bonus, but the personality of the solo cellist – presumably from the orchestra – in *Silent woods* is not very strong, though he plays well enough.

After their splendid début recording of Rossini overtures – see below – this is disappointing. The Orpheus Chamber Orchestra is a band of talented New York musicians who work extremely successfully without a conductor. Here, however, though performances are refined they lack the bite and commitment to make them fully compelling. The *String serenade* starts with a disconcertingly limp and wayward account of the first movement at a very slow speed, and there is little feeling for the bright folk element. Surprisingly, the *Wind serenade* lacks bite too, though the often fast speeds bring impressively clean ensemble. Good recording in all three formats.

Serenade for strings in E, Op. 22; Symphonic variations, Op. 78.
(M) *** Ph. Seq. 412 360-1/*4*. LSO, Sir Colin Davis.

The *Symphonic variations* – little performed – is one of Dvořák's finest orchestral works; and Sir Colin Davis's account is strong, direct and sympathetic, with first-rate playing from the LSO. He has a genuine feeling for the work and keeps a firm grip on the structure. There is no finer version in the catalogue. The *Serenade* also comes off well. The 1968 Philips sound was comparatively lack-lustre on the original premium-priced LP, but emerges with remarkable freshness in this new mid-price transfer. The tape too is first class, vivid and well detailed.

Serenade for wind in D min., Op. 44.
(*) HM Orfeo Dig. **C 051831A; S 051831A [id.]. Mun. Wind Ac., Brezina – GOUNOD: *Petite symphonie.***(*)

The sumptuously weighty ensemble of Munich players at the opening of Dvořák's first movement sets the scene for a performance that is altogether more robust than Marriner's, yet no less well played. The *Andante*, slightly self-conscious in its spaciousness, lacks Marriner's lighter touch, but the very entertaining scherzo is quite bucolic in its deft and spirited articulation. The finale goes well, too. The recording made in St Stephen's Church, Munich, is amply textured throughout, yet detail is not clouded and there is individuality and character in the solo playing. The CD brings fine presence, but is short on playing time – there would have been plenty of room for another piece alongside the Gounod coupling.

Slavonic dances Nos 1–16, Opp. 46 and 72.
(M) *** DG Gal. 419 056-1/*4* [id.]. Bav. RSO, Kubelik.
(*) Sup. Dig. **C37 7491 [id.]. Czech PO, Neumann.
(*) Chan. Dig. **CHAN 8406; ABRD/*ABTD* 1143 [id.]. SNO, Järvi.
(*) Decca Dig. **411 735-2; 411 735-1/*4* (2). RPO, Dorati – *American suite.****
(B) ** Ph. On Tour *416 219-4* [id.]. Minneapolis SO, Dorati – BRAHMS: *Hungarian dances.***

Slavonic dances Op. 46/1–5.
(M) *** DG Walkman *413 159-4* [id.]. Bav. RSO, Kubelik – LISZT: *Hungarian rhapsodies* etc.; SMETANA: *Má Vlast* excerpts.***

Slavonic dances Nos 9–16, Op. 72; Slavonic rhapsody, Op. 45/1.
** Tel. **ZK8 42203**; AZ6 42203 [id.]. Czech PO, Neumann.

Kubelik's *Slavonic dances* are long admired; the recording dates from 1975 and is of excellent quality. Now at last, for the digitally remastered Galleria reissue, DG have managed to fit them on to two sides. The orchestral playing is first rate and the performances are infectiously full of flair. This is an obvious bargain.

Among the CDs, Neumann's latest Supraphon set, recorded in the House of Arists, Prague, is the obvious best buy, involving only one disc. Neumann's earlier Telefunken set had slightly more panache and the sound greater ambient glow, but the layout is uneconomical. The new set is very well played, with much felicitous detail from the Czech orchestra, who clearly have not grown tired of this engaging music. The recording is clear and naturally balanced, with no artificial digital brightness; it is also a little dry at the lower end, a truthful reflection of the acoustics of the recording site. But the alert vivacity of the music making is winning. One of the advantages of CD is that one can readily make one's own selection, rather than having them always in numerical sequence.

The Chandos CD also has the advantage of offering all sixteen *Slavonic dances* on a single disc; moreover, Järvi has the measure of this repertoire and he secures brilliant and responsive playing from the SNO. The recording, made in the SNO Centre, Glasgow, has the orchestra set back in an acoustic of believable depth, but the upper strings are brightly lit and fortissimos bring some loss of body and a degree of hardness on top, so that after a while the ear tends to tire. Unusually for Chandos, there is a noticeable loss of upper range in the treble on the chrome cassette; the sound is richer but has lost some of its sparkle.

Dorati's set involves two discs but offers the engaging *American suite* as a bonus. His performances have characteristic brio, the RPO response is warmly lyrical when necessary, and the woodwind playing gives much pleasure. Sparkle is the keynote and there is no lack of spontaneity. The Kingsway Hall venue with its natural resonance seems to have offered more problems than usual, and on CD the louder tuttis are not as sweet in the upper range of the strings as one would expect. The chrome cassettes, however, temper this effect, without loss of vividness.

Neumann's Telefunken *Slavonic dances* were originally issued in 1972 with the three *Slavonic rhapsodies*, the *Czech suite* and *The Wood dove* in a three-LP boxed set. Here Telefunken have reissued the eight Op. 72 *Dances* with the *First Slavonic rhapsody*. The performances are vivacious, with convincingly flexible rubato and the Czech Philharmonic on top form. The CD remastering seems to have removed some of the glare from the brightly lit original, which now has a better balance and greater depth. But this can hardly be recommended until the rest of the *Dances* appear, and even then, with the newer Supraphon issue offering all sixteen on a single CD, the Telefunken issue fails to compete.

Dorati's Philips set in fact has a Mercury source, the recording dating back to the beginning of the 1960s. The performances are vivid and sparkling, and the originally rather fierce recording has been tamed for this cassette reissue; now the sound is fuller, if less well defined. There is still enough brilliance at the top and this is good value at bargain price. However, this is not a tape to play all at one go.

The performances on the alternative Walkman cassette are part of an attractive compilation of popular Slavonic music (with Kubelik again conducting Smetana and Karajan in Liszt). Kubelik's accounts of the five *Slavonic dances* from Op. 46 offer polished, sparkling orchestral playing and very good sound.

Symphony No. 3 in E flat, Op. 10.
** Sup. Dig. **C37 7668** [id.]. Czech PO, Neumann.

This was the first of Dvořák's symphonies to show the full exuberance of his genius. When he wrote it in 1873 – eight years after the first two – he was very much under the influence of Wagner, but nowhere do the Wagnerian ideas really conceal the essential Dvořák. Even the unashamed crib from *Lohengrin* in the middle section (D flat major) of the slow movement has a Dvořákian freshness. This long slow movement is in any case the weakest of the three, but the outer movements are both delightful and need no apology whatever. The very opening of the symphony with its 6/8 rhythm and rising-scale motifs can hardly miss, and the dotted rhythms of the second subject are equally engaging. Neumann's directness of manner in Dvořák is more successful in this work than in some other of the early symphonies. The steady forward momentum of the first movement is attractive and the simple presentation of the second subject is helped by the fine orchestral playing. Again in the *Adagio* the flowing tempo is effective, with the restrained eloquence from the orchestra maintaining the tension consistently. After the climax, the delicate woodwind detail is nicely balanced by elegant string espressivo, with ardour never too overt to create a feeling of melodrama. This is left for the finale, which is thrustful, a trifle square but with crisp rhythms and excellent ensemble preventing heaviness. The recording is full and well detailed, if without the colour and glow of the finest Western CDs. Without a filler, however, the CD is poor value as it plays for only 38 minutes. Kertesz's Decca recording, coupled with the *Symphonic variations*, is far more recommendable (Jubilee JB/*KJBC* 112).

Symphony No. 4 in D min., Op. 13.
*(*) Sup. Dig. **C37 7442** [id.]. Czech PO, Neumann.

Compared with the exuberant symphonies which flank it on either side in the Dvořák canon, the *Fourth* is a disappointment. The opening theme – a fanfare-like idea – is not as characterful as one expects, but then the second subject soars aloft in triple time. The slow movement begins with so close a crib from the *Pilgrims' Music* in *Tannhäuser* that one wonders how Dvořák had the face to write it, but the variations which follow are attractive, and the scherzo has a delightful lolloping theme, which unfortunately gives way to a horribly blatant march trio with far too many cymbal crashes in it. The finale, despite rhythmic monotony, has at least one highly characteristic and attractive episode. Whatever the shortcomings of the work, however, there is much that is memorable. But it needs more coaxing than Neumann gives it. He is not helped by the rather stark acoustic of the Supraphon recording, which gives faithful detail without much overall bloom. The reading has plenty of thrust in the first movement, with the pacing in this new CD version distinctly faster than in his 1975 analogue account (the exposition repeat omitted on both occasions). The *Andante sostenuto* refuses to blossom and the Wagnerian quotation is curiously unexpansive. The most successful movement is the scherzo, and Neumann emphasizes its Lisztian associations without too much bombast. Overall, the dryness of the string timbre reduces the appeal of this issue, though the orchestral playing has plenty of character. Kertesz's Decca Jubilee issue, coupled with *In Nature's Realm*, remains a far better investment (JB/*KJBC* 113).

Symphony No. 6 in D, Op. 60.
*(*) Sup. Dig. **C37 7242** [id.]. Czech PO, Neumann.

If the three immediately preceding Dvořák symphonies reflect the influence of Wagner, this one just as clearly reflects that of Brahms, and particularly of Brahms's *Second Symphony*. Not only the shape of themes but the actual layout of the first movement has strong affinities with the Brahmsian model; Kertesz's performance, however, effectively underlines the individuality of the writing as well. This is a marvellous work that, with the *Fifth* and *Seventh*, forms the backbone of the Dvořák cycle. Unfortunately (or otherwise, depending on one's viewpoint), the Brahmsian influence is diminished in Neumann's recording. The acoustic is severe and the distinct lack of glowing warmth in the strings dilutes any expansiveness in the playing itself. Tuttis tend to be fierce, and this certainly gives brilliance to the *Furiant* scherzo which is played vivaciously and is the highlight of the performance. Elsewhere, the lack of amiable feeling is a great drawback. Once again Kertesz and the LSO on Decca are far more sympathetic, and they also offer the *My Home* overture (Jubilee JB/*KJBC* 115).

(i) *Symphonies Nos 7 in D min., Op. 70; 8 in G, Op. 88;* (ii) *Slavonic dances Nos 9, 10 and 15, Op. 72/1, 2 and 7.*
(B) *** DG Walkman *419 088-4* [id.]. (i) BPO; (ii) Bav. RSO; Kubelik.

This is one of the very finest Walkman bargains, and is worth obtaining even if it involves duplication. The recordings sound admirably fresh, full yet well detailed, the ambience attractive. Kubelik gives a glowing performance of the *Seventh*, one of Dvořák's richest inspirations. His approach is essentially expressive, but his romanticism never obscures the overall structural plan and there is no lack of vitality and sparkle. The account of the *Eighth* is a shade straighter, without personal idiosyncrasy, except for a minor indulgence for the phrasing of the lovely string theme in the trio of the scherzo. Throughout both works the playing of the Berlin Philharmonic is most responsive, with the polish of the playing adding refinement. The orchestral balance in the *G major Symphony* is particularly well judged. The recordings come from 1971 and 1966 respectively and sound in no way dated; nor do the beguilingly shaped *Slavonic dances*, from 1975, with the Bavarian orchestra on top form. They are used as encores following the close of each symphony.

Symphonies Nos 7–9 (*New World*).
(*) Ph. Dig. **412 542 (2) [id.]. Minnesota O, Marriner.

The effect of this Philips compact disc issue is to offer Sir Neville Marriner's Minnesota recordings of the last three Dvořák *Symphonies* at 'mid-price', for the three works are successfully encapsulated on two CDs. With the Minnesota Orchestra offering consistently responsive playing, Marriner's approach to Dvořák is mellow and warm-hearted, helped by the attractively rich textures of the Philips recording, with its agreeable ambient glow. Some might feel the *Seventh* is just a little too easy-going, although the first-movement climax is impressive enough. The *Poco adagio* flows pleasantly and, while the famous scherzo is spirited, other versions are rhythmically more infectious. The finale is positive and eloquent, but not overtly dramatic. The *Eighth* is the finest performance of the three, its sunny qualities most appealing. Though one might object in principle to the very relaxed espressivo manner in the first movement, Marriner's smiling lyricism is so persuasive that the joy and felicity are irresistible. The slow movement is both genial and elegant and the third has a delectable Viennese lilt. The finale very much breathes the air of the *Slavonic dances*, with fine rhythmic bite and no pomposity whatsoever. The *New World* is also available on a separate LP and cassette and is discussed in more detail below. It has an element of nostalgia consistent with the others – though certainly not lacking drama or spontaneity and beautifully played. Throughout the set the vivid digital recording, with CD definition never bringing excessive highlighting, adds to the listener's pleasure.

Symphony No. 7 in D min., Op. 70.
❀ ℂ *** Lodia **LO-CD 782**; LOD 782 [id.]. Philharmonic SO, Païta.
(*) Sup. **C37 7067; 1110 3139 [id.]. Czech PO, Neumann.
** DG Dig. **410 997-2**; 410 997-1/*4* [id.]. VPO, Maazel.
*(*) RCA Dig. **RD 85427 [RCD1 5427]**. Chicago SO, Levine.

Païta's recording is outstanding in every way, a performance of striking lyrical ardour, matching excitement with warmth and bringing spontaneity and freshness to every bar. The admirably balanced sound is demonstrably realistic and the ambience is ideal. Païta's own Philharmonic Symphony Orchestra produces playing of the first order, creating an immediate feeling of expectancy at the opening, moving to a climax of great excitement and then relaxing engagingly for the coda. There is comparable expressive fervour in the *Poco adagio*, and the lilting rhythms of the scherzo bring a ready parallel with the *Slavonic dances*. The 'comma' which is part of the presentation of the main idea is superbly articulated at the reprise – a moment of sheer delight – and the close of the movement brings a spontaneous burst of exuberance. This leads naturally to the thrustful finale which – while relaxing beguilingly for each appearance of the secondary theme – moves forward to generate steadily increasing excitement until its apotheosis. The orchestral playing here is quite riveting, and the performance as a whole has the kind of spontaneity one experiences only at the most memorable of live performances, helped by the extremely wide dynamic range captured so readily by the CD format.

Neumann is much more successful in his CD of the *Seventh* than in the earlier symphonies. The reading has a more positive character than Marriner's (see above), and is less histrionic than Païta's. There is fine, often superb playing from the Czech Philharmonic, with the most engaging response from the woodwind to the first movement's second subject. The slow movement is eloquent, the scherzo winningly light and vivacious in a specially Czech way and the finale steady and strong. The recording has less ambient glow than Marriner's and a fairly sharp focus, with orchestral timbres not lacking colour, and the overall balance realistic.

Maazel's reluctance to relax in Dvořákian happiness and innocence produces a powerful incisive performance, with the slow movement spacious and refined, though the bright DG recording fails to place the orchestra against any defined acoustic, making fortissimos rather aggressive. For some reason, the cassette is transferred at a disappointingly low level. Tape collectors are not given a great deal of choice in the symphony: first choice at present rests with Kertesz and the LSO (Decca Jub. JB/*KJBC* 116).

Using modern digital techniques, the Chicago engineers seem unable to capture the acoustic of Symphony Hall, Chicago, with the bloom and naturalness they achieved in the earliest days of analogue stereo. Levine's virile account of the *D minor Symphony* is hampered by a sound balance that makes tuttis seem aggressive (particularly the slow-movement climax) and the upper strings thin and febrile. The reading is direct and well played, but lacks charm: the sparkle of the scherzo is there, but Levine's inflection of the main idea is less affectionately subtle than Païta's.

Symphony No. 8 in G, Op. 88.
*** CBS **MK 42038** [id.]. Columbia SO, Bruno Walter – WAGNER: *Parsifal* excerpts.*** ❀
*** Sup. Dig. **C37 7073** [id.]. Czech PO, Neumann.
(M) **(*) DG Sig. 413 980-1/*4*. Chicago SO, Giulini.
** DG Dig. **415 205-2**; 2532/*3302* 034 [id.]. VPO, Maazel.

(i) *Symphony No. 8 in G, Op. 88;* (ii) *Carnaval overture, Op. 92.*
(B) **(*) ASV Dig. ABM/*ZCABM* 768 [id.]. (i) Royal Liverpool PO; (ii) LPO; Bátiz.

Symphony No. 8 in G, Op. 88; Nocturne for strings, Op. 40.
(*) Chan. Dig. **CHAN 8323; ABRD/*ABTD* 1105 [id.]. LPO, Handley.

Symphony No. 8 in G, Op. 88; Scherzo capriccioso, Op. 66.
ℭ *** Decca Dig. **414 422-2**; 414 422-1/*4* [id.]. Cleveland O, Dohnányi.

Walter's famous account of Dvořák's *Eighth* was one of the last he made (in 1962) during his CBS Indian summer just before he died. It has been in and out of the catalogue ever since. As with many of its companions in this CBS series, the improvement on CD is astonishing. The sound was always warm and full, but now is more naturally clear, the focus of all sections of the orchestra firmer with upper strings sweet (if with slightly less upper range than one would expect in a modern digital recording) and the violas, cellos and basses expansively resonant. It is a strong yet superbly lyrical reading; but the overall lyricism never takes the place of virility – as it sometimes seems to do in Giulini's performance – and Walter's mellowness is most effective in the *Adagio*. His pacing is uncontroversial until the finale, which is steadier than usual, more symphonic, although never heavy. With its inspired coupling of the *Prelude and Good Friday music* from *Parsifal*, this issue, like its *New World* companion, ranks high in the CBS legacy.

Rather like Kondrashin's splendid VPO version of the *New World*, Dohnányi's Decca Cleveland CD of the *Eighth* makes one hear it with new ears. As sound, it is superb, with a striking enhancement compared with the LP. Within the acoustics of the Masonic Hall, the Decca engineers have created an impression of realism thst places this well up on the list of demonstration orchestral CDs. The layout of the orchestra is convincingly natural, and the internal definition, achieved without any kind of digital edge, is remarkable. The various string groups, notably cellos and basses, are particularly firm, the woodwind, like the violins, given a fine bloom; and the brass, horns, trumpets and trombones, which are set back, still make a spectacular effect, as do the timpani. The performance is attractively alive and spontaneous, although it includes a few self-conscious nudgings here and there. But the playing of the Cleveland Orchestra is so responsive that the overall impression is of freshness, and in the coda there is the kind of interpretative freedom that can come off at a concert, but less often on record. Here it makes an exhilarating culmination. The coupling with the *Scherzo capriccioso* is apt, when the performance finds an affinity with the *Symphony* in bringing out the Slavonic dance sparkle, and moulding the lyrical secondary theme with comparable affectionate flair.

Neumann's *Eighth* is by the far the finest of his cycle. The firm momentum established at the opening does not produce any loss of expansive warmth, and the vigour is maintained throughout. The *Adagio* is particularly fine, with a feeling of creative spontaneity at the improvisatory central point of the movement, before the main theme returns on the woodwind against those delightful horn chugs, with elegant string decoration. The scherzo is vivacious, with a rustic Czech flavour from the woodwind in the trio; and the exciting finale rounds the performance off, the closing section especially vivid. Although there is a degree of blatancy from the Czech brass, the sound is otherwise excellent, convincingly balanced and realistic, with the woodwind colouring well conveyed.

With exceptionally full and brilliant sound, Handley's Chandos version – originally part of a Beecham tribute box – makes a strong, fresh impact. The manner is direct with the opening relatively straight, not eased in. Though some will miss a measure of charm, the life and spontaneity of the reading are most winning, with the CD brighter than the LP and with extra inner clarity. The *Nocturne* makes a most agreeable bonus and is beautifully played. There is an excellent chrome cassette, of Chandos's usual high standard.

Although this symphony is well served on LP and cassette mid-priced labels – notably on Decca Jubilee with Kertesz and the LSO (JB/*KJBC* 117) who offers also *The Water Goblin*; and Karajan with the VPO (JB/*KJBC* 71 [Lon. JL/*5*- 41043]) coupled less appropriately with Tchaikovsky's *Romeo and Juliet* – Giulini's Chicago performance might be considered reasonably competitive, even though it has no coupling. Reissued on DG's Signature label, it is an attractive performance, more relaxed than Handley or Walter, the phrasing broader, the rhythmic articulation more positive. The recorded sound is of DG's best quality and naturally balanced. Giulini's less pressing momentum brings some lovely soft-grained woodwind playing in the slow movement and a general sense of spaciousness, with the folksy quality of the scherzo material made obvious. The DG cassette is of high quality.

An excellent bargain version comes from Bátiz with consistently spirited playing from the Royal Liverpool Philharmonic Orchestra. The reading is direct, responsive and structurally sound and enjoyable in its easy spontaneity. The digital recording is vivid, yet does not lack warmth, although there is a touch of fierceness on climaxes. The overture is slightly less successful, but this is certainly good value.

Maazel's is a fierce performance, lacking the glow of warmth one associates with this work. Despite excellent incisive playing, the hardness of the reading is underlined by the recording balance, which favours a bright treble against a rather light bass. Though the trumpet fanfare heralding the start of the finale is wonderfully vivid, the sound lacks something in body.

Symphony No. 9 in E min. (From the New World), Op. 95.

© *** Decca Dig. **400 047-2**; SXDL/*KSXDC* 7510 [Lon. LDR/5-10011]. VPO, Kondrashin.
*** Ph. Dig. 412 224-1/*4* [id.]. Minnesota SO, Marriner.
*** CBS **MK 42039**. Columbia SO, Bruno Walter.
(*) HMV Dig. **CDC 747071-2 [id.]; EL 270104-1/*4* [Ang. DS/*4DS* 38140]. BPO, Tennstedt.
(M) **(*) Ph. 412 921-1/*4*. Concg. O, Sir Colin Davis.
(M) **(*) Ph. Seq. 412 003-1/*4*. LSO, Rowicki.
(B) **(*) Con. CC/*CCTC* 7579 [Lon. STS/5- 15567]. New Philh. O, Dorati.
** DG Dig. **415 509-2**; 415 509-1/*4* [id.]. VPO, Karajan – SMETANA: *Vltava*.**
** Decca Dig. **410 116-2**; 410 116-1/*4* [id.]. Chicago SO, Solti.
(M) ** EMI EMX 41 2051-1/*4*. LPO, Rostropovich.
(M) ** HMV EG 290275-1/*4* [Ang. AM/*4AM* 34700]. New Philh. O, Muti.
(**) RCA [mono **RCCD 1008**]. NBC SO, Toscanini – SMETANA: *Vltava*.(***)
*(*) RCA Dig. **RCD 14552 [RCD1 4552]**; RL 14248 [ARC1/*ARK1* 4552]. Chicago SO, Levine.
* Sup. Dig. **C37 7002** [id.]. Czech PO, Neumann.

Symphony No. 9; Carnaval overture.

(*) DG Dig. **410 032-2; 2532/*3302* 079 [id.]. VPO, Maazel.
** Erato **ECD 88036** [id.]. LPO, Conlon.

Kondrashin's Vienna recording of the *New World symphony* proved to be one of the first demonstration CDs, of many which subsequently came from Decca, and it can still hold its own with the best of them. Its impact is quite remarkable and no previous recording of the symphony can match its vividness. Recorded in the Sofiensaal, the range of the sound is equalled by its depth. The upper strings are brilliant, yet have body and sheen; the bass is rich and firmly defined, the woodwind is luminously clear, and the brass combines sonority with bite, the characteristic timbre of the Vienna trumpets unmistakable. The ambient effect of the hall prevents a clinical effect, yet every detail of Dvořák's orchestration is revealed, within a highly convincing perspective. Other performances of the first movement (exposition repeat included) may show a higher level of tension, but there is a natural spontaneity here and certainly no lack of excitement. In the *Largo* the Berlin Philharmonic may play even more beautifully for Tennstedt, but with Kondrashin the cor anglais solo is easy and songful, and there is an appealing simplicity in the way the music unfolds. But it is the finale that makes this version especially satisfying with the wide dynamic range bringing dramatic projection to climaxes, and the refinement and transparency of the orchestral texture uncovering the composer's ingenious reworking of ideas recalled from earlier movements. There are few better or more enjoyable demonstrations of the potential of the digital compact disc than this.

Sir Neville Marriner's rapport with his Minnesota players, already demonstrated in his recordings of the *Seventh* and *Eighth Symphonies*, is equally apparent in his *New World*, where his reading introduces a strong element of nostalgia, both at the opening and in the beautifully played *Largo*. Here the seamless cor anglais melody creates a mood of reverie, hardly interrupted by the burst of energy in the climax towards the end of the movement. Following on naturally, the scherzo is made to sound more contrasted than usual, vivacious and light-hearted, with an engaging lilt to the trio. The outer movements are fresh and strong without being heavy, with a spontaneous thrust of exuberance for the closing sections. There is a slightly self-conscious element in the phrasing of the famous second subject of the opening movement when the strings answer the flute melody, but Marriner's obvious affection makes this easy to accept. The vividness of the naturally balanced recording with its expansive dynamics, bright full string timbre, glowing woodwind and resonant brass is very persuasive. The effect is enhanced on CD (only available coupled with the *Seventh* and *Eighth Symphonies* – see above), but the LP is impressive in its own right. The cassette, with only marginally less range in the treble, has a more expansive bass response, and this gives the performance added weight.

Bruno Walter's *New World* dates from 1960 and was one of the first completely successful stereo versions. It is not a conventional reading; its recognizably Viennese roots lead to a more relaxed view of the outer movements than usual. However, as so often with Walter, there is underlying tension to knit the structure together, while detail is noted and affectionately shared with the listener – the coda of the first movement is typical of the conductor's individual touch. The *Largo* is played very beautifully, the strings radiantly tender, while the scherzo is lilting, with the introduction of the Trio lovingly prepared. The spacious finale finds dignity and stature without pomposity, and the result is more involving and satisfying than other rivals which have more surface excitement. The recording, very well balanced, emerges here registering freshly, yet without loss of the original body and warmth. Indeed the warm resonance of the sound is one of the CD's most attractive features, casting a glow over the proceedings without clouding. Inner detail is firm, the violins are fresh and sweet above the stave. The rich lower strings (a Walter hallmark), full-bodied horns and realistic timpani are well demonstrated in the very opening bars. This could be first choice for many, although a vestige of the original background hiss still remains.

Tennstedt's is a warm, romantic reading, freely expressive at generally spacious speeds, very much in the German rather than the Czech tradition. Though he fails to observe the important exposition repeat in the first movement, the symphonic weight of the work is powerfully conveyed with full, forward recording and outstanding playing from the Berlin Philharmonic, not least the soloists. The natural, easy warmth of the famous cor anglais solo at the start of the slow movement has a pure felicity that it would be hard to match. The CD adds clarity to the rich, full recording; however, it also adds a degree of shrillness on the treble in fortissimos.

Now reissued at mid-price, Sir Colin Davis's 1979 Philips version continues to hold its place near the top of the analogue list. It is completely free from egotistic eccentricity; the music is allowed to unfold in the most natural way, its drama vividly projected, and with beautiful orchestral playing throughout and outstanding recording (rich and full-blooded, well detailed yet with a natural bloom on the whole orchestra), this is very satisfying. For some listeners Davis's very directness may have its drawbacks. The cor anglais solo in the slow movement has an appealing simplicity, yet the effect is not very resilient, and later, when the horns echo the theme at the end of the opening section, the impression is positive rather than seductively nostalgic. The cassette transfer is well managed; though inner detail is not sharply defined, the overall balance is convincing.

Maazel's is a high-powered and superbly played reading, incisive to the point of fierceness (like his reading of No. 8) but with moments of affection, most strikingly in the poised and pure account of the slow movement. On compact disc the aggressive sound of Maazel's DG recording (lacking bloom on high violins in fast movements) cannot compare with Kondrashin's far warmer sound with the same orchestra on Decca – though here too the benefits of the new medium with its absence of background are considerable. The chrome cassette, transferred at only a modest level, is, however, comparatively mellow with much less sharply defined detail.

Rowicki is fresh and direct, somewhat lightweight in the first movement, although he observes the exposition repeat. The *Largo* is not as memorable as in some other versions, but the finale is particularly successful, and the relaxed mood at the centre of the scherzo brings out the rustic colouring of the scoring. The recording is first rate, bright and very well balanced, and it has transferred to tape admirably.

A recommendable bargain version on Contour from Dorati. This was originally recorded in 1968 using Decca's artificially balanced Phase Four system, with close microphones to bring everything vividly forward. Dorati's approach is spontaneously direct, the outer movements vigorous and alert, the *Largo* tenderly expressive and simply presented, and the scherzo strongly characterized. The bold primary colours of the recording undoubtedly heighten the dramatic effect and the sound, crisp and clear, is only a shade lacking in depth and bass resonance. There is an excellent chrome cassette.

Karajan's newest version of the *New World* is one of only three CDs offering a fill-up – and a substantial one too, in Smetana's *Vltava*. The recording, like Karajan's newest series of Beethoven and Tchaikovsky symphonies, has been made simultaneously on video, and is generally less precise in definition than the conductor's Berlin records. Moreover there is an element of edginess on strings and brass which compares unfavourably with Kondrashin's 1979 Decca CD with the same orchestra. The playing too is less refined than in Karajan's earlier accounts with the Berlin Philharmonic; in the slow movement the VPO wind soloists fail to match the beauty of timbre found in Tennstedt's Berlin recording. The Tennstedt and Karajan readings have much in common (with both conductors omitting the first-movement exposition repeat) and it need hardly be said that Karajan shows many positive qualities, not least an attractive air of relaxed spontaneity throughout the work. However, this cannot compare with the finest recent compact discs of this symphony, nor indeed with Karajan's earlier analogue LPs made in Berlin for both HMV and DG.

Solti's is a characteristically fierce reading, somewhat larger than life, recorded with rather aggressive brilliance, impressive but not too sympathetic. There is an excellent chrome cassette, but the CD, vivid though it is, does not match Kondrashin's version in beauty of texture and refinement of detail.

Rostropovich directs the weightiest reading imaginable. The very opening chords of the slow introduction suggest an epic view, and from then on, with generally expansive tempi, the performance presents this as a genuine '*Ninth*', a culmination to the cycle. In the first movement the exposition repeat brings a slight modification of treatment the second time, and some will resist such inconsistencies as that. The conscious weight of even the *Largo* is controversial too, though in all four movements Rostropovich contrasts the big tuttis – almost Straussian at times – with light pointing in woodwind solos. The recording is ample to match, and the cassette transfer is generally a close match for the disc, although its upper range is slightly limited.

Muti's is a sweet and amiable performance, unsensationally attractive but ignoring the minor textual points raised by Czech scholars which a true Dvořákian would have observed. Full, smooth recording, making the great cor anglais melody of the slow movement sound a little bland in simplicity. The tape is of good quality, bold and vivid, with plenty of body.

Toscanani's record was reissued at the end of the 1960s in pseudo stereo but didn't remain in the catalogue very long. For the CD, RCA have returned to the mono master tape, which is certainly clear but apparently flat and thin, with a shrill upper range. Toscanini's incisiveness is ever apparent and at its most telling in the finale. The *Largo* is kept moving but not helped by a nasal-sounding cor anglais solo. There is certainly no lack of vitality here, but it is a performance to admire rather than to love. The only real technical fault is a touch of wow at the very end of the slow movement. This CD is available in the UK only as a special import.

Conlan's is an essentially small-scale reading, with the refined presentation of the second subject of the first movement matched by the *Largo*, tender in its delicacy. The scherzo and finale are robust and straightforward, but the reading overall is short on weight and power. The overture goes well and the recording is good, but is no match for Kondrashin's Decca version.

Next to the finest CD versions Levine's is disappointing. The reading is lively and bright with some excellent playing – but the RCA recording, transferred at a relatively low level, is rough, with internal congestion in tuttis, giving the impression of a gauze in front of the orchestra.

Neumann's reading rarely rises above the routine. It gives a clear impression of over-familiarity (there is no exposition repeat), and though the Czech Philharmonic Orchestra make their presence felt, this cannot be considered as a serious alternative. The recording is good.

(i) *Symphony No. 9 (New World)*; (ii) *Scherzo capriccioso, Op. 66;* (iii) *Serenade for strings in E, Op. 22.*
(B) *** DG Walkman *413 147-4*. (i) BPO; (ii) Bav. RSO; (iii) ECO; Kubelik.

This bargain-priced (tape-only) reissue is self-recommending. Kubelik's version of the *New World* is outstanding in every way and the accounts of the *Scherzo capriccioso* and *String serenade* have a comparable freshness. The *Scherzo* is attractively spirited and colourful, while the account of the *Serenade* is beautifully lyrical, yet strong in impulse. The playing of the ECO here is attractively polished as well as resilient. The recording is brightly lit and, like the *Symphony*, somewhat dry in the bass, but the chrome-tape transfers are of DG's finest quality. The *Symphony* is offered without a break.

CHAMBER AND INSTRUMENTAL MUSIC

Piano quintets: in A, Op. 5; in A, Op. 81.
** Ph. Dig. **412 429-2**; 412 429-1/*4* (2/*1*) [id.]. Sviatoslav Richter, Borodin Qt.

The early *Quintet* comes from about 1872 when Dvořák was just over thirty and beginning to outgrow some of the worst excesses of his infatuation with Wagner. Later he revised it, not long before composing the famous Op. 81 *Quintet*. It is good to have it for the first time, even if it is by no means fully characteristic. Richter's recording was made at a public concert, this time in Prague at the 1982 Festival. The public is eminently well behaved, but the recording does tend to give excessive prominence to the pianist, and the Borodin Quartet do not have the tonal opulence and bloom which they possess in reality. The performance itself is a good one, though some may be worried by moments of waywardness in the onward flow of tempi; however, in general this is not as fine as Curzon's classic 1963 recording with the VPO Quartet (Decca Ace of Diamonds SDD 270) or Stephen Bishop's excellent version, recorded in Berlin (Ph. 6570/*7310* 571) which is coupled with a neglected masterpiece, the Op. 97 *String quintet* and which has an excellent tape equivalent. For LP collectors, with the Richter coupling there is a snag: these two works, together lasting just under seventy minutes, are accommodated on two LPs as opposed to one (technically admirable) cassette and one compact disc.

(i) *Piano quintet in A, Op. 81; String quartet No. 12 in F (American), Op. 96.*
* Denon Dig. **C37 7338** [id.]. (i) Josef Hála; Smetana Qt.

The coupling of the *A major Piano quintet* with Dvořák's most famous string quartet is an attractive idea, and it is surprising that it has not been offered before. In the event, however, these performances by the Smetana Quartet, with Josef Hála the pianist in Op. 81, are very disappointing. They were recorded live, and the balance produces a wan sound-picture, which is unflattering to the leader, Jiří Novák. The sense of urgency which one expects from live music-making is not apparent here and, with textures often meagre, the expressive side of the playing is under-projected. Allegros are spirited and the artists clearly appreciate the inherent dance rhythms, but the lack of ambient warmth robs the music of necessary body.

Piano trio No. 3 in F min., Op. 65.
*** Chan. Dig. **CHAN 8320**; ABRD/*ABTD* 1107 [id.]. Borodin Trio.
(M) *** Ph. 6503/*7303* 063. Beaux Arts Trio.

Dvořák's *F minor Trio* comes from the same period as the *D minor Symphony* and finds him at his most consistently Brahmsian. It is powerful in structure, but as Alec Robertson puts it in his *Master Musicians* monograph, 'the shape of the themes, the writing of the piano and the general feeling of the music "continually do cry" Brahms'. The playing of the Borodin Trio is little short of superb: they have great warmth and fire, such imperfections as there are arising from the natural spontaneity of a live performance, for one feels this is what it must have been, with few if any retakes. Rotislav Dubinsky is slightly under the note at the opening of the second group of the first movement; the pianist, Luba Edlina, is balanced rather forward. The wide-ranging Chandos recording has transferred with impressive presence to CD; the chrome tape too is very realistic, though there is a hint of edge on the violin timbre.

The Beaux Arts recording comes from the early 1970s, and the performance has great vitality and eloquence. The sound is vivid and truthful on cassette and disc alike. A good medium-priced LP and tape alternative.

Piano trio No. 4 in E min. (Dumky), Op. 90.
*** Chan. Dig. **CHAN 8445**; ABRD/*ABTD* 1157 [id.]. Borodin Trio – SMETANA: *Piano trio.****

Those unfamiliar with Dvořák's marvellous *E minor Piano trio* might think the sobriquet 'Dumky' indicates some kind of national dance. But instead it is the plural of the Russian word, *dumka* (a term also found in both Poland and Czechoslovakia) which can be broadly translated as a lament. Musically, it implies alternating slow and fast movements, with brightness lightening the melancholy. Dvořák's six-movement *Trio* follows this pattern, with contrasting sequences inherent in the structure of each. It is the spontaneous flexibility of approach to the constant mood changes that makes the splendid Borodin performance so involving, as well as the glorious playing from each of the three soloists. The recording is naturally balanced and the illusion of a live occasion is striking. Highly recommended in all formats, for the cassette is extremely well managed.

String quartet No. 10 in E flat, Op. 51.
*(*) Tel. Dig. **ZK8 43105**; AZ6/*CY4* 43105 [id.]. Vermeer Qt – VERDI: *Quartet.***

String quartets Nos 10 in E flat; Op. 51; 14 in A flat, Op. 105.
* Denon Dig. **C37 7235**. Kocian Qt.

The Kocian Quartet was formed in 1972 when three members of the Prague Symphony Orchestra joined forces with the violinist, Pravoslav Kohout. The *E flat Quartet*, Op. 51, comes from the period of the *Violin concerto*, when Dvořák was in his late thirties, and the wonderful *A flat Quartet* was written in 1896 after his return from Prague. They are lovely works but are given curiously lack-lustre readings by this Quartet, who command limited dynamic range and modest eloquence. The recordings are made in the somewhat unglamorous acoustic of the Domovina Studio in Prague, and are not particularly spacious or distinguished. There is no current alternative of Op. 105, but this is no more than a stopgap.

The Vermeer Quartet on Teldec have greater tonal bloom and play with finesse and more refined ensemble, though their playing is not as distinguished as in their Beethoven Opp. 130 and 133 on the same label. It sounds as if they are recorded in a small studio and the CD rather brings out its dryness. The leader's sniff, of which one commentator complained, did not trouble us; it is the overall sound that eventually proves tiring and which does not do full justice to the tone of this fine ensemble. This is something the clarity of the compact disc makes the more apparent, but it is almost equally true of the LP and matching cassette.

String quartets Nos 12 in F (American), Op. 96; 13 in G, Op. 106.
* Denon Dig. **C37 7234.** Kocian Qt.

String quartets Nos 12 in F, Op. 96; 14 in A flat, Op. 105.
*(*) Sup. Dig. **C37 7565** [id.]. Panocha Qt.

The Kocian Quartet couple Op. 96 with the late *G major Quartet*. The performances of both this and the *F major* are good but fall short of distinction, and the recording is made in the same unflattering acoustic as their Opp. 51 and 105. This does not represent a serious challenge to the best LP versions.

On Supraphon, the Panocha Quartet are balanced closely and, though their timbres are truthfully caught, one would have liked more space round the instruments. Their expressive playing is not unresponsive, yet the end effect is rather dry. The light articulation in the scherzo and finale of the *American quartet* is attractive, while the lively account of the second movement of Op. 105 (which Dvořák marked *molto vivace*) is spirited without being aggressive. The CD's presence is in no doubt, but a warmer ambience would have added to the effect of this music making.

Slavonic dances Nos 1–8, Op. 46.
(M) *** DG Sig. 413 984-1/*4* [id.]. Alfons and Aloys Kontarsky (piano duet) – BRAHMS: *Hungarian dances.****

Characteristically crisp and clean performances by the Kontarsky brothers of some of the most delectable piano duets ever written. More than they usually do, these pianists have allowed themselves the necessary rubato conveying affection and joy along with their freshness. Excellent recording and a splendid high-level chrome cassette, matching the disc very closely. These are every bit as enjoyable as the orchestral versions, for the spirit of the music is fully captured.

VOCAL AND CHORAL MUSIC

Stabat Mater, Op. 58.
(M) *** DG 415 178-1 (2) [id.]. Mathis, Reynolds, Ochman, Shirley-Quirk, Bav. R. Ch., and SO, Kubelik.

Dvořák's devout Catholicism led him to treat this tragic religious theme with an open innocence that avoids the sentimentality of other works which made their mark (as this one did) in Victorian England. Characteristically four of the ten movements are based on major keys, and though a setting of a relatively short poem which stretches to eighty minutes entails much repetition of words, this idiomatic DG performance, warmly recorded and with fine solo and choral singing and responsive playing, holds the attention from first to last. There are no cassettes.

Te Deum, Op. 103; Psalm 149, Op. 79; Heirs of the White Mountain, Op. 30.
(*) Sup. **C37 7230 [id.]. Beňačkova-Čápová, Souček, Prague Philharmonic Ch., Czech PO, Neumann.

Dvořák's exuberant setting of the *Te Deum* was written to be performed at the celebration of the 400th anniversary of Columbus's discovery of America, and the composer conducted its première in October 1892 in New York. It makes a powerful impression in this eloquent Czech performance with choral singing of inspired fervour and a fine solo contribution from Gabriela Beňačkova-Čápová, movingly serene in the *Sanctus*. Her colleague, Jaroslav Souček, is less distinctive, a little wobbly, if not seriously so. The sound has a wide dynamic range and the layout of chorus and orchestra is convincingly real, although detail is less refined than it would be in a Western recording. Neumann's eloquent direction and the fine playing of the Czech Philharmonic ensure that the music grips the listener throughout. The other two works are less distinguished but are sung with such conviction that the listener cannot fail to respond. This is one of Neumann's finest Dvořák records.

OPERA

Rusalka (complete).
*** Sup. Dig. **C37 7201/3** [id.]. Beňačková-Capova, Novak, Soukupová, Ochman, Drobkova, Prague Ch. and Czech PO, Neumann.

Dvořák's fairy-tale opera is given a magical performance by Neumann and his Czech forces, helped by full, brilliant and atmospheric recording which, while giving prominence to the voices, brings out the beauty and refinement of Dvořák's orchestration. Written right at the end of the composer's career in his ripest maturity but with Wagnerian influences at work, the piece has a unique flavour; where on stage it can seem too long for its material (though not in the highly imaginative version staged by the English National Opera at London's Coliseum), it works beautifully on record. The title role is superbly taken by Gabriela Beňačková. The voice is creamy in tone, characterfully Slavonic without disagreeable hooting or wobbling, and the famous *Invocation to the Moon* is enchanting. Vera Soukupová as the Witch is just as characterfully Slavonic in a lower register, though not so even; while Wieslaw Ochman sings with fine, clean, heroic tone as the Prince, with timbre made distinctive by tight vibrato. Richard Novak brings out some of the Alberich-like overtones as the Watersprite, though the voice is not always steady. The banding on compact disk is both generous and helpful.

Dyson, George (1883–1964)

(i) *Fantasia and ground bass for organ; 3 Choral hymns;* (ii) *Hierusalem;* (iii) *O praise God in his holiness; 3 Songs of praise.*
**(*) Hyp. A 66150 [id.]. (i) St Michael's Singers; Thomas Trotter (organ); (ii) with Valery Hill, RPO; (iii) with J. Rennert (organ).

This unpretentious record gives a delightful portrait of an academic who, as a venerable Principal of the Royal College of Music and afterwards in retirement, continued to write church and choral music to please. The most ambitious work is *Hierusalem*, based on a sixteenth-century hymn, a glowing product of his seventies, here most sympathetically performed. The *Three Choral hymns* and *Three Songs of praise* are attractive but far simpler in scale and expression. The organ *Fantasia*, also a late work, brings out Dyson's streak of toughness, again well played and recorded.

Einem, Gottfried von (born 1918)

String quartet No. 1.
** HMV Dig. EL 270100-1. Alban Berg Qt – STRAVINSKY: *Concertino* etc.***

Gottfried von Einem came into prominence after the war with his opera, *Dantons Tod*. His *First Quartet* is a late work, written in 1976, and pays overt tribute to the Viennese tradition, actually quoting Schubert in the last movement and Wolf's *Italian Serenade* in the first. As one might expect from this composer, it is expertly crafted and coherently structured, but ultimately rather anonymous. It is eloquently played by the Alban Berg Quartet and beautifully recorded.

Elgar, Edward (1857–1934)

3 Bavarian dances, Op. 27. Caractacus, Op. 35; Woodland interludes. Chanson de matin; Chanson de nuit, Op. 15/1 and 2. Contrasts, Op. 10/3. Dream children, Op. 43. Falstaff, Op. 68: 2 Interludes. Salut d'amour. Sérénade lyrique. (i) *Soliloquy for oboe* (orch. Jacob).
*** Chan. **CHAN 8371**; CBR/*CBT* 1016. Bournemouth Sinf., Del Mar, (i) with Goossens.

The real treasure in this superb collection of Elgar miniatures is the *Soliloquy* which Elgar wrote right at the end of his life for Leon Goossens. It was the only movement completed of a projected suite, a wayward improvisatory piece which yet has a character of its own. Here the dedicatee plays it with his long-recognizable tone colour and feeling for phrase in an orchestration by Gordon Jacob. Most of the other pieces are well known, but they come up with new warmth and commitment in splendid performances under Del Mar. The (originally RCA) recording is of high quality, full and vivid, and it has now been digitally remastered with great success to make a first-class CD. The LP too offers very good sound, and the chrome tape is virtually identical in quality.

(i) *Carissima; Chanson de matin, Op. 15/2; Chanson de nuit, Op. 15/1; Elegy for strings, Op. 58;* (ii) *Romance for bassoon and orchestra, Op. 62; Rosemary; Salut d'amour, Op. 12; Serenade for strings in E min., Op. 20; Sospiri, Op. 70;* (iii) *Pomp and circumstance marches Nos 1–5; Variations on an original theme (Enigma), Op. 36.*
(B) *(*) CBS DC 40146 (2). (i) ECO; (ii) with M. Gatt; (iii) LPO, Barenboim.

Another interesting example of CBS's paired discs, two for the price of one. In the miniatures Barenboim tends to dwell too affectionately on detail and the results are frankly schmaltzy. The recording is not the most natural in balance, though it is by no means unpleasing. For the *Pomp and circumstance marches*, by contrast, his tempi are surprisingly fast (though Elgar's own tend to be fast, too), and not all Elgarians will approve of his updating of Elgarian majesty. If only the recording were more sumptuous the interpretations would emerge more convincingly than they do. His view of the *Enigma variations* is full of fantasy, and its most distinctive point is its concern for the miniature element. Without belittling the delicate variations, Barenboim both makes them sparkle and gives them emotional point, while the big variations have full weight; and the finale brings extra fierceness at a fast tempo. The equivalent tape is to be avoided as it omits *Pomp and circumstance marches Nos 4* and *5*.

Caractacus: Triumphal march. Coronation march, Op. 65; Crown of India suite, Op. 66; Grania and Diarmid, Op. 42: Funeral march. Imperial march, Op. 32; The Light of Life, Op. 29: Meditation. Nursery suite; Severn suite, Op. 87.
(B) **(*) HMV *TCC2-POR 154590-9*. Royal Liverpool PO, Groves.

It is good to have these performances by Sir Charles Groves – recorded while he was principal conductor of the Royal Liverpool Philharmonic Orchestra – restored to the catalogue. This is all music that he understands warmly, and the results give much pleasure. One does not have to be an imperialist to enjoy any of the occasional pieces, and it is interesting to find the patriotic music coming up fresher than the little interlude from *The Light of Life*, beautiful as that is. The *Triumphal march* from *Caractacus* makes one want to try the complete recording of this major cantata. It is played with fine swagger. Both the *Nursery suite* (written for the Princesses Elizabeth and Margaret Rose) and the orchestral version of the *Severn suite* (written for a brass band contest) come from Elgar's very last period when his inspiration came in flashes rather than as a sustained searchlight. The completely neglected *Funeral march* was written in 1901 for a play by W. B. Yeats and George Moore. It is a splendid piece. The collection is gathered together on one of EMI's 'Portrait of the Artist' double-length tapes. The sound is of generally good quality, lacking the last degree of brilliance on top, but otherwise well balanced. The documentation, however, is poor, offering no information about the music except titles.

'90 Minutes': (i) *Chanson de matin;* (ii) *Dream children, Op. 43;* (iii) *Introduction and allegro for strings, Op. 47;* (iv) *Pomp and circumstance marches Nos 1–5;* (v) *Serenade for strings, Op. 20;* (vi) *Variations on an original theme* (*Enigma*), *Op. 36.*
(B) **(*) Decca *414 049-4*. (i) LPO, Boult; (ii) New SO, Agoult; (iii) ECO, Britten; (iv) LSO, Bliss; (v) ASMF, Marriner; (vi) LSO, Monteux.

This double-length tape compilation is much the same selection as was offered in the late 1970s on a pair of discs and tapes by Decca in their 'Favourite Composer' series but with the addition of Agoult's sensitive account of both Op. 43, *Dream children*, and the wholly advantageous substitution of Marriner's superb account of the *String serenade* (instead of a version by Cox and the RPO). Boult's *Chanson de matin* is a stereo transcription of a mono recording, but sounds well enough. Britten's performance of the *Introduction and allegro* needs no further advocacy from us. Both Bliss in *Pomp and circumstance* and Monteux's justly famous *Enigma* are very early stereo, but the original recordings were good in their day and don't sound too dated. The transfers, on iron-oxide stock, are well made and this is fair value.

Chanson de matin, Op. 15/2; Chanson de nuit, Op. 15/1; Elegy, Op. 58; Introduction and allegro, Op. 47; Serenade in E min., Op. 20; The Spanish Lady (suite).
(*) Nimbus **NIM 5008 [id.]. E. String O, William Boughton.

Boughton conducts warm, sympathetic performances of an attractive selection of shorter Elgar works – including the suite drawn from his unfinished opera, *The Spanish Lady*. The reverberant recording is less crisply detailed than is ideal – like the actual playing – but, with the clarification of CD, presents a pleasingly natural ensemble.

Cockaigne overture, Op. 40; Falstaff (symphonic study), *Op. 68; Introduction and allegro for strings, Op. 47.*
(B) *** CfP CFP 41 4476-1/*4* [id.]. LPO, Handley.

Vernon Handley directs a superb performance of *Falstaff*, one of Elgar's most difficult works, and the achievement is all the more remarkable because his tempi are unusually spacious (generally following the composer's markings), making the contrasted episodes more difficult to hold together. The playing of the LPO is warmly expressive and strongly rhythmic, and the recording is one of the finest to come from Classics for Pleasure, with an outstanding matching cassette. *Cockaigne* is also given a performance that is expansive yet never hangs fire. For this reissue, CfP have added Handley's later, digital recording of the *Introduction and allegro*, notable for a somewhat indulgent performance of the *Larghetto*.

Overtures: Cockaigne; Froissart; In the South. Overture in D min. (arr. from *Handel: Chandos anthem No. 2*).
*** Chan. **CHAN 8309**; ABRD/*ABTD* 1077 [id.]. SNO, Gibson.

Sir Alexander Gibson's Chandos collection is given a brilliantly truthful digital recording. The Scottish orchestra makes a vividly cohesive sound, although the strings are just a little lacking in richness of timbre. The picture of London is full of bustle and pageantry, with bold brass and flashing percussion, and the closing pages have striking impact. *In the South* does not lack impetus, and Gibson's directness serves *Froissart* and the Handel arrangement equally well. There is a touch of digital edge on the LP sound; as the chrome tape tempers this a little, while remaining of demonstration liveliness, many will prefer tape to disc. On both, the bass response is firm. The CD is very impressive, the treble smoother and the overall effect extremely vivid, with greater tangibility and body to the sound.

Cello concerto in E min., Op. 85.

❀ *** HMV **CDC 727329-2** [id.]; ASD/*TC-ASD 655* [(d.) Ang. S 36338]. Du Pré, LSO, Barbirolli – *Sea pictures*.*** ❀

*** CBS Dig. **MK 39541**; IM/*IMT* 39541 [id.]. Yo-Yo Ma, LSO, Previn – WALTON: *Concerto*.***

(*) Ph. Dig. **412 880-2 [id.]. Heinrich Schiff, Dresden State O, Marriner – DVOŘÁK: *Cello concerto*.

It was in the Elgar *Cello concerto* that Jacqueline du Pré first won world recognition, and the HMV recording gives a wonderful idea of how so young a girl captured such attention and even persuaded the Americans to listen enraptured to Elgar. Du Pré is essentially a spontaneous artist, no two performances by her are exactly alike; wisely, Barbirolli at the recording sessions encouraged her above all to express emotion through the notes. The style is freely rhapsodic. The tempi, long-breathed in first and third movements, are allowed still more elbow-room when du Pré's expressiveness requires it; in the slow movement, brief and concentrated, her 'inner' intensity conveys a depth of espressivo rarely achieved by any cellist on record. Brilliant virtuoso playing too in scherzo and finale. CD brings a subtle extra definition to heighten the excellent qualities of the 1965 recording, with the solo instrument firmly placed. In such a meditative work the absence of background is a special blessing.

In its rapt concentration Yo-Yo Ma's recording with Previn brings a version at last to set alongside the classic account of the young Jacqueline du Pré with Barbirolli. The dark, tear-laden quality of the work comes out from her performance as from no one else, yet Ma's concentration is just as keen, plus his sense of controlled spontaneity. The first movement is lighter, a shade more urgent, and in the scherzo he finds more fun, just as he finds extra sparkle in the main theme of the finale. The key movement with Ma, as it is with du Pré, is the *Adagio*, echoed later in the raptness of the slow epilogue, and there his range of dynamic is just as daringly wide with a thread of pianissimo at the innermost moment, poised in its intensity. Warm, fully detailed recording, finely balanced, with understanding conducting from Previn. It sounds even more refined on CD, and tape collectors will be glad to know that the chrome cassette is also first class.

Schiff gives a warm, thoughtful account, at his most successful in the lovely slow movement and the slow epilogue, both played with soft, sweet tone. Other readings may convey more of the structural cohesion, but this lyrical view has its place. The sound is superb, to match the orchestra's richness. The elegiac atmosphere at the opening of the *Concerto* is especially persuasive. The coupling of the Dvořák *Concerto* is generous, if less appropriate than the couplings of Du Pré and Yo-Yo Ma; but unfortunately Schiff is less impressive in Dvořák.

Violin concerto in B min., Op. 61.

❀ *** EMI Dig. **CDC 747210-2** [id.]; EMX 41 2058-1/*4*. Nigel Kennedy, LPO, Handley.

** DG Dig. **413 312-2**; 2532/*3302* 035 [id.]. Itzhak Perlman, Chicago SO, Barenboim.

Kennedy's is a commanding reading, arguably even finer than the long line of versions with star international soloists from outside Britain. With Vernon Handley as guide, it is at once the most centrally Elgarian of all those on record in its warm expressiveness; equally, in its steady pacing it brings out more than is usual the clear parallels with the Beethoven and Brahms concertos. That is particularly striking in the first movement and, both there and in his urgent account of the allegro in the finale, Kennedy has learnt more than any recorded rival from the example of the *Concerto*'s first great interpreter, Albert Sammons. Yet the example of Yehudi Menuhin is also clear, not least in the sweetness and repose of the slow movement and in the deep meditation of the accompanied cadenza which comes as epilogue. The recording, with the soloist balanced more naturally than is usual, not spotlit, is outstandingly faithful and atmospheric on LP, only slightly more impressive on CD. This made a worthy outright winner of the *Gramophone* Record Award, 1985. The LP, unlike the CD, comes at mid-price, but the CD, with its silent background, is worth the extra cost. The cassette is disappointing: the reverberation has produced a restriction of the upper range.

Perlman's ease in tackling one of the most challenging violin concertos ever written brings an enjoyable performance, though he misses some of the darker, more intense elements in Elgar's inspiration. The solo instrument is forwardly balanced and the recording is bright and vivid rather than rich, lacking some of the amplitude one expects in the Elgar orchestral sound. The CD emphasizes the presence of the soloist but confirms the lack of expansiveness in the orchestra.

Elegy for strings, Op. 58; Serenade for strings, Op. 20; Sospiri, Op. 70.
*** HMV Dig. EL 270146-1/*4* [Pathe id.]. City of L. Sinfonia., Hickox – PARRY: *English suite* etc.***

Hickox draws beautifully refined string-playing from his City of London Sinfonia, notably in the three elegiac movements, the slow movement of the *Serenade* as well as the two separate pieces. An excellent coupling for the rare Parry items on the reverse, excellently recorded. On the XDR tape, textures are ample, but the upper range is very smooth and the overall effect is slightly bland.

Falstaff, Op. 68; Variations on an original theme (Enigma), Op. 36.
**(*) HMV Dig. EL 270374-1/*4*. LPO, Mackerras.
** Lyr. SRCS 77. New Philh. O, Andrew Davis.

With recorded sound far more reverberant than is common in EMI's recordings of Elgar, Mackerras's powerful readings of the composer's own favourite among his orchestral works, together with the most popular, are given a comfortable glow, while losing some inner clarity. The reading of *Falstaff* is superb, among the most electrically compelling put on disc, but *Enigma* is marred by mannered and self-conscious phrasing in the opening statement of the theme and first variation, as well as in *Nimrod*. This is scheduled for CD issue during the lifetime of this book, as is Boult's set of the *Enigma variations*.

In the reissue from 1975 – still at full price – Lyrita also provides a generous coupling of two works which are both often paired with shorter items. With splendid, full-ranging recording the result should be a firm recommendation, but Andrew Davis suffers here as elsewhere from a degree of recording-studio reticence. These are intelligent, freshly-thought readings which yet fail in the last instance to catch fire. Handley's *Falstaff* is much more successful (see above) and is more reasonably priced.

Introduction and allegro for strings; Serenade for strings.
*** HMV ASD/*TC-ASD* 521 [Ang. S 36101]. Sinfonia of L., Allegri Qt, Barbirolli – VAUGHAN WILLIAMS: *Tallis fantasia* etc.*** ❀

Since our last edition, HMV have issued a first-class cassette of Barbirolli's outstanding versions of Elgar's string works, ideally coupled with an inspirational performance of Vaughan Williams's *Tallis Fantasia*. The 1963 sound, with its combination of clarity and ambient richness, remains in the demonstration class; this should be high on the EMI list for future CD issue.

Nursery suite; Wand of Youth suites Nos 1 and 2, Op. 1a and 1b.
*** Chan. Dig. **CHAN 8318**; ABRD/*ABTD* 1079. Ulster O, Bryden Thomson.

An admirable coupling. The Ulster Orchestra plays most beautifully and the ambience of the recordings is well suited to the music's moments of gentle nostalgia. Although Boult's performances of the more robust items from the *Wand of Youth* brought marginally more exuberance, the playing in Ulster is attractively spirited; in the gentle pieces (the *Sun dance*, *Fairy pipers* and *Slumber dance*) which show the composer at his most magically evocative, the music making engagingly combines refinement and warmth. The *Nursery suite* is strikingly well characterized and with first-class digital sound this is highly recommendable. Much of this music is delicately scored, and on CD it gains a great deal from the background silence and the refined detail at pianissimo level, while the dynamic range expands impressively when it needs to. There is just a hint of thinness in the upper string timbre, but this is more noticeable on the otherwise excellent chrome tape.

Serenade for strings in E min., Op. 20
(*) ASV Dig. **CDDCA 518; DCA/*ZCDCA* 518 [id.]. ASMF, Sir Neville Marriner – TIPPETT: *Fantasia concertante***; VAUGHAN-WILLIAMS: *Lark ascending* etc.**(*)

Sir Neville Marriner's recording of the *Serenade*, for ASV, offers well-defined and cleanly focused sound; perhaps it is just a little too 'present' and forward, though not unreasonably so. The performance adds nothing to his earlier recording on Argo, made in the late 1960s, which generates greater atmosphere (see above). Choice will doubtless be governed by the coupling required.

Symphony No. 1 in A flat, Op. 55.
*** Ph. Dig. **416 612-2**; 416 612-1/*4* [id.]. RPO, André Previn.
*** HMV **CDC 747204-2** [id.]; ASD/*TC-ASD* 3330. LPO, Boult.
*** RCA Dig. RL/*RK* 70748. BBC SO, Sir Colin Davis.
(M) ** EMI EMX 41 2084-1/*4*. Philh. O, Barbirolli.

Previn's version, first of a projected Elgar series, finds the conductor as idiomatic and understanding as he is in Walton and Vaughan Williams. His view of the first movement is spacious, with moulding of phrase and lifting of rhythm beautifully judged, to bring natural flexibility within a strongly controlled structure, steadier than usual in basic tempo. Previn's espressivo style tends towards accelerando rather than tenuto, towards fractional anticipation rather than hesitation, which makes for alert allegros and a slow movement that is warm but not self-indulgent. The syncopations of the scherzo/march theme have an almost jazzy swagger, and the reading is crowned by a flowing account of the finale. There Previn confirms his ability to point Elgarian climaxes with the necessary heart-tug, above all in the lovely passage where the main theme is augmented in minims on high violins, here achingly beautiful, neither too reticent nor too heavy-handed. The Philips sound is more refined and less beefy than the typical Elgar sound from EMI, but there is no lack of richness or bite. Particularly on CD, it is outstandingly full and open, but the chrome cassette too is splendidly managed and is most satisfying in its excellent body, range and definition.

Boult clearly presents the *First Symphony* as a counterpart to the *Second*, with hints of reflective nostalgia amid the triumph. Until this final version, made when Sir Adrian was eighty-seven, his recordings of the *First* had been among his less riveting Elgar performances. But the HMV disc, recorded with a suitable opulence, contains a radiantly beautiful performance, with no extreme tempi, richly spaced in the first movement, invigorating in the syncopated march rhythms of the scherzo, and similarly bouncing in the Brahmsian rhythms of the finale. Most clearly distinctive is the lovely slow movement, presented as a seamless flow of melody, faster, less 'inner' than with Previn, and above all glowing with untroubled sweetness. The CD is announced as we go to press. The cassette is rich and full-blooded, but needs a high-level replay to bring out the full detail and impact.

The lyrical spontaneity of Davis's version with the BBC Symphony Orchestra is very winning, an evocatively atmospheric live recording made at the Royal Albert Hall during a Concertaid event in May 1985. Live recording conditions evidently relaxed Davis to give a beautifully paced performance which is warmer in its expressiveness than his usual studio performances. Though in the finale ensemble is not as crisp as earlier and audience noises intrude in all four movements, this is persuasive in a way hard to achieve without an audience. The recording, though a little recessed, brings out the distinctive acoustic of the hall with a real Elgarian rasp on trombones. There is an excellent chrome cassette.

Barbirolli's 1963 recording still sounds well, not seriously dated, as the original recording had plenty of amplitude. It is a characteristically subjective reading, obviously deeply felt, but Barbirolli's tempi are controversial; apart from the very slow speed for the slow movement, there is a hint of heaviness in the first movement too, where after the march introduction the music should surge along. There is a good cassette, although the upper range is slightly restricted.

Still recommended: Vernon Handley's LPO version, beautifully paced, with the Elgar sound gloriously captured by the EMI engineers, remains a fine alternative choice on both LP and cassette, even making no allowances for price (CfP CFP/*TC-CFP* 40331).

Symphony No. 2 in E flat, Op. 63.

(*) HMV **CDC 747 299-2 [id.]. EL 270147-1/*4* [Ang. DS/*4DS* 38020]. Philh. O, Haitink.

Bernard Haitink gives Elgar's *Second Symphony* its CD début, and many Elgarians will want to make its acquaintance, even though the reading is controversial and the CD sound just a little disappointing. There is no doubt that he produces some altogether wonderful playing from the Philharmonia Orchestra and also offers valuable and fresh insights. There are many details to relish and beauties to discover – but there are also many wayward touches that fail to convince entirely on repeated hearing. Basically it is a straight, measured view, far from idiomatically Elgarian but always illuminating and often refreshing. It is a reading which clearly relates Elgar to Richard Strauss on the one hand but, more unexpectedly and more significantly, to Bruckner on the other. The way that Haitink keeps his eye on the culminating moment of climax with slow, steady speeds brings a very Brucknerian feeling to much of this music, and the control of transition passages has Brucknerian raptness. Elgarians will miss some of the usual spring in the 12/8 compound time of the first movement; the digital recording, more analytical and less full-blooded than one expects of Elgar sound from this source, adds to the unexpectedness of the performance. But for many, if not for dedicated Elgarians, it will be a revelation in its strength and lack of self-indulgence. As so often, the CD emphasizes the character of the recording, and the ear notices the more readily that the sound of the strings (middle and upper) is not as expansively opulent as expected, especially bearing in mind that the balance engineer was Christopher Parker, who has few peers in this repertoire.

Still recommended: For most collectors, Vernon Handley's outstanding LPO version, with its superb sense of Elgarian ebb and flow, makes an obvious first choice. Like his version of the *First*, this would be highly competitive at full price; as a bargain, there are few issues to match it (CfP CFP/*TC-CFP* 40350). Nevertheless, Boult's recording with the same orchestra (his fifth) is richly satisfying and, like Handley's, is splendidly recorded on both disc and cassette (ASD/*TC-ASD* 3266 [Ang. S 37218]).

Variations on an original theme (Enigma), Op. 36.

(M) ** Ph. Seq. 412 005-1/*4*. LPO, Haitink – BRAHMS: *St Anthony variations.****

Enigma variations; Crown of India: March of the Mogul Emperors; Pomp and circumstance marches Nos 1 and 2.
* DG Dig. **413 490-2**; 2532/*3302* 067 [id.]. BBC SO, Bernstein.

(i) *Enigma variations;* (ii) *Pomp and circumstance marches Nos 1 and 3.*
(B) *** DG Walkman *413 852-4* [id.]. (i) LSO, Jochum; (ii) RPO, Del Mar – HOLST: *Planets.****

The Walkman issue is an extraordinary bargain in combining Steinberg's exciting and sumptuously recorded complete set of the Holst *Planets* with Eugen Jochum's inspirational reading of *Enigma*, and – if that was not already remarkable value – adding as a bonus two of Del Mar's extremely spirited *Pomp and circumstance marches*. When Jochum recorded *Enigma* in 1975, he had not conducted it for several decades, but his thoughtful insight, in fresh study, produced an outstanding reading, consistently satisfying. The key to the whole work as Jochum sees it is *Nimrod*. Like others – including Elgar himself – Jochum sets a very slow *adagio* at the start, slower than the metronome marking in the score; unlike others, he maintains that measured tempo and, with the subtlest gradations, builds an even bigger, nobler climax than you find in *accelerando* readings. It is like a Bruckner slow movement in microcosm, around which revolve the other variations, all of them delicately detailed, with a natural feeling for Elgarian rubato. The finale has a degree of restraint in its nobility, no vulgarity whatever. The playing of the LSO and the recording match the strength and refinement of the performance. The chrome-tape transfer is not made at the highest level, but the sound does not seem to suffer.

Haitink's reading, thoughtfully direct and beautifully played, yet lacks the dynamism which welds the *Variations* into a unity. The blood never tingles, and clearly Haitink is much more naturally at home in the coupled Brahms *Variations*. The sound is good, fresher and livelier than the original issue on disc and tape alike.

Bernstein's is quite the most perverse reading of *Enigma* ever recorded, and most listeners will fail to respond to its outrageous self-indulgence – not least in *Nimrod*, which is dragged out to almost unimaginable lengths. Though wilful, Bernstein is always passionate, and with good playing and recording he may attract those who want to hear a fresh view or who enjoyed the television programme made at the time of the recording. Best of all are the fill-ups, bold and swaggering. The CD is impressive in its presence; but few Elgarians are likely to find the performance of the main work the kind that they can live with.

Still recommended: Barbirolli's reading of *Enigma* is special. The conductor was himself a cellist and, especially in the variations where the strings are given their full head, the music could have no more eloquent advocate. HMV's mid-priced Greensleeves reissue also finds room both for his inspired account of the *Introduction and allegro for strings* and for Elgar's richly painted canvas of Edwardian London, *Cockaigne*, which has a fine sweep and a Londoner's warmth of affection in Barbirolli's hands (ESD/*TC-ESD* 7169). This splendid record and its fine cassette equivalent were given a Rosette in our last edition. For some unaccountable reason, the American domestic equivalent, in Angel's Red Line series, omits the *Introduction and allegro* (RL/*4RL* 32127).

CHAMBER AND INSTRUMENTAL MUSIC

Music for wind quintet: *Adagio cantabile* (*Mrs Winslow's soothing syrup*); *Andante con variazione* (*Evesham Andante*); *4 Dances; Harmony music Nos 1–5; 6 Promenades.*
(M) ** Chan. CBR/*CBT* 1014–5. Athena Ens.

As a budding musician, playing not only the violin but also the bassoon, Elgar wrote a quantity of brief, lightweight pieces in a traditional style for himself and four other wind-players to perform. He called it 'Shed Music'; though there are few real signs of the Elgar style to come, the energy and inventiveness are very winning, particularly when (as here) the pieces – often with comic names – are treated to bright and lively performances. Excellent recording, with the cassettes in the demonstration class.

(i) *Piano quintet in A min., Op. 84;* (ii) *Wood magic* (spoken anthology about Elgar's music): excerpts (including Binyon: *The Fourth of August; The burning of leaves*).
*** Mer. **ECD 84082**; E 77082 [id.]. (i) Bingham, Medici Qt; (ii) Pasco and Leigh-Hunt (narrators).

The passion of the Medici performance comes out most strikingly in the central *Adagio*, taken daringly slowly with deliberately warm expressiveness. This is the movement which, in spite of the harmonic simplicity of the main theme, comes closest to earlier Elgar in the grandeur of the melody. In the outer movements too, the Medici players, with Bingham an understanding partner, perform with the red-blooded attack which earlier made their EMI records of Janáček and Haydn so enjoyable. Well-balanced recording set against an open but intimate acoustic. *Wood magic*, the phrase which Elgar's wife used for his late chamber music, is an entertainment using words as well as Elgar's music. Here, as a brief sample, before the first movement of the *Quintet*, Richard Pasco and Barbara Leigh-Hunt recite two poems by Laurence Binyon.

String quartet in E min., Op. 83.
*** ASV Dig. DCA/*ZCDCA* 526 [id.]. Brodsky Quartet – DELIUS: *Quartet.****

The young players of the Brodsky Quartet take a weightier view than usual of the central, interlude-like slow movement of Elgar's still-neglected *Quartet*, but with the ease and warmth of their playing amply justify it. The power of the outer movements, too, gives the lie to the idea of this as a lesser work than the two other chamber works, the *Piano quintet* and the *Violin sonata*, which Elgar also wrote at the very end of his creative career, not long before his wife died. First-rate recording, with an excellent matching cassette.

Violin sonata in E min., Op. 82.
(*) ASV Dig. DCA/*ZCDCA* 548 [id.]. McAslan, Blakely – WALTON: *Sonata.*(*)

Violin sonata in E min., Op. 82; Canto popolare; Chanson de matin; Chanson de nuit, Op. 15/1 and 2; Mot d'amour, Op. 13/1; Salut d'amour, Op. 12; Sospiri, Op. 70; 6 Easy pieces in the first position.
*** Chan. Dig. **CHAN 8380**; ABRD/*ABTD* 1099 [id.]. Nigel Kennedy, Peter Pettinger.

At the start of the *Sonata*, Kennedy establishes a concerto-like scale, which he then reinforces in a fiery, volatile reading of the first movement, rich and biting in its bravura. The elusive slow movement, *Romance*, inspired by a sinister clump of dead trees near Elgar's Sussex home, is sharply rhythmic in its weird Spanishry, while in the finale Kennedy colours the tone seductively. This is a warmer, more spontaneous-sounding performance than Hugh Bean's purer, more detached account on HMV. For coupling, Kennedy has a delightful collection of shorter pieces, not just *Salut d'amour* and *Chanson de matin* but such rare chips off the master's bench as the *Six very easy pieces in the first position*, written for a favourite niece who was learning the violin. Even in their simplicity Kennedy finds genuine Elgar magic, and he is matched beautifully throughout the record by his understanding piano partner, Peter Pettinger. The recording is excellent, even more vivid and realistic in its CD version. The chrome cassette, too, is in the demonstration class.

Though Lorraine McAslan cannot match the virtuoso command and warmth of tone of Nigel Kennedy's Chandos recording of the *Sonata*, hers is an impressive and warm-hearted version, full of natural imagination, helped by the incisive playing of John Blakely. Good, forward recording which gives the violin tone less bloom than it might.

Organ sonata in G min., Op. 28.
*** ASV ALH/*ZCALH* 958 [id.]. Jennifer Bate (Royal Albert Hall organ) – SCHUMANN: *Four sketches.****

The Royal Albert Hall organ is just the instrument for Elgar's early *Sonata*, a richly enjoyable piece, full of characteristic ideas, not least the grand opening. Jennifer Bate plays with all the necessary flair, with her rubato only occasionally sounding unidiomatic, bringing out the dramatic contrasts of dynamic encouraged by this vast organ in its massive setting – emphasized by its special facility of causing the sound image to recede in quieter passages. The analogue recording provides good detail against the warm atmosphere, and there is a matching cassette.

VOCAL MUSIC

The Black Knight (symphony for chorus and orchestra); Part-songs: *Fly singing bird; The snow; Spanish serenade.*
*** HMV Dig. EL 270157-1/*4*. Liverpool PO Ch., Royal Liverpool PO, Groves.

The Black Knight was Elgar's first big choral work, written just after his marriage to Alice, the woman who effectively ensured that Elgar could, against the odds, become a great composer. The happiness and confidence of the writing is what comes over with winning freshness, even though the Elgarian must inevitably miss the deeper, darker, more melancholy overtones of his later, greater music. The subject, a tale of chivalry and a royal feast which brings disaster, is strikingly like that of Mahler's almost contemporary *Das klagende Lied*, but neurotic tensions are here far distant. Sir Charles Groves conducts a strong, fresh performance, not always perfectly polished in its ensemble but with bright, enthusiastic singing from the chorus. The three part-songs from the same period make an apt and attractive coupling. Clear, full recording which copes well with large forces. The tape transfer is well managed, with well-focused choral sound, and losing only a little of the extreme upper range.

The Dream of Gerontius, Op. 38.
❀ *** HMV SLS/*TC-SLS* 987 (2). Watts, Gedda, Lloyd, Alldis Ch., New Philh. O, Boult.

Sir Adrian Boult provided here the performance of *The Dream of Gerontius* for which Elgarians had waited since the advent of stereo recording. Listening to this wonderful set, one feels that this is the culmination of a long history of partial or complete recordings of this great masterpiece which stretches far back into the days of acoustic 78 r.p.m. discs. Boult's total dedication is matched by a sense both of wonder and of drama. The spiritual feeling is intense, but the human qualities of the narrative are fully realized, and the glorious closing pages are so beautiful that Elgar's vision is made to become one of the most unforgettable moments in all musical literature. Boult's unexpected choice of Nicolai Gedda in the role of Gerontius brings a new dimension to this characterization, which is perfectly matched by Helen Watts as the Angel. The dialogues between the two have a natural spontaneity as Gerontius's questions and doubts find a response which is at once gently understanding and nobly authoritative. It is a fascinating vocal partnership, and it is matched by the commanding manner which Robert Lloyd finds for both his roles. The orchestral playing is always responsive and often, like the choral singing, very beautiful. The lovely wind playing at the opening of Part 2 is matched by the luminosity of tone of the choral pianissimos, while the dramatic passages bring splendid incisiveness and bold assurance from the singers. The recording is very fine, and we look forward to the promised CD issue. The work is just too long to fit on a single CD and we understand it is to be coupled with *The Music Makers*.

(i) *The Music Makers, Op. 69. 3 Bavarian dances, Op. 27; Chanson de matin; Chanson de nuit, Op. 15/1–2; The Wand of Youth Suites Nos 1–2, Op. 1a–1b.*
(B) **(*) HMV *TCC2-POR 54291.* (i) Dame Janet Baker, LPO, Ch.; LPO, Boult.

Elgar's long-neglected cantata sets the Shaughnessy poem of the same name. It was a mature work, written soon after the *Symphonies* and *Violin concerto*, and is full of warm, attractive writing for both voices and orchestra. But it is some measure of the musical material that the passages which stand out are those where Elgar used themes from his earlier works. If only the whole piece lived up to the uninhibited choral setting of the *Nimrod* variation from *Enigma*, it would be another Elgar masterpiece. As it is, there are enough moments of rich expansiveness to make it essential for any Elgarian to hear, particularly as understanding a performance as this. Dame Janet Baker sings with dedicated mastery, though unfortunately her example is not always matched by the comparatively dull-sounding choir. It was a happy idea to include *The Music Makers* in EMI's 'Portrait of the Artist' series and place it complete on one side of an extended-length tape. The sound is good, losing only a little of the upper range (the chorus has rather more bite on disc). But to couple this with much slighter music, however attractively performed, is more controversial. Even so, Boult's performances of the *Wand of Youth suites* are well worth having, for they capture both the innocence and the fragile charm of this music. The orchestral playing is first rate and the sound is good, though not as transparent as the Chandos digital version (see above). The cassette, like the others in this series, offers no information whatsoever about the music, except titles and details of performers.

Sea Pictures (song cycle), *Op. 37.*
❀ *** HMV **CDC 747329-2** [id.]; ASD/*TC-ASD* 655 [(d.) Ang. S 36796]. Dame Janet Baker, LSO, Barbirolli – *Cello concerto.**** ❀

Sea Pictures hardly matches the mature inspiration of the *Cello concerto* with which it is coupled on HMV, but it is heartwarming here none the less. Like du Pré, Baker is an artist who has the power to convey on record the vividness of a live performance. With the help of Barbirolli she makes the cycle far more convincing than it usually seems, with words that are often trite clothed in music that seems to transform them. On CD, the voice is caught with extra bloom, and the beauty of Elgar's orchestration is enhanced by the subtle added definition.

Enescu, Georges (1881–1955)

Poème roumain, Op. 1; Roumanian rhapsodies, Op. 11/1 and 2.
** Erato Dig. NUM 75179 [id.]. Monte Carlo PO, Foster.

Roumanian rhapsody No. 1.
ℭ **(*) RCA Dig. **RCD 14439** [id.]. Dallas SO, Mata (with Concert.**(*) ℭ)

For the general musical public, Georges Enescu seems fated to remain a one-work composer, like Paul Dukas with his *Sorcerer's apprentice*. Enescu's chimerical *First Roumanian rhapsody* combines a string of glowing folk-derived melodies with glittering scoring, to make it the finest genre piece of its kind in laminating Eastern gypsy influences under a bourgeois orchestral veneer. The Dallas performance, with the help of superbly lustrous digital sound, brings out all the colour and much of the sparkle, although Mata does not quite find the flair and exhilaration in the closing pages which distinguish the best analogue versions (notably those by Dorati and Previn). But the RCA compact disc is truly demonstration-worthy in its natural vividness.

The *Second Rhapsody*, although still attractive, is not so indelible in its melodies as the *First*. The *Poème roumain* (Enescu's Op. 1), given by Lawrence Foster, it would seem, in its original form, is more ambitious in scale, but has something of the same nationalist colour and appeal. Not essential Enescu, perhaps, but worth investigating. The music is all well served by the Monte Carlo orchestra, and given the benefit of decent recorded sound, if not quite so spectacular as the RCA recording of *Rhapsody No. 1*.

Suites for orchestra Nos 1, Op. 9; 2 in C, Op. 20.
** Erato Dig. NUM/*MCE* 75118 [id.]. Monte Carlo PO, Foster.

Georges Enescu was an all-round musician, a great violinist, a hardly less fine pianist and conductor, and, it is argued, a composer of much greater range and imagination than emerges from the familiar *Rhapsodies*. Be that as it may, the first two of his three *Suites* are good without being in the very first rank: they are expertly laid out for the orchestra and have a charm and appeal that ought to ensure them a wider following than they have. Enescu conducted the première of the *First* when he was only twenty-one, and its successor followed more than a dozen years later in 1915. The idiom is overtly nationalist, though in the *Second* there is something of the delicacy of Reger in the *Gigue*. The *Air* is a richly imaginative piece which shows that the example of such contemporaries as Debussy, Strauss and Florent Schmitt was not lost on him. Good rather than distinguished playing from the Monte Carlo orchestra under Lawrence Foster, and eminently acceptable recording. However, this is worth a recommendation for the sake of the interesting repertoire.

7 Chansons de Clément Marot.
*** Unicorn Dig. **DKPCD 9035**; DKP/*DKPC* 9035 [id.]. Sarah Walker, Roger Vignoles – DEBUSSY: *Songs****; ROUSSEL: *Songs.***(*)

The set of Enescu songs, written in 1908, make a rare, attractive and apt addition to Sarah Walker's recital of French song. As a Rumanian working largely in Paris, Enescu was thinking very much in a French idiom, charming and witty as well as sweetly romantic. Ideal accompaniments and excellent recording, particularly vivid on CD.

Erkel, Ferenc (1810–93)

Hunyadi László (opera): complete.
*** Hung. **HCD 12581/3** [id.]. Gulyás, Sass, Molnár, Dénes, Sólyom-Nagy, Gáti, Hungarian People's Army Male Ch., Hungarian State Op. Ch. and O, Kovács.

Hunyadi László is a patriotic piece which, in 1844 at its first performance, aroused the sort of nationalistic fervour in Hungary that Verdi inspired in Italy with *Nabucco*. The end of Act I even brings a rousing chorus which, like *Va pensiero* in *Nabucco*, has all the qualities of a pop tune. Like the much later Erkel opera, *Bank ban*, *Hunyadi László* has never been out of the repertory in Hungary, and this live recording makes one understand why. Unlike its predecessor in the Hungaroton lists, it goes back to the original score instead of the corrupt reworking devised in the 1930s. Erkel's use of national music may not be as strikingly colourful as Smetana's in Czechoslovakia or Glinka's in Russia – both comparable figures – but the flavour is both distinctive and attractive, strongly illustrating a red-blooded story. Janos Kovács conducts with a vigour suggesting long experience of this work in the opera house. Denes Gulyás is a heroic, heady-toned hero, while Andras Molnár is equally effective as the villainous king, surprisingly another tenor role. Sylvia Sass is excellent as the hero's mother, in this version allowed to sing the beautiful prayer just before Laszlo's execution, excised from the earlier recording. First-rate sound. An excellent, unusual set, full of strong ideas, making easy listening.

Falla, Manuel de (1876–1946)

El amor brujo; The Three-cornered hat (ballet): complete.
❀ Ͼ *** Decca Dig. **410 008-2**; SXDL/*KSXDC* 7560 [Lon. LDR/5- 71060]. Boky, Tourangeau, Montreal SO, Dutoit.

El amor brujo: Ritual fire dance (only); *The Three-cornered hat* (ballet): complete.
*** Ph. Dig. **411 046-2**; 6514/*7337* 281 [id.]. Von Stade, Pittsburgh SO, Previn.

The Three-cornered hat (ballet): complete; *La vida breve: Interlude and dance*.
** Decca **414 032-2** [id.]; Contour CC/*CCTC* 7560. Berganza, SRO, Ansermet.

Dutoit provides the ideal and very generous coupling of Falla's two popular and colourful ballets, each complete with vocal parts. Few more atmospheric records have ever been made and, particularly in the compact disc version, the very opening, with the mezzo-soprano slightly distanced, with castanets, cries of *'Olé!'* and insistent timpani, is immediately involving. Performances are not just colourful and brilliantly played, they have an idiomatic feeling in their degree of flexibility over phrasing and rhythm. The ideal instance comes in the tango-like seven-in-a-bar rhythms of the *Pantomime* section of *El amor brujo* which is lusciously seductive. The sound is among the most vivid ever, whatever the format, but compact disc easily takes priority in its tangibility.

Previn's crisp and refreshing view of *The Three-cornered hat* provides a strong contrast with the sensuously beautiful Dutoit version. In its clarity and sharpness of rhythm it underlines the point that this Diaghilev ballet followed in the line of those of Stravinsky. The difference of approach is brought out at the very start, when von Stade's mezzo is presented very close, not distanced at all. Next to the Decca issue, the Philips fill-up is ungenerous, only a single item from *El amor brujo* instead of the whole ballet. Excellently clean-cut recording, although the relatively low-level chrome cassette has not quite the sparkle of the LP.

In *The Three-cornered hat* the Suisse Romande Orchestra play with vigour and spirit for Ansermet: even the occasional roughness of detail seems appropriate, and there is no lack of vividness. Berganza is a characterful soloist. The coupling is not generous. With vintage Decca sound from the 1960s, this seems competitive at bargain price on its Contour LP reissue. The compact disc, however, for all its added definition (and, because the recording is resonant, the gain is more marginal than usual), is surely over-priced and cannot possibly stand up to the competition from Dutoit on the same label.

Nights in the gardens of Spain.

ℭ *** Decca Dig. **410 289-2**; 410 289-1/*4* [id.]. De Larrocha, LPO, Frühbeck de Burgos – TURINA: *Rapsodia Sinfónica**** (with ALBÉNIZ: *Rapsodia española****).

(B) **(*) DG Walkman *413 156-4*. Margrit Weber, Bav. RSO, Kubelik – RODRIGO: *Concierto serenata* etc.**

** Ph. **416 443-2** [id.]. Clara Haskil, LOP, Markevitch – CHOPIN: *Concerto No. 2.***

Alicia de Larrocha has recorded the work before for Decca, but her compact disc newest version – made in Walthamstow Town Hall – has the advantage of superb digital sound, rich and lustrous, with refined detail. The piano image, although admirably tangible and truthful in timbre, is well forward, yet this allows the listener to relish the freshness and brilliance of the soloist's articulation in the work's latter sections. Miss Larrocha's playing has undoubted poetry and this beguiling and atmospheric performance makes for a very desirable issue indeed. There is a thoughtful, improvisatory quality about the reading (which has less thrust than Soriano's – see below) and the closing pages, consciously moulded, are particularly beautiful.

The DG recording is exceptionally vivid, with the performers going all out to bring the utmost grip and excitement to the score. With Margrit Weber giving a brilliant account of the solo part, particularly in the latter movements, the effect is both sparkling and exhilarating. A little of the fragrant atmosphere is lost, particularly in the opening section (where both De Larrocha and Soriano are gentler), but the performance, with its strong sense of drama, is certainly not without evocative qualities. This generously full Walkman cassette is in the main devoted to the music of Rodrigo, and the three coupled recordings are of mixed appeal, but those wanting Rodrigo's *Concierto serenata* for harp should not be disappointed with the Falla.

There is no lack of atmosphere in Clara Haskil's account with Markevitch, and the 1960 recording still sounds fresh and vivid, if not very transparent. This version would seem to be mainly of interest to admirers of the pianist, although the performance is by no means to be dismissed. At the same price, however, one can have De Larrocha's beautiful Decca CD.

(i; ii) *Nights in the gardens of Spain;* (ii) *El amor brujo: Ritual fire dance.* (iii; iv) *The Three-cornered hat* (ballet): complete; (iii; v) *La vida breve:* excerpts.
(B) **(*) HMV *TCC2-POR 154591-9.* (i) Soriano, (ii) Paris Conservatoire O, (iii) Los Angeles, (iv) Philh. O, (v) Higuero, Moreno, Ch., Nat. O of Spain; all cond. Frühbeck de Burgos.

An outstanding double-length tape collection, let down only by the (total) lack of provision of back-up documentation. It seems perverse to include a fascinating selection of excerpts from *La vida breve* and offer no information whatsoever about the scenario. Soriano gives a first-class account of the solo part in *Nights in the gardens of Spain* and Frühbeck de Burgos accompanies with a natural feeling for the subtleties of Falla's scoring. Apart from the opening *'Olés'* (which were recorded separately and dubbed on), the performance of the complete *Three-cornered hat* is highly recommendable, combining warmth with high spirits. Victoria de los Angeles does not sound quite earthy enough, but she sings splendidly and the sound is consistently vivid. In the attractive *Vida breve* excerpts there is demonstration presence.

Fantasia baetica.
** ASV ALH/*ZCALH* 949 [id.]. Alma Petchersky (piano) – ALBÉNIZ: *Suite española* **(*); GRANADOS: *Allegro di concierto.* **

Falla's masterly *Fantasia baetica* calls for more dramatic fire and projection than Alma Petchersky commands. But she is a musical and neat player, and the recording is far from unacceptable. There is a good cassette, clear and well balanced.

La vida breve (opera): complete.
(M) **(*) DG 410 936-1 [id.]. Berganza, Nafé, Carreras, LSO, Navarra.

La vida breve is a kind of Spanish *Cavalleria Rusticana* without the melodrama and with a conspicuously weak plot. The heroine dies of a broken heart when her lover deserts her for another, and it is hard to make her role sound convincing. Teresa Berganza may not have the light-of-eye expressiveness of her compatriot Victoria de los Angeles, who made two earlier recordings, but hers is a strong, earthy account which helps to compensate for Falla's dramatic weaknesses; and it is good to have so fine a singer as José Carreras in the relatively small tenor role of Paco. Reliant as the piece is on atmosphere above all, it makes an excellent subject for recording, and with vivid performances from the LSO and Ambrosian Singers, idiomatically directed, the result here is a convincing success. Recording balance is not always ideal, or consistent, but generally this is well worth exploring. Originally issued (in 1978) on three sides, it is now offered on two – about an hour of music. Good value at medium price. There is no tape.

Fauré, Gabriel (1845–1924)

Caligula, Op. 52; Les Djinns, Op. 12; Masques et bergamasques, Op. 112; Pavane, Op. 50; Pelléas et Mélisande, Op. 80; Pénélope: Prélude; Shylock, Op. 57.

(B) *** HMV *TCC2-POR 154596-9*. Bourbon Vocal Ens., Toulouse Capitole O, Plasson.

Although Fauré's most deeply characteristic thoughts are intimate rather than public, and his most natural outlets are the mélodie, chamber music and the piano, this set of his orchestral music nevertheless contains much that is highly rewarding. It includes the delightful *Masques et bergamasques* and the *Pelléas et Mélisande* and *Shylock* music as well as such rarities as *Les Djinns* and *Caligula*. The Orchestre du Capitole de Toulouse may lack the finesse and bloom of the leading Parisian orchestras, but Michel Plasson gets an alert and spirited response and is blessed with very decent orchestral sound. He shows a genuine feeling for the Fauréan sensibility, and the fine-spun lyricism of the *Nocturne* from *Shylock* is well conveyed. The collection derived from a set of three LPs (now deleted) which includes all Fauré's orchestral music. But by omitting the concertante works, EMI have been able to transfer the rest of Michel Plasson's Fauré anthology on to one double-length XDR ferric tape, which copes well with the warm resonance of the recording. Indeed the sound is consistently beautiful, catching voices as well as orchestra quite naturally and losing only a little of the upper range, although, with a slight drop in level, definition in the choral writing is slightly less clear on side two. Nevertheless this is highly rewarding music, and tape collectors should find this a worthwhile investment.

Élégie (for cello and orchestra), *Op. 24.*

*** Decca Dig. **CD 414 387-2**; 414 387-1/*4* [id.]. Harrell, Berlin RSO, Chailly – LALO: *Concerto*; SAINT-SAENS: *Cello concerto No. 2.****

A most distinguished performance of Fauré's *Elégie*, played with eloquence and restraint by Lynn Harrell and admirably accompanied by Chailly. The recording is extremely fine, and especially believable in its CD format. Fauré was pupil and friend of Saint-Saëns, and the coupling with his little-known *Second Cello concerto* is most apt.

(i) *Fantaisie for flute and orchestra, Op. 79* (orch. Aubert); *Masques et bergamasques, Op. 112; Pavane, Op. 50; Pelléas et Mélisande: suite, Op. 80.*
** Argo Dig. **410 552-2**; ZRDL/*KZRDC* 1003 [id.]. (i) Bennett; ASMF, Marriner.

This ASMF Fauré recital scores over its rivals in having excellent sound; detail is well defined and there is excellent body. The recording is most impressive on the compact disc version. Were the performances in quite the same league, this would be an indispensable issue for all lovers of the French composer. Not that the playing is second rate or routine, and William Bennett is most sensitive in the *Fantaisie*, but there could be greater freshness and charm. There is a chrome cassette which matches the LP very closely.

Pelléas et Mélisande: suite, Op. 80.
** Telarc Dig. **CD 80084** [id.]. Atlanta SO, Shaw – BERLIOZ: *Nuits d'été.***
(B) ** CBS DC 40143 (2). New Philh. O, Andrew Davis – GRIEG: *Peer Gynt; Songs;* PROKOFIEV: *Cinderella.***

Beautifully recorded in clear, natural sound, Robert Shaw and the Atlanta orchestra give a refined, beautifully shaped performance of Fauré's tenderly atmospheric suite, but it makes an odd and rather ungenerous coupling for the similarly reticent account of the Berlioz song-cycle.

Andrew Davis's performance with the New Philharmonia Orchestra is also freshly responsive and the recording is good. If the couplings are of interest, this two-disc CBS set is very reasonably priced.

Élégie, Op. 24; Papillon, Op. 77; Romance, Op. 69 (for cello and piano).
** ASV Dig. DCA/*DCDCA* 522 [id.]. Colin Carr, Francis Grier – DEBUSSY: *Sonata;* FRANCK: *Sonata.***

These three Fauré pieces make an attractive coupling for the more substantial sonatas on Carr's record of French cello music. The *Romance* was originally written for cello and organ, while *Papillon* was designed expressly as a contrasting companion piece for the celebrated *Élégie*, light and Mendelssohnian. The digital recording is truthful, but the ambience is rather dry. Cassette and disc are very closely matched.

Piano quartets Nos 1 in C min., Op. 15; 2 in G min., Op. 45.
❀ *** Hyp. **CDA 66166**; A/*KA* 66166 [id.]. Domus.
*** CRD Dig. **CRD 3403**; CRD 1103/*CRDC 4103* [id.]. Ian Brown, Nash Ens.

Lovely playing from all concerned in this immensely civilized music. Domus have the intimacy that this repertoire calls for, and their performances have the requisite lightness of touch and subtlety. Their nimble and sensitive pianist, Susan Tomes, can hold her own in the most exalted company (including Jean-Philippe Collard whose aristocratic accounts of these quartets both on record and in the concert hall resonate in the memory). This is really first-class chamber music playing, without any of the public concert-hall projection that is so prevalent nowadays. Their performances have just the right sense of scale and grasp of tempi. The recording is excellent, too, though the balance is a little close, but the sound is not airless. Some machines may cope less well than others with this; in any event, the playing is of such compelling quality that this qualification is of small account. The (iron-oxide) cassette is acceptable. Inner detail is less clearly defined than on disc, but is better on side two than on side one.

The Nash Ensemble on CRD appear to be recorded in a more open acoustic than the Domus on Hyperion and their performance is splendidly projected. Their readings are perhaps less inward and searching than the Hyperion team's, but they do not fall short of excellence, and the clarity and presence of the recording very much tell in its favour. The slow movement of the *G minor*, Op. 45, is played with particular eloquence and sensitivity, and the pianist, Ian Brown, is excellent throughout. A three-star issue then, in all three formats, but the wonderfully responsive Domus performance has something special which gives it preference.

Violin sonatas Nos 1 in A, Op. 13; 2 in E min., Op. 108.
❀ (M) *** Ph. 412 397-1/*4*. Arthur Grumiaux, Paul Crossley.

Four decades separate the two Fauré sonatas and they make a perfect coupling. The *First* is a richly melodious piece which, strangely enough, precedes the César Franck sonata by a dozen or so years, while the *E minor* was written in the same year as Debussy's (1917). They are immensely refined and rewarding pieces, with strange stylistic affinities and disparities: the second movement of the *E minor* actually uses a theme intended for a symphony that Fauré had discarded more than thirty years earlier. Although they have been coupled before (by Barbizet and Ferras, and Gallois-Montbrun and Hubeau), they have never been so beautifully played or recorded as on the Philips issue. Indeed, this is a model of its kind: there is perfect rapport between the two artists, and both seem totally dedicated to and captivated by Fauré's muse. Moreover, they are accorded recorded quality that is little short of superb. The two artists sound as if they are in the living-room; the acoustic is warm, lively and well balanced. The *Second* is not so readily accessible as the *First*, but it is difficult to imagine more persuasive advocacy than this. Reissued on Philips's 'Musica da camera' at mid-price, with an immaculately transferred equivalent cassette, this coupling is more desirable than ever. Fauré is not and never will be a popular composer, and it is doubtful whether this record will survive the lifetime of this *Guide*, so do not hesitate.

Barcarolles Nos 1–13 (complete).
**(*) CRD CRD 1122/*CRDC 4122* [id.]. Paul Crossley.

The *Barcarolles* encompass the best part of Fauré's creative life; the first dates from the 1880s and the last, Op. 116, comes from 1921. Paul Crossley is a fine interpreter of the gentle yet powerful French master. He has an instinctive grasp of the subtleties of this repertoire and is fully equal to its shifting moods. The CRD version was made in the somewhat reverberant acoustic of Rosslyn Hill Chapel, and is more vivid than the 1971 EMI recording of Jean-Philippe Collard (2C 069 11328). Honours are pretty evenly divided between the two players; at times Collard appears the more subtle of the two, at others Crossley. Collard gauges the temper of *No. 7 in D minor* more naturally than his English rival, but elsewhere Crossley's aristocratic sensibility seems the more completely attuned to Fauré's world. Both will give pleasure and, if Collard's account is not displaced, the CRD is still a strong challenger. It has the advantage of an excellent chrome-tape equivalent which catches the full bloom of the piano timbre and loses only a fraction of the sharpness of focus.

Requiem, Op. 48.
*** Ph. Dig. **412 743-2**; 412 743-1/*4* [id.]. Popp, Estes, Leipzig R. Ch., Dresden State O, Sir Colin Davis.

Requiem, Op. 48; Cantique de Jean Racine, Op. 11.
*** Conifer Dig. **CDCFRA 122**; CFRA/*MCFRA* 122 [id.]. Ashton, Varcoe, Cambridge Singers, L. Sinfonia (members), Rutter.
(*) HMV Dig. **CDC 747317-2; EL 270168-1/*4* [Ang. DS/*4DS* 38252], Hendricks, Van Dam, Orfeon Donastiarra, Toulouse Capitole O, Plasson.
(M) **(*) EMI EMX 41 2057-1/*4*. Burrowes, Rayner Cook, CBSO and Ch., Frémaux.

Rutter's Conifer disc, which won the choral prize in the *Gramophone* record awards, 1985, brings a revelation in returning to Fauré's original chamber instrumentation without violins and with a quartet of divided violas and cellos. Rightly, Rutter includes the two extra movements which Fauré added for a performance in 1983, along with two horns to augment the small ensemble. The result, in a fresh, understanding performance under Rutter with first-rate Cambridge singers, has extra intensity from the intimacy of ensemble and, far from seeming too small in scale, the periodic dynamic contrasts come out all the more sharply. The soloists are rightly presented as part of the ensemble, not as stars, the boyish-sounding soprano of Caroline Ashton very apt. The CD gives extra precision to an already well-balanced recording.

Sir Colin Davis uses the familiar orchestral version and the Philips recording is very well balanced, with the chorus believably recessed in a glowing acoustic aura which does not cloud detail. The choral singing is both warm and refined, pianissimos serene, climaxes swelling out with a natural eloquence. Lucia Popp provides a touchingly gentle *Pié Jesu*, her innocence contrasting with Simon Estes' highly dramatic contribution, operatic in feeling and hardly apt in style. Nevertheless, overall this is a movingly expansive account, with the moulded choral line ever responsive to the text, and projecting strong expressive feeling in the *Sanctus* and *Libera me*. The closing *In paradisum* has lyrical warmth yet remains ethereal in atmosphere. This makes a satisfying CD alternative to Rutter, larger in scale and essentially spacious in conception; one's only real quibble concerns the absence of a fill-up for a recording lasting about 40 minutes. There is an excellent cassette.

Michel Plasson's performance is even broader than Davis's in its basic conception, yet it is also more volatile. At the very opening Plasson's articulation is bolder, essentially dramatic; throughout the contrasts of dynamic are highlighted. The choir sing beautifully and, if some of the gentler moments seem rather withdrawn, climaxes are certainly powerful, as on the words *Hosanna in excelsis* in the *Sanctus* and in the transition from the *Agnus Dei* to the *Libera me*. Even the *In paradisum* has surges rising above its usually placid surface, although its loveliness is unimpaired. The sound is both fresh and atmospheric, with the acoustic setting admirably managed by the engineers. There is a bonus in the inclusion of the *Cantique*, an early work dating from 1885, to which Plasson and his choir bring passionate advocacy.

Frémaux's EMI version is attractively atmospheric, the recording comparatively recessed. Frémaux has a moulded style which does not spill over in too much expressiveness, and there is a natural warmth about this performance that is highly persuasive. Norma Burrowes sings beautifully; her innocent manner is most engaging. On tape, the backward balance means that the focus is not quite so clear as on the LP; but both sound well, and this makes a good mid-priced recommendation, as the recording is modern.

Ferguson, Howard (born 1908)

(i) *Partita for 2 pianos, Op. 5b; Piano sonata in F min., Op. 8.*
*** Hyp. A 66130 [id.]. Howard Shelley, (i) Hilary MacNamara.

Written in memory of his teacher, Harold Samuel, Ferguson's *Sonata* is a dark, formidable piece in three substantial movements, here given a powerful, intense performance. Though Ferguson with rare restraint decided later in life that he would write no more, here his creative urge is never less than purposeful in a romantic sonata well constructed, with a style which, for all the echoes of Rachmaninov, is quite individual. The *Partita* in its four movements is set in a neoclassical mould – overture, courante, sarabande and gigue – but is in no sense shallow in its expression, a large-scale piece full of good ideas in which, for this two-piano version, Howard Shelley is joined by his wife, Hilary MacNamara. Excellent, committed performances and first-rate recording.

Ferrari, Benedetto (*c.* 1604–81)

Queste pungenti spine (*cantata*); *Pur ti miro, pur ti godo* (Final duet for Monteverdi: *L'Incoronazione di Poppea*).
* HM **HMC 901129** [id.]. Concerto Vocale – MONTEVERDI: *Madrigals.**

Benedetto Ferrari was a Venetian composer, playwright and theorbo player, best remembered for a handful of operas and his three books of *Musiche varie*. His *Queste pungenti spine* is a spiritual cantata which comes from the 1637 book, and is accompanied on this record by the final duet from *L'Incoronazione di Poppea*, which he is thought to have written. Listening to the one, it is difficult to imagine that he really did compose the other. The Monteverdi madrigals with which these Ferrari pieces are coupled are on a much higher level of inspiration, but the singing on this issue is not of the very first order.

Fiala, Josef (1754–1816)

Cor anglais concerto in E flat.
(M) *** Ph. 412 354-1/*4*. Holliger, ECO, Leppard – J. C. BACH: *Oboe concerto;* HUMMEL: *Introduction and variations.****

Joseph Fiala was himself an oboe player and was admired by Mozart as a musician. His *Cor anglais concerto* is small in scale but most appealing, with an engaging *Adagio cantabile*, lasting under three minutes, and a spiritedly elegant finale. Holliger plays it beautifully and is attentively accompanied and well recorded. He provides his own cadenza for the first movement.

Fossa, François de (1775–?)

Guitar quartets, Op. 19/1–3.
*** Chan. ABRD/*ABTD* 1109 [id.]. Simon Wynberg, Gabrieli Qt (members).

The repertoire for the guitar is not extensive; these quartets by the French amateur, François de Fossa, form a useful addition to it. He was born in France in 1775 but emigrated to Spain at the outbreak of the revolution, where he served with distinction as a civil servant and in the army. These quartets make a useful alternative to those of Boccherini, whom de Fossa served as a copyist. These are interesting pieces, well worth reviving, and contain many individual touches. They are beautifully played by Simon Wynberg and the Gabrielis, and pleasingly recorded. Recommended.

Foulds, John (1880–1939)

Dynamic triptych for piano and orchestra.
*** Lyr. SRCS 130 [id.]. Shelley, RPO, Handley – VAUGHAN WILLIAMS: *Piano concerto.****

John Foulds was working in Paris in the late 1920s when he wrote this ambitious concerto, and the profusion of memorable ideas, not always well disciplined, makes for an attractive piece, particularly so in the last of the three movements, *Dynamic rhythm*, with its extrovert references to Latin-American rhythms and the American musical. The first movement, *Dynamic mode*, using a very individual scale, is lively too, a sort of toccata, but the very scheme limits harmonic variety. The second movement, *Dynamic timbre*, brings a loosely connected sequence of evocative ideas. Played with dedication and beautifully recorded, it makes an interesting coupling for the masterly and underestimated Vaughan Williams *Concerto.*

Françaix, Jean (born 1912)

Concertino for piano and orchestra.
(M) *** Ph. Seq. 412 028-1/*4*. Claude Françaix, LSO, Dorati – AURIC: *Overture;* MILHAUD: *Le Bœuf;* SATIE: *Parade.****

In general a highly recommendable account of Françaix's delectable four-movement *Concertino*. Dorati's touch is deliciously light in the outer movements, and the pianist is neat and accomplished. The scherzo is colourful too, but the gentle slow movement is taken a fraction too fast. (Kathleen Long in a famous Decca mono recording was preferable here.) Nevertheless, with the stereo adding a great deal to the delicate orchestral effects, particularly in the winsome finale, this is still highly recommendable, with its splendid couplings. The excellent tape is quite as impressive as the disc.

Franck, César (1822–90)

Symphony in D min.
❀ **(*) RCA Gold GL/*GK* 85261 [AGL1/*AGK1* 5261]. Chicago SO, Monteux.
(***) Ph. mono **416 214-2** [id.]. Concg. O, Mengelberg – R. STRAUSS: *Don Juan.*(***)
** DG Dig. **400 070-2**; 2532/*3302* 050 [id.]. O Nat. de France, Bernstein – SAINT-SAËNS: *Rouet d'Omphale.****
(B) * DG Walkman *413 423-4* [id.]. O de Paris, Barenboim – SAINT-SAËNS: *Symphony No. 3; Danse macabre.****

Monteux's stereo recording of the Franck *Symphony* was made in Chicago in January 1961. It has been absent from the British catalogues for nearly two decades, and during that period it has never been surpassed. Beecham's 1962 account is not quite its equal, nor are the Boult or Maazel versions from the same era, or indeed Karajan's (1970) – although all these are fine performances with insights of their own. Monteux exerts a unique grip on this highly charged Romantic symphony, and his control of the continuous ebband flow of tempo and tension is masterly, so that any weaknesses of structure in the outer movements are disguised. His reading brings a sense of mystery at the very opening while the *Andante* becomes a centrepiece of elegiac delicacy. The splendid playing of the Chicago orchestra is ever responsive to the changes of mood: the fervour of the thrusting chromatic secondary tune of the first movement is matched by the dynamism of the transformation of the main theme of the *Andante* when it reappears in the finale, before the superbly prepared apotheosis of the coda. Reissued in RCA's 'Legendary Performances' series (the sobriquet for once fully justified), the sound has been digitally freshened, but the harshness in the brass remains, and the added clarification has brought a degree of edge to the upper range at climaxes which need taming if listening is to be comfortable. Disc and tape are closely matched in this respect. However, the Chicago ambience provides an underlying fullness and weight, and in Monteux's hands Franck's work takes its place naturally alongside the great Romantic symphonies.

The Franck is one of the more desirable of the Mengelberg transfers to CD. In his hands, the *Symphony* is highly intense and dramatic and has one sitting on the edge of one's seat. The slow movement is very tautly held together and the playing of the incomparable Concertgebouw Orchestra incandescent. Whether one likes these interpretations or not, this is playing of the highest voltage whose current, thanks to the miracle of digital recording, triumphantly traverses four decades and glows with astonishing freshness. The sound is amazingly good, all things considered, and the Philips engineers have managed to secure excellent definition and detail.

Bernstein conducts a warmly expressive performance which, thanks in part to a live recording, carries conviction in its flexible spontaneity. It has its moments of vulgarity, but that is part of the work. Next to Monteux, the very opening may sound sticky, and the central *Allegretto* is unusually slow and drawn out, while the return of the *Allegretto* in the finale brings a vulgar slowing; but the reservations are of less importance next to the glowing positive qualities of the performance. The recording is vivid and opulent, but with the brass apt to sound strident. The compact disc version brings out the qualities the more positively and is specially valuable for its absence of background in the *Allegretto* and the expanses of the slow introduction. The chrome cassette is clear and very brilliant – the treble needs a little taming.

Barenboim's account is rather disappointing. He adopts a surprisingly plodding main tempo, the first subject lacking bite, with the strings sounding thin and unconvincing. There are places too where the reading is self-indulgent, though, in a generally fine account of the slow movement, the cor anglais solo is disappointingly wooden. The new couplings on this chrome Walkman tape, however, are two of Barenboim's finest performances on record, including his superlative version of the Saint-Saëns *'Organ' symphony*. The sound is very good.

CHAMBER MUSIC

Piano quintet in F min.
*(*) Erato STU 715502 (2). Hubeau, Viotti Qt – PIERNÉ: *Piano quintet in E min.* **; VIERNE: *Piano quintet.***

(i) *Piano quintet in F min.; Prélude, chorale and fugue.*
**(*) HMV Dig. EL 270159-1/*4*. Collard, (i) Muir Qt.

When one thinks of the popularity César Franck enjoyed during the 1940s and 1950s, it is amazing how rarely the *Piano quintet*, a cornerstone of French chamber music, has been recorded in recent years – indeed, there has been no really satisfactory version since Curzon's account with the Vienna Philharmonic quartet (Decca SDD 277). HMV offers a reading of this now unfashionable score of magisterial sweep and fire by Jean-Philippe Collard and the Muir Quartet, an American ensemble, and gives us an additional bonus in the form of the *Prélude, chorale and fugue*. These players convey all the ardour and intensity of the *Quintet* and may indeed be able to persuade listeners who find its unrelieved passion all a bit too overpowering. Jean-Philippe Collard's reading of the *Prélude, chorale and fugue* is let down by a rather hard and unsympathetic recording and, indeed, the *Quintet* itself, though well and clearly balanced, is not distinguished – certainly not by the standards of the Philips chamber music series. If the recording did it justice, this performance would rate a full three-star recommendation.

Jean Hubeau's performance with the Viotti Quartet is handicapped by being part of an interesting two-record package – but not so attractive if you only want the Franck. These artists give a faithful and committed account of the *Quintet* and are eminently well recorded, even if the much-respected pianist has not quite the same youthful ardour as Collard.

Violin sonata in A.
*** Decca **414 128-2** [id.]; SXL/*KSXC 6408* [Lon. CS 6628]. Perlman, Ashkenazy – BRAHMS: *Horn trio.****

Readers need have no hesitations about acquiring the recording by Perlman and Ashkenazy. The first movement catches the listener by the ears with its forward impulse, and the whole performance has the kind of spontaneity which is too rare in the recording studio. The passionate commitment of the playing in no way swamps the work's lyrical flow. The CD transfer is admirably done and the analogue sound is enhanced, although the warmly atmospheric ambience means that there is not the sharpness of detail one would expect in a digital recording. The resonance obviously offers problems with the tape transfer and the cassette, although acceptable, is by Decca standards slightly disappointing.

Cello sonata in A (arr. of *Violin sonata*).
** ASV Dig. DCA/*ZCDCA* 522 [id.]. Colin Carr, Francis Grier – DEBUSSY: *Sonata*; FAURÉ: *Élégie* etc.**

The Franck *Violin sonata* has come more and more to be performed and recorded in its optional cello version. Carr's recording, powerfully and warmly expressive, can be recommended to anyone wanting the Debussy and Fauré couplings. Clear, rather dry digital recording, on disc and tape alike. Those wanting this transcription, however, would do better to invest in the fine HMV digital version by Maisky and Argerich, with wonderfully eloquent playing and a warmer recorded sound (ASD 4334). There is no tape.

ORGAN MUSIC

Cantabile; Chorale No. 1; Fantaisie in C; Pièce héroïque; Prélude, fugue and variation.
**(*) Unicorn DKP/*DKPC* 9013 [id.]. Jennifer Bate.

3 Chorales; Pastorale, Op. 19; Prélude, fugue et variation, Op. 18.
Ɛ *** Argo Dig. **411 710-2**; 411 710-1/*4* [id.]. Peter Hurford.

3 Chorales; Pièce héroïque.
(M) *** Mercury SRI 75006 [id.]. Marcel Dupré.

Chorale No. 2 in B min.; Fantaisie in C, Op. 16; Grande pièce symphonique, Op. 17.
(*) Unicorn Dig. **DKPCD 9014; DKP/*DKPC* 9014 [id.]. Jennifer Bate.

Chorale No. 3 in A min.; Final in B flat, Op. 21; Pastorale, Op. 19; Prière in C sharp min., Op. 20.
** Unicorn Dig. **DKPCD 9030**; DKP/*DKPC* 9030 [id.]. Jennifer Bate.

Chorale No. 3 in A min.; Prélude, fugue et variation, Op. 18.
** ASV ALH 936 [id.]. Francis Grier – MESSIAEN: *L'Ascension.***

Peter Hurford is recorded on a Cavaillé-Coll at the Church of Saint-Sernin, Toulouse, and has the benefit not only of the right instrument but of the right engineers. His are masterly accounts of the three *Chorales* Franck composed in the last year of his life: these performances are beautifully shaped and grandly paced, and there is no real doubt that, among modern digital recordings, this leads the field in both compact disc and LP formats. The chrome cassette is very impressive too, though the sound is freer in its disc versions.

Jennifer Bate plays the Danion-Gonzalez organ at Beauvais Cathedral and is given the benefit of an excellent digital recording. The spacious acoustic contributes an excellent ambience to the aural image, and Miss Bate's brilliance is not in question. In general, however, Peter Hurford is musically more satisfying and every bit as well recorded. Nevertheless, the first of the Unicorn series offers fine accounts of the *Cantabile* and the *Pièce héroïque*, of which the latter seems rather well suited to the massive sounds which the Beauvais organ can command.

Throughout her series there are excellent chrome tapes to match the LPs fairly closely.

The Mercury recording of these Franck classics was made at St Thomas's Church, New York City, in 1959 and is so wide-ranging and realistic that one could be deceived into believing it was made a year or two ago; indeed, its presence and fidelity are little short of astonishing. The sound is exceptionally finely focused, vivid and bright, impressive even in these days of digital sound and compact discs. Marcel Dupré's playing itself has a vitality and imagination that are spellbinding. It is scarcely credible that it is a quarter of a century old.

In the third volume of Jennifer Bate's survey (**DKPCD 9030**) the digital sound is as impressive as in earlier issues, and the fine organ at Beauvais Cathedral is shown to best advantage. She rushes the opening of the *A minor Chorale*, some of whose detail does not register in this acoustic at the speed, though the *Pastorale* and the *Prière* fare better.

Francis Grier is recorded on the organ of Christ Church Cathedral, Oxford, in an acoustic that is unpleasingly dry. The performances in both of the Franck pieces are expert, and it is a tribute to Grier's artistry that the attention is held in spite of the unglamorous recording quality.

Fantaisie in A; Pastorale.
*** Telarc Dig. **CD 80096**; DG 10096 [id.]. Michael Murray (organ of Symphony Hall, San Francisco) – JONGEN: *Symphonie concertante.**** ℂ

Michael Murray plays these pieces very well and, although the San Francisco organ is not tailor-made for them, they are certainly effective as a fill-up for Jongen's engagingly spectacular *Symphonie concertante*. The Telarc recording is well up to standard.

Frescobaldi, Girolamo (1583–1643)

Canzoni: detta la Arnolfinia; detta la Bernardina; detta la Bianchina; detta la Diodata; detta la Moricona; detta la Nicolina; detta la Sardina; detta la Todeschina. Toccata. Arias: Così mi disprezzate?; Dunque dovrò del puro servir mio; La mia pallida faccia; Se l'aura spira tutta vezzosa. Sonetti spirituale in stile recitativo: Maddalena alla Croce; Ohimè, che fur, che sono.
(M) *** Ph. 9502/*7313* 111. Montserrat Figueras, Dickey, Canihac, Koopman, Coin.

This very well-produced anthology makes an ideal introduction to the music of Monteverdi's lesser-known contemporary. Both disc and tape (which are each in the demonstration class) are extremely well documented, with texts and translations of the vocal numbers and plenty of information about the music itself and its background. The recital includes selections from the First Book of Canzonas (Rome, 1628), the Florentian *Arie Musicali* (1630) and the Second

Book of Toccatas (Rome, 1627). Performances are first class; original instruments are featured without pain (although it is important not to set the volume level too high). The use of two cornetts adds piquancy to the instrumental items, but Ton Koopman's keyboard contribution is also distinguished, while Christopher Coin's bass continuo is enterprising. However, the star of the concert is undoubtedly Montserrat Figueras, whose beautifully focused soprano seems ideal for this repertoire. She is especially eloquent in the sonetto spirituale, *Ohimè, che fur*, and memorable in the aria, *Se l'aura spira tutta vezzosa* (When the breeze so gentle blows). Both here and in the final *Aria di romanesco* there are – not surprisingly – distinct echoes of Monteverdi. Highly recommended.

German, Edward (1862–1936)

Welsh rhapsody.
(M) *** HMV ED 290208-1/*4*. SNO, Gibson – HARTY: *With the Wild Geese;* MACCUNN: *Land of Mountain and Flood;* SMYTH: *The Wreckers overture.****

Edward German's *Welsh rhapsody*, written for the Cardiff Festival of 1904, makes a colourful and exciting finale for this enterprising collection of genre British tone-pictures. German is content not to interfere with the traditional melodies he uses, relying on his orchestral skill to retain the listener's interest, in which he is very successful. The closing pages, based on *Men of Harlech*, are prepared in a Tchaikovskian manner to provide a rousing conclusion. This is a good example of a tune with an inbuilt eloquence that cannot be improved upon. The cassette transfer is first class, the tape every bit the equal of the disc.

It is high time German's *Merrie England* returned to the catalogue. It no longer stands up on the stage but is consistently fresh melodically, and the famous *Sword and buckler by my side* is worthy to stand alongside the great patriotic melodies of Elgar.

Gershwin, George (1898–1937)

An American in Paris; Piano concerto in F; Rhapsody in blue.
(*) Ph. Dig. **412 611-2; 412 611-1/*4* [id.]. André Previn, Pittsburgh SO.

(i) *An American in Paris;* (ii) *Piano concerto in F;* (iii) *Rhapsody in blue.*
(B) **(*) DG Walkman *413 851-4* [id.]. (i) San Francisco SO, Ozawa; (ii) Szidon, LPO, Downes; (iii) Siegfried Stöckigt, Leipzig GO, Masur – BERNSTEIN: *West Side Story: Symphonic dances.****

An American in Paris; Cuban overture; Porgy and Bess: Symphonic picture (arr. Bennett).
** RCA Dig. **RCD 14551**; RL 14149 [ATC1/*ATK1* 4149]. Dallas SO, Mata.

An American in Paris; Cuban overture; Rhapsody in blue.
(M) *(*) Decca Jub. 414 067-1/*4* [Lon. id.]. Ivan Davis, Cleveland O, Maazel.

An American in Paris; Rhapsody in blue.
(*) Telarc Dig. **CD 80058; DG 10058 [id.]. List, Cincinnati SO, Kunzel.

An American in Paris; (i) *Piano concerto in F; Porgy and Bess: Symphonic picture* (arr. Bennett)*;* (i) *Rhapsody in blue.*
(B) (**) CBS *40-79024*. (i) Entremont; Phd. O, Ormandy.

Piano concerto in F; Rhapsody in blue; 2nd Rhapsody.
(*) MMG **MCD 10111 [id.]. Jeffrey Siegel, St Louis SO, Slatkin.

Rhapsody in blue; Prelude (for piano) *No. 2.*
(*) DG Dig. **410 025-2; 2532/*3302* 082 [id.]. Bernstein (piano and cond.), LAPO – BERNSTEIN: *West Side Story: Symphonic dances.****

André Previn's recording of Gershwin's triptych is in every way superior to his earlier HMV set (where the effect was too sophisticated – even cosy). Brightness and imagination are now the hallmarks, with Previn finding a skittish scherzando quality in his solo playing, both at the opening of the *Rhapsody* and in the first movement of the *Concerto* (which is a memorable performance overall). There is obvious affection too, as in the big tune of the *Rhapsody* (warm yet never schmaltzy) and in the graceful orchestral phrasing of the lyrical secondary themes of the outer movements of the *Concerto*. The *Adagio* is nostalgically poetic, with the solo trumpet outstanding, as in the great blues tune of *An American in Paris*, while the Pittsburgh woodwind play beautifully throughout both works. Previn knits the structure of Gershwin's Paris evocation convincingly together, yet his touch remains light-hearted, and the jazzy 'nightclub' sequence has a splendid rhythmic exuberance. The recording is very resonant; on CD the dynamic range is spectacularly wide, with the cymbals overwhelmingly prominent (the percussion-led opening of the *Concerto* certainly commands attention). Some might feel that the result is rather overblown in the *Rhapsody*, which comes over on a much larger scale than the composer's piano-roll version – see below. On the excellent chrome cassette, the dynamic contrast – though still wide – is slightly reduced and the enthusiastic cymbals are tempered by the smoother overall sound-picture which, nevertheless, retains its vividness.

The DG Walkman tape provides a mid-European slant on Gershwin, although the performance of the *Rhapsody* comes from further East, with the Leipzig Gewandhaus Orchestra under Masur providing a cultured accompaniment to the extremely lively account of the piano part by Siegfried Stöckigt. The jazzy flavour is enhanced by the blend of saxophone and string timbre in the big tune, which has an air of pre-1939 Berlin. The performance of the *Concerto* is even finer, with Robert Szidon treating the work as he would any other Romantic concerto; with rhythms superbly lithe and subtle tonal colouring, the result has both freshness and stature. The jazz idiom is seen here as an essential, but not overwhelmingly dominant, element. Downes and the LPO match the soloist in understanding and virtuosity. The softness of focus of Ozawa's account of *An*

American in Paris fits in well with this more restrained approach to Gershwin's genius, especially as the sound throughout this chrome tape is full as well as vivid. The Bernstein coupling is no less attractive.

Jeffrey Siegel's CD comes from a group of recordings he made for Vox in 1974. The performance of the *Rhapsody in blue* is among the finest, substantial yet full of those jazzy inflections which give the music its character and lift. The *Concerto* is a lightweight account, essentially lyrical but again very idiomatic, with the blues feeling in the slow movement obviously in the bones of the performers. The finale has plenty of zest. It was a pity that the *I got rhythm variations* was not chosen instead of the *Second Rhapsody*, but the performers do their best for the latter piece. The recording is sumptuous with a gorgeously resonant bass; the upper range has been slightly smoothed to remove the hiss, but the results are still very attractive.

Mata's performances are recorded in sumptuous digital sound and the compact disc offers gorgeously rich textures. But the conductor is not completely at home in this repertoire and the playing tends to lack vitality. The *Porgy and Bess symphonic picture* is the most successful piece here, but Dorati's CD is even finer – see below.

Eugene List has also recorded the *Rhapsody in blue* for Turnabout. On that occasion he used the original scoring; on Telarc he is accompanied by a full symphony orchestra and very sumptuously recorded indeed, in a glowingly resonant acoustic. Some of the work's rhythmically abrasive qualities are submerged, but the pianist does not lose the skittish character of the work's scherzando section. The rich sound is ideal for those who like to wallow in the melodic richness of *An American in Paris*. The blues tune certainly sounds expansive and there is no real lack of vitality, although in both works the hi-fi-conscious engineers have provided rather too much bass drum (a characteristic of Telarc CDs).

Maazel's performances (with Ivan Davis both brilliant and sophisticated in the *Rhapsody*) are in the last analysis disappointing. The recording does not help, being very brightly lit to the point of brashness. This makes the *Cuban overture* sound emptier and noisier than usual; and one feels also that the kernel of the two main works is missing. The great blues melody at the centre of *An American in Paris* sounds undernourished; it surely needs to be more sensuous than this. There is an outstanding tape transfer of this disc.

Besides being without proper documentation, Ormandy's cassette includes an unacceptable break in the middle of the *Rhapsody in blue*. Such an action, taken with the object of saving a few feet of tape, is obviously dictated by the commercial approach with which CBS have produced this double-length tape series. The original recordings were rather edgy on disc; this has been smoothed here to a considerable extent, but in its place there is some uncomfortable bass-drum resonance in the first movement of the *Concerto*. Otherwise the sound is quite good, and Ormandy's imaginative approach to the *Symphonic picture from Porgy and Bess* (with superb orchestral playing throughout) makes this piece sound uncommonly fresh, especially the atmospheric opening section. The blues tune in *An American in Paris* is played with a cultured lyrical warmth that is most pleasing and there are many individual touches in the accompaniments to the *Concerto* and the *Rhapsody*. Entremont plays well enough, but it is Ormandy's direction that is memorable here.

In his most recent recording for DG, Bernstein rather goes over the top with his jazzing of the solos in Gershwin. The encore too brings seductively swung rhythms, one of the three solo piano *Preludes*. Such rhythmic freedom was clearly the result of a live rather than a studio performance. The big melody in *Rhapsody in blue* is rather too heavily pointed for comfort (almost in the style of his reading of Elgar's *Nimrod*), but the effect of live recording is electric. The immediacy of the occasion is most compellingly projected on the compact disc, and there is also an excellent cassette, but this does not match Bernstein's inspired 1960 analogue coupling of the *Rhapsody* with *American in Paris*, which one day CBS will no doubt transfer to CD.

(i; ii) *Rhapsody in blue;* (iii) *Overtures: Girl crazy; Strike up the band.* (iv) *But not for me* (medley)*; Nice work if you can get it* (medley)*;* Songs: *Do, do, do it again; Fascinatin' rhythm; Foggy day; I've got a crush on you; The man I love; Sweet and low-down; Porgy and Bess: excerpts.*

(B) **(*) CBS *MGT 39488.* (i) Composer (from 1925 piano roll), (ii) Columbia Jazz Band; (iii) Buffalo PO; (iv) Sarah Vaughan; LAPO; cond. Tilson Thomas.

This admirable CBS tape anthology centres on the famous re-creation of the composer's own performance of *Rhapsody in blue* (taken from a piano roll) to which Michael Tilson Thomas added an exhilaratingly rooty-tooty accompaniment (1920s style) with the Columbia Jazz Band, using the original score. Tempi are almost breathlessly fast (Gershwin did not have an orchestra to consider when he cut the roll) and the effect, if controversial, is certainly refreshing. The Broadway overtures are also given expert and idiomatic performances, while Sarah Vaughan's contribution is an example of live recording at its most impressive. The intercommunication between Miss Vaughan and her audience brings singing of consistently high voltage (*Fascinatin' rhythm* is a *tour de force*). One can readily forgive the beat in the voice, when the projection is so huskily vibrant. The accompaniments are worthy of the occasion, with the orchestra under Tilson Thomas exciting in its own right. Often – as in *Porgy and Bess* – one just gets snippets of songs, but the programme is more generous than the above listing would indicate, the medleys including a number of favourites. With very acceptable sound (although iron-oxide stock is used) this is thoroughly worth while, even if the documentation is inadequate.

Catfish Row (suite from *Porgy and Bess*, arr. composer)*; Rhapsody in blue; Variations on I got rhythm.*

** HMV Dig. **CDC 747152-2** [id.]; ASD 143659-1/*4* [Ang. DS/*4DS* 38050]. Weissenberg, BPO, Ozawa.

Neither this pianist nor this orchestra would suggest themselves for this repertory, and Weissenberg sounds uncommitted in the *Rhapsody in blue*, rather better in the *Variations*. His role in Gershwin's own original suite from *Porgy and Bess* (for long overshadowed by Robert Russell Bennett's souped-up suite) is minimal, and he is unidiomatic in the *Jazzbo Brown* sequence. But *Catfish Row* is an important item, which is well played and recorded here.

Cuban overture. (i) *Second Rhapsody* (arr. McBride). *Porgy and Bess: Symphonic picture* (arr. Bennett).
** HMV Dig. **CDC 747021-2**; ASD/*TCASD* 3982 [Ang. DS 37773]. LSO, Previn, (i) with Ortiz.

Gershwin's *Cuban overture* is too long for its material, but the music has genuine vitality. Here Previn plays it with such gusto, and the digital recording is so infectiously brilliant, that one's reservations are almost swept aside. Similarly the *Second Rhapsody* cannot compare with the *Rhapsody in blue* for melodic appeal (Gershwin, like Hollywood, was not good at sequels); but this performance is very persuasive. The highlight here is of course the brilliant arrangement by Robert Russell Bennett of themes from *Porgy and Bess*, which has established a separate identity of its own. At the opening one fears the performance is going to be too self-conscious (although one can understand Previn revelling in the gorgeous LSO playing – *Summertime* is ravishing). But the music soon takes wing and again the ear revels in the glittering sonics. However, Previn unaccountably makes two cuts, notably the long slow introduction, which is so effective in Dorati's hands, and also in the storm sequence which separates *I've got plenty of nothin'* and *Bess, you is my woman now*.

Overtures: Funny face; Let 'em eat cake; Of thee I sing; Oh, Kay. Girl crazy: suite. Wintergreen for President (orch. Paul). *3 Preludes* (orch. Stone). (i) *Second Rhapsody*.
(M) ** Decca 411 835-1/*4* [Lon. id.]. Boston Pops O, Fiedler, (i) with Votapek.

Fiedler's performances are played with obvious idiomatic understanding, but they lack the zip of the Tilson Thomas versions. However, there are some valuable novelties here. *Wintergreen for President* quotes glibly from a number of other sources (including *The Pirates of Penzance*), and Fiedler catches its circus-style roisterous ambience. The *Second Rhapsody*, one of Gershwin's near misses, is given considerable fervour in its advocacy here, with Ralph Votapek's solo contribution sparking off a good orchestral response, but even so it remains obstinately unmemorable. The three piano *Preludes* do not readily transcribe for orchestra. The recording is forwardly balanced and brightly vivid, and the cassette matches the disc in its impact and brilliance.

Rhapsody in blue; Second Rhapsody; Preludes for piano; Short story (*1925*)*; Violin piece; For Lily Pons* (1933)*; Sleepless night* (1936)*; Promenade* (*Walking the dog*).

*** CBS Dig. **MK 39699**; IM/*IMT* 39699 [id.]. Michael Tilson Thomas (piano), LAPO.

Michael Tilson Thomas's newest Gershwin record supplements rather than displaces his earlier account of *Rhapsody in blue* accompanying the composer's 1924 piano roll (see above). There is no doubt that Tilson Thomas is an accomplished pianist, but there is not quite the same hell-for-leather excitement and zest for life that the earlier performance generated. Tilson Thomas has also taken the trouble to restudy the autographs of the *Second Rhapsody*, and the result of his researches brings us much closer to Gershwin's intentions. Even so, if it is not impertinent to dissent from the composer's own view, it is still far from being one of his best pieces. What, however, is a real discovery is *Sleepless night*, an altogether enchanting miniature, poignant and touching – and alone worth the price of the record. This and some of the other piano works that Tilson Thomas plays with such style are new to the catalogue. The *Violin piece* is previously unpublished, and Tilson Thomas in collaboration with Ira Gershwin has transcribed and expanded it. He gets very good results from the Los Angeles Philharmonic and is eminently well served by the CBS engineers. Strongly recommended. The CD is impressive in its presence, but the chrome tape, though fully acceptable, by its side sounds less sharply defined.

Porgy and Bess: Symphonic picture (arr. Bennett).
⊂ *** Decca Dig. **410 110-2**; 410 110-1/*4* [id.]. Detroit SO, Dorati – GROFÉ: *Grand Canyon suite*.*** ⊂

Robert Russell Bennett's famous arrangement of Gershwin melodies has been recorded many times, but never so beautifully as on this Decca digital version from Detroit. The performance is totally memorable, the opening evocatively nostalgic, and each one of these wonderful tunes is phrased with a warmly affectionate feeling for its character, yet never vulgarized. The sound is quite superb and on compact disc the strings have a ravishing, lustrous radiance that stems from the refinement of the playing itself, captured with remarkable naturalness. There is also a first-class chrome tape.

COLLECTION

'Fascinatin' Rampal': An American in Paris: excerpts; *Fascinatin' rhythm; A foggy day; I got rhythm; The man I love; Nice work if you can get it; 3 Preludes for piano; Someone to watch over me; Porgy and Bess: Bess, you is my woman; My man's gone; Summertime.*
⊂ **(*) CBS **MK 39700**; FM/*FMT* 39700 [id.]. Rampal, LAPO (members), Colombier.

Jean-Pierre Rampal is balanced closely, and his rich tone is seductively larger than life. Yet in the bright work he can display the lightest touch, and his stylish embroidery of *Fascinatin' rhythm* is most engaging, while *Nice work if you can get it* is attractively jaunty. His indulgently slow tempi in the lyrical tunes create a mood of languor, notably in *The man I love*, while *Summertime* is positively sultry. *An American in Paris* is a well-dovetailed potpourri of the main tunes from the piece, lasting about eight minutes, with the famous blues melody sounding unexpectedly elegant. The sophisticated accompaniments feature a small group of players from the Los Angeles Philharmonic, plus a synthesizer. The recording balance is essentially artificial within a warmly glowing acoustic, everything made clear by the microphones, and the results are certainly appealing, on both LP and the excellent chrome cassette. With the compact disc the presence of the accompanying group is extraordinarily tangible, and the ear revels in the cultured polish and sophistication of the playing. This is 'Pop' balancing at its most impressive, and one wishes that these fine musicians had been given more to do by the arranger, to provide greater variety of colour. As it is, the presentation tends to wear out its welcome after a few numbers because of the continuous domination of the flute timbre.

PIANO DUET

An American in Paris (original version).
** HMV Dig. **CDC 747044-2**; EJ 270122-1/*4* [Ang. DS/*4DS* 38130]. Katia and Marielle Labèque (pianos) – GRAINGER: *Fantasy*.**

The Labèque sisters here present the first recording of the composer's own two-piano score of his famous overture, in which several brief passages are included, later cut in the orchestral score. There is plenty of freshness and bite in the performance, if not much warmth. Recording to match, bright to the point of aggressiveness, and this clattery quality is unattractively accentuated on the tape.

Piano concerto in F; Rhapsody in blue (versions for 2 pianos).
(*) Ph. **400 022-2; 9500/*7300* 917 [id.]. Katia and Marielle Labèque.

Both the *Rhapsody in blue* and the *Concerto* were originally sketched out on four staves, and the *Rhapsody* and two movements of the *Concerto* were first performed on two pianos. Katia and Marielle Labèque are a highly accomplished duo actively interested in jazz, and they play with flawless ensemble and superb attack. These are sparkling accounts and are vividly recorded in all three formats. Anyone with an interest in this repertoire should consider this issue, although both works undoubtedly lose a good deal of colour without the orchestral contrast.

OPERA

Porgy and Bess (complete).

*** Decca **414 559-2** [id.]; SET 609-11/*K 3 Q28* [Lon. OSA/*5*- 13116]. White, Mitchell, Boatwright, Quivar, Hendricks, Clemmons, Thompson, Cleveland Ch., Children's Ch., Cleveland O, Maazel.

*** RCA **RD 82109** (3) [**RCD3 2109**]. Ray Albert, Dale, Andrew Smith, Shakesnider, Marschall, Children's Ch., Houston Grand Op. Ch. and O, DeMain.

If anyone was ever in doubt whether Gershwin in *Porgy and Bess* had really written an opera as opposed to a jumped-up musical, this superb recording with Cleveland forces conducted by Maazel establishes the work's formidable status beyond question. For one thing, Maazel includes the complete text, which was in fact cut even before the first stage presentation. Some half-hour of virtually unknown music, including many highly evocative passages and some striking choruses, reinforces the consistency of Gershwin's inspiration. It is not just a question of the big numbers presenting some of the most memorable melodies of the twentieth century, but of a grand dramatic design which triumphs superbly over the almost impossible conjunction of conventions – of opera and the American musical. With a cast that makes up an excellent team, there is no attempt to glamorize characters who are far from conventional, and the story is the more moving for that, with moments potentially embarrassing ('I's the only woman Porgy ever had,' says Bess to Crown in Act II) given genuine dramatic force à la Puccini. The vigour and colour are irresistible, and the recording is one of the most vivid that even Decca has produced. Willard White is a magnificent Porgy, dark of tone, while Leona Mitchell's vibrant Bess has a moving streak of vulnerability, and François Clemmons as Sportin' Life achieves the near-impossible by actually singing the role and making one forget Cab Calloway. But it is above all Maazel's triumph, a tremendous first complete recording with dazzling playing from the Cleveland Orchestra. The compact disc version is one of the most impressive transfers of an analogue original that Decca has yet issued, with the excellent balance and sense of presence intensified, and with none of the boominess that has afflicted some CD transfers from this source. Tape collectors will find that the cassettes are only marginally less wide-ranging.

The distinction is readily drawn between Maazel's Cleveland performance and John DeMain's equally complete and authoritative account on RCA. Where Maazel easily and naturally demonstrates the operatic qualities of Gershwin's masterpiece, DeMain – with a cast which had a riotous success with the piece on Broadway and elsewhere in the United States – presents a performance clearly in the tradition of the Broadway musical. There is much to be said for both views, and it is worth noting that American listeners tend to prefer the less operatic manner of the RCA set. The casts are equally impressive vocally, with the RCA singers a degree more characterful. Donnie Ray Albert, as Porgy, uses his bass-like resonance impressively, though not everyone will like the suspicion of hamming, which works less well in a recording than on stage. That underlining of expressiveness is a characteristic of the performance, so that the climax of the key duet, *Bess, you is my woman now*, has a less natural, more stagey manner, producing, for some ears, less of a frisson than the more delicate Cleveland version. For others, the more robust Houston approach has a degree of dramatic immediacy, associated with the tradition of the American popular theatre, which is irresistible. This basic contrast will decide most listeners' approach, and although the RCA recording has not quite the Decca richness it is strikingly vivid and alive. The RCA CD transfer is not quite so sophisticated as the Decca, but it readily creates a theatrical atmosphere. The sound has plenty of bloom and excellent presence, within a believable acoustic setting – it is as if one were sitting in the middle stalls.

Porgy and Bess: highlights.
(*) RCA **RD 84680; RL/*RK* 84680. Ray Albert, Dale, Andrew Smith, Shakesnider, Children's Ch., Houston Grand Op. Ch. and O, De Main.
(*) Ph. Dig. **412 720-2; 412 720-1/*4* [id.]. Estes, Alexander, Curry, Berlin R. Ch. and SO, Slatkin.

This highlights disc is taken from the robust and colourful, highly idiomatic complete recording made by RCA in the late 1970s. Donnie Ray Albert as Porgy has fine bass resonances but tends to underline expressiveness in a hammy way. That goes with the natural feeling in this performance for the tradition of the American musical, as distinct from grand opera. The recording gives fine projection to the voices, particularly on CD. There is an element of shrillness in the orchestral sound, and this is most striking on the otherwise faithfully transferred chrome cassette.

Slatkin's collection of highlights, opulently recorded, is totally geared to the glorious voices of Simon Estes and Roberta Alexander, both of them richer-toned than their opposite numbers in the complete sets. Naturally, each soloist sings numbers from several characters, not just hero (anti-hero?) and heroine. The rich darkness of Estes' voice is clearly operatic in style, but tough and incisive too, not just as Porgy but equally impressively as Sportin' Life in *It ain't necessarily so*. Only the Berlin Chorus lacks sharpness. Slatkin draws understanding playing from the orchestra, and the sound on CD is particularly rich. The chrome tape, too, is strikingly vivid and wide-ranging.

COLLECTION

But not for me (medley)*; Nice work if you can get it* (medley). Songs: *Do it again; Fascinating rhythm; A foggy day; I've got a crush on you; The man I love; My man's gone now; Sweet and low-down. Porgy and Bess: Overture and medley.*
*** CBS **MK 73650**; 73650/*40-* [M/*MT* 35205]. Sarah Vaughan and Trio; LAPO, Tilson Thomas.

This is live recording at its most impressive. The sound itself is vivid and the intercommunication between Miss Vaughan and her audience brings performances of consistently high voltage (*Fascinating rhythm* and *Strike up the band* are a *tour de force*). One can readily forgive the beat in the voice and the occasional strident moment. The accompaniments are worthy of the occasion, with the orchestra under Tilson Thomas exciting in its own right. Often – as in *Porgy and Bess* –one gets just snippets of the songs; but the programme is much more generous than the above listing would indicate, the medleys including many favourites. With any reservations about the soloist, not always at her best vocally, this remains a compelling musical experience.

Gesualdo, Carlo (*c.* 1560–1613)

Madrigals, Book 5 for 5 voices (1611).
*** O-L 410 128-1 [PSI id.]. Cons. of Musicke, Rooley.

Gesualdo's reputation as a madrigalist rests largely on the Fifth and Sixth Books, both for five voices and both dating from 1611. They were so successful that they were republished in score form, rather than as part books, only two years later; as David Butchart's note reminds us, contemporaries regarded them as 'outstanding for their artifice, range of harmony and chromaticism'. In performances with such perfect tonal blend and accurate intonation as these, the modulatory audacities and anguished suspensions of Gesualdo's music can register as they should. The record comprises twenty madrigals which are more varied in mood and expressive range than many realize. The documentation and presentation maintain the high standards of this label, and the sound-quality is admirably balanced and truthful. Of the Gesualdo recordings released in the last decade or so, this is easily the most distinguished.

Giannini, Vittorio (1903–66)

Symphony No. 3.
(M) **(*) Mercury SRI 75010 [id.]. Eastman Symphonic Wind Ens., Roller – HOVHANESS: *Symphony No. 4.* (***)

Vittorio Giannini studied in Milan and at the Juilliard, and was a prolific composer. His *Third Symphony* dates from 1958 and, though not strongly personal, has the benefit of good craftsmanship and is well laid out for the medium. Its idiom is distinctly neoclassical; on the whole, it makes pleasing if unmemorable listening. Its opening now seems dangerously reminiscent of a TV current affairs programme signature-tune, but there is a beautifully wrought slow movement and the piece is worth hearing for the sake of this. Unfortunately, the finale is somewhat facile and undoes the good work. The playing of the Eastman Wind Ensemble is stunningly expert and, as so often in this series, the recorded sound is quite astonishing.

Giordano, Umberto (1867–1948)

Andrea Chénier (opera): complete.

© **(*) Decca Dig. **410 117-2** (2); 410 117-1/*4* (3/*2*) [id.]. Pavarotti, Caballé, Nucci, Kuhlmann, Welsh Nat. Op. Ch., Nat. PO, Chailly.

The sound of the Decca set is so vivid and real, particularly on CD, that it often makes you start in surprise at the impact of fortissimos. Pavarotti may motor through the role of the poet-hero, singing with his usual fine diction but in a conventional barnstorming way; nevertheless, the red-blooded melodrama of the piece comes over powerfully, thanks to Chailly's sympathetic conducting, incisive but never exaggerated. Caballé, like Pavarotti, is not strong on characterization but produces beautiful sounds, while Leo Nucci makes a superbly dark-toned Gérard. Perhaps to compensate for the lack of characterization among the principals, a number of veterans have been brought in to do party turns: Hugues Cuénod as Fléville delightfully apt, Piero de Palma as the informer, Incredible, Christa Ludwig superb as Madelon, and Astrid Varnay well over the top caricaturing the Contessa di Coigny. Though this cannot replace the intermittently available RCA/Levine set with Domingo, Scotto and Milnes, it is a colourful substitute with its demonstration sound. The CD has the advantage of being on only two discs. The tape set is similarly tailored to four sides and is transferred up to Decca's usual high standard.

Glass, Philip (born 1937)

OPERA

Einstein on the beach (complete).

(***) CBS Dig. **M4K 38875**; M4/*MXT* 38875 (4) [id.]. Childs, Johnson, Mann, Sutton, Ch., Zukovsky (violin), Philip Glass Ens., Riesman.

As the surreal title implies, *Einstein on the beach* is more dream than drama. In this, his first opera, Glass, a leader in the minimalist movement, translated his use of slowly shifting ostinatos on to a near-epic scale. In the original stage production, the impact of the piece was as much due to the work of the avant-garde director, Robert Wilson, as to Glass's music. The opera takes significant incidents in Einstein's life as the basis for the seven scenes in three Acts, framed by five 'Knee Plays'. Einstein's life – starting with the child watching the trains go by – is then linked with related visual images in a dream-like way, reflecting the second half of the title, *On the Beach*, a reference to Nevil Shute's novel with its theme of nuclear apocalypse. The hallucinatory staging exactly reflected the music, which on its own conveys little. Other works of Glass, including the operas, are more communicative than this on record. Dedicated performances and first-rate recording. The booklet gives copious illustrations of the stage production. The four (!) CDs are announced as we go to press.

Satyagraha.
*** CBS Dig. 13M/*13T* 39672 [id.]. Perry, NY City Opera Ch. and O, Keene.

Like Glass's first opera, *Einstein on the beach*, this one takes scenes from the life of a great man as the basis of the 'plot' and sets them not in a narrative way but with hallucinatory music in Glass's characteristic repetitive style. The subject here is the early life of Mahatma Gandhi, pinpointing various incidents; and the text is is a selection of verses from the Bhagavadgita, sung in the original Sanskrit and used as another strand in the complex repetitive web of sound. The result is undeniably powerful. With overtones of Indian Raga at the very start, Glass builds long crescendos with a relentlessness that may anaesthetize the mind but which have a purposeful aesthetic aim. Where much minimalist music in its shimmering repetitiveness becomes static, a good deal of this conveys energy as well as power, notably the moving scene at the start of Act II in which Gandhi, attacked in the streets of Durban, is protected by Mrs Alexander, wife of the superintendent of police. The writing for chorus is often physically thrilling, and individual characters emerge in only a shadowy way. The recording, using the device of overdubbing, is spectacular. Warning has to be given of potential damage to loudspeakers from some of the sounds. The three tapes are handsomely packaged and well done, clearly documented; the sound is certainly vivid, if not quite as clean as the discs.

Glazunov, Alexander (1865–1936)

Violin concerto in A min., Op. 82.
(M) *** RCA Gold GL/*GK* 89833. Heifetz, RCA SO, Hendl – PROKOFIEV: *Concerto No. 2.****

Heifetz is incomparable here; his account is the strongest and most passionate (as well as the most perfectly played) in the catalogue. In his hands the *Concerto*'s sweetness is tempered with strength. It is altogether a captivating performance that completely absolves the work from any charge of synthetic sweetness. The RCA orchestra under Hendl gives splendid support, and although the 1963 recording is not beyond reproach, the disc is a must – as is the chrome cassette which sounds identical with it. The coupled Prokofiev is glorious, though the recording is earlier (1959). But these are truly 'legendary performances'.

Symphonies Nos 1 in E (Slavyanskaya), Op. 5; 2 in F sharp min., Op. 16; 3 in D, Op. 33; 4 in E flat, Op. 48; 5 in B flat, Op. 55; 6 in C min., Op. 58; 7 in F, Op. 77; 8 in E flat, Op. 83.
** Eurodisc 999 000 (8) [id.]. USSR RSO, Fedoseyev.

Glazunov composed his prodigious *First Symphony* in the early 1880s (it is not only remarkably accomplished but delightfully fresh) and the last in 1906 when he had just turned forty. In some ways the symphonies chart a decline in the loss of the natural musical innocence that makes Nos 1 and 2 so captivating and their command of resource so remarkable. Some of these performances by the USSR

Radio Symphony Orchestra under Vladimir Fedoseyev (those of the *Third, Sixth* and *Seventh*) have appeared on the HMV Melodiya label during the 1970s. The orchestral playing is eminently vital, even if the horns do bray in the Russian manner, and the recordings more than serviceable. Collectors wanting a complete survey may invest in these, but Glazunov's rather thick scoring would benefit from first-class digital sound and better-ventilated textures.

Symphonies Nos 1 in E, Op. 5; 5 in B flat, Op. 55; 8 in E flat, Op. 83; Overture solennelle, Op. 73; Wedding procession, Op. 21.
** Orfeo Dig. **CO 93842H**; SO/*MO* 93842H [id.]. Bav. RSO, Järvi.

The Glazunov symphonies have all been available at one time or another on LP though they tend to succumb quickly to deletion. This set of two records assembles three symphonies and two orchestral pieces in generally good performances by the Bavarian Radio orchestra under Neeme Järvi, in adequate but not spectacular sound. The *First Symphony* is a remarkable feat, being completed when Glazunov was barely sixteen years of age; in its freshness and assurance it showed a promise that was never entirely fulfilled. The *Fifth* and *Eighth Symphonies* are better known, the former having been recorded twice in the last decade or so. As so often in Glazunov, the scherzo is the best thing, full of delightful invention, but the remaining movements are also appealing. The *Eighth* is Glazunov's last completed symphony (there is a one-movement torso of a *Ninth*), dating from the middle of the first decade of the century, the period of the *Violin concerto*. It is a very considerable, well-constructed piece; like the *Seventh*, it deserves to be more popular.

Glinka, Mikhail (1804–57)

Ruslan and Ludmilla: overture.
(M) *** Decca Viva 411 838-1/*4* [Mobil 517]. LSO, Solti – BORODIN: *Prince Igor*: excerpts; MUSSORGSKY: *Khovantschina: Prelude* etc.***
(*) Andante **CDACD 85702 [Var./Sara. **VCD 42708**]. LSO, Tjeknavorian – RIMSKY-KORSAKOV: *Scheherazade*.**(*)

It is reported that, at the opening of the St Petersburg Conservatoire, Tchaikovsky dashed inside as soon as the doors were opened and played Glinka's *Ruslan and Ludmilla overture* from memory on the piano, to ensure that it was the first music to be heard in the new building. It certainly represents one of the earliest examples of what we now know as characteristic Russian orchestral music, with its energy and sparkle and vivid feeling for the orchestral palette. It is doubtful whether Tchaikovsky played the overture as fast as Solti. His spanking pace has the LSO on the very tips of their toes: a bravura performance, superbly articulated, which is irresistible; splendidly recorded on disc and cassette alike.

Tjeknavorian's account is also a lively one and makes a good, well-recorded filler for his CD of Rimsky-Korsakov's *Scheherazade*.

Grand sextet in E flat.
*** Hyp. **CDA 66163**; A/*KA* 66163. Capricorn – RIMSKY-KORSAKOV: *Quintet*.***

Glinka's *Sextet* dates from 1832 while he was still in Italy, where he came into contact with Mendelssohn, Bellini and Donizetti. It is not very individual but is very fluently written. The invention is rather engaging, particularly when played with such aplomb as it is here. The contribution of the pianist, Julian Jacobson, is brilliantly nimble and felicitous. The recording has an attractive ambience and is most naturally balanced, with an excellent matching cassette.

Gluck, Christoph (1714–87)

Alceste (complete).
** Orfeo Dig. SO 27823F (3) [id.]. Jessye Norman, Gedda, Krause, Nimsgern, Weikl, Bav. R. Ch. and SO, Baudo.

The French version of *Alceste*, quite different from the Italian, was for many years seriously in need of a complete recording; it was a great pity that the opportunity was not taken of recording Dame Janet Baker in the Covent Garden production conducted by Sir Charles Mackerras. However, this very well-cast set makes a valuable substitute, with Jessye Norman commanding in the title role, producing gloriously varied tone in every register. What is rather lacking – even from her performance – is a fire-eating quality such as made Dame Janet's performance so memorable and which comes out to hair-raising effect in Callas's recording of *Divinités du Styx*. Here it is beautiful but relatively tame. That is mainly the fault of the conductor, who makes Gluck's score sound comfortable rather than tense. The other protagonist is in effect the chorus, generally singing well but recorded rather distantly to reduce dramatic impact. The other principals sing stylishly; however, as a set, this does not quite rebut the idea that in Gluck 'beautiful' means 'boring'. Good, well-focused sound from Bavarian Radio engineers.

Iphigénie en Tauride (complete).
* Orfeo SO/*MO* 52833F (3) [id.]. Lorengar, Bonisolli, Groenroos, Fischer-Dieskau, Bav. R. Ch. and SO, Gardelli.

The brief contribution of Fischer-Dieskau in the unsympathetic role of Thoas underlines by contrast the serious disappointment of this set as a whole. His imagination and life provide quite a different perspective on the music from the rest, and Pilar Lorengar as recorded sounds so tremulous and uneven as the heroine that it is wearing to listen to. Bonisolli produces fine heroic tone but sings unimaginatively, and Walton Groenroos is gritty-toned as Oreste. A modern stereo recording of this masterly example of classical opera was seriously needed, but this is a total disappointment, despite the good recorded sound.

Orfeo ed Euridice (complete).
** Accent **ACC 48223/4D** (2). Jacobs, Kweksilber, Falewicz, Ghent Coll. Vocale, La Petite Bande, Kuijken.

With period instruments and a counter-tenor in the title role, Kuijken's set – using the original Italian version of 1762 – provides a fair alternative for those looking for an 'authentic' performance. Jacobs is especially impressive as Orfeo; however, exceptionally *Che farò*, taken very slowly, is disappointing, and not everyone will like his ornamentation. Marjanne Kweksilber makes an appealing Eurydice; but generally, with authentic style sounding a degree self-conscious, the whole performance lacks a necessary degree of involvement. This is *Orfeo* coolly dissected. Good recording.

Still recommended: The Erato version, directly based on the Glyndebourne production in which Dame Janet Baker made her very last stage appearance, has the advantage of the dramatic commitment and spontaneity of a live performance, allied to studio precision. Dame Janet's *Che farò* is unforgettable (NUM 740423 (3) [id.]).

Orfeo ed Euridice: highlights.
Ph. Dig **410 729-2** [id.]. Hofmann, Conwell, Mun. PO, Panzer.

The Philips CD of highlights comes from a disappointing set, unevenly sung and unimaginatively conducted. Not recommended.

Goldmark, Karl (1830–1915)

Overtures: Der gefesselte Prometheus, Op. 38; Im Frühling, Op. 36; In Italien, Op. 49; Sakuntala, Op. 13.
(*) Hung. Dig. **HCD 12552; SLPX/*MK* 12552 [id.]. Budapest PO, Korodi.

Goldmark is best remembered nowadays for his charming *Rustic wedding symphony*, the *Violin concerto*, and his opera, *The Queen of Sheba* – as well as being a teacher: his pupils included Sibelius. The overtures recorded here are expertly crafted and, in the case of *Im Frühling*, have good inventive ideas and no mean charm. Two of them, *Sakuntala* and *Der gefesselte Prometheus*, are longer than one would expect and, indeed, rather outstay their welcome. The playing of the Budapest orchestra under Andreas Korodi is very good; so, too, is the recording which has considerable depth. There is an acceptable cassette, although the high level of the transfer has made the upper string sound a little tight and on side two there is a hint that saturation point is near.

Gottschalk, Louis (1829–69)

Grande fantaisie triomphale sur l'Hymne Nationale Brésilien, Op. 69 (arr. Hazel).
*** Decca Dig. **414 348-2**; 414 348-1/*4* [id.]. Ortiz, RPO, Atzmon – ADDINSELL *Warsaw concerto*; LITOLFF: *Scherzo*; RACHMANINOV: *Concerto No. 2.****

Gottschalk's *Grand fantasia* has naivety and a touch of vulgarity, too, but the performers here give it an account which nicely combines flair and a certain elegance, and the result is a distinct success. The balance, within a resonant acoustic, places the piano backwardly; some might feel that there is a lack of glitter, but the CD emphasizes the naturalness, and the ambience is agreeably flattering.

Piano pieces: *Le Bananier* (chanson nègre); *The Banjo* (Grotesque fantaisie); *The Dying Poet* (méditation); *Grand scherzo; Le Mancenillier* (sérénade); *Manchega* (Étude de concert); *O ma charmante* (caprice); *Souvenirs d'Andalousie; Souvenir de Porto Rico; Suis moi; Tournament galop.*
(M) *** Decca Lon. Ent. 414 438-1/*4* [id.]. Ivan Davis.

Ivan Davis's collection of Gottschalk pieces is irresistible, for he is a fun pianist who warmly relishes – with just a hint of tongue-in-cheek – a consciously sentimental piece like *The Dying Poet*, and whose rhythmic pointing in *The Banjo* has fine wit. The result is that the composer's genuine imagination comes through far more keenly than in over-solemn performances. The recording is excellent, especially brilliant and immediate in its tape format.

Gounod, Charles (1818–93)

Faust: ballet music (*suite*).
(*) Decca Dig. **411 708-2 [id.]; 411 708-1/*4*. Montreal SO, Dutoit – OFFENBACH: *Gaîté Parisienne.***(*)

Gounod's attractive suite is warmly and elegantly played by the Montreal orchestra under Dutoit, although the conductor's touch is not as light as one would have expected. The CD sounds first rate, however, and there is an excellent chrome cassette.

Petite symphonie for wind in B flat.
(*) HM Orfeo Dig. **C 051831A; S 051831A [id.]. Mun. Wind Ac., Brezina – DVOŘÁK: *Wind serenade.***(*)

The playing of the Munich Academy is first class: they have an impressive overall blend and the solo contributions have plenty of individuality. The finale is especially engaging and the scherzo is deft. In the first two movements the musicians' geographical location is felt in the style, which is less vital and fresh than the famous Netherlands version under Edo de Waart – and it must also be noted that the Philips LP and tape, which offer the same basic coupling, also include an extra item by Schubert (Ph. 412 004-1/*4*). At mid-price, that record (or tape) is irresistible with its witty, civilized charm. Those insisting on CD will find that the Orfeo recording, made in a Munich church, is very believable, and the music itself is a delight.

Messe solennelle de Saint Cécile.
*** HMV Dig. **CDC747094-2** [id.]; EL 270134-1/*4* [Ang. DS/*4DS* 38145]. Hendricks, Dale, Lafont, Ch. and Nouvel O Philharmonique of R. France, Prêtre.

Gounod's *Messe solennelle*, with its blatant march setting of the *Credo* and sugar-sweet choral writing, may not be for sensitive souls, but Prêtre here directs an almost ideal performance, vividly recorded, to delight anyone not averse to Victorian manners. Prêtre's subtle rhythmic control and sensitive shaping of phrase minimize the vulgarity and bring out the genuine dramatic contrasts of the piece, with glowing singing from the choir as well as the three soloists: Barbara Hendricks aptly sensuous-sounding, Laurence Dale confirming in his first major recording the high promise of his stage and concert performances, and Jean-Philippe Lafont a clear, idiomatic baritone. In the wide-ranging recording, the organ-tone comes out most impressively, especially on CD. There is a good tape.

Roméo et Juliette (complete).
*** HMV Dig. EX 270142-3/*5* (3) [Ang. DSCX/*4D3X* 3960]. Alfredo Kraus, Malfitano, Van Dam, Quilico, Midi-Pyrenées Regional Ch., Capitole Toulouse Ch. and O, Plasson.

The Plasson set, well sung and vividly recorded, makes an excellent choice for an opera that has been unlucky on record. Kraus may no longer be youthful-sounding in the role of Roméo, but the range and finesse of expression are captivating, while Malfitano proves a delectably sweet and girlish Juliette. Excellent contributions too from Gino Quilico and José van Dam, beautifully set against ripely sympathetic playing from the Capitole orchestra and atmospherically recorded. Plasson's setting of scenes is most persuasive, whether in the love music or the big ensembles.

Grainger, Percy (1882–1961)

Blithe bells (Free ramble on a theme by Bach: Sheep may safely graze); Country gardens; Green bushes (passacaglia); Handel in the Strand; Mock morris; Molly on the shore; My Robin is to the greenwood gone; Shepherd's hey; Spoon River; Walking tune; Youthful rapture; Youthful suite; Rustic dance; Eastern intermezzo.
*** Chan. **CHAN 8377**; CBR/*CBT* 1022 [id.]. Bournemouth Sinf., Montgomery.

Among recent new anthologies of Grainger's music, this one stands out for the sparkling and sympathetic playing of the Bournemouth Sinfonietta and an engaging choice of programme. Among the expressive pieces, the arrangement of *My Robin is to the greenwood gone* is highly attractive, but the cello solo in *Youthful rapture* is perhaps less effective. The passacaglia on *Green bushes* is characteristically repetitive, yet the diversity in the inner parts shows Grainger's decorative imagination in full flight. Favourites such as *Country gardens*, *Shepherd's hey*, *Molly on the shore* and *Handel in the Strand* all sound as fresh as paint, and among the novelties the *Rustic dance* and *Eastern intermezzo* (in musical style a cross between Eric Coates and Edward German) have undoubted period charm. The recording is first class in all three media.

Fantasy on George Gershwin's Porgy and Bess.
** HMV Dig. **CDC 747044-2** [id.]; EJ 270122-1/*4* [Ang. DS/*4DS* 38130]. Katia and Marielle Labèque (pianos) – GERSHWIN: *American in Paris.***

The Labèque sisters in their tough way bring out the strong dramatic contrasts of Grainger's two-piano arrangement of passages from *Porgy and Bess*, a piece more obviously pianistic than the composer's own two-piano version of the overture on the reverse. A fair coupling, recorded with a brightness that threatens to become aggressive, with the tape even more clattery than the CD, the transfer level approaching saturation point.

Granados, Enrique (1867–1916)

Danzas españolas, Op. 37.
*** Decca **414 557-2** [id.]; SXL/*KSXC* 6980 [Lon. CS/*5*- 7209]. Alicia de Larrocha.

In this repertoire Alicia de Larrocha enjoys special authority; this fine Decca recording supersedes her earlier account on Erato. She has an aristocratic poise to which it is difficult not to respond, and plays with great flair and temperament. There have been other fine accounts, but this is undoubtedly the most desirable and best-recorded version in circulation. The transfer of the analogue master to CD has been very successful and the sound has enhanced presence. The cassette, too, is one of Decca's best, clear and wide-ranging, yet full and naturally coloured in the middle range.

Goyescas (complete).
*** Decca **411 958-2** [id.]; SXL 6785 [Lon. CS/5- 7009]. De Larrocha.

The Decca recording is most distinguished. Alicia de Larrocha brings special insights and sympathy to the *Goyescas*; her playing has the crisp articulation and rhythmic vitality that these pieces call for, and the overall impression could hardly be more idiomatic in flavour. These performances displace the alternative listing (Rajna on CRD), not least for the excellence of the recorded sound which is remarkably firm and secure.

Gregorian Chant

First Mass for Christmas; Third Mass for Christmas.
* DG Arc. Dig. **412 658-2**; 412 658-1/*4* [id.]. Benedictine Abbey Ch., Münsterschwarzach, Joppich.

As Rhabanus Erbacher points out in his interesting note, the celebration of Christmas is two hundred years younger than that of Easter. Thus the three masses for Christmas (for use at midnight, dawn and during the day) are of lesser antiquity, the plainsong melodies recorded here dating back to the ninth and tenth centuries. These two *Masses* originate from a five-LP set, recorded by the Choir of the Benedictine Abbey of Münsterschwarzach under Father Godehard Joppich, and which was the result of a fresh study of the earliest sources. Father Joppich's studies have led him to make some modifications of the melodic contour and rhythm, and these two *Masses* are very rich musically. The singing is another matter: the monks are rather forwardly balanced and the acoustic is neither as warm nor as spacious as one might expect; as a result, there is little sense of magic or atmosphere.

Grieg, Edvard (1834–1907)

Piano concerto in A min., Op. 16.
*** Ph. **412 923-2**; 412 923-1/*4*. Bishop-Kovacevich, BBC SO, Sir Colin Davis – SCHUMANN: *Piano concerto.****
*** Decca **414 432-2** [id.]; SXL/*KSXC* 6624. Lupu, LSO, Previn – SCHUMANN: *Piano concerto.***(*)
(*) HMV Dig. EL 270184-1/*4* [Ang. DS/*4DS* 38235]. Ousset, LSO, Marriner – MENDELSSOHN: *Piano concerto* No. 1.(*)
*(*) DG Dig. **410 021-2**; 2532/*3302* 043 [id.]. Zimerman, BPO, Karajan – SCHUMANN: *Piano concerto.***
*(*) RCA **RD 85363 [RCD1 5363]**. Rubinstein, O, Wallenstein – TCHAIKOVSKY: *Piano concerto No. 1.***(*)
(B) *(*) Ph. On Tour *412 906-4*. Arrau, Concg. O, Dohnányi – CHOPIN: *Andante*

*spianato***; SCHUMANN: *Piano concerto**(*); WEBER: *Konzertstück*.**

The freshness and imagination displayed in the coupling of the Grieg and Schumann *Concertos* by Stephen Bishop-Kovacevich and Sir Colin Davis offers a recording collaboration which – with the LP and cassette at mid-price – continues to dominate the catalogue. Whether in the clarity of virtuoso fingerwork or the shading of half-tone, Bishop-Kovacevich is among the most illuminating of the many great pianists who have recorded the Grieg *Concerto*. He plays with bravura and refinement, the spontaneity of the music making bringing a sparkle throughout, to balance the underlying poetry. The 1972 recording has been most successfully freshened, and now there is an extremely vivid chrome tape too, one of Philips's finest. Readers will note that this excellent cassette costs only a third of the price of the CD, which is nevertheless very welcome and sounds splendid.

Radu Lupu is given a bold, brightly lit analogue recording (one of Decca's very best, dating from 1974) and his performance is most enjoyable. There is both warmth and poetry in the slow movement; the hushed opening is particularly telling. There is a hint of calculation at the coda of the first movement, but the performance does not lack spontaneity, and the orchestral contribution under Previn is a strong one. The Schumann coupling is marginally less appealing. As usual with Decca, the transfer to compact disc is very successful and there is a first-class cassette.

Ousset's is a strong, dramatic reading, not lacking in warmth and poetry but, paradoxically, bringing out what we would generally think of as the masculine qualities of power and drive. The result, with excellent accompaniment recorded in very full sound, is always fresh and convincing. A good choice for anyone wanting this unusual coupling of the Mendelssohn *Concerto*. There is an excellent cassette.

Zimerman and Karajan do not seem an ideal partnership here. There are, of course, many things to admire from this remarkable young pianist, but neither concerto on this record conveys the sense that these artists are enjoying themselves very much, and there is a certain want of freshness. Judged by the standards he has set himself, Zimerman is neither as illuminating nor, indeed, quite so sensitive as one would expect in this most gentle and poetic of scores. The recording is admirably full and brilliant, especially in its CD format, and there is a matching chrome tape, but this version must be approached with caution.

Rubinstein usually has something interesting to say about any major concerto; it is a great pity that his partner here, Alfred Wallenstein, shows little sensitivity or imagination in his handling of the light-textured but all-important orchestral contribution. Nevertheless, Rubinstein produces some marvellously poetic and aristocratic playing towards the end of the slow movement, and the finale is both commanding and exciting, even if the orchestral response is aggressive. The remastering has produced a bold, if shallow, piano image, but the orchestral sound remains brashly two-dimensional. The coupled Tchaikovsky *Concerto* is infinitely finer in all respects.

On the Philips 'On Tour' compilation, Arrau's earlier (1964) recording with

Dohnányi is coupled with Chopin, Schumann and Weber. The appeal of these performances is variable. Arrau's view of the Grieg *Concerto* is not an idiomatic one. The reflective, studied calm of his reading of the first movement, presented within a mellow recording, is seriously lacking in vitality and sparkle. Although the performance is not without romantic feeling and integrity, its heaviness is out of character.

(i) *Piano concerto in A min., Op. 16;* (ii) *Elegiac melody: The last spring;* (iii) *Holberg suite, Op. 40;* (ii) *2 Norwegian melodies;* (iv) *Peer Gynt suite No. 1;* (ii) *Sigurd Jorsalfar: Homage march.*
(B) *(*) Decca *414 051-4.* (i) Katin, LPO, Sir Colin Davis; (ii) Nat. PO, Boskovsky; (iii) Stuttgart CO, Münchinger; (iv) LSO, Stanley Black.

(i) *Piano concerto in A min.* (ii) *Peer Gynt suites Nos 1 and 2.*
(B) ** DG Walkman *413 158-4* [id.]. (i) Anda, BPO, Kubelik; (ii) Bamberg SO, Richard Kraus – SIBELIUS: *Finlandia; Karelia; Valse triste.****

While both are generous, neither the Walkman nor the Decca '90 minutes' anthology is ideal. Anda's account of the *Concerto* is the more individual, although also the more wayward – but in an agreeable way: it has undoubted poetry, and the accompaniment has plenty of life. Katin's Decca performance is fresh and unhackneyed, but he seems loath to colour his playing with half-tones; the outer movements are the most successful, with Sir Colin Davis's brisk and masterly conducting adding to the feeling of a new work. The slow movement does not quite relax enough; Anda is more successful here. On the Walkman tape, a full selection from *Peer Gynt* is offered, vividly played, but the 1960 recording sounds a bit thin in the treble. The Sibelius couplings, however, are first rate, with two of the performances conducted by Karajan. On Decca, Boskovsky's contributions are somewhat unidiomatic, but very well recorded; Münchinger's *Holberg suite* is severe and unsmiling, and the recording of the upper strings is anaemic. However, Stanley Black's *Peer Gynt* suite has plenty of personality and vivid, forward sound.

Holberg suite, Op. 40.
*** DG Dig. **400 034-2**; 2532/*3302* 031 [id.]. BPO, Karajan – MOZART: *Serenade No. 13*; PROKOFIEV: *Symphony No. 1.****

Holberg suite, Op. 40; 2 Lyric pieces: Evening in the mountains; At the cradle, Op. 68/5.
(*) Ph. Dig. **412 727-2; 412 727-1/*4* [id.]. ASMF, Marriner – SIBELIUS: *Karelia; Swan.***

Karajan's performance of the *Holberg suite* is the finest currently available. The playing has a wonderful lightness and delicacy, with cultured phrasing not robbing the music of its immediacy. There are many subtleties of colour and texture revealed here by the clear yet sumptuous digital sound. Both LP and cassette are very successful, but it is the compact disc which presents this recording in the best light of all, with striking presence and detail.

Sir Neville Marriner's performance is more beautifully recorded than Karajan's, with more air round the string textures and a natural balance. However, his performance is less distinguished. Brisk tempi in the odd-numbered movements (with even a sense of hurry in the *Gavotte*) are not balanced by a comparable serenity in the *Sarabande* and *Air*, although the account of the latter is not without eloquence. The playing itself is fresh and committed, but the end result remains slightly disappointing. What makes this coupling worth considering is the pair of *Lyric pieces*. Each is highly evocative, with a memorable cor anglais solo from Barry Davis to create the atmosphere of an *Evening in the mountains*. The string group is strikingly tangible on CD, with the recessed balance adding to the realism, yet not obscuring detail. The high-level cassette transfer is strikingly successful, matching the LP very closely.

Cello sonata in A min.
** Ph. **412 962-2** (2) [id.]. Pierre Fournier, Jean Fonda – BRAHMS: *Sonatas*.*(*)

Although Fournier's playing at times lacks technical assurance (he was seventy-eight when this recording was made) there are moments when the old flair asserts itself, and the *Andante* is undoubtedly poetic, while the finale, the longest movement, shows both composer and performers at their best. The recording is very vivid, with the piano balance emphasizing Jean Fonda's assertive music-making.

PIANO MUSIC

Holberg suite, Op. 40; Lyric pieces from Opp. 12, 38, 43, 47, 54, 57, 68, 71; Norwegian dance No. 2, Op. 35; Peer Gynt: Morning.
₵ **(*) Tel. Dig. **ZK8.42925**; AZ6/*CX4*.42925 [id.]. Cyprien Katsaris.

As a glance at the above listing will show, Cyprien Katsaris draws on a wider range of Grieg's piano music than does the classic and, indeed, indispensable Gilels recital, which is drawn exclusively from the *Lyric pieces* (DG Acc. 2542/*3342* 142). Katsaris starts off the first side with *Morning mood* from *Peer Gynt*; his second side, apart from the opening ten minutes, is devoted to the suite *From Holberg's time* and one of the *Norwegian dances*, Op. 35. He is moreover accorded quite outstanding recording quality; the piano sound is particularly realistic and 'present', with plenty of range and colour. He plays with character and combines both temperament and sensitivity and is generally scrupulous in observing dynamic nuances. Of course, Gilels has poetic insights and an aristocratic finesse that are special; there are occasions here when this young artist is a shade impetuous, as in Op. 54, No. 3, or the middle section of *Home-sickness*, Op. 57, No. 6; but, for the most part, these are strong and idiomatic performances – perhaps too 'strong' in the *Holberg suite* where he is masterful and exuberant and where more finesse could be in order.

VOCAL MUSIC

Peer Gynt: extended excerpts.

(*) HMV Dig. **CDC 747003-2; ASD/*TCC-ASD* 143440-1/*4* [Ang. DS/*4XDS* 37968]. Popp. Amb. S., ASMF, Marriner.

(*) Ph. Dig. **411 038-2; 6514/*7337* 378 [id.]. Ameling, San Francisco SO, De Waart.

(M) **(*) HMV EG 290266-1/*4* [Ang. AM/*4AM* 34701]. Valjakka, Thaullaug, Leipzig R. Ch., Dresden State O, Blomstedt.

No disrespect is intended in calling Sir Neville Marriner's account of *Peer Gynt* serviceable, for the performance and recording are of good quality, the acoustic is pleasant and the sound agreeably fresh. No grumbles here, then, save for the fact that Lucia Popp sings in German – but then, so did Ilse Hollweg for Beecham. At the same time, this is not a performance that attains real distinction or character and, in spite of the excellence of the engineering, it does not displace Beecham. The compact disc is freshly detailed and glowing, but the music making does not really lift off here. There is a good cassette.

De Waart directs a warmly sympathetic reading of the *Peer Gynt* music, less sharply focused than the rival Marriner version on HMV. It brings an advantage in that Ameling, a fine soloist, sings in Norwegian, where Popp uses German. The *Wedding march* is not included, but the brief unaccompanied choral piece, *Song of the church-goers*, is. Otherwise the selection follows the now accepted expanded grouping of movements. Warm, full, not specially brilliant recording.

There is some splendid orchestral playing from the Dresden State Orchestra, with Joachim Ulbricht's folksy violin solos especially effective in the *Prelude*. The Leipzig chorus is spirited and vigorous, although the choral recording is not quite as clean as that of the orchestra. But in most respects the sound is lovely, warm and full, although the cassette focus is less sharp than the disc in the heavier climaxes. The two soloists sing strongly and dramatically, not always seeking to charm the ear. This is now offered at mid-price and it has modern recording, but for the same price one can have Beecham in a similar selection. His recording is much older, but he had a very special feeling for this score (HMV SXLP/*TC-SXLP* 30423 [Ang. RL/*4RL* 32026]).

Peer Gynt: Suites Nos 1, Op. 46; 2, Op. 55.

*** DG Dig. **410 026-2**; 2532/*3302* 068 [id.]. BPO, Karajan – SIBELIUS: *Pelléas et Mélisande.****

(M) *** DG Sig. 410 981-1/*4*. BPO, Karajan – SIBELIUS: *Finlandia; Valse triste.****

Peer Gynt: Suite No. 1; Suite No. 2. Ingrid's lament: Arab dance.

(*) Telarc Dig. **CD 80048; DG 10048 [id.]. St Louis SO, Slatkin – BIZET: *Carmen suites.***(*)

Grieg's perennially fresh score is marvellously played in Karajan's latest recording, though there are small differences between this and his earlier DG version with the same orchestra: Anitra danced with greater allure though no less elegance in 1973 and there was greater simplicity and repose in *Aase's Death*. The expressive portamenti in the latter may not be to all tastes, but the silkiness of the Berlin strings disarms criticism. The new recording is one of the best to have emerged from the Berlin Philharmonic, and the compact disc is particularly striking for its combination of presence, body and detail. Karajan's earlier analogue record remains available, reissued on the mid-priced Signature label, with an excellent matching cassette. The highly expressive performances were played with superlative skill and polish, and most listeners will be lost in admiration for the orchestral playing. The coupling is different so that any reader preferring the more popular Sibelius works will not be disappointed.

The Telarc digital recording is impressively vivid and clear. The over-resonant bass drum which muddies the fortissimos of the coupled incidental music from Bizet's *Carmen* is not troublesome here (although the climax of *In the Hall of the Mountain King* is not absolutely clean). The orchestral playing is good (*Morning* is not so evocative as in the finest versions), and the overall balance is natural. *Anitra's dance* is played by the first desks of the strings, which gives an intimate, chamber-scale presentation that is not ineffective.

Peer Gynt: Suites Nos 1, Op. 46; 2, Op. 55; 4 Norwegian dances, Op. 35.
(M) **(*) Ph. 412 922-1/*4*. ECO, Leppard.

Leppard's disc is very well recorded, the sound at once spacious and sparkling. The music making is fresh and has an air of thoughtfulness which will appeal to many, especially as the orchestral playing is so good. However, there is occasionally just a hint of a lack of vitality: *In the Hall of the Mountain King*, for instance, opens slowly and atmospherically, then does not build up quite the head of steam one expects. The *Four Norwegian dances* are splendidly done, with playing of vigour and showing a fine sense of colour.

Peer Gynt suites Nos 1 and 2; Songs: (i) *From Monte Pincio; Ich liebe dich; Lauf der Welt; The Princess; The Swan.*
(B) ** CBS DC 40143 (2). (i) Söderström, New Philh. O, Andrew Davis – FAURÉ: *Pelléas et Mélisande*; PROKOFIEV: *Cinderella.****

Bright, immediate recording goes with freshly thought performances of some of Grieg's most familiar music. A special attraction here is the singing of Elizabeth Söderström, not only in *Solveig's song* but in the orchestral songs (some of them with Davis's instrumentation) which make a delightful and original bonus. This pair of LPs is reasonably priced, although the couplings could hardly be more diverse. The equivalent cassette omits two songs (*Ich liebe dich* and *The Princess*), so cannot be recommended.

(i) *Sigurd Jorsalfar, Op. 22: incidental music; Funeral march in memory of Rikard Nordraak* (orch. Halvorsen); (i) *The Mountain spell, Op. 32.*
*** Unicorn KP/*KPC* 8003 [id.]. (i) Kåre Björköy; Oslo Philharmonic Ch., LSO, Per Dreier.

Grieg composed his incidental music for *Sigurd Jorsalfar* (Sigurd the Crusader) in 1872 for a production of Björnson's historical drama in Christiania (as Oslo was then known), though neither he nor the dramatist was particularly satisfied with it. The score comprised five movements in all (three instrumental pieces and two songs), from which Grieg drew the familiar suite; but there were additional sections as well, which are unfamiliar even to most Grieg enthusiasts: indeed, the *Prelude*, the *Horn calls* from Act II and *The King's Ballad* are all new to record and, more importantly, so is the moving *Funeral march in memory of Nordraak* which is given here in Halvorsen's orchestral transcription. Even though it does not claim to be a first recording, *Den Bergtekne* (*The Mountain spell*) for baritone, strings and two horns is something of a rarity, too. *The Mountain spell* (or 'thrall', as it is sometimes translated) is somewhat later than *Sigurd Jorsalfar* and was one of Grieg's favourite pieces. It is based on a ballad from Landstad's collection that is familiar to us through Keats' poem 'La Belle Dame sans Merci', and Grieg spoke of it once as 'possibly one of the few good deeds of my life'. It is a song of great beauty, and is alone worth the price of the record. The Oslo Philharmonic Choir give a spirited account of themselves, as do the LSO, who play sensitively for Per Dreier. Kåre Björköy is an excellent soloist with well-focused tone and is particularly impressive in *Den Bergtekne*. The recording is very good indeed: detail is well defined, and the texture clean and well ventilated, and the perspective is agreeably natural. There is an excellent chrome cassette.

Grofé, Ferde (1892–1972)

Grand Canyon suite.

€ *** Decca Dig. **410 110-2**; 410 110-1/*4* [id.]. Detroit SO, Dorati – GERSHWIN: *Porgy and Bess*.*** €

(M) ** Decca Viva 414 382-1/*4*. L. Fest. O, Stanley Black – BERNSTEIN: *Candide overture* etc.*(*)

Antal Dorati has the advantage of superlative Decca recording, very much in the demonstration class, with stereophonically vivid detail. Yet the performance combines subtlety with spectacle, and on compact disc the naturalness of the orchestral sound-picture adds to the sense of spaciousness and tangibility. With its outstanding coupling, this version is very much in a class of its own.

Stanley Black's recording was originally recorded using Decca's closely balanced Phase Four techniques. The sound is immensely vivid and in full technicolor throughout. Black secures lively and committed playing from his orchestra – and this is nothing if not spectacular (on both LP and tape), if lacking the subtlety of Dorati's recording. However, with an hour's music included at budget price this is certainly fair value.

Gulda, Friedrich (born 1930)

Ping-Pong for 2 pianos.
(**) Tel. Dig. **ZK8.42961**; AZ6/*CX4*.42961 [id.]. Corea, Gulda, Concg. O, Harnoncourt – MOZART: *Double concerto* *(*); COREA: *Fantasy*.**

Gulda's piece cannot be taken more seriously than its title and is in no way memorable, except for the noisy ending which does not lend itself to repetition. It is well played and the recording has plenty of presence. It makes a singularly unsatisfying coupling for the Mozart *E flat Double Piano concerto*.

Guy-Ropartz, Joseph (1864–1955)

Prelude, marine and chansons (for flute, violin, viola, cello and harp).
*** Decca 414 063-1/*4* [id.]. Ellis, Melos Ens. – RAVEL: *Intro. and allegro*; DEBUSSY: *Sonata*; ROUSSEL: *Serenade*.***

Guy-Ropartz's *Prelude, marine and chansons* makes a delightful bonus for a superb collection of French chamber music. The 1962 sound remains extremely full and vivid on both disc and cassette.

Halffter, Rodolfo (born 1900)

Violin concerto (rev. Szeryng).
** HMV Dig. EL 270151-1/*4* [Ang. DS/*4DS* 38258]. Szeryng, RPO, Bátiz – PONCE: *Violin concerto*.**

Rodolfo Halffter, not to be confused with his younger brother, Ernesto, who completed Falla's *Atlantida*, composed his *Violin concerto* in 1942, revising it a decade later in collaboration with the present soloist. Halffter was a considerable figure in Mexican musical life and head of the *Ediciones Mexicanas de Musica*, as well as editor of an important musical periodical. The *Concerto* is a well-crafted and colourful piece that is not unattractive. Szeryng gives a persuasive account of it and is well recorded. Performance and recording deserve a full recommendation – but the work does not; few listeners would, one suspects, return to it very often. There is a good XDR cassette.

Handel, George Frideric (1685–1759)

Ballet music: Alcina: overture; Acts I and III: suites. Il pastor fido: suite; Terpsichore: suite.
*** Erato Dig. **ECD 88084**; NUM/*MCE* 75169 [id.]. E. Bar. Sol., Eliot Gardiner.

As so often in the history of staged dance music, Handel wrote his ballet music for a specific dancer, in this case Marie Sallé, and her special skills demanded a high proportion of lyrical music. Handel rose to the challenge: the expressive writing here is very appealing; so is the scoring with its felicitous use of recorders. John Eliot Gardiner is just the man for such a programme. He is not afraid to charm the ear, yet allegros are vigorous and rhythmically infectious. The bright and clean recorded sound adds to the sparkle, and the quality is first class in all media. A delightful collection, and very tuneful too.

Concerti grossi, Op. 3/1–6.
*** DG Arc. **413 727-2**; 413 727-1/*4* [id.]. E. Concert, Pinnock.
*** Ph. Dig. **411 482-2**; 6514/*7337* 114 [id.]. ASMF, Marriner.

Concerti grossi, Op. 3/1–6; Concerto grosso in C (Alexander's Feast).
** HMV Dig. EL 270245-3/*5* (2). Linde Consort, Linde.

Concerti grossi, Op. 3/1–6 & 4b; Oboe concerto No. 3 in G min.
** Tel. **ZA8. 35545**; EX6. 35545 (2) [id.]. VCM, Harnoncourt.

The six Op. 3 *Concertos* with their sequences of brief jewels of movements find Pinnock and the English Concert at their freshest and liveliest, with plenty of sparkle and little of the abrasiveness associated with 'authentic' performance. For a version on period instruments, this could hardly be bettered with its realistic, well-balanced sound. The playing has breadth as well as charm. While the CD is particularly striking in its presence, the chrome cassette too is a state-of-the-art issue.

In Sir Neville Marriner's latest version with the Academy, tempi tend to be a little brisk, but the results are inspiring and enjoyable. The playing is of the usual high standard that we take for granted from this ensemble, with the wind playing particularly distinguished. The continuo is divided between organ and harpsichord, though the latter is reticently balanced; otherwise, the recording is altogether excellent, clean and well detailed with an agreeable ambience. This should well suit CD collectors who are not 'authenticists'; textures are fuller here than on Pinnock's competing Archiv recording, and the CD quality is admirably fresh. One regrets the absence of real grandeur and breadth which earlier LP versions such as the Mainz Chamber Orchestra under Günther Kehr found, or the flair which Thurston Dart brought to the harpsichord on his earlier recordings; however, there is much more to admire than to cavil at. The cassette is hardly less vivid than the disc, though the upper range has less bite.

Unlike many rivals, the Linde Consort take two LPs over the Op. 3 *Concerti*, offering the *Alexander's Feast* concerto as a make-weight. Given this undoubted handicap, it would have to offer special insights to justify the extra outlay, and it does not have the vitality or distinction of the finest rivals, either on period or on modern instruments. There are good things, of course, and at mid-price it might have been tempting but, for the most part, this is a *vin ordinaire*. It certainly is no match for Pinnock's Op. 3 on Archiv which has the merit of being on one compact disc.

Harnoncourt's version of Op. 3 is – like Linde's – presented very uneconomically, even if it includes the alternative version of the *F major Concerto* (No. 4b). It is spread over three and a half sides with the *Oboe concerto* as an (agreeable) make-weight. Tempi on the whole are relaxed – but the reason for the presentation has nothing to do with the pacing, but because each side contains only about twenty minutes of music. The performances are enjoyable in their easy-going way, the colouring of the baroque oboes distinctly attractive and the string sound unaggressive. Indeed, the sound is very good, but this cannot compete in a market crowded with excellence.

12 Concerti grossi, Op. 6/1–12.

❀ *** Ph. Dig. **410 048-2**; 6769/*7654* 083 (3) [id.]. ASMF, Iona Brown.
(M) *** Decca 414 260-1/*4* (3). ASMF, Marriner.
(*) DG Arc. Dig. **410 897-2; 410 897-1/*4* (1–4); **410 898-2**; 410 898-1/*4* (5–8); **410 899-2**; 410 899-1/*4* (9–12) [id.]. E. Concert, Pinnock.
** Tel. Dig. **ZB8.35603**; FR6.35603 (3) [id.]. VCM, Harnoncourt.

Handel's set of twelve *Concerti grossi*, Op. 6 – the high-water mark of Baroque orchestral music – has a distinguished recording history. The first successful complete set came in the early days of the mono LP era, on six 10″ discs (later transferred, less successfully, to three 12″), from Boyd Neel and his String Orchestra, and very fine it was. Others followed, notably from Menuhin, but it was Sir Neville Marriner's 1968 ASMF version, recorded under the guiding scholarship of Thurston Dart, which dominated the catalogue for over a decade and made the standards by which all others were judged. That has now reappeared, with the recording freshened and with excellent matching cassettes. It still makes a splendid mid-priced version and an apt memorial to Dart, both as performer (for he supplied the harpsichord continuo, in partnership with Andrew Davis on the organ) and as a scholar, with his rare and refreshing absence of pedantry. 'Marvellous music', he commented in the notes, and how right he was.

The young Iona Brown participated at Marriner's late-1960s recording sessions. She was soloist (among others, for the solo roles were shared, Marriner himself taking part) in the *Concerto No. 10 in D minor*, and she obviously absorbed a great deal from the experience of working with Thurston Dart. Her new Philips performances have much in common with the earlier set; tempi are sometimes uncannily alike, notably in Handel's marvellously entertaining fugues. But such similarities are deceptive, for the new readings have many new insights to offer and Miss Brown – while always remaining entirely at the service of the composer – sets her own personality firmly on the proceedings. In the expressive music (and there are some marvellous Handelian tunes here) she is freer, warmer and more spacious. Where allegros are differently paced, they are often slightly slower, yet the superbly crisp articulation and the rhythmic resilience of the playing always bring added sparkle. On recording grounds, the Philips set gains considerably: the sound is fuller and (on CD especially) fresher and more transparent. The contrast between the solo group and the ripieno (already extremely effective in Marriner's Decca balance) is even more tangible. Both sets remain indispensable (on occasion Marriner can bring a noble firmness of line to a lyrical phrase that is especially telling), but there is no doubt that the Philips is a clear first choice. It can be recommended strongly in all three media, for the chrome cassettes also represent the highest state of the art.

In his pursuit of authentic performance on original instruments, Pinnock finds a fair compromise between severe principle and sweetened practice. This set of Handel's most ambitious series of concertos, like Pinnock's set of Bach's *Brandenburgs*, adopts positive speeds which both give exhilaration and thrust to the fast movements (notably in the fugal writing) and provide an expressive feeling to slow movements. For all its 'authenticity', this is never unresponsive music-making, with fine solo playing set against an attractively atmospheric acoustic. Ornamentation is often elaborate – but never at the expense of line. However, these are performances to admire and to sample, but hardly to warm to. If listened through, the sharp-edged sound eventually tends to tire the ear and there is little sense of grandeur and few hints of tonally expansive beauty. It is difficult to believe that Handel's generation did not expect greater richness of texture in works of this kind. The recording is first class in all three media, and each of the three LPs, cassettes and CDs is available separately.

As the beginning of the *Concerto No. 1* demonstrates, Harnoncourt's version is eccentrically individual. After the rhythmically gruff opening flourish, the texture immediately lightens and the following allegro is fast and nimble. It is a performance of brutal contrasts, yet with the playing of the solo group often lingeringly expressive. Harnoncourt's insistence on continual dynamic change between phrases (and often within a phrase) gives the music a curiously restless feeling, with the emphatic fortissimos sometimes inelegantly heavy. There is much beautiful playing too, and the wonderfully refined recording, with its depth and natural detail, is among the finest this work has received on LP. This makes the overcharacterization the more frustrating, so that *Concerto No. 5*, one of the most inspired of the set, loses much of its humanity and repose, and the famous melody of the *Twelth*, fast and jaunty, is almost unrecognizable, while its forceful reprise reaches the point of ugliness. Vitality there is here in plenty (and the sound of the 'original' stringed instruments is more congenial than in the DG Archiv set), but in the last resort Harnoncourt's wilfulness misses the breadth and vision of Handel's instrumental masterpiece.

Concerto grosso, Op. 3/3 in G; Oboe concertos Nos 1–3; Sonata a cinque in B flat, for violin, oboe and strings.
(M) ** Ph. 9502/*7313* 113. Holliger, Sillito, ECO, Leppard.

Concerto grosso in C (Alexander's Feast); Oboe concertos Nos 1–3; Sonata a 5.
*** DG Arc. Dig. **415 291-2**; 415 291-1/*4* [id.]. E. Concert, Pinnock.

Rhythms are sprightly and Pinnock's performance of the *Alexander's Feast concerto* is as good as any now available. It has both vitality and imagination, and the string tone has clarity and body. (The wine has not turned to vinegar, as is so often the case with period string tone.) The *B flat Sonata* (HWV 288) is to all intents and purposes a concerto, and it is given with great sensitivity and taste by Simon Standage and his colleagues. David Reichenberg is the excellent soloist in the *Oboe concertos* (HWV 301, 302a, 287), the first of which is definitely Handel, while the authenticity of the others is less certain. Excellently balanced and truthful recording enhances the attractions of this issue on both LP and chrome tape, but particularly in the compact disc format. The only minor criticism is that the record could have been more generously filled.

Holliger, being a creative artist as well as a masterly interpreter, does not hesitate to embellish repeats; his ornamentation may overstep the boundaries some listeners are prepared to accept. His playing and that of the other artists in this recording is of the highest calibre, and the *Sonata a cinque* proves a particularly appealing work to set beside the three concertos. The Philips engineers produce a smooth and well-detailed recording which sounds fresher on this reissue than it did in its original form. The cassette matches the disc closely. However, for the *Oboe concertos* the collaboration of David Reichenberg and Pinnock is a clear first choice.

Concerti grossi, Op. 6/5 and 12; (i) *Organ concerto in F (Cuckoo and the nightingale).*
(B) **(*) DG Walkman *415 328-4* [id.]. Schola Cantorum Basiliensis, Wenzinger; (i) with Eduard Müller – VIVALDI: *Concertos.***(*)

Concerti grossi, Op. 6/10 and 12; (i) *Oboe concertos Nos 1–3.*
(M) ** HMV ED 290363-1/*4*. (i) Goossens; Bath Fest. O, Menuhin.

Wenzinger's *Op. 6 Concerti grossi* were recorded in 1964 and represent an early attempt at 'authenticity'; to present-day ears, however, the ample string timbres (and the total absence of vinegar) seem slightly anachronistic. That is not to suggest that the performances are unenjoyable. Indeed, Wenzinger secures some first-class playing and his expressive range is far wider than Menuhin's. *Concerto No. 5 in D major*, one of the very finest of the series, is especially well characterized, and the *Largo* of Op. 6, No. 12, has a heart-warming nobility of line. Eduard Müller's account of the most famous of Handel's organ concertos demonstrates the German approach at its most persuasive. The playing is sturdy but genially buoyant, and the registration is admirable. Again the sound (from 1966) is excellent. This Walkman tape is well worth considering with its phalanx of Vivaldi concertos as a coupling.

It is good to have two sample concertos from Menuhin's complete Op. 6, recorded in the early 1960s. He was the first in stereo to feature a double continuo of organ and harpsichord – although the organ makes little, if any, impression here. Thurston Dart's harpsichord, however, does come through. Throughout, the playing is warm and elegant rather than vivacious, and in the famous slow movement of *Concerto No. 12* Menuhin is expressively reticent, as if afraid of being accused of romanticism. Leon Goossens is in ravishing form in the *Oboe concertos*, but his recorded image is not as forward as is usual, with the integration into the string texture more in the nature of a concerto grosso. Menuhin accompanies sympathetically, but shows less vitality and imagination than Trevor Pinnock in his accompaniments for David Reichenberg – see above – and the effect of the music making is very slightly bland. The recording here is less dated in the matter of string timbre than in the *Concerti grossi* which were recorded two years later (in 1964). Cassette and disc are closely matched.

Concerto grosso in C (Alexander's Feast); Harp concerto, Op. 4/5; Concerto for lute and harp in B flat, Op. 4/6; Rodrigo: suite.
(M) *** Decca Ser. 414 052-1/*4*. [id.]. Ellis, Dupré, L. Philomusica, Granville Jones.

These recordings come from the earliest days of stereo (1959/60) but sound astonishingly undated. The *Rodrigo suite* has been added to fill out the original Oiseau-Lyre issue. They are wholly delightful performances and the recording is beautifully balanced. The cassette is splendidly managed, every bit the equal of the disc. A bargain.

Concerti a due cori: Nos 1 in B flat; 2 in F; 3 in F.
* O-L Dig. **411 721-2**; 411 721-1/*4* [id.]. AAM, Hogwood.

Tolerance is at times stretched by early music groups, even the most distinguished. The sounds produced by this band might have given pleasure to period ears – though in as hedonistic an age as the eighteenth century, this is doubtful – but they don't always to ours. Even by the standards of period-instrument groups, the noise is pretty vinegary and miserable, and there is some less-than-perfect ensemble. Of course there are some good things but, generally speaking, this record is only recommended *faute de mieux*. The quality of the recorded sound has razor-edged clarity to match the Academy's strings. The cassette has moments of roughness associated with the horns and is generally not as refined as the LP.

Guitar concerto in F (arr. from *Organ concerto, Op. 4/5*).
** CBS **MK 39560**; IM/*IMT* 39560 [id.]. Williams, ASMF, Sillito – BACH and MARCELLO: *Concertos.***

This concerto originated as a recorder sonata (Op. 1/11), but is best known in Handel's later version for organ and strings. In this further transcription the music is much less effective, and the use of modern string instruments does not help the balance. John Williams plays with his usual musicianship, but overall this cannot be said to be a great success.

Organ concertos, Op. 4/1–6; Op. 7/1–6; Second set: Nos 1 in F; 2 in A; Arnold edition: Nos 1 in D min.; 2 in F.

ᴄ *** Erato Dig. **ECD 881363** (3); NUM 75113 (4) [id.]. Ton Koopman, Amsterdam Bar. O.

Ton Koopman offers the complete sets of Opus 4 and Opus 7 plus four other *Concertos* on three CDs and rather sweeps the board, especially compared with Simon Preston's two packages (see below) which offer less music and involve an extra disc. In any case, Ton Koopman's recordings are generally preferable both as performances and as recordings. The playing has wonderful life and warmth, tempi are always aptly judged and, although original instruments are used, this is authenticity with a kindly presence, for the warm acoustic ambience of St Bartholomew's Church, Beek-Ubbergen, Holland, gives the orchestra a glowingly vivid coloration, and the string timbre is particularly attractive. So is the organ itself, which is just right for the music. Ton Koopman plays imaginatively throughout; no single movement sounds tired, while characterization is strong. The orchestral fugues emerge with genial clarity. Koopman directs the accompanying group from the keyboard, and the interplay between soloist and ripieno is a delight. The balance could hardly be better.

Organ concertos, Op. 4/1–6; in A, HWV 296.

*** DG Arc. Dig. **413 465-2**; 413 465-1/*4* (2) [id.]. Simon Preston, E. Concert, Pinnock.

Organ concertos, Op. 7/1–6; in F (Cuckoo and the nightingale); in D min., HWV 304.

*** DG Arc. Dig. **413 468-2**; 413 468-1/*4* (2) [id.]. Simon Preston, E. Concert, Pinnock.

Simon Preston's set of the Handel *Organ concertos* comes in two separate packages, with folders for the LPs, handsome slimline boxes for the chrome cassettes and 'jewel-boxes' for the CDs. Though in the first, containing the six Op. 4 works, plus the *A major* (the old No. 14), the balance of the solo instrument is not ideal, the playing of both Preston and the English Concert is admirably fresh and lively. Ursula Holliger is outstanding on a baroque harp in Op. 4, No. 6, and she creates some delicious sounds; however, it seems perverse not to include the organ version of this work, with the harp arrangement already available on other records. The second of the two boxes, containing the six Op. 7 works, plus the *'Cuckoo and the nightingale'* and the old *No. 15 in D minor*, was recorded on the organ at St John's, Armitage, in Staffordshire, and is even more attractive, not only for the extra delight of the works but for the warmth and assurance of the playing, which comes near the ideal for an 'authentic' performance. These are all recordings which positively invite re-hearing, with full, clear sound, all the fresher on CD, but sounding splendid, too, on the excellent chrome tapes.

Organ concertos, Op. 4/1 and 5; in F (Cuckoo and the nightingale): in A, HWV 296.
(M) ** HMV ED 100096-1/*4*. Simon Preston, Bath Fest. O, Menuhin.

These performances come from Simon Preston's complete set with Menuhin, made in the late 1960s, employing a variety of organs and using a new edition of the music prepared by Neville Boyling. The most striking feature to present-day ears – especially compared with Preston's Archiv set with Pinnock – is the way the lavish string textures almost swamp the organ, although the solo playing has plenty of personality and both artists communicate their enjoyment. The sound itself is first class and does not sound at all dated.

Overtures (ed. Bonynge)*: Ariodante; Arminio; Berenice; Deidamia; Faramondo; Giulio Cesare (Overture and Minuet); Radamisto; Rinaldo; Scipione; Sosarme; Teseo.*
(M) *** Decca Ser. 414 323-1. ECO, Bonynge.

This is a delightful record in every way. Bonynge uses his scholarship to produce results that are the very opposite of dry-as-dust. He may use double-dotting, *notes inégales* and added appoggiaturas beyond what other scholars would allow, but the Baroque elaboration is justified in the exuberance of the end result. The rarities included here are all delightful, and the recording is superbly vivid. There is no cassette.

Music for the Royal Fireworks (original wind scoring).
C *** Telarc Dig. **CD 80038**; DG 10038 [id.]. Cleveland Symphonic Winds, Fennell – HOLST: *Military band suites.**** C ❀

Music for the Royal Fireworks (original wind scoring)*; Concertos Nos 1 in F; 3 in D; Concerto a due cori No. 2 in F.*
(M) *** HMV ED 102894-1/*4* [Ang. S/*4XS* 37404]. *LSO, Mackerras.*

Music for the Royal Fireworks; Concerti a due cori Nos 1 and 2.
(*) Ph. Dig. **411 122-2; 411 122-1/*4*. E. Bar. Soloists, Gardiner.

Music for the Royal Fireworks; Concerti a due cori Nos 2 and 3.
*** DG Arc. Dig. **415 129-2**; 415 129-1/*4* [id.]. E. Concert, Pinnock.

Music for the Royal Fireworks; Concerto a due cori No. 2 in F; Concerto No. 1 in F.
** HMV Dig. EL 270128-1/*4*. Cappella Coloniensis, Linde.

Music for the Royal Fireworks; Water music (complete).
*** Argo **414 596-2**; ZRG/*KZRC* 697 [id.]. ASMF, Marriner.

Music for the Royal Fireworks; Water music: Suite in F.
*** O-L Dig. **400 059-2**; DSLC/*KDSLC* 595 [id.]. AAM, Hogwood.

Music for the Royal Fireworks; Water music: Suite in F; Solomon: Arrival of the Queen of Sheba.
** RCA Dig. **RD 85364**; RL/*RK* 85364 [HRC1 5364]. COE, Galway.

In 1959, Mackerras made an historic recording of Handel's *Fireworks music* with an enormous band of wind, including twenty-six oboes. That record is still available (PRT GSGC/*ZCGC* 2013). In 1977, HMV attempted to produce a comparable version with the benefit of modern stereo; a year later, in Severance Hall, Cleveland, Ohio, Frederick Fennell gathered together the wind and brass from the Cleveland Symphony Orchestra and recorded a new performance to demonstrate spectacularly what fine playing and digital sound could do for Handel's open-air score. Not all the sound is massive, of course: there is some refreshingly sprightly articulation in the *Bourrée*. But in the *Overture*, *La Réjouissance* and the closing section of the *Minuet*, the effect is remarkable. The record also includes an inflated account of Bach's *Fantasia in G*, but that is not an asset. The performance of the Handel represents one of the first great successes of digital recording, and the reading itself has genuine grandeur. The overall sound-balance tends to favour the brass (and the drums), but few will grumble when the result is as overwhelming as it is on the compact disc, with the sharpness of focus matched by the presence and amplitude of the sound image.

On HMV too, the martial music is formidably impressive, and the impact of Mackerras's version is vividly and powerfully caught. The *Concerto a due cori* is also impressive, with its antiphonal wind effects; the two other concertos with their anticipations of the *Fireworks music* make an apt fill-up. The sound on cassette is full-blooded, marginally less crisp and fresh than on the disc, but still good.

Pinnock does not attempt to compete with the outdoor performances, complete with added effects, except in spirit. He uses four flutes (for *La Paix*), three each of horns, trumpets, oboes and bassoons, and twenty-odd string players. The playing has tremendous spirit and zest, and for those wanting a period instrument version this is not only the safest but the best recommendation. The DG recording is among the finest Archiv has given us, sounding excellent in all three formats, although on the chrome cassette the focus slips just a little in some of the more spectacular moments in the *Fireworks music*.

For collectors wanting a coupling of the *Royal Fireworks* and *Water music* in first-class performances, but insisting neither on the original score in the former nor on the use of baroque instruments in the latter, the 1972 Argo issue by the Academy of St Martin-in-the-Fields remains an obvious choice. Marriner directs a sparkling account of the complete *Water music*. All the well-loved movements we once knew only in the Harty suite come out refreshed, and the rest is similarly stylish. Scholars may argue that textures are inaccurate, but for many listeners the sounds which reach the ears have a welcome freedom from acerbity. It is a substantial advantage that the compact disc (for the transfer is very successful) – unlike any of its rivals – also includes the complete *Fireworks music*. There

Marriner's interpretation is more obviously controversial, for he deliberately avoids a weighty manner, even at the magisterial opening of the overture. But with full, resonant recording, Sir Neville's generous coupling makes sound sense; and while other, more modern recordings may be more clearly defined, the digitally remastered Argo recording still sounds both full and fresh.

Those looking for 'authenticity' plus a coupling with the *Water music* can turn to the Academy of Ancient Music on Oiseau-Lyre who offer the Suite in F (with many familiar numbers) taken from Hogwood's complete set (DSLO/*KDSLC* 543 [id.]) which is not yet issued on CD. In the *Fireworks music* the Academy certainly make a vivid impact (if not creating the feeling of grandeur offered by Fennell on Telarc). The added clarity of the compact disc does emphasize some faults in balance; nevertheless, Hogwood's version can be counted among the best available and has lively rhythms and keen articulation. Hogwood gives a strong impression of the score, even if no attempt is made to reproduce the forces heard in 1749. In the *Water music*, the timbres of the original instruments are consistently attractive, with vibratoless string-tone never squeezed too painfully.

John Eliot Gardiner secures an excellent response from his players and, as one would expect from this conductor, rhythms are alive and well articulated, and phrasing is always musical. Tempi are a bit on the fast side: there are the usual string bulges favoured by period-instrument groups and wind intonation is good, though not always impeccable. The Philips recording is in the best traditions of the house on both LP and tape. Fine though this is, it does not displace Hogwood and the Academy of Ancient Music, or Pinnock and the English Concert on Archiv.

Linde and the Cappella Coloniensis give an eminently well-characterized account of the *Fireworks music*, and are well worth recommendation. There is some expert horn playing, but the performances are not as lean-textured or athletic as Pinnock's English Concert, and rhythms, particularly in the two *Concertos* (HWV 333 and 335b) are somewhat sluggish. The HMV digital recording is very well balanced and, though this is not a first choice, it is an eminently acceptable issue. There is a good XDR cassette, but the focus is somewhat less sharp than in the LP.

James Galway obtains polished and extremely spirited playing from the Chamber Orchestra of Europe. The sound is brightly vivid and the effect at times almost has an 'authentic' abrasiveness, created by sharp rhythms rather than spare textures. There is a good deal of fast music here, and the famous *Allegro* (the familiar opening movement of the old Harty suite) has surely never been more briskly paced on record. The result is invigorating, but in the end a little wearing, especially as, in the closing encore, the *Queen of Sheba* comes in at a gallop.

Music for the Royal Fireworks; Water music (both complete)*; Concertos Nos 1 in F; 3 in D.*
(B) **(*) Ph. On Tour *412 899-4* [id.]. ECO, Leppard.

(i) *Music for the Royal Fireworks; Water music* (both complete); (ii) *Harp concerto, Op. 4/6;* (iii) *Messiah: Sinfonia.*
(B) ** DG Walkman *413 148-4.* (i) BPO, Kubelik; (ii) Zabaleta, Kuentz CO, Kuentz; (iii) LPO, Karl Richter.

The Philips 'On Tour' chrome cassette which pairs Leppard's complete performances of both the *Royal Fireworks* and *Water Music* and adds the two orchestral concertos that are thematically associated with the former makes a good bargain and is generally preferable to the alternative Walkman compilation. In the *Fireworks music*, Leppard manages to combine point with a sense of ceremony, and the resonance of the acoustic adds a feeling of spectacle, even if it means that the tape transfer loses the last degree of sharpness of focus. In all three suites of the *Water music*, Leppard and the ECO are at their finest, giving elegant, beautifully turned and polished performances, with well-judged and truthful recording, admirably transferred here.

Kubelik's full-orchestral version of the complete *Water music* is freshly remastered for the Walkman reissue, and combines a sense of grandeur with liveliness. It is splendidly played, as is the *Fireworks music*, where the focus of the sound is slightly less clean. Zabaleta's approach to the *Harp concerto* is a trifle cool but eminently musical and the sound balance is excellent. But those looking for the complete *Fireworks* and *Water music* in a bargain-priced tape format will do better to stay with the Philips issue.

Music for the Royal Fireworks: suite; Water music; suite (both arr. Harty); *Overture in D min.* (arr. Elgar).
** Ph. Dig. **411 047**; 6514/*7337* 366 [id.]. Pittsburgh SO, Previn.

From Previn old-fashioned readings of the Harty arrangements, comfortable and well stuffed. Where Szell's vitality on Decca (see below under Collections) gave these period-piece orchestrations a new lease of life, Previn's way is indulgently amiable. So the *Water music Air* is taken slowly and expressively. Quick movements are crisp in the Previn manner, but overall mellowness – even in the brilliant Elgar arrangement with its elaborate percussion – is emphasized by the warm Pittsburgh recording, impressively spacious, yet well defined in its CD format. The chrome tape is transferred at quite a high level, but is generally less refined.

Music for the Royal Fireworks; Water music: suite in F (both arr. Howarth); *The Harmonious blacksmith* (arr. Dodgson). *Berenice: Minuet. Occasional oratorio: March. Solomon: Arrival of the Queen of Sheba. Xerxes: Largo* (arr. Archibald or Hazell).
*** Decca Dig. **411 930-2**; SXDL/*KSXDC* 7564. Philip Jones Brass Ens., Howarth.

This is a fun concert played with true Baroque spirit, combining polish with bravura, and spectacularly recorded. The *Arrival of the Queen of Sheba* initially needs a mental adjustment, but is disconcertingly vivid in its very different costume, while *The Harmonious blacksmith* stands at his anvil in similar bold relief. In the *Berenice Minuet* and the famous *Largo*, the sentiment of the bandstand is handsomely avoided, though the playing is warmly expressive, but it is the fast pieces with their intricately exhilarating detail that catch the ear. The sound is certainly spectacular in its CD format, but the LP is impressive too; the chrome cassette is slightly less sharply focused in the *Fireworks music*, where the wide range of dynamic is much more smoothly handled by the compact disc.

Water music: Suites Nos 1–3 (complete).
*** DG Arc. Dig. **410 525-2**; 410 525-1/*4* [id.]. E. Concert, Pinnock.
*** O-L DSLO/*KDSLC* 543 [id.]. AAM, Hogwood.
*** Erato **ECD 88005**; STU 71461 [id.]. E. Bar. Soloists, Gardiner.
*** ASV Dig. DCA/*ZCDCA* 520 [id.]. ECO, Malcolm.
(M) *** Ph. 412 924-1/*4*. ASMF, Marriner.
(*) HMV Dig. **CDC 747145-2 [id.]; EL 270156-1/*4* [Ang. DS/*4DS* 37857]. BPO, Muti.
(*) Chan. Dig. **CHAN 8382; ABRD/*ABTD* 1136 [id.]. Scottish CO, Gibson.
**(*) HMV Dig. EL 270091-1/*4*. Linde Cons., Linde.
** CBS Dig. M/*MT* 39066 [id.]. Grande Ecurie et la Chambre du Roy, Malgoire.
*(*) Tel. **ZK8.42368**; AZ6/*CY4*.42368 [id.]. VCM, Harnoncourt.

Handel's consistently inspired *Water music* which divides naturally into three suites is exceptionally well represented in the current catalogue on CD, LP and tape. For those wanting a performance featuring original instruments, choice lies between the Academy of Ancient Music and the English Concert under Trevor Pinnock (although the more idiosyncratic Gardiner version should also be considered). While the former is very attractive in its own special way, Pinnock's version on DG Archiv will be even more enticing for many. Speeds are consistently well chosen and are generally less controversial. One test is the famous *Air*, which is treated briskly by Hogwood, but here remains an engagingly gentle piece. The recording is beautifully balanced and clear, but with bloom on the sound, on disc and chrome cassette alike – although, on tape, when the brass enters on side two, the refinement of the transfer slips a little. On compact disc, the freshness and immediacy of the sound create a striking sense of presence and tangibility.

The Academy of Ancient Music has made many records for Oiseau-Lyre but few more immediately appealing than this account of music familiar in less 'authentic' renderings. Though it may come as a surprise to hear the well-known *Air* taken so fast – like a minuet – the sparkle and airiness of the invention have rarely been so endearingly caught on record. The timbres of original instruments are here consistently attractive, with vibratoless string-tone never squeezed too painfully. It was with this work that the Academy made its début at the Proms in the summer of 1978, and the joy of that occasion is matched by this performance, in which scholarship and imagination are convincingly joined. This version is not yet available on CD. The cassette transfer is lively but rather astringent in the treble. The upper partials could be cleaner, and the trumpets in the third suite are not free from discoloration.

Among performances on period instruments, Gardiner's is one of the more idiosyncratic, but its very oddities reflect a strong musical personality directing the performance with individuality. Some of his speeds are questionable – often slower than usual – but the life and sense of spontaneity in the performance are very winning, with excellent ensemble and balances. Strangely, he puts the *Overture* second in his scheme; but he has the bright solution, when Handel indicates 'three times' (first on strings, then on wind, finally all together), of doing each half separately, three times over, where normally, in effect, you get everything repeated six times in a movement such as the *Bourrée*. Almost everything he does has charm in it, and the Erato recording is first rate on both CD and LP.

Those whose taste does not extend to 'authentic' string textures should be well satisfied with George Malcolm's splendid new digital recording for ASV. The playing is first class, articulation is deft and detail is admirable. Decoration is nicely judged, and if the approach is lightweight, the alertness of the music making combined with the full, vivid sound makes a strong impact. There is a sense of delight in the music which makes this version especially appealing. There is as yet no CD version. The iron-oxide tape transfer is made at a high level, but the sound, though full and clear, loses something of the upper range of the disc.

The Philips account of the *Water music* brings Sir Neville Marriner's second complete recording – and characteristically he has taken the trouble to correct several tiny textual points read wrongly before. The playing too is even finer, helped by full-ranging, refined recording. For anyone wanting a version on a convincing scale, yet using modern instruments, this is highly recommendable at mid-price. It dates from 1980, but offers Philips's finest analogue sound quality, and the cassette is in the demonstration class.

As might be imagined, the playing of the Berlin Philharmonic Orchestra under Muti is of the highest calibre, polished and elegant. In the *Overture* of the first suite, a small instrumental group is featured as a neat counterpoint to the main ripieno; throughout, there is a strong emphasis on contrast, with instrumental solos often treated in a concertante manner. In the famous *Air*, some might feel that the element of light and shade is over-stressed, but the playing is very responsive and the strings generally display a light touch. The horns, however, are almost aggressive in their spirited vigour in the famous fanfare tune. With a full yet clear sound-picture, especially vivid on CD, this is easy to enjoy. The cassette too is one of EMI's best and is excellently focused.

Sir Alexander Gibson, like Muti, uses modern instruments. The Scottish Chamber Orchestra, competing directly against the Berlin Philharmonic, emerges with its head held high, not only in its sense of style and polish but also by the vigour and sparkle of the playing. Gibson's pacing of the allegros is brisk and he points the rhythms with infectious zest. There is fine lyrical playing too, notably from the principal oboe, while the horns are robust without being quite as emphatic as their counterparts in Berlin. The combination of energy and warmth comes as a welcome relief after prolonged exposure to period instruments. The ample acoustic of the Glasgow City Hall is attractive and, with excellent overall balance, the sound image is very believable, especially on CD which has splendid clarity and firmness of definition. The chrome tape is impressive, too, well up to the usual high Chandos standard. Neither here nor in Muti's version does the harpsichord make a strong impression – but that is inevitable in a recording of this kind. In all, this is a very likeable performance which could well be a first choice for many readers.

Using period instruments, the Linde Consort provides a gentler, more intimate alternative to the outstanding versions of Pinnock, Hogwood and Gardiner. The ensemble is not always so polished, but the easy warmth of the playing is most attractive, not least in the G major movements for flute, recorder, bassoon and strings which Linde (himself the flute- and recorder-player) turns into a separate suite after the groups in F major and D major. First-rate sound on both LP and tape to back up bright but unabrasive performances.

Malgoire has recorded the *Water music* before (in 1972); this new version is a great improvement on the old, with the period instruments under greater control and better balanced. The playing is robust and spirited, and not without finesse, though it does not match the Pinnock set, with which it is in direct competition. Its vigour and commitment, however, command attention; this sound is good, lively and full on LP and chrome cassette alike.

For Handel's tercentenary year, Telefunken brought out this digital transfer for CD of Harnoncourt's 1979 recording. The virtuosity of some of the playing is remarkable, not least that of the horns; but the sound of this ensemble is too often disagreeable as recorded here; other authentic performances are preferable, as well as providing better recorded sound.

Theatre music (arr. for woodwind): *Admeto: Da tanti affani. Amadigi di Gaula: Overture; Ballo. Ariodante: Gavotte. Esther: Overture. Il Parnasso in festa: Chaconne; Allegro. Rinaldo: Overture. Saul: Sinfonia. Scipione: Overture; Allegro.*
(M) ** Ph. 412 048-1/*4*. Philidor Ens.

Agreeable if hardly momentous arrangements for woodwind of excerpts from eight Handel operas. The attractive 'woody' sound of the baroque instruments gives the playing character; otherwise, it is a little bland. Pleasing wallpaper music, agreeably recorded on both disc and tape.

CHAMBER MUSIC

Flute sonatas, Op. 1/1a; in D; in A min., E min., and B min. (*Halle Nos 1–3*).
*** Ph. Dig. **412 606-2** [id.]. Bennett, Kraemer, Vigay.

These *Sonatas* were recorded in 1981 (the LP and cassette are now withdrawn). William Bennett's compact disc comprises the three *Halle sonatas* and two others: one from the Op. 1 set and the other a more recent discovery from a Brussels manuscript. Bennett uses a modern flute very persuasively, and Nicholas Kraemer and Denis Vigay provide admirable support. The CD transfer is altogether first class and brings to the aural image added freshness and presence.

Flute sonatas: Halle Nos 1–3; in D; Oboe sonatas, Op. 1/8; in B flat; in F; Recorder sonatas, Op. 1/2, 4, 7 and 11; in B flat; D min.; Violin sonatas, Op. 1/3, 6, 10, 12–15.

*** Ph. 412 444-1 (5) [id.]. Bennett, Black, Petri, Iona Brown, Kraemer, Vigay, Malcolm, Sheen.

Much of the material here has been issued before. Modern instruments are used, but there is an excellent sense of period style and accurate intonation. William Bennett is an excellent advocate of the *Halle Flute sonatas*, and in the works for violin Iona Brown plays with vigour and spirit. There is a welcome robustness and vitality about these performances; many will find it a relief to turn to the modern violin after the Gillette-like strains of the Baroque variety. The *Recorder sonatas* are beautifully played by Michala Petri, whose spirited approach is always infectious; the *Oboe sonatas* are also new to the catalogue and find an excellent response from the stylish and sensitive Neil Black.

Oboe sonatas (for oboe and continuo), *Op. 1/5 and 8; in B flat, HWV 357; Sinfonia in B flat for 2 violins and continuo, HWV 338; Trio sonatas: in E min. for 2 flutes, HWV 395; in F for 2 recorders, HWV 405.*

*** Ph. Dig. **412 598-2** [id.]. ASMF Chamber Ens.

Marvellously accomplished performances of the three oboe sonatas (Opp. 1, Nos 5 and 8, and the *B flat Sonata*, HWV 357) from Neil Black and the Academy team. Michala Petri and Elisabeth Selin shine in the *F major Sonata* (HWV 405); and the *B flat Sonata for two violins* (HWV 338) finds hardly less persuasive advocacy from Kenneth Sillito and Malcolm Latchem. William Bennett and Trevor Wye give a refreshing account of the *E minor* (HWV 395); and all receive excellent continuo support. No reservations whatsoever here about either the performance or the recording quality, which is among Philips's best.

Recorder sonatas, Op. 1/2, 4, 7; 9 in D min. (originally for flute), *11; in B flat; Oboe sonatas, Op. 1/8; in B flat; in F* (alternative of *Op. 1/5*)*; Trio sonata in F for 2 recorders and continuo; Flute sonata in D, HWV 378.*

*** CRD Dig. CRD 1077/8; *CRDC 4077/8* [id.]. L'Ecole d'Orphée.

Recorder sonatas, Op. 1/2, 4, 7, 9 and 11; in B flat.

*** Ph. Dig. **412 602-2** [id.]. Petri, Malcolm, Vigay, Sheen.

*** CRD Dig. **CRD 3412** [id.]. L'Ecole d'Orfée.

Michala Petri plays with her accustomed virtuosity and flair, and it would be difficult to imagine her performances being improved upon. She has the advantage of excellent rapport with her continuo players, and the Philips engineers have produced a natural and spacious sound that is particularly impressive in this compact disc format.

The CRD performances have already won much acclaim. There is some elegant and finished playing from the two recorder players, Philip Pickett and Rachel Becket. David Reichenberg deserves special mention for his contribution in the three *Oboe sonatas* on side four; and there are, as usual with this artist, some beguiling sounds from Stephen Preston. At times (the very opening of the *G minor Recorder sonata*, Op. 1) there is a slight air of inhibition or caution, but in faster movements there is genuine panache, and a real sense of style. The *Flute sonata in D*, HWV 378, is a recent discovery and was formerly attributed to Johann Sigismund Weiss (1690–1737): it has already been recorded by William Bennett. In any event, this represents a positive advance over the earlier volumes in this series; admirers of this ensemble can invest in it with confidence. The recording is excellent, well balanced and clean. The chrome cassettes are well engineered, but the transfer is very high and seems to be approaching saturation point in the *Oboe sonatas*. On CD the *Recorder sonatas* are grouped together and the sound is strikingly refined and realistic; this makes a rewarding alternative to Petri for those preferring 'authentic' timbres.

Trio sonatas, Op. 2/1–6; Op. 5/1–7; Sinfonia in B flat; Sonatas: in F; B; E min.; F; G min.; E; C.
*** Ph. Dig. 412 439-1 (4) [id.]. ASMF Chamber Ens.

On LP, Handel's *Trio sonatas* are gathered together in a box of four discs. Apart from the works published as Opp. 2 and 5, seven other sonatas are included, not all indisputably by Handel, four of which have been discovered only relatively recently. These recordings are all made using modern instruments and are expertly played, with sound well up to Philips's usual high standards. The CD issues are made separately and are discussed below.

Trio sonatas, Op. 2/1–6; Sonatas for 2 violins: in F, HWV 392; in G min., HWV 393.
*** Ph. Dig. **412 595-2** [id.]. ASMF Chamber Ens.

Trio sonatas, Op. 5/1–7; Sonatas for 2 violins: in E, HWV 394; in C, HWV 403.
*** Ph. Dig. **412 599-2** (2) [id.]. ASMF Chamber Ens.

This is most musical playing and is beautifully recorded. This makes an admirable change from the period instruments favoured by L'Ecole d'Orphée (see below). The performances from Michala Petri, William Bennett, Kenneth Sillito, Malcolm Latchem and others are wonderfully accomplished and have a refreshing vigour and warmth. In these sonatas, Handel's invention seems inexhaustible and it is difficult to imagine readers not responding to them. The compact discs are excellent in every way.

Trio sonatas, Op. 2/1–2 and 4; in D, HWV 385; in G min., HWV 393; in E min., HWV 395.

*(*) HMV Dig. EX 270083-3/*5*. Linde Cons. – BACH: *Trio sonatas.**(*)

For all their undoubted accomplishments, the Linde Consort are not wholly persuasive here, though they are very well recorded. They number some expert players among their ranks, including Han de Vries and Christopher Hogwood; surprisingly, however, the performances generally speaking are wanting in the flair and freshness one associates with their names.

Trio sonatas (for flute and violin), *Op. 2/1;* (for violins), *Op. 2/3; Op. 5/2 and 4; Violin sonata in A, Op. 1/3; Sonata for 2 violins in G min., HWV 393.*
*** DG Arc. Dig. **415 497-2**; 415 497-1/*4* [id.]. E. Concert, Pinnock.

This playing is wonderfully alive and fresh, and also excellently recorded. Rhythms are vital, and the playing of the two violinists (Simon Standage and Micaela Comberti) has enormous panache and style – as, for that matter, have the other contributors. The flautist, Lisa Beznosiuk, is particularly expert and imaginative in the *B minor Sonata*, Op. 2, No. 1; the whole enterprise gives pleasure and stimulus and can be recommended even to those normally unresponsive to period instruments or copies. On CD and LP, the recording has excellent ambience and warmth. On the otherwise excellent chrome cassette, the recording is slightly edgier in the treble.

Trio sonatas, Op. 2/3–4 and 5; Sonata in F; Rigaudon in D min., Bourrée in G min., March in G.
*(*) Denon **C37 7026** [id.]. Holliger, Bourgue, Thunemann, Christiane Jaccottet, Nagashima.

Not to be confused with the recording Heinz Holliger, Maurice Bourgue and Christiane Jaccottet made for Philips (9500 766 – now deleted). Needless to say, we have expert and lively performances from this distinguished team with what the notes endearingly describe as Christiane Jaccottet 'harpsichord and improvised of basso continuo'! The three dance movements only came to light after the war, when Karl Haas found them in the British Museum and the Fitzwilliam in Cambridge, plus the *F major Sonata*, which is not genuine Handel. The recordings have the merit of clarity, but are made in a relatively small studio whose dryness diminishes the pleasure given by these fine players. A strictly qualified recommendation.

Trio sonatas, Op. 5/1–7.
**(*) CRD CRD 1079-80/*CRDC 4079-80* [id.]. L'Ecole d'Orfée.

Those wanting baroque instruments in this repertoire will find the recordings by L'Ecole d'Orfée are well up to the high standard set by their series. As before, they are closely recorded, but the focus is firm and clean (on the excellent chrome cassettes as well as on the discs). The playing is expert and intonation is secure, as is the ensemble, with incisive articulation and lively tempi ensuring that the music is always vivid. The sound is undoubtedly astringent, and there is less geniality than in the Philips versions, but the approach is certainly committed and these performances are very good of their kind.

Violin sonatas, Op. 1/3, 6, 10, 12, 13–15; in D min., HWV 359a; in D min., HWV 367a; Fantasia in A, HWV 406.
*** Ph. Dig. **412 603–2** (2) [id.]. Iona Brown, Nicholas Kraemer, Denis Vigay.

Violin sonatas, Op. 1/3, 12, 13 and 15.
*(*) Denon Dig. **C37 7053** [id.]. Suk, Ruzickova.

These performances have been previously issued separately on LP (Philips 6769 022 – now withdrawn). They now reappear in compact disc format where they seem marvellously fresh, and are also included in the five-disc LP collection listed above. Iona Brown is on generally good form and is given excellent continuo support by Kraemer and Vigay. Like all the Handel instrumental recordings from members of the ASMF Chamber Ensemble, these can be given a prime recommendation.

Sturdy if old-fashioned performances by Josef Suk, full of warmth and vitality, though he does not blend ideally with Zuzana Ruzickova's harpsichord. Unfortunately, the recording is not ideal and the acoustic is rather cramped. While the CD catalogue can boast such beautifully recorded alternatives as those of Iona Brown on Philips, this has little chance, in spite of Suk's artistry.

Harpsichord suites Nos 2 in F; 3 in D min.; 5 in E; 6 in F sharp min.; 7 in G min.
(*) HM **HMC 90447 [id.]. Kenneth Gilbert (harpsichord).

This CD is compiled from Kenneth Gilbert's set of all eight harpsichord suites (HM 447/8). Gilbert is a scholar as well as a distinguished player. He uses a copy of a Taskin harpsichord by Bédard. Gilbert observes most first-half repeats but not the second, and he is as imaginative in the handling of decoration and ornamentation as one would expect. If one were to quibble, it would be merely that some grandeur, some larger-than-life vitality, is missing; but so much else is here that there is no case for qualifying the recommendation. The recording is much better balanced and more natural than recent rivals.

VOCAL AND CHORAL MUSIC

Acis and Galatea (masque).
(M) *** Argo 414 310-1/*4* (2/*1*). Sutherland, Pears, Galliver, Brannigan, St Anthony Singers, Philomus. O, Boult; Dart (harpsichord).

Boult provided the début stereo recording of Handel's masque (originally issued in 1960 on the Oiseau-Lyre label). It was written in the early 1730s for the Duke of Chandos and included such famous numbers as *O ruddier than the cherry* and *Love in her eyes sits playing.* The starry cast obviously relish the high level of Handel's inspiration; Joan Sutherland, in fresh, youthful voice, makes a splendid Galatea, sparkling in the florid passages, warmly sympathetic in the lyrical music. Peter Pears, too, is at his finest and although David Galliver is less striking, his contribution is still a good one, while Owen Brannigan was surely born to play Polyphemus, the genial one-eyed giant. We are given the opportunity to enjoy his splendid account of *O ruddier than the cherry* (where he makes a positive virtue of intrusive aspirates) on two occasions, for it is included as an appendix, in Handel's alternative version with treble recorder. Anyone hearing it who can resist a smile must be stony-hearted indeed. Boult's sympathetic direction ensures that the music making has a lift throughout; the recording sounds as vivid as ever, although the remastering has made the upper orchestral range sound thinner than it did, and this is most noticeable on the high-level chrome cassette. But the voices are given fine presence and the handy layout of the single extended-length tape (with full documentation) seems an ideal way of acquiring the piece. One wonders what Handel would have made of the suggestion that one day a performance of his masque could be carried comfortably in a jacket pocket. No doubt Marriner's set will also appear in due course at mid-price; meanwhile this Boult version is second to none in value.

Ah, che pur troppo è vero; Mi palpita il cor. Duets: *A miravi io son intento; Beato in ver chi può; Conservate, raddioppiate; Fronda leggiera e mobile; Langue, geme e sospira; No, di voi non vuo fidarni; Se tu non lasci amore; Sono liete, fortunate; Tanti strali al sen; Troppo cruda* (cantatas).
€ *** Hung. Dig. **HCD 12564-5**; SLPD/*MK* 12564/5. Zádori, Esswood; Falvay, Németh, Ella (cello, flute and harpsichord).

The two vocal soloists, the clear-voiced soprano Maria Zádori and the counter-tenor Paul Esswood, sing delightfully throughout this generous collection of very rare Handel duet cantatas, most of them charmers. Seven of them date from his Italian period in 1710, three more from thirty years later, and two solo ones are of unknown date. This is music aiming to delight an aristocratic audience, and it succeeds amply, when the singing is so sweet and accomplished and the coloratura so brilliantly turned. Excellent recording, particularly on CD. The chrome cassettes are also in the demonstration bracket, the voices most naturally focused and the accompaniment sounding very refined, with the harpsichord particularly realistic.

Alexander's Feast (with *Concerto grosso in F, Op. 3/4b*).
** Tel. **ZA8.35671** (2) [id.]. Palmer, Rolfe-Johnson, Roberts, Stockholm Bach Ch., VCM, Harnoncourt.

Reissued on CD as part of Telefunken's Handel Edition, Harnoncourt's 1978 recording of *Alexander's Feast* is variably successful. The team of soloists is first rate, with Felicity Palmer, Anthony Rolfe-Johnson and Stephen Roberts all very stylish, even if Roberts is too light of voice for the magnificent *Revenge, Timotheus cries*. The Stockholm choir is consistently lively, a splendid ensemble. The Concentus Musicus of Vienna play with excellent precision, but the edginess of authentic performance of this vintage is often disconcerting and not always well served by the variable recording. It also seems perverse to include the *Concerto grosso*, Op. 3/4b, as a fill-up rather than the obvious choice of the concerto which carries the name of the vocal work, and which was almost certainly played at its first performance.

L'Allegro, il penseroso, il moderato.

*** Erato **ECD 880752**; STU/*MCE* 71325 (2). Kwella, McLaughlin, Jennifer Smith, Ginn, Davies, Hill, Varcoe, Monteverdi Ch., E. Bar. Soloists, Gardiner.

Taking Milton as his starting point, Handel illustrated in music the contrasts of mood and character between the cheerful and the thoughtful. Then, prompted by his librettist, Charles Jennens, he added compromise in *Il moderato*, the moderate man. The final chorus may fall a little short of the rest (Jennens's words cannot have provided much inspiration), but otherwise the sequence of brief numbers is a delight, particularly in a performance as exhilarating as this, with excellent soloists, choir and orchestra. The recording is first rate.

Italian cantatas: *Alpestre monte; Mi palpita il cor; Tra le fiamme; Tu fedel? Tu costante?*

ϵ *** O-L Dig. **414 473-2**; 414 473-1/*4* [id.]. Emma Kirkby, AAM, Hogwood.

Emma Kirkby's bright, pure voice is perfectly suited to these brilliant but generally lightweight inspirations of the young Handel's Italian period. The four cantatas chosen, all for solo voice with modest instrumental forces, are nicely contrasted, with the personality of the original singer by implication identified with *Tu fedel*, a spirited sequence of little arias rejecting a lover. Even 'a heart full of cares' in *Mi palpita il cor* inspires Handel to a pastorally charming aria, with a delectable oboe obbligato rather than anything weighty, and even those limited cares quickly disperse. Light-hearted and sparkling performances to match. With generous cues, to give access to the many little arias and recitatives, the CD is particularly easy to use. The chrome-tape transfer is beautifully fresh and clear – in the demonstration class – and this is one of Emma Kirkby's finest recitals.

Amarilli vezzosa (*Il duello amoroso*); *Clori, mia bella Clori; O come chiare e belle* (cantatas).

*** Hyp. A 66155 [id.]. Kwella, Fisher, Denley, L. Handel O, Darlow.

The team which recorded the highly successful issue of Handel's *Aminta e Fillide* (see below) here tackles three more cantatas from Handel's Italian period. The most ambitious is *O come chiare e belle*, filling the whole of side one, a half-hour piece with allegorical overtones using all three voices and written to compliment Pope Clement XI during the War of the Spanish Succession. As in most of the cantatas, some of the ideas are familiar from later versions, as in *Tornami a vagheggiar*, used later in *Alcina*, and here brilliantly sung by Gillian Fisher. The two shorter cantatas are equally charming, *Clori, mia bella Clori* for one solo voice, the other a duet for soprano and contralto, well sung by Patrizia Kwella and Catherine Denley. Though Denys Darlow does not always lift rhythms enough, the freshness of the music is well caught.

Aminta e Fillide (cantata).
*** Hyp. **CDA 66118**; A/*KA* 66118 [id.]. Fisher, Kwella, L. Handel O, Darlow.

This was one of the longer cantatas which Handel composed during his years of work and self-education in Italy, learning above all how to write most effectively for the voice. Written for two voices and strings, it presents a simple encounter in the pastoral tradition over a span of ten brief arias which together with recitatives and final duet last almost an hour. The music is as charming and undemanding for the listener as it is taxing for the soloists. This lively performance, beautifully recorded with two nicely contrasted singers (who arguably should be cast the other way round with Fisher more boyish, Kwella brighter), delightfully blows the cobwebs off a Handel work till now totally neglected. The CD is all the fresher in its sound.

Brockes-Passion.
(M) ** DG 413 922-1 (3). Stader, Moser, Esswood, Haefliger, Jennings, Adam, Stämpfli, Regensburger Domchor, Schola Cantorum Basiliensis, Wenzinger.

Wenzinger's recording of the rare *Brockes-Passion* may be dated in both style of performance and sound but, until there is a better rival, it will be well worth hearing. At some date during his London period, Handel turned back to setting a relatively crude Passion text by Barthold Brockes (that was also set by other composers, including Telemann). It prompted a piece of some thirty or so arias, two duets and a trio, most of them brief, but full of superb ideas, many of which Handel raided for his later oratorios. Thus, the deeply moving duet between Christ and the Virgin Mary just before the *Crucifixion* later became the duet for Esther and King Ahasuerus in *Esther*. Generally, this degree of depth – worthy to be compared with Bach's Passion music – is missing, but there is still much to enjoy. The performance – without being specially distinguished – has no serious flaws, and the recording is fair for its period.

Cantatas: *Carco sempre di gloria; Splenda l'alba in oriente; Tu fedel? Tu costante?*
(M) ** Decca Ser. 414 053-1. Helen Watts, ECO, Leppard.

These performances by Helen Watts are sympathetic and enjoyable, direct in manner rather than especially subtle in the use of vocal colouring. But there is some fine music here, and Leppard ensures that the background for the voice is always well in the picture, at once alive and stylish. The recording (from 1962) still sounds well in this Decca Serenata reissue. There is no cassette.

Chandos anthems: As pants the hart; The Lord is my light.
(M) *** Argo 414 294-1/*4*. Cantelo, Partridge, King's College Ch., ASMF, Willcocks.

Handel wrote eleven anthems for his patron, the Duke of Chandos, to be performed at Canons, his country house near Edgware. Reflecting the period, they have grandeur but a direct unpretentiousness as well, and the elements of Italianate elaboration and German fugal complexity are married in them with an assurance that only Handel could achieve. These two, Nos 6 and 10, provide an attractive disc with all Teutonic pomposity avoided and the freshness of inspiration underlined. No. 6 includes a lovely Adagio chorus and beautiful soprano aria, while No. 10 is remarkable for some magnificent fugal writing. Excellent 1968 recording and a vivid chrome tape – very lively.

Chandos anthems: In the Lord put I my trust; I will magnify Thee.
(M) *** Argo 414 449-1/*4*. Friend, Langridge, King's College Ch., ASMF, Willcocks.

Here are two more of Handel's anthems (these are Nos 2 and 5) written for the Duke of Chandos, attractive for their freshness of inspiration, their economical vocal writing for small forces producing agreeably resilient textures. The choral singing here is well up to the King's standard, and the solo contributions have plenty of character; Philip Langridge is notable for his eloquence and simplicity of approach. With characteristically fine Argo recording, in the best King's tradition, this can be enthusiastically recommended.

Chandos anthems: Let God arise; O Praise the Lord with one consent.
(M) *** Argo 411 980-1/*4* [id.]. Vaughan, Young, Forbes Robinson, King's College Ch., ASMF, Willcocks.

The instrumentation here is simple, including only oboe and bassoon besides strings and continuo, and the choral writing effectively uses a small group of singers. The freshness of the idiom is delightful. The opening line of *O Praise the Lord with one consent* fits very nicely to the hymn tune we know as *O God our help in ages past*, but Handel only helps himself to this first line of the hymn and weaves his own music therefrom. This is an especially pleasing cantata with more than one reminder of *Messiah* (only the idiom less grandiose), and in this and its companion, *Let God arise*, the writing for the soloists is rewarding too. This latter work is marginally more conventional in style but redeems itself with a wonderfully imaginative chorus to the words *Praised be the Lord*. Excellent singing and recording from soloists and chorus alike, and a stylish accompaniment, all beautifully recorded, make this a most desirable disc for all Handelians. The chrome tape, too, is first class in every way, strikingly fresh and clear, with the King's acoustic offering no problems.

Coronation anthems (1, Zadok the Priest; 2, The King shall rejoice; 3, My heart is inditing; 4, Let Thy hand be strengthened).
*** DG Arc. Dig. **410 030-2**; 2534/*3311* 005 [id.]. Westminster Abbey Ch., E. Concert, Preston; Pinnock (organ).
(M) **(*) Argo 414 073-1/*4* [id.]. King's College Ch., ECO, Willcocks.

Coronation anthems (complete); *Judas Maccabaeus: See the conqu'ring hero comes; March; Sing unto God.*
ⅽ *** Ph. Dig. **412 733-2**; 412 733-1/*4* [id.]. ASMF Ch., ASMF, Marriner.

Coronation anthems (complete). *Solomon: From the censer, curling rise.*
(M) ** HMV ED 102057-1/*4*. Amb. S., Menuhin Fest. O, Sir Yehudi Menuhin.

The extra weight of the Academy of St Martin-in-the-Fields Chorus compared with the Pinnock version seems appropriate for the splendour of music intended for the pomp of royal ceremonial occasions, and the commanding choral entry in *Zadok the Priest* is gloriously rich in amplitude, without in any way lacking incisiveness. Throughout, the Academy Chorus set a perfect balance between expressive eloquence and fervour, and in *My heart is inditing* the four soloists (Joan Rodgers, Catherine Denley, Anthony Rolfe-Johnson and Robert Dean) create a stylish contrast, acting as a solo quartet in sequence with the ripieno of the main vocal group. The instrumental accompaniments are fresh and glowing, and those who can enjoy modern violin timbre in Baroque repertoire will find that the radiant orchestral sounds created by the Academy add much to the colour of the overall presentation. Sir Neville Marriner's direction is full of imaginative detail, and the Philips recording, with its wide dynamic range, is admirably balanced and excitingly realistic in its CD format. The chrome tape is very good too, but its upper focus is less sharp. The excerpts from *Solomon* are a delightful bonus with *See the conqu'ring hero* making an engaging change of mood after the closing section of the *Fourth Coronation anthem*. *Sing unto God* ends the concert with a final burst of exhilaration.

Those who prefer sparer, more 'authentic' textures can turn to Pinnock, where, although the overall effect is less grand, the element of contrast is even more telling. It is thrilling on the Archiv disc, after the lightness and clarity of the introduction to *Zadok the Priest*, to have the choir enter with such bite and impact, most strikingly of all in the compact disc version which underlines the freshness and immediacy. Though the Westminster Abbey Choir is not large, the recording gives ample sense of power, and the use of original instruments gives plenty of character to the accompaniments. An exhilarating version. Cassette collectors will find the chrome-tape transfer is of first-class DG quality.

On Argo, fine performances, brilliantly recorded, except in the matter of balance, and that is a problem inherent in the choral singing itself. This is stylish enough, but the kind of sound the choir makes is rather too light-textured for these large-scale ceremonial pieces. The result is that the orchestra tends to overwhelm the vocal sound, even though the engineering minimizes this as much as possible. However, even with reservations there is much to enjoy here, and the remastered 1963 recording is particularly successful in its tape format, the sound vivid and full-bodied and not clouded by the acoustic.

Although not as refined as the Argo King's College recording of the *Coronation anthems*, Menuhin's 1970 set is still an impressive account of some of Handel's finest ceremonial music. The chorus sing with striking vigour in the famous *Zadok the Priest*, and they are at their incisive best in *My heart is inditing*. No. 4 is let down just a little by its middle section, but the chorus from *Solomon* makes a splendid culmination. The recording is full and clear.

Cantata: *Crudel tiranno Amor*. Motet: *Silete venti*. *Giulio Cesare: E pur cosí in un giorno . . . Piangerò la sorte mia* (*Cleopatra's aria*).
(M) *** Ph. 9502/*7313* 114. Ameling, ECO, Leppard.

The delicacy, sparkle, precision and sweetness of Elly Ameling's voice make this a delightful record, with Leppard directing beautifully sprung accompaniments. One might object that *Cleopatra's aria* could be more dramatic, but as elsewhere the freshness here is most captivating, and the 1971 recording still sounds well in this mid-price reissue. The high-level cassette transfer is first class in every way. An issue not to be missed, whichever format is chosen.

Dettingen Te Deum; Dettingen anthem.
*** DG Arc. Dig. **410 647-2**; 410 647-1/*4* [id.]. Westminster Abbey Ch., E. Concert, Preston.

The *Dettingen Te Deum* was written to celebrate a famous victory during the War of the Austrian Succession. It is splendidly typical work and continually reminds the listener of *Messiah*, written the previous year. Arias and choruses alike are full of attractive invention, and one has the suspicion that Handel is knowingly capitalizing on the familiarity of his oratorio in almost plagiarizing himself. For the listener, nevertheless, the result is highly rewarding, particularly as the florid Baroque scoring, with liberal use of trumpets, gives so much pleasure in itself. Preston's new Archiv performance, with original instruments, from the English Concert makes an ideal recommendation with its splendid singing, crisp but strong (Stephen Varcoe does the two brief airs beautifully), excellent recording and a generous, apt coupling. This setting of *The King shall rejoice* should not be confused with the *Coronation anthem* of that name. It is less inspired, but has a magnificent double fugue for finale. The recording is first class in all media; the CD is especially fine, although the choral focus is occasionally very slightly blurred by the resonance.

Dixit Dominus; Zadok the Priest.
*** Erato **ECD 88072**; STU/*MCE* 71055. Palmer, Marshall, Brett, Messana, Morton, Thomson, Wilson-Johnson, Monteverdi Ch. and O, Gardiner.

Handel's *Dixit Dominus* dates from 1707 and was completed during his prolonged stay in Italy from 1706 to 1710. It divides into eight sections, and the setting, while showing signs of Handel's mature style in embryo, reflects also the Baroque tradition of contrasts between small and large groups. The writing is extremely florid and requires bravura from soloists and chorus alike. John Eliot Gardiner catches all its brilliance and directs an exhilarating performance, marked by strongly accented, sharply incisive singing from the choir and outstanding solo contributions. In high contrast with the dramatic choruses, the duet for two sopranos, *De torrente*, here beautifully sung by Felicity Palmer and Margaret Marshall, is languorously expressive, but stylishly so. Other soloists match that, and the analogue recording is first rate, proving ideal for CD remastering. The cassette quality is good on side one, although ultimately lacking upper range; but the sound is brighter and much more extended on side two.

Esther (complete).
(*) O-L Dig. **414 423-2; 414 423-1/*4* (2) [id.]. Kwella, Rolfe-Johnson, Partridge, Thomas, Kirkby, Elliott, Westminster Cathedral Boys' Ch., Ch. and AAM, Hogwood.

Hogwood presents *Esther*, Handel's first oratorio written in English, in a vigorous authentic performance. He has opted for the original 1718 score with its six compact scenes as being more sharply dramatic than the 1732 expansion, and he consistently brings out the composer's theatrical flair. Handel made this an oratorio rather than an opera only because biblical subjects were banned on the London stage at the time. Hogwood's rather abrasive brand of authenticity goes well with the bright, full recorded sound which unfortunately exaggerates the choir's sibilants. The Academy's own small chorus is joined by the clear, bright trebles of Westminster Cathedral Choir, and they all sing very well (except that the elaborate passage-work is far too heavily aspirated, at times almost as though the singers are laughing). The vigour of the performance is unaffected and the team of soloists is strong and consistent, with Patrizia Kwella distinctive and purposeful in the name-part. The cassettes are bright and clear, to match the CD and LP versions, with the astringency of the upper range very slightly underlined by the high-level transfer.

9 German arias; Violin sonata in F, Op. 1/12.
(*) HMV Dig. **CDC 747400-2 [id.]; EL 155359-1/*4* or EL 270392-1/*4* [Ang. DFO/*4DFO* 38265]. Emma Kirkby, London Baroque.

Handel's *Nine German arias* were published only in 1921 (they were omitted from Chrysander) and the accompaniment remains instrumentally conjectural. The present version will please authenticists, though timbres are meagre and the playing not strong on charm. However, the London Baroque have hit on a good idea for providing variety by interspersing the four movements of the *F major Violin sonata* in between the songs. They are beautifully sung, and the characteristic artless innocence of Emma Kirkby's style catches the spirit of Brockes' poems which, if pantheistic in subject matter, are religious in feeling. The LP, exasperatingly, is available under two alternative catalogue numbers, with different sleeves. The first depicts the artists. No doubt one or other will be deleted, and the collector will be frustrated in trying to order the version which remains available. Fortunately the CD, announced as we go to press, has no such ambiguity. There is a cassette; but the focus, though acceptable, is not ideally clean on top.

Israel in Egypt (complete).
(M) *** Argo 414 977-1/*4* (2). Gale, Watson, Bowman, Partridge, McDonnell, Watt, Christ Church Cathedral Ch., Oxford, ECO, Preston.

(M) ** DG 413 919-1/*4* (2) [id.]. Harper, Clark, Esswood, Young, Rippon, Keyte, Leeds Fest. Ch., ECO, Mackerras.

Simon Preston, using a small choir with trebles and an authentically sized orchestra, directs a performance of this great, dramatic oratorio which is beautifully in scale. He starts with the *Cuckoo and the nightingale organ concerto* – a procedure sanctioned by Handel himself at the first performance – and though inevitably the big plague choruses lack the weight which a larger choir gives them, the vigour and resilience are ample compensation, so that the text is illustrated with extra immediacy. Though Elizabeth Gale is not so firm a soprano as Heather Harper on the alternative Archiv issue, the band of soloists is an impressive one, and the ECO in splendid form. The recording, warmly atmospheric and realistically balanced, has been attractively freshened and now sounds especially well on cassette.

Although it has many merits, Mackerras's performance is in some ways disappointing. It represents a curious dichotomy of styles in using the English Chamber Orchestra, sounding crisp, stylish and lightweight in the opening overture (borrowed from *Solomon*), and the thick textures of the fairly large amateur choir, competent enough but lacking in incisive quality. Thus the work makes its effect by weight and grandiloquence rather than athletic vigour. The recording balance too reflects the problems of the basic set-up, with the chorus sometimes virtually drowning the orchestra in the epic pieces, and then suddenly coming forward for the lighter moments of the score. The solo singing is distinguished, but its style is refined rather than earthy and so again makes a contrast with the choral manner (although this contrast is not unfamiliar in the English tradition of live performance).

Jephtha.

(M) *** Argo 414 183-1/*4* (3). Rolfe-Johnson, Margaret Marshall, Hodgson, Esswood, Keyte, Kirkby, Ch. and ASMF, Marriner.

** Tel. **ZB8 35499** (3); GK 6.35499 (4) [id.]. Hollweg, Gale, Linos, Esswood, Thomaschke, Sima, Moz. Boys' Ch., Schoenberg Ch., VCM, Harnoncourt.

Jephtha, the last oratorio that Handel completed, is a strange and not always very moral tale. With the threat of blindness on him, the composer was forced to break off from writing for several months, but that threat seems only to have added to the urgency of inspiration; and Marriner's performance, helped by the bright tones of trebles in the choruses, is refreshing from first to last, well sprung but direct in style. The soloists are excellent, with Emma Kirkby nicely distanced in the role of the Angel, her clean vibratoless voice made the more ethereal. It is a very long oratorio, but in this performance it hardly seems so, with such beautiful numbers as Jephtha's *Waft her, angels* given a finely poised performance by Rolfe-Johnson. The recording is first rate, and the cassette transfer has a fine sparkle, with lively presence and detail.

Harnoncourt's pursuit of extra authenticity, with an orchestra using original instruments, will make his version an automatic choice for many; for the general listener, however, it has its snags, not just in the acid timbres of the strings. Harnoncourt takes a more operatic view of the work than Marriner on the rival version which appeared simultaneously, but he mars the impact of that by too frequently adopting a mannered style of phrasing. The soloists too are on balance far less impressive than those on the Marriner version. The recording acoustic, typically clean, is less helpful in its relative dryness next to the rival set. With a very full text this makes a long haul, although the CD format is on three discs against four LPs.

Judas Maccabaeus.
(M) *** DG 413 906-1/*4* (3) [id.]. Palmer, Baker, Esswood, Davies, Shirley-Quirk, Keyte, Wandsworth School Ch., ECO, Mackerras.

Judas Maccabaeus may have a lopsided story, with a high proportion of the finest music given to the anonymous soprano and contralto roles, Israelitish Woman (Felicity Palmer) and Israelitish Man (Dame Janet Baker); but the sequence of Handelian gems is irresistible, the more so in a performance as sparkling as this one under Sir Charles Mackerras. Unlike many versions, particularly those which in scholarly fashion attempt to restore Handel's original proportions, this holds together with no let-up of intensity, and though not everyone will approve of the use of boys' voices in the choir (inevitably the tone and intonation are not flawless) it gives an extra bite of character. Hearing even so hackneyed a number as *See, the conqu'ring hero* in its true scale is a delightful surprise. The orchestral group and continuo sound splendidly crisp; when the trumpets come in at *Sound an alarm*, the impact is considerable, just as it must have been for the original Handelian audience. Though some may regret the passing of the old-style fruity singing in the great tenor and bass arias, Ryland Davies and John Shirley-Quirk are most stylish, while both Felicity Palmer and Dame Janet crown the whole set with glorious singing, not least in a delectable sequence on the subject of liberty towards the end of Act I. The recording quality is outstanding, ideally fresh, vivid and clear, and the tape transfer too is of very high quality.

Lucrezia (cantata, ed. Leppard); *Giulio Cesare: Va tacito e nascosto.*
** HMV Dig. EL 270138-1/*4*. Ann Murray, Scottish CO, Leppard – MOZART: *Arias.***

Ann Murray's dramatic treatment of Handel's extended solo cantata, *Lucrezia*, wide-ranging in mood, brings a disadvantage on record whereby the microphone is unkind to her upper register under pressure, making it sound uncomfortably raw. The singing is sensitive and much easier on the ear after that initial outburst, but it is an unfortunate start to the disc. The splendid hunting aria from *Giulio Cesare* makes an attractive filler to the side, though done a little cautiously.

First-rate accompaniment and excellent recording, with a good XDR cassette, comfortably transferred.

Messiah (complete).

€ *** Ph. Dig. **411 041-2**; 6769/*7654* 107 (3) [id.]. Marshall, Robbin, Rolfe-Johnson, Brett, Hale, Quirke, Monteverdi Ch., E. Bar. Soloists, Gardiner.

€ *** Decca Dig. **414 396-2**; 414 396-1/*4* (2) [id.]. Te Kanawa, Gjevang, Keith Lewis, Howell, Chicago Ch. and SO, Solti.

(*) O-L **411 858-2; D189 D3/*K 189 K33* [id.]. Nelson, Kirkby, Watkinson, Elliot, Thomas, Christ Church Cath. Ch., Oxford, AAM, Hogwood.

(*) Erato **ECD 880503; NUM/*MCE* 751303 (3). Kweksilber, Bowman, Elliott, Reinhardt, the Sixteen, Amsterdam Bar. O, Koopman.

** Ph. Dig. **412 538-2**; 412 538-1/*4* (3) [id.]. Margaret Price, Schwarz, Burrows, Estes, Bav. R. Ch. and SO, Sir Colin Davis.

* Tel. Dig. **ZB8.35617**; FR6/*MU4*.35617 (3) [id.]. Gale, Lipovsek, Hollweg, Kennedy, Stockholm Chamber Ch., VCM, Harnoncourt.

The digital recording of *Messiah* directed by John Eliot Gardiner was the first to be issued on compact discs and it took the freshening process started by Sir Colin Davis and Sir Charles Mackerras in the mid-1960s a stage further. The momentum set off by these two famous recordings was continued by Marriner and Hogwood, both of whom attempted to re-create specific early performances and leave behind for ever the Victorian tradition of massive choral forces, exemplified by the Royal Choral Society and the famous Huddersfield Choir, directed in their halcyon years by Sir Malcolm Sargent. However, Gardiner's approach is not re-creative but essentially practical, with variants from the expected text rather the exception; thus the duet version of *He shall feed his flock* and the *Pastoral symphony* (with squeezed accents from the strings preventing the line from sounding too mellifluous) are both included. He chooses bright-toned sopranos instead of boys for the chorus, on the grounds that a mature adult approach is essential, and conversely he uses, very affectingly, a solo treble to sing *There were shepherds abiding*. Speeds are usually even faster and lighter than Hogwood's (or Davis's) and the rhythmic buoyancy in the choruses is very striking. There is drama and boldness, too. *Why do the nations* and *The trumpet shall sound* (both sung with great authority) have seldom come over more strongly. Perhaps most dramatic of all is the moment when, after a deceptively sedate opening, the *Amen chorus* suddenly bursts into full flood after the brief and gentle melisma from the violins, helped by the wide dynamic range of the recording. The soloists are all first class, with the soprano Margaret Marshall finest of all, especially in *I know that my Redeemer liveth* (tastefully decorated). There are times when one craves for more expansive qualities; the baroque string sound, though not so aggressively thin as it is under Hogwood, still can give cause for doubts. Yet there are some wonderful highlights, not least Margaret Marshall's angelic version of *Rejoice greatly*, skipping along in compound time. The set is admirably presented on three discs and cassettes, with each of the three parts complete on two sides. The CD layout follows the discs, with most items individually cued. The sound is outstandingly beautiful, fresh and natural, with some of the edge lifted from the baroque violins, so that, while the bite remains, there is beauty of texture too. Solo voices sound remarkably tangible, and the choral sound is wonderfully refined.

Surprisingly, Sir Georg Solti had never conducted *Messiah* before this recording, but he inspires the most vitally exciting reading on record. The Chicago Symphony Orchestra and Chorus respond to some challengingly fast but never breathless speeds, showing what lessons can be learnt from authentic performance in clarity and crispness. Yet the joyful power of *Hallelujah* and the *Amen chorus* is overwhelming. Dame Kiri Te Kanawa matches anyone on record in beauty of tone and detailed expressiveness, while the other soloists are first rate too, even if Anne Gjevang has rather too fruity a timbre. Brilliant, full sound on both LP and the splendid cassettes, but with even greater tangibility, breadth and clarity on the CDs. The layout on two discs, cassettes and compact discs also brings a special price, which is higher than the usual cost of two units, but a saving on the price of three.

By aiming at re-creating an authentic version – based meticulously on material from the Foundling Hospital, reproducing a performance of 1754 – Christopher Hogwood has managed to have the best of both worlds, punctilious but consistently vigorous and refreshing and never falling into dull routine. The trebles of Christ Church are superb, and though the soloists cannot match the tonal beauty of the finest of their rivals on other sets, the consistency of the whole conception makes for most satisfying results. As to the text, it generally follows what we are used to, but there are such oddities as *But who may abide* transposed for a soprano and a shortened version of the *Pastoral symphony*. The recording is superb, clear and free to match the performance, and the CD transfer is exceptionally successful, adding to the presence and immediacy within the resonant Christ Church acoustics. The cassettes too are very well managed.

With a small choir, an authentic baroque orchestra and clear-toned, lightweight soloists, Koopman's version provides an intimate view of what is usually presented in grandeur. The ease and relaxation of the approach, not at all abrasive in the way common with authentic performance, are attractive, helped by excellent recording which gives a fine sense of presence – but, inevitably, essential elements in Handel's vision are missing.

Sir Colin Davis's new digitally recorded set has some of the same electricity which made his classic 1967 recording with the LSO so refreshing, with fuller and richer sound on both disc and tape, and very impressive on CD. But there are notable snags. Hanna Schwarz, outstanding in the opera house, here sings painfully under the note with some ugly swooping, far less in style than her 1967 predecessor, Helen Watts. Other soloists are first rate, Margaret Price strong and pure and Simon Estes very distinctive with his clear, dark tone. The chorus is lively too, but the Bavarian Radio orchestra is a degree too smooth. This performance is far less well sprung rhythmically than Davis's earlier account, and so fails to convey the same freshness.

Harnoncourt's version was compiled from two public concerts in Stockholm in 1982 with ill-balanced sound that puts the choir at a distance, making it sound even duller than it is. With the exception of Elizabeth Gale, the soloists are poor, and Harnoncourt's direction lacks vigour. No competitor for other 'authentic' versions.

Messiah: highlights.

€ *** Ph. **412 267-2**; 412 267-1/*4* [id.] (from above set, cond. Gardiner).

*** 0-L **400 086-2**; DSLO/*KDSLC* 592 [id.] (from above set, cond. Hogwood).

(M) *** EMI EMX 41 2070-1/*4*. Harwood, Baker, Tear, Herincx, Amb. S., ECO, Mackerras.

(M) **(*) Pickwick Dig. **PCD 803**; CC/*CCTC* 7601. Lott, Finnie, Winslade, Herford, Scottish Philharmonic Singers, Scottish SO, Malcolm.

(*) ASV **CDDCA 525; DCA/*ZCDCA* 525 [id.]. Kwella, Cable, Kendal, Thomas Drew (treble), Jackson, Winchester Cathedral Ch., L. Handel O, Neary.

RCA Dig. **RCD 14622 [RCD1 4622]**. Blegen, Ciesinski, Aler, Cheek, Musica Sacra, Westerberg.

A fine selection from Gardiner's *Messiah*, demonstrating its merits, with the single caveat that *The trumpet shall sound* is missing. The *Amen chorus* is included, however, and rounds off a satisfying musical experience. The sound matches the complete set and the CD is eminently demonstration-worthy. The cassette is also first rate, although the final chorus shows the superiority of the CD format.

The digitally remastered compact disc of highlights from the Hogwood recording was issued before the complete set, and acts as an excellent sampler for it. There is just a little blurring at the top, caused by the resonance; but soloists and chorus alike (and of course the sharp-edged strings) are vividly projected against a virtually silent background. Listeners may immediately judge their reactions from the opening *Comfort ye* with its florid decorations. The solo singing is always fresh, David Thomas's *The trumpet shall sound* giving a robust reminder of an enduring style of presentation of this justly famous item. The recording is excellent; the cassette transfer is not quite so clean as the disc in reproducing the chorus.

Like Sir Colin Davis's Philips set, Sir Charles Mackerras's 1967 HMV recording was a landmark in its day, with the adoption of Handel's previously forgotten alternative versions of arias. Dame Janet Baker was outstanding in a fine team of soloists and, with robust choruses from the Ambrosian Singers, this very well-recorded selection makes a clear mid-priced recommendation on disc. The tape is good, too, but more restricted in the upper range.

Beautifully sung by excellent soloists (especially Felicity Lott) and choir, the Pickwick issue makes a good mid-priced CD, very naturally and beautifully recorded in warmly atmospheric sound, though the performance at times could be livelier.

Brightly if reverberantly recorded in Winchester Cathedral, Martin Neary's collection of excerpts gives a pleasant reminder of the work of one of our finest cathedral choirs. In its authentic manner Neary's style is rather too clipped to convey deep involvement, but the freshness is attractive, with some very good solo singing.

Wayward and sleepy, Westerberg's RCA collection of excerpts has little to recommend it, with elaborate ornamentation sounding all the stranger over perversely distorted rhythms. Fair recording.

Ode for St Cecilia's Day.

*** ASV Dig. **CDDCA 512**; DCA/*ZCDCA* 512 [id.]. Gomez, Tear, King's College Ch., ECO, Ledger.

** Tel. **ZK8.42349**; AZ6/*CY4* 42349. Palmer, Rolfe-Johnson, Stockholm Bach Ch., VCM, Harnoncourt.

An outstanding new version of Handel's splendid *Ode for St Cecilia's Day* from Ledger. With superb soloists – Jill Gomez radiantly beautiful and Robert Tear dramatically riveting in his call to arms, *The trumpet's loud clangour* – this delightful music emerges with an admirable combination of freshness and weight. Ledger uses an all-male chorus; the style of the performance is totally convincing without being self-consciously authentic. The recording is first rate, rich, vivid and clear, with better definition and greater presence in the CD format. The cassette is good, too, if not quite so sharp in its upper focus. Highly recommended.

Recorded with two of the same soloists as Harnoncourt's version of *Alexander's Feast*, his version of the *Ode* has most of the same merits and flaws, but it is worth noting that there is currently no rival using period instruments. The digital transfer, made as part of the Telefunken Handel Edition, clarifies the 1970s sound.

Samson.

*** Erato STU 71240 (4). Dame Janet Baker, Watts, Tear, Luxon, Shirley-Quirk, Burrowes, Lott, L. Voices, ECO, Leppard.

(M) ** DG 413 914-1 (4) [id.]. Young, Arroyo, Donath, Armstrong, Procter, Jennings, Stewart, Flagello, Mun. Bach Ch. and O, Karl Richter.

Leppard directs a highly dramatic account of Handel's most dramatic oratorio, one which translates very happily to the stage; its culmination, the exultant aria, *Let the bright seraphim*, is here beautifully sung by Felicity Lott, but for long was associated with Joan Sutherland at Covent Garden. The moment when the orchestra interrupts a soloist in mid-sentence to indicate the collapse of the temple is more vividly dramatic than anything in a Handel opera, and Leppard handles that and much else with total conviction. Robert Tear as Samson produces his most heroic tones – rather too aggressively so in *Total eclipse* – and the rest of the cast could hardly be more distinguished. Dame Janet Baker – not by nature a seductress in the Dalila sense – yet sings with a lightness totally apt for such an aria as *With plaintive notes*, and the others are in excellent voice. The recording is outstanding, atmospheric and well balanced.

Richter has a price advantage and excellent soloists: Alexander Young's Samson is impressive, and hardly less so are Norma Procter and Martina Arroyo, who makes a vivid Dalila. The least convincing part of the proceedings is

Richter's own heavy-handed conducting. He does not feel obliged to give us cadential trills or grace notes in recitatives and he is never particularly imaginative in his handling of detail. However, he does succeed in conveying the scale and majesty of the work and secures good playing from the Munich orchestra. The recording received wide praise at its first appearance in 1969, but it is now superseded by Leppard's Erato recording, which we hope will soon appear on CD.

Saul (complete).
(M) *** DG 413 910-1 (3) [id.]. Armstrong, Price, Bowman, Ryland Davies, English, Dean, McIntyre, Leeds Fest. Ch., ECO, Mackerras.

Few Handel choral works have been recorded with such consistent imagination as this fine performance conducted by Mackerras. With an excellent complement of soloists he steers an exhilarating course in a work that naturally needs to be presented with authenticity but equally needs to have dramatic edge. His scholarship is worn lightly, and the result is powerful on one hand, moving on another, sparkling on yet another. The contrast of timbre between Armstrong and Price, for example, is beautifully exploited, and Donald McIntyre as Saul, Ryland Davies as Jonathan, and James Bowman as a counter-tenor David are all outstanding, while the chorus willingly contributes to the drama. An outstanding set, beautifully recorded.

Solomon (complete).
⊛ ϵ *** Ph. Dig. **412 612-2** (2); 412 612-1/*4* (3) [id.]. C. Watkinson, Argenta, Hendricks, Rolfe-Johnson, Monteverdi Ch., E. Bar. Soloists, Gardiner.

This is among the very finest of all Handel oratorio recordings, triumphant proof that authentic performance can be the opposite of dry, detached and inexpressive; and the theatrical flair of the piece in its three sharply differentiated Acts is consistently brought out. With panache, Gardiner shows how authentic-sized forces can convey Handelian grandeur even with clean-focused textures and fast speeds that will have the older traditionalists jumping up in alarm. *Swell the full chorus*, they all sing at the end of Act II, after Solomon's Judgement, and with trumpets and timpani you could hardly imagine anything more joyful, a dance movement translated. The choruses and even more magnificent double-choruses stand as cornerstones of a structure which may have less of a story-line than some other Handel oratorios – the Judgement apart – but which Gardiner shows has consistent human warmth. Thus in Act I, the relationship of Solomon and his Queen is delightfully presented, ending with the ravishing Nightingale chorus, *May no rash intruder*, while the Act III scenes between Solomon and the Queen of Sheba, necessarily more formal, are given extra warmth by having in that role a singer who is sensuous in tone, Barbara Hendricks. She is one of the five excellent women principals, all strongly contrasted with one another. Carolyn Watkinson's pure mezzo, at times like a male alto, is very apt for Solomon himself (only after Handel's death did baritones capture it), while Nancy Argenta is clear and sweet as his Queen. In the Judgement scene Joan

Rodgers is outstandingly warm and characterful as the First Harlot, but the overriding glory of the set is the radiant singing of Gardiner's Monteverdi Choir. Its clean, crisp articulation matches the brilliant playing of the English Baroque Soloists, regularly challenged by Gardiner's fast speeds as in the *Arrival of the Queen of Sheba*. One big advantage from some judicious cutting of 'dead wood' is that the whole work, at 2 hours 20 minutes, is squeezed on to two CDs merely, and the sound is superb, coping thrillingly with the problems of the double choruses. There are three LPs and chrome cassettes, closely matched in sound, but the compact discs are even finer.

Utrecht Te Deum.
*(*) Tel. Dig. **ZK8.42955**; AZ6/*CY4*. 42955. Palmer, Lipovsek, Langridge, Vienna Boys' Ch., Schoenberg Ch., VCM, Harnoncourt – BACH: *Magnificat.**

Utrecht Te Deum and Jubilate.
*** O-L **414 413-2** [id.]; DSLO/*KDSLC* 582. Nelson, Kirkby, Brett, Elliot, Covey-Crump, Thomas, Ch. of Christ Church Cathedral, Oxford, AAM, Preston.

Handel wrote the Utrecht pieces just before coming to London, intending them as a sample of his work. Using authentic instruments and an all-male choir with trebles, Preston directs a performance which is not merely scholarly but characteristically alert and vigorous, particularly impressive in the superb *Gloria* with its massive eight-part chords. With a team of soloists regularly associated with the Academy of Ancient Music, the CD can be confidently recommended: the remastering from the original analogue recording is very successful. There is a good cassette, but there is some loss of refinement at the top.

Handel's magnificent *Utrecht Te Deum* makes a generous coupling for Bach's *Magnificat*, and in a relatively intimate acoustic Harnoncourt sometimes presents allegros briskly and lightly – but, as in the *Magnificat*, that is the exception. The characterful solo singing – the murky-sounding contralto apart – marries oddly with slow, heavy speeds and leaden rhythms, and the chorus, efficient enough, lacks brightness and rhythmic spring. Dryish recording.

OPERA

Atalanta (complete).
*** Hung. Dig. **HCD 12612/4**. Farkas, Bartfai-Barta, Lax, Bandi, Gregor, Polgar, Savaria Vocal Ens. and Capella, McGegan.

It is welcome to find Hungary producing – with the help of a British conductor and continuo-player, Nicholas McGegan – so stylish an authentic performance of a Handel opera on period instruments. The fresh precision of the string playing of the Capella Savaria demonstrates – even without the help of vibrato – what Hungarian string quartets have been proving for generations, a superfine ability to match and blend. Though it is odd that a Communist country should have lighted on an opera expressly written to celebrate a royal occasion (the wedding of Frederick, Prince of Wales, whose long-standing animosity towards Handel promptly evaporated) it proves an excellent choice, crammed with dozens of sparkling light-hearted numbers with no lull in the inspiration, the opposite of weighty Handel. Led by the bright-toned Katarin Farkas in the name-part, the singers cope stylishly, and the absence of Slavonic wobbles confirms the subtle difference of Magyar voices; Joszef Gregor with his firm, dark bass is just as much in style, for example, as he regularly is in Verdi. First-rate recording.

Giulio Cesare (complete).
(M) *(*) DG 413 897-1 (4) [id.]. Fischer-Dieskau, Troyanos, Hamari, Schreier, Crass, Mun. Bach Ch. and O, Karl Richter.

Julius Caesar (complete, in English).
*** HMV Dig. EX 270232-3/*5* (3). Dame Janet Baker, Masterson, Sarah Walker, Della Jones, Bowman, Tomlinson, E. Nat. Op. Ch. and O, Mackerras.

Julius Caesar, particularly in English translation, as in this set based on the ENO stage production at the Coliseum, really does bear out what specialists have long claimed concerning Handel's powers of characterization in opera. With Mackerras's lively and sensitive conducting, this is vivid and dramatically involving in a way rare with Handel opera on record. Dame Janet, in glorious voice and drawing on the widest range of expressive tone-colours, shatters the old idea that this alto-castrato role should be transposed down an octave and given to a baritone. Valerie Masterson makes a charming and seductive Cleopatra, fresh and girlish, though the voice is caught a little too brightly for caressing such radiant melodies as those for *V'adoro pupille* (*Lamenting, complaining*) and *Piangero* (*Flow my tears*). Sarah Walker sings with powerful intensity as Pompey's widow; James Bowman is a characterful counter-tenor Ptolemy and John Tomlinson a firm, resonant Achillas, the other nasty character. The ravishing accompaniments to the two big Cleopatra arias amply justify the use by the excellent ENO Orchestra of modern, not period, instruments. The full, vivid studio sound makes this one of the very finest of the invaluable series of ENO opera recordings in English sponsored by the Peter Moores Foundation.

Spread luxuriantly over four records (where Mackerras's ENO set achieves completeness on only three) Richter's version presents the German tradition of Handel opera performance in all its square solidity. The line-up of soloists is impressive, and Fischer-Dieskau sings with fine detail and formidable intensity; but it is a travesty of Handel to transpose down the original alto-castrato part. The sound is on the dry side, but clear and full.

Tamerlano (complete).
** CBS Dig. 13M/*13T* 37893 (3). Ledroit, Elwes, Van der Sluis, Jacobs, Poulenard, Reinhardt, La Grande Ecurie et la Chambre du Roy, Malgoire.

Tamerlano is one of Handel's most masterly operas and, though Malgoire's performance is not ideal, it fills an important gap. His style here is less abrasive than it has been on some other opera sets; but one looks in vain for an element of elegance or charm, despite some excellent work from a good band of soloists, with the two counter-tenors well contrasted – René Jacobs as ever a tower of strength – and with Mieke van der Sluis outstanding among the women. A warning ought to be given that this is a piece slow in starting but increasingly impressive over Acts II and III, with more ensembles than Handel customarily included. Some arias have been cut, but one has been added in Act I, well sung by the bass, Gregory Reinhardt. Good, clear sound, with the lavishly presented chrome cassettes matching the discs closely.

COLLECTIONS

Arias: *Judas Maccabaeus: Father of heaven. Messiah: O Thou that tellest; He was despised. Samson: Return O God of Hosts.*
❀ (***) Decca mono **414 623-2**; stereo 414 623-1/*4*. Kathleen Ferrier, LPO, Boult – BACH: *Arias.*(***)

Kathleen Ferrier had a unique feeling for Handel; these performances are unforgettable for their communicative intensity and nobility of timbre and line. She receives highly sympathetic accompaniments from Boult, another natural Handelian. While (here more than in the Bach coupling) there may be some who will prefer the more richly upholstered stereo orchestral sound of the LP and cassette with its fuller upper string timbre, there is no doubt that the direct derivation of the compact disc from the original mono master tape gives the voice greater freshness and realism. John Culshaw who produced the 1952 LP described this performance of *He was despised* as having 'a beauty and simplicity that I cannot think has been, or will be, surpassed'. On compact disc the deeply moving closing bars, when the orchestra drops away to leave the voice momentarily unaccompanied in the words 'He was despised . . . rejected', has an uncanny presence. There is, of course, pre-Dolby background noise, but it in no way detracts from the illusion of reality.

Opera arias: *Agrippina: Bel piacere. Orlando: Fammi combattere. Partenope: Funbondo spira il vento. Rinaldo: Or la tromba; Cara sposa; Venti turbini; Cor ingrato; Lascio ch'io piango mia cruda sorta. Serse: Frondi tenere; Ombra mai fù.*
(*) Erato Dig. **ECD 88034; NUM/*MCE* 75047. Marilyn Horne, Sol. Ven., Scimone.

Horne gives virtuoso performances of a wide-ranging collection of Handel arias. The flexibility of her voice in scales and trills and ornaments of every kind remains formidable, and the power is extraordinary down to the tangy chest register. The voice is spotlit against a reverberant acoustic. Purists may question some of the ornamentation, but voice-fanciers will not worry. The recording sounds well in all three media.

'Great choruses': Coronation anthem: Zadok the Priest. Israel in Egypt: He spake the word; He gave them hailstones. Jephtha: When his loud voice. Judas Maccabaeus: See the conqu'ring hero comes. Messiah: Hallelujah; For unto us a child is born; Worthy is the Lamb; Amen. Saul: Gird on thy sword. Solomon: May no rash intruder.

(B) ** Con. CC/*CCTC* 7611. Handel Op. Soc. Ch. and O, Farncombe.

An enjoyable concert, freshly sung and vividly recorded. It opens with an attractively buoyant account of *Hallelujah*, and there is an unexpected refinement in *For unto us a child is born*. Of the lesser-known choruses, *May no rash intruder* from *Solomon* with its evocative pastoral scene is particularly successful. The small orchestral group and indeed the excellent amateur choral singing readily make up in spontaneity for any lack of polish. The recording, originally made by Decca in their hi-fi-conscious Phase Four system, has been remastered to give greater projection, and has now lost some of its depth, especially on the clear, bright cassette.

'90 Minutes' (anthology): (i) *Music for the Royal Fireworks:* suite, arr. Harty); *Water music* (suite, arr. Harty); (ii) *Overture: Berenice; Solomon; Arrival of the Queen of Sheba.* Excerpts from: (iii) *Acis and Galatea;* (iv) *Israel in Egypt;* (iv; v) *Judas Maccabaeus;* (iv; vi) *Messiah;* (vii) *Samson;* (v) *Semele; Serse;* (viii) *Rodelinda;* (iv) *Zadok the Priest.*

❀ (B) *** Decca *414 048-4.* (i) LSO, Szell; (ii) ASMF, Marriner; (iii) Forbes Robinson; (iv) Handel Op. Soc. Ch. and O, Farncombe; (v) Kenneth McKellar; (vi) Kathleen Ferrier; (vii) Joan Sutherland; (viii) Bernadette Greevy.

This extraordinarily successful tape anthology – a model of its kind – is chosen with great skill to make an entertainment for a motorway journey, but also a splendid hour and a half of music making for domestic use. Centred on the Harty suites from the *Fireworks* and *Water music*, superbly played by the LSO under George Szell, the programme intersperses orchestral items with some of Handel's most attractive songs and arias, from Forbes Robinson's infectious *O ruddier than the cherry* and Joan Sutherland's *Let the bright seraphim*, to Kenneth McKellar's *Where'er you walk* and Kathleen Ferrier's *He was despised.* Choruses abound too, from *Messiah* and *Judas Maccabaeus* to *Zadok the Priest*; the collection also includes of course the lollipops like the *Minuet* from *Berenice* and the *Arrival of the Queen of Sheba.* With consistently good sound, this is far more than the sum of its parts and readily demonstrates both Handel's greatness and the universality of his inspiration.

Hartmann, Karl (1905–63)

Symphony No. 4 for string orchestra; Symphony No. 8.
(M) *** DG 413 650-1. Bav. RSO, Kubelik.

Karl Amadeus Hartmann enjoyed something of a vogue in Germany during the 1950s but has since fallen into neglect. The two symphonies recorded here make an excellent visiting card and give a good idea of his art. Rafael Kubelik gave the first performance of the *Eighth* (composed in 1962) in Cologne; these recordings were made not long after in 1968, but sound absolutely first class. The *Fourth, for strings*, dates from the immediate post-war years (1946–7) and has much the same post-expressionist language as the *Concerto funèbre*, also for strings. The *Eighth*, too, has a strongly post-expressionist feel to it, particularly the opening cantilena, but takes time before it reveals its true stature. His sound world is less richly imaginative, immediate and distinctive than Henze's but, even if at first this writing seems dense and unapproachable, one senses that it is music of substance. A strong recommendation to all who care about twentieth-century music. Most collectors would be better advised to investigate this version before going on to the complete set of the symphonies on Wergo (60086), which we have not been able to sample but which is available at some specialist outlets.

Harty, Hamilton (1879–1941)

(i) *Piano concerto in B min.;* (ii) *In Ireland* (*Fantasy for flute, harp and orchestra*); *With the wild geese.*
*** Chan. Dig. **CHAN 8321**; ABRD/*ABTD* 1084 [id.]. (i) Binns, (ii) Fleming, Kelly; Ulster O, Thomson.

This is the most engaging of the records issued so far in this enterprising series which is uncovering the art of a minor but rewarding talent. The *Piano concerto*, written in 1922, has strong Rachmaninovian influences (there are indelible associations with that composer's *Second Concerto* in both slow movement and finale). But the melodic freshness remains individual and in this highly sympathetic performance the work's magnetism increases with familiarity, in spite of moments of rhetoric. The *In Ireland fantasy* is full of delightful Irish melodic whimsy, especially appealing when the playing is so winning. Melodrama enters the scene in the symphonic poem, *With the wild geese*, but its Irishry asserts itself immediately in the opening theme. Again a splendid performance and on CD a high standard of digital sound. On the excellent chrome tape a slightly lower transfer level in the *Concerto* softens the edge on the upper strings very appropriately.

Violin concerto in D; Variations on a Dublin air.
*** Chan. **CHAN 8386**; ABR/*ABT* 1044 [id.]. Ralph Holmes, Ulster O, Thomson.

The *Violin concerto* is an early work and comes from 1908; it was written for Szigeti, who gave the first performance. Though it has no strongly individual idiom, the invention is fresh and often touched with genuine poetry. Ralph Holmes gives a thoroughly committed account of the solo part and is well supported by an augmented Ulster Orchestra under Bryden Thomson. The *Variations* are less impressive though thoroughly enjoyable, and readers who imagine that the orchestral playing will be indifferent (this was the début record of this provincial orchestra) will be pleasantly surprised. These are accomplished and well-recorded performances, the analogue masters successfully transferred to CD. The tape transfers are well balanced, but lack the last degree of range and sparkle in the treble.

An Irish symphony; A Comedy overture.
*** Chan. Dig. **CHAN 8314**; ABRD/*ABTD* 1027 [id.]. Ulster O, Thomson.

The *Irish symphony* dates from 1904 and arose from a competition for a suite or symphony based on traditional Irish airs, inspired by the first Dublin performance of Dvořák's *New World symphony*, 'founded upon negro melodies'! Harty's symphony won great acclaim for its excellent scoring and good craftsmanship. He revised it twice, and though it lays no claim to being a work of exceptional individuality, it is an attractive and well-wrought piece of light music. The scherzo is particularly engaging. It is extremely well played by the Ulster Orchestra under Bryden Thomson, and the overture is also successful and enjoyable. The recording is absolutely first class in every respect and sounds splendid in its CD format. The cassette is marginally less wide-ranging than the disc, but still yields excellent results.

With the wild geese (symphonic poem).
(M) *** HMV ED 290208-1/*4*. SNO, Gibson – GERMAN: *Welsh rhapsody*; MACCUNN: *Land of Mountain and Flood*; SMYTH: *The Wreckers overture*.***

With the wild geese, written in 1910 for the Cardiff Festival, is a melodramatic piece about the Irish soldiers fighting on the French side in the Battle of Fontenoy. The ingredients – a gay Irish theme and a call to arms among them – are effectively deployed; although the music does not reveal a strong individual personality, it is carried by a romantic sweep which is well exploited here. The 1968 recording, always vivid, has been freshened in this mid-priced reissue and sounds especially well in its tape format.

VOCAL MUSIC

The Children of Lir; Ode to a nightingale.
*** Chan. Dig. **CHAN 8387**; ABRD/*ABTD* 1051 [id.]. Harper, Ulster O, Thomson.

These two fine works span the full breadth of Harty's composing career. His setting of Keats' *Ode to a nightingale* written in 1907 reflects a time when a British (or Irish) composer could tackle boldly a grand setting of a poetic masterpiece almost too familiar. It says much for Harty's inspiration that the result is so richly convincing, a piece written for his future wife, the soprano, Agnes Nicholls. The other work, directly Irish in its inspiration, evocative in an almost Sibelian way, dates from 1939 and uses the soprano in wordless melisma, here beautifully sung by Heather Harper. The performances are excellent, warmly committed and superbly recorded, especially in their CD format. The cassette transfer of the symphonic poem on side one is made at only a modest level and lacks something in immediacy; the *Ode* is more effectively managed with a good vocal presence and natural balance.

Haydn, Josef (1732–1809)

6 Allemandes, Hob IX/12; 5 Contredanses: Minuet and Quadrille, Hob IX/24 and 29; 8 Gypsy dances, Hob IX/28; Ländler from The Seasons; Minuetti di ballo Nos 1–6, Hob IX/4; Notturni for 2 flutes and 2 horns, Hob II/D5.
*(*) HM Dig. **HMC 901057**. Bella Musica of Vienna Ens., Dittrich.

Although the music here is uneven, there is much of interest, not least the *Nocturnes* for flutes and horns and the first of the *Minuetti di ballo*, also attractively featuring flutes. The *Zingarese* only survive in a version for harpsichord, but Michael Dittrich has scored them traditionally, for a small group using a cymbalom; and one of the most appealing numbers is a solo for that characterful instrument, played very gently, and the more effective for the background silence of CD. However, in many of the pieces for the main group the dry acoustic and close microphones are unflattering to the violin timbre. It is not clear whether the players use 'original instruments', but the vinegar in the treble gives that impression, and robs the music making of a good deal of its charm.

Cello concerto in D, Op. 101, Hob VIIb/2.
** Denon Dig. **C37 7023** [id.]. Fujiwara, Netherlands CO, Inoue – BOCCHERINI: *Cello concerto.*
(B) ** DG Walkman *415 330-4*. Fournier, Lucerne Fest. O, Baumgartner – DVOŘÁK; BOCCHERINI: *Cello concertos.****

Cello concertos in C and D, Hob VIIb/1–2.
*** O-L Dig. **414 615-2**; DSDL/*KDSDC* 711 [id.]. Coin, AAM, Hogwood.

Cello concertos: in C, Hob VIIb/1; in D, Hob VIIb/4.
(*) Ph. Dig. **412 793-2; 412 793-1/*4* [id.]. Lloyd Webber with ECO.

(i) *Cello concerto in D;* (ii) *Trumpet concerto in E flat;* (iii) *Violin concerto in C.*
(*) CBS Dig. **MK 39310; IM/*IMT* 39310 [id.]. (i) Yo-Yo Ma, ECO, Garcia; (ii) Marsalis, Nat. PO, Leppard; (iii) Lin, Minnesota O, Marriner.

The discovery of Haydn's early *C major Cello concerto* in Prague in the early 1960s provided a marvellous addition to the limited cello repertory. For some, this concerto is even more attractive than the well-known D major work that for a time was fathered on Anton Kraft instead of Haydn. For those wanting the two concertos paired together, the young French soloist, Christophe Coin, provides a ready answer. He is a superb soloist and, provided the listener has no reservations about the use of original instruments, Hogwood's accompaniments are equally impressive. The style is not aggressively abrasive but gives extra clarity and point to the music, not least in the breathtakingly brilliant account of the finale of the *C major Concerto*. Certainly no fresher or more vital performance of these two works has been put on disc, although Coin's own cadenzas – undoubtedly stylish – are on the long side. Excellent sound on CD and LP; the upper range of the chrome cassette shows slight loss of refinement.

Yo-Yo Ma's approach to the more familiar *D major Concerto* is comparatively restrained in expression, gently moulded in the slow movement. But it is a reading of distinction, and its gentleness has a special appeal, when detail is so subtle. The account of the *Trumpet concerto* is discussed below and is certainly vivid. But Cho-Liang Lin's performance of the *Violin concerto* is less individual (see also below). The CBS recording has excellent clarity and its presence is very striking on CD. The orchestral sound is clear rather than warm – although on the chrome cassette, which is generally softer in focus, the balance is fuller.

Mari Fujiwara is a player of considerable quality, and collectors allergic to authentic-instrument recordings might like to consider this. The orchestral contribution under Michi Inoue, though not distinguished, is perfectly acceptable and the soloist is splendid. So, too, is the recording.

Fournier plays with style and polish; if Baumgartner's accompaniment is relatively unimaginative, the 1968 recording sounds better here than it has on some previous presentations. The Boccherini and Dvořák couplings are very attractive, and this Walkman chrome tape is certainly good value.

Lloyd Webber couples the *C major Concerto* with yet another newly discovered *Concerto in D*. This was originally published in a spurious 'improved' version by Grützmacher. The 'original edition' resurfaced in East Germany in 1948 and is claimed as authentic Haydn. This seems doubtful; although it is a substantial piece, it is of uneven appeal. Lloyd Webber's approach to both concertos is strong and committed, but rather heavy – he tends to overphrase. This is emphasized by a forward balance that makes the cello almost outweigh the orchestra. This larger-than-life impression is not the image this artist presents in the concert hall. In all other respects the recording is very good, especially on CD where, because of the clear definition, the ear accepts the presentation more readily.

(i) *Cello concerto in D, Hob VIIb/2;* (ii) *Piano concerto in D, Hob XVIII/2; Symphonies Nos* (iii) *59 in A* (*Fire*)*;* (iv) *100 in G* (*Military*).

(B) **(*) Ph. On Tour *412 900-4* [id.]. (i) Gendron, LOP, Casals; (ii) Haebler, Netherlands CO, Goldberg; (iii) ASMF, Marriner; (iv) VSO, Sawallisch.

In the *D major Cello concerto* Gendron is right on form, and the stylishness of his phrasing, coupled to complete security of intonation, makes for an admirable performance of this attractive work, with Pablo Casals's sympathetic handling of the orchestral contribution playing no little part in the overall success of the reading. Similarly, Ingrid Haebler sparkles attractively in Haydn's best-known *Piano concerto*. The two solo works are framed on this double-length chrome tape by Marriner's fresh and polished account of the *Fire symphony* (an unexpected, but welcome choice) and Sawallisch's straighter version of the *Military symphony*. The overall compilation works quite well, although the mix of artists and recording dates seems a little clumsy. The sound, always good, is a little variable, but not so inconsistent as to spoil listening in a continuous sequence.

Horn concertos Nos 1 in D, Hob VII/d3; 2 in D, Hob VIII/d4.

ꞓ *** Tel. Dig. **ZK8 42960**; AZ6/*CX4* 42960 [id.]. Clevenger, Liszt CO, Rolla – M. HAYDN: *Concertino.**** ꞓ

(M) *** HMV ED 290302-1/*4* [Ang. AM/*4AM* 34720]. Tuckwell, ECO – M. HAYDN: *Concertino.****

(i) *Horn concertos Nos 1–2;* (ii) *Trumpet concerto in E flat;* (i) *Divertimento a 3 in E flat.*

(*) Nimbus **NIM 5010 [id.]. (i) Thompson; (ii) Wallace; Philh. O, Warren-Green.

Dale Clevenger, principal horn with the Chicago Symphony, gives superb accounts of the two *Horn concertos* attributed to Haydn (the second is of doubtful lineage). He is especially good in the slow movements, a little solemn in the *First*, but eloquently so, with the *Adagio* of its companion given an air of gentle melancholy. This is a movement that can seem too long, but not here. The dotted main theme of the first movement, nicely pointed, is most engaging, and the performance projects a galant charm of the kind we associate with Hummel. The accompaniments are supportive, polished and elegant. These performances have fine spirit and spontaneity and on CD the Telefunken recording, made in a nicely judged and warm acoustic, is in the demonstration class: when Clevenger plays his solo cadenzas the tangibility of his presence is remarkable, yet the combination with the orchestra is hardly less convincing.

In his interesting notes for the Nimbus CD, Michael Thompson suggests that Haydn wrote his *First* and *Second Concertos* for his first and second horn players, Thaddaus Steinmüller and Carl Franz. Yet both works explore the widest range, and it was the *Divertimento*, an attractive bonus, that exploited Steinmüller's ability to slip easily into the stratosphere of the horn register. Thompson manages it too, with aplomb, and he gives bold, confident accounts of the two concertos, with a sprinkling of decoration. Christopher Warren-Green paces the slow movement of No. 1 only fractionally slower than Rolla, but his withdrawn, elegiac mood has a valedictory feeling. In contrast, the opening movement of the *Second Concerto* is slightly faster, but the orchestral playing is less precise (not helped by the reverberation) and the effect of the Clevenger performance is jauntier. John Wallace's trumpet timbre is strikingly brilliant, as recorded, and his playing in the *Trumpet concerto* is full of personality. He too likes to decorate and there are some attractive surprises in the finale. Again the pacing of the *Andante* is measured, but Wallace sustains the slower speed with nicely expressive phrasing. The recording was made in the resonant ambience of All Saints, Tooting, but the CD provides good definition under the circumstances, even if the harpsichord tends to get lost. This is very agreeable of its kind and, with 57′ of music, is better value than any of its competitors.

Barry Tuckwell has recorded these concertos before for Argo (ZRG 5498) but they are differently coupled. For HMV he shares the same Michael Haydn work chosen by Clevenger. Needless to say, his playing is first class, with the solo line of the *First Concerto* memorably eloquent. The orchestral support is crisp and classical in feeling; the phrasing has less finesse than on the Argo disc (under Marriner) but is neat and musical. The sound is good, and this makes an admirable mid-priced recommendation on both disc and cassette.

Oboe concerto in C.

(M) *** Ph. Seq. 6527/*7311* 190. Holliger, Concg. O, Zinman – MOZART: *Concerto.****

Haydn's *Oboe concerto* is of doubtful authenticity – but in this account, played by Holliger with wonderful finesse, Haydn surely would not have minded the attribution. Zinman's accompaniment is very well done and the 1979 recording is first class. There is an excellent matching cassette.

Organ concertos Nos 1–3 in C, Hob XVIII/1, 5 and 8.

(M) *** Ph. Seq. 6527/*7311* 200 [id.]. Chorzempa, German Bach Soloists, Winschermann.

Haydn's *Organ concertos* are not among his greatest works but, given spirited performances, they can sound attractively spontaneous. Daniel Chorzempa's playing of the organ at the Bergkirche, Eisenstadt, seems eminently suited to them; the acoustic of the church provides an attractive ambience for Winschermann's group, which makes the most of the accompaniments. The strings are appealingly fresh and phrasing is musical, while allegros are alert and vivacious. The overall balance is excellent, and as Chorzempa's registration is imaginative, this can carry a strong recommendation. The high-level tape is quite as vivid as the disc – indeed, it approaches demonstration standard – and the 1972 recording is in no way dated.

Trumpet concerto in E flat.

*** Delos Dig. **D/CD 3001** [id.]. Schwarz, New York 'Y' CO – HUMMEL: *Concerto.****

*** CBS **CD 37846**; 37846/*40*- [id.]. Marsalis, Nat. PO, Leppard – HUMMEL; L. MOZART: *Concertos.****

** Ph. Dig. **415 104-2**; 415 104-1/*4* [id.]. Herseth, Chicago SO, Abbado – MOZART: *Concertos for Bassoon; Horn; Oboe.***

Haydn's most famous concerto is well served on compact disc. Michael Thompson's brilliant and characterful account on Nimbus should not be forgotten – it is the most generously coupled of all, with three additional concertante works for the horn (see above). Marsalis's CBS compact disc also offers extra works, and his playing is much admired. But Schwarz's account on Delos is in many ways the finest on record since George Eskdale's famous 78 r.p.m. version – and he only recorded the last two movements. Indeed, Schwarz's stylish command, richly gleaming timbre and easy bravura are impossible to resist, and in the lovely *Andante* he adds a little decoration to the melody, played with a warm, serene elegance. The finale combines wit and sparkle. The recording is attractively reverberant without inflating the lively accompaniment which Schwarz himself directs (easier for a trumpeter to do than a keyboard player), with the CD giving the soloist tangible presence.

Marsalis is splendid too, his bravura no less spectacular, with the finale a *tour de force*, yet never aggressive in its brilliance. He is cooler than Schwarz in the slow movement, and this element of reserve perhaps stems from an anxiety not to carry over too much freedom from the jazz world with which he had hitherto been more familiar. This record became a best-seller in America and led to his recording a captivating follow-up anthology of Baroque trumpet music in partnership with Edith Gruberova (see Recitals below). Certainly his way with Haydn is eminently stylish, as is Leppard's lively and polished accompaniment. The CBS recording is faithful and the CD gives a very vivid projection, although the orchestral sound is slightly artificial in its immediacy.

Adolph Herseth's performance is characterful and thoroughly musical. It is part of a generous collection of wind and brass concertos (the remaining three by Mozart), recorded by principals from the Chicago Symphony Orchestra. There is no lack of accomplishment here; Abbado's accompaniment is predictably refined and the DG recording is excellent in all three formats. However, unless the couplings are especially suitable, this must be regarded as an also-ran.

Violin concerto in C, Hob VIIa/1.

€ *** Tel. Dig. **ZK8 42917**; AZ6 42917 [id.]. Zehetmair, Liszt CO – M. HAYDN: *Violin concerto.***(*)

(*) Ph. **412 718-2; 412 718-1/*4* [id.]. Van Keulen, Netherlands CO, Ros-Marba – MOZART: *Violin concerto No. 2.***(*)

** CBS Dig. **CD 37796**; 37796 [id.]. Lin, Minnesota O, Marriner – VIEUXTEMPS: *Concerto No. 5.***(*)

Haydn's *C major Violin concerto* is given a superb performance by the young Hungarian violinist, Thomas Zehetmair, stylish, strong and resilient. He also directs the accompaniments which are alert and spirited in outer movements and responsive in the lovely *Adagio*. On his bow this central movement has a touching lyrical serenity, essentially classical in spirit, yet expressively beautiful in timbre. The recording is first class, with the soloist given the most realistic presence on CD, yet with no sense that the microphones were placed too near. The orchestra is truthfully balanced within an attractively resonant acoustic.

Isabelle van Keulen was the European 'Young Musician of the Year' in 1984 when aged only eighteen; she gave an impressive account of herself in the Vieuxtemps *Fifth Concerto*. She is hardly less sweet-toned or persuasive here in the *C major* Haydn. She is particularly good in the slow movement, which shows her guilelessly lyrical phrasing to be as imaginative as her bowing is impeccable. The accompanying of the Netherlands orchestra under Antoni Ros-Marba is not, however, particularly distinguished. The recording is in the excellent traditions of the house, well balanced and truthful. The compact disc offers the usual gain in clarity and presence. The only possible grumble is that, at roughly twenty minutes a side, it offers short measure. The chrome cassette is surprisingly brightly lit for a Philips issue.

Cho-Liang Lin's performance has more strength and drive than Miss Van Keulen's and is not wanting in character, but it is almost entirely lacking in charm, notably in the slow movement. Moreover, the CBS coupling seems ill-considered, although the recording is impressive. It is made in a drier acoustic than the Philips and the balance is forward; but on CD every detail is clear and the solo image is very believable, with Lin's full timbre displayed to advantage. He plays the Vieuxtemps coupling with considerable flair.

Violin concerto in G, Hob VIIa/4.

(*) Sup. Dig. **C37 7571 [id.]. Josef Suk, Suk CO, Vlach – VAŇHAL: *Concerto.***(*)

Haydn's three violin concertos are all early works, written for Luigi Tomasini. The *G major* is less memorable than the *C major* (Hob VIIa/1), but Suk's advocacy is persuasive. He is forwardly balanced, but his image is truthful and the playing is warm yet classical in spirit and has plenty of vitality in the outer movements. He is well accompanied, with the orchestra effectively alert and crisply rhythmic in the finale. The background ambience is well judged, and the sound is full-bodied. With only 38′ 11″ offered here, this CD is not, however, very generous.

Overtures, Sinfonias and Ballet music: *Armida: Sinfonia; March. La fedeltà premiata: Sinfonia. L'incontro improviso: Overture; Intermezzo. L'infedeltà delusa: Overture. L'isola disabitata: Sinfonia. Il mondo della luna: Overture;* Act II: *Sinfonia; Ballet music; March. La vera costanza: Sinfonia.*

(M) *** Ph. Seq. 6527/*7311* 145. Lausanne CO, Dorati.

Taken from Dorati's series of complete opera recordings made in Lausanne, this collection of overtures (sinfonias) and ballet music can be warmly recommended. All those here were written between 1775 and 1783, when opera was Haydn's main concern at Esterháza. He may have been limited in his dramatic sense, but here in creating expectation and lively atmosphere he was a master. Splendid performances and first-rate recording, but the sleeve-notes are sadly uninformative. The cassette quality is always good, but suffers from variability in range and vividness between items.

SYMPHONIES

Symphonies Nos 6 in D (Le Matin); 7 in C (Le Midi); 8 in G (Le Soir).
*** Ph. Dig. **411 441-2**; 6514/*7337* 076 [id.]. ASMF, Marriner.

Although Sir Neville Marriner and the Academy can seem bland at times, this performance of the three symphonies Haydn composed not long after taking up his appointment at the Esterházy court in 1761 has plenty of character. This has been a popular coupling over the years, but the Marriner set is probably the best we have had for some time: it is generally fresher and more polished than the rival set from the Prague Chamber Orchestra and Bernhard Klee (now deleted). The CD is admirably balanced, with realistic detail, although the harpsichord is only just distinguishable. The tape is satisfactory but its upper range is less sharp than on the LP and compact disc.

Symphonies Nos 26 in D min. (Lamentatione); 41 in C; 43 in E flat (Mercury); 44 in E min. (Trauersinfonie); 48 in C (Maria Theresa); 52 in C min. Overture: Le Pescatrici.
**(*) CBS Dig. 13M/*13T* 39040 (3). L'Estro Armonico, Solomons.

Derek Solomons' project, to record the complete Haydn Symphonies in chronological as opposed to (Breitkopf and Hartel) numerical order, here reaches the dark period of the *Sturm und Drang* symphonies, six remarkable works, not just the named ones but the powerful No. 52 in C minor and the C major, No. 41. As in the early symphonies (available on Saga HAYDN 1, HAYDN 2 and CBS D3 37861) Solomons keeps his ensemble of period instruments very small, with six violins but only one each of the other string instruments. Recorded in the pleasingly atmospheric acoustic of St Barnabas Church, Woodside Park, the sense of lively, intimate music-making is delightful. The ensemble is not always as polished as in some authentic performances, but for the general listener the important point is that Solomons has modified his earlier approach to slow movements, which no longer have the squeezing, bulging style sometimes favoured by the 'authentic' movement. So the haunting slow movement of No. 44 (the *Trauer* or *Mourning symphony* – the one which Haydn wanted played at his own funeral) has a silky gentleness. As before, the intimacy of ensemble never prevents allegros from having the necessary bite and vigour. Not everyone will welcome such generous observance of repeats, but this makes a desirable and very distinct alternative to the Dorati series on Decca, the more stylish now that the players, with no sense of routine, have settled down to their marathon task. (The chrome cassettes are lavishly packaged; however, in spite of quite a high transfer level, the resonance clouds the upper range and the strings lack bite.)

Symphonies Nos 42 in D; 45 in F sharp min. (*Farewell*); *46 in B; 47 in G; 51 in B flat; 65 in A.*
**(*) CBS Dig. 13M/*13T* 39685 (3). L'Estro Armonico, Solomons.

This second volume of *Sturm und Drang* symphonies in Solomons' series centres round the musical marvel of No. 45 in the rare key (for Haydn's time) of F sharp minor. The picturesque story of the departing players in the finale tends to obscure the work's status as one of the most powerful of this rare, dark series of symphonies, not to mention the sheer originality (practical motives apart) of that amazing close. The other works in the box make a richly varied collection, all treated to Solomons' alert manner with no hint of routine in the playing. In virtuosity and stylishness, this series gathers ground as it progresses, and few reservations need be made if you fancy authentic performances using period instruments on a scale Haydn himself employed at Esterháza: six violins and one each of the other string instruments. Special mention must be made of the brilliant horn playing of Anthony Halstead, astonishing in the high horn melody of the slow movement of No. 51. Excellent recording, full of presence as in the earlier issues, although again the tape transfers are affected by the resonance which emphasizes the bass and gives a curious prominence to the horns, at the expense of the upper range of the strings.

Symphony No. 44 in E min. (*Trauersymphonie*).
Ꞓ (M) *** Pickwick Dig. **PCD 820.** O of St John's, Smith Square, Lubbock – MOZART: *Symphony No. 40.**** Ꞓ

The Orchestra of St John's are on their toes throughout this splendidly committed account of the *Trauersymphonie*. Outer movements are alert and vivacious – the finale has striking buoyancy and spring – and there is some lovely espressivo playing in the beautiful *Adagio* slow movement which brings out the forward-looking qualities of the writing. The recording too is in the demonstration class, the St John's ambience producing particularly fresh and natural violin timbre and a warm overall bloom, without blurring of detail. Although the coupled Mozart performance is less distinctive, this is worth considering on Pickwick's IMP mid-priced CD label.

Symphonies Nos 44 in E min. (*Trauersymphonie*); *77 in B flat.*
Ꞓ *** DG Dig. **415 365-2**; 415 365-1/*4* [id.]. Orpheus CO.

The Orpheus Chamber Orchestra is a conductorless group of twenty-six players from New York City who have been playing together since 1972. They certainly seem to be of one mind in the *Trauersymphonie*, which they give with great freshness and spirit. All the players are expert, and so keenly do they listen to each other that they blend, almost as if they had a fine conductor in front of them. They capture the urgency of feeling of the *Trauersymphonie*, and No. 77 in B flat is given with a lightness of touch and infectious high spirits. Its humour and vivacity are beautifully realized, and the DG engineers provide excellent recording, too. Strongly recommended in all three media, but the CD is especially believable.

Symphony No. 49 in F minor (*La Passione*).
(M) **(*) Pickwick Dig. **PCD 819.** O of St John's, Smith Square, Lubbock – SCHUBERT: *Symphony No. 5.***

John Lubbock's version of Haydn's *La Passione* is not quite so convincing as his fine account of No. 44. With the opening *Adagio* overtly expressive and the allegros boldly assertive in their fast, crisp articulation, this is certainly responsive playing, but there is at times a sense of over-characterization of an already powerfully contrasted work. The recording is first class.

Symphonies Nos 86 in D; 87 in A.
*** Ph. **412 888-2** [id.]. ASMF, Marriner.

Marriner's LP and tape set of the six Haydn *Paris symphonies* (Ph. 6725/*7655* 012) is distinguished by excellent ensemble and keen articulation. Nos 86 and 87 are digital recordings (the remainder being analogue) and have now been issued separately on CD. It is possible to imagine performances of greater character and personality than these (slow movements do bring a hint of blandness), but they have a certain charm and are, generally speaking, lively and musical. Moreover, they sound admirably vivid in their CD format.

Symphony No. 88 in G.
(***) DG mono **415 661-2** [id.]. BPO, Furtwängler – SCHUMANN: *Symphony No. 4; Manfred.* (***)

Furtwängler's coupling of Haydn's *Symphony No. 88* with Schumann's *Fourth* is deservedly one of his most famous records and can be universally recommended, even to those collectors who usually find his interpretations too idiosyncratic. Here the beauty of his shaping of the main theme of the slow movement is totally disarming and the detail of the finale, lightly sprung and vivacious, is a constant pleasure. The Berlin Philharmonic plays marvellously well for him and the 1951 recording, made in the attractive ambience of the Jesus Christ Church, West Berlin, needs no apology. It is digitally remastered and sounds admirably fresh, yet has body too.

Symphonies Nos 88 in G; 92 in G (*Oxford*).
(*) DG Dig. **413 777-2; 413 777-1/*4* [id.]. VPO, Bernstein.

A warmly glowing account of both symphonies with the full strings of the

Vienna orchestra and a richly upholstered recording. This is the kind of humane uncleaned-up Haydn one would have encountered in the pre-war era – not perhaps to all tastes nowadays. Bernstein observes the repeat of the development and restatement in the first movement of No. 88 and gives a romantic and really rather beautiful account of the *Largo*. Both performances emanate from concerts at the Musikvereinsaal, but the audiences are inaudible. An unqualified recommendation on CD and LP to admirers of Bernstein, but this will not enjoy universal approval. The cassette is not very satisfactory: there is a certain bass emphasis and a clouding of detail and absence of range on top; but the compact disc is strikingly fresh, with vivid presence.

Symphonies Nos 88 in G; 100 in G (Military).
*(*) CBS **MK 42047** [id.]. Columbia SO, Bruno Walter.

A disappointing CD transfer from 1961. The warm, naturally balanced recording belies its age, but the readings are disappointingly lacking in vitality, and the effect is rather one of a rehearsal than of a live performance. The glorious *Largo* of No. 88 drags, and the slow tempi of the *Military symphony* also bring heaviness. The finales of both works are the most successful movements. The focus of the CD transfer is not absolutely sharp, but the richness of the sound is attractive, even if its amplitude does not help to lighten the music making.

Symphonies Nos 91 in E flat; 92 in G (Oxford).
*** Ph. Dig. **410 390-2**; 410 390-1/*4* [id.]. Concg. O, Sir Colin Davis.

It is good to see that the success of their set of *London symphonies* has prompted Philips to continue with more Haydn with the Concertgebouw Orchestra under Colin Davis. The *Oxford* and its immediate predecessor in the canon, No. 91 in E flat, are given performances that are refreshingly crisp and full of musical life. It would be a sad day if Haydn were only to be heard on period instruments, for the sheer joy, vitality and, above all, sanity that these performances radiate is inspiriting and heart-warming. Excellent recorded sound, especially impressive on CD, though the quality is less transparent on tape and detail is not so sharply focused.

Symphonies Nos (i) *92 in G (Oxford);* (ii) *100 in G (Military); 101 in D (Clock).*
(B) **(*) DG Walkman *415 329-4* [id.]. (i) VPO, Boehm; (ii) LPO, Jochum.

On this Walkman tape Boehm conducts the *Oxford symphony* and he secures finely disciplined playing from the VPO. The recording too is excellent, but there is something rather unsmiling about Boehm's Haydn that inhibits a whole-hearted response. Jochum's performances are another matter. He too is well recorded and inspires the LPO to fresh, polished performances that do not miss the genial side of Haydn. The performance of the finale of the *Military symphony* is very good indeed and, throughout, the *Clock* is alert and sparkling. The sound, from the early 1970s, is naturally balanced and has transferred admirably in its tape format.

Symphonies Nos 93 in D; 94 (Surprise); 96 (Miracle).
*** Ph. Dig. **412 871-2** [id.]. Concg. O, Sir Colin Davis.

Finely paced and splendidly recorded in clean but warm digital sound, Sir Colin Davis's performances top the present lists for those listeners not requiring period instruments. They have something of the spirit of Beecham about them, and the playing of the Amsterdam Concertgebouw Orchestra cannot be faulted in any department. To the original LP coupling of Nos 93 and 94 the *Miracle* has been added, a refreshing and substantial bonus. Do not look to this CD for sharply defined inner detail, rather a very well-balanced ov rall perspective that gives a convincing illusion of the concert hall.

Symphonies Nos 94 in G (Surprise); 96 in D (Miracle).
❀ *** O-L Dig. **414 330-2**; 414 330-1/*4* [id.]. AAM, Hogwood.

Even more than in his compact disc of the *Military* and *London symphonies* (see below), Hogwood's coupling of the *Miracle* and *Surprise* brings striking revelations in the changes in texture and balance brought about by the use of original instruments. Moreover, the playing itself is superb: polished, feeling, and full of imaginative detail. The oboe solo in the Trio of the third movement of the *Miracle symphony* is a delight, and the sparkle in the finale with its crisp articulation and spirited pacing is matched by the elegance given to the engaging second subject of the first movement. The acid bottle has been abandoned by the strings who play expressively, without squeezing the timbre unmercifully. The account of No. 94 is particularly dramatic and in the *Andante* there is not just the one 'surprise' (and that pretty impressive, with the contrast afforded by gentle strings at the opening) but two more *forte* chords to follow at the beginning of each subsequent phrase – a most telling device. The presence of Hogwood's fortepiano can also be subtly felt here, and later the wind solos are full of character. The minuet is fast, but this follows naturally after the drama of the slow movement, while the finale makes a light-hearted culmination. With superb recording, full yet transparent, this can be strongly recommended in all three media, for while the CD has the usual advantages, the chrome cassette represents the highest state of the art. An issue to make converts to the creed of authenticity.

Symphonies Nos 94 in G (Surprise); 100 in G (Military).
** Decca Dig. **411 897-2**; 411 897-1/*4* [id.]. LPO, Solti.

The Decca recording is altogether superb, more analytical and transparent than most rivals currently on the scene. Solti stresses the brilliance and fire of the outer movements, which are a bit hard driven, but there is no lack of vitality or *joie de vivre*. The recording approaches demonstration standard and should really have three stars, but the performance will not be to all tastes. There is a very good chrome cassette, wide-ranging and full, with transparent detail.

Symphonies Nos 94 in G (Surprise); 101 in D (Clock).
(*) DG Dig. **410 869-2 [id.]. BPO, Karajan.

Karajan's recoupling of two popular named symphonies is on compact disc only. The emphasis of the performances is on breadth rather than geniality and charm, though No. 94 is not without humour. The sound made by the Berliners is always impressive, and there is a gain here (if only marginal) in firmness and transparency.

Symphonies Nos 94 in G (Surprise); 103 in E flat (Drum Roll); 104 in D (London).
(B) *** DG Walkman *413 424-4* [id.]. LPO, Jochum.

Like Jochum's companion Walkman coupling (see above), these performances derive from the complete set of *London symphonies* DG released in 1973, the *Surprise* having appeared the previous year as a trailer. The playing is elegant yet fresh, allegros marvellously crisp, slow movements warm and humane. This is among the musically most satisfying accounts of No. 104 in the catalogue; throughout, the recording is of DG's best analogue quality. A bargain.

Symphonies Nos 96 in D (Miracle); 100 in G (Military).
(*) DG Dig. **410 975-2 [id.]. BPO, Karajan.

DG have recoupled these two symphonies for compact disc. They certainly sound splendid in this form, with impressive body and range. As big-band Haydn goes, Karajan has much to recommend him; however, though these performances have grandeur and dignity, they lack the lightness of touch or humour of Sir Colin Davis on Philips. The minuet of No. 100 is heavy-handed, almost Prussian.

Symphonies Nos 97 in C; 98 in B flat.
**(*) DG Dig. 410 947-1/*4* [id.]. BPO, Karajan.

There is breadth and dignity here and, of course, splendid playing from the Berlin Philharmonic. Neither performance is to be preferred to the Concertgebouw and Sir Colin Davis, and the slow movement of No. 97 could perhaps have more tenderness and charm. As so often in this series, the minuet of No. 97 is very slow – here to admirable effect, since there is a splendid majesty about this. Good recording in both works.

Symphonies Nos 99 in E flat; 100 in G (Military).
**(*) DG Dig. 410 958-1/*4* [id.]. BPO, Karajan.

As we have noted above, Karajan is majestic but occasionally rather heavy-handed. The orchestral playing is, of course, glorious, and the recording very fine indeed, though not superior to Davis and the Concertgebouw on Philips. The tape transfer is vivid, but there is an element of roughness in the transfers of both symphonies, notably in the 'military' section of No. 100.

Symphonies Nos 100 in G (Military); 103 in E flat (Drum Roll).
(M) **(*) Ph. 412 925-1/*4*. ASMF, Marriner.

These are fine performances, with beautifully sprung rhythms and excellent detail. The atmosphere at the opening of the *Drum Roll* is caught wonderfully, and the first movement's second subject shows the fine pointing and lightness of touch which distinguish the music making throughout. The recording is sophisticated in balance and natural in timbre. In both symphonies Jochum evinces slightly more personality, although there is not a great deal to choose between them in terms of orchestral execution. The Philips recording is marginally smoother and more finely detailed, but for tape collectors Jochum offers better value (see above). Moreover, the Philips tape, though basically fresh, has problems with the 'military' section of No. 100.

Symphonies Nos 100 in G (Military); 104 in D (London).
*** Ph. **411 449-2** [id.]. Concg. O, Sir Colin Davis.
*** O-L Dig. **411 833-2**; 411 833-1/*4* [id.]. AAM, Hogwood.
(M) * HMV ED 290357-1/*4*. Philh. O, Klemperer.

Sir Colin Davis's coupling has genuine stature and can be recommended without reservation of any kind. It has better claims than any current rivals: the performances have breadth and dignity, yet are full of sparkle and character. The playing of the Concertgebouw Orchestra is as sensitive as it is brilliant, and Davis is unfailingly penetrating. The performances also benefit from excellent recorded sound, with fine clarity and definition. There is warmth and humanity here, and in either work collectors need look no further. The 1977 analogue recording has responded readily to digital remastering. The original LP is now withdrawn.

Those looking for performances on period instruments will find Hogwood's accounts are uncommonly good ones and offer much better playing than was the case in some of his Mozart cycle. The wind execution is highly accomplished and the strings well blended and in tune. The change in the balance in the orchestral texture is often quite striking, particularly where the bassoon cuts through the lower strings. The 'Turkish' percussion instruments in the *Military symphony* are most effectively placed, and the performances are not only vital but also splendidly paced. The recording has clarity and presence, in its compact disc form very much so. An altogether impressive issue. There is a very good chrome cassette, with the detail well handled and only slightly less well focused than on the disc.

There is little to recommend the Klemperer performances. Although the orchestral playing is of very high quality, there is a feeling of Teutonic weight here (most oppressive in the minuets) which denies the essential Haydn spirit, so readily revealed by Beecham, Jochum and Davis. The mid-1960s recordings have been remastered and sound brighter than on their first appearance, but there is now an element of congestion in the tuttis. As the opening of the *Military symphony* (the most attractively performed section of either of the two symphonies) shows, the cassette transfer is attractively fresh, but distortion sets in when Klemperer brings his troops on to the parade ground, later on in the work.

Symphonies Nos 100 in G (Military); 104 in D (London) (arr. Salomon for flute, string quartet and fortepiano).
*** O-L 414 434-1/*4* [id.]. Beznosiuk, Salomon Qt, Hogwood.

These engaging and ingenious arrangements were made by Salomon (long before the age of the gramophone) to enjoy Haydn's invention domestically. It is remarkable how much of the music's colour is caught in these sprightly, polished and by no means lightweight accounts. The sharp, clear and transparent sound (equally vivid on the disc and the admirable chrome cassette) enables detail to register consistently and the spirited music-making cannot help but give pleasure, even though the 'authentic' style is slightly astringent.

Symphonies Nos 101 in D (Clock); 102 in B flat; 103 in E flat (Drum Roll); 104 in D (London).
**(*) Erato Dig. NUM/*MCE* 751412 (2). Scottish CO, Leppard.

Symphonies Nos 101 in D (Clock); 104 in D (London).
(*) Erato Dig. **ECD 88079 [id.] (from above). Scottish CO, Leppard.

Eminently sane, likeable performances from Raymond Leppard and the Scottish Chamber Orchestra. These artists convey a pleasure in what they are doing, and that is more than half the battle. Not only do they bring geniality and high spirits to these symphonies, but also grace and considerable poetic feeling; the slow movement of No. 102 deserves special mention in this respect. The recording is agreeably natural and as fresh and warm as the performances themselves. A very useful chamber-sized alternative to the larger orchestras favoured in this repertoire by DG and Philips. There is an excellent CD, coupling two of the more popular symphonies.

Symphonies Nos 103 in E flat (Drum Roll); 104 in D (London).
*** DG Dig. **410 517-2**; 410 517-1/*4* [id.]. BPO, Karajan.

Karajan recorded these symphonies with the Vienna Philharmonic Orchestra for Decca at the beginning of the 1960s (VIV/*KVIC* 55 [Lon. STS/*5*- 15586]) and that recording still sounds extremely vivid. In the newer Berlin coupling, the first movement of No. 104 has greater weight and dignity, with altogether splendid string playing from the Berlin Philharmonic. As in his earlier Vienna account, Karajan observes the exposition repeat and refrains from any interpretative self-indulgence. The Minuet and Trio is even marginally faster than on the earlier record. No. 103 has comparable gravitas: there is an undeniable breadth and grandeur here, as well as magnificent orchestral playing. The difference between the excellent LP and the compact disc is marginal, for both are impressive.

CHAMBER MUSIC

Flute trios, Hob IV, Nos 1 in C; 2 in G; 3 in G; 4 in G (*London*). *Divertimentos, Hob IV, Nos 7 in G; 11 in D.*
*** CBS Dig. **MK 37786**; 37786/*40*- [id.]. Rampal, Stern, Rostropovich.

Eminently winning performances of some charming if minor pieces of Haydn's London years, as well as some earlier *Divertimenti*. These players convey a sense of enjoyment and pleasure, and the recording is perfectly acceptable. The LP enjoys a slight superiority over the cassette, but the latter is still admirably fresh and clean. However, on compact disc there is that extra degree of tangibility, so attractive with small instrumental groups.

String quartets Nos 1 and 6, Op. 1/1 and 6; 16–17, Op. 3/4–5; 32, 34–35, Op. 20/2, 4–5; 38 (*Joke*)*; 39* (*Bird*) *and 42, Op. 33/2, 3 and 6; 46 and 49, Op. 50/3 and 6; 57–59, Op. 54/1–3; 60 and 62, Op. 55/1 and 3; 65, 66 and 68, Op. 64/3–4 and 6; 69, Op. 71/1; 72–74, Op. 74/1–3; 76* (*Fifths*)*; 77* (*Emperor*)*; 78* (*Sunrise*)*, Op. 76/2–4; 81–82, Op. 77/1–2.*
⊛ (***) EMI Référence 290604-3 (9). Pro Arte Qt.

These are all mono recordings made for the HMV Haydn Quartet Society during the period 1931–8. Apart from the Busch, the Pro Arte was the most celebrated quartet of its day; it was good news that these classic accounts had been transferred to LP by Keith Hardwick. Surfaces are wonderfully tamed, and if the acoustic is on the dry side, one somehow never seems to find this worrying. The Pro Arte brought a classical poise and refinement to all these scores and their humanity and insight put these unrivalled performances very much in a class of their own. Even the early quartets are enlivened by many magical touches and have never sounded more enchanting. These records are to the Haydn *Quartets* what Schnabel was to the Beethoven *Sonatas* or what Beecham was to Delius: they bring one closer to the soul of this music and penetrate its genius in a very special way. Nothing in the stereo catalogue or on compact disc matches this as an overall achievement.

String quartets Nos 17 in F (*Serenade*)*, Op. 3/5; 76 in D min.* (*Fifths*)*; 77 in C* (*Emperor*)*, Op. 76/2–3.*
* Denon Dig. **C 37 7094.** Berlin Philh. Qt.

These performances are by the Philharmonia Quartet of Berlin, a relatively new ensemble whose first violin is leader of the Radio orchestra, and two of his colleagues come from the Philharmonic. Put alongside the finest now before the record-buying public, these accounts are serviceable rather than distinguished. Neither in vitality nor in musical imagination can they be said to match the Eder or Orlando, and readers who possess the Quartetto Italiano on LP need not make the change.

String quartets Nos 50–56 (*The Seven Last Words of our Saviour on the cross*)*, Op. 51.*
€ **(*) Ph. Dig. **412 878-2** [id.]. Kremer, Rabus, Causse, Iwasaki.

The Aeolian Quartet version on Decca (currently out of the catalogue) interspersed readings by Peter Pears between each of the movements, which enhances the impact of this work. This Philips account presents the seven movements without a break, as have all the preceding versions. Musically this does not displace the Aeolian, either as a performance or as a recording, but it is a useful addition to the catalogue, as no single-disc alternative is currently in the lists in any format. Moreover, the CD transfer brings sound of remarkable realism, recorded within a most attractive ambience. The background silence, too, greatly enhances the feeling of intensity in the playing.

String quartets Nos 61 in F min. (*Razor*), *Op. 55/2; 67 in D* (*Lark*), *Op. 65/4.*
*** O-L Dig. 414 172-1 [id.]. Salomon Qt.

As in their earlier records with Hyperion (see below), the Salomon Quartet use period instruments and vibratoless tone. They also observe repeats, including the minuet second time around. Their playing has plenty of character and personality and, both artistically and as far as recording quality is concerned, they maintain the high standards of the Opp. 71 and 74 sets.

String quartets Nos 71 in E flat, Op. 71/3; 72 in C, Op. 74/1.
*** Hyp. A 66098 [id.]. Salomon Qt.

String quartets Nos 73 in F; 74 in D min., Op. 74/2–3.
*** Hyp. A 66124 [id.]. Salomon Qt.

The Opp. 71 and 74 *Quartets* belong to the same period as the first set of *Salomon symphonies* (1791–2) and are grander and more 'public' than any of their predecessors. The appropriately named Salomon Quartet use period instruments, and the same verdict passed on their earlier issue of Op. 71, Nos 1–2 (Hyp. A 66065) must be echoed here. They are vibratoless but vibrant; the sonorities, far from being nasal and unpleasing, are clean and transparent. There is imagination and vitality here, and the Hyperion recording is splendidly truthful.

String quartets Nos 76 in D min. (*Fifths*)*; 77 in C* (*Emperor*)*; 78 in B flat* (*Sunrise*), *Op. 76/2–4.*
*** Tel. Dig. **ZK8 43110**; AZ6/*CY4* 43110 [id.]. Eder Qt.

The Eder is a Hungarian quartet who have only recently begun to make a name for themselves on records, even though public appearances have met with acclaim. The players command a refined and beautiful tone, with generally excellent ensemble and polish. These are elegant performances that are unlikely to disappoint even the most demanding listener, save perhaps in the finale of the *Emperor*, which they take a little too quickly. They are unfailingly thoughtful players whose internal balance and tonal blend are practically flawless. The recording is altogether excellent on CD and LP. The chrome tape, transferred at a high level, is very brightly lit in the treble, but the sound has excellent presence.

String quartet No. 77 in C (Emperor), Op. 76/3.
(*) DG Dig. **410 866-2; 410 866-1/*4* [id.]. Amadeus Qt – MOZART: *Quartet No. 17.***(*)

Although the recording is obviously more modern, the newest version of the *Emperor* by the Amadeus Quartet is not an improvement on the old (still available with the same coupling at mid-price – DG Acc. 2542/*3342* 122). The playing is expert, but there is an element of routine here, and the overall impression is a lack of communicative warmth. The recording has great presence on the compact disc, but also a touch of edginess; it sounds smoothest on the excellent chrome tape.

String quartets Nos 77 in C (Emperor), 78 in B flat (Sunrise), Op. 76/3–4.
(M) *** Ph. 416 241-1/*4* [id.]. Italian Qt.

These Italian performances are beautifully shaped, keenly alert and marvellously recorded. A self-recommending issue, especially at mid-price, with a first-class chrome cassette equivalent. There are few Haydn quartet issues to surpass this.

String quartets Nos 78 in B flat (Sunrise); 80 in E flat, Op. 76/4 and 6.
ℭ *** Ph. Dig. **410 053-2**; 6514/*7337* 204 [id.]. Orlando Qt.

One of the best Haydn quartet records currently available. The playing has eloquence, vitality and warmth; there is a keen sense of rhythm and phrases breathe with refreshing naturalness. Philips have given this fine ensemble first-rate recorded sound; the record can be recommended with enthusiasm, and so can the chrome cassette. This coupling also had the distinction of being the first Haydn chamber music to be issued on compact disc. The naturalness is enhanced; there is a striking body and realism to the sound image, especially in Op. 74, No. 6, which is very slightly smoother on top than its companion. What a wonderful work it is!

KEYBOARD MUSIC

Piano sonatas Nos 47 in B min., Hob XVI/32; 53 in E min., Hob XVI/34; 56 in D, Hob XVI/42; Adagio in F, Hob XVII/9; Fantasia in C, Hob XVII/4.
ℭ *** Ph. Dig. **412 228-2**; 412 228-1/*4* [id.]. Alfred Brendel.

Haydn's keyboard sonatas have been consistently underrated and need a powerful musical mind to do them justice. These performances are marvellously held together, self-aware at times, as many great performances are, but inspiriting and always governed by the highest intelligence. The *B minor Sonata* has a *Sturm und Drang* urgency, and Brendel's account has vitality and character. Moreover, the recording is splendidly realistic, particularly in the compact disc format. The two shorter pieces are a delight. The chrome tape is realistically balanced but lacks ultimate refinement in the extreme upper range, which robs the image of the presence and reality of the CD.

Piano sonatas Nos 58 in C, Hob XVI/48; 60 in C, Hob XVI/60; 61 in D, Hob XVI/51.
€ *** Ph. Dig. **411 045-2**; 6514/*7337* 317 [id.]. Alfred Brendel.

Brendel plays magnetically in these three mature and original works. He uses crisp, bright articulation which keeps the piano sound in scale, but in such movements as the opening *Andante con espressione* of No. 58(48) he conveys a Beethovenian intensity without overweighting the music with emotion. Rightly in the large-scale *allegro* of No. 60 Brendel takes repeats of both halves. The piano sound is among the most vivid ever, wonderfully real-sounding on compact disc with its silent background. The chrome cassette is transferred at quite a high level and is of good quality, but the upper range is less open than on either of the disc versions.

VOCAL MUSIC

The Creation (*Die Schöpfung*): complete.
(M) *** DG 410 951-1/*4* (2) [id.]. Janowitz, Ludwig, Wunderlich, Krenn, Fischer-Dieskau, Berry, V. Singverein, BPO, Karajan.
(*) DG Dig. **410 718-2; 2741/*3382* 017 (2) [id.]. Mathis, Araiza, Van Dam, V. Singverein, VPO, Karajan.
(*) Accent **ACC 58228/9D; ACC 8228 [id.]. Laki, Mackie, Huttenlocher, Ghent Coll. Vocale, La Petite Band, Kuijken.
(B) **(*) CfP CFPD 41 4444-3/*5* (2). Donath, Tear, Van Dam, Philh. Ch. and O, Frühbeck de Burgos.

The Creation has been a lucky work on records, with a number of very fine recordings (Marriner's relatively intimate account with his St Martin's team should not be forgotten – Philips 6769/*7699* 154 [id.]); but Karajan's 1969 set remains unsurpassed. Now reissued at mid-price with matching chrome cassettes of demonstration quality, this is a clear first choice in spite of two small cuts (in Nos 30 and 32). Here Karajan produces one of his most rapt choral performances. His concentration on refinement and polish might in principle seem out of place in a work which tells of religious faith in the most direct of terms. In fact the result is outstanding. The combination of the Berlin Philharmonic at its most intense and the great Viennese choir makes for a performance that is not only polished but warm and dramatically strong, too. The soloists are an extraordinarily fine team, more consistent in quality than those on any rival version. This was one of the last recordings made by the incomparable Fritz Wunderlich, and fortunately his magnificent contribution extended to all the arias, leaving Werner Krenn to fill in the gaps of recitative left unrecorded. The recording quality has a warm glow of atmosphere round it.

Karajan's later recording is taken from a live performance given at the Salzburg Festival in 1982. Not surprisingly, it cannot match the perfection of the earlier one either in musical ensemble or in recording balance, but there are many compensations, for there is greater warmth in the later version. For example 'the flexible tiger' (*der gelenkige Tiger*) bounces along more engagingly in Uriel's recitative, with Van Dam's bass firm and beautiful; and the choruses brim with joy at speeds generally a degree more relaxed. Edith Mathis cannot match her predecessor, Gundula Janowitz, in ethereal purity, but she gives a sweeter-toned performance than she did for Marriner on Philips, though the close balancing of voices is hardly flattering to any of the soloists. The sense of presence is what matters, and this is a fine memento of a powerful, glowing occasion, caught in wide-ranging digital sound. The chrome cassettes too are strikingly vivid, with the choral focus sharper in the second and third parts of the work. The compact discs offer a tangible presence – but also give more emphasis to the faults of balance. The choral focus too is less than ideal.

Recorded live at the Liège Festival in Belgium in 1982, Kuijken's version is admirably fresh, with period instruments adding a tang without sounding too aggressive. That is so, even though the top emphasis in the recording (brought out the more on CD) adds an edge to violins as well as to voices that is not quite natural, with sibilants exaggerated. The brightness and immediacy of the sound also means that performance noises are exceptionally clear, as though one were on stage with the performers. But the consistently clean tones of the soloists and the precision of the small chorus, coupled with Kuijken's happy choice of speeds and unfailing stylishness, will not disappoint anyone who fancies an 'authentic' performance. The aria we know as *With verdure clad* is particularly beautiful, relaxed in tempo and with the soprano Krzystina Laki singing with heavenly purity. Neil Mackie sings the tenor solos with heady clarity, and Philippe Huttenlocher makes an asset of a less heavyweight approach than usual.

Rafael Frühbeck de Burgos directs a genial performance, recorded with richness and immediacy. Though the Karajan version has even crisper ensemble in both chorus and orchestra, the easier pacing of Frühbeck provides an alternative which at bargain price remains very good value. The soloists are all excellent, and though Helen Donath is not so pure-toned as Janowitz on DG, with a hint of flutter in the voice, she is wonderfully agile in ornamentation, as in the bird-like quality she gives to the aria *On mighty pens*. The chorus might gain from a rather more forward balance. The cassette transfer is clear and vivid to match the LPs quite closely.

Mass No. 7 in C (*Paukenmesse*): *Missa in tempore belli*.
*(*) Ph. Dig. **412 734-2**; 412 734-1/*4* [id.]. Blegen, Fassbaender, Ahnsjö, Sotin, Bav. R. Ch. and SO, Bernstein.

Bernstein's rhythmic flair and feeling for dramatic contrast put him among the most compelling of Haydn conductors, as revealed in the fast numbers here. However, with muffled recording, which inflates the scale of the performance, with dangerously romantic treatment of slow sections, such as the introduction to the bass's *Qui tollis*, and with rough singing from the bass soloist (Hans Sotin well below form), the good qualities are quite cancelled out.

Still recommended: On Argo, George Guest provides a clean, brightly recorded account with good soloists, and as we go to press this has been reissued at mid-price (Argo 417 163-1/*4*).

Mass No. 9 in D min. (*Nelson*).

(*) Argo Dig. **414 464-2; 414 464-1/*4* [id.]. Howells, Rolfe-Johnson, Roberts, LSO Ch., City of L. Sinfonia, Hickox.

*(*) Claves **CD 508108**; 8108 [id.]. Graf, Piller, Haefliger, Stämpfli, Bern CO and Ch, Dähler.

Hickox conducts a lively, well-sung reading of the most celebrated of Haydn's late masses, most impressive in the vigorous, outward-going music which – with Haydn – makes up the greater part of the service. What is disappointing is the recessed sound of the choir, with inner parts less well defined than they should be. The soloists are good but, as recorded, Barbara Bonney's soprano has a thinness along with the purity. Enjoyable as this is, it falls short of the superb Argo version of twenty years earlier from Sir David Willcocks and King's College Choir, preferable even in its better-focused, more atmospheric sound (ZRG/*KZRC* 5325).

The Swiss performance on the Claves label lacks the necessary vigour for Haydn's most celebrated mass, and the recording balance, with the soloists very close and the rest too far away, rules it out still further, with technical flaws the more apparent in the CD version.

Mass No. 12 in B flat (*Harmonienmesse*).

(*) Hung. Dig. **HCD 12360; SLPD 12360 [id.]. Tokody, Takács, Gulyas, Gregor, Slovak Philh. O and Ch., Ferencsik.

With four of Hungary's outstanding singers as soloists (all increasingly well known on record), Ferencsik conducts for a recording of Haydn's last, masterly setting of the mass designed to celebrate the conductor's seventy-fifth birthday. The age of the conductor may have influenced his choice of speeds, generally on the slow side, and the weight of sound from the relatively large choir brings some lack of clarity, if no lack of vigour. The Argo LP version from St John's Choir, Cambridge (Argo ZRG 515), may be more buoyant, but Ferencsik gains in such a passage as the *Gratias* in the *Gloria*. The pure originality of the writing, with Haydn determined not simply to repeat himself in words he had set so often, is consistently brought out – as in the minor-key switch on *Et resurrexit* and the light, molto allegro *Benedictus*, not to mention the explosive triumph of the final *Donna nobis pacem*. It was almost as though the old man was at those points challenging himself to do the impossible. Excellent digital recording.

The Seasons (in German).

*** Ph. Dig. **411 428-2** (2); 6769/*7654* 068 (3) [id.]. Mathis, Jerusalem, Fischer-Dieskau, Ch. and ASMF, Marriner.

Sir Neville Marriner followed up the success of his resilient recording of *The Creation* with this superbly joyful performance of Haydn's last oratorio, effervescent with the optimism of old age. Edith Mathis and Dietrich Fischer-Dieskau are as stylish and characterful as one would expect, pointing the words as narrative. The tenor too is magnificent: Siegfried Jerusalem is both heroic of timbre and yet delicate enough for Haydn's most elegant and genial passages. The chorus and orchestra, of authentic size, add to the freshness. The recording, made in St John's, Smith Square, is warmly reverberant without losing detail. The transfer to CD brings two discs, instead of three LPs and cassettes (the latter with a disappointingly low transfer level), which is handsomely presented, with a pair of booklets (including full texts). The CD virtually transforms the sound, with added definition for both chorus and soloists, with cues for every individual item, and a total playing time of nearly two hours and a quarter. Highly recommended.

The Seasons: highlights.
(M) ** HMV 290567-1/*4*. Janowitz, Hollweg, Berry, Ch. of German Op., BPO, Karajan.

Karajan's 1978 complete recording of *The Seasons* offered a polished, often very dramatic performance with good soloists, but comparatively little charm. This selection is not ungenerous and includes several extended excerpts, but there are no dividing bands, which in the days of CD cueing is a distinct drawback. The remastered sound too is rather dry, not as richly expansive as the original, but it has transferred particularly successfully to the XDR cassette, which is strikingly vivid and well balanced.

Stabat Mater.
(*) Erato Dig. **ECD 88033; NUM/*MCE* 75025 [id.]. Armstrong, Murray, Hill, Huttenlocher, Lausanne Vocal Ens. and CO, Corboz.

Haydn's *Stabat Mater*, one of his first major masterpieces, showing him at full stretch, was written in his early years at Esterháza. Scored for strings with oboes, the work is far bigger in aim than that scale might suggest; some of the choruses include harmonic progressions which in their emotional overtones suggest music of a much later period. On Erato the thirteen movements – most of them slow – are squeezed neatly on to two sides merely, thanks in part to speeds brisker than usual. With an excellent quartet of soloists, fine choral singing of the kind we have come to expect of the Lausanne choir, and first-rate recording, it makes a most recommendable issue, even if in the Argo version on two LPs, coupled with the *Salve Regina* (ZRG 917/8), there is a more devotional manner. Those wanting a cassette version will find the Erato transfer of excellent quality, coping with the resonance with very little loss of refinement in the upper range.

COLLECTIONS

Ein' Magd ein' Dienerin (cantilena)*; Miseri noi, misera patria!* (cantata). Interpolation arias: *Chi vive amante* (for BIANCHI: *Alessandro nell' Indie*). *La moglie quando è buona* (for CIMAROSA: *Giannina è Bernadone*). *Il meglio mio carattere* (for CIMAROSA: *L'Impresario in Angustie*). *Ah, crudel! poi chè la brami* (for GAZZANIGA: *La Vendemmia*). *Sono Alcina* (for GAZZANIGA: *L'isola di Alcina*). *Son pietosa* (for pasticcio by Naumann).

*** Erato Dig. **ECD 88011**; NUM 75038 [id.]. Berganza, Scottish CO, Leppard.

Most of the items on this delightful recital disc are 'insertion' arias which Haydn wrote for productions of other composers' operas at Esterháza in the years between 1780 and 1790. They are generally short and tuneful, boasting of the singers' constancy in love or whatever, and Berganza with brilliant accompaniment sings them with delicious sparkle. The most substantial item is *Miseri noi, misera patria*, darker and more deeply expressive; and there, too, Berganza rises superbly to the challenge. Excellent Erato recording, most successfully transferred to compact disc, where both the voice and the accompanying group sound vivid within a natural perspective. Recommended.

'The prima donna in Haydn': arias from: *La fedeltà premiata; L'incontro improviso; L'infedeltà delusa; L'isola disabitata; Il mondo della luna; Orlando Paladino; La vera constanza.*

(M) *** Ph. Seq. 6527/*7311* 218 [id.]. Von Stade, Cotrubas, Jessye Norman, Donath, Zoghby, Margaret Marshall, Mathis, Auger, etc., Lausanne CO, Dorati.

Dorati's series of complete Haydn opera recordings made in Lausanne has never had the currency it deserves. These works may, as stage entertainment, miss the finesse of Mozart, but they contain innumerable gems. It was a splendid idea to gather some of the soprano arias sung in the Dorati series by a formidable array of star singers. Stylish, alert performances, excellent recording. Most welcome at mid-price, with a lively cassette equivalent.

Haydn, Michael (1737–1806)

Concertino for horn and orchestra in D.

ℂ *** Tel. Dig. **ZK8 42960**; AZ6/*CX4* 42960 [id.]. Clevenger, Liszt CO, Rolla – J. HAYDN: *Horn concertos.**** ℂ

(M) *** HMV ED 290302-1/*4* [Ang. AM/*4AM* 34720]. Tuckwell, ECO – J. HAYDN: *Horn concertos.****

Michael Haydn's *Concertino* is in the form of a French overture, beginning with a slow movement, followed by a fast one, and closing with a minuet and trio in which the soloist is only featured in the middle section. The music itself is attractive; the second-movement allegro is played with fine style by Dale Clevenger, whose articulation is a joy in itself. Rolla and his orchestra clearly enjoy themselves in the minuet, which they play with elegance and warmth and, in the absence of the soloist, the unnamed continuo player embroiders the texture gently and effectively. The recording, like the coupled concertos by Josef Haydn, is very realistic indeed, especially during the solo cadenzas which Dale Clevenger provides for the first two movements. An outstanding coupling.

Needless to say, Barry Tuckwell also plays the *Concertino* brilliantly and stylishly. The HMV recording is a modern one (1979) and sounds very well on both LP and tape. An excellent mid-priced recommendation.

Violin concerto in B flat.
Ͼ **(*) Tel. Dig. **ZK8 42917**; AZ6 42917 [id.]. Zehetmair, Liszt CO – J. HAYDN: *Violin concerto.**** Ͼ

A *Violin concerto* from Michael Haydn (written in 1760) makes an enterprising coupling for the better-known work by his brother, Josef. It is not melodically as memorable as Josef's but is a fine piece, with a lively first movement, rather briskly paced here, and a central *Adagio* of some depth. The finale is the weakest part, though not lacking in spirit. The performance with Thomas Zehetmair combining roles of soloist and conductor is strongly characterized and very well recorded. One's only reservation concerns a tendency for the phrasing – notably in the slow movement – to have squeezed emphases, so that the melodic line swells out dynamically, though this is not an alternative to the use of vibrato, as in 'authentic' performances.

Divertimenti: in C, P. 98; in C, P. 115.
*** Denon Dig. **C37 7119** [id.]. Holliger, Salvatore Qt – J. C. BACH: *Oboe quartet*; MOZART: Adagio.***

Josef Haydn's brother is seriously neglected on record. Both these *Divertimenti* contain captivating and original inspirations. The longer of the two, P. 98, has a fizzing first movement and a joyful *Presto* finale, while P. 115 brings unexpected timbres. Well coupled and vividly recorded.

Hebden, John (18th century)

6 Concertos for strings (ed. Wood).
(*) Chan. Dig. **CHAN 8339; ABRD/*ABTD* 1082 [id.]. Cantilena, Shepherd.

Little is known about John Hebden except that he was a Yorkshire composer who also played the cello and bassoon. These concertos are his only known works, apart from some flute sonatas. Although they are slightly uneven, at best the invention is impressive. The concertos usually feature two solo violins and are well constructed to offer plenty of contrast. The performances here are accomplished, without the last degree of polish but full of vitality. The recording is clear and well balanced and given good presence on compact disc; the chrome tape is wide-ranging but has a touch of edginess on top.

Henze, Hans Werner (born 1926)

Symphonies Nos 1–5.
(M) *** DG 410 937-1 (2) [id.]. BPO, composer.

Henze is not well represented in the UK catalogue (and what does appear, usually departs with alacrity), so the reissue of his 1967 recordings of the five *Symphonies* is most welcome. The product of a sophisticated imagination with a highly sensitive feeling for sonority, there is much nourishment and stimulus to be found in these scores. The *First* has a Stravinsky-like detachment and coolness, while the *Fifth* embraces the most violent angularity with passages of exquisite poignancy and tranquillity. The performances are brilliant and the vivid recording does not sound its age.

Hérold, Ferdinand (1791–1833)

La Fille mal gardée (ballet, arr. Lanchbery): complete.
*** Decca Dig. 410 190-1/*4* (2) [id.]. O of ROHCG, Lanchbery.

John Lanchbery's earlier record of extracts from this fizzingly comic and totally delightful ballet has been a treasured item in the catalogue for many years. Here, with sound of spectacularly high fidelity, he conducts an equally seductive account of the full score with the orchestra which plays it for ballet performances. The comic *Clog dance* for the widow, Simone (a male dancer in drag), must be among the most famous of all ballet numbers outside Tchaikovsky, and there is much else of comparable delight.

However, many may feel that two discs for this lightweight score is too much of a good thing; they are well served by Barry Wordsworth's scintillating account of a generous extended selection from the ballet, including all the important sequences. With playing from the Royal Liverpool Philharmonic Orchestra that combines refinement and delicacy with wit and humour (HMV ASD/*TC-ASD* 107770-1/*4*) this is also highly recommendable, with the HMV recording in the demonstration bracket. This record was awarded a Rosette in our last edition. The tape, however, is disappointingly lacking in transparency and sparkle; cassette collectors will need to turn to the complete Decca set which is brilliantly transferred, although the bright lighting on the upper strings is somewhat excessive.

Hildegard of Bingen (1098–1179)

Hymns and sequences: *Ave generosa; Columba aspexit; O Ecclesia; O Euchari; O Jerusalem; O ignis spiritus; O presul vere civitatis; O viridissima virga.*
*** Hyp. **CDA 66039**; A/*KA* 66039. Gothic Voices, Muskett, White, Page.

Abbess Hildegard of Bingen was one of the great mystics of her age and both Popes Gregory IX and Innocent IV proposed her canonization. From 1141 onwards she was Abbess of the Benedictine order at Disibodenberg near Bingen, twenty-five miles south-west of Mainz. She was naturalist, playwright and poetess as well as composer, and corresponded with many of the leading figures of the age, popes, emperors, kings, archbishops and so on. Her series of visions, *Scivias*, occupied her for the best part of a decade (1141–51); this record draws on her collection of music and poetry, the *Symphonia armonie celestium revelationum* – 'the symphony of the harmony of celestial revelations'. These hymns and sequences, most expertly performed and recorded, have excited much acclaim – and rightly so. A lovely record; an even finer CD. The cassette is of the highest quality, too, with good range and presence. The LP won the *Gramophone* Early Music award for 1983.

Hindemith, Paul (1895–1963)

Concert music for strings and brass, Op. 50; Mathis der Maler (Symphony).
(M) *** DG 413 651-1 [id.]. Boston SO, Steinberg.

The *Concert music for brass and strings* is one of Hindemith's most deeply characteristic utterances. Steinberg gives it a thoroughly committed performance and it is beautifully recorded. He also gives a well-controlled and spacious account of the *Mathis symphony*, and he has the advantage of excellently balanced 1972 DG recording. Some may find the balance a little distant but there is a spaciousness about the perspective and a consistency that is rewarding. Climaxes open out beautifully and the overall effect is unfailingly musical. The performance is on the sober side, which is not inappropriate in this music; it falls short perhaps of the inspired quality that Hindemith himself brought to it in his very first recording.

(i) *Violin concerto;* (ii) *Symphonic metamorphoses on themes of Weber.*
(M) *** Decca Lon. Ent. 414 437-1/*4* [id.]. (i) David Oistrakh; (i; ii) LSO; (i) composer; (ii) Abbado.

David Oistrakh's inspired 1963 recording of Hindemith's *Concerto* had a revelatory quality, turning what had hitherto seemed a somewhat dry work into an expansive lyrical utterance. The composer's own direction of the orchestral accompaniment has a matching passion, with the soloist providing many moments when the ear is ravished by the beauty of the phrasing and inflection.

Originally rather incongruously coupled with the *Scottish fantasia* of Max Bruch, the new pairing with the *Symphonic metamorphoses on themes of Weber* makes for one of the most enterprising of Decca's new mid-priced London Enterprise series. Abbado's account of the latter work is no less outstanding. It is a relief to find here a conductor content to follow the composer's own dynamic markings and who does not succumb to the temptation to score interpretative points at the music's expense. The stopped notes on the horns at the beginning of the finale, for example, are marked *piano* and are played here so that they add a barely perceptible touch of colour to the texture. The Decca engineers balance this so musically that this effect is preserved. This admittedly unimportant touch is symptomatic of the subtlety of the conductor's approach in a performance that in every respect is of the highest quality. The tape transfer is also strikingly successful, thrillingly vivid and admirably clear. The *Concerto* sounds particularly realistic.

Holst, Gustav (1874–1934)

A fugal overture, Op. 40/1.
(*) Lyr. SRCS 37. LPO, Boult – BAX: *November Woods* **(*); MOERAN: *Sinfonietta.**

Not one of Holst's most inspired compositions, but no one is likely to complain at its representation on record, particularly in so admirable a performance and recording. The main interest of this (full-priced) reissue lies in the Moeran coupling.

Invocation for cello and orchestra, Op. 19/2.
*** RCA Dig. RL/*RK* 70800. Lloyd Webber, Philh. O, Handley – DELIUS: *Concerto;* VAUGHAN WILLIAMS: *Folk songs fantasia.****

Holst's *Invocation for cello and orchestra* comes from 1911 and pre-dates *The Planets.* Indeed, in her book on her father, Imogen Holst spoke of it as 'trying out some of the ideas for the texture of Venus'. It is a highly attractive and lyrical piece well worth reviving, and a valuable addition to the growing Holst discography. Both the performance and recording are of admirable quality, with little to choose between LP and the excellent chrome tape. Strongly recommended.

Military band suites Nos 1–2.
❀ ☾ *** Telarc Dig. **CD 80038**; DG 10038 [id.]. Cleveland Symphonic Winds, Fennell – HANDEL: *Royal Fireworks music.**** ☾

Holst's two *Military band suites* contain some magnificent music – much underrated because of the medium – and they have been lucky on records. Frederick Fennell's famous Mercury recording, made at the beginning of the 1960s, is remembered nostalgically by many collectors and was a landmark in its day. His new versions have more gravitas though no less *joie de vivre*. They are magnificent, and the recording is truly superb – digital technique used in a quite overwhelmingly exciting way. Perhaps there is too much bass drum, but no one is going to grumble when the result is so telling. The *Chaconne* of the *First Suite* makes a quite marvellous effect here. The playing of the Cleveland wind group is of the highest quality, smoothly blended and full in slow movements, vigorous and alert and with strongly rhythmic articulation in fast ones. To be reproduced properly, the compact disc version needs amplifier and speakers that can easily handle the wide amplitude and range of the sound; then the result offers a most remarkable demonstration of spectacular sound reproduction that should convince even the most hardened sceptic of the full possibilities of this new format.

The Planets (suite), *Op. 32.*

*** HMV **CDC 747 160-2** [id.]; EG 290850-1/*4* [Ang. S/*4XS* 36991]. Amb. S., LSO, Previn.

(*) DG Dig. **400 028-2; 2532/*3302* 019 [id.]. Berlin Ch. and BPO, Karajan.

(B) **(*) DG Walkman *413 852-4* [id.]. Boston SO, Steinberg – ELGAR: *Enigma variations.****

(*) Decca **414 567-2 [id.]. LPO Ch., LPO, Solti.

(*) Chan. Dig. **CHAN 8302; ABRD/*ABTD* 1010 [id.]. SNO Ch., SNO, Gibson.

(M) **(*) Ph. Seq. 412 361-1/*4* [id.]. Amb. S., Concg. O, Marriner.

** CBS Dig. **CD 37249**; 37249 [id.]. O Nat. de France and Ch., Maazel.

The Planets was one of the first major orchestral works to be available in several different CD versions, with each demonstrating, to a greater or lesser extent, the problems of the early digital era. They were all recorded before engineers came to realize that only a completely natural sound-balance would be effective against a background silence, and that any misjudged microphone placing would be readily apparent, given the clarity and immediacy of the new system. Thus it is not surprising that the most desirable set of *Planets* to be issued so far on compact disc is Previn's digitally remastered EMI analogue recording of 1974. Though it may lack the remarkable range of the later Karajan or (notably) the Gibson/Chandos version, the focus is firmer than either, while the realistic perspective gives an impression of depth that is entirely believable. The brass sounds are both sonorous and thrilling, and the slowly graduated diminuendo into silence of the off-stage chorus at the end of *Neptune* is wonderfully atmospheric. Previn's interpretation is an outstandingly attractive one, with many of Holst's subtleties of orchestral detail telling with greater point than on many other versions. The performance is basically traditional, yet has an appealing freshness. As we go to press, the equivalent LP and cassette have been reissued (also remastered) at mid-price.

On Karajan's CD the sound is vividly wide-ranging. Indeed, the dynamic range is something to be marvelled at; the opening of *Mars* has remarkable bite, while the marvellously sustained pianissimo playing of the Berlin Philharmonic

– as in *Venus* and the closing pages of *Saturn* – is the more telling against a background of silence. But the 'digital edge' on the treble detracts from the overall beauty of the orchestra in fortissimos, and *Jupiter* ideally needs a riper body of tone. The bass is less resonant than in some digital recordings from this source, so that the organ pedals at the end of *Saturn* come through more positively in the old (Eminence) Sargent recording from the earliest days of stereo. However, one should not make too much of this. Both the ordinary LP and the chrome cassette are very impressive, and it would be perverse to suggest that the compact disc does not add to the impact and refinement of detail. Moreover, it is a thrilling performance that makes one hear Holst's brilliant suite with new ears. With the Berlin Philharmonic at peak form, Karajan improves even on the performance he recorded two decades earlier with the Vienna Philharmonic, modifying his reading to make it more idiomatic; for example, in *Jupiter* the syncopated opening now erupts with joy and the big melody has a natural flow and nobility. *Venus* has sensuous string phrasing, *Mercury* and *Uranus* have beautiful springing in the triplet rhythms, and the climax of that last movement brings an amazing glissando on the organ, made clear by the thirty-two-channel recording.

Recorded in the early 1970s, Steinberg's Boston set of *Planets* was another outstanding version from a vintage analogue period; this is now offered as a fine bargain in DG's Walkman series, placed uninterrupted on one side of a double-length chrome tape and coupled with Jochum's inspirational account of *Enigma*, plus a dash of *Pomp and circumstance* to balance out the side-lengths. Steinberg draws sumptuous playing from the Boston Symphony, and he is helped by reverberant recording that makes this a feast of sound. Anyone who wants to wallow in the opulence and colour of this extrovert work will certainly be delighted – the more so, one suspects, when Steinberg departs in certain respects from British convention. *Mars* in particular is intensely exciting. At his fast tempo he may get to his fortissimos a little early, but rarely has the piece sounded so menacing on record. The testing point for most will no doubt be *Jupiter*, and there Steinberg the excellent Elgarian comes to the fore, giving a wonderful nobilmente swagger. The transfer faithfully captures the richly vivid qualities of the recording, even though the resonance has brought a lower than usual level.

The Decca recording for Solti's Chicago version is extremely brilliant, with *Mars* given a vivid cutting edge at the fastest possible tempo. Solti's pacing is exhilarating to the point of fierceness in the vigorous movements; undoubtedly his direct manner is refreshing, the rhythms clipped and precise, sometimes at the expense of resilience. His directness in *Jupiter* (with the trumpets coming through splendidly) is certainly riveting, the big tune taken literally rather than affectionately. In *Saturn* the spareness of texture is finely sustained and the tempo is slow, the detail precise; while in *Neptune* the coolness is even more striking when the pianissimos are achieved with such a high degree of tension. The analogue recording has remarkable clarity and detail, and Solti's clear-headed intensity undoubtedly brings refreshing new insights to this multi-faceted score, even if some will prefer a more atmospheric viewpoint. The CD gives the orchestra great presence, but the digital remastering has brought an edge to the brightness of the upper range, and the performance is often made to sound too tense in the wrong way.

Gibson's version with the Scottish National Orchestra had the distinction of being the first set of *Planets* to be recorded digitally. The reading is characteristically direct and certainly well played. Other versions have more individuality and are more involving, but there is no doubt that the Chandos recording has fine bite and presence (slightly too much so in *Neptune*, with the chorus too positive and unethereal) and excellent detail, although even on the compact disc there are moments when one would have expected a greater degree of transparency. The CD format also has a marginal element of fierceness in *Mars* but gains at the lower dynamic levels from the absence of any kind of background interference. With this vivid sound, the impact of such a colourful score is enhanced – but undoubtedly Previn's analogue version brings a richer overall sound (notably in *Jupiter*) and more delicacy of texture in *Venus* and *Neptune*. The cassette is well managed but is less wide-ranging in the treble.

Marriner's LP is marked by splendid orchestral playing and richly spacious recording. The opulence and beauty of the sound are particularly striking, notably in *Venus* – taken faster than usual but richly refined, with a ravishing horn solo – and *Jupiter*, with the big tune given a slow but gloriously expansive presentation. In *Mars*, steadily paced, the flamboyant use of the tam tam increases the feeling of spectacle. The resonance gives an overall impression of weightiness; in *Neptune*, with beautiful singing from the Ambrosians, the final fade is not as distantly ethereal as in some versions, but the performance has many refreshing features. The high-level cassette has some problems with the resonance, and is less sharply focused than the LP.

Maazel's crisply disciplined performance, set against CBS's uncharacteristically diffused recording, makes for an attractive reading; though *Mars* is taken very slowly indeed, *Saturn* ends with a marked sense of happy release (strange response), and *Uranus* sounds spiky in a Stravinskian way. At the end of *Jupiter*, Maazel uses a military drum instead of the expected tambourine. The compact disc format impressively clarifies the texture against the reverberant acoustic, but this version cannot compare with the Previn CD.

(i) *The Planets; Egdon Heath; The Perfect Fool: suite.*

(B) **(*) HMV *TCC2-POR 54290*. LSO, Previn, (i) with Amb. S. – BUTTERWORTH: *The Banks of green willow;* VAUGHAN WILLIAMS: *Fantasia on Greensleeves.***(*)

Previn's fine version of *The Planets*, as on the CD above, is here offered without interruption on one side of EMI's 'Portrait of the Artist' cassette but with an attractive anthology of English music on the other. Previn's account of *Egdon Heath* is darkly intense, and the rip-roaring ballet music from *The Perfect Fool* presents a colourful contrast. Butterworth's idyll and the Vaughan Williams *Greensleeves Fantasia* add a suitably pastoral dimension to an attractive programme. The sound is good, but the CD of *The Planets* has a more sparkling upper range.

Suite de ballet in E flat, Op. 10.
*** Lyr. SRCS 120 [id.]. LSO, Braithwaite – WARLOCK: *Old song* etc.***

The *Suite de ballet*, written in 1900, is Holst's earliest published instrumental work, and already in this sequence of genre pieces – *Danse Rustique*, *Valse*, *Scène de Nuit* and *Carnival* – he showed his flair for brilliant and often unexpected orchestration. As a brass player himself, he often wrote for that section with particular daring, and this belated first recording will, one hopes, bring a bluff and attractive piece properly into the repertory. Excellent performance and recording.

Choral symphony, Op. 41.
(M) *** HMV ED 290378-1/*4*. Felicity Palmer, LPO Ch., LPO, Boult.

Though the Keats poems give a faded air to this ambitious work, Boult and his performers demonstrate the beauty and imagination of the writing. Holst even manages to set the *Ode on a Grecian Urn* without being overfaced; and until the finale the writing is always taut and intensely individual. The finale is altogether looser-limbed, but Boult in this totally unsentimental performance manages to draw it together. As samplers, try the strange *Prelude* with its monotone mutterings or the seven-in-a-bar energy of the *Bacchanal*. A fine and unjustly neglected work superbly performed and recorded.

Honegger, Arthur (1892–1955)

Concerto da camera.
** None. **CD 79018**; D/*D4* 79018 [id.]. Shostac, Vogel, LACO, Schwarz – R. STRAUSS: *Duet concertino.***

Honegger's *Concerto da camera* for flute, cor anglais and strings comes from 1949. It is a work of immediate charm and strong appeal, and is as civilized and atmospheric as the *Fourth Symphony*. Good though not distinguished playing and recording.

Symphony No. 1; Pastorale d'été; 3 Symphonic movements: Pacific 231; Rugby; No. 3.
*** Erato Dig. **ECD 88171**; NUM/*MCE* 75254 [id.]. Bav. RSO, Dutoit.

Honegger's *First Symphony* is a highly stimulating and rewarding piece: its level of energy is characteristic of the later symphonies, and the slow movement has a dignity and eloquence that foreshadow the corresponding movements of the *Second* and *Third*. Charles Dutoit gets an excellent response from the Bavarian Radio Symphony Orchestra who produce a splendidly cultured sound and particularly beautiful phrasing in the slow movement. The couplings are generous. Dutoit gives an atmospheric and sympathetic account of the *Pastorale d'été* and offers also the *Three Symphonic movements*, of which *Pacific 231* with its robust and vigorous portrait of a railway engine is by far the best known. All three are well done, although *Rugby* may be a little genteel by comparison with Bernstein's CBS version (60341). But the playing and recording are more than adequate compensation.

Symphonies Nos 2 for strings and trumpet; 3 (Liturgique).
❀ (M) *** DG 2543 805 [id.]. BPO, Karajan.

Symphonies Nos 2; 4 (Deliciae Basiliensis).
(*) Erato Dig. **ECD 88178; NUM/*MCE* 75259 [id.]. Bav. RSO, Dutoit.

Karajan's coupling of Nos 2 and 3 is an altogether marvellous record, arguably the finest version of any Honegger works ever recorded. The playing of the Berlin strings in the wartime *Second* is superb; the *Third* has never sounded more brilliant or poetic, and the coda is quite magical. The quality of the 1973 recorded sound is excellent.

Dutoit has the advantage of even better recording than Karajan. The perspective is completely natural and there is plenty of air around the various instruments, while detail is clean and well focused. He gets very cultured string playing from the Bavarian Radio orchestra in the dark, introspective *Symphony for strings*, and his performance is thoroughly meticulous in its observance of detail. But it is just a shade deficient in vitality and drive and does not match Karajan's splendid version. The *Deliciae Basiliensis* also has rather measured tempi. However, this beautifully recorded performance is superior to Ansermet's and serves to rekindle enthusiasm for a much underrated work whose sunny countenance and keen nostalgia bring unfailing delight.

Symphonies Nos 3 (Liturgique); 4 (Deliciae Basiliensis).
(M) ** Decca Lon. Ent. 414 435-1/*4* [id.]. SRO, Ansermet.

The *Fourth Symphony*, written for Paul Sacher and the Basle Chamber Orchestra (hence its title), is a charming work, full of character and invention, and probably the most relaxed, unpretentious and successful of the cycle. Quite frankly, the playing here does not do full justice to its lightness and wit; the orchestra is neither as alert nor as sensitive in its phrasing as one could wish. However, the 1969 Decca recording is extremely fine. The cassette, available for the first time, is also precise and vivid in its orchestral detail, yet the ambient effect remains very convincing.

Symphonies Nos 3 (Symphonie liturgique); 5 (Di tre re).
** Erato **ECD 88045** [id.]. Bav. RSO, Dutoit.

Neither the *Symphonie liturgique* nor the *Fifth Symphony* is otherwise represented on compact disc, so Charles Dutoit's performances on Erato are indeed welcome. The playing of the Bavarian Radio orchestra is alert and disciplined, and Dutoit gives thoroughly idiomatic accounts of both. Having said that, it must be stated that no one wanting the *Liturgique* should prefer this to Karajan's inspired Berlin version (DG 2543 805 [id.]) which has tremendous intensity and conviction. Indeed, it is difficult to imagine any challenge to its authority in the foreseeable future. In the *Fifth*, Dutoit does not galvanize his orchestra into playing of such volcanic fire and vitality as Serge Baudo secured from the Czech Philharmonic on Supraphon (110 1741/3), within his complete set of the five symphonies. Of course, the Erato recording is fresher and more detailed than the Supraphon, and those who require these works on compact disc can rest assured of their technical and artistic merits.

Horovitz, Joseph (born 1926)

Alice in Wonderland (ballet) complete.
*** Max Sound Dig. MSR 1/Dolby B: *MSCB 1*; Dolby C: *MSCC 1*. Northern Sinfonia, composer.

Horovitz wrote the score for Anton Dolin Festival Ballet's production of *Alice in Wonderland* in 1953. The music itself is amiable and elegant, nicely scored and surely ideal for its purpose. Its invention is melodious in an easygoing way, with one quite memorable idea to represent Alice. The performance by the Northern Sinfonia under the composer is first rate, responsive, polished and spontaneous, while the kindly acoustics of Leeds Grammar School, where the recording was made, are suitably flattering. There is even a choice in the matter of cassette equivalents, with both Dolby B and Dolby C available, ordered by different catalogue numbers. The Dolby C transfer has a marginally cleaner treble response and slightly less hiss, but both match the LPs pretty closely. Both disc and cassettes have admirable presentation. Horovitz's music may be slight, but it is very agreeable. The recording is published independently by a small Yorkshire firm called Max Sound.

Hovhaness, Alan (born 1911)

Symphony No. 4, Op. 165.
(M) (***) Mercury SRI 75010 [id.]. Eastman Symphonic Wind Ens., Roller – GIANNINI: *Symphony No. 3.****

The Mercury series has shown consistent enterprise and this imaginative issue should excite curiosity. A pupil of Frederick Converse and Martinů, Hovhaness developed a strong interest in Eastern music, in particular Armenian music. As a glance at the opus number will indicate, Hovhaness is enormously prolific and has fifty-odd symphonies to his credit. No. 4 is fairly static and uneventful, the invention thin and with very little sense of musical momentum. The playing of the Eastman Wind Ensemble is wonderfully expert and, as so often in this series, the recorded sound is quite astonishing.

Howells, Herbert (1892–1983)

(i) *Elegy for viola, string quartet and string orchestra. Merry Eye; Music for a prince: Corydon's dance; Scherzo in Arden.*
*** Lyr. SRCS 69. New Philh. O, Boult, (i) with Downes – BUTTERWORTH: *Banks of green willow* etc.***

Of these short Howells pieces the *Elegy* is much the most searching, a thoughtful and expressive inspiration playing on textural contrasts such as make Vaughan Williams's *Tallis fantasia* so moving in its restrained way. Written in 1917, it represents the sort of response to the First World War that one also finds in Vaughan Williams's *Pastoral symphony*. The other pieces are relatively slight, but present a welcome sample of the work of a highly discriminating composer. Excellent performances and recording.

(i) *Fantasy string quartet, Op. 25;* (ii) *Piano quartet in A minor, Op. 21;* (i; iii) *Rhapsodic quintet for clarinet and strings, Op. 31.*
*** Lyr. SRCS 68. (i) Richards Ens.; (ii) Richards Piano Qt; (iii) Thea King.

The *Piano quartet* was written in 1916, when Howells, still in his early twenties, was studying with Stanford. It may have its roots in a Brahmsian conception of the genre, but the inspiration is gloriously vital, and anyone not afraid to enjoy music composed without concern for fashion should sample a work that is far more than derivative and hardly immature. Within a year or so, when the young Howells had completed the other two works on the disc, the influence of the folksong movement had become more dominant. Though some of the youthful buoyancy has gone, this too is splendid music, warmly recommendable to anyone sympathetic to the English revival. The committed performances and fine recording add to the real joy of this disc. The original sound has been clarified in the remastered pressing.

Collegium Regale; St Paul's service.
(M) *** Argo 414 646-1/*4* [id.]. King's College, Cambridge, Ch., Willcocks; Andrew Davis (organ) – VAUGHAN WILLIAMS: *Songs*.***

The outstanding item in these reissued 1967 Argo performances of Howells's music is the setting of Anglican morning and evening services he wrote for this very choir of King's College, Cambridge (hence the title *Collegium Regale*). Few settings of Matins and Evensong rival it in the sensitivity and aptness of word treatment, and the *Gloria* is almost unequalled in Anglican church music for the exuberance and intensity of joy it conveys. Not that the King's Choir quite launch into the music as one knows from live performances in the past they can do. Even so, it is good to have this music so well performed, and the St Paul's setting of Evensong (more obviously influenced by the French impressionists) is welcome on record too, not to mention the other less well-known items. Excellent recording both on LP and on the impressive high-level cassette.

Hummel, Johann (1778–1837)

Trumpet concerto in E flat.

*** Delos Dig. **D/CD 3001** [id.]. Schwarz, New York 'Y' CO – HAYDN: *Concerto.****

*** CBS **CD 37846**; 37846/*40*- [id.]. Marsalis, Nat. PO, Leppard – HAYDN and L. MOZART: *Concertos.****

** Erato Dig. **ECD 88007**; NUM/*MCE* 75026 [id.]. André, Paris O Ens., Wallez – NERUDA and TELEMANN: *Concertos.***

Both Schwarz and Marsalis give fine accounts of Hummel's *Concerto*, but neither player quite catches its full galant charm. In matters of bravura, however, neither can be faulted; on Schwarz's lips the slow movement's melodic line is nobly contoured. Both artists relish the sparkling finale. If Marsalis is more reserved in the slow movement, he has the advantage of very fine accompaniment from Leppard, and the CBS record includes a substantial extra work. Both CDs give their respective soloists striking presence; the CBS orchestral sound is relatively dry by comparison with the more flatteringly resonant New York acoustic. Schwarz directs his own accompaniments very ably.

Needless to say, Maurice André is also an expert player; but Wallez's direction of the first movement is square and the genial jauntiness of its character is lost. None of these performances quite erases the memory of John Wilbraham's engaging account with Marriner and the ASMF, which is still available on Decca Serenata (410 134-1/*4*).

Introduction, theme and variations in F minor/major.

(M) *** Ph. 412 354-1/*4*. Holliger, ECO, Leppard – J. C. BACH: *Oboe concerto*; FIALA: *Cor anglais concerto.****

This is most appealing music, especially when played with such elegant virtuosity. Holliger holds the attention, whether in the ingenuous lyrical writing or the delicacy of his bravura; and with the accompaniment attractively scored, Leppard's contribution is equally enjoyable. Excellent recording on disc and tape alike.

Humperdinck, Engelbert (1854–1921)

Hänsel und Gretel (complete).

* Tel. Dig. **ZA8 35074** (2) [id.]. Springer, Hoff, Adam, Schröter, Schreier, Dresden Kreuzchor and State O, Suitner.

Suitner conducts a bright, direct reading of this fairy-tale opera, cleanly and forwardly recorded. There is little or no magic in the atmosphere, whether in the sound or the performance, and the often unsteady Gretel of Renate Hoff is most unconvincing. The Hänsel of Ingeborg Springer is much more effective; of the women singers, Gisela Schröter as the children's mother is the most characterful. The role of the witch is taken by a tenor, Peter Schreier. That device is dramatically unconvincing with so distinctively male a voice, but at least it avoids the usually exaggerated whining delivery which women singers generally assume in this role.

Still recommended: Karajan's classic 1950s set of Humperdinck's children's opera, with Schwarzkopf and Grummer peerless in the name parts, is enchanting. This was an instance when everything in the recording went right. The originally mono LP has been given a totally convincing stereo transcription (HMV SLS 5145). The alternative from CBS in true stereo is also beautifully cast, with Cotrubas and Von Stade both giving charming performances and the supporting cast exceptionally strong. Pritchard conducts sympathetically (CBS 79217/*40*-[M2-35898]).

Hurlstone, William (1876–1906)

Piano quartet in E min., Op. 43; Piano trio in G.
*** Lyr. SRCS 117 [id.]. Tunnell Piano Qt.
Hurlstone, who died at the age of thirty having suffered from ill-health all his life, was a sensitive, imaginative composer; his teacher, Stanford, thought him more promising than his contemporary, Vaughan Williams. Much of Hurlstone's most valuable music lies in his chamber works, superficially Brahmsian in manner, as with Stanford, but with a winning Englishry. The *Piano quartet* is the more vital of the two included here, but both are richly rewarding and very well played and recorded.

Ibert, Jacques (1890–1962)

Flute concerto.
(M) *** RCA Gold GL/*GK* 85448 [AGL1/*AGK1* 5448]. Galway, RPO, Dutoit – CHAMINADE: *Concertino*; FAURÉ: *Fantaisie*; POULENC: *Sonata.****
(M) *** Erato Presence EPR 15527 [Odys. Y 33906]. Rampal, Fr. R. O, Martinon – KHACHATURIAN: *Flute concerto.****

Ibert's high-spirited and inventive *Concerto* deserves the widest currency; it is full of charm and lyrical appeal, particularly when it is as well performed as it is here by James Galway and the RPO under Charles Dutoit. Moreover, it has the distinct advantage of highly attractive couplings. It will be difficult to supersede this version, which enjoys a clear, spacious recording on disc, and has been digitally remastered with a matching chrome tape. The cassette quality has a degree of edge on the flute timbre and the strings.

Jean-Pierre Rampal also gives a first-rate performance, bringing out all the

Concerto's wit. He is very well accompanied by the French ORTF Orchestra under Jean Martinon. The 1970 recording is extremely vivid, somewhat fuller in sound than the RCA balance for Galway. Rampal's coupling is less adventurous though not without piquancy, being a transcription for flute, made by Rampal himself with the composer's blessing, of Khachaturian's *Violin concerto.*

d'India, Sigismondo (*c.* 1582–c. 1630)

Amico hai vint'io; Diana (Questo dardo, quest' arco); Misera me (Lamento d'Olympia); Piangono al pianger mio; Sfere fermate; Torna il sereno zefiro.
*** Hyp. A 66106 [id.]. Emma Kirkby, Anthony Rooley (chitarone) – MONTEVERDI: *Lamento d'Olympia* etc.***

Two of these pieces are included in the Harmonia Mundi anthology by the Concerto Vocale (HM 1011), but otherwise they are rarities. They are also of very great interest. Sigismondo d'India's setting of the *Lamento d'Olympia* makes a striking contrast to Monteverdi's on the other side, and is hardly less fine. This is an affecting and beautiful piece and so are its companions on this side, particularly when they are as superbly sung and sensitively accompanied as they are here. This makes an admirable supplement to the Eighth Book of Madrigals on Oiseau-Lyre (DSDL 707).

Indian music

Ragas: Gara; Hameer; Mohan Kauns (Homage to Mahatma Gandhi). Talas: Farodast; Tintal. Improvisation on the theme of Rokudan.
(B) *** DG Walkman *415 621-4* [id.]. Ravi Shankar (sitar), Alla Rakha (tabla), Prodyot Sen (bass tanpura), Sunil Kumar Banerjee (treble tanpura), Mrs Jiban (2, 3), Mrs Widya (2–4) (tanpuras), Susumu Miyashita (koto), Horzan Tyamamoto (shakuhachi).

This recording comes outside our terms of reference, but undoubtedly Indian music has a fascination for many Western listeners, and its sounds, textures and tensions cannot fail to communicate when the performances are as authentic and committed as they are here. The recording gives the instrumentalists good presence and this is an inexpensive way of making a first exploration. It is a great pity that no proper documentation or background information is provided, to help the listener find his way about.

Ireland, John (1879–1962)

Concertino pastorale; Downland suite: Minuet and Elegy (only)*; Epic march; The Holy Boy: Prelude; A London overture.*
*** Lyr. SRCS 31. LPO, Boult.

The *Concertino pastorale* has a really beautiful *Threnody* for its slow movement, and the first movement is attractive too. The *Epic march*, with its patriotism tempered by the composer's essential distaste for bombast, deserves to be more popular. The pieces from the *Downland suite* are readily enjoyable; but clearly Ireland's best orchestral work was the *London overture*. The recording is even better defined in this reissue, and this is very enjoyable indeed.

The Forgotten Rite: prelude; (i) *Legend for piano and orchestra; Mai-Dun* (symphonic rhapsody); *Satyricon overture.*
**(*) Lyr. SRCS 32. LPO, Boult, (i) with Eric Parkin (piano).

The Forgotten Rite; Mai-Dun; (i) *These things shall be.*
(***) HMV mono EX 290107-3/5 (2). Hallé O, Barbirolli; (i) with Parry Jones, Hallé Choir – BAX: *Symphony No. 3*; DELIUS: *Aquarelles*; QUILTER: *Children's overture*.(***)

The reissue of Boult's 1966 collection is self-recommending, even if the music itself is uneven in inspiration, and the *Legend*, in particular, is rhapsodically diffuse. However, the performances are first class and the Lyrita recording sounds even fresher in this (full price) reissue.

Barbirolli's performances date from the 78 r.p.m. era; his set is enormously rewarding and an indispensable acquisition for lovers of English music, although some allowances have to be made for the sound. What a beautiful piece *The Forgotten Rite* is and how rapt and sensitive the string playing of the Hallé Orchestra under Sir John in this splendid recorded performance.

The Overlanders (suite) (arr. Charles Mackerras)*; Scherzo and Cortège on themes from 'Julius Caesar'* (arr. Geoffrey Bush)*; 2 Symphonic studies* (arr. Bush)*; Tritons* (symphonic prelude).
** Lyr. SRCS 45. LPO, Boult.

This disc obviously scrapes the bottom of the barrel of Ireland's existent orchestral music by including the very early *Tritons prelude*. Both the suite arranged by Sir Charles Mackerras and the *Symphonic studies* come from the incidental music Ireland wrote for the film *The Overlanders*. The *Symphonic studies* were arranged by Geoffrey Bush, who also turned a series of musical fragments into the *Julius Caesar* pieces. As can be seen, then, there are other hands besides Ireland's in the finished products, but admirers of his music will be glad to have this sympathetically played and well-recorded selection available again.

(i) *Sextet for clarinet, horn, and string quartet;* (ii; iii) *Fantasy-Sonata for clarinet and piano in E flat;* (iv; iii) *Cello sonata in G minor.*
**(*) Lyr. SRCS 59. (i) Melos Ens.; (ii) De Peyer; (iii) Parkin; (iv) Navarra.

The *Sextet* is an early work (1898), inspired by a performance of the Brahms *Clarinet quintet*. Its Brahmsian flavour is unmistakable, and the music has an attractive autumnal mood. The *Cello sonata* is both passionate and rhapsodic in feeling, and the performance here catches its romantic flair, even though the cello tone does not display much variety of colour, partly because of the close balance against a reverberant background. The performance of the *Fantasy-Sonata* is marvellously persuasive, and this emerges as the most memorable of the three works recorded here.

Violin sonatas Nos 1 in D min.; 2 in A min.
*** Lyr. SRCS 64. Yfrah Neaman, Eric Parkin.

John Ireland's *First Violin sonata* is an early work, dating from 1909. It is an attractive, spontaneous piece, with a fine slow movement and a characteristically gay, dance-like finale. The *Second Sonata* was composed during the First World War, and enjoyed a great success at its first performance, by Albert Sammons and William Murdoch in 1917. It is a splendid work; admirers of Ireland's *Piano concerto* are urged to discover its qualities in this very fine performance which catches so well the atmosphere of the first movement. This is genuinely inspired and shows the composer at his most imaginative. After the gentle eloquence of the song-like main theme of the slow movement, the lightweight finale may seem insubstantial, but its invention is attractive and the work as a whole is very rewarding. With dedicated performances and excellent recording this disc is highly recommendable.

Ives, Charles (1874–1954)

(i) *Orchestral set No. 2; Symphony No. 3* (*The Camp meeting*).
*** CBS Dig. **MK 37823**; IM/*IMT* 37823 [id.]. (i) Concg. Ch.; Concg. O, Tilson Thomas.

Symphony No. 3 (*The Camp meeting*).
*** Pro Arte Dig. **CCD 140**; (d.) PAD/*PDC* 140 [id.]. St Paul CO, Russell Davies – COPLAND: *Appalachian spring* etc.***

Tilson Thomas's version of Ives's most approachable symphony is the first to use the new critical edition, prepared with reference to newly available Ives manuscripts. Thanks to that and to Tilson Thomas's clear, incisive manner, it avoids any hint of blandness; the *Second Orchestral set*, with its three substantial atmosphere pieces, brings performances of a sharpness to back up the characteristically wordy titles – *An elegy to our forefathers*, *The rockstrewn hills join in the people's outdoor meeting* and *From Hanover Square North at the end of a tragic day the voice of the people again arose.* That last and most vivid of the pieces was written in 1915 as a direct response to the sinking of the *Lusitania.* First-rate recording to match the fine performances, especially refined and atmospheric on CD, but also sounding well on tape.

Russell Davies does not have the advantage of using the new edition of Ives's score; nevertheless, he gives a fine account of this gentlest of Ives's symphonies, with its overtones of hymn singing and revivalist meetings. It makes a good coupling for the fine Copland works on the reverse. Though the forward, relatively intimate acoustic may not evoke a church atmosphere at all, the beauty of the piece still comes over strongly.

Symphony No. 4.
(*) Chan. Dig. **CHAN 8397; ABRD/*ABTD* 1118 [id.]. John Alldis Ch., LPO, Serebrier.

(i) *Symphony No. 4; Central Park in the dark;* (ii) *Three places in New England.*
(M) ** DG 410 933-1 [id.]. Boston SO, (i) Ozawa; (ii) Tilson Thomas.

Ives's *Fourth Symphony*, scored for an immense orchestra, was not finally brought to the light of performance until long after the composer's death, when Stokowski and the All American Symphony Orchestra gave it in New York some half-century after it was written. American critics predictably greeted it as a masterpiece, and if it is hardly that (even by Ives's standards) it has a marvellous array of musical squibs and caprices that never let the listener go. The *Allegretto* second movement (not so much a scherzo as a bare-faced comedy) is another of Ives's mixed-up brass-band pieces, but for all the ingenuity and breathlessness of so many tunes being mixed together (with *Columbia, gem of the ocean* triumphing as usual) it does not quite match the best of the genre. The plain truth seems to be that Ives's most intense inspirations came when he limited himself to a single piece; though he was a big enough man to encompass symphony-length, it was difficult for him to fit the pieces together. Even so, no Ives enthusiast should miss this preposterous work. Stokowski's recording is currently not available in the UK.

José Serebrier acted as subsidiary conductor for Stokowski when he conducted the world première of this audacious and complex work in New York. In this English performance he somehow manages to find his way through multi-layered textures which have deliberately conflicting rhythms. The players respond loyally, and the movement representing *Chaos* is particularly colourful and dramatic in its sharp contrasts of dynamic, brutal but somehow poetic. *Order* is represented by a fugue, and the finale brings an apotheosis, a vivid, gripping work, but maybe not so great as some American commentators originally thought. For the record collector at least, it provides a store-house of fantastic orchestral sound, in a recording as vivid as this, particularly in its CD format. The chrome tape is impressive, too, though in the more spectacular moments the resonance brings a slight reduction in the sharpness of focus.

Ozawa's account of the *Fourth Symphony* is well recorded but, generally speaking, he does not effectively challenge the earlier version by Stokowski. The Boston orchestra plays quite magnificently, and the DG engineers produce a most musical balance. For the reissue, DG have added Michael Tilson Thomas's eloquent and poetic account of the *Three places in New England*, a much greater work. The performance is beautifully polished and sympathetic, and atmospherically recorded.

Piano trio.
(M) **(*) Ph. 412 402-1/*4* [id.]. Beaux Arts Trio – SHOSTAKOVICH: *Piano trio.***(*)

Listening to the extraordinary Ives *Trio*, it is difficult to believe that it was composed as long ago as 1904, so radical is its musical language. It was conceived during the same decade as the *Three places in New England* (1903–14) and the *Third Symphony* (1901–4, revised 1911). Ives subjected the *Trio* to revision during the following seven years: its first movement contains no indications of phrasing or dynamics, such matters being left to the discretion of the performers. It is a pretty weird piece, the scherzo (*Medley on the Campus Fence*) introducing the usual array of tunes, *Marching through Georgia*, *My old Kentucky home*, *In the sweet bye and bye* and so on. The Beaux Arts give a tremendously vital and idiomatic account of the piece, and the Philips recording which derives from the mid-1970s is absolutely first class. At mid-price, this deserves a fairly strong recommendation.

Songs: *Autumn; Berceuse; The cage; Charlie Rutlage; Down East; Dreams; Evening; The greatest man; The Housatonic at Stockbridge; Immortality; Like a sick eagle; Maple leaves; Memories: 1, 2, 3; On the counter; Romanzo di Central Park; The see'r; Serenity; The side-show; Slow march; Slugging a vampire; Songs my mother taught me; Spring song; The things our fathers loved; Tom sails away; Two little flowers.*
*** Etcetera Dig. **KTC 1020**; ETC/*XTC* 1020 [id.]. Roberta Alexander, Tan Crone.

Roberta Alexander presents her excellent and illuminating choice of Ives songs – many of them otherwise unavailable on record – in chronological order, starting with one written when Ives was only fourteen, *Slow march*, already predicting developments ahead. Sweet nostalgic songs predominate, but the singer punctuates them with leaner, sharper inspirations. Her manner is not always quite tough enough in those, but this is characterful singing from an exceptionally rich and attractive voice. Tan Crone is the understanding accompanist, and the recording is first rate.

Janáček, Leoš (1854–1928)

(i) *Capriccio for piano left hand, and wind instruments; Sonata 1.x.1905.*
*(*) Hyp. A/*KA* 66167 [id.]. Papadopoulos, (i) with RPO – STRAVINSKY: *Concerto for piano and winds.****

Marios Papadopoulos is a young Cypriot-born pianist who has made quite a name for himself as a soloist. He gives a ruminative, thoughtful account of the *Sonata* to which few will fail to respond. The *Capriccio for piano left hand*, which Papadopoulos directs from the keyboard, is less successful. The performance is less well held together and not quite incisive enough; memories of Firkusny are not effaced. The piano, recorded in Rosslyn Hill Chapel, is occasionally swamped by the brass and has an unpleasing twang. There is an acceptable cassette, but the resonance tends to blunt the focus.

Idyll for strings; Lachian dances.
** Erato Dig. **ECD 88095**; NUM/*MCE* 75191 [id.]. Rotterdam PO, Conlon.

(i) *Idyll for strings;* (ii) *Mládi for wind sextet.*
(*) None. Dig. **CD 79033; D/*D4* 79033 [id.]. (i) LACO, Schwarz; (ii) Los Angeles Wind Ens.

Mládi.
(*) DG Dig. **415 668-2; 415 668-1/*4* [id.]. Orpheus CO – BARTÓK: *Divertimento* etc.**(*)

Mládi (*Youth*) is a work of Janáček's old age and the *Idyll*, for strings, a product of his youth. The latter, written in 1878 when he was in his early twenties, springs from the tradition of Dvořák, though its thematic material lacks the spontaneity and freshness of that master. It is very persuasively played by the Los Angeles Chamber Orchestra, under Gerard Schwarz, and they are sensitive to dynamic nuances and shape phrases with imagination; the sound is very lifelike and clean. *Mládi* occupies the whole of the second side which at just under 17′ is short measure. The wind players of the Los Angeles Chamber Orchestra play marvellously and with altogether superb ensemble and blend. They show sensitivity, too, in the *Andante sostenuto* (particularly from fig. 6 onwards), though they are not helped by the recording balance. They are placed very forward, though the acoustic is warm and the detail remarkably clean.

On the DG version, the coupling is more generous than that offered by Schwarz, the playing is excellent and the recording very realistic. Tempi may at times seem brisker by comparison with some past performances on record, but the music is never made to seem hurried. This makes a fine alternative for those preferring the pairing with Bartók. While the CD sounds particularly impressive, the chrome cassette, too, is first class.

Idyll and the *Lachian dances*, both being early works, make a logical coupling; though neither is vintage Janáček, they have no want of appeal. James Conlon gets very good playing from the Rotterdam orchestra, but neither performance has quite the spirit and character one finds from native artists. These are capable and eminently well-recorded accounts that give pleasure but need not have high priority among Janáček collectors. Unfortunately the chrome cassette has been transferred at too high a level and the upper strings sound hard and shrill.

Sinfonietta.

(M) **(*) DG 410 993-1/*4* [id.]. Bav. RSO, Kubelik – BARTÓK: *Concerto for orchestra.***(*)

Sinfonietta; Taras Bulba (rhapsody).

*** Decca Dig. **410 138-2**; SXDL/*KSXDC* 7519 [Lon. LDR/5- 71021]. VPO, Mackerras.

*** EMI **CDC 747048-2**; ASD/*TC-ASD* 143522-1/*4* [Ang. DS/*4XS* 37999]. Philh. O, Rattle.

*** Sup. Dig. **C37 7056** [id.]. Czech PO, Neumann.

(B) **(*) CfP CFP 41 4469-1/*4*. Chicago SO, Ozawa; or RPO, Kubelik.

Mackerras's coupling comes as a superb supplement to his Janáček opera recordings with the Vienna Philharmonic. The massed brass of the *Sinfonietta* has tremendous bite and brilliance as well as characteristic Viennese ripeness, thanks to a spectacular digital recording. *Taras Bulba* too is given more weight and body than is usual, the often savage dance rhythms presented with great energy. The cassette has comparable brilliance and range, although on some machines the upper range is fierce and needs taming. The compact disc thrillingly combines tangibility and presence with atmosphere, and increases the sense of a natural perspective.

Simon Rattle and the Philharmonia give impressive performances that can hold their own with most rivals and will provide a fine CD alternative to Mackerras and the Vienna Philharmonic on Decca. Rattle gets an altogether first-class response from the orchestra and truthful recorded sound from the EMI engineers. The only quibble as far as recording is concerned (the excessively distant and pianissimo organ at bar 22 of *Taras Bulba*) still holds good in the compact disc format. The rival Decca recording is a hi-fi spectacular, with rather forward placing and a hint of aggression; many collectors may find the EMI sound more pleasing. The Decca has greater clarity and presence in its favour, as well as Mackerras's authority in this repertoire. However, honours are pretty evenly divided and neither is likely to disappoint. There is a good XDR cassette, slightly softer-edged than the disc, though the brass chorales in the *Sinfonietta* are well contained.

Neumann's recording with the Czech Philharmonic is also eminently recommendable. This conductor is often dull, but these performances have a distinctive flavour. The textures are marvellously transparent and light, and the Czech players have just the right colour and internal blend. Moreover, Neumann keeps a firm grip on the proceedings without ever seeming in the least inflexible. The recording is set back rather more than the current rivals, with some loss of immediacy but not of truthfulness. Those looking for the highest-fi and maximum impact will gravitate towards the Mackerras on Decca or Simon Rattle on HMV; but Neumann and the Czechs are a viable alternative, and some will actually prefer them for their complete naturalness.

Ozawa's account of the *Sinfonietta* is very brilliant and most vividly recorded. It comes from the early 1970s and now reappears for the first time at bargain price. It is excellent value, even if by the side of Rattle or Kubelik it sounds a little brash. Kubelik's *Taras Bulba* is of earlier vintage but still sounds amazingly fresh, and the performance is wonderfully idiomatic.

Rafael Kubelik's account of the *Sinfonietta* with the Bavarian Radio orchestra was originally – and more logically – paired with *Taras Bulba*. It is an authoritative and well-recorded performance, with plenty of warmth and detail. In a competitive field (and with both Rattle on HMV and Mackerras on Decca more appropriately coupled), this would not perhaps be a first recommendation. If the coupling is suitable, however, Kubelik's record represents excellent value. The cassette transfer is vivid, but with a degree of fierceness on the brass.

String quartets Nos 1 (*Kreutzer sonata*); *2* (*Intimate pages*).
*** Sup. Dig. **C37 7545** [id.]. Smetana Qt.

These performances come from 1976 and are so far the only versions of the Janáček *Quartets* to reach the CD medium. They are splendidly authoritative and intense accounts that can more than hold their own against opposition from the Gabrielis and the Medicis on LP. The aural image is boldly defined and the overall effect very realistic, though perhaps a richer sound could have been achieved.

VOCAL MUSIC

Amarus (cantata).
*** Sup. Dig. **C37 7735**; 1112 3576 [id.]. Němečková, Vodička, Zítek, Czech Philharmonic Ch. and O, Mackerras – MARTINŮ: *Field mass.****

Amarus is relatively early, coming from 1897, well before *Jenůfa*. It is a powerfully written piece, whose individuality was acknowledged by Dvořák to whom Janáček sent the score. It is full of atmosphere and has a real sense of movement. The choral writing is powerful and the orchestration skilful and imaginative. The performance is a fine one; the recording is excellent in both formats (and in particular on CD, which enjoys the usual advantages of the medium, greater range and body); and the only minor grumble is that the soloists are a little too closely balanced. But this is strongly recommended and supersedes the earlier version by Vaclav Neumann on all counts.

The Diary of one who disappeared (song cycle).
(*) Sup. Dig. **C37 7541** [id.]. Soukupová, Gedda, Prague R. Female Chamber Ch., Josef Páleníček (piano).

Janáček's haunting song-cycle is not otherwise represented in the current compact disc catalogue, but this 1985 account from Nicolai Gedda and Czech artists cannot be recommended. The voice is now sadly showing strain and has lost its vocal bloom, particularly at the top end of the register. Indeed, tonally there is none of the quality and lustre one recalls from the days of LP. The recorded sound is wonderfully clear and the contributions of the chorus and the pianist, Josef Páleníček, are admirable.

Still recommended: The earlier Czech version, made in 1978 with Libuše Márová and Vilem Přibyl, also with Josef Páleníček, is not ideal – the tenor is a less imaginative artist than his female colleague – but there is more to admire here than to cavil at (Sup. 1112 2414).

Glagolitic mass.

*** Sup. **C37 7448** [id.]. Söderström, Drobková, Livora, Novák, Prague Philharmonic Ch., Czech PO, Mackerras.

(M) *(*) DG 413 652-1. Lear, Rössl-Majdan, Haefliger, Crass, Bav. R. Ch. and SO, Kubelik.

Written when Janáček was over seventy, this is one of his most important and most exciting works, full of those strikingly fresh uses of sound that make his music so distinctive. The opening instrumental movement has much in common with the opening fanfare of the *Sinfonietta*, and all the other movements reveal an original approach to the church service. The text is taken from native Croatian variations of the Latin text, and Janáček himself said that he had village services in mind when he wrote the work. Not that this complex and often advanced music could be performed in any ordinary village church, but its vitality bespeaks a folk inspiration. Mackerras's new Czech version has the power and authority characteristic of his Janáček series. He secures superb singing, of great fervour and expressive eloquence, from the Czech choir; and the Czech Philharmonic Orchestra give an inspired accompaniment, whether in the rasping brass introduction or in the gentler pages at the opening of the *Sanctus*. The soloists too make a strong, if not always refined, team (the balance places them forwardly) and are obviously caught up in the excitement of the occasion. The recording, made in the House of Artists, Prague, has the right degree of resonance, although the sound is a little raw at times – but this only adds to the Slavonic bite. The layout is spacious, the overall perspective convincing.

The reissued DG version, which is perfectly acceptable, would have been welcome had there not been in existence not only the magnificent Czech performance under Mackerras but also, at medium-price, Kempe's excellent Decca version, with the Brighton Festival Chorus and the RPO singing and playing vividly. This does not have the snapping authenticity of Mackerras, but it is competitive in its price range and very well recorded on both disc and the comparably lively cassette (Decca Jub. 411 726-1/*4* [id.]).

OPERA

The Cunning little vixen (complete); *Cunning little vixen* (suite, arr. Talich).
ℂ *** Decca Dig. **417 129-2** (2) [id.]; (without suite) D257 D2/*K 257 K22* (2) [Lon. LDR/*5*- 72010]. Popp, Randová, Jedlická, V. State Op. Ch., Bratislava Children's Ch., VPO, Mackerras.

Mackerras's thrusting, red-blooded reading is spectacularly supported by a digital recording of outstanding demonstration quality in all three formats. His determination to make the piece more than quaint is helped by the Viennese warmth of the playing. That Janáček deliberately added the death of the vixen to the original story points very much in the direction of such a strong, purposeful approach. The inspired choice of Lucia Popp as the vixen provides charm in exactly the right measure, a Czech-born singer who delights in the fascinating complexity of the vixen's character: sparkling and coquettish, spiteful as well as passionate. The supporting cast is first rate, too. On CD, Talich's splendidly arranged orchestral suite is offered as a bonus in a fine new recording.

Suites: The Cunning little vixen; Fate; From the House of the Dead.
** Sup. Dig. **C37 7303** [id.]. Czech PO, Jílek.

Most Janáček lovers will want to have these operas undiluted, whether on CD, LP or cassette. However, those allergic to singers may welcome these transcriptions, which are eminently well played by the Czech Philharmonic under Frantisek Jílek. The *Cunning little vixen* suite is not the unforgettable Talich arrangement, which the great conductor recorded in the early 1950s, but concentrates on the interludes and parts of the last Act, while the excerpts from *Osud* comes mainly from the third Act. Not even *From the House of the Dead* loses much of its eloquence in this transcription. The Supraphon recording is of generally high quality.

Jenůfa (complete).
❀ ℂ *** Decca Dig. **414 483-2** (2); D276 D3 (3)/*K276 K32* (2) [Lon. LDR/*5*-73009]. Söderström, Ochman, Dvorský, Randová, Popp, V. State Op. Ch., VPO, Mackerras.

This is the warmest and most lyrical of Janáček's operas, and it inspires a performance from Mackerras and his team which is both deeply sympathetic and strongly dramatic. After Mackerras's previous Janáček sets it was natural to choose Elisabeth Söderström for the name part. Mature as she is, she creates a touching portrait of the girl caught in a family tragedy. Where this set scores substantially over previous ones is in the security and firmness of the voices, with no Slavonic wobblers. The two rival tenors, Peter Dvorský and Wieslav Ochman as the half-brothers Steva and Laca, are both superb; but dominating the whole drama is the Kostelnitchka of Eva Randová. For the first time on record one can register the beauty as well as the power of the writing for this equivocal central figure. Some may resist the idea that she should be made so sympathetic, but particularly on record the drama is made stronger and more involving. The layout on CD uses two discs only (to match the pair of excellent tapes). The compact discs give even greater clarity and better definition to the warm, wide-ranging Vienna recording, the voices caught with special vividness.

Jongen, Joseph (1873–1953)

Symphonie concertante, Op. 18.

⊂ *** Telarc Dig. **CD 80096**; DG 10096 [id.]. Murray, San Francisco SO, De Waart – FRANCK: *Fantaisie* etc.***

Jongen's harmonic idiom is not adventurous (the *Symphonie concertante* was written in 1926), but it is a very well-crafted piece, amiably eclectic in derivation and skilfully written for the medium. Anyone who likes the Saint-Saëns *Third Symphony* should enjoy this. Even if the music is on a lower level of inspiration, the passionate *Lento misterioso* and hugely spectacular closing *Toccata* make a favourable impression at first hearing and wear surprisingly well afterwards. The performance here is undoubtedly persuasive in its verve and commitment, and (as we know from his Bach records) Michael Murray has all the necessary technique to carry off Jongen's hyperbole with the required panache. He receives excellent support from Edo de Waart and the San Francisco Symphony Orchestra. The huge Ruffatti organ seems custom-built for the occasion and Telarc's engineers obviously had the time of their lives, capturing all the spectacular effects with their usual aplomb. A demonstration disc indeed, with the LP almost as good as the CD: the latter has a marginal gain in clarity, notably in dealing with the pedals.

Joplin, Scott (1868–1917)

Rags (arr. Perlman): *Bethena; The Easy Winners; Elite syncopations; The Entertainer; Magnetic rag; Pineapple rag; Ragtime dance; Solace; The strenuous life; Sugar cane rag.*

*** HMV **CDC 747170-2** [id.]; ASD/*TC-ASD* 3075 [Ang. S/*4XS* 37113]. Perlman, Previn.

Perlman and Previn letting their hair down present a winning combination in a whole sequence of Joplin's most naggingly haunting rags. This is very much Previn's country, and his rhythmic zest infects his brilliant partner. The naturally balanced 1975 sound is enhanced by the freshness of the CD transfer, and though the focus is not quite as sharp as one would expect in a more modern digital recording, the violin image is pleasingly without edge.

Josephs, Wilfred (born 1927)

Requiem, Op. 39.
*** Unicorn Dig. DKP/*DKPC* 9032 [id.]. Dawe, De Almeida, Adelaide Qt, Adelaide Ch. and SO, Measham.

It was this *Requiem* for baritone, chorus, string quintet and orchestra that first put Wilfred Josephs on the musical map, when in 1963 it won first prize in the city of Milan's first composers' competition, judged by a jury chaired by the conductor, Victor de Sabata. Subsequently it had more striking success in the United States than in Britain – where Josephs was regarded, unfairly, with suspicion by the musical establishment – and Carlo Maria Giulini, who conducted it in Chicago, pronounced it the most important work by a living composer. Even if that is an exaggeration, it is a piece well deserving of a recording; this one from Australia, conducted with keen commitment by a talented British musician, presents a very convincing account. Writing at exactly the same time as when Britten was composing his *War Requiem*, Josephs simultaneously had the idea of presenting the message of mourning on different levels. So, in commemoration of the Jewish dead of the Second World War, he frames a full choral setting of passages from the Kaddish, the lament for the dead, with darkly intense, mainly slow movements for string quintet alone. Stylistically, he makes a distinction between the Mahlerian anguish of the quintet movements and the plainer idiom of the choruses. It may be a dauntingly gloomy work, but the dedication of the performance, very well recorded, brings out the expressive warmth as well as the intensity of the inspiration, confidently matching an ambitious theme. There is an excellent chrome cassette, and this is music that needs to be heard without intrusive background noises.

Josquin des Prés (*c.* 1450–1521)

Motets: *Absolom, fili mi; Ave Maria gratia plena; De profundis clamavi; In te Domine speravi per trovar pietà; Veni, Sanctus Spiritus;* Chansons: *La déploration de la mort de Johannes Ockeghem; El grillo; En l'ombre d'ung buissonet au matinet; Je me complains; Je ne me puis tenir d'aimer; Mille regretz; Petite camusette; Scaramella va alla guerra; Scaramella va la galla.*
*** HMV Dig. ASD 143573-1/*4* [Ang. S/*4XS* 38040]. Hilliard Ens.

Josquin spent much of his life in Italy, first as a singer in the choir of Milan Cathedral and subsequently in the service of the Sforza family. Although Josquin research has become something of a light industry (to judge from the 1976 Congress in New York devoted to him), little of his vast output has reached the wider musical public and still less has been recorded. As Paul Hillier points out in his notes, 'in the carnival songs and frottole we encounter a native Italian style which composers such as Isaac and Josquin may have ennobled but which in turn had its own influence on this music. This fusion of learned polyphony and tuneful rhythmic gaiety laid the foundations of the Italian madrigal.' The chansons recorded here have both variety of colour and lightness of touch, while the motets are sung with dignity and feeling by the Hilliard Ensemble. Indeed, these performances will kindle the enthusiasm of the uninitiated as will few others. The recording is expertly balanced and eminently truthful, and there is a first-class cassette transfer.

Missa – Faisant regretz; Missa di dadi.
*** O-L 411 937-1 [id. PSI]. Medieval Ens. of London, Davies.

The two Josquin masses recorded here are both new to the catalogue; both are parody masses based on English music of the period. The *Missa di dadi* is among the earliest of Josquin's masses and takes for its cantus firmus the tenor part of the chanson *N'aray-je jamais mieulx* by Robert Morton; its companion, the *Missa – Faisant regretz*, draws for its cantus firmus on another by Walter Frye. The latter is among the shortest of Josquin's masses and acquires its name from the fact that its four-note cantus firmus occurs on the words, 'Faisant regretz', in the chanson *Tout a par moy*. They are both ingenious works and, more to the point, very beautiful, particularly when sung with such dedication and feeling as they are here. Nine singers are used for this recording, the number that would have been available in an average-size choir of one of the smaller religious establishments before the 1480s, the last decade when these masses could have been composed. The Medieval Ensemble of London sing superbly; they not only blend perfectly but are blessed with perfect intonation. This deserves the strongest recommendation to all with an interest in this period. There is no tape.

Missa – L'homme armé super voces musicales.
€ *** DG Arc. **415 293-2** [id.]. Pro Cantione Antiqua, Bruno Turner – OCKEGHEM: *Missa pro defunctis.****

This *Mass* on the *L'homme armé* theme is both one of the most celebrated of all mass settings based on this secular melody and at the same time one of Josquin's most masterly and admired works. It was written in the late 1480s or early '90s and is called *super voces musicales* to distinguish it from his *Missa L'homme armé in sexti toni* (in the sixth mode). In this *Mass*, the cantus firmus appears on all the natural degrees of the hexachord C–A, while the overall tonality remains Dorian. Jeremy Noble recorded its companion in 1973, and one hopes that it will not languish in oblivion, for it too deserves to be reissued. His edition is used in the present 1977 performance which must be numbered among the very finest accounts not only of a Josquin but of any Renaissance mass to have appeared on record. On CD, the transparency of each strand in the vocal texture is wonderfully clear and the singers are astonishingly present. An outstanding issue.

Three-part secular music: *Mon mari m'a diffamée; Ce povre mendiant/Pauper sum ego; De tous bien playne; Fortuna d'un gran tempo; La belle se siet; Je me*

complains; Que vous madame/In pace in idipsum; Cela sans plus, Je n'ose plus; Si j'avoys Marion; En l'ombre d'ung buissonet au matinet; Quant je vous voy; A la mort/Monstra te esse matrem; La Bernadina; Si j'ay perdu mon amy; Hélas, madame. La plus des plus. Ma dame, hélas, Ile fantazies de Joskin; Entré je suis en grant pensée; En l'ombre d'ung buissonet tout au loing d'une riviere.
*** O-L Dig. 411 938-1. Medieval Ens. of London, Davies.

This is an excellent companion disc to the Medieval Ensemble's accounts of the two Josquin masses, *Faisant regretz* and *Missa di dadi*, discussed above. The record purports to include all Josquin's secular music in three voices. Indeed, the performers have erred on the right side in including one or two pieces of doubtful authenticity. They have used new transcriptions by an eminent Josquin scholar, Jaap van Benthem. The performances are thoroughly alive and imaginative, and the sounds are altogether alluring and delightful. No reservations about the recording, which has the advantage of clarity and presence.

Kabalevsky, Dmitri (born 1904)

Cello concerto No. 1 in G min.
*** CBS Dig. **CD 37840**; 37840/*40*- [id.]. Yo-Yo Ma, Phd. O, Ormandy – SHOSTAKOVICH: *Cello concerto No. 1.****

Both of Kabalevsky's cello concertos have been recorded before, though neither with such persuasive force as Yo-Yo Ma brings to the *First*. This is an amiable piece to which great depth of feeling is quite alien. It opens very much in the manner of Prokofiev and Myaskovsky, and is well crafted and pleasing. The excellence of the performance is matched by a fine recording, and both the cassette and disc are equally distinguished. However, the CD, one of CBS's very best, adds considerably to the refinement and presence of the sound, and its vividness is such as to seem to add stature to the music itself.

Kálmán, Emmerich (1882–1953)

Countess Maritza: highlights (in English).
*** That's Entertainment **CDTER 1051**; TER/*ZCTER* 1051. Hill-Smith, Remedios, Barber, Livingstone, Tudor Davies, Moyle, New Sadler's Wells Op. Ch. and O, Wordsworth.

The label, 'That's Entertainment', has brought out an enterprising series of recordings of stage musicals. Here it adds a recording based on the New Sadler's Wells production (in English) of Kálmán's operetta. Voices are fresh, playing and conducting are lively and the recording excellent. Much recommended for those who prefer their operetta in English, for the CD has fine presence.

Ketèlbey, Albert (1875–1959)

Bank holiday; Bells across the meadow; The clock and the Dresden figures; Dance of the merry mascots; In a Chinese temple garden; In a monastery garden; In a Persian market; In the mystic land of Egypt; Sanctuary of the heart; With honour crowned.
(*) Ph. Dig. **400 011-2; 6514/*7337* 152 [id.]. Reeves, Dale, Amb. Ch., L. Prom. O, Faris.

It is appropriate that Ketèlbey, whose music has found a secure place in the gramophone catalogue since the earliest days of recording, should be represented among the first compact disc issues. The enterprise is in proper scale, the effect not too overblown and the contributions of Michael Reeves, Laurence Dale and the Ambrosian Chorus are tasteful. The recording too is excellent, best on the CD, the chrome cassette agreeable but not matching the other media in sparkle at the top. But the performances while enjoyable do not equal those under Lanchbery on HMV (ASD/*TC-ASD* 3542 [Ang. S/*4XS* 37843]) which is the best Ketèlbey collection available by a considerable margin.

Khachaturian, Aram (1903–78)

Violin concerto in D min.
*** HMV Dig. **CDC 747087-2** [id.]; EL 270108-1/*4* [Ang. DS/*4XS* 38055]. Perlman, Israel PO, Mehta – TCHAIKOVSKY: *Méditation.****

Khachaturian's splendid *Violin concerto* and the original score for *Gayaneh*, both of which date from the early 1940s, are probably his finest works. The *Concerto* has a liberal fund of melody and the sinuous secondary theme of the first movement, which returns in the finale, is memorable. Perlman's sparkling performance is superb in every way, lyrically persuasive in the *Andante* with its flavour of Armenian folk music, and displaying great fervour and rhythmic energy in the finale. He is well accompanied by Mehta; it is a pity that the comparatively dry Israeli acoustic does not provide an ideal bloom on the music making. On CD one's ear is drawn to the forward balance of the soloist, the timbre truthful and clearly focused. Orchestral detail is certainly tangible, but the bright lighting becomes rather fierce at the opening tutti of the last movement. Nevertheless the performance is admirable, and is unlikely to be bettered in the immediate future.

Flute concerto (arr. Rampal).
(M) *** Erato Presence EPR 15527 [Odys. Y 33906]. Rampal, Fr. R. O, Martinon – IBERT: *Concerto.****

Flute concerto (arr. Rampal/Galway); *Gayaneh: Sabre dance. Masquerade: Waltz. Spartacus: Adagio of Spartacus and Phrygia.*
*** RCA Dig. **RD 87010**; RL/*RK* 87010. Galway, RPO, Myung-Whun Chung.

Khachaturian's *Flute concerto* is a transcription of the *Violin concerto* made by Jean-Pierre Rampal, with the composer's blessing, and he gives a first-rate account of it, spirited and lyrically fluent. He is very well accompanied by the ORTF Orchestra under Martinon and the 1970 analogue recording is admirably full and vivid. This record is offered in the higher-mid-price range, and is attractively coupled with Ibert's witty *Concerto*.

Galway has prepared his own edition of the solo part 'which goes even further in its attempts to adapt the solo line to the characteristics of the flute'. He has the advantage of a more modern digital recording, but the resonant acoustic of Watford Town Hall tends to coarsen very slightly the orchestral tuttis, especially the big fortissimo flair-up towards the end of the slow movement, which is fierce – and especially so in the CD format. Needless to say, the solo playing is peerless. Galway's special gift is to make a transcription sound as if it was actually written for the flute; his radiant timbre in the engaging lyrical secondary theme of the first movement is matched by the dreamy languor of the sinuously beautiful *Andante*. In the finale, even Galway cannot match the effect Perlman makes with his violin, but the ready bravura is sparklingly infectious. As encores, he offers three of Khachaturian's most famous melodies. They are marvellously played, with the *Sabre dance* elegant rather than boisterously noisy. There is very little difference in quality between the LP and the excellent chrome cassette.

Gayaneh (ballet): *suite*.
(B) ** DG Walkman *413 155-4* [id.]. Leningrad PO, Rozhdestvensky – RIMSKY-KORSAKOV: *Scheherazade*; STRAVINSKY: *Firebird suite*.**

No one does the *Sabre dance* like the Russians, and with Rozhdestvensky it makes a sensational opening, exploding into the room at the end of Stravinsky's *Firebird suite*. The performance overall combines excitement with panache, and the original drawback of a rather fierce recording has been met here by the slight attenuation of the upper range of the chrome-tape transfer. But the sound remains vivid.

Gayaneh (ballet): *suite; Spartacus* (ballet): *suite*.
(*) HMV Dig. **CDC 747348-2; EL 270109-1/*4*. RPO, Temirkanov.

A new digital coupling of the major highlights from Khachaturian's two favourite scores was overdue; this recording – brightly lit and vivid, if just a little studio-ish in acoustic – gives considerable pleasure. Temirkanov opens *Gayaneh* with the boisterous but engaging *Gopak*, rather than the *Sabre dance* (which follows on soon enough); in the nine items from this ballet and the slightly shorter selection from *Spartacus* musical characterization is strong, rhythms are well sprung and the lyrical music is treated with contrasting tenderness. Most of Khachaturian's ideas are indelible, and the RPO respond with playing that is both alert and polished. In the famous *Adagio* from *Spartacus* Temirkanov refuses to go over the top – the composer's own recording was more passionate – but the element of slight reserve is not unattractive. The CD brings subtle enhancement of detail and confirms that the ambience is of the recording studio rather than the concert hall. The cassette is agreeably warm and vivid, but the upper range is more restricted.

Symphony No. 2 in C minor.
(M) **(*) Decca Lon. Ent. 414 169-1/*4* [id.]. VPO, composer.

This was a propaganda piece, written during the war when the composer was evacuated from Moscow. Khachaturian lays the Armenian colour on very thickly but, unlike the splendid *Violin concerto* of two years earlier, this does not develop into a coherent argument, let alone a genuinely symphonic one. The musical value is roughly in inverse proportion to the noise made, and it is a very loud score indeed. The performance is very fine and the magnificent quality of the 1962 recording deserves better material. There is a first-class chrome tape to match the disc.

Kim, Earl (born 1920)

Violin concerto.
*** HMV Dig. EL 270051-1 [Ang. DS 38011]. Perlman, Boston SO, Ozawa – STARER: *Violin concerto.****

Earl Kim is an American composer of Korean origin, now in his mid-sixties and professor of composition at Harvard. His *Violin concerto* was commissioned by Itzhak Perlman, who plays it with consummate mastery on this excellently engineered disc. It is an atmospheric work which begins evocatively and rather statically. Much of it is very quiet and reflective, like a still dawn in a mountain landscape. It seems to cultivate tranquillity and repose rather than the cut-and-thrust of the classical-romantic concerto. It is an interesting score, possibly more substantial than it might seem at first hearing, and leaves one wanting to explore other works by this composer.

Klemperer, Otto (1885–1973)

(i) *Symphony No. 2; Merry waltz.*
(M) ** HMV ED 290332-1/*4*. (i) New Philh. O; Philh. O; Klemperer – WEILL: *Threepenny opera*: suite.**(*)

Klemperer's *Symphony* is a fascinating reminder of an almost unknown creative side to the great conductor. Paradoxically for an interpreter whose structural control was so strong, this rather Mahlerian piece presents arguments far too full of disparate ideas for their own good, a string of beads rather than a co-ordinated whole. It remains well worth hearing, well played and recorded, with the unlikely *Merry waltz* (an inoffensive piece) an excellent makeweight along with the sharp Weill suite.

Knussen, Oliver (born 1952)

Where the Wild Things are (complete).
*** Unicorn Dig. **DKPCD 9044**; DKP/*DKPC* 9044 [id.]. Rosemary Hardy, Mary King, Herrington, Richardson, Rhys-Williams, Gallacher, L. Sinf., composer.

In a closely argued score, yet which communicates immediately and vividly, Oliver Knussen has devised a one-act opera that beautifully matches the grotesque fantasy of Maurice Sendak's children's book of the same name, with its gigantic monsters or Wild Things which prove to have hearts of gold, and make the naughty boy, Max, their king. On stage at Glyndebourne and elsewhere, the fun and ingenuity of Sendak's own designs and costumes tended to distract attention from the score's detailed concentration, but the record compensates here, while still presenting the piece with the bite and energy of a live performance. It helped that the sessions took place immediately after a series of stage performances. The final rumpus music, which Knussen managed to complete only after the rest, here feels like the culmination intended. Rosemary Hardy makes a superb Max, not just accurate but giving a convincing portrait of the naughty child with little or no archness. Mary King sings warmly in the small part of the Mother. The CD is particularly convenient to use, with no fewer than 26 separate bands. Any particular passage is promptly spotted, in a work of such detail, so that it feels far longer than 40 minutes. The brilliant recording vividly conveys a sense of presence and space with the LP and the excellent chrome cassette very closely matched.

Kodály, Zoltán (1882–1967)

(i) *Concerto for orchestra;* (ii) *Háry János: suite.*
** Hung. **HCD 12190**; SLPX 12190 [id.]. (i) Hungarian State O; (ii) Budapest PO, Ferencsik.

Ferencsik conducts the Budapest Philharmonic in a delightfully pointed and witty account of the *Háry János suite*, bringing out the narrative points in this brilliant sequence of characterful numbers. Rhythms are light and well sprung, ensemble crisp, and recording generally excellent. The *Concerto for orchestra*, an attractive coupling, is given a far less satisfactory performance and recording. Made in 1980, it is too reverberant to allow the detailed textures of this showpiece work to emerge, with much lost in a background haze.

Dances of Galánta; Dances of Marosszék; Variations on a Hungarian folksong (*Peacock*).
(*) Hung. Dig. **HCD 12252; SLPX 12252 [id.]. Budapest SO, Lehel.

Lehel conducts warmly idiomatic readings of three of Kodály's most colourful and approachable orchestral works, lacking only the last degree of virtuoso brilliance. The bright, immediate recorded sound makes up for that lack, with the instruments well defined within a helpful but hardly reverberant acoustic.

(i) *Dances of Marosszék;* (ii) *Háry János: suite;* (i) *Hungarian rondo.*
(M) *(*) Decca Viva 414 076-1/*4*. (i) Philh. Hungarica; (ii) Netherlands R. O, Dorati – PROKOFIEV: *Lieutenant Kijé.**

Háry János: suite.
*** HMV Dig. **CDC 747109-2** [id.]; EL 270021-1/*4*. LPO, Tennstedt – PROKOFIEV: *Lieutenant Kijé.****

Tennstedt might seem an unlikely conductor for Kodály's sharply characterized folk-based score, but his performance has sympathy as well as power and brilliance, drawing out the romantic warmth of the *Intermezzo*. Digital sound of the fullest, richest EMI vintage.

Dorati's recordings of the *Marosszék dances* and the *Hungarian rondo* come from his 1974 box, collecting all Kodály's major orchestral works. The *Rondo* was composed a decade before *Háry János* and draws on four different folksongs for its material. Both works are given strongly characterized performances, with the *Dances of Marosszék* excitingly vivid, although the remastered recording sounds thinner here than in the original. It was a pity that Decca chose not to include the Philharmonia Hungarica version of *Háry János*. The Netherlands account was recorded a year later, very forwardly balanced, in Decca's hi-fi-conscious Phase 4 system. Now the sound is bright but has an added shrillness which rather emphasizes the fact that the Netherlands orchestra is not one of the world's more polished ensembles, though they play with spirit. The cassette is, if anything, more piercing than the disc.

String quartets Nos 1 and 2.
(*) Hung. Dig. **HCD 12362; SLPX/*MK* 12362 [id.]. Kodály Qt.

Kodály's two fine quartets make an excellent coupling in warmly committed performances from this eponymous quartet. Though the playing is not so refined as from the most polished Hungarian quartet groups, the natural understanding brings out the sharply contrasted character of the two works very convincingly. Much the more ambitious and more passionate is the *First*, Kodály's Op. 2, written in 1909; in its luxuriant span it inhabits very much the same world as Bartók's *First Quartet* of the same period, yearningly lyrical but bitingly dramatic too, with its characteristic folk element. The *Second Quartet* of 1918 is altogether simpler and less intense, a delightful, compact piece, which reveals Kodály's own character more clearly, very different from that of his close colleague. Excellent, immediate recording.

(i) *Hymn of Zrinyi; Jesus and the traders; The aged; Norwegian girls; Too late; Ode to Liszt.*
** Hung. Dig. **HCD 12352-2**; SLPD 12352 [id.]. (i) Lajos Miller, Hungarian Radio-TV Ch., Ferencsik.

This is the first issue devoted to Kodály's choral music, conducted on this occasion by the late Janos Ferencsik. The longest work here is the *Hymn of Zrinyi* for baritone and *a cappella* choir, an ambitious ballad nearly twenty minutes in duration. The singing is first class throughout the set, but the recording, made presumably in the studio, could do with a richer acoustic. There are some beautiful pieces here, foremost among them *Too late*, to words of Endre Ady. The CD offers translations but no notes on the music itself.

Kreisler, Fritz (1875–1972)

Caprice viennois; Chanson Louis XIII (*La Précieuse*) *in the style of Couperin; La Gitana; Liebesfreud; Liebeslied; Marche miniature viennoise; Polichinelle serenade; Rondino on a theme of Beethoven; Scherzo alla Dittersdorf; Schön Rosmarin; Syncopation; Tambourin chinois;* Arrangements: (Bach) *Partita 3: Gavotte.* (Bizet) *L'Arlésienne: Intermezzo.* (Brandl) *The old refrain.* (Chopin) *Mazurka No. 45.* (Attrib. Corelli) *O Sanctissima.* (Dvořák) *Humoresque.* (Falla) *Jota; Danza española.* (Glazounov) *Serenade espagnole.* (Heuberger) *Midnight bells.* (Mendelssohn) *Song without words No. 25* (*A May breeze*). (Mozart) *Serenade No. 7* (*Haffner*): *Rondo.* (Poldini) *Poupée valsante.* (Rimsky-Korsakov) *Le coq d'or: Hymn to the sun. Sadko: Chanson hindoue.* (Schubert) *Rosamunde: Ballet in G.* (Scott) *Lotus Land.* (Tchaikovsky) *String quartet No. 1: Andante cantabile.* (Weber) *Violin sonata No. 1: Larghetto.* (Trad.) *Londonderry air.*
(M) (***) HMV mono EM 290556-3/5 (2). Fritz Kreisler with various accompanists.

Fritz Kreisler, one of the greatest of all soloists on the violin, is now remembered by the larger musical public by this series of encores which he either composed or arranged, to fill out his recitals. Here, taken from a series of 78 r.p.m. discs made between 1935 and 1938, he stylishly demonstrates his natural flair, charm and superb technique to sparkling effect. As transferred, the recordings have remarkable presence and clarity. There is sometimes a touch of edginess but the quality only very occasionally crumbles. Surface noise is seldom intrusive and, while the studio ambience is dry, the breadth of timbre is readily displayed, where appropriate. Full documentation is provided with both discs and tapes (the latter are packaged in an attractive double-depth hinged plastic 'library-box').

Caprice viennois; Liebesfreud; Liebeslied; Schön Rosmarin; Viennese rhapsodic fantasia; arr. of *Austrian Imperial hymn. Allegrettos* (in the style of Boccherini; Porpora). *La Chasse* (Cartier)*; Grave* (W. F. Bach)*; Praeludium allegro* (Pugnani)*; Sicilienne et Rigaudon* (Francoeur)*; Tempo di menuetto* (Pugnani).
**(*) ASV ALH/*ZCALH* 947 [id.]. Oscar Shumsky, Milton Kaye.

The subtitle for this first volume of Oscar Shumsky's Kreisler series for ASV is 'Viennese, and in the style of', presenting many of Kreisler's most popular trifles including *Caprice viennois*, *Liebeslied* and *Liebesfreud*, all played with masterly virtuoso flair. The second side contains six of the pieces that Kreisler first published with attribution to various eighteenth-century composers. The recording is clear and immediate, but the relative dryness brings an edge to the violin tone that may need a little taming. Disc and tape are closely matched in this respect.

Cavatina; La Gitana; Gypsy caprice; Recitative and scherzo caprice; Shepherd's madrigal; Toy soldiers' march. Arrangements: (Dvořák/Kreisler) *Humoresque; Indian lament* (from *Sonatina, Op. 100*); *3 Slavonic dances* (arr. from *Op. 46/2* and *Op. 72/1;* also from *Op. 72/2* and *8*); *Slavonic fantasy*.
**(*) ASV ALH/*ZCALH* 951 [id.]. Oscar Shumsky, Milton Kaye.

This second volume of Shumsky's Kreisler series is entitled *Dvořák/Kreisler and 'Original'*, with the first side rather more individual than the second. Within their limited salon style, each one of these 'original' trifles is full of charm, beautifully brought out by the violinist here, whose combination of technical mastery and musical flair is ideal for this music. The first of the three *Slavonic dances* is a re-creation, in which Kreisler assembles a 'new' piece out of the opening section of Op. 46, No. 2, and the middle section of Op. 72, No. 1, which works very well. The rather dry recording makes the violin timbre somewhat edgy – although this is slightly less striking on the tape – but the sense of presence is well caught.

Concerto in the style of Vivaldi (after Tartini); *Variations on a theme by Corelli* (from *Op. 5/10*, after Tartini). Arrangements: (Corelli) *La Folia, Sarabande and Allegretto*. (Tartini) *Devil's trill Sonata*.
**(*) ASV ALH/*ZCALH* 959 [id.]. Oscar Shumsky, Milton Kaye.

Shumsky's third disc of Kreisler includes some rather more ambitious pieces, not pastiche inventions, but arrangements of genuine eighteenth-century material. Shumsky, brightly recorded with some edge on the tone, plays in a warm, characterful style that Kreisler himself would have approved. This collection is especially useful in including the only readily available version of Tartini's *Devil's trill Sonata*. Kreisler's edition includes a realization of the continuo and, at a point indicated by the composer, he interpolates a cadenza of his own, more 'devilish' in its trilling than Tartini's original.

Kreutzer, Rodolphe (1766–1831)

Grand quintet in C.
*** Hyp. A66143. Sarah Francis, Allegri Qt – CRUSELL: *Divertimento*; REICHA: *Quintet*.***

This is the Kreutzer of the Beethoven sonata – not to be confused with Conradin (1780–1849) whose *Grand septet* is available on a splendid CRD disc and tape

(CRD 1090/*CRDC 4090*). The *Grand quintet* is thought to date from the 1790s; it is a rather bland but far from unpleasing piece when it is played as beautifully as it is here. None of the three works on this record is interrupted by a break, as Kreutzer shares the first side with Crusell.

Krommer, Franz (František) (1759–1831)

Flute concerto in G, Op. 30; Flute and oboe concertino, Op. 65; Oboe concerto in F, Op. 52.
** Claves **CD 8203**; D 8203 [id.]. Graf, Holliger, ECO.

Apart from being one of the most interesting of Beethoven's contemporaries, Krommer was very prolific, with more than 300 works to his credit. Although his music plumbs no great depths, it is delightfully fresh and vital. Krommer's harmonic sense was highly developed, as in the slow movement of the Op. 52 *Oboe concerto*; it is these unpredictable felicities that lend his work its charm. This issue does not duplicate any of the currently available Krommer. Peter-Lukas Graf is the flautist and directs the performance of the *Oboe concerto*, while in the *Concerto for flute* Heinz Holliger returns the compliment for him. The playing is expert, though the recording is not in the first flight: the soloists are a little too forward and there is a need for greater transparency, even in CD.

Octet-partitas: in F, Op. 57; in E flat, Op. 69; in E flat, Op. 79.
❀ (M) *** Ph. Seq. 412 362-1/*4* [id.]. Netherlands Wind Ens.

Exhilarating performances of these fresh and delightful pieces. The F major is given with great wit and virtuosity and, indeed, with all the sparkle of a good champagne. The Netherlanders make the most of the humour of the trio section of the Op. 57, so that one laughs out loud. This is highly entertaining music, which really deserves the widest currency; the performances derive from the late 1970s and are given superb Philips recording with plenty of body and impact, with the high-level tape sounding especially well.

Lalo, Édouard (1823–92)

Cello concerto in D min.
❀ *** CBS Dig. **MK 35848**; 35848 [id.]. Yo-Yo Ma, O Nat. de France, Maazel – SAINT-SAËNS: *Concerto No. 1.****❀
ℭ *** Decca Dig. **414 387-2**; 414 387-1/*4* [id.]. Harrell, Berlin RSO, Chailly – FAURÉ: Elégie; SAINT-SAËNS: *Cello concerto No. 2.****
*** RCA RL/*RK* 70798 [RCA ARL 1/*ARK 1* 4665]. Lloyd Webber, LPO, Lopez-Cobos – RODRIGO: *Concierto como un divertimento.****

Yo-Yo Ma is an artist who eschews overstatement, and his account of the Lalo

Concerto must rank as the finest now available. It has great sensitivity, beauty of tone and expressive feeling to commend it, and indeed it makes the work seem better than in fact it is. Moreover, Maazel and the Orchestre National de France give understanding support, matching the sensitivity of the soloist. The quality of the recorded sound is excellent, beautifully balanced and spacious, yet with detail well in focus on LP; it sounds even more refined in its CD format.

Lynn Harrell's Decca account was recorded within the attractive acoustic of the Jesus Christ Church, Berlin (the venue of many of Furtwängler's successful mono LPs of the 1950s). The orchestra is given vivid colour and presence. Chailly's accompaniment is attractively bold, more assertive than Maazel's for Yo-Yo Ma. Lynn Harrell's performance is an extremely fine one, perhaps less subtle but no less ardent than Ma's, and certainly no less convincing. While the playing remains refined in polish and detail, there is a yearning intensity in the *Intermezzo*, while the outer movements combine spontaneity and vigour. The cello image is very tangible on CD (though, like Yo-Yo Ma's, it is modest in scale) and while the orchestra creates a dramatic contrast, the balance remains totally believable. The LP is pleasingly atmospheric, but the overall focus is strikingly more present on CD, while timbres remain natural. Harrell's couplings are more generous than Ma's, including not only the attractive and virtually unknown *Second Concerto* of Saint-Saëns, but also a splendid account of Fauré's *Elégie*. The high level of the chrome cassette has brightened the upper range.

No complaints about Julian Lloyd Webber's account of the Lalo *Concerto*. It is played with style and feeling. The performance does not quite match that of Yo-Yo Ma on CBS, while Harrell has a finer recording, although the RCA is perfectly satisfactory, if less rich. But many may choose the attractive Rodrigo coupling, one of that composer's most endearing recent works. There is a first-class chrome cassette, strikingly refined in detail.

Scherzo for orchestra.
**(*) French Decca 1592 167. SRO, Ansermet – MAGNARD: *Symphony No. 3.* **(*)

This highly attractive little piece lasts no more than four and a half minutes but makes a useful addition to the catalogue, providing an appropriate fill-up to the rewarding Magnard *Symphony* which it follows on this record.

Symphonie espagnole, Op. 21.
*** DG Dig. **400 032-2**; 2532/*3302* 011 [id.]. Perlman, O de Paris, Barenboim – BERLIOZ: *Romance.****
*** Decca Dig. **411 952-2**; SXDL/*KSXDC* 7527 [Lon. LDR/*5*- 71029]. Kyung-Wha Chung, Montreal SO, Dutoit – SAINT-SAËNS: *Concerto No. 1.****
(*) HMV Dig. **CDC 747318-2 [id.]; EL 270176-1/*4*. Mutter, O Nat. de France, Ozawa – SARASATE: *Zigeunerweisen.* **(*)
(M) **(*) Ph. Seq. 412 363-1/*4* [id. PSI]. Szeryng, Monte Carlo Op. O, Van Remoortel – RAVEL: *Tzigane.* **(*)

Lalo's brilliant five-movement distillation of Spanish sunshine is well served here. While the compact disc version of Perlman's newest DG digital recording shows no marked improvement on the LP (if anything it emphasizes the degree of digital edge), the sound remains both vivid and refined. The very opening sets the style of the reading, with a strongly articulated orchestral introduction from Barenboim that combines rhythmic buoyancy with expressive flair. The lyrical material is handled with great sympathy, and the richness and colour of Perlman's tone are never more telling than in the slow movement, which opens tenderly but develops a compelling expressive ripeness. The brilliance of the scherzo is matched by the dancing sparkle of the finale. The recording is extremely lively – the chrome cassette matching the LP closely – and the forward balance of the soloist in no way obscures orchestral detail and impact.

Kyung-Wha Chung has the advantage of a first-class Decca digital recording (the CD technically preferable to either the DG or EMI alternatives), with a highly effective, natural balance. Hers is an athletic, incisive account, at its most individual in the captivatingly lightweight finale, with an element almost of fantasy. For some ears, the lack of sumptuousness of style as well as timbre may be a drawback; Miss Chung does not have quite the panache of Perlman. But Charles Dutoit's accompaniment is first class and the orchestral characterization is strong throughout. There is an excellent cassette.

Anne-Sophie Mutter's account is second to none, with its dazzling display of bravura, the first movement immediately commanding. The scherzo has an engaging element of fantasy; the finale is scintillating. Many will find the delicacy of her phrasing in the second subject of the first movement refreshing, with its absence of schmaltz, although Perlman is more sinuously beguiling here. Similarly, the opening of the slow movement is especially imaginative, with Ozawa's strong orchestral statement answered by the soloist with gentle, touching serenity. Both in the *Intermezzo* and *Andante* there is solo playing of passionate eloquence, the timbre richly expansive. While the orchestral detail is good, the balance projects the violin well to the front and the slightly-too-close microphones add a touch of shrillness to the upper range; a degree of digital edge affects the orchestra, too; on CD, the orchestral violins sound thin above the stave. In many ways this recording sounds its best in the tape format, which with its high-level transfer is admirably vivid but a little less fierce in the treble.

Szeryng was at the peak of his career when he made his record in 1971, and he gives a splendid performance with firm, full timbre and much subtlety of phrasing, with sparkling outer movements and an eloquent account of the *Andante*. Edouard van Remoortel gives strong support here, but the orchestral playing is generally less distinguished and not always helped by the not too well focused presentation of the recording. However, admirers of Szeryng will find this coupling throughly worthwhile. Disc and cassette have been freshly remastered and the quality of both is now most vivid.

Lassus, Orlandus (*c.* 1530–94)

Motets and Chansons: *Cum natus esset; In monte Oliveti; Stabat Mater. Bon jour mon coeur* (two versions)*; Fleur de quinze ans; J'ayme la pierre precieuse; Margot labourez les vignes; La nuict froide et sombre; Pour courir en poste a la ville; Susanne ung jour* (two versions).
*** HMV Dig. ASD/*TC-ASD* 143630-1/*4* [Ang. DS/*4XS* 38456]. Hilliard Ens., Hillier.

One side is devoted to motets, the other to chansons; both are sung one voice to a part. The tonal blend is as perfect as is usual with this ensemble and intonation is extraordinarily accurate, and there is no vibrato. The sacred pieces, and in particular the setting of the *Stabat Mater* which opens the first side, are most impressive. In some of the chansons, there is a discreet lute accompaniment to lend variety. Of the chansons, *La nuict froide et sombre* is quite magical and given with great feeling and colour. A useful addition to the Lassus discography and beautifully recorded, on disc and tape alike – indeed, the cassette is outstandingly firm and clear.

Lecocq, Alexandre (1832–1918)

Mam'zelle Angot (ballet, arr. Gordon Jacob).
*** Decca Dig. **411 898-2**; 411 898-1/*4* [id.]. Nat. PO, Bonynge – BERLIOZ: *Les Troyens: ballet***; WEBER: *Invitation to the dance.****

La Fille de Madame Angot was a highly successful operetta of the 1870s. The ballet originated for Massine's post-Diaghilev company and was first danced in New York in 1943. It found its definitive form, however, in a later Sadler's Wells production, also choreographed by Massine. The narrative line follows the story of the operetta, and much of the music is also drawn from that source; however, Gordon Jacob includes excerpts from other music by Lecocq. It is a gay, vivacious score with plenty of engaging tunes, prettily orchestrated in the modern French style. There are flavours from other composers too, from Adam to Sullivan, with Offenbach's influence strongly felt in the final carnival scene. Bonynge offers the first recording of the complete score, and its 39 minutes are consistently entertaining when the orchestral playing has such polish and wit. The Kingsway Hall recording offers demonstration quality on LP; the CD offers sharper detail and tangibility, especially at lower dynamic levels. The LP sound is slightly softer-grained and warmer, and some will prefer it. The chrome tape is extremely vivid, again with the strings brightly lit.

Lehár, Franz (1870–1948)

Waltzes: *Eva; Gold and silver; Gypsy love. The Count of Luxembourg: Luxembourg. Giuditta: Where the lark sings. The Merry Widow: Ballsirenen.*
(*) HMV Dig. **CDC 747020-2; ASD/*TC-ASD* 143540-1/*4* [Ang. DS/*4XS* 38025]. Johann Strauss O of Vienna, Boskovsky.

Gold and silver was Lehár's waltz masterpiece; the others are his arrangements, using melodies from the operettas. They are ravishingly tuneful; given such warmly affectionate performances and a recording which is both sumptuous and has sparkling detail, this is easy to enjoy. Lehár's scoring is often imaginative, but in the last resort one misses the voices. The CD is first class in every way. The XDR cassette, however, suffers from a resonance which tends to blunt the higher frequencies.

The Count of Luxembourg (highlights, in English).
*** That's Entertainment **CDTER 1050**; TER/*ZCTER* 1050. Hill-Smith, Jenkins, Tierney, Nicoll, Richard, New Sadler's Wells Op. Ch. and O, Wordsworth.

Like its companion disc of selections from Kálmán's *Countess Maritza*, this record from That's Entertainment presents lively and fresh performances from the cast of the New Sadler's Wells Opera production. Particularly in the general absence of records of operetta in English, this is very welcome. Bright digital sound, which is given plenty of presence on CD.

Giuditta (complete).
** HMV Dig. EX 270257-3 (2) [Ang. DS 3947]. Moser, Gedda, Baumann, Hirte, Mun. Concert Ch. and R. O, Boskovsky.

Written as a vehicle for Richard Tauber in 1934, *Giuditta* was Lehár's own favourite among his works. It may not have the easy tunefulness of *The Merry Widow* of a quarter-century earlier, and the Balkan flavours may be plastered on rather thick; but with its poignant, disillusioned close in place of the usual happy ending it is both charming and distinctive. As a young man, Willi Boskovsky played in the orchestra at the first performance; here he proves a persuasive advocate, though ensemble could be more polished. Gedda hardly shows his years in the Tauber role with half-tones as honeyed as ever, but Edda Moser is disappointing in the name-part. She may be glamorous to look at, but the voice is consistently too hard to sound seductive, even in the song, *Mein Lippen, sie küssen so heiss*, made so ecstatic by Schwarzkopf on her operetta record and by Hilde Gueden on the previous Decca set of *Giuditta*. Good recording, except that the spoken dialogue brings the performers suddenly much closer than the singing.

The Merry Widow (*Die lustige Witwe;* complete in German).
❀ © *** HMV **CDS 747178-8** [id.]; SLS 823 (2) [Ang. SBL 3630]. Schwarzkopf,

Gedda, Waechter, Steffek, Knapp, Equiluz, Philh. Ch. and O, Matacic.
(*) Denon Dig. **C37 7384/5** [id.]. Irosch, Minich, Prikopa, Koller, Karczykowski, Huemer, Ruzicka, V. Volksoper Ch. and O, Bibl.

Matacic provides a magical set, guaranteed to send shivers of delight through any listener with its vivid sense of atmosphere and superb musicianship. It is one of Walter Legge's masterpieces as a recording manager. He had directed the earlier *Merry Widow* set, also with his wife Elisabeth Schwarzkopf as Hanna, and realized how difficult it would be to outshine it. But outshine it he did, creating a sense of theatre that is almost without rival in gramophone literature. If the Decca approach to opera has always been to conceive it in terms of a new medium, Legge went to the opposite view and produced something that is almost more theatrical than the theatre itself. No other opera record more vividly conveys the feeling of expectancy before the curtain rises than the preludes to each Act here. The CD opens up the sound yet retains the full bloom and the theatrical presence and atmosphere are something to marvel at. The layout is less than ideal, however, and only two bands are provided on each CD, though there is generous indexing.

Recorded live in a stage performance given in Tokyo in 1982, the Vienna Volksoper version is easily idiomatic, but lacks the polish and finesse to make Lehár's charming operetta sparkle. With singing generally too rough to give much pleasure on record (shrill from the women, strained and wobbly from the men), the result is jolly but coarse. The recorded sound does not help, thin in the middle, lacking body. Banding is limited to beginnings of Acts, which is the more irritating when there is so much spoken dialogue to wade through.

The Merry Widow (English version by Christopher Hassall): abridged.
(B) ** CfP CFP 41 4485-1/*4*. Bronhill, Lowe, Glynne, McAlpine, Round, Dowling, Sadler's Wells Op. Ch. and O, William Reid.

The performance on HMV does not always have an *echt*-Viennese flavour; nevertheless it says much for the achievement of the Sadler's Wells production in the 1950s that their version is so successful. For many, the deciding factor will be the English words, sung in an admirable translation; but one is not sure that this is so important on a recording. The Sadler's Wells cast is strongly characterized: only in Howell Glynne's approach is there a suspicion of Gilbert and Sullivan. Thomas Round is an appropriately raffish Danilo, though it is a pity that the recording tends to exaggerate the unevenness in his voice. William McAlpine as the second tenor, Camille de Rosillon, comes over much better, and his *Red as the rose* is exquisitely sung. The chorus is outstandingly good (especially the men) in the big scenes. The 1959 recording sounds fresh but slightly dated. On tape, there is a touch of hardness on the voices at times.

The Merry Widow: highlights.
*(*) DG **415 524-2** [id.]. Harwood, Stratas, Kollo, Hollweg, Keleman, Grobe, Krenn, German Op. Berlin Ch., BPO, Karajan.

'Brahms's *Requiem* performed to the tunes of Lehár' was how one wit described the Karajan version of *The Merry Widow*, with its carefully measured tempi and absence of sparkle. Though Elizabeth Harwood is an appealing Widow, she seems relatively colourless beside Schwarzkopf. This CD selection of highlights is generous, some 68 minutes, and all the important numbers are included. The reverberant recording has been dried out a little, but this means that the choral focus is not always quite clean, although the solo voices have plenty of presence. There is a synopsis but no libretto.

Der Zarewitsch (complete).
*** Eurodisc **610 137**; 301 291 (2). Kollo, Popp, Rebroff, Orth, Hobarth, Bav. R. Ch., Mun. R. O, Wallberg.

Wallberg conducts a delightful and idiomatic performance of one of Lehár's later, more ambitious operettas which consciously extends the normal limits of the genre, and designedly provided a vehicle for the ever-charming Richard Tauber, the supreme operetta tenor of his day. René Kollo may not have the finesse of a Tauber, but he sings with a freshness and absence of mannerism that brings out the melodic beauty. Lucia Popp as the heroine, Sonya, sings ravishingly, and there is no weak link in the cast elsewhere. With two extra numbers given to the Grand Duke (Ivan Rebroff), both taken from Lehár's *Wo die Lerche singt*, sides are generously long, and the speed of the entertainment comes over all the more refreshingly in the excellent CD transfer. No text is given, only notes in German.

Leigh, Walter (1905–42)

(i) *Concertino for harpsichord and string orchestra; The Frogs: Overture and Dance; A Midsummer Night's Dream: suite; Music for string orchestra.*
*** Lyr. SRCS 126. (i) Pinnock; LPO, Nicholas Braithwaite.

Walter Leigh was a craftsman composer of the finest kind, one who aimed to make his music useful, hence his frequent essays in incidental music, like the fresh and attractive examples here. His studies with Hindemith helped to point him in that practical direction, but otherwise left little mark on his personal style, which remained very English, with frequent but gentle neoclassical overtones. It was a tragedy when he was killed in the Western Desert during the Second World War. His masterpiece remains the *Harpsichord concertino*, which has been recorded three times before, never so persuasively as by Kathleen Long, in the days of 78, using a piano. Pinnock's sensitive performance is the finest using a harpsichord, though the balance places the solo instrument too close. Otherwise the recording is excellent.

Leighton, Kenneth (born 1929)

Concerto for organ, strings and timpani, Op. 56.
(*) Hyp. A 66097 [id.]. Christopher Rathbone, Southern Pro Arte O, Peebles – BERKELEY: *Romance of the rose.**

Kenneth Leighton's *Organ concerto* is a predominantly sombre work, intense in expression, ambitious in scale, with a first movement entitled *Lament* leading to an urgent central *Toccata* (with echoes of Stravinsky), and a finale longer than either, a set of variations on a chorale theme that builds to a powerful conclusion. The argument and textures are complex – too much so for this modest-sized orchestra – but the emotional basis is clear and satisfying, an important addition to a limited repertory of organ concertos.

Lekeu, Guillaume (1870–94)

Adagio for strings, Op. 3; Fantaisie sur deux airs populaires angevins.
*** Erato Dig. NUM 75052 [id.]. Mouillère, Monte Carlo PO, Jordan – CHAUSSON: *Poème***; RABAUD: *Procession nocturne.****

Lekeu was Franck's last pupil and his death deprived French music (though he was Belgian in origin) of a potential master. The neglect of the *Adagio for strings* is altogether unaccountable, for it is a piece rich in elegiac feeling and eloquence. No doubt the composer's early demise at the age of twenty-four lends this dignified threnody an added poignancy. It enjoyed a modicum of popularity in the 1940s, thanks to Boyd Neel's set of 78s, but this is its first stereo recording. Anyone who is moved by the nobility of the Barber *Adagio* should acquire this beautiful piece and its almost equally attractive companion. Good performances and recording, though the performance of the Chausson *Poème* that fills up the second side is not special.

Leoncavallo, Ruggiero (1858–1919)

I Pagliacci (complete).
*(*) Ph. **411 484-2**; 411 484-1/*4* (2). Stratas, Domingo, Pons, Rinaldi, La Scala Milan Ch. and O, Prêtre.

The Prêtre version is taken from the soundtrack of Zeffirelli's film of the opera, and is principally remarkable for the large-scale heroic performance, superbly sung, of Placido Domingo as Canio. Singing of this calibre makes nonsense of the allegation that he fails to characterize his roles individually. Much of the rest is less recommendable. Juan Pons sings the Prologue impressively and exploits his fine baritone as Tonio; but Teresa Stratas and Alberto Rinaldi (Silvio) both suffer from uneven vocal production, with Stratas's earthy timbres going raw under pressure. The sound is good on both LPs and cassettes – but the format on four sides is very mean. The CD transfer, however, manages to place the opera complete on a single disc, although the extra clarity and presence only serve to underline the vocal flaws.

Still recommended: Karajan's set with Joan Carlyle, Carlo Bergonzi and Giuseppe Taddei is refined in its beauty, with passions underlying, and that somehow makes one appreciate the drama more. The 1966 recording still sounds impressive, and the set is coupled at medium price to an equally recommendable *Cavalleria Rusticana* (DG 413 275-1/*4* (3/*2*)).

Liadov, Anatol (1855–1914)

Polonaise, Op. 49.
(*) HMV Dig. EL 270050-1/*4* [Ang. DS/*4XS* 38090]. CBSO, Järvi – BALAKIREV: *Symphony No. 1.**

Liadov has much enchanting music to his credit – *The enchanted lake* and *Kikimora*, to name the two most obvious pieces. His *Polonaise*, Op. 49, which precedes the Balakirev *Symphony* on side one sounds like an amiable and not-too-distant relative of the *Polonaise* from *Eugene Onegin*. It is a rather feeble makeweight for an impressive symphony.

Lipkin, Malcolm (born 1932)

Clifford's Tower; Pastoral for horn and string quintet; String trio.
*** Hyp. A 66164 [id.]. Nash Ens.

Lipkin was born in Liverpool in 1932 and as a composer received encouragement from such figures as Boris Blacher and Georges Enescu before studying in the 1950s with Matyas Seiber. The most powerful work here is *Clifford's Tower*, a bleak and uncompromising score which takes its inspiration from William of Newbury's account of an incident in twelfth-century York: the Jewish population of the town, fleeing from an anti-semitic mob, was brutally massacred in Clifford's Tower where they had taken refuge and from which there was no escape. Scored for a wind quintet and string trio, it is a powerfully conceived, moving and highly imaginative score. So, too, is the earlier *String trio*, beautifully crafted, with a fine sense of movement and an appealing idiom. The *Pastoral* is hardly less successful, an evocative and atmospheric score, beautifully played by the Nash Ensemble and expertly recorded. This is the first record of Lipkin's music to come on to the market, and his long neglect is difficult to understand. His is a real voice and his work is far more substantial than his reputation would lead one to believe. Strongly recommended.

Liszt, Franz (1811–86)

Piano concerto No. 1 in E flat, G. 124.
(*) DG **415 061-2 [id.]. Argerich, LSO, Abbado – CHOPIN: *Concerto No. 1.***(*)

Piano concertos Nos 1 in E flat, G. 124; 2 in A, G. 125.
*** Ph. **412 006-2**; 412 006-1/*4* [id.]. Sviatoslav Richter, LSO, Kondrashin.
(M) **(*) RCA VL/*VK* 89036. Pennario, LSO, Leibowitz.

Piano concertos Nos 1–2; Hungarian fantasia, G. 123.
** Erato Dig. **ECD 88035**; NUM/*MCE* 75111. Duchable, LPO, Conlon.

Piano concertos Nos 1–2; Années de pèlerinages, Supplement: Venezia e Napoli, G. 162.
(M) *** DG Gal. 415 839-1/*4*. Lazar Berman, VSO, Giulini.

Piano concertos Nos 1–2; 3 Études de concert, G. 144.
*** Ph. **416 461-2**; (without *Études*) 412 926-1/*4* [id.]. Arrau, LSO, Sir Colin Davis.

Piano concertos Nos 1 and 2; Étude transcendante d'après Paganini, G. 140/2.
(B) **(*) DG Walkman *413 850-4* [id.]. Vásáry, Bamberg SO, Prohaska – RACHMANINOV: *Piano concerto No. 2* etc.**

Richter's 1962 recordings of the Liszt *Concertos* sweep the board. They are particularly distinguished, not only by the power and feeling of Richter's own playing and the obvious rapport between conductor and soloist, but also because of a similar and striking communication between Richter and the orchestra. The orchestral playing throughout is of the very highest order and achieves a remarkably poetic response when orchestral soloists are called on to share a melody with the piano. The recording, which is perhaps slightly below the finest modern standard, has been vividly remastered; this is the second time it has reappeared on LP and cassette at medium price. While the compact disc offers a marginal improvement in quality, the sound on the tape is very well managed, too – and it costs about a third the price of the CD.

Lazar Berman has the advantage of Giulini's sensitive and masterly accompaniment with the Vienna Symphony, and even if you feel that these scores hold no surprises for you, try to hear his record. Berman's playing is consistently poetic and he illuminates detail in a way that has the power to touch the listener. Some of his rapt, quiet tone would probably not register without the tactful assistance of the DG engineers, who enable all the detail to 'tell', but the balance is most musical and well judged. A very thoughtful account of No. 1 and a poetic reading of the *A major* make this a most desirable record. Giulini keeps a strong grip on the proceedings and secures an excellent response from his players. These performances do not eclipse Richter's but they are among the best currently available. The Galleria reissue has been digitally remastered with great success and the sound is rich and firm, with LP and chrome cassette virtually indistinguishable. The *Concertos* were recorded in 1966 and, to make the Galleria issue even more desirable, DG have added the three pieces which make up the *Années de pèlerinages Supplement*, with *Gondoliera* and the *Canzone* following the *First Concerto*, and *Tarantella* used as a final encore piece. There is more magnificent piano-playing here, and this is a bargain in every sense of the word.

Claudio Arrau made a stunning record of the *E flat Concerto* with Ormandy and the Philadelphia Orchestra in the 1950s, and this new account, made in his mid-seventies, is scarcely less fine. Even though some of the youthful abandon is tamed, Arrau's virtuosity is transcendental. There is a greater breadth in No. 1 here than in the earlier version, and there are many thoughtful touches throughout. This artist's Indian summer shows no loss of fire, and he brings plenty of panache to the *A major Concerto*. This does not displace Lazar Berman or, of course, Richter among the top recommendations but takes its place beside them. First-class sound, on both LP and cassette alike, which are are mid-price. Curiously, the remastering for CD has resulted in a very reticent triangle in the scherzo of the *First Concerto*; in fact one has to listen very carefully to hear it at all. The cassette has a similar effect. The CD adds Arrau's 1976 recordings of the three *Concert studies*, G. 144, of which the last, *Un sospiro*, has been a favourite since the days of 78s.

The generously coupled Walkman tape offers three concertos, plus solo items, and – while Vásáry's version of the Rachmaninov *C minor* is less impressive than his Liszt – this is still a bargain. His recording of Liszt's *E flat Concerto* still sounds very well indeed; the performance is distinguished by considerable subtlety and refinement, yet with no loss of impact, even if there is little barnstorming. His approach to the *A major*, too, is thoughtful and sensitive. The accompaniments under Prohaska are sympathetic, and the 1960 sound remains vivid, clear and full.

Pennario gives extremely brilliant, virtuoso performances, perhaps not penetrating too far beneath the surface of the music, but very enjoyable in their extrovert spontaneity. The recording is sparkling to match, with very vivid stereo to bring everything forward. The result is highly effective, with some superb, glittering bravura from the pianist and also plenty of excitement from the orchestra. The sound itself (mid-1960s vintage) is surprisingly fresh; and the closing pages of the *A major Concerto* are splendidly exhilarating, with the brashness put to the service of the music. This remains highly recommendable – it is a pity that RCA's latest reissue is not (like previous reincarnations on Camden and Victrola) in the bargain price-range: this costs more than Vásáry's Walkman.

Duchable's performances are flamboyantly extrovert, and the bold, forwardly balanced piano helps to underline that effect. The orchestra makes a strong impression, however, and Conlon matches his soloist with firm and vigorous accompaniments. On CD the *Second Concerto* comes first and is made to sound more melodramatic than usual. In both works, while the lyrical episodes do not lack expressive feeling, they are without the melting spontaneity of the famous

Richter versions. The dash and brilliance of the playing best suit the *Hungarian fantasia*. Certainly on CD the sound has plenty of presence.

A clear, direct, sometimes even fastidious approach to the *First Concerto*, coupled to Chopin, from Martha Argerich. She plays the *Larghetto* meltingly, and there is an excellent partnership between pianist and conductor. Both are agreed in minimizing the work's flamboyance without reducing the voltage. This is very much a performance to live with, and many should find it exactly to their taste, with the orchestra providing refined yet vivid detail under Abbado. The CD remastering of the 1969 recording is astonishingly successful, the sound hardly dated at all.

(i) *Piano concerto No. 1;* (ii) *Hungarian rhapsody No. 4;* (iii) *Les Préludes;* (iv) *Études de concert Nos 2* (*La Leggierezza*), *3* (*Un sospiro*); *Étude d'exécution d'après Paganini No. 3: La Campanella; Hungarian rhapsody No. 6; Liebestraum No. 3; Mephisto waltz; Valses oubliées Nos 1–2.*

**(*) Ph. On Tour *412 901-4* [id.]. (i) Sviatoslav Richter, LSO, Kondrashin; (ii) LOP, Benzi; (iii) LOP, Haitink; (iv) Dichter.

A good bargain-priced tape anthology, which, however, cuts across the acquisition of both concertos. Richter's account of the *First* needs no further advocacy here, while Haitink's unhistrionic account of *Les Préludes* is nicely balanced by Benzi's *Hungarian rhapsody*, which has plenty of flair. On side two, we are offered some fine solo playing from Misha Dichter, who gives intimate accounts of the *Liebestraum* and the equally famous third *Étude de concert* but displays no lack of dash in the *Mephisto waltz*, and makes *La Campanella* sparkle. There is a natural Lisztian sensibility here, even if the playing is at times somewhat withdrawn. The sound is very realistic and the recordings are well transferred throughout, on chrome tape.

Dante symphony, G. 109.

** Erato Dig. **ECD 88162**; NUM/*MCE* 75245 [id.]. Helmond Concert Ch., Rotterdam PO, Conlon.

* Andante Dig. **ACD 72401**; AD 72401 [id.]. Utah Ch. and SO, Kojian.

(i) *Dante symphony; Mephisto waltz No. 2; Les Préludes; Tasso, lamento e trionfo.*

(B) **(*) HMV *TCC2-POR 54292*. (i) Arndt, St Thomas's Ch., Leipzig; Leipzig GO, Masur.

This double-length iron-oxide tape, in EMI's 'Portrait of the Artist' series, offers a selection from Masur's distinguished integral recording of all Liszt's orchestral music. (A further compilation, on both mid-priced LP and cassette, which overlaps with this, is discussed below.) The *Dante symphony* is complete on one side without a break, and Masur proves as persuasive an advocate as any on record in this repertoire. The sound matches the original recordings in catching the rich sonorities of the Leipzig lower strings and the dark, perfectly blended woodwind timbre. The tape transfer is well detailed and convincingly balanced, but loses a little of the original sparkle on top.

Conlon's performance is atmospheric but a little lacking in charisma and grip: the Inferno sequence has more impact in Masur's hands, although the advantages of CD and a well-balanced digital recording cannot be disputed, and the Rotterdam account is well played and sung.

Kojian's performance of the *Dante symphony* does not represent a serious challenge to existing versions on LP and cassette. The Utah orchestra have good players, though they are not superior to the Leipzig Gewandhaus in any department. The Utah chorale is not as sensitively directed as it might be and does not always observe dynamic markings with the scrupulousness one finds in rivals such as Masur or Lopez-Cobos (Decca SXDL/*KSXDC* 7542). However enthusiastic one may be about the new medium, here is an instance where one should stay with the old.

Fantasia on Hungarian folk tunes, G. 123; Malédiction, G. 121; Totentanz, G. 126 (all for piano and orchestra).
ɕ *** Decca Dig. **414 079-2**; 414 079-1/*4* [id.]. Bolet, LSO, Ivan Fischer.

Bolet is the masterful soloist in a splendid triptych of concertante works, the second of which – using strings alone – is unjustly neglected. Bolet's performance, sensitive as well as brilliant, should do much to rectify that, and the accounts of the two well-known works, persuasive enough to paper over any structural cracks, bring out all of Bolet's characteristic bravura. Excellent accompaniments from the LSO under an understanding Hungarian conductor, and recording of demonstration quality, particularly impressive on CD, but with a chrome cassette also representing the highest state of the art.

(i) *Fantasia on Hungarian folk tunes, G. 123. Hungarian rhapsodies, G. 359/2, 4 and 5; Mazeppa, G. 100; Mephisto waltz No. 1; Les Préludes, G. 97; Tasso, lamento e trionfo, G. 96.*
❀ *** DG **415 967-2** (2). (i) Shura Cherkassky; BPO, Karajan.

For the CD collection, DG have added to the orchestral works offered on LP and tape (see below) Shura Cherkassky's glittering 1961 recording of the *Hungarian fantasia*. It is an affectionate performance with some engaging touches from the orchestra, though the pianist is dominant and his playing is superbly assured. Here as elsewhere the remastering for CD has impressively improved the range and body of the sound, with firm detail through the orchestra. The cellos and basses sound marvellous in the *Fifth Rhapsody* and *Tasso*, and even the brashness of *Les Préludes* is a little tempered. The quiet background for the coda of *Mazeppa* adds to the frisson-creating effect of the distanced brass. A superb achievement, showing Karajan and his great orchestra at their finest.

(i) *Fantasia on Hungarian folk tunes;* (ii) *Hungarian rhapsodies, G. 359/2, 4 and 6* (*Pest Carnival*); (iii) *Rákóczy march.*
** Hung. Dig. **HCD 12721-2** [id.]. (i) Jenö Jando, Hungarian State O, Ferencsik, (ii) Szeged SO, Pal, (iii) Németh.

The three *Hungarian rhapsodies* are well enough played by the Szeged orchestra under Tamas Pal, and there is no lack of paprika in the proceedings. Jenö Jando is rather closely balanced in the recording with the late János Ferencsik and the Hungarian State Orchestra, and sounds pretty thunderous at times. There is fine body and the sound is particularly rich and firmly defined in the bass. But this is not an outstanding issue in any way.

(i) *Faust symphony, G. 108; 2 Episodes from Lenau's Faust: Der Nachtliche Zug; Mephisto waltz No. 1, G. 110.*
*** Erato Dig. **ECD 880682** (without *Episodes*); NUM/*MCE* 751582 (2) [id.]. (i) John Aler; Slovak Philharmonic Ch.; Rotterdam PO, Conlon.
(M) *** DG 415 009-1/*4* (2) [id.]. Riegel, Tanglewood Fest. Ch., Boston SO, Bernstein – TCHAIKOVSKY: *Francesca da Rimini.**(*)

James Conlon secures extremely good results in the Erato version of the *Faust symphony* – and, for that matter, in the *Two episodes from Lenau's Faust* which come as a makeweight on the LP and cassette set (as they did with Ansermet's 1960s account on Decca). The CD fits the complete symphony on to two sides, and with an excellent sound-balance this makes an obvious best buy. On performance grounds alone, Muti's version on HMV (SLS/*TC-SLS* 143570-3/*5* [DSB/*42XS* 2928]) probably still remains first choice. As an ardent Tchaikovskian, Muti shows a natural sympathy for a piece which can readily seem overlong, and he finds obvious affinities in the music with the style of the Russian master; but that is not yet available on compact disc. The Erato LP coupling, however, makes Conlon's set more attractive (for most collectors will already have *Les Préludes*, which is Muti's fill-up). The Rotterdam orchestral playing is very alive and committed, and the recorded sound altogether excellent on LP, although the upper range of the chrome cassettes is rather fierce. The choral finale comes off impressively in all three media.

Bernstein recorded this symphony in the mid-1960s, but this newer version, made in Boston, is both more sensitive and more brilliant. It was the first modern recording to offer a serious challenge to Beecham's classic account made in the late 1950s (currently out of the catalogue). The *Gretchen* movement is most beautifully played here, with finely delineated detail and refined texture. The tenor soloist in the finale is excellent, and the Boston orchestra produce some exciting and atmospheric playing. The recording too is extremely fine, and it has transferred well to cassette. The only snag is that the new coupling for this mid-priced reissue is Tchaikovsky's *Francesca da Rimini*, with Bernstein conducting the Israel Philharmonic, which leaves something to be desired in the refinement of the orchestral playing.

Hungarian rhapsodies for orchestra Nos 1–6, G. 359.
(M) ** Ph. Seq. 6527/*7311* 202. LSO, Dorati.

Dorati's is undoubtedly the finest set of orchestral *Hungarian rhapsodies*. He brings out the gipsy flavour, and with lively playing from the LSO there is both polish and sparkle, but the music does not become urbane. The use of the cimbalom within the orchestra brings an authentic extra colouring. The 1961 recording has a Mercury source and is characteristically vivid, if a little thin on top. It sounds somewhat dated now. The tape transfer is first class.

Hungarian rhapsodies Nos 2 and 4; Les Préludes, G. 97.
(B) *** DG Walkman *413 159-4* [id.]. BPO, Karajan – DVOŘÁK: *Slavonic dances;* SMETANA: *Vltava* etc.***

Hungarian rhapsodies Nos 2, 4 and 5; Mazeppa, G. 100; Mephisto waltz No. 1; Les Préludes; Tasso, lamento e trionfo, G. 96 (see also above).
(M) **(*) DG 415 628-1/*4* (2) [id.]. BPO, Karajan.

Karajan is completely at home in this repertoire. He goes over the top in *Les Préludes*, not helped by a top-heavy recording balance which manages to make even the Berlin Philharmonic sound brash; but in the rest of the music here he secures marvellous playing and fine characterization. The approach to the *Hungarian rhapsodies* is somewhat urbane, yet there is plenty of sparkle; the orchestra produce their gravest manner for No. 5 (sub-titled *Héroïde-Elégiaque*). On the excellently engineered Walkman tape, the three most popular works are featured as part of a well-organized anthology of Slavonic music.

The two-disc/double-tape set collects together at medium price all Karajan's analogue recordings of Liszt's orchestral music. *Mazeppa* and the *Second Rhapsody* come from 1961, the *Fourth Rhapsody* and *Les Préludes*, 1968, and the rest of the programme was recorded in the 1970s. *Tasso* (1976), played with a convincing balance of power and refinement, is obviously more modern. The highlight of the set is *Mazeppa*, a great performance. It is superbly thrilling and atmospheric, with a moment to set the hairs at the nape of the neck tingling when, just before the final peroration, the magically distanced brass announce that the hero's rescue is at hand. The remastering for this mid-priced reissue has not been altogether advantageous, particularly on tape. In the earlier recordings the sound has lost some of its original depth, with the bass drier and the treble now brightly lit. On tape, *Les Préludes* is made to seem impossibly fierce and even the (originally) superbly balanced *Mazeppa* has lost a little of its ambient bloom.

Hunnenschlacht (symphonic poem), *G. 105.*
** Telarc Dig. **CD 80079**; DG 10079 [id.]. Cincinnati SO, Kunzel – BEETHOVEN: *Wellington's victory.***

A direct, unsubtle performance of a rarely recorded piece, not one of Liszt's finest works in the genre. The Telarc sound, however, is highly spectacular with the organ interpolation adding to the expansiveness of texture. Those wanting the *'Battle' symphony* of Beethoven won't be disappointed with this, although the CD is rather short measure.

Orpheus, G. 98; Mazeppa, G. 100; Les Préludes, G. 97; Tasso, lamento e trionfo.
(M) **(*) HMV EG 290495-1/*4*. Leipzig GO, Masur.

Orpheus, G. 98; Les Préludes, G. 97; Tasso, lamento e trionfo, G. 96.
** Hung. Dig. **HCD 12446-2**; SLPD/*MK* 12446 [id.]. Hungarian State O, Ferencsik.

Les Préludes, G. 97.
** HMV **CDC 747022-2** [id.]. Phd. O, Muti – RAVEL: *Boléro*; TCHAIKOVSKY: *1812.**

Masur offers one more work than Ferencsik in this generous helping from his complete recording of Liszt's orchestral music, issued by EMI in two 4-LP boxes (now deleted). The four works gathered here play for just over an hour and, although the digital remastering has robbed the sound of some of its rich sonority in the lower strings, the freshness of the new sound-balance has a different kind of appeal. Masur is not altogether at home in the melodrama of *Les Préludes* and *Mazeppa* – although the latter is excitingly done, if without the panache of Karajan (see above). He breezes through *Orpheus* at record speed, and misses the endearing gentleness that Beecham brought to it in the early 1960s. Nevertheless these performances are all strongly characterized and extremely well played. There is a very good XDR cassette, with the sound-balance rather fuller if less transparent than the LP. *Orpheus* and *Tasso* on side two sound especially well.

Janos Ferencsik is a sympathetic Lisztian; he gives a refined account of *Orpheus* and actually makes *Les Préludes* sound restrained. The image is well focused and has plenty of body, particularly at the bottom end of the register. All the same, these performances are not in any way superior to those of Haitink and the LPO on Philips, now available on the mid-price Sequenza label, and are not to be preferred to them. The same three pieces are offered on the Philips disc and tape (6527/*7311* 201 [id.]).

Muti's version of *Les Préludes* is suitably exuberant and the Philadelphia Orchestra are on top form. The recording, however, is far from ideal in the matter of sonority, suggesting that – as so often in this piece – the engineers were striving for brilliance above all. The Ravel and Tchaikovsky couplings sound even less congenial.

CHAMBER MUSIC

Elégies Nos 1 for cello, piano, harp and harmonium, G. 130; 2 for violin and piano, G. 131; La lugubre gondola for cello and piano, G. 134; La notte for violin and piano, G. 377a; Romance oubliée for viola and piano, G. 132.
*** Ph. 411 117-1/*4*. De Leeuw, Beths, Bijlmsa, Ockers, Bob Zimmerman.

A record of uncommon interest which assembles a number of chamber works from Liszt's last years. We don't think of him as a composer of chamber music; indeed, this music all exists, and is much better known, in its piano form. There is a notable recording of *La lugubre gondola* from Brendel, wonderfully concentrated in both feeling and atmosphere; and neither of the *Elégies* is *terra incognita*. Yet what an interesting arrangement the first *Elégie* is for the unusual combination of cello, piano, harp and harmonium – very strange and haunting it is, too. The artists distil an atmosphere of fragile, ghostly melancholy and there is a questing, troubled spirit about this music which is both moving and disturbing. The performances (from, among others, Reinbert de Leeuw, Vera Beths and Anner Bijlmsa, of whom we are accustomed to think in other musical contexts) are very persuasive; although the record is not well filled, it makes up for that deficiency in terms of sheer musical interest. The recorded sound is eminently truthful and vivid on LP and equally so on the excellent high-level chrome tape.

PIANO MUSIC

Années de pèlerinage, 1st Year (Switzerland), G. 160.
ɕ *** Decca Dig. **410 160-2**; 410 160-1/*4* [id.]. Jorge Bolet.

Winner of the instrumental prize in the *Gramophone* awards 1985, this recording of the Swiss pieces from the *Années de pèlerinage* represents Bolet at his very peak, in some ways even transcending his masterly achievement in earlier discs in the series, with playing of magical delicacy as well as formidable power. So *Au bord d'une source* brings playing limpid in its evocative beauty. The piano sound is outstandingly fine, set against a helpful atmosphere, and there is a very good cassette; the compact disc, however, gains greatly from its complete background silence.

Années de pèlerinage, 2nd Year (Italy), G. 161 (complete).
*** Decca Dig. **410 161-2**; 410 161-1/*4* [id.]. Jorge Bolet.
(M) *** Ph. Seq. 412 364-1/*4*. Alfred Brendel.

The pianistic colourings in this fine instalment in Bolet's Liszt series are magically caught here, whether in the brilliant sunlight of *Sposalizio* or the visionary gloom of *Il penseroso*. The *Dante sonata* brings a darkly intense performance, fresh and original and deeply satisfying. The piano sound is brilliant but not clangorous. On cassette, the wide range is impressively caught, but the focus is slightly less sharp than on CD and LP.

Brendel's performances are also of superlative quality. This was outstanding among Liszt records in the analogue era: not only is the playing highly poetic and brilliant but the 1973 recording offers Philips's most realistic quality. There is an excellent matching cassette.

Années de pèlerinages, Book 2. Supplement: Venezia e Napoli (Gondoliera; Canzone; Tarantella), G. 162; 3rd Year: Les jeux d'eau à la Villa d'este, G. 163/4; Ballade No. 2 in B min., G. 171; Harmonies poétiques et religieuses: Bénédiction de Dieu dans la solitude, G. 173/3.
*** Decca Dig. **411 803-2**; 411 803-1/*4* [id.]. Jorge Bolet.

Even in Bolet's prize-winning Liszt series, this sixth volume stands out for its performances, both brilliant and dedicated, of a group of the most colourful and popular pieces, 'a dazzling pendant to Liszt's Italian *Années de pèlerinage'*, as the sleeve-note describes them, and also of two of the weightiest, the *Bénédiction* and the *Ballade*, both spaciously conceived and far too little known. As he progresses in his series, so Bolet seems even more at ease in the studio; the concentration of the long pieces, as well as the magically sparkling textures of the sunny Italian pieces, is masterfully conveyed. Vivid and full piano recording. It has the usual added tangibility in its CD format, but the chrome tape too is another Decca issue to represent the highest state of the art.

Années de pèlerinage, 2nd Year, G. 161; Après une lecture du Dante (Dante sonata); 6 Chants polonais (Chopin), G. 480; Harmonies poétiques et religieuses, G. 173; Funérailles.
ϵ *** Ph. Dig. **411 055-2**; 6514/*7337* 273 [id.]. Claudio Arrau.

This is very distinguished playing, astonishing for an artist approaching his eightieth birthday. The *Dante sonata* is wonderfully commanding: it has a magisterial grandeur; and *Funérailles* is hardly less impressive. The transcriptions of Chopin songs are done with great charm and subtlety, too. The recording quality is totally realistic and splendidly focused – among the best recordings of the instrument we have had in the last year or so. The compact disc attains near-perfection by adding a reliably silent background.

Années de pèlerinages, 2nd Year, G. 161: Après une lecture de Dante. Concert paraphrases on Gounod's Faust, G. 407; Verdi's Rigoletto, G. 434; 6 Consolations, G. 172.
** Denon Dig. **C37 7332** [id.]. Jean-Yves Thibaudet.

Jean-Yves Thibaudet is a young French pianist of considerable prowess who has many prizes to his credit, including the French Radio prize which he won in 1977 when he was only fifteen. He has a formidable technique, which enables him to bestride the hurdles of the Faust paraphrase a little more readily than he encompasses the simplicity of the *Consolations*. He plays with plenty of brilliance and dramatic fire in the *Dante sonata* and is obviously an artist to watch. His recording, made in Japan, is splendidly vivid and truthful; no reader attracted by this programme need hesitate on this score. Dezsö Ránki recorded the *Dante sonata* for Denon in the 1970s when he was about the same age (see below), and the Hungarian's greater artistic maturity, freedom and excitement tell.

Concert paraphrases of Schubert Lieder: *Auf dem Wasser zu singen; Aufenthalt; Erlkönig; Die Forelle; Horch, horch die Lerch; Lebe wohl!; Der Lindenbaum; Lob der Tränen; Der Müller und der Bach; Die Post; Das Wandern; Wohin.*
*** Decca Dig. **414 575-2** [id.]; SXDL/*KSXDC* 7569. Bolet.

Superb virtuosity from Bolet in these display arrangements of Schubert. He is not just a wizard but a feeling musician, though here he sometimes misses a feeling of fun. First-rate recording on disc and chrome tape alike, with the CD adding the usual extra sense of presence, and gaining from the silent background.

Concert paraphrase of Verdi's: *Rigoletto, G. 434; Études d'exécution transcendante d'après Paganini: La Campanella, G. 140/6. Harmonies poétiques et religieuses: Funérailles, G. 173/7. Hungarian rhapsody No. 12, G. 244; Liebestraum No. 3, G. 541/3. Mephisto waltz No. 1, G. 514.*
ℭ *** Decca Dig. **410 257-2**; SXDL/*KSXDC* 7596 [LDR/5- 71096]. Jorge Bolet.

Bolet's is a superb collection of Liszt items, the first to be recorded of his current series. The playing is magnetic, not just because of virtuosity thrown off with ease (as here in the *Rigoletto* paraphrase) but because of an element of joy conveyed, even in the demonic vigour of the *Mephisto Waltz No. 1*. The relentless thrust of *Funérailles* is beautifully contrasted against the honeyed warmth of the famous *Liebestraum No. 3* and the sparkle of *La Campanella*. Even with the most hackneyed pieces, Bolet – superbly recorded – conveys complete freshness. Chrome tape and LP sound very much the same. The compact disc is thrillingly realistic in its spectacular sense of presence.

Concert paraphrases of Wagner: *Der fliegende Holländer: Spinning song, G. 440; Lohengrin: Bridal march, G. 445; Parsifal: Feierlicher Marsch, G. 450; Der Ring des Nibelungen: Valhalla, G. 449; Tannhäuser overture, G. 442; Tristan und Isolde: Liebestod, G. 447.*
(*) PRT **CDPCN 2. Michele Campanella.

Michele Campanella is an uncommonly fine Liszt player; although he does not quite solve the problems of the *Tannhäuser overture*, this remains a powerful reading. Here as elsewhere the pianist shows a splendid feeling not only for Wagner's musical line but also for the orchestral colour expressed in Liszt's pianistic terms. The *Spinning song* is most attractive, and the *Parsifal* music both eloquent and beautiful. The *Tristan Liebestod* is perhaps less directly passionate, but has underlying expressive feeling. The analogue recording has transferred well to CD, although the piano image is warm and full rather than brilliantly focused.

Études d'exécution transcendante, G. 139 (complete).
*** Ph. **416 458-2** [id.]. Claudio Arrau.

Arrau made this recording in 1977 and it was a formidable achievement for an artist in his seventies. Array plays always with great panache and musical insight, which more than compensate for the occasional smudginess of the recorded sound. On record both Lazar Berman and Cziffra (the latter now deleted) brought greater obvious virtuosity to these pieces, but both are much younger men. Arrau's playing is most masterly and poetic, and the recording, if too reverberant, is admirably truthful, and the CD transfer adds to the feeling of tangibility.

Études d'exécution transcendante Nos 1, Preludio; 2, in A min.; 3, Paysage; 5, Feux follets; 8, Wilde Jagd; 10, in F min.; 11, Harmonies du soir, G. 139; Mephisto waltz No. 1, G. 514.
** HMV Dig. EL 270177-1/*4*. Dmitri Sgouros.

Dmitri Sgouros possesses an amazing technical facility, remarkable in a player twice his age, and in this respect it would be ungenerous to deny him a high accolade. At the same time, prodigious feats of dazzling virtuosity which can carry an audience in the concert hall are very different from the musical achievement necessary for the repeated listening to which a record is exposed. His is a remarkable talent, of that there is no doubt; more than just promise, there is quite a lot of fulfilment here. However, by the harsh standards of the gramophone, the claims of this young lion have to be measured alongside those of Bolet and Brendel – to go no further in the alphabet – and he is not quite ready for that league. The recording has fine realism and presence on both LP and cassette.

Liebesträume Nos 1–3, G. 541.
*** DG **415 118-2** [id.]. Daniel Barenboim – MENDELSSOHN: *Songs without words****; SCHUBERT: *6 Moments musicaux.***

This is a recoupling from three different analogue LP sources. These famous Liszt pieces come from 1981 and are most naturally recorded. Barenboim plays them with unaffected simplicity and he is equally at home in Mendelssohn's *Songs without words*. The Schubert pieces are slightly more self-conscious but, taken as a whole, this is a rewarding CD.

Piano sonata in B min.; Années de pèlerinages, 2nd Year, G. 161: Sonetti del Petrarca Nos 47, 104 and 123; Après une lecture du Dante (Dante sonata).
** Delos **D/CD 3022** [id.]. John Browning.

Piano sonata in B min., G. 178; Années de pèlerinage, 2nd Year, G. 161: Après une lecture de Dante (Dante sonata). Mephisto waltz No. 1, G. 514.
₵ *** Denon Dig. **C37 7547** [id.]. Dezsö Ránki.

Piano sonata; Berceuse, G. 174; Étude de concert: Gnomenreigen, G. 145/2; Liebestraum No. 3, G. 541; Valse oubliée No. 1, G. 215/1.
(M) *** Decca Jub. 411 727-1/*4*. Clifford Curzon.

Piano sonata; Études d'éxécution transcendante d'après Paganini Nos 1–2, 3 (La Campanella), 4–6, G. 140.
*** HMV Dig. EL 270261-1/*4*. Cécile Ousset.

Piano sonata; Grand galop chromatique, G. 219; Liebesträume Nos 1–3, G. 541; Valse impromptu, G. 213.
*** Decca Dig. **410 115-2**; 410 115-1/*4*. Jorge Bolet.

Piano sonata; Harmonies poétiques et religieuses: Funérailles, G. 173/7.
(***) EMI Référence mono PM100100-1/*4*. Vladimir Horowitz – SCHUMANN: *Arabeske in C* etc.(***)

Piano sonata; 2 Légendes: (*St Francis of Assisi preaching to the birds; St Francis of Paulo walking on the waters*), *G. 175; Harmonies poétiques et religieuses: Bénédiction de Dieu dans la solitude, G. 173/3.*
** Erato Dig. **ECD 88091**; NUM/*MCE* 75177 [id.]. François-René Duchable.

Piano sonata; 2 Légendes, G. 175; La lugubre gondola, Nos 1 and 2, G. 200.
☾ *** Ph. Dig. **410 040-2**; 6514/*7337* 147 [id.]. Alfred Brendel.

Dezsö Ránki's performances come from 1975 and his anthology was one of the very earliest digital recordings to be made. His account of the *Dante sonata* is very impressive indeed, with real fire and a masterly control of dramatic pace. The *Mephisto waltz* and the *Sonata* are hardly less powerful in the hands of the young Hungarian master; indeed, the latter can hold its own with almost any of its rivals. The Denon recording is absolutely first class and has admirable clarity, body and presence. This is one of the best Liszt recital programmes currently available.

Curzon shows an innate understanding of the *Sonata*'s cyclic form, so that the significance of the principal theme is brought out subtly in relation to the music's structural development. There are only a few performances to compare with this and none superior, and Decca's 1963 recording matches the playing in its excellence. The shorter pieces too are imaginatively played. With an excellent tape, sounding every bit as good as the LP, this is superb value at mid-price.

Cécile Ousset enjoys an enviable reputation in the UK, and her following is unlikely to be disappointed with this Liszt recital. There is something of that hard steely tone in the first of the studies which does not enjoy universal appeal, but there is no denying that she has a formidable musical personality. Her account of the *B minor Sonata* is one of the finest now before the public; it is a thoroughly integrated view of this piece, played with extraordinary flair and forward drive. It is very impressive indeed and will appeal even to those who normally do not number themselves among her admirers. The recording on LP is little short of superb, and has plenty of space and presence. The cassette quality is slightly hard on top.

The power, imagination and concentration of Bolet are excellently brought out in his fine account of the *Sonata*. With the famous *Liebestraum* (as well as its two companions) also most beautifully done, not to mention the amazing *Grand galop*, this is one of the most widely appealing of Bolet's outstanding Liszt series. Excellent recording, especially on CD, but the cassette too is first class.

Horowitz's famous account of the *B minor Sonata* comes from 1932 and continues to dazzle. In this new transfer by Keith Hardwick, it is heard to greater advantage than in previous incarnations; in some ways, it still reigns supreme. The dated sound is forgotten almost immediately, so electrifying is this playing, and no serious collector should be without it. This classic version silences criticism and remains unsurpassed, even by Horowitz himself. His *Funérailles* offers a splendid makeweight. There is an excellent cassette.

Brendel's latest account of the *Sonata* has received wide acclaim; the critics of *Gramophone* magazine voted it the piano record of 1983. It is certainly a more subtle and concentrated account than his earlier version made in the mid-1960s – brilliant though that was – and must be numbered among the very best now available. There is a wider range of colour and tonal nuance, yet the undoubted firmness of grip does not seem achieved at the expense of any spontaneity. There have been many outstanding versions of this work in the past; this certainly ranks with them, among other reasons because of the striking excellence of the engineering, for it is amazingly well recorded. In its cassette format, the sound is hardly less vivid and matches the quality of the LP in almost every respect. On compact disc, the presence of the recording is enhanced by the absence of any intrusive noise, yet there is a feeling of ambience; although the balance is close, the effect is very realistic.

John Browning's Liszt recital offers good measure at 71′ 45″ and his performances are predictably brilliant. He gives us the last four of the Italian book of the *Années de pèlerinage* and the *B minor Sonata*. The only other pianist to couple the *Dante sonata* and the *B minor* together is Dezsö Ránki. Although Ránki's Denon recording is ten years old, it is not inferior, and artistically he gives the more satisfying performances. Browning, who gave us such inspired Ravel in the 1960s, has a searching intelligence and refined musicianship, but there are some disruptive agogic touches and he does not observe scrupulously all of Liszt's dynamic markings; Bolet, Brendel and Ránki do. Of course, there are many impressive and brilliant things here, though Browning's forte tone does at times harden a little.

François-René Duchable also gives a dashing account of the *B minor Sonata*; in terms of virtuosity, he is in the highest bracket. In a way, he allows his virtuosity to run away with him and dazzles rather than illuminates. Others have a greater musical impact, though this fine French pianist is often poetic, particularly in the third of the *Harmonies poétiques et religieuses*. The Erato recording is not as warm as the best of Philips (Brendel), Decca (Bolet) or HMV (Ousset), and on cassette the piano image is a little hard.

ORGAN MUSIC

Fantasia and fugue on 'Ad nos, ad salutarem undam', G. 259.

(*) DG Dig. **415 139-2; 415 139-1/*4* [id.]. Simon Preston (organ of Westminster Abbey) – REUBKE: *Sonata on the 94th Psalm.***(*)

Fantasia and fugue on 'Ad nos, ad salutarem undam'; Prelude and fugue on the name BACH, G. 260; Variations on Bach's 'Weinen, Klagen, Sorgen, Zagen', G. 673.
*** Pierre Verany Dig. **PV 783041** [id.]. Chantal de Zeeuw (organ of Aix-en-Provence Cathedral).

An impressive compact disc début. Mlle Chantal de Zeeuw plays Liszt's ripely romantic evocations of classical forms with striking flair and the resonant acoustic of Aix Cathedral helps to make a spectacular effect. The microphones are close enough to capture the organ's action noise, but the overall sound-picture remains convincing.

The organ in Westminster Abbey has a quite different character from the instrument in Aix, and the recording seeks an essentially atmospheric effect in an acoustic which prevents sharpness of detail. As in his previous analogue recording for Argo, Preston concentrates on colour (often dark-hued) and vivid contrasts, rather than extrovert excitement, although his playing is undoubtedly powerful. Those preferring the Reubke coupling will find that this sounds very impressive in all three formats, as long as one is willing to accept the blurred focus provided by the ambience of Westminster Abbey.

VOCAL MUSIC

Via Crucis, G. 53.
*** Ph. Dig. **416 649-2**; 416 649-1/*4* [id.]. Netherlands Chamber Ch., De Leeuw (piano).

This rarely heard work was written late in Liszt's career (1878/9). Its atmosphere is spare and austere. Short dramatic choruses are punctuated by imaginative keyboard solos which, as Reinbert de Leeuw shows, are highly effective played on the piano, although, when the choir is being accompanied, the use of the piano is less telling than the more usual organ with its ability to sustain. The baldness of the writing does not imply a lack of beauty or imaginative use of harmony, and the spacious simplicity of the presentation here, with very fine singing from the Netherlanders, is agreeably serene. The recording is first class and there is an excellent tape.

Litolff, Henri (1818–91)

Concerto symphonique No. 4, Op. 102: Scherzo.
*** Ph. Dig. **411 123-2**; 411 123-1/*4* [id.]. Dichter, Philh. O, Marriner (with Concert of concertante music***).
*** Decca Dig. **414 348-2**; 414 348-1/*4* [id.]. Ortiz, RPO, Atzmon – ADDINSELL: *Warsaw concerto*; GOTTSCHALK: *Grand fantaisie*; RACHMANINOV: *Concerto No. 2.****

Litolff's delicious *Scherzo*, famous since the days of 78 r.p.m. discs, receives its compact disc début from Misha Dichter, who gives it a scintillating account, played at a sparklingly brisk tempo. Marriner accompanies sympathetically and the recording is excellent in all three media.

Cristina Ortiz's version has less extrovert brilliance but an agreeable elegance. The intimacy of this account is emphasized by the balance which places the piano within the orchestral group, making the gentle central section especially effective. The pianism is assured in its delicacy and, with excellent – if reverberant – sound, this can be recommended alongside Dichter. The Decca couplings are more substantial and the CD is impressively natural.

Lloyd, George (born 1913)

(i) *Piano concerto No. 4; The lily leaf and the grasshopper.*
*** Conifer Dig. CFRA 119 [id.]. Kathryn Stott; (i) LSO, composer.

George Lloyd's bizarre career with its decades of total neglect has at last found some kind of fulfilment, with more recordings of major works than many composers receive. (Two of his symphonies are available in excellent recorded performances on Lyrita: No. 5 on SRCS 124 and No. 8 on SRCS 113, played by the Philharmonia Orchestra under Edward Downes.) This concerto, a late work, proves less rewarding than the symphonies so far recorded, though the dedicated performance makes out a persuasive case. The main trouble is the relative lack of memorability in the thematic material and Lloyd's tendency – not typical of his usual orchestral writing – to overload the score in busy textures. Nevertheless, the energy of the writing comes over well; Kathryn Stott gives a charming performance of the solo piano work that comes as fill-up. First-rate recording.

Lloyd Webber, Andrew (born 1948)

Requiem.
*** HMV Dig. **CDC 747146-2** [id.]; EL 270242-1/*4* [Ang. DFO/*4DS* 38218]. Brightman, Domingo, Miles-Kingston, Drew, Winchester Cathedral Ch., ECO, Maazel; J. Lancelot (organ).

Let no one be put off by the media hype that surrounded the first performances of this serious essay by a popular composer. This *Requiem* may be derivative at many points, with echoes of Carl Orff – not to mention the *Requiems* of both Verdi and Fauré – but, with Maazel conducting a performance of characteristic intensity, it certainly has a life of its own. The *Pié Jesu* – which rose to the top of the pop-singles at a time when the LP was listed in the pop-album charts – is a model of bridge-building, a melody beautiful and individual by any standard, which yet has all the catchiness of one of Lloyd Webber's tunes in a musical. Plainly the high, bright voice of Sarah Brightman (Mrs Lloyd Webber) was the direct inspiration, and the beauty of her singing certainly earns her this place alongside Placido Domingo contributing in a role rather less prominent. Radiant sounds from the Winchester Cathedral Choir, not least the principal treble, Paul Miles-Kingston. Above all, this is music to which one returns with increasing appreciation and pleasure. The CD gives extra presence and clarity to the excellent sound, while the cassette too is outstandingly successful, though the tape back-up documentation is a disgrace.

Lutoslawski, Witold (born 1913)

Concerto for orchestra.
(M) **(*) HMV ED 290134-1/*4* [Pathé, id.]. Chicago SO, Ozawa – BARTÓK: *Concerto for orchestra.***(*)

Concerto for orchestra; Funeral music for string orchestra (dedicated to the memory of Béla Bartók); Jeux venitiens (Venetian games) for orchestra.
(M) **(*) Ph. Seq. 412 377-1/*4*. Warsaw Nat. PO, Rowicki.

The Lutoslawski *Concerto* is (or ought to be) to the mid-1950s what Bartók's *Concerto* is for the mid-1940s. It is a brilliant, highly attractive and inventively scored work with great potential appeal. Its idiom is accessible and the ideas have character. It plumbs no great depths, it is true, but then nor do Lutoslawski's later and less accessible works. Rowicki gives a thoroughly idiomatic performance and secures playing of real brilliance from his fine orchestra. The recording is good, though not as vivid as that provided by HMV for Ozawa. It comes from 1965 and has been brightened for this reissue; this tends to date the sound in the lack of body of the string timbre. There is an excellent, lively tape. The Rowicki account is coupled with two other Lutoslawski works. The *Funeral music* is an angular and rather empty piece whose feelings seem to reside very much on the surface. *Jeux venitiens*, a work that contains aleatoric interpolations, is quite an attractive piece.

Ozawa's coupling is particularly generous and he offers music of wider appeal. The performance by the Chicago orchestra is absolutely dazzling, with its conductor seeming totally at home in the music's shallows. The recording is bright but well balanced. By the side of Rowicki's earlier version it sounds a bit flashy but thoroughly recommendable all the same. There is a first-class cassette, with excellent detail, body and range, in some ways preferable in balance to the LP. On some copies the two sides are mis-labelled: the Bartók *Concerto* is on the A side.

Variations on a theme of Paganini.
*** Ph. Dig. **411 034-2**; 6514/*7337* 369 [id.]. Argerich, Freire – RACHMANINOV: *Suite No. 2;* RAVEL: *La valse.****

Lutoslawski's *Variations* for piano duo date from 1941; they are exhilarating and played with great virtuosity by Martha Argerich and Nelson Freire. The recording is very realistic and natural on disc and tape alike. The compact disc makes more obvious the rather reverberant acoustic of the recording location.

Magnard, Albéric (1865–1914)

Symphony No. 3 in B flat min., Op. 11.
(*) French Decca 1592 167. SRO, Ansermet – LALO: *Scherzo.*(*)

It is indeed good news that moves are afoot to record all the Magnard symphonies in France, and that the revival of this composer's fortunes is at last gathering pace. The present recording dates from 1968 – though it still sounds altogether excellent in this immaculate new transfer. It has an inspired opening: there is a certain austerity about the wind writing that is quite original and an eloquence that makes his long neglect puzzling. The scherzo is inventive, and the third movement, *Pastoral*, is marvellously sustained. Let us hope that the coming year brings us this work in an up-to-date version on compact disc; but this is sufficiently well played and recorded to be far more than just a stop-gap. A fairly strong recommendation.

Symphony No. 4 in C sharp min., Op. 21; Chant funèbre, Op. 9.
(M) *** HMV EG 270150-1/*4* [Ang. Sera. *4XG 60421*]. Toulouse Capitole O, Plasson.

The *Fourth Symphony* dates from 1913, the year before the composer's death, and is a welcome addition to the catalogue. It has an impressive intellectual power. Like his countryman Guy-Ropartz, with whom he is often paired, Magnard is grievously neglected even in his home country; as is the case with the *Third Symphony*, his music is well crafted and there is no shortage of ideas. For all the appearance of academicism there is a quiet and distinctive personality here, and dignity too. The fill-up, the *Chant funèbre*, is an earlier work that has a vein of genuine eloquence. The Toulouse Capitole Orchestra under Michel Plasson play this music as if they believe in every note, as indeed they should, and the recording is sonorous and well defined. This is the first of his works to appear on cassette, and it is a very good one. Only the tape is available in the USA. In the UK, the success of both cassette and LP on an import label has prompted EMI to issue the recording at mid-price on the Greensleeve logo.

Mahler, Gustav (1860–1911)

Symphonies Nos 1–2 (Resurrection).
*** CBS M3P/*3PT* 39635 (3). Cundari, Forrester, Westminster Ch., Columbia SO or NYPO, Walter.

A welcome coupling of two of Bruno Walter's last Mahler recordings from the early 1960s. The remastered sound is impressive, and both are now available on compact disc (see below). The 1961 version of the *Resurrection symphony* is a classic of the gramophone. If anything, the excellent chrome cassettes are more impressive than the LPs, notably in the reproduction of the chorus.

Symphonies Nos 1; (i) *4 in G.*
**(*) DG 415 012-1/*4* (2) [id.]. (i) Elsie Morison; Bav. RSO, Kubelik.

This coupling of the two finest performances from Kubelik's late-1960s Mahler cycle with the Bavarian Symphony Orchestra is apt, for the lightness of his touch is appropriate in both symphonies. He gives an intensely poetic reading of No. 1, and the result could hardly be more glowing. The rubato in the funeral march is most subtly handled. In the *G major Symphony* the Bavarian orchestra phrase beautifully and their playing has great vitality. With generally faster tempi than is common, the effect is luminous, with a charming, boyish account of the final song from Elsie Morison. Other conductors favouring brisk pacing (Reiner, for instance) can be even more illuminating, and the slow-movement climax is without any sense of cataclysm; but with cleanly remastered sound which is virtually identical on the LPs and the tapes (which come in one of DG's cardboard flap-packs), this is certainly refreshing.

Symphony No. 1 in D (*Titan*).
*** Decca Dig. **411 731-2**; 411 731-1/*4* [id.]. Chicago SO, Solti.
(*) HMV Dig. **CDC 747032-2 [id.]; EL 270007-1/*4* [Ang. DS/*4DS* 38078]. Phd. O, Muti.
(*) CBS **MK 42031 [id.]. Columbia SO, Walter.
(*) Lodia **LO-CD 776; LOD/*LOC* 776 [id.]. RPO, Païta.
(*) Denon Dig. **C37 7537 [id.]. Frankfurt RSO, Inbal.
** DG Dig. **400 033-2**; 2532/*3302* 020 [id.]. Chicago SO, Abbado.
** CBS **CD 37373** [id.]. NYPO, Mehta.
(M) ** HMV EG 290496-1/*4* [Ang. S/*4XS* 37508]. LPO, Tennstedt.

Symphony No. 1 in D (original 5-movement version with *Blumine*).
(M) **(*) DG Sig. 410 845-1/*4*. Boston SO, Ozawa.

Solti's recording of 1969 with the LSO has rightly been a prime choice for many years; this has made it hard for him to match his earlier achievement, even with exceptionally high-powered playing from the Chicago orchestra and brilliant, crystal-clear digital recording. Particularly on CD, that very clarity takes away some of the atmospheric magic – the feelings of mists dispersing in the slow introduction, for example – but charm and playfulness in this *Wunderhorn* work emerge delightfully; one of the happiest of Solti's records, tinglingly fresh, with perfectly chosen speeds. The high-level chrome cassette is disappointing: the sound is very clear but the upper range is shrill.

Muti's version was the first recording made by the Philadelphia Orchestra in a new venue; though the sound does not have the sharpness of definition of Solti's Decca CD, this gives an excellent idea of the richness of timbre typical of this orchestra. Muti, like other conductors prone to fierceness, manages to relax most persuasively for the gentler *Wunderhorn* inventions, contrasted sharply against extrovert outbursts, with rhythms crisply pointed and solo playing exceptionally fine. Although the CD is obviously superior, the XDR cassette is certainly successful, weighty in the bass but with a bright upper range and with the resonance offering no problems.

Bruno Walter's 1961 record sounds splendid in its CD format. The compellingly atmospheric opening is magnetic, heard against the almost silent background, and Walter is at his most charismatic here. While the recording's range is obviously more limited than more recent versions, the balance and ambient warmth are entirely satisfying, emphasizing the Viennese character of the reading, with the final apotheosis drawn out spaciously and given added breadth and impact. The orchestral playing throughout is first class; other conductors have whipped up more animal excitement in the finale, but that is not Walter's way.

Carlos Païta's Latin view of Mahler is striking for its spontaneous qualities. This is a most enjoyable performance in spite of its extremes of tempo (particularly in the first movement, where there are some expressive lunges, whether in sudden rubatos or tenutos). The coda produces some scrambled ensemble, but otherwise the playing of the RPO is very good indeed, notably so in a beautiful account of the long-drawn melody in the finale. The recording is full and immediate and the transfer to CD highly successful in retaining the atmosphere and bloom of the first-class 1977 analogue recording (originally available on the Decca label).

Edited together from a couple of live performances, Inbal's Frankfurt version may not be as polished or high-powered as the finest from top international orchestras, but it has an easy-going charm which, coupled to recording that puts fine bloom on the sound, will please many. The happy expansiveness and gentle manners of the first three movements then lead to a powerful and urgent reading of the finale which is more tautly held together than usual. One point of detail: the CD has no fewer than 22 bands for the four movements, making it particularly easy to find any passage.

Abbado directs a pure and superbly refined reading, consistently well paced and recorded in excellent digital sound. By rights it should be an easy first choice – yet he misses some of the natural tension of a performance that communicates as in a live concert. In the *Wunderhorn* inspirations of the first two movements the music too rarely smiles. The funeral march of the slow movement is wonderfully hushed, more spontaneous-sounding than the rest. The chrome tape accommodates the wide dynamic range impressively, but the opening *pianissimo* is heard to finest effect on the excellent compact disc. The absolute silence does serve, however, to emphasize the lack of electricity during this sequence.

Mehta's is a dramatic reading, though the failure of the strings to play at a genuine *pianissimo* in the slow introduction points to a lack of finesse that prevents it from being a top competitor. Mehta's Viennese training comes out in the lilt of the Laendler second movement, and there is no lack of power. One of CBS's better New York recordings.

Tennstedt's manner in Mahler is somewhat severe, with textures fresh and neat and the style of phrasing generally less moulded than we have come to expect. This concentration on precision and directness means that when the conductor does indulge in rubato or speed changes it does not sound quite consistent and comes as a surprise, as in the big string melody of the finale. Most Mahlerians will prefer a more felt performance than this. The full, clear recording is first class and has transferred well to cassette.

The mid-price reissue of Ozawa's Boston version, a fresh, youthful account of the work, beautifully played, brings the bonus of having the simple, unpretentious movement, *Blumine*, included, which Mahler came to discard. The five-movement balance is questionable, but anyone attracted by its curiosity value can safely rely on the finely textured sensitivity of the performance as a whole, well recorded, though with Boston reverberation not always helpful. The cassette transfer is vivid and generally satisfactory, although the Boston resonance brings a degree of clouding, notably in the final peroration.

Symphony No. 2 in C min. (*Resurrection*).

*** DG 2707 094/*3370 015* (2) [id.]. Neblett, Horne, Chicago SO Ch. and O, Abbado.

(M) *** HMV SLS 802/*TCC2-POR 54293*. Schwarzkopf, Rössl-Majdan, Philh. Ch. and O, Klemperer.

*** Decca Dig. **410 202-2** [id.]; D 229 D 2/*K 229 K 22* [Lon. LDR/*5*- 72006]. Buchanan, Zakai, Chicago SO Ch. and O, Solti.

*** CBS **M2K 42032** (2) [id.]. Cundari, Forrester, Westminster Ch., NYPO, Bruno Walter.

(*) HMV Dig. **CDS 747041-8 [id.]; SLS/*TCC-SLS* 5243 (2/*1*) [Ang. DS/*4X2S* 3916]. Mathis, Soffel, LPO Ch., LPO, Tennstedt.

** CBS Dig. **M2K 38667**; 12M/*12T* 38667 (2) [id.]. Marton, Norman, VPO, Maazel.

** Telarc Dig. **CD 80081/2** [id.]. Battle, Forrester, St Louis Ch. and SO, Slatkin.

(M) *(*) DG 413 524-1/*4* (2). Mathis, Procter, Bav. R. Ch. and SO, Kubelik.

(B) *(*) DG Walkman *413 149-4* [id.] (from above recording, cond. Kubelik).

*(*) Denon Dig. **C37 7603/4**. Donath, Soffel, Frankfurt R. Ch. and SO, Inbal.

If on occasion Abbado has seemed to be a little too controlled on record, his collaboration with the Chicago orchestra in this, his first recording of a Mahler symphony, combines almost miraculous precision with electrifying urgency. The total conviction of the performance establishes itself in the very first bars, weighty yet marvellously precise on detail, with dotted rhythms sharply brought out. It proves a performance of extremes, with variations of tempo more confidently marked than is common but with concentration so intense there is no hint of self-indulgence. The delicacy of the Chicago orchestra in the second and third movements is as remarkable as its precision – the second movement is relatively fast, like an elegant minuet – while the great contrasts of the later movements prove a challenge not only to the performers but to the DG engineers, who produce sound of superlative quality – even if the actual range of dynamic may prove a problem to those anxious not to annoy the neighbours. Generally the singing is as splendid as the playing, but if there is even a minor disappointment it lies in the closing pages. There, other versions – such as Klemperer's or Solti's

– convey a more overwhelming emotional involvement, the triumph of Judgement Day itself, whereas Abbado keeps his sharpness of focus to the very end. This version is not yet available on compact disc, but it surely will be during the lifetime of this book. The chrome tapes encompass the wide dynamic range of the recording very successfully, but there is a degree of hiss apparent in the pianissimo passages.

Klemperer on HMV gives one of his most compelling performances on record, bringing out the music's ruggedness. The first movement, taken at a fairly fast tempo, is intense and earth-shaking, and that is surely as it should be in a work which culminates in a representation of Judgement Day itself. Though in the last movement some of Klemperer's speeds are designedly slow, he conveys supremely well the mood of transcendent heavenly happiness in the culminating passage, with chorus and soloists themselves singing like angels. The Last Trump brings a shudder of excitement to make one forget any prejudice against such literal representation. The less grand middle movements too have their simple charm under Klemperer, and the recording is among EMI's best. The cassette, issued quite separately in EMI's 'Portrait of the Artist' series, puts the symphony on one double-length tape. This cannot be recommended. In spite of quite a high transfer level, the orchestral recording is not well focused, with over-resonant, woolly bass, while the choral sound in the finale lacks bite. The discs have been impressively remastered and on LP the recording can still hold its own against most competition.

In digital sound of extraordinary power Solti has re-recorded with the Chicago orchestra this symphony which with the LSO was one of the finest achievements of his earlier Mahler series. Differences of interpretation are on points of detail merely, with a lighter, more elegant rendering of the minuet-rhythms of the second movement. Though the digital recording is not always so well balanced as the earlier analogue (Isobel Buchanan and Mira Zakai are too close, for example), the weight of fortissimo in the final hymn, not to mention the Judgement Day brass, is breathtaking. Interpretatively too, the outer movements are as fiercely intense as before, but it is only in the concluding passage of the last movement that Solti really outshines the DG performance of Abbado with the same orchestra, a reading that is more affectionate in all five movements without ever sounding mannered and featuring playing just as brilliant. The Decca cassettes are first class, sparklingly clear, full and wide-ranging. The compact discs with their extra precision make the brilliant sound of the Chicago orchestra even more immediate. In the last movement, the first cellist's groan before his solo – made more evident on CD – may worry some listeners.

Like Walter's other Mahler recordings, the 1958 CBS set of the *Resurrection symphony* is among the gramophone's indispensable classics. In the first movement there is a restraint and in the second a gracefulness which provides a strong contrast with a conductor like Klemperer. The recording, one of the last Walter made in New York before his series with the Columbia Symphony Orchestra, was remarkably good for its period and the dynamic range is surprisingly wide. In remastering for CD, the CBS engineers have sought to remove as much as possible of the pre-Dolby background noise, and the treble response is noticeably limited, with the attractively warm ambience tending to smooth internal definition. But the glowing resonance of the sound brings an evocative haze to the score's more atmospheric moments, and in the finale the balance with the voices gives the music making an ethereal resonance. If the choral focus is less than ideally sharp, the performance makes a profound impression, with the closing section thrillingly expansive.

Tennstedt's is a dedicated performance, not quite as well played as the finest, conveying Mahlerian certainties in the light of day and underplaying neurotic tensions. The recording on CD is impressively full and clear, though naturally balanced, and the work is also conveniently fitted on a single chrome tape of EMI's highest quality.

With full recording, clear and atmospheric, and no lack of presence, Maazel's Vienna version brings impressively weighty accounts of the vocal passages in the last part of the symphony, the vision of Judgement Day. But even there, Maazel's preference for a very steady pulse, varied hardly at all by rubato and tenuto, married to exceptionally slow speeds, undermines the keen intensity of the performance. Rhythmically the first movement becomes leaden and, paradoxically with the orchestra, the Viennese element in Mahler is minimized.

Superbly recorded, with even the weightiest and most complex textures, at once well detailed and well co-ordinated, and with fine, polished playing from the St Louis Orchestra, Slatkin's Telarc set yet lacks the sense of occasion essential in this work. The tension and weight needed in the first movement, for example, are not fully conveyed, and though the easy manners are attractive in their relative plainness, one really needs higher voltage. That higher voltage immediately makes itself felt when Maureen Forrester – a mezzo often chosen by Bruno Walter and a great stylist in Mahler – enters in the hushed opening of the fourth movement, *Urlicht*. In an instant, one can appreciate what has been missing; Kathleen Battle's contributions as the soprano soloist similarly bring an extra concentration. The engineers excel themselves in the great Judgement Day finale with even the organ textures clear, but the chorus's *pianissimo* entry is recorded so low that it is barely audible.

Kubelik's comparatively refined approach is enjoyable enough and he is certainly well recorded. But there is not enough thrust, and the performance fails to give any kind of monumental impression. The cassette transfer is one of DG's best, clear and vivid with an excellent choral focus. Kubelik's recording has additionally been issued at bargain price on a Walkman cassette, with the recording sounding strikingly vivid on chrome tape.

Inbal is a stylish and sympathetic Mahlerian, but the digital recording exposes both the limitations of the Frankfurt orchestra and detailed imprecisions of ensemble. The first movement lacks weight, and the rising violin theme of the second subject sounds thin, not sweet; while the second movement, taken at a very slow speed, brings a painstaking manner which undermines the scherzando quality. Doris Soffël, the same mezzo soloist as on Tennstedt's EMI recording, again sings characterfully in *Urlicht*; distractingly, in the finale the two soloists are placed far closer than the chorus and orchestra. That brings out all the more the sense of a less-than-monumental occasion, not helped by imperfect ensemble. Recording good, but not as clear as in the best rival versions.

Symphony No. 3 in D min.

*** DG Dig. **410 715-2**; 2741/*3382* 010 (2) [id.]. Norman, V. State Op. Ch., V. Boys' Ch., VPO, Abbado.

*** RCA **RD 81757**; RL/*RK* 81757 (2) [**RCD2 1757**; ARL2/*CRK2* 1757]. Horne, Ellyn Children's Ch., Chicago SO Ch. and O, Levine.

*** HMV Dig. **CDS 747405-8** (2); SLS/*TC-SLS* 5195 [Ang. DSB/*4D2S* 3902]. Wenkel, Southend Boys' Ch., LPO Ch. (Ladies), LPO, Tennstedt.

(*) Decca Dig. **414 268-2 [id.]; D281 D2/*K281* K22 (2) [Lon. LDR/*5*- 72014]. Dernesch, Glen Ellyn Children's Ch., Chicago SO Ch. and O, Solti.

(M) ** DG 413 525-1/*4*. Marjorie Thomas, Bav. R. Women's Ch., Tölz Ch., Bav. RSO, Kubelik.

* Sup. Dig. **C37 7288/9** [id.]. Ludwig, Prague Philharmonic Ch., Kühn Children's Ch., Czech PO, Neumann.

With sound of spectacular range, Abbado's performance is sharply defined and deeply dedicated. The range of expression, the often wild mixture of elements in this work, is conveyed with extraordinary intensity, not least in the fine contributions of Jessye Norman and the two choirs. The recording has even greater presence and detail on CD; the cassette transfer is not made at the highest level, however, and while the sound is generally very good, the *pianissimos* (the famous posthorn solos, for instance) lose a degree of projection and the background noise becomes apparent.

James Levine directs a superbly rhythmic account of the *Third Symphony*, with splendidly judged tempi which allow extra swagger (most important in the first movement), more lilt and a fine sense of atmosphere. The choral contributions, too, are outstanding. In the radiant finale Levine's tempo is daringly slow, but he sustains it superbly, though in that movement the recording has some congestion at climaxes; otherwise, the 1977 sound is nicely rounded, with the posthorn beautifully balanced in the third movement. On CD, refinement is enhanced by the virtually silent background: this is plainly not a digital recording, but it represents the highest analogue standards. The cassettes are splendid, too; like the LPs, though, they break the first movement for a turnover, which the CDs avoid by a slightly different layout.

Tennstedt too gives an eloquent reading, spaciousness underlined with measured tempi. With Ortrun Wenkel a fine soloist and the Southend boys adding lusty freshness to the bell music in the fifth movement, the HMV performance with its noble finale is very impressive, and it is splendidly recorded on both disc and cassette. The CDs are announced just as we go to press.

In Solti's earlier series of Mahler recordings for Decca with the LSO the *Third Symphony* brought disappointment, notably in the brassy and extrovert account of the last movement. In his Chicago version that movement is transformed, hushed and intense, deeply concentrated, building up superbly even though the hastening is a shade excessive towards the end. The other movements have brilliance, freshness and clarity, with Helga Dernesch a fine if rather detached soloist. Solti remains a bold Mahler interpreter, missing some of the *Wunderhorn* fun. The virtuoso playing of the Chicago orchestra is brilliantly caught by the wide-ranging recording, though the posthorn of the third movement is placed unatmospherically close; such a fault of balance is all the more striking on the otherwise very impressive CDs. The cassettes offer beautiful sound, refined, rich and clear. The focus is perhaps marginally less sharp than on the LPs, but there is little in it. The transfer level is not quite as high as usual from Decca.

There is a practical advantage to Kubelik's mid-priced version: the first movement is squeezed without a break on to the first side – but this is bought at the expense of tempo. As in the later Mahler symphonies, Kubelik is tempted to lighten the music with fast speeds, which certainly gives a mercurial element to the reading. With freshly vivid sound (on both disc and tape) the central movements are the most attractive, with fine contributions from Marjorie Thomas and the Tölz Boys' Choir. The recording is well balanced and sounds equally well on LP or the virtually identical chrome cassettes.

The rhythmic stodginess of Neumann's reading cancels out the many good qualities of a version from one of the great orchestras of Europe. Arguably, a plainer approach to Mahler than is common may be needed – but this example is far from persuasive, with necessary lightness missing even from the second-movement Minuet and the fifth-movement Bell Song, taken at a sluggish speed. The natural gravity of Christa Ludwig in *O Mensch*, the fourth movement, is negated by Neumann's squareness, not to mention wobbly horns. Fair recording.

Symphony No. 4 in G.

*** CBS Dig. **MK 39072**; IM/*IMT* 39072 [id.]. Kathleen Battle, VPO, Maazel.
*** DG **415 323-2**; 2531/*3301* 205 [id.]. Edith Mathis, BPO, Karajan.
*** Decca Dig. **410 188-2**; 410 188-1/*4* [id.]. Kiri Te Kanawa, Chicago SO, Solti.
*** Ph. Dig. **412 119-2**; 412 119-1/*4* [id.]. Roberta Alexander, Concg. O, Haitink.
*** HMV Dig. **CDC 747024-2** [id.]; ASD/*TCC-ASD* 4344 [Ang. DS/*4DS* 37954]. Lucia Popp, LPO, Tennstedt.
*** RCA **RD 80895 [RCD1 0895]**. Judith Blegen, Chicago SO, Levine.
(M) **(*) RCA Gold GL/*GK* 85256 [AGL1/*AGK1* 5256]. Della Casa, Chicago SO, Reiner.
** DG **413 454-2**; 2530/*3300* 966 [id.]. Frederica von Stade, VPO, Abbado.

As on LP, in the days of analogue stereo, Mahler's engagingly relaxed *Fourth Symphony* is well served on compact disc by a number of outstanding versions. Leading them is Maazel's VPO recording, unexpectedly the most completely successful issue so far in his developing cycle. The superbly refined and atmospheric recording enhances a performance that – unlike other Mahler from this conductor – reflects the Viennese qualities of the work while still conveying structural strength, above all in the beautiful, wide-ranging slow movement played with great inner intensity. Kathleen Battle with her radiant soprano brings aptly child-like overtones to the *Wunderhorn* solo in the finale, until the final stanza is given with rapt intimacy to match Maazel's whole reading. The chrome cassette offers pleasing sound but has not the range of the CD and LP.

With playing of incomparable refinement – no feeling of rusticity here – Karajan directs a performance of compelling poise and purity, not least in the slow movement, with its pulse very steady indeed, most remarkably at the very end. Karajan's view of the finale is gentle, wistful, almost ruminative, with the final stanzas very slow and legato, beautifully so when Edith Mathis's poised singing of the solo is finely matched. Not that this quest for refinement means that joy has in any way been lost in the performance; with glowing sound, it is a worthy companion to Karajan's other Mahler recordings, effectively transferred to CD, and also with an outstanding cassette.

Solti's version gives the lie to the idea of his always being fierce and unrelaxed. This sunniest of the Mahler symphonies receives a delightfully fresh and bright reading, beautifully paced and superbly played. The recording is bright, full and immediate in the Decca Chicago manner, without inflating the interpretation. Dame Kiri Te Kanawa sings beautifully in the child-heaven finale.

With outstandingly refined playing from the Concertgebouw superlatively recorded, Haitink's reading has a fresh innocence that is most winning. Thus the lovely *Adagio*, rather than conveying the deepest meditation, presents an ecstatic, songful musing in the long paragraphs of the main theme, and Roberta Alexander makes a perceptive choice of soloist for such a reading, both fresh and creamy of tone.

Tennstedt conducts a strong, spacious reading which yet conveys an innocence entirely in keeping with this most endearing of the Mahler symphonies. He makes the argument seamless in his easy transitions of speed, yet never deliberately adopts a coaxing, charming manner; in that, he is followed most beautifully by Lucia Popp, the pure-toned soloist in the finale. The peak of the work, as Tennstedt presents it, lies in the long slow movement, here taken very slowly and intensely. The recording is among EMI's finest, full and well balanced, and sounding splendid in its CD format. There is a good, though not outstanding, cassette.

James Levine, a thoughtful yet warmly committed Mahlerian, mature beyond his years, draws a superlative performance from the Chicago orchestra, one which bears comparison with the finest versions, bringing out not merely the charm but the deeper emotions too. The subtlety of his control of tempo, so vital in Mahler, is superbly demonstrated and, though he may not quite match the nobility of Szell's famous analogue CBS version in the great slow movement, he has the advantage of more modern (1975) recording. Blegen makes a fresh, attractive soloist. Szell's famous Cleveland version is available in the US on CD as a CBS/Sony Japanese import (**32CD 217**).

Reiner's version was made – like many of his famous recordings – in Orchestra Hall, Chicago, in December 1958. When it was first issued in stereo at the beginning of the 1960s, we were dismissive (in an early edition of the *Stereo*

Record Guide), partly on account of the recording balance and partly because of the idiosyncratic nature of the performance. The recording has been digitally remastered, with great improvement in the sound which remains brightly lit but has attractively vivid detail, naturally glowing within the acoustic bloom of the hall. The performance is certainly wayward, but lovingly so; and everything Reiner does sounds spontaneous. There is a mercurial quality in the first movement and plenty of drama, too; the second is engagingly pointed but with a balancing warmth, the Viennese influence strong. The slow movement has striking intensity, with its rapt closing pages leading on gently to the finale in which Lisa Della Casa, in ravishing voice, matches Reiner's mood. A highly individual reading. LP and tape are very closely matched, except that the slow-movement climax proves rather explosive on the chrome cassette.

After his superb performance of the Mahler *Second* with the Chicago orchestra, Abbado's recording of the *Fourth* is disappointing, above all in the self-consciously expressive reading of the slow movement. There is much beauty of detail, but the Vienna Philharmonic has played and been recorded better than this, even though the CD offers a more impressive sound than the LP.

Symphony No. 5 in C sharp min.

*** DG **415 096-2**; 2707 081/*3370 006* (2) [id.]. BPO, Karajan – *Kindertotenlieder.****

*** DG Dig. **415 476-2**; 415 476-1 (2)/*415 476-4* [id.]. Philh. O, Sinopoli – (on LPs only) *Jugendzeit Lieder*.

(*) Decca **413 321-2; 413 321-1/*4* [id.]. Chicago SO, Solti.

(B) ** DG Walkman *415 335-4* [id.]. Bav. RSO, Kubelik.

Symphony No. 5; Symphony No. 10 in F sharp: Adagio.

*** HMV **CDS 747104-8** [id.]; SLS/*TC-SLS* 5169 (2) [Ang. SZB/*4Z2S* 3883]. LPO, Tennstedt.

(*) RCA **RD 89205; RL/*RK* 82905 [ARL 2/*ARK 2* 2905]. Phd. O, Levine.

Karajan's characteristic emphasis on polish and refinement goes with sharpness of focus. His is at once the most beautiful and the most intense version available, starting with an account of the first movement which brings more biting funeral-march rhythms than any rival. Resplendent recording, rich and refined, admirably remastered on to CD to match the radiant playing of the Berlin Philharmonic. Christa Ludwig's warm singing in *Kindertotenlieder* makes a valuable fill-up. The cassette version, too, is of excellent quality.

Sinopoli's version, the first of his Mahler series with the Philharmonia Orchestra, draws the sharpest distinction between the dark tragedy of the first two movements and the relaxed *Wunderhorn* feeling of the rest. Thus, the opening *Funeral march* is tough and biting, expressive but moulded less than one associates with this conductor; here, as later, Sinopoli seems intent on not overloading the big melodies with excessive emotion. This comes out the more clearly in the central movements, where relaxation is the keynote, often with a pastoral atmosphere. The third-movement Ländler has the happiest of lilts, but leads finally to a frenetic coda, before the celebrated *Adagietto* brings a tenderly wistful reading, songful and basically happy, not tragic. If that seems understated and gentle compared to forcefully high-powered readings, it fits the more clearly with a *Wunderhorn* mood which returns in full joy in the finale, starting with a magical evocation of the Austrian countryside. Warmly atmospheric recording, not lacking brilliance, but – even on CD – not always ideally clear on detail. Both CD and tape share the advantage of being complete on two sides. The cassette, which is of a high technical standard, divides up the work conveniently so that the *Adagietto* opens side two. The LPs are less economical but have the advantage of a unique fill-up.

Tennstedt takes a ripe and measured view of this symphony; though his account of the lovely *Adagietto* lacks the fullest tenderness (starting with an intrusive balance for the harp), this is an outstanding performance, thoughtful on the one hand, warm and expressive on the other. The first movement of the *Tenth Symphony* makes an acceptable fill-up; the recording, not quite as detailed as in this conductor's later digital Mahler recordings with the LPO, is warm and full to match the performance. The sound is enhanced on CD. The cassettes, however, are rather patchy, not as cleanly focused as the best EMI transfers.

Solti's recording has been digitally remastered on to a single CD, LP and cassette; the 1971 analogue sound now has sharper detail without losing too much body – although the cassette is less successful than the other media, with the focus slipping a little in fortissimos and with a tendency for the strings to sound too brightly lit. The opening *Funeral march* sets the tone of Solti's reading. At a tempo faster than usual, it is wistful rather than deeply tragic, even though the dynamic contrasts are superbly pointed and the string tone could hardly be more resonant. In the pivotal *Adagietto*, Solti secures intensely beautiful playing, but the result lacks the 'inner' quality one finds so abundantly in Barbirolli's interpretation.

Apart from a self-consciously slow account of the celebrated *Adagietto*, Levine directs a deeply perceptive and compelling performance, one that brings out the glories of the Philadelphia Orchestra. The other movements are beautifully paced, and the fourth side offers a wonderfully luminous account of the first movement of the *Tenth Symphony*.

Kubelik in the opening *Funeral march* is gentle rather than tragic, and his relative lightness of manner, coupled with refined textures, misses the epic quality of the work. Nor does he succeed in disguising the patchwork structure of the last movement. As we go to press, this recording is available in three different formats: the bargain-priced Walkman issue as listed, a Signature LP and cassette (2543/*3343* 535) and in a three-sided version, coupled with Fischer-Dieskau's *Lieder eines fahrenden Gesellen* (415 015-1/*4*). In all cases the sound is excellent, with discs and tapes closely matched.

Still recommended: Barbirolli's recording of Mahler's *Fifth* is unique, one of the greatest and most warmly affecting performances ever committed to record; it brings on the fourth side a performance of the *Five Rückert Lieder* by Dame Janet Baker that achieves a degree of poetic intensity rarely heard on disc. When that set arrives on CD, it may supplant present recommendations (HMV SLS/*TC-SLS* 785).

Symphony No. 6 in A min.

*** DG **415 099-2**; 2707 106/*3370 026* (2). BPO, Karajan – *Rückert Lieder.***(*)

*** HMV Dig. **CDC 747050-8** [id.]; SLS/*TC-SLS* 143574-3/*5* [Ang. DSB/*4X2S* 3945]. LPO, Tennstedt.

*** Decca **414 674-2** [id.]; SET 469/70 [Lon. CSA 2227]. Chicago SO, Solti – *Lieder eines fahrenden Gesellen.****

(M) **(*) DG 413 528-1/*4* [id.]. Bav. RSO, Kubelik – *4 Rückert Lieder.****

(M) ** Ph. Seq. 412 034-1/*4* (2/*1*). Concg. O, Haitink.

With superlative playing from the Berlin Philharmonic, Karajan's reading of the *Sixth* is a revelation, above all in the slow movement which here becomes far more than a lyrical interlude. With this *Andante moderato* made to flower in poignant melancholy, and with a simpler lyrical style than Karajan usually adopts, it emerges as one of the greatest of Mahler's slow movements and the whole balance of the symphony is altered. Though the outer movements firmly stamp this as the darkest of the Mahler symphonies, in Karajan's reading their sharp focus – with contrasts of light and shade heightened – makes them both compelling and refreshing. Significantly, in his care for tonal colouring Karajan brings out a number of overtones related to Wagner's *Ring*. The superb DG recording, with its wide dynamics, adds enormously to the impact. It is further enhanced in the remastering for compact disc; Christa Ludwig's set of the *Five Rückert Songs* has been added as a bonus. These are not included with the LPs and cassettes, which are closely matched in sound, though the bass response is a little dry on tape.

Tennstedt's reading is characteristically strong, finding more warmth than usual even in this dark symphony. Thus, the third-movement *Andante* is open and songlike, almost Schubertian in its sweetness, though there is never any question of Tennstedt taking a sentimental view of Mahler. His expressiveness tends towards conveying joy rather than Mahlerian neurosis and, for some, that may make it too comfortable a reading. Karajan has more power and bite; his scale is bigger and bolder, the Berlin playing more brilliant. Naturally, in his digital recording Tennstedt gains from extra range in the recording of the famous hammer-blows of fate in the finale. The sound is full and the acoustic warm; the CD has added greater refinement of detail.

Solti draws stunning playing from the Chicago orchestra. This was his first recording with them after he took up his post as principal conductor, and, as he himself said, it represented a love-affair at first sight. The electric excitement of the playing confirms this; with brilliant, immediate but atmospheric recording, Solti's rather extrovert approach to Mahler is here at its most impressive. His fast tempi may mean that he misses some of the deeper emotions but – with an outstandingly successful performance of the *Wayfaring Lad* cycle on the fourth side (Yvonne Minton a splendid soloist) – this is a very convincing and attractive set. On CD the immediacy of the sound is the more striking, although the ambient effect tempers the brightness.

Kubelik, in one of his most successful Mahler recordings, directs a performance both refined and searching. Without ever coarsening the result, he allows himself generous ritardandi between sections, though ultimately the fineness of control gives a hint of reserve. The 1969 sound is fresh and clear, if a little light at the bass end; the coupling – from five years earlier – restores to the catalogue a valuable Fischer-Dieskau performance, four of the five *Rückert Lieder*. There is little to choose in quality between discs and tapes; if anything, the sound is marginally fuller on cassette.

Haitink takes a fast tempo for the first movement, but the reading is marked by refinement rather than fire. The whole performance reflects Haitink's thoughtful, unsensational approach to the composer. The 1970 recording has been remastered and brightened, not entirely to advantage, as the upper range is thinner; on the tape (a single extended-length cassette), it tends to shrillness.

Symphony No. 7 in E min.

*** DG Dig. **413 773-2**; 413 773-1/*4* (2) [id.]. Chicago SO, Abbado.

*** Decca **414 675-2** [id.]; SET 518/9 [Lon. CSA 2231]. Chicago SO, Solti – (CD only) *Des Knaben Wunderhorn* excerpts.***

(*) Ph. Dig. **410 398-2; 410 398-1/*4* [id.]. Concg. O, Haitink.

(*) RCA **RD 84581 [RCD2 4581; ARC2/*ARK2* 4581]. Chicago SO, Levine.

(M) ** DG 415 631-1/*4* (2). Bav. RSO, Kubelik – *Kindertotenlieder*.***

(B) *(*) CfP CFPD 41 4442-3/*5* (2) New Philh. O, Klemperer.

Abbado's command of Mahlerian characterization has never been more tellingly displayed than in this most problematic of the symphonies; even in the loosely bound finale, which might unkindly be described as ramshackle in structure, Abbado unerringly draws the threads together, while contrasting each section with the next in clear distinction. The contrasts in the earlier movements, too, are superbly brought out, with the central interludes made ideally atmospheric, as in the eeriness of the scherzo and the haunting tenderness of the second *Nachtmusik*. The precision and polish of the Chicago orchestra go with total commitment, and the recording is one of the finest DG has made with this orchestra. The CD version, besides having a degree more tangibility and presence, is generously banded within movements. There is an excellent chrome tape equivalent.

The sound of Solti's Decca issue is glorious, even riper and more brilliant than that of his two earlier Chicago recordings of Mahler and on CD much clearer. In interpretation, this is as successful as his fine account of the *Sixth Symphony*, extrovert in display but full of dark implications. The tempi tend to be challengingly fast – at the very opening, for example, and in the scherzo (where Solti is mercurial), and in the finale (where his energy carries shock-waves in its trail). The second *Nachtmusik* is enchantingly seductive, and throughout the orchestra plays superlatively well. On balance this is even finer than the Haitink version. For the CD issue, Yvonne Minton's fine performance of four Lieder from *Des Knaben Wunderhorn* has been added. (They were originally coupled with the *Fifth Symphony*, now reissued on a single disc.)

Beauty is the keynote of Haitink's newer, digitally recorded version of Mahler's *Seventh*. The superb playing of the Concertgebouw Orchestra is richly and spaciously caught; however, with spacious speeds to match, tensions have tended to ease since Haitink's earlier account; the vision of darkness is softened a degree. On CD, the wide dynamic range is very telling, with detail clarified. The chrome cassettes are refined and clear but transferred at a relatively modest level.

With a broad, warmly expressive account of the first movement and a riotously extrovert one of the finale, Levine's reading has many of the fine qualities of his other Mahler recordings but, with recording balances at times odd and some rhythmic self-indulgence, it cannot match the finest. At present this set is only available in the UK on compact disc.

Now coupled with Fischer-Dieskau's *Kindertotenlieder*, Kubelik's *Seventh* is attractively reintroduced to the medium-priced range. Kubelik is at his most impressive in what can be described as Mahler's *Knaben Wunderhorn* manner. The start of the second movement has an open-air innocence; conversely, however, Kubelik produces no sense of nocturnal mystery in the second *Nachtmusik*. The outer movements are characteristically refined and resilient, but something of Mahler's strength is missing. Clear, well-balanced recording, although on tape the high level of the transfer emphasizes the brightness of the treble.

Klemperer's is not one of his most convincing Mahler performances. The recording session caught him and the orchestra at less than their best, and one misses the concentrated sense of flow which normally ran through his performances, however magisterially slow. There is, nevertheless, a magically sensitive account of the second *Nachtmusik*. The sound is full and vivid, and the tapes are particularly successful.

Symphony No. 8 in E flat (*Symphony of 1000*).

❀ ₵ *** Decca **414 493-2** [id.]; SET 534-5/*KCET2 7006* [Lon. OSA/*5* 1295]. Harper, Popp, Augér, Minton, Watts, Kollo, Shirley-Quirk, Talvela, V. Boys' Ch., V. State Op. Ch. and Singverein, Chicago SO, Solti.

** Ph. Dig. **410 607-2**; 6769/*7654* 069 (2) [id.]. Robinson, Blegen, Sasson, Quivar, Myers, Riegel, Luxon, Howell, Tanglewood Fest. Ch., Boston Boys' Ch. and Boston SO, Ozawa.

*(*) Sup. Dig. **C37 7307/8** [id.]. Benačková-Cápová, Nielsen, Šounová, Soukupová, Márová, Moser, Schöne, Novák, Prague Philharmonic Ch., Czech R. Ch., Kühn Children's Ch., Czech PO, Neumann.

(i) *Symphony No. 8; Symphony No. 10: Adagietto.*

** DG 413 232-1/*4* (2). (i) Arroyo, Spoorenberg, Hamari, Mathis, Procter, Grobe, Fischer-Dieskau, Crass, Bav. N. and W. German R. Ch., Regensburg Ch., Bav. RSO, Kubelik.

The compact discs of Solti's set of Mahler's *Eighth*, like the LPs and the remarkably fine cassette, represent a triumph for everyone concerned, with greater detail than ever before and a remarkable sense of presence. Solti's is a classic recording. Challenged by the tightest possible recording schedule, the American orchestra and European singers responded to Solti at his most inspired with a performance that vividly captures the atmosphere of a great occasion – essential in this of all works. There is nothing cautious about the surging dynamism of the first movement, the electrifying hymn, *Veni Creator spiritus*; and the long second movement, setting the final scene of Goethe's *Faust*, proceeds through its contrasted sections with unrelenting intensity. In Solti's hands the hushed prelude is sharp-edged in pianissimo, not at all comforting, while the magnificent recording copes superbly with every strand of texture and the fullest range of dynamic – spectacularly so in the great final crescendo to the words *Alles vergängliche*.

Though the Philips digital recording is very good indeed, Ozawa's Boston reading of the *Symphony of a Thousand* rather lacks the weight and intensity of its finest rivals. It is a performance which has one thinking back to earlier Mahler of *Wunderhorn* vintage rather than accepting the epic scale. There is much beautiful singing and playing, recorded in a mellow acoustic, but this work needs a greater sense of occasion. On CD the refinement and beauty of the recording are particularly striking in the work's closing section.

Even in this massive symphony Kubelik concentrates on refinement, and the recording engineers faithfully match him. The result is crisp and clear but largely unexciting, giving little idea of a live occasion. Generally good solo singing. There is an excellent cassette transfer. The reissue with its added coupling of the *Adagietto* from the *Tenth Symphony* is fair value.

Neumann's version was recorded at live performances in Prague in February 1982. Though the start of *Veni Creator spiritus* is easy-going rather than tense and electric in the way that the epic theme demands, tensions build powerfully in that first movement. The long slow orchestral introduction to the second movement then brings another slackening of tension, with prosaic and unhushed playing. Inevitably with a live performance, there are moments which match the grandeur of Mahler's conception; but with soloists placed far closer than chorus or orchestra, with ensemble often slack, and with Neumann unable to point the necessary contrasts of mood, as when moments of *Wunderhorn* lightness are introduced, this is a poor competitor for Solti's magnificent reading with the Chicago orchestra, recorded in Vienna.

Symphony No. 9 in D min.

*** DG Dig. **410 726-2** (2) [id.]. BPO, Karajan.

*** Ph. **416 466-2** (with *Kindertotenlieder*); 6700 021 (2) [id.]. Concg. O, Haitink.

*** HMV **CDS 747113-8** [id.]; SLS/*TC-SLS* 5188 [Ang. SZB/*4Z2S* 3899]. LPO, Tennstedt.

*** CBS **M2K 42033** (2) [id.]. Columbia SO, Bruno Walter.

(*) Decca Dig. **410 012-2; D 274 D2/*K274 K22*. Chicago SO, Solti.

(M) ** DG 415 634-1/*4* (2). Bav. RSO, Kubelik – WAGNER: *Siegfried idyll* etc.***

*(*) Sup. Dig. **C37 7340/1** [id.]. Czech PO, Neumann.

Symphony No. 9; Symphony No. 10: Adagio.
(*) CBS Dig. **M2K 39721; 12M/*12T* 39721 (2) [id.]. VPO, Maazel.

Karajan's two recordings both transcend his earlier Mahler. In the 1980 analogue version (DG 2707 125/*3370 038* (2) [id.]) it is the combination of richness and concentration in the outer movements that makes for a reading of the deepest intensity, while the middle two movements bring point and humour as well as refinement and polish. In the finale Karajan is not just noble and stoic; he finds the bite of passion as well, sharply set against stillness and repose. Yet within two years Karajan went on to record the work even more compulsively at live performances in Berlin; it is this newer version which appears on CD. The major difference is that there is a new, glowing optimism in the finale, rejecting any Mahlerian death-wish, making it a supreme achievement. Despite the problems of live recording, the sound is bright and full, if somewhat close.

Haitink is at his very finest in Mahler's *Ninth*, and the last movement, with its slow expanses of melody, reveals a unique concentration. Unlike almost all other conductors he maintains his intensely slow tempo from beginning to end. This is a great performance, beautifully recorded, and with the earlier movements superbly performed – the first movement a little restrained, the second pointed at exactly the right speed, and the third gloriously extrovert and brilliant – this will be for many Mahlerians a first recommendation. The CD transfer freshens the 1969 recording, which still sounds highly impressive in its body and natural focus. Hermann Prey's early 1970s version of the *Kindertotenlieder* is added (the LPs are uncoupled), a fresh, intelligent account, yet lacking something in imagination and intensity of expression.

Tennstedt directs a performance of warmth and distinction, underlining nobility rather than any neurotic tension, so that the outer movements, spaciously drawn, have architectural grandeur. The second movement is gently done, and the third, crisp and alert, lacks just a little in adrenalin. The playing is excellent and the recording full, sharper in focus and better detailed on CD. The cassette version (on one double-length tape, but supplied in a box) is vivid and well detailed, although the upper range is a trifle over-bright and needs smoothing.

Walter's performance – recorded in 1961 during his retirement in California – lacks mystery at the very start, but through the long first movement Walter unerringly builds up a consistent structure, controlling tempo more closely than most rivals, preferring a steady approach. The middle two movements similarly are sharply focused rather than genial, and the finale, lacking hushed pianissimos, is tough and stoically strong. A fine performance, not at all the reading one would have predicted from Walter. The CD transfer, like the others in this fine series, is full and well balanced, if lacking ultimate range, although background noise has been minimized and the sound is still impressive.

Clear and certain from the first hushed murmur of the opening movement, Solti in his newest Chicago version – in forward and full digital sound – presents the power of the piece with total conviction. What he lacks in the outer movements is a sense of mystery; he is also short of charm in the central movements, which should present a necessary contrast. His earlier LSO reading was much warmer and more spontaneous-sounding, with recording balanced more naturally, and was outstanding for its time. The compact disc version brings considerable advantage in the absence of background, but with the sound so clearly focused there is even less feeling of mystery, and the lateral spread seems a fraction narrower. The range is formidable. The chrome cassettes are brilliant and clear. Though the balance is treble-orientated, it is very spectacular and free.

Maazel's superbly controlled Vienna version brings the obvious advantage of having a generous fill-up, a comparably powerful reading of the opening *Adagio* of the *Tenth*. Maazel may not have quite the gravity and masterful control of tension that mark the very finest versions – Karajan's, for example – but with glorious playing from the Vienna strings and with unexaggerated speeds it is hard to fault Maazel on any point. He steers a masterly course between the perils of being either too plain or too mannered. Though some may miss an element of temperament, this is one of the more satisfying in his Mahler series, and is extremely well recorded. The chrome cassettes are relatively soft-grained in the treble, but the string timbre is particularly beautiful. On CD, however, the spectacular sound quality with the widest range of dynamic does bring a feeling in the climaxes that the microphones were very near the orchestra.

Kubelik's restraint in the first movement means that the performance remains on a relatively low pitch of intensity. Though the result is in every way beautiful, it is only in the serenity of the finale that Kubelik achieves the sublimity to equal his finest rivals on record. However, with a new coupling of two outstanding Wagner performances it makes an interesting mid-price version; the recording is fresh and full, on both LPs and the chrome tapes.

The absence of hushed tension, together with the plain unmoulded style from the start, brands Neumann's version as lacking in a sense of occasion. The distinctive sound of the Czech Philharmonic, not to mention much distinguished solo work, are points in favour; however, when even in the crisp and clean accounts of the middle two scherzando movements Neumann's tempo relationships are often unconvincing, this is a disappointment. Even the glorious string tone at the hymn-like opening theme of the finale is marred by sluggish rhythmic control. The atmospheric recording is not ideally clear on detail.

Symphony No. 10 in F sharp (*Unfinished;* revised performing edition by Deryck Cooke).

*** HMV Dig. **CDS 747301-8** [id.]; SLS/*TC-SLS* 5206 (2/*1*) [Ang. DSB/*4D2S* 3909]. Bournemouth SO, Rattle – BRAHMS/SCHOENBERG: *Piano quartet* (on CDs only).***

(*) RCA Dig. **RD 84553 [RCD2 4553]; ARC2/*ARK2* 4553 (2). Phd. O, Levine.

With digital recording of outstanding quality in all three media, Simon Rattle's vivid and compelling reading of the Cooke performing edition has one convinced more than ever that a remarkable revelation of Mahler's intentions was achieved in this painstaking reconstruction. To Cooke's final thoughts Rattle has added one or two detailed amendments; the finale in particular, starting with its cataclysmic hammer-blows and growing tuba line, is a deeply moving experience, ending not in neurotic resignation but in open optimism. In the middle movements, too, Rattle, youthfully dynamic, has fresh revelations to make. The Bournemouth orchestra plays with dedication, marred only by the occasional lack of fullness in the strings. On the CDs, a generous filler has been added in Schoenberg's orchestration of Brahms's *Piano quartet No. 1 in G minor*. The tape box offers the *Symphony* laid out on a single double-length cassette.

Levine's complete Mahler symphony cycle will be the first to include the full five-movement version of the *Tenth Symphony*. The performance typically reveals Levine as a thoughtful and searching Mahlerian; the spacious account of the first movement is splendid, with refined Philadelphia string tone; however, the recording, digital or not, does not always do justice to the high violins which lack something in bloom, not least in the epilogue to the finale. The sound lacks a little in bass, too. These faults of balance remain on the CDs, although the sound overall is more refined and the silent background adds to the poignancy of the finale. However, although the playing is more polished than that of the Bournemouth orchestra on the rival HMV version, as a rule Levine is less intense, relaxing well in the jolly second movement, for example, but not quite conveying the same range of emotion as the work develops.

LIEDER AND SONG CYCLES

Lieder: *Ablösung in Sommer; Frühlingsmorgen; Nicht wiedersehen!; Selbstgefuhl; Um schlimme Kinder artig zu machen; Zu Strassburg auf der Schanz* (arr. Byrns).
*** DG Dig. 415 476-1 (2). Berndt Weikl, Philh. O, Sinopoli – *Symphony No. 5.****

These six early songs, most sensitively sung by Berndt Weikl, are orchestrations by Harold Byrns of five *Wunderhorn* settings, plus a poem of Richard Leander. Already, at the beginning of his career, Mahler's recognizable style was establishing itself. Excellent recording.

Kindertotenlieder.
(M) *** DG 415 631-1/*4*. Dietrich Fischer-Dieskau, BPO, Boehm – *Symphony No. 7.***
*** DG **415 096-2**; 2707 081/*3370 006* (2) [id.]. Christa Ludwig, BPO, Karajan – *Symphony No. 5.****

(i) *Kindertotenlieder;* (ii) *Lieder eines fahrenden Gesellen;* (i) *4 Rückert Lieder* (*Um Mitternacht; Ich atmet' einen linden Duft; Blicke mir nicht in die Lieder; Ich bin der Welt*).
*** DG **415 191-2** [id.]. Dietrich Fischer-Dieskau, (i) BPO, Boehm; (ii) Bav. RSO, Kubelik.

As one of the Fischer-Dieskau series that DG issued to celebrate the great baritone's sixtieth birthday, this CD of his Mahler performances makes an attractive collection, drawing on more than one LP to make up generous measure. Only four of the *Rückert Lieder* are included (*Liebst du um Schönheit* being essentially a woman's song), but otherwise this conveniently gathers Mahler's shorter and most popular orchestral cycles in performances that bring out the fullest range of expression in Fischer-Dieskau at a period when his voice was at its peak. The CD transfer gives freshness and immediacy to both the 1964 recording with Boehm and the 1970 recordings with Kubelik.

As can be seen, Fischer-Dieskau's superb account of the *Kindertotenlieder* is also available coupled with Kubelik's performance of Mahler's *Seventh Symphony*, while Christa Ludwig's performance is used as a fill-up for Karajan's Mahler *Fifth*. Her singing is characterful, if not so magical as Dame Janet Baker's whose generous anthology (including also the five *Rückert Lieder* and the *Lieder eines fahrenden Gesellen*) with Barbirolli, is an outstanding recommendation on both LP and cassette (HMV ASD/*TC-ASD* 4409).

Kindertotenlieder; Lieder eines fahrenden Gesellen.
** Decca **414 624-2** [id.]. Kirsten Flagstad, VPO, Boult – WAGNER: *Wesendonck Lieder.****

Flagstad sings masterfully in these two most appealing of Mahler's orchestral cycles, but she was unable to relax into the deeper, more intimate expressiveness that the works really require. The voice is magnificent, the approach always firmly musical (helped by Sir Adrian's splendid accompaniment), but this recording is recommendable for the singer rather than for the way the music is presented. The coupled *Wesendonck Lieder*, however, offers repertoire far more suited to her special artistry. The recording (late-1950s vintage) re-emerges with remarkable freshness.

Das klagende Lied (complete).
*** HMV Dig. **CDC 747089-2** [id.]; EL 270136-1/*4* [Ang. DS/*4DS* 38159]. Döse, Hodgson, Tear, Rea, CBSO and Ch., Rattle.

Das klagende Lied (complete); *Symphony No. 10: Adagio.*
(B) ** CBS DC 40155 (2). Söderström, Lear, Hoffman, Burrows, Haefliger, Nienstedt, LSO and Ch., Boulez.

Das klagende Lied (published version).
(M) *(*) Ph. Seq. 413 365-1/*4*. Harper, Procter, Hollweg, Netherlands R. Ch., Concg. O, Haitink.

The electricity of Simon Rattle as a recording conductor has rarely been more strikingly illustrated than in this fine recording of *Das klagende Lied*, complete with the dramatically necessary first part which Mahler came to discard. This is an amazing piece for a twenty-year-old to write, one which contains so much that is typical of the mature Mahler, not least the sense of drama and colour, and drawing on large-scale forces. Pierre Boulez was the first to record the work complete, a clean-cut and dramatic version that has been intermittently available from CBS. Like Boulez, Rattle brings out the astonishing originality but adds urgency, colour and warmth, not to mention deeper and more meditative qualities. So the final section, *Wedding Piece*, after starting with superb swagger in the celebration music, is gripping in the minstrel's sinister narration and ends in the darkest concentration on a mezzo-soprano solo, beautifully sung by Alfreda Hodgson. It adds to the attractiveness of this version that (on both LP and CD) the whole cantata is squeezed on to a single disc in vivid sound, thin only in the off-stage party music. The ensemble of the CBSO has a little roughness, but the bite and commitment could not be more convincing. The XDR tape, though full and pleasing, has less-refined detail than the LP, though the chorus is well focused in the wedding scene.

Boulez's version has now been reissued on two discs, costing about the same as HMV's single LP and tape. Boulez is a distinctive Mahlerian. His ear concentrates on precision of texture rather than warmth, and the chill at the heart of this gruesome story of the days of chivalry and knights in armour is the more sharply conveyed. Though the recording is not ideally atmospheric, it is not lacking in body, and the chorus, which sings well, is tellingly caught. The soloists are more uneven. The *Adagio* from the *Tenth Symphony* is used as a filler on the pair of LPs but is omitted on the equivalent tape.

Haitink's Sequenza record offers only the two regularly published sections, omitting *Waldmärchen*. The performance is not ideal, lacking urgency and a sense of imaginative imagery, but the recording remains very refined – it was a demonstration record in its day (1974). The cassette is impressive, too.

Des Knaben Wunderhorn: Das irdische Leben; Wo die schönen Trompeten; Urlicht. Rückert Lieder: Liebst du um Schönheit; Ich bin der Welt abhanden gekommen.
(M) **(*) Ph. 412 366-1/*4*. Jessye Norman, Irwin Gage – SCHUBERT: *Lieder.***(*)

Jessye Norman recorded these Mahler songs in 1971, towards the beginning of her career, and already the great voice was developing magically. There is less detail here than in more recent performances, but the magisterial sustaining of long lines at very measured speeds is impressive. Irwin Gage accompanies sensitively, though he cannot efface memories of the orchestral versions. Good recording for its period, with a satisfactory cassette.

Des Knaben Wunderhorn: excerpts (*Das irdische Leben; Verlor'ne Müh; Wo die schönen Trompeten blasen; Rheinlegendchen*).
(*) Decca **414 675-2 (2) [id.]. Minton, Chicago SO, Solti – *Symphony No. 7.****

Yvonne Minton, a singer whom Solti encouraged enormously in her career at Covent Garden, makes a splendid soloist in these colourful songs from *Des Knaben Wunderhorn*. They were originally coupled with the *Fifth Symphony* but now make an attractive bonus for the CD issue of the *Seventh*.

Das Lied von der Erde.
(M) *** Ph. 412 927-1/*4*. Baker, King, Concg. O, Haitink.

*** DG Dig. **413 459-2**; 413 459-1/*4* [id.]. Fassbaender, Araiza, BPO, Giulini.
*** HMV **CDC 747231-2** [id.]; EL 290440-1/*4* [Ang. S/*4XS* 38234]. Ludwig, Wunderlich, New Philh. O and Philh. O, Klemperer.
*** Decca **414 066-2**; Jub. 414 066-1/*4* [id.]. Minton, Kollo, Chicago SO, Solti.
(M) **(*) CBS **MK 42034** [id.]. Mildred Miller, Haefliger, NYPO, Walter.
(M) **(*) EMI EMX 41 2073-1/*4*. Fischer-Dieskau, Murray Dickie, Philh. O, Kletzki.
(**) Decca mono **414 194-2**; 414 194-1/*4*. Ferrier, Patzak, VPO, Walter.
** Ph. Dig. **411 474-2**; 6514/*7337* 112 [id.]. Norman, Vickers, LSO, Sir Colin Davis.

Dame Janet Baker's outstanding version continues to dominate the field; indeed, the combination of this most deeply committed of Mahler singers with Haitink, the most thoughtfully dedicated of Mahler conductors, produces radiantly beautiful and moving results, helped by refined and atmospheric recording. If usually these songs reflect a degree of oriental reticence, Dame Janet more clearly relates them to Mahler's other great orchestral songs, so complete is the sense of involvement, with the conductor matching his soloist's mood. The concentration over the long final *Abschied* has never been surpassed on record (almost all of it was recorded in a single take). Haitink opens the cycle impressively with an account of the first tenor song that subtly confirms its symphonic shape, less free in tempo than usual but presenting unusually strong contrasts between the main stanzas and the tender refrain, *Dunkel ist das Leben*. James King cannot match his solo partner, often failing to create fantasy, but his singing is intelligent and sympathetic. The balance with the tenor is realistic, but Dame Janet's voice is brought a shade closer; for this mid-priced reissue the sound has been brightened and made more vivid, at the expense of some of the original bloom and warmth. Yet the closing pages remain tellingly atmospheric. The chrome cassette matches the disc closely.

Giulini conducts a characteristically restrained and refined reading. With Araiza a heady-toned tenor rather than a powerful one, the line *Dunkel ist das Leben* in the first song becomes unusually tender and gentle, with rapture and wistfulness keynote emotions. In the second song, Fassbaender gives lightness and poignancy to the line *Mein Herz ist müde* rather than dark tragedy; and even the final *Abschied* is rapt rather than tragic, following the text of the poem. Not that Giulini fails to convey the breadth and intensity of Mahler's magnificent concept; and the playing of the Berlin Philharmonic could hardly be more beautiful. Warmer, more refined and more atmospheric recording than this orchestra has lately been receiving. There is a first-class chrome tape.

Klemperer's way with Mahler is at its most individual in *Das Lied von der Erde* – and that will enthrall some, as it must infuriate others. True, there is less case for Klempereran nobility in so evocative and orient-inspired a piece as *Das Lied* than there is in the symphonies; if the ear is open, however, Klemperer's preference for slow tempi and his refusal to languish reveal qualities far removed from the heaviness his detractors deplore. With slower speeds, the three tenor songs seem initially to lose some of their sparkle and humour; however, thanks to superb expressive singing by the late Fritz Wunderlich – one of the most memorable examples of his artistry on record – and thanks also to pointing of rhythm by Klemperer himself, subtle but always clear, the comparative slowness will hardly worry anyone intent on hearing the music afresh, as Klemperer intends. As for the mezzo songs, Christa Ludwig sings them with a remarkable depth of expressiveness; in particular, the final *Abschied* has the intensity of a great occasion. Excellent digitally remastered recording (1967 vintage), apart from a forward woodwind balance, sounding most impressive on CD. There is also a very good cassette, slightly less open at the top but retaining the bloom of the sound with very little loss of definition.

In sheer beauty of sound and precision of texture, few versions can match Solti's with the Chicago orchestra, helped by brilliant but refined 1972 recording. As an interpretation, it may lose something in mystery because of this very precision, but Solti's concentration, in a consciously less romantic style than normal, is highly compelling, above all in the final *Abschied*: slower than usual and in the final section bringing an unusually close observance of Mahler's *pianissimo* markings. Minton exactly matches Solti's style, consistently at her most perceptive and sensitive, while Kollo presents Heldentenor strength, combined with sensitivity. The recording has no need to give the tenor an unnaturally close balance, and the result is the more exciting, with the background quiet of the CD making everything seem more tangible. The LP and excellent tape are on Decca's mid-priced Jubilee label.

Though Bruno Walter's New York version does not have the tear-laden quality in the final *Abschied* that made his earlier Vienna account (in mono) with Kathleen Ferrier unique, that is its only serious shortcoming. Haefliger sparkles with imagination and Miller is a warm and appealing mezzo soloist, lacking only the last depth of feeling you find in a Ferrier; and the maestro himself has rarely sounded so happy on record, even in Mahler. The remastered recording has been considerably improved for CD and now sounds both warm and vivid.

At mid-price on a single disc, with first-rate playing and recording, the Kletzki version makes a good recommendation, particularly if you want to hear the optional baritone version of the second, fourth and sixth songs. Fischer-Dieskau – who went on to record them again later with Leonard Bernstein – is at his most sensitive, bringing ecstasy to the final murmurs of '*ewig*', no sadness. Murray Dickie – not a tenor who would normally sing this role in concert – sings very sympathetically within his limits of scale; and Kletzki draws a characteristically red-blooded performance from the Vienna Philharmonic. Disc and tape are closely matched.

It is a joy to have the voice of Kathleen Kerrier so vividly caught on CD – not to mention that of the characterful Patzak – in Bruno Walter's classic Vienna recording for Decca. It is also an enormous advantage having silent background with minimum tape-hiss, to be able to appreciate the radiance of the performance, not least in the ecstatic closing pages and the final murmurs of '*ewig*'. The sad thing is that the violin tone, by being given extra top, in high loud passages has acquired a very unattractive edge, not at all like the Vienna violins, and this makes for uncomfortable listening.

Sir Colin Davis rarely if ever recorded Mahler before his London reading of *Das Lied von der Erde*. Despite beautifully refined playing, the result is stiff and unpersuasive, lacking in tension. Vickers strains uncomfortably in the first song, gritty of tone, with no attempt at a *pianissimo* for *Dunkel ist das Leben*. Jessye Norman, as ever, is magnificent, deeply and naturally expressive, quite the finest element in the reading. Full and refined recording.

Lieder eines fahrenden Gesellen.
*** Decca **414 674-2** [id.]; SET 469/70 [Lon. CSA 2227]. Minton, Chicago SO, Solti – *Symphony No. 6.****
** CBS **MK 42025** [id.]. Mildred Miller, Columbia SO, Walter – BRAHMS: *Alto rhapsody* etc.**

Yvonne Minton's performance of the *Wayfaring Lad* cycle is outstandingly successful, and very well recorded too.

Mildred Miller sings well enough, although her vocal production is at times a little restricted and instead of long, resonant phrases the listener sometimes receives an impression of short-term musical thought. Yet Walter keeps the performance dramatically alive and there is superb orchestral detail, most vividly brought out by the excellent CD transfer, which is atmospheric and refined. The tangibility of both voice and orchestra is striking and the balance is first class.

5 Rückert Lieder.
(*) DG **415 099-2 [id.]. Christa Ludwig, BPO, Karajan – *Symphony No. 6.****
(M) ** DG 413 528-1/*4* (Nos 1, 3–5 only). Fischer-Dieskau, BPO, Boehm – *Symphony No. 6.***

Christa Ludwig's set of the *Rückert Lieder* is used as a makeweight for Karajan's CDs of the *Sixth Symphony*, but is not included on the equivalent LPs and tapes. Ludwig's singing has poise and character, but the microphone conveys some unevenness in the voice. It is the distinction and refinement of playing and conducting which stand out.

Fischer-Dieskau's performances are also available on a CD Lieder anthology – see above.

Marcello, Benedetto (1686–1739)

Guitar concerto in C min. (arr. Williams).
** CBS **MK 39560**; IM/*IMT* 39560 [id.]. Williams, ASMF, Sillito – BACH; HANDEL: *Concertos.***

Like the other arrangements on this disc, the change of solo instrument (in this instance the original was for oboe) is not an improvement, and although Williams is impressive in the *Adagio*, this collection will direct its main appeal to guitar enthusiasts and admirers of the soloist. The sound is good, with the chrome tape not so sharply defined as the LP and CD.

Psalm settings Nos 4, 10, 11, 29, 36, 42 and 46.
(M) *** Erato Presence EPR 15544/5. Soloists, Lausanne Chamber Vocal and Orchestral Ens., Corboz.

With Benedetto Marcello so poorly represented in the catalogue, these attractive Psalm settings are doubly welcome. They are miniature cantatas (about half as long as Bach's) though very Italian in feeling, with plenty of drama and sometimes mercurial changes of mood and tempo. Some of the finest music here is in duet form, for example the engaging piece for soprano and contralto in No. 4, another for two contraltos in No. 11 and for tenor and bass in No. 29. This also has a superb tenor aria, ravishingly sung by John Elwes with harp accompaniment. The soprano, Wally Staempfli, is given No. 46 as a solo cantata, but the most ambitious work is No. 36, which Corboz directs freshly and imaginatively. The 1975 recording is of excellent quality; at upper-mid-price, these two LPs are well worth exploring.

Martin, Frank (1890–1974)

(i) *Ballade for cello and piano;* (ii) *Ballade for flute and piano. 8 Préludes.*
(**) Jecklin mono 603 [id.]. Composer with (i) Henri Honegger; (ii) Robert Willoughby.

As a conductor Frank Martin recorded his *Violin* and *Harpsichord concertos*, the *Jederman* settings and excerpts from his opera, *The Tempest*. This record collects three performances in which he features as a pianist. The *Eight Préludes* were composed in 1947–8 for Dinu Lipatti, who alas never lived to perform them. The present account reveals Frank Martin as a very fine pianist though the mono recording is somewhat subfusc. Much the same must be said of the later records; the *Ballade for cello*, which dates from the period of the *Concerto for seven wind instruments* (1949), is an ambitious work. The recording derives from the archives of Süddeutscher Rundfunk, while the earlier *Ballade for flute* (1939) was taken from a public performance in New Hampshire in 1967. The recordings all call for some tolerance but like all such historic documents give a valuable insight into Martin's interpretative intentions.

Requiem.
*** Jecklin Jecklin 190. Speiser, Bollen, Tappy, Lagger (bass), Lausanne Ars Laeta Ch., Union Chorale and female voices, Lausanne, Luy, SRO, composer.

This is a recording of the première given in Lausanne Cathedral on 4 May 1973. It is one of the most searching and beautiful choral works composed since the Second World War, and it is a sorry comment on our times that music of this calibre and interest has so far attracted so little exposure. It was composed after a Mediterranean cruise the composer took in 1971, three years before his death, and inspired by three cathedrals: St Mark's in Venice, the Montreale in Palermo and the Greek temples of Paestum near Naples. The *Requiem* is scored for four soloists, mixed choirs and orchestral forces that include double woodwind, brass and an extensive percussion section, as well as harpsichord, harp and organ. Frank Martin possesses an Old Testament dignity, an exquisite feeling for pale textures and a 'cultured poise', as Robert Simpson put it. But there is more to this music than that. The *Requiem* has purity of utterance and real depth; it is distinguished by vision and elevation of spirit, and rises in the *In Paradisum* to something rare in contemporary music, inspiration. Indeed, the gently ecstatic setting of *In Paradisum* has an almost luminous quality – and a radiance that makes one catch one's breath. It really does persuade the listener that this is a glimpse of the beyond, so strong is its spell. Elsewhere there are familiar fingerprints: the opening of the offertorium, coming after an impressively powerful vision of the *Dies irae*, is scored for voices, strings and harpsichord; there are the same subtle shifts of colour and harmony one remembers from the *Petite symphonie concertante*, the *Violin concerto* and *Le vin herbé*. The octogenarian composer directs a performance that might well have been improved, here and there, in terms of ensemble or security, particularly in some of the choral singing, but which, in all important respects, is completely dedicated and authoritative. The Swiss Radio recording is generally well balanced and offers a natural enough acoustic, though it is not in the demonstration category. Strongly recommended.

Martinů, Bohuslav (1890–1959)

Double concerto for two string orchestras, piano and timpani; Les fresques de Piero della Francesca.
*** Sup. Dig. 1110 3393 [id.]. Prague RSO, Mackerras.

These two seminal Martinů works have been paired together before by Supraphon and make an excellent coupling. The *Concerto* has a brooding intensity that betrays the gathering war clouds, and its energy and power are marvellously conveyed by Sir Charles Mackerras and the fine Prague Radio orchestra. *Les fresques de Piero della Francesca* is a richly imaginative score, full of the almost mystical pantheism which one finds in this composer. While Mackerras does not efface memories of earlier recordings by Ančerl and Kubelik, his account can hold its own with theirs, and he has the advantage of excellent digital recording. An essential disc for anyone beginning a Martinů collection.

Field mass.
*** Sup. Dig. **C37 7735**; 1112 3576 [id.]. Zítek, Czech Philharmonic Ch. and O, Mackerras – JANÁČEK: *Amarus*.***

Martinů's *Field mass* is full of delightful and original sonorities, and this persuasive account under Mackerras shows it in the best possible light. The *Field mass* was intended for performance in the open air and is scored for the unusual combination of baritone, male chorus, wind instruments, percussion, harmonium and a piano, as well as a triangle and a number of bells. The resultant sounds are as fresh and individual as one could imagine, and so is Martinů's invention. The *Mass* was written in France in 1939 in the dark days of the war, yet it retains a life-enhancing quality and a sense of faith that is moving. It is very impressively performed by the Czech forces under Sir Charles Mackerras, and the recording is quite outstanding.

OPERA

Comedy on the Bridge (complete).
** Sup. Dig. 1116 3314. Krátká, Tuček, Novák, Krejčik, Hladík, Dufek, Kurfürst, Brno Janáček Ch., Opera O, Jílek.

Comedy on the Bridge is a radio opera; it tells of the plight of some travellers caught between two opposing armies, able neither to get to the far side (because their papers are not in order) nor to turn back (as they have no re-entry permit). The satire is a little heavy-handed – and reality was soon to overtake fantasy. The score is very lively but lightweight, its invention often pungent without ever really being Martinů at his very best. There are good performances from all concerned and the engineering is first class. Even if it is not top-drawer Martinů, *Comedy on the Bridge* is an entertaining and intelligent score that admirers of the composer will want to acquire.

Mascagni, Pietro (1863–1945)

Cavalleria Rusticana (complete).
*** RCA **RD 83091**; RL/*RK* 13091 [CRL1/*CRK1* 3091]. Scotto, Domingo, Elvira, Isola Jones, Amb. Op. Ch., Nat. PO, Levine.
*(*) Ph. **416 137-2**; 416 137-1/*4* (2) [id.]. Obraztsova, Domingo, Bruson, Gall, Barbieri, La Scala, Milan, Ch. and O, Prêtre.

(i) *Cavalleria Rusticana* (complete). *Guglielmo Ratcliffe: Intermezzo. Iris: Introduction and Hymn to the sun. Le Maschere: Overture.*
(B) ** EMI *TCC2-POR 290111-9* (i) Los Angeles, Corelli, Sereni, Lazzarini; Rome Opera Ch. and O, Santini.

There is far more than its compact disc format with a single CD (libretto included), and LP and cassette alternatives, to recommend the RCA version. On balance, in performance it stands as the best current recommendation, with Domingo giving a heroic account of the role of Turiddu, full of defiance. Scotto, strongly characterful too, though not always perfectly steady on top, gives one of her finest performances of recent years, and James Levine directs with a splendid sense of pacing, by no means faster than his rivals (except the leisurely Karajan), and drawing red-blooded playing from the National Philharmonic.

The recording is very good, strikingly present in its CD format, and the cassette transfer is first class, one of RCA's very best.

Taken from the soundtrack of a Unitel television film (like the companion version of *Pag.*) the Prêtre set can be recommended to those who want a reminder of the film, and maybe also to those who want to hear Domingo in ringing voice; but otherwise the flaws rule it out as a serious contender. Obraztsova's massive and distinctive mezzo is certainly characterful but hardly apt for the role, with its obtrusively edgy and uneven sounds. One or two moments are memorable – for example, the agonized utterance of the curse *A te la mala Pasqua*, not fire-eating at all – but she, like some of the others, equally unsteady, looked better than they all sound. Fedora Barbieri, a veteran of veterans among mezzos, makes a token appearance as Mamma Lucia. The recording is full and atmospheric with the sound-effects needed for television. The single-disc CD format brings a libretto in a slipcase. Both the LP and tape set (the latter of good quality) spread ungenerously over four sides.

On the EMI tape – very reasonably priced – an essentially lyrical performance. If the bitterness of Mascagni's drama is not a first consideration, this beautifully sung and warmly recorded set certainly gives scope for soaring Italianate singing of rich, memorable melodies. The three bonus items too are worth having. The sound is smooth, a little lacking in upper range but well balanced.

Massenet, Jules (1842–1912)

Le Carillon (ballet): complete. *Thaïs:* (i) *Meditation.*
*** Decca Dig. 410 189-1/*4* [id.]. (i) Nigel Kennedy; Nat. PO, Bonynge.

With his keen rhythmic sense and feeling for colour, Bonynge is outstanding in this repertory. With excellent playing and outstandingly brilliant recording this one-act ballet – written in the same year as *Werther* – makes a delightful offering, not always as lightweight as one might expect but with charming touches of humour. The cassette is one of Decca's very finest and loses little of the range and amplitude of the disc.

La Navarraise (opera): complete.
(B) *** CBS DC 40134 (2) [Col. M 33506]. Popp, Vanzo, Souzay, Sénéchal, Sardinero, Meloni, Ambrosian Op. Ch., LSO, Almeida – WOLF-FERRARI: *Il Segreto di Susanna.****

An outstanding bargain in CBS's 'Diamond' series offering two LPs for the price of one, in this case two complete operas, for the Massenet piece is happily coupled with a sparkling version of Wolf-Ferrari's *Susanna's secret. La Navarraise*, a compact 'lyric episode' lasting barely forty minutes, finds Massenet challenging the *verismo* school and succeeding convincingly. The flavour is of a cross between *Carmen* and *Cavalleria Rusticana* with a touch of *Il Tabarro.* To earn her dowry before marrying her beloved, the intrepid heroine penetrates the enemy lines in the Carlist wars and for money assassinates the Royalist general's direct adversary. By a misunderstanding the hero follows her and is mortally wounded. In despair the heroine promptly goes mad – a great deal of story for so short a piece. It says much for Massenet's dramatic powers that he makes the result as convincing as he does, and the score is full of splendid atmospheric effects. It was produced in the same year as *Thaïs* (1894), with a première at Covent Garden. Massenet originally had a heavyweight Carmen voice in mind, but here Lucia Popp, best known for her coloratura, is both moving and stylish, making the scalp tingle in the final mad scene. Alain Vanzo, long neglected on record, is impressive as the hero, singing sensitively and idiomatically. The rest of the cast sings well too, and Antonio de Almeida, apart from one or two passages where he presses on too hard, is warmly sympathetic in his conducting. Excellent atmospheric recording.

Werther (complete).
(M) **(*) DG 413 304-1/*4* (3/*2*) [id.]. Domingo, Obraztsova, Augér, Grundheber, Moll, Col. Children's Ch. and RSO, Chailly.

With a recording that gives a beautiful bloom to the sound of the Cologne orchestra, down to the subtlest whisper from pianissimo strings, the DG version makes a good medium-price recommendation, particularly as Chailly proves a sharply characterful conductor, one who knows how to thrust home an important climax as well as how to create evocative textures, varying tensions positively. Placido Domingo in the name part sings with sweetness and purity as well as strength, coping superbly with the legato line of the aria *Pourquoi me réveiller*. Elena Obraztsova is richer and firmer than she usually is on record, but it is a generalized portrait, particularly beside the charming Sophie of Arleen Augér. The others make up a very convincing team. The DG tape transfer uses two cassettes against three LPs (in one of this company's cardboard flap-packs). The sound is softer-grained than the LPs, and detail is less sharp.

Mathias, William (born 1934)

Lux aeterna, Op. 88.
*** Chan. Dig. ABRD/*ABTD* 1115 [id.]. Felicity Lott, Cable, Penelope Walker, Bach Ch., St George's Chapel Ch., Windsor, LSO, Willcocks; J. Scott (organ).

The influence of Benjamin Britten is strong in this multi-layered choral work, but the energy and sureness of effect make it far more than derivative, an attractively approachable and colourful piece, full of memorable ideas. Just as Britten in the *War Requiem* contrasted different planes of expression with Latin liturgy set against Wilfred Owen poems, so Mathias contrasts the full choir singing Latin against the boys' choir singing carol-like Marian anthems, and in turn against the three soloists, who sing three arias and a trio to the mystical poems of St John of the Cross. In the last section all three planes come together when the chorus chants the prayer *Lux aeterna*, and the boys sing the hymn, *Ave maris stella*, leaving the soloists alone at the end in a moving conclusion. There are choral and instrumental effects here which directly echo examples in Tippett and Messiaen, as well as Britten; but the confidence of the writing and of this excellent recorded performance reveal lessons well learnt. Outstanding recording, beautifully and atmospherically balanced.

Maxwell Davies, Peter (born 1934)

The Bairns of Brugh; (i) *Image, reflection, shadow. Runes from the Holy Island.*
*** Unicorn DKP/*DKPC* 9033 [id.]. (i) Knowles (cimbalom); Fires of London, composer.

Image, reflection, shadow is the major work in this collection, some 36 minutes long; it is evocative, like most of Maxwell Davies's Orkney pieces, of the impact of nature, not of storm or stress but of the play of light. It brings some of his happiest inspirations, with melody and thematic development more important than in most of his music. The third movement is particularly beautiful, developing on a meditative melody at the start into a dancing allegro and a cadenza for the cimbalom, an instrument that colours the chamber texture of the work consistently. The two shorter pieces make a valuable fill-up, *The Bairns of Brugh* a tender lament (viola over marimba) and *Runes* a group of brief epigrams. First-rate performances and recording.

Symphony No. 3.
*** PRT BBC Dig. **CD 560**; REGL 560. BBC Philharmonic O, Edward Downes.

Within six months of the first performance in Manchester by these same performers, Peter Maxwell Davies's *Symphony*, written for the fiftieth anniversary of the BBC Philharmonic (formerly the BBC Northern Symphony Orchestra) appeared in this excellent recording on the BBC Artium label. It presents a powerful case for a work which, more concerned with lyricism than its predecessors, yet builds a structure just as powerful. Where in the *First Symphony* Maxwell Davies's direct inspiration came from Sibelius, here he has taken his cue from the *Ninth Symphony* of Mahler, with two lighter scherzando movements in the middle and ending with a long *Lento* finale which calmly draws the many threads together to make a most satisfying conclusion. Downes coaxes playing from his Manchester orchestra of a commitment and brilliance to match any rival. Excellent recording.

Vesalii Icones.
*** Unicorn KPM/*UKC* 7016. Ward Clarke, Fires of London, composer.

Maxwell Davies has the great quality of presenting strikingly memorable visions, and this is certainly one, an extraordinary cello solo with comment from a chamber group. It was originally written to accompany a solo dancer in a fourteen-fold sequence, each dance based on one of the horrifying anatomical drawings of Vesalius (1543) and each representing one of the stations of the Cross. Characteristically Davies has moments not only of biting pain and tender compassion but of deliberate shock-tactics – notably when the risen Christ turns out to be Antichrist and is represented in a final jaunty foxtrot. This is difficult music, but the emotional landmarks are plain from the start, and that is a good sign of enduring quality. Jennifer Ward Clarke plays superbly, and so do the Fires of London, conducted by the composer. Excellent recording. The matching tape is admirably clear and vivid.

Mendelssohn, Felix (1809–47)

Piano concerto No. 1 in G min., Op. 25.
(*) HMV Dig. EL 270184-1/*4* [Ang. DS/*4DS* 38235]. Ousset, LSO, Marriner – GRIEG: *Concerto.*(*)

As in the Grieg on the reverse, Ousset gives a performance of power rather than poetry, not always bringing out Mendelssohn's sparkle and charm but in her robust way establishing this as a bigger work than its length suggests. Strong accompaniment, very well recorded. An excellent choice for those who fancy the rare coupling. There is a very good cassette, firm and clear.

Piano concertos Nos 1 in G min.; 2 in D min., Op. 40.
*** Decca Dig. **414 672-2** [id.]; SXDL/*KSXDC* 7623 [Lon. LDR/*5*- 71123]. András Schiff, Bav. RSO, Dutoit.

Schiff and Dutoit give Mendelssohn's engaging concertos their CD début. András Schiff plays marvellously, with great delicacy and fluency; his virtuosity is effortless and never pursued for the sake of personal display. There is plenty of poetic feeling, too. He is given excellent accompaniments by Dutoit and the Bavarian players, and the Decca recording is first class in all three media, though especially vivid and transparent in its CD transfer.

Violin concerto in E min., Op. 64.
*** Decca Dig. **410 011-2**; SXDL/*KSXDC* 7558 [Lon. LDR/*5* 71058]. Kyung-Wha Chung, Montreal SO, Dutoit – TCHAIKOVSKY: *Concerto.****
*** DG Dig. **400 031-2**; 2532/*3302* 016 [id.]. Mutter, BPO, Karajan – BRUCH: *Concerto No. 1.****
*** CBS Dig. **39007**; IM/*IMT* 39007 [id.]. Cho-Liang Lin, Philh. O, Tilson Thomas – SAINT-SAËNS: *Violin Concerto No. 3.****
(*) Denon Dig. **C37 7123. Kantorow, Netherlands CO, Ros-Marbà – BRUCH: *Concerto No. 1.***(*)
(M) **(*) RCA Gold GL/*GK* 85264 [AGL1/*AGK1* 5264]. Heifetz, Boston SO, Munch – TCHAIKOVSKY: *Concerto.***(*)

(***) HMV mono **CDC 747119-2** [id.]. Menuhin, BPO, Furtwängler – BEETHOVEN: *Concerto*.(***)
** RCA Dig. **RD 70111**. Ughi, LSO, Prêtre – BRUCH: *Concerto No. 1*.**
(M) ** Ph. 412 929-1/*4*. Accardo, LPO, Dutoit – BRUCH: *Concerto No. 1*.
* HMV Dig. **CDC 747074-2** [id.]; EL 270105-1/*4* [Ang. DS/*4DS* 38150]. Perlman, Concg. O, Haitink – BRUCH: *Concerto No. 1*.*
* CBS Dig **MK 37204**; 37204 [id.]. Stern, Boston SO, Ozawa – BEETHOVEN: *Romances*.*

(i) *Violin concerto in E min.; Octet in E flat, Op. 20* (ed. Zukerman).
** Ph. Dig. **412 212-2**; 412 212-1/*4* [id.]. (i) Zukerman, St Paul CO, Zukerman.

Chung favours speeds faster than usual in all three movements, and the result is sparkling and happy with the lovely slow movement fresh and songful, not at all sentimental. With warmly sympathetic accompaniment from Dutoit and the Montreal orchestra, amply recorded, the result is one of Chung's happiest records. Some may find the helter-skelter of the finale a little too breathless, but the exhilaration of a tight challenge superbly taken is very hard to resist. This is almost the reading that Heifetz might have recorded with speeds similarly fast but with the manner far sweeter and more relaxed. The Tchaikovsky coupling is generous. The compact disc version emphasizes the closeness of the soloist but, with its clarity and tangibility of atmosphere, the result is very real. On cassette, the sound is of high quality, but the focus of the solo instrument benefits from a slight treble cut.

Here even more than in her Bruch coupling, the freshness of Anne-Sophie Mutter's approach communicates vividly to the listener, creating the feeling of hearing the work anew. Her gentleness and radiant simplicity in the *Andante* are very appealing, and the closing pages have real magic, with Karajan catching the mood and scale in his accompaniment. Similarly, the second subject of the first movement has great charm, and the light, sparkling finale (again with the orchestral balance superbly managed) is a delight. The recording is most realistically balanced on both disc and tape. The sound on compact disc is refined but emphasizes the rather artificial microphone set-up. Mutter is given a small-scale image, projected forward from the orchestral backcloth, but the orchestral layout itself does not have the luminous detail of the Decca recording, with the wind tending to congeal slightly when playing together.

To judge from Cho-Liang Lin's account of the Mendelssohn *Concerto*, Yo-Yo Ma is not the only Chinese-American artist destined for greatness. His is a vibrant and keenly intelligent performance, breathtaking in its virtuosity, and always musical. Cho-Liang Lin also has the benefit of really excellent support from the Philharmonia Orchestra and Michael Tilson Thomas, and excellent CBS engineering. This is one of the best CD versions of the Mendelssohn on the market and is strongly recommended to those for whom the Saint-Saëns coupling is suitable, a comparably distinguished performance, full of flair. The chrome tape can also be recommended, the quality warm and pleasing, though not so sharply defined at either end of the sound spectrum. The compact disc, however, has splendid presence and definition.

Jean-Jacques Kantorow gives a fresh, bright account with well-chosen speeds, excellently recorded. The restrained poetry will appeal to those who are not looking for a powerfully individual reading – though Kantorow, winner of many prizes, has easy, natural flair, and plays with flawlessly pure tone. Understanding, if not inspired, accompaniment.

As one might expect, Heifetz gives a fabulous performance. His speeds are consistently fast, yet in the slow movement his flexible phrasing sounds so inevitable and easy, it is hard not to be convinced. The finale is a *tour de force*, light and sparkling, with every note in place. The recording has – like his comparable versions of the Beethoven and Brahms concertos – been successfully remastered digitally and the sound is smoother than before, on both LP and cassette, with the balance adjusted to some extent. There is still some lack of bloom but not enough to spoil enjoyment of music making which is rightly reissued in RCA's 'Legendary Performers' series.

Menuhin's unique gift for lyrical sweetness has never been more seductively presented on record than in his classic version of the Mendelssohn concerto with Furtwängler, recorded – like the Beethoven concerto with which it is coupled – only months before the conductor's death. The digital transfer is first rate, though not ideally clear. One hardly registers that this is a mono recording from the early 1950s.

Zukerman's performances, both of the *Concerto* – with the solo part technically impeccable – and of the *Octet* are to some extent controversial, though undoubtedly fresh. The atmosphere of the *Concerto* with its simple lyricism is surprisingly classical, the chamber scale of the accompaniment playing down the work's romanticism. In the finale the focus is unusually clear with superb articulation all round. The *Octet* is presented in Zukerman's own arrangement using varying numbers of strings, usually multiples in outer movements, but reserving the slow movement for eight soloists. The effect is attractive but adds nothing to Mendelssohn's original. The sound is truthful within a comparatively dry acoustic, with fine clarity on CD. There is also a very good tape.

Ughi gives a fresh, athletic reading, totally unsentimental, with well-chosen speeds and very well accompanied. He lacks only the final individuality of artists like Mutter or Chung. The recording quality is excellent, clean, well balanced and set against a believable atmosphere.

The freshness of Accardo's style is most appealing; the outer movements are lithe and sparkling, and the *Andante*, taken slower than usual, is expressive in an unforced way. However, in remastering the 1976 recording, the upper range has thinned out and this also affects the solo timbre. Nevertheless, the sound remains acceptable, which it does not on the Bruch coupling.

Perlman's later version with Haitink is disappointing, not nearly so fresh and spontaneous-sounding as his earlier recording with Previn, with phrasing in the slow movement too heavily expressive. Nor does the digital recording bring an improvement for, apart from its edginess, it is badly balanced with the soloist far too close and the orchestra thin.

Stern's newest digital recording of the Mendelssohn *Concerto* cannot be recommended. It is meagre of tone, and the close balance and clarity of CD only make matters worse. There are, of course, moments when Stern's authority reasserts itself – the end of the slow movement is nicely managed – but a romantic concerto needs riper playing than this.

(i) *Violin concerto in E min., Op. 64;* (ii) *Symphony No. 4 in A* (*Italian*)*, Op. 90;* (iii) *A Midsummer Night's Dream: Overture and incidental music.*
(B) *** DG Walkman *413 150-4*. (i) Milstein, VPO, Abbado; (ii) BPO, Maazel; (iii) Mathis, Boese, Bav. RSO with Ch., Kubelik.

(i; ii; iii) *Violin concerto in E min., Op. 64;* (ii; iv) *Symphony No. 4* (*Italian*)*;* (v) *A Midsummer Night's Dream: Overture; Scherzo; Nocturne; Wedding march.*
(B) ** Ph. On Tour *412 902-4*. (i) Grumiaux; (ii) New Philh. O; (iii) Krenz; (iv) Sawallisch; (v) Concg. O, Haitink.

This attractive compilation is one of the outstanding bargains in DG's Walkman series of double-length chrome tapes, aimed at collectors with miniaturized personal cassette reproducers. Milstein's 1973 account of the *Violin concerto* is highly distinguished. With excellent recording and balance this is worthy to rank with the best, and it is greatly enhanced by the sensitivity of Abbado's accompaniment. Maazel's *Italian* offers a fast, hard-driven but joyous and beautifully articulated performance of the first movement and equal clarity and point in the vivacious finale. The central movements are well sustained, and altogether this is highly enjoyable, the recording resonantly full-timbred. Kubelik's fairly complete version of the incidental music for *A Midsummer Night's Dream* is no less enjoyable and the sound is first class here, too.

The Philips 'On Tour' collection offers much the same programme as the DG Walkman tape. Grumiaux's performance of the *Concerto* with Krenz is slightly disappointing, well played but a little bland. Sawallisch's account of the *Italian symphony* is also comparatively reticent in style. A fast tempo in the first movement for once does not sound breathless, and Sawallisch observes the exposition repeat and so lets us hear a score of bars in the first-time lead-back often neglected. However, the DG tape finds room for more of the *Midsummer Night's Dream* incidental music, and is generally preferable.

2 Concert pieces for clarinet, bassett horn and orchestra, Opp. 113–14.
*** HMV Dig. EL 270220-1/*4*. Sabine Meyer, Wolfgang Meyer, Württemberg CO, Jörg Faerber – BAERMANN: *Adagio*; WEBER: *Clarinet quintet*.***

The Mendelssohn pieces are recorded in a slightly drier acoustic than the Baermann. They are arrangements either by Mendelssohn himself or by Baermann's son, Carl, of pieces originally written for clarinet, bassett horn and piano. They are also available on Hyperion (A 66022), but in a totally different coupling. They are high-spirited and delightful, and most expertly played by Sabine Meyer and her brother, Wolfgang.

Symphonies Nos 1–5; Overtures: Fair Melusina, Op. 32; The Hebrides (Fingal's Cave), Op. 26; A Midsummer Night's Dream, Op. 21; Octet, Op. 20: Scherzo.
*** DG Dig. **415 353-2** (4); 415 353-1/*4* (4/*3*) [id.]. LSO, Abbado (with Connell, Mattila, Blochwitz and LSO Ch. in *Symphony No. 2*).

Abbado's is a set to brush cobwebs off an attractive symphonic corner. He made his reputation as a Mendelssohn interpreter on record with an outstanding coupling of the two most popular symphonies, the *Scottish* and the *Italian*, fresh and athletic; it was an excellent idea to have him do a complete series with the same orchestra. If this time in the *Italian* the speed and exhilaration of the outer movements occasionally hint at breathlessness (some might feel that the pacing of the finale, like the allegro of the *Midsummer Night's Dream overture*, is too fast), there is pure gain in the more flowing speed for the pilgrim's march second movement. In the *Scottish* his view has changed relatively little, and the performance gains this time from having the exposition repeat observed in the first movement. Otherwise it is Abbado's gift in the lesser-known symphonies to have you forgetting any weaknesses of structure or thematic invention in the brightness and directness of his manner. Instead of overloading this music with sweetness and sentiment, as the Victorians came to do, he presents it more as it must have appeared at the very beginning, when on good evidence the composer himself was known to favour brisk, light allegros and crisp rhythms. So the youthful *First* has plenty of C minor bite. The toughness of the piece makes one marvel that Mendelssohn ever substituted the scherzo from the *Octet* for the third movement (as he did in London), but helpfully Abbado includes that extra scherzo, so that on CD, with a programming device, you can readily make the substitution yourself. The *Hymn of praise*, *Lobgesang*, with the chorus in glowing form, loses most of its saccharine associations, with *Watchman, what of the night?* coming over operatically. Elizabeth Connell is the weighty-toned soprano soloist, singing with fine purity as well as power; she is joined by Karita Mattila in *I waited for the Lord* (using the original German) and by a superb newcomer, Hans-Peter Blochwitz, as an attractively light, clean-toned tenor. The CD has 75 minutes of music on it. On LP the couplings are different, and the exposition repeat of No. 1 (observed on CD) is omitted. Good, bright recording, though not ideally transparent. The chrome tapes are first class in every way and well laid out, with the exposition repeat of No. 1 included, as on CD. The chorus in the *Hymn of praise* is impressively focused, and there are no problems with the spectacular closing pages of the *Reformation symphony*.

Symphonies Nos 3 (Scottish); 4 (Italian) and 5 (Reformation). Overture: The Hebrides.
(M) **(*) DG 415 018-1/*4* (2) [id.]. Israel PO, Bernstein.

This grouping of Bernstein's Israel performances of the later Mendelssohn symphonies makes sense. The recordings were all made at live concerts and have the spontaneity that comes with 'live' music-making. The loving account of the *Scottish* with expansive tempi runs the risk of overloading Mendelssohn's inspiration with Romantic heaviness, making the slow introduction and the slow movement sound almost Mahlerian. But the rhythmic lift of scherzo and finale makes amends. The performances of both the *Italian* and *Reformation* are sparkling and attractive, and avoid the exaggerated expressiveness found in the *Scottish symphony*. Though speeds are often challengingly fast, they never fail to carry the exhilaration of the occasion. In the *Reformation symphony*, Bernstein encourages the flute to give a meditative account of the chorale *Ein feste Burg*, but he makes it a revelation, not a distraction. The performance of *Fingal's Cave* is also very successful. The recording is convincingly atmospheric and well balanced and the tapes are good, too, though the resonance brings moments when the focus slips, notably in the finale of the *Reformation symphony*.

Symphony No. 3 in A min. (Scottish), Op. 56; Overture: The Hebrides (Fingal's Cave), Op. 26.
(*) Hung. Dig. **HCD 12660-2 [id.]. Hungarian State O, Ivan Fischer.

Symphony No. 3 in A min. (Scottish), Op. 56; A Midsummer Night's Dream: Overture, Op. 21.
*** DG Dig. **415 973-2**; 415 973-1/*4* [id.]. LSO, Abbado.
** Orfeo Dig. **C 089841A**; S 089841A [id.]. Bav. RSO, Sir Colin Davis.

Symphonies Nos 3 (Scottish); 4 (Italian).
(*) Argo **411 931-2; ZRG/*KZRC* 926 [id.]. ASMF, Marriner.
(M) ** HMV ED 290579-1/*4*. Philh. O, Klemperer.
*(*) Decca Dig. **414 665-2**; 414 665-1/*4* [id.]. Chicago SO, Solti.

Abbado's account comes from his complete set (see above). It is admirably fresh, brightly recorded and also has the advantage of including the first-movement exposition repeat. The *Overture* is briskly paced but beautifully played.

A beautifully played performance from Sir Colin Davis and the Bavarian orchestra, with the *Midsummer Night's Dream* music also impressive in its detail. The sound too is refined, but in the last resort this has not the sparkle of the finest analogue versions.

Helped by recorded sound that is exceptionally full and immediate, Fischer conducts strong and dramatic readings of both *Symphony* and *Overture*. Generally, the playing is fresh and alert rather than refined, with string sound not ideally sweet, but the clarity and precision of the scherzo are a delight and the close balance adds to the internal clarity as in the horn semiquavers, normally obscured. The slow movement is on the heavy side, at a relatively brisk speed, but in the main pacing is unexceptionable. The *Overture* is spaciously done.

In Marriner's Argo performance, the *Adagio* of the *Scottish* is so spacious (arguably too much so, since the middle section grows heavy) that the finale had to be put on side two of the original LP. This means that the *Italian* is given without the exposition repeat and the twenty-bar lead-back. The performances are stylish and well sprung but have no special individuality. The use of a smaller-scaled ensemble brings a crisper, more transparent effect than usual. The recording is excellent, especially in the CD format. The tape has a less cleanly focused upper range than the LP or CD.

Klemperer is broad and expansive in the *Scottish symphony*, the approach almost Brahmsian. There is no denying the feeling of authority here, and the colourful scherzo and beautifully played *Adagio* come off well. But the last movement is more controversial, with its weighty closing pages refusing to catch fire. The *Italian symphony* is altogether more convincing. Klemperer takes the first movement substantially slower than we are used to, but this is no heavily monumental and humourless reading. The playing sparkles and has an incandescence which tends to outshine almost all other versions. There is again a slowish speed for the second movement, but the way Klemperer moulds and floats the main theme over the moving bass defeats all preconceptions in its sustained beauty. A fast tempo in the minuet, but still with wonderful phrasing; and it is the beautiful shaping of a phrase that makes the finale so memorable. There is no lack of exhilaration, yet no feeling of being rushed off one's feet. The recording has been freshened and detail clarified. The cassette is particularly successful.

Solti recorded both these symphonies very successfully in the early days of LP, but these high-powered, glossy readings are unsympathetic with little or no Mendelssohnian sparkle. Speeds are often very fast. The first movement of the *Italian* is so rushed that there is little spring in the rhythm, while the 6/8 coda or epilogue to the *Scottish* gallops along at an absurd speed. The sound is larger than life, with high strings aggressively bright. The coupling is generous, with exposition repeats observed in both symphonies.

Symphony No. 4 in A (Italian), Op. 90.
ᑕ *** DG Dig. **410 862-2**; 410 862-1/*4* [id.]. Philh. O, Sinopoli – SCHUBERT: *Symphony No. 8.**** ᑕ ❀

Symphonies Nos 4 (Italian); 5 in D (Reformation), Op. 107.
*** DG Dig. **415 974-2**; 415 974-1/*4* [id.]. LSO, Abbado.
(***) RCA [mono **RCCD 1007**]. NBC SO, Toscanini.
** Hung. Dig. **HCD 12414-2** [id.]. Hungarian State O, Ivan Fischer.
(M) ** Ph. Seq. 412 008–1/*4*. New Philh. O, Sawallisch.

Symphony No. 4. A Midsummer Night's Dream: Overture, Op. 21; Incidental music, Op. 61: Scherzo; Nocturne; Wedding march.
(M) *** Ph. 412 928-1/*4*. Boston SO, Sir Colin Davis.

Sinopoli's great gift is to illuminate almost every phrase afresh. His speeds tend to be extreme – fast in the first movement, but with diamond-bright detail, and on the slow side in the remaining three. Only in the heavily inflected account of the third movement is the result at all mannered but, with superb playing from the Philharmonia and excellent Kingsway Hall recording, this rapt performance is most compelling. Like the disc, the chrome cassette is first class, but for refinement of detail, especially at lower dynamic levels, the compact disc is among the most impressive digital recordings to have come from DG. Interestingly, the engineers achieve here a brighter lighting for the upper strings than is usual in this venue.

Abbado's coupling comes from his complete set, discussed above. Both performances are admirably fresh, though the pacing of the outer movements of the *Italian* is very brisk. But with fresh sound, this makes an easy first choice if you want both works together on CD.

On Philips, Sir Colin Davis provides a delightful Mendelssohn coupling, an exhilarating but never breathless account of the *Italian symphony* (complete with exposition repeat), coupled with the four most important items from the *Midsummer Night's Dream* music. Unlike so many versions of this symphony, this is not one which insists on brilliance at all costs, and the recording is warm and refined. One recognizes that the Philips engineers are working in Boston. Again there have been more delicate readings of the *Midsummer Night's Dream* pieces, but the ripeness of the Boston playing is most persuasive. The freshened 1976 recording offers a full yet lively orchestral balance. The cassette is particularly successful.

Toscanini's Mendelssohn performances were among the last he recorded and, though the brass is coarse and dry in the *Reformation*, the sound in both symphonies is among the best he received in his NBC period. The first movement of the *Italian* is very fast but remains exhilarating in its sprung rhythm, and the finale too is light and brilliant, with superb articulation. These are not performances that allow the music to relax much; however, the electric intensity in both symphonies is consistently compelling, with the *Reformation* made to appear a stronger structure than it is. This CD, specially issued in the USA, is not currently available in the UK except through a specialist importer.

With full and immediate sound as in the companion version of the *Scottish symphony*, Ivan Fischer's coupling of Nos 4 and 5 brings generally clean and direct readings of both symphonies, lacking only a degree of individuality, with rhythms sometimes too square.

Sawallisch's comparatively reticent Mendelssohnian style suits these two fine works quite well. With the exposition repeat included, the *Italian* is admirably fresh and the *Reformation* is a symphony that gains from not being over-inflated. The opening slow introduction with its quotation of the *Dresden Amen*, later used by Wagner in *Parsifal*, may suggest Mendelssohn in pontifical mood, but this is belied by the rest of the symphony. The remastered recording is full and clean, with a tape to match. On cassette, the expansive climax of the *Reformation symphony* remains well in focus.

PIANO MUSIC

Andante and rondo capriccioso in E min., Op. 14; Prelude and fugue in E minor/major, Op. 35/1; Sonata in E, Op. 6; Variations sérieuses in D min., Op. 53.
*** CBS Dig. IM/*IMT* 37838 [id.]. Murray Perahia.

The *Sonata* is modelled on the Beethoven Op. 101 and occupies the first side, the remaining pieces being accommodated on the reverse. In terms of delicacy and poetic feeling, Perahia is perfectly attuned to Mendelssohn's sensibility and it would be difficult to imagine these performances being surpassed. In Perahia's hands, the *Variations sérieuses* have tenderness yet tremendous strength, and neither the popular *Rondo capriccioso* nor the *Prelude and fugue* have sounded more fresh or committed on record. An essential issue for all who care about nineteenth-century piano music and who may have written off Mendelssohn's contribution to this medium. The quality of the CBS recording is very good indeed.

Fantasia in F sharp min. (Sonata écossaise), Op. 28; 3 Fantaisies du caprices, Op. 16; Rondo capriccioso in E, Op. 14; Sonata in E, Op. 6.
(*) Chan. **CHAN 8326; ABRD/*ABTD* 1081 [id.]. Artymiw.

Lydia Artymiw is highly persuasive in the *Sonata* as she is in the other works, which are by no means inconsequential. The *Fantasia* is a considerable piece and the three movements which make up Op. 16 are delightful, as is the more famous *Rondo capriccioso*, which sparkles. This is an altogether excellent disc, very well recorded, although it must be said that, fine though Miss Artymiw's playing is, she does not quite match Perahia in quality of imagination or subtlety of dynamic gradation. His are the finer accounts of the Op. 6 *Sonata* and the *Rondo capriccioso* (see above).

Songs without words Nos 1–48 (complete).
(M) *** DG 419 105-1/*4* (2) [id.]. Daniel Barenboim.

Barenboim is the ideal pianist for what were once regarded (for the most part wrongly) as faded Victorian trifles. Whether in the earlier, technically more difficult pieces or in the later simple inspirations, Barenboim conveys perfectly the sense of a composer relaxing. He himself seems to be rediscovering the music, regularly turning phrases with the imagination of a great artist, relishing the jewelled passage-work of many of the pieces in simple, easy virtuosity. Originally coupled on three discs with other music, the complete set is now available on a pair of mid-priced LPs or tapes, on which the sound is virtually identical. With such fine recording quality, this is a set to charm any listener.

Songs without words, Op. 19/1; Op. 30/6; Op. 38/6; Op. 62/1 and 6; Spring song, Op. 62/6; Spinning song, Op. 67/4; Op. 67/5; Op. 102/6.
*** DG **415 118-2** [id.]. Daniel Barenboim – LISZT: *Liebesträume****; SCHUBERT: *Moments musicaux.***

An admirable selection from Barenboim's fine 1974 complete set of the *Songs without words*, coupled with Liszt and Schubert. The playing is fresh and imaginative, and the excellent recording has transferred most naturally to CD.

ORGAN MUSIC

Organ sonatas Nos 2 in C min.; 3 in A; 6 in D min., Op. 65/1–6. Preludes and fugues: in C min.; in G; in D min., Op. 37/1–3.

❀ *** Argo Dig. **414 420-2**; 414 420-1/*4* [id.]. Peter Hurford (organ of Ratzeburg Cathedral).

Hurford's performances of Mendelssohn bring the same freshness of approach which made his Bach series so memorable. Indeed, the opening of the *Prelude and fugue in C minor* is given a Baroque exuberance, and he finds a similar identification in his magnificent account of the *Sixth Sonata*. Here Mendelssohn more than pays homage to Bach in his splendidly imaginative set of choral variations (and fugue) on *Vater unser* (Our Father). Throughout the recital the throaty reeds of the characterful Ratzeburg organ prevent any possible hint of blandness, yet in the *Andantes* – essentially songs without words for organ – the registration has engaging charm. The recording is superb, as the majestic opening of the *Third Sonata* immediately demonstrates, with the CD giving marvellous presence. There is an excellent chrome tape, but the focus of the CD has added tangibility.

VOCAL MUSIC

A Midsummer Night's Dream: Overture, Op. 21; Incidental music, Op. 61.

*** HMV **CDC 747163-2** [id.]; ASD/*TC-ASD* 3377 [Ang. S/*4XS* 37268] (complete). Watson, Wallis, Finchley Children's Music Group, LSO, Previn.

*** Ph. Dig. **411 106-2**; 411 106-1/*4* [id.]. Augér, Murray, Amb. S., Philh. O, Marriner.

(M) *** DG Gal. 415 840-1/*4* [id.]. Mathis, Boese, Bav. R. Ch. and SO, Kubelik – WEBER: *Overtures*.***

(*) HMV **CDC 747230-2; SXLP/*TC-SXLP* 30196 [Ang. AE/*4AE* 34445]. Harper, Baker, Philh. Ch. and O, Klemperer.

** RCA Dig. **RD 82084 [RCD1 2084]**. Blegen, Von Stade, Mendelssohn Club Ch., Phd. O, Ormandy.

** DG **415 137-2**; 415 137-1/*4* [id.]: (excerpts). Blegen, Quivar, Chicago Ch. and SO, Levine – SCHUBERT: *Rosamunde*.**

*(*) Denon Dig. **C37 7564** [id.]. Toyoda, Ohkura, Tokyo Ch. and Met. SO, Maag.

Previn offers a wonderfully refreshing account of the complete score; the veiled pianissimo of the violins at the beginning of the overture and the delicious woodwind detail in the *Scherzo* certainly bring Mendelssohn's fairies into the orchestra. Even the little melodramas which come between the main items sound spontaneous here, and the contribution of the soloists and chorus is first class. The *Nocturne* (taken slowly) is serenely romantic and the *Wedding march* resplendent. The recording is naturally balanced and has much refinement of detail. The CD brings the usual enhancement, with the fairy music in the

Overture given a most delicate presence. A clear first choice in all three formats.

Marriner's disc is complete except for the inconsequential melodramas which separate the main items. The *Overture*, taken briskly, has the lightest possible touch, with the most delicate articulation from the strings; the *Scherzo* too is engagingly infectious in its gentle bustle, and there is a complementary sense of joy and sparkle from soloists and chorus alike. The *Nocturne* is rather broadly romantic, yet the *Wedding march* sounds resplendent when the quality is so vivid. There is a brief cut at the end of the *Intermezzo* but, this apart, the Philips recording, warm as well as refined in detail, has much to recommend it; the CD brings the usual enhancement. There is a good chrome tape.

Among reissues, that by the Bavarian Radio Orchestra takes pride of place. The playing and 1965 recording (equally clear and clean on disc and cassette, yet not lacking atmosphere) are both strikingly fresh. Even with the advantage of economy, however, this does not displace Previn where the performance has extra imagination and sparkle (the *Nocturne*, too, is more romantic); but at medium price the DG version is still very attractive. Although Kubelik omits the melodramas, this makes room for an appropriate coupling of the two finest Weber overtures, both also associated with magic, and *Oberon* drawing an obvious parallel with Mendelssohn.

Klemperer's recording (which dates from 1961) was made when the Philharmonia was at its peak, and the orchestral playing is superb, the wind solos so nimble that even the *Scherzo*, taken slower than usual, has a light touch. The contribution of soloists (Heather Harper and Dame Janet Baker) and chorus is first class and the disc has the advantage of including the *Fairy march* and *Funeral march*. The quality is remarkably fresh and transparent, yet there is no lack of body. However, the LP and excellent tape are offered at mid-price.

The distinctive point about Ormandy's version is that it uses the German translation of Shakespeare (which is of course what Mendelssohn originally set), so that *You spotted snakes* has a straight quaver rhythm when it becomes *Bunte Schlagen*. The Philadelphia Orchestra's playing is light and brilliant, if not quite so infectiously pointed as in some versions. Ormandy includes most of the extra melodramas, but not in the usual order. The 1978 recording is among RCA's best from this source and sounds quite fresh, if by no means outstanding, in its new format.

Instead of doing the *Midsummer Night's Dream* music absolutely complete, Levine offers the *Overture* and six main items (the *Scherzo*, *You spotted snakes*, *Intermezzo*, *Nocturne*, *Wedding march* and *Finale*), all well done and with excellent singing from soloists and chorus. This leaves room for three of Schubert's *Rosamunde* pieces. Recorded sound better than most from this source, most vivid on CD but with an excellent chrome tape.

Maag offers less music than Ormandy and, though he is better recorded (the Denon CD sounds impressive) and also uses the German text, otherwise the Japanese performance has less felicity, with unmemorable soloists. In the *Overture* there are some curious agogic pauses before certain emphatic chords, including some of Bottom's 'hee-haws'. The Japanese orchestral playing is meticulous rather than magical.

Psalms Nos 42: Wie der Hirsch schreit, Op. 42; 95: Kommt, lasst uns anbeten, Op. 46; 115: Nicht unserm Namen, Herr, Op. 31.
(*) Erato **ECD 88120 [id.]. Baumann, Silva, Brunner, Ihara, Blaser, Ramirez, Huttenlocher, Lisbon Gulbenkian Foundation Ch. and O, Corboz.

These performances appeared in the late 1970s on two different LPs (Psalms 42 and 95 on STU 71101, and 115 together with other pieces on STU 71123). The compact disc, which runs to 70 minutes, is able to accommodate all three – and very beautiful they are, too. They have been generally underrated by critics and scholars. The singers are mostly excellent, particularly Christiane Baumann in Nos 42 (*Wie der Hirsch schreit*) and 95 (*Kommt, lasst uns anbeten*); the only problem here is the vibrato of Pierre-André Blaser in Psalm 95 which will not enjoy universal appeal. Philippe Huttenlocher is however impressive in No. 115, and both the choral singing and the orchestral playing are of quality. The acoustic is warm and spacious, and the balance between the solo singers and the chorus and orchestra is excellently judged. The sound is not spectacular or in the demonstration category but, more important, it is musically satisfying.

Menotti, Gian-Carlo (born 1911)

(i) *The Medium* (complete); (ii) *The Telephone* (complete).
(**) CBS mono M2P/*MPT* 39532 (2/*1*) [Odys. Y2-35239]. (i) Marie Powers, Keller, Dame, Rogier, Mastice; (ii) Marilyn Cotlow, Rogier; O, Balaban.

In default of modern stereo versions, these mono recordings with the original Broadway cast of Menotti's double-bill fill an obvious gap, though the dryness of sound and absence of theatrical atmosphere expose the musical limitations of the scores and, apart from Marie Powers as the larger-than-life central character of *The Medium*, singing is undistinguished. *The Medium* may be the more striking of the two, but in most ways the charming duet-piece, *The Telephone*, is the more rewarding. The cassette transfer uses one extended-length tape, but *The Medium* is split between sides, so the advantage of this convenient layout is negated. The sound is clear.

Mercadante, Saverio (1795–1870)

Clarinet concerto in B flat.
*** Claves **CD 50-813** [id.]. Friedli, SW German CO, Angerer – MOLTER; PLEYEL: *Concertos.****

Mercadante's *Concerto* is the slightest of the three works played on this CD by Thomas Friedli, the excellent principal clarinettist of the Berne Symphony Orchestra. Its two movements consist of an *Allegro maestoso* and a *galant Andante with variations*. But the music is agreeably fluent and very well played by the soloist. An interesting collection of works, showing the development of the clarinet as a solo instrument.

Messager, André (1853–1929)

Les deux pigeons (ballet): complete.
**(*) HMV ASD 270038-1/*4* [id.]. Bournemouth SO, Lanchbery.

Messager's ballet (1886) was originally choreographed by Louis Merante, who had made his reputation with Delibes' *Sylvia*, and was based on a fable by Jean de la Fontaine. For the 1961 Royal Ballet production, Frederick Ashton discarded the original scenario in favour of a completely new narrative line with a nineteenth-century ambience. This involved considerable revision of the score; and the final scene, which contains some of the more memorable music, is a reconstruction by Lanchbery. The score overall is pretty but lightweight, but Act II is distinctly more rewarding than Act I. The performance is first class and the recording has an attractive warmth as well as a realistic overall balance. On tape, side one loses something in range and definition, but the level rises on the second side, giving added brightness and a sharper focus.

Still recommended: For most listeners the suite from *The Two Pigeons* encapsulates much of the best of the score; on HMV, Jacquillat's sparkling performance is generously coupled – at mid-price – with music from another attractive ballet, *Isoline*, plus Pierné's piquant *March of the little lead soldiers* and Berlioz's spectacular arrangement of *La Marseillaise* (all verses included) for soloists, choirs and orchestra (ESD 7048).

Messiaen, Olivier (born 1908)

L'Ascension.
** ASV ALH 936 [id.]. Francis Grier (organ) – FRANCK: *Chorale No. 3*.

Francis Grier is recorded on the organ of Christ Church Cathedral, Oxford; although his playing is altogether first class, he is handicapped by the dry acoustic which is unappealing. It is a tribute to his artistry that the performance sounds as atmospheric as it does.

Still recommended: Jennifer Bate's Unicorn recording of *L'Ascension* (on the organ of St Pierre de Beauvais Cathedral) is coupled with *L'Apparition de l'église éternelle* in performances of hypnotic concentration, superbly recorded (Unicorn DKP 9015 [id.]).

La Nativité du Seigneur (9 meditations)
(M) **(*) Decca Lon. Ent. 414 436-1/*4* [id.]. Simon Preston (organ of Westminster Abbey).

Simon Preston is a convinced advocate of this score and conveys its hypnotic power most successfully. The recording reproduces with great fidelity, although the organ and ambience of Westminster Abbey accommodate the music less readily than a French location. The high-level cassette gives the organ fine presence, although there is a touch of fierceness on fortissimos.

Still recommended: 'C'est vraiment parfait!' was the composer's comment after hearing Jennifer Bate's superb Beauvais recording of this work. The sound is of demonstration quality and the disc received a Rosette in our last edition. No doubt it will shortly appear on CD (Unicorn DKP 9005).

Préludes; Pièce pour le tombeau de Paul Dukas.
*** Unicorn Dig. DKP/*DKPC* 9037 [id.]. Peter Hill (piano).

The eight *Préludes* are early works written while Messiaen was studying composition at the Paris Conservatoire with Paul Dukas. Though there is a residual influence of Debussy, these *Préludes* still have a great deal of originality and are obviously the work of a strong personality. They are played with great sensitivity by Peter Hill, who is beautifully recorded. The sleeve announces that Peter Hill is engaged on recording the complete piano works of Messiaen for Unicorn Kanchana; if the remainder are as good as this, the set will be self-recommending. His approach is gentler and more contemplative than Michel Béroff's EMI set coupled with the *Études* (2C 069,16229), and the recording is certainly superior. It sounds particularly impressive in its chrome tape format, with the piano image completely truthful and very little background noise.

Milhaud, Darius (1892–1974)

Le carnaval d'Aix. Suite provençale, Suite française.
*(*) HMV Dig. EL 270088-1/*4* [Ang. DS/*4DS* 38121]. Béroff, Monte Carlo PO, Prêtre.

It is difficult to understand why Milhaud's *Le carnaval d'Aix* does not enjoy greater popularity: it has immense charm and an engaging easy-going Mediterranean sense of gaiety that never ceases to captivate. Michel Béroff's is the first recording of it for more than two decades, and it comes here with the endearing *Suite provençale* and the *Suite française* as companions. Earlier versions have never been entirely satisfying nor done it full justice, so on the face of it this is a welcome issue. In reality, however, it proves something of a disappointment: Béroff rattles off the solo part without a trace of charm and without that tenderness that is at times called for. The orchestral playing under Georges Prêtre is fairly brash too, and the sound does not really help very much: it is inclined to be dry and close. There is a faithful cassette.

Still recommended: Claude Helffer's 1962 recording of *Le carnaval* with the Monte Carlo orchestra under Frémaux (DG 2543 807) remains the best buy for this attractive work, coupled – at mid-price – with Roussel's *Bacchus and Ariadne suite No. 2* and Satie's *Parade*. The recording still sounds very good.

String quartets: Nos 2, 6 and 15.
*(*) Cybelia CY 653 [id.]. Arcana Qt.

The *Second String quartet*, dating from 1915, occupies the whole of one side and is a five-movement work which Milhaud dedicated to his friend, the poet Léon Latil, whose death later that year prompted the composition of the *Third*. The *Second* has good things in it and, in more persuasive hands, might make a stronger impression; but no such reservations extend to the *Sixth*, Op. 77, written at Aix-en-Provence in 1922 and dedicated to Poulenc. The three movements are all short and full of those tuneful scraps that periodically seem to collide with one another in a characteristic Milhaudesque fashion. It is a delightful piece and deserves a better performance. The *Fifteenth* is designed to be played either together with the *Fourteenth* or, as it is here, on its own. It dates from 1948 and is not Milhaud at his best. As in the companion records, the music is not given with great finesse or polish by the Arcana Quartet but there are no alternative versions currently available.

String quartets Nos (i) *3; 4, 9, 12, 14 and 17.*
*(*) Cybelia CY 651-2 [id.]. Arcana Qt; (i) with Nicole Oxombre.

It was Milhaud's declared ambition to compose eighteen string quartets, one more than Beethoven, an achievement he had already fulfilled by 1950. He was enormously prolific and his opus list extends to well over 400 entries. Needless to say, much of his music is uneven in quality and the limitations of the performances here do not help matters. The *Seventeenth Quartet*, Op. 307, of 1950 comes dangerously close to note-spinning. Generally speaking, the earlier quartets are the freshest and musically most rewarding. Readers who associate Milhaud exclusively with the carefree 1920s will find surprising depth in the *Third Quartet*, particularly in the sombre first movement. This is a moving and often beautiful lament for the poet, Léon Latil, and the second of the two movements sets one of his poems. Schoenberg had included a soprano in the last movement of his *Second Quartet* of 1908 but Milhaud was unacquainted with the Schoenberg piece at this time. It is possible to imagine a more sympathetic advocate of the vocal role than Nicole Oxombre. The *Fourth Quartet*, Op. 46 (1918), is quite different, and not dissimilar in style to the more familiar *Seventh*, which has been twice recorded before. It comes from the period when the composer was serving at the French Embassy in Rio de Janeiro as secretary to Paul Claudel. No. 9, Op. 140, comes from the following decade (1935) and is a beautiful and affecting piece, worth having for the gentle lyricism of its opening movement, though its successor degenerates into note-spinning. Milhaud wrote the *Twelfth Quartet*, Op. 252, to mark the centenary of Fauré's birth in 1945, and Nos 14 and 15 three years later. They share the same opus number, 291. They are better apart than together, though it must be admitted that they are stronger on ingenuity than inspiration. No 12, however, is a short and gentle piece, well worth a place in the repertoire. The Arcana Quartet unfortunately sound distinctly lacklustre and suffer from moments of queasy intonation. The recording, too, though acceptable, is not particularly flattering.

Milner, Anthony (born 1925)

Symphony No. 1, Op. 28; Variations for orchestra, Op. 14.
*** Hyp. A 66158 [id.]. BBC SO, Lionel Friend.

An important record. Anthony Milner is in his early sixties and has enjoyed little representation on disc. His *Variations for orchestra* date from the late 1950s and his *Symphony* (1965–71) was commissioned by the BBC. The *Symphony* is the more demanding work, but it is eminently approachable and full of haunting resonances. His work is infused with a strong religious fervour and there is also a keen feeling for nature. It has the luminous quality of Tippett, the same gravity of address and finished craftsmanship of such neoclassical figures as Walter Piston, Vagn Holmboe or Robert Simpson and (unlike much contemporary music) it leaves one wanting to hear it again. The *Symphony* is a most powerful score and its world grows more distinctive at each hearing. The *Variations* are highly inventive, and readers should investigate this music for themselves, for this is the work of a powerful musical mind. The BBC Symphony Orchestra give committed performances under Lionel Friend and the recording is clean and well balanced.

Moeran, Ernest J. (1894–1950)

Violin concerto.
*** Lyr. SRCS 10 [id.]. Georgiadis, LSO, Handley.

With more overtones of Delius than is usual in Moeran's music, this enjoyable *Violin concerto* may not be the most striking of his works but, in a performance as committed and stylish as this, the ambitious three-movement span makes an attractive rarity for anyone with a taste for an English idiom. Georgiadis, for years the outstanding leader of the LSO, here shows his virtuosity and expressiveness both in the lyrical outer movements and in the central scherzo; Vernon Handley is, as ever, the most sympathetic of concerto conductors. First-rate recording.

Symphony in G min.; Lonely Waters; Whythorne's Shadow.
(M) *** HMV ED 290187-1/4 [Pathé, id.]. E. Sinfonia, Dilkes.

Moeran's superb *Symphony in G minor* was written between 1934 and 1937. It is in the best English tradition of symphonic writing and worthy to rank with the symphonies of Vaughan Williams and Walton, with which it has much in common. But for all the echoes of these composers (and Holst and Butterworth too) it has a strongly individual voice. There is no question of the quality of the invention throughout the lyrical sweep of the first two movements, and in the rhythmically extrovert and genial scherzo. If the structure and atmosphere of the finale are unmistakably Sibelian – there is a striking passage very like the climax in *Tapiola* – it makes a cogent and satisfying close to a very rewarding work. Dilkes's fine, lusty performance is in many ways complementary to Boult's radiantly opulent Lyrita recording (SRCS 70), setting out more urgently, if without quite the subtlety of rubato that the veteran conductor draws from his bigger orchestra. With a smaller string band recorded relatively close, the sound is vivid and immediate, if lacking a little in atmosphere compared with the Lyrita disc. The two lovely orchestral miniatures are most beautifully played and recorded and make a very worthwhile bonus. Dilkes's reissue is at medium-price and excellent value – even if, for the *Symphony,* Boult's record remains first choice.

Cello sonata in A min.; Prelude for cello and piano. Piano pieces: *Bank Holiday; 2 Legends* (*A Folk Story; Rune*)*; Prelude and Berceuse; Stalham River; Toccata; The White Mountain.*
**(*) Lyr. SRCS 42. Peers Coetmore, Eric Parkin.

Peers Coetmore brings a dedicated intensity to the *Cello sonata,* which her husband wrote for her in 1948, not long before he died. It is thoughtful and introspective music, well worth getting to know. The piano pieces, which date from the 1920s, are less distinctive but fresh and enjoyable in their English adaptation of Debussian trends. Excellent 1972 recording.

Molter, Johann (1696–1765)

Clarinet concerto in D.
*** Claves **CD 50-813** [id.]. Friedli, SW German CO, Angerer – MERCADANTE; PLEYEL: *Concertos.****

Molter's *Concerto* is for D clarinet and its high tessitura means that it is a piece readily appropriated by trumpeters of the calibre of Maurice André. Heard on a modern version of the instrument for which it was written, the timbre sounds uncannily like a soft-grained trumpet – and very effective, too, especially when the playing is both expert and sympathetic. It is very much a Baroque concerto (with flavours of Bach and Handel) and well worth having on CD. The accompaniment is good rather than outstanding, and though the CD gives the soloist good projection, and both he and the orchestra are heard within a pleasing ambience, orchestral detail is not ideally clear and the harpsichord contribution is only just audible. Nevertheless, this remains a most enjoyable collection, for the coupled works are equally interesting.

Mompou, Federico (born 1893)

Cançons i dansas; Impresiones intimas; Música callada IV; Preludio VII a Alicia de Larrocha.
❀ *** Decca Dig. 410 287-1/*4*. Alicia de Larrocha.

The Catalan composer, Federico Mompou, is now in his mid-nineties and still living in Barcelona. This is gentle, reflective music which brings peace to the listener. Its quiet ruminative quality finds an eloquent exponent in Alicia de Larrocha, to whom Mompou in 1951 dedicated one of his preludes. The *Impresiones intimas* date from 1911–14 and is his first work of note. Like Falla and Turina, Mompou was drawn to Paris, and these pieces have absorbed something of the delicacy of Debussy. The French critic, Emile Vuillermoz, acclaimed him as a poet, who 'searches in his enchantments and spells wherewith to compound his magic songs. His formulae are short, concise, concentrated, but they possess a weird, hallucinating power of evocation.' This is a record to dip into rather than play all the way through: these quietly pensive musings can easily seem aimless and inconsequential if they are heard in an unsympathetic mood. Each piece needs to be savoured in its own right and in the proper framework before its poetic feeling or its fine detail and well-calculated proportions make their full effect. (When in Barcelona, R.L. was told that Mompou was still an active concert-goer until very recently – and claims never to have gone to bed before 3 a.m. for the whole of his life!) Alicia de Larrocha plays these poetic miniatures *con amore*, and the Decca recording is quite superb on both disc and tape. Let us hope that Decca will eventually release it on CD.

Monn, Georg Matthias (1717–50)

Cello concerto in D (arr. Schoenberg).
*** CBS Dig. **MK 39863**; IM/*IMT* 39863 [id.]. Yo-Yo Ma, Boston SO, Ozawa – STRAUSS, R.: *Don Quixote*.**(*)

As a fill-up to his *Don Quixote*, Yo-Yo Ma gives us an interesting rarity. In 1912 Guido Adler asked Schoenberg to edit a *Cello concerto* by Monn for publication in the *Denkmäler der Tonkunst in Oesterreich*. Two decades later, as a token of thanks for Casals' hospitality in inviting him to conduct the Barcelona Orchestra, Schoenberg made a free transcription for cello and orchestra of another Monn concerto, albeit for keyboard. His letter was at pains to stress that 'nowhere is it atonal'. In a sense it can be compared with Strauss's *Couperin suite*, though Schoenberg's scoring varies from a Regerian delicacy to altogether thicker sonorities. It is beautifully played and recorded.

Monteverdi, Claudio (1567–1643)

Ab aeterno ordinata sum; Confitebor tibi, Domine (3 settings); *Deus tuorum militum sors et corona; Iste confessor Domini sacratus; Laudate Dominum, O omnes gentes; La Maddalena: Prologue: Su le penne de venti. Nisi Dominus aedificaverit domum.*

❀ *** Hyp. Dig. **CDA 66021**; A/*KA* 66021. Kirkby, Partridge, Thomas, Parley of Instruments.

There are few records of Monteverdi's solo vocal music as persuasive as this. The three totally contrasted settings of *Confitebor tibi* (Psalm 110) reveal an extraordinary range of expression, each one drawing out different aspects of word-meaning. Even the brief trio *Deus tuorum militum* has a haunting memorability – it could become to Monteverdi what *Jesu, joy of man's desiring* is to Bach – and the performances are outstanding, with the edge on Emma Kirkby's voice attractively presented in an aptly reverberant acoustic. The accompaniment makes a persuasive case for authentic performance on original instruments. The cassette (issued some time after the disc had become something of a best-seller in its field) gives the performers a natural presence and is very well balanced. The CD does not differ greatly from the LP and cassette; in fact, this sounds superb in all three media.

Concerti spirituali: Audi caelum; Exsulta filia, Salve Regina. Madrigals: *Augellin che la voce al canto spieghi; Mentre vaga Angioletta; Ninfa che scalza il piede; O mio bene; Se vittorie si belle; Vaga su spina ascosa; Zefiro torna.*

** DG Arc. **415 295-2** [id.]. Nigel Rogers, Ian Partridge, Keyte, Ens. Jürgens.

All these recordings date from the early 1970s and are tenor duets with continuo support, with or without a bass. Nigel Rogers has great style and virtuosity – though there is a certain dryness about the vocal timbre that tires the ear. Ian Partridge and Christopher Keyte are no less skilled, but Jürgen Jürgens does opt for rather brisk tempi. A useful but not indispensable addition to the Monteverdi discography on CD. Good recorded sound.

Selva morale e spirituale: *Beatus vir a 6; Confitebor tibi; Deus tuorum militum a 3; Dixit Dominus a 8; Domine a 3; Jubilet tota civitas; Laudate dominum a 5; Laudate pueri a 5; Magnificat a 8; Salve Regina a 3.*

** HMV **CDC 747016-2** [id.]; ASD/*TC-ASD* 143539-1/*4* [Ang. S/*4XS* 38030]. Kirkby, Rogers, Covey-Crump, Thomas, Taverner Cons. Ch. and Players, Parrott.

There is some fine singing from Emma Kirkby and Nigel Rogers, and the recorded sound is very good. The performances really need more breadth and grandeur, and there is at times a somewhat bloodless quality about the singing of some of the pieces; but there is enough to admire, such as the attractive account of *Salve Regina* and the opening *Dixit Dominus*. The XDR cassette and

LP are virtually identical in sound, both offering the highest quality. The CD adds to the clarity and presence, but tends to emphasize minor faults of balance between instruments and voices, and suggest to the ear that a little more spaciousness in the acoustic would have given the music making (even with these comparatively small numbers) more amplitude. Even so, this collection is well worth considering.

Madrigals: *Bel pastor dal cui bel guardo; Lamento D'Arianna; Non è di gentil core; O come sei gentile; Ohimé, dov'é il mio ben?; Zefiro torna.*
* HM **HMC 901129** [id.]. Concerto Vocale – FERRARI: *Queste pungenti spine.**

These Monteverdi madrigals are not, as yet, well represented on CD; even so, these performances are not distinguished enough to displace the LPs most collectors will have on their shelves. Helga Müller-Molinari's approach is too redolent of grand opera to carry real conviction and does not readily blend with the instrumental support.

Canti amorosi: Mentre vaga Angioletta; Lamento della ninfa. Il combattimento di Tancredi e Clorinda. Ogni amante e guerrier.
(*) Tel. Dig. **ZK8. 43054; AZ6/*CX4*. 43054 [id.]. Hollweg, Schmidt, Palmer, Murray, Perry, Langridge, VCM, Harnoncourt.

Harnoncourt conducts sharply characterized readings of substantial items from Monteverdi's eighth Book of Madrigals plus two *Canti amorosi*. The substantial scena telling of the conflict of Tancredi and Clorinda is made sharply dramatic in a bald way. *Ogni amante a guerrier*, almost as extended, is treated with similar abrasiveness, made attractively fresh but lacking subtlety. The two *Canti amorosi* are treated quite differently, in a much warmer style, with the four sopranos of *Mentre vaga Angioletta* producing sensuous sounds. *Lamento della ninfa*, perhaps the most celebrated of all Monteverdi's madrigals, brings a luscious performance with the solo voice (Ann Murray) set evocatively at a slight distance behind the two tenors and a bass. On CD the recording is extremely vivid, with voices and instruments firmly and realistically placed. No translations are given, only the Italian text of *Tancredi e Clorinda*. This is not, however, included with the cassette, a very bright high-level transfer, putting a degree of edge on the male voices at higher dynamic levels.

Lamento d'Olympia; Maladetto sia l'aspetto; Ohimè ch'io cado; Quel sdengosetto; Voglio di vita uscia.
*** Hyp. A 66106. Emma Kirkby, Anthony Rooley (chitarone) – D'INDIA: *Lamento d'Olympia* etc. ***

A well-planned recital from Hyperion contrasts the two settings of *Lamento d'Olympia* by Monteverdi and his younger contemporary, Sigismondo d'India. The performances by Emma Kirkby, sensitively supported by Anthony Rooley, could hardly be surpassed and her admirers can be assured that this ranks among her best records. Its claims, apart from excellence, reside as much as anything else in the sheer interest of the pieces by Sigismondo d'India.

Vespro della Beata Vergine (*Vespers*).

*** HMV Dig. **CDS 747078-8** [id.]; EX 270129-3/*5* (2) [Ang. DSB/*4D2S* 3963]. Emma Kirkby, Nigel Rogers, David Thomas, Taverner Ch. Cons. and Players, Canto Gregoriano, Parrott.

*** Decca **414 572-2** [id.]; SET 593/4. Jill Gomez, Felicity Palmer, James Bowman, Robert Tear, Philip Langridge, John Shirley-Quirk, Michael Rippon, Monteverdi Ch. and O, Salisbury Cathedral Boys' Ch., Jones Brass Ens., Munrow Recorder Cons., Gardiner.

** Erato **ECD 88024** (2) [id.]. Jennifer Smith, Michael Evans, Elwes, Huttenlocher, Brodard, Lausanne Vocal Ens. and Instrumental Ens., Corboz.

Though Andrew Parrott uses minimal forces, with generally one instrument and one voice per part, so putting the work on a chamber scale in a small church setting, its grandeur comes out superbly through its very intensity. Far more than usual with antiphons in Gregorian chant it becomes a liturgical celebration, so that the five non-liturgical compositions or concerti are added to the main Vesper setting as a rich glorification. They are brilliantly sung here by the virtuoso soloists, above all by Nigel Rogers, whose distinctive timbre may not suit every ear but who has an airy precision and flexibility to give expressive meaning to even the most taxing passages. Fine singing from Parrott's chosen groups of players and singers, and warm, atmospheric recording, with an ecclesiastical ambience which yet allows ample detail; this is particularly beautiful and clear on CD, which is made more convenient to use by the banding. The high-level tape transfer is also first class.

'The grand quasi-theatrical design of this spectacular work has always seemed compelling to me,' says John Eliot Gardiner, and his fine set presents the music very much in that light. The recording was made in 1974, before Gardiner had been won over entirely to the claims of the authentic school. Modern instruments are used and women's voices, but Gardiner's rhythms are so resilient that the result is more exhilarating as well as grander. The whole span of the thirteen movements sweeps you forward with a sense of complete unity. Singing and playing are exemplary, and the recording is one of Decca's most vividly atmospheric. The digital remastering for CD is superb, with relatively large forces presented and placed against a helpful, reverberant acoustic. The grandeur, drama and incisiveness of Gardiner's reading are formidably reinforced, making this in many ways a safer recommendation than the more 'authentic' approach of Parrott on HMV.

Corboz's version is reverential rather than dramatic, genial and smooth with little feeling of grandeur, despite the spacious church acoustic. Like Parrott on his EMI version, Corboz includes antiphons, freshly sung by the boys of Notre Dame de Sion, and the team of soloists is a strong one, but rhythms are pointed consistently less crisply than in the two rival versions. The recording is full and atmospheric, though there are too few bands on the CDs.

OPERA AND OPERA-BALLET

Il Combattimento di Tancredi e Clorinda. L'Arianna: Lasciatemi Morire (*Ariadne's lament*) (with FARINA: *Sonata* (*La Desperata*). ROSSI: *Sonata sopra l'aria di Ruggiero.* FONTANA: *Sonata a tre violini.* MARINI: *Passacaglia a 4. Sonata sopra la Monica; Eco a tre violini.* BUONAMENTE: *Sonata a tre violini*).
(*) DG Arc. **415 296-2 [id.]. Watkinson, Rogers, Kwella, David Thomas, Col. Mus. Ant., Goebel.

Under Reinhard Goebel, the Cologne Musica Antiqua using original instruments has built up a formidable reputation on record, and these tasteful performances of two masterly Monteverdi settings, coupled with sonatas by Monteverdi's contemporaries, are welcome. Carolyn Watkinson's singing of the *Lament* is finely controlled and certainly dramatic. So too is the performance of the touching and powerfully imaginative narrative about the battle of Tancredi and Clorinda, which understandably moved the audience to tears at its première. The other pieces are of more mixed appeal. Highlights are Fontana's engaging *Sonata for three violins* and Marini's ingenious *Eco a tre violini*, which is performed here to great effect, with the imitations echoing into the distance. Elsewhere, the slightly spiky sounds produced by the string players, with the close microphones bringing a touch of edginess, may not appeal to all tastes. The transfers of the 1979 analogue recordings are impeccably managed. Full texts and notes are provided.

Ballet e balletti: *Orfeo: Lasciate i monti; Vieni imeneo; Ecco pur ch'a voi ritrno; Moresca. Tirsi e Clori: ballet. Scherzo musicali: Il ballo delle ingrate; De la bellezza la dovute lodi; Volgendo il ciel.*
(*) Erato **ECD 88032; NUM/*MCE* 75068 [id.]. Kwella, Rolfe-Johnson, Dale, Woodrow, Monteverdi Ch., E. Bar. Soloists, Gardiner.

This is in effect a Monteverdi sampler; while the mosaic from *Orfeo*, for instance, may not suit the specialist listener, it makes delightful listening when the singing is so fresh. The music from the famous *Il ballo delle ingrate* is very short (about 3½ minutes) and seems pointless out of context; but all the rest, notably the choral ballet from *Tirsi e Clori*, is most engaging with its changes of mood: sometimes dolorous, sometimes gay and spirited. Gardiner's direction, as always, is vivid and his pacing lively; there is much to titillate the ear in the spicy vocal and orchestral colouring. The balance is fairly close, but the overall perspective is well defined, within a warm acoustic. On CD, this sounds especially well.

Orfeo (opera): complete.
*** HMV Dig. **CDS 747142-8** [id.]; EX 270131-3/*5* (2) [Ang. DSBX/*4D2X* 3964]. Nigel Rogers, Patrizia Kwella, Emma Kirkby, Jennifer Smith, Stephen Varcoe, David Thomas, Chiaroscuro, L. Bar. Ens., L. Cornett and Sackbut Ens., Rogers and Medlam.
** Tel. **ZA8 35020** (2); FK 6.35020 (3) [id.]. Kozma, Hansmann, Katanosaka, Berberian, Rogers, Equiluz, Van Egmond, Villisech, Mun. Capella Antiqua, VCM, Harnoncourt.

*(*) Erato Dig. **ECD 88133**; NUM/*MCE* 75212 (2) [id.]. Quilico, Michael, Watkinson, Voutsinos, Tappy, Chapelle Royal Vocal Ens., Lyons Op. O, Corboz.

Nigel Rogers – who recorded the role of Orfeo ten years earlier for DG Archiv – in the EMI Reflexe version has the double function of singing the main part and acting as co-director. In the earlier recording under Kurt Jürgens, ample reverberation tended to inflate the performance but, this time in a drier acoustic, Rogers has modified his extraordinarily elaborate ornamentation in the hero's brilliant pleading aria before Charon, and makes the result all the freer and more wide-ranging in expression, with his distinctive fluttering timbre adding character. With the central singer directing the others, the concentration of the whole performance is all the greater, telling the story simply and graphically. The sound of thunder that fatefully makes Orpheus turn round as he leads Euridice back to earth is all the more dramatic for being drily percussive; and Euridice's plaint, beautifully sung by Patrizia Kwella, is the more affecting for being accompanied very simply on the lute. The other soloists make a good team, though Jennifer Smith as Proserpine, recorded close, is made to sound breathy. The brightness of the cornetti is a special delight, when otherwise the instrumentation used – largely left optional in the score – is modest. Excellent, immediate recording, at its finest on CD, but the cassettes too are outstanding. Transferred at the highest level they are very much in the demonstration class.

In Harnoncourt's version, the Ritornello of the Prologue might almost be by Stravinsky, so sharply do the sounds cut. He is an altogether more severe Monteverdian than Nigel Rogers. In compensation, the simple and straightforward dedication of this performance is most affecting, and the solo singing, if not generally very characterful, is clean and stylish. One exception to the general rule on characterfulness comes in the singing of Cathy Berberian as the Messenger. She is strikingly successful and, though slightly differing in style from the others, she sings as art of the team. Excellent restrained recording, as usual in Harnoncourt's remastered Telefunken CD series, projecting the performance even more vividly than on LP. The extra clarity and sharpness of focus – even in large-scale ensembles – adds to the abrasiveness from the opening *Toccata* onwards, and the 1969 recording certainly sounds immediate, with voices very realistic.

Corboz's version was recorded as a by-product of a successful staging of the piece at the Aix-en-Provence Festival, and the approach is more conventionally operatic than in most current versions, with the baritone, Gino Quilico, singing the name part in an almost verismo manner, so that *Possente spirito* is made lachrymose. Textures tend to be rich, opulent even, with sweet string-tone, and Corboz attempts, misguidedly, to exaggerate speeds in the dramatic interludes, ritornellos and sinfonias, but without making them sharp enough. The singing, solo and choral, is variably successful, with Carolyn Watkinson the most stylish as the Messenger, and Frangiskos Voutsinos the least effective in the two bass roles of Charon and Pluto. Ample recording, too reverberant for this music.

Collection: *Et è pur dunque vero; Ohimè ch'io cado; L'Incoronazione di Poppea: Disprezzata regina; Addio Roma.*
(*) Erato Dig. **ECD 88100; NUM/*MCE* 75183 [id.]. Frederica von Stade, SCO, Leppard – CAVALLI: *Arias.***(*)

Frederica von Stade sings these Monteverdi songs and arias stylishly and freshly. She is at her best in the delightful *Et è pur dunque vero*, while at the opening of *Addio Roma*, with its dramatic short pauses, the colouring of her lower register is telling. Here Leppard's accompaniment increases the tension, and elsewhere he gives admirable support. The recording gives the voice a strong presence and the overall balance is very good too, with an excellent chrome cassette to match the disc versions. Other accounts of the two *Poppea* excerpts have shown greater expressive ardour; however, this recital, with its attractive Cavalli coupling, still gives much pleasure. It would have been even greater had translations of the Italian texts been provided; as it is, the documentation is poor.

Moreno-Buendia, Manuel (born 1932)

Suite concertante (for harp and orchestra).
(*) Decca Dig. 411 738-1/*4* [id.]. Robles, Philh. O, Dutoit – RODRIGO: *Concierto de Aranjuez.**

Manuel Moreno-Buendia was a fellow student of Marisa Robles at the Madrid Royal Conservatory, and he wrote his *Suite* for her in 1958. The five movements are all titled: the opening *Portico* is brief and not sharply defined, the *Legend* is atmospheric; but the most memorable section is the fourth, *Troubadouresque*, which is quite imaginative. Overall, though pleasing, the music does not have the individuality of Rodrigo. Miss Robles is an eloquent advocate and she is attractively recorded, in a warm acoustic. There is an excellent chrome cassette.

Morgan, David (born 1933)

(i) *Violin concerto. Contrasts.*
*** Lyr. SRCS 97. RPO, Handley, (i) with Gruenberg.

David Morgan is an unashamed traditionalist. His *Violin concerto*, dating from 1967, is a warmly lyrical work in an expressively Waltonian idiom, and it comes as quite a surprise that the composer relates his inspiration darkly to the destruction of the individual, for ostensibly this is a work of protest. *Contrasts* consists of two movements only, the first slow, with a central scherzando section, the second a toccata-like finale. It almost makes a symphony but not quite; though the seriousness of Morgan's purpose is never in doubt (the Shostakovich initials D–S–C–H an important motif), the balance of sections is odd. Performances here are admirable, not least from the soloist in the *Concerto*, Erich Gruenberg, and the recording is well up to Lyrita's high standard.

Mozart, Leopold (1719–87)

Cassation in G: Toy symphony (attrib. Haydn). (i) *Trumpet concerto in D.*
*** Erato Dig. **ECD 88021**; NUM/*MCE* 75092. (i) Touvron; Paillard CO, Paillard – MOZART: *Musical Joke.****

One could hardly imagine this *Cassation* being done with more commitment from the effects department, while the music itself is elegantly played. The Minuet is particularly engaging, with its aviary of bird sounds plus a vigorous contribution from the toy trumpet; and the finale, with its obbligato mêlée, is despatched with an infectious sense of fun. After this, the more restrained approach to the excellent two-movement *Trumpet concerto* seems exactly right. The recording has plenty of presence and realism, with the balance very well judged, both for the solo trumpet and for the toy instruments in the *Cassation* – which are properly set back. An excellent CD début.

Mozart, Wolfgang Amadeus (1756–91)

Cassations Nos 1 in G, K.63; 2 in B flat, K.99; 3 (Serenade) in D, K.100; March in D, K.62.
(*) Erato Dig. **ECD 88101; NUM 75184 [id.]. Paillard CO, Paillard.

The range and command of instrumental colour displayed by these three *Cassations*, written in Salzburg in 1769 by the thirteen-year-old Mozart, are quite remarkable. Moreover, the delicate first *Andante* of K.99 is uncannily prophetic of a famous Trio in *Così fan tutte* both in mood and in its gentle string figurations. K.63 introduces a memorable *Adagio* cantilena featuring solo violin, and K.100 has two *Andantes*, of which the second – paced rather fast here – is also captivating. The performances are essentially orchestral in character and the slightly too resonant acoustic emphasizes this. But the CD ensures that detail is well caught, and while Paillard does not always show an instinctive feeling for exactly the right tempo, he secures committed and responsive playing throughout and his allegros are always alert. The music is what counts, and though Boskovsky showed more natural flair in his recordings on Decca (and also created a convincing chamber-music perspective), the Erato CD (with 61 minutes of music) is most welcome. The *March* is associated with and used to introduce K.100; the other two works have brief introductory marches as opening movements.

(i) *Bassoon concerto in B flat, K.191;* (ii) *Clarinet concerto in A, K.622.*
(B) ** CfP CFP 41 4484-1/*4*. (i) Nakanishi, (ii) Andrew Marriner; L. Moz. Players, Glover.

(i) *Bassoon concerto;* (ii) *Clarinet concerto;* (iii) *Flute concerto No. 1 in G, K.313;* (iv) *Oboe concerto in C, K.314.*

(B) *** Ph. On Tour *412 903-4* [id.]. (i) Chapman; (ii) Brymer; (iii) Claude Monteux; (iv) Black; ASMF, Marriner.

(i) *Bassoon concerto;* (ii) *Clarinet concerto;* (iii) *Flute concerto No. 1;* (iv) *Horn concerto No. 1 in D;* (v) *Oboe concerto.*
(M) **(*) DG 415 021-1/*4* (2). (i) Zeman; (ii) Prinz; (iii) Tripp; (iv) Högner; (v) Turetschek; VPO, Boehm.

An outstanding collection on Philips's 'On Tour' chrome tape. The performances of these concertos are among the finest available, and although the forward balance tends to make the soloists sound larger than life, the sound is otherwise realistic and eminently truthful in timbre. Michael Chapman plays with great spirit and verve and is stylishly supported. Jack Brymer's recording of the *Clarinet concerto* is the third he has made; in some ways it is his best, for he plays with deepened insight and feeling. The flute and oboe concertos are hardly less recommendable, and the tape transfers are admirably managed.

Zeman gives a highly competitive account of the *Bassoon concerto*, a distinguished performance by any standards; Prinz's account of the *Clarinet concerto* is beautifully turned. Both deserve a position of honour in the field. Tripp and Turetschek both give civilized performances (they are also available on compact disc – see below) and Högner's sturdy approach suits the *D major Horn concerto* very well. The linking factor is, of course, the warm, elegantly played accompaniments by the VPO under Boehm and DG's consistently truthful recording balance, within a pleasing acoustic. If you want these works all together, this mid-priced set – which sounds equally well on disc or tape – is fair value; however, the inclusion of a single horn concerto will inevitably involve duplication, if the other three are required. The bargain-priced Philips tape seems the obvious best buy.

Producing a beautifully even flow of warm tone, Andrew Marriner gives a distinguished performance of the *Clarinet concerto* which yet lacks a feeling of spontaneity, the forward thrust, the inspiration of the moment. It would be hard to find a more beautiful timbre in the slow movement, but nevertheless the effect remains placid. Nakanishi is a talented player who copes well with the technical problems of the *Bassoon concerto*, but he is more recessive still, and the orchestral playing adds to the feeling of a studio run-through rather than a live experience. However, at CfP's bargain price and with excellent sound the disc is fairly attractive. There is a good cassette, but its smooth upper range and warm bass response slightly increase the feeling of blandness.

(i) *Bassoon concerto;* (ii) *Horn concerto No. 3 in E flat, K.447;* (iii) *Oboe concerto.*
** DG **415 104-2**; 415 104-1/*4* [id.]. (i) Willard Elliot; (ii) Dale Clevenger; (iii) Ray Still; Chicago SO, Abbado – HAYDN: *Trumpet concerto.***

Anyone wanting this particular collection of Mozart concertos coupled with Haydn's *Trumpet concerto* should not be too disappointed, for the playing is expert, the recordings are truthful and well balanced and Abbado's accompaniments characteristically refined and elegant. However, while Ray Still's phrasing is nicely turned, and Willard Elliot plays a nimble bassoon, neither artist registers very strongly here as an instrumental personality, and even Dale Clevenger, who is so impressive in his Telefunken disc of Haydn's *Horn concertos*, proves less individual in Mozart, although his solo contribution is highly musical and technically effortless. The recordings sound best on CD and equally well on LP or tape.

(i) *Clarinet concerto;* (ii) *Flute and harp concerto in C, K.299.*
*** ASV Dig. **CDDCA 532** [id.]; DCA/*ZCDCA* 532. [id.] (i) Emma Johnson; (ii) Bennett, Ellis; ECO, Leppard.
*** DG **413 552-2** [id.]. (i) Prinz; (ii) Schulz, Zabaleta; VPO, Boehm.

(i) *Clarinet concerto;* (ii) *Flute concerto No. 1 in G, K.313;* (iii) *Flute and harp concerto.*
(B) *** DG Walkman *413 428-4* [id.]. (i) Prinz, VPO, Boehm; (ii) Linde, Mun. CO, Stadlmair; (iii) Schulz, Zabeleta, VPO, Boehm.

(i) *Clarinet concerto;* (ii) *Oboe concerto in C, K.314.*
*** O-L Dig. **414 399-2**; 414 399-1/*4* [id.]. (i) Antony Pay; (ii) Michel Piguet, AAM, Hogwood.

(i) *Clarinet concerto;* (ii) *Clarinet quintet in A, K.581.*
*** Hyp. Dig. **CDA 66199**; A/*KA* 66199 [id.]. Thea King, (i) ECO, Tate; (ii) Gabrieli Qt.

(i) *Flute concerto No. 1;* (ii) *Flute and harp concerto.*
(M) **(*) HMV EG 290304-1/*4* [Ang. AM/*4AM* 34723]. (i) Blau; (ii) Galway, Helmis; BPO, Karajan.

Thea King's coupling makes an outstanding choice in all three media, bringing together winning performances of Mozart's two great clarinet masterpieces. Thea King's earlier recording of the *Quintet* for Saga was for many years a top choice; here she again steers an ideal course between classical stylishness and expressive warmth, with the slow movement becoming the emotional heart of the piece. The Gabrieli Quartet is equally responsive in its finely tuned playing. For the *Clarinet concerto* Thea King – like Antony Pay in his period-instrument recording for Oiseau-Lyre – uses an authentically reconstructed basset clarinet such as Mozart wanted. Its extra range allows certain passages to be played as originally intended with octave jumps avoided. With Jeffrey Tate an inspired Mozartian, the performance – like that of the *Quintet* – is both stylish and expressive, with the finale given a captivating bucolic lilt. Excellent recording for both sides, with the cassette sounding extremely well, even though it uses iron-oxide stock.

Emma Johnson, the BBC's Young Musician of the Year in 1984 and an immediate and winning star on television through that competition, went on within months to record this performance in the studio. The result lacks some of the technical finesse of rival versions by more mature clarinettists, but it has a sense of spontaneity, of natural magnetism which traps the ear from first to last. There may be some rawness of tone in places, but that only adds to the range of expression, which breathes the air of a live performance, whether in the sparkle and flair of the outer movements or the inner intensity of the central slow movement, in which Emma Johnson plays magically in a delightfully embellished lead-back into the main theme. Leppard and the ECO are in bouncing form, as they are too for the *Flute and harp concerto* on the reverse, though there the two excellent soloists are somewhat on their best behaviour (not taking the risks that Emma Johnson does), until the last part of the finale sends Mozart bubbling up to heaven. First-rate recording, given the greater clarity on CD. There is an excellent cassette, too.

Antony Pay's version makes a good alternative choice for anyone wanting to hear this masterpiece on period instruments. In this instance the original instruments include the soloist's basset clarinet, with its extra range allowing Mozart's original solo lines to be followed. Pay is a more restrained, less warm-toned player than his main rivals, with a relatively cool account of the beautiful slow movement; but that is apt for the stylistic aims of the performance. The French oboist, Michel Piguet, is an equally stylish soloist in the *Oboe concerto* on the reverse, providing not a generous coupling but an attractive one. Clean, well-balanced recording, particularly on CD. The chrome tape is very well balanced in the *Clarinet concerto*, but in the *Oboe concerto* the bright upper range may need a little smoothing.

Prinz's 1974 recording of the *Clarinet concerto* is available in three formats: within a medium-priced set (see above); on an immaculately transferred CD, coupled with the *Flute and harp concerto*, which seems shorter measure; and on an excellent Walkman tape (at less than a third the price of the compact disc). Here there is a bonus, in the form of Linde's impeccably played account of the *G major Flute concerto*. It has a touch of rigidity in the outer movements, but in the slow movement the playing is beautifully poised and the melody breathes in exactly the right way. Boehm's *Flute and harp concerto* comes from 1976 and the performance could hardly be bettered. The balance, as far as the relationship between soloists and orchestra is concerned, is expertly managed, and this is altogether refreshing. The sound throughout these recordings is excellent, except that Linde's 1966 *Flute concerto* shows its earlier date in the quality of the string timbre.

Despite the superb artistry of James Galway and Fritz Helmis and the refined and highly polished response of the Berlin Philharmonic, this well-recorded performance of the *Flute and harp concerto* does not wholly escape the blandness that afflicted Karajan's HMV recordings of the wind concertos. Of course there are many details to enjoy and admire, and the HMV engineers produce a well-detailed sound-picture. Andreas Blau's account of the *Flute concerto* too is impeccably played and superbly accompanied. The recording has been remastered and freshened to good effect, and there is an excellent tape.

Flute concertos Nos 1 in G; 2 in D, K.313/4.
(M) *** Pickwick **PCD 807**; SHM/*HSC* 3010 [Quin. 3010]. Galway, New Irish Chamber Ens., Prieur.

Flute concertos Nos 1–2; Andante in C for flute and orchestra, K.315.
*** Eurodisc **610 130**. Galway, Lucerne Fest. O, Baumgartner.
(M) ** Ph. 416 244-1/*4*. Nicolet, Concg. O, Zinman.

To have modern recordings of Mozart's two *Flute concertos* played by James Galway available in the cheapest price-range is bounty indeed. On LP and cassette they are in the bargain catalogue; on the excellently transferred CD they are at mid-price. Moreover, the accompaniments, ably directed by André Prieur, are reasonably polished and stylish, and the recording (although it gives a rather small sound to the violins) is excellent, clear and with good balance and perspective. It might be argued that Galway's vibrato is not entirely suited to these eighteenth-century works and that his cadenzas, too, are slightly anachronistic. But the star quality of his playing disarms criticism. The slow movement of the *First Concerto* is beautifully paced; the timbre and phrasing have exquisite delicacy, and the pointed articulation in the finale (nicely matched by the orchestra) is a delight. In No. 2 Galway again floats the melodic line of the first movement with gossamer lightness, and after another enchanting slow movement the finale sparkles joyously, with the orchestra once more on top form. The sound is crisp, fresh and well balanced.

Galway's Lucerne performances, issued on the Eurodisc label, derive from the RCA catalogue; they also can be recommended with no reservations whatsoever. This playing, too, has spontaneity, virtuosity, charm and refinement. Galway is well supported by the Lucerne orchestra and the sound is good, though the resonant acoustic means that orchestral detail is less sharply defined. The orchestral playing itself is slightly more refined, but not more spirited. The advantage of this compact disc is that it includes a bonus in the way of the *Andante*, K.315. But it also costs more.

Although issued at mid-price, the Nicolet/Zinman disc and the excellent matching tape are new to the catalogue. The performances are very positive, with the flute balanced well forward and dominating the proceedings, though David Zinman's accompaniments are alert and strong. Both finales are particularly attractive, briskly paced, and the solo playing throughout is expert and elegantly phrased. However, Galway displays a lighter touch generally and is to be preferred.

(i) *Flute concerto No. 1 in G, K.313;* (ii) *Oboe concerto in C, K.314.*
(*) DG **413 737-2 [id.]. (i) Tripp, (ii) Turetschek; VPO, Boehm.

Highly musical performances, with Boehm in complete rapport with his soloists. But the 1975 sound shows its age a little in these CD transfers, with the string timbre more brightly lit than on LP.

(i) *Flute and harp concerto in C, K.299. Flute concerto in G, K.622G* (arrangement of *Clarinet concerto*, ed. Galway).
(M) **(*) RCA Gold GL/*GK* 85442 [AGL1/*AGK1* 5442]. Galway, LSO, Mata, (i) with Robles.

The *Flute and harp concerto* has seldom sounded as lively in a recording as it does here, with an engaging element of fantasy in the music making, a radiant slow movement, and an irrepressibly spirited finale. Marisa Robles makes a characterful match for the ubiquitous Galway. The balance of the soloists is forward, but not unrealistically so. The *Flute concerto* arranged from Mozart's masterpiece for clarinet is more controversial; the key of G major as well as Galway's silvery flute timbre make for even lighter results than one might have anticipated. The scintillating finale is especially successful. The recording is admirably bright and clear, the cassette matching the disc in vividness.

Flute and harp concerto in C, K.229; Andante for flute and orchestra in C, K.315; Horn concertos Nos 1–4; Concert rondo for horn and orchestra, K.371.
(B) **(*) Ph. On Tour *416 222-4* [id.]. Claude Monteux, Osian Ellis, Alan Civil; ASMF, Marriner.

The performance of the *Flute and harp concerto* is attractively warm and elegant but, as with the companion 'On Tour' tape of wind concertos, the solo instruments sound larger than life and the recording has an element of blandness, both here and in the *Horn concertos*, because of the resonance. Alan Civil's set of the *Horn concertos* is also available separately – see below – but this bargain-priced 'On Tour' tape is certainly the most economical way of acquiring them.

Horn concertos Nos 1–4; Concert rondo, K.371; Fragments: in E flat, K.370b; in D, K.514; in E, K.Anh.98a; Sinfonia concertante in E flat, K.297b; 3 Horn duets, K.487/1, 3 and 6; Horn quintet, K.407; Piano and wind quintet, K.452; (i) *Idomeneo: Se il padre perdei.*
**(*) Decca Dig. 410 283-1/*4* (3) [id.]. Tuckwell, ECO; Gabrieli Qt; John Ogdon; (i) Sheila Armstrong.

This box collects together a good deal of the Mozartian repertoire in which the horn has a solo or obbligato role – although why the (welcome) aria from *Idomeneo* should have been included yet nothing from *Così fan tutte* is curious. It is certainly well done by Sheila Armstrong, in her freshest voice. The four *Horn concertos*, together with the *Concert rondo* and the *Fragments*, are the highlight of the collection; their availability begs another question: why were they not all included on Tuckwell's compact disc, which is ungenerous in offering the concertos alone? However, they are a delight. The solo playing is engagingly fresh (even though Tuckwell has recorded them twice before): there is a sense of Mozartian joy here which continues the tradition established by the late Dennis Brain; moreover, the accompaniments have a comparably spontaneous feeling. Among the other items, the *Piano and wind quintet* is a little disappointing. This is an elusive work on records; Ashkenazy's earlier Decca version possesses an incandescence that eludes the present performers, with John Ogdon's pianism a trifle too sturdy. The *Horn quintet*, too, is somewhat severe in manner, although the *Sinfonia concertante* comes off very well. The recording is excellent throughout, though the high level of the tape transfer brings a tendency to shrillness in the upper strings and robs the timbre of bloom. The horn focus is slightly sharpened and given extra presence, without loss of body. The rather fierce string lighting on tape is especially noticeable in the chamber works.

Horn concertos Nos 1 in D, K.412; 2–4 in E flat, K.417, 447, 495.
*** Decca Dig. **410 284-2**; 410 284-1/*4* [id.]. Tuckwell, ECO.
*** Tel. **ZK8 41272**; AZ6 41272 [id.]. Baumann (natural hand-horn), VCM, Harnoncourt.
(*) Ph. Dig. **412 737-2; 412 737-1/*4* [id.]. Baumann, St Paul CO, Zukerman.
** DG **412 792-2** [id.]. Högner, VPO, Boehm.

Horn concertos Nos 1–4; Concert rondo in E flat, K.371.
(M) **(*) Ph. 412 930-1/*4*. Civil, ASMF, Marriner.
** Denon Dig. **C37 7432** [id.]. Zdeněk Tylšar, Prague CO.

(i) *Horn concertos Nos 1–4;* (ii) *Serenade No. 12 in C min., K.388.*
(B) *** CfP CFP 41 4488-1/*4*. (i) Civil, Philh. O; (ii) New Philh. O, Klemperer.

Barry Tuckwell has recorded the concertos previously for Decca; his 1962 set with the LSO under Maag still sounds marvellous on the mid-priced Jubilee label. Moreover, the earlier record (and tape) includes the fragment from the unfinished *Fifth Concerto* (JB/*KJBC* 70 [JL/*5*- 41015]). In this new digital set he plays as well as ever; he also directs the ECO in crisp, polished and elegant accompaniments. Tuckwell is a natural Mozartian and he is able to ensure that the string phrasing echoes the horn in every detail. The orchestra makes a perfectly scaled backcloth for solo playing which combines natural high spirits with a warmly expressive understanding for the Mozartian musical line. The recording is very well balanced and most realistic, with the CD adding a remarkable illusion of presence. The chrome tape too is outstandingly fine, particularly sweet on string timbre, yet retaining the presence of the solo instrument.

We are not convinced that the playing of 'original instruments' always demonstrates their full expressive potential and, in the case of the French horn, it would seem perverse to use a valveless instrument when a narrow-bore modern horn (of the kind used by Dennis Brain in his earliest recordings) can sound the same, produce uniformity of timbre, and stay in tune throughout its compass. Yet Hermann Baumann successfully uses the original hand-horn, without valves, for which the concertos were written, and the result is a *tour de force* of technical skill, not achieved at the expense of musical literacy or expressive content. Inevitably, this implies at least some alterations in timbre, as certain notes have to be 'stopped', with the hand in the bell of the instrument, if they are to be in tune. Herr Baumann is not in the least intimidated by this problem; he plays throughout with consummate tonal smoothness and in a totally relaxed manner.

He lets the listener hear the stopped effect only when he decides that the tonal change can be put to good artistic effect, as for instance in the rondo of No. 2 or in his own cadenza for No. 3. Here – in the cadenza – he also uses horn chords (where several notes are produced simultaneously by resonating the instrument's harmonics), but as a complement to the music rather than as a gimmick. The slow movement of No. 3 has one of Mozart's richest melodies and its touch of chromaticism is managed with superb flexibility and smoothness, so that one can only wonder at Baumann's artistry and skill. In short, these are remarkably satisfying performances by any standards. Baumann's execution in the gay rondos is a delight and his tone is particularly characterful. It is splendid to have such a successful representation of the horn timbre and technique that Mozart would have recognized, and which indeed all nineteenth-century composers would have expected. The 1974 recording has been digitally remastered for CD; while the horn is given added presence and tangibility, the brightness of the strings has brought some roughness of focus, as the original recording was mellow and reverberant. However, it is the astonishing horn playing that is the main interest here, and that is certainly well projected.

Like Barry Tuckwell, Alan Civil has recorded the Mozart concertos three times. The finest and freshest was his 1967 set with Kempe (EMI EMX/*TC-EMX* 2004) but his earlier (1961) partnership with Klemperer also worked very well, with the great conductor in essentially genial mood. Civil's tone production here has a quality which might affectionately be described as 'podgy' and his fluency of execution is matched by warmly lyrical phrasing and articulation of a character worthy of Dennis Brain. The recording still sounds good and is made doubly attractive in this bargain-priced reissue by the addition of Klemperer's magisterial account of the *Wind serenade*, K.388, very elegantly played by members of the Philharmonia. Tape and disc are closely matched.

Civil's most recent set was made in 1973 and includes the *Concert rondo*, an attractive extra piece which is seldom played in public. The recording is obviously more modern and the performances are highly enjoyable, with Sir Neville Marriner's polished and lively accompaniments giving pleasure in themselves. The balance has the effect of making the horn sound slightly larger than life, but the warmly resonant sound, now remastered, has better detail than originally, on both LP and the very good tape. However, tape collectors will note that these performances are available, more economically, on a bargain-priced 'On Tour' collection, coupled with the *Flute and harp concerto* – see above.

In his newest recording for Philips, Hermann Baumann uses a modern horn and he produces an agreeably broad and richly lyrical flow of sound. His articulation is especially attractive in the finales, which are robust and vigorous. There is no lack of expressive warmth here, but his use of light and shade is less subtle, less imaginative than with Civil or Tuckwell. The *Romanza* of K.495 is more melting in Civil's version. The most attractive performance is K.417, where the partnership with Zukerman is heard at its finest, with nicely pointed orchestral playing, genially echoed by the solo line. In the finale of K.412, Baumann again astonishes with a sumptuous series of horn 'chords' as part of his cadenza. The recording is of Philips's best quality, warmly resonant on LP and cassette, with the CD clarifying detail; this is certainly enjoyable, if not as fascinating as his earlier set using the Bohemian hand-horn.

Günter Högner also plays with much character; no one will be disappointed with the DG issue, which is well recorded and has splendid accompaniments from the VPO under Boehm. However, this would not be a first choice in a very competitive field.

Zdeněk Tylšar is also a stylish Mozartian and he is given neat accompaniments by the Prague orchestra. He is very well recorded, within a rather warmer acoustic than Tuckwell's Decca set. The effect of the performances is definitely on a chamber scale; though the solo playing by no means lacks personality (his neat articulation gives special pleasure), other accounts are rather more vivid. Moreover, the touch of vibrato on the lyrical melodies, although applied musically and judiciously, will not appeal to all Western ears.

Oboe concerto in C, K.314.
(M) *** Ph. Seq. 6527/*7311* 190. Holliger, New Philh. O, De Waart – HAYDN: *Concerto.****

This is Holliger's second recording of Mozart's charming *Oboe concerto*. It dates from 1971 and was originally issued coupled with the Richard Strauss *Concerto*. (At the time of going to press, that disc is still available.) Holliger's performance is even more masterly and more refined than the DG one he made in Munich. The recording is fresh, though not quite so full as the Haydn coupling. There is an excellent tape.

Piano concertos (for piano and strings) after J. C. Bach, *K.107, Nos 1 in D; 2 in G, 3 in E flat.*
*** CBS Dig. **MK 39222**; IM/*IMT* 39222 [id.]. Perahia, ECO – SCHRÖTER: *Piano concerto.****

Piano concertos: K. 107/1–3; Nos 1–6, 8, 9, 11–27; Concert rondos Nos 1–2, K.382 and 386.
❀ *** CBS **M13K 42055**; M 13 42055 (13) [id.]. Perahia, ECO (with SCHRÖTER: *Concerto*).

Piano concertos Nos 5, 6, 8, 9, 11–27; (i) *Double piano concertos, K.242 and K.365; Concert rondos 1–2.*
(*) Ph. **412 856-2 (10); 412 856-1/*4* (13/*9*) [id.]. Brendel, (i) Imogen Cooper, ASMF, Marriner.

Piano concertos Nos 5, 6, 8, 11, 15, 16, 21, 26; (i) *Double concertos K.242 and K.365.*
**(*) Ph. 412 970-1 (5) [id.]. Brendel, (i) Cooper (from above).

Piano concertos Nos 9, 12, 13–14, 17–20, 22–25, 27; Concert Rondos 1–2.
*** Ph. 6768 096 (8) [id.]. Brendel (from above).

Murray Perahia's cycle is the first complete set on compact disc. He not only includes the first four derived juvenile works but as an appendix (also available on a separate CD, LP and tape) the three concertos, written some time between 1765 and 1772, when Mozart would have been nine and fifteen. They are arrangements he made of keyboard sonatas by J. C. Bach. They are slight pieces which can sound quite unremarkable, but Perahia plays them with all the subtlety and poetic feeling they can bear. The results are quite charming, and readers normally unresponsive to them should hear them, particularly *No. 3 in E flat*, in such persuasive hands. The complete set is a remarkable achievement and it is difficult to imagine its being surpassed. In terms of poetic insight and musical spontaneity the performances are in a class of their own. There is a wonderful singing line and at the same time a sensuousness that is always tempered by spirituality. Schnabel's famous dictum, that Beethoven wrote music that was better than it can ever be played, applies to all great music – and every bit as much to Mozart. It is a measure of Perahia's imagination and achievement that, after listening to him in this repertoire, one wonders whether in this case it is true. The CBS recordings have improved since the cycle started and the more recent are excellent – although generally the sound Decca have afforded Ashkenazy has greater bloom and a firmer focus. Wagner spoke of Mozart as 'a genius of light and love'; although there are darker sides to these concertos, one is often reminded of these words in studying this set.

Turning to Brendel, one finds that apart from the compilation offering his recordings complete on ten CDs, thirteen LPs, or nine cassettes, there is also a supplementary box (on LP only) for those who have already collected his recordings of the fifteen concertos made in the 1970s (6768 096). Most of these are glorious; all are worth having. K.503 was recorded at a public concert in Strasbourg in 1978, but the remainder are all studio performances. Many of the performances in the five-disc box (412 970-1) are new and all show the vibrant intelligence of this artist. Brendel's performance of the *F major Concerto*, K.413, well serves to point the difference between his approach and that of Perahia: his tempo in the slow movement is perfectly judged, yet he does not cultivate quite the same tonal refinement, even though the playing has fine sensibility. Imogen Cooper is his elegant partner in the *E flat Concerto* and in the so-called *Lodron*, K.242, which is Mozart's own arrangement for two players of the three-piano concerto. There is a wise and penetrating note from Brendel himself: 'A Mozart player gives himself advice, in which he says: "A singing line and sensuous beauty, as important as they may be in Mozart, are not, however, the sole sources of bliss"'; he quotes Busoni's dictum: 'Mozart did not remain simple and did not grow over-refined.' In K.413 and elsewhere in the more recent recordings, Brendel seems more cautious of sensuousness and yet, in terms of articulation, does sometimes become a little over-refined. The playing of the Academy under Sir Neville Marriner is excellent and the recordings are in the best traditions of the house. The 'complete' box (which mixes the earlier analogue recordings with the ten he made digitally) does not include the four early concertos, K.37 and K.39–41, or the three based on J. C. Bach, K.107. The *Lodron concerto* and a handful of others (K.175, K.246, K.413, K.451 and the *Coronation*, K.537) are new; throughout, his thoughts are never less than penetrating. Where analogue recordings have been transferred to CD, the digital remastering has produced clean and successful results. The cassette layout is more controversial; the use of only nine cassettes is in no way advantageous: there is often more than one major work to a side, which is inconvenient, and K.414, K.450 and K.466 are split between sides to save a bit of tape, which is unacceptable. However, the transfers are consistently of the very highest quality.

Piano concertos Nos 1 in F, K.37; 2 in B flat, K.39; 3 in D, K.40; 4 in G, K.41.
*** CBS Dig. **MK 39225**; IM/*IMT* 39225. Murray Perahia, ECO.

The first four concertos which occupy the present issue date from the spring or summer of 1767, when Mozart was eleven. They draw for their thematic ideas on sonatas by Hermann Raupach, Leontzi Honauer, Schobart, Eckhard and Carl Philipp Emmanuel Bach. Of course, they are not the equal of any of his more mature concertos; however, played, as they are here, with such grace and affection, they make delightful listening. Throughout Murray Perahia's cycle with the ECO, the orchestral playing is imaginative and sensitive, and the CBS recordings are in the very first flight. On cassette, however, the orchestral bass is emphasized somewhat at the expense of the upper range.

Piano concertos Nos 5 in D, K.175; 25 in C, K.503.
*** CBS Dig. **MK 37267**; 37267/*40-* [id.]. Murray Perahia, ECO.

Murray Perahia never loses sight of the space and grandeur of the *C major*, K.503, and, like Bishop-Kovacevich on Philips and Brendel (particularly in his Vox recording from the 1960s), has the measure of its strength and scale as well as tenderness. Perahia invests the landscape with delicate and subtle colourings and there is a sparkle and poetry that is unfailingly affecting. The sheer refinement of keyboard sound is a joy in itself and never narcissistic; at only one point – the F major section of the finale (bar 163 onwards) – does the listener wonder whether Perahia and the wind players of the ECO caress the melodic line in a way that almost steps outside the sensibility of the period. A wonderful performance, however, and coupled with an account of the *D major*, K.175, which has an innocence and freshness that is completely persuasive. The recording is good without being as distinguished as the performance. On CD, the upper strings are a little fierce and not too cleanly focused. The chrome cassette is wide-ranging and clear, but again the treble is not completely refined.

Piano concertos Nos 6 in B flat, K.238; 13 in C, K.415.
*** CBS Dig. **MK 39223**; IM/*IMT* 39223 [id.]. Murray Perahia, ECO.

Perahia brings a marvellous freshness and delicacy to the *B flat Concerto*, K.238, but it is in the *C major* that he is at his most sparkling and genial. There have been fine accounts from Haskil, Barenboim and, more recently, Ashkenazy; but in its sense of character and its subtle artistry this is a first recommendation, even if Ashkenazy's Decca recording is better balanced. Perahia's piano is rather more forward and the acoustic ambience less spacious. However, the CBS sound is still very good indeed, although on cassette the bass resonance is emphasized somewhat and the upper range is slightly restricted.

Piano concertos Nos 8 in C, K.246; 9 in E flat, K.271.
** HMV EL 270071-1/*4*. Christian Zacharias, Polish CO, Maksymiuk.

Very good performances from Christian Zacharias in both the *C major*, K.246 (the so-called *Lützow concerto*), and in the *Jeunehomme*, K.271. The balance of the recording is rather forward and there needs to be far more air round the orchestra. Jerzy Maksymiuk turns in well-drilled accompaniments and gets generally alert and clean playing from the Polish Chamber Orchestra. In so competitive a market, however, this does not offer a serious challenge to Brendel, Perahia or Ashkenazy.

Piano concertos Nos 8, K.246; 22 in E flat, K.482.
*** CBS 76966/*40*- [IM/*IMT* 35869]. Murray Perahia, ECO.

Murray Perahia's version of the great *E flat Concerto* is second to none. He has the measure of its scale, and yet every phrase is lovingly shaped too. Perahia is an artist who blends unusual qualities of spirit with wonderful sensuousness; not only does he draw magical sounds from the keyboard, he also inspires the wind players of the ECO, who invest the serenade-like episodes in the slow movement with great eloquence. This is a reading of real stature. It is well recorded, though there is not quite the range and depth that distinguished Perahia's slightly earlier coupling of K.414 and K.595. The early *C major Concerto* is unfailingly fresh and elegant in his hands. The cassette, on chrome tape, is of good quality.

Piano concertos Nos 8, K.246; 27 in B flat, K.595.
* DG Dig. **410 035-2**; 410 035-1/*4* [id.]. Rudolf Serkin, LSO, Abbado.

Rudolf Serkin is an artist of keen musical intellect; older collectors will recall his K.449 with the Busch Chamber Players with both affection and admiration. This new cycle he is recording with Claudio Abbado and the LSO is not in that league. The opening of K.595 is very measured and spacious, and Serkin's contribution is wanting in the grace he once commanded. There are moments of inelegance (the theme of the slow movement is a case in point) and little real sparkle in the quicker movements. The orchestral playing is a little sluggish, too. The recording is excellent, in all three media.

Piano concertos Nos 9 in E flat, K.271; 11 in F, K.413.
*** DG Arc. Dig. **410 905-2**; 410 905-1/*4* [id.]. Malcolm Bilson, E. Bar. Soloists, Gardiner.

Malcolm Bilson's coupling is the first of a projected complete series of the Mozart keyboard concertos, featuring original instruments and including a copy of Mozart's own concert piano. Bilson may have made his reputation as an academic, but here he shows himself a lively and imaginative artist, well matched by the ever-effervescent and alert Gardiner. The recording, especially on CD, catches superbly the lightness and clarity of the textures, with the fortepiano sound not too twangy and with wind balances often revelatory. The darkness of the C minor slow movement of K.271 is eerily caught. The lightness of keyboard action encourages Bilson to choose fast allegros, but never at the expense of Mozart. There is a first-class chrome cassette, matching the LP closely.

Piano concertos Nos 9, K.271; 17 in G, K.453.
*(*) DG Dig. **415 206-2**; 2532/*3302* 060 [id.]. Rudolf Serkin, LSO, Abbado.

Serkin has a powerful musical mind – but his magisterial reputation should not obscure the fact that his playing is not so supple and refined as it once was. The second group of the first movement of the *G major Concerto*, K.453, is ungainly in presentation and there are other inelegances that diminish pleasure. There are no quarrels with the sound, however, which is very vivid and clear in CD, LP and cassette formats.

Piano concertos Nos 9, K.271; 21 in C, K.467.
*** CBS 76584 [M/*MT* 35462]. Murray Perahia, ECO.
** PRT **CDPCN 1**. Nina Milkina, O of St John's, Lubbock.

Perahia's reading of K.271 is wonderfully refreshing, delicate, with diamond-bright articulation, urgently youthful in its resilience. In the C minor slow movement, beautifully poised, Perahia finds gravity without weighing the music down. The famous *C major Concerto* is given a more variable, though still highly imaginative, performance. If the first movement is given charm rather than strength, it is the opposite with the slow movement and finale. Faithful, well-balanced recording. The cassette is less impressive than the disc, with the orchestral quality somewhat amorphous. K.467 is also available coupled with *No. 20 in D minor*, K.466 – see below.

Nina Milkina is a much-admired artist and a highly sensitive Mozartian. Tempi are well judged and passage-work immaculate. She is eminently stylish throughout, though she does limit her dynamic range (not without reason, of course); her playing sounds a shade small-scale as a result. The orchestral playing is better in K.467 than in K.271, where more polish would not come amiss. The acoustic is a little too reverberant and the piano not perfectly in focus in the first movement of K.271. The CD transfer has been unable to improve these matters.

Piano concertos Nos 11 in F, K.413; 20 in D min., K.466.
*** CBS 76651/*40-* [M/*MT* 35134]. Murray Perahia, ECO.

This is the most impressive of Perahia's Mozart concerto records so far. He plays both works with abundant artistry and imagination and is well served by the CBS engineers. These are finely integrated readings: the solo entry in the first movement of K.413 could hardly emerge more organically from the texture, and in the slow movement he is more withdrawn, more private than many of his colleagues. Here he is at the other end of the spectrum from Barenboim, whose reading is more outgoing and life-loving. Perahia brings less dramatic fire to

K.466 than some of his colleagues, but there is a strong case for this; too many artists view the work from the vantage-point of *Don Giovanni* rather than seeing it in terms of its own unique sensibility. None of the disturbing undercurrents goes unnoted, but at the same time the spiritual dimensions remain within the period: not the only way of looking at this work but a most convincing one. The cassette is not as wide-ranging as the disc but is satisfactorily balanced.

Piano concertos Nos 12 in A, K.414; 13 in C, K.415.
€ *** Decca Dig. **410 214–2**; SXDL/*KSXDC* 7556 [Lon. LDR/5-71056]. Vladimir Ashkenazy, Philh. O.

Vladimir Ashkenazy's account of K.414 and 415 must be numbered among the most successful of his cycle. The *A major* is well served on record, with splendid versions from De Larrocha (SXL/*KSXC* 6952 [Lon. CS/5- 7180]) and Perahia, both of which will give pleasure. Ashkenazy's account admirably combines expressive feeling with sparkle and conveys real enjoyment: he is moreover fortunate in having the benefit of well-defined and transparent recording, superior to that given Perahia. The *C major* has equally strong claims and readers collecting the Ashkenazy survey will not be disappointed. The compact disc is particularly impressive. The piano is forwardly balanced, but the naturalness of timbre and the bloom on the overall sound-picture are such as to confound criticism. The slow movement of K.414 is given memorable depth when the quality is so beautiful and the ambience so attractive.

Piano concertos Nos 12, K.414; 14 in E flat, K.449.
*** DG Arc. Dig. **413 463-2**; 413 463-1/*4* [id.]. Malcolm Bilson, E. Bar. Soloists, Gardiner.

Malcolm Bilson's coupling of the '*Little A major*', K.414, and the tough *Concerto in E flat*, K.449, amply confirms the wisdom of choosing him for the Archiv project of recording the Mozart concertos using a fortepiano. Though you might argue that authenticity would demand having no conductor, Gardiner and the English Baroque Soloists prove to be ideal accompanists, matching Bilson's expressiveness on the one hand while on the other relishing the very fast speeds he prefers in finales. The extra clarity of authentic instruments and the small scale here never prettify the music; rather, they make it seem all the stronger in its lean resilience. Excellent recording, fresh and clear in all three media.

Piano concertos Nos 12, K.414; 20 in D min., K.466.
*(*) DG Dig. **400 068-2**; 2532/*3302* 053 [id.]. Rudolf Serkin, LSO, Abbado.

Serkin made some distinguished Mozart concerto records way back in the days of shellac; he has now embarked on a new cycle at nearly eighty years of age. It would be a pleasure to report on the *A major* with enthusiasm, but Serkin's playing is far from elegant and, though there are flashes of authority, the ends of phrases are not beautifully turned. This offers no real challenge to De Larrocha, Ashkenazy and Perahia in K.414 or Brendel, Perahia and Bishop-Kovacevich in the *D minor*, K.466. The recording is clear and vivid, in both its LP and cassette format; those who are prepared to bear with the prosaic pianism for the sake of the musical insights that do emerge will have no quarrels with this issue technically. The compact disc offers the usual advantages.

Piano concertos Nos 12, K.414; 23 in A, K.488.
(*) Hung. Dig. **HCD 12472; SLPD/*MK* 12472 [id.]. Zoltan Kocsis, Liszt CO, Rolla.

Those wanting the two A major concertos could do worse than invest in the Hungaroton version from Zoltan Kocsis and the Franz Liszt Chamber Orchestra. In the 'little' *A major Concerto*, K.414, Zoltan Kocsis is marvellously sensitive and alert, and he is given excellent support by Janos Rolla. The small forces involved enhance the effect of intimacy, and Kocsis's participation in the orchestral ritornello is eminently discreet. As piano playing, this can hold its own with the best; the performance of K.488 is hardly less impressive. Kocsis is unfailingly vital and imaginative: he shapes the main theme of the second movement with all the finesse and subtlety of Barenboim on HMV, but without the slightest trace of self-indulgence. Unfortunately, the finale is completely rushed off its feet. The recording is a little wanting in opulence and bloom, yet even though it would not be a first choice, there is so much to delight the collector here that it must still have a fairly strong recommendation.

Piano concertos Nos 12, K.414; 27 in B flat, K.595.
*** CBS 76731/*40*- [M/*MT* 35828]. Murray Perahia, ECO.

Murray Perahia has the capacity to make the piano breathe and to persuade the listener that the sound he produces is almost independent of any physical agency. Yet this spiritual dimension harmonizes with a flesh-and-blood intensity and strongly classical instincts. Both these performances have great sparkle and a sense of naturalness and rightness: listening to the finale of K.414, one feels it could not be taken at any other speed or phrased in any other way. In K.595, Perahia produces some wonderfully soft colourings and a luminous texture, yet at the same time he avoids underlining too strongly the sense of valediction that inevitably haunts this magical score. There is a sublime simplicity to the slow movement in these artists' hands – for the ECO too seem as inspired as the soloist-director. The CBS sound is excellent, fresh-toned and well balanced. The cassette has less upper range than the disc, but with a bass cut the sound-balance is pleasing, and there is no muffling of the strings.

Piano concertos Nos 13 in C, K.415; 15 in B flat, K.450.
☾ *** DG Arc. Dig. **413 464-2**; 413 464-1/*4* [id.]. Malcolm Bilson, E. Bar. Soloists, Gardiner.

This third record in Bilson's projected complete series of Mozart piano concertos, using a fortepiano at low pitch in unequal temperament, completes the trilogy of work which Mozart wrote in the winter of 1782–3. Festive with trumpets, this last of the group makes a striking impact, despite the modest-sized forces (5, 4, 2, 2, 1 strings). Though Bilson opts for brisk allegros, which emerge with exceptional clarity, he and Gardiner relax well in the central andante and the two adagio episodes of the finale. K.450 brings woodwind to the fore, and the English Baroque players match their string colleagues in stylishness. The recording on CD, nicely balanced without spotlighting – there is a single crossover microphone over the conductor's head – is so vivid you can hear the clicking keys of the wind instruments. The chrome tape also represents DG's finest standard and is extraordinarily lifelike.

Piano concertos Nos 14 in E flat, K.449; 24 in C min., K.491.
*** CBS 76481/*40*- [M/*MT* 34219]. Murray Perahia, ECO.

Very distinguished playing from Perahia. K.449 is an immensely civilized reading, full of grace. This artist has the power to make each phrase sound freshly experienced and vibrant, though greater robustness might not be out of place. All the same, this is one of the best accounts of the concerto to have appeared recently. The slow movement of the *C Minor* is exquisitely played, and Perahia's control of keyboard colour and his sensitivity in matters of tonal nuance excite unstinted admiration. He also conducts and secures excellent results and responsive phrasing (though less than impeccable wind intonation in one place) from the ECO. His is an inward reading, not so full of the dramatic intensity as some rivals, but enormously rewarding. He is better served by the engineers than in any of his earlier records, but the cassette version offers poorer internal definition of the orchestra, although the piano timbre is fully acceptable.

Piano concertos Nos 15 in B flat, K.450; 16 in D, K.451.
*** CBS Dig. **MK 37824**; 37824/*40*- [id.]. Murray Perahia, ECO.
*** Decca **411 612-2**; SXL/*KSXC* 7010 [Lon. CS/*5*- 7254]. Vladimir Ashkenazy, Philh. O.

These two concertos, written for subscription concerts in March 1774, make an apt and attractive coupling. Perahia's are superbly imaginative readings, full of seemingly spontaneous touches and turns of phrase very personal to him, which yet never sound mannered. This is as near to live music-making as a record can approach. Perahia's version of the *B flat Concerto* has all the sparkle, grace and intelligence one would expect to encounter from this artist; both these performances uphold the special claims this cycle has of being to the 1980s what Edwin Fischer's Mozart concerto records were to the 1930s – that is to say, very special indeed. The recording is absolutely first rate, intimate yet realistic and not dry, with the players continuously grouped round the pianist. Trumpets and timpani in K.451 come out the more sharply. There is a refined chrome-cassette transfer.

Needless to say, Ashkenazy's performances also show characteristic sensibility. He takes a more direct view, yet there are many imaginative touches: both slow movements are played very beautifully yet without a trace of narcissism, and the finales sparkle. There is some splendid wind playing from the Philharmonia and the result is consistently clean and refreshing, but rather less individual than Perahia. The Decca sound is first rate, especially on CD, but also with a cassette in the demonstration class – yet it suggests a bigger scale, with the Kingsway Hall acoustic adding reverberation.

Piano concertos Nos 15, K.450; 21 in C, K.467.
*** Ph. Dig. **400 018-2**; 6514/*7337* 148 [id.]. Alfred Brendel, ASMF, Marriner.

Brendel is fine in K.450 and hardly less so in its companion. The outer movements of K.467 are brisk, but tempo is not in itself a problem. Each detail of a phrase is meticulously articulated, every staccato and slur carefully observed in an almost didactic fashion. The finale sounds over-rehearsed, for some of the joy and high spirits are sacrificed in the sense of momentum. However, it is curmudgeonly to dwell on reservations when there is so much to delight in these performances. The playing is very distinguished indeed, and so, too, is the recording. In the compact disc form the sound is more 'present' though the LP has excellent range and detail too. The cassette is of good quality – though by comparison with the LP, it is less transparent.

Piano concertos Nos 17 in G, K.453; 18 in B flat, K.456.
*** CBS Dig. **CD 36686**; 36686/*40*- [id.]. Murray Perahia, ECO.
** RCA Dig. RL/*RK* 84522 [ARC1/*ARK1* 4522]. Emanuel Ax, St Paul CO, Zukerman.
*(*) Decca Dig. **414 289-2**; 414 289-1/*4* [id.]. András Schiff, Salzburg Mozarteum Cam. Ac., Végh.

Perahia's cycle goes from strength to strength, and his account of the *G major Concerto* must rank among the very finest now before the public. It has all the sparkle, grace and finesse that one expects from him, and like its companion offers a thoroughly integrated view of the score. He has established a rapport with his players that recalls Edwin Fischer or Adolf Busch. An indispensable issue for Mozartians even if they already have other versions of these concertos. Good sound, clean yet not in any way lacking in warmth, and the chrome cassette offers a first-class transfer.

The sound in the RCA recording of Emanuel Ax and Pinchas Zukerman is very good on both LP and tape and the balance between soloist and orchestra well judged. The performances are accomplished and will give wide pleasure. At the same time they are not in any way special, and certainly not in the same class as Perahia or Ashkenazy.

András Schiff and Sandor Végh are rather ruled out of court because of the excessive resonance of the acoustic, in which the soloist seems lost. Schiff and Végh opt for a rather leisurely tempo in the opening movement of the *G major*, and not every reader will care for the staccato-like Alberti bass to which at times he reduces the accompaniment of the opening theme. The ensemble includes such distinguished figures as Aurèle Nicolet, Heinz Holliger and Klaus Thunemann; but the sound is too unfocused to compete alongside the best now available. There is a faithful equivalent tape.

Piano concertos Nos (i) *17, K.453;* (ii) *20 in D min., K.466;* (ii; iii) *Double piano concerto in E flat, K.365.*
(B) * CBS *MGT 39490.* Rudolf Serkin, (i) Columbia SO; (ii) Marlboro Fest. O; (iii) with Peter Serkin; all cond. Scheinder.

Serkin's CBS account of the *G major Concerto*, K.453, though at times dour by comparison with Edwin Fischer, Barenboim, Perahia and others, is still to be preferred to his more recent version with Abbado. The other two recordings were made at the Marlboro Festival and the performance of the *Double concerto*, in which Serkin is joined by his son, Peter, comes off well. However, the *D minor* is not so fine here as Serkin's superb Cleveland version, recorded with Szell a decade earlier. The latter is still available (CBS 60129/*40* [MY/*MYT* 37236]). The real snag with the present tape is the sound, which is fierce, with the violins' upper range made to sound shrill and with the piano timbre very dry.

Piano concertos Nos 17, K.453; 21 in C, K.467.
*** Decca **411 947-2**; SXL/*KSXC* 6881 [Lon. CS/*5*-7104]. Ashkenazy, Philh. O.

Ashkenazy's performances combine a refreshing spontaneity with an overall sense of proportion and balance. There is a fine sense of movement and yet nothing is hurried; detail is finely characterized, but nothing is fussy. Moreover, the recording is clear and lucid, with the balance between soloist and orchestra finely judged. The cassette transfer is made at the very highest level; although the sound is rich, very full and has striking range, there is just a hint of the refinement slipping marginally in tuttis.

Piano concertos Nos 17, K.453; 24 in C min., K.491.
** Ph. Dig. **412 524-2**; 412 524-1/*4* [id.]. André Previn, VPO.

These are the same two concertos that Previn recorded earlier for EMI with Sir Adrian Boult conducting; in these Philips performances, however, with his favourite Mozartian orchestra, the co-ordination is keener, bringing a natural interplay between soloist and players. Previn is generally a brisk Mozartian, fresh and direct with the crispest rhythmic pointing. The sparkle in the music making prevents the result from seeming rushed, even if some listeners may find the result lacking in charm. Previn offers comparatively little variety of keyboard colour, and dynamics are rarely reduced below *mezzo forte*. Compared with such strong keyboard personalities as Ashkenazy and Perahia, this seems slightly wanting in character, even though spontaneity is not lacking. Both piano and orchestra are superbly recorded in warm Vienna sound. The cassette is slightly less transparent in revealing orchestral detail than the CD and LP.

Piano concertos Nos 18 in B flat, K.456; 19 in F, K.459.
(*) DG Arc. Dig. **415 111-2; 415 111-1/*4* [id.]. Bilson, E. Bar. Sol., Gardiner.

The fourth of Malcolm Bilson's series brings an account of the *B flat Concerto* which is among the most attractive so far, with buoyantly spirited articulation in the outer movements, briskly paced but never sounding rushed, and the colour of the fortepiano made enticing in the *Andante*, by subtlety of inflection and imaginative dynamic shading. The performance of *No. 19 in F* is rather more controversial. Gardiner's fast, crisp tempo in the first movement is initially disconcerting and, with the *Allegretto* marking for the second movement observed to the letter, there is less contrast than usual. But again the sparkle of the finale rounds off a reading that is consistent in its freshness and momentum. The clear, naturally balanced recording adds much to the pleasure of this series, especially telling on CD, but very impressive on the outstanding chrome tape.

Piano concertos Nos 18 in B flat, K.456; 27 in B flat, K.595.
(M) *** Ph. 412 931-1/*4*. Alfred Brendel, ASMF, Marriner.

These are enchanting performances, beautifully recorded. There is immaculate and supremely intelligent playing in both concertos from Brendel and the Academy of St Martin-in-the-Fields. The slow movement of K.595 has not quite the breadth of Gilels, which remains in a class of its own. However, those collecting Brendel's cycle will need no prompting to add these splendid performances. Everything is deeply thought out, but retains its spontaneity. The remastered recording sounds equally refined on disc and tape.

Piano concertos Nos 19 in F, K.459; 22 in E flat, K.482.
*** Decca Dig. **410 140-2**; SXDL/*KSXDC* 7566 [Lon. 71066/5-]. De Larrocha, VSO, Segal.

Alicia de Larrocha can hold her own against most of her rivals both in terms of scale and sensitivity, though her K.482 is neither as completely integrated nor as touching as the Perahia which has particularly eloquent playing from the ECO wind. She is on good form, too, in the *F Major*; the Decca recording is beautifully transparent and clear, as well as being warmly resonant, which increases the tinge of romantic feeling in these performances. The sound on compact disc is particularly natural, with the upper range smooth yet well defined. Although the ear is slightly drawn to the forward balance of the woodwind, the piano image is most believable, the treble pellucid with no edge. The chrome cassette too is first class; even by comparison with the compact disc it loses little in refinement and range on top. Again the piano timbre is most impressive.

Piano concertos Nos 19, K.459; 23 in A, K.488.
❀ *** CBS Dig. **MK 39064**; IM/*IMT* 39064 [id.]. Murray Perahia, ECO.
*** DG **413 793-2**; 2530/*3300* 716 [id.]. Pollini, VPO, Boehm.

Murray Perahia gives highly characterful accounts of both concertos and a gently witty yet vital reading of the *F Major*, K.459. As always with this artist, there is a splendidly classical feeling allied to a keenly poetic sensibility. His account of K.488 has enormous delicacy and inner vitality, yet a serenity that puts it in a class of its own. There is however a robust quality about the finale and a fresh but controlled spontaneity. The slow movement has an elevation of spirit that reaffirms one's conviction that this version is one of the classics of the gramophone. Even in a series of such distinction, this performance stands out. On CD, the sound is particularly fresh and natural, but the chrome cassette has an excess of bass resonance.

The DG is also a distinguished record. Pollini is sparkling in the *F Major*, and in the *A Major* has a superbly poised, vibrant sense of line. Every phrase here seems to speak, and he is given excellent support from Boehm and the Vienna orchestra. There is no sense of haste in the outer movements; everything is admirably paced. Good, well-detailed and finely balanced analogue recording, which has transferred very well to CD, makes this one of the finest Mozart concerto records DG have given us. Among the K.488s, this must be ranked very highly. The transfer to cassette is also immaculate.

Piano concertos Nos 19, K.459; 24 in C min., K.491.
*** Decca **414 433-2** [id.]; SXL/*KSXC* 6947 [Lon. CS/*5*- 7174]. Ashkenazy, Philh. O.
*(*) ASV Dig. DCA/*ZCDCA* 541 [id.]. Osorio, RPO, Bátiz.

Ashkenazy's account of the *C minor Concerto* is a strong one, and must be numbered among the very finest now on the market. He has the measure of the work's breadth and emotional power; his playing, while showing all the elegance and poise one could desire, never detracts from the coherence of the whole. His is a balanced view of the first movement which avoids investing it with excessive intensity yet never loses impact. He is every bit as sensitive as his most formidable rivals (Barenboim and Perahia) in the middle movement and highly characterful in the finale. The *F major Concerto* also comes off effectively; it is subtle and sparkling. Clean, well-focused recording and an orchestral response that does almost as much credit to the pianist as his solo contribution. The cassette transfers are of Decca's highest quality: the *C minor Concerto* sounds particularly beautiful. The CD offers the usual advantages and the transfer of the analogue master cannot be faulted.

Jorge Fredrico Osorio is a young Mexican pianist who has been widely heard in America and Europe, and in BBC broadcasts in this country; he is obviously an artist of considerable talent. However, his excellently recorded account of the *F major Concerto*, although lively, misses the wit and sparkle of the score and suffers from a rather undervitalized accompaniment from Enrique Bátiz. On the reverse side, his *C minor Concerto* is small-scale by comparison with current rivals. Of course there are good things in both concertos but, generally speaking, this cannot carry an unqualified recommendation. There is an excellent cassette.

Piano concertos Nos 19, K.459; 25 in C, K.503.
*(*) DG Dig. **410 989-2**; 410 989-1/*4* [id.]. Serkin, LSO, Abbado.

If Serkin's 1984 Mozart was as good as the pre-war vintage – or, for that matter, some of the recordings he made at Marlboro in the 1960s – this would be a most valuable coupling. There is much to admire, including a clear and well-focused recording, but he is no match for the current competition; the insights this distinguished Mozartian brings to these concertos do not compensate for the ungainly passage-work and other infelicities. His vocal melisma is also slightly distracting, and this is just as striking on the excellent chrome tape as it is on the CD.

Piano concertos Nos 20 in D min., K.466; 21 in C, K.467.
*** CBS 74082/*40-*. Murray Perahia, ECO.

The Perahia is a recoupling of two already familiar performances: K.466 originally appeared in harness with the *F major*, K.413, and K.467 with the *Jeunehomme*, K.271, during 1977–8. They are discussed in greater detail in their original couplings. These readings are second to none and better than most.

Piano concertos Nos 20–21; 23 in A, K.488.
(B) ** Ph. On Tour *416 223-4* [id.]. Haebler, LSO, Galliera or Rowicki.

Ingrid Haebler's readings of the Mozart piano concertos are distinguished by a singular poise, meticulous finger control and great delicacy of touch. Bite and dramatic intensity are seldom much in evidence, but within her carefully delineated boundaries she undoubtedly gives pleasure by her restrained sensibility and musicianship. Her tempi in the *D minor Concerto* are warmly relaxed and on the leisurely side. She takes 34′ 35″ for the performance, which gives some idea of just how slow she is. She displays much delicate colouring, but more forward movement throughout and greater tautness in the finale would have been welcome. The first movement of K.467 is without the breadth and dignity that some artists have brought to it or the urgency one has from others. Neither soloist nor conductor can wholly escape the charge of prettifying the music. Haebler plays her own cadenzas – and very good they are – but in the heavenly slow movement she is not as imaginative as her finer rivals. Rowicki's direction is on the whole excellent, both here and in the *A major*, an enjoyable performance, though not on the level of Kempff or Perahia. What is impressive about this tape is the uniform excellence of the transfers, natural in timbre, very well balanced and with a very believable piano image. The recordings date from 1966–8 but they do not sound their age.

Piano concertos Nos 20–21; 24 in C min., K.491.
(B) *(*) HMV *TCC2-POR 54277*. Barenboim, ECO.

Barenboim's account of K.466 is among his finest Mozart recordings, and K.467 is also highly accomplished. The *C minor* is rather more controversial. The very first entry of the piano shows to what degree Barenboim wants to make it a romantic work. His conviction is unfailing; however, some may find the first two movements too heavy for their taste, while the finale is compensatingly fast and hectic. The layout of the three works on one extended-length cassette has the advantage of economy, but little else. The sound is generally good, although there is some loss of refinement in K.466 in the upper range of the orchestral tuttis; moreover, there is an irritating side-break after the first movement of K.467.

Piano concertos Nos 20–21; 26 in D (Coronation), K.537.
(B) *(*) DG Walkman *413 427-4* [id.]. Géza Anda, Salzburg Mozarteum O.

Anda's versions from the early 1960s are reasonably competitive in Walkman format. The recording sounds a little dated now in the matter of string timbre, but the piano is clear and truthful. The *D minor* is one of Anda's stronger performances, with solo playing that is stylish and spontaneous; No. 21 is notable for its poised introduction to the famous slow movement. One notices a certain rhythmic rigidity, and a lighter touch in the finale would have been acceptable; but on the whole this is satisfying. The *Coronation concerto*, however, is disappointing. Anda's performance lacks the magisterial quality of the finest accounts and there is a slightly routine feeling about the accompaniment.

Piano concertos Nos 20, K.466; 23 in A, K.488.
(M) *** Ph. Seq. 412 009-1/*4* [id.]. Alfred Brendel, ASMF, Marriner.

As a sampler for Brendel's Philips cycle, the Sequenza reissue could hardly be more enticing, coupling what always used to be regarded as the two most popular Mozart concertos – that is before K.467 was elevated by the inescapable film *Elvira Madigan*. Brendel here sounds more spontaneous than on some of his other Mozart records, notably in K.488, which is given a performance both strong and lyrical, with the F sharp minor slow movement intensely beautiful. The remastered recordings are more vivid than previously, although on tape the focus of No. 23 is not always absolutely sharp. However, there is a surprise bonus at the end of the cassette: the *Minuet* from the *Divertimento No. 17 in D*, K.334.

Piano concertos Nos 20, K.466; 24 in C min., K.491.
*** Ph. **412 254-2** [id.]. Clara Haskil, LOP, Markevitch.

These recordings, made shortly before her death in 1960, were last available on LP in a seven-record set devoted to Clara Haskil's Mozart; their reappearance on CD will give particular satisfaction to all her admirers. The poise she brought to Mozart and her effortless sense of style, with no straining after effect, are a source of wonder. Comparing the compact disc transfer with its last incarnation on LP, there is much greater body and clarity of detail – and, of course, greater range. The image is more firmly in focus. The orchestral sound from the Lamoureux Orchestra is certainly beefier than we are used to nowadays from the chamber forces favoured by artists such as Perahia and Ashkenazy, but the playing still remains rather special.

Piano concertos Nos (i) *20, K.466; 24 in C min., K.491;* (ii) *27 in B flat, K.595;* (iii) *Double concerto in E flat, K.365.*
(M) (*) HMV mono EX 290072-3/*5* (2). Artur Schnabel, (i) Philh. O, Susskind; (ii) LSO, Barbirolli; (iii) with Karl Ulrich Schnabel, LSO, Boult.

The two performances recorded with Susskind were made in 1948; the other two, with Sir John Barbirolli and Sir Adrian Boult, were pre-war. The transfers, made in 1982, are an improvement on earlier incarnations that appeared on French EMI. In Beethoven and Schubert, few pianists are more searching than Schnabel, but the very virtues that made him a great interpreter of Beethoven's Opp. 110 and 111 are less valid here. The originality of his mind is, of course, still extraordinary, and the cadenza he provides for the *C minor*, K.491, is positively mind-bending, modulating to remote key areas with the audacity of a Busoni. In K.466, the dramatic fires that he evokes are not those of *Don Giovanni*, but of Beethoven, and elsewhere his approach often sounds brusque. There is none of the pianistic elegance of a Casadesus, Gieseking or Lipatti; indeed, there are plenty of those impetuosities and moments of pianistic bad temper which are perfectly in character in Beethoven – but not here. Mozart's grace eludes him much of the time, and even in the slow movements of K.466 and K.595 he is rarely touching. The tape equivalents are cleanly transferred, though it is noticeable that in the *E flat Double concerto* the orchestral quality has less substance than in the solo concertos.

Piano concertos Nos 20, K.466; 27 in B flat, K.595.
❀ *** Decca **417288-2**; SXL/*KSXC* 7007 [Lon. CS/*5*- 7251]. Clifford Curzon, ECO, Britten.

In September 1970 Sir Clifford Curzon went to the Maltings at Snape, and there with Benjamin Britten and the ECO recorded these two concertos. K.595, the last concerto of all, was always the Mozart work with which he was specially associated; and not surprisingly – when he was the most painfully self-critical and distrusting of recording artists – he wanted to do it again. Just before he died in September 1982, sessions had been organized to make such a recording (as they had on previous occasions), but anyone hearing this magical record, full of the glow and natural expressiveness which always went with Britten's conducting of Mozart, will recognize both performances as uniquely individual and illuminating, with Curzon at his very finest. The coupling was kept from issue until after Sir Clifford's death, but it still sounds rich and beautiful, with the cassette matching the disc versions fairly closely, if a little soft-grained in the treble.

Piano concertos Nos 21 in C, K.467; 23 in A, K.488.
(M) **(*) RCA Gold GL/*GK* 85243 [AGL1/*AGK1* 5243]. Rubinstein, RCA Victor SO, Wallenstein.
** DG Dig. **410 068-2**; 2532/*3302* 095 [id.]. Serkin, LSO, Abbado.

Rubinstein brings his usual poise and beauty of phrasing to his coupling of two of

Mozart's finest concertos, and the slow movement of K.488 is especially beautiful. Alfred Wallenstein and his orchestra are well in the picture; they are more obviously in sympathy with their soloist here than in their companion coupling of the Grieg and Tchaikovsky *Concertos*. The recording was originally warm and spacious, but with the acoustic a little overblown. The remastering has refined the effect of the sound: it remains warm, but the upper strings are now very brightly lit. Rubinstein's timbre is clear and pearly. The woodwind is nicely balanced and retains its bloom. Disc and chrome tape sound very much the same.

It is sad that Serkin had to leave it until his eighties to attempt a full series of the Mozart concertos. Though his thoughtfulness as an artist is often clear, his playing is distressingly prosaic with no dynamic less than *mezzo forte*, scrappy passage-work and uneven scales. Refined accompaniment from Abbado and the LSO, but even there the styles clash. There are stronger and more sensitive accounts of both concertos, though few that are better recorded. The compact disc is of first-class quality, even if it reveals some of the soloist's vocal additions, and both LP and cassette formats are realistic.

Piano concertos Nos 23 in A, K.488; 24 in C min., K.491.
(M) **(*) HMV ED 290497-1/*4* [Ang. AM/*4AM* 34738]. Barenboim, ECO.

Barenboim's performance of the *A major Concerto* was the first to be recorded in his Mozart concerto series with the ECO, and the playing has all the sparkle and sensitivity one could ask for. There are times when the delicacy of fingerwork comes close to preciosity, as at the end of the opening theme in the slow movement, but it never goes over the edge. The orchestral accompaniment is admirably alive; one's only serious reservation concerns the somewhat fast tempo he adopts in the finale. K. 491 is altogether more controversial, heavily romantic. This is also available on a 'Portrait of the Artist' tape with two other *Piano concertos* (Nos 20 and 21) – see above. The sound of this reissue remains spacious and truthful.

Still recommended: Kempff's 1961 coupling of these two concertos with Leitner (a most perceptive partner) remains unsurpassed. The poetry of Kempff's playing is a constant joy, and the recording does not sound too dated (DG 2535/*3335* 204 [id.]).

Piano concertos Nos 23, K.488; 26 in D (Coronation), K.537.
** Tel. Dig. **ZK8.42970**; AZ6.42970 [id.]. Friedrich Gulda, Concg. O, Harnoncourt.

Like Zoltan Kocsis in his Hungaroton recording of K.488 (see above), Friedrich Gulda discreetly participates in the orchestral ritornelli. The playing of the Concertgebouw Orchestra for Nikolaus Harnoncourt is careful in handling both balance and nuances, and he is particularly successful in the *Coronation* concerto. Gulda gives an admirably unaffected and intelligent account of the *A major*, which is enjoyable – as, for that matter, is his reading of the *Coronation* – but it does not constitute a serious challenge to such rivals as Perahia or Brendel.

Piano concertos Nos 23, K.488; 27 in B flat, K.595.
*** Decca Dig. **400 087-2**; SXDL/*KSXDC* 7530 [Lon. LDR/*5*- 71007]. Ashkenazy, Philh. O.

Ashkenazy is on his finest form in both concertos and gets excellent results from both the keyboard and the Philharmonia Orchestra. His *A Major* is beautifully judged, alive and fresh, yet warm – one of the most satisfying accounts yet recorded. No quarrels either with the *B flat*, which is as finely characterized as one would expect. The recording focuses closely on the piano, but nevertheless no orchestral detail is masked and the overall impression is very lifelike, particularly in the excellent CD format. Along with Brendel, Perahia and Gilels, this is one of the best versions of the *B flat*. The quality on the chrome cassette is superb, luminous, rich and clear, with completely natural piano timbre. The CD is also very fine, but there is a slight edge on the strings; in many ways the cassette remains marginally preferable in its sound-balance.

Piano concertos Nos 24 in C min., K.491; 25 in C, K.503; 26 in D (Coronation), K.537; 27 in B flat, K.595.
(M) *(*) DG 413 532-1/*4*. Géza Anda, Salzburg Mozarteum O.

Géza Anda was the first to record the complete cycle in stereo in the 1960s, directing the Salzburg Mozarteum from the keyboard, and his set served us well for many years. Even if there are none of the refinements of nuance we have come to expect from Perahia and Ashkenazy, these are sane, straightforward accounts. To some, perhaps, his performances will seem strait-laced, very intelligent, but just a little short on poetry. The recording has long worn its years lightly but, after hearing many of the newest issues, it shows something of its age: the strings are a little wanting in bloom, particularly above the stave, and the orchestral recording is drier in this reissue. At its modest price, this is serviceable; unlike, say, the Kempff performances from this period, Anda is sound rather than special. The recordings are at their best in the tape format (issued in one of DG's cardboard flap-packs), with the quality fresh and clean.

Piano concertos Nos 25 in C, K.503; 26 in D (Coronation), K.537.
*** Decca Dig. **411 810-2**; 411 810-1/*4* [id.]. Ashkenazy, Philh. O.

Ashkenazy obviously sees K.503 as a 'big' concerto: his opening is on the grandest scale, emphasized by the weighty bass response of the recording. It is a strong reading, set in relief by the more delicate feeling of the *Andante*. Perahia establishes no less command but with a lighter orchestral texture, and his account is more imaginatively distinctive. However, Ashkenazy has much superior recording in every respect. Although the Philharmonia strings are brightly lit they are cleanly focused and woodwind detail is glowing, while the piano timbre is most beautiful. In the *Coronation concerto* Ashkenazy's approach to the first movement is comparably magisterial, while he produces some exquisitely shaded playing in the *Larghetto*, with the final *Allegretto* hardly less refined. Again the

Decca recording is of the highest quality, not only on CD, but on LP and the matching chrome tape. Perahia – though less beautifully recorded – is even finer, but those wanting Ashkenazy's coupling should not be disappointed.

Piano concerto No. 26 in D (Coronation), K.537; Concert rondos, Nos 1 in D, K.382; 2 in A, K.386.
*** CBS Dig. **MK 39224**; IM/*IMT* 39224 [id.]. Murray Perahia, ECO.

Perahia's award-winning account of the *Coronation concerto* is a performance of stature. He succeeds in making the work mean more than do most of his rivals, and the dignity and breadth of his reading are matched in the slow movement by enormous delicacy and sensibility. This is a magical performance in which the level of inspiration runs high. On LP and tape the *Concerto* is accommodated on one side, the other given over to superb accounts of the two *Concert rondos*, K.382 and K.386, which incorporates for the first time on record the closing bars newly discovered by Professor Alan Tyson. The recording is naturally balanced within a fairly resonant ambience, but on CD detail is refined and the piano image very tangible.

Piano concerto No. 27 in B flat, K.595; (i) *Double piano concerto in E flat, K.365.*
❀ (M) *** DG Gal. 419 059-1/*4* [id.]. Gilels, VPO, Boehm, (i) with Elena Gilels.

Gilels playing Mozart is in a class of his own. His is supremely lyrical playing that evinces all the classical virtues. No detail is allowed to detract from the picture as a whole; the pace is totally unhurried and superbly controlled. There is no point-making by means of agogic distortion or sudden rapt pianissimo; all the points are made by means of articulation and tone, and each phrase is marvellously alive. The slow-movement theme, for example, is played with a simplicity that is not arch as it is in some performances; nor is it over-refined in tone; the result gives added depth and spirituality. This is playing of the highest order of artistic integrity and poetic insight, while Boehm and the Vienna Philharmonic provide excellent support. The performance of the marvellous *Double concerto* is no less enjoyable. Its mood is comparatively serious, but this is not to suggest that the music's sunny qualities are not brought out, and the interplay of phrasing between the two soloists is beautifully conveyed by the recording without exaggerated separation. The quality both on disc and on tape is first class, and this is certainly one of the very finest Mozart piano concerto couplings in the catalogue. On this Galleria reissue it has been digitally re-mastered for later issue on compact disc.

Double piano concerto in E flat, K.365.
*(*) Tel. Dig. **ZK8.42961;** AZ6/*CX4*.42961 [id.]. Corea, Gulda, Concg. O, Harnoncourt – COREA: *Fantasy***; GULDA: *Ping-Pong*.(**)

On Telefunken, the spirited playing of the two soloists (who clearly enjoy themselves throughout) is not helped by Harnoncourt's aggressive direction of the first movement and his pacing of the finale which is too fast to achieve elegance as well as sparkle. But the accompanying notes (which are a collector's item) tell us that the artists were 'unanimous that the concerto should not be considered a *galant* trifle', so perhaps that explains the forcefulness of the direction. The recording derives from the Munich Klaviersommer Piano Festival of 1982, which accounts for the incredibly unsuitable couplings. The CD has plenty of immediacy.

Double piano concerto in E flat, K.365; (i) *Triple concerto in F, K.242.*
(M) ** Ph. Seq. 6527/*7311* 206. Haebler, Hoffman, (i) Bunge; LSO, Galliera.

These are fresh, unaffected readings, with Haebler dominating and producing characteristically fine playing in both slow movements. The recording is excellent, vivid and bold, on disc and tape alike. However, this is not in the class of the Gilels account of the *Double concerto* or the new Philips Brendel coupling below.

Double piano concerto in E flat, K.365; Triple piano concerto in F (Lodron), K.242 (arr. for 2 pianos).
*** Ph. **416 364-2**; 416 364-1/*4* [id.]. Brendel, Imogen Cooper, ASMF, Marriner.

Brendel chooses Mozart's own version of the so-called *Lodron triple concerto*, for two pianos, and couples it with the splendid *E flat Double concerto*. The playing is cultured and elegant, strikingly poised – particularly in K.242 – combining vigour with tonal refinement. Marriner's accompaniments are comparably polished and the Philips engineers afford the music making a most natural sound-balance, especially in the CD format, but also with a chrome tape of the highest quality. The analogue recording of K.365 dates from 1977; K.242 is digital and was made in 1984.

(i) *Triple harpsichord concerto in F, K.242; Harpsichord concertos* (after J. C. Bach) *K.107, Nos 1 in D; 3 in E flat.*
** Denon Dig. **C37 7600** [id.]. Dreyfus, (i) Baumont, Kiss; V. Capella Academica, Melkus.

There seems no special reason for preferring the so-called *Lodron triple concerto* on three harpsichords rather than on three fortepianos (or, indeed, pianos), but those attracted to the earlier keyboard instrument will find the present account is well managed and well recorded. The two solo works, based on sonatas by J. C. Bach, are admirably suited to the harpsichord, and Huguette Dreyfus plays them sympathetically. The accompaniments are sound and the balance is very good.

Violin concertos Nos 1–5.
(M) **(*) DG 413 203-1/*4* (2). Schneiderhan, BPO.

Schneiderhan's set with the Berlin Philharmonic Orchestra was made at the end of the 1960s. He plays with effortless mastery and a strong sense of classical proportion. The Berlin orchestra accompany well for him, though there is a slightly unsmiling quality at times. On two discs or tapes (in a DG flap-pack), this seems eminently worthwhile, as the recording remains of very good quality. On the chrome cassettes, the sound is suitably intimate for the first three concertos, then for No. 4 the level rises and gives the orchestra more presence, which seems appropriate.

Violin concertos Nos 1 in B flat, K.207; 2 in D, K.211; Rondo No. 1 in B flat, K.269.
*** Denon Dig. **C37 7506** [id.]. Kantorow, Netherlands CO, Hager.

Violin concerto No. 1; (i) *Sinfonia concertante in E flat for violin, viola and orchestra, K.364.*
** DG Dig. **413 461-2**; 413 461-1/*4* [id.]. Kremer, (i) Kashkashian, VPO, Harnoncourt.

Kantorow's coupling makes an excellent start to his Mozart series. He is given alert, stylish accompaniments by Leopold Hager and the Netherlands Chamber Orchestra, and the recording is eminently realistic, with the balance of the soloist only a trifle too close. Kantorow's full personality emerges gradually in the first movement of K.207, although he plays strongly with a fine classical spirit. The *Adagio* is beautifully done, and the presto finale sparkles. The account of K.211 is splendid in all respects, with a warmth and serenity in the *Andante* balanced by the character of the first movement and the elegant vivacity of the finale. The *B flat Rondo* makes an excellent bonus. Kantorow plays his own cadenzas – and very good they are. Highly recommended.

Neither of the Kremer performances is especially individual, though the playing is expert. For all the finesse of the soloist, the *B flat Concerto* is curiously uninvolving, and the digital recording is inclined to be fierce in the treble. There are much more rewarding accounts of the *Sinfonia concertante* available – see below.

Violin concerto No. 2 in D, K.211.
(*) Ph. Dig. **412 718-2; 412 718-1/*4* [id.]. Van Keulen, Netherlands CO, Ros-Marba – HAYDN: *Concerto in C.* **(*)

Violin concertos Nos 2, K.211; 4 in D, K.218.
*** HMV Dig. **CDC 747011-2** [id.]; ASD/*TCC-ASD* 4185 [Ang. DS/*4XS* 37904]. Mutter, Philh. O, Muti.

Violin concerto No. 2; (i) *Sinfonia concertante for violin and viola in E flat, K. 364.*
(*) Argo Dig. **411 613-2; 411 613-1/*4* [id.]. Iona Brown, (i) Suk; ASMF, Marriner.

Anne-Sophie Mutter followed up her famous record of the *G Major*, K.216, and *A Major*, K.219, with Karajan on DG – see below – with the two D major concertos on HMV and a different orchestra and conductor. The results are hardly less successful. She is given very sensitive support from the Philharmonia under Muti. Her playing combines purity and classical feeling, delicacy and incisiveness, and is admirably expressive. Its freshness too is most appealing and she is a strong contender in a very competitive field. The HMV recording is very good indeed; on CD the images are more sharply defined.

Iona Brown's account of the *D major Concerto* is also a fine one, even more positively classical in spirit, with striking vitality in the outer movements. The Brown/Suk partnership works well in the *Sinfonia concertante*, but there is an element of restraint in the slow movement which does not quite blossom here in the different ways one experiences with Zukerman and Perlman (on DG) or Brainin and Schidloff (on Chandos) – see below. Nevertheless these are both fine performances; if the coupling is more suitable, there are no grounds for complaint about the sound, which is fresh and clear. The CD gives realistic projection, but the ambience is not so warming as on some Argo recordings. There is a good tape.

Many readers will recall Isabelle van Keulen as the winner of the European young musician of the year in 1984 when, aged only eighteen, she gave an impressive account of a Vieuxtemps concerto. She is hardly less persuasive in Mozart, though there is formidable competition from Iona Brown and the Academy of St Martin-in-the-Fields on Argo. The Philips recording is excellently balanced and very vivid, particularly in the compact disc format, but the playing of the Netherlands Chamber Orchestra under Antoni Ros-Marba is a little deficient in character and vitality, by the side of Marriner's Academy. The agreeably warm ambience is more flattering than the Argo acoustic, with the cassette softer-grained than the CD and LP.

Violin concerto No. 3 in G, K.216.

(B) ** DG Walkman *415 332-4* [id.]. Schneiderhan, BPO – BEETHOVEN: *Triple concerto*; BRAHMS: *Double concerto.***

Violin concertos Nos 3; 4 in D, K.218.

*** CBS **MK 42030** [id.]. Francescatti, Columbia SO, Bruno Walter.

(M) **(*) HMV EG 290276-1/*4* [Ang. AM/*4AM* 34709]. D. Oistrakh, BPO.

(i) *Violin concerto No. 3;* (ii) *Sinfonia concertante in E flat, K.364.*

**(*) HMV Dig. EL 270355-1/*4*. (i) Oscar Shumsky, Scottish CO, Yan Pascal Tortelier; (ii) with Eric Shumsky.

*(*) Pickwick Con. CC/*CCTC* 7586. (i) Schneiderhan, BPO; (ii) Brandis, Cappone, BPO, Boehm.

Francescatti's coupling of the *Third* and *Fourth* Mozart *Concertos* is probably his finest record, and in their remastered CD format these fine performances from 1959 are given a new lease of life. The playing is at times a little wayward, but Bruno Walter accompanies throughout with his usual warmth and insight and falls into line sympathetically with his soloist. Both slow movements are beautifully played, albeit with an intensity that barely stops short of Romanticism, and the changing moods of the finale in the *G major Concerto* are admirably contrasted. In some ways the *D major* suits Francescatti's opulent style of playing best of all, and there is a warm glow about the second subject of the first movement – a sinuous and enchanting tune – that almost reminds one of Kreisler, while in both works the cadenzas are made a most attractive feature. The whole atmosphere of this music making represents the pre-authentic approach to Mozart at its most rewarding. The sound is just right for the music, warm and full with no apologies for the ample orchestral textures.

Shumsky is an artist of strong personality. His *G major Concerto* has an unhurried, musicianly non-virtuoso approach, a sweetness of tone and warmth of personality. This is likeable music-making of the old school, with nothing chromium-plated about it. The orchestral playing lacks the very last degree of polish, but Yan Pascal Tortelier produces eminently musical results. In the *Sinfonia concertante*, Shumsky is joined by his son, who produces splendidly rich tone. The slow movement is kept very flowing and may be a shade too fast for some tastes. At first it gives the impression of being almost matter-of-fact, but this soon proves deceptive. The interplay between the two soloists throughout is finely judged. Well-detailed, if not especially warm, recording, though the LP pressing of the *Sinfonia concertante* comes close to discoloration in tutti. The cassette is first class in every way, transferred at a high level with the sound vividly fresh.

Schneiderhan's is a finely wrought performance, strongly classical and well recorded for its period. He plays his own cadenzas and although there is a slight want of sparkle, and perhaps also the atmosphere is a shade cool, the reading is still throughly enjoyable. The Walkman tape is well engineered and offers generous couplings.

This Schneiderhan version is also available at bargain price (on both LP and tape), coupled to Boehm's 1966 *Sinfonia concertante*, K.364. This is let down ultimately by the slow movement, which is just a shade too brisk and prosaic; the finale is also a little unyielding. The two soloists have excellent style and are perfect in all matters of phrasing, intonation and so on, but Boehm's reading is lacking in personality by comparison with the finest versions.

Oistrakh's performances are taken from his 1972 complete set. The balance is close and Oistrakh is predictably strong and positive. He is well accompanied by the Berlin Philharmonic, although there is a touch of heaviness at times. But the remastering has lightened the orchestral sound and Oistrakh is at his finest in both slow movements, which are memorably expressive. There is a very good tape.

Violin concertos Nos 3 in G, K.216; 5 in A (Turkish) K.219.
*** DG **415 327-2**; Sig. 410 982-1/*4* [id.]. Mutter, BPO, Karajan.
*** HMV Dig. EL 270075-1/*4* [Ang. AE/*4AE* 34443]. Frank Zimmermann, Württemberg CO, Faerber.
(*) DG Dig. **410 020-2; 2532/*3302* 080 [id.]. Perlman, VPO, Levine.
(*) Denon Dig. **C37 7504 [id.]. Kantorow, Netherlands CO, Hager.
** Ph. **412 250-2** [id.]. Grumiaux, LSO, Sir Colin Davis.
*(*) CBS Dig. **CD 37290** [id.]. Zukerman, St Paul CO.

Extraordinarily mature and accomplished playing from Anne-Sophie Mutter, who was a mere fourteen years of age when this recording was made. Her instinctive mastery means that there is no hint of immaturity: the playing has polish, but fine artistry too and remarkable freshness. The lovely phrasing in the slow movements of both works is matched by an engaging spring in the first movement of K.219, with the 'Turkish' interlude in the finale also sparkling vividly. It goes without saying that she receives the most superb orchestral support from the Berlin Philharmonic. Karajan is at his most sympathetic and scales down the accompaniment to act as a perfect setting for his young soloist. The analogue recording is beautifully balanced, and on CD detail is enhanced and the imagery made firmer. There is also an excellent tape, which may be considered a very viable alternative to the CD which costs more than twice as much. Both LP and cassette are reissued on DG's mid-price Signature label.

Another most promising début comes from EMI. These are highly intelligent performances, thoughtful without being in the least self-conscious. In the slow movement of the *G major*, Frank Peter Zimmermann shows a keen and sensitive musical personality that augurs well for the future. Both concertos are very alive in feeling, with finely spun tone and keenly articulated rhythms: Zimmermann was still nineteen when these characterful performances were put on record. The recording is one of EMI's best and has warmth and body. The cassette is particularly fine, and both forms give great satisfaction.

With the violin balanced rather close, Perlman treats these two most popular of the Mozart violin concertos rather more as virtuoso showpieces than is common. For some the tone will be too sweet for Mozart, and though with sympathetic accompaniment these are both enjoyable performances, they have not quite the natural felicity that marks Perlman's finest work on record. Full digital recording which brings out the idiosyncrasy of the balance. This is equally noticeable on the lively chrome cassette and even more so on the compact disc, where one hears also that the woodwind is somewhat reticent. On CD the sound is strikingly clear and clean, but there is just a touch of digital edge on top.

Jean-Jacques Kantorow is a highly intelligent player and has obviously studied these scores with meticulous care. In his hands they come up very freshly indeed. Kantorow uses the Ysaye cadenzas, which are shorter. In a way his are the best thought-out of the present set, though in terms of personality and tonal beauty others are to be preferred. In this coupling, Perlman and Mutter (both on DG) and Frank Peter Zimmermann (on HMV) are front-runners.

Grumiaux's classic accounts date from the early 1960s and still sound excellent. His playing is beautifully finished and intonation is impeccable; Davis gives spirited support. However, while many collectors may feel tempted by these performances on mid-price LP, there will inevitably be some resistance to paying the full compact disc price when so many excellent newer versions of distinction are now available. The present coupling has been specially made for CD; on LP and tape, the *A major Concerto* is paired with No. 4 in D, K.218.

On CBS, Pinchas Zukerman directs as well as playing. His admirers will not be disappointed, though his sweet tone and effortless facility do not always engage one's sympathies. He languishes lovingly in the slow movements, particularly that of the *G major*, and is not always subtle in his projection of feeling. The St Paul's orchestra obviously consists of some fine players, and the CBS recording is very fine indeed. There is much to admire here, but this would not be a first choice.

Violin concertos Nos 4, K.218; 5 (Turkish), K.219.
*** Nimbus Dig. **NIM 5009**; 2140. Shumsky, Scottish CO, Yan Pascal Tortelier.

Shumsky's performances with the Scottish Chamber Orchestra have the advantage of being totally unaffected, natural and full of character. He seems to have an excellent rapport with Yan Pascal Tortelier who secures a very alive and thoroughly musical response from the Scottish Chamber Orchestra. They do not produce as sumptuous or as beautiful a sound as, say, the Vienna Philharmonic for Levine on Perlman's DG record of Nos 3 and 5, yet the results are every bit as enjoyable, because the players themselves convey enthusiasm and pleasure. The recording is nicely balanced.

Violin concerto No. 4 in D, K.218; Adagio in E, K.261; Rondos for violin and orchestra Nos 1 in B flat, K.269; 2 in C, K.373.
** CBS **MK 37839**; IM/*IMT* 37839 [id.]. Zukerman, St Paul CO.

Violin concerto No. 4; Adagio, K.261; Rondo No. 2, K.373; (i) *Concerto for violin and fortepiano, K. Anh. 56/315f* (fragment); (ii) *Sinfonia concertante in A, K. Anh. 104/320e* (fragment).
(*) Denon Dig. **C37 7505 [id.]. Kantorow, (i) Glen Wilson, (ii) Vladimir Mendelssohn, Mari Fujiwara; Netherlands CO, Hager.

Kantorow's account of the *D major Concerto* is well up to the standard of his fine Mozart series, with fresh, intelligent solo playing, essentially classical in spirit, and with an agreeable but not exaggerated warmth in the slow movement. The two shorter pieces are also splendidly done, the *Adagio*, K.261, particularly fine. There is undoubted interest in the inclusion of the two fragments, from an unfinished *Double concerto* and the *Sinfonia concertante*, featuring three soloists. However, they are disconcertingly short and break off abruptly. The recording is first class and very well balanced.

Zukerman's performance of the *Concerto* is unmannered and stylish, admirably direct in approach, although the *Andante* is taken rather slowly. The pacing of the last movement is also somewhat idiosyncratic. The shorter pieces are played with some flair, the *Adagio* most expressively. The accompaniments, which Zukerman also directs, are polished, the recording vivid and rather brightly lit. There is a touch of digital edge here, on both CD and LP; the chrome cassette, as so often with CBS, is smoother, yet realistic, although the focus occasionally slips in places.

Violin concerto No. 5, K.219; (i) *Sinfonia concertante in E flat, K.364.*
(M) **(*) HMV EG 290569-1/*4* [Ang. AM/*4AM* 34737]. David, (i) and Igor Oistrakh, BPO.

As in the new Oistrakh coupling of the *Third* and *Fourth Concertos*, the remastering has lightened and freshened the sound, and the touch of rhythmic heaviness in the otherwise fine accompaniments from the Berlin Philharmonic is mainly noticeable in the middle section of the finale of K.219. This is superbly played by David Oistrakh, with the slow movement particularly fine. He is joined by his son, Igor, in the *Sinfonia concertante*, and – as in their 1962 recording of the Bach *Double concerto* – there is a perfect symbiosis of timbre and phrasing. The outer movements are attractively vital; it is only in the *Andante* where the approach is rather too straight and unimaginative, although there is no lack of expressive feeling.

Concertone in C for 2 violins and orchestra, K.190; Sinfonia concertante in E flat for violin, viola and orchestra, K.364.
❀ *** DG **415 486-2**; 415 486-1/*4* [id.]. Perlman, Zukerman, Israel PO, Mehta.
ℭ *** Chan. Dig. **CHAN 8315**; ABRD/*ABTD* 1096 [id.]. Brainin, Schidlof, SNO, Gibson.
(*) Denon Dig. **C37 7507 [id.]. Kantorow, Olga Martinova, Vladimir Mendelssohn, Hans Meijer, Netherlands CO, Hager.
(B) *(**) CBS DC 40167 (2). Stern, Zukerman, ECO, Barenboim – PLEYEL and STAMITZ: *Sinfonias concertantes.***(*)

An obviously sensible coupling is well served on Chandos by excellent performances and sound of demonstration quality, made in the warmly flattering ambience of St Barnabas's Church in London. The responsive playing of Norbert Brainin and Peter Schidlof communicates readily, even if their expressive fervour does bring a degree of romanticism to the slow movement of the *Sinfonia concertante*, and their phrasing employs tenutos, at times rather indulgently. Yet there is no lack of vitality in outer movements, and Sir Alexander Gibson's accompaniments are stylish and strong. The *Concertone*, where Schidlof changes from viola to violin, is also very successful, with Neil Black making an elegant contribution in the concertante oboe role. This is a less inspired work but does not lack a sense of stature here. A most enjoyable issue, especially on CD, but sounding well on both LP and tape, the latter vivid but fractionally less refined.

The alternative DG version of the *Sinfonia concertante* was recorded in Tel Aviv at the Huberman Festival in December 1982. It is less successfully balanced, with the soloists a fraction too near the microphones and with orchestral detail not so clearly focused as on Chandos. This is slightly emphasized on CD, and many will find the quality on LP, and especially on the admirable chrome cassette, to be slightly smoother in its solo imagery, without loss of vividness. The performance is in a class of its own and is an example of 'live' recording at its most magnetic, with the inspiration of the occasion caught on the wing. On the bows of Perlman and Zukerman the slow movement has an unforgettable serenity and spiritual beauty. The two artists play as one, yet their timbres are marvellously contrasted, with the silvery image of the violin set against the dark, rich viola tone. After the elegiac close to the *Andante*, the joyful finale with its 'whoopsing' rhythms is a delight. Zubin Mehta is caught up in the music making and accompanies most sensitively, in the slow movement creating an almost ethereal pianissimo with his first violins. The *Concertone* is also splendidly done (with a fine oboe contribution from Chaim Jouval); the ear notices the improvement in the sound balance of the studio recording of this work. But the *Sinfonia concertante*, with the audience incredibly quiet, conveys an electricity rarely caught on record.

The second alternative, from Denon, offers performances which in character fall neatly between those offered on DG and Chandos. Kantorow forms an excellent partnership with Vladimir Mendelssohn in the *Sinfonia concertante*; in the *Concertone*, Olga Martinova, the violinist, and the fine oboist, Hans Meijer, distinguish themselves. In keeping with the style of Kantorow's concerto series, the playing is refined and classical in spirit. It has character and spontaneity, and the slow movement of the *Sinfonia concertante* does not stray outside the boundaries of Mozartian expressive feeling, while not lacking warmth. With recording which is naturally balanced and realistic (and in K.364 aurally more pleasing than on the DG), this Denon CD offers performances which give much pleasure in their freshness and natural responsiveness.

Stern recorded Mozart's *Sinfonia concertante* for CBS at least twice before the account with Zukerman and Barenboim, made in the early 1970s. The present account still stands among the finest available versions, presenting (as in the DG performance) two soloists of equally strong musical personality. The central slow movement is taken at a very expansive *Andante*, but the concentration intensifies the beauty, and the finale is sparkling and resilient. The recording, in its original format, had a tendency to sound aggressive, and this digitally remastered version is even more sharply etched, with the solo timbres given a degree of shrillness. The dryness of the acoustic also detracts from the charm of the *Concertone*, a work that can easily seem to go on too long for its material. Stern, Zukerman and Barenboim pay the *Andantino grazioso* the compliment of a very slow tempo to match that of the *Sinfonia concertante*, and again the concentration is superb. Whatever the shortcomings of the recording, the artistry of the soloists still communicates readily. These performances are adventurously coupled, at what amounts to bargain price, with *Sinfonias concertantes* by Pleyel and Stamitz – although the Pleyel work is omitted from the equivalent tape set, which is not recommended.

Divertimenti for strings Nos 1 in D; 2 in B flat; 3 in F, K.136–8; Serenade No. 6 in D (Serenata notturna), K.239.
ℭ *** Ph. Dig. **412 120-2**; 412 120-1/*4* [id.]. I Musici.

The three Salzburg *Divertimenti* date from early 1772, when Mozart was sixteen. They can be regarded as string quartets (and are indeed so listed in the *New Grove*), but more often than not are played by a fuller complement of strings, as they are here. The performances are finished and elegant and beautifully recorded. The compact disc is extremely vivid and clean, bringing the players before one's very eyes. The high-level chrome cassette is also exceptionally lively; I Musici have splendid presence and realism in the tape format.

(i) *Divertimenti for strings Nos 1 in D, K.136; 3 in F, K.138; Serenades Nos 6* (*Serenata notturna*); (ii) *13* (*Eine kleine Nachtmusik*); (iii) *Sinfonia concertante in E flat, K.297b.*
(B) **(*) DG Walkman *413 152-4*. (i) BPO, Karajan; (ii) VPO, Boehm; (iii) BPO, Boehm.

Karajan's performances of the two *String Divertimenti* and the *Serenata notturna* are beautifully played and as such they prompt the liveliest admiration. At the same time there is a predictably suave elegance that seems to militate against spontaneity. Cultured and effortless readings, beautifully recorded and well balanced, they somehow leave one untouched. There is too much legato and not always a balancing sparkle. Boehm's contribution to this generous bargain-priced Walkman tape is another matter. His 1976 VPO version of Mozart's *Night music* is among the finest available, polished and spacious, with a neat, lightly pointed finale. The account of the *Sinfonia concertante* is of superlative quality, sounding amazingly idiomatic and well blended, with the balance between soloists and orchestra nicely managed. This is altogether refreshing. The chrome-tape transfers are first class, except in *Eine kleine Nachtmusik* where the upper range lacks the last degree of freshness, although the quality remains full and clear in detail.

Divertimento for strings No. 1, K.136; A Musical Joke, K.522; Serenade No. 13 (*Eine kleine Nachtmusik*), *K.525.*
*** Ph. Dig. **412 269-2**; 412 269-1/*4* [id.]. ASMF Chamber Ens.

Three popular Mozart pieces given with elegance and polish by the Academy Chamber players and recorded with complete fidelity and splendid definition by the Philips engineers. All three will give pleasure. Readers wanting this particular coupling need not hesitate on either artistic or technical grounds. The compact disc conveys an excellent sense of presence and realism.

Divertimento for strings No. 3 in F, K.138; Serenade No. 13 (*Eine kleine Nachtmusik*), *K.525.*
*(*) Denon Dig. **C37 7178** [id.]. Lucerne Fest. Strings, Baumgartner – VIVALDI: *Concertos.**(*)

These are well-articulated, musical performances, played with a fine degree of polish and most realistically recorded. Baumgartner's touch is just a little severe, however, and the slow movement of the *Night music*, though not ungracious, fails to smile as it can.

Divertimento No. 11 in D for oboe, 2 horns and string quartet, K.251.
** Ph. Dig. **412 618-2**; 412 618-1/*4* [id.]. Holliger, Baumann, Gasciarrino, Orlando Qt, Guldemond – *Oboe quartet* etc.***

A disappointing performance of an attractive work. The playing itself is polished, alive and well integrated, as one might expect from this cast list, but the approach is rhythmically heavy at times – though the gentler movements come off well – not helped by the close balance. The sound is good, although the high-level cassette is less refined than the disc versions.

Divertimenti Nos 11 in D, K.251; 14 in B flat, K.270; Serenade No. 6 in D (Serenata notturna), K.239.
*** DG Dig. **415 669-2**; 415 669-1/*4* [id.]. Orpheus CO.

These are wholly admirable performances. Alert, crisply rhythmic allegros show consistent resilience, strong yet without a touch of heaviness, while slow movements are warmly phrased, with much finesse and imaginative use of light and shade. The minuet second movement of K.251 is particularly appealing in this respect, while the fourth movement, which is also a minuet but with three variations, has much engaging detail. The *Serenata notturna*, which can easily sound bland, has a fine sparkle here; while the *B flat Divertimento* with its scoring for 2 oboes, 2 horns and 2 bassoons makes an effective contrast. Here the oboe playing is particularly felicitous. This is another collection to confirm first impressions (from this group's début in Haydn and Rossini) that the Orpheus Chamber Orchestra is one of the world's finest, and perhaps the first to convince the listener that a conductor can be superfluous in certain repertoire. Impeccable in ensemble, this playing has no sense of anonymity of character or style. The recording, made in the Performing Arts Centre of New York State University at Purchase, is truthful but rather closely balanced. On the comparatively mellow LP and matching tape this offers no problems; but the more sharply defined CD brings a touch of edginess to the violins above the stave.

Divertimento No. 15 in B flat, K.287; Divertimento for strings No. 3, K.138.
*** Ph. Dig. **412 740-2**; 412 740-1/*4* [id.]. ASMF Chamber Ens.

The K.287 *Divertimento*, composed in Salzburg for the Countess Lodron, is a major six-movement piece, with an attractive theme with variations coming second and a central *Adagio*, led by the first violin, of considerable expressive intensity. The finale is witty and humorously based on a folksong ('The farmer's wife has lost the cat'). This piece was intended for solo instruments; the performance here, with a double bass and two horns added to a string quartet, is admirable and beautifully recorded (though the high-level tape loses some of the refinement of the CD and LP). The *String divertimento* makes an agreeable filler, less substantial, perhaps, but with a warmly appealing slow movement.

Divertimento No. 17 in D, K.334; March in D, K.445.
ⓒ *** Ph. Dig. **411 102-2**; 411 102-1/*4* [id.]. ASMF Chamber Ens.

Divertimento No. 17, K.334; Divertimento for strings No. 1, K.136.
ⓒ *** Denon Dig. **C37 7080** [id.]. Augmented Berlin Philh. Qt.

The engaging *D major Divertimento* with its famous Minuet has been frequently recorded in orchestral dress, but it is now more often given as a chamber version, as it is by the Academy. This is an expert performance with plenty of charm and a recording to match. In its compact disc format it is wonderfully lifelike and present; the cassette, however, is disappointing, with a loss of upper range and a balance which orientates to the middle and bass.

On Denon, a hardly less successful account from the augmented Berlin Philharmonia Quartet. The music making has the integrated feeling of outstanding ensemble playing, achieved without a conductor. It is polished, spirited and full of warmth. The famous Minuet is just a shade indulgent, but in all other respects this is first class. The *String Divertimento* is equally attractive and makes a more substantial encore than the *March*. With a particularly believable recording, this can be enthusiastically recommended alongside, though not in preference to, the ASMF version.

6 German dances, K.571; Les petites riens: ballet music, K.299b; Serenade No. 13 (Eine kleine Nachtmusik), K.525.
*** Erato Dig. **ECD 88014**; NUM/*MCE* 75091 [id.]. SCO, Leppard.

An excellent collection in every way. The performance of *Les petites riens* is delightful, spirited and polished, and the *German dances* are no less lively and elegant; the famous *Nachtmusik* is nicely proportioned and very well played. The sound is especially believable on CD, giving a tangible impression of the players sitting together out beyond the speakers.

A Musical joke, K.522.
*** Erato Dig. **ECD 88021**; NUM/*MCE* 75092 [id.]. Paillard CO, Paillard – LEOPOLD MOZART: *Cassation* etc.***

Happily paired with a high-spirited version of Leopold Mozart's *Toy symphony*, Paillard's account of Mozart's fun piece makes the most of its outrageous jokes, with the horns in the opening movement boldly going wrong and the final discordant clash sounding positively cataclysmic; yet it takes into account the musical values, too. The *Adagio cantabile* is very graciously played and the finale (famous as a TV signature tune) is articulated with infectious sparkle. The recording is excellent, the orchestral group being placed within a warm ambience which yet does not cloud inner detail. The overall effect may be less subtle than the Amadeus version (see below), but the more boisterous approach is not spoilt by clumsiness.

A Musical Joke, K.522; Serenade No. 13 in G (Eine kleine Nachtmusik), K.525.
*** DG **400 065-2**; 2531/*3301* 253 [id.]. Augmented Amadeus Qt.

Eine kleine Nachtmusik has rarely sounded so refreshing and exhilarating as here; the finale in particular is delectably resilient. The musical clowning in the *Musical Joke*, which can so often seem heavy and unfunny, is here given charm. The horn players, Gerd Seifert and Manfred Klier, are from the Berlin Philharmonic. The recording is first rate, although on the cassette the horns create slight problems of focus in the *Musical Joke* when they are playing loudly. The compact disc has fine presence and immediacy.

Notturno for four orchestras, K.286; Serenade No. 6 (Serenata notturna), K.239; Serenade No. 13 (Eine kleine Nachtmusik), K.525.
*** O-L Dig. **411 720-2**; 411 720-1/*4* [id.]. AAM, Hogwood.

Eine kleine Nachtmusik is usually given in the four-movement form that survives. Christopher Hogwood follows Dart's earlier example by adding the missing minuet, though – unlike Dart, who transcribed a minuet from a piano sonata – Hogwood uses a minuet that Mozart composed in collaboration with his English pupil, Thomas Attwood. All the repeats in every movement save one are observed – which is perhaps too much of a good thing. The performance is given one instrument to a part and is sprightly and alive. The *Serenata notturna* and the *Notturno for four orchestras* are for larger forces and are given with considerable panache. This record should in fact be investigated by those not normally responsive to period instruments as the musical results are certainly thought-provoking. Technically, this is first class, with clean and well-defined recorded sound and great presence, particularly in the compact disc format.

Overtures: La Clemenza di Tito; Così fan tutte; Don Giovanni; Die Entführung aus dem Serail; Idomeneo; Lucio Silla; Le Nozze di Figaro; Der Schauspieldirektor; Die Zauberflöte.
*** HMV Dig. **CDC 747014-2**; ASD/*TCC-ASD* 4101 [Ang. DS/*4XS* 37879]. ASMF, Sir Neville Marriner.

Overtures: La Clemenza di Tito; Così fan tutte; Don Giovanni; Die Entführung aus dem Serail; Idomeneo; Lo sposo deluso; Le nozze di Figaro; Der Schauspieldirektor; Die Zauberflöte.
(M) *** Ph. Seq. 6527/*7311* 204. BBC SO, LSO, or O of ROHCG, ASMF; Sir Colin Davis.

Marriner's collection is strongly characterized, emphasizing the spirit of the opera house, offering plenty of drama in *Don Giovanni* and *Idomeneo* and a sense of spectacle with the percussion effects in *Die Entführung*. *Così fan tutte* and *Figaro* bring a lighter touch; throughout, the ASMF playing is characteristically spirited and stylish, with the string detail nicely clean and polished. The digital recording is bright and bold, giving the upper strings a brilliant sheen. Chrome cassette and disc are closely matched. The CD, however, softens the focus and the sound is more natural.

Davis's complete recordings of Mozart operas made in the 1960s and 1970s stand the test of time well, and this collection of overtures, mainly taken from them, makes an attractive mid-price issue, well recorded, with a fresh, vivid cassette.

Serenade No. 3 in D, K.185; March in D, K.189.
(*) O-L Dig. **411 936-2; 411 936-1/*4* [id.]. Schröder, AAM, Hogwood.

Mozart's first large-scale *Serenade* dates from 1773 and is sometimes given the sobriquet '*Andretter*', after the name of its commissioner, a Salzburg military official who needed music for his son's wedding. In this work Mozart established the feature of including a miniature violin concerto as part of the structure, though here its movements are interspersed with others. This presents the only drawback to the present recording, for Schröder's account of the solo role in the *Andante* is rather too straight and direct, although he offers more charm later on when he contributes to the Trio of the Minuet. The performance overall is brimming with vitality, the finales especially neat and infectious, and those who do not object to the astringency of 'original' string timbres in a piece essentially intended to divert will find that the diversity of Mozart's invention is fully characterized. The recording is first rate in all three media.

Serenade No. 4 in D, K.203; March in D, K.237.
** German HM **IC 567 199989-2**. Collegium Aureum.

Serenade No. 5 in D, K.204; March in D, K.215.
** German HM **IC 567 199958-2**. Collegium Aureum.

These recordings date from the mid-1970s and have been digitally remastered for compact disc. Both *Serenades* encompass a three-movement violin concerto in their midst, played very well indeed by Franzjosef Maier. Although tempi are occasionally a bit problematic (the last Minuet of K.204 is positively funereal), there are enough good things to make both these performances enjoyable.

Serenades Nos 6 in D (Serenata notturna), K.239; 7 in D (Haffner), K.250; 9 in D (Posthorn), K.320; 13 in G (Eine kleine Nachtmusik), K.525.
(M) *** Decca Jub. 411 845-1/*4* (2). V. Moz. Ens., Boskovsky.

All but the *Serenata notturna*, which is more recent, come from the early 1970s, a vintage period for Boskovsky and the Decca engineers. They are economically recoupled, still at mid-price, on two discs and tapes, with excellent sound. Boskovsky's version of the *Haffner* is marvellously alive, full of sparkle and elegance, with admirable phrasing and feeling for detail. The *Posthorn serenade* (no longer available separately) is equally fine, with its natural musicality and sense of style. *Eine kleine Nachtmusik* sounds wonderfully fresh, and as a performance is unsurpassed in the present catalogue.

Serenade No. 7 in D (Haffner), K.250; March, K.249.
*** Ph. Dig. **416 154-2**; 416 154-1/*4* [id.]. I. Brown, ASMF, Marriner.
** Tel. Dig. **ZK8.43062**; AZ6/*CX4* 43062 [id.]. Zehetmair, Dresden State O, Harnoncourt.

A spacious, yet warm and polished account of the *Haffner serenade* from Marriner and his Academy players, with Iona Brown making a superb contribution in the concertante violin role. There is sparkle here as well as expressive grace. The Academy string tone is sweet and smooth, yet articulation is neat, with admirable rhythmic freshness in the outer movements. The recording is resonant, which increases the impression of a full orchestral performance rather than one on a chamber scale. As usual, the Philips engineers provide a natural sound-balance with rich, full textures, especially refined on CD but also sounding very well on the chrome tape. In terms of presence and realism, however, especially at lower dynamic levels, the compact disc takes the palm.

Like the *Posthorn serenade*, the *Haffner* enfolds a miniature violin concerto within its eight movements. As in his record of the former, Harnoncourt's soloist is Thomas Zehetmair who gives a splendid account of himself. Harnoncourt offers an eminently spacious and expressive view of the piece, at times a little idiosyncratic. (He puts the brakes on the trio sections of the Minuets of movements 3, 5 and 7, and the phrasing is mannered.) However, though the recording is very good on both disc and tape, this does not displace older versions, particularly Boskovsky's Decca LP (Jub. JB/*KJBC* 31) while on CD Marriner remains first choice.

Serenade No. 9 in D (Posthorn), K.320; 2 Marches, K.335.
*** Ph. Dig. **412 725-2**; 412 725-1/*4* [id.]. ASMF, Marriner.
*(*) Tel. Dig. **ZK8 43063**; AZ6/*CX4* 43063 [id.]. Dresden State O, Harnoncourt.

Serenades Nos 9 in D (Posthorn); 13 (Eine kleine Nachtmusik), K.525.
(*) Telarc **CD 10108; DG 10108 [id.]. Prague CO, Mackerras.
(*) DG Dig. **410 085-2; 2532/*3302* 098 [id.]. VPO, Levine.

Mozart's *Posthorn serenade* is well served on compact disc, but there is a clear first choice, unless a coupling of the *Night music* is essential. Marriner's performance is spacious, cultured and marvellously played. The posthorn, which gives the work its sobriquet, plays only a minor (if effective) role in the Trio of the second Minuet. The work's kernel is its central movements which – in the place of the usual miniature violin concerto – feature concertante wind in four pairs. The Academy wind players make a compelling case for modern instruments here, as do the strings in the lovely *Andantino* which follows, where the mood darkens. The outer movements are both spirited and strong, the minuets lively and resilient. Michael Laird's contribution on the posthorn is characterful yet elegant. The two marches are used as 'entrance' and 'exit' music, the first, with its jaunty oboe solo, setting an infectious atmosphere for the main work which is to follow. The recording, in a fairly resonant acoustic, adds to the feeling of breadth without blurring detail. The sound is first class in all three formats, but with a very slightly sharper focus on CD.

The Prague strings have great warmth and Mackerras gets vital results from his Czech forces. Rhythms are lightly sprung and the phrasing is natural in every way. The Telarc acoustic is warm and spacious with a wide dynamic range (some might feel it is too wide for this music), and most ears will find the effect more agreeable than the drier, brighter DG sound-balance. The performance of the *Posthorn serenade* here has slightly more character than Levine's, although in the *Night music* Levine's direct, elegant manner is in some ways more telling.

In the *Posthorn serenade* Levine's tempi are well judged, and the Vienna Philharmonic play with distinction. This performance is certainly among the best now available, and the coupling is no less persuasive. The recording is clean and well balanced, but with less warmth than the Telarc. Indeed, there is a sharpness of outlines on the DG compact disc which suggests that the microphones were a shade too close to the musicians, while on cassette there is a touch of edginess on the upper strings, more noticeable on side one.

Harnoncourt's soloist is Thomas Zehetmair – and very good he is, too. The ample acoustic of Dresden helps to inflate the performances, which are quite unlike those we are used to from this conductor. Marriner on Philips is more straightforward, less overtly charming and yet more winning, and the recording is cleaner and fresher.

Serenade No. 10 in B flat for 13 wind, K.361.
(M) **(*) EMI Dig. EMX 41 2059-1/*4*. LPO Wind Ens.
** German HM **IC 567 199919-2**. Collegium Aureum.
(**) Tel. **ZK8 42981**; AZ6 42981 [id.]. V. Moz. Wind Ens., Harnoncourt.

Outstanding playing from the wind ensemble of the London Philharmonic, richly blended, warmly phrased and full of character. The articulation and rhythmic feeling of the outer movements and the Theme and variations are particularly spontaneous; however, in the slower sections, notably the third-movement *Adagio*, one feels the need of a conductor's directing hand: there is some loss of character both here and, occasionally, elsewhere. Even so, with superb modern digital recording, attractively coloured by the ambience and refined in presence and detail, this is excellent value at lower-mid-price.

The Collegium Aureum version, like its companions listed above, dates from the mid-1970s and has been digitally remastered. It is an eminently satisfactory reading and has the advantage of a warm and truthful recording which has transferred most successfully to CD.

Harnoncourt's Telefunken version is more controversial. The actual playing of the Vienna Mozart Wind Ensemble is exemplary and the wind blend beautifully. The opening is double-dotted as authorized in the *Neue Mozart Ausgabe*, but tempi will doubtless worry many collectors. The *allegro* of the first movement is far from '*molto*' – but that in itself would not disturb those familiar with, say, Furtwängler's classic account. What renders this version unacceptable are the grotesque tempi of the third movement (*Adagio*) and (even more so) of the second Minuet. The treatment of the C minor section in the *Romance* is also very heavy-handed. The recording itself is absolutely first class – and so, needless to say, is the playing. But this is emphatically not a safe recommendation.

Serenades Nos 11 in E flat, K.375; 12 in C min., K.388.
*** ASV Dig. COE/*ZCCOE* 802 [id.]. COE, Alexander Schneider.
(*) Hung. Dig. **SLPD 12549 [id.]. Budapest Wind. Ens., Berkes.
(*) Tel. **ZK8 43097; AZ6/*CY4* 43097 [id.]. V. Moz. Wind Ens., Harnoncourt.
** Orfeo Dig. **C 134851A**; S/*M* 134851A [id.]. BPO Wind Ens.
** Chan. Dig. ABRD/*ABTD* 1144 [id.]. SNO Wind Ens., Järvi.

The talented young wind players of the Chamber Orchestra of Europe had made an impressive recording of the Dvořák *Wind serenade* before they turned their attention to these two supreme examples of wind music. With Schneider as a wise and experienced guide, they give performances which combine brilliance and warmth with a feeling of spontaneity. Where some older rivals are either on the one hand mannered or too tautly disciplined on the other, here Schneider very persuasively encourages the individuality of particular soloists, so that the result is both natural and compelling. K.375 in particular is a delight, as genial as it is characterful, conveying the joy of the inspiration. K.388 might have been more menacing at the C minor opening, but the result is most persuasive, with excellent digital sound set against a warm but not confusing acoustic. There is an excellent cassette.

The dry acoustic of the Hungaroton recording emphasizes the extraordinary precision of ensemble that marks the work of this group. Yet for all that precision, the result lacks the sort of fizz, the sense of spontaneous communication, which has been so striking a quality in the group's live performances. The studio conditions seem to have muted individuality a little, to make the results a shade machine-like. Nevertheless, it presents a fine, clean view of Mozart, beautifully paced, with no suspicion of mannerism, and with dazzling technical accomplishment.

Harnoncourt begins K.375 with an eccentrically slow tempo for the first movement, made to sound the more self-conscious by the agogic hesitations which also mar the slow movement. Though he regularly adopts a moulded style, he brings out the tonal contrasts between the instruments, never blending. Otherwise allegros are generally on the fast side, well pointed and with fine rhythmic flair; and the whole of K.388 is lively and colourful.

On Orfeo, elegantly turned performances, as one would expect from an ensemble which includes the clarinettist, Karl Leister, and the oboe of Hansjörg Schellenberger, who play their solos most imaginatively in the two slow movements, However, they are not quite as characterful or as spirited as the Chamber Orchestra of Europe on ASV, and accompaniment figures that are too metrical rob the music of resilience. Very good recording with plain, immediate sound.

The Chandos recording for the Scottish ensemble sets the players at a distance against a warm reverberation, not so much blunting the edge as lightening the effect. Passagework is delicate and neat, and these are enjoyable accounts, although ensemble is not as crisp as with most direct rivals. There is a characteristically faithful chrome cassette.

Serenade No. 13 in G (Eine kleine Nachtmusik), K.525.

ꞓ *** Ph. Dig. **410 606-2**; 6514/*7337* 370 [id.]. I Musici (with concert of Baroque music ***).

*** DG Dig. **400 034-2**; 2532/*3302* 031 [id.]. BPO, Karajan – GRIEG: *Holberg suite*; PROKOFIEV: *Symphony No. 1*.***

Recordings of Mozart's celebrated *Night music* are legion, coupled in various ways, but Boskovsky's should not be forgotten, an exceptionally successful mid-priced LP and tape version, paired with the *Serenade No. 3 in D*, K.185 (Decca Jub. JB/*KJBC* 19) and alternatively grouped with other serenades – see above. It was Karajan who gave the work its digital début in an early compact disc entitled 'Digital concert'. Apart from a self-conscious and somewhat ponderous minuet, it is a very fine performance, the playing beautifully cultured, with finely shaped phrasing and well-sprung rhythms. The digital sound, however, though well detailed and not without bloom, is a little sharp-edged; the CD shows this more readily than the disc or the excellent chrome tape.

First choice probably rests with the new version from I Musici, who play the music with rare freshness, giving the listener the impression of hearing the work for the first time. The playing is consistently alert and sparkling, with the *Romanze* particularly engaging. The recording is beautifully balanced, on both LP and the first-class high-level chrome tape. Obviously the CD brings a degree more refinement and presence, but this is in the demonstration class in all formats.

A fine alternative comes from Leppard and the Scottish Chamber Orchestra, coupled with a sparkling performance of *Les petites riens* ballet music – see above.

Symphonies Nos 1, 4–6, 7a, 8–20, 42–7, 55; in C. K.208/102; in D, K.45, 111/120, 141a and 196/121; in G.
*** Ph. **416 471-2** (6); 6769 054 (8). ASMF, Marriner.

Marriner's survey has a splendid Mozartian vitality and seems to combine the best qualities of previous sets by Boehm on DG and Kehr on Turnabout. The Academy play with great style, warmth and polish; the Philips engineers, having responded with alive and vivid recording, offer admirable (analogue) transfers into the new CD format. As with the set of later symphonies (see below), the layout is over six compact discs (offered for the price of five) as against eight LPs. These are altogether delightful records and can be strongly recommended.

Symphonies Nos 1 in E flat, K.16; in A min. (*Odense*), *K.16a; 4 in D, K.19; in F, K.19a.*
**(*) Unicorn Dig. DKP/*DKPC* 9039 [id.]. Odense SO, Vetö.

It was in Odense that the lost *Symphony*, K.16a, was discovered by the archivist, Gunnar Thygesen; to the local orchestra, an excellent band, under its permanent conductor, the Hungarian Tamás Vetö, went the honour of giving the first modern performance. Alas for everyone's hopes, it seems very unlikely, from stylistic evidence and even the key, A minor, that it is genuine Mozart. It remains a charming work in the *Sturm und Drang* manner, and is well coupled with an apt group of other early Mozart symphonies, done with warmer tone than those in the Hogwood complete set. First-rate recording on both disc and cassette.

Symphonies Nos 21–41 (complete).
*** Ph. **415 954-2** (6); 6769 032 (8) [id.]. ASMF, Marriner.

Marriner, following up the success of his splendid volume of the early symphonies, here presents the later works in comparably stylish, well-recorded performances. The layout, on six CDs, offers the symphonies in numerical sequence, with no single symphony divided between discs; the only exception to the ordering is No. 40, which is presented at the beginning of the second CD, immediately after the *'little' G minor* (No. 25). The transfers are of high quality; only in No. 40 and the *Haffner* (which date from 1970, nearly a decade before the rest) does a somewhat over-resonant bass betray the age of the originals. Perhaps when he reaches the *Jupiter*, Marriner fails to capture the full weight of Mozart's argument (exposition repeat not observed in the finale); but the wonder is that so many symphonies have been performed with no hint of routine.

Symphonies Nos 25 in G min., K.183; 26 in E flat, K.184; 27 in G, K.199.
**(*) O-L 414 472-1/*4* [id.]. AAM, Hogwood.

With all the repeats observed, the *'little' G minor* is no longer little, as Hogwood presents it. Taken from his complete Mozart series, this CD of three of the finest of the early symphonies follows the pattern and style of the rest, with the abrasive string tone of the Academy and its period instruments brightly caught, not a sound to relax to. Indeed, for some ears the razor-edged tuttis are very difficult to accept. On tape, the treble is slightly smoothed and the sound is more comfortable.

Symphonies Nos 25; 29; 31 (Paris); 33, 34; 35 (Haffner); 36 (Linz); 38 (Prague); 39; 40; 41 (Jupiter); Adagio and fugue, K.546; Masonic funeral music, K.477; Serenade No. 13 (Eine kleine Nachtmusik); Overtures: Così fan tutte; La Clemenza di Tito; Don Giovanni; Die Entführung aus dem Serail; Le Nozze di Figaro; Die Zauberflöte.
(M) **(*) HMV EX 290482-3/9 (6/*4*) [Ang. AEW 34470]. Philh. or New Philh. O, Klemperer.

Klemperer's Mozart recordings with the Philharmonia were made over a decade between 1957 (*No. 25 in G minor* – sounding a little rough in the remastered transfer) and 1966. His achievement was uneven. The spirit of Beethoven often makes its presence felt, beneficially in the large-scale symphonies, notably in Nos 38 and 39, but sometimes merely bringing heaviness, as in the *Haffner* and the *Linz* where the weightiness and portentous feeling step outside the boundaries of Mozartian sensibility. Yet, with wonderfully refined playing from the Philharmonia, usually in peak form, there are rare insights and moments of undoubted magic, as in the beautiful *Andante* of the *G minor* (No. 25) which has genuine incandescence. Nos 31 and 34 show Klemperer's sobriety at its most attractive. The finale of No. 34, with its scampering triplets, is the movement to try first: the rhythmic urgency makes it a delicious experience, unhurried but not at all heavy or too slow. Similarly, in the *Paris symphony* there is a gain in strength, not only in the outer movements but in the classical poise of the slow movement. Klemperer recorded the *40th, G minor, Symphony* twice in stereo and it is a pity that the earlier (late-1950s) version was not chosen instead of the – much better-recorded – 1963 performance, which is altogether heavier. The *Jupiter* lacks a sense of occasion: while alert and structurally impressive, it never really catches fire. The finest performances are undoubtedly the *Prague* and *No. 39 in E flat*, which combine virility and power in the outer movements with grace and elegance in the slow ones. Throughout, the orchestra respond with a spontaneous sense of joy that is irresistible. Klemperer gives characteristically sober and deeply felt performances of the *Adagio and fugue* and *Masonic funeral music*. Here his weighty style adds suitable gravitas to the music; in some of the overtures, however, his slow tempi will not appeal to everybody. While they are all fascinating examples of his art and are never boring, in the comic pieces the results are hardly sparkling; yet the woodwind felicities of *Così fan tutte*, the strong and positive seriousness of *Die Zauberflöte*, and the apocalyptic drama of *Don Giovanni* are all memorable. In *Eine kleine Nachtmusik*, the great conductor relaxes to give an unexpectedly warm and sunny performance, marvellously played and with the 1966 stereo revealing attractive antiphonal detail. The recorded sound, much freshened, is nearly always good or, in the later recordings, excellent. The actual quality varies between different items; this variability is emphasized on the cassettes, where the upper range at times can sound a bit thin, but at others is smoother than on the LPs. As on disc, the recordings made in the mid-1960s are impressively fresh and full. The layout – on four tapes – allots two of the earlier symphonies to a side but, from No. 36 onwards, offers a single major work per side, followed by shorter pieces.

Symphonies Nos 25 in G min., K.183; 35 in D (Haffner), K.385.
(B) ** Pickwick Con. CC/*CCTC* 7614. VPO, Kertesz.

This is a recoupling of Decca recordings made in the early 1970s. The reading of No. 25 was one of the best of the Kertesz series, giving this relatively early work considerable weight and strength, arguably too much so. However, it is superbly played. The account of the *Haffner symphony* is somewhat faceless, though again the orchestral playing and, indeed, Decca's engineering are of high quality. The recording has been remastered and freshened, with the upper range now much more brightly lit; this is the more striking on the high-level chrome tape.

Symphonies Nos 25 in G min., K.183; 40 in G min., K.550.
*** Erato Dig. **ECD 88078**; NUM/*MCE* 75119 [id.]. Scottish CO, Conlon.
*(*) Tel. Dig. **ZK8 42935**; AZ6/*CX4* 42935 [id.]. Concg. O, Harnoncourt.

Conlon's coupling of the *G minor Symphonies* is well up to the standard of his two previous issues in his Mozart series. The first movement of K.183 is particularly arresting and the *Andante* is beautifully played, serene in its sense of repose to make a striking contrast with the movements around it. The later symphony too is finely paced and well proportioned, spontaneous and alert. Those seeking a chamber scale yet wishing to avoid the astringencies and idiosyncrasies of the authentic style will find this very satisfying. Conlon's directness in no way prevents an imaginative approach to detail. Even the relatively relaxed speed for the first movement of No. 40 justifies itself in the crispness of rhythm and extra clarity. The sound is naturally balanced and clearly detailed within a convincing acoustic, though on the cassette the high level brings a very bright treble in K.550.

Harnoncourt secures fine playing from the Concertgebouw, but his coupling of the two G minor symphonies (in itself not a good plan) is only variably successful with some extreme speeds (as in the very brisk slow movement of No. 40) and an unsettled mood overall, hardly Mozartian. The sound on CD is bright and clear, with good presence, and there is a brilliant chrome tape.

Symphonies Nos 29 in A, K.201; 33 in B flat, K.319.
*** Ph. Dig. **412 736-2**; 412 736-1/*4* [id.]. E. Bar. Sol., Gardiner.

Although the opening is deceptively gentle, the first movement of John Eliot Gardiner's *A major Symphony* soon develops an athletic strength. Delicacy returns in the *Andante*, nicely proportioned and beautifully played. After a bright, crisp minuet, the finale has plenty of energy and bite, without being hurried. The account of *No. 33 in B flat* is outstandingly successful, the outer movements a delight, full of rhythmic character, with the good humour of the first nicely caught, and the secondary theme of the finale lilting and gracious. The *Andante* brings some slight squeezing of phrases, but overall this is authenticity with a winning countenance and without the abrasiveness of the Academy of Ancient Music in this repertoire. The recording is fresh and immediate and very well balanced, its tangibility striking on CD, but with an excellent chrome tape.

Symphonies Nos 29 in A, K.201; 35 in D (Haffner), K.385; Masonic funeral music, K.477.
(*) DG **413 734-2 [id.]. VPO, Boehm.

These performances, which first appeared not long before Boehm's death, are distinguished by finely groomed playing from the Vienna Philharmonic. The first movement of the *A major Symphony* is on the slow side but there is some lovely expressive playing in the second. Boehm's unashamedly nineteenth-century approach may at times seem heavy; however, although the performances are weightier than his earlier complete set made with the Berlin Philharmonic, they have a relaxed quality and a glowing resonance which make them endearing, mature products of octogenarian wisdom. They may sometimes lack the drive of other performances, but they remain compelling. The *Masonic funeral music*, darkly characterful, makes a worthwhile filler. The 1981 recordings have been superbly transferred to CD. Background noise is almost non-existent and the orchestral quality is warm, naturally balanced, yet tangible within its very attractive ambience.

Symphonies Nos 29 in A, K.201; 39 in E flat, K.543.
*(*) Tel. Dig. **ZK8 43017**; AZ6/*CY4* 43017 [id.]. Concg. O, Harnoncourt.

Although there is some fine orchestral playing, Harnoncourt's readings are unconvincing. Tempi are erratic: his pacing of the slow movement of No. 29 has little feeling of serenity or repose, and the Minuet of No. 39 is rushed, although the first movement of this symphony is well judged. The recorded sound is not always comfortable, resonant yet very bright; the cassette (which can sometimes adjust such matters of balance) is often fierce, notably in No. 29.

Symphonies Nos 31 in D (Paris), K.297; 33 in B flat, K.319; Andante, K.297.
(*) Tel. Dig. **ZK8 42817; AZ6/*CX4* 42817 [642817]. Concg. O, Harnoncourt.

Harnoncourt, when he stops conducting an orchestra of original instruments, may still favour speeds rather slower than usual, but the manner is relatively romantic in its expressiveness. This is the most successful of his Mozart records with the Concertgebouw, with beautiful, cleanly articulated playing. The alternative slow movements are given for the *Paris*, the second one much lighter in weight. In No. 33, Harnoncourt overdoes his slowness in the *Andante*, but adds to the breadth of the finale by giving the repeats of both halves. Very good recording. There is a vivid chrome cassette, although it makes the orchestral upper range sound rather dry. On compact disc the strings are given a very tangible presence, woodwind is somewhat more forward than under live concert-hall conditions, yet the bright vividness and realism of the sound are most impressive.

Symphonies Nos 31 in D (Paris), K.297; 34 in C, K.338; 39 in E flat, K.543; 40 in G min., K.550.
(B) *** HMV *TCC2-POR 154598-9*. ECO, Barenboim.

This is the second, as issued, of Barenboim's groupings of Mozart symphonies, taken from recordings made in the late 1960s. The first is discussed below. Both make distinguished and useful additions to HMV's 'Portrait of the Artist' tape series. There are no disc equivalents. Here the *Paris symphony* is given an outstanding performance, the contrasts of mood in the first movement underlined and the finale taken at a hectic tempo that would have sounded breathless with players any less brilliant than the modest-sized ECO. No. 34 (a later recording, dating from 1972) also has a vivacious finale and the playing is equally impressive with its consistently imaginative phrasing. Barenboim's approach to No. 39 is warmer, marginally more expressive than Sir Colin Davis's, and some may well prefer it for just these qualities. The responsive phrasing from the strings, both here and in the *G minor Symphony*, is matched by wind playing in which the colour is well brought out. The performances are thoughtful, yet spacious, alive and exciting too. The scale is right, and the warm, smooth recording, perhaps a little lacking in ultimate range at the top, is generally well balanced (only in the *Paris* does the bass resonance become a fraction too insistent at times).

Symphonies Nos 31 in D (Paris); 35 in D (Haffner); 40 in G min., K.550; 41 in C (Jupiter).
(B) **(*) DG Walkman *413 151-4*. BPO, Boehm.

These recordings date from between 1960 and 1966 and come from Boehm's complete Berlin cycle. The playing is first class, and the recordings sound well here. In the *G minor Symphony* Boehm's featuring of oboes in the place of clarinets (he uses Mozart's earlier version of the score) is hardly noticed, so mellifluous is the playing. This is excellent value at Walkman price, even if the later Vienna recordings (notably of Nos 40 and 41) have rather more character.

Symphonies Nos 31 in D (Paris), K.297; 40 in G min., K.550.
*** O-L **410 197-2**; DSDL/*KDSLC* 716. AAM, Schröder; Hogwood.

A fine sampler from the complete Mozart symphony set by the Academy, with original instruments at their freshest and brightest in crisp, clear interpretations with all possible repeats observed. The clarity and bite are made the cleaner and more immediate on compact disc. The chrome cassette too is of Decca's finest quality.

Symphonies Nos 31 in D (Paris), K.297; 41 in C (Jupiter), K.551.
*** Erato Dig. **ECD 88029**; NUM/*MCE* 75107 [id.]. SCO, Conlon.

This first of Conlon's Mozart symphony recordings for Erato brings an exceptionally fine account of the *Jupiter*, coupled with a fresh and resilient one of the *Paris symphony*. By fitting the earlier work on to only a part of a side, Conlon was able on LP to observe not only the exposition repeats in the outer movements but also the second-half repeat of the finale too, a positive gain with so weighty a movement. The sureness of focus of the orchestra, with the positioning of each instrument clearly defined within a believable acoustic, establishes the chamber scale very convincingly. As to Conlon's interpretations, the pacing cannot be faulted and the manner is never distractingly personal. The converse may be true: that the readings are not so distinctive as those from the finest rivals; for a sample, however, try the magically lilting account of the *Jupiter* Minuet. On CD the turnover in the *Jupiter symphony* is, of course, avoided, and the sound is even firmer and marginally more transparent.

Symphonies Nos 32, K.318; 35 (Haffner); 36 (Linz); 41 (Jupiter).
(B) *** HMV *TCC2-POR 54298*. ECO, Barenboim.

These Barenboim recordings were made towards the end of the 1960s and are not available in disc form. This extended-length ferric tape is of high quality, the sound full, clear and well balanced. Barenboim is at his finest in Mozart's last and longest symphony where he rightly focuses attention on the finale. He observes the second-half repeat as well as the first, to give Mozart's complex fugal design a majesty comparable only with Beethoven, and that at a brisk, swashbuckling tempo. The rest of the symphony is interpreted with equal compulsion. The *Haffner* is also strongly vigorous, the first movement bold almost to the point of brusqueness. In the *Prague*, Barenboim obviously intends the full weight of the imposing introduction to be felt. When the allegro arrives it is gracious and alive and the impetus is nicely judged. The finale too is light-hearted and gay, to make a foil with the rather serious-minded *Andante*. The account of Mozart's *'Italian overture' symphony* is straightforward and spirited. With an authentic-sized orchestra, playing very stylishly on modern instruments, this makes an attractive compilation.

Symphonies Nos 32 in G, K.318; 35 in D (Haffner), K.385; 39 in E flat, K.543.
*** HMV Dig. **CDC 747 327-2** [id.]; EL 270253-1/*4* [Ang. AE/*4AE* 34439]. ECO, Tate.
*** ASV Dig. DCA/*ZCDCA* 543 [id.]. ECO, Mackerras.

It is the gift of Jeffrey Tate to direct meticulously detailed readings of Mozart, full of stylish touches which never sound fussy or mannered, thanks to the natural electricity which he consistently reveals, whether in fast movements or slow. The phrasing of the first theme of the first-movement allegro in No. 39, for example, has the second and third beats meticulously slurred together, as marked, but the result remains fresh. As in his other late symphony recordings Tate is generous with repeats, and there is considerable gain from having both halves of the finale of No. 39 repeated, particularly when the ECO violins articulate so cleanly, more so than in most full orchestral versions. In the brief *Italian overture* of No. 32 and in the *Haffner*, Tate achieves comparable exhilaration at relatively spacious speeds, finding elegance on the one hand while bringing out dramatic contrasts on the other. Excellent sound, weighty but apt in scale. The high-level cassette is very brightly lit, especially on side one.

A decade after his series of Mozart symphony recordings for CfP, Sir Charles Mackerras began another series for ASV, of which this coupling of Nos 32, 35 and 39 was the first issue. With generally brisk speeds, the readings are attractively fresh and urgent. Mackerras rarely seeks to charm, but unfussily presents each movement with undistractingly direct manners. In places the fast speeds imperil ensemble a little, and the recording does not always capture the finest detail. These make excellent alternatives to the Tate coupling of the same symphonies, when the readings are so very distinct, with Tate regularly more spacious, more elegant and with marginally more polished playing from the same orchestra. The sound is bright and vivid, especially so on the high-level (iron-oxide) tape.

Symphonies Nos 33 in B flat, K.319; 40 in G min., K.550.
(B) ** ASV Dig. ABM/*ZCABM* 769 [id.]. Ac. of L., Richard Stamp.

The Academy of London is a new performing group with a nucleus of young American players, using modern instruments. Certainly their sparkling account of *Symphony No. 33 in B flat* makes an auspicious début, with its polished precision of articulation in outer movements and the gracious *Andante* which, together with the bright, rhythmically resilient Minuet, gives the performance a sunny, almost Beechamesque atmosphere. The pacing here is so finely judged that it is a disappointment to turn to the *G minor Symphony*, where the opening movement is so determinedly brisk that its underlying minor-key expressive qualities all but evaporate, although the rest of the work is attractive in a direct way. The ASV recording is naturally balanced and this issue is in the bargain range.

Symphonies Nos 34 in C, K.338; 35 in D (Haffner), K.385.
*(*) Tel. Dig. **ZK8 42703**; AZ6/*CX4* 42703. Concg. O, Harnoncourt.

With bright, clear digital recording – quite different from the sound which Philips engineers get from this orchestra – the Harnoncourt coupling provides refreshing, directly dramatic performances of these two symphonies, marked by unforced tempi. Charm is somewhat missing, and the coupling provides rather short measure; but the immediacy of sound compels attention. On compact disc, however, although the sound-picture is vividly clear, there is a dryness in tuttis which borders on harshness. This is much less attractive than the companion CD coupling Nos 31 and 33.

Symphonies Nos 34 in C, K.338; 41 in C (Jupiter), K.551.
(*) O-L **411 658-2; 411 658-1/*4* [id.]. AAM, Schröder; Hogwood.

This separate issue from Hogwood's complete set of the Mozart symphonies has all the merits of the series, but the abrasiveness of the string sound will not suit those who are in any way resistant to the idea of a performance on period instruments. Slow movements lack tenderness and elegance, but the weight of expression of the *Jupiter* comes over well, with every single repeat observed. First-rate, clear-textured recording, bright and clean on CD, and with the cassette also extremely lively.

Symphonies Nos 35 (Haffner); 36 (Linz); 38–40; 41 (Jupiter).
(M) *** CBS M3P/*3PT* 39627 (3). Columbia SO, Walter.

Walter's set of Mozart symphonies (alongside his Brahms) is one of the stereo gramophone's finest legacies from the early 1960s. The famous rehearsal record of the *Linz* demonstrates both his care in preparation and the response of the players – see below – and throughout the series these humane readings, tempi spacious but never dragging, demonstrate Walter's ability to bring out the noblest sounds from a Mozart score. The classical precision of the *Haffner* matches the deceptively simple approach to the *Linz*. The last symphonies have an added spaciousness and a sense of inevitability in their aptness of pacing and relaxed structural control, culminating in a highly satisfying *Jupiter*, still among the finest available. The remastered recordings have retained their fullness and bloom and sound especially well in the chrome-cassette format.

Symphonies Nos 35 in D (Haffner), K.385; 39 in E flat, K.543.
(*) CBS **MK 42026 [id.]. Columbia SO, Bruno Walter.

Walter gives a beautifully crisp, classical performance of the *Haffner*, a symphony whose brilliance at times belies its intensity. The slow movement and finale are outstanding in a reading where natural expressive warmth of phrasing is matched by alert, sparkling articulation. There is a breadth about his mature and reflective reading of K.543 which balances with the music's inherent energy. The main theme of the first movement is nobly moulded and the remainder of the work reflects Walter's warmly human approach to Mozart. Pacing has a sense of inevitability in the way each movement relates to the others in Walter's overall conception. Fine playing and a wide-ranging recording, although the resonance and brightness on top bring a touch of fierceness to the high violins in fortissimos.

Symphonies Nos 35 (Haffner); 40 in G min., K.550; March in D, K.408/2.
(M) *** Ph. Seq. 412 367-1/*4* [id.]. ASMF, Marriner.

Marriner's stylish coupling uses original scorings of both works – minus flutes and clarinets in the *Haffner*, minus clarinets in No. 40. The *March* is included as makeweight, since (having the same K. number) it has long been associated with the *Haffner symphony*. Marriner's readings are finely detailed but dynamic too, nicely scaled against refined recording. The cassette is well managed.

Symphonies Nos 35 in D (Haffner), K.385; 41 in C (Jupiter), K.551.
*** DG Dig. **415 305-2**; 415 305-1/*4* [id.]. VPO, Bernstein.

The *Jupiter* brings one of the finest of all of Bernstein's Mozart recordings, edited together from live performances and exhilarating in its tensions. This is one of the very few recordings to observe the repeats in both halves of the finale, making it almost as long as the massive first movement; but Bernstein's electricity sustains that length, and one welcomes it for establishing the supreme power of the argument, the true crown to the whole of Mozart's symphonic output. Pacing cannot be faulted in all four movements, and the *Haffner* brings a similarly satisfying reading until the finale, when Bernstein in the heat of the moment breaks loose with a speed so fast that even the Vienna violins find it hard to articulate exactly. It remains exciting and, with recording on CD only slightly cloudy in heavy tuttis, far better than most taken from live performance; it makes an excellent recommendation, not so heavy in texture as most using regular symphony orchestras. There is a good, high-level tape, perhaps marginally less refined than the LP, but vivid enough.

Symphony No. 36 in C (Linz); 'The birth of a performance' (rehearsals and performance).
(B) *** CBS DC/*DCT* 40182 (2). Columbia SO, Bruno Walter.

Some rehearsal records are witty (Beecham springs to mind), some are informative and others boring. But Walter's slow gestation of Mozart's *Linz symphony* is fascinating. It has long been out of the catalogue but now returns with the two LPs offered for the price of one. The thoroughness and attention to detail in an apparently straightforward classical score are balanced by Walter's obvious natural bond with the composer which he slowly and painstakingly instils into his players, so that the final performance is a culmination of all that has happened before.

Symphonies Nos 36 in C (Linz), K.425; 38 in D (Prague), K.504.
*** HMV Dig. **CDC 747442-2**; EL 270306-1/*4*. ECO, Tate.
(*) CBS **MK 42027 [id.]. Columbia SO, Bruno Walter.
(B) **(*) Pickwick Con. CC/*CCTC* 7581. ECO, Sir Colin Davis.
* Denon Dig. **C37 7051** [id.]. NHK SO, Suitner.

The coupling of the two Mozart symphonies named after central European cities is rare but apt; Tate directs characteristically strong and elegant readings of both works, bringing out the operatic overtones in the *Prague*, not just in the *Don Giovanni*-like progressions of the slow introduction but also in the menace of the development section and in the wonder of the chromatic progressions in the slow movement, as well as the often surprising mixing of timbres. In the *Linz*, Tate is again attractively individual, putting rather more emphasis on elegance and finding unusual tenderness in the slow movement, taken like the *Adagio* of the *Prague* at a very measured speed. With excellent sound, warm and full yet with detail brought out within an apt scale, it confirms the success of the whole series. On the high-level chrome tape the upper range is brightly lit, the overall effect slightly less warm than the LP.

It is appropriate that CBS should reissue Walter's (1960) account of the *Linz* on CD, with his famous rehearsal also again available (see above). His thoroughness and attention to detail in an apparently straightforward score are balanced by the natural flow of the phrasing, with the slow movement particularly fine. The (1959) *Prague* is another of Walter's finest performances. He achieves just the right balance of tempi in the two sections of the first movement and draws from the *Andante* all the sweetness and lyrical power of which he is capable. The finale is brilliantly played, but the pace is never forced; and if there are times when the tempo is slightly relaxed here and there, a careful listener will detect good musical reasons. The remastered recording is fresh and clear, with a strong, firm bass. It is not as full as we would expect today, and the violins are very brightly lit indeed above the stave, and lack body.

Sir Colin Davis's Contour record is a recoupling from the early 1960s. The *Linz* is strikingly successful. There is no forcing of the issue here but a direct and forthright account of the quick movements and a decorous moulding of the slow movement's shapely contours. The woodwind are very occasionally prominent in a way that would never happen in a concert hall, but otherwise the balance is admirable. Davis also captures the strength of the *Prague symphony*, with its obvious links with *Don Giovanni*, written at about the same time. His treatment of the slow movement steers an admirable course between classical poise and affection, and the ECO responds wonderfully well. The recording from the early 1960s is fully acceptable; this reissue, in the bargain price-range, is still attractive, although on tape the upper range is dry and rather fierce.

From Suitner fresh and plain readings, rhythmically too rigid and heavy-handed, with string playing lacking finesse. Good, immediate recording, with plenty of presence. Jeffrey Tate and the ECO are far preferable in this coupling.

Symphonies Nos 38 in D (Prague), K.504; 39 in E flat, K.543.
(*) Erato Dig. **ECD 88093; NUM/*MCE* 75180 [id.]. SCO, Conlon.
(*) DG **413 735-2 [id.]. VPO, Boehm.
(*) O-L Dig. **410 233-2; 410 233-1/*4* [id.]. AAM, Schröder; Hogwood.

With outstandingly realistic and firmly defined sound, Conlon presents readings of both symphonies which in their cleanly established chamber scale are satisfyingly fresh and direct. Speeds are consistently well chosen, with rhythms well sprung and textures made transparent. It is true that with this approach on this scale the tragic *Don Giovanni* overtones of the *Prague* are minimized, and some may feel that Conlon's directness makes for an undercharacterized reading, but both symphonies are undistractingly satisfying in sound that on CD is exceptionally faithful.

Boehm's versions, recorded when he had reached his mid-eighties, are sunnier and more genial than those he made as part of his complete Berlin Philharmonic series in the 1960s. Tempi are again spacious, but the results are less markedly magisterial. The glow of the performances is helped by the warm DG sound which has transferred strikingly well to CD. Detail is less sharp than on Conlon's digital alternative, but the balance is truthful and the effect pleasingly natural.

Those who prefer the acerbities of original instruments will find the Academy of Ancient Music coupling offers two splendid samples of this particular approach to the Mozart symphonies. The weight and scale of the *Prague* are the more keenly apparent in such a performance as this, with all repeats observed, even if Hogwood's and Schröder's determination not to overload slow movements with anachronistic expressiveness will disappoint some. Excellent, finely scaled recording in the CD format, although the chrome cassette is a minor disaster, with coarse sound in both works, in spite of a modest level of transfer.

Symphonies Nos 38 in D (Prague), K.504; 41 in C (Jupiter), K.551.
(**) Tel. Dig. **ZL8 48219** (2); DX6 48219 [id.]. Conc. O, Harnoncourt.

Harnoncourt's coupling was originally issued on two separate LPs, each at full-price, and although all repeats are included (even the *Prague* runs for 37′) the idea of offering these two symphonies on a *pair* of CDs seems extremely unrealistic. Harnoncourt turns out to be a much more romantic animal in Mozart. He secures superb playing from the Concertgebouw Orchestra, but the results in the *Jupiter* are on the heavy side, though the *Prague* is generally very successful.

Symphony No. 39 in E flat, K.543.
(B) **(*) DG Walkman *418 085-4* [id.]. BPO, Boehm – BEETHOVEN: *Symphonies Nos 1 and 4.***(*)

Boehm's 1966 recording of the *E flat Symphony* was one of the best of his earlier Berlin recordings, with effortlessly alert orchestral playing of great tonal beauty. The recording is warm and richly upholstered. This Walkman tape is much more generous in content and a third the price of Boehm's later Vienna coupling on CD (see above), but the Vienna performance has rather more grace and vitality.

Symphonies Nos 39 in E flat, K.543; 40 in G min., K.550.
(*) DG Dig. **413 776-2; 413 776-1/*4* [id.]. VPO, Bernstein.

Bernstein's coupling is inconsistent, with an electrifying account of No. 40, keen, individual and stylish, and a slacker, less convincing one of No. 39, recorded three years earlier. Though Bernstein's expressive manner is similar in the slow movements of both symphonies, the moulding of phrase sounds self-conscious in No. 39 – after a careless-sounding start to the movement – whereas it is totally convincing in No. 40. In the first movement of No. 39, the slow introduction is bitingly dramatic, but the relaxation for the main allegro loses necessary tension. It would be wrong to exaggerate the shortcomings of No. 39, when No. 40 is one of the finest versions available, keenly dramatic, with the finale delightfully airy and fresh. Considering the problems of making live recordings, the sound is first rate, lacking only the last degree of transparency in tuttis. The cassette too is well managed, smooth and full, yet quite vivid in the upper range.

Symphonies Nos 39 in E flat, K.543; 41 in C (Jupiter), K.551.
*** Ph. Dig. **410 046-2** [id.]. Dresden State O, Sir Colin Davis.

Imaginative playing from the Staatskapelle, Dresden, under Sir Colin Davis, finely paced and beautifully balanced. Arguably the finest account of the *E flat Symphony* currently on the market – if one leaves Beecham and Bruno Walter out of the reckoning. Davis has recorded the *Jupiter* more than once, and this newcomer is all that one would expect: alert, sensitive, perceptive and played with vitality and finesse. Philips also provide very good recording. A self-recommending coupling.

Symphony No. 40 in G min., K.550.
(*) Ph. Dig. **416 329-2; 416 329-1/*4* [id.]. O of 18th Century, Brüggen – BEETHOVEN: *Symphony No. 1*.**(*)
€ (M) **(*) Pickwick Dig. **PCD 820**. O of St John's, Smith Square, Lubbock – HAYDN: *Symphony No. 44*.*** €

Using only marginally fewer players than in the Beethoven on the reverse, Brüggen's live recording using period instruments is more warmly communicative than most authentic performances, without losing the benefits of clarity and freshness. Speeds are on the fast side without being stiff or eccentric. Good atmospheric recording but with some exaggeration of bass.

Although not as distinctive as the attractive Haydn coupling, Lubbock's is a pleasingly relaxed account of Mozart's *G minor Symphony*, well played – the Minuet particularly deft – and nicely proportioned. The last ounce of character is missing from the slow movement, but the orchestra is responsive throughout, and the recording is in the demonstration class. Excellent value on Pickwick's mid-priced CD label.

Symphonies Nos 40 in G min., K.550; 41 in C (Jupiter), K.551.
*** HMV Dig. **CDC 747147-2**; EL 270154-1/*4* [Ang. AE/*4AE* 34440]. ECO, Tate.
*** CBS **MK 42028** [id.]. Columbia SO, Bruno Walter.
*** DG **413 547-2**; 2530 780 [id.]. VPO, Boehm.
(M) *** EMI EMX 41 2074-1/*4*. ECO, Barenboim.
(*) Decca **414 334-2; 414 334-1/*4* [id.]. COE, Solti.
*(*) RCA Dig. **RCD 14413 [RCD1 4413]**. Chicago SO, Levine.

Symphony No. 41 (Jupiter); Serenade No. 13 (Eine kleine Nachtmusik).
*(*) HMV Dig. EL 270016-1/*4* [Ang. DS/*4DS* 38116]. O de Paris, Barenboim.

In his project to record a series of the late Mozart symphonies with the ECO, Jeffrey Tate entered at the deep end with the last two symphonies, and succeeded superbly. For the general listener this account of the *Jupiter* makes an excellent first choice, with an apt scale which yet allows the grandeur of the work to come out. On the one hand it has the clarity of a chamber orchestra performance, but on the other, with trumpets and drums, its weight of expression never underplays the scale of the argument, which originally prompted the unauthorized nickname. In both symphonies, exposition repeats are observed in outer movements, particularly important in the *Jupiter* finale, which with its miraculous fugal writing bears even greater argumentative weight than the first movement, a point firmly established by Tate. Those who like a very plain approach may find the elegant pointing in slow movements excessive, but Tate's keen imagination on detail, as well as over a broad span, consistently conveys the electricity of a live performance. The recording is well detailed, yet has pleasant reverberation, giving the necessary breadth; it is very impressive on CD. The XDR cassette transfer, made at the highest level with the sound wide-ranging and full, has just a hint of harshness on the upper strings at fortissimo level.

This is one of Walter's most treasurable couplings, although the symphonies were originally differently paired: the *G minor* was recorded in 1959 and has some excess of bass resonance, most noticeably in the last two movements, while the *Jupiter* has warmth without undue resonance, with the weight of sound entirely appropriate. Here the ear notices a slight lowering of the upper frequency ceiling in the *Andante* in order to produce the background quiet. Both performances are spacious, and with the leisurely pacing of K.550 comes a characteristic humanity. In the first movement the tempo seems exactly right, while the *Andante* spells enchantment and the Minuet takes on an added measure of dignity. The refusal to hurry in the finale brings nicely observed detail. In the

Jupiter neither the first-movement exposition nor the finale carry repeats, but Walter structures his interpretation accordingly and the reading has something of an Olympian quality. It makes a fitting peak to his cycle of late Mozart symphonies, a performance of indubitable greatness.

Boehm recorded this same coupling earlier with the Berlin Philharmonic as part of his complete Mozart cycle, but his Vienna versions, as well as being more vividly and immediately recorded, also present more alert, more spontaneous-sounding performances, with the octogenarian conductor sounding more youthful than before. Boehm takes a relatively measured view of the outer movements of No. 40, but the resilience of the playing rivets the attention and avoids any sort of squareness. Excellent recommendations for both symphonies, though in No. 41 the original single-sided LP format prevented the observance of exposition repeats which many count desirable in Mozart's most massive symphony. This is the only drawback to the CD transfer, which offers full, refined sound within a very attractive ambience.

The talented young players of the Chamber Orchestra of Europe, here recorded at the Alte Oper in Frankfurt, respond acutely to Solti's direction with finely disciplined ensemble, paradoxically producing an interpretation which in many places is uncharacteristic of the conductor, unforced and intimate rather than fiery. The middle movements of No. 40 are disappointing for opposite reasons, the *Andante* too self-consciously pointed, and the Minuet too heavy. The *Jupiter* is plainer and much more successful, brightly detailed and crisply articulated. Recording with plenty of bloom on the sound, as well as good detail.

Levine's performances cannot be recommended with any enthusiasm. The *G minor* is matter-of-fact and wanting in real warmth; while the *Jupiter* is more than routine, it is less than distinguished, given the reputation of the orchestra and the musicianship and insight of this conductor. The recording, made in the Medinah Temple, Chicago, has no want of clarity and presence, but its claims cannot be pressed over rival performances.

Barenboim's Paris version of the *Jupiter* is most disappointing, heavy and inflated, with recording that obscures detail. It is no match for his ECO version, reissued on the mid-price Eminence label in a generous coupling with No. 40. The sound of these earlier performances remains fully competitive on disc. The tape is variable, warm and slightly bass-heavy in No. 40, very brightly lit in the *Jupiter symphony*. They are also available coupled differently on two of EMI's 'Portrait of the Artist' cassette issues – see above.

CHAMBER MUSIC

Adagio in C for cor anglais, 2 violins and cello, K.580a.

*** Denon **C37 7119**. Holliger, Salvatore Qt – M. HAYDN: Divertimenti; J. C. BACH: Quartet.***

Though the shortest of the four works on Holliger's charming disc, this Mozart fragment – reconstructed when Mozart left the solo cor anglais part complete but not the string parts – is in a world apart, deeply expressive. The lively performances of the undemanding works by J. C. Bach and Michael Haydn make an attractive coupling. Excellent performances and recording. Since making this recording for Denon, Holliger has made another for Philips, and this is coupled, among other works, with the *Oboe quartet*, K.370 – see below.

(i) *Adagio and fugue in C min. K.546;* (ii) *Duos for violin and viola Nos 1 in G, K.423; 2 in B flat, K.424.*
(M) *** Ph. 412 059-1/*4*. (i) Italian Qt; (ii) Grumiaux, Pelliccia.

These performances derive from the Philips Mozart Edition and are of the highest quality; they are eminently well recorded, too. The Quartetto Italiano give a masterly account of the late *Adagio and fugue*, and Arthur Grumiaux and Arrigo Pelliccia are superb in the *Duos*. There is a splendid matching cassette.

Clarinet quintet in A, K.581.
*** Denon Dig. **C37 7038**; DG 410 670-1/*4* [id.]. Meyer, BPO Qt – WEBER: *Introduction, theme and variations.****

Clarinet quintet in A, K.581; Clarinet quintet fragment in B flat, K.516c; (i) *Quintet fragment in F for clarinet in C, basset-horn and string trio, K.580b* (both completed by Duncan Druce).
*** Amon Ra/Saydisc **CD-SAR 17**; SAR 17 [id.]. Alan Hacker, Salomon Qt, (i) with Lesley Schatzberger.

(i) *Clarinet quintet in A, K.581;* (ii) *Flute quartet No. 2 in G, K.285a.*
(B) **(*) Ph. On Tour *416 224-4* [id.]. (i) Brymer, Allegri Qt; (ii) Bennett, Grumiaux Trio – SCHUBERT: *Trout quintet.****

(i) *Clarinet quintet;* (ii) *Oboe quartet in F, K.370.*
*** Sequence SEQ 21101/*ZCSEQ 21501*. (i) Hacker; (ii) Miller, Arriaga Qt.
(M) *** Pickwick Dig. **PCD 810**. (i) Puddy; (ii) Boyd, Gabrieli Qt.

Mozart's *Clarinet quintet* is understandably the most popular and most frequently performed of all his chamber works, and it is very well represented in all price-ranges. Leading the compact disc versions (alongside Thea King's outstanding coupling with the *Clarinet concerto* on Hyperion – see above) is a superb new recording by Alan Hacker with the Salomon Quartet, using original instruments. Those fearing that the warm lyricism of Mozart's scoring might be spoiled by spiky string textures will find their fears immediately quashed by the lovely sounds created in the opening bars which encapsulate the kernel of the music's radiantly nostalgic spirit. Anton Stadler, the clarinettist for whom the work was written, possessed a timbre which was described as 'so soft and lovely that nobody who has a heart can resist it'. Alan Hacker's gentle sound on his period instrument has a similar quality, displayed at its most ravishing in the *Larghetto*. He is matched by the strings, and especially by the leader, Simon Standage, who blends his tone luminously with the clarinet. Tempi are wonderfully apt throughout the performance, the first movement pressing onward without haste, the second leisurely and expansive, and the robust Minuet making a fine contrast.

The rhythms of the finale are infectiously pointed and, following a passage of rhapsodic freedom from the soloist, there is a spirited closing dash. Hacker decorates the reprise of the *Larghetto* affectionately and adds embellishments elsewhere. His articulation in the second Trio of the Minuet is a delight; his chortling roulades in the last movement are no less engaging, the music's sense of joy fully projected. The recording balance is near perfect, the clarinet able to dominate or integrate with the strings at will; and the tangibility of the sound is remarkably realistic, with each of the stringed instruments clearly focused within a natural ambience. To add to the interest of this CD (which plays for over 60′), Alan Hacker includes a fragment from an earlier projected *Quintet*, probably written in 1787 (K.516c) and a similar sketch for a work featuring C Clarinet and basset-horn with string trio, possibly dating from the same year as the famous *A major Quintet* (1789). Both are skilfully completed by Duncan Druce. The work in B flat has a memorable principal theme and its structure is nicely judged (8′ 38″); the piece including the basset-horn is also well worth having, although, at 12′ 41″, it very nearly outstays its welcome.

Almost simultaneously with Alan Hacker's CD issue, an earlier analogue performance arrived on the new Sequence label (distributed by PRT), in which he is joined by the Arriaga Quartet, using modern instruments. The recording is made within a more resonant acoustic, the sound overall more opulent, the strings richer in texture and the clarinet image very slightly inflated, though not disagreeably so. The balance is excellent; the performance is undoubtedly persuasive, its lyrical warmth emphasized by the flattering ambience. Tempi are very similar to the CD version; Hacker's phrasing in the *Larghetto* is perhaps more consciously moulded, but only marginally so. Again he decorates the reprise and, in his solo in the second Trio of the Minuet, he neatly adds an extra embellishment. The analogue sound is first class and the coupling is an outstandingly fresh and imaginative account of the *Oboe quartet*, with Tess Miller the sprightly soloist, which is equally well balanced and recorded. The cassette is in the demonstration class; this most rewarding coupling offers a genuine alternative to the Amon Ra version.

Sabine Meyer was the young clarinettist whose appointment to the Berlin Philharmonic occasioned the open rift between Karajan and the orchestra that clouded their long relationship in early 1983. Judging from this account of the Mozart, she is a most gifted player whose artistry is of a high order. She produces a full, rich and well-focused tone that is a delight to the ear, and she phrases with great musicianship and sensitivity. The performance is one of the best in the catalogue and is well recorded. The balance is well judged, if placing the listener rather forward. However, the effect is eminently realistic and there is no qualification on technical grounds to stand in the way of a three-star recommendation. On the compact disc, which is issued by Denon, the sound is remarkably refined and natural, although, of course, the forward balance remains. The only drawback to Ms Meyer's version is the coupling, which though agreeable is neither very substantial nor generous.

The medium-priced Pickwick CD brings a re-recording of the Mozart by artists who earlier did it for CfP. As before, the reading of the *Clarinet quintet* is clean and well paced, lacking the last degree of delicacy in the slow movement, but never less than stylish. The young oboist, Douglas Boyd, then gives an outstanding performance in the shorter, less demanding work, with the lilting finale delectably full of fun. The digital recording is vividly immediate and full of presence, with even the keys of the wind instruments often audible.

Jack Brymer's interpretation is warm and leisurely. In some ways Brymer follows the famous Bavier recording from Decca's early mono days in choosing slow tempi throughout. He is nearly as successful as Bavier in sustaining them, although in the finale the forward flow of the music is reduced to a near-crawl. Even so, with smooth, believable sound this makes agreeable listening. As a bonus we are offered the two-movement *Flute quartet*, K.285a, in William Bennett's outstanding performance – see below. This generous bargain-priced tape is coupled with a very fine account of Schubert's *Trout quintet* (plus an *Impromptu*, played by Ingrid Haebler who leads in the chamber work). With such persuasive sound this is certainly an attractive collection.

Divertimento in E flat for string trio, K.563.
*** CBS Dig. **MK 39561**; IM/*IMT* 39561 [id.]. Kremer, Kashkashian, Yo-Yo Ma.
** DG Dig. 413 786-1/*4* [id.]. Amadeus Qt (members).

Gidon Kremer, Kim Kashkashian and Yo-Yo Ma turn in an elegant and sweet-toned account on CBS and are excellently recorded. Indeed, the sound is fresh and beautifully realistic. There are many perceptive insights, particularly in the *Adagio* movement which is beautifully done; even if there are one or two narcissistic touches from Kremer (which one does not find on Grumiaux's recording), his playing is still most persuasive. This is the most satisfying account of the *Divertimento* to appear since Grumiaux on Philips (6570/*7310* 572) which is still highly recommendable at medium price.

In the Amadeus performance Norbert Brainin's vibrato is a little sweet for some tastes and the distinguished trio's ardour leads to some traces of roughness. Indeed, though it has plenty of spirit and many musical insights, and is very well recorded, the performance as a whole does not have the polish or refinement of its finest rivals. The tape is exceptionally successful, strikingly 'present' and real.

Flute quartets Nos 1 in D, K.285; 2 in G, K.285a; 3 in C, K.285b; 4 in A, K.298.
*** Accent **ACC 48225D**. Bernhard and Sigiswald Kuijken, Van Dael, Wieland Kuijken.
(M) *** Ph. 412 058-1/*4* [id.]. Bennett, Grumiaux Trio.
**(*) ASV ALH/*ZCALH* 957 [id.]. Adeney, Melos Ens.
*(*) Denon Dig. **C37 7157** [id.]. Nicolet, Moz. String Trio.

Readers normally unresponsive to period instruments should hear these performances by Bernhard Kuijken, for they have both charm and vitality. Period instruments and the pedantic observance of the letter of performance practice – the trappings of a superficial authenticity – do not always go hand in hand with a comparable musical instinct. But these performances radiate pleasure and bring one closer to this music than many of their rivals. This record is rather special and cannot be too strongly recommended. The playing is exquisite and the engineering superb.

There seems general agreement about the merits of the William Bennett–Grumiaux Trio accounts of the *Flute quartets*. They are, to put it in a nutshell, exquisitely played and very well recorded, in every way finer than most other versions which have appeared and disappeared over the years. The freshness of both playing and the remastered 1971 recording gives very great pleasure. The tape transfer, too, is of admirable quality.

The performance by Richard Adeney with members of the Melos Ensemble is rather more extrovert in feeling, certainly vivid and enjoyable, even pert in the vivacious allegros. The balance treats the flute very much in a solo capacity. The effect is enjoyably spontaneous; with more modern (1978) recording, there is slightly more body and presence to the sound than the earlier Philips issue, on disc and tape alike. But the Philips balance is slightly more natural and has greater internal transparency. This ASV set was originally issued on the Enigma label and now seems expensive at full price, when Bennett is now offered at mid-price.

Nicolet plays stylishly and with both finesse and spirit to offer a reasonably recommendable CD version. But the accompanying Mozart String Trio is less subtle in matter of detail than either Grumiaux's group or the Melos Ensemble. The sound is truthful and 'present', with Nicolet balanced forwardly. They are eminently serviceable performances – it would be unfair to call them routine – but at the same time they do not inspire great enthusiasm.

(i) *Horn quintet in E flat, K.407;* (i–iii) *A Musical Joke, K.522;* (iii) *Serenade No. 13* (*Eine kleine Nachtmusik*), *K.525.*

** Denon Dig. **C37 7229** [id.]. (i) Hauptmann; (ii) with Klier; Berlin Philh. Qt; (iii) with Güttler.

Norbert Hauptmann phrases fluently and musically in the *Horn quintet*, but he misses the wit of the finale, and the approach is rather serious: more obvious pleasure in this spontaneous music could have been communicated. The horn balance dominates the sound, and string detail is far less present and clear than it should be in a digital recording. *Eine kleine Nachtmusik* (where the Berlin Philharmonia Quartet is joined by Wolfgang Güttler, double bass) is a well-made, polished account, rather lacking individuality. It is much better balanced and well recorded. The *Musical Joke*, however, is stiff and its humour determinedly Germanic.

Oboe quartet in F, K.370; Adagio in C for cor anglais, 2 violins and cello, K.580a.

*** Ph. Dig. **412 618-2**; 412 618-1/*4* [id.]. Holliger, Orlando Qt – *Divertimento 11.***

Holliger's performance has characteristic finesse and easy virtuosity; the Orlando support is first class and so is the Philips recording in all three media. The performance of the *Adagio* – a deeper, more expressive piece, is also eloquent, though not finer than Holliger's earlier version for Denon, differently coupled – see above. The *Divertimento* coupling here is less appealing.

Piano quartets Nos 1 in G min., K.478; 2 in E flat, K.493.
*** Ph. Dig. **410 391-2**; 410 391-1/*4* [id.]. Beaux Arts Trio with Giuranna.
(M) ** Ph. 412 399-1/*4*. Haebler, Schwalbé, Cappone, Borwitzky.

These are splendidly alive and vitally sensitive accounts that exhilarate the listener, just as the Curzon–Amadeus set did in the early days of LP. The Beaux Arts play them not only *con amore* but with the freshness of a new discovery. Incidentally, both repeats are observed in the first movements, which is unusual on record. The usual high standards of Philips chamber music recording obtain here; in its CD format, the sound (particularly that of the piano) is exceptionally lifelike. There are excellent rival LP versions from the Musikverein Quartet and Previn on Decca and from Walter Klien and the Amadeus on DG, but the Beaux Arts sweeps the board and must be the first recommendation.

Ingrid Haebler plays with elegance and grace and the Philips 1972 recording is first class, equally vivid on disc or cassette. Though not lacking character, this music making must yield to the Beaux Arts versions which have greater imaginative detail.

Piano trios Nos 1 in B flat (Divertimento), K.254; 5 in C, K.548.
** Hyp. A 66093 [id.]. London Fortepiano Trio.

Piano trios Nos 2 in G, K.496; 4 in E, K.542.
** Hyp. A 66148 [id.]. London Fortepiano Trio.

Piano trios Nos 3 in B flat, K.502; 6 in G, K.564.
** Hyp. A 66125 [id.]. London Fortepiano Trio.

For the specialist collector. Linda Nicholson plays a Schantz fortepiano of 1797 – and very well indeed; the string players may however pose problems for readers used to the more robust attack and articulation of modern performance practice. The muted sonorities and the tonal bulges and squeezes leave an initial impression of inhibition, but there is no doubt as to the refined musical intelligence and accomplishments of both artists. The recording is fairly well balanced, even if Linda Nicholson is just a little favoured at the expense of her two partners. The reason the performances take up three LPs instead of the Beaux Arts' two is principally because the London Trio are very generous indeed in the matter of repeats.

Still recommended: For most readers the Beaux Arts performances, using modern instruments, will remain first choice. Although these Philips performances were recorded in the late 1960s, they still sound amazingly vivid and wonderfully fresh, and the set reproduces particularly well in its alternative tape format. It was awarded a Rosette in our last edition (Philips 6768 032/*7650 017* (2)).

Piano and wind quintet in E flat, K.452.

*** CBS Dig. **MK 42099**; IM/*IMT* 42099 [id.]. Perahia, members of ECO – BEETHOVEN: *Quintet.****

** Telarc Dig. **CD 80114**; DG 10114 [id.]. Previn, V. Wind Soloists – BEETHOVEN: *Quintet.***

* Denon Dig. **C37 7090** [id.]. Kontarsky, BPO Wind Qt – BEETHOVEN: *Quintet.***

An outstanding account of Mozart's delectable *Piano and wind quintet*, with Perahia's playing wonderfully refreshing in the *Andante* and a superb response from the four wind soloists, notably Neil Black's oboe contribution. The pacing throughout is perfectly judged, especially the finale which is nicely relaxed. Clearly all the players are enjoying this rewarding music, and they are well balanced, with the piano against the warm but never blurring acoustics of The Maltings, at Snape. The first-movement exposition repeat is observed and so is the first half of the *Larghetto*. Highly recommended.

Previn leads admirably throughout this performance of one of the most engaging of Mozart's chamber works, but the wind support is robust rather than refined. The opening of the slow movement brings elegant playing from the pianist and a rather heavy response from his colleagues. Previn articulates the engaging main theme of the finale most attractively and here the effect is very spirited. The resonant acoustic tends to spread the sound, in spite of the digital recording, although the balance is otherwise well managed.

The Denon performance is very brusque and uncharming. Alois Kontarsky is the neat pianist; despite his undoubted brilliance, the effect is prosaic and two-dimensional. The recording is bright, forward and clear, rather lacking atmosphere, but the performance is plain and unsmiling.

String quartets Nos 1 in G, K.80; 2 in D, K.155; 3 in G, K.156; 4 in C, K.157; Adagio (originally intended for *Quartet No. 3, K.156*).

(M) *** Ph. 412 398-1/*4*. Italian Qt.

This reissue from the beginning of the 1970s gives us the very earliest of Mozart's quartets, the *G major*, K.80, composed when he was fourteen, and the so-called *Milan quartets*, written two years later. The playing is absolutely first class, everything perfectly matched, with beautifully homogeneous tone, spontaneous yet polished phrasing in a recording of striking naturalness and realism. There is now also a splendid tape, an exemplary transfer – in the demonstration class.

String quartets Nos 3 in G, K.156; 4 in C, K.157; 8 in F, K.168; 15 in D min., K.173.

*(*) None. Dig. **CD 79026**; D 79026 [id.]. Sequoia Qt.

These early quartets were composed when Mozart was sixteen and need the most elegant musical presentation. Predictably enough, the *D minor*, K.173, is the most impressive. The Sequoia Quartet give respectable enough accounts of these works, though they do not compare with the Quartetto Italiano on the Philips mid-price label; in terms of recorded sound, the Nonesuch issue is no match for the earlier Philips analogue sound-balance. However, the recordings by the Italian group are only available as a set of nine records (Philips 6747 097); the present issue stands unchallenged for those wanting these works in a separate format.

String quartets Nos 14 in G, K.387; 15 in D min., K.421; 16 in E flat, K.428; 17 in B flat (Hunt), K.458; 18 in A, K.464; 19 in C (Dissonance), K.465; 20 in D (Hoffmeister), K.499; 21 in D, K.575; 22 in B flat, K.589; 23 in F, K.590.
(M) ** DG 415 587-1 (5). Melos Qt of Stuttgart.

It is a sensible idea to present together the ten great Mozart *Quartets*, that is to say the six dedicated to Haydn, the last three written for the King of Prussia and the *Hoffmeister*, which are usually collected in miniature-score editions. These performances date from 1977 to 1984 and the six dedicated to Haydn (Nos 14–19) appeared first singly and then as a set. The Melos give eminently sound accounts of them, readings that are well conceived and finely executed. This judgement applies equally to the remaining four. Even if memories of the Quartetto Italiano on Philips are far from effaced, this is an eminently reliable and sound recommendation. It has the advantage of consistently good recording quality.

Reminder. The Italian Quartet's performances of the six *Haydn quartets* are available on three separate Philips discs with excellent tape equivalents: Nos 14 and 18 (6503/*7303* 067); Nos 15 and 19 (6570/*7310* 888); Nos 16 and 17 (6570/*7310* 922). They remain highly competitive at mid-price, even though the 1967 recording does now begin to show its age, producing a hint of edginess on top, particularly on the first two.

String quartets Nos 14 in G, K.387; 15 in D min., K.421.
*(*) Denon Dig. **C37 7228** [id.]. Kocian Qt.

Straightforward performances of both works, but there is nothing here to displace current LP recommendations. They are really somewhat bland without a wide range of colour or dynamics. Good recording.

String quartets Nos 14 in G, K.387; 21 in D, K.575 (Prussian No. 1).
** Tel. **ZK8 43122**; AZ6/*CY4* 43122 [id.]. Alban Berg Qt.

These performances, digitally remastered for CD, date from the mid-1970s and are very fine indeed. The playing has style and character, and there is no attempt to beautify or glamorize the music. The disc loses a star only because it is just too reverberant for comfort. The chrome cassette, transferred at a very high level, tends to be a little fierce in the treble.

String quartets Nos 15 in D min., K.421; 17 in B flat (Hunt), K.458.
*** Denon **C37 7003** [id.]. Smetana Qt.

These 1982 performances are both recorded in the House of Artists, Prague. The Smetana find just the right tempo for the first movement of the *D minor*, unhurried but forward-moving. *The Hunt*, which is placed first on the disc, is given a spirited performance and is rather more polished than its CD rivals. Not having enjoyed all of the Smetana Quartet's recent performances on this label, it is a pleasure to report with enthusiasm on these well-paced accounts.

String quartets Nos 16 in E flat, K.428; 17 in B flat (Hunt), K.458.
** Sup. Dig. **C37 7538** [id.]. Kocian Qt.

Good but not outstanding performances from this ensemble, formed in the early 1970s but little known outside Czechoslovakia. They are somewhat bland and do not penetrate deep below the surface in the sublime slow movement of the *E flat Quartet*, K.428. These are certainly not as characterful or as beautifully played as such LP versions as the Quartetto Italiano on Philips.

String quartet No. 17 (Hunt), K.458.
(B) *** DG Walkman *413 854-4* [id.]. Amadeus Qt – SCHUBERT: *Trout quintet***; BEETHOVEN: *Ghost Trio.***(*)
(M) ** DG Dig. **410 866-2**; 410 866-1/*4* [id.]. Amadeus Qt – HAYDN: *Quartet No. 77.***

String quartets Nos 17 (Hunt), K.458; 19 in C (Dissonance), K.465.
(M) ** DG Sig. 413 988-1/*4* [id.]. Melos Qt.

The earlier Amadeus account of the *Hunt quartet*, recorded in the mid-1960s, was one of their popular successes. It is, generally speaking, a most satisfying performance, well recorded. On the Walkman tape it receives a most agreeable new transfer and is recoupled with Schubert and Beethoven.

The Amadeus CD repeats the original coupling (with the Haydn *Emperor*) rather less attractively than before. There is a distinct absence of charm. Moreover, the sound, although with striking presence, is not ideally smooth in the treble. It sounds most impressive on the equivalent chrome cassette.

The Melos performances are admirably shaped, with finely integrated tone and much beauty of phrasing. They are very well recorded; indeed, the sound is the most convincingly balanced of any of these issues. The playing, however, lacks the sense of spontaneity and poetic imagination that distinguishes their finest rivals (notably the series by the Italian Quartet on Philips).

String quartets Nos 20 in D (Hoffmeister), K.499; 21 in D, K.575.
** DG Dig. 410 998-1 [id.]. Melos Qt.

Very accomplished playing, with all the musical intelligence and expertise that one expects from this ensemble. They move things along in the first movement of the *Hoffmeister* with the right feeling of musical continuity and rhythmic momentum, but do so at the cost of a certain grace – and this strikes the listener more forcibly in the wonderful minuet. One regrets the passing of the humane virtues of grace and tenderness in some modern quartet playing. Needless to say, the Melos possess many virtues: fine internal balance between the players, a keen responsiveness, superb ensemble and great beauty of sound. The recording is excellent. There is no tape.

String quartets Nos 21 in D, K.575; 22 in B flat, K.589.
*** Ph. Dig. **412 121-2**; 412 121-1/*4*. Orlando Qt.

This Orlando recording comes from 1983 (before their change of personnel) and must be numbered among their most successful. Their account of the *B flat major*, K.589, is wonderfully unhurried and this generally relaxed approach extends to its companions – which makes a pleasant change from the high-powered and 'public' style of quartet playing which is now the norm. The same naturalness is to be found in the *D major*, K.575, which is placed second. This is generally to be preferred to the Alban Berg, good though that is, as it has more modern recording which is spacious yet with excellent definition and fine detail. There is an excellent chrome cassette.

String quintets Nos 1–6.
*** Ph. **416 486-2** (3). Grumiaux Trio with Gerecz, Lesueur.

No reservations about the Grumiaux ensemble's survey of the *String quintets*: immensely civilized and admirably conceived readings. Throughout the set the vitality and sensitivity of this team are striking, and in general this eclipses all other recent accounts. The remastering of the 1973 recordings for CD is astonishingly successful. There is added presence – the tangibility of solo playing is remarkable – and the overall blend remains natural.

String quintets Nos 1 in B flat, K.174; 2 in C min., K.406.
(M) *** Ph. 412 057-1/*4*. Grumiaux Ens.

The Grumiaux series of Mozart's *Quintets* is self-recommending and has the advantage of refined and truthful recording, now with an excellent tape equivalent. This is the last of the three separate issues on LP and cassette.

String quintets Nos 1 in B flat, K.174; 5 in D, K.593.
** Sup. Dig. **C37 7075** [id.]. Smetana Qt with Suk.

Vigorous performances, recorded in Japan in 1983. The sound is forward but perfectly acceptable. The Grumiaux set is still the more polished, particularly in K.174, but this is undoubtedly enjoyable.

String quintets Nos 2 in C min., K.406; 6 in E flat, K.614.
(*) Denon **C37 7179; Sup. 1111 3159 [id.]. Smetana Qt with Suk.

The *C minor Quintet*, K.406, is of course an arrangement of the *Serenade for wind octet*, K.388, which Mozart made in 1787; the *E flat Quintet*, K.614, is his last important chamber work, written in the year of his death. The Smetana Quartet and Josef Suk give extremely fine accounts of both works, though they do not quite have the same lightness of touch of the Grumiaux series. They are accorded very realistic sound; the disc, a co-production with Nippon Columbia, Tokyo, can be warmly recommended, though not in preference to Grumiaux. The Denon CD possesses the usual advantages compared with the Supraphon LP.

String quintets Nos 3 in C, K.515; 4 in G min., K.516.
*(*) Hung. Dig. **HCD 12656-2**; SLPD 12656 [id.]. Takacs Qt, Koromzay.

The Takacs are a young and gifted Hungarian quartet who came into prominence in the 1970s. Their recordings of the two great Mozart *Quintets* with Denes Koromzay as second viola (though he plays first in the *C major*) have spontaneity and warmth, but there are drawbacks which inhibit a wholehearted recommendation. There could be a greater sensitivity to dynamic range, particularly at the *piano* end of the spectrum. There is some rough-and-ready intonation from Denes Koromzay, too. Readers will be better off with the Grumiaux coupling of the same works on LP and tape which will doubtless reach the new format in due course (Philips 6570/*7310* 574).

Violin sonatas Nos 17 in C, K.296; 18 in G, K.197; 19 in E, K.302; 20 in C, K.303; 21 in E min., K.304; 22 in A, K.305; 23 in D, K.306; 24 in F, K.376; 25 in F, K.377; 26 in B flat, K.378; 27 in G, K.379; 28 in E flat, K.380; 32 in B flat, K.454; 34 in A, K.526; Six variations on Hélas, j'ai perdu mon amant, K.360.
(*) Ph. Dig. **412 121-2 (4); 412 121-1/*4* (5/*3*) [id.]. Arthur Grumiaux, Walter Klien.

The Grumiaux/Klien LP set runs to five LPs, while there are four CDs and three high-quality matching cassettes. There is a great deal of sparkle and some refined musicianship in these performances, and pleasure remained undisturbed by the balance, which in the 1981 recordings favours the violin. The later records from 1982 and 1983 are much better in this respect. It goes without saying that there is some distinguished playing in this set, even if the players are not quite so completely attuned as were Grumiaux and Haskil. Some may be troubled by the occasional portamento but, for the most part, this can only give pleasure. Walter Klien is always an intelligent partner and the results in the slow movements of the later sonatas are invariably moving. Now that the fine Decca series by Szymon Goldberg and Radu Lupu has been deleted, this is a strong front-runner. It is, so far, the only complete set on compact disc, though DG are gradually recording this glorious music with Perlman and Barenboim (see below).

Violin sonatas Nos 17 in C, K.296; 22 in A, K.305; 23 in D, K.306.
*** DG Dig. **415 102-2**; 415 102-1/*4* [id.]. Itzhak Perlman, Daniel Barenboim.

These three sonatas are the first of what Alfred Einstein described as Mozart's concertante sonatas; even here, however, the piano is dominant, a point reflected in the fact that, for all Perlman's individuality, it is Barenboim who leads. This is playing of a genial spontaneity that conveys the joy of the moment with countless felicitous details. Three sonatas on a full disc is far from generous measure for a compact disc, but the recording is undistractingly good, with the violin balanced less forwardly than is usual with Perlman. to everyone's advantage. There is an excellent tape, transferred at the highest level, but avoiding edginess.

Violin sonatas Nos 18–21, K.301–4.
*** DG Dig. **410 896-2**; 410 896-1/*4* [id.]. Perlman, Barenboim.

Some very distinguished playing here from Perlman and Barenboim, with fine teamwork and alert and vital phrasing. The recording, too, is extremely lifelike on both disc and chrome tape (it will perhaps be too forward for some tastes) but it is amazingly clean and vivid, particularly in its CD form.

Violin sonatas Nos 18 in G, K.301; 19 in G, K.302; 21 in E min., K. 304; 24 in F, K. 376; 26 in B flat, K.378.
*** Ph. mono **412 253-2** [id.]. Arthur Grumiaux, Clara Haskil.

Violin sonatas Nos 32 in B flat, K.454; 34 in A, K.526.
*** Ph. mono **416 478-2** [id.]. Arthur Grumiaux, Clara Haskil.

These sonatas come from the box of seven LPs devoted to Clara Haskil which appeared two or three years ago and from which the *D minor* (K.466) and *C minor* (K.491) *Piano concertos* with Markevitch are taken (see above). This was a celebrated partnership and these classic accounts, which have excited much admiration over the years (and which will doubtless continue so to do), have been transferred excellently. Mozartians should not hesitate. The original mono recordings come from the late 1950s, yet the sound is remarkably vivid and true and background noise has been virtually vanquished. The performances represent the musical yardstick by which all later versions are judged. Highly recommended.

Violin sonatas Nos 21 in E min., K.304; 23 in D, K.306; 26 in B flat, K.378; Sonata movement in B flat, K.372.
**(*) ASV ALH/*ZCALH* 944 [id.]. Oscar Shumsky, Artur Balsam.

Violin sonatas Nos 24 in F, K.376; 27 in G, K.379; 12 variations on La bergère Célimène, K.359; 6 variations on Hélas, j'ai perdu mon amant, K.360.
**(*) ASV ALH/*ZCALH* 950 [id.]. Oscar Shumsky, Artur Balsam.

Violin sonatas Nos 25 in F, K.377; 28 in E flat, K.380; 29 in A, K.402; 30 in C, K.403; 31 in C, K.404.
**(*) ASV ALH/*ZCALH* 954 [id.]. Oscar Shumsky, Artur Balsam.

Violin sonatas Nos 32 in B flat, K.454; 33 in E flat, K.481.
**(*) ASV ALH/*ZCALH* 964 [id.]. Oscar Shumsky, Artur Balsam.

Violin sonata No. 34 in A, K.526; Violin sonatina in F, K.547.
**(*) ASV ALH/*ZCALH* 967 [id.]. Oscar Shumsky, Artur Balsam.

This is warm, glorious playing of the old style and is wonderfully inspiriting. Unfortunately, these performances were recorded in a rather dry acoustic which, though not in itself unpleasing, tires the ear after some length of time. Balsam is the always intelligent partner, though he does not encompass as wide a dynamic range or such delicacy of colour as did Lupu for Goldberg. There is some fine music-making here and, were the acoustic warmer, this would carry an unqualified recommendation. The cassettes match the discs faithfully enough, with just a hint of edge on the violin timbre.

Piano sonatas Nos 1–18 (complete)*; Fantasia in C min.*
*** HMV **CDS 747336-8** (6) [Ang. **CDCF 47335**]; EX 270324-3 (3) [Ang. DS 3987]: (*Nos 1–7, 9, 10, 12*); EX 270327-3 (3) [Ang. DS 3988]: (*Nos 8, 11, 13–18; Fantasia*). Daniel Barenboim.

Barenboim, while keeping his playing well within scale in its crisp articulation, refuses to adopt the Dresden china approach to Mozart's *Sonatas*. Even the little *C major*, K.545, designed for a young player, has its element of toughness, minimizing its 'eighteenth-century drawing-room' associations. Though – with the exception of the two minor-key sonatas – these are relatively unambitious works, Barenboim's voyage of discovery brings out their consistent freshness, with the orchestral implications of some of the allegros strongly established. The recording, with a pleasant ambience round the piano sound, confirms the apt scale.

Piano sonatas Nos 1 in C, K.279; 14 in C min., K.457; 17 in D, K.576.
ɕ *** Ph. Dig. **412 617-2**; 412 617-1/*4* [id.]. Mitsuko Uchida.

One of the later issues in Mitsuko Uchida's series, this is well up to the standard set previously. The *D major Sonata*, K.576, is fresh and alert, and the *C minor Fantasia* and *Sonata* have stature too. So far these recordings have achieved genuine distinction, and readers who have invested in any of them will need no further reassurances. The sound is first class, especially realistic on compact disc, but very impressive on cassette, too.

Piano sonatas Nos 6 in D, K.284; 14 in C min., K.457; Fantasia in C min., K.475.
(*) Erato Dig. **ECD 88062; NUM/*MCE* 75167 [id.]. Maria Joao Pires.

Maria Joao Pires is a gifted Mozartian who is making an excellent reputation for herself. She is a sensitive and intelligent player, who is well recorded here, too. It would be a pity if her cycle, which is now under way, were to be totally eclipsed by Uchida, for it would make a very acceptable alternative choice.

Piano sonatas Nos 7 in C, K.309; 8 in A min., K.310; 9 in D, K.311.
ꞓ *** Ph. Dig. **412 741-2**; 412 741-1/*4* [id.]. Mitsuko Uchida.

Beautiful playing, elegant, never superficial, finely structured and admirably paced. The slow movements bring the kind of sensibility we associate with Perahia in the *Concertos*. As in the rest of this fine series the piano recording is completely natural, slightly distanced in an ideal ambience. While the CD offers a degree of added presence, the chrome cassette is in every way an acceptable alternative, representing Philips's highest standards of transfer.

Piano sonatas Nos 8 in A min., K.310; 14 in C min., K.457.
(**) Ph. Dig. **412 525-2**; 412 525-1/*4* [id.]. Alfred Brendel.

The pianism is masterly, as one would expect from this great artist, but both performances strike one as the product of excessive ratiocination. There is no want of inner life, the texture is wonderfully clean and finely balanced, but the listener is all too aware of the mental preparation that has gone into it. The first movement of the *A minor* has immaculate control but is more than a little schoolmasterly, particularly in the development. The staccato markings in the slow movement are dreadfully exaggerated, by the side of Lipatti's 1950 record or, among modern pianists, Ashkenazy; and the movement as a whole is unsmiling and strangely wanting in repose. Any great artist who is widely acclaimed is always under pressure from within to renew his vision, to explore new dimensions of his familiar repertoire; and the result is often to focus unnatural attention on detail. In an article in the *New York Review of Books*, Brendel speaks of his conviction that the first movement of the *A minor* is orchestral; for all that, he seems intent on refusing to seduce us by beauty of sound. Self-conscious playing, immaculately recorded, though the cassette is not as impressive as Uchida's series.

Piano sonatas Nos 9 in D, K.311; 10 in C, K.330; 11 in A, K.331; Rondo in A min., K.511.
(*) Denon Dig. **C37 7388 [id.]. Maria Joao Pires.

Maria Joao Pires is a clean and intelligent player with a lively mind and alert sensibility. She is less fastidious than Mitsuko Uchida and in some places is quite thought-provoking. Her account of the *A minor Rondo* is curiously fast and does not make any effort to search out hidden depths. The recording, made in Japan in the mid-1970s, is bright but somewhat dry, and is not really in the same class as the sound Philips provide for Uchida. Incidentally, each of the variations in the first movement of K.331 is separately indexed.

Piano sonatas Nos 10 in C, K.330; 13 in B flat, K.333; Adagio in B min., K.450; Eine kleine Gigue in G, K.574.
ꞓ *** Ph. Dig. **412 616-2**; 412 616-1/*4* [id.]. Mitsuko Uchida.
The marvellous *B minor Adagio* is given an appropriately searching reading. Erik Smith's note reminds us that recent research has established both sonatas

to be later than had been supposed: K.330 was written in Vienna in 1781 (rather than in Paris in 1778), while its companion on this record, K.333, was almost certainly composed in Linz in 1783, along with the *Linz symphony*. The two sonatas are immaculately played and beautifully recorded in all three media.

Piano sonatas Nos 11 in A, K.331; 12 in F, K.332; Fantasia in D min., K.397.
ϲ *** Ph. Dig. **412 123-2**; 412 123-1/*4* [id.]. Mitsuko Uchida.

Mitsuko Uchida's first record to be issued in her Mozart series brings playing of fine sense and sound sensibility. There is no trace of pianistic narcissism, but every indication that this will supersede earlier Mozart surveys, such as those of Gieseking, Haebler and Eschenbach. Every phrase is beautifully placed, every detail registers, and her realization of the closing bars of the *D minor Fantasia* combines taste and a refined musical judgement. The recording is particularly realistic, even judged by the very highest standards. A demonstration disc both sonically and artistically. The cassette is very good, too, although the transfer level might have been higher.

Piano sonatas: in F, K.533/494; No. 15 in C, K.545; Rondo in A min., K.511.
ϲ *** Ph. Dig. **412 122-2**; 412 122-1/*4* [id.]. Mitsuko Uchida.

The first issue in Mitsuko Uchida's cycle of Mozart *Sonatas* – see above – inspired enthusiasm; its successor, which offers two more *Sonatas*, the *F major*, K.533/494, and the *C major*, K.545, is no less captivating. As for the *Rondo in A minor*, K.511, which completes the second side, Mitsuko Uchida delivers a reading that is so haunting and subtle that one can hardly rest until one replays it. This has impeccable style and is strongly recommended. What superb sound the Philips engineers give us too, with the tape as well as the compact disc in the demonstration class.

Piano sonatas Nos 16 in B flat, K.570; 17 in D, K.576; Adagio in B min., K.540.
*(**) Ph. Dig. **411 136-2**; 411 136-1/*4* [id.]. Claudio Arrau.

Arrau's Mozart is the product of enormous thought and a lifetime's wisdom. Yet these readings are highly personal – some would say idiosyncratic. He brings greater sonority and weight to them than do most artists, and his K.570 is powerful and compelling, much bigger in conception than that of most rivals. There are also some unusual agogic touches. Indeed, these accounts are so personal that they call for a specialist rather than a general recommendation, for admirers of this great pianist first, rather than to those starting out building a Mozart sonata collection. The recording is first class, with an excellent tape.

Double piano sonata in D, K.448.
*** **CBS MK 39511**; IM/*IMT* 39511 [id.]. Murray Perahia, Radu Lupu – SCHUBERT: *Fantasia in D min.****

The partnership of two such individual artists as Perahia and Lupu produces magical results, particularly when it was set up in the context of the Aldeburgh Festival, playing at The Maltings concert hall, where this Mozart *Sonata*, like the Schubert *Fantasia*, was recorded live. With Perahia taking the primo part, his brightness and individual way of illuminating even the simplest passagework dominate the performance, challenging the more inward Lupu into comparably inspired playing. Pleasantly ambient recording, beautifully caught on CD. The chrome cassette is 'plummier' in the middle range and less fresh on top.

VOCAL AND CHORAL MUSIC

Concert arias: *Ah, lo previdi . . . Ah, t'invola, K.272; Bella mia fiamma . . . Resta oh cara, K.528; Chi sa, K.582; Nehmt meinen Dank, ihr holden Gönner, K.383; Non più . . . Non temer, K.490; Oh temerario Arbace! . . . Per quel paterno amplesso, K.79/K.73d; Vado, ma dove, K.583.*
*** Decca **411 713-2**; SXL/*KSXC* 6999 [Lon. OS 26661]. Te Kanawa, V. CO, György Fischer.

Kiri Te Kanawa's set of Mozart's concert arias for soprano makes a beautiful and often brilliant recital. Items range from one of the very earliest arias, *Oh temerario Arbace*, already memorably lyrical, to the late *Vado, ma dove*, here sung for its beauty rather than for its drama. Atmospheric, wide-ranging recording, which has transferred well to CD. The cassette is lively and wide-ranging too, although there is a touch of edge on the voice.

Ave verum corpus, K.618; Exsultate, jubilate, K.165; Kyrie in D minor, K.341; Vesperae solennes de confessore in C, K.339.
(*) Ph. **412 873-2; 6500 271/*7300 173* [id.]. Te Kanawa, Bainbridge, Ryland Davies, Howell, LSO Ch., LSO, Sir Colin Davis.

This disc could hardly present a more delightful collection of Mozart choral music, ranging from the early soprano cantata *Exsultate, jubilate*, with its famous setting of *Alleluia*, to the equally popular *Ave verum*. Kiri Te Kanawa is the brilliant soloist in the cantata, and her radiant account of the lovely *Laudate Dominum* is one of the highspots of the *Solemn vespers*. That work, with its dramatic choruses, is among the most inspired of Mozart's Salzburg period, and here it is given a fine responsive performance. The 1971 recording has been remastered for the CD issue; the original was very resonant and the choral sound is not ideally focused, though the Philips engineers were right not to try and clarify the sound artificially. The balance is otherwise truthful and the ear soon adjusts to the slightly cloudy ambience. Dame Kiri's voice is freshly caught.

(i; ii) *Ave verum corpus;* (ii; iii; iv) *Mass No. 16 in C* (*Coronation*), *K.317;* (iii; v) *Requiem mass, K.626;* (vi; i; ii) *Vesperae solennes de confessore, K.339: Laudate Dominum.*

(B) *** Ph. On Tour *416 225-4* [id.]. (i) LSO Ch.; (ii) LSO; (iii) John Alldis Ch.; (iv) Donath, Knight, Davies, Dean; (v) Donath, Minton, Davies, Nienstedt, BBC SO; (vi) Kiri Te Kanawa; all cond. Sir Colin Davis.

One of the very finest (if not *the* finest) of the various collections in Philips's bargain 'On Tour' tape series. The transfers are first rate and demonstrate the best features of the original recordings which date from between 1967 and 1972. Sir Colin Davis's account of the *Coronation mass* is strong and intense and he has excellent soloists; the *Requiem*, with a smaller choir, is more intimate and here the soloists are more variable, yet this is still a satisfying version in its less ambitious way. The *Ave verum* and Kiri Te Kanawa's *Laudate Dominum* are discussed above. A bargain.

Concert arias: *Il burbero di buon cuore: Chi sà. Vado, ma dove, K.583. Exsultate, jubilate, K.165.* Arias: *La Clemenza di Tito: Parto, parto. Idomeneo: Ch'io mi scordi . . . Non temer, amato bene. Le Nozze di Figaro: Al desio di chi t'adore; Un moto di gioia mi sento.*
*** Erato **ECD 88090**; NUM/*MCE* 75176 [id.]. Dame Janet Baker, Scottish CO, Leppard.

In a Mozart programme which extends well beyond the normal mezzo-soprano repertory, Dame Janet Baker sings with all her usual warmth, intensity and stylishness, hardly if at all stretched by often high tessitura. The biggest challenge is the most taxing of all Mozart's concert arias, *Ch'io mi scordi di te*, with Leppard a brilliant exponent of the difficult piano obbligato part. There Dame Janet, so far from being daunted by the technical problems, uses them to intensify her detailed rendering of words. The two *Figaro* items are alternative arias for Susanna, both of them delightful. Sesto's aria from *Clemenza di Tito* presents another challenge, magnificently taken, as does the early cantata, *Exsultate, jubilate*, with its famous *Alleluia.* The other two arias were written for Louise Villeneuve – Dorabella to be – as an enrichment for her part in an opera by Soler, more delightful rarities. Excellent sound and warmly sympathetic accompaniment. Although the CD has ultimate presence, the high-level chrome cassette too is both truthful and vivid.

Concert arias: *Clarice cara, K.256; Con ossequio, K.210; Misero! O sogno . . . Aura, che intorno spiri, K.431; Or che il dover . . . Tali e cotanti sono, K.36; Per pietà, non ricercate, K.420; Se al labbro mio non credi, K.295; Si mostra la sorte, K.209; Va dal duror portata, K.421.*
*** Decca Dig. 414 193-1/*4* [id.]. Gösta Winbergh, Vienna CO, György Fischer.

Winbergh is an exceptionally stylish Mozart tenor, and though his collection includes a few items of less than vintage Mozart, he rises splendidly to the challenge of such magnificent arias as K.420 and K.431, using his clean, heady tenor very effectively, if without the final degree of individuality. First-rate accompaniment and excellent sound on LP. However, the cassette, transferred at the highest level, tends to make the upper vocal range sound peaky.

Exsultate, jubilate, K.165 (Salzburg version); Motets: *Ergo interest, K.143; Regina coeli* (2 settings), *K.108, K.127.*

€ *** O-L Dig. **411 832-2**; 411 832-1/*4* [id.]. Emma Kirkby, Westminster Cathedral Boys' Ch., AAM Ch. and O, Hogwood.

The boyish, bell-like tones of Emma Kirkby are perfectly suited to the most famous of Mozart's early cantatas, *Exsultate, jubilate*, culminating in a dazzling account of *Alleluia.* With accompaniment on period instruments, that is aptly coupled with far rarer but equally fascinating examples of Mozart's early genius, superbly recorded. A most refreshing collection and sounding very well indeed on tape, although the CD is finest of all, giving the singer a most realistic presence.

Masses Nos 10 in C (Spatzenmesse), K.220; 16 in C (Coronation), K.317. Inter natos mulierum in G, K.72.

(*) Ph. Dig. **411 139-2; 411 139-1/*4* [id.]. Jelosits, Eder, V. Boys' Ch., VSO, Harrer.

This coupling of the two of the C major masses that Mozart wrote as part of his duties in Salzburg will please those who prefer performances authentically using an all-male band of singers – if with a modern orchestra. The *Spatzenmesse* (Sparrow mass) owes its nickname to the chirping of violins in the *Pleni sunt coeli*, a setting even more compressed than most. The *Coronation mass* is the most famous of the period, well sung and played, with the two named soloists joined by two lusty boy singers, making a well-matched quartet. A fair recommendation for those who fancy the coupling, but there are more distinctive versions of K.317, notably Karajan's (DG 2530/*3300* 704 [id.]). Atmospheric recording, generally well balanced. There is a good cassette.

Masses Nos 12 in C (Spauer), K.258; 14 in C (Missa longa), K.262.

(*) Ph. Dig. **412 232-2; 412 232-1/*4* [id.]. Shirai, Schiml, Ude, Polster, Leipzig R. Ch., Dresden PO, Kegel.

Kegel with his brilliant Leipzig Radio Chorus conducts attractive performances of two of Mozart's rarer settings of the mass, with Mitsuko Shirai outstanding among the soloists. Neither mass reveals Mozart at his most inspired, but the *Spaurmesse*, much the shorter of the two, is the more consistent, the *Missa longa* the one with sharper contrasts. The recording is good, but places the singers too far in front of the orchestra. The high-level cassette reflects this in its focus, which is excellent for the soloists, slightly less sharp for the chorus – though better in K.258 than in K.262.

Masses Nos 16 in C (Coronation), K.317; 17 (Missa solemnis), K.337.

(*) Argo Dig. **411 904-2; 411 904-1/*4*. Margaret Marshall, Murray, Covey-Crump, Wilson-Johnson, King's College Ch., ECO, Cleobury.

Stephen Cleobury, inheritor of the King's choral tradition, imaginatively couples the well-known *Coronation mass* with the very last of the fifteen settings that Mozart wrote for Salzburg, a work just as inspired, with a similar anticipation of the Countess's music for *Figaro* in the *Agnus Dei* (reminding us of *Dove sono* in K.317, of *Porgi amor* in K.337). Though rhythmically this is not as lively as the finest versions of K.317, the coupling can be warmly recommended, with its excellent soloists and fresh choral singing all beautifully recorded, though the chrome tape has some problems with the King's resonance and the focus slips a little at peaks.

(i) *Mass No. 16 in C (Coronation), K.317;* (ii) *Requiem Mass in D min., K.626.*
**(*) DG Walkman *419 084-4* [id.]. (i) Mathis, Procter, Grobe, Shirley-Quirk, Bav. R. Ch. and SO, Kubelik; (ii) Mathis, Hamari, Ochman, Ridderbusch, V. State Op. Ch., VPO, Boehm.

A characteristically generous Walkman coupling, with good sound throughout. Both recordings were made in the early 1970s. Kubelik draws a fine, mellow-toned performance of the *Coronation mass* from his Bavarian forces, lacking something in exuberance, but still alive and well sung. Boehm's account of the *Requiem* is also spacious but has more power, and the majesty of the closing *Agnus Dei* is very involving. This is also available on CD (see below), but the recording loses little in its chrome tape transfer and is strikingly well balanced; moreover, in this format it costs less than a third as much, and offers more music.

Mass No. 18 in C min. (Great), K.427.
*** DG Dig. **400 067-2**; 2532/*3302* 028 [id.]. Hendricks, Perry, Schreier, Luxon, V. Singverein, BPO, Karajan.
(M) *** HMV EG 290277-1/*4* [Ang. AM/*4AM* 34710]. Cotrubas, Te Kanawa, Krenn, Sotin, Alldis Ch., New Philh. O, Leppard.
(*) Tel. Dig. **ZK8 43120; AZ6/*CY4* 43120 [id.]. Láki, Dénes, Equiluz, Holl, V. State Op. Ch. Soc., VCM, Harnoncourt.
(M) ** Ph. 412 932-1/*4*. Marshall, Palmer, Rolfe-Johnson, Howell, Ch. and ASMF, Marriner.

Karajan gives Handelian splendour to this greatest of Mozart's choral works, and though the scale is large, the beauty and intensity are hard to resist, for this, unlike much of Karajan's Mozart, is strongly rhythmic, not smoothed over. Solo singing is first rate, particularly that of Barbara Hendricks, the dreamy beauty of her voice ravishingly caught. Though woodwind is rather backward, the sound is both rich and vivid, and the compact disc is even more impressively realistic, though, as the opening shows, the internal balance is not always completely consistent. On CD the thirteen movements are all separately banded. The chrome tape is of good quality but not as clear in detail as some of DG's digital issues, though side two is slightly sharper in focus than side one.

Raymond Leppard uses the Robbins Landon edition, rejecting the accretions which were formerly used to turn this incomplete torso of a work into a full setting of the liturgy. He uses a modest-sized professional choir and his manner is relatively affectionate, which many will prefer, even in this dark work. The sopranos are the light-givers here, and the partnership of Ileana Cotrubas and Kiri Te Kanawa is radiantly beautiful. Fine, full, clear recording, more naturally balanced than Karajan's digital version. On cassette, the upper range is slightly less extended and the choral focus not as sharp as on disc.

Harnoncourt's version, using period instruments, is strongly characterized, with authentic performance used not to smooth away dramatic contrasts but to enhance them. The emphatic rhythmic style in both slow and fast passages will not please everyone, but with a well-chosen quartet of soloists and responsive choral singing this fills an obvious gap. Reverberant recording is not always helpful to detail.

Neville Marriner secures a good response from his artists, though this performance falls short of being really inspired. Marriner's is a well-thought-out and conscientious reading, and there is some fine singing. His account does not quite communicate the sense of stature this music calls for.

Requiem mass (No. 19) in D min., K.626.

*** Ph. Dig. **411 420-2**; 6514/*7337* 320 [id.]. Margaret Price, Schmidt, Araiza, Adam, Leipzig R. Ch., Dresden State O, Schreier.

** Argo **417 133-2**; ZRG/*KZRC* 876 [id.]. Cotrubas, Watts, Tear, Shirley-Quirk, Ch. and ASMF, Marriner.

** DG **413 553-2** [id.]. Mathis, Hamari, Ochman, Ridderbusch, V. State Op. Ch., VPO, Boehm.

*(*) Tel. Dig. **ZK8 42756**; AZ6/*CX4* 42756 [id.]. Yakar, Wenkel, Equiluz, Holl, V. State Op. Ch., VCM, Harnoncourt.

*(*) HMV Dig. **CDC 747342-2** [id.]; EL 270194-1/*4* [Ang. DS/*4DS* 38216]. Battle, Murray, Rendall, Salminen, Ch. and O de Paris, Barenboim.

Peter Schreier's is a forthright reading of Mozart's valedictory choral work, bringing strong dramatic contrasts and marked by superb choral singing and a consistently elegant and finely balanced accompaniment. The recording is exceptionally well balanced and the orchestral detail emerges with natural clarity. The singing of Margaret Price in the soprano part is finer than any yet heard on record, and the others make a first-rate team, if individually more variable. Only in the *Kyrie* and the final *Cum sanctis tuis* does the German habit of using the intrusive aitch intrude. Altogether this is the most satisfying version currently available. It sounds best of all on the compact disc, where the refinement of detail is even more striking; but there is also a good tape, where the focus does not cloud.

Marriner, who can usually be relied on to produce vigorous and sympathetic performances on record, generates less electricity than usual in the *Requiem*. It is interesting to have a version which uses the Beyer Edition and a text which aims at removing the faults of Süssmayr's completion, amending points in the harmony and instrumentation; but few will register any significant differences except in such points as the extension of the *Osanna*. Solo singing is good, but the chorus could be more alert. Good, atmospheric recording.

Boehm's is a spacious and solemn view of the work, with good solo singing and fine choral and orchestral response. It is not as dramatic a reading as Schreier's, though it is immensely polished in every way. The recording dates from 1972 and sounds well in its new format; however, this is not as satisfying as the Schreier Philips CD. It is also available, sounding extremely well, on a Walkman chrome tape, coupled with the *Coronation mass* at a fraction of the price of the CD.

Harnoncourt's distinctive view of Mozart – heavier than you would expect from one so wedded to authenticity – is here negated by the washiness of the recording of voices. The chorus might have been performing in a swimming bath, and though ambience adds some glamour to the solo voices, a good team, it is disconcertingly inconsistent to have an orchestra of original instruments in all its clarity set against vocal sound so vague. Disc and chrome tape are much the same. The compact disc only serves to emphasize the flabbiness of the choral focus.

Since he recorded it earlier for EMI with an even more distinguished quartet of soloists, Barenboim's view of the Mozart *Requiem* has broadened and become more obviously romantic in manner. Set in a reverberant church acoustic, this is really too weighty for Mozart, a good performance but not one to compete with the finest. Even on CD, the sound is not especially clear.

Requiem Mass (*No. 19*) *in D min.* (edited Maunder).
(*) O-L Dig. **411 712-2; 411 712-1/*4* [id.]. Emma Kirkby, Watkinson, Rolfe-Johnson, David Thomas, Westminster Cathedral Boys' Ch., AAM Ch. and O, Hogwood.

Hogwood's version is strictly incomparable with any other, using as it does the edition of Richard Maunder which aims to eliminate Sussmayr's contribution to the version of Mozart's unfinished masterpiece that has held sway for two centuries. So the *Lacrimosa* is completely different, after the opening eight bars, and concludes with an elaborate *Amen*, for which Mozart's own sketches were recently discovered. The *Sanctus*, *Osanna* and *Benedictus* are completely omitted as being by Sussmayr and not Mozart. This textual clean-out goes with authentic performance of Hogwood's customary abrasiveness, very fresh and lively to underline the impact of novelty, and to divide Mozartian opinion. With fine solo singing from four specialists in baroque performance and bright choral sound, brilliantly recorded, it can be recommended to those who welcome a new look in Mozart. While the CD has the usual advantages, the chrome tape, too, is strikingly vivid and clear in focus.

Thamos, King of Egypt (incidental music), *K.345*.
(*) Tel. Dig. **ZK8 42702; AZ6/*CX4* 42702 [642702]. Perry, Mühle, Van Alterna, Thomaschke, Van der Kemp, Netherlands Chamber Ch., Concg. O, Harnoncourt.

Harnoncourt directs a spirited account of the *Thamos* incidental music, now thought to date from rather later than originally estimated and here made to seem strong and mature in incisive, sharply articulated performances. Playing is excellent, and though chorus and soloists are rather backwardly placed in a reverberant acoustic, the singing is enjoyable too.

OPERA

Così fan tutte (complete).
(*) O-L Dig. **414 316-2; 414 316-1/*4* (3) [id.]. Yakar, Resick, Nafé, Winberg, Krause, Feller, Drottningholm Court Theatre Ch. and O, Östman.

Arnold Östman has established a formidable reputation conducting authentic performances of Mozart in the beautiful little court opera house at Drottningholm, near Stockholm. Except that soloists of international standing have been introduced – an aptly fresh-voiced team, stylishly Mozartian – this recording aims to reproduce one of the most successful of his productions. The point initially to marvel at is the hectic speed of almost every number. The wonder is that with light-toned period instruments and with singers sufficiently agile, the anticipated gabble does not take place, and Östman refreshingly establishes a valid new view. Few Mozartians would want to hear *Così fan tutte* like this all the time, but with no weak link in the cast and with the drama vividly presented, it can be recommended to those who enjoy authentic performance and to all who are prepared to listen afresh. With ample cueing, the CD is particularly convenient to use, and the sound is even clearer and more immediate. The chrome cassettes, too, are extremely vivid, but Mozartians are warned that those seeking the charm and humane geniality that Boehm finds in this work will discover that Östman's set is less ingratiating, though it remains compulsive listening thoughout.

Still recommended: Boehm's classic recording with Schwarzkopf, Ludwig, Steffek, Kraus, Taddei and Berry remains first choice, with its Rosette still unfaded (HMV SLS/*TC-SLS* 5028 [Ang. SCLX 3631]).

Don Giovanni (complete).
*** HMV Dig. **CDS 747037-8** [id.]; SLS/*TC-SLS* 143665-3/*9* (3) [DSX-*4D3X* 3953]. Thomas Allen, Vaness, Ewing, Gale, Van Allan, Keith Lewis, Glyndebourne Ch., LPO, Haitink.
(***) HMV mono EX 290667-3/*9*. Siepi, Schwarzkopf, Edelmann, Grümmer, Berger, Dermota, Berry, V. State Op. Ch., VPO, Furtwängler.

Haitink's set superbly captures the flavour of Sir Peter Hall's memorable production at Glyndebourne, not least in the inspired teamwork. The only major change from the production on stage is that Maria Ewing (Lady Hall) comes in as Elvira, vibrant and characterful, not ideally pure-toned but contrasting characterfully with the powerful Donna Anna of Carol Vaness and the innocent-sounding Zerlina of Elizabeth Gale. Keith Lewis is a sweet-toned Ottavio, but it is Thomas Allen as Giovanni who – apart from Haitink – dominates the set, a swaggering Don full of charm and with a touch of nobility when, defiant to the end, he is dragged to hell – a spine-chilling moment as recorded here. Rarely has the Champagne aria been so beautifully sung, with each note articulated – and that also reflects Haitink's flawless control of pacing, not always conventional but always thoughtful and convincing. Excellent playing from the LPO – well practised in the Glyndebourne pit – and warm, full recording, far more agreeable than the actual sound in the dry auditorium at Glyndebourne. The CD with its ample cueing brings extra convenience as well as even cleaner sound than the LPs. The cassettes are very successful, too; this version shares the top recommendation with Giulini's famous analogue set with Waechter, Schwarzkopf, Sutherland, Sciutti, Alva and Taddei (HMV SLS/*TC-SLS* 5083 [Ang. SCL/*4X3X* 3605]).

The historic Furtwängler performance was recorded by Austrian Radio live at the Salzburg Festival in 1954, barely three months before the conductor's death. Though the mono sound is limited and stage noises are often thunderous, the voices come over with amazing clarity, while the orchestra is given Mozartian refinement. Though Furtwängler's speeds are often slower than we would expect today, he is a far more stylish Mozartian than most of his romantic contemporaries. Rhythms are crisply lifted to make even the slow speed for Leporello's catalogue aria seem charmingly individual. With the exception of a wobbly Commendatore, this is a classic Salzburg cast, with Cesare Siepi a fine, incisive Don, dark in tone, Elisabeth Schwarzkopf a dominant Elvira, Elisabeth Grümmer a vulnerable Anna, Anton Dermota a heady-toned Ottavio and Otto Edelmann a clear, direct Leporello. There are excellent cassettes.

Don Giovanni: highlights.
(M) *** Ph. Seq. 412 016-1/*4* [id.]. Wixell, Arroyo, Te Kanawa, Freni, Ganzarolli, Burrows, Van Allan, ROHCG Ch. and O, Sir Colin Davis.

The mid-price highlights from Sir Colin Davis's set are most attractive, a generous selection, well chosen, well performed and well recorded. Wixell's Don is intelligent and stylish, if not always seductive in tone; there is no serious weakness in the cast, though Arroyo's weight does not always go with Mozartian delicacy. Davis's direction is fresh and invigorating. The very lively cassette transfer brings sharply focused solo voices but with some edginess on the orchestral sound.

Die Entführung aus dem Serail (complete).
*** Tel. Dig. **ZB8 35673**; GK6/*MR4* 35673 (3). Kenny, Watson, Schreier, Gamlich, Salminen, Zurich Op. Ch. and Moz. O, Harnoncourt.

Based on a celebrated stage production in Zurich with these same forces, Harnoncourt's version establishes its uniqueness at the very start of the overture, tougher and more abrasive than any previous recording. What Harnoncourt contends is that Mozart wanted more primitive sounds than we are used to in his

Turkish music, with the jingle of cymbals, Turkish drums and the like more than living up to the nickname 'kitchen department', with the stove itself seemingly included. It is not a comfortable sound, compounded by Harnoncourt's often fast allegros, racing singers and players off their feet. Another source of extra abrasiveness is the use of a raw-sounding flageolet instead of a piccolo. Once you get used to the sound, however, the result is refreshing and lively, with the whole performance reflecting the fine rapport built up in stage performance. Slow passages are often warmly expressive, but the stylishness of the soloists prevents them from seeming excessively romantic, as in Schreier's charming singing of *O wie ängstlich* in Act I. The other men are excellent, too: Wilfried Gamlich both bright and sweet of tone, Matti Salminen outstandingly characterful as an Osmin who, as well as singing with firm dark tone, points the words with fine menace. Yvonne Kenny as Konstanze and Lillian Watson as Blonde sound on the shrill side – partly a question of microphones – but they sing with such style and point that one quickly accepts that. *Martern aller Arten* prompts the most brilliant coloratura from Kenny, with the coda including some extra bars, now authorized by scholarship, but doubtfully effective, one of the many textual niceties of the set. Good, clean, dryish recording. The cassettes are excellently transferred and, by providing a special plastic wallet within the box, Telefunken are able to fit in the admirably printed libretto designed for the CD set.

La finta semplice (complete).

*** Orfeo Dig. SO 85844K (4) [id.]. Donath, Rolfe-Johnson, Berganza, Holl, Ihloff, Moser, Lloyd, Salzburg Mozarteum O, Hager.

La finta semplice is an astonishing achievement for a twelve-year-old, but variably successful as an *opera buffa*. The heroine, Rosina, is the 'feigned simpleton' of the title, and it is she who has many of the most distinctive numbers, some of them very beautiful, including an echo aria in Act I, with an oboe solo following the voice, and with the orchestra including two cor anglais. Under Hager's stylish direction the singing is consistently satisfying with no weak link in the cast. For anyone who wants to investigate a Mozart rarity, the set can be strongly recommended, with excellent recording.

Idomeneo (complete).

(*) Tel. **ZB8 35547; GX6/*MU4* 35547 (3) [id.]. Hollweg, Schmidt, Yakar, Palmer, Zurich Op. O, Harnoncourt.

Using a text very close to that of the Munich première of Mozart's great *opera seria*, and with the role of Idamante given to a soprano instead of being transposed down to tenor register, Harnoncourt presents a distinctive and refreshing view, one which in principle is preferable to general modern practice. The vocal cast is good, with Hollweg a clear-toned, strong Idomeneo, and no weak link. Felicity Palmer finds the necessary contrasts of expression as Elettra. On LP, the voices are sometimes given an unpleasant edge, and the sharp articulation of the recitatives is initially disconcerting but, with the CD remastering, the sound is transformed and the edginess smoothed without loss of presence. The cassettes, too, are smoother than the LPs. It is surprising that, in an account which aims at authenticity, appoggiature are so rarely used. This is hardly a performance to warm to, but it is refreshing and alive.

Le Nozze di Figaro (complete).

*** Decca Dig. **410 150-2** (3) [id.]; D267 D4/*K267 K42* (4/*2*) [Lon. LDR/*5-74001*]. Te Kanawa, Popp, Von Stade, Ramey, Allen, Moll, LPO and Ch., Solti.

*** DG **415 520-2** [id.]; 2740 204/*3371 005* (3) [2711 007/id.]. Janowitz, Mathis, Troyanos, Fischer-Dieskau, Prey, Lagger, German Op. Ch. and O, Boehm.

(M) **(*) HMV EX 290017-3/*9* (3). Jurinac, Sciutti, Stevens, Bruscantini, Calabrese, Ian Wallace, Cuenod, Glyndebourne Fest. Ch. and O, Gui.

It is important not to judge Solti's effervescent new version of *Figaro* by a first reaction to the overture. It is one of the fastest on record (matching Karajan in the 'egg-timer' race). Elsewhere Solti opts for a fair proportion of extreme speeds, slow as well as fast, but they rarely if ever intrude on the quintessential happiness of the entertainment. Rejecting the idea of a bass Figaro, Solti has chosen in Samuel Ramey a firm-toned baritone, a virile figure. He is less a comedian than a lover, superby matched to the most enchanting of Susannas today, Lucia Popp, who gives a sparkling and radiant performance to match the Pamina she sang in Haitink's recording of *Zauberflöte*. Thomas Allen's Count is magnificent too, tough in tone and characterization but always beautiful on the ear. Kurt Moll as Dr Bartolo sings an unforgettable *La vendetta* with triplets very fast and agile 'on the breath', while Robert Tear far outshines his own achievement as the Basilio of Sir Colin Davis's amiable recording. Frederica von Stade, as in the Karajan set, is a most attractive Cherubino, even if *Voi che sapete* is too slow; but crowning all is the Countess of Kiri Te Kanawa, challenged by Solti's spacious tempi in the two big arias, but producing ravishing tone, flawless phrasing and elegant ornamentation throughout. With superb, vivid recording this now makes an excellent first choice for a much-recorded opera, especially vivid on the three CDs but also sounding extremely well on the chrome cassettes which offer the ideal layout with one Act complete on each of four sides.

Boehm's earlier version of *Figaro* was once available on the cheap Fontana Special label, but unlike that sprightly performance this newer one gives a complete text, with Marcellina's and Basilio's Act IV arias included. This is among the most consistently assured performances available. The women all sing most beautifully, with Janowitz's Countess, Mathis's Susanna and Troyanos's Cherubino all ravishing the ear in contrasted ways. Prey is an intelligent if not very jolly-sounding Figaro, and Fischer-Dieskau gives his dark, sharply defined reading of the Count's role. All told, a great success, with fine playing and recording, enhanced on CD which offers fresh, clean sound and an excellent perspective. There are generous cues, giving access to all the important points of the score.

Recorded originally to celebrate the Mozart Bicentenary in 1956, Gui's Glyndebourne set superbly captures the flavour of productions of the period under Carl Ebert, with a cast featuring many Glyndebourne favourites, including Sena Jurinac's enchanting Countess, Sciutti's sparkling Susanna, Sesto Bruscantini's amiable Figaro, Ian Wallace's orotund Bartolo and – not least – the delectably pointed Basilio of Hugues Cuenod, an indestructible tenor who nearly thirty years later as an octogenarian sang memorably as Don Curzio in the Glyndebourne 50th-anniversary production of the opera. The great merit of the set is not just the light touch of Gui but the way the story is told so clearly with light, brisk recitatives and stereo production which remains a model of its kind. This remastering freshens sound, which is excellent for its period. There are good cassettes, with Acts tailored to side-ends.

Reminder. Mozart's opera is extremely well served on both disc and tape; other fine versions include Giulini's classic HMV set with its star-studded cast including Schwarzkopf, Moffo, Taddei, Waechter and Cossotto (HMV SLS/*TC-SLS* 5152 [Ang. SCL/*4X3X* 3608]); Sir Colin Davis's sparklingly paced Philips recording with Freni, Norman, Minton, Ganzarolli and Wixell (6707 014/*7699 053* [id.]); and not least the outstandingly successful tape transfer of Erich Kleiber's mid-1950s recording with Gueden, Danco, Della Casa, Poell, Corena and Siepi (Decca *K79 K32* [Lon. OSA/*5*- 1402]).

Le Nozze di Figaro: highlights.
(M) *** Ph. Seq. 412 017-1/*4* [id.]. Freni, Norman, Minton, Ganzarolli, Tear, Wixell, BBC SO and Ch., Sir Colin Davis.

The selection from Davis's outstanding complete set is well balanced and attractive – though what disc could possibly contain every favourite item from such an opera? The sound has been brightened, and on tape the male vocal timbres are more notable for presence than mellowness.

Die Zauberflöte (complete).
*** HMV Dig. SLS/*TCC-SLS* 5223 (3). Popp, Gruberová, Lindner, Jerusalem, Brendel, Bracht, Zednik, Bav. R. Ch. and SO, Haitink.
*** DG Dig. **410 967-2**; 2741/*3382* 001 (3) [id.]. Mathis, Ott, Perry, Araiza, Hornik, Van Dam, German Op. Ch., BPO, Karajan.
(*) Decca **414 568-2 (3) [id.]; SET 479-81/*K2 A4* [Lon. OSA/*5*- 1397]. Lorengar, Deutekom, Burrows, Fischer-Dieskau, Prey, Talvela, V. State Op. Ch., VPO, Solti.
*(*) Ph. Dig. **411 459-2**; 411 459-1/*4* (3) [id.]. Margaret Price, Serra, Schreier, Moll, Melbye, Venuti, Tear, Dresden Kreuzchor, Leipzig R. Ch., Dresden State O, Sir Colin Davis.

Haitink in his first ever opera recording directs a rich and spacious account of *Zauberflöte*, superbly recorded in spectacularly wide-ranging digital sound.

There is a sterling honesty in Haitink's approach to every number. With speeds generally a shade slower than usual, the point of the playing and the consistent quality of the singing present this as a Mozart masterpiece that is weighty as well as sparkling. The dialogue – not too much of it, nicely produced and with sound effects adding to the vividness – frames a presentation that has been carefully thought through. Popp makes the most tenderly affecting of Paminas (as she did in the Salzburg production) and Gruberová has never sounded more spontaneous in her brilliance than here as Queen of the Night: she is both agile and powerful. Jerusalem makes an outstanding Tamino, both heroic and sweetly Mozartian; and though neither Wolfgang Brendel as Papageno nor Bracht as Sarastro is as characterful as their finest rivals, their personalities project strongly and the youthful freshness of their singing is most attractive. The Bavarian chorus too is splendid, and the recording's perspectives featuring the chorus are extraordinarily effective, particularly in the superb Act I finale. The chrome cassettes are no less outstanding technically than the discs, offering sound of remarkable range, body and presence. Some readers will certainly prefer Karajan's more urgent, more volatile Berlin version, but the gravitas of Haitink's approach does not miss the work's elements of drama and charm, though nothing is trivialized. We look forward to the compact disc issue of this set, which we assume will arrive during the life of this book.

Zauberflöte has also inspired Karajan to one of his freshest, most rhythmic Mozart performances, spontaneous-sounding to the point where vigour is preferred to immaculate precision in ensembles. The digital recording is not always perfectly balanced, but the sound is outstandingly fresh and clear, on disc and chrome cassettes alike. The CDs add presence and refine detail but also underline the variable balances. There are numbers where the tempi are dangerously slow (Tamino's *Dies Bildnis*, both of Sarastro's arias and Pamina's *Ach, ich fühl's*), but Karajan's concentration helps him to avoid mannerism completely. The choice of soloists may seem idiosyncratic, and in principle one would want a darker-toned Sarastro than José van Dam, but the clarity of focus and the fine control, not to mention the slow tempi, give the necessary weight to his arias. Francisco Araiza and Gottfried Hornik make impressive contributions, both concealing any inexperience. Karin Ott has a relatively weighty voice for the Queen of the Night, but in his tempi Karajan is most considerate to her; and the Pamina of Edith Mathis has many beautiful moments, her word-pointing always intelligent.

If one is looking for Mozartian charm in this most monumental of Mozart's operas, then plainly Solti's reading must be rejected. It is tough, strong and brilliant, and it is arguable that in this opera those are the required qualities above all; but even so the absence of charm has a cumulative effect. The drama may be consistently vital, but ultimately the full variety of Mozart's inspiration is not achieved. On the male side the cast is very strong indeed, with Stuart Burrows assuming his international mantle easily with stylish and rich-toned singing. Martti Talvela and Fischer-Dieskau as Sarastro and the Speaker respectively provide a stronger contrast than usual, each superb in his way, and Hermann Prey rounds out the character of Papageno with intelligent pointing of words. The cast of women is less consistent. Pilar Lorengar's Pamina is sweetly attractive as long as your ear is not worried by her obtrusive vibrato, while Cristina Deutekom's Queen of the Night is technically impressive, though marred by a curious warbling quality in the coloratura, almost like an intrusive 'w' where you sometimes have the intrusive 'h'. The Three Ladies make a strong team (Yvonne Minton in the middle), and it was a good idea to give the parts of the Three Boys to genuine trebles. The brilliant and lively 1971 recording has been transferred to CD with the utmost vividness and there are ample cues to provide internal access to the opera. However, the adjective we originally applied to the LP libretto (sumptuous) hardly applies to the CD booklet. The coloured illustrations have reduced effectively to the smaller size, but the libretto itself is in small type, and not very bold.

The last of Sir Colin Davis's recordings of Mozart's major operas, and the only one made outside Britain, is also the least successful. With speeds often slower than usual and the manner heavier, it is a performance of little sparkle or charm, one which seems intent on bringing out serious, symbolic meanings. Thus, although Margaret Price produces a glorious flow of rich, creamy tone, she conveys little of the necessary vulnerability of Pamina in her plight. Luciana Serra sings capably but at times with shrill tone and not always with complete security; while Peter Schreier is in uncharacteristically gritty voice as Tamino, and Mikael Melbye as Papageno is ill-suited to recording, when the microphone exaggerates the throatiness and unevenness of his production. The greatest vocal glory of the set is the magnificent, firm and rich singing of Kurt Moll as Sarastro. The recording is excellent, with first-class matching tapes.

Die Zauberflöte: highlights.
*** HMV Dig. **CDC7 47008-2** (from above recording, cond. Haitink).
*** DG Dig. **415 287-2**; 2532/*3302* 004 [id.] (from above set, cond. Karajan).
** RCA Dig. **RCD 14621**. Donat, Cotrubas, Kales, Tappy, Talvela, Boesch, V. State Op. Ch., VPO, Levine.

Haitink's selection has at present no LP or cassette equivalents, but the compact disc has all the virtues of the new system, giving an added sense of presence and atmosphere. The selection is well made to include many favourites, with the Papageno/Papagena music well represented to make a contrast with the lyrical arias and the drama of the Queen of the Night.

This selection from the Karajan set concentrates on the major arias, and very impressive it is. The buoyancy as well as the spaciousness of Karajan's reading come over well on CD, helped by the bright digital recording. The cassette transfer is not made at the highest level but retains the immediacy and range of the complete set.

The RCA highlights CD is generous in offering fifteen excerpts and has a certain charm in detailing each in a lurid English translation; thus the Queen of the Night's second aria (*Die Hölle Rache*) is given as 'The vengeance of Hell boils in my heart'. It is variably sung. Zdzislawa Donat's contribution is one of the few outstanding performances here, alongside Cotrubas's Pamina – her aria

Ach, ich fühl's is equally fine. Neither artist is named on the insert leaflet; however, this does provide a synopsis of 'The Plot'. There is nothing special about the CD sound, apart from the background silence. However, the dialogue which weighs down the complete set is omitted here.

Highlights from: (i) *Così fan tutte;* (ii) *Don Giovanni;* (iii) *Le Nozze di Figaro;* (iv) *Die Zauberflöte.*
(B) * DG Walkman *415 613-4* [id.]. (i) Janowitz, Fassbaender, Prey, Schreier, Panerai, VPO; (ii) Berry, Milnes, Mathis, Tomowa-Sintow, Zylis-Gara, VPO; (iii) Prey, Troyanos, Janowitz, Mathis, Fischer-Dieskau, German Op. O, Berlin; (iv) Wunderlich, Lear, Fischer-Dieskau, Peters, Crass, BPO; all cond. Boehm.

The Walkman cassette format, with its extended length, at bargain price, would be an admirable way of offering a really comprehensive set of highlights from a single opera, or in some cases two – but certainly not four. In each of these selections the overture is included, which leaves room for merely five vocal items from *Così* and *Figaro*, and only four each from *Don Giovanni* and *Die Zauberflöte*. Although the selection includes obvious favourites, the flaws of the complete sets from which the items are taken (recorded between 1965 and 1979) are also apparent, and the music included is too piecemeal to be satisfactory. No synopses or translations are offered; although the sound is satisfactory, this is not really recommendable even as a sampler.

MISCELLANEOUS VOCAL RECITALS

Concert arias: *Ah! lo previdi, K.272; Ch'io mi scordi di te, K.490; Misera, dove son, K.369. Idomeneo: Padre germani addio! Lucio Silla: Frai pensier più funesti di morte. Le Nozze di Figaro: Dove sono. Die Zauberflöte: Ach, ich fühls.*
(*) HMV Dig. **CDC 747122-2 [id.]; EL 270127-1/*4*. Barbara Hendricks, ECO, Tate.

Barbara Hendricks with her distinctive, characterful soprano tackles a challenging range of arias, including the most demanding of the concert arias, *Ch'io mi scordi di te*, interestingly done with violin instead of the usual piano obbligato, a valid alternative. Though with her flickering vibrato the voice is not always ideally suited to individual items, the warmth and intensity are very compelling, helped by strong and stylish accompaniment. Excellent sound particularly on CD, although the XDR tape is also first class.

Concert arias: *Un bacio di mani, K.541; ich möchte wohl der Kaiser sein, K.539.* Arias: *Così fan tutte: Donne mie la fate a tante. Don Giovanni; Metà di voi quà vadano; Deh, vieni alla finestra; Finch'han dal vino. Le Nozze di Figaro: Non più andrai; Bravo signor padrone . . . Se vuol ballare; Hai gia vinta la causa . . . Vedrò, mentre io sospiro; Tutto e isposto . . . Aprite un po' quegl'occhi. Zaïde: Nur mutig mein Herze. Die Zauberflöte: Der Vogelfänger bin ich ja; Ein Mädchen oder Weibchen.*

*** HMV Dig. EL 270137-1/*4* [Ang. DS/*4DS* 38043]. Thomas Allen, Scottish CO, Armstrong.

There have been few recitals of Mozart baritone arias to match Thomas Allen's, stylish vocally with firm, characterful tone and with an engaging range of characterization. To the predictable favourite arias from the operas, Allen effectively adds the little concert aria, *Un bacio di mano*, which provided Mozart with a theme for the *Jupiter symphony*, and the swaggering song about the Kaiser. Excellent accompaniment and recording, with a particularly successful XDR tape giving fine vocal presence.

Arias: *Ch'io mi scordi di te, K.505; Chi sà, chi sà qual sia, K.582; Misera dove son, K.369; Vado, ma dove, K.583. Così fan tutte: Temerari! . . . Come scoglio. Don Giovanni: Batti, batti, o bel Masetto; Vedrai carino. Le Nozze di Figaro: Non so più; Giunse alfin . . . Deh vieni, non tardar; Voi che sapete.*
(M) **(*) Ph. Seq. 412 368-1/*4*. Elly Ameling, ECO, de Waart; Baldwin.

Performances of great charm and vocal freshness. The operatic excerpts are perhaps a shade under-characterized, with no great differences made in the arias for Susanna, Zerlina and Cherubino, but they are delightfully sung. The scene from *Così fan tutte* is, however, much more dramatic. Miss Ameling is very much at home in the concert arias. Her performances have not quite the distinction of Schwarzkopf but the singing is so assured, sensitive and accurate that it cannot fail to give pleasure. *Misera dove son* is especially telling. Excellent recording, though the vivid cassette transfer approaches saturation point on side two and peaks are less refined than on disc.

Arias: La Clemenza di Tito: Non più di fiori vaghe catene. Così fan tutte: Come scoglio. Don Giovanni: In quali eccessi . . . Mi tradì quell'alma ingrata. Crudele? non mi dir bell' idol mio. Die Entführung aus dem Serail: Welcher Kummer . . . Traurigkeit ward mir zum Lose. Idomeneo: Solitudini amiche . . . Zeffiretti lusinghiere. Le Nozze di Figaro: Voi che sapete; Giunse al fin il momento . . . Deh vieni; Porgi amor. Il re pastore: L'amerò, sarò costante.
** HMV Dig. **CDC 747019-2**; ASD 146787-1/*4* [Ang. DS/*4XS* 38023]. Lucia Popp, Mun. R. O, Slatkin.

Lucia Popp was perhaps mistaken at this stage in her career to have attempted to assume such a wide variety of Mozartian roles within a single recital. She is an enchanting Susanna – *Deh vieni* is the highlight of the disc – but while her portrayal of Cherubino (*Voi che sapete*) is fresh and light, her characterization of the Countess (*Porgi amor*) lacks maturity of feeling. The *Don Giovanni* excerpts although impressive both musically and technically are made to sound almost like concert arias, and *Come scoglio* lacks fire. The recording is generally flattering with the CD adding presence and the XDR cassette well managed.

Arias, duets and trios: (i) *La Clemenza di Tito: Ah perdonna al primo affetto;*

S'alto che lagrime. (i; ii) *Così fan tutte: Soave sia il vento.* (ii) *Don Giovanni: Là ci darem la mano; Batti, batti; Vedrai carino;* (iii) *Per queste tue manina. Le Nozze di Figaro:* (ii; iv) *Cosa sento! Tosto andate;* (ii) *Crudell! perchè finora; Giunse alfin . . . Deh vieni. Il re pastore: L'amerò sarò costante. Zaïde: Ruhe sanft.* (ii) *Die Zauberflöte: Bei Männern.*
(M) *** Decca Grandi Voci GRV/*KGRC* 23. Lucia Popp, with (i) Fassbaender; (ii) Krause; (iii) Bacquier; (iv) Krenn.

With many of these items taken from Decca's two-disc 'Mozart Festival' issue (SET 548-9, long deleted) conducted by Istvan Kertesz, the sweetness, brightness and charm of Popp's singing in well-chosen arias from the early years of her career are superbly demonstrated. Though more recently she may have intensified her characterizations, there are few more attractively varied Mozart soprano recitals. Excellent recording for its period; though the cassette (issued after the LP) is transferred at a very high level and there are few hints of peaking, the upper range has an extra degree of treble emphasis.

Arias: *La Clemenza di Tito: S'altro che lagrime. Così fan tutte: Ei parte . . . Sen . . . Per pieta. La finta giardiniera: Crudeli fermate . . . Ah dal pianto. Idomeneo: Se il padre perdei. Lucio Silla: Pupille amate. Il re pastore: L'amerò sarò costante. Zaïde: Ruhe sanft, mein holdes Leben. Die Zauberflöte: Ach ich fühl's es ist verschwunden.*
*** Ph. Dig. **411 148-2**; 6514/*7337* 319 [id.]. Te Kanawa, LSO, Sir Colin Davis.

Kiri Te Kanawa's is one of the loveliest collections of Mozart arias on record, with the voice at its most ravishing and pure. One might object that Dame Kiri concentrates on soulful arias, ignoring more vigorous ones, but with stylish accompaniment and clear, atmospheric recording, beauty dominates all.

Arias: *La Clemenza di Tito: Ecco il punto . . . Non più di fiori; Parto, parto. Don Giovanni: Vedrai carino. Le Nozze di Figaro: Non so più; Voi che sapete.*
(M) *** Ph. 416 250-1/*4* [id.]. Von Stade, Rotterdam PO, de Waart – ROSSINI: *Arias.****

Frederica von Stade was first heard in Britain as a uniquely compelling Cherubino, and the Mozart side of her 1977 recital begins splendidly with the page's two arias, followed by an equally charming account of Zerlina's aria. She shows rather less imagination in the arias from *La Clemenza di Tito*. Excellent recording, although the cassette is inclined to be rather peaky.

Arias: *La Clemenza di Tito: Parto, parto. Lucio Silla: Il tenero momento. Mitridate: Lungi da te, mio bene.*
** HMV Dig. EL 270138-1/*4*. Ann Murray, Scottish CO, Leppard – HANDEL: *Lucrezia* etc.**

Ann Murray's group of three Mozart arias – *Parto, parto* much better known than the other two – comes as coupling to Handel performances including the cantata *Lucrezia*. Happily the rawness which afflicts her in that cantata is hardly at all apparent in Mozart, but the microphone still fails to capture warmth in her distinctive sound. First-rate obbligato playing from the SCO soloists with splendid, full-ranging recording and a good XDR cassette.

'The prima donna in Mozart': arias from: *La Clemenza di Tito; Così fan tutte; Don Giovanni; Die Gärtnerin aus Liebe.*

(M) *** Ph. Seq. 6527/*7311* 219. Yvonne Minton, Mirella Freni, Jessye Norman, Dame Kiri Te Kanawa, Edith Mathis, Ileana Cotrubas, Montserrat Caballé, Lucia Popp, Frederica von Stade, Dame Janet Baker; cond. Sir Colin Davis; Klee.

An attractive compilation at mid-price of arias taken mainly from Davis's complete opera sets for Philips, but also from *Die Gärtnerin aus Liebe* (*La finta giardiniera*) conducted by Bernhard Klee. Whether or not you query the description 'prima donna' for mezzo sopranos as well as for sopranos, the singing here from a distinguished group is both characterful and stylish, and the sound remains remarkably consistent.

COLLECTION

'Favourite Mozart': excerpts from: *Clarinet concerto, K.622; Flute concerto, K.313; Flute and harp concerto, K.299; Horn concerto, K.495; Piano concertos Nos 21, K.467; 23, K.488; Violin concertos, K.218 and K.219. Overtures: Don Giovanni; Le Nozze de Figaro;* excerpts from: *Eine kleine Nachtmusik; Symphony No. 40, K.550; Piano sonata in A, K.331. Rondo in D, K.485.*

(B) ** Ph. On Tour *412 904-4*. Brymer, Claude Monteux, Ellis, Civil, Bishop-Kovacevich, Brendel, Szeryng, Haebler; ASMF, Marriner and cond. Sir Colin Davis, Gibson, I Musici.

It is curious that a tape compilation subtitled *'Eine kleine Nachtmusik'* should include only the final rondo from this work. However, this makes a most agreeable anthology for in-car use, with a distinguished cast and fairly consistent sound. The layout, too, is satisfactory. Mozart's individual movements are so complete in themselves that they can be enjoyable heard out of context in a sequence of this kind.

Mundy, William (*c.* 1529–*c.* 1591)

Vox Patris caelestis.

*** Gimell **CDGIM 339** [id.]; CfP CFP/*TC-CFP* 40339 [Ang. RL/*4RL* 32122]. Tallis Scholars, Phillips – ALLEGRI: *Miserere*; PALESTRINA: *Missa Papae Marcelli.****

Mundy's *Vox Patris caelestis* was written during the short reign of Queen Mary (1553–8). While it is almost exactly contemporary with Palestrina's *Miss Papae*

Marcelli, its florid, passionate polyphony is very different from that of the Italian composer. This is emphasized by Peter Phillips's eloquent performance, which presses the music onwards to reach an exultant climax in the closing stanza with the words *'Veni, veni, veni, caelesti gloria coronaberis'*. The work is structured in nine sections in groups of three, the last of each group being climactic and featuring the whole choir, with solo embroidery. Yet the music flows continuously, like a great river, and the complex vocal writing creates the most spectacular effects, with the trebles soaring up and shining out over the underlying cantilena. The imaginative force of the writing is never in doubt, and the Tallis Scholars give an account which balances linear clarity with considerable power. The recording is first class and the digital remastering for CD further improves the focus, adding firmness of outline and detail. The effect is wonderfully involving: this work is comparable with Tallis's famous motet, *Spem in alium*, in its power; it suggests that William Mundy's music deserves further exploration. The excellent LP and the virtually identical cassette are offered at bargain price and cost only a quarter of the outlay for the CD.

Mussorgsky, Modest (1839–81)

Night on the bare mountain (arr. Rimsky-Korsakov); *Khovanshchina: Prelude.*
(M) *** Decca 411 838-1/*4* [Mobile 517]. LSO, Solti – BORODIN: *Prince Igor excerpts*; GLINKA: *Russlan: overture.****

Solti also recorded these items in a rare session with the Berlin Philharmonic Orchestra (originally Decca SPA 257, now withdrawn), and the Berlin account of the *Khovanshchina Prelude* was marginally more lyrically persuasive; but the LSO account is beautifully played and recorded. *Night on the bare mountain* can stand up to all competition, with its vintage 1967 recording projecting the music with fine amplitude and brilliance. The couplings are superbly done – the Glinka overture is electrifying – and this remains one of Solti's finest analogue discs, with a matching tape hardly less vivid.

Night on the bare mountain (arr. Rimsky-Korsakov); *Pictures at an exhibition* (orch. Ravel).
ⓒ *** Telarc Dig. **CD 80042**; DG 10042 [id.]. Cleveland O, Maazel.
(B) *** DG Walkman *413 153-4*. Boston Pops O, Fiedler; Chicago SO, Giulini – TCHAIKOVSKY: *1812* etc.**(*)
* Ph. Dig. **411 473-2**; 9500 744/*7300 829* [id.]. Concg. O, Sir Colin Davis.

Night on the bare mountain; Pictures at an exhibition; Khovanschina: Prelude.
** Decca **413 139-2** [id.]. SRO, Ansermet.

All current versions of this coupling rest under the shadow of the magnificently recorded Telarc disc, one of the first great successes of the early digital era. The quality of the recording is apparent at the very opening of *Night on the bare mountain* in the richly sonorous presentation of the deep brass and the sparkling yet unexaggerated percussion. With the Cleveland Orchestra on top form, the *Pictures* are strongly characterized; this may not be the subtlest reading available, but each of Mussorgsky's cameos comes vividly to life. The opening trumpets are more robust than in the Philadelphia version (see below), and *The old castle* is particularly evocative. The chattering children in the Tuileries are matched in presence by the delightfully pointed portrayal of the cheeping chicks, and if the ox-wagon (*Bydlo*) develops a climax potent enough to suggest a juggernaut, the similarly sumptuous brass in the *Catacombs* sequence cannot be counted as in any way overdramatized. After a vibrantly rhythmic *Baba-Yaga*, strong in fantastic menace, the closing *Great Gate of Kiev* is overwhelmingly spacious in conception and quite riveting as sheer sound. On compact disc, the background silence enhances the realism, although detail is not so sharply outlined as in the fine Abbado alternative – see below. With the Cleveland set, the ear is conscious of the warm, glowing ambience of Severance Hall, although often individual wind solos have a luminous realism. The record's producer, Robert Woods, and the sound engineer, Jack Renner, continue their love affair with the bass drum, which is occasionally allowed to dominate the orchestral texture. But it is the richness and amplitude of the brass which make the work's final climax unforgettable. The programme notes provided with the CD are fully adequate, but a simple list of titles would have been useful; moreover, the *Pictures* are not separately banded. However, within the technical information supplied is the laudable claim that 'it is Telarc's philosophy to employ additional microphones *only* when the size of the performing forces is greater than can be accommodated appropriately by the basic three'. This recording impressively bears out the success of Telarc's refusal to embrace close multi-microphone techniques, much beloved in Europe at present, and which often produce the most unnatural effects.

It is interesting that Giulini's very successful account of the *Pictures* should use the Chicago orchestra, thus repeating Reiner's success of the early days of stereo. The modern recording, however, is noticeably more refined and detailed, with brilliant percussive effects (a superb bass drum in *The hut on fowl's legs*). With superlative orchestral playing and strong characterization, this is highly recommendable; the tape transfer is generally of excellent quality. It is here paired with an excitingly volatile account of *Night on the bare mountain*, directed by Fiedler. Both sound well on this bargain-price Walkman tape, generously coupled with Tchaikovsky.

Ansermet's compact disc is an astonishing technical achievement. His set of the *Pictures* dates from 1959, but in this digitally remastered format the ear would never guess that the recording was not quite modern – it sounds far more vivid than Sir Colin Davis's 1981 digital version. The performance itself takes a little while to warm up, but Ansermet's fastidious ear for detail is telling in the later portraits, with *The hut on fowl's legs* unforgettably sharp in characterization. *Night on the bare mountain* and the *Khovanschina Prelude* come from the mid-1960s, and the former can stand alongside any of the modern versions. In the *Prelude* the translucent clarity of the sound reveals some less-than-perfect wind intonation, but Rimsky's marvellous scoring (especially in the closing section) still creates a magical effect. It is a pity that this record is over-priced, but aficionados will still want to consider it. There is uncannily little background noise.

Sir Colin Davis's coupling was the first digital recording from Philips (issued early in 1981) and proved technically a disappointment on both LP and the bass-heavy cassette. The CD with its greater body and immediacy is an improvement, but is no match for the Telarc issue, for Davis's performances are strangely short on brilliance. The speeds are often on the slow side, which makes the music sound tame and under-characterized rather than weighty.

Pictures at an exhibition (orch. Ravel).

*** DG Dig. **410 033-2**; 2532/*3302* 057 [id.]. LSO, Abbado – RAVEL: *La valse*.**(*)

*** HMV **CDC 747099-2** [id.]; ASD/*TC-ASD* 3645 [Ang. S/*4XS* 37539]. Phd. O, Muti – STRAVINSKY: *Firebird suite*.***

*** Decca Dig. **400 051-2**; SXDL/*KSXDC 7520* [Lon. LDR/5- 10040]. Chicago SO, Solti – RAVEL: *Tombeau de Couperin*.**

(B) **(*) Pickwick Con. CC/*CCTC* 7676. New Philh. O, Maazel – PROKOFIEV: *Symphony No. 1*.**(*)

(B) ** Ph. On Tour *416 221-4* [id.]. Concg. O, Haitink – TCHAIKOVSKY: *Capriccio Italien*; RIMSKY-KORSAKOV: *Scheherazade*.***

*(*) CBS **MK 76880 [MK 35165]**. NYPO, Mehta – RAVEL: *La valse*.*(*)

Abbado takes a straighter, more direct view of Mussorgsky's fanciful series of pictures than usual, less consciously expressive, relying above all on instrumental virtuosity and the dazzling tonal contrasts of Ravel's orchestration. He is helped by the translucent and naturally balanced digital recording; indeed, the sound is first class, making great impact at climaxes yet also extremely refined, as in the delicate portrayal of the unhatched chicks. Abbado's speeds tend to be extreme, with both this and *Tuileries* taken very fast and light, while *Bydlo* (the Polish ox-cart) and *The Great Gate of Kiev* are slow and weighty. Both readily demonstrate the recording's wide dynamic range. The fullness and clarity are especially impressive in the compact disc version which, although not as sumptuous as the famous Telarc disc, is among the finest of DG's issues in the new format. The digital effect is brilliant and sharply defined, but not as aggressive in the way that the Decca sound is for Solti's Chicago version. There is also an excellent DG cassette.

Muti's reading is second to none. Any comparison is only with the finest previous versions (Toscanini, Koussevitzky, Karajan); given the excellence of its recorded sound, it more than holds its own. Moreover, it was one of the first records to do justice to the Philadelphia sound (although the balance is forward and perhaps not all listeners will respond to the brass timbres at the opening). But it is a far richer and more full-blooded quality than we have been used to in the 1960s and '70s from this source. The lower strings in *Samuel Goldenberg and Schmuyle* have extraordinary body and presence, and *Baba-Yaga* has an unsurpassed virtuosity and attack, as well as being of a high standard as a recording. Putting the LP and CD versions side by side, there is no doubt that the new format offers the greater range and firmness of texture. The coupling is no less thrilling. On the cassette, the focus is marginally less clean than on the disc, but remains impressive. This can be recommended even to those readers who have not always responded to later records from this conductor.

Solti's performance is fiercely brilliant rather than atmospheric or evocative. He treats Ravel's orchestration as a virtuoso challenge, and with larger-than-life digital recording it undoubtedly has demonstration qualities. The cassette is one of Decca's very finest, matching the LP closely, but softening the edge of the sound-picture very slightly, without losing detail. It is no less demonstration-worthy than the disc; many might feel that its focus is more natural. Whether heard on disc or tape, however, this is a listening experience that tingles with energy and electricity. The Ravel fill-up makes an original coupling, although here the brilliantly forward sound-balance is less appropriate. On CD, the orchestral clarity has an almost X-ray precision, and the transparency of texture, given the forward balance, provides quite startling clarity.

Though the characterization is less subtle than Abbado's or Muti's, Maazel's is an immensely vivid reading, brilliantly recorded. It dates from 1972 and was originally made by Decca in their hi-fi-conscious Phase Four system. But the orchestral layout does not lack depth, and the sound has fine amplitude to balance the brightness on top. It has responded well to remastering, and there is an excellent chrome cassette. At bargain price, this is worth considering, although Giulini's Walkman version is even better value if the couplings are suitable – see above.

Haitink's account is part of a generous but not distinctive 'On Tour' tape anthology. It is somewhat lacking in electricity, but the playing of the Concertgebouw Orchestra is evocative and cultured. *Cum mortuis in lingua* is wonderfully serene. There is plenty of atmosphere, but the bite of the performance is somewhat blunted by the resonant acoustics of the Concertgebouw, although the tape transfer is otherwise well managed.

Mehta's CBS version is hardly in the running. It is a 1980 analogue recording; the balance is surprisingly recessed for CBS and lacks vividness of detail. The orchestral playing is excellent; certain portrayals are very effective, with the 'Unhatched chicks' and *Goldenberg and Schmuyle* notable among them. But this cannot be recommended above the rival performances; in the coupled *La valse*, Mehta is far less subtle than Abbado.

Pictures at an exhibition: (i) orch. Ashkenazy; (ii) original piano version.
(*) Decca Dig. **414 386-2 [id.]. (i) Philh. O, Ashkenazy; (ii) Ashkenazy (piano).

A side-by-side comparison between Mussorgsky's original piano score and the orchestral version is always instructive; but here the orchestration is Ashkenazy's own, which he made after finding dissatisfaction with Ravel's transcription, 'guided by the deeper undercurrents of this predominantly dark-coloured piece'. His arrangement concentrates on a broader orchestral tapestry – helped by the richness of the Kingsway Hall acoustic – and he does not attempt to match Ravel in subtlety of detail or precision of effect. The character of the pictures is not always very individual, although Ashkenazy finds plenty of Russian feeling in the music itself. The recording is brightly opulent rather than glittering. Ashkenazy's digital solo account of the *Pictures* does not differ in its broad essentials from his earlier analogue recording. It is distinguished by spontaneity and poetic feeling but lacks something of the extrovert flair with which pianists like Richter or Berman can make one forget all about the orchestra. The piano focus is clear with fine presence, if not quite natural in balance.

Pictures at an exhibition (original piano version). *Au village; En Crimée; Impromptu passionné; Méditation; Scherzo; Un larmé.*
* Denon Dig. **C37 7177** [id.]. Jacques Rouvier.

A disappointing alternative of Mussorgsky's original version. The piano is very closely balanced and its percussive character emphasized. The individual pictures are made to sound like boldly-lined cartoons. The six miniatures offered as a fill-up are more relaxed in feeling, but again the sound is unflattering.

OPERA

Boris Godunov (original version; complete).
(*) Ph. **412 281-2 (3); 412 281-1/*4* (4/*3*). Vedernikov, Arkhipova, Koroleva, Shkolnikova, Sokolov, USSR TV and R. Ch. and SO, Fedoseyev.

Fedoseyev conducts a powerful performance of Mussorgsky's masterpiece in its original scoring, using the composer's own 1872 revision, as near an 'authentic' solution as one can get with a problematic score that never reached definitive form. Some may miss the brilliance of the Rimsky-Korsakov revision, which still generally holds sway in the opera house and did so for a generation on record; but the earthy strength of the score comes over superbly, far more bitingly than it did in EMI's disappointing version recorded in Poland, now deleted. Ideally for records, one needs a firmer singer than the mature Vedernikov as Boris, but this is a searingly intense performance which rises commandingly to the big dramatic moments, conveying the Tsar's neurotic tensions chillingly. Arkhipova is also too mature for the role of Marina, but equally her musical imagination is most convincing. The rest of the cast is a mixed bag, with some magnificent Russian basses but a few disappointing contributions, as from the whining tenor, Vladislav Piavko, as the Pretender. Though the recording was made over a period of years, the sound is full and satisfying, if not always ideally balanced.

The Marriage.
*** Chant du Monde LDX 78785. Khrulen, Podbolotiv, Kolmakova, Tibasenko, USSR SO, Rozhdestvensky.

As an experiment in putting music to words, Mussorgsky did this setting, almost word for word, of Gogol's comedy, *The Marriage*, but got no further than the first Act which makes a delightful piece on its own. The distinctive way in which he copied the stresses and inflections of the Russian language in his vocal lines for four soloists led finally to the revelation of *Boris*. Rightly, Rozhdestvensky in his arrangement has not tried to inflate a delicate fragment by imitating Mussorgsky's later, heavier style, but has pointed the original piano sketch with chamber instrumentation. The fun of the comedy is sharpened; it is a pity that this Chant du Monde set includes only a French translation of the Russian text. The performance is colourfully idiomatic from soloists and players alike, the recording clean to match.

Mysliveček, Josef (1737–81)

Violin concertos in C; D; E; F.
** Sup. Dig. 1110 4031/2 [id.]. Ishikawa, Dvořák CO, Pešek.

Violin concertos in C; E.
*(*) Sup. Dig. **C37 7285** [id.]. Ishikawa, Dvořák CO, Pešek.

Josef Mysliveček was Czech born, but spent much of his life in Italy where many of his operas were produced. The four *Violin concertos* offered on this pair of LPs are slight in musical substance but are, for all that, pleasing examples of the genre at a transitional stage from the Baroque to the Classical period. Mozart heard and admired him and praised his sonatas: 'They will no doubt delight everyone: they are easy to memorize and very effective when played with proper precision.' The same applies here, as these concertos are played with great sweetness of tone and flawless technical command by the young Japanese violinist, Shizuka Ishikawa, who has lived in Czechoslovakia since her student years; she is given adequate support by the Dvořák Chamber Orchestra under Libor Pešek. These concertos have some original and interesting touches – though no one in their right mind would play them in preference to Mozart; these have the manner of Mozart but no depth whatever. The recording, made in the highly resonant House of Artists, Prague, is good rather than outstanding. Supraphon miss a trick in being bound by the LP layout; instead of accommodating three of the concertos on the compact disc, they give us only two, which together last a little over 37′. Needless to say, the improvement in definition and transparency of detail is very marked – but only the most dedicated enthusiast will be willing to invest so considerable an outlay for such lightweight music.

Neruda, Jan (1708–*c.* 1780)

Trumpet concerto in E flat.
** Erato Dig. **ECD 88007**; NUM/*MCE* 75026 [id.]. André, Paris Ens., Wallez – HUMMEL; TELEMANN: *Concertos.***

The *Trumpet concerto* by the Czech composer, Jan Neruda, is flexible of line and exploits the possibilities of its solo instrument in a conventional way, without producing music that is in any way memorable. Maurice André gives an expert performance and is well enough accompanied. The digital recording is good without being especially vivid, though it is fully acceptable in all three formats.

Nielsen, Carl (1865–1931)

(i) *Clarinet concerto, Op. 57;* (ii; iii) *Symphony No. 2* (*The Four Temperaments*), *Op. 16;* (ii; iv) *Symphony No. 4* (*Inextinguishable*), *Op. 29;* (ii; v) *Symphony No. 5, Op. 50.*
(M) (***) HMV mono ED 290444-3/*5* (2). (i) Cahuzac, Copenhagen Op. O, Fransden; (ii) Danish State R. O, (iii) Jensen; (iv) Gröndahl; (v) Tuxen.

Danish recordings of the post-war period were uncommonly fresh; these, which come from 1947–51, still make an astonishingly vivid impression. Nielsen himself made no records of his own music, and these are the next best thing, since Thomas Jensen, Launy Gröndahl and Erik Tuxen all played under him. Jensen's feeling for Nielsen's tempi was said to be particularly strong and he apparently remembered them with unerring accuracy. Launy Gröndahl's account of the *Fourth Symphony* has a fire and spirit that carries all before it and captures the very essence of this work. It does not have the finesse, polish or rich sonority of the 1982 Karajan, but it is an indispensable complement to it. Erik Tuxen's pioneering account of the *Fifth*, made a few months before he presented it at the 1950 Edinburgh Festival, was soon superseded by Thomas Jensen's Decca version which had, of course, the advantage of greater clarity and presence and, in some ways, was more tautly held together. Yet Tuxen secures the more powerfully distilled atmosphere, particularly in the opening pages, and the sound has slightly greater warmth. Cahuzac's pioneering version of the *Clarinet concerto* is hardly less fine; the transfer has considerable transparency and detail, and no obtrusive surfaces. Listening to these performances, one realizes why we were all so enthusiastic about Nielsen in the 1950s, for there is such blazing commitment about them. There are good equivalent cassettes.

Flute concerto.
*** Ph. Dig. **412 728-2**; 412 728-1/*4* [id.]. Nicolet, Leipzig GO, Masur – BUSONI: *Divertimento*; REINECK: *Concerto.****

Nielsen's *Flute concerto* is a late work, written about the same time as Sibelius's *Tapiola* – and moreover in the same country, Italy. It is a wonderfully subtle and affecting piece whose light spirits hide a vein of keen poetic feeling. Nicolet's performance is first rate in every way, fully catching the work's rhapsodic, indeed chimerical mood changes; he is given splendid support by the fine Leipzig orchestra under Masur. Moreover, the Philips recording is ideally balanced so that the various dialogues between the soloist and the orchestral woodwind are interchanged within a most believable perspective. The sound itself is beautiful, within an attractive ambience which does not blur detail. This can be strongly recommended in all three media, for while the compact disc is subtly clearer, the chrome cassette, too, is extremely successful.

Symphony No. 2 (*The Four Temperaments*)*; Aladdin suite, Op. 34.*
*** **BIS CD 247**; LP/*MC* 247. Gothenburg SO, Myung-Whun Chung.

Myung-Whun Chung has a real feeling for this repertoire and his account of the *Second Symphony* is very fine. The Gothenburg Symphony Orchestra proves an enthusiastic and responsive body of players; Chung, who studied with Sixten Ehrling at the Juilliard, does not put a foot wrong. The recording in all three formats is impressive too (the chrome cassette is excellent) and can be recommended with enthusiasm. There is no current alternative version of the *Aladdin* music. The Gothenburg orchestra plan to record all of Nielsen's output – as well as the complete Sibelius and a complete Stenhammar – and if the rest of the symphonies are as good, this will be a very distinguished set.

Symphony No. 4 (Inextinguishable), Op. 29.
*** DG Dig. **413 313-2**; 2532/*3302* 029 [id.]. BPO, Karajan.

Symphony No. 4 (Inextinguishable); Helios overture, Op. 17.
* CBS Dig. **MK 42093;** IM/*IMT* 42093. Swedish RSO, Esa-Pekka Salonen.

Symphony No. 4 (Inextinguishable); Pan and Syrinx, Op. 49.
**(*) HMV Dig. EL 270260-1/*4*. CBSO, Rattle.

By far the best performance of Nielsen's *Fourth* ever recorded comes from Karajan. The orchestral playing is altogether incomparable and there is both vision and majesty in the reading. The strings play with passionate intensity at the opening of the third movement, and there is a thrilling sense of commitment throughout. The wind playing sounds a little over-civilized by comparison with the pioneering record from Launy Gröndahl and the Danish State Radio Orchestra, made in the early 1950s – but what exquisitely blended, subtle playing this is. It is excellently recorded, too; there is a distinct gain in presence and realism in the CD format. The sound on cassette is bright and vivid, but rather light in the bass.

Simon Rattle has the measure of this work and it is an undeniably powerful performance. The very opening has a splendid breadth and grandeur; his tempo is broader and less urgent than Gröndahl's newly reissued 1951 version, and much less so than Thomas Jensen's inspiring 1952 broadcast on Danacord. The gain in grandeur is at the loss of a certain incandescence, though the Birmingham orchestra play with splendid intensity and conviction. The heavens are not stormed, as they are in Gröndahl's performance. The HMV recording is more present and detailed; moreover, it has the advantage of a makeweight in the form of *Pan and Syrinx*. This has, of course, been recorded by Blomstedt and, before him, by Ormandy, but Simon Rattle's version is vastly superior to either; it has great delicacy of texture and feeling for atmosphere. *Pan and Syrinx* is among the most refined and inspired of Nielsen's works, and it is unlikely that this account will be bettered in the immediate future. On cassette, *piano* and *pianissimo* detail is well defined, but at *fortissimo* level the ear notices that the upper range is slightly restricted.

There is no doubt that Esa-Pekka Salonen gets an excellent sonority from the Swedish Radio Symphony Orchestra and that the CBS and Swedish Radio engineers, working in the Berwald Hall in Stockholm, produce a very natural and well-balanced sound, with both clarity and space. Nor is there any question that this young Finnish conductor is a real musical personality, with an ear for orchestral balance, who in the fullness of time will become a conductor of stature. However, his account of this marvellous symphony simply will not do. The opening has an imposing grandeur and a genuine sweep that promise well – but then disaster suddenly strikes, with a disruptive application of the brakes immediately after the second subject group. There is a further destructive pull-back at the end of this A major section, and the result is insupportably inflated and egocentric. The second movement is well done, though woodwind intonation is far from impeccable. The slow movement, too, nearly collapses at one point. This is a pity since there is so much else that is right about this performance, in particular the authentic atmosphere that is evoked. The playing is totally committed, and the climax, with the famous dialogue between the two timpani, is vividly exciting. However, the eccentricities prove as irksome on repetition as they do on first hearing.

Symphonies Nos 4 (Inextinguishable), Op. 29; 5, Op. 50; Helios overture, Op. 17; Saga-drøm, Op. 39.
(B) **(*) HMV *TCC2-POR 154593-9*. Danish RSO, Blomstedt.

Tape collectors should find this double-length 'Portrait of the Artist' cassette worth acquiring. Each symphony is complete on one side, with one of the two shorter works as a filler. The sound is full and brilliant. Blomstedt's version of the *Fourth* is excellent with some fine wind playing from the Danish orchestra. In the *Fifth* Ole Schmidt is to be preferred (see below), but with two major works offered for the price of one, this is good value.

Symphony No. 5, Op. 50.
**(*) HMV Dig. EL 270352-1/*4*. Danish RSO, Kubelik.
* Ph. 412 069-1/*4* [id.]. Concg. O, Kondrashin – SIBELIUS: *Symphony No. 5*.*

Kubelik's well-recorded account of the *Fifth Symphony* emanates from a public performance from the Danish Radio Concert Hall in 1983. He gives us the most leisurely view of it yet committed to disc. However, his is a performance of some vision, and obviously the product of deep feeling for this symphony. He secures the most rapt *pianissimo* tone from the strings at the very opening and, indeed, gets extremely fine playing from them throughout. The impassioned threnody towards the end of the work has enormous eloquence – though, further on, some will find the very closing bars more than a little inflated. In the first movement, the gain in breadth is at the cost of a certain impetus, and many listeners will want things moved on. But the leisurely tempo lends a sense of space and atmosphere to the movement which is rather special. The march section has a menacing power that is impressive, and there is real mystery in the sparsely scored middle episode (fig. 21–26) that seems almost to evoke a chilling lunar landscape. Those who like their Nielsen to be very taut and concentrated may not derive great satisfaction from this interpretation, but it is none the less a humane, deeply musical reading. Ole Schmidt remains the safer recommendation, and has the additional advantage of being at mid-price. Kubelik's is a more personal view of the symphony than its immediate rivals, but it is obviously a deeply considered one; though it would probably not be the sole version of the work in one's collection, it is an enriching performance. There is a good cassette, though the resonance brings some blurring in climaxes.

On the face of it, the Philips record offers good value: both symphonies normally take a record each. The performances derive from the concert hall rather than the recording studio and there are moments when audience noise is obtrusive – but this is less of a stumbling block than Kondrashin's tempi, which are consistently hurried. In the first movement of the Nielsen *Symphony*, the *Tempo giusto* is much faster than the metronome marking (crotchet = 100), thus diminishing its sense of space and mystery. Not really recommendable. The tape equivalent is well transferred.

Still recommended: Ole Schmidt's account is first class and the LSO respond positively to his direction. The cassette is double-length, coupled with the *Fourth Symphony* (Unicorn KPM 7006/*UKC 7460*).

Complete choral music: *6 Canons; 4 Songs for male choir (1887); 3 Motets, Op. 55; 2 School songs (1929); Miscellaneous songs (1899–1926).*
*** Danachord DMA 061/2 [id.]. Canzone Ch., Rasmussen.

The set does not include such works as *Hymnus Amoris* or *Sleep* or the various cantatas Nielsen composed to commission but the shorter *a cappella* compositions, some of which, at under one minute in duration, are too numerous to list here. Most of them are simple and many are slight, but all have a good deal of charm. The best-known works in this set are the *Three Motets*, Op. 55. They are given most persuasively and with great eloquence by this accomplished ensemble and are recorded in an agreeably spacious acoustic ambience. The singing of the Canzone Choir conducted by Frans Rasmussen is very fine indeed. The set is handsomely presented, with complete texts and translations and an authoritative essay by the leading Nielsen scholar of the day, Torben Schousboe.

Novák, Vítézslav (1870–1949)

Pan (tone-poem), Op. 43.
** Sup. 1111 3427. František Rauch (piano).

Pan is a five-movement piece with descriptive sub-titles, distinctly pantheistic in spirit and Lisztian in the rhapsodic character of much of its piano writing. Novák subsequently scored it but, insofar as it is heard at all outside Czechoslovakia, it has been in its original form. While it does not have the depth of his masterpiece, *The Storm*, or the charm of the *Slovak suite*, it makes a powerful impression in František Rauch's hands. The Supraphon recording is serviceable without being in any way out of the ordinary.

Nystroem, Gösta (1890–1966)

Sinfonia concertante for cello and orchestra.
*** Cap. Dig. CAP 1272 [id.]. Lavotha, Stockholm PO, Göran Nilsson – CARLID; *Mass for strings.****

For many years Nystroem lived in Paris and pursued a dual career as painter as well as musician. He belonged to the same artistic colony as Dardel and Grünewald, and the sleeve reproduces one of his (rather attractive) paintings. His Parisian sympathies tell in this *Sinfonia concertante for cello and orchestra*, arguably his finest composition. It is a wartime work (1940–44) and without question one of much beauty. There is a melancholy and eloquence strongly reminiscent of Honegger or Sauguet, though one is momentarily also reminded even of Bloch. The finale opens with a haunting siciliano theme and the movement is well sustained. It is infinitely more rewarding than the grossly overrated *Sinfonia del mare*. There can be no grumbles about the excellent soloist, Elemér Lavotha, or the Stockholm Philharmonic who play with conviction under Göran Nilsson. A lovely record, beautifully engineered and balanced.

Ockeghem, Johannes (*c.* 1410–97)

Requiem (*Missa pro defunctis*).
*** DG Arc. **415 293-2** [id.]. Pro Cantione Antiqua, Hamburger Bläserkreis für alte Musik, Turner – JOSQUIN DES PRÉS: *Missa – L'homme armé.**** ©

Requiem (*Missa pro defunctis*); *Missa Mi-Mi* (*Missa quarti toni*).
**(*) HMV Dig. EL 270098-1/*4*. Hilliard Ens., Hillier.

Ockeghem's *Missa pro defunctis* is the first surviving polyphonic *Requiem*. The *Missa Mi-Mi* is his most widely performed mass and survives in three different sources in the Vatican Library; in one it is called *Missa Quarti Toni* and in another *My-My*, which is assumed to derive from the short motif that appears in the bass section at the beginning of each main section and consists of a descending fifth. These HMV performances have the expertise, secure intonation, blend and ensemble that one expects from these singers, and the music itself has an austere and affecting simplicity. Although it has had a qualified welcome from specialists in this field, and despite a certain blandness, it would be curmudgeonly not to welcome such generally persuasive accounts of both works. They make an eminently serviceable introduction to the sacred music of this composer and are very well recorded, too. As usual with HMV's early music series, the XDR-tape transfer is sophisticated and the high level gives the voices a natural presence and realism. This is quite the equal of the disc.

The DG Archiv version of the *Missa pro defunctis* was originally recorded in Hamburg in 1973. The Pro Cantione Antiqua was unmatched at this period (with such artists as James Bowman and Paul Esswood as their countertenors, this is hardly surprising), and Bruno Turner's direction has both scholarly rectitude and musical eloquence to commend it. They do not cultivate the white, somewhat virginal and vibrato-less tone favoured by Early Music groups in the 1980s. For most of the *Requiem* (though not in the Josquin with which it is coupled), the lines are at times doubled by the excellent Hamburger Bläserkreis für alte Musik. The *Requiem* is currently available on LP only as part of a five-record set, *The Flowering of Renaissance Polyphony*. It is an eminently welcome addition to the compact disc catalogue and is more involving than the alternative Hilliard version on HMV.

Offenbach, Jacques (1819–80)

Gaîté parisienne (ballet, arr. Rosenthal): complete.
*** Ph. Dig. **411 039-2**; 6514/*7337* 367 [id.]. Pittsburgh SO, Previn.
(*) Decca Dig. **411 708-2; 411 708-1/*4*. Montreal SO, Dutoit – GOUNOD: *Faust: ballet music*.**(*)

Previn's digital recording sweeps the board. He realizes that tempi can remain relaxed, and the music's natural high spirits will still bubble to the surface. The orchestral playing is both spirited and elegant, with Previn obviously relishing the score's delightful detail. The rhythmic spring is captivating, as is the gentle lilt in the *Barcarolle*, Ländler and Waltz movements (from *La Belle Hélène*, for instance). The fizzing effervescence does not prevent a minor sense of gravitas when necessary, and this is mirrored by the Philips sound-balance which has substance as well as atmosphere and brilliance. Perhaps the tuba thumping away in the bass is a shade too present, but it increases one's desire to smile through this engagingly happy music. The CD sounds splendid. The chrome cassette tends to be bass-orientated, but with adjustment of the control can be made to produce good results.

Dutoit has the advantage of sound that is brighter and has rather more projection than Previn's Philips disc, though the acoustic is resonant and detail is no clearer. But the recording is undoubtedly out of Decca's top drawer. He opens the music racily and there are many admirable touches, yet as the ballet proceeds there is a hint of blandness in the lyrical moments, and the *Barcarolle* is somewhat disappointing. Some might like the extra feeling of breadth Dutoit generates, but Previn catches the spirit of the score more naturally. The Decca record has the advantage of including also the *Faust* ballet music, warmly and elegantly played, but here also Dutoit's touch is a shade heavy. The feeling in both works is redolent of the concert hall rather than the ballet theatre, and this effect is enhanced on the excellent CD. The chrome cassette is also very successful and preferable to Previn's Philips tape.

Gaîté parisienne (ballet, arr. Rosenthal): suite.
(M) **(*) DG Sig. 413 983-1/*4*. BPO, Karajan – BIZET: *Carmen suite***(*); RAVEL: *Boléro*.***
(B) ** CBS DC 40149 (2). O Nat. de France, Maazel – DUKAS: *L'apprenti sorcier*; SAINT-SAËNS: *Danse macabre*; RAVEL: *Alborada* etc.**

Karajan's selection is generous (only Nos 3–5, 7 and 19–21 are omitted). The Berlin Philharmonic playing has an attractively racy brilliance; its polish and sparkle produce a style which combines elegance in the *Barcarolle* with boisterous high spirits in the *Can-can*. The 1972 recording is vivid and undated, with disc and chrome tape virtually indistinguishable.

With the French orchestra making a suitably tangy sound, Maazel's, too, is a highly vivacious account which includes most of the important numbers. The brightly lit recording suits the style of the music making. The equivalent extended-length tape omits two items from the generous LP anthology and is not recommended. The two discs are offered for the price of one.

Overtures: *Barbe-Bleue; La Belle Hélène; Les deux Aveugles; La Fille du tambour-major; La Grande-Duchesse de Gérolstein; Orphée aux enfers* (*Orpheus in the Underworld*)*; La Périchole; La Vie parisienne.*
*** Ph. Dig. **411 476-2**; 6514/*7337* 098 [id.]. Philh. O, Marriner.

Where Karajan in his Offenbach collection – see below – tended to use inflated versions of these operetta overtures by hands other than the composer's, Marriner prefers something nearer to the original scale, even though *Orpheus*, *Belle Hélène* and *La Périchole* are not originals. This music suits the sprightly, rhythmic style of Marriner splendidly, and the Philharmonia responds with polished playing, very well recorded. The CD sparkles attractively. The chrome cassette is less lively than the LP.

Overtures: *La Belle Hélène; Bluebeard; La Grande-Duchesse de Gérolstein; Orpheus in the Underworld; Vert-vert. Barcarolle* from *Contes d'Hoffmann.*
(*) DG Dig. **400 044-2; 2532/*3302* 006 [id.]. BPO, Karajan.

Other hands besides Offenbach's helped to shape his overtures. Most are on a pot-pourri basis, but the tunes and scoring are so engagingly witty as to confound criticism. *La Belle Hélène* is well constructed by Haensch, and the delightful waltz tune is given a reprise before the end. Karajan's performances racily evoke the theatre pit, and the brilliance is extrovert almost to the point of fierceness. But the Berlin playing is very polished and, with so much to entice the ear, this cannot fail to be entertaining. The demonstration item is *Vert-vert*, which is irresistibly tuneful and vivacious. The digital recording is extremely vivid and there is no appreciable difference between disc and cassette: both have plenty of range and immediacy. The compact disc emphasizes the dryness of the orchestral sound; the effect is rather clinical, with the strings lacking bloom. This is disappointing.

La Belle Hélène (complete).
*** HMV **CDS 747157-8** [id.]; EX 270171-3/*5* (2) [Ang. DS/*4DS* 3981]. Norman, Alliot-Lucaz, Aler, Burles, Bacquier, Lafont, Capitole Toulouse Ch. and O, Plasson.

The casting of Jessye Norman in the name part of *La Belle Hélène* may seem too heavyweight, but the way that the great soprano can lighten her magisterial voice with all the flexibility and sparkle the music calls for is a constant delight, and her magnetism is irresistible. John Aler, another American opera-singer who readily translates to the style of French operetta, makes a heady-toned Paris, coping superbly with the high tessitura in the famous Judgement couplets and elsewhere. The rest of the cast is strong too, not forgetting Colette Alliot-Lugaz as Oreste, who had such dazzling success in the central role of Chabrier's *L'étoile* in John Eliot Gardiner's brilliant recording. Michel Plasson here produces similarly fizzing results, with excellent ensemble from the choir and orchestra of the Capitole. Excellent recording, less reverberant than in some other discs from this source, and especially lively and present in its CD format. Indeed, with the compact discs it is very important not to set the volume level too high or the spoken dialogue will seem unrealistically close. The XDR tapes, however, are disappointingly lacking in sparkle.

Orpheus in the Underworld: abridged version (in English).
(M) **(*) HMV ED 290354-1/*4*. Bronhill, Shilling, Miller, Weaving, Steele, Nisbett, Thurlow, Crofoot, Sadler's Wells Op. Ch. and O, Faris.

With a single reservation only, this is an enchanting disc. Without visual help the recording manages to convey the high spirits and genuine gaiety of the piece, plus – and this is an achievement for a non-Parisian company – the sense of French poise and precision. June Bronhill in the *Concerto duet* is infectiously provocative about her poor suitor's music. One's only complaint is that Alan Crofoot's King of the Boeotians is needlessly cruel vocally. The sound is full and brilliant, with plenty of atmosphere, and there is no doubt that this reissue of a vintage recording dating from 1960 is very successful. The cassette transfer, made at a high level, is very well managed, lively, yet avoiding edginess on the voices.

Orff, Carl (1895–1982)

Carmina Burana (cantata).
*** HMV **CDC 747411-2** [id.]; ASD/*TC-ASD* 3117 [Ang. S/*4XS* 37117]. Armstrong, English, Allen, St Clement Danes Grammar School Boys' Ch., LSO Ch., LSO, Previn.
(*) RCA Dig. **RCD 14550; RL 13925 [**RCD1 4550**; ATC1/*ATK1* 3925]. Hendricks, Adler, Hagegard, Boys of St Paul's Cathedral, LSO Ch., LSO, Mata.
(*) HMV **CDC 747100-2 [id.]; ASD/*TC-ASD* 3900 [Ang. SZ/*4ZS* 37666]. Augér, Summers, Van Kesteren, Southend Boys' Ch., Philh. Ch. and O, Muti.

** Decca Dig. **411 702-2**; 411 702-1/*4* [id.]. Greenberg, Bowman, Roberts, Berlin R. Ch. and SO, Chailly.
** DG Dig. **415 136-2**; 415 136-1/*4* [id.]. Anderson, Creech, Weikl, Glen Ellyn Children's Ch., Chicago Ch. and SO, Levine.
** Telarc Dig. **CD 80056** [id.]. Blegen, William Brown, Hagegard, Atlanta Ch. and SO, Shaw.

Previn's 1975 analogue version, richly recorded, still leads the available recorded performances of Orff's most popular work. It is strong on humour and rhythmic point. The chorus sings vigorously, the men often using an aptly rough tone, and if there is at times a lack of absolute precision, the resilience of Previn's rhythms, finely sprung, brings out a strain not just of geniality but of real wit. This is a performance which swaggers along and makes you smile. The recording captures the antiphonal effects impressively, better even in the orchestra than in the chorus. Among the soloists, Thomas Allen's contribution is one of the glories of the music making, and in their lesser roles the soprano and tenor are equally stylish.

Mata's RCA version is otherwise the most convincing as an overall performance and it also offers first-class sound. It is a volatile reading, not as metrical in its rhythms as most; this means that at times the LSO Chorus is not as clean in ensemble as it is for Previn. The choristers of St Paul's Cathedral sing with perfect purity but are perhaps not boyish enough; though the soloists are first rate (with John Adler coping splendidly, in high refined tones, with the Roast Swan episode), the LP recording – digital, but lacking a little in bass – does not put a very persuasive bloom on their voices. This, however, is corrected in the compact disc which has fine warmth of atmosphere and no lack in the lower range. *Pianissimo* choral detail is not sharply defined, but in all other respects the sound is superb, the background silence adding a great deal, especially when the tension is not as consistently high as in some versions.

The digital remastering of Muti's 1980 analogue recording is slightly disappointing. The LP was remarkable for bringing out the fullest weight of bass (timpani and bass drum most spectacular at the opening) but had a balancing brilliance. This seems less obvious on the compact disc, although the orchestra is affected less than the chorus and soloists, who seem to have lost a degree of immediacy. There is a compensating advantage in that every one of the twenty-five sections of the work is cued (against Decca's fifteen access points). Muti's is a reading which underlines the dramatic contrasts, both of dynamic and of tempo, so the nagging ostinatos are as a rule pressed on at breakneck speed; the result, if at times a little breathless, is always exhilarating. The soloists are first rate: Arleen Augér is wonderfully reposeful in *In trutina* and Jonathan Summers in his first major recording characterizes well. The Philharmonia Chorus is not quite at its most polished, but the Southend Boys are outstandingly fine. This is a performance which may lose something in wit and jollity but is as full of excitement as any available. On cassette, the choral sound is satisfyingly full-bodied, but the wide dynamic range has brought serious recession of image when the soloists are singing quietly.

Using the Jesus-Christuskirche (a far more sympathetic Berlin venue for recording than the Philharmonie), Chailly's Decca performance brings outstandingly full and brilliant recording, particularly impressive on CD. The performance is strong and dramatic in a direct, clean-cut way, with fast allegros relatively unpointed and lacking in detail. Chailly compensates in his expressive treatment of the gentle moments, as in the final section, *The Court of Love*, in which Sylvia Greenberg's light, bright soprano has a girlish, innocent quality. James Bowman, for all his imagination, misses some of the comedy of the tenor role when, as a countertenor, he is singing falsetto all the time, instead of simply as a tenor's strainful expedient, which is what Orff intended. Stephen Roberts, another excellent singer, is also miscast, too gritty and too thin of tone for the baritone role. On cassette, although *pianissimo* detail is not particularly sharp, the richness and amplitude of the recording, combined with the wide dynamic range, produce a satisfying overall sound-picture.

Levine's Chicago account is enjoyable enough; on CD, the recording is spectacular, with greatly enhanced detail compared with the LP which is not cut at the highest level. Even so, the Chicago Chorus match neither Previn's group in their lusty projection of joyous vigour, nor Muti's Philharmonia Chorus in weight. The Chicago soloists are less distinctive, too – though Bernd Weikl's Abbot's drinking song is a highlight. Philip Creech's portrayal of the Roasted Swan is less comfortable, but no doubt the roughness is part of the characterization. Levine makes a good deal of the atmosphere of the score and obviously responds to the earthy sentiment of the love poems; he is certainly expansive in the work's latter sections. There is a very good tape.

Telarc characteristically present exceptionally full and brilliant sound, though hardly more so than the analogue sound given to Previn on HMV. Like Muti, Robert Shaw (for some years Toscanini's choirmaster) prefers speeds on the fast side, though his manner is more metrical. In *The Court of Love* one wants more persuasive treatment, though the choral singing – recorded rather close in analytical sound – is superb. The soloists are good, but the Atlanta boys cannot quite match their rivals on most European versions. The compact disc issue is on two sides (as against three for the original LP set), but the recorded sound is unflattering to the soloists – notably the baritone, Hakan Hagegard – although the choral and orchestral sound is certainly spectacular.

Osborne, Nigel (born 1948)

(i) *Concerto for flute and chamber orchestra;* (ii) *Remembering Esenin* (for cello and piano); (iii) *I am Goya;* (iv) *The sickle.*

*** Unicorn DKP/*DKPC* 9031 [id.]. (i) Dobing; (ii) Kitt, Hill; (iii) Varcoe; (iv) Manning; with City of London Sinfonia, Hickox.

This well-chosen group of four works gives an excellent musical portrait of a composer of the middle generation, whose habitual language may be thorny and complex, but whose feeling for energy and colour and at times expressive warmth give even the unprepared listener the necessary landmarks. The two vocal works, setting Russian poems by Esenin and Voznesensky, are the more immediately striking, with Jane Manning superb in *The sickle*, the Esenin setting, and Stephen Varcoe equally intelligent in *I am Goya*. The work of lament for Esenin uses both cello and piano very originally; the *Flute concerto*, with Duke Dobing a brilliant soloist, is the lightest and most approachable of the pieces, with Hickox drawing committed playing from the City of London Sinfonia. Excellent recording.

Paganini, Niccolò (1782–1840)

Andante amoroso; Larghetto con passione; Moto perpetuo in C, Op. 11; Sonata for grand viola; Variations on The carnival of Venice; Variations on a theme from Rossini's Mosè.

*** HMV Dig. EL 270062-1/*4* [Ang. DS/*4DS* 38127]. Accardo, COE, Tamponi.

Balletto campestre (*Variations on a comic theme*), orch. Tamponi*; Polacca with variations in A; Sonata Maria Luisa in E; Sonata Varsavia.*

*** HMV Dig. EL 270063-1/*4* [Ang. DS/*4DS* 38128]. Accardo, COE, Tamponi.

With his usual expertise and flair, Accardo here explores the byways of Paganini's concertante music for violin and orchestra. The assurance of the playing in itself gives pleasure, and much of the virtuosity is stunning. As can be seen from the listings, Paganini's favourite device was a set of variations on a simple, often ingenuous theme, alternating galant lyricism with fiendish bravura. Accardo is equally at home in both; his virtuosity in the *Balletto campestre* and the *Polacca* is breathtaking, although he is no less impressive in the more famous *Carnival of Venice*, the *Moto perpetuo*, or the *Mosè variations* (where for added bite he tunes his G string a minor third higher and uses it throughout!). The orchestral accompaniments are of minimal interest, but are warmly supportive; the flattering ambience of the recording and the good balance ensure that the sounds reaching the listener are pleasingly believable, and this applies equally to the discs and the tapes.

Violin concerto No. 1 in D, Op. 6.

❀ *** HMV **CDC 747101-2** [id.]; ASD 2782 [Ang. S/*4XS* 36836]. Perlman, RPO, Foster – SARASATE: *Carmen fantasy*.*** ❀

Itzhak Perlman demonstrates a fabulously clean and assured technique. His execution of the fiendish upper harmonics in which Paganini delighted is almost uniquely smooth, and with the help of the EMI engineers, who have placed the microphone in exactly the right place, he produces a gleamingly rich tone, free from all scratchiness. The orchestra is splendidly recorded and balanced too, and Lawrence Foster matches the soloist's warmth with an alive and buoyant orchestral accompaniment. Provided one does not feel strongly about Perlman's traditional cuts, there has been no better record of the *D major Concerto*, and when it is played with this kind of panache the effect is irresistible. The Sarasate *Carmen fantasy* offered as a bonus is quite stunning. Though this sounds well enough on LP, the CD enhances the presence of the recording and emphasizes the success of the original sound-balance (analogue – 1972) which is far more believable and natural than many of Perlman's more recent digital recordings, where the soloist is often unattractively spotlit.

Violin concertos Nos 1 in D, Op. 6; 2 in B min., Op. 7.
*** DG **415 378-2** [id.]. Accardo, LPO, Dutoit.

Violin concertos Nos 1 in D, Op. 6; 2 in B min., Op. 7; Le Streghe (Witches' dance); 4 Caprices, Op. 1.
*** DG Walkman *413 848-4* [id.]. Accardo, LPO, Dutoit.

Paganini's concertos can too often seem sensationally boring, or the scratchy upper tessitura can assault rather than titillate the ear. But, as Perlman has shown in the *First Concerto* – see above – when the recording balance is well managed and the playing and musicianship first class, they can be very entertaining. Accardo, like Perlman, has a formidable technique, marvellously true intonation and impeccably good taste and style; it is a blend of all these that makes these performances so satisfying and enjoyable. The recordings are taken from the complete set he made in the mid-to-late 1960s. He is beautifully accompanied by the LPO under Dutoit and the sound is very good. The two concertos are obviously shown in their best light in the CD format, although the transfer seems to have generated some excess of bass resonance; however, DG's alternative Walkman tape costs a fraction of the price of the compact disc and offers more music. The recording's resonance has meant that DG's tape transfer is rather lower than usual, but the image has not lost its immediacy. Apart from the witchery of *Le Streghe*, Accardo includes also four *Caprices*, including the most famous, on which the multitude of variations are based. A real bargain for all tape collectors.

24 Caprices, Op. 1.
*** HMV **CDC 747171-2**; ASD 3384 [Ang. S/*4XS* 36860]. Perlman.
(*) DG Dig. **415 043-2; 2532/*3302* 042 [id.]. Mintz.

These two dozen *Caprices* probably represent the peak of violinistic difficulty, even though more than a century has gone by since their composition, and many new works continue to exploit the extraordinary range of effects possible on one four-stringed instrument. Perlman's playing is flawless, wonderfully assured and polished, yet not lacking imaginative feeling. Moreover, such is the magnetism of his playing that the ear is led on spontaneously from one variation to the next, even though with CD it is possible to programme any given selection from the set. The 1972 recording is extremely natural and the transfer to CD brings a very convincing illusion of realism, without the microphones seeming too near the violin.

Shlomo Mintz is often dazzling, as are most of the violinists who have recorded these astonishing pieces. There are many breathtaking things to admire, and plenty of colour and life in the set as a whole. He is recorded with admirable clarity and definition in good digital sound, though the overall effect is not as warm as Perlman's HMV record which is, if anything, more dazzling. There are times (*No. 17 in E flat* is an example) when one could wish that he had not been in quite so much of a hurry, for the characterization would gain as a result. On the other hand, others such as the *F major, No. 22*, could hardly be improved upon. The CD emphasizes the closeness of the balance at the expense of the surrounding ambience.

Palestrina, Giovanni da (*c.* 1525–94)

Missa Papae Marcelli.
*** Gimell **CDGIM 339** [id.]; CfP CFP/*TC-CFP* 40339 [Ang. RL/*4RL* 32133]. Tallis Scholars, Phillips – ALLEGRI: *Miserere*; MUNDY: *Vox Patris caelestis.****

Missa Papae Marcelli; Tu es Petrus (motet).
*** DG Arc. **415 517-2**; 415 517-1/*4* [id.]. Westminster Abbey Ch., Preston (with ANERIO: *Venite ad me omnes*; NANINO: *Haec dies*; GIOVANNELLI: *Jubilate Deo****) – ALLEGRI: *Miserere.***(*)

Palestrina's *Missa Papae Marcelli* has a famous historical reputation for its influence on decisions made at the Council of Trent. The Catholic hierarchy had become concerned that the elaborate counterpoint of much church music, and the interpolation of non-liturgical texts, was obscuring the ritual purpose of the Mass itself. Palestrina's work, with its syllabic style and clear text, supposedly demonstrated that great music need not cover the religious message, and so influenced the decision not to ban polyphony altogether. If the story is apocryphal, there is no doubt that Palestrina's settings satisfied the authorities, while the quality of his music, and the memorability of the *Missa Papae Marcelli* in particular, are equally certain. With its apparent simplicity of line and serene beauty which disguises an underlying emotional power, it is not a work which lends itself readily to performers with an Anglican background. The account by the Westminster Abbey Choristers, however, transcends any such stylistic limitations. It is a performance of great fervour, married to fine discipline, rich in timbre, eloquent both at climaxes and at moments of serenity. The singing is equally fine in the hardly less distinctive motet, *Tu es Petrus*, also in six voices, written in 1573. Felice Anerio, Giovanni Bernardino Nanino and Ruggiero Giovannelli represent the following generation of composers in straddling the end of the sixteenth and beginning of the seventeenth century. Their contributions to this collection are well worth having, particularly Giovanelli's *Jubilate*

Deo which makes a splendid closing item. The digital recording is first class. All Saint's, Tooting, was used, rather than the Abbey, and the acoustics are both intimate and expansive, while detail is beautifully caught, especially against the background silence of CD, although the chrome cassette, which costs less, also represents the highest state of the art.

The Gimell/CfP alternative is an analogue recording from 1980, but the digital remastering produces extremely fine sound, firm, richly blended and not lacking internal detail. The acoustics of Merton College, Oxford, are admirably suited to this music; while the recording sounds its best on CD, the LP and excellent tape are splendid too and are available at a quarter the price of the compact disc. The singing has eloquence, purity of tone, and a simplicity of line which is consistently well controlled. The contrasts between serenity and power are striking, and this can be considered alongside the Preston version. Both the Allegri and Mundy couplings are outstandingly successful.

Motet and Mass – Tu es Petrus.
(*) Argo Dig. **410 149-2; 410 149-1/*4* [id.]. King's College Ch., Cleobury – VICTORIA: *O quam gloriosum.*

Fine performances, positively shaped, with plenty of tonal weight and a natural flowing eloquence, with the blend secure, the voices given extra presence on CD. The King's style adapts well to this repertoire without achieving an entirely Latin feeling. But Palestrina's six-part *Mass* still projects impressively.

Pallis, Marco (20th century)

Nocturne de l'ephémère (cantata).
** Pearl SHE 583 [id.]. Underwood, Southern O Pro Arte, Dods – BERKELEY, M.: *Oboe concerto.****

Pallis, best known as an exponent of the viol and colleague of Arnold Dolmetsch, has here set a poem in French by his brother (the title translated on the sleeve as *The Mayfly's evensong*) in a mixture of neoclassical styles with naïve unconcern for structure. Its very amiability reflects the composer's own joy, though the performance is rather rough. An odd coupling for the fine Berkeley *Oboe concerto*, similarly well recorded.

Parry, Hubert (1848–1918)

An English suite; Lady Radnor's suite.
*** HMV Dig. EL 270146-1/*4* [Pathé id.]. City of L. Sinfonia, Hickox – ELGAR: *Elegy* etc.***

An English suite; Lady Radnor's suite; Overture to an unwritten tragedy; Symphonic variations.
*** Lyr. SRCS 48 [id.]. LSO, Boult.

Lyrita's 1970 recording of these Parry pieces wears its years well, and Boult's performances are as near definitive as could be. If anything, he is sharper in the *Symphonic variations* than he was in his later EMI recording. It is a superb work, worthy precursor of the *Enigma variations*, while the *Overture*'s only flaw is in having such a mouthful of a title, a brilliant piece. The two suites for strings bring pastiches of the kind that Grieg devised in the *Holberg suite*; they might justly be compared with that work in colour and energy.

On HMV, Parry's two elegant and beautifully crafted suites make an unusual and very apt coupling for the Elgar string music on the reverse. The combination of straightforward, warm expression with hints of melancholy below the surface is very Elgarian. Both suites were written later than the Elgar *Serenade*, with *An English suite* published only after the composer's death. The Bach tributes in *Lady Radnor's suite* are surface-deep; the slow minuet for muted strings is particularly beautiful. Refined playing and first-rate recording. On the XDR cassette, textures are as rich and pleasing as on LP, but inner definition is less sharply defined, and there is an element of blandness.

Violin sonata in D, Op. 103; Fantasia-sonata in B, Op. 75; 12 short pieces.
*** Hyp. A 66157. Erich Gruenberg, Roger Vignoles.

Much of Parry's prolific output still lies buried; this attractive collection gives a fair sample of the distinguished quality. The *Fantasie sonata*, an early work written at high speed just after Parry had left his job in the City at Lloyd's to become a full-time composer, provides a fascinating example of cyclic sonata form, earlier than most, but also echoing Schumann. The three-movement *Sonata in D* is another compact, meaty piece, again written fast, the strongest work on the disc. The *Twelve short pieces*, less demanding technically, are delightful miniatures dedicated to Parry's wife and daughters, some of them later providing material for larger-scale works. Gruenberg and Vignoles prove persuasive advocates, and the recording is first rate.

Penderecki, Krisztof (born 1933)

(i) *De natura sonaris II; Fluorescences;* (ii) *Threnody for the victims of Hiroshima;* (i) *Kosmogonia* (for soloists, chorus and orchestra).
(M) *** Ph. Seq. 412 030-1/*4*. Woytowicz, Pustelak, Ladysz, Warsaw Nat. PO and Ch., (i) Markowski; (ii) Rowicki.

Penderecki's *Threnody for the victims of Hiroshima* is the best known of his shorter works; here it is coupled, in warmly committed performances, with later works that similarly aim at direct communication to a wide audience. That is a rare and admirable ambition these days, except that he does not always avoid an inflated tone of voice, with rhetoric and effect taking the place of genuine passion. Fine recording successfully captures the distinctive textures; and there is an extremely vivid tape.

Pergolesi, Giovanni (1710–36)

Stabat Mater.

*** DG **415 103-2**; 415 103-1/*4* [id.]. Margaret Marshall, Valentini Terrani, LSO, Abbado.

** Hung. **HCD 12201**; SLPX 12201 [id.]. Kalmar, Hamari, Hungarian R. and TV Ch., Liszt CO, Gardelli.

Abbado's account brings greater intensity and ardour to this piece than any rival, and he secures marvellously alive playing from the LSO – this without diminishing religious sentiment. Margaret Marshall is an impressive singer; her contribution combines fervour with an attractive variety of colour, while Lucia Valentini Terrani – who is also on Scimone's Erato version – is an excellent foil. The DG recording has warmth and good presence – especially on CD, which is better defined than the LP – and the perspective is thoroughly acceptable. The chrome tape is of DG's finest quality with a high level bringing almost comparable presence, yet the voices are smoothly focused. This is now a clear first choice, for although Scimone's Erato issue (with Cotrubas) includes also the *Salve Regina in C minor* and brings out the devotional side of the music, the recording is not ideally clear (STU 71119).

Gardelli conducts a sweet, smooth and well-mannered performance of a work that might be counted too sweet already. The soloists Magda Kalmar and Julia Hamari are both aptly pure-toned, but the concentration on smoothness allows few words to emerge. However, the use of a women's chorus does add greater variety of texture to the score, even if the singing here, though well drilled, lacks bite. The 1981 analogue recording has been transferred well, but unless the choral contribution is vital, Abbado's version has greater character and is preferable.

Pierné, Gabriel (1863–1937)

Piano quintet in E min., Op. 41.

** Erato STU 715502 (2). Hubeau, Viotti Qt – FRANCK: *Piano quintet**(*); VIERNE: *Piano quintet.***

It is good that the French are at long last paying some attention to Pierné, some of whose finely-scored orchestral pieces have been recorded in recent years on Pathé-Marconi. The *Piano quintet* is quite a powerful piece, well worth getting to know; though written in the period of the First World War, it was not published until after the composer's death in 1937. Were this to be unharnessed from the Franck, it would be to the advantage of both. This is good enough music to stand in its own right.

Reminder. Two highly rewarding collections of Pierné's orchestral music are available on imported EMI LPs: Dervaux conducts the Loire Philharmonic

Orchestra in the *Images*, Op. 49, and *Paysages franciscains* (2C 069 16302), while Mari and the Paris Opéra Orchestra offer *Cydalise et le chèvre-pied*, the ballet which is the source of the *Entry of the Little Fauns* (2C 069 14140). Attractive music, very well played and recorded.

Pleyel, Ignaz (1757–1831)

Clarinet concerto in C.
*** Claves **CD 50-813** [id.]. Friedli, SW German CO, Angerer – MERCADANTE; MOLTER: *Concertos.****

Pleyel's *Concerto* is written for C clarinet. Thomas Friedli uses a modern instrument and it does not sound greatly different from the familiar B flat clarinet. Pleyel's *Concerto* is obviously post-Mozart and his debt to that master is obvious. The work is engagingly inventive throughout, with the finale especially attractive (it has a striking secondary theme), and it is altogether a well-made piece. Friedli plays it skilfully and sympathetically and gets good if not outstanding support from Angerer. The CD gives good presence to the soloist, but orchestral detail is a little clouded by the resonance. Nevertheless, in the interest of the repertoire one can make allowance for this, for the overall sound is very pleasing.

Sinfonia concertante in E flat for violin, viola and orchestra, Op. 29.
(B) **(*) CBS DC 40167 (2). Stern, Zukerman, ECO, Barenboim – MOZART: *Sinfonia concertante* etc.*(**); STAMITZ: *Sinfonia concertante.***(*)

This work, unearthed in Paris during the 1970s by the oboist James Brown, is in two extended movements – an ambitious *Maestoso* followed by a gently playful rondo. Though it goes on rather too long for its material, it provides splendid opportunities for Stern and Zukerman to display their artistry. The recording, however, is rather dry and (in remastered form) not very flattering to the soloists. Nevertheless, this two-disc set is imaginatively compiled and is offered for the cost of one premium-priced LP. The equivalent extended-length cassette omits the Pleyel work from the collection altogether.

Ponce, Manuel (1882–1948)

Violin concerto.
** HMV Dig. EL 270151-1/*4* [Ang. DS/*4DS* 38258]. Szeryng, RPO, Bátiz – HALFFTER: *Violin concerto.***

Ponce is well known for his guitar music; he was the leading Mexican composer of his day. The *Violin concerto*, like that of Rodolfo Halffter, with which it is coupled, was composed in 1942, six years before his death, and first performed by Szeryng with Carlos Chavez conducting. It has a dazzlingly brilliant solo part and its invention is amiable and pleasing. However, unlike Ponce's *Variations and fugue on La Folia de España*, it is not a work of great substance. The distinguished soloist makes out a strong case for it and the performers are well served by the HMV engineers, on both LP and cassette.

Canción Gallega; Sonatina meridional; Suite in A; Teme variada y final; Trópico; Variations on a theme of Cabézon.
*** BIS LP 255 [id.]. Jukka Savijoki (guitar).

This recital of Ponce forms a useful supplement to John Williams's classic account of the *Variations and fugue on Folia de España* and shorter pieces on CBS (76730/*40*- [M 35820]). Jukka Savijoki offers us Ponce's last work, the *Variaciones sobre un tema de Cabézon*, written in the last year of his life. The *Suite in A*, the pastiche he attributed to Weiss, and the early *Sonatina meridional* are played with elegance and finesse by the young Finnish guitarist who is obviously an artist to be reckoned with. He is eminently well recorded, though in a somewhat resonant acoustic. However, this is a distinguished record of worthwhile music. In time, doubtless this and John Williams's marvellous record will be transferred to compact disc.

Ponchielli, Amilcare (1834–86)

La Gioconda (complete).
*** Decca Dig. **414 349-2** [id.]; D 232 D 3/*K 232 K 33* (3) [Lon. LDR/*5*- 73005]. Caballé, Baltsa, Pavarotti, Milnes, Hodgson, L. Op. Ch., Nat. PO, Bartoletti.

The colourfully atmospheric melodrama of this opera gives the Decca engineers the chance to produce a digital blockbuster, one of the most vivid opera recordings yet made, with CD enhancing the presence of both voices and orchestra to involve the listener strongly. The casting could hardly be bettered, with Caballé just a little overstressed in the title role but producing glorious sounds. Pavarotti, for long immaculate in the aria *Cielo e mar*, here expands into the complete role with equally impressive control and heroic tone. Commanding performances too from Milnes as Barnaba, Ghiaurov as Alvise and Baltsa as Laura, firm and intense all three. Bartoletti proves a vigorous and understanding conductor, presenting the blood and thunder with total commitment but finding the right charm in the most famous passage, the *Dance of the hours*. The chrome cassettes match the LPs closely (there is very little loss of focus, despite the resonance), but the smaller libretto supplied with the tape box is much less attractive to read.

Poulenc, Francis (1889–1963)

(i) *Aubade* (*Concerto choréographique*); (ii) *Concert champêtre for harpsichord and orchestra;* (iii) *Double piano concerto in D min.*
(M) *** HMV Green. ESD/*TC-ESD* 7165. (i) Tacchino; (ii) Van de Wiele; (iii) composer and Fevrier; Paris Conservatoire O, Prêtre.

At medium price this is self-recommending. The composer may only have been an amateur pianist, but his interpretation (with partner) of his own skittish *Double concerto* is infectiously jolly. One could never mistake the tone of voice intended. In the imitation pastoral concerto which forms the principal coupling Prêtre is not ideally flexible, but the finale has the right high spirits. The *Aubade* is an exhilarating work of great charm. It dates from the late 1920s and is a send-up of Mozart, Stravinsky, etc. The performance is admirably pointed and fresh and the recording quality, from the mid-1960s, is excellent. There is a good high-level cassette transfer.

Aubade (*Concerto choréographique*); *Piano concerto in C sharp min.;* (i) *Double piano concerto in D min.*
*** Erato Dig. **ECD 88140**; NUM/*MCE* 75203 [id.]. Duchable, (i) Collard; Rotterdam PO, Conlon.

Like EMI's compilation from the 1960s – see above – Erato offer excellent value in providing three works on one CD, LP and tape. The 1985 recording is of altogether excellent quality, with splendid presence and a wide range, especially at the bottom end of the spectrum. The performances of the two solo works by François-René Duchable and the Rotterdam orchestra have a certain panache and flair that are most winning. The *Double concerto* too captures all the wit and charm of the Poulenc score, with the 'mock Mozart' slow movement particularly elegant. The balance is almost perfectly judged. Perhaps in the solo works Duchable is a shade too prominent, but not sufficiently so to disturb a strong recommendation. There is an excellent chrome cassette, the quality slightly drier in the bass than the disc versions, but vivid, wide-ranging and clear.

(i) *Les Biches* (ballet suite); (ii) *Concerto for organ, strings and timpani;* (iii) *Deux Marches et un intermède; Les Mariés de la Tour Eiffel; La Baigneuse de Trouville; Discours du Général; Sinfonietta; Suite française d'après Claude Gervaise.*
(B) *** HMV *TCC2-POR 54289*. (i) Paris Conservatoire O; (ii) Duruflé, French Nat. R. O; (iii) O de Paris; Prêtre.

A splendid representation for Georges Prêtre in this tape-only issue in the 'Portrait of the Artist' series, one of the most imaginatively programmed of any double-length cassette of its kind. All the music is attractive; the little-known *Sinfonietta* has much in common with Prokofiev's *Classical symphony*, while the scoring of the *Suite française* is attractively quirky. All the performances are good ones, notably the *Organ concerto*. The ambience for *Les Biches* is somewhat over-resonant but, throughout, the tape transfer is of high quality; this compilation is not to be missed, even if it means duplicating the ballet suite with Prêtre's later complete version of *Les Biches* to which we gave a Rosette in our last edition (HMV ASD/*TCC-ASD* 4067 [Ang. DS/*4XS* 37848]).

(i) *Concert champêtre for harpsichord and orchestra;* (ii) *Concerto in G min. for organ, strings and timpani.*

(*) Erato Dig. **ECD 88141; NUM/*MCE* 75210 [id.]. (i) Koopman; (ii) Alain, Rotterdam PO, Conlon.

The *Organ concerto* has never come off better in the recording studio than on this Erato recording, made in Rotterdam's concert hall, the Doelen, with its excellent Flentrop organ. Marie-Claire Alain is fully equal to the many changes of mood (it is structured in seven contrasting sections), and her treatment of the *Allegro giocoso* racily catches the music's rhythmic humour. The balance is very well managed and the CD is in the demonstration bracket in this work. The *Concert champêtre* always offers problems of balance, as it is scored for a full orchestra, nor are they solved on this occasion. The resonance makes the orchestral tapestry sound very imposing indeed, against which the harpsichord seems almost insignificant. Those who like such a strong contrast will not be disappointed, for the performance is most perceptive, with a particularly elegant and sparkling finale. James Conlon provides admirable accompaniments.

The matter of balance in the *Concert champêtre* is handled better on the alternative analogue recordings, notably another Erato issue with Robert Veyron-Lacroix the stylish soloist and Marie-Claire Alain equally successful in the *Organ concerto* (STU 70637). Alternatives, from HMV with Simon Preston assuming the solo role in both works, accompanied by the LSO under Previn (ASD/*TC-ASD* 3489 [Ang. S/*4XS* 37441]) and, at mid-price on Decca Jubilee, where the joint soloist is George Malcolm (410 172-1/*4*) are also recommendable, with the harpsichord image in the latter notably realistic in perspective.

(i) *Concert champêtre for harpsichord and orchestra;* (ii) *Double piano concerto in D min.*

*(*) HMV Dig. EG 270148-1/*4* [Ang. DS/*4DS* 38122]. (i) Brosse; (ii) Tacchino, Ringeissen; Monte Carlo PO, Prêtre.

A disappointing coupling. This new version of the *Concerto for two pianos* by Gabriel Tacchino and Bernard Ringeissen is less satisfying than its predecessor – see above – with the results brash and hard-driven. The *Harpsichord concerto* fares much better, its charm and tenderness effectively conveyed by Jean-Patrice Brosse. The Monte Carlo orchestra is well enough recorded – but this new issue does not displace the earlier record and tape which, apart from being cheaper, have the bonus of the delightful *Aubade*.

Sonata for flute and orchestra (orch. Berkeley).
(M) *** RCA Gold GL/*GK* 85448 [AGL1/*AGK1* 5448]. Galway, RPO, Dutoit – CHAMINADE: *Concertino;* FAURÉ: *Fantaisie;* IBERT: *Concerto.****

Poulenc's *Flute sonata*, composed in the mid-1950s towards the end of his life, deserves to be widely popular, so beguiling is its delightful opening theme. Yet so far it remains relatively neglected in the British catalogue (though not in the American one) and this is the only version currently available. Let us hope that Sir Lennox Berkeley's delightful arrangement and James Galway's persuasive advocacy will bring it to a larger public. The performance is elegant and polished and the orchestration highly successful. The recording is admirably spacious and well detailed and the tape transfer is clear and clean although, with a rise of level on the second side, the upper range is given a cutting edge in the treble.

Sextet for piano, flute, oboe, clarinet, bassoon and horn. Clarinet sonata; Flute sonata; Oboe sonata; Villanelle for piccolo and piano.
** Erato Dig. **ECD 88044** [id.]. Chamber Music Society of Lincoln Center.

The resonant acoustic of St Bartholomew's Episcopal Church of White Plains, New York, is less than ideal for this programme, although the balance is faithful within the limitations of the blurring acoustic. In the *Sextet* the playing is boisterously spirited and the humour of the second-movement *Divertissement* is not lost on the performers. The three solo sonatas are very well done, with Gervase de Peyer especially memorable in the *Romanza* of the *Clarinet sonata*. The flautist, Paula Robinson (her instrument sounding somewhat larger than life), gives an engaging account of the piece for flute and also provides an attractive encore at the end with the *Villanelle* which takes a mere 1′ 40″.

VOCAL MUSIC

(i; ii) *Le Bal masqué* (*cantate profane*)*; Le Bestiare* (*ou Cortège d'Orphée*)*;* (iii) *Gloria;* (iv) *Quatre motets pour le temps de pénitence;* (ii; iv; v) *Stabat mater*.
(B) ** HMV *TCC2-POR 154597-9*. (i) Benoît; Maryse Charpentier (piano); (ii) Paris Conservatoire O; (iii) Carteri, Fr. Nat. R. TV Ch. and O; (iv) René Duclos Ch.; (v) Crespin; all cond. Prêtre.

A thoroughly worthwhile tape-only anthology, let down by inadequate documentation (only music titles and performers' names are indicated) and the use of iron-oxide instead of chrome tape, plus variable transfer levels. The choral sound in the *Stabat mater* on side one is not transparent and the recording has less than ideal definition. The *Motets* which follow are rather more effectively projected and *Le Bestiare*, admirably presented by Jean-Christophe Benoît, has more presence. Side two with an outstanding version of the *Gloria* – recorded in the presence of the composer – is more vivid; and the forward balance of *Le Bal masqué* with its witty accompaniment, offering an obvious musical similarity to Ravel's *L'Enfant et les sortilèges*, comes off best of all in terms of clarity and liveliness.

Gloria.
*(*) Telarc Dig. **CD 80105**; DG 10105 [id.]. McNair, Atlanta Ch. SO, Shaw – STRAVINSKY: *Symphony of psalms.**(*)

Helped by brilliant and well-balanced recording, Robert Shaw conducts a brightly sung and finely disciplined performance, yet which misses both the electricity and the necessary lightness of Poulenc's vision. Sylvia McNair is a disappointingly unsteady soloist.

Still recommended: Until a satisfactory CD version arrives, readers can choose between Bernstein's vibrant account, coupled with an equally impressive performance of Stravinsky's *Symphony of psalms* (CBS 76670 [M/*MT* 34551]) or Prêtre's fine 1960s recording, coupled with the *Organ concerto* (HMV ASD 2835 [Ang. S 35953)].

Stabat Mater; Litanies à la vierge noire; Salve regina.
*** HM Dig. **HMC 905149**; HMC 5149 [id.]. Lagrange, Lyon Nat. Ch. and O, Baudo.

Stabat Mater; Quatre motets pour un temps de pénitence.
** HMV Dig. EL 270259-1/*4* [Ang. DS/*4DS* 38107]. Hendricks, O Nat. de France, Prêtre.

Apart from an LP by Frémaux, Poulenc's *Stabat Mater* has not been recorded for almost two decades; this excellent account on Harmonia Mundi fills the gap with some measure of distinction. The recording is well detailed and made in a good acoustic. Serge Baudo is perhaps a more sympathetic interpreter of this lovely score than was Prêtre in his earlier record, and gets more out of it. He certainly makes the most of expressive and dynamic nuances; he shapes the work with fine feeling and gets good singing from the Lyons Chorus. Michèle Lagrange may not efface memories of Régine Crespin on Prêtre's 1964 version (still available on cassette), but she has a good voice and is an eminently expressive soloist. The coupling differs from its rival and offers the short *Salve Regina* and the *Litanies à la vierge noire*, an earlier and somewhat more severe work, written on the death of the composer, Ferroud. A welcome and worthwhile issue.

Georges Prêtre's second recording of the *Stabat Mater* and the *Quatre motets pour un temps de pénitence* has the benefit of digital sound. From the very beginning of the *Stabat Mater*, however, one is struck by the less than distinguished choral singing. The playing of the Orchestre National de France is committed enough and detail is in good perspective. Readers who have the older version will find Barbara Hendricks a little hard-edged and lacking the warmth of Régine Crespin. There is a fair but not outstanding tape of the newer version.

OPERA

La voix humaine (complete).
** Chan. Dig. **CHAN 8331** [id.]. Farley, Adelaide SO, Serebrier.

This virtuoso monodrama, just one woman and a telephone, is ideally suited to a record if, as here, the full text is provided. Where on stage few singers can project the French words with ideal clarity to make every detail apparent, both the brightness of Carole Farley's soprano and the recording balance present the whole scena in vivid close-up. Ms Farley's French is clear but not quite idiomatic-sounding, and that rather applies to the playing of the Adelaide orchestra, crisply disciplined and sharply concentrated as it is. The result has little of French finesse. The fifteen bands of the CD are very helpful for finding one's way about the piece.

Praetorius, Michael (1571–1621)

Dances from Terpsichore (Suite de ballets; Suite de voltes). (i) Motets: *Eulogodia Sionia: Resonet in laudibus; Musicae Sionae: Allein Gott in der Höh sei Ehr; Aus tiefer Not schrei ich zu dir; Christus der uns selig macht; Gott der Vater wohn uns bei; Polyhymnia Caduceatrix: Erhalt uns, Herr, bei deinem Wort.*
(M) *** HMV EG 290570-1/*4* [Ang. AM/*4AM* 34728]. Early Music Cons. of L., Munrow, (i) with Boys of the Cathedral and Abbey Church of St Alban.

One of the great pioneers of the 'authentic' re-creation of early music, David Munrow was never one to put scholarly or theoretical considerations before his main purpose which was to bring the music fully to life and, at the same time, imaginatively to stimulate the ear of the listener. This record, made in 1973, is one of his most successful achievements. It is especially welcome in this mid-priced reissue, well documented on both LP and tape. The cassette, however, needed chrome stock to cope with the resonance of the recording; as it is, the sound lacks sharpness of focus in this format, although the LP remains excellent in all respects.

Terpsichore is a huge collection of some three hundred dance tunes used by the French-court dance bands of Henry IV. They were enthusiastically assembled by the German composer Michael Praetorius, who also harmonized them and arranged them in four to six parts. Moreover, he left plenty of advice as to their manner of performance, although he would not have expected any set instrumentation – this would depend on the availability of musicians. Any selection is therefore as arbitrary in the choice of items as it is conjectural in the matter of their orchestration. David Munrow's instrumentation is imaginatively done (the third item, a *Bourrée* played by four racketts – a cross between a shawm and comb-and-paper in sound – is fascinating), even if the playing itself sometimes seems too refined in manner. But one must not exaggerate this. The collection is still a delightful one, the motets on side two reminding one very much of Giovanni Gabrieli.

Prokofiev, Serge (1891–1953)

Cinderella (ballet; complete), *Op. 87.*
*** Decca Dig. **410 162-2**; 410 162-1/*4* [id.]. Cleveland O, Ashkenazy.

Prokofiev's enchanting score had been neglected in recent years until 1983 saw two new sets arrive, both by artists who are completely inside the Prokofiev idiom. No doubt Previn's HMV recording with the LSO (SLS/*TC-SLS* 143595-3/*5* [Ang. DSB/*4X2S* 3944]) will appear on CD in due course. Honours are very evenly divided between the two: they both occupy two discs and they are very well played. As the Previn is not yet to hand, compact disc collectors can safely invest in Ashkenazy without fear of disappointment. Some dances come off better in one version than in the other, and there is an element of swings and roundabouts in assessing them. Detail is more closely scrutinized by the Decca engineers; Ashkenazy gets excellent results from the Cleveland Orchestra. There are many imaginative touches in this score – as magical indeed as the story itself – and the level of invention is astonishingly high. On CD, the wonderful definition noticeable on the LPs is enhanced and the bright, vivid image is given striking projection. The Decca tapes are on chrome stock; with only a relatively modest level of transfer possible, because of the Kingsway Hall resonance, the sound, though beautifully refined, loses a little of the range and sharpness of focus so noticeable on compact disc.

Cinderella (ballet): highlights.
(*) RCA Dig. **RD 85321; RL/*RK* 85321 [**RCD1 5321**; ARC1/*ARK1* 5321]. St Louis SO, Slatkin.

Slatkin's disc is listed as a 'suite', but the twenty numbers (from the fifty of the complete score) follow the ballet's action comprehensively. There is an excellent note by Richard Freed placing the music in its historical perspective in relation to other settings of the *Cinderella* story. Within the flattering St Louis acoustic, the orchestra is naturally balanced and the sound is vividly spectacular. The upper range is brightly lit but the CD has marginal added amplitude and bloom so that, while the violins above the stave at *fortissimo* are brilliant, there is no edginess. The orchestral playing is sympathetic, polished and committed; the wide dynamic range of the recording produces a riveting climax towards the end of the ballet when, at midnight, the stereoscopically ticking clock dominates the orchestra dramatically. Slatkin then creates an attractively serene contrast with the closing *Amoroso*. Earlier in the work, Slatkin's characterization is just a little tame, and the detail and rhythmic feeling of the music making has, at times, an element of blandness.

Those wanting a single-disc set of highlights will find this enjoyable enough, but readers are reminded that there is a marvellous shorter selection from the ballet by the RPO under Robert Irving, with excitingly vivid playing and the 1958 recording hardly sounding its age. This is coupled with a finely shaped set of excerpts from *Romeo and Juliet* from the Philharmonia under Efrem Kurtz.

This is equally desirable on disc or tape and is offered at mid-price (HMV ESD/*TC-ESD* 7151).

Cinderella: suites Nos 1, Op. 107; 2, Op. 108: excerpts.
(B) ** CBS DC 40143 (2). LSO, Andrew Davis – GRIEG: *Peer Gynt; Songs;* FAURÉ: *Pelléas et Mélisande.***

On one and one-third sides of an LP, Andrew Davis provides a fair selection of items from the two suites which the composer concocted from his complete ballet, often joining totally unrelated excerpts. The performances are fresh, straightforward and well played; the recording is clear and well balanced. The two discs (offered for the price of one) include attractive music by Grieg and Fauré, and this is good value, though the equivalent extended-length tape is not recommended as it omits two of the Grieg songs.

(i) *Piano concerto No. 1 in D flat, Op. 10. Romeo and Juliet* (ballet): *suite, Op. 75* (arr. composer). *Suggestion diabolique.*
(M) *** HMV EG 290326-1/*4* [AM/*4AM* 34715]. Gavrilov; (i) LSO, Rattle.

Piano concerto No. 1 in D flat; Piano sonata No. 5 in C, Op. 38.
*** ASV Dig. DCA/*ZCDCA* 555 [id.]. Osorio, RPO, Bátiz – RAVEL: *Left-hand concerto* etc.***

A dazzling account of the *First Concerto* from the young Soviet pianist Andrei Gavrilov, who replaced Richter at Salzburg in 1975 and has astonished audiences wherever he has appeared. This version is second to none for virtuosity and for sensitivity: it is no exaggeration to say that this exhilarating account is the equal of any we have ever heard and superior to most. Apart from its brilliance, this performance scores on all other fronts, too; Simon Rattle provides excellent orchestral support and the EMI engineers offer vivid recording. The original coupling was the *Scene and dance of the young girls* from *Romeo and Juliet*, plus Ravel's *Left-hand Piano concerto* and *Pavane*. Now one needs to acquire an extra record to get the Ravel *Concerto*. In its place, Gavrilov's selection from the composer's piano arrangement of *Romeo and Juliet* has been expanded (and these pieces, even in their monochrome form, sound abundantly characterful in his hands), while the *Suggestion diabolique* makes a – by no means lightweight – encore after the *Concerto*. On cassette, the reverberation brings slight blunting of the transients, but otherwise the sound is good. At mid-price, the disc remains first-class value.

Jorge-Fredrico Osorio is a gifted Mexican player whose excellently recorded account of the Prokofiev *Concerto* challenges the EMI Gavrilov coupling with the Ravel *Left-hand concerto*, now at mid-price. However, ASV offer us generous and interesting fill-ups in the form of the Prokofiev *Fifth Sonata* which Osorio does in its post-war revised form. It is an interesting piece from the 1920s and a welcome addition to the catalogue. Osorio copes splendidly with the *Concerto* and is not so percussive a pianist as Gavrilov. Readers wanting this coupling need not fear that this is second best. It may be less dazzling but is not less perceptive.

Piano concertos Nos 2 in G min., Op. 16; 3 in C, Op. 26.
(M) *** HMV EG 290261-1/*4* [AM/*4AM* 34705]. Béroff, Leipzig GO, Masur.

A satisfying mid-priced coupling. Michel Béroff plays masterfully: he is a pianist of genuine insight where Prokofiev is concerned, and Masur gives him excellent support. Béroff is free from some of the agogic mannerisms that distinguish Ashkenazy in the slow movement of the *Third* and he has great poetry. The balance is good; although the overall sound-picture is not wholly natural, it is certainly vivid, and the timbre of the piano is sympathetically captured.

Piano concerto No. 3 in C, Op. 26.
*** DG **415 062-2** [id.]. Argerich, BPO, Abbado – TCHAIKOVSKY: *Piano concerto No. 1.****
*** Decca **411 969-2** [id.]. Ashkenazy, LSO, Previn – BARTÓK: *Concerto No. 3.****

Martha Argerich made her outstanding coupling of the Prokofiev and Ravel concertos in 1968, while still in her twenties, and this record helped to establish her international reputation as one of the most vital and positive of women pianists. There is nothing ladylike about the playing, but it displays countless indications of feminine perception and subtlety. The Prokofiev *C major Concerto*, once regarded as tough music, here receives a sensuous performance, and Abbado's direction underlines that from the very first, with a warmly romantic account of the ethereal opening phrases on the high violins. When it comes to the second subject the lightness of Argerich's pointing has a delightfully infectious quality, and surprisingly a likeness emerges with the Ravel *G major Concerto*, which was written more than a decade later. This is a much more individual performance of the Prokofiev than almost any other available and brings its own special insights. The recording remains excellent, though there is less presence and immediacy than with the Ashkenazy CD, and a certain amount of the original tape hiss remains for keen ears to spot. Argerich's coupling is the finest version of the Tchaikovsky *B flat Concerto* yet issued on CD; with nearly 63 minutes' music offered, this is fair value, even if both concertos are also available (differently coupled) on LP and cassette, costing far less.

Ashkenazy's account of the *Third Concerto* is keen-edged and crisply articulated, and he is very sympathetically supported by Previn and the LSO. One's only reservation concerns the slow movement: Ashkenazy's entry immediately after the theme is uncharacteristically mannered. Yet his virtuosity remains thrilling and this is still a fine performance. The Prokofiev was recorded six years earlier than the Bartók coupling, yet the sound in the compact disc transfer is clearer and more transparent, if with a touch of thinness on violin tone.

Piano concerto No. 5 in G, Op. 55.
*** DG **415 119-2** [id.]. Sviatoslav Richter, Warsaw PO, Witold Rowicki – RACHMANINOV: *Piano concerto No. 2.****

Richter's account of the *Fifth Piano concerto* is a classic. It was recorded in 1959, yet the sound of this excellent CD transfer belies the age of the original in its clarity, detail and vividness of colour. In any event it cannot be too strongly recommended to all admirers of Richter, Prokofiev and great piano playing. The coupling has also been very successfully remastered.

Violin concertos Nos 1 in D, Op. 19; 2 in G min., Op. 63.
© *** DG Dig. **410 524-2**; 410 524-1/*4* [id.]. Mintz, Chicago SO, Abbado.
*** HMV Dig. **CDC 747025-2**; ASD/*TCC-ASD* 4098 [Ang. DS/*4XS* 37800]. Perlman, BBC SO, Rozhdestvensky.

Prokofiev's two *Violin concertos* are eminently well served in the present catalogue. Mintz's performances are as fine as any; he phrases with imagination and individuality – the opening of the *G minor* is memorably poetic – and if he does not display quite the overwhelming sense of authority of Perlman, there is an attractive combination of freshness and lyrical finesse. He has the advantage of Abbado's sensitive and finely judged accompaniments. Abbado has a special feeling for Prokofiev's sound-world, and here there is much subtlety of colour and dynamic nuance, yet the music's vitality is undiminished. In short this partnership casts the strongest spell on the listener and, with recording which is both refined and full, and a realistic – if still somewhat forward – balance for the soloist, this record and the excellent equivalent tape must receive the strongest advocacy. The compact disc is in the demonstration league, one of the most impressive to come from DG, adding to the presence and range of the sound-picture without overemphasis.

Perlman's performances bring virtuosity of such strength and command that one is reminded of the supremacy of Heifetz. Though the HMV sound has warmth and plenty of bloom, the balance of the soloist is unnaturally close, which has the effect of obscuring important melodic ideas in the orchestra behind mere passagework from the soloist, as in the second subject of the *First Concerto*'s finale, and this is even more apparent on CD. Nevertheless, in their slightly detached way these performances are impossible to resist: one is left in no doubt that both works are among the finest violin concertos written this century. Apart from the balance, the recording is very fine, with a matching cassette of very good quality.

Violin concerto No. 2 in G min., Op. 63.
(M) *** RCA Gold GL/*GK* 89833. Heifetz, Boston SO, Munch – GLAZOUNOV: *Concerto.****

Heifetz made the first recording of this work in the 1930s under Koussevitzky. His newer (1959) version uses the same Boston orchestra and Munch proves a worthy successor to the Russian conductor. In the *arioso*-like slow movement,

Heifetz chooses a faster speed than is usual, but there is nothing unresponsive about his playing, for his expressive rubato has an unfailing inevitability. In the spiky finale he is superb, and indeed his playing is glorious throughout. The recording is serviceable merely, though it has been made firmer in the current remastering. But no one is going to be prevented from enjoying this ethereal performance because the technical quality is dated. In the USA this is available on CD, coupled with both the Sibelius and the Glazounov *Concertos* – treasure trove indeed ([RCA **RCD1 7019**]). We must hope this is soon issued in Britain; meanwhile the cassette will serve, as it sounds identical with the LP.

Lieutenant Kijé (incidental music), *Op. 60: suite.*
*** HMV Dig. **CDC 747109-2** [id.]; EL 270021-1/*4* [Ang. DS/*4DS* 38095]. LPO, Tennstedt – KODÁLY: *Háry János.****
(M) * Decca Viva 414 076-1/*4*. Netherlands R. O, Dorati – KODÁLY: *Háry János* etc.*(*)

Prokofiev's colourful suite drawn from film music makes the perfect coupling for Kodály's *Háry János*, similarly brilliant and with a comparable vein of irony. Tennstedt's reading, in repertory with which he is not usually associated, is aptly brilliant and colourful, with rhythms strongly marked. Excellent recording, especially vivid and present in its CD format.

Dorati's Decca Viva coupling is even more generous in including also Kodály's *Marosszek dances* and *Hungarian rondo.* The performance of the *Kijé suite* is characteristically direct, with everything boldly characterized. But the – originally Phase Four – recording sounds thin in remastered form, with the tape shrill, the strings lacking body.

Lieutenant Kijé (suite), *Op. 60; Love of Three Oranges* (suite).
*** RCA Dig. **RD 85168**; RL/*RK* 85168 [**RCD1 5168**; ARC1/*ARK1* 5168]. Dallas SO, Mata – STRAVINSKY: *Suites.**** ©

There are no finer performances of these two colourful suites available than on Mata's RCA LP (and its impressive chrome-tape equivalent) and the Stravinsky coupling is equally attractive. Both LP and cassette open with *Kijé*, and the distanced cornet solo immediately creates a mood of nostalgia. The orchestral playing, both here and in the suite from *Love of Three Oranges*, is vividly coloured and full of character, and the ambience of the Dallas auditorium adds bloom and atmosphere. The CD is marginally brighter and sharper in definition, not entirely to advantage. Here, the order of the music is reversed so that the more acerbic opera suite comes first. Whichever format is chosen, however, the music making is of the highest order, and Mata shows an instinctive rapport with both these scores.

Lieutenant Kijé (suite)*; Love of Three Oranges* (suite)*; Symphony No. 1 in D* (*Classical*).
(*) CBS Dig. **MK 39557 [id.]. O Nat. de France, Maazel.

After a brilliant account of the *Classical symphony*, well played and brightly lit,

Maazel gives exceptionally dramatic and strongly characterized accounts of Prokofiev's two colourful suites. Though he does not miss the romantic colouring of *Love of Three Oranges* or the nostalgia of *Kijé*, it is the pungency of the rhythms and the sharp pointing of detail that register most strongly, helped by the resonant acoustic which adds an effective degree of edge to Prokofiev's bolder scoring. Inner detail registers vividly at all dynamic levels; while Maazel is clearly seeking a strong projection rather than refinement, the committed orchestral response is exhilarating.

Lieutenant Kijé (suite); *Romeo and Juliet:* excerpts; *Symphony No. 1 in D* (*Classical*); (i) *Alexander Nevsky* (cantata), *Op. 78.*
(B) *** HMV *TCC2-POR 54278*. LSO, Previn, (i) with Reynolds, LSO Ch.

EMI could hardly have chosen better to represent Previn in their 'Portrait of the Artist' double-length tape series. The performances of the *Kijé suite* and the *Classical symphony* are among the finest available. *Alexander Nevsky* is currently not available in the UK in disc format (it is issued in the USA, however, on [Ang. RL/*4RL* 32081]) and here it is presented without a break on one side of the cassette. All the weight, bite and colour of the score are captured; though the timbre of the singers' voices may not suggest Russians, they cope very confidently with the Russian text; and Previn's dynamic manner ensures that the great *Battle on the ice* scene is powerfully effective. Anna Reynolds sings the lovely lament for the dead most affectingly. The transfers are sophisticated throughout, the sound vivid with excellent range and a good choral focus.

Peter and the wolf, Op. 67.
*** Ph. Dig. **412 559-2**; 412 559-1/*4* [**412 556-2**, with Dudley Moore]. Terry Wogan, Boston Pops O, John Williams – TCHAIKOVSKY: *Nutcracker suite.****
*** DG **415 351-2** [id.]. Hermione Gingold, VPO, Boehm – SAINT-SAËNS: *Carnival.****
(*) HMV Dig. **CDC 747067-2 [id.]; EL 270125-1/*4* [Ang. DS/*4DS* 38190]. Perlman, Israel PO, Mehta – SAINT-SAËNS: *Carnival of the animals.***(*)*
(*) RCA **RD 82743 [id.]; ARL 1/*ARK 1* 2743]. Bowie, Phd. O, Ormandy – BRITTEN: *Young person's guide.***

Terry Wogan's amiably fresh narration is a great success. Any listener expecting a degree of archness or too much Irish whimsy will soon be disarmed by the spontaneity of the story telling and the way the added asides point the gentle irony of the tale and the involvement of its characters. The little bird shrugs its shoulders ('not an easy thing for a bird to do'); the hunters – against the thundering kettledrums – 'shoot at everything that moves' while, at the end, after Peter has caught the wolf without their aid, Wogan comments characteristically, 'I don't think the hunters liked Peter.' Perhaps the camped-up voice of Grandfather sounds a shade self-conscious, but the humour of the grumpy old man is nicely caught. All in all, this is the most endearing version of the tale since

Sir Ralph Richardson's classic Decca performance with Sir Malcolm Sargent (Decca SPA/*KCSP* 90 [Lon. STS/5- 15114]). John Williams provides the most imaginative orchestral backing, full of atmosphere and with marvellous detail, so that one hears Prokofiev's miraculous score as if for the first time. The entry of the wolf is particularly telling, sinister in effect, and he is certainly portrayed as the villain of the piece. By contrast, the wolf's capture has a deliciously light touch, with the final procession then played very grandly indeed. One small editing criticism: in the introductory section, which is agreeably less stilted than usual, the frequent repetition of the word 'tune' is not very felicitous; but this is a small point, not likely to worry younger listeners. The recording is superb, with the nicely resonant Boston acoustic bringing an attractive overall bloom (reminding one of Decca's very first mono LP, made in the Kingsway Hall, by John Culshaw with Frank Phillips and the LPO under Malko). The CD emphasizes the difference in acoustic between the separate recordings of voice and orchestra, but this is not a disadvantage for, within his cleaner ambience, Terry Wogan is able to use a *sotto voce* technique, even a whisper, to great effect. The chrome cassette is first class, though the level of transfer is a little low. In the American edition, Dudley Moore replaces Terry Wogan as narrator.

On DG, Hermione Gingold's narration is certainly memorable and the orchestral playing under Boehm is of a superlative standard. Some might find Miss Gingold a trifle too camp in her presentation of the text (which was amended and embellished by Edward Greenfield, so comment on our part is perhaps inappropriate). However, it is difficult to resist the strength of Miss Gingold's personality and her obvious identification with the events of the tale. Boehm gives a straightforward accompaniment, but is attentive to every detail, and the performance is beautifully characterized. The 1976 orchestral recording was considered to be of demonstration standard in its day; it is remarkably transparent and truthful. The voice itself is a little larger than life, but has such presence and such a well-judged background ambience that one cannot quibble.

Itzhak Perlman makes Prokofiev's story very much part of his own culture; Peter's grandfather, an engaging character, is obviously Jewish as well as Russian. The whole presentation has a sense of transatlantic hyperbole and, in his involvement with the drama, Perlman nearly goes over the top, with the episode of the duck being swallowed very dramatic indeed. Some will also resist the rather schmaltzy opening with its 'gorgeous oboe' and the 'three mean horns' representing the wolf. Yet one succumbs to the strong personality of the story telling, and Mehta, who opens the proceedings a little cosily, is soon caught up in the action. The recording is clear and close, notably so on CD, but the cassette, too, is very clean and sharply defined.

David Bowie's narration has undoubted presence and individuality. He makes a few additions to the text and colours his voice effectively for the different characters. He has the face to ask, 'Are you sitting comfortably?' before he begins; on the whole, the narration seems aimed at a younger age-group. The manner is direct and slightly dead-pan, but definitely attractive. Ormandy accompanies imaginatively and the orchestral players enter fully into the spirit of the tale. The recording is generally excellent (David Bowie's voice is very close, but admirably real), and the remastering for CD produces clear and clean sound, if not the ambient glow of the Philips version.

Romeo and Juliet (ballet), *Op. 64:* complete.
(B) **(*) CfP CFPD 41 4452-3/*5* (2). Bolshoi Theatre O, Zuraitis.

Though Zuraitis's version takes only two discs instead of three, he includes an important supplement in addition to the usual complete ballet score. Having studied the original manuscript material, he adds three movements finally omitted in the ballet, the *Nurse and Mercutio* (using familiar material), a sharply grotesque *Moorish dance* and a so-called *Letter scene* which provides a sketch for what eight years later became the scherzo of the *Fifth Symphony*. Zuraitis has scored this last with reference to the symphony. The performance generally may lack something in rhythmic flair and orchestral refinement compared with those of Previn and Maazel, with the Russian brass uninhibitedly brazen, but in its direct way it is warm and committed, with digital sound of colour and power, not always perfectly balanced. The chrome cassettes match the discs closely, and are well laid out, with Acts tailored to side-ends.

Reminder. Previn and Maazel (almost simultaneously) made outstanding complete sets of Prokofiev's ballet in 1973. Previn's is perhaps the more seductive performance, with the LSO on their best form (HMV SLS/*TCC-SLS* 864 [Ang. SC/*4X3S* 3802]); by contrast, Maazel will please those who believe that this score should above all be bitingly incisive (Decca SXL 6620-2/*K20 K 32* [Lon. CSA/*5*-2312]). Both recordings are first class, but on tape the Maazel/Cleveland set is a clear first choice.

Romeo and Juliet: Suites Nos 1–2, Op. 64a/b.
(*) DG Dig. **410 519-2; 2532/*3302* 087 [id.]. Nat. SO of Washington, Rostropovich.
*(*) HMV Dig. **CDC 747004-2**; ASD/*TCC-ASD* 4068 [Ang. DS/*4XS* 37776]. Phd. O, Muti.

Rostropovich gives a carefully prepared account, thoroughly attentive to details of dynamic markings and phrasing, but symphonic rather than balletic in approach. At no time does the listener feel tempted to spring into dance. Nevertheless the effect is atmospheric in a non-theatrical way, and to some ears the feeling of listening almost to an extended tone-poem is most rewarding, though to others the effect of Rostropovich's approach is ponderous at times. To be fair, some movements give no cause for complaint. Friar Lawrence is even enhanced by the slower tempo, and the *Dance* (No. 4 of the *Second Suite*) has no want of momentum or lightness of touch. The recording is clean with sharply focused detail (even on cassette, where the wide dynamic range has brought only a modest transfer level); and it makes a thrilling impact on the compact disc which is far more successful than Muti's, where the glossily brilliant sound tends to weary the ear.

Multi gives us the *First Suite* as published, and then in the *Second* he omits the *Dance* that forms the fourth number and the penultimate *Dance of the girls with lilies*. There is very impressive virtuoso playing from the Philadelphia Orchestra, and a full-blooded digital recording. There are some magical moments, such as the opening of the *Romeo and Juliet* movement of the *First Suite* but, for the most part, the performance is overdriven. Had Muti relaxed a little, the gain in atmosphere and charm would have been enormous. Other versions bring one closer to the heart of this wonderful score; Muti leaves us admiring but unmoved. The chrome cassette is wide in range though there is a degree of glassiness on the strings, but the sound is in every other respect brilliantly clear. On CD the sharpness of detail and the 'digital edge' on the upper strings in fortissimo increase the feeling of aggressiveness.

Romeo and Juliet: Suites Nos 1 and 2: excerpts.
❀C *** Telarc Dig. **CD 80089** [id.]. Cleveland O, Yoel Levi.
(B) *** DG Walkman *413 430-4* [id.]. San Francisco SO, Ozawa – TCHAIKOVSKY: *Sleeping Beauty; Swan Lake*.**(*)

Levi offers by far the finest single disc of excerpts from Prokofiev's masterpiece, to provide a fitting legacy of his four-year term as resident conductor at Cleveland, 1980–84. The recording, made at Severance Hall in 1983, combines the spectacular and natural qualities we associate with Telarc in this venue: the strings sumptuous, the brass given a thrilling sonority and bite, and luminous woodwind detail registering within a believable overall balance. Levi draws wonderfully eloquent playing from his orchestra, its virtuosity always at the service of the music. He seems to have a special affinity with Prokofiev's score, for pacing is unerringly apt and characterization is strong. The high drama of the very opening is matched later by the power and thrust of the *Death of Tybalt*. There are some wonderfully serene moments, too, as in the ethereal introduction of the flute melody in the first piece (*Montagues and Capulets*), and the delicacy of the string playing in *Romeo at Juliet's tomb* – which explores the widest expressive range – is touching. The quicker movements have an engaging feeling of the dance and the light, graceful articulation in *The child Juliet* is a delight. Levi draws on both suites but intersperses the movements to create contrast and make dramatic sense. His telling portrayal of *Friar Lawrence* (violas and bassoons) is affectionately sombre; but the highlights of the performance are the *Romeo and Juliet love scene* (Suite 1, No. 6) and *Romeo at Juliet's before parting* (Suite 2, No. 5), bringing playing of great intensity, with a ravishing response from the Cleveland strings leading on from passionate yearning to a sense of real ecstasy.

This is also one of Ozawa's finest recordings. He draws warmly committed playing from the San Francisco orchestra, helped by vividly rich recording and this shorter selection from Prokofiev's ballet is well chosen. In his coupled excerpts from *Swan Lake* the music making is at a lower voltage, but Rostropovich's companion suite from the *Sleeping Beauty* is marvellous. At Walkman price, with excellent transfers, this is good value.

Romeo and Juliet: excerpts; *Symphony No. 1 in D* (*Classical*), *Op. 25*.
*(*) Decca Dig. **410 200-2**; SXDL/*KSXDC* 7587. Chicago SO, Solti.

Solti compiles a selection of his own from *Romeo and Juliet*. He is wholly unmannered and secures a brilliant response from the Chicago orchestra. The outer movements of the *Symphony* could do with more spontaneity and sparkle; the slow movement, however, has an occasional moment of charm. As far as the sound is concerned there is spectacular presence and impact, a wide dynamic range and maximum detail. Alas, there is little distance to lend enchantment and many collectors will find everything fiercely overlit, especially on CD. Neither work comes anywhere near the top of the recommended list.

Symphony No. 1 in D (*Classical*), *Op. 25*.
*** DG Dig. **400 034-2**; 2532/*3302* 031 [id.]. BPO, Karajan – GRIEG: *Holberg suite*; MOZART: *Eine kleine Nachtmusik*.***
*** Delos Dig. **D/CD 3021** [id.]. LA CO, Schwarz – SHOSTAKOVICH: *Piano concerto No. 1***(*); STRAVINSKY: *Soldier's tale*: suite.*** ⊛
(B) **(*) Pickwick Con. CC/*CCTC* 7576. LSO, Abbado – MUSSORGSKY: *Pictures*.**(*)

Karajan's performance is predictably brilliant, the playing beautifully polished, with grace and eloquence distinguishing the slow movement. The outer movements are wanting in charm alongside Marriner. The recording is bright and clearly detailed, though the balance is not quite natural. The compact disc has the upper strings very brightly lit, with a touch of digital edge, but the ambience is attractive.

Schwarz's version, if not quite as brilliant as Karajan's, is a nicely paced performance, the slow movement particularly pleasing in its relaxed lyricism and the finale sparkling with high spirits. It is very well played; the orchestra is naturally balanced within a fairly resonant acoustic which provides plenty of air round the instruments. The couplings are unusual and attractive.

On the bargain-priced Contour disc, Abbado's Prokofiev sounds very mellow, coming immediately after the finale of Maazel's brilliant version of Mussorgsky's *Pictures at an exhibition*. It is fresh and beautifully played, but the reading has not quite the sparkle of Marriner. The sound is warm and naturally balanced, although on tape there is a middle and bass orientation and a lack of bite in the treble.

Still recommended: Marriner's famous 1973 recording (coupled with an equally felicitous account of the Bizet *Symphony*) sounds marvellously fresh in its Jubilee reissue (Decca 410 167-1/*4* [id.]). Marriner's tempi are comparatively relaxed, but the ASMF are in sparkling form. The sound remains in the demonstration class, on LP and cassette alike.

Symphonies Nos 1 in D (*Classical*); *4 in C, Op. 112* (revised 1947 version).
*** Chan. Dig. **CHAN 8400**; ABRD/*ABTD* 1137 [id.]. SNO, Järvi.

Unlike the *Third*, the *Fourth Symphony* does not have quite the same independence, and its balletic origins are obvious, both in terms of the melodic substance and its organization. Prokofiev himself recognized this and drastically revised the score later in life. The extent of this overhaul, made immediately after the completion of the *Sixth Symphony*, can be gauged by the fact that the 1930 version takes 23′ 08″ and the revision 37′ 12″. The first two movements are much expanded; indeed, in playing time the first is doubled, and the *Andante* is half as long again. The orchestration is richer; among other things, a piano, which Prokofiev had used in the *Fifth* and *Sixth Symphonies*, is added. Not all of Prokofiev's afterthoughts are improvements, but Järvi succeeds in making out a more eloquent case for the revision than many of his predecessors. He also gives an exhilarating account of the *Classical symphony*, one of the best on record. The slow movement has real *douceur* and the finale is wonderfully high-spirited. On CD, the recording has fine range and immediacy, but in the *Fourth Symphony* the upper range is a little fierce in some of the more forceful climaxes. The splendid chrome cassette, which is also extraordinarily vivid, seems slightly smoother, yet there is no sense of loss of range or detail.

Symphonies Nos 1 (*Classical*)*; 7 in C sharp min., Op. 131; Lieutenant Kijé: suite, Op. 60.*
(M) *** HMV EG 290298-1/*4* [Ang. AM/*4AM* 34711]. LSO, Previn.

In both symphonies (a popular coupling since the earliest days of LP) Previn is highly successful. He produces much inner vitality and warmth, and the EMI engineers provide a strikingly integrated sound. The *Classical symphony* is more successful here than in Previn's earlier version on RCA. It is genuinely sunlit and vivacious. Previn is obviously persuaded of the merits of the underrated and often beguiling *Seventh Symphony*. As a substantial bonus for this mid-priced reissue, Previn's colourful, swaggering performance of the *Lieutenant Kijé suite* has been added, yet the recording retains its full vividness and sparkle. The tape is very good too and although there are slight problems with the bass drum in *Kijé* and the *Seventh Symphony*, many will like its warmer middle range.

Symphony No. 2 in D min., Op. 40; Romeo and Juliet (ballet)*: suite No. 1, Op. 64.*
(*) Chan. Dig. **CHAN 8368; ABRD/*ABTD* 1134 [id.]. SNO, Järvi.

The *Second Symphony* reflects the iconoclastic temper of the early 1920s; the violence and dissonance of its first movement betray Prokofiev's avowed intention of writing a work 'made of iron and steel'. It is obvious that Prokofiev was trying to compete with Mossolov and the *style mécanique* of Honegger or Horace Victorieux in orchestral violence, even if the unremitting and sustained *fortissimo* writing is at times self-defeating. In its formal layout (but in no other respect), the symphony resembles Beethoven's Op. 111, with two movements, the second of which is a set of variations. It is this movement that more than compensates for the excesses of its companion. It is rich in fantasy and some of the variations are wonderfully atmospheric. Chandos accommodate this densely written score on to one side, thus leaving room for the whole of the first *Romeo and Juliet suite*. Neeme Järvi produces altogether excellent results from the Scottish National Orchestra and has great bite and character; indeed, he has a real flair for this composer. The Chandos recording has admirable detail and body, but is naturally cut at a lower level than its past rivals. In its CD form it is impressively detailed and vivid. The *Romeo and Juliet suite* comes off well; the SNO play with real character, though the quality of the strings at the opening of the Madrigal is not luxurious. On the chrome cassette, the sound in the *Symphony*, though vivid, is also rather fierce, but in *Romeo and Juliet* a slight drop in the level brings a mellower balance, entirely to advantage.

Symphony No. 3, Op. 44.
* Ph. 412 070-1/*4* [id.]. Concg. O, Kondrashin – BORODIN: *Symphony No. 2*.*(*)

Symphony No. 3, Op. 44; Love of Three Oranges: suite, Op. 33a.
**(*) DG Dig. 410 988-1/*4* [id.]. Junge Deutsche Philharmonie, Riccardo Chailly.

Such is the sheer accomplishment of so many of the youth orchestras on the present scene that one ceases to be amazed. The Junge Deutsche Philharmonie are outstanding by any standards and make a far better sound for Chailly than the Moscow Radio Orchestra did for Rozhdestvensky! The digital recording has impressive range and presence; the only reservation to note is a certain opaque quality. A brief comparison with Abbado and the LSO on Decca (now deleted) leaves no doubt that the earlier analogue disc had the greater transparency and detail, without in any way wanting weight or presence. The new DG version is still pretty impressive, even if Abbado was more deeply inside this music and responsive to its demonic atmosphere and sense of mystery. However, the fill-up, the suite from the *Love of Three Oranges*, is marvellously played. The DG cassette is little short of superb.

Kondrashin is an authoritative interpreter of Prokofiev, but his fine account of the *Third Symphony* must be ruled out of court. It emanates from a 1975 performance at the Concertgebouw and, although there are one or two audience noises, these are not in themselves worrying; but there is, alas, a disruptive – indeed, ruinous – noise a bar after the magical string entry at fig. 71. This completely spoils the atmosphere and would prove insupportable on repeated hearing. The performance is a very fine one and the recording eminently satisfactory, though not as impressive as its rivals. However, it does have the advantage of a more substantial fill-up in the form of Borodin's *Second Symphony*.

Symphonies Nos 3 in C min., Op. 44; 4 in C, Op. 47 (original 1930 version).
*** Chan. Dig. **CHAN 8401**; ABRD/*ABTD* 1138 [id.]. SNO, Järvi.

Neeme Järvi's account of the *Third* can more than hold its own with the opposition. He is particularly successful in the *Andante*, which derives from the last Act of the opera, *The Fiery Angel*, and succeeds in conveying its sense of magic and mystery. The opening idea is austere but lyrical, and the music to which it gives rise is extraordinarily rich in fantasy and clothed in an orchestral texture of great refinement and delicacy. In the scherzo, said to have been inspired by the finale of Chopin's *B flat minor Sonata*, he secures a very good response from the SNO strings. If one had made the acquaintance of the expanded version first, the original of the *Fourth Symphony* would possibly seem more like a ballet suite than a symphony: its insufficient tonal contrast tells. Neither version has the degree of organic cohesion or symphonic drama of Nos 5 and 6, but both have delightful and characteristic ideas. The scherzo, drawn from the music for the Temptress in *The Prodigal Son* ballet, is particularly felicitous. Prokofiev at his second best is infinitely superior to many of his contemporaries at their very best. The chrome tape is first class.

Symphony No. 5 in B flat, Op. 100.
(M) *** DG Sig. 410 992-1/*4* [id.]. BPO, Karajan.
(*) CBS Dig. **CD 35877 [35877/*HMT*]. Israel PO, Bernstein.
(*) RCA Dig. **RD 85035; RL/*RK* 85035 [**RCD1 5035**; ARC1/*ARK1* 5035]. St Louis SO, Slatkin.

Symphony No. 5 in B flat, Op. 100; Waltz suite, Op. 110.
*** Chan. Dig. **CHAN 8450**; ABRD/*ABTD* 1160 [id.]. SNO, Järvi.

Even at full price, Karajan and the Berlin Philharmonic would still sweep the board, and at its new mid-price level it is a clear first choice; fifteen years after its first release it still remains incomparable. The playing has wonderful tonal sophistication and Karajan judges tempi to perfection so that the proportions seem quite perfect. The recording, too, is extremely well balanced and has excellent ambience; the new pressing is smoother and more refined than the original. There is an excellent cassette. Only one other account can be named in the same breath – Koussevitzky and the Boston Symphony Orchestra, made not long after the first performance. No rival version begins to match this in distinction and stature.

Järvi's credentials in this repertoire are well established and his direction unhurried, fluent and authoritative. His feeling for the music is unfailingly natural. Although Karajan's version remains in a class of its own, for those seeking a modern digital recording on CD Järvi would be a good choice. The three *Waltzes* which derive from various sources are all elegantly played. The Chandos recording is set just a shade further back than some of its companions in the series, making a little more of the hall's ambience. Yet at the same time every detail is clear, and the upper range is more telling than in either the RCA or CBS rivals. There is an excellent chrome cassette.

It would be easy to underestimate Bernstein's version. Edited from live performances, it is a consistently powerful reading, but with the romantic expressiveness underlined. Bernstein is superb at building climaxes and the playing has great concentration, but for some ears there is too much emotional weight. The recording is bold and full, with a strong, firm bass line in its CD format.

Slatkin's account is superbly recorded. On CD, the sound has a very wide dynamic range, and the acoustic glow of the hall does not prevent detail from emerging vividly. The chrome cassette, too, is extremely successful. Slatkin's performance has an attractive freshness, and its directness is appealing, especially when the orchestral playing is both polished and responsive (though no match for Karajan's Berliners in the Scherzo). But it would be idle to pretend that Slatkin's reading – for all its volatile freedom – has the power of Bernstein's, nor is it as imaginative. The climax of the slow movement is greatly helped by the expansive RCA recording, but there is more grip in the Israel account. Even so, its lyrical innocence is certainly engaging, when the recording is so warmly flattering, especially in its CD format.

Symphony No. 6 in E flat min., Op. 111. Waltz Suite, Op. 110, Nos 1, 5 and 6.
*** Chan. Dig. **CHAN 8359**; ABRD/*ABTD* 1122 [id.]. SNO, Järvi.

Though it lags far behind the *Fifth* in popularity, the *Sixth Symphony* goes much deeper than any of its companions; indeed, it is perhaps the greatest of the Prokofiev cycle. Neeme Järvi has an instinctive grasp and deep understanding of this symphony; he shapes its detail as skilfully as he does its architecture as a whole. The various climaxes are expertly built and related to one another, and the whole structure is held together in a way that recalls the most distinguished precedents. At times, however, one longs for greater sonority from the strings, who sound distinctly lean at the top and wanting in body and weight in the middle and lower registers, even in quieter passages. This may seem churlish when in all other respects the orchestra rises so magnificently to the challenges of this score and is obviously playing with such commitment. These artists have the measure of its tragic poignancy more than almost any of their predecessors on record. A word about the balance: it has the distinct merit of sounding well blended and in good perspective, at whatever dynamic level you choose to play it. If you want the impact of a forward place in the hall, a high-level setting does not disturb the effect of overall naturalness and warmth. The bass is particularly rich, finely detailed and powerful. There is a first-class matching chrome cassette. The fill-up, as its title implies, is a set of waltzes, drawn and adapted from various stage works: Nos 1 and 6 come from *Cinderella* and No. 5 from *War and Peace*.

Symphony No. 7 in C sharp min., Op. 131; Sinfonietta in A, Op. 5/48.
*** Chan. Dig. **CHAN 8442**; ABRD/*ABTD* 1154 [id.]. SNO, Järvi.

Neeme Järvi's account of the *Seventh Symphony* is hardly less successful than the other issues in this cycle. He gets very good playing from the SNO and has the full measure of this repertoire. Earlier recordings of the *Seventh* from Nicolai Malko, Rozhdestvensky and Previn have coupled it with the *Classical*, but Chandos are more enterprising, offering the early *Sinfonietta*. There is no current alternative of either work on compact disc but, even on LP, Järvi would be a first choice – save for the additional advantage that the Previn version enjoys of being at mid-price. However, the Chandos digital recording has greater range and, given the attractions of the coupling (what a sunny and charming piece it is!), must be a first choice. There is a superb chrome cassette, handling the wide dynamic range and resonant ambience with spectacular realism.

CHAMBER AND INSTRUMENTAL MUSIC

Cello sonata in C, Op. 119.
*** Chan. Dig. **CHAN 8340**; ABRD/*ABTD* 1072 [id.]. Turovsky, Edlina – SHOSTAKOVICH: *Sonata.****

Yuli Turovsky and Luba Edlina are both members of the Borodin Trio; they are eloquent advocates of this *Sonata*, which is a late work dating from 1949 not currently available in any alternative form. Rostropovich and Richter recorded it in the days of mono LP, but its subsequent appearances on record have been few. A finely wrought and rewarding score, it deserves greater popularity, and this excellent performance and recording should make it new friends. The balance is particularly likelike on CD. The chrome cassette has fine presence, but the high-level transfer brings a rather dry timbre to the cello's upper range.

Violin sonatas Nos 1 in F min., Op. 80; 2 in D, Op. 94a.
*** Chan. Dig. **CHAN 8398**; ABRD/*ABTD* 1132 [id.]. Mordkovitch, Oppitz.

Lydia Mordkovitch and Gerhard Oppitz are the first artists to offer the two Prokofiev *Sonatas* on CD; though their accounts do not displace earlier versions by Oistrakh and Richter or Perlman and Ashkenazy from the memory, neither is readily available at the time of writing. In any case the new performances make a worthy successor. They are both thoughtful readings with vital contributions from both partners. They have the measure of the darker, more searching side of the *F minor*, and are hardly less excellent in the companion. They also have the benefit of well-balanced Chandos recording. Both artists bring insights of their own to this music that make these performances well worth having. Tape collectors will find that the sound on the chrome cassette has good presence and realism, and that the slight spiky quality on top – notably in No. 1 – is easily smoothed.

Piano sonata No. 6 in A, Op. 82.
❀ *** DG Dig. **413 363-2**; 2532/*3302* 093 [id.]. Pogorelich – RAVEL: *Gaspard de la nuit.****

Pogorelich's performance of the *Sixth Sonata* is quite simply dazzling; indeed, it is by far the best version of it ever put on record and arguably the finest performance of a Prokofiev sonata since Horowitz's hair-raising account of the *Seventh*. It is certainly Pogorelich's most brilliant record so far and can be recommended with the utmost enthusiasm, especially in its CD format. There is a faithful chrome cassette, though the transfer level is not especially high.

Alexander Nevsky (cantata), *Op. 78.*
(*) Decca Dig. **410 164-2; 410 164-1/*4* [id.]. Arkhipova, Cleveland Ch. and O, Chailly.

Chailly has the advantage of full-blooded Decca digital sound, and its richness adds to the emotional weight of the opening sections. The *Battle on the ice* is characteristically impulsive and, with Irina Arkhipova touchingly expressive in her elegiac aria, Chailly finds an effective exuberance in the work's closing pages. The recording is not always ideally clear on detail, even on CD, although it is not short on spectacle and the chorus projects well. As a performance, Previn's version (currently available only on tape – see above) is preferable.

(i) *Alexander Nevsky, Op. 78;* (ii) *Seven, they are seven* (cantata), *Op. 30; Festival song* (*Zdravitsa*), *Op. 85.*
(*) Chant du Monde **LDC 278389 [id.]. (i) Avdeyeva, RSFSR Russian Ch., USSR SO, Svetlanov; (ii) Elnikov, Ch., Moscow R. O, Rozhdestvensky.

Svetlanov's is a vigorous, earthy performance, given fine bite and presence in the remastering for CD, which gains enormously from the authentic sounds of a Russian chorus. The recording is not refined but has plenty of weight and body; though the ensemble does not match that of the best performances from the West, the urgency of the inspiration is most compelling, and the *Battle on the ice* sequence has a splendid cutting edge. What makes this CD doubly attractive is the inclusion of two important bonuses. *Seven, they are seven* is one of Prokofiev's most adventurous and original scores. It consists of a series of contrasting episodes in which the mood changes from venomous violence to mysteriously sombre evocation, with undertones of an ageless ritual. The effect is hallucinatory and immensely involving when the performance is so powerful. By contrast, the *Festival song* (*Zdravitsa*) is radiantly life-enhancing. By setting folk-texts from the various provinces, Prokofiev achieves an energetic kaleidoscope of peasant life, with a beautiful Ukrainian lullaby providing radiant contrast. The fervour of the performance is remarkable; and the CD brings a sharp focus to the singers, without loss of body.

Puccini, Giacomo (1858–1924)

Capriccio sinfonico; Crisantemi; Minuets Nos 1–5; Preludio sinfonico; Edgar: Preludes, Acts I and III. Manon Lescaut: Intermezzo, Act III. Le Villi: Prelude; La Tregenda (*Act II*).
ϾΙ *** Decca Dig. **410 007-2**; SXDL/*KSXDC* 7607 [Lon. LDR/5- 71107]. Berlin RSO, Chailly.

In a highly attractive collection of Puccinian juvenilia and rarities, Chailly draws opulent and atmospheric playing from the Berlin Radio Symphony Orchestra, helped by outstandingly rich and full recording. The compact disc version is of demonstration quality; the chrome cassette, too, is admirably fresh and clear. The *Capriccio sinfonico* of 1876 brings the first characteristically Puccinian idea in what later became the opening Bohemian motif of *La Bohème*. There are other identifiable fingerprints here, even if the big melodies suggest Mascagni rather than full-blown Puccini. *Crisantemi* (with the original string quartet scoring expanded for full string orchestra) provided material for *Manon Lescaut* as did the three little *Minuets*, pastiche eighteenth-century music.

Messa di Gloria.

*** Erato Dig. ECD 88022; NUM/*MCE* 75090 [id.]. Carreras, Prey, Ambrosian S., Philh. O, Scimone.

Puccini's *Messa di Gloria*, completed when he was only twenty, some 15 years before his first fully successful opera, has a vigour and memorability to put it within hailing distance (but no more) of the masterpiece which plainly inspired it, Verdi's *Requiem*, first given only six years earlier. The bold secularity of some of the ideas, as for example the brassy march for the *Gloria* itself, is very much in the Italian tradition, perilously skirting the edge of vulgarity. Scimone and a fine team are brisker and lighter than their predecessors on record, yet effectively bring out the red-bloodedness of the writing. José Carreras turns the big solo in the *Gratias* into the first genuine Puccini aria. His sweetness and imagination are not quite matched by the baritone, Hermann Prey, who is given less to do than usual, when the choral baritones take on the yearning melody of *Crucifixus*. Excellent, atmospheric sound.

OPERA

La Bohème (complete).

*** HMV **CDS 747235-8**; SLS/*TC-SLS* 896 (2) [Ang. Sera. SIB/*4X2G* 6099]. Los Angeles, Bjoerling, Merrill, Reardon, Tozzi, Amara, RCA Victor Ch. and O, Columbia Boychoir, Beecham.

(*) Decca **411 868-2 (2) [id.]; 411 868-1/*4* [Lon. JL/*5*- 42002]. Tebaldi, Bergonzi, Bastianini, Siepi, Corena, D'Angelo, St Cecilia Ac. Ch. and O, Rome, Serafin.

(B) ** HMV *TCC2-POR 1545999*. Freni, Gedda, Adani, Sereni, Rome Op. Ch. and O, Schippers.

As we go to press, EMI announce that the famous Beecham *La Bohème* is scheduled for CD issue, and the catalogue number is listed above. Beecham recorded his classic interpretation of *Bohème* in 1956 in sessions in New York that were arranged at the last minute. It was a gamble getting it completed, but the result was incandescent, a unique performance with two favourite singers, Victoria de los Angeles and Jussi Bjoerling, challenged to their utmost in loving, expansive singing. The present LPs and tapes certainly sound attractively atmospheric, although with such a performance one hardly notices the recording. It has always been rumoured that three of the four Acts had been recorded in stereo, although the LPs claim only 'transcription stereo'. It will be interesting to hear the results of the digital remastering.

It seems astonishing that Decca should have chosen to offer for their first *La Bohème* on CD a 27-year-old recording, instead of their newest version with

Freni and Pavarotti under Karajan. Certainly the earlier Decca set with Tebaldi and Bergonzi was technically outstanding in its day, and its vividness and sense of stage perspective are enhanced on CD, with minimal residue tape-hiss, not at all intrusive. However, the cassettes, too, are very lively and offer almost comparable quality – and they cost only slightly more than a third the price of the pair of CDs. Vocally, the performance achieves a consistently high standard, Tebaldi as Mimi the most affecting: she offers some superbly controlled singing, but the individuality of the heroine is not so indelibly conveyed as with Los Angeles, Freni or Caballé. Carlo Bergonzi is a fine Rodolfo; Bastianini and Siepi are both superb as Marcello and Colline, and even the small parts of Benoit and Alcindoro (as usual taken by a single artist) have the benefit of Corena's magnificent voice. The veteran Serafin was more vital here than on some of his recordings.

HMV have reissued the Schippers 1964 *Bohème* on a single extended-length tape. The use of iron-oxide stock, even with the XDR monitoring system, means that the upper range is not quite so sharply focused as on the discs (which are still available in the USA), but the resonant acoustic is attractive and there is no lack of vividness. The presentation includes a plot summary instead of a libretto, but with the four Acts pairing neatly between the two sides (with only two seconds' difference in their combined timing) the layout is convenient and this is a bargain. Freni's characterization of Mimi is so enchanting that it is worth ignoring some of the less perfect elements. The engineers placed Freni rather close to the microphone, which makes it hard for her to sound tentative in her first scene; but it is the beauty of the voice that one remembers and, from there to the end, her performance is conceived as a whole, leading to a supremely moving account of the death scene. Nicolai Gedda's Rodolfo is not rounded in the traditional Italian way, but there is never any doubt about his ability to project a really grand manner of his own. Thomas Schippers's conducting starts as though this is going to be a hard-driven, unrelenting performance, but quickly after the horse-play he shows his genuinely Italianate sense of pause, giving the singers plenty of time to breathe and allowing the music to expand.

Still recommended: Karajan's spacious but electrically intense performance has Pavarotti an inspired Rodolfo, with comic flair and expressive passion, and Freni just as seductive a Mimi as she was in the Schippers set of ten years earlier. Karajan's version, like Beecham's, must take precedence over the earlier Decca CD performance (Decca SET 565-6/*K2 B5* [Lon. OSA/*5-* 1299]).

La Fanciulla del West (*The Girl of the Golden West;* complete).

(M) *** DG 413 285-1/*4* (3/*2*). Neblett, Domingo, Milnes, Howell, ROHCG Ch. and O, Mehta.

Like *Madama Butterfly*, '*The Girl*', as Puccini called it in his correspondence, was based on a play by the American David Belasco. The composer wrote the work with all his usual care for detailed planning, both of libretto and of music. In idiom the music marks the halfway stage between *Butterfly* and *Turandot*, and the first audience must have been astonished at the opening of an Italian opera dependent on the whole-tone scale in a way Debussy would have recognized as akin to his own practice. Nevertheless, it produces an effect wildly un-Debussian and entirely Puccinian.

DG took the opportunity of recording the opera when Covent Garden was staging a spectacular production in 1977. With one exception the cast remained the same as in the theatre and, as so often in such associated projects, the cohesion of the performance in the recording is enormously intensified. The result is magnificent, underlining the point that – whatever doubts may remain over the subject, with its weeping goldminers – Puccini's score is masterly, culminating in a happy ending which brings one of the most telling emotional coups that he ever achieved.

Mehta's manner – as he makes clear at the very start – is on the brisk side, not just in the cakewalk rhythms but even in refusing to let the first great melody, the nostalgic *Che faranno i viecchi miei*, linger into sentimentality. Mehta's tautness then consistently makes up for intrinsic dramatic weaknesses (as, for example, the delayed entries of both heroine and hero in the first Act). Sherrill Milnes as Jack Rance was the newcomer to the cast for the recording, and he makes the villain into far more than a small-town Scarpia, giving nobility and understanding to the first-Act *arioso*. Domingo, as in the theatre, sings heroically, disappointing only in his reluctance to produce soft tone in the great aria *Ch'ella mi creda*. The rest of the Covent Garden team is excellent, not least Gwynne Howell as the minstrel who sings *Che faranno i viecchi miei*; but the crowning glory of a masterly set is the singing of Carol Neblett as the Girl of the Golden West herself, gloriously rich and true and with formidable attack on the exposed high notes. Rich atmospheric recording to match, essential in an opera full of evocative offstage effects. These very distant effects have only fractionally less sharpness of focus on tape than on disc, and this medium-priced reissue is a bargain, whichever format is chosen. However, in re-editing the set to fit on a pair of chrome tapes (against three LPs) Acts have not been tailored to fit side-ends. The tape libretto is clear.

Gianni Schicchi (complete).

(*) Hung. Dig. **HCD 12541 [id.]. György Melis, Magda Kalmar, Denes Gulya, Hungarian State Op. O, Ferencsik.

Ferencsik conducts all-Hungarian forces in an energetic and well-drilled account of Puccini's comic masterpiece which makes up for some unidiomatic rigidity with red-blooded commitment. The singing is variable, with the incidental characters including some East European wobblers. György Melis is not always perfectly steady, but his is a fine, characterful reading, strongly projected; though Magda Kalmar sounds too mature for the girlish Lauretta, the tone is attractively warm and finely controlled, as is Denes Gulya's tenor in the role of Rinuccio. It is a pity that the CD has no banding whatever.

Still recommended: The combination of Maazel and Gobbi in this most scintillating of Puccini's scores is irresistible and, with Domingo giving a swaggering performance of his big aria, this CBS LP version remains first choice for American readers ([M 34570]), although it has been withdrawn in the UK. The CBS box of *Il Trittico*, however, remains available – see below.

Madama Butterfly (complete).

(*) Decca **411 634-2 (2); 411 634-1/*4* [id.]. Tebaldi, Bergonzi, Cossotto, Sordello, St Cecilia Ac. Ch. and O, Serafin.

(B) **(*) CfP CFPD 41 4446-3/*5* (2). Los Angeles, Bjoerling, Pirazzini, Sereni, Rome Op. Ch. and O, Santini.

** Hung. **HCD 12256-7**; SLPX/*MK* 12256-8 [id.]. Kincses, Dvorský, Takács, Miller, Hungarian State Op. Ch. and O, Patanè.

Though it is sad not to have the superb Karajan version as a first CD issue of this favourite opera from Decca, Serafin's sensitive and beautifully paced reading from the beginning of the stereo era makes a welcome substitute, with Tebaldi at her most radiant. Though she was never the most deft of Butterflys dramatically (she never actually sang the role on stage before recording it), her singing is consistently rich and beautiful, breathtakingly so in passages such as the one in Act I where she tells Pinkerton she has changed her religion. The excellence of Decca engineering in 1958 is amply proved in the CD transfer, with one serious exception. The very opening with its absence of bass brings a disagreeably shrill and thin sound, promptly corrected once the orchestration grows fuller, with voices very precisely and realistically placed. Each of the two CDs has over 70 minutes of music and is generously banded.

In the late 1950s and early 1960s, Victoria de los Angeles was also memorable in the role of Butterfly, and her 1960 recording displays her art at its most endearing, her range of golden tone-colour lovingly exploited, with the voice well recorded for the period, though rather close. Opposite her, Jussi Bjoerling was making one of his very last recordings, and though he shows few special insights, he produces a flow of rich tone to compare with that of the heroine. Mario Sereni is a full-voiced Sharpless, but Miriam Pirazzini is a disappointingly wobbly Suzuki; while Santini is a reliable, generally rather square and unimaginative conductor who rarely gets in the way. With recording quality freshened, equally bright and clear on LPs and tapes, this set has been successfully remastered on to two discs and two cassettes in the lowest price-range; it makes a bargain comparable with the finest of the Walkman tape series. There is no libretto.

Recorded in 1981 in analogue sound, vividly remastered for CD, the Hungaroton set presents a warm, idiomatically conducted reading with dramatically convincing performances from the principals. Peter Dvorský's clear, fresh tenor takes well to recording; he gives an attractively lyrical performance as Pinkerton, sweet and concerned rather than an ardent lover in Act I. He remains a recessive character next to the Butterfly of Veronika Kincses who emerges as an attractively girlish figure with facial expression made clear in every phrase. For all the natural vibrancy there is no suspicion of a wobble, and it is only when the voice is pressed in the upper register that the tone hardens in vocal as well as dramatic terms from girlish tones through increasing warmth and on to growing maturity in Act II. Sadly, the least attractive singing comes in the final suicide aria, but Patanè's commitment carries one over that. Lajos Miller makes a young-sounding Sharpless, pleasing of tone, while Klara Takács is a fruity, positive Suzuki and József Gregor a firmly resonant Bonze, impressive in the curse.

Still recommended: Karajan's 1975 Decca set remains a clear first choice for this opera. Karajan inspires singers and orchestra to a radiant performance which brings out all the beauty and intensity of the score; Freni is an enchanting Butterfly, Pavarotti an intensely imaginative Pinkerton, while Christa Ludwig is a splendid Suzuki. The recording is equally recommendable on disc or cassette (Decca SET 584-6/*K2 A1* [Lon. OSA/*5*- 13110]).

Manon Lescaut (complete).

*** DG Dig. **413 893-2** (2); 413 893-1/*4* (3/*2*) [id.]. Freni, Domingo, Bruson, ROHCG Ch., Philh. O, Sinopoli.

(M) (***) HMV mono **CDC 747393-8**; EX 290041-3/*5* (2). Callas, Di Stefano, Fioravanti, La Scala Milan Ch. and O, Serafin.

After years of neglect from the record companies, Sinopoli's brilliant version of Puccini's first fully successful opera provides in almost every way the answer most Puccinians have been waiting for. With his concern for detail, his love of high dramatic contrasts, and the clear pointing of changes of mood, along with sharp control of tension, the plan of each Act is presented with new precision, reflecting the composer's own careful crafting. This is also the most sensuous-sounding reading on record, thanks also to the fine playing of the Philharmonia, taking over in what is in most respects a recording of the Covent Garden production. Plainly the chorus has benefited from having also worked with Sinopoli in the opera-house, and Placido Domingo's portrait of Des Grieux is here far subtler and more detailed, with finer contrasts of tone and dynamic, than in his earlier EMI recording opposite Caballé. The nicely shaded legato of *Donna non vidi mai* in Act I contrasts with an Othello-like outburst on *No, no pazzo son*, making a shattering conclusion to Act III. Freni, taking the place of Kiri Te Kanawa in the stage production, proves an outstanding choice. Her girlish tones in Act I rebut any idea that she might be too mature. *In quelle trine morbide*, in Act II, retains freshness of tone with fine concern for word detail, while the long duet and aria of the last Act present a most moving culmination, not feeling like an epilogue. Freni and Sinopoli together bring a ravishing change of mood on the unexpected modulation from F minor to D flat on *Terra de pace* in that scene, a wonderful moment of stillness to heighten the impact of *Non voglio morir*. Of the others, a first-rate team, Renato Bruson nicely brings out the ironic side of Lescaut's character, and having Brigitte Fassbaender just to sing the madrigal adds to the feeling of luxury, as does John Tomlinson's darkly intense moment of drama as the ship's captain, bringing the happy resolution in Act III. The voices are more recessed than is common, but they are recorded with fine bloom, and the brilliance of the orchestral sound comes out particularly impressively on CD, which has the benefit of being on two discs, instead of three for LP. There are excellent cassettes.

The early La Scala mono set partnering Callas and Di Stefano has striking individuality and dramatic power. It is typical of Callas that she turns the final scene – which often seems an excrescence, a mere epilogue after the real drama – into the most compelling part of the opera. Serafin, who could be a lethargic recording conductor, is here electrifying, and Di Stefano too is inspired to one of his finest complete opera recordings. The cast-list even includes the young Fiorenza Cossotto, impressive as the singer in the Act II madrigal. The recording – still in mono, not a stereo transcription – minimizes the original boxiness and gives good detail. The CDs are announced just as we go to press.

La Rondine (complete).
Ⓒ *** CBS Dig. **M2K 37852**; D2 37852/*40-D2* [id.]. Te Kanawa, Domingo, Nicolesco, Rendall, Nucci, Watson, Knight, Amb. Op. Ch., LSO, Maazel.

Even more than usually, the gains in vividness and immediacy and the sense of the singers' presence is striking when comparing CD with LP in this fine CBS set. The precision of the vocal placing is determined with striking realism, so that the interplay between the characters is very tangible against the background silence. The orchestra too is beautifully caught, while off-stage effects are nicely managed. *La Rondine* was a product of the First World War, and though in subject nothing could be less grim than this frothy tale told in Viennese operetta-style, the background to its composition and production may have had their effect. It has never caught on, and a recording like this will almost certainly surprise anyone at the mastery of the piece, with a captivating string of catchy numbers. The story is based on a watered-down *Traviata* situation, culminating not in tragedy but in a sad-sweet in-between ending such as the Viennese (for whom it was written) loved. It is not just a question of Puccini taking Viennese waltzes as model but all kinds of other suitable dances such as tangos, foxtrots and two-steps. Not aggressively at all, for, as with so much that this most eclectic of composers 'cribbed', he commandeered them completely, to make the result utterly Puccinian. If there is a fault, it lies in the inability of the story to move the listener with any depth of feeling, but a recording does at least allow one to appreciate each tiny development with greater ease than in the theatre.

Maazel's is a strong, positive reading crowned by a superb, radiant Magda in Dame Kiri Te Kanawa, mature yet glamorous. From the stratospheric phrases in *Il sogno di Doretta* which are headily beautiful, her performance has one spellbound. Domingo, by age too mature for the role of young hero, yet scales his voice down most effectively in the first two Acts, expanding in heroic warmth only in the final scene of dénouement. Sadly the second pair are far less convincing, when the voices of both Mariana Nicolesco and David Rendall take ill to the microphone. Others in the team are excellent, and though Maazel launches the very opening too aggressively, the rest is most sympathetically done, with fine playing from the LSO. One's only real criticism is the lack of access within the opera itself. Acts I and II are on the first disc, Act III on the second, but there are no cues to find individual arias.

Suor Angelica (complete).
(*) Hung. Dig. **HCD; SLPD *TC-SLPD* 12490 [id.]. Tokody, Poka, Barlay, Takacs, Hungarian State Op. Ch. and O, Gardelli.

Gardelli conducts a beautifully paced reading, marked by effective characterization from the Hungarian cast (suggesting stage experience) and vivid, lifelike digital sound. Ilona Tokody makes an attractively girlish-sounding Angelica, but above the stave her voice is shrill. The Zia Principessa of Eszter Poka is breathy and wobbly and not even formidable, the one unconvincing characterization.

Still recommended: As with *Gianni Schicchi*, Maazel's CBS recording is the strongest on record, although in the UK it is only available within *Il Trittico* – see below. In the USA, it is still also available separately ([M 34505]).

Tosca (complete).
❀ *** HMV **CDS 747175-8** [id.]; EX 290039-3/*5* (2) [Ang. BLX/*4X2X* 3508]. Callas, Di Stefano, Gobbi, Calabrese, La Scala Milan Ch. and O, De Sabata.
*** DG **413 815-2**; 2707 121/*3370 033* (2) [id.]. Ricciarelli, Carreras, Raimondi, Corena, German Op. Ch., BPO, Karajan.
*** Ph. **412 885-2** (2) [id.]. Caballé, Carreras, Wixell, ROHCG Ch. and O, Sir Colin Davis.

There has never been a finer recorded performance of *Tosca* than Callas's first, with Victor de Sabata conducting and Tito Gobbi as Scarpia. One mentions the prima donna first because, in this of all roles, she was able to identify totally with the heroine and turn her into a great tragic figure, not merely the cipher of Sardou's original melodrama. Gobbi too makes the unbelievably villainous police chief into a genuinely three-dimensional character, and Di Stefano as the hero, Cavaradossi, was at his finest. The conducting of De Sabata is spaciously lyrical as well as sharply dramatic, and the recording (originally mono, here stereo transcription) is superbly balanced in Walter Legge's fine production. The CD remastering brings an extension of range at both ends of the spectrum, with a firm, full bass to balance the extra brightness and clarity in the treble. Though there is inevitably less spaciousness than in a real stereo recording, there is no lack of bloom even on the violins, and the voices are gloriously caught. Only in the big *Te Deum* scene at the end of Act I does the extra clarity reveal a hint of congestion, and this is minimal. One's only real complaint is the absence of comprehensive cueing throughout the set.

Karajan's alternative, superbly unified reading for DG presents *Tosca* as very grand opera indeed, melodrama at its most searingly powerful. For Karajan, the police chief, Scarpia, seems to be the central character, and his unexpected choice of singer, a full bass, Raimondi, helps to show why, for this is no small-time villain but a man who in full confidence has a vein of nobility in him – as in the *Te Deum* at the end of Act II or the closing passage of the big solo addressed to Tosca, *Già mi dicon venal.* Detailed illumination of words is most powerful, and Karajan's coaching is evident too in the contribution of Katia Ricciarelli –

another singer who had not taken the role on stage before the recording. She is not the most individual of Toscas, but the beauty of singing is consistent, with *Vissi d'arte* outstanding at a very slow tempo indeed. Carreras is also subjected to slow Karajan tempi in his big arias and, though the recording brings out an unevenness in the voice (this is not as sweet a sound as in the performance he recorded with Sir Colin Davis for Philips), it is still a powerful, stylish one. The recording is rich and full, with the stage picture clearly established and the glorious orchestral textures beautifully caught. The difference between LPs and tapes is only marginal (the discs are fractionally sharper in focus). The CD transfer improves definition further but also, and more importantly, increases the feeling of spaciousness, putting more air round the voices and adding bloom to the orchestral sound. The wide dynamic range, however, means that care has to be taken to select a playing level which strikes a compromise between general immediacy and containment of the expansive climaxes. There are 15 separate cues on the first CD, 16 on the second.

Pacing the music naturally and sympathetically, Sir Colin Davis proves a superb Puccinian, one who not only presents Puccini's drama with richness and force but gives the score the musical strength of a great symphony. Davis rarely if ever chooses idiosyncratic tempi, and his manner is relatively straight; but it remains a strong and understanding reading, as well as a refreshing one. In this the quality of the singing from a cast of unusual consistency plays an important part. Caballé may not be as sharply jealous a heroine as her keenest rivals, but with the purity of *Vissi d'arte* coming as a key element in her interpretation, she still presents Tosca as a formidable siren-figure ('*Mia sirena*' being Cavaradossi's expression of endearment). Carreras reinforces his reputation as a tenor of unusual artistry as well as of superb vocal powers. Though Wixell is not ideally well focused as Scarpia, not at all Italianate of tone, he presents a completely credible lover-figure, not just the lusting ogre of convention. The 1976 analogue recording is full as well as refined, bringing out the beauties of Puccini's scoring. It is given a strikingly successful CD transfer, with three-dimensional placing of voices. The overall effect is more consistent and certainly more spacious than on the remastered Karajan set – especially noticeable at the big choral climax at the end of Act I.

Il Trittico: (i) *Il Tabarro;* (ii) *Suor Angelica;* (iii) *Gianni Schicchi.*

**(*) CBS 79312 (3) [Col. M3 35912]. Maazel, (i; ii) Scotto, (i; iii) Domingo, (i) Wixell, Sénéchal, (ii) Horne, (ii; iii) Cotrubas, (iii) Gobbi, Amb. Op. Ch., (ii) Desborough School Ch., (i; ii) Nat. PO, (iii) LSO.

(M) ** Decca 411 665-1/*4* (3). Tebaldi, Del Monaco, Simionato, Merrill, Corena, Maggio Musicale Fiorentino Ch. and O, Gardelli.

Puccini's three one-Act operas show him musically and dramatically at the peak of his achievement. They are balanced like the movements of a concerto: *Il Tabarro*, sombre in its portrait of the cuckolded bargemaster, but made attractive by the vividness of the atmosphere and the sweetness of the love music; *Suor Angelica*, a lyrical slow movement with its picture of a nunnery, verging on the syrupy but never quite falling; *Gianni Schicchi*, easily the most brilliant and witty one-Act comedy in the whole field of opera.

Hearing Maazel's performances of the three *Trittico* operas together underlines his consistency. *Il Tabarro* may most seriously lack atmosphere, but his directness is certainly refreshing, and in the other two operas it results in powerful readings; the opening of *Gianni Schicchi*, for example, has a sharp, almost Stravinskian bite. In the first two operas, Scotto's performances have a commanding dominance, presenting her at her finest. In *Gianni Schicchi* the veteran Tito Gobbi gives an amazing performance, in almost every way as fine as his HMV recording of twenty years earlier – and in some ways this is even more compelling. The generally close recording has a pleasantly full range.

On grounds of recording, the alternative Decca set is very impressive, but the performances are more variable. Fernando Corena's Schicchi is too coarse-grained, both vocally and dramatically. This is buffo-bass style with too much parlando 'acting' and Gobbi is to be preferred every time. Neither is Tebaldi entirely at home in the open-eyed part of the young Lauretta, though she sings *O mio babbino caro* very sweetly. She is more at home in the role of Sister Angelica and gives a rich-voiced and affecting portrayal, only slightly troubled by the top notes at the end. Simionato makes a fine firm Zia Principessa; one can really believe in her relentlessness, while Gardelli keeps the performance moving gently but firmly, and in a somewhat static piece this is most important. The scene of *Il Tabarro* is set on a barge on the banks of the Seine, in Paris, and though the Decca recording captures all of Puccini's background effects the result has not so much a Parisian flavour as the acoustic of an empty opera-house. Merrill sings very strongly as the cuckolded bargemaster, and Tebaldi and del Monaco are good in a conventional, whole-hogging Italian way. The recording has been effectively remastered and sounds a shade drier than when first issued, but voices are vivid and the sense of atmosphere remains. The tapes are particularly successful, and are consistently clear in focus.

Turandot (complete).

*** Decca **414 274-2** (2) [id.]; SET 561-3/*K2 A2* (3/2) [Lon. OSA/*5*- 13108]. Sutherland, Pavarotti, Caballé, Pears, Ghiaurov, Alldis Ch., Wandsworth School Boys' Ch., LPO, Mehta.

*** DG Dig. **410 096-2**; 2741/*3382* 013 (3) [id.]. Ricciarelli, Domingo, Hendricks, Raimondi, V. State Op. Ch., V. Boys' Ch., VPO, Karajan.

** CBS **M2K 39160** (2); 13M/*13T* 39160 (3) [id.]. Marton, Ricciarelli, Carreras, Kerns, V. State Op. Ch. and O, Maazel.

On compact disc (two CDs, well banded, as opposed to three LPs) the Mehta set, in vividness, clarity and immediacy of sound, brings an astonishing tribute to Decca engineering in the early 1970s. In every way it outshines the later digital recordings of Karajan and Maazel, and the reading remains supreme. The role of Turandot, the icy princess, is not one that you would expect to be in Joan Sutherland's repertory, but here on record she gives an intensely revealing and appealing interpretation, making the character far more human and sympathetic than ever before. This is a character, armoured and unyielding in *In questa reggia*, whose final capitulation to love is a natural development, not an incomprehensible switch. Sutherland's singing is strong and beautiful, while Pavarotti gives a performance equally imaginative, beautiful in sound, strong on detail. To set Caballé against Sutherland was a daring idea, and it works superbly well; Pears as the Emperor is another imaginative choice. Mehta directs a gloriously rich and dramatic performance, superlatively recorded; on tape, too, the sound is richly atmospheric and deals with the moments of spectacle without strain.

Karajan takes a characteristically spacious view of Puccini's last opera. His tempi are regularly slower than those in rival versions, yet his concentration is irresistible and he relishes the exotic colourings of the sound, just as he puts an unusual slant on the vocal colouring as well as the dramatic balance by his distinctive casting of the two contrasted heroines. Both the Liù of Barbara Hendricks and the Turandot of Katia Ricciarelli are more sensuously feminine than is usual. With her seductively golden tone, Hendricks is almost a sex-kitten, and one wonders how Calaf could ever have overlooked her. This is very different from the usual picture of a chaste slave-girl. Ricciarelli is a far more vulnerable figure than one expects of the icy princess, and the very fact that the part strains her beyond reasonable vocal limits adds to the dramatic point, even if it subtracts from the musical joys. By contrast, Placido Domingo is vocally superb, a commanding prince; and the rest of the cast presents star names even in small roles. The sound is full and brilliant, if at times rather close in the manner of DG engineers working in the Berlin Philharmonie. Ensemble is not always quite as flawless as one expects of Karajan with Berlin forces, though significantly the challenge of the manifestly less inspired completion of Alfano has him working at white heat. Admirably laid out on three cassettes – one to each Act – the chrome-tape set offers DG's finest quality, clear, with natural perspectives (witness the opening of Act III) and the widest dynamic range. The climaxes have great impact. Even finer are the compact discs which bring added presence, although not all ears will find the balance completely satisfactory.

Turandot brings the warmest and most sensuous performance in Maazel's Puccini series, thanks in good measure to its being a live recording, made in September 1983 at the Vienna State Opera House. Applause and stage noises are often distracting, and the clarity of CD tends to make one notice them the more. Recording balances are often odd, with Carreras – in fine voice – suffering in both directions, sometimes disconcertingly distant, at others far too close. Karajan's Turandot here becomes Liù, and the result is predictably heavyweight, though the beat in her voice is only rarely apparent. The strengths and shortcomings of Eva Marton as the icy princess come out at the very start of *In questa reggia*. The big, dramatic voice is well controlled, but there is too little variation of tone, dynamic or expression; she rarely shades her voice down. In the closing Act, during the Alfano completion, Marton's confidence and command grow impressively, with her heroic tone ever more thrilling. Recommendable to those who relish a live performance. Annoyingly, the CDs contain no bands within the Acts. There are excellent chrome cassettes, lavishly produced.

Arias: *La Bohème: Quando m'en vo' soletta. Gianni Schicchi: O mio babbino caro. Madama Butterfly: Un bel dì. Manon Lescaut: In quelle trine morbide. La Rondine: Chi il bel sogno. Tosca: Vissi d'arte. Le Villi: Se come voi.*
*** CBS Dig. **CD 37298**; 37298/*40*- [id.]. Kiri Te Kanawa, LPO, Pritchard – VERDI: Arias.***

The creamy beauty of Kiri Te Kanawa's voice is ideally suited to these seven lyrical arias – including rarities like the little waltz-like song from *Le Villi.* Expressive sweetness is more remarkable than characterization, but in such music, well recorded, and sounding especially believable on CD, who would ask for more? The chrome tape is transferred at a low level, which leaves the voice sounding pure and natural but does not afford a great deal of presence to the orchestra, which is backwardly balanced in relation to the voice.

Arias: *Manon Lescaut: Cortese damigella . . . Donna non vidi mai; Presto! In filia! . . . Guardate, pazzo son. Turandot: Non piangere Liù . . . Ah! Per l'ultima volta; Nessun dorma.*
*** DG Dig. **413 785-2**; 413 785-1/*4* [id.]. Placido Domingo – VERDI: Arias.***

These Puccini items, taken, like the Verdi, from earlier recordings made by Domingo for DG, make a fine heroic supplement, when he was challenged to some of his finest, most imaginative singing by Sinopoli and Karajan. The sound is consistently vivid in all three media.

'Heroines': (i) *La Bohème: Musetta's waltz song;* (ii) *Sì, mi chiamano Mimì.* (iii) *Edgar: D'ogni dolor.* (i) *Gianni Schicchi: O mio babino caro. Madama Butterfly: Un bel dì. Manon Lescaut: In quelle trine morbide;* (iii) *Sola perduta abbandonata.* (i) *La Rondine: Chi il bel sogno di Doretta.* (iii) *Suor Angelica: Senza mamma, o bimbo.* (i) *Tosca: Vissi d'arte.* (iv) *Turandot: Tu che di gel sei cinta* (Death of Liù)*;* (v) *In questa reggia.* (i) *Le Villi: Se come voi.*
(*) CBS **MK 39097; M/*MT* 39097 [id.]. (i) Kiri Te Kanawa; (ii) Ileana Cotrubas; (iii) Renata Scotto; (iv) Katia Ricciarelli; (v) Eva Marton; (iv; v) José Carreras.

The CBS compilation of Puccini 'heroines' neatly gathers together some fine performances out of its series of complete Puccini opera sets, plus other items such as the two *Bohème* arias taken from recitals. Vocally these are not always immaculate performances, but the quintet of sopranos represented is exceptionally characterful, contrasting strongly with one another, where Puccini recitals from a single soprano can lack variety. However, the layout does not make as much as possible of the interplay of different voices, as Kiri Te Kanawa's seven contributions are all placed together at the start of the collection. They come from her recital with Pritchard – see above – and have the character of concert performances. Ileana Cotrubas's assumption of Mimi has greater feeling of the opera-house; other highlights include Katia Ricciarelli's *Death of Liù* and Renata Scotto's beautiful *Senza mamma* from *Suor Angelica.* The thrilling climax of *In questa reggia* (Eva Marton and José Carreras) is spoiled by a fade-out at the end, particularly unfortunate as it is the closing item. The CD gives the voices plenty of presence, but the variations in ambience and balance are made the more striking.

Purcell, Henry (1658–95)

Come, ye Sons of Art; Funeral music for Queen Mary (1695).
*** Erato **ECD 88071**; STU/*MCE* 70911 [id.]. Lott, Brett, Williams, Allen, Monteverdi Ch. and O, Equale Brass Ens., Gardiner.

Come, ye Sons of Art, the most celebrated of Purcell's birthday odes for Queen Mary, is splendidly coupled here with the unforgettable funeral music he wrote on the death of the same monarch. With the Monteverdi Choir at its most incisive and understanding, the performances are exemplary, and the recording, though balanced in favour of the instruments, is clear and refined. Among the soloists Thomas Allen is outstanding, while the two counter-tenors give charming performance of the duet, *Sound the trumpet*. The *Funeral music* includes the well-known *Solemn march* for trumpets and drums, a *Canzona* and simple anthem given at the funeral, and two of Purcell's most magnificent anthems setting the *Funeral sentences*. There is a good cassette: the *Funeral music* on side two sounds especially impressive on tape, with sonorous brass and a good choral focus.

Ode on St Cecilia's Day (*Hail! bright Cecilia*).
(*) Erato Dig. **ECD 88046; NUM/*MCE* 75049. Jennifer Smith, Stafford, Gordon, Elliott, Varcoe, David Thomas, Monteverdi Ch., E. Bar. Soloists, Eliot Gardiner.

Gardiner's characteristic vigour and alertness in Purcell come out superbly in this delightful record of the 1692 *St Cecilia Ode* – not as well known as some of the other odes he wrote, but a masterpiece. Soloists and chorus are outstanding even by Gardiner's high standards, and the recording excellent. The transfer to CD is made at a very high level and there is a degree of roughness in the sound when the trumpets enter. This effect is also noticeable on the cassette.

Songs: *Ah! cruel nymph; As Amoret and Thirsis lay; The fatal hour; I lov'd fair Celia; Pious Celinda.* Elegies: *Upon the death of Mr Thomas Farmer; Upon the death of Queen Mary.* Arias: *Hail bright Cecilia: 'Tis Nature's voice. History of Dioclesian: Since from my dear Astrea's sight. History of King Richard II: Retir'd from any mortal's sight. Oedipus: Music for a while. Pausanias: Sweeter than roses.*
(*) Accent **ACC 57802D; ACC 7802 [id.]. René Jacobs, W. Kuijken, K. Jünghanel.

René Jacobs's distinctive counter-tenor is well suited to Purcell; with unusually wide range, he sings this selection, weighted in favour of solemn songs, very beautifully – if with too little feeling for variety of mood. The most ambitious song is the elegy on the death of Queen Mary to Latin words, a superb piece too little known. First-rate recording.

Songs: *Ah! How sweet it is to love; The earth trembled; An evening hymn; If music be the food of love; I'll sail upon the dog star; I see she flies me ev'rywhere; Let the night perish; Lord, what is man; Morning hymn; A new ground.* Arias: *Birthday ode for Queen Mary: Crown the altar. Bonduca: Oh! Lead me to some peaceful gloom. History of Dioclesian: Since from my dear Astrea's sight. The Indian Queen: I attempt from love's sickness to fly. The Mock marriage: Man that is for woman made. Oedipus: Music for a while. Pausanias: Sweeter than roses. The Rival sisters: Take not a woman's anger ill.*
*** ASV ALH/*ZCALH* 963 [id.]. Ian Partridge, George Malcolm.

Appropriately titled 'Sweeter than Roses', this is a warmly sympathetic collection of favourite Purcell songs from a tenor whose honeyed tones are ideally suited to recording. The style smoother than we have come to expect latterly – this is a reissue of an earlier Enigma issue – but with ever-sensitive accompaniment from George Malcolm, who also contributes one brief solo, this is an excellent recommendation for those who resist the new style of authenticity. Atmospheric recording, with the voice well forward. There is an outstandingly faithful cassette, with the voice caught in its presence and natural bloom and the harpsichord image believable and nicely focused.

Songs and airs: *Bess of Bedlam; Evening hymn; If music be the food of love; Lovely, lovely Albina; Not all my torments; Olinda in the shades unseen; The Plaint; O, Urge me no more; When first Amintas sued for a kiss.* Arias: *Birthday ode for Queen Mary: Crown the altar. The Fairy Queen: Hark! hark!; O, O let me weep; Ye gentle spirits of the air. The Indian Queen: I attempt from love's sickness to fly. Pausanias: Sweeter than roses. The Tempest: Dear pritty youths. Timon of Athens: The cares of lovers.*
ϵ *** O-L Dig. **417 123-2** [id.]; DSLO/*KDSLC* 713. Kirkby, Rooley, Hogwood.

The purity of Emma Kirkby's soprano – as delightful to some ears as it is disconcerting to others – suits this wide-ranging collection of Purcell songs splendidly, though you might argue for a bigger, warmer voice in the *Bess of Bedlam* song. The *Evening hymn* is radiantly done, and so are many of the less well-known airs which regularly bring new revelation. Excellent recording, if with the voice forward, given striking extra presence on CD. The chrome cassette is superbly managed, the voice sounding every bit as fresh as on LP, and the accompaniments naturally balanced and clear.

Songs: *Come, let us drink; A health to the nut brown lass; If ever I more riches; I gave her cakes and I gave her ale; Laudate Ceciliam; The miller's daughter; Of all the instruments; Once, twice, thrice I Julia tried; Prithee ben't so sad and serious;*

Since time so kind to us does prove; Sir Walter enjoying his damsel; 'Tis women makes us love; Under this stone; Young John the gard'ner.
*** HM **HMC 90242**; HM/*40* 242 [id.]. Deller Cons., Deller.

One section of this charming and stylish collection has a selection of Purcell's catches, some of them as lewd as rugby-club songs of today, others as refined as *Under this stone* – all of which the Deller Consort take in their stride. The final two pieces are extended items; *If ever I more riches*, a setting of Cowley, has some striking passages. The remastering for CD has greatly improved the sound, with voices fresh and first-rate recording of the instruments. There is a good cassette.

Songs: *The fatal hour comes on apace; Lord, what is man?; Love's power in my heart; More love or more disdain I crave; Now that the sun hath veiled his light; The Queen's Epicedium; Sleep, Adam, sleep; Thou wakeful shepherd; Who can behold Florella's charms.* Arias: *History of Dioclesian: Since from my dear Astrea's sight. The Indian Queen: I attempt from love's sickness to fly. King Arthur: Fairest isle. Oedipus: Music for a while. Pausanias: Sweeter than roses. The Rival Sisters: Take not a woman's anger ill. Rule a wife and have a wife: There's not a swain.*
*** Etcetera Dig. **KTC 1013**; ETC/*XTC* 1013 [id.]. Andrew Dalton; Uittenbosch; Borstlap.

Andrew Dalton has an exceptionally beautiful counter-tenor voice, creamy even in its upper register to make the extended '*Hallelujahs*' of *Lord, what is man?* and *Now that the sun* even more heavenly than usual. One side has sacred songs, some of them less well known, the other secular, including various favourites. Many of them require transposition, but only in some of the soprano songs such as *Fairest isle* does that distract. A delightful disc, well recorded.

STAGE WORKS AND THEATRE MUSIC

Dido and Aeneas (complete).
*** Ph. Dig. **416 299-2**; 416 299-1/*4* [id.]. Norman, McLaughlin, Kern, Allen, Power, ECO and Ch., Leppard.
*** Chan. Dig. **CHAN 8306**; ABRD/*ABTD* 1034 [id.]. Kirkby, Nelson, Thomas, Taverner Ch. and Players, Parrott.
*(*) Tel. Dig. **ZK8 42919**; AZ6/*CX4* 42919 [id.]. Yakar, Murray, Scharinger, Schmidt, Köstlinger, Gardow, Schoenberg Ch., VCM, Harnoncourt.

'Like *Tristan und Isolde* in a pint pot', says Raymond Leppard of *Dido and Aeneas*, here providing crisply disciplined backing for the most magnificently expansive rendering of *Dido* since Kirsten Flagstad recorded it over thirty years ago. Authenticists should keep away, but Jessye Norman amply proves that this amazingly compressed setting of the epic *Aeneid* story has a dramatic depth and intensity to compare with Berlioz's setting – or, for that matter, with Wagner's

Tristan. The opening phrase of *Ah Belinda* brings the most controversial moment, when Norman slows luxuriantly. But from then on the security and dark intensity of her singing make for a memorable performance, heightened in the recitatives by the equally commanding singing of Thomas Allen as Aeneas. The range of expression is very wide – with Jessye Norman producing an agonized whisper in the recitative just before Dido's *Lament* – but the unauthentic element must not be exaggerated. By most yardsticks this is finely poised and stylish singing, even if in the last resort Norman cannot match Dame Janet Baker in conveying the aching vulnerability of the love-lorn Dido. Marie McLaughlin is a pure-toned Belinda, Patrick Power a heady-toned Sailor, singing his song in a West Country accent, while Patricia Kern repeats her performance as the Sorceress, using conventionally sinister expression. The warm-toned counter-tenor, Derek Ragin, makes the Spirit Messenger into an eerie, other-worldly figure. Leppard's direction this time is a degree plainer and more direct than it was in his Erato version, again with some slow speeds for choruses. Excellent recording in all three formats.

Andrew Parrott's concept of a performance on original instruments has one immediately thinking back to the atmosphere of Josias Priest's school for young ladies where Purcell's masterpiece was first given. The voices enhance that impression, not least Emma Kirkby's fresh, bright soprano, here recorded without too much edge but still very young-sounding. It is more questionable to have a soprano singing the tenor role of the Sailor in Act III; but anyone who fancies the idea of an authentic performance need not hesitate. The compact disc is exceptionally refined, the sound well focused, with analogue atmosphere yet with detail enhanced. The tape transfer, too, is fresh and clean, retaining the recording's bloom. There is just the faintest hint of peaking on one or two of Miss Kirkby's high notes.

Harnoncourt's idiosyncratic rhythmic style in Purcell, often in exaggerated marcato, as well as his extreme speeds in both directions, undermines the effectiveness of the whole performance, presenting the authentic view far less imaginatively than the Parrott set on Chandos. Ann Murray sings beautifully as Dido, but has to struggle against the funereal speed for the *Lament*. The chorus is excellent, and the other soloists consistently good, well trained in English but still distractingly foreign-sounding, even the heady-toned sailor of Josef Köstlinger. Rachel Yakar is an agile Belinda, but she does not always blend well with Dido, and Trudeliese Schmidt a resonant, fire-eating Sorceress.

Still recommended: No doubt Decca have plans to transfer one of the two recordings starring Dame Janet Baker to compact disc, either the famous 1962 Oiseau-Lyre version which established her as a recording star of the front rank (O-L SOL 60047 [id.]) or the mature Decca account, made sixteen years later with Peter Pears and Norma Burrowes (Decca SET/*KCET* 615 [Lon. OSA/*5*-1170]).

King Arthur (complete).

*** Erato **ECD 880562**; STU/*MCE* 751272 (2) [id.]. Jennifer Smith, Gillian Fischer, Priday, Ross, Stafford, Elliott, Varcoe, E. Bar. Soloists, Eliot Gardiner.

It is a tragedy that this magnificent work presents such difficulties of staging, not to mention textual problems, that it is unlikely to be given publicly as often as it deserves. Gardiner, with his combination of stylishness and electricity of the highest voltage, presents a performance on record which in almost every way provides the clear modern answer. *King Arthur* may be cumbersome on stage, but here its episodic nature matters hardly at all; one can simply relish the wealth of sharply inspired and colourful numbers. Gardiner's solutions to the textual problems carry complete conviction, as for example his placing of the superb *Chaconne in F* at the end instead of the start. Solo singing for the most part is excellent, with Stephen Varcoe outstanding among the men. As the Cold Genius he helps Gardiner to make the Frost scene far more effective than usual. He is also one of the trio that give a delightfully roistering account of *Harvest home*. *Fairest isle* is treated very gently after that, with Gill Ross, boyish of tone, reserved just for that number. Throughout, the chorus is characteristically fresh and vigorous, and the instrumentalists marry authentic technique to pure, unabrasive sounds beautifully. The recording vividly captures a performance in an aptly intimate but not dry acoustic, with the cueing of the CD making it very convenient to use.

Quilter, Roger (1877–1953)

A children's overture.
(M) (***) HMV mono EX 290107-3/5 (2). Hallé O, Barbirolli – BAX: *Symphony No. 3*; IRELAND: *Forgotten rite* etc.; DELIUS: *Aquarelles*.(***)

It seems extraordinary that the only available recording of Roger Quilter's highly engaging *Children's overture* should be Barbirolli's affectionate version recorded with the Hallé Orchestra in the 1940s. The sound is more obviously dated here than in the indispensable couplings, but the performance is marvellously fresh.

Rabaud, Henri (1873–1949)

La Procession nocturne, Op. 6.
*** Erato Dig. NUM 75052. Monte Carlo PO, Jordan – CHAUSSON: *Poème***; LEKEU: *Adagio for strings* etc.***

Henri Rabaud is best known as Fauré's successor at the Paris Conservatoire and as the composer of the opera *Marouf, savetier de Caire*. He made his début, however, as a symphonic writer with two symphonies and the present work, *La Procession nocturne*, which was inspired by the same literary theme as Liszt's *Die Nächtliche Zug*. It is an atmospheric piece with some most imaginative and effective writing in it. Neglected by the gramophone since the composer's own recording, it is well performed here and, like the Lekeu with which it is coupled, is a most valuable addition to the catalogue.

Rachmaninov, Sergei (1873–1943)

Piano concerto No. 2 in C min., Op. 18.
*** DG **415 119-2** [id.]. Sviatoslav Richter, Warsaw PO, Wislocki – PROKOFIEV: *Concerto No. 5.****
*** Decca Dig. **414 348-2**; 414 348-1/*4* [id.]. Ortiz, RPO, Atzmon – ADDINSELL: *Warsaw concerto*; LITOLFF: *Scherzo*; GOTTSCHALK: *Grande fantaisie.****
(*) Decca Dig. **414 475-2; 414 475-1/*4* [id.]. Ashkenazy, Concg. O, Haitink – *Concerto No. 4.****

The power and authority of Richter's performance of Rachmaninov's most popular piano concerto remain totally commanding; the digital remastering of the mid-1960s recording for CD has firmed up the orchestral image and increased the feeling of presence for the boldly realistic piano timbre. Richter has strong, even controversial ideas about speeds in this concerto. The long opening melody of the first movement is taken abnormally slowly, and it is only the sense of mastery which Richter conveys in every note which prevents one from complaining. One ends by admitting how convincing that speed can be in Richter's hands; away from the magic, however, one realizes that this is not quite the way Rachmaninov himself intended it. The slow movement too is spacious – with complete justification this time – and the opening of the finale lets the floodgates open the other way, for Richter chooses a hair-raisingly fast allegro, which has the Polish players, scampering after him as fast as they are able. Richter does not, however, let himself be rushed in the great secondary melody, so this is a reading of vivid contrasts. The coupling is Richter's classic account of Prokofiev's *Fifth Concerto*, so this CD combines two of Richter's very finest performances for the gramophone.

Cristina Ortiz's account has the advantage of splendid Decca digital sound. Recorded in Walthamstow Assembly Hall, the piano is realistically distanced and, although the ambience is resonant, the orchestral layout is believable, with attractively rich string textures and an excitingly expansive dynamic range. The performance is warmly romantic, the first-movement climax satisfyingly expansive and the *Adagio* glowingly poetic, with the orchestral response under Atzmon matching the sensibility of the solo playing. A similarly successful partnership in the finale brings sparklingly nimble articulation from Ortiz and a fine expressive breadth from the strings in the famous lyrical melody. The CD offers a subtle extra degree of presence, although the reverberation means that detail is not always sharply registered.

Unfortunately, Ashkenazy's new account cannot quite match his hauntingly poetic earlier reading with Previn. The opening theme is a touch ponderous this time, and elsewhere too the yearning passion of the work is rather muted, even in the lovely reprise of the main theme in the slow movement, which sounds much cooler than in the hands of Cristina Ortiz. Those reservations are relative; admirers of Ashkenazy who fancy this generous coupling with the *Fourth Con-*

certo, about which there are no reservations, need not be too hesitant. The Decca sound is excellent, especially on CD, but the cassette too is first class. The Amsterdam acoustic makes the strings sound wonderfully warm and sumptuous.

(i) *Piano concerto No. 2 in C min.;* (ii) *Preludes Nos 3 in B flat; 8 in C min., Op. 23/2 and 7; 13 in B flat min., Op. 32/2.*
(B) ** DG Walkman *413 850-4* [id.]. (i) Vásáry, LSO, Ahronovich; (ii) Sviatoslav Richter – LISZT: *Concertos Nos 1 and 2* etc.**(*)

Vásáry and Ahronovich make quite an effective partnership in the *C minor Concerto* and the performance of the first movement has a fine climax. But after that the voltage is lower and the *Adagio* does not distil the degree of poetry which makes the Ashkenazy/Previn analogue account so beautiful (this couples both *First* and *Second Concertos* in performances of the highest distinction; on balance, the finest available versions of both works: Decca SXL/*KSXC* 6554 [Lon. CS/*5-* 6774]). Vásáry's DG recording is bold and colourful, but the piano timbre is drier for Richter's masterly performances of the three *Preludes* which are used as a makeweight on this generously full Walkman chrome cassette.

Piano concerto No. 2; Rhapsody on a theme of Paganini, Op. 43.
(B) *** CfP Dig. CFP/*TC-CFP* 4383. Tirimo, Philh. O, Levi.
*** HMV Dig. EL 270103-1/*4* [Ang. DS/*4DS* 38087]. Ousset, CBSO, Rattle.
(M) ** Ph. Seq. 6527/*7311* 208. Orozco, RPO, De Waart.
(M) ** EMI Dig. EMX 41 2083-1/*4*. Fowke, RPO, Temirkanov.
*(*) CBS Dig. **CD 38672**; 38672/*40-* [id.]. Cécile Licad, Chicago SO, Abbado.

Concentrated and thoughtful, deeply expressive yet never self-indulgent, Tirimo is outstanding in both the *Concerto* and the *Rhapsody*, making this the most desirable version of this favourite coupling, irrespective of price. Speeds for the outer movements of the *Concerto* are on the fast side, yet Tirimo's feeling for natural rubato makes them sound natural, never breathless, while the sweetness and repose of the middle movement are exemplary. The digital recording is clear, brilliant and well balanced. An outstanding bargain, with disc and cassette very close in sound-quality.

Cécile Ousset gives powerful, red-blooded performances of both works in the grand manner, warmly supported by Simon Rattle and the CBSO. Her rubato may often be extreme, but it never sounds studied, always convincingly spontaneous, though the big melody of the eighteenth variation is on the heavyweight side. Ousset is second to none in urgency and excitement, brought out the more here by extreme range of dynamic, with the opening of both the first two movements of the *Concerto* intensely hushed and poetic. The EMI recording copes well with that extreme range, but the inner textures are not ideally clear.

Rafael Orozco is a fine player and an understanding Rachmaninovian, and he is sympathetically accompanied by the RPO under Edo de Waart. The *Rhapsody* (also available on an 'On Tour' compilation – see below) is vividly characterized, and the slow movement of the *Concerto* is eloquently expressive. The recording too is good. But Tirimo's performances on Classics for Pleasure are even finer.

Philip Fowke gives tasteful, well-mannered performances, ultimately lacking the fire and bravura needed in both these display works. With good modern digital recording and an excellent matching tape, it makes a generous bargain – but from the same source on the even cheaper CfP label is Martino Tirimo's excellent coupling of the same two works, also in first-rate digital sound and with more red-blooded performances.

Cécile Licad opens the *Concerto* very squarely, with slow deliberation, the superfine Chicago orchestra sounding heavyweight, almost Germanic. The climax is well built but, at its peak, rhythmic articulation again seems heavy. The slow movement is diffuse, and Licad does not match her finest rivals in intensity of poetic feeling. At a fast speed, the finale is brilliant and exciting, but no more so than in rival versions. The *Rhapsody* also suffers from an absence of sparkle, and the earlier variations lack a feeling of momentum. At the eighteenth the performance comes to life, but overall this cannot compare with the best versions of this much-recorded work. The recording is not sharply focused but is more tangible on CD and is pleasantly atmospheric, if in no way distinctive.

Piano concertos Nos (i) *2 in C min.;* (ii) *3 in D min.;* (iii) *Rhapsody on a theme of Paganini, Op. 43.*

(B) (***) Ph. On Tour *416 226-4* [id.]. (i; ii) Byron Janis, (i) Minneapolis SO; (ii) LSO; (i; ii) Dorati; (iii) Orozco, RPO, De Waart.

This potential bargain in Philips's 'On Tour' series is all but ruined by misguided engineering. Byron Janis established himself at the beginning of the 1960s as a Rachmaninovian of distinction and made outstanding Mercury recordings of both the *Second* and *Third Concertos*. At that time, Mercury were experimenting with the use of 35-mm film instead of tape for their master recording, and this led to a higher level of background noise alongside higher fidelity and a wider dynamic range. Once before in the mid-1960s Philips tried to filter this out with disastrous results. For the present reissue they have made the same mistake and robbed the orchestral sound of much of its life. Byron Janis's account of the *Second Concerto* is splendidly full-blooded and can rank alongside the finest. The playing is full of conviction and always sounds spontaneous. His performance of the *Third* is unsurpassed in the present catalogue by any other version, save those of Horowitz. In both works Dorati is very much an equal partner, but the limitation on the upper frequencies damps down the orchestral response. This is all the more noticeable when the *Rhapsody on a theme of Paganini* opens, with its extended treble and natural brilliance adding to the vitality of Orozco's brilliant playing.

Still recommended: The Janis/Dorati recordings remain available separately in undoctored sound and can be strongly recommended. No. 2 is coupled with the Tchaikovsky *Piano concerto No. 1* (Mercury SRI/*MRI* 75032) and No. 3 is on Mercury SRI/*MRI* 75068. In both cases discs and equivalent tapes are closely matched.

Piano concerto No. 3 in D min., Op. 30.
*(**) RCA **RD 82633 [RCD1 2633**; CRL1/*CRK1* 2633]. Horowitz, NYPO, Ormandy.
❀ (M) (***) RCA mono Gold GL/*GK* 85272. Horowitz, RCA SO, Reiner.
(*) Decca Dig. **414 671-2 [id.]; SXDL/*KSXDC* 7609 [Lon. LDR/*5*- 71109]. Bolet, LSO, Fischer.
*(*) HMV Dig. **CDC 747031-2** [id.]; EL 270020-1/*4* [Ang. DS/*4DS* 38105]. Sgouros, BPO, Simonov.

(i) *Piano concerto No. 3; Prelude in C sharp min., Op. 3/2; Vocalise, Op. 34/14* (arr. Kocsis).
** Ph. Dig. 412 213-1/*4* [id.]. Kocsis, (i) San Francisco SO, De Waart.

Piano concertos Nos 3; 4 in G, Op. 40.
*(**) Ph. Dig. **411 475-2** [id.]. Kocsis, San Francisco SO, De Waart.

Horowitz's legendary association with Rachmaninov's *D minor Concerto* daunted even the composer. Horowitz made it virtually his own property over half a century. Inevitably there are rosy memories of his first 78 r.p.m. recording with Albert Coates, but in most respects the mono LP, made in Carnegie Hall in May 1951, represents the highwater mark of his achievement. In January 1978 he was persuaded to re-record the work in stereo, again in Carnegie Hall, but this time at a live concert, with Ormandy drawing a committed and romantically expansive accompaniment from the New York Philharmonic Orchestra. Perhaps just a little of the old magic is missing in the solo playing but it remains prodigious, and Horowitz's insights are countless. The outer movements have undoubted electricity and there is a powerful climax to the *Adagio*, but it is the fascination of the detail that draws one back to this remarkable recorded document. Not all the playing is immaculate and there is some rhythmic eccentricity in the finale; but the communicative force of the reading is unquestionable. The snag is the recording, which was originally very dry and clinical, the piano timbre lacking bloom. For CD, the remastering has radically altered the sound-picture, considerably softening the focus, to bring a more romantic aura to the music making. The result is that at lower dynamic levels the image appears to recede, while the climaxes of the second and third movements expand very dramatically, with the rise in dynamic level immediately accompanied by a brighter, freer upper range. The effect is disconcerting – but one can adjust to it, and certainly the effect is more agreeable than the 'bare bones' of the original LP sound quality.

RCA have also reissued the 1951 mono version, on both LP and an excellent matching cassette. For many listeners, this provides an even more rewarding experience, even though the orchestral detail is at times all but masked by the forwardly balanced piano. But the partnership with Fritz Reiner (also at the height of his powers) is inspirational and, if the piano dominates the texture throughout, the strings sing their Rachmaninovian melodies with heart-warming lyrical fervour. The opening of the slow movement is ravishingly played; despite the occasionally subfusc wind focus and woolly bass, Reiner makes his orchestral presence felt in every bar. The opening statement of the main theme by the piano has a magical flowing simplicity and, for all the thrilling bravura of the first-movement cadenza and the breathtaking finale, it is Horowitz's expressive response that one remembers most. Within the ambience of the empty hall, the piano timbre, though less cleanly focused than in the later recording, blooms readily and every nuance of colour is telling. One readily forgives the compression and the limited sound, when so much that is memorable is revealed in the solo playing itself. Even more than the stereo version, this is one of the great recorded concerto performances of all times.

Bolet brings out the heroic side of this formidable concerto, and the recording of the piano – digitally bright to the point of clangorousness – underlines that. The clarity of articulation and bravura is breathtaking, but some of the work's romantic tenderness is lost, with the orchestra tending to sound aggressive; if anything, this is emphasized by the added presence of the CD.

Zoltán Kocsis's recording with Edo de Waart and the San Francisco Symphony has had a bad press and, in so far as he rushes through the first movement, deservedly so. All the same, there is some very exciting playing here – and he earns one listener's thanks for opting for the shorter cadenza in the first movement. This he plays with electrifying brilliance. The *Fourth Concerto* is a good deal less rushed, though it is full of excitement and virtuosity, when this is required. Indeed, there is much thrilling playing here, but there are moments in both concertos when one feels Kocsis should perhaps rein in his fiery high spirits. The Philips recording places him rather far forward but there is no lack of orchestral detail and there is plenty of range. On LP, the *C sharp minor Prelude* is placed before the *Third Concerto* and the *Vocalise* acts as a contrasting pendant, both effectively played; but one would not always want to hear the music in this order. There is a good, if not outstanding tape equivalent.

Dmitri Sgouros possesses an altogether remarkable technique – not only for his tender years but, one is tempted to say, for any age. It would be ungenerous not to give his first concerto recording a welcome, for much of the piano playing is pretty dazzling as such. But, however remarkable it may be for a boy of fifteen, the standards of the gramophone differ from those of the concert hall; much of the musical meaning seems to escape him and the bravura work often loses its meaning. Compare the main theme in the hands of a Rachmaninov or a Horowitz: it is evident that Sgouros is an artist of enormous facility and promise, rather than of fulfilment. He plays the second cadenza first recorded by Ashkenazy rather than the shorter one chosen by Rachmaninov himself. The recording itself is serviceable rather than distinguished. It is certainly not in the demonstration class, even in the compact disc format. The Berlin Philharmonic does not produce its characteristic rich string sonority for Yuri Simonov. Not a front runner.

Piano concerto No. 4 in G min., Op. 40.

*** Decca Dig. **414 475-2**; 414 475-1/*4* [id.]. Ashkenazy, Concg. O, Haitink – *Concerto No. 2.***(*)

Ashkenazy gives a superb account of the *Fourth Concerto*, strong and dramatic and warmly passionate, with Haitink and the Concertgebouw establishing the work as more positively characterful than is often appreciated. As in Michelangeli's classic account of the 1950s, this becomes far more than a poor relation of the earlier concertos. Splendid Decca sound, with the Concertgebouw acoustics making a warmly resonant framework, yet with the CD ensuring refinement of detail. The cassette too is of high quality.

The Isle of the Dead, Op. 29; Symphonic dances, Op. 45.
*** Decca Dig. **410 124-2**; 410 124-1/*4* [id.]. Concg. O, Ashkenazy.

The Isle of the Dead, Op. 29; Symphonic dances, Op. 45; Aleko: Intermezzo and Women's dance. Vocalise, Op. 34/14.
(M) *** HMV EG 290531-1/*4* [Ang. AM/*4AM* 34741]. LSO, Previn.

Symphonic dances, Op. 45; Aleko: Intermezzo. Vocalise, Op. 34/14.
(*) DG Dig. **410 894-2; 410 894-1/*4* [id.]. BPO, Maazel.

Ashkenazy's is a superb coupling, rich and powerful in playing and interpretation. One here recognizes *The Isle of the Dead* as among the very finest of Rachmaninov's orchestral works, relentless in its ominous build-up, while at generally fast speeds the *Symphonic dances* have extra darkness and intensity too, suggesting no relaxation whatever at the end of Rachmaninov's career. The splendid recording, especially fine on CD, but also ample and brilliant on LP and chrome cassette alike, highlights both the passion and the fine precision of the playing.

Previn's original full-priced issue (from 1976) offered the same coupling as Ashkenazy, but now it has been remastered, and the *Aleko* excerpts plus a fine, lyrical account of the *Vocalise* added, to make a generous mid-priced collection playing for over 70′. In Previn's hands the dark progress of Rachmaninov's scene-painting after Boecklin is given a slow formidable increase of tension, while the *Symphonic dances*, as with Ashkenazy, bring generally fast tempi and sharp rhythms to underline the vitality (and in the middle movement the dance-like flexibility). With full recording, now sounding rather drier than originally and not as subtle in detail as Ashkenazy's Decca, this is excellent value, with the encores used to lighten the mood after the tone poem. The cassette is well managed but has a more restricted upper range than the disc.

Maazel's is a crisp, light-textured reading of the *Symphonic dances*. Brilliance is there in plenty, but full warmth of lyricism is lacking, as it is too in the *Vocalise*. Bright, spacious recording, among the best made in the Philharmonie in Berlin. The chrome tape too is one of DG's finest, vivid and wide-ranging, yet with plenty of body. On compact disc the detail and focus of the sound are the more striking and the precision of ensemble is given added freshness and projection. But Maazel comes into competition with Ashkenazy, who offers an equally fine (if fascinatingly different) reading of the *Symphonic dances*, plus a much more substantial coupling.

Rhapsody on a theme of Paganini, Op. 43.
(M) *** RCA Gold GL/*GK* 85205 [AGL1/*AGK1* 5205]. Rubinstein, Chicago SO, Reiner – FALLA: *Nights in the gardens of Spain.****
(*) Ph. Dig. **410 052-2; 6514/*7337* 164 [id.]. Davidovich, Concg. O, Järvi – SAINT-SAËNS: *Concerto No. 2.****

Rubinstein's scintillating account of the *Rhapsody* dates from the end of the 1950s when the maestro was at the height of his powers. The recording, too, comes from a vintage RCA era; in this digitally remastered form, its age is effectively disguised, with the Chicago ambience casting an agreeable glow over the music making. The sparkle of the great pianist's articulation is a constant delight, and Reiner prepares the famous eighteenth variation with considerable subtlety so that when it arrives the romantic blossoming is all the more telling. There is no finer account in the catalogue and the sound is equally impressive on the excellent tape.

Bella Davidovich is given the benefit of natural and vivid recorded sound with genuine warmth and space round the various instruments. She plays with fleet-fingered fluency and no want of either brilliance or poetry, and Neeme Järvi gives excellent support. This is a likeable performance, but the characterization is romantically relaxed and other versions show deeper insights. The compact disc offers richly atmospheric quality, with the Concertgebouw acoustic bringing an ambient glow and flattering the piano timbre. The chrome cassette is rather middle- and bass-orientated.

Symphony No. 1 in D min., Op. 13.
*** Decca Dig. **411 657-2**; SXDL/*KSXDC* 7603 [Lon. LDR/*5*- 71031]. Concg. O, Ashkenazy.

Symphony No. 1; The Rock (fantasy), Op. 7.
*** DG Dig. 413 784-1/*4* [id.]. BPO, Maazel.

Ashkenazy's is an outstanding version, volatile and extreme in its tempi, with the Concertgebouw players responding in total conviction. In the first movement the cellos and basses articulate their comments on the first theme with phenomenal clarity. This was the last of Ashkenazy's Rachmaninov symphony series to be recorded and it is the most convincing of all. The digital recording is most beautiful, for the sound is full, atmospheric and brilliant. It is superb on CD, with nothing to choose between LP and chrome tape. Though the weight of the opening of the finale is magnificent, the relentless hammering rhythms are presented vividly in scale, where they can easily seem oppressive. The scherzo at a very fast speed has Mendelssohnian lightness, the flowing *Larghetto* is presented as a lyrical interlude.

Maazel's is also a superb performance, in which he characteristically makes Rachmaninov's often thick orchestration beautifully transparent, consistently clarifying detail. He may lack something in Slavonic passion but, with a generous fill-up, the fascinating, early fantasy, *The Rock*, the positive strength of the reading stands well against any rival. In the famous opening theme of the finale, once used as a signature tune for *Panorama* on BBC Television, Maazel is almost genial, where Ashkenazy on the outstanding Decca version makes the music swagger more brazenly. The recording, drier than the Decca, is one of the finest that DG engineers have produced in the Philharmonie in Berlin, with a first-class chrome tape.

Symphony No. 2 in E min., Op. 27.

(*) HMV **CDC 747159-2 [id.]; ED 290498-1/*4* [Ang. AM/*4AM* 34740]. LSO, Previn.

(*) Decca Dig. **400 081-2; SXDL/*KSXDC* 7563 [Lon. LDR/*5*- 71063]. Concg. O, Ashkenazy.

(*) Telarc Dig. **CD 80113; DG 10113 [id.]. RPO, Previn.

** HMV Dig. **CDC 747062-2** [id.]; EL 270052-1/*4* [Ang. DS/*4DS* 38100]. LAPO, Rattle.

Previn's 1973 recording of the *Second Symphony* has dominated the catalogue for over a decade. Its passionate intensity combines freshness with the boldest romantic feeling, yet the music's underlying melancholy is not glossed over. With vividly committed playing from the LSO and a glorious response from the strings, this remains a classic account, unlikely to be surpassed. Unfortunately, the digital remastering for this mid-priced reissue produces a much drier sound-balance with the middle and bass response less expansive. The rich sumptuousness of the strings, so striking on the full-priced original LP, has been replaced by clean, full textures with noticeably reduced amplitude and ambient bloom. On CD, inner detail is undoubtedly fresher, and the orchestra generally has enhanced presence. The bass is firm. But the upper strings are thinner and there is a touch of shrillness in climaxes of the outer movements. In the *Adagio* the LSO violins are inspired to provide such weight and intensity of timbre that climaxes still retain an impressive weight of tone. The tape matches the LP fairly closely and is perhaps slightly more expansive.

Ashkenazy began his Rachmaninov series with the Concertgebouw on this most popular of the symphonies; though the result is most impressive, a performance of high contrasts, there are signs that the Dutch players had not fully adjusted to their guest conductor. In the *Adagio* third movement, the clarinet line is less smooth than in either of the Previn versions. Nevertheless, Ashkenazy's reading has a romantic urgency and drive that are missing from Previn's Telarc version, with the climaxes of the outer movements far more gripping. In the scherzo too, the Amsterdam strings are tauter in ensemble; there is a vibrant impulse about the performance as a whole which is very Russian in its intensity. The Decca recording is full-bodied but with a degree of edge on the strings, and this extra bite suits Ashkenazy's approach; the CD has a balancing depth and richness. The chrome tape has all the fullness and bloom of the LP yet softens the edge on top a little. It is very much in the demonstration class.

The greater feeling of spaciousness of Previn's 1985 Telarc recording is apparent at the very opening. The whole reading is more moderately paced than before, with long-breathed phrases moulded flexibly, with far less urgency and none of Ashkenazy's impetuosity (Ashkenazy's first movement is over two minutes shorter). Previn's *Adagio* is even more relaxed (17′ 17″ against Ashkenazy's 14′ 15″). This expansiveness is enhanced by the finely sustained playing of the RPO strings and the sumptuous Telarc recording with its luxuriant resonance. However, the comparative lack of drive in the scherzo and the finale, with full reserves held back for the ultimate climax, emphasizes the reflective nature of the performance. With such superbly rich sound there are some ravishing moments, but in the last resort the lack of electricity – compared with the earlier LSO version – brings a degree of disappointment, and on CD Ashkenazy offers the more satisfying musical experience.

Rattle's first recording with the Los Angeles Philharmonic is also a disappointment. The problems of recording in the orchestra's home, the Chandler Pavilion, have brought sound that is clear but lacks body in the string section, with violins made to sound emaciated. All this comes out the more clearly on CD. Rattle's performance also lacks urgency, with spacious speeds often without necessary tensions, particularly in the finale, which is unexciting compared with the finest rivals.

Symphony No. 3; Youth Symphony (1891).
*** Decca Dig. **410 231-2**; SXDL/*KSXDC* 7531 [Lon. LDR/5- 71031]. Concg. O, Ashkenazy.

Ashkenazy's is a performance of extremes, volatile and passionate in a very Russian way. In the first movement the varying speeds are contrasted far more than usual, the allegros faster, the slow, lyrical passages (notably the great melody of the second subject) slower with copious rubato. The finale is fast and hectic to the point of wildness, but the Concertgebouw players respond superbly and the digital recording is full, rich and brilliant. The fragment of a projected symphony – with its first subject plainly indebted to Tchaikovsky's *Fourth* – was written when Rachmaninov was only nineteen. It is an enjoyable and unusual makeweight. The glorious sound is even more impressive on compact disc, while the chrome tape is outstanding, offering a beautiful overall bloom, refined detail and natural string timbre.

CHAMBER AND INSTRUMENTAL MUSIC

Trio élégiaque in G min. (1892); Trio élégiaque in D min., Op. 9.
*** Chan. Dig. **CHAN 8341**; ABRD/*ABTD* 1101 [id.]. Borodin Trio.

The *G minor Trio* was composed when Rachmaninov was nineteen; its successor, the *D minor*, Op. 9, comes from the following year and was written in memory of Tchaikovsky. The first is a pensive one-movement piece lasting no more than a quarter of an hour, while Op. 9 is on a much larger scale, in three movements, the first alone lasting almost 20 minutes and the second not much less. They are both imbued with lyrical fervour and draw from the rich vein of melancholy so characteristic of Rachmaninov. The performances by the Borodin Trio are eloquent and masterly, and the recording is admirably balanced and has plenty of warmth. While the CD has the usual subtle gain in presence and definition, there is also a chrome cassette of the highest standard. The reverberant acoustic offers no transfer problems, the sound clear and realistic.

Études-tableaux, Opp. 33 and 39.
*** Hyp. A 66091 [id.]. Howard Shelley.

Howard Shelley is a powerful and convincing Rachmaninov interpreter, not afraid to take an individual line. The conviction and thoughtfulness of the playing, coupled with excellent modern sound, make this convenient coupling a formidable rival to Ashkenazy's classic versions, which on LP come on two separate records. This makes a fine supplement to Shelley's outstanding set of the Rachmaninov *Preludes*, also for Hyperion (A 66081/2).

Reminder. Ashkenazy's fine set of the *Études-tableaux*, Op. 33, comes coupled with the original 1931 version of the *Piano sonata No. 2*, Op. 36 (Decca SXL 6696 [Lon. CS/5- 7236]); while the superb account of the Op. 39 set is coupled with the *Variations on a theme of Corelli*, Op. 42 (Decca SXL 6604 [Lon. CS 6822]). Both are given first-class recordings.

Études-tableaux, Op. 33/5, 6 and 9; Op. 39/1–4, 7 and 9.
*** MMG Dig. **MCD 10031** [id.]. Sviatoslav Richter – TCHAIKOVSKY: *The Seasons*: excerpts.***

As might be expected, Richter gives marvellously authoritative and individual performances of the *Études-tableaux*, offering many insights and playing that is physically involving with its wide range of dynamic, yet at times with the timbre shaded right down. He chooses a selection from both Opp. 33 and 39 but makes up for the absent items by adding four of the most attractive of Tchaikovsky's *Seasons*, playing with comparable character. These begin the recital and are treated more intimately, so that when he opens the Rachmaninov group with Opus 33 No. 9, the change of mood is commanding. The recording stems from Melodiya but was engineered in Munich in April 1983. The sound is first class, with the piano very tangible.

24 Preludes (complete); *Piano sonata No. 2 in B flat min., Op. 36.*
*** Decca **414 417-2** (2) [id.]. (*Preludes* only) 5BB 221-2/*KSXC2 7038* [CSA/5-2241]. Ashkenazy.

Considering his popularity and their quality, it is odd that Rachmaninov's *Preludes* have not been recorded complete more often. Ashkenazy's are the first to appear on CD, with the excellent recording further enhanced. There is superb flair and panache about this playing. As a bonus, the compact discs offer the *Second Piano sonata*, with Ashkenazy generally following the 1913 original score but with some variants. He plays with great virtuosity and feeling and the result is a *tour de force.*

Preludes Nos 3 in B flat; 5 in D; 6 in G min.; 8 in C min., Op. 23/2, 4–5 and 7; 12 in C; 13 in B flat min., Op. 32/1–2.
(M) *** DG Gal. 419 068-1/*4*. Sviatoslav Richter – TCHAIKOVSKY: *Piano concerto No. 1.*(**)

Richter's marvellous performances make one still hope that we shall have a complete set from him in stereo. Anyone who has heard him play the *Preludes* in the concert hall will count it a truly memorable experience, for his insights are many and his playing generates much physical excitement as well as the widest emotional range. The present recordings are a little dry but fully acceptable, with disc and tape sounding virtually identical.

Suite No. 2, Op. 17.
*** Ph. Dig. **411 034-2**; 6514/*7337* 369 [id.]. Argerich, Freire – LUTOSLAWSKI: *Paganini variations*; RAVEL: *La valse.****

Argerich and Freire give a dazzling virtuoso account of the *Suite*, rushing the waltzes off their feet (the movement is marked *presto* but they play it *prestissimo*). They are as fresh, idiomatic and thoughtful as their Decca rivals (Ashkenazy and Previn) and their performance is thoroughly exhilarating. They are well recorded and can be recommended alongside the Decca team who perhaps find more in the inner movements (Decca SXL 6697 [Lon. CS 6893]). The only drawback to the recording is the reverberation which seems a trifle excessive, even for an expansively romantic score, and this is even more striking on the excellent compact disc.

VOCAL MUSIC

Vespers, Op. 37.
(***) Chant du Monde **278 552** [id.]. Korkan, Ognevoi, RSFSR Ac. Russian Ch., Sveshnikov.

Rachmaninov's *Vespers* (1915) must be counted among his most profound and fascinating works. The fifteen movements are superbly written and are as dark, deeply affecting and richly sonorous as any Orthodox Church music. The performances can only be called superlative, and it will be a long time before they are superseded. The basses in particular have incredible richness (at one point they sing a low B flat) and the recording is in an appropriately resonant acoustic. The recording has plenty of atmosphere. The digital remastering produces very little background noise; but some of the liveliness of the original LP has been lost, and pianissimos tend to recede, though climaxes are expansive. However, the real snag about the CD edition is that, by some kind of transfer error, the last three sections of the score are omitted.

Rameau, Jean Philippe (1683–1764)

Les Indes galantes: excerpts (harpsichord transcriptions).
*** HM **HMC 901028**; HM/*40* 1028. Kenneth Gilbert.

These transcriptions are Rameau's own, made some time after the success scored by his first opera-ballet, *Les Indes galantes*, in 1735. He grouped a number of items into four suites or '*concerts*', and these included not only dance numbers and orchestral pieces but arias as well. Kenneth Gilbert, playing a fine instrument in contemporary tuning, reveals these miniatures as the subtle and refined studies that they are. He could not be better served by the recording engineers, and the CD brings added presence and background quiet. The cassette is transferred at a very high level indeed and, while the quality is excellent, the image tends to be right on top of the listener unless care is exercised with the controls.

Grand motets: *In convertendo; Quam dilecta laboravi.*
*** HM **HM 90 1078**; HM/*40* 1078 [id.]. Gari, Monnaliu, Ledroit, De Mey, Varcoe, Chapelle Royale Ch., Ghent Coll. Vocale, Herreweghe.

These two motets are among Rameau's finest works and come from the years preceding his first opera in 1733. The recordings are made in the Carmelite Church in Ghent which has a warm, reverberant acoustic, and the Ghent Collegium Vocale is stiffened by forces from La Chapelle Royale in Paris. They produce excellent results and the soloists are also very fine indeed. In his book on the composer, Girdlestone speaks of *In convertendo* as Rameau's greatest piece of church music, and this record makes out the most persuasive case for it. The instrumental ensemble includes several members of La Petite Bande and so its excellence can be almost taken for granted.

OPERA-BALLET AND OPERA

Anacréon (complete).
*** HM **HMC 90190**; HM/*40* 1090 [id.]. Schirrer, Mellon, Feldman, Visse, Laplénie, Les Arts Florissants, Christie.

Rameau composed two works on the theme of the ancient Greek poet, Anacreon, famed for his devotion to Cupid and Bacchus! This is the second, originally designed as an *acte de ballet* to a libretto by P.-J. Bernard and composed in 1757. The music has charm, even if it is not Rameau at his most inventive; the performance is as authoritative and stylish as one would expect from William Christie's group. It is not essential Rameau, but readers with an interest in the period will want it – and it has moments of great appeal. The recording is admirable in its disc formats; but on cassette, although the generally high level of transfer produces lively results, there are moments of peaking on solo voices.

Dardanus: suite.
(*) Erato **ECD 88013; NUM/*MCE* 75040 [id.]. E. Bar. Soloists, Gardiner.

John Eliot Gardiner offers a substantial selection from the orchestral music of both versions of Rameau's opera (the 1739 score and the score for the 1744 revival which involved radical rewriting of the last two Acts). There is plenty of variety here, from lightly scored dance music to the powerful closing *Chaconne*. Some of the music is slight and, out of context, does not make its full effect, but as a sampler this might tempt some listeners to try the whole work (only available on LP). The CD offers fine if not remarkable sound, with good presence but without the depth of perspective of the best recordings from this source. There is also a sharply focused chrome cassette.

Zoroastre (complete).
**(*) HM HM 1999813 (4) [id.]. Elwes, De Reyghere, Van Der Sluis, Nellon, Reinhart, Bona, Ghent Coll. Vocale, La Petite Bande, Kuijken.

Zoroastre was the last but one of Rameau's tragédies lyriques. It appeared 15 years before his final masterpiece, *Les Boréades*; but the original 1749 score was drastically revised to produce the text of 1756, recorded here. *Zoroastre* may not have quite the inspiration of *Les Boréades* in modifying once rigid conventions; but frequently, as in the monologue of the villain, Abramane, in Act III, Rameau was clearly taking a leaf out of Gluck's book in the dark originality of the instrumentation, here made transparent in finely detailed recording. Though Kuijken's characteristically gentle style with his excellent authentic group, La Petite Bande, fails to give the piece the bite and urgency that John Eliot Gardiner brings to *Les Boréades* in his Erato recording, it is a fine presentation of a long-neglected masterpiece, with crisp and stylish singing from the soloists, notably John Elwes in the name part and Gregory Reinhart as Abramane. The Ghent Collegium Vocale, placed rather close, sings with vigour in the choruses, but the individual voices fail to blend. The five Acts (with Rameau here abandoning the old convention of an allegorical Prologue) are spread none too generously over four discs. The libretto has a facsimile-style reproduction of the French text, but no English translation, only a summary.

Reminder. Gardiner's outstanding set of *Les Boréades* is still available on Erato (STU 715343).

Ravel, Maurice (1875–1937)

Alborada del gracioso; Une barque sur l'océan; Menuet antique; Ma Mère l'Oye (*Mother Goose*)*: complete ballet; Pavane pour une infante défunte; Le Tombeau de Couperin; Valses nobles et sentimentales.*
(M) ** DG 413 535-1/*4* (2). Boston SO, Ozawa.

The attraction of Ozawa's generous two-disc collection is that, by omitting *Boléro* and *Daphnis et Chloé* (which most collectors will have already acquired), it offers, economically, much of the rest of Ravel's orchestral output, except *Rapsodie espagnole, La valse* and the concertos. Moreover, the recording is first class, beautifully balanced with the hall ambience colouring the textures most naturally. Chrome tapes (in a cardboard flap-pack) are virtually indistinguishable from the LPs. Ozawa is at his finest in catching the atmosphere of *Une barque sur l'océan* and throughout he secures admirable orchestral playing. Yet in general the performances are wanting the last degree of character. *Ma Mère l'Oye* is really quite cool and that limits the appeal of the set overall.

Alborada del gracioso; Boléro, Daphnis et Chloé (ballet)*: suite No. 2. Pavane pour une infante défunte; Rapsodie espagnole; La valse; Valses nobles et sentimentales.*
(B) **(*) CBS *MGT 39012.* Cleveland O and Ch.; NYPO, Boulez.

This double-length CBS cassette assembles Boulez's Ravel performances recorded in New York and Cleveland in the early 1970s, and they are very impressive. Detail is sensitively observed and both orchestras respond with splendid virtuosity to his direction. His *Rapsodie espagnole* is very well shaped; Boulez's Spain is brilliant and well lit. *Daphnis* too is beautifully done, and there is a sense of magic in the *Valses nobles et sentimentales*. The *Alborada* is superbly brilliant. The range is wide, though one could wish for more expansive textures on climaxes. The tape transfers are well managed at a high level and only the very last degree of refinement is missing. The very gentle drum taps at the opening of *Boléro*, however, are almost inaudible against the background noise not entirely removed by the Dolby pre-emphasis.

Alborada del gracioso; Boléro; Ma Mère l'Oye: suite; La valse.
** Erato Dig. **ECD 88159**; NUM/*MCE* 75201 [id.]. SRO, Jordan.

This is not an issue that need deter collectors unless the actual programme offered is essential. Armin Jordan secures good playing from the Suisse Romande Orchestra, but the performances have no special distinction. It is good to have *Boléro* beginning at a real *pianissimo* against a silent background and moving to a climax not heightened by artificially brilliant sound, as with Muti, but here the problem is the reverberation of the hall which, in spite of the excellent CD definition, still clouds the articulation of the *Alborada* and provides a degree of inflation to the textures of *La valse*. Its rhythms are affectionately inflected, but the rubato is a shade conventional. *Ma Mère l'Oye* is without the sense of gentle ecstasy that Dutoit finds, and *Le jardin féerique* makes a disappointing conclusion.

Alborada del gracioso; Boléro; Pavane pour une infante défunte; Rapsodie espagnole; La valse.
(M) *** HMV ED 290162-1/*4*. O de Paris, Martinon.

These performances are taken from Martinon's (deleted) 1975 complete collection of Ravel's orchestral music and are among the very best things he has given us. The virtuosity and expressive response of the Orchestre de Paris give great pleasure and the recording is both atmospheric and full, with excellent detail. An outstanding mid-priced collection.

Alborada del gracioso; Boléro; Rapsodie espagnole.
(*) RCA Dig. **RCD 14438; RL 13686 [ARC1/*ARK1* 3686]. Dallas SO, Mata.

Mata has helped to build the Dallas orchestra into a splendid band, and it gives impressive performances of these virtuoso showpieces. There are more distinguished accounts of each work, but the coupling is certainly recommendable, helped by digital recording of great range. *Boléro* develops from a whisper of pianissimo at the start to a formidably loud climax, though the detailed balancing is not always consistent. The compact disc is impressive, but this cannot compare with Dutoit's even finer (and more generous) collection – see below.

Alborada del gracioso; Boléro; Rapsodie espagnole; La valse.
ⓒ *** Decca **410 010-2**; SXDL/*KSXDC* 7559 [Lon. LDR/5- 71059]. Montreal SO, Dutoit.
** CBS **MK 37289** [id.]. O Nat. de France, Maazel.
(B) ** CBS DC 40149. O Nat. de France, Maazel – OFFENBACH: *Gaîté parisienne*; DUKAS: *L'apprenti sorcier*; SAINT-SAËNS: *Danse macabre*.**

Even if you possess alternative versions of the works on this Decca record, you should consider this anthology, for it is a model of its kind. Not only is the playing of the Montreal orchestra under Charles Dutoit absolutely first class and thoroughly atmospheric, the recorded sound has a clarity, range and depth of perspective that are equally satisfying. This recording defines the state of the art and, apart from the sumptuous music-making, has impressive refinement and a most musically judged and natural balance. Outstanding on both LP and chrome tape, while the compact disc version has even greater immediacy and refinement of detail and texture.

As can be seen, Maazel's collection, digitally recorded in 1984, is available either in CD format or in a double-LP set offered at the cost of one premium-priced disc. Thus the CD in effect costs about three times as much – assuming the collector wants the Offenbach, Dukas and Saint-Saëns pieces that fill the accompanying LP. The performances are brilliantly played, and Maazel's extrovert sentience in the *Rapsodie* is certainly involving. *La valse* is high-powered, with an indulgent treatment of the climax. The sound is resonant and brightly lit. Frankly, this is not in the same league as Dutoit.

Alborada del gracioso; Boléro; Rapsodie espagnole; La valse; Valses nobles et sentimentales.
** Decca **414 046-2** [id.]. SRO, Ansermet.

The offering is generous, but clearly this CD is overpriced when Dutoit's Montreal recordings of this repertoire are available, offering superior orchestral playing and more subtle sound. Yet Ansermet aficionados will be glad to discover how remarkably fine these recordings were, mostly from the early 1960s. Only the *Rapsodie* (1958) is dated by the thin string timbre in the *Prélude à la nuit*; yet in the other movements the vivid orchestral colours give pleasure and Ansermet's sense of detail is matched by the rhythmic energy of the playing.

Boléro is a strikingly well-graduated performance, and the sound and range are enhanced as they are in the two waltz pieces. The *Valses nobles* are rather slow but have a certain sensuous allure, while *La valse* is excellent in its combination of poise and momentum. The resonance takes a little of the edge off the *Alborada*, which scintillates in the Dutoit version; generally, however, one can only register amazement at the overall fidelity of this digitally remastered analogue quality. There is minimal background noise.

(i) *Alborada del gracioso; Daphnis et Chloé* (ballet)*: Suite No. 2;* (ii) *Pavane pour une infante défunte; Rapsodie espagnole.*
(M) **(*) EMI EMX 41 2076-1/*4*. (i) Philh. O; (ii) New Philh. O, Giulini.

The *Alborada* and *Daphnis* come from 1960, yet the recording has an extraordinarily wide range and the ecstatic climax of *Daybreak* is unforgettable. Throughout the suite there is superlative playing from the Philharmonia at the height of its powers, the solo flute particularly memorable. The *Alborada* is no less spectacular, and this reissue is worth getting for these two works alone. The sound is amazingly good, but there is a touch of rawness on the upper strings, which is slightly smoothed on the tape. In all other respects the cassette is the equal of the disc. The other two performances were recorded in 1966. The *Pavane* is beautifully serene, and the *Rapsodie* has fine delicacy and atmosphere, but here Giulini is distinctly cooler and the orchestral response lacks the spontaneous excitement of the 1960 sessions. The sound is fuller, less glitteringly clear at the climax of the *Feria*. Here the LP is slightly more sharp in focus than the cassette.

Alborada del gracioso; Menuet antique; Rapsodie espagnole; Valses nobles et sentimentales.
(M) **(*) Ph. Seq. 412 010-1/*4*. Concg. O, Haitink.

The playing of the Amsterdam orchestra is eminently polished and civilized, and all four works are finely shaped. The *Rapsodie espagnole* lacks the last ounce of dash in the *Feria*, but the *Habanera* is lazily seductive. Likewise, the *Valses nobles et sentimentales* just fall short of the magic that Martinon achieves. But to say this is not to deny the excellence of the orchestral response or the general sensitivity of Haitink's direction. Fine performances, very well recorded indeed, with the remastered pressings improved in firmness of outline, without loss of atmosphere or bloom. The cassette transfer, too, is very successful.

Boléro.
(M) *** DG Sig. 413 983-1/*4* [id.]. BPO, Karajan – OFFENBACH: *Gaîté parisienne*; BIZET: *Carmen suite.***(*)
* HMV **CDC 747022-2** [id.]. Phd. O, Muti – LISZT: *Les Préludes***; TCHAIKOVSKY: *1812.**

Karajan's 1964 *Boléro* (reissued appropriately on the Signature label) is a very characteristic performance, marvellously controlled, hypnotic and gripping, with the Berlin Philharmonic at the top of its form. The sound is still very fine, with disc and chrome tape closely matched.

Muti sets a measured tempo and almost lingers in his expressve treatment of the opening statements of the theme. By the time the climax is in sight, however, the upper range has a harsh digital edge and the strings sound glassy; the final *fortissimo* is very fierce indeed.

Boléro; (i) *Daphnis et Chloé: Suite No. 2; Pavane pour une infante défunte.*
*** HMV **CDC 747162-2**; ASD/*TC-ASD* 3912 [Ang. SZ/*4ZS* 37670]. LSO, Previn.
*(*) Telarc Dig. **CD 80052**; DG 10052 [id.]. St Louis SO, Slatkin, (i) with Ch.

Though an analogue recording, Previn's coupling of favourite Ravel pieces provides wonderfully rich, full and atmospheric sound for performances full of sparkle and flair. *Daphnis et Chloé* is sensuously beautiful (good augury for the complete recording of the ballet which Previn went on to make within months – see below), and *Boléro*, at a slow and very steady tempo rather like Karajan's, sounds splendidly relentless. The cassette quality too is outstandingly good, clear and full-bodied at the big climax of *Boléro*. On CD, the sound is spectacular, both brilliant and full, with detail enhanced. It must be counted a disadvantage, however, that there are no dividing bands within the *Daphnis et Chloé* suite. Moreover, the playing time at 41′ 15″ is distinctly ungenerous.

Slatkin directs capable performances of the Ravel showpieces, but they are lacking in rhythmic flair and the digital recording is, by Telarc standards, unspectacular, with a relatively limited range of dynamic.

Boléro; Daphnis et Chloé: suite No. 2; Pavane pour une infante défunte; Rapsodie espagnole.
* HMV **CDC 747356-2** [id.]. O de Paris, Munch.

Although Munch's CD offers one more piece than Previn's collection (see above), there is nothing to detain the listener here. The readings serve well enough, though they lack magnetism, but the orchestral playing is acceptable merely, with moments of suspect intonation; although the *Rapsodie* comes off quite well, Munch increases the pace of *Boléro*, albeit subtly. The analogue recording – from 1969 – has an element of harshness.

Boléro; Daphnis et Chloé: Suite No. 2; Pavane pour une infante défunte; La valse.
(*) DG Dig. **400 061-2; 2532/*3302* 041 [id.]. O de Paris, Barenboim.

At a slow speed *Boléro* brings fine balancing and smooth solos. The *Pavane* and *La valse* too are both on the slow side, but the seductive phrasing makes them sound lusciously idiomatic. The *Daphnis suite* brings the most persuasive performance of all. The recorded sound is sumptuous to match, but it could have more air round it, qualities the more easily appreciable on compact disc. There is a good chrome cassette with side two sharper in focus than side one.

Boléro; Pavane pour une infante défunte; Le Tombeau de Couperin; La valse.
(M) ** Ph. 412 934-1/*4* [id.]. Concg. O, Haitink.

Fine performances, distinguished by instinctive good judgement and taste. The orchestral playing has refinement and finish, and the engineers produce a sound to match; the perspective is truthful and the overall effect most pleasing. Yet Haitink's *La valse* fails to enchant and captivate the listener as do the finest versions, and there is not quite enough atmosphere in *Le Tombeau de Couperin*. The cassette is not as vivid as the disc.

Piano concerto in G; Piano concerto for the left hand in D.
* HM Forlane Dig. **UCD 16522**; UM 6552 [id.]. El Bacha, O Philharmonique du Pays de Loire, Soustrot.

(i) *Piano concerto in G; Piano concerto for the left hand. Une barque sur l'océan; L'éventail de Jeanne (Fanfare); Menuet antique.*
(*) Decca Dig. **410 230-2; SXDL/*KSXDC* 7592 [Lon. LDR/*5* 71092]. (i) Rogé; Montreal SO, Dutoit.

Piano concerto in G; Piano concerto for the left hand in D; Pavane pour une infante défunte; Jeax d'eau; (i) *La valse* (version for 2 pianos).
❀ *** HMV **CDC 747386-2** [id.]; ASD/*TC-ASD* 3845 [Ang. SZ 37730] (without *Pavane*; *Jeux d'eau*; *La valse*). Collard; (i) Béroff; O Nat. de France, Maazel.

Superbly vivid recording quality on HMV while Jean-Philippe Collard gives a meticulous, sparkling and refined account of the *G major Concerto* and a marvellously brilliant and poetic account of the *Left-hand concerto*. He brings great *tendresse* to the more reflective moments and there is real delicacy of feeling throughout. Maazel gives thoroughly sympathetic support, and the Orchestre National play superbly. In the *Left-hand concerto* Collard does not quite match the dash and swagger of Gavrilov's altogether dazzling account (see below), but he runs him pretty close. This is undoubtedly the best version of this coupling to have appeared for many years, and it will be difficult to surpass. The cassette transfer is extraordinarily vivid in projection with impressively crisp transients. The CD further refines the recorded sound and adds three piano items (two solos and one duet) not on LP or tape: the *Pavane*, *Jeux d'eau* and *La valse*, all beautifully played.

Pascal Rogé brings both delicacy and sparkle to the *G major Concerto*, which he gives with his characteristic musical grace and fluency. He produces unfailing beauty of tone at every dynamic level – as indeed does Collard on HMV, who is more incisive in the outer movements. Rogé brings great poetry and tenderness to the slow movement but in the *Left-hand concerto* he is a good deal less dynamic. There is a certain want of momentum here, even though there is much to admire in the way of pianistic finesse – and charm. The Decca recording offers excellent performances of three short orchestral pieces as a makeweight, which may tip the scales in its favour for some collectors.

The Forlane issue was not well received in the specialist press and its claims on the allegiance of collectors seem slight. Abdel Rahman El Bacha has to meet stiff competition on CD from Pascal Rogé on Decca and, above all, from Jean-Philippe Collard on HMV. The slow movement of the *G major* does not have the requisite serenity or magic (and in any event is far too fast). Nor is the orchestral contribution of outstanding quality. In fact this is all *vin ordinaire*.

(i) *Piano concerto for the left hand; Gaspard de la nuit; Pavane pour une infante défunte.*
(M) *** HMV EG 290325-1/*4* [Ang. AM/*4AM* 34725]. Gavrilov; (i) LSO, Rattle.

(i) *Piano concerto for the left hand. Miroirs: Alborada del gracioso.*
*** ASV Dig. DCA/*ZCDCA* 555 [id.]. Osorio, RPO, Bátiz – PROKOFIEV: *Piano concerto No. 1* etc.***

Gavrilov's recording of the *Left-hand concerto* is altogether dazzling. He plays with effortless virtuosity, brilliance and, when required, great sensitivity. This is at least the equal of any of the classic accounts either on 78s or LP. The *Pavane* is also very distinguished; apart from the strangely impulsive closing bars, this too is beautiful playing. This was originally coupled with Gavrilov's equally dazzling account of Prokofiev's *First Concerto*, but now *Gaspard de la nuit* is substituted, taken from a 1978 solo recital. The performance is not quite as distinctive as Ashkenazy's: both *Ondine* and *Le gibet* have an element of reserve. But *Scarbo* has superb dash, and the whole performance has impeccable style. The recording is excellent on both disc and cassette, although in the *Concerto* the tape is less open at the top.

Jorge-Fredrico Osorio's account of the *Left-hand concerto* can hold its own with the best, and it can certainly withstand comparison with the excellent Decca Rogé version on all counts. He gives a crisp and colourful performance of the *Alborada*, too.

(i) *Piano concerto in G. Pavane pour une infante défunte; Ma Mère l'Oye* (complete)*; Le Tombeau de Couperin; Valses nobles et sentimentales.*
(B) **(*) HMV *TCC2-POR 154600-9*. O de Paris, Martinon; (i) with Ciccolini.

These recordings are all taken from Martinon's 1975 (deleted) LP box and it is a pity that Ciccolini's version of the *Piano concerto* was included, as it is in no way distinctive. The rest of the programme, however, affords much pleasure; the slightly softened focus of the transfer suits Martinon's ravishingly beautiful account of *Ma Mère l'Oye*. *Le Tombeau de Couperin*, too, is one of the finest versions available, the orchestral playing refined, and with plenty of bloom on the recording.

Daphnis et Chloé (ballet; complete).
❀ ℂ *** Decca Dig. **400 055-2**; SXDL/*KSXDC* 7526 [Lon. LDR/*5*- 71028]. Montreal SO and Ch., Dutoit.
(M) *** HMV Green. ED 290799-1/*4*. Paris Nat. Op. Ch., O de Paris, Martinon.

*** HMV Dig. **CDC 747123-2** [id.]; ASD/*TCC-ASD* 4099 [Ang. S/*4XS* 37868]. LSO and Ch., Previn.

(B) **(*) DG Walkman *415 336-4* [id.]. Boston SO, and Ch., Ozawa – STRAVINSKY: *Petrushka*.***

** DG Dig. **415 360-2**; 415 360-1/*4* [id.]. V. State Op. Ch., VPO, Levine.

The compact disc of the Dutoit/Montreal *Daphnis et Chloé* immediately established itself as a demonstration disc *par excellence* in the new medium, from the opening *pianissimo* bringing a new dimension to sound recording. The sensation that a subtle veil is being withdrawn from the orchestral image persists throughout the performance which is sumptuously evocative, with Dutoit and his splendid orchestra creating the most ravishing textures. He adopts an idiomatic and flexible style, observing the minute indications of tempo change but making every slight variation sound totally spontaneous. The final *Danse générale* finds him adopting a dangerously fast tempo, but the Montreal players – combining French responsiveness with transatlantic polish – rise superbly to the challenge, with the choral punctuations at the end adding to the sense of frenzy. The digital recording is wonderfully luminous, with the chorus ideally balanced at an evocative half-distance. It is a pity that Decca do not provide cues to guide access to the main sections of the score. Tape collectors will be glad to know that the cassette, too, is in the demonstration class.

The reissue on Greensleeve of Martinon's superb Paris recording of the complete ballet is a real bargain. Collectors who have yet to go over to compact disc need look no further, for this is as magical an account of Ravel's glorious score as any, sumptuously recorded and beautifully played. It is the equal of any now before the public – and half the price of most of them. It is to be preferred to all the current CD versions, save only for Dutoit on Decca. The performance originates from the five-LP box of Ravel's complete orchestral music that EMI made with Martinon in the mid-1970s, first issued in quadraphony and now digitally remastered. This is a great performance. There is an excellent tape, not quite as sharply defined as the LP, but its slightly mistier quality and warm amplitude suit the music, and the percussion effects are not blunted.

With rhythm more important than atmosphere, Previn directs a very dramatic performance, clear-headed and fresh, an exciting alternative to the superlative Dutoit version. It is made all the more vivid in the excellent CD transfer, with textures sharply defined. It is regrettable that the opportunity was not taken to insert a full quota of bands, for the listener will obviously not always want to play the complete score from beginning to end. The tape equivalent originally used chrome stock, but newer copies are likely to be XDR iron-oxide cassettes.

Ozawa's 1975 *Daphnis* is not as distinctive as Dutoit's or Previn's, but it is superbly played; the flattering Boston acoustic adds to the glowing sense of rapture in *Daybreak*, while not blunting the sparkle of the finale. The tape transfer is particularly successful; as it is coupled with Dutoit's outstanding 1977 complete recording of *Petrushka*, this makes another fine Walkman bargain.

With ripe Viennese horns adding opulence to Ravel's rich textures and with recording that brings an uncomfortably wide dynamic range, Levine's reading could hardly be higher-powered, with superb playing from the Vienna Philharmonic. He has a natural feeling for Ravelian rubato, but what the reading consistently lacks is poetry, for in even the gentlest moments there is a want of evocative warmth. Despite the excessive contrasts between loud and soft and some hardness on violin tone, the recording is one of the most brilliant that DG engineers have made recently in Vienna. The tape has not quite the breadth of dynamic of the CD, but certainly does not lack vividness.

Daphnis et Chloé (ballet)*: Suites 1 and 2.*
*(*) ASV Dig. DCA/*ZCDCA* 536 [id.]. LSO, Nowak – BARTÓK: *Dance suite.****

The young Polish conductor, Grzegorz Nowak, making his début recording in two brilliant showpieces is far less successful here in Ravel than in the Bartók on the reverse. It is a worthy, undynamic account of richly atmospheric music, helped a little by fine recording. There is an excellent cassette.

Ma Mère l'Oye (complete ballet).
*** Ph. Dig. **400 016-2**; 9500/*7300* 973 [id.]. Pittsburgh SO, Previn – SAINT-SAËNS: *Carnival of the Animals.****

Ma Mère l'Oye (complete)*; Le Tombeau de Couperin; Valses nobles et sentimentales.*
❀ ☾ *** Decca Dig. **410 254-2**; 410 254-1/*4* [id.]. Montreal SO, Dutoit.

A few bars of this Decca record leave no doubt as to its quality. Charles Dutoit and the Montreal orchestra offer *Ma Mère l'Oye* complete, together with *Le Tombeau de Couperin* and the *Valses nobles et sentimentales*, recorded, as have been its companions in the Decca Ravel series, in St Eustache, Montreal. This offers demonstration quality, transparent and refined, with the textures beautifully balanced and expertly placed. The CD is altogether outstanding: here is another instance where one could speak of the gauze being removed, for the CD has even more translucent detail, firmer focus and presence than the LP – but both are superb. The performances too are wonderfully refined and sympathetic. *Ma Mère l'Oye* is ravishingly beautiful, its special combination of sensuousness and innocence perfectly caught. Tape collectors will find that the chrome cassette is hardly less sophisticated and desirable.

In Previn's version of the complete *Mother Goose* ballet, played and recorded with consummate refinement, the quality of innocence shines out. The temptation for any conductor is to make the music exotically sensuous in too sophisticated a way, but Previn keeps a freshness apt for nursery music. The recording is superb, with the Philips engineers refusing to spotlight individual instruments but presenting a texture of luminous clarity. Those qualities come out the more impressively on compact disc. The chrome cassette sounds well, too; but the disc versions have more refined detail.

Le Tombeau de Couperin.
** Decca Dig. **400 051-2**; SXDL/*KSXDC* 7520 [Lon. LDR/5- 10040]. Chicago SO, Solti – MUSSORGSKY: *Pictures.****

Recorded with very different microphone placing from the main Mussorgsky work on the disc, *Le Tombeau de Couperin* in Solti's reading sounds hard and brilliant rather than classically elegant. The recording is partly to blame, with close-up sound reducing the sense of ambience (on both compact disc and LP). Nevertheless, it makes an original coupling for the Ravel arrangement of Mussorgsky. The cassette transfer is softer-edged than the disc and the effect more atmospheric; many will prefer it.

Tzigane (for violin and orchestra).
*** Decca **417 118-2** [id.]; SXL/*KSXC* 6851 [Lon. CS/*5- 7073*]. Kyung Wha Chung, RPO, Dutoit – CHAUSSON: *Poème*; SAINT-SAËNS: *Havanaise* etc.***
(M) **(*) Ph. Seq. 412 363(1/*4* [id.]. Szeryng, Monte Carlo Op. O, Van Remoortel – LALO: *Symphonie espagnole.***(*)

With its seemingly improvisatory solo introduction, *Tzigane* is a work which demands an inspirational artist, and Kyung Wha Chung is ideally cast, coupling this elusive piece with other concertante works too often neglected. Accompaniments and recordings are both excellent; the cassette needs a slight smoothing of the treble to sound its best.

Szerying was at the height of his powers when he recorded this splendidly strong and committed account of Ravel's *Tzigane*, flexible and responsive as well as brilliant in execution. The recording spotlights him, so that the orchestral contribution emerges less strongly; however, this is not too serious as the support is rather less distinguished, although well held together by Eduard van Remoortel. In remastered form, the sound is extremely vivid on both disc and tape, and this coupling makes very enjoyable listening.

La Valse.
(*) DG Dig. **410 033-2; 2532/*3302* 057 [id.]. LSO, Abbado – MUSSORGSKY: *Pictures.****
*(*) CBS **MK 76880** [**MK 35165**]. NYPO, Mehta – MUSSORGSKY: *Pictures.**(*)

Though detail is not so needle-sharp for this Ravel fill-up as for the Mussorgsky–Ravel *Pictures* with which it is coupled, Abbado directs a fluent and incisive account, not quite ideally idiomatic and lilting in its dance rhythms, but with a thrilling surge of adrenalin in its closing pages. The digital recording is outstanding on LP and chrome tape alike, with the palm going to the compact disc, one of DG's best. The recording, however, has a shade too much resonance to be ideal, and this is even more obvious on the CD.

Mehta's performance is in no way really distinctive, though it is well played. Abbado is subtler in shaping and rubato.

CHAMBER MUSIC

Introduction and allegro for harp, flute, clarinet and string quartet.
(M) *** Decca 414 063-1/*4*. Osian Ellis, Melos Ens. – DEBUSSY: *Sonata;* GUY-ROPARTZ: *Prelude, marine and chansons;* ROUSSEL: *Serenade.****

The beauty and subtlety of Ravel's sublime septet are marvellously realized by the 1962 Melos account, originally on Oiseau-Lyre and now reissued on Decca. The interpretation has great delicacy of feeling, and the recording, excellent in its day, shows its age only slightly in the upper range, which has lost a little of its bloom in this remastered format. There is an excellent high-level tape, not previously available.

Piano trio in A min.
*** Ph. Dig. **411 141-2**; 411 141-1/*4*. [id.]. Beaux Arts Trio – CHAUSSON: *Piano trio.****

The most recent Beaux Arts account of the Ravel *Trio* is little short of inspired – as inspired as this music itself – and even finer than their earlier record of the late 1960s. The recording, too, is of high quality, even if the piano is rather forward and – if one is going to quibble – the bottom end of the instrument looms too large in the aural picture. But there is no doubt that this is a most distinguished chamber-music issue and must carry the strongest recommendation in all formats.

String quartet in F.
(*) HMV **CDC 747347-2 [id.]; EL 270356-1/*4*. Alban Berg Qt – DEBUSSY: *Quartet.***(*)*
** Ph. Dig. **411 050-2**; 6514/*7337* 387 [id.]. Orlando Qt – DEBUSSY: *Quartet.**
** Delos Dig. **D/CD 3004** [id.]. Sequoia Qt – BARTÓK: *String quartet No. 3.***

Superb, indeed incomparable playing from the Alban Berg Quartet, and splendidly rich and sonorous recording from the EMI engineers, particularly on compact disc, though there is an excellent cassette, too. Yet while this is marvellously polished and has such excellence in terms of ensemble and tonal blend, there is a want of spontaneity that ultimately weighs against it. In a sense the Alban Berg beautify the work and, although Ravel's glorious *Quartet* must have polish, it must be a polish that enables one to forget the physical aspects of the music making and become totally immersed in the music itself. Although this is marvellous in its way, collectors who have invested in the old Melos Quartet of Stuttgart version on DG need not make the change. Despite one's reservations, however, it is difficult not to prefer the Alban Berg to its rivals on CD.

The Orlando Quartet are wonderfully passionate and possess glorious tone and ensemble. They press the Ravel to greater expressive extremes than do the Melos Quartet of Stuttgart; though the Orlando play with superb artistry and feeling, some will find the greater restraint of the Melos more telling, particularly in the slow movement. There is a sudden lurch in pitch in this movement, though it is not quite so ruinous as is the case in the Debussy on the reverse side. There is an excellent cassette. However, the Melos remain unsurpassed (DG 2531/*3301* 203 [id.]).

Good though they are, the Sequoia Quartet are not quite in the top league. Their account of the Ravel, ungenerously coupled with Bartók's shortest *Quartet*, is accomplished enough, but they slightly exaggerate shifts of tempo. A very acceptable but not distinguished performance that inspires more respect than enthusiasm.

PIANO DUET

Ma Mère l'Oye; Rapsodie espagnole; La valse.
**(*) CRD Dig. CRD 1124/*CRDC 4124* [id.]. Eden and Tamir.

Ma Mère l'Oye; Rapsodie espagnole; Entre cloches; Frontispiece.
(M) *(*) DG 415 006-1/*4*. Alfons and Aloys Kontarsky – DEBUSSY: *Two-piano music.**(*)

Eden and Tamir celebrate a long partnership of more than thirty years and their expertise and musicianship are always in evidence here. For all their excellence, they must yield in *La valse* to Argerich and Freire on Philips (see below). Their *Ma Mère l'Oye* has some lovely things in it, as has *Rapsodie espagnole* – though they are a little lacking in electricity and excitement in the *Feria*. But the piano sound is beautiful – the resonant acoustic casts a pleasing ambient glow on the music making – and overall this set gives much pleasure. The chrome tapes are excellent, too.

The Kontarsky brothers play these famous Ravel pieces and the two short rarities with unfailing fleetness of finger but the results are somewhat prosaic and unmagical – though it must be difficult to produce a poetic effect in so cramped an acoustic. The interest and value of the set is considerable, particularly as it offers a Debussy curiosity, an early symphonic movement he wrote in 1880.

La valse.
*** Ph. Dig. **411 034-2**; 6514/*7337* 369 [id.]. Argerich, Freire – LUTOSLAWSKI: *Paganini variations*; RACHMANINOV: *Suite No. 2.****

The transcription is Ravel's own and was first heard in this form played by the composer himself and Alfredo Casella in Vienna in 1920. Indeed, the first idea of such a work came as early as 1906. This one is the only single issue of it. Brilliant, atmospheric playing and good recording.

SOLO PIANO MUSIC

À la manière de Borodin; À la manière de Chabrier; Gaspard de la nuit; Jeux d'eau; Menuet antique; Menuet sur le nom de Haydn; Miroirs; Pavane pour une infante défunte; Prélude; Sérénade grotesque; Sonatine; Le Tombeau de Couperin; Valses nobles et sentimentales.
*** CRD Dig. CRDD 1083-5/*CRDDC 4083-5* [id.]. Paul Crossley.

Paul Crossley is the only English pianist at present represented on record in the complete Ravel piano music. His is a fastidious musical personality, well attuned to Ravel's sensibility; his accounts of all these works are beautifully fashioned and can hold their own with the available competition. Crossley is aristocratic, with an admirable feeling for tone colour and line, and rarely mannered (the end of *Jeux d'eau* is an exception). His version of *Le Tombeau de Couperin* has a classical refinement and delicacy that is refreshing. The CRD recording is very good indeed and this fine set deserves the warmest welcome. CRD merit congratulations in giving recognition to this much underrated player. The chrome cassettes are of high quality, softer-grained in the treble than is sometimes the case with CRD, which suits the music admirably, for definition is very good.

À la manière de Borodin; À la manière de Chabrier; Menuet antique; Prélude; Le Tombeau de Couperin; Valses nobles et sentimentales.
(*) Nimbus **NIM 5011; (d.) 2103 [id.]. Vlado Perlemuter.

Gaspard de la nuit; Jeux d'eau; Miroirs; Pavane.
(*) Nimbus **NIM 5005; (d.) 2101 [id.]. Vlado Perlemuter.

Perlemuter, pupil and friend of Ravel himself, was asked by Nimbus to record the complete piano music, when he had reached his seventies. Though his technical command was not so complete as it had been, he gives delightful, deeply sympathetic readings; the sense of spontaneity is a joy. There may be Ravel recordings which bring more dazzling virtuoso displays, but none more persuasive. If the articulation in *Alborada del gracioso*, from *Miroirs*, is not so spectacular as from some younger pianists, the rhythmic vigour and alertness, the flair with which dance rhythms are presented, make this just as involving and exciting. The original three-LP set has here been transferred to two CDs, with the analogue sound freshened and clarified. Nimbus's preference for an ample room acoustic makes the result naturally atmospheric on CD, with light reverberation presenting a halo of sound.

Gaspard de la nuit.
*** DG Dig. **413 363-2**; 2532/*3302* 093 [id.]. Pogorelich – PROKOFIEV: *Sonata No. 6.**** ❀

Pogorelich's *Gaspard* is out of the ordinary. In *Le gibet*, there is the self-conscious striving after effect that mars his Schumann *Études symphoniques* and attention soon wanders from the ends to the means. We are made conscious of the pianist's refinement of tone and colour first, and Ravel's poetic vision afterwards. But for all that, this is piano playing of astonishing quality and, despite the touches of narcissism, this is a performance to relish. His control of colour and nuance in *Scarbo* is dazzling and its eruptive cascades of energy and dramatic fire have one sitting on the edge of one's seat. The coupling, Prokofiev's *Sixth Sonata*, is quite simply stunning.

Gaspard de la nuit; Menuet sur le nom d'Haydn; Prélude; Sonatine; Valses nobles et sentimentales.
(*) Hung. Dig. **HCD 12317-2 [id.]. Dezsö Ránki.

On compact disc this fine Hungarian pianist faces formidable competition in *Gaspard* and the *Valses nobles* from Ashkenazy on Decca and, in the former, from Pogorelich on DG. Even so, Ránki acquits himself well and shows a keen sympathy for this repertoire. He is thoroughly attuned to the Gallic sensibility, and in the last of the *Valses nobles* – each is separately indexed on the CD – his playing has wonderful atmosphere and poignancy. Unfortunately, his recording is not quite as good as the sound given to his rivals – the piano is rather forward in a reverberant acoustic, and does not altogether flatter him.

Gaspard de la nuit; Valses nobles et sentimentales; Pavane pour une infante défunte.
*** Decca Dig. **410 255-2**; 410 255-1/*4* [id.]. Vladimir Ashkenazy.

Fresh from his nearly-completed Chopin series and various triumphs on the podium, Vladimir Ashkenazy has now returned to Ravel. His earlier version of *Gaspard* (Decca SXL 6215) was in its day a yardstick by which others were judged, and is still pretty impressive. While there is no doubt as to the dazzling virtuosity and amazing control of colour and mood in Ivo Pogorelich's remarkable DG account, he is self-conscious, particularly in *Le gibet*, and his record is not for everyday listening. Ashkenazy's new account is hardly less impressive than the old and is in no way narcissistic. It does not altogether efface memories of the Argerich (see above), though there is not a great deal to choose between them. His *Valses nobles* are splendidly refined and aristocratic. The recording has marvellous range and is extremely vivid and open, but the slightly less bright sound of his earlier *Gaspard* is rather more pleasing. The newer issue offers somewhat short measure for CD. The cassette is wide-ranging, with striking presence, but there is a hint of metal in the treble.

Miroirs; Le Tombeau de Couperin.
(*) BIS Dig. **CD 246; LP 246. Yukie Nagai.

Yukie Nagai is a young Japanese pianist who has settled in Munich. She won the 1977 International Prize in Geneva and, as is the case with so many Oriental artists, obviously has a real feeling for French music. Her account of *Noctuelles* is marvellously refined, and her range of colour at the *piano* and *pianissimo* end of the range is particularly lovely. Her account of *Oiseaux tristes* is very slow and altogether magical in atmosphere, and she is hardly less impressive elsewhere.

This is distinguished playing. The recording is good – though without being quite as wide-ranging as Bolet's Liszt records for Decca or Kocsis for Philips; it sounds as if it is made in a small studio, yet there is no lack of ambience.

VOCAL MUSIC

Mélodies: *Ballade de la Reine; Morte d'Aimer; Canzone italiana; Chanson du rouet; Chanson espagnole; Chanson français; Chanson hébraïque; Chansons madécasses; Cinq mélodies populaires grecques; Deux épigrammes de Clément Marot; Deux mélodies hébraïques; Don Quichotte à Dulcinée; Un grand sommeil nuit; Les grands vents venus d'outremer; Histoires naturelles; Manteau de fleurs; Noël des jouets; Rêves; Ronsard à son âme; Sante; Scottish song; Shéhérazade* (complete)*; Si morne!; Sur l'herbe; Tripatos; Trois poèmes de Stéphane Mallarmé; Vocalise en forme de Habanera.*

*** HMV EX 270139-3/*9* (3) [Ang. DSCX/*4D3X* 3965]. Norman, Mesplé, Lott, Berganza, Van Dam, Bacquier, Capitole Toulouse O or Paris CO, Plasson; Dalton Baldwin (piano).

With a composer whose expressive range in song-form (or mélodie) might have seemed limited, it is an excellent idea in the HMV set to have six strongly contrasted singers, each given an apt area to cover. So Teresa Berganza as well as singing *Shéhérazade* has two songs inspired by Spain, the *Vocalise in the form of an Habanera* and the *Chanson espagnole* from the set of five *Chants populaires*, each of which is allotted to a different singer. Felicity Lott's *Chanson écossaise* is a rarity, *Ye banks and braes* sung in a convincing Scots accent. For all the shallowness of Mady Mesplé's voice, it works well in the *Mélodies populaires grecques*, while Jessye Norman, rich-toned if not quite so characterful as usual, has the *Chansons madécasses* as well as lesser-known songs. It is the contribution of the two men that provides the sharpest illumination: José van Dam magnificently dark-toned in the *Don Quichotte* songs and the *Mélodies hébraïques* (making *Kaddish* thrillingly powerful in its agony of mourning), while Gabriel Bacquier twinkles in Figaro tones in the point songs. Excellent sound on both disc and tape.

Chansons madécasses; Don Quichotte à Dulcinée; Epigrammes de Clément Marot; Histoires naturelles; Deux mélodies hébraïques; Cinq mélodies populaires grecques.

(M) *** Ph. Seq. 6527/*7311* 154 [id.]. Gérard Souzay, Dalton Baldwin.

A distinguished recital from 1968, when Gérard Souzay was in his prime. His sensibility in this repertoire is matched by consistently sympathetic accompaniments from Dalton Baldwin. The recording is admirably balanced, with a smooth matching tape.

(i) *Chansons madécasses;* (ii) *Don Quichotte à Dulcinée; Cinq mélodies populaires grecques;* (iii) *Trois poèmes de Stéphane Mallarmé;* (iv) *Shéhérazade.*

*** CBS Dig. M/*MT* 39023 [id.]. (i) Norman, Ens. InterContemporain; (ii) José van Dam; (iii) Jill Gomez; (iv) Heather Harper; BBC SO, Boulez.

With four characterful and strongly contrasted soloists, Boulez's collection of Ravel's songs with orchestra (including arrangements) makes a delightful disc. This is an important supplement to the EMI set of Ravel's complete songs, when the *Don Quichotte* and the *Greek popular songs* (both with José van Dam as soloist) are rarely heard in this orchestral form. Van Dam may not be as relaxed as he is with piano on the HMV set, but the dark, firm voice is just as impressive. Excellent sound, on both LP and tape, with translations provided in both formats.

Shéhérazade (song cycle).
© *** Ph. Dig. **410 043-2**; 6514/*7337* 199 [id.]. Elly Ameling, San Francisco SO, De Waart – DEBUSSY: *La damoiselle élue*; DUPARC: *Songs*.*** ©
(*) Ph. **412 493-2; 9500 783/*7300 857* [id.]. Jessye Norman, LSO, Sir Colin Davis – BERLIOZ: *Nuits d'été*.**(*)
** HMV Dig. **CDC 747111-2** [id.]; EL 270135-1/*4* [Ang. DS/*4DS* 38061]. Dame Kiri Te Kanawa, Belgian Nat. Op. O, Pritchard – DUPARC: *Songs*.**
** Decca Dig. **411 895-2**; 411 895-1/*4* [id.]. Hildegard Behrens, VSO, Travis – BERLIOZ: *Nuites d'été*.*(*)

Elly Ameling has a voice of innocence, pure of tone; however, when she sings Gershwin for example, she can colour it sensuously; and so it is here in Ravel's evocative song-cycle. Other versions may delve deeper into the exotic emotions behind the poems by 'Tristan Klingsor', but in its sweetness and beauty (enhanced by the orchestral playing and radiant recording) this has a place too, particularly when the coupling is apt and unusual. On the superb compact disc the effect is ravishing, the voice seemingly floating against a wonderfully luminous orchestral backcloth. Compact disc collectors may feel that this even takes precedence over the classic Baker version. There is also a good chrome cassette.

Jessye Norman seems more at home in Ravel's song-cycle than in the coupled account of the Berlioz, although she and Sir Colin Davis are languorous to the point of lethargy in *L'Indifférent*. With the voice very forward, the balance is less than ideal, though otherwise the sound is rich and atmospheric. Ameling, however, has special qualities to offer which Miss Norman does not match. The CD transfer enhances the presence of the recording while emphasizing the balance. There is a faithful tape, but made at rather a low level.

Unlike some of her colleagues, Dame Kiri elects to couple Ravel's glorious triptych with Duparc songs rather than the usual *Les Nuits d'été* favoured by Norman and Behrens. She is somewhat bland by comparison with her most formidable rivals, and despite good orchestral playing from the Belgian National Opera Orchestra under Sir John Pritchard and good EMI recording, this is not among the most memorable recorded versions of the cycle.

Behrens's version is rich-toned and evocative, with the weight of the voice adding to the impact – though the pure beauty of these songs has been more ravishingly caught in other versions. As in the disappointing account of the Berlioz on the reverse, the recording is outstandingly vivid and approaches demonstration standard not only on CD but on LP and cassette too.

OPERA

L'Enfant et les sortilèges.
*** HMV Dig. **CDC 747169-2** [id.]; ASD/*TCC-ASD* 4167 [Ang. DS/*4XS* 37869]. Wyner, Augér, Berbié, Langridge, Bastin, Amb. S., LSO, Previn.

Previn's dramatic and highly spontaneous reading of *L'Enfant* brings out the refreshing charm of a neglected masterpiece. Helped by a strong and stylish team of soloists, this makes superb entertainment. On CD, the precision and sense of presence of the digital recordings come out the more vividly, with subtle textures clarified and voices – including the odd shout – precisely placed. That precision goes well with Previn's performance, crisply rhythmic rather than atmospherically poetic. It is a pity that the 44-minute piece has only one band, divided only by index markings, unusable on many machines. LP and tape too are extremely vivid.

Rawsthorne, Alan (1905–71)

Piano concertos: No. 1 (1942); No. 2 (1951).
*** Lyr. SRCS 101 [id.]. Malcolm Binns, LSO, Braithwaite.

Rawsthorne's star has waned since his untimely death in 1971, but his musical language is always highly distinctive and the finest of his works, such as the *Symphonic Studies* and the *First Symphony*, have real substance. The two *Piano concertos* are the product of an immensely fertile mind; and it must be said that these 1978 recordings supersede all earlier versions. The *First*, written in 1939, is the more haunting and atmospheric of the two; it was originally scored for piano, strings and timpani but was subsequently rescored (1942) for larger forces where its ideas are heard to greater effect. The *Second*, written for the 1951 Festival of Britain and recorded by both Clifford Curzon and Denis Matthews, wears its years less lightly, and some of its ideas are just a bit facile. However, the two *Concertos* make a logical and welcome coupling and Malcolm Binns gives a most persuasive account of both scores. He finds a Prokofiev-like contrast between jagged figuration and lyrical warmth and brings out the expressiveness of the music, particularly in the *First Concerto* with its hushed slow movement and interlude in the middle of the final *Tarantella*. There is plenty of vigour in both dance finales (the second has its quota of Latin American rhythms). The LSO play excellently for Nicholas Braithwaite, and the Lyrita recording is extremely fine.

Reich, Steve (born 1936)

Eight lines; Vermont counterpoint.
*** HMV Dig. EL 270291-1/*4* [Ang. DS/*4XS* 37345]. Solisti New York, Wilson – ADAMS: *Grand pianola music.****

Steve Reich's *Vermont counterpoint* is aurally fascinating, with its flute-dominated textures – Ransom Wilson here soloist as well as musical director – and the longer *Eight lines* is also ingeniously scored. But this is minimalist music with a vengeance, with the textural alterations relatively insignificant over a fairly long time-span, and the listener might be forgiven the impression that the recording is 'stuck in the groove'. Both performances are admirably fresh however, and the hypnotic effect of the music is undeniable. The recording is first class and the XDR tape is clear and vivid.

Variations for winds, strings and keyboard.
*** Ph. **412 214-2**; 412 214-1/*4* [id.]. San Francisco SO, De Waart – ADAMS: *Shaker loops.****

Reich's *Variations*, written for the San Francisco orchestra in 1980, marked a new departure in the writing of this leading minimalist, using a large orchestral rather than a small chamber scale. The repetitions and ostinatos, which gradually get out of phase, are most skilfully used to produce a hypnotic kind of poetry, soothing rather than compelling. With the excellent Adams coupling and first-rate performance and recording, it can be warmly recommended to anyone wanting to sample minimalism. There is an excellent tape, catching the engaging sounds Reich creates as freshly as the LP. The CD does not add a great deal because of the resonant ambience, but the background silence increases the feeling of tension.

Reicha, Antonin (1770–1836)

Oboe quintet in F, Op. 107.
*** Hyp. A 66143 [id.]. Sarah Francis, Allegri Qt – CRUSELL: *Divertimento*; KREUTZER: *Grand quintet.****

Born in the same year as Beethoven, Antonin Reicha was an enormously productive composer, as well as a respected teacher whose pupils included Liszt and Berlioz. The *F major Quintet*, Op. 107, dates from the first half of the 1820s and is spectacularly unmemorable but always amiable. None of the three pieces on this record is interrupted, this *Quintet* occupying all of the second side. The present performance is of high quality and is very well recorded.

Reinecke, Carl (1824–1910)

Flute concerto in D, Op. 283.
*** Ph. Dig. **412 728-2**; 412 728-1/*4* [id.]. Nicolet, Leipzig GO, Masur – BUSONI: *Divertimento*; NIELSEN: *Concerto*.***

Carl Reinecke was a great figure in Leipzig's musical life; for many years he was conductor of the Gewandhaus Orchestra and director of the Leipzig conservatoire. In his youth he served as pianist to the Danish court. His *Flute concerto* is a late work, as its vast opus number might indicate, written in 1908 when he was in his mid-eighties. It could have been written in the mid-1850s and is very much in the tradition of Mendelssohn; it has considerable charm and warmth as well as personality. The elegiac slow movement has real eloquence and is beautifully written; this *Concerto* will come as something of a discovery. Aurèle Nicolet plays it with effortless ease and is admirably supported by the Leipzig orchestra. The recording, made in a reverberant acoustic, is also excellent; even if the soloist is a shade too forward, the balance is well judged. Because of the resonance, the CD improves the definition only marginally over the very fine LP and chrome tape.

Respighi, Ottorino (1879–1936)

(i) *Ancient airs and dances: Suites Nos 1–3;* (ii) *The Birds; 3 Botticelli pictures.*
(B) *** HMV *TCC2-POR 54276*. (i) LACO; (ii) ASMF, Marriner.

An admirable compilation chosen to represent Neville Marriner in HMV's 'Portrait of the Artist' double-length tape series. The account of the suite of dances is attractively light and gracious, offering an almost French elegance with pleasingly transparent textures. The performances of *The Birds* and the *Trittico Botticelliano* are no less delightful and beautifully recorded. The score for the *Botticelli pictures* is less well known and understandably so, for its inspiration is less assured; with presentation of this standard, however, the music is certainly enjoyable. The tape transfer is of high quality, with the sound fresh and pleasing; *The Birds* and the *Botticelliano* are notably warm and refined, yet there is excellent detail.

Ancient airs and dances for lute (arr. for orchestra): *Suites Nos 1–3. Feste romane; The Fountains of Rome; The Pines of Rome* (symphonic poems).
(M) **(*) DG 413 206-1/*4* (2). Boston SO, Ozawa.

Ozawa was the first to offer Respighi's Roman triptych on a single disc (see below); though the sides are well filled, the quality of the recording stands up well alongside Karajan's LP which omits *Feste romane*. Ozawa is at his best in *The Fountains of Rome*; this performance is as good as any in the catalogue; the other works have plenty of atmosphere, too, *Feste romane* vivid without being noisy. The orchestral playing is very fine throughout and DG's recording captures the resonant Boston acoustic impressively: the climax of *The Pines* is overwhelmingly powerful. The complete set of *Ancient airs and dances* is only marginally less distinctive. Ozawa displays an attractive lightness of touch, though rhythms are firm. He is at his best in the *Second Suite*, where the luminous wind playing combines with plentiful contrasts of pacing and dynamic to good effect. The *Third Suite* is more memorable in Karajan's hands. But with excellent recording throughout (the discs and chrome tapes – in a cardboard flap-pack – sound virtually identical) this is good value at mid-price. However, with the three Roman symphonic poems now available again separately on Galleria, the attraction of the present set is slightly diminished.

Ancient airs and dances: Suite No. 3; The Fountains of Rome; The Pines of Rome.
*** DG **413 822-2**; (without *Ancient airs and dances*) 2531/*3301* 055 [id.]. BPO, Karajan.

On CD, Karajan's highly polished, totally committed performances of the two most popular Roman pieces are well supplemented by the third suite of *Ancient airs and dances*, just as brilliantly done and with 1970s' analogue recording just as beautifully transferred, more impressive in sound than many more recent Karajan recordings. In the symphonic poems Karajan is in his element, and the playing of the Berlin Philharmonic is wonderfully refined. The evocation of atmosphere in the two middle sections of *The Pines of Rome* is unforgettable. A distanced and magically haunting trumpet solo is matched by the principal clarinet who is no less poetic. In *The Fountains* the tension is rather less tautly held, but the pictorial imagery is hardly less telling when the orchestral response is so magical. Both LP and the closely matching cassette omit the *Ancient airs and dances*.

Belkis, Queen of Sheba: suite. Metamorphoseon modi XII.
€ *** Chan. Dig. **CHAN 8405**; ABRD/*ABTD* 1142 [id.]. Philh. O, Simon.

Geoffrey Simon follows up the success of his earlier Respighi recording (coupling *Church windows* and *Brazilian impressions*) with two even rarer pieces, one of which gives a surprising slant on a composer who often seems just an atmosphere man, a colourist rather than a musical arguer. The ballet-suite *Belkis, Queen of Sheba*, taken from a full-length ballet written in the early 1930s, is just what you would expect: a score that set the pattern for later Hollywood biblical film music; but *Metamorphoseon* is a taut and sympathetic set of variations. It has been ingeniously based on a medieval theme, and though a group of cadenza variations relaxes the tension of argument in the middle, the brilliance and variety of the writing have much in common with Elgar's *Enigma*. Superb playing from the Philharmonia, treated to one of the finest recordings that even Chandos has produced, outstanding in every way. This is very attractive music and the sound is certainly in the demonstration bracket in all three media. The chrome cassette is quite astonishing.

The Birds; The Fountains of Rome; The Pines of Rome (symphonic poems).
** Ph. Dig. **411 419-2**; 6514/*7337* 202 [id.]. San Francisco SO, De Waart.

The Birds is an evocative and beautifully scored work; it makes a less usual coupling for Respighi's two finest symphonic poems associated with Rome. De Waart conducts brilliant and sympathetic performances, but an unnatural brilliance in the recording with unrealistic placing of instruments is underlined on the finest reproducers, not least in the compact disc version.

Brazilian impressions; Church windows (*Vetrate di chiesa*).
ϵ *** Chan. Dig. **CHAN 8317**; ABRD/*ABTD* 1098 [id.]. Philh. O, Simon.

Respighi's set of musical illustrations of church windows is not among his finest works (the second stained-glass portrait, representing St Michael, is the most memorable, with its extrovert colouring) but is well worth having when the recording is impressively spacious and colourful. Geoffrey Simon is sympathetic and he secures very fine playing from the Philharmonia. The superb digital recording and the useful coupling (which avoids duplication with Respighi's more famous works) will be an added incentive to collectors. On CD, the wide dynamic range and a striking depth of perspective create the most spectacular effects, and this is very much in the demonstration class. The chrome tape, too, has very good definition within the atmospheric acoustic.

Feste romane; The Fountains of Rome; The Pines of Rome (symphonic poems).
*** HMV Dig. **CDC 747316-2** [id.]; EL 270312-1/*4* [Ang. DS/*4DS* 38219]. Phd. O, Muti.
ϵ *** Decca Dig. **410 145-2**; SXDL/*KSXDC* 7591 [Lon. LDR/*5*- 71091]. Montreal SO, Dutoit.
(M) *** DG Gal. 415 846-1/*4* [id.]. Boston SO, Ozawa.
(***) RCA mono [**RCCD 1010**]; Gold GL/*GK* 85226 (without *Feste Romane*). NBC SO, Toscanini.

Muti gives warmly red-blooded performances of Respighi's Roman trilogy, captivatingly Italianate in their inflections. With brilliant playing from the Philadelphia Orchestra and warmly atmospheric recording, far better than EMI engineers have generally been producing in Philadelphia, these are exceptional for their strength of characterization. Each scene is vividly dramatized, and the most impressive of the three is the most brazen of a brazen trio of works, *Feste romane*. Muti flouts the idea of vulgarity, and produces a reading that is well 'over the top', but all the more captivating for it. In the final orgiastic jubilation of *La Befana*, the jazzy jollity and outrageous intrusions of popular music are so exuberant they are enough to make you laugh. The CD version clarifies the reverberant recording very effectively, with individual soloists cleanly placed. Each of the four sections in each piece is separately banded. There is a fair cassette, but it does not match the CD in definition and range.

Dutoit as in other brilliant and colourful pieces draws committed playing from his fine Montreal orchestra. Where many interpreters concentrate entirely on brilliance, Dutoit finds a vein of expressiveness too, which – for example in the opening sequence of *The Pines of Rome* – conveys the fun of children playing at the Villa Borghese. There have been more high-powered, even more polished performances on record, but none more persuasive. The recorded sound is superlative, most of all on compact disc, where the organ pedal sound is stunning and where the format avoids the break in *Roman festivals* inevitable on LP. Cassette collectors too should be well satisfied, for the standard of tape transfer is remarkably fine.

Ozawa's 1979 record has been digitally remastered for its Galleria reissue and remains very competitive at mid-price, with an excellent matching chrome tape, although while sharpening the focus and refining detail the brighter treble has brought a hint of harshness to the loudest fortissimos.

The *Pines* and *Fountains of Rome* were among Toscanini's most famous recordings. They were made in Carnegie Hall in 1953 and 1951 respectively and thus have a more flattering ambience than Toscanini's notorious studio sessions. Even so, to judge from these digitally remastered records, it seems that the conductor (or the engineers) still insisted on a top-heavy sound-balance, with very little of the expansive resonance in the bass which is the natural feature of that auditorium. The CD transfers exaggerate this imbalance still further and put an edge on the treble which, at the opening of *The Pines* and the piercingly shrill transients at the turning-on of the Triton fountain, assault the ear-drums unmercifully. The LP and tape are much more comfortable (there is little to choose between them) although they omit *Feste Romane* where Toscannini, apart from securing orchestral playing of stunning bravura, shows a nice feeling for the atmosphere of his homeland in the gaudy detail of *The night before Epiphany*. (One wonders why this is omitted, for side two of the LP plays for only 14′ 58″.) Although Toscanini does not have the advantage of stereo (nor indeed have the RCA engineers exploited the possibilities of mono techniques with the skill of a Walter Legge), in *The Pines* and *Fountains* he manages to convey more colour than some maestros who do. The last of the four fountains, *La fontana di Villa Medici al tramonte*, has an intense nostalgia that suggests this music meant a very great deal to him. *The Pines* flourish equally well and come vividly to life in a virtuoso performance which exhilarates, electrifies and, in the moments of repose, touches. The recording brings improved definition at lower dynamic levels, although the lack of bass support in the climax of the *Trevi* sequence is a drawback. The CD is not yet issued in the UK and we must hope that, before it is, RCA will have found a way to minimize the aggressiveness of the treble.

OPERA

La Fiamma (complete).

*** Hung. Dig. **HCD 12591/3**; SLPD/*MK* 12591/3 [id.]. Tokody, Kelen, Takács, Sólyom-Nagy, Hungarian R. and TV Ch., Hungarian State O, Gardelli.

La Fiamma, a tale of witchcraft and the early church set in seventh-century

Ravenna, might be described as Puccini updated – though the setting does also give Respighi plenty of opportunities to draw on his medievalist side, not just his love of exotic sounds. Richly atmospheric with choruses and ensembles both mysterious and savage, it makes a fine impact in this excellent first recording, idiomatically conducted by Lamberto Gardelli. The Hungarian cast is impressive, with Ilona Tokody producing Callas-like inflections in the central role of Silvana, the young wife of the exarch, Basilio. She falls in love with her son-in-law, shocks her husband into falling down dead, and then cannot find tongue to deny a charge of witchcraft. Sándor Sólyom-Nagy is impressive as Basilio, Peter Kelen is aptly light-toned as the son-in-law, but it is the formidable Klára Takács as the interfering Eudossia who personifies the grit in the oyster, providing high melodrama. The playing is warmly committed and, apart from some distancing of the chorus, the sound is first rate, atmospheric but also precisely focused.

Reubke, Julius (1834–58)

Sonata in C min. on the 94th Psalm.
*** DG Dig. **415 139-2**; 415 139-1/*4* [id.]. Simon Preston (organ of Westminster Abbey) – LISZT: *Fantasia and fugue on 'Ad nos salutarem'.****

Julius Reubke (son of an organ builder) studied under Liszt at Weimar and modelled his *Sonata* on Liszt's *Fantasia and fugue* (which is the appropriate coupling). He gave its première in 1857 and died the year after, only twenty-four years of age. His monothematic piece is powerfully conceived and ingeniously wrought; its three sections can be regarded either as separate movements or as different facets of a single structure. Simon Preston's performance is of the first rank and his playing is superbly recorded, with LP and cassette equally impressive, and with the CD adding a degree of extra definition. The acoustic of Westminster Abbey seems especially suited to the sombre *Adagio-Lento*, which is superbly eloquent in Preston's hands. In the outer sections the characteristic blurring created by the acoustics of the Abbey cannot be blamed on the engineers, but in the closing fugue Preston thrusts forward and the complex detail is welded into the texture. Here the CD comes into its own with its thrilling weight and projection.

Rimsky-Korsakov, Nikolay (1844–1908)

Capriccio espagnol, Op. 34.
(B) *** DG Walkman *413 422-4* [id.]. BPO, Maazel – BIZET: *L'Arlésienne*; *Carmen*; DUKAS: *L'apprenti sorcier*; CHABRIER: *España*.**(*)

Capriccio espagnol, Op. 34; May night overture; Russian Easter festival overture, Op. 36; Sadko, Op. 5.
* ASV Dig. DCA/*ZCDCA* 549 [id.]. Mexico City PO, Bátiz.

Maazel's 1960 recording of the *Capriccio espagnol* has never been surpassed. With gorgeous string and horn playing, and a debonair relaxed virtuosity in the *Scene e canto gitano* leading to breathtaking bravura in the closing section, every note in place, this is unforgettable. The remastering for the Walkman tape has smoothed the treble a little, but otherwise the sound remains vivid. With Claudio Abbado's splendid account of Bizet's *L'Arlésienne* and *Carmen suites*, this is worth acquiring, even if some duplication may be involved with the other items.

Bátiz's performances have plenty of spirit, but on the evidence of this LP the Mexico City Philharmonic Orchestra cannot produce a rich enough body of string timbre to do justice to the *Capriccio*, though the horns are good and there is a fine trombone solo in the *Russian Easter festival overture*. *Sadko* comes off best, with Bátiz obviously in sympathy with its atmosphere. The digital recording is brilliant, but artificially balanced, with sometimes fierce brass and the *Festival overture* dominated by the percussion.

Capriccio espagnol; May night overture; Sadko, Op. 5; (i) *The Snow Maiden: suite.*

** Ph. Dig. **411 446-2**; 6514/*7337* 306 [id.]. Rotterdam PO, Zinman; (i) with Alexander and Ch.

Zinman secures some quite lustrous playing from his Rotterdam orchestra in the *Capriccio*, and he finds both atmosphere and colour in *Sadko* and the *May night overture*. But this is music that needs more than refined orchestral playing: there is a lack of charisma here, and the adrenalin only begins to flow at the very end of the Spanish piece. In the *Danse des oiseaux* (from *The Snow Maiden*) there is an effective vocal contribution. Even on compact disc, the recording, though naturally balanced, has no special presence, though it is full and pleasing. The chrome tape only produces satisfactory results if played back at a very high level.

Christmas eve (suite); Le Coq d'or: suite; Legend of the invisible city of Kitezh: suite; May night: overture; Mlada: suite; The Snow Maiden: suite; The Tale of the Tsar Saltan: suite.

ℭ *** Chan. Dig. **CHAN 8327-9**; DBRD/*DBTD* 3004 (3) [id.]. SNO, Neeme Järvi.

Much of the more memorable writing in Rimsky-Korsakov's fairy-tale operas is for orchestra alone, which the composer uses with enormous flair to create the background atmosphere for the exotic events of the narrative. There is an essential pantheism in Rimsky's art. The *Prelude* to *The invisible city of Kitezh* is described as a hymn to nature, while the delights of the *Christmas eve suite* (an independent work) include a magical evocation of the glittering stars against a snow-covered landscape and, later, a flight of comets. The plots, drawn on Gogol and Ostrovsky, are peopled by picaresque human characters. In *Le Coq d'or* the bumbling King Dodon has his counterpart in the alluring Queen

Shemakha for whom Rimsky wrote one of his most sensuously languorous melodies, an idea – like so many here – of great memorability. Apart from the feast of good tunes, the composer's skilful and subtle deployment of the orchestral palette continually titillates the ear. Within the ideal resonance of their Glasgow home, Neeme Järvi draws the most seductive response from the SNO (who clearly relish the feline delicacy of Queen Shemakha's seduction of the King); he consistently creates orchestral textures which are diaphanously sinuous. Yet the robust moments, when the brass blazes or the horns ring out sumptuously, are caught just as delectably. LPs and chrome tapes are both in the demonstration class (the latter slightly smoother in the treble but with an impressive range and amplitude), but the CDs have that extra degree of presence while the focus is that bit more natural. This Chandos set achieves new standards in this repertoire and the listener is assured that this is music that survives repetition uncommonly well.

Le Coq d'or: suite; The Tale of Tsar Saltan: suite.
** Ph. Dig. **411 435-2**; 6514/*7337* 163 [id.]. Rotterdam PO, Zinman.

While new digital recordings of this repertoire are welcome and the Rotterdam orchestra plays with appealing freshness, Zinman's approach seems over-refined; while there is no lack of colour, the sinuously sentient qualities of *Le Coq d'or* are minimized, and there is a lack of real sparkle elsewhere. The chrome tape, as usual with Philips, has less brilliance on top. On CD, the sound approaches demonstration standard. But Zinman's performances are much less enticing than Järvi's with the SNO, on Chandos.

Scheherazade (symphonic suite), *Op. 35.*
*** Ph. **400 021-2**; 9500 681/*7300 776* [id.]. Concg. O, Kondrashin.
(M) *** Ph. 416 861-1/*4* [id.]. LPO, Haitink.
*** HMV Dig. **CDC 747023-2**; ASD/*TCC-ASD* 4188 [Ang. DS/*4XS* 37851]. Phd. O, Muti.
(*) Ph. Dig. **411 479-2; 6514/*7337* 231 [id.]. VPO, Previn.
(*) Andante **CDACD 85701 [Var/Sara. **VCD 47208**]. LSO, Tjeknavorian – GLINKA: *Russlan overture.****
**(*) JVC/Target VCD 519. Moscow RSO, Fedoseyev.
(B) **(*) DG Walkman *413 155-4* [id.]. Boston SO, Ozawa – STRAVINSKY: *Firebird suite*; KHACHATURIAN: *Gayaneh.***(*)
** Decca **414 124-2** [id.]. SRO, Ansermet – BORODIN: *Polovtsian dances.***
** DG Dig. **415 512-2**; 415 512-1/*4* [id.]. BPO, Maazel.
(B) ** Ph. On Tour *416 221-4* [id.]. LSO, Markevich – MUSSORGSKY: *Pictures*; TCHAIKOVSKY: *Capriccio italien.***

Scheherazade; Capriccio espagnol, Op. 34.
(*) Decca Dig. **410 253-2; 410-253-1/*4* [id.]. Montreal SO, Dutoit.

Kondrashin's version with the Concertgebouw Orchestra has the advantage of marvellous recorded sound, combining richness and sparkle within exactly the right degree of resonance. Here the personality of Hermann Krebbers (the orchestra's concertmaster) very much enters the picture, and his gently seductive portrayal of Scheherazade's narrative creates a strong influence on the overall interpretation. His exquisite playing, especially at the opening and close of the work, is cleverly used by Kondrashin to provide a foil for the expansively vibrant contribution of the orchestra as a whole. The first movement, after Krebbers's tranquil introduction, develops a striking architectural sweep; the second is vivid with colour, the third beguilingly gracious, while in the finale, without taking unusually fast tempi, Kondrashin creates an irresistible forward impulse leading to a huge climax at the moment of the shipwreck. On CD, one notices that inner detail is marginally less sharp than it would be with a digital recording, but the analogue glow and naturalness more than compensate, and the richness of texture is just right for the music. Unfortunately the cassette transfer, although well balanced, lacks the ultimate range and sparkle of the LP.

Haitink's LPO record dates from 1974 when it was the finest account of *Scheherazade* to appear for more than a decade. Compared with the Kondrashin, the recording shows its age just a little in the string timbre, but in all other respects it is exceptionally truthful in both sound and perspective. It is relief to hear a solo violin sounding its natural size in relation to the orchestra as a whole. Yet Rodney Friend, who plays the solos subtly – like Krebbers with Kondrashin – dominates the performance, with his richly sinuous picture of Scheherazade herself as narrator of each episode. The playing of the LPO is both sensitive and alert, Haitink's interpretation is wholly unaffected and totally fresh in impact, with no lack of excitement in the finale. The recording has been remastered with great success, and now there is a first-class chrome tape, every bit as vivid as the LP. For those not requiring a CD, this makes a splendid recommendation in the mid-price range.

Muti's reading is colourful and dramatic in a larger-than-life way that sweeps one along. The bravura has one remembering that this was the orchestra which in the days of Stokowski made this a party-piece. The great string theme of the slow movement has all the voluptuousness one expects of Philadelphia strings in one of the best of HMV's latterday Philadelphia recordings, more spacious than usual, though not ideally balanced. There is a glare in the upper range to which not all ears will respond, even if the racy finale, with its exciting climax, carries all before it. The CD emphasizes the brightness of the treble, especially in climaxes; this digital emphasis is much less congenial than the Philips sound for Kondrashin. On tape, there is a slight loss of refinement, if not of impact.

Previn in his Vienna version opts for spacious speeds and a direct, unsentimental view of the fairy-tale suite. With his characteristic rhythmic flair and sumptuous playing from the Vienna Philharmonic, the result can be recommended to those wanting a more restrained reading than usual. Excellent, finely balanced sound on LP, with improved definition and presence on CD. The chrome cassette lacks sparkle and the finale is bass-heavy. But even on compact disc, in spite of the advantages of digital recording, this does not match Kondrashin in excitement and the recording is only marginally more effective.

Tjeknavorian's is an arresting performance and, with extremely brilliant and detailed recording, its sharpness of detail will certainly appeal to some ears. The overall sound-balance is bright rather than richly sumptuous, yet the bass response is strong and clear. Tjeknavorian paces the music briskly throughout: the first movement has a strong, passionate climax, and the slow movement has less repose than usual, sounding more elegant, less sensuous, its 6/8 rhythmic pattern readily apparent. The finale has a furious basic tempo, but the LSO players obviously revel in their virtuosity and the result is consistently exhilarating, with (for the most part) amazingly clear articulation. The climax has a brilliance to make the ears tingle, with a hint of fierceness in the recording itself.

The brilliant Russian digital recording projects the sound of the Moscow Radio orchestra faithfully enough, with its rather febrile string timbre, braying brass and robust woodwind. The balance also favours the percussion, and in the finale the cymbals are almost overwhelming at times. There is no lack of adrenalin here, even the sinuous melody of the slow movement is kept moving; however, though the overall effect is undoubtedly exciting and very Russian in feeling, elegance is almost entirely absent. The CD transfer has both weight and fullness to underpin the brightness on top, yet inner definition is not especially clear.

Ozawa's version is available on a Walkman cassette, making a bargain alternative if the couplings, Maazel's early stereo recording of the *Firebird suite* and Rozhdestvensky's *Gayaneh*, are suitable. It is an attractive performance, richly recorded. The first movement is strikingly spacious, building to a fine climax; if the last degree of vitality is missing from the central movements, the orchestral playing is warmly vivid. The finale is lively enough, if not earth-shaking in its excitement; the reading as a whole has plenty of colour and atmosphere, however, and it is certainly enjoyable. The chrome-tape transfer is sophisticated.

Dutoit offers an exceptionally generous coupling; the long sides of the LP have no adverse effect on the recording, which is characteristic of the Montreal acoustic, full and warm, with luminous detail. There is an equally impressive chrome tape. However, this is a relaxed, lyrical reading at speeds slower than usual; essentially an amiable view, lacking in virtuoso excitement. The *Capriccio espagnol* compensates to some extent for this shortcoming, again given a genial performance – though one not lacking in brilliance. On compact disc, in spite of the impressive Decca recording, first choice remains with Kondrashin.

Ansermet's CD is of a historic recording of 1961; though the sound is impressive for its period, the rasp of the brass at the start and the occasional fuzz in heavy tuttis are revealed the more clearly as incipient distortion. As to the interpretation, Ansermet's skill as a ballet conductor comes out persuasively. The outer movements with their undoubted sparkle are the finest: the first is dramatic, and in the last the final climax makes a considerable impact. The music's sinuous qualities are not missed and every bar of the score is alive. However, this is also available on LP at bargain price on Contour in a clean, new master which seems a more sensible way of acquiring the performance (CC 7501). In hi-fi terms, the CD issue is hardly viable (unlike the companion collections of Debussy, Mussorgsky and Ravel), although the *Polovtsian dances*, complete with chorus - not included on the LP – comprise a reasonably attractive makeweight.

There is nothing to detain the collector in Maazel's DG version. The playing of the Berlin Philharmonic Orchestra is, of course, peerless, and in the slow movement they make some gorgeous sounds (though the acoustics of the Philharmonie are not entirely flattering on CD). But Maazel's reading is essentially spacious and the outer movements are wanting in electricity. The chrome cassette offers a comfortable sound-balance and does not match the LP in range and sparkle.

There are generous couplings on the Philips 'On Tour' cassette, but Markevich's *Scheherazade* fails to generate the degree of vivid colour or sheer excitement that the music needs. The slightly dry recording has transferred well to tape and does not lack immediacy. There is some good orchestral playing here, but it is doubtful if *Scheherazade* would have lasted 1001 nights at this temperature.

Symphonies Nos 1 in D min., Op. 1 (second version); *2* (*Antar*), *Op. 9; 3 in C, Op. 32. Russian Easter festival overture, Op. 36.*
** Chant du Monde (without *Overture*) **CD 278771/3** (2); LDX/*K4* 78771/3 [id.]. USSR Nat. O, Svetlanov.

Symphony No. 3 in C, Op. 32; Skazka (*Fairy tale*), *Op. 29.*
**(*) ASV Dig. DCA/*ZCDCA* 538 [id.]. LSO, Butt.

These symphonies have been recorded before on Melodiya (issued here by HMV), but not to such substantial effect. The *First* was sketched in 1860–61 but was not completed until 1865, only to be revised in its present format in the spring of 1884. So it falls between two stools, lacking the youthful spontaneity of, say, Bizet's *Symphony*, but without the mastery of maturity. Yet it has some good ideas and, not surprisingly, some effective orchestration. It has a sombre *Andante tranquillo*, which Svetlanov shapes impressively, and the finale is good-humoured and not too rhetorical. The *Second Symphony* is better known under its sub-title, *Antar*, a powerful precursor of *Scheherazade*. Its memorable themes and dramatic orchestral effects illustrate a story from mythology whose heroine (as characterized in Rimsky's sinuous descriptive orientalism) has a good deal in common with Queen Shemakha in *Le Coq d'or*.

The *Third Symphony* is not one of the composer's strongest works but remains distinctly appealing, especially in Svetlanov's hands, where it becomes weightier and more symphonically commanding than in the ASV version under Yondani Butt. Throughout the Chant du Monde set the orchestral playing has great character, the strings are eloquent and produce a fine body of timbre, and woodwind solos have plenty of colour. If the brass tend to bray a bit, that is part of any Russian performance and there is, overall, a lyrical fervour that is especially telling in music which is not always structurally strong. The recording itself is very bright, combining a warm hall ambience with a degree of dryness brought by the fairly close microphones. There is an element of harshness in the louder tuttis and a patch of congestion in the slow movement of the *First Symphony*, but no lack of weight, and the percussion effects bring a proper Rimskian glitter, notably in the *Russian Easter festival overture*. This is omitted on the pair of CDs.

The ASV recording of the LSO is altogether more sophisticated and Butt's performance, if lightweight, is also persuasive. In the *Andante*, with its characteristic sequential climaxes, Svetlanov is stronger; but overall Butt has a degree more charm. Moreover, he has the advantage of an interesting fill-up, *Skazka*, a somewhat Lisztian but highly inventive piece that has been out of the catalogue since Fistoulari's mono recording on Parlophone. With a good matching cassette, this can certainly be recommended as an alternative to the complete set, especially to those who already have *Antar*.

Tsar Saltan, Op. 57: March.

*** Telarc Dig. **CD 80107**; DG 10107 [id.]. RPO, Previn – TCHAIKOVSKY: *Symphony No. 5.****

The crisp, stylized *March* from *Tsar Saltan*, a fairy-tale piece, makes a delightful bonne-bouche, a welcome fill-up for Previn's fine account of the Tchaikovsky *Fifth Symphony*, equally well played and recorded.

Piano and wind quintet in B flat.

*** CRD CRD 1109/*CRDC 4109* [id.]. Nash Ens. – ARENSKY: *Piano trio No. 1.****

*** Hyp. A/*KA* 66163 [id.]. Capricorn – GLINKA: *Grand Sextet.****

Rimsky-Korsakov's youthful *Quintet for piano, flute, clarinet, horn and bassoon* is a thoroughly diverting piece. In an earlier edition we described it as being like a garrulous but endearing friend whose loquacity is readily borne for the sake of his charm and good nature. The main theme of the finale is pretty brainless but singularly engaging, and the work as a whole leaves a festive impression. It has been out of the catalogue since the deletion of the Vienna Octet account on Decca, but the Nash Ensemble give a spirited and delightful account of it on CRD that can be warmly recommended for its dash and sparkle.

Capricorn is a young group, formed in the 1970s, who have been making a name for themselves in recent years. Their account of the Rimsky-Korsakov *Quintet* has great vivacity and is excellently recorded. There is not a great deal to choose between them and the Nash, though the excellence of the pianist, Julian Jacobson (formerly Dawson Lyall), should be noted: he contributes a rare sparkle to the proceedings. Personal requirements concerning the respective couplings may be safely left to decide matters. Both are rarities, and the Arensky is a delicious period piece. There is an excellent matching cassette.

Rodrigo, Joaquín (born 1902)

A la busca del más allá; (i) *Concierto de Aranjuez; Zarabanda lejana, y Villancico.*
(M) **(*) EMI Dig. EMX 41 2068-1/*4* [Ang. DS/*4XS* 37876]. LSO, Bátiz; (i) with Moreno.

The *Zarabanda lejana* (Distant sarabande) was Rodrigo's first work for guitar (1926), written in homage to Luis Milan. He later orchestrated it and added the *Villancico* to make a binary structure, the first part nobly elegiac, the second a gay dance movement, with a touch of harmonic astringency, but having something of the atmosphere of a carol. The symphonic poem, *A la busca del más allá* (In search of the beyond) was written as recently as 1978 but, like all Rodrigo's music, its idiom is in no way avant-garde. It could easily be dismissed as film music without a film, yet it is evocative and powerfully scored and makes a curiously indelible impression. Bátiz plays it with strong commitment, as he does the earlier piece, and the vividly brilliant, forwardly balanced digital sound produces a considerable impact on both disc and the boldly transferred cassette. Unfortunately the performance of the ubiquitous *Concierto de Aranjuez*, although bright and sympathetic, is in no way outstanding, which reduces the attractions of this issue, even at mid-price.

(i) *Concierto Andaluz;* (ii) *Concierto madrigal.*
*** Ph. **400 024-2** [id.]. (i) Los Romeros; (ii) P. and A. Romero, ASMF, Marriner.

Los Romeros and the Academy make the very most of the *Concierto Andaluz*, with infectious spirit in the outer sections and plenty of romantic atmosphere in the slow movement. The *Concierto madrigal* was also written for the Romero family; the performance here is definitive and beautifully recorded. Each of the twelve miniatures that make up this engaging work springs vividly to life. Sir Neville Marriner's contribution to both concertos has real distinction. The analogue recordings, originally first class, have responded most convincingly to digital remastering.

Concierto de Aranjuez; Fantasia para un gentilhombre.
ℭ *** Decca Dig. **400 054-2**; SXDL/*KSXDC* 7525 [Lon. LDR/*5*- 71027]. Carlos Bonell, Montreal SO, Dutoit.
*** CBS Dig. **CD 37848**; IM/*IMT* 37848 [id.]. John Williams, Philh. O, Frémaux.
*** Ph. **411 440-2** [id.]. Pepe Romero, ASMF, Marriner.
(M) *** HMV EG 290300-1/*4* [Ang. AM/*4AM* 34716]. Angel Romero, LSO, Previn.
(B) *** CBS *MGT 39017*. John Williams, ECO, Barenboim – CASTELNUOVO-TEDESCO: *Concerto***(*); VILLA-LOBOS: *Concerto.****
(*) DG **413 349-2 [id.]. Narciso Yepes, Philh. O, Navarro.

The great success of the digital Decca issue is due not only to the exceptionally clear and well-balanced digital recording (as realistic and demonstration-worthy on cassette as on LP) and to Bonell's imaginative and inspired account of the solo part, but equally to the strong characterization of the orchestral accompaniments by Charles Dutoit and his excellent Montreal orchestra. In the *Concierto*, the series of vivid interjections by the orchestral wind soloists (cor anglais, bassoon and trumpet) is projected with the utmost personality and presence, and a feeling of freshness pervades every bar of the orchestral texture. Soloist and orchestra combine to give an outstandingly eloquent account of the famous slow movement, and the climax retains its clarity of texture. The finale has irresistible sparkle. In the *Fantasia*, the balance between warmly gracious lyricism and sprightly rhythmic resilience is no less engaging; here again, the orchestral solo playing makes a strong impression. This is a clear first choice for this coupling, especially on compact disc, where the ambient warmth counters the bright upper range.

John Williams's newest version of the *Concierto* (his third) also has the advantage of first-class digital recording. The balance is most believable, the soloist a little forward but with the guitar image admirably related to the orchestra, where inner detail is impressively clear. The acoustic, however, is a little dry compared with the Decca issue; this is emphasized on CD which also suggests that the woodwind is a shade too forward. Nevertheless, this is technically superior to Williams's previous analogue partnership with Barenboim – see below – and the performance is even finer. The slow movement is wonderfully atmospheric, with the soloist's introspective yet inspirational mood anticipated and echoed by Frémaux who secures most beautiful orchestral playing. The finale is light and sparkling with an element of fantasy and much delicacy of articulation in the accompaniment. The performance of the *Fantasia* is no less memorable. Its relaxed opening dialogue between soloist and orchestra is engagingly spontaneous and refined in feeling; later, when the music becomes more energetic, Frémaux brings out the Renaissance colours in the scoring most vividly. This is altogether a most winning coupling, not as extrovert as the Bonell/Dutoit partnership, but no less distinguished.

Pepe Romero's CD is digitally remastered from high-quality analogue recordings dating from 1979 and 1976 respectively. The performance of the *Concierto de Aranjuez* is as satisfying as any available, with a strong Spanish flavour and the musing poetry of the slow movement beautifully caught. The account of the *Fantasia* is warm and gracious, with the Academy contributing quite as much as the soloist to the appeal of the performance. The success of the CD transfer is remarkable; although inner detail is less sharply focused than on either the Bonell or Williams digital versions, it hardly matters, for the warm beauty of the analogue atmosphere emphasizes the Mediterranean feeling; indeed, many will like the softer-grained Philips quality. Background noise is virtually eradicated.

The Previn/Romero issue is undoubtedly very successful, too; it might also be considered at mid-price by those who prefer a recording that favours atmospheric warmth to crystal clarity (though the Decca version does not lack ambient effect). Angel Romero does not emerge as such a strong personality as John Williams, but the skill and sensibility of his playing are in no doubt, and Previn is obviously so delighted with the orchestral scores that he communicates his enthusiasm with loving care for detail. Thus, although the solo guitar is slightly larger than life in relation to the orchestra, Previn is still able to bring out the delightful woodwind chatter in the outer movements of the *Concierto*. The famous slow movement is very beautifully played indeed; the opening is especially memorable. The approach to the *Fantasia* is vividly direct, missing some of the essentially Spanish graciousness that marks the Marriner version (see above), but its infectious quality is more than enough compensation. The spacious recording has transferred well to tape (which is marginally mellower than the LP). The short patch of less than perfectly focused *tutti* at the end of the slow movement is common to both LP and cassette.

John Williams's second analogue recording of the *Concierto*, with Barenboim, made in 1975, is superior to his earlier version with Ormandy. The playing has marvellous point and spontaneity; the *Adagio* had rarely before been played with this degree of poetic feeling. There is a hint of rhythmic overemphasis in the finale, but in general the performance is first class, and if the digital version on CD – see above – is even finer, this remains fully satisfying. The *Fantasia* too is impeccably played and thoroughly enjoyable, with Barenboim making the most of the vivid orchestral colouring. With an outstanding version of the Villa-Lobos *Concerto* and a very good one of the Castelnuovo-Tedesco, this is an unbeatable bargain in CBS's '90 Minute' tape series. The transfer level is high and the sound vivid, and it is generally preferable to the *tape* equivalent of the newest digital coupling of the two Rodrigo works.

Yepes' 1980 version of the *Concierto de Aranjuez* is an improvement on his recording of a decade earlier with the Spanish Radio and TV Orchestra – see below – mainly because of the superior accompaniment. Even here, however, there is a lack of vitality in the outer movements, although the poetic element of the *Adagio* is well managed. The performance of the *Fantasia*, too, has character and refinement, and in both works the analogue recording balance is clear and immediate. But Yepes comes into competition with more attractive versions in all price ranges and his coupling would not be a first choice. The CD transfer is in no way distinctive.

(i) *Concierto de Aranjuez; 3 Piezas españolas* (*Fandango; Passacaglia; Zapateado*)*; Invocation and dance* (*Homage to Manuel de Falla*).
*** RCA Dig. **RD 84900 [RCD1 4900]**. Julian Bream, COE, Gardiner.

Bream's recording of the *Concierto* has a personality all its own. With outer movements offering strong dynamic contrasts and some pungent accents (from orchestra as well as soloist) the music's flamenco associations are underlined and the famous *Adagio* is played in a very free, improvisatory way, with some highly atmospheric wind solos in the orchestra. The whole presentation is immensely vivid, with the orchestration in the outer movements made to sparkle.

The balance is more natural than usual, with the guitar set slightly back and heard in a convincing perspective with the orchestra. The only slight snag is that the resonance adds a touch of harshness to the emphatic orchestral tuttis. What makes this issue especially valuable, however, is the inclusion of the *Tres Piezas españolas*, of which the second, *Passacaglia*, is one of Rodrigo's finest shorter works. No less involving is his *Invocation* for Manuel de Falla, with both performances showing Bream at his most inspirationally spontaneous.

Concierto de Aranjuez (arr. for harp and orchestra).
*** Decca Dig. 411 738-1/*4* [id.]. Marisa Robles, Philh. O, Dutoit – MORENO-BUENDIA: *Suite concertante.**(*)*

The glowing acoustic of St Barnabas Church, London, creates an attractively romantic aura for Marisa Robles' magnetic and highly atmospheric account of the composer's own arrangement for the harp of his famous concerto. Miss Robles is so convincing an advocate that for the moment the guitar original is almost forgotten, particularly when, with inspirational freedom, she makes the beautiful slow movement sound like a rhapsodic improvisation. It is a haunting performance and the sound is first rate. One's only regret is that she does not offer the obvious coupling of the *Concierto serenata* which Rodrigo actually wrote for her instrument. The equivalent chrome tape is well up to Decca's finest standard.

Concierto como un divertimento (for cello and orchestra).
*** RCA RL/*RK* 70798 [ARL1/*ARK1* 4665]. Lloyd Webber, LPO, Lopez-Cobos – LALO: *Concerto.****

One suspects that Julian Lloyd Webber, in commissioning this new concerto, may not have known of the existence of the earlier *Concierto en modo galante* (written in 1949) as recorded by Robert Cohen (but now deleted). If so, the gain is considerable, for the new work is delightful, and even more Spanish in feeling than the old. The style of writing is familiar, with a sinuously atmospheric *Adagio nostalgico* sandwiched between sparklingly inventive outer sections. The moto perpetuo finale has an engaging lyrical strain and the first movement, too, has a catchy main theme. It is all characteristically friendly music, and Lloyd Webber is obviously attuned to its spirit and completely equal to its technical demands. The sound is clear and fresh on disc and vividly transferred to tape, which is refined, quite the equal of the disc.

Concierto para una fiesta (for guitar and orchestra).
*** Ph. **411 133-2**; 411 133-1/*4* [id.]. Pepe Romero, ASMF, Marriner – ROMERO: *Concierto de Málaga.***

Rodrigo's second solo guitar concerto dates from 1982 and was commissioned (in an excellent musical tradition that goes back to Mozart and before) by the McKay family of Fort Worth, Texas, for the social début of their two daughters. It had its first performance, with Pepe Romero the soloist, in March 1983. The recording followed soon after and has all the freshness of new discovery, with Romero playing with striking spontaneity and Marriner and his Academy providing an accompaniment that is characteristically polished as well as thoroughly committed. If Rodrigo does not quite repeat the success of the *Concierto de Aranjuez*, the first movement with its contrasting Valencian themes is highly engaging, and the *Andante calmo* has a hauntingly ruminative introspection, with its sombre main theme involving the dark-timbred cor anglais. The dance rhythms of the finale introduce an Andalusian sevillanas as the principal idea, and the effect is unashamedly brash, in contrast to what has gone before. The recording is most natural and beautifully balanced in all three formats.

Concierto pastoral (for flute and orchestra); *Fantasia para un gentilhombre* (arr. Galway for flute and orchestra).
*** RCA Gold GL/*GK* 85446 [AGL1/*AKL1* 5446]. Galway, Philh. O, Mata.

The *Concierto pastoral* was composed for James Galway in 1978. Its spikily brilliant introduction is far from pastoral in feeling, but the mood of the work soon settles down. At first hearing, the material seems thinner than usual, but Rodrigo's fragmented melodies and rhythmic ostinatos soon insinuate themselves into the listener's memory. The slow movement is especially effective, with a witty scherzando centrepiece framed by the *Adagio* outer sections. James Galway's performance is truly superlative, showing the utmost bravura and matching refinement. He is beautifully recorded, and the small accompanying chamber orchestra is well balanced. The arrangement of the *Fantasia* is a very free one, necessitating re-orchestration, exchanging clarinet and horn instrumentation for the original scoring for trumpet and piccolo. The solo part too has been rewritten and even extended, apparently with the composer's blessing. The result is, to be honest, not an improvement on the original. But Galway is very persuasive, even if there is a persistent feeling of inflation. Tape and disc are virtually identical in the *Fantasia*; there is just a fractional loss of refinement in the *Concierto* tape version, but it is of minor importance.

(i) *Concierto pastoral;* (ii) *Concierto serenata.*
*** HMV Dig. EL 270363-1/*4* [Ang. DS/*4DS* 38278]. (i) Hansen, (ii) Allen, RPO, Bátiz.

These two attractive concertos are already available in first-class performances by their commissionees – see above and below. However, neither coupling is particularly advantageous (although both issues are economically priced), while the pairing on this superbly recorded new HMV digital disc seems ideal. If neither performance is quite as distinctive of those of Galway and Zabaleta respectively, both are spontaneously affectionate and full of engaging touches from the two soloists and the RPO is in sparklingly refined form under Enrique Bátiz. In the *Concerto for harp*, Nancy Allen is rather reticent – she nearly disappears altogether in the first-movement cadenza. But she beguiles the ear with her gentleness, and Bátiz scales down his support to produce a successful partnership in this winning piece (the very opening, with its cascade of trickling notes, is wonderfully inviting). In terms of sheer bravura, Lisa Hansen is not quite James Galway's equal in the *Flute concerto*, but she is a fine player and is particularly sympathetic in the slow movement. The flawless recording, beautifully balanced and immaculately clear, is enhanced by the silent surfaces of the LP; the cassette is second best, with the freshness of the upper range slightly blunted in the XDR iron-oxide transfer; this needed chrome stock, because of the resonant acoustic. We look forward to the CD.

(i) *Concierto serenata* (for harp and orchestra); (ii) *Concierto de Aranjuez; Fantasia para un gentilhombre.*
(B) ** DG Walkman *413 156-4*. (i) Zabaleta, Berlin RSO, Marzendorfer; (ii) Yepes, Spanish R. and TV O, Alonso – FALLA: *Nights in the gardens of Spain.***(*)

Zabaleta himself commissioned the *Concierto serenata*, which has an unforgettable piquancy and charm in both its invention and its felicity of scoring. It is superbly recorded, with the delicate yet colourful orchestral palette entrancing the ear in charming contrast to the beautifully focused timbre of the harp. The performance has great virtuosity and flair and (with the tape transfer in the demonstration class) still deserves the Rosette we awarded to the original LP issue (coupled with a different and much better version of the *Concierto de Aranjuez*). The present recordings of the *Guitar concerto* and the *Fantasia para un gentilhombre* are disappointingly lacking in sparkle. These two works have been recorded in a studio with an unattractively dry acoustic which seems to have damped the spontaneity out of the performances, except in the slow movement of the *Concierto* which seems indestructible. However, this inexpensive double-length tape is worth considering for the *Harp concerto* alone.

Romero, Celedonio (born 1918)

Concierto de Málaga (for guitar; orch. Torroba).
** Ph. **411 133-2**; 411 133-1/*4* [id.]. Pepe Romero, ASMF, Marriner – RODRIGO: *Concierto para una fiesta.****

Romero's *Concierto* originated as an *Andalusian suite* for solo guitar and was orchestrated by Moreno Torroba. Its material is slight and its structure more so; it will appeal most to those who like the passionate guitar-strumming effects of flamenco music, from which it is essentially derived. Pepe Romero creates a strong sense of involvement and is suitably atmospheric when called for, and the accompaniment is well managed. But this work is not on the level of its Rodrigo coupling.

Rosenberg, Hilding (1892–1985)

(i) *Cello concerto No. 2* (*1953*); *Symphony No. 8* (*1980*).
** Cap. Dig. CAP 1283 [id.]. Swedish RSO, Westerberg, (i) with Ola Karlsson.

The one-movement *Eighth Symphony* initially dates from 1974 when, as a free symphonic fantasy, it prefaced a cantata based on poems by Vilhelm Ekelund, commissioned by the Malmö Concert Society. In 1980, when he was approaching his eighty-ninth year, Rosenberg reworked this opening movement so that it should stand on its own feet as a symphony. It is not quite as strong as the *Sixth*, which was once in the catalogue on the Vox Turnabout label, but the score shows some measure of resource and is well worth investigating, even if its abrupt close does not wholly convince. The *Cello concerto No. 2* does not represent Rosenberg at his most inspired. As always with this composer, it has many episodic beauties but does not always seem to have a firm sense of direction. The very opening is imaginative and there is a gently lyrical slow movement. The soloist, Ola Karlsson, plays with an aristocratic poise and refinement, and the recording is outstanding.

Rossini, Gioacchino (1792–1868)

La Boutique fantasque (ballet, arr. Respighi; complete).
*** Decca Dig. **410 139-2**; SXDL/*KSXDC* 7549 [Lon. LDR/*5*- 71039]. Nat. PO, Bonynge – BRITTEN: *Matinées; Soirées*.***

A complete digital recording of *La Boutique fantasque*, one of the great popular triumphs of Diaghilev's Ballets Russes, is an essential part of the CD catalogue. (We hope CBS have plans to issue Andrew Davis's glowing account with the Toronto Symphony Orchestra on compact disc.) Respighi's masterly scoring, glittering and sumptuous, transmutes his relatively slight source-material into a magical tapestry, which on the Davis LP (CBS 35842) sounds superbly atmospheric.

The Decca compact disc has even greater brilliance and also registers remarkable inner detail. Against the silent background the opening bass pizzicatos nearly re-create the magic of Ansermet's famous early mono LP; throughout, the orchestral colours glitter and glow within the attractive resonance of Kingsway Hall, although the digital recording does also produce an edge on the treble. Bonynge goes for sparkle and momentum above all; Davis is more relaxed (as was Ansermet) but Bonynge's exuberance is certainly exhilarating when the sound is so spectacular. The LP is first class too, but the chrome tape is transferred at a modest level to accommodate the very wide dynamic range, and its transients are more subdued. Whichever format is chosen, this issue is much more generous than the CBS; the Britten arrangements are highly engaging and the Decca record plays for over an hour.

Introduction, theme and variations in C min. for clarinet and orchestra.
*** ASV Dig. **CDDCA 559**; DCA/*ZCDCA* 559 [id.]. Emma Johnson, ECO, Groves – CRUSELL: *Concerto No. 2* ❀; BAERMANN: *Adagio*; WEBER: *Concertino.****

On ASV, Sir Charles Groves immediately sets the atmosphere as for a Rossini opera aria, and this performance delectably combines wit with expressive freedom. As in all her recordings, Emma Johnson's lilting timbre and sensitive control of dynamic bring imaginative light and shade to the melodic line. Brilliance for its own sake is not the keynote, but her relaxed pacing is made to sound exactly right. Vivid recording, with a good matching tape.

Overtures: *Il Barbiere di Siviglia; La cambiale di matrimonio; L'inganno felice; L'Italiana in Algeri; La scala di seta; Il Signor Bruschino; Tancredi; Il Turco in Italia.*
❀ ℂ *** DG Dig. **415 363-2**; 415 363-1/*4* [id.]. Orpheus CO.

The Orpheus Chamber Orchestra displays astonishing unanimity of style and ensemble in this splendid collection of Rossini overtures, played without a conductor. Not only is the crispness of string phrasing a joy, but the many stylish wind solos have an attractive degree of freedom, and one never senses any rigidity in allegros which are always joyfully sprung. *La scala di seta* is an especial delight, and the opening string cantilena of *Il Barbiere* is agreeably gracious. These are performances that in their refinement and apt chamber scale give increasing pleasure with familiarity. The DG recording is marvellously real and, when the perspective is so perfectly judged, the background silence gives the wind added tangibility. The string timbre is sweet and natural and entirely without edge in tuttis. A demonstration CD par excellence and one that displays admirable group musicianship put entirely at the service of the composer. The chrome tape is very well managed too, even if it does not match the CD in refined sharpness of detail. But in all three formats this is a clear first choice among presently available collections of Rossini overtures.

Overtures: *Il Barbiere di Siviglia; La cambiale di matrimonio; Otello; Semiramide; Le siège de Corinthe; Tancredi; Torvaldo e Dorliska.*
*** Decca Dig. **414 407-2**; 414 407-1/*4* [id.]. Nat. PO, Chailly.

This is Chailly's second collection of Rossini overtures; it shows a distinct improvement in offering cleaner ensemble and more polished detail, while retaining the high spirits and geniality of the first CD – see below. The novelties, *Otello* – played with great dash – and *Torvaldo e Dorliska*, with its witty interchanges between wind and strings, are among the highlights. *Semiramide* is also elegantly played and *The Barber* is nicely stylish. As before, detail is wonderfully clear in the music's gentler sections, but the vivid tuttis bring a touch of aggressiveness on the fortissimo strings. However, this can be tamed, and the performances are undoubtedly infectious.

Overtures: *Il Barbiere di Siviglia; La Cenerentola; La gazza ladra; L'Italiana in Algeri; Otello; La scala di seta: Semiramide; William Tell.*
*** Ph. **412 893-2** [id.]. ASMF, Marriner.

These eight overtures, playing for about 70 minutes, are the best known, taken from Sir Neville Marriner's 'complete' survey, recorded in the late 1970s, which included two dozen in all. Original orchestrations are used and the performances are characteristically neat and polished. In the remastering for CD, while the sound remains beautifully natural and refined, there has been a fractional loss of transient sparkle in achieving a virtually silent background. However, the balance remains excellent; if the last degree of presence is missing, compared with DG's Orpheus recordings, this is still very enjoyable.

Overtures: *Il Barbiere di Siviglia; La gazza ladra; Semiramide; William Tell.*
(*) DG **415 377-2 [id.]. BPO, Karajan – SUPPÉ: *Overtures.* **(*)

These performances are taken from Karajan's 1971 collection and offer orchestral playing of supreme polish and bravura. The recording is extremely realistic at *piano* and *mezzoforte* levels, with inner detail refined, but the digital remastering has made the treble sound slightly fierce in tuttis and the focus is not always quite clean.

Overtures: *Il Barbiere di Siviglia; La scala di seta; Semiramide; Le siège de Corinthe; Il viaggio a Reims; William Tell.*
(*) HMV **CDC 747118-2 [id.]; EG 290278-1/*4* [AM/*4AM* 34707]. Philh. O, Muti.

Muti, following the Rossini style of his great compatriot Toscanini, generally adopts fast tempi for these sparkling overtures. The performances are brilliant and thrustful, helped by large-scale recording, but at times they are just a little short on wit and delicacy. The CD version gives fine precision to the original 1980 analogue sound, with firm placing of instruments but some thickening of textures in tuttis. The LP and cassette are in the mid-price range and cost less than half the price of the CD. The tape is full-bodied and lively and matches the LP closely.

Il Barbiere di Siviglia: Overture and highlights. Overtures: *Corradino; L'Italiana in Algeri; Semiramide* (arr. for wind by Wenzel Sedlak).
(M) ** Ph. Seq. 412 369-1/*4*. Netherlands Wind Ens.

Marvellously polished playing and beautiful recorded sound (which has transferred most naturally to tape) ensure undoubted enjoyment here. But not all the wit of the *Barber of Seville* vocal numbers comes over; one keeps waiting for the voices to come in. The overtures on side two are the most rewarding items, particularly *Corradino*.

Overtures: *La Cenerentola; La gazza ladra; Le siège de Corinthe; Semiramide; Il viaggio a Reims; William Tell.*
(M) *** Ph. 412 935-1/*4*. ASMF, Marriner.

Sparkling, lively performances that should give wide pleasure to collectors. The sound is pleasing and the balance musically judged. There is no shortage of recommendable anthologies of Rossini overtures, but this is certainly among them. *The Siege of Corinth* and *The Journey to Rheims* are particularly delectable. These particular overtures are not included in the CD collection from the same source – see above. The cassette transfer too is successful, although inner detail is less sharply defined than on LP, and the *Galop* from *William Tell* lacks something in sheer sonic brilliance.

Overtures: *La gazza ladra; L'Italiana in Algeri; La scala di seta; Il Signor Bruschino; Il Turco in Italia; Il viaggio a Reims; William Tell.*
*** Decca Dig. **400 049-2**; SXDL/*KSXDC* 7534 [Lon. LDR/*5*- 71034]. Nat. PO, Chailly.

This was the first compact disc of Rossini overtures and among the finest of the first generation of recordings in this medium. The balance is truthful, with the orchestral layout very believable. Each of the solo woodwind is naturally placed within the overall perspective, the violins have a clean focus, with pianissimo detail given striking presence. At times there is a degree of digital edge on tuttis, but the bustle from the cellos is particularly engaging. The background silence is especially telling when Rossini's scoring is so light and felicitous, while the overall bloom afforded by the Kingsway Hall acoustic completes the concert-hall effect. The solo playing is fully worthy of such clear presentation: the cellos at the opening of *William Tell* and the principal oboe and horn in *The Italian Girl* and *Il Turco in Italia* (respectively) all demonstrate that this is an orchestra of London's finest musicians. The wind articulation in *La scala di seta* is admirably clean, although the bow tapping at the opening of *Il Signor Bruschino* is rather lazy. Just occasionally elsewhere the ensemble slips when the conductor, Riccardo Chailly, lets the exhilaration of the moment triumph over absolute discipline and poise. But if you want precision and virtuosity alone, go to Karajan; under Chailly the spirit of the music making conveys spontaneous enjoyment too, especially in *The Thieving Magpie* and the nicely paced account of *William Tell*. Incidentally, *Il viaggio a Reims* had no overture at its first performance, but one was put together later, drawing on the ballet music from *Le siège de Corinthe*.

String sonatas Nos 1–6.
*** Tel. Dig. AZ6/*CY4* 43099 [id.]. Liszt CO, Rolla.

String sonatas Nos 1 in G; 4 in B flat; 5 in E flat; 6 in D.
*** Tel. Dig. **ZK8 43099** [id.]. Liszt CO, Rolla (from above).

String sonatas Nos 1 in G; 3 in C; 4 in B flat; 5 in E flat.
⊛ *** DG Dig. **413 310-2**; 413 310-1/*4* [id.]. Bern Camerata, Füri.

String sonatas Nos 1 in G; 3 in C; 5 in E flat; 6 in D.
(B) **(*) CfP CFP 41 4483-1/*4*. Polish CO, Maksymiuk.

These sonatas are the astonishing work of the twelve-year-old Rossini and are prodigious indeed. Although they were intended to be played one instrument to a part, with the composer himself as second violin, they are nearly always given by a small string ensemble.

The merits of the Liszt Chamber Orchestra and Janos Rolla who directs from the first desk are by now well known. On LP and the excellent matching chrome tape, their version of these sonatas has the distinct advantage of completeness and may well be a serious contender on that count alone. They are hardly less virtuosic than the Camerata Bern under Thomas Füri, and have the advantage of very natural recorded sound. There have been many fine records of these enchanting pieces, and there is little to choose between this Hungarian performance and the best of its rivals. The CD offers the usual advantages, but against the small gains in presence and definition must be set the fact that two of the sonatas are omitted. However, that applies also to the DG issue by the Bern Camerata.

These Bern performances have an elegance, virtuosity and sparkle that it is going to be very difficult to beat. The playing is pretty dazzling and they are accorded recording quality of the highest order. In its compact disc form, the sound is particularly fresh and vividly focused; overall, the balance is very satisfying. This is a record that will give enormous pleasure, and the chrome tape is also in the demonstration bracket.

The freshness and virtuosity of the Polish Chamber Orchestra under Jerzy Maksymiuk have been much admired in earlier editions of the *Guide*. As so often, Maksymiuk opts for rather fast tempi; as a result, the music loses just a little of its natural flow and becomes a display vehicle. However, this qualification only surfaces in some of the quicker movements; at budget price, this version of these sonatas has the merit of economy. The earlier of the recordings (*Sonatas* Nos 3 and 5) date from the late 1970s and have been digitally remastered. Both they and the more recent recordings are very good indeed, with a first-class matching cassette, fresh and cleanly focused.

Petite messe solennelle.
*** Eurodisc **610 263** (2). Lovaas, Fassbaender, Schreier, Fischer-Dieskau, Münchner Vokalisten, Hirsch, Sawallisch (pianos), Baffalt (harmonium), Sawallisch.
*** HMV Dig. **CDS 747482-2** [id.]; EX 270316-3/*5* (2) [Ang. DS/*4D2S* 3976]. Popp, Fassbaender, Gedda, Kavrakos, King's College, Cambridge, Ch., Katia and Marielle Labèque (pianos), Briggs (harmonium), Cleobury.

(i) *Petite messe solennelle;* (ii) *Mosè in Egitto: Preghiera.*
** Ph. Dig. **412 548-2** (2); (without *Preghiera*) 412 124-1/*4* (2). (i) Ricciarelli, Zimmermann, Carreras, Ramey, Amb. S., Sheppard, Berkowitz (pianos), Nunn (harmonium); (ii) Anderson, Fisichella, Raimondi, Amb. Op. Ch., Philh. O; Scimone.

Rossini's *Petite messe solennelle* must be the most genial contribution to the church liturgy in the history of music. The description *Petite* does not refer to size, for the piece is comparable in length to Verdi's *Requiem*; rather it is the composer's modest evaluation of the work's 'significance'. But what a spontaneous and infectious piece of writing it is, bubbling over with characteristic melodic, harmonic and rhythmic invention. The composer never overreaches himself. 'I was born for *opera buffa*, as well Thou knowest,' Rossini writes touchingly on the score. 'Little skill, a little heart, and that is all. So be Thou blessed and admit me to paradise.' The Sawallisch performance would surely merit the granting of the composer's wish. The soloists are first rate, the contralto outstanding in the lovely *O salutaris* and *Agnus Dei*. Good choral singing, and fine imaginative playing from the two pianists. The – originally Ariola – recording, now available on Eurodisc, dates from the early 1970s and is of high quality.

Recorded, not in King's College Chapel – which would have been too reverberant for Rossini's original chamber textures – but in the Music Faculty at Cambridge, the EMI verson provides a different and contrasted view from Swallisch's. The use of the refined trebles of King's College Choir brings a timbre very different from what Rossini would have expected from boys' voices – but, arguably, close to what he would have wanted. That sound is hard to resist when the singing itself is so movingly eloquent. The work's underlying geniality is not obscured, but here there is an added dimension of devotional intensity from the chorus which, combined with outstanding singing from a fine quartet of soloists and beautifully matched playing from the Labèque sisters, makes for very satisfying results. The recording, too, attractively combines warmth with clarity. The tape issue is on a single extended-length cassette, supplied in a slimline box. The quality is admirable, clear in detail and with a natural overall bloom. A pity that the reduced size of the booklet means that the translation is in such small print.

Scimone conducts a sober performance of this highly attractive and original work, taking too much note of the adjective *solennelle*, instead of remembering that in effect this was yet another of what Rossini called his 'sins of old age'. Though the recording is clean and faithful with a pleasant bloom on it in all three formats, the different tonal elements, including the highly distinctive sound of the harmonium, fail to coalesce, rather as the performance fails to add up to the sum of its parts. The team of soloists is strong, but even the stylish José Carreras sounds strained, and the accompanying instrumentalists sound dutiful rather than sympathetic. The fill-up (on CD only), the *Preghiera* from Act III of *Mosè in Egitto*, with Ruggero Raimondi, Salvatore Fisichella and June Anderson as soloists, is taken from Scimone's earlier complete set of that opera, a brief but welcome makeweight.

Stabat Mater.

(*) DG Dig. **410 034-2; 2532/*3302* 046 [id.]. Ricciarelli, Valentini-Terrani, Gonzalez, Raimondi, Philh. Ch. and O, Giulini.

** HMV Dig. **CDC 747402-2** [id.]; [Ang. DS/*4XS* 37901]. Malfitano, Baltsa, Gambill, Howell, Ch. and O of Maggio Musicale Fiorentino, Muti.

Rossini loses nothing of his natural jauntiness in setting a religious text, and generally conductors treat this music simply as an offshoot of Rossini opera. Giulini, however, takes a refined and dedicated view, one that lacks something in robust qualities. Some will feel that Rossini's broad, clean-cut tunes and strong rhythms should be presented more directly, but there is much here to enjoy in the singing of the chorus as well as of the soloists, though Ricciarelli is at times ungainly on top. This appeared simultaneously with Muti's Florence version for HMV, and it is a pity that the qualities of each could not have been shared. The DG version has much the more refined and atmospheric recording, and it has transferred exceptionally well to chrome tape, which captures the wide dynamic range with striking sophistication and clarity of focus. But the compact disc is even more impressive, the acoustics richly atmospheric, the ambience adding a great deal to the choral sound and giving the listener a convincing concert-hall effect, even though the balance of the soloists is well forward.

Muti's view of the *Stabat Mater* is a dramatic one, and it is sad that he did not record it with the Philharmonia (the orchestra for Giulini's DG version) or with the Vienna Philharmonic, with whom he gave a memorable reading at the 1983 Salzburg Festival. As it is, the Florence Festival forces are at times rough – notably the orchestra – and the singing at times unpolished, though the solo quartet is a fine one. Warm but rather unrefined recording. The LP and cassette have been withdrawn in the UK.

OPERA

Il Barbiere di Siviglia (complete).
*** Ph. Dig. **411 058-2**; 6769/*7654* 100 (3) [id.]. Baltsa, Allen, Araiza, Trimarchi, Lloyd, Amb. Op. Ch., ASMF, Marriner.
(*) DG **415 695-2 (2); 2709 041/*3371 003* (3) [id.]. Berganza, Prey, Alva, Montarsolo, Amb. Ch., LSO, Abbado.

Il Barbiere di Siviglia: highlights.
*** Ph. Dig. **412 266-2**; 412 266-1/*4* [id.] (from above set cond. Marriner).

Sir Neville Marriner, conducting his first complete opera recording, finds a rare sense of fun. His characteristic polish and refinement – beautifully caught in the clear, finely balanced recording – never get in the way of urgent spontaneity, the sparkle of the moment. So for example in the big Act II quintet, when the wool is being pulled over Don Basilio's eyes, there is an ideal balance between musical precision and dramatic presentation. Thomas Allen as Figaro – far more than a *buffo* figure – and Agnes Baltsa as Rosina – tough and biting, too – manage to characterize strongly, even when coping with florid divisions, and though Araiza allows himself too many intrusive aitches, he easily outshines latterday rivals, sounding heroic, not at all the small-scale tenorino, but never coarse either. Fine singing too from Robert Lloyd as Basilio. On compact disc, the theatrical feeling and sense of atmosphere are enhanced, with the placing of the singers strikingly clear. There is extensive cueing of individual numbers. Though there is some reduction of range on top, the chrome-tape transfer is refined and of Philips's best quality. However, no attempt is made to lay out each Act on a single cassette. The libretto is clear, but in small print.

The highlights are well chosen and admirably reflect the qualities of the complete set. While the CD has the usual gain in presence and immediacy, the chrome cassette is first class too, the sound particularly sparkling in the delightful Act II finale.

Abbado directs a clean and satisfying performance that lacks the last degree of sparkle. Berganza's interpretation of the role of Rosina remains very consistent with her earlier performance on Decca, but the Figaro here, Hermann Prey, is more reliable, and the playing and recording have an extra degree of polish. The text is not absolutely complete, but this means that the DG engineers have been able to fit the opera on to a pair of CDs. With fresh recorded sound and plenty of immediacy, this is certainly competitive; but Marriner has a stronger cast plus modern digital sound, and his version is more enjoyable on almost all counts.

La Cenerentola (complete).

** DG **415 698-2**; 2709 039 (3) [id.]. Berganza, Alva, Montarsolo, Capecchi, Scottish Op. Ch., LSO, Abbado.

** CBS 79359/*40-* (3) [M3/*M3T* 38607]. Valentini-Terrani, Araiza, Dara, Trimarchi, Ravaglia, W. German R. Male Ch., Cappella Coloniensis, Ferro.

La Cenerentola has not been lucky on record, and the DG set, although enjoyable, lacks the extrovert bravura and sparkle of an ideal performance. The atmosphere in places is almost of a concert version, with excellent balance between the participants, helped by the fine recording. The recitative in general has plenty of life, particularly when Dandini (Renato Capecchi) is involved. Berganza, agile in the coloratura, seems too mature, even matronly, for the fairy-tale role of Cinderella. Alva sings well enough but is somewhat self-conscious in the florid writing. Abbado, though hardly witty in his direction, inspires delicate playing throughout. The CD transfer of the 1972 analogue recording brings an admirable feeling of freshness, with plenty of presence for the voices, and a good balance with the lively orchestral sound. Cueing is provided for all the major arias; the Act I finale, for instance, is given three access points.

Ferro, one of the ablest of Rossini scholars who earlier recorded *L'Italiana in Algeri* impressively, here conducts an easy-going, at times pedestrian account of *La Cenerentola*, well played and well sung but lacking some of the fizz essential in Rossini. Even the heroine's final brilliant aria hangs fire, and that in spite of warm, positive singing from Valentini-Terrani, whose stylish contribution is marred only by a high quota of intrusive aitches. The rest of the cast is strong and, apart from backward placing of the orchestra, the digital recording is full and realistic; but the set cannot take precedence over the best earlier versions. The chrome cassettes, lavishly packaged, are of good quality, although the resonance has taken off some of the transient sparkle.

La Donna del lago (complete).
*** CBS Dig. 13M/*13T* 39311 (3) [id.]. Ricciarelli, Valentini-Terrani, Gonzalez, Raffanti, Ramey, Prague Philharmonic Ch., COE, Pollini.

La Donna del lago – adapted with extreme freedom from Scott's *Lady of the Lake*, published not long before – may doubtfully be effective on stage, as the 1985 Covent Garden production suggested; on record, in a lively and understanding performance, it is a Rossini rarity to cherish. Philip Gossett, the Rossini scholar, has described it as 'by far the most romantic of Rossini's Italian operas and perhaps the most tuneful'. With Rossini echoing if not quoting the inflections of Scottish folksong, whether in the Scottish snaps in the jolly choruses or the mooning melodies given to the heroine, it is certainly distinctive. Maurizio Pollini, forsaking the keyboard for the baton, draws a fizzing performance from the Chamber Orchestra of Europe, suggesting fascinating foretastes not just of Donizetti but of Verdi: of the *Anvil chorus* from *Il Trovatore* in the Act I March and of the trombone unisons of *La forza del destino* later in the finale. Though Pollini keeps his singers on a tight rein, there are three outstanding and characterful performances. Katia Ricciarelli in the title-role of Elena, Lady of the Lake, has rarely sung so stylishly on record, the voice creamy, with no suspicion of the unevenness which develops under pressure, and very agile in coloratura. Lucia Valentini-Terrani with her warm, dark mezzo is no less impressive in the travesti role of Elena's beloved, Malcolm; while Samuel Ramey as Elena's father, Douglas, makes you wish the role was far longer with his darkly incisive singing. Of the two principal tenors, Dalmacio Gonzalez, attractively light-toned, is the more stylish; but Dano Raffanti as Rodrigo Dhu copes with equal assurance with the often impossibly high tessitura. The recording, made at the end of a series of performances in the 1983 Rossini Festival in Pesaro, is clear and generally well balanced. On cassette, the range is softer-grained than on disc, but the voices are naturally caught.

L'Italiana in Algeri (complete).
*** CBS Dig. M3/*M3T* 39048 (3) [id.]. Valentini-Terrani, Ganzarolli, Araiza, Col. R. Ch., Cappella Coloniensis, Ferro.

Like the Erato set conducted by Claudio Scimone, this fine CBS version uses the critical edition of the score published by the Fondazione Rossini in Pesaro; it goes further towards authenticity in using period instruments including a fortepiano instead of harpsichord for the recitatives (well played by Georg Fischer).

Though Ferro can at times be sluggish in slow music (even in the opening of the overture), he is generally a sparkling Rossinian, pacing well to allow a rhythmic lift to be married to crisp ensemble. The set also gains from forward and bright digital recording, more immediate than in previous sets, and the cast is at least as fine as in rival versions. Lucia Valentini-Terrani here gives her finest performance on record to date with her rich, firm voice superbly agile in coloratura. She may not be so tough and forceful as Marilyn Horne on the Erato set but, with a younger, sunnier voice, she is far more seductive, helped by greater consideration and imagination from the conductor. Francisco Araiza as Lindoro peppers the rapid passagework with intrusive aitches – but not too distractingly – and the strength of the voice makes the performance heroic with no suspicion of the twittering of a tenorino. Ganzarolli treats the role of the Bey, Mustafa, as a conventional *buffo* role, with a voice not ideally steady but full of character; the rest of the cast is strong, too. CBS, unlike Erato, provides an English translation for the libretto. On balance a good first choice, on both LP and the excellent cassettes, which are lavishly packaged.

Maometto II (complete).
*** Ph. Dig. **412 148-2**; 412 148-1/*4* (3) [id.]. Anderson, Zimmermann, Palacio, Ramey, Dale, Amb. Op. Ch., Philh. O, Scimone.

Claudio Scimone here repeats the success of his earlier set for Philips of *Mosè in Egitto*. But where he chose the most compressed of Rossini's three versions of that opera, here he chooses the most expansive early version of a work which the composer also radically revised for Paris as *Le Siège de Corinthe*. There are cogent reasons for approving Scimone's preference in each instance. This account of *Maometto II* has Samuel Ramey magnificently focusing the whole story in his portrait of the Muslim invader in love with the heroine. The nobility of his singing makes Maometto's final self-sacrifice all the more convincing, even if the opera is made the less tense dramatically from having no villain. The other singing is less sharply characterized but is generally stylish, with Margarita Zimmermann in the travesti role of Calbo, June Anderson singing sweetly as Anna, not least in the lovely prayer which comes as an interlude in a massive Trio or Terzettone in Act I. Laurence Dale is excellent in two smaller roles, while Ernesto Palacio mars some fresh-toned singing with his intrusive aitches. Excellent recording, made the more attractive on CD. The well-chosen banding adds to one's enjoyment of an exceptionally long opera. The tape transfer is very well managed, with voices and orchestra sounding fresh and immediate.

Tancredi (complete).
** CBS 13M/*13T* 39073 (3) [id.]. Horne, Cuberli, Palacio, Zaccaria, Di Nissa, Schuman, Ch. and O of Teatro la Fenice, Weikert.

The chief glory of this live recording from Venice is the enchanting singing of Lella Cuberli as the heroine, Amenaide. The purity and beauty of her tone, coupled with immaculate coloratura and tender expressiveness, make it a memorable performance, confirming the high opinions she won from the DG set of *Il viaggio a Reims*. Marilyn Horne, though not quite as fresh-sounding as earlier in her career, gives a formidable performance in the breeches role of Tancredi, relishing the resonance of her chest register, but finding delicacy too in her first big aria, *Di tanti palpiti*. Ernesto Palacio is an accomplished Rossini tenor, commendably agile in the role of Argirio, but the tone tends to grow tight; and Ernesto Zaccaria as Orbazzano sings with fuzzy, sepulchral tone. The conducting is efficient rather than inspired, failing to make the music sparkle or to bring the drama to life. The recording gives a realistic idea of a dryish theatre acoustic.

Il viaggio a Reims (complete).

*** DG Dig. **415 498-2** (2); 415 498-1/*4* (3/*2*) [id.]. Ricciarelli, Valentini-Terrani, Cuberli, Gasdia, Araiza, Gimenez, Nucci, Raimondi, Ramey, Dara, Prague Philharmonic Ch., COE, Abbado.

This fizzing piece of comic nonsense, which Rossini wrote as a gala piece for the coronation of Charles X in Paris, was painstakingly reconstructed and given its first modern performances at the 1984 Pesaro Festival. This recording was edited together from various performances which the DG engineers put on tape; the result is one of the most sparkling and totally successful live opera recordings available, with Claudio Abbado in particular freer and more spontaneous-sounding than he generally is on disc, relishing the sparkle of the comedy. The piece has virtually no story, with the journey to Rheims never actually taking place, only the prospect of it. The wait at the Golden Lily hotel at Plombières provides the opportunity for the ten star characters each to perform in turn: and one hardly wonders that after the first performances Rossini refused ever to allow a revival, on the grounds that no comparable cast could ever be assembled. Instead, he used some of the material in his delectable comic opera, *Le comte Ory*, and it is fascinating here to spot the numbers from it in their original form. Much else is delightful, and the line-up of soloists here could hardly be more impressive, with no weak link. Established stars like Lucia Valentini-Terrani, Katia Ricciarelli, Francisco Araiza, Samuel Ramey and Ruggero Raimondi, not to mention the *buffo* singers, Enzo Dara and Leo Nucci, hardly need commendation; in addition, there are two formidable newcomers in principal roles, Cecilia Gasdia as a self-important poetess (a nice parody of romantic manners) and, even finer, Lella Cuberli as a young fashion-crazed widow. The rich firmness and distinctive beauty of Cuberli's voice, coupled with amazing flexibility, proclaims a natural prima donna, and Karajan plans to record Bellini's *Norma* with her. Inconsequential as the sequence of virtuoso numbers may be, ensembles as well as arias, the inspiration never flags, and Abbado's brilliance and sympathy draw the musical threads compellingly together with the help of superb, totally committed playing from the young members of the Chamber Orchestra of Europe. The pair of CDs bring extra precision and clarity, where the LP is ungenerously spread over three discs. The chrome tape transfer is sophisticated, but the reverberant acoustic takes away some of the sharpness of focus, though climaxes expand impressively.

Arias: *Il Barbiere di Siviglia: Una voce poco fa. La Cenerentola: Nacqui all'affanno. Otello: Assisa a'piè d'un salice.*
(M) *** Ph. 416 250-1/*4* [id.]. Von Stade, Rotterdam PO, De Waart – MOZART: *Arias.****

Superbly sung, finely characterized, these performances of Rossini arias can hardly be faulted, whether it be Rosina's *Una voce poco fa* or the rare *Willow song and prayer* from Rossini's idiosyncratic version of *Otello*. Excellent recording, although the cassette does not avoid moments of peakiness.

Arias: *La Donna del lago: Mura felici; Tanti affetti. L'assedio di Corinto* (*Le siège de Corinthe*): scenes: *Avaziam . . . Non temer d'un basso affeto! . . . I destini tradir ogni speme . . . Signormche tutto puio . . . Sei tu, che stendi; L'ora fatal s'appressa . . . Giusto ciel.*
(M) **(*) Decca Grandi Voci 411 428-1/*4*. Marilyn Horne, Amb. Op. Ch., RPO, Lewis.

With typical versatility and brilliance, Marilyn Horne takes on the arias of both travesti heroes and heroines in this selection from two Rossini operas long neglected. Effectively she lightens her voice for the higher tessitura of heroine's music. The early 1970s, when this reissue was first recorded, found her in magnificent vocal form, both agile and powerful. First-rate sound for the period. *L'assedio di Corinto* is the Italian translation of *Le siège de Corinthe*, the Paris revision of what had started as *Maometto II*, though Horne includes one item found only in *Maometto*.

COLLECTION

Il Barbiere di Siviglia: (i) *Overture;* (ii) *Storm music;* (iii) *Largo al factotum;* (iv) *Una voce poco fa;* (v) *La calunnia. La Cenerentola:* (vi) *Un soave no so che; Nacqui all'affanno al pianto* (Finale). *La gazza ladra:* (vii) *Overture. L'Italiana in Algeri:* (viii) *Overture. La scala di seta: Overture. Semiramide:* (ii) *Overture. William Tell: Overture;* (viii) *Soldier's dance.*
(B) ** DG Walkman *413 486-4* [id.]. (i) Bav. RSO, Bartoletti; (ii) Rome Op. O, Serafin; (iii) Prey; (iv) Berganza; (v) Paolo Montarsolo; (vi) Berganza and Alva; (vii) LSO, Abbado; (viii) Monte Carlo Op. O, Frémaux.

This compilation begins well with Abbado's crisply stylish account of *La gazza ladra overture*; he also directs excerpts from several complete sets, with Hermann Prey, Teresa Berganza (brilliant rather than charming) and Luigi Alva. The rest of the programme is more piecemeal, with rather less distinguished orchestral contributions from the Rome and Monte Carlo ensembles. The sound is variable. This is quite lively and entertaining, but not distinctive.

Roussel, Albert (1869–1937)

Bacchus et Ariane (complete ballet), *Op. 43; Le festin de l'araignée: symphonic fragments.*
*** HMV Dig. **CDC 747376-2** [id.]; EL 270333-1/*4* [Ang. DS/*4DS* 38263]. O Nat. de France, Prêtre.

Le festin de l'araignée: suite.
** Sup. Dig. 1110 3404 [id.]. Czech PO, Košler – CHAUSSON: *Symphony.***

Bacchus et Ariane is a relatively late score, composed in 1931, immediately after the *Third Symphony*. The ballet was originally choreographed by Lifar and had designs by Chirico but never captured the public imagination in quite the same way as *Le festin de l'araignée*. The music teems with life and is full of rhythmic vitality and richness of detail. It has perhaps less of the poetic feeling of *Le festin* but is nevertheless an exhilarating score. The recording, made in the generous acoustic of the Salle Wagram, is a shade too reverberant at times but no essential detail is masked. Georges Prêtre obtains an excellent response from the Orchestre National de France in both scores. This supersedes Martinon's albeit excellently balanced earlier version on Erato (EPR/*MCE* 15540) which merely contained the two suites (or acts) of the ballet and had no fill-up. The CD freshens detail a little, although the resonance means that the improvement is relatively limited. However, the background silence is certainly an asset in *The spider's feast*. The cassette is well managed, losing a little in transparency, but not blurred by the reverberation.

On Supraphon, Zdenek Košler offers the suite (or symphonic fragments). Košler is not quite as atmospheric as some earlier accounts, particularly the Cluytens from the mid-1960s, though his performance is well held together and idiomatic. The recording offers good detail and a somewhat closer balance than in the Chausson *Symphony* on the reverse. All things considered, this is a recommendable issue, particularly for the Chausson, and would be thoroughly recommendable were the recording richer in sonority.

Symphony No. 3 in G min., Op. 42; Bacchus et Ariane: suite No. 2.
** Forlane Dig. **UCD 16529** [id.]. O de Bordeaux Aquitaine, Benzi.

On Forlane a useful coupling of Roussel's tautly written *Third Symphony* and parts of his imaginative score to *Bacchus et Ariane*. Benzi has the full measure of the *Symphony*. The outer movements have plenty of vigour and thrust, and the exciting climax of the *Adagio* is made the more telling by the expansive dynamic of the digital recording. The scherzo has plenty of spirit and there is some attractively delicate woodwind articulation both here and in the joyously energetic finale. The ballet suite is not short on atmosphere, and again there is fine solo playing from the woodwind. The strings of the Bordeaux Aquitaine Orchestra lack body under pressure above the stave, but they play with fervour and, despite a degree of shrillness on top, the recording balance is convincing, with the orchestra set back within the resonant acoustic of the Church of Notre Dame, Bordeaux.

Serenade for flute, violin, viola, cello and harp, Op. 30.
(M) *** Decca 414 063-1/*4*. Melos Ens. – RAVEL: *Introduction and allegro*; DEBUSSY: *Sonata*; GUY-ROPARTZ: *Prelude, marine and chansons.****

The Melos version has held its place in the catalogue for more than two decades. It is an inspired account and very well engineered, though beginning now to sound its age. It is part of a concert which includes an equally memorable account of Ravel's *Introduction and allegro*. There is now, for the first time, an excellent tape.

Songs: *Jazz dans la nuit; Mélodie, Op. 19/1: Light; 2 Mélodies, Op. 20; 2 Poèmes chinoises, Op. 35.*
(*) Unicorn **DKPCD 9035; DKP/*DKPC* 9035 [id.]. Sarah Walker, Roger Vignoles – DEBUSSY; ENESCU: *Songs.****

Sarah Walker may not plumb the full emotions of some of the deceptively deep songs in her Roussel group – *Light* for example – but the point and charm of *Jazz dans la nuit* are superbly caught, and the group makes an attractive and generous coupling for the Debussy and Enesco songs, all superbly recorded, with Vignoles a most sensitive accompanist.

Rubbra, Edmund (1901–86)

Symphony No. 2, Op. 45; Festival overture, Op. 62.
**(*) Lyr. SRCS 96 [id.]. New Philh. O, Handley.

Rubbra's *Second Symphony* dates from 1937, only a year after the turbulent and somewhat overscored *First*. As always with this composer, seriousness of purpose and contrapuntal mastery are immediately evident, and in the slow movement there is real tranquillity. Here we have music of a deep originality, that derives from Holst and Sibelius in certain respects, but which is like neither in its overall impact. It inhabits a northern – but not a Scandinavian – world and its landscape is unlike anything else in English music at the time. Except in the slow movement, the scoring of the work is consistently thick; but if one puts orchestral colour on one side and concentrates on the linear development and organic growth of this music, it is a rewarding experience. It is eloquently played by the New Philharmonia under Vernon Handley and the recording, which first appeared in 1978, while not state-of-the-art, is very fine. The *Festival overture* is a post-war piece and more extrovert. Commissioned for the 1947 Elgar Festival at Malvern, it is not one of the composer's strongest works.

Symphony No. 10 (Sinfonia da camera), Op. 145; Improvisations on virginal pieces by Giles Farnaby, Op. 50; A tribute to Vaughan Williams on his 70th birthday (Introduction and danza alla fuga), Op. 56.
*** Chan. **CHAN 8378**; CBS/*CBT* 1023 [id.]. Bournemouth Sinf., Schönzeler.

Rubbra's *Tenth Symphony* is for chamber orchestra and dates from 1975. It is a work of considerable substance whose language employs a received but distinctive vocabulary, consistent with the growth of Rubbra's musical personality. Nothing ever detracts from the musical argument and the gradual unfolding of the symphonic plan. It is a short one-movement work, whose opening has a Sibelian seriousness and a strong atmosphere that grip one immediately. It has moreover the advantage here of the convinced advocacy of the performers and a well-balanced recording. Schönzeler is scrupulously attentive to dynamic nuance and internal balance, while keeping a firm grip on the architecture as a whole. The 1977 recording has been impressively remastered. It has a warm acoustic and reproduces natural, well-placed orchestral tone. The upper range is crisply defined. The *Farnaby variations* is a pre-war work whose charm Schönzeler effectively uncovers, revealing its textures to best advantage. *Loath to depart*, the best-known movement, has gentleness and vision in this performance. Strongly recommended, especially on CD; though there is also an excellent cassette, and the LP and tape are in the mid-price range.

Saint-Saëns, Camille (1835–1921)

Carnival of the animals.
*** Ph. Dig. **400 016-2**; 9500/*7300* 973 [id.]. Villa, Jennings, Pittsburgh SO, Previn – RAVEL: *Ma Mère l'Oye.****

Carnival of the animals (with verses by Ogden Nash).
*** DG **415 351-2** [id.]. Hermione Gingold, Alfons and Aloys Kontarsky, VPO, Boehm – PROKOFIEV: *Peter.****
(*) HMV Dig. **CDC 747067-2 [id.]; EL 270125-1/*4* [Ang. DS/*4DS* 38190]. Perlman, Katia and Marielle Labèque, Israel PO, Mehta – PROKOFIEV: *Peter.***(*)

In the bargain range, the CfP LP or tape (conducted by Sir Alexander Gibson with Peter Katin and Philip Fowke) of Saint-Saëns's delightful zoological fantasy remains highly competitive for those not willing to go to a premium-priced issue (CFP/*TC-CFP* 40086 – coupled with Ravel's *Ma Mère l'Oye* and Bizet's *Jeux d'enfants*). On CD, Previn's version makes a ready first choice, particularly when the coupling is outstanding and both are recorded in superbly rich and atmospheric sound. On some machines the bass resonance of the somewhat larger-than-life pianos may seem slightly excessive but, that apart, the quality has remarkable bloom. On chrome tape, the bass overbalances the treble. The music is played with infectious rhythmic spring and great refinement. It is a mark of the finesse of this performance – which has plenty of bite and vigour, as well as polish – that the great cello solo of *Le Cygne* is so naturally presented, with the engineers refusing to spotlight the soloist. The shading of half-tones in Anne Martindale Williams's exquisitely beautiful playing is made all the more tenderly affecting. Fine contributions too from the two pianists. The compact disc brings out all these qualities even more strikingly than the LP.

Not everyone will care for the inclusion of Ogden Nash's verses (Saint-Saëns's music stands up admirably without them), but those who do will find Miss Gingold's narration is splendidly performed – every inflection of that superb voice is to be relished. Marvellous playing from the Kontarskys and the Vienna Philharmonic, and splendid 1976 analogue recording. The voice, the pianists, and the orchestra are all caught in perfect focus and natural sound.

Ogden Nash's often outrageous rhymes for Saint-Saëns's gently humorous masterpiece could have no more committed advocate than Perlman, and his diction and vocal inflections combine clarity with nice timing. Too often, however, Nash's metaphor falls short of wit and such a dialogue – unlike the music – can lose its freshness. The performance overall is lively, with the Labèque duo in scintillating form and good support from Mehta. The acoustic is rather dry and the balance close, emphasized by the CD, but this does mean that the cassette is very clean and clear.

(i) *Carnival of the animals;* (ii) *Piano concertos Nos 2 in G min., Op. 22; 4 in C min., Op. 44. 6 Études for the left hand only, Op. 135.*
(B) *** HMV *TCC2-POR 154595-9*. Ciccolini, with (i) Weissenberg and Prêtre; (ii) O de Paris, Baudo.

Tape collectors should be more than satisfied with this generous compilation, which offers very good sound. Ciccolini's performances of the two favourite *Concertos* are in every way distinguished; they combine elegance with spirit. No. 4 is especially fine. With the six *Études* thrown in as an attractive bonus (Saint-Saëns was a superb miniaturist), this is all most enjoyable.

Cello concerto No. 1 in A min., Op. 33.
*** CBS Dig. **MK 35848**; 35848 [Col. IM/*HMT* 35848]. Ma, O Nat. de France, Maazel – LALO: *Concerto*.*** ❀
*** Decca Dig. **410 019-2**; SXDL/*KSXDC* 7568 [Lon. LDR/5- 71068]. Harrell, Cleveland O, Marriner – SCHUMANN: *Concerto*.***

Yo-Yo Ma's performance of the Saint-Saëns *Concerto* is distinguished by fine sensitivity and beautiful tone. As in the Lalo, one is tempted to speak of him as being 'hypersensitive', so fine is his attention to light and shade; yet there is not a trace of posturing or affectation. The Orchestre National de France respond with playing of the highest quality throughout. Superb recorded sound which reflects great credit on the engineers, with added refinement and transparency of texture on CD.

Harrell's reading of the Saint-Saëns, altogether more extrovert than Yo-Yo Ma's, makes light of any idea that this composer always works on a small scale.

The opening is positively epic, and the rest of the performance is just as compelling, with the minuet-like *Allegretto* crisply neoclassical. This coupling of Saint-Saëns and Schumann challenges comparison with the classic recording of Du Pré and Barenboim (now deleted), even if in warmth and commitment it cannot quite match that model. Recording is outstanding, beautifully balanced, with the compact disc version particularly fine. The chrome cassette is slightly less refined at the top than the disc versions, but is otherwise full and vivid.

Cello concerto No. 2 in D min., Op. 119.
*** Decca Dig. **414 387-2**; 414 387-1/*4* [id.]. Harrell, Berlin RSO, Chailly – LALO: *Concerto*; FAURÉ: *Elégie*.***

Saint-Saëns wrote his *Cello Concerto No. 2* in 1902 when he was at the height of his powers. It has an attractive spontaneity and its ideas are memorable, notably the strongly rhythmic opening theme of the first movement – which returns to cap the finale – and the very engaging melody of the *Andante* (which is linked to the opening movement). At its close, Harrell refines his timbre to an exquisite half-tone and the effect is ravishing, with a gentle muted horn decoration. Chailly's accompaniment is sympathetic, polished and full of character; the attractive ambience of the Jesus Christ Church, Berlin, makes a convincing backcloth for the music making. On CD, the cello image is very tangible, and the balance is near perfect, while the orchestral sounds are glowing and vivid. The LP is atmospheric, but detail is less sharp. A most welcome recording début – in all three media: the work has not previously appeared in the British catalogue, although it has been available in France. The cassette is bright, clear and vivid.

Piano concertos Nos 1–5; La Jeunesse d'Hercule, Op. 50.
*** Decca **417 351-2** [id.] (without *La Jeunesse*) (2); D 244 D 3/*K 244 K 33* (3). Rogé, Philh. O, LPO or RPO, Dutoit.

Played as they are here, these concertos can exert a strong appeal: Pascal Rogé brings delicacy, virtuosity and sparkle to the piano part and he receives expert support from the various London orchestras under Dutoit. Altogether delicious playing and excellent piano sound from Decca, who secure a most realistic balance. On the sixth side there is a rarity in the shape of *La Jeunesse d'Hercule*, Saint-Saëns's final tone-poem. In every respect, this set outclasses Aldo Ciccolini's survey of the early 1970s, good though that was. The cassettes sound splendid too. On CD the five *Concertos* are successfully accommodated on two discs; *La Jeunesse d'Hercule*, used as a filler on the LPs, is omitted; but Decca tell us this will reappear later in a CD anthology of Saint-Saëns's orchestral works under Dutoit.

Piano concertos Nos 1 in D, Op. 17; 2 in G min., Op. 22; 3 in E flat, Op. 29.
(M) *** HMV EG 290591-1/*4*. Ciccolini, O de Paris, Baudo.

There may be little development of style between the first concerto, written when the composer was twenty-three, and the later works, but this is first-rate gramophone material. Beethoven, Bach and Mendelssohn all get their due in the *First Concerto*. The *Second* is already well known; only No. 3 falls short in its comparatively banal ideas – and even in that there is a hilarious finale which sounds like a Viennese operetta turned into a concerto. Ciccolini's performances are very enjoyable, and they are well recorded, too. The cassette is transferred at the highest level and the sound is projected with great vividness. There is about 81 minutes of music on this issue.

Piano concerto No. 2 in G min., Op. 22.

(*) CBS Dig. **MK 39153; IM/*IMT* 39153 [id.]. Cécile Licad, LPO, Previn – CHOPIN: *Piano concerto No. 2.***(*)

(*) Ph. Dig. **410 052-2; 6514/*7337* 164 [id.]. Davidovich, Concg. O, Järvi – RACHMANINOV: *Rhapsody on a theme of Paganini.***(*)

Piano concertos Nos 2; 4 in C min., Op. 44.

** Erato Dig. **ECD 88002**; STU/*MCE* 71460. Duchable, Strasbourg PO, Lombard.

Cécile Licad and the LPO under Previn turn in an eminently satisfactory reading of the *G minor Concerto* that has the requisite delicacy in the scherzo and seriousness elsewhere. It is a pleasing and persuasive performance of strong contrasts, with both power and thoughtfulness in the opening movement and a toccata-like brilliance of articulation in the finale. The recording is well balanced but a little diffuse, even in its CD format – although the centrally placed piano certainly dominates the proceedings.

Bella Davidovich also gives a most sympathetic account of the *G minor Concerto*; she has the advantage of excellent orchestral support from the Concertgebouw Orchestra. The recording is very natural and Davidovich draws most sympathetic tone-quality from the instrument, even if she lacks the brilliance that Licad brings to the scherzo. This is warmly attractive music-making, but in the last resort it has less flair and life than Licad's version, although on compact disc the richly atmospheric sound is very persuasive. The chrome tape, however, lacks something in sparkle at the top.

Saint-Saëns's two most popular piano concertos are also offered by Ciccolini, either coupled with the *First* (at medium price) or – on tape only – in an attractive EMI collection together with the *Carnival of the animals* (see above). The Erato pairing is less winning, even with the advantage of CD sophistication. The piano is forwardly balanced and Duchable's bold assertiveness in outer movements brings character of the wrong sort to music making which at times sounds aggressive. There is little charm; while the first movement of No. 2 is stronger than usual and the playing is never thoughtless or slipshod, this does not match the Licad version in character and flexibility of mood.

Still recommended: Pascal Rogé has made an outstanding analogue coupling of these two concertos for Decca with the RPO under Dutoit, and we hope that will soon appear on CD. Rogé is both sparkling and elegant, and the Decca sound is vivid and luminous in colouring (SXL/*KSXC* 7008 [Lon. CS/*5*- 7253]).

Violin concerto No. 1 in A, Op. 30.
*** Decca Dig. **411 952-2**; SXDL/*KSXDC* 7527 [Lon. LDR/5- 71029]. Kyung Wha Chung, Montreal SO, Dutoit – LALO: *Symphonie espagnole.****

Saint-Saëns's *First Violin concerto* is a miniature, playing for only eleven and a half minutes. It was written for Sarasate, and if it seems somewhat insubstantial, Kyung Wha Chung makes the most of the lyrical interludes and is fully equal to the energetic bravura of the outer sections. With a clear yet full-blooded digital recording and an excellent accompaniment from Charles Dutoit, this is persuasive. The cassette is of very good quality, matching the LP closely. The CD, as in all Decca's Montreal recordings, refines detail and increases the feeling of natural presence.

Violin concerto No. 3 in B min., Op. 61.
*** CBS Dig. **MK 39007**; 39007/*40*- [id.]. Cho-Liang Lin, Philh. O, Tilson Thomas – MENDELSSOHN: *Violin concerto.****
*** DG Dig. **410 526-2**; 410 526-1/*4* [id.]. Perlman, O de Paris, Barenboim.

Cho-Liang Lin's account of the *B minor Concerto* with the Philharmonia Orchestra and Michael Tilson Thomas is exhilarating and thrilling; indeed, this is the kind of performance that prompts one to burst into applause. Bernard Shaw's famous remark about the Saint-Saëns *Concerto* as consisting of 'trivially pretty scraps of serenade music sandwiched between pages from the great masters' has always seemed almost on target, but Cho-Liang Lin manages to persuade one otherwise. He is given excellent recording from the CBS engineers and, in terms of both virtuosity and musicianship, his version is certainly second to none and is arguably the finest yet to have appeared. The CD format is admirably 'present'. The chrome tape, however, is a little disappointing. A relatively modest transfer level, because of the resonance, has brought some restriction of the upper range, while the bass response remains full.

On DG, Perlman achieves a fine partnership with his friend Barenboim who provides a highly sympathetic accompaniment in a performance that is both tender and strong. They join together in finding an elegiac quality in the *Andantino*, while Perlman's verve and dash in the finale are dazzling. The forward balance is understandable in this work, but orchestral detail could at times be sharper. There is an excellent cassette.

Violin concerto No. 3 in B min., Op. 61; Havanaise, Op. 86; Introduction and rondo capriccioso, Op. 28.
(M) ** Ph. 412 011-1/*4*. Szeryng, Monte Carlo Op. O, Van Remoortel.

Clean, immaculate performances from Szeryng, whose approach is aristocratic rather than indulgent. The orchestral contribution is adequate, but is not helped by the recording balance which spotlights the violin and tends to dim the colour in the important woodwind solos. In the finale of the *Concerto*, the brass chorale lacks resonance; but there is no doubt that Szeryng's solo playing gives this collection a distinct character: in the *Havanaise* and *Introduction and rondo* capriccioso the bravura and sense of style make for impressive results. There is a good matching cassette, but as sound this is less impressive than Szeryng's companion coupling of Lalo and Ravel.

Havanaise, Op. 83; Introduction and rondo capriccioso, Op. 28.
*** Decca **417 118-2** [id.]; SXL/*KSXC* 6851 [Lon. CS/5-7073]. Kyung Wha Chung RPO, Dutoit – CHAUSSON: *Poème*; RAVEL: *Tzigane*.***

On Decca the fireworks in two Saint-Saëns showpieces provide the necessary contrast for the more reflective works with which they are coupled. In both, Kyung Wha Chung shows rhythmic flair and a touch of the musical naughtiness that gives them their full charm. As in the other nicely matched pieces Dutoit accompanies most sympathetically, and the recording is excellent.

Symphony No. 3 in C min., Op. 78.
*** Decca Dig. **410 201-2**; SXDL/*KSXDC* 7590 [Lon. LDR/5- 71090]. Hurford, Montreal SO, Dutoit.
*** ASV Dig. **CDDCA 524**; DCA/*ZCDCA* 524 [id.]. Rawsthorne, LPO, Bátiz.
*(*) Telarc Dig. **CD 80051**; DG 10051 [id.]. Phd. O, Ormandy.
* Ph. Dig. **412 619-2**; 412 619-1/*4* [id.]. Guillou, San Francisco SO, De Waart – WIDOR: *Symphony No. 6: Allegro*.**
* DG Dig. **400 063-2**; 2532/*3302* 045 [id.]. Cochereau, BPO, Karajan.

(i) *Symphony No. 3;* (ii) *Danse macabre, Op. 40.*
(B) *** DG Walkman *413 424-4*. (i) Chicago SO; (ii) O de Paris, Barenboim (with FRANCK: *Symphony**(*)).

(i) *Symphony No. 3;* (ii) *Danse macabre; Le Déluge: Prélude, Op. 45; Samson et Dalila: Bacchanale.*
(M) *** DG Gal. 415 847-1/*4*[id.]. (i) Chicago SO; (ii) O de Paris, Barenboim.

(i) *Symphony No. 3;* (ii) *Danse macabre; Le Rouet d'Omphale.*
(M) *** HMV Green. ESD/*TC-ESD* 173191-1/*4*. (i) French Nat. R.O, Martinon; (ii) O de Paris, Dervaux.

With Bátiz's fine new ASV version of Saint-Saëns's popular *Organ symphony* technically disappointing in its CD format, first choice on compact disc lies with Dutoit's Decca version. However, collectors should remember that Barenboim's inspirational 1976 recording is now available on a Walkman chrome tape which includes a fine account of *Danse macabre*. While the Franck *Symphony* used as coupling is much less recommendable, this remains a bargain, costing considerably less than a premium-priced LP and offering the Saint-Saëns work uninterrupted. Barenboim's is a superlative performance which glows with warmth from beginning to end. In the opening 6/8 section the galloping rhythms are irresistibly pointed, while the linked slow section has a poised stillness in its soaring lyricism which completely avoids any suspicion of sweetness or sentimentality. A brilliant account of the scherzo leads into a magnificent energetic conclusion, with the Chicago orchestra excelling itself in radiant playing in every section. The tape transfer is admirably managed and it has the advantage of continuity. This is not shared by the Galleria reissue which, although it offers three generous bonuses including an exciting *Bacchanale* from *Samson et Dalila*, brings a turnover in the *Symphony*, immediately before the organ entry at the beginning of the finale, spoiling the element of dramatic surprise. The sound has been digitally remastered, which is not wholly advantageous. While detail is sharper (most effectively so in the scherzo), the massed violins above the stave sound thinner; in the finale, the attempt to clarify the fairly resonant acoustic has lost some of the bloom, and the focus is not necessarily cleaner. LP and chrome tape sound virtually identical.

Dutoit brings his usual gifts of freshness and a natural sympathy to Saint-Saëns's attractive score. There is a ready spontaneity here. The recording is very bright, with luminous detail, the strings given a thrilling brilliance above the stave. One notices a touch of digital edge, but there is a balancing weight. The reading effectively combines lyricism with passion. In the finale, Hurford's entry in the famous chorale melody is more pointed, less massive than usual, although Dutoit generates a genial feeling of gusto to compensate. With its wide range (cassette and disc are closely matched) and bright lighting, this is a performance to leave one tingling after Dutoit's final burst of adrenalin. The compact disc shows no very striking improvement on LP or tape, although the background silence is certainly telling.

The magnificent ASV recording can be strongly recommended only in its LP and tape formats. Present copies of the CD (mastered in Japan) have added an unattractive digital edge to the strings, and while the impact of the organ remains, the sound has lost some of its ambient bloom in this format. Under an inspirational Bátiz, the orchestral playing is exhilarating in its energy and commitment, while the *Poco adagio* balances a noble elegiac feeling with romantic warmth. On LP, the recording (made in Guildford Cathedral) brings an attractive overall bloom, yet registers detail naturally and vividly. After the vivacious scherzo, the entry of the organ in the finale is a breathtaking moment, and the sense of spectacle persists, bringing an unforgettable weight and grandeur to the closing pages. The cassette is successful too, matching the disc fairly closely and losing only a fraction of the dynamic range. The tape, however, has to compete with Barenboim's Walkman.

Martinon's Greensleeve reissue has the advantage (besides being economically priced) of two extra pieces, very well played by the Orchestre de Paris under Pierre Dervaux. *Omphale* acts as a delicate curtain-raiser for the *Symphony*, creating an aptly evocative mood, while the *Danse macabre* is a suitably extrovert encore, with its faintly abrasive violin solo at the opening making a nice foil for the preceding spectacle. Martinon's account of the *Symphony* is in every way distinguished, the first movement alert and sparkling, the *Poco adagio* warmly romantic (with wonderfully rich recording), yet with a touch of nobility at the close. The organ entry in the finale is massively buoyant, but detail registers admirably so that both here and in the vivacious scherzo the rippling piano figurations are clearer than usual. In fact the recording, with its attractive ambient glow, is almost ideally balanced, and this record is very competitive.

There is a good cassette, but the level drops on side two and the effect becomes more subdued than the disc.

Ormandy's Telarc performance is curiously lacking in vitality. It is not helped by the recessed, over-resonant recording, in which the microphones place the organ in a forward concerto-like position. Orchestral detail is poor and the piano contribution barely audible. In the finale, the closing climax is effectively balanced, but elsewhere the performance makes little real impact. On CD, the organ entry is spectacular and some may like the overall sumptuousness.

Edo de Waart's Rotterdam account is unimpressive and uncompetitive. The recording is bright and well detailed, but curiously two-dimensional. The first movement does not lack vigour, but the reticent *Poco adagio* is uninvolving, while the finale, rhythmically positive like the scherzo, is entirely without a sense of occasion.

Karajan's version is superbly played and obviously has its insights. But the recording is artificially balanced and the edginess of the sound turns into a fierce harshness in the finale when Pierre Cochereau opens up his big guns. Some equipment may respond more kindly to this than others, but this can hardly be recommended. The CD is a considerable sonic improvement on the LP, but the fierceness remains.

Sarasate, Pablo (1844–1908)

Carmen fantasy, Op. 25.

❀ *** HMV **CDC 747101-2** [id.]; ASD 2782 [Ang. S/*4XS* 36836]. Perlman, RPO, Foster – PAGANINI: *Concerto No. 1.****❀

This is the filler for Perlman's account of Paganini's *First Violin concerto*, but what a gorgeous filler. Sarasate's *Fantasy* is a selection of the most popular tunes from *Carmen*, with little attempt made to stitch the seams between them. But played like this, with superb panache, luscious tone and glorious recording, the piece almost upstages the concerto with which it is coupled. The recording balance is admirable; the truthfulness of the sound is the more apparent on CD, with the quality far preferable to many of Perlman's more recent digital records.

Zigeunerweisen (Gypsy airs), Op. 21.

(*) HMV Dig. **CDC 747318-2; EL 270176-1/*4*. Mutter, O Nat. de France, Ozawa – LALO: *Symphonie espagnole*.**(*)

A sparkling performance of Sarasate's gypsy potpourri from Anne-Sophie Mutter, given good support from Ozawa. There are some dazzling fireworks; but some may feel her playing in the famous principal lyrical melody too chaste; others will enjoy the total absence of schmaltz. The balance places the solo violin well forward, and the timbre is very brightly lit. The cassette is slightly smoother on top and in that respect is preferable to the sharp definition of the CD.

Satie, Erik (1866–1925)

Avant-dernières Pensées; Embryons desséchés; Enfantillages pittoresques; 3 Gnossiennes; 3 Gymnopédies; Heures séculaires et instantanées; 3 Nocturnes; Passacaille; Peccadilles importunes; Pièces froides I–III.
(M) **(*) Decca Jub. 414 064-1/*4* [Deram 18036]. Camarata Contemporary Chamber Group.

Rather nicely sub-titled 'The velvet gentleman', after Satie's mode of dress during his 'Bohemian' period, this collection needs to be approached with some caution. The Camarata players are expert instrumentalists and they show a natural response to this music, particularly the lyrical pieces which are given a melancholy languor that readily communicates. The scoring is free and includes a synthesizer, often used very effectively – but not always without a degree of (probably intended) vulgarity. Such an approach attempts a cross-over to appeal to listeners who would not approach Satie's music via the recital-room, and it is undoubtedly successful. The recording is extremely vivid in both formats. On tape, there is one uncomfortable moment when a brass climax becomes too piercing, but otherwise disc and cassette are closely matched. This is an inexpensive collection and it should make the composer new friends.

(i) *Les aventures de Mercure* (ballet)*; La belle excentrique; Gymnopédies 1 and 3* (orch. Debussy)*; Jack-in-the-box* (orch. Milhaud)*;* (ii) *Parade* (ballet, arr. Camarata).
(M) (*) Decca Viva 411 839-1/*4*. (i) LPO or L. Fest. Players, Herrmann; (ii) Camarata and instrumentalists.

Originally recorded in Decca's hi-fi Phase Four system, the sound is characteristically vivid with a forward balance. Although Bernard Herrmann is not an unsympathetic Satie advocate, his performances are not distinguished, and the jaunty manner misses the mordant wit of these scores; moreover the *Gymnopédies* by contrast take languor to the point of lassitude. In his version of *Parade*, Camarata has updated the special effects (which Satie intended to be laminated on to the score); besides the authentic pistol-shot, typewriter and siren, he has added a jet plane, crowd noises, plus a chorus reciting *The Lord's Prayer*, nightclub strippers' music, the voice of Hitler, and even the atom bomb! The performance of the music itself is laboured. Of novelty value only.

Music for piano, 4 hands: *Aperçus désagréables; La belle excentrique; Cinéma; Trois Morceaux en forme de poire; Parade* (ballet).
** Denon **C37 7487** [id.]. Takahashi, Planès.

Satie's music for piano duet is not widely represented on disc, and this collection is a good introduction to it. In *La belle excentrique*, the pianists are joined by Juji Murai (clarinet) and Kuji Okasaki (bassoon), a particularly crazy touch. *Parade* in this somewhat monochrome format loses a little of its music-hall character but is none the less entertaining. Well-pointed performances from both artists, and satisfactory though not outstanding recording.

Avant-dernières pensées; (i) *Choses vues à droite et à gauche; Descriptions automatiques; Embryons desséchés; Préludes flasques* (*pour un chien*); *Sonatine bureaucratique; Sports et divertissements; 3 Valses distinguées du précieux dégoûté; Véritables préludes flasques* (*pour un chien*).
** Denon Dig. **C37 7486** [id.]. Yuji Takahashi, (i) with Keiko Mizuno.

These recordings were made in 1979 and, like Yuji Takahashi's earlier recital (**C37 7485** – see below), suffer from a very dry recording acoustic, which may theoretically suit music of dry humour but does not beguile the ear. Takahashi's playing is certainly stylish, but some of this repertoire is already duplicated by Pascal Rogé whose Decca recording is much more agreeable and flattering.

Avant-dernières pensées; Embryons desséchés; Fantaisie-Valse; 3 Gnossiennes; 3 Gymnopédies; Jack-in-the-Box; Je te veux; Le Piccadilly; Poudre d'or; Prélude en tapisserie; Sports et divertissements; Les trois valses distinguées du précieux dégoûté; Valse-ballet.
(M) *(*) EMI EMX 41 2071-1/*4*. Angela Brownridge.

This gifted player has other records to her credit, and there is much to admire here. It replaces a similar and sensitive compilation from Peter Lawson and is intelligently planned and excellently recorded; all the same, something of the essential melancholy and poetry of this music eludes her. There is some fluent playing, but one is rarely touched in the *Gnossiennes* and the *Gymnopédies*. The cassette is faithful and full in timbre, but the recording is resonant and the upper range is less sharply focused than on disc. Pascal Rogé's recital on Decca (see below) is worth the extra outlay.

Danses gothiques; 6 Gnossiennes; Petite ouverture à danser; Prélude de la porte héroïque du ciel.
(*) Ph. Dig. **412 243-2 [id.]. Reinbert de Leeuw.

This CD offers a not especially generous programme, taken from Reinbert de Leeuw's three-LP set concentrating on Satie's earlier music (6768 269). He is a sensitive player and thoroughly attuned to Satie's sensibility. He takes the composer at his word by playing many of the pieces *très lente*; indeed, he overdoes this at times, though this impression may be caused by listening to too much slow music all at once. But if one occasionally feels the need for more movement (and, on occasion, for greater dynamic nuance), these are admirable performances, and any blame must partly lie with the producer of this CD in not seeking greater variety. There is no doubt that the playing creates and maintains a mood of poetic melancholy; this is helped by the beautiful recorded quality, the more effective on compact disc, when the piano image is so believable and the background is silent.

Embryons desséchés; 6 Gnossiennes; 3 Gymnopédies; Je te veux; Nocturne No. 4; Le Piccadilly; 4 Préludes flasques; Prélude en tapisserie; Sonatine bureaucratique; Vieux sequins et vieilles cuirasses.
*** Decca Dig. **410 220-2**; 410 220-1/*4*. Pascal Rogé.

Pascal Rogé gave Satie's music its compact disc début in a fine recital which is splendidly caught by the microphone. Rogé has real feeling for this repertoire and conveys its bitter-sweet quality and its grave melancholy as well as he does its lighter qualities. He produces, as usual, consistent beauty of tone, and this is well projected by the recording in all three formats. This remains the primary recommendation on CD for this repertoire.

Gnossiennes 1–3; Gymnopédies 1–3; Prélude de la porte héroïque du ciel; Je te veux; Nocturnes 1–5; Pièces froides: Airs à faire fuir 1–3; Danses de travers 1–3. Ragtime parade.
** Denon **C37 7485** [id.]. Yuji Takahashi.

Yuji Takahashi recorded these pieces in the mid-1970s and his strong rhythmic feeling and sense of style won him some considerable praise in the BBC's 'Record Review'. The snag is the forward balance and the cramped, dry acoustic of the Denon recording. If you can accept that (and the piano has undoubted presence), then there is much to admire here. But Pascal Rogé's softer contours and more sophisticated colouring, as recorded by Decca, sound much more sensuous.

Scarlatti, Alessandro (1660–1725)

Sinfonie di concerti grossi Nos 1–6.
*** Ph. Dig. **400 017-2** [id.]. Bennett, Lenore, Smith, Soustrot, Elhorst, I Musici.

These performances are taken from the complete set of twelve (originally issued on LP as 6769 066, now withdrawn). All are elegantly and stylishly played. All are scored for flute and strings; in No. 2 there is a trumpet as well, in No. 5 an oboe and in Nos 1 and 5 a second flute. No complaints about the performances, which are lively and attractive and eminently well recorded. The harpsichord is a little reticent, even on CD, but few will fail to derive pleasure from the music making here.

Motets: *Domine, refugium factus es nobis; O magnum mysterium.*
(M) **(*) Argo 411 981-1/*4*. Schütz Ch. of London, Norrington – D. SCARLATTI: *Stabat Mater.***(*)

These two motets are fine pieces that show how enduring the Palestrina tradition was in seventeenth-century Italy. They are noble in conception and are beautifully performed here, making an excellent fill-up to the Domenico Scarlatti *Stabat Mater.*

Scarlatti, Domenico (1685–1757)

Keyboard sonatas, Kk. 8, 13, 20, 87, 107, 109, 132, 184, 193, 233, 247, 450, 481, 531, 544.
* DG Dig. **415 511-2**; 415 511-1/*4* [id.]. Alexis Weissenberg.

An uncompetitive issue. There is an abundance of fine pianists, both on and off record, who can play Scarlatti on the piano with elegance and sensitivity (not least Horowitz – see Recitals, below). Alexis Weissenberg's recital falls short of distinction and has little to recommend it but good recording in all three media.

Keyboard sonatas, Kk. 9, 115, 124, 132–3, 206, 208–9, 238–9, 259–60, 308–9, 394–5, 402–3, 429–30, 446, 460–1, 481, 490–2, 513.
(M) *** Ph. 412 421-1 (2). Blandine Verlet (harpsichord).

With sonatas in the same key authentically juxtaposed, slow against fast, and playing of exceptional subtlety and point with delightful harpsichord registration, these are among the most enjoyable records of Scarlatti sonatas in the catalogue, the more attractive on the Philips mid-price label. The sonatas chosen include some of the most sharply original, dark and even tragic as well as brilliant. Excellent 1976 recording. (The two discs were originally issued separately but are now together in a double-sleeve.)

Keyboard sonatas, Kk. 39, 87, 96, 118, 124, 162, 183, 193, 208–9, 296, 318–19, 322, 380–1, 386, 434, 436, 454–5, 460, 466–7, 475, 481, 516–17, 531, 533, 544, 551.
(M) *** HMV Dig. EX 290349-3 (3). Christian Zacharias (piano).

These recordings have been made over the period 1979–84. The high standards of taste and expertise of the music making are to be found throughout. Zacharias is splendidly alert, his articulation crisp and clean, and rhythms buoyantly alive. Indeed, anyone wanting a good cross-section of Scarlatti sonatas on the piano would have to go a long way to beat this beautifully recorded anthology.

Keyboard sonatas (arr. for guitar)*: Kk. 32, 34, 42, 64, 77, 146, 238, 283, 322, 377, 446, 474.*
** DG Dig. 413 783-1/*4* [id.]. Narciso Yepes (guitar).

Agreeable performances of undoubted sensibility, improvisatory in character and very well recorded on both LP and tape. Those who like Scarlatti sonatas on the guitar will find this agreeable for the late evening. Even if the style is free and a shade romantic, it carries its own conviction.

Stabat Mater.
*** Erato Dig. **ECD 88087**; NUM/*MCE* 75172 [id.]. Monteverdi Ch., E. Bar. Soloists, Gardiner – *Concert: 'Sacred choral music'*.***

(M) **(*) Argo 411 981-1/*4*. Schütz Ch. of London, Norrington – A. SCARLATTI: *Motets.***(*)

The *Stabat Mater* is an early work, written during Scarlatti's sojourn in Rome (1714–19) when he was maestro di cappella at S. Giulia, and it shows him to be a considerable master of polyphony. It is extended in scale and taxing to the performers. This new version from John Eliot Gardiner has nothing to fear from any comparison you might care to make: the singing is never less than excellent. The *Stabat Mater* has been written off by some critics as bland and wanting in individuality; though it falls off in interest towards the end, yet it possesses eloquence and nobility – and it is far less bland than Pergolesi's setting. Gardiner's fine performance couples three motets of interest, by Cavalli, Gesualdo and Clément, which are also splendidly done. The recording is very good indeed, notably fresh in its CD format but also sounding first class on the excellent chrome cassette.

Norrington's Argo account is competitively priced and is also admirable, though not always impeccable in matters of tonal balance. The recording is good, even if it suffers from a certain want of focus at the top. But the coupling of motets by Alessandro Scarlatti is in itself of interest.

Schmidt, Franz (1874–1939)

Symphony No. 3 in A.
**(*) Sup. Dig. 1110 3394. Slovak PO, Pešek.

So far the *Fourth* is the only one of Schmidt's symphonies to have reached the domestic catalogues (Decca SXL 6544 [Lon. CS 6747]); this recording of its immediate predecessor, composed in 1928, is a welcome alternative to its only rival which was released in 1977 on an obscure American label (Austrian Radio Orchestra under Carl Melles). The idiom is eminently approachable, firmly in the tradition of Schubert, Bruckner and Reger, but the ideas have nobility and character that are all Schmidt's own. Libor Pešek gets eminently satisfactory results from the Slovak orchestra; however, the recording, though an improvement on its predecessor, is not top-drawer and could be more detailed in climaxes. But such is the interest of the work that it would be wrong not to give this a strong recommendation.

Piano quintet, Op. 51.
(*) Accord **149528**. Bärtschi, Berne Qt.

Schmidt's *Piano quintet* was written between 1905 and 1908, but revised later and republished in 1919. It is conceived on the largest scale, sprawling out for a full 55 minutes, and its romantic atmosphere is permeated with *fin de siècle* decadence. Nevertheless it has its impressive moments, notably the opening of the slow movement which is quite haunting. It needs a better performance than this to be convincing. Though Werner Bärtschi is thoroughly at home in the piano part, the Berne Quartet sound uncomfortable, producing edgy timbre and suspect intonation, although the playing is committed, even passionate. The compact disc is only too clear, and this disc gives little pleasure.

String quartet in A.
* Preiser SPR 3062. Wiener Konzerthausquartett.

The *Quartet in A major* dates from 1925, the year in which Schmidt became Director of the Vienna Staatsakademie, though the score was not published until 1962. It is a work of much nobility of feeling and beauty, whose consummate craftsmanship is a joy in itself. The opening bars prompt one's thoughts to stray to Reger, Strauss and perhaps Pfitzner, but one soon comes to recognize Schmidt's distinctive voice and to admire the richness and quality of the invention and mastery of musical design. In the absence of any alternative recordings, the collector seeking this *Quartet* has no choice but to invest in this issue. Neither the performance nor the quality of the recorded sound is very distinguished. Tonally it is lacklustre, thanks to the dry acoustic of the small Austrian Radio studio from which it emanates. It does not sound of recent provenance: the sleeve gives no date but merely notes that the recording derives from the Austrian Radio Archives.

Schmitt, Florent (1870–1958)

The Haunted palace, Op. 49.
*** HMV Dig. EL 270158-1/*4* [Ang. DS/*4DS* 38168]. Monte Carlo PO, Prêtre – CAPLET: *Masque***(*); DEBUSSY: *Chute de la maison Usher*.***

Florent Schmitt, like Debussy and Caplet in the works used for coupling, found the inspiration for his *Étude* in Edgar Allan Poe. It is young man's music (written in 1904, shortly before the Caplet *Masque of the Red Death*) for though Schmitt was in his mid-thirties when he completed it, he used his years in Rome as a student-winner of the Prix de Rome for the composition. It is a richly evocative piece, some twelve minutes in length, and is given an enthusiastic performance under Prêtre. The recording is excellent, on both disc and tape; the work undoubtedly adds to the interest of an issue which is an indispensable acquisition for all Debussians.

Schnittke, Alfred (born 1934)

(i) *Violin concerto No. 2;* (ii) *Piano quintet.*
*** Ph. Dig. 411 107-1/*4* [id.]. (i) Kremer, Basle SO, Holliger; (ii) Bashkirova, Kremer Ens.

The second of Schnittke's four *Violin concertos* dates from 1966 and enjoys the expert advocacy of Gidon Kremer and the Basle Symphony Orchestra under Heinz Holliger. Schnittke is a much-respected figure, and this is a work which would seem somewhat beholden to the Polish avant-garde of the 1960s. The *Concerto* offers some carefully calculated and often remarkable effects. Of course, many of the expressive devices seem derived from without, rather than arising naturally from within – yet one must admit that one's attention is held completely. Whether or not one is wholly drawn into its world is another matter – but at least there is a world there into which one could be drawn. The *Piano quintet* of 1972 strikes one as having greater substance: its bleak and uncompromising sounds call to mind the late Shostakovich quartets, and there is no doubt as to its seriousness of feeling. Repeated hearings of the *Concerto* will perhaps reveal further depths and a purpose and direction that are not apparent on one or two playings. The actual sound is absolutely superb; the balance is perfectly judged and the clarity and definition, particularly on the outstanding cassette, are of demonstration standard. Indeed, recording – whether of the *Concerto* or of the *Quintet* – doesn't come much better than this, on disc and cassette alike.

Violin sonata No. 1; Sonata in the olden style.
*** Chan. Dig. ABRD/*ABTD* 1089 [id.]. Dubinsky, Edlina – SHOSTAKOVICH: *Violin sonata.****

Schnittke is now over fifty and has achieved prominence as one of the leading Soviet composers of the middle generation. In the early 1950s he composed a number of relatively conventional works, including *Nagasaki* and *Songs of War and Peace*, but after steeping himself in the idiom of Shostakovich and Prokofiev, he became attracted to the more exploratory musical idiom of the Western avant-garde who built their foundations on the Second Viennese School. The *First sonata* dates from 1963 when he was still in his late twenties; it is a well-argued piece that seems to unify his awareness of the post-serial musical world with the tradition of Shostakovich. It is linked on this version with a pastiche of less interest, dating from 1977. Excellent playing from both artists and very good recording too. The chrome cassette matches the disc in presence and realism.

Schoenberg, Arnold (1874–1951)

Chamber symphony, Op. 9; Variations, Op. 31.
(M) *** Decca Lon. Ent. 414 440-1/*4* [id.]. LAPO, Mehta.

It is good to have two Schoenberg masterpieces (one from early in his career and one from the very peak, arguably his finest instrumental work) coupled in brilliant performances from a virtuoso orchestra. It was, after all, to Los Angeles that Schoenberg moved to settle in his last years, and it would have gladdened him that his local philharmonic orchestra had achieved a degree of brilliance to match that of any other orchestra in America. The Op. 31 *Variations*, among the most taxing works Schoenberg ever wrote, somehow reveal their secrets, their unmistakable greatness, more clearly when the performances have such a sense of drive, born of long and patient rehearsal under a clear-headed conductor. The *First Chamber symphony* is also given a rich performance, arguably too fast at times, but full of understanding for the romantic emotions which underlie much of the writing. Brilliant 1969 recording, though the high-level tape (available for the first time) is shrill.

Pelleas und Melisande, Op. 5.
(M) *** DG 410 934-1 [id.]. BPO, Karajan.

The Straussian opulence of Schoenberg's early symphonic poem has never been as ravishingly presented as by Karajan and the Berlin Philharmonic in this superbly recorded version. The gorgeous tapestry of sound is both rich and full of refinement and detail, while the thrust of argument is powerfully conveyed in Karajan's radiant performance.

Variations for orchestra, Op. 31; Verklaerte Nacht, Op. 4.
❀ *** DG **415 326-2**; 2530 627 [id.]. BPO, Karajan.

Verklaerte Nacht, Op. 4.
*** Decca Dig. **410 111-2**; 410 111-1/*4* [id.]. ECO, Ashkenazy – WAGNER: *Siegfried idyll.****

Karajan's version of *Verklaerte Nacht* is altogether magical and very much in a class of its own. There is a tremendous intensity and variety of tone and colour: the palette that the strings of the Berlin Philharmonic have at their command is altogether extraordinarily wide-ranging. Both these masterly performances are classics of the Karajan discography; their transfer to compact disc cannot be too strongly welcomed: the sound is firmer and more cleanly defined, and the increased range that the new medium offers enables both interpretations to be heard to even better advantage than before. It is to be hoped that Karajan's other records of twentieth-century music (including the Berg *Orchestral pieces*, Op. 6, and the Honegger *Symphonie liturgique* and *Symphony for strings*) will soon take their place in the CD catalogue.

Ashkenazy conducts an outstandingly warm and lyrical reading, one which brings out the melodic richness of his highly atmospheric work, with passionate playing from the ECO. Full and brilliant recording. The compact disc brings an extra edge to the sound, not always quite comfortable on high violins.

String trio, Op. 45; Verklaerte Nacht, Op. 4.
** DG Dig. 410 962-1/*4* [id.]. LaSalle Qt (with McInness and Pegis).

Suite, Op. 29; Verklaerte Nacht, Op. 4.
*** CBS IM/*IMT* 39566 [id.]. Ens. InterContemporain, Boulez.

Boulez has already recorded *Verklaerte Nacht* in the version for full strings with the New York Philharmonic for CBS; and this beautifully played account for solo strings is hardly less impressive. Here he is billed as supervising, rather than directing the performance as he does for Op. 29. Yet the precision of ensemble and refinement of balance suggest just such a strong but deeply sympathetic guiding hand. The neoclassical *Suite* – with Boulez this time conducting a mere seven players – reveals a totally different side of the composer, never so light as he himself must have intended in its very Germanic humour, but a spiky piece presented at its sharpest in this reading. There is no lack of intimacy and expressive feeling. The CBS recording is absolutely first class in every way and the splendid cassette is in the demonstration class, full and atmospheric, yet well defined.

The LaSalle Quartet give a superbly efficient, virtuosic account of *Verklaerte Nacht*, though there is no want of expressive feeling. They are superbly recorded by the DG engineers, but they are at times inclined to rush things; the overall effect is by no means as impressive as in Boulez. The *String trio*, composed almost half a century later, is played with an effortless mastery by Walter Levin, Peter Kammitzer and Lee Fiser, and again is superbly recorded, with a high-quality matching cassette.

Still recommended: On Nonesuch, the Sante Fe Chamber Music Festival Ensemble offer the same coupling as DG. This group includes such fine players as Walter Trampler and Ralph Kirschbaum. Both performances are marvellously eloquent and beautifully recorded. This is preferable to the DG issue, and *Verklaerte Nacht* has perhaps marginally more warmth than Boulez's fine version (Nonesuch Dig. D/*D4* 79028 [id.]).

VOCAL MUSIC

De Profundis, Op. 50b; Dreimal tausend Jahre, Op. 50a; 3 Folksongs, Op. 49; 3 Folksongs for mixed chorus; Friede auf Erden, Op. 13; 4 Pieces, Op. 27; 6 Pieces for male chorus, Op. 35; 3 Satires for mixed chorus, Op. 28.
*** Ph. Dig. 411 088-1 (2). Netherlands Chamber Ch., De Leeuw – ZEMLINSKY: *Psalm 23.****

The Netherlands Chamber Choir on its two-disc set gathers together a whole series of important and neglected vocal works, many of them more approachable than is common with this master. Ensemble is finely controlled, though speeds are often on the cautious side; it is, however, surprising that the purely tonal folksong settings inspire the least concentrated performances. The matching of voices is as fine as the refined and well-balanced recording.

Die eiserne Brigade (march for string quartet and piano); (i) *Ode to Napoleon* (for reciter, string quartet and piano); (ii) *Serenade, Op. 24; Weihnachtsmusik.*
*** Decca Lon. Ent. 414 171-1/*4* [id.]. (i) Gerald English; (ii) John Shirley-Quirk, members of London Sinf., Atherton.

These varied pieces of Schoenberg in lighter – or at least more approachable –

mood are taken from an outstanding set of Schoenberg chamber recordings made in 1974 in connection with a festival celebrating the centenary of Schoenberg's birth. With excellent recording each item can be warmly recommended, not just the neoclassical *Serenade* and the haunting *Ode to Napoleon*, using words by Byron, but also the two brief pieces, written when Schoenberg was conscripted into the Austrian army, which deliberately use banal and popular ideas in an almost Ivesian way. A most welcome reissue on the mid-price Enterprise label. The tape, however, has been transferred at marginally too high a level. On side one especially, the upper range is excessively bright, while in the *Ode* the voice is over-projected, with consonants emphasized.

Gurrelieder.

*** Ph. **412 511-2**; 6769 038/*7699 124* [id.]. McCracken, Norman, Troyanos, Arnold, Scown, Tanglewood Fest. Ch., Boston SO, Ozawa.

Ozawa directs a gloriously opulent reading of Schoenberg's *Gurrelieder*, one which relates it firmly to the nineteenth century rather than pointing forward to Schoenberg's own later works. The playing of the Boston Symphony has both warmth and polish and is set against a resonant acoustic; among the soloists, Jessye Norman gives a performance of radiant beauty, at times reminding one of Flagstad in the burnished glory of her tone colours. As the wood-dove, Tatiana Troyanos sings most sensitively, though the vibrato is at times obtrusive; and James McCracken does better than most tenors at coping with a heroic vocal line without barking. Other versions have in some ways been more powerful – Boulez's, for one – but none is more sumptuously beautiful than this. The luxuriant textures are given a degree more transparency, with detail slightly clearer on CD. The cassettes match the LPs closely, encompassing the wide dynamic range without difficulty until the short but massive closing chorus, which lacks the open quality of the LP and CD.

Pierrot Lunaire, Op. 21.

*** Chan. ABR/*ABT* 1046 [id.]. Jane Manning, Nash Ens., Rattle – WEBERN: *Concerto.****

Jane Manning is outstanding among singers who have tackled this most taxing of works, steering a masterful course between the twin perils of, on the one hand, actually singing and on the other of simply speaking. As well as being beautifully controlled and far more accurate than is common, her sing-speech brings out the element of irony and darkly pointed wit that is an essential too often missed in this piece. In a 1977 recording originally made for the Open University, Rattle draws strong, committed performances from the members of the Nash Ensemble and, apart from some intermittently odd balances, the sound is excellent. Unlike those of some rivals, the disc contains an important fill-up in the late Webern piece.

OPERA

Moses und Aaron.

Ⓒ *** Decca Dig. **414 264-2**; 414 264-1/*4* [id.]. Mazura, Langridge, Bonney, Haugland, Chicago Ch. and SO, Solti.

Recorded in conjunction with concert performances, working very much against the clock and with the whole opera completed in fourteen hours, Solti gives Schoenberg's masterly score a dynamism and warmth which set it firmly – if perhaps surprisingly – in the grand Romantic tradition. This is no mere intellectual exercise or static oratorio, as it can seem, but a genuine drama. Solti instructed his performers to 'play and sing as if you were performing Brahms', and here *Moses und Aron* can almost be regarded as the opera which Brahms did not write – if with the 'wrong notes'.

Particularly when two fine previous versions remain unavailable – Boulez on CBS, Gielen on Philips – Solti's broad romantic treatment presents a splendid alternative. This is a performance which in its greater variety of mood and pace underlines the drama, finds an element of fantasy and, in places – as in the *Golden Calf* episode – a sparkle such as you would never expect from Schoenberg. It is still not an easy work. The Moses of Franz Mazura may not be so specific in his sing-speech as was Gunter Reich in the two previous versions – far less sing than speech – but the characterization of an Old Testament patriarch is the more convincing. As Aron, Philip Langridge is lighter and more lyrical, as well as more accurate than his predecessor with Boulez, Richard Cassilly. Aage Haugland with his firm, dark bass makes his mark in the small role of the Priest; Barbara Bonney too is excellent as the Young Girl. Above all, the brilliant singing of the Chicago Symphony Chorus matches the playing of the orchestra in virtuosity. More than ever the question-mark concluding Act II makes a pointful close, with no feeling of a work unfinished. The brilliant recording shows little or no sign of the speed with which the project was completed, and the CD adds an even sharper focus. The cassettes are also of a state-of-the-art standard, catching the full ambient bloom yet retaining inner clarity.

Schröter, Johann (1752–1788)

Piano concerto in C, Op. 3/3.

*** CBS Dig. **MK 39222**; IM/*IMT* 39222 [id.]. Murray Perahia, ECO – MOZART: *Piano concertos Nos 1–3, K.107.****

Johann Samuel Schröter was born in Poland and was four years older than Mozart. He made his début in Leipzig in 1767 and then appeared in London at the Bach–Abel concerts; he eventually succeeded J. C. Bach as music master to the Queen in 1782, six years before his death. It was Schröter's widow for whom Haydn developed an attachment on his first visit to London. He was a highly accomplished pianist, and this sparkling little concerto explains why he was so successful. Murray Perahia gives it all his care and attention without overloading it with sophistication. Delightful in every way and beautifully recorded, it sounds particularly fresh and present in its CD form.

Schubert, Franz (1797–1828)

Konzertstück, D.345; Polonaise in B flat, D.580; Rondo in A, D.438.
(M) *** DG Sig. 410 985-1/*4*. Kremer, LSO, Tchakarov – BEETHOVEN: *Concerto movement* etc.***

Like Beethoven in the *Concerto movement* Schubert was twenty when he wrote these three concertante pieces, none of them specially individual, but all attractive in performances so sweetly sympathetic. Excellent recording.

Symphonies Nos 1–3; 4 (Tragic); 5–7; 8 (Unfinished); 9 in C (Great); 10 in D, D.936a; Symphonic fragments in D, D.615 and D.708a (completed and orch. Newbould).
*** Ph. Dig. **412 176-2** (6); 412 176-1/*4* (7/5) [id.]. ASMF, Marriner.

Marriner's excellent set gathers together not only the eight symphonies of the regular canon but two more symphonies now 'realized', thanks to the work of Professor Brian Newbould of Hull University. For full measure, half a dozen fragments of other symphonic movements are also included, orchestrated by Professor Newbould. Those fragments include the four-movement outline of yet another symphony – scherzo complete, other movements tantalizingly cut off in mid-flight. Though you can often appreciate what snags the young composer was finding in particular ideas, the authentic charm is consistently there. Newbould's No. 7 is based on a sketch which quickly lapsed into a single orchestral line, now devotedly filled out. That work proves less rewarding than 'No. 10', written in the last months of Schubert's life, well after the *Great C major*, which now appears to have been written a year or so earlier. This *Tenth*, in three movements, has a heavenly slow movement, with some bald Mahlerian overtones and a last movement that starts as a scherzo and then satisfyingly ends as a finale.

Sir Neville's readings of the first six symphonies, recorded earlier, bring sparkling examples of the Academy's work at its finest, while the bigger challenges of the *Unfinished* (here completed with Schubert's scherzo filled out and the *Rosamunde B minor Entr'acte* used as finale) and the *Great C major* are splendidly taken. These are fresh, direct readings, making up in rhythmic vitality for any lack of weight. The recordings, all digital, were made between 1981 and 1984; particularly on CD, they present consistent refinement and undistractingly good balance. The tape transfers too are of Philips's best standard. There seems slight clouding of the middle frequencies in Nos 1 and 4 on the first cassette, but the upper range is not restricted; elsewhere, inner detail is good, if marginally less sharp than on the CDs.

Symphonies Nos 1 in D, D.82; 4 in C min. (Tragic), D.417.
*** Ph. Dig. 6514/*7337* 261 [id.]. ASMF, Marriner.

The style of Marriner and the Academy, their polish and point, is ideally suited to early Schubert. Even No. 4 is far less weighty than its subtitle suggests, and this performance captures the stirrings of romanticism (particularly in the outer movements) while keeping the results totally Schubertian in their lightness. Fine recording. The chrome tape is agreeable, but rather bass-orientated.

Symphonies Nos 2 in B flat, D.125; 6 in C, D.589.
*** Ph. Dig. 6514/*7337* 208 [id.]. ASMF, Marriner.

Marriner and the Academy gain over almost every rival in the lightness and clarity of articulation as well as the apt and refreshing choices of speeds – particularly important in No. 6 which is a demanding work interpretatively. An outstanding issue like the others in Marriner's Schubert series, very well recorded. The chrome cassette is generally pleasing, though it tends to be bass-heavy.

Symphonies Nos 2 in B flat, D.125; 8 in B min. (*Unfinished*), *D.759.*
(*) CBS Dig. **MK 39676; IM/*IMT* 39676 [id.]. BPO, Barenboim.

With fine playing from the Berlin Philharmonic, particularly brilliant in the perpetuum mobile finale of No. 2, in which the repeat is observed, Barenboim offers an unusual coupling for the *Unfinished.* It can be recommended with reservations to those who fancy the youthful work alongside the mature masterpiece, but the recording does not clarify textures sufficiently for No. 2, which becomes rather too inflated. Barenboim's approach to the *Unfinished* is fresh, yet thoughtfully expressive. Even with the added clarification of CD, the orchestral sound remains very weighty in the middle and bass registers, and the chrome cassette too has a noticeable resonance at the bass end.

Symphonies Nos 3 in D, D.200; 5 in B flat, D.485.
❀ *** HMV SXLP/*TC-SXLP* 30204. RPO, Beecham.
*** Ph. 6514/*7337* 149 [id.]. ASMF, Marriner.

Beecham's are magical performances in which every phrase breathes. There is no substitute for imaginative phrasing, and each line is shaped with affection and spirit. Sunny, smiling performances with beautifully alive rhythms and luminous textures. The recording is faithful in timbre, well balanced and spacious. This is an indispensable record for all collections. The cassette transfer too is of excellent quality.

Stylish, fresh and beautifully sprung performances from Marriner and the Academy, superbly played and recorded. The classic Beecham coupling of the same two symphonies brought one or two extra touches of magic, but for charm and sparkle these performances are unsurpassed among modern versions. On the chrome cassette, detail and focus are soft-grained; the disc is far preferable.

Symphonies Nos 3 in D, D.200; 8 in B min. (*Unfinished*), *D.759.*
(*) DG **415 601-2; 2531/*3301* 124 [id.]. VPO, Carlos Kleiber.

Carlos Kleiber is a refreshingly unpredictable conductor; sometimes, however, his imagination goes too far towards quirkiness, and that is certainly so in the slow movement of No. 3, which is rattled through jauntily at breakneck speed. The effect is bizarre even for an *Allegretto*, if quite charming. The minuet too becomes a full-blooded scherzo, and there is little rest in the outer movements. The *Unfinished* brings a more compelling performance, but there is unease in the first movement, where first and second subjects are not fully co-ordinated, the contrasts sounding a little forced. The recording brings out the brass sharply, and is of pleasantly wide range. This is the more striking in the CD transfer. On cassette, the pianissimos of the *Unfinished* tend to recede a little; otherwise the transfer is of sophisticated quality and strikingly clear.

Symphonies Nos 4 in C min. (Tragic), D.417; 5 in B flat, D.485.
*** Ph. Dig. **410 045-2** [id.]. ASMF, Marriner.

For the compact disc issue, the coupling is different from LP and cassette. The sound remains warm and luminous, but the refinement of the presentation against the silent background makes the ear realize that the balance is not quite ideal in the relationship of wind and strings and the recording is not as clearly defined internally as one might expect, with the overall focus less than sharp. Nevertheless, this remains a highly desirable issue.

Symphonies Nos 4 in C. min. (Tragic), D.417; 8 in B min. (Unfinished), D.759.
*(*) Erato **ECD 88008**; NUM/*MCE* 75063. Basle SO, Jordan.

Jordan's coupling is well played but the readings are not distinctive. The *Unfinished* lacks biting drama, nor does it have any special romantic feeling; while the *Tragic symphony* is undercharacterized until the finale which suddenly springs to life. The recording is full and atmospheric but in no way special. A disappointing issue.

Symphony No. 5 in B flat, D.485.
(M) ** Pickwick Dig. **PCD 819.** O of St John's, Smith Square, Lubbock – HAYDN: *Symphony No. 49.***(*)

With tempi fractionally on the brisk side, Lubbock's pacing is nevertheless convincing; the playing is responsive, if not as polished as on Beecham's famous version. There is no want of character here and the recording is first class, but ultimately this is not a performance to resonate in the memory, though the slow movement has grace. Very good sound, and the price is competitive.

Symphonies Nos 5 in B flat, D.485; 8 in B min. (Unfinished), D.759.
*** Decca Dig. **414 371-2**; 414 371-1/*4* [id.]. VPO, Solti.
*** CBS **MK 42048** [id.]. Columbia SO or NYPO, Bruno Walter.
(M) **(*) HMV EG 290572-1/*4* [Ang. AM/*4AM* 34730]. BPO, Karajan.
(M) **(*) HMV 290460-1/*4* [Ang. RL/*4RL* 32038 or AE/*4AE* 34444]. Philh. O, Klemperer.

** Denon Dig. **C37 7156** [id.]. Berlin State O, Suitner.
(M) * Ph. Seq. 412 370-1/*4* [id.]. Concg. O, Haitink.

As with Solti's fresh, resilient and persuasive reading of the *Great C major* with the Vienna Philharmonic, his coupling of Nos 5 and 8 brings one of his most felicitous recordings. There have been more charming versions of No. 5 but few that so beautifully combine freshness with refined polish. The *Unfinished* has Solti adopting measured speeds but with his refined manner keeping total concentration. Excellent recording.

Bruno Walter brings special qualities of warmth and lyricism to the *Unfinished.* Affection, gentleness and humanity are the keynotes of this performance; while the first movement of the *Fifth* is rather measured, there is much loving attention to detail in the *Andante*. The 1961 recording emerges fresh and glowing in its CD format and, like the rest of the Walter series, completely belies its age. The sound is richly expansive as well as clear, and the CD is in every way satisfying.

Karajan's EMI coupling is taken from the complete cycle of Schubert symphonies which he recorded in the late 1970s. The performance of the *Unfinished* may lack the mystery and dark intensity of his DG recording of the work (see below), but both No. 5 and No. 8 here find Karajan at his freshest and least complicated. The mannered style which sometimes mars his Schubert is completely absent. With full, undistracting sound and superb playing, it makes a good mid-price coupling.

Rugged performances from Klemperer, very characteristic of him in their almost total lack of charm; but with open-air freshness, thanks to alert rhythmic control, to fine playing from the Philharmonia at its peak, and to recording which is excellent for its period. A valuable memento in the mid-price Klemperer centenary series.

With strings recessed as in the companion disc of the *Great C major*, the start of Suitner's account of the *Unfinished* is murky, not just dark, and though the picture clarifies later, the fresh, direct reading is let down by some indifferent playing. In both movements the boomy bass exaggerates low pizzicatos without defining the sound, a distracting effect. Suitner's reading of No. 5 is fresh and bright, not very subtle, again marred by variable string playing and oddly balanced recording.

Disappointingly dull performances from Haitink, with slow tempi the rule. It is a bad sign when one does not welcome the exposition repeat in the first movement of the *Unfinished.*

Symphony No. 8 in B min. (*Unfinished*), *D.759.*

❀ ₵ *** DG Dig. **410 862-2**; 410 862-1/*4* [id.]. Philh. O, Sinopoli – MENDELSSOHN: *Symphony No. 4.**** ₵

(M) *** DG Sig. 413 982-1/*4* [id.]. BPO, Karajan – SCHUMANN: *Symphony No. 4.****

** Telarc Dig. **CD 80090** [id.]. Cleveland O, Dohnányi – BEETHOVEN: *Symphony No. 8.***(*)

* CBS **CD 36711** [id.]. VPO, Maazel – BEETHOVEN: *Symphony No. 5.*

Sinopoli here repeats a coupling made famous by Cantelli with the same orchestra (his World Records reissue, now withdrawn). Sinopoli secures the most ravishingly refined and beautiful playing; the orchestral blend, particularly of the woodwind and horns, is magical. It is a deeply concentrated reading of the *Unfinished*, bringing out much unexpected detail, with every phrase freshly turned in seamless spontaneity. The contrast, as Sinopoli sees it, is between the dark – yet never histrionic – tragedy of the first movement, relieved only partially by the lovely second subject, and the sunlight of the closing movement, giving an unforgettable, gentle radiance. The exposition repeat is observed, adding weight and substance. This takes its place among the recorded classics. The warmly atmospheric recording, made in Kingsway Hall, is equally impressive on LP and chrome tape; but on CD the opening pages of each movement are wonderfully telling, with pianissimo orchestral tone projected against the silent background. The refinement of detail is matched by the drama inherent in the wide dynamic range. This is one of the finest compact discs yet to come from DG.

Karajan's 1966 recording of the *Unfinished* had a long catalogue life at full price and is now fully recommendable in the mid-range. Its merits of simplicity and directness are enhanced by the extraordinary polish of the orchestral playing, lighting up much that is often obscured. The first movement is extremely compelling in its atmosphere; the slow movement too brings tinglingly precise attack and a wonderful sense of drama. The recording was originally first rate; it sounds fresher still in remastered form. There is a splendid cassette.

If Dohnányi's reading lacks a little in poetry and magic, it presents a fresh and direct view, beautifully played. He omits the exposition repeat in the first movement. Like the Beethoven symphony on the reverse, this one is treated to a rather less bright recording than one expects from Telarc.

Although Maazel's *Unfinished*, recorded in Japan, comes off rather better than its Beethoven coupling, with the recording reasonably atmospheric if never clear, this remains one of the most undistinguished CDs in the catalogue.

Symphony No. 8 (*Unfinished*), *D.759*, including completed *Scherzo* and *Allegro* from *Rosamunde, D.797* (arr. Newbould); *Symphonic fragments, D.708a* (completed and orch. Newbould).
*** Ph. **412 472-2** [id.]. ASMF, Marriner.

Symphony No. 8 (*Unfinished*), *D.759* (completed by Newbould); *Symphonic fragments in D, D.615* (arr. Newbould).
*** Ph. 411 439-1/*4* [id.]. ASMF, Marriner.

On CD, LP and the matching cassette, the *Unfinished* from Marriner and the Academy – as it does in their boxed set – comes with a completion suggested by Professor Brian Newbould in which the scherzo is filled out and the *B minor Entr'acte* from *Rosamunde* is used as finale. Where on LP and cassette the two brief fragments labelled *D.615* are provided as makeweight, the CD has a much more generous offering in the four-movement outline of a complete *Symphony*, also in D, D.708a. All are immaculately done.

Symphony No. 8 (Unfinished), D.759; Rosamunde: Overture (Die Zauberharfe), D.644; Ballet music Nos 1 and 2; Entr'acte in B flat.
(*) Ph. Dig. **410 393-2; 410 393-1/*4* [id.]. Boston SO, Sir Colin Davis.

Symphony No. 8 (Unfinished), D.759; Rosamunde: Ballet music Nos 1 and 2.
(B) **(*) DG Walkman *413 157-4*. BPO, Boehm – SCHUMANN: *Symphony No. 1* etc.**(*)

(i) *Symphony No. 8 (Unfinished), D.759;* (ii) *Rosamunde: Overture, Ballet music and Entr'actes;* (iii; iv) *Piano quintet in A (Trout): Theme and variations* (only); (iii) *Impromptus D.899/3 and 4; D.935/2.*
(B) ** Ph. On Tour *412 905-4* [id.]. (i) Dresden State O, Sawallisch; (ii) Concg. O, Haitink; (iii) Haebler; (iv) Grumiaux Qt.

Sir Colin Davis offers a strong, direct account of the *Unfinished*, the first movement taken briskly but beautifully played. The magic of the disc is concentrated on the second side where the refined, nicely sprung performances of the *Rosamunde* music are consistently refreshing. Warm Boston recording, made a degree clearer in the compact disc version, but sounding well on both LP and tape (where the transfer of the *Symphony* is made at quite a high level).

Boehm conducts a glowing performance of the *Unfinished*, a splendid sampler of the Schubert cycle he recorded with the Berlin Philharmonic around 1960. The opening of the development in the first movement – always a key moment – gives the perfect example of Boehm magic. It is coupled with Kubelik's Schumann on the bargain-priced Walkman tape. Only two items from *Rosamunde* are included and, with a fairly long stretch of blank tape at the side-end, one wonders why the *Overture* could not have been added. The sound is excellent.

The Philips 'On Tour' compilation concentrates on Schubert, but the programme is somewhat piecemeal. Sawallisch's *Unfinished* has character; the slow tempi are supported by eloquent orchestral playing and natural phrasing. The recording is less expansive than Boehm's. Haitink's *Rosamunde* items are very successful in their simplicity and natural sensitivity, while the variations on the famous theme from the *Trout quintet* and the *Impromptus* are agreeably fresh. The transfers are excellent throughout.

Symphonies Nos 8 in B minor (Unfinished), D.759; 9 in C (Great), D.944.
(*) Ph. mono **416 212-2** [id.]. Concg. O, Willem Mengelberg.

These recordings emanate from 1939 and 1940. Mengelberg always secures playing of enormous intensity from the Concertgebouw which more than compensates for the odd agogic eccentricity. However, by the side of other historic recordings from Furtwängler and Walter, these will not do. The sound is coarse and the slow movement of the *Unfinished* is ruined by an obtrusive background swish. Nor as interpretations are they particularly impressive: the *Great C major symphony* is terribly fast throughout. This gives little pleasure.

Symphony No. 9 in C (Great), D.944.
C *** Decca Dig. **400 082-2**; SXDL/*KSXDC* 7557 [Lon. LDR/*5*-71057]. VPO, Solti.

*** Ph. 416 245-1/*4* [id.]. Concg. O, Haitink.
(*) CBS **MK 42049 [id.]. Columbia SO, Bruno Walter.
(M) **(*) HMV ED 290426-1/*4* [Ang. AE/*4AE* 34463]. Philh. O, Klemperer.
(*) DG Dig. **413 437-2; 413 437-1/*4* [id.]. Chicago SO, Levine.
** Denon Dig. **C37 7371** [id.]. Berlin State O, Suitner.
** Telarc Dig. **CD 80110**; DG 10110 [id.]. Cleveland O, Dohnányi.
*(*) Hung. Dig. **HCD 12722-2** [id.]. Budapest Fest. O, Ivan Fischer.

Symphony No. 9 in C (*Great*); *Rosamunde: overture* (*Die Zauberharfe*), *D.644*.
(***) DG mono **413 660-2** [id.]. BPO, Furtwängler.

Sir George Solti is not the first conductor one thinks of as a Schubertian, but the *Great C major symphony* prompted him to one of the happiest and most glowing of all his many records, an outstanding version, beautifully paced and sprung in all four movements and superbly played and recorded. It has drama as well as lyrical feeling, but above all it has a natural sense of spontaneity and freshness, beautifully caught by the richly balanced recording, outstanding on both LP and chrome tape, but finest of all on compact disc. Here the slow movement in particular has wonderful refinement of detail so that one hears things even missed at a live performance, yet there is no sense that the added clarity is in any way unnatural. The silence which follows the central climax is breathtaking, and towards the end, when the melody is decorated by pizzicatos running through the orchestra, the feeling of presence is uncanny. Few of the first generation of CDs show more readily the advantages of the new technology than this, at the same time confirming the Vienna Sofiensaal as an ideal recording location.

Haitink's too is a fresh and beautiful performance, marked by superb playing from the Concertgebouw. The interpretative approach is generally direct, so that the end of the first movement brings fewer and less obvious rallentandos than normal, with the result sounding natural and easy. The slow movement, more measured than usual, is lightened by superb rhythmic pointing, and the 1976 recording is both full and refined. The tape transfer is generally very successful. There is a slight bass emphasis but this can be corrected, and the upper range is fresh.

Furtwängler gives the *Great C major* a glowing performance, if a highly individual one. The first movement brings an outstanding example of his wizardry, when he takes the recapitulation at quite a different speed from the exposition and still makes it sound convincing. In the *Andante*, his very slow tempo is yet made resilient by fine rhythmic pointing. The CD brings a sizeable bonus in *Rosamunde*, not as well recorded as the *Symphony*, the sound boxier, though clear enough; however, Furtwängler springs the main allegro with an attractive jauntiness. No apologies need be made for the sound in the *Symphony*. The mono recording dates from 1951 and, like Furtwängler's Haydn/Schumann coupling, was made in the Jesus Christ Church in West Berlin. The sound is fresh and very well balanced, with the dynamic range in the slow movement strikingly wide.

Bruno Walter's 1959 CBS recording has been impressively enhanced on CD;

the warm ambience of the sound – yet with no lack of rasp on the trombones – seems ideal for his very relaxed reading. The performance has less grip than Furtwängler's, while Solti shows greater spontaneity; but in the gentler passages there are many indications of Walter's mastery, not least in the lovely playing at the introduction of the second subject of the *Andante*. The mannered reading of the slow introduction gets the work off to a bad start, but the overall pacing of the outer movements has a firm momentum, and the closing section of each is very well managed. With much affectionate detail in the slow movement and an attractive Schubertian lilt to the scherzo, there is much to admire, even if this never quite achieves the distinction of the conductor's earlier recordings of this symphony.

Klemperer's measured performance is highly individual, deliberately literal and rather heavy, particularly in the first movement, with few pianissimos. Once the speeds and severe approach are accepted, however, the fascination of the performance is clear. There is superb playing from the Philharmonia, with a delectable oboe solo in the slow movement. First-rate sound for its period.

Levine conducts a refined performance, beautifully played and excellently recorded, especially on CD, which is commendably free from mannerism, yet may on that account seem undercharacterized. He omits the exposition repeats in the outer movements (just as was universally done till recently). Conversely, all the repeats in the scherzo are observed, which unbalances the structure. On tape, the focus is slightly less clean than on the LP, although otherwise the transfer is well managed.

Recorded in East Berlin, Suitner's version brings a plain and direct reading, remarkable mainly for observing every single repeat, even the exposition in the finale, with the total time close on an hour. With the sound of the strings pleasantly recessed to give an agreeable bloom, the recording is faithful without being spectacular. The violins are not always consistent, sounding feeble in the scherzo but cleanly resilient in the finale.

Dohnányi paces the first movement briskly and is not subtle enough to accommodate the second subject flexibly within his conception. The slow movement is beautifully played. In the scherzo Dohnányi is less generous with repeats than Levine (and Suitner), and the overall effect of the reading is lightweight. The Telarc sound is warm and spacious but not brightly lit; the woodwind solos, though placed in believable perspective, lack vividness.

Although Ivan Fischer's reading is very relaxed and does not generate much excitement, it has the underlying tension of a live performance. Tempi are controlled very freely and not always convincingly; but in its easy-going way this would be quite enjoyable if the recording had been clearer and more vivid. As it is, the resonance clouds the middle range. At the end of the slow movement the pizzicato strings, which are so telling on Solti's CD, make a very diminished effect.

CHAMBER AND INSTRUMENTAL MUSIC

Arpeggione sonata, D.821 (arr. for cello).

Ͼ *** Ph. Dig. **412 230-2**; 412 230-1/*4* [id.]. Maisky, Argerich – SCHUMANN: *Fantasiestücke* etc.*** Ͼ

(M) ** Ph. 412 061-1/*4*. Gendron, Françaix – BEETHOVEN: *Variations*.**

The Arpeggione enjoyed too brief a life for it to have an extensive literature, and Schubert's *Sonata* is about the only work written for it that survives in the repertoire. To put it mildly, it is not one of Schubert's most substantial works; but even those who do not care for it should hear Mischa Maisky and Martha Argerich play it, for they make more of it than any of their rivals. Their approach may be relaxed, but they bring much pleasure for their variety of colour and sensitivity. The Philips recording is in the very best traditions of the house in all three formats (the cassette is strikingly realistic).

Maurice Gendron and Jean Françaix are on the mid-price Philips label and their recording is a reissue from the late 1960s. The playing is eminently musicianly and fine-grained, but there is a formidable competitor here in the shape of Maisky/Argerich. However, if the coupled Beethoven *Variations* are wanted, this is fair value. There is an excellent equivalent tape.

Arpeggione sonata in A min. (arr. for flute)*; Introduction and variations on Trock'ne Blumen* from *Die schöne Müllerin; Schwanengesang: Ständchen, D.957/4.*

(*) RCA Dig. **RD 70421; RL 70421 [HRC1/*KRC1* 5303]. James Galway, Phillip Moll.

This record is obviously addressed to Galway's many admirers. The *Arpeggione sonata* transcribes surprisingly well for the flute, and is played with skill and some charm by this partnership. The *Introduction and variations on Trock'ne Blumen* are designed for the medium and are as neatly played. Not an important issue, but those who enjoy Galway's music making will not be disappointed by this pleasing and well-recorded recital.

Octet in F, D.803.

*** Ph. **416 497-2**; 9500 400/*7300 613* [id.]. ASMF Chamber Ens.

* Accord **149 510**. Lucerne Camerata.

The Chamber Ensemble of the Academy of St Martin-in-the-Fields offer one of the very best versions of this endearing work. Everything is vital, yet polished and sensitive. The recording is beautifully balanced, and the performance has a warmth and freshness that justify the acclaim with which this issue was greeted when it was first issued in 1978. The analogue recording is smoothly realistic but lacks something in clarity of internal definition compared with a modern digital recording, although the compact disc transfer retains all the bloom of the original LP.

On this showing the Lucerne Camerata are a pretty charmless lot – though, to be fair, they are handicapped by a balance that does not do justice to the strings.

Piano quintet in A (*Trout*)*, 0.667.*

*** Decca Dig. **411 975-2;** 411 975-1/*4* [id.]. Schiff, Hagan Qt.

***Ph. **400 078-2**; 9500 422/*7300 648* [id.]. Brendel, Cleveland Qt.

*** HMV Dig. **CDC 747009-2**; ASD/*TCC-ASD* 4032 [Ang. DS/*4XS* 37846]. Sviatoslav Richter, Borodin Qt.
(B) **(*) CfP CFP 41 4466-1/*4*. Moura Lympany, principals of LSO.
(B) ** DG Walkman *413 854-4* [id.]. Demus, Schubert Qt – BEETHOVEN: *Ghost trio*; ** MOZART: *Hunt quartet*.***
(M) **EMI EMX 41 2078-1/*4*. H. Menuhin, Amadeus Qt – BEETHOVEN: *Ghost piano trio*.**

(i) *Piano quintet* (*Trout*); *String quartet No. 12* (*Quartettsatz*), *D.703*.
(*) DG **413 453-2; 2530/*3300* 646 [id.]. (i) Gilels; Amadeus Qt (augmented).

(i) *Piano quintet* (*Trout*); *Impromptu in C min., D.899/1*.
(B) **(*) Ph. On Tour *416 224-4* [id.]. Ingrid Haebler; (i) Grumiaux Ens. – MOZART: *Clarinet quintet* and *Flute quartet*.**(*)

András Schiff with the talented young players of the Hagan Quartet – a family group from Austria of exceptional promise – gives a delectably fresh and youthful reading of the *Trout quintet*, full of the joys of spring, but one which is also remarkable for hushed concentration, as in the exceptionally dark and intense account of the opening of the first movement. Schiff, unlike many virtuosi, remains one of a team, emphatically not a soloist in front of accompanists; particularly on CD, the recording balance confirms that, with the piano rather behind the strings but firmly placed. The scherzo brings a light, quick and bouncing performance, and there is extra lightness too in the other middle movements. Unlike current rivals, this version observes the exposition repeat in the finale, and with such a joyful, brightly pointed performance one welcomes that. The cassette is also extremely realistic and vivid, though on some reproducers the violin timbre may need a little soothing.

The Brendel/Cleveland performance may lack something in traditional Viennese charm, but it has a compensating vigour and impetus, and the work's many changes of mood are encompassed with freshness and subtlety. The second-movement *Andante* is radiantly played, and the immensely spirited scherzo has a most engagingly relaxed trio, with Brendel at his most persuasive. His special feeling for Schubert is apparent throughout: the deft pictorial imagery at the opening of the variations is delightful. The recording is well balanced and truthful on LP and tape alike, although on the cassette there is a hint of edginess in the upper strings. The compact disc is smooth and refined, but lacks something in upper range and sharpness of detail.

Richter dominates the HMV digital recording of the *Trout quintet*, not only in personality but in balance. Yet the perfomance has marvellous detail, with many felicities drawn to the attention that might have gone unnoticed in other accounts. The first movement is played very vibrantly indeed, and the second offers a complete contrast, gently lyrical. The variations have plenty of character; taken as a whole, this is very satisfying, even though other versions are better balanced and are stronger on Schubertian charm. The cassette, like the disc, gives striking presence to the piano, but adds just a hint of edginess to the strings, although this is more noticeable on side one. The CD emphasizes the somewhat artificial balance but is certainly not lacking in projection. However, the upper string sound is thin and rather lacking substance.

Also among the full-price *Trouts* that have claims for consideration is the DG issue which includes an excellent account of the *Quartettsatz*. In the main work there is a masterly contribution from Gilels, and the Amadeus play with considerable freshness. The approach is very positive, not as sunny and springlike as in some versions, but rewarding in its seriousness of purpose. On CD, the 1976 analogue recording is enhanced in presence and the balance is convincing. The cassette has less range and naturalness in the strings.

The Haebler/Grumiaux account of the *Trout* is small-scale, but nevertheless very enjoyable. There is some admirably unassertive and deeply musical playing from Miss Haebler and from the incomparable Grumiaux; it is this freshness and pleasure in music making that render this account memorable. These artists do not try to make 'interpretative points' but are content to let the music speak for itself. The balance is not altogether perfect, but the quality of the recorded sound is good and the tape transfer is natural in timbre and detail. As an encore, Miss Haebler plays the *Impromptu in C minor*. Attractively coupled with two rewarding Mozart performances (if a somewhat leisurely one of the *Clarinet quintet*), this is one of the best issues in Philips's bargain 'On Tour' series.

Moura Lympany's performance sets off in a brisk manner, the playing lively and fresh. In the second movement, the interpretation relaxes and the variations are attractively done. The matter-of-fact approach is enhanced by the overall spontaneity of the music making. The balance favours the piano with the first violin seeming backward – in his decorations of the 'Trout' theme he is too distant, with less body to his tone, as recorded, than the lower strings. But in most respects this is a lively and enjoyable account, not wanting in perception; the 1974 recording is of good quality. The cassette is excellent, smoother on top than the disc, to advantage.

An agreeable if not distinctive performance on the Walkman tape, with Demus dominating, partly because the piano recording and balance are bold and forward and the string tone is thinner. There is – as befits the name of the string group – a real feeling for Schubert, and the performance has spontaneity. The first movement is especially arresting, and the *Theme and variations* are well shaped. The tape transfer is well managed; however, the Amadeus recording of the first movement of Mozart's *Hunt quartet* follows immediately after the end of the *Trout*, and their string timbre, fuller and firmer, emphasizes the relative lack of body of the Schubert recording.

The EMI version at medium price has a generous coupling in the shape of Beethoven's *Ghost trio*. The record is produced in tribute to the late Hephzibah Menuhin and the performance dates from 1960. The balance is not wholly ideal, though the recording wears its years lightly. There are moments of charm here, and the performance will give pleasure. Hephzibah Menuhin was an intelligent but not always subtle player. Repeats have been excised from this performance so as to accommodate an ample fill-up. This is not a disc that displaces the existing mid-price or newer recommendations. The cassette transfer is clear, but rather dry.

Piano trios Nos 1–2; Notturno in E flat, D.897; Sonata in B flat, D.28.
** Ph. Dig. **412 620-2**; 412 620-1/*4* (2) [id.]. Beaux Arts Trio.

Collectors who have the older Beaux Arts recordings of the Schubert *Trios* (or indeed the splendid Suk performance of the *B flat Trio* coupled with the *Notturno* on Supraphon 1111 896) need look no further, for although this new set is much better recorded, the performances are not quite as fresh and spontaneous as the earlier issues. Notwithstanding the benefits of the new technology, the older and less expensive records or cassettes are the ones to go for. The *E flat Trio* is discussed below; the *B flat* and *Notturno* were reissued first (Ph. 6503/*7303* 069). The earlier performance of the *B flat Trio* is perhaps on the lightweight side, although Manahem Pressler is always sharply imaginative and the string playing is sensitively spontaneous in line and phrase. The slow movement has a disarming simplicity. The *Notturno* is played most eloquently. The sound, from the late 1960s, is a little dated in the matter of upper string timbre, although this is more noticeable on the cassette (successfully transferred at quite a high level).

Piano trio No. 1 in B flat, D.898.
** Chan. Dig. **CHAN 8308**; ABRD/*ABTD* 1064 [id.]. Borodin Trio.
** CRD Dig. **CRD 3438**; CRD 1138/*CRDC 4138* [id.]. Israel Piano Trio.

The Borodin Trio gives a warm and characterful interpretation, with natural expressiveness only occasionally overloaded with rubato. The impression is very much of a live performance, though in fact this is a studio recording marked by full and open sound. As the compact disc shows, the microphone balance is a little close, giving a slightly resiny focus to the strings. Otherwise there is fine presence and most realistic separation. This applies also to the chrome cassette, although here the upper range is slightly more abrasive.

The CRD version with the Israel Piano Trio does not materially affect current recommendations. It is all thoroughly musical: a broadly conceived and straightforward account, very well recorded in all three media but offering no special illumination. No disrespect is intended by saying that playing of this order can be heard in any good concert hall anywhere in the world. Having heard and enjoyed it once, one would not rush to hear it again. This and the Borodin Trio are the only two at present on compact disc, but neither match the Suk Trio (Supraphon) or the Beaux Arts (Philips) on LP.

Piano trio No. 2 in E flat, D.929.
(*) Chan. Dig. **CHAN 8324; ABRD/*ABTD* 1045. Borodin Trio.

Piano trio No. 2; Sonata for piano trio in B flat, D.28.
(M) *** Ph. 412 060-1/*4*. Beaux Arts Trio.

The Beaux Arts Trio's ensemble is superbly polished here, and the pianist's contribution is consistently imaginative, with the cellist, Bernard Greenhouse, bringing simple dedication to such key passages as the great slow-movement melody of the *B flat Trio*. The extra item gives this disc an added appeal. Written during Schubert's student days, the attractive early *Sonata in B flat* has the same kind of fluency as Beethoven's *First Piano trio*, although the lyrical flow has the unmistakable ring of Schubert. The 1967 recording has fine freshness and immediacy.

The Borodin Trio gives a strong and understanding performance of the *B flat Trio*, generally preferring spacious tempi. The outer movements are made the more resilient, and only in the scherzo does the reading lack impetus. The speed for the slow movement is nicely chosen to allow a broad, steady pulse. The pianist is not always at her most subtle, but there is a sense of enjoyment here to which one responds. Good though the LP is, the compact disc is even more lifelike and present. The cassette is admirably clear and well balanced, though the sound seems drier in the treble than on the LP.

String quartets Nos 10 in E flat, D.87 (finale only)*; 14 in D min.* (*Death and the Maiden*)*, D.810.*
** Sup. Dig. **C37 7546** [id.]. Smetana Qt.

The Supraphon version was recorded by the Smetana Quartet at a concert performance in Japan in November 1978, the finale of the early *E flat Quartet* being an encore. It is just a little disappointing: theirs is predictably a good, straightforward performance but with less warmth and freshness than one expects from this illustrious ensemble. Nor is it as beautifully recorded as the finest rivals now on offer.

String quartets Nos 12 in C min. (*Quartettsatz*)*, D.703; 14 in D min.* (*Death and the Maiden*)*, D.810.*
*** Tel. Dig. **ZK8 42868**; AZ6 42868 [id.]. Vermeer Qt.
*** ASV Dig. DCA/*ZCDCA* 560 [id.]. Lindsay Qt.
(M) *** Ph. 412 936-1/*4*. Italian Qt.
*** MMG Dig. **MCD 10004** [id.]. Tokyo Qt.
(*) DG Dig. **410 024-2; 2532/*3302* 071 [id.]. Amadeus Qt.
(B) **(*) DG Walkman *415 333-4* [id.]. Amadeus Qt – BEETHOVEN: *Archduke trio*.**(*)

String quartets Nos 13 in A min., D.804; 14 in D min. (*Death and the Maiden*)*, D.810.*
(*) HMV Dig. **CDC 747333-2 [id.]; EL 270248-1/*4* [Ang. DS/*4DS* 38233]. Alban Berg Qt.

String quartet No. 14 in D min. (*Death and the Maiden*)*, D.810.*
** Ph. Dig. **412 127-2**; 412 127-1/*4* [id.]. Orlando Qt.

The Vermeer Quartet offer a serious challenge to the much (and rightly) admired Quartetto Italiano on Philips. They have thought deeply and to good effect about this *Quartet*, and are thoroughly scrupulous in observing both the spirit and the letter of the score. Indeed, there is nothing in the least routine about this reading: it has a splendid grasp of architecture – yet it is not over-intellectual, but conveys something of the grace of the slow movement. In every way – not least the recording quality – this is an impressive disc that can stand along with the best. The reverberation on the very last chord of the finale is unfortunately cut short.

The Lindsays do not yet have the advantage of CD, but many listeners may count them first choice when they do. Their intense, volatile account of the first movement of the *Death and the Maiden* quartet, urgently paced, played with considerable metrical freedom and the widest range of dynamic, is balanced by an equally imaginative and individual set of variations with a similar inspirational approach. The hushed opening for the presentation of the famous theme is deceptive, for the tune is made to expand eloquently before the variations begin, while the coda is equally subtle in preparation and realization. The finale has a winning bustle and energy; and the *Quartettsatz*, which acts as the usual filler, is unusually poetic and spontaneous in feeling. The recording is excellent on disc, but the (iron-oxide) tape transfer is less than ideal, with the high level bringing a touch of shrillness on the first side; side two is fuller and smoother, but with the upper range more restricted.

The Italian Quartet have made two recordings of this coupling and both are currently available. This is the more recent, made in 1980. The Italians again bring great concentration and poetic feeling to this wonderful score, and they are free of the excessive point-making to be found in some rival versions. The sound of the reissue is first class on LP, though the high-level cassette transfer has brought a touch of unwanted pungency to the upper range.

The playing of the Tokyo Quartet is also first class. The performance has tension of the right kind in abundance, and phrasing is eloquent. The first movement has plenty of thrust and there is some imaginative characterization in the variations, while the finale has fine brio. With well-balanced, truthful recording this can be recommended alongside, though not in preference to, the Vermeer coupling.

The HMV issue offers very good value for money. The *Death and the Maiden quartet* usually occupies a whole disc with the *Quartettsatz* thrown in for good measure, but here we are offered two major quartets, marvellously played and truthfully recorded on one disc. In all, there is more than 70 minutes of music, and the only loss is the exposition repeat in the first movement of *Death and the Maiden*. The sleeve note gives no details of the 'original version' which the title billing claims, and it is difficult to determine in what significant way it differs textually from any other. The *A minor Quartet* is beautifully played, though the slow movement (with the theme of the *Rosamunde entr'acte*) is very fast indeed. All the same, even if the playing is breathtaking in terms of tonal blend, ensemble and intonation, one remains strangely unmoved, except perhaps in the minuet and trio of the *A minor*. The clear, clean recording is very brightly lit in its CD format with the sound certainly 'present', but also with a slightly aggressive feeling on fortissimos.

The 1983 Amadeus version of *Death and the Maiden* offers much to admire. The performance has a powerful momentum and though there is some rough playing from Brainin, there is relatively little sentimentality. The actual sound is not as pure as in their very first mono recording, when their blend was superb and the leader's vibrato unobtrusive. Good though it is, this does not displace the Italian Quartet. The compact disc brings impressive presence to the sound, but the balance seems a trifle close.

The Walkman cassette offers the earlier (1960) Amadeus stereo recording. The Quartet gives a wonderful impression of unity as regards the finer points of phrasing, for example at the very beginning of the variations in D.810. This is a worthwhile issue, even if this account of *Death and the Maiden* cannot match that of the Italians. The recording still sounds well, and the chrome-tape transfer is well managed.

The Orlando Quartet is superbly recorded on Philips, even if there is a certain hardness on the LP, less striking on the compact disc and cassette. Their approach is impassioned, even a little rhetorical, with very pronounced dynamic extremes, and not wholly free from traces of affectation. There are exaggerated expressive touches (hushed pianissimos which draw attention to themselves) which might make this record irksome to replay. It robs Schubert of some of the grace and innocence that are central to his sensibility. It would be difficult to prefer this to the versions by the Vermeer or Italian Quartets. Without a coupling, this issue seems uncompetitive generally.

String quartet No. 15 in G, D.887.
(M) *** Ph. 412 401-1/*4*. Italian Qt.
(M) *** HMV EG 290294-1/*4* [Ang. AM/*4AM* 34713]. Alban Berg Qt.

Now the Italians are at mid-price, though they do not offer any makeweight, they are a strong front-runner in this field. The conception is bold, the playing is distinguished by the highest standards of ensemble, intonation and blend, and the recording is extremely fine. The Italians take a very broad view of the first movement, and they shape the strong contrasts of tempo and mood into an impressively integrated whole. The playing is no less deeply felt elsewhere in the work, making this one of the most thought-provoking accounts of the *Quartet* now before the public. The cassette transfer is made at an excessively high level, bringing an unnatural degree of astringency to the upper range.

In some ways, the Alban Berg players are the most dramatic and technically accomplished of all in this outstanding work. Indeed, they tend to overdramatize: pianissimos are the barest whisper and ensemble has razor-edge precision. They are marvellously recorded, however, and beautifully balanced; but it is the sense of over-projection that somehow disturbs the innocence of some passages. They do not observe the exposition repeat in the first movement.

String quintet in C, D.956.
*** ASV Dig. **CDDCA 537**; DCA/*ZCDCA* 537 [id.]. Lindsay Qt with Douglas Cummings.
*** Decca Dig. **417 115-2** [id.]; SXDL/*KSXDC* 7571 [Lon. LDR/*5*- 71071]. Fitzwilliam Qt with Van Kampen.
*** HMV Dig. **CDC 747018-2** [id.]; ASD/*TC-ASD* 143529-1/*4* [Ang. DS/*4XS* 38009]. Alban Berg Qt with Schiff.

*** CBS Dig. **MK 39134**; IM/*IMT* 39134 [id.]. Cleveland Qt with Yo-Yo Ma.
(B) *** CfP CFP 41 4480-1/*4*. Chilingirian Qt with J. Ward Clark.
(M) ** Ph. 412 200-1/*4*. Grumiaux Quintet.
*(*) Denon Dig. **C37 7601** [id.]. Berlin Philh. Qt with Finke.

The Lindsay version gives the impression that one is eavesdropping on music making in the intimacy of a private home. Although there is plenty of vigour and power, there is nothing of the glamorized and beautified sonority that some great quartets give us. (The two cellos in the Lindsay version, incidentally, are both by the same maker, Francesco Rugeri of Cremona.) They observe the first-movement exposition repeat (as do the Fitzwilliam on Decca, but not so the Alban Berg), and the effortlessness of their approach does not preclude intellectual strength. The first movement surely refutes the notion that Schubert possessed an incomplete grasp of sonata form, an idea prompted by the alleged discursiveness of some of the sonatas. It is surely an amazing achievement, even by the exalted standards of Haydn, Mozart and Beethoven; and the Lindsays do it justice, as indeed they do the ethereal *Adagio*. Here they effectively convey the sense of it appearing motionless, suspended, as it were, between reality and dream, yet at the same time never allowing it to become static. The Lindsays may not enjoy quite the splendour or richness of the Alban Berg, nor in terms of tonal blend do they altogether match their homogeneity, but they have a compelling wisdom. Their reading must rank at the top in both the LP and CD formats, and for those who find the Alban Berg account 'too perfect', the Lindsays' will be an obvious first choice. The compact disc is well worth the extra outlay, for it has the additional presence, range and realism this medium offers. The cassette is of only moderate quality; it is inclined to be slightly shrill on top.

The Fitzwilliam Quartet with Van Kampen give a reading exceptionally faithful to Schubert's markings, yet one which, with freshness and seeming spontaneity, conveys the work's masterly power and impulse, too. They observe the exposition repeat in the first movement and play the second group with effortless elegance and lovely pianissimo tone. The melody is the more affecting in its simple tenderness when played, as here, exactly as the composer intended. The reading overall is deeply thoughtful, never exaggerated in expressiveness but naturally compelling. The great *Adagio* has a hushed intensity, played without affectation, and the last two movements are taken challengingly fast. Some might feel tempi are too brisk, yet the scherzo is the more exhilarating when played presto as marked, and the finale keeps its spring to the very end. Just occasionally in this performance the leader is not absolutely dead in the centre of the note, though intonation is never a serious problem at any time. The recording is outstanding, superbly full and atmospheric. It has remarkable presence, both on LP and on the splendid chrome cassette. But as usual the CD gives the group even greater tangibility, against the silent background.

Few ensembles offer timbre as full-bodied or richly burnished as that produced by the Alban Berg and Heinrich Schiff, whose recording has impressive sonority and bloom. Admirable though the Fitzwilliams are on Decca, the Alban Berg have the advantage of wonderfully homogeneous tone and, given the sheer polish and gorgeous sound that distinguish their playing, theirs must rank high among current recommendations. The performance is strongly projected and they have the advantage of excellent recording. However, unlike the Lindsays or the Fitzwilliams, they do not observe the first-movement exposition repeat.

The Cleveland Quartet and Yo-Yo Ma have won golden opinions for their account of the *Quintet* on CBS. They are scrupulous in observing dynamic markings (the second subject is both restrained and *pianissimo*) and they also score by making all repeats. Their performance has feeling and eloquence, as well as a commanding intellectual grip. Moreover, they are admirably recorded and thus present a strong challenge to both the Lindsays and the Fitzwilliam Quartet on Decca. There is an excellent chrome cassette.

Vividly recorded, with clear placing of instruments in a smallish but not dry hall, the Chilingirian version presents a most compelling account, totally unmannered and direct in style but full of concentration and spontaneity. So one consistently has the sense of live performance, and the great melody of the second subject emerges without any intrusive nudging or overexpressiveness. The slow movement too has natural intensity, though the closeness of the recording rather prevents one from registering a really soft *pianissimo*. An outstanding bargain on disc. The cassette is smooth and natural, but one notices the reduced dynamic contrasts more, and there is less range at the top.

Grumiaux and colleagues give a consciously expressive performance which runs the risk of sounding mannered in its marked rubato and hesitations. The ensemble is most refined, but there are more rewarding performances than this, just as well recorded, though few with a more successful matching cassette.

The Philharmonia Quartet of Berlin all come from the BPO and the second cellist here, Eberhard Finke, is one of its senior members, having been their first soloist since 1950. Their account of the Schubert *Quintet* is very decently played and the recording is well balanced and truthful. Rarely, however, does one feel during the course of the record that theirs is a performance of real stature that would reveal greater depths on repeated playing. The middle section of the slow movement and the opening of the finale are pedestrian by the side of the Lindsays. And surely if one does not come away from a performance of this *Quintet* feeling that it has been a rather special experience, then one might as well have not heard it at all. This is no real match for its rivals on compact disc or, for that matter, any of the classic LP accounts, from the 1952 Hollywood account onwards.

PIANO MUSIC

Fantasy in C (Grazer), D.605a; Piano sonata No. 18 in G, D.894.
**(*) Chan Dig. ABRD/*ABTD* 1075 [id.]. Lydia Artymiw.

The *Grazer-Fantasy* is thought to date from 1817–18; it acquired its title simply because it was discovered in the 1960s among manuscripts once belonging to Schubert's friend, Huttenbrenner. Lydia Artymiw plays it with great expressive freedom and real feeling; she gives an equally romantic account of the *G major Sonata*. Here she is up against Lupu and Ashkenazy, who both recorded the work for Decca in the 1970s and have perhaps a stronger grip on its architecture.

Nevertheless, this is a useful addition to the catalogue, and the Chandos engineering is quite superb, wide in dynamic range and truthful in timbre.

Fantasia in C (Wanderer), D.760.
(M) *** DG 410 983-1/*4* [id.]. Maurizio Pollini – SCHUMANN: *Fantasia in C.****

Pollini's account is outstanding and, though he is not ideally recorded (and the tape, too, is rather dry in timbre), the playing shows remarkable insights. Moreover, the coupling is equally fine.

Fantasia in D min., D.940.
*** CBS Dig. **MK 39511**; IM/*IMT* 39511 [id.]. Murray Perahia, Radu Lupu – MOZART: *Double piano sonata.****

Recorded live at The Maltings during the Aldeburgh Festival, the performance of Lupu and Perahia is full of haunting poetry, with each of these highly individual artists challenging the other in imagination. Where in the Mozart coupling Perahia plays primo, here it is the more recessive Lupu adding to the mellowness of this most inspired of all piano duet works, one of Schubert's supreme masterpieces. Warmly atmospheric recording, caught most naturally on CD, though the chrome tape is less fresh and rather middle-orientated.

Impromptus Nos 1–4, D.899; 5–8, D.935.
*** CBS Dig. **CD 37291**; 37291/*40-* [id.]. Murray Perahia.
*** Ph. **411 040-2**; 9500 357/*7300 587*. Alfred Brendel.
*** Decca Dig. **411 711-2**; SXDL/*KSXDC* 7594. Radu Lupu.
(B) *** Pickwick Con. CC/*CCTC* 7583. Christoph Eschenbach.
(M) *** Ph. Seq. 412 012-1/*4*. Ingrid Haebler.

Perahia's account of the *Impromptus* is very special indeed and hardly falls short of greatness. Directness of utterance and purity of spirit are of the essence here. As one critic has put it, Perahia's vision brings the impression of a tree opening out, whereas Brendel's suggests the moment of full bloom. The CBS recording is very good, truthful in timbre, with an increase in firmness on CD and added presence. Chrome cassette and LP are fairly closely matched.

Brendel's complete set of *Impromptus* on Philips was previously split into two separate groups (each coupled with other music of Schubert). Now they are joined and the result is truly magical. The recording is very natural and rich, with a glowing middle range and fine sonority. It is difficult to imagine finer Schubert playing than this; to find more eloquence, more profound musical insights, one has to go back to Edwin Fischer – and even here comparison is not always to Brendel's disadvantage. The cassette is no less recommendable than the disc, with the focus a little softer. The compact disc has been digitally remastered, but the piano image remains slightly diffuse.

Lupu's account of the *Impromptus* is of the same calibre as the Perahia and Brendel versions, and he is most beautifully recorded, especially ion CD. Indeed, in terms of natural sound this is the most believable image of the three. Lupu brings his own special insights to these pieces. Sometimes his rubato is almost

Chopinesque in its delicacy; but the playing can also be robust and lyrically powerful. Perahia displays a fresher innocence; Brendel is more direct and wonderfully warm, but Lupu is compelling in his own way; and these performances yield much that is memorable. His musing, poetic romanticism in the *G flat Impromptu* (D.899/3) is wonderfully telling, when the piano timbre is so ravishingly caught by the engineers. The cassette is superbly managed, quite the equal of the LP. Choice between the CBS, Philips and Decca versions is very difficult (we each have our own preferences) and the lack of a Rosette suggests that we might be inclined to award one to all three.

Eschenbach's playing is quite outstandingly masterful. There are moments when he is a trifle self-conscious in his phrasing, but never is there any doubt that this is playing of the highest distinction. True, his tempo in the *A flat major Impromptu* (No. 6) is far slower than the *allegretto* marking, and some may well feel that it is far too slow; likewise the *C minor* (No. 1) is measured. However, the sensitivity, refinement and intelligence behind this reading are formidable, and he is very well recorded. The cassette is immaculately transferred. A bargain.

Ingrid Haebler, at medium price, is even more beautifully recorded, and her performances are so natural and musical that hers has strong claims to be numbered the finest budget-priced recording. It certainly deserves to be recommended alongside Eschenbach's and shows different but no less impressive insights. At times her playing has the most disarming innocence, at others great maturity and poise; she often surprises the listener, for instance by her direct way with the famous *A flat Impromptu*, D.935/2. The natural Philips recording is beautifully transferred to tape, sounding warm and full.

Moments musicaux Nos 1–6, D.780.

(M) *** Decca JB/*KJBC* 145 [Lon. STS 15483]. Curzon – *Piano sonata No. 17.****

** DG **415 118-2** [id.]. Barenboim – LISZT: *Liebesträume*; MENDELSSOHN: *Songs without words.****

Moments musicaux Nos 1–6, D.780; Impromptus (Klavierstücke), D.946, Nos 1–3.

(M) *** Ph. Seq. 6527/*7311* 110. Brendel.

Both Curzon and Brendel on Philips give superb performances of the *Moments musicaux*. These readings are among the most poetic now in the catalogue, and the recording in both cases is exemplary. Brendel recorded the same coupling earlier for Turnabout, but this reissue offers marginally more natural sound. The three *Klavierstücke* are also welcome, but Curzon's coupling is far more substantial, equally well recorded on disc and cassette alike.

In the *Moments musicaux* there is much to admire in Barenboim's performances. His mood is often thoughtful and intimate; at other times we are made a shade too aware of the interpreter's art, and there is an element of calculation that robs the impact of freshness. There are good things, of course, but this does not challenge Brendel or Curzon. The recording is excellent and has fine presence in its CD format. The Liszt and Mendelssohn couplings show Barenboim at his finest.

Piano sonata No. 4 in A min., D.537.
** DG Dig. **400 043-2**; 2532/*3302* 017 [id.]. Michelangeli – BRAHMS: *Ballades*.***

Piano sonatas Nos 4 in A min., D.537; 13 in A, D.664.
*(*) Ph. Dig. **410 605-2**; 6514/*7337* 282 [id.]. Brendel.

Michelangeli's Schubert is less convincing than the Brahms coupling. He rushes the opening theme and rarely allows the simple ideas of the first movement to speak for themselves. Elsewhere his playing, though aristocratic and marvellously poised, is not free from artifice, and the natural eloquence of Schubert eludes him. Splendid recording on both disc and chrome cassette, which approaches demonstration standard on the compact disc.

Brendel's account of the *A minor Sonata* sounds a little didactic: the gears are changed to prepare the way for the second group, and this sounds unconvincing on the first hearing and more so on the repeat. He broadens, too, on the modulation to *F major* towards the end of the exposition, only to quicken the pulse in the development. The result is curiously inorganic. The *A major* is given with less simplicity and charm than one expects from this great artist. There are also some disruptive and studied agogic fluctuations which are not always convincing. Clear, well-focused recording, which sounds wonderfully natural in its compact disc format.

Piano sonata No. 13 in A, D.664.
(*) ASV ALH/*ZCALH* 948 [id.]. Shura Cherkassky – BRAHMS: *Piano sonata No. 3*.(*)

The *A major Sonata* has great tenderness and poetry in Cherkassky's hands. Like the Brahms *F minor Sonata*, with which it is coupled, the Schubert was recorded in 1968 at a recital in London's Queen Elizabeth Hall with an unusually rapt audience, as well they might be. There is a finger slip in the heavenly slow movement, as if to remind us that one is still on earth. In every way a performance of great artistic insight and real distinction. The sound is from a truthful and well-balanced broadcast, but not as good as the best modern studio recordings. The cassette transfer has plenty of life, but the upper range of the piano timbre is somewhat shallow in fortissimos.

Still recommended: Ashkenazy's Decca recording of the *A major Sonata* is magnificent in every respect, and his version has splendid range and fidelity. It is coupled with *No. 14 in A min.*, D.784, and some lighter Schubert dance pieces (Decca SXL 6260 [Lon. CS 6500]).

Piano sonata No. 15 in C (Reliquie), D.840.
*** Ph. **416 292-2**; 416 292-1/*4* [id.]. Sviatoslav Richter.

Richter's approach to Schubert's unfinished *Sonata* is both dedicated and strong. He treats the opening movement very spaciously indeed, both in his slow pacing and in observing the exposition repeat, to extend it to 22½ minutes. The following *Andante* is comparably thoughtful. The recording was made at a live performance and captures the spontaneity of the occasion and the full range of the pianist's dynamic (which is considerable). Indeed, the sound is most realistic. With its aristocratic assurance this is a very considerable account and it ends abruptly where the composer stopped, leaving the rest to the listener's imagination. The CD provides a remarkable feeling of presence (the balance is close) and, mercifully, the audience is unobtrusive. The cassette is excellent but slightly softer-grained. This recording is also available as a coupling with Peter Schreier's *Winterreise*, in its CD format only – see below.

Piano sonata No. 17 in D, D.850.
(M) *** Decca Jub. JB/*KJBC* 145 [Lon. STS 15483]. Curzon – *Moments musicaux.****

The passage to try first in the *Sonata* is the beginning of the last movement, an example of the Curzon magic at its most intense, for with a comparatively slow speed he gives the rhythm a gentle 'lift' which is most captivating. Some who know more forceful interpretations (Richter did a marvellous one) may find this too wayward, but Schubert surely thrives on some degree of coaxing. Curzon could hardly be more convincing – the spontaneous feeling of a live performance better captured than in many earlier discs. The Jubilee reissue is very generously coupled and the recording remains of Decca's finest analogue quality. The high-level cassette is bold and clear, matching the disc closely, perhaps a fraction harder-edged.

Piano sonata No. 20 in A, D.959; 12 German dances, D.790.
** Ph. **411 477-2** [id.]. Alfred Brendel.

Brendel's late Schubert records are among his finest, but the *A major Sonata* suffers from rather more agogic changes than is desirable. Some listeners will find these interferences with the flow of the musical argument a little too much of a good thing. The coupling, however, is delightful and particularly beautifully played. The 1973 analogue recording is of Philips's best quality; it is enhanced on CD, where the dynamic range is made to seem even more dramatic than on the original LP, yet the timbre retains its colour and bloom.

Piano sonata No. 21 in B flat, D. 960; Impromptus, D.899/2–3.
(*) Denon Dig. **C37 7488 [id.]. Dezsö Ránki.

Piano sonata No. 21 in B flat; Impromptus, D.899/3 and 4; D.935/2.
❀ (M) *** Decca Jub. JB/*KJBC* 140 [Lon. CS 6801]. Curzon.

Curzon's is perhaps now the finest account of the *B flat Sonata* in the catalogue. Tempi are aptly judged, and everything is in fastidious taste. Detail is finely drawn but never emphasized at the expense of the architecture as a whole. It is beautifully recorded, and the piano sounds marvellously truthful in timbre. For the Jubilee reissue, the coupling has been extended to include the three most memorable Schubert *Impromptus*, the playing no less distinguished. This is a truly magical disc, and the cassette is equally recommendable.

Denon claim their CD as an early digital recording, but apologize for 'some minute noises' in the pianissimo music. These are hard to spot and the recording has the usual digital advantages of a most realistic presence and background quiet. The piano timbre has a bold outline (there is a not inappropriate hint of fortepiano tone at times, notably in the scherzo), yet the bass has a full resonance, so important in the *B flat Sonata*. Dezsö Ránki was twenty-four when he made this record in 1975 and it is a performance impressive in its concentration. It must be counted controversial that Ránki begins with a very expansive pacing of the opening theme, far slower than his basic speed later, and he consistently returns to this slow tempo when the famous melody recurs. The effect is to make the first movement unusually volatile, but it is also spontaneous, and he has clearly thought deeply about this approach. The slow movement is intensely poetic, played with a lovely singing legato, and the middle section produces another bold contrast. With a nimbly articulated scherzo and a finale which balances sparkle with strength, this is a very considerable reading and it is matched by the two *Impromptus* which are beautifully played and nicely characterized.

VOCAL MUSIC

Lieder: *Abendbilder; Am Fenster; Auf der Bruck; Auf der Donau; Aus Heliopolis; Fischerweise; Im Frühling; Liebesläuschen; Des Sängers Habe; Der Schiffer; Die Sterne; Der Wanderer; Wehmut; Das Zügenglöcklein.*
(M) *** DG Sig. 410 979-1/*4* [id.]. Fischer-Dieskau, Sviatoslav Richter.

Recorded live in 1978, this beautifully balanced selection of Schubert songs displays the singer's enormous range of expression as well as the acute sensitivity of the pianist in responding. The songs have been grouped almost in a cycle, starting with a biting expression of self-torment (perhaps too aggressively sung here), but gradually the mood lightens from melancholy to brighter thoughts. Not many of these songs are well known, but it is a programme to delight aficionado and newcomer alike, atmospherically recorded with remarkably little interference fom audience noises. On tape, there is slight recession of the image at pianissimo levels, but otherwise the quality is clear and well balanced.

Lieder: *Abendbilder; An die Musik; An den Mond; Bertas Lied in der Nacht; Die Blumensprache; Erster Verlust; Frühlingssehnsucht; Der Knabe; Nachthymne; Schwestergruss; Sei mir gegrüsst; Die Sterne; Wiegenlied.*
ɕ *** Ph. Dig. **410 037-2**; 6514/*7337* 298 [id.]. Ameling, Baldwin.

Elly Ameling's is a fresh and enchanting collection of Schubert songs, starting with *An die Musik* and including other favourites like the *Cradle song* as well as lesser-known songs that admirably suit the lightness and sparkle of Ameling's voice. This was the first Lieder record to appear on compact disc, and it deserved our accolade, for the new medium with its absence of background enhances a recording already beautifully balanced. It gives astonishing sense of presence to the singer, with the bright top of the voice perfectly caught and the piano unusually truthful. Some ears, however, may notice that the microphone is just a little close.

Lieder: *Abendstern; Am Grabe Anselmo's; Am See; Auflösung; Bei Dir!; Gondelfahrer; Heidenröslein; Der Jüngling an der Quelle; Liebesbotschaft; Die Rose; Sehnsucht; Wanderers Nachtlied I and II; Wehmut; Wiegenlied; Das Zügenglöcklein.*
*** Etcetera ETC 1009 [id.]. Elly Ameling, Dalton Baldwin.

Elly Ameling's 'Bouquet of Schubert' could hardly be more delightful. Not only is the voice caught (by a rather close recording) at its very sweetest, the 'face' behind each sharply characterized performance comes over vividly. From the very first song, *Liebesbotschaft*, one is immediately caught in a live-sounding experience, with Dalton Baldwin an exceptionally understanding accompanist. The piano is placed relatively backward, but otherwise the recording is excellent.

Lieder: *Die Allmacht; An die Natur; Auf dem See; Auflösung; Erlkönig; Ganymed; Gretchen am Spinnrade; Der Musensohn; Rastlose Liebe; Suleika I; Der Tod und das Mädchen; Der Zwerg.*
*** Ph. Dig. **412 623-2**; 412 623-1/*4* [id.]. Jessye Norman, Philip Moll.

It is remarkable that, with so magnificently large a voice, Jessye Norman manages to scale it down for the widest range of tone and expression in this beautifully chosen selection of Schubert songs. The characterization of the four contrasting voices in *Erlkönig* is powerfully effective, and the reticence which once marked Norman in Lieder has completely disappeared. The poignancy of *Gretchen am Spinnrade* is exquisitely touched in, building to a powerful climax; throughout, the breath control is a thing of wonder, not least in a surpassing account of *Ganymed*. Fine, sympathetic accompaniment from Philip Moll and first-rate recording. The chrome cassette is well balanced and the sound is pleasing; compared with the CD, however, it is as if a fine gauze lies between the artists and the listener.

'Favourite Lieder': An die Geliebte; An die Musik; An die Nachtigall; An mein Klavier; Auf dem Wasser zu singen; Ave Maria; Claudine von Villa Bella: 3, Hin und wieder fliegen Pfeile; 6, Liebe schwärmt. Du bist die Ruh'; Der Einsame; Des Fischers Liebesglück; Fischerwise; Die Forelle; Frühlingsglaube; Frühlingsträume; Geheimes; Gretchen am spinnrade; Heidenröslein; Das Heimweh; (i) *Der Hirt auf dem Felsen. Horch! Horch! die Lerche; Im Abendroth; Die junge Nonne; Der Jüngling an der Quelle; Der Jüngling und der Tod; Lachen und Weinen; Liebhaber*

in allen Gestalten; Litanei; Das Lied im Grünen; Das Mädchen; Mignon Lieder: 3, So lasst mich Scheine; 4, Nur wer die Sehnsucht kennt. Musensohn; Nacht und Träume; Nachtviolen; Nähe des Geliebten; Die Post; Rosamunde: Der Vollmond strahlt. Der Schmetterling. Die schöne Müllerin: Des Baches Wiegenlied. Schwanengesang: Liebesbotschaft. Seligkeit; Das sie hier gewesen; Die Vögel; Der Vollimond; Wiegenlied: Schlafe, schlafe, holder, süsser Knabe; Wohin?
❀ (M) (***) HMV mono EX 290359-3/5 (2). Elisabeth Schumann, Moore, Alwin, Coleman, Reeves; O, cond. Rosenek; (i) with R. Kell.

The enchanting art of Elisabeth Schumann, with an angelically pure and characterful voice married to unfailing charm and keen musical imagination, is superbly illustrated in this Schubert collection. Schumann's Lieder-style does not always quite match today's stylistic taste, but the immediacy of her expression is unfailingly winning. The earliest recordings were made in 1927, the last in 1949, but few sopranos have remained so consistent in vocal quality over so long a span. It is particularly good to have Schumann's only recording of *An die Musik*, which previously had limited circulation. Good transfers by Keith Hardwick, but with a few surface blemishes on individual items. Full translations are provided, plus superb notes and a personal appraisal by Desmond Shawe-Taylor which are consistently illuminating in their joint consideration of the songs and performances. The tapes, which are similarly documented, are transferred at a high level and the earliest recordings (1927–33) are made to sound rather peaky. Also our second tape had moments of pre- and post-echo. Other than that, the vocal quality is very good.

Lieder: *An die Musik; An Sylvia; Ave Maria; Die Forelle; Gretchen am Spinnrade; Heidenröslein;* (i) *Der Hirt auf dem Felsen; Lachen und Weinen; Lied der Mignon; Nacht und Träume; Seligkeit; Wiegenlied.*
*(*) Decca Dig. 410 259-1. Gabriele Fontana, György Fischer (i) with P. Schmidl.

The promising young soprano Gabriele Fontana brings together an attractive collection of favourite Schubert songs, including the relatively rare *Shepherd on the rock* with its swooping clarinet obbligato, but the voice does not take kindly to the microphone, and the readings are too often misjudged, as when she treats *An die Musik* unduly heavily.

Lieder: *An die Nachtigall; An mein Klavier; Auf dem Wasser zu singen; Geheimnis;* (i) *Der Hirt auf dem Felsen; Im Abendrot; Ins stille Land; Liebhaben in allen Gestalten; Das Lied im Grünen; Die Mutter Erde; Romanze; Der Winterabend.*
*** HM Orfeo **C 001811 A** [id.]. Margaret Price, Sawallisch; (i) with H. Schöneberger.

Consistent beauty of tone, coupled with immaculately controlled line and admirably clear diction, makes Margaret Price's Schubert collection a fresh and rewarding experience. Right at the beginning of her recording career she made a similar recital record for CfP (see below), but the performances on the Orfeo disc are even more assured and benefit from modern digital recording. Sawallisch as ever shows himself one of the outstanding accompanists of the time, readily translating from his usual role of conductor. The rather reverberant recording gives extra bloom to the voice.

Lieder: *An mein Herz; An Sylvia; Auf dem Wasser zu singen; Der Einsame; Fischerweise; Der Fluss; Die Forelle; Fülle der Liebe; Gretchen am Spinnrade; Die junge Nonne; Der Jüngling an der Quelle; Der Knabe; Die Rose; Der Schmetterling; Seligkeit; Der Wanderer an den Mond.*
*** HMV Dig. EL 270067-1/*4* [Ang. DS/*4DS* 38139]. Lucia Popp, Irwin Gage.

The charm, sparkle and silvery beauty of voice displayed by Lucia Popp make hers an outstanding Schubert collection. The choice of songs is delightful, and not always predictable; though the voice momentarily loses some of its natural sweetness under pressure, this is memorably beautiful singing, most sympathetically accompanied. For sample, try *Der Jüngling an der Quelle*, hauntingly lovely.

Lieder: *Auflösung; Der Einsame; Gesänge des Harfners; Gruppe aus dem Tartarus; Herbst; Hippolits Lied; Im Abendrot; Nachtstück; Nacht und Träume; Über Wildemann; Der Wanderer; Der Wanderer an den Mond.*
*** Ph. Dig. **411 421-2**; 6514/*7337* 384 [id.]. Dietrich Fischer-Dieskau, Alfred Brendel.

The combination of Fischer-Dieskau and Brendel is particularly compelling in the dark or meditative songs which make up the majority of items here. A delicate song like *Der Einsame* loses something in lightness, but the intensity remains. A lifetime of experience in this repertoire brings a magical degree of communication from the great baritone, made the more immediate on compact disc, but the atmospheric recording, naturally balanced, also sounds impressively realistic on LP and chrome cassette (transferred at a good level).

Lieder: *Auf der Riesenkoppe; Der blinde Knabe; Du bist die Ruh'; Die Forelle; Das Geheimnis; Gretchen am Spinnrade; Heidenröslein;* (i) *Der Hirt auf dem Felsen; Der König in Thule; La Pastorella; Schwanengesang: Die Wehmut.*
(B) **(*) CfP CFP 41 4491-1/*4*. Margaret Price, James Lockhart; (i) with Jack Brymer.

Recorded in 1971 at the beginning of her career, the selection here displays Margaret Price's rich voice to admirable effect. The simpler songs, *Die Forelle*, the sustained *Der König in Thule* and *Gretchen am Spinnrade*, come off beautifully, as does *La Pastorella* (a charming song). Elsewhere there is an operatic sense of drama, as in the opening recitative of *Auf der Riesenkoppe*. In the famous *Shepherd on the rock*, the clarinet is rather backwardly balanced and, although the two artists work well together, the full voice tends slightly to dwarf the clarinet. But at bargain price this makes a splendid introduction to some of Schubert's finest songs. James Lockhart accompanies sensitively, but he is reticently balanced in relation to the soaring vocal line. The cassette is vivid but on side two the level of transfer reaches saturation point.

Lieder: *Ave Maria; Jäger, ruhe von der Jagd; Raste Krieger!; Schwestergruss; Der Zwerg.*

(M) **(*) Ph. 412 366-1/*4*. Jessye Norman, Irwin Gage – MAHLER: *Lieder.***(*)

These five Schubert songs come as fill-up to Jessye Norman's early (1971) recording of songs from Mahler's *Des Knaben Wunderhorn*, all sensitively done, if with less detail than she would later have provided. Good recording for its period on both disc and tape.

Rosamunde: Overture (*Die Zauberharfe, D.644*) *and incidental music, D.797.*

*** Ph. Dig. **412 432-2**; 412 432-1/*4* [id.]. Ameling, Leipzig R. Ch., Leipzig GO, Masur.

Rosamunde: Overture (*Die Zauberharfe, D.644*)*; Entr'acte No. 3 in B flat; Ballet music No. 2 in G, D.797.*

** DG Dig. **415 137-2**; 415 137-1/*4* [id.]. Chicago SO, Levine – MENDELSSOHN: *Midsummer Night's Dream.***

(**) Ph. mono. **416 210-2** [id.]. Concg. O, Willem Mengelberg – BRAHMS: *Symphony No. 1.*(**)

Masur's fine new recording of the *Rosamunde Overture and incidental music* is a worthy replacement for Haitink's 1965 LP and tape which have dominated the catalogue for two decades. As with the Concertgebouw recording, the resonance of the Leipzig Gewandhaus seems over-reverberant for scoring designed for the theatre pit. Even on CD, the choral items are not very sharply focused and the bass is diffuse. Yet the ambient effect gives strings and woodwind a nice bloom and detail is not obscured. The superb Leipzig orchestra provides its usual cultured response to the music's drama as well as its lyricism – the second *Entr'acte* only just stops short of melodrama – and the innocent eloquence of Elly Ameling's contribution is matched by the direct vigour of the chorus of spirits, with affinities found with Mozart's *Die Zauberflöte* as well as with Weber. This can be recommended in all three formats, for the high-level chrome cassette is only fractionally less clear than the LP and CD.

From Levine, three favourite items from *Rosamunde*, all well – if not outstandingly – done, to provide a fair makeweight for a generous selection of *Midsummer Night's Dream* pieces. There is a good cassette.

On the Philips historical reissue from the 78 r.p.m. era, the Schubert excerpts, coupled with Mengelberg's account of the Brahms *First Symphony*, are rather poignant and beautifully played; the portamenti serve as a reminder of an orchestral style that has totally disappeared.

Die schöne Müllerin (song cycle), *D.795.*

*** DG **415 186-2**; 2530 544 [id.]. Dietrich Fischer-Dieskau, Gerald Moore.

(M) *** Ph. Seq. 412 013-1/*4*. Gérard Souzay, Dalton Baldwin.

(*) DG Dig. **415 347-2; 415 347-1/*4* [id.]. Francisco Araiza, Irwin Gage.

(M) **(*) DG Sig. 413 990-1/*4*. Peter Schreier, Walter Olbertz.

With an excellent digital transfer to CD barely giving an indication of its analogue source back in 1972, Fischer-Dieskau's classic version remains among the very finest ever recorded. Though he had made several earlier recordings, this is no mere repeat of previous triumphs, combining as it does his developed sense of drama and story-telling, his mature feeling for detail and yet spontaneity too, helped by the searching accompaniment of Gerald Moore. It is a performance with premonitions of *Winterreise*.

Souzay made this recording in his prime in 1965; his lyrical style is beautifully suited to this most sunny of song-cycles. Fischer-Dieskau may find more drama in the poems, but Souzay's concentration on purely musical values makes for one of the most consistently attractive versions available, with the words never neglected and Dalton Baldwin giving one of his most imaginative performances on record. The Pears/Britten version (on Decca Jubilee 411 729-1/*4*) has even more imaginative accompaniment, but Pears's voice is for once rather gritty. Fischer-Dieskau has Gerald Moore, of course; but on this occasion Baldwin provides an interesting alternative view. The sound belies the recording's age; there is a naturally balanced cassette, the quality mellow rather than sparkling, but clear, and kind to the voice.

It says much for the versatility of the Spanish opera tenor, Francisco Araiza, that he gives such a stylish performance of *Die schöne Müllerin*, rarely if ever revealing that he is not a born German-speaker. There is youthful exuberance in the reading, coupled with a strong, heroic vocal tone which yet under pressure is less sweet than this music really demands. The closing songs, however, are particularly beautiful. Sensitive accompaniment from Irwin Gage and excellent recording. The chrome cassette is not transferred at the highest level but the voice is naturally caught and the balance is excellent. The CD thrusts the voice strikingly forward.

Schreier is a thoughtful and sensitive interpreter of Schubert, and though his account of *Die schöne Müllerin* is less intense than some of his finest performances on record, it will certainly please his admirers. The tone, well caught by the recording, sometimes loses its natural freshness. There is an excellent cassette.

Schwanengesang (Lieder collection), *D.957*.
*** Ph. Dig. **411 051-2**; 6514/*7337* 383. Dietrich Fischer-Dieskau, Alfred Brendel.

Schwanengesang (Lieder collection), *D.957;* Lieder: *An die Musik; An Sylvia; Die Forelle; Heidenröslein; Im Abendrot; Der Musensohn; Der Tod und das Mädchen.*
*** DG **415 188-2** [id.]. Dietrich Fischer-Dieskau, Gerald Moore.

Fischer-Dieskau's DG version with Moore, though recorded ten years before his CD with Brendel, brings excellent sound in the digital transfer, plus the positive advantages, first that the voice is fresher, and then that the disc also contains seven additional songs, all of them favourites. Taken from Fischer-

Dieskau's monumental complete set of the Schubert songs, these performances represent a high-water mark in his recording of Schubert, and are all the more cherishable in the new medium.

Fischer-Dieskau's newest version offers deeply reflective performances, both from the singer and from his equally imaginative piano partner. His voice is not as fresh as on the earlier DG set but, particularly with the clarity and immediacy of compact disc, this is a beautiful, compelling record. The chrome cassette is good too, though it offers slightly less presence (it is transferred at a rather lower level than the companion Fischer-Dieskau/Brendel digital compilation of miscellaneous Lieder – see above).

Winterreise (song cycle), *D.911.*
*** DG **415 187-2** [id.]. Dietrich Fischer-Dieskau, Gerald Moore.
** Denon Dig. **C37 7240** [id.]. Hermann Prey, Philippe Bianconi.
*(*) BIS **CD 253/4** (1); LP 253/4 (2) [id.]. Martti Talvela, Ralf Gothoni.

(i) *Winterreise, D.911; Piano sonata No. 15 in C, D.840.*
*** Ph. Dig. **416 289-2** (2); (without *Sonata*) 416 194-1/*4* (2) [id.]. Peter Schreier, Sviatoslav Richter.

Taken from the collected recording of Schubert songs that Fischer-Dieskau made with Gerald Moore in the early 1970s, this DG version, now clarified and freshened in an excellent digital transfer to CD, is arguably the finest of his readings on record. At this period the voice was still at its freshest, yet the singer had deepened and intensified his understanding of this greatest of song-cycles to a degree where his finely detailed and thoughtful interpretation sounded totally spontaneous. Moore exactly matches the hushed concentration of the singer, consistently imaginative without drawing attention to himself with any waywardness. The single-CD format is an obvious benefit, with the enclosed leaflet containing lyrics and translation.

Recorded live at the newly restored Semper opera house in Dresden just after its reopening in February 1985, Schreier's is an inspired version, both outstandingly beautiful and profoundly searching in its expression, helped by magnetic, highly individual accompaniment from Richter, a master of Schubert. Speeds are not always conventional, indeed are sometimes extreme – but that only adds to the vivid communication which throughout conveys the inspiration of the moment. Rarely has the agonized intensity of the last two songs been so movingly caught on record, the more compellingly when the atmosphere of a live occasion is so realistically captured; it is a small price to pay that the winter audience makes so many bronchial contributions. A more serious snag is that the cycle – which can usually be contained on a single CD – spreads over on to a second, thanks to the slow speeds. Though the Schubert *Sonata* brings a comparably inspired performance from Richter (recorded live at Leverkusen in West Germany in December 1979), not everyone will want the coupling. Nevertheless, the two CDs provide generous measure at a total of 122 minutes' playing time. The sound in the *Sonata* recording – though it has striking presence – is drier than the cycle, but is less troubled by audience noise. The pair of LPs and the first-class matching cassettes offer the song-cycle only.

Prey's is a positive, intelligent reading which misses the meditative depth of this greatest of song-cycles. With often brisk speeds and light-of-day accompaniment, the tension of live communication is generally missing and the result sounds almost casual, though the final songs bring greater intensity. The sound is clean and faithful. The single disc comes in a separate box, together with a booklet with lyrics and translation.

Though Martti Talvela does wonders in lightening his big dark bass voice, making it surprisingly agile where necessary, it never sounds really comfortable, with the vibrato exaggerated in an ugly way. There is keen intensity in his reading, and the darkness in the cycle comes over well; but, with often prosaic accompaniment, poetry is lacking. The recording is very immediate, giving a striking vocal presence in the CD format, which is on single disc as against a pair of LPs.

Schuman, William (born 1910)

American festival overture.

*** DG Dig. **413 324-2**; 2532/*3302* 083 [id.]. LAPO, Bernstein – BARBER: *Adagio;* BERNSTEIN: *Candide: Overture;* COPLAND: *Appalachian spring.****

Schuman's overture is the least known of the four representative American works making up this attractive disc. It is rather like a Walton comedy overture with an American accent, and is played here with tremendous panache. Close, bright and full recording on both disc and cassette, which are closely matched. Highly recommended – this collection is more than the sum of its parts.

Schumann, Robert (1810–56)

Cello concerto in A min., Op. 33.

*** Decca Dig. **410 019-2**; SXDL/*KSXDC* 7568 [Lon. LDR/5- 71068]. Harrell, Cleveland O, Marriner – SAINT-SAËNS: *Concerto No. 1.****

The controversial point about Harrell's reading is that he expands the usual cadenza with a substantial sequence of his own. His is a big-scale reading, strong and sympathetic, made the more powerful by the superb accompaniment from the Cleveland Orchestra. The digital recording is outstandingly fine, with the compact disc version presenting a vividly realistic sound spectrum. The chrome cassette, too, is impressively wide-ranging, though here the treble is marginally less refined in focus.

Piano concerto in A min., Op. 54.

(M) *** Ph. **412 923-2**; 412 923-1/*4*. Bishop-Kovacevich, BBC SO, Sir Colin Davis – GRIEG: *Concerto.****

*** Ph. **412 251-2**; 9500 677/*7300 772* [id.]. Brendel, LSO, Abbado – WEBER: *Konzertstück*.***

(B) *** DG Walkman *419 087-4* [id.]. Kempff, Bav. RSO, Kubelik – BRAHMS: *Concerto No. 2*.***

(*) CBS **MK 42024 [id.]. Istomin, Columbia SO, Walter – BRAHMS: *Double concerto*.**(*)

(*) Decca **414 432-2 [id.]; SXL/*KSXC* 6624. Lupu, LSO, Previn – GRIEG: *Concerto*.**(*)

** Decca Dig. **411 942-2**; 411 942-1/*4* [id.]. Schiff, Concg. O, Dorati – CHOPIN: *Concerto No. 2*.**

** DG Dig. **410 021-2**; 2532/*3302* 043 [id.]. Zimerman, BPO, Karajan – GRIEG: *Concerto*.*(*)

(B) *(*) Ph. On Tour *412 906-4* [id.]. Janis, Minneapolis SO, Skrowaczewski – GRIEG: *Concerto**(*); CHOPIN: *Andante spianato*; WEBER: *Konzertstück*.**

This much-recorded favourite concerto has proved less successful than some comparable works in the recording studio. The fusing together of its disparate masculine and feminine Romantic elements has proved difficult, even for the finest artists. Thus our primary recommendation remains with the successful symbiosis of Stephen Bishop-Kovacevich and Sir Colin Davis who give an interpretation which is both fresh and poetic, unexaggerated but powerful in its directness and clarity. More than most, Bishop-Kovacevich shows the link between the central introspective slow movement and the comparable movement of Beethoven's *Fourth Concerto*; and the spring-like element of the outer movements is finely presented by orchestra and soloist alike. The sound has been admirably freshened for its mid-price reissue and the 1972 recording date is quite eclipsed. There is now also an outstanding chrome cassette, vivid and clear, to match the disc in excellence – far preferable to the original full-priced tape. The CD, of course, costs about three times as much as the LP or cassette, but the sound is warm and beautiful, and naturally balanced.

Of recent accounts, Brendel's is easily the best; it is a thoroughly considered, yet fresh-sounding performance, with meticulous regard to detail. There is some measure of coolness, perhaps, in the slow movement, but on the whole this is a most distinguished reading. The orchestral playing under Abbado is good, and the occasional lapse in ensemble noted by some reviewers on its first appearance is not likely to worry anyone. The recorded sound is up to the usual high standards of the house and is especially fine on CD. The cassette offers rather less transparent sound than the disc. Overall, this does not efface memories of the fresh and poetic account by Bishop-Kovacevich and Sir Colin Davis but remains an attractive alternative, if the coupling is suitable.

After a rather solid account of the opening chords of the *Concerto*, Kempff proceeds characteristically to produce an unending stream of poetry. His tempi are generally leisurely, and he is richly supported by Kubelik and the Bavarian Radio Symphony Orchestra. The 1974 recording is full and resonant, with warm piano timbre. On this Walkman chrome tape, coupled with Gilels's masterly version of the Brahms *Second Concerto*, the bargain is obvious.

Istomin's distinguished performance, recorded in 1960, is unfamiliar in the UK. The reading attractively combines strength and poetry, with bold contrasts in the first movement, a nicely lyrical *Intermezzo* and a fluent, well-paced finale. Bruno Walter's directing personality is strong: there is a natural flow in the outer movements, with the tempo flexing easily to accommodate the dialogues between piano and woodwind, which are beautifully managed. The recording sounds remarkably fine in its digital remastering, the warm ambience preventing any feeling of aggressiveness being generated by the dramatic tuttis. The piano timbre is fuller in colour than one expects from CBS recordings of this period. Indeed, Istomin's contribution is most appealing and, while the orchestral texture is less transparent than one would expect in a more modern version, Walter ensures that detail registers to the fullest effect. If the coupling is suitable, this is excellent value, offering 62′ of music.

Lupu's performance with André Previn is also a fine one. The clean boldness of approach to the first movement is appealingly fresh, but the poetry is more unevenly apparent than with Bishop-Kovacevich. The end of the slow movement is less magical than it might be; in general, the balance between the work's expressive and dramatic elements is not managed with complete success. The digital CD transfer is especially telling in the quieter moments, but tuttis are less transparent than with a digital recording – although the sound overall is excellent and there is a first-class cassette.

András Schiff's is an exceptionally gentle and lyrical reading, full of poetic insight. On CD, the recorded sound brings the same soft focus from distancing as in the Chopin on the reverse, but there is more bite of contrast both in Schiff's playing and in that of the Concertgebouw, giving necessary power to the work. The cassette offers Decca's very best quality, wide-ranging and full, with a most believable piano image.

Zimerman gives a big-boned performance, bold rather than delicate. There is consummate pianism from this most aristocratic of young artists, and Karajan draws fine playing from the Berlin orchestra. The sound is full and brilliant, strikingly present in its CD format. The cassette lacks something in refinement and transparency. However, there is an unyielding quality here in place of a natural romantic spontaneity, and this performance would not be a primary choice.

There is nothing special about Byron Janis's account. It has a Mercury source and dates from 1964. It is coupled with Arrau's heavily romanticized Grieg, but the Chopin and Weber items are fresher.

(i) *Piano concerto in A min., Op. 54; Symphony No. 3 in E flat* (*Rhenish*), *Op. 97.*
(*) DG Dig. **415 358-2; 415 358-1/*4* [id.]. Justus Frantz, VPO, Bernstein.

Bernstein draws excellent playing from the Vienna Philharmonic on DG and, although there are some expressive indulgences, these are by no means as disruptive in the *Rhenish symphony* as some reviews have indicated. The performances derive from concerts given in 1984 in the Grossersaal of the Musikverein and have the electricity and immediacy of live music-making. There is some slight exaggeration in the fourth movement (said to be inspired by the sight of Cologne Cathedral), but there is no want of dignity and nobility. Justus Frantz's account of the *Piano concerto* does seem a little wanting in spontaneity and does not have quite the delicacy of feeling or subtlety of nuance that Bishop-Kovacevich commands. The recording is full-bodied yet clear, although on the chrome cassette there is occasionally a degree of clouding in the lower frequencies.

Violin concerto in D min., Op. posth.
(*) HMV Dig. **CDC 747110-2 [id.]; ASD/*TC-ASD* 143519-1/*4* [Ang. DS/*4XS* 37957]. Kremer, Philh. O, Muti – SIBELIUS: *Concerto.***

The Schumann *Violin concerto* has had a generally bad press since it resurfaced in 1937. Kulenkampff and Menuhin were among its earliest champions. Its vein of introspection seems to suit Gidon Kremer, who gives a generally sympathetic account of it and has very good support from the Philharmonia Orchestra under Riccardo Muti. It is not Schumann at his most consistently inspired, but there are good things in it, including a memorable second subject and a characteristic slow movement. The recording is full-bodied and vivid; while the CD, with its added firmness, slightly emphasizes the forward balance of the soloist (the violin timbre strikingly tangible), the integration with the orchestra is also more positive. LP and tape are impressive too, closely matched in quality.

Symphonies Nos 1–4; (i) *Overtures: Genoveva, Op. 81; Manfred, Op. 115.*
(*) Ph. Dig. **412 126-2 (without overtures) (2); (i) 412 852-1/*4* (3) [id.]. Concg. O, Haitink.

Haitink conducts thoughtful and unexaggerated readings of all four symphonies, beautifully paced, with refined playing from the Concertgebouw Orchestra. His chosen speeds are never controversial, and the playing is both polished and committed, to make these consistently satisfying performances. The only snag is the recording quality which, with works that from the start are thick in their orchestration, is too reverberant. It is an ample, pleasing sound, but something sharper would have helped more to rebut criticism of Schumann's orchestration. On CD, the Overtures are omitted, but the four Symphonies are comfortably accommodated on two discs as against the triple LP or tape format.

Still recommended: As we have said in earlier editions of the *Penguin Stereo Record Guide*, Karajan's set of the Schumann Symphonies is undoubtedly the best, among the most impressive ever committed to disc, combining poetic intensity with intellectual strength (DG 2740 129 [2709 036]).

Symphony No. 1 in B flat (Spring), Op. 38; Manfred overture, Op. 115.
(B) **(*) DG Walkman *413 157-4*. BPO, Kubelik – SCHUBERT: *Symphony No. 8* etc.**(*)

Symphony No. 1 in B flat (Spring), Op. 38; Manfred overture, Op. 115; Overture, scherzo and finale, Op. 52.
(*) Capriccio **CD 10 063; C27/*CC27* 078. Stuttgart RSO, Marriner.

Symphonies Nos 1 in B flat (Spring), Op. 38; 3 in E flat (Rhenish), Op. 97.
(M) *** DG Sig. 2543/*3343* 504 [id.]. Chicago SO, Barenboim.

Symphonies Nos 1 (Spring); 4 in D min., Op. 120.
(M) *** DG Gal. 419 065-1/*4* [id.]. BPO, Karajan.
(*) DG Dig. **415 274-2; 415 274-1/*4* [id.]. VPO, Bernstein.

Karajan provides beautifully shaped performances, with orchestral playing of the highest distinction. The sound has been digitally remastered ready for a later CD issue and is full, yet detail is sharper. No. 4 is especially fine: this can be classed alongside Furtwängler's famous record – similarly inspirational – with the same orchestra. Karajan's versions dominate all other modern readings of these symphonies.

Barenboim's record is a recoupling of two fine performances from his earlier complete set. Freshness and high spirits mark both performances, though there is no lack of Germanic weight from this German-orientated American orchestra. No. 3 is particularly impressive for the superb horn playing; characteristically, the Cologne Cathedral movement is taken slowly and heavily. The forward and opulent recording matches the interpretations. The chrome cassette is first class, combining fullness with a lively upper range. This coupling represents the best features of Barenboim's cycle.

Like the coupling of the *Piano concerto* with the *Rhenish symphony*, these VPO versions of Nos 1 and 4 have the extra voltage which comes with live music-making at its most compulsive; it is a pity that Bernstein, who displays a natural response to Schumann, seeks to impose personal idiosyncrasies on the performances less convincingly than Karajan and Furtwängler. Both symphonies have portentous openings, and tempi are not always consistently controlled. The first movement of the *Spring symphony* is pushed hard, while the outer movements of No. 4 are not allowed to move forward at a steady pulse. The big transitional climax before the finale of the *Fourth* is massively conceived, yet has not the spine-tingling sense of anticipation that Furtwängler generates at this point. Even so, with splendid orchestral playing and much engaging detail, there is a great deal to admire here; both slow movements have striking warmth and humanity, even if the phrasing at the opening of the *Romance* of No. 4 has an element of self-consciousness. The recording has an attractive ambience and is full and well balanced, with the woodwind attractively coloured. On tape, there is occasionally a slight thickening of the lower end of the sound spectrum, but textures remain unclouded.

Alongside Bernstein's performance, the bright directness of Marriner's reading of the *First Symphony* is the more striking, and there is certainly a spring-like freshness in the outer movements, with the finale sparkling in an almost Schubertian way. The string ensemble is first rate, with rhythms nicely sprung and the phrasing of the *Larghetto* agreeably songful. There is perhaps a lack of Romantic weight, but throughout Sir Neville lets the music speak for itself and avoids interfering with the onward flow to register expressive emphases. The *Overture, scherzo and finale* is strongly characterized, again very well played, with the closing apotheosis lyrically powerful without melodrama. The *Manfred overture* too is eloquently done. Throughout, one's ear is drawn to the fine internal balance of the Stuttgart Radio Orchestra, with woodwind beautifully blended (the colouring of the second subject of the first movement of the *Symphony* is particularly telling), while the brass are firm and incisive, never blatant. The digital recording is first class within a kindly studio ambience that allows detail to register admirably, yet is not too dry.

Kubelik's account of the *Spring symphony* dates from 1963 and the recording sounds well on this Walkman chrome tape. Both performances here have a sympathetic lyrical impulse; if the coupling is suitable, this should not disappoint, for the price is very competitive.

Symphony No. 2; Manfred overture.
(*) DG Dig. **410 863-2; 410 863-1/*4* [id.]. VPO, Sinopoli.

Sinopoli's is a performance of extremes, consciously designed to reflect the composer's own mental torment. Even the lovely slow movement broods darkly rather than finding repose. The Vienna Philharmonic play with the necessary bite, with the recording providing some mellowness. On CD, the strings are given added bite and brilliance and wind detail is clarified, but the overall balance is not always completely convincing. LP and tape are closely matched.

Symphony No. 3 in E flat (*Rhenish*)*, Op. 97; Manfred overture, Op. 115.*
*** DG Dig. **400 062-2**; 2532/*3302* 040 [id.]. LAPO, Giulini.
(*) Ph. Dig. **411 104-2; 411 104-1/*4* [id.]. Concg. O, Haitink.

Despite the aristocratic qualities that distinguish his performances and the spirituality that is in evidence, Giulini can often obtrude by the very intensity of his search for perfection; as a result, while the sound he produces is of great beauty, he does not always allow the music to unfold effortlessly. This *Rhenish* is, however, completely free of interpretative exaggeration and its sheer musical vitality and nobility of spirit are beautifully conveyed. The Los Angeles players produce a very well-blended, warm and cultured sound that is a joy to listen to in itself. The recording is extremely fine, too, and reproduces well in its cassette format. This is among the best of recent versions and is particularly impressive in its compact disc format where the focus is marginally sharper and detail clearer.

Haitink's is a characteristically strong and direct reading, beautifully played with outstandingly resonant and rich brass – most important in this of all the Schumann symphonies. Speeds are finely chosen, with the slower movements nicely flowing. Good Concertgebouw sound, lacking a little in brilliance but allowing textures to be registered in fair detail. The high-level cassette does not quite achieve the inner definition of the LP and compact disc, but still sounds well.

Symphony No. 4 in D min., Op. 120.
(M) *** DG Sig. 413 982-1/*4*. BPO, Karajan – SCHUBERT: *Symphony No. 8.****

Symphony No. 4 in D min., Op. 120; Manfred overture, Op. 115.
(***) DG mono **415 661-2** [id.]. BPO, Furtwängler – HAYDN: *Symphony No. 88.*(***)

There is little doubt that this is one of Furtwängler's really great records. Even those who find this conductor's tampering with speeds too personal and wilful can hardly fail to be moved by the richness of his conception of Schumann's *Fourth Symphony*. The appearance of the first movement's secondary theme is an unforgettable moment, while the *Romance* is freshly spontaneous in its simplicity; but it is perhaps in the finale where the lack of a firm forward tempo is most striking – and equally (from the magnificently prepared 'Wagnerian' transition passage onwards) where the conductor is most successful in giving a sense of creation in the actual performance. There is superb playing from the Berlin Philharmonic, especially in the brass and strings. The recording has been remastered and the string timbre is clear rather than rich; but there is a supporting weight so that the ear readily adjusts, for the original 1953 mono recording (made in the Berlin Jesus Christus Church) was well balanced, with a fine ambience. *Manfred* – recorded in 1949 at a public performance – has rather less congenial sound, and the strings sound thinner. Moreover, there are audience noises to interrupt the rapt concentration of the closing pages. It is a characteristically Romantic reading, but convincingly controlled. With its splendid Haydn coupling, this is one Furtwängler CD to recommend without reservation to all readers.

Karajan is totally attuned to Schumann's sensibility in the *Fourth Symphony*; one is reminded of the pre-war Bruno Walter LSO recording. The performance is beautifully shaped, with orchestral playing of the highest distinction. The recording from the early 1970s is fresh and clear, but does not lack weight in its remastered form. With a splendid coupling, this is a bargain in DG's mid-priced Signature series; the sobriquet is wholly appropriate, for Karajan's personality is at its strongest in both works. The chrome cassette transfer is one of DG's finest – the tape matches the disc very closely, with no appreciable loss of range or detail.

Piano trio No. 1 in D min., Op. 63.
(*) CRD **CRD 3433; CRD 1133/*CRDC 4133* [id.]. Israel Piano Trio – BRAHMS: *Piano trio No. 2.***(*)

The *D minor Trio* dates from 1847 and is not otherwise represented on compact disc, though there is a good LP and cassette by Kyung Wha Chung, Tortelier and Previn; this is coupled with the Mendelssohn *D minor Trio*, Op. 49, and is given a more humane and relaxed reading (HMV ASD/*TC-ASD* 3894). The Israel Piano Trio give a powerfully projected account; the pianist is at times rather carried away, as if he were playing a Brahms concerto. The scherzo is too emphatically – indeed, almost brutally – articulated and as akin to the world of Schumann as are the skyscrapers of Manhattan or Tel Aviv. There are, however, some sensitive and intelligent touches; and there is at present no CD alternative. The recording is first class and there is an extremely realistic cassette.

Fantasiestücke, Op. 73; 5 Stücke in Volkston, Op. 102.
☪ *** Ph. Dig. **412 230-2**; 412 230-1/*4* [id.]. Maisky, Argerich – SCHUBERT: *Arpeggione sonata.**** ☪

Mischa Maisky and Martha Argerich give relaxed, leisurely accounts of these pieces that some collectors may find almost self-indulgent. Others will luxuriate in the refinement and sensitivity of this playing, coupled with an unusual and musically perceptive account of the *Arpeggione sonata*; an altogether outstanding Philips recording in all three formats, but especially tangible on CD.

PIANO MUSIC

Allegro, Op. 8; Novelette, Op. 21; Romance No. 2 in F sharp, Op. 28/2; Sonata No. 3 in F min., Op. 14.
*** Decca Dig. 414 035-1/*4* [id.]. Marc Raubenheimer.

Poignant testimony to the talents of the South African pianist, Marc Raubenheimer (1951–84), this recital was recorded in 1983, not long after he had won the Santander competition and shortly before his untimely death in a plane crash. He has the measure of this music and conveys a refreshing impression of spontaneity, almost as if one is encountering its questing improvisatory spirit for the first time. With the deletion of Horowitz's RCA account, there is no alternative version of the *Sonata* currently available in any form. The recording is eminently faithful.

Arabeske, Op. 18; Carnaval, Op. 9; Études symphoniques, Op. 13; Kinderscenen (Scenes from childhood), Op. 15; Papillons, Op. 2; Waldscenen, Op. 82.
(M) **(*) DG 413 538-1/*4* (2). Wilhelm Kempff.

These recordings come from a box of six LPs of Schumann's music, issued to celebrate Kempff's eightieth birthday; all the performances have the blend of poetry and intellect that marks this great pianist's style. Kempff is in his element in the *Arabeske*, *Papillons* and *Waldscenen*. The comparatively extrovert style of *Carnaval* suits him less well; if the reading of the *Études symphoniques* misses some of the heroism of the music, it is still marvellously persuasive, giving a clear illusion of a live performance. The only relative disappointment is *Kinderscenen*, unexpectedly not one of the pianist's more compelling performances. The recordings have good timbre and presence, although the quality is a trifle dry. There is little to choose between discs and the matching chrome tapes.

Arabeske in C, Op. 18; Études symphoniques, Op. 13.
*** DG Dig. **410 916-2**; 410 916-1/*4* [id.]. Maurizio Pollini.

Pollini's account has a symphonic gravitas and concentration: it has the benefit of excellent recorded sound from DG. If, in terms of tenderness and poetic feeling, Perahia remains a first choice on LP, this newcomer has great strength. Pollini includes the five additional variations that Schumann decided against including in either of the editions published during his lifetime, placing them as a group between the fifth and sixth variations, rather than as a kind of appendix or *Anhang* as Perahia does. Perahia also offers a more substantial fill-up than the *Arabeske* in the shape of *Papillons* (CBS 76635/*40*- [M/*MT* 34539]). However, Pollini's is a most impressive record by any standards. The CD has fine presence, but the balance of the chrome cassette is a little orientated towards the bass end of the spectrum, though the upper range is clear and the timbre is agreeably full.

Arabeske in C, Op. 18; Fantasiestücke: Traumeswirren, Op. 12/7. Presto passionato in G min.; Toccata in C, Op. 7.
(***) EMI Référence mono PM 100100-1/*4*. Vladimir Horowitz – LISZT: *Sonata* etc.(***)

These famous performances all date from the 1930s and reappear in improved transfers with a good, clear matching cassette. The playing can only be described as stunning, and reservations about the faded sound are soon dissipated. The Schumann pieces accompany Horowitz's transcendental account of the Liszt *Sonata* and are essential listening for any serious collector. Not to be missed.

Davidsbündlertänze, Op. 6; Fantasiestücke, Op. 12.
*** CBS 73202/*40-76202* [M 32299]. Murray Perahia.

Perahia has a magic touch, and his electric spontaneity is naturally caught in the studio. In works of Schumann which can splinter apart, this quality of concentration is enormously valuable, and the results could hardly be more powerfully convincing, despite recording quality which lacks something in bloom and refinement. The chrome cassette is very well managed, with good definition. The treble is smoothed a little to advantage, without loss of presence.

Études symphoniques; Toccata, Op. 7.
*(*) DG Dig. **410 520-2**; 2532/*3302* 036 [id.]. Iv. Pogorelich – BEETHOVEN: *Piano sonata No. 32.***(*)

Pogorelich opens his performance of the *Études symphoniques* with a grotesquely self-conscious and studied presentation of the theme. This is pianism of the first order, but the listener's attention tends to be drawn from the music to the pianism, which is too wilful to be considered alongside Pollini's eloquent account (see above) or the fresh and ardent version by Murray Perahia. The recording is vivid and truthful, and has striking presence on compact disc.

The chrome cassette is full, wide-ranging and well focused, but slightly dry in timbre.

Fantasia in C, Op. 17.
(M) *** DG 410 983-1/*4* [id.]. Maurizio Pollini – SCHUBERT: *Wanderer fantasia.****

Fantasia in C, Op. 17; Fantasiestücke, Op. 12.
*** Ph. Dig. **411 049-2**; 6514/*7337* 283 [id.]. Alfred Brendel.

Pollini's account of the *Fantasia* (now recoupled at mid-price with Schubert) is as fine as Richter's now deleted version. The playing throughout has command and authority on the one hand and deep poetic feeling on the other that instantly hold the listener spellbound. The recording is good, but not remarkable, slightly dry in timbre. Disc and tape are closely matched.

Brendel's coupling is also outstanding. As the very opening of the *Fantasiestücke* demonstrates, this is magically spontaneous playing, full of imaginative touches of colour, strong as well as poetic. The compact disc has a greater range and presence than the already impressive LP and cassette formats. The actual sound is rather more forward than one would encounter in the recital room, but it serves Brendel well and truthfully conveys the depth of timbre.

Kinderscenen (Scenes from childhood), Op. 15; Kreisleriana, Op. 16.
*** Ph. 9500/*7300* 964 [id.]. Brendel.
*(**) DG Dig. **410 653-2**; 410 653-1/*4* [id.]. Martha Argerich.

Keenly intelligent and finely characterized playing from Brendel here. He is better recorded than most of his rivals, and though certain details may strike listeners as less spontaneous the overall impression is strong. The *Kinderscenen* is the finest for some years and is touched with real distinction. On cassette, the sound has slightly less sharpness of focus than on disc, but remains very good.

There is no doubting the instinctive flair of Argerich's playing or her intuitive feeling for Schumann. However, she is let down by an unpleasingly close recording that diminishes pleasure somewhat, no less in CD format than on LP and cassette.

4 Sketches, Op. 58.
(*) ASV ALH/*ZCALH* 958 [id.]. Jennifer Bate (Royal Albert Hall organ) – ELGAR: *Sonata.*(*)

The *Four Sketches* were originally written for a piano with pedal attachment, and are here arranged for organ by E. Power Biggs. Each of the pieces is in 3/4 time, but the writing is attractively diverse. They are pleasant trifles, pleasing enough as a coupling for the fine Elgar performance on the reverse. Rich, atmospheric recording with fair detail, and an excellent matching tape.

VOCAL MUSIC

Dichterliebe (song cycle), *Op. 48; Liederkreis* (song cycle), *Op. 39; Myrthen Lieder, Op. 25.*

*** DG **415 190-2** [id.]. Dietrich Fischer-Dieskau, Christoph Eschenbach.

Fischer-Dieskau's Schumann recordings made with Christoph Eschenbach in the mid-1970s provide an attractive coupling of an outstandingly fine *Dichterliebe* (the voice still fresh) and the magnificent Op. 39 *Liederkreis*, made the more attractive on CD by the generous addition of seven of the *Myrthen* songs, making 39 items in all. Though a thoughtfully individual artist in his own right, Eschenbach here provides consistently sympathetic support for the singer. He is imaginative on detail without ever intruding distractingly. Very good sound for the period.

Frauenliebe und Leben, Op. 42; Liederkreis, Op. 24; 3 Heine Lieder (*Abends am Strand; Lehn' deine Wang' an meine Wang'; Mein Wagen rollet langsam*). *Tragödie, Op. 64/3.*

*** DG Dig. **415 519-2**; 415 519-1/*4* [id.]. Brigitte Fassbaender, Irwin Gage.

Positively characterized with a wide range of expression and fine detail but little sense of vulnerability, Fassbaender's reading conceals the underlying sentimentality of the poems of *Frauenliebe*. There is little attempt to beautify the voice, though it is a fine, consistent instrument, for clear exposition of the words is the singer's prime aim. Passionate involvement also marks Fassbaender's singing of the Heine *Liederkreis*, of which there are surprisingly few recordings. The three songs of *Tragödie* and the three separate Heine settings make an important supplement. Irwin Gage is the understanding accompanist. The recording is well balanced with fine presence, and there is a first-class chrome cassette.

Reminder. Dame Janet Baker's early Saga recording of *Frauenliebe und Leben* with its extraordinarily expressive range remains paramount (Saga 5277). This has also been issued on a double-length tape (*SAGD 2*) combining with the Brahms and Schubert Lieder featured on the above LP a fine collection of English songs also recorded at the beginning of Dame Janet's career.

Requiem in D flat, Op. 148; Requiem für Mignon, Op. 98b.

*** HMV Dig. ASD 146756-1. Donath, Lindner, Andonian, Soffel, Georg, Gedda, Fischer-Dieskau, Düsseldorf Musical Soc. Ch., Düsseldorf SO, Klee.

Written in 1852, Schumann's *Requiem* was the very last work to which the composer assigned an opus number; like Mozart, he was unable to shake off the conviction that the *Requiem* was for himself. The opening *Requiem aeternam* is affecting and dignified, and the final *Benedictus* has a haunting eloquence. Bernhard Klee extracts a very sympathetic response from his distinguished team of soloists and the fine Düsseldorf chorus and orchestra. They also give an attentive and committed account of the 1849 *Requiem for Mignon*, Op. 98b, which completes the second side. The EMI recording is natural and well balanced; collectors with a special interest in Schumann should lose no time in acquiring this enterprising issue.

Schütz, Heinrich (1585–1672)

Motets: *Auf dem Gebirge; Der Engel sprach; Exultavit cor meum; Fili mi Absalon; Heu mihi Domine; Hodie Christus natus est; Ich danke Dir, Herr; O quam tu pulchra es; Die Seele Christi, heilige mich; Selig sind die Todten.*
** ASV ALH/*ZCALH* 960 [id.]. Pro Cantione Antiqua, Edgar Fleet.

An eminently useful and well-recorded anthology of Schütz motets that offers such masterpieces as *Fili mi Absalon* (for bass voice, five sackbuts, organ and violone continuo) and the glorious *Selig sind die Todten* in well-thought-out and carefully prepared performances under Edgar Fleet. This first appeared in 1978 to a respectful rather than enthusiastic press, but these accounts have a dignity and warmth that make them well worth considering. Moreover, the cassette is splendidly managed, the sound rich and clear, every bit the equal of the disc.

Deutsches Magnificat. Motets: *Ach, Herr, straf mich nicht* (Psalm 6)*; Cantate Domino* (Psalm 96)*; Herr unser Herrscher* (Psalm 8)*; Ich freu mich des* (Psalm 122)*; Unser Herr Jesus, wie lieblich* (Psalm 84).
(M) *** Argo 414 532-1/*4*. Heinrich Schütz Ch., Symphoniae Sacrae Ens. and continuo, Norrington.

This is a valuable reissue from 1971 and one of the most successful records these artists have given us. The choral singing is impressively firm and the recording does justice to the antiphonal effects. The *Deutsches Magnificat* is given with admirable authority, and this splendid example of Schütz's last years (he was eight-five when he wrote it) is one of the best things on the disc. The instrumental playing is fully worthy of the singing, and there need be no qualification in recommending this to all who have discovered this remarkable composer. The *Cantate Domino*, by the way, may well be by Giovanni Gabrieli, with whom Schütz studied in Venice in the early years of the seventeenth century. The recording has been remastered and freshened; it is clearer but there is a slight loss of sonority. On tape, the high level has also brought some loss of refinement and the balance is disappointingly light in the bass.

Easter oratorio: The Resurrection of our Lord Jesus Christ.
*** Argo 414 072-1/*4*. Pears, Tear, Shirley-Quirk, Heinrich Schütz Ch., Elizabethan Cons., L. Cornett and Sackbut Ens., Norrington.

Schütz's masterly setting of the Resurrection story will not appeal to all tastes. It will seem too uneventful and austere for some, but its rewards are rich. Part of its musical success depends on the artistry of the Evangelist, sung here by Peter Pears, who has impressive authority and insight and is given admirable support by the soloists and instrumentalists. The 1970 recording is both full and detailed.

Italian Madrigals, Book 1 (complete).
*** German HM 1C 067 1695271. Cons. of Musicke, Rooley.
*** HM **HMC 901162**; HMC/*HMC40*- 1162. Concerto Vocale, René Jacobs.

Schütz's first and only Book of Italian Madrigals comes from his study years in Venice (1608–11) and reflects his encounter with the music of Giovanni Gabrieli and Monteverdi. As one would expect, Anthony Rooley's record with The Consort of Musicke has the advantage of impeccable intonation and blend, and the performances are all beautifully prepared and recorded.

The Concerto Vocale led by the counter-tenor, René Jacobs, are hardly less fine than their cross-Channel rivals, The Consort of Musicke. The latter are unaccompanied whereas the Concerto Vocale employ a theorbo which provides aural variety, and at times they offer a greater expressive and tonal range. They omit the very last of the madrigals, the eight-part *Vasto mar*, to which The Consort of Musicke do full justice on their disc. On balance, either version serves this repertoire more idiomatically than the somewhat heavy-handed Capella Lipsiensis version on Philips, which is now displaced. Those who require a compact disc will note that, at the time of writing, only the Concerto Vocale is available in this format.

Psalms of David Nos 115; 128; 136; 150; Canzon: Un lob, mein Seel; Concerti: Lobe den Herren; Zion spricht; Jauchzet dem Herren; Motets: Ist nicht Ephraim; Die mit Tranen saen.
*(*) DG Arc. **415 297-2** [id.]. Regensburger Domspatzen, Hamburg Wind Ens., Ulsamer Coll., Schneidt.

The Psalms of David formed Schütz's first sacred work, published in 1619. There are twenty-six settings of Psalms plus two other biblical texts, written for single, double or triple chorus, with ad lib instrumental support. The last ten of these works are gathered together here, and in nine of them Schütz has indicated the required instrumentation. The performances here are more than adequate, quite well sung and played, although pacing tends to be brisk and the approach rather stiff. Unfortunately the 1972 recording is poorly focused: at the opening of Psalm 150 the impression is of 'fluff on the stylus', not an effect one expects from a digitally remastered CD.

Musikalische Exequiem; Psalm 136: Danket dem Herren, dem er ist freudlich.
*** HMV EL 270342-1/*4*. Nigel Rogers Vocal Ens., Basle Boys' Ch., Schola Cantorum Basiliensis, Linde.

Schütz's *Musikalische Exequiem* comes from 1635; it was written in response to a commission from Prince Heinrich Reuss for performance at his funeral, which the Prince planned in detail during his lifetime. The first part, subtitled 'Concert in the form of a burial Mass', is based on verses from the Bible and hymns which Reuss had ordered to be placed on his coffin; the second is the motet *Herr, wenn ich nur dich habe*, and the third the *Song of Simeon* from St Luke's Gospel, which was to be sung at the beginning of the burial. The present recording was made in 1979 and has been digitally remastered to excellent effect. The solo group of singers includes Jennifer Smith, Patrizia Kwella, James Bowman and Ian Partridge, as well as Nigel Rogers himself, and the instrumental team is hardly less distinguished. The fill-up, *Psalm 136* for two solo groups, chorus, and brass, comes from the *Psalms of David* (1619) and is an imposing piece in the Venetian style. This now becomes a first recommendation and displaces the mid-price Dresden version under Mauersberger on Philips. As usual with this series, the tape transfer is first class, the sound full and clear.

St Matthew Passion.
*** HMV Dig. EL 270018-1/*4* [Ang. DS/*4DS* 38167]. Hilliard Ens., Hillier.

Schütz's setting of the Passion Story, composed in 1666 when he was in his eighties, is exclusively vocal; its austerity extends to the absence not only of instrumental support but of any additional hymns or arias. Peter Pears's (now deleted) account with Roger Norrington's Heinrich Schütz Choir and John Shirley-Quirk as Jesus was recorded in the early 1970s; this new version from the Hilliard Ensemble and Paul Hillier, who takes the bass part of Jesus, makes an admirable successor. The solo parts are on the whole admirable and the restraint of Paul Elliot's Evangelist is impressive. The soloists double in the choral sections, which is less than ideal; in that respect, the Norrington version was to be preferred. In all others, however, there is no need to fault this excellently balanced and finely produced HMV version. The sound on the cassette is especially beautiful – in the demonstration class – and this is music that needs to be enjoyed against a background free from noise.

Der Schwanengesang (reconstructed by Wolfram Steude).
*** HMV Dig. EX 270275-3/*5* (2). Hilliard Ens., Hannover Knabenchor, London Baroque, Hennig.

Schütz's *opus ultimum* is a setting of Psalm 119, the longest psalm in the psalter, which he divides into eleven sections. He finishes off this thirteen-part motet cycle with his final setting of Psalm 100, which he had originally composed in 1662, and the *Deutsches Magnificat*. Wolfram Steude's note recounts the history of the work, parts of which disappeared after Schütz's death; and his reconstruction of two of the vocal parts is obviously a labour of love. The project was undertaken in celebration of the European Music Year in 1985 and the recording a co-production with NDR (North German Radio). The performance is a completely dedicated one, with excellent singing from all concerned and good instrumental playing, and the conductor, Heinz Hennig, secures warm and responsive singing from his Hannover Knabenchor. The acoustic is spacious and warm, and the recording balance well focused. The cassettes too are extremely well managed, the sound firm, clear and sonorous.

Scriabin, Alexander (1872–1915)

Symphony No. 1 in E, Op. 26.
*** HMV Dig. **CDC 747349-2**; EL 270270-1/*4* [Ang. DS/*4DS* 38260]. Toczyska, Myers, Westminister Ch., Phd. O, Muti.

Scriabin's *First Symphony* is a long, six-movement work dating from 1900, a highly rhapsodic score whose harmonic processes betray keyboard habits of mind, and whose lines are highly characteristic of Art Nouveau. It has been recorded before, by Svetlanov and Inbal; but neither commands the luxurious orchestral playing or the superb quality of the new EMI recording. Indeed, this inspired version eclipses all rivals and will be hard to beat. Muti brings great refinement of dynamic nuance and plasticity of phrasing to this score, showing its many beauties to the best possible advantage. It would be difficult to overpraise the sensitivity and polish of the Philadelphia wind or the sumptuous tone of the strings. The vocal contributions from Stefania Toczyska and Michael Myers in the last movement, a setting of Scriabin's own words, are also excellent. It is less overheated than the later symphonies and its lush pastures are brought wonderfully to life. This is undoubtedly one of Muti's best records in recent years and should acquire classic status. It sounds superb on CD and there is a good cassette, though the effect on tape is spacious, with definition less sharp than on the disc versions.

Symphony No. 3 in C min. (*Le divin poème*), *Op. 43.*
*** BBC Dig. **CD 520**; REGL/*ZCF* 520. BBC SO, Pritchard.
*** Etcetera **KTC 1027**; ETC/*ETX* 1027 [id.]. Concg. O, Kondrashin.

Scriabin's mammoth *Third Symphony* calls for vast forces: the scoring includes quadruple woodwind, eight horns (the BBC recording has nine), five trumpets, and so on. The work dates from 1903 and with its long, swirling lines is typical of the Art Nouveau. The commentator gives hostages to fortune by calling it 'one of the finest works of art created in its time or at any period in the history of music', but there is no doubt that it is original, both in layout and in substance. The BBC Symphony Orchestra play for Sir John Pritchard with commitment and give a thoroughly convincing account of this complex and at times inflated score. The recording, too, unravels the complexities of Scriabin's scoring with considerable success, though it is the compact disc that has the greater clarity and definition – and conveys the greater illusion of space. There is impressive range, particularly at the bottom end of the aural spectrum. Moreover, in so far as the symphony is played without a break, the CD has the obvious advantage of continuity.

Kondrashin and the Concertgebouw Orchestra recorded the *Third Symphony* at a public concert in 1976, and the performance has a certain authority and intensity that eludes its rival. This, too, is well recorded – though not quite so well as either the analogue Inbal account on Philips (available only as part of the complete set on 6769041) or the digital BBC version. It is just announced on compact disc. Collectors for whom the clarity and definition of digital recording are a first priority should go for the BBC account in its CD format, but others should note that honours are pretty well divided between the three LP versions, with Kondrashin's having a slight edge as an interpretation.

Preludes, Op. 11, Nos 2, 4–6, 8–14, 16, 18, 20, 22, 24; Op. 13, Nos 1–3; Op. 15, Nos 1 and 5; Op. 16, Nos 2 and 4. Prelude for the left hand in C sharp min., Op. 9/1; Étude in C sharp min., Op. 42/5. Piano sonata No. 4 in F sharp, Op. 30.
*** HMV Dig. **CDC 747346-2** [id.]; EL 270090-1/*4* [Ang. DS/*4DS* 38161]. Andrei Gavrilov.

Gavrilov does not give us any set of the *Preludes* or *Studies* complete but picks and chooses – which is no doubt ideal in a piano recital designed to show his sympathies, but less desirable from the point of view of a record collector. We have all the even-numbered *Preludes* of Op. 11, most of them exquisitely played, plus Nos 5, 9, 11 and 13, and a handful of preludes drawn arbitrarily from Opp. 9, 13, 15 and 16, one of the Op. 42 *Études* and the *Fourth Sonata*, Op. 30, which is about the finest account on record. At times the playing is impetuous and dynamics can be exaggerated: Op. 11, No. 20 begins *ff* when the marking is merely *mf*, and there are numerous such instances where a *piano* becomes *piano-pianissimo*. But playing of this order is still pretty remarkable, and imperfections – the odd ugly *ff* and a not particularly pleasing instrument – should be overlooked. The balance is not too close, yet the CD brings a tangible presence and the piano timbre is naturally caught.

Shostakovich, Dmitri (1906–75)

Chamber symphony in C min., Op. 110a (arr. Barshai from *String quartet No. 8, Op. 11*); *Symphony for strings in A flat, Op. 118a* (arr. from *String quartet No. 10, Op. 118*).
*** Phoenix Dig. DGS 1038 [id.]. Phoenix CO, Julian Bigg.

Rudolf Barshai's string orchestral arrangement of the *Eighth Quartet* – the best-known of the cycle and the one with graphic wartime overtones and the 'DSCH' motif obsessively worked on – is deservedly well known. The parallel arrangement of the equally intense *Quartet No. 10* is also surprisingly effective in the larger-scale medium, particularly when, as here, you have lively, committed performances from a youthful band of players under a talented young conductor. One may miss some of the incisiveness of the original quartets (particularly with a warm, reverberant recording) but, if anything, the weight and urgency are intensified.

Cello concerto No. 1 in E flat, Op. 107.
*** CBS Dig. **CD 37840**; 37840/*40*- [id.]. Yo-Yo Ma, Phd. O, Ormandy – KABALEVSKY: *Cello concerto No. 1.****

Ͼ *** Chan. Dig. **CHAN 8322**; ABRD/*ABTD* 1085 [id.]. Raphael Wallfisch, ECO, Geoffrey Simon – BARBER: *Cello concerto*.*** Ͼ

Cello concertos Nos 1 in E flat, Op. 107; 2, Op. 126.
Ͼ *** Ph. Dig. **412 526-2**; 412 526-1/*4* [id.]. Heinrich Schiff, Bav. RSO, Maxim Shostakovich.

Yo-Yo Ma on CBS brings an ardent musical imagination to the *First Cello concerto*. He plays with an intensity that compels the listener and, as befits an artist who has been acclaimed as one of the greatest cellists now before the public, can hold his own with any competition, though the Philadelphia Orchestra play here at a slightly lower voltage than they did (also under Ormandy) a quarter of a century ago for Rostropovich. The CBS recording has ample presence and warmth, with the balance slightly favouring the soloist, but very well judged overall. The CD adds presence and refines detail, while the chrome-tape transfer is one of CBS's very best.

Wallfisch's version on Chandos also has the advantage of an interesting coupling, the *Cello concerto* of Samuel Barber, a work of great freshness and charm. He handles the first movement splendidly, though there is not quite the same sense of momentum as in Yo-Yo Ma's account. However, Raphael Wallfisch gives a sensitive account of the slow movement and has thoughtful and responsive support from the ECO. The soloist is forward – but then so is Ma on CBS, and neither is unacceptably larger than life. The Chandos recording is outstandingly fine in all three formats and, technically, the CD can more than hold its own alongside its rivals. The chrome tape has striking pianissimo detail.

Heinrich Schiff on Philips is the only cellist so far to couple the two concertos. Schiff's superbly recorded account does not displace Yo-Yo Ma in the *First*, but it can hold its own, and interest inevitably centres on its companion. The *Second Concerto* comes between the *Thirteenth* and *Fourteenth Symphonies*, neither of which endeared Shostakovich to the Soviet Establishment. The concerto did not meet with the enthusiastic acclaim that had greeted No. 1; nor has it established itself in the repertory to anywhere near the same extent as its predecessor, perhaps because it offers fewer overt opportunities for display. It is a work of eloquence and beauty, inward in feeling and spare in its textures, rhapsodic, even fugitive in character, yet the sonorities have the asperity so characteristic of Shostakovich. A haunting piece, essentially lyrical, it is gently discursive, sadly whimsical at times and tinged with a smiling melancholy that hides deeper troubles. In all three formats – and particularly on CD – the recording is enormously impressive. The chrome tape is exceptionally well managed and is not inferior to the LP.

Piano concerto No. 1 in C min., for piano, trumpet and strings, Op. 35.
(*) Delos Dig. **D/CD 3021 [id.]. Rosenberger, Burns, LACO, Schwarz – PROKOFIEV: *Symphony No. 1****; STRAVINSKY: *Soldier's tale*.*** Ͼ

Piano concertos Nos (i) *1, Op. 35;* (ii) *2 in F, Op. 102.*
(M) *** CBS 60504/*40*- [MP/*MPT* 38892]. NYPO, Bernstein, with (i) Previn, Vacciano; (ii) Bernstein (piano).

Piano concertos Nos 1–2; 3 Fantastic dances, Op. 5.
(M) **(*) HMV ED 290210-1/*4* [Ang. S 37109]. Ortiz, Bournemouth SO, Berglund.

Piano concerto No. 2 in F, Op. 102; Symphony for strings in A flat, Op. 118a.
(*) Chan. Dig. **CHAN 8443; ABRD/*ABTD* 1155 [id.]. Dmitri Shostakovich, I Musici de Montreal, Montreal SO (members), Maxim Shostakovich.

In the early summer of 1975, CBS and HMV simultaneously apprehended the need for a good coupling of the two Shostakovich *Piano concertos*; now both these LPs have been almost simultaneously reissued at mid-price. Bernstein's radiant account of No. 2 on CBS is shrewdly re-coupled with Previn's equally striking reading of No. 1. Though these New York performances bring somewhat dated recording, both pianists have a way of turning a phrase to catch the imagination, and a fine balance is struck between Shostakovich's warmth and his rhythmic alertness. There is a good tape.

Cristina Ortiz gives fresh and attractive performances of both concertos, a degree undercharacterized, but very well recorded and with a fine accompaniment from the Bournemouth orchestra. This music making is not so individual as that on the CBS disc, but there is compensation in the EMI sound, and this disc offers a small bonus in the *Three Fantastic dances*, which are played with splendid character.

There have been more witty accounts of the *First Concerto* than Rosenberger's, but the extra degree of gravitas in the first movement adds an unexpected depth to the music, and the *Lento* is beautifully played, with a fine expressive response from the strings of the Los Angeles Chamber Orchestra. The finale, taken fast, makes a brilliant contrast, though here the humorous vulgarity is not emphasized, though the trumpet-playing has plenty of dash. The recording is resonant, the piano balanced more forwardly than would be ideal, but the CD certainly has splendid presence.

Maxim Shostakovich, who gave the *Second Piano concerto* its première in 1957, on Chandos directs a performance in which his son is soloist, which ensures authenticity, and yet one must register a degree of disappointment. The outer movements are firm and crisply rhythmic, and the *Andante* avoids any suggestion of sentimentality. Its opening mood is elegiac, but the piano figurations, refusing to linger in any kind of romanticism, are a shade too straight, and the closing toccata is also somewhat anonymous in its very energetic progress. The *Symphony for strings*, arranged by Rudolf Barshai from the *String quartet No. 10*, is certainly not lacking incisiveness in the account by I Musici de Montreal, although this does not seem an apt coupling for the *Concerto* and is rather more convincingly done by the Phoenix Chamber Orchestra – see above. The

Montreal account is well, rather than outstandingly, played. The recording is impressively vivid in both works, although the acoustics of the Church of St Madeleine, Outremont, Montreal, are rather resonant for this music. This is most striking on the faithful chrome cassette.

Still recommended: Dmitri Alexeev's coupling of the two Shostakovich *Piano concertos*, offered at bargain price, remains a clear first choice in this repertoire. Artistically he has more personality than most of his rivals, and he has the advantage of sensitive and idiomatic support from the ECO under Jerzy Maksymiuk. He offers as a fill-up a kind of Soviet *Warsaw concerto* (though without the tune!) from a film-score called *The Unforgettable Year 1919*. The digital recording is in every way excellent on both disc and tape (CfP CFP 41 4416-1/*4* [Ang. AE/*4AE* 34489]).

Symphonies Nos 1–15 (complete).
(M) **(*) HMV Dig. EX 290387-3 (12). Moscow PO, Kondrashin; with Eisen, RSFSR Ac. Ch. (in No. 13); Tselovalnik, Nesterenko (in No. 14).

EMI have replaced their mid-1970s set of the complete Shostakovich symphonies with a digitally remastered cycle under Kirill Kondrashin. Kondrashin had, of course, conducted the bulk of the earlier set, though Nos 5 and 15 were allotted to Svetlanov, 12 to Yevgeni Mravinsky and 14 to Rudolf Barshai. The earliest recording here is of the *Fourth*, made in 1962 not long after its first performance, and the most recent (1975–6) are Nos 7 (*Leningrad*), 14 and 15. Generally speaking, Kondrashin favours brisk tempi and the impact of Nos 6 (recorded in 1968) and 8 (1963) was somewhat reduced on that count. Nos 1–4 are very good indeed; the latter sounds impressive, in spite of its relative age, as indeed do Nos 11 and 12, though neither displace the wonderful recordings Mravinsky made in the early 1960s. Kondrashin gave the first performance of No. 13; his 1972 recording of it (he made three in all) is altogether excellent – among the best things in the box. Of the newcomers, No. 10, recorded in 1974, has much to recommend it: Kondrashin allows the first movement time to breathe, and the same goes for the *Allegretto*. He captures the dark brooding quality of the introduction to the finale extremely well, even if the main body of the movement is a bit rushed; the recording is admirably faithful and vivid. His account of No. 5 comes from the mid-1960s; here again, tempi are distinctly on the fast side, both in the first movement and in the *Largo*; indeed this, the most popular of the symphonies, is the least acceptable. The first movement of the *Sixth* is also far too fast to do full justice to its breadth and depth, and even the *Ninth* suffers this fate. (His Concertgebouw performances on Philips are similarly flawed.) Oddly enough, the quicker one takes slow music, the longer it seems! The last three symphonies are undeniably the best: No. 15 is admirably characterized and splendidly recorded; along with No. 14, which has two distinguished soloists who make memorable contributions, it is really as good as any so far issued. Those who have the earlier box (now deleted) need not make the change; for other collectors, however, this is a useful compilation and at mid-price is eminently recommendable, even if the recommendation cannot be unqualified.

Symphonies Nos 1 in F, Op. 10; 6 in B min., Op. 54.
(*) Chan. Dig. **CHAN 8411; ABRD/*ABTD* 1148 [id.]. SNO, Järvi.

Symphonies Nos 1 in F min., Op. 10; 9 in E flat, Op. 70.
*** Decca Dig. **414 677-2**; SXDL/*KSXDC* 7515 [Lon. LDR/5- 71017]. LPO, Haitink.

Haitink's reading of the brilliant *First Symphony* may lack something in youthful high spirits (the finale does not sound quirky enough in the strange alternation of moods), but it is a strong, well-played performance none the less, and it is coupled with a superb account of No. 9, a symphony that has long been written off as trivial. Without inflation Haitink gives it a serious purpose, both in the poignancy of the waltz-like second movement and in the equivocal emotions of the outer movements, which here are not just superficially jolly, as they can so easily seem. The recording is outstandingly clean and brilliant, notably so on CD, with the cassette matching the LP closely.

Järvi's account of the *First Symphony* is strikingly more volatile than Haitink's in the outer movements – there is no lack of quirkiness in the finale, while the *Largo* is intense and passionate. The *Sixth* has comparable intensity, with an element of starkness in the austerity of the first movement, even if the reading is not quite as powerful as Berglund's, while the SNO strings do not command the body of tone produced by the Concertgebouw players under Haitink. The scherzo is skittish at first, but like the finale has no lack of pungent force. In both symphonies this is emphasized by the reverberant acoustics of Glasgow City Hall, bringing an element of brutality to climaxes (which are spectacularly expansive). This is less appropriate in the *First Symphony*. The CD underlines the wide dynamic range, affords striking presence to the wind soloists, but confirms the lack of amplitude in the massed strings. Yet these readings remain very convincing, and many will prefer Järvi's chimerical response to the changing moods of the *First Symphony* to Haitink's more serious manner. There is a very good chrome tape which copes remarkably well with the resonance.

Symphonies Nos 2 (October Revolution), Op. 14; 3 (The First of May), Op. 20.
*** Decca Dig. SXDL/*KSXDC* 7535 [Lon. LDR/5- 71035]. LPO Ch. and O, Haitink.

Shostakovich was still in his early twenties when he composed these symphonies, neither of which shows him at his most inspired, even if the opening of the *Second Symphony* enjoyed a certain avant-garde interest in its day. Admirable performances and excellently balanced sound with great presence and body. Those collecting Haitink's cycle need not hesitate. The cassette too is first class.

Symphony No. 4 in C min., Op. 43.
**(*) Decca SXL/*KSXC* 6927 [Lon. CS/5- 7160]. LPO, Haitink.

If the *Fourth Symphony* usually seems overweight in its scoring, with the vehement brutality explaining why it remained on the shelf for so long, Haitink brings out an unexpected refinement in the piece, a rare transparency of texture. He is helped by recording of demonstration quality on both disc and tape. Detail is superbly caught; yet the earthiness and power, the demonic quality which can make this work so compelling, are underplayed. One admires without being fully involved.

Symphony No. 5 in D min., Op. 47.

€ *** Decca Dig. **410 017-2**; SXDL/*KSXDC* 7551 [Lon. LDR/*5*- 71051]. Concg. O, Haitink.

*** Telarc Dig. **CD 80067**; DG 10067 [id.]. Cleveland O, Maazel.

*** CBS **CD 35854**; 35854/*40*- [id.]. NYPO, Bernstein.

** DG Dig. **410 509-2**; 2532/*3302* 076 [id.]. Nat. SO of Washington, Rostropovich.

Haitink is eminently straightforward and there are no disruptive changes in tempo. It comes as a breath of fresh air after the Rostropovich, and the playing of the Concertgebouw Orchestra and the contribution of the Decca engineers are beyond praise. There could perhaps be greater intensity of feeling in the slow movement, but, whatever small reservations one might have, it is at present a first recommendation artistically and a long way ahead in terms of sheer sound. The compact disc is superb and makes the LP, itself a demonstration disc, sound like a carbon copy by comparison. The presence, range and body of the sound in both forms is impressive, and the CD is one of the very best yet to appear. There is, however, an element of fierceness in the upper strings on the chrome tape.

Brilliant in performance, spectacular in recorded sound, like all of Maazel's Cleveland recordings for Telarc, this Shostakovich reading is also warm, with the Cleveland violins sweet and pure in the long-legged melody of the second subject in the first movement. Though Maazel is faster than is common in the exposition section, he allows himself less stringendo than usual in the build-up of the development. The other three movements are also on the fast side, with little feeling of Laendler rhythm in the scherzo and a sweet rather than rarefied reading of the *Largo* slow movement. This fits neatly between the spacious but rather severe reading of Haitink and the boldly expressive Bernstein.

Recorded in Tokyo in 1979, when Bernstein and the New York Philharmonic were on tour there, the CBS version is the weightiest on record, partly because of the interpretation but also because of the digital sound, which is particularly rich in bass. Unashamedly Bernstein treats the work as a Romantic symphony. The very opening makes an impact rarely possible in the concert hall; then, exceptionally, in the cool and beautiful second-subject melody Bernstein takes a slightly detached view – though as soon as that same melody comes up for development, after the exposition, the result is altogether more warmly expressive. Yet the movement's central climax, with its emphasis on the deep brass, injects a powerful element of menace, and the coda communicates a strongly Russian melancholy – which is perhaps why the composer admired Bernstein above other American interpreters of his music. The *Allegretto* becomes a burlesque, but its Mahlerian roots are strongly conveyed. The slow movement is raptly beautiful (marvellously sustained pianissimo playing from the New York Philharmonic strings), and the finale is brilliant and extrovert, with the first part dazzlingly fast and the conclusion one of unalloyed triumph, with no hint of irony. The chrome cassette is one of CBS's finest, carrying all the brilliance and weight of the disc. On CD, the bass is made to sound even fuller and richer than on LP, and the slight distancing of the sound (compared with many CBS recordings) places the orchestra within a believable ambience. Even so, this does not match the quality of Haitink's Decca CD.

Rostropovich's account is too idiosyncratic to be recommended without qualification. He secures a refined, cultured string-tone, capable of searing intensity and strength, and all sections of the orchestra play with excellent attack and ensemble. The opening is given with hushed *ppp* intensity (the marking is in fact *piano*) and all promises well until, as is so often the case with this great Russian musician, he disturbs the natural musical flow for the sake of expressive effect. The brakes are abruptly applied in the scherzo (at fig. 56), just before the horn figure is repeated, and he pulls other phrases around, too. He wrings the last ounce of intensity out of the finale, which is undoubtedly imposing, but there is also a hectoring quality which is distinctly unappealing (like being lectured by Solzhenitsyn on the moral decline of the West). The recording is on the whole good, even if it is a multi-mike, somewhat synthetic balance; and the CD will impress all who hear it as strikingly 'present'. It is only when the Decca CD is put alongside it that its limitations strike the listener. The cassette is wide-ranging and full-bodied, but slightly fierce on top.

Symphonies Nos 6 in B min., Op. 54; 9 in E flat, Op. 70.
*(*) Ph. 412 073-1/*4* [id.]. Concg. O, Kondrashin.

Kondrashin's account with the Concertgebouw Orchestra of the *Sixth* and *Ninth Symphonies* of Shostakovich disappoints, despite some superb playing. As in his earlier version with the Moscow Radio orchestra, he robs the first movement of the *Sixth* of its tragic breadth by too brisk an opening tempo. The marking (quaver = 76) is probably a bit on the slow side, but neither Reiner in his post-war Columbia recording nor Mravinsky are quite that slow – but they do convey the right feeling and power. The fast movements of the *Ninth*, fast in his earlier recordings, are still too headlong, except, perhaps, in the case of the finale. The second movement is another matter: the strings are sumptuous and the feeling of other-worldly melancholy is eloquently conveyed. The recordings, which date from 1968, are good without really being in the front rank. The cassette is very well managed, with refined detail at pianissimo level and climaxes only fractionally blurred by the Concertgebouw reverberation.

Symphonies Nos 6 in B min., Op. 54; 11 in G min. (1905), Op. 103.
*** HMV SLS 5177 (2). (B) *TCC2-POR 54286.* Bournemouth SO, Berglund.

Symphonies Nos 6 in B min., Op. 54; 11 in G min. (1905), Op. 103; Overture on Russian and Kirghiz folk themes, Op. 115.
*** Decca Dig. **411 939-2**; (without *Overture*) 411 939-1/*4* (2) [id.]. Concg. O, Haitink.

Berglund gives new tragic depth to the *Sixth* and, with similar rugged concentration, demonstrates the massive power of the *Eleventh*, a work which, with its programme based on the abortive 1905 uprising in Russia, usually seems far too thin in material. Shostakovich's pessimism in both works is underlined, with hardly a glimmer of hope allowed. In the *Sixth*, the very measured tempo for the first movement, taken direct and with little *espressivo*, points the link with the comparable movement of the *Eighth Symphony*; the remaining two movements are made ruthlessly bitter by not being sprung as dance movements, as is more usual. No Soviet optimism here. In the *Eleventh* too, even more daringly, Berglund lets the music speak for itself, keeping the long opening *Adagio* at a very steady, slow tread, made compelling by the hushed concentration of the Bournemouth playing. With superb recording, Berglund's art has never been more powerfully conveyed on record. On tape, this is issued at bargain price in HMV's 'Portrait of the Artist' series. Although iron-oxide stock is used, there is only marginal loss of range and the sound retains its weight and power and most of its bite. A splendid bargain!

Haitink's two-disc coupling of Nos 6 and 11 brings characteristically refined and powerful performances of two symphonies that have often been underestimated. With superb playing from the Concertgebouw, particularly the strings, the textures have an extra transparency, helped also by the brilliant and atmospheric Decca recording in all three formats. Haitink's structural control, coupled with his calm, taut manner, also brings out the weight and power of the big slow movements which open both works; the *Largo* of No. 6 is particularly impressive, containing, as it does, the main symphonic meat of the work, anticipating the comparable movement of No. 8. Nevertheless, in comparison with the rival set coupling these same two works, from Berglund and the Bournemouth orchestra, Haitink seems almost detached, marginally lacking the concentrated tension of a genuine performance. Berglund's commitment makes the vast slow expanses of No. 11 even more compelling and moving. On the Decca set, the CDs include the *Overture*, Op. 115, as a bonus.

Symphony No. 7 (Leningrad); Age of Gold: suite, Op. 22.
*** Decca Dig. D 213 D 2/*K 213 K 22* (2) [Lon. LDR/*5*- 10015]. LPO, Haitink.

Symphonies Nos 7 (Leningrad); 12 (The Year 1917), Op. 112.
*** Decca Dig. **412 392-2** (2). LPO or Concg. O, Haitink.

With his characteristic refinement and avoidance of bombast Haitink might not seem an apt conductor for the most publicized of Shostakovich's wartime symphonies, but in effect he transforms it, bringing out the nobility of many passages. One sees that the long first-movement *ostinato* – now revealed as having quite different implications from the descriptive programme suggested by the Soviet propaganda-machine in the war years – is almost an interlude in a work which otherwise in its deep seriousness challenges comparison with the other wartime symphony, the epic *Eighth*. The recording is of demonstration quality, and the fill-up, the joky *Age of Gold suite*, provides comparable brilliance. The cassette transfer is equally sophisticated, though the focus of the thundering side-drums slips just a little in the first-movement climax. As can be seen, the compact disc format includes also the *Twelfth Symphony* – see below – a very generous coupling. Moreover, the pairing is particularly well designed in putting together two symphonies that have been seriously underestimated. The first compact disc contains the whole of No. 12, played without a break, as the composer wanted, followed by the long first movement of the *Leningrad*, some 72 minutes in all. The CD transfer brings the usual enhancement and greater sense of presence.

Symphony No. 8 in C min., Op. 64.
*** Decca Dig. **411 616-2**; SXDL/*KSXDC* 7621 [Lon. LDR/5- 71121]. Concg. O, Haitink.
*** HMV Dig. EL 270290-1/*4*. Bournemouth SO, Barshai.

The *Eighth Symphony*, written in response to the sufferings of the Russian people during the Second World War, is one of Shostakovich's most powerful and intense creations, starting with a slow movement almost half an hour long, which emerges as not only emotionally involving but cogent in symphonic terms too. The sharp unpredictability of the remaining movements, alternately cajoling and battering the listener, shows Shostakovich at his most inspired.

Haitink characteristically presents a strongly architectural reading of this war-inspired symphony, at times direct to the point of severity. After the massive and sustained slow movement which opens the work, Haitink allows no lightness or relief in the scherzo movements, and in his seriousness in the strangely lightweight finale (neither fast nor slow) he provides an unusually satisfying account of an equivocal, seemingly uncommitted movement. The playing of the Concertgebouw Orchestra is immaculate and the digital recording full, brilliant and clear on both disc and chrome cassette (though on tape the upper strings have marginally less body than on LP). The compact disc has the usual virtues of added presence and definition, although it is marginally less impressive than the companion CD of the *Fifth Symphony*.

Barshai holds up surprisingly well against the competition it faces from its outstanding Decca rival. The noble symphonic *Adagio* which opens the work is marvellously sustained and the playing of the Bournemouth orchestra is extremely fine in all departments. In one or two exposed passages the strings do not quite match the bloom and lustre of their celebrated Dutch colleagues, but no apologies need to be made for the Bournemouth Symphony Orchestra these days. This is a finely paced and powerful reading which, particularly in the first movement, has a wonderfully brooding intensity and eloquence. In the *Allegretto*, Barshai adopts the recommended crotchet = 132, and most listeners will at first think this too slow; Haitink is appreciably faster. However, it is what the composer asks for, and the result inevitably seems weightier. In the third movement Barshai is less successful in sustaining tension and momentum. The *Passacaglia* is very powerful and has a real epic sweep. As far as sound quality is concerned, the balance could hardly be improved upon, and the excellent acoustic is used to splendid and often thrilling effect. The perspective is consistent and well judged, and detail is wonderfully present. If the Haitink/Concertgebouw account on Decca must remain the preferred version, this is still a very formidable competitor. The cassette too is very successful, vividly detailed and only losing a little of the sharpness of focus of the LP in the most spectacular climaxes.

Symphony No. 10 in E min., Op. 93.
*** DG Dig. **413 361-2**; 2532/*3302* 030 [id.]. BPO, Karajan.
(B) **(*) CfP CFP 41 4472-1/*4*. LPO, Andrew Davis.

Already in his 1967 recording Karajan had shown that he had the measure of this symphony; this newer version is, if anything, even finer. In the first movement he distils an atmosphere as concentrated as before, bleak and unremitting, while in the *Allegro* the Berlin Philharmonic leave no doubts as to their peerless virtuosity. Everything is marvellously shaped and proportioned. The *allegro* section of the finale is taken up to speed (176 crotchets to the minute), faster than Mitropoulos and much faster than most other rivals. The digital sound is altogether excellent, and this must now rank as a first recommendation. It has greater intensity and grip than Haitink (the LPO's playing is not quite in the same league), and though Mitropoulos's pioneering account is still to be treasured, this 1982 Berlin version is marvellously powerful and gripping. The CD enjoys the usual advantages of greater range and presence; but the cassette too is of demonstration quality, with splendid range, body and detail.

Andrew Davis draws a fresh and direct reading from the LPO, not so powerfully individual as Karajan's or Haitink's (Decca SXL/*KSXC* 6838 [Lon. CS/*5*- 7061]), but consistently compelling both in the long paragraphs of the first and third movements and in the pointedly rhythmic second and fourth. Excellent recording quality. A first-rate bargain, with a very good equivalent cassette.

Mravinsky's Leningrad recording remains available on Saga (5228). The virtues of this performance are well known: it has impressive authority, a masterly grasp of architecture and great depth of feeling. However, the recording was not good even in its day. The primitive sound will present a major obstacle to the collector, even though the pressing is exemplary. The frequency range of this Russian recording, made in the mid-1950s at about the same time as the 1954 Mitropoulos account, is very limited and climaxes suffer from distortion. Even if something of the stature of the performance can still be glimpsed, it is not really possible to recommend it.

Symphony No. 12 in D min. (*The Year 1917*), *Op. 112; Overture on Russian and Kirghis folk themes, Op. 115.* (See also under *Symphony No. 7.*)
*** Decca Dig. SXDL/*KSXDC* 7577 [Lon. LDR/5- 71077]. Concg. O, Haitink.

The *Twelfth* is most strikingly recorded by the Decca team, even judged by the high standards of the house. Indeed, the sheer quality of sound and the superb responsiveness and body of the Concertgebouw Orchestra might well seduce some listeners and make friends for a work that has so far found little favour. For while the finest of the symphonies have the epic, panoramic sweep of the great Russian novelists, the more 'public' works, among which the *Twelfth* must be numbered, come closer to the patriotic and more repetitive Eisenstein films. There is much of the composer's vision and grandeur but also his crudeness. The slow movement, however, has a marvellous sense of atmosphere which is well conveyed in this new performance – as it was, to be fair, in Mravinsky's pioneering account with the Leningrad Philharmonic. The control is masterly and the great Amsterdam orchestra play as if they believe every crotchet, though not even their eloquence can altogether rescue the finale. However, there is no doubt that this is the most successful version so far of No. 12 and it supersedes all its predecessors – and, moreover, offers a fill-up in the shape of the *Overture on Russian and Kirghis folk themes* from the same period. The chrome cassette is exceptionally wide-ranging and vivid, although, as with other tape issues in this Concertgebouw series, the upper range needs a little taming. On CD, this *Symphony* is coupled – very appropriately – with the *Leningrad symphony* (see above).

Symphony No. 13 in B flat min. (*Babi-Yar*), *Op. 113.*
Ͼ *** Decca Dig. **417 261-2** [id.]. Rintzler, Concg. Male Ch. and O, Haitink.

(i) *Symphony No. 13;* (ii; iii) *From Jewish Folk Poetry, Op. 79;* (ii) *6 Poems of Marina Tsvetaeva, Op. 143a.*
*** Decca Dig. 414 410-1/*4* (2) [id.]. Concg. O, Haitink, with (i) Rintzler and Male Ch.; (ii) Wenkel; (iii) Söderström, Wenkel, Karcykowski.

The often brutal directness of Haitink's way with Shostakovich works well in the *Thirteenth Symphony*, particularly in the long *Adagio* first movement, whose title, *Babi-Yar*, gives its name to the whole work. That first of five Yevtushenko settings boldly attacking anti-semitism in Russia sets the pattern for Haitink's severe view of the whole. The second movement, *Humour*, is made an unrelenting dance of death, missing something in irony; and the third movement, with its picture of women queueing in the snow outside a grocer's store, is less atmospheric than austere. Rintzler with his magnificent, resonant bass is musically superb but, matching Haitink, remains objective rather than dashingly characterful. The resolution of the final movement, with its pretty flutings surrounding a wry poem about Galileo and greatness, then works beautifully. Outstandingly brilliant and full sound, remarkable even for this series. The CD offers the *Symphony* alone; the LPs and matching cassettes (hardly less demonstration-worthy) include the two song-cycles that on CD are to be coupled with the last two symphonies (which are scheduled for issue during the lifetime of this book). Both cycles are splendidly sung; though they too are often sombre, as always with Shostakovich there are moments of tenderness and humour – even happiness, as in the last of the Jewish cycle. Ryszard Karcykowski brings vibrant Slavonic feeling to his contribution to the latter work which, with its wide variety of mood and colour, and imaginative eloquence, has a scale to match the shorter symphonies.

Symphony No. 14, Op. 135.
*** Decca Dig. SXDL/*KSXDC* 7532 [Lon. LDR/5- 71032]. Varady, Fischer-Dieskau, Concg. O, Haitink.

The *Fourteenth* is Shostakovich's most sombre and dark score, a setting of poems by Lorca, Apollinaire, Rilke, Brentano and Küchelbecker, all on the theme of death. It is similar in conception (though not in character) to Britten's *Nocturne* or *Spring symphony*, and is in fact dedicated to him. Earlier recordings under Barshai, Ormandy and Rostropovich have all been in Russian, but this version gives each poem in the original. This is a most powerful performance under Haitink, and the outstanding recording is equally impressive on disc and the excellent chrome tape.

Symphony No. 15 in A, Op. 141.
❀ *** Decca SXL/*KSXC* 6906 [Lon. CS 7130]. LPO, Haitink.
*(*) Melodiya **VCD 528**. USSR SO, Rozhdestvensky.

This was the second issue in Haitink's Shostakovich series and it brings a performance which is a revelation. Early readings of the composer's last symphony seemed to underline the quirky unpredictability of the work, with the collage of strange quotations – above all the *William Tell* gallop, which keeps recurring in the first movement – seemingly joky rather than profound. Haitink by contrast makes the first movement sound genuinely symphonic, bitingly urgent. He underlines the purity of the bare lines of the second movement; after the Wagner quotations which open the finale, his slow tempo for the main lyrical theme gives it heartaching tenderness, not the usual easy triviality. The playing of the LPO is excellent, with refined tone and superb attack, and the recording is both analytical and atmospheric, as impressive on cassette as on disc. Although the textures are generally spare, the few heavy tuttis are difficult for the engineers, and Decca sound copes with them splendidly.

Rozhdestvensky's Melodiya issue brings a sharply Slavonic reading, full of the idiomatic feeling for rhythm and phrase that comes from an orchestra of players seemingly born to this music. Rozhdestvensky, the inspirer, equally brings out the quirkiness of the composer's last symphony, while holding the structure tautly together. Sadly, the recording with its harshness and unnatural highlighting of particular instruments harks back to the bad old days of Russian recording.

CHAMBER AND INSTRUMENTAL MUSIC

Cello sonata in D min., Op. 40.
*** Chan. Dig. **CHAN 8340**; ABRD/*ABTD* 1072 [id.]. Turovsky, Edlina – PROKOFIEV: *Sonata.****
** Denon Dig. **C37 7563** [id.]. Fujiwara, Rouvier – STRAVINSKY: *Suite italienne*; DEBUSSY: *Cello sonata.***

Yuli Turovsky and Luba Edlina play the *Cello sonata* with great panache and eloquence. At times, in the finale, they almost succumb to exaggeration in their handling of its humour – no understatement here. However, they are totally inside this music and the recording reproduces them truthfully. The record is also of particular value in restoring the Prokofiev *Sonata* to circulation after an absence of some years. The chrome cassette, made at the highest level, gives the artists great presence, but the balance gives slight exaggeration to the upper partials of the cello timbre.

The coupling will probably decide matters for most readers as far as the Denon version is concerned. Fujiwara and Rouvier are quite brisk in the opening movement but slow up considerably for the second subject. Spirited though their playing is, they do not displace the Chandos CD by Turovsky and Edlina.

Piano quintet, Op. 57; Piano trio No. 2 in E min., Op. 67.
(*) Chan. Dig. **CHAN 8342; ABRD/*ABTD* 1088 [id.]. Borodin Trio, Zweig, Horner.
**(*) ASV ALH/*ZCALH* 929 [id.]. Music Group of London.

(i) *Piano quintet, Op. 57; String quartets Nos 7 in F sharp min., Op. 108; 8 in C min., Op. 110.*
**(*) HMV Dig. EL 270338-1/*4*. (i) Sviatoslav Richter; Borodin Qt.

Piano trio No. 2 in E min., Op. 67.
(M) **(*) Ph. 412 402-1/*4*. Beaux Arts Trio – IVES: *Piano trio.***(*)

The Chandos and ASV discs bring together two of Shostakovich's most important chamber works. The Chandos version of the *Quintet* is bolder in character and more concentrated in feeling than either of the rival versions. There are one or two moments of vulnerable intonation but these are of little account, given the intensity of this playing. The Music Group of London show rather less panache but are still impressive, and in their hands the *Trio* is affectingly played. This is a particularly painful and anguished work, dedicated to the memory of a close friend, Ivan Sollertinsky, who died in the year of its composition. Excellent balance and good recording quality make this ASV disc an attractive proposition, although on performance alone the Chandos issue remains first choice. Here the sound is vivid, though the microphones are rather close and there is too much reverberation round the piano, an effect the more noticeable on CD. On tape, the presence is no less striking, although the string focus is not absolutely clean. The ASV tape is of good quality, and the resonance brings only very slight clouding to the piano focus.

A powerful performance by Richter and the Borodins of the *Piano quintet*, recorded at a public concert at the Moscow Conservatoire, and it goes without saying that the two *Quartets* are superbly played, too. Although the quality of the recorded sound is on the dry side in Nos 7 and 8, it is by no means as dry as some of the others in the complete set listed below, and it produces a first-class cassette transfer. This coupling contains 70 minutes of music and is at full price. It is, of course, included in the seven-record complete set at mid-price.

The Beaux Arts version of the *Second Piano trio* comes from the mid-1970s and has the advantage of excellent Philips engineering. The performance is dedicated and deeply felt: the Beaux Arts have its measure, and readers not whole-heartedly committed to compact disc may well prefer this mid-price account to the Borodins on Chandos. There is a good tape.

String quartets Nos 1–15; (i) *Piano quintet in G min., Op. 57.*
(M) **(*) HMV Dig. EX 270339-3 (7). (i) Sviatoslav Richter; Borodin Qt.

The Borodin Quartet recorded a complete cycle in the period from the late 1960s to the early 1970s; they could not, of course, include the last two quartets, which were not composed until 1973–4. (They subsequently repaired this omission, but their accounts, while available on the Continent, were not issued in the UK.) This newcomer naturally includes them all – and the *Piano quintet* for good measure, in an imposing performance with Sviatoslav Richter, recorded at a public concert in 1983. The layout of the new set is superior in one small but not unimportant respect: whereas their earlier set involved side-breaks in Nos 2 and 3 (and the Fitzwilliams have side-breaks in Nos 2, 3 and 13), every quartet in the new set can be enjoyed without interruption. The Shostakovich *Quartets* thread through his creative life like some inner odyssey and inhabit terrain of increasing spiritual desolation. The Borodins are masterly guides throughout, and listening to this set over a fairly long period reaffirms admiration for this impressive cycle. The performances altogether can only be described as masterly. Two of them, apart from the *Quintet*, derive from concerts, but the audience is commendably attentive and their presence is only momentarily betrayed in the slow movement of the *Sixth*. The very first thing that strikes the ear, however, is the somewhat drier acoustic of this recording. In this respect the earlier set is to be preferred – and so, of course, is the Fitzwilliam on Decca, Oiseau-Lyre. The ear soon adjusts, although in the *Fifth Quartet* the sound seems significantly drier and harder than before. This is a pity since this is an altogether compelling account, and its quieter moments are particularly moving. In No. 6, comparison with the earlier Borodin set shows that though the earlier performance is not so eloquent, the recording is undoubtedly warmer. Readers who have already invested in the Fitzwilliam set need not feel that their allegiance has been misplaced. The Borodins possess enormous refinement, an altogether sumptuous tone, and a perfection of technical address that is almost in a class of its own, and the complete set is offered at mid-price. This mundane (but hardly insignificant!) factor may well be decisive for some collectors, in spite of the fact that the Borodins are not so well served in terms of recorded sound. There is no cassette version.

Reminder. The Fitzwilliam set remains available on Decca Oiseau-Lyre (D 188 D 7).

Violin sonata, Op. 134.
*** Chan. Dig. **CHAN 8343**; ABRD/*ABTD* 1089 [id.]. Dubinsky, Edlina – SCHNITTKE: *Sonata No. 1* etc.***

Shostakovich composed his *Sonata* for Oistrakh's sixtieth birthday, and since his pioneering record, issued in the early 1970s, there have been versions by Kremer, Gavrilov and Lubotsky, also coupled with Schnittke, which all succumbed (like the Oistrakh/Richter version) to rapid deletion. The *Sonata* is a bitter and at times arid score, thought-provoking and, unusually in this composer, not totally convincing. Rostislav Dubinsky's account is undoubtedly eloquent, and Luba Edlina makes a fine partner. The recording is excellent too, with vivid presence, especially on CD, although it is balanced a shade closely. The Chandos chrome tape is clear and well focused and should provide a satisfying alternative in this medium.

Sibelius, Jean (1865–1957)

The Bard, Op. 64; The Dryad, Op. 45/1; En Saga, Op. 9; Finlandia, Op. 26; (i) *Luonnotar, Op. 70; Night ride and sunrise, Op. 55; The Oceanides, Op. 73; Pohjola's daughter, Op. 49; Tapiola, Op. 112; Varsäng* (*Spring song*)*, Op. 16.*
(*) Chan. **CHAN 8395/6; CBR/*CBT* 1027/8 [id.]. SNO, Gibson, (i) with Phyllis Bryn-Julson.

Sir Alexander Gibson's analogue recordings of the Sibelius tone-poems date from the late 1970s and were originally issued by RCA. The recordings have been digitally remastered with great success; the slightly distant sound balance is admirably suited to the music, with the spacious acoustic of Glasgow City Hall generally flattering the orchestra and creating a suitable ambient atmosphere. Gibson's affinity with the Sibelius idiom is at its most convincing here, particularly in the more elusive pieces, like *The Bard* and the *The Dryad*, although *En Saga*, which opens the collection, is also both evocative and shows an impressive overall grasp. Sometimes one would have welcomed a greater degree of dramatic intensity, and both *Pohjola's daughter* and *Tapiola* fall a little short in this respect, while *Night ride and sunrise* does not fully blossom until the closing section. Nevertheless there is much that is impressive here, and the fine playing and natural perspectives of the recording contribute a great deal to the music making in all formats. In *Luonnotar* the soprano voice is made to seem like another orchestral instrument; while there have been more histrionic versions, the singing is tonally beautiful, sensitive and well controlled. The LPs and the excellent cassettes are at mid-price. However, on CD the recordings sound particularly fine: the strings are given a lovely freshness and bloom in *The Bard* and *The Dryad*, and have diaphanous delicacy of texture in *The Oceanides*. Although both ends of the sound spectrum are less sharply focused than in a true digital recording (most noticeable in *En Saga*) climaxes are made excitingly expansive, with the brass superbly sonorous: *Night ride and sunrise*, *Pohjola's daughter* and *Tapiola* are all enhanced.

Violin concerto in D min., Op. 47.

(M) *** RCA Gold GL/*GK* 89832. Heifetz, Chicago SO, Hendl – BRUCH: *Scottish fantasia.****

*** HMV **CDC 747167-2** [id.]; ASD/*TC-ASD* 3933 [Ang. SZ/*4ZS* 37663]. Perlman, Pittsburgh SO, Previn – SINDING: *Suite.****

(*) Erato **ECD 88109 [id.]. Amoyal, Philh. O, Dutoit – TCHAIKOVSKY: *Violin concerto.***(*)

(*) PRT **CDPCN 14. Yaron, LPO, Soudant – TCHAIKOVSKY: *Concerto.***

** HMV Dig. **CDC 747110-2** [id.]; ASD/*TC-ASD* 143519-1/*4* [Ang. DS/*4XS* 37957]. Kremer, Philh. O, Muti – SCHUMANN: *Concerto.***(*)

Heifetz's performance of the Sibelius *Concerto* with the Chicago Symphony Orchestra under Walter Hendl set the standard by which all other versions have come to be judged. It is also one of his finest recordings; in remastered form the sound is vivid, with the Chicago ambience making an apt setting for the finely focused violin line. The purity and luminous beauty of the violin tone at the opening put the seal on this as an interpretation of unusual depth, consummate technique and supreme artistry. At medium price this should be in every collection, with disc and tape sounding virtually identical; but CD collectors will note that in the USA this is already available on compact disc, coupled with Heifetz's equally indispensable accounts of the Glazounov and the Prokofiev *Second* [**RCD1 7019**].

Itzhak Perlman first recorded this concerto in the mid-1960s with Leinsdorf and the Boston Symphony for RCA. Here he plays the work as a full-blooded virtuoso showpiece, and the Pittsburgh orchestra under André Previn support him to the last man and woman. In the first movement his tempo is broader than that of Heifetz, and in the rest of the work he seems more expansive than he was in the earlier record. The new version takes 32′ 00″, whereas his Boston performance took 29′ 15″ (and fitted on one LP side). He is at his stunning best in the first cadenza and makes light of all the fiendish difficulties in which the solo part abounds. Perlman takes a conventional view of the slow movement, underlining its passion, and he gives us an exhilarating finale. The balance places Perlman rather forward. On both disc and cassette the sound is marvellously alive and thrilling, while the CD has the usual improvement in presence and definition, though the forward balance is even more apparent.

Admirers of Pierre Amoyal will not be surprised to learn that his interpretation can hold its own with most now available. He brings a splendid ardour, refined taste and great purity of tone to the concerto; and it goes without saying that he surmounts its many technical hurdles with aplomb. He is free from that slight suggestion of the *zigeuner* that disfigures Belkin's account with Ashkenazy on Decca (SXL 6953) and has greater spirituality than Kremer. The finale perhaps lacks the sheer excitement of Heifetz, whose pupil he was in the late 1960s; nevertheless it is good, and in the slow movement Amoyal has nobility and warmth. The recording is very natural, with a decent perspective and balance.

Yuval Yaron won the Sibelius Prize in Helsinki in 1975; the young Israeli violinist made this analogue recording in 1978. It is a more inward-looking reading than Perlman's, opening gently, and Yaron is persuasively poetic. The *Adagio* blossoms eloquently, with good support from Soudant who elsewhere is markedly less passionate than Previn or Muti, although the urgency of the solo playing is not inhibited. The analogue recording is atmospheric and more naturally balanced than either of the HMV versions, but not nearly as vividly detailed. Overall, it is an account easy to enjoy but not distinctive enough to recommend as a first choice. Moreover, the Tchaikovsky coupling has rather less tension.

Kremer presents the *Concerto* essentially as a bravura showpiece and his is a vibrantly extrovert reading. While the recording balance places the soloist well forward, the orchestral texture has plenty of impact and good detail, and the fortissimo brass blaze out excitingly. There is undoubted poetry in the slow movement, and throughout Muti gives his soloist splendid support. However, their version does not displace Perlman nor, for that matter, the Chung account, which is beautifully subtle and warm (Decca SXL/*KSXC* 6493 – not yet available on CD). Both are more searching than Kremer and have more character, albeit in very different ways. Generally speaking, they all have more attractive couplings. The HMV XDR cassette matches the LP closely. The CD adds presence and sharpens detail, with the solo timbre very real and tangible, but the ear notices that the bass might be fuller in relation to the bright upper range.

(i) *Violin concerto; Symphony No. 5 in E flat, Op. 82; Tapiola, Op. 112.*
(B) **(*) DG Walkman *415 619-4* [id.]. (i) Ferras; BPO, Karajan.

Christian Ferras's account of the *Violin concerto* is a very good one and is well recorded. Although he begins the work with a winningly golden tone, when he is under stress, at the end of the first movement and in the finale, his intonation and general security are less than impeccable. However, there is still much to enjoy, and Ferras again develops a rich romantic tone for the main tune of the slow movement. The couplings, also from the mid-1960s, are outstanding. *Tapiola* is a performance of great intensity and offers superlative playing. The

1964 recording of the *Fifth Symphony* is undoubtedly a great performance. The orchestral playing throughout is glorious and the effect is spacious and atmospheric. Karajan finds an engrossing sense of mystery in the development section of the first movement, and there is jubilation in the finale. The only snag is that this Walkman tape is transferred at the highest level and there is a degree of harshness in the climaxes of the *Symphony*. The recording sounds freer and altogether more impressive in its CD format (coupled with the *Seventh Symphony* – see below), but this tape remains a formidable bargain.

Canzonette, Op. 62a; Impromptu for string orchestra; Kuolema: Scene with cranes; Valse triste, Op. 44/2–3. Presto. Romance for string orchestra, Op. 42; Suite caractéristique, Op. 100; Suite champêtre, Op. 98b; Suite mignonne, Op. 98a; Valse romantique, Op. 62b.
*** Finlandia FAD 354 [id.]. Finlandia Sinf., Hellasvuo.

A useful anthology of lighter Sibelius pieces, some of which (the *Impromptu for string orchestra*, *Presto* and *Suite caractéristique*, Op. 100) are not otherwise available. The Finlandia Sinfonietta are all members of the Helsinki Philharmonic – and very good they are, too. The material of the *Presto* (1894) is in fact of earlier provenance and is a transcription of the scherzo movement of the *B flat Quartet*, Op. 4, while its companion, the *Impromptu for strings*, is an arrangement of the fifth and sixth *Impromptus* for piano of 1894. The two *Suites*, Op. 98, could without much exaggeration be called Tchaikovsky with a Sibelian accent. The later Op. 100, written in 1922, is poor stuff – worlds removed from the level of inspiration and poetry of the *Scene with cranes*. The performances are very well shaped by Pekka Hellasvuo, and while Rattle distils the stronger atmosphere in the *Scene with cranes* (the fill-up to his account of the *Second Symphony* – see below), there is not a great deal in it. The recording is cleanly focused and well balanced.

(i) *Finlandia, Op. 26;* (ii) *Karelia suite, Op. 11;* (i) *Kuolema: Valse triste, Op. 44.*
(B) *** DG Walkman *413 158-4* [id.]. (i) BPO, Karajan; (ii) Helsinki R.O, Kamu – GRIEG: *Piano concerto*; *Peer Gynt.***

Finlandia, Op. 26; Kuolema: Valse triste, Op. 44.
(M) *** DG Sig. 410 981-1/*4*. BPO, Karajan – GRIEG: *Peer Gynt.****

These are familiar performances from the mid-1960s. *Valse triste* is played very slowly and in a somewhat mannered fashion. *Finlandia* is one of the finest accounts available, with eloquent playing from the Berliners, although on the Signature LP one notices that the digital remastering has brightened the sound and that it has rather less body than originally, though it is still impressive. Disc and tape are virtually identical.

The bargain Walkman tape adds to the Karajan performances Kamu's splendid *Karelia suite*, as fine as any available, the outer movements atmospheric and exciting and the *Ballade* eloquently played, without idiosyncrasy. The sound is very good, too; Karajan's *Finlandia* has slightly more body here than on the

Signature issue. If the couplings are suitable (and Géza Anda's account of the Grieg *Piano concerto*, if not among the finest available, is certainly enjoyable), this is excellent value.

Finlandia, Op. 26; Karelia suite, Op. 11; Kuolema: Valse triste, Op. 44; Legend: The Swan of Tuonela, Op. 22/2; Pohjola's daughter, Op. 49.
** D Sharp **DSDC 1002**; DSLP/*DSMC* 1002. LSO, Rozhdestvensky.

Finlandia, Op. 26; Karelia suite, Op. 11; Kuolema: Valse triste, Op. 44; Legend: The Swan of Tuonela, Op. 22/2.
(M) ** Ph. Seq. 412 014-1/*4*. Boston SO, Sir Colin Davis.

Rozhdestvensky's performances, very well played, are highly individual but often wayward in their control of the music's pulse. The opening of *Finlandia* is very grand and portentous, the overall conception spacious, but the ritenutos in *Valse triste* are rather indulgent. The central *Ballade* of the *Karelia suite* is very measured, though evocative, yet the *Alla marcia* has a fine climax. Rozhdestvensky is at his most convincingly poetic in the rhapsodic *Swan of Tuonela* (with a memorable solo from the cor anglais), and the opening and closing sections of *Pohjola's daughter* are also tellingly atmospheric, although again one misses a consistent forward momentum. The recording, made in EMI's No. 1 Studio, is impressively balanced to give a concert-hall effect, with a warm ambience. On CD, the slightly sharper focus makes plain, however, that this is a studio venue.

Davis's *Finlandia* is impressively expansive and *The Swan of Tuonela* has a powerful atmosphere. In *Karelia*, however, the sound is rather clouded by the resonance, and the tempo for the *Intermezzo* seems rather too deliberate. The cassette reflects the disc faithfully.

Finlandia; Karelia suite, Op. 11. Kuolema: Valse triste. Legends: Lemminkäinen's return, Op. 22/4; Pohjola's daughter, Op. 49.
(M) **(*) HMV EG 290273-1/*4* [Ang. AM/*4AM* 34712]. Hallé O, Barbirolli.

Although the orchestral playing is not as polished as that of a virtuoso orchestra, it is enthusiastic and has the advantage of excellent recording. *Pohjola's daughter* is extremely impressive, spacious but no less exciting for all the slower tempi. *Lemminkäinen's return* is also a thrilling performance. Overall, a desirable introduction to Sibelius's smaller orchestral pieces, with admirable stereo definition, although the cassette lacks something in glitter on top, which affects the percussion transients. The original recording dates from the mid-1960s but has been effectively remastered digitally.

Finlandia, Op. 26; Kuolema: Valse triste, Op. 44; Legends: The Swan of Tuonela, Op. 22/2. Tapiola, Op. 112.
*** DG Dig. **413 755-2**; 413 755-1/*4* [id.]. BPO, Karajan.

Karajan first recorded *Tapiola* with the Philharmonia Orchestra, then again in

1965 and 1977, on both occasions with the Berlin Philharmonic. This is his fourth and undoubtedly his greatest account of this score, for it has the full measure of its vision and power. Never has it sounded more mysterious or its dreams more savage, and the wood-sprites weaving their magic secrets come vividly to life. The great classic accounts from Kajanus, Koussevitzky and Beecham are all imaginative in their very different ways; however, while they may offer different insights, they are not superior to the new Karajan. Nor has the build-up to the storm ever struck such a chilling note of terror: an awesomely impressive musical landscape. *The Swan*, Karajan's third account on record, is powerful and atmospheric; and the remaining two pieces, *Valse triste* and *Finlandia*, reinforce the feeling that this Berlin/Karajan partnership has never been equalled, not even by Toscanini and the NBC Symphony Orchestra. As a recording, this does not surpass the Philharmonia version under Ashkenazy, coupled with the *Fourth Symphony* and *Luonnotar* on Decca, but it does not fall far short; the orchestral playing is, of course, really in a class of its own.

Karelia suite, Op. 11; Legend: The Swan of Tuonela, Op. 22/2.
** Ph. **412 727-2**; 412 727-1/*4* [id.]. ASMF, Marriner – GRIEG: *Holberg suite*; *Lyric pieces*.**(*)

Marriner's performance of *Karelia* is curiously subdued (though on CD, against the background silence, the pianissimo opening of the *Intermezzo* is very telling) and the closing *Alla marcia* could be more exuberant. Even the central *Ballade* seems to lack momentum, though the cor anglais solo is beautifully played by Barry Griffiths, who is no less eloquent in *The Swan of Tuonela*. The recording is most naturally balanced. The cassette is generally excellent, though in *Karelia* the percussion is less telling in the tape format.

4 Legends, Op. 22 (*Lemminkäinen and the maidens of Saari; The Swan of Tuonela; Lemminkäinen in Tuonela; Lemminkäinen's return*).
*** BIS Dig. **CD 294**; LP 294. Gothenburg SO, Järvi.
*** Chan. **CHAN 8394**; CBR/*CBT* 1026 [id.]. SNO, Gibson.

Choice between the only two current versions of the *Legends* is not straightforward. On LP and cassette, Gibson has the advantage of economy, but Järvi offers modern digital sound. As far as recording quality is concerned, the latter's issue is very impressive, with splendid range and presence and a wonderfully truthful balance. How good it is to hear solo violins sounding so naturally life-size – and not larger than life! The bass drum sounds impressively realistic, too – not just on compact disc but on LP as well. Järvi gives a passionate and atmospheric account of the first *Legend*. One small reservation concerning internal balance comes in its closing paragraph, where the sustained chords on horns and trombone are obtrusively loud, thus masking the woodwind cries and robbing the coda of much of its atmosphere. Järvi's account of *The Swan of Tuonela* is altogether magical, one of the best in the catalogue. He takes a broader view of

Lemminkäinen in Tuonela than many of his rivals and builds up an appropriately black and powerful atmosphere, showing the Gothenburg brass to excellent advantage. The slight disappointment is *Lemminkäinen's homeward journey* which, though exciting, hasn't the possessed, manic quality of Beecham's very first record, which sounded as if a thousand demons were in pursuit.

In many ways this is the finest Sibelius recording Gibson has given us. The recording – originally issued by RCA – dates from 1979 and the distanced balance is particularly suitable for these scores, especially as the digital remastering has refined inner detail. The Scottish orchestra play freshly and with much commitment. *The Swan of Tuonela* has a darkly brooding primeval quality, and there is an electric degree of tension in the third piece, *Lemminkäinen in Tuonela*. The two outer *Legends* have ardent rhythmic feeling, and altogether this is highly successful. The recorded sound is excellent in both formats. The CD is announced as we go to press; but the LP and first-class cassette sound very well indeed and are offered in the medium-price range.

Pelléas et Mélisande: suite.

*** DG Dig. **410 026-2**; 2532/*3302* 068 [id.]. BPO, Karajan – GRIEG: *Peer Gynt suites 1 and 2.****

At last a version of Sibelius's subtle and atmospheric score that can compare with the classic Beecham version, originally dating from 1957. Indeed in certain movements, *By the spring in the park* and the *Pastorale*, it not only matches Sir Thomas but almost surpasses him. The *Pastorale* is altogether magical, and there is plenty of mystery in the third movement, *At the seashore*, omitted from the Beecham set. Some may find the opening movement, *At the castle gate*, a little too imposing, but the fervour and eloquence of the playing should win over most listeners. The recording, particularly on compact disc, is very striking indeed, with greater clarity and presence. Although Beecham's record (HMV SXLP 30197) will remain indispensable for most Sibelians, the Karajan must now be a prime recommendation.

Rakastava (suite), *Op. 14; Scènes historiques, Opp. 25, 66; Valse lyrique, Op. 96/1.*

*** Chan. **CHAN 8393**; CBR/*CBT* 1025 [id.]. SNO, Gibson.

Written for a patriotic pageant, the *Scènes historiques* are vintage Sibelius; some of them (the *Scena*, Op. 25, No. 2, and the *Love song*, Op. 66, No. 2) plumb real depths of feeling, while others, like *The Chase*, Op. 66, No. 1, have a sense of the sweep and grandeur of nature. In the *Love song* Gibson strikes the right blend of depth and reticence, while elsewhere he conveys a fine sense of controlled power. Convincing and eloquent performances that have a natural feeling for the music. Gibson's *Rakastava* is beautifully unforced and natural, save for the last movement, which is a shade too slow. The *Valse lyrique* is not good Sibelius, but everything else certainly is. Gibson plays this repertoire with real commitment. The recorded sound is excellent, with the relationships between the various sections of the orchestra very well judged. The digital remastering (the original dates from 1977) is very successful, with the orchestral layout, slightly distanced, most believable. As with the other issues in Gibson's series of Sibelius orchestral music, the LP and the excellent tape are offered at mid-price. The CD is announced as we go to press.

Symphony No. 1 in E min., Op. 39; Finlandia, Op. 26.
** **BIS CD 221**; LP 221. Gothenburg SO, Järvi.

Symphony No. 1 in E min., Op. 39; Karelia suite, Op. 11.
ℭ *** Decca Dig. **414 534-2;** 414 534-1/*4* [id.]. Philh. O, Ashkenazy.

Symphony No. 1 in E min., Op. 39; The Oceanides, Op. 73.
**(*) HMV Dig. EL 270309-1/*4* [Ang. DS/*4DS* 38264]. CBSO, Rattle.

Symphonies Nos 1 in E min., Op. 39; 7 in C, Op. 105.
*(*) Chan. Dig. **CHAN 8344**; ABRD/*ABTD* 1086 [id.]. SNO, Gibson.

As a recording, Ashkenazy on Decca is quite simply the best of all. It has superb detail and clarity of texture, and there is all the presence and body one could ask for. The bass-drum rolls are particularly realistic! Moreover, it is as successful artistically as it is in terms of recorded sound, and further evidence – if such be needed – of Ashkenazy's growing mastery as a conductor. It is well held together and finely shaped; it is every bit as committed as Simon Rattle's with the CBSO but free from the occasional mannerism that disfigures his account. Ashkenazy is exactly on target in the scherzo (dotted minim = 104), fractionally faster than Karajan and much more so than Rattle, who is far too measured here. The resultant sense of momentum is exhilarating. The very opening of the work is strongly projected and boldly contrasted with the movement which grows out of it. Throughout, however, the sheer physical excitement that this score engenders is tempered by admirable control. Only at the end of the slow movement does one feel that Ashkenazy could perhaps have afforded greater emotional restraint. The playing of the Philharmonia Orchestra is of the very first order. The *Karelia* suite is very good too, the middle movement, *Ballade*, fresh and imaginative. As for the *Symphony,* while allegiances to Karajan's earlier Berlin Philharmonic account remain (HMV ASD/*TCC-ASD* 4097 [Ang. DS/*4DS* 37811]), this Decca version must remain the preferred recommendation.

Rattle can hold his own against most of the competition. In his hands, if the whole symphony was as fine as the first movement this would be a clear first recommendation. Rattle has a powerful grasp of both its structure and character, and elicits an enthusiastic response from his players. The slow movement is for the most part superb, with excellent playing from the wind and brass of the Birmingham orchestra; but he makes too much of the commas at the end of the movement, which are so exaggerated as to be disruptive. An effect that is successful in the concert hall can sound exaggerated on a record, and such is the case in this peroration. The scherzo has splendid character but is a good deal slower than the marking; he also makes the *Lento* at letter H correspondingly – and unacceptably – slower, for Sibelius marks it *ma non troppo*. Sibelius composed *The Oceanides* in 1914 for his visit to America (incidentally, it is his only tone-poem not directly inspired by the *Kalevala*). The Oceanides were the nymphs who inhabited the waters of Homeric mythology, and the opening of the piece has an atmosphere that is altogether ethereal. Simon Rattle has its measure and conveys all its mystery and poetry. The refinements of dynamics are scrupulously observed, so that the differences between *pp* and *ppp* really tell, and serve to produce the right delicacy of colouring and transparency of texture. This is a subtle and masterly performance. There is an excellent cassette.

No one would pretend that the Gothenburg Symphony ranks alongside the great orchestras that have recorded this symphony (Vienna, Berlin, Boston, and the Philharmonia), but heaven forbid that this repertoire should be the sole preserve of the virtuoso orchestras. The Gothenburg strings are clean, well focused in tone, lean and lithe; the wind are well blended and the clarinet solo at the beginning is sensitively played; and there is an excellent sense of atmosphere. The first movement is finely shaped, and preparation for the return of the first group in the restatement is handled with impressive power. The slow movement is restrained and all the more effective on this count; the *Symphony* on the whole, one or two touches apart, is commendably straightforward. Neeme Järvi pulls back and is overemphatic at one bar after letter F in the finale. Better characterized than Gibson and very well recorded.

On the generous Chandos coupling there is plenty of enthusiasm in the first movement of No. 1, and there is no doubt that Sir Alexander is an 'echt Sibelian' through and through. Moreover, the actual sound is first rate by any standards, extremely vivid and present. However, the pitch discrepancy at letter S in the first movement of the *First Symphony* is worrying. In the long run, the playing does fall short of real distinction. The excellence of the Chandos sound on CD cannot disguise the want of tension and power that troubles the *Seventh*. It would be perverse to recommend this performance in preference to its rivals currently in the lists; in the *Seventh Symphony* it cannot displace (even on sonic grounds) Ashkenazy and the Philharmonia – though it should in fairness be added that the Decca, coupled with a powerful account of *Tapiola*, offers the shorter playing time.

Symphony No. 2 in D, Op. 43.
(*) Decca Dig. **410 206-2; SXDL/*KSXDC* 7513 [Lon. LDR/5- 10014]. Philh. O, Ashkenazy.
(*) Chan. Dig. **CHAN 8303; ABRD/*ABTD* 1062 [id.]. SNO, Gibson.

Symphony No. 2 in D, Op. 43; Finlandia, Op. 26.
* Telarc Dig. **CD 80095**; DG 10095 [id.]. Cleveland O, Levi.

Symphony No. 2 in D, Op. 43; Kuolema, Op. 44: Scene with cranes.
**(*) HMV Dig. EL 270160-1/*4* [Ang. DS/*4DS* 38169]. CBSO, Rattle.

Symphony No. 2 in D, Op. 43; Romance for strings in C, Op. 42.
*** BIS Dig. **CD 252**; LP 252. Gothenburg SO, Järvi.

From BIS a thought-provoking and excellent-sounding issue with plenty of presence and body. Not only is it very interesting; it is often a powerful performance of much honesty and directness. Järvi is very brisk in the opening *Allegretto*: he is every bit as fast as Kajanus in his pioneering account of 1930 which enjoyed the composer's own imprimatur. This Gothenburg version has more sinew and fire than its rivals, and the orchestral playing is more responsive and disciplined than that of the SNO on Chandos. Throughout, Järvi has an unerring sense of purpose and direction and the momentum never slackens. Of course, there is not the same opulence as the Philharmonia under Ashkenazy on Decca, but the BIS performance is concentrated in feeling and thoroughly convincing. The *Romance for strings* is not otherwise available in the CD format, though there is an alternative LP account by Sir Charles Groves, to which this has no reason to yield.

We are divided in our response to the Ashkenazy version. There are no doubts about the quality of the recorded sound, which is superb. It is atmospheric, beautifully rounded in tone, and has splendid clarity, definition and depth. As for the performance, it is a passionate, volatile reading, in many ways a very Russian view of Sibelius, with Ashkenazy finding a clear affinity with the Tchaikovsky symphonies. At the very opening, the quick, flexible treatment of the repeated crotchet motif is urgent, not weighty or ominous as it can be. Ashkenazy's control of tension and atmosphere makes for the illusion of live performance in the building of each climax, and the rich digital sound (recorded in the ideal acoustic of the Kingsway Hall) adds powerfully to that impression. Yet some listeners may find it more difficult to respond positively to this reading; like R.L., they may feel the performance is wanting in firmness of grip, especially in the slow movement, with the dramatic pauses lacking spontaneity and unanimity of response. The cassette matches the disc in richness and bloom, but the biggest climaxes seem marginally less expansive on tape. The compact disc is very impressive, though not quite as fine as Ashkenazy's *Fourth Symphony*.

The *Second* is among the best of the Gibson cycle; it scores, thanks to the impressive clarity and impact of the recording. Sir Alexander has been a doughty champion of Sibelius ever since the early 1960s, and this version of the *Second* is honest and straightforward, free of bombast in the finale. Tempos are well judged and there is at no time any attempt to interpose the personality of the interpreter. The first movement is neither too taut nor too relaxed: it is well shaped and feels right. The strings do not possess the weight or richness of sonority of the Berlin Philharmonic or the Philharmonia, and the performance as a whole does not displace the first recommendations on CD or LP (see below). The cassette is first rate, full, vivid and clean, though side two (in the copy we sampled) is transferred at a lower level and needs a higher setting to make the maximum effect. The CD is impressive, among the finest to come from Chandos, and is extremely vivid.

The CBSO play with fervour and enthusiasm for Simon Rattle except, perhaps, in the first movement where the voltage is lower – particularly in the development, which is not easy to bring off and which can easily sound laboured. Rattle's is not the *Allegretto* of the pioneering Kajanus record, let alone Järvi's more recent CD version. Indeed, he is in fact slightly broader than Karajan in either of his recordings and the playing is less fine-grained. The slow movement is full-blooded and gutsy, convincing even when Rattle arrests the flow of the argument by underlining certain points. The scherzo is bracing enough, though in the trio the oboe tune is caressed a little too much and is in danger of sounding sentimentalized. However, the transition to the finale is magnificent and Rattle finds the *tempo giusto* in this movement. The Birmingham strings, incidentally, produce a splendidly fervent unison here – and elsewhere in the *Symphony*. The recording is very alive, though the perspective needs greater depth and more air round the various orchestral sections. As a fill-up, Simon Rattle and the CBSO give an imaginative and poetic account of the *Scene with cranes* from the incidental music to *Kuolema*. A good record but not one that sweeps the board. The XDR cassette is full-bodied but lacks sparkle at the top.

Levi's is a plainspun reading, essentially spacious, though with moments when he forces the pace. The Cleveland Orchestra play well for him, but the electricity sparks only fitfully, and overall the result fails to grip the listener. *Finlandia*, too, is unimpressive, although the rich Telarc sound (made in Cleveland's Masonic Auditorium) gives a fine body and bloom to strings and brass alike.

Reminder. Karajan's 1981 version with the Berlin Philharmonic provides an essentially spacious reading; throughout all four movements there is splendour and nobility and some glorious sounds from the Berlin strings and brass (HMV ASD/*TC-ASD* 4060 [Ang. DS/*4ZS* 37816]). Maazel's mid-priced Decca account leans towards a Romantic view of the work with the Tchaikovskian inheritance stressed, but is richly recorded and beautifully played by the VPO (Decca Jubilee JB 43).

Symphony No. 3 in C, Op. 52; King Kristian II suite, Op. 27.
*** BIS Dig. **CD 228**; LP 228. Gothenburg SO, Järvi.

Symphonies Nos 3 in C, Op. 52; 6 in D min., Op. 104.
*** Decca Dig. **414 267-2**; 414 267-1/*4* [id.]. Philh. O, Ashkenazy.
** Chan. Dig. ABRD/*ABTD* 1097 [id.]. SNO, Gibson.

Neeme Järvi's version of the *Third Symphony* comes as part of an ambitious series that he is undertaking with the Gothenburg Symphony Orchestra to record the complete orchestral output of Sibelius for BIS. Although Sir Alexander Gibson and he do not differ more than fractionally, there is more sense of the epic in Järvi's hands. There is, on the other hand, great excitement in the Gibson, and many may respond more positively to the sense of forward movement here. But in Gothenburg, the slow movement is first class and the much more leisurely tempo adopted here by the Estonian conductor is just right. Neeme Järvi's coupling is the incidental music to *King Christian II*, and at present he has the field virtually to himself, the only rival being Paavo Berglund and the Bournemouth orchestra on HMV. Neeme Järvi has much greater poetic feeling; his account is splendidly committed throughout and free from the literalness that seems at times to distinguish this Finnish conductor. This is very beautifully played and recorded. Järvi's account of the *Third* can hold its own with any in the catalogue; though it is not to be preferred to the currently deleted account from Okko Kamu and the Finnish Radio Orchestra, there is no doubt it is better recorded.

Vladimir Ashkenazy and the Philharmonia Orchestra give a first-class account of both the *Third* and *Sixth Symphonies*. In the first movement of the *Third*, Ashkenazy is a shade faster than the metronome marking, and so there is no want of forward momentum and thrust, either here or in the finale. The tempi and spirit of the *Andantino* are well judged, though the withdrawn passage in the slow movement (at fig. 6) could perhaps have more inwardness of feeling; Ashkenazy is not helped, however, by the balance, closer than ideal, which casts too bright a light on a landscape that should be shrouded in mystery. It is clear that Ashkenazy has great feeling for the *Sixth* and its architecture. There is no lack of that sense of communion with nature which lies at the heart of the slow movement or the sense of its power which emerges in the finale. He is a good deal broader than Karajan – though that performance has an altogether special atmosphere – and Ashkenazy lets every detail tell in the *Poco vivace* third movement. Indeed, this is possibly the most successful in the current Decca cycle, with the *Seventh* as a close runner-up, technically impressive in all three media. Early in the present century, Sibelius enjoyed the championship of another great Russian pianist-conductor, Alexander Siloti, in whose concerts the *Third Symphony* was heard as early as 1909. In Ashkenazy he has found a natural heir and a worthy successor.

Sir Alexander Gibson and the Scottish National Orchestra last recorded the *Third Symphony* way back in the 1960s, coupling it with the *Seventh*; but this is his first recording of the *Sixth*. The SNO is in very good form, even though the 'cross-hatched' string writing in the slow movement of the *Sixth* does show their limitations. The first movement of the *Third* has real momentum. Gibson's tempo is a good deal brisker now than it was in his earlier recording, though the steadier pulse that he set in the 1960s is to be preferred. Yet the SNO play with genuine fire and enthusiasm and the recording is outstanding. The slow movement is another matter; here, Sir Alexander, as Anthony Collins before him, loses much of the inwardness and some of the fantasy of this enigmatic movement by pressing ahead too rapidly – and faster than the marking. Still, readers who are collecting the Gibson cycle will find there is more to admire than to cavil at. Both accounts are likeable; at the same time, it would be idle to pretend that as performances they displace Ashkenazy's coupling or, in the case of the *Sixth Symphony*, Karajan and the Berlin Philharmonic on DG, even if the Chandos recording is more vivid and better detailed. The cassette is hardly less impressive than the disc.

Symphony No. 4 in A min., Op. 63; Canzonetta, Op. 62/1; The Oceanides, Op. 73.
(*) BIS Dig. **CD 263; LP 263. Gothenburg SO, Järvi.

Symphony No. 4 in A min., Op. 63; Finlandia, Op. 26. (i) *Luonnotar, Op. 70.*
℄ *** Decca Dig. **400 056-2**; SXDL/*KSXDC* 7517 [Lon. LDR/5- 71019]. Philh. O, Ashkenazy, (i) with Söderström.

Ashkenazy achieves great concentration of feeling in the *Fourth*. The brightness of the Philharmonia violins and the cleanness of attack add to the impact of this baldest of the Sibelius symphonies, and Ashkenazy's terracing of dynamic contrasts is superbly caught in the outstanding digital recording. Like his other Sibelius readings, this one has something of a dark Russian passion in it, but freshness always dominates over mere sensuousness; as ever, Ashkenazy conveys the spontaneity of live performance. There is splendid drama and intensity throughout, and this is a very impressive performance. The couplings add to the special attractions of this issue; *Finlandia* is made fresh again in a performance of passion and precision, and Elisabeth Söderström is on top form in *Luonnotar*, a symphonic poem with a voice (although some ears may find her wide vibrato and hard-edged tone not entirely sympathetic). The cassette offers impressively rich sound but has slightly less range at the top: the transients in *Finlandia* are less telling. The compact disc has most impact of all, with the silent background adding to the dramatic impact of the performance and the dynamic contrasts even more effective. The close balancing of certain instruments is more noticeable, but the Kingsway Hall acoustic is demonstrated as ideal for this score, with the brass both biting and sonorous. The voice of Söderström in *Luonnotar* is given extra immediacy.

The sound of the BIS recording is splendidly fresh and vivid, thanks to the celebrated acoustic of the Gothenburg Concert Hall and the expertise of the engineering. Neeme Järvi takes a very broad view of the first movement – and conveys much of its brooding quality. There is perhaps more introspection here, and less of the stoicism of Beecham or the granite-like density of Karajan's performance. The scherzo has a splendid strength, even if Järvi allows the pace to slacken far too much towards the end. Both Järvi and Karajan portray the bleak yet other-worldly landscape of the slow movement to excellent effect, but the tension between phrases in the Karajan makes his the more powerful experience. In the finale Järvi opts for the tubular bells rather than the glockenspiel, which Sibelius wanted. As a fill-up, he gives us the *Canzonetta for strings*, Op. 62a, which derives from the music to *Kuolema*. It has great allure and charm and is beautifully played by the Gothenburg strings. *The Oceanides* is a very fine performance, too, though less subtle than Rattle's, particularly in its observance of dynamic nuances.

Symphonies Nos 4 in A min., Op. 63; 5 in E flat, Op. 82.
(M) *** HMV EG 290613-1/*4* [Ang. AM/*4AM* 34734]. BPO, Karajan.

Symphonies Nos 4 in A min., Op. 63; 6 in D min., Op. 104.
❀ *** DG **415 107-2** [id.]. BPO, Karajan.

Symphonies Nos 4 in A min., Op. 63; 7 in C, Op. 105.
*** HMV Dig. **CDC 747443-2** [id.]; EL 270099-1/*4* [Ang. DS/*4XS* 38135]. Helsinki PO, Berglund.

Karajan's twenty-year-old recording of the *Fourth Symphony* is only marginally less powerful than Ashkenazy on Decca, and his performance is of real stature. Having found it too well groomed on first acquaintance in the mid-1960s, many collectors have come to discover its depths and to value its sense of mystery. Although one is bowled over by the Ashkenazy at first, it is the Karajan that has the greater concentration and tension. DG also offer his glorious account of the *Sixth Symphony* which remains almost unsurpassed among recent accounts. Among its predecessors, only the famous Beecham record offers more distinctive insights. Although this DG transfer does not quite have the range and body of the BIS and Decca versions, it sounds more vivid than on its earlier appearances and, like that of No. 4, the performance is a great one.

In some ways Karajan's re-recording of the *Fourth Symphony* for HMV must be counted controversial. He gives spacious – and highly atmospheric – accounts of the first and third movements, a good deal slower than his earlier DG version. He conveys eloquently the other-worldly quality of the landscape in the third movement. The first undoubtedly has great mystery and power. Again, in the HMV *Fifth* the opening movement is broader than the earlier DG account, and he achieves a remarkable sense of its strength and majesty. The transition from the work's first section to the 'scherzo' is slightly more abrupt than in the 1965 recording; tempi generally in the work's first half are rather more extreme. The variety of tone-colour and, above all, the weight of sonority that the Berlin Philharmonic have at their command is remarkable, and the bassoon lament in the development section finds the Berlin strings reduced to a mere whisper. Both the slow movement and finale are glorious and have real vision, and the recording is excellent. However, the digital remastering has brought drier, less opulent textures than in the original full-priced issues; there is now a degree of thinness on the string timbre above the stave, not apparent when the two symphonies were issued separately – although this is much less noticeable on the otherwise excellent cassette. In both works the earlier DG versions (each differently coupled) are even finer, but at mid-price this HMV disc offers formidable value.

Paavo Berglund has recorded both symphonies before: indeed, this is his third account of the *Fourth*, and it is legitimate to question the need for a newcomer. However, these are both performances of considerable stature; indeed, the *Seventh* is arguably one of the finest now before the public: it has a real nobility and breadth, and Berglund has the full measure of all the shifting changes of mood and colour. Moreover, the Helsinki orchestra play magnificently and seem to have a total rapport with him. The *Fourth* is hardly less imposing and has a stark grandeur that resonates in the mind. Both his earlier versions had a certain grim intensity but the slow movement in neither matches this newcomer in its brooding power and poetic feeling. It has a mystery that perhaps eludes him in the development of the first movement, though the opening is marvellous in his hands. There are one or two things worth noting: there is not a great deal of *vivace* in the second movement. (Ashkenazy gets the tempo of this movement absolutely right – and he, too, is spectacularly well recorded.) The finale is superb, even if some collectors may find the closing bars insufficiently cold and bleak. However, these are both excellent versions and must have strong claims on the collector. The HMV compact disc is announced as we go to press.

Symphony No. 5 in E flat, Op. 82.
* Ph. 412 069-1/*4* [id.]. Concg. O, Kondrashin – NIELSEN: *Symphony No. 5.**

Symphony No. 5 in E flat, Op. 82; Andante festivo; Karelia overture, Op. 10.
*(*) BIS **CD 222**; LP 222. Gothenburg SO, Järvi.

Symphony No. 5 in E flat; Karelia suite, Op. 11.
(B) *(*) Pickwick Con. CD/*CCTC* 7603. LSO, Gibson.

Symphony No. 5; Night ride and sunrise, Op. 55.
⊛ *** HMV Dig. **CDC 747006-2**; ASD/*TC-ASD* 4168 [Ang. DS/*4XS* 37883]. Philh. O, Rattle.

Symphony No. 5; En Saga.
⊛ *** Decca Dig. **410 016-2**; SXDL/*KSXDC* 7541 [Lon. LDR/*5*- 71041]. Philh. O, Ashkenazy.

Symphonies Nos 5 in E flat, Op. 82; 7 in C, Op. 105.
(*) DG **415 108-2 [id.]. BPO, Karajan.

Simon Rattle's record of the *Fifth Symphony* has collected numerous prizes in Europe – and deserves them all. Right from the very outset, one feels that he has found the *tempo giusto*. Ashkenazy conducting the same orchestra is fractionally more measured, and that slight difference is enough to affect the sense of flow. Moreover, one notices that the woodwind are better blended in the HMV version, whereas in the Decca the clarinets obtrude slightly. Rattle is scrupulous in observing every dynamic nuance to the letter and, one might add, spirit. What is particularly impressive is the control of the transition between the first section and the scherzo element of the first movement, where the listener is often made all too conscious of the changing of gears and releasing of levers. This relationship is ideally balanced and enables Rattle to convey detail in just the right perspective. There is a splendid sense of atmosphere in the development and a power unmatched in recent versions, save for the Karajan. The playing is superb, with the recording to match. *Night ride* is very good but not quite as outstanding; however, this is undoubtedly an exceptional *Fifth*. The cassette quality is rather soft-grained, the upper range less open than the disc. The CD gains on the LP in range, depth and presence. It is strikingly natural and vivid, one of the best compact discs to come from EMI.

Ashkenazy's performance is outstandingly well recorded, with fine, spacious and well-detailed digital sound. His reading is a thoroughly idiomatic one and disappoints only in terms of the balance of tempi between the two sections of the first movement. This is a fine rather than a great performance. Ashkenazy's *En*

Saga is the best version of that work now in the catalogue; when one considers also the outstanding excellence of the recording, this issue will obviously have strong appeal. The chrome cassette is also very impressive, although in *En Saga* the bass is not as cleanly focused as on the disc. The compact disc must be listed among the best of Decca's earlier releases. The entry of the horns in the finale – perhaps the most impressive part of the performance – is especially telling; overall, the fullness of the sound is matched by its immediacy and warmth of atmosphere, with no trace of digital edginess, although the brass has bite as well as richness of sonority.

Such is the excellence of the classic Karajan DG *Fifth* that few listeners would guess its age. It is a great performance, and this 1964 version is indisputably the finest of the four he has made (two with the Philharmonia for Columbia and the 1977 Berlin account for HMV). Impressive though it is, his *Seventh* is not quite in the same class, and must yield both technically and even artistically to the Ashkenazy, which is very powerful and coupled with an impressive *Tapiola*. However, the virtues of the *Fifth* are well known and its appearance on compact disc more than welcome.

Neeme Järvi is broad and spacious in the first movement; indeed, he almost calls to mind the Tuxen account with the Danish Radio Orchestra from the early days of LP. There is, however, insufficient sense of mystery in the development movement, and the slow movement is a bit laboured. At the same time, it is a useful issue in that it also includes the *Andante festivo* (1922), a broad dignified piece for strings (the only work that Sibelius himself recorded), and the *Karelia overture*, not otherwise available at the time of writing. The Gothenburg orchestra has the advantage of a superb acoustic: it has both warmth and clarity.

Gibson's 1960 (Decca) recording still sounds well. Though the first-movement climax is impressively sustained and the reading is not without moments of excitement, there is generally a lack of tautness. The *Karelia* coupling is disappointing too, rather lacking spontaneity. Bargain-hunters would do far better with Karajan's HMV coupling of the *Fourth* and *Fifth Symphonies*.

In Kondrashin's reading, the first movement of the *Fifth* begins at a good tempo, but the slow movement really is too taut for comfort, and the finale is absurdly rushed. Needless to say, the Concertgebouw Orchestra generally play well for him, their virtuosity never in doubt, and the recording is perfectly truthful. The performances derive from live concerts, and audience noise is obtrusive. Not really recommendable.

Symphony No. 6 in D min., Op. 104; Pelléas et Mélisande: suite, Op. 46.
(*) BIS Dig. **CD 237; LP 237 [id.]. Gothenburg SO, Järvi.

The response of the Gothenburg orchestra to Järvi's direction is whole-hearted; one warms to the eloquence of the opening string polyphony and the impassioned finale. Järvi takes the main section very fast, much in the manner of the 1934 record by Schnéevoigt who is headlong in this section. There are one or two overemphatic gestures in the closing paragraphs of the slow movement, but on the whole this is well thought out and often impressive. It can hold its own with most competition and can be recommended, albeit not in preference to the classic Karajan version, though it is better recorded. Both *Pelléas et Mélisande* and the *Symphony* are in the CD catalogue from Karajan, the former being altogether magical and likely to reign as the unchallenged classic for as long as did the celebrated Beecham version. Järvi produces a very atmospheric account of this score, in particular the brief but concentrated *By the sea*. Yet it would be idle to pretend that it can be preferred to the Berlin performance.

Symphony No. 7; Tapiola.
ℭ *** Decca Dig. **411 935-2**; SXDL/*KSXDC* 7580 [Lon. LDR/5- 71080]. Philh. O, Ashkenazy.

Magnificent sound and very impressive playing. Ashkenazy's accounts of both the *Symphony* and *Tapiola* have many insights; the Decca recording is of the very highest quality, with altogether splendid range and presence. Ashkenazy does not build up the *Symphony* quite as powerfully as Berglund, but he has the measure of its nobility. His *Tapiola* is atmospheric and keenly dramatic; the only quarrel one might have is with his frenetic storm, whose very speed diminishes its overall impact and detracts from the breadth and grandeur that otherwise distinguish this reading. Apart from these minor qualifications, there is much to admire – indeed, much that is thrilling – in these interpretations; in any event, it is difficult to imagine the recorded sound being surpassed for a long time to come. It is especially impressive on CD; but the chrome cassette, too, is one of Decca's finest, with radiant strings and rich brass and a glowing overall bloom which in no way blurs internal detail.

String quartets: in A min. (*1889*)*; in B flat, Op. 4.*
(*) Finlandia **FACD 345; FAD 345. Sibelius Ac. Qt.

Voces intimae, the quartet he composed in Paris and London during 1908–9, is not Sibelius's only essay in the medium. Here, for the first time on record, are two early quartets, the *A minor*, written in 1889, his last year as a student, in Helsinki, and the *B flat*, composed the following year. Only the first violin part of the *A minor Quartet* was thought to survive, but a complete set of parts was recently discovered by Erik Tawaststjerna. There are many prophetic touches, as well as plenty of what Professor Tawaststjerna calls 'the fragile Nordic melancholy linked stylistically to Grieg'. It is interesting to see that the highly developed feeling for form we recognize from the mature Sibelius is already evident in these quartets. New ideas emerge at just the right moment (with the possible exception of the rather primitive fugal episode in the first movement of the *A minor*) and, given the fact that these are student works, the music is excellently paced. The playing of the Sibelius Academy Quartet is sympathetic and intelligent, very good rather than impeccable. The rather close balance of the recording does not do full justice to their dynamic range or tone colour and, despite the reverberant ambience, the sound does not really expand. Don't, however, be put off by this reservation; if the recording is not ideal, it is perfectly acceptable, and there is no doubt as to the commitment or expertise of the performances. An issue of great interest to all Sibelians.

Reminder. There is an outstanding record of the *D minor Quartet* (*Voces intimae*) by the Fitzwilliam Quartet, coupled with Delius. The recording is superb (O-L DSLO 47 [Lon. CS 7238]).

CHORAL MUSIC

(i) *Kullervo symphony, Op. 7; Scènes historiques: suite No. 1, Op. 25.*
(B) *** HMV *TCC2-POR 54287*. Bournemouth SO, Berglund, (i) with Kostia, Viitanen, Helsinki University Male Voice Ch.

Kullervo symphony, Op. 7; Oma maa (Our native land), Op. 92; The Origin of fire, Op. 32.
*** HMV Dig. **CDS 747496-8** [id.]; EX 279336-3/*5* (2). Naumanen, Hynninen, Estonian State Ac. Ch., Helsinki University Male Voice Ch., Helsinki University Ch., Helsinki PO, Berglund.

The *Kullervo symphony* is an ambitious five-movement work for two soloists, male-voice choir and orchestra, some seventy or so minutes long, which Sibelius wrote at the outset of his career in 1892. It brought him national fame and a commission from Kajanus that resulted in *En Saga*. After its first performance Sibelius withdrew the score and it was never performed in its entirety until 1958, a year after his death. It is revealed as an impressive work, full of original touches, particularly in its thoroughly characteristic opening. Naturally there are immaturities: the slow movement is over-long and overtly Tchaikovskian. What impresses, however, is the powerful vocal writing, and there are many exciting facets of Sibelius's early style to be found in this rewarding score.

Berglund's 1971 recording is available on LP only, as part of a mid-priced seven-record set of the complete symphonies (HMV SLS/*TC-SLS* 5129). But on tape it is available separately, well transferred on a single bargain-priced 'Portrait of the Artist' double-length cassette. The first thing collectors will want to know is whether this new issue represents a decisive improvement over the old. Berglund's basic conception of the score remains unchanged, save for a somewhat steadier fourth movement; overall, there is a much greater lyrical intensity in the shaping of phrases and altogether greater fantasy in the treatment of detail. He digs deeper into the score and conveys more of its epic power and, above all, its poetry than he did in his earlier account. This reading makes more of dynamic contrast and grips one far more than did its predecessor; it is fresher and comes more from the heart. This recording also has the advantage of two very fine soloists, Eeva Liisa Naumanen and the incomparable Jorma Hynninen, while the male choirs from Helsinki University and from Estonia produce a splendidly firmly-focused and black tone-colour. The only area in which this does not represent a striking improvement is in the recording, which is in the same expert hands of Brian Culverhouse as before. Not that the new recording is anything but very fine – and, of course, there is the richer bass and range of digital recording – but the acoustic of the 1971 version (Guildhall, Southampton) definitely has greater warmth and offers greater transparency and detail than the slightly drier Helsinki venue, and this difference is even more marked on cassette, where the newer recording sounds relatively opaque, with the choral focus less sharp than in Bournemouth.

The newest issue also brings us two rarities: *Oma maa* (*Our native land*), written in 1918 between the *Fifth* and *Sixth Symphonies*, which has not been recorded before, and *Tulen synty*, Op. 32, otherwise known as *The Origin of fire* or *Ukko the Firemaker*. This comes from the period of the *Second Symphony* and was revised at the time the composer was working on the *Fourth*. *The Origin of fire* is a powerful piece; as Professor Erik Tawaststjerna puts it, it 'comes close to being one of Sibelius's masterpieces'. There is more in it that belongs closer to the darker world of the *Fourth Symphony* than to 1902. The solo part is marvellously sung here by Jorma Hynninen, while Berglund gives us a performance of great atmosphere and of brooding intensity. If one were asked to place *Our native land*, one's thoughts would turn more to the 1890s than to 1918, and it is certainly no match for its companion on this side. The performance is a good one, though the sopranos of Helsinki University Choir are not quite as distinguished as the men. Another *Kullervo* is promised soon from Gothenburg under Neeme Järvi, also with Jorma Hynninen and a Finnish choir. This will appear on compact disc as well as LP. It might be wiser to wait for this, but no one investing in the EMI should be disappointed. The EMI CDs are announced just as we go to press.

Complete songs: *5 Christmas songs, Op. 1. Arioso, Op. 3. 5 Songs of Runeberg, Op. 13. 7 Songs, Op. 17. Jubal, Teodora, Op. 35. 6 Songs, Op. 36. 5 Songs, Op. 37. 5 Songs, Op. 38. 6 Songs, Op. 50. 8 Songs of Josephson, Op. 57. 4 Songs, Op. 72. 6 Songs, Op. 86. 6 Songs of Runeberg, Op. 90. Serenade (1888). Segelfahrt (1899). Souda, souda, sinisorsa (1899). Hymn to Thaïs (1900). Erloschen (1906). Narcissen (1918). Små flickorna (1920). King Christian II, Op. 27 – Serenade of the Fool. Pelléas et Mélisande, Op. 46 – Les trois soeurs aveugles. Two songs from Twelfth Night, Op. 60.*

*** Argo 411 739-1 (5) [id.]. Söderström, Krause, Ashkenazy or Gage; Bonell (guitar).

Many of these songs (including two of the very greatest, *Jubal* and *Teodora*) have never been recorded before. Sibelius the symphonist has, understandably enough, overshadowed the achievement of the song composer. Indeed the songs have been written off by many music-lovers whose knowledge of them does not extend far beyond the popular handful: *Black roses*, *The maid came from her lover's tryst* (*Flickan kom ifrån sin älsklings möte*) and *Sigh, sedges, sigh* (*Säv, säv, susa*). As with Grieg, the most popular of the songs are not necessarily the best and have served to hinder the music-lover from exploring the rest. Another cause for their neglect is the relative inaccessibility of the Swedish language as far as non-native singers are concerned for, again like those of Grieg or Mussorgsky, the songs of Sibelius do not sound well in translation. Only a handful (quite literally five) of the songs are in Finnish: the bulk are inspired by the great Swedish nature romantics: Runeberg, Rydberg, Fröding and Tavaststjerna. Apart from the familiar handful, there are so many riches here to take one by surprise: songs like *Soluppgång* (*Sunrise*) and *Lasse Liten* (*Little Lasse*) are finely characterized, with some of the concentration and atmosphere you find in his finest miniatures. *On a balcony by the sea* (*På verandan vid havet*), more familiar from Flagstad's record, is almost a miniature tone-poem; it shows a very different side of Sibelius's world and its dark, questing lines look forward to the bleak contours and landscape of the *Fourth Symphony*. Both *Autumn evening* (*Höstkväll*) and *On a balcony by the sea* are great songs by any standards and can be mentioned in the most exalted company, but neither is new to record, whereas both *Jubal* and *Teodora*, the two songs comprising Op. 35, are. The first, *Jubal*, is to a poem of the Swedish poet and painter, Josephson, who inspired the Op. 58 settings. As often in Sibelius, the piano part is fairly simple, and the burden of the musical argument rests with the voice – the reverse of Wolf. But what a vocal part it is. It ranges with great freedom over a compass of almost two octaves; indeed, so intense is this writing and that in its companion, *Teodora*, and so full of dramatic fire that, in spite of *The maiden in the tower*, one wonders whether he could not have become an operatic composer. *Teodora* will come as a revelation to many Sibelians, for in its over-heated expressionism it comes close to the Strauss of *Salome* and *Elektra*. Krause is superb here and indeed throughout this set. The vast majority of these songs falls to him and Irwin Gage, the remaining dozen or so coming from Söderström and Ashkenazy. Krause's voice has lost some of its youthful freshness and bloom but none of its black intensity. If you put his earlier accounts of, say, *Vilse* (*Astray*) or *Narcissen* (*Narcissus*), both delightful songs, alongside the new, you will notice the firmer focus of the voice in the earlier but will also find this offset by the keener interpretative insight and feeling for character of the complete set. The performances throughout are authoritative and majestic. Apart from Swedish and Finnish, Sibelius set a number of German poets before the First World War. They are not in the same class as the best of the Runeberg settings, but none of them is second-rate: *Im Feld ein Mädchen singt* is undoubtedly an eloquent song. However, the real masterpiece in this set is its companion, *Die stille Stadt*, which has the concentration of mood and strong atmosphere of a miniature tone-poem: indeed, its serenity, beauty of line and sense of repose mark it out from the others. It is a song of great distinction and refinement of feeling. The Op. 61 set, composed in the close proximity of the *Fourth Symphony*, has some of Sibelius's most searching thoughts. One song here is grievously neglected; it alone is almost worth the price of this set: *Långsamt som kvällsyn* (*Slowly as the evening sun*) which haunts the listener with its intensity and concentration of mood. It is a setting of Karl August Tavaststjerna, to whom Sibelius turns for four other poems in this set. None is quite so searching and inward in feeling, but nevertheless they all find the composer at his most individual. *Romeo*, for example, is a most subtle and brilliant song which shows that he knew his Debussy well; and the *Romans* has strong atmosphere, too. (His diaries from this period record that Sibelius had been studying both Debussy and Rachmaninov.) This is one of the pleasures of this set, that one finds new delights in the songs each time one turns to them, and a piece that one at first thought unremarkable turns out to be very special. In terms not just of ambition but also of achievement, this box is a major event, not dissimilar to that of the Hugo Wolf Society volumes. Very few of the songs (*Segelfahrt* is an example) are wanting in interest; most of them are very rewarding indeed, and there are many more masterpieces than is commonly realized. This is a veritable treasure-house, which will be a revelation to many who think they already know their Sibelius.

Songs with orchestra: *Arioso; Autumn evening* (*Höstkväll*)*; Come away, Death!* (*Kom nu hit Död*)*; The diamond on the March snow* (*Diamanten på marssnön*)*; The fool's song of the spider* (*Sången om korsspindeln*)*; Luonnotar, Op. 70; On a balcony by the sea* (*På verandan vid havet*)*; The Rapids-rider's brides* (*Koskenlaskian morsiammet*)*; Serenade; Since then I have questioned no further* (*Se'n har jag ej frågat mera*)*; Spring flies hastily* (*Våren flyktar hastigt*)*; Sunrise* (*Soluppgång*).
*** **BIS CD 270**; LP 270 [id.]. Jorma Hynninen, Mari-Anne Häggander, Gothenburg SO, Panula.

This record collects all the songs that Sibelius originally composed for voice and orchestra, together with those for voice and piano that he himself subsequently orchestrated. The great find here is a newly discovered song of haunting beauty, *Serenade*, which begins the record. Not to put too fine a point on it, this is one of Sibelius's very greatest and most subtle songs. (It was recently discovered by Professor Erik Tavaststjerna.) The *Serenade* dates from 1895, the period of the *Lemminkäinen Legends*, and has the greatest delicacy and atmosphere: its whispering pizzicato strings are wonderfully suggestive. Jorma Hynninen is a great interpreter of this repertoire, and it is strange that he has had such little exposure in this country. His singing can only be called glorious. Mari-Anne Häggander manages the demanding tessitura of *Arioso* and *Luonnotar* with much artistry, and her *Luonnotar* is certainly to be preferred to Söderström's. Her vibrato is minimal and her pitch dauntingly accurate. She succeeds beautifully, too, in achieving *pp* tone on the top B, towards the end of the piece. Jorma Panula proves a sensitive accompanist and secures fine playing from the Gothenburg orchestra. In any event, this is an indispensable complement to the Decca complete Sibelius songs.

Songs with orchestra: *Arioso; Diamenten på marssnon; Den första kyssen; Flickan kom ifrån sin älsklings möte; Höstkväll; Kom nu hit; Men min fågel märks dock icke; Om kvällen; På verandan vid havet; Säf, säf, susa; Se'n har jag ej frågat mera; Svarta Rosor; Var det en dröm; Våren flyktar hastigt.*
(M) *** Decca 414 443-1/*4*. Flagstad, LSO, Fjeldstad.

Some of the songs here were orchestrated by the composer, but seven of them remained in their original form (voice and piano) until transformed, usually with great skill, by such arrangers as Jalas, Pingoud, Fougsted, and Hellman. This recording, made in the early days of stereo, still sounds astonishingly good, and

Sibelius-singing doesn't come like this any more! These classic performances give a magnificent impression of Sibelius's not inconsiderable range as a song composer, and will perhaps tempt the listener to explore further in this repertoire.

Songs: *Astray; Black roses; Come away, Death; Driftwood; In the field a maiden sings; King Christian II: The Fool's song of the spider. Kullervo's lament; The maiden came from her lover's tryst; On a balcony by the sea; Pelléas et Mélisande: The three blind sisters; Sigh, sedges, sigh; Spring flies speedily; Swim, duck, swim!; To evening; Twelfth Night: 2 Songs. Was it a dream?; When that I was.*
*** HM HMC/*40* 5142. Jorma Hynninen, Ralf Gothoni.

Jorma Hynninen has altogether superb vocal artistry at his command; his powerful, finely-focused voice always rings in the memory long after the turntable has come to rest; indeed, he is one of the finest Finnish singers now before the public. The recording, made as long ago as 1975 but not released in the UK until recently, is eminently well balanced, with the piano excellently placed. The performances are of a high order vocally and interpretatively, and Hynninen and his fine partner colour the words beautifully. The Shakespeare settings have wonderful atmosphere and are rightly given in Hagberg's Swedish translation: they do not fit the English at all. Readers who baulk at the prospect of buying the complete Decca/Argo set will welcome this issue, as will all lovers of good singing.

The maiden in the tower (opera). *Karelia suite, Op. 11.*
*** BIS Dig. **CD 250**; LP 250. Häggander, Hynninen, Hagegård, Kruse, Gothenburg Ch. and SO, Järvi.

Sibelius abandoned his first operatic venture, *Veneen luominen* (*The building of the boat*) after visiting Bayreuth in 1894, only two years after *Kullervo*, though some of its material found its way into the *Lemminkäinen Legends*; indeed, the first version of *The Swan of Tuonela* originally served as its Prelude. Only two years later came the present work, which was performed in Helsinki in 1897 and never revived in the composer's lifetime. The feeble libretto has been blamed for the opera's failure, but this is only part of the problem. The plot itself does not rise above Victorian melodrama and the layout of the opera is scarcely convincing. It falls into eight short scenes and lasts no more than 35 minutes. Its short Prelude is not unappealing but does not promise great things – any more than the ensuing scene delivers them. But the orchestral interlude between the first two scenes brings us the real Sibelius, and the second scene is undoubtedly impressive; there are echoes of Wagner, such as we find in some of the great orchestral songs of the following decade, and the vocal line has the wide tessitura and dramatic flexibility of such masterpieces as *Höstkväll* and *Jubal*. All the same, Sibelius's refusal to permit its revival was perfectly understandable, for it lacks something we find in all his most characteristic music: quite simply, a sense of mastery. Yet even if it must be admitted that this is neither good opera nor good Sibelius, there is enough musical interest to warrant the attention of more than just the specialist collector. There are telling performances, too, from Mari-Anne Häggander and Jorma Hynninen and the Gothenburg orchestra. Neeme Järvi's account of the *Karelia suite* is certainly original, with its opening rather impressive in its strange way. It is difficult to imagine a more spacious account of the *Intermezzo*, which is too broad to make an effective contrast with the ensuing *Ballade*. Järvi's account of this movement is so slow that it sags. However, this is obviously a record that the Sibelian will want to investigate, and BIS have put us in their debt by making it.

Simpson, Robert (born 1921)

String quartets Nos 7 (1977); 8 (1979).
*** Hyp. A 66117. Delmé Qt.

The *Quartets* of Robert Simpson have so far been represented on commercial records only by No. 1, a work of great natural eloquence. The appearance of two relatively recent works, Nos 7 and 8, both from the late 1970s, is therefore something of an event, for they greatly enrich the repertoire. The *Seventh* has a real sense of vision and something of the stillness of the remote worlds it evokes. It is dedicated to Susi Jeans, the organist and widow of the astronomer, and reflects the composer's own passion for astronomy; he speaks of the universe, 'quiet and mysterious yet pulsating with energy'. The *Eighth* turns from the vastnesses of space to the microcosmic world of insect-life. Indeed, this provides a superficial link with Bartók, but, as with so much of Simpson's music, there is a concern for musical continuity rather than beauty of incident. Excellent playing by the Delmé Quartet, and very good recorded sound too.

String quartet No. 9.
*** Hyp. A 66127. Delmé Qt.

What an original and, in its way, masterly conception the *Ninth Quartet* is! It is quite unlike anything in the literature of chamber music: a set of thirty-two variations and fugue on the minuet of Haydn's *Symphony No. 47*. Like the minuet itself, all the variations are in the form of a palindrome; some of the earlier ones derive from an early piano work, thus finding an even more natural habitat in the quartet medium. Many will find it a tough nut to crack, and it certainly calls for – and repays – concentrated study. It is a mighty and serious work, argued with all the resource and ingenuity one expects from this composer. A formidable achievement in any age, and a rarity in ours. The Delmé Quartet cope with its difficulties splendidly, and the performance carries the imprimatur of the composer. The recording is very good.

Sinding, Christian (1856–1941)

Suite, Op. 10.
*** HMV **CDC 747167-2** [id.]; ASD/*TC-ASD* 3933 [Ang. SZ/*4ZS* 37663]. Perlman, Pittsburgh SO, Previn – SIBELIUS: *Concerto.****

Heifetz recorded this dazzling piece in the 1950s, and it need only be said that Perlman's version is not inferior. Sinding's *A minor Suite* was originally composed in 1888 for violin and piano, and subsequently scored for double woodwind, two horns, strings and (in the finale) a harp. Its blend of archaism and fantasy sounds distinctively Scandinavian of the 1890s yet altogether fresh – and quite delightful. Such is the velocity of Perlman's first movement that one wonders whether the disc is playing at the right speed. Stunning virtuosity and excellent recording, which gains in immediacy in its CD format. The cassette too is brilliantly clear, its forward balance matching the LP and CD.

Smetana, Bedřich (1824–84)

Má Vlast (complete).
(M) **(*) HMV EG 290860-1/*4*. Dresden State O, Berglund.
** Sup. Dig. **C37 7241**; 1110 3431/2. Czech PO, Smetáček.

(i) *Má Vlast* (complete); (ii) Symphonic poems: *Carnival in Prague; Haakon Jarl*, Op. 16; Wallenstein's Camp, Op. 14.
(M) *** DG 419 111-1/*4* (2) [id.]. (i) Boston SO; (ii) Bav. RSO, Kubelik.

Má Vlast (complete)*; The Bartered Bride: Overture; Furiant; Dance of the comedians.*
(*) Tel. **ZA8 35672 (2) [id.]. Leipzig GO, Neumann.

Kubelik's DG set has dominated the catalogue for a decade and a half; in its remastered form, the 1971 recording has been transformed, the string tone (so important in *Vltava*) full and fresh, woodwind vivid, brass sonorous, and the ambience warm and spacious. The performances of the two unquestioned masterpieces of the cycle, *Vltava* and *From Bohemia's woods and fields*, are particularly fine, and the orchestral playing throughout is first class. Kubelik is careful to temper the bombast which too readily comes to the surface in this music (in *Tábor* and *Blaník* especially) and his skill with the inner balance of the orchestration brings much felicitous detail. For the mid-priced reissue three symphonic poems, which he recorded a year later with his Bavarian orchestra, make a worthwhile bonus. *Carnival in Prague* was written in 1883; the others are much earlier works dating from around 1860. The music is cast in the mould of the more famous cycle, with a flavour of Dvořák, if without quite the imaginative flair of that master. The most spectacular is *Wallenstein's Camp* with its opportunities for offstage brass fanfares – well managed here – although the most distinguished is *Haakon Jarl*, which has a strong vein of full-blooded romanticism. The playing is first class in all three, the performances fresh and committed, and the recording exemplary, often spectacular in range and sonority. There are excellent matching chrome tapes (in a cardboard 'flap-pack').

The Telefunken recording of *Má Vlast* dates from 1968 and runs to 81 minutes, just too long to fit on a single CD. But Neumann is on his best form and the Leipzig orchestra produce some superb playing for him. His is not the most dramatic reading, but *Vyšehrad*, with its evocative opening harp solo, is warmly romantic and both *Vltava* and *From Bohemia's woods and fields* bring much lovely detail, with glowing woodwind and a rich string sheen, although the violins remain very brightly lit. The music making has fine spontaneity throughout, and the recorded sound is first class in this digitally remastered form, with the Leipzig acoustic casting an agreeable ambient glow while never blurring detail. The *Bartered Bride* overture and dances are splendid, attractively combining spirit with polish. However the *Bartered Bride* items play for just under a quarter of an hour.

Berglund's 1979 *Má Vlast* has been digitally remastered from three LP sides to two, playing for 39′ 31″ and 38′ 02″ respectively. But such economy has not been achieved without some loss of range, and the recording now sounds slightly constricted in fortissimos. While it has not lost its bloom, it is a pity that originally superb sound has been degraded to ensure that the record remains competitive. On performance grounds the set has a great deal to commend it: the playing of the Dresden orchestra is magnificent. If *Vltava* is slightly undercharacterized, *Vyšehrad* is full of lyrical evocation and atmosphere, and *Tábor* and *Blaník* are jubilant rather than rhetorical, so that the very end of the cycle has a feeling of joyous release. At mid-price this is an obvious bargain, but because of the restricted sound it is less satisfying than Kubelik's recording.

Smetáček's approach is broad and spacious, seeking to emphasize the music's epic qualities rather than finding sharpness of characterization. There is certainly an absence of melodrama, and the closing pages of *Blaník* have a feeling of apotheosis. The orchestral playing is assured; the resonant ambience is warmly attractive, and the CD brings enhanced detail, with the brass brightened and percussive transients sharpened, while string timbres remain natural. In the last resort, this is not among the more memorable versions of Smetana's cycle. However, it does have the advantage of fitting on to a single CD, which makes it a much more economical proposition than the Telefunken set, even if *Vltava* and *From Bohemia's woods and fields* are far more imaginative under Neumann.

Má Vlast: Vltava; Vyšehrad.

(B) *** DG Walkman *413 159-4* [id.]. Bav. RSO, Kubelik – DVOŘÁK: *Slavonic dances*; LISZT: *Hungarian rhapsodies; Les Préludes.***(*)

Part of a generally attractive collection of Slavonic music. Kubelik's excellent performances come from his complete set (DG Privilege 2726 111) and are splendidly played and very well recorded, although the acoustic is slightly dry.

Má Vlast: Vltava.

** DG Dig. **415 509-2**; 415 509-1/*4* [id.]. VPO, Karajan – DVOŘÁK: *Symphony No. 9.***

(***) RCA mono [**RCCD 1008**]. NBC SO, Toscanini – DVOŘÁK: *Symphony No. 9.* (***)

Although the recording sounds a degree more expansive than the coupled *New World symphony*, there is also a bass emphasis that affects the overall naturalness. The performance is not without spontaneity, but it does not match Karajan's earlier analogue versions made in Berlin nor his more recent digital Berlin Philharmonic account – see Concerts section below (DG **413 587-2**; 413 587-1/*4*).

Toscanini sees *Vltava* as a symphonic structure rather than a descriptively evocative symphonic poem; though the playing in the moonlight sequence is ravishing in effect, that is because the music itself is beautiful. In the Wedding sequence on the river bank, the poor dancing peasants are rushed off their feet. If one forgets the programme, the performance is attractive enough, and the spacious and masterly gathering together of the music's threads at the climax shows the maestro at his most compelling. The sound is acceptable, with only a hint of congestion.

Piano trio in G min., Op. 15.

*** Chan. Dig. **CHAN 8445**; ABRD/*ABTD* 1157 [id.]. Borodin Trio – DVOŘÁK: *Dumky trio.****

The composition of Smetana's only *Piano trio* is closely related to the death of the composer's four-year-old daughter from scarlet fever, which left him beside himself with grief. The writing of the *Trio* acted as a catharsis, so it is not surprising that it is a powerfully emotional work. Although it has an underlying melancholy, it is by no means immersed in gloom: there is serenity too, and the powerful finale ends with a sense of lyrical release. The writing gives fine expressive opportunities for both the violin and cello, which are taken up eloquently by Rostislav Dubinsky and Yuli Turovsky, and it need hardly be said that the pianist Luba Edlina is wonderfully sympathetic, too. In short, a superb account given a most realistic recording balance. Highly recommended in all three media.

String quartets Nos 1 in E min. (*From my life*); *2 in D min.*

(*) Sup. Dig. **C37 7339; 4112 130. Smetana Qt.

These performances date from 1976. They are authoritative, idiomatic and fresh and, in a mid-price LP format, warranted a strong recommendation. This compact disc transfer is at a much higher price, and whether it is worth the additional outlay will depend on individual priorities. There is an undoubted gain in background silence and a slight gain in definition when one puts the two together, but the sound could do with a little more warmth, and there is a certain glassiness above the stave. So far there is no alternative compact disc version of these two quartets, but few performances are likely to be much better.

OPERA

The Bartered Bride (complete, in Czech).
*** Sup. Dig. **C37 7309/11**; 1116 3511/3 [id.]. Beňácková, Dvorský, Novák, Kopp, Jonášová, Czech Philharmonic Ch. and O, Košler.

The digital Supraphon set under Košler admirably supplies the need for a first-rate Czech version of this delightful comic opera. The recording acoustic may be rather reverberant for comedy, but the orchestral sound is warm and the voices are given good presence, while the performance sparkles from beginning to end with folk rhythms crisply enunciated in an infectiously idiomatic way. The cast is strong, headed by the characterful Gabriela Beňácková as Mařenka and one of the finest of today's Czech tenors, Peter Dvorský, as Jeník. Miroslav Kopp in the role of the ineffective Vašek sings powerfully too. As Kecal the marriage-broker, Richard Novák is not always steady, but his swaggering characterization is most persuasive. The CDs offer some of the best sound we have yet had from Supraphon, fresh and lively. The voices are placed well forward in relation to the orchestra, and there is occasionally just a hint of digital edge on the vocal peaks. But the effect overall has fine presence. The discs are generously banded. The libretto is of poor quality, badly printed in minuscule type, offering a choice of Czech, English and Japanese.

Libuše (complete).
(*) Sup. Dig. **C37 7438/40 [id.]. Beňačkova-Čápová, Zítek, Švorc, Vodička, Prague Nat. Theatre Ch. and O, Košler.

Recorded live at the Prague National Theatre in 1983, this has many of the advantages of live recording, not least the communicated fervour of its nationalist aspirations, more convincing when shared with an audience. But this opera, written for the opening of the National Theatre of Prague in 1881, has a limited appeal for the non-Czech listener, with a plot essentially concerned with the Czech royal dynasty. The cast here is even stronger than that of the previous recording under Krombholc, with Gabriela Beňačková-Čápová as Libuše memorable in her prophetic aria in Act III, while Václav Zítek as Přemysl, her consort, provides an attractive lyrical interlude in Act II which, with its chorus of harvesters, has affinities with *The Bartered Bride*. In Act I there is some Slavonic wobbling, notably from Eva Děpoltová as Krasava, but generally the singing is as dramatic as the plot-line will allow. Košler directs committedly; with the stage perspectives well caught, an unintrusive audience, and no disturbing stage noises (the events being fairly static), the recording is very satisfactory. The libretto booklet is clear, even if the typeface is minuscule. But with only 16 cues provided to an opera playing for not far short of three hours, internal access is less than ideal. This issue is for the specialist, rather than the ordinary opera-lover.

Soler, Vicente Martín y (1754–1806)

Canzonette: *Amor e gelosia; La costanza; L'innozenza; La mercede; La natura; La preghiera; La semplice; La volubile; Una cosa rara* (opera): *Consola le pene mia vita; Dolce mi parve un di.*
*** Ph. Dig. **411 030-2**; 411 030-1/*4* [id.]. Teresa Berganza, José Morenzo – SOR: *Seguidillas.****

Not to be confused with Antonio Soler, best known for his keyboard music, Vicente Martín y Soler in the generation immediately following was regarded as a rival of Mozart, who even quoted a bar or two of his in *Don Giovanni.* These songs and one aria are charming enough in their modest way, making a fair coupling for the more characterful Sor *Canzonette* on the reverse. Fine performances, well recorded.

Sor, Fernando (1778–1839)

12 Seguidillas for voice and guitar; Andante (from *Divertimento, Op. 2/3*).
*** Ph. Dig. **411 030-2**; 411 030-1/*4* [id.]. Teresa Berganza, José Morenzo – SOLER, Martín y: *Canzonette.****

Fernando Sor, best remembered for his guitar music, here provides a striking example of his equally characterful vocal style in twelve *Canzonette* which with their Spanish flavour admirably match the sharpness of the words. Berganza, well accompanied and well recorded, relishes their individuality.

Spohr, Ludwig (1784–1859)

Symphonies Nos 6 in G (*Historical*), *Op. 116; 9 in B min.* (*The Seasons*), *Op. 143.*
** Orfeo **C 094841A**; S 094841A [id.]. Bav. RSO, Rickenbacher.

Spohr wrote ten symphonies, of which he subsequently discarded the first and the last. Nos 2–5, dating from between 1820 and 1837, show a personal voice. They were admired by Schumann and established the composer's symphonic reputation. No. 6, written in 1839, reminds us of the Mikado's Gilbertian quip about 'Spohr interwoven with Bach and Beethoven'. The first movement sets a Baroque atmosphere, with fugal Bach contrasting genially with a Handelian pastoral style. Karl Rickenbacher has its full measure and the Bavarian orchestra play it most engagingly. The element of pastiche continues throughout, but the other movements are less successful, with the third utterly failing to evoke the energy of a Beethoven scherzo and producing watered-down Schumann instead. Indeed, Schumann's influence is also strong in the *Spring* movement of No. 9 (which comes second). The first, *Winter*, lacks strength of purpose, but the *Largo* of *Summer* is pleasingly warm, if a little bland. The finale, with its echoes of the hunt, is marked (like the finale of No. 6) *Allegro vivace*, and both movements suffer from

Rickenbacher's easy-going manner. A more alert, vivacious approach might have brought these two symphonies more fully to life, although the playing of the Bavarian Radio Orchestra is always responsive and cultured, and the attractive ambience of the recording, sounding especially natural in its CD format, gives pleasure in itself. Despite reservations, this is a coupling of great interest, and we hope the earlier symphonies will follow in due course.

Nonet in F, Op. 31; Octet in E, Op. 32.
(M) **(*) Decca Lon. Ent. 414 439-1/*4* [id.]. Vienna Octet (members).

Spohr's *Octet* is a work of great charm; the variations on Handel's *Harmonious blacksmith* which form one of the central movements offer that kind of naïveté which (when played stylishly) makes for delicious listening. The playing is expert here, the five strings blending perfectly with the two horns and clarinet; and altogether this is a most winning performance. The recording, from 1959, still sounds extremely well, fresh and open, with the right kind of resonance, equally effective on disc or cassette. The *Nonet* is also very attractive. Spohr's invention is again at its freshest and his propensity for chromaticism is held in reasonable check. The performance, however, is less spontaneous than in the coupling. The scherzo comes off well but the *Adagio*, taken very slowly, could be more smiling. The 1968 sound is less attractively balanced than the earlier recording; in the remastering, the upper range has been brightened and on cassette is a little edgy. The CRD version of this coupling by the Nash Ensemble (CRD 1054/*CRDC 4054*) offers elegant performances and more modern recording.

Stainer, John (1840–1901)

The Crucifixion.
*** HMV Dig. EL 270410-1/*4*. Tear, Luxon, Westminster Singers, John Scott, Hickox.
(M) *** Argo SPA/*KCSP* 267. Lewis, Brannigan, St John's College, Cambridge, Ch., Brian Runnett, Guest.
** Hyp. A/*KA* 66035 [id.]. Griffett, George, Peterborough Cathedral Ch., Andrew Newberry, Vann.

The newest HMV digital recording of *The Crucifixion* differs from its predecessors in using mixed voices in the choir rather than the men and trebles of the Anglican tradition, well represented by the Argo Cambridge version, made two decades earlier, which is a vintage recording of the highest analogue quality. Stainer arranged further contrast by including five hymns in which the congregation are invited to join, and this device is used in both recordings. However, Hickox is freer in their treatment, which will be a plus point for some listeners, although the greater simplicity favoured by Guest is by no means a drawback. The devotional atmosphere of the contribution of the Westminister Singers is impressive and they rise well to the famous *Fling wide the gates, the Saviour waits* (even if this is not the happiest choice of rhyme). The organist, John Scott, makes a fine contribution here – as indeed he does elsewhere. Robert Tear and Benjamin Luxon are a well-matched pair of soloists, especially in their duet *So Thou liftest Thy divine petition*. But Richard Lewis and Owen Brannigan worked well together for Argo, with the effect rather more dramatic, and preference will be a matter of taste. The HMV recording is scheduled for CD release during the lifetime of this book and already has a good cassette equivalent. But the fine Argo version, which is also now available on tape, has a considerable price advantage.

The Peterborough account was originally issued on Enigma in the late 1970s. The performance is sincere and eloquent in a modestly restrained way, using the choir for both choruses and hymns. In his efforts not to overdramatize the narrative, Stanley Vann falls into the opposite trap of understatement, and there is a lack of vitality at times. The two soloists make a stronger contribution, and James Griffet is pleasingly lyrical. However, the style of presentation does not wholly avoid hints of the sentimentality that hovers dangerously near all performances of this work. The recording is atmospheric, the choral sounds warm rather than incisive. There is a good cassette.

Stamitz, Karl (1745–1801)

Sinfonia concertante in D (for violin, viola and orchestra).
(B) **(*) CBS DC 40167 (2). Stern, Zukerman, ECO, Barenboim – MOZART: *Sinfonia concertante**(**); PLEYEL: *Sinfonia concertante*.**(*)

A relatively lightweight but enjoyable fill-up for a very fine account of Mozart's great *Sinfonia concertante* – again giving these vital artists an opportunity to strike musical sparks off each other. The unnaturally forward balance, plus a degree of edginess on the sound, is the main drawback to an otherwise highly recommendable pair of discs. The equivalent tape omits the Pleyel coupling and is not recommended in consequence.

Stanford, Charles (1852–1924)

Piano concerto No. 2 in C min., Op. 126.
*** Lyr. SRCS 102 [id.]. Malcolm Binns, LSO, Braithwaite.

Anyone who fancies a virtuoso concerto in the grand manner, which has flavours of Brahms on the one hand, Rachmaninov on the other, and with an Irish tang to some of the themes, will be delighted with this ambitious work, here given a strong performance, very well recorded. Stanford wrote it late in his career, in 1911, when Rachmaninov was already established, but it had to wait for some years to be performed, by which time the taste for Romantic concertos had faded. The Irish flavour is particularly strong in some of the yearning melodies of the central slow movement, with plentiful harp arpeggios in the texture, and the finale opens with a jolly Irish folk-tune treated in Brahmsian manner.

Irish rhapsody No. 4 in A min.
*** Lyr. SRCS 123 [id.]. LPO, Nicholas Braithwaite – BANTOCK: *Oedipus Colonnus.***(*)

Though not as distinctive as the Stanford symphonies, *Irish rhapsody No. 4* – given its first performance under no less a conductor than Willem Mengelberg – is a rich and atmospheric piece, masterfully scored. It starts memorably with a cor anglais playing a mournful fisherman's song over muted strings, and slow music predominates, with a stormy interlude in the middle. Besides the fisherman's song, the piece quotes a jolly Ulster marching tune and a tune called *The death of General Wolfe*. Braithwaite's performance is most persuasive, and the recording excellent.

Stanley, John (1712–86)

6 Organ concertos, Op. 10.
*** CRD **CRD 3409**; CRD 1065/*CRDC 4065* [id.]. Gifford, Northern Sinfonia.

John Stanley published these six concertos in 1775, towards the end of his long career as organist and composer. He gave the option of playing the solo part on the harpsichord or fortepiano, but this is essentially organ music, and these bouncing, vigorous performances, well recorded as they are on the splendid organ of Hexham Abbey, present them most persuasively. No. 4, with its darkly energetic C minor, is particularly fine. The recording is natural in timbre and very well balanced. The CD gives the attractive organ sounds added tangibility, although the 1979 recording stems from an analogue master. The only disappointment is the lack of bands for individual movements. There is a first-class cassette.

Starer, Robert (born 1924)

Violin concerto.
*** HMV Dig. EL 270051-1 [Ang. DS 38011]. Perlman, Boston SO, Ozawa – KIM: *Violin concerto.****

Robert Starer was born in Vienna and spent his formative years in Jerusalem where he was a pupil of Josef Tal. He subsequently went to the Juilliard and studied with Copland; he settled in America in 1957. He has composed three operas, ballet scores for Martha Graham and three piano concertos. His *Violin concerto*, like that of Earl Kim, with which it is coupled, was commissioned by Itzhak Perlman who plays it with dazzling virtuosity, great sympathy and beauty of tone. The playing of the Boston Symphony Orchestra under Ozawa is no less superb and the recording itself is sumptuous. There is a distinctly Middle-Eastern flavour and a strong atmosphere, even if an individual personality is slow to discern.

Stenhammar, Wilhelm (1871–1927)

Symphony No. 2; Overture, Excelsior!, Op. 13.
ꞓ *** BIS **CD 251**; LP 251. Gothenburg SO, Järvi.

The acoustic of the Gothenburg Concert Hall is justly celebrated and enables the orchestra to be heard at its very best. They play with tremendous enthusiasm in *Excelsior!* and the CD produces sound of striking realism. This is a completely truthful and well-balanced recording that conveys to the listener exactly what it is like to be there. *Excelsior!* improves enormously on acquaintance and deserves to become a repertoire work, even if there is a lot of Strauss and Wagner in it. The *Symphony* gets an immensely lively and spirited performance under Järvi, even if its first movement will be too fast for some tastes. The aural image is so 'present' and its range and body so impressive on CD that it is an even more desirable issue than before.

The Song, Op. 44.
*** Cap. Dig. CAP 2185 [id.]. Sörenson, Von Otter, Dahlberg, Wahlgren, Adolf Fredrik Music School Children's Ch., State Ac. of Music Chamber Ch., Swedish R. Ch. and SO, Blomstedt.

Stenhammar's symphonic cantata, *Sången* (*The Song*) is his last major work and this its first recording. It is a noble and, at times, inspired piece which will appeal to readers who love their Elgar. Indeed, Stenhammar occupies a not dissimilar place in Swedish music to that of Elgar in England, and has something of his dignity and nobility. Save for this present work, *The Song* (1920–21), only minor pieces such as the magical score for Tagore's *Chittra* were to follow. *The Song* was commissioned in 1920 by the Swedish Academy of Music to mark its 150th anniversary. Its second performance, in Gothenburg, must have been quite an occasion: Stenhammar conducted *The Song* in the second half, while Nielsen conducted his *Helios overture* and *Hymnus Amoris* before the interval. The first half is a great fantasy in which four different sections can be discerned, and is Stenhammar at his best and most individual; the choral writing is imaginatively laid out and the contrapuntal ingenuity never seems contrived but always at the service of poetic ends. There are some felicitous orchestral touches reminiscent of the earlier orchestral *Serenade*. The second half of the cantata is a lively choral allegro in the style of Handel – diatonic, yet ingenious and imposing; however, it is less interesting than the first half. The solo and choral singing is superb and the whole performance has the total commitment one would expect from these fine choirs and orchestra. The superbly engineered recording does them full justice.

Still, Robert (1910–70)

(i) *Symphony No. 3;* (ii) *Symphony No. 4.*
** Lyr. SRCS 46. (i) LSO, Eugene Goossens; (ii) RPO, Fredman.

Robert Still was a gifted composer and a very considerable musician. His *Third Symphony* is an expertly written piece (the opening sounds a bit Prokofievian and is undeniably attractive), though the slow movement is lacking in depth. It is extremely well played and recorded. Not a work perhaps that one would wish to hear often but not by any means a negligible piece. The *Fourth Symphony* is inspired by a psychological case-history and reflects the composer's interest and specialized knowledge of psychiatry. The RPO respond well for Myer Fredman and are well recorded. A useful reissue from 1971, though still at full price.

Stockhausen, Karlheinz (born 1928)

Goldstaub.
** DG 410 935-1 [id.]. Ensemble directed by composer.

Predominantly meditative, like *Stimmung*, the far greater work which preceded this by a few weeks, *Goldstaub* (*Gold dust*) presents a sequence of powerful and often memorable effects, which however outstay their welcome. The taped material mixes spoken and sung effects (shrieks and the like) with the basic instrumental 'score'. This is a reissue of a 1974 recording, good for its time.

Stimmung (1968).
*** Hyp. A 66115 [id.]. Singcircle, Gregory Rose.

Gregory Rose with his talented vocal group directs an intensely beautiful account of Stockhausen's minimalist meditation on six notes. Expansively it spreads to a full 70 minutes, but it is the variety of effect and response within the sharply limited parameters which comes out in a performance as intense as this, making one concentrate. Though the unsympathetic listener might still find the result boring, this explains admirably how Stockhausen's musical personality can magnetize even with the simplest of formulae. Excellent recording.

Atmen gibt das Leben . . . (choral opera).
*** DG Dig. 410 857-1 [id.]. N. German R. Ch. and SO, composer.

Atmen gibt das Leben . . . (*Breathing gives life*) is among the more approachable and less protracted of Stockhausen's later works, a choral opera in three parts setting a weird collection of texts from Haikus to quotations from Socrates, St Thomas's Gospel and the composer himself. The first part, written before the rest, sets the aphorism, *Breathing gives life, but only singing gives form*; the supplementary parts elaborate that in their stylized presentation of topics: God and man, body and soul, man and nature. Definitive performance and recording to capture atmospheric and distinctive sounds. Stockhausen's DG records do not usually survive in the catalogue for long, so interested readers should snap this one up before it too succumbs to the deletions axe.

Strauss, Johann, Snr (1804–49)

Strauss, Johann, Jnr (1825–99)

Strauss, Josef (1827–70)

Strauss, Eduard (1835–1916)

(All music listed is by Johann Strauss Jnr unless otherwise stated)

Egyptischer Marsch. Overtures: *Die Fledermaus. Der Zigeunerbaron; Perpetuum mobile.* Polkas: *Annen; Auf der Jagd; Pizzicato; Tritsch-Tratsch.* Waltzes: *An der schönen blauen Donau; Geschichten aus dem Wiener Wald; Kaiser; Rosen aus dem Süden; Wiener Blut.*
(B) **(*) DG Walkman *413 432-4* [id.]. Berlin R. O, Fricsay; BPO, Karajan; VPO, Boehm.

This Walkman tape juxtaposes the contrasting personalities of Ferenc Fricsay, Boehm and Karajan – all effective Johann Strauss exponents – in a generous collection of favourites. Fricsay's volatile temperament brings individuality to the *Blue Danube* and *Emperor waltzes*, and he is at his most charismatic in *Tales from the Vienna Woods* and in registering the changing moods of the *Fledermaus overture*. Boehm and Karajan are at their most exuberant in *Roses from the South* and *Vienna blood*, respectively, while the *Egyptian march* has striking panache in Karajan's hands. The recordings come from the 1960s, the earliest 1961; while the sound is variable, it does not seem obviously dated.

Egyptischer Marsch. Overture: *Der Zigeunerbaron. Perpetuum mobile.* Polkas: *Auf der Jagd; Pizzicato; Neue Pizzicato.* Waltzes: *An der schönen blauen Donau; Fledermaus; Frühlingsstimmen; Geschichten aus dem Wiener Wald; Kaiser; Rosen aus dem Süden; 1001 Nacht; Wiener Blut.*
(B) *** Decca *KMC2 9001.* VPO, Boskovsky.

An irresistible ninety-minute tape from Decca's vintage period of Strauss recordings in Vienna at the end of the 1960s. The sound is remarkably vivid and the performances leap out from the speakers to grab the listener with lilting *joie de vivre.* The spontaneity of the playing is a joy throughout; many later Strauss recordings cannot match this for the combination of polish and sparkle. Highly recommended to brighten up any motorway journey.

Napoleon march. Perpetuum mobile. Die Fledermaus: Quadrille. Waltzes: *Geschichten aus dem Wiener Wald; Wiener Blut.* STRAUSS, Johann, Snr: *Radetzky march.* STRAUSS, Josef: Waltzes: *Delirien; Sphärenklänge.*
*** DG Dig. **410 027-2**; 2532/*3302* 027 [id.]. BPO, Karajan.

This collection shows Karajan at his finest, with magically evocative openings to each of the four waltzes, and outstanding performances of *Sphärenklänge, Delirien* and (especially) *Wiener Blut. Perpetuum mobile* and the engaging *Fledermaus quadrille* make a piquant contrast as centrepieces of each side. The brilliant digital recording is equally impressive on disc and cassette. The compact disc, however, adds comparatively little, but emphasizes detail, not entirely to advantage.

Persischer Marsch. Die Fledermaus: overture. Polkas: *Eljen a Magyar; Leichtes Blut; Unter Donner und Blitz.* Waltzes: *Accelerationen; An der schönen blauen Donau; Künstlerleben.*
(*) DG Dig. **400 026-2; 2532/*3302* 025 [id.]. BPO, Karajan.

A superbly played selection. The virility and flair of the waltzes (especially *Künstlerleben*) are matched by the exuberance of the polkas, and the *Fledermaus overture* sparkles so vividly it sounds like a new discovery. This compact disc, however, sounds somewhat clinical in its added detail; the slightly less sharply defined LP and matching chrome tape convey the atmosphere of the occasion more readily.

Persischer Marsch. Polkas: *Annen; Auf der Jagd; Pizzicato* (with Josef); *Unter Donner und Blitz.* Waltzes: *An den schönen blauen Donau; Geschichten aus dem Wiener Wald; Kaiser; Wiener Blut.* STRAUSS, J. Snr: *Radetzky march.*
(M) *** DG Gal. 415 852-1/*4*[id.]. BPO, Karajan.

These recordings are drawn from a pair of LPs, originally issued in 1967 and 1971. The digital remastering has brightened the sound, of the violins especially, but the resonant ambience means that the effect is warmer, with detail clear and less clinical than in the later recordings made in the Philharmonie. The offering is generous and many will like a selection that includes the three greatest waltzes. All the music is beautifully played; there are one or two indulgences (notably in *Wiener Blut*) but effective ones, when the results are still made to sound spontaneous, with the orchestra clearly enjoying their own spirited response. Disc and chrome tape sound virtually identical.

Marches: *Persischer; Russischer. Perpetuum mobile.* Polkas: *Annen; Explosionen; Unter Donner und Blitz.* Waltzes: *Accelerationen;* (i) *An der schönen blauen Donau; Morgenblätter.* STRAUSS, Josef: Polka: *Feuerfest!* Waltzes: *Delirien; Sphärenklänge.*
ɕ *** Decca **411 932-2** [id.]. VPO, Boskovsky; (i) with V. State Op. Ch.

Digitally remastered from recordings made in the 1970s (the earliest from 1971, the last 1976 – though the ear registers very little difference in quality), the results are astonishingly successful, and this makes an easy first choice for compact disc collectors in this repertoire. There is a glorious ambient warmth; the upper range gives the cymbals the right metallic sparkle, yet the strings are naturally clear and lustrous. Detail is refined and the analogue warmth and ambient bloom are most beguiling. The novelty here is the inclusion of the Vienna State Opera Chorus in the original choral version of the *Blue Danube*. These are not the original words (which caused a political storm at the time), but new lyrics introduced in 1890. The effect is rather more robust than the version for the orchestra alone, but the performance has an infectious lilt, with the singers conveying their enjoyment. The rest of the programme is up to the highest Boskovsky standard; the two Josef Strauss items are particularly successful, with the orchestra on top form. There is just about an hour of music here, the background is virtually silent, and the whole concert wonderfully spirited and life-enhancing.

'The Spirit of Vienna': Eine Nacht in Venedig overture. Polkas: *Champagne; Eljen a Magyar; Im Krapfenwald; Neue Pizzicato*. Waltzes: *An der schönen blauen Donau; Geschichten aus dem Wiener Wald; Kaiser; Künstlerleben; Rosen aus dem Süden; Wiener Blut; Wo die Zitronen blüh'n.*
(B) ** HMV *TC2-MOM 102*. Johann Strauss O of V., Boskovsky.

The Boskovsky recordings offered on this 'Miles of Music' double-length tape date from the early 1970s. The performances are genial and stylish; there is no lack of lilt in the phrasing, and the control of rubato is effective. Yet the playing is less memorable and individual than on Boskovsky's Decca VPO tape (see above). With warm, agreeably resonant recording, the effect in the ear is pleasing, and this certainly makes entertaining and undistracting background entertainment for a long journey. At home, the reproduction lacks something in brilliance and detail, but still sounds very acceptable.

New Year concert, 1983. Overtures: *Eine Nacht in Venedig; Indigo und die vierdig Räuber*. Polkas: *Eljen a Magyar; Freikugeln; Wiener bonbons*. Waltzes: *Geschichten aus dem Wiener Wald; Wo die Zitronen blüh'n*. STRAUSS, Josef: Polkas: *Aus der Ferne; Die Libelle; Vélocipède.*
** DG Dig. **410 516-2**; 410 516-1/*4*. VPO, Maazel.

After the noisy applause at the opening, the warmly recessed orchestral image is most welcome. The atmosphere is intimate and Maazel obviously seeks to beguile the ear rather than impress with energetic brilliance. But he goes to the opposite extreme, and both major waltzes are very mellow (although the indulgent opening piece, which gives the record its title, is certainly effective). The account of the *Night in Venice overture*, however, is noticeably self-conscious. In spite of the audience, the spontaneity of the occasion is only sporadically projected, although the orchestral playing is always assured. The recording is smooth without loss of detail, but this is not among the more memorable Strauss collections currently available.

Der Zigeunerbaron overture. Polkas: *Annen; Auf der Jagd; Tritsch-Tratsch*. Waltzes: *Kaiser; Rosen aus dem Süden; Wein, Weib und Gesang*.
(*) DG Dig. **410 022-2; 2532/*3302* 026 [id.]. BPO, Karajan.

This is less attractive than the companion Karajan collections (see above). After a refined introduction, the *Emperor* does not achieve the zest of some of the other waltzes, and although the playing is not without elegance, the noble contour of the principal melody is less potent here than in some versions. The polkas go well, and the overture is a highlight. The digital sound is full and brilliant, and the chrome tape is of excellent quality. On compact disc, the wide dynamic range at the opening of the *Emperor* emphasizes the bright digital sheen on the upper strings. Detail is impressive, although ideally the recording could do with a little more warmth in the lower-middle range.

(i) *Perpetuum mobile*. Polkas: *Champagne;* (ii) *Tritsch-Tratsch;* (i) *Unter Donner und Blitz*. Waltzes: *An der schönen blauen Donau;* (ii) *Kaiser*. (iii) *Casanova: Nuns' chorus*. (iv) *Die Fledermaus: Overture; Bruderlein und Schwesterlein;* (v) *Chacun à son goût;* (vi) *Mein Herr Marquis*. (i) STRAUSS, Johann Snr: *Radetzky march*.
(B) *** CfP CFP 41 4499-1/*4*. (i) Hallé O, Barbirolli; (ii) Philh. O, Henry Krips; (iii) Schwarzkopf, Philh. Ch. and O, Ackermann; (iv) V. State Op. Ch., VPO, Boskovsky, (v) with Brigitte Fassbaender; (vi) Renate Holm.

A splendid collection, played and sung with style and panache, and vividly recorded; the cassette, however, has not always the sharpness of focus of the disc, notably in the *Die Fledermaus* items. These come from Boskovsky's admirable complete set and include the beguilingly sung *Champagne chorus*, Brigitte Fassbaender's superb *Chacun à son goût* (never bettered on record since) and Renate Holm's charming *Mein Herr Marquis*. Barbirolli's splendid performances come from 1967, while the other two equally individual orchestral contributions were recorded most persuasively by the Philharmonia under Henry Krips in 1961. Elisabeth Schwarzkopf's uniquely seductive contribution to the *Nuns' chorus* rounds off a fine entertainment.

Polkas: *Auf der Jagd; Banditen* (*galop*)*; Champagne; Pizzicato* (with Josef)*; Unter Donner und Blitz*. Waltzes: *An der schönen blauen Donau; Geschichten aus dem Wiener Wald*. STRAUSS, Johann Snr: *Radetzky march*. STRAUSS, Josef: *Feuerfest polka*. STRAUSS, Eduard: *Bahn Frei polka*.
* Telarc Dig. **CD 80098**; DG 10098 [id.]. Cincinnati Pops O, Kunzel.

This collection is strictly for those who think the special effects are more important than the music. The accompanying booklet prints a warning in red letters cautioning the listener to 'read page 10 before playing!'. The *Explosions polka* then opens with a cannon shot across the bows which could offer problems to small speaker cones, and other items here are also used as an excuse for various bangs. At the end of the closing *Thunder and lightning polka* the final cannonade is left to echo in the distance. In the overall balance the orchestra is relegated to the background and, within the very resonant acoustic of Music Hall, Cincinnati, much detail is lost, so that the pianissimo plucks of the *Pizzicato polka* recede into inaudibility. Kunzel's performances are plainspun, occasionally rhythmically mannered (as in *Tales from the Vienna Woods*) and in no way memorable, although Josef Strauss's *Feuerfest polka* shows his approach at its most convincingly spectacular.

Polkas: *Episode; I'Tipferl.* Waltzes: *Feuilleton; Flugschriften; Gedankenflug; Die Leitartikel; Morgenblätter.* STRAUSS, Josef: Polkas: *Buchstaben; Sport.*
**(*) HMV Dig. EL 270111-1/*4* [Ang. DS/*4DS* 38146]. Johann Strauss O of V., Boskovsky.

The programme here has a journalistic theme (*Morning papers* and *Leading article* are but two examples) and contains some attractive novelties. Boskovsky is in good form and the performances are spirited, if without the finesse and magic of his famous VPO collections of an earlier era. The sound is excellent, vivid and lively with a good cassette, and the offering is generous. The two items by Josef Strauss are particularly welcome, with the engaging *Buchstaben* making a link with the printing press.

Waltzes: *An der schönen blauen Donau; Frühlingsstimmen; Geschichten aus dem Wiener Wald; Kaiser; Künstlerleben; Rosen aus dem Süden; Wiener Blut.*
(*) HMV Dig. **CDC 747052-2 [id.]; ASD/*TCC-ASD* 4178 [Ang. DS/*4XS* 37892]. Johann Strauss O of V., Boskovsky.

This is Boskovsky's most impressive Strauss collection since his Decca era. From the very opening of the *Blue Danube* the playing balances an evocative Viennese warmth with vigour and sparkle. Each performance is freshly minted, rhythmic nuances are flexibly stylish and the spontaneity is enjoyably obvious. The digital sound is full and vivid and on LP sounds agreeably rich. On CD, however, the string timbre has less bloom, and the resonant acoustic is emphasized. The tape was originally chrome, but is now XDR iron oxide, with an inevitable loss in the upper range. But the spirit of the dance is strikingly present throughout these enjoyable performances.

Waltzes: *An der schönen blauen Donau; Geschichten aus dem Wiener Wald; Kaiser; Rosen aus dem Süden; Wein, Weib und Gesang; Wiener Blut.*
* Ph. Dig. **411 119-2**; 411 119-1/*4* [id.]. V. Volksoper O, Bauer-Theussl.

Franz Bauer-Theussl's performances are well played and the excellent zither player (Karl Swoboda) is given a credit. But with a resonant acoustic emphasizing the lazy tempi, and lack of rhythmic lift or sparkle, this is not tempting, in spite of the good sound.

Die Fledermaus (complete).
*(*) Denon Dig. **C37 7305/6** [id.]. Irosch, Holliday, Juster, Koller, Kmentt, Granzer, Karczykoski, Drahosch, Kraemmer, V. Volksoper Ch. and O, Binder.

In June 1982, Denon engineers recorded this complete performance of *Fledermaus* on stage at the Sun Palace in Fukuoka during the Vienna Volksoper's visit. It is warm, idiomatic and involving, but there are even more snags than in most live recordings. The slabs of spoken dialogue in German sometimes last for four, five or even six minutes at a time, and hardly one of the principals matches in vocal standard what one expects in studio recordings of operetta. As a Viennese veteran, Waldemar Kmentt gives a vividly characterful portrait of Eisenstein, but the voice is painfully strained for much of the time, sometimes not even able to sustain a steady note. The other men are capable but often raw of tone, at times producing sing-speech. Mirjana Irosch as Rosalinde suffers from a pronounced vibrato, though the weight of voice is apt. Melanie Holliday is a tinkly Adele in traditional mould; the voice is not always sweet enough, but she rises well to her big numbers. Dagmar Koller as Prince Orlofsky might be a parody of the traditional mezzo in this role, with Greta Garbo-like tones in her spoken dialogue erupting into a wobbly and fruity singing voice. Binder's brisk conducting is consistently sympathetic. The overture brings exceptionally vivid orchestral sound but, with the addition of stage microphones for the performance proper, the orchestra recedes. There is a great deal of clomping and banging on stage, and the audience applauds at every conceivable moment. Using the discs is made much less convenient when there is no banding, or even indexing, except at the beginnings of Acts.

Still recommended: Boskovsky's Viennese set with a splendid cast (Rothenberger, Holm, Gedda, Fischer-Dieskau, Berry and Fassbaender) has just been withdrawn, no doubt for later reissue at mid-price; Karajan's 'Gala performance' remains on Decca, a sparkling account but with an uneven singing cast, compensated for by vintage contributions from many famous artists (ranging from Joan Sutherland's *Il Bacio* to Simionato and Bastianini going over the top in *Anything you can do, I can do better*) in the interpolated party scene (D247 D3/*K247 K32* [Lon. OSA 1319]).

Wiener Blut (complete).
** Denon Dig. **C37 7430/1** [id.]. Martikke, Kales, Dallapozza, Dönch, V. Volksoper Ch. and O, Bibl.

This warmly idiomatic performance by the company of the Vienna Volksoper was recorded live in 1982 in Tokyo. Though the fun of the occasion comes over well, the performance is too flawed to give consistent pleasure, and the extended dialogue will please only fluent German speakers, though it is well acted. Both the principal women soloists are shrill of voice, Elisabeth Kales very edgy as the seductive dancer, Franzi, Siegrid Martikke fluttery as the Countess. Dallapozza as the Count gives the most accomplished performance, though even he overacts. Karl Dönch, veteran bass, also director of the Volksoper, makes a welcome appearance in the character role of the princely Prime Minister. The full text is given, together with translations in minuscule print, but no very relevant information about the operetta itself. There is no banding nor even any index points, except at the beginning of Acts. The recording is dry but realistic enough, not helpful to the singers.

Strauss, Josef (1827–70)

Polkas: *Feuerfest; Frauenherz; Im Fluge; Jockey; Ohne Sorgen; Die Schwätzerin; Vorwärt.* Waltzes: *Aquarellen; Delirien; Dorfschwalben aus Österreich* (*Village swallows*)*; Dynamiden; Mein Lebenslauf ist Lieb und Lust.*
*** HMV Dig. ASD 143616-1/*4* [Ang. DS/*4DS* 38077]. Johann Strauss O of Vienna, Boskovsky.

Willi Boskovsky topped off his series of analogue Johann Strauss recordings for Decca with a 1976 LP devoted entirely to the music of brother Josef. His affection for this repertoire plus a sense of freshness of discovery came over vividly on that occasion, helped by refined playing from the Vienna Philharmonic and splendid Decca sound. The disc was given a Rosette in an earlier edition of the *Guide*. It has long disappeared, but we hope that it will re-emerge on CD in due course. This new digital concert is also very enjoyable, generously offering nearly an hour of Josef's music. Boskovsky again communicates both his affection and his special feeling for Josef's music and he secures a committed response from his players, notably in the *Delirien waltz* which has fine zest. The sound is excellent on both disc and the very well-managed cassette; this can be strongly recommended, for many of these pieces are able to stand alongside all but the most inspired of Johann's works. However, the finesse and subtlety of detail of the earlier collection resonate in the memory.

Strauss, Richard (1864–1949)

An Alpine symphony, Op. 64.
*** DG Dig. **400 039-2**; 2532/*3302* 015 [id.]. BPO, Karajan.
*** Ph. Dig. **416 156-2**; 416 156-1/*4* [id.]. Concg. O, Haitink.
*** Decca **414 676-2** [id.]; SXL 6959 [Lon. CS 7189]. Bav. RSO, Solti.

The *Alpine symphony* has all the rhetoric, confidence and opulence of the great Strauss tone-poems, but, judged by the finest of them, its melodic invention is less fresh and its gestures sometimes ring a hollow note. But there is much to relish and enjoy.

Karajan's account is recorded digitally, but orchestral detail is less analytical than in Solti's Decca version with the Bavarian Radio orchestra, which is fresher and more transparent and has not the slight edge to the upper strings that is a feature of the DG digital recording. But it would be wrong to give the impression that the DG sound is less than first class and, as a performance, the Karajan is in the highest flight. It is wonderfully spacious, beautifully shaped and played with the utmost virtuosity. This is certainly one of the finest accounts now available, though Kempe's version (see below) has more breadth and majesty and no less atmosphere. The compact disc increases the recording's presence and clarity and has a firmer, better-defined bass response. The DG chrome cassette matches the

LP closely, although side one has fractionally less sparkle at the top than side two. However, the edge noticeable on the disc is softened on tape.

Haitink's account on Philips is a splendid affair, a far more natural-sounding recording than the Karajan on DG, more spacious and less frenetic than Solti on Decca, and strongly characterized throughout. The offstage horns sound suitably exciting, the perspective is excellent, and there is plenty of atmosphere, particularly in the episode of the calm before the storm. Above all, the architecture of the work as a whole is impressively laid out and the orchestral playing is magnificent. This does not quite displace Karajan (or Kempe – see below), but it can hold its own with the best. There is a first-class cassette.

The Bavarian Radio orchestra under Solti, recorded in the Herkulessaal in Munich, could hardly sound more opulent, with brass of striking richness. That warmth of sound and the superb quality of the 1980 analogue recording tend to counterbalance the generally fast tempi. Many of them are in principle too fast, but with such sympathetic and committed playing in such a setting, the results are warm rather than frenetic. The CD transfer is highly successful.

An Alpine symphony; Ein Heldenleben.
(B) **(*) HMV *TCC-2 POR 54279*. Dresden State O, Kempe.

With no break in continuity in either work, this is one of the best-conceived issues in EMI's 'Portrait of the Artist' series; though the reverberant acoustic has brought minor problems, with transients not absolutely clean, in all other respects this is a success. The richness of tone provided by this splendid orchestra is captured in all its sumptuousness and both performances are glowing with life, under one of the most distinguished Straussians of our time.

Also sprach Zarathustra, Op. 30.
ၦ *** Ph. Dig. **400 072-2**; 6514/*7337* 221 [id.]. Boston SO, Ozawa.
(*) CBS **CD 35888 [IM/*HMT* 35888]. NYPO, Mehta.

Also sprach Zarathustra; Don Juan, Op. 20.
*** DG Dig. **410 959-4**; 410 959-1/*4* [id.]. BPO, Karajan.

Also sprach Zarathustra; Macbeth, Op. 23.
(*) Decca Dig. **410 146-2; SXDL/*KSXDC* 7613 [Lon. LDR/*5*- 71113]. Detroit SO, Dorati.

Also sprach Zarathustra; Till Eulenspiegel, Op. 28. Salome: Salome's dance.
(M) *** DG Gal. 415 853-1 (without *Salome's dance*)/*415 853-4* [id.]. BPO, Karajan.

In its compact disc version, Ozawa's warmly persuasive version of *Also sprach Zarathustra* became one of the first demonstration records for the new medium, when the depth and unforced firmness of the organ pedal sound leading on to an extraordinary crescendo over the spectacular introduction gave clear indication of its extra potential. The solo strings are balanced rather close, but otherwise this is a wonderfully warm and natural sound, with both a natural bloom and fine inner clarity. Ozawa as a Strauss interpreter goes for seductive phrasing and warmth rather than high drama or nobility. The chrome cassette also offers an impressive sound-balance, without a hint of distortion at the opening, but this has been achieved by using a very low transfer level with attendant hiss.

Karajan's 1974 version of *Also sprach Zarathustra* has now been reissued at mid-price, coupled with his vividly characterized performance of *Till Eulenspiegel* from the same period, also played with stunning virtuosity. This account of *Also sprach* has long held sway and up to now would be a strong first recommendation, in spite of the excellence of many of its rivals. His 1984 version has, of course, the advantage of the new technology and, as far as the compact disc is concerned, can offer greater dynamic range and presence, particularly at the extreme bass and treble. As a performance, this newcomer will be very hard to beat and, looking at it solely from the viewpoint of a CD collector, it could well be a first choice. The playing of the Berlin Philharmonic Orchestra is as glorious as ever; its virtuosity can be taken for granted along with its sumptuous tonal refinement, and in Strauss, of course, Karajan has no peer. As a recording it is very good indeed, though it does not offer the spectacular definition and transparency of detail of the Dorati CD version on Decca. But the playing, it goes without saying, is in a totally different league. Of course, couplings also come into it and Dorati offers a rarity in the form of *Macbeth*, whereas both Ozawa and Mehta are handicapped by having no coupling at all. Karajan offers an exciting account of *Don Juan* and this performance is generally preferred to its current CD rivals (see below). To sum up, this new issue is a strong recommendation for CD collectors, while the chrome tape too is clear and refined, losing little in range and definition. But otherwise, Karajan's great 1974 recording is not displaced. Put the CD alongside the LP, not of the present version but of Karajan's 1974 account, and you will be surprised to discover how well the latter holds up in its digitally remastered format, even though the now more brightly lit upper strings have lost something of their original sumptuousness. The Galleria chrome cassette avoids the LP side-break in the middle of *Also sprach Zarathustra* and fills up the space on side two with Karajan's powerfully voluptuous account of *Salome's dance*. In sound quality the tape matches the LP closely, for the transfer is outstandingly clear and clean.

There are no doubts as to the greater transparency and presence of the Decca recording, which has wider range and more detail on both disc and tape. Yet it does not set out merely to produce a sonic spectacular: the sound is vivid and brilliant, without being overlit. However, the Detroit orchestra is no match for the Berlin Philharmonic in terms of richness of sonority, homogeneity of tone and ensemble, and Maazel has the greater grip and keener vitality. Splendid though it sounds on its own, as soon as it is placed side by side with the DG version, Dorati's *Zarathustra* does not sound so firmly held together and *Macbeth* is not as well characterized. It is an early work whose first version appeared in 1887 when Strauss was barely twenty-three; but the composer revised it at the instigation of von Bülow and it was completed in its definitive form after *Don Juan* – hence the later opus number. It is powerful and does not quite deserve the neglect it suffers in the concert hall. The best current version is Maazel's (DG 410 597-1/*4* – not available on CD). In *Zarathustra*, Karajan remains unsurpassed.

Mehta's CBS account is predictably exciting and the recording is brilliantly clear and positive. There is some superbly eloquent horn playing, and the forceful thrust of Mehta's reading brings undoubted exhilaration at climaxes; the appearance of the midnight bell at the apotheosis of the *Tanzlied* makes a spectacular effect, and the closing *Nachtwanderlied* is tenderly played. But Karajan finds more mysticism in the score than Mehta, and the bright sheen on the New York strings is less telling than the Berlin string timbre in the 'Yearning' and 'Passion' sequences.

Also sprach Zarathustra; Don Juan; Ein Heldenleben, Op. 40.
(M) ** DG 415 637-1/*4* (2). BPO or VPO, Boehm.

Also sprach Zarathustra; Don Juan; Till Eulenspiegel.
(*) Decca **414 043-2 [id.]. Chicago SO, Solti.

Also sprach Zarathustra; (i) *Don Quixote, Op. 35.*
(M) *** HMV Green. ED 290801-1/*4*. (i) Tortelier; Dresden State O, Kempe.

(i) *Also sprach Zarathustra;* (ii; iii) *Ein Heldenleben;* (iv; iii) *Till Eulenspiegel.*
(B) **(*) DG Walkman *413 431-4* [id.]. (i) Boston SO, Steinberg; (ii) VPO; (iv) BPO; (iii) Boehm.

Kempe's 1974 *Also sprach Zarathustra*, though powerful in its emotional thrust, is completely free of the sensationalism that marks so many newer performances. It is admirably paced and, while the Dresden orchestra may yield in virtuosity – though not much – to the Berlin Philharmonic under Karajan whose Galleria version was made in the same year, the HMV digital remastering retains the opulence of the Dresden acoustic and the orchestral sound has more body and bloom than the Galleria reissue (see above). Moreover, the coupling is extraordinarily generous: the total playing time of this Greensleeve disc and tape is 73′ 12″. Kempe's 1973 performance of *Don Quixote* is one of the very finest available. The balance gives the cellist an exaggeratedly forward projection, so that the work is made to sound almost like a cello concerto at times, but Paul Tortelier's contribution is a very fine one; the overall orchestral balance combines vividness with a rich, Straussian homogeneity of texture which is warmly appealing. The tape transfer is particularly satisfying; the slight loss in the upper range is not serious, for detail is unimpaired, the cello focus is excellent and the big climaxes of *Also sprach* are sumptuously accommodated without strain.

Boehm's version of *Also sprach Zarathustra* is undoubtedly distinguished, passionate and finely structured. But the 1958 recording is dated by its upper string timbre. *Don Juan* (1964) is much more successful technically, and is admirably vivid (glorious leaping strings and rich thrusting horns). For *Ein Heldenleben*, Boehm turns to the VPO and, although the orchestral playing is first class, the reading lacks the dash and fire of its companions. He is a shade dour and a little too conscious of his dignity by comparison with the swaggering hero created by Karajan.

This performance is common to the Walkman cassette, with the 1974 *Till Eulenspiegel*, another of Boehm's finest Strauss readings, offered instead of *Don Juan*. Steinberg's 1972 *Also sprach Zarathustra* is sumptuously recorded, with the orchestra slightly recessed within the warm Boston acoustic, which adds to the sentient feeling of what is essentially a lyrical account, of considerable ardour. It has been well transferred to tape and, if Boehm's *Ein Heldenleben* is acceptable, this is excellent value.

Solti's performances come from analogue originals of the mid-1970s and the coupling is apt and generous. Solti is ripely expansive in *Also sprach Zarathustra* and throughout there is glorious playing from the Chicago orchestra in peak form. This is Solti at his strongest, with this most Germanic of American orchestras responding in the manner born. The transfer to CD is impressive, even if the finest digital versions aerate the textures more.

Le bourgeois gentilhomme: suite, Op. 60.
*** RCA Dig. **RD 85362**; RL/*RK* 85362 [HRC1/*HRK1* 5362]. Canadian Nat. Arts Centre O, Mata – WIRÉN: *Serenade*.***

Strauss's delightful suite with its beguiling post-*Rosenkavalier* atmosphere is admirably suited to Mata's talents; he gives a persuasively warm and elegant account – the finest yet to have appeared on record. The orchestra is a chamber group, led by Walter Prystawski whose playing of the violin obbligatos is wholly admirable. The recording ambience is perhaps a shade too resonant, but the effect is so pleasing, bathing the orchestra in a glowing ambient bloom, that criticism is disarmed. The CD refines detail and adds the considerable advantage of background silence, but the cassette is first class too, though the resonance means that detail is less sharp.

Horn concertos Nos 1 in E flat, Op. 11; 2 in E flat.
(*) Ph. Dig. **412 237-2; 412 237-1/*4* [id.]. Baumann, Leipzig GO, Masur – WEBER: *Concertino*.***

Dennis Brain made these concertos his own and we hope that one day his superlative performances will be issued on compact disc. Baumann is at his finest in the first movement of the *Second Concerto* (which comes first on the CD), where his glowing phrasing of the lyrical main theme is very engaging. His broad stream of tone and consummate technique bring much pleasure throughout both works, and the florid finale of the *Second Concerto* is articulated with enviable ease. But this easy-going quality also brings some relaxation of normal tensions. The bold contrasting episode at the centre of the slow movement of Op. 11 ideally needs a kind of *Don Juan*-like fervour to make its best effect, as Dennis Brain demonstrated. The soloist here is most truthfully caught, but the orchestra, slightly recessed in the reverberant Leipzig acoustic, loses some of its edge in the brilliant tuttis, while inner detail is not sharp. However, if you enjoy an essentially lyrical approach to these very tuneful concertos, this will be no disappointment, for the sound is consistently warm and flattering.

Death and Transfiguration, Op. 24.
(*) HMV Dig. **CDC 747013-2 [id.]; ASD/*TCC-ASD* 4182 [Ang. DS/*4XS* 37887]. LPO, Tennstedt – *4 Last songs.****

Tennstedt's account of *Death and Transfiguration* is a direct yet impressively spacious performance, very well played and recorded, and the CD transfer is both full and clear. The tape was originally transferred on chrome stock, but has now reverted to iron-oxide XDR. This is a less than ideal coupling for Lucia Popp's irresistible account of the *Four last songs*, for Tennstedt would not be first choice in the symphonic poems.

Death and Transfiguration; Don Juan; (i) *Don Quixote, Op. 35.*
(B) *** DG Walkman *419 090-4* [id.]. (i) Fournier; BPO, Karajan.

Death and Transfiguration; Don Juan; Metamorphosen for 23 solo strings; Till Eulenspiegel; Salome: Dance of the seven veils.
(B) **(*) HMV *TCC2-POR 54296*. Philh. O, Klemperer.

Death and Transfiguration; Don Juan; Till Eulenspiegel; Salome: Dance of the seven veils.
(M) **(*) HMV ED 290616-1/*4*. Philh. O, Klemperer.

Karajan's superlative analogue version of *Death and Transfiguration* can still be regarded as a showpiece, even among Karajan's earliest set of analogue Strauss recordings with the Berlin Philharmonic. Like *Don Juan* it dates from 1973; although, in its Walkman incarnation, textures are slightly leaner than in the latter piece, the sound is both vivid and refined in its detail. The thrilling account of *Don Juan*, played with stunning virtuosity, offers sound of striking fidelity in its Walkman transfer, with gloriously full violins above the stave and excellent overall clarity within an ambience that seems near ideal. In *Don Quixote*, Fournier's partnership with Karajan is outstanding. His portrayal of the Don has no less nobility than his previous rivals, and he brings great subtlety and (when required) repose to the part. The finale and Don Quixote's death are very moving in Fournier's hands, while Karajan's handling of orchestral detail is quite splendid. The 1963 recording has been remastered and sounds remarkably fresh and transparent, though the sound is less sumptuous than the Kempe/Tortelier Dresden version on HMV – see above – which is a comparable bargain.

This double-length tape in EMI's 'Portrait of the Artist' series admirably assembles Klemperer's Richard Strauss recordings in convenient form at a reasonable price. In his hands it is the *Metamorphosen* and *Death and Transfiguration* that excite the greatest admiration. With Klemperer the work for strings has a ripeness that exactly fits Strauss's last essay for orchestra, while *Death and Transfiguration* is invested with a nobility too rarely heard in this work. Not everyone will respond to Klemperer's spacious treatment of the other works. His account of *Salome's dance* is splendidly sensuous, but the ennobled *Till* lacks something in boisterous high spirits, and *Don Juan* is clearly seen as 'the idealist in search of perfect womanhood'. But with marvellous Philharmonia playing and a recording which still sounds sumptuous this collection is certainly not lacking in strength of characterization. The level of the tape transfers might have been higher (especially in *Metamorphosen*, where the cello line is not always very clear) but generally detail is good.

As can be seen, four of the Klemperer performances are also available on a mid-priced LP and tape, digitally remastered, with detail clarified, but the inclusion of *Metamorphosen* makes the double-length cassette more attractive and the cost is only marginally greater.

Death and Transfiguration; Don Juan; Till Eulenspiegel.
*** Ph. Dig. **411 442-2**; 6514/*7337* 228 [id.]. Concg. O, Haitink.
*** DG Dig. **410 518-2**; 2532/*3302* 099 [id.]. LSO, Abbado.
(*) CBS Dig. **CD 35826 [IM/*IMT* 35826]. Cleveland O, Maazel.
(*) Decca Dig. **400 085-2; SXDL/*KSXDC* 7523 [Lon. LDR/*5*- 71025]. Detroit SO, Dorati.

Among recent versions of this most popular coupling, Haitink's takes the palm. The Philips digital recording is less analytical than the sound pictures DG provide for Abbado or Decca for Dorati (which is exceptionally clear) but the ambient bloom of the Concertgebouw is admirably suited to Strauss's rich orchestral tapestries and detail is naturally defined. The CD enhances the overall effect, and the opening of *Death and Transfiguration* is particularly telling against the silent background. Haitink's performances are undoubtedly distinguished, superbly played, persuasively and subtly characterized. Even Karajan hardly displays more dash. He and the Berlin Philharmonic have a unique authority in this repertoire, but Haitink finds added nobility in *Death and Transfiguration*, while there is no lack of swagger in the characterizations of both the Don and Till. The easy brilliance of the orchestral playing is complemented by the natural spontaneity of Haitink's readings, seamless in the transition between narrative events, without loss of the music's picaresque or robust qualities. When the sound is so full and spacious as well as vivid (on the excellent chrome tape as well as the CD and LP) this must receive the strongest recommendation.

The performances under Claudio Abbado have plenty of dash and their brilliance is tempered with sensitivity. Some may feel that *Don Juan* veers too much towards the exuberant showpiece and vehicle for display, but both this and *Till Eulenspiegel* must be numbered among the best available. Abbado's *Death and Transfiguration* is scarcely less impressive than Karajan's and has a marvellously spacious opening. The strings produce some splendidly silky tone and there is much sensitive wind playing too. Haitink and Karajan still reign supreme in this work, but Abbado runs them very close and he is equally well recorded. On the chrome tape *Don Juan* and *Till* present a rather recessed image, though *Death and Transfiguration* has more projection and brilliance, while compared with the Philips Concertgebouw sound for Haitink, the DG upper range on CD is less smoothly natural.

Maazel repeats a coupling made famous by George Szell at the peak of his era with the Cleveland Orchestra. Szell's performances had tremendous vitality and electricity and are issued in their enhanced CD format on a CBS/Sony compact disc (**32DC 216**, available only in Japan or, to special order and at a price, from some specialist sources in the USA). Maazel's approach is entirely different from Szell's. With superbly committed support from his players, he takes an extrovert view of *Death and Transfiguration*; the mortal struggle is frenzied enough, but there is comparatively little feeling of menace, and when the transformation comes, the opulent climax is endearingly rose-tinted. The portrayal of *Till* is warmly affectionate, but the reading is exhilaratingly paced and has excellent detail. *Don Juan* too is made totally sympathetic, with Maazel relishing every moment. In the famous love scene, the oboe solo is glowingly sensuous; the final climax is ecstatic, the tempo broadened when the strings rapturously take up the great horn tune. On CD, the CBS digital sound is sumptuous, richly glowing, but does not lack clarity, and the brass has telling bite and sonority. The chrome cassette too (transferred at a high level) has comparable body.

Dorati's Decca recording is also digital and its internal clarity is striking. Dorati's approach to *Death and Transfiguration* is more austere than Maazel's; there is plenty of atmosphere, a certain dignity in the struggle and a sense of foreboding before the release at the end, where the climax has real splendour (and a magnificent breadth of sound). Dorati's view of *Don Juan* is heroic, the sensuality played down by the sound-balance, brilliant rather than sumptuous. After a central love scene which is tenderly delicate, there is satiety and disillusion at the end. *Till* is essentially a picaresque portrait, not without humour and well paced, but a little lacking in affectionate involvement. In spite of a transfer level that is lower than usual from Decca, there is no appreciable difference in sound between disc and cassette. On CD, the dazzling brilliance of detail and focus is even more telling.

Death and Transfiguration; Metamorphosen for 23 solo strings.
❀ *** DG Dig. **410 892-2**; 2532/*3302* 074 [id.]. BPO, Karajan.

Karajan made the pioneering record of *Metamorphosen* with the Vienna Philharmonic in 1947 and brings a special authority to this valedictory work. His new digital account has even greater emotional urgency than the 1971 record he made with the Berlin Philharmonic and there is a marginally quicker pulse (in 1971 he took 27′ 30″ as opposed to 26′ 11″ in this 1983 version). The sound is fractionally more forward and cleaner (though some may find the richer ambience of the earlier analogue disc more appealing). The newer version, however, still sounds sumptuous and the account of *Death and Transfiguration* is quite electrifying. The recording balance is not so spectacular as Dorati's on Decca, nor so spacious as Tennstedt's on HMV (see above), but there is no lack of vividness, and the playing of the Berliners is in itself thrilling. It would be difficult to improve on this coupling by the greatest Strauss conductor of the day. The compact disc of the later recording is in a class of its own, bringing a marginally firmer image than the LP and greater range, while the background silence is especially telling in the *Metamorphosen*.

Don Juan, Op. 20.
(***) Ph. mono **416214-2** [id.]. Concg. O, Mengelberg – FRANCK: *Symphony*.(***)

Mengelberg gave many Strauss first performances, and this account of *Don Juan* penetrates to the very heart of its heroic fervour and its alternating virtuosity and tenderness. Listening to this performance leaves no doubt as to why the great German-born conductor exercised so strong a hold over audiences in the inter-war years. The Concertgebouw Orchestra has always been of legendary quality; its debt to Mengelberg, who guided its fortunes from 1895 until the end of the Second World War, is obvious. Mengelberg achieves songful, powerfully shaped lines whose lyrical intensity and dramatic fire still strike home, even through the inevitably dated sound.

Don Juan; Ein Heldenleben, Op. 40.
*(**) RCA **RD 85408 [RCD1 5408]**; GL/*GK* 85257. Chicago SO, Reiner.

Reiner's versions of both these Strauss showpieces are among the finest ever. *Don Juan* has a superbly thrilling climax where the great horn theme leaps out unforgettably. For its 1950s vintage the RCA early stereo of the time was outstanding. This generous coupling makes a valuable addition to the 'Legendary Performers' series, but in clarifying the rather muddy originals the digital transfer does not quite convey the full body of sound needed.

Don Quixote, Op. 35 (see also above, under *Also sprach Zarathustra* and *Death and Transfiguration*).
(*) CBS Dig. **MK 39863; IM/*IMT* 39863 [id.]. Yo-Yo Ma, Boston SO, Ozawa – MONN: *Cello concerto*.**(*)

Yo-Yo Ma's portrait of the Don is masterly and, as always, he plays with impeccable taste and refined tone, though at times pianissimos are exaggerated and affectation comes dangerously close. Ozawa is a shade cautious in matters of characterization, as if he is determined not to be thought brash. Karajan's performance has more panache, and the opening theme is a shade more idiomatic in his hands. Although Ozawa pays scrupulous attention to detail (the encounter with the sheep is marvellously done), the very last ounce of Straussian braggadocio is wanting. At the moment this is the only version available on CD, and the CBS recording has a lot going for it: tonally it is very natural and the balance between cello and orchestra is true to life. The orchestral texture is transparent and detail is excellent, though there is a trace of hardness evident when reproduced at a high level setting. There is a good chrome cassette, losing only a little of the transparency of the disc versions.

Duet concertino for clarinet, bassoon, strings and harp.
** None. Dig. **79018-2**; D/*D4* 79018 [id.]. Shifrin, Munday, LACO, Schwarz – HONEGGER: *Concerto da camera*.**

The Strauss work appeared within a year or two of the Honegger with which it is coupled, and so it is a late piece. It is very nicely played here, though the performance does not obliterate memories of the deleted Kempe version included in the Dresden Strauss complete-concertos box on HMV, which had greater warmth both as a performance and as sound. The present issue is nevertheless a perfectly likeable account.

Ein Heldenleben, Op. 40.
*** Denon Dig. **C37 7561** [id.]. Dresden State O, Blomstedt.
(M) *** Ph. Seq. 6527/*7311* 128 [id.]. Concg. O, Haitink.
(*) DG Dig. **415 508-2; 415 508-1/*4* [id.]. BPO, Karajan.
(*) Decca Dig. **414 292-2; 414 292-1/*4* [id.]. Cleveland O, Ashkenazy.
(*) Ph. Dig. **400 073-2 [id.]. Boston SO, Ozawa.
** CBS **MK 76675** [id.]. Cleveland O, Maazel.
* CBS **MK 37756**; IM/*IMT* 37756 [id.]. NYPO, Maazel.

Strauss's *Ein Heldenleben* is already well served on CD but, in any assessment, Haitink's analogue Concertgebouw version must be remembered, for it is outstanding as a recording as well as for the distinction of the performance. Among the CDs, curiously, the Blomstedt disc with the Dresden Staatskapelle for Denon comes close to the sound we used to associate with DG in the analogue era, warm, with articulate detail, but great tonal homogeneity. Blomstedt shapes his performance with both authority and poetry. One can tell from the outset that this is the real thing, for there is a genuine heroic stride and a sense of dramatic excitement here, while the Dresden orchestra, which has a long Strauss tradition, creates glorious Straussian textures. The melodic lines always mean something (as indeed they do in the Karajan and Ashkenazy accounts), and the whole edifice is held together in a way that commands admiration. The violinist, Peter Mirring, is the finest of the players on the CD versions under review and worthy to be discussed alongside Michel Schwalbé in the earlier Karajan analogue version (DG 2535 194) or Herman Krebbers in the Haitink. The recording, though not as transparent as Ashkenazy's Decca, is warm and wide-ranging. The measure of a great Strauss conductor lies in his capacity to produce sumptuous, refined and well-balanced sonorities, to ensure that colours and expressive detail remain in the right perspective and, above all, to pace the score so that each climax registers at the right level. In these respects, Blomstedt's account is the most completely satisfying CD.

Haitink's 1971 version of *Ein Heldenleben* is one of his very finest records. He gives just the sort of performance, brilliant and swaggering but utterly without bombast, which will delight those who normally resist this rich and expansive work. With a direct and fresh manner that yet conveys consistent urgency, he gives a reading which makes even such fine rival versions as Karajan's or Ashkenazy's sound a little superficial. In the culminating fulfilment theme, a gentle, lyrical 6/8, Haitink finds a raptness in restraint, a hint of agony within joy, that links the passage directly with the great Trio from *Der Rosenkavalier*.

The Philips sound – freshened in this reissue – is admirably faithful, refined but full and brilliant too. The cassette is outstanding, one of Philips's best, matching the disc closely.

Karajan's new *Heldenleben* is his third on records (and his second for DG), being separated from the first by no less than a quarter of a century. His reading of this score has tremendous sweep and all the authority and mastery we have come to expect – and, indeed, take for granted. Nor is the orchestral playing anything other than glorious – indeed, in terms of sheer virtuosity the Berlin players have never surpassed this. It is the architectural mastery, the sheer grip that Karajan exerts over the canvas as a whole that is so impressive, together with his tremendous command of the long-arched melodic line. There is also a dramatic fire and virtuosity that are quite electrifying. Leon Speirer gives a highly characterized account of the long solo cadenzas, with which some might quarrel, emphasizing the domineering and shrewish quality of Pauline; Michel Schwalbé in the 1959 Karajan set undoubtedly had the greater finesse and portrayed a more cultured Hero's Companion. Even with the advantage of CD, the recording falls a little short of the highest of present-day standards, though it has no want of firmness and body. The upper strings, however, are a little lacking in bloom and a shade congested. Comparing the 'Critics' section with the 1959 recording and making allowances for the difference in frequency range and dynamic spectrum, one is struck by the greater space around each instrument, the deeper perspective and the richer bloom on the strings on the earlier disc. The new DG recording is neither as transparent nor as finely detailed as Decca's for Ashkenazy – or, for that matter, as Philips for Haitink. The chrome cassette transfer, however, is extremely well managed.

The Decca version from Vladimir Ashkenazy and the Cleveland Orchestra is predictably the best recording *per se*. Of the CDs, the Decca has the greatest range and transparency of detail and the firmest definition. Ashkenazy gives a refreshing reading, with fast speeds the rule and a volatile element regularly dispelling any hint of pomposity. It has much to commend it, though something of the grandeur, the broad canvas and the sense of drama that the greatest Strauss conductors have found in it is missing. However, there is much more to admire than to deprecate, and it is, particularly in its compact disc form, the most impressive of recordings. The cassette too, transferred at the highest level, is extremely fine technically although, like all the other cassettes of this work (except Kempe's – coupled with the *Alpine symphony* – see above), it suffers from a side-break as distracting as anything experienced in the days of 78 r.p.m. discs.

Ozawa's view of *Heldenleben* is free-flowing, lyrical and remarkably unpompous. He consistently brings out the joy of the virtuoso writing, and though the playing of the Boston orchestra is not quite so immaculate as in the companion version of *Zarathustra*, the richness and transparency are just as seductive, superbly caught by the Philips engineers. The compact disc version adds significantly to the sense of presence and reality. The chrome cassette is full and clear, though not as wide-ranging on top. But there is attendant hiss, occasioned by the relatively low transfer level.

Lorin Maazel is basically a perceptive and idiomatic Straussian, and it goes without saying that the playing of the Cleveland Orchestra is impressive under his direction – as it is, too, for Ashkenazy on Decca. Moreover, the breadth of his reading with its unhurried pace and thoroughly idiomatic feel is to be admired. But on CD, as in the LP version, the sound of the orchestra is cloaked in an opulent reverberation, the very opposite of an analytical recording. Even so, the overall effect is just a little unnatural, for the wind are not quite in perspective, and one remains aware of the multi-mike technique. Taken in isolation, the sound is far from unacceptable; but put alongside the best rival recordings, this lacks real transparency.

Generally speaking, the alternative Mehta version on CBS offers a very acceptable sound, with good body and a sense of space, though it is not among the most distinguished from this source. As a performance, it is not outstanding at all, though it starts out very well. However, it lacks breadth or any sense of vision. The players don't always attack the score with real appetite. As far as the balance is concerned, there are some oddities: the pizzicato E flat from the violas five bars after fig. 6 leaps out of the aural picture quite unnaturally, and the clarinet is far too close. For all the bombast, there is a certain dignity about Strauss's hero – and this does not come across in Mehta's hands. Mehta drools over certain details and the final coda reeks with sentiment. All in all, this is a far less impressive account than his earlier Decca one with the Los Angeles Philharmonic Orchestra which, if it lacked subtlety, had a satisfying directness and thrust.

Symphonia domestica, Op. 53; Macbeth, Op. 20.
** DG Dig. **413 654-2**; (*Symphonia* only) 413 460-1/*4* [id.]. VPO, Maazel.

A tone-poem rather than a symphony, Strauss's *Symphonia domestica* is the second in what one assumes is going to be a new Strauss series from the Vienna Philharmonic and Maazel. Ten years have elapsed since the last *Domestica* appeared, so it obviously figures low in popular esteem. It has come in for some pretty harsh criticism in its day: Newman called the attempts at realism 'pitiably foolish', and Romain Rolland called the erotic scene 'in extremely bad taste'; yet those who grew up with Clemens Krauss's inspiring performance in the early days of mono LP will need no reminder that there is more richness and humanity in this work than many interpreters discover. Karajan has called it one of Strauss's greatest works, and on his 1974 record the Berlin orchestra played as if they loved every semiquaver of it. Maazel's is a very good performance, too, and the recording is altogether admirable. It may be a counsel of perfection but, for all its excellence, comparison with the Karajan is not to Maazel's advantage; both Karajan and, for that matter, Kempe touched the listener more in this music. The LP and cassette formats offer only the symphony, but the CD gives us a bonus in the shape of *Macbeth*, which appeared on LP and tape coupled with Maazel's finely played *Also sprach Zarathustra* (DG 410 597-1/*4*). The performance of *Macbeth* is highly polished and superbly played. The chrome tape – albeit not transferred at the highest level because of the wide dynamic range – is very well managed though, like the LP, it does not represent good value: side two plays for a mere 14′ 28″.

Symphony for wind in E flat (*The happy workshop*).
** Orfeo **C 004821A** [id.]. Mun. Wind Ac., Sawallisch.

Strauss's *Wind symphony* is a late work, dating from 1944. The composer preferred to call it a sonata, and it was the publisher who decided on the title change. As suggested by the subtitle, it is essentially a genial piece, though the finale opens sombrely before the mood lightens. This comes off quite well, as does the nicely played *Andantino*, but the focus of the first movement is less sure and the music making often lacks a necessary smiling quality. The recording, though full and homogeneous in texture, does not display the inner clarity one would expect from a digital source; the CD is poor value, playing for only 38½′. There was certainly room here for another of Strauss's wind pieces.

Piano sonata in B min., Op. 5; 5 Pieces, Op. 3.
*** CBS **CD 38659**; 38659/*40*- [id.]. Glenn Gould.

This was Glenn Gould's last record, made in New York in September 1982. It is one of his finest, and many will be willing to accept the inevitable vocalise, for the interest of the repertoire and the mastery of the playing. The recording too is first rate, especially on CD, where the image is strikingly firm and believable, but also on the excellent chrome tape where the piano timbre is fully coloured, yet the focus is clear. Strauss wrote the *Sonata* (his third) when he was sixteen, and its maturity and structural strength are remarkable. True, it quotes – freely and rather engagingly – from the first movement of Beethoven's *Fifth Symphony* in the first movement, but the rest of the invention is fresh, if with no hints of the orchestral Strauss to come. The *Five Pieces*, from the same period, although very well wrought, are less distinctive, even if the opening *Andante* is most appealing. Gould characterizes them strongly, with superb articulation in the brilliant scherzo, and the *Largo* played slowly and thoughtfully. All Straussians should try this, while admirers of Gould will find no better example of his recording skills.

VOCAL MUSIC

Lieder, Opp. 10; 15; 17; 19; Schlichte Weisen, Op. 21; Lieder, Opp. 26–27; 29; 31–32; 36–37; 49; 56; 67; Kleine Lieder, Op. 69; Gesänge, Op. 87.
*** DG 413 455-1 (3) [id.]. Dietrich Fischer-Dieskau, Wolfgang Sawallisch.

This selection is not quite so generous as on Fischer-Dieskau's previous three-disc LP set of Strauss songs, recorded for EMI (*Zueignung*, *Waldseligkeit*, and *Die Nacht* among the favourites now missed out), and inevitably the voice is less fresh than it was. Even so, no one can match Fischer-Dieskau among male singers in conveying the depth and intensity of these songs, often glowingly beautiful, distinctive within the whole genre. This time *Ruhe, meine Seele*, for example, is even darker and more intense than before; *Heimliche Aufforderung* is even more uninhibited, with a wider range of dynamic; and *Morgen* is slower and more inward. In that last song, Wolfgang Sawallisch is masterly in his legato phrasing and hushed concentration, at a very slow speed and with serenade-like spreading of chords. Excellent sound.

8 Lieder, Op. 10; 3 Liebeslieder (*Songs of Roses*) *without opus number*. Lieder: *Für fünfzehn Pfennige; Hat gesagt; Heimkehr; Leise Lieder; Leises Lied; Meinem Kinde; Schlagende Herzen; Schlechtes Wetter; Weissen Jasmin; Wiegenlied.*
*** HMV Dig. EL 270255-1/*4* [Ang. DS/*4DS* 38256]. Lucia Popp, Wolfgang Sawallisch.

The bright-eyed charm, the ability to communicate word-meaning with vivid intensity, makes Popp's Strauss recital a delightful one, helped by accompaniment from Sawallisch that is comparably inspired, as in the dreamily beautiful accompaniment to *Die Georgine*. Including a number of less well-known songs as well as many favourites, it can be warmly recommended to aficionados and newcomers alike. The full, digital recording at times brings out an edge at the top of the voice, when it is under pressure, but otherwise the sweetness of the Popp sound adds to the delight. The XDR tape is extremely well managed, softening the upper vocal range a little without loss of presence.

5 Lieder, Op. 32; Gefunden; Heimkehr; Heimliche Aufforderung; Ich liebe dich; Morgen!; Die Nacht; Nichts; Ruhe, meine Seele!; Schlechtes Wetter; Schlichte Weissen, Op. 21/1–5; Ständchen; Traum durch die Dämmerung; Waldesfahrt; Winternacht.
*** DG Dig. **415 470-2**; 415 470-1/*4* [id.]. Dietrich Fischer-Dieskau, Wolfgang Sawallisch.

A delightful collection, taken from the complete three-LP set reviewed above, with the benefits of CD specially valuable in the hushed intimacy of Lieder-singing. The selection includes a fair proportion not only of the favourite Strauss songs but of Fischer-Dieskau's (and Sawallisch's) finest and most beautiful performances. First-rate sound, in all three media. While the CD has added presence, the chrome cassette, too, is one of DG's best.

Lieder: *Des Dichters Abendgang; Freundliche Vision; Heimliche Aufforderung; Ich trage meine Minne; Liebeshymnus; Morgen!; Das Rosenband; Ständchen; Traum durch die Dämmerung; Verführung; Waldseligkeit; Zueignung.*
*** Ph. Dig. 6514/*7337* 321 [id.]. Siegfried Jerusalem, Leipzig GO, Masur.

Starting with an account of *Heimliche Aufforderung* that is both heroic and glowingly beautiful, Siegfried Jerusalem's collection of Strauss Lieder in orchestral arrangements provides a male counterpart to Jessye Norman's magnificent disc, also recorded with Masur and the Leipzig Gewandhaus Orchestra (see below). The shading of tone which Jerusalem commands is most delicate, as in *Morgen* or in a finely delicate rendering of *Ständchen.* Naturally balanced recording, warmly reverberant to bring out the ravishing beauty of Strauss's orchestrations. The tape transfer, however, is bass-heavy, with the lower end of the orchestral spectrum emphasized at the expense of the upper. The voice is naturally caught.

Mädchenblumen, Op. 22; 3 Lieder, Op. 29; 4 Lieder, Op. 27; 8 Lieder aus letzte Blätter, Op. 10.
** Etcetera Dig. **KTC 1028**; ETC 1028 [id.]. Roberta Alexander, Crone.

Although the Etcetera recording is too reverberant, the range and beauty of Roberta Alexander's voice come over well, particularly in the fuller and more dramatic songs, where her operatic experience is an obvious asset. Otherwise, by the standards of her finest rivals, these are readings rather lacking in perception and detail, with words not always clear. It makes a neat package, having four opus numbers of songs recorded complete; but the leaflet inconveniently puts English translations after the German, not alongside.

Four Last songs (*Vier letzte Lieder*).
*** HMV Dig. **CDC 747013-2**; ASD/*TCC-ASD* 4182 [Ang. DS/*4XS* 37887]. Lucia Popp, LPO, Tennstedt – *Death and Transfiguration.***(*)

Four Last songs; Lieder: *Das Bächlein; Freundliche Vision; Die heiligen drei Könige; Meinem Kinde; Morgen; Muttertändelei; Das Rosenbande; Ruhe, meine Seele; Waldseligkeit; Wiegenlied; Winterweihe; Zueignung.*
❀ ☾ *** HMV **CDC 747276-2** [id.]. Elisabeth Schwarzkopf, Berlin RSO, or LSO, Szell.

Four Last songs; Lieder: *Befreit; Einerlei; Ich wollt' ein Strausslein binden; Schlechtes Wetter. Ariadne auf Naxos: Es gibt ein Reich. Capriccio: Wo ist mein Bruder* (closing scene).
(M) (***) Decca mono 411 660-1 [id.]. Lisa della Casa, VPO, Boehm or Hollreiser; Karl Hudez (piano).

Four Last songs; Lieder: *Befreit; Morgen; Muttertändelei; Ruhe, meine Seele; Wiegenlied; Zueignung.*
(*) CBS **MK 76794; 76794 [M/*MT* 35140]. Kiri Te Kanawa, LSO, Andrew Davis.

Four Last songs; Lieder: *Cäcilie; Meinem Kinde; Morgen; Ruhe, meine Seele; Wiegenlied; Zueignung.*
❀ ☾ *** Ph. Dig. **411 052-2**; 6514/*7337* 322 [id.]. Jessye Norman, Leipzig GO, Masur.

Strauss's publisher Ernest Roth says in the score of the *Four Last songs* that this was a farewell of 'serene confidence', which is exactly the mood Jessye Norman conveys. The power of her singing reminds one that the first ever interpreter (with Furtwängler and the Philharmonia Orchestra at the Royal Albert Hall in May 1950) was Kirsten Flagstad. The start of the second stanza of the third song, *Beim Schlafengehen*, brings one of the most thrilling vocal crescendos on record, expanding from a half-tone to a gloriously rich and rounded forte. In concern for word-detail Norman is outshone only by Schwarzkopf (unique in conveying the poignancy of old age), but both in the *Four Last songs* and in the orchestral songs on the reverse, the stylistic as well as the vocal command is irresistible, with *Cäcilie* given operatic strength. The radiance of the recording matches the interpretations, the more fully and immediately on compact disc.

For the CD version of Schwarzkopf's raptly beautiful recording of the *Four Last songs*, EMI has generously added not just the old coupling of Strauss orchestral songs but also the extra seven which she recorded three years later in 1969, also with George Szell conducting but with the LSO instead of the Berlin Radio Orchestra. There are few records in the catalogue which so magnetically capture the magic of a great performance, with the intensity of Schwarzkopf's singing in all its variety of tone and meaning perfectly matched by inspired playing. In the deep meditations of the *Four Last songs* it is especially valuable on compact disc to have background noise eliminated, with the precise balances of the original recording marking a high-water mark of the art of engineering.

Lucia Popp, too, gives a ravishingly beautiful performance of the *Four Last songs*. With the voice given an ethereal glow, naturally balanced in a warmly atmospheric digital recording, the radiance of texture is paramount. This is an orchestral performance rather than a deeply illuminating Lieder performance, and that matches the coupling, the early tone-poem on death which is quoted by the dying composer in the last of the songs. Tennstedt is a direct rather than a persuasive Straussian. The beauty of sound is unfailing, with a first-class matching chrome cassette. However, as the CD readily shows, the Philips recording for Jessye Norman has even more atmospheric warmth.

Lisa della Casa in the 1950s and '60s was a rival to Schwarzkopf herself in radiant performance of this Strauss repertory. This generous coupling in the mid-price 'Grandi Voci' series brings together what had previously appeared on two discs; though the mono sound is limited, the creamy beauty of the singing comes over beautifully, whether in the *Four Last songs* (poised and immaculate, if not as detailed as Schwarzkopf's), the orchestral Lieder, *Ariadne's Lament* or the closing scene from *Capriccio*.

Dame Kiri Te Kanawa gives an openhearted, warmly expressive reading of the *Four Last songs*. If she misses the sort of detail that Schwarzkopf uniquely brought, her commitment is never in doubt. Her tone is consistently beautiful, but might have seemed even more so if the voice had not been placed rather too close in relation to the orchestra. The orchestral arrangements of other songs make an excellent coupling (as a comparable selection does in the Schwarzkopf version); and Andrew Davis directs most sympathetically, if not with the sort of rapt dedication that Szell gave to Schwarzkopf.

OPERA

Arabella (complete).
(M) ** DG 415 385-1/*4* (3/*2*). Della Casa, Rothenberger, Fischer-Dieskau, Malaniuk, Paskuda, Bav. State Op. Ch., Bav. State O, Keilberth.

Recorded live at a performance celebrating the opening of the restored Munich Opera House, the Keilberth set gives a highly atmospheric picture of a great occasion, with Keilberth conducting most sympathetically. There are inevitable flaws of detail, both musically and in stage and audience noises (though applause is curiously muted). The set hardly stands comparison with its principal mid-priced rival (Decca GOS 571/3) in which Lisa della Casa was creamily beautiful, in her recording with Solti; while Fischer-Dieskau was even more perceptive and subtler in his later assumption of the role of Mandryka on HMV, with Julia Varady characterfully tender as the heroine and Helen Donath charming as the younger sister (HMV SLS 5224 [Ang. DSCX 3917]). Nevertheless, the Munich version has the spontaneity of a live occasion and there is much to enjoy. Della Casa sings her Act I soliloquy very beautifully, and her voice blends unusually well with that of Anneliese Rothenberger (an excellent Zdenka). The Act II love duet is also touching, although the background detail of the ballroom scene is diffuse and the orchestra sounds insubstantial. It is a pity the tape layout does not attempt to tailor breaks more satisfactorily, with the Act III introduction beginning at the very end of the third side, for otherwise the pair of well-transferred cassettes is very convenient, with its neat, clearly printed libretto.

Capriccio: closing scene; *Daphne:* closing scene.
*(*) Chan. Dig. **CHAN 8364**; ABRD/*ABTD* 1127 [id.]. Carole Farley, RTBF SO, Serebrier.

This couples two of the loveliest soprano passages from Strauss's later operas, potentially a magical coupling, but not when Carole Farley's voice is imperfectly controlled, too edgy and fluttery for this music. She is balanced close to make every word clear; the orchestral sound is vividly caught, though the fruity horn at the start of the *Capriccio* momentarily makes it sound like a brass band playing softly. Texts and translations are given. There is an excellent matching chrome cassette.

Reminder. The HMV set of *Daphne* is highly recommended, with Lucia Popp an enchanting girlish nymph, wooed by the heroic Apollo of Reiner Goldberg, and exceptionally rich, refined recording (SLS 143582-3 [Ang. DXS 3941]).

Elektra (complete).
* HM Rodolphe **RPC 32420/21**; RP1/*RPK2* 2420/1. Vinzing, Rysanek, Forrester, Hiestermann, Norup, Schaer, French R. Ch., O Nat. de France, Perick.

The Harmonia Mundi set brings a live recording of a middling performance, well conducted but with too little dramatic bite, when with one exception the singing is undistinguished and often poor, and words are often masked in the cloudy acoustic. The exception is the Klytemnestra of the veteran contralto, Maureen Forrester, not always vocalized perfectly in the stress of the moment, but always projecting superbly a larger-than-life character. All the others, including Ute Vinzing as Elektra and Leonie Rysanek as Chrysothemis (sounding old now), suffer from varying degrees of unsteadiness. In every way, Solti's Decca set is preferable (SET 354-5/*K 124 K 22* [Lon. OSA/5- 1269]).

Feuersnot (complete).
**(*) Acanta 4023530 (2). Varady, Weikl, Berger-Tuna, Engen, Tölz Boys' Ch., Bav. R. Ch., Mun. R. O, Fricke.

There are many weaknesses in the curious libretto for this second of Strauss's operas, not least that the hero, the sorcerer Kunrad who casts a spell on the city of Munich, and heroine, the proud Diemut who finally concedes that she loves him, have only one on-stage duet. Happily, Strauss's opulent use of the orchestra provides the luscious duetting denied the singers, and there are many ripe moments worthy of the later Strauss, with a children's chorus (the splendid Tölz Boys' Choir) adding to the sparkle and charm. The two principal roles are both strongly taken, with Julia Varady emphasizing the heroine's arrogance (symbolic of the philistinism of Munich, where Strauss's first opera had been rejected) and Bernd Weikl in fine heroic voice as the baritone hero. Textures are not ideally clear (partly the fault of the conductor), but this is still a most welcome set.

Die Frau ohne Schatten (complete).
*** DG **415 472-2**; 415 472-1/*4* (3) [id.]. Nilsson, Rysanek, Hesse, King, Berry, V. State Op. Ch. and O, Boehm.

Boehm's live recording of Strauss's most ambitious, most Wagnerian opera was edited together from two performances at the Vienna State Opera in October 1977, and provides a magnificent reminder of the conductor at his very finest. Though the Decca set of the mid-1950s – also conducted by Boehm in Vienna but recorded in the studio – still sounds amazingly well, with early stereo very well focused, the new one glows far more warmly. It is a performance to love rather than just to admire, with the opera-house acoustic handled persuasively by the engineers of Austrian Radio to give the solo voices plenty of bloom without losing precision. Inevitably, there are stage noises and the balance of the singers varies, but this is outstanding among live recordings. The stage cuts are an irritation, but at least they allow the hour-long Acts to be accommodated each on a single disc, whether on CD or LP. The cast is an excellent one, with Birgit Nilsson making the Dyer's Wife a truly Wagnerian character, richer as well as subtler than her Decca predecessor, Christel Goltz. As before, Leonie Rysanek sings the role of the other heroine, the Empress, musically almost as demanding; amazingly, if anything the voice has grown firmer and rounder between the mid-1950s and 1977. Barak the Dyer is sung by Walter Berry, not always as firmly Sachs-like as Paul Schoeffler was before, but searchingly expressive; and James King in the Heldentenor role of the Emperor is just as remarkable for his finely shaded pianissimo singing as for heroic moments, where he is occasionally strained. Until a full, uncut studio recording of this rich and grand if occasionally pretentious opera is recorded (one hopes one day with Solti, the keenest of advocates), this historic Boehm version stands as the most welcome of substitutes. Although, on CD, definition is marginally sharper, the chrome cassettes are also outstandingly well managed, with splendid range and detail, and the perspectives impressively caught at all levels of dynamic.

Die Frau ohne Schatten: symphonic fantasy; *Der Rosenkavalier:* concert suite (arr. Dorati).
** Decca Dig. **411 893-2**; 411 893-1/*4* [id.]. Detroit SO, Dorati.

In his *Rosenkavalier* suite, Dorati has strung together most of the sweetest lollipops from the opera, keeping Strauss's orchestration but giving vocal lines to various instruments. The result may not appeal to the lover of the opera itself – particularly when Strauss's delicate final pay-off is substituted with a coarse return to the big waltz theme – but performance and recording are aptly opulent. Strauss's own symphonic fantasy on his biggest, most ambitious opera is artistically far more valuable, a piece compiled in his last years with nostalgia for some magnificent ideas. The digital recording is formidably impressive in its range and richness. The CD approaches the demonstration bracket and the chrome tape is excellent too.

Guntram (complete).
*** CBS Dig. 12M/*12T* 39737 (3) [id.]. Goldberg, Tokody, Sólomon-Nagy, Gati, Bándi, Hungarian Army Ch. and State O, Queler.

Strauss's very first opera suffers from an undramatic libretto written by the composer, a sloppy tale of knights-in-armour chivalry. Musically, however, the piece provides a marvellous musical wallow, with the young Strauss echoing *Don Juan* and other early symphonic poems in sumptuous orchestral writing. Even when he consciously adopts a Wagnerian stance, the music quickly turns sweet, often anticipating the more lyrical side of *Salome*. Heading the cast as the eponymous knight is Rainer Goldberg, on record the most reliable and open-toned of today's Heldentenoren, only occasionally strained. Otherwise the cast is Hungarian, with Ilona Tokody strong and firm, if rarely beautiful, in the taxing role of the heroine, Freihild, originally written with Strauss's wife-to-be, Pauline, in mind. Warmly sympathetic conducting from Eve Queler. The recording acoustic too is attractively rich; this means that on the chrome tapes the quality is warm and smooth with the voices well projected, but the upper range is a little blurred by the resonance which affects the orchestral focus. The cassettes, as is usual with CBS, are handsomely packaged, with a fairly large libretto, folded to fit in the slimline box.

Der Rosenkavalier (complete).

❀ *** HMV EX 290045-3/9 (4) [Ang. SDLX/*4CDX* 3970]. Schwarzkopf, Ludwig, Edelmann, Waechter, Philh. Ch. and O, Karajan.

(*) DG Dig. **413 163-2; 413 163-1/*4* [id.]. Tomowa–Sintow, Baltsa, Moll, Hornik, Perry, VPO Ch. and O, Karajan.

** Denon Dig. **C37 7482/4** [id.]. Pusar-Joric, Walther, Stejskal, Dresden State Op. Ch., Dresden State O, Vonk.

One of the great peaks in the history of opera recording, this 1956 EMI Karajan recording now comes with the substantial benefit of a digital remastering. The clear, firm balances of the original stereo are now focused more satisfyingly than ever, making it far preferable in sound to the recent DG digital version from Karajan, despite a little audible tape-hiss. One can only hope that copyright problems will soon be sorted out, to allow a CD version as well. As to the performance, it is in a class of its own, with the patrician refinement of Karajan's spacious reading combining with an emotional intensity that he has rarely equalled, even in Strauss, of whose music he remains a supreme interpreter. Matching that achievement is the incomparable portrait of the Marschallin from Schwarzkopf, bringing out detail as no one else can, yet equally presenting the breadth and richness of the character, a woman still young and attractive. Christa Ludwig with her firm, clear mezzo tone makes an ideal, ardent Octavian and Teresa Stich-Randall a radiant Sophie, with Otto Edelmann a winningly characterful Ochs, who yet sings every note clearly.

When Karajan re-recorded this opera in preparation for the 1983 Salzburg Festival with this same DG cast, inevitably he invited comparison with his own classic 1956 recording. The new set brings few positive advantages, not even in recorded sound: for all the extra range of the modern digital recording, the focus is surprisingly vague, with the orchestra balanced too far behind the soloists. One advantage there certainly is: the Vienna Philharmonic, having been brought up with a natural feeling for waltz rhythm, is a degree more idiomatic in providing a genuine Viennese lilt, if it is also at times less precise. The orchestral balance adds to the impression of relative lightness, and so does the casting. As successor to Schwarzkopf, Karajan chose one of his favourite sopranos, the Bulgarian Anna Tomowa-Sintow; the refinement and detail in her performance present an intimate view of the Marschallin, often very beautiful indeed, but both the darker and more sensuous sides of the Marschallin are muted. *Da steht der Bub* she sings in the great Act III Trio, and the voice conveys pure maternal joy, hardly any regret for her own loss. The Baron Ochs of Kurt Moll, firm, dark and incisive, is outstanding, and Agnes Baltsa as Octavian makes the lad tough and determined, if not always sympathetic. Janet Perry's Sophie, charming and pretty on stage, is too white and twittery of tone to give much pleasure. For all the flaws, Karajan is once more presented as a supreme Straussian, even more daringly spacious than before (which will not please everyone). The benefits of CD in this opera are considerable, not only in the extra clarity of sound but in the way the new medium can contain Acts II and III on a single disc each, without a break, with Act I then divided in the middle on the first two discs. However, the splendid chrome cassettes – representing the highest state of the art – are even more conveniently laid out, with one Act complete on each of three tapes. The sound is superb on tape, the only snag being that the slimline libretto presents a small typeface, though the printing is clear.

In the USA, Bernstein's Vienna recording is available through specialist dealers (though at a high premium price), digitally remastered on three imported Japanese CBS/Sony CDs (**82DC 328-30**). This commemorates a great theatrical occasion at the beginning of the 1970s when the Viennese were swept off their feet – much to their surprise – by the magic of the American conductor. His direction of this opera at the Vienna State Opera was an almost unparalleled success; his recorded version captures much of the ripeness in the fine, mature Marschallin of Christa Ludwig, which plainly owes much to the example of Schwarzkopf (for whom, on the EMI Karajan set, Ludwig was Octavian). Lucia Popp makes a charming Sophie and Walter Berry a strong, expressive Ochs, less limited in the lower register than one might expect. But Gwyneth Jones's Octavian, despite the occasional half-tone of exquisite beauty, has too many raw passages to be very appealing, a bad blot on the set. Bernstein follows traditional cuts. Surprisingly, when Decca engineers were responsible for the recording itself, the quality is more variable than one would expect, with vulgarly close horn balance.

The Denon set, recorded live at the opening of the reconstructed Semper Opera House in Dresden, also brings the obvious benefit of being on only three CDs, one per Act. Stage and audience noises are often obtrusive and the orchestra is balanced well behind the solo singers, but this can still be recommended to those who want a plain, generally brisk view, with plenty of atmosphere. Vonk's rather metrical manner affects even the waltzes, but the orchestral playing is superb, particularly from the horns. The Yugoslav soprano, Ana Pusar-Joric, has a warm, vibrant voice, and her fresh characterization brings delightful pointing of words; but too often she sits under notes, or slides up to them. Ute Walther is an attractively ardent Octavian and Margot Stejskal a thin-toned Sophie, shrill and fluttery at times. Theo Adam's characterful Ochs is marred by too much gritty, ill-focused tone.

Der Rosenkavalier: highlights.
(*) DG Dig. **415 284-2; 415 284-1/*4* [id.] (from above set with Tomowa-Sintow, cond. Karajan).

This highlights disc, taken from Karajan's re-recording of the complete opera, provides a generous sample of excerpts, incorporating most of the favourite passages, and includes the tenor aria, lightly sung by Vinson Cole. The richness and beauty of the score are hardly in doubt, but the flaws noted above are just as apparent.

Salome (complete).
*** Decca **414 414-2**; SET 228-9/*K 111 K 22* [Lon. OSA/5- 1218]. Nilsson, Stolze, Hoffman, Waechter, Kmentt, VPO, Solti.

Solti's recording of *Salome*, originally issued in 1962, was one of the most spectacular of the opera recordings produced by John Culshaw at the Sofiensaal in Vienna. It used what was called the Sonicstage technique – with the sound of Jokanaan's voice in the cistern recorded from another acoustic very precisely – and that sharpness of focus, coupled with opulence of texture, comes out with extraordinary brilliance in the digital transfer on CD. The additional absence of background makes the final scene, where Salome kisses the head of John the Baptist in delighted horror (*I have kissed thy mouth, Jokanaan!*), all the more spine-tingling, with a vivid close-up effect of the voice whispering almost in one's ear. Nilsson is splendid throughout; she is hard-edged as usual but, on that account, more convincingly wicked: the determination and depravity are latent in the girl's character from the start. Of this score Solti is a master. He has rarely sounded so abandoned in a recorded performance. The emotion swells up naturally even while the calculation of impact is most precise. Waechter makes a clear, young-sounding Jokanaan. Gerhardt Stolze portrays the unbalance of Herod with frightening conviction, and Grace Hoffman does all she can in the comparatively ungrateful part of Herodias. The cassettes as well as the CDs show Decca's technology at its most impressive, and the sound on tape is also extraordinarily vivid.

Stravinsky, Igor (1882–1971)

Apollo (*Apollon Musagète*): ballet (complete).
*** DG **415 979-2** [id.]. BPO, Karajan – *Rite of spring*.***
*** Decca Dig. **414 457-2**; 414 457-1/*4* [id.]. Detroit SO, Dorati – COPLAND: *Appalachian spring*.*** ₠

Though Stravinsky tended to disparage Karajan's approach to his music as not being rugged enough, here is a work where Karajan's moulding of phrase and care for richness of string texture make for wonderful results. This neoclassical score is strong enough to stand such individual treatment, and the writing is consistently enhanced by the magnificent playing of the Berlin Philharmonic Orchestra. The recording dates from 1973 and sounds excellent in its CD format, if not quite as wide-ranging and 'present' as Dorati's newer digital version for Decca.

Although the playing of the Detroit orchestra cannot match the polish of the Berlin account under Karajan, Dorati's performance has an attractive vitality, while the variations of Terpsichore and Apollo are genially characterized and the splendid *Pas de deux* – one of Stravinsky's most memorable inspirations – is warmly played. The recording is first class, spacious and with strikingly realistic detail, not only on the fine CD but also on the first-class cassette, which is slightly smoother on top.

Reminder. Marriner's famous 1968 ASMF recording of *Apollo*, ideally coupled with the *Pulcinella suite*, is available at mid-price, with a first-class matching tape; and it remains highly recommendable, with playing that is both refined and vivid, and demonstration sound (Decca Jub. 411 728-1/*4* [id.]).

Le baiser de la fée (ballet; complete). Tchaikovsky (arr. Stravinsky): *Sleeping Beauty: Bluebird pas de deux.*
*** Chan. **CHAN 8360**; ABRD/*ABTD* 1123 [id.]. SNO, Järvi.

Le baiser de la fée is a remarkable symbiosis of Tchaikovskian tuneful charm (as instanced by the unforgettable rhythmic theme for the horns, taken from a piano piece) and Stravinskian twentieth-century neoclassicism. Stravinsky was only occasionally a memorable tunesmith himself (Arthur Rubinstein once demonstrated in a TV interview how virtually all the famous melodies in the three great ballets are derived from Russian folk-themes). But he could illuminate and refine the invention of others more gifted in that respect, adding also a firm lamination of his own musical personality. The scoring here is a constant delight, much of it on a chamber-music scale; and its delicacy, wit and occasional pungency are fully appreciated by Järvi, who secures a wholly admirable response from his Scottish orchestra. The ambience seems exactly right, bringing out wind and brass colours vividly; the CD adds a degree of extra definition, alongside the background silence. However, both the LP and the splendid chrome tape are also first class. The condensation of the scoring of the *Sleeping Beauty pas de deux*, made for a wartime performance when only limited forces were available, also shows Stravinsky's orchestral individuality – he even introduces a piano.

Le baiser de la fée (Divertimento); (i) *Fanfare for a new theatre; Suites for orchestra: Nos 1 and 2; Octet;* (ii) *3 Pieces for clarinet solo.*
Ⓒ *** Decca Dig. **417 114-2**; 417 114-1/*4* [id.]. L. Sinf., Chailly; (i) Watson; Archibald; (ii) Pay.

Ansermet made a famous mono LP (1951) of the four-movement *Divertimento*, which Stravinsky distilled from the complete ballet in 1934. The Swiss conductor re-recorded it later in stereo, but the second account proved rhythmically less taut and was not as well played. Chailly's version, admirably fresh, cannot be criticized on either of these counts. It is superbly played and Decca's recording is in the finest traditions of the house, especially in its CD format. After the gently nostalgic opening, Chailly's approach to the *Sinfonia* is dramatic and strong: clearly, he sees this movement in terms of the concert hall, rather than the ballet theatre. Stravinsky's dominance over the music is emphasized; later and especially in the scherzo and *Pas de deux* the Tchaikovskian influences rise more readily to the surface. Chailly's pacing throughout is splendidly judged, rhythms are resilient – the pointing of the lighter rhythmic patterns is especially effective – and the espressivo playing is at once responsive and slightly cool, a most engaging combination. The rest of the programme is imaginatively chosen. The jagged *Fanfare*, written in 1964 for the opening of the State Theatre in New York's Lincoln Center, lasts a mere 0′ 43″; the three miniatures for solo clarinet are no less original and characteristic. They are splendidly played by Anthony Pay who readily responds to taxing writing over the instrument's full range, with the bravura of the finale despatched with an assured geniality. The two *Orchestral suites*, vivid orchestrations of *'Easy' pieces* for piano, provide a kaleidoscopic series of colourful vignettes. Unfortunately, on CD the individual movements are not banded. Finally, and very welcome indeed, the 1922 *Octet* is restored to the catalogue, a considerable piece for flute, clarinet, two bassoons – used to great effect – two trumpets, trombone and bass trombone. It is given a performance of infectious virtuosity, with individual bravura matched by polished ensemble and fine tonal blending. The second-movement *Theme and variations*, with its bizarre quotations of the *Dies irae*, is particularly memorable. Throughout the programme, the CD is very much in the demonstration class, with the tangibility and presence of the imagery enhanced by the background silence (the bass drum featured with rare subtlety). The overall bloom, without any clouding, again testifies to the ideal acoustic properties of London's Kingsway Hall. The cassette transfer is sophisticated in its detail and range, although the high level has added brightness to the treble.

Le Chant du rossignol (symphonic poem); *Fireworks, Op. 4.*
** Decca Dig. **414 078-2**; 414 078-1/*4* [id.]. Berlin RSO, Chailly – *Symphony of Psalms.***

Le Rossignol is an underrated Stravinsky opera; its derivative opening, with overtones of *Nuages*, and its Rimskian flavour have led to its virtues being undervalued. Among them is its extraordinarily rich fantasy and vividness of colouring; the symphonic poem that Stravinsky made from the material of this work deserves a more established place in the concert repertoire. Its exotic effects and glittering colours sound lustrously delicate in the ecclesiastical ambient glow of the Jesus Christus Church in West Berlin; but Chailly does not have this score in his bones and he tends to force the pace and overdramatize the music, instead of letting it blossom naturally. *Feux d'artifice* makes a curious encore, and the coupled *Symphony of Psalms* also suggests that this is not repertoire with which Chailly is naturally sympathetic, although the response of the Berlin Radio Symphony Orchestra is impressive throughout this collection.

Concerto for piano and winds.
*(*) Hyp. A/*KA* 66167 [id.]. Marios Papadopoulos, RPO – JANÁČEK: *Capriccio for piano left hand; Sonata.**(*)

Marios Papadopoulos is a young Cypriot-born pianist whose first record this is. He is obviously an accomplished player, though his view of the Stravinsky *Concerto*, which he directs from the keyboard, is perhaps a little too neat and not quite savage enough. The recording errs in the right direction as far as the balance between piano and wind is concerned, but there are times when the soloist seems a little too overwhelmed by the orchestral forces. Bishop-Kovacevich and the BBC Symphony Orchestra on Philips is to be preferred (6527/*7311* 160); this is coupled with the *Violin concerto* (Grumiaux) and there is a good tape. The Hyperion tape lacks something in bite because of the resonance.

Concerto for strings in D; Danses concertantes; Dumbarton Oaks concerto in E flat.
(M) *** Decca Lon. Ent. 414 168-1/*4* [id.]. ECO, Sir Colin Davis.

The *Danses concertantes* date from early in Stravinsky's Hollywood period. Despite the name, the work was not planned as a ballet; but the dancing quality of much of the music has since attracted choreographers. Like the other two works on the disc, it is one of Stravinsky's most light-hearted pieces, and the highly original scoring is a constant delight, particularly when recorded as brilliantly as here. The *Concerto for strings in D* was written in 1946, and the *Dumbarton Oaks concerto* in 1938, the year Stravinsky settled in America. Their neoclassicism need not deter anyone who has ever enjoyed Bach's *Brandenburgs*. Indeed, Stravinsky himself admitted that the *Brandenburgs* were his starting-point for the earlier work. Colin Davis brings enormous vitality as well as the right degree of humour, and this splendid reissue of a 1962 recording sounds as fresh as the day it was made, with tape as well as LP approaching demonstration standard. Detail is crisp and the ambience exactly right for the music.

Violin concerto in D.
*** DG **413 725-2**; 2531/*3301* 110 [id.]. Perlman, Boston SO, Ozawa – BERG: *Concerto*.***

Perlman's precision, remarkable in both concertos on this disc, underlines the neoclassical element in the outer movements of the Stravinsky. The two *Aria* movements are more deeply felt and expressive, presenting the work as a major twentieth-century concerto. The balance favours the soloist, but no one will miss the commitment of the Boston orchestra's playing, vividly recorded. The CD subtly adds to the definition and presence of the recording, but the tape transfer is first rate, matching the LP closely. Until Kyung Wha Chung's fine Decca version (coupled with Walton on SXL 6601 [Lon. CS 6819]) is transferred to CD, the Perlman has the field to itself.

Danses concertantes; Pulcinella (ballet): *suite.*
*** Chan Dig. **CHAN 8325** [id.]; ABRD/*ABTD* 1065 [id.]. ECO, Gibson.

Gibson and the ECO are very well recorded on Chandos and give highly enjoyable accounts of both works. The *Pulcinella* suite does not quite eclipse the Marriner on Argo (see above), but it is still very lively, and the *Danses concertantes* scores even over the composer's own in terms of charm and geniality. The CD is especially impressive in its firmness of detail. The chrome cassette is vivid and very bright on top; indeed, it may call for a little taming, especially in *Pulcinella*.

The Firebird (ballet): complete.
*** Ph. **400 074-2**; 9500/*7300* 742 [id.]. Concg. O, Sir Colin Davis.
⊛ *** Decca Dig. **410 109-2**; 410 109-1/*4* [id.]. Detroit SO, Dorati.

(*) Decca **414 141-2 [id.]. Pickwick Con. *CC/CCTC* 7500 [Lon. STS/5-15139]. New Philh. O, Ansermet.
(*) HMV Dig. **CDC 747017-2 [id.]. Boston SO, Ozawa.

With superb analogue sound Sir Colin Davis directs a magically evocative account of the complete *Firebird* ballet, helped not just by the playing of the Concertgebouw Orchestra (the strings outstandingly fine) but by the ambience of the hall, which allows the finest detail yet gives a bloom to the sound, open and spacious, superbly co-ordinated. This is finer even than Haitink's splendid LPO version, and is probably the most satisfying account of the *Firebird* score ever committed to disc. The cassette is of good quality, but the transfer level is unadventurous, and in some of the pianissimo passages the tape has not the sharpness of focus of the LP. The compact disc has been digitally remastered, which has sharpened up detail, somewhat at the expense of the magical analogue atmosphere. While there is more depth and bite, it is not all gain; although the brass has greater presence, the high violins sound less natural. Background noise has been virtually eliminated.

Dorati's Detroit version has the benefit of spectacular digital recording. The clarity and definition of dark, hushed passages is amazing, with the contra-bassoon finely focused, never sounding woolly or obscure, while string tremolos down to the merest whisper are uncannily precise. There is plenty of space round woodwind solos, and only the concertmaster's violin is spotlit. The performance is very precise, too; though Dorati's reading has changed little from his previous versions with London orchestras, there is a degree more of caution. Individual solos are not so characterful and *Kaschei's dance* lacks just a degree in excitement, but overall this is both a strong and beautiful reading, even if the Mercury account, an electrifying example of 1960s analogue engineering, is not entirely superseded (SRI 75058). The somewhat literal quality of the Decca performance, lacking a degree of magic and intensity, is brought out the more on CD, though the vividness and impact of the sound are most impressive.

Ansermet's New Philharmonia version offers more polished playing than the performance he recorded earlier with his own Suisse Romande Orchestra, but generally the interpretations were amazingly consistent, with the principal difference lying in the extra flexibility of the London players. The firmness and precision of the sound with a vividly realistic (Kingsway Hall) acoustic make the 1968 recording very impressive in its CD transfer, even today. The brilliance sometimes brings a touch of hardness, and the growling basses at the start are not as sharply defined as they are in Dorati's digital recording, but the sense of presence is startling. However, the equivalent LP is available at bargain price on Pickwick's Contour label at about a quarter of the cost of the CD, and this seems the most sensible way to approach this famous interpretation, as the LP pressing is strikingly clean. The chrome cassette is less reliable; the sound clouds in the closing climax because of the very high level of the transfer.

Ozawa's Boston version is more refined than his Paris record, also for HMV; but with the extra precision has come a degree of detachment, chill even. *Kaschei's dance* is less an orchestral showpiece than a delicate tapestry, relatively light and transparent, with dance rhythms well sprung and the bite of fortissimo reserved for sforzando chords. On LP the brass lacked a little in body. The CD is much firmer, however, and brings satisfying weight to the brass. Nevertheless, as a recording this is less brilliant than Ansermet's, let alone Dorati's; and Sir Colin Davis remains first choice on grounds of interpretation, while the Philips analogue sound is in many ways as impressive as the digital balance the EMI engineers give Ozawa.

The Firebird: suite (1919 version).
*** HMV **CDC 747099-2** [id.]; ASD/*TC-ASD* 3645 [Ang. S/*4XS* 37539]. Phd. O, Muti – MUSSORGSKY: *Pictures.****
(*) Telarc Dig. **CD 80039; DG 10039 [id.]. Atlanta SO, Shaw – BORODIN: *Prince Igor excerpts.****
(B) ** DG Walkman *413 155-4* [id.]. Berlin RSO, Maazal – KHACHATURIAN: *Gayaneh*; RIMSKY-KORSAKOV: *Scheherazade.***

Muti gets excellent playing from the Philadelphia Orchestra and, though their response is admirably disciplined, they are not quite as overdriven as in some of the later records Muti has made in Philadelphia. Indeed, there is delicacy and poetry in the *Dance of the princesses* and the *Berceuse* in *Firebird*, and the colours of this score are heard in full splendour. Putting the CD and LP versions side by side, there is no doubt that the new format offers the greater range and firmness. A welcome issue which can be recommended even to those readers who do not always respond to some of the later records from this conductor.

The *Firebird suite* has been recorded by the finest orchestras in the world; excellent as is the Atlanta Symphony, it would not claim to be of their number. Nevertheless Robert Shaw, the thoroughly musical conductor, achieves an atmospheric and vivid reading of Stravinsky's famous suite. The *Round dance of the princesses* is played very gently to maximize the shock of the entry of Kaschei. The very wide dynamic range of the digital recording achieves the most dramatic impact both here and in the closing pages of the finale. With its spectacular coupling this issue is designed to appeal to those wanting to show off their reproducer, and that it will certainly do. This applies especially to the CD, but the LP is very impressive, too.

Maazel's reading of the *Firebird suite* has an enjoyable éclat and he has the advantage of the most beautiful woodwind playing; indeed the Berlin Radio Orchestra is consistently on top form. The recording dates from 1960 and tended to betray its age by the sound of the massed upper strings. However, in the present transfer the DG engineers have smoothed off the upper partials and in consequence the recording, although still impressive, has lost some of its bite.

The Firebird: suite (1919 version); *Petrushka* (ballet; 1911 score; complete); *The Rite of spring* (complete).
(M) *** DG 413 209-1/*4* (2) [id.]. LSO, Abbado.

The Firebird: suite (1919 version); *The Rite of spring* (complete).
(M) *** DG Gal. 415 854-1/*4* [id.]. LSO, Abbado.

The highlight here is *Petrushka*, almost certainly the finest available version, while the *Firebird suite* is also given a stunning performance of great vitality. There is a degree of detachment in Abbado's reading of *The Rite of spring*, but on points of detail it is meticulous; and an orchestra whose members have sometimes claimed they could play this score without a conductor revels in the security given by the conductor's direction. The recording is extremely brilliant, with a range of dynamic exceptionally wide, even by latterday standards. In the flap-pack box containing the pair of cassettes a somewhat unadventurous transfer level means that the upper range has less bite on tape than on disc in the *Firebird* and *Petrushka*, although *The Rite of spring* has strikingly more projection.

For the later Galleria reissue the recordings have been digitally remastered in preparation for a probable CD issue in 1987/8.

The Firebird: suite (rev. 1945 version); *Petrushka* (concert suite); *The Rite of spring* (complete).
(B) *** CBS *MGT 39015* [id.]. Columbia SO, composer.

The composer's own performance of *The Rite of spring* stands out among all others. Its authority in matters of balance and detail brings a remarkable documentary value to this recording – and yet this a mere bonus to a performance which in its vividness and sheer excitement leads all rivals. The recording dates from the beginning of the 1960s and will no doubt appear on CD during the lifetime of this book. It is also available on LP (CBS 60285 (MP 38765]); but the value of the present double-length bargain tape issue is formidable. It is a pity that the complete *Petrushka* was not chosen instead of the concert version with the shortened ending, but now that most recordings of the *Firebird suite* use the original score, the composer's account of the revised 1945 edition is doubly welcome. The tape transfers are vivid and lack only the last degree of refinement.

The Firebird: suite (1919 version); *Pulcinella* (ballet; rev. 1947 version): *suite*.
* DG Dig. **415 127-2**; 415 127-1/*4* [id.]. Israel PO, Bernstein.

Bernstein's version of Stravinsky's *Firebird* and *Pulcinella* with the Israel Philharmonic proves something of a disappointment. The dryness of the acoustic is all too evident at the end of the opening *Sinfonia* of *Pulcinella*, though less disturbing in *Firebird*. Like his *Petrushka*, the performances are neither as well executed nor as fully characterized as his earlier highly atmospheric accounts with the New York Philharmonic. The Israel Philharmonic is not in the same league, and the strings in the *Tarantella* of the *Pulcinella suite* sound pretty scrappy and lacklustre.

Petrushka (ballet; 1911 score; complete).
*** DG Dig. **400 042-2**; 2532/*3302* 010 [id.]. LSO, Abbado.

(B) *** DG Walkman *415 336-4* [id.]. LSO, Dutoit – RAVEL: *Daphnis et Chloé.***(*)
(M) *** Ph. Seq. 412 371-1/*4* [id.]. LPO, Haitink.

Petrushka (1947 score; complete).
*** Decca SXDL/*KSXDC* 7521 [Lon. LDR/5- 71023]. Detroit SO, Dorati.
** HMV Dig. **CDC 747015-2**; ASD/*TCC-ASD* 4069 [Ang. DS/*4XS* 37822]. Phd. O, Muti.
(B) *(*) Pickwick Con. CC/*CCTC* 7605. VPO, Dohnányi.

Petrushka (1947 score; complete); *Circus polka; Fireworks, Op. 4.*
(*) ASV Dig. **CDDCA 542; DCA/*ZCDCA* 542 [id.]. RPO, Bátiz.

Petrushka (1947 score; complete); *Scènes de ballet.*
** DG Dig. **410 996-2**; 410 996-1/*4* [id.]. Israel PO, Bernstein.

Petrushka (1947 score; complete); *Scherzo à la russe.*
** CBS **CD 37271** [id.]. Philh. O, Tilson Thomas.

Abbado's version of the 1911 *Petrushka* has the advantage of extremely fine digital sound, even though it is not quite as overwhelming sonically as Decca's for Dorati. The performance is strongly characterized, and the LSO play marvellously. Abbado combines refinement and a powerful sense of dramatic atmosphere (he is especially sympathetic in the central tableaux) with a kaleidoscopic brilliance. The recording has impressive range and colour, with the chrome tape very close to the disc. The compact disc, however, is slightly disappointing. It emphasizes the virtues of the LP by its clarity and silent background, but there is a degree of digital edge on the upper strings which is certainly not entirely natural.

Dorati's Decca recording is also digital, but not yet issued on CD. It is based on the 1947 version, though at certain points Dorati reverts to the original 1911 scoring, in accordance with his recollections of a conversation he had with Stravinsky himself. *Petrushka* has always been a vehicle for the virtuosity of recording engineers, right from the early days of LP, when Decca put the famous first Ansermet mono LP on to the market. Dorati's version creates a comparable digital landmark. The sound is breathtakingly vivid and clean, yet remains naturally balanced and transparent. The performance does not always have the refinement of Abbado's, but it is immensely dramatic and also very telling in the scene where the frustrated Petrushka is confined to his cell. Dorati is at his finest in the final tableau, bringing out the robust Russian earthiness of the dancing peasants. Abbado's account also has splendid physical exuberance here, but the projection of the Decca sound is even more striking. The Decca cassette is up to the highest standards of the house, extraordinarily vivid and clear, to match the disc very closely indeed.

For a bargain tape version the Walkman is unbeatable. Charles Dutoit recorded *Petrushka* for DG in 1977 before he had become a star conductor on the Decca roster. Interestingly, it was made almost impromptu: a planned opera recording fell through and sessions were hastily reallotted with little advance planning. The result is triumphantly spontaneous in its own right, with rhythms that are incisive yet beautifully buoyant, and a degree of expressiveness in the orchestral playing that subtly underlines the dramatic atmosphere, and is especially magical in the Third Tableau. The final section too is strongly coloured, so that the gentle closing pages make a touching contrast to the gaiety of the early part of the scene. The recording is rich and atmospheric, the only fault of balance being the prominence of the concertante piano soloist, Tamás Vásáry. In its Walkman chrome-tape format detail is less sharply etched than in some versions, but the combination of drama and evocation is most satisfying. Coupled with an excellent complete *Daphnis and Chloé* under Ozawa, this is formidable value.

Haitink's recording dates from 1974 but has been remastered with great success. There is a sense of expansion of the dynamic range and the performance is given added projection. Though not as dramatic as Dutoit, it is a very involving account, with detail imaginatively delineated. The rhythmic feeling is strong, especially in the Second Tableau and finale where the fairground bustle is vivid. The LPO wind playing is especially fine; the recording's firm definition and the perfectly proportioned and truthful aural perspective make it a joy to listen to. The resonance means that the cassette is not quite so sharply focused as the disc, but it is still impressive. On both disc and tape the ballet's closing pages are very telling.

With bright, forward, well-detailed recording, the Bátiz issue brings a performance of comparatively little sparkle or charm, more emphatic than usual, but therefore looking forward illuminatingly to the *Rite of spring*. The crispness of ensemble, the resilience of rhythms and the distinction of much of the solo work (notably the first flute) lightens what could have been too heavy, with some speeds slower than usual. The two lightweight fill-ups are certainly too heavily done, but are worth having as makeweights. The otherwise good cassette is made unacceptable by a turnover break in the middle of the Third Tableau.

Sonic limitations qualified the enthusiasm with which Bernstein's version of *Le Sacre* could be greeted; his *Petrushka* was recorded in the same unglamorous acoustic of the Mann Auditorium, Tel Aviv. However, the results are by no means as unpleasing, though still too dry and unventilated. Bernstein coaxes some highly responsive playing from the Israel Philharmonic and secures much pleasing string tone – not always to be found from this body. Perhaps this *Petrushka* is not as touching as his earlier New York account made in the 1960s, surely one of the most vital and sensitively characterized versions of the work (CBS 61020/*40*- [MY/*MYT* 37221]), but it is still vividly projected and keenly felt. Moreover, this record is particularly welcome for its coupling, the *Scènes de ballet* of 1944, which the Israeli orchestra play with something approaching elegance. This is a charming and underrated piece, not otherwise available at present save in the composer's own account. The CD draws the ear to the acoustic dryness of the recording, but the upper range is clear and clean and not edgy. On tape, the resonance agreeably smooths the treble, and the transfer is otherwise well managed.

Michael Tilson Thomas can hold his own with the available competition artistically. He shows a keen imaginative insight and much poetic feeling in *Petrushka* and his reading has the merit of freshness. However, in its CD format it still sounds bottom-heavy, lacking the transparency and well-integrated balance of some of its rivals. The *Scherzo à la russe* is a much less generous fill-up than Bernstein's but it is played with much character.

Muti secures playing of stunning virtuosity from the Philadelphians; but if their response is breathtaking, his reading can best be described as breathless. There is unremitting drive here, with the *Danse russe* taken at breakneck speed and everything far too regimented. The recording has splendid impact and clarity, but there is too little tenderness and magic in this overdriven account. The chrome tape is comparably vivid. The compact disc is extremely brilliant, but though the sound has 'hi-fi' vividness, there is an aggressive sharpness of focus to the sound-picture which emphasizes Muti's forcefulness.

Christoph von Dohnányi's measured approach has a certain warmth, matched by the playing of the VPO, for whom the score is an obvious novelty. The sound is rich but not very sharply detailed. The lack of drama and bite (the trumpet flourishes at the close, so effective with Haitink, are curiously laboured) is a serious drawback and there is no compensating imaginative feel for the work's atmosphere. The solo pianist (Horst Gobel) provides a very mundane contribution. This LP is offered at bargain price and has modern (Decca) recording, but Dutoit's DG Walkman is obviously better value for tape collectors. The Contour tape, like the disc, has its turnover break in the middle of the Third Tableau.

The Rite of spring (complete ballet).
(M) *** HMV **CDC 747102-2**; ED 290265-1/*4* [Ang. AM/*4AM* 34708]. Phd. O, Muti.
*** DG **415 979-2** [id.]. BPO, Karajan – *Apollo.****
*** Decca Dig. **400 084-2** [id.]; SXDL/*KSXDC* 7548 [Lon. LDR/5-71048]. Detroit SO, Dorati.
(M) *** DG Sig. 413 975-1/*4*. LSO, Abbado.
(*) Telarc Dig. **CD 80054; DG 10054 [id.]. Cleveland O, Maazel.
(B) **(*) DG Walkman *413 160-4* [id.]. Boston SO, Tilson Thomas – ORFF: *Carmina Burana.****
** DG Dig. **410 508-2**; 2532/*3302* 075 [id.]. Israel PO, Bernstein.

The Rite of spring (complete); *Symphonies of wind instruments.*
** Decca Dig. **414 202-2**; 414 202-1/*4* [id.]. Montreal SO, Dutoit.

Among his recordings of his major ballets, Stravinsky's own of the *Rite of spring* is indispensable. It is available on a bargain-priced CBS tape, coupled with the 1945 revised version of the *Firebird suite* and the *Petrushka concert suite* (see above), also on a single LP and tape (CBS 60285/*40*- [MP/*MPT* 38765]) and will no doubt appear on CD in due course. Among other versions those of Muti, Karajan and Boulez (CBS 60151/*40*-[MY/*MYT* 37764]) stand out. Muti's account is in a Philadelphia line stretching back to Stokowski and has been re-issued on LP and tape, digitally remastered, at mid-price. It is a performance of

Stravinsky's barbaric masterpiece which is aggressively brutal yet presents the violence with red-blooded conviction. Muti generally favours speeds a shade faster than usual, and arguably the opening bassoon solo is not quite flexible enough, for metrical precision is a key element all through. There are signs that Muti has studied the last of Stravinsky's own recordings of *The Rite* (by far the most convincing of the three he made), and it is good to have the amendment to the horn part sanctioned in it in the *Sacrificial dance* (two bars before fig. 75). The recording, not always as analytically clear as some rivals, is strikingly bold and dramatic, with brass and percussion exceptionally vividly caught. Like the disc, the tape has great impact, but the CD is finest of all, spacious yet with fine bite and amplitude. The effect is very exciting, without being fierce. There are no additional cues, however, only one at the beginning of Part 2.

Karajan's first recording of the *Rite of spring* came in for criticism from the composer, who doubted whether the Berlin Philharmonic tradition could encompass music from so different a discipline. In this 1977 version, tougher, more urgent, less mannered, Karajan goes a long way towards rebutting Stravinsky's complaints, and the result is superb, perhaps more civilized than some versions; but Karajan is at his finest: persuasive still but never obtrusively so, and above all powerfully dramatic. The analogue recording has neither the bite of the Muti version nor the presence of Dorati's, but its spaciously rich sound certainly has no lack of impact. Generously coupled with a superb version of *Apollo*, the CD is certainly good value.

However, in terms of recorded sound, Dorati's *Rite* with the Detroit orchestra scores over almost all its rivals. This has stunning clarity and presence, exceptionally lifelike and vivid sound, and the denser textures emerge more cleanly than ever before. It is a very good performance too, almost but not quite in the same league as those of Karajan and Muti, generating plenty of excitement. The only let-down is the final *Sacrificial dance*, which needs greater abandon and higher voltage. The Detroit strings too are not as sumptuous as those of the Berlin orchestra and sound distinctly undernourished in places. Yet too much should not be made of this. Although Dorati does not match the atmosphere of his finest rivals, the performance is so vivid that it belongs among the very best – for those primarily concerned with recorded sound, it will probably be a first choice, especially in its compact disc format. The chrome cassette too is in the demonstration bracket.

Abbado's version, having first reappeared on the above Signature label, has subsequently been reissued, generously coupled with the *Firebird* suite, in DG's new Galleria series, in digitally remastered form, ready for a later CD format – see above.

The sound on the Cleveland Orchestra version conducted by Lorin Maazel is pretty spectacular. Indeed, it is superior in terms of balance to that of the Detroit version when the two CD versions are juxtaposed. However, there are a number of sensation-seeking effects such as excessive ritardandi in the *Rondes printanières* so as to exaggerate the trombone glissandi (fig. 53) which are vulgar. Compare, too, the opening of the second part in this version with that of Karajan and one is in a totally different world.

Michael Tilson Thomas's reading is dramatic enough but warmly expressive too, missing some of the music's bite. The amply reverberant acoustic emphasizes his approach but, with fine playing from the Boston orchestra and the advantage of continuity, this Walkman tape is well worth considering, as it also contains Jochum's outstanding account of Orff's *Carmina Burana*, which has the composer's imprimatur.

Dutoit's Montreal CD offers sumptuous, finely detailed sound with a realistic balance and plenty of presence and body, and, of course, a marvellous dynamic range. This compact disc will, no doubt, be widely demonstrated for its sonic splendours. The playing of the Montreal Symphony Orchestra is first rate in every department: the strings are rich in sonority, the wind playing flawless, and phrasing throughout is sensitive. Yet Dutoit has little of that blazing intensity which one finds in the composer's own 1961 record, while if the Dutoit account is put alongside Karajan at the opening of the *Sacrifice*, the greater atmosphere of the latter is immediately apparent. In short, this Montreal version is unsurpassed as a recording, but the performance falls short of the highest voltage. The fill-up, the *Symphonies of wind instruments*, the work Stravinsky composed in 1920 in memory of Debussy, is given a very effective and crisp performance by the excellent Montreal wind.

Stravinsky hailed Bernstein's earlier record of *The Rite* with the New York Philharmonic with an amazed 'Wow!' Now, a quarter of a century later, he has re-recorded the score with the Israel orchestra. Unfortunately the recording is made in a dry acoustic ambience (at the Mann Auditorium, Tel Aviv) and though there is no lack of clarity, there is a loss of atmosphere. Each strand in the texture is clearly audible and the dynamic perspective is perfectly judged, but the overall result sounds synthetic. The same criticism could be applied to the Dorati version on Decca, but there is a much livelier acoustic in which to operate. In its CD format, the clarity is quite stunning but the dryness of the acoustic even more striking. The strings of the Israel orchestra are not in the same league as those of the NYPO nor, for that matter, are some of the wind.

The Soldier's tale: suite.

ʗ *** Delos Dig. **D/CD 3021** [id.]. LACO, Schwarz – PROKOFIEV: *Symphony No. 1****; SHOSTAKOVICH: *Piano concerto No. 1.***(*)

A splendid CD début for a work which is surprisingly little recorded. The acoustic is ideal for the music and the sound is wonderfully realistic and present. The performance makes a nice balance between pungency and the underlying lyricism; there is some splendid solo playing from Paul Shure (violin) and the superb trumpeter, Tony Plog, whose easy virtuosity and fine timbre add much to the music's appeal. Recommended, especially as the couplings are imaginative.

Suites Nos 1 and 2 for small orchestra.

ʗ *** RCA Dig. **RD 85168**; RL/*RK* 85168 [**RCD1 5168**; ARC1/*ARK1* 5168]. Dallas SO, Mata – PROKOFIEV: *Lieutenant Kijé* etc.***

Arranged by the composer from piano duets – 'Easy pieces' that are not so easy – these eight witty orchestral miniatures are a delight. They are played with marvellous finesse and point, and superbly recorded. Here the slight extra edge given by the CD is entirely apt, and the recording has presence and vividness.

Symphony in E flat, Op. 1; Symphony in C; Symphony in 3 movements; Ode (*Elegiacal chant in 3 parts*).
*** Chan. Dig. **CHAN 8345/6**; DBRD/*DBTD* 2004 (2). SNO, Gibson.

Even compared with the composer's own performances, this collection by the Scottish National Orchestra – in excellent form – under Sir Alexander Gibson stands up well. The vividness of the digital recording makes up for any slight lack of sparkle, and while the *Symphonies for wind instruments* might have seemed a more obvious makeweight for the three major works, it is good to have the *Ode* in memory of Natalia Koussevitzky, which has an extrovert, rustic scherzo section framed by short elegies. On CD, the bloom on the instruments in the amply atmospheric Glasgow acoustic is the more realistically caught. The sound is first class, with the reverberation rarely if ever obscuring detail. The cassettes are of generally good quality but use iron-oxide stock and on side four (in the *Symphony in 3 movements*) the upper woodwind partials are not as clean as on LP. The accompanying leaflet, too, is poorly produced – but that is not unusual with tape sets.

Symphony in C; Symphony in 3 movements.
*** Decca Dig. **414 272-2** [id.]; SXDL/*KSXDC* 7543 [Lon. LDR/5-71043] SRO, Dutoit.
** DG Dig. **415 128-2**; 415 128-1/*4* [id.]. Israel PO, Bernstein.

Although the Suisse Romande Orchestra is not in the very first rank, it is in much better shape than when it last recorded these symphonies in the 1960s for Ansermet, whose record has been reissued on Decca (Lon. Ent. 414 062-1/*4* [id.]). The brilliant recording they now receive from the Decca team and the alert direction of Charles Dutoit make this a very winning coupling. These are both exhilarating pieces and Dutoit punches home their virile high spirits and clean-limbed athleticism. The sound is first class, even if the woodwind may strike one at times as just a shade forward. No matter, this is a splendid issue and unlikely to be superseded for a while. The fullness of the Geneva recording (made in the Victoria Hall) is the more impressive on CD, when the bass register is so firmly and cleanly caught, and the spaciousness of the acoustic brings clarity without aggressiveness. The tape is fresh and clear, though the transfer level could have been higher.

While they may not be the last word in elegance and finish, Bernstein's performances have spirit. The orchestra is in good form and in the *Symphony in three movements* they play with freshness and immediacy. Although both performances have plenty of character, that of the *Symphony in C* is lightweight and at times (in the first movement particularly) there is the air of the ballet theatre, which also emerges in the lighter sections of the companion piece. Those who regard these as essentially sharp-edged works may find the orchestra's rhythmic attack not biting enough, particularly when Bernstein's speeds are often relatively slow. The recorded sound is not top-drawer, but at least it is present and vivid. The chrome cassette is well managed but is not as sharply defined as the CD. But the Tel Aviv acoustic is dry and unflattering alongside Decca's Dutoit coupling, and this is still the version to have.

CHAMBER MUSIC

Concertino for string quartet; Double canon in memoriam Raoul Dufy; 3 Pieces.
*** HMV Dig. EL 270100-1. Alban Berg Qt – EINEM: *Quartet.****

This record collects all of Stravinsky's output for the quartet medium with the sole exception of the *In memoriam Dylan Thomas.* The quartet as such was never really congenial to his sensibility, and it is significant that even the *Three pieces* and the *Concertino* were subsequently transcribed for other forces. Needless to say, the Alban Berg Quartet have the measure of Stravinsky's spare textures and are beautifully recorded. This repertoire is more logically coupled, however, by the Ensemble InterContemporain under Boulez on DG with, among other things, the *Ebony concerto* and the *Eight Miniatures for 15 players* (2531 378).

Suite italienne.
** Denon Dig. **C37 7563** [id.]. Fujiwara, Rouvier – DEBUSSY: *Cello sonata*; SHOSTAKOVICH: *Cello sonata.***

Stravinsky made several transcriptions of movements from *Pulcinella*, including the *Suite italienne* for violin and piano. This was arranged in 1932 with the aid of Piatigorsky and, with the exception of the first movement which is a little too sober, Mari Fujiwara and Jacques Rouvier give a very characterful account of these engaging pieces. They have the field to themselves on both CD and LP.

VOCAL MUSIC

Le Roi des étoiles (The King of stars); Symphony of Psalms.
** Decca Dig. **414 078-2**; 414 078-1/*4* [id.]. Berlin R. Ch. and SO, Chailly – *Le Chant du rossignol; Fireworks.***

Symphony of Psalms.
*(*) Telarc Dig. **CD 80105**; DG 10105 [id.]. Atlanta Ch. and SO, Shaw – POULENC: *Gloria.**(*)

The Decca recording is first class, but the ambience of the Jesus Christus Church in West Berlin emphasizes the expressive lyricism of Chailly's approach; although the *Laudate Dominum* has a spectacular dynamic expansion, overall this performance is soft-centred. Bernstein's splendid account on CBS (76670 [M/*MT*

34551]) has far more grip; it is significant that while Chailly's overall timing is 20′ 17″ (against Bernstein's more expansive 24′ 15″), the greater bite and concentration of the CBS performance by the English Bach Festival Chorus and LSO give the impression of more forward thrust. The inclusion by Chailly of the short but dramatic motet *Le Roi des étoiles* is most welcome; this piece has greater intensity. The Decca CD is very impressive as sound (with an excellent matching cassette), but the Bernstein LP has a grandeur and a powerful sense of atmosphere that elude Chailly.

Like the Poulenc on the reverse, Robert Shaw's Atlanta version is well disciplined and brilliantly recorded, but it misses the energetic bite and sharpness of focus so necessary in this work, before it finds its resolution at the end in heavenly *Alleluias*.

Oedipus Rex (opera/oratorio).
*** Orfeo Dig. S/*M* 071831A [id.]. Moser, Norman, Nimsgern, Bracht, Piccoli (nar.), Bav. R. Male Ch. and SO, Sir Colin Davis.

Recorded live in Munich in 1983, Davis's Orfeo performance is unerringly paced, with rhythms crisply sprung and detail finely touched in. Though the low-level sound is no help, the orchestral playing is first rate, and the cast is excellent, with Jessye Norman a commanding figure as Jocasta, firm and dramatic, making one wish the role was longer. Thomas Moser is both expressive and cleanly faithful to Stravinsky, and it is only partially his fault that the culminating moment of *Lux facta est* is rather understated. Michel Piccoli as narrator uses the original Cocteau text in French with fine dramatic emphasis. All in all, this is the most satisfactory recording available of Stravinsky's opera/oratorio, and we hope it will soon find its way on to CD.

The Rake's progress (complete).
(*) Decca Dig. **411 644-2; 411 644-1/*4* (2) [id.]. Langridge, Pope, Walker, Ramey, Dean, Dobson, L. Sinf. Ch. and O, Chailly.

Riccardo Chailly draws from the London Sinfonietta playing of a clarity and brightness to set the piece aptly on a chamber scale without reducing the power of this elaborately neoclassical piece, so cunningly based on Mozartian models by the librettists, W. H. Auden and Chester Kallman. Philip Langridge is excellent as the Rake himself, very moving when Tom is afflicted with madness. Samuel Ramey as Nick, Stafford Dean as Trulove and Sarah Walker as Baba the Turk are all first rate, but Cathryn Pope's soprano as recorded is too soft-grained for Anne. Charming as the idea is of getting the veteran Astrid Varnay to sing Mother Goose, the result is out of style. The recording is exceptionally full and vivid in all three media, but the balances are sometimes odd. The orchestra recedes behind the singers and the chorus sound congested, with little air round the sound. As an interpretation, the composer's own version is more subtly varied and therefore more dramatic (CBS 77304 [M3S-710]).

Suk, Josef (1874–1935)

Asrael symphony, Op. 27.
*** Sup. Dig. **C37 7404** [id.]. Czech PO, Neumann.

It is astonishing that a work of this stature has been so neglected outside Czechoslovakia. Only a few months after the first performance of his *G minor Fantasy* in 1904, Suk suffered a double bereavement: first, the death of Dvořák the same year, quickly followed by that of his wife, Dvořák's daughter, Otilia. Suk poured all his grief into this *Symphony*, which is a work of rare vision and compelling power. In its organization it owes a good deal to the 'cyclic' principle fashionable at the end of the last century. A sense of numbness in the face of grief comes across, yet there is much that is fiery, vigorous and exciting. Asrael is the Angel of Death – hence the title – and touches real depths; but it is more than a moving human document, it is a great work. The predominant influences, apart from his countrymen, are Liszt and, above all in the scherzo, Mahler. The performance is a very fine one; though those who have Vaclav Talich's classic account will surely never part with it; this is its first recording for almost thirty years and a must for all serious collectors.

A Fairy-tale, Op. 16; Praga (symphonic poem), Op. 26.
*** Sup. Dig. **C37 7509** [id.]. Czech PO, Libor Pešek.

Suk's *A Fairy-tale* is a concert suite drawn from the incidental music to Julius Zeyer's fairy-tale drama, *Raduz and Nahulena.* The music comes from 1898 and tells of a prince and princess, subjected to all sorts of trials; it must have appealed to the young composer then poised on the brink of marriage. The invention is full of charm and originality, and is as persuasively played here as it is on Jiři Bělohlávek's 1978 analogue LP (Sup. 1410 2699). On this compact disc it is coupled with *Praga* (1904), a patriotic tone-poem reflecting the more public, out-going figure than *Asrael*, which was to follow it. Libor Pešek secures an excellent response from the Czech Philharmonic; the recordings, which date from 1981–2, are reverberant but good. A reminder that Jiři Bělohlávek's record of *A Fairy-tale*, coupled with the deliciously high-spirited *Fantastic scherzo*, Op. 25, is now available on a cassette as well as on LP and should not be overlooked. The *Fantastic scherzo* is to Suk what the *Scherzo capriccioso* is to Dvořák.

(i) *Fantasy in G min. for violin and orchestra, Op. 24; Symphony in E, Op. 14.*
*** Sup. Dig. **C37 7540** [id.]. Czech PO, Neumann; (i) with Josef Suk.

A well-filled record (the *Symphony* takes 46′ 06″ and the *Fantasy* 22′ 30″). The *Symphony in E major* comes from 1898 when Suk was in his mid-twenties, and he took great trouble over its composition. For the third movement, for instance, he wrote no fewer than three scherzos before deciding on this one – all one can say is that he made a splendid choice. He likewise rejected his first thoughts for the second movement in favour of the present *Adagio*. The *Symphony* sounds marvellously fresh; though much of it is Dvořákian in outward appearance, there is much that one recognizes from Suk's maturity. This is a delightfully inventive and astonishingly accomplished *Symphony* that will captivate all who enjoy Dvořák, who became his father-in-law during the latter stages of its composition. The *G minor Fantasy*, Op. 24, was first performed in 1904; Josef Suk first recorded it for Supraphon way back in the late 1960s, and this is a worthy successor. It is an ardent, life-loving work – a kind of one-movement concerto, full of imaginative ideas and variety of invention. Suk is rather forwardly placed, but the somewhat reverberant recording is generally well balanced and the performance is very good indeed.

Sullivan, Arthur (1842–1900)

Pineapple Poll (ballet music, arr. Mackerras).
*** Ara. **Z 8016** [id.]. HMV ESD 7028 [Ara. 8016/*9016*]. RPO, Mackerras.

Pineapple Poll; Overture: Di Ballo.
*** Decca Dig. SXDL/*KSXDC* 7619. Philh. O, Mackerras.

Pineapple Poll (ballet suite, arr. Mackerras).
(B) *** CfP CFP 41 4490-1/*4*. LPO, Mackerras – VERDI: *Lady and the Fool.****

The new Decca digital recording of *Pineapple Poll* was made in the Kingsway Hall, and its glowing ambience casts a pleasing bloom over the spirited and elegantly polished playing of the Philharmonia Orchestra. Mackerras conducts with great warmth and finds space for a delightful performance of *Di Ballo*, showing a fine delicacy of approach. The chrome cassette is first class. We look forward to a CD version in due course.

Mackerras's earlier record is not entirely superseded. Considered definitive in its day (1962), it is still striking for its sheer brio. The RPO is in excellent form and the HMV recording still sounds extremely well. At mid-price this remains competitive; the playing has a real feeling of the ballet theatre, even if the later version gains in breadth and atmosphere. As can be seen, the enterprising Arabesque company have made a CD of this earlier account for the American market and this is available in the UK as an import from D Sharp. The transfer is remarkably successful. Most of the background noise has been vanquished and the bright, vivid sound suits the music, while in the lyrical sections (*Poll's solo* and *Jasper's solo*, scene ii) the strings retain their body. However, the fortissimos have a degree of hardness on top, the string sound is tighter and there is a touch of shrillness at times, though not beyond control. This makes an excellent stopgap until the Decca recording arrives in CD format.

Mackerras recorded the suite (and it is a very generous one, including nearly all the important music) for Classics for Pleasure in 1978. It is played with great élan, and the remastered recording sounds modern in all respects; it has a wide amplitude and the balance is admirable, combining vividness with warmth. With its attractive, but little-known Verdi coupling (also arranged by the conductor), this is a real bargain, on LP. The tape, unfortunately, loses a fair degree of brightness in the upper range because of the resonance, so the disc is much to be preferred in music that demands sparkle.

OPERAS

The suspension of the D'Oyly Carte Opera Company as a continuing theatrical enterprise, after creating a century-old tradition, gives a unique documentary value to Decca's series of authentic stereo recordings made, for the most part, in the late 1950s and early 1960s under the inspired direction of Isidore Godfrey. In its last years the company received much (often ill-informed) criticism for perpetuating a style of performance which Gilbert would have recognized. That seems ironic during a time when the 'authentic' movement in relation to music from an earlier era was gaining strength. Over a period of thirty years the company's musical standards were steadfastly maintained by Godfrey. It must be remembered that only a small group of key orchestral players travelled with the singers, so that at each city visited the orchestra needed considerable augmentation from the local pool of freelance musicians, some of limited accomplishment. With infinite patience Godfrey consistently directed rehearsals as if for a première performance, and his ability to inject the operas with freshness never flagged. Company salaries were never high, even for famous principals, yet the quality of solo singing was maintained at a remarkable, if variable level, while the chorus blossomed in the last years before Godfrey died.

While aficionados remember cast-lists from earlier recordings (for the D'Oyly Carte history is synonymous with that of the gramophone), the soloists in Decca's stereo series were given the task of setting the mould for the various famous roles before the final curtain fell. No doubt in the course of time the earlier sets will also find their way on to CD; meanwhile Decca are currently remastering their series and the first compact discs have already appeared.

The Gondoliers (complete, with dialogue).
*** Decca 417 254-1/*4* (2). Reed, Skitch, Sandford, Round, Styler, Knight, Toye, Sansom, Wright, D'Oyly Carte Op. Ch., New SO of L., Godfrey.

One welcomes back *The Gondoliers* to the catalogue, especially as it is now complete on two discs and tapes, whereas previously it needed a third. Isidore Godfrey's conducting is vividly alive; alongside *HMS Pinafore* and *The Pirates*, this is the finest Gilbert and Sullivan he gave us on record. Decca provided a large and excellent orchestra and a spacious recording. The solo singing throughout is consistently good. Jeffrey Skitch and Jennifer Toye are a well-matched pair of lovers, and the two Gondoliers and their wives are no less effective. Thomas Round sings *Take a pair of sparkling eyes* very well indeed. The ensemble singing is very well balanced and always both lively and musical. The *Cachucha* is captivating and goes at a sparkling pace. Everywhere one can feel the conductor's guiding hand. The dialogue is for the most part well spoken, and Kenneth Sandford, who is a rather light-voiced Don Alhambra, makes much of his spoken part, as well as singing his songs with fine style. John Reed is a suitably dry Duke of Plaza-Toro: he makes the part his own and is well partnered by Gillian Knight. All in all, a considerable achievement. This is scheduled for CD issue and should appear during the lifetime of this book.

HMS Pinafore (complete, with dialogue).
❀ (M) *** Decca 414 283-1/*4* (2) [OSA/*5*- 1209]. Reed, Skitch, Round, Adams, Hindmarsh, Wright, Knight, D'Oyly Carte Op. Ch., New SO of London, Godfrey.

There is a marvellous spontaneity about the invention in *Pinafore* and somehow the music has a genuine briny quality. It would be difficult to imagine a better-recorded performance than the 1960 Decca D'Oyly Carte set. It is complete with dialogue, and here it is vital in establishing the character of Dick Deadeye, since much of his part is spoken rather than sung. Donald Adams is a totally memorable Deadeye and his larger-than-life personality underpins the whole piece. Among the others, Jeffrey Skitch is a first-class Captain; Jean Hindmarsh is absolutely convincing as Josephine (it was a pity she stayed with the company for so short a time), and she sings with great charm. Thomas Round is equally good as Ralph Rackstraw. Little Buttercup could be slightly more colourful, but this is a small blemish; among the minor parts, George Cook is a most personable Bill Bobstay. The choral singing is excellent, the orchestral playing good and Isidore Godfrey conducts with marvellous spirit and lift. The recording has splendid atmosphere and its vintage qualities are very apparent in this remastered form. The sound is bright and open, words are clear and the ambience is splendidly calculated. The tapes (two of them, packed in a double-width hinged library box) use only iron-oxide stock and, though the transfers are good, the relatively modest level means that the upper range does not quite match the discs.

Iolanthe (complete, with dialogue).
(M) *** Decca 414 145-1/*4* (2). Sansom, Reed, Adams, Round, Sandford, Styler, Knight, Newman, D'Oyly Carte Op. Ch., Grenadier Guards Band, New SO, Godfrey.

This was the first (1960) stereo *Iolanthe*, not the later and generally inferior remake under Nash. Even though Decca's budget had not yet stretched to the Royal Philharmonic Orchestra, the production was given added panache by introducing the Grenadier Guards Band into the *March of the Peers*, with spectacular effect. The only real gain in the later version was that John Reed had refined his portrayal of the Lord Chancellor, but here the characterization is wittily immediate, and the famous *Nightmare song* undoubtedly has greater freshness. (There is still a hint that its virtuosity is not surmounted without considerable concentration.) Mary Sansom is a very convincing Phyllis, and if her singing has not the sense of style Elsie Morison brought to the Sargent HMV set (SXDW/*TC-SXDW* 3034) she is marvellous with the dialogue. Her discourse with the two Earls – portrayed to perfection by Donald Adams and

Thomas Round – at the beginning of side four is sheer delight. Alan Styler makes a vivid personal identification with the role of Strephon. To create a convincing portrayal of an Arcadian shepherd is no mean feat in itself, but the individuality of Styler's vocal personality and inflections is curiously appropriate to this role. Iolanthe's final aria (sung by Yvonne Newman) is a shade disappointing: it is a lovely song and it needs a ravishing, melancholy timbre, whereas here the voice does not sound quite secure. But this is a minor lapse in a first-rate achievement. The chorus is excellent, and the orchestral detail has the usual light Godfrey touch. Indeed, his spirited direction keeps the whole cast on their toes, and the engaging Act I finale (with both composer and librettist at their most inspired) is wonderfully infectious. The remastering is very successful, the sound bright, but with an admirable acoustic ambience which allows every word to project clearly. Tapes and discs are very closely matched.

The Mikado (complete; without dialogue).

*** Decca **417 296-2** (2) [id.]; SKL 5158-9/*K 22 K 22* [Lon. OSA/5- 12103]. Ayldon, Wright, Reed, Sandford, Masterson, Holland, D'Oyly Carte Op. Ch., RPO, Nash.

**(*) Decca 414 341-1/*4* (2) [Ara. 8051/*9051*]. Adams, Round, Pratt, Sandford, Hindmarsh, Drummond-Grant, D'Oyly Carte Op. Ch., New SO, Godfrey.

The 1973 stereo re-recording of *The Mikado* by the D'Oyly Carte company directed by Royston Nash is a complete success in every way and shows the Savoy tradition at its most attractive. The digital remastering for CD adds to the brightness: its effect is like a coat of new paint, so that the G. & S. masterpiece emerges with a pristine sparkle. Musically this is the finest version the D'Oyly Carte company have ever put on disc. The choral singing is first rate, with much refinement of detail. The glees, *Brightly dawns* and *See how the fates*, are robust in the D'Oyly Carte manner but more polished than usual. The words are exceptionally clear throughout. This applies to an important early song in Act I, *Our great Mikado*, which contains the seeds of the plot and is sometimes delivered in a throaty, indistinct way. Not so here: every word is crystal clear. Of the principals, John Reed is a splendid Ko-Ko, a refined and individual characterization, and his famous *Little list* song has an enjoyable lightness of touch. Kenneth Sandford gives his customary vintage projection of Pooh Bah – a pity none of his dialogue has been included. Valerie Masterson is a charming Yum-Yum; *The sun whose rays* has rarely been sung with more feeling and charm, and it is followed by a virtuoso account of *Here's a how-de-do* which one can encore, for each number is separately cued (there are 37 separate bands on the two CDs). Colin Wright's vocal production has a slightly nasal quality, but one soon adjusts to it and his voice has the proper bright freshness of timbre for Nanki-Poo. John Ayldon's Mikado has not quite the satanic glitter of Donald Adams's classic version, but he provides a laugh of terrifying bravura. Katisha (Lyndsie Holland) is commanding, and her attempts to interrupt the chorus in the finale of Act I are superbly believable and dramatic. On CD the singers are given striking presence, though the bright lighting of the sound has brought more noticeable sibilance; and many will feel that a judicious cutting back of the treble is useful in giving more emphasis to the lower middle range, though the overall ambient effect is theatrically convincing. As a CD transfer, this is less successful than *The Pirates of Penzance*.

The earlier (1958) Godfrey set is enjoyable enough and well cast but the later Nash recording is preferable in almost all respects. The one exception is Donald Adams's formidable portrayal of the Mikado himself, outstanding in its authority and resonance, which John Ayldon did not match in the later recording. Thomas Round, too, is a very good Nanki-Poo and Peter Pratt an enjoyably lightweight Ko-Ko (though John Reed's portrayal is even more memorable). Jean Hindmarsh is a petite Yum-Yum and Ann Drummond-Grant a compelling Katisha, with both her arias movingly sung. Kenneth Sandford is common to both sets. Isidore Godfrey conducts with characteristic point and sparkle, and the lively transfer seldom betrays the age of the original. There are excellent matching tapes.

Patience (complete, with dialogue).
(M) **(*) Decca 414 429-1/*4* [Lon. OSA 1217]. Sansom, Adams, Cartier, Potter, Reed, Sandford, Toye, D'Oyly Carte Op. Ch. and O, Godfrey.

Patience has some charming music, but the Act I finale is slightly disappointing, and elsewhere one is led to feel that Sullivan is better with primary colours than pastel shades. Certainly *When I first put this uniform on* and *The soldiers of the Queen* are among the very best of all Sullivan's military numbers, and Donald Adams is a worthy successor to Darrell Fancourt in these. Patience herself is well characterized by Mary Sansom, but her singing is less impressive: she is thoroughly professional and excellent in the dialogue, but her songs lack style, although they are not without moments of charm. All the dialogue is included, and it is very important to the action. Unfortunately the poems are spoken with too much intensity, whereas they need throwing off, if the barbs of the satire are to be lightly pointed, as Gilbert intended. In all other respects both Bunthorne and Grosvenor are well played. Both chorus and orchestra have never sounded better; Isidore Godfrey displays his usual skill with the accompaniments, which have a splendid bounce. The remastering is first class in every way, fuller than some in this series but just as crisp and clear, with cassettes and LPs closely matched.

Still recommended: The HMV set of *Patience* was one of the great successes of the Sargent recordings, with hand-picked soloists and the Glyndebourne Festival Chorus. It is in almost every way preferable to the Decca version. Although there is no dialogue (or poems), there is more business than usual from HMV and a convincing theatrical atmosphere. The opening scene is more effective than on Decca, and so is the Act I finale. Elsie Morison's Patience, George Baker's Bunthorne and John Cameron's Grosvenor are all admirably characterized, while the military men are excellent, too. The recording sounds extremely well on disc but on our review copy the tape transfer (on one double-length cassette) was over-modulated, bringing a treble emphasis which overstressed consonants and thin strings. However, this may have been corrected by the time of publication (SXDC/*TC2-SXDW* 3031).

The Pirates of Penzance (complete, with dialogue).
*** Decca **414 286-2**; 414 286-1/*4* [Lon. OSA 1277]. Reed, Adams, Potter, Masterson, Palmer, Brannigan, D'Oyly Carte Op. Ch., RPO, Godfrey.

For compact disc issue, Decca have chosen the second (1968) D'Oyly Carte recording, and Isidore Godfrey is helped by a more uniformly excellent cast than was present on the earlier set. The dialogue is included, theatrical spontaneity is well maintained, and the spoken scenes with the Pirate King are particularly effective. Donald Adams has a great gift for Gilbertian inflection – some of his lines give as much pleasure as his splendidly characterized singing. Christine Palmer's Ruth is not quite so poised, but her singing is first rate – her opening aria has never been better done. John Reed's characterization of the part of the Major General is strong, while Valerie Masterson is an excellent Mabel; if her voice is not creamy throughout its range, she controls it with great skill. Her duet with Frederick, *Leave me not to pine alone*, is enchanting, sung very gently. Godfrey has prepared us for it in the overture, and it is one of the highlights of the set. Godfrey's conducting is as affectionate as ever, more lyrical here without losing the rhythmic buoyancy; one can hear him revelling in the many touches of colour in the orchestration, which the Royal Philharmonic Orchestra present with great sophistication. But perhaps the greatest joy of the set is Owen Brannigan's Sergeant of Police, a part this artist was surely born to play. It is a marvellously humorous performance, yet the humour is never clumsy; the famous *Policeman's song* is so fresh that it is almost like hearing it for the first time. The recording is superbly spacious and clear throughout, with a fine sense of atmosphere. The cassettes are also of excellent quality, although only iron-oxide stock is used. The CD transfer is remarkable in its added presence. While a slight degree of edge appears on the voices at times, the sense of theatrical feeling is greatly enhanced and the dialogue interchanges have an uncanny realism. This is markedly more successful technically than the companion CD transfer of *The Mikado*.

Princess Ida (complete, without dialogue).
*** Decca 414 126-1/*4* [Lon. OSA 1262]. Harwood, Sandford, Adams, Skitch, Reed, D'Oyly Carte Op. Ch., RPO, Sargent.

Sir Malcolm Sargent is completely at home here, and his broadly lyrical approach has much to offer in this 'grandest' of the Savoy operas. Elizabeth Harwood in the name part sings splendidly, and John Reed's irritably gruff portrayal of the irascible King Gama is memorable. He certainly is a properly 'disagreeable man'. The rest of the cast is no less strong, and with excellent teamwork from the company as a whole and a splendid recording, spacious and immediate, this has much to offer, even if Sullivan's invention is somewhat variable in quality. The cassette transfer is outstanding, one of Decca's best.

The Sorcerer (complete, with dialogue).
*** Decca 414 344-1/*4* (2) [Ara. 8068L/*9068L*]. Palmer, Reed, Adams, Masterson, D'Oyly Carte Op. Ch., RPO, Godfrey.

John Reed's portrayal of the wizard himself is one of the finest of all his characterizations. The plot, with a love potion administered to the whole village by mistake, has considerable potential, but it drew from Sullivan a great deal of music in his fey pastoral vein. Returning to this freshly remastered set, however, one discovers how many good and little-known numbers it contains. By 1966, when the set was made, Decca had stretched the recording budget to embrace the RPO, and the orchestral playing is especially fine, as is the singing of the D'Oyly Carte chorus, at their peak. The entrance of John Wellington Wells is an arresting moment; John Reed gives a truly virtuoso performance of his famous introductory song, while the spell-casting scene is equally compelling. The final sequence in Act II is also memorable. While the score is undoubtedly uneven in invention, the best numbers are not to be dismissed, especially in a performance so dedicated. The sound is well up to Decca's usual high standard, though on our copy the transfer level of the first of the two cassettes seemed excessively high to bring a few moments of discoloration; however, this may have been corrected by the time we are in print.

Utopia Ltd: complete. *Imperial march.*
**(*) Decca 414 359-1/*4* [Lon. OSA/*5*- 12105]. Field, Holland, Ayldon, Reed, Sandford, Ellison, Buchan, Conroy-Ward, D'Oyly Carte Op. Ch., RPO, Nash.

Utopia Ltd was first performed in 1893, ran for 245 performances and then remained unheard (except for amateur productions) until revived for the D'Oyly Carte centenary London season in 1974, which led to this recording. Its complete neglect is unaccountable; the piece stages well, and if the music is not as consistently fine as the best of the Savoy operas, it contains much that is memorable. Moreover, Gilbert's libretto shows him at his most wittily ingenious, and the idea of a Utopian society *inevitably* modelled on British constitutional practice suggests Victorian self-confidence at its most engaging. Also the score offers a certain nostalgic quality in recalling earlier successes. Apart from a direct quote from *Pinafore* in the Act I finale, the military number of the First Light Guards has a strong flavour of *Patience*, and elsewhere *Iolanthe* is evoked. *Make way for the Wise Men*, near the opening, immediately wins the listener's attention, and the whole opera is well worth having in such a lively and vigorous account. Royston Nash shows plenty of skill in the matter of musical characterization, and the solo singing is consistently assured. When Meston Reid as Captain Fitz-Battleaxe sings 'You see I can't do myself justice' in *Oh, Zara*, he is far from speaking the truth – this is a performance of considerable bravura. The ensembles are not always as immaculately disciplined as one is used to from the D'Oyly Carte, and *Eagle high* is disappointingly focused: the intonation here is whole are irresistible. As there is no overture as such, the recording uses Sullivan's less than secure. However, the sparkle and spontaneity of the performance as a

Imperial march, written for the opening – by the Queen – of the Imperial Institute, five months before the première of the opera. It is an effective enough piece, but not a patch on the *March of the Peers* from *Iolanthe*. The cassettes, which have been remastered, are curiously uneven in quality for Decca. The first two sides are transferred at fractionally too high a level, bringing a hint of peakiness on climaxes; the second two go to the other extreme and lack something in presence and clarity in the upper range.

COLLECTION

'Here's a how-de-do!': excerpts from: *Cox and Box; The Gondoliers; The Grand Duke; Haddon Hall; H M S Pinafore; Iolanthe; The Mikado; Patience; Ruddigore; The Sorcerer; Utopia Ltd; The Yeomen of the Guard.*
**(*) HMV Dig. EL 270170-1/*4* [Ang. DS/*4DS* 38147]. Armstrong, Tear, Luxon, Northern Sinf., Hickox.

Benjamin Luxon is very much the star of this collection and it is he who introduces the principal novelty, *I've heard it said* from *Haddon Hall*, a vintage Sullivan number, even though the words are not by Gilbert. He sings it in a beguilingly relaxed manner and is no less engaging in *When you find you're a broken-down critter* from *The Grand Duke*. He partners well with Robert Tear in duets from *Ruddigore*, *The Gondoliers* and *Cox and Box*, but Tear tends at times to over-project his solos. Sheila Armstrong is heard at her best in *For love alone* from *The Sorcerer*; when the three artists sing together, however, the last touch of polish is missing, as in the pay-off of *Here's a how-de-do!* Hickox provides understanding accompaniments and the recording is vivid, though the tape has a hint of edginess now and then.

Reminder. An earlier HMV partnership between Robert Tear and Valerie Masterson produced the finest Gilbert and Sullivan anthology in the catalogue and perhaps the most attractive recital of its kind ever recorded. We gave it a Rosette in our last edition (HMV ASD/*TCC-ASD* 4392 [Ang. DS/*4DS* 37996]).

Suppé, Franz von (1819–95)

Overtures: *Beautiful Galathea; Fatinitza; Jolly robbers; Light cavalry; Morning, noon and night in Vienna; Pique dame; Poet and peasant.*
*** Decca Dig. **414 408-2**; 414 408-1/*4* [id.]. Montreal SO, Dutoit.

Decca have previously relied on Solti for their Suppé overtures – indeed, he was first disconcertingly asked to record this repertoire, when he would have much preferred Wagner. As we know, that came later. Dutoit's approach could hardly be further removed from Solti's electrifyingly hard-driven performances. There is no lack of bravura but, as the dignified opening of *Poet and peasant* demonstrates, there is breadth, too. Indeed, the pacing is splendid, combining warmth and geniality with brilliance and wit, as in the closing galop of *Fatinitza*. The orchestral playing is admirably polished, the violins sounding comfortable even in the virtuoso passages of *Light cavalry*, one of the most infectious of the performances here. It is difficult to imagine these being bettered, even by Karajan, while the Decca sound is superb, well up to the usual Montreal standards. The tape, however, does not always retain the sharpness of focus of the CD and LP.

Overtures: *Light cavalry; Morning, noon and night in Vienna; Poet and peasant.*
(*) DG **415 377-2 [id.]. BPO, Karajan – ROSSINI: *Overtures.***(*)

Karajan's performances are taken from a 1970 collection and are coupled with four Rossini overtures. The playing is swaggeringly brilliant, but the sound is just a little fierce at fortissimo level, although the overall balance is warm and natural.

Swayne, Giles (20th century)

Cry (1978/9).
*** BBC Dig. REF/*ZCD* 550. BBC Singers, John Poole.

Using simply a choir of 28 voices electronically treated, Swayne produces an astonishing range of expression, very unconventional but ear-tickling in its originality, and obviously relished by the virtuoso members of the BBC Singers. His ambitious theme is nothing less than to illustrate the seven days of Creation, following the Bible account in Genesis and using only three words and no connected sentences. Though it is not always easy to relate the different moments to their titles, the exuberance of Swayne's inspiration reflects pure enjoyment in creation, both that of God and that of the composer on his own level. Finally breaking from his fragmentary patterns, Swayne allows himself simple triads used modally, a symbol for Order arriving out of Chaos. The ever-inventive vocal orchestration is brilliantly realized by the BBC Singers, and the sound is vividly atmospheric.

Szymanowski, Karol (1882–1937)

Symphonies Nos 2 in B flat, Op. 19; (i) *3* (*Song of the Night*), *Op. 27.*
*** Decca Dig. SXDL/*KSXDC* 7524 [Lon. LDR/5- 71026]. Detroit SO, Dorati, (i) with Karczykowski, Jewell Chorale.

This is the first Western commercial record of either of these Szymanowski symphonies. *The Song of the Night* is one of his most beautiful scores, a setting (made in the period 1914–16) of a poem by the great Persian Sufi mystic Djelaleddin Rumi. It is finely performed here, and the detail and opulence of the orchestral texture are revealingly captured by the digital recording. The *Second* is not so rewarding a symphony as the *Third*, but this is a most valuable issue, with a good equivalent cassette. We hope it will appear on CD during the lifetime of this book.

String quartets Nos 1 in C, Op. 37; 2, Op. 56.
*** Pavane ADW 7118. Varsovia Qt.

Szymanowski's *Quartets* are separated by a decade: the first dates from 1917 and its successor from 1927. Both open with inspired ideas and immediately establish a highly charged and distinctively personal atmosphere: both are short and concentrated, lasting just under 20 minutes. The *First* comes in the wake of the *First Violin concerto* and its opening has something of the same sense of ecstasy and longing. It is only let down by the somewhat Milhaudesque *Scherzando alla burlesca*, which is neither a completely successful scherzo nor a sufficiently weighty finale. However, the beauties of the work more than outweigh its flaws; so original is its sound-world that its almost total neglect these days seems unaccountable. Of course, it has much exposed and demanding writing above the stave which calls for the most accurate intonation, and the Varsovia Quartet rises to the challenge. This is a subtle and deeply felt performance, and much the same must be said of their account of No. 2. Again the subtle scents and the exotic luxuriance we find in the *Third Symphony* and the two *Violin concertos* are present, yet the colours are still intense and refined. The opening of the *Second Quartet* is like listening to the Ravel *Quartet* in a moonlit garden. The idiom derives from Ravel and, of course, Debussy; yet there are darker shadows, and the scudding ostinato demisemiquavers produce an almost unearthly effect. Like so much Szymanowski, it is steeped in nostalgia, a vision of a vanishing world. There are magical things in both works, and the Varsovia play them with real poetic feeling and deep commitment. They are excellently recorded.

Reminder. The two *Violin concertos* are available on an imported EMI disc, persuasively performed by Kulka and the Polish Radio Symphony Orchestra under Maksymiuk (1C 065 03597).

Tallis, Thomas (*c.* 1505–85)

Derelinquat impius; Ecce tempus idoneum; In jejunio et fletu; In manus tuas; O nata luz; Salvator mundi; Spem in alium (40-part motet)*; Te lucis ante terminum* (settings 1 and 2)*; Veni Redemptor gentium.*
(M) *** Decca 411 722-1/*4* [id.]. King's College Ch., Cambridge University Musical Soc. Ch., Willcocks.

The 1965 Argo recordings – now reissued at mid-price on Decca – hold an honoured place in the catalogue. In the 40-part motet, the Cambridge University Musical Society joins forces with King's to give an eloquent and powerful performance, while the simpler hymn-settings are no less impressive, with performances and recording equally distinguished. The King's acoustic is mistier than that of Merton College (see below), but the sound is still very fine on LP; however, the tape, transferred at marginally too high a level and using iron-oxide stock, produces roughness at climaxes.

Gaude gloriosa; Loquebantur variis linguis; Miserere nostri; Salvator mundi, salva nos, I and II; Sancte Deus; Spem in alium (40-part motet).

❀ *** Gimell **CDGIM 006**; 1585-06/*1585T-06* [id.]. Tallis Scholars, Peter Phillips.

On the splendid Gimell issue the Tallis Scholars at once celebrate the Quatercentenary of the composer's death and provide a Tallis collection for the CD era to match – and surpass – the Argo recordings of the 1960s. Within the admirably suitable acoustics of Merton College Chapel, Oxford, they give a thrilling account of the famous 40-part motet, *Spem in alium*, in which the astonishingly complex polyphony is spaciously separated over a number of point sources, yet blending as a satisfying whole to reach a massive climax. The *Gaude gloriosa* is also a magnificent piece, while the soaring *Sancte Deus* and the two very contrasted settings of the *Salvator mundi* are hardly less beautiful. Throughout, the music is paced spontaneously, the vocal line is beautifully shaped and the singing combines ardour with serenity. On CD, the breadth and depth of the sound is spectacular; the LP is first class too, and the cassette is a model of its kind, full and smooth, with the focus never slipping.

The Lamentations of Jeremiah the Prophet, Motets: *Sancte Deus; Videte miraculum. Organ lesson.*

(M) **(*) Argo 414 367-1/*4*. King's College Ch., Willcocks; Andrew Davis (organ).

The Lamentations of Jeremiah the Prophet; Spem in alium (40-part motet).

(M) ** Pickwick Dig. **PCD 806**; CC/CCTC 7602. Pro Cantione Antiqua, Mark Brown – ALLEGRI: *Miserere*. **

The Argo performances – a reissue from 1962 – are authentic, using men's voices only, and the singing, without being inexpressive, has the right element of restraint. The two motets are for full choir; here the balance is less than ideal, giving over-prominence to the trebles. Andrew Davis provides an excellent account of the *Lesson* for organ, and the recording itself is natural and atmospheric. On cassette, the sombre *Lamentations* are successfully transferred, but a higher level on side two brings a loss of focus at peaks.

On Pickwick, a strong, generally well-sung performance (although there are moments in the motet when intonation is not absolutely secure). Tempi are well judged but there is less light and shade than would be ideal. The microphone balance brings a thickening of tone to the expansive climax of *Spem in alium* and less than ideal transparency of texture. But this CD comes at mid-price and may be counted good value. The LP is even better value, as it is in the bargain range; but the chrome cassette is over-modulated to the point of distortion.

Tartini, Giuseppe (1692–1770)

Violin concertos: in G, D.78; A, D.96; in B, D.117.
(M) **(*) Ph. 412 403-1/*4*. Salvatore Accardo, I Musici.

Tartini is most famous as an innovator of violin technique; as these three concertos (chosen from a complete collection of 125 works) show, the quality of his invention was often considerable. Accardo is an excellent soloist – the *Largo andante* of the *G major Concerto* is particularly beautiful. The accompaniments are sympathetic and have plenty of life. The 1974 recording is clear, fresh and well balanced, though perhaps a little lacking in body. There is an excellent cassette. A pleasant choice for undemanding late evening listening.

Tavener, John (born 1944)

Funeral Ikos; Ikon of Light; Carol: The Lamb.
*** Gimell 1585-05/*1585T-05* [id.]. Tallis Scholars, Chilingirian Qt, Phillips.

Both the major works on the disc, *Funeral Ikos* and *Ikon of Light*, represent Tavener's more recent style at its most compelling, simple and consonant to the point of bareness but with sensuous overtones. *Ikon of Light*, first performed at the Cheltenham Festival in 1984, is a setting of Greek mystical texts, with chant-like phrases repeated hypnotically. The string trio provides the necessary textural variety. More concentrated is *Funeral Ikos*, an English setting of the Greek funeral sentences in six linked sections, often yearningly beautiful. Both in these and in the brief setting of Blake's *The Lamb*, the Tallis Scholars give immaculate performances, atmospherically recorded in the chapel of Merton College, Oxford.

Taverner, John (*c.* 1495–1545)

Missa gloria tibi Trinitas; Audivi vocem (responsory); ANON.: *Gloria tibi Trinitas.*
*** Hyp. A 66134 [id.]. The Sixteen, Harry Christophers.

Missa gloria tibi Trinitas; Dum transisset sabbatum; Kyrie a 4 (*Leroy*).
*** Gimell Dig. **CDGIM 004**; 1585-04/*1585T-04* [id.]. Tallis Scholars, Peter Phillips.

This six-voice setting of the Mass is one of the great glories of Tudor music, richly varied in its invention (not least in rhythm) and expressive in a deeply personal way very rare for its period. Harry Christophers and The Sixteen underline the beauty with an exceptionally pure and clear account, superbly recorded, and made the more brilliant by having the pitch a minor third higher than modern concert pitch.

Phillips and the Tallis Scholars give an intensely involving performance of this glorious example of Tudor music. The recording may not be so clear as on the rival Hyperion version, with textures sometimes thickened, but Phillips rejects all idea of reserve or cautiousness of expression; the result reflects the emotional basis of the inspiration the more compellingly. The motet, *Dum transisset sabbatum*, is then presented more reflectively, another rich inspiration.

Tchaikovsky, Peter (1840–93)

Andante cantabile, Op. 11; Nocturne, Op. 19/4; Pezzo capriccioso, Op. 62 (1887 version); *2 Songs: Legend; Was I not a little blade of grass; Variations on a rococo theme, Op. 33* (1876 version).
*** Chan. Dig. **CHAN 8347**; ABRD/*ABTD* 1080 [id.]. Wallfisch, ECO, Simon.

This delightful record gathers together all of Tchaikovsky's music for cello and orchestra – including his arrangements of such items as the famous *Andante cantabile* and two songs. The major item is the original version of the *Rococo variations* with an extra variation and the earlier variations put in a more effective order, as Tchaikovsky wanted. The published version, radically different, was not sanctioned by him. Geoffrey Simon, following up the success of his record of the original version of the *Little Russian symphony*, draws lively and sympathetic playing from the ECO, with Wallfisch a vital if not quite flawless soloist. Excellent recording, with the CD providing fine presence and an excellent perspective. The cassette transfer approaches demonstration standard on side one, but is much softer-grained on side two, which rather suits the music. Rostropovich's analogue recording, with Karajan, of the *Rococo variations* is also available on CD – see below – but he uses the published score.

Capriccio italien, Op. 45.
© *** RCA Dig. **RCD 14439**. Dallas SO, Mata (with Concert ***).
(B) ** Ph. On Tour *416 221-4* [id.]. Concg. O, Haitink – MUSSORGSKY: *Pictures*; RIMSKY-KORSAKOV: *Scheherazade*.**

Capriccio italien; 1812 Overture; Marche slave.
** DG Dig. **400 035**; 2532/*3302* 022 [id.]. Chicago SO, Barenboim.
*(*) Decca **414 494-2** [id.]. Detroit SO, Dorati.

Capriccio italien; 1812 Overture; Hamlet (fantasy overture), Op. 67a; Marche slave.
** DG Dig. **415 379-2**; 415 379-1/*4* [id.]. Israel PO, Bernstein.

Capriccio italien; 1812 Overture; Mazeppa: Cossack dance.
** Telarc Dig. **CD 80041**; DG 10041 [id.]. Cincinnati SO, Kunzel.

(i) *Capriccio italien;* (ii) *Francesca da Rimini;* (iii) *Symphony No. 4, Op. 36.*
(B) DG Walkman *415 617-4* [id.]. (i) BPO, Rostropovich; (ii) Leningrad PO; Rozhdestvensky, or (iii) Mravinsky.

(i) *Capriccio italien; Marche slave; Mazeppa: Gopak. Romeo and Juliet* (fantasy overture); (ii) *Sleeping Beauty: Waltz and Polacca.* (i) *Suite No. 3 in G, Op. 55.*
(B) ** HMV *TCC2-POR 290114-9.* (i) LPO; (ii) RPO, Boult.

Tchaikovsky's *Capriccio italien* is given an extraordinarily successful compact disc début on Mata's Dallas disc. The concert-hall effect of the recording is very impressive indeed with the opening fanfares as sonically riveting as the silences, when the reverberation dies away naturally. The performance is colourful and exciting, and the piece is issued within an attractive compilation of favourite orchestral showpieces (see our Concerts section below).

Haitink's account of the *Capriccio* is warm-blooded, with some elegantly turned string-playing from the Concertgebouw Orchestra. The restatement of the main theme at the end is given tremendous weight – to be honest, it sounds rather phlegmatic played like this; it also means that the coda gets underway too slowly. However, this is enjoyable in its fashion; the acoustic, warm and spacious, matches the reading, although the tape transfer tends to blunt the transients a little.

Even more than in Bernstein's Stravinsky series, here the Tel Aviv acoustic is too dry for music which needs a warmly expansive resonance. The performances have plenty of excitement and are well paced, although the oboe solo in *Hamlet* could have been more beguiling. The CD is greatly preferable to the LP; with the extra presence and definition, the ear can accept – though not revel in – the chosen ambience. At the end of *1812* the cannon make a spectacular effect, though the sudden peal of bells near the end seems contrived. Overall, this cannot be recommended with great enthusiasm. The cassette is well managed, although it has problems with the cannon.

Barenboim gives a slinkily persuasive account of the *Capriccio* but *1812* is disappointingly done and, by Chicago standards, poorly played. The chrome cassette matches the disc fairly closely, although the opening trumpet fanfare of *Capriccio italien* is not quite clean. The compact disc only confirms that the recording is not ideally balanced, with the end of *1812* sounding constricted, while the violin sound has a distinct digital edge. The *Capriccio* is more agreeable; overall, however, this is an acceptable issue rather than a memorable one.

Both the Telarc compact disc and LP give due warning that on this record the cannon dwarf the orchestra in *1812* – indeed, at the time of the sessions many windows nearby were shattered. So if you need a recording of cannon, plus *1812*, and your speakers can accommodate the dynamic range and amplitude, both impressively wide, then this issue is for you. In the *Capriccio* there are no cannon – so the engineers substitute the bass drum, which is very prominent. The orchestral contribution throughout is lively but not memorable, and the playing simply does not generate enough adrenalin to compensate for the relative lack of projection of the orchestral tone. At the end of *1812*, Tchaikovsky's carefully contrived climax, with its full-blooded scalic descent, seriously lacks weight. The most enjoyable item here is the lively *Cossack dance*.

Dorati's coupling is not a digital recording and the sound-quality does not compare with his more recent Decca CDs. It represented the return of the Detroit orchestra to the international recording scene at the beginning of 1979. The performance of the *Capriccio* is not without elegance, but the steadily paced *Marche slave* seems rather sombre until the coda, which is taken briskly. This is underlined by an over-emphasis to the bass response. The account of *1812* is not especially exciting, nor is it helped by the lack of a really sharp focus in the sound. The original LP was excessively bright; this has now been tempered in the remastering. There are guns and bells at the end, all well contained.

At the time of writing, Boult's 'Portrait of the Artist' double-length tape offers the only available recording of Tchaikovsky's *Third Orchestral suite*, with its famous *Theme and variations*. Boult displays less than his usual flair in this final section of the work, although the first three movements are lyrically persuasive. *Romeo and Juliet* was one of his best Tchaikovsky recordings, but the other performances are unexpectedly idiosyncratic at times, quite volatile in their control of the forward momentum, especially *Marche slave*. The recording is resonant, which means that the focus is smooth rather than sharp; on our copy, the opening trumpet solo of the *Capriccio italien* produced a moment of discoloration. Otherwise the sound is good.

The Walkman tape offers what is potentially a most attractive collection, but (unusually for DG) it has been ruined by inept engineering. Rostropovich's (1979) *Capriccio* has marvellous flair, with decoratively elegant playing by the Berlin Philharmonic and full recording, but Rozhdestvensky's very exciting (1961) *Francesca da Rimini* sounds rather fierce. The tape is put out of court by Mravinsky's *Fourth Symphony*, where the sound has been brightened and the underlying harmonic distortion, inherent in the original master-tape, is now uncomfortably emphasized: in the first big climax the distortion is unacceptable.

Piano concerto No. 1 in B flat min., Op. 23.

*** DG **415 062-2** [id.]. Martha Argerich, RPO, Dutoit – PROKOFIEV: *Piano concerto No. 3.****

(M) *** DG Sig. 410 978-1/*4*. Lazar Berman, BPO, Karajan.

(*) DG Dig. **415 122-2; 415 122–1/*4* [id]. Ivo Pogorelich, LSO, Abbado.

(*) CBS Dig. **CD 36660; 36660/*40*- [id.]. Emil Gilels, NYPO, Mehta (with Bach: *Well-tempered Clavier: Prelude No. 10*, arr. Siloti ***).

(*) RCA **RD 85363 [RCD1 5363]. Artur Rubinstein, Boston SO, Leinsdorf – GRIEG: *Concerto.**(*)

(*) Ph. Dig. **411 057-2 [id.]. Martha Argerich, Bav. RSO, Kondrashin.

(M) (**) DG Gal. 419 068-1/*4*. Sviatoslav Richter, VSO, Karajan – RACHMANINOV: *Preludes.****

Argerich's 1971 recording of the Tchaikovsky *First Piano concerto* with Dutoit makes a clear first choice on CD. Not quite all the background hiss has been eliminated, and the digital remastering cannot provide the inner clarity which is more apparent in her 1980 version for Philips. Nor are the strings as rich in timbre as on the new DG/Pogorelich version. But the sound is firm, with excellent presence, and its ambience is more attractive than the later version. The weight of the opening immediately sets the mood for a big, broad performance, with the kind of music making in which the personalities of both artists are complementary. Argerich's conception encompasses the widest range of tonal shading. In the finale she often produces a scherzando-like effect; then the orchestra thunders in with the Russian dance theme to create a real contrast. The tempo of the first movement is comparatively measured, but satisfyingly so; the slow movement is strikingly atmospheric, yet delicate, its romanticism light-hearted. On LP and cassette the coupling is different, with a highly individual account of the Liszt *First concerto*, instead of Prokofiev. However, this is offered at mid-price, so that it is about a third of the cost of the CD (DG Sig. 2543/*3343* 503 [id.]). The Argerich performance is also available on a particularly attractive Walkman tape (see below) where the couplings are even more generous.

Berman's 1976 recording with Karajan has been reissued at mid-price, without a coupling, on DG's Signature label; no doubt this outstanding version will also appear on CD in due course. It is interesting that credit for its incandescence must go almost as much to the conductor as to the pianist – and yet the conductor is Karajan, who has sometimes seemed too aloof as a concerto accompanist. Berman's character is firmly established in the massive chords of the introduction (though, curiously, he hustles the first group of all); from there his revelling in dramatic contrast – whether of texture, tone colour, dynamic or tempo – makes this one of the most exciting readings ever put on record. It is not just a question of massive bravura but of extreme delicacy too, so that in the central scherzando of the slow movement it almost sounds as though Berman is merely breathing on the keyboard, hardly depressing the notes at all. The ripe playing of the Berlin Philharmonic backs up the individuality of Berman's reading, and the recording is massively brilliant to match. The cassette is well balanced, but not as brilliant as the disc, though the finale is brighter and the climax expands satisfactorily.

The opening of the Pogorelich/Abbado account has an impressive sweep and, provided one accepts the forward balance of the piano – on CD it is so tangible that one feels almost able to reach out and touch it – the recording is superbly full-bodied and wide-ranging. The orchestra, set back in the spacious acoustic of Watford Town Hall, makes an impressive impact, even if pianissimos seem a shade recessed. The dramatic contrasts of the first movement are thus underlined, with the poetic secondary material beautifully and thoughtfully played by soloist and orchestra alike. But after the first big climax, Pogorelich puts the brakes on; here, and again in the cadenza, his ruminative (some might say narcissistic) introspection holds up the music's forward flow. The movement overall takes 23′ 18″, which must be something of a record. The *Andante* is a delight, with the delicately agile LSO strings matching the soloist's nimbleness in the central *Prestissimo*; and the finale is similarly exhilarating in its crisp articulation, producing no real barnstorming until the closing section after Abbado's very positive broadening for the final statement of the big tune. The charisma of the performance is undeniable and, in spite of Pogorelich's eccentricities, his partnership with Abbado is a convincing one; but many will find the first movement too wilful to live with – and with no fill-up, the CD seems poor value running for only 37 minutes. There is a very good chrome cassette, but the CD is supreme in its range and immediacy.

Any Gilels record is an event, and his CBS recording appears a quarter of a century after his first account with Fritz Reiner and the Chicago Symphony Orchestra (see below). Gilels has an outsize musical personality, and this is a performance of leonine calibre, with nobility and fire. There is no want of virtuosity – the double octaves leap off the CD – and there are the inward-looking qualities we associate with Gilels, too. The music making was recorded live at Carnegie Hall, and the claims of Gilels's artistry have to be weighed against less than distinguished recorded sound and second-rate orchestral playing: the wind (bar 186) are not in tune and do not blend, and at no point does the orchestra respond as alertly or sensitively as it did in the days of Bernstein. The digital recording reproduces clean detail – the high-level tape transfer has striking range and brilliance, although the upper string timbre is rather crude – and the relationship between soloist and orchesta is well balanced. But the sound is not top-drawer. The compact disc offers very marginally greater refinement and the obvious advantage of background silence, but otherwise the difference between this and the LP is minimal. However, Gilels is Gilels, and the quality of his playing cannot be too highly praised. The Siloti arrangement of the Bach *Prelude* was his encore on the occasion of the recording, and it is affecting in its direct eloquence.

Many older readers will remember Rubinstein's famous 78 r.p.m. recording of this work. The present account is no less magnetic, with fine bravura in the outer movements and a poetic *Andante*. There is a mercurial quality here, not only in the central section of the slow movement but also in the finale. Leinsdorf is obviously caught up in the music making and the orchestra opens the work splendidly and provides plenty of excitement throughout. The 1963 recording is less than ideal, but the digital remastering has taken some of the brashness out of the close-microphoned strings and provided a piano image impressively bold and clear. The result is very enjoyable.

Argerich's Philips issue comes from a live performance given in October 1980, full of animal excitement, with astonishingly fast speeds in the outer movements. The impetuous virtuosity is breathtaking, even if passagework is not always as cleanly articulated as in her superb studio performance for DG. That earlier version also brings more variety of tone; but you will find few more satisfying performances on record than either of these. The CD version clarifies and intensifies the already vivid sound.

Unlike his partnership with Lazar Berman, Karajan's 1963 recording with Richter was not a success. The element of struggle for which this work is famous is only too clear, with soloist and conductor each choosing a different tempo for the second subject of the finale and maintaining it in spite of the other. In both the dramatic opening and closing pages of the work they are agreed, however, on a hugely mannered, bland stylization which fails to convince. Elsewhere in the first movement, both conductor and pianist play havoc with any sense of forward tempo (though they produce some real bursts of excitement here and there), and Richter's excessive rubato in the lyrical second-subject group is unspontaneous. Clearly two major artists are at work here, but it is difficult to praise the end product as a convincing reading. The recording has been digitally remastered; it sounds clearer and fresher, but slightly less full-bodied, with a firm piano image, and is now coupled with some highly recommendable Rachmaninov *Preludes*.

Piano concertos Nos 1; 3 in E flat, Op. 75.
(M) **(*) EMI Em. EMX/*TC-EMX* 2001. Emil Gilels, New Philh. O, Maazel.
(B) ** CfP CFP 41 4470-1/*4*. Philip Fowke, LPO, Boettcher.
*(*) Decca Dig. **410 112-2;** 410 112-1/*4* [id.]. Victoria Postnikova, VSO, Rozhdestvensky.

At medium price, this EMI reissue is worth investigating for the *Third Concerto* alone, a comparatively lightweight piece but not lacking in memorable ideas. Gilels plays it with authority and freshness. The account of No. 1 is in many ways distinguished also and is much better recorded than Gilels's CBS CD. It has a very fast opening, exhilarating in its way, but many Tchaikovskians will feel that this – one of his most famous melodies – needs a broader treatment. The performance as a whole has undoubted insights, but it is less commanding and magisterial than the CBS version. The balance places the piano well forward; that said, the sound is first class, although the cassette has noticeably less range at the top than the disc, especially on side two.

It is a pity that the least successful part of Philip Fowke's two performances is the grand introduction to the *First Concerto*, plain and four-square at a stolid tempo. After that, much of the first movement is plain too, lacking in sparkle; paradoxically, however, the bravura passages with their extra challenge lift the performance, and the soloist promptly sounds more relaxed and spontaneous. The slow movement is coolly presented, effectively so, with the central scherzando delightfully clean and light; but it is the finale which really sets the performance alight, with the orchestra, like the soloist, warming to the exuberance of inspiration. Fowke then gives a dazzling performance of the *Third Concerto*, full of joyful bravura. At CfP price, this alone is worth the money, and the digital recording is excellent on LP, though disappointingly the cassette lacks brightness in the upper range.

The collaboration of wife and husband in the Postnikova/Rozhdestvensky performances makes for very personal readings, marked by spacious speeds. The very introduction is disconcertingly slow and so is the basic tempo for the central *Andante*. There and in other places Postnikova's expressive fluctuations sound studied, but the clarity of articulation will for some make up for the lack of adrenalin. The long single movement of the *Third Concerto* also needs more consistently persuasive treatment, though the dactylic dance-theme is delectably pointed. Close balance for the piano in a firm, clear recording, enhanced on CD – but the performances remain unenticing.

(i) *Piano concerto No. 1;* (ii) *Violin concerto in D, Op. 35.*
(M) *(**) RCA Victrola VL/*VK* 89043. (i) Gilels, Chicago SO, Reiner; (ii) Szeryng, Boston SO, Munch.

These recordings come from 1958 and 1960 respectively and are inevitably dated, especially in terms of the orchestral sound. The reverberant Chicago acoustics bring a touch of coarseness, but Gilels is at his most commanding: this is a very exciting, full-blooded account, including a beautifully gentle reading of the outer sections of the slow movement, with mercurial brilliance in its central episode. When it first appeared at full price, Szeryng's performance of the *Violin concerto* was widely accounted to provide the ideal combination of brilliance, warmth and subtlety. The purity of the solo playing is still remarkable, for quite apart from his effortless sense of bravura, he is able to bring all the lyrical sweetness and Slavonic yearning needed for Tchaikovsky's big melodies. The timbre is made to sound thinner in this remastering, but the quality of the phrasing still comes over with ravishing effect. The Boston orchestra give first-rate support, and we hope that when this is issued on CD in RCA's 'Legendary Performers' series, the sound can be smoothed on top in the manner of the Heifetz Brahms *Concerto.*

(i) *Piano concerto No. 1;* (ii) *Violin concerto in D, Op. 35;* (iii) *Serenade for strings: Waltz;* (iv) *Variations on a rococo theme, Op. 33.*
❀ (B) *** DG Walkman *413 161-4.* (i) Argerich, RPO, Dutoit; (ii) Milstein, VPO, Abbado; (iii) BPO, Karajan; (iv) Rostropovich, Leningrad PO, Rozhdestvensky.

This extended-length (ninety-minute) chrome tape is the jewel in the crown of DG's Walkman series, always generous, but here exceptionally so, both in quality of performances and recording, as well as the amount of music offered. We award it a Rosette as the outstanding Tchaikovsky bargain. Argerich's account of the *B flat minor Piano concerto* is second to none; Milstein's (1973) performance of the *Violin concerto* is equally impressive, undoubtedly one of the finest available, while Abbado secures playing of genuine sensitivity and scale from the Vienna Philharmonic. Rostropovich's earlier (1961) version of the *Rococo variations* offers playing with just the right amount of jaunty elegance as regards the theme and the first few variations; and when the virtuoso fireworks are let off, they are brilliant, effortless and breathtaking in their éclat. Indeed, Rostropovich needs no superlatives and his accompanist shows a mastery all his own. Karajan provides a stylishly polished account of one of Tchaikovsky's most memorable (and original) waltzes, here an elegant interlude between the *Variations* and the first movement of the *Piano concerto.* The only slight drawback is that the turnover then follows, before the *Andantino.* But it is difficult to see how this could have been avoided within the chosen format. The sound is first class.

(i) *Piano concerto No. 1;* (ii) *Marche slave; Symphony No. 6* (*Pathétique*).
(B) * Ph. On Tour *412 907-4* [id.]. (i) Haas, Monte Carlo Op. O, Inbal; (ii) Concg. O, Haitink; (iii) O de Paris, Ozawa.

The Philips 'On Tour' compilation does not compare in value with DG's Walkman tape centring on concertante works. Werner Haas's 1970 recording of the *Piano concerto* has a good solo contribution, but the support from the Monte Carlo orchestra under Inbal is less impressive. Haitink's *Marche slave* comes off well, but Ozawa's *Pathétique* is too lightweight to reward continued listening, although its balletic feel is certainly individual. The sound quality is acceptable; but this is uncompetitive.

Piano concerto No. 2 in G, Op. 44.
*(*) Decca Dig. **410 113-2**; 410 113-1/*4* [id.]. Postnikova, VSO, Rozhdestvensky.

Though it provides the full text of the *Second Concerto*, complete with the piano trio passages of the slow movement, and though the recording is exceptionally vivid, Postnikova's version can be recommended only with serious reservations. Speeds are consistently slow and rhythms lumbering, so that the very opening sounds more like a rehearsal and the 25-minute span of that first movement tends to fall apart. Postnikova is more poetic in the slow movement, and the lightheartedness of the finale is attractive, but more is needed. The CD enhances the presence and richness of the recording, made in the Vienna Sofiensaal, and there is a good tape; but this is little more than a stopgap.

Violin concerto in D, Op. 35.
*** Decca Dig. **410 011-2;** SXDL/*KSXDC* 7558 [Lon. LDR/*5*– 71058]. Kyung Wha Chung, Montreal SO, Dutoit – MENDELSSOHN: *Concerto.****
(M) *** DG Gal. 419 067-1/*4* [id.]. Milstein, VPO, Abbado – MENDELSSOHN: *Concerto.****
(M) **(*) RCA Gold GL/*GK* 85264 [AGL1/*AGK1* 5264]. Heifetz, Chicago SO, Reiner – MENDELSSOHN: *Concerto.***(*)
(*) Erato **ECD 88109 [id.]. Amoyal, Philh. O, Dutoit – SIBELIUS: *Violin concerto.***(*)
** PRT **CDPCN 14.** Yaron, LPO, Soudant – SIBELIUS: *Concerto.***(*)
(B) ** Ph. On Tour *416 227-4* [id.]. Accardo, BBC SO, Sir Colin Davis – BRUCH: *Violin concerto No. 1; Scottish fantasia.**

Violin concerto in D, Op. 35; Sérénade mélancolique, Op. 26.
(*) HMV **CDC 747106-2 [id.]. Perlman, Phd. O, Ormandy.
** DG Dig. **400 027-2;** 2532/*3302* 001 [id.]. Kremer, BPO, Maazel.

Violin concerto in D, Op. 35; Sérénade mélancolique, Op. 26; Mélodie, Op. 42/3.
(*) CBS Dig. **MK 39563; IM/*IMT* 39563 [id.]. Zukerman, Israel PO, Mehta.

Violin concerto; Sérénade mélancolique, Op. 26; Valse-scherzo, Op. 34.
(M) **(*) Ph. 412 015-1/*4*. Accardo, BBC SO, Sir Colin Davis.

Chung's earlier recording of the Tchaikovsky *Concerto* with Previn conducting has remained one of the strongest recommendations for a much-recorded work ever since it was made, right at the beginning of her career. The remake with Dutoit is amazingly consistent. Though on the concert platform she is so volatile a performer, responding to the inspiration of the moment, she is a deeply thoughtful interpreter. Here, as before, she refuses to sentimentalize the central *Canzonetta*, choosing a flowing, easily songful speed. The result is the more tenderly affecting, though this time the violin is balanced more closely than before. The finale has, if anything, even more exhilaration, with technical problems commandingly overcome at a very fast speed. Like other recent versions, this opens out the tiny cuts traditional in the finale. Excellent recording, warm and atmospheric. As in the Mendelssohn coupling, the compact disc is even more vivid. There is a very good chrome cassette too, although here the treble needs a degree of smoothing – it is not quite as refined as the disc versions in the higher partials.

Milstein's fine 1973 version with Abbado is more attractively coupled on the Walkman cassette – see above – but those for whom the Mendelssohn *Concerto* is more suitable will find that on Galleria the recording has been digitally remastered, bringing greater clarity, although the sound on the Walkman tape is fuller.

Zukerman's Israel version with Mehta was recorded at a live performance, which inevitably makes it marginally less perfect on detail and overall less disciplined than the superb account he recorded in London (also for CBS) at the very beginning of his recording career. However, that was relatively disappointing technically, while this new CD sounds extremely well. The sound is less dry and enclosed than in most recordings made in the Mann Auditorium in Tel Aviv; while on LP the tuttis fail to open out clearly, on CD the sound is greatly enhanced, freer, better defined and with more bloom. The soloist is balanced closely, but only at one point in the first movement is the impact of bow on string given a touch of aggressiveness, while in the cadenza the violin image is very tangible indeed. The new reading of the central *Canzonetta* is certainly preferable to the old – faster, less heavily expressive – but the first movement is more self-indulgent in its expressive lingering. Yet Zukerman's warmth is endearing and the intensity of the live music-making prevents the result from being slack. Zukerman, unlike most other soloists in recent versions, does not open out the once-traditional tiny cuts in the finale, but the playing here certainly conveys the excitement and thrills of a live performance, with extremes of speed in both directions – although the soloist's habit of stamping his foot may irritate some listeners. The fill-ups are brief, if apt, and are tenderly played: Zukerman's G string tone in the *Sérénade mélancolique* is ravishing, without being too schmaltzy. All in all, a most rewarding issue. There is a first-class chrome tape.

Taken from an analogue original of the late 1970s, Perlman's Philadelphia version sounds all the fuller and more natural in its CD format, with the soloist balanced less aggressively forward than usual; but in clarity and openness, however, it cannot match the finest digital recordings on compact disc. Perlman's expressive warmth goes with a very bold orchestral texture from Ormandy and the Philadelphia Orchestra, and anyone who follows Perlman – in so many ways the supreme violin virtuoso of our time – is not likely to be disappointed. The coupling is not very generous, though beguilingly played.

Heifetz's recording was made in the earliest years of stereo (1957). He was balanced very near the microphone; on the original LP, this tended to make the performance sound over-intense and also provided the listener with some uncomfortable sounds, as bow met strings in the many florid moments in which this concerto abounds. Now the recording (like the Brahms, made during the same period) has been digitally remastered for RCA's 'Legendary Performers' series and, with the upper range smoothed and the orchestral presence enhanced, the magic of Heifetz can be enjoyed more fully. There is some gorgeous lyrical playing and the slow movement marries deep feeling and tenderness in ideal proportions, while the finale scintillates. Reiner accompanies understandingly, producing fierily positive tuttis. The quality is equally impressive on LP or cassette; we hope RCA have plans to issue this outstanding coupling on compact disc in the near future.

Pierre Amoyal gives a fine account of the Tchaikovsky, though while Salvatore Accardo and Chung open out the traditional cuts, Amoyal observes them. However, there is an aristocratic quality about his playing and great warmth, too. The Philharmonia Orchestra under Charles Dutoit are in excellent form and eminently well recorded. Erato scores over such rivals as Perlman and Kremer, both coupled with the *Sérénade mélancolique*, in offering the Sibelius *Concerto*.

Salvatore Accardo's account combines poise and freshness with flair. He has a keen lyricism and a fine sense of line, as one would expect, and he is sensitively accompanied by Sir Colin Davis and the BBC Symphony Orchestra. He plays the *Concerto* complete; an additional attraction is that he includes both the *Sérénade mélancolique* and the *Valse-scherzo*. Accardo's reading of the *Concerto* has a refinement and restraint that mark it off from the traditional virtuoso approach; no doubt for some collectors it will lack the passionate sweep they look for. Accardo has a marvellous purity, and if the (1977) recording was as good it would carry a three-star grading. As it is, the soloist is a shade too close to the microphone to do his tone full justice. However, the tape transfer is very successful – the violin timbre is slightly smoother than on the disc (though not quite all the edge is removed) and the orchestral detail remains vivid.

Accardo's account is also available on a Philips 'On Tour' tape with the Bruch *G minor Concerto* and *Scottish fantasia*. The slight edge to the solo timbre is here slightly more noticeable and the coupled Bruch works also have an element of shrillness in the upper range.

Yuval Yaron gives an impressive performance. Like Zukerman, he takes the first movement at a comparatively spacious tempo and revels in its lyrical detail; however, unlike Zukerman, he does not enjoy the extra intensity engendered by a live performance. The *Canzonetta* is played most tenderly – he uses a mute at the opening – and is given an elegiac atmosphere; then Soudant prepares the finale rather deliberately, so that the start of the allegro makes a striking contrast. The woodwind interchanges in the finale are very relaxed, and the soloist too brings out the lyricism of these interludes between the bravura very pleasingly. Thus the performance as a whole is imaginatively thought out and individual.

Yaron is balanced well forward, but his technique stands up to the spotlight thus provided. The 1978 analogue recording has been successfully remastered; but those seeking a coupling with the Sibelius will find that Amoyal's more modern version on Erato is even finer, though that also has an analogue source.

Kremer's was the first digital recording of the concerto and the first CD version. This artist blends keen nervous energy with controlled lyrical feeling, and it goes without saying that his virtuosity is impressive. Self-regarding agogic distortions are few (bars 50–58 and the first-movement cadenza are instances), and there is no lack of warmth. Yet both here and in the *Sérénade mélancolique* there is something missing. A great performace of this work refreshes the spirit and resonates in the mind. Here, although both the recording and the playing of the Berlin Philharmonic for Maazel are undoubtedly excellent, there is not the special kind of humanity and perception that are needed if a newcomer is to displace the superb versions already available.

1812 Overture, Op. 49.
* HMV **CDC 747022-2** [id.]. Phd. O, Muti – LISZT: *Les Préludes***; RAVEL: *Boléro*.*

1812 Overture; Francesca da Rimini; Marche slave.
(M) **(*) Ph. 416 247-1/*4*. Concg. O, Haitink.

1812 Overture; Francesca da Rimini; Marche slave; Eugene Onegin: Polonaise.
(*) HMV Dig. **CDC 747375-2 [id.]; EL 270237-1/*4* [Ang. DS/*4DS* 38200]. BPO, Ozawa.

1812 Overture; Marche slave.
*(*) CBS **CD 37252** [IM/*IMT 37252*]. V. State Op. Ch., VPO, Maazel – BEETHOVEN: *Wellington's victory*.**

(i) *1812 Overture;* (ii) *Marche slave;* (iii) *Romeo and Juliet.*
(B) **(*) DG Walkman *413 153-4*. (i) Boston Pops O, Fiedler; (ii) BPO, Karajan; (iii) San Francisco SO, Ozawa – MUSSORGSKY: *Pictures* etc.***
(M) ** Pickwick Dig. **PCD 801;** CC/*CCTC* 7551. LSO, Ahronovich.

(i) *1812 Overture; Marche slave; Romeo and Juliet; Swan Lake, Act I: Waltz.*
* ASV Dig. DCA/*ZCDCA* 544 [id.]. City of Mexico PO, Bátiz, (i) with Marina Symphonic Band.

(i) *1812 Overture; Romeo and Juliet;* (ii) *Eugene Onegin: Polonaise; Waltz; Écossaise. The Oprichnik: Dances.*
*** Ph. **411 448-2** [id.]. (i) Boston SO, with Tanglewood Fest. Ch. (in *1812*); (ii) ROHCGO; Sir Colin Davis.

Sir Colin Davis is not renowned as a Tchaikovskian, yet here he provides one of the most satisfying versions of *1812* ever recorded. Though he departs from the original score – to great effect – by including a chorus, it is musical values rather than any sense of gimmickry that make this version so successful. Men's voices alone are used to introduce softly the Russian hymn at the opening, with the ladies freshening the reprise. In the closing spectacle, the chorus soars above the bells, and the effect is exhilarating. The music in between is splendidly played and satisfyingly alert. On CD, the initial choral entry is enhanced by the absence of background and the balance in the closing peroration is superbly managed, the choral sound a little thicker than it would be in a digital master, but impressively full-bodied; and the very believable cannon are superbly placed. What is especially striking is how the resonantly firm support of the middle and lower strings adds to the effect of the Tchaikovsky sound, to make a consistently satisfying impact throughout, as it does in *Romeo and Juliet*. This is a slightly reserved performance, but one which in its minor degree of introversion misses neither the noble passion of the lovers nor the clash of swords in the feud sequences. The elegiac closing pages are particularly telling. The colourful operatic dances are a generous makeweight and are played with élan; while the two most famous *Eugene Onegin* items tend to overshadow what follows, the *Oprichnik* excerpts show the composer's orchestral skill at its most felicitous. Here the ear notices, slightly more than in *Romeo and Juliet*, that the recording balance has lost just a degree of sparkle in the upper range, with the removal of virtually all the background noise.

Ozawa's *1812* has the advantage of strikingly vivid digital recording, full-blooded, but not without a degree of edge on the brass. The reading is thrustful and certainly exciting, with the Berlin Philharmonic strings singing their lyrical melodies eloquently. The cannon are very spectacular: their first fusillade is so engulfing that one is surprised to discover the orchestra still sitting in their places afterwards, to reassert the musical line! In the final cannonade, however, the joyous bells are drowned, unlike the Davis/Philips version where all the 'ad lib' additions to the orchestra are well balanced. Ozawa's *Marche slave* is nicely paced, dignified yet spirited, and the *Eugene Onegin Polonaise* is attractively buoyant. The reading of *Francesca da Rimini*, however, is essentially neurotic. Tchaikovsky's portrayal of Dante's Inferno is vividly realized, with superb bravura playing from the orchestra. The beautifully scored middle section is also seductive, but Ozawa begins his accelerando much too early (at the cor anglais scalic figure) and, while what follows is undeniably thrilling, it turns Tchaikovsky's construction into melodrama. On CD the sound is enhanced at both ends of the spectrum, the bass full and firm, the upper range just as clear but with added body and smoothness. This approaches demonstration quality, but the cannon in *1812* remain overwhelmingly noisy.

Haitink is more brilliantly recorded than usual. The acoustics of the Concertgebouw slightly cloud the final climax of *1812*, but the unfocused resonance of the bells is effective. *Francesca da Rimini* is superbly played, especially its melting central episode where the woodwind solos are lovely. In the closing pages, a greater degree of compulsive excitement would not have come amiss, although the effect is far from uninvolving. *Marche slave* is the most successful piece here, most convincingly paced: clearly Haitink and his orchestra are enjoying themselves. The cassette matches the disc closely on side one, but in *Francesca da Rimini* the reverberation brings a loss of inner definition and range.

Fiedler's account of *1812* has plenty of adrenalin and is brilliantly recorded, with the effective display of pyrotechnics at the end adding spectacle without drowning the music. The direct manner of the performance does all Tchaikovsky asks, if with no special individuality. Nevertheless, with Karajan's *Marche slave* and Ozawa's excellent *Romeo and Juliet* and first-class sound throughout, this Walkman chrome tape coupled with Mussorgsky is certainly good value.

The Pickwick CD is offered at mid-price, and the recording is very spectacular. The balance is truthful, the ambience a little dry but with a convincing perspective. The dynamic range is wide and the fusillade of cannon at the end of *1812* impressively realistic, without ruining the musical focus. Yuri Ahronovich's readings are extremely wilful. He moulds the lyrical music idiosyncratically and drives on the allegros with the acceleration in constant flux. The LSO ensemble suffers, but the thrust is undeniable. There is no doubt that this music making creates bursts of excitement, and the sound is physically very involving. The CD is far superior to either the LP or cassette in this respect.

Maazel's performance of *1812* is in no way distinctive, with the chorus failing to add a *frisson* of excitement at the opening, as it does in Sir Colin Davis's Philips version. Moreover, the CD adds little to one's enjoyment, serving only to emphasize the relative lack of ambient richness, with brass sharply defined and upper strings very brightly lit. The closing pages, with chorus, orchestra and cannon, certainly make a spectacle, but there is nothing really involving about the music making itself. *Marche slave* is rather more successful; but there are other, better versions, not least Ozawa's.

Muti gives an urgent, crisply articulated version of *1812*, concentrated in its excitement. The Philadelphia Orchestra takes the fast speed of the main allegro in its stride, and the coda produces a spectacular climax. The snag is the recording which – like the coupled *Boléro* – has a shrill upper range in its CD format, with the violins glassy above the stave, and the brilliance sounding wholly artificial.

From Bátiz and the City of Mexico Philharmonic, an agreeably spirited *1812* with an enthusiastic fusillade of gunfire at the close. *Marche slave*, too, has plenty of impetus, the brass pungent in an almost Russian way. But while there is passion in *Romeo and Juliet*, the lack of refinement in the orchestral playing, with intonation at times suspect, is more serious here. The spontaneity of the music making is never in doubt throughout this concert, but for repeated listening one needs a higher degree of polish. The recording is impressively brilliant, but there is too much bass drum in the *Swan Lake Waltz*.

(i) *1812 Overture; Serenade for strings, Op. 48; Eugene Onegin: Polonaise and waltz.*
(M) **(*) DG Gal. 415 855-1/*4* [id.]. (i) Don Cossack Ch.; BPO, Karajan.

This is a reshuffling of performances from the late 1960s and early 1970s, digitally remastered. The sound has undoubtedly been enhanced in range and clarity. *1812* is exciting, finely played, but the chorus used to open the piece is not very sonorous and the closing pages have the cannon added with calculated precision, although the fusillade is certainly spectacular. Karajan's reading of the *Serenade* is brilliantly played but lacks charm. The *Waltz* is suavely done, and the main points of the slow movement are made without expressive underlining, but

Karajan seems relatively uninvolved. This impression may partly be caused by the recorded sound, which is very brightly lit, although the tempi of the outer movements are notably brisk. The two *Eugene Onegin* dances are played with fine panache.

Eugene Onegin (ballet, arr. and orch. Kurt-Heinz Stolze): excerpts.
(M) ** EMI Dig. EMX 41 2080-1/4. Sydney SO, Lanchbery.

To have a Tchaikovsky-derived ballet score that manages consistently to avoid including memorable tunes is quite an achievement, while to re-score Tchaikovsky seems something of a liberty. The *Waltz* and *Polonaise* included here are not the famous examples from the opera; when a familiar melody finally turns up at the end, it derives from *Francesca da Rimini*. Perhaps most remarkable of all, Tatiana's bedroom scene is able to avoid any quotation from the famous letter song. The music is agreeable in an inconsequential way, is obviously suitable as an accompaniment for dancing and is very well played and sumptuously recorded, with disc and tape sounding virtually identical.

Festival overture on the Danish national anthem, Op. 15. (i) *Hamlet: Overture and incidental music, Op. 67 bis. Mazeppa: Battle of Poltava and Cossack dance; Romeo and Juliet* (fantasy overture; 1869 version); *Serenade for Nikolai Rubinstein's saint's day.*
❀ *** Chan. Dig. **CD 8310/1**; DBRD/*DBRT* 2003 (2) [id.]. LSO, Simon, (i) with Janis Kelly, Hammond-Stroud.

The credit for the appearance of this enterprising set, indispensable for any true Tchaikovskian, lies with Edward Johnson, a keen enthusiast and Tchaikovsky expert. He spent many months trying to persuade one of the major recording companies to make an investment in this repertoire, and it was Chandos which finally responded, producing a resplendent digital recording fully worthy of the occasion. Tchaikovsky himself thought his *Danish Festival overture* superior to *1812*, and though one cannot agree with his judgement it is well worth hearing. The *Hamlet* incidental music is another matter. The overture is a shortened version of the *Hamlet Fantasy overture*, but much of the rest of the incidental music (which occupies two well-filled LP sides) is unknown, and the engaging *Funeral march* and the two poignant string elegies show the composer's inspiration at its most memorable. Ophelia's mad scene is partly sung and partly spoken, and Janis Kelly's performance is most sympathetic, while Derek Hammond-Stroud is suitably robust in the *Gravedigger's song*. The music from *Mazeppa* and the tribute to Rubinstein make engaging bonuses, but the highlight of the set is the 1869 version of *Romeo and Juliet*, very different from the final 1880 version we know so well. It may be less sophisticated in construction, but it uses its alternative ideas with confidence and flair. It is fascinating to hear the composer's early thoughts before he finalized a piece which was to become one of the most successful of all his works. The performances here under Geoffrey Simon are excitingly committed and spontaneous; the orchestral playing is nearly always first rate, and the digital recording has spectacular resonance and depth to balance its brilliance. The cassette transfer is of the highest quality, matching the discs very closely. Edward Johnson provides the excellent notes and a translation of the vocal music, which is sung (as the original production of *Hamlet* was performed) in French. The compact discs are among Chandos's most impressive, with the strings in the *Hamlet* incidental music sounding attractively refined, although the forward balance of the vocal soloists is made more noticeable. Orchestral tuttis are given added weight and range.

Francesca da Rimini, Op. 32.
(M) *(*) DG 415 009-1/*4* (2) [id.]. Israel PO, Bernstein – LISZT: *Faust symphony.****

Francesca da Rimini, Op. 32. Romeo and Juliet (fantasy overture).
(M) ** DG Sig. 410 990-1/*4* [id.]. Israel PO, Bernstein.
*(*) Decca Dig. **414 159-2**; 414 159-1/*4* [id.]. Cleveland O, Chailly.

Bernstein's approach to *Francesca da Rimini* certainly conveys the passion of the story and the outer sections are powerful and exciting. But the Israel Philharmonic's wind players provide a disappointing response in the idyllic central episode, while Bernstein's pacing is more idiosyncratic here. *Romeo and Juliet* is not really memorable, although its romanticism is involving and the climax is strong. Similarly, the closing pages of *Francesca* make a spectacular impression, with a thrilling accelerando in the coda. Here the wide-ranging sound, with bass drum and tam tam adding to the impact, is well accommodated on the LP, but the chrome tape has problems with the high level, and the quality disintegrates.

Chailly's coupling is superbly recorded in Decca's best manner, the sound wonderfully vivid and spacious, with the spectacle of the Tchaikovskian climaxes even more telling on CD. But Chailly, who secures excellent playing from the Cleveland Orchestra, especially in the middle section of *Francesca da Rimini*, displays no interpretative flair in this repertoire. *Romeo and Juliet* is not without life and ardour, yet the performance lacks individuality, while the outer climaxes of *Francesca* are underpowered, and the overall effect gives the impression as much of the ballet as of a symphonic poem.

Manfred symphony, Op. 58.
*** HMV Dig. **CDC 747412-2** [id.]; ASD/*TCC-ASD* 4169 [Ang. DS/*4XS* 37752]. Philh. O, Muti.

Muti's recording of Tchaikovsky's *Manfred*, released in 1982, was one of EMI's spectacular early digital LPs (though the tape did not quite match the excellence of the disc). Recorded in Kingsway Hall, it remains one of this company's most impressive digital issues. At the close of the first movement, Tchaikovsky's memorable climactic statement of the principal Manfred theme heard on the massed strings (*sul G*) brings a tremendous physical excitement, and when it is similarly reprised in the finale, capped with cymbals, the effect is electrifying. The weight of the sound emphasizes the epic style of Muti's reading, forceful and boldly dramatic throughout. Muti's scherzo has a quality of exhilarating bravura, rather than concentrating on delicacy; the lovely central melody is given a sense of joyous vigour. The *Andante*, after a refined opening, soon develops a passionate forward sweep; in the finale the amplitude and brilliant detail of the recording, combined with magnificent playing from the Philharmonia Orchestra, brings a massively compulsive projection of Tchaikovsky's bacchanale and a richly satisfying dénouement. The CD is scheduled for release soon after publication of this book.

Meditation (for violin and orchestra, arr. Glazounov), *Op. 42/1.*
*** HMV **CDC 747087** [id.]; EL 270108–1/*4* [Ang. DS/*4DS* 38055]. Perlman, Israel PO, Mehta – KHACHATURIAN: *Violin concerto.****

A charming Tchaikovskian trifle, arranged for violin and orchestra by Glazounov, makes an agreeable balm to the ear, following on, as it does, after the brilliant finale of the Khachaturian *Concerto.*

The Nutcracker (ballet), *Op. 71* (complete).
*** HMV **CDS 747267-8** (2). Amb. S., LSO, Previn.
(B) ** CBS DC 40188 (2) [M2-35189]. Nat. PO, Schermerhorn.

HMV have scheduled the complete Previn *Nutcracker* for release as we go to press. It was recorded in 1972 and has been chosen in preference to the Lanchbery digital set of a decade later. The performance is affectionate and polished, the Transformation scene is richly done, and the famous dances of Act II show the LSO consistently on their toes. The originally warm and sumptuous sound should lend itself readily to the freshening that usually accompanies digital remastering for CD.

Kenneth Schermerhorn's complete *Nutcracker* dates from 1978. The sleeve does not indicate the source of the National Philharmonic. It seems to have only a modest-sized string section but, within the attractive recording ambience, the effect is intimate, with the performance itself amiable rather than dramatic. However, the absence of histrionics is not necessarily a drawback, for the playing is polished and sympathetic, the reading has momentum and the characteristic dances have plenty of colour. The recording was made in conjunction with an American Ballet Theatre production. This is the least expensive *Nutcracker* available, with two discs, in a folder, offered for the price of one. With good sound, it is quite a bargain, though the Previn HMV set is worth the extra cost.

The Nutcracker: suite, Op. 71a; Suite No. 2.
*** Ph. 412 938–1/*4*. Concg. O (with chorus), Dorati.

Dorati offers a second suite to supplement Tchaikovsky's own selection. This is taken from his splendid Philips complete set (at present out of the catalogue); with refined playing and Dorati's warm attention to detail, this makes a clear first choice for a single-LP compilation. It was recorded in the ample acoustic of the Concertgebouw, and the resonance has brought a low-level tape transfer, which reduces the sparkle of the cassette sound. But the remastered LP sounds fresh and most vivid.

Nutcracker suite, Op. 71a.
ℂ *** Ph. Dig. **412 559–2 [412 556–2]**; 412 559–1/*4*. Boston Pops O, John Williams – *Peter and the wolf.**** ℂ

A vividly crisp performance of Tchaikovsky's marvellous score from John Williams and the Boston Pops. Tempi are brisk and the style is rather metrical, but the playing has plenty of rhythmic lift and only in the closing *Waltz of the flowers* is there a slight lack of lyrical freedom, but not of flair. The characteristic dances are strong on character: the piccolo in the *Chinese dance* provides superb bravura, and the freely sinuous wind solos in the *Arab dance* are equally engaging. The *Russian dance* is exhilarating, and the Sugar plum fairy is gently seductive. With vivid three-dimensional recording within the glowing Boston acoustic, this makes a first-rate coupling for a splendid version of *Peter and the wolf.*

Nutcracker suite; Romeo and Juliet.
(*) DG Dig. **410 873–2; 410 873-1/*4*. BPO, Karajan.
(*) Telarc Dig. **CD 80068; DG 10068. Cleveland O, Maazel.

Originally designed to accompany a picture biography of Karajan, this surprisingly rare Tchaikovsky coupling brings superbly played performances. The suite is delicate and detailed, yet perhaps lacks a little in charm, notably the *Arab dance* which, taken fairly briskly, loses something of its gentle sentience. The overture is both polished and dramatic, but Karajan draws out the climax of the love theme with spacious moulding, and there is marginally less spontaneity here than in his earlier recordings. The sound, characteristic of Berlin, is truthfully balanced; but alongside greater clarity, the CD brings a certain dryness of timbre in *Romeo and Juliet*, while adding a degree of hardness on the high violins in the *Nutcracker*, although the wind and brass solos have good definition and presence.

With vivid orchestral playing and bright, crisply focused recording within a natural ambience, Maazel's *Nutcracker suite* is enjoyably colourful. His manner is affectionate (especially in the warmly lilting *Waltz of the flowers*), and the only idiosyncrasy is the sudden accelerando at the close of the Russian dance. *Romeo and Juliet* is given a spaciously romantic performance, reaching a climax of considerable passion. However, the almost overwhelming impact of the percussion in the (undoubtedly exciting) feud music is obviously designed for those who like to say 'Listen to that bass drum!' Others may feel that the balance is not exactly what one would experience in the concert hall.

Nutcracker suite; Serenade for strings.
** Ph. Dig. **411 471–2**; 6514/*7337* 265 [id.]. ASMF, Marriner.

A good if not especially individual account of the *Nutcracker suite* is here coupled with a new version of the *Serenade* which is no match for Sir Neville Marriner's Decca account, recorded when the Academy was at an early peak (Jubilee JB/*KJBC* 131). By the side of this, the new performance, though well played, seems a routine affair. The recording is vivid and full-bodied, with detail slightly more refined on the CD, though the difference is not very striking.

(i) *Nutcracker suite;* (ii) *Sleeping Beauty: suite;* (iii) *Swan Lake: excerpts.*
(B) ** Ph. On Tour *416 228–4* [id.]. (i) LSO, Fistoulari; (ii) VSO, Ančerl; (iii) LSO, Monteux.

Nutcracker suite; Swan Lake: excerpts.
(*) Pro Arte Dig. **CDD 121; PAD/*PCD* 121 [id.]. Minnesota SO, Slatkin.

Nutcracker suite; Swan Lake: suite.
** Decca Dig. **410 551–2** [id.]; SXDL/*KSXDC* 7505 [Lon. LDR/*5*– 10008]. Israel PO, Mehta.

This 'On Tour' triptych is certainly good value. The highlight is Fistoulari's *Nutcracker suite*, recorded in 1963, with the characteristic dances piquantly colourful and the *Waltz of the flowers* elegantly vivacious. The *Sleeping Beauty suite* is less distinctive, but has plenty of life, while Monteux's extended selection from *Swan Lake* (from 1962) has also stood the test of time, with an excellent response from the LSO.

Splendid playing from the wind soloists in the excellent Minnesota orchestra and attractively vivid recording, with a very wide dynamic range, the orchestra attractively set out in a concert-hall acoustic. The usual *Swan Lake suite* is augmented to include eight items and, in the closing *Wedding dance*, Slatkin's hitherto spirited direction becomes positively boisterous. There is much attractive detail in both *Suites*, although in the Swan Queen's famous orchestral duet the principal violin (Lea Foli) displays more poetic flair than the cellist (Robert Jamieson). The cornet soloist in the *Neapolitan dance* perhaps slightly overdoes the rubato, while Slatkin's rhythms in the *Waltz of the flowers* are a shade metrical; but otherwise this is a most enjoyable coupling and the playing is generally more spontaneous and imaginative than Mehta's Decca selection.

Mehta's compact disc is markedly superior to the LP recording of the same performances. The sound is fuller and much more refined and, in the *Nutcracker*, textures have more delicacy. The Mann Auditorium in Tel Aviv, where this recording was made, does not usually provide a flattering ambience, but on the CD it is caught most successfully. Climaxes swell up thrillingly and the brass is especially vivid. On LP, the cellos sound rather buzzy at times and there is a curious bass-drum sound in *Swan Lake*. Even with the help of CD brilliance, however, the performances are not distinctive enough to command a strong recommendation: there are better versions of both *Suites*.

Serenade for strings in C, Op. 48.
€ *** DG Dig. **400 038-2**; 2532/*3302* 012 [id.]. BPO, Karajan – DVOŘÁK: *Serenade.****
(B) *** CfP CFP 41 4482-1/*4*. Sinf. of L., Faris (with BACH: Air from *Suite No. 3, BWV 1068*; BOCCHERINI: *Minuet* from *Quintet, Op. 13/5*; HANDEL: *Berenice: Minuet***).

A vigorously extrovert reading from Karajan, with taut, alert and superbly polished playing in the first movement, an elegant *Waltz*, a passionately intense *Elegy* and a bustling, immensely spirited finale. The compact disc is one of the finest yet to come from DG. Although there is just a hint of digital edge on the violins, this is offset by the extension of the middle and lower range which is gloriously full and resonant, far superior to the LP. The refinement of inner detail is remarkable. Tchaikovsky often wrote antiphonally (when he was not using his strings in unison), and so clear is the definition that the effect almost becomes visual as ideas move back and forth within the string groupings. The LP is distinctly second-best, brightly lit on top, with some lack of warmth in the middle range. The chrome tape, however, while retaining the inner clarity, is slightly fuller and softer-grained in the treble.

Faris's recording dates from 1960 but it is extraordinarily fine for its period, rich and well detailed, with disc and tape closely matched. The reading of the first movement has lithe clean lines. It has no special individuality, but throughout the playing is polished and sensitive. In the *Elegy* the commitment of the players is obvious, but the reading is comparatively restrained, while the *Waltz* is neat and the finale rhythmically plain. But the lack of idiosyncrasy is a plus point when the music is allowed to speak for itself. The sparkle and sonority of the sound make this a good bargain alternative when the three popular fill-ups are also very successful in their straightforwardness.

Sleeping Beauty (ballet), *Op. 66:* highlights.
(B) ** Pickwick Con. CC/*CCTC* 7612. SRO, Ansermet.

This lively selection from Ansermet's 1959 complete set comes up amazingly freshly in Pickwick's remastered bargain-priced LP and equivalent chrome tape. The character of the music making triumphs over any inadequacies of the orchestral playing, and the personality of the conductor projects as strongly as ever. The Act II music is especially vivid.

(i) *Sleeping Beauty: suite*; (ii) *Swan Lake, Op. 20*: excerpts.
(B) **(*) DG Walkman *413 430–4* [id.]. (i) BPO, Rostropovich; (ii) Boston SO, Ozawa – PROKOFIEV: *Romeo and Juliet*.***

Sleeping Beauty: suite; Swan Lake: suite.
(*) HMV Dig. **CDC 747075–2 [id.]; EL 270113-1/*4* [Ang. DS/*4DS* 38117]. Phd. O, Muti.
(M) *** EMI EMX 41 2067-1/*4*. Philh. O, Karajan – MUSSORGSKY: *Khovantschina: Dance of Persian slaves*.***

Rostropovich's *Sleeping Beauty suite* is highly distinguished, as fine as any in the catalogue. The recording is wonderfully expansive and the performances admirably combine Slavonic intensity with colour. The whimsical portrait of the cats contrasts with the glorious *Panorama* melody, floated over its gently rocking bass with magical delicacy. The collection of *Swan Lake* excerpts from Ozawa is generous. Here the sophistication of playing and recording, within the warm Boston acoustic, is impressive; while the individual items have less individuality of approach than with Rostropovich, the orchestral response is first class and the final climax expands magnificently. Combined with an excellent selection from Prokofiev's *Romeo and Juliet*, this Walkman tape is splendid value.

From HMV, one of the first recordings made by the Philadelphia Orchestra in the Fairmount Park Memorial Hall, which at last provides a flattering ambience for this great orchestra. The layout has a convincing concert-hall perspective so that the placing of the solo string players in the beautifully phrased *Swan Queen's dance* is naturally distanced. The only snag (if it is that) is the very wide dynamic range, which means that when one achieves a satisfactory level for the violin/cello duet the spectacular climaxes are almost overwhelming. The order of items in *Swan Lake* is unconventional, ending with the Act III *Mazurka* instead of the (perhaps more suitable) grandiloquent finale. Muti's approach is essentially spacious and he concentrates on the elegance of the music, achieving an excellent response from his orchestra. There is not the Slavonic intensity of Rostropovich here, nor quite the electricity of Karajan in the *Rose Adagio*, yet the recording makes a thrilling effect at fortissimo level, and its amplitude is considerable. The CD is transferred at the highest level; this increases the presence of the orchestra even further and emphasizes the resonance of the loudest moments, with the textures glowingly rich. There is also an outstanding XDR cassette, one of EMI's best, strikingly clean in detail.

Karajan has recorded this coupling three times in stereo, and this, the first (1959), derives from Walter Legge's Columbia label, with the Philharmonia Orchestra in peak form. The recording was admirably balanced and still sounds splendid. The sound has a rich ambient bloom and the very slight lack of upper range is more noticeable in *Swan Lake* than in *Sleeping Beauty*. The orchestral playing in such items as the violin/cello duet and the dapper *Dance of the little swans* in *Swan Lake*, or the lustrous *Rose Adagio* and seductive *Panorama* of *Sleeping Beauty*, makes this issue especially desirable.

Swan Lake (ballet), *Op. 20* (complete).
(*) DG **415 367-2 (2) [id.]. Boston SO, Ozawa.

This is the first major Tchaikovsky ballet to be issued complete on CD. Ozawa omits the Act III *Pas de deux* but otherwise plays the original score as Tchaikovsky conceived it. It is now generously fitted on to a pair of CDs, against the three LPs of the original issue. The performance was by no means a first choice in its LP format: Lanchbery (HMV), Bonynge (Decca) and Previn (HMV) all have rather more character. But the playing of the Boston orchestra is strikingly polished and sympathetic, and there are many impressive things here, with wind (and violin) solos that always give pleasure. The 1979 analogue recording is spectacular and wide-ranging, and it has been enhanced in this transfer to CD, but the end result is just a little faceless, without quite the verve of Lanchbery and Bonynge (on Decca) , or the seductive sumptuousness of Previn (on HMV).

Swan Lake (ballet), *Op. 20*: highlights.
(M) *** HMV EG 290305-1/*4* [Ang. AM/*4AM* 34722]. LSO, Previn.
** Denon Dig. **C37 7479** [id.]. VSO, Soltesz.

Previn's selection is both generous and felicitous. It is superbly played and shows the very best qualities of his complete set (SLS 5070 [Ang. SCLX/*4X3S* 3834]), with splendid solo wind playing and a rich-toned contribution from the violinist, Ida Haendel. The recording has been digitally remastered; the quality is full, slightly drier than the original, but still impressive. At mid-price, this is highly recommendable on both LP and cassette.

The Hungarian-born Stefan Soltesz is Viennese by upbringing and is a former soloist in the Vienna Boys' Choir. As conductor of the Vienna National Opera Ballet, he is obviously familiar with this repertoire; he secures meticulously rehearsed playing from the VSO, which has no lack of life. The orchestral solo contributions are sensitive, if not displaying the personality of the LSO under Previn, and at times the music making is just a little lacking in flair. The recording is wide-ranging and its ambience pleasing. The selection is fairly generous, but CD collectors will find that Muti's coupling of the suite with music from the *Sleeping Beauty* (see above) is more rewarding than this.

Symphonies Nos 1 (*Winter daydreams*)*; 2* (*Little Russian*)*; 3 in D* (*Polish*)*, Op. 29.*
(B) *** DG 415 024-1/*4* (2) [id.]. BPO, Karajan.

Having recorded the last three Tchaikovsky symphonies three times over in little more than ten years, Karajan finally turned to the earlier symphonies (before returning for the fourth time to the later works, with video in mind, this time using the VPO – see below). In the first three of the Tchaikovsky canon, displaying the same superlative refined qualities he produced performances with the great Berlin orchestra which proved equally illuminating. The orchestral playing is marvellous and it is typical that, though the opening *Allegro tranquillo* of the first movement of No. 1 is taken fast, there is no feeling of breathlessness, as there usually is: it is genuinely *tranquillo*, though the rhythmic bite of the syncopated passages, so important in these early symphonies, could hardly be sharper. The high polish may give a hint of the ballroom to some of the dance movements, with the folk element underplayed, but no finer versions have ever been recorded. In the *Little Russian*, everything is in perfect scale; the tempo for the engaging *Andante* is very nicely judged and the outer movements have plenty of drama and fire, with the articulation in the finale a joy. In the *Polish*, Karajan's first movement is full of flair while in the central movements he is ever conscious of the variety of Tchaikovsky's colouring. He even finds an affinity with Brahms in the second movement, and yet the *Andante* is full of Tchaikovskian fervour. In the finale, the articulation of the *Polacca* – like the fugato in No. 1 – brings a sense of symphonic strength often lacking in other versions, besides being both vigorous and joyful. The recording quality throughout is clear and naturally balanced, if a little lacking in ambient bloom. Nevertheless, when issued at what amounts to bargain price, with the three symphonies on two mid-priced LPs, this set should not be ignored by any true Tchaikovskian, however wedded to the new CD format. The matching chrome cassettes are issued in DG's flap-pack style.

Symphony No. 1 in G min. (*Winter daydreams*), *Op. 13.*
❀ *** Chan. Dig. **CHAN 8402**; ABRD/*ABTD* 1139 [id.]. Oslo PO, Jansons.

Refreshingly direct in style and for the most part avoiding the romantically expressive moulding common in Tchaikovsky interpretations, Jansons with his brilliant orchestra gives an electrically compelling performance of this earliest of the symphonies. The focus is sharp, both of the playing and of the recording, which is both brilliant and atmospheric. Structurally strong, the result tingles with excitement, most of all in the finale, faster than usual, with the challenge of the complex fugato passages superbly taken. Jansons' directness is conveyed with such involvement that there is no question of the performance sounding cold, least of all in the lyrical outpouring of the slow movement. The recording is highly successful in all three media. Our Rosette is a token not only of this performance but also of the others in Jansons' outstandingly successful Chandos cycle of the Tchaikovsky *Symphonies*, a remarkable combined achievement for conductor, orchestral players and recording engineers alike.

Symphony No. 2 in C min. (*Little Russian*), *Op. 17* (original 1872 score).
*** Chan. Dig. **CHAN 8304**; ABRD/*ABTD* 1071 [id.]. LSO, Simon.

This is the first recording of Tchaikovsky's original score of the *Little Russian symphony* and probably the first performance outside Russia. It was prompted (like the earlier Chandos set of rare Tchaikovsky – see above) by the enterprising enthusiasm of Edward Johnson, who provides an admirably exhaustive sleeve-note (included with the cassette too). Although the 1872 score gained considerable success at its early performances, it gave the composer immediate and serious doubts, principally about the construction of the first movement and the length of the finale. Fortunately the work had only been published in piano-duet form, and so in 1879 Tchaikovsky retrieved the score and immediately set to work to rewrite the first movement. He left the *Andante* virtually unaltered, touched up the scoring of the scherzo, made minor excisions and added repeats, and made a huge cut of 150 bars (some two minutes of music) in the finale. He then destroyed the original. (The present performance has been possible because of the surviving orchestral parts.) There can be no question that Tchaikovsky was right. The reworked first movement is immensely superior to the first attempt and the finale – delightful though it is – seems quite long enough shorn of the extra bars. However, to hear the composer's first thoughts (as with the original version of *Romeo and Juliet*) is fascinating, and this is an indispensable recording for all Tchaikovskians.

The original first movement begins and ends much like the familiar version with its andante horn theme based on the folksong, *Down by Mother Volga*, but the first subject of the exposition offers unfamiliar lyrical material. The working out is more self-consciously 'symphonic', and clearly there is more rhetoric than development. There are some exciting moments of course, but in the end one remains unconvinced. Geoffrey Simon secures a committed response from the LSO, there is some splendid string playing in the finale, and the brass is bitingly sonorous as recorded. Indeed, the sound is first class and the chrome tape is very impressive, too, in its range and impact. The compact disc is striking in its inner orchestral detail and freshness, and although the lower range is without the resonant richness of some CDs, the balance remains very good and the bass drum is telling without swamping the fortissimos.

Symphony No. 2 in C min. (*Little Russian*), *Op. 17; The Tempest, Op. 18.*
(*) CBS Dig. **MK 39359; IM/*IMT* 39359 [id.]. Chicago SO, Abbado.

Abbado's version is the first in a projected new Tchaikovsky series from CBS, and its first substantial advantage over direct rivals is the generosity of its fill-up, Tchaikovsky's large-scale *Fantasy* on Shakespeare's *The Tempest* – not to be confused with the much less ambitious piece, based on Ostrovsky's *The Storm.* In that work, Abbado's performance, dramatic and passionate as well as evocative in the opening seascape, is likely to be unrivalled on record: in the *Symphony*, too, he is most persuasive, with virtuoso playing from the Chicago orchestra. With speeds generally faster than usual, he conveys lightness and sparkle, so that the *Andantino marziale* of the second movement becomes a sharply pointed miniature march and in the scherzo the cross-rhythms are incisively sprung. Only in the finale does he adopt a restrained basic speed; effectively so, except that he slows perceptibly in the jaunty syncopated counter-subject. On LP, the recording is warm with the sound a little distanced, natural and undistracting but not ideally clear on detail. The CD, disappointingly, brings no improvement, with the lower range not too well focused and the bass drum balanced too prominently at times, especially in the finale of the *Symphony*. There are no dividing bands for individual movements. The chrome tape is middle- and bass-heavy and poorly defined.

Symphony No. 3 in D (*Polish*), *Op. 29.*
*** Chan. Dig. **CHAN 8463**; ABRD/*ABTD* 1179 [id.]. Oslo PO, Jansons.

Jansons' performance of Tchaikovsky's least tractable symphony glows with freshness and vitality; it certainly deserves its share of the token Rosette given to the companion performance of the *Winter daydreams symphony*. Like that account, the *Third* is given a clear, refreshingly direct reading, totally unsentimental, yet conveying the warmth as well as the exuberance of Tchaikovsky's inspiration. The likeness with *Swan Lake* in the first movement is delectably pointed, but it is the irresistible sweep of urgency with which Jansons builds the development section that puts his performance apart, with the basic tempo varied less than usual. The second movement is beautifully relaxed, light and lilting in *Alla tedesca*. The *Andante elegiaco* brings a heartwarming performance, expressive, tender and refined. The fourth-movement scherzo has a Mendelssohnian elfin quality, but it is the swaggering reading of the finale, always in danger of sounding bombastic, which sets the seal on the whole performance. Even the anthem-like second subject has a lightness of touch, avoiding any sense of squareness or coarseness. Though the recording does not convey a genuinely hushed pianissimo for the strings, it brings full, rich and brilliant sound, like the others in the series. The CD adds a touch of extra precision in the overall focus, but the LP and cassette sound very impressive too, the latter strikingly warm and full, yet not lacking range and transparency, and with particularly convincing violin tone.

Symphonies Nos 4–6 (*Pathétique*).
(B) **(*) DG 413 541-1/*4* (2) [id.]. Leningrad PO, Mravinsky.
(B) ** HMV EM 290282-3/*9* (2). Philh. O, Klemperer.
(B) ** CBS DC 40161 (2). Cleveland O, Maazel.

The classic Mravinsky performances come from 1961 and have now been transferred on to four LP sides, or to a pair of tapes which sound virtually identical. The performances are striking for their fervour and Slavonic intensity; these extremely volatile readings will appeal to some more than to others. They are superbly played and always convincingly spontaneous. The snags include a wobbly horn solo in the *Fifth* and a breakneck pace for the finale of the *Fourth* which, though exhilarating, sounds positively inebriated. The recording, too, though full and vivid, suffers from slight underlying harmonic distortion. This is nothing to do with the compression on to four sides but stems from the master tapes. At what amounts to bargain price, however, many will feel able to accept these reservations when the performances are so involving.

Klemperer recorded the three major Tchaikovsky symphonies in 1962/3; throughout, he secured polished, responsive playing from the Philharmonia Orchestra. The digitally remastered recordings have lost none of their warmth and bloom, and the slight lack of range at the top is far preferable to thin strings. The performances are more controversial. In the *Fourth*, Klemperer's first movement is weighty yet relaxed. The basic dotted rhythm here sometimes recalls Beethoven's *Seventh* (an unexpected association), but the coasting along does not really catch the almost barbaric Russian spirit that other conductors find in this movement. There are no complaints elsewhere, and the scherzo is particularly attractive. The *Fifth* is surprisingly successful in a way that one would not perhaps expect: there is an expanding emotional warmth in the treatment of the opening movement, with the second subject blossoming in a ripely romantic way. The slow movement, too, if not completely uninhibited, is played richly, with a fine horn solo from Alan Civil. The *Waltz* is marginally disappointing, but the finale has splendid dignity. The *Sixth* is the least satisfactory. The opening goes well; it has poise and dignity, and the beginning of the allegro sounds spontaneous. Later, the climaxes are restrained without losing their underlying intensity, and the coda is convincingly moulded. But the *Allegro con grazia* has a heavy melancholy, without grace; and in the third movement all suggestions of a scherzo evaporate and the coda is given a weightily Teutonic climax. The finale has considerable eloquence.

Maazel, who had already recorded the *Fourth* with outstanding success for Decca and went on to record it again, digitally, for Telarc – see below – made this set for CBS between 1982 and 1984. The *Fourth* remains the most successful of the three, the interpretation very like that on Telarc with its direct thrust and concern for detail. The recording here, however, though fully acceptable, has less amplitude than the earlier Decca version and is certainly far less impressive than the spectacular Telarc sound. The *Fifth* is rather lightweight, with a slow movement that lacks the degree of momentum that distinguishes the *Fourth*. The *Pathétique* is altogether more successful, with a volatile first movement, moving to an impressive climax, a swiftly paced but effective *Allegro con grazia*, a brilliant scherzo/march and a convincing finale. The sound throughout is obviously modern, but acceptable rather than in any way notable; however, with the three symphonies offered for the price of a single premium-priced LP, this is the least expensive way of acquiring a reasonably satisfactory set of the last three Tchaikovsky symphonies. The orchestral playing is excellent throughout. The equivalent double-length tape (at the same price) cannot be considered as it omits the *Pathétique symphony*.

Symphony No. 4 in F min., Op. 36.
*** Chan. Dig. **CHAN 8361**; ABRD/*ABTD* 1124 [id.]. Oslo PO, Jansons.
(*) DG Dig. **415 348-2; 415 348-1/*4* [id.]. VPO, Karajan.
(*) Telarc Dig. **CD 80047; DG 10047 [id.]. Cleveland O, Maazel.
** Ph. Dig. **400 090-2** [id.]. Pittsburgh SO, Previn.
** Decca Dig. **414 192-2**; 414 192-1/*4* [id.]. Chicago SO, Solti.

In his outstanding Tchaikovsky series with the Oslo Philharmonic, Jansons conducts a dazzling performance of the *Fourth*, unusually fresh and natural in its expressiveness, yet with countless subtleties of expression, as in the balletic account of the second-subject group of the first movement. So idiomatic-sounding is Jansons' handling that the transitions between sections are totally unobtrusive, with steady rather than fluctuating speeds. The *Andantino* flows lightly and persuasively, the scherzo is very fast and lightly sprung, while the finale reinforces the impact of the whole performance: fast and exciting, but with no synthetic whipping-up of tempo. That is so until the very end of the coda, which finds Jansons pressing ahead just fractionally as he would in a concert, a thrilling conclusion made the more so by the wide-ranging, brilliant and realistic recording in which the reverberant background brings warmth of atmosphere and little or no obscuring of detail. The CD adds impressively to the orchestra's sense of presence within the characterful ambience of the Oslo Philharmonic Hall, although the lower end of the sound spectrum is less expansive than Maazel's Telarc Cleveland recording. The chrome cassette is highly successful; tape collectors can be assured that its loss of range and clarity of detail, compared with the LP and CD, is marginal.

The *Fourth* is the most successful of the last three Tchaikovsky symphony recordings which Karajan made in 1985 in connection with the Telemodial video project. Although the playing of the Vienna orchestra does not match that of the Berlin Philharmonic in earlier versions, the performance itself has greater flexibility and more spontaneity. The freer control of tempo in the first movement brings a more relaxed second-subject group, while in the *Andantino* the Vienna oboist is fresher (though the timbre is edgier) than his Berlin counterpart, the phrasing less calculated. The scherzo is attractively bright, if less precise, and the finale has splendid urgency and excitement. With the extra depth in the bass that CD can provide, the sound is fuller than before, and the warmly resonant acoustic is attractive, even if detail remains a little clouded. But the Chandos version has even greater electricity and the Oslo recording is richer still, and clearer.

Maazel's Telarc Cleveland disc was one of the first digital recordings of any Tchaikovsky symphony; in its initial LP format it established a reputation for sound of spectacular depth and brilliance within natural concert-hall acoustics. The CD is even more impressive in its amplitude and range. It was made, not in the Severance Hall – scene of other Telarc early successes – but in the Masonic Auditorium. Maazel's reading is very similar to his 1965 Decca record (last available as JB 23, but currently withdrawn), and only in the finale does the new version differ markedly from the old, by seeking amplitude and breadth in preference to uninhibited extrovert excitement. Maazel's is a less subtle approach than Jansons', but it generates a strong forward momentum in the first movement and is consistently involving in its directness. Yet he lightens the tension effectively (like Jansons) by his balletic approach to the second-subject group. The slow movement, with a plaintive oboe solo, is distinctly appealing, and at the *Più mosso* Maazel makes a swift, bold tempo change, whereas here Jansons makes the transition more flexibly. On the whole, Jansons' is the more imaginative reading, and his finale generates more adrenalin, but the Cleveland Orchestra produces not only a richer body of timbre in the upper strings but has a fuller, more resonant response from the lower strings and brass. This is immediately apparent at the first big fortissimo chord at the end of the – comparatively mellow – opening fanfare of the first movement.

Previn's view is distinctive. His preference in Tchaikovsky is for directness and no mannerism: with unusually slow speeds for the first three movements, this produces little excitement and some lack of charm, however. The finale makes up for that with a very fast tempo, which is a formidable challenge for the Pittsburgh orchestra, here distinguishing itself with fine playing, well recorded. The CD is a major improvement on the original LP issue, the sound brighter and fresher, with no unnatural edge on the violins; but other versions are more involving.

Solti's basic speed for the first movement is surprisingly slow, yet it remains a clear-headed, straightforward reading rather than an affectionate one. The *Andantino* is then slow to the point of sounding sluggish, while in the third and fourth movements, taken very fast, he finally goes for brilliance at all costs. In brilliant sound, lacking a little in depth and perspective, emphasized on CD, it is not a version to warm to. There is an extremely faithful chrome cassette.

Symphony No. 5 in E min., Op. 64.

*** Chan. Dig. **CHAN 8351**; ABRD/*ABTD* 1111 [id.]. Oslo PO, Jansons.

*** Telarc Dig. **CD 80107**; DG 10107 [id.]. RPO, Previn – RIMSKY-KORSAKOV: *Tsar Saltan*: *March*.***
(B) *** CfP CFP 41 4478-1/*4*. BPO, Kempe.
(*) DG Dig. **415 094-2; 415 094-1/*4* [id.]. VPO, Karajan.
** ASV Dig. DCA/*DCDCA* 550 [id.]. LPO, Bátiz.
** Decca Dig. **410 232-2**; SXDL/*KSXDC* 7533 [Lon. LDR/*5*- 71033]. VPO, Chailly.
** CBS Dig. **CD 36700** [IM/*IMT* 36700]. Cleveland O, Maazel.
** Delos **D/CD 3015** [id.]. Phd. O, Ormandy.
*(*) Denon **C37 7100** [id.]. Berlin SO, Sanderling.
*(*) Target Melodiya **VDC 512** [id.]. Moscow RSO, Fedoseyev.

Symphony No. 5, Op. 64; The Voyevoda, Op. 78.
*** CBS Dig. IM/*IMT* 42094 [id.]. Chicago SO, Abbado.

With speeds fast but never breathless and with a manner fresh and direct but never rigid, Jansons conducts the Oslo Philharmonic in a brilliant and exciting performance which is full and vivid in its sound. This was the first to be recorded in an outstanding Tchaikovsky series, in which Jansons, Leningrad-trained, revealed something of the debt he held to the example of Evgeni Mravinsky, a master among Russian interpreters. Jansons is notably less wilful than Mravinsky tended to be, but is no less intense and electrifying. In the first movement, Jansons' refusal to linger never sounds anything but warmly idiomatic, lacking only a little in charm. The slow movement again brings a steady tempo, with climaxes built strongly and patiently but with enormous power, the final culmination topping everything. In the finale, taken very fast, Jansons tightens the screw of the excitement without ever making it a scramble, following Tchaikovsky's notated slowings rather than allowing extra rallentandos. The sound is excellent, specific and well focused within a warmly reverberant acoustic, with digital recording on CD reinforcing any lightness of bass. A warm recommendation – unless charm or wayward sensuousness are essentials. There is an excellent chrome cassette.

Previn's version brought his first recording with the RPO, the orchestra of which he was already the musical director designate, and the quality of the playing is a tribute to a fast-blossoming relationship. Previn's fine concern for detail is well illustrated by the way that the great horn melody in the slow movement (superbly played by Jeff Bryant with firmly focused tone and immaculate control of phrasing) contains the implication of a quaver rest before each three-quaver group, where normally it sounds like a straight triplet. In the first movement rhythms are light and well sprung, and the third movement is sweet and lyrical yet with no hint of mannerism, for Previn adopts a naturally expressive style within speeds generally kept steady, even in the great climax of the slow movement which then subsides into a coda of breathtaking delicacy. Not that Previn misses any of the drama or excitement; and the finale, taken very fast indeed, crowns an outstandingly satisfying reading. The Telarc recording is full and wide-ranging, not as detailed as some, but very naturally balanced. The Rimsky-Korsakov coupling makes a delightful fill-up, brief but charming.

Abbado's Chicago version is admirably fresh and superbly played. All Tchaikovsky's markings are scrupulously yet imaginatively observed, and the reading is full of contrast. Thus, in the second subject group of the first movement, the firmly articulated crotchet/quaver motive is the more striking in its emphasis, leading, as it does, to the lyrical legato of the *Molto più tranquillo*. Other versions of the slow movement have more extrovert passion, but Abbado shows that the climaxes can be involving without being histrionic. After an elegant Waltz, with the orchestra in sparkling form, the finale has fine energy and momentum. If it does not have quite the gripping excitement of Jansons' version, the moment of the composer's self-doubt, before the *Poco più animato*, is the more effectively characterized. *The Voyevoda* was discarded by Tchaikovsky after an unsuccessful première, and he was probably right to do so. It is a melodramatic piece, lacking strong thematic interest. The plot has something in common with *Francesca da Rimini* – only here it is the betrayed husband who (literally and audibly) gets the bullet at the end, instead of the wife's lover. The CBS recording is made in a convincingly resonant acoustic; if inner detail is not always sharply defined, the balance is very good, with full strings and a supporting weight in the bass; but it is less rich than the Jansons Chandos version.

Kempe's reading from 1961 is highly individual, marvellously played and ideal for those seeking a fresh slant on Tchaikovsky's masterpiece. There is an underlying melancholy which is only dispelled with the final jubilation of the coda of the last movement, matching Tchaikovsky's own doubts which he finally cast aside. Kempe hammers home the last four chords, like a closing reminder from Fate. From the very opening, when the clarinet's velvety chalumeau leads to an elegiac statement of the main theme, Kempe is slightly withdrawn, yet at the reprise the second subject is finally allowed to blossom. The slow movement opens tragically and the climaxes, given fervour by the expansive Berlin strings, have depth without hysteria. The Waltz is elegant, slightly doleful, beautifully played, and the finale too opens sombrely, with the clouds not finally lifting until the closing bars. The whole performance flows naturally, and the recording – on disc and tape alike – has a warm amplitude which is right for the performance.

Karajan's latest version of the *Fifth* brings a characteristically strong and expressive performance; however, neither in the playing of the Vienna Philharmonic nor even in the recorded sound can it quite match his earlier Berlin Philharmonic version for DG. Like Karajan's most recent recordings of the Beethoven symphonies, this was done with video as part of the project; though the long takes have brought extra spontaneity, the recording of the strings in the Musikvereinsaal (a difficult venue for the engineers) is inconsistent, with front-desk players sharply focused but not the whole body of strings behind them, and with woodwind set at a distance. The slack ensemble and control of rhythm in the waltz movement is specially disappointing. All this is emphasized with the extra definition of the CD, although both LP and cassette are impressively clear. Karajan's earlier analogue versions are still available, the earlier from 1967 (on Accolade: 2542/*3342* 108) slightly more self-conscious than the 1976 recording which is more physically exciting but more dryly recorded (DG Galleria 419 066-1/*4*).

Bátiz's performance is enjoyably direct and exciting, and he secures a lively response from the LPO. It is an extrovert reading, and his control of the music's ebb and flow of tension has an attractive ardour. The recording, though made in a resonant hall with the orchestra set back, has, however, a degree of harshness on the massed violins and brass, and the brass response is not ideally expansive.

Chailly's is a relatively lightweight and somewhat idiosyncratic reading which gives the impression of inexperience in this repertoire. There are some attractive things here, notably the exhilarating tempo for the finale, but the reading does not make a very convincing whole. The VPO playing is not always immaculate, and the horn solo in the slow movement is not really distinguished. Yet the lyrical momentum of the performance is certainly enjoyable; the Decca digital recording, which has considerable richness and brilliance, is very attractive, especially in its enhanced CD format. The chrome-tape transfer is first rate in every way.

Though the reading remains direct, Maazel's Cleveland version is less fresh-sounding than his earlier Vienna version for Decca (also rather lightweight, and now deleted). Cleveland virtuosity is impressive but, with a disappointing slow movement and aggressive digital recording, the result is cold. The CD is unimpressive, with poorly focused strings. Chailly's Decca version has far superior sound.

Ormandy in his heyday was an outstanding Tchaikovskian, warmly expressive but always keeping emotion firmly under control. This Delos version, recorded not long before he died, characteristically has plenty of excitement and no hysteria, but the fires were burning lower and the recorded sound takes away the bite that might have been there, with textures unattractively thick. The one benefit of that is that for once the horn solo in the slow movement is not spotlit.

Sanderling in his years with the Leningrad orchestra became a masterly interpreter of Tchaikovsky; but with indifferent playing from the Berlin Symphony Orchestra, leaden rather than exciting, and with variable sound, his Denon version cannot be recommended.

Fedoseyev can be an imaginative and illuminating interpreter of Tchaikovsky, but here the voltage is relatively low. At slowish speeds, with fallible ensemble and with the inevitable drawback of a whining French horn in the big solo of the slow movement, it is not competitive, and the sound brings some congestion in tuttis.

Symphonies Nos 5–6 (*Pathétique*).
(B) *** HMV *TCC2-POR 54284*. Phil. O, Muti.
(B) **(*) DG Walkman *413 429-4*. LSO, VPO, Abbado.

Muti's recordings of these two symphonies are both highly successful, the *Fifth* strong, direct and exciting, the *Pathétique* persuasive in its easy expressiveness (see below). This double-length tape in EMI's 'Portrait of the Artist' series allows each work to be heard uninterrupted. The transfers are both first class, the wide dynamic range admirably caught, with the sound vivid and full throughout.

The Walkman chrome cassette couples Abbado's lightweight but refreshingly individual DG accounts of Tchaikovsky's two most popular symphonies. The performance of the *Fifth* is both sophisticated and sparkling: there is lyrical intensity and the outer movements have plenty of vigour; the finale is genuinely exciting, yet with no sense of rhetoric. There are more powerful accounts available but none more spontaneously volatile. The *Pathétique* is also slightly underpowered but may have many attractions for those who prefer a reading that is not too intense. There is a strong impulse throughout, with the third movement essentially a scherzo, the march-rhythms never becoming weighty and pontifical. The recordings have transferred well to tape, that of the *Fifth* richer than the *Sixth*, which is slightly dry.

Symphony No. 6 in B min. (*Pathétique*), *Op. 74.*
*** Decca **411 615-2**; SXL/*KSXC* 6941 [Lon. CS/*5*- 7170). Philh. O, Ashkenazy.
(M) *** Ph. 412 937-1/*4* [id.]. Concg. O, Haitink.
(M) *** HMV EG 290499-1/*4* [Ang. AM/*4AM* 34739]. Philh. O, Muti.
(*) Lodia Dig. **LO-CD 778 [id.]. Nat. PO, Païta.
(*) DG **415 095-2; 415 095-1/*4* [id.]. VPO, Karajan.
** DG Dig. **400 029-2**; 2532/*3302* 013 [id.]. LAPO, Giulini.
** Target Melodiya **VDC 502** [id.]. Moscow RSO, Fedoseyev.
*(*) Delos **D/CD 3016** [id.]. Phd. O, Ormandy.
* Denon Dig. **C37 7062** [id.]. Berlin SO, Sanderling.
RCA Dig. **RD 85355**; RL/*RK* 85355 [**RCD1 5355**]. Chicago SO, Levine.

After an arresting account of the sombre introduction, the urgency with which Ashkenazy and his Philharmonia players attack the *Allegro* of the first movement of the *Pathétique* belies the composer's *non troppo* marking. The directness and intensity of the music making are supported by remarkably crisp articulation, producing an electrifying forward thrust. The emergence of the beautiful second subject offers the more striking contrast, with Ashkenazy's characteristic lyrical ardour bringing a natural warmth to the great melody. As in his other Tchaikovsky records, this whole performance is pervaded with freshness and spontaneity, through the balletic 5/4 movement, with its essentially Russian quality of melancholy, and the vigorous scherzo/march, rhythmically buoyant and joyful rather than relentlessly high-powered, as under Karajan. The finale combines passion with tenderness, and the total absence of expressive hysteria brings a more poignant culmination than usual. With superb Decca Kingsway Hall sound, this is among the finest *Pathétiques* ever recorded. The Philharmonia is on peak form and, although the Berlin Philharmonic playing under Karajan is even more polished, the Decca version gains by its greater amplitude, warmth and colour. The CD retains the analogue atmosphere while detail is clarified and intensified. The chrome cassette loses a little of the sparkle at the top, but remains excellently balanced.

Whether in terms of interpretation or of execution, it would be hard to distinguish between Haitink's later (1980) reading here and his splendid earlier account. Their confident strength and natural expressiveness, allied to a degree of restraint, make them both most satisfying for repeated listening on the gramophone. Where the second version gains is in the fullness and warmth of the recording. On cassette, the sound-balance is comparably full and wide-ranging.

Muti adopts characteristically fast tempi, yet the result is fresh and youthful, not over-hectic. The lyrical second subject, flowing faster than usual, has easy expressiveness without a hint of mannerism, and the 5/4 movement, also taken at a speed faster than usual, is most persuasive. The march, for all its urgency, never sounds brutal; though the recording does not quite match the fine fullness which marks the others in Muti's series, it hardly detracts from a most refreshing reading. The cassette is also successful; however, on tape for about the same price one can have Muti's coupling of both the *Fifth* and *Sixth Symphonies* in EMI's 'Portrait of the Artist' series – see above.

The Païta account has considerable spontaneity, though the reading is individual. The recording balance, with the orchestra set back in the familiar ambience of the Kingsway Hall, is appealing, especially as detail is vivid, without spotlighting. Païta makes a degree of expressive emphasis at the very opening, but the *Allegro* is fresh and lightly articulated, and there is an elegiac feel to the first appearance of the second subject. The development brings sharper articulation from the strings, but at the climax a degree of fierceness in the brass adds an aggressive touch; while the string playing has real fervour, the actual body of timbre suggests a smaller number of players than usual. The coda, with dignified brass, is eloquent yet restrained. The central movements go especially well; the 5/4 *Allegro con grazia* has more lift and grace than with Karajan's VPO account; and the buoyantly spirited scherzo/march has a fine climax, with the timpani dramatically underlining the final peroration. The finale is flexibly passionate, and the close is sombre, returning to the elegiac mood of the beginning of the first movement.

Recorded, like the VPO *Fourth* and *Fifth*, with video as part of the project, Karajan's latest version of the *Pathétique* has many characteristically strong points; however, although the reading is not without intensity or spontaneity, it lacks the grip of the earlier Berlin Philharmonic recordings and, with the Vienna ensemble noticeably slacker than that of the Berliners, it is a flawed experience. The 5/4 movement is slower than before and rather heavy in style; though the speed of the march movement remains as fast as previously, the result is less tense, breathless rather than exuberant in virtuosity. The sound is curiously inconsistent, with violins edgy in tuttis, while the heavy brass jangles aggressively. There are distracting knocks and rustles in the *pppppp* passage at the end of the exposition just before the fortissimo start to the development. On tape, the resonance brings clouding at the climax of the third movement. Of the two earlier recordings for DG, the more recent (1977) has the most brilliant – though not the most sonorous – recording; nevertheless the effect of the performance on the listener is tremendously powerful and strong, with the Berlin Philharmonic, who share Karajan's special affinity with this work, producing the most precise articulation, yet matching the conductor's passionate involvement (2530/*3300* 774). For some ears, the 1964 recording is even finer, more consistent and less impetuous in its overall control of tension. The fervour of the first-movement climax here sends a shiver down the spine, and the playing of the orchestra in the scherzo/march is demonic in its aggressive force, with the close of the finale, for all its sense of despair, finding a release from previous tensions. The sound has rather more bloom than on the later version, especially on cassette (2542/*3342* 154).

Giulini's digital *Pathétique* is curiously lightweight, the mood set with the almost *scherzando* quality of the opening *Allegro*. The 5/4 movement is relatively unlilting, and though the march is impressive, it is no match for the Ashkenazy version. The finale does not lack eloquence, but Giulini's Philharmonia version of two decades earlier had more individuality than this. The digital recording is impressive, if slightly dry. The compact disc tends to emphasize rather than disguise the recording's faults, especially the close balance. LP and cassette are closely matched.

Fedoseyev is at his most distinctive in the outer movements, light and elegant in the first movement's main subject, with the big *Andante* melody similarly restrained, sweetly reflective rather than passionate. In the slow finale he takes a hushed and intimate view, making it an inner lament not an open tragedy. Against this, Fedoseyev builds powerful contrasting climaxes, with the first-movement development taken fast and furiously but with fine control. His remains a distinctive view but, with sound that grows congested in fortissimos, it is not a general recommendation.

Ormandy made several fine recordings of the *Pathétique* before this final account for Delos which found the veteran conductor lacking some of his earlier fire. The reading remains warmly romantic, strong and unexaggerated, with steady, generally rather measured speeds. Only in the yearning lyricism of the slow finale is there the full flavour of Ormandy in his prime. The recording is dull, strangely damped down and restricted on top.

Like the companion disc of No. 5, Sanderling's version is disappointing, intensely so when one remembers what fine performances of Tchaikovsky he directed with the Leningrad Philharmonic. The playing of the Berlin Symphony is uninspired and the recording poor. Indeed, it is difficult to believe this is digital sound.

Levine's reading is dramatic and direct, but his version is totally ruled out by the indifferent quality of the recording, strident on the brass, scratchy on high violin timbre.

Variations on a rococo theme for cello and orchestra, Op. 33.

*** DG **413 819-2;** 139 044/*923 098* [id.]. Rostropovich, BPO, Karajan – DVOŘÁK: Concerto.***

No grumbles about Rostropovich's performance. He plays as if this were one of the greatest works for the cello, and he receives glowing support from Karajan and the Berlin Philharmonic. The *Rococo variations* is a delightful work, and it has never sounded finer than it does here. Rostropovich uses the published score, not Tchaikovsky's quite different original version as played by Wallfisch on Chandos, who also has the advantage of modern digital sound, whereas the DG version is analogue from as early as 1969. But it is rich and refined and sounds fresh in its digitally remastered form (if much less transparent than its competitor). Those seeking the Dvořák coupling should be well satisfied.

CHAMBER AND INSTRUMENTAL MUSIC

Album for the young, Op. 39: (i) original piano version; (ii) trans. for string quartet by Dubinsky.
*** Chan. **CHAN 8365**; ABRD/*ABTD* 1129 [id.]. (i) Luba Edlina; (ii) augmented Borodin Trio.

These twenty-four pieces are all miniatures, with many playing for approximately a minute only, but they have great charm; their invention is often memorable, with quotations from Russian folksongs and one French, plus a brief reminder of *Swan Lake*. Here they are presented twice, both in their original piano versions, sympathetically played by Luba Edlina, and in effective string quartet transcriptions arranged by her husband, Rostislav Dubinsky. Some of the arrangements are more telling on the piano, but others transcribe so well that one could imagine that was how their composer conceived them. The Borodin group play them with both affection and finesse. The CD has plenty of presence; this collection is rather attractive, however, in its excellent cassette format, for late evening listening or as a background in the car.

Piano trio in A min., Op. 50.
(M) *(**) HMV EG 270228-1/*4* [Ang. S/*4XS* 38196]. Barenboim, Zukerman, Du Pré.
(M) ** Ph. 412 062-1/*4*. Beaux Arts Trio.
** Chan. Dig. **CHAN 8348**; ABRD/*ABTD* 1049 [id.]. Borodin Trio.

Tchaikovsky's *Piano trio*, with its huge set of variations acting as slow movement and finale combined, is not an easy work to bring off on record. Ideally, it needs the sense of bravura and flair that characterizes the playing of Russian virtuosi. The newest HMV release was a fortieth-birthday tribute to Jacqueline du Pré. It is a recording of a concert given in 1972 at the Mann Auditorium, Tel Aviv, made by the Israel Broadcasting Authority and digitally remastered by the EMI engineers. The playing has great ardour and all the immediacy of a real performance, and that more than compensates for the odd inelegance that might have been corrected in the recording studio or the occasional moment of impetuosity from the pianist in the formidable piano part. There is nothing routine about Daniel Barenboim's playing: he takes plenty of risks and is unfailingly imaginative; it is a pity that the instrument itself is not worthy of him, for it sounds less than fresh. Zukerman also sustains a high level of intensity and at times comes close to schmalz. However, this is without doubt a high-voltage performance. Incidentally, the traditional cut sanctioned by the composer is observed here. Regrettably the recorded sound produced by the Israeli and EMI engineers is by no means as good as the Beaux Arts on Philips: it is dryish and lacks the depth and frequency range of the best studio recordings.

The Beaux Arts recording dates from 1972. It is naturally balanced and the sound is still fresh (with an excellent matching tape). The playing is both polished and eloquent, offering much pleasure in its care for detail, but the effect is rather lightweight. The fugue (Variation 8) is cut from the second movement.

The alternative from Chandos is less appealing. The clear digital recording serves to spotlight the string sounds, which are less polished and less rich than on the finest rival versions. The variations have spontaneity and are not without charm, but the first movement is less convincing. There are two major cuts. This is the only CD so far: its added presence is undeniable but, ideally, one needs a warmer string timbre to balance the large-scale piano writing.

The Seasons, Op. 37a.
(*) Chan. Dig. **CHAN 8349; ABRD/*ABTD* 1070 [id.]. Lydia Artymiw.

The Seasons, Op. 37a; Scherzo à la Russe, Op. 1; Song without words, Op. 2/3; Swan Lake: Pas de quatre (arr. Wild).
*** Dell'Arte DBS 7003. Earl Wild.

The Seasons: January; May; June; November.
*** MMG Dig. **MCD 10031** [id.]. Sviatoslav Richter – RACHMANINOV: *Études-Tableaux.****

Tchaikovsky's twelve *Seasons* (they would better have been called months) were written to a regular deadline for publication in the St Petersburg music magazine, *Nuvellist*. They are lightweight but attractively varied in character and style. Earl Wild has their full measure. He is especially good in the pieces (*August*, for instance) that call for swift light articulation; yet in the expressive writing he is no less appealing, simple in his approach, never sentimental, so that *May* (*Starlit nights*) is no less memorable than the better-known *June*. The encores make an attractive bonus and include Wild's own transcription of the *Dance of the Little Swans* from *Swan Lake*; and the recital ends with a dazzling account of the *Russian Scherzo*.

It is the gentler, lyrical pieces that are most effective in the hands of Lydia Artymiw, and she plays them thoughtfully and poetically. Elsewhere, she sometimes has a tendency marginally to over-characterize the music, which is slight, but she also notices and brings out the orchestral feeling in fuller-sustained textures, and she is rhythmically alert and sparkling. The digital recording is truthful, and on CD the fairly close balance (pedal noises are faintly audible) gives striking presence to the piano which might ideally have been a little further back; but the image is real enough. The chrome tape, too, has excellent body and realism.

Richter chose four very contrasting movements, including the most famous, *June*, a Barcarolle. He plays each of them with great character and enhances their stature. The 1983 Melodiya recording is excellent; the internal focus is not always absolutely sharp, but the piano timbre is naturally coloured and the instrument given realistic presence.

OPERA

Yolanta (complete).

(*) Erato Dig. **ECD 88147; NUM/*MCE* 75207 (2) [id.]. Vishnevskaya, Gedda, Groenroos, Petkov, Krause, Groupe Vocale de France, O de Paris, Rostropovich.

We still await Decca's fine Solti set of *Eugene Onegin* (SET 596-8/*K 57 K 32* [Lon. OSA 13112]) in its CD format. Meanwhile Tchaikovsky's operatic CD début is made by Erato with the much later (1892) one-act opera *Yolanta* (*Iolanthe*).

Recorded at a live concert performance in the Salle Pleyel in December 1984, with excellent, spacious sound, Rostropovich's performance has a natural expressive warmth to make one tolerant of vocal shortcomings. This is the fairy-tale story of a blind princess in medieval Provence who is finally cured by the arrival of the knight who falls in love with her. The libretto may be flawed but the lyrical invention is a delight. Though Vishnevskaya's voice is not naturally suited to the role of a sweet young princess, she does wonders in softening her hardness of tone, bringing fine detail of characterization. Gedda equally by nature sounds too old for his role, but again the artistry is compelling, and ugly sounds few. More questionable is the casting of Dimiter Petkov as the King, far too wobbly as recorded.

Telemann, Georg Philipp (1681–1767)

Concerto for flute, oboe d'amore and viola d'amore in E; Concerto polonois; Double concerto for recorder and flute in E min.; Triple trumpet concerto in D; Quadro in B flat.

*** O-L Dig. **411 949-2**; DSDL/*KDSDC* 701. AAM with soloists, Hogwood.

In the early years of the eighteenth century, Telemann had served as kapellmeister to Count Erdmann II of Promnitz at Sorau in Poland. During the summer the Court moved to Pless, one of the Promnitz estates in Upper Silesia, and the folk music he heard there made a great impression on him. 'An attentive observer could gather from these folk musicians enough ideas in eight days to last a lifetime,' he wrote; in three of the concertos recorded here, Polish ideas are to be found – indeed, one of the pieces is called *Concerto polonois*. As always, Telemann has a refined ear for sonority and the musical discourse with which he diverts us is unfailingly intelligent and delightful. The performances are excellent and readers will not find cause for disappointment in either the recording or presentation. The CD has slightly better definition, but the difference is marginal. The chrome tape, however, is over-modulated and there is distortion at peaks.

Horn concerto in D ; Double horn concerto in D; Triple horn concerto in D; Suite in F for 2 horns and strings; Tafelmusik, Book 3: *Double horn concerto in E flat.*
*** Ph. Dig. **412 226-2**; 412 226-1/*4* [id.]. Baumann, Timothy Brown, Hill, ASMF, Iona Brown.

The *E flat Concerto* comes from the third set of *Tafelmusik* (1733) and is the best-known of the four recorded here. The playing here and in the other concertos is pretty dazzling, not only from Hermann Baumann but also from his colleagues, Timothy Brown and Nicholas Hill. Mention should also be made of the concertante contributions from the two violinists. Telemann's invention rarely fails to hold the listener, and the recording has warm ambience and excellent clarity in all its three forms. The usual advantages of compact disc must be noted and readers with an interest in this much underrated and unfailingly intelligent composer should acquire this rewarding issue. The chrome cassette is less recommendable; the amplitude of the horns brings problems and the focus is less clean than on the LP.

Oboe concertos: in C min.; D; D min.; E min.; F min.
*** Ph. Dig. **412 879-2**; 6514/*7337* 232. Holliger, ASMF, Iona Brown.

The *C minor Concerto* with its astringent opening dissonance is the most familiar of the concertos on Holliger's record and the *E minor* has also been recorded before, but the remaining three are all new to the catalogue. Telemann was himself proficient on the oboe and wrote with particular imagination and poignancy for this instrument. The performances are all vital and sensitively shaped and a valuable addition to the Telemann discography. Well worth investigation. The high-level chrome tape is in the demonstration class.

Double concerto in F, for recorder, bassoon and strings; Double concerto in E min., for recorder, flute and strings; Suite in A min., for recorder and strings.
*** Ph. Dig. **410 141-2**; 6514/*7337* 165. Petri, Bennett, Thunemann, ASMF, Iona Brown.

The *E minor Concerto* for recorder, flute and strings is also included on the Academy of Ancient Music's anthology (**411 949-2**) but is played on modern instruments on the Philips record. This is a delightful piece and is beautifully played, even though period instrument addicts will doubtless find William Bennett's tone a little fruity. The playing throughout is highly accomplished and the *Suite in A minor*, Telemann's only suite for treble recorder, comes off beautifully. Excellently played and recorded throughout, with a matching first-class cassette. The compact disc brings out the forward balance of the soloists in the *Double concerto*, but the effect is not unattractive. The orchestral focus is not absolutely clean, though quite agreeable.

Concerto for 3 trumpets, 2 oboes and strings.
** Erato Dig. **ECD 88007**; NUM/*MCE* 75026 [id.]. M. André, Touvron, L. André, Arrignon, Chavana, Pontet, Paris O Ens., Wallez – HUMMEL; NERUDA: *Concertos.***

This Telemann work has some very attractive textures and the invention is fresh. The soloists, led by Maurice André, are excellent but the orchestral support is less impressive. The recording is good, though not as clearly defined as one usually expects from a digital source.

Overtures (Suites): in C; D.
(*) Tel. **ZK8 42989; AZ6 42989 [id.]. VCM, Harnoncourt.

One hundred and thirty-four *Overtures* (or *Suites*) by Telemann survive, though he composed many more. The two recorded here were first issued during 1981, the tercentenary of his birth, and are given sparkling performances by the Concentus Musicus under Harnoncourt. Don't be put off by what appears to be the heavy hand of pedantry right at the opening *Grave* of the *D major Suite*, for what follows is much lighter in accent and eminently keen in both sensibility and spirit. Indeed, the oboe playing is really distinguished. The balance is rather close, which emphasizes the nasal tone of the strings, and in tutti sections the recording has a trace of roughness.

Overtures (Suites): in G min.; D min.
(*) Tel. **ZK8 42986; AZ6 42986 [id.]. VCM, Harnoncourt.

A companion issue to the above; it comes from the same set which first appeared during the tercentenary celebrations in 1981. The music, as always with Telemann, has elegance and intelligence in abundance, the ideas being fresh and inventive. The performances have plenty of liveliness to recommend them; they fully communicate the vitality and wit of this music. As always, Telemann's invention has freshness and intelligence, and at times unpredictability: there is, for example, an extraordinary modulation in the *Loure* of the *D minor*, from B minor to F major in its middle section.

Suite in A min. for flute and strings.
(B) ** CBS *MGT 39493*. Rampal, Jerusalem Music Centre CO – VIVALDI: *Four Seasons* and *Double concertos*.**

Telemann's *Suite in A minor*, which has so much in common with Bach's *B minor Suite*, is available on CD in a splendid performance by Michala Petri with the ASMF – see above. Rampal is very spirited, even racy, even if his performance is not authentic in style (the orchestra is distinctly big band). Not for purists by any means, and it is perhaps too brisk and wanting in dignity to enjoy the widest appeal. But the couplings are generous and this is fair value. The sound is good, if a little over-bright.

Water Music (Hamburger Ebb and Flow); Concertos in A min.; B flat; F.
*** DG Arc. Dig. **413 788-2**; 413 788-1/*4* [id.]. Col. Mus. Ant., Goebel.

Telemann's *Water Music* was written for the centenary celebrations of the Hamburg Admiralty in 1723, and this lively and inventive suite was performed during the festivities. It is one of Telemann's best-known works and, save for the very opening *overture*, is given a very lively performance, with sprightly rhythms and vital articulation. The eccentric opening is less than half the speed of Marriner's version on Argo (ZRG 837) or Wenzinger's famous old Archiv account. Of particular interest are the three concertos on the reverse side of the LP, two of which (in F major and A minor) are new to records. The invention is of unfailing interest as is the diversity of instrumental colouring. The balance is admirably judged and the recording excellent on LP, with the compact disc offering additional presence. The chrome tape is disappointing, over-modulated to saturation point and producing congestion.

CHAMBER MUSIC

Essercizii musici: Solo (Sonata) in E min.; (i) *Sonata (Trio) in E flat. Partita in G min. Tafelmusik: Solo (Sonata) in G min.*
❀ (M) *** Ph. 412 404-1/*4* [id.]. Holliger, Jaccottet, Sax, Mermoud; (i) with Hostettler.

This is an enchanting collection, beautifully played, with a recording balance that is as near perfect as could be imagined. The sound is so good on the cassette that one might think it was a CD, for background noise is minimal. The *Partita in G minor* is a seven-movement piece of considerable substance. Holliger is in superb form and his phrasing and articulation are a constant delight. Manfred Sax, the bassoonist, plays a major part in the continuo, and he too gives constant pleasure in the delicacy of his timbre and the skilful way he balances his line to blend with the oboe. The *Sonata in E flat* has an obbligato keyboard part, played here on the spinet by Nicole Hostettler; its finale, which is part fugue, part imitation, is wonderfully infectious.

Essercizii musici: Sonata in B flat. Der getreue Musik-Meister: Suite in G min. Die kleine Kammermusik: Partita No. 2 in G. Tafelmusik: Sonata in G min.
** Accent **ACC 48013D**; ACC 8013. Dombrecht, Kuijken, Kohnen.

This recital of oboe music by Telemann first appeared in 1980 and has been digitally remastered for the new medium. Paul Dombrecht is a sensitive player who offers pieces from the *Tafelmusik* and *Der getreue Musik-Meister* as well as a rather remarkable *Sonata in B flat* from the *Essercizii musici* of 1739. Enthusiasts will doubtless want everything; for a basic Telemann collection, however, the non-specialist collector will probably turn first to Holliger's anthology from *Der getreue Musik-Meister* listed below, particularly as there is the occasional insecurity of intonation here. Generally speaking, however, these are good performances and are well recorded.

Der getreue Musik-Meister: Nos 4, 7, 13, 20, 28, 31, 35, 50, 53, 59, 62.
*** Denon Dig. **C37 7052** [id.]. Holliger, Thunemann, Jaccottet.

In the mid-1960s, Archiv recorded a complete set of *Der getreue Musik-Meister*, the musical periodical Telemann began publishing in 1728, which offers a rewarding wealth of invention. This compact disc offers three of the most important works for oboe and continuo, two *Sonatas* and a *Suite*, as well as the *F minor Sonata*, designated for recorder or bassoon and played here by Klaus Thunemann. They are interspersed with various miniatures, all well played and recorded. Holliger's playing is unusually expressive and his eloquence makes this selection alone worth having. Those who don't possess the complete set might well consider obtaining this selection.

VOCAL MUSIC

Der Schulmeister (cantata).
*** Hung. Dig. SLPD 12573 [id.]. Gregor, Boys of Schola Hungarica, Corelli CO, Pal – CIMAROSA: *Il maestro di capella.****

Telemann's cantata featuring a stupid schoolmaster is much more heavily Germanic in its comedy than the Cimarosa piece on the reverse, but Gregor's strong personality and magnificently firm, dark bass, coupled with enthusiastic contributions from the boys of the Schola Hungarica (a rowdy bunch, to judge by the decibel-level), make its simple humour endearing. An excellent and apt, if ungenerous coupling for the Cimarosa. Excellent recording.

Tiomkin, Dimitri (1894–1979)

Film music: *The Fall of the Roman Empire: Overture: Pax Romana. The Guns of Navarone: Prologue-Prelude; Epilogue. A President's country. Rhapsody of steel. Wild is the wind.*
(*) Unicorn **DKPCD 9047; DKP/*DKPC* 9047 [id.]. Royal College of Music O, Willcocks; D. King (organ).

Dimitri Tiomkin was one of a number of émigré musicians who made a considerable contribution to the music of Hollywood. He was born in the Ukraine, studied under Glazunov and was still in St Petersburg at the time of the Russian Revolution. Later in Berlin he was a pupil of Busoni and made appearances as a solo pianist with the Berlin Philharmonic. His musical pedigree, then, is impressive and it is not surprising that his film career was distinguished. He contributed scores to some of the most famous movies of all time, for Hitchcock and Frank Capra among others. But it was Carl Foreman's *High noon* that produced his most memorable idea, and he quotes its famous theme, among others, in *A President's country*, a well-crafted medley used as background music for a documentary about President Johnson's Texas. *Wild is the wind* is another familiar melody; Christopher Palmer's arrangement makes a tastefully scored showcase. The latter has arranged and orchestrated all the music here except *Rhapsody of steel*, a complex pseudo-symphonic score written for another documentary, which lasts some 22 minutes. It is an ambitious piece; while aficionados of this repertoire will welcome its inclusion, others may decide that the rhetoric outbalances the fresher material: this includes a nonchalant theme in the style of a popular song and a scherzando section which comes about halfway through. The music for *Pax Romana* has the robust character of a typical epic Hollywood costume spectacular, featuring a bold contribution from the organ. All the music is played with obvious enjoyment by the Orchestra of the Royal College of Music; no apologies need be made for their technique, which is fully professional. Sir David Willcocks conducts with understanding of the idiom and great personal conviction. The music could hardly be better presented. The recording is very impressive too, though the balance gives brass and percussion rather too much prominence. Such a degree of spectacle obviously has a maximum effect in the CD format, and the chrome tape is a little disappointing, lacking ultimate brilliance, though wide in amplitude.

Tippett, Michael (born 1905)

(i) *Concerto for double string orchestra;* (ii; iii) *Piano concerto;* (iv) *Fantasia concertante on a theme of Corelli;* (v) *String quartet No. 1;* (ii) *Piano sonatas 1–2.*

(M) *** HMV EX 290228-3/*5* (2). (i) Moscow CO and Bath Fest. CO, Barshai; (ii) John Ogdon; (iii) Philh. O, Sir Colin Davis; (iv) Bath Fest. O, composer; (v) Edinburgh Qt.

This two-disc collection of EMI recordings made mainly in the 1960s was compiled as a tribute to Sir Michael on his eightieth birthday in January 1985. Though the choice of works is rather arbitrary, depending on what was in the company's archive, these are all fascinating examples of Tippett's individual imagination at its keenest; the performances are all first rate and the sound hardly shows its age. An excellent set for anyone desiring this rare material that reflects one of the most imaginative and original musical figures of our time. The cassettes are also extremely vivid.

Concerto for double string orchestra; Fantasia concertante on a theme of Corelli; Little music for strings.

*** Argo ZRG/*KZRC* 680 [id.]. ASMF, Marriner.

Concerto for double string orchestra.

(B) *** CfP CFP 41 4489-1/*4*. LPO, Handley – BRITTEN: *Violin concerto.****

Concerto for double string orchestra; The Midsummer Marriage: Ritual dances.

** HMV Dig. **CDC 747330-2**; EL 270273-1/*4*. Bournemouth SO, Barshai.

The *Concerto for double string orchestra*, on any count one of the most beautiful of twentieth-century works for strings, receives on Argo performance more sumptuous and warm-hearted than any before on record. With utter commitment Sir Neville Marriner and his colleagues allow the jazz inflections of the outer movements to have their lightening effect on the rhythm; in the heavenly slow movement, the slowish tempo and hushed manner display the full romanticism of the music without ever slipping over the edge into sentimentality. The *Corelli fantasia*, a similarly sumptuous work but without quite the same lyrical felicity, and the *Little music* provide an ideal coupling. The recording is outstanding; since our last edition, it has also been issued in an excellent tape equivalent.

Tippett's eloquent *Concerto* is also well served by this bargain-priced 1977 performance by Handley and the LPO. The playing is strong and committed; no one could here overlook the passion behind both the sharp rhythmic inspirations of the outer movements and the glorious lyricism of the central slow movement. The recording is excellent and there is a very good tape, vivid and wide-ranging.

In 1963 Rudolf Barshai made a fine recording of the *Concerto for double string orchestra* with the combined Moscow Chamber and Bath Festival orchestras (see above), but this 1985 Bournemouth version brings a slowing and a thickening which take away the natural impulse of the music and even undermine the radiant lyricism of the slow movement. The *Ritual dances* sound cautious, too, and the weight of brass obscures the detail in other sections. Nevertheless, the digital recording is weightily impressive, exceptionally full and realistic, and there is an excellent tape equivalent.

Concerto for orchestra; Suite for the birthday of Prince Charles.
(M) *** Ph. Seq. 412 378-1/*4* [id.]. LSO, Sir Colin Davis.

The *Concerto for orchestra* was a by-product of the opera *King Priam*; even more successfully than the opera, it exploits a new thorny style, tough and sinewy, hardly at all lyrical in the manner of Tippett's earlier music. To study such a piece on record is immensely rewarding, especially when the performance is powerful and dedicated and the 1965 recording remains fresh. The occasional piece used as coupling is altogether less substantial, but entertaining enough. There is a vivid tape equivalent, given one of Philips's best transfers, clear and well projected.

Fantasia concertante on a theme of Corelli.
** ASV Dig. **CDDCA 518**; [id.]. ASMF, Marriner – ELGAR: *Serenade***; VAUGHAN WILLIAMS: *Tallis fantasia* etc.**(*)

The *Fantasia concertante of a theme of Corelli* is the first Tippett work to appear on CD and the ASV recording has fine clarity and detail. The new performance is certainly successful – but the earlier Argo account is finer still and has preferable couplings.

(i) *Fantasia on a theme of Handel;* (i; ii) *The Vision of St Augustine.*
*** RCA RL 89498. LSO, composer, with (i) Margaret Kitchin (piano); (ii) Shirley-Quirk, LSO Ch.

The Vision of St Augustine is a masterpiece of Tippett's later, thorniest period to set beside *The Midsummer Marriage*, culmination of his euphonious years. It is nothing short of an attempt to convey the impossible – a momentary glimpse of heaven itself, taking the narrative of St Augustine. Where most composers would kneel humbly and purify their style in the face of heaven, Tippett carries in his thorny, complex textures the fanaticism of a mystic. The result is not easy music, but in this magnificent performance and recording, burning with intensity from beginning to end, few will miss the excitement of the work even at a first hearing, and this is amply confirmed by repetition. The *Fantasia* is essentially a much easier piece to come to grips with, similarly complex, but less jagged. It makes a generous coupling for an imaginatively conceived project. Again the performance and recording quality are first class.

(i) *Symphony Nos 1–2;* (i; ii) *Symphony No. 3;* (iii) *Symphony No. 4.*
*** Decca 414 091-1/*4* (3). (i) LSO, Sir Colin Davis; (ii) with Heather Harper; (iii) Chicago SO, Solti.

All four symphonies have been available separately, the *First* and *Third* on Philips, the *Second* on Argo, and the *Fourth* on Decca itself. One welcome result of the Polygram merger is this kind of venture, marking the composer's eightieth birthday, which enables all four symphonies to be accommodated in one box, albeit shorn of their original couplings. (Since possessing the *First* and *Fourth* originally involved duplication as they were both coupled with the *Suite for the birthday of Prince Charles*, this new format is obviously attractive, particularly as the *Suite* has now been re-coupled with the *Concerto for orchestra*.) There is also now a first-class tape equivalent.

Piano sonatas Nos 1 (Fantasy sonata); 2; 3; 4.
*** CRD Dig. CRD 1130/1/*CRDC 4130/1* (2) [id.]. Paul Crossley.

More than two decades separate the first two sonatas, and the remaining two have appeared at ten-year intervals. The *Fantasy sonata* is one of Tippett's very first published works and was written in 1937. The two middle sonatas are related to other Tippett works: the *Second* (1962) to the opera, *King Priam*, from which it quotes; and the *Third* (1973) comes from the same world as the *Symphony No. 3.* Paul Crossley had been strongly identified with the Tippett sonatas; he recorded the first three for Philips in the mid-1970s: indeed, No. 3 was written for him. The *Fourth* and most recent (1983–4) started life as a set of five bagatelles. Crossley contributes an informative and illuminating note on the sonata and its relationship with, among other things, Ravel's *Miroirs*; his performance has all the lucidity and subtlety one would expect from him. These masterly accounts supersede the earlier recording and their excellence is matched by truthful and immediate sound quality, with chrome cassettes of matching high quality.

OPERA

The Knot Garden (complete).
(M) *** Ph. 412 707-1 (2) [id.]. Herincz, Minton, Gomez, Barstow, Carey, Tear, Hemsley, ROHCGO, Sir Colin Davis.

As Tippett has grown older, so his music has grown wilder. Those who have enjoyed the ripe qualities of *The Midsummer Marriage* (Philips 6703 027) may be disconcerted by the relative astringency of this later opera, a garden conversation piece to a libretto by the composer very much in the style of a T. S. Eliot play. The result characteristically is a mixture, with the mandarin occasionally putting on a funny hat, as in the jazz and blues passages for the male lovers Dov and Mel. The brief central Act, called *Labyrinth*, has characters thrown together two at a time in a revolving maze, a stylized effect which contributes effectively to Tippett's process of psychiatric nerve-prodding. Sir Colin Davis draws a superb performance from his Covent Garden cast, and the recording, a little dry, is vivid.

Tjeknavorian, Loris (born 1937)

Othello (ballet): symphonic suite.
*** HMV Dig. EL 270322-1/*4*. LSO, composer.

Loris Tjeknavorian's *Othello* was composed for the Northern Ballet Theatre (based in Manchester) and was first performed in London in 1985. The symphonic suite is drawn from both Acts of the ballet and is re-scored for a larger orchestra than the original. The problem for any composer/conductor is the unconscious assimilation of the styles of others, and so it is here. The music is well laced with Prokofievian and Stravinskian influences, among others, although the later part of the work seems to be more personal. The eclecticism does not prevent vividness of invention, although it must be admitted that much of this sounds more like film music than a 'symphonic' suite. It is all extremely colourful, and every bar is alive in this committed and authoritative performance under the composer, with the LSO kept on their toes throughout. The recording too is spectacular – very much in the demonstration class – and there is a splendid tape equivalent.

Tubin, Eduard (1905–82)

Concerto for balalaika and orchestra.
*** Cap. Dig. CAP 1180 [id.]. Zwetnow, Stockholm PO, Ingebretsen.

Tubin's *Concerto for the balalaika* is a characteristically inventive and interesting piece; it is as beautifully played by Nicolaus Zwetnow and the Stockholm

Philharmonic Orchestra under Kjell Ingebretsen and as expertly recorded as one expects from this label. Apart from being one of the leading exponents of the balalaika, Nicolaus Zwetnow studied music and medicine in Oslo and is now professor of neurosurgery in Stockholm. The *Concerto* is coupled with various solo works by Nikolai Budazhkin, Boris Goltz, Boris Trojanovsky, Sven-Eric Johansen and the enterprising soloist himself. Many of these pieces are fun and make the most of the resources and the unusual sonorities of the instrument. Not the least impressive of them is Zwetnow's own piece, *Cadenza.*

Violin concerto No. 1; Suite on Estonian dances for violin and orchestra; Prélude solennel.
** BIS Dig. **CD 286**; LP 286 [id.]. Lubotsky, Gothenburg SO, Järvi.

All the music on the present disc derives from the period before Tubin settled in Sweden in 1944: the *Suite* (1943) is a rather slight and folksy piece, originally for violin and piano, which Tubin scored later in life. But no one approaching this *Suite* or the empty and bombastic *Prélude solennel* without foreknowledge of any of Tubin's other music should judge him on either of these pieces. The *Violin concerto No. 1* is a good deal better – though, again, it is no match for the *Fourth Symphony*, composed only a year later. The solo line is lyrical and the melodic ideas are not unappealing or lacking in character, but the orchestra often provides rather simple harmonic support and the writing is somehow wanting in interest. It was recorded at a public concert in Gothenburg, and both the performance and sound engineering are eminently acceptable. However, this is emphatically not Tubin at his best.

Symphonies Nos 2 (The Legendary); 6.
*** BIS **CD 304**; LP 304 [id.]. Swedish RSO, Järvi.

Eduard Tubin was an Estonian who fled his country in 1944 and settled in Sweden, where he suffered relative neglect. All ten of his symphonies are being recorded; the *Fourth*, written when he was still living in Estonia in 1943, is already available, conducted by Neeme Järvi on LP (BIS LP 227). The *First Symphony*, composed in 1931–4 when Tubin was in his late twenties, apparently caused something of a stir on its first performance in Tallinn, and – if it is anything like its successor – it is not hard to see why. His *Second Symphony*, together with the *Sixth*, makes a more fully representative introduction to his musical personality. Both are the work of an original and highly inventive musical mind with a deep feeling for the symphonic process. The *Second* was written during the summer of 1937 which Tubin spent on the north-east coast of Estonia; despite its title, it has no specific programme. Its opening is quite magical: soft, luminous string chords that evoke a strongly powerful atmosphere. The *Sixth* (1954) has obvious resonances of Prokofiev, even down to instrumentation, and yet the rhythmic vitality and melodic invention are quietly distinctive. There is always a sense of movement – the music pursuing a purposeful course – and the ear is always engaged by the diversity of musical incident. The Swedish Radio Symphony Orchestra play with great commitment under Neeme Järvi, who has put us deeply in his debt by his tireless championship of Tubin; and the engineers have done a magnificent job. The recording, made in the Berwald Hall, Stockholm, has splendid range, clarity and definition, and there are reasonable pauses between movements.

Symphony No. 9 (*Sinfonia semplice*); *Estonian dance suite; Toccata.*
*** BIS LP 264 [id.]. Gothenburg SO, Järvi.

The *Ninth Symphony* is a work of striking and compelling power and was recorded at a concert performance. It dates from 1969 and is in two movements; its mood is elegiac, and a restrained melancholy permeates the slower sections. Its musical language is direct, tonal and (once one has got to grips with it) quite personal. If its spiritual world is clearly Nordic, the textures are transparent and luminous, and its argument unfolds naturally and cogently. It is strong in both concentration of feeling and melodic invention, and the playing of the Gothenburgers under Järvi is totally committed in all sections of the orchestra. Unfortunately, it has not been coupled with music of comparable stature: the early *Estonian suite* (1938) is a pleasant, more or less conventional piece of nationalism – a kind of Estonian *Dances of Galánta* (and no harm in that) – but it is by no means Tubin at his best. The *Toccata for orchestra* (1937) is more individual and inventive. However, neither of these pieces is remotely comparable in quality of invention or nobility of feeling with the *Symphony*. The performances are authoritative and the recording altogether excellent and, as one has come to expect from this source, the surfaces are impeccable. Collectors who enjoy composers like Stenhammar, Bax and Prokofiev should investigate this.

Turina, Joaquín (1882–1949)

Rapsodia sinfónica, Op. 66.
*** Decca Dig. **410 289-2**; 410 289-1/*4* [id.]. De Larrocha, LPO, Frühbeck de Burgos – FALLA: *Nights in the gardens of Spain*; ALBÉNIZ: *Rapsodia*.***

Turina's *Rapsodia sinfónica* has been recorded by others, but in the hands of Alicia de Larrocha it is played with such éclat that it becomes almost memorable and thoroughly entertaining. The Falla coupling is poetic and atmospheric, while the delightfully chimerical Albéniz companion piece glitters most engagingly. Excellent, vivid sound out of Decca's top drawer, especially on the splendid CD.

Tye, Christopher (born *c.* 1500)

Euge bone mass in 6 parts; Western wind mass.
(M) *** Argo 412 707-1/*4*. King's College Ch., Willcocks.

Tye was born five years before Tallis, and his style is less personal than that of Fayrfax, Tallis or Taverner. But the *Euge bonę mass* for six voices is one of the glories of early Tudor music, amazingly rich and complex. Like Taverner and Sheppard, Tye also wrote a Mass using the secular song, *The Western wind*, as basis. Both these works are beautifully sung and recorded in this reissued 1973 recording. Both have also reappeared on more recent records (from HMV and CRD respectively), but not coupled together, an excellent idea. The cassette has been transferred at fractionally too ambitious a level and the focus of the choir almost roughens at the opening of the *Euge bone mass*.

Vaňhal, Jan (1739–1813)

(i) *Double bassoon concerto in F; Sinfonias: in A min.; F.*
** BIS **CD 288**; LP 288 [id.]. (i) Wallin, Nilsson; Umeå Sinf., Saraste.

The best thing here is the *Concerto*, which is an arresting and inventive piece. The opening allegro is conceived on a broader canvas than one expects, and the slow movement has real distinction, and touching a deeper vein of feeling than anything else on this record. The work is not only beautifully crafted and well laid out, which one expects, but its invention is fresh. It is not too fanciful to detect in some of the harmonic suspensions the influence of Gluck, with whose music he came into contact in the late 1760s. The two *Sinfonias* are less musically developed but far from uninteresting: the minuet of the *F major* has a distinctly '*Sturm und Drang*' feel to it: Vaňhal's symphonies may well have paved the way for Haydn at this period; they were certainly given by Haydn while Kapellmeister at the Esterhazy palace. The recording is good, as one has come to expect from this source, and detail is clean and fresh, even if the acoustic is on the dry side. The playing of the Umeå ensemble is eminently respectable, even if the upper strings occasionally sound a little lacking in bloom. The balance is well judged, though perhaps the accomplished young soloists are placed just a little too forward.

Violin concerto in G.
(*) Sup. Dig. **C37 7571 [id.]. Josef Suk, Suk CO, Vlach – HAYDN: *Concerto in G.***(*)
Jan Vaňhal was Haydn's contemporary, Bohemian by birth but active in Vienna. His *G major Concerto* is every bit as good as Haydn's in the same key – which, of course, is not saying a great deal. In fact, it is quite an engaging little work, with a busy first movement, a rather solemn *Adagio* which Suk plays with characteristic warmth, and a brilliant presto finale, which both soloist and orchestra dive into with great vivacity and spirit. The recording is truthful if forwardly balanced, but this is short measure for CD – room could easily have been found for a third concerto.

Varèse, Edgar (1885–1965)

Arcana; Intégrales; Ionisation.
(M) *** Decca Lon. Ent. 414 170-1/*4* [id.]. LAPO, LA Percussion Ens., Mehta.

Déserts; (i) *Ecuatorial; Hyperprism; Intégrales; Octandre;* (ii) *Densité;* (iii) *Offrandes.*
*** CBS Dig. IM/*IMT* 39053 [id.]. InterContemporain Ens., Boulez, with (i) Ch. of R. France; (ii) Beauregard; (iii) Yakar.

These exploratory and innovative works are eminently well served both by the Ensemble InterContemporain and Pierre Boulez and by the CBS engineers, who provide outstanding recording quality on both LP and cassette. All these extraordinary pieces from the earliest, *Hyperprism* (1922–3), to the much later *Déserts* (1945–54) sound as modern as most radical music of the 1960s, and are certainly more substantial. These performances are meticulously prepared and completely idiomatic; the exceptionally wide range of the recording does justice to every dynamic subtlety. One point worth noting is that Boulez omits the electronic interpolations that Varèse inserted into *Déserts*, an omission that does have the authority of the composer.

The earlier and less generous Decca collection comes from 1972. It includes *Arcana*, a substantial (18′ 40″) and spectacular piece, and only duplicates *Intégrales. Arcana* uses a large string section and thirty-nine percussion instruments, and was first performed by Stokowski in 1927. Its mood can be determined from the quotation from Paracelsus' *Hermetic Astronomy* which heads the score: 'One star exists higher than all the rest. This is the apocalyptic star; the second star is that of the ascendant. The third is that of the elements, and of these there are four, so that six stars are established. Besides these there is still another star, imagination, which begets a new star and a new heaven.' *Ionisation* for thirteen percussionists (and including eerily used sirens) dates from 1931. Mehta's performances have a dramatic spontaneity plus an easy expressiveness that come from close and warm acquaintance by the players. The recording is first class, with an excellent high-level chrome tape matching the LP closely. At mid-price on this London Enterprise reissue, it may be considered a worthwhile supplement to the Boulez collection.

Vaughan Williams, Ralph (1872–1958)

Concerto grosso; (i) *Oboe concerto; Fantasia on Greensleeves; Fantasia on a theme of Thomas Tallis; Five variants of Dives and Lazarus.*
(*) Nimbus Dig. **NIM 5019 [id.]. (i) Bourgue; E. String O, Boughton.

Recorded in the spacious acoustic of the Great Hall of Birmingham University, Boughton's sympathetic performances of an attractive group of Vaughan

Williams works are presented amply and atmospherically. That is particularly effective in the *Tallis fantasia*, and the *Greensleeves fantasia* – with the flute solo nicely distanced – is equally beautiful. Though the reverberation thickens the textures of the *Concerto grosso*, reducing its neoclassic lightness, that too loses little from the weight of sound. More questionable is the *Oboe concerto* with the superb French soloist, Maurice Bourgue, balanced too close, so that the strings in the background do little more than comment distantly. Nevertheless Bourgue's playing, rich in tone and sharply rhythmic, makes a persuasive case for a neglected piece.

Piano concerto in C.
*** Lyr. SRCS 130 [id.]. Howard Shelley, RPO, Handley – FOULDS: *Dynamic triptych.****

The heavyweight piano textures and thorny counterpoint (whether Bach-like or Hindemithian) led the composer to revise his *Piano concerto* of 1931 as a two-piano concerto, in which form it has also been recorded (see below). This, however, is the first recording of the *Concerto* in solo form, not quite as originally written, because the definitive score, published only recently and giving the alternatives of one or two pianos, opts for ending with a serene coda instead of the original brief dispatching coda of ten bars. That is certainly an improvement, and the wonder is that though the solo piano writing is hardly pianistic, the very challenge to as fine an exponent as Shelley brings out an extra intensity to a highly individual score, written when Vaughan Williams was at the peak of his powers, at the time of *Job* and just before the *Fourth Symphony*. Despite the thick textures, there is lightheartedness in much of the writing, whether the urgently chattering *Toccata* or the *Alla tedesca* which emerges out of the toughly chromatic fugue of the finale. A fascinating, long-neglected piece, here given an outstanding performance and recording.

(i) *Double piano concerto in C; The Wasps: Overture and suite;* (ii) *Fantasia on the old 104th Psalm tune.*
(M) *** HMV ED 290653-1/*4*. (i) Vronsky and Babin; (ii) Katin, LPO Ch.; LPO, Boult.

This arrangement for two pianos was made when Vaughan Williams decided that his solo concerto (see above), which was originally written for Harriet Cohen, might be more effective in a new form. The revised version prepared with the help of Joseph Cooper was first performed by Cyril Smith and Phyllis Sellick in 1946, but in the event it has not found a place in the repertoire. It remains one of RVW's less tractable works, with its characteristic first-movement *Toccata*, but Vronsky and Babin are very persuasive, with the help of Boult's authority. The thick texture is well handled by the engineers. The *Fantasia* (*quasi variazione*) *on the old 104th Psalm tune* is not an entirely successful work. The piano introduces the psalm theme and then creates an obbligato for the chorus, but is given its own interludes, both poetic and dramatic. Katin is admirably fresh and the LPO Chorus sing eloquently. The *Wasps overture* is well known; the other items in the suite are delightful, too, not least the *March of the kitchen utensils*. The recordings, made between 1968 and 1970, all sound well; the cassette is also very successful, with good choral focus on side one. This is timed at just over 40 minutes, and the collection as a whole plays for well over an hour, which makes it excellent medium-price value.

Fantasia on Sussex folk tunes for cello and orchestra.
*** RCA Dig. RL/*RK* 70800. Lloyd Webber, Philh. O, Handley – DELIUS: *Cello concerto*; HOLST: *Invocation.****

The *Fantasia on Sussex folk tunes* is new to the gramophone. It was composed for Casals, who gave its first performance in 1930 at a Royal Philharmonic Society concert, and comes from the same period as *Job* and the *Piano concerto*. The piece has lain neglected since its first performance, and it proves something of a discovery. This is a highly appealing work, most persuasively performed too by Lloyd Webber and the Philharmonia and Vernon Handley. The recording is first class on both disc and tape.

Fantasia on Greensleeves.
(M) *** HMV *TCC2-POR 54290*. LSO, Previn – BUTTERWORTH: *Banks of green willow*; HOLST: *The Planets* etc.***

Fantasia on Greensleeves; Fantasia on a theme of Thomas Tallis.
❀ *** HMV ASD/*TC-ASD* 521 [Ang. S 36101]. Sinf. of L., Allegri Qt, Barbirolli – ELGAR: *Introduction and allegro; Serenade.****

Fantasia on Greensleeves; Fantasia on a theme of Thomas Tallis; Five Variants of Dives and Lazarus; (i) *The Lark ascending.*
*** Argo **414 595-2**; ZRG 696/*KZRC 15696* [id.]. ASMF, Marriner (i) with Iona Brown.

Fantasia on a theme of Thomas Tallis; (i) *The Lark ascending.*
(*) ASV Dig. **CDDCA518; DCA/*ZCDCA* 518 [id.]. (i) Iona Brown; ASMF, Marriner – ELGAR: *String serenade;* TIPPETT: *Fantasia concertante.***

The rich projection of the theme when it first appears in full, after the pizzicato introduction, sets the seal on Barbirolli's quite outstanding performance of the *Tallis fantasia*, one of the great masterpieces of all music. The wonderfully ethereal and magically quiet playing of the second orchestra is another very moving feature of this remarkable performance. HMV should be very proud both of the excellence of their stereo effect and of the warm realism of the string textures on both disc and cassette. The delightful *Greensleeves fantasia* makes a pleasing bonus. We hope this will soon appear on CD.

On Argo, superbly balanced and refined performances of four favourite Vaughan Williams works, which with the help of full, clear recorded sound here have great power and intensity. A richly rewarding record, made in 1972, but strikingly enhanced in its CD format, while the excellent cassette offers three songs (*Linden Lea; Orpheus with his lute;* and *The Water mill*) as a bonus, admirably sung by Robert Tear. On CD, detail is more refined and the fullness retained, but the massed upper strings now have a slight edge in climaxes.

On ASV, Iona Brown offers her second recording of *The Lark ascending* and she has the advantage here of digital recording. The present version, though not finer than the old, is both eloquent and evocative; the silent background of the CD, plus the internal clarity, makes it highly competitive. The *Tallis fantasia* is beautifully played too, but the effect here is relatively bland beside the earlier Argo account, now also transferred to CD. The acoustic is warm but not quite as expansive as the Argo and HMV versions. Couplings are also important with a record of this kind (called 'The English connection'), and neither shows these artists at their very best.

Previn's excellent account of the *Greensleeves fantasia* is part of a double-length tape in HMV's 'Portrait of the Artist' series, of which the major contents are by Holst. The sound is first rate.

Fantasia on a theme of Thomas Tallis; Job (masque for dancing).
(M) (***) HMV mono ED 290800-1/*4*. BBC SO, Boult.

Job is undeniably one of Vaughan Williams's greatest works; it shows his inspiration at its most deeply characteristic. Boult is its dedicatee, and he recorded it four times. This first version, transferred with great skill from 78 r.p.m. discs by Peter Brown, dates from 1946; its dramatic power is undeniable, although the recording, with its remarkably wide range of dynamic, tends to harden in fortissimos; and while this brings added bite to the invocation of Satan, the lyrical climaxes are made to sound less than ideally expansive. Even so, the achievement is considerable and the nobly restrained account of the *Tallis fantasia* – recorded in the Colston Hall, Bristol, six years earlier – also sounds remarkably well. But Boult's later 1971 stereo version of *Job* is exceptionally successful, dignified in its lyricism as well as pungently dramatic, and the balance has striking range and truthfulness – one of the very best analogue recordings among Boult's many fine discs (HMV ASD 2673). There is also a remarkable digital successor, with the LPO playing with inspired fervour under Vernon Handley, one of his major achievements in the EMI studios (EMX/*TC-EMX* 41 2056 [id.]).

Five variants of Dives and Lazarus; (i) *The Lark ascending; The Wasps: Overture and suite.*
(M) *** EMI Dig. EMX 41 2082-1/*4*. (i) David Nolan; LPO, Handley.

Handley, like his mentor, Sir Adrian Boult, is an outstanding interpreter of Vaughan Williams, and here on the Eminence label he conducts an unusual and attractive collection in which rarities spice the two central, popular items, *The Lark ascending* and *The Wasps overture*. The immediacy of the brilliant, full recorded sound allows no mistiness in the former piece, but it is still a warm, understanding performance. The overture is here spaciously conceived and it leads to charming colourful accounts of the other, less well-known pieces in the suite, tuneful and lively. The *Five Variants of Dives and Lazarus* find Vaughan

Williams using his folksong idiom at its most poetic, here superbly played and recorded. The cassette transfer is highly successful, with rich string textures, yet retaining a lively treble response.

(i) *Flos campi. Old King Cole* (ballet music); *The Poisoned kiss: overture; Serenade to music* (orchestral version).
*** HMV Dig. EL 270060-1/*4* [Ang. DS/*4DS* 38129]. N. Sinfonia of England, Hickox; (i) with Andrew Williams and Sinfonia Ch.

Though the *Serenade to music* loses something in its orchestral version, Hickox conducts a warmly atmospheric performance, and it provides a good makeweight for the other three works: the masterly *Flos campi* – with Andrew Williams a most sympathetic soloist and the Northern Sinfonia Chorus equally understanding – the ballet music, *Old King Cole* – lively and radiant, full of charm – and the tuneful overture to the sadly neglected opera, *The Poisoned kiss*. All are pieces that deserve to be far better known; they receive from Hickox excellent performances, superbly recorded. There is a very good tape, wide-ranging and well focused.

2 Hymn-tune preludes: Eventide; Dominus regit me. (i) *The Lark ascending; Prelude: 49th Parallel; Prelude on an old carol tune; The running set; Sea songs: Quick march.* (ii) *5 Mystical songs.*
*** HMV Dig. EL 270305-1/*4* [Ang. DS/*4DS* 38244]. N. Sinfonia of England, Hickox, with (i) Bradley Creswick; (ii) Stephen Roberts and Sinfonia Ch.

Hickox conducts lively and sympathetic performances of a delightful collection of Vaughan Williams rarities, almost all of them occasional pieces written for particular events or projects, such as the *Prelude* to the film *49th Parallel. The Lark ascending*, the best-known work, is rather the exception, one of the composer's most poetic visions, here beautifully achieved. The most substantial work is the set of *Five Mystical songs* to words by George Herbert, sensitively sung by Stephen Roberts, but with too gritty a vibrato. Excellent contributions there from the Sinfonia Chorus and first-rate recording. The tape is also well transferred, with a good vocal focus; only in the two bright orchestral pieces, *The running set* and the *Quick march*, would the extra sparkle of a chrome transfer have brought an obvious gain.

In the Fen Country. (i) *The Lark ascending. Norfolk rhapsody No. 1.* (ii) *Serenade to music.*
*** HMV ASD/*TC-ASD* 2847 [Ang. S/*4XS* 36902]. LPO, Boult, with (i) Bean; (ii) 16 vocal soloists.

An attractive coupling of four works that originally appeared as fill-ups to Boult versions of the symphonies, all beautifully performed and recorded. Hugh Bean understands the spirit of *The Lark ascending* perfectly and his performance is wonderfully serene. Since our last edition, this collection has been issued on cassette, with generally good transfers, though the use of iron-oxide stock means that the vocal focus in the *Serenade to music* is less clear and refined than on the LP.

Suite for viola and orchestra; (i) *Flos campi.*
(*) Chan. **CHAN 8374; CBR/*CBT* 1019. Riddle, Bournemouth Sinf., Del Mar; (i) with Ch.

Originally issued in 1978 by RCA, this valuable coupling has been digitally remastered by Chandos with the choral sound enhanced on CD. Neither work is over-familiar and the evocation of the Song of Solomon contained in *Flos campi* shows Vaughan Williams at his most rarefied and imaginative. The *Suite* is lightweight but engaging, unpretentious music to be enjoyed, with its charming *Carol* and quirky *Polka mélancolique*. Frederick Riddle is an eloquent soloist, even if the playing is not always technically immaculate, and Norman Del Mar directs sympathetically. On the otherwise good chrome tape the choral sound is a little misty. However, the LP and tape are in the mid-price range.

A Sea symphony (*No. 1*).
(M) *** RCA Gold GL/*GK* 89689 [AGL1/*AGK1* 4212]. Harper, Shirley-Quirk, LSO Ch., LSO, Previn.

Previn's is a fresh, youthful reading of a young composer's symphony. If his interpretation lacks some of the honeyed sweetness that Boult brings to music he has known and loved for half a century and more, Previn's view provides a clearer focus. His nervous energy is obvious from the very start. He does not always relax as Boult does, even where, as in the slow movement, he takes a more measured tempo than the older conductor. In the scherzo, Boult concentrates on urgency, the emotional surge of the music, even at the expense of precision of ensemble, where Previn is lighter and cleaner, holding more in reserve. The finale similarly is built up over a longer span, with less deliberate expressiveness. The culminating climax with Previn is not allowed to be swamped with choral tone, but has the brass and timpani still prominent. The *Epilogue* may not be so deliberately expressive, but it is purer in its tenderness and exact control of dynamics. Even if Vaughan Williams devotees will disagree over the relative merits of the interpretations, Previn has clear advantages in his baritone soloist and his choir. The recording has been digitally remastered and detail clarified, yet the rich ambience remains, with the performers set slightly back, which means that the famous opening section is more spacious but has a less dramatic bite than in Boult's version. The chrome cassette matches the disc closely and loses very little of the inner definition, although the soloists are slightly more present on LP.

Reminder. Boult's warm, relaxed reading also remains available at mid-price, with a good cassette, fractionally less open at the top than the disc (HMV ESD/*TC-ESD* 7104).

A London symphony (*No. 2*).
(M) *** RCA Gold GL/*GK* 89690. LSO, Previn.

(i) *A London symphony (No. 2); Fantasia on Greensleeves.*
(M) **(*) EMI EMX 41 2087-1/*4*. (i) Hallé O; Sinf. of L., Barbirolli.

A London symphony (No. 2); Fantasia on a theme by Thomas Tallis.
*** HMV **CDC 747213-2**; ED 290331-1/*4* [Ang. AE/*4AE* 34438]. LPO, Boult.

Previn underlines the greatness of this work as a symphony, as more than a sequence of programmatic impressions. Though the actual sonorities are even more subtly and beautifully realized here than in rival versions, the architecture is equally convincingly presented, with the great climaxes of the first and last movements powerful and incisive. Most remarkable of all are the pianissimos which here have new intensity, a quality of *frisson* as in a live performance. The LSO play superbly and the digitally remastered recording, made in Kingsway Hall, is beautifully balanced and refined, coping perfectly with the widest possible dynamic range. The cassette transfer is very successful, full and well detailed – in fact the difference between disc and tape is minimal.

Boult's 1970 LP has also been remastered; though detail is sharper and the sound remains spacious, the upper strings sound less rich than before. On the XDR tape the slight loss of range at the top means that they seem smoother and fuller, though the focus is slightly less clear-cut. The orchestral playing is outstandingly fine. The outer movements are expansive, less taut than in his much earlier mono version for Decca. The central *tranquillo* episode of the first movement, for instance, is very relaxed; but here, as in the slow movement, the orchestra produces lovely sounds, the playing deeply committed; and criticism is disarmed. The scherzo is light as thistledown and the gentle melancholy which underlies the solemn pageantry of the finale is coloured with great subtlety. With Boult's noble, gravely intense account of the *Tallis fantasia* offered as a coupling, this remains an attractive mid-price alternative to Previn. The CD impressively refines textures (especially in *Tallis*), but lightens the bass.

Barbirolli's HMV recording dates from 1963 and the sound is a considerable advance on his earlier Pye record. In remastered form it is most impressive, vivid in detail with a wide dynamic range. Although broad in conception, the first movement has plenty of vitality – indeed, it has slightly more grip than Boult's version – and towards the end the threads are drawn together with striking majesty and power. The slow movement gains in spaciousness and atmosphere but its climax has less fervour than the earlier Pye account. The scherzo is controversial: it is played lightly and gracefully, but the pacing is much less brisk than before and there is a lack of boisterousness in the 'street dance' sequence. The powerful finale and finely graduated closing pages of the *Epilogue* make a strong impression. The attractive bonus is taken from a highly recommended HMV disc listed above.

(i) *A London symphony;* (ii) *Symphony No. 5 in D.* (iii) *Fantasia on Greensleeves.*
(B) *** HMV *TCC2-POR 54280*. (i) Hallé O; (ii) Philh. O; (iii) Sinf. of L., Barbirolli.

This is among the finest of HMV's enterprising 'Portrait of the Artist' tape-only series. Barbirolli was a great Vaughan Williams conductor, and his account of the *Fifth Symphony* is unforgettable, with the Philharmonia strings and brass making the most ravishing sounds. The account of the *London symphony* is more uneven but still rewarding, and *Greensleeves* is offered as an attractive encore at the end of the latter work. Both symphonies are heard without a break. The XDR transfers have lost a little of the sharpness of detail of the original LPs, but the sound remains very good.

(i) *A Pastoral symphony* (*No. 3*); (ii) *Tuba concerto in F min.*
(M) *** RCA Gold GL/*GK* 89691 [LSC 3281]. LSO, Previn, with (i) Harper; (ii) Fletcher.

One tends to think of Vaughan Williams's pastoral music as essentially synonymous with the English countryside, and it is something of a shock to discover that in fact the *Pastoral symphony* was sketched in Northern France while the composer was on active service in 1916, and the initial inspiration was a Corot-like landscape in the sunset. But the music remains English in essence, and its gentle rapture is not easily evoked.

Previn draws an outstandingly beautiful and refined performance from the LSO, the bare textures sounding austere but never thin, the few climaxes emerging at full force with purity undiminished. In the third movement the final coda – the only really fast music in the whole work – brings a magic tracery of pianissimo in this performance, lighter, faster and even clearer than in Boult's version. The digitally remastered recording adds to the beauty in its atmospheric distancing, not least in the trumpet cadenza of the second movement and the lovely melismas for the soprano soloist in the last movement. Cassette and disc are very closely matched. In the *Tuba concerto* John Fletcher's nimble and sensitive playing fully justifies the composer's choice of this apparently unwieldy instrument for a concertante piece. This is a first-class performance of an attractive and imaginatively conceived work.

(i) *A Pastoral symphony* (*No. 3*); *Symphony No. 6 in E min.*
(M) **(*) HMV ED 290480-1/*4*. New Philh. O, Boult, (i) with M. Price.

In the *Pastoral symphony* Boult is not entirely successful in controlling the tension of the short but elusive first movement, although it is beautifully played. The opening of the *Lento moderato*, however, is very fine, and its close is sustained with a perfect blend of restraint and intensity. After the jovial third movement, the orchestra is joined by Margaret Price, whose wordless contribution is blended into the texture most skilfully. There is also an element of disappointment in discussing Boult's re-recording of the powerful *Sixth Symphony*; perhaps one expected too much. The performance is without the tension of the earlier mono recording Boult made for Decca, with the composer present. The sound of that record cannot of course compare with that of the newer version, but Boult's comparative mellowness here means that the reading is not as searching as the score demands. The strange finale is beautifully played, with a finely sustained pianissimo from wind and strings alike, but the atmosphere, if not without a sense of mystery, is somehow too complacent. Both recordings have been remastered for this very generous reissue, and the value is obvious. The cassette matches the LP fairly closely. There is a slight loss of bite in No. 6, but the gain of a background free from intrusive noises more than compensates.

Symphony No. 4 in F min.; (i) *Concerto accademico for violin and orchestra in D min.*
(M) **(*) RCA Gold GL/*GK* 89692. LSO, Previn, (i) with Buswell.

Symphony No. 4; Norfolk rhapsody No. 1.
(M) *** HMV ED 290417-1/*4*. New Philh. O, Boult.

Boult's was the first stereo recording of the *Fourth*; although it would be possible to imagine a performance of greater fire and tenacity, few will find much to disappoint them in this persuasive account. Sir Adrian procures orchestral playing of the highest quality from the New Philharmonia, and the slow movement, one of the composer's finest inspirations, is particularly successful. The recording, too, is first class; in this remastered form it sounds admirably fresh and combines body and clarity with spaciousness. There is now an excellent matching cassette, losing only a little of the upper range of the LP. The *Norfolk rhapsody* (in spite of its number, there is no No. 2) is a lovely work and this, its first stereo recording, could not be bettered. It dates from the years immediately preceding the First World War, and despite its obvious indebtedness to the English folk-music tradition, it has great freshness and individuality and in its pensive moments a genuine delicacy of feeling. Boult evokes the most eloquent playing from the New Philharmonia; and the HMV engineers give us a well-focused, musically balanced and beautiful sound.

Previn secures a fine performance of the *F minor Symphony*; only the somewhat ponderous tempo he adopts for the first movement lets it down. But on the whole this is a powerful reading, and it is vividly recorded. A good alternative to Boult's version, though not superior to it. The *Concerto* makes an attractive bonus. The sound on cassette is virtually identical with the LP.

(i) *Symphonies Nos 4 in F min.; 6 in E min.*
(M) **(*) EMI EMX 41 2072-1/*4*. (i) RPO; Bournemouth SO, Berglund.

Berglund directs a rugged, purposeful account of the *Fourth Symphony*, one which refuses to relax even in the more lyrical passages. Berglund follows the composer himself in preferring an unusually fast speed in the first movement, while the second movement is superbly sustained at a very slow tempo. The playing of the RPO may not match that of the Previn and Boult versions in polish, but Berglund's extra bite is fair compensation, not to mention his more modern recording. The account of the *Sixth Symphony* is also direct and strong; the long, unrelieved pianissimo finale has a hushed concentration which rightly presents it as one of the composer's most cogent arguments. The Bournemouth strings lack a little in weight and refinement, but with such a generous coupling this is certainly recommendable. Both recordings are more recent than the Boult equivalents and the fullness of the sound is especially telling in the famous lyrical melody in the first movement of the *Sixth*. There is an excellent cassette.

Symphony No. 5; The Wasps: Overture.
❀ (M) *** RCA Gold GL/*GK* 89693. LSO, Previn.
(M) *** HMV ED 290418-1/*4*. LPO, Boult.

If anyone has ever doubted the dedication of Previn as an interpreter of Vaughan Williams, this glowing disc will provide the clearest rebuttal. In this most characteristic – and many would say greatest – of the Vaughan Williams symphonies, Previn refuses to be lured into pastoral byways. His tempi may – rather surprisingly – be consistently on the slow side, but the purity of tone he draws from the LSO, the precise shading of dynamic and phrasing, and the sustaining of tension through the longest, most hushed passages produce results that will persuade many not normally convinced of the greatness of this music. In the first movement Previn builds the great climaxes of the second subject with much warmth, but he reserves for the climax of the slow movement his culminating thrust of emotion, a moment of visionary sublimity, after which the gentle urgency of the *Passacaglia* finale and the stillness of the *Epilogue* seem a perfect happy conclusion. It is some tribute to Previn's intensity that he can draw out the diminuendi at the ends of movements with such refinement and no sense of exaggeration. This is an outstanding performance, superbly recorded. The cassette is of high quality, but the very wide dynamic range of the recording has meant a slightly lower transfer level than the rest of the series, so that definition is slightly less clear than on the disc.

Boult gives a loving performance of the *Fifth Symphony*, one which links it directly with the great opera *The Pilgrim's Progress*, from which (in its unfinished state) the composer drew much of the material. It is a gentler performance, easier, more flowing than Previn's, and some may prefer it for that reason, but the emotional involvement is a degree less intense, particularly in the slow movement. There is an excellent cassette equivalent, with the sound fresh and clear.

(i) *Symphony No. 6* (includes original and revised Scherzo); (ii) *The Lark ascending*; (iii) *Song of thanksgiving*.
(M) (***) HMV ED 290258-1/*4*. (i) LSO; (ii) Pougnet, LPO; (iii) Dolemore, Speaight (nar.), Luton Ch. Soc. and Girls' Ch., LPO; Boult.

This is a compilation of Sir Adrian Boult's early post-war recordings of Vaughan Williams's music, issued first on 78 r.p.m. discs, but sounding surprisingly well in excellent transfers. The recording of the *Symphony No. 6* was made very soon after the first performance in 1948, so soon that it was originally done with the unrevised version of the scherzo. As soon as the revision was written, Sir Adrian re-recorded that movement alone, and that is why this historic disc includes both, with the original version as a supplement. Jean Pougnet, leader of the

LPO at the time, with his exceptionally pure tone, is a natural soloist for *The Lark ascending*; the *Song of thanksgiving*, originally entitled *Thanksgiving for victory*, is an attractive period-piece designed for victory celebrations after the Second World War. It proved rather more than an occasional piece, but has never been recorded since.

Symphonies Nos 6; 8 in D min.
(M) **(*) RCA Gold GL/*GK* 89694 [AGL1/*AGK1* 5067]. LSO, Previn.

Previn's is a sensible and generous coupling. The *Sixth Symphony*, with its moments of darkness and brutality contrasted against the warmth of the second subject or the hushed intensity of the final other-worldly slow movement, is a work for which Previn has a natural affinity. In the first three movements his performance is superbly dramatic, clear-headed and direct with natural understanding. His account of the mystic final movement with its endless pianissimo is not, however, on the same level, for the playing is not quite hushed enough, and the tempo is a little too fast. In its closely wrought contrapuntal texture this is a movement which may seem difficult to interpret, but which should be allowed to flow along on its own intensity. Boult here achieves a more vital sense of mystery, even though his account is not ideal. Previn's account of the *Eighth* brings no such reservations, with finely pointed playing, the most precise control of dynamic shading, and a delightfully Stravinskian account of the bouncing scherzo for woodwind alone. Excellent recording, which has been opened up by the digital remastering and made to sound more expansive. Disc and tape are very closely matched.

Sinfonia antartica (*No. 7*).
*** HMV Dig. EL 270318-1/*4* [Ang. DS/*4DS* 38251]. Armstrong, LPO, Haitink.
(M) **(*) RCA Gold GL/*GK* 89695. Harper, Amb. S., LSO, Previn; Richardson (nar.)

With stunningly full and realistic recording, among the finest EMI has ever produced, Haitink directs a revelatory performance of what has long been thought of as merely a programmatic symphony. Based on material from RVW's film music for *Scott of the Antarctic*, the symphony is in fact a work which, as Haitink demonstrates, stands powerfully as an original inspiration in absolute terms. When it first appeared in 1953, its avoidance of conventional symphonic argument seemed a weakness; however, in a performance whose generally measured speeds and weighty manner bring out the inherent power of the writing, merely structural points seem irrelevant in the face of so strong a concept. Only in the second movement does the 'penguin' music seem heavier than it should be, but even that acquires new and positive qualities, thanks to Haitink. There is a first-class cassette equivalent.

In its relatively distant balance, as well as in Previn's interpretation, the RCA recording concentrates on atmosphere rather than drama in a performance that is sensitive and literal. Because of the recessed effect of the sound (which is virtually identical on disc and cassette), the portrayal of the ice fall (represented by the sudden entry of the organ) has a good deal less impact than on Boult's old Decca mono LP. Before each movement Sir Ralph Richardson speaks the superscriptions written by the composer on his score.

Symphonies Nos 8 in D min.; 9 in E min.
(M) *** HMV ED 290239-1/*4* [Pathé, id.]. LPO, Boult.

The coupling of Vaughan Williams's *Eighth* and *Ninth Symphonies* is generous and apt, both having been seriously underestimated. Boult's account of the *Eighth* is an essentially genial one. It may not be so sharply pointed as Previn's version, but some will prefer the extra warmth of the Boult interpretation with its rather more lyrical approach. The *Ninth* contains much noble and arresting invention, and Boult's performance is fully worthy of it. He gets most committed playing from the LPO, and the recording is splendidly firm in tone. There is an excellent XDR cassette; both transfers are very successful.

Symphony No. 9 in D min.; The England of Elizabeth: suite.
(M) *** RCA Gold GL/*GK* 89696. LSO, Previn.

The *Ninth*, Vaughan Williams's last symphony, stimulates Previn to show a freshness and sense of poetry which prove particularly thought-provoking and rewarding. He secures smooth contours in the first movement and, as a result of refined string playing, he produces attractively transparent textures. The RCA recording is highly successful, and the string tone is expansive, well balanced in relation to the rest of the orchestra and free from the slight hint of hardness that sometimes disturbs this cycle. Listening to this reading reinforces the view that the critics of the day were unfairly harsh to this fine score. On the whole, this version is finer than Boult's HMV account. The *England of Elizabeth suite* is a film score of no great musical interest but is undoubtedly pleasant to listen to; both performance and recording are first class. The LP and cassette sound much the same, but the disc has just a fraction better definition in the upper range.

The Wasps: Overture. Serenade to music (orchestral version).
€ *** Chan. **CHAN 8330**; ABRD/*ABTD* 1106 [id.]. LPO, Handley – DELIUS: *Collection.**** €

Exceptionally well recorded and vividly impressive on CD, Handley's readings of the *Wasps overture* and the *Serenade to music* in its orchestral version are most sympathetically done. The overture is here more urgent than in Handley's more recent version for Eminence (as part of the complete suite), and though the *Serenade* inevitably lacks a dimension without voices, this is most persuasive, beautifully played by the LPO. As usual with Chandos, the chrome-tape transfer is exceptionally sophisticated, the sound beautifully refined, yet firm.

VOCAL MUSIC

Blessed Son of God; 2 Elizabethan part songs; (i) Fantasia on Christmas carols; 3 Shakespeare songs; The turtle dove.

(M) *** Argo 414 646-1/*4* [id.]. King's College, Cambridge, Ch., Willcocks; (i) with Hervey Alan, LSO – HOWELLS: *Collegium Regale*.***

A delightful compilation of vocal music from King's recordings, mainly from the 1960s. The *Three Shakespeare songs* (*Full fathom five, The cloud capp'd towers* and *Over hill, over dale*) show the composer at his most imaginative and are strikingly atmospheric here, while the closing *Blessed Son of God* has great expressive beauty yet a telling simplicity. The *Fantasia on Christmas carols* is comparatively short. It was written for performance in 1912 in Hereford Cathedral, so again the acoustic at King's is well chosen. The orchestral recording sounds a little dated in this piece, but otherwise the sound quality throughout is first class. The Howells couplings are no less desirable. The high-level cassette is generally impressive, though there are moments when saturation point is approached and the choral focus slips.

(i) *Flos campi;* (ii) *5 Mystical songs;* (iii) *O clap your hands;* (iv) *5 Tudor portraits.*

(B) *** HMV *TCC2-POR 54294*. (i) Aronowitz, Jacques O; (ii) Shirley-Quirk; (i; iii) King's College Ch.; (iii) ECO; (iv) Bainbridge, Carol Case, Bach Ch., New Philh. O, Willcocks.

In our last edition, we dismissed this imaginative issue in EMI's 'Portrait of the Artist' tape series for poor technology. We are glad to report that the XDR reissue has been remastered and now sounds well. The performances are admirable, with the *Five Tudor portraits* particularly attractive, very well performed and recorded, and not otherwise available.

(i) *On Wenlock Edge*; (ii) *Songs of travel* (song-cycles).

*** HMV EL 270059-1/*4* [Ang. DS/*4DS* 38089]. (i) Robert Tear; (ii) Thomas Allen, CBSO, Rattle.

Orchestral arrangements of two song-cycles originally written for lighter accompaniment make an attractive and apt coupling. The more revelatory is the collection of *Songs of travel*, to words by Robert Louis Stevenson, originally written with piano accompaniment and here discreetly orchestrated. The orchestral version brings home the aptness of treating the nine songs as a cycle, particularly when the soloist is as characterful and understanding a singer as Thomas Allen. Only in 1960 was the epilogue song finally published (after the composer's death), drawing together the two sets of four songs that had previously been published separately. The Housman settings in the other cycle are far better known, and Robert Tear – who earlier recorded this same orchestral version with Vernon Handley and the Birmingham orchestra – again proves a deeply perceptive soloist, with his sense of atmosphere, feeling for detailed word-meaning and flawless breath control. Warm, understanding conducting and playing, and excellent sound.

Verdi, Giuseppe (1813–1901)

Overtures and Preludes (complete): *Aïda* (Prelude)*; Alzira; Aroldo* (Overtures)*; Attila; Un Ballo in maschera* (Preludes)*; La Battaglia di Legnano; Il Corsaro* (Sinfonias)*; Ernani* (Prelude)*; La Forza del destino; Un Giorno di regno; Giovanna d'Arco* (Sinfonias)*; Luisa Miller* (Overture)*; Macbeth; I Masnadieri* (Preludes)*; Nabucco* (Overture)*; Oberto, Conte di San Bonifacio* (Sinfonia)*; Rigoletto; La Traviata* (Preludes)*; I vespri siciliani* (Sinfonia).
(M) *** DG 413 544-1/*4* (2). BPO, Karajan.

Make no mistake, this playing is in a class of its own and has an electricity, refinement and authority that sweep all before it. Some of the overtures are little known (*Aroldo*, *Alzira* and *La Battaglia di Legnano*), and all are given with tremendous panache and virtuosity. These are performances of real spirit and are vividly recorded, even if the climaxes could expand more. There is an equivalent cassette issue in one of DG's 'flap-packs', offering sophisticated chrome-tape transfers which match the discs closely.

Overtures: *Aïda* (reconstructed and arr. Spada)*; Aroldo; La Forza del destino; Luisa Miller; Nabucco; I Vespri siciliani.*
*** RCA Dig. **RCD 31378**; RL/*RK* 31378. LSO, Abbado.

Overtures and Preludes: *Aïda; Attila; Un Ballo in maschera; La Forza del destino; Luisa Miller; Nabucco; La Traviata: Preludes, Acts I and III; I vespri siciliani.*
*** DG **411 469-2**; 411 469-1/*4* [id.]. VPO, Sinopoli.

Overtures: *Aroldo; La Forza del destino; Giovanna d'Arco; Luisa Miller; Nabucco; Oberto, Conte di San Bonifacio; I vespri siciliani.*
*** Decca Dig. **410 141-2**; SXDL/*KSXDC* 7595 [Lon. LDR/5-71095]. Nat. PO, Chailly.

Sinopoli's preference for sharp contrasts and precise rhythms makes for dramatic accounts of these Verdi overtures and preludes, which (like other rivals) include the four finest: *Forza*, *Vespri siciliani*, *Luisa Miller* and *Nabucco*. *Forza*, the finest of all, brings a less fierce account than one would have expected from this conductor, with delicate textures, rhythms and phrasing, but *Luisa Miller* is very characteristic, finely chiselled and exciting in its contrasts, with the Vienna cellos in particular adding lustre. The four items chosen for makeweight represent the most popular choice; those seeking a single-disc collection will note that only Sinopoli includes the famous *La Traviata Preludes*. The refined recording is matched by warm recorded sound, with the sweetness of string timbre the more striking on CD.

In his collection, Chailly has the advantage of brilliant Decca recording and a more generous list of overtures than Abbado, with the four most obviously desirable – *Nabucco*, *I vespri siciliani*, *Luisa Miller* and *Forza* – plus three rarities, including the overture to his very first opera, *Oberto*, and the most substantial of the early ones, *Aroldo*. Crisp and incisive, Chailly draws vigorous and polished playing from the National Philharmonic. The chrome cassette is extremely lively and wide-ranging; for some ears, the upper strings may need to be tamed a little. The admirable compact disc clarifies the texture without loss of bloom.

Abbado directs strong and brilliant performances of Verdi's most substantial overtures. The recording is brilliant and full, with resonant brass and a sparkling upper range on disc and cassette alike. The novelty is the introduction which Verdi originally wrote for the first Italian performance of *Aïda*, then subsequently rejected. It is a considerably extended piece; in Spada's reconstruction one can see why the composer wanted not to anticipate in instrumental terms effects far more telling in the full operatic setting; heard independently, however, it is most entertaining and deftly scored. The compact disc with its silent background brings extra magnetism to the pianissimos – especially in the opening of *Aïda*, but also strikingly in *I vespri siciliani*. However, the brightness of the upper range does produce a touch of shrillness on fortissimos.

The Lady and the Fool (ballet, arr. Mackerras): suite.
(B) *** CfP CFP 41 4490-1/*4*. LPO, Mackerras – SULLIVAN: *Pineapple Poll*.***

Mackerras's score for John Cranko's ballet *The Lady and the Fool* (1954) uses music from the lesser-known Verdi operas in much the same way as he drew upon Sullivan for *Pineapple Poll*. Here too the scoring is as colourful as it is witty, although the selection does not seem quite so inspired as the earlier work. It is very entertaining, but some ears may find there is rather a lot of boisterous music. It is all played with great flair and evident orchestral enjoyment here. The recording too is both vivid and atmospheric with fine bloom and warmth. There is an excellent cassette which matches the LP closely. The suite gives a very generous selection from the complete ballet.

String quartet in E min.
** Tel. Dig. **ZK8 43105**; AZ6/*CY4* 43105 [id.]. Vermeer Qt – DVOŘÁK: *Quartet No. 10*.*(*)

The Vermeer Quartet on Telefunken are coupled with the Dvořák *Quartet*, Op. 51, and give a well-groomed and affectionate account of Verdi's charming *E minor Quartet*. As was the case with the coupling, the acoustic is small and does not expand, and the CD rather enhances its dryness. However, the Vermeer have a splendid range of dynamics and colour, and their performance is persuasive.

Still recommended: On CRD, the Alberni Quartet give a strongly compelling performance of Verdi's *Quartet*, coupled with Puccini and Donizetti. The recording is first class on tape and disc alike (CRD 1066/*CRDC 4066*).

Requiem Mass.
*** Decca **411 944-2**; SET 374-5/*K 85 K 22* [Lon. OSA/*5*- 1275]. Sutherland, Horne, Pavarotti, Talvela, V. State Op. Ch., VPO, Solti.

(*) DG Dig. **415 091-2; 415 091-1/*4* [id.]. Tomowa-Sintow, Baltsa, Carreras, Van Dam, V. State Op. Concert Assoc. Ch., Sofia Nat. Op. Ch., VPO, Karajan.

*(*) DG **415 976-2**; 2707 120/*3370 032* (2) [id.]. Ricciarelli, Verrett, Domingo, Ghiaurov, La Scala, Milan, Ch. and O, Abbado.

Solti's Decca performance is not really a direct rival to any other for, with the wholehearted co-operation of the Decca engineers, he has played up the dramatic side of the work at the expense of the spiritual. There is little or nothing reflective about this account, and those who criticize the work for being too operatic will find plenty of ammunition here. The team of soloists is a very strong one, though the matching of voices is not always ideal. It is a pity that the chorus is not nearly so incisive as the Philharmonia on the HMV set – a performance which conveys far more of the work's profundity than this. But if you want an extrovert performance, the firmness of focus and precise placing of forces in the Decca engineering of 1967 make for exceptionally vivid results on CD. The detail is much clearer than on most modern versions, and signs of age are minimal. The cassettes are acceptable, but this was an early transfer and the *Dies irae* is not absolutely free from congestion; elsewhere, too, the choral peaks are not as open as on disc.

Recorded in conjunction with live performances in Vienna, Karajan's digital recording of 1984 certainly conveys a sense of occasion. With speeds slower than usual, the weight of the music is powerfully conveyed and much of its spiritual intensity. Though Karajan's smooth style has altered relatively little since he recorded this work before for DG, the overall impression is notably fresher – and would be even more so, were the recording more sharply focused and more consistent. Balances change between sections, though the soloists are more backwardly placed than is common, merging into the generally rich texture. The lack of brilliance in the recording also diminishes the element of Italian fire, so that the *Dies irae* is less sharply dramatic than in the finest versions. Soloists are good, naturally and warmly expressive. Though Tomowa-Sintow's un-Italian soprano timbre sometimes brings a hint of flutter, she sings most beautifully in the final rapt account of *Libera me*. The CDs bring sharper definition and an improvement in presence and range, but the basic recording faults remain. The chrome cassettes match the LPs closely. Karajan's earlier (1973) set, with Freni, Ludwig, Cossutta, Ghiaurov and the Vienna Singverein has also been reissued at mid-price with matching chrome tapes; but the conductor's smoothness within the mellow Berlin acoustic puts beauty of texture before drama (DG 413 215-1/*4*).

Abbado's version was recorded at La Scala, Milan, when an opera project was abandoned at the last moment. So far from making the result operatic – as, for example, Muti's highly charged version is – it seems to have sapped tensions. It is a pity that so intense a Verdian did not have a more committed team of performers. The choral entry on *Te decet hymnus* gives an early indication of the slackness and lack of bite, and though the *Dies irae* is exactly in place (unlike

Muti's hectic account) there is no excitement whatever, with the chorus sounding too small. The soloists too are often below their best, but, balances apart, the recording is very good. The CD transfer undoubtedly brings enhancement but the focus is not especially sharp at pianissimo level, although there is an attractive ambient bloom. There are good cassettes, although the tape transfer brings some recession of image at the lowest dynamic levels.

Still recommended: With spectacular analogue sound, the 1979 Muti version remains a general primary recommendation. Unashamedly this is from first to last an operatic performance, with a passionately committed quartet of soloists (Scotto, Baltsa, Luchetti and Nesterenko), and the Ambrosian Chorus given fine impact by the recording on both LP and tape (HMV SLS/*TC-SLS* 5185 [Ang. SZ/*4Z2S* 3858]). By the side of this, Giulini's 1964 Philharmonia recording is technically rather less satisfactory (and cannot be recommended in its cassette format). Yet Giulini's combination of refinement and elemental strength remains totally memorable. The array of soloists could hardly be bettered, with Schwarzkopf and Ludwig radiant and Gedda at his most reliable; while Ghiaurov with his really dark bass actually manages to sing the almost impossible *Mors stupebit* in tune without a suspicion of wobble (HMV SLS 909 [Ang. SBL 3649]). It is scheduled for CD issue, coupled with the *Four Sacred pieces*, on HMV **CDS 747257-8** (2).

4 Sacred pieces (*Ave Maria; Stabat Mater; Laudi alla Vergine; Te Deum*).
*** HMV Dig. **CDC 747066-2** [id.]; ASD/*TC-ASD* 143572-1/*4* [Ang. DS/*4DS* 3800]. Augér, Stockholm Chamber Ch., BPO, Muti.

4 Sacred pieces: Te Deum (only).
** Telarc Dig. **CD 80109**; DG 10109 [id.]. Morehouse-Spelman Ch., Atlanta Ch. and SO, Shaw – BERLIOZ: *Requiem*; BOITO: *Mefistofele: Prologue*.**

Verdi's *Four Sacred pieces* form his very last work – or, to be precise, group of works. There are echoes of the great *Requiem*, and many of the ideas have a genuine Verdian originality, but in general they mark a falling-off after the supreme achievement of the last two operas after Shakespeare, *Otello* and *Falstaff*.

Muti directs a characteristically dramatic yet thoughtful reading of these late pieces, keenly attentive to Verdi's markings. The two big outward-going pieces, the *Te Deum* and *Stabat Mater*, suit him perfectly, and the incisiveness of the professional Swedish choir, freshly yet atmospherically recorded, is an asset. In the first and third pieces the performances are hushed and devotional, without hint of sentimentality. The digital recording is full and bright, and the extra clarity of CD brings out the range more impressively, with the finely balanced choral singing made all the fresher and more beautiful.

Shaw conducts a finely disciplined reading of the Verdi *Te Deum* as the second of two generous fill-ups on the CD version of his recording of the Berlioz *Requiem*. As in the rest of the set, however, tension and mystery are lacking, despite firmly focused recording.

OPERA

Aïda (complete).

(M) *** Decca 414 087-1/*4* (3/*2*). Tebaldi, Bergonzi, Simionato, MacNeil, Van Mill, Corena, V. Singverein, VPO, Karajan.

(*) DG Dig. **410 092-2; 2741/*3382* 014 (3) [id.]. Ricciarelli, Domingo, Obraztsova, Nucci, Raimondi, Ghiaurov, Ch. and O of La Scala, Milan, Abbado.

The spectacular early Decca set with Karajan and the Vienna Philharmonic (dating from 1959) long stood unrivalled as a stereo version of this most stereophonic of operas. Of course Karajan is helped by having a Viennese orchestra, rather than an Italian one determined to do things in the 'traditional' manner. The chorus too is a very different thing from a normal Italian opera-house chorus, and the inner beauty of Verdi's choral writing at last manages to come out. Among the soloists, Bergonzi in particular emerges here as a model among tenors, with a rare feeling for the shaping of phrases and attention to detail. Cornell MacNeil too is splendid. Tebaldi's interpretation of the part of Aïda is well known and much loved. Her creamy tone-colour rides beautifully over the phrases, and she too acquires a new depth of imagination. Vocally there are flaws too, notably at the end of *O patria mia*, where Tebaldi finds the cruelly exposed top notes too taxing. Among the other soloists, Arnold Van Mill and Fernando Corena are both superb, and Simionato provides one of the very finest portrayals of Amneris we have ever had in a complete *Aïda*. The recording has long been famous for its technical bravura and flair. The control of atmosphere is remarkable, changing as the scene changes, and some of the offstage effects are strikingly effective in their microscopic clarity at a distance. Helped by Karajan, the recording team have managed, at the other end of the dynamic scale, to bring an altogether new clarity to the big ensembles, never achieved at the expense of tonal opulence. But the very wide dynamic range does offer problems for domestic listening. Even so, this is a comparatively small quibble and the set remains one of John Culshaw's outstanding achievements. At mid-price on three discs or a pair of tapes (with one Act complete on each side), it is a bargain.

Fresh and intelligent, unexaggerated in its pacing, Abbado's version from La Scala lacks a little in excitement. It is stronger on the personal drama than on the ceremonial. Domingo gives a superb performance as Radames, not least in the Nile scene, and the two bass roles are cast from strength in Raimondi and Ghiaurov. Leo Nucci makes a dramatic Amonasro, not always pure of line, while Elena Obraztsova produces too much curdled tone as Amneris, dramatic as she is. In many ways Ricciarelli is an appealing Aïda, but the voice grows impure above the stave, and floating legatos are marred. The digital recording – cleaner on compact disc than in the other formats – fails to expand for the ceremonial, and voices are highlighted, but it is acceptably fresh. The chrome tapes are satisfactory, but the sound is less open than the Karajan HMV set, and the big Act II choral scene sounds studio-bound and bass-heavy. The layout is improved on compact disc, but the increased clarity serves only to emphasize the confined acoustic.

Still recommended: Karajan's 1980 HMV version of *Aïda* is a performance that carries splendour and pageantry to the point of exaltation. With Freni singing the title role with tender beauty, Carreras a fresh and sensitive Radames, Raimondi a darkly intense Ramphis, Van Dam a cleanly focused King and Baltsa as Amneris crowning the whole performance, this superb account, conceived in conjunction with a Salzburg Festival production, is equally thrilling, sonically, on disc or cassette, with superbly believable perspectives. When it arrives on CD, it will surely sweep the board (HMV EX 290808-3/*5* [Ang. SZCX/*4Z3X* 3888]).

Aïda: highlights.
(*) DG Dig. **415 286-2; 2532/*3302* 092 [id.] (from above set, cond. Abbado).

DG have gathered together a generous selection of highlights from Abbado's set, lasting well over an hour, but the reservations remain as with the complete recording.

Attila (complete).
*** Ph. **412 875-2**; 6700 056 (2) [id.]. Raimondi, Deutekom, Bergonzi, Milnes, Amb. S., Finchley Children's Music Group, RPO, Gardelli.

It is easy to criticize the music Verdi wrote during his 'years in the galleys', but a youthfully urgent work like this makes you marvel not at its musical unevenness but at the way Verdi consistently entertains you. The dramatic anticipations of *Macbeth*, with Attila himself far more than a simple villain, the musical anticipations of *Rigoletto*, the compression which on record if not on the stage becomes a positive merit – all these qualities, helped by a fine performance under Gardelli, make this an intensely enjoyable set. Deutekom, not the most sweet-toned of sopranos, has never sung better on record, and the rest of the cast is outstandingly good. The 1973 recording is well balanced and atmospheric, but the remastering for CD has been able to make only a marginal improvement in definition, with the chorus less sharply focused than one would expect on a modern digital set. However, the absence of appreciable background noise and the access provided by the generous cueing are obvious advantages of the new format.

Un Ballo in maschera (complete).
*** Decca Dig. **410 210-2**; 410 210-1/*4* [id.]. Margaret Price, Pavarotti, Bruson, Ludwig, Battle, L. Op. Ch., Royal College of Music Junior Dept Ch., Nat. PO, Solti.
*** DG **415 685-2** (2); 2740 251/*3378 111* (3) [id.]. Ricciarelli, Domingo, Bruson, Obraztsova, Gruberova, Raimondi, La Scala, Milan, Ch. and O, Abbado.
(M) *** HMV EX 290710-3/*5* (2). Arroyo, Grist, Cossotto, Domingo, Cappucilli, ROHCG Ch., New Philh. O, Muti.

Shining out from the cast of Solti's set of *Ballo* is the gloriously sung Amelia of Margaret Price in one of her richest and most commanding performances on record, ravishingly beautiful, flawlessly controlled and full of unforced emotion. The role of Riccardo, pushy and truculent, is well suited to the extrovert Pavarotti, who swaggers through the part, characteristically clear of diction, challenged periodically by Price to produce some of his subtlest tone-colours. Bruson makes a noble Renato, Christa Ludwig an unexpected but intense and perceptive Ulrica, while Kathleen Battle is an Oscar whose coloratura is not just brilliant but sweet too. Solti is far more relaxed than he often is on record, presenting a warm and understanding view of the score. The recording is extremely vivid within a reverberant acoustic, with orchestra as well as singers given added presence on the pair of CDs against three LPs and cassettes, the latter vibrantly transferred to match the LPs closely, with the layout offering each of the three Acts on a single tape.

Abbado's powerful reading, admirably paced and with a splendid feeling for the sparkle of the comedy, remains highly recommendable. The cast is very strong, with Ricciarelli at her very finest and Domingo sweeter of tone and more deft of characterization than on the Muti set of five years earlier. Bruson as the wronged husband Renato (a role he again takes for Solti) sings magnificently, and only Obraztsova as Ulrica and Gruberova as Oscar are less consistently convincing. The analogue recording clearly separates the voices and instruments in different acoustics, which is distracting only initially and after that brings the drama closer. Certainly on the CD transfer the overall effect is marvellously vivid, with solo voices firmly placed and the chorus realistically full-bodied and clear. Internal access is excellent, with 26 cues provided over the two discs.

Muti's 1975 set makes an excellent mid-priced alternative, now digitally remastered on to four LP or cassette sides. On HMV the quintet of principals is also unusually strong, but it is the conductor who takes first honours in a warmly dramatic reading. His rhythmic resilience and consideration for the singers go with keen concentration, holding each Act together in a way he did not achieve in his earlier recording for HMV of *Aïda*. Arroyo, rich of voice, is not always imaginative in her big solos, and Domingo rarely produces a half-tone, though the recording balance may be partly to blame. The sound is opulent. The tape transfer is of good quality but has a more restricted upper range, though it is well balanced and clear, and retains the bloom of the LPs.

Un Ballo in maschera: highlights.
(M) **(*) Ph. Seq. 412 020-1/*4* [id.]. Caballé, Payne, Carreras, Wixell, Lloyd, ROHCG Ch. and O, Sir Colin Davis.

Davis's 1979 set, based on the Covent Garden production, was relatively lightweight, with Caballé and Carreras matching Davis's approach. This makes a good sampler, with an excellent cassette equivalent.

Don Carlos (complete).
(*) DG Dig. **415 316-2; 415 316-1/*4* (4) [id.]. Ricciarelli, Domingo, Valentini-Terrani, Nucci, Raimondi, Ghiaurov, La Scala, Milan, Ch. and O, Abbado.

For the dedicated Verdian, Abbado's set brings new authenticity and new revelation. This is the first recording to use the language which Verdi originally set, French; in addition to the full five-Act text in its composite 1886 form including the Fontainebleau scene (recorded twice before), there are half a dozen appendices from the original 1867 score, later cut or recomposed. These include a substantial prelude and introduction to Act I, an introduction and chorus to Act III, the Queen's ballet from that same Act (15 minutes long), a duet for the Queen and Eboli in Act IV (even longer), and extra material for the finales of Acts IV and V. By rights, this should be the definitive recording of the opera, for, as has often been promised, the French text brings an apt darkening of tone compared with the open sounds of Italian, and Abbado is a masterly interpreter of Verdi. The first disappointment lies in the variable quality of the sound, with odd balances, so that although the Fontainebleau opening, with its echoing horns, is arrestingly atmospheric, the Auto da fé scene lacks bite, brilliance and clarity. In addition, the very weight of the project, the extra stress on soloists and chorus working on music they know in a language they do not, has tended to prevent the drama from taking flight. Large-scale flair and urgency are missing; once that is said, however, the cast of singers is a strong one (even if they are variable in their French), with Placido Domingo outstanding. Domingo easily outshines his earlier recording with Giulini (in Italian), while Katia Ricciarelli as the Queen gives a tenderly moving performance, if not quite commanding enough in the Act V aria. Ruggero Raimondi is a finely focused Philip II, nicely contrasted with Nicolai Ghiaurov as the Grand Inquisitor in the other black-toned bass role. Lucia Valentini-Terrani as Eboli is warm-toned if not very characterful, and Leo Nucci makes a noble Posa. Whatever the reservations, this most costly of all opera recordings to date remains a fine historic document. The three chrome cassettes represent the highest state of the art, vividly transferred and having no problems with the varying perspectives.

Still recommended: Karajan, in his HMV recording based on a Salzburg Festival production, opts firmly for the later four-Act version of the opera, merely opening out the cuts he adopted on stage. The results could hardly be more powerfully dramatic, one of his most involving opera performances, comparable with his vivid HMV *Aïda*. Both Carreras and Freni are most moving, Baltsa is a superlative Eboli and Cappuccilli an affecting Rodrigo. Raimondi and Ghiaurov as the Grand Inquisitor and Philip II (exchanging the roles they occupy in the Abbado set) here provide the most powerful confrontation. There is no doubt that Karajan's is the most effective of the complete recordings; it is vivid as sound, too, on both discs and cassettes (HMV SLS/*TC-SLS* 5154 [Ang. SZDX/*4ZX4* 3875]).

Ernani (complete).

(*) HMV Dig. **CDS 747083-2 [id.]; SLS/*TC-SLS* 143584-3/*9* (3/*2*) [Ang. DSCX/*4X3X* 3942]. Domingo, Freni, Bruson, Ghiaurov, Ch. and O of La Scala, Milan, Muti.

** Hung. Dig. **HCD 12259/61**; SLPD 12259/61 [id.]. Lamberti, Sass, Kovats, Miller, Takacs, Hungarian State Op. Ch. and O, Gardelli.

Ernani, the fifth of Verdi's operas, was the first to achieve international success.

At this stage of his career Verdi was still allowing himself the occasional imitation of Rossini in a crescendo, or of Bellini in parallel thirds and sixths; but the control of tension is already masterly, the ensembles even more than the arias giving the authentic Verdian flavour. The great merit of Muti's set, recorded live at a series of performances at La Scala, is that the ensembles have an electricity rarely achieved in the studio. The results may not always be so precise and stage noises are often obtrusive with a background rustle of stage movement rarely absent for long, but the result is vivid and atmospheric. The singing, generally strong and characterful, is yet flawed. The strain of the role of Elvira for Mirella Freni is plain from the big opening aria, *Ernani involami*, onwards. Even in that aria there are cautious moments. Bruson is a superb Carlo, Ghiaurov a characterful Silva, but his voice now betrays signs of wear. Ernani himself, Placido Domingo, gives a commandingly heroic performance, but under pressure there are hints of tight tone such as he nowadays rarely produces in the studio. The recording inevitably has odd balances which will disturb some more than others. The CD version gives greater immediacy and presence, but also brings out the inevitable flaws of live recording the more clearly. The iron-oxide tapes are of quite good quality, but less wide-ranging at the top than the discs, though this is more noticeable in the final two Acts than at the beginning of the opera. The layout on four sides (against six on LP) is generally preferable.

Gardelli's conducting is most sympathetic and idiomatic in the Hungarian version, and like Muti's it is strong on ensembles. Sylvia Sass is a sharply characterful Elvira, Callas-like in places, and Lamberti a bold Ernani, but their vocal flaws prevent this from being a first choice. Capable rather than inspired or idiomatic singing from the rest. The digital recording is bright and well balanced, although the CD transfer brings out the fact that the recording acoustics are very resonant.

Ernani: highlights.
** Hung. Dig. **HCD 12609** [id.] (from above recording, cond. Gardelli).

A useful selection of items from the complete Hungaroton set, flawed but most sympathetically conducted.

Falstaff (complete).
*** DG Dig. **410 503-2** (2); 2741/*3382* 020 (3) [id.]. Bruson, Ricciarelli, Hendricks, Egerton, Valentini-Terrani, Boozer, Los Angeles Master Ch., LAPO, Giulini.
(*) Ph. Dig. **412 263-2 (2); 6769/*7654* 060 (3). Taddei, Kabaivanska, Perry, Panerai, Ludwig, Araiza, V. State Op. Ch., VPO, Karajan.
(M) **(*) Decca 417 168-1/*4* (2). Sir Geraint Evans, Ligabue, Freni, Kraus, Elias, Simionato, RCA Italiana Op. Ch. and O, Solti.

Recorded at a series of live performances in the Chandler Pavilion in Los Angeles, Giulini's reading combines the tensions and atmosphere of live performance with a precision normally achieved only in the studio. This was Giulini's first essay in live opera-conducting in fourteen years, and he treated the piece with a care for musical values which at times undermined the knockabout comic element. On record that is all to the good, for the clarity and beauty of the playing are superbly caught by the DG engineers, and though the parallel with Toscanini is an obvious one – also recorded at a live performance – Giulini is far more relaxed. Here the CD emphasizes the success of the engineers in the matter of balance, besides adding to the refinement of detail and the tangibility of the overall sound-picture. The voices are given fine bloom but in a contrasted stage acoustic. Bruson, hardly a comic actor, is impressive on record for his fine incisive singing, giving tragic implications to the monologue at the start of Act III after Falstaff's dunking. The Ford of Leo Nucci, impressive in the theatre, is thinly caught, where the heavyweight quality of Ricciarelli as Alice comes over well, though in places one would wish for a purer sound. Barbara Hendricks is a charmer as Nanetta, but she hardly sounds fairy-like in her Act III aria. The full women's ensemble, though precise, is not always quite steady in tone, though the conviction of the whole performance puts it among the most desirable of modern readings.

Karajan's second recording of Verdi's last opera, made over twenty years after his classic Philharmonia set, has lower standards of precision, yet conveys a relaxed and genial atmosphere. With the exception of Kabaivanska whose voice is not steady enough for the role of Alice, it is a good cast, with Ludwig fascinating as Mistress Quickly. Most amazing of all is Taddei's performance as Falstaff himself, full and characterful and vocally astonishing from a man in his sixties. The recording is not so beautifully balanced as the Philharmonia set, but the digital sound is faithful and wide-ranging, though on LP the level of cut is on the low side. The CD version, however, captures the bloom of the original, reverberant recording so vividly, one worries less about any oddities of balance, while textures are to a degree clarified. There are a pair of CDs against three LPs and cassettes. The chrome tapes are of Philips's highest quality: the sound has striking range, depth and atmosphere.

The combination of Solti and Sir Geraint Evans is irresistible. Their 1964 set, originally issued by RCA, comes up as sparkling as ever in this Decca reissue at a very modest price. There is an energy, a sense of fun, a sparkle that outshines most rival versions, outstanding as they may be. Sir Geraint has never sounded better on record, and the rest of the cast admirably live up to his example. Solti drives hard, and almost any comparison with the ancient Toscanini set will show his shortcomings, but it is still an exciting and well-pointed performance, the rest of the cast well contrasted.

Still recommended: In response to his newer digital recording on Philips, EMI reissued Karajan's 1957 HMV set, refreshing the sound which loses nothing from its remastering on to two instead of three LPs (and cassettes). Led by Gobbi's sharp characterization of Falstaff, the rest of the cast is a delight, with Schwarzkopf a tinglingly dominating Mistress Ford, Anna Moffo sweet as Nanetta, and Rolando Panerai a formidable Ford. The whole production is a vintage example of the work of Walter Legge (HMV SLS/*TC-SLS* 5211 [Ang. SBL/*4X2X* 3552]). In the USA, Bernstein's Toscanini-inspired set with Fischer-Dieskau as Falstaff, Panerai singing superbly as Ford, Regina Resnik as Mistress

Quickly, Ilva Liabue, Graziella Sciutti and Juan Oncina is available (expensively) as an imported CBS/Sony Japanese CD set (**64DC 312/3**). Bernstein always conveys a sense of fun, while in relaxed passages he allows a full rotundity of phrasing.

I Lombardi (complete).

(*) Hung. Dig. **HCD 12498/500; SLPD 12498/500 [id.]. Kovats, Sass, Lamberti, Misura, Gregor, Jasz, Janosi, Hungarian R. & TV Ch., Hungarian State Opera O, Gardelli.

The Hungaroton set, like the earlier Philips set conducted by Lamberto Gardelli with warmth and finesse, makes a very acceptable alternative to that fine version, bringing the benefit of modern digital recording and a CD alternative. One of the principal glories of the Budapest performance is the brilliant and committed singing of the chorus, turning the Crusaders Hymn of Act II into a sort of Verdian *Csardas*. The big ensembles have a warmth and thrust to suggest stage experience, and though the line-up of principals is not quite as strong as on the rival set (Philips 6703 032), there is no serious weakness; Sylvia Sass, singing with a new evenness and purity, is certainly preferable to the fluttery Deutekom on Philips. Giorgio Lamberti as the hero is no match for Placido Domingo, heroic of tone but unsubtle; similarly, Kolos Kovats as the Hermit has a glorious natural voice, a really firm bass, but musically is no rival to Raimondi on the earlier set. The sound is excellent, clean and well balanced, but not a substantial improvement on the excellent 1971 Philips recording.

Macbeth (complete).

*** Ph. Dig. **412 133-2**; 412 133-1/*4* (3) [id.]. Zampieri, Bruson, Shicoff, Lloyd, German Op. Berlin Ch. and O, Sinopoli.

*** DG **415 688-2**; 2709 062/*3371 022* (3) [id.]. Cappuccilli, Verrett, Ghiaurov, Domingo, Ch. and O of La Scala, Milan, Abbado.

A vital element in Sinopoli's conducting of Verdi – maybe the Toscanini inheritance – is an electrifying fierceness of expression. Here it has one sitting up in surprise over the choruses for witches and murderers, but equally relishing the absence of apology. Even more than his finest rivals, Sinopoli presents this opera as a searing Shakespearean inspiration, scarcely more uneven than much of the work of the Bard himself. In the Banqueting scene, for example, he creates extra dramatic intensity by his concern for detail and by his preference for extreme dynamics, as in the vital stage-whispered phrases from Lady Macbeth to her husband, marked *sotto voce*, which heighten the sense of horror and disintegration over the appearance of the ghost. Detailed word-meaning is a key factor in this, and Renato Bruson and Mara Zampieri respond vividly. Zampieri's voice may be biting rather than beautiful, occasionally threatening to come off the rails but, with musical precision as an asset, she matches exactly Verdi's request for the voice of a she-devil. Neil Shicoff as Macduff and Robert Lloyd as Banquo make up the excellent quartet of principals, while the high voltage of the whole performance clearly reflects Sinopoli's experience with the same chorus and orchestra at the Deutsche Oper in Berlin. Some of the unusually slow speeds for the big ensembles make the result all the more tellingly ominous. CD adds vividly to the realism of a recording that is well balanced and sharply focused but atmospheric. The cassettes too are of outstanding quality, in range and presence; this is one of the best opera sets to come from Philips in this format. However, better planning of the layout could have prevented the awkward side-break at the end of side two.

In Abbado's scintillating performance the diamond precision of ensemble also has one thinking of Toscanini. The conventional rum-ti-tum of witches' and murderers' choruses is transformed, becomes tense and electrifying, helped by the immediacy of sound. At times Abbado's tempi are unconventional, but with slow speeds he springs the rhythm so infectiously that the results are the more compelling. Based on the Giorgio Strehler production at La Scala, the whole performance gains from superb teamwork, for each of the principals is far more meticulous than is common about observing Verdi's detailed markings, above all those for *pianissimo* and *sotto voce*. Verrett, hardly powerful above the stave, yet makes a virtue out of necessity in floating glorious half-tones, and with so firm and characterful a voice she makes a highly individual, not at all conventional Lady Macbeth. As for Cappuccilli, he has never sung with such fine range of tone and imagination on record as here, and José Carreras makes a real, sensitive character out of the small role of Macduff. Excellent, clean recording, impressively remastered for CD but sounding well in all three formats.

Nabucco (complete).

*** DG Dig. **410 512-2** (2); 2741/*3382* 021 (3/*2*) [id.]. Cappuccilli, Dimitrova, Nesterenko, Domingo, Ch. and O of German Op., Berlin, Sinopoli.

(*) HMV **CDS 747488-8 (2). Manuguerra, Scotto, Ghiaurov, Luchetti, Obraztsova, Amb. Op. Ch., Muti.

This was Sinopoli's first opera recording and it suggests in its freshness, its electricity and its crystal clarification the sort of insight that Toscanini must once have brought. Sinopoli makes Verdi sound less comfortable than traditional conductors, but he never lets the 'grand guitar' accompaniments of early Verdi churn along automatically. One keeps hearing details normally obscured. Even the thrill of the great chorus *Va, pensiero* is the greater when the melody first emerges at a hushed pianissimo, as marked, sounding almost offstage. Strict as he is, Sinopoli encourages his singers to relish the great melodies to the full. Dimitrova is superb in Abigaille's big Act II aria, noble in her evil, as is Cappuccilli as Nabucco, less intense than Gobbi was on Gardelli's classic set for Decca, but stylistically pure. The rest of the cast is strong too, including Domingo in a relatively small role and Nesterenko superb as the High Priest, Zaccaria. Bright and forward digital sound, less atmospheric than the 1966 Decca set with Gobbi and Suliotis, conducted by Gardelli (SET 298-300/*K126 K32* [OSA/*5*-1382]), which will no doubt appear on CD in due course. The CD layout of the Sinopoli recording is on two discs (against three on LP) and brings added presence and sharper detail, while emphasizing the dramatic dynamic range. The cassettes are also laid out over four sides and the sound is vivid and full. Only in the big choruses does the upper range fall slightly short of the LPs. This is more noticeable on the first tape than the second, where the level rises slightly.

Muti's 1978 set is also scheduled for CD reissue on HMV, but the performance does not match either Sinopoli's newest DG version or the Gardelli set on Decca, which will no doubt also arrive on compact disc in due course. The HMV cast, as impressive as could be gathered at the time, with Manuguerra an imaginative choice as Nabucco, failed nevertheless to equal the three-dimensional characterizations of its competitors. Renata Scotto sang well but was not entirely inside her role; Manuguerra proved strong and reliable but lacked something in flair. Even the recording quality failed to improve on the earlier Decca set.

Nabucco: highlights.
*** DG Dig. 413 321-1/*4* [id.] (from above recording, cond. Sinopoli).

A useful collection of highlights from Sinopoli's strong, dramatic and individual complete set, brightly recorded like the original. The cassette needs a high level for satisfactory reproduction, while pianissimos tend to recede.

Oberto (complete).
*** Orfeo **C 105843 F**; S/*M* 105843 F (3) [id.]. Dimitrova, Bergonzi, Panerai, Baldani, Bav. R. Ch., Mun. R. O, Gardelli.

It was left to the enterprising Orfeo label to round off the series of early Verdi operas, with Gardelli conducting, that Philips for so long promoted. In every way this issue matches the success of those other recordings, despite the change of venue to Munich. Gardelli is a master of pacing and pointing Verdi effortlessly; here he presents a strong case for this first of the Verdi canon, revealing in such ensembles as the Trio towards the end of Act I clear forecasts of full mastery to come. Otherwise there is much that reflects the manners and style of Donizetti, as one would expect of a 26-year-old writing in Italy at the time; but the underlying toughness regularly provides a distinctive flavour. Gardelli successfully papers over the less convincing moments, helped by fine playing from the orchestra, an outstanding chorus and first-rate principals. Ghena Dimitrova makes a very positive heroine, powerful in attack in her moment of fury in the Act I finale, but also gently expressive when necessary. Only in cabalettas is she sometimes ungainly. The veterans, Carlo Bergonzi and Rolando Panerai, more than make up in stylishness and technical finesse for any unevenness of voice, and Ruza Baldani is a warm-toned Cuniza, the mezzo role. First-rate recording.

Otello (complete).
*** RCA **RD 82951** (2) [**RCD2-2951**]. Domingo, Scotto, Milnes, Amb. Op. Ch., Boys' Ch., Nat. PO, Levine.

(M) **(*) HMV EX 290137-3/*9* (3) [Ang. SCLX/*4X3X* 3742]. McCracken, Gwyneth Jones, Fischer-Dieskau, De Palma, Amb. Op. Ch., Upton House Boys' Ch., Hammersmith County School Girls' Ch., New Philh. O, Barbirolli.

Levine's is the most consistently involving version of *Otello*; on balance, it has the best cast and is superbly conducted, as well as magnificently sung. Levine combines a Toscanini-like thrust with a Karajan-like sensuousness, pointing rhythms to heighten mood, as in the Act II confrontration between hero and heroine over Cassio. Domingo as Otello combines glorious heroic tone with lyrical tenderness. If anyone thought he would be overstrained, here is proof to the contrary: he himself has claimed that singing Otello has helped and benefited his voice. Scotto is not always sweet-toned in the upper register, and the big ensemble at the end of Act III brings obvious strain; nevertheless, it is a deeply felt performance which culminates in a most beautiful account of the all-important Act IV solos, the *Willow song* and *Ave Maria*, most affecting. Milnes too is challenged by the role of Iago. His may not be a voice which readily conveys extremes of evil, but his view is far from conventional: this Iago is a handsome, virile creature beset by the biggest of chips on the shoulder. The recording has been fitted on to a pair of CDs. The digital remastering has opened up the sound and, while it could be fuller, the balance between voices and orchestra is excellent.

Recorded not long before he died, Barbirolli's highly distinctive version of *Otello* makes a welcome reissue at mid-price. Guided by the memories of his father and grandfather (both of whom played in the orchestra at the opera's first performance), he takes a very expansive view and produces glowing results. His concentration readily justifies this warmer, more lyrical view of the work, less forcefully dramatic than usual. The strength and intelligence of the singing form a powerful asset, with Fischer-Dieskau's malevolent portrait of Iago, the complete smiling villain, as distinctive as Barbirolli's conducting. McCracken as Otello is powerfully heroic, though he strains occasionally and *Dio mi potevi* brings histrionic sobbing. Gwyneth Jones gives one of her most beautiful recorded performances. Her voice still spreads under pressure, but the range of expression is finely controlled in a tenderly perceptive characterization. Richly expressive playing from the New Philharmonia, a recording that was of demonstration quality in 1969, and still sounds well.

Rigoletto (complete).

*** Ph. Dig. **412 592-2** (2); 412 592-1/*4* (3) [id.]. Bruson, Gruberova, Shicoff, Fassbaender, Lloyd, Rome St Cecilia Ac. Ch. and O, Sinopoli.

*** Decca **414 296-2** (2) [id.]; SET 542-4/*K2A3* (3) [Lon. OSA/*5*- 13105]. Milnes, Sutherland, Pavarotti, Talvela, Tourangeau, Amb. Op. Ch., LSO, Bonynge.

(*) DG **415 288-2 (2); 2740 225/*3371 054* (3) [id.]. Cappuccilli, Cotrubas, Domingo, Obraztsova, Ghiaurov, Moll, Schwarz, V. State Op. Ch., VPO, Giulini.

(M) **(*) Decca 411 880-1/*4* (2). Sutherland, MacNeil, Cioni, Rome St Cecilia Ac. Ch. and O, Sanzogno.

(M) *(*) DG 413 294-1/*4* (3/*2*). Scotto, Bergonzi, Fischer-Dieskau, Vinco, La Scala, Milan, Ch. and O, Kubelik.

Sinopoli conducts a tensely dramatic reading which, in its detailed concentration from first to last, brings out the unity of Verdi's inspiration. Unlike many other conductors who present Verdi freshly at white heat, Sinopoli here has close concern for his singers, with full potential drawn from each in what is on record the most consistent cast yet. Edita Gruberova might have been considered an unexpected choice for Gilda, remarkable for her brilliant coloratura rather than for deeper expression, yet here she makes the heroine a tender, feeling creature, emotionally vulnerable yet vocally immaculate. As a stickler for the text, Sinopoli eliminates a top note or two, as in *Caro nome*. Similarly, Renato Bruson as Rigoletto does far more than produce a stream of velvety tone, detailed and intense, responding to the conductor and combining beauty with dramatic bite. Even more remarkable is the brilliant success of Neil Shicoff as the Duke, more than a match for his most distinguished rivals. Here the Quartet becomes a genuine climax as it rarely has been in complete recordings. Like the others, Shicoff brings out unexpected detail, as does Brigitte Fassbaender as Maddalena, sharply unconventional but vocally most satisfying. Sinopoli's speeds, too, are unconventional at times, but the fresh look he provides makes this one of the most exciting of recent Verdi operas on disc, helped by full and vivid recording, consistently well balanced and particularly impressive on CD, fitted on two discs as against three LPs. Cassettes follow the layout of the LPs, with no attempt to tailor Acts to side-ends. However, the quality is outstandingly vibrant and clear, comparing very favourably with the LPs.

Just over ten years after her first recording of this opera, Sutherland appeared in it again – and this set was far more than a dutiful remake. Richard Bonynge from the very start shows his feeling for the resilient rhythms; the result is fresh and dramatic, underlining the revolutionary qualities in the score which we nowadays tend to ignore. Pavarotti is an intensely characterful Duke: an unmistakable rogue but an unmistakable charmer, too. Thanks to him and to Bonynge above all, the Quartet, as on the Sinopoli set, becomes a genuine musical climax. Sutherland's voice has acquired a hint of a beat, but there is little of the mooning manner which disfigured her earlier assumption, and the result is glowingly beautiful as well as being technically supremely assured. Milnes makes a strong Rigoletto, vocally masterful and with good if hardly searching presentation of character. Urgently enjoyable, the digital transfer on two compact discs is exceptionally vivid and atmospheric, underlining the excellence of the original engineering with its finely judged balances, but also enhancing the superimposed crowd noises and the like, which not everyone will welcome. There are excellent equivalent tapes.

Giulini, ever thoughtful for detail, directs a distinguished performance. Speeds tend to be slow, phrases are beautifully shaped and, with fine playing from the Vienna Philharmonic, the dynamics are subtle rather than dramatic. The conductor seems determined to get away from any conception of *Rigoletto* as melodrama; however, in doing that he misses the red-blooded theatricality of

Verdi's concept, the basic essential. Although it may be consistent with Giulini's view, it further reduces the dramatic impact that Cappuccilli with his unsinister voice makes the hunchback a noble figure from first to last, while Domingo, ever intelligent, makes a reflective rather than an extrovert Duke. Cotrubas is a touching Gilda, but the close balance of her voice is not helpful, and the topmost register is not always comfortable. The recording, made in the Musikverein in Vienna, has the voices well to the fore, with much reverberation on the instruments behind. CD focuses the voices even more vividly than before, but that makes the closeness of balance all the more apparent, even if the orchestral sound is cleaner. The cassettes are transferred at a relatively low level to accommodate the recording's wide dynamic range; while the vocal presence is good, some of the pianissimo orchestral detail is less cleanly defined than it might be, though the opening, with recessed stage band, is given impressive perspective.

Sutherland's earlier version of *Rigoletto* (recorded in June 1961, her first complete opera set for Decca) found her at her dreamiest. This welcome reissue on two mid-price discs and cassettes is well worth hearing for her alone. Though there are hints of her mooning manner, with *Caro nome* softened and far less bright than in her '*Art of the Prima Donna*' recording of 1960 (see Recitals, below), the flawless control and sheer beauty have rarely been matched. The final top B of that aria is a vocal marvel, sung pianissimo and breathtakingly drawn out, ten seconds of trill followed by ten seconds of sustained note. In florid music Sutherland is exquisitely light. Otherwise Cornell MacNeil is a sound rather than an imaginative Rigoletto and Renato Cioni similarly undistinguished, while the conducting of Sanzogno is undistracting. The sound is very good for its period.

Reaction to the mid-priced 1965 DG set will depend very much on reaction to Fischer-Dieskau's singing of the name part. There is no denying the care and sensitivity with which he approaches the music, and almost every phrase has the nicety of Lieder-singing, but the end result is oddly unconvincing and mannered. It is partly that Fischer-Dieskau's voice was just too young-sounding then for the old jester: you cannot quite believe in him as a grief-stricken father. Bergonzi's Duke is beautifully sung, but the Gilda of Renata Scotto is disappointing. On this showing, the engineers seem to find it impossible to capture the special tangy quality which had made her stage appearances so attractive; instead, the sound has a throaty quality. Kubelik's conducting is frankly dull, and the set can only be recommended to those who want Fischer-Dieskau as Rigoletto. There is a satisfactory tape equivalent.

Simon Boccanegra (complete).

❀ *** DG **415 692-2** (2); 2740 169/*3371 032* (3) [2709 071/*id.*]. Cappuccilli, Freni, Ghiaurov, Van Dam, Carreras, Ch. and O of La Scala, Milan, Abbado.

Abbado's 1977 recording of *Simon Boccanegra*, directly reflecting the superb production which the La Scala company brought to London at the time, is one of the most beautiful Verdi sets ever made, and the virtual background silence of the CDs enhances the warmth and beauty of the sound, the orchestra fresh and glowing in ambient warmth, the voices vivid and the perspectives always believable. From this one can appreciate not just the vigour of the composer's imagination but the finesse of the colouring, instrumental as well as vocal. Under Abbado the playing of the orchestra is brilliantly incisive as well as refined, so that the drama is underlined by extra sharpness of focus. The cursing of Paolo after the great Council Chamber Scene makes the scalp prickle, with the chorus muttering in horror and the bass clarinet adding a sinister comment, here beautifully moulded. Cappuccilli, always intelligent, gives a far more intense and illuminating performance than the one he recorded for RCA earlier in his career. He may not match Gobbi in range of colour and detail, but he too gives focus to the performance; and Ghiaurov as Fiesco sings beautifully too, though again not so characterfully as Christoff on the deleted HMV set. Freni as Maria Boccanegra sings with freshness and clarity, while Van Dam is an impressive Paolo. With electrically intense choral singing too, this is a set to outshine even Abbado's superb *Macbeth* with the same company. The cassettes – because of the modest transfer level – have not quite the sharpness of detail of the discs, but solo voices are naturally caught and the distant choral perspectives are convincing. The CD layout, on two discs, is more economical, however, and is well worth the extra cost, with 29 access points provided by the internal cueing. The libretto is clear, if in small print.

Simon Boccanegra: highlights.
** Hung. Dig. **HCD 12611** [id.]. Kincses, Nagy, Miller, Gregor, Hungarian State Op. Ch. & O, Patane.

Though the complete set from which these excerpts are taken (LP only) is a non-starter compared with Abbado's masterly DG version, this makes a useful collection on CD, bringing together some of the finest passages of a still-undervalued masterpiece. Lajos Miller as Boccanegra gives the only performance of real stature, strong and expressive if not always smooth of tone; and the admirable bass, Josef Gregor, sings Fiesco. Disappointing singing from soprano and tenor, but excellent recording.

La Traviata (complete).
*** Decca Dig. **410 154-2** (2) [id.]; D 212 D 3/*K212 K 32* (3/2) [Lon. LDR/*5*-73002]. Sutherland, Pavarotti, Manuguerra, L. Op. Ch., Nat. PO, Bonynge.
(*) HMV Dig. **CDS 747059-8 [id.]; SLS/*TCC-SLS* 5240 (3) [Ang. DSCX/*4X3X* 3920]. Scotto, Kraus, Bruson, Amb. Op. Ch., Philh. O, Muti.
(B) **(*) CfP CFPD 41 4450-1/*4* (2) [Ang. SCL 3623]. Los Angeles, Del Monte, Sereni, Ch. and O of Rome Op., Serafin.
(*) DG **415 132-2; 2707 103/*3370 024* (2) [id.]. Cotrubas, Domingo, Milnes, Bav. State Op. Ch. and O, Carlos Kleiber.
(M) **(*) Decca 411 877-1/*4* (2) [Lon. JL/*5*- 42010]. Sutherland, Bergonzi, Merrill, Ch. and O of Maggio Musicale Fiorentino, Pritchard.
(M) ** DG 415 392-1/*4* (2). Scotto, Raimondi, Bastianini, Ch. and O of La Scala, Milan, Votto.

Sutherland's second recording of the role of Violetta has a breadth and exuberance beyond what she achieved in her earlier version of 1963 conducted by John Pritchard. This *Traviata* is dominated by the grand lady that Sutherland makes her. Some of the supremely tender moments of her earlier recording – *Ah dite alla giovine* in the Act II duet with Germont, for example – are more straightforward this time, but the mooning manner is dispelled, the words are clearer, and the richness and command of the singing put this among the very finest of Sutherland's later recordings. Pavarotti too, though he overemphasizes *Di miei bollenti spiriti*, sings with splendid panache as Alfredo. Manuguerra as Germont lacks something in authority, but the firmness and clarity are splendid. Bonynge's conducting is finely sprung, the style direct, the speeds often spacious in lyrical music, generally undistracting. The digital recording is outstandingly vivid and beautifully balanced. The difference between the sound of LP and CD is marginal because of the resonant acoustic, but the use of two discs brings improved layout. The CD booklet is a reduction and is not ideal. The cassettes, too, in the main, offer Decca's best quality and the layout is ideal, with Acts tailored to side-ends. Surprisingly, however, there is some peaking on vocal climaxes, notably in *Ah fors'è lui*; and the libretto supplied with the cassettes is below this company's highest standard, with noticeably small print, especially in the notes.

Muti as a Verdi interpreter believes in clearing away performance traditions not sanctioned in the score, so cadential top notes and extra decorations are ruthlessly eliminated; Muti, with no concern for tradition, insists on speeds, generally fast, for which he quotes the score as authority. Thus, at the start of the Act I party music, he is even faster than Toscanini, but the result is dazzling; and when he needs to give sympathetic support to his soloists, above all in the great Act II duet between Violetta and Germont, there is no lack of tenderness. Overall, it is an intensely compelling account, using the complete text (like Bonynge), and it gains from having three Italy-based principals. Scotto and Kraus have long been among the most sensitive and perceptive interpreters of these roles, and so they are here; with bright digital recording, however, it is obvious that these voices are no longer young, with Scotto's soprano spreading above the stave and Kraus's tenor often sounding thin. Scotto gives a view of Violetta which even amid the gaiety of Act I points forward to tragedy, with wonderful expansion in *Ah fors'è lui* on the phrase *Ah quell'amor*. Kraus takes *Dei miei bollenti spiriti* slowly but effectively so, with plenty of extra expression. Bruson makes a fine, forthright Germont, though it does not add to dramatic conviction that his is the youngest voice. Small parts are well taken and the stage picture is vivid. The breadth and range of sound, as well as the firm placing of instruments and voices, are the more present on CD, with the pleasant reverberation clarified. The chrome cassettes are sophisticated, with the perspective in which voices and orchestra are placed more natural than usual, while everything is clear.

Even when Victoria de los Angeles made this EMI recording in the late 1950s, the role of Violetta lay rather high for her voice. Nevertheless, it drew from her much beautiful singing, not least in the coloratura display at the end of Act I which, though it may lack easily ringing top notes, has delightful sparkle and flexibility. As to the characterization, Los Angeles was a far more sympathetically tender heroine than is common; though neither the tenor nor the baritone begins to match her in artistry, their performances are both sympathetic and feeling, thanks in part to the masterly conducting of Serafin. All the traditional cuts are made, not just the second stanzas. The sound on both tape and LP is vivid and clear, seldom betraying the age of the recording. Reissued on only two discs or cassettes at CfP's extreme budget price, the set makes an outstanding bargain, both for newcomers and for those who have another set already, though no libretto is provided.

For some, Cotrubas makes an ideal heroine in this opera; but what is disappointing in the DG recording is that the microphone-placing exaggerates technical flaws, so that not only is her breathing too often audible but also her habit of separating coloratura with intrusive aitches is underlined, and the vibrato becomes too obvious at times. Such is her magic that some will forgive the faults, for her characterization combines strength with vulnerability. But Carlos Kleiber's direction is equally controversial, with more than a hint of Toscanini-like rigidity in the party music, and an occasionally uncomfortable insistence on discipline. The characteristic contributions of Domingo and Milnes, both highly commendable, hardly alter the issue. The recording suggests over-reliance on multi-channel techniques, and the closeness of the microphone-placing, spotlighting not only the soloists but members of the orchestra, is the more apparent on CD, underlining the fierce side of Kleiber's conducting which contrasts strongly with his ripely romantic side. The cassettes are very closely matched to the LPs, admirably clean and clear.

Opinions on Sutherland's earlier recording are sharply divided, and this characteristic performance from her will not win over her determined critics. It is true that her diction is poor, but it is also true that she has rarely sung on record with such deep feeling as in the final scene. The *Addio del passato* (both stanzas included and sung with an unexpected lilt) merely provides a beginning, for the duet with Bergonzi is most winning and the final death scene, *Se una pudica vergine*, is overwhelmingly beautiful. This is not a sparkling Violetta, true, but it is more perfect vocally than almost any other in a complete set. Bergonzi is an attractive Alfredo and Merrill an efficient Germont. Pritchard sometimes tends to hustle things along, with too little regard for shaping Verdian phrases, but the 1963 recording quality is outstandingly good, and this mid-price reissue makes an excellent bargain.

It is worth having the DG Votto set just for the moving and deeply considered singing of Renata Scotto as Violetta, fresher in voice than in her later HMV set. In a role which has usually eluded the efforts of prima donnas on record, she gives one of the most complete portraits, and it is sad that the rest of the cast is largely undistinguished, with even Bastianini roaring rather unfeelingly, and the conductor giving routine direction. But on only two mid-price discs (usual stage cuts observed) this should not be dismissed. The tape transfer is made at a high level, which has brought some shrillness to the sound and edginess to the voices.

La Traviata: highlights.
*** Decca Dig. **400 057-2** [id.]; SXDL/*KSXDC* 7562 [Lon. LDR/5-71062] (from above set with Sutherland, cond. Bonynge).

This Decca highlights disc was the first operatic issue on compact disc, and pointed forward to the extra immediacy possible with the new medium. One item is omitted compared with the LP – Germont's *Di Provenza* – but it remains an outstandingly generous selection at just on an hour of music; CD irresistibly brings the sense of being face to face with the singers even while it brings out the forward balance of voices against orchestra. Pavarotti is less individual than Sutherland, but well placed, and the whole selection brings highly enjoyable performances. There is a vivid chrome cassette, losing only a fraction of the focal clarity on top.

Il Trovatore (complete).
*** DG Dig. **413 355-2**; 413 355-1/*4* (3) [id.]. Plowright, Domingo, Fassbaender, Zancanaro, Nesterenko, Ch. and O of Rome St Cecilia Ac., Giulini.
(M) ** DG 415 389-1/*4* (2). Stella, Cossotto, Bergonzi, Bastianini, La Scala, Milan, Ch. and O, Serafin.

In an intensely revelatory performance, one which is richly red-blooded but which transforms melodrama into a deeper experience, Giulini flouts convention at every point. The opera's white-hot inspiration comes out in the intensity of the playing and singing, but the often slow tempi and refined textures present the whole work in new and deeper detail, product of the conductor's intense study of the work afresh. Even Giulini has rarely matched this achievement among his many fine Verdi records. More than any previous conductor on record, Giulini brings out the kinship between *Il Trovatore* and *La Forza del destino*, above all in the heroine's music, in which inspired casting presents Rosalind Plowright triumphantly in her first international opera recording. Sensuous yet ethereal in *Tacea la notte*, she masterfully brings together the seemingly incompatible qualities demanded, not just sweetness and purity but brilliant coloratura, flexibility and richly dramatic bite and power. Placido Domingo sings Manrico as powerfully as he did in the richly satisfying Mehta set on RCA (perhaps still a safer choice for the unadventurous), but the voice is even more heroic in an Otello-like way, only very occasionally showing strain. Giorgio Zancanaro proves a gloriously firm and rounded Count di Luna and Evgeny Nesterenko a dark, powerful Ferrando, while Brigitte Fassbaender, singing her first Azucena, finds far greater intensity and detail than the usual roaring mezzo, matching Giulini's freshness. The recording is warm and atmospheric with a pleasant bloom on the voices, naturally balanced and not spotlit. The CD is all the firmer and more vivid.

The mid-priced reissue on a pair of records or tapes of the 1963 La Scala set under Serafin is most welcome. It is immensely enjoyable in the contributions of Cossotto as Azucena and Carlo Bergonzi as Manrico, both highly satisfying. The conducting of Serafin is stylish and, though both Antonietta Stella and

Ettore Bastianini give flawed performances, they have their impressive moments. The recording is excellent for its period. The high-level cassettes are just a little edgy, but the sound is given fine presence and impact.

Decca have also reissued their early Tebaldi/Del Monaco set under Erede, not one of the most recommendable of their recordings. Tebaldi, as always, has some lovely moments; in the last resort, however, there is some lack of imagination in her interpretation. Del Monaco has exactly the right heroic tone-colour for Manrico – it is the greatest of pities that he fails so lamentably to do much more than bawl away. The best singing in the set comes from the rich-voiced Simionato. The conducting too does not have quite the lift and dramatic tension this opera calls for, and this does not compete at mid-price with the DG Serafin set (Decca 411 874-1/*4*).

Il Trovatore: highlights.
*** DG Dig. **415 285-2**; 415 285-1/*4* [id.] (from above recording, cond. Giulini).
(*) Ph. Dig. **411 447-2; 412 019-1/*4* [id.]. Ricciarelli, Toczyska, Carreras, Lloyd, ROHCG Ch. and O, Sir Colin Davis.

This generous and well-chosen DG collection of excerpts celebrates Giulini's masterly and highly individual interpretation, with the sound again excellent, but the warning given in the *Gramophone* review might be repeated: 'listening to these highlights may make you regret not having invested in the whole set'.

Sir Colin Davis's complete set (Philips 6769/*7654* 063) is a refreshing and direct reading, refined in sound but rather wanting in dramatic impact. A highlights disc seems an excellent way to approach it; however, while the CD has superior sound, the LP and tape are issued in the mid-price range, and as the cassette is admirably vivid and costs a third the price of the CD, it makes an obvious choice. Ricciarelli's Leonora is most moving and if Carreras lacks the full confidence of a natural Manrico, he is at his best in the more lyrical moments.

RECITALS

Arias: *Aïda: Ritorna vincitor. Un Ballo in maschera: Ecco l'orrido . . . Ma dall' arrido stelo divulsa. La Forza del destino: Son giunta . . . Madre pietosa vergine; Pace, pace, mio Dio. Macbeth: Ambizio spirto . . . Vieni t'affretta! La luce langue; Una macchia è qui tuttora. Nabucco: Ben io t'invenni . . . Anch'io dischiuso.*
(M) **(*) Decca 411 885-1/*4*. Birgit Nilsson; cond. Solti and others.

This recital in the 'Grandi Voci' series has been compiled from various recordings that Nilsson made for Decca in the early 1960s, including the complete *Ballo in maschera* conducted by Solti. The magnificent voice, dramatically incisive, rarely rounded, does not always sound comfortable in Verdi, but the power and command are formidable, reminding us that she was not just an heroic Wagner singer. The recording is consistently vivid, strikingly so on the excellent tape.

Arias: *Aïda: Se quel guerrier io fossi! . . . Celeste Aïda; Pur ti riveggo, mia dolce Aïda . . . Tu! Amonasro! Don Carlos: Fontainebleau! Forêt immense et solitaire . . . Je l'ai vue; Écoute. Les portes du couvent . . . Dieu, tu seras dans nos âmes. Nabucco: Che si vuol? Il Trovatore: Quale d'armi . . . Ah! si, ben mio . . . Di quella pira.*

*** DG Dig. **413 785-2**; 413 785-1/*4* [id.]. Placido Domingo with various orchestras and conductors – PUCCINI: *Arias.****

Domingo's Verdi recital, supplemented by Puccini items from *Manon Lescaut* and *Turandot*, brings an excellent collection of recordings taken from different sources. When working on a complete opera recording there is no danger of big arias like this simply being churned out without apt characterization. The sound is most vivid throughout, not only in the disc formats but also on the really excellent chrome cassette.

Arias: *Aïda: Ritorna vincitor; Qui Radames verrà! . . . O patria mia. Don Carlos: Tu che le vanità. Macbeth: Nel dì della vittoria . . . Vieni! t'affretta. Otello: Era più calmo . . . Piangea cantando . . . Ave Maria.*

(M) *** Decca 414 442-1/*4*. Dame Gwyneth Jones, ROHCG O, Downes.

Recorded early in Dame Gwyneth's career, this recital brought one of her finest recordings, with any suspicion of squalliness quickly suppressed and with legato lines finely controlled. A valuable addition to Decca's 'Grandi Voci' series, well recorded. There is an extremely vivid cassette.

'World stars sing Verdi': arias from *Attila; I due Foscari; I Lombardi; I Masnadieri.*

(M) *** Ph. Seq. 6527/*7311* 192. Bergonzi, Carreras, Domingo, Milnes, Cappuccilli, Wixell, Raimondi, Amb. S., various orchestras, Gardelli.

Compiled, like the companion record of soprano arias (see below), from the Philips series of early Verdi opera sets, this varied collection can be warmly recommended to collectors who would like to explore this area of Verdi's output without going to the expense of complete sets. With such a starry cast, it is not surprising that these are consistently fine performances, very well recorded.

Arias: *Un Ballo in maschera: Ecco l'orrido . . Ma dall'arido stelo divulsa; Morro ma prima in grazia. Don Carlos: Tu che le vanità. La Forza del destino: Son giunta! Madre, pietosa vergine. Giovanna d'Arco: Oh, ben s'addice . . . Sempre all'alba. Otello: Mia madre . . . Ave Maria. Il Trovatore: Tacea la notte.*

(M) **(*) Decca 411 886-1/*4*. Renata Tebaldi, New Philh. O, Fabritiis; other orchestras and conductors.

Vintage performances from Tebaldi with her rich, warm and consistently beautiful tone finely controlled. A suspicion of intrusive aitches in the *Giovanna d'Arco* cabaletta is among the few technical flaws. That and other items come from a recital record of the mid-1960s, but consistency was her forte, and the whole collection can be warmly recommended as a fine portrait in Decca's 'Grandi Voci' series.

Arias: *Don Carlo: Tu che le vanità. La Traviata: Ah fors'è lui. Il Trovatore: Timor di me.*
*** CBS Dig. **CD 37298**; 37298/*40*- [id.]. Te Kanawa, LPO, Pritchard – PUCCINI: *Arias.****

The Verdi side of Kiri Te Kanawa's Verdi–Puccini recital brings three substantial items less obviously apt for the singer, but in each the singing is felt as well as beautiful. The coloratura of the *Traviata* and *Trovatore* items is admirably clean, and it is a special joy to hear Elisabetta's big aria from *Don Carlo* sung with such truth and precision. Good recording, enhanced on CD. The chrome tape is transferred at a low level. The voice sounds well, but the orchestra is recessed.

'The Prima Donna in Verdi': arias from*: I due Foscari; Un giorno di Regno; I Masnadieri; Stiffelio.*
(M) *** Ph. Seq. 6527/*7311* 220. Caballé, Norman, Cossotto, Sass, Ricciarelli, Deutekom, Connell, Amb. S., various orchestras, cond. Gardelli.

This collection marries up nicely with the similar compilation of male arias, also taken from Philips's excellent series of early Verdi recordings under Gardelli (see above). Many of the items are rare and overall this makes an unusual and attractive recital, generally very well sung and recorded.

Choruses: *Aïda: Triumphal march and ballet music. Attila: Urli rapine. La Battaglia di Legnano: Giuriam d'Italia. I Lombardi: O Signore dal tetto natio. Nabucco: Gli arredi festivi; Va pensiero. Otello: Fuoco di gloria. Il Trovatore: Vedi! le fosche; Squilli, echeggi.*
(M) **(*) Decca 411 834-1/*4*. Ch. and O of St Cecilia Ac., Rome, Carlo Franci.

When this collection was first issued in 1965 we wondered (in the first *Penguin Stereo Record Guide*) whether the engineers had brightened the sound artificially. This impression still remains with the remastered reissue, for the upper range of chorus and orchestra has an unnatural brightness, and this applies to both disc and tape. In all other respects the quality is very good, inner detail is sharp and the big climaxes open up well. The performances are vivid, with a willingness to sing softly and, indeed, sometimes a degree of refinement in the approach surprising in an Italian chorus. The *I Lombardi* excerpts at the end of side one are especially appealing, but all the little-known items come up freshly. The trumpets in the *Aïda* Triumphal scene get the full stereo treatment.

Choruses: *Aïda: Gloria all'Egitto. Don Carlo: Spuntato ecco il dì. Ernani: Si, ridesti il leon di Castiglia. I Lombardi: Gerusalem. Macbeth: Patria oppressa. Nabucco: Gli arredi festivi; Va, pensiero. Otello: Fuoco di gioia. Il Trovatore: Vedi, le fosche.*
*(**) DG **413 448-2** [id.]. Ch. and O of La Scala, Milan, Abbado.

The combination of precision and tension in these La Scala performances is riveting, and the recording has a strikingly wide dynamic range. The diminuendo at the end of the *Anvil chorus* is most subtly managed, while the rhythmic bounce of *Si, ridesti* is matched by the expansive brilliance of the excerpts from *Aïda* (with fruity trumpets) and *Don Carlo*, and by the atmospheric power of *Patria oppressa* from *Macbeth*. One's praise, however, has to be tempered with disappointment, for this is one instance when the analogue recording from the mid-1970s has lost something in its digital remastering for CD. On the original LP and cassette, pianissimo detail registered convincingly and the upper range was free and open. On CD, definition at lower dynamic levels is disappointingly dim, and there is a fierce edge on fortissimos, though the pleasing ambience remains.

Choruses: *Aïda: Gloria all'Egitto. Don Carlos: Spuntato ecco il dì. I Lombardi: Gerusalem!; O Signore, dal tetto natio. Macbeth: Patria oppressa! Nabucco: Va, pensiero; Gli arredi festivi. Otello: Fuoco di gioia! Il Trovatore: Vedi! le fosche; Or co' dadi . . . Squilli, echeggi.*

(*) Ph. Dig. **412 235-2; 412 235-1/*4* [id.]. Dresden State Op. Ch. and State O, Varviso.

Varviso's collection of choruses brings polished but soft-grained performances, beautifully supported by the magnificent Dresden orchestra. Gentler choruses are excellent, but the dramatic ones lack something in bite. One of the highlights is the *Fire chorus* from *Otello* in which the choral and woodwind detail suggests the flickering flames of bonfires burning in Otello's honour. The recording is warmly atmospheric, successful in all three media, with CD adding a degree more presence and definition.

OTHER COLLECTIONS

Arias, duets and choruses from: *Aïda; Un Ballo in maschera; Don Carlo; Falstaff; La Forza del destino; Luisa Miller; Nabucco; Otello; Rigoletto; La Traviata; Il Trovatore.*

(B) ** Decca *414 050-4*. Artists include: Bergonzi, Pavarotti, Sutherland, Crespin, Simionato, Tebaldi, Bumbry, Sir Geraint Evans.

Highlights and *Preludes* from: *Aïda; Un Ballo in maschera; Don Carlo; La Forza del destino; Nabucco; Otello; Rigoletto; La Traviata; Il Trovatore; I vespri siciliani.*

(B) * DG Walkman *413 433-4* [id.]. Various artists include: Arroyo, Bergonzi, Cossotto, Di Stefano, Raimondi, Scotto, Fischer-Dieskau; La Scala, Milan, Ch., Abbado.

There are some fine performances on this Decca extended-length tape compilation, but this selection does not match the companion Bach and Handel anthologies. Although the sound is vivid (if not always absolutely refined), the juxtaposition of items could be more felicitous. However, for those wanting a

Verdi programme for the car, this does range over a reasonably wide choice of repertoire and is far preferable to DG's comparable Walkman.

With the wealth of marvellous Verdi performances in their catalogue, one would have thought that DG could have found a more rewarding selection than that offered on this Walkman Verdi. There are one or two memorable items, of course: for instance Fiorenza Cossotto's *O don fatale*, Giuseppe di Stefano's *Celeste Aïda*, and some favourite choruses recorded at La Scala under Abbado. But most of the rest is undistinguished; though the sound is always good, this cannot be recommended with any enthusiasm.

Victoria, Tomás Luis de (*c.* 1548–1611)

Ascendens Christus (motet)*; Missa Ascendis Christus in altum; O Magnum mysterium* (motet)*; Missa O Magnum mysterium.*
*** Hyp. Dig. A/*KA* 66190 [id.]. Westminster Cathedral Ch., David Hill.

Missa Ave maris stella; O quam gloriosum est regnum (motet)*; Missa O quam gloriosum.*
❀ ☾ *** Hyp. **CDA 66114**; A/*KA* 66114 [id.]. Westminster Cathedral Ch., David Hill.

Winner of a *Gramophone* award in 1984, David Hill's superb coupling of *Ave maris stella* and *O quam gloriosum* gives Tomás Luis de Victoria a splendid CD début. The Latin fervour of the singing is very involving; some listeners may be surprised initially at the volatile way David Hill moves the music on, with the trebles eloquently soaring aloft on the line of the music. *Ave maris stella* is particularly fine, Hill's mastery of the overall structure producing a cumulative effect as the choir moves towards the magnificent closing *Agnus Dei.* The recording balance is perfectly judged, with the Westminster acoustic adding resonance in both senses of the word to singing of the highest calibre, combining a sense of timelessness and mystery with real expressive power. Throughout, the choral line remains firm without clouding. While the CD with its silent background marginally increases the tangibility of the sound, the cassette transfer also is flawless – this too is in the demonstration class.

The companion disc and tape are hardly less recommendable, the singing at once fervent and serene. Tempi are consistently fresh. The spirited presentation of the motet *Ascendens Christus in altum* prepares the way for a performance of the mass that is similarly invigorating. The spontaneous ebb and flow of the pacing is at the heart of David Hill's understanding of this superb music, and the listener is thrillingly involved when the sound so successfully combines immediacy and body, yet remains admirably coloured by the Westminster resonance. Again the cassette is of demonstration standard.

Mass and Motet – O quam gloriosum.
(*) Argo Dig. **410 149-2; 410 149-1/*4* [id.]. King's College Ch., Cleobury – PALESTRINA: *Tu es Petrus.***(*)

This coupling with Palestrina offers eloquent, if slightly reserved performances in the King's tradition, the voices finely blended to produce an impressive range of sonority. The recording is admirably faithful and, while there is an element of introspection here, the singing also offers moments of affecting serenity. The CD adds slightly to the presence of the LP, but the recording is basically 'live' and well balanced. However, by the side of David Hill's Westminster Cathedral performance, the King's approach sounds relatively static.

Vierne, Louis (1870–1937)

Piano quintet in C min., Op. 42.
** Erato STU 715502 (2) [id.]. Hubeau, Viotti Qt – PIERNÉ: *Piano quintet***; FRANCK: *Piano quintet.**(*)

As organist of Notre Dame, Louis Vierne is best known for his music for that instrument, which includes six symphonies. However, he wrote a quantity of chamber music, violin and cello sonatas, string quartets and the present *Quintet*. This is a civilized and deeply felt piece composed in 1917–18; it has a tragic intensity not dissimilar to Franck, whose pupil he was. Thoroughly committed performances from Hubeau and the Viotti Quartet, and very acceptable recording.

ORGAN MUSIC

Suite No. 3, Op. 54: Carillon de Westminster.
*** DG Dig. **413 438-2**; 413 438-1/*4* [id.]. Simon Preston (organ of Westminster Abbey) – WIDOR: *Symphony No. 5.****

The Vierne *Carillon de Westminster* is splendidly played by Simon Preston and sounds appropriately atmospheric in this spacious acoustic and well-judged recording. It makes an attractive makeweight to the Widor *Fifth Symphony*. There is an excellent cassette.

Vieuxtemps, Henri (1820–81)

Violin concertos Nos 4 in D min., Op. 31; 5 in A min., Op. 37.
*** HMV **CDC 747165-2** [id.]; ASD 3555 [Ang. S/*4XS* 37484]. Perlman, O de Paris, Barenboim.

Vieuxtemps wrote six violin concertos, and it is surprising that so few violinists have attempted to resurrect more than the odd one. This coupling of the two best-known is not only apt; it presents superbly stylish readings, with Perlman both aristocratically pure of tone and intonation and passionate of expression.

In his accompaniments Barenboim draws warmly romantic playing from the Paris Orchestra. The 1978 recording, balancing the soloist well forward, now sounds a little dated in its clear, clean CD transfer.

Violin concerto No. 5 in A min., Op. 37.
(*) CBS Dig. **CD 37796; 37796 [id.]. Lin, Minnesota O, Marriner – HAYDN: *Concerto.***

Cho-Liang Lin is a Taiwanese-born player whose formidable technique is well able to meet the demands of this concerto. He plays it with flair and zest, and is well supported by Sir Neville Marriner and the Minnesota Orchestra. The recording is first class, and the enhancement provided by the CD is striking. However, the coupling, though well played, is not a very appropriate one. Now that Lin's reputation has been established by his splendid CD of the Mendelssohn and Saint-Saëns concertos, CBS would do well to find another pairing for his Vieuxtemps.

Villa-Lobos, Heitor (1887–1959)

Bachianas brasileiras Nos (i) *1* (*Prelude* only)*;* (ii) *2* (includes *The little train of the Caipira*)*;* (i; iii) *5* (*Aria* only)*;* (iv) *Cirenda of the seven notes, for bassoon and strings;* (v) *Chôro No. 4, for 3 horns and trombone.*
(**) Chant du Monde **278 644** [id.]. (i) Rostropovich with Cello Ens.; (ii) USSR SO, Bakarev; (iii) Vishnevskaya; (iv) Pecherski, Leningrad CO, Gozman; (v) Bouyanovski, Evstigneyev, Sukorov, Benglovski.

Although this collection looks enticing and the cast list is strong, the results are often less than captivating. The digital remastering has brought a pungency to the treble response which affects the strings adversely in the most substantial item, the *Bachianas brasileiras No. 2*, and also makes the percussive effects in *The little train of the Caipira* sound tinselly. The result is unevocative. The programme opens with Vishnevskaya's unlovely account of the *Aria* from *No. 5*, which is made the more abrasive by the forward balance and the edgy sound. Rostropovich languishes ravishingly in his solo in the *Prelude* to *No. 1* and here the recording is much more agreeable, as it is in the attractive brass quartet and the *Cirenda*, a fine piece, very well played. Thus the latter half of the concert, which includes these three items together, is far more attractive than the earlier part; it was not a good idea to open the disc with Vishnevskaya.

Bachianas brasileiras No. 5 for soprano and cellos.
*** Decca Dig. **411 730-2**; 411 730-1/*4* [id.]. Te Kanawa, Harrell and Instrumental Ens. – CANTELOUBE: *Songs of the Auvergne.****

The Villa-Lobos piece makes an apt fill-up for the Canteloube songs completing Kiri Te Kanawa's recording of all five books. It is, if anything, even more sensuously done, well sustained at a speed far slower than one would normally expect. Rich recording to match.

Guitar concerto.
(B) *** CBS *MGT 39017.* John Williams, ECO, Barenboim – CASTELNUOVO-TEDESCO: *Concerto* **(*); RODRIGO: *Concierto; Fantasia.****

The invention of this concerto is not very strong, relying a good deal on texture and atmosphere; but John Williams makes the most of its finer points, especially the rhapsodic quality of the *Andantino.* The CBS recording is lively and immediate, and this extended-length tape is an undoubted bargain.

Vivaldi, Antonio (1675–1741)

L'Estro armonico, Op. 3 (complete).
*** O-L **414 554-2** [id.]; D245 D2/*K 245 K 22* (2). Holloway, Huggett, Mackintosh, Wilcock, AAM, Hogwood.
*** Ph. Dig. **412 128-2**; 412 128-1/*4* [id.]. Carmirelli, I Musici.

Even those who normally fight shy of 'authentic' performances of Baroque music, with their astringent timbres and deliberate avoidance of romantic gestures, will find it hard not to respond to the sparkling set of Vivaldi's Op. 3 from the Academy of Ancient Music, directed by Christopher Hogwood. The captivating lightness of the solo playing and the crispness of articulation of the accompanying group bring music making that combines joyful vitality with the authority of scholarship. Textures are always transparent, but there is no lack of body to the ripieno (even though there is only one instrument to each part). Hogwood's continuo is first class, varying between harpsichord and organ, the latter used to add colour as well as substance. The balance is excellent, and the whole effect is exhilarating. While some listeners may need to adjust to the style of playing in slow movements, the underlying expressive feeling is never in doubt, and in the allegros the nimble flights of bravura from the four soloists are a constant delight. The recording is superb: apart from the truthfulness of individual timbres, there is a striking depth of acoustic, with the solo instruments given a backward and forward perspective as well as the expected antiphonal interplay. The extra range that the compact disc can encompass helps to give the aural image the impression of greater definition. The cassettes are excellent too, although the upper partials are cleaner in the CD and LP versions.

Readers allergic to the Academy of Ancient Music are well served, too. I Musici are thoroughly fresh and alive, and few will find much to quarrel with in their interpretation. They may not have the dash and sparkle of the Academy – but they do not have any rough edges either. The Philips recording has great warmth and the texture is well ventilated, allowing detail to register clearly within a realistic perspective. The non-specialist collector will find much to enjoy here. Recommended alongside – but not in preference to – the Academy.

L'Estro armonico: Double violin concerto in A min.; Quadruple violin concerto in B min.; Triple concerto in D min., for 2 violins and cello, Op. 3/8, 10 and 11. Triple violin concerto in F.

(M) **(*) Pickwick Dig. **PCD 809** [id.]. Soloists, SCO, Laredo.

The three concertos from *L'Estro armonico* are among Vivaldi's finest; they receive vigorous performances from members of the Scottish Chamber Orchestra, with their director, Jaime Laredo, again creating the lively spontaneity that informs his successful version of *The Four Seasons.* While the solo playing occasionally lacks the last touch of polish, there is an excellent team spirit, and the phrasing has more light and shade than in Laredo's companion collection of wind concertos. The recording is a shade overbright, but there is a firm supporting bass line and the acoustic is attractive, adding ambience and warmth without blurring detail. The *Triple concerto in F* has an unusual pizzicato-based *Andante*, showing the composer at his most imaginative. On Pickwick's pioneering mid-priced CD label, this seems excellent value.

L'Estro armonico: Double violin concerto No. 8 in A min.

** CBS Dig. **CD 37278**; 37278/*40*- [id.]. Zukerman, Stern, St Paul CO, James – BACH: *Double concertos.***

This lovely *Double concerto* makes an apt coupling for the two Bach *Double concertos* on this record from Minnesota, but the same reservations have to be made about the excessive weight of bass, alongside comparable praise for the solo playing.

The Trial between harmony and invention (Il Cimento dell'armonia e dell' invenzione), Op. 8 (complete).

(*) Tel. **ZK8 42985; AZ6/*CY4* 42985 (1–6, incl. *4 Seasons*). **ZK8 43094**; AZ6 43094 (7–12) [id.]. Alice Harnoncourt, Schaeftlein, VCM, Harnoncourt.

The Trial between harmony and invention, Op. 8/5–10.

(*) CRD **CRD 3410; CRD 1048/*CRDC 4048* [id.]. Simon Standage, E. Consort, Pinnock.

(i) *The Trial between harmony and invention, Op. 8/11–12.* (ii) *Cello concerto in B min., RV 424;* (iii) *Flute concerto in D, RV 429.*

(*) CRD **CRD 3411; CRD 1049/*CRDC 4049* [id.]. (i) Standage; (ii) Pleeth; (iii) Preston; E. Concert, Pinnock. – C. P. E. BACH: *Harpsichord concerto.***(*)

The first four concertos of Op. 8 are a set within a set, forming what is (understandably) Vivaldi's most popular work, *The Four Seasons.* Their imaginative power, their eloquence and their tunefulness tend slightly to dwarf the remaining eight concertos, but there is some splendid music throughout the whole work which is well worth exploring. The Telefunken complete set is undoubtedly original in approach and full of character; there is, however, an element of eccentricity in Harnoncourt's control of dynamics and tempi, with allegros often aggressively fast and chimerical changes of mood that are not always convincing. Alice Harnoncourt's timbre is leonine, and her tone production somewhat astringent, bringing out the pithiness of timbre inherent in her baroque instrument. The dramatic style of the solo playing is certainly at one with the vivid pictorialism of Vivaldi's imagery. The shepherd's dog in *Spring* barks vociferously, and the dance rhythms at the finale of the same concerto are extremely invigorating. The interpretative approach throughout emphasizes this element of contrast. The languorous opening of *Summer* makes a splendid foil for the storm and the buzzing insects, yet the zephyr breezes are wistfully gentle. The continuo uses a chamber organ to great effect, and picaresque touches of colour are added to the string textures. Concertos Nos 9 and 12 are played on the oboe by Jurg Schaeftlein, who makes a first-class contribution; and this choice of instrumentation further varies the colouring of Vivaldi's score. The sound is bright, vivid and clean, if dry-textured and sometimes fierce in the Telefunken manner. As can be seen, this 1978 analogue recording has been reissued on a pair of CDs, digitally remastered. The two discs are available separately; the first includes *The Four Seasons* plus two other characterful works: No. 5, subtitled *La Tempesta di mare*, and No. 6, called, with no special significance, *Il piacere*. The first six concertos are also available on a technically excellent chrome cassette.

CRD have anticipated the needs of many collectors, who either may not wish to duplicate *The Four Seasons* or may prefer to choose an alternative account, by making available the remaining eight concertos on two CDs, filling up the available space with two other Vivaldi works, and on CD offering a harpsichord concerto by C. P. E. Bach as a bonus. The *Flute concerto* (played by Simon Preston on a baroque flute) is particularly attractive. These 1981 performances are alert and full of character; they established a new style, using original instruments, which was to become even more famous when Pinnock and his English Concert later moved over to DG's Archiv label. Slow movements remain expressively eloquent, and a chamber organ is used in the continuo to add extra colour, although without the imaginative touches or sense of fantasy which Marriner finds in this repertoire. Indeed, the playing is a little short on charm. On the LPs and cassettes, the sound has a certain astringency, but in the remastering for CD this has been slightly smoothed off, and in tuttis there is at times some loss of focus. The separate concertos are banded, but there is no cueing of individual movements. *The Four Seasons* from this set are available on LP and cassette only (CRD 1025/*CRDC 4025*).

The Four Seasons, Op. 8/1–4.
*** Argo **414 486-2**; ZRG/*KZRC* 654 [id.]. Loveday, ASMF, Marriner.
*** DG Arc. Dig. **400 045-2**; 2534/*3311* 003 [id.]. Standage, E. Concert, Pinnock.
*** Ph. Dig. **410 001-2**; 6514/*7337* 275 [id.]. Carmirelli, I Musici.
(M) *** Pickwick **PCD 800**; CC/*CCTC* 7575. Jaime Laredo, SCO.
*** DG **413 726-2**; 2531/*3301* 287 [id.]. Kremer, LSO, Abbado.
*** O-L Dig. **410 126-2**; 410 126-1/*4* [id.]. Hirons, Holloway, Bury, Mackintosh, AAM, Hogwood.
(*) CBS **CD 36710 [id.]. Zukerman, St Paul CO.

(*) HMV Dig. **CDC 747319-2; EL 270023-1/*4* [Ang. DS/*4DS* 38123]. Perlman, Israel PO.

(M) **(*) Ph. 412 939-1/*4*. Michelucci, I Musici.

(*) DG **415 301-2 [id.]. Schwalbé, BPO, Karajan – ALBINONI: *Adagio*: CORELLI: *Concerto grosso, Op. 6/8*.**

(M) **(*) DG Sig. 415 201-1/*4* (as above, Schwalbé; Karajan) – ALBINONI: *Adagio*; PACHELBEL: *Canon*.**

(*) HMV Dig. **CDC 747043-2 [id.]; EL 270102-1/*4* [Ang. DFO/*4DFO* 38160]. Mutter, VPO, Karajan.

** Delos Dig. **D/CD 3007** [id.]. Oliveira, LACO, Schwarz.

*(*) Erato **ECD 88003**; NUM/*MCE* 75054 [id.]. Toso, Sol. Ven., Scimone.

*(*) Denon Dig. **C37 7013** [id.]. Larsens, Lucerne Fest. Strings, Baumgartner.

Vivaldi's *Four Seasons* is currently the most often recorded of any piece of classical music. It seems extraordinary that Sir Neville Marriner's 1970 Academy of St Martin-in-the-Fields version with Alan Loveday, having dominated the LP and tape catalogues for a decade and a half, should now establish its place at the top of the list of recommended compact discs. It was made during a vintage Argo recording period and the digital remastering has been completely successful, retaining the fullness and bloom of the original, besides slightly refining its inner detail, already excellent on the original LP. The performance is as satisfying as ever, and will surely delight all but those who are ruled by the creed of authenticity. It has an element of fantasy that makes the music sound utterly new; it is full of imaginative touches, with Simon Preston subtly varying the continuo between harpsichord and organ. The opulence of string tone may have a romantic connotation, but there is no self-indulgence in the interpretation, no sentimentality, for the contrasts are made sharper and fresher, not smoothed over. The cassette is not quite as clean as the LP (especially on side two), but is still thoroughly recommendable alongside it.

The Archiv version by Simon Standage with the English Concert, directed from the harpsichord by Trevor Pinnock, has the advantage of using a newly discovered set of parts found in Manchester's Henry Watson Music Library – which has additionally brought the correction of minor textual errors in the Le Cène text in normal use. The Archiv performance also (minimally) introduces a second soloist and is played on period instruments. The players create a relatively intimate sound, though their approach is certainly not without drama, while the solo contribution has impressive flair and bravura. The overall effect is essentially refined, treating the pictorial imagery with subtlety. The result is less voluptuous than with Marriner and less vibrant than the version under Abbado, but it finds a natural balance between vivid projection and atmospheric feeling. The digital recording is first class on disc and chrome tape alike, while the compact disc offers the usual additional virtues of background silence, added clarity and refinement. Authenticists should be well satisfied.

The new Philips digital recording is the third in stereo by I Musici, and it is undoubtedly the finest of the three. Musical values as ever are paramount; this time, however, there is more vitality and the programmatic implications are more strikingly realized (indeed, the bark of the shepherd's dog in *Spring* is singularly insistent). Yet Pina Carmirelli's expressive playing maintains the lyrical feeling and beauty of tone for which I Musici versions are remembered, and he combines it with attractively alert and nimble bravura in the allegros. The gentle breezes are as effectively caught as the summer storms, and the slow movement of *Autumn* (helped by especially atmospheric recording) makes an elegiac contrast. The opening of *Winter* is certainly chilly. The recording is outstandingly natural on both LP and the excellent chrome tape, but is most impressive of all on CD, with its added refinement of detail.

Jaime Laredo's Pickwick CD is a fine bargain. The performance has great spontaneity and vitality, emphasized by the forward balance which is nevertheless admirably truthful. The bright upper range is balanced by a firm, resonant bass. Jaime Laredo plays with bravura and directs polished, strongly characterized accompaniments. Pacing tends to be on the fast side; although the reading is extrovert, and the lyrical music – played responsively – is made to offer a series of interludes to the vigour of the allegros, the effect is exhilarating rather than aggressive. There is a first-class chrome tape which, alongside the excellent LP, costs considerably less than the CD; but the compact disc gives extra tangibility to the soloist and slightly more body to the orchestra.

In the DG version by Gidon Kremer with the LSO under Claudio Abbado, it is obvious from the first bar that Abbado is the dominating partner. This is an enormously vital account, with great contrasts of tempo and dynamic. The dramatization of Vivaldi's detailed pictorial effects has never been more vivid; the vigour of the dancing peasants is surpassed by the sheer fury and violence of the summer storms. Yet the delicacy of the gentle zephyrs is matched by the hazy somnolence of the beautiful *Adagio* of *Autumn*. After a freezingly evocative opening to *Winter*, Abbado creates a mandolin-like pizzicato effect in the slow movement (taken faster than the composer's marking) to simulate a rain shower. The finale opens delicately, but at the close the listener is almost blown away by the winter gales. Kremer matches Abbado's vigour with playing that combines sparkling bravura and suitably evocative expressive moments. Given the projection of a brilliantly lit recording, the impact of this version is considerable. Leslie Pearson's nimble continuo, alternating organ and harpsichord, sometimes gets buried, but drama rather than subtlety is the keynote of this arresting account. The 1982 analogue recording has been effectively remastered for CD, sounding fresh and clean, its brilliance very apparent, and there is an excellent cassette.

With a different soloist for each of the four concertos, Hogwood directs the Academy of Ancient Music in lively performances with exceptionally imaginative use of continuo contrasts, guitar with harpsichord in *Spring* and *Autumn*, lute and chamber organ in *Summer* and *Winter*. These performances have a high place among authentic versions, a shade more abrasive than most; however, they cannot quite match the subtly responsive approach of Trevor Pinnock's Archiv set with the English Concert. The CD has striking presence; the chrome cassette, too, is exceptionally clear and clean, although the upper range is very brightly lit indeed.

Another fine modern version comes from Zukerman. The playing has character throughout, with the music's programmatic associations well observed but not overemphasized. The conception has a strong lyrical feeling; perhaps the relaxed approach does minimize the drama, but there is a compensating refinement and, as with I Musici, musical values are paramount here. The sound of the orchestra gives a degree of bass emphasis, but the continuo comes through well and the overall effect is believable with the added presence afforded by CD.

Fine as was Perlman's 1977 recording of the *Four Seasons*, a modern virtuoso performance that held the sequence together with perceptive artistry and immaculate virtuosity, he decided he wanted to record the four concertos again. There are certainly gains, in that the harpsichord continuo is more readily audible, but the closeness of sound, as recorded in the Mann Auditorium in Tel Aviv, also brings an unwanted harshness on LP. However, as so often with recordings made in this venue, the CD brings a remarkable improvement. The balance remains close, but the sound is opened out, the effect much more natural and congenial. The accompanying string group has more body and the imagery is altogether more believable. As an interpretation, this is a masterly example of a virtuoso's individual artistry, but the account does not convey quite the warmth and spontaneity of the earlier set, which had many passages of magic, notably the central *Adagio* of *Summer*. This is also beautifully played in the new recording, but is less memorable. For LP collectors, the 1977 version remains a primary recommendation (HMV ASD/*TC-ASD* 3293 [Ang. S/*4XS* 37053]).

Philips have also reissued Michelucci's 1970 version at mid-price, sounding extremely well on both LP and cassette. I Musici must have played this work countless times and probably find it more difficult than most groups to bring freshness to each new recording. Roberto Michelucci is a first-class soloist, displaying bursts of bravura in the outer movements but often musingly thoughtful in the slower ones. His expressiveness is finely judged, and the group are naturally balanced, with the harpsichord coming through in the right way, without exaggeration. The last degree of spontaneity is sometimes missing, but this is certainly enjoyable.

Karajan's 1973 version was an undoubted success, even if unlikely to appeal to authenticists. Its tonal beauty is not achieved at the expense of vitality and, although the harpsichord hardly ever comes through, the overall scale is acceptable. Michel Schwalbé is a memorable soloist. His playing is neat, precise and very musical, with a touch of Italian sunshine in the tone. His sparkling playing is set against polished Berlin Philharmonic string textures, although in the digital remastering the sound seems to have been dried out a little and is not as expansive or as natural-sounding as before. Choice lies between the CD and a Signature LP and its closely matching cassette which costs around a third as much. The couplings are slightly different, although Albinoni's *Adagio* is common to both.

As with his previous recording, made in Berlin, Karajan's HMV version offers much to admire, not least the beautiful playing of his young soloist. A reduced string group from the Vienna orchestra is used, but the warmly reverberant acoustic makes the sound plushy, although the effect is richly agreeable. The balance sometimes drowns the continuo (to which Karajan contributes himself); detail registers more clearly on the CD, but this medium serves also to emphasize the anachronism of the conception. On tape, the quality is rich and full, but with the overall focus marginally less sharp.

The Delos recording by Elmar Oliveira and the excellent Los Angeles Chamber Orchestra under Gerard Schwarz made the digital début of *The Four Seasons* in 1980. The recording is extremely brilliant, the sharp spotlighting of the soloist bringing a degree of steeliness to his upper range. Tempi too are extremely brisk throughout: extrovert bravura is the keynote here, rather than atmosphere. The recording balance ensures that the continuo comes through well. But – as the opening of *Winter* demonstrates – this is not an especially imaginative version, although the alert vivacity of the playing of soloist and orchestra alike is undoubtedly exhilarating, and slow movements are expressive and sympathetic.

Piero Toso and Scimone made a previous analogue recording in the early 1970s that was notable for its extremes of dynamic and wayward tempi. The new version still favours plenty of rubato and mercurial speed changes and although, as before, the music making sounds alive, the results are not always convincing. Modern instruments are used; while Toso provides some judicious ornamentation, in essence the style is somewhat old-fashioned. Further variety of timbre is achieved by introducing a pair of theorbos and an organ, besides a harpsichord, into the continuo. The resonant recording is clarified on CD, but the new format also picks up some intrusive studio background noises.

On Denon, Gunars Larsens is a first-class soloist, stylish, very assured technically, and giving pleasure in his lyrical phrasing. But Baumgartner accompanies in a doggedly po-faced way and takes not a great deal of account of the work's descriptive intentions. With an unimaginative continuo, this account has little that is new to contribute, and the bright but rather dry recording is not especially congenial.

(i) *The Four Seasons; Violin concertos, Op. 8 Nos 5* (*La Tempesta di mare*)*; 6* (*Il piacere*)*; 10* (*La caccia*)*;* (ii) *in E* (*L'amoroso*)*, RV 271.*
(B) ** Ph. On Tour *412 908-4*. (i) Ayo; (ii) Carmirelli; I Musici.

The Four Seasons; (i) *Double concertos* (*arr.*) *for violin and flute: in C min; D min.*
(B) ** CBS *MGT 39493*. Stern, (i) (with Rampal), Jerusalem Music Centre CO – TELEMANN: *Suite in A min.***

(i; ii) *The Four Seasons;* (iii) *Recorder concerto in C, RV 443;* (ii) *Double violin concerto in A* (*Echo*)*, RV 552.*
(B) **(*) DG Walkman *413 142-4*. (i) Schneiderhan; (ii) Lucerne Fest. Strings, Baumgartner; (iii) Linde, Emil Seiler CO, Hofmann (with: ALBINONI: *Adagio* (arr. Giazotto). CORELLI: *Concerto grosso in G min.* (*Christmas*)*, Op. 6/8.* PACHELBEL: *Canon and Gigue in D****).

Schneiderhan favours fast tempi in the *Seasons*, but his playing is assured and the performance has plenty of character. The recording, from the beginning of the 1960s, is rather light in the bass. On the Walkman tape the couplings are generous and include Vivaldi's ingenious *Echo concerto*, where the echo effects are not just confined to the soloists but feature the ripieno too; plus the engaging *Concerto for sopranino recorder*, RV 552. Then to make the concert doubly generous, this bargain-priced Walkman tape offers three other Baroque favourites. Performances are of high quality throughout and the transfer is consistently vivid, although there is a slight edge on the solo violin in *The Four Seasons*.

Felix Ayo's version of *The Four Seasons* was I Musici's first stereo recording, and although it dates from 1959 the warmly resonant sound does not seem dated. The only snag is that its ambient warmth casts a sentient spell over the proceedings, to suggest that this particular set of seasons is located in a semi-tropical climate. The solo playing is stylish, but *Winter* is far from severe, and even the shepherd's dog in *Spring* seems to be barking in his sleep. There is much more vitality in the additional works, three of which also come from Op. 8. Pina Carmirelli takes over the solo role in *L'amoroso*. An agreeable tape for late evening but not a strong recommendation for the main work.

Isaac Stern creates a novelty in the slow movement of *Spring* by his decoration of the reprise of the solo line. Otherwise, this is a strong, bravura reading, with plenty of orchestral bustle to support the soloist. Stern's articulation is impressively brilliant and he provides serene contrast in slow movements. But with bright sound this has few moments of real individuality, although the opening of *Winter* is suitably icy. What makes this CBS double-length tape more interesting is the inclusion of a pair of *Double concertos*, originally for two violins, but here arranged for violin and flute. Stern is joined by Rampal, and the partnership is a sparkling one, especially in the D minor work. The sound is good throughout.

The Four Seasons, Op. 8/1–4 (arr. for flute and strings).
*** RCA **RD 70161**; RL/*RK* 70161 [**RCD1 2264**; LRL1/*LRK1* 2284]. Galway, I Solisti di Zagreb.

James Galway's transcription is thoroughly musical and so convincing that at times one is tempted to believe that the work was conceived in this form. The playing itself is marvellous, full of detail and imagination, and the recording is excellent, even if the flute is given a forward balance, the more striking on CD. The LP and cassette are closely matched.

6 Flute concertos, Op. 10 (complete).
*** O-L **414 685-2**; DSLO/*KDSLC* 519 [id.]. Preston, AAM.
*** Ph. **412 874-2**; 9500/*7300* 942 [id.]. Petri, ASMF, Marriner.
** CBS Dig. **MK 39062**; IM/*IMT* 39062 [id.]. Rampal, Sol. Ven., Scimone.
** RCA Dig. **RD 85316**; RL/*RK* 85316 [**RCD1 5316**; HRC1/*HRE1* 5316]. Galway, New Irish CO.

Stephen Preston plays a period instrument, a Schuchart, and the Academy of Ancient Music likewise play old instruments. Their playing is eminently stylish, yet both spirited and expressive, and they are admirably recorded, with the analogue sound enhanced further in the CD format. The cassette has marginally less refinement in the upper range but is otherwise of good quality.

Whereas Stephen Preston uses a baroque flute and Jean-Pierre Rampal a modern instrument, the young Danish virtuoso Michala Petri uses a modern recorder. At least this, like Rampal's set, gives us the opportunity of hearing these concertos at present-day pitch. Michala Petri plays with breathtaking virtuosity and impeccable control, and she has the advantage of superb recording. In the slow movements – and occasionally elsewhere – there is more in the music than she finds, but the sheer virtuosity of this gifted young artist is most infectious. She uses a sopranino recorder in three of the concertos. Generally speaking, this Philips recording is to be preferred to either of the recent newcomers, Rampal on CBS or Galway on RCA, and sounds even fresher on the digitally remastered compact disc. The cassette matches the LP closely. The upper orchestral range has slightly less bite, but the solo recorder has fine naturalness and presence.

Jean-Pierre Rampal was one of the first to record these concertos, way back in the early 1950s, but this CBS account, his third for LP, is rather more glamorized than its predecessors. Dynamic contrasts are rather extreme and the results a little overblown. Of course, as flute playing this is pretty spectacular; if you want a frankly modern virtuoso approach, rather than a more scaled-down reading with a greater sense of period, this excellent recorded version will not disappoint. The CD has the advantage of a digital master and sounds admirably fresh and transparent.

James Galway directs the New Irish Chamber Orchestra from the flute – and to generally good effect. The playing is predictably brilliant but the sweet vibrato is all a bit too much. This record is directed towards the broader public, and it is for Galway rather than Vivaldi that one will want it. No complaints about the recording quality or the orchestral contribution, but those who do buy it are warned that the pauses between movements are absurdly short. There is a faithful chrome cassette.

Chamber concertos: in A min., RV 86; in C, RV 87; in D, RV 92 and 95 (La Pastorella); in G, RV 101; in G min., RV 103 and RV 105; in A min., RV 108.

*** Ph. Dig. **411 356-2**; 411 356-1/*4* (2) [id.]. Petri, Holliger, Ayo, Pellegrino, Jaccottet, Thunemann, Demenga, Rubin.

These are what later generations might have called concertante works, concertos exploiting the interplay of several soloists. They are all given performances of the highest accomplishment and recordings that are natural in both timbre and perspective. As usual, Philips give us warm, excellently focused sound with admirable detail and realism, particularly in the compact disc format, which is delightfully fresh and immediate. The playing of these artists is eminently fine, though in one or two of the slow movements there is just a suggestion of the routine. However, so rich is Vivaldi's invention and resource and so brilliant are these performances, that it would be curmudgeonly to deny them a warm recommendation. The equivalent chrome tapes have splendid presence and realism.

(i) *Flute concertos: in D, R V 84 and R V 89; in G, R V 102;* (ii) *Recorder concerto in A min., R V 108* (with (ii) VALENTINE: *Recorder concerto in B flat;* SARRI: *Recorder concerto in A min.).*
* DG Arc. **415 299-2** [id.]. (i) Hazelzet; (ii) Heyens, Col. Mus. Ant., Goebel.

Both Gudrun Heyens and Wilbert Hazelzet are masters of their authentic instruments. With fast pacing from Goebel, their bravura is in no doubt either. But the edgy accompaniments, using only a string quartet plus continuo, are not helped by a recording focus that is less than sharp, and there is a total absence of charm here, with allegros made to sound aggressiv · by the close balance. The concertos by Roberto Valentine (1680–1735) and Domenico Sarri (1679–1744), each of four movements, open the concert, with the Sarri work the more attractive of the two. But the lack of bloom on the recording does not entice the listener to return to them.

Flute concertos: in D, R V 429; in G, R V 435; Sopranino recorder concerto in C, R V 443; Treble recorder concertos: in A min., R V 108; in F, R V 434.
(M) *** HMV EG 290303-1/*4* [Ang. Sera. S 60362]. Linde, Prague CO.

The West German flautist Hans-Martin Linde has an attractively fresh tone both on the flute and on the two sizes of recorder he uses for three of these concertos. Two of the regular Op. 10 works are included – No. 4, expressly written for transverse flute, and No. 5, expressly written for treble recorder, as it is played here. Rhythmically lively, Linde is splendidly accompanied by the excellent strings of the Prague Chamber Orchestra. The sound is full and clear.

Guitar concertos: in D, R V 93; in A min. (from Op. 3/6), R V 356; in C, R V 425. Double guitar concerto in G, R V 532; Quadruple guitar concerto in B min. (from Op. 3/10), R V 580.
*** Ph. Dig. **412 624-2**; 412 624-1/*4* [id.]. Los Romeros, ASMF, Iona Brown.

Two of these concertos are transcriptions from *L'Estro armonico* and, though they are in themselves pleasing, they are probably more enjoyable in their original form, particularly the slow movements with their sustained melodic lines. However, no less a composer than Bach transcribed them for keyboard, and there is no doubting the expertise and musicianship of the four Romeros and the Academy, nor the excellence of the Philips engineering. The other concertos for lute and mandolin come off excellently. Not an issue that would probably have high priority in a Vivaldi collection, but none the less enjoyable. The chrome cassette is perhaps not so sharply defined as the CD, but its intimate atmosphere is most attractive, and this could provide evocative listening for the late evening. The *Largo* of R V 93, which ends the programme, is particularly haunting.

Guitar concertos in D, R V 93; in B flat, R V 524; in G, R V 532. Trios: in C, R V 82; in G min., R V 85.
*** DG Dig. **415 487-2**; 415 487-1/*4* [id.]. Söllscher, Bern Camerata, Füri.

Four of these works are for mandolin (RV 532) or lute (RV 82, 85, 93), and the remaining two are for two violins (RV 524) and two cellos (RV 532). Göran Söllscher further enhances his reputation both as a master-guitarist and as an artist on this excellently recorded issue, in which he has first-class support from the Camerata Bern under Thomas Füri. In RV 532, Söllscher resorts to technology and plays both parts. Throughout, this gifted young Swedish artist plays with the taste and intelligence one has come to expect from him. The DG balance is admirably judged, and in the compact disc format the results are remarkably clean and finely focused.

Mandolin concerto in C, RV 425; Double mandolin concerto in G, RV 532; (Soprano) Lute concerto in D, RV 93; Double concerto in D min. for viola d'amore and lute, RV 540. Trios: in C, RV 82; in G min., RV 85.
*** Hyp. **CDA 66160**; A/*KA* 66160 [id.]. Jeffrey, O'Dette, Parley of Instruments, Goodman and Holman.

These are chamber performances, with one instrument to each part, and this obviously provides an ideal balance for the *Mandolin concertos*. There are other innovations, too. An organ continuo replaces the usual harpsichord, and very effective it is; in the *Trios* and the *Lute concerto* (but not in the *Double concerto*, RV 540) Paul O'Dette uses a gut-strung soprano lute. This means that in passages with the lute doubling the violin, the two instruments play in unison and the effect is piquant, with the lute giving a delicate edge to the more sustained string articulation. The *Double concerto* features a normal baroque lute, and Peter Holman argues the case for the use of these alternatives in his interesting notes. Any practice of this kind is bound to be conjectural, but the delightful sounds here, with all players using original instruments or copies, are very convincing. Certainly the mandolin concertos are more telling (plucked with a plectrum) than they are in guitar transcriptions. The recording is realistically balanced within an attractively spacious acoustic, and the scale is most convincing. There is an excellent tape.

Oboe concertos: in C, RV 446 and RV 452; in D min. (from Op. 8), RV 454; in G for oboe and bassoon, RV 545.
*** Ph. Dig. **411 480-2**; 411 480-1/*4* [id.]. Holliger, Thunemann, I Musici.

A collection of this kind is self-recommending. Holliger is in superb form, matching his expressive flexibility with infectious bravura in allegros and providing nicely judged ornamentation. All the music is attractively inventive, especially the *Double concerto for oboe and bassoon* which is nicely scored and has a memorable slow movement. The recording is balanced most realistically and sounds especially well in its newest compact disc format – the LP and matching cassette were issued first in 1982.

Piccolo concertos: in C, RV 433; in C min., RV 441; in C, RV 444; in A min., RV 445.
** Denon Dig. **C37 7076** [id.]. Dünschede, augmented Berlin Philh. Qt.

These are chamber performances using modern instruments, and the resonance of the sound adds substance to the accompanying string quintet, plus harpsichord, without in any way blurring inner detail. The playing is eminently musical, tempi are steady, articulation is clean and Hans Wolfgang Dünschede plays expertly and adds judicious ornamentation. But four piccolo concertos in a row is not very good planning, particularly when two are in C major, and the performances have no striking flair to render them individual or give them special charm. Michael Copley's rather similar collection, using recorders – see below – is a much better recommendation.

Recorder concertos: in C min., RV 441; in F, RV 442; in C, RV 443 and RV 444; in A min., RV 445.
*** DG Dig. **415 275-2**; 415 275-1/*4* [id.]. Copley, Bern Camerata, Füri.

The first two concertos (RV 441–2) are for alto recorder and strings, the remaining three are for an instrument Vivaldi called the *flautino*, which the majority of expert opinion believes to be the sopranino recorder. This plays an octave above the alto recorder. The music is not to be taken at one sitting but, as always with this composer, one is often taken by surprise by the quality and range of the invention. The *F major*, RV 442, is a delight, the material of all three movements deriving from operatic arias written twenty years earlier in the 1720s. The slow movement in particular is quite inspired. These performances by Michael Copley and the Camerata Bern lack nothing in virtuosity and dash; and the recording is excellent in every way, well balanced and truthful in perspective. The cassette nearly matches the CD in clarity and presence, but the opening concerto (RV 444) has a trace of roughness in the orchestra, stemming from the high transfer level. The remainder of the collection seems to be unaffected.

Violin concertos: L'Estro armonico: in A min., Op. 3/6; La Stravaganza: in A, Op. 4/5; in C min. (Il Sospetto), RV 199; in G min., Op. 12/1.
*** HMV Dig. **CDC 747076-2** [id.]; EL 270012-1/*4* [Ang. DS/*4DS* 38080]. Perlman, Israel PO.

Virtuoso performances of a representative set of Vivaldi violin concertos, given with Perlman's customary aplomb and effortless virtuosity. Unlike, say, Galway or Rampal in the Op. 10 *Flute concertos*, Perlman scales down the virtuoso display, and those who want sweet modern string-tone and warmth in the slow movements need look no further. The string playing of the Israel Philharmonic is expressive without becoming overladen with sentiment. The only handicap is the somewhat dryish acoustic, a factor that is underlined in the clarity achieved on compact disc, which also lends a trace of hardness in tutti. However, the ear rapidly adjusts and it is worth stressing that this is not sufficiently disturbing to stand in the way of a strong recommendation.

Violin concertos: in E flat (La Tempesta di mare), Op. 8/5, RV 253; in E (L'Amoroso), RV 271; in E min. (Il Favorito), RV 277; in A, RV 253.
*(*) ASV ALH /*ZCALH* 953 [id.]. Monica Huggett, L. Vivaldi O.

This collection is strictly for confirmed authenticists. Monica Huggett has a justified reputation in this repertoire, but the playing here, with spiky timbres and squeezed phrasing, is charmless, lacking any feeling of Italian sunshine in works that can sound highly beguiling. The sound on LP is clear and full, with a resonant bass, but the cassette transfer is poorly focused.

Violin concertos: in D min. (*Senza cantin*), *RV 243; in E* (*Il Riposo*), *RV 270; in E min.* (*Il Favorito*), *RV 277; in F* (*Per la solennità di San Lorenzo*), *RV 286.*
*** HMV Dig. EL 270133/-1/*4*. Accardo, I Solisti delle Settimane Musicali Internazionali di Napoli.

Salvatore Accardo plays each of the four concertos on this record on different instruments from the collection of the Palazzo Communale, Cremona. He plays the *E major*, *Il riposo*, on the Niccolo Amati, *Il Favorito* on the Cremonose of 1715, the darker-hued *Concerto senza cantin* (without using the E string) on the Guarnieri del Gesù, and the *Concerto per la solennità di San Lorenzo* on the Andrea Amati of Charles IX of France. But this is more than a record for violin specialists; it offers playing of the highest order by one of the finest violinists of our time. Accardo himself directs the excellent ensemble, and the EMI recording is first class in every respect. A very distinguished record and an essential LP for any Vivaldi collection. The tape quality is dry and clear, but somewhat lacking in bloom.

Double concerto for violin and oboe in G min., RV 576; Violin concerto in D (*per la S.S.ma Assontione di Maria Vergine*), *RV 582.*
(*) Ph. Dig. **411 466-2; 6514/*7337* 311 [id.]. Holliger, Kremer, ASMF – BACH: *Double concerto* and *Sinfonia.****

As in the Bach coupling, Holliger dominates the performance of the *Double concerto*, especially in the slow movement, where Kremer's timbre is expressively less expansive. But Kremer comes into his own in the delightful *D major concerto*, showing Vivaldi at his most inspired and imaginative. This features a double orchestra in the accompaniment sometimes used antiphonally and, although the effects are well brought off here, the stereo separation is not as clear as might have been expected. Otherwise the sound, clear and resonant, is finely judged; Kremer's sparkling articulation in the allegros is balanced by his serenely beautiful playing in the delicate cantilena of the central *Largo*.

MISCELLANEOUS COLLECTIONS

Bassoon concerto in A min., RV 498; Flute concerto in C min., RV 441; Oboe concerto in F, RV 456; Concerto for 2 oboes, bassoon, 2 horns and violin, RV 369.
(M) *** Decca Ser. 414 056-1/*4*. Gatt, Bennett, Black, Nicklin, Timothy Brown, Robin Davis, ASMF, Marriner.

This Decca Serenata reissue gives great pleasure. The playing is splendidly alive and characterful, with crisp, clean articulation and well-pointed phrasing, free from over-emphasis. The work for oboes and horns is agreeably robust; the *A minor Bassoon concerto* has a delightful sense of humour, while the flute and the oboe concertos, if not showing Vivaldi at his most inventive, are still very compelling and worthwhile. The recording is a model of clarity and definition. It stems from the Argo catalogue and dates from 1977. For those who enjoy the sound of modern wind instruments in this repertoire, it is one of the finest Vivaldi collections on LP or tape made during the analogue era. The cassette transfer is on iron-oxide stock, but the sound quality is very good.

(i) *Bassoon concerto in E min., RV 584;* (ii) *Double horn concerto in F, RV 539;* (iii) *Double trumpet concerto in D, RV 537; Concerto for 2 violins, 2 cellos in D, RV 564;* (iv) *Concerto for 2 violins and lute, RV 93.*

*(*) Erato Dig. **ECD 88009**; NUM/*MCE* 75009 [id.]. (i) Allard; (ii) Magnardi, Both; (iii) Touvron, Boisson; (iv) Hubscher (lute), Sol. Ven., Scimone.

A disappointing collection, often lacking in vitality. The most characterful of the soloists is Maurice Allard (bassoon) whose woody timbre is attractive; he finds a nice balance between geniality and lyricism. The two string concertos are also well done, with plenty of antiphonal interplay; much use is made of echo phrasing. The string soloists are drawn from the orchestra, while Jürgen Hubscher's lute adds an extra constituent to RV 93. The 1981 recording does not provide the presence and inner definition one would expect from a digital master, though it is naturally balanced.

Double cello concerto in G min., RV 531; Double flute concerto in C, RV 533; Concertos for strings in D min. (*Madrigalesco*), *RV 129; in G* (*Alla rustica*), *RV 151; Double trumpet concerto in C, RV 537; Concerto for 2 violins and 2 cellos in D, RV 564.*

*** O-L **414 588-2** [id.]; DSLO/*KDSLC* 544. AAM, Hogwood.

Not everything in this issue is of equal substance: the invention in the *Double trumpet concerto*, for example, is not particularly strong; but for the most part it is a rewarding and varied programme. It is especially appealing in that authenticity is allied to musical spontaneity. The best-known concertos are the *Madrigalesco* and the *Alla rustica*, but some of the others are just as captivating. The *Concerto for two flutes* has great charm and is dispatched with vigour and aplomb. Readers with an interest in this often unexpectedly rewarding composer, whose unpredictability continues to astonish, should not hesitate. Performances and recording alike are first rate, with added clarity and presence on CD. The cassette, however, is coarsened by too high a transfer level.

(i) *Flute concerto in F* (*La Tempesta di mare*), *Op. 10/1;* (ii) *Oboe concertos: in C* (*from Op. 8/12*), *RV 449; in D min., RV 454;* (i) *Recorder concerto in C, RV 444; Concertos for strings: in D min., RV 127; in A, RV 158.*

(*) Chan. Dig. **CHAN 8444; ABRD/*ABTD* 1156 [id.]. (i) Hutchins, (ii) Baskin; I Musici di Montreal, Turovsky.

I Musici di Montreal is a new Canadian group that has been working under its present conductor since the autumn of 1983. They are recorded in the resonant acoustic of St Madeleine's Church, Montreal, and the balance produces a fresh bright sound from the fourteen strings, just a shade lacking in body. Their spirited musicianship brings plenty of life to the two attractive string concertos, while the rather beautiful *Largo* of the *A major*, RV 158, enjoys a nicely judged expressive response. The programme opens buoyantly with Timothy Hutchins's brilliant account of *La Tempesta di mare*, expertly presented on a sopranino recorder; but the highlight of the concert is the pair of oboe concertos, beautifully played by Theodore Baskin. Like Hutchins, he is a principal of the Montreal Symphony. Readers who possess Dutoit's Montreal Ravel recordings will not be surprised to discover that he is a superb soloist in every respect. His articulation of allegros is a delight, while phrasing in slow movements combines elegance and finesse with a stylish approach to ornamentation. The recording places him realistically in relation to the accompaniment; allowing for the reverberation, the sound is first class.

(i) *Flute concerto in D (Il Cardellino), Op. 10/3; Triple violin concerto in F, RV 551.*

*(*) Denon Dig. **C37 7178** [id.]. Susan Milan; Lucerne Fest. Strings, Baumgartner – MOZART: *Divertimento, K.138* etc.*(*)

Recorded very realistically in the attractive ambience of the new Symphony Hall in Osaka, Baumgartner and his group give eminently musical accounts of these two concertos. However, the German manner in Vivaldi is not always totally convincing, and in the slow movement of the *Flute concerto* the soloist's phrasing seems very deliberate. Acceptable, but not really distinctive, in spite of the excellent sound.

Double flute concerto in C, RV 533; Double oboe concerto in D min., RV 535; Double horn concerto in F, RV 539; Double trumpet concerto in C, RV 537; Concerto for 2 oboes, 2 clarinets and strings, RV 560.

(M) **(*) Pickwick Dig. **PCD 811**. Soloists, SCO, Laredo.

An attractive mid-priced compilation, with soloists and orchestra set back in good perspective in a believable acoustic. The resonance tends to make the trumpet timbre spread, but otherwise the sound is very good. The solo playing is accomplished, although rather more light and shade between phrases would have made the performances even more enticing, while Jaime Laredo's direction of the slow movements is not especially imaginative. But there is some highly engaging music here, not least the outer movements of RV 560 where the sounds of oboes and clarinets chatter in alternation like excited children chasing each other. In RV 539, the horn playing is robust; while modern instruments are used, the effect is not over-sophisticated, though remaining secure.

Double flute concerto in C, RV 533; Double horn concerto in F, RV 539; Double mandolin concerto in G, RV 536; Double oboe concerto in A min., RV 536; Concerto for oboe and bassoon in G, RV 545; Double trumpet concerto in D, RV 563.
*** Ph. Dig. **412 892-2**; 6514/*7337* 379 [id.]. Soloists, ASMF, Marriner.

This collection repeats the success of the Academy's recordings of Vivaldi wind concertos made in the late 1970s for Argo and currently reissued at mid-price on Decca's Serenata label (see above and below). Apart from the work for two horns, where the focus of the soloists lacks a degree of sharpness, the recording often reaches demonstration standard. On CD, the concerto featuring a pair of mandolins is particularly tangible, with the balance near perfect, the solo instruments in proper scale yet registering admirable detail. The concertos for flutes and oboes are played with engaging finesse, conveying a sense of joy in the felicity of the writing. Throughout, the accompaniments are characteristically polished and especially imaginative of their use of light and shade in alternating phrases. In this respect the music making here is of a different calibre from the Scottish collection on Pickwick – see above – but, as it happens, only two of the concertos are duplicated. Once again Marriner makes a very good case for the use of modern wind instruments in this repertoire. The cassette is transferred at the highest level – indeed, the horn and trumpet works are obviously taking the tape near saturation point, although the other concertos sound excellent.

Double horn concerto in F, RV 539; Double oboe concerto in D min., RV 535; Concerto in F for 2 oboes, bassoon, 2 horns and violin, RV 574; Piccolo concerto in C, RV 443.
(M) *** Decca Ser. 414 324-1/*4*. Soloists, ASMF, Marriner.

The musical substance may not be very weighty, but Vivaldi was rarely more engaging than when, as here, he was writing for wind instruments, particularly if he had more than one in his team of soloists. This delectable record makes a splendid supplement to the earlier one in the series (Decca 414 056-1/*4* – see above). Both originally stem from the Argo catalogue and are notable for vivid and excellently balanced recording. The equivalent tape is also very well managed, although iron-oxide stock is used.

Double concerto for oboe and violin in B flat, RV 548; Triple concerto in C for violin, oboe and organ, RV 554; Double concertos for violin and organ: in D min., RV 541; in C min. and F, RV 766–7.
*** Unicorn Dig. **DKPCD 9050**; DKP/*DKPC* 9050 [id.]. Francis, Studt, Bate, Tate Music Group, Studt.

An engaging clutch of concertos, two of which (RV 766–7) are first recordings. The works featuring the organ in a concertante role are in the concerto grosso tradition and are notable for their imaginative juxtaposition of colours – which is not to say that they lack vitality of invention. The highlight is RV 541 with its fine *Grave* slow movement and exhilaratingly busy finale, while the *Double* concerto for oboe (in the ascendant role) *and violin* is hardly less engaging, and offers some captivating oboe playing from Richard Studt, whose timbre seems exactly right for this repertoire. The recording is very attractive in ambience and the balance is admirable, with the sound first class in all three media – the chrome cassette is outstandingly realistic.

(i) *L'Estro armonico: Violin concerto in G, Op. 3/5;* (ii) *Mandolin concerto in C, RV 425;* (iii) *Recorder concerto in G min. (La Notte), Op. 10/2;* (iv) *Double trumpet concerto in C, RV 537;* (v) *Concerto for viola d'amore and guitar in D min., RV 540.*

(B) **(*) DG Walkman *415 328-4* [id.]. (i) Prystawski, Lucerne Fest. Strings, Baumgartner; (ii) Ochi, Kuentz CO, Kuentz; (iii) Linde, Zurich Coll. Mus., Sacher; (iv) André, ECO, Mackerras; (v) Frasca-Colombier, Yepes, Kuentz CO, Kuentz – HANDEL: *Concertos.***(*)

A diverse and enjoyable collection offering expert solo-playing (Maurice André – by electronic means – takes both parts in the *Double trumpet concerto* and the bravura is spectacular). There is plenty of vitality. The close balance in RV 425 produces a jumbo-sized mandolin, and the very high level of the transfers veers close to, but does not quite reach, saturation point. With its excellent Handel coupling, this is worth its modest cost.

VOCAL MUSIC

Beatus vir, RV 597; Dixit dominus, RV 594.

*** Argo Dig. **414 495-2**; 414 495-1/*4* [id.]. Buchanan, Jennifer Smith, Watts, Partridge, Shirley-Quirk, King's College Ch., ECO, Cleobury.

When discussing this issue in *Gramophone*, the reviewer, Nicholas Anderson, recalled the mono LP début of this setting of *Beatus vir*, conducted on Vox by the late Hans Grischat. We remember it too, and especially the discovery of Vivaldi's magically gleaming phrase on the trebles with which the piece opens so memorably. Those were the days when the gramophone was just beginning to reveal the genius and diversity of a composer whose music had lain largely unperformed for well over two centuries. In the early 1950s even *The Four Seasons* was fresh to most ears, and there was so much else to come; nothing, however, more refreshing than these two delightfully spontaneous and original psalm settings. *Dixit dominus* cannot fail to attract those who have enjoyed the better-known *Gloria.* Both works are powerfully inspired and are here given vigorous and sparkling performances with King's College Choir in excellent form under its latest choirmaster. The soloists are a fine team, fresh, stylish and nimble – for much of the florid music calls for technical bravura – and the reverberant recording remains atmospheric, without detail becoming clouded. There is plenty of clean articulation from the choristers, nicely projected, especially in the CD format, with its extra sharpness of definition. The chrome cassette is impressive too, but less clean and refined on top.

Gloria in D, RV 589.
*** O-L **414 678-2** [id.]. Nelson, Watkinson, Christ Church Cathedral Ch., AAM, Preston – BACH: *Magnificat.****

The freshness and point of the Christ Church performance of the *Gloria* are irresistible; anyone who normally doubts the attractiveness of authentic string technique should sample this, for the absence of vibrato adds a tang exactly in keeping with the performance. The soloists too keep vibrato to the minimum, adding to the freshness, yet Carolyn Watkinson rivals even Dame Janet Baker in the dark intensity of the Bach-like central aria for contralto, *Domine Deus, Agnus Dei.* The choristers of Christ Church Cathedral excel themselves and the recording is outstandingly fine. For the CD issue, the performance has been re-coupled, more generously, with the original version of Bach's *Magnificat,* and the sound brings a marked improvement in definition and presence compared with the analogue LP.

Gloria in D, RV 588; Gloria in D, RV 589.
*** Argo Dig. **410 018-2**; ZRDL/*KZRDC* 1006. Russell, Kwella, Wilkens, Bowen, St John's College, Cambridge, Ch., Wren O, Guest.

The two settings of the *Gloria* make an apt and illuminating coupling. Both in D major, they have many points in common, presenting fascinating comparisons, when RV 588 is as inspired as its better-known companion. Guest directs strong and well-paced readings, with RV 588 the more lively. Good, warm recording to match the performances. On compact disc the added clarity is never clinical in sharpening detail, and the overall ambient atmosphere is most appealing. There is also a vivid chrome cassette, but the upper choral focus is not as clean as the LP, and needs a treble cut to smooth the sound.

(i) *Nisi Dominus* (*Psalm 126*), *RV 608; Stabat Mater, RV 621; Concerto for strings in G min., RV 153.*
(*) O-L Dig. **414 329-2 [id.]; DSLO/*KDSLC* 506. AAM, Hogwood; (i) with Bowman.

These performances are vital enough and there is no want of stylistic awareness. James Bowman is a persuasive soloist. But since Vivaldi probably wrote these for the Pietà, a Venetian orphanage for girls, readers might prefer to turn to Helen Watts in the *Nisi Dominus*, although her beautiful Erato version is not yet available on compact disc (STU 71200). The *Concerto* is an engaging work whose charms benefit from the authentic instruments. While on LP the recording – cut at a higher level than usual – does not always reproduce with maximum smoothness, the CD is altogether excellent, bringing a marked improvement. The sound is marvellously fresh and present. The cassette too is of very good quality, smooth, yet clear; but the CD is finer still.

OPERA

Catone in Utica (partially complete).
*(*) Erato Dig. **ECD 88142**; NUM 75204 (2) [id.]. Gasdia, Schmiege, Zimmermann, Lendi, Palaccio, Sol. Ven., Scimone.

When so few Vivaldi operas have been recorded, it is disappointing that this set can be given only a limited recommendation. It is a curious choice, when the first Act is missing, and the other two Acts are not so rich musically as other Vivaldi operas. Cecilia Gasdia sings impressively, and Scimone conducts a fair, middle-of-the-road interpretation, but more is needed if the cause of the music is to be argued effectively. Good sound.

Wagner, Richard (1813–83)

Overtures: Die Feen; Der fliegende Holländer; Tannhäuser (with *Bacchanale*).
** Ph. Dig. **400 089-2** [id.]. Concg. O, De Waart.

The special interest here is the rarely heard (and rarely recorded) *Die Feen overture*, written when Wagner was twenty for his first completed opera (see below). It is agreeable music, cast in the same melodic mould as *Rienzi*, if less rumbustious in feeling. All the performances here are warmly spacious, lacking something in electricity (the *Flying Dutchman* – which uses the original ending – sounds too cultured). The digital recording faithfully reflects the acoustic of the Concertgebouw, with its richly textured strings and brass, and resonant lower range; but some listeners might feel a need for a more telling upper range.

Overtures: Polonia; Rule Britannia. Marches: Grosser Festmarsch; Kaisermarsch.
*(*) HK/Impetus Dig. HK6/*HK4* 220114 [id.]. Hong Kong PO, Kojian.

The *Polonia overture* (1836) is the best piece here. Although its basic style is Weberian, there is a hint of the Wagner of *Rienzi* in the slow introduction. The *Grosser Festmarsch* (*American Centennial march*) was commissioned from Philadelphia, and for this inflated piece Wagner received a cool five thousand dollars! The *Rule Britannia overture* is even more overblown and the famous tune, much repeated, outstays its welcome. The *Kaisermarsch* is also empty and loud. The Hong Kong orchestra play all this with great enthusiasm, if without much finesse. The recording is vividly bright – but if this appears on CD, it is not a priority item, even for the most dedicated Wagnerian.

'Brass at Valhalla': Grosser Festmarsch. Götterdämmerung: Siegfried's funeral march. Lohengrin: Prelude to Act III; Bridal chorus. Die Meistersinger: Prelude to Act III. Das Rheingold: Entry of the Gods into Valhalla. Tannhäuser: Grand March.
* Decca Dig. **414 149-2**; 414 149-1/*4* [id.]. Philip Jones Ens., Howarth.

This collection gets off on the wrong foot by opening with the pompous rhetoric of the *Grosser Festmarsch*, played without cuts, and lasting for nearly fourteen weary minutes. The highlight of the collection is the *Act III Prelude* to *Lohengrin*, long beloved of brass bands – and rightly so, for it transcribes admirably. But the *Act III Prelude* to *Die Meistersinger* is another matter, losing much of its character in transcription. The *Götterdämmerung* and *Rheingold* excerpts are more successful, and of course everything is superbly played. But, even with the added presence of CD, only the *Lohengrin* piece is memorable, for after the opening fanfares the *Grand march* from *Tannhäuser* needs its chorus.

Siegfried idyll.
*** Decca Dig. **410 111-2**; 410 111-1/*4* [id.]. ECO, Ashkenazy – SCHOENBERG: *Verklaerte Nacht.****
*** Ph. **412 465-2** (2) [id.]. Concg. O, Haitink – BRUCKNER: *Symphony No. 8.****
(*) CBS **M2K 42036 (2) [id.]. Columbia SO, Walter – BRUCKNER: *Symphony No. 7.***

Siegfried idyll; Lohengrin: Prelude to Act I.
(M) *** DG 415 634-1/*4* (2). BPO, Kubelik – MAHLER: *Symphony No. 9.***

The honeyed warmth of Wagner's domestic inspiration, its flow of melodies and textures that caress the ear, are superbly brought out by Ashkenazy. Warm, full recording to match the playing, especially on compact disc. The chrome-cassette transfer too is one of Decca's best, matching the LP closely.

Haitink gives a simple, unaffected reading and draws playing of great refinement from the Concertgebouw Orchestra. Like Karajan's version – not yet available on CD – this has a simplicity of expression and a tenderness that will leave few listeners unmoved. The sound is first class, with the 1980 analogue recording most successfully remastered.

Walter's is essentially a gentle performance; the opening is quite lovely, and though the 1963 recording loses just a little of its bloom at the climax – which has no lack of ardour – the rapt quality of the closing ritenuto is magical, with the ambience just right for the music.

There is marvellous playing from the Berlin Philharmonic on Kubelik's 1963 recording. If the *Siegfried idyll* is a little cool at the opening, it is beautifully shaped and, like the *Lohengrin Prelude*, the central climax is satisfyingly placed in relation to the whole. The recording still sounds very well in both LP and tape formats.

ORCHESTRAL EXCERPTS FROM THE OPERAS

Siegfried idyll. Götterdämmerung: Siegfried's Rhine journey, death and Funeral music. Lohengrin: Preludes to Acts I and III. Die Meistersinger: Overture. Siegfried: Forest murmurs. Tannhäuser: Overture and Venusberg music. Tristan und Isolde: Prelude and Liebestod. Die Walküre: Ride of the Valkyries.
(***) Fonit Cetra mono **CDC3 A/B** (2) [id.]. NBC SO, Toscanini.

Toscanini in Wagner was incandescent. Though the early 1950s mono sound on these live recordings is hard and rarely allows a true pianissimo, the brightness and clarity convey the electric intensity of the maestro, bringing out the white heat but also underlining the point that in Wagner Toscanini was rarely if ever rigid. At spacious speeds, he regularly drew out melodic lines with Italianate warmth, while preserving Germanic strength. Fortissimos with brass tend to blare – not just the fault of the recording – and string tone is not always sweet; but the sensuous beauty that Toscanini could elicit is superbly illustrated in the *Siegfried idyll.* The recordings have been digitally remastered by Fonit Cetra and this two-CD set is at present available only through specialist import sources.

Der fliegende Holländer: Overture. Götterdämmerung: Siegfried's Rhine journey. Die Meistersinger: Overture. Rienzi: Overture.
** Telarc **CD 80083;** DG 10083 [id.]. Minnesota SO, Marriner.

Marriner is at his best in the earlier overtures and notably in *Rienzi*, played with plenty of spirit, with the Minneapolis Hall adding richness and bloom. However, in *Die Meistersinger*, while the effect is agreeably spacious, the contrapuntal detail in the middle section is clouded in a way one does not expect in a digital recording. The overall perspective is truthful, but the muddying of the resonance is not ideal. *Siegfried's Rhine journey* is very well played, but is in no way distinctive.

Der fliegende Holländer: Overture. Lohengrin: Prelude to Act I. Die Meistersinger: Overture. (i) *Tannhäuser: Overture and Venusberg music.*
*** CBS **MK 42050** [id.]. Columbia SO, Bruno Walter, (i) with Occidental College Ch.

These performances all date from 1959. When the *Tannhäuser Overture and Venusberg music* was first issued at the beginning of the 1960s, we described it – in an early edition of the *Stereo Record Guide* – as one of Walter's greatest recordings. The years have not diminished its impact. The poise of the opening of the *Pilgrim's chorus* is arresting, and the reprise of this famous melody, before the introduction of the Venusberg section, is wonderfully gentle. With the central section thrillingly sensuous, the closing pages – the Occidental College Choir distantly balanced – bring a radiant hush. In digitally remastered form, the recording is most impressive. The sound in the *Flying Dutchman* and the *Mastersinger overtures* is fiercer in the upper range and, ideally, the latter could do with more amplitude; but the performances are mellowed by the conductor's spacious approach. The detail in the fugato middle section of *Die Meistersinger* is characteristically affectionate, and all the threads are satisfyingly drawn together in the expansive closing pages. The *Lohengrin Prelude* is rather relaxed, but beautifully controlled. With fine orchestral playing throughout, this stands among the most rewarding of all available compilations of Wagnerian orchestral excerpts.

Der fliegende Holländer: Overture. Lohengrin: Preludes to Acts I and III. Tristan und Isolde: Prelude and Liebestod.
(*) DG **413 733-2 [id.]. VPO, Boehm.

This companion to Boehm's earlier collection of Wagner overtures and preludes (see below) follows very much the same spacious pattern, with speeds broad rather than urgent. Not all the balances seem quite natural, but sound quality is not one's first concern in one of Boehm's last records. However, although the CD transfers are successful, this is not especially generous measure.

Overtures: Der fliegende Holländer; Die Meistersinger; Tannhäuser (original version). *Tristan und Isolde: Prelude and Liebestod.*
(*) Decca **411 951-2; SXL 6856 [Lon. 7078]. Chicago SO, Solti.

A quite attractive collection of Wagner overtures, very well played. Except for the *Flying Dutchman overture*, these are newly made recordings, not taken from Solti's complete opera sets. So this is the self-contained *Tannhäuser overture* from the Dresden version, and the *Liebestod* comes in the purely orchestral version. Perhaps surprisingly, comparison between Solti in Chicago and Solti in Vienna shows him warmer in America. The compact disc has been digitally remastered and emphasizes the different recording balances: *Fliegende Holländer* very brightly lit, *Die Meistersinger* appropriately mellower, *Tannhäuser* somewhat two-dimensional, and *Tristan* the most effective, with an impressive ambience. Overall, however, this is not a compilation to show any striking advantages from CD remastering.

Der fliegende Holländer: Overture. Die Meistersinger: Overture. (i) *Tannhäuser: Overture and Venusberg music. Tristan: Prelude and Liebestod.*
(M) *** HMV EG 290411-1/*4* [Ang. AM/*4AM* 34724]. BPO, Karajan; (i) with German Op. Ch.

This mid-priced collection is assembled from two LPs quadraphonically recorded by Karajan in 1975, one slightly more successful than the other in terms of electricity and excitement. All the music is superbly played, but the *Overture and Venusberg music* from *Tannhäuser* (Paris version, using chorus) and the *Prelude and Liebestod* from *Tristan* are superb. In the *Liebestod* the climactic culmination is overwhelming in its sentient power, while *Tannhäuser* has comparable spaciousness and grip. There is an urgency and edge to *The Flying Dutchman overture*, and *Die Meistersinger* has weight and dignity, but the last degree of tension is missing. Moreover, the digitally remastered sound produces a touch of fierceness in the upper range of these pieces; the *Tannhäuser* and *Tristan* excerpts are fuller, though some of the original bloom has gone. But the glorious playing of the Berlin orchestra still ensures a firm recommendation at mid-price.

Götterdämmerung: Siegfried's funeral music. Die Meistersinger: Overture.

Parsifal: Good Friday music. Tannhäuser: Overture. Tristan und Isolde: Prelude and Liebestod.
(**) DG mono **415 663-2** [id.]. BPO, Furtwängler.

Furtwängler's account of the *Tristan Prelude and Liebestod* is electrifying, and the 1954 recording is good. However, the collection opens with a 1949 version of the *Mastersingers overture* (notable for a memorably spacious broadening at the close) and a 1951 *Tannhäuser overture* (with splendidly clean articulation from the Berlin strings, but rather blatant brass), where the recording is no more than acceptable, and the harsh timbres are at odds with the music's amplitude. The *Parsifal* and *Götterdämmerung* excerpts sound much better, and again offer characteristic tension, but the bronchial afflictions of the audience in the *Good Friday music* are disturbingly intrusive.

Götterdämmerung: Prelude, Dawn, Siegfried's Rhine journey; Siegfried's funeral music; Finale. Siegfried: Forest murmurs. Die Walküre: Ride of the Valkyries.
** DG 410 893-1/*4* [id.]. O de Paris, Barenboim.

In long preparation before his appearances conducting the *Ring* cycle, Daniel Barenboim here recorded a useful collection of *Ring* excerpts with idiomatic warmth. The snag is that the Paris Orchestra – particularly the brass section, with its excessive vibrato – does not sound quite authentic, and the recording acoustic is not helpful, failing to give the necessary resonance to the deeper brass sounds. There is a satisfactory cassette equivalent.

Götterdämmerung: Dawn and Siegfried's Rhine journey; Siegfried's death and funeral march. Das Rheingold: Entry of the gods into Valhalla. Siegfried: Forest murmurs. Die Walküre: Ride of the Valkyries; Wotan's farewell and Magic fire music.
(*) HMV Dig. **CDC 747007-2; ASD/*TCC-ASD* 3985 [Ang. DS/*4XS* 37808]. BPO, Tennstedt.
** **CBS MK 37795** [id.]. NYPO, Mehta (with Peter Wimberger in the *Magic fire music*).

This HMV Berlin Philharmonic CD was the first digital orchestral collection from *The Ring*, and it was recorded with demonstrable brilliance. With steely metallic cymbal clashes in the *Ride of the Valkyries* and a splendid drum thwack at the opening of the *Entry of the gods into Valhalla*, the sense of spectacle is in no doubt. There is weight too: the climax of *Siegfried's funeral march* has massive penetration. There is also fine detail, especially in the atmospheric *Forest murmurs*. The playing itself is of the finest quality throughout and Tennstedt maintains a high level of tension. But the brass recording is rather dry and at times the ear feels some lack of amplitude and resonance in the bass. However, the grip of the playing is extremely well projected, and the degree of fierceness at the top is tameable. The compact disc seems to emphasize the dryness in the bass, and while detail is clear there is a lack of richness and bloom. The XDR tape has less glitter and bite than the LP (the cymbal transients demonstrably less telling), but the balance overall is fuller, without much loss of detail.

Mehta's performances are spacious and there is plenty of surface excitement. The playing of the New York Philharmonic has fervour; in the *Magic fire music* from *Die Walküre*, the orchestra is joined briefly by Peter Wimberger as Wotan, which has the effect of increasing the level of tension. *Siegfried's funeral music* is paced slowly with a sombre pianissimo at the opening, but Mehta's grip here is not ideally taut. Elsewhere, the very brilliant CBS sound gives a brashness to the brass which is not always quite comfortable.

In the USA, Szell's comparable collection made with the Cleveland Orchestra at the end of the 1960s is available on a 'Great Performances' CD (**MYK 36715**). The orchestral playing is superb and Szell's *Funeral march* (and indeed his atmospheric account of the *Forest murmurs* from *Siegfried*) is far finer than Mehta's; and his concert ends with a thrilling account of the immolation climax from *Götterdämmerung*. However, once again the CBS sound-balance is shrill on top, and Tennstedt remains a better choice.

Götterdämmerung: Siegfried's funeral music; Final scene. Das Rheingold: Entry of the gods into Valhalla. Siegfried: Forest murmurs. Die Walküre: Ride of the Valkyries; Wotan's farewell and Magic fire music.
Decca Dig. **410 137-2**; SXDL/*KSXDC* 7612. VPO, Solti.

There is nothing at all distinguished about Solti's 1983 compact disc of *Ring* excerpts – issued to coincide with the opening of his *Ring* at Bayreuth. The effect is of an unmusically balanced hi-fi spectacular. Brilliance and high dynamic contrasts, with every strand made artificially clear, emphasize unattractively aggressive performances, notably the first item, the *Ride of the Valkyries*, with none of the bloom and flair which marked John Culshaw's classic *Ring* production of over twenty years earlier. The performances – with vocal parts at times transcribed for instruments – are bold and strong, but show little warmth of any kind. The crystal-clear CD is even less attractive in demonstrating that crude brilliance is not enough in these scores.

Götterdämmerung: Siegfried's Rhine journey. Die Meistersinger: Overture. Parsifal: Good Friday music. Rienzi: Overture.
* Erato **ECD 88015**; NUM 75066 [id.]. Basle SO, Jordan.

This is well recorded, the acoustic is spacious and the CD has the usual virtues, not least a silent background for the *Good Friday music*. Jordan's pacing is well judged – but the Basle Symphony Orchestra is not the Berlin Philharmonic: the wind playing is unrefined (especially in the *Parsifal* excerpt) and the trumpeter at the opening of *Rienzi* sounds nervous.

Lohengrin: Preludes to Acts I and III. Die Meistersinger: Overture. Rienzi: Overture. Tannhäuser: Overture.
(*) HMV Dig. **CDC 747030-2 [id.]; ASD/*TC-ASD* 143578-1/*4* [Ang. DS/*4XS* 37990]. BPO, Tennstedt.

Klaus Tennstedt here shows something of the Klemperer tradition with these essentially broad and spacious readings, yet the voltage is consistently high. The opening and closing sections of the *Tannhäuser overture* are given a restrained nobility of feeling (and there is absolutely no hint of vulgarity) without any loss of power and impact. Similarly the gorgeous string melody at the opening of *Rienzi* is elegiacally moulded, and later when the brass enter in the allegro there is no suggestion of the bandstand. In the Act I *Lohengrin Prelude*, Tennstedt lingers in the pianissimo sections, creating radiant detail, then presses on just before the climax, a quite different approach from Furtwängler's, but no less telling. The Berlin Philharmonic are on top form throughout and the digital recording is both refined and brilliant, if without a glowing resonance in the middle and bass frequencies. This is emphasized by the CD which adds clarity of detail, brightens the treble, and makes the ear aware that a greater overall richness and amplitude would have been welcome. But these are fine performances, superbly played. The XDR cassette is generally faithful, though inner detail is less sharp: it isn't really a serious alternative to the compact disc.

Die Meistersinger: Overture. Parsifal: Prelude to Act I. Rienzi: Overture. Tannhäuser: Overture.
(*) DG **413 551-2 [id.]. VPO, Boehm.

Under Boehm the Vienna Philharmonic play beautifully in a choice of overtures spanning Wagner's full career from *Rienzi* to *Parsifal.* The performance of *Rienzi* has striking life and vigour; *Die Meistersinger* has both grandeur and detail, the *Parsifal Prelude* is superbly eloquent and spacious in feeling, and both show a compulsive inevitability in their forward flow. The recording is full, but its beauty is slightly marred by the aggressiveness of trumpet tone, although this is slightly less disturbing on CD. The programme is not very generous either.

Die Meistersinger: Prelude to Act III. Tannhäuser: Overture and Venusberg music. Tristan und Isolde: Prelude and Liebestod.
(*) DG Dig. **413 754-2; 413 754-1/*4* [id.]. BPO, Karajan.

HMV issued much the same compilation from Karajan and the Berlin Philharmonic in the mid-1970s in qudraphony, the difference being that on the present occasion the *Prelude* to Act III of *Die Meistersinger* replaces that to Act I of *Lohengrin*, and the Dresden rather than the Paris version of the *Venusberg music* is used in *Tannhäuser*. As can be seen above, EMI have reissued the earlier *Tannhäuser* and *Tristan* performances at mid-price in a different collection, with the digitally remastered sound a good deal less opulent than the original. In the new CD concert the orchestral playing, as before, is altogether superlative; artistically, there need be no reservations here. But the upper strings lack an ideal amount of space in which to open out and climaxes are not altogether free. The overall effect is slightly more clinical in its detail, instead of offering a resonant panoply of sound. But Brangaene's potion still remains heady, and the playing is eloquent and powerful. The chrome-cassette transfer is particularly successful – a state-of-the-art issue, losing nothing in detail even at pianissimo levels.

Parsifal: Prelude and Good Friday music.
Ͼ *** CBS **MK 42038** [id.]. Columbia SO, Bruno Walter – DVOŘÁK: *Symphony No. 8.****

A glorious account of the *Prelude and Good Friday music* from Walter, recorded in 1959, but with the glowingly rich recording never hinting at its age. The digital remastering is a superb achievement. This is one of the most beautiful orchestral recordings of Wagner yet available on CD, and the sound-balance is preferable to nearly all the modern digital collections of Wagner orchestral excerpts. The coupling with Walter's outstanding account of Dvořák's *Eighth Symphony* – another very fine performance and recording – makes this CD an indispensable acquisition for any admirer of this great conductor.

Tristan und Isolde: Prelude and Liebestod.
(*) Lodia Dig. **LOCD 783/4 [id.]. New Philh. O, Païta - BRUCKNER: *Symphony No. 8.***(*)

Recorded over twelve years before the Bruckner symphony with which it is coupled, Païta's urgent reading of the *Prelude and Liebestod* originally won a *Grand Prix du Disque*; it still sounds well, though after the symphony the tape hiss is noticeable, and the bass is at times boomy.

VOCAL MUSIC

Wesendonk Lieder.
*** Decca **414 624-2** [id.]. Kirsten Flagstad, VPO, Knappertsbusch – MAHLER: *Kindertotenlieder; Lieder eines fahrenden Gesellen.***

Wesendonk Lieder. Tristan und Isolde: Prelude and Liebestod.
(*) Ph. **412 655-2; 9500 031 [id.]. Jessye Norman, LSO, Sir Colin Davis.

Flagstad's glorious voice is perfectly suited to the rich inspiration of the *Wesendonk Lieder. Im Treibhaus* is particularly beautiful. Fine accompaniment, with the 1956 recording sounding remarkable for its vintage and skilfully remastered to give the voice added character and presence. However, the Mahler couplings recorded during the same period are rather less successful.

The poised phrases of the *Wesendonk Lieder* drew from Jessye Norman in this 1976 recording a glorious range of tone-colour, though in detailed imagination she falls short of some of the finest rivals on record. The coupling is most apt, since two of the *Wesendonk* songs were written as studies for *Tristan*. Though the role of Isolde would no doubt strain a still-developing voice, and this is not the most searching of *Liebestods*, it is still the vocal contribution which crowns this conventional linking of first and last in the opera. Good, refined recording, made the more vivid on CD with an excellent digital transfer and silent background.

OPERA

Die Feen (complete).

*** Orfeo Dig. S 063833F (3) [id.]. Gray, Lovaas, Laki, Studer, Alexander, Hermann, Moll, Rootering, Bracht, Bav. R. Ch. and SO, Sawallisch.

Wagner was barely twenty when he wrote *Die Feen*, his first opera, a story of a fairy who marries a mortal and is threatened with separation from him. It is amazing how confident the writing is, regularly echoing Weber but stylistically more consistent than Wagner's next two operas, *Das Liebesverbot* and *Rienzi*. The piece is through-composed in what had become the new, advanced manner, and even when he bows to convention and has a buffo duet between the second pair of principals, the result is distinctive and fresh, delightfully sung here by Cheryl Studer and Jan-Hendrik Rootering.

This first complete recording was edited together from live performances given in Munich in 1983, and has few of the usual snags of live performance and plenty of its advantages. Sawallisch gives a strong and dramatic performance, finely paced; and central to the total success is the singing of Linda Esther Gray as Ada, the fairy-heroine, powerful and firmly controlled. John Alexander as the tenor hero, King Arindal – finally granted immortality to bring a happy ending – sings cleanly and capably; the impressive cast list boasts such excellent singers as Kurt Moll, Kari Lovaas and Krisztina Laki in small but vital roles. Ensembles and choruses – with the Bavarian Radio Chorus finely disciplined – are particularly impressive, and the sound is generally first rate.

Der fliegende Holländer (complete).

*** HMV Dig. **CDS 747054-8** (3) [id.]; EX 270013-3/*9* (3) [Ang. DSCX/*4D3X* 3958]. Van Dam, Vejzovic, Moll, Hofmann, Moser, Borris, V. State Op. Ch., BPO, Karajan.

(*) Decca **414 551-2 (3) [id.]; D 24 D 3/*K 24 K 32* (3/*2*) [Lon. OSA/*5*- 13119]. Bailey, Martin, Talvela, Kollo, Krenn, Isola Jones, Chicago SO Ch. and O, Solti.

(M) ** DG 413 291-1/*4* (3/*2*). Gwyneth Jones, Wagner, Stewart, Ridderbusch, Ek, Bayreuth Fest. (1971) Ch. and O, Boehm.

The extreme range of dynamics in EMI's recording for Karajan, not ideally clear but rich, matches the larger-than-life quality of the conductor's reading. He firmly and convincingly relates this early work not so much to such seminal earlier works as Weber's *Der Freischütz* as to later Wagner, *Tristan* above all. His choice of José van Dam as the Dutchman, thoughtful, finely detailed and lyrical, strong but not at all blustering, goes well with this. The Dutchman's Act I monologue is turned into a prayer as well as a protest in its extra range of expression. Van Dam is superbly matched and contrasted with the finest Daland on record, Kurt Moll, gloriously biting and dark in tone yet detailed in his characterization. Neither the Erik of Peter Hofmann, nor – more seriously – the Senta of Dunja Vejzovic matches such a standard, for Hofmann has his strained and gritty moments and Vejzovic her shrill ones. They were both better cast in

Karajan's *Parsifal* recording. Nevertheless, for all her variability Vejzovic is wonderfully intense in *Senta's Ballad* and she matches even Van Dam's fine legato in the Act II duet. The CD version underlines the heavyweight quality of the recording, with the *Sailors' chorus* for example made massive, but effectively so, when Karajan conducts it with such fine spring. The banding is not generous, making the issue less convenient to use than most Wagner CD sets.

Solti's first Wagner opera recording in Chicago marked a change from the long series he made in Vienna. The playing is superb, the singing cast is generally impressive, and the recording is vividly immediate to the point of aggressiveness. What will disappoint some who admire Solti's earlier Wagner sets is that this most atmospheric of the Wagner operas is presented with no Culshaw-style production whatever. Characters halloo to one another when evidently standing elbow to elbow, and even the Dutchman's ghostly chorus sounds very close and earthbound. But with Norman Bailey a deeply impressive Dutchman, Janis Martin a generally sweet-toned Senta, Martti Talvela a splendid Daland, and Kollo, for all his occasional coarseness, an illuminating Erik, it remains well worth hearing. The brilliance of the recording is all the more striking on CD, but the precise placing so characteristic of the new medium reinforces the clear impression of a concert performance, not an atmospheric re-creation. The cassettes offer vibrant, vivid sound, if slightly less refined than the LPs.

The fact that Boehm's 1971 Bayreuth recording is from a live performance detracts from its appeal, for the chorus, poorly disciplined in their singing, are noisy on the stage and this is distracting. Gwyneth Jones sings beautifully in pianissimo passages but develops a wobble which worsens as she puts pressure on the voice. Thomas Stewart is better focused in tone than he sometimes is. Boehm's searching interpretation is well worth hearing, but on balance this is a disappointing set. The mid-priced reissue is on three LPs or a pair of chrome cassettes; although the tape transfer is vivid, the tailoring is not ideal, with a long stretch of blank tape on side four. The libretto is poorly produced.

Götterdämmerung (complete).

*** Decca **414 115-2** (4); 414 115-1/*4* (5/*4*) [id.]. Nilsson, Windgassen, Fischer-Dieskau, Frick, Neidlinger, Watson, Ludwig, V. State Op. Ch., VPO, Solti.

*** DG **415 155-2** (4) [id.]; 2740 148 (6) [2716 001]/*3378 048* [*id.*] (coupled with *Das Rheingold*). Dernesch, Janowitz, Brilioth, Stewart, Kelemen, Ludwig, Ridderbusch, German Op. Ch., BPO, Karajan.

*** Ph. **412 488-2** (4) [id.]. Windgassen, Nilsson, Greindl, Mödl, Stewart, Neidlinger, Dvořáková, Bayreuth Fest. (1967) Ch. and O, Boehm.

*** Eurodisc **610081** (5); 301/*501* 817 (6). Kollo, Altmeyer, Salminen, Wenkel, Nocker, Nimsgern, Sharp, Popp, Leipzig R. Ch., Berlin R. Ch., Dresden State Op. Ch., Dresden State O, Janowski.

In Decca's formidable task of recording the whole *Ring* cycle under Solti, *Götterdämmerung* provided the most daunting challenge of all; characteristically, Solti, and with him the Vienna Philharmonic and the Decca recording team under John Culshaw, were inspired to heights even beyond earlier achievements. Even the trifling objections raised on earlier issues have been eliminated here. The balance between voices and orchestra has by some magic been made perfect, with voices clear but orchestra still rich and near-sounding. On CD, the weight of sound in this 1964 recording comes out with satisfying power in its digital transfer, so giving the brilliance of the upper range its proper support. The big ensembles come over particularly well, and Culshaw's carefully planned, highly atmospheric sound staging is the more sharply focused, exhilaratingly so in the fall of the Gibichung Hall at the end. Access to the set is first class, with rather more generous cueing than in rival versions. Solti's reading had matured before the recording was made. He presses on still, but no longer is there any feeling of over-driving, and even the *Funeral march*, which in his early Covent Garden performances was brutal in its power, is made into a natural, not a forced, climax. There is not a single weak link in the cast. Nilsson surpasses herself in the magnificence of her singing: even Flagstad in her prime would not have been more masterful as Brünnhilde. As in *Siegfried*, Windgassen is in superb voice; Frick is a vivid Hagen, and Fischer-Dieskau achieves the near impossible in making Gunther an interesting and even sympathetic character. As for the recording quality, it surpasses even Decca's earlier achievement. No more magnificent set has appeared in the whole history of the gramophone, and Decca have also surpassed themselves in the excellence of the tape transfer: the cassettes are quite the equal of the LPs, with remarkably little background noise.

Recorded last in Karajan's *Ring* series, *Götterdämmerung* has the finest, fullest sound, less brilliant than Solti's on Decca but with glowing purity in the CD transfer to match the relatively lyrical approach of the conductor, with Helge Dernesch's voice in the Immolation scene given satisfying richness and warmth. His singing cast is marginally even finer than Solti's, and his performance conveys the steady flow of recording sessions prepared in relation to live performances. But ultimately he falls short of Solti's achievement in the orgasmic quality of the music, the quality which finds an emotional culmination in such moments as the end of Brünnhilde's and Siegfried's love scene, the climax of the *Funeral march* and the culmination of the Immolation. At each of these points Karajan is a degree less committed, beautifully as the players respond, and warm as his overall approach is. Dernesch's Brünnhilde is warmer than Nilsson's, with a glorious range of tone. Brilioth as Siegfried is fresh and young-sounding, while the Gutrune of Gundula Janowitz is far preferable to that of Claire Watson on Decca. The matching is otherwise very even. The balance of voices in the recording may for some dictate a choice: DG brings the singers closer, gives less brilliance to the orchestral texture. Nevertheless, next to Solti's Decca set, such scenes as the summoning of the vassals in Act II lack weight. On tape, the Karajan *Götterdämmerung* is issued in a 'chunky' box together with *Das Rheingold* at what is virtually bargain price. The transfers are of good quality but made at a generally lower level than the Decca Solti recordings, which are fuller and more vivid in sound.

Boehm's urgently involving reading of *Götterdämmerung*, very well cast, is crowned by an incandescent performance of the final Immolation scene from

Birgit Nilsson as Brünnhilde. Small wonder that she herself has always preferred this version to the fine one she recorded three years earlier for Solti in the studio. It is an astonishing achievement that she could sing with such biting power and accuracy in a live performance, coming to it at the very end of a long evening. The excitement of that is matched by much else in the performance, so that incidental stage noises and the occasional inaccuracy, almost inevitable in live music-making, matter hardly at all. This recording, which appeared on LP in the early 1970s, has been transformed in its CD version. The voices are well forward of the orchestra, but the result gives a magnetically real impression of hearing the opera in the Festspielhaus, with the stage movements adding to that sense of reality. Balances are inevitably variable, and at times Windgassen as Siegfried is less well treated by the microphones than Nilsson. Generally his performance for Solti is fresher – but there are points of advantage, too. Josef Greindl is rather unpleasantly nasal in tone as Hagen, and Martha Mödl as Waltraute is unsteady; but both are dramatically involving. Thomas Stewart is a gruff but convincing Gunther and Dvořáková, as Gutrune, strong if not ideally pure-toned. Neidlinger as ever is a superb Alberich. Anyone preferring a live recording of the *Ring* will find Boehm's final instalment the most satisfying culmination.

With sharply focused digital sound, Janowski's studio recording hits refreshingly hard, at least as much so as in the earlier *Ring* operas. Speeds rarely linger but, with some excellent casting – consistent with the earlier operas – the result is rarely lightweight. Jeannine Altmeyer as Brünnhilde rises to the challenges not so much in strength as in feeling and intensity, ecstatic in Act I, bitter in Act II, dedicated in the Immolation scene. Kollo is a fine heroic Siegfried, only occasionally raw-toned, and Salminen is a magnificent Hagen, with Nimsgern again an incisive Alberich on his brief appearances. Despite an indifferent Gunther and Gutrune and a wobbly if characterful Waltraute, the impression is of clean vocalization matched by finely disciplined and dedicated playing, all recorded in faithful studio sound with no sonic tricks. On the five CDs the background silence adds to the dramatic presence and overall clarity, which is strikingly enhanced, but on ten sides the layout is less satisfactory than that of its rivals, to say nothing of the price disadvantage this incurs. The chrome cassettes too are impressive, although some will count it a disadvantage that the layout follows the discs. However, the wide range of the recording and its excellent detail are admirably captured. The brightly lit sound gives a brilliant sheen to the strings and an exciting edge to the brass, even if the voices are at times slightly hard.

Götterdämmerung: Siegfried's Rhine journey, death and Funeral music. Immolation scene and Finale.

** Lodia **LO-CD 785** [id.]. Ute Vinzing, James King, Philharmonic SO, Païta.

Païta generates a volatile, thrustful excitement in the *Rhine journey*, but the pacing of the *Funeral music* and the final scene is less convincing, and the closing section lacks the feeling of spacious apotheosis which Solti brings to it.

Ute Vinzing's Brünnhilde is dramatic but the performance is not really memorable enough to stand on its own away from a complete set. The Kingsway Hall recording is clear and well balanced, but not as sumptuous as one might have expected.

Lohengrin (complete).
(M) ** DG 419 029-1/*4* (5/3). Janowitz, King, Gwyneth Jones, Stewart, Ridderbusch, Bav. R. Ch. and O, Kubelik.

Kubelik's dedicated and thoughtful reading of *Lohengrin* is most welcome in this medium-price reissue (on five LPs or three matching tapes). Gundula Janowitz's ravishing performance as Elsa makes this an essential set for Wagnerians to hear, and James King is an imaginative Lohengrin; but Thomas Stewart's Telramund has nothing like the dramatic intensity ideally required, and Gwyneth Jones as the wicked Ortrud makes a sad showing. First choice remains with the wonderfully rapt account directed by Kempe on HMV (SLS 5071 [Ang. SEL 3641], which has never been surpassed on record. The intensity of Kempe's conducting lies even in its very restraint, and the singers too seem uplifted, with Jess Thomas, Elisabeth Grümmer and Gottlob Frick all in superb form. But it is the partnership of Christa Ludwig and Dietrich Fischer-Dieskau as Ortrud and Telramund that sets the seal on this marvellous performance.

Die Meistersinger von Nürnberg (complete).
*** DG **415 278-2** (4) [id.]; 2740 149/*3378 068* (5) [2713 011/*id.*]. Fischer-Dieskau, Ligendza, Lagger, Hermann, Domingo, Laubenthal, Ludwig, Ch. and O of German Op., Berlin, Jochum.

Jochum's is a performance which, more than any, captures the light and shade of Wagner's most warmly approachable score, its humour and tenderness as well as its strength. The recording was made at the same time as live opera-house performances in Berlin, and the sense of a comedy being enacted is irresistible. With Jochum the processions at the start of the final Festwiese have sparkling high spirits, not just German solemnity, while the poetry of the score is radiantly brought out, whether in the incandescence of the Act III *Prelude* (positively Brucknerian in hushed concentration) or the youthful magic of the love music for Walther and Eva. Above all, Jochum is unerring in building long Wagnerian climaxes and resolving them – more so than his recorded rivals. The cast is the most consistent yet assembled on record. Though Caterina Ligendza's big soprano is a little ungainly for Eva, it is an appealing performance, and the choice of Domingo for Walther is inspired. The key to the set is of course the searching and highly individual Sachs of Fischer-Dieskau, a performance long awaited. Obviously controversial (you can never imagine this sharp Sachs sucking on his boring old pipe), Fischer-Dieskau with detailed word-pointing and sharply focused tone gives new illumination in every scene. The Masters – with not one woolly-toned member – make a superb team, and Horst Laubenthal's finely tuned David matches this Sachs in applying Lieder style. The recording balance favours the voices, but on CD they are made to sound just slightly ahead of the orchestra. There is a lovely bloom on the whole sound and, with a recording which is basically wide-ranging and refined, the ambience brings an attractively natural projection of the singers.

Parsifal (complete).

❀ ℂ *** DG Dig. **413 347-2** (4); 2741/*3382* 002 (5) [id.]. Hofmann, Vejzovic, Moll, Van Dam, Nimsgern, Von Halem, German Op. Ch., BPO, Karajan.

ℂ *** Decca **417 143-2** (4) [id.]; SET 550-4/*K 113 K 54* (5/*4*) [Lon. OSA/*5*- 1510]. Kollo, Ludwig, Fischer-Dieskau, Hotter, Kelemen, Frick, V. Boys' Ch., V. State Op. Ch., VPO, Solti.

(*) Ph. **416 390-2 (4); 6747 250 (5). Jess Thomas, Dalis, London, Talvela, Neidlinger, Hotter, Bayreuth Fest. (1962) Ch. and O, Knappertsbusch.

**(*) HMV Dig. EX 270178-3/*5* (5) [Ang. DSB 3972]. Ellsworth, Meier, Joll, Gwynne, McIntyre, Folwell, Welsh Nat. Op. Ch. and O, Goodall.

Communion, musical and spiritual, is what this intensely beautiful Karajan set provides, with pianissimos shaded in magical clarity and the ritual of bells and offstage choruses heard as in ideal imagination. If, after the Solti recording for Decca, it seemed doubtful whether a studio recording could ever match in spiritual intensity earlier ones made on stage at Bayreuth, Karajan proves otherwise, his meditation the more intense because the digital sound allows total silences. The playing of the Berlin orchestra – preparing for performance at the Salzburg Easter Festival of 1980 – is consistently beautiful; but the clarity and refinement of sound prevent this from emerging as a lengthy serving of Karajan soup. He has rarely sounded so spontaneously involved in opera on record. Kurt Moll as Gurnemanz is the singer who, more than any, anchors the work vocally, projecting his voice with firmness and subtlety. José van Dam as Amfortas is also splendid: the *Lament* is one of the glories of the set, enormously wide in dynamic and expressive range. The Klingsor of Siegmund Nimsgern could be more sinister, but the singing is admirable. Dunja Vejzovic makes a vibrant, sensuous Kundry who rises superbly to the moment in Act II where she bemoans her laughter in the face of Christ. Only Peter Hofmann as Parsifal leaves any disappointment; at times he develops a gritty edge on the voice, but his natural tone is admirably suited to the part – no one can match him today – and he is never less than dramatically effective. He is not helped by the relative closeness of the solo voices, but otherwise the recording is near the atmospheric ideal, a superb achievement. The four CDs, generously full and offering an improved layout, are among DG's finest so far, with the background silence adding enormously to the concentration of the performance. The cassette transfer on chrome tapes is also of the very highest quality, losing little if anything in comparison with the LPs.

It was natural that, after Solti's other magnificent Wagner recordings for Decca, he should want to go on to this last of the operas. In almost every way it is just as powerful an achievement as any of his previous Wagner recordings in Vienna, with the Decca engineers surpassing themselves in vividness of sound and the Vienna Philharmonic in radiant form. The singing cast could hardly be stronger, every one of them pointing words with fine, illuminating care for detail. The complex balances of sound, not least in the *Good Friday music*, are beautifully caught; throughout, Solti shows his sustained intensity in Wagner. There remains just one doubt, but that rather serious: the lack of that spiritual quality which makes Knappertsbusch's live version so involving. However, the clear advantage of a studio recording is the absence of intrusive audience noises which, in an opera such as this with its long solos and dialogues, can be very distracting. The remastering for CD, as with Solti's other Wagner recordings, opens up the sound, and the choral climaxes are superb. The tapes are generally as impressive, though there is slight lack of refinement at times. The layout on tape is superior both to LPs and to CDs; on CD, the break between the second and third discs could have been better placed. Cueing is generous but the libretto is poor, the typeface minuscule and in places no pleasure to read.

Knappertsbusch's expansive and dedicated reading is superbly caught in the Philips set, arguably the finest live recording ever made in the Festspielhaus at Bayreuth, with outstanding singing from Jess Thomas as Parsifal and Hans Hotter as Gurnemanz. Though Knappertsbusch chooses consistently slow tempi, there is no sense of excessive squareness or length, so intense is the concentration of the performance, its spiritual quality. This of all operas is one that seems to gain from being recorded live, and the sound has undoubtedly been further enhanced in the remastering for CD. The snag is that the stage noises and coughs are also emphasized and the bronchial afflictions are particularly disturbing in the *Prelude*. However, the recording itself is most impressive, with the choral perspectives particularly convincing and the overall sound warmly atmospheric.

Goodall in his plain, unvarnished, patiently expansive reading characteristically finds deep intensity in a strong, rough-hewn way. He may lack the ethereal beauties of Karajan, for here *Parsifal* is brought down to earth, thanks not just to Goodall but to the full, immediate recording and a cast which with one exception stand up well to international competition. It was plainly a help that these same singers had appeared together under Goodall on stage in the Welsh National Opera production. Donald McIntyre gives one of his very finest performances as Gurnemanz, with more bloom than usual. Waltraud Meier's powerful, penetrating voice suits the role of Kundry well, while the American, Warren Ellsworth, has power and precision, if little beauty, as Parsifal. Only the ill-focused Amfortas of Phillip Joll is disappointing, too gritty of tone, though he too makes the drama compelling. The cassettes are splendidly transferred, catching the full bloom of the recording and its perspectives, with an excellent choral focus. The layout on five tapes follows the LPs. The slimline libretto is poorly produced for the cassette issue, with minuscule print.

Das Rheingold (*complete*).

€ *** Decca **414 101-2**; 414 101-1/*4* (3/*2*). London, Flagstad, Svanholm, Neidlinger, VPO, Solti.

(*) DG **415 141-2 [id.]; 2740 145 (3) [2709 023]/*3378 048* [*id.*] (coupled with *Götterdämmerung*). Fischer-Dieskau, Veasey, Stolze, Kelemen, BPO, Karajan.

(*) Ph. **412 475-2 (2) [id.]. Adam, Nienstedt, Windgassen, Neidlinger, Talvela, Böhme, Silja, Soukupová, Bayreuth Fest. (1967) Ch. and O, Boehm.

(*) Eurodisc Dig. **610058; 301/*501* 137 (3). Adam, Nimsgern, Stryczek, Schreier, Bracht, Salminen, Vogel, Buchner, Minton, Popp, Priew, Schwarz, Dresden State O, Janowski.

The first of Solti's cycle, recorded in 1958, *Rheingold* remains in terms of engineering the most spectacular, an ideal candidate for transfer to CD, with its extra clarity and range. Noises and movements in the lowest bass register, virtually inaudible on LP, become clearly identifiable on CD; but the immediacy and precise placing of sound are thrilling, while the sound-effects of the final scenes, including Donner's hammer-blow and the Rainbow bridge, have never been matched since. The sound remains of demonstration quality, to have one cherishing all the more this historic recording with its unique vignette of Flagstad as Fricka. Solti gives a magnificent reading of the score, crisp, dramatic and direct. He somehow brings a freshness to the music without ever over-driving or losing an underlying sympathy. Vocally, the set is held together by the unforgettable singing of Neidlinger as Alberich. Too often the part – admittedly ungrateful on the voice – is spoken rather than sung, but Neidlinger vocalizes with wonderful precision and makes the character of the dwarf develop from the comic creature of the opening scene to the demented monster of the last. Flagstad learnt the part of Fricka specially for this recording, and her singing makes one regret that she never took the role on the stage; but regret is small when a singer of the greatness of Flagstad found the opportunity during so-called retirement to extend her reputation with performances such as this. Only the slightest trace of hardness in the upper register occasionally betrays her, and the golden power and richness of her singing are for the rest unimpaired – enhanced even, when recorded quality is as true as this. As Wotan, George London is sometimes a little rough – a less brilliant recording might not betray him – but this is a dramatic portrayal of the young Wotan. Svanholm could be more characterful as Loge, but again it is a relief to hear the part really sung. Much has been written on the quality of the recording, and without a shadow of a doubt it deserves the highest star rating. Decca went to special trouble to produce the recording as for a stage performance and to follow Wagner's intentions as closely as possible. They certainly succeeded. An outstanding achievement, and so is the cassette version, complete on four sides.

Karajan's account is more reflective than Solti's; the very measured pace of the *Prelude* indicates this at the start, and there is often an extra bloom on the Berlin Philharmonic playing. But Karajan's very reflectiveness has its less welcome side, for the tension rarely varies. One finds such incidents as Alberich's stealing of the gold or Donner's hammer-blow passing by without one's pulse quickening as it should. Unexpectedly, Karajan is not so subtle as Solti in shaping phrases and rhythms. There is also no doubt that the DG recording managers were not so painstaking as John Culshaw's Decca team, and that too makes the end-result less compellingly dramatic. On the credit side, however, the singing cast has hardly any flaw at all, and Fischer-Dieskau's Wotan is a brilliant and memorable creation, virile and expressive. Among the others, Veasey is excellent, though obviously she cannot efface memories of Flagstad; Gerhard Stolze with his flickering, almost *Sprechstimme* as Loge gives an intensely vivid if, for some, controversial interpretation. The 1968 sound has been clarified in the digital transfer, but while the compact discs bring out the beauty of Fischer-Dieskau's singing as the young Wotan the more vividly, generally the lack of bass brings some thinness. The cassettes are well managed, but do not compare with the Decca transfer in vividness. On cassette, the DG set is coupled with *Götterdämmerung*.

The transfer to CD of Boehm's 1967 live recording made at Bayreuth is outstandingly successful. His preference for fast speeds (consistently through the whole cycle) here brings the benefit that the whole of the *Vorabend* is contained on two CDs, a considerable financial advantage. The pity is that the performance is marred by the casting of Theo Adam as Wotan, keenly intelligent but rarely agreeable on the ear, at times here far too wobbly. On the other hand, Gustav Neidlinger as Alberich is superb, even more involving here than he is for Solti, with the curse made spine-chilling. It is good too to have Loge cast from strength in Wolfgang Windgassen, cleanly vocalized; among the others, Anja Silja makes an attractively urgent Freia. Though a stage production brings nothing like the sound-effects which make Solti's set so involving, the atmosphere of the theatre is in its way just as potent.

The Eurodisc set of *Das Rheingold*, also part of a complete cycle, comes from East Germany, with Marek Janowski a direct, alert conductor of the Dresden State Orchestra, and more recently of the Royal Liverpool Philharmonic. This performance is treated to a digital recording totally different from Solti's. The studio sound has the voices close and vivid, with the orchestra rather in the background. Some Wagnerians prefer that kind of balance, but the result here rather lacks the atmospheric qualities which make the Solti *Rheingold* still the most compelling in sound, thanks to the detailed production of the late John Culshaw. With Solti, Donner's hammer-blow is overwhelming; but the Eurodisc set comes up with only a very ordinary 'ping' on an anvil, and the grandeur of the moment is missing. Theo Adam as Wotan has his grittiness of tone exaggerated here, but otherwise it is a fine set, consistently well cast, including Peter Schreier, Matti Salminen, Yvonne Minton and Lucia Popp, as well as East German singers of high calibre. The CDs sharpen the focus even further, with clarity rather than atmosphere the keynote. The cassettes match the LPs closely, although there is an element of hardness on top.

Der Ring des Nibelungen: complete.

❀ *** Decca [**414 100-2**] (15); 414 100-1/*4* (16/*12*). cond. Solti (for details see under each opera).

(M) (***) HMV mono EX 290670-3 (14) [Ang. Sera. IN 6148]. Mödl, Suthaus, Frantz, Patzak, Neidlinger, Windgassen, Konetzni, Jurinac, RAI Ch. and Rome SO, Furtwängler.

The Decca set – one of the great achievements of the gramophone – has been reissued in a special edition at medium price in the UK on sixteen LPs and twelve equivalent cassettes. As we go to press, the cost works out at about £4 for each disc. In the USA, the CD version is also available as a boxed set on fifteen compact discs, and no doubt this will become available here in the lifetime of this book.

When in 1972 EMI first transferred the Italian Radio tapes of Furtwängler's studio performances of 1953, the sound was disagreeably harsh, making sustained listening unpleasant. In this latest digital transfer, the boxiness of the studio sound and the closeness of the voices still take away some of the unique Furtwängler glow in Wagner, but the sound is acceptable and actually benefits in some ways from extra clarity. Each Act was performed on a separate day, giving the advantage of continuous performance but with closer preparation than would have been otherwise possible. Furtwängler gives each opera a commanding sense of unity, musically and dramatically, with hand-picked casts including Martha Mödl as a formidable Brünnhilde, Ferdinand Frantz a firm-voiced Wotan and Ludwig Suthaus (Tristan in Furtwängler's recording) a reliable Siegfried. In smaller roles you have stars like Wolfgang Windgassen, Julius Patzak, Rita Streich, Sena Jurinac and Gottlob Frick.

Siegfried (complete).

*** Decca **414 110-2** (4); 414 110-1/*4* (4/*3*). Windgassen, Nilsson, Hotter, Stolze, Neidlinger, Böhme, Hoffgen, Sutherland, VPO, Solti.

*** Ph. **412 483-2** (4) [id]. Windgassen, Nilsson, Adam, Neidlinger, Soukupová, Köth, Böhme, Bayreuth Fest. (1967) Ch. and O, Boehm.

(*) Eurodisc Dig. **610070; 301/*501* 810 (5). Kollo, Altmeyer, Adam, Schreier, Nimsgern, Wenkel, Salminen, Sharp, Dresden State O, Janowski.

** DG **415 150-2** (4) [id.]; 2740 147 (5) [2713 003]/*3378 049* [*id.*] (coupled with *Die Walküre*). Dernesch, Dominguez, Jess Thomas, Stolze, Stewart, Kelemen, BPO, Karajan.

Culshaw tackled this second recording in Solti's *Ring* series after a gap of four years from *Das Rheingold.* By then he was using what he called the 'Sonicstage' technique, which on compact disc makes the sepulchral voice of Fafner as Dragon all the more chilling. On CD, this 1962 recording comes out very well, with full brilliance and weight as well as extra clarity. The gimmicks may be made the more obvious, but they are good ones. *Siegfried* has too long been thought of as the grimmest of the *Ring* cycle, with dark colours predominating. It is true that the preponderance of male voices till the very end, and Wagner's deliberate matching of this in his orchestration, gives a special colour to the opera, but a performance as buoyant as Solti's reveals that, more than in most Wagner, the message is one of optimism. Each of the three Acts ends with a scene of triumphant optimism – the first Act in Siegfried's forging song, the second with him in hot pursuit of the woodbird, and the third with the most opulent of love duets. Solti's array of singers could hardly be bettered. Windgassen is at the very peak of his form, lyrical as well as heroic. Hotter has never been more impressive on records, his Wotan at last captured adequately. Stolze, Neidlinger and Böhme are all exemplary, and predictably Joan Sutherland makes the most seductive of woodbirds. Only the conducting of Solti leaves a tiny margin of doubt. In the dramatic moments he could hardly be more impressive, but that very woodbird scene shows up the shortcomings: the bird's melismatic carolling is plainly intended to have a degree of freedom, whereas Solti allows little or no lilt in the music at all. But it is a minute flaw in a supreme achievement. With singing finer than any opera house could normally provide, with masterly playing from the Vienna Philharmonic and Decca's most opulent recording, this is a set likely to stand comparison with anything the rest of the century may provide. The tape transfer is of outstanding quality. Decca have digitally remastered the recording on cassette as well as on disc, and the quality of the tapes is by no means inferior to the LPs, with an almost silent background and remarkable overall clarity.

The natural-sounding quality of Boehm's live recording from Bayreuth, coupled with his determination not to let the music lag, makes his account of *Siegfried* as satisfying as the rest of his cycle, vividly capturing the atmosphere of the Festspielhaus, with voices well ahead of the orchestra. Windgassen is at his peak here, if anything more poetic in Acts II and III than he is in Solti's studio recording, and just as fine vocally. Nilsson, as in *Götterdämmerung*, gains over her studio recording from the extra flow of adrenalin in a live performance; and Gustav Neidlinger is unmatchable as Alberich. Erika Köth is disappointing as the woodbird, not sweet enough, and Soukupová is a positive, characterful Erda. Theo Adam is at his finest as the Wanderer, less wobbly than usual, clean and incisive.

Dedication and consistency are the mark of the Eurodisc *Ring*, recorded with German thoroughness in collaboration with the East German state record company. The result – with Janowski, direct and straight in his approach, securing superb playing from the Dresdeners – lacks a degree of dramatic tension, but he does not always build the climaxes cumulatively, so there is no compensation for any loss of immediate excitement. So the final scene of Act II just scurries to a close, with Siegfried in pursuit of a rather shrill woodbird in Norma Sharp. The singing is generally first rate, with Kollo a fine Siegfried, less strained than he has sometimes been, and Peter Schreier a superb Mime, using Lieder-like qualities in detailed characterization. Siegmund Nimsgern is a less characterful Alberich, but the voice is excellent; and Theo Adam concludes his portrayal of Wotan/Wanderer with his finest performance of the series. The relative lightness of Jeannine Altmeyer's Brünnhilde comes out in the final love-duet more strikingly than in *Walküre*. She may be reduced from goddess to human, but the musical demands are greater. Nevertheless, the tenderness and femininity are most affecting as at the entry of the idyll motif, where Janowski in his dedicated simplicity is also at his most compelling. Clear, beautifully balanced digital sound, with voices and instruments firmly placed. On CD, the opera's dark colouring is given an even sharper focus against the totally silent background, but the layout on five compact discs, against four for all the competitors, is a distinct disadvantage. The cassettes follow the discs in layout (which brings at least one clumsy side-break that could have been avoided). But the transfer itself is very sophisticated, though not at the highest level.

When Siegfried is outsung by Mime, it is time to complain, and though the DG set has many fine qualities – not least the Brünnhilde of Helga Dernesch – it hardly rivals the Solti or Boehm versions. Windgassen on Decca gave a classic performance, and any comparison highlights the serious shortcomings of Jess Thomas. Even when voices are balanced forward – a point the more apparent on CD – the digital transfer helps little to make Thomas's singing as Siegfried any more acceptable. Otherwise, the vocal cast is strong, and Karajan provides the seamless playing which characterizes his cycle. Recommended only to those irrevocably committed to the Karajan cycle. The tapes are issued coupled to *Die Walküre* at a very reasonable price, but the transfer lacks the flair and immediacy of the Decca or Eurodisc versions.

Tannhäuser (Paris version; complete).

*** Decca **414 581-2** (3) [id.]; SET 506-9/*K 80 K 43* [Lon. OSA/*5* 1438]. Kollo, Dernesch, Ludwig, Sotin, Braun, Hollweg, V. State Op. Ch., VPO, Solti.

Tannhäuser (Dresden version; complete).

(M) ** DG 413 300-1/*4* (3/*2*). Windgassen, Nilsson, Fischer-Dieskau, Adam, German Op., Berlin, Ch. and O, Gerdes.

** HMV Dig. **CDS 747296-8** (3) [id.]; EX 270265-3/*5* [Ang. DSB 3982]. König, Popp, Weikl, Meier, Moll, Jerusalem, Bav. R. Ch. and O, Haitink.

Solti provides an electrifying experience, demonstrating beyond a shadow of doubt how much more effective the Paris revision of *Tannhäuser* is, compared with the usual Dresden version. The differences lie mainly – though not entirely – in Act I in the scene between Tannhäuser and Venus. Wagner rewrote most of the scene at a time when his style had developed enormously. The love music here is closer to *Walküre* and *Tristan* than to the rest of *Tannhäuser*. The hero's harp song enters each time in its straight diatonic style with a jolt; but this is only apt, and the richness of inspiration, the musical intensification – beautifully conveyed here – transform the opera. The Paris version has never been recorded before, and that alone should dictate choice. Quite apart from that, however, Solti gives one of his very finest Wagner performances to date, helped by superb playing from the Vienna Philharmonic and an outstanding cast, superlatively recorded. Dernesch as Elisabeth and Ludwig as Venus outshine all rivalry; and Kollo, though not ideal, makes as fine a Heldentenor as we are currently likely to hear. The compact disc transfer reinforces the brilliance and richness of the performance. The sound is outstanding for its period (1971), and Ray Minshull's production adds to the atmospheric quality, with the orchestra given full weight and with the placing and movement of the voices finely judged; this is all the more apparent on CD. The tape transfer is extremely brilliant, not quite so smooth and sweet on the top as in some Decca opera sets, but very vivid. The distant choral effects are impressively atmospheric; the moments of spectacle come off well, though there is just a hint of roughness at times (in the *Grand*

March scene, for instance). But that is judging by Decca's own very high standards: this is still first class.

Gerdes – formerly one of DG's recording managers – gives a crisp, dramatic reading of the Dresden version of *Tannhäuser*, lacking in finer points of interpretation but fair enough in support of an excellent singing cast. Windgassen is not ideally sweet-toned, but Fischer-Dieskau makes a superb Wolfram, deeply expressive in *O star of eve*. The controversial point for many will be the choice of Birgit Nilsson, undoubtedly the leading Wagner soprano of her generation, to sing the roles of both Venus and Elisabeth. Vocally, the result is firmly satisfying, but Nilsson is suited by neither temperament nor quality of voice to either the voluptuous Venus or the pure Elisabeth. She copes very intelligently – but one admires rather than being moved. Good, atmospheric 1970 recording. At mid-price, this is worth hearing; the tape format (on a pair of chrome cassettes) seems a good way of approaching it, as the sound quality is very good.

Haitink's unexpected pursuit of lightness and refinement, almost as though this is music by Mendelssohn, makes for a reading which, for all its beauties, lacks an essential dramatic bite. Consistently he refines the piece, until you can hardly believe that this is an opera which deeply shocked early Victorians with its noisy vulgarity. Haitink's performance tends to sound like a studio run-through, carefully done with much intelligence, but largely uninvolved. It is not helped by a strained hero in Klaus König and a shrewish-sounding Venus in Waltraud Meier. The serious disappointment of the first Act then tends to colour one's response to the rest too, though Lucia Popp, stretched to the limit in a role on the heavy side for her, produces some characteristically beautiful singing as Elisabeth. Bernd Weikl is an intelligent but uningratiating Wolfram. Finely balanced sound, the more impressive on CD, beautifully atmospheric in the processional scenes. Banding is sparse, with limited index points added.

Tristan und Isolde (complete).

*** Ph. Dig. **410 447-2** (5); 6769/*7654* 091 (5/*3*) [id.]. Hofmann, Behrens, Minton, Weikl, Sotin, Bav. R. Ch. and SO, Bernstein.

(***) HMV mono **CDS 747322-8** (4) [**CDCD 47321**]; EX 290684-3/*9* (4/*3*) [Ang. Sera. IE/*4X5G* 6134]. Flagstad, Suthaus, Thebom, Greindl, Fischer-Dieskau, ROHCG Ch., Philh. O, Furtwängler.

(M) ** DG 415 395-1/*4* (5/*3*) [id.]. From Bayreuth Fest. (1966) production (with rehearsal sequence): Windgassen, Nilsson, Ludwig, Talvela, Waechter, Bayreuth Fest. Ch. and O, Boehm.

Bernstein's was the first *Tristan* on CD; worthily so, though at that point the art of fitting Wagner operas on to four discs was not pursued and, beside most other Wagner offerings in the new medium, this five-disc set is not only expensive but cumbersome in five separate 'jewel-boxes'. Nevertheless, the fine quality of the recording is all the more ravishing in the transfer, the sound rich, full and well detailed, a tribute to the Bavarian engineers working in the Herkulesaal in Munich. 'For the first time someone dares to perform this music as Wagner wrote it,' was Karl Boehm's comment when he visited Bernstein during rehearsals for this *Tristan* recording, made live at three separate concert performances. The surprise is that Bernstein, over-emotional in some music, here exercises restraint to produce the most spacious reading ever put on disc, more expansive even than Furtwängler's. His rhythmic sharpness goes with warmly expressive but un-exaggerated phrasing, to give unflagging concentration and deep commitment. The love-duet has rarely if ever sounded so sensuous, with supremely powerful climaxes – as at the peak of *O sink'hernieder*. Nor in the *Liebestod* is there any question of Bernstein rushing ahead, for the culmination comes naturally and fully at a taxingly slow speed. Behrens makes a fine Isolde, less purely beautiful than her finest rivals but with reserves of power giving dramatic bite. The contrast of tone with Yvonne Minton's Brangäne (good, except for flatness in the warning solo) is not as great as usual, and there is likeness too between Peter Hofmann's Tristan, often baritonal, and Bernd Weikl's Kurwenal, lighter than usual. The King Mark of Hans Sotin is superb. The cassette layout is generally preferable to that of the LPs and CDs, though irritatingly the end of Act II is carried over to the third cassette. The transfer level, too, might have been higher, though the sound itself is of high quality.

It was one of the supreme triumphs of the recording producer, Walter Legge, when in 1952 with his recently formed Philharmonia Orchestra he teamed the incomparable Wagnerian, Wilhelm Furtwängler, with Kirsten Flagstad as the heroine in *Tristan und Isolde*. It was no easy matter, when Furtwängler was resentful of Legge at the time for sponsoring his rival, Karajan, and he agreed to the arrangement only because Flagstad insisted. The result has an incandescent intensity, typical of the conductor at his finest, and caught all too rarely in his studio recordings. The concept is spacious from the opening *Prelude* onwards, but equally the bite and colour of the drama are vividly conveyed, matching the nobility of Flagstad's portrait of Isolde. Some of the sensuousness of the character is missing, but the richly commanding power of her singing and her always distinctive timbre make it a uniquely compelling performance. Suthaus is not of the same calibre as Heldentenor, but he avoids ugliness and strain, which is rare in Tristan. Among the others, the only remarkable performance is from the young Fischer-Dieskau as Kurwenal, not ideally cast but keenly imaginative. One endearing oddity is that – on Flagstad's insistence – the top Cs at the opening of the love-duet were sung by Mrs Walter Legge (Elisabeth Schwarzkopf). The Kingsway Hall recording was admirably balanced, catching the beauty of the Philharmonia Orchestra at its peak. The CDs have opened up the original mono sound and it is remarkable how little constriction there is in the biggest climaxes, mostly shown in the *fortissimo* violins above the stave. The voices ride triumphantly over the orchestra (the balance is superbly judged) and at *mezzo forte* and *piano* levels there is striking atmosphere and bloom, with the vocal timbres firm and realistically focused. CD cueing is not especially generous (24 bands over the four discs) and the libretto typeface, though clear, is minuscule. The cassettes are superbly managed and the layout, on six sides, is preferable to CD and LP alternatives. The sound, too, is wonderfully warm and natural, very like stereo in its amplitude, with the slight loss of range at the top almost always beneficial. The voices have a natural bloom and the strings are gloriously full, so that the final *Liebestod* is radiant in its glowing expansiveness. Many will prefer these tapes to the CDs, and their cost is far less. Moreover, the slimline libretto is preferable to the CD booklet, clearer and easier to read.

Boehm's set, now available at medium price in the UK, was taken from a live performance at Bayreuth, but apart from such passages as the *Prelude* and concluding *Liebestod*, where the experience is vivid, the performance too often acquires tensions of the wrong sort, and Boehm's speeds are surprisingly fast. Nilsson is here more expressive but less bright-toned than in her Decca set, and Windgassen – in his time an incomparable Tristan – begins to show signs of wear in the voice. The recording favours the voices, suffering inevitably from live recording conditions. The cassette transfer is undoubtedly vivid.

Tristan und Isolde: highlights.
**(*) DG Dig. 410 534-1/*4* [id.]. Kollo, Margaret Price, Fischer-Dieskau, Moll, Dresden State O, Carlos Kleiber.

A useful selection from a set which, for all its many merits – notably the radiantly beautiful Isolde of Margaret Price – is hardly a first choice. The recording is rather variable but it has transferred well to tape (there is slight recession at pianissimo levels, but otherwise the wide dynamics are very well captured) and this makes a useful sampler.

Die Walküre (complete).
*** Decca **414 105-2** (4); 414 105-1/*4* (4/*3*) [id.]. Nilsson, Crespin, Ludwig, King, Hotter, Frick, VPO, Solti.
*** Ph. **412 478-2** (4) [id.]. King, Rysanek, Nienstedt, Nilsson, Adam, Burmeister, Bayreuth Fest. (1967) Ch. and O, Boehm.
*** Eurodisc **610064**; 301/*501* 143 (5). Altmeyer, Norman, Minton, Jerusalem, Adam, Moll, Dresden State O, Janowski.
(*) DG **415 145-2 (4) [id.]; 2740 146 (5) [2713 002]/*3378 049* [*id.*] (coupled with *Siegfried*). Crespin, Janowitz, Veasey, Vickers, Stewart, Talvela, BPO, Karajan.

Recorded last in Solti's series, *Die Walküre* in some ways had the most refined sound, to make the CD version particularly impressive, amazingly fine for 1965, with voices and orchestral detail all the more precisely placed. Solti's conception is more lyrical than one would have expected from his recordings of the other three *Ring* operas. He sees Act II as the kernel of the work, perhaps even of the whole cycle. Acts I and III have their supremely attractive set-pieces, which must inevitably make them more popular as entertainment, but here one appreciates that in Act II the conflict of wills between Wotan and Fricka makes for one of Wagner's most deeply searching scenes. That is the more apparent when the greatest of latterday Wotans, Hans Hotter, takes the role, and Christa Ludwig sings with searing dramatic sense as his wife. Before that, Act I seems a little underplayed. This is partly because of Solti's deliberate lyricism – apt enough when love and spring greetings are in the air – but also (on the debit side) because James King fails both to project the character of Siegmund and to delve into the word-meanings as all the other members of the cast consistently do. Crespin has never sung more beautifully on record, but even that cannot cancel out the shortcoming. As for Nilsson's Brünnhilde, it has grown mellower, the emotions are clearer, and under-the-note attack is almost eliminated. Some may hesitate in the face of Hotter's obvious vocal trials; but the unsteadiness is, if anything, less marked than in his EMI recordings of items done many years ago. Like the CDs and LPs, the cassettes have been remastered and, with background virtually eliminated, the sound compares very favourably indeed with the LPs.

Anyone wondering whether to invest in the Boehm *Ring* cycle, recorded live at Bayreuth in 1967, should sample the end of Act I of this account of *Die Walküre*, where the white heat of the occasion makes the scalp prickle. When Siegmund pulls the sword, Nothung, from the tree – James King in heroic voice – the Sieglinde, Leonie Rysanek, utters a shriek of joy to delight even the least susceptible Wagnerian, matching the urgency of the whole performance as conducted by Boehm. Rarely if ever does his preference for fast speeds undermine the music; on the contrary, it adds to the involvement of the performance, which never loses its concentration. Theo Adam is in firmer voice here as Wotan than he is in *Rheingold*, hardly sweet of tone but always singing with keen intelligence. As ever, Nilsson is in superb voice as Brünnhilde. Though the inevitable roughnesses of a live performance occasionally intrude, this presents a more involving experience than any rival complete recording. The CD transfer transforms what on LP seemed a rough recording, even if passages of heavy orchestration still bring some constriction of sound.

The Eurodisc *Ring* cycle is one for Wagnerians who want to concentrate on the score, undistracted by stereo staging or even by strongly characterful conducting. Janowski's direct approach matches the relative dryness of the acoustic, with voices fixed well forward of the orchestra – but not aggressively so. That balance allows full presence for the singing from a satisfyingly consistent cast. Jessye Norman might not seem an obvious choice for Sieglinde, but the sound is glorious, the expression intense and detailed, making her a superb match for the fine, if rather less imaginative Siegmund of Siegfried Jerusalem. The one snag with so commanding a Sieglinde is that she overtops the Brünnhilde of Jeannine Altmeyer who, more than usual, conveys a measure of feminine vulnerability in the leading Valkyrie even in her godhead days. Miss Altmeyer, born in Los Angeles of a German father and an Italian mother, may be slightly overparted, but the beauty and frequent sensuousness of her singing are the more telling, next to the gritty Wotan of Theo Adam. With its slow vibrato under pressure, his is rarely a pleasing voice, but the clarity of the recording makes it a specific, never a woolly sound, so that the illumination of the narrative is consistent and intense. Kurt Moll is a gloriously firm Hunding, and Yvonne Minton a searingly effective Fricka. On CD, the drama and urgency of the recording have even greater bite; but, as with the others in this series, the use of five discs is uncompetitive. The chrome cassettes, similarly, follow the LP layout and are of high quality in all respects.

The great merits of Karajan's version in competition with those of Solti are the refinement of the orchestral playing and the heroic strength of Jon Vickers as Siegmund. With that underlined, one cannot help but note that the vocal shortcomings here are generally more marked, and the total result does not add up to quite so compelling a dramatic experience: one is less involved. Thomas Stewart may have a younger, firmer voice than Hotter, but the character of Wotan emerges only partially; it is not just that he misses some of the word-meaning, but that on occasion – as in the kissing away of Brünnhilde's godhead – he underlines too crudely. A fine performance, none the less; and Josephine Veasey as Fricka matches her rival Ludwig in conveying the biting intensity of the part. Gundula Janowitz's Sieglinde has its beautiful moments, but the singing is ultimately a little static. Crespin's Brünnhilde is impressive, but nothing like as satisfying as her study of Sieglinde on the Decca set. The voice is at times strained into unsteadiness, which the microphone seems to exaggerate. The DG recording is good, but not quite in the same class as the Decca – its slightly recessed quality is the more apparent in the CD transfer. The bass is relatively light, but an agreeable bloom is given to the voices, set in an atmospheric acoustic, all made the more realistic on CD. The cassettes are well managed but hardly match the Decca tapes in vividness, being transferred at a relatively low level. They are issued competitively priced, coupled with *Siegfried.*

VOCAL COLLECTIONS

Der fliegende Holländer: Senta's ballad. Götterdämmerung: Brünnhilde's immolation scene. Tannhäuser: Dich teure Halle. Tristan und Isolde: Prelude and Liebestod.

*(*) CBS **CD 37294**; 37294/*40*-. Caballé, NYPO, Mehta.

There are moments of tender intensity in Caballé's recital, illuminatingly perceptive of detail; but the singing is too often flawed, when the voice is not well suited to the heavier roles, and Caballé disguises her weakness in mannerism. The recording is only fair; and this is a collection for Caballé admirers, rather than for the general collector.

Der fliegende Holländer: Die Frist ist um. Parsifal: Mein Sohn, Amfortas, bist du am Amt . . . Wehel Wehe der Qual! Die Walküre: Lass isch's verlauten . . . Was keinem in Worten ich hünde; Leb wohl du kühnes herrliches Kindl.

*** Ph. Dig. **412 271-2**; 412 271-1/*4* [id.]. Simon Estes (with Bundschuh, Reeh), Berlin State Op. O, Fricke.

Simon Estes with his dark bass-baritone has proved an impressive Dutchman at Bayreuth, and the firmness and tonal clarity of his singing contrast strongly with the woolly Wagner sound often delivered in these roles. His enunciation of German is excellent, but the relative youthfulness of the timbre may disconcert some who expect Wotan or Amfortas or even the Dutchman to sound old. Variety of expression is a little limited; but it is rare for the music to be heard with such freshness and clarity in all four of these substantial excerpts – *Wotan's Narration* 25 minutes long. Eva-Maria Bundschuh as Brünnhilde in that passage and Hein Reeh as Titurel in *Amfortas's Lament* provide capable support, as does the Berlin State Opera Orchestra. First-rate recording, particularly clear and vivid on CD. The chrome cassette, too, is of high quality.

Lohengrin: In fernem Land. Die Meistersinger: Fanget an!; Morgenlich leuchtend im rosigen Schein. Rienzi: Allmacht'ger Vater. Siegfried: Nothung! (i) *Tannhäuser: Unbrunst im Herzen. Die Walküre: Ein Schwert verhiess mir der Vater; Winterstürme wichen dem Wonnemond.*
(*) CBS Dig. **CD 38931; 38931 [id.]. Peter Hofmann, Stuttgart RSO, Ivan Fischer; (i) with Doernberger.

Hofmann's Wagner recital, extending over a wide range of heroes, is as fine as any from today's Heldentenoren. The voice as recorded is a little gritty in lyrical music, and the high tessitura of Walther's *Prize song* brings strain, but the heroic power is impressive in everything. The *Tannhäuser* excerpt is not limited to the hero's solo but also includes his exchanges with Wolfram (Victor Doernberger). Sympathetic accompaniment, not brilliant in ensemble or sound.

OTHER COLLECTIONS

(i) *Siegfried idyll;* (ii) *Der fliegende Holländer: Overture; Lohengrin:* (i) *Prelude to Act I;* (iii) *Bridal Chorus;* (i) *Die Meistersinger: Prelude;* (iv) *Tannhäuser: Overture;* (i) *Tristan und Isolde: Prelude and Liebestod;* (v) *Die Walküre: Ride of the Valkyries.*
(B) **(*) DG Walkman *413 849-4* [id.]. (i) BPO, Kubelik; (ii) Bayreuth Fest. O, Boehm; (iii) Bayreuth Fest. Ch., Pitz; (iv) cond. Gerdes; (v) cond. Karajan.

This Wagner Walkman tape centres on some fine performances made in 1963 by Kubelik and the Berlin Philharmonic, including the *Siegfried idyll* (also available coupled with Mahler – see above). Karajan contributes a lively *Ride of the Valkyries* (taken from his complete *Die Walküre*); Gerdes's *Tannhäuser overture* also comes from his complete set; while the *Bridal chorus* from *Lohengrin* has a Bayreuth hallmark, although in fact recorded in the studio. The sound is generally very good; only the opening *Flying Dutchman overture*, actually made at Bayreuth under Boehm, sounds slightly less refined than the rest of the concert.

Waldteufel, Emil (1837–1915)

Waltzes: *Dolores; España; Estudiantina; Les Patineurs; Plus de diamants; Les Sirènes; Très jolie.*
(*) Ph. Dig. **400 012-2; 6514/*7337* 069 [id.]. V. Volksoper O, Bauer-Theussl.

Waltzes: *Dolores; España; The Grenadiers; Mon Rêve; Les Patineurs; Pomone; Toujours ou jamais.*
(M) *** Decca VIV/*KVIC* 32 [Lon. STS/*5*- 15572]. Nat. PO, Gamley.

Waldteufel's waltzes have a direct, breezy vivacity. They lack the underlying poetic feeling that takes the works of Johann Strauss into the concert hall, but their spontaneity and wit more than compensate for any lack of distinction in the tunes. Undoubtedly *The Skaters* is Waldteufel's masterpiece, but *Pomone*, *Mon Rêve* and the less well-known *Toujours ou jamais* all show the composer at his best. *España* is, of course, a direct crib from Chabrier, but is enjoyable enough, even if it does not match the original score in exuberance.

Franz Bauer-Theussl's performances with the excellent Vienna Volksoper Orchestra are amiable and recorded in a generously warm acoustic. The effect is pleasing, but slightly bland. Moreover, the opening of *Les Patineurs* is truncated. The famous horn solo is omitted; instead, there is just a snatch of the main theme on the cello. The compact disc makes admirable if rather expensive background music, but does not differ a great deal from the LP; the chrome tape is agreeable too, though it has slightly less sparkle on top. But Gamley's Decca disc costs about a third the price and has far more brio and style. Rhythmic zest and vitality are the keynote of these performances. Gamley does not forget that Waldteufel was French. There is just the right degree of sophistication and affection in the phrasing, and the fine Decca recording, made in a well-chosen resonant acoustic, has both brilliance and bloom. The cassette transfer is very successful.

Walton, William (1902–83)

Capriccio burlesco; The Quest (ballet suite); *Scapino overture;* (i) *Sinfonia concertante for orchestra with piano.*
*** Lyr. SRCS 49. LSO, composer, (i) with Katin.

The reissue of this 1971 collection is most welcome with no other recording of the *Sinfonia concertante* available, though this admittedly has not the bite and dash of the immediate post-war recording. But what is even more valuable is *The Quest*, an attractive score not otherwise represented on record, so that this disc will be eagerly sought by admirers of Walton's music. The performances have the composer's authority, though there are the odd untidinesses here and there. On the whole, though, good playing and truthful recording.

Cello concerto.
*** CBS Dig. **MK 39541**; IM/*IMT* 39541 [id.]. Yo-Yo Ma, LSO, Previn – ELGAR: *Concerto.****

Yo-Yo Ma and Previn give a sensuously beautiful performance. With speeds markedly slower than usual in the outer movements, the meditation is intensified to bring a mood of ecstasy, quite distinct from other Walton. In turn, with spacious outer movements, the toughness and power of the central allegro is made the more marked. It becomes the symphonic kernel of the work, far more than just a scherzo. In the excellent CBS recording the soloist is less forwardly and more faithfully balanced than is common. The CD is one of CBS's most impressive, refining detail and increasing tangibility. Though Tortelier's version, more openly extrovert in its emotional response, offers a highly involving alternative approach (HMV ESD/*TC-ESD* 107763-1/*4*), Ma's reading takes pride of place, especially as the coupling of the Tortelier issue, Ida Haendel's similarly ripe account of the *Violin concerto*, is now available coupled with Britten – see below.

Violin concerto.

(M) *** HMV ED 290353-1/*4*. Ida Haendel, Bournemouth SO, Berglund – BRITTEN: *Violin concerto.****

The *Violin concerto*, written for Heifetz in 1939, shows Walton at his most distinctively compelling. Even he has rarely written melodies so ravishingly beautiful, so hauntedly romantic, yet his equally personal brand of spikiness has rarely if ever been presented with more power. A sunny, glowing, Mediterranean-like view of the *Concerto* comes from Ida Haendel, with brilliant playing from the soloist and eloquent orchestral support from the Bournemouth orchestra under Paavo Berglund. Kyung Wha Chung's version (Decca SXL/*KSXC* 6601) is wirier and in some ways more in character, but many collectors will respond equally (or even more) positively to Miss Haendel's warmth. There is an unrelieved lyricism about her tone that may not be to all tastes but, given the quality of both playing and recording (as well as the interest of the no less successful performance of the Britten coupling), this is an eminently desirable issue. On the cassette, which is generally impressively transferred, the resonance does slightly cloud some of the more exuberant orchestral tuttis, but the soloist is beautifully caught.

(i) *Façade* (complete); (ii) *A Song for the Lord Mayor's table.*

(M) * Decca Lon. Ent. 414 664-1/*4* [id.]. (i) Peggy Ashcroft, Paul Schofield, L. Sinf. (members), composer; (ii) Harper, Hamburger.

Walton's own recording of *Façade* is a near-disaster, not for the musical side (which sadly can barely be heard behind the speakers) but for the utter miscasting of Paul Scofield, the slowest and least rhythmic of reciters. Dame Peggy Ashcroft is more aptly characterful, but she also lags behind the best. She is recorded so close that her breath is constantly in one's ear.

Peter Pears and Edith Sitwell herself still provide the finest available performance of the complete entertainment (Decca Eclipse ECS 560). This is not real stereo, but the transcription is astonishingly successful, clear and atmospheric. No doubt this will be issued on CD one day.

Film music: *Hamlet: Funeral march; Hamlet and Ophelia* (*A poem for orchestra*, arr. Mathieson). *Henry V: suite. Richard III: Prelude and suite.*

**(*) HMV Dig. EL 270118-1/*4* [Ang. DS/*4DS* 38088]. Royal Liverpool PO, Groves.

The orchestral glory of ceremonial Walton richly deserves the splendour of modern digital recording, to make this selection of his Shakespeare film music very welcome. *Hamlet and Ophelia* is a 13-minute 'Poem for orchestra' drawn from the *Hamlet* music in an arrangement by Muir Mathieson, mainly using material for Ophelia's scenes, not least her drowning. The *Hamlet Funeral march*, expanded here by Mathieson, is much more substantial, as are the other items, earlier recorded by Walton himself with the Philharmonia. Groves's performances rarely match the composer's own in flair and panache, but the richness of sound, with fine bloom on the brass, is some compensation. There is also a very good XDR cassette, with good amplitude, range and detail; the strings sound especially full and natural. The composer's own collection remains available at mid-price (HMV SXLP 30139 [Ang. Sera. S 60205]).

Symphony No. 1 in B flat min.
** Chan. Dig. **CHAN 8313**; ABRD/*ABTD* 1095. SNO, Gibson.
(M) (***) Decca mono 414 659-1/*4*. LSO, Sir Hamilton Harty.

Gibson's is a convincingly idiomatic view, well paced but with ensemble not always bitingly precise enough for this darkly intense music (malice prescribed for the scherzo, melancholy for the slow movement). Recording first rate, but with less body than usual from Chandos and with timpani resonantly obtrusive. The compact disc is somewhat disappointing, bringing out the thinness on top and this probably sounds best in its excellent cassette format. This is only a stop-gap until Previn's intermittently available RCA version is transferred to CD.

Made in December 1935 within a month of the first complete performance of Walton's *Symphony*, Sir Hamilton Harty's historic recording, transferred from 78 r.p.m. discs, brings a more overtly emotional reading than any recorded since. The passionate warmth and bite of the performance, remarkable when orchestral standards in London hardly approached those of today, are a tribute to his mastery. He is a conductor too little represented on L P. The surface hiss is high but is steady enough to be unobtrusive, once the ear adjusts to it. Though the dynamic range is limited and the acoustic dry, the electricity of the playing comes over superbly.

Violin sonata.
(*) ASV Dig. DCA/*ZCDCA* 548 [id.]. McAslan, Blakely – ELGAR: *Sonata.*(*)

Lorraine McAslan gives a warmly committed performance of Walton's often wayward *Sonata*, coping well with the sharp and difficult changes of mood in both of the two long movements. The romantic melancholy of the piece suits her well, and though the recording does not make her tone as rounded as it should be, she produces some exquisite pianissimo playing, making this a most impressive début recording. John Blakely is a most sympathetic partner, particularly impressive in crisply articulated scherzando passages.

(i) *Belshazzar's Feast; Henry V (film score): suite.*
*** ASV Dig. **CDRPO 8001**; RPO/*ZCRPO* 8001 [id.]. (i) Luxon, Brighton Fest. Ch., L. Coll. Mus., RPO, Previn.

André Previn's new digital version of Walton's oratorio was the first issue on the Royal Philharmonic Orchestra's own RPO label, providing a first-class start to the project in a performance even sharper and more urgent than his fine earlier version for EMI with the LSO. The recording is spectacular, bringing out details of Walton's brilliant orchestration as never before. The chorus, singing with biting intensity, is set realistically behind the orchestra, and though that gives the impression of a smaller group than is ideal, clarity and definition are enhanced. Benjamin Luxon – who earlier sang in Solti's Decca version – is a characterful soloist, but his heavy vibrato is exaggerated by too close a balance. The five-movement suite from Walton's film music for *Henry V* makes a generous and attractive coupling. Previn is the first conductor on record since Walton himself to capture the full dramatic bite and colour of this music, with the cavalry charge at Agincourt particularly vivid. The iron-oxide cassette cannot be recommended. The transfer level is low and there is little choral bite with the upper range blunted.

Warlock, Peter (1894–1930)

(i) *An old song;* (ii) *Capriol suite; Serenade for strings.*
*** Lyr. SRCS 120 [id.]. (i) LPO, Boult; (ii) LSO, Nicholas Braithwaite – HOLST: *Suite de ballet.****

An old song – a piece in which Warlock boldly echoes Delius's *First cuckoo* – here brings the last completely new recording of Sir Adrian Boult to be issued. Derivative as it is, it makes a charming item, well matched with Warlock's most celebrated orchestral piece, the captivating *Capriol*, and the single movement that was completed of the *String serenade*. All three performances are excellent, and so is the recording – well up to Lyrita's usual high standard.

Wassenaer, Unico (1692–1766)

6 Concerti armonici.
*** Argo Dig. **410 205-2**; ZRDL/*KZRDC* 1002. ASMF, Marriner.

Sir Neville Marriner and the Academy of St Martin-in-the-Fields are nothing if not spacious. They bring both dignity and warmth to these remarkable pieces, and they are sumptuously recorded, too. They combine opulence of tone with genuine feeling and make a clear first choice in this repertoire. The compact disc is also first class, though it is not markedly superior to the LP. The chrome cassette is very well managed, its upper focus fractionally less clean than CD and LP. But the sound still combines fullness with delicacy of detail.

Weber, Carl (1786–1826)

Clarinet concertino in C min., Op. 26.

*** ASV Dig. **CDDCA 559**; DCA/*ZCDCA* 559 [id.]. Emma Johnson, ECO, Groves – CRUSELL: *Concerto No. 2* ❀; BAERMANN: *Adagio*; ROSSINI: *Intro. theme and variations.****

Emma Johnson is in her element in Weber's delightful *Concertino*. Her phrasing is wonderfully beguiling and her use of light and shade agreeably subtle, while she finds a superb lilt in the final section, pacing the music to bring out its charm rather than achieve breathless bravura. Sir Charles Groves provides an admirable accompaniment, and the recording is eminently realistic and naturally balanced. There is a good tape.

Clarinet concertos Nos 1 in F min., Op. 73; 2 in E flat, Op. 74; Concertino in C min., Op. 26.

(*) Chan. **CHAN 8305; ABRD/*ABTD* 1058 [id.]. Hilton, CBSO, Järvi.
(*) HM Orfeo **CO 67831A; SO 67831A. Brunner, Bamberg SO, Caetani.

Clarinet concerto No. 2.

*** Hyp. **CDA 66088**; A/*KA* 66088 [id.]. Thea King, LSO, Francis – CRUSELL: Concerto No. 2.***

Stylish, understanding performances of both concertos from Janet Hilton, spirited and rhythmic (particularly in No. 1), but erring just a little on the side of caution next to her finest virtuoso rivals. With full, well-balanced digital recording and nice matching between soloist and orchestra, it certainly outshines its main competitor in sound, with an excellent matching cassette. This record is generous in including the engaging *Concertino* alongside the two concertos, a piece made famous in far-off 78 r.p.m. days by a Columbia record by the Garde Républicain Band of France, the solo part played with great bravura by all members of the first clarinet line in unison.

Eduard Brunner offers the same coupling as Janet Hilton. His performances are often more romantically ardent, with a firmer line. Both slow movements come off especially well, with the horn chorale in the *Adagio* of the *First Concerto* producing some lovely playing from the Bamberg orchestra. However, articulation of the fast running passages is sometimes less characterful and Janet Hilton finds rather more humour in the finales, especially the *Alla Polacca* of No. 2. Yet Brunner is at his best in the last movement of the *Concertino*, his bravura agreeably extrovert here. Where the Chandos issue scores is in the recording which, especially on the compact disc, is more open and transparent, whereas on the Orfeo CD orchestral textures are thick in tuttis.

Readers content with the *E flat Concerto* alone will find the Hyperion coupling with Crusell a delectable combination. Thea King with her beautiful range of tone-colours is an outstandingly communicative artist on record and here gives a totally delightful account of the second of the two Weber concertos, particularly lovely in the G minor slow movement and seductively pointed in the *Polacca* rhythms of the finale, never pressed too hard. She is admirably accompanied by Alun Francis and the LSO in a warmly reverberant recording that CD makes very realistic indeed.

Horn concertino in E min., Op. 45.
*** Ph. Dig. **412 237-2**; 412 237-1/*4* [id.]. Baumann, Leipzig GO, Masur – R. STRAUSS: *Horn concertos.***(*)

Baumann plays Weber's opening lyrical melody so graciously that the listener is made to feel this is a more substantial work than it is. At the end of the *Andante* Baumann produces an undulating series of chords (by gently singing the top note as he plays) and the effect is spine-tingling, while the easy virtuosity of the closing *Polacca* is hardly less breathtaking. The bravura is essentially easy-going, and Masur's accompaniment has matching warmth, while the Leipzig Hall adds its usual flattering ambience. The soloist is given fine presence on CD.

Introduction, theme and variations (for clarinet and orchestra).
*** Denon **C37 7038**; DG 410 670-1/*4* [id.]. Meyer, Berlin Philh. Qt – MOZART: *Clarinet Qt.****

This piece attributed to Weber is now known to be the work of Joseph Küffner (1777–1856) and is listed here for convenience. It is an effective but unimportant brief display work, essentially lightweight. The recording by Sabine Meyer and the Berlin Philharmonia is first rate, very well balanced and recorded. As can be seen, the compact disc comes from Denon, while DG have mastered the LP and the excellent equivalent cassette.

Invitation to the dance (orch. Berlioz).
*** Decca Dig. **411 898-2**; 411 898-1/*4* [id.]. Nat. PO, Bonynge – BERLIOZ: *Les Troyens ballet***; LECOCQ: *Mam'zelle Angot.****

Bonynge's account has elegance and polish and the waltz rhythms are nicely inflected. The Kingsway Hall recording is first class, slightly sharper in focus on CD, with the LP mellower, not to disadvantage. The cassette, too, is of high quality. The Lecocq coupling is vivaciously tuneful; but the Berlioz ballet sequence is not really memorable heard out of context.

Konzertstück in F min., Op. 79.
*** Ph. **412 251-2**; 9500 *677*/*7300 772* [id.]. Brendel, LSO, Abbado – SCHUMANN: *Piano concerto.****
(B) ** Ph. On Tour *412 906-4*. Magaloff, LSO, Sir Colin Davis – CHOPIN: *Andante spianato***; GRIEG; SCHUMANN: *Concertos.**(*)

Weber's programmatic *Konzertstück* is seldom heard in the concert hall these days, and it is a rarity in the recording studio. This Philips version is very brilliant indeed and finds the distinguished soloist in his very best form: he is wonderfully light and invariably imaginative. In every respect, including the recording quality, this is unlikely to be surpassed for a long time. As in the case of the Schumann concerto with which it is coupled, on CD Weber emerges in brighter, firmer focus than on LP; collectors wanting this delightful work in the new format need not hesitate. The cassette is acceptable, but less transparent than the LP.

Magaloff's account with the LSO under Sir Colin Davis is sound and thoroughly musical, and it is well recorded on this Philips tape. But it comes in harness with other concertante works in recordings of mixed vintage, and even more mixed appeal.

Overtures: *Abu Hassan; Beherrscher der Geister; Euryanthe; Der Freischütz; Oberon; Peter Schmoll. Invitation to the dance* (orch. Berlioz), *Op. 65*.
(M) *** DG Gal. 419 069-1/*4* [id.]. BPO, Karajan.

A self-recommending reissue from 1973, digitally remastered. The performances have great style and refinement. Weber's overtures are superbly crafted and there are no better examples of the genre than *Oberon* and *Der Freischütz*. While epitomizing the spirit of the operas which they serve to introduce, each also shows the composer's special feeling for the romantic possibilities of the French horn, heard as soloist in *Oberon* and in a marvellously crafted quartet in *Der Freischütz*. Here, by scoring the four parts for a pair each of horns, crooked in C and F, Weber achieves a lengthy four-part melody, with almost every note available on the natural harmonics of the valveless instrument of his time. Needless to say, the Berlin horn playing is peerless. For this reissue, Karajan's stylish performance of another Weberian innovation, the *Invitation to the dance* (in Berlioz's orchestration), makes a valuable bonus.

Overtures: *Der Freischütz; Oberon*.
(M) *** DG Gal. 415 840-1/*4* [id.]. Bav. RSO, Kubelik – MENDELSSOHN: *Midsummer Night's Dream*.***

Kubelik offers Weber's two greatest overtures as a fine bonus for his extended selection from Mendelssohn's *Midsummer Night's Dream* incidental music. The playing is first class and compares favourably with the Karajan versions.

Symphony No. 1 in C.
(M) *** Ph. Seq. 412 374-1/*4*. New Philh. O, Boettcher – CHERUBINI: *Symphony*.***

Symphonies Nos 1 in C; 2 in C.
*** ASV Dig. **CDDCA 515**; DCA/*ZCDCA* 515 [id.]. ASMF, Marriner.
(*) Orfeo **C 091841A; S 091841A [id.]. Bav. RSO, Sawallisch.

Weber's two symphonies were written within a period of two months between December 1806 and the end of January 1807. Curiously, both are in C major, yet each has its own individuality and neither lacks vitality or invention. Sir Neville Marriner has their full measure; these performances combine vigour and high spirits with the right degree of gravitas (not too much) in the slow movements. The orchestral playing throughout is infectiously lively and catches the music's vibrant character. The recording is bright and fresh, with excellent detail. It is full in the bass, but the bright upper range brings a touch of digital edge to the upper strings, which is slightly more apparent on the CD. The cassette is smoother on top, yet still bright and full.

Sawallisch's is also a fine, well-played coupling. His approach is more romantic, with rather more atmosphere. Allegros are alert; and both slow movements go well, although there is heaviness in the minuet of No. 2, taken rather ponderously. On the whole, Marriner is fresher and the Academy playing has greater resilience. The Orfeo recording is smoother on top but not so clear.

LP and tape collectors content with the *First Symphony* only, coupled with Cherubini, will find that this delightful work is well served both by the New Philharmonia under Boettcher and by the Philips engineers. The 1971 recording sounds admirably fresh in this reissue, and there is a vivid matching cassette, transferred at the highest level.

Clarinet quintet in B flat (arr. for clarinet and string orchestra).
*** HMV Dig. EL 270220-1/*4*. Meyer, Württemberg CO, Faerber – BAERMANN: *Adagio;* MENDELSSOHN: *Concert pieces.****

(i) *Clarinet quintet in B flat, Op. 34;* (ii) *Grand Duo concertante, Op. 48; 7 Variations on a theme from Silvana, Op. 33.*
(*) Chan. Dig. **CHAN 8366; ABRD/*ABTD* 1131 [id.]. Hilton, (i) Lindsay Qt; (ii) Keith Swallow.

Weber's *Clarinet quintet* was written for Baermann, whose *Adagio* is one of the couplings on the HMV issue. The *Quintet* is recorded in an orchestral transcription, a course which Weber himself authorized. Sabine Meyer is, of course, the highly accomplished clarinettist whom Karajan invited to join the Berlin Philharmonic, and her account of this quintet leaves no doubts as to her expertise and musicianship. The recording is warm and bright, and the balance between soloist and orchestra well judged.

On LP, Anthony Pay with the Nash Ensemble (CRD CRD 1098/*CRDC 4098*) and Alan Hacker with the Music Party, using original instruments (O-L DSLO 533), lead the field in the *Quintet*; but neither is available on compact disc, so the Chandos issue with Janet Hilton and the Lindsays is self-recommending. She plays with considerable authority and spirit though she is not always as mellifluous as her rivals. On LP, this version does not entirely sweep the board even though it is very good indeed. Janet Hilton's account of the *Grand Duo concertante*, which Weber wrote for himself and Baermann to play, is a model of fine ensemble, as are the *Variations on a theme from Silvana*, of 1811, in which Keith Swallow is an equally expert partner. At times the acoustic seems almost too reverberant in the two pieces for clarinet and piano, but the sound in the *Quintet* is eminently satisfactory. There is a first-class cassette.

Folksong settings: *The gallant troubadour; John Anderson; My love is like a red, red rose; O poor tithe cauld and restless love; Robin is my joy; A soldier am I; The soothing shades of gloaming; True hearted was he; Yes, thou may'st walk; Where he'e ye been a' the day.*
*** HMV EL 270323-1/*4* [Ang. DS/*4DS* 37352]. Robert White, Sanders, Peskanov, Rosen, Wilson – BEETHOVEN: *Folksongs*.***

It was an inspiration for Robert White to unearth, as an ideal coupling for Beethoven, ten of the folksong settings which Weber in the last months of his life composed (like Beethoven before him) for the Scottish publisher, George Thomson. This first recording, winningly sung with heady tenor tone and fine characterization, brings out the poetry and imagination that the dying composer gave to his well-paid commission. *The gallant troubadour* is a lilting setting of the Walter Scott poem; but just as attractive – with specially original use of the flute obbligato – are such items as the four Burns settings, including a honeyed one of *My love is like a red, red rose*. Warm, helpful recording, with a first-class cassette.

OPERA

Euryanthe (complete).
*** HMV EX 290698-3/*5* (3). Norman, Hunter, Gedda, Krause, Leipzig R. Ch., Dresden State O, Janowski.

Much has been written about the absurdity of the plot of *Euryanthe*, as unlikely a tale of the age of chivalry and troubadours as you will find; but, as this fine recording bears out, the opera is far more than just an historic curiosity. The juxtaposition of the two sopranos, representing good and evil, is formidably effective, particularly when as here the challenge is taken by singers of the stature of Jessye Norman and Rita Hunter. Hunter may not be the most convincing villainess, but the cutting edge of the voice is marvellous; as for Jessye Norman, she sings radiantly, whether in her first delicate cavatina or the big aria of Act III. Tom Krause as the villain, Lysiart, has rarely sung better, and Nicolai Gedda, as ever, is the most intelligent of tenors. Good, atmospheric recording (as important in this opera as in *Freischütz*) and direction from Marek Janowski which makes light of any longueurs. The cassettes are very disappointing, middle- and bass-heavy with a restricted upper range, caused by the resonance and the use of iron-oxide stock.

Der Freischütz (complete).
(*) Decca **417 119-2 (2) [id.]; D235 D3/*K235 K 32* (3/*2*) [Lon. OSA/*5*- 13136]. Behrens, Donath, Meven, Kollo, Moll, Brendel, Bav. R. Ch. and SO, Kubelik.

****(*)** Denon Dig. **C37 6433/5** [id.]. Smitková, Ihle, Goldberg, Wlaschiha, Adam, Dresden State Op. Ch. and O, Hauschild.

Kubelik takes a direct view of Weber's high romanticism. The result has freshness but lacks something in dramatic bite and atmosphere. There is far less tension than in the finest earlier versions, not least in the Wolf's Glen scene which, in spite of full-ranging brilliant recording, seems rather tame, even with the added projection of CD. The singing is generally good – René Kollo as Max giving one of his best performances on record – but Hildegard Behrens, superbly dramatic in later German operas, here seems clumsy as Agathe in music that often requires a pure lyrical line. The 1981 recording has been vividly remastered on to a pair of CDs. The tape quality is also crisp and clear. The cassette layout on four sides is preferable to that on LP.

On 13 February 1985 the Semper opera house in Dresden was re-opened, lovingly rebuilt and restored after wartime destruction thirty years earlier. Japanese engineers from Denon worked with East German colleagues to record this first performance in the theatre, capturing the atmosphere very vividly. Those who like live recordings of opera will not mind the occasional odd balance and the bouts of coughing from the audience, but the conducting of Wolf-Dieter Hauschild is not always electrifying enough to make compensation. The Wolf's Glen scene, when the magic bullets are cast, lacks the full tingle of horror, though Ekkehard Wlaschiha as Kasper and Rainer Goldberg are both first rate. Jana Smitková makes a tender and vulnerable Agathe, though she is not always steady of tone. Much of the rest of the singing is indifferent, though the chorus work is lively. Moreover, the set is uneconomically laid out on three CDs.

Reminder. The DG set with Janowitz, Mathis, Schreier, Adam, Vogel and Crass is much more enjoyable. Carlos Kleiber may have his extreme tempi in places, but his is an electrifying reading of an opera that must be played and sung for all it is worth. No doubt this version will appear on compact disc during the lifetime of this book (DG 2720 071/*3371 008* [2709 046/*id.*]).

Oberon: complete.
(M) *** DG 419 038-1/*4* (2). Grobe, Nilsson, Domingo, Prey, Hamari, Augér, Schimil, Bav. R. Ch. and SO, Kubelik.

Rarely has operatic inspiration been squandered so cruelly on impossible material as in Weber's *Oberon.* We owe it to Covent Garden's strange ideas in the mid-1820s of what 'English opera' should be that Weber's delicately conceived score is a sequence of illogical arias, scenas and ensembles strung together by an absurd pantomime plot. Though even on record the result is slacker because of that loose construction, one can appreciate, in a performance as stylish and refined as this, the contribution of Weber. The original issue included dialogue and a narration spoken by one of Oberon's fairy characters. In the reissue this is omitted, cutting the number of discs required from three to two, yet leaving the music untouched. With Birgit Nilsson commanding in *Ocean, thou mighty monster*, and excellent singing from the other principals, helped by

Kubelik's ethereally light handling of the orchestra, the set can be recommended without reservation, for the recording remains of excellent quality. The enchanting *Mermaids' song*, with its decorative horn motif, ravishingly sung here by Arleen Augér, is one of Weber's most memorable ideas. The set now appears for the first time on chrome cassettes of excellent quality (in a cardboard flap-pack with a miniature but clearly printed libretto).

Webern, Anton (1883–1945)

Concerto for nine instruments, Op. 24.
*** Chan. ABR/*ABT* 1046 [id.]. Nash Ens., Rattle – SCHOENBERG: *Pierrot Lunaire.****

This late Webern piece, tough, spare and uncompromising, makes a valuable fill-up for Jane Manning's outstanding version of Schoenberg's *Pierrot Lunaire*, a 1977 recording originally made for the Open University. First-rate sound.

Weill, Kurt (1900–50)

Symphonies Nos 1–2.
(M) *** Decca Lon. Ent. 414 660-1/*4*. BBC SO, Bertini.

Both of these symphonies are fascinating works. The *Symphony No. 1* was a student piece, written in Berlin in 1921, when Weill was still a Busoni pupil. Fortunately the influences were mainly from Mahler and Schoenberg rather than Busoni (hence the master's disapproval), and though the thickness of texture has its dangers, the youthful urgency and imagination of the argument in a complex interlinked form carry the work off most successfully. The *Symphony No. 2* of 1933–4 is an obviously more mature work, with three colourful and effective movements which have much in common with the Soviet symphonies that Shostakovich, Kabalevsky and others were beginning to write at the time. Behind the characteristic ostinatos and near-vulgar melodies, there is a lurking seriousness – reflection of Weill's personal trials as he left Germany for American exile – and some assess this as the first really important symphony in the Austro-German tradition after the death of Mahler. The performances are committed, but could be better disciplined. Good late-1960s recording. The cassette is extremely vivid. The upper range is a little dry, but it suits the music well.

Silverlake (complete).
** None. Dig. **CD 79003**; DB 79003 (2) [id.]. Grey, Neill, Hynes, Bonazzi, NY City Opera Ch. and O, Rudel.

Textually this is a travesty of Weill's intentions in *Der Silbersee,* the play in three Acts 'with extensive musical score' which he wrote to a text by Georg Kaiser. For a highly successful production at the New York City Opera, *Silverlake* was given an entirely new book by Hugh Wheeler with lyrics by Lys Symonette, who also drew on Weill's earlier incidental music for a Strindberg play to provide support for spoken dialogue. Such is the vitality of Weill's inspiration, much of the authentic bite comes over in this lively performance, which is presented in recorded sound as in performing style on the lines of a Broadway musical. The acoustic is dry and unflattering, the placing of voices and instruments close.

The Threepenny opera: suite.
(*) HMV ED 290332-1/*4*. Philh. O, Klemperer – KLEMPERER: *Symphony No. 2* etc.

Klemperer reminds us of his early allegiance to the music of Weill in the tangy and characterful suite drawn from the composer's most successful piece. It may be rather straight-faced for latter-day taste but, well recorded, it makes a good coupling for the Klemperer *Symphony* on the reverse.

Widor, Charles-Marie (1844–1937)

Organ symphony No. 5 in F min., Op. 42/1.
*** DG Dig. **413 438-2**; 413 438-1/*4* [id.]. Simon Preston (organ of Westminster Abbey) – VIERNE: *Carillon de Westminster.****

Organ symphonies Nos 5; 10 (Romane), Op. 73.
*** Ph. Dig. **410 054-2**; 6769/*7654* 085 (2) [id.]. Chorzempa (organ of Saint-Sernin Basilica, Toulouse).

Simon Preston gives a masterly account of the Widor *Fifth Symphony*, with a fine sense of pace and command of colour. The Westminster Abbey organ may lack something of the Gallic acerbity of the Cavaillé-Coll used by Chorzempa, but there is a marvellous sense of space in this DG recording. On compact disc, detail seems far more sharply focused and one benefits from the wider dynamic range CD encompasses. However, cassette collectors will find that DG's chrome tape also sounds most realistic.

Daniel Chorzempa provides a massive demonstration of compact-disc opulence which should send the neighbours scurrying for cover if this CD is played at full volume. He chooses some agreeable registration for the amiable earlier music of the *Fifth Symphony*; but at times one wonders if he does not overdo the dynamic range for domestic listening, for the gentle music is distanced and atmospheric to a great degree. Nevertheless, he provides a highly energetic account of the famous *Toccata* which exudes a nice mixture of power and exuberance. The *Tenth Symphony* has its structure bound together by the Easter plain-chant, *Haec Dies*, and after a pleasant *Cantilène* third movement the composer gathers up the threads of the music for another weighty finale; then the rhetoric suddenly evaporates and the piece ends gently. Chorzempa makes much of this effect (and the CD background silence helps) and seems entirely at home in this repertoire. The Cavaillé-Coll organ is well chosen; the recording is excellent on LP as well as CD, although on the chrome tapes there are moments when the focus roughens under pressure. However, the single CD is a more economical format than the pair of tapes or LPs.

Organ symphony No. 5: Toccata.
ℭ *** Argo Dig. **410 165-2**; ZRDL/*KZRDC* 1011 [id.]. Hurford (organ of Ratzburg Cathedral) – *Recital.**** ℭ

Those wanting the *Toccata* alone could not do better than choose Peter Hurford's exhilarating version, recorded with great presence and impact on a most attractive organ, and giving demonstration quality, whether compact disc, LP or chrome cassette is chosen.

Organ symphonies: No. 5: Toccata (only); *6 in G min., Op. 42/2; 9 in C min. (Gothic), Op. 70.*
*** Erato ECD 88111. Marie-Claire Alain (Cavaillé-Coll organs).

Marie-Claire Alain plays Cavaillé-Coll organs, using the instrument at Orléans Cathedral for the famous *Toccata* (recorded in 1980) and the organ of Saint Germain-en-Laye for the later symphonies. Her performances are first class, that of the *Toccata* spacious and bold, rather like the composer's own 78 r.p.m. version. Both the later symphonies are much more impressive works than the earlier group of Op. 13. The *Gothic symphony* has a specially fine third movement, where a Christmas chant (*Puer natus est nobis*) is embroidered fugally. The final section is a set of variations, and in the closing *Toccata* the Gregorian chant is reintroduced on the pedals. Both this and the hardly less inventive *Sixth Symphony* were recorded in 1977, but the analogue master yields splendid results. However, the *Symphonie gothique* is cut at a lower level than the *Toccata*, and having raised the volume it is important to remember to turn it down again, otherwise one is engulfed in a flood of sound at the opening of No. 6.

Organ symphony No. 6 in G min., Op. 42/2: Allegro.
** Ph. Dig. **412 619-2**; 412 619-1/*4* [id.]. Jean Giullou – SAINT-SAËNS: *Symphony No. 3.**

Although well played and recorded, this excerpt friom Widor's *Sixth Symphony* is merely a filler for an indifferent version of the Saint-Saëns *Organ symphony*.

Wieniawski, Henryk (1835–80)

Violin concertos Nos 1 in F sharp min., Op. 14; 2 in D min., Op. 22.
*** HMV **CDC 747107-2** [id.]; ASD 2870 [Ang. S/*4XS* 36903]. Perlman, LPO, Ozawa.

Violin concerto No. 2 in D min., Op. 22.
*** DG Dig. **410 526-2**; 410 526-1/*4* [id.]. Perlman, O de Paris, Barenboim – SAINT-SAËNS: *Violin concerto No. 3.****

Those who have enjoyed the relatively well-known *Second Concerto* of this contemporary of Tchaikovsky should investigate this coupling of his two concertos. The *First* may not be as consistently memorable as the *Second*, but the central *Preghiera* is darkly intense, and the finale is full of the showmanship that was the mark of the composer's own virtuosity on the violin. Perlman gives scintillating performances, full of flair, and is excellently accompanied. The recording, from 1973, has similar admirable qualities to the companion remastered CD, from the same period, of Paganini's *First Concerto*. The sound is warm and vivid and well balanced, and all the clearer and more realistic in its compact disc format. It is preferable to Perlman's digital re-make of the *Second Concerto*. This offers playing that is effortlessly dazzling, while he and Barenboim create an attractively songful *Andante*, so that the scintillating bravura of the *moto perpetuo* finale sounds even more dashing by contrast. Generally good recording, with a moderately forward balance for the soloist. The compact disc offers the usual advantages but, as so often with DG, emphasizes that the balance is artificially contrived, with the soloist too close.

Williams, Grace (1906–77)

Ave maris stella; The Dancers; Harp song of the Dane women; Mariners' song. The 6 Gerard Manley Hopkins poems.
*** Chan. Dig. ABRD/*ABTD* 1116 [id.]. Eiddwen Harrhy, Helen Watts, Thomas, Richard Hickox Singers, City of L. Sinfonia, Hickox.

Hickox presents a delightful collection of the choral music of Grace Williams, one of the most sensitive of Welsh composers. With overtones of Britten and early Tippett, the writing yet has freshness and originality, with rich textures supporting open melodies, often crisply rhythmic. The resonant acoustic does not always allow for ideally clear textures, but the performances are as fresh as the inspirations. Helen Watts is the eloquent contralto soloist in the Hopkins cycle with its complex rhythmic patterning.

Williams, John (born 1932)

Close encounters of the third kind: suite; Star Wars: suite.
(*) RCA **RCD 13650. Nat. PO, Gerhardt.

Film music: *Close encounters of the third kind; E.T.; Raiders of the lost ark; Star Wars trilogy; Superman* (with COURAGE: *Star Trek: theme*).
** Telarc Dig. **CD 80094** [id]. Cincinnati Pops O, Kunzel.

Gerhardt has the full measure of this music and the National Philharmonic plays marvellously for him: the sweeping strings have an eloquence in the best Hollywood tradition. He shows particular skill in the *Close encounters* sequence, creating genuine tension and evocative feeling. In *Star Wars*, the theme for

Princess Leia includes a horn solo which is played quite gorgeously, while the closing section has a *nobilmente* swagger. The RCA recording is bright and well balanced, but it could ideally be richer.

The Telarc recording is certainly spectacular and the concert has a synthesized prologue and epilogue to underline the sci-fi associations. The inclusion of the famous *Star Trek* signature theme (a splendid tune) is wholly appropriate. The orchestra plays this music with striking verve, and the sweeping melody of *E.T.* is especially effective; but the overall effect is brash, with the microphones seeking brilliance in the sound-balance.

Wirén, Dag (1905–83)

Serenade for strings, Op. 11.
*** RCA Dig. **RD 85362**; RL/*RK* 85362 [HRC1/*HRK1* 5362]. Canadian Nat. Arts Centre O, Mata – R. STRAUSS: *Le Bourgeois gentilhomme.****

An unexpected but welcome coupling for a very attractive account of Strauss's delectable *Bourgeois gentilhomme*. Mata's touch is a light one: this is essentially a chamber performance, but it is very well played and recorded in all three formats. There is an alternative version by the Stockholm Sinfonietta on BIS (**CD 285** – see Concerts, below) using a larger string group, where the conductor, Salonen, gives even more point to the famous *Alla marcia* at a slightly faster tempo; but Mata's account remains attractive in its smaller scale.

String quartets: Nos 3, Op. 18; 4, Op. 28.
**(*) Phono/Suecia Dig. PS 16. Fresk Qt.

Dag Wirén's reputation rests firmly on one work: the famous *Serenade for strings* of 1937 which put this likeable Swedish composer on the map. Otherwise his admittedly small output has enjoyed scant exposure on record. Both *Quartets* are new to the international catalogue, though the *Fourth* was recorded in the early 1960s on the Swedish Radio's label. No. 3 dates from 1945 and its successor from 1952–3, the same period as his *Fourth Symphony*, once available on Vox-Turnabout. As usual with this modest but fine composer, there is a strong sense of atmosphere, a keen feeling for nature and its changing moods, and a pervasive melancholy which is quite distinctive. His invention tends to be short-breathed and ideas are reiterated, rather than developed to any real extent; and the overall effect is of a limited sensibility. The *Third Quartet* is in some ways closer to the world of the *Serenade*, and the second group of the first movement is obviously from the same stable. At times one longs for a greater variety of melodic substance, but the overall effect is sympathetic and congenial, and less intense than the somewhat darker *Fourth*. The Fresk Quartet give generally persuasive accounts of both works, though they fall short of real distinction. They are excellently recorded, with plenty of presence and detail in a good acoustic setting.

Wolf, Hugo (1860–1903)

Goethe-Lieder: Anakreons Grab; Erschaffen und Beleben; Frech und Froh I; Ganymed; Kophtisches Lied I and II; Ob der Koran; Der Rattenfänger; Trunken müssen wir alle sein. Mörike-Lieder: Abschied; An die Geliebte; Auf ein altes Bild; Begegnung; Bei einer Trauung; Denk' es, O Seele!; Er ist's; Der Feuerreiter; Fussreise; Der Gärtner; In der Frühe; Jägerlied; Nimmersatte Liebe; Selbstgeständnis; Storchenbotschaft; Der Tambour; Verborgenheit.
*** DG **415 192-2** [id.]. Dietrich Fischer-Dieskau, Daniel Barenboim.

This generous collection of seventeen of Wolf's Mörike songs and nine Goethe settings (65 minutes in all, with each song separately banded) was issued on CD to celebrate the singer's sixtieth birthday, a masterly example of his art. Barenboim's easily spontaneous style goes beautifully with Fischer-Dieskau's finely detailed singing, matching the sharp and subtle changes of mood. The mid-1970s analogue recording has been very well transferred, with the voice vividly immediate. Full texts and translations are given in the accompanying booklet.

Italian Lieder Book (complete).
(M) *** Ph. 412 391-1/*4* (2) [id.]. Elly Ameling, Gérard Souzay, Dalton Baldwin.

The recordings come from the early 1970s; though not as fine as the unforgettable version by Schwarzkopf and Fischer-Dieskau with Gerald Moore, currently out of the catalogue, this Philips set is welcome back in its mid-price format. Elly Ameling, delicately sweet and precise, contrasts well with Souzay, with his fine-drawn sense of line. The charm and point of these brief but intensely imaginative songs are well presented here, with perceptive accompaniments from Dalton Baldwin. The whole presentation has striking spontaneity and freshness. The cassette equivalent is on a single extended-length tape of Philips's highest quality and well documented. The reproduction has excellent presence and realism.

Mörike-Lieder: *An eine Aeolsharfe; Auf eine Christblume I and II; Begegnung; Bei einer Trauung; Elfenlied; Er ist's; Gebet; Die Geister am Mummelsee; In der Frühe; Der Knabe und das Immlein; Lebe wohl; Lied vom Winde; Nimmersatte Liebe; Nixe Binsefuss; Rat einer Alten; Schlafendes Jesuskind; Selbstgeständnis; Ein Stündlein wohl vor Tag; Das verlassene Mägdlein.*
(M) ** Ph. 412 027-1/*4*. Elly Ameling, Dalton Baldwin.

Elly Ameling possesses a voice of great charm, and her readings here are unfailingly musical. Her diction is clean and her interpretations intelligent. Yet there is a certain uniformity of colour and mood that makes listening to the recital as a whole less satisfying than choosing individual songs. There is, needless to say, much to enjoy, and the recording cannot be flawed. Dalton Baldwin is a little prosaic at times, but against this must be balanced some highly musical and carefully thought-out details. There is some marvellous music in this recital and it is on this count that it must be recommended. There is an excellent equivalent cassette.

Das Spanische Liederbuch (complete): *Geistliche Lieder* (*Sacred Songs*) *1–10; Weltliche Lieder* (*Secular songs*) *1–34*.
(M) **(*) DG 413 226-1/*4* (2). Schwarzkopf, Fischer-Dieskau, Moore.

The advantage of this set lies in its variety. The *Spanische Liederbuch* was not intended as a cycle, and there are few people, one imagines, who would wish to hear it from end to end at one sitting. However, the set, with its ten sacred and thirty-four secular songs, naturally gains from the variety of vocal timbre; both Schwarzkopf and Fischer-Dieskau are in excellent form here, even if the former will disappoint some of her admirers by sounding just a little mannered, even arch, at times. The recording is very good, and Gerald Moore's accompanying is predictably perceptive in its musicianship. This set is now also available for the first time on tape, and although the voices lack something in presence, the reproduction is smooth and natural. Full texts are provided.

Wolf-Ferrari, Ermanno (1876–1948)

Il segreto di Susanna (complete).
(B) *** CBS DC 40134 (2). Scotto, Bruson, Philh. O, Pritchard – MASSENET: *La Navarraise*.***

Susanna's secret is that she smokes, in secret (and against Edwardian convention), and she sings a rare aria describing the bliss of the tobacco addict: 'Oh what joy to follow with half-closed eyes the fine cloud that rises in blue spirals, more delicately than a veil.' But her husband's detection of the unmistakable fumes persuades him that he has a rival for his wife's favours. Of course all is resolved at the end in a moonlit scene, as the reconciled partners go up in smoke together. Considering the fragile plot, the music itself is surprisingly dramatic, though pleasingly lyrical too, even if nothing is quite as memorable as the scintillating overture. Scotto and Bruson make the very most of their opportunities and Sir John Pritchard and the Philharmonia keep everything sparkling. The recording, from 1981, is first rate and, coupled with Massenet's *La Navarraise* and with the two discs offered for the price of one, this is a bargain.

Zamfir, Gheorghe (born 1941)

Concerto No. 1 in G for panpipes and orchestra; Rumanian rhapsody (*Spring*)*; Autumn colours; Black waltz*.
(*) Ph. Dig. **412 221-2; 412 221-1/*4* [id.]. Zamfir, Monte Carlo PO, Foster.

Gheorghe Zamfir is famous, not only as a virtuoso of the panpipes which he plays with unique flair and skill, but also as performer/composer, notably providing a haunting score for the Australian film, *Picnic at Hanging Rock*. These two concertante works are fluently written, tunefully based on folk material. Unfortunately, the *Rumanian rhapsody* outlasts its welcome; but the *Concerto* is better judged and more economically constructed. It is entertaining, if lightweight. Of the two encores, the *Black waltz* is almost indelible and reminds one of Khachaturian. The recording is first class – though, understandably, the soloist dominates the sound picture. There is also a very good cassette.

Zelenka, Jan (1649–1745)

Requiem in C min.

(*) Claves Dig. **CD 50-8501; D 8501 [id.]. Brigitte Fournier, Balleys, Ishii, Tüller, Berne Chamber Ch. and O, Dahler.

The DG Archiv recordings of the orchestral works and the *Trio sonatas* (currently withdrawn) left no doubt as to the individuality of Zelenka's mind. This record of the *Requiem in C minor*, like the settings of the *Lamentations of the Prophet Jeremiah* which Supraphon recorded in the late 1970s, confirms his originality. *The Last Trump*, for example, is a thoughtful soprano solo without any of the dramatic gestures one might expect; and the *Agnus Dei* is quite unlike any other setting of his period – or of any other – austere, intent and mystical. There is hardly a moment that is not of compelling interest here; the only qualification that needs to be made concerns the balance, which places the solo singers too forward. The performance is well prepared and thoroughly committed. On CD, one might have expected the choral focus to be sharper, but in all other respects the sound is very good, with the ambience nicely judged.

Zemlinsky, Alexander von (1871–1942)

Psalm 23, Op. 14.

*** Ph. 411 088-1 (2) [id.]. Netherlands Chamber Ch., De Leeuw – SCHOENBERG: *Choral music.****

Zemlinsky's incongruous setting of *Psalm 23*, beginning and ending in pastoral mood, provides an interesting makeweight to the important set of Schoenberg choral pieces from the Netherlands Chamber Choir, taking up the last half-side. This was music originally written for the concerts Schoenberg promoted in his Society for Private Musical Performances.

Collections

Concerts of Orchestral and Concertante Music

Academy of Ancient Music, Hogwood or Schröder

PACHELBEL: *Canon and gigue.* VIVALDI: *Concerto in B min. for 4 violins, Op. 3/10. Double trumpet concerto in C, RV.537.* GLUCK: *Orfeo: Dance of the Furies; Dance of the Blessed Spirits.* HANDEL: *Solomon: Arrival of the Queen of Sheba. Berenice: Overture; Minuet. Water music: Air; Hornpipe.*
** O-L **410 553-2**; DSLO/*KDSLC* 594.

It seems a curious idea to play popular Baroque repertoire with a severe manner. Pachelbel's *Canon* here sounds rather abrasive and lacking charm; and the *Arrival of the Queen of Sheba* is altogether more seductive in Beecham's or Marriner's hands. But those who combine a taste for these pieces with a desire for authenticity at all costs should be satisfied. The highlight here is the pair of Gluck dances, very strongly characterized and making a splendid foil for each other. The sound is extremely vivid, especially on compact disc. On tape, there is an extra degree of spikiness on side one of the cassette.

'Christmas concertos': CORELLI: *Concerto grosso Op. 6/8.* WERNER: *Christmas pastorella.* GOSSEC: *Christmas suite* (with chorus). HANDEL: *Messiah: Pifa* (*Pastoral symphony*). VEJVANOVSKY: *Sonata Natalis.* BACH: *Christmas oratorio.* TORELLI: *Concerto grosso, Op. 8/6.*
(*) O-L Dig. **410 179-2; DSDL/*KDSDC* 709.

For those needing a touch of acerbity to prevent their Christmas pastorellas becoming too bland, the present collection provides the answer. The playing has a suitably light touch (the Corelli especially so) and the programme is imaginative, though the invention in some of the lesser-known pieces is somewhat ingenuous, notably the Vejvanovský (which has the compensation of trumpets to add colour), or the Gossec, which surprises with a chorus of shepherds as its finale. The sound is first class (though the tape loses a degree of refinement with the entry of the trumpets), with the compact disc adding extra presence.

Academy of St Martin-in-the-Fields, Marriner

HANDEL: *Solomon: Arrival of the Queen of Sheba; Berenice: Minuet. Messiah: Pastoral symphony.* BACH: *Cantatas Nos 147: Jesu, joy of man's desiring; 208: Sheep may safely graze; Christmas oratorio: Sinfonia.* GRIEG: *Holberg suite: Prelude.* SCHUBERT: *Rosamunde: Entr'acte No. 2.* GLUCK: *Orfeo: Dance of the Blessed Spirits.* BORODIN: *Nocturne for strings* (arr. Marriner).
(*) HMV **CDC 747027-2 [id.]; ASD/*TC-ASD* 143642-1/*4* [Ang. DS/*4DS* 38056].

The sound of Sir Neville Marriner's CD is a striking improvement on the equivalent LP, fresher and more transparent – indeed, it is very good indeed – and while the two Bach chorales are still given considerable warmth of texture, the suggestion of romanticism is less overt than on the more ample-sounding LP. The cassette too is strikingly clear and vivid. As a whole, however, this programme is less memorable than many earlier Academy analogue collections. Handel's Queen of Sheba trots in very briskly but the polished playing prevents a feeling of breathlessness. The *Pastoral symphony* is stylish and the noble contour of the famous *Berenice* melody is warmly phrased. But it is the Schubert *Entr'acte* and the passionately expressive Borodin *Nocturne* that resonate in the memory.

'The French connection': RAVEL: *Le Tombeau de Couperin.* DEBUSSY: *Danses sacrée et profane* (with Ellis, harp). IBERT: *Divertissement.* FAURÉ: *Dolly suite, Op. 56.*
*** ASV Dig. **CDDCA 517**; DCA/*ZCDCA* 517 [id.].

An excellent collection. The spirited account of Ibert's *Divertissement* is matched by the warmth of Fauré's *Dolly suite* in the Rabaud orchestration. The remainder of the record is hardly less appealing. Ravel's *Le Tombeau de Couperin* is nicely done, though the *Forlane* is kept on too tight a rein and one feels the need for a slightly bigger body of strings. But though not a first choice, there is no denying that it is very well played indeed, as is the Debussy *Danses sacrée et profane.* One would welcome more space round the orchestra and, considering the disc was made in Studio One, Abbey Road, greater use could have been made of its ambience. This apart, however, everything is very clear with the sound even more refined and present on CD. The cassette has slightly less bite than the LP.

'The English connection': ELGAR: *Serenade for strings, Op. 20.* TIPPETT: *Fantasia concertante on a theme of Corelli.* VAUGHAN WILLIAMS: *Fantasia on a theme of Thomas Tallis; The Lark ascending* (with Iona Brown).
(*) ASV Dig. **CDDCA 518; DCA/*ZCDCA* 518 [id.].

Sir Neville Marriner's newer performances of the Elgar *Serenade* and the *Tallis Fantasia* are less intense (and less subtle) than his earlier versions; the highlight of this concert is Iona Brown's radiant account of *The Lark ascending*. The sound is rich and very well defined, especially in its CD format, while the cassette is only marginally less sharply detailed. Readers will note, however, that Marriner's 1972 Argo recordings of the Vaughan Williams *Tallis fantasia* and *The Lark ascending* (also with Iona Brown) are also available on CD (see above under the composer).

'Famous Baroque concertos': VIVALDI: *L'Estro armonico, Op. 3: Concerto No. 10 in B min. for 4 violins. Double trumpet concerto, RV 537.* CORELLI: *Concerto grosso (Christmas), Op. 6/8.* HANDEL: *Concerto grosso, Op. 3/1; Organ concerto in F (Cuckoo and the nightingale).* TELEMANN: *Viola concerto.* BACH: *Flute concerto in G min., BWV 1056; Concerto for violin and oboe, BWV 1060.*
(B) *** Decca *411 891-4*.

All the recordings on this double-length (iron-oxide) tape were made in the 1970s during the Academy's vintage Argo period. The solo playing is expert and full of personality, the accompaniments polished and alive, and the sound is consistently fresh and vivid. A strong recommendation on all counts.

French music: BERLIOZ: *Damnation de Faust: Hungarian march.* DUKAS: *The sorcerer's apprentice.* SAINT-SAËNS: *Danse macabre, Op. 40.* DEBUSSY: *Prélude à l'après-midi d'un faune.* CHABRIER: *Joyeuse marche.* RAVEL: *Pavane pour une infante défunte.*
(*) Ph. Dig. **412 131-2; 412 131-1/*4* [id.].

Marriner may not have quite the panache of Beecham in lollipops like these, but with the Academy's 'big band' it makes a succulent collection, if ungenerous in length (42 minutes). The Saint-Saëns, taken fast, has brilliant solo work from Alan Loveday; the Debussy and Ravel are sensuously beautiful; and the Chabrier is full of flair, the most Beechamesque of the performances here. By comparison, the Berlioz lacks something in spectacle, neat and rhythmic rather than expansive (though on CD the bass drum is impressively caught). *L'apprenti sorcier* has a sparkling scherzando quality, though rather less of a sense of drama, and the tempo could be more consistent. The sound is the more transparent on compact disc; but the cassette is less impressive and has problems with the bass drum.

'Famous overtures': STRAUSS, J. Jnr: *Die Fledermaus.* SUPPÉ: *Morning, noon and night in Vienna.* AUBER: *Fra Diavolo.* SMETANA: *The Bartered bride.* OFFENBACH: *La Belle Hélène.* SULLIVAN: *The Mikado.*
*** Ph. Dig. **411 450-2**; 411 450-1/*4* [id.].

Sparkling performances, the pacing often brilliantly fast, with *Die Fledermaus* convincing in its dash, even though tempi are wayward. The effect is exhilarating, particularly in the bustle of *The Bartered bride*, where string detail is attractively refined, as it is at the engaging opening of *Fra Diavolo*. It is good to have Sullivan included. Even if the overture to *The Mikado* was not one of his best, it receives most persuasive advocacy here. For the Offenbach piece, Sir Neville uses an arrangement by Alan Boustead which is less effective than the Haensch version that we usually hear. However, with playing of much finesse and extremely vivid sound, approaching demonstration standard, this is all most enjoyable. While the CD has the usual advantages, the chrome tape is also very well managed, one of Philips's best.

'Scandinavian music': GRIEG: *Holberg suite; 2 Elegiac melodies, Op. 34.* SIBELIUS: *Kuolema: Valse triste, Op. 44. Rakastava, Op. 14.* NIELSEN: *Little suite, Op. 1.* WIRÉN: *Serenade for strings, Op. 11.*
*** Argo **417 132-2** [id.].

A splendid collection of appealing and attractive music from the north. It gives us a splendid account of Sibelius's magical *Rakastava* (there is an eloquent version by the Finnish Chamber Ensemble on BIS) as well as the perennially fresh Dag Wirén *Serenade.* These are good, vividly recorded performances from 1980, to which the splendid vintage (1970) version of the *Holberg suite* has been added for the CD issue.

Adni, Daniel (piano)

'Music from the movies' (with Bournemouth SO, Alwyn): ADDINSELL: *Warsaw concerto.* WILLIAMS: *The Dream of Olwen.* ROZSA: *Spellbound concerto.* BATH: *Cornish rhapsody.* GERSHWIN: *Rhapsody in Blue.*
(B) **(*) CfP CFP 41 4493-1/*4*.

By far the finest of these film 'concertos' is Addinsell's *Warsaw concerto,* written for *Dangerous Moonlight.* The other pieces here have less distinction but are taken seriously and presented with commitment and flair. The performance of the Gershwin *Rhapsody* (also used in a biopic of the same title) is not as distinctive as the rest of the programme. Excellent, vivid sound on LP; on cassette, however, the warmly resonant acoustic blunts the upper range.

All Star Percussion Ensemble, Farberman

BIZET: *Carmen fantasy.* BEETHOVEN: *Symphony No. 9: Scherzo.* PACHELBEL: *Canon.* BERLIOZ: *Symphonie fantastique: March to the scaffold.*
* MMG Dig. **MCD 10007** [id.].

This CD certainly has novelty value in offering the *Scherzo* from the *Choral symphony* featuring a vibraphone, among other exotic timbres. But the novelty wears pretty thin in the 20-minute selection from *Carmen.* The sound itself is vivid and clear.

André, Maurice (trumpet)

Trumpet concertos (with ASMF, Marriner): STÖLZEL: *Concerto in D*. TELEMANN: *Concerto in C min. Concerto in D for trumpet, 2 oboes and strings* (with Nicklin and Miller). VIVALDI: *Double trumpet concerto in C, RV 537* (with Soustrot); *Double concerto in B flat for trumpet and violin, RV 548* (with I. Brown).
*** HMV Dig. **CDC 7 47012-2**; ASD/*TCCASD* 143530-1/*4* [Ang. DS/*4XS* 37984].

Maurice André has recorded a number of such collections for EMI but they have all been swiftly deleted. He is peerless in this kind of repertoire and the accompaniments under Marriner are attractively alert and stylish. The Academy provides expert soloists to match André in the concertante works by Telemann (*in D*) and Vivaldi (*RV 548*) which come together on the second side and offer much the most interesting invention. The concerto by Stölzel is conventional, but has a fine slow movement. Throughout, André's smooth, rich timbre and highly musical phrasing give pleasure. The recording is first class, with the CD adding extra definition and presence. The cassette is very good, too, only very occasionally less clean in its focus of the solo instrument.

Baroque suites and concertos (with Paris O Ens., Wallez): MOURET: *Suites de symphonies*. VIVALDI: *Concertos: in C, RV 534; in D min., RV 535*. LALANDE: *Symphonies pour les souper du Roy: 1st Caprice*; STÖLZEL: *Concerto grosso in D*. TORELLI: *Sinfonia a 4 in C*.
** HMV Dig. **CDC 747140-2** [id.].

Maurice André plays here as brilliantly as ever. However, in the Vivaldi arrangements (the works were conceived for a pair of oboes), for all the combined balancing skill of the soloist and the engineers, the effect is not completely convincing. The CD offers brilliant sound and a forward balance and is best not played in a single session. Either of André's other compact discs are more rewarding than this, where at times the dominating trumpet timbre becomes a little tiring.

Concertos (with Philh. O, Muti.): BACH: *Brandenburg concerto No. 2 in F, BWV 1047*. TELEMANN: *Concerto in D*. TORELLI: *Concerto in D*. HAYDN: *Concerto in E flat*.
*** HMV Dig. **CDC 747311-2** [id.]; EL 270269-1/*4* [Ang. DS/*4DS* 38220].

André is a big star on the continent, which accounts for the allocation of a third compact disc to him in EMI's still relatively sparse CD catalogue. It seems a curious idea to include the Bach *Brandenburg*, for, although André plays the solo part most stylishly and the balance with his Philharmonia colleagues is expertly managed, most collectors will have already acquired this work within a complete set. Otherwise this is an admirable concert, for André's performance of the Haydn is particularly pleasing, with a gentle *Andante* to offset the sparkle of the outer movements; the Telemann is also a fine piece. With first-class accompaniments throughout and an excellently balanced recording, this is all enjoyable. While first choice rests with the CD for its added presence, the cassette, too, is one of EMI's best, giving a clear focus to the soloist and a most attractive orchestral sound, warm, yet clear.

'Trumpet concertos' (with ECO, Mackerras): HANDEL: *Concerto in D minor* (reconstituted and orch. Thilde). ALBINONI: *Concertos: in B flat; in D* (arr. Paumgartner). TELEMANN: *Concerto in D* (ed. Töttcher-Grebe). HERTEL: *Concerto in E flat.*
(M) ** HMV EG 290494-1/*4*.

Arrangements of concertos originally written for flute or oboe obviously call for high bravura when played on the trumpet, and Maurice André is on top form here. The works by Albinoni sound perhaps excessively robust in these transcriptions, but the Telemann concerto is particularly agreeable. For trumpet fans this should prove a worthwhile anthology.

'Trumpet Festival' (with Rouen CO, Beaucamp; Wind and String Ens., Birbaum; Masson Trombone Qt; Paris Clarinet Sextet): MOZART, L.: *Concerto in D.* MARCELLO: *Largo and Allegretto.* CORELLI: *3 Country dances.* HANDEL: *Sonata in C min., Op. 1/8.* ALBINONI: *Concerto in D min.* (transcriptions of *Church sonatas for organ*); *Concerto in A for trumpet and clarinet sextet* (*St Mark*). VIVALDI: *Trumpet concerto in D.* TELEMANN: *Concerto in F min.; Divertissement in D.* STÖLZEL: *Concerto in D.* CLARKE: *Trumpet voluntary.* PURCELL: *Cibell: Trumpet tune. Dance suite.*
*(**) Ph. On Tour *416 231-4*.

A fascinating collection, let down by variable technology. Even though chrome tape is used, the varying sources and altering acoustics have at times defeated the Philips transfer engineers. The opening concerto of Leopold Mozart was recorded in a very reverberant hall and the orchestral image is overblown and blurred. At other times the trumpet focus is less than ideally clean, notably in the splendid Stölzel *Concerto* and in the Purcell *Trumpet tune*, where the accompaniment is made up of four horns, two trombones and timpani. The most intriguing sound, however, is the Albinoni *A major Concerto* (*St Mark*), here transcribed for trumpet and a sextet of clarinets, to piquant effect. André plays superbly throughout, and many of the other items offer novel textures. In the closing Telemann *Divertissement*, both solo parts are managed by one soloist, with electronic aid. For those willing to accept the variable sound quality, there is much of interest here.

Backhaus, Wilhelm (piano)

Concertos: MOZART: *Piano concerto No. 26 in D (Coronation), K.537* (with Berlin City O, Zaun). BRAHMS: *Piano concerto No. 1 in D min., Op. 15* (with BBC SO, Boult). GRIEG: *Piano concerto in A min., Op. 16* (with New SO, Barbirolli).
(M) (**) HMV mono EX 290343-3 (2).

Undoubtedly the best thing in this set is the Brahms *D minor Concerto*, made in 1932 with Dr Adrian Boult (as he then was) and the newly formed BBC Symphony Orchestra. It is a commanding account though even here, in the slow movement for example, Backhaus has surely been surpassed in terms of poetic insight, inwardness of feeling and spirituality by such artists as Gilels, Arrau and Curzon. The 'massive technique' of which Harold Schonberg speaks in *The Great Pianists* is always in evidence, and there is a certain magisterial strength in the outer movements. The Mozart *Concerto*, recorded in 1940, has a marmoreal quality, a surface beauty that somehow leaves one unmoved. The Grieg (from 1933) is charmless and curiously lacking in freshness. There is obviously a powerful musical mind at work here, but also a sensibility short on tenderness.

Ballet

'Ballet favourites' (with (i) LSO, Monteux; (ii) SRO, Ansermet; (iii) Paris Conservatoire O, Maag; (iv) ROHCGO, Lanchbery or (v) Morel; (vi) Israel PO, Solti): excerpts from: (i) TCHAIKOVSKY: *Sleeping Beauty*; (ii) *Nutcracker;* (v) *Swan Lake.* CHOPIN: (iii) *Les Sylphides.* (iv) HÉROLD: *La Fille mal gardée.* (vi) ROSSINI–RESPIGHI: *La Boutique fantasque.*
(B) ** Decca *KMC2 9004.*

This 90-minute tape selection is well engineered, although the sound is vivid and robust rather than refined. Performances are vintage ones from the early Decca stereo catalogue, and are lively and characterful, although the Monteux selection from *Sleeping Beauty* includes his curiously insensitive, swiftly paced *Panorama.* Otherwise there is little to complain of. The highlight is undoubtedly the selection from *La Fille mal gardée* in which the full, sparkling sound belies the age of the recording.

'Nights at the ballet' (with (i) RPO, Weldon; (ii) Philh. O; (iii) Kurtz; (iv) Irving; (v) RPO, Fistoulari; (vi) CBSO, Frémaux; (vii) New Philh. O, Mackerras): excerpts from: (i) TCHAIKOVSKY: *Nutcracker; Swan Lake.* (ii; iii) PROKOFIEV: *Romeo and Juliet.* (ii; iv) ADAM: *Giselle.* (v) LUIGINI: *Ballet Égyptien* (suite). (vi) SATIE: *Gymnopédies Nos 1 and 3.* (vii) DELIBES: *Coppélia.* GOUNOD: *Faust* (suite).
(B) *** EMI *TC2-MOM 111.*

Here (on tape only) is nearly an hour and a half of some of the most tuneful and colourful ballet music ever written. Kurtz's three excerpts from *Romeo and Juliet* are most distinguished, the inclusion of the Fistoulari recording of *Ballet Égyptien* is most welcome, and Mackerras is at his sparkling best in the *Coppélia* and *Faust* selections. Weldon's Tchaikovsky performances lack the last degree of flair, but they are alert and well played. The sound is admirable both for home listening and in the car.

'Ballet memories' (with (i) LSO, Monteux: (ii) Concg. O, Fistoulari; (iii) VPO, Knappertsbusch; (iv) SRO, Ansermet; (v) Paris Conservatoire O, Maag or (vi) Martinon): excerpts from: TCHAIKOVSKY: (i) *Sleeping Beauty*; (ii) *Swan Lake*; (iii) *The Nutcracker*. DELIBES: (iv) *Coppélia; Sylvia*. (v) CHOPIN: *Les Sylphides*; (vi) ADAM: *Giselle*.
(B) ** Decca 414 077-1/*4*.

This follow-up to Decca's *'Ballet favourites'* (above) is available on LP as well as tape. It offers much the same mixture as before, with vivid sound and performances of mixed though always acceptable quality. Highlights are the Fistoulari *Swan Lake* excerpts and the items from Martinon's early stereo recording of *Giselle*, currently out of the catalogue.

Baroque concertos

VIVALDI: *Quadruple violin concerto in B min. Op. 3/10: Flute concerto in F* (*La tempesta de mare*), *Op. 10/1; Double mandolin concerto in G, RV 532.* LOCATELLI: *Violin concerto in D, Op. 3/1.* ALBINONI: *Oboe concerto a 5 in D min., Op. 9/2* (soloists incl. Gazzelloni and Holliger with I Musici). HANDEL: *Oboe concerto No. 3 in G min.* (Holliger, ECO, Leppard): *Organ concerto in F* (*Cuckoo and the nightingale*) (Chorzempa, Concerto Amsterdam, Schröder).
(B) *** Ph. On Tour *412 909-4*.

A highly successful anthology, one of the best issues in Philips's 'On Tour' series. If you enjoy this repertoire, none of these performances will disappoint – some, especially those by Holliger and Gazzelloni, are extremely fine – and the sound is of consistently high quality.

'Baroque favourites'

Baroque music (with (i) I Musici and (ii) Gazzelloni; (iii) Ursula Holliger, Pepin, Harmanjat; (iv) André, Holliger, Ayo; (v) ASMF, Marriner and (vi) Wilbraham; (vii) Kaine; (viii) Smithers): (i) PACHELBEL: *Canon and gigue.* (ii) VIVALDI: *Flute concerto in G min.* (*La Notte*), *Op. 10/2.* (iii) HANDEL: *Concerto in B flat, Op. 4/6* (for harp, 2 flutes). (iv; ii) BACH: *Brandenburg concerto No. 2 in F, BWV*

1047. (v) *Suite No. 3, BWV. 1068: Air.* (vi) CLARKE: *Trumpet voluntary.* (vii) VIVALDI: *Concerto per molti stromenti in D, RV 562a.* HANDEL: *Solomon: Arrival of the Queen of Sheba.* PURCELL: *Abdelazer: Rondeau.* (viii) *The Indian Queen: Trumpet overture.* WASSENAER: *Concertino No. 4 in F min.* RAMEAU: *La Poule.*
(B) (*) Ph. On Tour *416 230-4.*

The opening I Musici account of Pachelbel's *Canon* is rather staid, but most of these performances are good ones, although the Handel *Flute and harp concerto* could have more life. The snag is the recorded sound: the transfers are made at a very high level, yet on side one the focus is not very sharp and the *Brandenburg concerto* is unrefined. Side two reaches saturation point in the Vivaldi *Concerto*, and here the quality is very rough.

Baroque music

'The sound of baroque' (with (i) Royal Liverpool PO, Groves; (ii) Scottish CO, Tortelier; (iii) LPO, Boult; (iv) Menuhin, Ferras, Bath Fest. O; (v) Bournemouth Sinf., Montgomery; (vi) Reginald Kilbey and Strings; (vii) RPO, Weldon; (viii) ASMF, Marriner): (i) ALBINONI: *Adagio for strings and organ* (arr. Giazotto). (ii) BACH: *Suite No. 3 in D, BWV 1068: Air.* (iii) *Brandenburg concerto No. 3 in G, BWV 1048.* (iv) *Double violin concerto in D, BWV* 1043. (i) GLUCK: *Orfeo: Dance of the Blessed Spirits.* (v) HANDEL: *Messiah: Pastoral symphony. Berenice overture.* (v) *Solomon: Arrival of the Queen of Sheba.* (vi) *Serse: Largo.* (vii) *Water music: suite* (arr. Harty). (viii) PACHELBEL: *Canon.*
(B) *** EMI *TC2-MOM 103.*

One of the first of EMI's 'Miles of Music' tapes, planned for motorway listening as well as at home, and offering about 80 minutes of favourite baroquerie, this is recommendable in every way. The sound is lively, the performances are first class, with Bach's *Double violin concerto* and *Brandenburg No. 3* (Boult) bringing substance among the lollipops.

Bavarian Radio Symphony Orchestra, Salonen

TCHAIKOVSKY: *1812 overture, Op. 49.* BALAKIREV: *Islamey* (oriental fantasy, arr. Lyapunov). BORODIN: *In the Steppes of Central Asia; Prince Igor: Polovtsian dances* (with Bav. R. Ch.). GLINKA: *Russlan and Ludmilla: overture.*
*(*) Ph. **412 552-2**; 412 552-1/*4* [id.].

Not a very successful *1812.* After a dramatic pause, Esa-Pekka Salonen begins the main allegro sturdily as if it was a concerto grosso. At the end the orchestra is (to paraphrase John Betjeman) submerged by bells. Balakirev's *Islamey* is played in Lyapunov's orchestral transcription, but sounds much more convincing in its original piano format. The *Polovtsian dances* have plenty of vigour and the *Russlan Overture* is also paced very fast; however, unlike Solti, Salonen does not avoid the feeling that the music is rushed, though the Bavarian orchestra play well for him. *In the Steppes of Central Asia* is refined rather than voluptuous. With resonant recording that tends to cloud detail – even on CD, but notably on cassette, so that one cannot decipher the words of the Bavarian Radio Chorus in Borodin's dances – this is not a very recommendable concert.

Berlin Philharmonic Orchestra, Karajan

'Digital concert': GRIEG: *Holberg suite, Op. 40.* MOZART: *Serenade No. 13 in G* (*Eine kleine Nachtmusik*), *K.525.* PROKOFIEV: *Symphony No. 1 in D* (*Classical*), *Op. 25.*
*** DG Dig. **400 034-2**; 2532/*3302* 031 [id.].

Some of the rustic freshness of Grieg eludes these artists: this is not unaffected speech. But how marvellous it sounds all the same! This is a great orchestral partnership 'making something' of the *Holberg suite*, perhaps, yet the music survives any over-sophistication and has never sounded more sumptuous and luxurious. Apart from a self-conscious and somewhat ponderous minuet, *Eine kleine Nachtmusik* sounds good, too; the playing is beautifully cultured, with exquisitely shaped phrasing and wonderfully sprung rhythms. Only in the Prokofiev does one feel the want of charm and sparkle, except perhaps in the slow movement, which has grace and eloquence. The digital recording is excellent, though the balance in the Prokofiev is not entirely natural. Nevertheless a most desirable issue, particularly on account of the Grieg, especially in its compact disc format.

ALBINONI: *Adagio in G min.* (arr. Giazotto). VIVALDI: *Flute concerto in G min.* (*La Notte*), *Op. 10/3, RV 439.* BACH: *Suite No. 3 in D: Air.* PACHELBEL: *Canon and Gigue in D.* GLUCK: *Orfeo: Dance of the Blessed Spirits.* MOZART: *Serenata notturna, K.239.*
** DG Dig. **413 309-2**; 413 309-1/*4*.

Karajan's digital Baroque collection is given the benefit of beautiful sound, rich and refined. His mood is solemn, both in the famous *Adagio* and in his stately, measured view of the Pachelbel *Canon*, with the *Gigue* sprightly to provide contrast. The rest of the programme is very polished, but the effect is enervating rather than spirited. The CD is exceptionally vivid, approaching demonstration standard. The chrome cassette, too, is of high quality, smooth, yet full and clear.

'Encore': WEBER: *Invitation to the dance, Op. 65* (arr. Berlioz). SMETANA: *Má Vlast: Vltava.* ROSSINI: *William Tell: overture.* LISZT: *Les Préludes, G.97; Hungarian rhapsody No. 5, G. 359.*
(*) DG Dig. **413 587-2; 413 587-1/*4* [id.].

Karajan has recorded all these pieces before, so *'Encore'* is an appropriate title. Moreover the concert plays for over 63 minutes and is generous value. Karajan is at his finest in *Vltava:* there is some radiant playing from the Berlin orchestra in the moonlit stillness before the river approaches the St John's Rapids. *Les Préludes* is vibrant, but a little brash; however, the dark colouring of the *Fifth Hungarian rhapsody* is finely caught. The *William Tell overture* has fine panache, and *Invitation to the dance* a characteristic suave elegance. The Berlin Philharmonie provides a less flattering ambience than in some of Karajan's earlier analogue recordings; and some may prefer the slightly more diffuse quality of the LP, and matching tape, to the sharper, brighter image of the compact disc.

Opera intermezzi and ballet music: PONCHIELLI: *La Gioconda: Dance of the hours.* Intermezzi from: MASCAGNI: *Cavalleria Rusticana; L'amico Fritz.* GIORDANO: *Fedora.* SCHMIDT: *Notre Dame.* MUSSORGSKY: *Khovantschina.* MASSENET: *Thaïs: Méditation* (with Schwalbé). VERDI: *Aïda: ballet suite.* BERLIOZ: *Damnation de Faust: Danse des Sylphes; Menuet des Follets.* SMETANA: *Bartered bride: Polka.* GOUNOD: *Faust: Waltz.*
(M) *** DG Gal. 415 856-1/*4* [id.].

This generous and attractive programme (63 minutes) is assembled from recordings made between 1968 and 1972. The playing is marvellous and Karajan consistently displays both warmth and flair: the *Dance of the hours* is captivating, as are the two Berlioz pieces and the *Polka* from the *Bartered Bride* with its affectionate rubato. The various intermezzi sound wonderfully fresh and vivid, and in the *Thaïs Méditation* Michel Schwalbé plays the violin solo exquisitely. In short, this is more than the sum of its parts; and the analogue recordings, although brightly lit in their digitally remastered form, have the advantage of a more flattering and congenial ambience than many of Karajan's more recent sessions made digitally in the Philharmonie. LP and chrome cassette sound virtually identical.

'Popular German overtures': MENDELSSOHN: *The Hebrides (Fingal's Cave), Op. 26.* NICOLAI: *The Merry Wives of Windsor.* WEBER: *Der Freischütz.* WAGNER: *Der fliegende Holländer. Lohengrin (Prelude to Act I).*
(M) *** EMI EMX/*TC-EMX* 41 2052-1/*4* [Ang. AE/*4AE* 34429].

This collection dating from the early 1960s is outstanding in every way. The performance of *Der Freischütz* included here is most exciting, while the *Lohengrin Prelude* moves with a compelling inevitability to its great central climax. *Fingal's Cave* too is played most beautifully, its effect enhanced by the resonantly spacious acoustic, which also prevents the recording from sounding too dated. The cassette transfer is very successful, in spite of the reverberation.

Black Dyke Mills Band, Major Peter Parkes

'Blitz' BOURGEOIS: *Blitz, Op. 65.* BALL: *Journey into freedom* (rhapsody). HOWELLS: *Pageantry* (suite). WRIGHT: *Tam O'Shanter's ride.*
ɕ *** Chan. Dig. **CHAN 8370;** BBRD/*BBTD* 1014 [id.].

These are all test-pieces designed to show the prowess of the English brass band movement over a period of half a century (the Howells suite dates from the 1930s and *Blitz* was featured in 1981). Dennis Wright and Eric Ball are famous names in the brass band world and both show great skill in scoring for their medium, while Bourgeois's *Blitz* is as spectacular as it sounds. Each piece displays a lyrical facility as well as an imaginative use of brass sonorities; but the invention of the three-movement *Pageantry* is markedly more individual than the other pieces. The playing of the Black Dyke Mills Band is superb, and Major Parkes is a convincing advocate of this repertoire. The Chandos sound is in the demonstration bracket throughout, featuring much engaging antiphonal interplay; in the last resort, however, the interest of the music itself is limited by the conventional harmonic idiom.

'Boléro'

Spanish music: (i) Chicago SO, Solti; (ii) LAPO; (iii) SRO; (iv) Lopez-Cobos; (v) Montreal SO, Dutoit; (i) RAVEL: *Boléro,* (ii; iv) FALLA: *Three-cornered Hat: 3 Dances.* RIMSKY-KORSAKOV: *Capriccio espagnol.* CHABRIER: *España* (rhapsody). (iii; iv) TURINA: *Danzas fantásticas: Orgía.* (v) FALLA: *El amor brujo: Ritual fire dance.*
*(*) Decca **411 928–2** [id.].

A reasonably generous CD anthology with a playing time of just under an hour. Apart from the last two items, however, the performances are rather mixed in quality and are not primary recommendations, and the digital remastering produces a spectacular impact rather than refinement. Solti's *Boléro* reaches a fierce climax, and the Los Angeles recordings have a somewhat thick bass response. The *Ritual fire dance* at the end, under Dutoit and with a digital master, shows up the rest of the programme.

Boston Pops Orchestra, Fiedler

'The best of the Boston Pops': RAVEL: *Boléro.* GINASTERA: *Estancia: Danza final* (*Malambo*). KHACHATURIAN: *Gayaneh: Sabre dance.* DEBUSSY: *Suite bergamasque: Clair de lune.* STRAUSS, J. jnr; *Gypsy Baron: March; Fairy tales from the Orient* (waltz); *Emperor waltz.* COPLAND: *Outdoor overture.* JOPLIN: *The Entertainer.* MACDERMOT: *Hair: medley.* SAINT-SAËNS: *Danse macabre.*

HANDEL: *Messiah: Hallelujah chorus.* BACH: *Violin Partita No. 3, BWV 1006: Prelude in E.* SOUSA: *The Stars and Stripes forever.*
(B) ** DG Walkman *415 620-4* [id.].

A characteristic if slightly incongruous mixture from the end of Fiedler's Boston recording career. The layout prevents too much of a cultural clash between Scott Joplin and Handel's *Hallelujah chorus* (a pointless transcription). All the music is expertly played and given plenty of life. The highlight is Copland's *Outdoor overture.* The sound is lively, tending at times to over-brilliance. At Walkman price, this is fair value.

Boston Pops Orchestra, Williams

'Pops round the world': KABALEVSKY: *Overture: Colas Breugnon.* SUPPÉ: *Overture: Boccaccio.* AUBER: *Overture: The bronze horse.* GLINKA: *Overture: Russlan and Ludmilla.* WILLIAMS: *Overture: The Cowboys.* ROSSINI: *Overture: L'Italiana in Algeri.* BERNSTEIN: *Overture: Candide.*
(*) Ph. Dig. **400 071-2; 6514/*7337* 186 [id.].

During the 78 r.p.m. era, Arthur Fiedler created in the Boston 'Pops' a musical tradition, enduring and influential, comparable with, though quite different from, Sir Henry Wood's London Promenade Concerts. In assuming Fiedler's role, John Williams brings not only his brilliant talents as a composer of film music, but a natural understanding of the lighter orchestral repertoire, whether derived from the European concert hall and musical theatre, or from the rhythm and blues tradition of American popular music. This lively collection, played and recorded with brash brilliance, brings together a fizzing musical cocktail. There are subtler versions of most of these pieces, but Williams can in no way be faulted for lack of bounce or vigour. The bright, extrovert qualities of performance and recording come out even more vividly on compact disc. The chrome cassette is of good quality but does not match the LP, let alone the CD, in sparkle.

'Out of this world': STRAUSS, R.: *Also sprach Zarathustra: Introduction.* WILLIAMS: *E. T.: Adventures on earth. Return of the Jedi: suite.* GOLDSMITH: *Alien: Closing title. Star Trek – The Motion Picture: Main Title.* COURAGE: *Star Trek: TV theme.* PHILIPS: *Battlestar Galactica: Main title.* CONSTANT: *Twilight zone: Theme and variations.*
** Ph. Dig. **411 185-2**; 411 185-1/*4* [id.].

Music of much flamboyance, very well played and spectacularly recorded within a flattering acoustic. Apart from Alexander Courage's quite memorable TV signature theme for *Star Trek*, John Williams's own contributions are clearly superior to the rest. There is a melodic sweep and a sense of purpose that – for all the eclectic derivations of style – put these scores in a class of their own, even if the suite from *Return of the Jedi* is less memorable than the music for

E.T. The CD offers an agreeable bloom on the sound, which is vivid but lacking something in brilliance in the upper range. However, the ambient warmth is very agreeable. The chrome cassette could ideally have been transferred at a higher level, but still sounds well.

'On stage': BERLIN: *There's no business like show business.* HAMLISCH: *A Chorus line: Overture.* MANN/WEIL: *Here you come again.* ELLINGTON: *Sophisticated lady; Mood indigo; It don't mean a thing.* STRAYHORN: *Take the 'A' train.* LLOYD WEBBER: *Cats: Memory.* BERLIN: *Top hat, white tie and tails.* YOUMANS: *The Carioca.* SCHWARZ: *Dancing in the dark.* KERN: *I won't dance.* CONRAD: *The Continental.* RODGERS: *On your toes: Slaughter on 10th Avenue* (arr. Bennett).
*** Ph. **412 132–2**; 412 132-1/*4* [id.].

John Williams is completely at home in this repertoire. He is especially good in bringing out detail in the *Overture* for *A Chorus line*, and in the ballet score, *Slaughter on 10th Avenue*, which is heard complete and contains two of the most memorable tunes the composer ever wrote – fully worthy of Gershwin. The other items are offered in groups, tailored sophisticatedly as tributes to Duke Ellington and Fred Astaire; but equally enjoyable is the highlight of Bob Fosse's *Dancin'*, the engaging *Here you come again.* Splendid orchestral playing and excellent sound (with a very good tape), although the body of strings is not made to seem sumptuous, and this is even more striking on CD. Even so, this is a highly recommendable collection.

'Swing, swing, swing': OLIVER: *Opus one.* PORTER: *Begin the beguine.* CARLE: *Sunrise serenade.* DASH: *Tuxedo Junction.* ELLINGTON: *Satin doll.* GARLAND: *In the mood.* PRIMA: *Sing. sing, sing.* SAMPSON: *Stompin' at the Savoy.* MILLER: *Moonlight serenade.* GRAY: *String of pearls.* COATES: *Sleepy lagoon.* RIMSKY-KORSAKOV (arr. Sebesky): *Song of India.* THORNHILL: *Snowfall.* WILLIAMS: *Swing, swing, swing.*
** Ph. Dig. **412 626-2**; 412 626-1/*4* [id.].

This collection of swing band repertoire, in which John Williams might have been in his element, is unexpectedly disappointing. Great trouble has been taken with the arrangements (although *Moonlight serenade*, heard on soupy strings without a hint of the famous clarinet/saxophone voicing, is a travesty). So much else obstinately refuses to sound authentic; although the direction has plenty of vigour, the irresistible bounce of the big-band era is too often missing. Williams is at his best in the gently syncopated numbers like Frankie Carle's *Sunrise serenade* and Gerry Gray's *String of pearls.* The whole programme is tuneful and the recording spectacular, but the expansive Boston ambience gives a 'symphonic' inflation to the presentation, in spite of crisp brass playing and no lack of enthusiasm from the rhythm department. The sound is impressive in all three media.

'America, the dream goes on' (with Tanglewood Fest. Ch.): GOULD: *American salute.* WARD: *America the beautiful.* GUTHRIE: *This land is your land.* COPLAND: *Rodeo: Hoe down. Fanfare for the common man.* WILLIAMS: *America, the dream goes on.* STEFFE: *Battle hymn of the Republic.* BERNSTEIN: *On the Town: New York, New York; Lonely town. West Side Story: America.* Arr. MAY: *When the Saints go marching in.* TRAD.: *Prayer of thanksgiving.*
** Ph. Dig. **412 627-2**; 412 627-1/*4* [id.].

The inclusion of rather soupy choral versions of the transatlantic equivalents of our *Land of hope and glory* and *Jerusalem* will limit the appeal of this compilation for British collectors, even though *America the beautiful* and the *Battle hymn of the Republic* have agreeable conviction and fervour. The opening *American salute* (based on *When Johnny comes marching home*) is a splendid genre piece, and the Bernstein items are self-recommending. The sound is excellent too, though the cassette, transferred at only a modest level, does not match the CD in sparkle and presence.

'We wish you a merry Christmas': TRAD.: *We wish you a merry Christmas.* ANDERSON: *Medley: Christmas festival.* BURT: *Medley: A Christmas greeting.* MAY: *Medley: Holiday cheer.* IVES: *A Christmas carol.* DAVIS: *Carol of the drum.* Arr. MAY: *The twelve days of Christmas.*
*** Ph. Dig. **416 287-2**; 6302/*7144* 125 [id.].

Leroy Anderson's arrangements of nine famous carols are predictably stylish and lively. There are also some attractive cross-over carols by Alfred Burt plus a group more positively derived from the idiom of the Pop world by Billy May. The piece by Ives was an interesting choice; but what makes this CD irresistible is Billy May's tongue-in-cheek version of *The twelve days of Christmas* featuring orchestral instruments as the gifts: 'three French horns; four golden strings . . . and a bell high up in a pear tree'. The whole conception is delightfully witty and not too long. With splendid choral singing (though the words could be clearer) in the warm Boston ambience, this is a most attractive entertainment for Christmas Eve.

Bournemouth Sinfonietta, Hurst

'English music for strings': HOLST: *St Paul's suite, Op. 29/2.* ELGAR: *Serenade for strings, Op. 20.* WARLOCK: *Capriol suite.* IRELAND: *Concertino pastorale.*
(*) Chan. **CHAN 8375; CBR/*CBT* 1020 [id.].

The novelty here is Ireland's *Concertino pastorale,* a gently persuasive piece, perhaps a shade long for its unambitious material, but always attractive. It is very sympathetically presented. The rest of the programme is well played but less strongly characterized. There are better versions of the Elgar and Warlock suites available, although the *St Paul suite* of Holst is most enjoyable, with the outer sections of the *Intermezzo* beautifully done. The 1977 sound has plenty of body and atmosphere, but detail at pianissimo level is not as clear as one would have in a modern digital recording, and this is especially true of the pizzicato section of the *Capriol suite*. There is an excellent cassette which costs a good deal less than the CD, as both LP and tape are in the medium-price range.

Burns, Stephen (trumpet)

'Music for trumpet and strings' (*with Ensemble*): PURCELL: *Sonata No. 1 in D.* STANLEY: *Trumpet voluntary* (from *Organ Voluntary, Op. 6/5*, arr. Bergler). CLARKE: *Suite in D.* CORELLI: *Sonata in D.* BALDASSARE: *Sonata in F.* TORELLI: *Sonata a cinque in D, G. 1.*
*** ASV Dig. **CDDCA 528**; DCA/*ZCDCA* 528 [id.].

Stephen Burns plays a rotary piccolo trumpet in the East German style by Scherzer, and his freedom and smoothness of timbre in the instrument's highest tessitura are breathtaking. With crisp ornamentation (often florid, in short decorative bursts of filigree), the playing is attractively stylish: the timbre gleams and the exhilarating articulation of the allegros is balanced by a natural expressive lyricism in slow movements. Whether in the beautiful *Grave* sections of the Corelli and Torelli *Sonatas* or in the faster movements of the latter piece, this is playing to delight the ear, with its combination of sensitivity and bravura. The opening of Purcell's *Sonata* is marked 'Pomposo' and Burns catches its character perfectly: it is a most engaging work overall, as is the *Suite* of Jeremiah Clarke which includes the *Trumpet voluntary* (entitled *The Prince of Denmark's march*). The other movements are inventive too, notably the *Prelude*, another catchy march for the Duke of Gloucester. The recording balances the soloist well forward and the CD projects him almost into one's room, although it also emphasizes the rather insubstantial sound of the accompaniment and the ineffective harpsichord balance. But this collection is Stephen Burns' triumph, and it would be churlish to withhold the fullest recommendation. Alongside the Marsalis/Gruberova CBS compact disc this is strongly recommended to trumpet aficionados.

Cantilena, Shepherd

'Encore': HANDEL: *Solomon: Arrival of the Queen of Sheba.* PACHELBEL: *Canon.* VIVALDI: *Concerto in A, P.231.* TELEMANN: *Viola concerto in A.* PEZEL: *Suite a 5.* BACH, J. S.: *Suite No. 3, BWV 1068: Air.* MUFFAT: *Concerto grosso* (*Delirium amoris*): PEPUSCH: *Chamber symphony in D min.*
** Chan. Dig. **CHAN 8319**; ABRD/*ABTD* 1069.

The Pepusch and Muffat pieces are welcome rarities, no less charming than the other 'Baroque encores' included on this disc. The performances are not immaculate but are always fresh and well sprung, with no sentimentality in slower pieces like the Bach. First-rate recording, but the chrome cassette, with its slightly smoother upper range, is preferable to the CD, which has a touch of digital edge on the violins. (It also costs less.) With an attractive ambience, this is enjoyable in an unostentatious way. The opening *Arrival of the Queen of Sheba* is especially engaging. The Telemann *Viola concerto* is the most substantial work and comes off very well. The programme plays for about an hour.

Chamber Orchestra of Europe, Judd

'Music of the Masters': BEETHOVEN: *Creatures of Prometheus overture, Op. 43.* MOZART: *Divertimento No. 1 in D for strings, K.136.* ROSSINI: *Il Barbiere di Siviglia:* overture. FAURÉ: *Pavane, Op. 50.* WAGNER: *Siegfried idyll.*
(M) **(*) Pickwick Dig. **PCD 805**; CC/*CCTC* 7574.

An enjoyable and well-balanced programme with first-class ensemble from these young players and excellently balanced digital recording. The presence and naturalness of the sound are especially striking in the Fauré *Pavane* (with a beautiful flute solo) and the *Siegfried idyll*, using only a small string group. James Judd brings stylish, thoroughly musical direction, although the overall presentation is a shade anonymous. The CD is offered at mid-price; the LP and cassette are in the bargain range and cost less than half as much.

Chandos: 'The special sound of Chandos'

Digital demonstration recordings: (i) SNO, Gibson; (ii) Janis Kelly, LSO, Simon; (iii) J. Hilton, CBSO, Järvi; (iv) Taverner Players, Parrott; (v) Ulster O, Thomson; (vi) J. Strauss O, Rothstein; (vii) Cantilena, Shepherd; (viii) ECO, Gibson; (ix) BBC SO, Schurmann: (i) HOLST: *The Planets: Jupiter.* (ii) TCHAIKOVSKY: *Hamlet: Scène d'Ophélie.* (iii) WEBER: *Clarinet concertino, Op. 73: Finale.* (iv) PURCELL: *Dido and Aeneas: Overture.* (v) HARTY: *Irish symphony: 3rd movt.* (i) ARNOLD: *Tam O'Shanter, Op. 51.* (vi) STRAUSS, J. jnr: *Egyptian march.* (vii) HANDEL: *Solomon: Arrival of the Queen of Sheba:* (viii): STRAVINSKY: *Pulcinella: Serenata and Scherzino.* (ix) SCHURMANN: *6 Studies: No. 5.*
Ͼ *** Chan. Dig. **CHAN 8301**; CBRD/*CBTD* 1008.

It is surprising that a smaller company should make the first digital demonstration issue in compact disc form, rather than one of the majors. The result is a spectacular success. All the recordings are impressive (though the Purcell sounds spiky, and the oboes are balanced too closely in the *Arrival of the Queen of Sheba*). On CD, there is a thrilling impact and sense of orchestral presence in the pieces by Holst and Malcolm Arnold, while the delightful Tchaikovsky vocal scena (a perfect item for a musical quiz), the Harty excerpt from the *Irish symphony* (*In the Antrim Hills*) and the Johann Strauss *March* are equally impressive and enjoyable with their different kinds of evocation. The sound is demonstration-worthy on the LP and the chrome cassette too, but the CD is breathtaking in its vividness.

Chicago Symphony Orchestra, Barenboim

SMETANA: *Má Vlast: Vltava.* DVOŘÁK: *Slavonic dances, Op. 46/1 and 8.* BRAHMS: *Hungarian dances Nos 1, 3 and 10.* BORODIN: *Prince Igor: Polovtsian dances.* LISZT: *Les Préludes.*
(M) *** DG Gal. 415 851-1/*4* [id.].

When this collection was first issued at the end of the 1970s, we commented that the measure was short. For the reissue, DG have added the *Polovtsian dances* which has splendid life and impetus. Indeed one hardly misses the chorus, so lively is the orchestral playing. Both *Vltava* and *Les Préludes* show Barenboim and the Chicago orchestra at their finest. *Vltava* is highly evocative – especially the moonlight sequence – and beautifully played; *Les Préludes* has dignity and poetry, as well as excitement. The Brahms and Dvořák *Dances* make attractive encores (especially the delightfully phrased *Hungarian dance No. 3 in F*). The only slight snag is that, in the digital remastering, the recording has lost some of its original glow and the strings sound thinner above the stave. But this is only striking in the violin timbre of the big tune of *Vltava*. There is a first-class cassette equivalent

Cincinnati Pops Orchestra, Kunzel

'Time warp': DORSEY: *Ascent.* STRAUSS, R.: *Also sprach Zarathustra: Opening.* GOLDSMITH: *Star Trek the Movie: Main theme. The Alien: Closing title.* COURAGE: *The Menagerie: suite.* PHILIPS: *Battlestar Galactica: Main theme.* WILLIAMS: *Superman: Love theme. Star wars: Throne room and end-title.* STRAUSS, J. Jnr: *Blue Danube waltz.* KHACHATURIAN: *Gayaneh: Adagio.*
C *** Telarc **CD 80106**; DG 10106.

This sumptuously recorded CD is well established as a demonstration disc *par excellence* and needs no fillip from us. Sufficient to say that the playing is first class and the sound superb, the rich ambient effect just right for this music, with particularly gorgeous string and brass timbres, Telarc's concert-hall balance at its most impressive. There are plenty of indelible tunes too and John Williams's music for *Superman* and *Star wars* (the latter in the Elgar/Walton nobilmente tradition) has never been recorded to more telling effect. Aficionados of *Star Trek* (who are not already knowledgeable Trekkies) will be interested to read in the excellent sleeve-notes that *The Menagerie* was the hour-long pilot for the series and that the only familiar face in its cast was that of Leonard Nimoy: the others all came later. Alexander Courage's music is of excellent quality. The collection opens with an electronic spectacular to put the Cincinnati orchestra in orbit.

'Orchestral spectaculars': RIMSKY-KORSAKOV: *Mlada: Procession of the nobles. Snow Maiden: Dance of the tumblers.* DUKAS: *L'apprenti sorcier.* WEINBERGER: *Svanda the Bagpiper: Polka and fugue.* SAINT-SAËNS: *Samson et Dalila: Bacchanale.* LISZT: *Les Préludes.*
(*) Telarc Dig. **CD 80115; DG 10115 [id.].

Some of the earlier records made by the Cincinnati orchestra in their Music Hall have been ineffectively balanced by the Telarc engineers, but this collection is very successful. The title is not belied by the sound, which has a sparkling but not exaggerated percussive constituent. The side drum which introduces the colourful Rimsky *Procession of the nobles* is strikingly well focused, and this clarity comes within a believable overall perspective. There is much fine orchestral playing, with the string detail in the *Svanda Polka and fugue* particularly pleasing, and the horns sounding agreeably strong and rich-timbred in the introductory Rimsky-Korsakov piece. The Saint-Saëns *Bacchanale* has plenty of adrenalin, with the timpani and bass drum adding to the climax without swamping it. The account of *Les Préludes* is lightweight until the end, which is almost solemn in its spacious broadening. The one disappointment is *The Sorcerer's apprentice*, an elusive piece in the recording studio, here bright and well paced, but lacking cumulative excitement. The CD has a subtle added presence and the advantage of background silence, but the LP sounds very impressive, too.

City of Birmingham Symphony Orchestra, Dods

'British music for film and TV': ADDISON: *A Bridge Too Far: March.* BENNETT: *Yanks: Theme. Lady Caroline Lamb: Theme.* WALTON: *Battle of Britain: Battle in the air.* BENJAMIN: *An Ideal Husband: Waltz.* BLISS: *Christopher Columbus: Suite.* FARNON: *Colditz: March.* MORLEY: *Watership Down: Kehaar's theme.* IRELAND: *The Overlanders: Romance; Intermezzo.* GOODWIN: *Frenzy: Theme.* BAX: *Malta, G.C.: Introduction and march.*
(M) *** HMV Green. ED 290109-1/*4* [id.].

An excellent and imaginative anthology, ranging wide from the concert-hall style of Bliss's *Christopher Columbus* to the modern 'themes', with their concentrated romanticism, intended to catch the ear at the first whiff of melody. Walton's *Battle in the air* sequence makes a splendid little descriptive scherzo, while the amiable Benjamin *Waltz* from *An Ideal Husband* has a rather similar flavour to Constant Lambert's *Horoscope* ballet music. Farnon's *Colditz* march is both stirring and instantly memorable. The performances are well played and full of character, as is the recording balance, everything clear and vivid yet not overblown.

Cleveland Symphonic Winds, Fennell

'Stars and stripes': ARNAUD: *3 Fanfares*. BARBER: *Commando march*. LEEMANS: *Belgian Paratroopers*. FUČIK: *Florentine march, Op. 214*. KING: *Barnum and Bailey's favourite*. ZIMMERMAN: *Anchors aweigh*. STRAUSS, J. snr: *Radetzky march*. VAUGHAN WILLIAMS: *Sea songs; Folk songs suite*. SOUSA: *The Stars and Stripes forever*. GRAINGER: *Lincolnshire posy*.
Ꞓ*** Telarc Dig. **CD 80099**; DG 10099 [id.].

This vintage collection from Frederick Fennell and his superb Cleveland wind and brass group is one of the finest of its kind ever made. Severance Hall, Cleveland, has ideal acoustics for this programme and the playing has wonderful virtuosity and panache. Leo Arnaud, the composer of the opening *Fanfares* (which are agreeably concise), flew to Cleveland 'with his side drum under his arm' to make a personal contribution, and the result is most attractive. What is also unusual about the programme is its variety. Both the Barber and Leemans pieces mix subtlety with spectacle; the Barnum and Bailey circus march is predictably exuberant; while *The Stars and Stripes* is not overblown, with the piccolo solo in natural perspective. Add, to all this, digital engineering of Telarc's highest calibre – and you have a very special issue, with the Grainger and Vaughan Williams suites adding just the right amount of ballast.

Cologne Musica Antiqua, Goebel

Baroque concert: PACHELBEL: *Canon and Gigue*. HANDEL: *Sonata for 2 violins and continuo in G, Op. 5/4*. VIVALDI: *Sonata in D min.* (*La Follia*) *for 2 violins and continuo, RV63*. BACH: *Suite No. 2 in B min. for flute and strings, BWV 1067* (with W. Hazelzet).
*(*) DG Arc. Dig. **410 502–2** [id.].

The Pachelbel *Canon* taken fast with squeezed notes and buzzy decoration will not be everyone's idea of fun, and the closely balanced sound is scratchy. It improves in the Bach *Suite* and this is an enjoyably fresh, lightweight performance. The Vivaldi is successful too, in its way, though the timbre here is the opposite of mellow. The recording focus in fact is rather variable and this compact disc seems to have few of the obvious virtues of the new system, except background silence.

'Le Parnasse français': MARAIS: *La Sonnerie de Saint-Geneviève du Mont de Paris*. REBEL: *Tombeau de Monsieur de Lully*. COUPERIN: F.: *Sonata: La Sultane*. LECLAIR: *Ouverture, Op. 13/2*. BLAVET: *Concerto a 4 parties*. CORRETTE: *Les Sauvages et la Fürtstemberg* (*Concerto Comique No. 25*).
** DG Arc. **415 298-2** [id.].

The performances date from various periods between 1978 and 1983 and are representative of this accomplished group. The Marais piece, *La Sonnerie de Saint-Geneviève du Mont de Paris*, has plenty of wit; so, too, does their elegant playing in the charming *Les Sauvages et la Fürtstemberg* of Michel Corrette. However, those who recall the warmth and nobility of the old Oiseau-Lyre performance by Merckel, Ales, Frécheville and Gerlin will find something missing in this account. The opening emerges sadly diminished in breadth and dignity, and the now mandatory bulges and nasal tone disturb the sense of line. Still, there are other pieces which benefit from the more transparent textures and lighter accents this ensemble have. The refurbishing for compact disc is excellent and, if the Couperin gives scant pleasure, there is much in this issue that gives more.

Copenhagen Music Society Chamber Orchestra, Hansen

'Invitation to Baroque music': ALBINONI: *Adagio in G min.* (arr. Giazotto). BACH: *Suite No. 3: Air.* PURCELL: *Chaconne in G min.* HANDEL: *Berenice: Minuet. Concerto grosso, Op. 6/12: Aria.* SAMMARTINI: *Sonata in A min., Op. 1/4: Andante amoroso.* MARCELLO, A.: *Oboe concerto in C min.: Adagio.* BACH: *Harpsichord concerto in F min., BWV 1056: Largo.* PACHELBEL: *Canon and Gigue.*
*(*) Denon Dig. **C 37 7037** [id.].

This is nearly all slow music and tempi are stately, performances restrained; string timbre is not opulent. The music itself is all of high quality, and there are some famous melodies here; but the performances are not distinctive enough to justify a top-price CD. The documentation too leaves something to be desired in identifying the correct source of the items included.

'Country gardens'

English music (various artists, including Bournemouth SO, Silvestri; Hallé O, Barbirolli; Royal Liverpool PO, Groves; E. Sinfonia, Dilkes): VAUGHAN WILLIAMS: *The Wasps: Overture. Rhosymedre.* WARLOCK: *Capriol suite.* DELIUS: *Summer night on the river. A Song before sunset.* GRAINGER: *Country gardens. Mock Morris; Shepherd's Hey.* arr. BRIDGE: *Cherry Ripe.* COLERIDGE TAYLOR: *Petite suite de concert* (excerpts). GERMAN: *Nell Gwyn: 3 Dances.* COATES: *Meadow to Mayfair: In the country. Summer Days: At the dance. Wood Nymphs.* ELGAR: *Chanson de matin. Salut d'amour.*
(B) **(*) EMI *TC2-MOM 123.*

A recommendable tape-only collection, essentially lightweight but never trivial. Barbirolli's Delius and Neville Dilkes's *Capriol suite* are among the highlights, and certainly it makes a most entertaining concert for use on a long journey, with the lively Grainger, Coates and German pastoral dances providing an excellent foil for the lyrical music. On domestic equipment the quality is slightly variable, with side two noticeably brighter than side one. Thus the opening *Wasps overture* is a little bass-heavy and the attractive *Capriol suite* has a more restricted upper range here than when it appears on EMI's companion tape collection *'Serenade'* (see below). But the rest of the programme sounds well.

Dallas Symphony Orchestra, Mata

Concert: MUSSORGSKY: *Night on the bare mountain.* DUKAS: *L'apprenti sorcier.* TCHAIKOVSKY: *Capriccio italien.* ENESCU: *Rumanian rhapsody No. 1.*
ϵ *** RCA Dig. **RCD 14439** [id.].

One of the outstanding early digital orchestral demonstration CDs. The acoustic of the Dallas Hall produces a thrilling resonance without too much clouding of detail. The opening of Tchaikovsky's *Capriccio italien* is stunning in its amplitude, with lustrous string timbres and brass fanfares riveting in their impact. The silences when the music pauses are hardly less telling, both here and in the equally sumptuous Enescu *Rhapsody.* These are the two most effective performances; the Mussorgsky piece is rather lacking in menace when textures are so ample. *The Sorcerer's apprentice* is spirited and affectionately characterized, yet there is no sense of real calamity at the climax. But the Tchaikovsky and Enescu are richly enjoyable, even if the latter lacks the last degree of unbuttoned exuberance in its closing pages.

'Ibéria': DEBUSSY: *Images: No. 2, Ibéria.* RIMSKY-KORSAKOV: *Capriccio espagnol, Op. 34.* TURINA: *Danzas fantásticas: Orgía.*
*(*) Telarc Dig. **CD 80055**; DG 10055 [id.].

A disappointing collection. The recording is certainly vivid, but in *Ibéria* detail registers at the expense of a panoramic view; as an extrovert performance, this does not match Stokowski's sparklingly sensuous account with the French National Radio Orchestra (deleted, alas), which is equally impressive as a recording. Here, Rimsky-Korsakov's *Capriccio* has neither sumptuousness nor a compensating electricity, and one wonders why room could not have been found for all three of Turina's *Danzas fantásticas.*

Dichter, Misha (piano), Philharmonia Orchestra, Marriner

Concertante works: ADDINSELL: *Warsaw concerto.* GERSHWIN: *Rhapsody in blue.* LITOLFF: *Concerto symphonique, Op. 102: Scherzo.* CHOPIN: *Fantasia on*

Polish airs, Op. 13. LISZT: *Polonaise brillante* (arr. of WEBER: *Polacca brillante, Op. 72*).
*** Ph. Dig. **411 123-2**; 411 123-1/*4* [id.].

Addinsell's indelible pastiche is here promoted up-market, away from the usual film-music anthologies into a collection of pieces written for the concert hall, and how well it holds its own. Never before has the orchestral detail emerged so beguilingly on record as it does under Marriner; he and Misha Dichter combine to give the music genuine romantic memorability, within a warmly sympathetic acoustic. Gershwin's famous *Rhapsody* is hardly less successful, the performance spirited yet glowing. To make a foil, the Litolff *Scherzo* is taken at a sparklingly brisk tempo and projected with great flair. The Chopin *Fantasia* has a lower voltage, but the closing Liszt arrangement of Weber glitters admirably. The sound is first rate (with an excellent tape) and is very believable in its CD format.

Dresden State Orchestra, Marriner

Orchestral showpieces: CHABRIER: *España* (rhapsody). GLINKA: *Jota aragonesa.* RAVEL: *Boléro.* TCHAIKOVSKY: *Capriccio italien.*
* Ph. Dig. **410 047-2**; 6514/*7337* 235.

The Dresden orchestra produces some excellent playing, but there is a cosiness of style in Marriner's readings that ill suits music of this kind. The sound is not especially vivid either, although the compact disc sounds fresher than the LP, and *Boléro* obviously gains from the opening background silence. But there is no drama in its dynamic expansion.

Dresden State Orchestra, Varviso

Overtures and Intermezzi: ROSSINI: *La gazza ladra: overture.* PONCHIELLI: *La Gioconda: Dance of the hours.* MASCAGNI: *Cavalleria Rusticana: Intermezzo.* PUCCINI: *Manon Lescaut: Intermezzo.* BIZET: *Carmen: Prelude to Act I.* SAINT-SAËNS: *Samson et Dalila: Bacchanale.* SCHMIDT: *Notre-Dame: Intermezzo.* MASSENET: *Thaïs: Méditation* (with Peter Mirring). OFFENBACH: *Contes d'Hoffmann: Barcarolle.*
ɕ **(*) Ph. Dig. **412 236-2**; 412 236-1/*4* [id.].

The highlight here is a splendid version of the *Dance of the hours*, the most beguiling in the catalogue. The rich Dresden ambience adds to the colour of the elegant woodwind chirruping, and the recording provides a fine dynamic expansion for the climax before the scintillating finale. Otherwise, the mood is very relaxed and atmospheric; in the ripely romantic account of the *Thaïs Méditation* (with a fine violin solo from Peter Mirring), the Dresden State Opera Chorus creates a soupily religiose backing. The atmospheric timbre of the strings and the warmly sentient playing are certainly very agreeable; and if the Saint-Saëns *Bacchanale* only becomes unbuttoned at the very close, the *Carmen Prelude* does not lack dash. With the background silence especially telling in the Ponchielli ballet, the CD enhances refinement of detail, although the LP is excellent, too; and so is the chrome tape, even if not transferred at the highest level.

English Concert, Pinnock

PACHELBEL: *Canon and Gigue in D.* VIVALDI: *Sinfonia in G min., RV 149.* ALBINONI: *Concerto a cinque in D min. for oboe and strings, Op. 9/2.* PURCELL: *Chacony in G min.* HANDEL: *Solomon: Arrival of the Queen of Sheba.* AVISON: *Concerto Grosso No. 9 in A min.* HAYDN: *Concerto for harpsichord in D, Hob. XVIII/2.*
*** DG Arc. Dig. **415 518-2**; 415 518-1/*4* [id.].

The English Concert is one of the acceptable faces of the authentic-instrument movement, and these vital accounts will give unalloyed pleasure. There are many good things here, particularly the Albinoni *Concerto* (with David Reichenberg as the eloquent soloist) and the Avison, which comes from the set that draws on Scarlatti keyboard sonatas. Although there are popular items too, such as Handel's *Arrival of the Queen of Sheba* from *Solomon* and the Pachelbel *Canon*, there are others of considerable substance, the Purcell *Chacony* and Haydn's *D major Concerto* brilliantly played on the harpsichord by Trevor Pinnock. The performances are crisp and thoroughly alive, and beautifully recorded. The chrome cassette is lively, but not always as cleanly focused as the disc versions.

European Community Chamber Orchestra, Faerber

'The Symphony in Europe', 1785': BOCCHERINI: *Symphony in B flat, G. 514.* MALDERE: *Symphony in G min., Op. 4/1.* SCHWINDL: *Symphony périodique in F.* WESLEY, Samuel: Symphony No. 5 in A.
(*) Hyp. Dig. **CDA 66156; A/*KA* 66156 [id.].

Four amiable symphonies, written at about the same time, but otherwise chosen arbitrarily from four different European countries, given lively, polished but not especially distinctive performances. The Maldere, in the unusual key of G minor, is quite an impressive little work; the Schwindl *Symphony périodique* is certainly a charming, if lightweight, piece; but on the whole the English work, Samuel Wesley's No. 5, is as attractive as any, and its *Brillante* finale is in the form of a rondo with a main theme that remains in the memory. The recording is good, but the acoustic of St James's Church, Clerkenwell, is perhaps a shade too resonant. There is, nevertheless, a good cassette.

'Fantasia on Greensleeves'

English music (with (i) Boston Pops O, Fiedler; (ii) ASMF, Marriner; (iii) ECO, Britten or (iv) Steuart Bedford): VAUGHAN WILLIAMS: (i) *English folksongs suite*; (ii) *Fantasia on Greensleeves*. TRAD: *The oak and the ash*. (iii) ELGAR: *Introduction and allegro for strings, Op. 47*. DELIUS: *2 Aquarelles*. BRIDGE: *Sir Roger de Coverley*. GRAINGER: *Shepherd's Hey*: (iv) *Green bushes; Molly on the shore*.
(M) *** Decca 411 639-1/*4*.

An attractive anthology centring on Britten's ECO recordings made in 1968 at The Maltings. In the Delius, the delicacy of evocation is delightful; while the *Introduction and allegro* is a fascinating performance, with the structure of the piece brought out far more clearly than is common and the music deeply felt. Among the lighter pieces, Frank Bridge's delicious arrangement of *Sir Roger de Coverley* is particularly memorable with its unexpected introduction of *Auld lang syne* near the end. The sound is admirably fresh on disc and cassette alike.

Film music: 'Great Film Music'

(i) Nat. PO, Herrmann; (ii) L. Fest. O and Ch., Black: (i) BAX: *Oliver Twist: Fagin's romp; Finale*. VAUGHAN WILLIAMS: *49th Parallel: Prelude*. BLISS: *Things to come: suite*. WALTON: *Escape me never: Ballet. Richard III: Prelude*. (ii) *The First of the Few: Spitfire prelude and fugue. Henry V: excerpts*.
(M) * Decca Viva 411 837-1/*4*.

Bernard Herrmann was a successful composer of film music in his own right (the score for Alfred Hitchcock's *Psycho* comes readily to mind), so it is surprising that his performances of this music by Bax, Walton and Bliss are so leaden. Vaughan William's memorable theme for *The 49th Parallel* is certainly spacious, but in Bliss's suite for the H. G. Wells *Things to come* the famous March is given such exaggerated nobilmente treatment that it almost comes to a halt. The music Walton wrote for *The First of the Few* and *Henry V* is more attractively presented by Stanley Black, complete with chorus and whistling arrows in the spectacular Agincourt sequence. The sound throughout is vivid and very forwardly balanced, with a comparable matching tape.

'Finlandia'

Scandinavian music: (with (i) Nat. PO, Boskovsky; (ii) RPO, Weller; (iii) New Philh., Kord; (iv) SRO, Stein; (v) ASMF, Marriner): (i) GRIEG: *Holberg suite, Op. 40; Norwegian melodies, Op. 63*; (ii) *Peer Gynt: suite No. 1*. (iii)

SIBELIUS: *Finlandia;* (*iv*) *Legend: The swan of Tuonela.* (v) *Kuolema: Valse triste.*
*(*) Decca **411 933-2** [id.].

Boskovsky produces performances that are essentially undistinguished, lacking the point and refinement one expects of this orchestra. Boskovsky's rhythmic flair is less apparent here than in his home repertory, both in the *Holberg suite* and the *Norwegian dances*. Weller's *Peer Gynt suite* is far more imaginative. The Sibelius performances are variable in appeal, although, as in the Grieg, the recordings (all of which are analogue and come from between 1975 and 1980) sound extremely vivid, with an impressive richness of sonority from the brass in *Finlandia*.

Galway, James (flute)

'Song for Annie' (with (i) Nat. PO, Gerhardt; (ii) Marisa Robles Harp Ens.; (iii) Kevin Conneff, Irish drum): (i) MARAIS: *Le Basque.* VILLA-LOBOS: *Bachianas Brasileiras. No. 5: Aria.* FAURÉ: *Dolly suite: Berceuse.* MOZART: *Piano sonata No. 15 in C, K.545: Allegro.* DENVER: *Annie's song.* HASSE: *Tambourin.* DEBUSSY: *La plus que lente.* TRAD.: (ii) *Brian Boru's march.* (iii; played on a tin whistle) *Belfast hornpipe.* (i) BIZET–BORNE: *Carmen fantasy.* TRAD.: *Spanish love song.*
** RCA **RCD 25163**; RL/*RK* 25163 [**RCD1 3061**; ARL1/*ARK1* 3061].

This collection, dedicated to Galway's wife, includes the John Denver song which took him into the charts (quite an achievement for a modest flute!); but otherwise the one totally memorable item here is the opening *Le Basque* of Marais. Its simple *moto perpetuo* theme registers with indelible charm and remains in the memory long after the disc has finished playing. The rest of the programme is a characteristically fetching array of clever arrangements by either Galway or Gerhardt; but one would not give this collection a first place among Galway's anthologies, of which there are a number on both LP and tape. The present digital remastering is successful, although the gain compared with the LP is marginal. The flute is admirably caught, even though the balance is larger than life.

'Nocturne' (with Nat. PO, Measham): DEBUSSY: *Suite bergamasque: Clair de lune. Petite suite: En bateau.* CHOPIN: *Nocturne in E flat, Op. 9/2.* HALISCH: *Dreamers.* MOUQUET: *Pan and the birds.* MASSENET: *Thaïs: Méditation.* STRAVINSKY: *Firebird: Berceuse.* FAURÉ: *Dolly: Berceuse.* BOULANGER: *Nocturne.* FIELD: *Nocturne No. 5.* LISZT: *Consolation No. 3.* GRIEG: *Peer Gynt: Morning.*
** RCA Dig. **RCD 25463**; RS/*RK* 9012 [ARL1/*ARK1* 4810].

With a very forward balance to make a jumbo-sized flute, dwarfing the accompaniment, the result here is lusciously soporific, and items like the *Berceuse* from Stravinsky's *Firebird* and Grieg's *Morning* from *Peer Gynt* lose their freshness. The *Nocturnes* of Field and Boulanger are the most effective items. Disc and chrome tape are closely matched in quality and, because of the character of the recording, the CD does not add a great deal, except the advantage of background silence.

'In the Pink' (with Nat. PO, Mancini): MANCINI: *The Pink Panther. The Thorn Birds: Meggie's theme; Theme. Breakfast at Tiffany's. The Molly Maguires: Pennywhistle jig; Theme. Victor Victoria: Crazy world. The Great Race: Pie in the face polka. Baby elephant walk. Two for the road. Speedy Gonzales. Medley: Days of wine and roses – Charade – Moon river. Cameo for flute 'for James'.*
❀ *** RCA Dig. **RCD 85315** [RCD 1 5315].

Of the several fine composers who have dominated post-war film music (including Ron Goodwin, John Williams and John Barry) Henry Mancini stands out in providing the most indelible melodies of all. If Sir Arthur Bliss was the pioneer with his famous *March* for the H. G. Wells film, *Things to come* (1936), it was Max Steiner who, in *Gone with the Wind* (1939), first established the idea of associating a film in the public mind with an unforgettable musical 'theme' (in this case representing Tara, the home of the heroine – from which all the action derives). More recently came Maurice Jarre's *Dr Zhivago*, where the music (as David Lean commented appreciatively) had the effect of drawing the public – who had heard the music first – into the cinema to see the film. But the prolifically talented Henry Mancini has provided a whole string of superb musical ideas. It is interesting to reflect that a century ago he and his colleagues would have found an outlet for their invention in the ballet theatre and concert hall. But today's avant garde, often surrounded by musical barbed wire, eschews (or is incapable of) the direct musical communication of melody. Mancini's tunes are often unashamedly romantic (*Moon River* and *Charade* are superb examples); but the delicate *Meggie's theme* from *The Thorn Birds* or the similar *Theme* from *The Molly Maguires* (which Galway phrases with magical Irish inflection) have an agreeable understated lyricism. Other, no less striking examples make their impact with a quirky rhythmic felicity: no one easily forgets *The Pink Panther* or *The Baby Elephant Walk*. Mancini is admirably served here by Galway's superb artistry. His advocacy is wonderfully stylish and sympathetic to the melodic lines, while he can add an attractive touch of Irish whimsy to a piece like the *Pennywhistle jig*. Mancini himself directs the accompaniment using an orchestra of top London sessions players and creating an appropriately silky string timbre. The atmospheric recording is nicely balanced, Galway forwardly miked in the Pop manner, and the whole concoction makes a delightful entertainment, with an encore especially written for the soloist.

Gazzelloni, Severino (flute), **I Musici**

MERCADANTE: *Flute concerto in E min.* VIVALDI: *Concerto in D* (*Il Cardellino*), *Op. 10/3.* BOCCHERINI: *Concerto in D, Op. 27.* TELEMANN: *Suite in A min, for flute and strings.* TARTINI: *Concerto a 5 in G.*
(B) **(*) Ph. On Tour *412 910-4.*

This collection certainly cannot be criticized on grounds of the quality of performances or recordings, for the playing is expert and highly musical and the sound excellent. Moreover, the inclusion of the fine Telemann *Suite* and the delightful *Il Cardellino* of Vivaldi – which Gazzelloni presents with admirable flair – gives substance to the programme. However, the opening Mercadante concerto is more conventional and it must be admitted that 87′ of concertante flute music tends to wear out its welcome. Taken in small sections, this is enjoyable enough.

'Greensleeves'

English music (with (i) Sinfonia of L. or Hallé O, Barbirolli; (ii) New Philh. O, LPO or LSO, Boult; (iii) Williams, Bournemouth SO, Berglund; (iv) E. Sinfonia, Dilkes): (i) VAUGHAN WILLIAMS: *Fantasia on Greensleeves.* (ii) *The lark ascending* (with Hugh Bean). (iii) *Oboe concerto in A min.* (ii) *English folksongs suite.* (i) DELIUS: *A Village Romeo and Juliet: Walk to the Paradise Garden. On hearing the first cuckoo in spring.* (iv) BUTTERWORTH: *The banks of green willow.* (ii) ELGAR: *Serenade for strings, Op. 20.* (iii) MOERAN: *Lonely Waters.*
(B) *** EMI *TC2-MOM 104.*

Looking at the programme and artists' roster, the reader will hardly need the confirmation that this is a very attractive tape anthology. Performances never disappoint, the layout is excellent, and for the car this is ideal. On domestic equipment the sound is a little variable, although the tape has been remastered since its first issue and now sounds pleasantly smooth on top. Often the quality is both vivid and rich, as in the title-piece and the Elgar *Serenade.* Vaughan Williams's *Oboe concerto*, stylishly played by John Williams, is admirably fresh. This is excellent value.

English music (with (i) ASMF, Marriner; (ii) ECO, Britten; (iii) New SO, Collins; (iv) LSO, Bliss; (v) Boston Pops O, Fiedler; (vi) RPO, Cox; (vii) LSO, Monteux): (i) VAUGHAN WILLIAMS: *Fantasia on Greensleeves;* (v) *English folksongs suite.* (i) ELGAR: *Introduction and allegro for strings, Op. 47;* (iv) *Pomp and Circumstance marches Nos 1 and 4;* (vi) *Serenade for strings, Op. 20;* (vii) *Enigma variations: Nimrod.* (i) DELIUS: *On hearing the first cuckoo in spring;* (ii) *2 Aquarelles.* BRIDGE: *Sir Roger de Coverley.* (i) WARLOCK: *String serenade.* (iii) BALFOUR GARDINER: *Shepherd fennel's dance.* (i) BUTTERWORTH: *The banks of green willow.* (ii) BRITTEN: *Simple symphony: Playful pizzicato.*

(B) *** Decca *KMORC 9003*.

In several respects the Decca 'Greensleeves' compilation is even more attractive than the HMV one. The sound is consistently vivid and wide-ranging. The ASMF performances are outstanding, as are those by the ECO under Britten; and the music is skilfully chosen to give variety and yet make a sensible programme. The Bridge and Balfour Gardiner dances are especially welcome, and Britten's *Playful pizzicato* is a delight. Highly recommended and equally successful in the car or at home.

Grimethorpe Colliery Band, Howarth

'Classics for brass': HOLST: *A Moorside suite*. IRELAND: *A comedy overture*. ELGAR: *Severn suite, Op. 87*. BLISS: *Kenilworth*.
(M) *** Decca 414 644-1/*4*.

This reissue from the late 1970s is most welcome, although it now comes into competition with a modern compilation on CRD from the London Collegiate Brass which duplicates three of the four works. But the character of the performances is different: this is a brass band – which implies the use of vibrato, often to good expressive effect, though in the Bliss, less tellingly. It is still a fine performance of a resplendent piece which seeks to conjure up the pageantry of the visit of Queen Elizabeth I to Kenilworth Castle in 1575. The highlight of the concert is Holst's *Moorside suite*, written for the national championship contest at Crystal Palace in 1929. It is superbly played, with great vigour and refinement of detail and quite the equal of the London Collegiate version. Ireland's *Comedy overture* was later transcribed for orchestra and retitled *A London overture*; but here the composer's first thoughts are no less convincing. Elgar's *Severn suite* is given an admirably direct performance, but Elgar Howarth's reading is direct and exciting, with less swagger in the memorably broad opening theme than that of James Stobart on CRD. The recording has outstanding clarity and fine sonority throughout. The cassette is in the demonstration bracket.

Grumiaux, Arthur (violin)

'Violin romances' (with New Philh. O, De Waart): BEETHOVEN: *Romances Nos 1 in G, Op. 40; 2 in F, Op. 50*. BERLIOZ: *Rêverie et Caprice, Op. 8*. TCHAIKOVSKY: *Sérénade mélancolique, Op. 26*. WIENIAWSKI: *Violin concerto No. 2 in D min., Op. 22: Romance* (2nd movt). *Légende, Op. 17*. SVENDSEN: *Romance in G, Op. 26*.
(M) *** Ph. Seq. 412 373-1/*4*.

This is a splendid anthology, offering solo playing of superlative quality. There have been very few finer performances of the Beethoven *Romances*, and the account of the Berlioz *Rêverie et Caprice* is no less distinguished. Of the slighter pieces, the delightful Svendsen *Romance* (which some readers may remember from 78 r.p.m. days) is presented with style and charm. The soloist's warmth for such a perfectly made miniature is understandable. The accompaniment is well in the picture throughout, although the balance treats the solo violin and the orchestral backing on equal terms, which rather reduces the effect of light and shade. There is an excellent high-level cassette. However, tape collectors will find many of these performances included on an outstanding Philips 'On Tour' anthology which costs no more than this and offers a great deal of extra music (see below, under *'Romance'*).

Harvey, Richard (recorder)

Chamber concertos (with Huggett, Goodman, Caudle, Roberts, or Ross), VIVALDI: *Recorder concerto in A min., RV 108.* BASTON: *Concerto No. 2 in C for descant recorder.* NAUDOT: *Concerto in G for treble recorder.* TELEMANN: *Concerto in G min. for treble recorder.*
(*) ASV **CDDCA 523; DCA/*ZCDCA* 523 [id.].

Both the Naudot *Concerto for treble recorder* and the delightful Baston piece for descant recorder have also been recorded by Michala Petri, although they are in two separate collections. She is accompanied by the ASMF, whereas the present performances are on a more intimate scale, with one instrument to each part. However, the solo balance is forward; and this is especially striking on the CD, which is very clearly focused, so the feeling of a chamber partnership is diluted. The performances have strong character and the Telemann *Concerto*, a fine piece, comes off especially well. The cassette uses iron-oxide stock and in consequence the focus is less sharp.

Heward, Leslie (conductor)

'The art of Leslie Heward' (with LPO or Hallé O, and (i) Eileen Joyce): MOERAN: *Symphony in G min.* IRELAND: (i) *Piano concerto in E flat.* GERMAN: *Nell Gwyn dances.* ELGAR: *Salut d'amor.* DVOŘÁK: *Nocturne in B, Op. 40.* LALO: *Aubade No. 1.* SIBELIUS: *Rakastava suite, Op. 14. King Christian II: Elegy.* SHOSTAKOVICH: (i) *Concerto No. 1 for piano, trumpet and strings.* BORODIN: *Prince Igor: Overture.*
(M) (***) HMV mono EM 290462-3/*5* (2).

Leslie Heward did not live long enough to achieve media canonization, and his name will inevitably be unfamiliar to younger readers and to collectors outside the UK; his reputation scarcely had time to penetrate beyond these shores. His pioneering account of the Moeran *Symphony* is marvellously vivid and powerfully held together, and so are the two wartime recordings he made with Eileen

Joyce of the Ireland *Piano concerto* and the Shostakovich *First concerto for piano, trumpet and strings*. Listening to them reinforces the conviction that first recordings have special insights and a freshness of impulse that are only rarely recaptured. Both the Moeran and the two concertos were relatively fresh from their composers' pens, and these performances convey much the same ring of conviction and fervour as did Koussevitzky's Prokofiev *Fifth* or Kajanus's *Tapiola*. Judging from his *Rakastava*, Heward must have been a formidable Sibelian, and his reading of Dvořák's *Notturno* is wonderfully affecting, beautifully phrased and with rapt string-tone. This set deserves the warmest recommendation.

'Invitation to the dance'

Music of the dance (with (i) Berlin RSO, Fricsay; (ii) BPO, Leitner or (iii) Karajan; (iv) Berganza, Davies, Shirley-Quirk, LSO, Abbado): (i) WEBER: *Invitation to the dance* (orch. Berlioz). (ii) TCHAIKOVSKY: *Nutcracker suite*. (iii) DELIBES: *Coppélia: suite*. (iv) STRAVINSKY: *Pulcinella:* excerpts.
(B) ** DG Walkman *415 618-4* [id.].

Both Fricsay's attractively volatile *Invitation to the dance* and Leitner's beautifully played *Nutcracker suite* were recorded at the beginning of the 1960s, but the sound is very good. Karajan's suave yet sparkling account of the *Coppélia suite* is slightly less refined in recorded quality, because here the high transfer level almost reaches saturation point. The piecemeal selection from Stravinsky's *Pulcinella* is less effective, with the vocal contributions playing such a major part – it would have been far better to have included the orchestral suite played complete.

Johann Strauss Orchestra, Rothstein

'Vienna premiere': MILLÖCKER: *Die Sieben Schwaben* (march). *Jonathan* (march). STRAUSS, J. jnr: *Concurrenzen waltz; L'Inconnue* (polka); *Hoch Österreich!* (march); *Alexandrine polka; Die Fledermaus: New Czardas*. STRAUSS, E.: *Knall und Fall* (polka); *Leuchtkäferln waltz; Hectograph* (polka). STRAUSS, JOSEF: *Frohes Leben* (waltz). *Vorwärts!* (polka); *Nachtschatten* (polka); *Elfen* (polka).
** Chan. Dig. **CHAN 8381**; ABRD/*ABTD* 1087.

Quite apart from the variety offered, virtually none of this repertoire is otherwise available. The present record was sponsored by the Johann Strauss Society of Great Britain. Jack Rothstein gives polished, spirited performances, with rhythms well sprung and touches of rubato nicely sophisticated. He uses a comparatively small orchestral group; the recording is balanced fairly well forward, so that, even though the ambient effect is good, the strings are made to sound very bright and not too full-bodied, though detail is admirably clear. The result tends to be aurally tiring and this is best taken a few items at a time. Not all the music is inspired, although the highlights (such as the *Vorwarts!* and *Elfen* polkas of Josef Strauss) are well worth a hearing. Marilyn Hill Smith makes a brief appearance to sing an alternative *Czardas* for *Die Fledermaus* (distinctly inferior to the famous one); the microphone is not too kind to her voice, although the performance has plenty of character.

(Philip) Jones Brass Ensemble

'Lollipops': LANGFORD: *London miniatures.* RIMSKY-KORSAKOV: *Flight of the bumble bee.* ARBAN: *Variations on a Tyrolean theme.* KOETSIER: *Little circus march, Op. 79.* GRIEG: *Norwegian dance, Op. 35/2.* JOPLIN: *Bethena.* PARKER: *A Londoner in New York.* TRAD. (arr. Iveson): *Song of the Seahorse.*
C *** Claves **CD 50 8503**; D/*MC-D* 8503 [id.].

Recorded in St Luke's Church, Hampstead, this Claves CD makes an ideal demonstration showcase for the superb British group that is in some ways the brass equivalent of the Academy of St Martin-in-the-Fields. A collection of 'originals' – music written or arranged specifically for these players, the concert is admirably framed by two suites of descriptive miniatures, both considerable additions to the brass repertoire. In between come many entertaining examples of musical bravura, including Rimsky's descriptive piece, sounding like a jumbo-sized bumble bee on John Fletcher's incredibly nimble tuba, and Arban's more conventional, but no less breathtaking *Variations on a Tyrolean theme*, where the horn player Frank Lloyd is featured; while Jan Koetsier's *Kleiner Zirkusmarsch* has wonderfully deft articulation from the whole group. Gordon Langford's set of six *London miniatures* shows this composer at his most inventive. Each cameo catches the spirit of a famous London landmark, with Nelson dominating *Trafalgar Square* in an ingenious kaleidoscope of sea-songs. The contrasting *Elegy*, evoking the Cenotaph, is touchingly sombre, while the brilliant *Horse Guards Parade* march is in the best Eric Coates tradition. Jim Parker's *A Londoner in New York* provides a transatlantic mirror-image in his five-movement suite, with lively jazzy imagery not only in the second movement, *Harlem* (with a strong Scott Joplin flavour), but also in the finale, *Radio City*, which provides an exuberant contrast after the nostalgic little waltz representing *Central Park*. Tony Faulkner, the recording producer, deserves a credit for the wonderful tangibility of the sound balance, which combines bite and clarity with fine, rich sonority. The presence of the instrumentalists on CD is very real.

'Brass splendour': HANDEL: *Royal fireworks music: excerpts.* BACH: *Christmas oratorio:* excerpts. GABRIELI, G.: *Sonata pian' e forte.* CLARKE: *Trumpet voluntary.* BYRD: *The Battell.* PURCELL: *Trumpet tune and air.* SCHEIDT: *Galliard battaglia.* BACH, C. P. E.: *March, Wq. 188.* STRAUSS, R.: *Festmusik der Stadt Wien.* DVOŘÁK: *Humoresque, Op. 101.* TCHAIKOVSKY: *Sleeping Beauty: Waltz.*

COPLAND: *Fanfare for the common man.* MUSSORGSKY: *Pictures: Baba Yaga; The great gate of Kiev.*
(*) Decca Dig. **411 955-2; Jub. 411 955-1/*4*.

This selection is made from the various anthologies recorded by the Philip Jones Ensemble for the Argo label between 1973 and 1980. The analogue sound has been successfully remastered and the quality is now impressively vivid and clear, if not of the calibre of the newer digital issue from Claves. The programme ranges wide, with Gabrieli's *Sonata pian' e forte*, Scheidt's *Galliard battaglia* and the C. P. E. Bach *March* (both with striking antiphonal effects) among the highlights. Tchaikovsky's *Sleeping Beauty waltz* is played by the inimitable John Fletcher (with electronic aid) as a tuba quartet, but this is a novelty rather than a rewarding repeat experience: the music lies too low and sounds lugubrious. Copland's *Fanfare* is resplendent, but the Mussorgsky *Finale* loses something on the orchestral version. In its LP and tape form, this is issued at mid-price on Decca's Jubilee label; the LP is probably the best buy. The tape is well managed and brilliant, but the amplitude of the *Fireworks music* and the bass drum in the Copland *Fanfare* brings slight loss of focus.

Kantorow, Jean-Jacques (violin), **New Japan Philharmonic Orchestra, Michi Inque**

CHAUSSON: *Poème, Op. 25.* SARASATE: *Zigeunerweisen, Op. 20.* SAINT-SAËNS: *Introduction and Rondo capriccioso.* RAVEL: *Tzigane.* BEETHOVEN: *Romance in F, Op. 50.*
** Denon Dig. **C37 7005**.

Although he opens Chausson's *Poème* with persuasive romantic feeling, Kantorow's approach to all this music is as an opportunity for virtuoso display. He is fully up to the fireworks, but a little more relaxation would have given more contrast in the lyrical writing. The recording is first class and well balanced, but its clarity in relation to the orchestral playing is not always flattering.

Kremer Ensemble

Viennese dance music: LANNER: *Die Weber, Op. 103; Marien Waltz; Steyrische-Tänze.* STRAUSS, J. Snr: *Eisele und Beisle Sprünge (polka). Kettenbrücke Waltz; Beliebte Annen-Polka; Wiener Gemüts Waltz; Schwarz'sche Ball-Tänze.* KLAUSER: *Nationalländler Nos 1, 2, 5–6, 12.*
*** Ph. **410 395-2**; 410 395–1/*4* [id.].

Gidon Kremer, not just a brilliant and individual virtuoso, is a devotee of chamber-playing. It is good to have such superb performances of this charming Viennese dance repertoire using an authentic small-scale group. Much of the music is slight, and Johann Strauss senior emerges as the strongest musical personality, with his *Eisele und Beisle Sprüng polka* – delivered here with great élan – and the engaging *Kettenbrücke Waltz* among the more memorable items. The recording is most realistic in its CD format although somewhat dry, and its intimacy is heard most effectively if the volume control is not too high. There is an excellent tape.

Lloyd Webber, Julian (cello)

'Cello man' (with Nat. PO, Gerhardt): CANTELOUBE: *Baïléro*. FALLA: *Ritual fire dance*. SAINT-SAËNS: *Samson et Dalila: Softly awakes my heart*. BRIDGE: *Scherzetto*. FAURÉ: *Élégie*. VILLA-LOBOS: *Bachianas Brasileiras No. 5*. BACH: *Arioso*. PÖPPER: *Gavotte No. 2*. DELIUS: *Hassan: Serenade*. BRUCH: *Kol Nidrei*.
** RCA RL/*RK* 70797.

Flatteringly recorded, with the cello forward and the orchestra in a very resonant acoustic, this programme is soupily romantic and will not be to all tastes, though the playing is lushly effective. But a song like *Baïléro* loses its innocence with such treatment, and the arrangement of the *Ritual fire dance* for cello and orchestra is pointless. The Pöpper, Delius and Bruch pieces are the highlights. The chrome tape matches the disc closely.

'Travels with my cello' (with ECO, Cleobury): STRAUSS, J. Jnr: *Pizzicato polka*. LEHAR: *Vilja*. DEBUSSY: *Golliwog's cakewalk*. SCHUMANN: *Träumerei*. ALBÉNIZ: *Puerta de tierra*. SAINT-SAËNS: *The swan*. BACH/GOUNOD *Ave Maria*. LLOYD WEBBER: *Andante*. ALBINONI: *Adagio*. KHACHATURIAN: *Sabre dance*. GRAINGER: *Londonderry air*. RIMSKY-KORSAKOV: *Flight of the Bumble bee*.
(*) Ph. Dig. **412 231-2; 412 231-1/*4* [id.].

This collection is issued in connection with Julian Lloyd Webber's autobiographical book, which shares the same title. The colourful orchestral arrangements were specially made by Christopher Palmer; the recording balance, by not projecting the cello too far forward, ensures that orchestral detail is very good. The solo playing has considerable flair, although the swooping lyrical style in *Vilja* and, notably, *The swan* may not appeal to all tastes. But there is no lack of personality here.

'Pieces' (with LSO, Mike Batt): *'Pieces:'* HAYWARD: *Nights in white satin*. ANDERSSON: *I know him so well*. MACCOLL: *The first time I saw your face*. MASSER: *Tonight I celebrate my love*. RICHIE: *Hello*. BACH: *Suite 3: Air*. SAINTE-MARIE: *Up where we belong*. BURGON: *Theme from Brideshead Re-*

visited. BATT: *Theme from The Yellow Book; Bright eyes.* DVOŘÁK: *Symphony No. 9 (New World): Largo: Theme.* MYERS: *Cavatina (Theme from The Deer Hunter).*
** Polydor Dig. **827 352-2.**

Here the crossover is almost complete, with only two 'classical items'. Those apart, most of the melodic ideas are short-breathed, though Mike Batt's arrangements extend them as far as possible. The cello, a little larger than life, is placed forward, against a pleasantly washy orchestral backing. This is quite agreeable as late-evening wallpaper music if you enjoy the solo cello non-stop for about three-quarters of an hour. Bach's famous *Air* is romanticized, yet Dvořák's *Largo* is paced more like an *Andante.* Mike Batt's own *Theme from the Yellow Book*, alongside the Myers *Cavatina*, is among the more memorable items.

Locke Brass Consort, Lake

'Miniatures for brass': PEZEL: *Suite.* SPEER: *Sonata No. 1.* HOLBORNE: *3 Pieces.* BRADE: *Suite.* STEELE-PERKINS: *Intrada.* GRIEG: *Bridal song. Op. 17/24; Ballad, Op. 65/5; Wedding day in Troldhaugen, Op. 65/6.* GUBBY: *The great Panathenaea.* BARTÓK: *For Children: 3 Pieces.* WALTON: *2 Duets for children.*
**(*) Chan. Dig. ABRD/*ABTD* 1038 [id.].

Although expertly presented, with admirable use of dynamic light and shade, the early (seventeenth-century) music has an element of blandness played on modern brass instruments. Yet its invention remains attractive. The twentieth-century items are all most entertaining. Alan Civil's Grieg arrangements, too, are highly diverting; and throughout the second side of this record (and the equally impressive chrome cassette) the sparkle of the music making combines with sound of vivid realism to give much pleasure.

London Collegiate Brass, Stobart

ELGAR: *Severn suite, Op. 87* (arr. Geehl and Brand). VAUGHAN WILLIAMS. *Henry V overture.* HOLST: *A Moorside suite.* IRELAND: *A comedy overture.*
*** CRD Dig. **CRD 3434**; CRD 1134/*CRDC 4134.*

Elgar's *Severn suite* was a late work, commissioned as a brass band test piece in 1930. He was aided in the scoring by Henry Geehl, but the performing version was lost for half a century. When it was rediscovered, in 1980, it was found to be in a key a tone higher than the published score. The piece was then further edited by Geoffrey Brand, who favoured the original pitch but took into account the composer's own revisions made for his orchestral arrangement. The result is very convincing and here the opening theme is given a swagger and feeling of pageantry that remain obstinately in the memory. The rest of the work is also impressive, though the quality of the music is uneven. Vaughan Williams's *Henry V overture* dates from 1933/4 but remained unpublished until 1981, again in an edited version by Roy Douglas. It stirringly quotes both French and English traditional melodies. Holst's *Moorside suite* demonstrates the composer's usual mastery when writing for wind and brass; while John Ireland's jaunty *Comedy overture*, played with striking rhythmic felicity, also shows the composer at his finest. The performances here (by a group drawn mainly from the London music colleges, and using trumpets rather than cornets, French horns rather than the tenor horns of the brass band world) produce a fine rich sonority. The execution has impressively polished ensemble; timbres are vibratoless to give an orchestral character to the sound. CRD's recording is superbly spacious and realistic, and the focus is only slightly less sharp on the chrome tape which handles the wide amplitude impressively. Even on CD the upper range, at times, seems not absolutely clean, probably an effect created by the reverberation.

(i) **London Philharmonic Orchestra**; (ii) **London Symphony Orchestra**; (iii) **Sir Adrian Boult**; (iv) **the composer**

'Concert of British music': (i) BERKELEY–BRITTEN: *Mont Juic* (*suite of Catalan dances*), *Op. 12* (cond. Berkeley). (ii; iv) BLISS: *Mêlée fantasque*. (ii; iii) HOLST: *Japanese suite, Op. 33*. (i; iv) WALTON: *Music for children*.
*** Lyr. SRCS 50.

An outstanding reissue from the beginning of the 1970s, when each composer was invited to direct his own music. Berkeley directs the *Catalan dances*, vivid and likeable pieces which he produced jointly with Benjamin Britten, while Sir Adrian steps in to deputize for Holst. His *Japanese suite*, dating from 1915, offers exotic scoring and a characteristic style of melody, and generates the vivid orchestral palette which makes *The Planets* so memorable. Walton's *Music for children* is a set of eight miniatures, originally written for piano duet, wittily scored. (They have something in common with Stravinsky's orchestral versions of his *Easy Piano Pieces*.) Bliss's *Mêlée fantasque*, somewhat eclectic in style, produces an unexpected melodic sweep in its central section then seems to make an almost direct quote from Stravinsky's *Rite of spring* towards the close. With first-class Lyrita recording, atmospheric but sparkling, this is most attractive; but even after all this time, it is still offered at full price.

London Symphony Orchestra, Ahronovich

'Russian spectacular': KHACHATURIAN: *Gayaneh: Sabre dance. Spartacus: Adagio of Spartacus and Phyrigia. Masquerade: Waltz.* PROKOFIEV: *Lieutenant Kijé: Troika. Love of 3 Oranges: March.* BORODIN: *Prince Igor: Polovtsian dances.* GLINKA: *Overture: Russlan and Ludmilla.* MUSSORGSKY: *Night on the bare mountain.* SHOSTAKOVICH: *Gadfly: Folk festival.*
(M) **(*) Pickwick Dig. **PCD 804**; CC/*CCTC* 7557.

An excellent collection of characteristically vivid Russian orchestral genre pieces, played with plenty of spirit and polish by the LSO who are in excellent form. Yuri Ahronovich may not be a subtle conductor, but his pacing here is notably convincing in Mussorgsky's *Night on the bare mountain*, while the piquant Prokofiev *March* is crisply rhythmic and nicely pointed. The *Sabre dance* and *Polovtsian dances* have no lack of energy and fire. The recording combines brilliance with weight; this CD is excellent value in Pickwick's mid-priced series, even though the ambience is a little dry. The LP and cassette are at bargain price.

London Symphony Orchestra, Gould

RAVEL: *Boléro.* SHOSTAKOVICH: *Festival overture, Op. 96.* GINASTERA: *Estancia: ballet suite, Op. 8a.* WEINBERGER: *Svanda the Bagpiper: Polka and fugue.*
(B) **(*) ASV Dig. ABM/*ZCABM* 763 [id.].

Spanish dance music: FALLA: *La vida breve: Dance No. 1. El amor brujo: Pantomime; Ritual fire dance. Three cornered hat: Final dance.* TURINA: *Danzas fantásticas: Orgia.* GRANADOS: *Goyescas: Intermezzo.* ALBÉNIZ: *Iberia: Fête-Dieu a Seville; Triana.*
(B) **(*) ASV Dig. ABM/*ZCABM* 766 [id.].

Both these concerts derive from the Varese Sarabande catalogue and, with modern digital recording, are good value on ASV's bargain label. Morton Gould brings a composer's insights to his direction of both programmes and there is no lack of imaginative touches, while the LSO plays well for him, if not always providing the crispest ensemble. The Spanish collection has its full measure of sun-drenched colours, and the recording sparkles vividly without developing too much digital edge; there is good supporting weight and the ambience is well judged. In the USA, a special CD compilation has been made, using the whole content of the first LP plus the Turina and Granados items from the collection of Spanish music [Var./Sar. **VCD 47209**].

London Symphony Orchestra, Yan-Pascal Tortelier

RAVEL: *Boléro*. RIMSKY-KORSAKOV: *Sadko: Song of India*. SHOSTAKOVICH: *The Gadfly: Romance*. PROKOFIEV: *Romeo and Juliet:* excerpts.
** D Sharp Dig. **DSCD 1001**; DSLP/*DSMC* 1001.

This is agreeable but in no way distinctive. The recording was made in EMI's Abbey Road Studio yet has a concert-hall atmosphere which suits performances that do not generate a great deal of electricity. There is attractively refined wind-playing in Ravel's *Boléro*, but the climax is not greatly compulsive. Overall, Tortelier's approach is lyrical rather than dramatic, and the Rimsky-Korsakov and Shostakovich items sound rather soupy. We have not heard the CD.

Los Angeles Chamber Orchestra, Schwarz

'American string music': BARBER: *Serenade, Op. 1*. CARTER: Elegy. DIAMOND: *Rounds*. FINE: *Serious song*.
*** None. Dig. **CD 79002** [id.].

The Barber *Serenade* was first recorded in the 1960s, but its long absence from the catalogue is at last rectified by this excellent issue. It is a winning piece with all the freshness of youth. The *Rounds* for strings by David Diamond is another fertile and inventive piece, which has not been available since the early days of LP. Elliot Carter's *Elergy* was originally written for cello and piano, then arranged for string quartet, and dates from 1939. It is a long-breathed and noble piece, while Irving Fine, like Carter a pupil of Boulanger and Walter Piston, composed his *Serious song* in the mid-1950s. A worthwhile issue for all who have inquiring tastes, excellently played and recorded.

'Lyrita Lollipops'

English music (with (i) RPO, Myer Fredman; (ii) LSO, Bliss; (iii) LPO, Walton): (i) BENJAMIN: *Italian comedy overture*. (ii) BLISS: *Adam Zero* (*ballet suite*). (i) DELIUS: *A Village Romeo and Juliet: Walk to the paradise garden*. (iii) WALTON: *Portsmouth Point: overture; Siesta*.
*** Lyr. SRCS 47.

Another worthwhile Lyrita reissue of English music (from 1971), with Walton's own version of *Portsmouth Point* (a surprisingly under-recorded piece) a highlight. Benjamin's *Italian comedy overture* is less substantial, but deliciously scored. With Sir Arthur Bliss giving an authoritative account of *Adam Zero* and making it sound like film music, this is an enjoyable collection given Lyrita's best analogue sound, sparkling and atmospheric.

Marsalis, Wynton (trumpet), **Edith Gruberova** (soprano)

'Let the bright Seraphim' (with ECC Leppard): FASCH: *Concerto for trumpet and 2 oboes in D.* TORELLI: *2 Sonatas for trumpet and strings a 5.* HANDEL: *Samson: Let the bright Seraphim. Birthday Ode for Queen Anne: Eternal source of Light divine.* PURCELL: *Come ye sons of art: Sound the trumpet; Chaconne. Indian Queen: Trumpet overture; Intrada; Air. King Arthur: Trumpet tune.* MOLTER: *Concerto No. 2 in D.*
*** CBS Dig. **MK 39061**; IM/*IMT* 39061 [id.].

Although Edith Gruberova makes an important contribution to the success of this anthology, it must be listed here, rather than in the vocal section, for Wynton Marsalis is clearly the star. His superb, sometimes slightly restrained virtuosity is ideal for this programme and his cool sense of classical style brings consistently memorable results. So often in a trumpet anthology the ear wearies of the timbre, but never here. Marsalis scales down his tone superbly to match the oboes in the delightful Fasch *Concerto* (especially as they are backwardly balanced), and he plays the *Sonatas* of Torelli and the sharply characterized Purcell miniatures with winning finesse. With Edith Gruberova he achieves a complete symbiosis in *Sound the trumpet* from *Come ye sons of art*, with the voice and instrumental melismas uncannily imitative; and he forms a comparable partnership in the two Handel arias, where Gruberova's agile and beautifully focused singing is hardly less admirable. The recording balance is excellent and the CD, as usual, adds an indefinable extra sense of presence, making the trumpet very tangible, especially in the upper tessitura of the Molter *Concerto*, where the solo playing makes the hairs at the nape of one's neck tingle.

Menuhin, Yehudi and **Stéphane Grappelli** (violins)

'For all seasons' (with Instrumental Ens. and rhythm): HARRIS: *Winter set.* HENDERSON: *Button up your overcoat.* BERLIN: *I've got my love to keep me warm; Heat wave.* JOHNSTON: *I'll remember April.* LOESSER: *Spring will be a little late this year.* GRAPPELLI: *Giboulées de Mars; Automne.* DUKE: *April in Paris.* McHUGH: *On the sunny side of the street.* STYNE: *The things we did last summer.* WARREN: *September in the rain.* KOSMA: *Autumn leaves.* DUKE: *Autumn in New York.*
*** HMV Dig. **CDC 747144-2** [id.]; EL 270112-1/*4*.

The unexpected but rewarding collaboration of Menuhin and Grappelli has produced a whole series of highly individual 'crossover' records of which this is the first on CD (although the sixth overall). It returns to the original, more intimate format where, in Menuhin's words, he and Grappelli 'exchange comments and solo passages with others, accompanied by the incredibly intense, precise rhythmic commentary'. The others include Martin Taylor and Marc Fosset (guitars) and David Snell (harp), plus a small instrumental group of strings and horns. The arrangements are by Max Harris and in two numbers Grappelli makes a contribution on the piano. Everything combines to make an excellent example of the sweet-sour genre, and the many hits are spiced with some unusual items. There is no better example of this fruitful partnership than Irving Berlin's *Heat wave*, with plenty of warmth generated by the interplay of these two quite different musical personalities. On CD, the recording is full and forwardly balanced, with plenty of presence. There is also a good matching tape.

Messiter, Malcolm (oboe)

'Oboe fantasia' (with Nat. PO, Mace): PASCULLI: *Concerto on themes from Donizetti's 'La Favorita'*. DEBUSSY: *Rêverie*. SCARLATTI, D.: *Sonata in C, Kk.159*. SAINT-SAËNS: *The Swan*. MUSSORGSKY: *Ballet of the unhatched chicks*. NOVAČEK: *Perpetual motion*. DELARUE: *Compte à rebours: Adagio*. PUCCINI: *Gianni Schicchi: O mio babbino caro*. KREISLER: *Caprice viennois*. JOSEPHS: *Enemy at the Door: Song of freedom*. POULENC: *Mouvements perpétuels No. 1*. YOUNG: *Stella by Starlight*.
(M) **(*) RCA Gold GL/*GK* 70799.

With a showcase issue of this kind RCA are obviously trying to promote Malcolm Messiter as a star oboist to catch the public fancy and match the achievement of James Galway's silver flute. Certainly Messiter can charm the ear, as in Debussy's *Rêverie*; he can also produce impressive bravura, as in Pasculli's reworking of tunes from Donizetti's *La Favorita*. There is sparkle in Kreisler's *Caprice viennois*, and an eloquent operatic line in Puccini; but in the last resort, this playing has neither the memorability nor quite the technical flair of Galway's. Messiter is at his best in the slighter material. The recording is faithful, the oboe well forward, the orchestral strings sometimes sounding thin. The cassette matches the LP very closely, if anything slightly smoother at the top.

Mexico City Symphony Orchestra, Bátiz

'Music of Mexico! Vol. 3: GALINDO: *Sones de Mariachi*. HALLFTER: *Obertura festiva*. REVUELTAS: *Janitzio; Cuauhnáhuac*. JIMÉNEZ: *Tres cartas de México (suite sinfonica)*.
(M) *** HMV Dig. ED 270229-1/*4*.

This is the third of a series of LPs Bátiz is making of Mexican orchestral music; among the items offered, Galindo's *Sones de Mariachi* stands out. The music derives from the Mariachi groups which originated in the composer's native

State of Jalison, and the orchestration roisterously suggests their enthusiastic folk-style. By comparison, Hallfter's *Festival overture* sounds a trifle bland, but Revueltas's two musical picture postcards of Janitzio have a dazzling orchestral palette and plenty of brash rhythms. The *Three letters* of Jiménez are more subtle in their orchestral atmosphere, though the folk element remains, with marimba and guitars included in the scoring. The Orquesta Sinfónica de la Ciudad de Mexico are clearly at home in this repertoire and play with enjoyable gusto, yet also with moments of pictorial refinement. Bátiz directs with panache, and the extremely vivid digital recording captures all these exotic sounds without the music sounding impossibly noisy.

Milwaukee Symphony Orchestra, Lukas

'American festival': BERNSTEIN: *Candide overture.* SCHUMAN: *Newsreel.* IVES: *The unanswered question; Circus band march.* RUGGERI: *If . . . Then.* COPLAND: *Fanfare for the common man; Appalachian spring: Variations.* BARBER: *Adagio for strings.* COWELL: *Saturday night at the Firehouse.*
** Pro Arte Dig. **CDD 102** [id.].

The Milwaukee players are at their finest in William Schuman's *Newsreel*, a sharply characterized set of five miniatures. They play atmospherically in Ives's famous enigma, although here, as in the Barber *Adagio*, the voltage is not too high. Only 3′ 30″ are included of *Appalachian spring*. The exhilarating Bernstein overture is undoubtedly a success, as is the Cowell *Saturday night at the Firehouse*; and many will find this unusual programme well worth investigating. The sound has a resonant concert-hall acoustic, but the overall effect is spectacular and realistic.

Monte Carlo Philharmonic Orchestra, Foster

BARBER: *Adagio for strings, Op. 11.* KHACHATURIAN: *Spartacus: Adagio.* SCHMIDT: *Notre Dame: Intermezzo.* GRIEG: *Peer Gynt: Morning.* SIBELIUS: *Kuolema: Valse triste, Op. 44.* MASCAGNI: *Cavalleria Rusticana: Intermezzo.* RACHMANINOV: *Vocalise, Op. 34.* SATIE: *Gymnopédies 1 and 3* (orch. Debussy).
(*) Erato Dig. **ECD 88103; ERA/*MCE* 9271.

By concentrating on atmosphere, Lawrence Foster – aided by the warmly resonant sound – sets and maintains here a mood of evocative romanticism, though the last degree of electricity is missing from the climax of the Barber *Adagio*. The *Spartacus* climax is effective, without too much in the way of histrionics; although *Valse triste* seems a shade lethargic at first, the performance is not without character. Excellent playing from the Monte Carlo strings; and a CD which, with its wide dynamic range and background silence, is well balanced and realistic.

I Musici

ALBINONI: *Adagio in G min.* (arr. Giazotto). BEETHOVEN: *Minuet in G, WoO.10/2.* BOCCHERINI: *Quintet in E, Op. 13/5: Minuet.* HAYDN (attrib.): *Quartet, Op. 3/5; Serenade.* MOZART: *Serenade No. 13 in G* (*Eine kleine Nachtmusik*), *K.525.* PACHELBEL: *Canon.*
C *** Ph. Dig. **410 606-2**; 6514/*7337* 370 [id.].

An exceptionally successful concert, recorded with remarkable naturalness and realism. The compact disc is very believable indeed, but the LP and cassette also offer demonstration quality. The playing combines warmth and freshness, and the oft-played Mozart *Night music* has no suggestion whatsoever of routine: it combines elegance, warmth and sparkle. The Boccherini *Minuet* and (especially) the Hofstetter (attrib. Haydn) *Serenade* have an engaging lightness of touch.

'Christmas concertos': CORELLI: *Concerto grosso in G min., Op. 6/8.* TORELLI: *Concerto in G min.* (*in forma di pastorale per il Santissimo Natale*)*, Op. 8/6.* MANFREDINI: *Concerto in C, Op. 3/12.* LOCATELLI: *Concerto in F min., Op. 1/8.*
(*) Ph. Dig. **412 739-2; 412 739-1/*4*.

These concertos sustain a similar mood and atmosphere; together, they fail to offer a great deal of variety. Performances are warmly responsive, and I Musici bring greater lightness of touch to this Christmas anthology than do their Polish colleagues in the same programme under Jerzy Maksymiuk – see below. While some listeners will prefer this repertoire in more self-consciously 'authentic' performances, there is still much to be said for the richer sonority and body that this expert ensemble bring to bear on these concertos. The recording is excellent, though the chrome cassette is less transparent than the disc versions.

National Philharmonic Orchestra, Stokowski

'Stokowski spectacular': SOUSA: *Stars and stripes forever.* MUSSORGSKY: *Khovantschina: Entr'acte to Act V.* STRAUSS, J., jnr: *G'schichten aus dem Wiener Wald* (*Tales from the Vienna Woods*)*, Op. 325.* IPPOLITOV-IVANOV *Caucasian sketches, Op. 10: Procession of the Sardar.* CHABRIER: *España* (rhapsody). HAYDN: *String quartet No. 17, Op. 3/5: Andante cantabile.* SAINT-SAËNS: *Danse macabre, Op. 40.* BRAHMS: *Hungarian dance No. 1 in G min.* TCHAIKOVSKY: *Solitude, Op. 73/6.* BERLIOZ: *Damnation de Faust, Op. 24: Hungarian march.* (All items arr. Stokowski.)
*** **PRT CDPCN 4** [id.].

Although this is digitally remastered from a 1976 analogue recording, the sound often approaches demonstration quality, especially in the opening Sousa march, which has irresistible élan and even includes a zylophone. Throughout the programme, the Stokowski charisma is heard at its most magnetic, not least in *Tales from the Vienna Woods*, which is genially relaxed; with rhythms nicely lilting and pointed, even though every repeat is observed it does not sound a bar too long. The rubato in Chabrier's *España* is rather more self-conscious, and the Brahms *Hungarian dance* and Tchaikovsky's *Solitude* are soupily over-romantic, yet even here Stokowski is persuasive by the sheer force of his personality. Elsewhere there is plenty of sparkle and consistent orchestral finesse. The reverberant acoustic undoubtedly adds glamour, but it means that the compact disc brings only minor improvement in definition. However, with background noise minimized, the overall impact is undoubtedly enhanced.

'Great overtures': BEETHOVEN: *Leonora No. 3.* SCHUBERT: *Rosamunde* (*Die Zauberharfe*). BERLIOZ: *Le carnaval romain.* MOZART: *Don Giovanni.* ROSSINI: *William Tell.*
(*) **PRT CDPCN 6; Dell'Arte DA 9003.

Stokowski made this record just before his ninety-fourth birthday, yet, as with so many of the recordings made during his 'Indian summer', the electricity crackles throughout. The Beethoven is immensely dramatic, while *Rosamunde* combines high romanticism with affectionate warmth. Dissatisfied with Mozart's ending to *Don Giovanni*, Stokowski extends this piece to include music from the opera's finale. The pacing in *William Tell* is fast but, here as elsewhere, the players obviously relish the experience, and if ensemble slips a little, the music making is enjoyably infectious. The sound is extremely vivid, too. Readers will note that the LP is published on the Dell'Arte label, whereas the digitally remastered CD comes from PRT.

New Philharmonia Orchestra, Leppard

'Eighteenth-century overtures': PERGOLESI: *L'Olimpiade.* HANDEL: *Il Pastor Fido.* GRÉTRY: *Le jugement de Midas.* RAMEAU: *Pygmalion.* BONONCINI: *Polifemo.* SACCHINI: *Oedipe à Colone.* MEHUL: *Le chasse de jeune Henri.* SCARLATTI, D.: *Sinfonia in B.*
(M) *** Ph. 412 406-1/*4*.

A remarkably interesting anthology of eighteenth-century overtures. All these pieces are full of surprises: Rameau's *Pygmalion* is a delight. *La chasse de jeune Henri* with its horn calls was one of Beecham's favourites, and the artistry and lightness of touch that distinguish Raymond Leppard's direction of the New Philharmonia Orchestra are at times worthy of Sir Thomas. The recording, from 1968, has been freshened on disc, but the tape is transferred at a very high level which brings some fierceness in the high violins.

New York Philharmonic Orchestra, Bernstein

'Favourite overtures': HÉROLD: *Zampa.* THOMAS: *Raymond; Mignon.* REZNIČEK: *Donna Diana.* SUPPÉ: *Poet and peasant; Beautiful Galatea; Light cavalry.* ROSSINI: *William Tell.* OFFENBACH: *Orpheus in the Underworld.* NICOLAI: *The merry wives of Windsor.* BERNSTEIN: *Candide.*
(B) *(**) CBS *MGT 39492.*

This collection of bandstand overtures shows Bernstein and the NYPO in top virtuoso form and obviously enjoying themselves hugely, a superb demonstration of a fine orchestra under a great conductor all letting their hair down, yet retaining an overall discipline. The addition of the fizzing account of Bernstein's own *Candide* is particularly welcome. It is a great pity that this issue was made before CBS moved over to chrome tape, for the quality, though brilliant, is not ideally refined. But the performances are marvellously exhilarating.

(i) New York Philharmonic Orchestra, Bernstein; (ii) Philadelphia Orchestra, Ormandy

'Romantic favourites for strings': (i) BARBER: *Adagio, Op. 11.* VAUGHAN WILLIAMS: *Fantasia on Greensleeves.* BIZET: *L'Arlésienne: Adagietto.* TCHAIKOVSKY: *Serenade, Op. 48: Waltz.* MAHLER: *Symphony No. 5: Adagietto.* (ii) BORODIN: *Nocturne.* TRAD.: *Londonderry air.* MASCAGNI: *Cavalleria Rusticana: Intermezzo.* BACH: *Air; Arioso.* FAURÉ: *Pavane.* RACHMANINOV: *Vocalise.* GRIEG: *Notturno.*
** CBS *MGT 39020.*

A good double-length tape showing the New York Philharmonic and Philadelphia Orchestras at the peak of their respective forms during the Bernstein and Ormandy eras. The recording is full and generally spacious; Bernstein is heard at his most impressive in the Mahler *Adagietto* and the Barber *Adagio*, while Ormandy and the Philadelphia strings are suitably expansive in Borodin and Rachmaninov. The programme is well put together for continued listening.

New York Trumpet Ensemble

'Art of the trumpet': Music by: MOURET; VALENTINE; WILBYE; BIBER; MARTINI; FRESCOBALDI; Giovanni and Andrea GABRIELI.
* MMG Dig. **MCD 10001.**

Among the many current trumpet anthologies, this does not stand out. The highlights are the Biber *Sonata a 7* and the music by the two Gabrielis, which is admirably sonorous. The sound too is first class; but a little of the rest goes a long way.

New York Trumpet Ensemble, 'Y' Chamber Orchestra, Schwarz

'The sound of trumpets': ALTENBURG: *Concerto in D for 7 trumpets.* VIVALDI: *Double trumpet concerto, RV 537.* BIBER: *Sonata* (*Sancti Polcarpi*). TORELLI: *Sonata a 5.* TELEMANN: *Concerto in D.*
(*) Delos Dig. **D/CD 3002 [id.].

As we know from his outstanding version of the Haydn *Trumpet concerto*, Gerard Schwarz is an accomplished soloist and musician, and both the Telemann and Vivaldi performances (where he is joined by Norman Smith) are first class. The Altenburg *Concerto* features seven soloists, the Biber *Sonata* eight, in two antiphonal groups. Both come off splendidly: neither is too long to outstay its welcome. The balance places the brass well forward, but the chamber orchestra is backward and detail might have been better defined. Otherwise the sound is very good.

Paillard Chamber Orchestra, Paillard

Baroque music: PACHELBEL: *Canon.* BACH: *Erbarm' dich, BWV 721; Jesu, joy of man's desiring* (*from BWV 147*)*; Ihr Menschen rühmet Gottes Liebe* (*from BWV 167*)*; Wachet auf* (*from BWV 140*)*; Die Elenden sollen essen; Sinfonia* (*from BWV 75*)*; Bleib bei uns, denn es will Abend Werden* (*from BWV6*). ALBINONI: *Adagio* (arr. Giazotto). BONPORTI: *Andante* (*from Concerto, Op. 11/5*). MOLTER: *Double trumpet concerto in D: Adagio.*
*(*) Erato **ECD 88020**; NUM/*MCE* 75093.

Opening with a stately and effective version of Pachelbel's *Canon*, its crescendos nicely controlled, and including an eloquent and a quite imaginative account of the Albinoni/Giazotto *Adagio*, this disc is dominated by its Bach chorales, played very soberly. The instrumentation is at times less than ideal, especially where the trumpet is used for the melodic line and the overall effect is rather square. The sound is full and pleasing, but not particularly transparent, even on CD.

Perlman, Itzhak (violin)

'Popular violin repertoire' (with (i) RPO, Foster; (ii) S. Sanders; (iii) A. Previn; (iv) ECO, Barenboim): (i) SARASATE: *Carmen fantasy, Op. 25.* (ii) TARTINI/KREISLER: *Variations on a theme of Corelli.* NOVAČEK: *Perpetuum mobile.* (iii) JOPLIN: *The Entertainer.* (iv) BACH: *Violin concerto No. 2 in E, BWV 1042.* PAGANINI: *Caprices, Op. 1/9 and 24.*
(B) *** CfP CFP 41 4492-1/*4*.

A self-recommending issue, and a real bargain for those who enjoy this kind of collection. The Sarasate and Bach concertante pieces have already received high praise (above) in their original full-priced formats. The encores are hardly less agreeable, with the account of Scott Joplin's *Entertainer*, in which Perlman is partnered by André Previn, particularly enticing. The two solo *Caprices* of Paganini are dazzling: No. 24 is the source of many famous sets of variations, including those by Brahms, Rachmaninov and Lloyd Webber. The sound is excellent, although the tape is softer-grained in the upper range.

Petri, Michala (recorder), **ASMF**

Recorder concertos (directed I. Brown): VIVALDI: *Sopranino recorder concerto in C, RV* 443. SAMMARTINI: *Descant recorder concerto in F.* TELEMANN: *Treble recorder concerto in C.* HANDEL: *Treble recorder concerto in F* (arr. of *Organ concerto, Op. 4/5*).
*** Ph. **400 075-2**; 9500 714/*7300 808* [id.].

Michala Petri plays her various recorders with enviable skill, and her nimble piping creates some delightful sounds in these four attractively inventive concertos. This is not a record to be played all at once; taken in sections, it has unfailing charm; the sound is of demonstration quality on disc and cassette alike. The CD retains the analogue ambient warmth, while detail seems marginally cleaner. While the upper range is not quite as open as on recordings with digital source, the quality remains very impressive.

'English concertos' (directed K. Sillito): BABEL: *Concerto in C for descant recorder, Op. 3/1.* HANDEL: *Concerto in B flat for treble recorder and bassoon, Op. 4/6* (with G. Sheene). BASTON: *Concerto No. 2 for descant recorder in D.* JACOB: *Suite for treble recorder and strings.*
❀ ☾ *** Ph. Dig. **411 056-2**; 6514/*7337* 310 [id.].

The *Concerto* by William Babel (*c.* 1690–1723) is a delight, with Petri's sparkling performance of the outer movements full of good humour and high spirits, matched by Kenneth Sillito's alert accompaniments. The Handel is yet another arrangement of Op. 4/6, with the organ part felicitously re-scored for recorder and bassoon. The two instruments are nicely balanced and thus a familiar work is given an attractive new look. Not a great deal is known about John Baston, except that he lived in eighteenth-century London. But his *Concerto* has individuality, its *Adagio* has distinct charm, and the finale is quirkily infectious. Gordon Jacob's *Suite* of seven movements balances a gentle bitter-sweet melancholy in the lyrical writing with a rumbustious extrovert quality in the dances. Altogether a highly rewarding concert, beautifully played and recorded. The chrome tape is in the demonstration class, as of course is the compact disc. On CD, the quality of the string timbre in the Gordon Jacob *Suite* is especially real and beautiful.

Recorder concertos (directed K. Sillito): VIVALDI: *Concerto in C, RV 44.* MARCELLO: *Concerto in D min.* TELEMANN: *Concerto in F.* NAUDOT: *Concerto in G.*
(*) Ph. **412 630-2; 412 630-1/*4* [id.].

The Vivaldi *Concerto* is the most familiar work for sopranino recorder and has been frequently recorded, though never more winningly than here. The Marcello is better known in its original format for oboe; Michala Petri plays it convincingly on the descant recorder and makes it her own. The Telemann is also a good piece, but the Naudot is rather less memorable. Admirers of this fine artist will be glad to have this new collection, notable for splendid accompaniments, with slow movements particularly attractive in their expressive warmth, without being romanticized. Overall, however, this is a less memorable programme than the collection listed above. The recording is excellent, with the compact disc adding marginally to the clarity of detail within a pleasing ambience. There is a very good tape.

Polish Chamber Orchestra, Maksymiuk

Christmas concertos: CORELLI: *Concerto grosso in G min., Op. 6/8.* MANFREDINI: *Concerto grosso (per il santissimo natale) in C, Op. 3/12.* TORELLI: *Concerto a quattro (in forma di pastorale) in G min., Op. 8/6.* LOCATELLI: *Concerto grosso in F min., Op. 1/8.*
(M) *(*) HMV Dig. ED 270022-1/*4*.

Although Jerzy Maksymiuk gets excellent playing from the Polish Chamber Orchestra in this anthology of popular Christmas concertos, pleasure is not unalloyed. As is often the case with this conductor, faster movements are a shade overdriven and breathless. Highly contrasted dynamics also draw attention to themselves and seem pasted on, rather than emerging naturally from the music making. While there is no doubting the expertise and vitality of these players or the excellence of the recording, these performances are short on grace and charm.

'Pomp and circumstance'

English music (with (i) Royal Liverpool PO, Groves; (ii) King's College Ch., Camb., University Music Soc., New Philh. O, Ledger): (i) ELGAR: *Pomp and Circumstance marches Nos 1 and 4. Imperial march. Coronation march. Enigma variations: Nimrod.* (ii) *Land of Hope and Glory.* (i) ARNE: *Rule, Britannia* (with Anne Collins, Liverpool PO Ch.). *The British Grenadiers.* WALTON: *Spitfire prelude and fugue. Orb and Sceptre. Crown Imperial.* COATES: *Dambusters march.* (ii) PARRY: *I was glad.* (i) WALFORD DAVIES: *RAF March past.*
(B) ** EMI *TC2-MOM 105.*

Such an unrelenting stream of musical patriotism is more suitable for keeping up the spirits on the motorway than for a continuous domestic concert, although Sir Charles Groves's sturdy performances never lack character. The transfer is not too well calculated and the high level brings patches of roughness, notably at the opening of the *Spitfire prelude*, and occasionally in the choral music. This is barely noticeable in the car.

Famous marches (LPO, Solti or Weller; Chicago SO or LSO, Bonynge; VPO, Dohnányi; Nat. PO or Detroit SO, Dorati; Montreal SO, Dutoit): ELGAR: *Pomp and circumstance marches 1 and 4.* Marches from: PROKOFIEV: *Love of three oranges.* BERLIOZ: *Symphonie fantastique; Damnation de Faust.* MEYERBEER: *Le Prophète.* MENDELSSOHN: *Athalia.* TCHAIKOVSKY: *Nutcracker suite. Marche slave.* RESPIGHI: *Pines of Rome.*
** Decca **411 954-2**.

A wide variety of sources here; although all the recordings are analogue, the digital remastering consistently produces spectacular sound: in Solti's Elgar one can feel the bite of bow on string. There is never a dull moment, but the consistent energy and brilliance becomes wearing and this is best taken in small doses.

Ragossnig, Konrad (lute), **Ulsamer Collegium, Ulsamer**

'Terpsichore': Renaissance dance music by: ATTAINGNANT; DALZA; PETRUCCI; NEUSIDLER; SUSATO; GERVAISE; PHALESE. *Early Baroque dance music by:* MAINERIO; RESARD; MOLINARO; DA VENOSA; CAROSO; CAROUBEL; HOLBOURNE; DOWLAND; SIMPSON; GIBBONS; PRAETORIUS; HAUSSMANN.
*** DG Arc. **415 294-2** [id.].

There are in all 43 items on this compact disc which collects material from the recordings made by this ensemble, issued on two LPs in 1971 and 1972. Although on the face of it this music is of specialist interest, it is in fact highly attractive and could (and should) enjoy wide appeal. The performances are crisp and vital, and the DG engineers have made a first-class job of the digital remastering. Readers who recall the originals will not hesitate, and newcomers will find it full of delights.

'Romance'

Music for violin and orchestra (with: (i) Grumiaux; (ii) Accardo; (iii) Szeryng; (iv) Kremer (various orchestras and conductors): (i) BEETHOVEN: *Romances Nos 1 in G, Op. 40; 2 in F, Op. 50.* SAINT-SAËNS: *Havanaise, Op. 83; Introduction and*

Rondo capriccioso, Op. 28. WIENIAWSKI: *Légende, Op. 17.* SVENDSEN: *Romance in G, Op. 26.* (ii) TCHAIKOVSKY: *Sérénade mélancolique, Op. 26; Valse-Scherzo, Op. 34.* (iii) RAVEL: *Tzigane.* (iv) CHAUSSON: *Poème, Op. 25.*
(B) *** Ph. On Tour *412 911-4* [id.].

This is an outstanding anthology of its kind and is recommended to all tape collectors. The offering is generous, the programme is well laid out and the performances are splendid, as is the sound. There is plenty of attractive music here, much of it lightweight but none of it trivial, and these are some of the finest versions available.

(The) Romeros

'Guitar Festival' (with Angel, Celedonio, Pepe and Celin Romero; (i) San Antonio SO, Alessandro; (ii) Corigliano, Saltarelli, Bella): (i) VIVALDI: *Quadruple guitar concerto in B min. (from Op. 3/10); Guitar concerto in C, RV 425; Double guitar concerto in G. RV 532*; (ii) *Sonata in A for guitar, violin, viola and cello, RV 82.* TELEMANN: *Concerto in D for 4 guitars.* SCARLATTI, D.: *Sonata in D, Kk, 391.* BACH: *Prelude in D min., BWV 99. Flamenco music* (suite).
(B) ** Ph. On Tour *416 232-4.*

The Romero family are all fine players; the Vivaldi performances are good, if not distinctive. In spite of a high level of transfer, the warm acoustic does not provide a very sharp focus for the solo instruments, and the result is at times rather bland. The *Quadruple concerto* was written for four violins, and the composer had mandolins in mind for the other two. The rest of the programme is pleasant enough, but the resonance remains. The whole of the second side is given over to a selection of Flamenco music, played with considerable flair by Pepe Romero; here, the guitar image is much more firmly focused.

Royal Philharmonic Orchestra or (i) French National Radio Orchestra, Beecham

'Popular French repertoire': CHABRIER: *Marche joyeuse.* DEBUSSY: *L'enfant prodigue: Cortège et Air de danse. Prélude à l'après-midi d'un faune.* SAINT-SAËNS: *Samson et Dalila: Danse des prêtresses de Dagon; Bacchanale. Le rouet d'Omphale, Op. 31.* GOUNOD: *Roméo et Juliette: Le sommeil de Juliette.* (i) FAURÉ: *Dolly suite, Op. 56; Pavane, Op. 50.*
❀ (M) *** EMI EMX 41 2077-1/4.

This is an enchanting record, full of the imaginative and poetic phrasing that distinguishes the best Beecham performances. The delicacy of the wind playing (notably the flute) in *Le rouet d'Omphale* and Debussy's *Cortège et Air de danse* is exquisite, but this is only one of many delights to be found here. Both the

Saint-Saëns *Bacchanale* and the *Marche joyeuse* of Chabrier have wonderful dash and flair, and one can visualize the twinkle in Sir Thomas's eye. After Delius, this is repertoire which showed him at his very finest. The recording is always good and sometimes excellent. The cassette is first class in every way, quite the equal of the LP; but this is a prime candidate for compact disc issue.

Russian orchestral music

'1812 overture and other Russian pops' (with (i) Bournemouth SO; (ii) LPO; (iii) RPO; (iv) Philh. O; (v) Silvestri; (vi) Boult; (vii) Sargent): (i; v) TCHAIKOVSKY: *Overture 1812. Capriccio italien.* (iii; vii) *Marche slave.* (i; v) BORODIN: *In the Steppes of Central Asia.* (ii; vi) RIMSKY-KORSAKOV: *Mlada: Procession of the nobles. Capriccio espagnol.* (i; v) MUSSORGSKY (arr. Rimsky-Korsakov): *Night on the Bare Mountain.* (iv; v) GLINKA: *Overture: Russlan and Ludmilla.*
(B) ** EMI *TC2-MOM 107.*

Levels have been successfully manipulated here to avoid coarseness without too much loss of dynamic range, and even at the end of *1812* (with cannon) the sound does not disintegrate as it often does in cassette versions of this piece. Silvestri's performances are good but neither especially individual nor exciting.

St Louis Symphony Orchestra, Slatkin

VAUGHAN WILLIAMS: *Fantasia on a theme of Thomas Tallis.* BARBER: *Adagio for strings.* GRAINGER: *Irish tune from County Derry.* FAURÉ: *Pavane, Op. 50.* SATIE: *Gymnopédies Nos 1 and 3.*
** Telarc Dig. **CD 80059**; DG 10059 [id.].

This was the digital début of both Vaughan Williams's *Tallis fantasia* and the Barber *Adagio.* Both are given spacious performances and are well structured with strong central climaxes, although there are more distinctive accounts available of both works. The recording too is both rich and clear. The rest of the programme is beautifully played but, with Slatkin favouring slow tempi, the overall effect is a little lacking in vitality; this applies especially to the *Londonderry air.* The sound on CD is much the same as the LP, but with the added gain of background silence, which is especially telling in the Vaughan Williams and the Barber.

Russian music: TCHAIKOVSKY: *Marche Slave, Op. 31.* RIMSKY-KORSAKOV: *Russian Easter festival overture, Op. 36.* GLINKA: *Russlan and Ludmilla overture.* BORODIN: *In the Steppes of central Asia.*
*(*) Telarc Dig. **CD 80072**; DG 10072 [id.].

These are effective but in no way memorable performances; while the Telarc sound has plenty of lustre, it is lacking in glitter for such a vividly volatile programme. In playing time, this is distinctly ungenerous.

PACHELBEL: *Canon.* BORODIN: *Nocturne for strings* (arr. Sargent). VAUGHAN WILLIAMS: *Fantasia on Greensleeves.* TCHAIKOVSKY: *Serenade for strings in C, Op. 48.*
(*) Telarc **CD 80080; DG 10080 [id.].

A winning account of Tchaikovsky's *Serenade* from Slatkin, essentially sunny, with the *Elégie* warmly controlled, the histrionics not emphasized. The finale is nicely prepared; if it lacks the last degree of incandescent energy, its good-humoured mood fits in with the overall conception, as does the genially elegant account of the Waltz. The Borodin *Nocturne* is volatile, with accelerando treatment of the middle section to point the contrast. *Greensleeves* is slow and stately, in the American manner, endearingly respectful in its spaciousness. There are two climaxes in Pachelbel's *Canon*, which some may feel is one too many – but better this than the unimaginative approach of some German performances. All in all, a successful concert, given a rich, naturally balanced concert-hall sound-balance, slightly recessed, with inner detail less than ideally sharp.

Savijoki, Pekka (saxophone), **New Stockholm Chamber Orchestra, Panula**

LARSSON: *Concerto for saxophone and string orchestra, Op. 14.* GLAZOUNOV: *Concerto in E flat, Op. 109.* PANULA: *Adagio and allegro for string orchestra.*
*** **BIS CD 218**; LP 218 [id.].

The find here for most collectors outside Scandinavia will be Lars-Erik Larsson's *Saxophone concerto*, written in the 1930s for Sigurd Rascher (and indeed recorded by him in the days of 78s, but neglected since). It is a very fine and inventive work; the slow movement with its beautiful canonic opening is of particular distinction. The Glazunov, written at the same time, is more original and imaginative than it first appears. Accomplished performances and good recording.

Scottish Chamber Orchestra, Laredo

'String masterpieces': ALBINONI: *Adagio in G min.* (arr. Giazotto). HANDEL: *Berenice: Overture. Solomon: Arrival of the Queen of Sheba.* BACH: *Suite No. 3, BWV 1068: Air. Violin concerto No. 1 in A min., BWV 1041: Finale.*

PACHELBEL: *Canon.* PURCELL: *Abdelazer: Rondo. Chacony in G min.*
(M) *** Pickwick Dig. **PCD 802**; Con. Dig. CC/*CCT* 7597.

An excellent issue. The playing is alive, alert, stylish and committed without being overly expressive, yet the Bach *Air* has warmth and Pachelbel's *Canon* is fresh and unconventional in approach. The sound is first class, especially spacious and convincing on CD, and with little to choose between disc and cassette, the former very slightly brighter, but both well detailed without any clinical feeling. The Purcell *Rondo* is the tune made familiar by Britten's orchestral guide; the *Chaconne* is played with telling simplicity.

Scottish National Orchestra, Gibson

'Land of the mountain and the flood': MENDELSSOHN: *The Hebrides overture (Fingal's Cave], Op. 26.* BERLIOZ: *Waverley overture, Op. 2.* ARNOLD: *Tam O'Shanter overture.* VERDI: *Macbeth: Ballet music.* MACCUNN: *Overture: Land of the Mountain and the Flood.*
ꞓ **(*) Dig. **CHAN 8379**; ABRD/*ABTD* 1032.

The MacCunn overture, made popular by a television programme (*Sutherland's Law*), here provides an attractive foil for the Scottish National Orchestra's collection of short pieces inspired by Scotland. These performances are not as refined as the best available versions – significantly, the most dashing performance is of Arnold's difficult and rumbustious overture – but make an attractive recital. On CD, the spectacularly vivid orchestration of *Tam O'Shanter* produces sound that is in the demonstration bracket; and the MacCunn piece is pretty impressive, too. The Berlioz is vivid, and Gibson's approach to *Fingal's Cave* attractively romantic. The cassette transfer is of good quality, but the comparatively unadventurous level brings a less sparkling upper range than the LP.

'Serenade for strings'

Serenades (with (i) Philh. O, Colin Davis; (ii) LSO, Barbirolli; (iii) Northern Sinfonia, Tortelier; (iv) RPO, Sargent; (v) E. Sinfonia, Dilkes; (vi) Bournemouth Sinf., Montgomery; (vii) LPO, Boult): (i) MOZART: *Serenade No. 13 in G (Eine kleine Nachtmusik), K.525.* (ii) TCHAIKOVSKY: *String serenade, Op. 48: Waltz.* (iii) GRIEG: *Holberg suite, Op. 40. Elegiac melody: Heart's wounds, Op. 34/1.* (iv) DVOŘÁK: *String serenade, Op. 22:* 1st and 2nd movts. (v) WARLOCK: *Capriol suite.* (vi) WIRÉN: *String serenade, Op. 11: March.* (vii) ELGAR: *Introduction and allegro for strings, Op. 47.*
(B) *** EMI *TC2-MOM 108.*

This was the finest of EMI's first release of 'Miles of Music' tapes with an attractive programme, good (and sometimes distinguished) performances and consistent sound quality, slightly restricted in the upper range, but warm, full and clear. Tortelier's Grieg and Boult's complete version of Elgar's *Introduction and allegro* are obvious highlights, and this certainly makes an attractive background for a car journey, yet can be enjoyed at home too.

'Showpieces for orchestra'

(i) LPO, Boult; (ii) RPO; (iii) Sargent; (iv) Colin Davis; (v) CBSO, Frémaux; (vi) Bournemouth SO; (vii) Silvestri; (viii) Berglund: (i) BRAHMS: *Academic Festival overture*. (ii; iii) SMETANA: *Má Vlast: Vltava*. MENDELSSOHN: *The Hebrides overture*. WAGNER: *Die Meistersinger overture*. (ii; iv) ROSSINI: *William Tell overture*. (V) DEBUSSY: *Prélude à l'après-midi d'un faune*. CHABRIER: *España*. BERLIOZ: *Le Carnaval romain overture*. (vi; vii) SAINT-SAËNS: *Danse macabre*. (vi, viii) GRIEG: *Peer Gynt suite No. 1: Morning; In the hall of the Mountain King*.
(B) *(*) EMI *TC2-MOM 109*.

These are all acceptable performances, but the recording, though full, is somewhat lacking in sparkle, and overall this seems an arbitrary collection that does not add up to a satisfying whole. Sargent's *Marche slave* has a lively impetus, and Boult's versions of the Rimsky-Korsakov *Capriccio* and *Procession* show plenty of character, even if there is some lack of exuberance in the closing pages of the *Capriccio*. The richly resonant recording here is well contained in this transfer. Silvestri's account of Tchaikovsky's *Capriccio italien* has a curiously clumsy quickening of tempo in the coda.

Smith, Daniel (bassoon), **English Chamber Orchestra, Ledger**

Three Bassoon concertos: VIVALDI: *Concerto in C. RV 472*. BACH, J. C.: *Concerto in B flat*. GRAUPNER: *Concerto in G*.
*** ASV Dig. DCA/*ZCDCA* 545 [id.].

Anyone thinking that a combination of three bassoon concertos might be a shade dull will be pleasantly surprised by this entertaining ASV collection. Daniel Smith is principal with the New York Virtuosi Chamber Symphony and a well-known orchestra player on the East Coast of the USA. He is also a first-class concerto soloist with a strong musical personality, an enviable technical command and a mastery of colour and mood. The J. C. Bach *Concerto* is the most substantial piece here, but the work by Christopher Graupner (1683–1760) springs readily to life when played so winningly. With alert, responsive accompaniments from the ECO under Philip Ledger and vivid sound on both LP and the excellent tape, (although the soloist is balanced perhaps a shade too forwardly), this can be strongly recommended.

Steele-Perkins, Crispian (trumpet)

Six trumpet concertos (with ECO, Halstead): HAYDN: *Concerto in E flat.* TORELLI: *Concerto in D.* HAYDN, M.: *Concerto No. 2 in C.* TELEMANN: *Concerto for trumpet and 2 oboes in D* (with N. Black and J. Brown). NERUDA: *Concerto in E flat.* HUMPHRIES: *Concerto in D, Op. 2/12.*
(M) ** Pickwick Dig. **PCD 821**.

The highlight of this collection is the Telemann *Triple concerto* which features a pair of oboes alongside the solo trumpet. In the engaging central movement (*Grave–Aria–Grave*) the trumpet is silent and the atmospheric resonance brings an element of fantasy to the texture of the two wind instruments plus a distant continuo. Elsewhere, the very reverberant acoustic clouds orchestral detail. The trumpet, placed forward, has plenty of presence, but the solo part at times masks what is going on in the background. The lack of a sharply focused orchestral presence is not helpful in the opening movement of the Haydn *Concerto*, and there is an element of heaviness in the accompaniment, while the *Andante* too is very measured. The works by Michael Haydn and Telemann are more successful, but neither the Neruda nor the piece by John Humphries is really memorable, although the latter is given a fine, crisp performance by Steele-Perkins.

Stern, Isaac (violin)

'Sixtieth anniversary celebration' (with Perlman, Zukerman, NYPO, Mehta): BACH: *Double violin concerto in D min., BWV 1043.* MOZART: *Sinfonia concertante in E flat, K.364.* VIVALDI: *Triple violin concerto in F, RV 551.*
(*) CBS Dig. **CD 36692; 36692/*41*- [Col. IM 36692/*MT 37244*].

At a time when the pursuit of authenticity has accustomed us to pinched sound in Bach and Vivaldi it is good to have such rich performances as these, recorded live at Stern's sixtieth-birthday concert in the autumn of 1980. Stern nobly cedes first place to Perlman in the Bach *Double concerto*, and in the Vivaldi he plays third violin, though there he has the bonus of playing the melody in the lovely slow movement. With Zukerman on the viola this account of the *Sinfonia concertante* is even more alive than the studio recording made ten years earlier by the same artists, heartfelt and beautifully sprung. The recording is a little thin, but digitally clear. Mehta and the New York orchestra are not ideal in this music, but the flavour of the live occasion is most compelling. The chrome cassette is extremely lively, matching the disc with its close balance and larger-than-life solo images although it does not lack fullness.

Stockholm Sinfonietta, Salonen

'A Swedish serenade'. WIRÉN: *Serenade for strings, Op. 11.* LARSSON: *Little serenade for strings, Op. 12.* SÖDERLUNDH: *Oboe concertino* (with Alf Nilsson, oboe). LIDHOLM: *Music for strings.*
Ⓒ *** BIS Dig. **CD 285**; LP 285 [id.].

The most familiar piece here is the Dag Wirén *Serenade for strings*, which is well represented on LP but not so well on CD. Lille Bror Söderlundh will be a new name to collectors. He began his career in the world of light music, and it was some time before he gained acceptance (albeit limited) as a more serious composer in the 1950s. The *Concertino for oboe and orchestra* comes from 1944, when he was in his early thirties: he died just over a decade later in 1957. By far the best movement is the lovely *Andante*, whose melancholy is winning and has a distinctly Gallic feel to it. By contrast, the finale is rather thin and naïve, but the piece is still worth hearing and is certainly played with splendid artistry by Alf Nilsson and the Stockholm Sinfonietta, one of the best small chamber orchestras in the Nordic countries. The Lidholm piece, the *Music for strings* (from 1952) is somewhat grey and anonymous though it is expertly wrought. It reveals a greater debt to Bartók than is desirable. Esa-Pekka Salonen gets good results from this ensemble and the recording lives up to the high standards of the BIS label, with the CD enjoying an impressive immediacy and presence. It is forwardly balanced but has splendid body and realism.

Stuttgart Chamber Orchestra, Münchinger

Baroque music: PACHELBEL: *Canon.* GLUCK: *Orfeo: Dance of the Blessed Spirits.* HANDEL: *Water music: suite No. 3; Organ concerto in F* (*Cuckoo and the nightingale*; with Martin Haselböck). MOZART, L.: *Toy Symphony.* ALBINONI: *Adagio in G min.* (arr. Giazotto). BACH: *Suite No. 3, BMV 1068: Air.* BOCCHERINI: *Minuet* (from *String quintet in E. Op. 13/5*).
Ⓒ **(*) Decca Dig. **411 973-2**; 411 973-1/*4* [id.].

Beautifully recorded – the CD is particularly fine – this is an attractive concert with a very well played suite from Handel's *Water music*, and the engaging *Cuckoo and the nightingale Organ concerto* (with Martin Haselböck an excellent soloist) to give a little ballast. The performance of Pachelbel's *Canon* is a little heavy-handed, but the strongly expressive account of Albinoni's *Adagio* is convincing. The *Toy symphony* has some piquant special effects, and the shorter lollipops are quite elegantly played. The overall mood is a trifle serious, but that is Münchinger's way. The cassette is transferred at a high level and the upper range is less smooth than the disc versions; although the sound is vivid, the violins are slightly fierce above the stave.

Thompson, Michael (horn)

'The golden echo' (with (i) Richard Watkins; Philh. O, Warren-Green): VIVALDI: (i) *Double concerto in F, RV 539.* ROSETTI: *Horn concerto in D min.* MOZART: L.: *Horn concerto in D.* HAYDN (attrib): (i) *Double concerto in E flat.*
*(**) Nimbus Dig. **NIM 5018** [id.].

Like the companion Nimbus trumpet anthology, this was recorded in the very resonant acoustic of All Saints, Tooting; while the warmly reverberant acoustic lends a romantic aura to the horn timbre, it muddles detail in the orchestra and also tends to cause blurring of the solo lines in the double concertos. Michael Thompson is a superb soloist – he surmounts the high tessitura of the Leopold Mozart *Concerto* with thrilling ease, and when he is joined by Richard Watkins the interplay is infectious. The attributed Haydn work is most attractive, whoever wrote it (both Rosetti and Michael Haydn have been suggested), especially the gay finale. The collection runs for about an hour (including pauses).

Touvron, Guy and **Bernard Soustrot** (trumpets)

Trumpet concertos (with Lucerne Festival Strings, Baumgartner): HAYDN: *Concerto in E flat.* MANFREDINI: *Double concerto in D.* HAYDN, M.: *Concerto in C.* ALBINONI: *Concerto a cinque, Op. 9/9.*
(*) Denon Dig. **C37 7544 [id.].

A generally attractive collection, recorded in Zurich. Both soloists are French, and the style of their playing is admirable in all respects, with no intrusive vibrato. Guy Touvron's account of Joseph Haydn's famous concerto is fresh, lightly articulated and pleasingly stylish. Bravura is always at the service of the music, the nicely paced *Andante* has a hint of melancholy and the finale is contrastingly gay. The Manfredini is a more conventional piece but, like Michael Haydn's two-movement work, also has a memorable finale, despatched with easy flair by Soustrot. Albinoni's *Concerto a cinque* was intended for a pair of solo violins, but the trumpeters make it seem otherwise and the overlapping imitation of the *Adagio* and finale is particularly effective. The Denon recording is well balanced and orchestral detail is good (although the harpsichord is almost inaudible), while the soloists are given a fine presence against a suitably resonant acoustic.

Vienna Philharmonic Orchestra, Maazel

'New Year's concert' (1980): STRAUSS, J., Jnr: *Die Fledermaus: overture; Czárdás. Neue Pizzicato polka. Perpetuum mobile. Wiener Blut. Banditen Galop. Rettungs-Jubel march. Fata Morgana polka. An der schönen blauen Donau.* STRAUSS, Josef: *Eingesendet polka.* OFFENBACH: *Orpheus in the Underworld: overture.* ZIEHRER: *Loslassen.* STRAUSS, J., Snr: *Radetzky march.*
** DG Dig. **400 040-2**; 2532/*3302* 002 [id.].

This record of the 1980 Viennese New Year Concert is generously full, with applause faded quickly between items. The famous *Radetzky march* sets the pattern for the concert: the performance is crisply brilliant, with well-disciplined hand-claps from the audience. Maazel is at his best in the *Rettungs-Jubel march*, written for the Kaiser, which is infectiously volatile. The performance of *The Blue Danube* departs from the sharply rhythmic manner and is unashamedly indulgent. But charm is not a strong point here, and the brightly lit recording underlines the vigour of the playing. The sound has striking presence and detail, but the ambience is a little dry; ideally, one would like a little more resonant glow, such as the Decca engineers found for Boskovsky in this repertoire.

Vienna Volksoper Orchestra, Bauer-Theussl

'Famous waltzes': WEBER: *Invitation to the dance, Op. 65* (arr. Berlioz). LANNER: *Die Schönbrunner.* IVANOVICI: *Donauwellen* (*Waves of the Danube*). KOMZAK: *Bad'ner Mad'ln.* STRAUSS, Josef: *Dynamiden.* ZIEHRER: *Herreinspaziert* (arr. Schönnherr).
(*) Ph. Dig. **400 013-2; 6514/*7337* 067 [id.].

The first of two collections, this record admirably gathers together some waltzes from contemporaries of the Johann Strauss family. Each has a striking main theme and the performances, if sometimes lacking the last degree of vitality, have an agreeable warmth. Franz Bauer-Theussl's rubato is not always subtle but is often effective in its way. He is good with the atmospheric openings – indeed, he shapes the main theme of Ivanovici's *Donauwellen* (*Danube waves*) very persuasively. *Invitation to the dance* lacks the last degree of characterization although, like the rest of the programme, it is well played. The resonant acoustic is effective and the digital recording ensures good detail, although the CD adds comparatively little to the LP quality, apart from the silent background. The chrome tape is pleasing, if a little lacking in sparkle.

'Famous waltzes', Vol. 2: ZIEHRER: *Faschingskinder; Wiener Burger.* LEHÁR: *Gold and silver; Ballsirenen.* ROSAS: *Uber den Wellen.* LANNER: *Hofballtänze; Der Romantiker.*
(*) Ph. Dig. **412 883-2; 6514/*7337* 068 [id.].

There is some worthwhile repertoire in Volume 2, and Franz Bauer-Theussl and his excellent Vienna Volksoper Orchestra are warmly sympathetic. The rhythmic emphasis is perhaps a little stylized, but there is an engaging geniality of spirit and the phrasing of the lyrical melodies (and there are some memorable ones) is both polished and nicely timed. The recording is within an attractively resonant acoustic and the excellent digital recording provides good detail, with LP and CD sounding very similar. This should bring a ready response from listeners familiar with the music of the Strauss family wanting to do a little exploring in the Viennese hinterland. Ziehrer and Lanner were accomplished tune-masters, and the Lehár waltzes are first rate. The chrome tape has only marginally less upper range and, like the discs, offers quality of considerable richness and lustre.

'Violin favourites'

(i) Hoelscher, Mun. RO, Wallberg; (ii) Menuhin, Philh. O; (iii) Pritchard; (iv) Goossens; (v) Haendel, Parsons; (vi) Ferras, Barbizet: (i) SARASATE: *Carmen fantasy. Zigeunerweisen.* (ii; iii) BEETHOVEN: *Romances Nos 1 and 2.* (ii; iv) SAINT-SAËNS: *Introduction and rondo capriccioso. Havanaise.* (v) MENDELSSOHN: *On Wings of Song.* SARASATE: *Habañera.* SCHUBERT: *Ave Maria.* (vi) RAVEL: *Tzigane.*
(B) **(*) EMI *TC2-MOM 118.*

A reasonably attractive collection, not as enticing as some in this 'Miles of Music' series, but well recorded throughout. The highlights are Menuhin's superb Saint-Saëns performances and the more lushly recorded Sarasate, played with panache by Ulf Hoelscher. Ida Haendel is in excellent form in her transcriptions, and Ferras gives an impressive account of Ravel's *Tzigane* (in the version for violin and piano).

Wallace, John (trumpet)

'Man – the measure of all things' (with Philh. O, Warren-Green): MONTEVERDI: *Orfeo: Toccata.* TORELLI: *Sinfonia a 4 in C.* ALBINONI: *2 Concerti a 6 in C; Sonata di concerto a 7 in D.* VIVALDI: *Double concerto in C.* FRANCHESCINI: *Sonata in D.* PURCELL: *Sonata in D.* BONONCINI: *Sinfonia decima a 7.* ALBERTI: *Sinfonia teatrale a 4.*
(*) Nimbus Dig. **NIM 5017 [id.].

The title of this collection aims to epitomize the spirit of the Italian Renaissance, which produced a great flowering of the arts. The collection covers a period of nearly two centuries of trumpet music. The total playing time (at nearly 67′) almost defeats its own object of showing the diversity of baroque style, for during this period trumpet devices did not change very much. The music explores all the possibilities of one, two and four trumpets, and the ear finds welcome relief in Albinoni's *Concerto a 6* for trumpet, oboes and bassoon. John Wallace is a splendid soloist; in the multiple works he is joined by John Miller, David Mason and William Stokes, who play with comparable bravura. The recording was made in the resonant acoustics of All Saints, Tooting, which tend to blur the opening Monteverdi *Toccata* and the following Torelli *Sinfonia*, which features all four soloists. On another occasion, in an Albinoni *Grave*, the harpsichordist is left sounding lonely in the distance, against reiterated string chords. But for the most part the reverberation colours the music attractively.

Waltzes

'Famous Waltzes' (played by: (i) VPO, Boskovsky; (ii) Nat. PO, Bonynge; (iii) ASMF, Marriner; (iv) Nat. PO, Gamley; (v) Paris Conservatoire O, Maag; (vi) LSO, Bonynge: (vii) VPO, Maazel): (i) STRAUSS, J. Jnr: *An der schönen blauen Donau; Accelerationen; Wein, Weib und Gesang.* LEHÁR: *Gold and silver.* (ii) TCHAIKOVSKY: *Sleeping Beauty: Waltz. Nutcracker: Waltz of the flowers. Swan Lake: Waltz.* (iii) *String serenade: Waltz.* (iv) WALDTEUFEL: *The Skaters; España.* (v) CHOPIN: *Les Sylphides: Grande valse brillante.* (vi) OFFENBACH: *Le Papillon: Valse des rayons.* (vii) STRAUSS, R.: *Der Rosenkavalier: 1st Waltz sequence.*
(B) ** Decca *410 292-4.*

An attractive double-length tape compilation, with generally distinguished performances, notably those from Boskovsky (*Gold and silver* as attractive as the Johann Strauss items), Marriner and Gamley. The very high level of the transfer, however, robs the sound of complete refinement at times, with the resonance sometimes clouding the bass at fortissimo levels. However, this sounds well enough on a smaller player or in the car.

Wickens, Derek (oboe)

'The classical oboe' (with RPO, Howarth): VIVALDI: *Oboe concerto in A min., RV 461.* MARCELLO, A.: *Oboe concerto in D min.* HAYDN: *Oboe concerto in C.*
*** ASV **CDDCA 1003**; ACA/*ZCACA* 1003 [id.].

The Haydn concerto may be spurious, but it makes an attractive item in this collection, and the Vivaldi, a lively, compact piece, and the Marcello (by Alessandro, not his more famous brother Benedetto), with its lovely slow movement, make up a good mixture. During his years with the RPO, Wickens repeatedly demonstrated in yearningly beautiful solos that he was one of the most characterful of London's orchestral players. Though at times he seems to be looking for his back desk rather than his solo spot, his artistry comes out vividly on this well-recorded disc, with the CD providing believable projection for the oboe against Howarth's sympathetic accompaniments. The tape too is outstandingly vivid, to match the LP closely.

Zukerman, Pinchas (violin)

'Three Favourite Violin concertos' (with (i) LAPO, Mehta; (ii) NYPO, Bernstein; (iii) LSO, Dorati): (i) BRUCH: *Concerto No. 1 in G min., Op. 26.* (ii) MENDELSSOHN: *Concerto in E min., Op. 26.* (ii) TCHAIKOVSKY: *Concerto in D, Op. 35.*
(B) **(*) CBS *MGT 39016.*

Zukerman has re-recorded both the Mendelssohn and Tchaikovsky concertos (for Philips and CBS respectively – see above), but his earlier 1960s versions were very successful and now, coupled with the Bruch on an extended-length tape, they make a real bargain. The account of the Bruch is passionately extrovert, tempered by a genuine tenderness in the slow movement. The bright recording increases the sense of fiery energy in the outer sections, and the excitement of the solo playing and strongly committed accompaniment combine to make this very involving. In the Mendelssohn, Zukerman gives a sweet-toned but never cloying reading. His playing is impeccable from the technical point of view and the support he receives from Bernstein and the New York orchestra is thoroughly sympathetic. The Tchaikovsky is comparably fine, and again his tone is clean and sweet. The sound balance is less than ideal, but there is no lack of vividness, and the tape transfer is well managed.

Concertos (with (i) RPO, Foster: (ii) Sillito, Garcia, Tunnell, ECO): BLOCH: *Baal Sheem: No. 2, Nigun.* KABALEVSKY: *Violin concerto, Op. 48.* WIENIAWSKI: *Violin concerto No. 2, Op. 22.* (ii) VIVALDI: *Double violin concertos: in A min., RV 522; in D min., RV 565; Triple violin concerto in F, RV 551. Quadruple violin concerto in B min., Op. 3/10.*
(B) **(*) CBS DC 40158 (2).

This pair of LPs, offered together at bargain price, admirably demonstrates the breadth of Zukerman's range. The Vivaldi collection was originally issued in quadraphonic form, with the soloists very forward; the normal analogue version, though providing good sound, is unable to give a natural relationship between soloists and orchestra because of this artificial balance. However, the ear adjusts, and all these multiple concertos are stylishly performed, with fine contributions from Philip Ledger as continuo player – what you can hear of him. The improvisatory second movement of Bloch's *Baal Shem suite*, with its dark colouring and dramatized mood-changes, is well understood by Zukerman who plays with intensity and a fine sense of atmosphere. He projects the gay, extrovert Kabalevsky *Concerto* with panache and is agreeably tender in the fine slow movement. The Wieniawski No. 2 is also first class, with the central *Romance* again given with much warmth. Close-up recording. The equivalent extended-length tape cannot be recommended as it omits the Bloch piece.

Baroque concert (with St Paul CO): VIVALDI: *Violin concerto in E flat* (*La tempesta di mare*), *Op. 8/5*. PURCELL: *Chaconne in G min*. HANDEL: *Concerto grosso, Op. 6/1; Solomon: Arrival of the Queen of Sheba*. PACHELBEL: *Canon and gigue in D*. TELEMANN: *Viola concerto in G*. RAMEAU: *Pieces en clavecin: Tambourin en rondeau*.
** Ph. Dig. **412 215-2**; 412 215-1/*4* [id.].

There is plenty of dash in these performances. The sparkle and vitality of the *Concerto, La tempesta di mare*, are highly attractive, but Handel's *Concerto grosso*, Op. 6, No. 1 is rather hard-driven. In the Telemann *Concerto*, Zukerman takes up the viola and gives a winning performance, producing the richest timbre, so one easily forgives the sound balance being somewhat larger than life. The recording is otherwise excellent throughout, full-bodied and lively, with the CD gaining a little in refinement at both ends of the spectrum. For some reason the final Rameau item is slightly less transparent in texture than the rest of the programme.

Instrumental Recitals

Accardo, Salvatore (violin)

'Famous encores' (with Bruno Canino): RIES: *Perpetuum mobile*. PARADIS: *Sicilienne*. SGAMBATI: *Serenate napoletana*. VIEUXTEMPS: *Romance, Op. 7/2*. GLAZOUNOV: *Méditation, Op. 32*. TCHAIKOVSKY: *Scherzo, Op. 42/2*. WIENIAWSKI: *Souvenir de Moscou*. SCHUBERT: *Die Biene*. FAURÉ: *Après un rêve*. ZARZYCKI: *Mazurka, Op. 26*. PAGANINI: *Cantabile; Moto perpetuo*. ALBÉNIZ: *Chant*. SMETANA: *From my homeland*.
*** HMV Dig. EL 270186-1/*4*.

Salvatore Accardo plays all these pieces with natural flair, easy virtuosity and a musical refinement which never regards the music as merely a vehicle for display. The layout of the programme is designed to afford maximum variety, and although much of the content is slight, nothing is made to sound trivial, while the Glazounov and Tchaikovsky items are particularly appealing. The recording is eminently realistic.

(i) Adni, Daniel; (ii) John Ogdon (piano)

'Piano favourites': (i) CHOPIN: *Revolutionary study in C min. Fantaisie-Impromptu*. (ii) *Waltz No. 6 in D flat* (*Minute*). *Polonaises Nos 3* (*Military*); *6* (*Heroic*). RACHMANINOV: *Prelude in C sharp min*. (i) GRAINGER: *Country Gardens; Handel in the Strand*. DEBUSSY: *Clair de lune*. BRAHMS: *Rhapsoy in G min*. (ii) SINDING: *Rustle of Spring*. LISZT: *Liebestraum No. 3. La Campanella*. BEETHOVEN: *Für Elise*. CHAMINADE: *Autumn*. (i) MENDELSSOHN: *The Bees' Wedding*. SCHUBERT: *Impromptu in A flat. Moment musical in F min*. GRIEG: *To the Spring. Wedding Day at Troldhaugen*.
(B) ** EMI *TC2-MOM 101*.

'More piano favourites': (ii) BACH: *Well-tempered Clavier: Prelude No. 5. Jesu, joy of man's desiring*. MOZART: *Fantasia in D min., K.397*. BEETHOVEN: *Andante favori*. CHOPIN: *Mazurka No. 17 in B flat min*. (i) *Scherzo No. 3 in C sharp min., Op. 39. Waltz No. 1 in E flat, Op. 18. Ballade No. 3 in A flat, Op. 47*. (ii) SCHUMANN: *Nachtstück in F, Op. 23/4*. (i) DEBUSSY: *L'Isle joyeuse. Reflets dans l'eau*. (ii) SCOTT: *Lotus Land*. LISZT: *Hungarian rhapsody No. 15*. GRANADOS: *Goyescas. The Maiden and the nightingale*. ALBÉNIZ: *Tango*. (i) GRIEG: *Lyric pieces: Album leaf; Butterfly; Shepherd's boy*.
(B) **(*) EMI *TC2-MOM 113*.

There are some distinguished performances here. On the first tape, Daniel Adni is heard at his best in the music of Grainger, Schubert and Grieg and John Ogdon is impressive in Liszt; on the second, Adni is on top form in Chopin and Debussy, while Ogdon communicates strongly in Bach and Mozart and again plays Liszt with great flair. The original recordings were of high quality and these tapes sound well in the car, but at home one notices some lack of focus on the first collection, though timbres are full. The second recital is technically more successful. Though the upper range is soft-grained, the quality is pleasing, the piano tone not too dry.

'Piano moods': (i) CHOPIN: *Scherzo No. 2, Op. 32. Waltzes in A flat and A min., Op. 34/1 and 2. Études: in A flat and G flat, Op. 25/1 and 9; in G flat, Op. 10/5.* (ii) *Mazurkas Nos 5 in B flat, Op. 7/1; 23 in D, Op. 33/2.* LISZT: *Paganini study No. 2. Étude de concert No. 3. Valse oubliée No. 1. Mephisto waltz No. 1.* (i) GRIEG: *March of the Dwarfs.* SCHUMANN: *Arabesque, Op. 18.* DEBUSSY: *Poissons d'or. Arabesque No. 1.* MENDELSSOHN: *Songs without words: Venetian gondola song, Op. 62/5; Spring song.* RAVEL: *Alborada del gracioso.*
(B) ** EMI *TC2-MOM 122.*

There is some impressive playing again here, John Ogdon on top form in Liszt, and Daniel Adni poetic and commanding in Chopin and Debussy. But the high-level recording is dry and some of the bloom of the originals is lost.

American Brass Quintet

Renaissance, Elizabethan and Baroque music: SCHEIDT: *Battle suite.* FERRABOSCO: *Almayne; Dovehouse pavane.* MORLEY: *Joyne hands.* HOLBORNE: *Widow's myte; Why are you ladies staying.* WEELKES: *Hark I hear some dancing.* SIMPSON: *Allemande.* DOWLAND: *Volta.* BACH: *Art of fugue: excerpts.* SPEER: *Sonata a 4; Sonata for 2 cornetts and 3 trombones.* STÖRL: *Sonata No. 1.* COPRARIO: *Al primo giorno; Fancie a 5.* GABRIELI, A.: *Ricercar del sesto tono.* GABRIELI, G.: *Canzon per sonare a 5; Canzon per sonare* (*La Spiritata*).
ϵ ** (*) Delos Dig. **D/CD 3003** [id.].

Elizabethan music always sounds excessively robust when arranged for brass, but much of the music included here is rewarding as arranged for these fine players, notably the *Sonatas* by Speer and Störl, while the Scheidt *Battle suite* is undoubtedly a highlight. Most memorable of all are the Gabrieli pieces, which show the fine ensemble and blending to excellent effect. The Quintet is recorded in the ideal ambience of the Masonic Temple auditorium in New York City and the imagery is superbly realistic – one almost feels able to reach out and touch the players. Their integration of texture has the homogeneity of a string quintet, and the use of dynamic shading and fine phrasing emphasizes the comparison.

Amsterdam Loeki Stardust Quartet

'Virtuoso recorder music': ANON.: *Istampita: Tre Fontane.* PALESTRINA: *Ricercar del secundo tuono.* FRESCOBALDI: *Canzon prima.* MERULA: *Canzon: La Lusignuola.* VIVALDI: *Recorder concerto in C, RV 443.* LOCKE: *Suite in G min.* GIBBONS: *In Nomine.* SIMPSON: *Ricercar: Bonny Sweet Robin.* BLACK: *Report upon When shall my sorrowful sighing slake.* JOHNSON: *The Temporiser.* BYRD: *Sermone blande.*
*** O-L Dig. **414 277-2**; 414 277-1/*4* [id.].

The Amsterdam Loeki Stardust Quartet are superbly expert players: their blend is rich in colour and their ensemble wonderfully polished. There are many piquant sounds here: the virtuosity of Robert Johnson's transcribed lute piece, *The Temporiser*, is a delicious *tour de force* with the following *Sermone blande* of Byrd aptly named; the Vivaldi *Concerto* transcribes successfully to an all-recorder group. It is surprising – although this is not a collection to be played all at once – that the ear does not readily weary of the timbre, even after several pieces heard consecutively. The recording has striking presence and realism, though on tape there is the occasional suspicion that the transfer level is near saturation point.

Backhaus, William (piano)

Solo piano recordings: ALBÉNIZ: *Tango.* BACH: *Christmas oratorio: Pastorale.* BRAHMS: *Variations on a theme of Paganini, Op. 35.* CHOPIN: *Études Op. 10/1–12; Op. 25/1–12.* DELIBES: *Naïla: Waltz.* HANDEL: *Harmonious Blacksmith.* LISZT: *Liebestraum: Hungarian Rhapsody No. 3.* RACHMANINOV: *Prelude in C sharp min., Op. 3/2.* SCHUMANN: *Fantasia in C, Op. 17; Nachstücke No. 4. Fantasiestück No. 2.*
(M) *(*) HMV mono EX 290845-3 (2).

Wilhelm Backhaus was a much-admired Beethoven interpreter before and after the Second World War, and we tend not to associate his name with Chopin and Schumann – rightly, one is tempted to add, after hearing this set. 'Unsmiling and solid' were the adjectives chosen by one reviewer of this set, and it must be admitted that there is too little real warmth or poetic feeling here. Very good transfers, but they can be recommended only to committed admirers of this artist.

Barere, Simon (piano)

'The complete HMV recordings 1934–6': LISZT: *Étude de concert, G.144/2. Années de pèlerinage, 2nd Year (Italy): Sonetto 104 del Petrarca, G.161/5.*

Gnomenreigen, G.145/2. Réminiscences de Don Juan, G.418 (2 versions). *Rapsodie espagnole, G.254; Valse oubliée No. 1, G.215.* CHOPIN: *Scherzo No. 3 in C sharp min., Op. 39; Mazurka in F sharp min., Op. 59/3; Waltz in A flat, Op. 42.* BALAKIREV: *Islamey* (2 versions). BLUMENFELD: *Étude for the left hand.* GLAZUNOV: *Étude in C, Op. 31/1.* SCRIABIN: *Étude in C sharp min., Op. 2/1; Étude in D sharp min., Op. 8/12* (2 versions). LULLY: *Gigue.* RAMEAU (arr. Godowsky): *Tambourin.* SCHUMANN: *Toccata in C, Op. 7* (2 versions).
❀ (M) (***) Archive Piano Recordings mono APR 7001 (2).

Although the new medium has embraced Furtwängler, Bruno Walter and Horowitz, it will be a long time before we can expect the compact disc catalogue to get round to Simon Barere, whose complete HMV recordings from 1934 to 1936 now surface on Archive Piano Recordings. His finger-work is quite astonishtaking, and his virtuosity almost in a class of its own. Younger readers who know only the name should lose no time in obtaining this modestly priced and quite outstanding pair of discs. The set contains an absolutely stunning account of the *Réminiscences de Don Juan* and a performance of Balakirev's *Islamey* so breathtaking that it is difficult to imagine it ever being equalled, let alone surpassed. Nor is there any want of poetry, as witness the delicacy of the Scriabin *C sharp minor Étude* or Liszt's *La leggierezza.* No superlative is strong enough to convey adequately the quality of this playing. One of the most important functions of the gramophone is to chart performance traditions that would otherwise disappear from view, and this set is one to celebrate.

Bate, Jennifer (organ)

Organ of St James's Church, Muswell Hill, London: *'Two centuries of British organ music':* STANLEY: *Voluntary in F.* RUSSELL: *Voluntary in A min.* WESLEY, Samuel: *A Scrap.* WESLEY, Samuel Sebastian: *Holsworthy Church bells; Introduction and fugue in C sharp min.* WOOD: *Prelude on St Mary's.* STANFORD: *Prelude and postlude on a theme of Orlando Gibbons, Op. 105/2; Andante tranquillo; Allegro non troppo e pesante, Op. 101/4 and 2.*
*** Hyp. Dig. **CDA 66180**; A/*KA* 66180 [id.].

French organ music is currently very fashionable, but this fine collection of British repertoire can stand alongside most French compilations for quality and variety of invention. The *Voluntaries* of Charles John Stanley (1713–86) and William Russell (1777–1813) are most personable, and their cheerfulness is striking. Samuel Wesley's *Scrap for organ*, a delightful moto perpetuo in binary form, is even more fetching; and the set of rather gentle variations on *Holsworthy Church bells* by his son, Samuel Sebastian, has great charm. The *Introduction and fugue* is strongly argued and very well structured, but less flamboyant than the comparable piece of Parry. Charles Wood's *Prelude on St Mary's* opens elegiacally and brings an association with the opening of Elgar's *First Symphony*. The three Stanford pieces are strongly characterized and round the collection off satisfyingly. The organ of St James, Muswell Hill, is perfectly chosen for the programme, the effect warmly atmospheric yet vivid and clear; and Jennifer Bate's choice of tempi and registration is admirable, with all the music sounding spontaneous. The excellent recording sounds equally well on LP and the very impressive cassette.

Organ of Beauvais Cathedral: *'Virtuoso French organ music'*: BOËLLMANN: *Suite gothique*. GUILMANT: *Cantilène pastorale; March on 'Lift up your heads'*. SAINT-SAËNS: *Improvisation No. 7*. GIGOUT: *Toccata in B min.; Scherzo; Grand choeur dialogué*.
**(*) Unicorn Dig. DKP/*DKPC* 9041 [id.].

The playing here has enormous flair and thrilling bravura. Jennifer Bate's imaginative touch makes Boellman's *Suite gothique* sound far better music than it is. In the closing *Toccata*, as in the spectacular Guilmant march based on Handel's famous chorus, the panache and excitement of the playing grip the listener firmly, and the clouding of the St Beauvais acoustic is forgotten. But in the swirling Saint-Saëns *Improvisation* and the Gigout *Scherzo*, much detail is masked. In the massive *Grand choeur dialogué*, the clever timing makes the firm articulation register, but although the Unicorn engineers achieve a splendidly sumptuous sound-image, elsewhere there is much blurring caused by the wide reverberation of the empty cathedral. The LP and the excellent chrome tape are closely matched.

Bergen Wind Quintet

BARBER: *Summer music, Op. 31*. SAEVERUD: *Tunes and dances from Siljustøl, Op. 21a*. JOLIVET: *Serenade for wind quintet with principal oboe*. HINDEMITH: *Kleine Kammermusik, Op. 24/2*.
ℭ *** BIS **CD 291**; LP 291 [id.].

Barber's *Summer music* is a glorious piece dating from the mid-1950s; it is in a single movement. Saeverud's *Tunes and dances from Siljustøl* derive from piano pieces of great charm and sound refreshing in their transcribed format. Jolivet's *Serenade* is hardly less engaging, while Hindemith's *Kleine Kammermusik*, when played with such character and finesse, is no less welcome. Throughout, the fine blend and vivacious ensemble give consistent pleasure, and the recording seems ideally balanced within an ambience that brings bloom and atmosphere without being too reverberant. On CD, the illusion of realism is very striking. Highly recommended.

Bonell, Carlos (guitar)

'Baroque guitar works': PURCELL (arr. Bonell): *The Fairy Queen: Rondeau; Dance of the fairies. Chaconne.* WEISS: *Tombeau sur la mort de Monsieur Comte de Logy.* VISÉE: *Suite in G major.* BACH: *Suite in A minor, BWV 997.*
** ASV ALH/*ZCALH* 962 [id.].

Carlos Bonell recorded this recital in 1977, some years before the Decca record of Rodrigo's *Concierto de Aranjuez* which established his international reputation. As we know, he is a bold player and here he characterizes the music strongly. This is emphasized by the close microphone placing of the recording (originally made for Enigma and now reissued by ASV). This tends to reduce the light and shade; but the sound is clean and has good presence. This Baroque programme is certainly attractive, though the presentation is direct rather than displaying expressive subtleties.

Boyd, Liona (guitar)

'The best of Liona Boyd' (with E. Robertson, synthesizer, and rhythm): MARTINI: *Plaisir d'amour.* MYERS: *Cavatina* (*Theme* from *The Deer Hunter*). TRAD.: *Greensleeves. Spanish romance* (*Theme* from *Forbidden games*). LECUONA: *Malaguena.* MAZA: *Campanas de Alba.* ALBÉNIZ: *Asturias.* GALILEI: *Saltarello.* MUDARRA: *Fantasy.* BACH: *Prelude and Bourrée. Jesu, joy of man's desiring.* SAGRERAS: *The Hummingbird.* SATIE: *Gymnopédie No. 1.* TARREGA: *Recuerdos de la Alhambra.* VIVALDI: *Guitar concerto in D: Largo.* PAYET: *Lejania.* BOYD: *Cantarell.*
*** CBS FM/*FMT* 37788 [id.].

This is an unashamedly Romantic recital, with a synthesizer used to fill out textures in Bach as well as in Myers' haunting *Cavatina*. But most of the music is unaccompanied, and Liona Boyd's playing has great magnetism and charisma. The balance is forward in the CBS manner but the image is not overblown; with the whole programme so atmospheric and the playing so accomplished and full of character, this makes very agreeable late-evening listening, though perhaps not for purists. The chrome cassette is the obvious format to choose: technically it is excellent.

Bream, Julian (guitar)

'Homage to Segovia': TURINA: *Fandanguillo, Op. 36; Sevillana, Op. 20.* MOMPOU: *Suite compostelana.* TORROBA: *Sonatina.* GERHARD: *Fantasia.* FALLA: *Homenaje pour le tombeau de Claude Debussy; Three-cornered hat: Miller's dance.* OHANA: *Tiento.*
€ *** RCA Dig. **RD 85306**; RL/*RK* 85306

Readers who have already acquired Bream's earlier digital recital concentrating on the music of Albéniz and Granados (see the Composer section, above) will find this hardly less impressive, both musically and technically. The programme here is even more diverse, with the Gerhard *Fantasia* adding a twentieth-century dimension while Ohana's *Tiento* has a comparable, imaginative approach to texture. The Mompou *Suite compostelana* is most attractive in its diversity and the Tórroba *Sonatina* is perhaps this composer's finest work for guitar. Throughout, Bream plays with his usual flair and spontaneity, constantly imaginative in his use of a wide dynamic range and every possible colouristic effect. The recording has the most tangible realism and presence and, while the background silence of the compact disc adds much, the cassette too is first class.

'Guitarra': MUDARRA: *Fantasias Nos 10 and 14.* MILAN: *Fantasia No. 22.* NARVAEZ: *La canción del Emperador; Conde Claros.* SANZ: *Galliardas; Pasacalles; Canarios.* GUERAU: *Villano; Canario.* MURCIA: *Prelude and allegro.* BOCCHERINI: *Fandango.* SOR: *Sonata in D, Op. 14. Variations on a theme by Mozart, Op. 9.* AQUADO: *Rondo in A, Op. 2/3.* TARREGA: *Study in A; Prelude in A min; Recuerdos de la Alhambra.* GRANADOS: *La Maja de Goya. Danza española No. 5.* ALBÉNIZ: *Suite española: Cádiz. Cantos de España: Córdoba.* TORROBA: *Sonata in A.* TURINA: *Fandanguillo.* FALLA: *Homenaje pour le tombeau de Claude Debussy. Three-cornered hat: Miller's dance.* RODRIGO: *Concierto de Aranjuez: Adagio* (with CO of Europe, Eliot).
€ *** RCA Dig. **RD 85417**; RL/*RK* 85417 (2) [CRL2/*CRK2* 5417].

A wholly admirable survey of Spanish guitar music covering four hundred years and featuring four different instruments, all especially built by José Ramanillos: a Renaissance guitar, vihuela, baroque guitar and a modern classical guitar. Bream's natural dexterity is matched by his remarkable control of colour and unerring sense of style. Many of the early pieces are quite simple but have considerable magnetism. Some of the items included in the latter part of the recital come from his Albéniz/Granados coupling reviewed in the Composer section, others from the shorter collection above dedicated to Segovia, notably the exciting Turina *Fandanguillo*, a real highlight. It was a happy idea to end the recital with the Rodrigo *Adagio* from the *Concierto de Aranjuez*, the most famous piece ever written for the instrument. The presence of the recording is remarkable, the focus sharp and believable; while one again registers the background silence of the CD as bringing a subtle additional sense of realism, the pair of chrome cassettes is also in the demonstration bracket, with very little background and a completely faithful transfer. An excellent, beautifully printed booklet accompanies both the discs and the tapes, with extensive notes setting the music in its historical context.

Bream, Julian, and **John Williams** (guitars)

'Together': LAWES: *Suite for 2 guitars.* CARULLI: *Duo in G, Op. 34.* SOR: *L'Encouragement, Op. 34.* ALBÉNIZ: *Córdoba.* GRANADOS: *Goyescas: Intermezzo.* FALLA: *La vida breve: Spanish dance No. 1.* RAVEL: *Pavane pour une infante défunte.*
*** RCA **RD 83257**; RL/*RK* 83257.

'Together again': CARULLI: *Serenade, Op. 96.* GRANADOS: *Danzas españolas Nos 6 and 11.* ALBÉNIZ: *Bajo la Palmera, Op. 32. Iberia: Evocación.* GIULIANI: *Variazioni concertanti, Op. 130.*
*** RCA **RD 80456**; RL 80456.

In this case two guitars are better than one; these two fine artists clearly strike sparks off each other. In the first recital, Albéniz's *Córdoba* is hauntingly memorable and the concert closes with a slow, stately version of Ravel's *Pavane* which is unforgettable. Here Bream justifies a tempo which he did not bring off so effectively in his solo version (now deleted). On the second disc, it is again music of Albéniz that one remembers for the haunting atmosphere the two artists create together. The sound of these reissues is truthful and atmospheric, although the digital remastering for CD does not succeed in removing all the background hiss. This is distinctly noticeable in the first collection, but in the second is only very slight, and the effect is not intrusive. Moreover, the digital remastering of **RD 80456** brings striking presence.

'Live': JOHNSON: *Pavane and Galliard.* TELEMANN: *Partie polonaise.* SOR: *Fantaisie, Op. 54.* BRAHMS: *Theme and variations, Op. 18* (trans. Williams). FAURÉ: *Dolly suite, Op. 56.* DEBUSSY: *Rêverie. Children's Corner: Golliwog's cakewalk. Suite bergamasque: Clair de lune.* ALBÉNIZ: *Castilla.* GRANADOS: *Spanish dance No. 2* (*Oriental*).
(*) RCA **RD 89645; RL/*RK* 83090 (2) [ARL2/*ARK2* 3090].

This recital was recorded live in Boston and New York during a North American tour. The recording is well balanced and eminently realistic, but the drawback is the applause which, though shortened in the editing, is still very intrusive on repeated hearings. The playing is of the highest quality although perhaps at times slightly self-conscious (the Granados encore has an almost narcissistic tonal beauty). As a whole there is not quite the electricity of this team's other recitals. Fauré's *Dolly suite* sounds a little cosy and the transcription of the *Variations* from Brahms's *B flat major Sextet* is not entirely effective. But the *Golliwog's cakewalk* and the Albéniz *Castilla* are highly enjoyable. The compact disc transfer provides a very quiet but not absolutely silent background (though the very slight hiss is not distracting); it offers the contents of the pair of LPs or tapes on a single disc (over 70′), so is good value; and the documentation is adequate.

Brendel, Alfred (piano)

Recital. BERG: *Sonata, Op. 1;* BUSONI: *Toccata.* LISZT: *Années de pélerinage, 1st Year: Vallée d'Obermann, G.160/6; 2nd Year: Sposalizio, G.161/1: Harmonies poétiques et religieuses: Funérailles, G.173/7; Bagatelle without tonality, G.216a.*
**(*) Ph. 416 319-1/*4* [id.].

This record is issued in aid of Amnesty International; it assembles some impressive concert performances, including a powerful Berg Op. 1 *Sonata.* The recordings emanate from Amsterdam, Vienna and London and are variable in quality. The playing has no lack of authority and virtuosity when required, though the occasions on which these performances were given do not find the instruments all perfectly in tune. There are some ugly octaves – and this is quite disturbing at times in the Berg and the Liszt pieces. However, this is playing of stature. The cassette is faithfully transferred, matching the LP closely.

Byzantine, Julian (guitar)

'Baroque guitar music': BACH: *Lute suite No. 1 in E min., BWV 996; Prelude, fugue and allegro in D, BWV 998.* WEISS: *Tombeau sur la mort de M. Compte De Logy; Fantasie; Suite No. 14: Passacaille.* SCARLATTI, D.: *Keyboard sonatas: in A, Kk. 332; in E, Kk. 380.*
(B) ** CfP Dig. CFP 41 4486-1/*4*.

Julian Byzantine's thoughtful, somewhat self-effacing style produces a thoroughly musical account of the Bach *Suite* and in the Weiss *Tombeau sur la mort de M. Compte De Logy* his restraint is telling. Overall, however, one would have liked a little more projection of personality, although the music making itself, if somewhat considered, is never lifeless. The digital recording is eminently realistic and well balanced, with little to choose in quality between disc and tape, though the background quiet of the latter is an obvious advantage.

Cambridge Buskers

'Classic Busking'
(B) *** DG Walkman *415 337-4.*

This highly diverting collection is an ideal entertainment for a long car journey – though, for all its effervescence and wit, it is best taken a side at a time. The Cambridge Buskers are a duo, Michael Copley (who plays the flute, piccolo and various recorders, with often astonishing bravura) and Dag Ingram, the hardly less fluent accordionist. They met at Cambridge, and these recordings date from the end of the 1970s. There are thirty-four items here, including a remarkably wide range of classical lollipops. The recital immediately establishes the stylistic credentials of the players by opening with an engaging account of the *Rondo* from Mozart's *Eine kleine Nachtmusik*. The programme ranges from Chopin and Praetorius to Bach and Vivaldi, with ear-tickling operatic excerpts by Bizet, Gluck, Rossini, Mozart and Verdi. With tongue-in-cheek irreverence, they manage to include not only the Quartet from *Rigoletto*, but even the *Ride of the Valkyries* – which sounds a good deal more enticing than some overenthusiastic orchestral versions. The players clearly delight in their more outrageous transcriptions, and they are such natural musicians that good taste comes easily. With crisp, clean recording and 83 minutes of music, this is certainly value for money.

'The explosive sound of the Cambridge Buskers'
**(*) DG Dig. 415 443-1/*4*.

There are some enjoyable trifles here, not least a survey of the Beethoven symphonies in 3′ 19″, an engagingly delicate *Pomp and circumstance No. 1* and the reason for the explosive title, a 5′ 21″ condensation of *1812*, complete with pyrotechnic effects. Two items from Tchaikovsky's *Nutcracker suite* are also agreeably felicitous. But with twenty vignettes included, and no great advantage gained from the digital recording, this seems less desirable at full-price while the Walkman concert remains available, although the sound here is first class, on both LP and cassette. Fritz Spiegl's witty descriptive notes are, however, a delight in themselves.

'Handel, Bach and other stock baroquers'
** DG Dig. 415 469-1/*4* [id.].

Though there is some engagingly light-hearted playing here and some of the items surprise the ear by their effectiveness, the touches of humour are a little heavy, notably an all-too-obvious joke to accompany the *Water music* and an account of the *Hallelujah chorus* that doesn't really bear repetition. However, among the twenty items the successes far outweigh the failures. The recording has admirable presence and the chrome cassette is strikingly successful. Fritz Spiegl again provides a running commentary in the back-up notes.

Cherkassky, Shura (piano)

BALAKIREV: *Islamey*. BARTÓK: *Sonata*. BENNETT, Richard Rodney: *5 Études*. STRAVINSKY: *Petrushka*.
**(*) ASV ALH/*ZCALH* 965 [id.].

This recital comes from 1968 (when it enjoyed a brief life-span on the Philips Fourfront label), and brings a rather odd assortment of pieces. Collectors who know Simon Barere's classic account of *Islamey* (see above) will find Cherkassky rather cautious and distinctly slow; and though his *Petrushka* is also slow by comparison with Pollini and has one or two minor inaccuracies, he produces some splendidly felicitous and vital characterization. Textures are splendidly clean, as they are in the impressive performance of Richard Rodney Bennett's *Five Études* and the Bartók *Sonata*. The sound-quality is admirably clean and, at mid-price, this deserves a recommendation to all readers wanting this particular compilation.

Chorzempa, Daniel (organ of Cadets' Chapel, West Point, New Jersey)

WAGNER: *Die Meistersinger: Overture, Die Walküre: Ride of the Valkyries. Tannhäuser: Pilgrims' chorus.* GIGOUT: *Grand choeur dialogué.* RHEINBERGER: *Sonata No. 11 in D min., Op. 148: Cantilena.* BOËLLMANN: *Suite gothique.* CD only: VIERNE: *Scherzetto and Berceuse, Op. 31/14 and 19.*
*(*) Ph. Dig. **416 159-2**; 416 159-1/*4* [id.].

The West Point instrument is a spectacularly large one, with 18,000 pipes comprising 286 ranks. Perhaps understandably, Daniel Chorzempa turns to Wagner transcriptions to show its resources of colour and wide range of dynamic. However, his account of the *Ride of the Valkyries* is rhythmically awkward and unexciting, and *Die Meistersinger overture* is much too spacious, with the music nearly coming to a halt in its middle section (it takes about 2 minutes longer than an average orchestral performance). Chorzempa is clearly at home in the simplistic but effective Boëllmann *Suite gothique* and the rather engaging Rheinberger *Cantilena*, but Gigout's *Grand choeur dialogué* is too heavy and deliberate. The highlights of the programme are the two Vierne *Pièces en style libre*, well played and nicely contrasted, but these are offered only on the CD. The sound is impressively clear, spacious and free in all three media (the chrome cassette quite the equal of the LP), with the CD offering a marginal gain at the far ends of the sound-spectrum, plus a degree more tangibility.

'Clair de lune'

Favourite piano music (with (i) Joseph Cooper; (ii) Katchen; (iii) Gulda; (iv) Rogé; (v) Katin): (i) DEBUSSY: *Clair de lune.* (ii) BACH: *Jesu, joy of man's desiring.* MOZART: *Piano sonata No. 15 in C, K.545:* 1st movt. BEETHOVEN: *Piano sonata No. 8* (*Pathétique*)*:* 2nd movt. (i) *Für Elise;* (iii) *Piano sonata No. 14* (*Moonlight*). (ii) MENDELSSOHN: *On wings of song.* BRAHMS: *Hungarian dance No. 5; Intermezzo in E flat, Op. 117/1.* (v) *Rhapsody in G min., Op. 79/2.* (ii) CHOPIN: *Polonaise in A flat, Op. 53;* (v) *Waltzes in D flat and C sharp min., Op. 64/1 and 2;* (i) *Nocturne in E flat, Op. 9/2; Prelude, Op. 28/15* (*Raindrop*). DVOŘÁK: *Humoresque in G flat, Op. 101/7.* (iv) LISZT: *Liebestraum No. 3 in A flat;* (v) *Consolation No. 3.* SCHUMANN: *Romance, Op. 28/2.*
(B) **(*) Decca *KMC2 9002.*

This is generally a most attractive recital, truthfully engineered, offering distinguished playing of a wide-ranging and nicely contrasted 90-minute programme. The only disappointment is Gulda's version of the *Moonlight sonata*, which has an excessively deliberate opening movement and rather 'plummy' recording. Otherwise the sound is bright and clear, without lacking depth and atmosphere. Some of these performances are very good indeed.

Drake, Susan (harp)

'Echoes of a waterfall': HASSELMANS: *La Source, Op. 44; Prelude, Op. 52; Chanson de mai, Op. 40.* ALVARS: *Divertissement, Op. 38.* GODEFROID: *Bois solitaire; Étude de concert in E flat min., Op. 193.* GLINKA: *Variations on a theme of Mozart.* THOMAS: *Echoes of a waterfall: Watching the wheat; Megan's daughter.* SPOHR: *Variations on Je suis encore, Op. 36.*
*** Hyp. **CDA 66038**; A/*KA* 66038.

The music is lightweight and sometimes facile, but the young Welsh harpist, Susan Drake, is a beguiling exponent, and her technique is as impressive as her feeling for atmosphere. Those intrigued by the title of the collection will not be disappointed by the sounds here (the recording is excellent) which balance evocation with a suitable degree of flamboyance when the music calls for it. The Thomas evocation of watery effects is certainly picturesque, as is Hasselmans' charming *La Source*, and both the Spohr and (especially) the Glinka *Variations* have considerable appeal. This is a case where the background quiet of the CD must be an advantage, but the cassette too has little background noise and manages the resonance well; the sound is warm and mellow, yet definition remains quite good.

Ensemble Wien–Berlin

HAYDN: *Divertimento in B flat, Hob. II/46.* DANZI: *Wind quintet in B flat, Op. 51/1.* BOZZA: *Scherzo for wind, Op. 48.* IBERT: *Trois pièces brêves.* VILLA-LOBOS: *Quintet en forme de chôros.*
*** CBS Dig. **MK 39558** [id.].

The Vienna/Berlin Ensemble happily combine elegance and a lightness of touch with technical polish, and it is difficult to imagine these pieces being better played. Haydn's *Divertimento* is engaging, if not of the calibre of similar works by Mozart, but its main interest is in indicating the source of the chorale used in Brahms's famous orchestral variations. It has great character heard in Haydn's original wind scoring. The Danzi is facile but pleasing, the Bozza *Scherzo* highly felicitous, even memorable. Probably the best work is the set of *Pièces brêves* of Ibert (given here with considerable flair); the most original, though not the most agreeable – it is a little spiky – is the Villa Lobos *Chôros*. The recording is first class, well balanced and eminently realistic.

Equale Brass

'Baccanales': WARLOCK: *Capriol suite* (arr. Gout). POULENC: *Suite* (arr. Jenkins): *Mouvement perpétuel No. 1; Novellette No. 1 in C; Impromptu No. 3; Suite française*. ARNOLD: *Brass quintet*. COUPERIN, F.: *Suite* (arr. Wallace). BARTÓK: *4 Hungarian pictures* (arr. Sears).
Ͼ *** Nimbus **NIM 5004**.

This was one of the first Nimbus compact discs to be issued without an LP equivalent. It offers sound of striking presence and realism and the programme (56′ including the silences between items) is quite generous and certainly imaginative. The arrangements are cleverly scored and produce highly diverting results. Warlock's *Capriol suite* and the music of François Couperin seem unlikely to adapt well for brass, yet they are the highlights of the programme, alongside the engaging Poulenc *Movement perpétuel* and the colourful Bartók *Hungarian pictures*. The Equale Brass is a quintet (two trumpets, horn, trombone and tuba), and besides immaculate ensemble their playing is infectiously spirited and readily conveys the enjoyment of the participants so that the music making has the atmosphere of a live concert. Each of the twenty-one items is banded. A demonstration issue.

Fernandez, Eduardo (guitar)

Recital: LEGNANI, Luigi: *10 Caprices, Op. 20*. GIULIANI: *3 Giulianate, Op. 148* (*Il Sentimentale; La Melancolia; L'Allegria*). SOR: *Variations on a theme from Die Zauberflöte of Mozart, Op. 9*. DIABELLI: *Sonata in F*. PAGANINI: *Sonata in A*.
Ͼ *** Decca Dig. **414 160-2**; 414 160-1/*4* [id.].

All the composers represented on this recital were guitarists, and each well understood the instrument. The Giuliani triptych is characteristically innocent of any real depth of feeling, but is very engaging nevertheless. But the find here is undoubtedly the *Caprices* of Luigi Legnani (who was also a singing teacher). There are thirty-six in all, and Fernandez has made a personal choice of ten of them. His advocacy is persuasive, especially in No. 25, *Andante grazioso*, which, when heard against the background silence of the CD, is quite haunting in its simplicity. Fernandez is in excellent form and the recording gives him a most realistic presence, although it is important not to set the volume level too high. The cassette too is first class, with very little background noise.

Spanish music: TURINA: *Homenaje a Tárrega*. GRANADOS: *La maja de Goya*. ALBÉNIZ: *Torre bermeja; Rumores de la caleta; Cádiz*. TORROBA: *Sonatina*. RODRIGO: *2 Spanish Pieces*. FALLA: *Homenaj pour le tombeau de Claude Debussy. Three-cornered hat: Miller's dance*.
Ͼ *** Decca Dig. **414 161-2**; 414 161-1/*4* [id.].

Eduardo Fernández is a thoughtful, often intimate player and while he creates less sheer electricity than Julian Bream in much of this recital, the playing has fine musicianship and is always alive. He sees the Torroba *Sonatina* as classical in feeling and makes the very most of the variety within the *Passacaglia*, second of the two *Spanish Pieces* of Rodrigo. Then he treats the last two items, Albéniz's *Cádiz*, played with great charm, and the spectacular *Miller's dance* of Falla, which is dramatically arresting, as encores, and the latter would surely receive an ovation at a live recital. The recording is most believable, the acoustic somewhat drier than that favoured by Bream and Williams on RCA, but this increases the feeling of intimacy without detracting from the immediacy and realism on CD. The chrome cassette, too, has splendid presence and is also in the demonstration bracket.

'Guitar favourites'

(i) Diaz; (ii) Parkening; (iii) Angel Romero; (iv) Costanto: (i) RODRIGO: *Concierto de Aranjuez* (with Professors of Spanish Nat. O, Frühbeck de Burgos). SOR: *Variations on a theme from Die Zauberflöte*. (ii) BACH: *Jesu, joy of man's desiring. Sheep may safely graze. Sleepers, awake.* (iii) GRANADOS: *La maja de Goya.* RODRIGO: *Fandango.* ALBÉNIZ: *Tango.* (iv) VILLA-LOBOS: *Preludes Nos 1–3.* TURINA: *Sevillana. Fandanguillo. Rafaga. Homenaje a Tarrega.* (i) MOMPOU: *Canción.*
(B) *** EMI *TC2-MOM 117.*

At the centre of this tape-only collection is a warmly attractive performance of Rodrigo's *Concierto de Aranjuez* from Alirio Diaz and a Spanish orchestral ensemble. Diaz is good too in the Sor and Mompou items. The contribution from Angel Romero has less electricity, but Christopher Parkening's group of Bach transcriptions is most enjoyable, especially *Sleepers, awake*, which is presented with great flair. Irma Costanto provides the most memorable playing of all, her style very free but compellingly spontaneous and full of atmosphere and colour. The sound is excellent throughout.

Hardenberger, Háken (trumpet)

'The virtuoso trumpet' (with Roland Pöntinen): ARBAN: *Variations on themes from Bellini's 'Norma'.* FRANÇAIX: *Sonatine.* TISNÉ: *Héraldiques.* HONEGGER: *Intrada.* MAXWELL DAVIES: *Sonata.* RABE: *Shazam!.* HARTMANN: *Fantasia brillante on the air Rule Britannia.*
Ͼ **(*) BIS **CID 287**; LP 287 [id.].

This collection includes much rare and adventurous repertoire, not otherwise available and very unlikely to offer frequent access in live performance. Moreover, Hardenberger is a superb trumpeter, playing with electrifying bravura in the Maxwell Davies *Sonata* and the virtuoso miniatures. Antoine Tisné's five *Héraldiques* are eclectic but highly effective on the lips of such an assured player; *Scandé* and the following *Elégiaque* are notably characterful. Two sets of nineteenth-century airs with variations are used to flank the serious content: they are agreeably ingenuous and, like Folke Rabe's florid *Shazam!*, are quite entertaining when presented with such flair. But easily the most memorable item is the Françaix *Sonatine* (originally for violin and piano) in which two deliciously brief outer movements frame a pleasing central *Sarabande*. Honegger's improvisatory *Intrada* is an effective encore piece. The recording is eminently realistic, with the CD giving superb presence, so that at the finale of the Tisné suite one almost believes the trumpet to be in the room. The balance with the piano is expertly managed.

Herrick, Christopher (organ of Westminster Abbey)

'Organ fireworks': BONNET: *Variations de concert, Op. 1.* GUILMANT: *Grand choeur triomphale in A, Op. 47/2; March upon Handel's 'Lift up your heads', Op. 16.* WHITLOCK: *Fanfare.* BREWER: *Marche héroïque.* MONNIKENDAM: *Toccata.* JOHNSON: *Trumpet tune in D.* WIDOR: *Symphony No. 7: Finale.* PRESTON: *Alleluyas.* HOVLAND: *Toccata on 'Now thank we all our God'.*
** Hyp. **CDA 66121**; A/*KA* 66121.

Fireworks there are in plenty in Egil Hovland's *Toccata*, based on *Now thank we all our God*, where the florid brilliance in the treble counteracts the wide Westminster reverberation. The performance is a *tour de force* of dexterity, but Christopher Herrick is less exciting than Jennifer Bate (see above) in Guilmant's treatment of Handel. Those who like a hugely expansive organ sound, with thundering pedals, will be well satisfied here, while the Whitlock *Fanfare*, which depends on the trumpet stop, brings a welcome relief in its brighter, lighter texture. The engineering is faultless, and there is a remarkably good cassette.

Hilton, Janet (clarinet), **Keith Swallow** (piano)

'Rhapsodie': POULENC: *Sonata.* RAVEL: *Pièce en forme d'habanera.* DEBUSSY: *Première Rhapsodie.* SAINT-SAËNS: *Sonata, Op. 167.* ROUSSEL: *Aria.* MILHAUD: *Duo concertante, Op. 351.*
** Chan. Dig. ABRD/*ABTD* 1100 [id.].

There are some highly beguiling sounds here, and the languorous style adopted throughout is emphasized by the reverberant acoustic, which is less than ideal, in creating the feeling of an empty hall. The Ravel and Debussy are given an evocative sentience and the Poulenc comes off very well, too; overall, however, there is a feeling that a little more vitality and a more sharply focused sound-picture would have been advantageous. In spite of the resonance, the chrome cassette is first class in every way.

Horowitz, Vladimir (piano)

'At the Met.': SCARLATTI, D.: *Sonatas: in A flat, Kk.127; in F min., Kk.184 and 466; in A, Kk.101; in B min., Kk.87; in E, Kk.135.* CHOPIN: *Ballade No. 4 in F min., Op. 52; Waltz No. 9 in A flat, Op. 69/1.* LISZT: *Ballade No. 2 in B min., G.171.* RACHMANINOV: *Prelude No. 6 in G min., Op. 23/5.*
*** RCA Dig. **RCD 14585**; RL 14260 [ATC1 4260].

The sound Horowitz makes has not previously been fully captured on record, particularly in some of his RCA mono issues of the 1940s and 1950s. The playing is in a class of its own and all one needs to know is that this recording (especially on compact disc) reproduces the highly distinctive tone-quality he commands. This recital, given at the Metropolitan Opera House and issued here at the time of his London Festival Hall appearance in 1982, comes closer to the real thing than anything else on record, except his DG recitals – see below. The quality of the playing is quite extraordinary.

'In London': God save the Queen (arr. Horowitz). CHOPIN: *Ballade No. 1 in G min., Op. 23; Polonaise No. 7 in A flat* (*Polonaise-Fantasie*)*, Op. 61.* SCHUMANN: *Kinderszenen, Op. 15.* SCRIABIN: *Étude in D sharp min., Op. 8/12.*
*** RCA Dig. **RD 84572**.

Highlights from the memorable London recital Horowitz gave in 1982, though omitting the elegant Scarlatti sonatas he played on that occasion, doubtless because it would duplicate *'Horowitz at the Met.'* – see above. However, room could surely have been found for the Rachmaninov *Sonata*, or his encores, as the CD is not generously filled. As those who attended this electrifying recital will know, there were idiosyncratic touches, particularly in the *Kinderszenen* (and also in the Chopin *Ballade*), but this is remarkable testimony to his wide dynamic range and his refined *pianopianissimo*. There are many fascinating points of detail in both works (but notably the Chopin) which give one the feeling of hearing the music for the first time.

Recital: BACH/BUSONI: *Chorale prelude: Nun komm der Heiden Heiland.* MOZART: *Piano sonata No. 10 in C, K.330.* CHOPIN: *Mazurka in A min., Op. 17/4; Scherzo No. 1 in B min., Op. 20; Polonaise No. 6 in A flat, Op. 53.* LISZT: *Consolation No. 3 in D flat.* SCHUBERT: *Impromptu in A flat, D.899/4.* SCHUMANN: *Novellette in F, Op. 21/1.* RACHMANINOV: *Prelude in G sharp min., Op. 32/12.* SCRIABIN: *Étude in C sharp min., Op. 2/1.* MOSZKOWSKI: *Étude in F, Op. 72/6* (recording of performances featured in the film *Vladimir Horowitz –The Last Romantic*).
*** DG Dig. **419 045-2**; 419 045-1/*4* [id.].

Possibly the best recording Horowitz has received so far, in all three media, though his RCA compact discs have also given a splendid sense of his *pp* tone. Recorded when he was over eighty, this playing betrays remarkably little sign of frailty. The Mozart is beautifully elegant and the Chopin *A minor Mazurka*, Op. 17, No. 4, could hardly be more delicate. The only sign of age comes in the *B minor Scherzo* which does not have the leonine fire and tremendous body of his famous 1950 recording. However, it is pretty astonishing for all that.

'The studio recordings': SCHUMANN: *Kreisleriana, Op. 16.* SCARLATTI, D.: *Sonatas: in B min., Kk. 87; in E, Kk. 135.* LISZT: *Impromptu (Nocturne) in F sharp; Valse oubliée No. 1.* SCRIABIN: *Étude in D sharp min., Op. 8/2.* SCHUBERT: *Impromptu in B flat, D.935/3.* SCHUBERT/TAUSIG: *Marche militaire, D.733/1.*
⊛ *** DG **419 217-2**; 419 217-1/*4*.

Those who have watched Horowitz's televised recitals will be familiar with much of this music. He plays it in the studio just as if he were in front of an audience, and the freshness and accuracy would be astonishing if we had not already heard him repeating the trick. The pianism is marvellous. The subtle range of colour and articulation in the Schumann is matched in his Schubert *Impromptu*, and the Liszt *Valse oubliée* offers the most delicious, twinking rubato. Hearing Scarlatti's *E major Sonata* played with such crispness, delicacy and grace must surely convert even the most dedicated authenticist to the view that this repertoire can be totally valid in terms of the modern instrument. The Schubert–Tausig *Marche militaire* makes a superb encore, played with the kind of panache that would be remarkable in a pianist half Horowitz's age. With the passionate Scriabin *Étude* as the central romantic pivot, this recital is uncommonly well balanced to show Horowitz's special range of sympathies. Only Mozart is missing, and he is featured elsewhere. The recording is extremely realistic and present in its CD format. It belies the suggestion, made to support the harsh timbre of some of the pianist's older American recordings, that he sought a dry, close sound-balance.

Hurford, Peter (organ)

Ratzeburg Cathedral organ: *'Romantic organ music':* WIDOR: *Symphony No. 5, Op. 42: Toccata.* VIERNE: *Pièces en style libre: Berceuse.* ALAIN: *Litanies.* FRANCK: *Chorale No. 3.* KARG-ELERT: *Marche triomphale; Nun danket alle Gotte, Op. 65.* BRAHMS: *Chorale preludes; O wie selig, seid, ihr doch; Schmücke dich; Es ist ein' Ros' entsprungen, Op. 122.* MENDELSSOHN: *Organ sonata in A, Op. 65/3.* REGER: *Introduction and passacaglia in D min.*
ℭ *** Argo Dig. **410 165-2** [id.]; ZRDL/*KZRDC* 1011.

There are not many records of Romantic organ music to match this in colour, breadth of repertory and brilliance of performance, superbly recorded. The ever-popular Widor item leads to pieces just as efficient at bringing out the variety of organ sound, such as the Karg-Elert or the Alain. These are performances which defy all thought of Victorian heaviness, and the Ratzeburg organ produces piquant and beautiful sounds. The result is first class on disc and chrome cassette alike, with plenty of edge on climaxes. On CD the presence and range are breathtaking.

Sydney Opera House organ: *'Great organ works'*: BACH: *Toccata and fugue in D min., BWV 565; Jesu, joy of man's desiring.* ALBINONI: *Adagio* (arr. Giazotto). PURCELL: *Trumpet tune in D.* MENDELSSOHN: *A Midsummer Night's Dream: Wedding march.* FRANCK: *Chorale No. 2 in B min.* MURRILL: *Carillon.* WALFORD DAVIES: *Solemn melody.* WIDOR: *Organ symphony No. 5: Toccata.*
ϵ **(*) Argo Dig. **411 929-2** [id.]; ZRDL/*KZRDC* 1016.

Superb sound here, wonderfully free and never oppressive, even in the most spectacular moments. The Widor is spiritedly genial when played within the somewhat mellower registration of the magnificent Sydney instrument (as contrasted with the Ratzeburg Cathedral organ – see above), and the pedals have great sonority and power. The Murrill *Carillon* is equally engaging alongside the Purcell *Trumpet tune*, while Mendelssohn's wedding music has never sounded more resplendent. The Bach is less memorable, and the Albinoni *Adagio,* without the strings, is not an asset to the collection either.

Jacobs, Paul (piano)

American piano music: BOLCOM: *3 Ghost rags.* COPLAND: *4 Piano blues.* RZEWSKI: *4 North American Ballads.*
** None. Dig. **CD 79006**; D 79006 [id.].

The death in 1983 of Paul Jacobs robbed us of a versatile and enterprising artist, who has enriched the catalogue with much out-of-the-way material. The best music here is the Copland, also available in Leo Smit's two-record Copland set on CBS, and Jacobs plays these pieces with thoroughly idiomatic style; the most interesting is Frederick Rzewski's brilliant and effective *Ballads.* The composer, now in his forties, is new to the catalogue and is eminently worth watching. The Bolcom *Rags* are not particularly strong pieces, but Jacobs makes out as persuasive a case for them as he can. Good recording, slightly reverberant but given convincing presence on CD.

Kremer, Gidon (violin)

'A Paganini': MILSTEIN: *Paganiniana.* SCHNITTKE: *A Paganini.* ERNST, Heinrich: *Étude No. 6: Die letzte Rose.* ROCHBERG, George: *Caprice variations Nos 5, 7–8, 16, 18–19, 21, 23–25, 31, 34–36, 38, 41–46, 49–51.*
ϵ *** DG Dig. **415 484-2**; 415 484-1/*4* [id.].

This is playing of extraordinary virtuosity and command. The programme, in a real sense, starts where Paganini left off. The recital begins and ends with the famous *Caprice No. 24* which has inspired so much subsequent music by others, of which Milstein's is an entertainingly lightweight example, with seven variations very much in the Paganini manner. Heinrich Ernst's *Variations* on *The last rose of summer* show the nineteenth-century inheritance of the format quite pleasingly, while Alfred Schnittke and George Rochberg bring the music's ethos into the twentieth century. In his mighty set of 51 variations (of which 24 are included here) Rochberg moves backwards and forwards in his eclecticism: some of his variations (like the opening *Nocturnal*) are relatively avant garde; others are more conventional. The variety of the music here is remarkable, and so is Gidon Kremer's identification with it. The recording gives him an absolutely natural presence (though it is important not to set the volume level too high) which is very tangible indeed on CD. The chrome cassette is excellent too, but leaves a thin veil between the artist and the listener.

Kroumata Percussion Ensemble

CAGE: *Second construction.* COWELL: *Pulse.* LUNDQUIST: *Sisu.* TAÏRA: *Hiérophonie.*
ⓒ *** BIS Dig. **CD 232**; LP 232 [id.].

A well-constructed programme (lasting only 39′ 29″ – but perhaps that is long enough), demonstrating the range of a percussion group performing without other 'melodic' instruments. That is not perhaps strictly true, for the Lundquist piece introduces simplistic melodic ideas (rather attractively) using xylophone, vibraphone, xylorimba and marimba. Cage relies on imaginative textures, and as his piece is not too extended (6′ 44″) it is very successful. The Cowell is not dissimilar, but the *Hiérophonie* of Yoshihisa Taïra is another matter. The CD draws attention to the layout of the music on the disc, with the Cage quietly atmospheric, but warns that this final piece has a very wide dynamic range. The work opens with vigorous and highly involved shouts, making an interplay with the percussive sounds, and one cannot help but associate the effect with Kung Fu. The structure moves steadily and strongly towards a spectacular climax whose sheer physical thrill is undeniable, even if the listener might feel a lack of patience on the way, as the experience lasts 19′ 32″. But the skill and commitment of the performers are very impressive throughout this collection, which is a classic of its kind. The recording itself is superbly realistic, with the instruments set back in an atmospheric acoustic. The sound engineers have resisted the temptation to emphasize the transient bite.

'Music with flute' (with Manuela Wiesler): JOLIVET: *Suite en concert for flute and percussion.* HARRISON, Lou: *Concerto No. 1 for flute and percussion.* CAGE: *Amores.* SANDSTRÖM: *Drums.*
ⓒ **(*) BIS Dig. **CD 272**; LP 272 [id.].

It is the gentle music which comes off best here, with the many delicate *piano* and *pianissimo* passages greatly enhanced by the silent background of the CD. Not many readers would expect that an avant garde piece by a composer like John Cage would be suitable atmospheric listening for the late evening, but his four-part *Amores* has an ear-tickling fascination, especially the two central *Trios* for nine tom-toms and pod rattle (!) or seven woodblocks, 'not Chinese', respectively, used with the utmost discretion. Of the two works featuring the concertante flute, the Jolivet has a haunting second-movement *Stabile* and an improvisatory *Calme* finale, where flute and exotically soft percussion sounds make a memorable impression; similarly, Lou Harrison's *Concerto* had a middle movement, marked *Slow and poignant*, which is quite indelible. All this music is lightweight, in both implications of the adjective; however, the final item, which (at 14′ 40″) is far too long, makes a thunderous contrast. Even the most resilient pair of speaker cones will surely shudder at the weight of *fortissimos* heaped upon them by Sandström's *Drums*: it is all physically thrilling in projecting animal vitality, but its only real purpose is surely to provide hi-fi buffs with noisy demonstration sound, *par excellence*. The recording handles the widest dynamic ranges with the utmost realism throughout the concert.

Labèque, Katia and **Marielle** (piano duet)

'Glad rags': GERSHWIN/DONALDSON: *Rialto ripples*. MAYERL: *Honky-tonk*. JOHNSON: *Carolina shout*. JOPLIN: *The Entertainer; Antoinette; Magnetic rag; Maple leaf rag; Elite syncopations; Strenuous life; Stop-time; Bethena*.
*** EMI Dig. **CDC 747093-2** [id.]; EMD/*TC-EMD* 5541 [Ang. S/*4 XS 37980*].

The Labèque duo play with irresistible bravura and dash. Scott Joplin may have frowned on their tempi (he favoured slow speeds), but the playing has such wit and conveyed enjoyment that criticism is silenced. The recording has sparkle but depth too and fine presence on CD. The cassette – although not chrome – is of a high standard, too. This is by far the most generally recommendable collection of this repertoire.

Lhévinne, Josef (piano)

'Ampico recordings', Vol. 1: SCHUMANN: *Papillons, Op. 2*. RUBINSTEIN: *Kamennoy-Ostrow* (*Rêve Angélique*), *Op. 10/22*. CHOPIN: *Études: in E flat, Op. 10/11; in G flat, Op. 25/9; Nocturne in B, Op. 9/3; Polonaise in A, Op. 53*. SCHUTT: *À la bien-aimée, Op. 59/2*.
(M) *** O-L 414 097-1/*4* [id.].

'Ampico recordings', Vol. 2: SCHUBERT/LISZT: *Soirée de Vienne No. 6*. MENDELSSOHN/LISZT: *On wings of song*. LISZT/BUSONI: *La Campanella*.

LISZT: *Gondoliera; Liebestraum No. 3.* TAUSIG: *Fantasia on Hungarian gypsy songs.* CUI: *Causerie Étude in F, Op. 40/6.*
(M) *** O-L 414 121-1/*4* [id.].

'Ampico recordings', Vol. 3: SCHUBERT/TAUSIG: *Marche militaire.* BEETHOVEN: *Piano sonata No. 14 (Moonlight), Op. 27/2.* ALBÉNIZ: *Suite espagnole: Sevilla. Chants d'espagne: Córdoba.* SINDING: *Rustle of spring.* SCHULZE-EVLER: *Concert arabesques on 'The Blue Danube' waltz by Johann Strauss.*
(M) *** O-L 414 123-1/*4* [id.].

Joseph Lhévinne (1874–1944) had an enormous reputation in his lifetime and possessed a phenomenal technique. He is said to have produced such extraordinary beauty of tone that he could move his listeners to tears. Some years ago, Argo in collaboration with the BBC transferred to LP some of the Ampico piano rolls of celebrated pianists, including Lhévinne. Along with the Welte and the Duo-Art, the Ampico piano was the most successful of its day, and these recordings certainly testify to its remarkably high standards. Lhévinne's extraordinary technique and delicacy come across in these astonishing records and matching cassettes, which have the merit of sounding as if they were made only yesterday. Great care has gone into the preparation of the rolls and the piano mechanism, and the only reservation that could be made concerns the somewhat thicker, slightly wooden bass sonority. What a pianist, though!

'Liebesträume'

'Romantic piano music': (i) Bolet; (ii) Ashkenazy; (iii) De Larrocha; (iv) Lupu: (i) LISZT: *Liebestraum No. 3; Étude de concert No. 3 (Un sospiro).* (ii) RACHMANINOV: *Prelude in C sharp min., Op. 3/2.* CHOPIN: *Nocturne in F min., Op. 55/1; Étude in E, Op. 10/3.* BEETHOVEN: *Piano sonata No. 14 in C sharp min. (Moonlight).* (iii) CHOPIN: *Prelude No. 15 in D flat (Raindrop).* SCHUBERT: *Impromptu in A flat, D.899/4.* SCHUMANN: *Romance, Op. 28/2.* (iv) BRAHMS: *Rhapsody in G min., Op. 79/2.*
*** Decca **411 934-2** [id.].

Jorge Bolet's warmly romantic account of Liszt gives this specially assembled compact disc its title and is also the only true digital recording included in the programme. But the sound is generally excellent and the digital remastering, if producing a rather forward image, offers truthful quality throughout. The performances are distinguished and there is passionate contrast in Ashkenazy's Rachmaninov. Lupu's Brahms is rather less extrovert in feeling; generally, the recital has a nicely relaxed atmosphere.

Lindeberg, Christian (trombone), **Roland Pöntinen** (piano)

'The Romantic trombone': GUY-ROPARTZ: *Pièce in E flat min.* MERCADANTE: *Salve Maria.* SAINT-SAËNS: *Cavatina, Op. 114.* GAUBERT: *Morceau symphonique.* JONGEN: *Aria and polonaise, Op. 128.* STOJOWSKI: *Fantaisie.* ALFVEN: *Herdsmaiden's dance.* WEBER: *Romance.*
** BIS Dig. **CD 298**; LP 298.

Those collectors with a special interest in the trombone will find that this BIS CD brings admirable presence and reality to Christian Lindeberg and his erstwhile accompanist. The music they have to play is thin stuff: the Saint-Saëns *Cavatina* is unexpectedly disappointing; the most interesting items are those by Gaubert, Jongen and Stojowski, but if one never heard them a second time the musical loss could be borne without regret. The arrangement of Alfven's *Herdsmaiden's dance* serves to demonstrate Lindeberg's fine articulation and easy bravura; elsewhere, his firm, rich timbre and musical sense of line and phrasing are always in evidence.

Longhurst, John (Mormon Tabernacle organ, Salt Lake City)

Recital: GIGOUT: *Grand choeur dialogué; Toccata.* HERON: *Trumpet voluntary.* WIDOR: *Symphony No. 9 (Gothique), Op. 70: Andante.* VIERNE: *Carillon de Westminster.* CLARKE: *Trumpet voluntary.* HANDEL: *Xerxes: Largo.* FRANCK: *Pièce héroïque.* BACH: *Chorale prelude: Wachet auf, BWV 645; Jesu, joy of man's desiring. Bist du bei mir.*
*** Ph. Dig. **412 217-2**; 412 217-1/*4* [id.].

Although John Longhurst is a most accomplished organist who plays and registers with admirable taste and understanding of the potential of his instrument, it is the huge Mormon Tabernacle organ that is the star here (flattered by the Tabernacle ambience). There is spectacle when called for – in the Franck, for instance – but one is never overwhelmed. Most enjoyable of its kind: the LP and cassette are both excellent; the CD adds a little tangibility.

Mandozzi, Graziano (synthesizer)

'Bach/Handel 300': excerpts from: BACH: *Brandenburg concerto No. 2; Double violin concerto; Orchestral suite No. 2 in B min.; Cantatas Nos 41 and 147. Prelude, BWV 934; Bist du bei mir; Minuet in G.* HANDEL: *Water music; Sonata, Op. 1/11; Messiah; Sonata a 5 in B flat; Solomon; Viola da gamba sonata in C. Concerto in B flat, Op. 4/6. The harmonious blacksmith; Country dance in G min.*
** DG Dig. **415 110-2**; 415 110-1/*4* [id.].

Without the finesse or subtlety that Wendy (formerly Walter) Carlos brings to this repertoire, the sounds here are agreeably cheerful – and if the effect is outrageously vulgar, it is still infectious. Chirruping and whoopsing noises decorate the background at times, to show that Graziano Mandozzi's tongue is firmly in his cheek. The wild arrangement of Handel's *Harmonious blacksmith*, and the *Hallelujah chorus* complete with synthesized voices, are characteristic of the extrovert confidence of the simulations. The sound is bright and immediate; and this is most effective in its cassette format as a distraction for a journey on the motorway.

Oortmerssen, Jacques van (organ)

'The Arp Schnidtger organ, St Cosmae's Church, Stade': SCHEIDEMANN: *Preambulum in D; Magnificat VIII Toni.* BUXTEHUDE: *Chorale variations on Vater unser im Himmelreich, BuxWV 207; Prelude and fugue in A min., BuxWV 153.* WECKMANN: *Magnificat II Toni.* BRUHNS: *Choral fantasia: Nun komm der Heiden Heiland.* LÜBECK: *Preambulum.*
** Denon Dig. **C37 7005** [id.].

As usual with Denon organ recitals, this is generous in content; the character of the organ at St Cosmae's, Stade, is well caught, with its sometimes throaty reeds and full-blooded pedals. The programme concerns itself with the North German organ school, from Scheidemann (1596–1663) to Lübeck (1654–1740). The music is interesting and well wrought rather than adventurous. The most impressive piece is the closing Lübeck *Preambulum*, actually written for this organ (and impressively registered by Van Oortmerssen), although the Buxtehude and Bruhns chorale variants and the Scheidemann *Magnificat* also bring plenty of opportunities to demonstrate the instrument's palette.

Organ music

'Great organ favourites' (with (i) Danby (organ of Blenheim Palace); (ii) Bayco (Holy Trinity, Paddington); (iii) Willcocks (King's College, Cambridge); (iv) Preston (Westminster Abbey); (v) Thalben-Ball (Temple Church); (vi) Jackson (York Minister)): (i) BACH: *Toccata and fugue in D min., BWV 565.* (ii) *In dulci jubilo.* (iii) *Wachet auf.* (i) CLARKE: *Trumpet voluntary.* WIDOR: *Symphony No. 5, Op. 42/1: Toccata.* ELGAR: *Enigma variations: Nimrod.* GIGOUT: *Scherzo.* FRANCK: *Choral No. 3 in A min.* (iv) MURRILL: *Carillon.* (ii) MENDELSSOHN: *A Midsummer Night's Dream: Wedding march.* LEMARE: *Andantino.* HOLLINS: *Spring song.* WAGNER: *Lohengrin: Bridal chorus.* WOLSTENHOLME: *Allegretto.* BOËLLMANN: *Prière à Notre Dame.* HANDEL: *Water music: Air.* (v) PURCELL: *Voluntary on the Old 100th.* (vi) COCKER: *Tuba tune.*
(B) ** EMI *TC2-MOM 115.*

Obvious care has been taken with the engineering of this mixed bag of excerpts (one of the tape-only 'Miles of Music' series), but occasionally the reverberant acoustic brings moments when the focus slips a little. For the most part, however, the sound is impressive. The programme begins well with excellent versions of the Widor, Gigout, Franck's *Third Choral* and Murrill's engaging *Carillon*, but on side two Frederick Bayco, who provides the lighter fare, is sometimes unstylish: he is very mannered in the famous *Wedding march*. But how many drivers want organ music as a background for a car journey?

Parker-Smith, Jane (organ of Coventry Cathedral)

'Popular French Romantics': WIDOR: *Symphony No. 1: March pontifical. Symphony No. 9 (Gothique), Op. 70: Andante sostenuto.* GUILMANT: *Sonata No. 5 in C min., Op. 80: Scherzo.* GIGOUT: *Toccata in B min.* BONNET: *Elfes, Op. 7.* LEFÉBURE-WÉLY: *Sortie in B flat.* VIERNE: *Pièces de fantaisie: Clair de lune, Op. 53/5; Carillon de Westminster, Op. 54/6.*
*** ASV Dig. **CDDCA 539**; DCA/*ZCDCA* 539 [id.].

The modern organ in Coventry Cathedral (built by Harrison and Harrison of Durham) is surprisingly well suited to French repertoire. Its bright, full-blooded tutti, with just a touch of harshness, adds a nice bite to Jane Parker-Smith's very pontifical performance of the opening Widor *March* and creates a blaze of splendour at the close of the famous Vierne *Carillon de Westminster*, the finest performance on record. The detail of the fast, nimble articulation in the engagingly Mendelssohnian *Elfes* of Joseph Bonnet is not clouded; yet here, as in the splendid Guilmant *Scherzo* with its wider dynamic range, there is a nice atmospheric effect, too. Hardly less enjoyable is the robustly jocular *Sortie* of Lefébure-Wély, which is delivered with fine geniality and panache. Overall, a most entertaining recital, made the more vivid on the boldly focused compact disc.

Petri, Michala (recorder), **George Malcolm** (harpsichord)

Recorder sonatas: VIVALDI: *Il Pastor fido: Sonata No. 6 in G min., RV 58.* CORELLI: *Sonata in C, Op. 5/9.* BIGAGLIA, Diogenio: *Sonata in A min.* BONONCINI: *Divertimento da camera No. 6 in C min.* SAMMARTINI: *Sonata in G, Op. 13/4.* MARCELLO, B.: *Sonata in F, Op. 2/1.*
❀ ℂ *** Ph. Dig. **412 632-2**; 412 632-1/*4* [id.].

Six recorder sonatas in a row might seem too much of a good thing, but the playing is so felicitous and the music has such charm that the collection is immensely enjoyable, even taken complete, and if sensibly dipped into is a source of much delight. There are many individual highlights. The Corelli *Sonata* has a memorable *Tempo di gavotta* as its finale which reminds one a little of Handel's *Harmonious blacksmith*; the work in A minor by the composer with the unlikely name of Diogenio Bigaglia (*c.* 1676–*c.* 1745) is a winner, with a nimble minuet and sparkling finale. Bononcini's *Divertimento da camera* alternates slow and fast sections, and in the third-movement *Largo* George Malcolm makes the delicate accompaniment sound like a harp. Sammartini's *Sonata* is enchanting, with its opening *Andante* in siciliano form and three more delectable movements to follow. Throughout, Michala Petri's playing is wonderfully fresh: she has made many records for Philips, but none more enticing than this. George Malcolm proves an equally imaginative partner, and both artists embellish with admirable flair and taste, never overdoing it. The music making combines geniality and finesse with spontaneity and a direct communication of pleasure in a lightweight but consistently rewarding programme. The Philips recording is quite perfectly balanced and wonderfully tangible in all formats, for there is a superb cassette.

Piano: 'Golden piano music'

Recital (with (i) Ivan Davis; (ii) Ashkenazy; (iii) De Larrocha; (iv) Kempff; (v) Curzon; (vi) Bolet; (vii) Lupu; (viii) Cherkassky; (ix) Schiff; (x) Rogé; (xi) Backhaus): (i) CHOPIN: *Waltz in D flat ('Minute'), Op. 64/1;* (ii) *Études: in E, Op. 10/3; in C min. (Revolutionary), Op. 10/12.* (iii) *Prelude in D flat (Raindrop), Op. 28/15;* (iv) *Berceuse, Op. 57.* (v) LISZT: *Liebesträume No. 3;* (vi) *Étude de concert, G.144/3.* (v) SCHUBERT: *Moment musical No. 3.* (vii) BRAHMS: *Rhapsody in G min., Op. 79/2; Ballade in G min.* (viii) RUBINSTEIN: *Melody in F.* (ix) MOZART: *Sonata No. 11 in A, K.331: Rondo alla Turca.* (x) DEBUSSY: *Suite bergamasque: Clair de lune.* (xi) BACH: *French suite No. 5: Gavotte.* MENDELSSOHN: *Spring song.* (iii) GRANADOS: *Danza española No. 5.*
(M) *** Decca Jub. 414 498-1/*4*.

A generous and exceptionally distinguished collection. Don't be put off by the excessively forward balance of the piano in Ivan Davis's glittering opening Chopin *Waltz*; after that the sound is very good and often excellent – although on tape the overall quality seems a little drier on side one than on side two which has slightly more bloom. However, such a collection needs the background quiet of a cassette rather than LP. Many of the individual performances are memorable: Ashkenazy's *'Revolutionary' Study* is enormously commanding, while the magic of Kempff's *Berceuse* is matched by the sensitive rubato of Alicia de Larrocha's *'Raindrop' Prelude*, while Pascal Rogé's account of Debussy's *Clair de lune* is wonderfully poetic. The programme is pleasingly arranged to provide contrast; overall, it is most rewarding.

Piano: 'Virtuoso piano showpieces'

Recital (with (i) Jorge Bolet; (ii) Eden and Tamir; (iii) Rhondda Gillespie; (iv) Ilana Vered; (v) Shura Cherkassky; (vi) Julius Katchen; (vii) Ivan Davis): (i) CHOPIN/GODOWSKI: *Étude, Op. 10/1.* (ii) ARENSKY: *Suite for 2 pianos, Op. 15: Waltz.* LISZT: Transcription of *Rossini's La Danza.* (iii) *Hungarian rhapsody No. 15 (Rákóczi march);* (iv) *Hungarian rhapsody No. 2.* CHOPIN: *Étude Op. 10/12 (Revolutionary).* (v) STRAUSS, J. jnr/GODOWSKY: *Wein, Weib und Gesang.* (vi) FALLA: *El amor brujo: Ritual fire fance.* (vii) GOTTSCHALK: *Souvenirs de Porto-Rico; Souvenirs d'Andalousie.* RIMSKY-KORSAKOV/RACHMANINOV: *Flight of the bumble bee.* LISZT: *Paraphrase on Mendelssohn's Wedding march and Dance of the Elves.*
(M) **(*) Decca Viva 411 836-1/*4*.

This collection effectively demonstrates the virtuosity of Decca's roster of pianists over the stereo era from the late Julius Katchen, whose *Ritual fire dance* is boldly commanding, through to Jorge Bolet, who plays one of Godowsky's embellishments of Chopin which adds nothing to the appeal of the original: does Chopin really need more notes? Cherkassky sparkles in the Strauss waltz, a much better example of Godowsky's embellishments, and Ilana Vered, an underrated artist, provides a glittering account of Liszt's *Hungarian rhapsody No. 2*. But the highlights are all from Ivan Davis whose virtuosity is irresistible, whether in Gottschalk or the deliciously delicate fairy music from Mendelssohn's *A Midsummer Night's Dream*. The sound varies a little, but not distractingly; it is always good and usually excellent. The cassette is admirably faithful. It brings out the differences of acoustic and balance rather more obviously than the LP.

Pinnock, Trevor (harpsichord)

'The harmonious blacksmith': HANDEL: *Suite 5: The Harmonious blacksmith.* FISCHER: *Urania: Passacaglia in D min.* COUPERIN: *Les baricades mystérieuses.* BACH: *Italian concerto in F, BWV 971.* RAMEAU: *Gavotte in A min.* SCARLATTI, D.: *2 Sonatas Kk.380/1.* FIOCCO: *Suite 1: Adagio in F.* DAQUIN: *Le Coucou.* BALBASTHE: *La Suzanne in E min.*
(*) DG Arc. **413 591-2; 413 591-1/*4* [id.].

A delightful collection of harpsichord lollipops, superbly and stylishly played and brilliantly – if aggressively – recorded. If one samples the famous title-piece, being careful to set the volume control at a realistic level, in the CD format the presence and tangibility of the instrument are spectacular. However, the bright sharpness of focus can become just a little tiring if the recital is taken all at once. The cassette softens the upper range, but too much so and, although agreeable, is much less realistic.

Pöntinen, Roland (piano)

Russian piano music. STRAVINSKY: *3 Movements from Petrushka.* SCRIABIN: *Sonata No. 7 in F sharp* (*White Mass*), *Op. 64.* SHOSTAKOVICH: *3 Fantastic dances.* RACHMANINOV: *Études-tableaux, Opp. 33 and 39.* PROKOFIEV: *Toccata.* KHACHATURIAN: *Toccata.*
*** BIS Dig. **CD 276**; LP 276 [id.].

Roland Pöntinen is a young Swedish pianist of twenty-three who is beginning to make a name for himself. The name sounds Finnish rather than Swedish: his father hails from the Baltic and settled in Sweden in 1946. He gives a suitably ardent and inflammable account of the *Seventh Sonata*, the so-called '*White Mass*', and is fully attuned to the Scriabin sensibility, conveying its wild, excitable character to real effect. His playing has real temperament and a good sense of colour, and this well-recorded recital shows his very considerable technique and prowess to good advantage. A very enjoyable programme.

Preston, Simon (organ)

'Great organ works' (organs of King's College Chapel, Cambridge, or Westminster Abbey): WIDOR: *Symphony No. 5: Toccata.* BACH: *Chorale preludes: Wachet auf, BWV 645; Kommst du nun, BWV 650.* MOZART: *Fantasia in F min. K.608.* FRANCK: *Choral No. 2; Pièce héroïque.* BRAHMS: *Chorale prelude: Es ist ein Ros entsprungen.*
(M) *** Decca Viva 411 840-1/*4*.

An excellent and generous lower-mid-priced recital, taken from recordings made between 1961 and 1964. The performances are distinguished. It might be argued that these organs are not ideal for the French repertoire, and Preston uses a very wide range of dynamic so that pianissimos are recessed though clearly focused (noticeably so in Brahms and Mozart, as well as Widor). But the Franck *Pièce héroïque* certainly has a fine impact, while the Bach *Chorale preludes* are successful in providing contrast. In their remastered form these recordings sound exceptionally well, with neither the Westminister Abbey nor King's reverberation offering any problems either on disc or on tape. Moreover, Simon Preston has seldom sounded more spontaneously involved than here.

English organ music (organ of Colston Hall, Bristol): ELGAR: *Organ sonata in G, Op. 28.* LEIGHTON, Kenneth: *Paen.* BRIDGE: *Adagio in E.* HOWELLS: *Rhapsody in C sharp min., Op. 17/3.* TIPPETT: *Preludio al vespro di Monteverdi.* BRITTEN: *Prelude and fugue on a theme of Vittoria.*
(M) **(*) Argo 414 647-1/*4*.

This is an admirable collection of English organ works, with a far wider appeal than most such programmes. The Elgar *Sonata*, a ripely expansive piece dating from 1895 (in the period leading up to the *Enigma variations*), takes up a whole side, a richly inspired work that might sound well in a full symphonic orchestration. Here Simon Preston gives a somewhat too detached interpretation which loses some of the ripeness, particularly on a clean-sounding modern organ of a kind that Elgar can hardly have had in mind. On the reverse the performances are richer and more committed, with Howells again demonstrating his feeling for the Anglican cathedral tradition and Tippett and Britten characteristically using the instrument with fine textural cunning. The excellent (1967) recording is almost too clean for some of the music, but it has transferred admirably to cassette.

English organ music (with organs of (i) Knole Chapel, Sevenoaks, (ii) St John the Baptist, Armitage; (iii) with Trevor Pinnock): (i) ANON.: *I smile to see how you devise*. BYRD: *Fantasia in C*. TOMKINS: *Voluntary* (*Fancy*) *in C*. GIBBONS: *Fantasia in A min*. PURCELL: *Voluntary in G*. FARRANT: *Felix namque*. BULL: *Prelude in D min*. and *In nomine in A min*. (ii) STANLEY: *Voluntary in A min*. GREENE: *Voluntary in G*. BOYCE: *Voluntary in D*. (ii; iii) WESLEY: *Duet in C*.
*(**) DG Arc. Dig. **415 675-2**; 415 675-1/*4* [id.].

An attractive idea, but one that will offer aural problems for some listeners. The programme played on the Knole Chapel organ with its engagingly bright timbre is attractive enough, although none of the music is of great moment. The Armitage organ, however, has a very individual temperament so that the major thirds are all slightly wider than pure, and the fifths down from C are slightly wider than those upwards. This produces an 'out of tune' impression in some of the music, and while the very personable *Voluntary* of Maurice Greene (with its effective exploitation of the cornet stop) is a highlight, the Wesley *Duet* (where Simon Preston is joined at the keyboard by Trevor Pinnock) produces some clashes of tuning that some may find piquant but other ears will resist.

Rachmaninov, Sergei (piano)

Ampico recordings, Vol. 1: RACHMANINOV: *Barcarolle in G min. Op. 10/3; 5 Morceaux de fantaisie, Op. 3* (*Elégie; Prélude; Mélodie; Polichinelle; Sérénade*); *Études-tableaux; in B min. and A min., Op. 39/4 and 6; Humoresque in G, Op. 10/5; Lilacs, Op. 21/5; Prelude in G min., Op. 23/5*.
(M) *** O-L 414 096-1/4 [id.].

'Ampico recordings', Vol. 2: CHOPIN/LISZT: *Mädchens Wunsch* from *Op. 74*. BIZET: *L'Arlésienne: Minuet*. PADEREWSKI: *Minuet in G, Op. 14/1*. KREISLER: *Liebeslied; Liebesfreud*. MUSSORGSKY: *Hopak*. RUBINSTEIN: *Barcarolle*. RIMSKY-KORSAKOV: *Flight of the bumble bee*. TCHAIKOVSKY: *Troika, Op. 37/11; Waltz in A flat, Op. 40/8*. RACHMANINOV: *Polka de V. R.*
(M) *** O-L 414 099-1/*4* [id.].

'Ampico recordings', Vol. 3: BACH: *Partita No. 4: Sarabande.* BEETHOVEN: *Ruins of Athens: Turkish march.* GLUCK (arr. Sgambati): *Mélodie dell'Orfeo.* MENDELSSOHN: *Spinning song, Op. 67/4.* HENSELT: *Si oiseau j'étais.* SCHUBERT/LISZT: *Das Wandern.* SCHUBERT/RACHMANINOV: *The brooklet; Wohin.* SCHUBERT: *Impromptu in A flat, D.899/4. Arr.* RACHMANINOV: *The Star-spangled Banner.* CHOPIN: *Scherzo No. 2 in B flat min., Op. 31; Nocturne in F, Op. 15/1; Waltzes: in E flat Op. 18; in F Op. 34/3.*
(M) *** O-L 414 122-1/*4* [id.].

An invaluable appendix to the five-volume set of all Rachmaninov's recordings, both acoustic and electrical, issued by RCA in the 1970s (not currently available). The breathtaking technical address, the poetry and finesse come across with even greater immediacy in these astonishing records which sound as if the master had come into the studio only yesterday. As was the case in the Lhévinne set, enormous care has gone into the preparation of the rolls and the piano mechanism. Again the somewhat thicker, slightly wooden bass sonority is the only evidence of their provenance: the last of the three LPs contains the least appealing performances. There are excellent cassettes.

Rawsthorne, Noel (organ of Coventry Cathedral)

'Organ spectacular': VERDI: *Aïda: Grand march.* CLARKE: *Trumpet voluntary.* BACH: *Suite No. 3 in D; Air.* SCHUBERT: *Marche militaire.* SULLIVAN: *The lost chord.* MENDELSSOHN: *Midsummer Night's Dream: Wedding march.* SOUSA: *The Stars and stripes forever.* ELGAR: *Pomp and circumstance march No. 1.* TRAD.: *Londonderry air.* HANDEL: *Messiah: Hallelujah.* WAGNER: *Die Walküre: Ride of the Valkyries.*
*** HMV Dig. EL 270165-1/*4*.

This collection is aptly named, for the digital recording captures some splendid sounds from the modern Coventry organ. With all the transcriptions arranged by Rawsthorne himself, obviously with the instrument in mind, he shows great flair in both playing and registration. It is a frankly popular programme, well laced with marches, balancing expansive tunes with opportunities for bravura, as in the *Aïda* march or the boisterous *Stars and stripes*. The resonance is well controlled by player and engineers alike, and this should be very impressive on CD – it is pretty spectacular on LP.

Romero, Pepe (guitar)

'Famous Spanish guitar music': ANON.: *Jeux interdits.* ALBÉNIZ: *Asturias.* MALATS: *Serenata española.* TARREGA: *Capricho Ababe.* SOR: *Introduction and variations on a theme of Mozart, Op. 9.* TARREGA: *Recuerdos de la Alhambra; Tango (Maria); Marieta; Las dos hermanitas.* TÓRROBA: *Romance de los pinos.*

ROMERO, Celedonio: *Malagueña; Fantasia.*
(*) Ph. Dig. **411 033-2; 6514/*7337* 381.

A thoroughly professional and immaculately played collection of favourites. The effect is rather calculated and sometimes a little chocolate-boxy – the virtuoso showing his paces in familiar vehicles. Of course a bravura piece like Tarrega's *Recuerdos de la Alhambra* cannot fail to make a strong impression, and the Tórroba *Romance* is very beguiling too. The Flamenco-based pieces by the composer's father, Celedonio, bring a sudden hint of fire, but for the most part the easy style of the playing does not generate a great deal of electricity. The recording is very natural and sounds well in all three formats, but even the compact disc gives a touch of blandness to the focus. No information is provided about the music (except titles).

Romero, Pepe, and **Celin Romero** (guitars)

'Famous Spanish dances': GRANADOS: *Danzas españoles, Op. 37, Nos. 2, 4, 5 and 10. Goyescas: Intermezzo.* ALBÉNIZ: *Suite española, Op. 47: Granada, Recuerdos de viaje, Op. 71: Rumores de la caleta. España, Op. 165: Tango; Malagueña.* FALLA: *El amor brujo: Ritual fire dance; Three-cornered hat: Miller's dance.*
** Ph. Dig. **411 432-2**; 6514/*7337* 182.

Here two guitars are not appreciably better than one, for these two artists blend their music making rather cosily together, rather than striking sparks off each other as do Julian Bream and John Williams. The music for the most part is rather gently projected (witness the opening Granados *Spanish dance*, which does not have the electrifying impact of Julian Bream's solo version) but not necessarily the worse for that, for the playing is musical and quite spontaneous. An enjoyable collection for late-evening listening, then, well recorded on CD, LP and tape alike, although the last is transferred at an astonishingly low level.

(Los) Romeros

BIZET: *Carmen suite.* CHAPI: *La Revoltosa: Overture.* FALLA: *La vida breve: Spanish dance No. 1. Three-cornered hat: Danza del corregidor; Danza del molinaro. Spanish popular songs by Jota; Nana; Polo.* TÓRROBA: *Sonatina brianera for four guitars and castanets.*
** Ph. Dig. **412 609-2**; 412 609-1/*4* [id.].

In the extended suite from *Carmen* (including six of the opera's most familiar numbers, alongside the Prélude to Act I) the combined guitars of Angel, Celedonio, Celín and Pepe are joined by Angelita on the castanets, but the effect is curiously cosy, even bland in the *Toreador song*, although the marvellous tunes sound very well in their guitar colouring. The following *Overture* from Ruperto Chapi's sainete (a one-Act zarzuela) has much more spirit, and the famous Falla pieces come off quite well. The recording is eminently realistic, although perhaps there is a shade too much resonance. There is a good tape.

Rosenthal, Moriz (piano)

'Ampico recordings': Vol. 1: CHOPIN: *Étude in G sharp min., Op. 25; Waltz in A flat, Op. 42.* CHOPIN/LISZT: *Chant polonnaise in G flat, Op. 74/5.* MENDELSSOHN: *Songs without words (Spring song), Op. 62/30; Op. 19/1.* RUBINSTEIN: *Valse-caprice.* ALBÉNIZ: *Oriental, Op. 232/2.* ROSENTHAL: *Carnaval de Vienne; Prelude in F sharp min.; Papillons.* BORTKIEWICZ: *Étude in D flat, Op. 15/8.*
*** O-L 414 098-1/*4* [id.].

Moriz Rosenthal (1862–1946) was a Liszt pupil in the mid-1870s. His reputation was legendary though he made fewer commercial records than, say, Rachmaninov. Apart from exciting the admiration of fellow pianists and musicians, Rosenthal gained the plaudits of critics as far apart in time and sensibility as Hanslick and Cardus: the latter spoke of 'his touch as almost aromatic and he distils fine fragrance', and admired the exquisite melancholy of his Chopin. Some of his poetry and all of his dazzling technical mastery come across in these superb transfers. While the caveat noted in Lhévinne's and Rachmaninov's Ampico recordings must be made, this is of little account when offset against the astonishing clarity and delicacy of so much on this record.

Smith, Daniel (bassoon)

English music for bassoon and piano (with Roger Vignoles): HURLSTONE: *Sonata in F.* ELGAR: *Romance, Op. 62.* JACOB: *4 Sketches.* ARNE (arr. Craxton/Mather): *Sonata No. 5 in G.* DUNHILL: *Lyric suite.* VAUGHAN WILLIAMS: *6 Studies in English folk song.* AVISON (arr. Atkinson): *Sonata in F.*
*** ASV Dig. DCA/*ZCDCA* 535 [id.].

An interesting collection of English bassoon music, sympathetically played, with a number of attractive rarities. The Arne and Avison are transcriptions, but nearly all the rest are original bassoon pieces, with the Elgar and Jacob in particular revealing special understanding for the instrument. Elgar shows his special vein of nostalgia (the *Romance* dates from 1910, the period of the *Violin concerto* and *Second Symphony*), and Gordon Jacob catches, in two out of the four movements, the instrument's humorous character. Vaughan Williams's six brief vignettes are melodically succinct and suit the bassoon rather well, though the composer wrote with the cello in mind. Daniel Smith's woody timbre has strong presence; it is caught with the utmost realism by the digital recording which helps a very convincing balance with the piano, very much in the picture. There is a first-class matching cassette. A worthwhile issue, though not to be played all at once.

Söllscher, Göran (guitar)

'Greensleeves': ANON./CUTTING: *Greensleeves*. ANON.: *Kemp's jig; Packington's round; Frog galliard*. GALILEI: *Toccata corrente; Volta*. WEISS: *Fantasie; Ciacona*. BACH (trans. Segovia): *Chaconne* (from *Violin partita No. 2*). SOR: *Variations on Marlborough s'en va-t-en guerre, Op. 28*.
** DG Dig. **413 352-2**; 2532/*3302* 054.

Söllscher is a fine player and he is beautifully recorded, with the background silence of the CD especially helpful. His playing is very positive, but not always relaxed enough to charm. He is at his finest in the famous Bach *Chaconne*, where his firm control and impeccable technique serve the music well, and then he relaxes attractively for the final item – the Sor *Variations* – and closes the recital with engaging communication. There is an excellent cassette.

'Cavatina': MYERS: *Cavatina; Portrait*. ALBÉNIZ: *Granada*. TÁRREGA: *Maria; Rosita*. BARIOS: *Villancico de Navidad*. YOCOH: *Sakura*. LLOBET: Arr. of Catalan folksongs: *La filla del marxant; La canço del lladre; El noi de la mare*. LAURO: *El Marabino*. CRESPO: *Norteña*. PATIÑO: *Nevando está*. NEUMANN: *Karleksvals*. CARMICHAEL: *Georgia on my mind*. ANON.: *Romance d'amour*.
*** DG Dig. **413 720-2**; 413 720-1/*4*.

Göran Söllscher is at his finest here. The programme is essentially Romantic and very tuneful and atmospheric. The indelible opening Myers *Cavatina* is of course the justly famous *Deerhunter theme*, while even the anonymous *Romance* will be familiar. Whether in the attractive Llobet arrangements of Catalan folksongs, the two evocative portraits from Tárrega, or Yocoh's colourful *Sakura* (from Japan), this is the kind of music making that remains in the memory, for even while the playing is relaxed there is no doubt about Söllscher's magnetism. Hoagy Carmichael's *Georgia on my mind* gives the feeling of a final lollipop as the stylish closing encore. The sound is most naturally balanced, and the immediacy and realism are apparent in all three formats, for the cassette is expertly transferred.

Stern, Isaac (violin), **Alexander Zakin** (piano)

BRAHMS: *F.A.E. Sonata: Scherzo*. SCHUMANN: *F.A.E. Sonata: Intermezzo*. DVOŘÁK: *Romantic Pieces, Op. 75*. ENESCU: *Sonata No. 3, Op. 25*.
*** CBS 74118/*40*- [M 39114].

In this record Isaac Stern pays tribute to his lifelong keyboard partner, Alexander Zakin, and offers some of the finest recordings they have made over the years. For collectors this is of particular value in restoring to circulation the *Third Violin sonata* of Enescu, a visionary work which in its ecstatic sound-world is almost reminiscent of Szymanowski. It is beautifully played here, particularly the demanding piano part, and is well worth a place in any collection. The Enescu was recorded in 1967 – but few would guess as much without having been told.

Tortelier, Paul (cello)

'Encores' (with Shuki Iwasaki, piano): SAINT-SAËNS: *Carnival of the Animals: The swan.* RAVEL: *Pièce en forme de habanera.* FAURÉ: *Papillon, Op. 77. Après un rêve.* MASSENET: *Elégie, Op. 10.* TORTELIER: *Pisanetto.* GRANADOS: *Goyescas: Intermezzo.* SARASATE: *Zapateado.* VALENTINI: *Violoncello sonata No. 10 in E major.* PAGANINI: *Moto perpetuo. Variations on a theme of Rossini.* DVOŘÁK: *Rondo in G minor, Op. 94.* CHOPIN: *Prelude in E minor, Op. 28/4.*
(M) *** HMV Green. ED 290209-1/*4*.

Tortelier is on top form here: Saint-Saëns's noble portrayal of *The swan*, which opens the recital, is beautifully played, and later the upper-register histrionics demanded by the display pieces of Sarasate and Paganini evoke an equally impressive bravura. Eloquent phrasing is matched by good taste, if this kind of programme appeals, it could hardly be better done. The recording spotlights the cello at the expense of the piano accompaniments, but in a programme of this nature that is not a serious drawback.

Turovsky, Eleonora (violin), **Yuli Turovsky** (cello)

French music for violin and piano: RAVEL: *Sonata.* RIVIER, Jean: *Sonatine.* HONEGGER: *Sonatine.* MARTINŮ: *Duo.*
*** Chan. Dig. **CHAN 8358**; ABTD/*ABRD* 1121 [id.].

An enterprising issue, albeit one that is unlikely to top the charts. Yuli Turovsky is best known as the cellist of the Borodin Trio, but his partner is hardly less fine. The most substantial piece here is the Ravel *Sonata*, which opens magically and is beautifully played by these two artists. Jean Rivier is little known outside France though his *Third* and *Fifth Symphonies* were recorded in the 1950s. His *Sonatine* lasts ten minutes and is slight but charming; while the Honegger and Martinů works are more challenging. There is over an hour's music here, repertoire that one seldom encounters in the concert hall. A very well-recorded programme, designed rather for the connoisseur of French music than for the wider record-collecting public, but well worth investigating. Tape collectors will find that the chrome cassette is admirably smooth and faithful.

Williams, John (guitar)

'Spanish music': ALBÉNIZ, I.: *Asturias; Tango; Córdoba.* SANZ: *Canarios.* RODRIGO: *Fandango.* TORROBA: *Nocturno.* GRANADOS: *Valses poeticos; La Maja de Goya.* ALBÉNIZ, M.: *Sonata in D.* FALLA: *Danse du Corregidor; Fisherman's song; Miller's dance.* TORROBA: *Madranos.* TRAD. (Catalan): *La nuit de Nadal: El noy de la mare.*
'Music from Japan, England and Latin America': YOCOH: *Theme and variations on 'Sakura'.* DODGSON: *Fantasy-Divisions.* PONCE: *Sonatina Meridional.* VILLA-LOBOS: *Chôros No. 1.* LAURO: *Valse criollo.* CRESPO: *Nortena.* SOJO: *5 Venezuelan pieces.* BARRIOS: *Danza Paraguaya.*
(B) *** CBS DC 40140 (2).

This CBS double-album combines two of John Williams's finest analogue recitals. Now offered for the price of one, they represent a real bargain, for the sound-balance has admirable realism and presence. The playing in the Spanish collection is often electrifying, including a marvellous performance of the delightful *Sonata in D* by Mateo Albéniz (not the more famous Isaac). The companion collection is more exotic. The Dodgson piece is by no means lightweight and it makes a good foil for the Villa-Lobos *Chôros* which it follows. The Venezuelan pieces are inventive and colourful too, while the *Sakura variations* transcribe effectively from the Japanese koto to the Western instrument. Throughout, Williams is a superbly assured and stylish advocate, and his interplay of mood is created with the spontaneity of a live recital. The equivalent cassette omits the Albéniz *Cordoba.*

Yepes, Narciso (guitar)

Spanish guitar music: TÁRREGA: *Recuerdos de la Alhambra; Capricho arabe; Serenata; Tango; Alborada; Marieta mazurka.* SOR: *Theme and variations, Op. 9; Minuet in G, Op. 11/1. Variations on Marlborough, Op. 28;* SANZ: *Spanish suite.* RODRIGO: *En los Trigales.* GRANADOS: *Spanish Dance No. 4.* ALBÉNIZ: *Rumores de la Caleta; Malaguena, Op. 165. Suite española: Asturias* (*Leyenda*). arr. LLOBET: *La canço del liadre; La filla del marzant* (Catalan folksongs). SEGOVIA: *El noi de la mare.* YEPES: *Forbidden games* (film score): *Romance.* VILLA-LOBOS: *Prelude No. 1.* RUIZ PIPO: *Canción and Danza No. 1.*
❀ *** DG Walkman *413 434-4.*

This can be recommended with the utmost enthusiasm to anyone wanting an inexpensive, generous (88 minutes) and representative programme of Spanish guitar music. Narciso Yepes is not only an outstanding exponent of this repertoire, he also has the rare gift of consistently creating electricity in the recording studio, and all this music springs vividly to life. In popular favourites like the famous opening *Recuerdos de la Alhambra* of Tárrega, the exciting transcription of Falla's *Miller's dance*, the earlier Baroque repertoire (the *Suite* of Sanz is particularly appealing), and in the communicative twentieth-century items by Rodrigo and Ruiz Pipo, Yepes' assured and always stylish advocacy brings consistent pleasure. The tape transfer level is quite high and the attendant hiss is not a problem. A real bargain in every sense of the word.

Zabaleta, Nicanor (harp)

'Harp music of 5 centuries': CABEZÓN: *Diferencias sobre la Gallarda Milanesa.* RODRIGUEZ: *Toccata No. 2 for harp.* HANDEL: *Theme and variations in G min.* BACH, C. P. E.: *Sonata, Wq.139.* VIOTTI: *Sonata in B flat.* SPOHR: *Variations, Op. 36.* CAPLET: *Divertissement.* SALZEDO: *Chanson dans la nuit.*
(M) *** DG Sig. 410 995-1/*4*.

The title stretches the point a little, for it was more likely that the fine Cabezón piece was intended for the vihuela; nevertheless, Zabaleta plays it with noble restraint. His taste is impeccable throughout this programme, finally producing the glissandos we associate with the modern instrument in the Salzedo *Chanson dans la nuit*. The C. P. E. Bach *Sonata* is well worth having, and the Spohr *Variations* have characteristic charm. The programme is well designed and Zabeleta's artistry gives consistent pleasure. He is recorded in an admirably chosen acoustic which has just the right degree of resonance; and the sound is faultless on both LP and cassette.

Vocal Recitals and Choral Collections

(John) Alldis Choir, LSO, Davis

'Festival of Christmas carols': MENDELSSOHN: *Hark the herald angels sing.* TRAD.: *Coventry carol; in dulci jubilo; God rest ye merry, gentlemen; The holly and the ivy; What child is this?; The first nowell; Good King Wenceslas; Deck the hall; O Tannenbaum; Patapan; I saw three ships; I wonder as I wander; Away in a manger;* HANDEL: *Joy to the world.* GRÜBER: *Silent night.* HOPKINS: *We three kings of orient are.* READING: *O come all ye faithful.*
(M) *** Ph. 416 249-1/*4*.

The arranger of this collection, Peter Hope, tells us in the notes: 'my purpose is to give pleasure, with arrangements that are easy to listen to without being trivial, and colourful without being tasteless'. He has succeeded and the colourful orchestrations give much delight, not least the flute-led woodwind in *Silent night* and the horns in *Tannenbaum*. The profusion of memorable tunes here cannot help but delight the ear in such vivid scoring; but this is primarily an orchestral collection in pot-pourri style, with the chorus entering only occasionally (and to great effect). The sound is first class on both LP and cassette; at Christmas this could be very enjoyable, interspersed with an all-vocal carol collection. Sir Colin Davis directs throughout with great affection, and the LSO respond most sensitively.

Ameling, Elly (soprano)

'Serenata' (with Rudolf Jansen, piano): TOSTI: *La Serenata.* CASTELNUOVO-TEDESCO: *Ninna nanna.* DOWLAND: *Weep you no more, sad fountaines.* QUILTER: *Weep you no more.* NAKADA: *Watakushi no kono kami.* MARX: *Hat dich die Liebe berührt.* SCHUMANN: *Du bist wie eine Blume.* WOLF: *Verborgenheit.* SATIE: *La diva de L'Empire.* HAHN: *L'amité; La vie belle.* BIZET: *Adieux de l'hôtesse arabe.* GOUNOD: *Viens! Les gazons sont verts!* CHABRIER: *L'île heureuse.* OBRADORS: *Del cabello mas sutil; El vito.* CIMAGLIA: *Niebla portena.*
*** Ph. Dig. **412 216-2**; 412 216-1/*4* [id.].

The charm of the Dutch soprano in lighter music is vividly caught in this attractive collection, taking its title from the song which receives the most memorable performance, Tosti's *Serenade*, enchantingly done. With an obvious exception in the Satie song, most items are slow, but the variety of expression makes up for that. Warm recording. On tape, a relatively modest transfer level brings sound-quality which is atmospheric rather than vividly detailed.

'Sentimental me' (with Louis van Dijk, piano, John Clayton, double bass): GERSHWIN: *I've got a crush on you; But not for me.* GOEMANS: *Aan de Amsterdames gratchen.* PORTER: *I get a kick out of you; What is this thing called love?; You do something to me; Begin the beguine; Night and day.* KERN: *All the things you are.* SONDHEIM: *Can that boy foxtrot!.* JOBIM: *Garota de Ipanema.* GIRAUD: *Sous le ciel de Paris.* ELLINGTON: *Caravan; Sophisticated lady; Solitude; It don't mean a thing; In a sentimental mood.*
*** Ph. Dig. **412 433-2**; 412 433-1/*4* [id.].

If anyone thought of Elly Ameling as just a staid singer in the Dutch manner, this frothy 'crossover' collection completely counters that. More than most who attempt to turn popular numbers into art songs, she finds a happy stylistic compromise. Although she is most obviously at home in a song like *Aan de Amsterdames gratchen*, numbers like *Night and day* and *Begin the beguine* bring an idiomatic response; and she is particularly good in the Ellington items. The recording is suitably intimate and atmospheric, and the balance with the piano is nicely judged. The sound is very good in all three media.

Anderson, Marian (contralto)

'The art of Marian Anderson' (with O, Collingwood; Kosti Vehanen, piano): HANDEL: *L'Allegro, il Penseroso ed il Moderato: Lass mich Wandernd. Siroe, Re di Persia: Ch'io mai vi possa. He was despised.* SCHUBERT: *Der Tod und das Mädchen; Ave Maria.* SIBELIUS: *Aus banger Brust; Långsamt som Kvällsskyn.* Arr. PALMGREN: *Läksin minä. Arr.* VEHANEN: *Tuku, tuku.* SAINT-SAËNS: *Samson et Dalila: Samson recherchant ma présence . . . Amour! viens aider ma faiblesse; Mon coeur a ta voix.* VERDI: *Don Carlo: O don fatale.* Spirituals: *I don't feel no ways tired; Deep river; Dere's no hiding place; Ev'ry time I feel de spirit; I can't stay away; Were you there?*
(M) **(*) HMV mono EG 290016-1/*4*.

Marian Anderson's career spanned five decades; her achievement was more than just vocal: she had the distinction in 1955 of being the first black artist to sing in opera on the stage of the New York Met. Her fame was world-wide but in England she was best known for her marvellous recordings of spirituals. Six are included here; in their humanity and innocent simplicity they generate the utmost magic. The vocal charisma is immediately apparent in the opening Handel aria (an unexpected choice for a 78 r.p.m. disc in 1936). Indeed, the range of material here is enterprisingly wide. Not everything is equally successful: the Saint-Saëns is far more impressive than the Verdi; but the Sibelius songs are especially worth having. The voice is clearly focused and truthful in timbre, even if at times one feels the balance of sound includes a little too much treble, to bring a touch of hardness on top. There is an excellent tape, which shares the full documentation of the LP.

Atlanta Chorus and Symphony Orchestra, Robert Shaw

'The many moods of Christmas' (arr. R. Russell Bennett): *Good Christian men, rejoice; Patapan; O come all ye faithful; O Sanctissima; Away in a manger; Fum fum fum; March of the Kings; What Child is this?; Bring a torch, Jeanette, Isabella; Angels we have heard on high; The first nowell; I saw three ships; Deck the halls.* GRÜBER: *Silent night.* MENDELSSOHN: *Hark the herald angels sing.* BACH: *Break forth, O beauteous heav'nly light.* REDNER-BROOKS: *O little town of Bethlehem.*
Ɛ *** Telarc **CD 80087**; DG 80087 [id.].

The carols here are arranged into four groups, each lasting about 12 minutes, and the scoring and use of both chorus and orchestra is as flamboyantly imaginative as one would expect from a musician of the calibre of Robert Russell Bennett. Moreover, the dynamic range of the recording is dramatically wide and the expansion of sound for the climaxes of *O come all ye faithful* and *Hark the herald angels sing*, with thrillingly realistic brass, is almost overwhelming. The chorus is backwardly balanced and with some choral pianissimos the words are barely audible, but the musical effect remains impressive. This is not a concert that can be treated as background music; one has to stop and listen, whether to the gentle solo lute playing of the *Greensleeves* melody by George Petsch (*What Child is this?*), the charming detail in *Bring a torch Jeanette, Isabella*, or the impressive choral interplay in the splendid arrangement of *Angels we have heard on high*. Technically this is vintage Telarc, with the hall's ambience seen as of primary importance in its warm colouring of the colourful sounds from voices and instrumentalists alike. Highly recommended on all counts.

Baker, Janet (mezzo-soprano)

Song recital: BERLIOZ: *Nuits d'été: Villanelle. Les Troyens: Pluton, semble, m'être propice.* FAURÉ: *Clair de lune.* GOUNOD: *Sérénade.* MASSENET: *Crépuscule.* CHABRIER: *Villanelle des petits canards.* CAMPION: *Fain would I wed.* TRAD.: *Drink to me only; I know where I'm going.* ELGAR: *Sea pictures: Where corals lie.* MENDELSSOHN: *Elijah: O rest in the Lord.* BACH: *Cantata No. 82: Aria: Ich habe genug.* STRAUSS, R.: *Morgen.* MAHLER: *Ich bin der Welt abhanden gekommen.*
❀ (B) *** CfP CFP 41 4487-1/*4*.

Compiled from some of Dame Janet's finest records of the 1960s and early 1970s, including some – like the Strauss – long unavailable, this CfP collection is a total delight. The variety of expression combined with keenly consistent intensity makes this a superb portrait of a great artist. The sound is transferred with commendable consistency, with an excellent matching tape. An outstanding bargain.

'Songs for Sunday' (with Philip Ledger, piano): BRAHE: *Bless this house.* PARRY: *Jerusalem.* TRAD.: *Were you there.* PLUMSTEAD: *A grateful heart. Close thine eyes.* EASTHOPE MARTIN: *The holy child.* THOMPSON: *The knights of Bethlehem.* LIDDLE: *How lovely are Thy dwellings. The Lord is my shepherd. Abide with me.* VAUGHAN WILLIAMS: *The call.* FORD: *A prayer to Our Lady.* BACH–GOUNOD: *Ave Maria.* WALFORD DAVIES: *God be in my head.*
(M) *** EMI EMX 41 2089-1/*4*.

Dame Janet Baker's total dedication makes this a moving experience, transforming songs that would as a rule seem merely sentimental. Sensitive accompaniment and excellent recording by Philip Ledger, which has transferred admirably to tape, where the atmospheric sound remains clear, with only slight loss of definition at the top.

Ballads: 'World of Favourite Ballads'

(i) Stuart Burrows; (ii) Felicity Palmer; (iii) Norman Bailey; (iv) Forbes Robinson; (v) Robert Tear; (vi) Benjamin Luxon: (i) BALFE: *Come into the Garden, Maud.* MURRAY: *I'll walk beside you.* (ii) MOLLOY: *Love's old sweet song.* HAYDNWOOD: *A brown bird is singing.* BISHOP: *Home, sweet home.* (iii) BRAHE: *Bless this house.* MOSS: *The floral dance.* RASBACH: *Trees.* (iv) SPEAKS: *On the road to Mandalay; Sylvia.* (v) VAUGHAN WILLIAMS: *Linden Lea.* ANON.: *And yet I love her till I die.* (vi) CAPEL: *Love, could I only tell thee.* WOODFORDE-FINDEN: *Kashmiri song.*
(M) *** Decca 411 642-1/*4*.

An attractive and generous collection that adds variety of vocal timbre and presentation to a well-mixed programme. Highlights include Norman Bailey's splendidly lively *Floral dance* and Stuart Burrows' honeyed *I'll walk beside you*, with Forbes Robinson's *On the road to Mandalay* and Benjamin Luxon's *Kashmiri song* adding a strong period flavour. The excellent accompanists include John Constable, Geoffrey Parsons and Philip Ledger. The recording is extremely vivid, but on tape the transfer level is too high and climaxes become peaky.

Berganza, Teresa (mezzo-soprano)

Venetian concert (with Yasunori Imamura, lute, theorbo, chitarra; Joerg Ewald, harpsichord or organ; and continuo): STROZZI: *Non ti doler mio cor; Rissolvetevi pensieri.* SANCES: *Misera, hor si ch'il pianto; O perduti diletti.* MONTEVERDI: *Confitebor tibi Domine.* MILANUZZI: *Ut re mi.* FONTEI: *Auree stelle.* MINISCALCHI: *Fuggir pur mi convien; Fuggir voglio.* LAMORETTI: *Bell'il vana tua beltade.* (Instrumental): MOLINARO: *Fantasia nono.* PALESTRINA: *Vestiva i colli.* RORE: *Anchor che col partire.*
*** Claves **CD 8206**; D 8206 [id.].

Teresa Berganza is the star of this attractive concert of Venetian music, with little of the included repertoire at all familiar. The vocal contributions are characteristically intelligent and stylish – but expressively telling, too. The instrumental numbers provide suitable contrast and are very well done; the recording has fine presence, although the CD offers only a marginal gain on the LP – except in the matter (not a small one here) of freedom from intrusive background noises. The collection is well documented.

'Grandi voci': HAYDN: *Arianna a Naxos* (cantata). MOZART: *Così fan tutte: Ah! scostati! . . . Smanie implacabili; E amore un ladroncello. La Clemenza di Tito: Parto, parto.* ROSSINI: *Il Barbiere di Siviglia: Una voce poco fa; Contro un cor. L'Italiana in Algeri: Cruda sorte! Amor titanno!; Pur lui che adoro; Amici, in ogni evento . . . Pensa alla patria.*
(M) *** Decca 414 612-1/*4* [id.].

A fine collection, mostly recorded early in the singer's career and revealing her at her freshest and brightest, producing golden tone along with brilliance in coloratura. The Rossini items come from a dazzling recital recorded in 1959, the *Così fan tutte* arias from Sir Georg Solti's complete recording of 1974. The Haydn cantata, with Felix Lavilla at the piano, recorded in 1977, is issued for the first time. Excellent transfers. The high-level cassette is bright, fresh and clear.

'Signature' BIZET: *Carmen: Havanaise; Duet; Seguidilla; Les tringles des sistres tintaient.* ROSSINI: *Il Barbiere di Siviglia: Una voce poco fa; Contro un cor; Dunque io son. La Cenerentola: Tutto è deserto. Una violta c'era.* PERGOLESI: *Stabat Mater: Quae morebat; Fac, ut portem.* MOZART: *La Clemenza di Tito: Deh per questo istante.*
(M) **(*) DG Sig. 415 444-1/*4* [id.].

The Bizet and Rossini excerpts come from Berganza's complete sets under Abbado. She is a seductive if a somewhat straightfaced Carmen, but here, as in her Rossini characterizations, the agility and reliability of the singing give much pleasure. The timbre is warm, too – though charm is not always a strong point. Overall, this is an attractive collection, vividly recorded, though on the high-level tape there are a few moments of peaking.

Bergonzi, Carlo (tenor)

'Signature': VERDI: *Il Trovatore: Quale d'armi . . . Di quella pira. Rigoletto: Questa o quella; Ella mi fu rapita . . . Possente amor; La donna è mobile; Quartet* (with Scotto, Cossotto, Fischer-Dieskau). MASCAGNI: *Cavalleria Rusticana:* Finale: *Mamma, quel vino.* LEONCAVALLO: *I Pagliacci: Un tal gioco; Vesti la giubba; No! Pagliaccio non son.*
(M) **(*) DG Sig. 415 445-1/*4* [id.].

One of the most consistent and stylish of Italian tenors, in vintage performances of favourite items taken from complete opera sets of the 1960s. A collection directed mainly at admirers of this artist, the programme includes only standard repertoire.

Berlin German Opera Chorus and Orchestra, Sinopoli

Opera choruses: MOZART: *Die Zauberflöte: O Isis und Osiris.* BEETHOVEN: *Fidelio: O welche Lust.* WEBER: *Der Freischütz: Huntsmen's chorus; Viktoria! Viktoria!* WAGNER: *Tannhäuser: Grand march.* VERDI: *Nabucco: Va, pensiero. I Lombardi: O Signore, dal tetto natio. Macbeth: Patria oppressa. Il Trovatore: Anvil chorus. Aïda: Gloria all'Egitto . . . Vieni, o guerriero vindice.*
*** DG Dig. **415 283-2**; 415 283-1/*4* [id.].

A splendid collection of choruses, full of character, the atmosphere of each opera distinctive. The pianissimo at the beginning of the famous *Fidelio Prisoners' chorus* has striking intensity, while the exuberant *Hunting chorus* from *Freischütz* is irresistible in its buoyancy. On the other hand, Sinopoli's broadening of the sustained tune in the short *Aïda* excerpt may for some seem too deliberate. Needless to say, the orchestral playing is first class; the balance, with the orchestra placed vividly forward and the chorus set back within a warmly resonant acoustic, is most convincing, although words are not always sharply clear. A well-balanced and rewarding compilation in all other respects, especially vivid in its compact disc format, slightly less clear on cassette, but still impressive.

Buchanan, Isobel (soprano), Ronald Maconaghie (baritone)

Scottish and Irish folk songs (with Sharolyn Kimmorley, piano)*: Ye banks and braes; The crooked bawbee; The wee wee cooper o' Fife; Island spinning song; Air Falalalo; Ho-reem Ho ro my little wee girl; Westering home; The rowan tree; Marie's wedding; Turn ye to me; The Keel row; Dashing white sergeant; Flight of the Earls; The green bushes; Believe me, if all those endearing young charms; Molly Brannigan; Love's young dream; She moved thro' the fair; Next market day; I know where I'm going; The harp that once through Tara's halls; The young May moon; Londonderry air.*
(B) *** CfP CFP 41 4497-1/*4*.

A simply and eloquently sung collection that cannot fail to give pleasure. Some of the songs are unaccompanied and, without the piano, the hint of the concert hall (that some might count a disadvantage elsewhere) disappears. Isobel Buchanan's voice is heard at its most beautiful in the Irish repertoire, such as *She moved thro' the fair* and *I know where I'm going*; and *The green bushes* sung as a duet shows the partnership at its most felicitous. With excellent recording and fine accompaniments from Sharolyn Kimmorley, this collection, which derives from the Australian Broadcasting Corporation, is among the finest of its kind currently available. There is a good matching tape, only a little less free in the upper range than the disc.

Burchuladze, Paata (bass)

Arias (with ECO, London Opera Chorus, Edward Downes): MUSSORGSKY: *Boris Godunov: Coronation scene; Monologue; Clock scene; Death of Boris.* VERDI: *Simon Boccanegra: A te l'estremo addio . . . Il lacerato spirito. Macbeth: Studia il passo . . . Come dal ciel precipita. Don Carlo: Ella giamma m'amò. Ernani: Che mai vegg'io! . . . Infelice! . . . Infin che.*
*** Decca Dig. **414 335-2**; 414 335-1/*4*.

This exciting Russian bass from Georgia sings each one of these items with gloriously firm tone from top to bottom of the register. In every sense a great voice is revealed, and the repertory could hardly be more apt, one side comprising Verdi's finest bass arias, the other Boris's principal solos. If little depth of feeling is conveyed as yet, the sensuous beauty of the sound is enough to make this a very special bass recital record, strongly accompanied by Downes and his team and brilliantly recorded in all three media.

Burrows, Stuart (tenor)

'Operetta favourites' (with Nat. PO, Stapleton): LEHÁR: *Land of Smiles: You are my heart's delight. Frederica: O maiden, my maiden. Frasquita: Farewell, my love. Paganini: Girls were made to love and kiss. Czarevitch: Alone, always alone. Giuditta: Comrades, this is the life for me.* SIECZYŃSKY: *Vienna . . . city of my dreams.* ROMBERG: *The Student Prince: Serenade.* TAUBER: *Old Chelsea: My heart and I.* STOLZ: *Don't ask me why.* NOVELLO: *Glamorous Night: Shine through my dreams.* KUNNEKE: *The Cousin from Nowhere: I'm only a strolling vagabond.*
(M) *** Decca 414 643-1/*4*.

Stuart Burrows' collection is a tribute to Richard Tauber, and he shows himself an excellent successor in this repertoire, with his headily beautiful tenor tone and direct charm. The sound is excellent and this is strongly recommendable on LP. The high-level cassette, however, is rather fierce and the transfer takes the bloom off the orchestral strings.

Caballé, Montserrat (soprano)

'Signature': GOUNOD: *Faust: Song of the King of Thule; Jewel song. Roméo et Juliette: Je veux vivre dans le rêve.* MEYERBEER: *Les Huguenots: O beau pays.* CHARPENTIER: *Louise: Depuis le jour.* BIZET: *Carmen: Micaela's aria.* STRAUSS, R.: *Salome: Es ist kein Laut zu vernehmen.* PUCCINI: *Manon Lescaut: Tu, tu, amore? Tu?* (with Placido Domingo).
(M) **(*) DG Sig. 415 446-1/*4* [id.].

The French arias come from a 1971 recital, with the Meyerbeer and *Carmen* arias the highlights. The voice is caught with full bloom but this account of *Depuis le jour* is not quite so memorable as Cabellé's performance on a Spanish-made RCA record (now withdrawn), made even earlier in her career. The version of the final scene of *Salome* with Bernstein came more than a decade after she had recorded the complete opera (also for RCA) with Leinsdorf, and the singing has much of the same imagination. The *Manon Lescaut* duet with Domingo is a live recording and has fine immediacy.

Callas, Maria (soprano)

'Mad scenes and Bel canto arias' (with Philh. O, Rescigno): DONIZETTI: *Anna Bolena: Piangete voi; Al dolce guidami. La figlia del reggimento: Convienpartir. Lucrezia Borgia: Tranquillo ei possa . . . Come' è bello. L'Elisir d'amore: Prendi, per me sei libero.* THOMAS: *Hamlet: À vos jeux; Partagez-vous mes fleurs; Et maintenant écoutez ma chanson.* BELLINI: *Il Pirata: Oh! s'io potessi . . . Col sorriso d'innocenza; Sorgete, Lo sognai ferito esangue.*
*** HMV **CDC 747283-2** [id.].

If, as ever, the rawness of exposed top-notes mars the sheer beauty of Callas's singing, few recital records ever made can match, let alone outshine, her collection of mad scenes in vocal and dramatic imagination. This is Callas at her very peak; Desmond Shawe-Taylor suggested this as the collection which, more than any other, summed up the essence of Callas's genius. For the CD reissue further arias have been added, notably excerpts from Donizetti's *La figlia del reggimento*, *L'Elisir d'amore* and *Lucrezia Borgia* (from the mid-1960s), a fair example of the latter-day Callas, never very sweet-toned, yet displaying the usual Callas fire. However, the singing here is less imaginative and there are few phrases that stick in the memory by their sheer individuality. Nevertheless, the main part of the recital is indispensable; the digital remastering has enhanced the originally excellent recordings and given the voice striking presence.

Cambridge Schola Gregoriana, Berry

'Anglo Saxon Easter' (Chants and Tropes for the Mass on Easter Day from the Winchester Troper).
*** DG Arc. Dig. 413 546-1/*4*.

It comes as a surprise to find so grand a setting of the Easter service dating from over a thousand years ago. Mary Berry and her scholarly group have together reconstructed the outlines suggested in manuscripts and produced a service that is both dramatic and moving. Such a reconstruction requires much scholarly detective work. The notation of most of the two Winchester manuscripts consists of neumes which do not indicate a precise pitch. To prepare a performing edition, it was necessary to locate either at home (including Worcester, Canterbury, Downpatrick sources) or abroad (Dijon, Chartres, Nevers), and it was even found possible to include the early two-part harmonic device of organum. The result is astonishingly effective and memorable and brings this centuries-old music fully alive within a vividly atmospheric ecclesiastical acoustic. The chrome cassette is in the demonstration class, the focus splendidly firm and clear, and – until this appears on CD – is the preferred format, with its freedom from intrusive background noise.

Canterbury Cathedral Choir, Allan Wicks

'I was glad' (with Philip Jones Brass Ens.): VAUGHAN WILLIAMS: *O clap your hands; O taste and see; Valiant for truth; Old Hundredth; Sine nomine.* IRELAND: *Greater love hath no man.* PARRY: *I was glad; My soul there is a country; Jerusalem.* STANFORD: *Gloria in excelsis.* ELGAR: *Give unto the Lord, Op. 73; Ave verum, Op. 2/1.*
**(*) Argo Dig. 411 714-1/*4*.

A well-chosen collection of English church music from the early years of the century, done with freshness and vigour. With brass contributing to four of the twelve items, the sound is spectacular, though words are not ideally clear. LP and cassette are closely matched.

Carreras, José (tenor)

French opera arias (with ROHCG O, Jacques Delacôte): GOUNOD: *Faust: Salut! Demeure chaste. Roméo et Juliette: L'Amour! Polyeucte: Source délicieuse.* MASSENET: *Le Cid: O Souverain. Sapho: Ah! qu'il est loin, mon pays. Hérodiade: Adieu donc, vains objets.* HALÉVY: *La Juive: Rachel! quand du Seigneur.* MEYERBEER: *L'Africaine: O paradis.* LALO: *Le roi d'ys: Vainement ma bien aimée.* BIZET: *Carmen: La fleur que tu m'avais jetée.*
**(*) HMV Dig. EL 270262-1/*4* [Ang. DS/*4DS* 38103].

Carreras's collection of French arias includes rarities like the *Sapho*, *Hérodiade* and *Polyeucte* items, all beautifully if rather strenuously done. Carreras's thoughtfulness and fine musicianship come over consistently. Though this artist may not always match the finest rivals of the past, the disc, well recorded, fills a valuable niche. The cassette, although smoothly transferred, lacks range and sparkle in the treble.

Neapolitan songs (with ECO, Muller): DENZA: *Funiculi, funicula; I'te vurria vasà*. CARDILLO: *Core 'ngrato*. D'ANNIBALE: *'O paese d'o sole*. FALVO: *Dicitencello vuie*. LAMA: *Silenzio cantatore*. MARIO: *Santa Lucia luntana*. DI CURTIS: *Tu, ca nun chiagne! Torna a Surriento*. DI CAPUA: *'O sole mio*. BOVIO/TAGLIAFERRI: *Passione*. CIOFFI: *'Na sera 'e maggio*. CANNIO: *'O surdato 'nnamurato*.
(*) Ph. Dig. **400 015-2; 9500/*7300* 943 [id.].

José Carreras produces refined tone here. The performances have plenty of lyrical fervour and are entirely lacking in vulgarity. The opening *Funiculi, funicula* is attractively lilting, but elsewhere some listeners will wish for a more gutsy style. The recording is first class. The compact disc combines naturalness with added presence, yet the sound remains warmly atmospheric. The chrome tape is smooth and kind to the voice but is less sharply defined.

'You belong to my heart' (with ECO, Asensio): LARA: *You belong to my heart*. LEONCAVALLO: *Mattinata*. BELLINI: *Fenesta che lucive*. LECOUNA: *Siboney*. ROSSINI: *La danza*. GARDEL: *El Día que me quieras*. BARGONI: *Concerto d'autonno*. GREVER: *Te quiero*. D'HARDELOT: *Because*. ROIG: *Quiéreme mucho*. EPOSITO: *Anema e core*. MENENDEZ: *Aquellos ojos*.
(*) Ph. Dig. **411 422-2; 411 422-1/*4* [id.].

Following his rivals Domingo and Pavarotti, Carreras here presents a collection of love-songs coming from European popular repertoire as distinct from the American-derived rhythm-and-blues idiom represented below. They are all done with commendable taste and attractively presented – if with only a few hints of their earthier, more robust side. The recording is bright and lively in all three media; the cassette gives good projection of the voice and bright string timbre.

'Love is' (with O, Farnon): BRODSZKY: *Because you're mine*. HUPFELD: *As time goes by*. FAIN: *Love is a many-splendoured thing*. HAMLISCH: *The way we were*. BERNSTEIN: *West Side story: Tonight*. GROSS: *Tenderly*. STEINER: *My own true love*. MANDEL: *The sandpiper*. LLOYD WEBBER: *Cats: Memory*. LEGRAND: *The summer knows*. DARION: *Man of La Mancha: The impossible dream*. FRANÇOIS: *My way*.
(*) Ph. Dig. **412 270-2; 412 270-1/*4* [id.].

The potency of such a splendid tenor voice unleashed in standards like *The impossible dream* and *My way* is undeniable, yet José Carreras is most impressive of all in the ballads, bringing considerable nostalgia to *The way we were*. The very opening number is given a feeling of Hollywood kitsch by his slight accent, yet lyrics are admirably clear throughout, and *Tonight* from *West Side story* projects splendidly. Robert Farnon's accompaniments are stylishly made and the recording is first class in all three formats.

Opera arias (with LPO, Lopez-Cobos): VERDI: *I vespri siciliani: E di Monforte il cenno . . . Giorno di pianto. Rigoletto: Ella mi fu rapita . . . Parmi veder le lagrime. Ernani: Mercè, diletti amici . . . Come rugiada al cespite. Attila: Qui del convegno è il loco . . . Che non avrebbe il misero.* DONIZETTI: *L'Elisir d'amore: Una furtiva lagrima. Roberto Devereux: Ed ancor la Tremenda porta . . . A te dirò.* ROSSINI: *Stabat Mater: Cuius animam gementem. Guglielmo Tell: Non mi lasciare . . . O muto asil del pianto.*
(M) **(*) Ph. 416 248-1/*4*.

Though the voice is one of the most beautiful among tenors today, and the selection of items is attractively varied, Carreras here shows the occasional sign of wear and only in *Una furtiva lagrima* from *L'Elisir d'amore* is there really hushed singing. Even so, the performances are strong and committed, with *Cujus animam* from Rossini's *Stabat Mater* bringing a fine top D-flat. Well-balanced and vivid (1981) recording on both LP and tape, with full translations provided. This is good value at mid-price.

Arias: VERDI: *Il Corsaro: Come liberi . . . Tutto parea; Eccomo prigionero. I due Foscari: Notte, perpetua notte . . . Non maledirmi.* PUCCINI: *Tosca: E lucevan le stelle.* ROSSINI: *Elisabetta Regina d'Inghilterra: Dell cieca fortuna . . . Sposa amata.* DONIZETTI: *Lucia di Lammermoor: Tombe degl'avi mei . . . Fra poco a me ricovero.*
(M) *** Ph. 6527/*7311* 193 [id.].

This analogue Carreras collection is compiled mainly from contributions to complete opera sets. It makes an attractive, mid-price tenor recital, spiced as it is with rarities. The sound is consistently vivid on LP, although the tape is a little lacking in brilliance. But the vocal timbre is truthful, and projection and detail remain good.

Choral music

'Great choral classics' (sung by various artists): excerpts from: HANDEL: *Messiah.* BERLIOZ: *L'Enfance du Christ. Requiem.* BACH: *Cantata 147. St Matthew Passion.* FAURÉ, VERDI, MOZART: *Requiems.* POULENC: *Gloria.* ORFF: *Carmina Burana.* VIVALDI: *Gloria.* GOUNOD: *St Cecilia Mass.* BRAHMS: *German Requiem.* WALTON: *Belshazzar's Feast.* MENDELSSOHN: *Elijah.* BEETHOVEN: *Missa solemnis.* PURCELL: *Rejoice in the Lord.*
(B) ** EMI *TC2-MOM 116*.

A wide-ranging programme, quite imaginatively selected as entertainment for the car. The changing acoustic and degrees of reverberation bring less variation than might be expected in clarity of focus. Even the *Dies irae* from the Berlioz *Requiem* (surely ideal for playing in a traffic jam) avoids congestion. The opening excerpts from *Messiah* sound a little dry, and it is a pity that Muti's (rather than Previn's) *O fortuna* from *Carmina Burana* was chosen, as the quieter moments lack clarity in the tape version. Also the King's acoustic in *Jesu, joy of man's desiring* brings a rather mushy choral quality. Highlights include the *Sanctus* from Muti's Verdi *Requiem*, the delightful *Shepherds' chorus* from *L'Enfance du Christ* and the vivid *Praise ye the God of Gold* from Previn's *Belshazzar's Feast*. Purcell's anthem *Rejoice in the Lord* is heard complete.

Circa 1500

Renaissance music from the Courts of Mantua and Ferrara. Music by: CARA; TROMBONCINO; SPINACINO; DIOMEDES; ROMANO; ANON.
** Chan Dig. **CHAN 8333**; ABRD/*ABTD* 1110 [id.].

Circa 1500 is a mixed consort of soprano, flute, viola da gamba, lute and guitar. Their performances here, of some very attractive music, are fresh if sometimes a little over-refined. The main burden falls on Emily Van Evera who is a most accomplished singer with a clear, pure vocal line. She is highly musical, never squally, but she seldom sings dramatically; and one could ask for more variety of colour. The instrumental sounds might also with advantage have sought a more robust effect. However, the recording is eminently realistic and the collection is well documented.

Crespin, Régine (soprano)

'Grandi voci' (with SRO or V. Volksoper O, Alain Lombard or Georges Sebastian): GLUCK: *Iphigénie en Tauride: Cette nuit . . . O toi qui prolongeas.* BERLIOZ: *La damnation de Faust: D'amour l'ardente flamme.* GOUNOD: *Sapho: O ma lyre.* SAINT-SAËNS: *Ascanio: Le chanson de Scozzone.* MASSENET: *Werther: Air des lettres: Va! laisse couler mes larmes; Ah! mon courage m'abandonne! . . . Seigneur Dieu!* BIZET: *Carmen: Habañera; Seguidilla.*
(M) *** Decca 414 444-1/*4*.

This is a reissue of the operatic half of a superb early-1970s two-disc collection, which revealed Crespin at her most commanding and characterful. Though as ever the microphone brings out the unevennesses in the vocal production, the ringing vibrancy is consistently compelling, a fine portrait of a great artist, helped by excellent recording on both LP and cassette. We hope Decca have plans to reissue the operetta section of this recital in their *Grandi voci* series, as this is even more delectable. Two of the items are already included in the *'Golden Operetta'* anthology – see below.

Dawson, Peter (bass-baritone)

'On stage': excerpts from: SULLIVAN: *The Pirates of Penzance; Patience; Iolanthe; The Mikado; The Yeomen of the Guard; The Gondoliers;* and from operetta and musical comedy, including: *The Arcadians; Merrie England; Our Miss Gibbs; Chu Chin Chow; Maid of the Mountains; Southern Maid; Show Boat* and other Jerome Kern musicals.
(*) HMV mono EM 290573-3/*5* (2).

A disappointing selection. Many of these recordings are primitive, and in cutting down the background noise the engineers have taken the brightness off the voice; moreover, the other singers who join Peter Dawson in the concerted numbers are frequently undistinguished. The Gilbert and Sullivan excerpts generally sound dim, and many of the excerpts from musical comedy will sound terribly dated, except perhaps to aficionados prepared to make allowances. Every so often there is a song (and there are surprisingly few) where the voice suddenly comes alive and projects splendidly, as in *The Yeomen of England* on side two, or Fraser-Simson's *Call of the sea* from *A Southern maid. The Cobbler's song* from Chu Chin Chow is also memorable, as is an unlikely 'Tchaikovsky' duet (with Bessie Jones) called *The lily and the sun*, a garbled version of the famous melody from the first movement of the *Pathétique symphony. Ol' man river*, which ends the recital, is impressive too – but so much else is not. Tapes and discs are closely matched and excellent documentation is also provided with the cassette box.

Reminder. *'The art of Peter Dawson'* includes the widest range of Peter Dawson recordings made between 1906 and 1934. The sound is admirably vivid, and this fine collection cannot be too strongly recommended. Dawson's career spanned virtually the whole 78 r.p.m. era, and the size of his vocal personality and the famous clarity of diction are equally well demonstrated (HMV mono RLS/ *TC RLS* 107705-3/*5* (2)).

Deller, Alfred (counter-tenor)

'Grandi voci': CAMPION: *Never weatherbeaten sail; Most sweet and pleasing are thy ways; Author of light; To music bent.* ANON.: *Miserere my maker.* BUXTEHUDE: *Jubilate domino.* PURCELL: *Come ye sons of art* (excerpts). BACH: *Magnificat: Esurientes.* HANDEL: *Sosarme: Alle sfere; in mille dolci modi; M'Opporro da generoso.*
(M) (***) Decca mono 411 661-1/*4*.

Compiled from Oiseau-Lyre mono recordings of the 1950s, this fine collection of favourites and rarities explains how Alfred Deller, distinctive in timbre and style, established the counter-tenor voice with a wider public than ever before. Good transfers, and a nicely laid-out recital. The voice is given a most realistic presence, both on LP and on the excellent cassette; the only snag is that some of the accompaniments are made to sound thin; and in the set of excerpts (9′ 21″) from *Come ye sons of art* on side two the chorus and orchestra are constricted.

Dimitrova, Ghena (soprano)

Opera arias (with Munich R.O., Gardelli): VERDI: *Aïda: Ritorna vincitor. I Lombardi: Salve Maria. Attila: Oh! Nel fuggente nuvolo. Macbeth: Viene! t'affretta!* PONCHIELLI: *La Gioconda: Suicidio!* CILEA: *Adriana Lecouvreur: Io son l'umile ancela; Poveri fiori.* GIORDANO: *Andrea Chénier: La mamma morta.* CATALANI: *La Wally: Ne andrò lontano.* PUCCINI: *Turandot: in questa reggia.*
*** HMV Dig. EL 270041-1/*4* [Ang. DS/*4DS* 38074]

With her powerful, lyric-dramatic voice, Dimitrova is here at her finest in a wide-ranging collection of items, with fire-eating performances of Lady Macbeth's and Turandot's arias. Vocal production is not always firm enough on top, and the engineers have problems over focusing the voice, but with Gardelli the most perceptive accompanist, this is consistently exciting, the finest recording this uneven singer has yet made.

Domingo, Placido (tenor)

Verdi, Puccini, Gounod, Boito: VERDI: *Aïda: Se quel guerrier . . . Celeste Aïda; Pur ti riveggo . . . Fuggiam gli ardori inospiti. Don Carlo: Su cacciator . . . Fontainebleau!; Al chiostro di San Giusto . . . Dio che nell'alma. Un Ballo in maschera: Su, profetessa . . . Di' tu se fedele; Teco io sto; Non sai tu che se l'anima; Forse la soglia attinse . . . Ma se m'è forza perderti. Giovanna d'Arco: Il Re! . . . Sotto una quercia . . . Pondo è letal.* PUCCINI: *Tosca: Dammi i colori . . . Recondita armonia; È lucevan le stelle; O dolce mani. Manon Lescaut: Donna non vidi mai; Ah, sarò la più bella . . . Tu, tu amore . . . Taci, taci; Ah, Manon, mi tradisce; Presto! In fila . . . No! no! Pazzo son.* GOUNOD: *Faust: Rien! En vain j'interroge; Quel trouble inconnu me pénètre . . . Salut! Demeure chaste et pure; Il se fait tard.* BOITO: *Mefistofele; Dai campi, dai prati; Forma ideal Purissima.*
(M) *** HMV EX 143448-3/*5* (2) [Ang. AVB 34024].

Compiled from Domingo's contributions to EMI opera sets in the 1970s, this excellent two-disc collection is a resounding tribute to his remarkable consistency as a musician, not just to his magnificent voice. If he has since recorded such items as the *Manon Lescaut* aria and duet more perceptively, and if his singing of *Faust* here is less stylish than it usually is in French music, the range of achievement is formidable and the beauties great. Excellent transfers, both on discs and on a pair of tapes packaged in EMI's new-style plastic box with good back-up documentation. The tapes lose only a little at the top, with both voice and orchestra given attractive bloom, yet remaining vivid. At mid-price, this is splendid value.

Operatic recital (*1970–80 recordings*): VERDI: *Aïda: Se quel guerrier . . . Celeste Aïda. Giovanna d'Arco: Sotto una quercia . . . Pondo è letal, martiro. Un Ballo in maschera: Forse la soglia . . . Ma se m'è forza perderti. Don Carlo: Fontainebleau!*

. . . *Io la vidi, al suo sorriso; Ascolta! . . . Dio che nell'alma infondere.* GOUNOD: *Faust: Quel trouble inconnu . . . Salut! Demeure chaste et pure; Il se fait tard.* BOITO: *Mefistofele: Dai campi, dai prati.* PUCCINI: *Manon Lescaut: Donna non vidi mai! Ah, Manon, mi tradisce. Tosca: Dammi i colori . . . Recondita armonia; È lucevan le stelle; Ah! Franchigia a Floria Tosca . . . O dolci mani . . . Amaro.*
*** HMV Dig. **CDC 747257-2** [id.].

This is taken from the above two-disc/two-tape set and includes some 71 minutes of music. The remastering for CD brings the advantage of negligible background noise, but otherwise there is no great gain in presence, though the sound is admirably clear and well balanced. The Puccini items sound especially real, combining a fresh clarity with a pleasing atmosphere.

'Ave Maria' (with Vienna Boys' Choir, VSO, Froschauer): HERBECK: *Pueri concinite.* TRAD.: *Adeste fidelis.* FRANCK: *Panis angelicus.* SCHUBERT: *Ave Maria.* KIENZL: *Der Evangelimann: Selig sind, die Verfolgung leiden.* HANDEL: *Xerxes: Ombra mai fù.* EYBLER: *Omnes de Saba venient.* BACH–GOUNOD: *Ave Maria.* FAURÉ: *Crucifix.* BIZET: *Agnus Dei.* LUTHER: *A mighty fortress is our God* (*Ein feste Burg*).
*** RCA **RD 70760 [RCD1 3835]**.

This collection dates from 1979 and can be recommended unreservedly. Domingo is in freshest voice and these famous religious 'pops' are sung with golden tone and a simple eloquence that is most engaging. Nothing sounds routine and the Vienna Boys make a considerable contribution, not only by providing a treble soloist to share Schubert's *Ave Maria* but in the dialogue of the excerpt from Kienzl's *Evangelimann* (an attractive novelty and a highlight of the programme). In the closing chorale (*Ein feste Burg*) the Chorus Viennensis join the group to excellent effect. Attractively atmospheric recording with Domingo's voice given fine presence and bloom.

'Bravissimo, Domingo!': VERDI: *Il Trovatore: Di quella pira. Un Ballo in maschero: Teco io sto* (with Leontyne Price). *Rigoletto: La donna è mobile. Otello: Ah! Mille vite; Si, pel ciel marmoreo giuro! Don Carlo: Dio, che nell'alma infondere* (both with Sherrill Milnes). *Aïda: Se quel guerrier io fossi . . . Celeste Aïda. La Traviata: Lunge da lei . . . De miei bollenti spiriti.* PUCCINI: *Tosca: È lucevan le stelle. Manon Lescaut: Oh, sarò la più bella!; Tu, tu, amore tu?* (with Leontyne Price). *Turandot: Non piangere Liù.* LEONCAVALLO: *Pagliacci: Recitar! Mente preso . . . Vesti la giubba.* CILEA: *Adriana Lecouvreur: L'anima ho stanco.* GOUNOD: *Roméo et Juliette: L'amour! L'amour! Ah! Lève-toi, soleil. Faust: Quel trouble inconnu; Salut! Demeure chaste et pure.* GIORDANO: *Andrea Chénier: Un di all'azzurro spazio.* MASCAGNI: *Cavalleria rusticana: Mamma; mamma! Quel vino è generoso.* BIZET: *Carmen: Flower song.*
*** RCA **RD 87020**.

This selection of recordings ranges wide over Domingo's recording career. The opening items come from complete sets and *Di quella pira* immediately establishes the ringing vocal authority. The excerpts from *Cav.* and *Pag.* are equally memorable, as are the duets with Sherrill Milnes. With over 72 minutes offered, this is generous enough; although the remastered recordings sometimes show their age in the orchestra, the voice always remains fresh.

'Always in my heart' (The songs of Lecuona) (with RPO, Holdridge): *Siboney; Noche azul; Andalucia; Siempre en mi corazón; Maria la o; Canto Karabali; Juventud; Malagueña; Damisela encantadora; La Comparsa.*
** CBS **CD 38828**; FM/*FMT* 38828 [id.].

Domingo is obviously at home in this repertoire and sings with a nice rhythmic feeling as well as plenty of fervour. But the bright, forward recording lacks a seductive atmosphere, and the lively numbers come off better than the languorous ones. The cassette approaches over-modulation on side one.

'Great love scenes' (with Renata Scotto, Kiri Te Kanawa, Ileana Cotrubas): PUCCINI: *Madama Butterfly: Love Duet. La rondine: Tu madre!* CILEA: *Adriana Lecouvreur: La dolcissima effigie.* MASSENET: *Manon: Toi!* GOUNOD: *Roméo et Juliette: Va je t'ai pardonne.* CHARPENTIER: *Louise: Vois la ville qui s'eclair.*
*** CBS **MK 39030**; M/*MT* 39030 [id.].

This compilation from various CBS opera sets brings an attractively varied group of love duets, with Domingo matched against three splendid heroines. Scotto is the principal partner, better as Adriana than as Butterfly, Juliette or Manon, but still warmly individual, responding to the glory of Domingo's singing, which is unfailingly beautiful and warmly committed. The wonder is that his exceptional consistency never falls into routine; these are all performances to have one wanting to go back to the complete operas. Good recording, though the chrome cassette is over-modulated and produces roughness at climaxes.

'Gala opera concert' (with LAPO, Giulini): DONIZETTI: *L'Elisir d'amore: Una furtiva lagrima. Lucia di Lammermoor: Tombe degl'avi miei . . . Fra poco.* VERDI: *Ernani: Mercé, diletti amici . . . Come rugiada; Dell'esilio nel dolore . . . O tu che l'alma adora. Il Trovatore: Ah si, ben mio; Di quella pira. Aïda: Se quel guerrier io fossi . . . Celeste Aïda.* HALÉVY: *La Juive: Rachel, quand du Seigneur.* MEYERBEER: *L'Africaine: Pays merveilleux . . . O Paradis.* BIZET: *Les Pêcheurs de perles: Je crois entendre encore. Carmen: La fleur que tu m'avais jetée* (with R. Wagner Chorale).
*** DG Dig. **400 030-2**; 2532/*3302* 009 [id.].

Recorded in 1980 in connection with a gala in San Francisco, this is as noble and resplendent a tenor recital as you will find. Domingo improves in detail even on the fine versions of some of these arias he had recorded earlier, and the finesse of the whole gains greatly from the sensitive direction of Giulini, though the orchestra is a little backward. Otherwise excellent recording, and the chrome transfer is first rate too, with tingling digital brass in the *Aïda* excerpt; however, the sound has a more dramatic range on side two than side one (with a rise in level). But it is on the compact disc that the honeyed beauty of the voice is given the greatest immediacy. The orchestra too gains resonance in the bass and this added weight improves the balance.

'French opera arias': BIZET: *Les Pêcheurs de perles: Je crois entendre encore. Carmen: Flower song.* HALÉVY: *La Juive: Rachel, quand du Seigneur.* MEYERBEER: *L'Africaine: Pays merveilleux . . . O Paradis.* MASSENET: *Werther: Je ne sais . . . O Nature; Pourquoi me reveiller.* BERLIOZ: *Béatrice et Bénédict: Ah! je vais l'aimer, mon coeur. La Damnation de Faust: Invocation à la Nature.* OFFENBACH: *Contes d'Hoffmann; Legend of Kleinzach.* SAINT-SAËNS: *Samson et Dalila: Vois ma misère . . . Samson, qu'as-tu fait du Dieu de tes pères . . .* DE LISLE: *La Marseillaise* (with chorus).
(M) *** DG Sig. 410 991-1/*4* [id.].

Taken from complete DG sets with the jolly addition of the Berlioz setting of *La Marseillaise*, this recital demonstrates what a rare insight into the French repertory Domingo has, far more at home here than almost any rival from the Italian discipline. At mid-price an excellent issue, with sound well transferred, equally vivid on LP and the first-class chrome cassette, with the closing *Marseillaise* exhilarating in its immediacy.

'Be my love' (with LSO, Loges; Marcel Peters, piano): LEHÁR: *The Land of Smiles: Dein ist mein ganzes Herz.* Popular and Neapolitan songs.
** DG **413 451-2**; 2530/*3300* 700 [id.].

This collection does not show Domingo at his best. The performances are lusty and the recording is not very refined, the voice projected forward and the whole presentation without subtlety.

'The best of Domingo': VERDI: *Aïda: Se quel guerrier . . . Celeste Aïda. Rigoletto: La donna è mobile. Luisa Miller: Oh! fede negar . . . Quando le sere. Un Ballo in maschera: Forse la soglia . . . Ma se m'è forza perderti; Dì tu se fedele. La Traviata: Lunge da lei . . . De'miei bollenti spirit.* BIZET: *Carmen: Flower song.* FLOTOW: *Martha: Ach so fromm.* DONIZETTE: *L'Elisir d'amore: Una furtiva lagrima.* OFFENBACH: *Contes d'Hoffmann: Legend of Kleinzach.*
*** DG **415 366-2**; 2531/*3301* 386 [id.].

A popular recital showing Domingo in consistent form, the voice and style vibrant and telling, as the opening *Celeste Aïda* readily shows, followed by an agreeably relaxed *La donna è mobile*. In the lyric arias, the *Flower song* and the excerpts from *Martha* and *L'Elisir d'amore* there is not the honeyed sweetness of a Gigli, but in the closing *Hoffmann* scena the sheer style of the singing gives special pleasure. The sound is vivid throughout and the CD brings the usual enhancement, though marginally. There is a very good cassette.

Opera arias from: DONIZETTI: *Lucia di Lammermoor.* VERDI: *Aïda; Un Ballo in maschera; Don Carlos; Ernani; I Lombardi; Luisa Miller; Macbeth; Nabucco;*

Rigoletto; La Traviata; Il Trovatore. PUCCINI: *La Fanciulla del West; Manon Lescaut; Turandot.* MEYERBEER: *L'Aficaine.* HALÉVY: *La Juive.* BERLIOZ: *La Damnation de Faust.* OFFENBACH: *Contes d'Hoffmann.* BIZET: *Carmen; Les Pêcheurs de perles.* SAINT-SAËNS: *Samson et Dalila.* MASSENET: *Werther.* WAGNER: *Die Meistersinger von Nürnberg.*
(M) *** DG 415 583-1 (3) [id.].

If EMI can compile a superb recital set from complete opera recordings, DG here shows that its archives have just as formidable a collection of Domingo recordings. Items here are taken mainly – though not entirely – from complete opera sets, and as ever bear witness to the great tenor's astonishing ability to produce consistently strong and thoughtful performances in the studio over the widest range of repertory. It is good to have a sample of his distinctive contribution to the Jochum set of *Meistersinger*, even if Germans tend to object to his pronunciation. Admirers of this artist will not want to be without this box; for the normal collector, however, the shorter compilations are more obviously recommendable. For the price of this box one could buy a complete opera.

Domingo, Placido (tenor), **Pilar Lorengar** (soprano)

Zarzuela duets (with ORFSO, Navarro): excerpts from: SOUTULLO/VERT: *La Leyenda del Beso.* SERRANO: *La Dolorosa; El trust de Los Tenorios.* BRETÓN: *La Dolores.* LUNO: *El nino Judio.* TORROBA: *Luisa Fernanda.* GIMÉNEZ: *La Boda de Luis Alonso* (orchestral interlude). CABALLERO: *El duo de la Africana.*
* CBS Dig. IM/*IMT* 39210 [id.].

Although the repertoire is rare and valuable, this recording, made live at the Salzburg Festival, suffers from a poor orchestral balance and intrusive applause; indeed, the audience seem to cheer every item, quite irrespective of the quality of the performance – and Miss Lorengar's contribution has little vocal bloom or charm. Full translations are provided.

Early Music Consort of London, Munrow

'Music of the Gothic era': Notre Dame period: LEONIN: *Organum Viderunt omnes.* PEROTIN: *Organum Viderunt omnes.* Ars Antiqua: *Motets from the Bamberg and Montpellier Codices* by Petrus de Cruce, Adam de la Halle and Anon. Ars Nova: *Motets from the Roman de Fauvel. Chantilly/Ivrea Codices* by Machaut: De Vitry.
*** DG Arc. **415 292-2**.

This issue draws on the fine three-LP set, *'Music of the Gothic Era'*, made by the late-lamented David Munrow just before his death in 1976. It offers two items from the first LP, one each by Leonin and Perotin, and gives us more from the other two, from the so-called *Ars antiqua* (1250–1320) and includes two motets of Adam de la Halle, and the *Ars nova* (1320–80), representing such figures as Philippe de Vitry and Machaut. David Munrow had exceptional powers both as a scholar-performer and as a communicator, and it is good that his work is remembered on compact disc. The performances are wonderfully alive and vital, and the digital remastering as expert as one would expect. A strong recommendation.

Estes, Simon (bass-baritone)

Spirituals (with Howard Roberts Chorale, O, Roberts): *Ride on, King Jesus; Swing low, sweet chariot; Ezekiel saw thy wheel; City called Heaven; Plenty good room; Let us break bread together; Go down, Moses; No hiding place; Nobody knows the trouble I've seen; Every time I feel the spirit; Steal away to Jesus; Witness; Sometimes I feel like a motherless child; Standin' in the need of prayer; He's got the whole world in His hands.*
(*) Ph. Dig. **412 631-2; 412 631-1/*4*.

With his heroic baritone, Estes makes this an outstanding recital of spirituals, tastefully done, if with the accompaniment overblown in some items. First-rate sound, although the highly modulated cassette sounds opaque and slightly bass-orientated compared with the LP. Some listeners may feel that the music, with the chorus consistently acting as a ripieno to the solo voice, is over-arranged.

Ferrier, Kathleen (contralto), **Bruno Walter** (piano)

Edinburgh Festival recital, 1949: SCHUBERT: *Die junge Nonne. Rosamunde: Romance. Du liebst mich nicht; Der Tod und das Mädchen; Suleika; Du bist die Ruh'.* BRAHMS: *Immer leiser wird mein Schlummer; Der Tod das ist die kuhle Nacht; Botschaft; Von ewiger Liebe.* SCHUMANN: *Frauenliebe und Leben, Op. 42.*
(M) (***) Decca mono 414 611-1/*4*.

Though the mono recording – taken from a BBC tape of 1949 – is rather dim with the piano sound often hazy, this historic issue gives a wonderful idea of the intensity of a Ferrier recital. Her account here of *Frauenliebe* is freer and even more compelling than the studio performance she also recorded. Walter's accompaniments may not be flawless, but they are comparably inspirational. The recital is introduced by a brief talk on Walter and the Edinburgh Festival given by Ferrier.

Fischer-Dieskau, Dietrich (baritone)

'The Lieder singer' (with Gerald Moore, Daniel Barenboim, Hertha Klust, Karl Engel, Wolfgang Sawallisch, Sviatoslav Richter, Herman Reutter, A. Reimann): Lieder by: HAYDN; MOZART; BEETHOVEN; SCHUBERT; SCHUMANN; FRANZ; CORNELIUS; BRAHMS; WOLF; LISZT; NIETZSCHE; Richard STRAUSS; PFITZNER; SCHOECK; DEBUSSY; REGER; WEBER; REIMANN.
(M) *** HMV EX 290429-3 (3) [Ang. AVC 34027].

'The opera singer' Arias from: *Nozze di Figaro; Alfonso und Estrella; Zwillingsbruder; Merry wives of Windsor; Wildschütz; Zar und Zimmerman; Genoveva Margarethe; Tales of Hoffmann; Fledermaus Intermezzo; Fliegende Holländer; Tannhäuser; Tristan; Parsifal; Die Walküre; Il Trovatore; Rigoletto; Don Carlo; Il Ballo; Otello; Falstaff; I vespri siciliani.*
(M) *** HMV EX 290432-3 (3) [Ang. AVC 34028].

'The concert singer': Arias by PURCELL; CLERAMBAULT; BACH. HANDEL: *Cantata: Cuopre tal volta.* HAYDN: Duet: *Schlaf in deiner Engen* (with Los Angeles). MOZART: *Notturno; Canzonetta.* BEETHOVEN: *Irish and Welsh songs.* Lieder by SCHUBERT; SCHUMANN. MENDELSSOHN: Excerpts: *St Paul; Elijah.* Also RHEINBERGER; FAURÉ; PFITZNER; MAHLER: *Lieder.*
(M) *** HMV EX 290435-3 (3) [Ang. AVC 34029].

Issued to celebrate Fischer-Dieskau's sixtieth birthday in 1985, these three boxes provide astonishing evidence of the singer's commanding versatility, his unique mastery in the widest range of repertory. It is a pity that the Lieder box does not contain some of his first 78 r.p.m. recordings for EMI; but in these recordings, made between 1956 and 1975, early recordings from the 1950s and 1960s predominate, demonstrating the poise and refinement of his singing then, rather less dramatic or explosive than later. As well as the wide range of solo items, it is good to have Schumann and Brahms duets recorded live with Dame Janet Baker; though some will be disappointed that only one side is devoted to Schubert, it is good to have the last side including songs by Reger, Weber and Reimann, as well as just one French song, by Debussy.

The operatic selection, recorded between 1953 and 1978, includes two sides each devoted to Wagner and Verdi. If the Verdi items – mainly taken from a 1959 recital – in their meticulous concern for detail often sound unidiomatic, these performances are unfailingly illuminating. The Wagner choice is splendid, with a sample of his young Kurewenal in the Furtwängler *Tristan* and superb excerpts from *Tannhäuser* and *Fliegende Holländer* recorded in 1960 and 1961. It is interesting too to have Fischer-Dieskau in *Wotan's Farewell* – not the most comfortable performance – recorded in 1978. The first disc of the box is nicely varied, with rare Schubert and Schumann as well as Lortzing, Gounod's *Faust* in German and samples of both Strausses, Johann and Richard, all intensely individual.

The concert-singer box ranges from Purcell and Telemann to Pfitzner and

Rheinberger, with the last side devoted to Fischer-Dieskau's magnificent account of the *Abschied* from Mahler's *Das Lied von der Erde* with Kletzki conducting. Equally welcome is the *Fahrenden Gesellen* cycle with Furtwängler conducting, recorded in 1952. Duets and trios with Schwarzkopf and Los Angeles – taken from Gerald Moore's farewell – provide variety, as well as Beethoven duets with Los Angeles, recorded in the studio. Typically with Fischer-Dieskau, oratorio numbers by Mendelssohn (*Elijah* and *St Paul*) are made tough and strong.

The accompanying booklet is the same in all three boxes, giving full details of the recording sources but no texts. First-rate transfers.

'Grandi voci': MOZART: *Le Nozze di Figaro: Hai gia vinta . . . Vedro mentrio sospiro.* HAYDN: *Acis and Galatea: Tergi i vezzosi rai.* VERDI: *Macbeth Perfidi! all' angelo contro me v'unite. La Traviata: Di provenza il mar. Don Carlo: O Carlo ascolta.* PUCCINI: *Tosca: Tre sbirri . . . Una carrozza.* SCHUMANN: *Scenes from Faust* (excerpt). WAGNER: *Parsifal: Ja, wehe! wehe!. Götterdämmerung: Brünnhilde, Die hehrste Frau . . . Gegrüsst sei teurer Held.* MAHLER: *Das Lied von der Erde: Von der Schonheit.* BRITTEN: *War Requiem: After the blast of the lightning from the East.*
(M) *** Decca GRV/*KGRC* 7 [Lon. 414 198-1/*4*].

This generous collection provides superb evidence within the limits of a single LP or cassette of the enormous span of Fischer-Dieskau's artistry, including as it does unexpected corners of the repertory. His keenly intelligent and stylish command, whether as the Count in *Figaro*, as Macbeth, as Scarpia or in the Britten recording of Schumann's *Faust scenes*, is extraordinary. It was imaginative to include the passage from Britten's *War Requiem*. First-rate recording. The cassette, transferred at the highest level, has a hint of fierceness – though this is more obvious on side one than on side two.

Ghiaurov, Nicolai (bass)

Russian arias (with LSO and Chorus, Downes): GLINKA: *A life for the Tsar: Susasin's aria.* RUBINSTEIN: *The Demon: Demon's aria.* TCHAIKOVSKY: *Iolanta: René's aria. Eugene Onegin: Prince Gremin's aria.* BORODIN: *Prince Igor: Konchak's aria; Galitzky's aria.* RIMSKY-KORSAKOV: *Sadko: Song of the Viking quest.* MUSSORGSKY: *Boris Godunov: Pimen's monologue.* RACHMANINOV: *Aleko: Aleko's cavatina.*
(M) **(*) Decca Grandi Voci 414 441-1/*4* [id.].

Nicolai Ghiaurov's recital in Decca's *Grandi voci* series is compiled from two previous collections, issued in 1963 and 1965, with all the Russian arias now gathered together. The first appeared just after a recital by Boris Christoff of bass arias and, though his voice is just as rich and the Decca recording considerably more brilliant, Ghiaurov still has to yield to his fellow Bulgarian in sheer artistry, particularly on detail. He is at his best in the comparatively straightforward arias; but the voice quality is what matters, and this is all magnificent singing. The recording too is excellent, with a first-class matching cassette.

Gothic Voices, Christopher Page

'The Garden of Zephirus' (*Courtly songs of the 15th century*, with Imogen Barford, medieval harp): DUFAY: *J'atendray tant qu'il vous playra; Adieu ces bons vins de Lannoys; Mon cuer me fait tous dis penser.* BRIQUET: *Ma seul amour et ma belle maistresse.* DE CASERTA: *Amour ma' le cuer mis.* LANDINI: *Nessun ponga speranza; Giunta vaga bilta.* REYNEAU: *Va t'en mon cuer, avent mes yeux.* MATHEUS DE SACTO JOHANNE: *Fortune, faulce, parverse.* DE INSULA: *Amours n'ont cure le tristesse.* BROLLO: *Qui le sien vuelt bien maintenir.* ANON.: *N'a pas long temps que trouvay Zephirus; Je la remire, la belle.*
*** Hyp. **CDA 66144**; A/*KA* 66144 [id.].

Most of this repertoire is unfamiliar, with Dufay the only famous name, but everything here is of interest and the listener inexperienced in medieval music will be surprised at the strength of its character. The performances are naturally eloquent and, although the range of colour is limited compared with later writing, it still has immediacy of appeal, especially if taken in short bursts. The recording balance is faultless and the sound first rate, with a splendid matching cassette. With complete security of intonation and a chamber-music vocal blend, the presentation is wholly admirable. There is full back-up documentation.

Gruberova, Edita (soprano)

(see also Orchestral Concerts under Marsalis, Wynton)

Italian and French opera arias (with Munich R.O, Kuhn): DELIBES: Lakmé: *Bell song.* MEYERBEER: *Les Huguenots: Nobles seigneurs, salut!* GOUNOD: *Roméo et Juliette: Waltz song.* THOMAS: *Hamlet: Mad scene.* DONIZETTI: *Lucia di Lammermoor: Mad scene.* ROSSINI: *Semiramide: Bel raggio lusinghier. Il Barbiere di Siviglia: Una voce poco fa.*
*** HMV Dig. **CDC 747047-2** [id.].

Gruberova, for long type-cast in the roles of Queen of the Night and Zerbinetta, here formidably extends her range of repertory in a dazzling display of coloratura, impressive not only in the Italian repertory but in the French too, notably the *Hamlet* mad scene. The agility is astonishing, but the tone as recorded often hardens on top. CD provides extra fullness and clarity. The LP and tape have now been withdrawn.

Song recital (with Friederich Haider, piano): MOZART: *Als Luise; Das Veilchen; Der Zauberer; Oiseaux si tous les ans; Dans un bois solitaire.* DEBUSSY: *Pantomime; Clair de lune; Apparition; Pierrot.* WOLF: *Der Gärtner; Zintronenfalter; Mausfallensprüchlein; Nixe Binsefuss; Elfenlied; Storchenbotschaft; Er ist's; Jägerlied; Auf einer Wanderung; Erstes Liebeslied.*
** CBS Dig. **MK 42002**; IM/*IMT* 42002.

Gruberova's bright voice is not entirely an asset in this wide-ranging recital. She succeeds in varying the tone more than one would expect, and there are many delightful items, notably among the Mozart French songs and the Debussy; but the overall effect does not avoid monotony. The recording is rather too reverberant for the intimate genre of Lieder. No texts or translations are given.

Gueden, Hilde (soprano)

'Operetta favourites' (with V. State Op. Ch. and O, Robert Stolz): KÁLMÁN: *Gräfin Mariza: Entry of Mariza; Sag ja.* BENATSKY-STOLZ: *White Horse Inn: Mein Liebeslied muss ein Walzer sein.* LEHÁR: *Der Zarewitsch: Kosende Wellen. Zigeunerliebe: Hör ich Cymbalklänge.* FALL: *Madame Pompadour: Heut' könnt' einer sein Gluck.* STRAUSS, J. Jnr: *Casanova: Nuns' chorus. Die Fledermaus: Mein Herr Marquis. Wiener Blut: Wiener Blut.* STOLZ: *Der Favorit: Du sollst der Kaiser.* ZELLER: *Der Obersteiger: Sei nicht bös.* STRAUS, Oscar: *The Chocolate soldier: Held meiner Träume* (*My hero*).
(M) *** Decca Grandi Voci 414 176–1/*4*.

Hilde Gueden's many delightful gramophone contributions to operetta tended, quite unfairly, to rest in the shadow of Elisabeth Schwarzkopf, who brought a Lieder-like skill with words even to relatively banal lyrics. Gueden's approach was more direct, but she had this repertoire in her very being; a lilting feel for a Viennese melodic line and her lovely voice combine here to enchanting effect in a recital dating from 1961, when the full vocal bloom was winningly apparent. Decca's vintage recording, too, still sounds first class, on both disc and tape. There are some especially good things on side two, notably the numbers from *Die Fledermaus* and *The Chocolate soldier*. The splendidly alive and sympathetic accompaniments under Robert Stolz add a great deal to the collection, which is a classic of its kind. It deserves consideration for future CD issue alongside Schwarzkopf's famous record of similar material. The engaging *Sei nicht bös* (with chorus) and the vivacious *Mein Herr Marquis* are also rightly included in Decca's *'Golden operetta'* collection – see below.

Hendricks, Barbara (soprano), **Dmitri Alexeev** (piano)

Spirituals: *Deep river; Ev'ry time I feel the spirit; Fix me, Jesus; Git on boa'd little child'n; His name is so sweet; Hold on!; Joshua fit de battle of Jericho; Nobody knows de trouble I've seen; Oh what a beautiful city!; Plenty good room; Roun' about de mountain; Sometimes I feel like a motherless child; Swing low, sweet chariot; Talk about a child that do love Jesus; Were you there?; When I lay my burden down.*
*** HMV Dig. **CDC 747026-2**; ASD/*TC-ASD* 173168-1/*4*.

So often spirituals can be made to seem too ingenuous, their deep reserve of feeling degraded into sentimentality. Not so here. Barbara Hendricks' vibrant identification with the words is thrilling, the jazz inflections adding natural sophistication, yet not robbing the music of its directness of communication. Her lyrical singing is radiant, operatic in its eloquence of line, yet retaining the ecstasy of spirit, while the extrovert numbers – *Joshua fit de battle of Jericho* a superb example – are full of joy in their gutsy exuberance. Dmitri Alexeev accompanies superbly and the very well-balanced recording has remarkable presence on disc and tape alike. A rare example of a record that feels like a 'live' experience. *Roun'about de mountain* is unforgettable in its impact, although on CD the forward projection of the voice almost overdoes the sense of presence.

Hilliard Ensemble, Paul Hillier

'The Singing Club': RAVENSCROFT: *A round of three country dances; There were three ravens.* HILTON: *Call George again, boys.* LAWES, William: *Drink to the knight of the moonshine bright; She weepeth sore in the night; Dainty, fine aniseed water; Gather ye rosebuds.* WILSON: *Where the bee sucks.* PURCELL: *'Tis woman makes us love; Sir Walter enjoying his damsel.* BATTISHILL: *Epitaph.* ARNE: *The singing club; To soften care; Elegy on the death of Mr Shenstone; Sigh no more, ladies.* BISHOP: *Foresters sound the cheerful horn.* SMITH, J. S.: *The Ancreontick song.* PEARSALL: *There is a paradise on earth; O who will o'er the down so free.* BARBY: *Sweet and low.*
€ **(*) HM Dig. **HMC 901153**; HMC 1153 [id.].

This collection of part-songs, glees, catches and rounds embraces a period of English song stretching from the beginning of the seventeenth century to the end of the nineteenth. The Hilliard Ensemble are particularly at home in the earlier songs: their blending and intonation cannot be faulted and they shows a nice feeling for the gentle melancholy of the period. They manage the more robust glees with panache, notably the *Wedding night song* of Inigo Jones, whose lyrics make a ribald pun on the writer's name, and Purcell's risqué narrative based on a true story of Sir Walter Raleigh's first conquest in the woods. Words are admirably clear throughout and the recording, made in London's Henry Wood Hall, gives a very real impression of the group standing back just behind the speakers. In some of the later nineteenth-century items the style, though not insensitive, is just a little pale.

Hill Smith, Marilyn (soprano), Peter Morrison (baritone)

'Treasures of operetta' (with Concert O, Barry): ZIEHRER: *Der Schatzmeister: Do re mi fa sol la si.* STRAUSS, J. jnr: *Casanova: O Queen of my delight.* KÁLMÁN: *Gypsy Princess: Let me dance and let me sing.* STRAUS: *Chocolate Soldier: My*

hero. TAUBER: *Old Chelsea: My heart and I.* MESSAGER: *Veronique: Trot here and there.* HERBERT: *Naughty Marietta: Tramp! tramp! tramp!* LEHÁR: *The Merry Widow: Love unspoken; I'm off to Chez Maxim. Giuditta: On my lips every kiss is like wine.* ZELLER: *Der Obersteiger: Don't be cross.* MONCKTON: *The Arcadians: Charming weather.*
(*) Chan. Dig. **CHAN 8362; LBRD/*LBTD* 013 [id.].

One has to make an initial adjustment to a style of performance which is very English, evoking memories of the Palm Court tradition of Anne Ziegler and Webster Booth. Marilyn Hill Smith sings freshly and often very sweetly, and she is genially partnered by the warm, easy-going baritone of Peter Morrison. Moreover, the orchestral accompaniments have plenty of flexibility and lilt, and the resonantly rich recording is exactly right for the music. With almost every number a 'hit', this is very attractive of its kind. While the voices are given slightly more presence on CD, the chrome cassette too is first class and costs considerably less.

Horne, Marilyn (mezzo-soprano)

French opera arias (with Monte Carlo PO, Lawrence Foster): AUBER: *Zerline: O Palerme! O Sicile.* SAINT-SAËNS: *Samson et Dalila: Mon coeur s'ouvre à ta voix.* OFFENBACH: *La Grande Duchesse de Gérolstein: Ah! que j'aime les militaires.* GOUNOD: *Sapho: O ma lyre immortelle; Héro sur la tour solitaire.* GODARD: *La Vivandière: Viens avec nous, petit.* MASSENET: *Hérodiade: Venge-moi d'une suprême offense.* DONIZETTI: *La Favorite: L'ai-je bien entendu? . . . Oh, Mon Fernand.* CHERUBINI: *Médée: Ah! nos peines.*
*** Erato Dig. **ECD 88085**; NUM/*MCE* 75170 [id.].

With a fair proportion of rare items, Horne's French recital is highly recommendable. The voice may have lost some of the firm focus that was so impressive at the beginning of her career, but the brilliance and command are unfailing over the widest range of repertory. The classical poise of the Cherubini aria is as impressive as the zest of the Offenbach or the rich resonance of the Massenet. Excellent sound, made the more vivid on CD.

'*Grandi voci*': BIZET: *Carmen: Habañera: Seguidilla.* SAINT-SAËNS: *Samson et Dalila; Mon coeur s'ouvre à ta voix; Printemps qui commence.* MEYERBEER: *Le Prophète: O prêtres de Baal . . . O toi qui m'abandonnes; Ah! mon fils.* MASSENET: *Werther: Air de lettres Va! Laisse couler mes larmes.* THOMAS: *Mignon: C'est moi ... me voici dans son boudoir; Elle est là! près de lui!* GOUNOD: *Sopho: Où suis-je . . . O ma lyre immortelle.*
(M) *** Decca 417 110-1/*4* [id.].

Unlike Horne's Erato recital of French arias (which overlaps in the Saint-

Saëns and Gounod items), this collection has been compiled from vintage recordings made in 1964 and 1967. With sound excellent for its period, the voice comes over superbly, bringing out both the imagination and the total security of the singing. Particularly impressive in its range of expression is the aria from *Le Prophète*. There is a first-class cassette, projecting the voice vividly.

'Italian opera favourites'

LEONCAVALLO: *I Pagliacci: Prologue* (Gobbi); *Vesti la giubba* (Corelli). PUCCINI: *La Bohème: Sì, mi chiamano Mimì; Una terribil tosse* (Freni, Gedda). *Madama Butterfly: Love duet; Flower duet; Humming chorus* (Bjoerling, Los Angeles, Pirazzini, Rome Op. Ch., Santini). *Manon Lescaut: Donna non vidi mai* (Fernandi); *In quelle trine morbide* (Cavalli). *Turandot: In questa reggia* (Shuard). VERDI: *Il Trovatore: Di quella pira* (Corelli); *Soldiers' chorus* (Rome Op. Ch., Schippers). *Aïda: Qui Radames verrà! . . . O patria mia* (Cavalli); *Ritorna vincitor* (Shuard). *Rigoletto: Questa o quella; La donna è mobile* (Fernandi); *Caro nome* (*Grist*); *Zitti zitti* (Rome Op. Ch., Molinari-Pradelli); *Bella figlia* (Grist, Gedda, Di Stasio, MacNeil). *Otello: Ave Maria* (Gwyneth Jones). MASCAGNI: *Cavalleria Rusticana: Mamma, mamma* (Fernando). BELLINI: *I Puritani: A te, o cara* (Corelli).
(B) ** EMI *TC2-MOM 120.*

Recorded loudly and vibrantly, at times rather fiercely, for maximum impact in the car, this is a generous collection of operatic purple patches. The finest performances are from Gobbi (*Pagliacci*), Freni as Mimì, Gwyneth Jones in *Otello* and the excellent excerpts from the Los Angeles/Bjoerling set of *Madama Butterfly*. Corelli makes several appearances, and his singing is best described as lusty.

Kanawa, Kiri Te (soprano)

'Come to the fair' (with Medici Qt; Nat. PO, Gamley): EASTHOPE MARTIN: *Come to the fair.* LAMBERT: *She is far from the land.* TRAD: *Early one morning; The last rose of summer; Island spinning song; The ash grove; The Keel Row; Comin' thro' the rye; Annie Laurie; O can ye sew cushions; The Sally gardens; Greensleeves; The gentle maiden; I have a bonnet trimmed with blue; Danny Boy.*
*** HMV Dig. **CDC 747080-2**; EL 270040-1/*4* [Ang. DS/*4DS* 38097].

Very much following in the Kathleen Ferrier tradition, Dame Kiri Te Kanawa sings this repertoire with infectious charm. She can be exhilaratingly robust, as in the title piece and *The Keel Row*, yet at the next moment provide a ravishing lyricism, as in *The last rose of summer* or *The Sally gardens*. The orchestral accompaniments are decorative but simple (*Greensleeves*, a highlight, is especially felicitous). The recording has splendid presence, especially on the compact disc but the high-level cassette is very lively too. A captivating recital in every way.

'Ave Maria' (with St Paul's Cathedral Choir, ECO, Rose: GOUNOD: *Messe solennelle à Sainte Cécile: Sanctus. O divine Redeemer.* MOZART: *Ave verum, K. 618; Solemn Vespers: Laudate Dominum.* FRANCK: *Panis angelicus.* HANDEL: *Solomon: Let the bright Seraphim; Let their celestial concert.* MENDELSSOHN: *On wings of song.* BACH: *Jesu, joy of man's desiring.* SCHUBERT: *Ave Maria.*
(*) Ph. Dig. **412 629-2; 412 629-1/*4* [id.].

Countless music-lovers who heard Dame Kiri sing *Let the bright Seraphim* at the wedding of the Prince and Princess of Wales have been waiting for this record to appear, and they will not be disappointed, for the trumpet playing, too, is suitably resplendent. This comes at the end, and the rest of the programme lacks something in variety, although the voice always sounds beautiful and the naturally expressive singing gives much pleasure. The chorus, backwardly balanced, might have been more clearly focused, however. Obviously the recording producer intended to sustain a devotional atmosphere throughout, and in this he has succeeded. The CD hardly improves the definition. There is an excellent cassette.

'Blue skies' (with Nelson Riddle and his orchestra): BERLIN: *Blue skies.* WEILL: *Speak low.* RODGERS: *It might as well be spring; I didn't know what time it was.* VAN HEUSEN: *Here's that rainy day.* KERN: *Yesterdays; The folk who live on the hill.* PORTER: *So in love; True love.* LEWIS: *How high the moon.* WRUBEL: *Gone with the wind.* ROMBERG: *When I grow too old to dream.*
*(*) Decca Dig. **414 666-2**; 414 666-1/*4* [id.].

This is disappointing – more a disc for those who like crossover records than for the general devotee of Dame Kiri. Nelson Riddle provides characteristic arrangements of the numbers, but there is a curious lack of vitality. The tempi lack sufficient variety and what is intended to sound sultry too often becomes soporific; *True love*, for instance, is much too languorous. There is plenty of atmosphere (helped by the background silence of the CD) but a curiously inert feeling overall.

King's College, Cambridge, Choir, Cleobury

ALLEGRI: *Miserere mei, Deus.* FRESCOBALDI: *Messa sopra l'aria della Monica.* MARENZIO: *Magnificat.* NANINO: *Adoramus te, Christe.* UGOLINI: *Beata es Virgo Maria.*
(*) HMV **CDC 747065-2 [id.]; EL 270095-1/*4* [Ang. DS/*4DS* 38086].

An attractively planned concert of Renaissance choral music. The opening *Adoramus te, Christe* is movingly serene, and both Marenzio's fine *Magnificat* and the stirring *Beata es Virgo Maria* of Ugolini (a contemporary of Allegri) make a strong impression – the latter reminding the listener of Andrea Gabrieli. The performances are generally excellent and the King's acoustic provides its usual beautiful aura. The account of Allegri's *Miserere*, although effective, lacks the ethereal memorability of the finest versions; its treble soloist, Timothy Beasley-Murray, is made to sound almost over-confident, with his upward leap commandingly extrovert. The CD gains much from the background silence, but the choral focus is mistier than one might have expected.

'O come all ye faithful' (with David Briggs, organ): *Once in Royal David's city; Up! good Christian folk; On Christmas night; Ding dong merrily on high; O little town of Bethlehem; in the bleak midwinter; The first nowell; Away in a manger; The seven joys of Mary; The infant king; God rest ye merry, gentlemen; The holly and the ivy; I saw three ships; O come all ye faithful;* GRÜBER: *Silent night.* MENDELSSOHN: *Hark! the herald angels sing.*
*** Decca Dig. **414 042-2**; 414 042-1/*4* [id.].

King's College Choir make their digital Christmas début with a programme of tested favourites. The usual opening is varied, with *Once in Royal David's city* done not as a processional but as an interplay between the treble solo and full choir. The atmosphere overall is slightly subdued; but *Hark the herald angels* comes in a spectacular arrangement by Philip Ledger, and Stephen Cleobury's version of *Silent night* takes an original turn after the opening verse. The digital recording does not seek to clarify textures but concentrates on capturing the ambient atmosphere, which means that the cassette is not always ideally focused, though pleasing enough.

King's College, Cambridge, Choir, Ledger and Willcocks

'Christmas carols from King's College': Once in Royal David's city; O little town of Bethlehem; The first nowell; I saw three ships; Personent Hodie; Myn Lyking; A spotless rose; Away in a manger; I sing of a maiden; O come, O come Emanuel; While shepherds watched; Up! Good Christian folk; In the bleak midwinter; Silent night; The holly and the ivy; It came upon the midnight clear; Three kings; On Christmas night; A child is born in Bethlehem; In dulci jubilo; O come all ye faithful; Hark! the herald angels sing.
(M) *** HMV EG 290701-1/*4*.

With over an hour of music and twenty-two carols included, this is formidable value. The recordings were made between 1969 and 1976 and have been digitally remastered. The sound is excellent on LP, although the tape focus is not always absolutely clean; but this is an ideal programme for cassette listening and the

King's acoustic is generally well caught in both media. The closing two carols are made particularly resplendent.

King's College, Cambridge, Choir, Willcocks

Settings by Byrd (of each piece) and also by the composer listed: PALESTRINA: *Haec dies; Tu es Petrus*. PHILIPS, Peter: *Ave verum corpus*. GABRIELI, G.: *Miserere mei*. VICTORIA: *O quam gloriosam*. LASSUS: *Iustorum animae*.
(B) **(*) CfP CFP 41 4481-1/*4*.

This is an imaginatively devised collection of motets in which settings of Latin texts by Byrd are directly contrasted with settings of the same words by some of his greatest contemporaries. As was the intention, the juxtaposition makes one listen to the individual qualities of these polyphonic masters the more keenly and to register their individuality. It is not a question of a contest between composers but of the greatness of each being underlined. The 1965 recording was one of the first made by EMI at King's College; it is not as freshly transparent as later ones from this source, but the beauty of the singing is never in doubt. There is a very good cassette.

ALLEGRI: *Miserere*. PALESTRINA: *Magnificat in 8 parts* (*Primi toni*); *Stabat Mater*. BLOW: *Let Thy hand be strengthened; Behold, O God, our defender*. CROFT: *Burial service*. TALLIS: *Spem in alium* (40-part motet – with Cambridge University Musical Society Chorus).
(M) *** Argo 417 160-1/*4*.

This new collection is assembled mainly from King's recordings of the 1960s, although the two fine, if briefly succinct anthems of John Blow are much more recent. They are agreeably spirited and make an excellent foil to the more serene music of Croft and Palestrina. In the famous 1963 version of Tallis's motet, *Spem in alium*, the second choir is drawn from other universities; and the combination is a fruitful one, with the music's power and rich textures producing thrilling climaxes. The 1964 recording of Allegri's *Miserere* with its soaring treble line, marvellously sung by Master Roy Goodman, remains as riveting now as the day it was made, and the misty King's acoustic suits the presentation, with the second choir and its soloists slightly distanced. The sound is excellent throughout.

King's Singers

'*A Tribute to the Comedian Harmonists*' (with Emil Gerhardt, piano): JURMANN: *Veronika, der Lenz ist da*. HEYMANN: *Liebling, mein Herz; Das ist die Liebe der*

Matrosen; Wenn der Wind weht über das Meer. PORTER: *Night and day*. REISFELD: *Mein kleiner grüner Kaktus*. ELLINGTON: *Creole love call*. ABRAHAM: *Eins, zwei, drei, vier*. ARLEN: *Stormy weather*. ROSSINI: *Overture: Il Barbiere di Siviglia* (abridged and arr. Runswick). RIMSKY-KORSAKOV: *Flight of the bumble bee*. FRIML: *The Firefly: Donkey serenade*. SCHMIDSEDER: *Gitarren spielen auf*. YOUMANS: *No no Nanette: Tea for two*. DOUGHABY: *Du armes Girl vom Chor*. AGER: *Wochenend und Sonnenschein*.
**(*) EMI EJ 270247-1/*4*.

The Comedian Harmonists reigned supreme as a highly original German vocal group from 1927 to 1935, when events overtook them: not only were some of their members Jewish, but the vocal style essentially belonged to the special atmosphere of pre-Nazi Germany. The King's group features six singers (against the original quintet) and this is a tribute rather than a re-creation: only *Stormy weather* attempts actually to simulate the original arrangement. Thus this collection may fall between two stools, as admirers of the German group could be disappointed and aficionados of the usual King's style could resist the use of the German language, however impeccable. (The American songs are sung in English.) Nevertheless, there are some memorable highlights here, notably the delectable Reisfeld novelty about a cactus plant which falls off a balcony, and the infectious nonsense song, *Eins, zwei, drei, vier* (which could be a marvellous encore piece), while the voicing of Duke Ellington's *Creole love call* is tellingly instrumental, in colour and effect. The *Donkey serenade* is a shade lacking in élan and some may resist the languorously nostalgic version of *Tea for two*. The recording is first class; the arrangements, by Daryl Runswick, Emil Gerhardt, Andrey Leroy and Paul Kuhn, are often brilliantly imaginative, and Gerhardt's own piano contribution to rather more than half of the items is nicely done. The cassette is faithful but could ideally have had more sparkle at the top. One looks forward to the extra presence of the CD.

'Watching the white wheat': Lamorna; Barbara Allen; Bobby Shaftoe; Early one morning; Jack the Jolly Tar; Oak and the ash; O waly waly; Raggle taggle gypies; She moved through the fair; Migildi Hagildi; Watching the white wheat; Star of the County Down; Londonderry air; Dance to my daddy; O my love is like a red red rose; There's nae luck.
*** HMV Dig. EL 270249-1/*4*.

As in their live concerts, the King's Singers spice their selection of folksong settings with witty and pointed arrangements, full of fun. This is as varied a collection as one could wish for, brilliantly done with superfine ensemble and excellent recording and excellent recording on LP. The cassette is pleasant but lacks sparkle and range.

Kollo, René (tenor)

'Opera gala' (with DDR R. O): BIZET: *Carmen: Flower song.* MEYERBEER: *L'Africaine: Pays merveilleux.* CILEA: *L'Arlesiana: E'la solita storia.* GIORDANO: *Andrea Chénier: Come un bel dì di maggio; Vicino a te* (with Katia Ricciarelli). VERDI: *Otello: Niun mi tema. Aïda: Se quel guerrier io fossi . . . Celeste Aïda. Il Trovatore: Ah, si ben mio.* MASCAGNI: *Cavalleria Rusticana: O Mamma, quel vino a generoso.* PUCCINI: *Madama Butterfly: Addio, fiorito asil. Turandot: Nessun dorma.*
*(*) RCA **RD 70585.**

Kollo's heroic, very German-sounding voice is not well suited to much of this repertory, and his singing frequently coarsens in tone. But his admirers will welcome having a CD. Other collectors should approach this with caution.

Lear, Evelyn (soprano), **Thomas Stewart** (baritone)

'Romantic duets' (with Erik Werba, piano): SCHUBERT: *Mignon und der Harfner.* WEBER: *Va', ti consola, addio.* MENDELSSOHN: *Herbstlied; Maiglöckchen und die Blümenlein; Abendlied.* SCHUMANN: *Schön Blümelein; So wahr die Sonne scheinet.* BRAHMS: *Die Meere; Weg der Liebe.* DVOŘÁK: *Možnost* (*Hoping in vain*)*; Slavíkovský polečko malý* (*Pledge of love*). TCHAIKOVSKY: *Evening.* GRETSHANINOV: *Baju bai; Ai dudu.* SAINT-SAËNS: *Pastorale.* FOSTER, Stephen: *Beautiful dreamer; Hard times come again no more; I dream of Jeanie with the light brown hair.*
(M) *** DG Sig. 415 448-1/*4*.

A charming and unusual collection with the two singers consistently sympathetic over the widest range of repertory, responding to each others' musical imagination. Diction is excellent in five languages. An attractive mid-price offering, well recorded.

Lott, Felicity (soprano), **Graham Johnson** (piano)

Mélodies on Victor Hugo poems: GOUNOD: *Sérénade.* BIZET: *Feuilles d'album: Guitare. Adieux de l'hôtesse arabe.* LALO: *Guitare.* DELIBES: *Eclogue.* FRANCK: *S'il est un charmant gazon.* FAURÉ: *L'absent; Le papillon et la fleur; Puisqu'ici bas.* WAGNER: *L'attente.* LISZT: *O quand je dors; Comment, disaint-ils.* SAINT-SAËNS: *Soirée en mer; La fiancée du timbalier.* WHITE, M. V.: *Chantez, chantez jeune inspirée.* HAHN: *Si mes vers avaient des ailes. Rêverie.*
*** HM **HMC 901138**; HMC/*40* 1138.

Felicity Lott's collection of Hugo settings relies mainly on sweet and charming songs, freshly and unsentimentally done, with Graham Johnson an ideally sympathetic accompanist. The recital is then given welcome stiffening on side two with fine songs by Wagner and Liszt, as well as two by Saint-Saëns that have a bite worthy of Berlioz.

Miles-Kingston, Paul (treble)

'Music from Winchester Cathedral' (with vocal quartet; Martin Neary, organ): FRANCK: *Panis angelicus;* (Organ) *Pièce héroïque; Pastorale, Op. 19.* TRAD.: *I wonder as I wander.* WARLOCK: *Balalow.* FAURÉ: *Requiem: Pié Jesu.* DURUFLÉ: *Requiem: Pié Jesu.* VIERNE: *Suite No. 2, Op. 53: Toccata.* HOLST: *Lullay my liking.* MARTIN: *The Lord's prayer.* BURGON: *Nunc Dimittis* (with Crispian Steele-Perkins, trumpet). BACH: *Bist du bei mir.*
** HMV Dig. EL 270372-1/*4*.

Paul Miles-Kingston came to fame as the treble solist chosen to participate in the première and recording of Andrew Lloyd Webber's *Requiem.* Away from the influence of such a special occasion his vocal style, while retaining its purity and innocence (effectively demonstrated in Fauré's *Pié Jesu* and the Burgon *Nunc Dimittis* – made famous on TV), is very direct and simple and lacking in a strong projecting personality. In the Duruflé excerpt, Martin Neary's organ decoration adds much to the effect, and he fills out the recital with two solos by Franck and one by Vierne. Among the more memorable items are the carols of Holst and Warlock in which Paul Miles-Kingston is joined by a vocal quartet and the effect is agreeably intimate. Overall, however, this is a curiously chosen programme.

Milnes, Sherrill (baritone)

ROSSINI: *Il Barbiere di Siviglia: Largo al factotum.* BELLINI: *I Puritani: Or dove fuggo io mai . . . Ah per sempre io ti perdei.* DONIZETTI: *La Favorita: Jardins de l'Alcazar . . . Leonore viens!* VERDI: *Ernani: Mi lascia . . . O de'verd' anni miei; O sommo Carlo. Don Carlos: C'est moi, Carlos . . . C'est mon jour suprême; Pour moi la vengeance du Roi . . . Ah! je meurs. Otello: Inaffia l'Ugola . . . Brindisi; Non ti crucciar . . . Credo.* PONCHIELLI: *La Gioconda: Pescator, affonda l'esca.* PUCCINI: *La Fanciulla del West: Minnie dalla mia casa.*
(M) *** Decca 411 976-1/*4* (id.].

This *'Grandi Voci'* disc brings a welcome reissue at mid-price of Milnes's formidable 1974 recital, a fine display of versatility, with the lighter items like the *Figaro* aria as impressively done as the darker arias. Specially impressive is the fine contrast drawn between the *Credo* of Iago and that of Jack Rance in *Fanciulla del West*, the one inward, the other extrovert. First-rate sound, and a splendid cassette.

Monteverdi Choir, English Baroque Soloists, Gardiner

'Sacred choral music': SCARLATTI, D.: *Stabat Mater*. CAVALLI: *Salve regina*. GESUALDO: *Ave, dulcissima Maria*. CLÉMENT: *O Maria vernana rosa*.
*** Erato Dig. **ECD 88087;** NUM/*MCE* 75172 [id.].

This collection is centred round Domenico Scarlatti's *Stabat Mater*, which is praised in the Composer section. The shorter works which fill out this collection are no less worthwhile, notably the rewarding Gesualdo motet from the *Sacrae cantiones*, whose remarkably expressive opening has few precedents in its harmonic eloquence, and another Marian motet by Jacques Clément, better known as Clemens non Papa. The recording is very good indeed in all three media, without being in the demonstration bracket.

New College, Oxford, Choir, Higginbottom

'Carols from New College': O come all ye faithful; The angel Gabriel; Ding dong merrily on high; The holly and the ivy; I wonder as I wander; Sussex carol; This is the truth; A Virgin most pure; Rocking carol; Once in Royal David's city; ORD: *Adam lay y bounden;* BENNETT: *Out of your sleep*. HOWELLS: *A spotless rose; Here is the little door*. DARKE: *In the bleak midwinter*. MATHIAS: *A babe is born; Wassail carol*. WISHART: *Alleluya, a new work is come on hand*. LEIGHTON: *Lully, lulla, thou little tiny child*. JOUBERT: *There is no rose of such virtue*.
*** CRD **CRD 3443;** CRD 1143/*CRDC 4143* [id.].

A beautiful Christmas record, the mood essentially serene and reflective. Apart from the lovely traditional arrangements, from the Czech *Rocking carol* to the Appalachian *I wonder as I wander*, many of the highlights are more recently composed. Both the Mathias settings are memorable and spark a lively response from the choir; Howells' *Here is the little door* is matched by Wishart's *Alleluya* and Kenneth Leighton's *Lully, lulla, thou little tiny child* in memorability. In some of these and in the opening *O come all ye faithful* and the closing *Once in Royal David's city*, Howerd Moody adds weight with excellent organ accompaniments, but fifteen out of the twenty-one items here are sung unaccompanied, to maximum effect. The recording acoustic seems ideal and the balance is first class. The documentation, however, consists of just a list of titles and sources – and the CD (using the unedited artwork from the LP) lists them as being divided on to side one and side two!

Norman, Jessye (soprano)

'Sacred songs' (with Ambrosian Singers, RPO, Gibson): GOUNOD: *Messe solennelle à Sainte Cécile: Sanctus. O Divine Redeemer.* FRANCK: *Panis angelicus.* ADAMS: *The Holy City.* ANON.: *Amazing grace. Greensleeves. Let us break bread. I wonder.* MAGGIMSEY: *Sweet little Jesus Boy.* YON: *Gesù Bambino.*
€ *** Ph. Dig. **400 019-2**; 6514/*7337* 151 [id.].

Miss Norman's restraint is very telling here; she sings with great eloquence, but her simplicity and sincerity shine through repertoire that can easily sound sentimental. The Gounod *Sanctus* is especially fine, but the simpler traditional songs are also very affecting. First-class recording and an excellent tape transfer. The compact disc, however, is very much in the demonstration class, strikingly natural and giving the soloist remarkable presence, especially when she is singing unaccompanied.

'With a song in my heart' (with Boston Pops O, Williams): RODGERS: *Falling in love with love; Spring is here; With a song in my heart.* PORTER: *In the still of the night; I love Paris; I love you.* KERN: *I'm old fashioned; The song is you; All the things you are.* ARLEN: *The sleeping bee.* GERSHWIN: *Love is here to stay; Love walked in.*
*(*) Ph. Dig. **412 625-2**; 412 625-1/*4* [id.].

Though the big, rich voice is as glorious to hear as ever, this crossover record is a disappointment, with the singer caught between operatic and pop styles, and the accompaniments generally too aggressive. Bright, forwardly balanced recording, effective in all three media.

Opera choruses

'Celebrated opera choruses' (sung by: (i) Leipzig Radio Ch., Carlos Kleiber, or (ii) Boehm; (iii) Berlin RIAS Ch., Boehm; (iv) Ambrosian Singers, Abbado; (v) Elisabeth Brasseur Ch., Markevitch; (vi) Bayreuth Festival Ch., Pitz; (vii) La Scala, Milan, Ch., Abbado, or (viii) Votto, or (ix) Karajan; (x) Württemberg State Opera Ch., Stuttgart, Leitner): (i) WEBER: *Der Freischütz: Huntsmen's chorus.* (ii) BEETHOVEN: *Fidelio: Prisoners' chorus.* (iii) MOZART: *Die Zauberflöte: O Isis und Osiris.* (iv) BIZET: *Carmen: Children's march and chorus; Entry of the Toreadors.* (v) BERLIOZ: *Damnation de Faust: Soldiers' chorus.* (vi) WAGNER: *Der fliegende Holländer: Sailors' chorus. Tannhäuser: Entry of the guests; Pilgrims' chorus. Lohengrin: Bridal procession to the cathedral; Bridal chorus. Parsifal: Entry of the Knights of the Grail.* (vii) VERDI: *Nabucco: Gli arredi festivi; Va, pensiero. Otello: Fuoco di gioia. Aïda: Triumphal march. Don Carlo: Spuntato ecco il dì d'esultanza. Il Trovatore: Anvil chorus. Macbeth: Che faceste? dite su!* (viii) *La Traviata: Matadors' chorus.* (ix) LEONCAVALLO: *Pag-*

liacci: Bell chorus. MASCAGNI: *Cavalleria rusticana: Gli aranci olezzano; Beato voi . . . Regina coeli laetare.* (X) PUCCINI: *Madama Butterfly: Humming chorus.*
(M) *** DG 419 114-1/*4* (2).

A superb anthology. Most of the favourites from the standard repertoire are included and the performances are consistently distinguished. Carlos Kleiber's huntsmen from *Der Freischütz* open the concert with invigoratingly crisp articulation, and among the highlights are some splendid Wagner items, stirringly sung by the 1958 Bayreuth Festival Chorus under their distinguished chorus master, Wilhelm Pitz, and Abbado's La Scala Verdi collection. This is also available on CD but sounds better here, especially on the chrome tapes which are exceptionally vivid throughout. There is not a single disappointing item included: Markevitch's French soldiers sound very French indeed and Ferdinand Leitner at Stuttgart magics the lovely *Humming chorus* from *Madama Butterfly.*

Opera: 'Golden opera'

'Golden opera' Vol. 1: DELIBES: *Lakmé: Viens Mallika . . . Dôme épais le jasmin* (Sutherland; Berbié). BIZET: *Carmen: Habañera* (Horne). *Les Pêcheurs de perles: Au fond du temple saint* (Pavarotti, Ghiaurov). ROSSINI: *Il Barbiere di Siviglia: Largo al factotum* (Milnes). MOZART: *Così fan tutte: Soave sia il vento* (Popp, Fassbaender, Krause). CATALANI: *La Wally: Ne andrò lontana* (Tebaldi). VERDI: *La Traviata: Prelude, Act I* (Pritchard); *Brindisi* (Sutherland, Bergonzi). *Aïda: Celeste Aïda* (Bergonzi). PUCCINI: *Madama Butterfly: Un bel dì* (Crespin). *Tosca: Recondita armonia* (Corelli). *Gianni Schicchi: O mio babbino caro* (Tebaldi). OFFENBACH: *Contes d'Hoffmann: Barcarolle* (Sutherland, Tourangeau).
(M) *** Decca Jub. 414 205-1/*4*.

Decca have a reputation for arranging this kind of anthology well; the order of items here is felicitous, with the recital (and the end of side one) opening and closing with well-chosen duets, and plenty of good things in between. There is nothing to disappoint and much to give pleasure, not least Milnes as a resoundingly good-humoured Figaro in Rossini's *Il Barbiere* and Tebaldi's ravishing *O mio babbino caro*. The sound is consistently vivid on LP and tape alike. Recommended – with the caveat that no background information is given about the content, only titles.

'Golden opera', Vol. 2: DELIBES: *Lakmé: Bell song* (Sutherland). MOZART: *Le nozze di Figaro: Voi che sapete* (Berganza). *Don Giovanni: Il mio tesoro* (Burrows). VERDI: *Nabucco: Va pensiero* (V. State Op. Ch., Gardelli). *Rigoletto: La donna è mobile* (Pavarotti). DONIZETTI: *La Favorita: O mio Fernando* (Cossotto). *Lucia di Lammermoor: Chi me frena* (Sutherland, Miles, Pavarotti, Ghiaurov, Tourangeau, Davies). TCHAIKOVSKY: *Eugene Onegin: Waltz* (Weikl, Burrows, Ch. and O of ROHCG, Solti). SAINT-SAËNS: *Samson et Dalila: Mon coeur s'ouvre à ta voix* (Horne). BIZET: *Carmen: Votre toast . . . Toreador* (Krause, Resnik).

PUCCINI: *Tosca: Vissi d'arte* (Price). *È lucevan le stelle* (Di Stefano). *Madama Butterfly: Vogliatemi bene* (*Love duet*) (Tebaldi, Bergonzi).
(M) *** Decca Jub. 414 497-1/*4*.

Volume 2 offers a less obvious arrangement of items, but some splendid performances, notably Sutherland's scintillating *Bell song* from *Lakmé*, and the justly famous Stuart Burrows *Il mio tesoro*. Marilyn Horne is superb in *Softly awakes my heart* from *Samson and Delilah* and Leontyne Price's *Vissi d'arte* is as unforgettable as the earlier *Love duet* from the 1958 *Madama Butterfly*, with Tebaldi in ravishing voice. The recordings all sound well, although the sound is a little variable from item to item. The tape handles the transfers vividly, and only in the *Bell song* is there an occasional hint of peaking.

Opera: 'Nights at the Opera'

'Nights at the opera': VERDI: *Aïda: Celeste Aïda* (Corelli); *Triumphal march. Don Carlos: O don fatale* (Verrett). *Il Trovatore: Anvil chorus; Miserere* (Tucci, Corelli). *La Traviata: Brindisi; Ah, fors' è lui* (Monte, Los Angeles). *Nabucco: Chorus of Hebrew slaves.* MASCAGNI: *Cavalleria Rusticana: Easter hymn* (Tinsley). DONIZETTI: *L'Elisir d'amore: Una furtiva lagrima* (Alva). PUCCINI: *Madama Butterfly: Un bel dì* (Scotto). *La Bohème: Che gelida manina; O soave fanciulla* (Gedda, Freni); *Musetta's waltz song* (Adani). *Turandot: Nessun dorma* (Corelli). *Gianni Schicchi: O mio babbino caro* (Los Angeles). *Tosca: Recondita armonia; È lucevan le stelle* (Bergonzi); *Vissi d'arte* (Callas). ROSSINI: *Il Barbiere di Siviglia: Largo al factotum* (Bruscantini).
(B) ** EMI *TC2-MOM 112*.

This is generally a preferable eighty minutes to the collection of *Italian opera favourites* in the same tape series (see above). Sometimes the performances are robust rather than endearing (Corelli's *Celeste Aïda* is vibrant but clumsily phrased). But there are many good things, notably the contributions of Luigi Alva, Victoria de los Angeles and Callas's *Vissi d'arte*. Vivid sound throughout, with a high transfer level, yet little roughness. However, some of the excerpts, taken from complete sets, have to be faded out quickly at the end, which tends to unsettle one's listening in an anthology of this kind.

Operatic Duets: 'Duets from famous operas'

Duets sung by: (i) Nicolai Gedda, (ii) Ernest Blanc, (iii) Jussi Bjoerling and Victoria de Los Angeles, (iv) Carlo Bergonzi, (v) Maria Callas, (vi) Mirella Freni, (vii) Eberhard Waechter and Graziella Sciutti, (viii) Tito Gobbi, (ix) Gabriella Tucci, (x) Franco Corelli, (xi) Evelyn Lear and D. Ouzounov, (xii) Antonietta Stella: (i; ii) BIZET: *Les Pêcheurs de perles*: *Au fond du temple saint*, (iii) PUCCINI; *Madama Butterfly*: *Bimba dagli occhi;* (iv; v) *Tosca: O dolci mani;*

(i; vi) *La Bohème: O soave fanciulla.* (vii) MOZART: *Don Giovanni: Là ci darem la mano.* (v; viii) ROSSINI: *Il Barbiere di Siviglia: Dunque io son.* (ix; x) VERDI: *Il Trovatore: Miserere d'un'alma già vicina.* (xi) MUSSORGSKY: *Boris Godunov: O Tsarevich I beg you.* (x; xii) GIORDANO: *Andrea Chénier: Vicini a te.*
(B) **(*) CfP CFP 41 4498-1/*4*.

There are not many operas that hold their reputation in the public memory by means of a male duet, but *The pearl fishers* is one, and a sturdy performance of *Au fond du temple saint* makes a suitable opening for side two of this collection of purple duos. Side one, however, opens with the genial lyricism of *Là ci darem la mano*, from the 1961 Giulini set of *Don Giovanni* with Eberhard Waechter and Graziella Sciutti singing most winningly. The star quality of the artists is noticeable through most of these extracts. Highlights include this beautifully relaxed *Là ci darem*, the short Rossini item, and the *La Bohème* duet (which seldom fails). The record ends in a blaze of melodrama with *Andrea Chénier*. As a programme, the effect of a series of such full-blooded passionate vocal embraces is perhaps a little wearing. But otherwise, with generally lively recording, few will be disappointed. The cassette is smoothly transferred, if without quite the upper range of the LP.

Operetta: 'Golden operetta'

'Golden operetta': STRAUSS, J. Jnr: *Die Fledermaus: Mein Herr Marquis* (Gueden); *Csardas* (Janowitz). *Eine Nacht in Venedig: Lagunen waltz* (Krenn). *Wiener Blut: Wiener Blut* (Gueden). *Der Zigeunerbaron: O habet Acht* (Lorengar). *Casanova: Nuns' chorus* (Sutherland, Ambrosian Singers). ZELLER: *Der Obersteiger: Sei nicht bös* (Gueden). LEHÁR: *Das Land des Lächelns: Dein ist mein ganzes Herz* (Bjoerling). *Die lustige Witwe: Vilja-Lied* (Sutherland); *Lippen schweigen* (Holm, Krenn). *Schön is die Welt: Schön ist die Welt* (Krenn). *Der Graf von Luxemburg: Lieber Freund . . . Bist du's, Lachendes Gluck* (Holm, Krenn). *Giuditta: Du bist meine Sonne* (Kmentt). LECOCQ: *Le Coeur et la main: Bonsoir Perez le capitaine* (Sutherland). OFFENBACH: *La Périchole: Letter song. La Grande Duchesse de Gérolstein: J'aime les militaires* (Crespin).
(M) *** Decca Jub. 414 466-1/*4*.

A valuable and generous anthology, not just for the obvious highlights: Joan Sutherland's *Vilja* and the delightful contributions from Hilde Gueden – notably a delicious *Sei nicht bös* – recorded in 1961 when the voice was at its freshest; but also Régine Crespin at her finest in Offenbach – the duchess reviewing her troops, and the charming *Letter song* from *La Périchole*. In their winningly nostalgic account of the *Merry widow waltz* Renate Holm and Werner Krenn hum the melody, having sung the words, giving the impression of dancing together. The recording throughout is very good, the tape only marginally less refined than the LP.

Pavarotti, Luciano (tenor)

'The world's favourite arias' from: LEONCAVALLO: *I Pagliacci.* FLOTOW: *Martha.* BIZET: *Carmen.* PUCCINI: *La Bohème; Tosca; Turandot.* VERDI: *Rigoletto; Aïda; Il Trovatore.* GOUNOD: *Faust.*

(*) Decca **400 053-2; SXL/*KSXC* 6649 [Lon. OSA/5- 26384].

As one would expect from Pavarotti, there is much to enjoy in his ripe and resonant singing of these favourite arias, but it is noticeable that the finest performances are those which come from complete sets, conducted by Karajan (*Bohème*), Mehta (*Turandot*) and Bonynge (*Rigoletto*), where with character in mind Pavarotti's singing is more intense and imaginative. The rest remains very impressive, though at under forty minutes the measure is short. The transfer to compact disc has involved digital remastering, which has resulted in slight limitation of the upper range to take out background noise. However, the vividness of the voice is enhanced in the process. The cassette is slightly more uneven in quality than LP or CD, most noticeably in the *Turandot* excerpt where the chorus is none too clear.

'Digital recital' (with Nat. PO, Chailly or Fabritiis): GIORDANO: *Fedora: Amor ti vieta. Andrea Chénier: Colpito qui m'avete . . . Un dì all'azzuro spazio; Come un bel dì di maggio; Si, fui soldata.* BOITO: *Mefistofele: Dai campi, dai prati; Ogni mortal . . . Giunto sul passo estremo.* CILEA: *Adriana Lecouvreur: La dolcissima effigie; L'anima ho stanca.* MASCAGNI: *Iris: Apri la tua finestra!* MEYERBEER: *L'Africana: Mi batti il cor . . . O Paradiso.* MASSENET: *Werther: Pourquoi me réveiller.* PUCCINI: *La Fanciulla del West: Ch'ella mi creda. Manon Lescaut: Tra voi belle; Donna non vidi mai; Ah! non v'avvicinate! . . . No! No! pazzo son!* (with Howlett).

(*) Decca Dig. **400 083-2; SXDL/*KSXDC* 7504 [Lon. LDR/5- 10020).

This first digital recital record from Pavarotti has the voice more resplendent than ever. The passion with which he tackles Des Grieux's Act III plea from *Manon Lescaut* is devastating, and the big breast-beating numbers are all splendid, imaginative as well as heroic. But the slight pieces, Des Grieux's *Tra voi belle* and the Iris *Serenade*, could be lighter and more charming. The compact disc gives the voice even greater projection, with its full resonance and brilliance admirably caught, but it does also make the listener more aware of the occasional lack of subtlety of the presentation. The cassette transfer is vibrant and clear, if losing a little of the CD projection.

Neapolitan songs (with Ch. and O of Teatro Communale, Bologna, Guadagno, or Nat. PO, Chiaramello): DI CAPUA: *O sole mio. Maria, Marì.* TOSTI: *A vuchella. Marechiare.* CANNIO: *O surdato 'nnamurato.* GAMBARDELLA: *O Marenariello.* ANON.: *Fenesta vascia.* DE CURTIS: *Torna a Surriento. Tu, ca nun chiagne.* PENNINO: *Pecchè . . .* D'ANNIBALE: *O paese d'o sole.* TAGLIAFERRI: *Piscatore 'e pusilleco.* DENZA: *Funiculi, funicula.*

*** Decca **410 015-2**; SXL/*KSXC* 6870 [Lon. OSA/5- 26560].

Neapolitan songs given grand treatment in passionate Italian performances, missing some of the charm but none of the red-blooded fervour. The recording is both vivid and atmospheric. The tape transfer is well managed although there is slight loss of presence in the items with chorus. This certainly does not apply to the compact disc, where the recording is most successfully digitally remastered.

'Mamma' (Italian and Neapolitan popular songs with O and Ch., Henry Mancini): BIXIO: *Mamma; Vivere; Mia canzone al vento; Parlai, d'amore.* DE CURTIS: *Non ti scordar di me.* BUZZI-PECCIA: *Lolita:* excerpts. GASTALDON: *Musica proibita.* CESARINI: *Firenza sogna.* KRAMER: *In un palco della scala.* RIVI: *Addio, sogni di gloria!* D'ANZI: *Voglio vivere cosi.* DI LAZZARO: *Chitarra romana.* DE CRESCENZO: *Rondine al nido.* TRAD.: *Ghirlandeina.* CALIFONA: *Vieni sul mar'.* ARONA: *Campana di San Giusto.*
(*) Decca Dig. **411 959-2; 411 959-1/*4* [id.].

Larger-than-life arrangements by Henry Mancini of popular Italian and Neapolitan songs with larger-than-life singing to match. Vulgarity is welcomed rather than skirted, which is fair enough in this music. Larger-than-life recording, too.

'O Holy night' (with Wandsworth School Boys' Ch., Nat. PO, Adler): ADAM: *Cantique noël* (*O holy night*). STRADELLA: *Pieta Signore.* FRANCK: *Panis angelicus.* MERCADANTE: *Parola quinta.* SCHUBERT: *Ave Maria.* BACH–GOUNOD: *Ave Maria.* BIZET: *Agnus Dei.* BERLIOZ: *Requiem: Sanctus.* TRAD.: *Adeste fidelis.* YON: *Jesù bambino.* SCHUBERT, arr. Melichar: *Mille cherubini in coro.*
(*) Decca **414 044-2; SXL/*KSXC* 6781.

It is a long-established tradition for great Italian tenors to indulge in such songs as these, most of them overtly sugary in their expression of (no doubt) sincere religious fervour. Pavarotti is hardly a model of taste, but more than most of his rivals (even a tenor as intelligent as Placido Domingo) he avoids the worst pitfalls; and if this sort of recital is what you are looking for, then Pavarotti is a good choice, with his beautiful vocalizing helped by full, bright recording. Note too that one or two of these items are less hackneyed than the rest, for instance the title setting by Adam, Mercadante's *Parola quinta* and the *Sanctus* from Berlioz's *Requiem mass.* The analogue recording has transferred well to CD; the cassette too is admirably clear and clean, the chorus naturally caught.

'Mattinata': CALDARA: *Alma del core.* CIAMPI: Tre giorni. BELLINI: Vaga luna che inargenti. DURANTE: *Danza danza, fanciulla.* GIORDANI: *Caro mio ben.* ROSSINI: *La promessa.* GLUCK: *Orfeo: Che farò.* TOSTI: *L'alba separa; Aprile; Chanson de l'adieu; L'Ultima canzone.* DONIZETTI: *Il barcaiolo.* LEONCAVALLO: *Mattinata.* BEETHOVEN: *In questo tomba.*
(*) Decca **414 454-2 [id.]; SXL/*KSXC* 7013 [Lon. OSA/*5*- 26669].

Pavarotti is at home in the lightweight items. *Caro mio ben* is very nicely done and the romantic songs have a well-judged ardour. *Che farò* is rather less impressive. The tone is not always golden, but most of the bloom remains. The recording is vividly faithful in all three media.

'Pavarotti's greatest hits': PUCCINI: *Turandot: Nessun dorma. Tosca: Recondita armonia; È lucevan le stelle. La Bohème: Che gelida manina.* DONIZETTI: *La fille du régiment: O mes amis . . . Pour mon âme. La Favorita: Spirito gentil. L'Elisir d'amore: Una furtiva lagrima.* STRAUSS, R.: *Der Rosenkavalier: Di rigori armato.* LEONCAVALLO: *Mattinata.* ROSSINI: *La danza.* DE CURTIS: *Torna a Surriento.* BIZET: *Carmen: Flower song.* BELLINI: *I Puritani: A te O cara. Vanne, O rose fortunata.* VERDI: *Il Travatore: Di qual tetra . . . Ah, si ben, mio; Di quella pira. Rigoletto: La donna è mobile; Questa o quella. Requiem: Ingemisco. Aïda: Celeste Aïda.* FRANCK: *Panis angelicus.* GOUNOD: *Faust: Salut! Demeure.* SCHUBERT: *Ave Maria.* LEONCAVALLO: *I Pagliacci: Vesti la giubba.* PONCHIELLI: *La Gioconda: Cielo e mar.* DENZA: *Funiculi, funicula.*
*** Decca **417 011-2** (2) [id.]; D236 D2/*K236 K22* [PAV/*5*- 2003/4].

This collection of 'greatest hits' can safely be recommended to all who have admired the golden beauty of Pavarotti's voice. Including as it does a fair proportion of earlier recordings, the two discs demonstrate the splendid consistency of his singing. Songs are included as well as excerpts from opera, including *Torna a Surriento, Funiculi, funicula*, Leoncavallo's *Mattinata* and Rossini's *La Danza*. The sound is very good on LP, especially vibrant on CD, but sometimes a little fierce on cassette.

'Passione' (with Bologna Teatro Comunale O, Chiaramello): TAGLIAFERRI: *Passione.* COSTA: *Era de maggio.* ANON.: *Fenesta che lucive; La Palummella; Te voglio bene assaje.* NARDELIA: *Chiove.* FALVO: *Dicitencello vuie.* DE CURTIS: *Voce 'e notte.* DI PAPUA: *I 'te vurria vasa.* MARIO: *Santa Lucia luntana.* LAMA: *Silenzio cantatore.* CARDILLO: *Core 'ngrato.*
*** Decca Dig. **417 117-2**; 417 117-1/*4* [id.].

With the advantage of first-class recording, this perhaps is the most attractive of Pavarotti's Neapolitan collections. The voice sounds fresh, the singing is ardent and the programme is chosen imaginatively. The great tenor obviously identifies with this repertoire and sings everything with the kind of natural response that skirts vulgarity. The orchestrations by Giancarlo Chiaramello show a feeling for the right kind of orchestral colour: they may be sophisticated, but they undoubtedly enhance the melodic lines. If the title of the collection suggests hyperbole, there is in fact a well-judged balance here between passionate romanticism and concern for phrasing and detail. There is an excellent high-level cassette.

Pears, Sir Peter (tenor)

'Grandi voci': PURCELL: *Morning hymn.* SCHUTZ: *Venite ad me.* BACH: *Christmas oratorio: Frohe Hirten.* HANDEL: *L'Allegro ed il penseroso: There let Hymen oft appear. Acis and Galatea: Love in her eyes sits playing; Love sounds th'alarm.* SCHUBERT: *An die Laute; Geheimes; Die Taubenpost.* HAYDN: *Sailor's song.* BRITTEN: *Serenade: Nocturne. Peter Grimes: Go there!; The Foggy dew; Sally in our alley; Lincolnshire poacher.*
(M) *** Decca 411 919-1.

A splendidly varied collection, mainly of Sir Peter's earlier recordings, to bring out his versatility and consistent stylishness. It is good to have a nicely chosen selection of Britten items including folksong settings; the Schubert songs with Britten accompanying at the piano mark another high spot. The Handel items may come from old Oiseau-Lyre recordings but the sound, of whatever vintage, has been very well remastered.

Price, Leontyne (soprano), **Marilyn Horne** (mezzo-soprano).

'In concert at the Met' (with NY Met. Op. O, Levine): MOZART: *Così fan tutte: Ah guarda sorella. Le nozze di Figaro: Dove sono.* HANDEL: *Rodelinda: Vivi tiranno!; Rinaldo: Fermati! No crudel!* VERDI: *I vespri siciliani: Overture. Aïda: Silenzio! Aïda verso noi s'avanza. La forza del destino: Pace, pace.* ROSSINI: *L'Assedio di Corinto: Non temer.* BELLINI: *Norma: Sinfonia; Mira o Norma.* MEYERBEER: *Les Huguenots: Non, non, non . . . vous n'avez jamais, je gage.* PUCCINI: *La Rondine: Chi il bel sogno di Doretta. Madama Butterfly: Flower duet.*
* RCA Dig. **RD 84609** (2).

This is a complete, unedited recording of an afternoon celebrity concert at the Met. on 28 March 1982, and it offers all the disadvantages and few of the advantages of live recording. The microphones are unflattering to the voices, which are made to sound bright and hard; and the orchestral sound is most unattractive, with unacceptably shrill violins in the *Norma Sinfonia.* Marilyn Horne demonstrates her formidable technique in the *Rodelinda* aria, but the duets are without charm and the famous *Mira, o Norma* would not have been passed in the studio. By far the most attractive items are the three encores with the excerpt from *Les Huguenots* treated as a fun piece and Leontyne Price heard at something like her best form in the excerpt from *La Rondine*. The enthusiastic audience bursts in with applause at the end of each aria, and this becomes increasingly irritating.

Royal College of Music Chamber Choir and Brass Ensemble, Willcocks

Carols for Christmas, Volumes 1 and 2: Vol. 1: MENDELSSOHN: *Hark the herald angels.* REDNER: *O Little town of Bethlehem.* WILLIS: *It came upon the midnight clear.* TRAD.: *Good Christian men, rejoice; Angels we have heard on high; Away in a manger; Good King Wenceslas; The first nowell.* BACH: *O little one sweet.* TRAD.: *Bring a torch, Jeanette, Isabella; Boar's head carol.* SMART: *Angels from the realms of Glory.* TRAD.: *Wassail; Coventry carol; God rest you merry; Sans day carol; Deck the hall; Joseph dearest, Joseph mine; Sussex carol.* GRÜBER: *Silent night.* HOLST: *In the bleak midwinter.*

Vol. 2: TRAD.: *The holly and the ivy.* PRAETORIUS: *Lo, how a rose.* HANDEL: *Joy to the world.* TRAD.: *O come, O come, Emmanuel; Infant holy; I saw three ships.* GAUNTLETT: *Once in Royal David's city.* WADE: *O come all ye faithful.* CORNELIUS: *The three kings.* TRAD.: *Here we come a-wassailing; Rocking carol; While shepherds watched their flocks; Patapan; Whence comes this rush of wings?; The twelve days of Christmas; What Child is this?; O Christmas tree; Ding dong, merrily on high. We wish you a merry Christmas.* HOPKINS: *We three kings of orient are.*
(*) [RYKO (RCA/CBS) **RCDI 0004/5.].

This pair of CDs covers most of the more familiar carols and was specially produced for Christmas 1985 when it proved very successful in the USA. It is not yet available in the UK. Obviously made on a shoestring budget, it features a chamber choir of eighteen, plus a brass ensemble, piano, organ and a few ad lib additions. The use of just a piccolo and side-drum in *Patapan* is a good example where economy is highly effective, but the piano is much less welcome, adding nothing whatsoever to *I saw three ships*, and is an irritant in *The twelve days of Christmas*. Fortunately many of the carols are sung a cappella and the small group is very telling in simple inspirations like *Silent night, Deck the hall* and *What Child is this?* (to the tune of *Greensleeves*). Equally the brass adds an extra dimension, with quite basic part-writing, to the *Sussex carol* and *God rest ye merry*, for instance, and the organ is always nicely balanced. The performances have an agreeable freshness and simplicity, and many will welcome the absence of florid arrangements, when the music making is so effectively presented in a kindly but not too resonant ambience.

Royal occasions: 'Music from Great Royal Occasions'

Coronation, 1953: BULLOCK: *Fanfare.* PARRY: *I was glad.* HOWELLS: *O God our defender.* HARRIS: *Let Thy prayer come into Thy presence.* HANDEL: *Zadok the Priest* (cond. Dr William McKie). Wedding of Princess Anne and Captain

Mark Phillips, 1973: VAUGHAN WILLIAMS: *Let all the world in every corner sing*. BASHFORD: *Fanfare: Toccata for trumpets*. WIDOR: *Organ Toccata in F*. STRAUSS, J. snr: *Radetzky march* (Westminster Abbey Ch., Guest; Timothy Farrell (organ)). Wedding of the Prince of Wales and Lady Diana Spencer, 1981: JACKSON: *Fanfare*. CLARKE: *Trumpet voluntary*. MATHIAS: *Let the people praise Thee, O God*. Arr. Willcocks: *National anthem*. HANDEL: *Occasional oratorio: March. Samson: Let the bright seraphim; Let their celestial concerts all unite*. RICHARDS: *Fanfare: Rejoicing*. ELGAR: *Pomp and circumstance march No. 4* (St Paul's Cathedral Ch., Barry Rose; Kiri Te Kanawa, Bach Ch., Willcocks; O, Sir Colin Davis. Christopher Dearnley (organ); State trumpeters.
**** BBC CD 470.**

This is essentially a memento collection, for many of the individual items can be obtained elsewhere in more satisfactory studio recordings. The early mono sound from the 1953 Coronation is remarkably clear and well balanced, but the later stereo recordings are far more impressive in capturing the acoustics of Westminster and St Paul's. Dame Kiri Te Kanawa seems (understandably) nervous in *Let the bright seraphim* and her Philips studio recording – see above – is a far superior performance. The State Trumpeters make some resplendent sounds and Timothy Farrell is suitably high-spirited in the famous Widor *Toccata*, but the inevitable editing between items makes a less than satisfactory experience for continuous listening.

St George's Canzona, John Sothcott

'Merry it is while summer lasts': RAIMBAUT DE VAQUEIRAS: *Kalenda maya*. MONIOT D'ARRAS: *Ce fut en mai*. LANDINI: *L'alma mia piange*. WALTER VON DER VOGELWEIDE: *Unter den Linden*. ANON.: *Estampie reale; Miri it is while summer ilast; Ye have so long keepyt o; Me lyketh ever the lenger the bet; Chominciamento di gioia; Amor me fa cantar*. TRAD.: *Cuckoo's nest; Morris dance; Trunkles; The cuckoo; The merry Sherwood rangers*.
*** CRD CRD 1112/*CRDC 4112* [id.].

Primarily this conveys a convivial medieval view of summer, but while the main programme is made up of music dating from between 1200 and 1400, the last four traditional items are more up to date. This is the most attractive collection from the St George's Canzona so far. They show great flair in matching voices with instrumental colour and do not seek to simulate authenticity with poor intonation. So much of this repertoire has indelible character. The very opening item with its unexpected melodic progression is delightfully piquant and its drone bass gives it a hurdy-gurdy flavour. By contrast *Ce fut en mai* is lyrically serene while the *Estampie reale*, featuring the bagpipes, is infectiously spirited. The second group opens with an elaborate treatment of *Unter den Linden*, an indelible tune, with instrumental as well as vocal variants, while the florid singing of the group's counter-tenor, Derek Harrison, is most appealing in *Amor mi fa cantar* and *L'alma mia piange*, two very contrasted love songs. The recording, made at St James, Clerkenwell, is splendidly vivid and clear, and the chrome cassette is in the demonstration bracket. A most entertaining dip into the distant and not so distant past. Excellent back-up documentation.

Medieval songs and dances: Lamento di Tristano; L'autrier m'iere levaz. 4 Estampies real; Edi beo thu hevene quene; Eyns ne soy ke plente fu; Tre fontane; PERRIN D'AGINCOURT: *Quant voi en la fin d'este.* Cantigas de Santa Maria: *Se ome fezer; Nas mentes senper teer; Como poden per sas culpas; Maravillosos et piadosos.*
*** CRD **CRD 3421;** CRD 1121/*CRDC 4121* [id.].

As so often when early music is imaginatively re-created, one is astonished at the individuality of many of the ideas. This applies particularly to the second item in this collection, *Quant voi en la fin d'este*, attributed to the mid-thirteenth century trouvère, Perrin d'Agincourt, but no less to the four Cantigas de Santa Maria. The fruity presentation of *Como poden per sas culpas* ('As men may be crippled by their sins, so they may afterwards be made sound by the Virgin') is admirably contrasted with the strong lyrical appeal of the following *Maravillosos et piadosos*, directly extolling the virtues and compassion of Saint Mary. Among the four *Estampies real* the one presented last (band 11 on the CD) is haunting in its lilting melancholy. The instrumentation is at times suitably robust, but does not eschew good intonation and subtle effects. The group is vividly recorded and the acoustics of St James, Clerkenwell, are never allowed to cloud detail. The sound is admirably firm and real in its CD format, but the cassette is very lively and clear also. The documentation is first class.

Sass, Sylvia (soprano)

'Grandi voci': PUCCINI: *Turandot: In questa reggia. Tosca: Vissi d'arte. Manon Lescaut: In quelle trine morbide; Sola perduta, abbandonata. Madama Butterfly: Un bel dì.* VERDI: *Aïda: Ritorna vincitor. Macbeth: Una macchia è qui tutt'ora! I Lombardi: O madre dal cielo . . . Se vano, se vano è il pregare.*
(M) *** Decca 414 175-1/*4*.

This début recital was made in 1977. Glamorous and vibrant in personality and appearance as well as of voice, Sylvia Sass immediately established her star status at the very start of Turandot's big aria, *In questa reggia.* The Puccini excerpts stand any kind of competition in their range and expression, searching as well as beautiful, and though the Verdi items occasionally betray tiny chinks in the technical armour, there have been few more exciting soprano recital recordings in recent years. The recording is vivid and clear, and the refinement of detail creates the most beautiful orchestral textures in the introductions to the scenes from *Macbeth* and *I Lombardi*. There is a first-class cassette.

Schoeffler, Paul (bass-baritone)

(*Grandi voci'*: MOZART: *Le nozze di Figaro: Non più andrai. Don Giovanni: Madamina.* VERDI: *Otello: Era la notte; Credo in un Dio crudel.* STRAUSS, R.: *Arabella: Der Richtige, so hab'ich still zu mir.* WAGNER: *Die Meistersinger: Fliedermonolog; Wahnmonolog. Die Walküre: Wotan's farewell and Magic fire music.*
(M) (**) Decca Grandi Voci mono 414 543-1.

Paul Schoeffler was a highly distinctive contributor to a number of Decca opera issues of the 1950s, and this *'Grandi voci'* issue collects some of the more striking, notably the Wagner items; his portrait of Hans Sachs has rare geniality. Though the Italian items do not suit him so well, this makes a welcome historic issue.

Schumann, Elisabeth (soprano)

'Treasury' (recordings from 1926–45): Excerpts from: BACH: *Mass in B min.; St Matthew Passion.* HANDEL: *Joshua.* MOZART: *Il re pastore; Le nozze di Figaro; Don Giovanni; Die Zauberflöte. Exsultate jubilate.* HUMPERDINCK: *Hänsel und Gretel.* ZELLER: *Der Obersteiger; Der Vogelhändler.* HEUBERGER: *Der Opernball.* OFFENBACH: *Contes d'Hoffmann.* STRAUSS, J. Jnr: *Die Fledermaus.* Songs by Mozart; Haydn; Beethoven; Ziehrer.
(M) (***) HMV EX 290541-3/5 (2).

Few sopranos have sung with such sparkle and charm as Elisabeth Schumann, and those qualities shine out at full voltage in superb transfers of recordings she made between 1926 and 1945. Though neither Schubert nor Richard Strauss is represented – other reissues cover her recordings of them – the range here is wide. The bright, strong personality expressed through the characterful but always delicate silver of her voice is ideal both for Mozart – Susanna, Cherubino and Zerlina all enchantingly portrayed – as well as for Viennese waltz songs. But the Bach items on side one and songs like Beethoven's *Wonne der Wehmut* reveal how her ability to inflect a phrase with personal magic could be turned to far more than charm. The Bach is not to today's taste stylistically, but it is above all fresh and alive. The duets from the *B minor Mass*, for example, underline her personal imagination, when she is set against such strong, forthright British singers as Margaret Balfour and Walter Widdop. Schumann was a virtuoso whistler too, as demonstrated in the first of the *Hänsel und Gretel* items and in Zeller's *Nightingale Song*. In the second *Hänsel* item as well as in the Offenbach

Barcarolle she sings duets with herself, but, owing to primitive recording techniques, surface noise is doubled. There is end-of-side roughness on one of the *B minor Mass* items. Otherwise the transfers are outstanding. The usual excellent documentation appears in a valuable booklet.

Schwarzkopf, Elisabeth (soprano)

'Elisabeth Schwarzkopf sings operetta' (with Philharmonia Ch. and O, Ackermann): HEUBERGER: *Der Opernball: Im chambre séparée.* ZELLER: *Der Vogelhändler: Ich bin die Christel; Schenkt man sich Rosen. Der Obersteiger: Sei nicht bös.* LEHÁR: *Der Zarewitsch: Einer wird kommen. Der Graf von Luxemburg: Hoch Evoë, Heut noch werd ich Ehefrau. Giuditta: Meine Lippen.* STRAUSS, J. jnr: *Casanova: Nuns' chorus; Laura's song.* MILLÖCKER: *Die Dubarry: Ich schenk mein Herz; Was ich im Leben beginne.* SUPPÉ: *Boccaccio: Hab ich nur deine Liebe.* SIECZYŃSKY: *Wien, du Stadt meiner Träume* (*Vienna, city of my dreams;* song).
❀ ₠ *** HMV **CDC 747284-2** [id.]; ASD/*TC-ASD* 2807 [Ang. S 35696].

This is one of the most delectable recordings of operetta arias ever made, and it is here presented with excellent sound. Schwarzkopf's 'whoopsing' manner (as Philip Hope-Wallace called it) is irresistible, authentically catching the Viennese style, languor and sparkle combined. Try for sample the exquisite *Im chambre séparée* or *Sei nicht bös*; but the whole programme is performed with supreme artistic command and ravishing tonal beauty. This outstanding example of the art of Elisabeth Schwarzkopf at its most enchanting is a disc which ought to be in every collection. The compact disc transfer enhances the superbly balanced recording even further, manages to cut out nearly all the background, give the voice a natural presence, and retain the orchestral bloom. Cassette collectors, too, will find that the tape transfer is beautifully managed.

Scottish Early Music Consort, Edwards

'Songs and Dances from the time of Mary Queen of Scots.'
** Chan. Dig. **CHAN 8332**; ABRD/*ABTD* 1103 [id.].

The idea of this anthology is to assemble songs and dances that, while not necessarily associated with her, could have been heard at the Court and in the noble households of the time of Mary Queen of Scots. The recital is arranged in roughly chronological order, opening with music from Mary's childhood and ending with two laments adapted to music by Byrd. The contents are varied: some of the pieces have charm (there is a Sermisy chanson adapted to Scottish words); others are less interesting, and performances are generally accomplished even if intonation is not always true. Good recording quality in all media.

Siepi, Cesare (bass)

'Grandi voci': VERDI: *Don Carlos: Ella giammai m'amò. Nabucco: Vieni, O Levita! . . . Tu sul labbro dei Veggenti. Ernani: Che mal vegg'io . . . Infelice! è tu credevi. Simon Boccanegra: Il lacerato spirito.* GOMES: *Salvator Rosa: Di sposo, di padre.* HALÉVY: *La Juive: Si la rigueur.* MEYERBEER: *Les Huguenots: Seigneur . . . Piff, paff. Robert le Diable. Nonnes qui reposez.*
(M) (**) Decca mono 411 659-1.

This is a straight reissue of a recital recorded in mono in the early days of LP, showing Siepi's dark bass at its firmest and most resonant. The characterizations in these items are not as individual as one expects from this singer. So many bass arias together makes a sombre collection, but the magnificent voice is splendidly presented.

Souzay, Gérard (tenor)

Opera arias (with LOP, Baudo): MONTEVERDI: *La Favola d'Orfeo: Tu sei morta mia vita.* HANDEL: *Partenope: Combattono il mio core dover . . . Furibondo spira il vento.* GLUCK: *Orfeo ed Euridice: Che puro ciel!; Cara Sposa! . . . Che farò senza Euridice.* MOZART: *Le nozze di Figaro: Hai già vinta . . . Vedro mentr'io sospiro. Don Giovanni: Deh vieni alla finestra; Fin ch'han dal vino.* BIZET: *Les Pêcheurs de perles: L'orage s'est calmé . . . O Nadir. La jolie fille de Perth: Quand la flamme.* GOUNOD: *Roméo et Juliette: Mab, la reine des mensonges.* MASSENET: *Thaïs: Voilà donc la terrible cité. Manon: Les grands mots que voilà . . . Epouse quelque brave fille.* THOMAS: *Hamlet: O vin, dissipe ma tristesse.*
(M) ** Ph. 412 373-1/*4*.

Unlike Souzay's collection of Baroque opera arias, one of his finest contributions to the gramophone (9502/*7313* 081) this wider-ranging collection, made in 1966, shows less individuality of approach. The voice itself sounds splendid, for the recorded sound is excellent on LP and cassette alike, but the Italian arias are less telling than the French, though Souzay's articulation of Handel is very stylish. Unusually for Philips, the issue is poorly documented, with no translations or details about the music itself.

Stade, Frederica von (mezzo-soprano)

'Portrait': MOZART: *Le nozze di Figaro: Non so più.* ROSSINI: *Semiramide: Bel raggio lusinghier.* THOMAS: *Mignon: C'est moi . . . Me voici.* MASSENET: *Cendrillon: Que mes soeurs.* OFFENBACH: *La Grande Duchesse: Dites-lui.* CHAUSSON: *Chanson perpétuelle.* SCHUMANN: *Botschaft; Das Glück.* BRAHMS: *6 Duets* (both with Judith Blegen).
*** CBS **MK 39315**; M/*MT* 39315 [id.].

This *'Portrait'*, compiled from a variety of sources, gives a good idea of the wide range of this characterful and charming singer. Though she is appreciated most as a superb Cherubino, the French items are the ones that stand out here for their extra intensity. The Chausson and the items taken from the complete sets of *Cendrillon* and *Mignon* are enchantingly done, while the Offenbach brings out the full fun of the piece lightly with point and wit. Intelligent singing too in Rossini and the duets with Blegen. Recording from different sources is generally well transferred on both LP and chrome cassette with the CD improving definition and presence.

'Stars of the Vienna Opera'

Vienna opera recordings 1918–1945 (with Maria Cebotari, Maria Jeritza, Jan Kiepura, Anni Konetzni, Selma Kurtz, Lotte Lehmann, Lauritz Melchior, Jarmila Novotna, Alfred Piccaver, Maria Reining, Elisabeth Schumann, Leo Slezak, Richard Tauber, Marcel Wittrisch and others) singing music by: Gluck; Mozart; Beethoven; Donizetti; Verdi; Wagner; Thomas; Goldmark; J. Strauss Jnr; Smetana; Offenbach; Puccini; R. Strauss; Korngold; Lehár; Weinberger and other composers.
(M) (***) HMV mono EX 290131-3/*5* (3) [Sera. IC 6140].

Though many of the singers in this fascinating collection had important international careers outside Vienna, together they give a vivid idea of the house's special qualities between the two World Wars. Even the disappointing Puccini items add to the flavour. Alfred Piccaver – always a favourite tenor in Vienna – is uncharacteristically coarse in *Ch'ella mi creda*, recorded in 1914; while Jan Kiepura is lachrymose in *Non piangere Liù*, both sung in German. Conversely, Maria Cebotari and Marcel Wittrisch singing in German for the Act I *Bohème* duet are a delight. Verdi in German is also a variable quantity, with Rosvaenge stridently exciting and unstylish in *Di quella pira*, but Leo Slezak superb in Otello's *Ora e per sempre* (in Italian). Singers often disappointing on record like Maria Jeritza and Maria Reining are here represented at their very finest, and from an older generation Selma Kurtz sings ravishingly in a Goldmark item. Anni Konetzni is a magnificent Brünnhilde, as recorded in 1933, explaining her legendary reputation; and Jarmila Novotna accompanied by Lehár himself in an item from *Giuditta* conveys an exotic Slavonic tang. Lotte Lehmann, Lauritz Melchior, Elisabeth Schumann and Richard Tauber are all well represented (the last unexpectedly in an aria from *Mignon*), but the many less well-known singers are the ones who provide the distinctive flavour. Excellent transfers and first-rate documentation.

Stefano, Giuseppe di (tenor)

'Signature' (with Maggio Musicale Fiorentino O, Bartoletti): VERDI: *Aïda: Se quel guerrier . . . Celeste Aïda. Luisa Miller: Oh! fede negar potessi . . . Quando le sere. Otello: Dio! mi potevi scaglier; Niun mi tema.* BOITO: *Mefistofele: Giunto sul passo estremo.* MEYERBEER: *L'Africana: Mi batte il cor . . . O paradiso.* PONCHIELLI: *La Gioconda: Cielo e mar.* PUCCINI: *Fanciulla del West: Or son sei mesi.* CILEA: *Adriana Lecouvreur: La dolcissima effigie.* LEONCAVALLO: *La Bohème: Musette! O gioja della mia dimora.* GIORDANO: *Fedora: Amor ti vieta.* PIETRI: *Maristella: Io conosco un giardino.* PIZZETTI: *Il Calzard d'argento: Davvero, quanto grande è la miseria.*
(M) ** DG Sig. 415 447-1/*4* [id.].

Giuseppe di Stefano's singing is not strong on subtlety, and while the voice rings out freely and thrillingly in this 1963 recital which is extremely vividly recorded on LP and cassette alike, the listener is made to reflect that a little more restraint would have greatly enhanced this programme. As it is, Bruno Bartoletti aids and abets his soloist with vibrant accompaniments, and the result is a little wearing. But the voice itself is in fine shape, and admirers of this artist should find the selection characteristic of his power and undoubted charisma.

Streich, Rita (soprano)

'Portrait': Arias from: DONIZETTI: *Don Pasquale; Lucia di Lammermoor; Linda di Chamounix.* ROSSINI: *Il Barbiere.* VERDI: *Un Ballo in maschera; I vespri siciliani; Rigoletto; Falstaff.* MEYERBEER: *Les Huguenots; Dinorah.* MOZART: *Zaïde; Die Entführung; Così fan tutte; Die Zauberflöte; Nozze di Figaro. Concert arias.* BELLINI: *I Capuletti ed i Montecchi.* PUCCINI: *Gianni Schicchi.* OFFENBACH: *Contes d'Hoffmann.* BIZET: *Les Pêcheurs de perles.* DELIBES: *Lakmé.* MASSENET: *Manon.* WEBER: *Der Freischütz.* NICOLAI: *Die lustigen Weiber von Windsor.* DVOŘÁK: *Rusalka.* RIMSKY-KORSAKOV: *Le coq d'or.* STRAUSS, J. Jnr: *Die Fledermaus.* Waltzes. Lieder by: Schubert; Wolf; R. Strauss; Schumann; Brahms.
(M) (***) DG 413 824-1 (6).

Prepared for the French market with notes only in French, except for one general article in English, this six-record box gives a comprehensive view of an artist whose records have not had the circulation they deserve. Internationally, Streich first came to attention on record in the mid-1950s as the most brilliant Zerbinetta in Strauss's *Ariadne auf Naxos*, as well as a fordmidable Queen of the Night in *Zauberflöte*. The *Ariadne* performance (EMI) has had to be excluded from this set, but the *Zauberflöte* arias are here, along with much more Mozart, all equally bright and clear. If in the opera house the voice was not always strong enough to ride the orchestra, it was an ideal instrument for the recording studio.

Though the range of expression is inevitably limited, with a relatively small, bright and flexible voice, Streich does wonders in such items as the *Lucia* Mad scene, even if it is not advisable to play all twelve sides at one sitting. Each area of the repertory reveals keen intelligence and finely polished technique, to remind one that, like Elisabeth Schwarzkopf, Streich was taught by Maria Ivogün. The items of opera and Lieder are leavened by two sides devoted to lollipops, labelled with the French expression 'bis'. Transfers are good, though on some sides the brightness of the voice is exaggerated with top emphasis.

Reminder. Rita Streich's single-disc and tape *'Portrait'* as published by DG (Privilege 2535/*3335* 367) was recorded in the earliest days of stereo when her voice was at its freshest. It is an irresistible collection of vocal lollipops, offering dazzling coloratura and winning charm; and it rightly earned a Rosette in our last edition.

Sutherland, Joan (soprano)

'The art of the prima donna', Vol. 1: ARNE: *Artaxerxes: The soldier tir'd.* HANDEL: *Samson: Let the bright seraphim.* BELLINI: *Norma: Casta diva; I Puritani: Son vergin vezzosa; Qui la voce; La Sonnambula: Come per me sereno.* ROSSINI: *Semiramide: Bel raggio lusinghier.* GOUNOD: *Faust: Jewel song. Roméo et Juliette: Waltz song.* VERDI: *Otello: Willow song; Rigoletto: Caro nome; Traviata: Ah, fors è lui; Sempre libera.* MOZART: *Die Entführung aus dem Serail: Marten aller Arten.* THOMAS: *Hamlet: Mad scene.* DELIBES: *Lakmé: Bell song.* MEYERBEER: *Les Huguenots: O beau pays.*

❀ *** Decca **414 450-2**; 414 450-1/*4* (2) [id.].

This ambitious early two-disc recital (from 1960) remains one of Joan Sutherland's outstanding gramophone achievements, and it is a matter of speculation whether even Melba or Tetrazzini in their heyday managed to provide sixteen consecutive recordings quite so dazzling as these performances. Indeed, it is the Golden Age that one naturally turns to rather than to current singers when making any comparisons. Sutherland herself by electing to sing each one of these fabulously difficult arias in tribute to a particular soprano of the past, from Mrs Billington in the eighteenth century, through Grisi, Malibran, Pasta and Jenny Lind in the nineteenth century, to Lilli Lehmann, Melba, Tetrazzini and Galli-Curci in this, is asking to be judged by the standards of the Golden Age. On the basis of recorded reminders she comes out with flying colours, showing a greater consistency and certainly a wider range of sympathy than even the greatest Golden Agers possessed. The sparkle and delicacy of the *Puritani Polonaise*, the freshness and lightness of the Mad scene from Thomas's *Hamlet*, the commanding power of the *Entführung* aria and the breathtaking brilliance of the Queen's aria from *Les Huguenots* are all among the high spots here, while the arias which Sutherland later recorded in her complete opera sets regularly bring performances just as fine – and often finer – than the later versions. The freshness of the voice is caught superbly in the recording, which on CD is amazingly full, firm and realistic, far more believable than many new digital recordings. The cassettes, too, are very well managed and at mid-price cost considerably less than the CDs.

Sutherland, Joan, and **Luciano Pavarotti** (tenor)

Operatic duets (with National PO, Bonynge) from: VERDI: *La Traviata; Otello; Aïda* (with chorus). BELLINI: *La Sonnambula*. DONIZETTI: *Linda di Chamounix*. *** Decca **400 058-2**; SXL/*KSXC* 6828 [Lon. OSA/*5*- 26437].

This collection offers a rare sample of Sutherland as Aïda (*La fatale pietra . . . O terra, addio* from Act IV), a role she sang only once on stage, well before her international career began; and with this and her sensitive impersonations of Desdemona, Violetta and the Bellini and Donizetti heroines, Sutherland might have been expected to steal first honours here. In fact these are mainly duets to show off the tenor, and it is Pavarotti who runs away with the main glory, though both artists were plainly challenged to their finest and the result, with excellent accompaniment, is among the most attractive and characterful duet recitals. The recording is admirably clear and well focused, and the sophistication of orchestral detail is striking in the *Otello* and *Aïda* scenes which close the recital, and this is especially striking on the compact disc which, though a remastered analogue recording, gives the artists remarkable presence. The cassette too is extremely well managed.

Vienna Boys' Choir

'Folksongs and songs for children' (with V. CO, Harrer; Farnberger; Miller). *** Ph. Dig. **400 014-2**; 6514/*7337* 188 [id.].

Here are some two dozen songs, many traditional and all of great charm. They are presented artlessly, but the singing is polished and the simply scored accompaniments are very effective. The recording is admirably natural, with the CD offering a marginal improvement in definition. The chrome tape sounds well too (although it has rather a low transfer level). There is a good deal of moderately paced music here, and sometimes one feels that the direction could be more spirited; yet the overall effect is undoubtedly beguiling and, not taken all at once, this recital will give much pleasure. With the CD comes an excellent booklet, complete with all translations.

Walker, Sarah (mezzo-soprano), **Thomas Allen** (baritone)

'The Sea' (with Roger Vignoles, piano): IRELAND: *Sea fever*. HAYDN: *Mermaid's song; Sailor's song*. DIBDIN: *Tom Bowling*. WALTON: *Song for the Lord Mayor's table; Wapping Old Stairs*. WOLF: *Seemanns Abschied*. FAURÉ: *Les Berceaux; Au cimetière; L'horizon chimérique*. SCHUBERT: *Lied eines Schiffers an die Dioskuren*. BORODIN: *The Sea; The Sea Princess*. DEBUSSY: *Proses lyriques: De grêve*. IVES: *Swimmers*. SCHUMANN: *Die Meerfee*. BERLIOZ:

Nuits d'été: L'île inconnue. MENDELSSOHN: *Wasserfahrt.* BRAHMS: *Die Meere.* TRAD.: *The Mermaid.* Arr. BRITTEN: *Sail on, sail on.*
❀ *** Hyp. A 66165.

With Roger Vignoles as master of ceremonies in a brilliantly devised programme, ranging wide, this twin-headed recital celebrating The Sea is a delight from beginning to end. Two outstandingly characterful singers are mutually challenged to their very finest form, whether in solo songs or duets. As sample, try the setting of the sea-song, *The Mermaid*, brilliantly arranged by Vignoles, with hilarious key-switches on the comic quotations from *Rule Britannia*. Excellent recording.

Westminster Abbey Choir, Preston

Christmas carols: TRAD.: *Up! awake!; There stood in heaven a linden tree; The holly and the ivy; Ding dong merrily on high; Up! good Christian folk; In dulci jubilo; Rocking; Illuminare Jerusalem; Good King Wenceslas.* OLDHAM: *Remember O thou man.* WISHART: *Alleluya, a new work.* CHARPENTIER: *Salve puerule.* POSTON: *Jesus Christ the apple tree.* PRAETORIUS: *Resonet in laudibus.* MAXWELL DAVIES: *Nowell* (*Out of your sleep arise*). HAMMERSCHMIDT: *Alleluja! Freuet euch.* MENDELSSOHN: *Hark! the herald angels sing.* SCHEIDT: *Puer natus.* GARDNER: *Tomorrow shall be my dancing day.* BRITTEN: *Shepherd's carol.*
*** DG Dig. **413 590-2**; 413 590-1/*4*.

An excellent concert in every way. The programme is nicely balanced between old favourites and rewarding novelty, the traditional material spiced with modern writing, which readily captures the special essence that makes a carol instantly recognizable as a Christmas celebration. Fresh singing of fine vigour, expressively responsive, is combined with first-class sound in all three media, the ambience nicely judged.

Westminster Cathedral Choir, Hill

'Treasures of the Spanish Renaissance': GUERRERO: *Surge propera amica mea; O altitudo divitiarum; O Domine Jesu Christe; O sacrum convivium; Ave, Virgo sanctissima; Regina caeli laetare.* LOBO: *Versa est in luctum; Ave Maria; O quam suavis est, Domine.* VIVANCO: *Magnificat octavi toni.*
*** Hyp. **CDA 66168**; A/*KA* 66168 [id.].

This immensely valuable collection reminds us vividly that Tomas Luis de Victoria was not the only master of church music in Renaissance Spain. Francisco Guerrero is generously represented here, and the spacious serenity of his polyphonic writing (for four, six and, in *Regina caeli laetare*, eight parts) creates the most beautiful sounds. A criticism might be made that tempi throughout this collection, which also includes fine music by Alonso Lobo and a superb eight-part *Magnificat* by Sebastian de Vivanco, are too measured, but the tension is well held, and David Hill is obviously concerned to convey the breadth of the writing. The singing is gloriously firm, with the long melismatic lines admirably controlled. Discreet accompaniments (using Renaissance double harp, bass dulcian and organ) do not affect the essentially a cappella nature of the performances. The Westminster Abbey acoustic means the choral tone is richly upholstered, but the focus is always firm and clear. There is an excellent cassette which shares the excellent documentation of the other formats.

White, Robert (tenor)

(with Nat. PO, Mace): LOHR: *Little grey home in the West.* HAWTHORNE: *Whispering hope.* DIX: *The Trumpeter.* RASBACH: *Trees.* CLAY: *I'll sing thee songs of Araby.* FOSTER: *I dream of Jeanie with the light brown hair.* BALFE: *Come into the garden, Maud.* JACOBS-BOND: *Just a-wearyin' for you.* WHITE: *Two blue eyes.* ADAMS: *Thora.* MARTINI: *Plaisir d'amour.* MURRAY: *I'll walk beside you.* FRASER-SIMPSON: *Christopher Robin is saying his prayers.*
(M) *** RCA GL/*GK* 70734.

The reissue of this attractive recital at mid-price is most welcome. Here Robert White turns to popular ballads and sings them with characteristic artless charm. He can be dramatically vivid, as in Dix's *The Trumpeter*, or phrase a simple melody with ravishingly warm tone. In the duet *Whispering hope* (one of the gramophone's earliest million-sellers in its 78 r.p.m. recording by Alma Gluck and Louise Homer) he sings with himself (by electronic means), disguising the colour of the 'second' voice so that it sounds like a light baritone, yet blends marvellously with the 'tenor'. A fascinating sleeve-note tells of White's childhood when one of an 'enormous collection' of John McCormack's records would go on the phonograph every time his mother put the kettle on for tea. This recital contains many favourites (described enthusiastically by White as 'belters'), and they are sung superbly. The accompaniments under Ralph Mace are stylishly sympathetic, although the orchestral group is thin in numbers, perhaps appropriately. The cassette transfer is first class, matching the excellent disc closely.

MORE ABOUT PENGUINS, PELICANS, PEREGRINES AND PUFFINS

For further information about books available from Penguins please write to Dept EP, Penguin Books Ltd, Harmondsworth, Middlesex UB7 0DA.

In the U.S.A.: For a complete list of books available from Penguins in the United States write to Dept DG, Penguin Books, 299 Murray Hill Parkway, East Rutherford, New Jersey 07073.

In Canada: For a complete list of books available from Penguins in Canada write to Penguin Books Canada Limited, 2801 John Street, Markham, Ontario L3R 1B4.

In Australia: For a complete list of books available from Penguins in Australia write to the Marketing Department, Penguin Books Australia Ltd, P.O. Box 257, Ringwood, Victoria 3134.

In New Zealand: For a complete list of books available from Penguins in New Zealand write to the Marketing Department, Penguin Books (N.Z.) Ltd, Private Bag, Takapuna, Auckland 9.

In India: For a complete list of books available from Penguins in India write to Penguin Overseas Ltd, 706 Eros Apartments, 56 Nehru Place, New Delhi 110019.

PENGUIN REFERENCE BOOKS

☐ ***The Penguin Dictionary of Troublesome Words*** £2.50

A witty, straightforward guide to the pitfalls and hotly disputed issues in standard written English, illustrated with examples and including a glossary of grammatical terms and an appendix on punctuation.

☐ ***The Penguin Guide to the Law*** £8.95

This acclaimed reference book is designed for everyday use, and forms the most comprehensive handbook ever published on the law as it affects the individual.

☐ ***The Penguin Dictionary of Religions*** £4.95

The rites, beliefs, gods and holy books of all the major religions throughout the world are covered in this book, which is illustrated with charts, maps and line drawings.

☐ ***The Penguin Medical Encyclopedia*** £4.95

Covers the body and mind in sickness and in health, including drugs, surgery, history, institutions, medical vocabulary and many other aspects. Second Edition. 'Highly commendable' – *Journal of the Institute of Health Education*

☐ ***The Penguin Dictionary of Physical Geography*** £4.95

This book discusses all the main terms used, in over 5,000 entries illustrated with diagrams and meticulously cross-referenced.

☐ ***Roget's Thesaurus*** £3.50

Specially adapted for Penguins, Sue Lloyd's acclaimed new version of Roget's original will help you find the right words for your purposes. 'As normal a part of an intelligent household's library as the Bible, Shakespeare or a dictionary' – *Daily Telegraph*

A CHOICE OF PENGUINS

☐ ***The Complete Penguin Stereo Record and Cassette Guide***
Greenfield, Layton and March £7.95

A new edition, now including information on compact discs. 'One of the few indispensables on the record collector's bookshelf' – *Gramophone*

☐ ***Selected Letters of Malcolm Lowry***
Edited by Harvey Breit and Margerie Bonner Lowry £5.95

'Lowry emerges from these letters not only as an extremely interesting man, but also a lovable one' – Philip Toynbee

☐ ***The First Day on the Somme***
Martin Middlebrook £3.95

1 July 1916 was the blackest day of slaughter in the history of the British Army. 'The soldiers receive the best service a historian can provide: their story told in their own words' – *Guardian*

☐ ***A Better Class of Person*** **John Osborne** £2.50

The playwright's autobiography, 1929–56. 'Splendidly enjoyable' – John Mortimer. 'One of the best, richest and most bitterly truthful autobiographies that I have ever read' – Melvyn Bragg

☐ ***The Winning Streak*** **Goldsmith and Clutterbuck** £2.95

Marks & Spencer, Saatchi & Saatchi, United Biscuits, GEC . . . The UK's top companies reveal their formulas for success, in an important and stimulating book that no British manager can afford to ignore.

☐ ***The First World War*** **A. J. P. Taylor** £4.95

'He manages in some 200 illustrated pages to say almost everything that is important . . . A special text . . . a remarkable collection of photographs' – *Observer*

A CHOICE OF PENGUINS

☐ ***Man and the Natural World*** **Keith Thomas** £4.95

Changing attitudes in England, 1500–1800. 'An encyclopedic study of man's relationship to animals and plants . . . a book to read again and again' – Paul Theroux, *Sunday Times* Books of the Year

☐ ***Jean Rhys: Letters 1931–66***
Edited by Francis Wyndham and Diana Melly £4.95

'Eloquent and invaluable . . . her life emerges, and with it a portrait of an unexpectedly indomitable figure' – Marina Warner in the *Sunday Times*

☐ ***The French Revolution*** **Christopher Hibbert** £4.95

'One of the best accounts of the Revolution that I know . . . Mr Hibbert is outstanding' – J. H. Plumb in the *Sunday Telegraph*

☐ ***Isak Dinesen*** **Judith Thurman** £4.95

The acclaimed life of Karen Blixen, 'beautiful bride, disappointed wife, radiant lover, bereft and widowed woman, writer, sibyl, Scheherazade, child of Lucifer, Baroness; always a unique human being . . . an assiduously researched and finely narrated biography' – *Books & Bookmen*

☐ ***The Amateur Naturalist***
Gerald Durrell with Lee Durrell £4.95

'Delight . . . on every page . . . packed with authoritative writing, learning without pomposity . . . it represents a real bargain' – *The Times Educational Supplement.* 'What treats are in store for the average British household' – *Daily Express*

☐ ***When the Wind Blows*** **Raymond Briggs** £2.95

'A visual parable against nuclear war: all the more chilling for being in the form of a strip cartoon' – *Sunday Times*. 'The most eloquent anti-Bomb statement you are likely to read' – *Daily Mail*